NORWICH CATHEDRAL

LOMBARDIC ARCHITECTURE
ITS ORIGIN DEVELOPMENT AND DERIVATIVES By G. T. RIVOIRA

VOLUME II

HACKER ART BOOKS

NEW YORK, N.Y. 1975

First published London: Heineman, 1910
Revised edition Oxford: Clarendon Press, 1933

Reissued New York: Hacker Art Books, 1975

Library of Congress Catalogue Card Number 73-76789
ISBN 0-87817-137-1

Printed in the United States of America

CONTENTS OF VOLUME II

LIST OF ILLUSTRATIONS

The great majority of the illustrations which appear in this book are derived from photographs taken expressly for the work. Many of those in Volume II are by Lionel Johnson, Esq. For a few the author and editors are indebted to Miss P. Bruce, Miss A. Bulwer, Dr. T. Ashby, A. W. Clapham, Esq., Prof. Camille Enlart, Dr. Paul Gauckler, Dr. Henry Gee, Harold Johnson, Esq., Dr. G. Lindsay Johnson, H. G. Leask, Esq., F. Tuckett, Esq., and J. R. H. Weaver, Esq.; to all of whom sincere thanks are offered.

VOLUME II

LIST OF ILLUSTRATIONS

LIST OF ILLUSTRATIONS

LIST OF ILLUSTRATIONS

LIST OF ILLUSTRATIONS

LIST OF ILLUSTRATIONS

LIST OF ILLUSTRATIONS

LIST OF ILLUSTRATIONS

LIST OF ILLUSTRATIONS

PART II

INTRODUCTION

HAVING traced the origins of the Lombardic vaulted basilica, I now proceed to reconstruct the history of its principal derivatives in the countries north of the Alps. In doing so I shall confine myself to giving the main outlines, leaving to others the task of indicating the secondary ones. These outlines will be based on original monuments which have come down to us in a state of complete or partial preservation, or of which we have descriptions or drawings; so that students of medieval architecture may have some clue to guide them in the labyrinth where at present they have lost their way.

The views of writers on the origins and development of the great styles of ecclesiastical architecture practised in the Transalpine lands between the epoch of 1000 and the first appearance of the Pointed style show immense divergence. Round these origins and round this development there has grown up such a dense growth of 'influences'—Syrian, Roman, Gallo-Roman, Byzantine, Barbarian, Arabic—having their source, when evidence fails, in the imagination, that it is no easy matter to unwind the tangle. And the difficulty has been intensified by the erroneous belief that the East was the chief inspirer and authoritative guide of all the medieval Christian systems, from the Romano-Ravennate down to the Pointed style.

The leading idea of this part of my book is as follows. With the appearance of the Lombardic basilica, a spring-tide of new styles of building burst forth north of the Alps, the chief being the Lombardo-Norman and the Lombardo-Rhenish, as I prefer to call them. I do so because the terms 'Romanic' and 'Romanesque', applied to this great art of the Middle Ages, do not seem to me to be justified; for we might equally well call the Byzantine style 'Romanesque', seeing that the Byzantine vaulted basilica in its supreme expression, St. Sophia at Constantinople, had its origin in the great Baths of Rome, as I have explained.

It was the monks of St. Benedict who acted as the sponsors of these styles; it was under their protection that they were nurtured; it was to the Benedictine services that they were adapted. Brought into conformity with the tendencies and peculiar character of the peoples among whom they were introduced, and even modified to suit their climates, clothed in new forms, and treated with variety of conception, these two styles made remarkable progress, and were diffused far and wide by the agency of the Benedictine monks.

In the course of my argument I shall again have to shatter more than one legend about the real origins of the chief characteristics which go to make up Lombardic architecture; and I shall have to apply the same treatment to other legends concerning the birth and growth of the principal styles which derived from it their life and sustenance.

The illustrations provided to explain and confirm the text will, as before, be, in the main, reproductions of photographs. Mere drawings, in which the artistic element is emphasized at the expense of truth, have in the past lent themselves too readily to illusion; and though they may thereby satisfy the taste of the dilettantes of architecture, they only lead real students astray.

I

THE BEGINNINGS OF THE LOMBARDO-NORMAN STYLE IN BURGUNDY[1]

THE first solid foundations of the Lombardic-Norman style were not laid, to judge by the buildings which have come down to us, in Burgundy, as some think, but in Normandy. Burgundy, however, can claim the credit of having provided the field for the free exercise and consolidation of the forces which later helped to lay those foundations, and of having produced the first flowers of the new style.

The soul of this work of preparation was the Benedictine monk, William of Volpiano (961–1031), born on the island of San Giulio in the Lake of Orta, brought as a youth to Cluny by Majolus abbot of that monastery (948–994), and afterwards appointed abbot of Saint Bénigne at Dijon (990) by Bruno bishop of Langres (981–1016). With regard to this man of great learning, of iron will, a great reformer of the monastic orders, architect and builder of churches and convents, the diffuser of Italian culture in Burgundy and Normandy, we know, among other things, that he took in hand the erection of the new abbey church of St. Benignus at Dijon (1002–1018), and also built the abbey of Fruttuaria in Piedmont, founded in 1003 and consecrated in 1006.[2]

Of this preparatory work the famous church at Dijon, in which some of the characteristics of the Lombardic basilica appeared for the first time, was the highest, most solemn expression. Let us turn to it.

THE CHURCH OF SAINT BÉNIGNE AT DIJON, built by St. Gregorius bishop of Langres (507–539) above a crypt which he raised in height,[3] was renewed in 871 by Isaac bishop of the same diocese (859–880). Having fallen into decay, and part of it being in ruins, it was rebuilt by William of Volpiano, the extreme eastern part of the previous structure being preserved. The rebuilding was begun in 1002, and the dedication took place in 1018.

The church, however, was unfortunate. In 1096 the central tower fell, and was rebuilt. Following this operation and the repairs of the damage caused by the catastrophe came a second dedication performed by Pope Paschal II in 1107. In 1136 the whole building suffered considerably from the terrible conflagration which devastated Dijon, and the restoration necessitated thereby must have been far-reaching inasmuch as it involved a second reconsecration at the hands of Pope Eugenius III in 1146. In 1271 the rebuilt tower over the crossing again collapsed, injuring not only its immediate surroundings but other parts of the church as well.[4] After this disaster the portions that had suffered most were rebuilt in the new or Pointed style, thus satisfying the passion for innovation which followed the appearance of the new architecture. Under these circumstances, all that was left of William's church was the rotunda, with the

---

[1] [The most recent work on the Burgundian School, CHARLES OURSEL, *L'Art roman de Bourgogne. Études d'histoire et d'archéologie* (Dijon and Boston, 1928), is reviewed by L. Bréhier in the *Revue Archéologique*, 5 S., xxix (1929), 291–316. See also M. Aubert in DE LASTEYRIE, op. cit., p. 782. (R.)]

[2] MABILLON, *Acta SS. Ord. S. Benedicti*, vol. vii, pp. 291, 292. *Vita S. Guillelmi abbatis Divionensis auctore Glabro Rodulfo monacho*; Id., ibid., p. 307;

D'ACHERY, *Spicilegium* (Paris, 1723), vol. ii, pp. 383–6. *Chronica S. Benigni Divionensis*; SAVIO, op. cit., p. 195. [On the relation of William of Volpiano to this and other buildings see Appendix I at the end of this chapter.]

[3] *Mon. Germ. Hist.*, *Historia Francorum*, p. 523, *Gregorii ep. Turonensis liber in gloria martyrum*.

[4] *Mon. Germ. Hist.*, *Script.*, vol. v, p. 50. *Annales S. Benigni Divionensis*.

ancient chapel of St. John Baptist at one end of it, and a considerable part of the termination of the basilica at the other. Finally, in 1792 the pickaxe demolished everything of his church that still remained above ground. The part below ground, with its vaulting broken in, and degraded into a receptacle for rubbish, has been restored in recent years to the condition which it now presents.

The chronicle of Saint Bénigne[1] contains a description of the interior of the church, though it is not without omissions and inaccuracies. Plancher[2] has furnished interesting particulars about the portions still surviving in the first half of the eighteenth century,

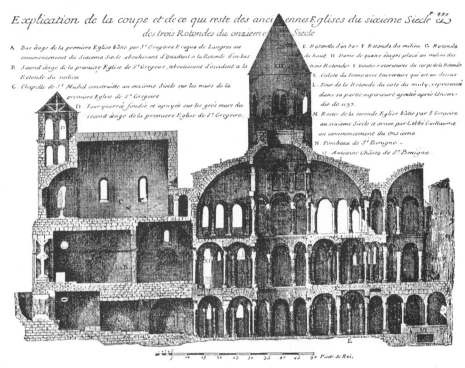

Fig. 386. Dijon. Saint Bénigne. Section of the eastern end (1002–1018, and 6th and 9th centuries).
(From PLANCHER, *Histoire générale et particulière de Bourgogne*, vol. i, p. 498)

and of these he gives two ground plans, a section of the elevation, and two views of the exterior.

The structure consisted of a basilica, terminated towards the east by a rotunda. Both basilica and rotunda were of three stories, one being underground. The latter or crypt was composed of a circular vaulted structure consisting of two concentric circles of columns enclosed by an outer wall with half-columns, lighted by four windows splayed on the inside, and with a chapel at the eastern end used as a chancel. Over the central space rose a kind of open octagonal tower, having three series of arcades one above the other, the two lower supported by columns, the uppermost by piers. It was crowned by a cupola with a circular opening at the top (fig. 386).

To the west of the rotunda was another structure, shaped like a ⊤ (in the underground part), consisting of a nave and a transept or cross nave, both of the same length, and separated in either case from aisles by two rows of columns. The nave and aisles

[1] D'ACHERY, *Spicilegium*, vol. ii, p. 383. *Chronica S. Benigni Divionensis.*

[2] *Histoire générale et particulière de Bourgogne,* 4 vols. (Dijon, 1739), i, pp. 81, 499 ff.

were flanked by closed vestibules forming outer aisles, and terminated in an arcaded apse which contained the tomb and altar of St. Benignus. On the eastern side of either arm of the transept was a rectangular chapel with an apse, and a semicircular recess taken out of the thickness of the wall. This arrangement was based on the lines of the previous church, in the form which it acquired in the ninth century; a fact which has come to light in the recent restoration.

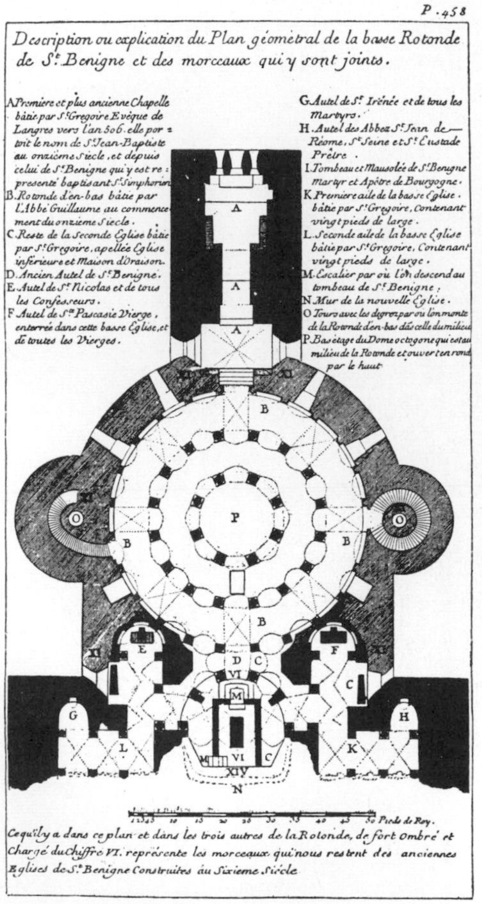

Of this underground church there survives the rotunda with its eastern adjunct, the chapel containing the tomb of St. Benignus, and the eastern end of the basilica (fig. 387).[1]

In the rotunda (fig. 388) the isolated shafts are surmounted by Pre-Lombardic cubicles, hollowed out at the angles, each of which is filled by a smooth pointed leaf, while the faces are left plain. There are two exceptions in the middle row of columns, with the faces bearing a human figure, sometimes of very curious character, in the act of supporting with its arms a conventional abacus (fig. 389). The crosses roughly engraved on two of the angle leaves of one of these capitals are a later addition. The figures are worked in rather round relief, and without undercutting. Design and execution alike are barbarous and elementary.

In the outer circle of columns, opposite to the tomb of St. Benignus, are two more capitals[2] carved with animals of rude but robust design, boldly conceived, treated with variety of action (and not a uniform one, like the human figures on the two capitals just described), strongly, and sometimes completely undercut (figs. 390, 391). These belong to a period considerably later than the rebuilding of the early eleventh century. They may probably be connected with the restoration necessitated by the fall of the central tower in 1096, and this is the date to which an experienced eye would be inclined to assign them. From the capitals spring round arches.

The vaulting, which has been rebuilt on the pattern of the few old portions which survived, is of barrel form over the inner annular aisle, and alternately of barrel and intersecting form over the outer one. The barrel vaults are constructed of radiating oblong blocks of stone, roughly cut. The central space, originally open at the top, is now covered by a cupola.

In the arcaded apse round the tomb of St. Benignus still stand six original columns with Pre-Lombardic cubical capitals hollowed out at the angles, and with plain faces.

Fig. 387. Dijon. Saint Bénigne. Underground plan of the eastern end (1002–1018, and 6th and 9th centuries). (From PLANCHER, *Histoire générale et particulière de Bourgogne*, vol. i, p. 484)

[1] [See V. FLIPO, *La Cathédrale de Dijon (Petites Monographies des grandes Édifices de la France*).]

[2] [DE LASTEYRIE, *L'Architecture religieuse en France à l'Époque romane*, p. 156, refers to these capitals without distinguishing between an earlier and a later type, and, while agreeing with Viollet-le-Duc that they may well be earlier than the 11th century, suggests that the eventual conclusion may be that they are anterior to the age of Charlemagne. (H. T.)]

The southern area of the east end of the basilica, to the side of the saint's tomb, is divided into aisles, the vaulting of which has recently been replaced; and here are seven capitals of the same date as the two carved ones facing the tomb. One of them shows foliage and monsters. Another has grooved leaves. Another has similar foliage and interlacings, with four heads at the angles each holding in its mouth a leaf which takes the place of a volute. These heads are by the same hand that executed those at the angles of one of the capitals about the tomb. A fourth is ornamented with large volutes at the angles, roses, palm leaves, and animals (fig. 392). The fifth is carved, partly with plain leaves the tips of which are divided and curl over in volutes (i.e.

Fig. 388. Dijon. Saint Bénigne. Crypt of the Rotunda (1002–1018)

crockets), and partly with curiously wrought foliage and interlacing wicker work. The two remaining ones show a double row of stiff plain leaves. Those of the bases which are old are stepped, and differ in form from those in the rotunda belonging to the time of William of Volpiano. They are clearly of another period.

In the northern arm, only a portion of which survives, two original capitals may be observed, one cubical with the faces left plain, the other the fellow of the two which we pointed out in the central circle of the rotunda.

The presence in this arm and in the arcade round the tomb of St. Benignus, i.e. in the most important part of the rotunda, of rudely executed Pre-Lombardic capitals of the type which prevails all through the crypt, is a clear proof that the elaborately worked capitals which we assigned to the end of the eleventh century are certainly not of the same date as the crypt itself.

The chapel of St. John Baptist consists of a rectangular chamber, regularly orientated, roughly built of stones with very thick joints. The cross vaulting has been rebuilt. Beyond it is another rectangular chamber, even more rudely constructed, showing a mortar which differs from the other. Here again the barrel vault has been replaced.

The difference between the masonry of the walls of the two chambers, and also of the outer wall of the rotunda, makes it certain that the three structures are not of the same date. And seeing that this adjunct to the termination of Saint Bénigne is mentioned about the year 938, when the dedication to St. Mary took place,[1] we must ascribe it, for the present, to the restoration of the church in 871. Then, when we take into

Fig. 389. Dijon. Saint Bénigne. Crypt of the Rotunda. Capital (1002–1018)

Fig. 390. Dijon. Saint Bénigne. Crypt of the Rotunda. Capital (1096–1107)

Fig. 391. Dijon. Saint Bénigne. Crypt of the Rotunda. Capital (1096–1107)

Fig. 392. Dijon. Saint Bénigne. Capital at east end of the underground church (1096–1107)

consideration the barrel vault of the chamber at the eastern extremity of the church, the method of covering regularly adopted for the earliest Christian oratories in France, and in presence of the greater rudeness of the masonry of this chamber, and also of the persistence with which it was preserved, evidently as being a spot of peculiar sanctity, through the two rebuildings of the original church of St. Gregory, bishop of Langres, in the ninth and eleventh centuries, we may fix the date of this oldest chamber

[1] CHOMTON, *Histoire de l'église Saint-Bénigne de Dijon*, p. 76.

at a period earlier than the ninth century, and perhaps in the time of the said bishop, while the other chamber may be ascribed to the ninth century.

On the ground floor, or church proper, the rotunda had the same plan as in the crypt; but in the outer wall were engaged whole, and not half columns.

The basilica was in the form of a cross, with aisles and galleries, and was some 210 ft. long and 85 ft. wide. The height was about 50 ft. in every part of the interior except the nave, which was some 65 ft. It was supported by massive quadrangular piers and columns, with shafts at the angles of some of the piers in the galleries. The nave, terminated by an arcaded apse, was flanked by vaulted double aisles ending in two chapels and two recesses like those of the underground church. Over the crossing rose a broad tower of stone.

On the first floor the rotunda was in the form of a crown, with a smaller circle of isolated columns, and a larger one of columns engaged in the outer wall. So far as one can judge from Plancher's sectional view, the capitals belonging to these columns, and to those of the upper story of the rotunda, were of the cubical shape to be seen in the underground part.

Interesting details of the two stories above ground are furnished by two paintings of the eighteenth century, preserved in the sacristy of the present Saint Bénigne, which represent the rotunda in process of demolition.

In the upper story of the rotunda a chapel projected towards the east, above the square sanctuary of which rose a low tower of the same form, heightened in the twelfth century. This story communicated with the two below it by means of two spiral staircases, rising as high as the roof, contained within two round towers, also increased in height in the twelfth century, placed to the north and south of the rotunda, and forming part of its structure. The elevation of these towers was little more than that of the rotunda, as may be seen in the two pictures referred to, and in another which goes with them, giving a view of the interior of Saint Bénigne before 1792. At the foot of each spiral stair two passages started, connecting the rotunda with two arcaded galleries, and also with two spiral staircases which gave access to the roof and a way protected by a parapet all round the outside. Two other staircases, formed symmetrically in the front wall of the church, connected the galleries with the aisles below them. The building was provided with eight towers, in which other columns occurred, and had three entrances.

The exterior of the original portions of William's church still existing when Plancher wrote, and when the pictures mentioned in the sacristy of the present Saint Bénigne were executed, was decorated with blank arcading and arched corbel courses, in some cases continuous, in others broken by lesenas.

Such are the main features of the church as it has been described to us. About the rotunda we know enough to form a clear idea of what it was like. Not so of the basilica, where too much essential information as to its statical, constructive, and decorative features is wanting for us to be able to reproduce its real character even approximately. Nor are the inferences which we may draw from the various data, and from a comparison with other relevant buildings, sufficient to throw much light on the subject. A few considerations will show this.

It is known that, in the portion which formed the junction between the rotunda and the basilica, the walls of the central body rose very little above the horizontal line of the aisle roofs (fig. 393); whence it might be inferred that the walls of the nave of the basilica were constructed in the same way. It is equally clear from Plancher's evidence that the nave was vaulted. We are also informed by a statement in the Dijon

Chronicle that the aisles were vaulted as well. So that we might infer the same for the galleries, and consequently that the entire building was vaulted. This would account for the remarkable thickness (over 5½ ft.) of the outer walls, and also for the adoption of the plan of keeping the walls of the nave low, with the object of resting the vaulting on them in such a way that the thrust should be resisted by the gallery vaulting and by the outer walls. This idea would be suggested by a fear in the minds of the architect and builders of compromising the stability of the nave if its walls were raised high enough to admit of windows: a fear which is not difficult to understand when we consider the condition of statical science as applied to vaulting at the beginning of the eleventh century.

Veue de la Rotonde de St Benigne de Dijon du côté du Septentrion et des restes des anciens Batimens qui y sont joints regardez du même côté

Fig. 393. Dijon. Saint Bénigne. Elevation of the eastern end (1002–1018, and 6th and 9th centuries). (From PLANCHER, *Histoire générale et particulière de Bourgogne*)

On the other hand, the clear reference in the Chronicle to the parts of the basilica which had vaulting (very probably rude cross vaults like those in Ste. Marie at Bernay, founded in 1013, and also designed and built by William of Volpiano), viz. the aisles (' . . . geminas porticus dupliciter transvolutas'), the very serious damage suffered by the church in the fire of 1136, and, thirdly, the fact that William had provided mainly wooden ceilings for the nearly contemporary church at Bernay, are all things which lead one to believe that originally the basilica had its nave, transept, and gallery roofed with timber in the same fashion as the church of Bernay, and also that of Cerisy la Forêt, rebuilt in 1030 either from the plans or under the immediate influence of William of Volpiano. In that case, the wooden ceilings of Saint Bénigne must have been substituted for a solid roof of masonry in the course of the restorations occasioned by the fire referred to, involving a reduction in height of the previously lofty walls of the nave so as to bring them into relation with the new conditions of equilibrium established for the structure. It is impossible to suppose that these walls were at first blank and windowless, as Plancher's views would suggest, since the maximum height of the church (some 65 ft.) mentioned in the Dijon Chronicle (where the height of the nave and not of the central tower, as has been suggested, must be referred to) presupposes a lofty wall space for windows above the galleries, as at Bernay and Cerisy la Forêt.

The doubt as to how the basilica was roofed may be extended to the piers between the nave and the aisles. For while, on the one hand, one might imagine that they were alternately larger and smaller, on the other, the supports of uniform size in the church at Bernay, known to have been built by the same architect, makes one suspect with good grounds that the same design was followed in both buildings.

It has been a common view that the plan of Saint Bénigne, in joining a basilica on to a rotunda, was suggested by the Holy Sepulchre at Jerusalem. This, however, is an erroneous idea, based on plans of the original church of Constantine which are partly imaginary, like De Vogüé's,[1] though the world has shut its eyes and accepted them, and exhibit a basilica ending in a semicircle with an aisle round it and three apses. In other cases the theory is based on statements which have no facts to support them. This is not surprising when we consider that the history, at any rate up to the time of the Crusades, of the complex of buildings which make up what is commonly called the Church of the Holy Sepulchre at Jerusalem is still involved in obscurity. And as I feel that it is a very desirable thing to try to remove that obscurity, I therefore undertake the task, so far as the incompleteness of the historical documents allows, and the absence of much essential information as to its construction and decoration which might throw light on the changes through which this famous sanctuary has passed.

THE CHURCH OF THE HOLY SEPULCHRE[2] was only just founded by St. Helena in the year before her death, 327, when she went on pilgrimage to the Holy Places in the hope of forgetting the tragedies which had taken place in her family. The building was erected by Constantine the Great, and dedicated in 335.

It consisted of the 'Anastasis', or Church of the Resurrection, at the west, containing the Holy Sepulchre; and the great Constantinian basilica, or 'Martyrion', at the east. Between them came the sanctuary of Calvary (in Cyril of Jerusalem [fourth century] 'Golgotha' means two things: the entire hill, and the summit or mound on which the cross was planted[3]), which was a space open to the sky, enclosed by a silver railing.[4] On this spot, brought into prominence by Constantine's levelling operations,[5] a chapel was erected by the younger Melania († 439).[6]

About the Church of the Resurrection all that we know is: on the authority of the 'Jerusalem Breviary' (of about 530 according to one view, or about 420 according to another), that it was in the form of a rotunda; from the evidence of Eusebius, that it contained magnificent columns; and, thirdly, from the statement of Antiochus,[7] that it must have had a wooden roof, as it was set on fire by the Persians (614).

Constantine's basilica is described by Eusebius as follows. It excited wonder by its dimensions. The nave was supported by columns, and flanked by double aisles with

[1] *Les églises de la Terre-Sainte*, pp. 118–232, plate vi.

[2] [RIVOIRA, *La Chiesa del Santo Sepolcro*, in *Dissertazioni della Pontificia Accademia Romana di Archeologia*, ser. 2, vol. vii (1916), pp. 181–93; PP. VINCENT and ABEL, *Jérusalem* (Paris, 1914–26), vol. ii, pp. 105 ff.; cp. CLAPHAM, *Antiquaries Journal*, i (1921), pp. 3 ff.]

[3] MIGNE, *Patr. Gr.*, vol. 33, *Descriptio et historia basilicae Resurrectionis*, col. 1261 B.

[4] *Perigrinatio Etheriae* (under Theodosius I, 379–95), first published (as by St. Silvia) by J. F. GAMURRINI (2nd ed., Rome, 1888, p. 65). Cp. DUCHESNE, *Christian Worship* (5th ed.), pp. 490 ff., 559. EUSEBIUS,

Vita Constantini (ed. Heikel), iii. 33 ff.; TOBLER et MOLINIER, *Itinera Hierosolymitana*, *S. Eucherii epitome de Locis aliquibus Sanctis* (about 440) (Geneva, 1877), p. 52; Id., op. cit., *Breviarius de Hierosolyma*, p. 57; Id., op. cit., *Antonini martyris perambulatio Locorum Sanctorum* (about 570), p. 101.

[5] WILSON, *Golgotha*, p. 82, note 2.

[6] *Analecta Bollandiana* vol. viii (1889), p. 46, *Vita S. Melaniae iunioris*.

[7] MIGNE, *Patr. Gr.*, vol. 89, *Epistola Antiochi monachi Laurae Sabae abbatis ad Eustachium*, col. 1427 B.

galleries over them. The interior was lined with marbles of various colours, while the exterior was faced with stone so finely wrought and adjusted that it did not yield in beauty to the marble. It terminated towards the west in a hemispherical apse, the interior of which was encircled by twelve columns symbolizing the Apostles, each supporting a silver vase—an arrangement like that of an exedra in the Thermae of Trajan.[1] The ceilings of nave and aisles glistened with gold. The front of the church was turned towards the east, and contained three doors. Before it extended a spacious atrium.

This orientation is a confirmation of my statement that the Basilica Ursiana at Ravenna (370–384) was the first to have the apse placed at the east. Another piece of evidence is the basilica erected by Constantine at Baalbek in the middle of the great court of the temple of Jupiter (138–249), with nave and aisles separated by rectangular piers; where the three semicircular apses (the lateral ones being terminated by little sacristies) are at the west, while in the transformation which the basilica subsequently underwent, the principal apse (semicircular internally but pentagonal externally in the manner of Ravenna) was placed at the east after the Ravennate model. This has been made clear by the excavations recently carried out in the great buildings of Heliopolis, which I have had an opportunity of examining personally.[2]

The external appearance of the basilica, with its gabled roof, the façade with its three doors, and the rotunda, is represented in the important mosaic from the church of Madaba, which gives a map of Egypt and the Holy Places, and is considered to belong to the early years of the sixth century,[3] or, more probably, to the time of Justinian (527–565).[4] The church of Madaba, with its apse semicircular both internally and externally, shows that, at the time when it was built, the Ravennate plan of apses polygonal on the outside had not yet penetrated to the region east of the Jordan. In other parts of Syria, too, long after Christianity had become the official religion with Constantine, churches had apses in the form of round half-towers, as for instance the basilicas of Tafkha (ascribed to the fourth or fifth century) and Sueida (believed to be of the fifth). In the Syrian lands it seems that apses, curvilinear internally and polygonal externally, did not appear before the sixth century. Two of the earliest examples are St. George at Ezra[5] (515–516) and the cathedral of Bosra (511–512).

In the mosaic referred to the artist represented in flattened perspective ('proiezione ribaltata') the essential features of the individual buildings which made up the vast complex of Constantine's sanctuary of the Holy Sepulchre, as they would appear to a spectator standing facing the propylaea. He has omitted the cloistered forecourt of the basilica, the enclosing wall, and Golgotha, which he was unable to include in his view (fig. 394). He shows the propylaea which precede the forecourt, with the great flight of steps; the pedimented façade of the basilica with its three doors; the gabled roof of the basilica; and, last of all, the dome of the Anastasis which is represented in the same cadmium-yellow and orange-yellow tint used for the surface of all the pediments of basilicas figured on the mosaic. The perspective of the main body of the church hides the apse and a portion of the rotunda.

The fate suffered by the buildings connected with the Holy Sepulchre when

[1] PALLADIO, op. cit., pl. viii (see fig. 174 above).

[2] PUCHSTEIN, SCHULZ, KRENCKER, ERSTER, *Jahresbericht über die Ausgrabungen in Baalbek*, in *Jahrbuch des Deutschen Archäologischen Instituts*, vol. xv (1901), pp. 133–60. [BUTLER, op. cit., pp. 72–3.]

[3] PP. CLEOPHAS et LAGRANGE, *La mosaïque géographique de Mâdabâ*, in *Revue Biblique*, vol. vi, pp. 165–230.

[4] [For the map of Madaba see also DALTON, *East Christian Art*, p. 295 with references. (R.)]

[5] [See RIVOIRA, *Moslem Architecture*, figs. 59, 105; *Roman Architecture*, fig. 155.]

Jerusalem in 614 fell into the hands of the Persian king, Chosroes II (591–628) (who was joined by the Jews of Ptolemais and the Galilaean mountains[1]), is well known: they were destroyed by fire. Afterwards, the patriarch Modestus set about rebuilding them (616–626): 'he raised up again the venerable churches of our Saviour Jesus Christ which had been burned; viz. Calvary, and the Resurrection, and the venerable sanctuary of the precious Cross, the mother of churches, &c.'[2]

Some light, though incomplete, is shed on the results achieved, by the evidence of an eye-witness, Arculf. From the description which he dictated to Adamnan,[3] and from the ground plan of the buildings which he has preserved (fig. 395), we learn that between the Anastasis and the Martyrion was interposed the church of Golgotha, having on its right another church of the same form, dedicated to St. Mary; and we gather that the principal church was no longer, as in the time of Constantine, the basilica but the rotunda. Lastly, we learn that the rotunda ('mira rotunditate') was annular, and that its dome was sustained by twelve columns 'mirae magnitudinis'. At the east were two entrances, each with four openings. In the centre of the building stood a circular isolated *tugurium* or chamber containing the actual Sepulchre.

Fig. 394. Portion of mosaic in the church of Madaba (6th century)

Adamnan described it as being 'tota lapidea', from which one would infer that the church was entirely constructed of masonry, and, consequently, that the main walls survived the disaster of 614, and were only restored by Modestus. But this was not the case, for we learn from Eutychius[4] that the dome seen by Arculf was of wood, and that it was restored by Thomas, patriarch of Jerusalem, who imported the materials from Cyprus. And so Constantine's church of the Ascension, also rebuilt by the patriarch Modestus, which was in the form of a rotunda with concentric aisles,[5] had a wooden roof except over the central space, which was open to the sky. Another seventh-century building at Jerusalem with a wooden roof was the octagon known as the Mosque of Omar, erected in the precinct of the ancient Jewish Temple between 684 and 687 by the Caliph Abd-el-Melek.

For though the existing dome is the result of a rebuilding (1022) of the original one destroyed by an earthquake (1016), still it must have been copied from it. It has also been observed before now that there were other ancient buildings in Syria with wooden domes, as the thinness of the supporting drums indicates. Among them was the cathedral of Bosra;[6] and the same is said to have been the case in the church of St. George at Ezra, where the present conical cupola of light concrete construction resting on raccords (the rest of the church being built of dressed stone set without mortar) is clearly of later origin.

[1] RAMPOLLA DEL TINDARO, *Santa Melania Giuniore senatrice Romana* (Rome, 1905), p. 283.

[2] MIGNE, *Patr. Gr.*, vol. 89, *Epistola Antiochi monachi*, p. 1427 B.

[3] TOBLER et MOLINIER, op. cit., *Arculfi relatio de Locis Sanctis, scripta ab Adamnano* (about 670), pp. 146, 149.

[4] MIGNE, *Patr. Gr.*, vol. cxi, *Eutychii patriarchae Alexandrini annales* (10th cent.), p. 1130 C.

[5] [See K. A. C. CRESSWELL in *The Origin of the Plan of the Dome of the Rock* (British School at Jerusalem, 1924). The researches of PP. Vincent and Abel have shown that the church of the Ascension was octagonal with an interior ring of columns, not a rotunda, as previously supposed on the strength of Arculf's diagram. (R.)]

[6] TEXIER and PULLAN, op. cit., p. 136. [DE LASTEYRIE, op. cit., 739.]

A short description of Holy Places in Palestine, thought to be of the seventh century, incorporated in the *History of Agvan* compiled by Moses Kagankavatsi probably at the end of the tenth century,[1] throws additional light to that provided by Arculf on the round church of the Resurrection, and some quite new light on the basilica of the Invention of the Cross or 'Martyrion'. The domed rotunda was one hundred cubits both in diameter and height. It contained two concentric circles of columns, with above them two ranges of twelve columns each. The Martyrion, separated from the Anastasis by a space of at least twenty cubits, also had ranges of columns one above the other, the number of shafts being sixty-five or seventy-five. This limited number of supports, in the case of a basilica with ranges of columns in two stories, suggests the small proportions of the Martyrion as restored by Modestus on a diminished scale; and this explains why Adamnan in his plan gave more space to the rotunda as compared with the basilica.

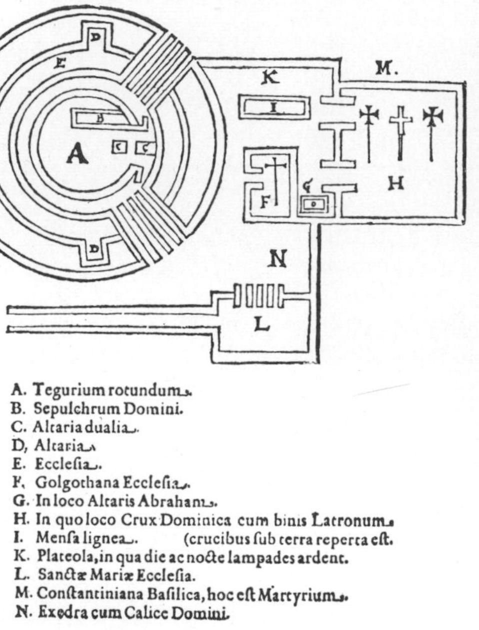

These structures are mentioned about 720 by the Venerable Bede.[2] It is known that in 812 they were sacked by the Arabs from Egypt, and that the patriarch Thomas restored them between 813 and 833 in the days of the Caliph Mamun. It was after his restoration that they were visited by the monk Bernard.[3] We know, too, that they were damaged by a fire in 936. But the most serious disaster happened in 1010. Hakem, the Fatimite Caliph of Egypt (996–1021), commanded the destruction of the rotunda; and the order was so scrupulously carried out by the governor of Ramleh that, as we learn from William of Tyre,[4] Radulphus Glaber,[5] and Ademar,[6] it was levelled with the ground. A new rotunda was erected in 1048 by direction of the Emperor Constantine X Monomachus (1042–1054). This was built 'politis et quadris lapidibus', according to the statement of Radulphus Glaber, and was supported by twelve monolith columns and six piers. It had six doors, and galleries with sixteen columns. The roof was of wood, with a circular opening in the centre. Next to it on the east was an atrium containing various chapels, later put under cover by the Crusaders and connected with the rotunda, thus forming the basilica of the Holy Sepulchre. Other chapels flanked it on the south.[7]

A. Tegurium rotundum.
B. Sepulchrum Domini.
C. Altaria dualia.
D. Altaria.
E. Ecclesia.
F. Golgothana Ecclesia.
G. In loco Altaris Abraham.
H. In quo loco Crux Dominica cum binis Latronum.
I. Mensa lignea.   (crucibus sub terra reperta est.
K. Plateola, in qua die ac nocte lampades ardent.
L. Sanctæ Mariæ Ecclesia.
M. Constantiniana Basilica, hoc est Martyrium.
N. Exedra cum Calice Domini.

Fig. 395. Jerusalem. Plan of the buildings connected with the Holy Sepulchre in the 7th century. (From GRETSER, *Adamanni Scotohiberni de situ Terrae Sanctae* (Ingolstad, 1619), lib. iii, p. 13))

[1] *Palestine Exploration Fund, Quarterly Statement,* October 1896: (NISBET BAIN), *Armenian description of the Holy Places in the seventh century,* pp. 346–9.

[2] TOBLER et MOLINIER, op. cit., *De Locis Sanctis* (about 720), p. 216.

[3] Id., op. cit., *Itinerarium* (about 870), p. 314.

[4] Op. cit.

[5] GLABER, *Historiae sui temporis. De eversione templi Hierosolymorum, &c.* (BOUQUET, *Recueil,* &c., vol. x, p. 34).

[6] *Ex chronico Ademari Cabannensis* (BOUQUET,

Recueil, vol. x, p. 152).

[7] BOURGOGNE et MARTINET, *Recueil de Voyages et de mémoires publié par la Société de Géographie,* Paris. *Relatio de peregrinatione Saewulfi ad Hierosolymam et Terram Sanctam, A.D.I. MCII et MCIII,* vol. iv, 2, pp. 817, 854; DE KHITROWO, op. cit., *Vie et pèlerinage de Daniel, hégoumène russe* (1106–1107), pp. 12, 13; TOBLER et MOLINIER, op. cit., *Qualiter sita est Jerusalem* (before 1096), p. 347; William of Tyre, op. cit.

The date at which the buildings connected with the Holy Sepulchre began to undergo the alterations made by the Crusaders is not precisely known. It is, however, certain that it was later than the years 1102–1103 and 1106–1107, the dates of the pilgrimages to Jerusalem of Saewulf and of the Russian Hegumenus Daniel, respectively. The latter credits the Crusaders only with the construction of the isolated chapel or *tugurium* over the tomb of the Redeemer. And the alterations must have been effected shortly before the decade 1155–1165, for we gather from John of Würzburg[1] that the construction of the new church, and the alteration of the rotunda necessitated by putting the two buildings in direct communication, were a recent event. As a matter of fact the dedication took place in 1143.[2] For the church thus produced by the conjunction of

Fig. 396. Jerusalem. Rotunda of the Holy Sepulchre in 1586. (From ZUALLARDO, *Il devotissimo viaggio di Gerusalemme* (Roma, 1587), p. 189)

the rotunda of Constantine Monomachus (1048) with the new church (twelfth century), the principal entrance was made on the south, approached through a 'mout bel place'[3]— alas, how different nowadays!

In course of time the sanctuary was remodelled, tampered with, partially rebuilt, and for the most part concealed by structures of every description. In the rotunda, of which I give a view taken in 1586 (fig. 396), the three lofty semicircular recesses can only just be made out. The one to the south has been broken through at the bottom, and each has three windows in the half-dome.

A conspicuous piece of evidence about the church, in spite of its injuries, is the façade (fig. 397). It was all built at one time, and of tufa, not limestone like the Constantinian building, remains of which may be seen in the Russian Convent. The hand of time has given this façade of the twelfth century a uniform patina, alike in the constructive and decorative elements, thus indicating that it all belongs to one date. Against it in course of time was erected a bell-tower, 'li clochiers del Sepucre'[4] or

---

[1] TOBLER, *Descriptiones Terrae Sanctae* (Leipzig, 1874), *Johannes Wirziburgensis, Descriptio Terrae Sanctae*, p. 150.

[2] MARITI, *Viaggi per l'isola di Cipro e per la Siria e Palestina* (Florence, 1769–71).

[3] MICHELANT et RAYNAUD, *Itinéraires à Jerusalem et description de la Terre-Sainte* (Geneva, 1882), p. 35; ERNOUL, *L'estat de la cité de Jherusalem* (about 1231).

[4] TOBLER, op. cit., *La citez de Jherusalem* (about 1187), p. 203.

'li clokiers del Sepulcre'[1] or 'li closchierz del Sepulcre',[2] first mentioned by Theodoricus of Würzburg about 1172.[3] By the year 1586 this tower had lost its top (fig. 398).[4]

The façade exhibits four archivolts with fluted voussoirs, recalling the Futuh Gate (1087) at Cairo. The motive is copied on the front of the existing church of St. Anne

Fig. 397. Jerusalem. Façade of the Church of the Holy Sepulchre (12th century)

at Jerusalem (fig. 399), which some would take back to a rather early date (for instance, in the period before the Crusades),[5] though in reality it cannot be older than the taking of Jerusalem by the Crusaders (1099). This is proved by the compound piers, designed, like the corresponding half-piers and external buttresses, under the potent influence of the Lombardic School; and also by the Lombardic doorway in the façade. More

[1] MICHELANT et RAYNAUD, op. cit.; ERNOUL, op. cit., p. 35.

[2] Id., *Le continuateur anonyme de Guillaume de Tyr, La sainte cité de Jherusalem, &c.* (1261), p. 147.

[3] TOBLER, *Theodorici Libellus de Locis Sanctis editus circa A.D. 1172* (St. Gallen, 1865), pp. 27 and 183 n.

[4] ZUALLARDO, *Il devotissimo viaggio di Gerusalemme* (Roma, 1587), p. 186.

[5] MAUSS, *La piscine de Bethesda à Jérusalem.*

evidence is provided by a capital (supposing it to be old) in the transept, carved with the motive of shallow truncated and inverted half-cones, with pointed leaves in the free spaces, which was imported from the West and may be seen in the abbey church of St. George at Boscherville (eleventh and twelfth centuries). And in any case it is not credible that the architect of St. Anne, who came, it seems, from France[1] (it has been suggested that the building was of local execution, but that the plans were brought from Europe), endowed Palestine with a more developed system of construction than existed at home. And in St. Anne (where the arches are pointed) the transept has barrel vaults coming up to the central conical cupola, which rests on spherical pendentives, while the nave and aisles have cross vaulting with visible transverse arches.

Fig. 398. Jerusalem. Façade of the Church of the Holy Sepulchre in 1586.
(From Zuallardo, *Il devotissimo viaggio di Gerusalemme* (Roma, 1587), p. 186)

So that we shall be within the truth if we fix its date (as De Vogüé[2] has already done) in the second half of the twelfth century, and, to be more exact, after Judith, daughter of Baldwin II (1118–1131), had taken the veil there (1130). The building, partly constructed of materials which bear masons' marks belonging to the age of the Crusades, was not long after (1192) turned into a school by the great Saladin, who had recaptured Jerusalem in 1187.

After this short digression we resume our subject. The existing Church of the Holy Sepulchre, so far as one can judge from what is visible, does not contain any decorative fragment from the first foundation. Thus the four capitals with foliage and cauliculi springing from a basket of woven wickerwork, now used in the chapel of St. Helena (fig. 400) and mutilated in order to make them fit, are detached specimens of the epoch of Justinian, analogous to similar ones in the mosque 'al Aqsa',[3] taken from the magnificent basilica of the Virgin completed by Justinian[4] and described by Procopius.[5] Again, the detached Corinthian capital having sharply cut acanthus leaves with the

---

[1] De Luynes, *Voyage d'exploration à la Mer Morte, à Petra, et sur la rive gauche du Jourdain*, vol. i, p. 63.

[2] *Les Églises de la Terre-Sainte*, pp. 242, 243.

[3] [See Rivoira, *Moslem Architecture*, figs. 10, 11.]

[4] Conder, *The City of Jerusalem*, p. 223.

[5] *De aedificiis. Corpus Script. Hist. Byz.* (Bonn, 1838), vol. iii, pp. 183–5.

points turned over and a carved torus (fig. 401), now to be seen on the ground floor of the northern limb of the church, belongs to the same period, as shown by its close relationship to Justinian's Corinthian capitals in the Church of the Virgin just mentioned, and also to the capitals of the same order belonging to the so-called Golden Gate near that church.

The same thing is true of the Byzantine capital formed of a basket of wicker-work, completely undercut, from which spring cauliculi at the sides of a wreath, with leaves below, to be found close to the other one we have just described in the Church of the Holy Sepulchre. This, too, may be compared with the similar ones in the mosque 'al Aqsa' (fig. 402), and is to be ascribed to the sixth century, and in fact to the long reign of Justinian I (527–565), when magnificent constructions made Jerusalem the most splendid city of the East after Constantinople. This basket capital of the Holy Sepulchre must be distinguished from another of the same kind (fig. 403) surmounting a half wall-column at the entrance to the court in front of the church, because, in spite of the similarities between them, they differ in composition, design, and execution. Moreover, the latter is carved in the same sort of stone as the façade, and belongs to the same date.

Fig. 399. Jerusalem. Church of St. Anne (12th century)

In the fifth century at Jerusalem the art of carving would not have been equal to the production of the capitals described above; not to speak of the fact that it was only in that century that the basket capital was created by the School of Salonica. One of the earliest examples at Jerusalem would be a capital which is believed to have belonged to the church of St. Stephen, erected by the Empress Eudoxia, wife of Theodosius the Younger, and dedicated by her in 460,[1] supposing it were undoubtedly proved that the basilica with nave and aisles recently discovered really goes back to the days of that empress.

Moreover, in the fourth century, that is to say in the reign of Constantine the Great, the design and carving of capitals followed the type still to be seen in the Church of the Nativity at Bethlehem (fig. 404), founded by the Empress Helena (327) but erected by Constantine.[2] For the existing basilica, with its nave and double aisles, ending in a choir with three apses (a Latin plan, previously employed in the basilica

[1] P. LAGRANGE, Sainte-Étienne et son sanctuaire à Jérusalem, p. 70.

[2] [For a full description and discussion see The Church of the Nativity at Bethlehem, edited by W. SCHULTZ (Byzantine Research Fund, London, 1910), where Prof. Lethaby also maintains the Constantinian date of the building; PP. VINCENT and ABEL, Bethléem, le Sanctuaire de la Nativité (Paris, 1914). (R.)].

of St. Paulinus at Nola, which must have been built after 394, the year when Paulinus settled in the 'Cemetery' of Nola, for the work was finished by 402), roofed with timber in all parts except the three apses, lighted by large round-headed windows some of which have been blocked up or altered, is the result of a remodelling carried out

Fig. 400. Jerusalem. Church of the Holy Sepulchre. Capital in the chapel of St. Helena (6th century)

Fig. 401. Jerusalem. Church of the Holy Sepulchre. Capital (6th century)

Fig. 402. Jerusalem. Mosque 'al Aqsa' Capital (6th century)

Fig. 403. Jerusalem. Church of the Holy Sepulchre. Capital in the entrance court (12th century)

under Justinian I, and not of a complete rebuilding, which that emperor had indeed in his mind but did not carry out. Hence his anger with his deputy, whom he caused to be beheaded.[1] The result is fortunate for us, as it has preserved the nave colonnades of the original church up to the point where the choir begins.

In them the shafts are formed of a yellowish stone from the local quarries, and were

[1] MIGNE, *Patr. Gr.*, vol. cxi, *Eutychii patriarchae Alexandrini annales* (10th cent.), col. 1072 B.

made, with the bases and capitals, expressly for the church. The bases are Attic; the capitals Corinthian, the body slightly moulded into a bell shape, but without a torus forming part of it. The acanthus leaves have not their tips arched over, but still retain a classical character, while the flower on the abacus is marked with a cross. The execution is so uniform that they seem to have come not merely from one stone-yard but from a single chisel, wielded by a hand which was fairly skilful though somewhat lacking in power.

These colonnades cannot be assigned to the age of Justinian, for, like the nave of the old Vatican basilica (fourth century), they are surmounted by architraves and not by arches. Nor can the capitals. Very different were the capitals of the days of Justinian

Fig. 404. Bethlehem. Nave of the Church of the Nativity (327)

in Palestine, as those of the mosque 'al Aqsa' and of the so-called Golden Gate at Jerusalem (fig. 405) tell us. De Vogüé[1] thought that this structure might belong to the fifth century, or at latest to the sixth; but it must be assigned to the latter, and in fact to the time of Justinian, that is to say to the golden age of Byzantine art. The determining feature is the obvious relationship between its Corinthian capitals and those of the same order and style in the mosque referred to.

It has been suggested,[2] on the strength of the description of the Holy Places referred to before as contained in the *History of Agvan*,[3] that the existing church of the Nativity retains hardly anything of the edifice of Helena and Constantine, and that the latter was vaulted, like the Basilica Nova at Rome (the work of Maxentius and Constantine), and afterwards destroyed by fire during the revolt of the Samaritans in 642. But the stone vaulting mentioned in that description must refer to the choir apses. Besides, it is not even remotely conceivable that a colonnaded basilica could carry the very heavy vaulting of that period; and the same account speaks of ninety marble columns. One has only to think of the complex, ponderous system of supports which

[1] *Le Temple de Jérusalem*, p. 64.
[2] P. Barnabé (of Alsace), *Le prétoire de Pilate et la*
forteresse Antonia, p. 180.
[3] *Palestine Exploration Fund*, loc. cit. (*supra*, p. 14).

the architect of the Basilica Nova was obliged to adopt for carrying his complete roof of masonry, in order to see that my view agrees with the facts. It is also confirmed by the circumstance that the architect of the nearly contemporary Basilica Julia in the Forum at Rome, having employed simple cruciform piers, vaulted his aisles, but did not venture to do so for the nave, and had to be content with a wooden roof. When the builders of the Constantinian age did construct vaulting over colonnades, it was only in the case of circular buildings. And, on the other hand, the Samaritans would never have been able to destroy by fire a structure covered, like the Basilica Nova, with barrel and cross vaults of great thickness, with the roof tiles resting directly on the extrados.

And now we will conclude our story of the Holy Sepulchre with a few brief observations.

The plan of a tomb standing close to a church erected over a place of martyrdom is a Roman idea, followed at Rome by the Byzantines themselves, as is shown by the Imperial Mausoleum, which formerly stood to the left of the old St. Peter's in the Vatican. It is also illustrated by the sepulchral church or mausoleum of St. Helena[1] on the ancient Via Labicana (now Casilina) (fig. 406), erected in a region where, among numerous other sacred memorials, stood the tombs of Saints Peter and Marcellinus, in the cemetery 'ad duas lauros', over which Constantine, after his official recognition of the Church (313), built a basilica in honour of the two martyrs.[2] This structure belongs to the same class as the magnificent example in the Licinian Gardens at Rome (253–258),[3] compared with which, though the masonry of the walls is less finished, and even contains fragments of a dentilated cornice, it shows

Fig. 405. Jerusalem. Golden Gate (6th century)

a notable advance in the principles of construction. Thus the organic structure of the cupola is different from that of the Licinian edifice. There is no longer (as in the latter) a hemispherical vault, with its framework composed of radiating ribs meeting in the crown, resting on a lofty polygonal drum lighted by large windows, and strengthened on the outside by powerful buttresses corresponding to the re-entrant angles inside, and raised somewhat by means of steps above the impost of the cupola in order to be the better able to resist its thrust. Here, on the contrary, we get a vaulted dome, lightened by concentric rings of amphorae. Owing to the relief which this provided,

[1] [See RIVOIRA, *Roman Architecture*, pp. 230 ff.]

[2] ARINGHI, *Roma subterranea novissima*, p. 365; CAETANI-LOVATELLI, *Varia, Una gita a Tor Pignattara*, p. 228; MARUCCHI, *La cripta storica dei santi Pietro e Marcellino* in *Nuovo Bullettino di Archeologia Christiana*, 1898, pp. 137, 193; TOMASSETTI, *Della campagna Romana*, Archivio della R. Società romana di storia patria, 1902, p. 79.

[3] [See RIVOIRA, *Roman Architecture*, pp. 182 ff.]

the dome of the mausoleum of St. Helena was able to be set up, without any buttressing, upon a lofty drum, lightened by niches on its exterior, and pierced by windows. And this fixes its date to a period later than the Licinian Nymphaeum, in other words to the early years of the fourth century, and after the death of Maxentius (312), when Constantine the Great was undisputed master of the Empire.[1] The edifice was the regal monument destined to receive the body of his octogenarian mother; for it is to Rome, as Duchesne has proved,[2] that Eusebius refers in his Life of Constantine when he mentions the burial, seeing that in those days the Emperor had not yet turned his eyes to Byzantium.[3] The works necessary to convert the latter into the seat of government were only begun in 328, and Constantinople was not dedicated till 330.[4]

Fig. 406. Rome. Mausoleum of St. Helena (4th century)

The aisled rotundas of the West were not copied from the Holy Sepulchre at Jerusalem, i.e. the earliest example of the form which the East can show, as is the general idea. Rather they were adapted from the plans of Nymphaeums and tombs at Rome, which was their place of birth, and formed a natural centre for their development, since no other city, or rather country, could ever show so large, or so varied, or so imposing a series of circular buildings, evolved from the germ of the round Etruscan tomb. And to those structures at Rome all others of the kind in the Roman Empire have to give place.

We are acquainted with the form given to sepulchral monuments in Palestine and the other districts of Syria before the time of Constantine. There is, for instance, among many others, the so-called 'Tomb of the Kings' near Jerusalem, believed to be the burial-place of the queen of Adiabene (about the middle of the first century A.D.). It is cut out of the rock, and the front was originally supported by two columns and decorated with festoons of leaves and fruit and with palm branches. There are also

[1] [RIVOIRA, Roman Architecture, pp. 230–37.]
[2] Le liber pontificalis, vol. i, p. 198[90].
[3] BOSIO, Roma sotterranea (Roma, 1650), p. 347.

[4] VAN MILLINGEN, Byzantine Constantinople, pp. 15, 33–4.

the so-called 'Tomb of the Judges' (fig. 407) and the 'Tomb of Absalom' (fig. 408), both regarded by De Vogüé[1] as belonging to the three centuries before the destruction of the city by Titus (70), while others think that they belong to about the first half of the first century A.D.[2] Then there is the tomb of Roman type at Qasr al Nuwayjis (fig. 409) of the second century, and that of Hamrath with square base and stepped pyramidal roof at Sueida, thought to belong to the end of the first century B.C. Next comes the tomb of Aemilius Reginus (195) at Katura, surmounted by pairs of columns. Lastly, there are the tower-tombs, the most remarkable specimens of which are to be seen at Palmyra (fig. 410); and the typical examples at Petra (the most important being the Khasneh Firun or 'Treasury of Pharaoh') belonging to the age of the Empire. Any one who can find earlier examples in this part of Asia, or in Greece or any other Mediter-

Fig. 407. Jerusalem. 'Tomb of the Judges' (1st century A.D.)

ranean country, of structures of the type of the Licinian Nymphaeum, or of the Mausoleum of St. Helena, and of aisled rotundas with solid cupolas resting on isolated supports, like Santa Costanza, will be heartily welcomed.[3] I was never so fortunate.

In the Asiatic provinces, vaulted and domed rotundas with aisles were an importation from Rome, and originally were roofed with timber. This is shown by the celebrated church erected by Constantine in the middle of Antioch, which, according to Eusebius,[4] was octagonal, with galleries round the interior.[5] It is not certain whether these were used as a matroneum, seeing that (as De Vogüé also noticed[6]) it may be gathered from a homily of John Chrysostom, presbyter of Antioch, and afterwards patriarch of

---

[1] *Le Temple de Jérusalem*, p. 43.

[2] SPIERS, ANDERSON, and ASHBY, *The Architecture of Ancient Rome*, p. 129.

[3] [K. A. C. CRESSWELL in *The Origin of the Plan of the Dome of the Rock* (British School at Jerusalem, 1924), pp. 19 ff., remarks that as there is no evidence for the existence of a rotunda in Syria or Palestine earlier than Constantine's church of the Holy Sepulchre, with the solitary exception of the Marneion at Gaza (see G. F. HILL, *Life of Porphyry, Bishop of Gaza*, p. 85), Rivoira's thesis of its Roman origin is undoubtedly correct in so far as the evolution of the annular rotunda, with columns or piers, crowned by a dome, is concerned. But it does not go far enough,

as it ignores the further evolution of the type. He goes on to show that the links in the chain of development which culminated in the Dome of the Rock were forged in Syria. The plan of the Dome of the Rock is based on that of the cathedral of Bosra, where Butler showed that there was an inner octagon with intermediate columns between the piers. The plan of the Dome of the Rock may therefore be regarded as Syrian, although the first steps in the evolution of annular rotundas took place in Rome. (R.)]

[4] *Vita Constantini* (ed. Heikel), iii. 59.

[5] See *Moslem Architecture*, pp. 60, 61.

[6] *Syrie centrale*, p. 15.

Constantinople (398–404), that in the churches of the old seat of the patriarchate of the Eastern Church the men were placed on one side of the building and the women on the other, in enclosures formed by barriers of wood or more permanent material.[1] This church at Antioch, built probably after the death of the Empress Helena, and even after the dedication of Constantinople (330), as it is mentioned by Eusebius after those events, must have been entirely ceiled with wood, and devoid of vaulting and a central cupola. As a matter of fact, Chrysostom, preaching in the principal church at Antioch, rebukes his hearers for finding his sermons too long, seeing that they are comfortably seated with a magnificent ceiling over their heads, whereas they were content to stand for a whole day in the circus, exposed to sun and rain, without ever complaining of the length of the performance.

Fig. 408. Jerusalem. 'Tomb of Absalom'
(1st century A.D.)

Among the examples which still exist, the mausoleum at Rome known as Santa Costanza,[2] erected between 324 and 326[3] (fig. 411), is to be looked upon as the prototype of the vaulted aisled rotunda. This structure, which, as Duchesne says,[4] both research and the best accredited opinions refer without a shadow of doubt to the time of the Constantinian dynasty, is separated by only a short interval from the sepulchre of St. Helena. The cupola of the latter and its circular drum (both rising in stepped outline from a ground floor of similar plan, with exedras) have only to be set on an open arcade, and you have the aisled rotunda of Santa Costanza.

And any one who has the wish and the ability to investigate the difficult subject of Roman architectonic science in what is regarded as the age of decadence, but really marks the culminating point of that science, as though the architecture of Pagan Rome, before sinking into the long slumber from which it was to be roused at a later time by the efforts of the Popes and the surrounding artistic influences, concentrated itself in one last ray of dazzling light—any one, I say, who makes that investigation will readily perceive how, in the course of the strivings of the 'Urban' builders after the solution of the most difficult problems of equilibrium, the architect of the Basilica Nova had already indicated to his successor of Santa Costanza the conception of raising a great central dome on isolated supports by the aid of barrel vaults.

The rotunda of Santa Costanza—another instance of a circular mausoleum close to a basilica erected by Constantine, in this case over the tomb of St. Agnes—in which the masonry in the original parts of the facing, formed of bricks of every quality and size, with thick joints, resembles that of St. Helena, must have been built before the works at Constantinople were begun. To take part in those works, destined to fit Byzantium for becoming the seat of government, craftsmen were invited who would

[1] MIGNE, *Patr. Graeca*, vol. 58, *Homiliae in Matthaeum*, p. 712.

[2] [For a full description see RIVOIRA, *Roman Archi-tecture*, pp. 238 ff.]

[3] *Supra*, vol. i, p. 9.

[4] *Le liber pontificalis*, vol. i, p. 196[80].

represent the best from every part of the Empire. In Lydus[1] we read of a portico said to have been built by Campanians and marble-workers from Naples and Puteoli. And it must have been finished before the Roman School, already weakened when Maximian made Milan his capital, was, so to speak, deprived of its vitality by the drain caused by the works of 'New Rome', and before the progress in the science of construction and equilibrium, which had reached its climax in the days of Diocletian (284–305), Maximian (286–310), and Maxentius (306–312), had received its death-blow. This fatal event readily explains the sudden arrest of the splendid development which was leading to ever newer and bolder systems of vaulting—systems now recognized as worthy of the rulers of the world[2]—and the appearance of structures, of great dimensions indeed, but made up of old materials, and only roofed with timber. Such were the first great Christian basilicas, or occasionally a public market like that on the Celian at Rome (of the second half of the fourth century), later converted into the church of Santo Stefano Rotondo (468–483). (Cf. *supra*, i. 12.)

Fig. 409. Tomb at Qasr al Nuwayjis (2nd century). (From a photograph provided by the 'Palestine Exploration Fund')

Any one who cares to give even a passing glance at the illustrations of Montano[3] or Bramantino,[4] or at Pauvinio's copies from Ligorio's drawings in the Vatican,[5] will find specimens of every kind of Roman sepulchral annular rotundas. Some have a central cupola buttressed by barrel vaults, with the basement of the outer wall broken by a series of curved or rectangular recesses; while the inner concentric circle presents in some cases twelve or sixteen columns, either single or in pairs, on a common plinth, in others eight cruciform piers, in a third kind twelve square piers with half-columns. And if he wishes, he may at the same time verify, especially in Palladio[6] and Serlio,[7] the fact that the buildings of ancient Rome offer in their amazing variety (due to a large extent to the use of concrete) every one of the plans which we are told must have come from the

Fig. 410. Palmyra. Tomb

[1] *De Magistratibus. Corp. Script. Hist. Byz.* (Bonn, 1837), p. 266.
[2] BLOMFIELD, *The Mistress Art*, pp. 241 ff.
[3] Op. cit., lib. iii, *passim*.
[4] Op. cit., *passim*.
[5] Vatican Library, *Cod. Lat.* 3439.
[6] Op. cit., *passim*.   [7] Op. cit., lib. iii, *passim*.

East, but which, on the contrary, the East borrowed from the West. For if the reverse had been the case, the East ought to have been able to show all that variety of plan in examples of earlier date than those of the Rome of the Empire; and this is certainly not the case.

Fig. 411. Rome. Santa Costanza (4th century)

Before leaving this subject of the Holy Sepulchre, I must draw attention to two sketches of ancient Roman circular buildings which I have noticed in the Uffizi, and have had photographed for the first time (figs. 413, 414). One of them is very interesting, not only because the internal facing is entirely in brick, but also on account of the form of the piers of the arcade which carries the cupola, and of the construction of the cupola itself. The latter shows on its intrados bands which intersect and form lozenge-shaped spaces filled in with horizontal brick courses.

And now to resume our subject. More than one feature of the church of Saint Bénigne is clearly derived from preceding buildings.

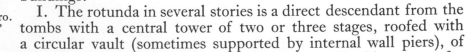

Fig. 412. Coin of Nero. 'Macellum Augusti'

I. The rotunda in several stories is a direct descendant from the tombs with a central tower of two or three stages, roofed with a circular vault (sometimes supported by internal wall piers), of which Rome affords so many examples. Any one who wants to verify this may go for examples to Montano[1] and Bramantino.[2]

II. The termination of the basilica, with its lateral niches and the rotunda behind, recalls the plan of the Pantheon at Rome (120–124), which must have been before the mind of Abbot William when making his design, seeing that the rotunda was dedicated to the Virgin (the basilica had been previously dedicated to St. Benignus) precisely on the anniversary day of the consecration of Hadrian's famous structure to 'Sancta Maria ad Martyres', on its conversion into a church by Pope Boniface IV (608–615).

[1] Op. cit., lib. iii, plates 25, 32, 35, 37, 40, 41, 44.   [2] Op. cit., plates 23, 24, 36, 40, 65.

Fig. 413. Sketch by Salvestro Peruzzi (Uffizi, no. 683), probably from the coin
of Nero representing the Macellum Magnum, here reproduced (fig. 412)

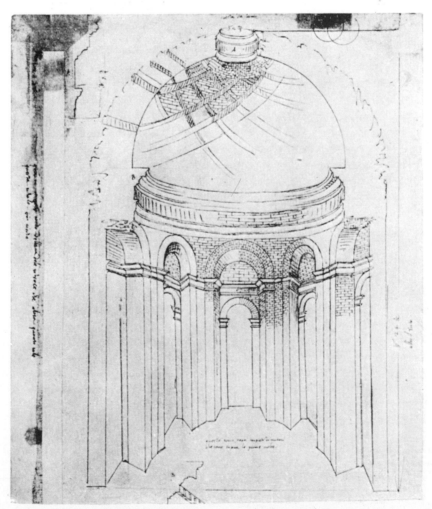

Fig. 414. Sketch of circular Roman building (Uffizi, no. 1330 *v.*)

III. The arrangement of towers incorporated with the façade had been a feature of the Cluniac system from the time when Abbot Majolus introduced it in Saint Pierre le Vieux (982). The two round staircase towers flanking the rotunda, and its encircling aisles and gallery, are suggested by San Vitale at Ravenna (526–547).

IV. The idea of a tower raised over the crossing (applied shortly before in Saint Pierre le Vieux at Cluny) is derived from structures such as the mausoleum of Galla Placidia at Ravenna (about 440), or, more probably, from the ancient church of Santa Croce (about 449) in the same place. In France it was used from very early times, its presence there in the sixth century being disclosed by passages in Gregory of Tours and Venantius Fortunatus.

I ought here to put on record the fact that the oldest example that can be produced of a church with a lantern tower rising over the chancel, and, moreover, with a solid roof, is that of San Salvatore at Spoleto. It will be convenient to give a short account of it at this point.

THE BASILICA OF SAN SALVATORE OR DEL CROCIFISSO, IN THE CAMPOSANTO AT SPOLETO, had been dedicated to the Saviour by 815, but was known as San Concordio in 1158.[1] It is a basilica with nave and aisles, which were originally more lofty than at present, the nave having been supported at first by columns carrying an architrave, after the fashion still to be seen in the presbytery (fig. 415). It was also provided with low galleries, like Santa Maria in Cosmedin at Rome after Hadrian I's (772–795) rebuilding, as may be inferred from the remains of arches in the north wall of the nave. The apse, raised above the presbytery, is flanked by two square sacristies, each provided with a small apse, which is a later addition.[2] Above the presbytery rises a tower (fig. 416) strengthened by buttresses at the corners. The transition from the square to the octagon is managed by means of four clumsy triangular raccords, almost like sloping pieces of wall. Everything suggests that they were made to carry a spherical dome, for which the present octagonal cupola has been substituted. The façade is finished off by a pediment and two half-pediments. Its upper part is decorated with four pilasters, reaching nearly to the cornice. The capital of one of them has been found and is now kept in the church.

There has been great variety of opinion about the date and origin of this very ancient church. Thus, for instance, Hübsch[3] thinks it belongs to the beginning of the Constantinian age, and that it was a Christian church from its inception, though the columns were taken from some Pagan building. But he is surprised to find the square bay between the apse and the triumphal arch, with a cupola rising above it. De Rossi,[4] on the other hand, regards it as the result of the conversion of a Pagan temple into a church, preserving the part which forms the sanctuary of the Christian building, with the addition of the nave and aisles and their façade. This transformation would have taken place in the time of Theodosius I (378–395) and his sons.

Grisar's[5] idea is this. Originally a Pagan building adapted to Christian uses, it was given its present form in the twelfth century. It contains no traces of work belonging to the Constantinian, Theodosian, or Gothic periods. The cupola is neither Pagan nor Early Christian. The only possible remains of the original Pagan structure which

[1] SANSI, *Degli edifici e dei frammenti storici delle antiche età di Spoleto* (Foligno, 1869), p. 226.

[2] [TOESCA, op. cit., pp. 143 n., 34, also believes the two minor apses of San Salvatore at Spoleto to be later.]

[3] Op. cit., p. 4.

[4] *Bull. di arch. cristiana*, 1871, pp. 138, 139, *Spicilegio d'archeologia cristiana nell'Umbria, Della basilica del Salvatore presso Spoleto.*

[5] *Nuovo bull. di arch. cristiana*, 1895, p. 43. *Il tempio del Clitunno e la chiesa spoletina di San Salvatore.*

occupied the site are the plain jambs of the main door in the façade; and these were either set there in the twelfth century, or else kept in their original position.

In my view, this extremely important building is the work of one period, as is shown by the original masonry, not excluding the façade, which is intimately connected with the nave, and forms an integral part of the basilica. It also possessed a central tower with a solid roof, a fact revealed by the masonry, and also by the pains taken by the architect to ensure its stability.

Fig. 415. Spoleto. Church of San Salvatore or the Crocifisso. Chancel (4th century)

The period of erection must be rather early, in view not only of the two sacristies flanking the apse, but also of the architraves which carry the nave walls. Additional reasons are, the rudimentary form of the pendentives by means of which the square of the tower passes into an octagon, and the large round-headed unsplayed windows. The period is, perhaps, that subsequent to the age of Constantine. I say this, not because it was only then that Pagan buildings began to be robbed of materials to build churches, for that practice had begun as soon as Constantine had conquered Maxentius, as we see from, among other instances, Santa Costanza outside the walls of Rome. My reason rather is the character of the carvings executed expressly for the façade. They certainly do not exhibit the power of the chisels of the time of Constantine, but, on the other hand, there is not as yet the poverty, hardness, want of clearness both in design and execution, which characterize Italian work of the fifth century. Nor do they exhibit the typical features (and this applies equally to the capitals in the three windows of the façade) of sixth-century carving. It is enough to compare the way in which the bead and reel mouldings and the ovolos are treated in either case.

The decoration of the doorway in the front of the church inspired in after times, among others, Melioranzio, the artist of the well-known central entrance to the cathedral of Spoleto (twelfth century), who, though he may have been superior in force to the carver who worked at San Salvatore, was inferior to him in delicacy of execution.

Fig. 416. Spoleto. Church of San Salvatore or the Crocifisso (4th century)

The adoption in this singular building of the Ravennate plan of an apse at the eastern end, of which the Basilica Ursiana at Ravenna (370–384) is the prototype,[1] was made necessary by the nature of the site.

To return to Saint Bénigne:

V. The arcaded choir appears to be derived from the very early open apse of San Sebastiano outside the walls of Rome (366–384), which is the prototype of this arrangement. Or it may have been suggested by the apse with three arches opening into an ambulatory, in the basilica of Severus at Naples (367, and about 387). Other open apses that may have formed the model are those of the basilica of St. Paulinus at Cimitile near Nola (394–402); the basilicas of Santa Maria Maggiore (fourth or fifth century) and SS. Cosma e Damiano (526–530) at Rome; the Basilica Vincentiana, now San Giovanni Maggiore, at Naples (554–577); Santo Stefano at Verona (tenth century); and, lastly, the cathedral of Ivrea (973–1001 or 1002).

VI. The introduction of galleries in the basilica merely indicates the adoption of an arrangement which had become the fashion in Italy at the time, as applied in a building of almost the same date as Saint Bénigne, and certainly familiar to William of Volpiano —I mean the cathedral of Ivrea. It was an arrangement which did not originate then, any more than it originated in the days when San Salvatore at Spoleto (fourth century) and the suburban basilicas of Sant' Agnese and the SS. Quattro Coronati erected by Honorius I (625–638), or San Lorenzo by Pelagius II (579–590), were provided with galleries.[2] Nor did it originate under Byzantine influence, as is commonly supposed.

It is indeed inconceivable that the Italian builders should have felt the need of such influence, when their forefathers had, as long ago as the year 179 B.C., provided the Basilica Fulvia Aemilia with a gallery, as we are informed by the reverse of a coin

[1] See *Roman Architecture*, p. 263.   [2] See p. 147 *infra*.

published by Babelon[1] and Cohen,[2] also reproduced by Hülsen.[3] Or, again, when they had before their eyes examples of civil basilicas, even divided by piers into nave and aisles, and with a gallery above the vaulting of the latter, as was the case with the Basilica Julia in the Roman Forum, which, even before its rebuilding by Augustus (A.D. 12), possessed a gallery occupied, on the occasion of important trials, by the two sexes separately.[4] At a later date, too, after its reconstruction by Diocletian (284–305) and restoration by the City Prefect Probianus in 416, it still exhibited its gallery carried by the cruciform piers and the vaulting.

The fact about galleried basilicas is this. When the Easterns began to erect Christian basilicas, and introduced women's galleries into them, as in the churches at Tafkha (fourth and fifth centuries) and Kanawat (fourth century), they derived the suggestion from the civil galleried basilica which had been developed (e.g. the second- or third-century example at Chaqqa) under the influence of Pagan Rome, which was its creator.

The Chronicle of the Abbey tells us who was the architect and director in chief of the works of Saint Bénigne, so far at least as his many and various duties and long absences allowed: 'Et reverendus Abbas, magistros conducendo, et ipsum opus dictando . . .'[5] It also informs us that the prior Arnulf, from the diocese of Toul, took part in the work of supervision. Many, indeed, from an incorrect interpretation of another passage, would give this supervision, but restricted to matters of decoration, to the monk Unald, of whom they make an accomplished carver. But the Chronicle, though mentioning the assistance which he gave to Abbot William ('ad omnia quippe quae sibi erant necessaria, praedicti fratris iuvabatur solertia'), states that he was entrusted with the care of the church, and performed his duties with such zeal that almost all the ritual ornaments were gathered together by his efforts: in other words he was the Sacrist or Apocrisarius of the church: 'Denique iniunxit illi curam huius sacri periboli, quam tanta prosecutus est cura, ut paene totum quicquid fuit ornamentorum in hac basilica, eius studio sit aggregatum.'

As to the workmen, there are different opinions. If we are to believe Cordero,[6] they were Italians. His opinion is based on the Chronicle. But although it describes a remarkable emigration of Italians to Burgundy about the epoch of 1000 ('Coeperunt denique ex sua patria, hoc est Italia, multi ad eum convenire; aliqui litteris bene eruditi, alii diversorum operum magisterio docti, alii agriculturae scientia praediti, quorum ars et ingenium huic loco profuit plurimum'), it makes it equally clear what was the result, namely, to increase the number of monks under the rule of William ('Crescebat ergo quotidie multitudo monachorum sub eius magisterio degentium'). But there is no suggestion of Cordero's statement that William laid the foundations of the new church of the monastery of St. Benignus 'with the aid of a band of Italian craftsmen'.

On the other hand, our limited knowledge of the constructive, static, and decorative elements of the original building does not give much help in answering the question. However, I feel that we shall not go far wrong if we ascribe the erection of the church

---

[1] *Description historique et chronologique des monnaies de la République Romaine*, vol. i, p. 129, no. 25.

[2] *Description générale des monnaies de la République Romaine*, plate i.

[3] [*The Roman Forum* (Rome, 1909), p. 128, fig. 62, and still better in RIVOIRA, *Moslem Architecture*, p. 10, fig. 6. The date of this coin is, however, about 65 B.C., and the reference is probably to a restoration of 78 B.C. (PLATNER and ASHBY, *Topographical Dictionary*, p. 72). There is, however, no reason why the gallery should not date from the original construction. Indeed, if precedents for galleries were required, one could go back to the temple of Neptune at Paestum. (A.)]

[4] LANCIANI, *The Ruins and Excavations of Ancient Rome*, pp. 273, 275.

[5] D'ACHERY, *Spicilegium*, vol. ii, p. 383, *Chronica S. Benigni Divionensis*.

[6] Op. cit., pp. 159–60.

to Italian master builders, associated with Burgundian masons and workmen. Burgundy cannot have been entirely without such, for the tradition of the art of building had never been interrupted there. Without going back to still earlier times, as long ago as the partition (768) of the kingdom of Pippin III (752–768) between his sons Charles (768–814) and Carloman (768–771), opportunities of one sort or another had not been wanting to the craftsmen of those countries for practising the art of building, either in the form of the erection of new ecclesiastical edifices, or of the renewal and restoration of old ones. And this, notwithstanding the frequent family and civil wars which followed the division of the Empire made at Aachen in 817 by Louis the Pious (814–840), and culminated in the period between the death of Lothair (840–855) and the deposition and death of Charles the Fat (887). That partition marked in France (and equally so in Germany) the extinction of the family of Charles the Great. For Charles the Simple was held to be the bastard son of Louis the Stammerer (877–879), and the last sovereign of this illegitimate line was Louis the Fainéant (986–987).

Nor was building prevented by the raids of the Saracens or, what were more serious, those of the Danes or Normans who, after the battle of Fontenay (841) had opened the way for the destruction of the Frankish Empire, and the treaty of Verdun (843) had brought it about, made themselves master of most of the French rivers, and spread terror, desolation, and death in every direction.

Further, the builders of Burgundy had not been without opportunities of going to Italy for training (if they felt the need of it) in the art of construction, in the days of Louis III King of Provence (887–928), of Rudolf II King of Transjuran Burgundy (911–937), of Hugo Duke of Provence (911–947) and his son Lothair (946–950), who were elected Kings of Italy respectively in the years 900, 922, 926, and 946. And so, the character of the barrel vaulting in the crypt of the rotunda of Saint Bénigne (rebuilt, as we saw, on the original lines) suggests the school of builders who constructed the similar vaulting in the staircase of the campanile of San Benigno at Fruttuaria (1003–1006). The arched corbel courses divided into groups, by lesenas, which decorated the towers of the rotunda, point to the gilds of Upper Italy who were the first to apply (in the tower of San Satiro at Milan, of 876) this form of architectural decoration to towers, and had used it with good effect, not long before, on the towers of the cathedral of Ivrea. I have searched in vain through France for a tower of certain date with this decorative treatment, older than the rebuilding of Saint Bénigne.

The Pre-Lombardic cubical capitals are clearly the work of the school whence came the chisels which wrought the nearly contemporary original capitals in the crypt and ambulatory of the cathedral of Ivrea (973–1001 or 1002), and the one of the same date in the crypt of the cathedral of Aosta (eleventh century).

Then there are the Pre-Lombardic figure capitals in the Lombardic style, the earliest specimens of certain date to be found north of the Alps. In those countries, from Merovingian times onwards, the only previous example I can point to is a capital in the crypt of Saint Pierre de la Couture at Le Mans (997),[1] with water leaves, those at the angles being of crocket form, and on each face a human head, infantile in execution and design, taking the place of the flower. But these capitals, with their representation of a man supporting the abacus, reveal a chisel from Cisalpine Gaul. This motive was dear to the Lombard gilds, and was borrowed by them from the Romans, who used to represent living figures supporting with head or hand the abacus of a capital; or

[1] [The date 997 is suggested by the fact that Sigenfrid, bishop of Le Mans, who died about 996–997, was buried in the church. But this is not conclusive evidence for architectural purposes. (H. T.)]

they may have taken it from the Etruscans, who sometimes in their designs of squares in carving figured a man supporting the frame above him with his hands, as shown in fig. 152, and again on a sculptured stone of the archaic Etruscan period in the Archaeological Museum at Florence, in which one of the figures is a telamon holding up the interlaced top of a square compartment.

All these details prove that Piedmontese craftsmen trained in the Lombardic School took part in the works of Saint Bénigne at Dijon, or possibly some Lombard gild, but not one of the best, considering the exceptional poverty and rudeness of the capitals in the rotunda compared with the markedly superior art of capitals produced by those gilds about the same time, e.g. those in the crypt of the parish church of San Vincenzo at Galliano (1007), and others in the church of San Babila at Milan (eleventh century).

But, granting this, we cannot believe that Burgundian builders were not given some share in the work, either restricted to duties of secondary importance, or even entrusted with those of a higher order under the direction of experienced master builders from the Italian side of the Alps. It is well known that the erection of Saint Bénigne was aided by the moral and material support of the Court of Burgundy, of Bishop Bruno who was related to the reigning family, and of Majolus the powerful abbot of Cluny. It is therefore quite reasonable to infer that local craftsmen were invited to take part in the work, and the best, inasmuch as the subject was a church regarded in those days, as Radulphus Glaber says,[1] as the most magnificent in France, and demanding a degree of knowledge of the principles of construction which was for that age remarkable. Still, the local builders could not have possessed an experience equal to that of the craftsmen who came from the south of the Alps; otherwise there would have been no need to summon the latter to France.

The employment of Burgundian workmen was also made desirable by the financial difficulties with which from time to time Abbot William had to contend in the course of his operations—difficulties which were certainly not of a character to encourage him to rely exclusively on the more expensive services of builders of his own nationality. The presence of skilled Italian workmen tells its tale as to the real capacity of the Burgundian builders, and further informs us that, as they were not capable of venturing upon operations which demanded a considerable knowledge of the principles of construction, the religious buildings erected in their own country in the days before they were reached by Italian artistic influence must have been of a modest character so far as those principles were concerned.

In addition to builders, Burgundy must have contained carvers. Then there arises this dilemma. Either the carving of the original capitals in William's crypt was by Italian hands, and, as we said, certainly not hands of great experience; and in that case, barbarous as it is, it was beyond the powers of the local chisels, for otherwise they could have been entrusted with the work; or else it is the product of French hands (not, of course, of the monk Unald, as we showed just now), and then these capitals represent the best that French artists could do at the beginning of the epoch of about 1000, and give us a standard of their ability in the treatment of the human figure.

At the time of the erection of Saint Bénigne, and indeed throughout the first quarter of the eleventh century, the carvers both of Burgundy and of France generally were at a very low level in the treatment of the figure in sculpture—the capital in Saint Pierre de la Couture at Le Mans (997) tells us how low. It is only by unduly moving back the dates of buildings that so many writers have been able to prove the contrary. Thus the imposing two-storied porch of the monastic church of Saint Benoît sur Loire is

---

[1] *Supra*, p. 5, n. 1.

dated by Gailhabaud[1] and others in the two years following the fire of 1026 under Abbot Gauzlinus, Archbishop of Bourges (1014–1020–1030), who began the erection of a tower of squared stone which he was unable to finish.[2] But the capitals carved with figures of realistic or fanciful character, and other figure sculpture on the exterior (very different both in design and execution from, I will not say the very unfavourable specimens in Saint Bénigne, but from those in the monastic church of Cerisy la Forêt [1030–1066], which show some improvement), point to a much more advanced period, certainly decidedly later than the first half of the eleventh century. The fact is that, so far as the church is concerned, the work of Gauzlinus was confined to mere restoration, and the rebuilding had to be undertaken by Abbot William, who was cut off before he saw its completion: 'Ecclesiam multis incendiis devastatam et senio praegravatam novo iacto aedificare coepit fundamento.' The new structure was finished in 1108 under Abbot Simon, and King Philip I (1060–1108) was present at the dedication,[3] and was buried in the church in the same year.

There are writers who are surprised that Saint Bénigne, being so conspicuous as it was, did not serve as a model for many other churches. But this is easy to explain when we remember that the form of the building, besides being too complicated, was not that on which the Latin Church had set its seal. It was out of touch with the artistic traditions of the Western peoples, nor was it the best fitted for the requirements of Western ritual. And so it came about that even its own author did not repeat it.

Then, there are others who would see in it the first or one of the first specimens of Lombardo-Norman architecture in France. But this is not in accordance with the facts. The result, as it was, of the Roman, Romano-Ravennate, Byzantino-Ravennate, and Pre-Lombardic monuments seen by its architect in the course of his long journeyings in Italy, the church at Dijon, to judge by what we know of it, did not present one of the original and distinctive characteristics of the Lombardo-Norman style, which we shall specify by degrees in the course of our work.

But it had the merit of giving its designer the opportunity of putting into practice on a large scale, and with a difficult problem to solve, his ideas of construction, and the monks who were his assistants experience in directing the works of a great building. Thirdly, it gave the local workmen the advantage of taking part in the erection of an edifice of exceptional importance for that time and place, and of acquiring familiarity with the very difficult art of vault construction, complex forms of which were here presented.

From its underground part originated one characteristic feature of the Lombardo-Norman basilica; I mean the chapels projecting from the transept. It appears in the Norman and English churches erected from the plans of William of Volpiano, or if not from his plans, certainly from those of his disciples and under his advice. In other cases the plans came from his pupils, or from Lanfranc of Pavia.

Here, too, was seen for the first time in France the Pre-Lombardic cubical figure capital. Previously, and as far back as the time of Pippin III (752–768), the Pre-Lombardic type had been seen, and even in a decorated form, but not with figures. Instances are to be found in the crypt of the abbey church of Flavigny (755–768), the churches of Germigny des Prés (801–806) and Saint Pierre at Jumièges (940), and the chapel of Sainte Blandine in Saint Martin d'Ainay at Lyons (about 966).

---

[1] L'architecture du Ve au XVIIe siècle, vol. i, Paris, 1858.

[2] Ex libello Hugonis Floriacensis. De Modernis Francorum Regibus (BOUQUET, Recueil, vol. xii, p. 794).

[3] Id., Ex chronico S. Petri vivi Senonensis (BOUQUET, Recueil, vol. xii, p. 282. [For illustrations of the capitals see Congrès Arch., Orléans (1930), 569 ff., where M. Aubert also assigns the tower to Abbot William's rebuilding (1067–80). (R.)]

Such facts, combined with other pieces of evidence, put into our hands the main clues to the history of the buildings erected in Burgundy and the neighbouring provinces before the epoch of the year 1000. Their rarity is due, not so much to Saracen, Norman, or Hungarian ravages, as to the passion for innovation in the eleventh century, referred to by Radulphus Glaber,[1] which spread over the whole of France, and destroyed so many buildings in order to reconstruct them in a form more consonant with the new fashions. It is true there are writers who will not admit their almost universal disappearance. Thus, for instance, Revoil,[2] led astray by the erroneous idea that the Lombardic style, which he regards as the source of the Carolingian, had reached maturity centuries before it was born, has dated in the centuries from the eighth to the tenth a whole batch of religious structures in southern France. But what must we think of attributions such as the following?

The chapel of Saint Gabriel near Tarascon is regarded as belonging to the first years of the ninth century, and identified with one mentioned about 858 in a charter of Charles the Bald and his first wife Hirmentrudis. And this in the face of its pointed barrel vaulting, and the rose window enclosed within a pointed arch in its front. Yet the pointed arch did not appear in European churches before the second half of the eleventh century. And so, not only in the first half of that century, and in the same district as Saint Gabriel, do we find the chapel of the Holy Cross at Montmajour, near Arles (1018), still presenting only arches which are round and not pointed like the transverse ones in the nave and the one in the gable front of Saint Gabriel, but as late as 1063 the chapel of Saint Trophime near Arles was built with arches and vaulting of semicircular form. Rose windows, again, were not invented till the next century, and that is the date indicated by the carving in the chapel.

The abbey church of Saint Guilhem du Désert (originally the church of Gellone) is still believed to be the one founded by William, Duke of Aquitaine, which must have been finished in 806.[3] Later it was restored or altered under Louis the Pious by Juliofredus, its first abbot.[4] But a glance at the apse (fig. 417) with its range of deep arched niches, decorated in front with shafts and enclosing arches springing from heads, or at its Lombardic portal, and the ribbed vaulting of the porch, is sufficient to show that they are not earlier than the twelfth century. And as the side walls of the nave (fig. 418) have facing of different and less regular masonry than that at the end of the building, and, moreover, as even the plan of the church suggests that there has been some alteration, one may infer that the side walls are older than the twelfth century. But their date cannot be that of the original foundation, for the church of Duke William was a mere oratory paved with precious marbles, which formed a beginning for his monastic foundation, and was hastily finished.[5] It was no basilica with nave and aisles over 42 feet wide. To settle the two periods of construction we have the assistance of two dates connected with important facts. The first is the year 1076, when the altar of St. William was solemnly dedicated in the presence of the Papal Legate Amatus, and the consecration of the church followed.[5] With this date we may connect the rebuilding of the church, which took place after the confirmation of the privileges (1066) and the immunity (1068) granted to the

[1] GLABER, *Historiarium sui temporis, De innovatione ecclesiarum in toto orbe* (BOUQUET, *Recueil*, vol. x, p. 29 f.).

[2] *Architecture romane du midi de la France*, Paris, 1867, *passim*.

[3] *Ermoldi Nigelli Exulis Carminis, De rebus gestis Ludovici Pii* (BOUQUET, *Recueil*, vol. vi, p. 15, note e).

[4] Id., *Vita Hludowici Pii imperatoris* (BOUQUET, *Recueil*, vol. vi, p. 95 and note); *Diplomata Ludovici Pii* (BOUQUET, *Recueil*, vol. vi, p. 454, note b).

[5] MABILLON, *Acta Sanct. Ord. S. Benedicti, Vita S. Willelmi ducis ac monachi Gellonensis in Gallia*, vol. v, pp. 72, 84.

monastery.[1] The other date is 1138, when the second translation of the relics of the saint took place.

Fig. 417. Saint Guilhem du Désert. Apse of church (12th century)

The corbel courses grouped by lesenas on the side walls of the church suit well a period not far removed from the first date (1076). The ecclesiastical buildings erected north of the Alps in the days of Charles the Great had no external decoration of that kind, as we may see from the abbey church of Saint Riquier or Centula (793–798) according to a view of it preserved for us by Mabillon,[1] from the Palatine Chapel at Aachen (796–804), and from Theodulf's church of Germigny des Prés (801–806). The earliest certain example of the treatment in France is presented by the two stair-case towers of Saint Bénigne at Dijon, and there only by virtue of Lombardic influence. And it was not till the twelfth century that any very extensive use was made of it,

as on the magnificent bell-tower of Saint Théodorit at Uzès, and that of Saint Trophime at Arles.

Nor shall we offend against logic or probability if we assign the alterations, for instance, those in the apse and the porch, to the years immediately pre-ceding the second date, 1138. The decorative scheme of a range of deep arched niches, applied to the apses of churches, rotundas, and baptisteries, created in the case of Sant' Ambrogio at Milan between 789 and 824, con-tinued, and that too in the land of its birth, to lack the adjunct of shafts up to the time of its transformation into open galleries. In the centre of the world that created them, there are only rectangular piers for the ranges of niches in the basilica and baptistery of Agliate (824–860); the basilicas of San Vincenzo in Prato (835–859), San Calimero (ninth or tenth century), Sant' Eustorgio (tenth century), San Celso (996), and San Babila (eleventh century) at Milan; the Rotonda at Brescia (eleventh or twelfth century); the baptisteries of Biella (tenth cen-tury) and Novara (tenth century). For

Fig. 418. Saint Guilhem du Désert. Side of the church (11th century)

this reason it must have been long after the erection of San Babila at Milan and of the Rotonda at Brescia, and only when the Lombard gilds had transformed their ranges of arched niches into open galleries with small shafts, exhibited for the first time in San Giacomo at Como (1095–1117), that the niches of Saint Guilhem du Désert, with their compound supports and enclosing arches resting on heads, can have been constructed.

As for the portal, we know that this kind of doorway had its beginnings about the year 1032 in Sant' Andrea at Montefiascone. Shortly after the middle of the eleventh century we find it in a still modest garb in Saint Étienne at Caen (1066–1086), and at the beginning of the twelfth, when it had been discovered that it was more effective in proportion as the orders were multiplied, in a fairly advanced shape and sumptuous attire at Cluny (1089–1130), Vézelay (1096–1132), and other churches.

Lastly, there is the ribbed vaulting in the porch. We know that cross vaulting with

[1] *Acta Sanct. Ord. S. Benedicti, Vita S. Angilberti abbatis Centulensis in Gallia*, vol. v, p. 106.

diagonal arches or ribs makes its first unquestioned appearance in San Flaviano at Montefiascone (1032), and that it was afterwards used in the cathedral of Aversa, in Sant' Ambrogio at Milan, and in the church of Rivolta d'Adda, all structures of the eleventh century. But north of the Alps it was not seen till about the end of that century; and Durham Cathedral, the first stone of which was laid in 1093, affords the earliest dated example.

The church of Saint Quenin near Vaison, in its oldest part—the chancel—is supposed to have been built by order of Charles the Great or his successors; but we have only to notice the ribbed vault of the apse, and the crouching animal carved on the keystone of the vaulting, to see that we have to deal with a building of the twelfth century. It was towards the end of the eleventh century that the carving of keystones in vaulting started in Italy. There is a rudely carved lamb at the intersection of the diagonal arches in the nave of the church at Rivolta d'Adda. North of the Alps it appears with the rise of Pointed architecture, and in some cases in the very first churches in that style. Thus the cross vaulting with moulded ribs in the western towers (1134–1144) of the cathedral of Chartres has the point of intersection left plain, while the main vaulting of similar type in the cathedral of Sens (1130)[1] is ornamented by a rosette at the intersections.

It is appropriate to notice here that an archaic example of ornament applied to a keystone of vaulting is afforded by the well-known Etruscan tomb of the Volumnii near Perugia (believed to be of the third century B.C.), where the head of a Gorgon appears in the middle of the stepped squares which form the ceiling.

The cupola of the church of Notre Dame des Doms at Avignon, together with the other parts of the structure, is thought to be a work of the time of Charles the Great.[2] Now this cupola rises from Campano-Lombardic hooded pendentives, a form of Italian origin which did not migrate to other countries till about the middle of the eleventh century, when it had reached its full development. It appears as a conchiform squinch in the western towers of Jumièges (1040–1066), though not long after there are good specimens in the transept towers at Cluny.

In the cathedral of Vaison, the apse with the bay in front, and the apsidal chapels, are reputed to belong to the Merovingian age. The three bays before the latter are supposed to be of the early Carolingian period; and the whole was probably restored by Bishop Humbert I (996), who will have added the bell-tower which rises above one of the minor apses. And all this though we know from Boyer, the historian of the church of Sainte Marie de Vaison, that it was built by the said bishop, and though the existing structure is, from its vaulting, evidently of the twelfth century, when the east end of the original church was preserved in an altered form.[3] As a matter of fact, Choisy[4] considers the body of the church to be the result of a rebuilding following the destruction of the city in 1160.

Having made these observations we will now return to our subject, and pass in review some of the very rare buildings still surviving in Burgundy and the neighbouring districts, which really belong to the Merovingian (481–752) and Carolingian (752–987)

---

[1] [CHARTRAIRE, La cathédrale de Sens, p. 12.]

[2] [See DE LASTEYRIE, op. cit., pp. 411, 412. The theory of a Carolingian date for any part of the building has long been abandoned. The church was entirely rebuilt, and was consecrated in 1069; and there is strong architectural evidence for a second reconstruction c. 1150, to which the porch and cupola are now generally assigned. (H. T.)]

[3] [DE LASTEYRIE, op. cit., p. 411, considers the apse and minor chapels at Vaison to be possibly Merovingian, but regards the nave as an 11th-century structure remodelled in the 12th century, when the vaulting was added. (H. T.)]

[4] Histoire de l'architecture (Paris, 1903), vol. ii, p. 214.

ages and the years up to the epoch of 1000, and retain sufficient constructive and decorative elements to form the basis for profitable comparisons and reasonable dating of other edifices which have been wrongly classified.

THE CHAPEL (NOW CRYPT) OF SAINT LAURENT AT GRENOBLE.—Below the presbytery of the present church of Saint Laurent (considered to belong to the eleventh century) is situated a small church which forms its crypt. It is a three-lobed structure, with the addition of a fourth arm in the end or western wall (fig. 419). Over the central part is a barrel vault. The half-domes of the subordinate apses in the transverse portion are formed by concave sections carried by small arches. The principal apse at the eastern end has a similar vault, and the angles of its face are decorated with single shafts, above which are doubled shafts. The large apse at the west end was probably added when the three-lobed chamber was turned into a crypt: in any case, it is the result of an alteration in the structure. In the body of the chapel we notice the stylobate on which stand the shafts with capitals carrying high Ravennate pulvins (fig. 420) supporting a plain architrave. The carving of these capitals recalls that on two of the Visigothic period, with leaves, water-lilies, stars, and crosses, at the principal entrance of the Mosque at Cordova,[1] founded by Abderrahman in 786, to which they were brought from the church dedicated to the deacon-martyr, St. Vincent (304), built after King Reccared's conversion to Catholicism (586–601).

Fig. 419. Grenoble. Crypt of Saint Laurent
(6th century)

The date of the chapel of Saint Laurent, which I regard as the oldest church in France, is unknown. The general view is that it may be ascribed to the seventh century. I believe, on the other hand, that the proper date is the second half of the sixth century, and perhaps the period when the see of Gratianopolis was held by Bishop Isicius (573–601). A date near to the sixth century has already been suggested.[2]

The Ravennate figure pulvins must follow close on the archetypes of the kind for western Europe, to be seen in San Vitale at Ravenna (526–547). At the same time they must be earlier than the moulded specimens in the Merovingian crypt of Jouarre (653). The capitals, too, cannot be assigned to the time of King Pippin (752–768) or later, because, as we shall see when we come to the crypt of the church of Flavigny (755–768), a different type of capital was then in vogue in France.

[1] [See RIVOIRA, *Moslem Architecture*, p. 336.]
[2] *Bulletin archéologique*, 1893, REYMOND et GIRAUD, *La chapelle Saint-Laurent à Grenoble*, p. 10. [Reymond's theory that the chapel was a family mausoleum subsequently converted into a crypt, which appears to be accepted in the text, is contested by DE LASTEYRIE, op. cit., p. 46. (H. T.)]

Fig. 420. Grenoble. Crypt of Saint Laurent. Capitals (6th century)

Fig. 421. Rome. So-called 'Tempio di Siepe' (2nd century). (From GIOVANNOLI, *Roma Antica*, lib. vii, no. 23; lib. iii, no. 34 of the 2nd edition and no. 39 of the later edition)

This chapel presents two notable characteristics. The first is that of the three segmented half-domes, the earliest specimen of the form that I have met with north

Fig. 422. Tivoli. Villa of Hadrian. Interior of the Vestibule of the Piazza d'Oro (125–135)

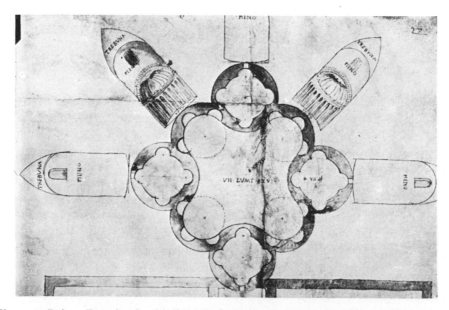

Fig. 423. Baiae. Drawing by Giuliano da Sangallo of a Thermal building (2nd century)

of the Alps. The idea of breaking up the intrados of a cupola is said to be of Eastern origin, though really it was a Latin invention, of the time of Hadrian (117–138). Thus, the intrados of the dome of the building known as the 'Tempio di Siepe' at Rome[1] was

[1] [A rectangular hall with a semi-domed apse forming part of the group of buildings of which the   Templum Matidiae was the most important (HÜLSEN in *Oesterr. Jahreshefte*, xv (1912), pp. 124–42). A plan

composed of a succession of concave sections (fig. 421). Another interesting feature of this dome was the round openings with which it was pierced—the earliest example of such treatment that I know.

Another example of a segmented cupola is the hemispherical vault of the Serapeum in Hadrian's Villa at Tivoli,[1] from which the architect of SS. Sergius and Bacchus at Constantinople derived his inspiration. We find it again in the dome of the octagonal vestibule (fig. 422) in the so-called 'Piazza d'Oro' of the Villa.[2] Again, a group of circular thermal buildings (second century), preserved in Sangallo's Vatican sketchbook,[3] had segmented domes (fig. 423). The form appears again in the half-dome at the end of a hall close to the circular mausoleum in the Villa of the Gordians (third century) on the Via Praenestina near Rome.[4] And the round building called 'Tempio di Venere Sallustiana' has a similar cupola.[5]

Fig. 424. Part of elevation of wall in a Roman Bath. (G. B. Sangallo, Uffizi, 1656; reproduced by BARTOLI, *Mon. Ant. di Roma nei disegni degli Uffizi*, pl. cccxii, fig. 522)

In the Byzantine world the earliest example of a dome with continuous concave segments (i.e. not alternating with flat bands as in SS. Sergius and Bacchus) with which I am acquainted is the one in the convent church of Myrelaion, also at Constantinople (919–945).[6]

The second characteristic is that of the two tiers of shafts which decorate the apses. This motive was suggested by the two tiers of columns sometimes employed by the Roman architects in the decorative treatment of walls in their Thermae (fig. 424). We have not found it applied to apses before its appearance in this chapel at Grenoble.

CRYPT OF THE ABBEY CHURCH OF FLAVIGNY.—The abbey of Flavigny in the Duchy of Burgundy, which in 1626, as Robert says,[7] lay '. . . ruinis et ruderibus pene sepultum', was, according to the same authority, founded about the year 606. Ansart, on the other hand, states that the date of its foundation is not known. In the next place, Courtépée cautiously remarks that the foundation with its dedication to St. Praejectus, bishop of Clermont, cannot have taken place till after his martyrdom at Volvic, which happened in 674.[8] Mabillon[9] puts it exactly in the year 722; while Plancher[10] fixes it in the time of Theuderich IV (720–737).

Whatever may be the truth, the translation of the relics of St. Praejectus from Volvic to Flavigny, and the erection of the church under his patronage, did not take place till

is given in RIVOIRA, *Moslem Architecture*, p. 69, fig. 58, from a drawing in the Uffizi at Florence (no. 2976) and reproduced in RIVOIRA, *Roman Architecture*, p. 136, fig. 154. (A).]

[1] [PIRANESI, *Vedute di Roma*, ed. HIND, plate 90 (RIVOIRA, *Roman Architecture*, p. 139, fig. 158); *infra*, p. 106.]

[2] [*Roman Architecture*, pp. 132–3; and *infra*, p. 106.]

[3] [MS. Barb. Lat. 4424, f. 7a; HÜLSEN, *Il libro di Giuliano da Sangallo*, p. 13; *Roman Architecture*, pp. 133, 134. There is, however, no reason for supposing that this building was situated at Baiae, except that the other two buildings drawn on the same leaf are

still in existence there. (A.)]

[4] [PIRANESI, *Antichità Romane*, vol. ii, pls. 59, 60; LUGLI in *Bull Com.*, vol. xliii (1915), pp. 158–60.]

[5] [*Roman Architecture*, pp. 96 ff. (where it is attributed to the period of Vespasian).]

[6] [*Supra*, vol. i, p. 283.]

[7] *Gallia Christiana* (Paris, 1626), p. 579 C.

[8] MABILLON, *Acta Sanct. Ord. S. Benedicti, Vita s. Praejecti episcopi Arvernensis et martyris*, vol. ii, p. 616.

[9] *Annales Ord. S. Benedicti*, vol. ii, p. 64.

[10] Op. cit., vol. i, p. 108.

the time of Abbot Manasses (755–788) and King Pippin (753–768).[1] According to Hugh of Flavigny it was in 880 that the consecration of the church was performed by Pope John VIII (872–882). This function must be connected with the translation to Flavigny in 864 of the body of Sainte Reine d'Alise,[2] and with the alterations or rebuilding carried out in the church.

It does not appear that the building was destroyed by the Normans in their raid of 887 mentioned by the annalist Hugh.

Fig. 425. Flavigny. Crypt of the old abbey church (755–768)

In the course of the thirteenth century it was rebuilt in the Pointed style, though the old sanctuary and the parts connected with it were preserved. In the seventeenth and eighteenth centuries far-reaching restorations and alterations were carried out. In the last century it was deserted and fell into ruin. The materials were carried away, and the only parts preserved were the crypt with a corridor flanking it, a portion of the sanctuary, and a few arches of the nave.[3]

The only part of the original church standing is the crypt (fig. 425), popularly known as the prison of Sainte Reine. The passage flanking it on the south, and, above ground, the remains of the choir with open and blank arcades, one above the other (fig. 426), which were also preserved in the rebuilding of the thirteenth century, are works of a later date, as is shown by the masonry and the carving. This date may very well be the second half of the eleventh century, as is suggested;[4] and then the new works will have followed on the reform effected by King Robert (996–1031) in 1025 or 1026.[5] Belonging to the isolated columns in the crypt there still survive three of the original Pre-Lombardic cubical capitals, of even ruder character than those in the crypt of Saint Laurent at Grenoble.

Some would have it that the crypt was rebuilt or restored in the eleventh and twelfth centuries. This view is quite untenable. The vaulting and the outer wall are manifestly of the same date, and the capitals, with their abaci, have been made on purpose to fit the vaulting; so that piers, vaulting capitals, and abaci form a single architectural whole of one date. Moreover, the remarkable rudeness of the vault construction would

[1] MIGNE, *Patr. Lat.*, vol. 154, *Hugonis abbatis Flaviniacensis chronicon*, p. 139; ROBERT, *Gallia Christiana*, p. 580 c.

[2] MIGNE, *Patr. Lat.*, vol. 154, *Hugonis abbatis Flaviniacensis chronicon*, p. 168 D.

[3] BORDET et GALIMARD, *Restes de l'ancienne basilique de l'abbaye bénédictine de Flavigny* in *Bulletin d'Histoire, de Littérature et d'Art Religieux du Diocèse de Dijon*, Jan., Fev. 1906, p. 4.

[4] Ibid., op. cit., pp. 14–16.

[5] *Roberti regis diplomata* (BOUQUET, *Recueil*, vol. x, p. 611, note a).

ill agree with the quality of French masonry in the ninth and tenth centuries, not to say that of the eleventh and twelfth. The capitals, again, whether on account of their form or the rudeness of the execution, cannot by any means be ascribed to the time of the successors of Charles the Great, and still less to a later period. Lastly, the occurrence on two of the capitals of the letter **M**, believed to be the initial of Manasses the Great (755–788), the builder of the crypt,[1] is another piece of evidence which confirms the date of the building.

Fig. 426. Flavigny. Abbey church. Remains of the choir
(11th century)

Fig. 427. British Museum. Phoenician
carving. No. 520

The crypt of Flavigny, or so much of it as is left, is that erected on the occasion of the translation of the relics of St. Praejectus (755), and was the necessary consequence of that event; for crypts were constructed with the special object of containing the bodies of saints.

It is the oldest dated building in France exhibiting Pre-Lombardic cubical capitals. These are earlier than the examples in the church of Germigny des Prés (801–806). The importation of the type into these regions was perhaps one of the results of Pippin's descents on Italy. The conquest of the Lombard kingdom by Charles the Great did the rest, and the form spread all over his Empire. It is a Lombardic creation of the second half of the seventh century. Before that time capitals of this type were not produced.

[1] BORDET et GALIMARD, op. cit., pp. 12–13.

At the most, and then only very rarely, they were used in a decorative way, like those for instance (to which I am the first to call attention) to be seen in the representation of a temple on a Phoenician stone-carving from Carthage in the Semitic Room at the British Museum (fig. 427).

In the next place, the intersecting vaulting of the crypt, with the vaulting arches incorporated in it, shows that the device of visible arches, which had long been practised by the builders of Rome, Ravenna, and Constantinople, was not yet followed in France.

THE CHAPEL OF SAINTE BLANDINE IN SAINT MARTIN D'AINAY AT LYONS.— With regard to the monastery of Ainay at Lyons we are told by Mabillon[1] that Queen Brunhildis (566–613) restored an earlier one known by the name of Interamnis, founded in the fifth century by Romanus abbot of Condat (†460). Choppin,[2] however, says that it was erected by Brunhildis in 612, and afterwards destroyed by the Hungarians; while Robert[3] only states that the queen was the foundress of the monastery at Ainay dedicated to St. Martin. Additional information is given by Mabillon,[4] who relates that it was restored by the Abbot Aurelian, afterwards archbishop of Lyons (875–876–895). And Robert[3] states that Abbot Amblard, who also became archbishop (957–978), rebuilt it in consequence of the damage done by the Hungarians in 937.[5]

It is to this last renewal, which took place about 966, that the existing chapel of Sainte Blandine belongs. Recent restorations have revealed the existence of work of two dates. In the

Fig. 428. Lyons. Saint Martin d'Ainay. Chapel of Sainte Blandine (about 966)

oldest, that at the end of the building, the mortar contains pounded pottery, while in other parts it is made with sand from the bed of the Rhone. The former will belong to the work of Aurelian, while the large blocks of stone in the front of the existing church of Saint Martin may come from the building of Brunhildis.

The existing church is the result of rebuilding by Abbot Gaucerannus in 1102,[6] consecrated by Pope Paschal II in 1107.[7] Later it was altered by the addition of outer

[1] *Annales Ord. S. Benedicti*, vol. i, p. 13.
[2] *Monasticon* (Frankfort-s.-M., 1744).
[3] *Gallia Christiana*, p. 525 D.
[4] *Acta Sanct. Ord. S. Benedicti, S. Aureliani episcopi Lugdunensis elogium historicum*, vol. vi, pp. 512–13; *Annales Ord. S. Benedicti*, vol. iii, p. 16 C.
[5] *Annales Ord. S. Benedicti*, vol. iii, p. 435 A.
[6] SAMMARTHANUS, &c., *Gallia Christiana, Ecclesia Lugdunensis, Athanaeum* (Paris, 1728), vol. iv, p. 236 C.
[7] JAFFÉ, *Regesta pontificum romanorum*, vol. i, p. 728.

aisles and a dome; by the substitution of sham barrel vaulting for the original wooden ceiling; and by the conversion of the three round-headed doorways of the west front into entrances with pointed arches.

The chapel of Sainte Blandine is of rectangular plan, with a sanctuary of similar form (fig. 428). Two columns are inserted in the angles of the frontal arch of this sanctuary, while its side walls are decorated with blank arcading springing from columns. All these columns have Pre-Lombardic cubical capitals, which tell us that this type, introduced into France in the time of Pippin, was still the fashion in the southern parts of the country in the tenth century.

APPENDIX

By Prof. A. HAMILTON THOMPSON

UPON the claims of William of Volpiano to consideration as an architect see R. de Lasteyrie, op. cit., pp. 486–7. The chronicler of St. Bénigne describes the contributions of the bishop of Langres and of William himself to the building of the abbey church at Dijon in the words, 'in cujus basilice miro opere domnus presul expensas tribuendo, ac columnas marmoreas ac lapideas unde-cumque adducendo, et reverendus abbas *magistros conducendo, et ipsum opus dictando*, insudantes dignum divino cultui templum construxerunt'. The reputation of William as an architect is founded upon the phrase italicized in this passage. The statement is simply that he hired master-craftsmen and gave them orders for the work, and may be pressed to imply more than it actually means; and de Lasteyrie's comment, 'il n'avait pas besoin d'être architecte pour dresser le programme des travaux, *opus dictare*, ou pour traiter avec des maîtres maçons, *magistris conducere*', suggests the true interpretation of the words. The administrative supervision of the work may be attributed to William, but it is reasonable to conclude that, while he no doubt communicated his wishes to the *magistri*, as a modern client does to his architect, details of design and execution were left to them. There is no hint that William himself was a magister.

It should also be noted that no indication is given of the districts from which William of Volpiano obtained his *magistri*. After a visit to Rome in 995 or 996, his community at Dijon was augmented by many Italians, some of whom were well learned in letters, others 'diversorum operum magisterio docti', to the great advantage of the monastery. These artist monks, however, are not to be con-founded, for obvious reasons, with the *magistri* hired in 1001, and of the nationality of the latter nothing is said. As regards their style of work, conclusions must be qualified by the statement of the chronicler that the bishop procured columns of marble and stone for the church from all parts, which implies that he collected these from older buildings for re-use in the new church. If this is so, the *magistri* had much ready-made material to their hand, which limited their originality in design.

William's architectural influence in Normandy (p. 70) is not emphasized in any way by his bio-graphers. Of his work at Fécamp, Raoul Glaber (Migne, *P.L.* cxlii. 710) says: 'praefatum locum . . . taliter claustris atque officinis regularibus, caeterisque bonorum copiis adornavit, ut prae caeteris illius provinciae felicibus semper floreat incrementis.' This is very general, and implies no more than that, like other prelates, he instigated and furthered with benefactions the building of his monastery. The later writers, quoted on p. 70, can hardly be said to do more than repeat this implication. With the exception of the single passage with regard to his work at St. Bénigne, from which his interest in architecture may be inferred, the biographers represent him as, before every-thing else, a reformer of discipline. The author of the *Chron. Fiscamnense* (Migne, *P.L.* cxli. 849) praises his culture and ecclesiastical learning: 'liberalibus artibus apprime eruditum, atque disciplinis ecclesiasticis, cunctisque spiritualibus officiis . . . virtutum gratia imbutum et illuminatum.' Of architectural training there is no word; and Odilo's reference to him (*Vita Maioli*, Migne, *P.L.* cxlii. 954) as a monk at Cluny, 'ut pace spiritualium artificum in eadem fabrica laborantium dicam, unus praecipue refulsit', is a metaphor from which it would be unsafe to conjecture an allusion to his gifts as an *artifex* in fabrics of a temporal kind.

As in the case of William of Volpiano, so in that of Lanfranc, p. 90, the texts have been made to bear a meaning which is to say the least extremely doubtful. The administrator has been turned into an architect. I think that it is necessary to examine the passages on which this confusion rests. William of Jumièges (vi. 9) describes the coming of Lanfranc to Bec, then a struggling monastery. This led to a great increase in its resources and numbers, so that Lanfranc pressed Herluin to rebuild it on a larger scale. He now became the life and soul of the work: 'coepti operis institutor', the real founder of the new building. In this connexion, however, 'inchoavit' is used, not only of Lanfranc, but of Herluin, so that, if we are to read into this word the authorship of the design, Herluin has as good a claim as Lanfranc to be styled the architect. But the fact is that no phrase is used in these passages which implies more than the moral energy and practical activity of the men who were at the back of the whole work as *duces et auspices*, and of whom it might be said therefore that they built the monastery: 'novam ecclesiam quam beatus Herluinus, ejusdem loci gloriosus abbas, Lanfrancus, et Anselmus, viri magne auctoritatis, aedificaverant' (*Chronicon Beccense*).

Such men as William of Volpiano, Lanfranc, and Anselm no doubt brought strong architectural tastes from Italy and encouraged building as part of their work; and it is possible that more than one of them attracted Lombard masons to Normandy. But it is dangerous to assume that they brought with them a fully developed architectural style which they imposed upon the churches which they were instrumental in founding, especially when throughout France at this period builders were working out the solution of the problem of vaulting churches with well-marked local characteristics. These considerations here advanced may be applied equally to the claims of Suger (p. 129), Saxulf (p. 139), and Gundulf (p. 226) to be regarded as architects.

On the other hand, it is an interesting fact that, in the laws of Rotharis, *operam dictare* is used in a context which may place it among the professional tasks of a *magister*: 'Si quis magistrum comacinum unum aut plures rogaverit aut conduxerit ad operam dictandum aut solatium diurnum praestandum inter suos servos ad domum aut casam faciendam.' Here, however, the second part of the sentence, which couples *praestandum* with *dictandum*, makes it more probable that the *dictatio operis* belongs to the employer than the employee, i.e. 'If any one invites or hires one or more mastermasons to give them directions for their work, or furnish them with daily refreshment among his servants, in order that they may make a building or dwelling-house.' This corresponds exactly to the description of the relations between William of Volpiano and his *magistri* at Dijon, and marks the distinction between employer and architect.[1]

---

[1] For a further discussion see HAMILTON THOMPSON, *Cathedral Builders of the Middle Ages*, in *History*, vol. x (1925), pp. 139 ff., and R. DE LASTEYRIE, op. cit., pp. 486–7.

II

THE LOMBARDO-NORMAN STYLE IN NORMANDY

THE foundations of the new church of Saint Bénigne at Dijon had scarcely been laid when Richard II, Duke of Normandy (996–1026), invited William of Volpiano to come to Fécamp and reform the abbey of the Trinity. The latter, remembering the negative results of a previous attempt by Majolus the abbot of Cluny (948–994), at first tried to avoid the duty, on the ground of the barbarous and savage character of the Norman dukes, who were more inclined to destroy than to build churches, and more likely to drive monks away than gather them together in monasteries.[1] But at last, in consequence of a fresh and urgent entreaty, he gave way and started on his mission.

At the dawn of the eleventh century Normandy was no longer in the miserable conditions which had prevailed during the period between the settlement, in the days of Louis the Pious (814–840), of the sea-kings' hordes on the island of Noirmoutier, the centre from which they started, plundering, burning, slaughtering, in every direction, and the treaty of Saint Clair sur Epte. By that treaty Charles the Simple (893–929) assured to Rollo (911–931) the possession of Rouen and the lower valley of the Seine, from the Epte to the sea. And though we have no documentary information about the early days of the Norman dukedom, founded in 911 or perhaps not till 921, still, we know that, after the Normans had obtained a foothold and given the country their name, an epoch of depredation and ruin was succeeded by one of security and internal development.

It is also certain that, with the accession of Richard II, and after the peasant revolt had been crushed by Rudolf, Count of Evreux (997), in the manner described by William of Jumièges,[2] the country had become so strong internally that it felt itself capable of engaging in a series of expeditions against other territories, which culminated in the conquest of England. Moreover, what is known about Richard is far from confirming the charges brought by William against the Norman princes; so that we must suppose, either that these were instigated by the desire of putting Richard's intentions to the proof, and obtaining his support in all things necessary, or else were based on the low opinion he had of the religious sincerity of the dukes. The latter point was not devoid of some element of truth, at any rate in the case of the improvised Christianity of Rollo, or the skin-deep faith of Richard I 'the Fearless' (943–996).

There is, indeed, some discrepancy in the accounts given by the chronicles of the conduct of Rollo the Rover after his baptism (912) by Franco, archbishop of Rouen; so that, while we read in Ademar[3] that, on the one hand, he sacrificed his Christian prisoners to the Scandinavian idols, and, on the other, made donations to churches ('Christianos captivos centum ante se decollari fecit in honore quae coluerat idolorum, et demum centum auri libras per ecclesias distribuit Christianorum in honore veri Dei'), Dudo of Saint Quentin,[4] on the contrary, tells us that he was a good and pious ruler, and a protector of the Church. All the same, there is good reason for thinking

---

[1] MABILLON, *Acta Sanct. Ord. S. Benedicti*, vol. vii, p. 313. *Vita s. Guillelmi abbatis, Excerpta ex libro de revelatione, aedificatione, et auctoritate monasterii Fiscamnensis.*

[2] DUCHESNE, *Historiae Normannorum scriptores*

antiqui (Paris, 1619), *Historia Normannorum*, p. 249.

[3] *Mon. Germ. Hist.*, ADEMARUS, *Historiarum libri IV a saec. V–1028*, p. 123.

[4] MIGNE, *Patr. Lat.*, vol. 141, *De moribus et actis primorum Normanniae ducum*, p. 628.

that at the bottom of his heart he remained the pagan he was before baptism ('idolisque contemptis, quibus ante deservierat').[1] And with regard to sacred buildings, if Rollo gave largely to the churches of Rouen, Evreux, Bayeux, Jumièges, Mont Saint Michel, and Saint Denis, at his baptism, as we are told by Dudo and William of Jumièges, he does not seem to have undertaken any general restoration of the churches destroyed during the wars as these chroniclers would have us believe ('templa frequentia paganorum destructa restauravit'), seeing that one of them, Jumièges, was, with the adjoining monastery, still a heap of ruins in the days of William I 'Longsword' (931–943). Again, in the case of Richard I (943–996), though the 'Benedictine Annals' and the two historians just referred to mention sundry religious buildings as restored or founded by him, on the other hand we know that, on the occasion of the invasion of Normandy by King Sihtric (943), when a large number of Normans headed by Thurmod returned to paganism, he followed their example. This sudden relapse, which may find an excuse in the duke's youth, is confirmed by the clear testimony of Flodoard.[2]

Fig. 429. Rouen. Apse of the old Saint Ouen (11th and 12th centuries)

However this may be, William of Volpiano, immediately on his arrival at Fécamp and institution as abbot, took in hand the reformation of that and other monasteries (e.g. Jumièges, Mont Saint Michel, and Saint Ouen at Rouen), founded new ones, restored or rebuilt the old ones, and was in every case made their superior. The virtues and enterprise of the new abbot of Fécamp and his assistants speedily fanned into flame a real religious revival which made its influence felt in every direction. This revival, the result of a movement which is natural to peoples in an elementary stage of culture, was accompanied by an intellectual efflorescence produced by the establishment, in the abbeys subject to the supreme control and authority of William, of schools open to every class of society. The Benedictines were well aware that letters, aided by the arts, are one of the most effective weapons for fighting barbarism. In this way the abbeys became seats of public instruction; and this was especially the case at Fécamp, where William took a personal share in the work of education.

Having given this brief sketch of the conditions under which the work of William of Volpiano and his successors was begun, let us see what was the state of the arts of architecture and carving in Normandy in the century preceding the epoch of 1000.

Of the very rare ecclesiastical buildings erected by order of the Norman dukes of that period, the only one of which there are sufficient remains to provide material for study and observation is the old church of Saint Pierre at Jumièges (940).

The oldest portions of the church at Fécamp, viz. the chapels of St. Peter and St. Nicholas, and the round arches springing from continuous Lombardic capitals ornamented with scroll work and undercut foliage in the ambulatory of the existing church in the Pointed style, have nothing to do with the church of the Trinity founded

[1] LE PRÉVOST, *Orderici Vitalis historia ecclesiastica*, vol. ii, p. 8.

[2] *Mon. Germ. Hist., Script.*, vol. iii, pp. 389–90; FLODOARDUS, *Annales*.

by Richard I in 990. Of that structure, with its nave and aisles, Dudo of Saint Quentin has left a brief but valuable description, in which he mentions the master builder who acted as its architect ('petrarum fabro architectoria arte perito'), and also the material of which it was constructed. The fragments just referred to must be assigned to the rebuilding carried out by William de Ros, third abbot of Fécamp (1087–1107), and described by Ordericus Vitalis. 'Nam cancellum veteris Ecclesiae, quam Richardus Dux construxerat, deiecit, et eximiae pulchritudinis opere in melius renovavit, atque in longitudine ac latitudine decenter augmentavit. Navem quoque Basilicae, ubi Oratorium sancti Frodmundi habetur, eleganter auxit.'[1]

Fig. 430. Jumièges. Church of Saint Pierre (about 940)

No trace remains of the rebuilding of the church of the Mother of God at Rouen, carried out in the days of Rollo, Duke Richard I, and Bishop Robert I (989–1037).[2] Nor is anything preserved above ground of the reconstruction in the time of Archbishop Maurilius (1055–1067), who consecrated the new work in 1063. It is to a later date that we must assign the remains of piers and shafts under the pavement to the left of the presbytery of the present cathedral, which was begun after the fire of 1200.

The same may be said of the church of Saint Ouen, also at Rouen, founded under the invocation of SS. Peter and Paul by Archbishop Flavianus (533–542) in the reign of Clotaire I, the name being changed to Saint Ouen in the eleventh century.[3] It was rebuilt, if not built, by the said duke according to Ordericus Vitalis and William of Jumièges. For the most ancient part of the present church, viz. the apse in two stories marked off on the outside by a billet course, each of which contains a window with angle shafts and Corinthianesque capitals, is not older than the rebuilding carried out between 1064 and 1126 (fig. 429).

CHURCH OF SAINT PIERRE AT JUMIÈGES.—It has been thought by some[4] that the relics of this church which survive belong to the first foundation (654) by St. Philibert with the aid of Chlodovech II (638–656) and his queen Bathildis. Really what we see is a rebuilding of the original structure (burned with the adjoining convent by Hasting in 851) carried out by Duke William I, it seems, in 940,[5] while Gonthardus was archbishop of Rouen (919–942). The greater part of it was destroyed to make way for the

[1] LE PRÉVOST, *Orderici Vitalis hist. eccl.*, vol. iv, p. 270.
[2] [But see J. BILSON, *Les vestiges de la cathèdrale de Rouen du XIe siècle, Bull. Mon.* 1927, p. 251, and DE LASTEYRIE, op. cit., p. 800. (R.)]
[3] ROBERT, *Gallia Christiana*, p. 526 C.

[4] LOTH, *Histoire de l'abbaye royale de Saint-Pierre de Jumièges* (Rouen, 1882–5, *Soc. hist. Norm.*), vol. i, p. 18.
[5] LE PRÉVOST, *Orderici Vitalis hist. eccl.*, vol. ii, p. 9, note.

new construction of the fourteenth century; and what was left was damaged in the sixteenth, and finally reduced in the early years of the last century to the deplorable state in which it now appears.

In the small surviving fragment of the original building, which had a nave and aisles (fig. 430), two features are to be noticed. One is the triforium gallery, with groups of arches enclosed within a relieving arch after the Romano-Ravennate manner, thus confirming our idea as to the date of the building. This did not become the fashion north of the Alps before the time of Charles the Great (768–814). The Pre-Lombardic cubical capitals (fig. 431) also confirm the date. Very different were the capitals in vogue in the north of France in the seventh century, and precisely in the time of Chlodovech II and Queen Bathildis, as the crypt of Jouarre (653) tells us.

Fig. 431. Jumièges. Capital in church of Saint Pierre (about 940)

The remains of Saint Pierre inform us how low was the standard of building in Normandy in the tenth century. Nor was this confined to the Duchy, but must also have prevailed in the adjoining districts, to judge by the remains of the old cathedral of Beauvais.

THE OLD CATHEDRALE OF BEAUVAIS is popularly known as the 'Basse Œuvre'. There are those who would take it back to Merovingian times (481–752), while others regard it as a work of the eighth or ninth century. A third view places it in the time of Bishop Hervé (987–997). It is this last date which suits it best, as Robert[1] shows; and it explains Viollet-le-Duc's[2] statement that the church was in existence in 990.

Of the original structure, mutilated when the new cathedral was built in the Pointed style (thirteenth century), there is preserved the front, and the first three bays of the nave and aisles. They have wooden roofs, and are separated by piers of octagonal or quadrangular section without capitals or impost mouldings. The octagonal ones are hollowed out on four sides in order to fit the springers of the arches. These piers are the precursors of the more elaborate ones still surviving in the ruins of Saint Martin at Angers (fig. 432), which are fitted to their imposts by being hollowed out at the angles, each hollow being occupied by a coarse leaf. Saint Martin was rebuilt, with the assistance of Count Fulco III Nerra (1012–1040) and his wife Hildegarde, before the year 1020,[3] and dedicated by Hubert, bishop of Angers (1010–1047), in 1030.[4]

In the old cathedral of Beauvais the window archivolts, with alternate voussoirs of stone and brick enclosed by a ring of bricks laid horizontally (fig. 433), recall those at Agliate (824–860) and in the palace of Constantine VII Porphyrogenitus (912–958) at Constantinople (fig. 434). The large window in the front, richly decorated with stars in low relief, is the result of an alteration (fig. 435). Ornament of this kind was revived by the Lombardo-Roman style, which borrowed it from buildings of the Roman period.

We will now supplement our account of the two buildings just discussed by that of five others of an earlier date: the crypt of Jouarre (653), the baptistery of Poitiers

[1] *Gallia Christiana* (Beauvais, 1626), vol. i, col. 262; cf. ed. 1715, vol. ix, col. 704.
[2] Op. cit., vol. iv, p. 418. [The church finished by Hervé was the old cathedral of St. Peter, not Notre-Dame de la Basse Œuvre, which was built in the 8th century, patly of Roman materials. M. AUBERT in DE LASTEYRIE, op. cit., p. 766. (R.)]
[3] GUSTAVE D'ESPINAY, *Notices archéologiques*. Première série. Angers, 1876, p. 124 and note.
[4] GAMS, op. cit., p. 489.

(seventh century), the church of Germigny des Prés (801–806), and the crypts of Saint Aignan (814–840) and Saint Avit (ninth century) at Orleans. We are thus provided with a group of buildings of the Merovingian (481–752) and Carolingian (752–987) ages which, with the addition of the three of the same periods described in the first chapter of the Second Part, and of Angilbert's basilica at Saint Riquier (Centula) (793–798) as preserved in a view in Mabillon,[1] may furnish us with typical examples which

Fig. 432. Angers. Remains of church of Saint Martin (1030)

Fig. 433. Beauvais. Old Cathedral (987–997)

will enable us to form an idea, incomplete perhaps, but certain so far as it goes, of the state of ecclesiastical architecture in France at those periods and up to the epoch of 1000.

THE CRYPT OF THE CHURCH OF SAINT PAUL AT JOUARRE was built (653) by St. Ado,[2] placed under the rule of St. Columban, and endowed by Queen Bathildis (649–680).[3] It exhibits work of three distinct dates. The first is that of the original foundation, and to this belongs the northern part of the structure with its Corinthianesque and Composite capitals (fig. 436). To the second is to be ascribed the enlargement of the primitive crypt, represented by a chapel built against it, dedicated to St. Ebrigisilus, bishop of Meaux (seventh or eighth century). This enlargement is to be connected with the translation of the relics of St. Potentianus to Jouarre (874).[4] As a matter of fact, a pulvin carved with foliage, recalling specimens in the abbey church of Mettlach (987–1000),

[1] *Acta Sanct. Ord. S. Benedicti*, vol. v, p. 105, *Vita S. Angilberti abb. Centulensis, auctore Hariulfo*.

[2] DELISLE, *Aimoini monachi Floriacensis, De gestis regum Francorum* (BOUQUET, *Recueil*, vol. iii, p. 138).

[3] *Mon. Germ. Hist., Script. rerum Merov.*, vol. ii,

p. 492, *Vita Sanctae Bathildis*.

[4] MABILLON, *Acta Sanct. Ord. S. Benedicti*, vol. vii, p. 227, *De translatione Sancti Potentiani in Coenobium Jotrense*.

Fig. 434. Constantinople. Palace of Constantine Porphyrogenitus (912–958)

Fig. 435. Beauvais. Old Cathedral. (987–997)

and others in the small chapel under the south aisle of the Castle church of Quedlinburg (997–1021), may be assigned, on account of its form and the quality of the carving, to the Carolingian age, and in it to a period later than the reign of Charles the Great. To the third date belongs a final enlargement to the south-west, forming a pendant to the chapel referred to (fig. 437). This event may be connected[1] with the installation in the eleventh century of a chapter of secular canons which is mentioned by Mabillon.[2] This date suits the Lombardic capitals, some of them having figures, a result of the Lombardo-Norman influence in art which made itself felt after the epoch of 1000. Earlier than this, Lombardic figure capitals are not to be found in France. From the

Fig. 436. Jouarre. Original Crypt in the church of Saint Paul (653)

Merovingian age onwards the only dated French figure capital that I can oint to is the one to which I have already called attention in the crypt of St. Pierre de la Couture at Le Mans (997) (p. 32).

On the one hand, the carved heads on the capitals at Jouarre are, to judge by the one which is well preserved, poor work, and earlier than the twelfth century; but, on the other hand, a date not before the eleventh century is disclosed by the Attic spurred bases in this part of the crypt, for this Lombardic motive did not cross the Alps till about the middle of that century.

This third phase was accompanied by a general alteration of the building, and by the construction of the unraised cross vaulting. For the vaults belonging to the eleventh-century building are evidently made to fit the supports, and those of the seventh century in the crypt are of just the same character. Moreover, the cross vaulting in the crypt of Saint Pierre at Flavigny tells us that in France, during the Dark Ages, cross vaulting was of the continuous type, and not supported by visible arches, as at Jouarre. I should

[1] ENLART, *Manuel d'archéologie française depuis les temps mérovingiens jusqu'à la Renaissance, Architecture religieuse*, partie i, pp. 170, 171.

[2] *Annales Ord. S. Benedicti*, vol. v, p. 423 C.

mention here that Rohault de Fleury[1] thinks that the first church had only a flat roof, and that the vaulting was added in the tenth or eleventh century.

The most important things in the crypt are the Merovingian capitals. They display an artistic quality which one would look for in vain in Italian Lombardic capitals of the seventh century, and can only be compared (making allowance for the difference of type) with the contemporary productions of the School of Ravenna.[2] Another note-worthy object is the shrine of St. Theodechildis, the original parts of which have carvings of scroll work with grapes, roses, lilies, and scallop shells, all finely executed (see fig. 436).

This revival of art in France in the seventh century is not difficult to understand when we remember the assistance it received in the form of the foundation and endowment of ecclesiastical institutions by a whole series of royal personages, from the pious Radegund (538–587) to the great but unfortunate Brunhildis (566–613), who protected the mission sent by Pope Gregory I to convert England, and was so important a patroness of architecture that a large number of buildings with which she had no connexion were ascribed to her.[3] And the series goes on from her to Sigibert III (638–650), and the virtuous and capable Bathildis.

THE BAPTISTERY OF SAINT JEAN AT POITIERS was erected over a Gallo-Roman sepulchral edifice. It consists of two parts, the baptistery proper and the narthex. The plan is an oblong, with apses projecting from the three free sides (fig. 438). The

Fig. 437. Jouarre. Additions to original Crypt of Saint Paul (9th and 11th centuries)

roof is of wood, except in the case of the two subordinate apses to the north and south. The principal apse, and the north, south, and east walls of the body of the building, are decorated internally with arcading. On the outside it is ornamented with small pilasters, round and triangular pediments, &c. (fig. 439).

The front and the narthex were probably rebuilt after the conflagration which devastated Poitiers in 1018.[4] Traces of fire may still be seen in the building.

With regard to this most interesting of the earliest French churches we are entirely without authentic documentary evidence for fixing the date of its construction. The

[1] *La Messe*, vol. ii, p. 116.

[2] [DE LASTEYRIE (op. cit., 113) thought they were of Italo-Byzantine origin. (R.)]

[3] *Mon. Germ. Hist., Script.*, vol. xvii, p. 37,

Annales Wormatienses.

[4] *Mon. Germ. Hist., Ex chronico Ademari Cabanensis.*

most likely date appears to be the time of Bishop Ansoald (682–696),[1] one of the most important holders of the see. Structural works are generally to be connected with characters capable of large undertakings, and Ansoald was one of the most notable bishops of Poitiers.

The presence of capitals brought from elsewhere, which, though more bevelled, recall by their nearly equal rudeness those in the chapel of Saint Laurence at Grenoble, and may

Fig. 438. Poitiers. Baptistery of Saint Jean (7th, 11th, and 13th centuries)

well date from the long and prosperous reign of Theodoric the Visigoth (449–451), fixes the erection of the baptistery in Merovingian times. Now, in that period, the most favourable moment for its construction was certainly the time of Radegund; yet there is no mention of the event, which, considering the purpose of the building, would be an important one, either by Venantius Fortunatus[2] who was intimate with her, and was afterwards bishop of Poitiers (599–600), or by the nun Baudonivia,[3] or by their contemporary,

[1] C. DE LA CROIX, *Étude sommaire du baptistère Saint-Jean de Poitiers* (2nd ed., 1904). [DE LASTEYRIE (op. cit., p. 126) agrees to a 7th century date. (R.)]
[2] *Mon. Germ. Hist., Auct. Antiquiss.*, vol. iv, p. 38,
De Vita sanctae Radegundis.
[3] *Mon. Germ. Hist., Script. rerum Merov.*, vol. ii, p. 377, *Vita Radegundis reginae Francorum.*

Gregory of Tours (573–595). So that we are obliged to ascribe it to a later date, viz. the seventh century, in which the period that suits it best is the episcopate of Ansoald.

The most notable features of the baptistery of Poitiers are its architectural decoration, both internal and external; the triple frontal arch of the principal apse; the blank arcading in the apse, which leads the way for that in the church of Germigny des Prés (801–806) and the chapel of Sainte Blandine at Lyons (966); and, lastly, the triangular-headed arches and pediments, like the apertures in a dove-cot.

Fig. 439. Poitiers. Baptistery of Saint Jean (7th, 11th, and 13th centuries)

THE CRYPT OF THE CHURCH OF SAINT AIGNAN AT ORLEANS.—The crypt beneath the choir of the present church of Saint Aignan exhibits in its oldest parts the remains of a structure which may be referred to the time of the Emperor Louis the Pious (814–840), and was the result of a visit paid by him to the place,[1] and also to the rebuilding of the church by King Robert, the dedication taking place in 1029[2] (fig. 440).

To the ninth century belong the wall-arches on the north and south, the cubical capitals of which, as being artistically inferior to the original ones of the same form in Theodulf's church at Germigny des Prés, must be dated later than the first years of that century.

To the beginning of the eleventh century belong the two capitals (one with foliage, the other with figures) on the half-columns in the west wall. They are rudely executed, especially the one with figures.

THE CHURCH OF GERMIGNY DES PRÉS was erected by Theodulf, abbot of Fleury and bishop of Orleans (788–821), between 801 and 806.[3] It was regarded at the time as

[1] ERMOLDUS NIGELLUS, *Carmen elegiacum de rebus gestis Ludovici Pii* (BOUQUET, *Recueil*, vol. vi, p. 43 and note f).
[2] HELGALDUS, *Epitoma vitae Regis Roberti Pii*

(BOUQUET, *Recueil*, vol. x, p. 110 and note). [Plan in DE LASTEYRIE, op. cit., fig. 164.]
[3] PRÉVOST, *La basilique de Théodulfe et la paroisse de Germigny-des-Prés*, pp. 6–14.

a wonderful achievement—in the words of one writer: 'ecclesiam mirifici operis construxit, ut nullum in tota Neustria inveniri potest aedificii opus quod ei valeret aequari.'[1] Another account says: 'Theodulfus igitur episcopus inter cetera suorum operum basilicam miri operis . . . aedificavit in villa quae dicitur Germiniacus.'[2] Its fame was evidently derived from the wealth of decoration lavished on the interior, where mosaics and stucco-work adorned the walls, and the pavement was rich with marbles. For we cannot suppose that, in spite of its peculiar plan and complete system of vaulting, the building, with its modest dimensions and ostentatiously bare exterior, could of itself have excited so much admiration as it did among the inhabitants of Neustria, i.e. the western part of France. Nevertheless, and in spite of much new work introduced in the restoration which it underwent between 1867 and 1870, Theodulf's church is a monument of the first rank.

Fig. 440. Orleans. Saint Aignan. Crypt (9th and 11th centuries)

The plan (fig. 441) may be described as a cross inserted in a square, the centre marked by four quadrangular isolated piers which carry the dome, while the arms end in apses, each of which is larger than a semicircle and has the form of a horse-shoe. The western apse disappeared when the church became a priory in 1067, and was enlarged by the addition of a nave.

The elevation, with its square tower, recalls the sepulchral chapel of Galla Placidia at Ravenna (about 440), and the external shape (fig. 442) is derived from San Lorenzo Maggiore at Milan (sixth century).[3] The square body, with an exedra projecting from each side, exactly reproduces, with the exception of the front wall, the external form of San Lorenzo. Other features copied from it are the buttresses at the angles continuing the lines of the outer walls, and those which strengthen the apses. So that we may assume that these two structures were present to the mind of the architect.

A skilful courtier, Theodulf had sung in verse the praises of the chapel at Aachen; and he now made choice of the architectural type followed in that edifice, viz. the Byzantino-Ravennate, for which it seems that Charles the Great had a special liking, with the object of attracting a contribution from him towards the heavy expenses demanded by the costly decorations of the new church and the high grade of the artists capable of being entrusted with their execution.

A palaeographical comparison of the abbreviations in the dedicatory inscription (cut

---

[1] BALUZIUS, *Miscellanea, Catalogus abbatum Floriacensium* (Paris, 1678), lib. i, p. 492.
[2] *Ex miraculis s. Maximini abbat. Miciacensis* (BOUQUET, *Recueil*, vol. v, p. 469).
[3] *Supra*, vol. i, pp. 30, 81, and figs. 42, 114.

on the capitals of the two piers nearest to the principal apse),[1] with similar abbreviations in Italian inscriptions and manuscripts of the eighth and ninth centuries, supports the generally accepted view that Theodulf, a Goth by origin, but an Italian by birth ('erat Theodulfus natione Italus'[2]), procured from Italy the craftsmen qualified to erect and decorate the church which was his pleasure and his pride. These craftsmen must, of course, have had French assistants. This is confirmed by the capitals, clumsy adaptations of Corinthian, used in the internal adornment of the church (I am speaking of those that are original, for the modern ones are devoid of the characteristic stamp of the cubical capitals of the time of Charles the Great), and also by the narrow double-splayed windows in the eastern apse, and the still narrower slits in the other parts of the church, except the dome where the windows are fairly large. Both of these features are characteristic of the contemporary School of Lombardy.

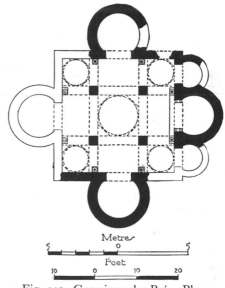

Fig. 441. Germigny des Prés. Plan of church (801–806)

More evidence is to be found in the capitals of the shafts belonging to the sanctuary arch, the arcading round the apse, the triple window openings in the central space, &c., all displaying the Pre-Lombardic manner of the eighth and ninth centuries. Among these capitals, the old ones still preserved, and the casts taken of the others before they were re-worked, suggest a Lombard hand. Unless, indeed, some French carver had learned to handle his chisel in Lombardic fashion, after the introduction of the Pre-Lombardic cubical capital in the crypt of Flavigny (755–768), where, as some think, it was due to imitation of foreign models, or actually to the work of Lombard masters.[3]

Again, there are the remains of the mosaics in the half-dome of the principal apse, which are believed to be original.[4] We must remember that when Theodulf's church was erected, mosaic work still maintained a position of some importance in Italy, as is shown by the precious examples in the Roman basilicas of Santa Cecilia, Santa Maria in Domnica, and Santa Prassede, all put up by Pope Paschal I (817–824), and as would be illustrated, had they survived, by the mosaics, probably the work of artists from Ravenna, with which not a few sumptuous structures of the Lombard age were originally decorated.

Then there is the arcading which decks the interior of the sanctuary apse (fig. 443), an arrangement perhaps derived from the pairs of arcades in the sanctuary of the baptistery at Poitiers (seventh century), which in their turn may have come from the arcading round the apse of San Giovanni Evangelista at Ravenna (425).

Lastly, there are the pairs of decorative angle shafts in the sanctuary arch, a feature taken from the chapel (now crypt) of Saint Laurent at Grenoble (sixth century), where it was employed just about the time when the architect of the basilica at Kalb-Lauzeh (sixth century) was springing the outer archivolt of his chancel arch from shafts supported by brackets.

---

[1] [The part of the inscription with the date 806 has been shown to be a modern forgery. *Bull. Arch.*, 1923, pp. 197 ff. Cp. DE LASTEYRIE, op. cit. 763. (R.)]

[2] MABILLON, *Annales Ord. S. Benedicti*, vol. ii, p. 314 C.

[3] BORDET et GALIMARD, op. cit., pp. 12, 13.

[4] PRÉVOST, op. cit., pp. 73–82.

Fig. 442. Germigny des Prés. Church (801–806)

But though we may infer that Theodulf's basilica was raised by the combined efforts of Italian and French workmen, we may also be allowed to believe that it was carried out under the advice of an architect from the East, perhaps the one who designed the chapel at Aachen in accordance with the wishes of Charles the Great.[1] This would

Fig. 443. Germigny des Prés. Church (801–806)

explain the presence of domes and barrel vaults in the church, and also the feature of horse-shoe arches. For though recesses of this form occur (sporadically) in the ruins of the villa known as the 'Sette Bassi' on the Via Latina near Rome (second century), the type came from the East. I may notice that the sides of a sarcophagus in Sant' Apollinare in Classe (not earlier than the second half of the eighth century, owing to the motive of branches ending in leaves joined at the centre of each group by a boss

[1] [For Strzygowski's theory of Armenian influence in this church see DALTON, *East Christian Art*, pp. 156, 158, &c. (R.)]

so as to form a sort of series of wheels: a motive which does not appear in Italy before that time) afford an early decorative example of horse-shoe arches for Italy and the lands beyond the Alps. The oldest instance in the West is furnished by the well-known sarcophagus formerly in the grounds of the Villa Mattei on the Caelian at Rome representing Muses and poets (third century) in arcades which have arches larger than semicircles (fig. 444).

Fig. 444. Rome. Museo Nazionale (No. 80711). Detail from sarcophagus (3rd century)

THE CRYPT OF SAINT AVIT AT ORLEANS.—This is a miniature basilica, with nave and aisles divided by four octagonal piers surmounted by polygonal capitals chamfered at the angles. The vaulting has been reconstructed (fig. 445). It is reached through an ante-crypt with intersecting vaulting springing from two cylindrical columns with capitals in the same style as those just mentioned.

The history of this structure is not known. Some think that it belongs to the days of Childebert I (511–558), others that it is of the Carolingian period. With this latter view I am in agreement, and the most probable date will be the reign of Charles the Fat (881–887), and later than the crypt of Saint Aignan, inasmuch as the art displayed in the mouldings of Saint Avit is more decadent than that of the capitals of the latter.

Let us now proceed to review the distinguishing characteristics of the French ecclesiastical buildings of Merovingian or pre-Merovingian and Carolingian times.

I. Up to the time of Charles the Great (768–814) chapels were covered with barrel vaulting, while structures of larger size, such as aisled basilicas, had timbered roofs. Thus, barrel vaults occur in the chapel of Saint Laurent at Grenoble (sixth century), and in the oldest part of the chapel of St. John Baptist in Saint Bénigne at Dijon, going back to an earlier period than the ninth century, and possibly even belonging to the age of Gregory, bishop of Langres (507–539).[1] For though the vaulting of the chapel

---

[1] *Mon. Germ. Hist.*, *Gregorii episcopi Turonensis historia Francorum*, pp. 82, 129.

at Grenoble has been restored, and that of the one at Dijon rebuilt, its form was not altered in either case.

On the other hand, to take a few instances, there were wooden ceilings in the basilicas of St. Martin at Tours as erected by Bishop Perpetuus (460–490), and of SS. Peter and Paul, also founded by him there. The same was the case with the church built by St. Namatius (446–462) at Clermont;[1] and with that of Holy Cross and St. Vincent (Saint Germain des Prés) at Paris, erected by King Childebert (511–558), and conse-crated in 558 by St. Germanus, which was of cruciform plan and had its roof sheeted with gilded copper.[2] Again, the baptistery of Saint Jean at Poitiers (seventh century), not excepting the sanctuary, had, apparently, a wooden roof; for when the scheme of painting was carried out in the twelfth century, the decoration was confined to the side walls, whereas in the re-decoration of the following century the paintings extended over the vaulting, so that we must infer that the latter was not in existence in the twelfth century.

In all these wooden-roofed buildings the apse must be excepted. Apart from one here and there, of more complex form, and presenting greater difficulties in construction, like the eastern apse of the baptistery at Poitiers, they must have had half-domes in masonry, though Gregory of Tours never mentions such.

The lantern-tower over the crossing, where there was one, must also have had a wooden roof. Gregory, in fact, says in his account of the destruction of the tower over the altar of the basilica of St. Antolianus at Clermont, that the

Fig. 445. Orleans. Crypt of Saint Avit (9th century)

operation began with the removal of the timbers of the roof: 'iussit tegnos asseresque vel tegulas amoveri.'[3]

The crypts mentioned by him are described as vaulted. The one at Dijon stands for all. Later, those of basilica form, of the age of Pippin (752–768), had continuous unraised cross vaulting springing from isolated supports or wall shafts, after the manner seen in the crypt of Saint Pierre at Flavigny (755–768).

In the reign of Charles the Great, churches of central plan, as his palace chapels appear to have been generally, were vaulted, as we see at Germigny des Prés; while those of basilica plan had wooden roofs over nave and aisles. The abbey church of Saint Riquier, built by Angilbert between 793 and 798[4] ('fulgentissima ecclesia,

[1] *Mon. Germ. Hist., Gregorii episcopi Turonensis historia Francorum,* pp. 82, 129.

[2] D'ACHERY, *Acta Sanct. Ord. S. Benedicti, Vita s. Droctovei abbatis basilicae S. Vincenti in suburbio;* MABILLON, *Annales Ord. S. Benedicti,* vol. i, p. 135.

[3] *Mon. Germ. Hist., Historia Francorum, Liber in gloria martyrum,* p. 532.

[4] [DE LASTEYRIE, op. cit. 142, 763; A. CLAPHAM, *English Romanesque Architecture,* p. 78.]

omnibusque illius temporis ecclesiis praestantissima'[1]), was supported by columns brought from Rome, and had a wooden roof, which accounts for its destruction in 1131.

The two large round towers of this church, one in front of the apse, the other between the church and its vestibule, had imbricated wooden roofs with an opening at the top, over which rose light structures, also of wood, in three stages with corresponding roofs.

Fig. 446. Saint Riquier (Centula). View of the Churches (793–798). (From the *Acta Sanct. Ord. S. Benedicti* (Venice, 1733–1738), saec. iv, pars i, p. 106)

An identical tower, but of smaller dimensions, stood beside the adjacent church of St. Mary, also built by Angilbert, as may be seen in the priceless view of the monastery of Centula, preserved for us by D'Achery[2] (fig. 446). This type of very lofty towers with wooden spires, passing from an interior square base into a circular form on the exterior, is of Frankish origin. Venantius Fortunatus,[3] describing the new cathedral of Nantes, erected by Bishop Felix (552–582) about the year 570, mentions a tower-like structure, square below and round above, rising to a point, and soaring into the air with a series of arcaded stories:

'*In medium turritus apex super ardua tendit*
Quadratumque levans crista rotundat opus.
Altius, ut stupeas, arce ascendente per arcus
Instar montis agens aedis acumen habet.'

Cross vaulting continued to be without visible transverse arches, as is proved by that of the ground floor of the Palatine Chapel at Aachen (796–804)—not indeed a French building, but the most famous structure of its time. Such arches do appear in the upper story, but in connexion with barrel vaults and vault cells.

After the time of Charles the Great the practice of vaulting only the sanctuary continued. The first of the two chambers forming the chapel of St. John Baptist in Saint Bénigne at Dijon (ninth century) has an unraised intersecting vault. The chapel, too, of Sainte Blandine at Lyons (about 966) was given an unbroken barrel vault. Basilicas also still had wooden roofs. The abbey church of St. Gall (822–829) (outside

[1] D'ACHERY, *Spicilegium, Chronicon Hariulfi monachi S. Richarii Centulensis*, vol. ii, p. 303.
[2] D'ACHERY, *Acta Sanct. Ord. S. Benedicti, Vita s. Angilberti abbatis Centulensis*, vol. i, p. 106.
[3] *Mon. Germ. Hist., Venantius Fortunatus, Carmina*, lib. iii. 31–4.

France like the rotunda at Aachen), which was a colonnaded basilica, had a roof of this nature.

It was only after the advent of the Capets (987) that aisles of churches were occasionally vaulted. Thus, for instance, while the old cathedral of Beauvais (987–997) had its nave and aisles roofed with timber, the church of Saint Front at Périgueux, founded later than the year 988, had a wooden roof over the nave, but ramping barrel vaults in the aisles.

It is true that it has been suggested that the abbey church of Saint Pierre de la Couture at Le Mans had a cross-vaulted ambulatory with radiating chapels. The rebuilding of this church is chronicled by Mabillon under the year 997[1] at the hands of Abbot Gauzbert I (990–1007) (apparently in consequence of a donation by Hugo Count of Le Mans in 990[2]), replacing the older church erected by Bishop Bertram (587–623), and still standing in 996 when Bishop Segenfrid of Bellême (971–996) was buried in it.[3] But the oldest parts of the church of 'La Couture' must be subjected to a fresh examination, for the only fragment of the rebuilding of 997 which survives is the crypt, and that is no longer in its original condition.

Fig. 447. Angers. Church of Notre Dame de la Charité. Capital (1028)

Whether the works begun by Gauzbert I were interrupted, and then resumed with a fresh architectural design by his successor Ingelbaud (1010); or whether, at a later date, the choir above the crypt was pulled down in order to rebuild it with an ambulatory and radiating chapels, it is impossible to say. It is certain, however, that the shafts barely touching the outer walls of the crypt, with their stilted arches, are a later addition. The capitals, too, belonging to similar shafts and to the corresponding half-wall-piers, are different from the others in the crypt, and must have been set up in the second quarter of the eleventh century, and that will be the date of the remodelled ambulatory with its ring of chapels—a date, in other words, later than that of the original capitals in the crypt and in the abbey church of Notre Dame de la Charité or 'du Ronceray' at Angers, founded by Fulco III Nerra (1012–1040) and his wife Hildegarde, and consecrated in 1028. And we say this while taking into account the absence of extreme archaic character in the animal figures in the ambulatory of 'La Couture' compared with those in 'La Charité'. These latter, being original, exhibit foliage, birds, quadrupeds either in pairs facing one another in a threatening manner (fig. 447) or engaged in throttling a dove, human figures in a circle holding hands, a man into whose ear the Holy Spirit whispers in the form of a dove, the Flight into Egypt. The representation of the living beings reveals a lower stage of art than that of the contemporary capitals in San Flaviano at Montefiascone.

We may observe here that the crypt of Saint Martin au Val at Chartres belongs in our opinion to almost the same date, viz. the episcopate of the celebrated Fulbert (1007–1029). The church itself was destroyed by the Normans in 911, and again by Duke Richard I (943–996) in 965.[4] As a matter of fact, its Lombardic capitals belong to the first quarter of the eleventh century, with the exception of one here and there of

[1] *Annales Ord. S. Benedicti*, vol. iv, p. 110 B.
[2] *Cartulaire des abbayes de Saint-Pierre de la Couture et Saint-Pierre de Solesmes, publié par les Bénédictins de Solesmes*, Le Mans, 1881, pp. 6–8.

[3] *Ex actibus pontificum Cenomannensium* (BOUQUET, *Recueil*, vol. x, p. 385).
[4] CLERVAL, *Chartres* (Guide Chartrain), p. 16. [DE LASTEYRIE, op. cit., p. 161.]

the Merovingian age, which has been utilized: e.g. a Composite capital with handles, recalling another of the same kind in the crypt of Saint Paul at Jouarre (653).

II. The buildings of the Merovingian age illustrate a whole new Grammar of Ornament. One fresh motive is that of shafts placed one above the other to decorate the sanctuary arch, in the manner we noticed in the chapel of Saint Laurent at Grenoble (sixth century). Entirely new, again, are the coupled blank arcades in the sanctuary of the baptistery of Poitiers (seventh century), which were the model for the continuous arcades of the principal apse in Theodulf's church at Germigny des Prés (801–806), and the variant in the apse of the chapel of Sainte Blandine at Lyons (about 966). Original, too, is the form of the triple arch enclosing the frontal arch of the principal apse of the baptistery just mentioned. Of quite new design and conception are the two

Fig. 448. Rome. Sarcophagus in the Lateran Museum (4th century)

blank arches with a triangular-headed one between them, suggested by the colonnades of alternate arches and pediments, or arches, architraves, and pediments, which sometimes decorate the fronts of sarcophagi belonging to the first Christian centuries[1] (fig. 448), and also tombstones.[2] Possibly this architectural and decorative pediment design of the baptistery at Poitiers may have given suggestions to the French builders of the epoch of 1000; unless, indeed, they got the idea from some structure of the Gallo-Roman age, for the Romans were acquainted with the motive of a series of isolated or continuous pediments, as we saw in our account of San Giovanni at Ravenna. In the same way, the design of blank triangular-headed arcading may have given the idea to the German builders of the ninth century.

In Italy, where the round arch has always been in favour, and has formed the basis of all the chief architectural styles, examples of this motive are very rare in medieval buildings, and have only a secondary importance.

In France the pediment motive may be seen employed on the exterior of the nave of the church at Saint Généroux, of the origin or history of which nothing is known, though some think that it was built before the Norman invasions, while others, with Gailhabaud,[3] believe that it probably belongs to the reign of Charles the Bald (843–

[1] MARUCCHI, *I monumenti del Museo Cristiano Pio-Lateranense*, pl. xxiii. 3 and p. 18.

[2] RAMSAY, *The Cities of St. Paul*, p. 390. [Also better, MISS RAMSAY, *Studies in Art and History of the Eastern Provinces*, pp. 22 ff.]

[3] *L'architecture du Vᵉ au XVIIᵉ siècle*, vol. i.

877). I should place it, approximately, in the last years of the tenth or the first of the eleventh century, on the grounds suggested by Choisy[1] and by Dehio and Von Bezold.[2] In any case it is certain that it is not earlier than the reign of Louis III the Saxon (876–882). In the time of Charles the Great (768–814) and Louis the Pious (814–840) ecclesiastical buildings had no external architectural ornament, and decoration was confined to the interior. Thus, the exterior of the rotunda at Aachen is plain, with the exception of the drum of the dome, where the angle buttresses form part of the construction. And the exteriors of the original church at Saint Riquier (Centula), and of the existing ones at Germigny des Prés and Steinbach near Michelstadt (815–819), and of the sepulchral rotunda at Fulda (812–822), were equally unadorned. North of the Alps the first building exhibiting a scheme of architectural decoration on its outer face was the chapel at Lorsch (876–882).

Moreover, the presence of dentils, not of the ordinary oblong form, but cylindrical (i.e. billets), in the moulding which frames the windows and runs below the gables in the church at Saint Généroux, suggests a date which, though not the ninth century, when a decorative member of that form was unknown, is not far from the revival of art which dawned on France at the opening of the epoch of 1000. These billet mouldings were largely used in the exterior decoration of churches in the Lombardo-Norman style.

III. As late as the reign of Pippin (752–868) capitals were either Roman ones used over again, or else imitations of them so far as could be achieved in that more or less disturbed period. But under Pippin the Pre-Lombardic cubical capital came on the scene. This characteristic member, with or without chamfering of the lower part, the earliest Transalpine example of which exists in the crypt of Saint Pierre at Flavigny (755–768), soon became the fashion in France, and in the days of Charles the Great we find it in full possession at Germigny des Prés. It remained so all through the tenth century: the old church of Saint Pierre at Jumièges (940), and the chapel of Sainte Blandine in Saint Martin d'Ainay at Lyons (966), still contain capitals of the purest Pre-Lombardic type.

The typical Pre-Lombardic cubical capital in France before the epoch of 1000 was embellished with foliage, flowers, interlacing, cauliculi, but not human or animal figures, whether real or imaginary. For these the French had to wait till they were imported from Lombardy; and the first results of this importation we saw in Saint Bénigne at Dijon.

After this preliminary study we will now proceed to examine the few but important churches built from the designs of William of Volpiano or his pupils, and with their help to trace the gradual development of the Lombardo-Norman style which marked the revival of architecture in Normandy.

THE ABBEY CHURCH OF BERNAY was founded and dedicated to the Mother of God in 1013 by Judith (1008–1017), wife of Duke Richard II (996–1026). The convent was dependent on the abbey of Fécamp, and placed under the supreme authority of William of Volpiano. The work was completed by the Duke, who gave the abbey a liberal endowment.[3]

With all its mutilations and alterations; reduced at one time to a barrack, and now permanently converted into a corn exchange, a fire-engine house, shops, a prison, &c.;

[1] *Histoire de l'architecture*, vol. ii, p. 164.
[2] Op. cit., vol. ii, p. 256. [DE LASTEYRIE, op. cit. 151.]
[3] DU MONSTIER, *Neustria Pia* (Rouen, 1663), pp. 398–9. [DE LASTEYRIE, op. cit., pp. 487 (plan), 800. J. BILSON, *La date et construction de l'église abbatiale de Bernay* in Bull. Mon., 1911, p. 403.]

partly concealed by structures which have grown up against it, this ill-starred Lombardo-Norman church still forms, in spite of the great difficulty of making an even incomplete examination of the structure, a very valuable piece of evidence, dealing as we are with the earliest known specimen of the Lombardo-Norman style in its infancy.

To begin with, it had the form of a perfect Latin cross ('crux immissa', in which the

Fig. 449. Bernay. Nave of Abbey Church (1013)

transept is not placed at the extremity of the upright limb but cuts it some way below the top), and was divided into nave and aisles which were continued east of the crossing. The nave ended in a semicircular apse. Each arm of the transept has an apse projecting from its eastern side.

All that is left standing of the original structure is the nave arcades of five arches on either side, and the corresponding southern aisle; the south arm of the transept, and the crossing; and, thirdly, the south aisle of the presbytery. The northern one has been altered and spoiled, and all that can be seen on the outside is a fragment of wall and a window. The northern aisle of the nave has been rebuilt in the style of the fourteenth century, probably after the damage which the church is believed to have suffered in the siege of 1357, when the parish church of Sainte Croix, adjoining the fort within which the abbey stood, was destroyed. It was rebuilt in 1374. An old view[1] shows the church reduced to five bays and deprived of its apse.

The interior has an effect of rugged, severe majesty (fig. 449). The nave has a wooden roof, and the piers are compound with two engaged columns. The vaulting in the south aisle is work of the eighteenth century. Above the aisles are galleries covered by very low roofs, and originally lighted from the nave by two-light openings enclosed by an arch. Above the arches of the crossing rose the lantern tower, now destroyed.

The south arm of the transept, which belongs to the original construction, has on its west side a passage or service gallery with lofty open arches (fig. 450); while the similar one on the eastern side has low arches. An ace of hearts is carved on the face of one of the piers belonging to the latter. With regard to this decorative motive of the ace of hearts, sometimes taking the form of an ace of spades, I may remark that it has been derived,[2] at least when it occurs later than the fifth century, from Syria. But this is not the case. These aces of spades and hearts, which are merely reproductions of the conventionalized outline of ivy or vine leaves with or without the stalk, had been used by Christian artists in the West from the earliest times of Christianity, either as a symbol, or as a full stop, or in separating or abbreviating words. A defective tablet, with an in-

Fig. 450. Bernay. Abbey Church. South arm of transept (1013)

scription of 269,[3] still exhibits ten aces of clubs, and originally fourteen or more. Nor was there any need for these artists to go to the distant East (e.g. the temple of Baalsamin at Siah founded about 23 B.C.) to find conventionalized ivy or vine leaves for there were plenty of examples in the West. They appear, to take one instance, on a mosaic of the Romano-British period discovered at Silchester (Calleva Atrebatum) (fig. 451).[4] And in Italy, not to mention the Romans, the Etruscans had used them in their tomb decorations from early times (fig. 452).

The nave and aisles are continued for two bays east of the crossing, the central space having a wooden roof, while the aisles had roughly constructed cross vaulting (fig. 453).

The original rude capitals in the nave and choir are Corinthianesque, with stiff, plain,

[1] PEIGNÉ-DELACOURT, *Monasticon Gallicanum*, vol. ii, pls. 109, 110.

[2] COURAJOD, *Origines de l'art gothique*, p. 56.

[3] DE ROSSI, *Inscriptiones Christianae urbis Romae*, vol. i, p. 18.

[4] ST. JOHN HOPE and FOX, *Excavations on the site of the Roman city at Silchester, Hants, in 1895*, in *Archaeologia*, vol. lv, part i (1896), p. 225 and pl. xii.

crocket leaves which take the place of the angle volutes.¹ Some have a crown of leaves, with a boss or rude human head instead of the flower (fig. 454). Some of them have been re-worked, probably in the days when the abbey was ruled by Vitalis (1060–1076), originally a monk at Fécamp and afterwards abbot of Westminster (1076–1082), when it attained its greatest prosperity. Some have even been treated with drapery, knobs, and cherubim heads, in the fantastic baroque style of the eighteenth century.

Fig. 451. Silchester. Portion of Roman mosaic. (From *Archaeologia*, vol. lv, pl. xii)

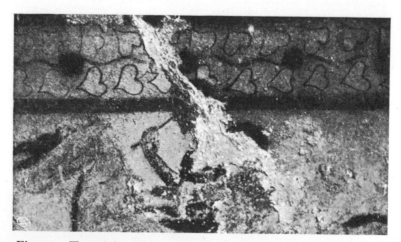

Fig. 452. Tarquinia. Wall painting in the Tomba del Letto Funebre

To judge by what is left, the external decoration of the building (fig. 455) was confined to a stringcourse at the foot of the windows, and occasionally billet mouldings round the archivolts. The walls were entirely without buttresses. In short, it was a structure of noble proportions, but poor in mouldings and carving.

The architect was William of Volpiano ('Haec enim auctore Guillelmo abbate Fiscannensi . . .'),² who personally directed the works at their outset ('qui in locandis

---

¹ [One of the capitals at Bernay has the name of the carver inscribed upon it: ME FEC[IT] ISEMBARDVS. (H. T.)]

² SAMMARTHANUS, &c., *Gallia Christiana*, *Abbatiae dioecesis Lexouiensis*, *Bernaicus* (Paris, 1759), vol. xi, p. 830ᵉ.

fundamentis non modicum praestiterat consilii auxilium').[1] As to the builders, I imagine they were masons and workmen from Normandy, assisted by Italian or Burgundian master builders, and acting under their direction. What has survived of the work of Norman builders at a date not far removed from that of the erection of this church (e.g. at Jumièges) is more than sufficient to prove the impossibility of their undertaking a structure of this extent, or of constructing the vaulting which we see in the presbytery aisles at Bernay. A letter sent from Fécamp to Dijon in the time of Abbot William[2]

mentions the sending of master builders to Fécamp, that is to the centre of the religious, intellectual, and artistic life of Normandy. 'De artificibus aedificiorum nostrorum quae coepimus, vos obsecramus quod . . . mittere ad nos festinetis, quia valde nobis necessarii sunt.' This request must have been due to the small numbers and, still more, the lack of skill of the Norman workmen.

As for the carving (I refer, of course, only to the original work) I think we shall be right in ascribing it to Norman artists, perhaps inspired by artists among the monks who had learned how to handle the chisel during the erection of the great Burgundian edifice. At any rate, it is not from an Italian hand. The crocket leaf is characteristic of the Norman School, which introduced it subsequently into England.

This church provides material for the following interesting observations:

I. The plan of a Latin cross may come from that of SS. Peter and Paul, now Sant' Abondio outside

Fig. 453. Bernay. Abbey Church. South aisle of presbytery (1013)

Como (fifth century), that of the mausoleum of Galla Placidia (about 440), and, even more probably, that of Santa Croce (about 449) at Ravenna. These buildings, in their turn, were derived from cruciform Roman structures with a central cupola supported by a circle of columns, such as one illustrated in Montano.[3] In our case the plan shows two features worth notice.

The first is that of the aisles prolonged beyond the crossing. There was a precedent for the idea in the church of the Nativity at Bethlehem (fourth and sixth centuries), where the aisles were continued into the choir.

The other is that of the subordinate apses projecting from the transept outside the line of the choir aisles. This arrangement seems to have some relation to the recesses

---

[1] Du Monstier, op. cit., *Bernayum*, p. 400.
[2] Paris, Bibliothèque Nationale, Coll. de Bourgogne, tom. xi. [3] Op. cit., lib. ii, pl. 6.

taken out of the thickness of the eastern walls in the transept of the underground church of Saint Bénigne at Dijon; if indeed it were not borrowed from the Constantinian

Fig. 454. Bernay. Capital in the Abbey Church (1013)

Fig. 455. Bernay. South side of Abbey Church as seen from the prison yard (1013)

Fig. 456. Rome. Imperial Walls near the Porta Pinciana (4th century)

Vatican Basilica, where, as we learn from the plan made and published by Alfarano in 1590, the transept had niches on its western side (the side of the high altar), and in the end walls, all used for chapels and altars (see fig. 776).

These two features were afterwards copied in the great abbey churches built under

William of Volpiano's immediate supervision, or produced under the influence of the School of Fécamp, of which he was the founder and for many years the director.

II. The church affords the earliest instance of an arcaded wall-passage. Such passages, designed partly for purposes of communication, and partly for decorative effect, were suggested by passages like those in the Imperial walls of Rome (fig. 456).[1] There is no trace of them in any church earlier than Bernay. Later, when they had been put at the level of the clerestory, in imitation of the arcading in the interior of San Pietro at Toscanella (739), and embellished, they formed one of the most striking and truly original features of Lombardo-Norman ecclesiastical architecture.

Fig. 457. Florence. Baptistery (11th century)

It has been suggested, indeed, that in the interior of the Baptistery of Florence a wall-passage with pairs of openings (fig. 457) was constructed between the last years of the fourth century and the early ones of the fifth.[2] But this celebrated building was really a result of the material prosperity and religious zeal exhibited by Florence about the end of the tenth century.[3] It was not finished by 1057 or 1058, for otherwise it would have been consecrated by Pope Victor II (1054–1057) or his successor Stephen IX (1057–1058), both of whom died at Florence. The date of its completion was 1059, on the 6th of November of which year it was consecrated by Pope Nicholas II (1059–1061); and the dedication festival is still kept on that day.[4]

The pairs of openings have no intimate connexion with the masonry of the building, and are therefore a later addition. The assertion that the presence of Ionic capitals in these openings is decisive against a medieval origin both for this baptistery and for all the other structures in Italy and the various European countries where they occur,[4] is wrong. I will only mention here the Ionic capitals made expressly for the positions they occupy in the portico of San Lorenzo outside the walls (1216–1227) at Rome, and in the external open galleries of the façades of San Pietro (twelfth century) and Santa Maria Maggiore (1206) at Toscanella.

[1] [For the walls of Rome see I. A. RICHMOND, *The City Wall of Imperial Rome*; also RIVOIRA, *Roman Architecture*, p. 200.]

[2] NARDINI DESPOTTI MOSPIGNOTTI, *Il duomo di San Giovanni oggi battistero di Firenze*, p. 66.

[3] VILLARI, *I primi due secoli della storia di Firenze*, p. 69.

[4] NARDINI DESPOTTI MOSPIGNOTTI, *Il duomo di San Giovanni oggi battistero di Firenze*, pp. 83, 37.

III. The church of Bernay tells us, thirdly, that in Normandy at the beginning of the eleventh century great churches built in the new style, which was still in its infancy, had wooden roofs, except for the ground floor of the aisles. And further, that the characteristic Lombardic compound piers made their appearance in Normandy only after they had been in use for years in Italy, where they were first produced.

THE ABBEY CHURCH OF MONT SAINT MICHEL is known under the names of St. Michael 'in monte tumba', St. Michael 'in periculo maris', and St. Michael 'de monte'

Fig. 458. Mont Saint Michel in the 11th century. (From the Bayeux Tapestry)

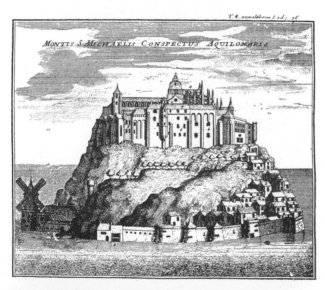

Fig. 459. Mont Saint Michel in the 18th century. (From the *Annales Ordinis S. Benedicti*, vol. iv, p. 75)

(figs. 458, 459, 460). Originally a mere chapel or oratory built by St. Aubert (about 708), bishop of Avranches, it was rebuilt after a fire (1001) in the time of Abbot Maynard II (991–1009) with a subsidy from Duke Richard II (996–1026), and was re-founded in 1020, when Hildebert II, a disciple of William of Volpiano, was abbot (1017–1022). This date, coming between the building of Bernay (1013) and the rebuilding of the church of Cerisy la Forêt (1030), would be considerably more important for us than it is had not the erection of the fabric been connected with dissensions between the monks of Mont Saint Michel and the abbot of Fécamp, which delayed its completion, and had it not in course of time undergone extensive alteration and rebuilding.

Suppo, abbot of Fruttuaria, was appointed (1023) by William of Volpiano to succeed Hildebert II. But the opposition of the Norman monks, who objected to the rule of a foreigner (and Suppo was William's nephew), prevented his taking possession, and Almodus (1023–1031) and Theodoric (1031–1033), another nephew of William, were appointed to administer the abbey. His installation did not take place till 1033 by Johannelinus, abbot of Fécamp (1029–1078). Suppo remained abbot, in spite of the continual opposition of the monks, till 1048, when he went back to Fruttuaria.

These events were not of a kind to facilitate the progress of the new buildings then in course of erection. The works, in themselves, had already demanded a great deal of time and trouble, on account of the massive substructions required for carrying out Hildebert's design of constructing on the summit of the conical rocky eminence a platform on which the church and conventual buildings were to stand. So that in 1048 the choir was hardly finished, and, in fact, Abbot Raoul de Beaumont (1048–1058) was still engaged in 1058 in erecting the piers and arches for the central tower. Abbot Ranulphe I de Bayeux (1060–1084) worked on the nave (according to some he entirely finished it),[1] which his successor, Roger I (1084–1106), completed in its upper part (Labbe[2] says that he put on the roof), only to see the north side collapse (1103),[3] Huynes stating that the nave fell down on that side.[3] The disaster was repaired by Roger II (1106–1123), under whom the abbey was set on fire by lightning (1112), the vaulting and walls being left without any covering. Bernard de Bec (1131–1149) raised a bell-tower above the four piers of the crossing, and Robert de Torigni (1154–1186)

Fig. 460. Mont Saint Michel in 1904

built two western towers, one of which fell shortly afterwards, and added a porch to the west front.

Such is, in brief, the generally accepted history of the church of Mont Saint Michel in the eleventh and twelfth centuries, as it may be found in the latest publications on the subject.[4] Of this church (in the form of a perfect Latin cross, like William's design for Bernay), damaged on several occasions by fire, by the fall of the central tower and of the choir which was rebuilt in the Pointed style of the fifteenth and sixteenth centuries, deprived in the eighteenth of three out of the seven bays of the nave and aisles which threatened to collapse, the only portions that survive are the transept and the four easternmost bays of the nave and aisles.

[1] SAMMARTHANUS, &c., Gallia Christiana, Abbatiae dioecesis Abrincensis, S. Michael in periculo maris, vol. xi, p. 515 D.

[2] Nova bibliotheca manuscriptorum librorum (Paris, 1657), De abbatibus M.S. Michaelis in periculo maris, vol. i, p. 351.

[3] ROBILLARD DE BEAUREPAIRE, Huynes, Histoire générale de l'abbaye du Mont Saint-Michel au Péril de la mer, p. 164.

[4] GOUT, Le Mont Saint-Michel: Histoire de l'Abbaye et de la ville, étude archéologique et architecturale des monuments (Paris, 1910), vol. i, Introduction, and second part: Les temps anciens: Le moyen âge. CORROYER, Description du Mont Saint-Michel, pp. 181, 183, 186.

This history requires correction in one point, viz. as to the works carried out under the eighth abbot, Raoul de Beaumont, originally a monk at Fécamp, and appointed

by William of Volpiano in 1028 to take charge of the abbey of Bernay. For Raoul's operations cannot have been confined to the piers and arches forming the central bay or crossing, but must have extended to a part of the body of the building, in order to abut the piers and enable them to resist the weight and thrust of the arches. An examination of the structure during the last restoration has in fact made it clear to me that the two bays nearest to the crossing are, owing to various features which they present, evidently the work of a different period from that of the next bays; and this period is nearer to the first than the second half of the eleventh century.

Fig. 461. Mont Saint Michel. Abbey Church. Capital (1048–1058)

In these bays, the imposts of the two-light openings in the south gallery have a different outline from that in the next bays. Further, one of the original crocket capitals with a human head (fig. 461) is very similar to the earlier

ones at Bernay (1013) and Cerisy la Forêt (1030–1066); while it is itself clearly older than those in the crypt of the Trinité (1064–1066), and others in Saint Étienne at Caen (1066–1086), and must therefore be dated before 1064.

The body of the church is divided into nave and aisles (fig. 462) by cruciform piers of uniform size. The nave had a wooden roof, while the aisles have rudely constructed unraised cross vaulting. The triforium (fig. 463) gets its light from the nave, and is covered by a sloping roof. The exterior is marked by lesenas which to some extent have suffered from alteration (fig. 464).

The low triforium without direct lighting, more lofty, however, than the one at Bernay, which is also without windows, but not of large size with windows in the aisle walls which are carried up above the vaulting, as at Cerisy la Forêt; and the absence of wall-passages in the clerestory, as at Bernay, while that system of communication and decoration is employed at Cerisy la Forêt, prove that in the construction of the body of the church the design of the original

Fig. 462. Mont Saint Michel. Abbey Church (11th and 12th centuries)

choir (1020) was followed. And that is the reason why we deal with the building in this place, so that it may form a link in the chain of the history of the Lombardo-Norman basilica.

Mont Saint Michel was the work of the School of Fécamp founded by William of

Fig. 463. Mont Saint Michel. Triforium in Abbey Church (11th and 12th centuries)

Fig. 464. Mont Saint Michel. South side of Abbey Church
(11th and 12th centuries)

Volpiano, and was modelled on the abbey church of Bernay, from which it differs by its piers with roofing shafts, not only in the choir but in the transept and the whole of the nave; by the lesenas which strengthen the walls on the outside; by the triforium with its pairs of two-light instead of single openings, and greater space gained by carrying up the aisle walls; and by the absence of wall-passages in the transept. It exhibits only one advance in scientific construction over its original, viz. the use of buttresses

Fig. 465. San Michele della Chiusa. Abbey Church (12th century)

at the points most in need of support, with the object of compensating for the reduced thickness of the outer walls.

We will conclude by remarking incidentally that of the two well-known churches with the title of Mount St. Michael—the one just described, and that at Chiusa (fig. 465) on the summit of the Monte Pircheriano in the Val di Susa—the latter no longer provides any materials for our studies. Of the original church on Monte Pircheriano, founded, according to some, in 966, or between 999 and 1002 according to others, by Hugues de Montboissier, all that is left is the plan of a basilica of small dimensions and irregular outline, with nave and aisles ending in apses, beneath the floor of the present church, which was erected about the second half of the twelfth century.

THE ABBEY CHURCH OF CERISY LA FORÊT was erected in 1030 by order of Duke Robert II, called by some 'the Magnificent' and by others 'the Devil' (1028–1035), to replace the church founded by St. Vigor, bishop of Bayeux (514–537),[1] and destroyed by the Normans. It was dedicated to him in 1032. The primary operations were directed by the abbot Durandus (1030–1033), previously a monk of St. Ouen at Rouen, and after him by Almodus (†1033), who had been in charge of the abbey of Mont Saint Michel (1023–1031). After the death of Robert II the building was continued and finished (with the exception of the west front, where the towers were left incomplete) by Duke William II, the Bastard (1035–1066), afterwards King William I, the Conqueror (1066–1087), through the instrumentality of the third abbot Garin (1032–1066), who had been a monk of Mont Saint Michel.

Fig. 466. Cerisy la Forêt. Abbey Church. Capital in the nave (1030–1066)

Altered in the thirteenth century by the vaulting of the presbytery, nave, and transept, at which time the west front was modified by the addition of a porch; damaged in the eighteenth century by the collapse of a part of the north arm of the transept, and by lightning in the sixteenth, seventeenth, eighteenth, and nineteenth centuries, it was partly demolished in 1811, and reduced to its present condition.[2]

Generally speaking, its plan is a copy of those of Bernay and Mont Saint Michel. The only difference is the feature of the piers which bisect the extremities of the transept and carry galleries. Of the structure of Robert II and William II there remain three of the eight original bays of the nave, the last of which was flanked by the two western towers, the whole of the upper limb of the cross, and the transept, of which the northern arm has been mutilated.

In the nave the arches spring from compound piers, alternately larger and smaller, cruciform in section with four half-columns and the same number of angle shafts. The capitals are Lombardo-Norman Corinthianesque, not continuous, however like the Lombardic, but confined to the columns.

Fig. 467. Cerisy la Forêt. Abbey Church. Triforium (1030–1066)

They occasionally recall those with figure subjects in San Flaviano at Montefiascone, and the vegetable forms are treated fairly well, though without

---

[1] Du Monstier, op. cit., *Cerasium*, p. 429. [2] [De Lasteyrie, op. cit., pp. 503, 774.]

much undercutting. The animal representations, however, are very barbarous, especially those of human beings (fig. 466).

The aisles have cross vaulting. Over them extends a spacious triforium with wooden roofs (fig. 467). Above, in the clerestory, a service gallery is constructed, with triplet openings enclosed by a single arch after the Ravennate fashion, and this runs the whole way round the building. The nave and choir had originally a wooden roof, and the walls were not tied together by transverse arches as some have imagined.[1] Any one can satisfy himself of this who takes the trouble to mount to the present vaulting. The

Fig. 468. Cerisy la Forêt. Abbey Church. South arm of the transept (1030–1066)

Fig. 469. Cerisy la Forêt. Choir of Abbey Church (1030–1066)

two lowest stages of the central tower belong to the original work. The south arm of the transept (fig. 468) still retains its gallery carried on arches, and terminates on the east in an apsidal chapel opening out of both floors, not in its original condition.

The aisles and triforium extend for two bays east of the crossing. The deep semi-elliptical apse (fig. 469) has a range of blank arcading round its base. The middle stage contains a wall-gallery in continuation of the triforium, while round the clerestory runs a service gallery. Originally it had a wooden roof, but this was replaced in the thirteenth century by vaulting in radiating sections.

The great display of tiers of multiplied arches in this apse, giving it an effect of severe majesty, has a decorative as well as a practical object which, it seems to me, was suggested, on the one hand, by the desire to give a magnificent appearance to the most sacred part of the church, and, on the other, by the difficulty of procuring marbles

[1] DEHIO and VON BEZOLD, op. cit., vol. ii, p. 286; FARCY, *Abbayes de l'évêché de Bayeux*, 1er fasc., p. 41.

for lining the walls, or artists capable of decorating the vault with adequate paintings or mosaics. The motive of lofty arches to decorate the internal wall of an apse is an old one. The apse of the 'Bishop's chapel',[1] going back to the time of Frugiferus, first bishop of Trieste (524–about 568) and founder of the cathedral,[2] provides an instance of a range of arches supporting the half-dome (fig. 470).[3]

Fig. 470. Trieste. Duomo. 'Bishop's chapel' (524–about 568)

The church is lighted by round-headed windows, splayed on the inside. The walls of the exterior (figs. 471, 472) show frequent use of herring-bone work, and are strengthened by buttresses. The lantern tower is embellished with blank arcading. The fact that this is partly hidden by the main roofs of the church has suggested the idea[4] that the nave and transept had originally a flat roof covered with sheets of lead on the outside, and with a ceiling within. But the eleventh-century builders certainly used gabled roofs in such cases; and the architect would never have followed any other plan,

[1] [See note 2, vol. i, p. 237.]
[2] GAMS, op. cit., p. 319.
[3] [It should, however, be noted that the mosaics belong to the 12th, and the frescoes to the 14th century. (A.)]
[4] FARCY, loc. cit.

3274.2

M

considering the region in which the church was situated with all its rain and snow, under whose weight a flat roof might have given way.

It is not known whether the plans for Cerisy la Forêt were made by Durandus, or by him with suggestions from William of Volpiano, who, just at the time when the rebuilding was begun, had come back from Fruttuaria to Fécamp, where John of Aglié, called 'Johannelinus', was then abbot (1029–1078), and where William himself died in 1031.

Fig. 471. Cerisy la Forêt. South side of Abbey Church (1030–1066)

It is, however, certain that the designs were modelled on two buildings of the School of Fécamp, Bernay, and Mont Saint Michel, from which it proclaims its direct and immediate descent.

The builders were apparently Normans; at least, there are no signs of any Italian gild in any part of the work, from the rough, unraised, and heavy cross vaulting, to the carving on the capitals. The craftsmen of Normandy were at last, for better or worse, self-sufficing, though they may have had the aid of carvers who were monks or came from some other part of France, e.g. Anjou, where as early as 1028 representations of living beings were being produced, as we noticed in the church of Ronceray. Very different was the cross vaulting produced at the same period in Italy, sometimes with bold ribs after the Lombardic fashion, as in San Flaviano at Montefiascone (1032), which is nearly contemporary with Cerisy. Very different, too, was the carving, as San Flaviano again bears witness.

Cerisy shows a notable advance over Mont Saint Michel in organic forms, by the adoption of two of the typical characteristics of the Lombardic church. On the one hand, the triforium is lighted directly from the raised outer walls, which by their additional weight strengthen the lower part corresponding to the aisles. The other Lombardic feature is the alternation of large and small piers. Lombardic influence is

Fig. 472. Cerisy la Forêt. Abbey Church from the south-east (1030–1066)

further illustrated by the characteristic arcaded wall-passages. And, finally, it appears in the two stages of wall-passages round the apse, continuing the triforium and clerestory passages. It thus marks another notable step towards the perfection of the Lombardo-Norman basilica.

The characteristic arcaded clerestory passages of the nave, choir, and apse, which combine their immediate utilitarian object with a constructive and static purpose, viz. that of diminishing the weight of the upper part of the walls, and also with a decorative intention, have the merit of absolute novelty. We saw their beginnings at Bernay and in San Pietro at Toscanella (739). Before the erection of Saint Vigor, service passages were either mere gangways protected by a railing, carried along projecting cornices above the architraves of colonnades and galleries in large naves, or else below the impost lines of domes and half-domes. Such passage-ways are illustrated by the old St. Peter's at Rome (fourth century) (fig. 473), and by St. Irene (eighth century) and St. Sophia (532–537) at Constantinople.

Another novelty at Cerisy is the arcaded passage formed in the thickness of the apse walls, and continuing the triforium. It was suggested by apsidal galleries like the upper

Fig. 473. Rome. Old St. Peter's (4th century). (From BONANNI, *Templi Vaticani Historia*)

stage of the apse of Santo Stefano at Verona (tenth century), and by the blank arcade in the apse at Germigny des Prés (801–806).

We should also notice the feature of the transept galleries, which first appeared in the Lombardo-Norman basilica, and was suggested by the two porticoes at the ends of the transept in the Constantinian Vatican basilica.

In the same way we should note the first appearance in Normandy of animal figures on capitals. In Italy, after making a timid display in San Babila at Milan early in the eleventh century, they had attained considerable development by 1032 in San Flaviano at Montefiascone; but in France they did not appear till somewhat later. Notre Dame de la Charité at Angers, consecrated in 1028, affords a very early dated example. If its capitals betray Lombardic influence, the handiwork of French carvers is no less obvious. To mention only one point, the crocket leaves were not the work of any Italian chisel.

THE ABBEY CHURCH OF JUMIÈGES, begun in 1040 by the well-known Robert II, one of the advisers of Edward the Confessor (1042–1066), for a short time bishop of London (1044), afterwards archbishop of Canterbury (1051–1052), and from 1037 onwards abbot of Jumièges, was finished in 1066 and consecrated in 1067, in the presence of William the Conqueror (1066–1087),[1] by Maurilius, archbishop of Rouen (1055–1067), a disciple of William of Volpiano and an Italian by birth according to one account, though others say that he was born at Rheims.

Fig. 474. Jumièges. West front of Abbey Church (1040–1066)

After the alterations of the fourteenth century, and the destruction in the first years of the nineteenth, all that is left of the original building is the west front (fig. 474), the body of the church as far as the crossing, and a portion of the latter and the central tower (figs. 475, 476).[2] Within the front, flanked by a pair of very lofty towers, a narthex of two stories is formed. The carving of the two Lombardic capitals (fig. 477) in the upper one is later. In the towers, the square base passes into an octagon, and the octagon into a circle, by means of conchiform squinches or hood-shaped raccords. The nave, which was designed for a wooden ceiling, has eight round arches on either side, and square piers with three half-columns attached (the half-piers of Pointed character on the nave side are a fourteenth-century addition), alternating with cylindrical piers which are not tapered. In all these supports, and the corresponding ones in the outer wall, the columns are surmounted by quadrangular funnel-shaped cubical capitals, which sometimes have a ridge down the middle, and the angles hollowed out. The left aisle still retains its original unraised cross vaulting of rough construction, above which is the triforium with similar vaulting. The latter, on the nave side, has triple openings enclosed by a single arch after the Ravennate fashion.

On the outside, the north wall of the aisle and triforium, which is visible and in good preservation, is strengthened by massive buttresses corresponding to the wall

---

[1] *Rolls Series*, 90, *Willelmi Malmesbiriensis monachi gesta regum Anglorum*, p. 145; DU MONSTIER, op. cit., *Gemeticum*, p. 310; LOTH, *Histoire de l'abbaye royale de Saint-Pierre de Jumièges*, vol. i, pp. 189–90.

[2] [The foundations of the ambulatory of the 11th-century apse, which had no projecting chapels, have now been uncovered. See G. LANFRY, *Fouilles et découvertes à Jumièges: le déambulatoire de l'église romane*, in *Bulletin Monumental*, vol. lxxxvii (1928), pp. 107–37. Cp. DE LASTEYRIE, op. cit., 800, 801. (R.)]

piers within (fig. 478). Their present stepped form is the result of later alterations. The central tower, which is square and not octagonal as stated by Cordero,[1] had originally a wooden roof. The ruins of the transept show that the side walls were pierced in their highest part by passages.

Fig. 475. Jumièges. Nave of Abbey Church (1040–1066)

Notwithstanding all the injuries inflicted by time and human agency, the latter being by far the most serious, enough is left of this impressive church to compel the spectator on the first view to pause and admire, not indeed the elegance of its decoration or the grace of its forms, but its severe lines, its noble proportions, and the grandeur of the whole effect.

The church of Jumièges, rude but excellent example as it is of the method of building prevalent in Normandy about the middle of the eleventh century, displays a marked advance on the way towards the perfection of the Lombardo-Norman basilica, by

[1] Op. cit., p. 142.

the extension of cross vaulting to the aisles and triforium, the angle thrust being met
by substantial buttresses outside. Choisy[1] speaks of this as a risky undertaking, and
one that must appear so when we think of the depression of the vaulting and the consequent increase of thrust, and also of the time when it was done. And it could only be
carried out at the expense of the direct lighting of the triforium.

Next, we may notice the hood-shaped raccords in the western towers, the earliest

Fig. 476. Jumièges. Nave and transept of Abbey Church (1040–1066)

instance of this form north of the Alps to which I can point. The central tower is also
notable because, though the explosives intended to destroy it at one blow in 1802 have
spared only one of its four sides, what remains makes it clear that it had a roof of wood
and not of masonry, and, with the traces left of the nave roof, enables us to restore its
form and that of the ceiling below it—details which are of interest for the history of
Norman architecture.

Nor should we omit to notice the presence of a decorative form not previously used
in ecclesiastical architecture, viz. the bands of chequer pattern, so frequently reproduced
later in Normandy and England, and finally by the architect Lanfrancus to the capitals
in the cathedral at Modena (1099–1106). This chess-board motive was a favourite one

[1] *Histoire de l'architecture* (Paris, 1903), vol. ii, pp. 189–90.

with the Etruscan artists, who often employed it in tomb-paintings (fig. 479). The Romans applied it specially in mosaics.

On the other hand, we must not ignore the retrograde step taken by the designer in going back to some of the forms of the church at Bernay (e.g. the absence from the nave piers of roofing shafts rising to the point where they could carry the main beams of the roof, and the lack of wall-passages with open arches springing from thick piers), which are a negation of the progress we remarked at Mont Saint Michel and Cerisy la Forêt. This retrogression may, perhaps, have been due to the theories of construction which Robert II had learned in the school of William of Volpiano, and also, in the case of the piers, to the desire of keeping the nave freer by suppressing the wall shafts with their bases, and relying on the considerable thickness of the nave walls and the substantial buttresses outside for resisting the weight and thrust of the main beams of the roof.

Fig. 477. Jumièges. Abbey Church. Capital in upper narthex (11th or 12th century)

Lastly, we must notice the alternation of massive piers with squat, untapered columns, an arrangement which demands some remark.

The organic conception of supports alternately substantial and slight, which was introduced in the first Lombardic vaulted churches, had no connexion with the device of pairs or triplets of columns alternating with piers, as in Santa Maria in Cosmedin and Santa Prassede at Rome, in spite of the reiterated assertions to the contrary of so many writers, one of whom, Enlart,[1] adds that the expedient was the origin of a whole constructive system. For the last restoration of Santa Maria in Cosmedin has revealed the fact that the church of Hadrian I (772–795) was rebuilt in the twelfth century, only some of the oldest parts being preserved. And the piers in Paschal I's (817–824) church (in the shape of a 'crux commissa' where the transept forms the horizontal limb of a T) are the result of one of the remodellings which the building underwent. The alternate large and small supports found in Normandy are really due to Lombardic influence. In Italy it occurs as early as 985 in SS. Felice e Fortunato near Vicenza, and in 1013 at San Miniato near Florence.

The church of Jumièges forms the climax of the series of Lombardo-Norman buildings erected under the auspices of William of Volpiano. We have now to watch the rise of another series, essentially as important as the first, and superior to it in the intrinsic value of its results; one, too, in the course of which the style in question will be seen to take fresh and important steps towards completion.

Lanfranc, born at Pavia (1005) and educated in its venerable and flourishing school, the centre of Latin culture at the time, had left his home for France accompanied by a band of colleagues and disciples, and opened a school at Avranches (1039). Then, quite unexpectedly, he abandoned teaching, shut himself up in the monastery of Bec (1042), erected about that time by Herluin, previously abbot of Burneville (1034), and there received the coarse habit of a Benedictine monk. Thanks to him, this obscure convent soon became the intellectual centre of the Christian world. To the school which he there opened, and of which he was the life and soul, laymen of every station flocked from the most distant regions; the great sent their sons to it; the most famous

[1] Op. cit., p. 168.

Fig. 478. Jumièges. North side of Abbey Church (1040–1066)

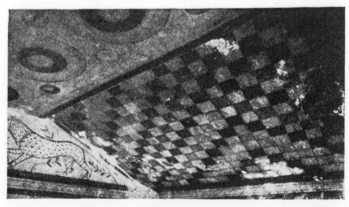

Fig. 479. Tarquinia. Painting in the Tomba dei Leopardi

masters, the most profound dialecticians regarded it as a special privilege to be allowed to frequent it.[1]

Herluin's buildings at Bec being found too small for such a concourse, new and more spacious ones took their place, and were consecrated in 1077. Lanfranc,[2] who had been appointed prior (1045–1066), designed them and began the work, which was finished by Anselm.[3] Nothing is left of this new structure, which is all the more to be regretted because it was the first essay in architecture of the creator of Saint Étienne at Caen and many other famous churches. And so it comes about that we are obliged to make

Fig. 480. Caen. Abbey Church of the Trinité. Crypt (1064–1066)

Fig. 481. Caen. Abbey Church of the Trinité. Capital in the crypt (1064–1066)

Saint Étienne itself the point of departure for the architectural epoch which succeeded that of William of Volpiano, and must be called the epoch of Lanfranc.

THE ABBEY CHURCH OF THE TRINITÉ AT CAEN.—The exact date of its erection is not known. Du Monstier[4] puts it in 1064. It was dedicated in 1066.[5] But the dedication clearly implied by the well-known charter of Duke William[6] ('coniux mea Mathildis . . . construxit basilicam') can only refer to the choir and crypt beneath it. It must have been finished by 1082, for in the deed of foundation which appears in Du Monstier we read that William the Conqueror and Queen Matilda had built the church ('ecclesiam . . . pro salute animarum nostrarum coaedificavimus'), and by the same deed the abbey was endowed with a noble revenue for its support.

The only part of the original building preserved intact is the crypt (figs. 480, 481). The church as a whole (speaking of the parts that are old) is the result of a general remodelling in the twelfth century (figs. 482, 483).

[1] DUCHESNE, *Hist. Normann. script. antiqui* (Paris, 1619), *Willelmi Calculi historia Normannorum*, pp. 261, 262[a]; LE PRÉVOST, op. cit., vol. ii, pp. 210–11; MABILLON, *Acta Sanct. Ord. S. Benedicti, Crispinus Milo, Vita B. Lanfranci*, vol. ix, pp. 633–4.
[2] [See appendix to Chapter I, *supra*, p. 47.]

[3] MIGNE, *Patr. Lat.*, vol. 150, *Chronicon Beccensis abbatiae*, p. 646 A.
[4] Op. cit., *Cadomus*, p. 625.
[5] LE PREVOST, op. cit., vol. ii, p. 163, note.
[6] SAMMARTHANUS, &c., *Gallia Christiana*, vol. xi, p. 59 B, C, *Instrumenta Ecclesiae Baiocensis*.

Fig. 483. Caen. Abbey Church of the Trinité (12th century)

Fig. 482. Caen. Abbey Church of the Trinité (12th century)

THE ABBEY CHURCH OF SAINT ÉTIENNE AT CAEN was, like the Trinité, founded in expiation of the marriage contracted by Duke William II with Matilda of Flanders in face of the prohibition decreed by the Council of Rheims (1049). About the dates when it was begun and when it was consecrated, there is disagreement among the contemporary writers and chroniclers. Du Monstier [1] places the former in 1064. But seeing

Fig. 484. Caen. Abbey Church of Saint Étienne (1066–1086)

that Lanfranc, the architect of the building (his subordinate was his pupil Ralph, afterwards prior of Caen), was appointed the first abbot of Saint Étienne in 1066, [2] we may infer that the latter year is the more probable date, if not of laying the first stone, at any rate of the beginning of building operations on a large scale. As to the consecration, the date 1077, given by Ordericus Vitalis, [3] must be that of the choir, transept, and part of the nave; while that of 1081 or 1086, which appears in Du Monstier,

[1] Op. cit., *Cadomus*, p. 625.   [2] LE PRÉVOST, op. cit., vol. ii, p. 126.   [3] Ibid., p. 128 and note.

will refer to some minor ceremony [1] relating to the completion of the building and the alterations effected in the west front and the towers.

What is left of the original church comprises the western limb of the cross with the west front and internal narthex and the transept. The eastern limb (except part of the triforium) and the apse, together with the apsidal chapels in the transept were sacrificed to the rage for the Pointed style.

The body of the church, entered through a two-storied narthex confined between the western towers, is divided into nave and aisles by an arcade with compound piers alternately larger and smaller (fig. 484). The half-columns belonging to these supports (fig. 485) and those in the triforium (fig. 486) are surmounted by Corinthianesque capitals supporting a continuous abacus, and ornamented with plain crocket leaves,

Fig. 485. Abbey Church of Saint Étienne. Capitals in nave (1066–1086)

Fig. 486. Caen. Abbey Church of Saint Étienne. Capitals in triforium (1066–1086)

carved foliage, projections either plain or graduated, and with human or semi-human heads. These capitals, though their conventional treatment betrays a want of imagination in the carvers, are nevertheless well designed, with free movement and bold relief, but not completely undercut. The same, however, cannot be said of the figures; for no sooner do the carvers leave the treatment of foliage than they fail and become clumsy. The heads, something between man and beast, with erect pointed ears, should be noticed, for this stylistic representation, with another which we shall see on the piers of the central tower, crossed the Channel, and served as a model for the carvers of Great Britain, e.g. those who worked in Durham Cathedral (1093–1133).

The aisles, originally covered by unraised cross vaulting, have triforium galleries over them, roofed by ribbed half-barrel vaults (fig. 487). If this barrel vaulting is not original, everything shows that it merely replaced an older roof of the same kind. Nor can Ruprich-Robert's [2] idea that it was unnecessary be maintained, for at Jumièges (1040–1066) it was precisely the triforium that was vaulted, while the nave had a timbered roof. Its object is easily explained by the architect's desire to increase the stability of the nave walls, which, though about 4 feet 6 inches thick, were considerably weakened by the wall-passages with their wide arches, and also by the external blank

[1] FREEMAN, *The History of the Norman Conquest of England*, vol. iii, p. 108.
[2] *Les voûtes de l'abbaye-aux-hommes à Caen* (*Bulletin de la Société des Beaux-Arts de Caen*, vol. ii, 1862 p. 412; vol. iii, p. 33).

arcading. The expedient adopted at Saint Étienne was afterwards followed by Serlo in the choir of Gloucester, rebuilt in 1089.

Above the triforium on either side runs a clerestory passage with triplet openings, the result of an alteration which is believed to have been carried out in the twelfth century, when the existing vaulting was substituted for the original ceiling of the nave and choir. In the course of this, new clerestory arches were opened lower down, with the object of enabling the walls to offer more resistance to the thrust of the vaulting. Their capitals are in the form of truncated and inverted half-cones and wicker baskets, or else they show monsters with serpents' tails, foliage, interlacings, monsters with demon heads and limbs ending in cauliculi. The archivolts are ornamented with an embattled moulding sunk in the thickness of the wall. All the instances of the embattled and zigzag moulding which appear on the interior walls of the church are later additions. At the same time was inserted the continuous course of billet moulding carried round the capitals of the vaulting shafts; and the capitals themselves were carved. The half wall-piers were also converted into shafts from which to spring the ribs of the groining.

Fig. 487. Caen. Abbey Church of Saint Étienne. Triforium (1066–1086)

Above the present vaulting may still be seen the continuous impost cornice at the height of the original ceiling; and in the north wall there are traces of two of the original openings of the service passage, each of four lights, with roll mouldings, and uniform in size like those at Cerisy la Forêt.

In the central tower, the arches of which are not in their original state, the capitals of the piers exhibit, besides the usual single or combined leaves, a human head, and another characteristic semi-human one with pointed ears and no lower jaw, but a row of dog's teeth in the upper one.

The ends of the transept are occupied by galleries with unraised cross vaulting (fig. 488). Here the figure carvings are barbarous in design and no less rude in execution, and teach us that if the Norman craftsmen had by this time learned to treat pure decoration with some grace, they were still far from being at home in dealing with the human form.

In the triforium of the existing choir are to be seen part of an arch parallel to the axis of the building, and some Corinthianesque capitals, both belonging to the original work.

Bouet[1] states that the original choir had cross vaulting, but with this I do not agree.

The exterior of the nave, aisles, triforium, and central tower is embellished with blank arches and arcading (fig. 489). The west front (fig. 490) contains three Lombardic portals (fig. 491) which have been partly rebuilt. The three stages of the towers, with their wall arcading, must be assigned to between 1081 and 1086; the upper portions were completed at later dates.

[1] *Analyse architecturale de l'abbaye de Saint-Étienne de Caen*, p. 18, note.

Saint Étienne, though, on the whole, it belongs to the type established by William of Volpiano, presents certain organic and decorative features which differentiate it from that type; and some of these mark a new step towards the completion of the Lombardo-Norman basilica.

In this church Lanfranc remained content to carry the vaulting shafts up to the roof, hinting at a desire to cover the nave with cross vaulting, which, however, he never fulfilled (in spite of Bouet's[1] idea to the contrary), deterred perhaps by the inefficiency

Fig. 488. Caen. Abbey Church of Saint Étienne.
Gallery in north arm of transept (1066–1086)

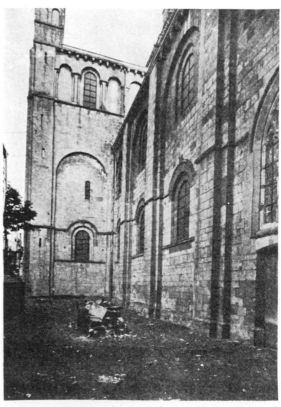

Fig. 489. Caen. North side of Abbey Church
of St. Étienne (1066–1086)

of his master masons. For the primatial church of Canterbury, which he began shortly after (1070), had a wooden roof; and similar roofs, without even the support of transverse arches, were provided for the first great churches built in England by his pupils. With this new arrangement goes that of the single arch openings of the triforium. Other peculiarities are the following:

I. The Ravennate motive of external arcading corresponding to the nave arches in the interior. Such applied arcading appeared in Saint Bénigne at Dijon, but it does not occur in the naves of the great Norman abbeys.

II. The blank external galleries forming a finish to the side walls of the church. I cannot remember any earlier example of this feature in Normandy. In another part of France, an older instance is presented by the abbey church of Ronceray at Angers

[1] BOUET, *Seconde lettre à M. de Caumont au sujet des voûtes de Saint-Étienne de Caen* in *Bulletin Monu-* *mental publié par la Société française d'Archéologie*, Caen, vol. 29 (1863), pp. 770, 774.

(1028). Some writers give the Normans credit for its invention, whereas it is a creation of the Lombardo-Ravennate style.

III. The arched corbel course forming a continuous cornice, the first of its kind to appear in a Lombardo-Norman church.

IV. Lastly, there are the portals of the west front. This is the first occasion on which we can verify their appearance in a building of the Lombardo-Norman style.

Fig. 490. Caen. West front of Abbey Church of Saint Étienne (1066–1086)

Fig. 491. Caen. Abbey Church of Saint Étienne. Portal in west front (1066–1086)

Further, we must not omit to notice the remarkable progress shown in the carved foliage of the capitals in Saint Étienne, compared with work of the same kind in earlier Norman buildings. These capitals are differentiated by their artistic quality, not only from the contemporary ones in the crypt of the Trinité at Caen, but also from those of the same date in the crypt of the cathedral of Bayeux, rebuilt by Bishop Hugh about the year 1044, finished and decorated by Odo I (1050–1097), and finally reconstructed after the fire of 1105.

This later crypt is not the work of Hugh or Odo, as has been thought,[1] some[2] actually believing that the existing church is Hugh's work and not a reconstruction.

---

[1] MYLNE, *The Cathedral Church of Bayeux*, p. 43; FREEMAN, op. cit., vol. ii, p. 214.

[2] BÉZIERS, *Mémoires pour servir à l'état historique et géographique au diocèse de Bayeux*.

Of the time of Hugh or Odo I (who was, according to Gams,[1] the builder of the church, which he consecrated in 1080) nothing is left save the outer walls, and some of the isolated supports with their bases and capitals showing plain, stiff, turn-over leaves and crocket leaves. In some cases they have been re-worked and embellished by carving the leaves. The rest is a reconstruction carried out by Bishop Philippe d'Harcourt

Fig. 492. Bayeux. Cathedral (12th and 13th centuries)

(1142–1164), and of this there remains the Lombardo-Norman part of the nave (fig. 492), the church having been largely rebuilt in the thirteenth century. To the time of Bishop Philip belong, for instance, a capital with foliage and human heads with cauliculi protruding from their mouths, and another with inverted half-cones surmounted by a denticulated cornice, this last type of capital not having been introduced when the crypt was built, as it appears in France for the first time at Boscherville. To the same date belong the bases of Pointed character and the beautiful continuous unraised

---

[1] Op. cit., p. 507. [Cp. DE LASTEYRIE, op. cit., p. 800, note 7.]

cross vaulting. The Norman builders of the eleventh century, though fairly skilful on the whole, were still indifferent constructors of vaulting. Ruprich-Robert[1] has called attention to their weakness in this respect, even during the next century.

THE CHURCH OF SAINT NICHOLAS AT CAEN, though not erected from the designs of Lanfranc, is immediately derived from his church of Saint Étienne, and is traditionally said to have been planned by monks who were his pupils, the same builders being employed who erected the abbey church. It will, then, be convenient to describe it next after the latter.

Fig. 493. Caen. Saint Nicholas. South aisle (1080–1093)

It is said to have been begun about the year 1080,[2] when the work on the west front of the neighbouring Saint Étienne was being brought to a conclusion, and is believed to have been finished in 1093. It is now a military store.

The plan shows that it belongs to the type which we connect with the name of William of Volpiano. It has a nave and aisles of seven bays, divided by six compound piers similar in section to those at Cerisy la Forêt. The capitals have foliated volutes or crockets, and crowns of leaves going all the way round, with projections representing the flower. This type of capital prevails all through the building. Occasionally we find a human or half-animal head with erect ears (rough work, evidently from the same chisel that produced those in Saint Étienne), that of a lion, and of some indefinable creature.

The aisles (fig. 493) have unraised cross vaulting. In the fifteenth century the timbered roofs of the nave and transept were replaced by Pointed vaulting. The interior of the central tower is embellished with two tiers of wall-passages. The transept, on the other hand, has ranges of deeply recessed arches without communication, just below the clerestory. Similar blank arcading decorates the apsidal chapels which project from their eastern sides (fig. 494). The choir, together with the nave, has a sham triforium corresponding to the aisle roofs, and has cross vaulting like the aisles. The apse has arcading in two tiers, one of which forms a passage. The exterior of the church is strengthened by substantial buttresses, and is decorated with arcading (figs. 495, 496). The west front is flanked by two towers, originally left unfinished.

Saint Nicholas marks another step towards the perfection of the Lombardo-Norman basilica by having the parts east of the crossing covered by cross vaulting with visible arches springing from compound piers, and supported by buttresses outside. Further, it exhibits an entirely new feature in the triforium, which is not an open gallery but

[1] Op. cit., vol. ii, p. 410.
[2] BOUET, *Analyse architecturale de l'abbaye de Saint-Étienne de Caen*, p. 17.

a mere series of tall, narrow openings, almost like loops. This arrangement (followed at Boscherville), which had the advantage of consolidating the walls by the omission of wide openings, combined with the shortness of the eastern limb, and the support provided by the adjoining transept and central tower (in itself an important element of stability), must have given confidence to the architect and builders in taking the step, which for them was a bold one, of covering the whole of the eastern limb of the church with cross vaulting. Lastly, in the apse we find for the first time the decorative

Fig. 494. Caen. Saint Nicholas. Chapel in south arm of transept (1080–1093)

Fig. 495. Caen. Saint Nicholas. South side (1080–1093)

treatment of large arches enclosing pairs of smaller blank ones. It was copied immediately afterwards at Boscherville, and later in other churches.

THE ABBEY CHURCH OF SAINT GEORGES AT BOSCHERVILLE.—As Saint Étienne was the parent of Saint Nicholas at Caen, so Saint Georges at Boscherville is the immediate descendant of the latter, and that is the reason for its inclusion in our survey.

Some writers would make out that the existing building is identical with the cruciform church mentioned in a well-known deed,[1] executed between 1053 and 1066, of Duke William II (1035–1066), and believed to have been erected about the year 1050 by Raoul de Tancarville to replace an earlier chapel, of uncertain age, dedicated to St. George. Others, on the contrary, regard it as a reconstruction of Raoul's

[1] BESNARD, *Monographie de l'église et de l'abbaye de Saint-Georges de Boscherville*, pp. 3–4.

church, carried out either when the Benedictine monks of Saint Évroult d'Ouche were installed in it (1114), or in the last quarter of the eleventh century.[1]

The ground plan (fig. 497) follows the type of William of Volpiano: a Latin cross; nave and choir with apsidal termination; aisles prolonged east of the crossing, and flanking the prebytery; a transept with minor apses projecting from the east side, and galleries at the ends. With the exception of the clerestory above the triforium, the

Fig. 496. Caen. Saint Nicholas. Apse (1080–1093)

scheme is a copy of that of Saint Nicholas at Caen: the same triforium, without direct light and formed under the slope of the roof, and similar vaulting for the choir.

The piers of the nave arcades have the same section as those at Cerisy la Forêt and Saint Nicholas at Caen. The pillars in some cases have Lombardic cubical capitals of the Sant' Abondio (1013–1095) type, but mainly capitals of a new pattern derived from a combination of the cubical Byzantine melon form and the aforesaid Lombardic capital. This form, with an entirely new inspiration, displays, in place of the segments of a melon, a sort of undulation consisting of shallow inverted semicones in relief. The primitive form of this capital is to be traced to England, where it appears in the Anglo-

[1] [For a recent account see *Congrès archéologique, Rouen*, 1926.]

Lombardic cubical capitals of St. Albans (1077–1088). There we find cubical capitals with each face exhibiting not a single half round, as in the Lombardic type, but two portions of rounds. This new capital (the real origin of which has not hitherto been pointed out), described in France as 'godronné' and in England as 'scalloped', while my name for it is the Anglo-Lombardic cubical capital, appears in its earliest form in the abbey church of St. Albans, and in more elegant and perfect shape in Gloucester Cathedral. The oldest instance of a scalloped capital, though without the refinement of that at Gloucester, which I can point to in France is to be found on the cruciform piers which carry the first transverse arch in the parish church of Saint Valentin at Jumièges (fig. 498), built by Abbot Ursus (1101–1127),[1] and original from the west front as far as the said arch.

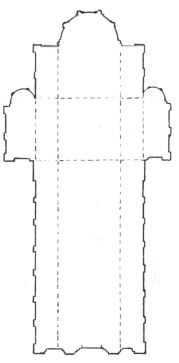

The new capitals of Boscherville, in some cases merely blocked out, are either quite plain, or else exhibit pointed, stiff, smooth leaves, stars, studs, and other ornaments. We also notice capitals decorated with the usual crockets, bunches of cauliculi, human heads, stylistic palmettos, interlaced circles, disks, cables, and monsters of all sorts. The foliage is fairly well treated, but not undercut; the figures, on the other hand, are very uncouth and barbarous. The bases, in some cases decorated with zigzags and other ornaments, are almost all provided with angle-spurs in the shape of claws, leaves, disks, &c.

The body of the church (fig. 499) was originally spanned by transverse arches with the object of resisting any inward tendency of the walls. Its roof was of timber, the present vaulting having been constructed in the thirteenth century. The side aisles had from the beginning unraised cross vaulting. Above the aisles runs a shallow triforium, constructed under the sloping roof, and originally lighted by narrow oblong openings contained within arcades of four arches to a bay. These have spurred bases and capitals ornamented with semi-cones, foliage, human and animal heads. These openings were blocked up later, perhaps when the present Pointed vaulting was constructed. A service passage is formed in the clerestory. The galleries

Fig. 497. Boscherville. Plan of Abbey Church (11th and 12th centuries)

at the ends of the transept (fig. 500) have interesting figure capitals (fig. 501).

The deep apse, encircled by blank and open arcading, was originally covered with a half-dome, to which ribs have been added at a later date. The two bays of the choir in front of it have ordinary unraised cross vaulting.

The most remarkable features of the exterior (figs. 502, 503) are the west front (fig. 504) with its Lombardic portal, the chief ornament of the church, and the arcaded apse.

And now let us turn to the vexed question of the date of Saint Georges. Attempts to fix it in an approximately definitive or, at any rate, an acceptable manner have hitherto been generally unsuccessful owing to a failure to bring the right buildings into comparison with it.

In my opinion, the existing church is certainly not the one mentioned in the foundation charter, which must have been a building of modest dimensions, but a new structure, carried out on a larger scale and under more advanced artistic conditions,

[1] Loth, op. cit., vol. i, p. 237.

Fig. 498. Jumièges. Church of Saint Valentin (12th century)

Fig. 499. Boscherville. Abbey Church (11th and 12th centuries)

before the year 1114, i.e. while the Augustinian Canons were still in possession, and after the completion of Saint Nicholas at Caen (1080–1093); in other words, between the last years of the eleventh and the first of the next century. With the exception of the west front, it was built all of a piece, and on a predetermined plan: the roll mouldings employed throughout are sufficient to prove this. The violent contrasts sometimes exhibited by the carvings are the result of later work, executed when the west front was erected under a new artistic impulse.

It must be later than Saint Nicholas at Caen, as it shows an advance in construction beyond that church in the form of the transverse arches of the nave. Its Anglo-Lombardic scalloped capitals must be later than the erection of the cathedral of St. Albans (1077–1088), where their primitive form appears for the first time. Moreover, the date of the body of the church is earlier than that of the west front. There is too great a gulf between the carvings of the latter with their free movement, and the clumsy forms in the church itself, for them to be contemporary. The front in its turn is considerably later than that of Saint Étienne at Caen, for the carvings of the portal of Saint Georges (which exhibits multiplied mouldings of much greater richness than the doors of

Fig. 500. Boscherville. Abbey Church. North arm of transept (11th and 12th centuries)

Fig. 501. Boscherville. Abbey Church. Capital in transept (11th and 12th centuries)

Lanfranc's church) reveal a more developed art and a surer hand than the doorways of Saint Étienne. It is also decidedly later than the chapter-house of the abbey, erected by Abbot Victor (1157–1211) after 1157, where (making allowances for the Pointed forms of the structure) the beautiful carved foliage and figures are very different both in style and execution from the work on the portal in question. Hence we may reasonably assign it to the first years of Abbot Louis (1114–1157) ('. . . ingenii sanctitatisque fama celeberrimum clarissimumque . . .'[1]); and to it, together with the re-working of some of the carving in the church, will refer the words 'ecclesiam ampliare et meliorare' in the well-known charter of Henry I of England (1100–1135).[2]

Saint Georges marks an advance in the principles

[1] *Gallia Christiana*, vol. xi, col. 268.
[2] Deville, *Essai hist. et descript. sur l'église et* *l'abbaye de Saint-Georges-de-Bocherville, près Rouen* (Rouen, 1827), p. 24.

Fig. 502. Boscherville. North side of Abbey Church
(11th and 12th centuries)

of equilibrium and construction beyond Saint Nicholas at Caen. The introduction of cross arches with walling above them served to bind the walls together, and also to provide a solid support for the roof; in case of fire, too, they would prevent the flames from spreading, and the nave walls from falling in. A very early instance of such arches, which form the germ of a revolution in the system of covering a church—the substitution of stone for timber—is to be seen in San Miniato al Monte, near Florence (1013); and the primitive church of SS. Felice e Fortunato, near Vicenza (985), provided a still older one.

We should notice also on the bases the free use of the characteristic protective spurs, which are not met with in Normandy before the second half of the eleventh century.

Lastly, the blank arcading which decorates both the interior and exterior of the apse of Saint Georges recalls an ancient circular structure treated in the same way —the vestibule of the 'Piazza d'Oro'[1] in Hadrian's Villa at Tivoli (125–135) (fig. 505). This vestibule is of no small importance in the history of architecture, for we may be sure that some Roman building of the same kind, derived from that in Hadrian's Villa, was the original which served as a model to the builders of the first medieval apses decorated with blank arcading.

The mention of Hadrian induces me to lay before the reader an original view of the Emperor and of the manner in which he influenced the buildings erected by him. My object is to bring into relief one of the eminent qualities of an illustrious ruler whose deficiencies are usually more noticed than his estimable sides, viz. his ability as a master architect.[2] This has, indeed, been previously suggested,[3] but as yet the facts have never been established.

Fig. 503. Boscherville. East end of Abbey Church
(11th and 12th centuries)

[1] [RIVOIRA, *Roman Architecture*, p. 134; and *supra*, vol. i, p. 23.]
[2] [Cf. RIVOIRA, *Roman Architecture*, pp. 118 ff.]
[3] LANCIANI, *The Ruins and Excavations of Ancient Rome*, p. 481.

Aelius Spartianus[1] states that Hadrian was well versed in arithmetic, geometry, and painting. His capacities as a geometrician and an artist are confirmed by other ancient authorities.[2] From a passage in Dio Cassius,[3] where he relates that Hadrian sent his plans for the Temple of Venus and Rome to Apollodorus, we learn that he made his own designs for his buildings. There is therefore no room for doubt as to his architectural endowments.

Among the structures, wholly or partially preserved, which he created and erected, the most important is the Pantheon at Rome, proved by recent investigations to be the result of a rebuilding carried out between 120 and 124. The fact might have been arrived at long ago if the formulas used by Spartianus—'instauravit, fecit, aedificavit, exaedificavit, extruxit'—had been correctly interpreted. For the Pantheon falls under the formula 'instauravit', which is used by Spartianus in the sense of 'restoration' only in the case of the Forum of Augustus. 'Romae instauravit Pantheum, Saepta, basilicam Neptuni, sacras aedes plurimas, forum Augusti, lavacrum Agrippae.' Whereas, in the case of the other pre-existing buildings which we are told that he rebuilt, it has the meaning of 'building afresh' or 'reconstruction'. As a matter of fact, rebuilding took place in the case of

Fig. 504. Boscherville. West front of Abbey Church
(11th and 12th centuries)

the Pantheon, which had been finished by Agrippa in 27 B.C.;

the Saepta Julia, begun by Julius Caesar and completed by Agrippa in the last-named year;

the Basilica of Neptune, another work of Agrippa of the year 26 B.C.;

the Baths of Agrippa, erected by him in 19 B.C.

The other expressions, on the contrary, are used for the structures of which Hadrian was the creator as well as the builder. Such, for instance, as

his Mausoleum with the bridge leading to it (136);

the Temple of Trajan in that Emperor's Forum;

his Villa at Tivoli (125–135);

the Basilica which he erected in honour of Plotina near Nîmes;

the monument raised by him to the memory of Pompey at Pelusium.

The lofty dome of the Pantheon was an object of admiration from ancient times onwards. Ammianus Marcellinus[4] bears testimony to this in his account of the notable things seen at Rome in 357 by the Emperor Constantius (337–361). The investigation

[1] *Script. Hist. Aug. Vita Hadriani*, 14, 9.
[2] *Incert. Auct. Epit. de Caes.*, 14, 2.
[3] *Dionis Cassii Cocceiani Historia Romana* (ed. Teubner), lib. lxix. 15.
[4] AMMIANUS MARCELLINUS, *Res gestae*, lib. xvi. 10, 14.

of its organic structure made in 1892 and 1893[1] revealed the masterly system of relieving arches which rendered possible the construction and ensured the stability of the wonderful pile (figs. 506, 507). I will only remark that, so far as my researches have gone, I have never found in a dome or half-dome of earlier date than the Pantheon any use of relieving arches or even of mere ribs; so that the employment of a skeleton framework in vaults of circular form is due to Hadrian.

Next to the Pantheon, in the new constructive and static features which it presents,

Fig. 505. Tivoli. Villa of Hadrian. Vestibule of the 'Piazza d'Oro' (125–135)

Fig. 506. Rome. Pantheon. System of relieving arches (120–124). (From BELTRAMI, *Il Pantheon*)

comes the Villa Tiburtina, which excited the wonder of Spartianus. Among them we note:[2]

I. The idea of cross vaulting springing from corbels, to be seen in the Large Baths, for which we may refer to fig. 123.

II. The half-dome in the Serapaeum,[3] with alternate concave and flat compartments. There is no record of any earlier instance of this treatment. And we cannot accept the suggestion that it is a reproduction of some original in the temple of Serapis at Canopus. It is true that Hadrian derived his general idea from the famous Egyptian sanctuary, but that does not imply that he copied it in every detail. Spartianus, in fact, does not refer to any such slavish imitation. 'Tiburtinam villam mire exaedificavit, ita ut in ea et provinciarum et locorum celeberrima nomina inscriberet, velut Lycium, Academian, Prytanium, Canopum, Picilem, Tempe vocaret. Et, ut nihil praetermitteret, etiam inferos finxit.'[4]

[1] BELTRAMI, *Il Pantheon*, pp. 37, 75.
[2] [See RIVOIRA, *Roman Architecture*, pp. 132 ff.]
[3] *Supra*, p. 42, and vol. i, p. 89.
[4] Ibid., 26, 5.

III. The conical raccords to which I have called attention in connexion with the baptistery of Galliano.[1]

IV. The vestibule of the 'Piazza d'Oro'. It is an octagonal hall, with recesses alternately round and rectangular, two of which form the entrance and exit. The plan reproduces that of two rooms in the 'Domus Augustana' on the Palatine. In the interior, the re-entrant angles contained shafts (now gone, but the sockets remain) supporting the semicircular arches which carried the compartments of the cupola. The latter was pierced by a round opening in the centre. On the outside, corresponding to the shafts within, are piers (about 1 ft. 4 in.×1 ft.), from which spring arches rising as high as the base of the cupola. These arches served four purposes. They met the oblique thrust of the arches inside; they strengthened the cupola at its base; they formed a facing to the walls, supplementing their very moderate thickness of some 1 ft. 8 in., with considerable economy of materials and expense; and they added grace and elegance to the structure.

I am unable to point to any earlier vaulted building in which such sound principles of making the forces of resistance depend on their distribution and not on mass were illustrated. Nor can I refer to any earlier example of a dome composed entirely of compartments.

On the model of the vestibule rose another work of Hadrian's (in all probability), which would naturally follow the first experiment made at Tivoli, viz. the semidome, called by Alò Giovannoli[2] in a view published in 1616 the 'Tempio di Siepe', which stood near

Fig. 507. Rome. Pantheon (120–124)

Hadrian's Temple of Neptune. This building was converted into Santo Stefano del Trullo, and demolished in the time of Pope Alexander VII (1655–1667).[3]

Lastly comes the Temple of Venus and Roma at Rome (121–135), which was finished by Antoninus Pius, damaged by fire in 307, and restored by Maxentius[4] (307–312).

The singular plan of two sanctuaries with their apses back to back, strengthened at their point of contact with massive buttresses, and the roof formed throughout of barrel vaulting some 68 ft. in diameter, make up a whole of absolute originality for that age, so far as temple architecture is concerned. And it is not difficult to understand the unfavourable judgement passed on it by Apollodorus when Hadrian, during the progress of the work, sent him the plans in order that he might see that buildings on a vast scale could be erected at Rome without his assistance. Some ill-feeling already existed between them. We may be sure that Hadrian had not forgotten or forgiven the insult he had received in the presence of Trajan when, according to the story in Dio Cassius, the Syrian, unaware of the young man's genius, had told him to 'go away and paint pumpkins'.

[1] Vol. i, pp. 217 ff.

[2] *Supra*, p. 41.

[3] [So LANCIANI (*Ruins and Excavations*, p. 490: *Storia degli Scavi*, i. 132); but HÜLSEN (op. cit., p. 40: *Le Chiese di Roma nel Medio Evo*, p. 485), maintains that a Renaissance document and other indications show that S. Stefano del Trullo was situated in the Piazza di Pietra, where the modern Via dei Bergamaschi enters it. (A.)]

[4] [RIVOIRA, *Roman Architecture*, pp. 131, 215.]

Moreover, the Greek architect brought up in the theory of elegant flat-roofed architectural compositions, so far as basilicas and temples were concerned, of which he had produced so notable an example in the Forum of Trajan at Rome ('singularem sub omni caelo structuram'[1]), must have thought the design conceived and the constructive methods adopted by the Imperial architect at least inharmonious and possibly extravagant. And this quite apart from the unfavourable criticisms which Dio tells us he made on the building.

Here was more than a quarrel between two great architects: it was a battle between two schools, the Roman and the Greek, placed as they were at opposite poles. The one, the representative of a new people, serious, sturdy, practical; capable of conquering a world and impressing a unity upon it: the other, the expression of an old race, restless, unstable, but penetrated with the sense of proportion and beauty. It was the clash of two architectural styles. The one new, finding its chief expression in Baths and Palaces; based essentially on vaulting and its combination, stability, and equilibrium; deriving its source of vitality from its own nature and not from the liberal aid of the minor arts; capable of inexhaustible development leading to the production of new styles. The other, mainly an architecture of temples, carried by the Greeks to a superlative degree of beauty, but by this time fossilized and incapable of giving birth to new treatments.

The buildings raised by Hadrian which we have examined are the main exponents of vaulted construction, carried out scientifically, in the Roman Empire during the second century. And it was to the impulse given by the Emperor-architect to the building art ('in omnibus paene urbibus aliquid aedificavit'[2]) that a feature of capital importance for vaulted architecture was due. For it was in the time of Hadrian (who has been described as the only man of genius among the Roman Emperors[3]) that the ribs which had previously been used by the Romans in arches and barrel vaults were first applied to cross vaulting. And this is not all. These diagonal ribs, very interesting examples of which are provided by the substructions of the Palace of Septimius Severus[4] (203) and the Imperial *Pulvinar* looking on to the Circus Maximus at Rome, with double or single 'chains' of brick, while the Baths of Diocletian present striking instances with two chains and compartments in brickwork filled in with rubble, were also used in a new way by making them stand out on the intrados of the vault, as may be seen in the 'Sette Bassi'[5] Villa near Rome. And this form was the precursor of the principle of vaulting in the Lombardic and Pointed styles.

Our account of the Norman churches must be supplemented by the description of another which, though not in Normandy but close to the borders of southern Burgundy, nevertheless belongs to the Lombardo-Norman style, and was the work of the same monastic order which produced the founder of that style, William of Volpiano. This building, as being the most complete expression· of the science of construction as practised by the Cluniac monks and French builders at the close of the eleventh and the opening of the following century, furnishes a sure guide for estimating the real conditions of French ecclesiastical architecture at that time, and also for testing the much-vaunted influence of the School of Cluny and of French art generally on the evolution and perfection of the vaulted Lombardic basilica.

---

[1] *Ammianus Marcellinus*, xvi. 10, 15.

[2] *Script. Hist. Aug.*, *Vita Hadriani*, 19, 2.

[3] STUART JONES, *The Roman Empire* (London, 1908), p. 195.

[4] [RIVOIRA, *Roman Architecture*, p. 164.]

[5] [Ibid., p. 140; *supra*, vol. i, p. 281.]

THE ABBEY CHURCH OF CLUNY.[1]—The original church of the abbey, founded in 910[2] by William the Pious, Duke of Aquitaine (887–918), and the Abbot Berno (910–927), was a mere chapel. When this became too small for the ever-growing community, a larger structure (still preserving the old one) was begun under Abbot Aymar (942–965), finished by Majolus (944–994), and dedicated in 981. Known in later times as 'Saint Pierre le Vieux', it remained standing, though it had suffered a good deal, till the abbey's destruction. This church, in addition to its central tower, had two flanking the west front, an idea which Majolus may have derived from the bell-towers of the northern façade of St. John Lateran at Rome, at least as old as the time of John XIII (965–972).

Fig. 508. Cluny. Abbey Church. South arm of main transept (1089–1130)

But even this in course of time no longer sufficed for the great concourse of monks for whom room had to be found in the choir, nor was it consonant with the splendour of the monastery. It was under these circumstances that Abbot Hugo (1049–1109) took in hand (1088) the erection of the colossal edifice which forms our subject. The monk Hezzel, formerly a canon of Liége, is said to have the credit of being the author of the designs. In 1095 Pope Urban II (1088–1099) consecrated the high altar, which stood a little east of the second crossing—a fact throwing light on the progress of the works, which, according to Marrier, took twenty years to finish. Really they must have taken longer, seeing that the dedication by Innocent II (1130–1143) only took place in 1130, though one of his predecessors, Callixtus II (1119–1124), had been at Cluny in 1120.[3] In front of Hugo's church Abbot Roland I added in 1220 a narthex like a church with nave and aisles.

Of the building, the largest monastic church in Christendom, and once thought fit to be a 'deambulatorium angelorum', as well as of Roland's addition, the whirlwind of the Revolution in the eighteenth century swept away like dust so large a part that in 1811 all that remained was the portal of the west front of the narthex with its rose window flanked by two square towers, some arches of the nave vaulting, three bell-towers, the columns of the choir, the apse almost perfect, and some of the chapels which had been added to the aisles.[4]

[1] [*Archaeologia*, vol. lxxx (1930), pp. 143 ff.; R. GRAHAM and A. W. CLAPHAM, *The Monastery of Cluny*. Reports of the American excavations by K. J. CONANT in *Speculum* (Mediaeval Academy of America, Cambridge, Mass.), iv–vi (1929–31); summary in *Revue de l'Art*, lx (1931), 141, 154, He dates the choir and capitals before 1095, main transept *c.* 1100, nave 12th cent., narthex (finished) 2nd half of 12th cent. (R.)]

[2] BRUEL, *Recueil des chartes de l'abbaye de Cluny* (Paris, 1876), vol. i, p. 124.

[3] JAFFÉ, *Regesta pont. Rom.*, vol. i, pp. 791, 844.

[4] MARRIER, *Bibliotheca Cluniacensis* (Paris, 1614), *Vita sanctissimi patris Hugonis abbatis Cluniacensis*,

At the present day Hugo's church is represented by so much of the south arm of the main transept as projects beyond the line of the outer aisle, with its octagonal tower and staircase tower; the angle where the outer aisle wall meets the south arm of the lesser transept, and some remains of the latter. The main transept (fig. 508) is decorated with arcading, and has a barrel vault. From its eastern face one of the two original apses still projects. The octagonal tower belonging to it rests on hood-shaped pendentives. The capitals are Corinthianesque with conventional foliage, and, in some cases, roses and monsters. These figures disprove the arbitrary assertion that the monster figures of the Lombardic School were excluded by the School of Cluny. The capitals are designed and carved with freedom, and are boldly and sometimes completely undercut. One in particular, with foliage and rampant monsters, is admirable.

On the exterior (fig. 509) the tower is enriched with arcading and arched corbel courses. The surviving apse, on the other hand, has shafts round its circumference, while the side walls of the transept have lesenas in their upper part. A large staircase tower projects from its south-west angle.

With these data, with the illustrations and only too brief description of Mabillon[1] (fig. 510), and with the information given by Lorain,[2] we may form a clear idea of Hugo's basilica. It consisted of a nave and choir with double aisles, regularly orientated, and had the form of a double cross, i.e. it possessed two transepts, one larger than the other. The length from the west front to the end of the apse was some 443 ft., and the breadth about 131 ft. The nave was about 32 ft. wide between the piers, the inner aisles over 19 ft., and the outer about 13 ft. They were separated by compound piers with a uniform diameter of about 8 ft. The nave, which had pointed arches, was covered by a barrel vault rising to a height of over 98 ft. above the floor of the church. Over each of the longitudinal arches were two tiers of round-headed arcading, three arches to a bay. According to Lorain, the lower, which contained windows, had piers, and the upper, which was blind, had shafts. The inner aisles also had barrel vaults nearly 60 ft. high, and pointed arches. The same was the case in the outer aisles, which

Fig. 509. Cluny. Abbey Church. South arm of main transept (1089–1130)

vol. i, p. 458 B; MABILLON, *Annales Ord. S. Benedicti*, vol. v, pp. 252, 455; LORAIN, *Essai historique sur l'Abbaye de Cluny* (Dijon, 1839), pp. 81 ff.; PIGNOT, *Histoire de l'Ordre de Cluny*, vol. ii, p. 504; SACKUR, *Die Cluniacenser*, vol. ii, p. 372.

[1] MABILLON, op. cit., vol. v, p. 252. [2] Op. cit.

were over 39 ft. high. Vaulting of the same kind (though Pignot[1] erroneously talks of cross vaulting) was continued in both transepts, of which the larger measured over 217 ft. by about 32 ft., while the smaller was above 108 ft. long, and somewhat wider than the other. The tiling of the roof rested directly on the extrados of the vaulting without any intervening timber work. The presbytery, with an apsidal termination, was supported by lofty ancient columns brought from Italy, with pointed arches springing from them, and was covered by a barrel vault and half-dome.

The pointed arch was used for all the structural parts of the building, while the round arch was confined to the doors, windows (splayed on both sides), and internal arcading.

From the ambulatory surrounding the presbytery and forming a prolongation of the inner aisles opened five radiating chapels, each vaulted with an elongated half-dome. Three towers rose on the line of the main transept: a square one exactly over

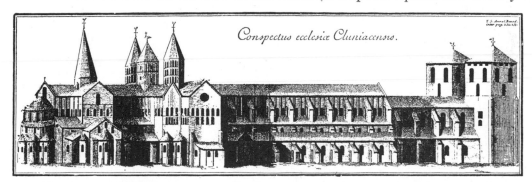

Conspectus ecclesiæ Cluniacensis.

Fig. 510. Cluny. Abbey Church (1089–1130). (From the *Annales Ordinis S. Benedicti*)

the crossing, and two octagonal ones above the arms. The latter, to judge from the one that remains, formed at their base an octagonal cupola resting on hood-shaped pendentives. In the case of the square tower the dome was probably circular, and at a height of about 118 ft. above the floor of the church. A single tower rose above the second crossing which formed the upper bar of the cross. All these towers had pyramidal roofs covered with slating.

The exterior of the walls of the nave, lesser transept, and part of the larger one, was broken by pilasters. Both nave and aisles were strengthened by substantial vertical buttresses corresponding to the arcades within. Those of the nave and outer aisles were further supported by flying buttresses, added, it is thought, in the thirteenth century to increase the resistance to the pressure of the vaulting, over-weighted by the tiled roof resting directly upon it, and consequently of weakened stability.

Of the three towers of the principal transept, the surviving one has been described above. The view in Mabillon[2] shows that the corresponding tower over the north arm had three stages of arcading, instead of only two like the southern, and that the central tower also had two. The tower over the minor crossing was of one story only, and undecorated.

The west front contained a Lombardic portal with four jamb shafts on either side, surmounted by a range of arcading resting on pilasters, of which the central arch was pierced and lighted a small chapel formed in the thickness of the wall, while part of it projected into the nave. The arches on either side of it formed niches. This range of blank arcading was the earliest appearance of this form of decoration on a church front in France.

[1] Op. cit., vol. ii, p. 499.   [2] Op. cit., p. 252.

Having completed our description, let us see what new features are presented by Hugo's basilica. I confess that I cannot discover a single one. The double transept is not one; here due to the necessity of providing room for a large number of monks in the choir. As a matter of fact, the view of Angilbert's basilica of Saint Riquier in Mabillon[1] makes it clear that the two great lantern towers, flanked in either case by a turret staircase, rose above the crossing of two transepts, which were obviously of the same date as the central towers, as both show the same motive of 'oculi', these being blank in the towers and open in the transepts, and also the same type of roof. Again, the church of Saint Remi at Rheims, rebuilt by Archbishop Turpin (756–802) and finished by Hincmar (845–882), who dedicated it, according to Flodoard, in 852, had two transepts, one of which included a tower, and a large two-storied tower at the west front, as we learn from an illustration of a bas-relief on the tomb of the said Hincmar (reproduced in Marlot's 'Mémoires', published in 1895 by the Academy of

Fig. 511. Coin of St. Martin of Tours (768–800)

Rheims) which appears to represent the dedication, and contains a figure of the Emperor Charles the Bald (843–877) holding a model of the church. Lastly, St. Michael at Hildesheim, completed in 1033, possesses two transepts with, in each case, a tower over the crossing.

Nor is the arrangement of chapels radiating from the arcaded ambulatory round the apse original, for its prototype is to be found in the destroyed basilica of Saint Martin at Tours, the most famous sanctuary in the whole of Gaul, though not the church erected by Bishop Perpetuus (460–490) to replace the earlier one built over the tomb of St. Martin, first bishop of Tours (371–397), by St. Britius (396–443), and dedicated about the year 470—the subject of the eulogies of Sidonius Apollinaris,[2] and of a brief description by Gregory of Tours.[3] For though the testimony of the Frankish historian shows that the 'absida tumuli', or 'absida corporis', or 'absida sepulchri' in the church was surrounded by an atrium—'hoc in atrio quod absidam corporis ambit'[4]—it does not follow that the atrium itself was surrounded by radiating apsidal chapels, as has been imagined.[5] Perhaps this 'absida' was something like the 'absida lignea'[6] over the tomb of St. Benignus at Dijon, but constructed in masonry, seeing that, during the fire of 796, Alcuin was able to prostrate himself on the pavement in front of the saint's tomb and pray that the flames might be stayed, without receiving any harm.[7] Unless, indeed, the 'absida' were an arcaded apse enclosed by an ambulatory, after the fashion of that in San Sebastiano outside the walls of Rome (367–384). In any case, only one apse projected from the body of the basilica of St. Martin, and that formed the chancel. This alone is mentioned by Gregory of Tours, and its existence is implied in the story of the robbers who broke into the church and carried off a rich booty.[8]

The church of Perpetuus, which suffered from fire in the time of Bishop Euphronius (555–572) and was restored by him, was sacked by the Saracens in 732. Scarcely had it been restored, when a new fire damaged it in the days of Alcuin, who had been prefect

[1] *Acta Sanct. Ord. S. Benedicti*, vol. i, p. 106, *Vita S. Angilberti abbatis Centulensis*.

[2] *Mon. Germ. Hist.*, Sidonius Apollinaris, *Carmina*, p. 69, vv. 1–20.

[3] *Mon. Germ. Hist.*, Gregorius episcopus Turonensis, *Historia Francorum*, pp. 81–2.

[4] Migne, *Patr. Lat.*, vol. 71, *S. Georgii Florentii Gregorii de miraculis S. Martini episcopi*, p. 988 D.

[5] C. Chevalier, *Les fouilles de Saint-Martin de Tours*, p. 127.

[6] D'Achery, op. cit., vol. ii, p. 384, *Chronica S. Benigni Divionensis*.

[7] *Mon. Germ. Hist.*, *Script.*, vol. xv, pars i, p. 194, *Vita Alcuini*.

[8] Op. cit., p. 255. [De Lasteyrie, op. cit., p. 185 and fig. 163 (plan of the 10th cent. apse).]

of the palace of Charles the Great, and afterwards became abbot of Tours. He gave it a new roof.

A coin of the time of Charles before his coronation as Emperor (768–800)[1] shows the front of the church as it existed in the second half of the eighth century (fig. 511). Later, the Emperor himself rebuilt it, but not entirely, as may be inferred from another coin struck under Louis the Pious (814–840), showing the same church front as that of the days when Charles the Great was still only a king. On this occasion a lofty bell-tower was erected,[2] which some would make out to be identical (except for the topmost story) with the existing 'Tour Charlemagne' (fig. 512) which stands near the present church of Saint Martin.[3] This, however, is due neither to the Emperor, nor to the treasurer Hervé, as others argue, but is rather one of the results of the work undertaken after the fire of 1096. The architectural and artistic decoration of the two stages above the basement exactly suits the last years of the eleventh and the first of the next century. The highest stage in the Pointed style is the result of alterations in the thirteenth or fourteenth centuries.

On several later occasions Saint Martin was set on fire and injured by the Normans between 853 and 903, and consequently several times repaired, and between 904 and 918 radically restored or rather rebuilt, as was the monastery. A coin struck in the time of Charles the Simple (893–929) shows quite a different front from that of the eighth and ninth centuries, and implies a reconstruction (fig. 513). The basilica of the time of Charles the Simple was devasted by a fire in 994, according to Maan;[2] but Hervé de Buzançais, treasurer of Saint Martin from 1014 onwards,[4] at once took in hand its rebuilding, and the new structure was dedicated by Bishop Hugo (1007–about 1023) in 1014, or, according to Ademar, 1020.[5] Mosnier[6] states that Hervé rebuilt only that part of the basilica which covered the saint's tomb, i.e. the east end. Maan, on the contrary, describes the old walls being pulled down before the new church was built up. However this may be, what is of importance for us to notice is that to Hervé must be assigned the oldest traces of the choir with its five radiating chapels, which came to light during the recent erection of the new Saint Martin, when I was able to inspect them.

Fig. 512. Tours. So-called 'Tour Charlemagne' (11th, 12th, and 13th or 14th centuries)

Maan, again, can scarcely be trusted when he refers to an increase of length in the new church. This choir was afterwards rebuilt, first after the fire of 1096, then again after 1175, and finally after 1202. In Italy the plan does not occur till 1032,

[1] C. CHEVALIER, op. cit., pp. 108–9.
[2] MAAN, *Sancta et metropolitana ecclesia Turonensis sacrorum pontificum suorum ornata virtutibus ...* (Tours, 1667), p. 81.
[3] [On the 27th March 1928 the 'Tour Charlemagne' split in two, and almost the whole of the northern face fell. *Bulletin Monumental*, lxxxvii (1928), p. 168. See also *The Builder*, 20th Sept. 1929, p. 458. (R.)]
[4] U. CHEVALIER, *Répertoire des sources historiques du moyen âge*, 2137.
[5] *Mon. Germ. Hist.*, ADEMARUS, *Historiae*, p. 139.
[6] *Historia S. Martini.*

in an elementary form, in San Flaviano at Montefiascone, and fully developed at Aversa.

Nor was there anything original in the small apses which formed the termination of the transepts. Rome and Roman Italy afford very ancient examples of cruciform buildings with the arms ending in a curved projection. Montano[1] shows several such.

To my mind, an impartial estimate of the church of Cluny reveals nothing really notable except its imposing proportions and the immense vaulted space covered by it —immense, however, only in the sense of length, for the nave was not so wide as that of Sant' Ambrogio at Milan.[2] But this does not detract from the great achievement of Hezzel in raising at that date a building of such size entirely in masonry. The carving is also remarkable.

The church itself, then, shows that the influence which it is supposed to have exercised on the development and completion of the Lombardic organism is imaginary.

Fig. 513. Coin of St. Martin of Tours (893–929)

But there were directions in which it had an influence, sometimes of considerable importance.

Thus, the free use of the conical pendentive, which previously had barely made an insignificant appearance at Jumièges (1040–1066), was the starting-point for its diffusion through the country, where in the district between the Loire and the Garonne it prevails. It is precisely to the end of the eleventh century that the cupola of Saint Étienne at Nevers (1097) with its pendentives of this type belongs; while in the twelfth century we get them in Notre Dame at Avignon, Saint Philibert at Tournus, Notre Dame at Beaune, the church at La Charité, Notre Dame du Port at Clermont, Saint Hilaire at Poiters (which originally had a wooden roof), &c.

The use of the pointed arch, though it was anomalous and not systematic, gave rise to the Transitional or Lombardo-Pointed style, and was thus the starting-point for the Pointed style proper.

Again, we may be sure that the lofty walls of the nave, with their two tiers of arcading rising above arches of excessive height, formed a subject of study, of reflection, of imitation, for the earliest architects of churches in the Pointed style with their soaring naves, quasi-triforiums, and wall galleries.

As for the carving, to judge by the little that has been preserved, it is certainly, in the case of some of the figure subjects, not a whit inferior to the best Italian work of the same date. I refer especially to the capitals, eight superb ones among them, now collected in the Museum near the site of Roland I's narthex.[3] They are of Corinthian type with figures, the conventional foliage being treated in high relief or completely undercut, and are executed in a very easily worked stone.

On one of them appear Adam and Eve before the Fall, wearing the characteristic

---

[1] Op. cit., lib. ii, pls. 5, 6, 8, 36, 37.

[2] [L. Bréhier in his review of Oursel's *Art roman de Bourgogne* (*Rev. Arch.*, 5th ser. xxix, 299) thus sums up the contribution of Cluny: 'En laissant de côté les proportions grandioses qui n'ont jamais été reproduites dans l'art roman, on peut dire qu'on trouvait réunis pour la première fois dans l'église de Cluny les éléments suivants: l'élévation de la nef en un triple étage comportant les arcades en tiers-point, le triforium, les hautes fenêtres; la superposition des ordres Classiques; la couverture de la nef par un berceau brisé longitudinal.' (R.)]

[3] [E. Mâle, *L'Art religieux du XIIᵉ siècle en France* (2nd ed., 1924), p. 320, explains the subjects of the capitals as the Seasons, Virtues, and Sciences. Prof. Conant (*Rev. de l'Art*, lx. 198) follows the suggestion of L. Bréhier (*Rev. Arch.*, 5th ser. xxix (1929), 311 ff.) that they are 'une traduction iconographique' of a letter from Peter Damiani to Abbot Hugo in 1063, describing the virtues of the monks (Migne, *Patr. Lat.*, cxliv. 374), and believes that they were in place by 1095. For an 11th century date see also A. Gardner, *Medieval Sculpture in France*, pp. 86 ff., and S. Casson in *Burlington Magazine*, lxi (1932), 266, 273. (R.)]

cylindrical Jewish cap, also to be seen on the common head belonging to the bodies of a pair of winged centaurs carved on a capital in the old part of the crypt of the cathedral at Modena (1099–1106) (fig. 514), and represented on many of the sculptured sarcophagi in the Lateran Christian Museum. The motive of two quadrupeds with a single head was derived from the Etruscans, who employed it not only on vases but also on carved panels.[1] One of the compartments of a piece of archaic Etruscan carving in the Archaeological Museum at Florence[2] contains a pair of lions with a single head (fig. 515). The

Fig. 514. Modena. Duomo. Crypt (1099–1106)

Romans also used it, as may be seen on a capital illustrated by Montano,[3] showing two winged animals united by a single head which takes the place of the flower on the abacus.

On another capital, which seems to me the finest of all, a man is represented playing the harp (fig. 516).[4] The figure is treated with grace, in an easy and lifelike manner, showing refinement and correct proportions, especially in the extremities. The pose is natural, and the drapery intelligently arranged. Taken all in all it is not inferior to the figures of the same date executed by Wiligelmus or Guglielmus for the façade of the cathedral of Modena (fig. 517). In these, while we can admire, for instance in the

[1] [On these pairs of animals with single head see E. Mâle, op. cit., p. 357, referring to E. Pottier's derivation of them from primitive Greek (Mycenean) and Chaldean art. Prof. Mâle considers that the motive as it appears in Romanesque carving was probably taken directly from Oriental (Moslem) textiles. For the influence of these Eastern stuffs on Romanesque sculpture see also P. Deschamps, *Bull. Mon.*, 1925, p. 73, who refers to L. Bréhier's *Études sur l'histoire de la sculpture byzantine*. (R.)]

[2] Milani, *Museo Topografico d'Etruria* (1898), p. 104.

[3] Op. cit., lib. i, p. 38.

[4] [It represents the third tone of Plainsong. Cp. Gardner, op. cit., p. 89. (R.)]

subjects from the beginning of Genesis, the grand style and majestic air of the figures, which sometimes (e.g. Cain killed by Lamech's arrow) have a natural look not found in the faces of the figures at Cluny with their more forced expression, on the other hand one cannot help noticing the general lack of proportion between the heads and bodies,

Fig. 515. Florence. Archaeological Museum. Portion of Etruscan carving from Tarquinia

Fig. 516. Cluny. Museum. Capital from Abbey Church (1089–1130)

Fig. 517. Modena. Sculpture on the façade of the Duomo (12th century)

and also in the feet, even when covered. Moreover, they have a rigidity from which the figure at Cluny is free. In a third capital, with God calling Adam after the Fall (fig. 518), the figures are inferior both in quality of line and modelling to the best of the work at Modena.

The church of Cluny was not alone in its failure to show any contribution towards the evolution and perfection of the Lombardic vaulted basilica; for the same thing is true of the rest of the French ecclesiastical buildings. And this we shall have to substantiate by the evidence of some of the most important dated churches of the country in the eleventh and early years of the following century, though not in the Norman districts which we have hitherto dealt with. These we shall briefly compare, taking note of their chronology and special features, with the Lombardic buildings of Italy; thus obtaining tangible proof that all these French churches were behind the times so far as that development is concerned, when confronted with the creations of the Lombard gilds which showed the way.

THE ABBEY CHURCH OF SAINT PHILIBERT AT TOURNUS is the result of Abbot Bernerius's rebuilding between 1008 and 1019 (the latter being the year of the consecration) of the previous church erected by Abbot Stephen between 960 and 980, and damaged, together with the adjoining convent, by a fire in 1006 in the days of Abbot Vago.[1] This tenth-century church in its turn replaced an earlier one.[2]

Fig. 518. Cluny. Museum. Capital from Abbey Church (1089–1130)

Five bays of the church of Bernerius remain. The choir with its crypt, and the two-light openings on the interior face of the two-storied narthex, indicate with their Corinthianesque and varied Composite capitals the partial rebuilding in the early years of the twelfth century mentioned by Robert,[3] and followed by the dedication performed by Calixtus II (1119–1124). The original bays are divided into nave and aisles by very lofty cylindrical piers, each of which carries above its capital a vaulting shaft (fig. 519). From these shafts spring the uncouth transverse arches which support the barrel vaults over the nave. The aisles, which are of great height, have roughly constructed, ramping, unraised cross vaulting. The side walls are strengthened by external buttresses corresponding to the piers within (fig. 520).

The church of Tournus is important not only for its place in the history of the development of vaulting, but also because it presents two features, one of which is worthy of special notice.

The first and most important is that of the great cylindrical piers which separate the nave from the aisles. This form influenced the builders of Sant' Abondio at Como (1013–1095) and of Jumièges (1040–1066), and it was copied at Malvern (1085), where it became the model which was reproduced in so many abbey and priory churches of Great Britain.

The second is the arrangement of the vaulting shafts. It was used later by the builders of Sant' Ambrogio at Milan on the piers, with the object of supporting an arched corbel course to decorate the nave. Afterwards the architects of the cathedrals

---

[1] [The usual dates assigned to Tournus are highly problematic, and it is an extremely perplexing church, whose history remains to be written. It seems doubtful whether the date 1008–1019 can be accepted for the nave; the choir, with its three radiating rectangular chapels, in the walls of which is much herring-bone work, was consecrated in 1120. The fact that there are cylindrical piers at Malvern and Gloucester is no evidence of a derivation from Tournus (see below, p. 234). (H. T.) The latest writer, C. OURSEL (L'Art roman de Bourgogne), ascribes the crypt and the choir with its ambulatory and radiating chapels to Abbot Stephen, while the two-storied narthex was built between 980 and 1000. The nave was rebuilt after the fire of 1007 by Abbot Bernerius, but its transverse barrel vaults will be the work of Peter I (1066–1107). Their purpose was to avoid interference with the high clerestory windows. Cf. L. BRÉHIER in *Rev. Arch.*, 5th ser. xxix (1929), p. 295. (R.)]

[2] MEULIEN, *Histoire de la ville et du Canton de Tournus* . . . (Société des Amis des Arts de Tournus, 1893), pp. 12–13.

[3] *Gallia Christiana, Tornusium*, p. 652 D.

of Worms and Mainz employed it in the form of half-piers from which to spring the pairs of wall-arches in the nave.

The chief value of Saint Philibert consists in its system of construction and equilibrium. As we saw, the second church had to be rebuilt after little more than a quarter of a century; and the reason, as the injury caused by fire suggests, was that it had a wooden roof. It was accordingly decided to rebuild it completely in masonry. And it is this decision which demonstrates the real merit of the Burgundian builders.

Anxious to give their work a character distinct from that of the Lombardic style, which at that time was being illustrated by Saint Bénigne at Dijon, then in course of erection (1002–1018), and San Babila at Milan, and desirous of lighting the nave directly, but afraid to spring a longitudinal vault from such elongated piers, they fell back on the inartistic but more stable device of springing from the transverse arches of the nave as many barrel vaults as there were bays, the nave walls being strengthened by buttresses corresponding to the arches. This system, which is of very rare occurrence, had been already followed in the original church of Saint Front at Périgueux, the erection of which was begun[1] by Bishop Froterius (988–991), who was buried in it,[2] a proof that the work must have been then well advanced. The dedication took place in 1047 during the episcopate of Geraldus, who died in 1059. The facts are that the parts of this church preserved in the later rebuilding show that while the nave, which was barely 17 ft. wide, had a wooden roof, the aisles were covered with ramping barrel vaults, one to each bay, parallel to one another and

Fig. 519. Tournus. Saint Philibert (1008–1019)

at right angles to the nave, and resting on transverse arches springing from isolated piers and half wall-piers.[3]

It was undoubtedly from Saint Front that the architect of Saint Philibert derived his idea when he adopted ramping vaulting in the aisles. Its function in the latter case was to abut the transverse arches of the nave, while at the same time the nave was not affected by its thrust. The result was a three-lobed framework of resistance and of thrust ('trilobo di forza') discharged on to the outer walls, almost without need of intermediate supports.

The present church of Saint Front[4] is a new erection of 1120, and not identical with

[1] SAMMARTHANUS, &c., *Gallia Christiana*, vol. ii, p. 1457 A.

[2] ROBERT, *Gallia Christiana*, p. 443 AB.

[3] VERNEILH, *L'architecture byzantine en France* (Paris, 1851), p. 91.

[4] [DE LASTEYRIE, op. cit., pp. 466–72, advances strong arguments against the usual view that St. Front and the cupola churches of Aquitaine generally were derived from Byzantine and Venetian sources. The argument for this derivation rested in no small degree upon the mistaken supposition that the present church is identical with that of Froterius. (H. T.)]

the fabric of 1047 as some even recent writers imagine.[1] The church of Froterius was burned, together with the whole of the wooden-roofed convent, in the terrible fire of 1120, when even the bells were melted.[2] The only parts which escaped were the vaulted aisles.

And all said and done, San Babila at Milan, but little older, already possessed aisles with beautiful raised cross vaulting springing from compound piers, while the nave (though without windows) had a barrel vault, and the thrust of the ribs which interrupted it and supported the other vaulting, was met by an original and scientific system of buttressing.

A great deal of water will have to run down the rivers of France before the French builders succeed in covering directly lighted naves with longitudinal barrel vaulting. And when this does happen, the hour will have almost struck for them to abandon a foreign style, and devote all their energies to the creation, under the guidance of the ruling principles of the Lombardic basilica, and with the assistance of the improvements in vaulting introduced in the nave of Durham Cathedral, of a new national architecture, viz. the Transitional Lombardo-Pointed, out of which the Pointed style pure and simple was developed.

Fig. 520. Tournus. Saint Philibert. North side (1008–1019)

THE CHURCH OF SAINT HILAIRE AT POITIERS was rebuilt[3] after the disastrous fire which destroyed most of the churches of the city in 1018,[4] and dedicated in 1049.[5] Originally it consisted of a nave with double aisles, the former separated from the latter by compound piers and columns alternately, and had a wooden roof. The aisles were separated by columns, and had cross vaulting. The interior face of the side walls presents a cluster of three shafts corresponding to the nave piers, from which spring transverse arches, and a shaft answering to the columns of the aisles and nave, to support the cross vaulting. On the outside these wall-supports are met by buttresses alternately larger and smaller.

When, in 1130,[6] it was decided to vault the nave, owing to the fact that it was some 46 ft. wide, the plan was adopted of lining its interior with arcades resting on clustered piers connected by transverse arches at the level of the clerestory, which was

[1] PEYRE, *Histoire générale des beaux-arts*, p. 294.

[2] *Ex chronico S. Maxentii* (BOUQUET, *Recueil*, vol. xii, p. 407); *Ex fragmento de Petragoricensibus episcopis* (BOUQUET, *Recueil*, vol. xii, p. 392).

[3] *Ex fragmento historiae Monasterii Novi Pictavensis* (BOUQUET, *Recueil*, vol. xi, p. 119).

[4] *Ademari Cabannensis Chronicon*, ed. Chavanon (Paris, 1897), p. 182.

[5] *Ex chronico S. Maxentii* (BOUQUET, *Recueil*, vol. xi, p. 218); LABBE, op. cit., *Chronicon S. Maxentii*, vol. ii, p. 209.

[6] ENLART, op. cit., p. 316 (1919).

strengthened by an additional facing, and then raising over each bay of this inner structure an octagonal cupola resting on hood-shaped pendentives (fig. 521).

It is obvious that the only Lombardic features presented by Saint Hilaire are the alternate large and small supports, and the form of the piers, the capitals of which, however, are neither continuous nor Lombardic. The figure capitals (where old) must

Fig. 521. Poitiers. Saint Hilaire (11th and 12th centuries)

be ascribed to the twelfth century. The original ones were of two kinds: those with plain crocket leaves, and those with similar foliage above a continuous crown of leaves.

THE ABBEY CHURCH OF SAINT SAVIN was erected in the time of Duke William III (980–1030) and Abbot Gumbald (†1040).[1] It was designed with nave and aisles separated by cylindrical piers, and the aisles had cross vaulting (which, being the result of the intersection of two perfectly semicircular barrel vaults, is without transverse arches) springing from the nave piers and the corresponding half wall-piers, the latter being strengthened externally by powerful buttresses. The nave, on the other hand, is covered with a continuous barrel vault rising from very low nave walls, and

---

[1] *Gallia Christiana*, vol. ii, p. 1287. [MAILLARD, *Saint-Savin* (*Petites Monographies*, 1926).]

therefore without windows, the thrust of which is met by the aisle vaulting. The whole is covered by a single gabled roof.

The only Lombardic feature in this church is the familiar idea, derived from the Roman tradition, of strong external buttresses to resist the thrust of the cross vaulting.

Fig. 522. Rheims. Saint Remi (11th and 12th centuries)

Whereas, in the contemporary San Flaviano at Montefiascone we already find used in the aisles the essential element of Lombardic architecture—diagonal ribs applied to the cross vaulting.

THE CHURCH OF SAINT REMI AT RHEIMS was rebuilt by Abbot Theoderic (1036–1048) in the fifth year from his appointment, after demolishing, owing to its excessive size, the portion of the structure begun by his predecessor Airardus (1005) to replace the older church which had been completed by Hincmar (845–882) in 852. This demolition spared nothing but some of the foundations: 'quam basilicam Theodericus, destructa ob nimiam aedificii molem ea quae ab Airardo incoepta fuerat, aedificare aggressus, Herimaro successori perficiendam reliquit.'[1] It was finished by his successor Herimar, who completed the north arm of the transept and erected the southern one. He also constructed the roof. The consecration was performed by Pope Leo IX in 1049.[2] The church was enlarged by Abbot Pierre de Celles[3] (1162–1182), who replaced the narthex by two bays. He also remodelled the west front, raised the side walls of the nave, and threw across them, as also in the transept, Pointed vaulting, which involved an alteration in the nave piers. Lastly, he rebuilt the choir.[4]

Of the original church there survive the nave, the transept, and the remains of the choir. The nave and aisles are separated by massive pillars formed of a number of shafts clustered within a circle, and two compound piers, preceded by two bays in the

Fig. 523. Rheims. Saint Remi. Capitals in the nave (11th century)

Pointed style (fig. 522). Everything indicates, as has been suggested, that the piers were, at first plain and cylindrical instead of being encircled by clustered shafts as now. This would explain the difference between the rude capitals with triangular indentations (fig. 523) and those with foliage and figures which would be the result of alterations between 1049 and 1162, when also the single-arch openings of the triforium springing from rectangular piers were divided into two by shafts with foliage capitals evidently of another date, though earlier than the capitals of the time of Pierre de Celles.

The aisles (fig. 524), which were afterwards cross vaulted and bear traces of alteration on two occasions, originally had wooden roofs like the triforium. The vaulting we see in the nave is not that of Abbot Pierre, but a sham vault put up in the last century, when at the same time some bays of the transept vaulting were rebuilt, as well as considerable part of that in the aisles and triforium.

The transept also has aisles, with galleries above. The piers were originally either cylindrical or quadrangular with attached members: in the one case a half-column and a pilaster, in the other a simple pilaster. The ground floor had barrel vaulting interrupted by transverse arches springing from cylindrical or quadrangular piers. The galleries and central space had timbered roofs.

The aisles terminated at the east in small apses (partly destroyed) flanking the rectangular sanctuary.

Externally, the south side of the nave (the only one that is free) is strengthened by semi-cylindrical buttresses, which were altered when the nave walls were raised for the construction of the vaulting. At the same time the range of round windows was formed at the top (fig. 525).[5]

---

[1] MABILLON, *Annales Ord. S. Benedicti*, vol. iv, p. 408 c.
[2] *Ex Orderici Vitalis Historiae Ecclesiasticae* (BOUQUET, *Recueil*, vol. xii, p. 606); and *Ex libello Hugonis Floriacensis monachi* (BOUQUET, *Recueil*, vol. xii, p. 796).
[3] *Ex historia dedicationis ecclesiae S. Remigii* (BOUQUET, *Recueil*, vol. xi, p. 464); *Petri Cellensis, episcopi Carnotensis elogium* (ibid., vol. xiv, p. 487).
[4] MARLOT, *Metropolis Remensis historia* (Rheims, 1679), vol. ii, pp. 90–3; GOSSET, *La basilique de Saint-*

Remy à Reims (Paris, 1900), pp. 24, 29. [DE LASTEYRIE, op. cit., 158, 766.]
[5] [During the bombardment of Rheims in 1918 St. Remi suffered severely, the wooden vault of the nave being burnt; and in 1919 the south wall of the nave collapsed. The nave has now been restored, with stone vaulting, and reopened, but the restoration of the choir and transepts is still in progress. In the course of the work the plan of Hincmar's church, with an apse at either end, came to light. *Revue Archéologique*, 5th ser., vol. xxxiv (1931), p. 189. (R.)]

Fig. 524. Rheims. Saint Remi. South aisle of nave (11th and 12th centuries)

Fig. 525. Rheims. Saint Remi. South side (11th and 12th centuries)

The old Saint Remi exhibits no Lombardic features, displays an art which is old-fashioned compared with that of the contemporary church at Cerisy la Forêt (1030–1066), and contains no element of service to the Italian gilds for the development of the Lombardic vaulted basilica. We find, however, one feature which is new for France: the transept aisles and galleries continuing those of the nave. This arrangement must have been suggested by St. Maria im Capitol at Cologne, which, though it too was consecrated in 1049, appears to have been rebuilt between 1024 and 1030.

THE MONASTIC CHURCH OF SAINT SERNIN AT TOULOUSE was rebuilt after the Cluniac monks in 1083 took the place of the canons, and was consecrated in 1096 by Pope Urban II.[1] Its plan is that of a nave and choir with double aisles, divided by piers of uniform thickness with an engaged vaulting shaft to carry the transverse arches of the nave. The latter is barrel vaulted and without windows. The aisles have ordinary cross vaulting. The transverse arches over the two outer ones started from piers and half wall-piers strengthened by substantial buttresses outside. Above the inner aisles is a triforium covered by a half barrel vault which meets the thrust of the nave vaulting. The outer aisles have half barrel vaults springing from the floor level, forming dark spaces. To each arch of the nave corresponds a double opening above, divided by a shaft, and enclosed by a single arch. Round-headed windows light the outer aisles.

THE MONASTIC CHURCH OF SAINT ÉTIENNE AT NEVERS was rebuilt by William I, Count of Nevers (1040–1097), and given, with the convent, to Cluny in 1097.[2] Its plan is that of a nave and choir separated from aisles by compound piers of uniform size, consisting of a square pier with four engaged half-columns corresponding to which are wall-shafts and external buttresses. The aisles have ordinary cross vaulting, but the nave is covered by a barrel vault divided into sections by large transverse arches kept up by buttresses outside. The nave walls from which it starts are carried up high enough to allow of windows, formed partly in the walls and partly in the base of the vault. Over the aisles runs a triforium with a semicircular vault, which opens on the nave by pairs of arches, divided by a column, and enclosed by another arch.

The church of Rivolta d'Adda had already been given to Pope Urban II (1088–1099), and Sant' Ambrogio at Milan was nearing completion, when Saint Sernin at Toulouse and Saint Étienne at Nevers were finished. Now, any one can see at the first glance how different was the organic and constructive conception in the minds of the architects of the two Lombardic churches from that which was before the authors of the two French ones, and how far ahead the former were of the latter in constructive and statical knowledge. This is abundantly proved by the rational system of buttressing employed in the church of Rivolta, which has maintained the integrity of the building in such a wonderful way through the centuries; whereas the cracks in Saint Étienne at Nevers are evidence of unsound construction. And so we have reached the close of the eleventh century without having found a single building of certain date in France which can be said to have in any respect shown the way in the creation of the Lombardic style.

THE ABBEY CHURCH AT LA CHARITÉ appears to have been begun by the prior Girardus, who was also its architect, in 1056,[3] or 1069,[4] and was dedicated in 1107.[5] It was

[1] JAFFÉ, *Regesta pontificum Romanorum*, vol. i, p. 687.

[2] MARRIER, op. cit., *Carta fundationis seu dotationis Monasterii S. Stephani Nivernensis*, vol. ii, *Notae ad Bibliothecam*, p. 174.

[3] *Ex chronico Andegavensi altero* (BOUQUET, *Recueil*, vol. xi, p. 169); *Ex chronica Willelmi Godelli, monachi S. Martialis Lemovicensis* (BOUQUET, *Recueil*, vol. xi, p. 283).

[4] *Ex chronico S. Maxentii* (BOUQUET, *Recueil*, vol. xi, p. 221).

[5] *Sugerius, abbat. S. Dionysii. De Vita Ludovici Grossi regis* (BOUQUET, *Recueil*, vol. xii, p. 19).

erected with ordinary cross vaulting for the aisles, supported by internal and external buttresses; while the nave had a barrel vault, crossed by transverse arches, and starting above the clerestory with its round-headed windows.

THE ABBEY CHURCH OF THE MADELEINE AT VÉZELAY, erected by Abbot Artald (1096–1106), was dedicated in 1104. It was damaged by a terrible fire in 1120,[1] but repaired by Abbot Rainald of Semur (1106–1128). The narthex, built and dedicated about 1132,[2] must have been the work of his successor.

The body of the church, which belongs to the original work, is divided into nave and aisles (figs. 526, 527) by compound piers of uniform size, and has unraised cross

Fig. 526. Vézelay. Abbey Church of the Madeleine. Nave (11th and 12th centuries)

vaulting. The bases of the piers are in some cases ornamented with foliage, ovolos, cauliculi, fluting, animals, scroll-work, &c. The Corinthianesque capitals display, besides foliage, real or imaginary animals of every description, demons, human beings in repose or conflict, and scenes from sacred story.[3] These carvings, evidently the work of the same school which produced those at Cluny, with complete undercutting in some cases, while they will not bear comparison with those of the cathedral of Modena (1099–1106), are superior to those at Rivolta d'Adda and in Sant'Ambrogio at Milan, though we must of course remember the rather easily worked stone used for the church of Vézelay.

The representations of monsters and of hunting and fighting scenes, which run riot on the capitals, show how entirely without foundation is the assertion that the School of Cluny avoided such subjects. On a capital of the first pier to the right, near the west end, and therefore of about 1104, a centaur has the characteristic cylindrical cap which we noticed in the Museum at Cluny and in the crypt of Modena cathedral.

[1] *Ex chronico S. Maxentii* (BOUQUET, *Recueil*, vol. xii, p. 407); *Ex chronologia Roberti monachi S. Mariani Autissiodorensis* (ibid., p. 291).

[2] PETIT, *Descriptions des villes et campagnes du département de l' Yonne*; ANTHYME SAINT-PAUL, *Viollet-le-Duc, ses travaux d'art*, etc. (Paris, 1881), p. 134. [DE LASTEYRIE, op. cit., 425, 823.]

[3] [GARDNER, *Medieval Sculpture in France*, pl. x and figs. 75, 76.]

On the outside, the walls had simple pilasters, converted later into the present massive buttresses.

Fig. 527. Vézelay. Abbey Church of the Madeleine. South aisle (11th and 12th centuries)

Fig. 528. Vézelay. Abbey Church. Portal (12th century)

The imposing portal of the nave, divided after the French fashion by a central pier to relieve the weight of the lintel (fig. 528), shows a marked advance artistically over the carvings inside the church, and is to be referred to the beginning of the works on the narthex. For the fineness of its sculpture its only rivals in Italy are the contemporary portal of the cathedral at Ferrara (fig. 529), dated by the inscription on the inner-most arch in 1135, and that of the church of San Zeno Maggiore at Verona, the rebuild-ing of which was finished in 1138,[1] both works of Master Nicholas. The front of San Zeno was afterwards pierced by a large rose window (the middle cornice being cut through for the purpose) symbolizing the wheel of Fortune, the carvings of which are certainly to be referred to the works carried out before 1178. This rose window is one of the earliest to be found in Italy, the birthplace of this type of opening. Santa Maria del Vescovado at Assisi furnishes an example of 1163. It was only in 1220 that the church of Cluny received one in the west front of Abbot Roland's narthex.

The two-storied narthex at Vézelay is constructed with arches some of which are round and others pointed, Lombardic piers, and ordinary cross vaulting con-structed in rubble, either groined or else ribbed. The narthex has a portal of its own, almost entirely re-worked, the outer archivolt of which rests on the back of a lion with a monster between its paws on one side, and a bull surrounded by foliage on the other. It is the oldest example of an arch supported by half-figures ('protome'), after the Etruscan (as we shall see when we come to Deerhurst) and Lombardic fashion, that France can show.

Some of the capitals in the church and narthex have a suggestion of the Pointed style in the play of the foliage. Similar capitals, still more advanced in character, are found in the cathedral at Modena (a fact to which attention has hitherto not been called), which, with the slender bell and the play of the foliage, anticipate or may even be said to be treated in the manner characteristic of the Pointed style (figs. 530, 531, 532).

Fig. 529. Ferrara. Portal of Duomo (1135)

It cannot be said that the first attempt made by the School of Cluny to cover an entire structure of considerable size with cross vaulting achieved a perfectly happy result, for not only did the vaulting of the nave develop cracks and have to be held in by tie-rods, the attachments of which are still to be seen, but it became necessary, after the lapse of little more than a hundred years, to secure the stability of the entire structure by the external buttressing to which we have already called attention. While, on the other hand, the church of Rivolta d'Adda, with its ribbed raised cross vaulting, concave at the crown, lighted by windows in the lunette wall spaces, and with its ramp-ing buttresses pierced by arches, still stands to bear witness to its inherent soundness.

Some have wanted to make out that the idea of covering the nave of Vézelay with cross vaulting came from Palestine. On the contrary, it was the natural solution of

[1] CIPOLLA, *Per la storia d'Italia e de' suoi conquistatori nel medio evo più antico, ricerche varie* (Bologna, 1895), p. 634.

a problem which was always stimulating the energies and efforts of the School of Cluny, eager as it was to pursue an independent course, and anxious to carry out, by ways and means distinct from those laid down by the great Lombardic School, the revolution in the principles of construction and equilibrium which the North Italian gilds had brought about in the Latin basilica. The fact rather is that it was the monks of Cluny who carried the idea to Palestine. New styles of architecture are not produced by magic. Now, neither Palestine nor Syria afford, after the Roman period, a single dated example of a basilica completely covered by cross vaulting in which the cells are constructed in coursed and dressed masonry, and the piers are of the Lombardic type, as for instance in St. Anne's at Jerusalem before their introduction by the Franks after their capture of the city, for there can be no question that they were the builders (with the assistance perhaps of local workmen) of the churches there which have roofs of that kind. We can

Fig. 530. Modena. Duomo. Capital in the crypt (1099–1106)

Fig. 531. Modena. Duomo. Capital in the façade (1099–1106)

Fig. 532. Modena. Duomo. Capital in the façade (1099–1106)

thus explain the appearance in Palestine of such structures of perfected type, without having to look there for earlier ones illustrating the necessary gradual development.

The abbey church of Vézelay is a proof that the School of Cluny was still in the first stages of the solution of the problem how to cover churches of large size with a complete system of cross vaulting, at a time when the church of Rivolta d'Adda was ready to serve as the introduction to the first chapter of pointed-arch construction. It was only at the dawn of the Pointed style that this much-vaunted School resolutely entered upon the difficult path leading to the proper arrangement of simple or ribbed cross vaulting; and that period, so far as the northern countries are concerned, did not begin in France, but rather in England. France may lay claim to the imperishable honour of having seen how to unite the Lombardic organism to that fusion of the pointed arch with ribbed cross vaulting which was achieved in Durham Cathedral between 1129 and 1133, perfecting and transforming it in a transitional system which later found its perfect balance and entire harmony in the Pointed style.

Of this Transitional style I will, in conclusion, indicate a few typical examples.

(1) The western towers of the cathedral of Chartres as rebuilt after the fire of 1134. The northern tower was begun in the same year, and it is known that about 1144 the works on the southern one were in progress.[1] The two cross vaults of the ground floor are ribbed, the ribs having a moulding of three rolls.

[1] CLERVAL, op. cit., p. 19.

(2) The abbey church of Saint Denis, founded by King Dagobert about the year 630, refounded by Pippin and Charles the Great, and erected by Abbot Suger (1122–1152), who was also the architect ('instauravit ecclesiam eo schemate').[1] The narthex, which was the first work undertaken, and the choir were finished in 1140 and 1144 respectively, while the nave was built later than 1144.[2]

Fig. 533. Angers. Cathedral (12th century)

(3) The cathedral of Sens, begun about 1130.[3]
(4) The cathedral of Angers (fig. 533). The vaulting over the aisleless nave, which is nearly 50 ft. wide, was constructed by the bishop Normand de Doué (1149–1153).[4]

[1] [See appendix to Chapter I, supra, p. 47.]
[2] ROBERT, Gallia Christiana, p. 568 A; SUGER, Histoire de Suger, abbé de Saint Denis [by A. F. GERVAISE], 3 vols., Paris, 1721, vol. iii, pp. 53, 96, 97 ff.; MIGNE, Patr. Lat., clxxxvi, pp. 1239, 1254, Sugerius abb. S. Dionysii, Libellus de consecratione ecclesiae a se aedificatae; ibid., 1227-31, Liber de rebus in administratione sua gestis. [DE LASTEYRIE, op. cit., 158, 766.]
[3] LEFÈVRE-PONTALIS, L'Architecture religieuse dans l'ancien diocèse de Soissons, vol. i, p. 63, and note.
[4] TRESVAUX DU FRAVAL, Histoire de l'église et du diocèse d'Angers. [DE LASTEYRIE, op. cit., p. 479.]

III

ECCLESIASTICAL ARCHITECTURE IN ENGLAND FROM CONSTANTINE TO THE NORMAN CONQUEST

THERE is little to be said about the ecclesiastical architecture of Britain in the period between Constantine's Edict of Milan (313) giving peace to the Christians, and the withdrawal of the Roman legions from the island (411) by the Emperor Honorius's rescript of 410, and from this to the invitation given to the Anglo-Saxons (449).[1] The only vestige that has survived is the remains, barely rising above the ground,

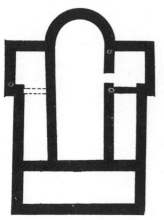 of the small basilica which in old days stood near the Forum of the Roman town of Calleva Atrebatum (Silchester). It followed the early Latin plan of a cross without the upper limb and with a very short transept, like the old St. Peter's at Rome.[2] The nave and aisles were reached through a narthex, and the former terminated in a semicircular apse, while the latter were closed by two sacristies at the upper end.

The basilica at Silchester, the plan (fig. 534) of which unquestionably indicates the Christian purpose for which it was erected, has been dated between 313 and 411,[3] and I think rightly, particularly on the ground of the orientation, for it was only after the erection of the Basilica Ursiana at Ravenna (370–384) that the new Ravennate arrangement of the apse at the east end was generally adopted. On the other hand, Britain was rapidly christianized in the course of the fourth century.[4]

Fig. 534. Silchester. Plan of Christian Basilica (4th or 5th century)

The church of Silchester affords a very early specimen of an apse flanked by two 'secretaria'. In Italy it is illustrated by three examples, also of early date, two of which have been already mentioned: the Basilica Pammachiana at Porto near Rome (about 398), and the large Basilica of St. Symphorosa on the Via Tiburtina, thought to be not later than about the fifth century. The third is San Salvatore at Spoleto, which belongs to the fourth century.

We are able to say even less about church building in the years following the calling in of the barbarians down to the arrival of the monk Augustine and his companions (597). The feeble ray of light (one might almost say moonlight) shed by the remains of

---

[1] [See CLAPHAM, *English Romanesque Architecture*, pp. 9–14, for other early churches in Gaul and Britain; and cf. *supra*, i, p. 31. The discovery of the prototype of the vaulted basilica, with apse, nave, aisles, and narthex (RIVOIRA, *Roman Architecture*, p. 34), just outside the Porta Maggiore in Rome itself, has of course entirely altered the whole state of the question. It is doubtful whether, as there suggested, it can be as early as the reign of Augustus; and it most probably belongs to the first century after Christ, and perhaps to the middle of that century (PLATNER and ASHBY, *Topographical Dictionary of Ancient Rome*, p. 71 and reff.). (A.)]

[2] [The similarity of the plan of the basilica at Silchester to that of the old St. Peter's is somewhat

qualified by the fact that the 'transept' at Silchester consisted of two separate rooms, as noted below, at the ends of the aisles, instead of forming an uninterrupted cross-aisle. (H. T.)]

[3] *Archaeologia*, vol. liii (1893), FOX and ST. JOHN HOPE, *Excavations on the Site of the Roman City at Silchester, Hants, in 1892*. [HAVERFIELD's latest pronouncement was that its remains cannot be dated (*The Roman Occupation of Britain*, ed. G. Macdonald, p. 206), while Sir C. R. PEERS (*Antiquity*, iii (1929), p. 65) thinks that it is probably of 4th-century date. (A.)]

[4] HARNACK, *The Mission and Expansion of Christianity in the First Three Centuries*, vol. ii, p. 411.

the little suburban church of St. Martin at Canterbury is insufficient to dissipate the settled darkness which envelops the conditions of the art of building during the period when the unhappy country was being trampled under foot by its new masters. Those remains are in all probability to be referred to the work of Queen Bertha,[1] and this explains the dedication of the church to the wonder-working saint of Tours.[2]

When Bertha, daughter of Charibert I (561–567), was married to Ethelbert King of Kent (560–616),[3] a condition was made, according to Bede,[4] that she should be accompanied by Liudhard so that she might keep her Christian faith. Hence, it is natural that as Ethelbert had a sanctuary for his pagan worship, his wife should demand another

Fig. 535. Canterbury. Old Church of St. Martin. South side (6th century)

for her Christian service; and so St. Martin's was erected on the spot where she was wont to offer her prayers. This supposition would be confirmed by the eastern orientation of the structure, a fact which is fatal to Bede's assertion that it was built in the days of the Roman occupation. Whatever its form may have been, the chancel was certainly at the east end. It has been thought[5] that it was semicircular, on account of traces of buttresses belonging to the original building discovered at the south-east angle; but the evidence is insufficient, though it is quite true that everything is in favour of an apsidal end. Moreover, the use of Roman bricks in the construction suggests a date

[1] MICKLETHWAITE, *Something about Saxon Church building*, in *The Archaeological Journal*, liii (1896), p. 295.

[2] [In *Antiquity*, iii (1929), 65 ff., Sir C. R. PEERS has conveniently summarized the facts about the seven earliest churches (SS. Peter and Paul, St. Mary, and St. Pancras at Canterbury, St. Andrew at Rochester, St. Mary at Lyminge, St. Peter at Bradwell, and St. Mary at Reculver), all of which were in existence before the end of the 7th century, and show an obvious similarity of plan, which may be considered as a revival of the classic tradition illustrated by the supposed Christian basilica at Silchester. They are also dealt with by Mr. CLAPHAM, op. cit., pp. 17 ff., who points out that St. Martin of Canterbury stands by itself. (R.)]

[3] *Rolls Series*, 23, *The Anglo-Saxon Chronicle*, p. 16.

[4] *Historia Ecclesiastica gentis Anglorum*, i. 25 (ed. Plummer, vol. i, p. 45).

[5] ROUTLEDGE, *The Church of St. Martin, Canterbury*, Appendix C.

contemporary or nearly so with St. Pancras at Canterbury, built by Augustine.[1] Unless the traces of a junction with the south wall of the church, near the second door, and the remains of a pavement in front of the latter, belong to a porch,[2] in which case the church itself would date from the time of Augustine, and belong to the type which has been conveniently named 'Augustinian'.[3]

Of the primitive church there remains the rectangular nave (fig. 535), which has been tampered with and originally extended farther west. It forms the chancel of the present Anglo-Saxon Church, probably built after a bishop was established there by the primate Theodore (668–690), as we are told in 'The Black Book of the Archdeacons of Canterbury'. This episcopal see is also mentioned by Dugdale.[4]

St. Martin's contains a font which may be supposed to have been originally a well-head, and belongs to the twelfth century. The decorative motives on it are derived from the simple arcading found as an ornament on other well-heads, e.g. the one in the cloister of St. John Lateran at Rome (fig. 536), the execution of which indicates the same date as that of the *puteal* in the ancient atrium of San Giovanni a Porta Latina, in other words, the tenth century.

Fig. 536. Rome. Well-head in cloister of St. John Lateran (10th century)

We are more fortunate when we come to the years after 597 and the constructive period of the time of Augustine and his companions, for here we have important descriptions and remains of building.

THE CATHEDRAL OF CANTERBURY.[5]—We know from Bede[6] that the monk Augustine, afterwards first Archbishop of Canterbury,[7] recovered, with the help of Ethelbert, a church said to have been built on the site by Roman Christians, and dedicated it to the Saviour. Augustine's work, however, cannot

---

[1] ST. JOHN HOPE, *Excavations at St. Austin's Abbey, Canterbury*, in *The Chapel of St. Pancras*, in *Archaeologia Cantiana*, vol. xxv, p. 235.

[2] PEERS, *On Saxon Churches of the St. Pancras type*, *The Archaeological Journal*, vol. lviii (1901).

[3] [In his latest treatment of the subject (*Antiquity*, iii (1929), p. 67) Sir C. R. PEERS maintains that 'as it exists to-day it shows two periods of early work, in the nave and in the western part of the chancel, the latter being demonstrably the older of the two. Its walls are thin and built of Roman brick: 'the rectangular nave to which they belonged was 14 feet wide, but neither its east nor its west end remains. In its south wall is a lintelled opening 3·6 feet wide, which gave access to a small square chamber now destroyed. To the west of this building, and overlapping it to some extent, the present nave of St. Martin's was built, at a date which may well fall within the 7th or

8th centuries.' As to what is meant by 'early work', he says 'St. Martin's church was given to them (Bertha and Liudhard); the suggestion is that it had been in existence for some time, and Bede says that it was built of old while the Romans still occupied Britain.' CLAPHAM (op. cit., pp. 24, 33, 42) agrees in the main with this dating, thinking that the earlier part may have been rebuilt before the time of Augustine. (A.)]

[4] *Monasticon Anglicanum* (new ed., London, 1817–30), i. 81.

[5] [CLAPHAM, op. cit., pp. 85 ff.]

[6] *Hist. eccl.*, i. 33 (ed. Plummer, vol. i, p. 70).

[7] [The date of Augustine's archiepiscopate, properly speaking, is the year of the consecration of Mellitus and Justus to the suffragan sees of London and Rochester. He died shortly after on 26 May 604. (H. T.)]

have been confined to a consecration, but must have taken the form of rebuilding, for the altar was at the east end, an arrangement which shows that the church cannot have been erected before the Anglo-Saxon conquest. And we cannot suppose that in the years between that conquest and 597 the Christians would have erected, under Pagan rule, a church of such importance, which was a reproduction, up to a certain point, of St. Peter's at Rome. As a matter of fact, Mabillon[1] mentions the rebuilding of the previous church, and places it in 602. Goscelin[2] also confirms the fact of a construction by Augustine; and a short description of it is given by Eadmer.[3] According to this it consisted of a nave and choir with aisles. The apsidal chancel at the east, raised above a crypt or *confessio* formed in imitation of that in St. Peter's at Rome, and reached through the choir, was faced at the west end by a chapel dedicated to the Virgin, also elevated above the floor of the church, and containing the primatial chair. From the aisles, at a point more than halfway down the church towards the west, projected two towers, which at first must have been mere porches, afterwards raised in height by Archbishop Odo (942–959), when he increased the walls of the church to a height of 50 ft. There is no record of tower porches in England before the tenth century. The southern tower contained an altar dedicated to Pope Gregory, while the northern had an altar of St. Martin.

On these main facts, and some secondary ones derived from Gervase, Professor Willis[4] based a plan of Augustine's church, imagination supplying the gaps where Eadmer's description fails. But we shall deal with this when we come to discuss St. Mary's at Abingdon (675).

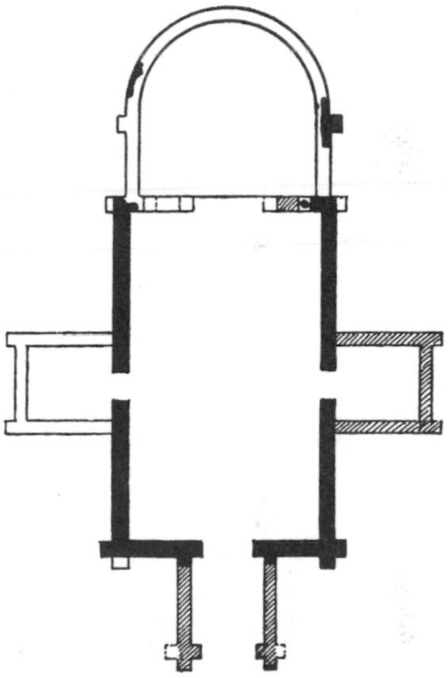

Fig. 537. Canterbury. Plan of St. Pancras (6th or 7th century)

THE CHURCH OF ST. PANCRAS AT CANTERBURY.—Thorne[5] and Elmham[6] say that this was a pagan temple which Augustine converted into a church and dedicated to St. Pancras.[7] This transformation ('quod phanum ... mutavit in ecclesiam') certainly took the form of rebuilding, for the existing remains show no trace of a temple, but belong to a church with an elongated apse at the east end.

The little church had an aisleless nave terminating in a semicircular apse with a bay in front of it, separated from the nave by four columns (fig. 537). It possessed three porches, on the west, north, and south sides. What remains visible above ground consists of the body of the church, and very scanty relics of the presbytery and apse (fig. 538).

The plan of St. Pancras, with its apsidal chancel projecting by more than a semicircle

[1] *Annales Ord. S. Benedicti*, vol. i, p. 270.
[2] MABILLON, *Acta Sanct. Ord. S. Benedicti, Vita s. Augustini episcopi Cantuariensis primi Anglorumque apostoli*, vol. i, p. 513.
[3] *Rolls Series*, 73, *Gervasii Cantuariensis opera historica*, i, pp. 7–9.
[4] WILLIS, *The architectural history of Canterbury Cathedral* (1845), p. 27, fig. 2.
[5] TWYSDEN (1652), *Historiae anglicanae scriptores decem. Chronica Guill. Thorne monachi S. Augustini Cant.*, col. 1760.
[6] *Rolls Series*, 8, THOMAS ELMHAM, *Historia monasterii S. Augustini Cantuariensis*, pp. 79–80.

[7] [Sir C. R. PEERS (loc. cit., p. 68) says 'this is only valuable as showing that its early date was recognized at the time (14th century) when the Chronicle was written'. He also describes the church of St. Peter and St. Paul, which was begun at the end of the 6th century and finished early in the 7th, being in plan very similar to the late Roman building at Silchester; its east end was destroyed in the middle of the 11th century to make room for the octagon built by Abbot Wulfric (*infra*, p. 149), and the rest at the end of the century to make room for the Norman church whose remains are to be seen to-day. Also the scanty remains of the similar church of St. Mary (about A.D. 620). (A.)]

from the outer nave wall to provide room for a presbytery; with its chancel, divided from the nave by a row of columns; with its small porch at the west front, and the side chapels or porches, exercised a notable influence on the form of later English churches, right up to the Norman Conquest. The origin of the plan is involved in great obscurity, and we shall endeavour to give an explanation which may throw some light on it. The idea of a row of columns dividing the nave from the sanctuary was borrowed from a church with which the monk Augustine must have been well acquainted, as it stood but a few steps from his monastery of San Gregorio *ad Clivum Scauri* at Rome.[1] This church, the relationship of which to the other has not hitherto been suggested, is the building which some archaeologists identify with

Fig. 538. Canterbury. Remains of St. Pancras (6th or 7th century)

THE PALATINE CHURCH OF SAN CESARIO.—The 'Ecclesia S. Caesarii in Palatio' is first mentioned in the reign of Phocas (603), and for the last time in the fourteenth century. Though its site has not been identified, Lanciani[2] is inclined to place it in the ruins of the so-called Baths of Heliogabalus on the Via Sacra (third century). Others think that it was an oratory of the fourth century fitted up in the 'Domus Augustana', and afterwards converted into a church.[3] Without attempting to decide between such conflicting views, we will confine ourselves to the simple statement that a church was undoubtedly fitted up in these ruined buildings about the end of the fifth century. The rough construction of the inserted masonry, consisting of alternate courses of used-up bricks and blocks of tufa, with a liberal use of mortar, points definitely to the period following the days of Leo I (440–461) and the terrible sack of the city by Genseric's Vandals (455), and preceding the revival of building under Theodoric (493–526). The remains of Santo Stefano on the Via Latina, erected in the time of that great pontiff, are very instructive in this connexion, for they show the same style of masonry as the inserted walls of the reputed San Cesario,[4] though it is not so rough.

[1] [Mr. CLAPHAM (op. cit., p. 31) compares the triple arch shown in a mosaic from a church at Tabarka (Tunis) and the sixth-century chapel of the Episcopio at Parenzo. (R.)]

[2] *The Ruins and Excavations of Ancient Rome*, pp. 169, 170.

[3] BARTOLI, *Scoperta dell'oratorio e del monastero di San Cesario sul Palatino, Nuovo Bull. di Archeologia Cristiana*, 1907, pp. 200 ff.

[4] [HÜLSEN, *Misc. Ehrle*, ii (*Studi e Testi*, vol. 36), pp. 377 ff., now puts the church of S. Cesario in the so-called Hippodromus of the Domus Augustiana; cf. PLATNER and ASHBY, *Topographical Dictionary of*

Ancient Rome, p. 164: while he identifies this building with S. Maria de Metrio (*Chiese di Roma nel Medio Evo*, pp. 345, 346). See, however, LUGLI, *The Classical Monuments of Rome and its Vicinity*, vol. i, *The Zona Archeologica*, p. 164, who revives MIDDLETON's doubts (*Remains of Ancient Rome*, vol. i, p. 227) as to its having been a church at all. (A.) Cf. C. R. PEERS in *Archaeologia*, lxxvii (1928), p. 210, on St. Augustine's, Canterbury: 'There seems no ground for the idea that Augustine's church was directly inspired from any church in Rome itself—where indeed nothing closely resembling it has yet come to light.' (R.)]

The fragmentary remains of the church in question, of which I append an approximate plan (fig. 539) as it appeared when excavated in 1872, consist of a nave ending in
a spacious presbytery marked off by two columns and two pilasters (fig. 540). The
presbytery is flanked by two sacristies, as in the large basilica of St. Symphorosa on
the Via Tiburtina, and is provided with an apse having a passage round it behind the
altar. An exactly similar arrangement is presented by an
ancient dated example, the basilica at Benian in Algeria
(434–439).[1] Facing the apse at the farther end of the church
is the tank for baptism.

It will be readily seen that this church is related to those
of the Anglo-Saxon period, not only by its pillared chancel
screen, but also by the cruciform shape given to the presbytery and found, for instance, in the churches of Repton
(tenth or eleventh century), Deerhurst (tenth century), and
St. Mary's in the Castle at Dover (eleventh century). Another
point of contact is the prolongation of the apse, a feature
already presented by St. Symphorosa.

The large rectangular chambers at the sides of the presbytery of the reputed San Cesario, transferred to the aisleless
nave of St. Pancras, form the typical chapels which some
English writers[2] believe to be the germ of the transept of
later times, ignoring the fact that the Romans had constructed
not only buildings in the form of a Latin cross, but also
cruciform structures with a dome over the crossing, as may
be seen in Montano[3] and other sources. And they were
followed in this by the builders of Ravenna, as may still be
seen in the mausoleum of Galla Placidia (about 440), and as
might have been seen a few centuries ago in the church of
Santa Croce (about 449). Consequently there was no occasion
to evolve the idea afresh by means of tentative experiments.

With regard to the external buttresses of St. Pancras, we
know how this form of support had been already developed
in Italy. The single-bay porch at the west end was derived
from the one in front of the portico of the Constantinian
St. Peter's.[4] Lastly, as to the two side porches, we may
remark that the scheme of giving more than one portico to
a building had been already introduced by the Romans.
Montano[5] and Bramantino[6] give illustrations of buildings
with several entrances each approached through a porch
(fig. 541). We may also remember that before this time an example of two lateral
porches is presented by the celebrated

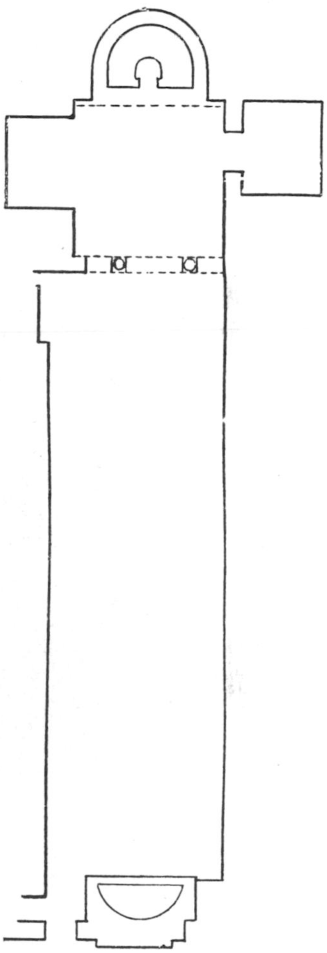

Fig. 539. Rome. Plan of so-
called San Cesario al Palatino
(5th century)

CHAPEL KNOWN AS THE TEMPLE OF THE CLITUMNUS, NEAR SPOLETO.—It consists of
a cella measuring inside about 15 ft. by 10 ft., with a semicircular recess at the east
end, and a vestibule or narthex flanked by two porches which have been damaged.

[1] GSELL, *Les monuments antiques de l'Algérie*,
vol. ii, p. 179.
[2] F. BOND, *Gothic Architecture in England*, p. 222;
PRIOR, *A History of Gothic Art in England*, p. 52.
[3] Op. cit., lib. ii, pls. 3, 5, 6, 8, 21, 37, 45; lib. iii,

[4] [See RIVOIRA, *Roman Architecture*, pp. 223, 224.]
[5] Lib. ii, pls. 4, 23; lib. iii, pl. 4.
[6] Op. cit., pls. 58, 72, 73.

Cella, narthex, and porches, all have barrel vaults, while the apsidal recess is covered by a half-dome. The walls are constructed of squared blocks of limestone, and have been tampered with at the sides. At the top runs a dentil cornice. The cella was originally lighted by an opening above the entrance: the windows on the south side have been made later (figs. 542, 543).

Inside, above the small apse (partly buried under the modern road to Foligno), is a tympanum with the decussate cross-monogram among scroll-work with roses. An

Fig. 540. Rome. Remains of so-called San Cesario al Palatino (5th century)

elaborate cornice runs round the base of the half-dome at the impost line. The pediment above the exterior of the apse contains the cross-monogram between scrolls with roses, bunches of grapes, poppy heads, and vine leaves.

The elaborate pediment of the façade is supported by four marble columns, two of spiral design and two covered with imbricated water-leaves, and two pilasters. They are surmounted by Corinthian capitals with acanthus leaves, or with stiff leaves combined with acanthus, or, in a third case, with palmetto leaves, acanthus, and scroll-work with roses. The pediment contains the cross-monogram, between scroll-work bearing roses, vine leaves, clusters of grapes, and poppy heads.

De Rossi[1] regarded this architectural gem as a pagan sanctuary transformed into

---

[1] *Bull. d'arch. cristiana*, 1871, p. 143, *Spicilegio d'archeologia cristiana nell'Umbria, Del tempietto sulle rive del Clitunno, consecrato al culto cristiano.*

a Christian church in the Theodosian age (378–450). Grisar,[1] on the other hand, believes it to be a building of the pre-Christian period, constructed in its lower part of old materials, and afterwards rebuilt by Umbrian 'marmorarii' in the twelfth century.

My view, on the contrary, is that it is a structure of one date, and that of Christian times, and contemporary with the basilica of San Salvatore or the Crocifisso at Spoleto, i.e. perhaps the reign of Constantine. Thus, though its original masonry is composed of materials taken from earlier buildings, it is obviously the result of a single constructive effort. The architectural ornaments, too, were executed at one and the same time. A comparison of the carving on the façade with that in the interior above the apse is quite enough to prove this. And the capitals of the vestibule, in spite of their differences in design, were executed at the same moment.

These carvings, in their turn, are obviously contemporary with those in San Salvatore. Compare the continuous impost cornice of the altar recess in our chapel with that in the apse and those in the central square space of San Salvatore, and the correctness of my statement will at once become apparent. Moreover, the surviving Corinthian capital belonging to one of the pilasters on the front of San Salvatore is clearly of the same date as the two imbricated columns in the chapel by the Clitumnus. And the carving on the front of the chapel is, on comparison, seen to be contemporary with that on the front of San Salvatore. At the most one might say that the latter has a slightly more classical air about it.

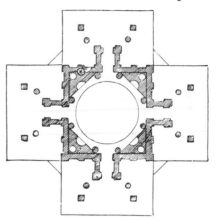

Fig. 541. Rome. Plan of tomb on the Via Appia. (From MONTANO, *Li Cinque libri di architettura*, iii. 4)

Before leaving the subject we should notice that here, as in the case of San Salvatore at Spoleto, topographical reasons were responsible for the eastern orientation, as the chapel was built against the steep cliff, with its front turned to the ancient Roman road which must have run below it.

THE CATHEDRAL OF ROCHESTER.—The church of St. Andrew at Rochester was built (604) by King Ethelbert for Justus its first bishop (604–624), subsequently archbishop of Canterbury (624–627).[2] Of this earliest cathedral, as is supposed—for there is no record of any rebuilding—the foundations of part of the east end were discovered in 1889 below the west front of the present cathedral and the roadway before it. The remains showed an aiseless nave ending in an apse at the east; but there was no indication whether or no they were separated by a row of columns.[3]

THE CATHEDRAL OF YORK.—We learn from Bede[4] that King Edwin (617–633) began to build (627), under the direction of Paulinus, the first bishop of York (625–633), a basilica dedicated to St. Peter, which his death at the battle of Hatfield prevented him from finishing. This was done by King Oswald (634–642).

In the course of the works undertaken after the fire of 1829 a large part of the area occupied by the church of Paulinus came to light. It was found to be a cruciform

---

[1] *Nuovo bull. d'arch. cristiana*, 1895, p. 127, *Il tempio del Clitunno e la chiesa spoletina di San Salvatore*.
[2] BEDA, *Hist. eccl.* II. iii.
[3] [The probability that a row of columns divided the apse from the nave at Rochester is indicated by the existence of a sleeper wall across the chord of the apse. See BALDWIN BROWN, ii. 99, 100, and G. M. LIVETT's article in *Archaeol. Cantiana*, xviii. 261–78. (H. T.)]
[4] Op. cit., II. xiv (ed. Plummer, vol. i, p. 114).

building with a very short transept. As no traces of the sanctuary were discovered it is not known whether the cross was, as is very probable, imperfect, i.e. without the topmost limb, or of the perfect 'Latin' form.[1]

The cathedral of York is supposed to have served as a model for the primitive St. Peter's at Peterborough,[2] founded by Peada, king of Mercia (655–656 or 657), and erected by the first abbot Saxulf. Burned by the Danes in 870, it was rebuilt with the help of King Edgar (957–975) by Ethelwold, bishop of Winchester (963–984);[3] and it is not possible, in their present state, to date with certainty the remains of transept and presbytery walls of some early church existing underneath the present cathedral.

THE CHURCH OF ST. MARY AND ST. ETHELBURGA AT LYMINGE (KENT) was built by Queen Ethelburga after the death of her husband, Edwin of Northumbria (633), or, to be precise, in the year 640.[4] There exist near the present church, which is ascribed to Dunstan, some remains of its foundations showing that the nave and chancel were separated by two columns.[5]

Following the type of the buildings which we have described was erected

THE CHURCH OF ST. PETER ON THE WALL AT YTHANCAESTIR (BRADWELL) IN ESSEX, of which the walls of the aisleless nave still exist. It is supposed that these remains belong to the church erected by Cedd of Lindisfarne, bishop of the East Saxons (654–664).[6] This view we cannot accept.[7] We learn from Bede that

Fig. 542. Temple of Clitumnus near Spoleto
(4th century)

[1] [Prof. BALDWIN BROWN remarks (Anglo-Saxon Architecture, rev. ed., p. 75): 'The earliest actual remains are to be seen in the crypt of the present Minster, and consist in two masses of herring-bone masonry, one on each side of the crypt at its W. end.... The general appearance of the work accords with an Early Norman date, and there is nothing about it that looks Saxon.' For remains in the choir crypt, possibly belonging to Abp. Albert's church (about 770), see PEERS in The Antiquaries Journal, xi (1931), 116ff.(R.)]

[2] [For plan and description of the remains at Peterborough see BALDWIN BROWN, op. cit., pp. 168–71; cf. also CLAPHAM, p. 91, who attributes them to 970–972, inasmuch as they contain re-used material.]

[3] Rolls Series, 23, The Anglo-Saxon Chronicle, pp. 25, 60, 93; BEDA, Hist. eccl. IV. vi; SPARKE, Historiae anglicanae scriptores varii (1723), Chronicon Angliae per Iohannem abbatem Burgi S. Petri, pp. 27,

30; Hugonis Candidi coenobii Burgensis historia, p. 17.

[4] Rolls Series, 8, ELMHAM, Hist. monasterii S. Augustini Cantuariensis, p. 176.

[5] [PEERS, Antiquity, iii, p. 70, with plan. He writes as follows: 'There are in the churchyard at Lyminge, to the south of the parish church, the foundations of a small church with an eastern apse, and rectangular nave, built of Roman brick, with some evidence of chambers to the north and south of the east end of the nave, and overlapping the apse. The opening between nave and apse seems to have been divided into three, and the general arrangements have so much in common with the Canterbury churches that a date in the second quarter of the 7th century may be not unreasonably claimed for them.' (A.)]

[6] BEDA, Hist. eccl. III. xxii (ed. Plummer, i, p. 173).

[7] [The fabric and date of the church of St. Peter on the Wall are discussed by BALDWIN BROWN, op. cit.,

the church of the monastery at Lastingham, founded by Cedd himself (648), was constructed of wood, and that it was only later that a stone church was built in honour of the Virgin, into which the body of the founder was transferred. We can hardly imagine that, when he had used timber for the church of Lastingham, which was so near to his heart, he would go on to erect another in masonry after the Augustinian type of St. Pancras at Canterbury. We must not forget the tenacity with which the Irish missionaries clung to wooden construction, even when they went to Italy and were in contact both with ancient buildings and with the rising Lombardic School. It is far more likely that the first church at Ythancaestir was of wood, and that later it was rebuilt in stone under the influence of Canterbury, after the Synod of Whitby (664).

Some writers (Amico Ricci[1] and Merzario[2] among them) state that the churches built at the time of Augustine's mission were the work of Italian craftsmen, particularly those belonging to the Lombard gilds, who followed him together with the missionaries sent by Gregory the Great. This, however, is an arbitrary assertion. The Pope sent with Augustine monks only ('misit servum Dei Augustinum et alios plures cum eo monachos timentes Dominum'), not monks and craftsmen. The 'operarii', whose small numbers compared with the abundant harvest of converts had been deplored by Augustine in the message sent through Peter and Laurence, were

Fig. 543. Temple of Clitumnus near Spoleto. Side view (4th century)

not material workmen but missionaries, and it was of such that Gregory sent him a fresh supply (601) ('. . . misit cum praefatis legatariis suis plures cooperatores ac verbi ministros') to the fullest extent that was in his power ('exhaurit monasteria sua et ecclesias, et quidquid potest eruditorum ac religiosorum virorum in opus Evangelii efflagitare . . . certat delegare').[3] The fact is these buildings must have been designed and carried out by the monks. Saxulf, the first abbot of St. Peter's at Medeshamstede (Peterborough), is actually described in Bede[4] as the 'constructor' of the monastery founded by Peada.[5] And though it is reasonable to suppose that, in consequence of the wars and disorder prevailing after the Anglo-Saxon invasion, England became practically devoid of any national art, and the tradition of beautiful things was lost as the artists

101–5. His ascription of the building to the 7th century is positive, but he doubts whether it can be attributed to Cedd, whose Celtic traditions seem to forbid his adoption of the St. Pancras type of plan and the apsidal chancel. See description and plan in *Hist. Mon. Comm., Inv. Essex*, iv. 15, 16. (H. T.) Mr. CLAPHAM (op. cit., p. 22) thinks that it is St. Cedd's Church. (R.)]

[1] Op. cit., vol. i, p. 183.
[2] Op. cit., vol. i, pp. 87–8.
[3] BEDA, *Hist. eccl.* I. xxix ; D'ACHERY, *Appendix ad illustranda B. Lanfranci opera, Chronicon Beccensis Abbatiae* (MIGNE, *Patr. Lat.* cl, col. 752, no. 62).
[4] *Hist. eccl.* IV. vi (ed. Plummer, i, p. 218).
[5] [See Appendix to Chapter I, p. 47.]

of the old time went down to the grave without imparting any lessons to their successors, yet we cannot imagine that a school of builders, however rude, did not continue to exist; still less that the very stamp of it had perished. We may therefore fairly assume that the builders of the structures in question were English. In any case the entire absence of architectural ornaments and carving excludes the presence of Italian or French artists in these works, and so confirms the opinion expressed above.

When Oswald became King of Northumbria (634–642) there was a pause in the extension of the influence of the Church of Rome, while the activity of the Irish Church was correspondingly accentuated. The latter dated from the fifth century, its first two bishops being Palladius (431–432) and Patrick (432–461).[1] Oswald as a boy had found refuge within the walls of the monastery founded by Columba (†597) in the island of Iona, where he had taken up his abode about the year 563, and whence he drew Aidan and other clergy belonging to the Celtic rite in which he had been baptized. The foundation of the monastery at Lindisfarne followed. Here Aidan fixed his episcopal seat (635–651), and from it soon issued bands of missionaries who spread over the realm of Oswald (where with his help they erected churches) and the various other states, but not over Kent, which belonged to the Roman obedience.

Oswald's death at the battle of Maserfield and the consequent supremacy of the pagan king, Penda (626–654 or 655), retarded for a space the activity of the missionaries, but it became more lively than ever the moment that Penda was dead and Oswy had ascended the throne (642–670). So that the North of England, so far as it was christianized, had for its primate, not the archbishop of Canterbury, in spite of the rights which he asserted, but the abbot of Iona.[2] At length the Synod of Whitby (664) inflicted a mortal blow on the flourishing Celtic community; and the Latin Church obtained a firm seat in the island with no rival to dispute her sway.

Of the churches erected by the missionaries of Iona and Lindisfarne or its daughter monasteries I have not been able to find traces of any one constructed of masonry. Perhaps this is because they were all built 'in the Celtic fashion' or 'in the Scotch fashion', that is to say of wood, like the cathedral erected by Finan (651–661) at Lindisfarne ('quam tamen more Scotorum non de lapide sed de robore secto totam composuit atque arundine texit'), the reed and thatch roof of which Bishop Eadbert (687–698) replaced by a complete covering of sheets of lead ('ablata arundine plumbi laminis eam totam, hoc est et tectum et ipsos quoque parietes eius cooperire curavit').[3]

We need not be surprised at the Irish clergy erecting structures of this kind in England, when we remember that the church built by Columban (†615) in Italy at Bobbio, in the reign of the Lombard king, Agilulf (590–615), was also of wood: 'ecclesiam in honore almae Dei genitricis semperque Virginis Mariae ex lignis construxit.'[4] It has been suggested[5] that the church of Lindisfarne was rebuilt in stone by King Ecgfrid (670–685), and that its tri-apsidal arrangement was due to Theodore, archbishop of Canterbury (668–690). But the account in Bede, who lived about the same time (677–735) and was familiar with the place and circumstances, is fatal to the theory. The remains of a stone church, which had, as a matter of fact, three apses, discovered to the east of the eleventh- to twelfth-century priory church, must be assigned to a date

---

[1] BURY, *The Life of St. Patrick and his place in History*, pp. 431–60.

[2] [There is no historical evidence for the exercise of any actual primacy by the abbot of Iona. (H. T.)]

[3] BEDA, *Hist. eccl.* III. xxv.

[4] MABILLON, *Acta Sanct. Ord. S. Benedicti,* Miracula Columbani scripta a monacho Bobbiensi, vol. ii, p. 37.

[5] PARK HARRISON, *On an early illuminated manuscript at Cambridge, Archaeologia Oxoniensis,* 1893, pp. 167–8.

after its second destruction by the Danes (867), and probably to the reign of Athelstan (924 or 925–940), who was such a benefactor to Lindisfarne,[1] or even later.[2]

The struggle for supremacy between the Latin and the Celtic Churches in Northumbria was conducted on the side of Rome by two energetic champions, Benedict Biscop and Wilfrid, the latter being the most prominent. And it was carried on with a policy clear-sighted, determined, at times even high-handed, at least in the case of Wilfrid, who was always more inclined to carry war than peace in the folds of his tunic; but also with the aid of one of the arts which is more closely connected than others with the instincts, the ideas, the progress, the needs of a people—I mean architecture. And so they set themselves to erect churches in the country, the work of builders of more skill than could be found at home, and recruited beyond the Channel: churches with glass windows, a new thing in Great Britain, and sometimes paintings brought from Rome and intended to form a 'biblia pauperum' to teach the unlearned the facts of the sacred story. One of these churches was constructed in so elaborate a fashion as to make it the most notable of which the district could boast for a long time to come. Let us see what remains of them.[3]

THE CHURCH OF ST. PETER, MONKWEARMOUTH, was built in 675 by Benedict Biscop, first abbot of Wearmouth and Jarrow, near the monastery which he had founded (674) at the mouth of the Wear with the aid of King Ecgfrid (670–685). Bede[4] informs us that the church was built of stone in the Roman style, which was always preferred by Benedict, certainly as against the Celtic fashion of wooden construction. And it was carried out by workmen brought on purpose from France.

Of the original building, which took but a year to finish, there remains only the west front and its two-storied porch (figs. 544, 545), the outline of whose gable can still be seen in the third stage of the present tower. The western opening of this porch is sustained by short baluster shafts (fig. 546), turned on the lathe, standing on high plinths ornamented with intertwined serpents, whose long, beak-like jaws interlace, like some of the winged creatures on the famous Bayeux Tapestry (eleventh century). In the tower which rises above, the upper part is no doubt due to the restoration carried out in 1075[5] by the monk Aldwin, with the assistance of Walcher, bishop of Durham (1071–1080), after the destruction caused by the Scottish king, Malcolm III (1054–1093), and certainly before 1083, when the monks of Jarrow and Monkwearmouth were transferred to Durham. It has, indeed, been suggested that the addition to the tower belongs to the years between the foundation of the church and the devastations of the Danish hordes (867), who burned the monasteries of Monkwearmouth, Jarrow, Tynemouth, Lindisfarne, and Whitby. But, as we shall see when we come to the abbey church of Ramsey, the characteristic western tower makes its first appearance in connexion with datable English churches only in the tenth century, and then as an importation from France.

The tower at Monkwearmouth is closely related to that of St. Cuthbert's, Billingham

---

[1] Rolls Series, 75, Symeonis monachi opera omnia, Historia ecclesiae Dunelmensis, vol. i, p. 75.

[2] [The theory that the remains of the early east end of the priory church at Lindisfarne contain Saxon work has now been abandoned, as it is impossible to fit them in with any scheme of building at so early a period. See BALDWIN BROWN, vol. ii, p. 468. (H.T.)]

[3] [See CLAPHAM, op. cit., pp. 38–46, who includes the church at Escomb (infra, p. 186) in the early Northumbrian group which he contrasts with the Kentish group described above. (A.)]

[4] Historia abbatum, 5 (Opera historica, ed. Plummer, vol. i, p. 368).

[5] Rolls Series, 75, Symeonis monachi hist. eccl. Dunelm., vol. i, p. 113; ibid., vol. ii, pp. 201, 68, Symeonis monachi historia Regum.

(fig. 547), which must not be identified with the church of Ecgred, bishop of Lindis-farne (831–846),[1] but was erected after the Conqueror had given back Billingham to

Fig. 544. Monkwearmouth. West end of church (7th century)

St. Cuthbert (1072).[2] It is also related to those of St. Mary, Ovingham, and St. Mary

[1] *Rolls Series*, 75, *Symeonis monachi historia Regum*, vol. ii, pp. 201, 68.

[2] *Rolls Series*, *Symeonis monachi hist. eccl. Dunelm.*, vol. i, p. 198. [There is no positive evidence that Ecgred founded a church at Billingham. The refer-ences in Symeon of Durham state merely that he founded (*condidit*) and built (*aedificavit*) the vill of Billingham (Surtees Soc. li, 68, 142). In both places the statement follows the definite mention of the church which he built at Gainford on the Tees (*aedificavit*

Fig. 545. Monkwearmouth church. Interior of west end (7th century)

Fig. 546. Monkwearmouth church. Baluster shafts in outer west door (7th century)

Fig. 547. Billingham. Tower of St. Cuthbert's (11th century)

Fig. 549. Athens. Acropolis. Base of monument to Agrippa (1st century B.C.)

Bishophill Junior at York, which belongs to the time of the Conqueror's building of St. Mary's Abbey, York.[1] All the towers with two-light openings enclosed by a common arch standing out from the face of the wall, or framed by a single arch within a rectangular recess, are later than the Conquest, which ushered in their appearance in England. Monkwearmouth, Jarrow, and Billingham provide instances.

Before leaving Monkwearmouth I should like to say a word about the baluster shafts.[2] I have never been able to discover any of earlier or even contemporary date with these.

Fig. 548. Edinburgh. Museum. Top of Roman altar from Birrens.

They seem to me to reveal the co-operation of native workmen in the construction of the church. The use of supports of this form for decorative purposes was of great antiquity in the island. An altar of the Roman period discovered at Birrens (Dumfriesshire), and now in the Museum at Edinburgh,[3] has a carved representation of an arched doorway with the jambs formed as baluster shafts (fig. 548). Another small Roman altar from Lanchester[4] in the Cathedral Library at Durham has also been mentioned in this connexion, but the pediment of the shrine represented on it does not rest on baluster shafts, but on a bead and reel and cable moulding.[5]

ecclesiam apud villam quae vocatur Gegnford, ibid., p. 142, and see p. 171 below); and, though the foundation and building of a vill may imply those of a church, yet at Gainford the vill apparently preceded the church. Although the later date here assigned to the tower of Billingham is on general grounds highly probable, it cannot be assumed to be absolutely certain. (H. T.)]

[1] DUGDALE, op. cit., iii. 529. [The date of the tower of St. Mary Bishophill Junior, like that of the tower of Billingham, is conjectural, although a date as late as 1088 is not impossible (see note on p. 142). St. Mary's Abbey, York, was actually founded shortly before this time: the settlement of the monks who came there from Whitby possibly may have taken place in 1085, after their intermediate settlement at Lastingham.

The date of the type of tower to which belong the examples referred to in the text has been variously stated. Its most frequent occurrence is in the northeast of England, and there are several groups of such towers in Lincolnshire. The characteristic features are the absence of angle-buttresses, the tall lower stage, sometimes battering slightly, and divided by an offset from the belfry stage, and the peculiar construction of the double window openings in the latter. This, not noted in the text, is their division by a shaft, usually monolithic and roughly shaped, set in the middle of the thickness of the wall: the capital is frequently carved with volutes or rough crockets, and above it is a through-stone impost from which the arched heads of the openings spring. The enclosing arch, where it occurs, is a purely ornamental frame of strip-work, and in most instances is omitted. E. A. FREEMAN (*English Towns and Districts*) laid down the principle that the type indicates the work of English builders after the Conquest, and it is probable that his general contention is true, and that the type, late Saxon in origin, was preserved by English builders

for some time afterwards. Dr. JOHN BILSON has made a notable contribution to the dating of these towers in his paper on *Wharram-le-Street Church, Yorkshire, and St. Rule's Church, St. Andrews* (*Archaeologia*, lxxiii. 55–72), and the whole question of the 'Saxo-Norman overlap' is fully discussed by BALDWIN BROWN, ii, ch. xiii, in the light of the most recent evidence. The northern examples of the older type mentioned in the text, to which may be added the tower of Bywell St. Andrew, are all classified by Baldwin Brown as belonging to the late Saxon period: the use of large stones in their construction favours this date. Usually such towers are of rubble with small quoin-stones. (H. T.)]

[2] [On baluster shafts see BALDWIN BROWN, op. cit., 59 (possible Roman origin), 257, and CLAPHAM, op. cit., 116. STRZYGOWSKI derives them from the turned woodwork of North European timber-architecture (*Early Church Art in Northern Europe*, p. 98). (R.)]

[3] [*Proc. Soc. Ant. Scot.*, 1896, p. 51, fig. 9.]

[4] [See HAVERFIELD and GREENWELL, *Catalogue of the Sculptures and Inscribed Stones in the Cathedral Library, Durham* (Durham, 1899), p. 20, no. xxiii.]

[5] [St. Peter, Monkwearmouth, was cited by Comm. RIVOIRA in the first edition of this book as providing the earliest example in Great Britain of the so-called 'long-and-short work', in which the stones at the salient angles and the jambs of the openings are set alternately horizontally and vertically. It has now been established that there is no trace of the alternation of horizontally with vertically set stones which constitutes long-and-short technique, nor does the latter appear in English churches which may be attributed to the period at which Monkwearmouth was probably built. The long-and-short treatment of the jambs of openings, seen at Escomb, is a different matter: see note 4 on p. 186. (H. T.)]

[In connexion with Monkwearmouth, Comm.

ST. PAUL'S CHURCH, JARROW, founded by Benedict Biscop and Abbot Ceolfrid, with the assistance of King Ecgfrid (670–685), was consecrated in 685.[1] The nave of the original building still exists forming the present chancel (figs. 550, 551).[2] It was restored

Fig. 550. Jarrow. Nave of the original church (7th century)

in the course of Bishop Walcher's[3] work carried out after 1074, at the same time as the erection of the existing porch with its tower.[4] In the north porch of the present church

RIVOIRA added in the first edition the following general discussion of long-and-short work: 'A Byzantine origin has been sought for this form, and a pedestal (fig. 549) on the Acropolis at Athens has been produced as evidence; but this structure belongs to a monument erected in honour of M. Vipsanius Agrippa in 27 B.C., and has nothing in common with the work in question. Bonding of this kind, used in the angles of irregular masonry, and forming a source of weakness rather than of strength, was undoubtedly a product of barbarism in the art of quoining. Its introduction into Britain, to judge by what we know, must have been due to French craftsmen, perhaps from Poitou, as there is no other locality where we find its use so deeply rooted and with the tradition of a thousand years behind it; for instance, at Poitiers, where the interior of the narthex of the baptistery of Saint Jean exhibited it as early as the first years of the 11th century, and masonry, both ancient and modern, in secular buildings still provides numerous illustrations of it for the observer to-day. In this connexion it is interesting to note that, just at the time of Benedict Biscop, there is evidence of direct contact between the North of England and Poitou in a fragment of the will of Ansoald, bishop of Poitiers (682–696), from

which we learn that he appointed a bishop called Romanus from the land of the Scoti, accompanied by a band of his countrymen, to govern and occupy the monastery of Mazerolles sur Vienne, which had been restored by him.' (CHAMARD, *Histoire ecclésiastique du Poitou*, p. 157.)]

[1] BEDA, *Hist. Abbatum*, 7. [The date of the consecration of the church at Jarrow is not given by Bede; but the inscribed stone now in the east wall of the nave gives the date as *VIIII kal. Mai.* in the fifteenth year of Ecgfrid and the fourth year of Ceolfrid (23 April 685). It may be noted that this inscription does not necessarily refer to the existing fabric of the chancel. Jarrow is briefly discussed by BALDWIN BROWN, op. cit., pp. 133–5: see also the articles by C. C. HODGES in *The Reliquary*, July 1893, and by H. E. SAVAGE in *Archaeol. Aeliana*, 2nd ser., vol. xxii, pp. 30–6. (H.T.)]

[2] [But cf. CLAPHAM (op. cit., p. 39), who says that it is uncertain whether the dedicatory inscription of 685 applies to the existing chancel. (R.)]

[3] *Rolls Series*, 75, *Symeonis monachi hist. eccl. Dunelm*, vol. i, p. 9.

[4] [There is no definite evidence for any architectural work furthered by Walcher at Jarrow, though it is very probable that a large portion of the adjacent

in the Pointed style are preserved some ancient baluster shafts and fragments of a string-course with miniature balusters and vertical rolls of sausage shape in relief, of the same date as similar fragments belonging to Wilfrid's church at Hexham, now in the Cathedral Library at Durham. There are also various pieces of carving, some of which may be ascribed to the French artists brought over by Benedict Biscop. They consist of a fragment with interlacing and birds, and another exhibiting interlacing with part of a recumbent figure, and also a man disentangling himself from the interlacing. They go with another fragment at Hexham, and part of a cross from Jarrow at Durham.

Fig. 551. Jarrow Church. South side of the original nave and later tower (7th and 11th centuries)

THE BASILICA OF ST. ANDREW AT HEXHAM[1] was erected by Wilfrid (634–709) between 672 and 678. Its dedication is the same as that of the church built by Gregory the Great in his monastery near the Clivus Scauri, from which came the missionaries who evangelized the Anglo-Saxons. Eddius Stephanus,[2] the biographer and chaplain of the energetic bishop, has left a short account extolling the size ('mirabilique longitudine et altitudine') and splendour of the building ('neque ullam domum aliam citra Alpes montes talem aedificatam audivimus'); but these eulogies must be discounted, as it is easy to see that language of this kind originated in the great poverty of ecclesiastical structures which might serve as standards for contemporary descriptions. These characteristics are confirmed by Richard of Hexham[3] (who has left a fairly detailed account, though with some omissions, of Wilfrid's church), Simeon of Durham,[4] William of Malmesbury,[5] and Eadmer.[6]

Of the original church, which still retained its beauty in the time of William of Malmesbury (twelfth century), as he himself says in his *Gesta pontificum Anglorum*, but of which the east part must have been removed early in the next century to make way for the present choir and transept, there is preserved the crypt, above which rose the sanctuary, as we learn from the metrical biographer of Wilfrid, Frithegode.[7] It consists of a chamber reached through a vestibule, with three passages for entrance and exit. There are also some remains of the apse.

monastic buildings was the result of the settlement of Aldwin of Winchcombe here in or after 1075. The tower with its substructure (the west porch, which now opens on the west into the modern nave) does not seem to have been completed till later. (H. T.)]

[1] [For the Hexham churches see Prof. G. BALDWIN BROWN, *The Arts in Early England*: vol. ii, *Anglo-Saxon Architecture* (new ed., London, 1925), ch. ii and pp. 100 ff.; CLAPHAM, op. cit., pp. 44 ff.]

[2] *Rolls Series*, 71, *The historians of the Church of York and its archbishops*, *Vita S. Wilfridi episcopi*, vol. i, p. 33.

[3] TWYSDEN, op. cit., *De statu et episcopis Hagustaldensis Ecclesiae*, cols. 290–1.

[4] *Rolls Series*, 75, *Hist. Regum.*, vol. ii, p. 52.

[5] *Rolls Series*, 52, *Gesta pontificum Anglorum*, vol. i, p. 255.

[6] *Rolls Series*, 71, *The historians of the Church of York and its archbishops*, *Vita S. Wilfridi episcopi*, vol. i, p. 185.

[7] *Rolls Series*, 71, *The historians of the Church of York and its archbishops*, *Vita S. Wilfridi episcopi*, vol. i, p. 128.

With regard to the actual builders of St. Andrew's we are informed in general terms that Wilfrid procured them from the Continent ('adductis secum ex partibus transmarinis artificibus'—'De Roma quoque et Italia et Francia et de aliis terris ubicumque invenire poterat, cementarios et quoslibet alios industrios artifices secum retinuerat').[1] But we are also told explicitly that they were brought from Rome ('sed et cementariorum, quos ex Roma spes munificentiae attraxerat, magisterio . . .'), which finds its natural explanation in the fact that the Roman workmen, accustomed as they were from the time of Constantine onwards to erect colonnaded basilicas with ancient materials, were the best fitted for carrying out the bishop's ideas.[2]

Fig. 552. Rome. Basilica of Sant' Agnese outside the walls (7th century)

For the works which they were engaged in executing under his direction he had formed a clear idea during his sojourns in Rome, where, as early as his first visit (about 654), he was able to admire, among other things, the galleried basilicas of Sant' Agnese fuori le mura (fig. 552) and the Santi Quattro Coronati (fig. 553), recently rebuilt by Pope Honorius I (625–638).[3]

The 'title' of the Santi Quattro is mentioned as far back as the time of Gregory the Great, and dates, according to some authorities, from the fifth century. Duchesne[4] believes that the church goes back to the fourth century, which would explain its western orientation, unless indeed this is the result of reasons connected with the site. It was rebuilt by Honorius I, Leo IV, and lastly, after the Norman fire, by Paschal II, who began his work on it in 1111, and consecrated it in 1116. It was remodelled and redecorated in the fifteenth, sixteenth, and seventeenth centuries.[5]

In my opinion the traditional history of the Santi Quattro does not quite correspond with the facts; and the reconstructions under Leo IV and Paschal II consisted, in the former case, of restorations and new additions, in the latter, of mutilations and additions, preserving in part the arrangements of the church of Honorius I. This view is confirmed by the apse, in which the untouched masonry of the exterior belongs to the work of Honorius up to a point above the large original windows with their double ring of bricks.

[1] TWYSDEN, op. cit., col. 293.

[2] MABILLON, Acta Sanct. Ord. S. Benedicti, Vita S. Wilfridi episcopi auctore anonimo sec. XII., vol. iii, p. 205; Rolls Series, Willelmi Malm. monachi gesta pontificum Anglorum, p. 255.

[3] [See A. MUÑOZ, Il restauro della chiesa dei SS. Quattro Coronati (Rome, 1914).]

[4] Le Liber pontificalis, vol. i, p. 326[13].

[5] DE ROSSI, Bull. d'arch. cristiana, 1879, pp. 88–9; LANCIANI, Storia degli scavi di Roma, pp. 5, 6; ARMELLINI, Le chiese di Roma, pp. 498–9.

If we compare it with the brickwork of the time of Leo IV (i.e. the ninth century) to be seen in the apses of Santa Cecilia in Trastevere (817–824), and San Giorgio in Velabro (827–844), and in the nave of Santa Prassede (817–824), all apparently the work of the same masons, we shall notice a less marked decadence, and in any case a difference in date. In the next place, no one would ascribe it to Paschal II. Very different were the exteriors of buildings of his time, especially in the treatment of the windows, as we see from the circular and round-headed specimens in the nave of Santi Giovanni e Paolo, which he restored after the Norman fire, and those in San Clemente, the rebuilding of which was started before 1126 or 1128. All that he did to the apse of the Santi Quattro was to repair it, and insert the range of consoles derived from some ancient building.[1] At Rome, the apses of Christian buildings earlier than the epoch of about 1000 never have any but borrowed consoles, and it is a mistake to assign to the sixth century[2] the eaves cornice on the apse of San Martino ai Monti (498–523), formed of carved consoles supporting sculptured slabs and panels with masks and other ornaments, for it is made up of ancient materials.

Fig. 553. Rome. Basilica of the Santi Quattro Coronati (12th century)

The apse of the Santi Quattro at a later date was raised to its present height. As for the body of the church, Paschal II abandoned the two old aisles, and walled up their colonnades; shortened the nave, within the width of which he constructed a new nave and two aisles; and in the latter repeated the arrangements of galleries as it existed in the church of Honorius I.[3] It was not till the times of Pelagius II (579–590), as in the case of his transformation of the Constantinian basilica of San Lorenzo in Agro Verano (fig. 554), Honorius I, and Hadrian I (as Santa Maria in Cosmedin showed), that galleried basilicas, with two stories of colonnades after the pagan type, were erected in Rome.

To return to Hexham. The three churches of Pelagius II and Honorius I referred to must have formed the models for Wilfrid's structure, for it was provided with just the same colonnades in two stories, a feature indicated by a passage of Prior Richard's chronicle: 'parietes autem quadratis et variis et bene politis columpnis suffultos, et tribus tabulatis distinctos immensae longitudinis et altitudinis erexit.' And this explains William of Malmesbury's[4] reference to the likeness between St. Andrew's and churches at Rome: 'Nunc qui Roma veniunt idem allegant, ut qui Haugustaldensem fabricam vident ambitionem Romanam se imaginari jurent.'

[1] [Muñoz (op. cit., p. 28) attributes them to the 9th century.]
[2] Mazzanti, op. cit., p. 20.

[3] [Muñoz, op. cit., p. 22, attributes their first introduction in this church to Paschal II.]
[4] [Rolls Series, Gesta Pontif. Anglorum, p. 255.]

We have still to consider who executed the carving. I do not include, of course, the figured capitals mentioned by Prior Richard, because I believe they were Roman antiques brought from elsewhere. Britain, in Roman times, could not have been barren of capable executants of figure subjects (fig. 555). On the other hand, in the seventh century the chisels of Rome and France, which it seems were at work on Hexham, did not produce figure capitals (I say capitals and not pulvins), for there is not a single specimen in existence.[1]

Some of the carving from Hexham is preserved in Durham Cathedral Library. It includes three fragments of stringcourse showing upright balusters, cable mouldings, and rolls arranged either horizontally or in zigzag fashion (fig. 556). The rudeness of both design and execution, as well as the style of ornamentation, suggest that they are

Fig. 554. Rome. Old Basilica of San Lorenzo in Agro Verano (6th century)

the work of British hands, with whom baluster shafts were a favourite feature as far back as the Romano-British period. We cannot imagine that Wilfrid would have taken the trouble to bring artists from beyond the seas in order to produce work of this kind. These fragments go with others of the same kind preserved in St. Paul's, Jarrow, and the portion of a stringcourse with a roll between two cables now in the north arm of the transept of the existing church of Hexham.

Of the carving executed by Continental artists for Hexham we have no specimens which can be identified with certainty. We may, however, ascribe to them some of the fragments gathered in the north arm of the transept, though their provenance can only be said to be Hexham and not definitely the church. Among them are three Lombardic cubical capitals (fig. 557), which have been made to pass for Anglo-Saxon, but are really later than the Conquest (1066). One might search in vain among dated buildings in England for capitals of similar type till we come to the abbey church of St. Augustine at Canterbury as rebuilt by Abbot Scotlandus (1070–1087). The earliest trace of simple hemispherical capitals that I have been able to find in this country is the representation of an arcade with two bulbous capitals and one of hemispherical form in the well-known manuscript 'Liber Geneseos, caeteraeque historiae sacrae' in the British Museum, which is thought to be rather earlier than 1066.

[1] [On capitals in general see CLAPHAM, op. cit., pp. 124, 125.]

To the time of Wilfrid may be assigned a fragment with vine foliage showing a cock, and the legs and one arm belonging to two human figures (fig. 558), all in low relief. The composition, design, and technique show that it comes from the same school, and possibly from the same hand, as that which produced the two fragments with scroll-work, birds, and human beings, which we noticed at Jarrow.[1]

With the carving of the time of Wilfrid and Benedict Biscop executed by foreign artists may be connected the very decayed portions of the upright limb of a cross,

Fig. 555. Bath. Museum. Mask of Sol

Fig. 556. Durham. Cathedral Library. Fragments of carving from St. Andrew's, Hexham (7th century)

Fig. 557. Hexham. Capital in St. Andrew's (11th century)

Fig. 558. Hexham. Church of St. Andrew. Fragment of carving (7th century)

supposed to be that of Acca, bishop of Hexham (709–740), or rather one of the two crosses which stood at the head and foot of his grave: 'Duaeque cruces lapideae mirabili celatura decoratae positae sunt, una ad caput alia ad pedes eius.'[2] The fragments, covered with a very intricate vine stem design, have been set up in the Cathedral Library at Durham, to which they were brought from Hexham (fig. 559). The date of the carving may be that which is generally assigned to it. We know that Acca embellished St. Andrew's,[2] and we need not be surprised if the foreign artists of Wilfrid's

[1] [Dr. J. BRØNDSTED in *Early English Ornament* (London and Copenhagen, 1924) states that the vine pattern with its regular curves, grape-clusters, and birds or animals, so characteristic of ornamentation in the North of England in the 7th and 8th centuries, originated in an Oriental conventionalization of a decorative subject first found in Hellenistic-Roman art (p. 17). The home of the vine pattern is Syria and Egypt (p. 28). In its oldest form (of which fig. 558 is an example) both plant and animals are true to nature, and only in the laying out of the pattern does conventionalizing appear. (R.)]

[2] *Rolls Series*, 75, *Symeonis monachi hist. Regum.*, vol. ii, pp. 33–52.

time were followed by others at a later date who produced these gravestones. It is clear that the carving belongs to a period which, if not that of Wilfrid, is not far removed from it; and it is equally clear that it comes from a French hand. I say this because the carvers of Rome and Ravenna, at that date the best in Italy, did not produce such complicated interlacings; and those of Lombardy, though very fond of employing them, were unable to treat them with the grace shown by the cross from Hexham.

All this carving in relief is quite different, both in composition, design, and technique, from that of the well-known tall cross at Ruthwell, Dumfriesshire, which cannot be dated earlier than the first half of the twelfth century (fig. 560).[1]

Lastly, we can connect with Wilfrid's work the ancient episcopal chair (fig. 561) known as 'the Frith stool', cut out of a single block of stone, which may be seen in St. Andrew's. The front is outlined by roll mouldings, and on the arms are carved interlacings ending in knots. The way in which the framing is executed, and the simple character of the interlacing, suggest a Roman hand; especially the mouldings, which recall works of the Roman and Ravennate schools, beginning with the well-known screen panels in San Clemente at Rome (fig. 562).

In connexion with the better carving of the time of Benedict Biscop, Wilfrid, and Acca, it has been suggested that in the days of Theodore of Tarsus, archbishop of Canterbury (668–690), artists from the East came to Britain to ply their trade. But there is no mention of such in the chroniclers, and in the course of my long and frequent wanderings up and down England I have never been able to recognize their hand in any of the early carving still in existence.

Fig. 559. Durham. Cathedral Library. Fragment of cross from Hexham (8th century)

The presence of such artists in the island may, then, be relegated to the domain of fable.[2] Others there are who would attribute it to Irish chisels. Ireland, they say, in the seventh, eighth, and ninth centuries, was not only a great school of missionaries but also of art; and as evidence they produce the illuminated manuscripts of the period—for instance, the 'Book of Dimma',[3] written by a scribe of the name, who is supposed to be the same[4] as the Dimanus mentioned in a letter of Pope John IV

[1] [The author restated and developed his views on the Ruthwell and Bewcastle crosses in *Antiquities of St. Andrews, Burlington Magazine*, xxi (1912), p. 24. See Appendix to this chapter, where the subject is discussed.]

[2] [Dr. BRØNDSTED is of a different opinion. After mentioning the five Syrian Popes (686–731) and Theodore of Tarsus, he continues (op. cit., p. 31): 'France during the same period was saturated from south to north with Oriental industry and trade; it was a time when the art and ornamentation of the East were advancing everywhere in southern and western Europe. Is it then any wonder that the new style which is introduced into and strikes root in Northumberland in the latter part of VII should be purely Oriental, should be the Syrian vine pattern?' See also DALTON, *East Christian Art*, p. 62, and CLAPHAM, op. cit., p. 64. (R.)]

[3] Now at Trinity College, Dublin.

[4] [Mr. J. S. GROGAN, Librarian of Trinity College, Dublin, kindly states that the signatures to the manu-

(640–642).[1] Here we see simple interlacing framing figures of the Evangelists John and Matthew. Or there are the 'Lindisfarne Gospels',[2] written by Edfrid, as is supposed, before he became bishop of Lindisfarne (698–721), and illuminated by his successor Ethelwold (724–740). Here the interlacing is sometimes very complicated, and better drawn than in the 'Book of Dimma'. The latter is also surpassed by the 'Lindisfarne Gospels' in the representation of figures, showing a more advanced stage of art.[3] Or, again, there is the 'Book of Durrow',[4] dated in the seventh century; but its more complicated interlacing and the representations of animals differentiate it somewhat from the 'Book of Dimma', and suggest that it belongs to the second half of the eighth century. A noticeable peculiarity is the long beak-like jaws of the animals, a feature recalling the serpents carved by some French artist in the porch of St. Peter's at Monkwearmouth (675). Another example is the 'Psalterium charactere Hibernico' in the British Museum, believed to be of the ninth century, with interlacing, simple in some cases, and very intricate in others. Or, lastly, there is the 'Book of Kells',[4] the most important palaeographical and artistic monument existing in Ireland, and regarded as belonging to the eighth century.[5] But though the style of its interlacings connects it with the 'Evangelistarium of Mac Regol' (†820) in the Bodleian Library, on the other hand the quality of the drawing suggests that it is later than the 'Book of Durrow'. Its date will therefore fall in the years immediately subsequent to the foundation of Kells (802–815) by Cellach, who, with the Columban community, had fled from Iona through fear of the Danes.

Fig. 560. Ruthwell Cross (12th century)

But the interlacing in the 'Book of Dimma' is evidently derived from Romano-British mosaic decoration. There was no lack in Britain of public and private buildings of that period, rich in polychrome mosaics. The existence, and also, except in the representations of living beings, the fine quality of the mosaics, is proved by, to give only two or three instances, those recently discovered at Calleva Atrebatum (Silchester) and Venta Silurum (Caerwent). We may mention, too, the mosaic found in 1805 under the site of the Bank of

script are now considered to be forgeries: and the manuscript was, it has been proved, written about the time of Dimma, son of Fringus, abbot of Roscrea (800–816). See R. I. Best in *Hermathena*, no. xliv, p. 84.]

[1] Gilbert, *National Manuscripts of Ireland*, vol. i (1874), p. xii.

[2] British Museum; Cotton MS. Nero D. iv.

[3] [The Lindisfarne Gospels are treated by Baldwin Brown, op. cit., vol. v, in connexion with their relation to the sculpture at Bewcastle and Ruthwell.]

[4] Trinity College, Dublin.

[5] Abbott (T. K.), *Celtic ornaments from the Book of Kells*, p. iv.

England, and now on the north wall of the Roman Gallery of the British Museum, which displays, besides knot work and lotus flowers, a circle enclosing eight branches arranged in the form of the so-called Maltese cross.[1]

Mosaics of this kind might have provided suggestions for the Anglo-Saxon artists, and, if necessary, for the Irish as well. The fact remains, however, that they did not do so, for neither England, Ireland, nor Scotland contain any datable carving of the same type as that which we have classed as the work of foreign artists in the time of Benedict Biscop, Wilfrid, and Acca, going back to the years between the calling in of the Northern barbarians (449) and the coming of the craftsmen invited or brought from the Continent by Benedict and Wilfrid.

Fig. 561. Hexham. St. Andrew's. Episcopal chair (7th century)

The real worth of the carvers at work in Northumbria before 675, or even after that date but continuing the old style, appears to me to be shown by the well-known gravestones in Durham Cathedral Library, the Black Gate Museum at Newcastle-upon-Tyne, and the British Museum, which were unearthed from the ancient cemetery of the convent of St. Hilda at Hartlepool, founded by Heiu before 650[2] and destroyed by the Danes. Each of these gravestones shows a characteristic rude cross enclosed in a circle, and has a semicircular top; while the lettering of the inscriptions corresponds to that of the Irish manuscripts of the seventh century. The fact that a specimen of this rare type of gravestone has come to light in St. Peter's at Lindisfarne, and that others have been found at Glendalough and Clonmacnoise in Ireland, demonstrates its Celtic origin.

Fig. 562. Rome. San Clemente. Pluteus from the choir (6th century)

The highly complicated interlacing of the Lindisfarne Gospels (even granting that the illumination comes from an Irish hand, though the name 'Ethelwold' sounds Anglo-Saxon) was done at a time when the Lombard gilds had long been accustomed to produce patterns of the most varied and intricate character in carving. And it was executed under the influence of centres of Latin culture like Jarrow, Monkwearmouth, and Hexham, where Benedict Biscop, Ceolfrid, and Wilfrid had formed libraries with books brought from Rome. And this influence extended in the same way to the artists of the other illuminated manuscripts mentioned above.

Another source of influence, especially in the case of the intricate interlacing sometimes with heads of animals which occurs in the 'Psalterium charactere Hibernico',

---

[1] [The mosaic at Woodchester, near Stroud, may also be added.]   [2] BEDA, *Hist. eccl.*, iv. 23

the 'Book of Kells', and the 'Evangelistarium of Mac Regol', may have been the School of St. Gall, which was in touch with the Lombard gilds on the one side, and on the other kept up relations with the clergy of Great Britain and Ireland. I have, in fact, seen in that celebrated monastery several manuscripts (one, of local origin, being of the eighth century) with very involved interlacing closely related to that of the English and Irish manuscripts previously referred to. I may mention an 'Evangelium S. Iohannis' (eighth century), the 'Quattuor Evangelia' (eighth century), the 'Homiliae S. Gregorii' (ninth century), and the 'Psalterium Folchardi' (ninth century).

On the other hand, there is no proof that the artists of that age derived ideas for carving from the illuminated manuscripts, and still less that they were Irish. It would indeed have been a singular anomaly if people who were so little used to stone buildings as to go on erecting wooden structures in the 'Celtic' fashion through the seventh and

Fig. 563. British Museum. Side of whalebone casket (8th century)

eighth centuries had been capable of producing carving of so advanced a character as we find at Monkwearmouth, Jarrow, and Hexham.

Moreover, had not Britain and Ireland suffered from a positive sterility of artists, Benedict Biscop and Wilfrid would never have incurred the heavy expense of engaging the services of foreigners. It is more reasonable to believe, as I do, that it was the instruction and the light derived from the examples left behind them by the Continental artists which guided the Anglo-Saxon carvers in the work which they undertook as their successors, resulting in the founding of a National School.

Certain it is that the productions of the Anglo-Saxon School, particularly in Northumbria, where the said National School was formed, are quite distinct from the foreign work which provided it with models. In the treatment of figures, and especially of the human form, there is nothing short of a gulf between them, both as regards design and execution. A convincing proof of this is furnished by the important whalebone box known as 'the Franks Casket' in the British Museum (figs. 563, 564). The missing portion (fig. 565) belongs to the National Museum at Florence. This casket, Northumbrian work of the eighth century with Runic inscriptions, betrays foreign influence, e.g. in the scene of the wolf with Romulus and Remus, and in the canopy with supports showing interlaced ornament and a knot in a spandrel, evidently derived from a Pre-Lombardic source.[1] The Adoration of the Magi recalls the precious remains of the oak coffin which

[1] [Comparison with animal forms in 8th-century Merovingian manuscripts has persuaded Dr. BRØND- STED that the casket is work of the South of England of that period, strongly influenced by Merovingian art circles (*Early English Ornament*, pp. 134–6). But the Northumbrian origin is supported by Mr. O. M.

once held the body of St. Cuthbert, now fitted together and exhibited under glass in Durham Cathedral Library, with its representations of Christ between the Emblems of the Evangelists, the Archangels, the Virgin and Child, and the Apostles, poor in drawing but freely cut with the knife or graver, and accompanied by legends in Roman and Runic characters. Any one who looks at the human heads represented full face on the British Museum casket will not fail to perceive the relationship, especially in the

Fig. 564. British Museum. Side of whalebone casket (8th century)

Fig. 565. Florence. National Museum. Missing side of whalebone casket in British Museum (8th century)

oval outline of the head, between them and those on the remains of St. Cuthbert's coffin. The latter may very well belong to the year 698, or perhaps 696, as has been suggested.[1] In any case it cannot belong to a date later than 995, when his relics, carefully preserved during the wanderings of the community of Lindisfarne after their departure in the ninth century, were brought to Durham, the view being, on every ground, quite untenable which would place it in 1104, the year of the translation of

DALTON (*Catalogue of Ivories in the British Museum*), Mr. REGINALD SMITH (*Archaeologia*, lxxiv, p. 233), and Prof. BALDWIN BROWN (op. cit., vol. vi, part i, p. 38: 'the date not far from 700'); and a similar conclusion is reached by Prof. L. BRÉHIER in his recent valuable treatment of the subject, *Le coffret*

d'Auzon (Brioude, 1931). (R.)]

[1] *The Victoria History of the County of Durham*, i. 248. (KITCHIN, *The Contents of St. Cuthbert's shrine*.) [See also HAVERFIELD and GREENWELL, *Catalogue*, &c., pp. 133 ff.; CLAPHAM, op. cit., p. 43.]

the relics of the sainted bishop of Lindisfarne to the shrine at the east end of the new church, whose foundation had been laid in 1093.

The productions of the Anglo-Saxon School, as reflected in motives of ornament, are also to be recognized by an interesting feature which distinguishes English work between the eighth and eleventh centuries. This is the typical complicated interlacing

Fig. 566. Hexham. St. Andrew's.
Fragment of carving

Fig. 567. Mawgan in Pyder. Wheel-head
cross (10th century)

Fig. 568. Peterborough. Cathedral.
Portion of tombstone in the transept
(before the 12th century)

Fig. 569. Hexham. St. Andrew's. End of top
of 'hog-backed' tomb (Pre-Conquest)

in which the bands are not given a triangular or merely rounded surface but have the appearance of intestines. Numerous specimens are scattered about England, but the best are to be found in Northumbria because it was there that, under foreign influence, the School had its origin. We may mention a few of these examples, the date of which is not always easy to fix, as this treatment of interlaced work is not confined to the Anglo-Saxon period but sometimes occurs as late as the fifteenth century.

(1) The examples preserved at Monkwearmouth, Jarrow, Hexham (fig. 566), and in

Durham Cathedral Library, which contains the most important collection of Anglo-Saxon carving in England.

(2) A sepulchral cross with a Runic inscription commemorating one Cynibalth, from the churchyard of St. Mary's, Lancaster: now in the British Museum, and assigned to the late Anglo-Saxon period.

(3) A wheel-head cross brought from the parish of Gwinear, and now standing outside the church of Mawgan in Pyder (fig. 567). It is considered to be the finest example of a carved cross in Cornwall, and might be ascribed to the period following the submission of the British Church in Cornwall to the see of Canterbury in the reign of Athelstan (925–940), and the consequent introduction of Anglo-Saxon influence.

Fig. 570. Rome. Santo Stefano al Celio (4th and 5th centuries)

(4) Fragments of sepulchral slabs from the ancient graveyard of Peterborough Cathedral, found in 1887 under the floor of the north arm of the transept. One of them (fig. 568) shows the characteristic Gallic cross, interesting and very early examples of which in different forms may be seen carved on the tombstones collected in the baptistery of Saint Jean at Poitiers. This form of cross was probably imported from France, as were also the tombstones of the type of that at St. Andrew's, Bolam, with its cross and fish-bone ornament. National English work can also be recognized in the characteristic tops of tombstones (difficult to date) of Northumbrian origin, known as 'hog-backed stones', ornamented with crosses, circles, arcading, animal heads, interlacing. Interesting specimens can be seen in Durham Cathedral Library, and another in St. Andrew's church, Hexham (fig. 569).

CHURCH OF ST. MARY AT HEXHAM.—Prior Richard of Hexham[1] describes the form of this church, which was founded by Wilfrid about 680 A.D., and formerly stood near St. Andrew's: 'in modum turris erecta et fere rotunda, a quatuor partibus totidem porticus habens.' In other words, it was a structure of polygonal plan with four porches or vestibules, like the Roman edifice illustrated in fig. 541.

It appears, then, that St. Mary's at Hexham was also copied from a Roman building, either one of the type to which we have just referred, or else a church with which the bishop had become familiar in the course of his travels, Santo Stefano on the Caelian,[2]

[1] TWYSDEN, op. cit., *De statu et episc. Hagust. Eccl.*, col. 291.　　　[2] [*Supra*, p. 25.]

just remodelled by Pope Theodore I (642–649)[1] on the occasion of his translation of the bodies of the martyrs Primus and Felicianus from a catacomb on the Via Nomentana (fig. 570). It was a concentric circular building with a tower, and four inserted courts, one of which was made into a chancel. Or the plan may have been derived from the octagonal Lateran Baptistery with its three chapels and narthex.[2] In any case it is clear that St. Mary's was not, as has been suggested, an equal-armed cross with a central polygonal tower, for this does not agree with Prior Richard's brief description, and is inconsistent with William of Malmesbury's account of the new style of Athelney Abbey, of which we shall treat presently; unless the shape of a Greek cross was produced

Fig. 571. Perugia. Sant' Angelo (6th century)

by three porches or chapels and an apsidal chancel, as in the round church of Sant' Angelo at Perugia (fig. 571), which the latest discoveries show was provided with four projecting arms of this kind.[3]

THE CHURCH OF ST. PETER AT RIPON was erected according to Eddius[4] by Wilfrid between 671 and 678. We gather from his account and that of William of Malmesbury that it was a basilica with two tiers of arcades with columns, like St. Andrew's at Hexham. Destroyed by the Danes in the ninth century,[5] it was rebuilt from the foundations by Roger of Pont l'Évêque (1154–1181), archbishop of York, but Wilfrid's crypt

[1] LANCIANI, *The Ruins and Excavations of Ancient Rome*, p. 357.

[2] [See RIVOIRA, *Roman Architecture*, pp. 222, 263.]

[3] [Other examples of English round or polygonal churches were: the abbey church of Abingdon as rebuilt 959–975; a circular tomb chapel at Bury St. Edmunds for the body of the martyr, the remains of which were found in 1275; the octagon at Canterbury erected by Wulfric about 1060 (*infra*, p. 212, note 1); and the cathedral at Hereford re-erected by Robert of

Lorraine about 1080 after the pattern of Charlemagne's church at Aachen. See CLAPHAM, op. cit., pp. 144 ff. (A.) The last may be the square central-plan chapel on the south of the cloister, destroyed in 1737. *R. Comm. Hist. Monuments, Herefordshire*, i (1931), pp. 90, 115. (R.)]

[4] *Rolls Series*, 71, *The historians of the Church of York and its archbishops, Vita S. Wilfridi episcopi*, vol. i, p. 25.

[5] *Rolls Series*, 52, *Willelmi Malm. monachi gesta pontif. Anglorum*, p. 244.

was retained. This consists of a rectangular chamber with a barrel vault, approached through a rectangular vestibule with a half barrel vault.[1] Both communicate with two passages roofed with stone slabs.[2]

ST. ANDREW'S CHURCH, CORBRIDGE, is first mentioned by Simeon of Durham under the year 786.[3] It is supposed that it was built by Wilfrid,[4] and some remains of the

Fig. 572. Corbridge. West end of
St. Andrew's (7th century)

Fig. 573. Corbridge. St. Andrew's. Interior of
west end (7th century)

original structure support this. They consist of the porch, the walls of which have been raised, and the aisleless nave, to which aisles were added at a later date (fig. 572). There is a large opening in the west end (fig. 573), the arch of which must have been transferred bodily from the neighbouring Roman town of Corstopitum, or from the Roman Wall, and built into the church—an operation which suggests the presence of the foreign masons who worked on St. Andrew's at Hexham.

While the churches which we have just considered were being erected through the

[1] [In 1930 it was discovered that the barrel vault was constructed with splayed ribs. *The Antiquaries Journal*, xi (1931), p. 116. (R.)]

[2] [The similarity of design between the crypts of Ripon and Hexham points to their identity of date and origin. Some interesting suggestions with regard to their relation to the plan of the churches to which they belonged were advanced by J. T. MICKLE-THWAITE (*Archaeol. Journal*, xxxix (1882), 347–54).

His arguments for a western orientation, however, are unsupported. For a recent examination of these structures see also Sir C. PEERS in *The Antiquaries Journal*, xi (1931), pp. 113 ff. (H. T.)]

[3] *Rolls Series*, 75, *Hist. Regum*, vol. ii, p. 51.

[4] *The Reliquary*, vii (1893), p. 12, HODGES, *The pre-conquest churches of Northumbria—Corbridge, St. Andrew's Church*. [BALDWIN BROWN, op. cit., p. 142.]

action of the Latin Church in Northumbria, which under Oswald, Oswy, and Ecgfrid, was the most important state in the island, others were rising, or were about to rise, through the same influence in the southern districts and in Mercia.

Fig. 574. Canterbury. Columns from Reculver in the Cathedral Close (669) [recently removed to the crypt]

THE CHURCH OF RECULVER was erected by Bassus under the patronage of Egbert, king of Kent (664–673) in 669.[1] There survive the foundations, and some fragment of walls above ground.[2]

The original church consisted of a nave, with a corresponding apse,[3] in front of which was a short presbytery, separated from the nave by three arches supported by two columns which are now set up on the north side of Canterbury Cathedral (fig. 574): on each side of the nave, and overlapping its junction with the chancel, is an oblong chamber, and others were added a little later against the remaining parts of the nave walls, including a west porch.

Its importance consists in these columns on account of the capitals which surmount them; for though the shafts and bases go back to late Roman times, the capitals are the work of Anglo-Saxon hands.[4] They, too, were originally Roman, but were afterwards re-worked by keeping the base and reducing the body of the capital to the form of three graduated abaci, chamfered at the angles. The barbarous way in which this transformation has been carried out is an indication of the abyss of decadence into which the British carvers had fallen, and also explains why Benedict Biscop and Wilfrid had recourse to foreign chisels.

[1] *Rolls Series*, 23, *The Anglo-Saxon Chronicle*, p. 30.
[2] [For the results of the excavation of the site in 1926–7 see Sir C. PEERS in *Archaeologia*, lxxvii (1928), pp. 241 ff. (R.)]
[3] [It may be noted that the apse was polygonal (seven sides) externally and semicircular internally. Sir C. PEERS points out that though in the other early churches of the south-eastern group no evidence of this form has survived (the apse at Lyminge is semicircular), the foundation courses alone remain, whereas at Reculver the polygonal form ends at the ground-level, and has semicircular foundations without as well as within, so that the possibility that some others of these early apses were polygonal must be borne in mind. For the fragments of an early sculptured cross from Reculver see note on the Ruthwell Cross given in an appendix to this chapter, *infra*, p. 209. (R.)]
[4] [PEERS (p. 246) and CLAPHAM (p. 122) consider the bases to be contemporary with the capitals.]

THE ABBEY CHURCH OF ST. MARY AT ABINGDON, founded in 675 by it first abbot Heane with the assistance of a local chieftain Cissa, had the peculiar feature of two apses at opposite ends of the building: 'et erat rotundum tam in parte occidentali quam in parte orientali.'[1] It was the first church in England to exhibit this arrangement. For though the plan of the first cathedral of Canterbury given by Willis shows a western apse, it is a gratuitous addition of his. Eadmer makes no mention of it: 'Finis ecclesiae ornabatur oratorio. Ad quod, quia structura eius talis erat, non nisi per gradus cuiusvis patebat accessus,'[2] and his words simply mean that the church ended at the west in a chapel, which could only be reached by several steps.

The plan is of very ancient origin. For instance, the magnificent Basilica Ulpia in Trajan's Forum at Rome (112–114) had a hemicycle at either end. Montano[3] gives the plan of a Pagan Roman sepulchral edifice ending in three apses, the principal one of which is faced by a corresponding one at the opposite end of the structure (fig. 575); and his work contains other examples of buildings with aisleless naves and two apses, facing one another. Again, recent excavations at Silchester have brought to light the remains of a civil basilica with a hemicycle at either end.[4] And so the architect of St. Mary's at Abingdon would not have had to go to distant lands in search of the arrangement, for Silchester is only just outside the confines of Berkshire in which Abingdon is situated.

In Christian buildings it had been used as far back as the fifth century in the basilica of St. Reparatus near Orléansville in Algeria (324), when a new counter-apse was erected to contain the tomb of the bishop of that name (475).[5] And later, when the vestibule (in which an altar of St. Andrew had already been introduced) of the Imperial Mausoleum near St. Peter's at Rome was transformed into the basilica of Sant'

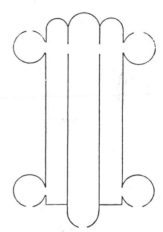

Fig. 575. Rome. Plan of sepulchral edifice. (From MONTANO, *Le cinque libri d'architettura*, iii. 14)

Angelo,[6] the latter presented, as indeed it always had done, two apsidal ends facing one another. It has been suggested[7] that it was St. Boniface (†755) who carried the plan to Germany, but there is no evidence in existence to support the idea.

BRIXWORTH CHURCH was built about 680, in the time of Cuthbald, second abbot of Peterborough.[8] The surviving parts of the original structure are the nave (now forming

[1] *Rolls Series*, 2, *Chronicon monasterii de Abingdon*, Appendix II, *De abbatibus Abbendoniae*, vol. ii, p. 272. [Cf. ibid., p. 277, for the round church built by Ethelwold ('cancellus rotundus erat, ecclesia et rotunda duplicem habens longitudinem quam cancellus; turris quoque rotunda erat'), *supra*, p. 158, n. 3. (A.)]

[2] *Rolls Series*, 73, *Gervasii Cant. opera historica*, vol. i, p. 8.

[3] Op. cit., iii. 14.

[4] Fox and ST. JOHN HOPE, *Excavations on the site of the Roman city of Silchester, Hants, in 1892*, in *Archaeologia*, vol. liii, part 2 (1893), p. 549.

[5] GSELL, op. cit., vol. ii, pp. 339–40.

[6] DE ROSSI, *Inscriptiones christianae urbis Romane*, vol. ii, p. 225[3].

[7] MICKLETHWAITE, *Something about Saxon church building*, Archaeological Journal, liii (1896) 296, n. 2.

[8] SPARKE, op. cit., *Hugonis Candidi Coenobii Bur-

gensis Historia*, p. 9. [For an architectural description of Brixworth church see *Archaeol. Journal*, lxix (1909), pp. 505–10, also BALDWIN BROWN, vol. ii, pp. 106–14, Sir HENRY DRYDEN's paper *On the Chancel of Brixworth Church* (Assoc. Archit. Soc. Reports, xx, 343–52), and CLAPHAM, op. cit., pp. 33 ff. In addition to the points noted in the text should be mentioned (1) the traces of the transverse arcade, which, as in churches of the St. Pancras type, divided the nave from the presbytery; (2) the use of Roman tiles in the arcades of the nave and the arches of tower and chancel; and (3) the sunken passage, now open to the air, which encircles the foundations of the apse, and was originally entered by doorways on either side of the chancel arch. This passage, in the outer wall of which are two recesses for tombs, seems to have been intended as the ambulatory of a crypt, of which no other indications remain. The apse, externally polygonal, with shallow the body of the church) and portions of the presbytery and western porch (figs. 576, 577). The internal face of the west end (fig. 578) contains high up a three-light opening (a later addition), the arches of which are carried by baluster shafts with Pre-Lombardic cubical capitals bevelled in the lower part, surmounted by an abacus of barbarous form. The balusters do not follow the characteristic type of those at Monkwearmouth and Jarrow, but belong to a Roman type, and are the oldest specimens of the kind (for those in St. Andrew's, Hexham, are only used for a decorative purpose) employed in a church that I have discovered in England. The Pre-Lombardic cubical capitals are also the

Fig. 576. Brixworth Church (about 680)

earliest examples of their kind in the country. Balusters of this type must have made their appearance about the end of the tenth century, and have come into fashion in the first part of the eleventh, as we find them represented in English manuscripts just at that period. I may refer to one in the British Museum (Cottonian MS., Claudius B. IV), described in the catalogue, and I think rightly, as rather earlier than the Norman Conquest, exhibiting specimens of baluster shafts, bulbous capitals formed by truncated

angle-buttresses, was certainly rebuilt at some period after the Danish invasions, and the employment of tufa in its walling points to a date contemporary with the upper part of the tower, in which tufa is also used. The heightening of the tower included the blocking-up of the original west doorway of the porch by the construction of an external stair-turret, three-quarters of a circle in projection, in which there is a considerable amount of herring-bone work. As described in the text, the walls of the porch were probably raised somewhat earlier, when the triple-arched opening (fig. 578) was inserted in the west wall above the blocked opening from the original chamber above the porch. The upper story of the tower was much altered in the 14th century, when the spire was added. The unusual size of this basilican church gives it a claim to be considered the most remarkable example of its early date in England, and the highly developed clerestory of the nave is unique among existing remains of the architecture of the period. Recent researches tend to establish some alliance between the rebuilding of the apse and the construction of the apses of Wing and Deerhurst. (H. T.)]

inverted pyramids, and arcading with alternate round and triangular heads, thus showing how the activity in building in the time of Edgar, Canute, and Edward the Confessor, was reflected in the illuminations of sacred volumes.

The walls of the porch were raised and the tower built some time after 870, when the church suffered at the hands of the Danes the same fate which befell the mother-church of Peterborough, but before the Norman Conquest. The former probably took place during the peaceful reign of Edgar (959–975), who was such a benefactor to Peterborough; the latter, in the course of the new invasion of the Danes, who in 1010 had burned the neighbouring town of Northampton, and made it urgently necessary to fortify Brixworth Church.

Fig. 577. Brixworth Church. East end (about 680)

With the organization of the Church in England carried out by Archbishop Theodore (668–690) and Abbot Hadrian (669–708)—a Church which became a national institution and prepared the way for the political unity of the country—the direct action of Rome through her missionaries came to an end, and the stream of Christian culture emanating from the City was stayed till we come to the days of Lanfranc (1070–1089) and Anselm (1093–1109). The primatial chair of Canterbury, which from the time of Augustine had been filled, except for a few years under Deodatus (655–664), by Italians and a Romanized Greek, received no more foreigners till 1070. And the same was the case with York, occupied till now, with the exception of Ceadda's and Bosa's tenure of the see, by an Italian, Paulinus (625–633), and an Anglo-Saxon educated on Italian lines, Wilfrid.

The withdrawal of direct Italian influence involved the cessation of the activity of the French and Italian builders and carvers, which had passed like a meteor over Northumbria. There were no longer monks from Italy to superintend the construction of ecclesiastical buildings. Architecture in England must now pursue its own course with the local means at its disposal and, apparently, without external aid. And this lasted till the time of Alfred the Great (871–901), when the relations of England with the Continent once more became intimate, particularly with France, whence the learned king drew most of the intellectual influences by which he strove to raise the culture of his subjects from the low level at which he found it. These relations were resumed afresh, and with more tangible results, in the time of Dunstan's tenure of the see of Canterbury (960–988), when a new current of foreign artistic influence passed over England. A similar current was felt in the reign of Ethelred II (978 or 979–1016) and Canute (1014–1035 or 1036), and becoming stronger and stronger, and finally carrying all before it, resulted in the appearance under Edward the Confessor (1041 or 1042–1066) of the 'New style' of Architecture, viz. the Lombardo-Norman. Its introduction did something to vivify the inert ecclesiastical architecture of England

Fig. 578. Brixworth Church. West end (about 680)

with its barbaric ornamentation, but at the same time it sounded its knell; for the moment had come for the old, uncomely forms to make way for a new creation of youth and vigour, backed up as it was by the strong hand.

However, we must not anticipate our conclusion; and first, let us take a rapid historical survey of three dark centuries barely illuminated as it were by the spasmodic, flickering light of an aurora borealis, so that we may take stock of the conditions existing in these lands, and set out the evidence relating to their ecclesiastical monuments which is to be found in the annalists, and contains matter of interest for our purpose.

In the eighth century the history of England is a tale of perpetual wars for conquest and supremacy between the various states into which the nation was divided. Such was the story of intestine struggles in the kingdom of Wessex, which compelled Ine (688–728) to abandon his throne and go on a pilgrimage to Rome, where he ended his days; and this in spite of his successes in the field, the civil organization which he devised for his subjects, and the religious awakening brought about by Aldhelm, bishop of Sherborne (705–709). The result was that Wessex fell into the power of Ethelbald, king of Mercia (716–755). In the kingdom of Northumbria, again, Eadbert (737 or 738–757), resigning the sceptre to his son Oswulf (757), after the example of his predecessor Ceolwulf (731–737), retired to the monastery of Lindisfarne, while the country became the scene of discord, revolt, and slaughter; evils accentuated by fire, pestilence, famine, and, to crown all, by the Danish inroads described by Simeon of Durham.[1] A state of things like this was not exactly favourable for the practice of architecture.

These disorders were brought to an end by the Mercian supremacy under Ethelbald, Offa (755–794 or 796), and Cenwulf (796–819 or 822), though, at the same time, it fell to pieces through the intervention of the Frankish kings in the affairs of England. Indeed, with the establishment of Eardwulf on the Northumbrian throne (795–806) and of Egbert on that of Wessex (800–836), and the outbreak of civil war in Mercia

[1] *Rolls Series*, 75, *Hist. Regum*, vol. ii, pp. 55, 56, 70–6.

itself after the death of Cenwulf, the supremacy broke up, and the extensive kingdom which he left at his death was divided.

The supremacy of Mercia was succeeded in the ninth century by that of Wessex under Egbert, brought about by the submission of Mercia and Northumbria, and his conquest of Cornwall. But it was not of long duration. Even before his accession, and that of his successor Ethelwulf (836–855 or 856), the Danes had begun their raids, in alliance with the Britons of the West. Ethelwulf could not do more than repress these raids for a time, for in 866 the pirates, after wintering in East Anglia, first invaded North-umbria, next subdued the eastern kingdom and put to death its king Edmund (870), then the lands of Mercia, and lastly Wessex, where, however, they were compelled by the sword of the liberator, Alfred the Great (871–901), to come to terms at Wedmore (878). The last years of the ninth century were spent in more fighting between Alfred and the Danes, and the tenth opened with the determined attempt of his daughter Ethelfleda (910–918 or 922) to subdue the Danish Confederation, the 'Denlag' or 'Danelaw', which had taken the place of the old kingdom of Mercia and been recognized by the Peace of Wedmore. This object was achieved by Edward the Elder (901–925), who received the voluntary submission of Scotland, Northumbria, and Wales, and of the Britons in Strath-clyde. Then came the wars of Athelstan (925–940) with the confederate kingdoms and with the Danes, brought to an end by his victory at Brunanburh (937), which initiated an era of peace in a reign made illustrious by the courage, firmness, and wisdom of the monarch. There followed Edmund's (940–946) reconquest of the Danish Confederation which had taken up arms against him, and Edred's (946–955) subjugation of Northumbria.

After the misgovernment of Edwy (955–959), a long period of peace succeeded in the days of Edgar (959–975). Under his rule, and with the co-operation of Dunstan, Ethelwold, and Oswald (who had been a monk at Fleury), the triad which was the source of the splendour of the reign, his people saw the restoration of order and justice, the promotion of trade and agriculture, the multiplication of abbeys, instituted not only for monastic purposes but also as places of education, which, in spite of the impulse given by Alfred the Great, was well-nigh extinct. The century ended amidst famine, internal conflicts, wars between the states, and fresh Danish invasions, with their attendant rapine, fire, and slaughter, which marked the reigns of Edward the Martyr (975–978 or 979) and Ethelred II (978 or 979–1016).

The eleventh century opened with Sweyn's revenge for the massacre of St. Brice's day (1002); and this was followed by repeated invasions of the Danes and finally by their conquest of England (1013), when the barbarian chief assumed the crown, and Ethelred took refuge in Normandy. Recalled in 1014, the latter made various efforts to recover the sceptre of which he had shown himself so unworthy, and his son Edmund (1016) took measures to oppose the power of Canute (1014–1035 or 1036); but the Dane, after the battle of Assandun and the death of his rival, obtained a firm seat on the throne, and in the course of a peaceful reign conferred such benefits on his subjects that Edgar's work was almost forgotten. He well deserved his title of Great. The disturbed reigns of Harold I (1035 or 1037–1039 or 1040) and Hardecanute (1039 or 1040–1041 or 1042) followed, and then we come to the time of Edward the Confessor (1041 or 1042–1066) and the end of the period.

When we draw up the list of ecclesiastical buildings which we know were founded, rebuilt, or restored during the epoch which we have just outlined, we find that the majority of these belong (1) to the long reign of Ine (688–728); (2) to that of Edgar (959–975), the founder or rebuilder of forty-four monasteries,[1] mainly through the

---

[1] SPARKE, op. cit., *Chronicon Johannis abb. S. Petri de Burgo*, p. 28.

instrumentality of Dunstan (960–988), Ethelwold (963–984), and Oswald (961–992); and (3) to the reigns of Canute and the Confessor, as William of Malmesbury testifies.[1] This is a perfectly natural result, the history of art exactly coinciding with the social and political history, and even more with that of religion.

Of these buildings some were merely wooden structures, like the monastery church of Doulting in Somersetshire, where Aldhelm ended his life.[2] Others were built of stone, and in some cases were so notable in that age and country that William of Malmesbury describes the church of his own abbey, St. Mary's (whether the original church erected by Aldhelm himself, as we learn from the 'Gesta Pontificum', or a reconstruction by Aelfric, who became abbot in 970), as 'vincens decore et magnitudine quicquid usquam ecclesiarum antiquitus factum visebatur in Anglia';[3] while Alcuin[4] is lost in admiration of the new cathedral of York built by Archbishop Albert (767–780) under the direction of Eanbald and Alcuin himself, to replace the old one burned in 741.[5]

With regard to the form of some of these churches and their architects very instructive information has come down to us. We know, for instance, that Winchester Cathedral, founded in 639, at the desire of Cynegils King of Essex (611–642 or 643) and with the permission of his son Cenwalh (642 or 643–672), by Bishop Birinus, who had been sent by Honorius I to convert the West-Saxons,[6] was in 863 reached through an atrium which had a tower rising from the middle of the side parallel to the front of the church.

> *Turris erat rostrata tholis, quia maxima quaedam,*
> *Illius ante sacri pulcherrima limina templi,*
> *Eiusdem sacrata Deo sub honore hierarchi.*
> *Inter quam templique sacram pernobilis aulam*
> *Corpore vir Domini sanctus requievit humatus,*[7]

.   .   .   .   .   .

Whether this tower went back to the time of Birinus or was erected later, we do not know. In connexion with it I would remark that in the old St. Peter's at Rome the façade of the atrium showed an entrance flanked by a bell tower built by Stephen II (752–757), who gave it three bells.[8]

It is also stated that the little church of the monastery at Athelney, founded by Alfred the Great (871–901), was built in a new style ('Fecitque ecclesiam, situ quidem pro angustia spatii modicam, sed novo edificandi modo compactam'[9]) and with a plan somewhat like that of the church at Germigny des Prés (801–806): 'quattuor enim postes solo infixi totam suspendunt machinam, quattuor cancellis opere sperico in circuitu ductis.'[9] Its architect, too, is known to us, for there can be little doubt that the

---

[1] *Rolls Series*, 90, *Gesta regum Anglorum*, vol. ii.

[2] *Rolls Series*, 52, *Willelmi Malm. monachi gesta pontificum Anglorum*, p. 382, note 4; id., p. 361–2.

[3] Id., pp. 361–2.

[4] *Rolls Series*, 71, *The historians of the Church of York and its archbishops, De pontificibus et sanctis Ecclesiae Eboracensis carmen*, vol. i, p. 394.

[5] *Rolls Series*, 75, *Symeonis monachi Historia Regum*, vol. ii, p. 38.

[6] *Rolls Series*, 36, *Annales monasterii de Wintonia*, vol. ii, p. 5; *Rolls Series*, 23, *The Anglo-Saxon Chronicle*, p. 24.

[7] MABILLON, *Acta Sanct. Ord. S. Benedicti* (Venice, 1738), *De S. Swithuno episcopo Wintoniensi, eiusque translatione et miraculis*, vol. vi, p. 71.

[8] DUCHESNE, *Le liber pontificalis*, vol. i, pp. 404, 454, 503; Manuscript plan by Alfarano in the Archivio Capitolare of St. Peter's (CERRATI, *Tiberii Alpharani de Basilicae Vaticanae antiquissima et nova structura* (*Studi e Testi*, vol. 26), pl. i, no. 15; cf. text, pp. 127, 128); it was engraved in 1589–1590. [See RIVOIRA, *Roman Architecture*, p. 223; and A. SERAFINI, *Torri Campanili medioevali di Roma e del Lazio* (Rome, 1927), who considers that it was this very tower that is shown in so many Renaissance drawings and was only demolished in the 17th century; cf. vol. i, p. 55. (A.)]

[9] *Rolls Series*, 52, *Willelmi Malm. monachi gesta pontificum Anglorum*, p. 199.

John, presbyter and monk, a native of Old Saxony, who was invited from his convent of Corbie by Alfred to become abbot of Athelney, may reasonably be regarded as responsible for the building, knowing as we do that he was 'in omnibus disciplinis litteratoriae artis eruditissimus et in multis aliis artibus artificiosus'.[1] I believe, in default of proof to the contrary, that this church marks the introduction of the central cupola plan into England, for we must imagine that the four isolated supports carried a square tower over the crossing.

Again, we know that Ramsey Abbey Church, founded in 969 by Oswald, bishop of Worcester (961–992) and archbishop of York (972–992), with the assistance of Earl Ailwin, and consecrated in 974, was of cruciform plan with two towers, one over the crossing and the other at the west end. 'Duae quoque turres ipsis tectorum culminibus eminebant, quarum minor versus occidentem in fronte basilicae pulchrum intrantibus insulam a longe spectaculum praebebat, maior vero in quadrifidae structurae medio columnas quatuor, porrectis de alia ad aliam arcubus sibi invicem connexas, ne laxe defluerant, deprimebat.'[2] Oswald himself was the architect of the building, the idea of which he may have derived from the church of Germigny des Prés, situated only a few miles from the convent of Fleury at Saint Benoît sur Loire, with which Ramsey Abbey was closely connected for several centuries. Fleury was a centre of instruction in the liberal arts, as the Ramsey Chronicle tells us: '. . . virum nominatissimum Abbonem, qui liberalium artium notitiam imis hauserat medullis, de coenobio Floriacensi evocatum.' Now Theodulf's church, besides the existing central tower, had another, used for the bells, rising above the porch at the entrance, thus described in an account printed by Baluze: 'Porro in matherio (read 'narthecio' or 'atrio') turris de qua signa pendebant, huiuscemodi inseruit versus argenteo colore expressos.'

Haec in onore Dei Theodulfus templa sacravi,
Quae dum quisquis ades oro memento mei.[3]

The church at Saint Riquier (Centula) (793–798) also possessed a tower in front of the apse, and another between the church and its narthex. Again, St. Remi at Rheims, as rebuilt by Archbishop Turpin (756–802) and finished by Hincmar in 852, had a large tower at its western end. The western tower of the church at Blandigny, consecrated in 979,[4] may have been suggested by the examples at Saint Riquier and Rheims.

Soon after the central tower of Ramsey was finished it threatened to fall, and had to be reconstructed. This was carried out by Abbot Eadnoth the younger under the advice of Oswald, and the whole church was rebuilt in 991. Ramsey had an aisleless nave. Aisled churches with central towers, as has been pointed out,[5] did not make their appearance in Great Britain before the time of Edward the Confessor. The example of Winchester brought forward by Prof. Willis and others is imaginary.[6] The rebuilding of the cathedral was begun by Ethelwold during his tenure of the see (963–984), and the dedication took place in 980;[7] but apparently it was finished by his

[1] MABILLON, *Acta Sanct. Ord. S. Benedicti, Venerabilis Johannis abbatis Aethelingiensis elogium historicum*, vol. vi, p. 514.

[2] *Rolls Series*, 83, *Chronicon abbatiae Rameseiensis*, pp. 41, 43, 44; *Rolls Series*, 71, *The historians of the Church of York and its archbishops, Vita Oswaldi archiep. Eboracensis*, vol. i, p. 434.

[3] *Miscellanea, Catalogus abbatum Floriacensium*, p. 492.

[4] *Mon. Germ. Hist. Script.*, vol. v, p. 25, *Annales Blandinienses*.

[5] *The Archaeological Journal*, vol. liii (1896), MICKLETHWAITE, *Something about Saxon church building* (p. 326).

[6] [*Proc. Archaeological Institute*, Winchester meeting, 1845, pp. 14–16: 'The evidence for the early tower depends entirely on literature, and this in turn gives no hint where the tower was situated. Can it, like Dunstan's tower at Glastonbury, have been at the west end?']

[7] WHARTON, *Anglia Sacra*, T. RUDBORNE, *Historia maior Wintoniensis* (London, 1691), parte i, p. 223;

successor Alphege (984–1005), as may be gathered from a letter addressed to the latter by the monk Wulstan.[1] All we know about it is that it had a tower and atrium with chapels on its north and south sides: we hear nothing about a nave with aisles.

As Athelney is the first recorded cruciform church with a central tower in Great Britain, so Ramsey is the earliest recorded example of a western tower. Nevertheless, the arrangement of a tower in the middle of the west front may be traced back to the reign of Edward the Elder (901–925), for on a coin of his time struck by one Wlfgar there appears what looks like an aisleless church with a frontal tower rather higher than the nave (fig. 579). And here I may say that towers are frequently represented on Edward's coins, which is to be explained by the fact that he and his sister Ethelfleda backed up their operations against the Danes by the construction of strongholds in many places (figs. 580, 581).

Nor were these the only churches erected in an important foreign style during the period we are discussing—the style introduced into the Frankish Empire in the days

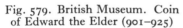

Fig. 579. British Museum. Coin   Fig. 580. British Museum. Coin   Fig. 581. British Museum. Coin
of Edward the Elder (901–925)   of Edward the Elder (901–925)   of Edward the Elder (901–925)

of Charles the Great. The original church at Abingdon (675) having been seriously damaged by the Danes in the ninth century, Athelstan gave orders for its reconstruction, and this was carried out under Edgar (959–975) by Ethelwold, who had been a monk at Glastonbury, and was now abbot of Abingdon: 'Erat namque Atheluuoldus magnus aedificator'[2]—'tot et tanta monasteria fecit quod vix modo credibile videatur.' The new church of St. Mary at Abingdon is thus described: 'Cancellus rotundus erat, ecclesia et rotunda duplicem habens longitudinem quam cancellus; turris quoque rotunda erat.'[3] This implies that it was a round church, with an apse and a round central tower.

The abbey church of Exeter (a cathedral after 1050) as rebuilt by Canute in 1019, in place of the one erected by Athelstan and destroyed by the Danes in 1003, possessed not only a central tower, but also two others which flanked the west front. The evidence for this is the obverse of a seal of the old Chapter of Exeter attached to a document of 1133.[4] This church of SS. Mary and Peter is the first historical instance in England of a pair of western towers. I have found another and nearly contemporary representation of a church front with two towers in the 'Poems of Caedmon',[5] assuming that the manuscript belongs to the first half of the eleventh century. The adoption of this arrangement was due to the influence of the Lombardo-Norman style which had by this time made its appearance in William of Volpiano's church at Bernay (1013). His employment of it goes back to the erection of Saint Bénigne at Dijon

MABILLON, *Acta Sanct. Ord. S. Benedicti, Vita S. Ethelwoldi episcopi*, vol. vi, p. 608.

[1] Id., pp. 616–17.

[2] *Rolls Series*, 2, *Chronicon monasterii de Abingdon*, Appendix I, *Vita S. Aethelwoldi*, vol. ii, p. 259.

[3] *Rolls Series*, 2, *Chronicon monasterii de Abingdon*, Appendix II, *De abbatibus Abbendoniae*, vol. ii, pp. 277–8.

[4] OLIVER, *Lives of the Bishops of Exeter* (Exeter, 1861), p. 189, pl. 14. [See H. E. BISHOP and E. K. PRIDEAUX, *The Building of Exeter Cathedral* (Exeter, 1922), p. 21, for the discovery of possible Saxon foundations. Cf. CLAPHAM, op. cit., p. 95, note 2. (R.)]

[5] Bodleian Library, Oxford (MS. Junian).

(1002–1018), where we know that a pair of staircases were formed in the wall of the west front (the 'pariles scalas' of the Abbey Chronicle) communicating with the galleries of the church. And William, in his turn, derived it from the mother-church of Cluny, dedicated in 982.

This influence, showing itself in the form selected for the church at Exeter, is explained, as is the case with all the English buildings erected between 1000 and the Norman Conquest (1066), by the consequences resulting from the marriages of Ethelred II (1012) and of Canute (1017) with Emma (1002–1052), the daughter of Richard the Fearless, Duke of Normandy (943–996). These events opened the way for the Normans to get a foothold in the island, and made possible its ultimate conquest.

Let us now pass in review the dated churches, wholly or partially preserved, or at least known to us by descriptions or drawings, which have escaped not so much the destructive hand of time as the violence of human passions, the rage for novelty which came in with the Norman Conquest and the invention of the Pointed style, and last but not least, all the crimes committed in the name of 'restoration' during the last century.

St. Michael's Church, St. Albans, was built by Abbot Wulsin about the year 950.[1] It consisted of a nave ending in a rectangular chancel, and a tower at the west end. All that is left of this, after successive alterations and the deplorable ill-treatment inflicted under the pretext of restoration, is the remodelled nave (which has been lengthened westwards, involving the demolition of the tower) and the chancel (figs. 582, 583). The only notable

Fig. 582. St. Albans. Church of St. Michael. Nave (about 950)

feature presented by the church is the double splay of the windows, the earliest dated instance to be found in England. It is evident that this form of aperture, of Roman origin, as we saw when dealing with the church at Bagnacavallo, was late in making its appearance in England.[2]

Church of SS. Mary and Ethelburga at Lyminge (Kent).—Queen Ethelburga's church[3] (640), which had been practically destroyed by the Danes (804), was rebuilt

[1] *Rolls Series*, 28, *Tho. Walsingham, Gesta abbatum monasterii S. Albani*, vol. iv[a], p. 22. [The attribution of a pre-Conquest date to St. Michael's, St. Albans, has been rejected by Baldwin Brown, vol. ii, p. 440, chiefly on the ground of the thickness of the walls (4 ft.), which is a strong argument against its probability. The double-splayed window opening, though unusual after the Conquest, is not necessarily a criterion of Saxon work: it occurs, e.g., in the remains of the chapel on the south side of the cloister at Hereford cathedral, for which a pre-Conquest date cannot be assumed. The remarkable series of double-splayed windows above the 12th-century arcades at Tredington, Worcs. (Baldwin Brown, vol. ii, p. 483: illustration, ibid., p. 425), occur in walls 2 ft. 10 in. thick. Cf. also Clapham, op. cit., pp. 113, 114. (H. T.)]

[2] See Clapham, op. cit., pp. 113, 114.

[3] *Supra*, p. 138.

by Archbishop Dunstan in 965.[1] What remains of his work consists of the aisleless nave, altered on the north side by the addition of an aisle, and with a rebuilt west front; and the rectangular chancel (fig. 584).[2] It is the earliest dated instance in England of an undoubted rectangular and not apsidal sanctuary.

Fig. 583. St. Albans. Church of St. Michael (about 950)

Fig. 584. Lyminge Church (965)

DURHAM CATHEDRAL.—As the original church (998) ('honesto nec parvo opere'[3]) of Bishop Aldhun (990–1018) has given place to the existing cathedral, the work of Bishop William of St. Carilef (1081–1096), it would not concern us further were it

[1] JENKINS, *A Sketch of the Life of St. Ethelburga the Queen, Foundress of the Church of Lyminge*, p. 27; G. GILBERT SCOTT, *Essay on the History of English Church Architecture*, p. 40. [For remains of Ethelburga's church see CLAPHAM, op. cit., p. 21 and fig. 8. (R.)]

[2] [BALDWIN BROWN, vol. ii, p. 469, admits the possible existence of early fragments in the walling of the church at Lyminge, but assigns the present building to a later date. The walls contain much herringbone coursing. (H. T.)]

[3] *Rolls Series*, 75, *Symeonis monachi hist. Eccl. Dunelm.*, vol. i, p. 81.

not for the recent discovery in the foundations of the Chapter House, demolished in 1796, of the heads of four sculptured grave-crosses. These are now to be seen in the Cathedral Library, and show representations of, among other things, the Crucifixion, Baptism, and the Agnus Dei. As we can date them with certainty, they are very valuable for purposes of comparison, and this is why they are deserving of our attention. We give illustrations of two of the fragments which, in spite of the rudeness of the ornamentation and the elementary treatment of the figures, are nevertheless of great interest both in their general outline and in the details, and provide us with definite information about the style of carving in an important religious centre of Northumbria (figs. 585, 586).

These relics of the primitive cathedral recall another carving preserved in the Library, a portion of a figure cross (fig. 587) brought from St. Mary's, Gainford, built by Ecgred,

Fig. 585. Durham. Cathedral Library. Head of cross (10th or 11th century)

Fig. 586. Durham. Cathedral Library. Head of cross (10th or 11th century)

bishop of Lindisfarne (830–845), for the monastery which existed as early as 801, and given to Durham by Bishop Aldhun.[1] For though it presents analogies with the Durham fragments, there are differences in the treatment of the drapery; and this, together with its ruder character, makes me think that the Gainford Cross belongs to the eleventh or tenth century, and before the reign of Edgar.

I would remark at this point that we have reached the age of Dunstan without having met with any dated English building showing the characteristic long and short work which we first noticed at Monkwearmouth (675).[2] We may, then, reasonably infer that this feature did not gain a new lease of life and become the fashion till after the erection of St. Michael's at St. Albans, and of Lyminge Church. But it must not be supposed that it was confined to the Anglo-Saxon period, for it is well known that there are instances of it in Norman times.

THE CATHEDRAL OF OXFORD.—Christ Church, Oxford, the old convent church of St. Frideswide, originally founded by Didanus and his daughter Frideswide about the year 727, and burned in 1002, was rebuilt by Ethelred the Unready (978 or 979–1016) after 1004.[3] Of the church of Didanus and Frideswide nothing is left that can be

---

[1] *Rolls Series*, 75, *Symeonis monachi Historia Regum*, vol. ii, p. 65; *Historia Eccl. Dunelm.*, vol. i, p. 63; *Historia de S. Cuthberto*, vol. i, p. 213.

[2] [See above, p. 144, n. 5.]

[3] *Rolls Series*, 52, *Willelmi Malm. gesta pontificum Anglorum*, pp. 315–16; DUGDALE, op. cit., ii, p. 134.

seen.[1] The remains of a three-apsed east end, which came to light in 1887, are to be assigned to Ethelred's work (fig. 588). This plan is not found in England before the eleventh century; unless, indeed, the relics of the ancient church at Lindisfarne can be referred to the time of Athelstan (925–940), a date which has still to be demonstrated. Ethelred's masonry is coarse and irregular. Until the contrary has been proved, we may say that his church was the first to have the three-apsed plan in England. It was an arrangement of Pagan Roman origin, as we saw when discussing St. Mary's, Abingdon.

Fig. 587. Durham. Cathedral Library. Fragment of cross from Gainford (9th or 10th century)

Fig. 588. Oxford. Cathedral. Frontal arch of lateral apse of old church of St. Frideswide (11th century)

Shortly after the erection of Ethelred's church at Oxford another English structure came into existence, interesting for the material of which it is constructed. This is the chapel set up near Aungre (Chipping Ongar) on the occasion of Alwin's translation of the relics of St. Edmund from London, which took place in 1013, or perhaps not until 1020, when Canute installed Benedictine monks at Bury St. Edmunds and erected a stone church there, consecrated in 1032, to replace the original wooden one.[2]

The chapel still exists as the nave of Greenstead Church (fig. 589), its walls formed of oak trunks sawn in half and set upright side by side with the plane surface inwards.

---

[1] *The Archaeological Journal*, vol. liii (1896), p. 333; MICKLETHWAITE, *Something about Saxon church building*. [See the paper by J. PARK HARRISON, *Recent Discoveries in Oxford Cathedral* (*Archaeol. Journ.*, xlv (1888), pp. 271–83). This, first published in 1888, was succeeded by other papers in which Mr. Harrison sought to prove a Saxon origin for a considerable amount of work in the church for which no claim can be substantiated. (H. T.)]

[2] BALDWIN BROWN, op. cit., p. 39; DUGDALE, op. cit., vol. iii, p. 99; *Rolls Series*, 96, *Memorials of St. Edmund's Abbey*, vol. ii, pp. 218–19; vol. i, p. 47.

It enables us to realize what English timber construction was like in the Anglo-Saxon period.[1]

ST. MARY'S CHURCH, STOW (LINCOLNSHIRE),[2] was built by Eadnoth II, bishop of Dorchester (1034–1049), about the year 1040, with the assistance of Earl Leofric (†1057) and his wife Godiva. Remigius, bishop of Dorchester and Lincoln (1067–1092), introduced Benedictine monks before 1076, and rebuilt the church for them.[3] Though there is no documentary evidence, some[4] consider the upper limb of the cross to be work of the twelfth century, belonging to the time of Bishop Alexander of

Fig. 589. Greenstead Church (11th century)

Lincoln (1123–1148), or perhaps erected after the fire from which Stow is believed to have suffered[5] in 1156.

The oldest portions of St. Mary's are the result of three separate operations. It is

[1] [STRZYGOWSKI explains the timber construction, which he says is similar to that of the Norwegian 'mast-churches' (*Early Church Art, &c.*, p. 116). For a detailed description see BALDWIN BROWN, op. cit., pp. 39–41; *Royal Commission on Historical Monuments, Essex*, vol. ii, p. 112. (R.)]

[2] [The tradition that the church at Stow was the cathedral church of the see of Lindsey, which led to the general adoption of the idea that its oldest portions belong to a date far earlier than that accepted in the text, has no historical foundation. It may be remarked, however, that the present central tower is entirely of the 15th century, and rests upon piers and arches inserted behind the earlier work. The quoins of the lower part of the first tower, which rose directly from the ground, with arches in its four walls, remain as high as the roof-eaves in the angles between nave, chancel, and transept. The arch shown in fig. 591 is clearly later than the jambs: its mouldings and its construction with a rubble core are characteristically Norman, and have no connexion with the rough

shafting and strip-work on the west face of the wall below. It may be assigned to the work of reconstruction under Remigius; and, while the work beneath it may be accepted as belonging to the church of 1040, the uncouthness of effect noticed on p. 174 is due, not to the inferior artistic conditions of a single period, but to the disparity between an arch built by Norman workmen and the rude if imposing substructure to which it was added. It may be doubted whether the tower begun in 1040 was actually completed until the arches were added about half a century later. BALDWIN BROWN, vol. ii, p. 356, notes this difference of date, and gives a sketch-plan of the tower. (H. T.)]

[3] *Rolls Series*, 52, *Willelmi Malm. gesta pontificum Anglorum*, p. 312 and note 7; *Rolls Series*, 75, *Symeonis monachi historia regum*, vol. ii, p. 173.

[4] *Journal R.I.B.A.*, Third Series, vol. vi (March 25, 1899), BILSON, *The beginnings of Gothic Architecture.*

[5] MADOX, *The History and Antiquities of the Exchequer of the Kings of England* (2 vols. 1769), vol. i, p. 342, and note.

a cruciform church with central tower (fig. 590). The windows and doors show long and short work in the jambs. The imposing arch with multiplied moulded archivolts (fig. 591), forming the communication between the aisleless nave and the crossing, has bulbous bases like the striking examples in the Bodleian 'Caedmonis Paraphrasis Poetica' (where the capitals are also of the same form), believed to have been executed later than the epoch of 1000, but before the Conquest. And there are other instances in the 'Liber Geneseos' in the British Museum, to which we have already referred, dated rather before 1066.

Fig. 590. Stow Church. South side of transept and choir (11th and 12th centuries)

Fig. 591. Stow Church. Crossing and choir (11th and 12th centuries)

Stow Church affords the earliest dated examples in England of protuberant bulbous bases. The employment of this characteristic feature in the form of substantial roll mouldings in the north and west doors of the church, and its presence in the oldest part of the crypt of St. Servatius at Quedlinburg (936), show how cautious we should be in attributing buildings where it occurs to the Anglo-Saxon period.

Further, it provides the earliest surviving dated instance in England of a compound arch with roll mouldings. The design was of Norman origin, for in the Lombardo-Norman style extensive use was made of it. The somewhat uncouth manner in which it is introduced at Stow is explained by the different artistic conditions of the two countries,

THE CHAPEL OF THE TRINITY AT DEERHURST was built in 1056 by Duke Odda, as we are told by an inscription in the Ashmolean Museum at Oxford, whither it was removed in 1675. It consists of a rectangular space opening at the east into a chancel of the same form, of which only portions remain. The surviving door on the north side and the chancel arch diminish in width towards the top and have a hood mould over them. The jambs are constructed with long and short work (fig. 592).

ST. GREGORY'S CHURCH, KIRKDALE, NEAR KIRBY MOORSIDE (YORKSHIRE), was rebuilt by Orm in the reign of Edward the Confessor, and when Tosti was Earl of Northumbria (1055–1065), as we are informed by an inscription on either side of the sun-dial inserted in the wall above the south door.[1]

The original structure consisted of an aisleless nave with rectangular chancel. On the outside various carved fragments from the ancient 'minster' of St. Gregory may be observed, which have been used in the building of the church. The most important is a gravestone built into the wall near the ground on the north side, with part of a cross surrounded by scroll-work. In spite of its decayed state we are still able to see that it is of high quality, though the hand of the carver was not very sure. The intestinal treatment of the interlacing induces us to ascribe the work to an English carver under the influence of the Continental artists of the time of Benedict Biscop and Wilfrid, and before the Danish ravages of 867. The evidence is too slight and uncertain to support the suggestion that it is the gravestone of Oidilwald, King of Deira (651–660); and, moreover, he was buried at Lastingham.

In the jambs of the west door are inserted two shafts with Pre-Lombardic cubical capitals hollowed out at the angles and carrying two high, moulded impost blocks from which spring the multiplied archivolts. It forms the prototype for doorways of this kind in Great Britain, and

Fig. 592. Deerhurst. Chapel (11th century)

its capitals are the earliest dated specimens in the country of the Pre-Lombardic cubical type with chamfered angles. An older though only approximately dated example exists at Brixworth in the capitals of the three-light opening in the inner face of the west end.

THE ABBEY CHURCH OF ST. PETER, WESTMINSTER.—The exact date of the building which the Confessor intended to be the chief monument of his reign is unknown. According to Mabillon[2] it was erected between 1060 and 1065. Freeman,[3] on the other hand, puts it between 1051 and 1065. Micklethwaite,[4] in his turn, relying on the oldest description we possess of the church, contained in a life of the king[5] written after the battle of Stamford Bridge (1066) and before the death of Queen Edith (1043–1075),

[1] [See CLAPHAM, op. cit., pp. 103, 104 (with plan).]
[2] Annales Ord. S. Benedicti, vol. iv, p. 671ᶜ.
[3] Op. cit., vol. ii, p. 509.
[4] The Archaeological Journal, vol. li (1894), pp. 1 ff.,
Further notes on the abbey buildings at Westminster.
[5] Rolls Series, 3, Lives of Edward the Confessor, Vita Aeduuardi regis, pp. 417–18.

believes that at Edward's death only the eastern part of the structure begun in 1055 was in existence. It appears to me that this date would be confirmed by Edward's transfer of some of the property of Pershore to Westminster between 1054 and 1056. The building will have been finished afterwards, i.e. some time before 1150; so that the later description in another Life of Edward, dedicated to Eleanor of Provence, wife of Henry III (1216–1272), and written about 1245,[1] will refer to the whole period between 1055 and 1150.

It is my belief that the surest evidence as to the date of Edward's work is to be found in the Bayeux Tapestry. This important relic, which I have examined on several

Fig. 593. Bayeux. Detail from the Tapestry
(11th century)

occasions, can only belong to the reign of William I, the chief figure in the great drama of the Conquest of England, whose defence and glorification are the main purpose of all the scenes therein unrolled. Moreover, it must have been made in the time of Odo I, bishop of Bayeux (1050–1097), the rebuilder of the cathedral to which the tapestry belonged, and in the nave of which it was exhibited in past times, as we learn from an inventory of 1476. To be precise then, it was made between the battle of Hastings (1066) and the consecration of the cathedral. To a period practically contemporary with the battle, and anterior to the death of the Conqueror (1087), belong the coats of mail worn by the figures, with the sleeves only reaching to the elbow (fig. 593), whereas soon after 1087 they were made longer, so as to come down to the wrist, and at the same time wider than the sleeves of 1100 to 1120. I derive this statement from a communication made to me by Professor Oman of Oxford, and from one of his works.[2] The numerous representations of buildings never show the pointed arch, the great characteristic of the last third of the twelfth century, to which (contrary to the general opinion placing it between 1066 and 1080) the Tapestry has been assigned[3] on the supposition that it was inspired by the 'Roman de Rou' of Wace, without taking account of the possibility of Master Wace having derived his ideas from the facts recorded on the tapestry in Bayeux Cathedral of which he was for nineteen years a prebendary.[4]

The date thus established is confirmed by the pictorial representation, partly in section and partly in elevation, of Westminster Abbey, which the tapestry contains (fig. 594). Though the figure of a man engaged in fixing a weather-cock as a finial on the sanctuary roof is an allusion to the consecration, and while the central tower is reproduced with elaborate detail, there is no sign of the two western towers mentioned in the Life of Edward dedicated to Queen Eleanor:

En miliu dresce une tur,
E deus en frunt del Occident.

[1] *Rolls Series*, 3, *La estoire de Saint Aedward le Rei*, p. 90.
[2] *A History of the Art of War*, vol. ii, p. 3.
[3] MARIGNAN, *La tapisserie de Bayeux* (Paris,

1902), p. 8.
[4] TAYLOR, *Master Wace, his Chronicle of the Norman Conquest from the Roman de Rou* (London, 1837), pp. xvii–xviii.

So that we may infer that the church was unfinished when the tapestry was worked, and this also explains why the author of the oldest Life makes no mention of the western towers. The incomplete state in which the building was left seems to me to be also shown by the liberal endowment, on a larger scale than that of Edward, given by the Conqueror to the Abbey.[1]

Edward's church was of cruciform plan, with a central tower, nave and aisles, chapels in two stories projecting from the transepts, and an apsidal choir with ambulatory. We learn the last detail from the fact that in 1220 the old Lady Chapel was added at the east end of the choir, so that the latter must have been provided with an ambulatory, if there was to be access to the chapel.[2] All that is left under the floor of the present presbytery is three bases of the compound piers of the choir, which with

Fig. 594. Bayeux Tapestry. Representation of the old church of Westminster (11th century)

their shallow mouldings recall those at Jumièges. Some idea of its construction is given by the so-called Chapel of the Pyx in Westminster Abbey, with its rude unraised cross vaulting. In this chapel the foliage capital of the wall pier on the south side is work of the twelfth century.

The name of the architect has not come down to us, but we learn that the church was in a new style: 'Ecclesiam aedificationis genere novo fecit.'[3] Now, seeing that a new architectural style is not born in a day, and that, after the erection of Ramsey Abbey Church (969), the cruciform plan with aisleless nave was reproduced in England with monotonous regularity, while the Latin cross plan with central tower and aisled nave, of which the Normans had made a speciality, did not make its appearance there until the building of the church at Westminster, it is quite certain that it was from Normandy and from the Benedictine Order that the Confessor derived the design of his building.

The ties uniting the last survivor of the race of Cerdic with the country and the Order which had received him as a fugitive (1013) in the days of his boyhood, with his mother Emma and his brother Alfred, were too strong for him not to indulge his love of monasticism by the erection of a sanctuary which was to be the expression of all that

[1] *Rolls Series*, 52, *Willelmi Malm. gesta pontificum Anglorum*, p. 141.

[2] [The remains of the early east end indicate that the church terminated in three apses *en échelon*, and show no signs of an ambulatory plan. See *Archaeologia*, lxii (1910), 81 ff.; lxix (1920), 38 ff. The addition of a Lady Chapel in 1220 does not postulate the existence of an original ambulatory, as access to the new chapel could be made by removing the apsidal chapels at the end of the aisles. (H. T.)]

[3] *Rolls Series*, 52, *Willelmi Malm. gesta pontificum Anglorum*, p. 141.

was dearest to his heart, and of his affection for Normandy and the Benedictine Order. To carry out this design who would be more fitted than some monk of the School of Fécamp, whose abbot, John of Aglié, stood so high in the favour of the English king, or else some member of the abbey of Bec, which the genius of Lanfranc was at that moment rendering so conspicuous?

Westminster Abbey was not only the first church in England planned as a Latin cross, with nave and aisles and a tower rising above the crossing; it was also the first example of an apsidal choir surrounded by an ambulatory.

We will now proceed to describe some well-known churches, about which we possess incomplete or misleading historical notices, but which are still regarded by universal consent as belonging to the Anglo-Saxon period. Our object is to endeavour to date them within limits of greater precision, and, so far as may be, with certainty.

St. Wistan's Church, Repton.—In 850 the body of St. Wistan was deposited in the church at Repton, but it was afterwards moved by Canute to Evesham about 1034.[1] The erection of the church is ascribed to the Scotsman Diuma, bishop of Mercia, one of the missionaries brought by King Peada (656–657) from Lindisfarne to help in the conversion of his subjects. When Repton fell into the hands of the Danes in 874,[2] it must have succumbed to the fate which befell all Christian buildings in the districts conquered by these barbarians, and there is every probability that the church dates from the reign of Edgar (959–975).[3]

Of the building thus assigned to the tenth century there survive incorporated in the present church, though not in their original condition, the rectangular chancel with the crypt beneath it, besides some traces of the aisleless nave and transept.[4] On the exterior the original parts of the chancel have a stringcourse supporting slim lesenas ending in curious capitals consisting of inverted truncated pyramids with a rude necking (fig. 595). I remarked some of the same pattern in the Bodleian 'Caedmonis Paraphrasis Poetica'.

Here I would note, if only in the interest of facts, as against the statements of various writers, that lesenas were not a German creation, their origin being Italian, just as their name is Italian—a fact already noticed by Hübsch.[5] The truth is that, long before their appearance in German lands, they had been used, first of all by the Romans in the manner that may be seen on the exterior of the so-called Praetorium in Hadrian's Villa at Tivoli (125–135) (fig. 596), then by the architects of Ravenna, and thirdly by the Lombard gilds.[6]

In the south porch of the church are preserved two shafts[7] which unquestionably belong to the church. They have rude capitals like those in the crypt. This crypt (fig. 597) has rough vaulting sustained by pillars which swell out as if compressed by the spiral band which encircles them. They have bulbous bases, and rudimentary capitals chamfered off to fit the shafts. The fact that the walls of the chancel slightly

[1] *Rolls Series*, 29, *Chronicon abbatiae de Evesham*, p. 83.

[2] *Rolls Series*, 23, *The Anglo-Saxon Chronicle*, p. 62.

[3] Cox, *Notes on the churches of Derbyshire*, 4 vols. (Chesterfield, 1875–1879), vol. iii, p. 434. [For recent accounts of Repton see Baldwin Brown, op. cit., pp. 312 ff.; Clapham, op. cit., p. 157.]

[4] [With regard to the transeptal plan of the east end of the church at Repton, see the comparison made on p. 135 above. The area of the transept is now included in the aisled nave. The masonry above the chancel arch, rebuilt at the same time as the nave, indicates that the walls of the transept-crossing rose into a tower. (H. T.)]

[5] Op. cit., p. 263.

[6] [Clapham (op. cit., p. 109) fully agrees.]

[7] [The shafts mentioned here were removed into the porch at a 19th-century restoration. An early 19th-century water-colour drawing, preserved in the church, shows that before that date they stood at the east end of the north arcade, supporting a round arch with un-moulded edges, which has now disappeared. (H. T.)]

impinge on the vaulting of the crypt has given rise to a suggestion that they are not of the same date, but the capitals mentioned above make this impossible.

Assuming the church and the crypt to be contemporary, let us proceed to the question of date, which we can fix with approximate certainty by a process of elimination.

Before the time of Augustine (597–604) there is no record in England of a crypt with columns under a chancel. The crypt of Christ Church, Canterbury, was copied from the one in St. Peter's at Rome,[1] that is to say it had an ambulatory or corridor

Fig. 595. Repton. East end of the church
(10th or 11th century)

Fig. 596. Tivoli. Villa of Hadrian.
Praetorium (125–135)

following the curve of the apse, from the centre of which started a passage at right angles to the chord of the apse leading to the chamber over the tomb of St. Peter.[2] It was on the model of the crypts of St. Peter's at Rome and Christ Church, Canterbury, that those constructed by Wilfrid at Hexham and Ripon were planned,[3] for they, too, had underground passages leading to a space which communicated with the chamber containing the relics. But this does not make it even remotely possible that the earliest church at Repton, which was probably of wood, as it was erected under the influence of Lindisfarne, possessed a crypt with aisles separated by columns. So that we are obliged to date it in the days of Athelstan, after the battle of Brunanburh (937); or more probably in the peaceful reign of Edgar, after Edmund (943) had broken the back of the fresh Danish rebellion, but in the last years of the reign, inasmuch as St. Michael's at

[1] *Rolls Series*, 73, *Gervasii Cantuariensis opera historica*, vol. i, p. 7.

[2] Rohault de Fleury, *La Messe, études archéologiques sur ses monuments*, vol. ii, p. 92; De Rossi, *Inscriptiones christianae urbis Romae*, vol. ii, p. 235.

[3] [For these and other early crypts see Clapham, op. cit., pp. 154 ff.]

St. Albans (about 950) and Dunstan's church at Lyminge[1] (965) still exhibit a system of absolutely plain wall surfaces.

The introduction into England of wall decoration by lesenas, and later by arcading, or by a combination of arcading and lesenas, was due, I believe, to the influence of buildings such as the abbey church of Gernrode (968), in which the eastern apse is

Fig. 597. Repton. Crypt of the church (10th or 11th century)

decorated with a range of pilasters and another of engaged columns, while the western towers are embellished with arcades of round and triangular-headed arches.[2] The marriage of the devout Edith (†947), daughter of Edward the Elder (901–925), with Otto the Great (936–973) must have brought the Anglo-Saxon clergy into communication with Old Saxony and its monuments; and it is thence that they may have derived the idea of such decorative motives rather than from Italy (though it remains true that it was in Italy that lesena and arcade decoration was created), seeing that, though triangular-headed arcading appears in Italian carved representations, it is very rare to find it used there in the decoration of buildings. Moreover, the capitals at Repton of inverted, truncated, pyramid form, or with barbarous, rude mouldings, and also the bulbous bases and spiral columns, suggest German influence derived from the crypts of St. Wipertus (936) and St. Servatius at Quedlinburg (936). However, it is certain that, so far as arcading is concerned, if we confine ourselves to existing dated monuments, on the one hand, England has no architectural decoration of this kind to show before the close of Edgar's long reign, while, on the other, it made lavish use of it before the Norman invasion. And so, English buildings which show this treatment are to be dated between 965 and 1066; and as the disastrous reign of Ethelred II was anything but favourable to architectural development, we may reasonably suppose that such embellishments began to be used under Edgar, and that they were afterwards elaborated in the times of Canute and of the Confessor.

We will conclude by remarking that the church and crypt of Repton were certainly built before 1034, the year in which Canute removed the relics of St. Wistan, for we

[1] [Cf. however, *supra*, p. 170, note 2.]   [2] Fig. 764.

know that crypts were constructed on purpose to receive the bodies of saints. And therefore the date must be fixed some time in the second half of the tenth, or at latest in the first years of the next century.

THE ABBEY CHURCH OF ST. MARY, DEERHURST.[1]—We know that the abbey was certainly in existence in 804; that it was destroyed by the Danes; that Alphege, bishop of Winchester (984–1005) and archbishop of Canterbury (1005–1012), there received the monastic habit; that it was still an abbey in 1006; that Edward the Confessor deprived it of its possessions in order to endow the abbeys of Westminster and Saint Denis at Paris; and that finally it became a cell of the latter between 1054 and 1056.[2] It is also stated that in 1016 Canute and Edmund had a meeting there, though there is some disagreement among the annalists about the locality, the Anglo-Saxon Chronicle placing it at Alney, near Deerhurst.[3]

The presence of Alphege at Deerhurst proves that the abbey had been restored after the damage which it had suffered from the Danes, and this probably took place in the reign of Edgar, to which we may assign the oldest portions of the church (though no longer in their original condition), that is to say, the aisleless nave with two quasi-transept chapels, and a tower porch.[4] The suggestion that the whole was rebuilt by the Confessor, and

Fig. 598. Deerhurst Church (10th century)

consecrated in 1056[5] cannot be entertained, for that date belongs to the chapel of the Trinity which we have described above.

The nave terminated in an apsidal sanctuary, of which traces remain, and though

[1] [The church at Deerhurst has been recently examined by Mr. W. H. KNOWLES: see his paper in *Archaeologia*, lxxvii (1927), pp. 141–64; also BALDWIN BROWN, op. cit., pp. 205–20, and CLAPHAM, op. cit., p. 92, &c. BALDWIN BROWN dates it in the earlier rather than the later part of the 10th century: otherwise their conclusions do not differ substantially from those in the text. (R.)]

[2] DUGDALE, op. cit., vol. iv, p. 664; WHARTON, op. cit., OSBERN, *Vita s. Elphegi arch. Cantuariensis*, part ii, p. 123; BUTTERWORTH, *A short account of the ecclesi-*

astical buildings at Deerhurst, Gloucestershire (Tewkesbury, 1891), pp. 3 ff.; *Rolls Series*, 51, *Chronica magistri Rogeri de Houedene*, vol. i, p. 66.

[3] *Rolls Series*, 23, p. 124.

[4] [The nave was aisled about 1200. Above the second arch from the west end are small triangular openings like the lower one in the west wall (fig. 600), which indicate that the nave had lateral porches or chapels with upper chambers. (H. T.)]

[5] DUGDALE, op. cit., vol. iv, p. 664.

Fig. 599. Deerhurst Church. Chancel arch
(10th century)

Fig. 600. Deerhurst Church. West end (10th century)

these show a different style of masonry from that of the rest of the original structure (fig. 598) they are none the less contemporary with it.[1]

The regular western tower had originally a double porch, of which only the outer is left intact. Here may be seen a sculptured panel with two nimbed figures, apparently the Virgin and Child, under a canopy which seems to be supported by three pillars with stepped bases and capitals. There is no evidence of a central tower rising between the chapels, and therefore we are unable to say whether it was a case of a real or only of a pseudo-transept. The whole of the church was roofed with timber.

The artistic details of the church point to a single date and the hand of a single carver of low quality. For instance, the hood mould round the sanctuary arch (fig. 599), resting on rude animal heads, is contemporary with a similar one in the wall separating the two halves of the porch, while the stepped supports of the canopy described above, and the piers of the two-light triangular-headed opening on the inner face of the west end (fig. 600), are treated in precisely the same way.

[1] [Considerable portions of the south wall of the apse remain outside the east end of the present church. Within recent years this wall has been stripped of plaster. The carving of a winged angel then found is illustrated by BALDWIN BROWN, op. cit., p. 219. The wall contains much herringbone work, which is a sign that it is unsafe to accept without qualification the modern doctrine that such coursing invariably is of post-Conquest date. Indeed, in England herring-bone work appears to be distinctive of no particular locality or period, but recurs at intervals, apparently as the convenience of local builders dictates its use. At the present time, it is used for walling in English country places from time to time, without reference to any historic tradition: within the last few years I have seen field-walls in Yorkshire and Devon being constructed in this way. All that can be said is that, at certain times, it appears as a common method, e.g. during the 11th century in England, where it seems to have developed before the Norman Conquest, and was freely used soon after that period in the walls of the earlier stone-built castles. (H. T.)]

The lofty western tower,[1] which originally must have been still higher as the bell-chamber has disappeared, tells us that the church, for reasons already stated, cannot be earlier than the reign of Edward the Elder (901–925). But if it had been erected at that date, so much of it would not have survived as is the case, for then it must have passed unscathed through the struggles between the Anglo-Saxons and Danes which

Fig. 601. Volterra. Porta dell' Arco

desolated Mercia up to 941; so that we are obliged to come down to the reign of Edgar (959–975), which saw a revival of religious zeal among the Anglo-Saxons now that they were freed from the pagan Danish yoke, in order to find a state of things favourable to its reconstruction.

On the other hand, it is known that the abbey was in existence in 1006, and we cannot suppose that Edward the Confessor rebuilt it before he impoverished it. Besides, the masonry of his time in Gloucestershire was very different, as the walls of the chapel of the Trinity at Deerhurst tell us.

[1] [Cf. CLAPHAM, op. cit., pp. 96, 118, 119.]

Deerhurst Church contains the earliest English example of the hood mould of an arch springing from heads,[1] a feature of which considerable use was made in the Lombardic style, though it was of Etruscan origin. Indeed, the Etruscans used projecting heads

Fig. 602. Rimini. Arch of Augustus

not only on the imposts and keystones of arches, but even inserted them in the spandrels of arches. Thus the 'Porta dell' Arco' at Volterra (fig. 601), which, though not in its original state, has not changed sensibly from its original appearance,[2] exhibits three

---

[1] [The heads at Deerhurst are suggested by BALDWIN BROWN, op. cit, pp. 205, 206, to be of Scandinavian origin, on the ground of their likeness to similar carvings in wood and metal found in Nordic art. (H. T.)]

[2] MARTHA, L'art étrusque, p. 240.

heads in relief, one on the keystone of the arch, the others on the imposts. The gate known as the 'Arco di Augusto' at Rimini (fig. 602) has two heads in the spandrels, while the Porta Marzia at Perugia (fig. 603) displays the remains of heads of the Dioscuri in the spandrels, and another, thought to be that of a horse, on the keystone of the arch.[1] At Faleri the 'Porta di Giove'[2] and the 'Porta di Bove' have keystones carved with the heads of Jupiter and of a bull respectively.

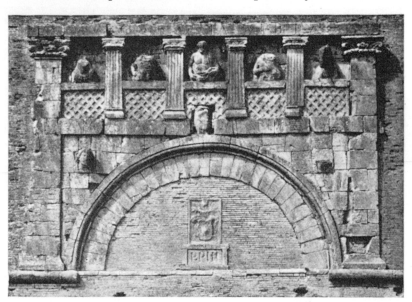

Fig. 603. Perugia. Arch of the Porta Marzia

THE CHURCH OF ST. LAURENCE, BRADFORD-ON-AVON.[3]—We learn from William of Malmesbury[4] that in his time there was standing at Bradford-on-Avon a small church said by tradition to have been built in honour of St. Laurence by Aldhelm, abbot of Malmesbury (680–705), Frome, and Bradford, and bishop of Sherborne (705–709). 'Et est ad hunc diem eo loci ecclesiola, quam ad nomen beatissimi Laurentii fecisse predicatur.' It is on this statement that the idea of so many writers, even some of the more recent,[5] is based, that the existing structure is the work of the sainted abbot and bishop. In my opinion, however, the account preserved by the historian was only a legend. And we are not the first to have doubts about the remote date assigned to St. Laurence, for they are shared by others.[6]

The church, in spite of the injuries and mutilation which it has suffered, is still, as a whole (excepting the west front), such as it was designed by its architect. It consists of a rectangular nave with a chancel of the same form attached to it (fig. 604). The

[1] [The Eumenides according to G. BELLUCCI, L'ipogeo della famiglia etrusca Rufia presso Perugia, p. 39.]

[2] [RIVOIRA, Roman Architecture, p. 58, fig. 64.]

[3] [The church at Bradford-on-Avon is described by BALDWIN BROWN, op. cit., pp. 296–305, who inclines to a late 10th-century date, while CLAPHAM, op. cit., pp. 108 ff., puts it in the early part of the century. There is a parallel to the unusual external arcading in the triangular-headed arcading which remains above the later nave arches at Geddington, Northants. There is no mention in the text of the lateral porches, of which that on the north side remains, or of the sculptured angels above the chancel arch, which bear some affinity in technique to the angel at Deerhurst (see note on p. 182, supra). These figures are referred to on p. 269 below, where the late date assigned to them calls for revision. (H. T.)]

[4] Rolls Series, 52, Gesta pontificum Anglorum, p. 346.

[5] HODGKIN, The History of England from the earliest times to the Norman Conquest, p. 658.

[6] BALDWIN BROWN, op. cit., pp. 296–305.

exterior is decorated with lesenas, small clustered shafts, and blank arcading (fig. 605). This ornamentation is by some thought to be a later addition, but any one who looks carefully at it will see at once this is not the case.

The most remarkable feature is the blank arcading. I have never come across any church in East or West, of Aldhelm's age or earlier, with this decorative treatment, continued, moreover, round the front and the chancel. Therefore we must conclude that Aldhelm, brought up at Canterbury in the School of Abbot Hadrian (669–708) ('qui esset fons litterarum, rivus artium'[1]), cannot have learned from a foreigner, of African origin but brought over from a convent of Campania, a new form of architectural decoration; and for the same reason he cannot have acquired it during his visit to Rome. Ranges of arches, either blank, or open and forming passages, were not employed in this extended form before the eleventh century; and in England, judging from dated buildings, they do not make their appearance till after the Norman Conquest. It is inconceivable that Aldhelm should have introduced them on his church, and so freely too, at so remote a date, and that then the model should have remained for centuries a mere isolated phenomenon, ignored, never copied, and presenting a striking contrast to the appearance of other English churches. On the other hand, we cannot imagine that William of Malmesbury, who lived, roughly speaking, from 1095 to 1143, would have recorded the tradition about the antiquity of the church if it had only just been rebuilt in his time.

Fig. 604. Bradford-on-Avon. Church of St. Laurence. Chancel arch (11th century)

Another important point to be noticed is the double splay of the windows, a feature which, as we have remarked already, did not appear in England before the time of Dunstan.[2]

I believe that the only period in which we can date St. Laurence is that of Edward the Confessor, under the influence of the artistic movement of the epoch of 1000, or, perhaps, with greater likelihood, the first years of the reign of the Conqueror, at a time when Saint Étienne at Caen (1066–1086) was being designed with its double encircling range of large blank arches and blank arcading of an elaborate nature. This would explain the mixture of Anglo-Saxon (the plan and the doorways) and Lombardo-Norman features (the blank arcading) in the church. Nor need we be surprised that, after an interval of more than half a century, William of Malmesbury should have recorded, in his 'Gesta Pontificum Anglorum', finished in 1125, an erroneous tradition about its origin; for, as has been remarked,[3] fifty years do not pass, even in our own time, without the invention, even on the spot, and propagation of false ideas about the origin of buildings; and my own long and varied experience in such matters entirely confirms this opinion.

St. John's Church, Escomb (Durham).[4]—Though we have no information about

[1] *Rolls Series*, 52, *Willelmi Malm. gesta pontificum Anglorum*, p. 334.　　[2] [See p. 169, note 1.]

[3] *Archaeological Journal*, lv (1898), Micklethwaite, *Some further notes on Saxon Churches*, second series, vol. v, p. 342.

[4] [Escomb Church is described by Baldwin Brown, op. cit., pp. 136–42, and Clapham, pp. 39, 40. The argument for the early date, rejected in the text,

the origin of this church, we are not altogether ignorant of its history. We know, for instance, that 'Ediscum', one of the possessions of St. Cuthbert, was alienated by force, with other lands and churches, from Bishop Aldhun (990–1019), but afterwards restored to him.[1]

It consists of a nave with rectangular chancel (fig. 606). The lofty, narrow chancel arch, with long and short work in the jambs, should be noticed (fig. 607). In the chancel is a slab carved in high relief with a rude cross ornamented with studs (fig. 608), which recalls another on a gravestone in St. Andrew's, Auckland (alienated, like Escomb, with other lands and churches belonging to St. Cuthbert from Aldhun[2]), more elaborately

Fig. 605. Bradford-on-Avon. Church of St. Laurence. Chancel (11th century)

treated, but of the same type, and ornamented with pellets in the upper corners of the field—a style of decoration of which there are but few examples in England.

Escomb Church is generally regarded as of great antiquity; for instance, as belonging to the age of Benedict Biscop and Bede, or of about the year 800.[3] We do not share these views, but believe it to have been erected after its restoration to Aldhun, and very probably after Canute had made his generous donation to St. Cuthbert; for it does not

is strengthened by the fact that Roman stonework is freely re-used in the structure, and that the chancel arch, with its long and short jambs, composed of large through-stones set alternately horizontally and vertically, is almost unquestionably a Roman arch rebuilt stone for stone, like the arch at Corbridge (fig. 573). It is noteworthy that no long and short quoining is employed at the angles of the church, where large stones set on edge are used in the alternating fashion found at Monkwearmouth (see note 5 on p. 144). This is entirely different from the long and short technique of the jambs of the chancel arch and of the two doorways (now blocked) in the north walls of the chancel arch and nave, for which there are parallels in Roman and Byzantine work (see BALDWIN BROWN, op. cit., pp. 52, 53, and cf. fig. 549 above). This type of work may have had some

influence upon the long and short quoining of the later Saxon churches, but at Escomb, where no other characteristics, such as the use of strip-work or 'lesenas', occur which usually accompany such quoining, it cannot be taken as positive evidence of late date. Nor is the square-ended chancel conclusive: the theory that the form is of Celtic origin, and is therefore likely to have entered the north of England early, must be taken into account. (H. T.)]

[1] *Rolls Series*, 75, *Symeonis monachi hist. de S. Cuthberto*, vol. i, p. 213; *Rolls Series*, 75, *Symeonis monachi hist. Eccl. Dunelm*, vol. i, p. 82.

[2] *Rolls Series*, 75, *Symeonis monachi hist. de S. Cuthberto*, vol. i, p. 213; *Rolls Series*, 75, *Symeonis monachi hist. Eccl. Dunelm*, vol. i, p. 82.

[3] [Professor BALDWIN BROWN argues for a seventh-century date (op. cit., pp. 136 ff.). (R.)]

Fig. 606. Escomb Church (11th century)

Fig. 607. Escomb Church. Chancel arch (11th century)

seem possible that the original structure, probably of wood, like the cathedral at Chester-le-Street before 1042, can have survived, almost untouched, the dark days of the Danish invasions. We must also take account of the following reasons:

(1) The earliest dated example of an English church with a rectangular chancel which can be certainly instanced is SS. Mary and Ethelburga at Lyminge (965). I believe that it was in the time of Dunstan that the plan came into fashion. Nor need we wonder that the square chancel, which was certainly not the plan favoured by the Roman Church, obtained a firm footing under Dunstan, if we remember the spirit of independence which distinguished him, and even carried him to the length of disobeying a Papal order.[1] Its adoption may have been due to reasons of expense. The builders of that age were obliged to choose straight walls, which were easy and simple of construction, in preference to curvilinear ones, which require specially prepared materials and a higher degree of skill. Or it may have been dictated by the small dimensions of some churches, which were too narrow to allow of the throwing out of an apse large enough to contain the altar and provide room for the free movement of the celebrant.

Fig. 608. Escomb Church.
Carving (Pre-Conquest)

(2) The feature of long and short work, which we first noticed in St. Peter's, Monkwearmouth (675)[2], does not prove, to judge by existing remains, that its use was general in England as a constructive or decorative device, or both combined, and introduced, either only in the windows, or at the angles of the building as well, before the reign of Edgar (959–975). It was a feature which, together with that of lesenas, appears to me to have reached its highest expression as a form of decoration at the end of the Anglo-Saxon period.

St. Mary's Church, Norton (Durham).—The Durham 'Book of Life' tells us that 'Northtun' was given, or rather given back, to St. Cuthbert about the end of the tenth century. In 1083 the church was made collegiate, at the same time as Auckland and Darlington, in order to receive the canons ejected by Bishop William of St. Carilef from Durham.

Its plan was cruciform, with an aisleless nave and central tower (figs. 609, 610). The nave has been rebuilt on the old lines, and the chancel reconstructed on a larger scale. The eastern and western arches of the crossing have been rebuilt, and those on the north and south have lost the innermost archivolt. The only portions of the original structure left are the transept walls, those on the north being almost intact, while the south arm has been altered in quite recent times. The tower is also original, though the upper part is no longer in its primitive state.

This is the only early cruciform church with a central tower in Northumbria. This feature shows that it is later than Alfred the Great's (871–901) church at Athelney, and the church at Ramsey (969), that is to say, the two earliest examples in England; while the remaining square-headed window in the transept reminds one of Escomb. Lastly, the outer archivolt of the tower arches recalls the chancel arch at Stow Church (about 1040), the plan and elevation of which suggest analogies with

[1] *Rolls Series*, 63, *Memorials of St. Dunstan, arch. of Canterbury, Epistola Adelardi ad Elfegum arch. de vita S. Dunstani*, p. 67.   [2] [But see note 5, p. 144.]

Norton.[1] We regard it as a reconstruction, like Escomb, following the donation of Canute; carried out perhaps, in the days of Bishop Egelric of Durham (1042–1056), who rebuilt in stone the primitive wooden cathedral at Chester-le-Street.[2]

BOSHAM CHURCH (SUSSEX) is represented, though only in a conventional way, on the Bayeux Tapestry, with Harold on the point of entering the door, followed by a travelling companion (fig. 611). Originally it consisted of an aisleless nave with a tower at the west end (fig. 612), and at the east a chancel which appears to have been of rectangular

Fig. 609. Norton Church (11th century)

Fig. 610. Norton Church (11th century)

shape. The nave walls were afterwards cut through to admit of aisles, and the end of the chancel was pulled down in order to increase its length.

The most interesting feature in the church is the chancel arch (fig. 613), with its half compound piers surmounted by rude continuous capitals of bulbous form, and a common abacus, from which spring multiplied archivolts. The rude bases are formed of rolls and hollow mouldings, and rest on a large roll moulding common to all the members, and the plinth.[3]

Bosham Church must be rather earlier than Harold's visit to Normandy (about 1064), and had, perhaps, been recently erected, either by Godwin (†1053), the owner of Bosham, or by Harold himself, when he went there to pay his devotions.

The developed art shown in the chancel arch, with the grouping of the shafts at the

[1] HODGES, *Norton: St. Mary the Virgin's Church, The Reliquary*, vol. viii (1894), p. 9. [The comparison of Norton with Stow is worked out by BALDWIN BROWN, op. cit., pp. 356–8. (H. T.)]

[2] HODGES, *Chester-le-Street: St. Mary and St. Cuthbert's Church, The Reliquary*, vol. viii (1894), p. 75.
[3] [Cf. BALDWIN BROWN, op. cit., p. 399.]

Fig. 611. Bayeux Tapestry. Representation of Bosham Church (11th century)

Fig. 612. Bosham Church. Tower (11th century)

Fig. 613. Bosham Church. Chancel arch (11th century)

sides, and the way in which they correspond to the archivolts above, and also the character of the capitals and bases as compared with the original tower arch at Stow, fix the date of the church in the years after 1040, and during the reign of the Confessor.

To his reign may also be assigned the original portions of the nave and the square chancel attached to it of Wittering Church (Northants).[1]

With the evidence of the churches which we have just examined, and with the light shed by the proper comparisons, let us now see whether we can find our way among the obscurities of those which are quite undated, though they present features which have caused them to be assigned to the Anglo-Saxon period. It will appear, I think, that the

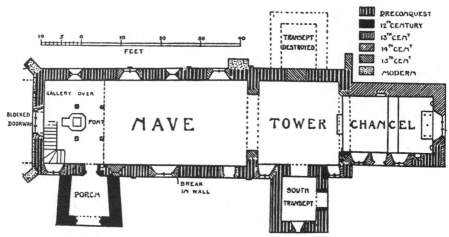

Fig. 614. Breamore Church (10th century). Plan (CLAPHAM, op. cit., fig. 26)

meagre list of buildings of that age, which since the time of Rickman[2] has gone on growing to excessive dimensions, will have to be reduced.

ST. MARY'S CHURCH, BREAMORE (HANTS), is of cruciform plan, with aisleless nave and rectangular chancel, but has lost the north arm of the transept (fig. 614). The form of the quasi-transept, the arms of which are not open, but closed like two chapels, access being given by an arch in either case (fig. 615),[3] connects the church with those of Deerhurst, Worth, St. Mary's, Dover, and Repton; while its poor and meagre artistic features, confined nowadays to the cable moulding on two impost courses, and the roughness of the masonry (fig. 616), relieved neither by arcading nor lesenas, lead one to place it about the same date as the church at Lyminge (965), and before Repton.

As approximately contemporary with it we must regard the nave of Britford Church (Wilts.),[4] which has two arches in the side walls, probably giving access originally to two lateral chapels. The arch on the north side has the intrados ornamented by a band

---

[1] [The long and short quoins remain at all four angles of the nave at Wittering, aisled in the 12th century. The curious chancel arch, with its massive imposts, is illustrated by BALDWIN BROWN, vol. ii, p. 400. Here the arch has a soffit-roll, as at Bosham, and there is a rough correspondence between arch and jambs. Neither here nor at Bosham, where the only distinctively Saxon feature is the bases of the jamb-shafts, is there anything like the remarkable discrepancy between the archivolts and jambs at Stow. (H. T.)]

[2] *Studies of the Styles of English Architecture*, Appendix, pp. iv, xxxiii.

[3] [The Saxon inscription above the south arch, shown in fig. 615, should also be noted. See BALDWIN BROWN, op. cit., pp. 351, 335. (H. T.)]

[4] [Britford is discussed by BALDWIN BROWN, op. cit., pp. 220–5, with several considerations which are of remarkable interest; cf. CLAPHAM, op. cit., pp. 49, 50. (H. T.)]

Fig. 615. Breamore Church. Arch of south arm of transept (10th century)

Fig. 617. Britford Church. Carving in north opening (8th–10th centuries)

Fig. 616. Breamore Church (10th century)

with plain sunk panels at intervals, while the jambs are made up with fragments of carving which may belong to any time between the eighth and tenth centuries (fig. 617).[1]

THE TOWER OF BARNACK CHURCH (NORTHANTS).—Of the original western tower (fig. 618) only two stages are left. They are of stepped outline, separated by a stringcourse, and striped vertically by rude narrow lesenas of varying dimensions. Some of the windows have round, others triangular heads. Two of them are filled

Fig. 618. Barnack Church. Tower (11th century)

Fig. 619. Barnack Church. Tower arch (11th century)

with *transennae* of interlacing circles. The west window on the ground floor had, apparently, a projecting figure ('protome') above it, remains of which may be seen.

The door, on the south side, with a hood mould, recalls the original arches which carry the tower of St. Mary's, Norton. Above it is a window with two birds in the spandrels, facing one another, of barbarous design and execution; and at the top a circle with rudely represented flowers. Three carved slabs may be noticed built into the north, west, and south sides respectively of the upper stage. On each is represented a tree with branches of scroll-work. The carving is in fairly high relief and shows some vigour, though of rude design. Above one of the pieces is a cock, and in another case a bird which is decayed beyond identification.

The tower of Barnack belongs to the same family as that of Earl's Barton, but is an elder sister, as is proved by its greater rudeness both in construction and decoration. It may[2] have been erected after the Danish ravages in Northamptonshire in 1010,

[1] [Cf. BALDWIN BROWN, op. cit., pp. 220 ff., and for the carving, p. 207.]

[2] [The details (BALDWIN BROWN, op. cit., pp. 273–83) show no reason for supposing that the tower is

and very likely in the early years of Canute's reign (1014–1035, or 1036), and after the building of Repton Church, which, though it also shows decorative treatment with plain lesenas, has ruder masonry. And it will come before Stow (about 1040), for the tower arch (fig. 619) is less developed than the surviving original one in that church.

ST. PETER'S CHURCH, BARTON-ON-HUMBER (LINCS.), originally consisted of a square tower (figs. 620, 621), the ground floor of which served as a nave, and east and west of this two projecting structures, the former, of rectangular shape, being the chancel.

Fig. 620. Barton-on-Humber. Tower of the church (11th century)

Fig. 621. Barton-on-Humber Church. East side of the tower (11th century)

This has now disappeared, but remains of the foundations were discovered recently. In the tower, to which a story has been added, the two-light openings of the original parts have mid-wall baluster shafts with pulvins. Those in the added story which have not been rebuilt are divided by moulded shafts—a sort of combination of the shaft and the baluster, like those in the tower of Glentworth Church (Lincs.)—and in one case by an ordinary shaft. The capitals (two with a crocket at each angle) are of Pre-Lombardic cubical type, with each face ornamented by a semicircle, and carry pulvins.

Apart from the singular plan of the church, we may notice two features, the baluster shafts and pulvins, and the arcaded decoration, as likely to throw some light on the date which has, by some authorities, been put in the last part of the tenth century.[1]

later than the 10th century, on the assumption that its peculiar technique is characteristic of the artistic revival under Edgar the Peaceful. These remarks apply equally to the earlier portion of the tower at Barton-on-Humber (ibid., vol. ii, pp. 288–91). See

Appendix II to this Chapter, p. 209, on the periods of Saxon work. (H. T.)]

[1] [BALDWIN BROWN, op. cit., pp. 288 ff., and CLAPHAM, op. cit., p. 115, plate 41 and fig. 31 (plan).]

With regard to the moulded corbel pulvins, if we are to judge by buildings of certain or approximately certain date, this impost member did not make its appearance in England before the reign of the Confessor. And in their earliest form they consist simply of a flat upper face and a straight chamfer, which is exactly what we find at Barton-on-Humber. Later, they were given a hollow chamfer profile, and curl over at the ends, as at Sompting and Jarrow, or take other forms. If they occasionally appear

Fig. 622. Rome. Santa Pudenziana. Campanile
(12th or 13th century)

Fig. 623. Rome. Santa Maria in Cappella.
Campanile (1090)

as mere square-edged oblong blocks, as at Worth, this must be due to the incapacity of the workman or the economy of his employer.

We may remark here that, though pulvins of Ravennate origin served as models or suggestions for the builders of other countries, corbel pulvins of elongated form and considerably flattened at the sides did not appear for the first time in the ninth century on the campanile of Santa Pudenziana at Rome (fig. 622),[1] for the Lombardo-Roman bell-towers, derived as they were from those of Lombardy, the prototype being represented by San Satiro at Milan (876), did not appear in Rome till about the end of the eleventh century, and the archetype is to be found in the little church of Santa Maria in Cappella ('Sancta Maria ad Pineam') (fig. 623), dedicated in 1090, as may be read in the well-known inscription built into the inner face of the entrance wall. The campanile of Santa Pudenziana is an addition made in the time of Innocent III (1198–1216), who restored the church of Siricius (384–399).

[1] [See SERAFINI, op. cit., pp. 96, 185.]

The triangular and round-headed arcading on the tower of Barton-on-Humber recalls and must be an echo of that on the two western towers of the abbey church of Gernrode (tenth century).[1] We have noticed similar arcading, alternating with a range of round arches, represented in one of the Cottonian MSS. (Claudius B. IV) in the British Museum.

Hence, taking everything into account, and remembering, as we pointed out when discussing Repton Church, that the earliest appearance in England of the decorative use of lesenas was not before the time of Dunstan or the year 965, though it must come before 1034, and considering that the architectural decoration of the church shows an advance on that of Repton, we shall not be far wrong if we date Barton-on-Humber Church later than Repton, and, to be as exact as may be, in the first years of Edward's reign (1041 or 1042–1066).

Fig. 624. Bracebridge Church. Tower (12th century)

The baluster shafts and rude pulvins in the tower carry one's thoughts to St. Michael's, Oxford, where the two-light openings in both stories have balusters surmounted by rude moulded pulvins. I believe with Freeman[2] that the tower was built by Robert d'Oily the Elder. And, indeed, the original masonry, external as well as internal, showing as it does long and short work at the angles, differs widely from the remains of Ethelred II's work in Oxford Cathedral (after 1004) by its less barbarous and less irregular character. While, on the other hand, the era of building activity which marked the time of Robert, forms a very appropriate setting for the tower of St. Michael's, in spite of its display of Anglo-Saxon details—details which we know were perpetuated by English builders even after the Norman Conquest. For Robert, besides contributing to the reconstruction of Abingdon Abbey, erected at Oxford the Castle (1071), St. George's in the Castle (1074), a great bridge to the north of the city (1066–1087), and rebuilt some parish churches both within and without the walls.[3]

To return to Barton-on-Humber, the addition to the height of the tower must have been made under Norman influence and after 1066, for it was only then that Corinthian-esque crocket capitals, cubical crocket capitals, and cubical volute capitals were produced in England.

These capitals require a few words of explanation.[4] The reappearance of the Corinthianesque capital with crocket leaves at the angles after the decadence of the Dark Ages is to be ascribed to the revival which took place about 1000, when it was

[1] [Fig. 764.]

[2] Op. cit., vol. v, p. 636.

[3] *Rolls Series*, 2, *Chronicon monasterii de Abingdon*, vol. ii, pp. 24, 284; *Rolls Series*, 36, *Annales de Oseneia et chronicon Thomae Wykes*, vol. iv, pp. 9–10.

[4] [A large variety of these capitals from Lincoln-shire towers is illustrated by BALDWIN BROWN, op. cit., p. 408. The towers of the group generally are now accepted as characteristic of the 'Saxo-Norman overlap'. Only a few of the numerous examples are noted in the text. (H. T.)]

introduced as a novelty in the crypt of Saint Pierre de la Couture at Le Mans (997). It was not seen again in England (supposing that the Romans had introduced this Etrusco-Roman type of capital) till after the Norman Conquest, and then for the first time in the chapel of Durham Castle (1072), that is to say, if we are to trust the evidence of existing and dated English buildings. The English cubical crocket capital and cubical volute capital (i.e. a cubical capital having at the angles either the simple head of a crocket leaf or a double volute) are merely simplifications and corruptions of the Corinthianesque crocket capital.

Some comment is also demanded by the Lombardic cubico-spherical capital which made its first appearance in Sant' Abbondio at Como (1013–1095), and also by the scalloped capital. Of the first there is no trace in England before the Norman Conquest: the crypt of St. Augustine's, Canterbury, affords the oldest dated examples. The second appears in its rudimentary form in St. Albans Cathedral (1077–1088), as we shall see presently.

If we make use of these two touchstones it will not be difficult to ascertain the true age of certain English churches, regarded as pre-Conquest, but which really, until the contrary is proved, must be held to belong to the post-Conquest period. Such are the following:

Fig. 625. Dover. St. Mary in the Castle (11th century)

(1) The tower of St. Mary le Wigford, Lincoln, where the two-light windows have small Pre-Lombardic cubical capitals chamfered at the angles, and others of Corinthianesque form, recalling those in the smaller niches of the west front of the cathedral, surmounted by pulvins. Freeman[1] was right in assigning it, with the neighbouring church of St. Peter at Gowts, to the years between 1068 and 1086, and to the direction of the Conqueror's favourite, Colesvegen, who, having laid out the lower part of Lincoln across the Witham, was obliged to provide the new suburb with places of worship.

(2) The tower at the west end of Bracebridge Church, near Lincoln (fig. 624), having in its highest stage four tall two-light openings with mid-wall shafts (one of which is polygonal) bearing three scalloped capitals (ornamented with zigzags, stars, and studs) and corbel pulvins, and one volute capital. This structure is certainly later than St. Albans Cathedral, and not earlier than the close of the eleventh century, when the scalloped capital appeared in its embellished and perfect form.

(3) The tower at the west end of Branston Church (Lincs.), the ground floor of which is decorated with blank arcading having scalloped capitals. For the date of these what we have just said holds good.

[1] Op. cit., vol. iv, p. 219.

(4) The towers at the west ends of the churches of Clee and Scartho, near Grimsby, and that of Glentworth, in all of which the presence of the volute capital, sometimes with the addition of a row of rude leaves, betrays their Norman date. In connexion with Glentworth, a comparison has been made[1] with a capital in the Castle church at Quedlinburg, which must be the one with volutes formed by the prolongation of the interlacing bands and with pine cones at the angles, of which we shall give an illustration when we come to deal with it. But the church at Quedlinburg is not contemporary

Fig. 626. Worth Church (11th century)

with the Anglo-Saxon period; on the contrary, it is the result of rebuilding after the great fire of 1070. It is interesting to find at Glentworth the characteristic shaft partaking of the characters both of column and baluster which we noticed at Barton-on-Humber, for it shows that this form of support (which, moreover, is rare) was employed in England later than the Anglo-Saxon era.

(5) The tower at the west end of Great Hale Church, near Sleaford, the Norman date of which is proved by the occurrence of volute and scalloped capitals.

THE CHURCH OF ST. MARY IN THE CASTLE, DOVER, consists of a nave (fig. 625) with a tower rising above its eastern extremity, from the sides of which two chapels project and give it a cruciform shape.[2] To the east of this is a rectangular chancel. At the west end is a Roman lighthouse tower, which has suffered considerably.

[1] BALDWIN BROWN, op. cit., vol. ii, p. 430, and cf. p. 454.   [2] [See CLAPHAM, op. cit., fig. 28.]

This church is one of the most important Anglo-Saxon monuments that we possess. The fact of the central tower puts it later than Athelney (871–901), and the adaptation of the lighthouse as a western tower, the two being incorporated,[1] fixes the date as later than the erection of Ramsey Abbey Church (969–974), where this adjunct first appeared in England. Our choice, then, having to be made in the period between 969–974 and 1066, we decide for the time of Harold, who built a new castle at Dover.[2] In any case, it is certain that the church belongs to the Anglo-Saxon period, for while

Fig. 627. Worth Church. Chancel (11th century)

it exhibits the characteristic features of that period, e.g. the aisleless nave with a tower, a square chancel, the quasi-transept forming chapels, and a tower at the west end, it does not present a single Norman one. The large windows and plain brick arches may be due to imitation of openings in the Roman building from which the bricks were taken.

WORTH CHURCH (SUSSEX) forms a perfect Latin cross, with aisleless nave and a deep chancel, at the side of which rises a later bell-tower (figs. 626, 627). The form of the piers of the chancel arch connects it with Bosham, and the moulding of the impost course of the arch reveals Norman influence, which appears again in the broad lesenas on the exterior. The date must therefore be placed in the first years of the Conqueror's reign, or at earliest at the very end of the Confessor's, at a time when Westminster Abbey was in existence to suggest new ideas. Other writers have also suggested the eleventh century.[3]

THE TOWER OF EARL'S BARTON CHURCH (NORTHANTS) was the tower at the west end of a church which has been replaced by the existing one. It is still in its original condition, except for the embattled parapet (figs. 628, 629).

Apart from the good masonry, everything about it is of rude character, from the lesenas, unequal both in size and distribution, and the irregular blank arch courses and round heads of the windows, to the roughly worked and squat balusters and the clumsily carved crosses. The architectural decoration is, however, so varied, and shows such an effort after originality, though of a rather childish character, that it is effective.

Earl's Barton tower was the highest expression of an infantile art, doomed to disappear before the Lombardo-Norman style. It may be called the swan's song of Anglo-Saxon

[1] MICKLETHWAITE, *Something about Saxon church building*, in *The Archaeological Journal*, lvii (1896), p. 327.

[2] Freeman, op. cit., vol. iii, p. 535.

[3] F. M. SIMPSON, *A History of Architectural Development*, vol. ii, p. 239. [CLAPHAM, however (op. cit., p. 95, &c.), prefers a 10th-century date.]

Fig. 628. Earl's Barton Church. Tower (11th century)

architecture, in which some architect of the race combined in a sort of ill-ordered epitome all its leading characteristics, in order to form a kind of record for posterity.[1]

[1] [For Strzygowski (*Early Church Art in Northern Europe*, p. 98) the towers of Barnack and Earl's Barton are imitations in stone of old half-timber buildings. Of the latter he says: 'The upright posts connected in the lower parts by oblique pieces cut from oak are characteristic of half-timber work. More typical still of wood technique are the balusters on the sides of the six windows: they have come from the turnery.' The timber construction had been remarked by J. H. Parker long before (*Introduction to Gothic Architecture*, 2nd ed., 1861, p. 19; 14th ed., 1902, p. 27). Clapham (op. cit., pls. 38–40) dates them both to the 10th century. (R.)]

For there can be no doubt that it is to the end of the Anglo-Saxon or the dawn of the Norman epoch that the tower must be assigned, as it is somewhat later than the one at Barnack, which must have been its model, and displays an amount of architectural decoration, though of a quite different character, which is only equalled by that on St. Laurence at Bradford-on-Avon, with which it must be contemporary.[1]

WING CHURCH (BUCKS.) consists of a nave with aisles, the former terminated by a polygonal chancel (fig. 630), below which is a crypt in the form of an ambulatory, added later. The Pre-Lombardic capital in the two-light opening above the chancel arch, surmounting, not a baluster as at Brixworth, but a shaft as at Kirkdale (1055–1065), brings it into relation with the latter. The refinement of the supports of the arcading round the apse (fig. 631), which take the form of rolls instead of lesenas, points to the post-Saxon period and to Norman influence, which is further indicated by the two tiers of windows in the apse, and also by the basilica plan of the church. We know that, apart from a few of unusual importance, English churches of the tenth century and of the eleventh before 1066 (and Wing must belong to one or the other) had only aisleless naves and, possibly, a tower at the west end or over the crossing.

Fig. 629. Earl's Barton Church. Outer door in the tower (11th century)

The Anglo-Saxon feature of the church is the triangular-headed arcading; and therefore, on the whole, we are inclined to assign it, not so much to the last years of the Confessor's reign, as to the time of the Conqueror.[2]

The vertical rolls on the apse recall those on the tower of Sompting Church (Sussex), the roof of which was altered in 1727[3] (fig. 632). Here each face is bisected by a roll carried up to the highest point of the gable, and cut horizontally by a stringcourse with roughly moulded billets; while the windows consist of single or two-light openings, with round or triangular heads, and rude corbel pulvins, crutch-shaped, hollow chamfered, and curled at the ends. The prototype of this kind of pulvin is to be found at Mettlach (987: see p. 327).

Nevertheless, Sompting tower does not belong to the Anglo-Saxon age, as is generally believed.[4] Against that view are the semi-cylindrical form of the lesenas and the course

---

[1] Cf. BALDWIN BROWN, op. cit., pp. 283 ff.

[2] [Wing church is tentatively attributed by BALDWIN BROWN (pp. 321–3) to the reign of Canute. The apse seems to fall into line in point of date with those of Deerhurst and Brixworth. CLAPHAM (op. cit., p. 95, &c.) also makes it pre-Conquest. (H. T.)]

[3] BLOXAM, *The Principles of Gothic Ecclesiastical Architecture*, vol. i, p. 44.

[4] [The tower of Sompting is assigned by BALDWIN BROWN, op. cit., pp. 430–3, to the 11th century and the period of overlap. CLAPHAM, on the other hand (op. cit., p. 120), prefers the first half of the 11th century.]

Fig. 630. Wing Church (11th century)

Fig. 631. Wing Church (11th century)

of billets—a Norman idea. It is further opposed by the arch inside, springing from half-piers consisting of square-edged members and a half-column corresponding to the similar members and roll moulding of the archivolts; while the continuous capitals show two coarse turn-over leaves and cauliculi with berries. This arch, with its rational disposition of the supports, and the carving on the capitals, is separated by a considerable interval of time from those at Stow, Bosham, and Barnack, and by some interval from the one at Langford. All this suggests that the tower was built in the early part of the twelfth century, in spite of the triangular-headed windows, which, after all, only show that English craftsmen had not yet got rid of their traditional 'impedimenta'.

Fig. 632. Sompting Church. Tower (12th century)

The piece of carving inside the church, with the Saviour in the act of blessing, which is generally thought to be pre-Conquest, must be assigned to a period not earlier than the thirteenth century, on account of the form of the 'vesica piscis' containing the figure of the Redeemer, and also its drapery.

The chief interest of the tower is in the gable heads which determine the form of the roof. It was a type of German origin, which made its appearance with the Lombardo-Rhenish style, so that the oldest examples are not earlier than the twelfth century. Its nationality is proved by the fact that, while it had a relatively wide vogue in Germany, it only made rare and isolated appearances in other countries. Sompting is an instance of its sporadic employment, due to foreign importation. If it were not so we should not find among English buildings of the twelfth and thirteenth centuries, like an oasis in the desert, this solitary specimen of the 'helmed tower' at Sompting.

GREAT DUNHAM CHURCH (NORFOLK) has an aisleless nave with a tower at its eastern end (figs. 633, 634), beyond which was the chancel, rebuilt in later times. The sides of the nave are decorated internally with rough blank arcading, the supports being crowned by an abacus carved with stars, lozenges, and indentations. On the impost blocks of the arch (which has a hood mould) opening into the tower (original except the battlements) stars are carved in low relief, a motive of Romano-British tradition. Instances of the decorative use of stars, either singly or in groups, in carving have come to light in excavations on the Roman Wall.[1] The west door has a triangular head and two jambs ornamented with billets.

Great Dunham Church is a compound of Anglo-Saxon and Norman work. To the Saxon tradition belong the disposition of the corner stones, and the form of the west door; while the enrichment of the interior walls of the nave with blank arcading is due to Norman influence, for there is no dated record of such decorative treatment applied

[1] *The Builder*, June 11, 1898. [Altar of Jupiter Dolichenus from Great Chesters, now in the Black Gate Museum, Newcastle. *Archaeologia Aeliana* 4 ser., ii (1926), p. 60 and pl. vii.]

to the inside of an English building before the Conquest. To the same source are due the indented and billet mouldings. Moreover, the two-light openings of the tower, the elongated form of the shafts, the Pre-Lombardic cubical capitals each with its abacus and pulvin, and the bases consisting of two rolls (one of bulbous outline) separated by a hollow chamfer resting on a plinth, all point to the English craftsmen having been brought into contact with the work of their Continental brethren.

Fig. 633. Great Dunham Church (11th century)

For these reasons the church cannot be assigned to the Anglo-Saxon period. Its place is in the first years after the Norman Conquest, while the two-light windows may even be the result of an alteration carried out rather later, in the last quarter of the eleventh century. No weight need be given to the fact that there is a triangular-headed doorway, for this form continued to be used after the Conquest. An instance occurs in the tower of Jarrow, erected between 1074 and 1083.[1]

The tower of Great Dunham with its rounded openings above the two-light windows recalls that of St. Benet's, Cambridge (fig. 635), which we should assign to a

[1] [There is a triangular-headed doorway in the monastic buildings adjoining the church at Jarrow, which were begun c. 1075: this seems to be the doorway alluded to in the text. Other triangular-headed openings of Norman date occur in the gatehouse of Exeter castle. (H. T.)]

post-Conquest date (in spite of the long and short work at the angles), that is to say, to the time when the new town of Cambridge was rising in the reign of the Conqueror. The lions, for instance, from which spring the outer archivolts of its internal arch (fig. 636), point to Lombardic influence and a date which is not Anglo-Saxon. For, though as early as the first half of the eleventh century the Lombard gilds made use of animals flanking doorways to serve as supports, as we saw in San Flaviano at Montefiascone (1032), the English craftsmen before the Conquest only employed for this purpose

Fig. 634. Great Dunham Church. Tower (11th century)

Fig. 635. Cambridge. Tower of St. Benet's Church (11th century)

heads projecting from the wall, as we learn from the example of Deerhurst Church (tenth century).

THE TOWER OF ST. MATTHEW'S CHURCH, LANGFORD (OXON.), rests on two arches, that looking towards the nave having piers and two archivolts springing from an impost course, while the one on the chancel side has half-piers and archivolts with a roll moulding (fig. 637). It is lighted by single, double-splayed windows, and by pairs of openings outlined by sunk rolls with foliated capitals at the imposts (fig. 638). It has been thought to go back to the Anglo-Saxon age: perhaps to the early years of the eleventh century, or more probably to the reign of the Confessor.

We cannot accept this view. The arch, with its roll moulding, while recalling that at Bosham (which itself is subsequent to the Anglo-Saxon arch at Stow), is shown to be later by the more intelligent way in which the supports correspond to the archivolts, and by the more advanced art displayed in the carving of the continuous capitals.

Fig. 636. Cambridge. St. Benet's Church. Tower arch (11th century)

Fig. 637. Langford Church. Tower arches (11th century)

Fig. 638. Langford Church. Tower (11th century)

Fig. 639. Langford Church. Crucifix (11th century)

From another point of view, the well-executed foliage on the capitals of the two-light openings is decisive against an Anglo-Saxon date. We know what sort of capitals were produced by English chisels or axes. Nor is a pre-Conquest date indicated by the 'keyhole' windows, for there is no dated example of that period to point to. Moreover, the external facing, with the returned lesenas at the angles ending in flat imposts, has an air of finish which is not Anglo-Saxon.

Langford tower[1] must be put in the last quarter of the eleventh century, at a time when, under Norman influence, English carvers were beginning to produce foliated

Fig. 640. Romsey Church. Crucifix (12th century)

capitals. To the same date is to be assigned the headless crucifix now built into the outer wall of the south porch, a figure of such rude character that, with its drapery, it might be made of wood (fig. 639).[2] Some writers have compared it to the crucifix at Romsey (fig. 640). But this piece of sculpture, with its figure of the Redeemer, so much advanced beyond the figure capitals in the choir executed in the first half of the twelfth century, cannot possibly be earlier than the end of that century.[3]

---

[1] [BALDWIN BROWN (p. 463), while admitting a post-Conquest date for the tower, says that 'the advanced features are not characteristically Norman'. (H. T.)]

[2] [CLAPHAM (op. cit., pl. 52, &c.), while dating the tower as mid-11th century, considers the crucifix, pl. 61, to belong to the 10th century. This crucifix appears to be intended for a copy of the 'Volto Santo' of Lucca (E. MÂLE, L'art religieux du XIIe siècle en France, 2nd ed., Paris, 1924, p. 256), though this is disputed by Mr. CLAPHAM (op. cit., p. 138). Cf.

Transactions of the Bristol and Gloucester Archaeological Society, vol. liii (1931), p. 38, note 8. (R.)]

[3] [PRIOR and GARDNER, Figure Sculpture in England, uphold a pre-Conquest date for the Romsey crucifix. (H.T.) In Burlington Magazine, lxi (1932), 273 ff., Mr. STANLEY CASSON produces important evidence for a Saxon origin and date (not later than early 11th cent.), especially the Hand of God above the figure. (R.)]

APPENDICES

1. THE RUTHWELL CROSS

By G. McN. Rushforth

The question of the date of the cross at Ruthwell and of the kindred cross at Bewcastle in Cumberland has been discussed fully by Professor Baldwin Brown (*The Arts in Early England*, vol. v), the late Bishop G. F. Browne (*The Ancient Cross Shafts at Bewcastle and Ruthwell*, Cambridge, 1916), W. S. Calverley (*Notes on the Early Sculptured Crosses . . . in the present Diocese of Carlisle*, edited by W. G. Collingwood, Cumberland and Westmorland Ant. and Arch. Soc., Extra Series, vol. xi, 1899), W. G. Collingwood (*Northumbrian Crosses*, London, 1927), and Mr. Clapham (op. cit., pp. 55 ff.). Though their views differ in detail, they are united in rejecting the late date suggested in the text; and the general consensus of English scholars is in favour of one, if not contemporary with Wilfrid, at any rate not long after his time. The Runic inscriptions on both crosses, particularly that at Bewcastle, with its allusions to historical persons of the seventh century, furnish evidence which, if the later date (for which arguments have been produced by Professor A. Cook, *The Date of the Ruthwell and Bewcastle Crosses*, Yale, 1912) be accepted, it is impossible to explain satisfactorily: their form and language have been scientifically examined by Professor Blyth Webster, in collaboration with Baldwin Brown, with results in favour of the seventh-century ascription. The widespread remains of Anglo-Saxon sculpture in the north have been diligently investigated in Mr. W. G. Collingwood's illustrated *Catalogue raisonné of Anglian and Anglo-Danish Sculpture* in Yorkshire (*Yorks. Archaeol. Journal*, xix (1907), 267–413; xx, 149–213; xxi, 254–302; xxiii, 129–299).

These conclusions are confirmed by Professor Brøndsted, who, summarizing the results of the discussion about the date of the Ruthwell and Bewcastle crosses as pointing generally to an early date, maintains that the vine pattern on both belongs to the first stage of the English conventionalization of it, and therefore dates them soon after 700 (*Early English Ornament*, pp. 74–9). In this he is followed by Mr. Clapham, who gives illustrations of all the important examples, and suggests that the series of English sculptured stone monuments, which 'is unparalleled and largely unrepresented elsewhere in Europe in the same age', may have been due to the arrival (669) of Theodore and Hadrian.

Fragments of an early cross comparable to that of Ruthwell, and even more classic in the treatment of the figure-sculpture, have come to light at Reculver (Kent), and probably belong to the great cross seen in the church by Leland about 1540. Sir Charles Peers believes that it was set up by the first builder of the monastery at Reculver not much after the year 670 (*Archaeologia*, lxxvii (1928), 250–6). To these may now be added the fragments of the cross from Easby (Yorks.), recently collected in the Victoria and Albert Museum.[1]

2. THE CHRONOLOGY OF THE LATER SAXON CHURCHES

By Prof. A. Hamilton Thompson

The new edition of the volume on Anglo-Saxon Architecture in Professor Baldwin Brown's *The Arts in Early England* (vol. ii, 1925, fifteen years after the publication of *Lombardic Architecture*), to which constant allusion has been made in the notes, is a complete revision of the first edition, published in 1903. In his scheme of dating, however, and in the dates suggested for the numerous buildings included in his catalogue, the only important modification introduced is his admission of the overlap of Saxon architecture into the period after the Norman Conquest. In conclusions with regard to the date of certain churches, e.g. Escomb, his opinion differs widely from that of Signor Rivoira; and his study of plans and technique leads him to group together his examples with some degree of certainty. The point, however, in which he differs most materially from Signor Rivoira's conclusions is in his chronology of the later Saxon churches. Here Signor Rivoira speaks decisively in attributing

---

[1] Illustrated description by Miss M. Longhurst in *Archaeologia*, lxxxi (1931), 43–7; and see *Burlington Magazine*, lxi (1932), p. 267, where Mr. Stanley Casson compares the haloed heads with very similar sculpture (6th or 7th cent.) recently discovered in St. Mary Panachrantos, Constantinople.

the churches of which Barnack, Barton-on-Humber, and Earl's Barton are the best examples to an advanced date in the eleventh century. This group, the chief characteristics of which are long and short quoining and the decorative use of strip-work (lesenas), must belong to one of two periods, either that of ecclesiastical reform in the time of Edgar the Peaceful (959–975), which continued until the close of the tenth century, or to the epoch of church restoration under Canute, which was not seriously interrupted until the time of the Norman Conquest.

Signor Rivoira concluded, on grounds sufficiently stated in the text, that the later period was the *terminus a quo* for buildings with these distinctive marks of style. He relied much on the dates 950 and 965, which have been applied to the churches of St. Michael at St. Albans and Lyminge respectively; and in neither of these fabrics is there any approach in style to that of the buildings in question. On the other hand, examination of these structures goes far to show that in their present state they contain no work earlier than the Norman period, apart from possible fragments re-used from Saxon buildings. With the exception, therefore, of literary references, such as that to the building of the abbey church at Ramsey, we have no existing church of the late tenth century for which there is indisputable evidence. Baldwin Brown, who lays stress on the German influence discernible in the details of the churches of the Barnack group, believes that they may be assigned to this date and classifies them in his period C^1, as earlier than churches which may be placed tentatively in the age of Canute (C^2), and of which Wing is a possible example. It is certain that the type of decoration at Barnack, &c., represents a distinct period which, if identified with the earlier part of the eleventh century, must have developed rapidly and come to an end abruptly, as its features differ noticeably from those of undoubtedly eleventh-century churches. It is therefore reasonable to conclude that the date of these buildings may be placed in the age preceding the second period of Danish invasion, i.e. before 1002. This certainly makes later developments more easy to explain.

IV

THE LOMBARDO-NORMAN STYLE IN ENGLAND

WHEN the works of Saint Étienne at Caen were begun, Lanfranc was obliged to leave the scene of his achievements at Bec, and resign the prior's place to his pupil, Anselm of Aosta (1060–1066), in order to become abbot of the new monastery. The change was brought about by Duke William (1035–1066), anxious to have near him, in his favourite city, a trusty counsellor, capable of making clear and easy his way to the conquest of the crown, which on the death of Edward the Confessor had passed to Harold. That conquest was the common work of these two great men. Normandy was too small for the lion's grasp of the one, and the eagle's flight of the other.

Although it was the sword of the valiant, fearless warrior, William of Normandy, which, on the field of Hastings (1066), decided the fate of England, winning for him the title of Conqueror, and placing the long-coveted diadem on his head, nevertheless it was the mind of Lanfranc, the soul and spring of the whole enterprise, that moulded his conception of the invasion and conquest, correcting, supplementing, bringing it to perfection. In all this he received invaluable aid from the Benedictine monks and secular clergy of Normandy, and also the support of his pupil, Pope Alexander II (1061–1073), and of Hildebrand, afterwards Gregory VII (1073–1086). And after he became archbishop of Canterbury (1070–1089) he performed a work of the highest importance in organizing and consolidating the conquered country.

It was with Lanfranc, too, that the golden age of Lombardo-Norman architecture opened in England. And he was scarcely dead when William of Saint-Calais began the building of his great church at Durham, which was to mark the passing of the Lombardo-Norman forms into those of the Transition, and so lead the way to the Pointed style.

Lanfranc, uniting in himself the architect, the man of letters, the diplomat, the statesman, was, it appears to me, the most important figure in the ecclesiastical world of the eleventh century, with the exception of Hildebrand, who, however, was inferior to him in the perfect balance of his faculties. Placed at the summit of the hierarchical edifice, Gregory VII embraced in his view at once the vast horizon of the Catholic Church and the kingdoms of this world, in which he was the principal factor. But he did not know how to select the best ways and the most suitable means for carrying out his boundless designs. His insatiable ambition and ill-concealed restlessness were serious obstacles to his success; so that, if Lanfranc had not possessed the will and the skill to undo the mischief caused by the pontiff's lack of patience in dealing with William, the cry for separation from Rome would not have had to wait till the sixteenth century before it was raised. The triumph of Canossa would not have been repeated in the case of the Norman lion: the Conqueror was formed in a very different mould from the Emperor Henry IV. The last words said to have been uttered by Hildebrand—'Dilexi iustitiam et odivi iniquitatem, propterea morior in exilio'—words which are preserved in the 'Officium proprium Sancti Gregorii papae VII' of the Cathedral of Salerno, sum up the whole of his work. It is the confession of a man who has been beaten in the struggle against adverse fate.

THE ABBEY CHURCH OF ST. AUGUSTINE, CANTERBURY.—Recent excavations have revealed the scanty remains of the crypt of the church begun by the Norman abbot, Scotlandus (1070–1087),[1] after demolishing the new work of Wulfric (1047–1059), and finished in 1091 by his successor Vido (1087–1099).[2]

The body of the church was arcaded, and terminated in a semicircle surrounded by an ambulatory with three radiating chapels.[3] The arches of the body of the church were supported by piers, and the nave was separated from the aisles by columns. The ambulatory had cross vaulting with visible arches.

To judge by what I saw in 1903, the capitals of the supports were of the Lombardic cubical type; and among the bases were some of bulbous form in the Anglo-Saxon style, consisting of a plinth and a thick roll with a smaller roll above it. Such bases indicate that English craftsmen were employed in the works. When the first buildings in the Lombardo-Norman style were erected, the same thing must have happened in England which had taken place previously in Normandy in the days of William of Volpiano, as we explained in our account of the church at Bernay; that is to say, Anglo-Saxon workmen were put under the direction of Norman workmen, who also undertook the more difficult tasks, such as the cross vaulting. The artistic parts, e.g. the capitals, bases, stringcourses, cornices, were generally left to English hands, and this explains the poverty of the results.

As the plan of the crypt must have been repeated in the choir above, St. Augustine's affords the earliest certain instance in England of a choir ambulatory with radiating chapels.[4] For though we know that Westminster Abbey had an apsidal choir with surrounding aisle in the time of Edward the Confessor, it does not follow that it had a system of radial chapels.[5]

Related to this crypt is the one at Gloucester, as constructed by Serlo (1089).

Among the remains of the church at Canterbury, the presence of the Lombardic type of cubical capital should be noticed, for this is the earliest dated English building in which it occurs.

CANTERBURY CATHEDRAL.—The primitive church of Augustine, restored and increased in height by Odo (941–958),[6] and repaired by Canute after the Danes in 1011 had set fire to the roof,[7] was finally burned in the year 1067. Within seven years (1070–1077) Archbishop Lanfranc rebuilt the cathedral.[8] Under his successor Anselm (1093–1109), about the year 1096, Prior Ernulf, who had passed with Lanfranc from Bec to Caen, and had thence been summoned to Christ Church, Canterbury, demolished the eastern limb of the cathedral and began its reconstruction. It was completed by Prior Conrad, who gave his name to the choir, and the dedication followed in 1130.

In 1174 Conrad's choir, which had a painted wooden roof, was destroyed by fire.

---

[1] [Further excavations at St. Augustine's, Canterbury, since this passage was written, have revealed features of great importance, including the remains of the octagonal structure built at the east end of the nave by Wulfric. See W. H. St. John Hope, *Recent Discoveries in the Abbey Church of St. Austin at Canterbury* (*Archaeologia*, lxvi (1916), pp. 377–400), and C. R. Peers and A. W. Clapham, *St. Augustine's Abbey Church, Canterbury, before the Norman Conquest* (ibid. lxxvii (1927), 201–18). (H. T.)]

[2] *Rolls Series*, 8, Elmham, *Historia monasterii S. Augustini Cantuariensis*, p. 144; Mabillon, *Annales Ord. S. Benedicti*, vol. v, p. 288ᶜ; Twysden, op. cit., *Chronologia Augustinensis Cant.*, col. 2250.

[3] Routledge, *Excavations at St. Austin's Abbey,*

Canterbury, The Church of SS. Peter and Paul, p. 5.

[4] [It was probably, in some sort, a copy of S. Bénigne at Dijon (Clapham, op. cit., 149–51).]

[5] [It is now known that the apse of the Confessor's church was not surrounded by an ambulatory. *Archaeologia*, lxii (1910), pp. 92, 94, 99, and pl. xiv. See p. 177, note 2.]

[6] *Rolls Series*, 71, *The Historians of the Church of York and its Archbishops*, *Vita Oswaldi arch. Eboracensis*, vol. i, p. 407; Wharton, op. cit., Osborne, *Vita Odonis archiep. Cantuariensis*, part ii, p. 83.

[7] Wharton, op. cit., *Vita S. Elphegi archiep. Cant.*, part ii, p. 135.

[8] *Rolls Series*, 81, *Eadmeri historia novorum in Anglia*, p. 13.

It was rebuilt between 1175 and 1184 by the architects William of Sens, and William 'English by nation', who extended its length towards the east, incorporated part of the outer walls of the preceding church in the new work (as may readily be seen from fig. 641), and kept untouched only the crypt with its two lateral chapels. In the fourteenth century the nave and transept were rebuilt on the old lines, and in the fifteenth the great central tower was erected.

Gervase[1] tells us that Lanfranc's church was of cruciform plan with a central tower. The arches of the nave were carried on piers, and there were two lofty towers at its western end.[2] Each arm of the transept had a vaulted gallery or loggia, supported on three sides by the outer walls, and on the fourth by a pier. The choir was raised by several steps above the level of the rest of the church, and two flights of stairs led down to the crypt. The form of the choir and crypt is unknown, for Gervase did not see them, and was not acquainted with any description. But his account of the church, brief and imperfect as it is, makes it clear that Lanfranc's design was taken from his Saint Étienne at Caen.

Conrad's choir, we learn from Gervase, with Ernulf's new crypt beneath it, was of considerable length, with an apsidal end. It had arcades at the sides, with a triforium above them, and was provided with a secondary transept. Christ Church, Canterbury, is thus the first instance in England of a double transept. At the sides of the choir were two lofty towers, known as St. Andrew's and St. Anselm's, and at its extremity was a square chapel. This adjunct, and the similar one at Rochester, were the first 'Lady Chapels' in England.

Fig. 641. Canterbury Cathedral. South side (11th and 12th centuries)

A drawing made by the monk Edwin gives a view of the exterior of the new choir and the remains of Lanfranc's church.

Ernulf's crypt has come down to us almost untouched, and merely broken into at its junction with the other part of the crypt belonging to the late twelfth-century structure. Several of its Lombardic cubical capitals, as well as of those in the two lateral

[1] *Rolls Series*, 73, *Gervasii Cantuariensis opera historica*, vol. i, pp. 9–11.
[2] [Lanfranc's north-west tower survived till 1834, when it was destroyed and replaced by a copy of the 15th-century south-west tower. (R.)]

chapels (figs. 642, 643), were carved and ornamented in various ways in the course of the works carried out after the disaster of 1174. This may be inferred from the fact

Fig. 642. Canterbury Cathedral. Crypt. Chapel of St. John or St. Gabriel
(11th and 12th centuries)

Fig. 643. Canterbury Cathedral. Crypt. Capital in Chapel of
St. John or St. Gabriel (11th and 12th centuries)

that the capitals in Conrad's and Ernulf's building were left plain—'in capitellis veteribus opus erat planum, in novis sculptura subtilis', as Gervase says;[1] and also

[1] [The phrase quoted from Gervase refers only to the choir. There is no reason to assume that the carving of the crypt capitals illustrated in figs. 642, 643, was added after 1174. The *sculptura subtilis* of

from the advanced stage of art displayed by the carvings, which suits the period we have suggested.

Before leaving the subject I may remark that Edwin's view of the church is of the same date as the other illuminations in the Canterbury Psalter,[1] that is to say, of the

Fig. 644. Durham. Chapel in the Castle (1072)

twelfth and not the tenth century. This fact has not been previously observed, and it reduces the age of the Psalter, which has hitherto been studied only from the palaeographical and not from the architectural point of view, or by any one who was familiar with medieval buildings. The Psalter contains numerous representations of structures which indicate a date later than the Norman Conquest. We will only cite the instance

which Gervase speaks was of a very different kind, and applies only to the new work: there is no relation between the figure sculpture of the capitals in the crypt and the delicate Corinthianesque foliage for

which William of Sens found his models in Burgundy. (H. T.)]

[1] *Tripartitum Psalterium Eadwini* in the Library of Trinity College, Cambridge.

of a basilica with a central cupola decorated with two tiers of blank arcading separated by a band with lesenas at intervals. Now, it is known that, in England, lantern towers were not embellished with such arcading before Lanfranc's rebuilding of his cathedral, and that is why the central tower of Westminster Abbey was devoid of it, as shown by the Bayeux Tapestry. There is also another view of a church with arcading of a refined type running below the line of the aisle roof, a feature which appears on no dated English building earlier than the Conquest.

Fig. 645. Durham. Chapel in the Castle.
Capital (1072)

Fig. 646. Durham. Chapel in the Castle.
Capital (1072)

THE CHAPEL OF DURHAM CASTLE.—Durham Castle was begun in 1072, and the fruitless siege by the murderers of the unfortunate Bishop Walcher (1071–1080) shows that it had been finished before 1080. The fact that the canons of Waltham, whose church and lands had been given to the see of Durham by the Conqueror (1075), contributed in the days of Rannulf Flambard an annual payment towards the building of the castle, as we learn from the exemption which Queen Matilda obtained for them, only means that their subsidy went towards the important works executed by that energetic and restless prelate to increase the strength of both castle and city.

The castle chapel is the one described by the monk Laurence, afterwards prior of Durham (1149–1154), as 'non spatiosa nimis, sed speciosa satis'.[1] It is of rectangular form, divided into three aisles with unraised cross vaulting (fig. 644). The carving on the capitals of the columns is executed without undercutting, and the decorative elements are sometimes well treated; but the representations of living creatures are clumsy in design, and rude in execution (figs. 645, 646, 647). The chisels were, generally speaking, Norman, as is shown by the introduction of their characteristic crocket capital. One of the earliest instances in the North of England of this type is to be found in the crypt of Lastingham church, rebuilt about 1078.[2]

The Corinthianesque crocket capital, which has been wrongly described by some writers as Byzantine, is of remote origin. In the tomb of the Volumnii near Perugia is a marble cinerary urn in the form of a temple, believed to be of the age of Augustus,

[1] *Rolls Series*, 75, *Symeonis monachi hist. Regum*, vol. ii, p. 199; *Rolls Series*, 75, *Symeonis monachi hist. Eccl. Dunelm. continuatio*, vol. i; *Publications of the* Surtees Society, vol. 70 (1878), *Dialogi Laurentii Dunelmensis monachi ac prioris*, lib. i, p. 402.
[2] DUGDALE, op. cit., vol. i, p. 342.

in which the capitals of the pilasters have crocket leaves at the angles instead of volutes (fig. 648). Earlier still, leaves of this kind were used on the capitals of the 'Tomb of the Reliefs' at Cerveteri, and on those of a terra-cotta urn in the Museum at Perugia, dated respectively about the fourth century, and the second or third century B.C.

English carvers worked on the chapel at Durham as well as Norman ones, and this explains the low grade of art displayed by some of the results. I should, for instance, assign to Northumbrian artists the capitals with a grotesque human head, a siren, a stag, and a horse, all of which present various mutual analogies, while they are quite different from others of the living creatures represented, such as the strange animal head with protruding tongue, and the human figures holding up the abacus.

Fig. 647. Durham. Chapel in the Castle. Capital (1072)

Any one who compares the foliage of the best of these capitals with that in the cathedral on the capitals of the interior door near the south arm of the transept, and on the four capitals of the blank arcading in the nave aisles, will be at once struck by the inferiority of the artists who produced the foliated capitals in the cathedral. Noting this fact, and considering that the cubico-spherical is the prevailing type in the great church, we shall be safe in excluding any Norman artists from it, whether monastic or lay.

The masonry of the chapel may also be set down to Norman builders,

Fig. 648. Perugia. Tomb of the Volumnii. Cinerary urn (29 B.C.–A.D. 14)

as is shown by the cross vaulting. English masons were not yet capable of carrying out such work.

St. Albans Cathedral, founded as an abbey church in 793 by Offa, king of Mercia (755–794 or 796), was rebuilt between 1077 and 1088 (with help from the primate Lanfranc) by Abbot Paul (1077–1093), who had formerly been a monk of Saint Étienne at Caen.[1] Eadmer and Ralph de Diceto say that it was Lanfranc himself who carried out the rebuilding.[2]

[1] *Rolls Series*, 28, Walsingham, *Gesta abbatum monasterii S. Albani*, vol. iv[a], pp. 4, 53, 34; *Rolls Series*, 57, *Matthaei Parisiensis hist. Anglorum*, vol. i, p. 360; vol. ii, p. 16.

[2] *Rolls Series*, 81, *Historia novorum in Anglia*, p. 15; *Rolls Series*, 68, *Opera historica*, vol. i, p. 215.

Abbot John de Cella (1195–1214) pulled down the west front in order to make a new one. The work on the new front was continued by his successor, William of Trumpington (1214–1235), who altered the aisle windows in the new style and re-modelled the top of the central tower. Abbot John of Hertford took in hand the recon-struction of the choir, which, with its Lady Chapel, was completed in 1326 by Abbot Hugh of Eversden (1309–1327). In 1323 two of the piers on the south side of the nave collapsed, and five arches of the arcade had to be rebuilt. John of Wheathamstead

Fig. 649. St. Albans Cathedral. Nave
(1077–1088)

Fig. 650. St. Albans Cathedral. North arm of
transept (1077–1088)

(1420–1440, 1451–1464) made extensive changes. The restorations of recent years have to a considerable extent altered the original features of the church.

Of the Norman structure there survive, in a more or less altered state, the transept and central tower, the junction between this and the choir, and the body of the nave except the west front.

The nave (fig. 649) and transept (fig. 650) retain their wooden ceilings.[1] The aisles, to judge by what is left of the old choir, were originally covered with rude unraised cross vaulting.

In the transept may be noticed some baluster shafts which have been used over again. They have various mouldings, and are turned on the lathe. Possibly they were made in the second half of the tenth century, in the days of Abbot Eadmer, who cherished a design of rebuilding the church.[2] We may also observe some Lombardic cubical capitals with two half-rounds on each face.

---

[1] [The visible wooden ceiling of the nave is modern. (H. T.)]

[2] *Rolls Series*, 28, WALSINGHAM, op. cit., vol. iv[a], pp. 26, 28.

Though the design for St. Albans issued from the School of Lanfranc, English craftsmen and workmen were employed in its erection. The masonry (fig. 651), except for a larger use of bricks, is just like that of the neighbouring St. Michael's (about 950).[1] The design of the piers, consisting of mere rectangular supports without engaged shafts, and finished off by simple imposts instead of capitals, was, with its bare, monotonous

Fig. 651. St. Albans Cathedral (1077–1088)

simplicity, perfectly in keeping with the scanty skill of the Anglo-Saxon craftsmen and builders employed in the work. The inferior quality of these workmen is further betrayed by the poor character of the mouldings throughout the church, and the entire absence of carving. Moreover, the presence of English hands is indisputably proved by the use made in the transept of the characteristic baluster shafts which, being of irregular size, were made to fit their places by the addition of clumsy bases of Anglo-Saxon character; and their almost total unfamiliarity with the use of the chisel is shown by the fact that the cubical capitals and the shafts have been hewn with the axe.

[1] [According to more recent views, the date of St. Michael's is much nearer to that of the abbey church. See note 1 on p. 169. The simplicity of the pier design is qualified by the correct grammatical correspondence of the recessing of the piers to that of the arches, which English masons were slow to achieve. (H. T.)]

St. Albans Cathedral affords only one feature of importance: the cubical capitals with two half-rounds on each face; the earliest specimens of the sort, of certain date, that I can point to, and the representatives of the new Anglo-Lombardic type of cubical

Fig. 652. Lincoln Cathedral (12th and 13th centuries)

capital which, with some further embellishment, became the scalloped capital so largely employed by the English builders.

LINCOLN CATHEDRAL was founded in honour of the Virgin by Remigius, originally a monk of Fécamp, and afterwards bishop of Dorchester and Lincoln (1067–1092),[1] to replace an earlier church dedicated to St. Mary Magdalen. The foundation must

[1] *Rolls Series*, 52, *Willelmi Malmesbiriensis monachi gesta pontificum Anglorum*, p. 312.

have taken place when he transferred the see to Lincoln, that is to say, after his return from Rome (where, through the intercession of Lanfranc, Pope Alexander II had restored to him the pastoral staff and ring), and after the transfer had been decreed by the council held at Windsor in 1072.[1] We know that the building was finished in 1091,[2] and in 1092 it was dedicated.

Damaged by fire about 1141, the cathedral was brought up to date, and vaulted ('. . . egregie reparando lapideis fideliter voltis primus involvit') by the Norman bishop, Alexander (1123–1148).[3] The semi-elliptical outline remaining at the west end of the nave shows the kind of roof constructed. The terrible earthquake of 1185 rent the building from top to bottom,[4] and bishop Hugh of Avalon (1186 1200), who had been prior of Witham, took in hand its reconstruction in the Pointed style with Geoffrey de Noiers for his architect.[5] Of the two previous structures were retained: part of the west front with the two great towers, afterwards raised by the addition of a very lofty stage in the new style; the westernmost bay of the nave, with some alteration, repeated on a later occasion; and the walls of the aisles reduced to the form that they present to-day.

In the west front (fig. 652) the work earlier than Hugh's time at once strikes the eye.[6] It consists of the central portion, with two semicircular niches, three great recesses, and three doorways, and reaches as high as the two ranges of intersecting arcading above. It is the result of Bishop Alexander's alterations, which gave an exceptional thickness to the wall by adding a new facing to that

Fig. 653. Lincoln Cathedral. Central portal of west front (12th century)

[1] *Rolls Series*, 90, *Willelmi Malm. monachi gesta regum Anglorum*, vol. ii, p. 353.

[2] *Rolls Series*, 57, *Matthaei Parisiensis monachi S. Albani chronica maiora*, vol. ii, p. 31.

[3] WHARTON, *Giraldi Cambrensis liber de vitis episc. Lincolniensium*, part ii, p. 417.

[4] *Rolls Series*, 51, *Chronica magistri Rogeri de Houedene*, vol. ii, p. 303.

[5] *Rolls Series*, 37, *Magna vita s. Hugonis episcopi Lincolniensis*, p. 336.

[6] [The west front contains no work of the date of Hugh: the Pointed work of the upper part and sides belongs to the date of the rebuilding of the nave, which was begun about 1220 and finished towards 1250, to judge by the general character of the work. In the earlier portion, the three doorways may without doubt be ascribed to Alexander; but the recesses are unquestionably earlier than his time, and the quality of their work is quite different from that of the doorways. The archivolts of the lateral recesses are plain,

and the capitals of the lofty jamb-shafts are a variety of the early Norman crocketed type noted on p. 216 above. The gallery above these recesses, with its decoration of intersecting arches, is certainly later, and usually supposed to have been added in the time of Alexander, to which also the completion of the lower stages of the towers, with their gabled northern and southern annexes belongs. On Remigius' church see J. BILSON, *The Plan of the First Cathedral Church of Lincoln* (*Archaeologia*, lxii (1910), pp. 543–64). The treatment in the text of the Norman work in the west front as all of one date raises awkward problems. The foliage in the capitals of the apse-like niches is less advanced than is suggested; and the confinement of simple foliage to internal capitals is disproved, e.g. by the appearance of the Norman crocketed capitals in the outer doorways of the keeps of Richmond (formerly the gatehouse) and Colchester castles, which are both of the age of the Conqueror. (H. T.)]

built by Remigius, in order to enable the great recesses with their portals, and the two apsidal niches, to be formed within it. It is this which explains the fact that the towers, which originally formed part of the façade, no longer stand on the front line but behind it.

Before the twelfth century there was nowhere to be seen, not merely in England, but in no country of Europe, a portal with such deeply recessed and elaborate mouldings as the central one at Lincoln (fig. 653), nor did blank intersecting arcading appear in

Fig. 654. Winchester Cathedral. Part of the old crypt (1079–1093)

England before the end of the eleventh century. Moreover, it is quite inconceivable that Remigius can have ornamented the capitals in the two apse-like niches of the front with foliage in single or double ranks, while the most important abbey churches erected in the island in the course of the eleventh century and after the Norman Conquest contained only perfectly plain capitals, and merely, by way of exception, one here and there embellished with plain leaves at the angles, and then only where it occurred, not on the exterior, but inside the church.

Again, it is clearly to the twelfth century that we must assign the finished scalloped capitals in the portals, for this characteristic type did not see the light before that period. Lastly, it is quite impossible to ascribe the elaborate treatment of the doorways to the eleventh century. The results produced by English carvers in the last quarter of the eleventh century were of a very different character.

The great western towers, at least in their lower portions, and as far as the third stage, are also mainly the work of Bishop Alexander. The elaborate decoration of some of the arcading and stringcourses is of the same date as that on the west front, and we know that the blank intersecting arcading which embellishes the towers and their gabling cannot belong to the time of Remigius. In the much altered westernmost bay of the nave, now forming a kind of narthex, a fragment of his triforium may be observed, and also part of the wall passage made by Alexander.[1]

Lincoln Cathedral, though contributing no new element to the formation of the historical chain which it is our object to construct, is still worthy of attention as being the first instance in England, after Durham (1093–1131), of a nave on a great scale with a solid roof. Before taking leave of the church we may say that we shall discuss the important reliefs of the west front when we deal with the porch of Malmesbury Abbey.

Winchester Cathedral, rebuilt in 1079 by Bishop Walkelin (1070–1098), who had previously been a monk at Saint Étienne, Caen, and succeeded the deposed Stigand (1047–1069), was consecrated in 1093.[2] The lantern tower, owing to its defective construction, fell in 1107, but it was soon after rebuilt in the form which it still retains. In the twelfth, thirteenth, fourteenth, and fifteenth centuries various additions were made, and a general remodelling took place; so that all that is left of the original structure that is visible and in a fair state of preservation is the transept and the crypt.

The crypt consists of a rectangular central space ending in an apse, with surrounding ambulatory (figs. 654, 655). The central portion, which is supported by piers, is divided into two aisles by five

Fig. 655. Winchester Cathedral. Part of the old crypt (1079–1093)

short cylindrical pillars, each surmounted by a capital formed by a Doric ovolo and abacus, recalling the central pier of the Chapel of the Pyx in Westminster Abbcy, which belongs to the time of the Confessor. Like the ambulatory it has unraised cross vaulting. From the eastern end starts an elongated apse divided down the middle by columns carrying vaulting of the same kind.

The transept (figs. 656, 657), partly rebuilt after the fall of the central tower, was designed with a wooden ceiling for the central space and the triforium, and unraised cross vaulting in the aisles. The latter has been in part reconstructed with ribbing, or strengthened by the addition of ribs.[3]

We find here a form of support, new for England, consisting of a cylindrical pillar with a pilaster and a half-column attached to it from which to start a transverse arch and two springers for the groining. It was copied in Ely and Norwich Cathedrals. We may also note the blank arcading used as an interior decoration.

[1] [The wall passage alluded to is the clerestory passage of Remigius' nave. (H. T.)]

[2] *Rolls Series*, 36, *Annales monastici*, vol. ii, *Annales monasterii de Wintonia*, pp. 32, 37.

[3] [For the Winchester vaulting see C. H. Moore, *The Aisle Vaulting of Winchester Transept* (*Journal R.I.B.A.*, 3rd ser. xxiii. 313–20, 329–34), and J. Bilson on the same subject (ibid. xxiv. 65–9). (H. T.)]

Walkelin's church was a production of the School of Lanfranc so far as the general conception goes, but it was erected by Norman master masons in co-operation with English workmen. The presence of the former is indicated by the vaulting in the crypt, where the irregular forms of the bays demanded the services of skilled masons. The English element is revealed by the absence of carving, and by the bulbous bases of the transept piers; as also by the disaster which ultimately befell the central tower. The absence of Norman carvers, which we have already noticed at St. Albans, must have been due to the fact that, during the years when Abbot Paul's and Bishop Walkelin's churches were being built, the artists, perhaps not very numerous, were employed on Saint Étienne and the Trinité at Caen, the two favourite churches of the Conqueror and Queen Matilda, and also in the chapels of the castles which the Normans were steadily erecting in England.

Fig. 656. Winchester Cathedral. North arm of transept (1079–1093)

Winchester Cathedral, besides the singular form of pillar with attached half compound pier which we have noticed, affords the earliest English instance of the use of blank arcading at the base of the walls, and also of triplet arches with the middle one rising higher than the others (after the Ravennate manner), or sometimes groups of four, which appear here in the clerestory: a feature which afterwards was very freely used for the arcaded wall passages in the naves of Lombardo-Norman churches. The transept aisles, forming a continuation of the aisles of the nave, are another new feature in England. It was already to be found in St. Maria im Capitol at Cologne, and was afterwards copied in other Continental churches. In Italy an illustration is provided by the cathedral of Piacenza (fig. 658), rebuilt in 1122 after the earthquake of 1117 had destroyed the earlier church of St. Justina. Here Walkelin's conception is amplified in the sense that the aisles of the nave not only encircle the transept but are also prolonged into the choir. We may remark in passing that the form of the nave piers at Piacenza was derived from the type which we noticed in Saint Philibert at Tournus (1008–1019), and shall see used again in great English churches.

ST. JOHN'S CHAPEL IN THE TOWER OF LONDON.—We do not know the exact date of the erection of the fortress to which this chapel belongs. Though it is stated by William of Poitiers[1] that the Conqueror built a castle at London after his coronation (1066), it is thought that this means a mere palisade with a ditch, and that the masonry

[1] DUCHESNE, *Hist. norm. script. ant.*, *Gesta Guillelmi ducis Normannorum et regis Anglorum*, p. 208 B.

Fig. 658. Piacenza. Duomo (12th century)

Fig. 657. Winchester Cathedral. South arm of transept (1079–1093)

G g

construction was not begun till 1078 or 1080.[1] We hear of the new structure as the 'Tower of London' as early as 1097.[2]

The architect was Bishop Gundulf,[3] the capable builder[4] of the castle at Rochester.[5]

Fig. 659. Tower of London. St. John's Chapel (about 1080)

It is probable that it was not begun immediately after 1077 when he became bishop (having previously been Lanfranc's proctor), as he must have been deeply occupied in

[1] CLARK, *Mediaeval military architecture in England*, vol. ii, p. 205, note 2. [See also OMAN, *Castles*, p. 10.]

[2] SPARKE, op. cit., *Chronicon Angliae: per Johannem abbatem Burgi S. Petri*, p. 56.

[3] HEARNE, *Textus Roffensis* (Oxford, 1720), p. 212.

[4] [See Appendix to Chapter I, *supra*, p. 47.]

[5] WHARTON, op. cit., part i, p. 338, *Ernulfi episcopi*

Roffensis collectanea de rebus Ecclesiae Roffensis. [The tower known as Gundulf's is on the north side of the cathedral at Rochester. No part of the present castle at Rochester is as early as his day: the castle of his time was the earthwork structure of which the mound, called the Boley Hill, remains upon a site dismantled when the later castle was laid out. (H. T.)]

remedying the miserable state in which he found his bishopric, installing the Benedictines, and providing them with a monastery.[1] A likely date is 1080.

The chapel (fig. 659), which is on the first floor of the Tower, consists of a nave and
aisles, with an apsidal end. The nave is covered by barrel vaulting with a half-dome at
the end, and the aisles by unraised cross vaulting with a continuous barrel vault for the
triforium.

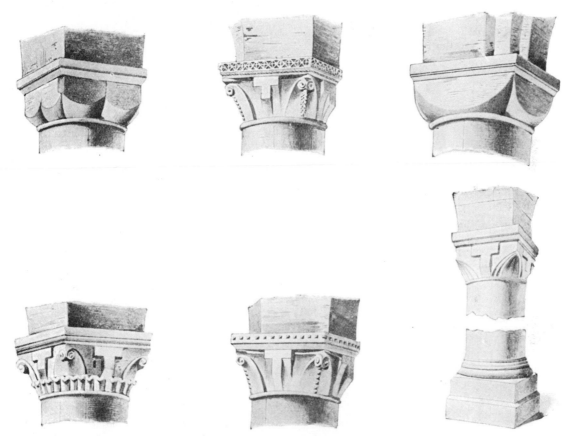

Fig. 660. Tower of London. Capitals in St. John's Chapel (about 1080)
(From sketches by Miss P. Bruce)

I believe it to have been the work of Norman builders and craftsmen, as, indeed, was
the whole of the Tower. The Normans being, as has been observed,[2] the importers
of this type of fortress into England, we cannot suppose that they employed inex-
perienced English masons on work that was quite unfamiliar to them. The presence of
Norman craftsmen is attested, apart from the form of the vaulting, which is unusual in
English Lombardo-Norman churches, by the artistic details (fig. 660), especially the
foliated capitals, quite alien to English taste at the time.

It may be noticed that the form of the chapel, with a central arcaded space encircled
by an ambulatory, reproduces Walkelin's crypt at Winchester.

ROCHESTER CATHEDRAL was rebuilt either by Lanfranc[3] or by his favourite pupil,

---

[1] WHARTON, op. cit., part ii, p. 280, *Vita Gundulfi
episc. Roffensis.*

[2] CLARK, op. cit., vol. i, pp. 39–41 ff.

[3] WHARTON, op. cit., part i, p. 50, *Excerpta ex*

Bishop Gundulf (1077–1108), with assistance from the archbishop.[1] This rebuilding is believed by some—and I agree with them—to have taken place about 1080 after the more pressing needs of the see and convent had been attended to, during which interval

Fig. 661. Rochester Cathedral. West front in 17th century. (From Dugdale, *Monasticon Anglicanum*, vol. i (1655), pl. 13)

the old church was left standing. It was not, however, completed till the time of Archbishop William I (1123–1136), when the consecration took place in 1130 or 1133, and

chronico Cantuariensi, de Roberti Winchelsey archiepiscopi rebus gestis; *Rolls Series*, 68, *Radulfi de Diceto decani Lundoniensis opera historica*, vol. i, p. 215; *Rolls Series*, 81, *Eadmeri historia novorum in Anglia*, p. 15. [For Rochester Cathedral see W. H. St. John Hope, *Cathedral Church and Monastery of St. Andrew at Rochester*, 1900, in which, however, the late Norman work of the nave and west front is considerably antedated in view of the advanced architectural details. (H. T.)]

[1] Wharton, op. cit., part ii, p. 280; and part i, p. 336, *Vita Gundulfi episcopi Roffensis authore monacho Roffensi coaetaneo. Ernulfi episcopi Roffensis collectanea de rebus Ecclesiae Roffensis.*

also the translation into the new church of the body of the bishop St. Ithamar (655), whence one may reasonably suppose that it was about then that the old church was demolished.

After suffering serious injuries from fire in 1137 or 1138 and 1177 or 1179,[1] and being repaired, altered, and partly rebuilt (fig. 661), the only portions that I have found

Fig. 662. Ely Cathedral. North arm of main transept (11th and 12th centuries)

surviving from the age of Gundulf, and therefore of interest for our subject, are the two western bays of the extensive existing crypt, and some remains of rude masonry. The bays of the crypt have short cylindrical piers, surmounted by funnel-shaped cubical capitals (imitations of Lombardic cubical capitals), hewn with the axe, and covered by a plain abacus. Below these piers are clumsy bases consisting of a plinth with thick ovolo, or else plinth, large half-roll, and necking. From them springs rough unraised cross vaulting without visible arches. Evidence of this kind both in construction and decoration clearly points to Anglo-Saxon handiwork. To the same source is due, as at

[1] *Rolls Series*, 73, *Gervasii monachi Cantuariensis* part i, pp. 343, 345, *Annales Ecclesiae Roffensis, ex opera historica*, vol. ii, p. 383; WHARTON, op. cit., *historia ecclesiastica Edmundi de Hadenham.*

St. Albans, the fact that the axis of the church points south-east, whereas the primitive church of the time of Justus, first bishop of Rochester, was correctly orientated.

We know that Gundulf's church was terminated by a rectangular space instead of an apse. Some think that this was the germ of the 'Lady Chapel' possessed by so many English cathedrals, whereas, as far back as 938, Saint Bénigne at Dijon had a square

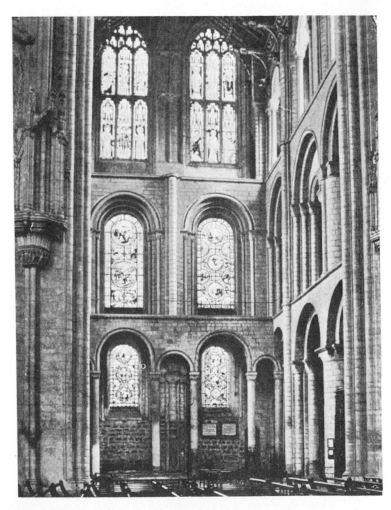

Fig. 663. Ely Cathedral. North arm of main transept (11th and 12th centuries)

chapel at its eastern extremity, dedicated to the Mother of God. It was a feature perhaps derived from the old St. Peter's at Rome, where behind the apse stood the mausoleum of the Anicii, or church erected by Sextus Anicius Petronius Probus, prefect of Rome in the second half of the fourth century.[1]

ELY CATHEDRAL.—The abbey church founded in 673 by Etheldreda, wife of Ecgfrid, king of Northumbria (670–685), and consecrated as abbess by Wilfrid, was burned by the Danes in 870 and rebuilt in 970 by Ethelwold, bishop of Winchester (963–984). Abbot Simeon (1081–1093), who had previously been a monk at Saint Ouen, Rouen,

[1] [Cf. RIVOIRA, *Roman Architecture*, p. 33.]

and prior of Winchester (where his brother Walkelin was bishop), took in hand its reconstruction in 1083. The work was completed in 1106 by Abbot Richard (1100–1107), formerly a monk of Bec ('ecclesiam suam a praedecessore suo incoeptam aedificavit'); and it was he who translated into it the body of St. Etheldreda.[1]

In 1109 the church became a cathedral. Bishop Geoffrey Ridel (1174–1189) erected the western transept, and a new west front with its tower nearly up to the roof; for

Fig. 664. Ely Cathedral. Nave (12th century)

this is surely the meaning of the words 'novum opus usque occidentem cum turre usque ad cumulum fere perfecit',[2] and not that he built the body of the church from the third bay west of the eastern crossing, or that he completed the west end of the old church, as has been suggested, for there is nothing in the building answering to such an interpretation.

Bishop Eustace (1198–1215) next added the narthex or Galilee to Ridel's work.[3] In the thirteenth century, under Bishop Northwold (1229–1254), the choir was lengthened;

[1] WHARTON, op. cit., part i, p. 613, *Thomae monachi Eliensis historia Eliensis.*

[2] WHARTON, op. cit., part i, p. 631, *Monachi Eliensis continuatio historiae Eliensis.*

[3] [The attribution of the Galilee at Ely to the period 1198–1215 rests on conjecture. The architectural details correspond more nearly with the advanced 13th-century work at the east end of the church. (H. T.)]

and the central tower, after its fall in 1322, was rebuilt as an octagon instead of a square, involving the demolition of two of the transept bays and the reconstruction of three of those of the choir. In this way all that was left of the work of the eleventh and twelfth centuries was the arms of the choir transept (figs. 662, 663), and the nave (fig. 664) as far as the western transept, the northern arm of which is wanting. The eastern transept is aisled. The central portion and the triforium had from the beginning wooden roofs, the aisles having unraised cross vaulting. The roofs of the nave and its aisles were treated on the same principle.

The general effect of Ely Cathedral recalls its elder sister, Winchester, and the hemispherical cubical capital predominates.

We do not share the theory that the nave of the church was completed by Bishop Ridel, or in the reign of Henry II (1154–1189). Besides being opposed to the statements of the Ely Chronicle, it is also at variance with the aspect of the building. The more recent parts of the eastern transept, which must be assigned to Abbot Richard—for the older, that is to say the plainer parts, belong, of course, to Simeon—show too strong analogies of organic structure, masonry, and decoration with the rest of the church for us not to recognize the single idea which informs it, and the impossibility of keeping that idea unchanged through the long series of years between 1106 and the reign of Henry II. The spirit, moreover, which animates Geoffrey Ridel's work is too distinct to allow us to regard it as a mere continuation of an unfinished structure left by his predecessors. On the contrary, the church must have been perfect and complete, as is indicated by the alterations required in order to fit the new work on to the old.

Fig. 665. Worcester Cathedral. Crypt (1084)

I think that the small Lombardic portal known as the 'Prior's doorway', a later insertion in the south aisle wall, should be ascribed to Ridel.[1] Its design is more in keeping with his time than with that of Eustace, in whose Galilee the pointed arch predominates.

Ely Cathedral was the first English church which exhibited the Romano-Ravennate decorative feature of an arched corbel course. But apart from this we have not discovered any other new element.

WORCESTER CATHEDRAL was rebuilt in 1084 by Bishop Wulstan II (1062–1095) in place of the church erected by Oswald, bishop of Worcester (961–992) and archbishop of

---

[1] [The doorway which communicated with the east, as the Prior's doorway with the west walk of the cloister, is of much the same date, but of very different design, with large medallion-shaped cusps with carved surfaces projecting from the intrados. This must belong to the latest years of the 12th century. (H. T.)]

York (972–992), which in its turn was the successor of the original structure (680) of the time of King Ethelred and Archbishop Theodore. It was seriously damaged by fire in 1113, and injured by the fall of the central tower in 1175; and the dedication did not take place till 1218.[1] The only parts of Wulstan's work spared by later reconstructions, which are of interest to us, are a considerable portion of the crypt under the choir, and a portion of the south-east pier of the central tower.

The crypt (fig. 665) consists of a rectangular central space, terminated by a semicircle with a surrounding ambulatory, flanked by two apsidal chapels. The capitals of the columns are of the Lombardic cubico-spherical type, occasionally chamfered off in the lower part in order to fit the shaft. Some of the bases are of Anglo-Saxon type, with two thick rolls and an ovolo.

What is left of the pier is interesting as illustrating the types of capital and base used in the church proper, which were the same as those in the crypt.

The remains of Wulstan's church contain no specially noteworthy feature. It was evidently the work of both Norman and Anglo-Saxon hands, the presence of the latter being betrayed by the fall of the central tower less than a century after its erection. The towers built by Norman masons did not share the fate which, as we have seen, befell the similar towers of Winchester and Ely. Norman hands are seen in the cross vaulting of the crypt, a task demanding skill only acquired by long practice in this difficult craft. The carvers employed were Anglo-Saxon, as can be seen from the clumsy attempts to decorate two of the plain capitals in the crypt, and also from the base mouldings. And this is confirmed by the decorative features of the arched passage or Slype (fig. 666) leading out of the west side of the cloister, where the bulbous capitals formed by a very large roll between two smaller ones (which inverted form the base as well), or by a curiously moulded bulbous roll, are surely of Anglo-Saxon character.

Fig. 666. Worcester Cathedral. Arcading in the Slype (1084)

THE PRIORY CHURCH, MALVERN, was founded by the monk Alvius or Aldwine in 1085.[2] The principal remains of the original church consist of the six arches on either side of the nave, supported by stout cylindrical piers (fig. 667) and their responds, with a portion of the wall above them; remains of the west front and south aisle; and the connexion between the latter and the transept. In the south wall there is also an original portal, the jamb shafts of which have bulbous

[1] *Rolls Series*, 36, *Annales monastici*, vol. iv, *Annales prioratus de Wigornia*, pp. 365, 370, 373, 375, 383, 409; *Rolls Series*, 52, *Willelmi Malm. monachi gesta pontificum Anglorum*, p. 283.

[2] *Rolls Series*, 36, *Annales monastici*, vol. iv, *Annales prioratus di Wigornia*, p. 373.

capitals and bases of the same shape, only inverted.   Both nave and aisles had wooden ceilings.

The construction of the church must be set down to Anglo-Saxon masons, whose presence is shown by the almost entire absence of ornament, and also by the decorative details of the portal.

Malvern Priory Church is noteworthy for an innovation in the form of the supports, that is to say, the employment of heavy cylindrical piers to carry the nave arches.[1] It is true that cylindrical piers had previously been used in the Chapel of the Pyx at

Fig. 667. Malvern. Priory Church (1085)

Westminster Abbey, in the crypt at Winchester, and the chapels of Durham Castle and the Tower of London; but all the same it was at Malvern that substantial supports of this form made their first appearance in an English monastic church of large size. From Malvern they spread over England, sometimes short and squat, in other cases elongated like their prototypes in St. Philibert at Tournus (1008–1019); in one place quite plain, in another decorated in various ways, and surmounted by the usual capital derived from the type we first found in the crypt at Winchester. They were either plain or else embellished with inverted truncated semi-cones, foliage, flowers, arcading, interlacing, lozenges, disks, and other ornamental motives. They occur in churches from London, where they appear in St. Bartholomew's, Smithfield, founded in 1123,[2] to Carlisle, where we find them in the Norman part of the cathedral (built when William Rufus restored the city in 1092) with spurs added at the corners of the base plinth, the earliest instance of this Lombardic feature known in England.

[1] [Dr. Bilson suggests that they were probably copied from the more important church of Gloucester. There is nothing to prove that the church at Great Malvern was begun as early as 1085. (R.)]

[2] E. A. WEBB, *The plan of St. Bartholomew's, West Smithfield, Archaeologia*, lxiv (1913), p. 165 ff.

These cylindrical piers had a long career, so that in the second half of the twelfth century we find them still employed, for instance, in the nave of Hereford Cathedral, belonging to the time of Bishop William de Vere (1186–1198). Or, again, in Waltham Abbey (fig. 668), founded as the Church of the Holy Cross and St. Laurence in 1062, and rebuilt by Henry II when he installed in it canons regular.[1] The original carving on the capitals of the south door exactly fits the second half of the twelfth century. Of the church consecrated in 1066 no trace is left.

GLOUCESTER CATHEDRAL.—St. Peter's Church, Gloucester, was originally founded in 681 by Osric, under a grant from Ethelred, king of Mercia (675–704). Another king

Fig. 668. Waltham Abbey Church (12th century)

of Mercia, Beornwulf (who according to Henry of Huntingdon[2] only reigned one year), rebuilt it in 823. Aldred, bishop of Worcester (1044–1061) and archbishop of York (1061–1069), rebuilt and dedicated it in 1058. Finally, Abbot Serlo (1072–1103), who had been a canon of Avranches and a monk at Mont Saint Michel, began to build it anew in 1089, not leaving one stone upon another of Aldred's work. The dedication took place in 1100.[3]

Extensive damage was done by the fire of 1102 ('ecclesia S. Petri Gloucestriae cum civitate igne cremata est'), and the church must have suffered again in 1122 when the monastery was burned.[4] At later dates it was again injured in parts by fire, suffered from an earthquake, lost one of its western towers, and was altered and partly rebuilt in the Pointed style.

The plan of Serlo's church is the usual one derived from William of Volpiano's design for Bernay (1013), that is to say a basilica of Latin cross form with nave and aisles, and two apses projecting from the eastern walls of the transept. The only

---

[1] *Rolls Series*, 36, *Annales mon.*, vol. ii, *Annales de Waverleia*, p. 241; LELAND, *Collectanea de rebus Britannicis* (London, 1770), vol. iii, tom. ii, pp. 208, 209.

[2] *Rolls Series*, 74, *Historia Anglorum*, pp. 132, 133.

[3] *Rolls Series*, 33, *Historia et cartularium monasterii S. Petri Gloucestriae*, vol. i, pp. 3–4, 9, 11, 12; DUGDALE, op. cit., i, p. 532.

[4] [Only the fire of 1122 damaged the church (information from Dr. Bilson). (R.)]

difference is in the two-storied ambulatory surrounding the choir, with three radiating chapels opening out of it.

The original crypt consisted of a central rectangular space with a semicircular end, enclosed by piers with arches. Columns divide it into three aisles, and it is encircled by

Fig. 669. Gloucester Cathedral. Capital in the crypt (1089–1100)

an ambulatory containing three radiating apsidal chapels. One of the capitals (fig. 669) has on one face a rude human head, as it were flattened, in very low relief without any undercutting. In the eastern radiating chapel the two columns which support the arch of the apse have capitals with four truncated inverted half-cones on the face, which form the archetype of the scalloped capital (fig. 670). At the entrance to the crypt are two more small chapels corresponding to those in the transept above.

The nave of the church is separated from the aisles by cylindrical piers (fig. 671). The first two bays, together with the west front, are work of the fifteenth century. The walls of the nave above the arches are pierced by pairs of two-light openings for the triforium (which has a wooden roof), divided by shafts with scalloped capitals. Above this runs the clerestory passage, altered when the wooden roof of the nave was replaced by vaulting.

The north aisle still retains its original unraised cross vaulting with moulded ribs. The awkward manner in which they meet the piers is due, not to the fact that the piers

Fig. 670. Gloucester Cathedral. Scalloped capital in the crypt (1089–1100)

were originally intended only for groined cross vaulting, but to the unfitness of cylindrical piers for receiving multiplied arches. For though such piers have over the Lombardic form the advantages of taking up less room and therefore facilitating circulation, and of permitting the passage of more light, they have at the same time the drawback of being ill adapted for carrying cross vaulting, which requires supports specially planned to receive it.

Considerable alterations were made in the transept in the course of the fourteenth and fifteenth centuries.

The choir has now lost its apse. The ambulatory is covered by unraised cross vaulting (fig. 672). Of the three radiating chapels which originally opened out of it, that on the south is well preserved. In it two rude wall-arches of pointed form should be noticed.

The interior of the choir now presents to the eye a facing of Perpendicular work, with a vaulted roof of the same style. No doubt it originally had a wooden roof. Wide spans were not vaulted in England till a much later date, and, moreover, if there had been vaulting it would have been preserved.[1]

[1] [It does not follow that, in a piece of work like that at Gloucester, which involved the complete transformation of the interior of the choir and an increase in height, the old vaulting would necessarily have been preserved. The possibility can hardly be assumed as a positive fact. (H. T.)]

The theory that the ramping barrel vaulting of the triforium was constructed to resist the thrust of the choir vault is readily disproved by the fact that, under exactly the same conditions, the nave of Saint Étienne at Caen had a wooden roof.

The ambulatory has an upper story, from which again three chapels originally opened. It has a half-barrel vault divided into sections by ramping transverse arches (fig. 673).

The Lombardo-Norman portions of Gloucester Cathedral belong to two different periods, and are the result of two distinct events, viz. Serlo's reconstruction, and the catastrophe of 1102. To the first belong the two-storied ambulatory of the choir and

Fig. 671. Gloucester Cathedral. Nave (12th century)

the crypt below it; to the second, the nave. Each period is revealed by characteristic features, which at the same time differentiate it from the other.

Thus the crypt and the choir have Lombardic cubical capitals, or else scalloped capitals, but not as yet perfected as in the body of the church. The choir arches, too, are in two orders, but not moulded. The unraised cross vaulting of the ambulatory is simply groined, and the transverse sustaining arches are clumsily fashioned. Moreover, ornament is in every case banished from the arches, and the wall supports consist of plain engaged shafts. Lastly, the choir has its ambulatory in two stories of the same width, and both vaulted. The choir and its junction with the transept are therefore to be regarded as undoubtedly the work of Serlo, for they are similar in style, and show a less advanced stage of art than the nave and aisles.

The body of the church, on the other hand, is the embodiment of constructive, statical, and decorative ideas which are diametrically opposed to all this. The squat piers of the choir are replaced by lofty ones, at the expense of the triforium stage, reduced to the smallest possible dimensions, and covered only by a sloping roof. The nave arches have mouldings and ornaments. In the aisle which remains the cross vaulting has moulded ribs, and is sustained, like the transverse arches, by half wall-piers with capitals, sometimes elaborately decorated, exhibiting carving which is superior both in design and execution to that of the ornamented capitals in the crypt.

It is easy to see that the choir and the nave of the cathedral are distinct from one another both in system and in date, a fact which has been remarked by others.[1] Accordingly, the nave is the result either of a rebuilding of Serlo's work which had been ruined by the fire of 1102, or of a completion of it after a new design. So sharp and marked a change in the work is inconceivable if the church had been begun and finished by the original architect. Moreover, that the nave was built after 1102 and not after 1122[2] is proved by the traces of fire still visible, which must be referred to the conflagration of 1122. Further, the transept turrets with their intersecting arcading are, in all

Fig. 672. Gloucester Cathedral. Ambulatory of choir (1089–1100)

probability, later than the days of Serlo, as this form of decoration did not appear in England before the erection of Durham Cathedral (1093).

Gloucester affords the earliest perfect specimens of the characteristic scalloped capital. We saw it in its elementary form at St. Albans, and now find it in its complete shape in the eastern chapel of the crypt, and in an embellished form in the body of the church.

It is also the earliest case in England of a choir and transept triforium entirely vaulted; while the two rude pointed arches in the south choir chapel are the earliest instance of the use of that form in construction. It was not long before it was employed in one of the monastic buildings connected with the church. The difference between the construction of the cross vaulting in the crypt and that in the lower choir ambulatory, and also the occurrence in the crypt of foliated capitals and of one with a human head, show that both Norman and English carvers and masons were employed. The Normans,

[1] F. Bond, *English cathedrals illustrated*, p. 95.

[2] [The use of chevron ornament in the arches of the main arcade and triforium points to the date of construction as after 1122; but the design may have been made and the eastern part of the nave begun earlier. The details show an advance upon those of the nave at Tewkesbury, which was probably begun, if not completed, by the time of the consecration of the church in 1121, and is otherwise identical in design with the nave at Gloucester, and shows a corresponding change in elevation from the choir. Which of the two churches originated the design is uncertain, but Tewkesbury was the first to bring it to completion. (H. T.)]

for instance, are responsible for the best of the vaulting in the crypt. The foliated capitals and the carved head must also be ascribed to them. Buildings erected in England in the eleventh century, after the Conquest, are almost devoid of artistic features of this kind, so common in Normandy; and this means that, for the time immediately following the Conquest, wherever we do not find Anglo-Lombardic or scalloped capitals and bulbous bases, there, in all probability, we may recognize Norman hands.

Before leaving Gloucester Cathedral we may observe that the Chapter House, altered at the east end, embellished internally with blank arcading, covered by a pointed barrel vault provided with transverse moulded ribs, and with traces of fire, seems to show

Fig. 673. Gloucester Cathedral. Upper ambulatory of choir (1089–1100)

the same decorative motives as the nave (zigzags and billets), and should be dated after the fire of 1102. To the same period belong the arched passage or Slype on the south side of the Chapter House, and some parts of the old Abbot's Lodging, the present Deanery, for instance, the rectangular room with a barrel vault and scalloped capitals.[1] These buildings, having solid roofs, may have escaped the disaster which destroyed the monastery in 1122.

NORWICH CATHEDRAL was founded with the dedication of the Holy Trinity in 1096 by the Norman bishop, Herbert Losinga (1094–1119),[2] originally prior of Fécamp, then abbot of Ramsey, and afterwards bishop of Thetford, whence he transferred the see to Norwich in 1094.[3] The greater part of it is his work.[4] The 'Registrum primum', preserved in the Cathedral Treasury, states how far the work of Herbert reached, viz. to the altar of the Cross or St. William on the north of the choir enclosure, though the writer's information was only derived from the tradition current in his time.

[1] [The room in the Deanery at Gloucester is probably later than 1122: the capitals are more like work of 1160–1170. (H. T.)]

[2] DUGDALE, op. cit., vol. iv, p. 1.

[3] WHARTON, op. cit., part i, p. 397, *Bartolomei de*

Cotton monachi Norwicensis annales Ecclesiae Norwi-censis.

[4] WHARTON, op. cit., part i, pp. 407, 409, *Historia de episcopis Norwicensibus.*

In the 'Anglia Sacra'[1] Bishop John of Oxford (1175–1200) is credited with the completion of the church, but the work of this prelate was really confined to the repairs necessitated by the fire of 1171. I believe that the cathedral was finished by Herbert Losinga's immediate successor, Everard (1121–1145), a view which is confirmed by the evidence of the building itself.

Norwich Cathedral, though it has lost two of the five choir chapels,[2] while a third has been altered, and though the choir has been tampered with, together with the transept (the chapel in the northern arm has disappeared), aisles, and lantern tower, while nave, choir, and transept have been vaulted in the Pointed style, nevertheless, on the whole, still retains its original form. The plan reproduces that of Gloucester,

Fig. 674. Norwich Cathedral. Choir (11th and 12th centuries)

with the variation that the choir chapels are lobed instead of being rectangular with apsidal end.

The original piers of the choir (fig. 674) consist of cylinders with engaged shafts and pilasters. The ambulatory has unraised cross vaulting of a superior character to that in a similar position at Gloucester. The triforium above has a wooden roof. Originally it must have contained ramping arches designed to give support to the lofty walls of the choir, which had a wooden roof before the construction in the fifteenth century of the present vaulting. The clerestory has been altered. The two-lobed chapels opening out of the ambulatory, and the outer walls of the choir, are decorated with blank arcading.

In the transept, which, again, had at first a wooden roof, may be seen ranges of blank arcading either simple or intersecting, with the arches in some cases surmounted by gables. A quasi-triforium is formed in the thickness of the wall, at the level of that in the choir. The openings for the clerestory passage are either single, in pairs, or in triplets with the centre one higher than the others.

[1] WHARTON, op. cit., part i, pp. 407, 409, *Historia de episcopis Norwicensibus*.

[2] [The two chapels which project at the springing of the curve of the ambulatory at Norwich remain. Neither of the chapels which projected from the east wall of the transept (probably included in the five chapels mentioned in the text) is left. The apsidal Lady chapel was superseded by another with a square end in the 13th century, which in its turn was destroyed in the 16th century. (H. T.)]

The interior of the tower has on each side an arcaded wall passage, above which is a range of pairs of blank arches, with a round opening at either end. The upper story, with its own wall passage, and elaborately ornamented, is an addition to Herbert's tower, as is shown by the difference of the original masonry.

Fig. 675. Norwich Cathedral. Nave (11th and 12th centuries)

The nave and aisles are divided by supports, alternately larger and smaller,[1] after the Lombardic fashion (fig. 675). Where they have not been refaced they consist alternately of compound piers and cylinders (either plain or with spiral grooving) for the first six arches: the rest are compound piers. The aisles have unraised cross vaulting, and are decorated with blank arcading.

[1] [The alternation of triple roof-shafts, the capitals of which were originally at the level of the clerestory stringcourse, with single shafts, whose capitals range with those of the triforium, is a feature of Norwich, which also existed in the Norman nave of Winchester, as may still be seen at the back of the later work. In the earlier part of the church the prevailing type of capital is the Norman crocketed type, which disappears in the western portions. (H. T.)]

We said that the erection of the cathedral, interrupted by the death of Bishop Herbert (1119), was completed by his successor Everard, and not by Bishop John of Oxford (1175–1200). If an interval of more than half a century had elapsed before the work was resumed, we should never have found that unity of conception and execution which pervades the building, a unity manifested by the masonry, the architectural decoration, and, with one exception, the arrangement of the church, and of so obvious a character that it takes a skilled eye to discover the line which divides the work of Herbert from that of Everard. That line is to be found in the sixth bay of the nave, for it is there that the cylindrical piers on the ground floor come to an end. Our dates for the two sets of building operations bring the statement of the Norwich Chronicle as to Herbert's share in the work into agreement with the account in the 'Registrum primum', and with the evidence of the structure itself.

Fig. 676. Rome. Tomb of Eurysaces (1st century B.C. or 1st century A.D.)

As we look at Norwich Cathedral we cannot but be impressed by the feeling that the exterior view of the choir and transept presents a whole of an imposing effect which is not equalled by that of any other church in the Lombardo-Norman style (see frontispiece to this volume).

The most notable features are the following:

(1) The circular openings, either closed or forming windows.

The combination and disposition of such round openings with a raised edge on the tower of Norwich is curiously reminiscent of the well-known tomb of Eurysaces and his wife Atistia, just outside the Porta Maggiore (Praenestina) at Rome (fig. 676), believed to belong to the end of the Republic or at latest to the first years of the Empire.[1] Or it may have been derived from the round openings of a campanile such as the early eleventh-century one belonging to San Francesco at Ravenna. It was only about the middle of that century that such circular openings, either forming windows or with a decorative purpose, began to appear in English towers, as the examples at Earl's Barton, Cambridge, and Great Dunham inform us. From Norwich it soon passed to Exeter, where the south tower of the cathedral, begun by Bishop William Warelwast (1107–1136) and finished by Bishop Henry Marshall (1194–1206), displays rows of these openings between smaller ones of the same form in groups of two, four, or five. From Exeter it travelled to Ely, where the great west tower has rows of circular openings each containing a

[1] CAETANI LOVATELLI, *Passeggiate nella Roma antica, Il sepolcro di Eurisace fuori della Porta Maggiore in Roma*, p. 151. [It is attributed to the end of the Republic by Mrs. STRONG, *Art in Ancient Rome* (London, 1929), vol. i, p. 94, and by PLATNER and ASHBY, *Topographical Dictionary of Ancient Rome*, p. 479. Despite the resemblance, the tomb of Eurysaces is not very likely to have influenced the builders of the tower at Norwich, for only a few of the large round vertical mixing bowls, to the depth of one row, were visible (see Sallustio Peruzzi's drawing in the Uffizi, no. 663 recto, reproduced by BARTOLI, op. cit., vol. iv, tav. ccclxxxiv). The semicircular tower erected by Honorius over the tomb had been in medieval times replaced, as regards its upper part, by a small rectangular turret, perched high up on it, but if the drawing is correct, its front and sides cannot have been 'almost completely disclosed' (RICHMOND, *City Wall of Imperial Rome*, p. 207; cf. PLATNER and ASHBY, *Topographical Dictionary of Ancient Rome*, pp. 413, 479—in the first passage the tower is wrongly attributed to Aurelian). (A.)]

quatrefoil. These smaller apertures had occurred previously in connexion with the five-light openings on the tower at Earl's Barton.

Round openings had already been used by the Roman builders to provide air and light for the wooden roofs of buildings and for the buildings themselves, as may be seen in the Temple of Ceres and Faustina, now Sant' Urbano, in the Valle Caffarella near Rome, erected by Herodes Atticus in the second century A.D., where the end of the building is pierced by a large round opening flanked by two windows. Their use was also extended to cupolas. Plenty of instances can be found, either in surviving remains or drawings of buildings which have disappeared. Such are the so-called 'Tempio di Siepe' (fig. 421) at Rome; the circular mausoleum in the Villa of the Gordians on the Via Praenestina near Rome; a presumable bath chamber shown in one of Bramantino's sketches reproduced by Mongeri;[1] a structure of uncertain character which appears as an illustration in our account of the Holy Sepulchre, and has its cupola lighted by a row of round openings (fig. 413); and, lastly, the so-called Tower of Boethius at Pavia (which fell in 1584), the appearance of which has been preserved for us by Sangallo[2] and Spelta (fig. 677).[3]

(2) The double-cone moulding, which reappears for the first time after the Romano-British age in this cathedral.

As we look at the exterior and seek for points of comparison, we are struck by the fact that, in spite of the lavish use of blank arcading, there is no suggestion of the external open galleries which had just at this time come into fashion in Italy. The explanation of their absence is to be found in the fact that when Herbert Losinga, before the transfer of the see to Norwich and the foundation of the cathedral there, visited Rome about the year 1093 in order to surrender the ring and pastoral staff which he had obtained by simoniacal means,[4] this architectural motive was only just making its appearance in its simplest form on the chapel of St. Aquilinus at Milan.

[1] [Op. cit., pl. ii.]   [2] Vatican Libr., *Barb. Lat.* 4424, f. 13ᵛ.
[3] *Historia de' fatti notabili occorsi nell'universo e in particolare nel Regno de' Gothi, ecc.* (Pavia, 1602), p. 106.
[4] *Rolls Series*, 68, *Radulfi de Diceto opera historica*, vol. i, p. 219.

Fig. 677. Pavia. Tower of Boethius

TEWKESBURY ABBEY CHURCH is believed to have been founded in 715 with a dedication to the Virgin, and must have been in existence in 800, for in that year (or in 802) Brihtric, king of Wessex, is said to have been buried in the chapel of St. Faith. It was refounded by Robert Fitz-Hamon, and put under Giraldus, abbot of Cranbourne, who now became the first abbot of Tewkesbury (1102–1109). The precise date of this new foundation is not known, but there are grounds for believing that it took place in 1102

Fig. 678. Tewkesbury Abbey Church (12th century)

when Giraldus and his monks at Cranbourne moved to Tewkesbury. The new church appears to have been dedicated in 1123.[1] It suffered from fire in 1178, and the new work visible at the top of the nave walls is to be explained by this disaster. It was not, however, 'redacta in pulverem' as the Winchester annalist says,[2] for traces of the fire

---

[1] *Rolls Series*, 51, *Chronica magistri Rogeri de Houedene*, vol. i, p. 28; DUGDALE, op. cit., ii, p. 54; *Rolls Series*, 36, *Annales monasterii de Theokesberia*, vol. i, pp. 44, 45. [The date 1123 for the dedication of Tewkesbury has been frequently accepted, as here, from the *Annales* of the monastery, a work which is of little historical value for that period; and it has been generally unrecognized that, on the day named in this chronicle, the bishop of Worcester, who is said to have officiated, was no longer alive. The real date, 1121, is given with details which put it beyond doubt, by 'Florence' of Worcester, who was a contemporary. (H. T.)]

[2] *Rolls Series*, 36, *Annales mon.*, vol. ii, *Annales de Wintonia*, p. 61.

are still to be seen on the fabric. In the course of the restoration the choir and transept were retouched, vaulting substituted for the wooden roof, and the form of nearly all the windows changed. Nevertheless, with the exception of the choir, the church remains as it was in the first quarter of the twelfth century (fig. 678). The plan is copied from that of Gloucester.[1]

Tewkesbury Abbey, built under the direction of a monk, whose name Alfred points to his being an Englishman, contains the following distinctive features:

Fig. 679. Tewkesbury Abbey Church. Nave (12th century)

(1) The spurred bases in the arcaded wall-passages of the nave (fig. 679); the second instance of this feature that we have met with in England, the first being at Carlisle.

(2) The great recess of the west front (fig. 680), apparently suggested by the one in a similar position in the Palatine Chapel at Aachen (796–804), copied again by Bishop Alexander (1123–1148) in his cathedral at Lincoln.[2]

(3) The unraised cross vaulting with square-edged ribs in the chapel on the ground floor of the transept, undoubtedly belonging to the early years of the twelfth century,

[1] [For the relation of the Tewkesbury design to that of Gloucester, see note 2 on p. 238. (H. T.)]

[2] [See note 6 on p. 221, for the probable date of the various parts of the west front of Lincoln. (H. T.)]

and probably to the time of Abbot Giraldus; consequently one of the first examples to be found in England.

On taking leave of Tewkesbury we may observe that the triforium-like passage with pairs of openings was derived[1] from the one in Chester Abbey Church (fig. 681) (which only became a cathedral in 1541), begun in 1093 by Hugh Lupus, Earl of Chester, who imported monks from Bec, and made Anselm's chaplain, Richard, their abbot (1093–1117), and finished by Abbot William (1121–1140). The foundation of Hugh Lupus

Fig. 680. Tewkesbury Abbey Church. West front
(12th century)

Fig. 681. Chester Cathedral. North arm of
transept (11th century)

replaced the original one of Wulfhere, king of Mercia (657–675), restored by Athelstan (925–940), and dedicated to St. Werburgh.[2]

The quasi-triforium of Tewkesbury also recalls the one in the transept of Pershore Abbey (the history of which is given by William of Malmesbury[3] and Dugdale[4]), which I believe does not represent the rebuilding of the wooden church burned in 1000, but belongs to the years immediately before the refounding of Tewkesbury.

SOUTHWELL CATHEDRAL.—We know on the authority of the chronicler Thomas Stubbs that the church of St. Mary, Southwell, was as old as the time of Kynsige, archbishop

---

[1] [The similarity of the triforium openings at Tewkesbury to the arcading at Chester may be admitted, but there is no proof of direct derivation. (H. T.)]

[2] *Rolls Series*, 52, *Willelmi Malm. monachi gesta*

pontificum Anglorum, p. 308[1].

[3] *Rolls Series*, 52, *Willelmi Malm. monachi gesta pontificum Anglorum*, p. 298.

[4] *Op. cit.*, vol. ii, p. 410.

of York (1051–1060), who gave it two large bells.[1] The same writer mentions it again in his account of Archbishop Aldred (1060–1069). The new foundation is generally admitted to have taken place under Thomas II, archbishop of York (1109–1114), for the 'Registrum Album' of the church contains a letter from an Archbishop Thomas to the people of his diocese in the County of Nottingham asking for a contribution of alms

Fig. 682. Southwell Cathedral. Nave (12th century)

towards the building. The writer cannot be either Thomas I (1070–1100) or Thomas III (1300–1304), for there is nothing in the structure answering to the dates of these prelates.

The new church (fig. 682) had its choir rebuilt in the thirteenth century: the rest retains its original form, though it has lost the two transept chapels.[2] The nave was designed with a wooden roof, while the aisles had unraised, ribbed cross vaulting (fig. 683).

Southwell Cathedral appears to me to be the result of two distinct sets of operations,

[1] *Rolls Series*, 71, *The historians of the Church of York—Chronica pontificum Ecclesiae Eboracensis: pars prima, auctore anonymo*, p. 344.

[2] [The north transept chapel at Southwell gave place to an aisle, containing two chapels in the 13th century. The blocked arch which communicated with the south transept chapel remains. (H. T.)]

during the first of which the building was finished as far as the nave, while the second saw the completion of the church. This would explain the change in the mouldings of the arches in the aisle vaulting. But there can have been only a short interval between them, for the structure is evidently the result of a single conception. The interruption may have been connected with the disturbed beginning of Thurstan's primacy (1114–1140).[1] The two operations fall within the period between 1108 and about 1125, and in any case they cannot belong to the time of Thomas I, on account of the great cylindrical piers with ornamented capitals, and of the ribbed cross vaulting. Still less can they fall in the years of Thomas III, for in that case Southwell would have been a church in the Pointed style.

Southwell, with Gloucester and Peterborough, proves that by the first quarter of the twelfth century Lombardic ribbed cross vaulting was diffused in England. Its other noteworthy features are these:

First come the round windows which light the nave and transept (fig. 684). This form of aperture, which we shall notice presently in the church of Steinbach near Michelstadt (815–819), and in the ninth-century cathedral of Cologne, had at this time come into fashion at Rome under Paschal II (1099–1118), as SS. Giovanni e Paolo, restored after the fire of Guiscard in 1084,[2] and San Clemente tell us. The form in which it occurs at Southwell was afterwards introduced in Waltham Abbey (1177).

Fig. 683. Southwell Cathedral. North aisle of nave (12th century)

Secondly, there is the pointed-arched arcading which decorates the south-western tower, the earliest example of the sort in England (fig. 685).

---

[1] [There seems little ground for connecting the disturbances, of a purely political character, which delayed Thurstan's consecration, with the interruption of architectural work in a church of his diocese. The changes at Southwell are more likely to have been caused by a change in master-masons. The direct influence of prelates on the fabrics of their churches is always questionable, apart from the encouragement and benefactions which they supplied: work once set on foot was not interrupted by their absence, and its continuity was subject mainly to the condition of funds. The actual employers of labour in such churches were the chapters who were their governing body, as appears clearly from surviving building accounts; and, although these are deficient for the 12th century, there is no reason to suppose that there was any difference between the normal organization then and at a later period. It is noteworthy that Gervase's account of the rebuilding of the choir of Canterbury contains no mention of the archbishop as in any way connected with the operations. (H.T.)]

[2] P. GERMANO DI S. STANISLAO, op. cit., p. 391.

Inside the church we should also notice the Corinthianesque 'storied' capitals, with crockets at the angles embellished with roses and other ornaments, belonging to the great eastern arch of the crossing (fig. 686). They exhibit subjects from sacred story, with figures of infantile design; and also display scroll-work, lilies, crosses, leaves, flowers, the symbolical lamb and cross, a dove, and a chaotic group of fanciful buildings with arches and round windows which seems to represent Jerusalem, and has been described, without the smallest foundation, as a church in the Byzantine style.[1]

Fig. 684. Southwell Cathedral (12th century)

It has been thought that these reliefs, now a good deal hidden by the organ, are Anglo-Saxon, because they have analogies with illuminations of the epoch about 1000 (forgetting that illumination is one thing and carving another), and that they were incorporated in the twelfth-century church,[1] without considering that these capitals exactly fit the shafts below them and were obviously made on purpose for them, and that the continuous abacus is of the regular Norman pattern, and, thirdly, that the crockets at the angles betray a similar origin.

Moreover, it is inconceivable that, at the end of the tenth century or the beginning of the eleventh, the Anglo-Saxon artists should have been capable of producing figure subjects, of rude character it is true, but at the same time of such broad artistic conception, while their successors, who had so many more opportunities for the practice of their chisels after the Conquest, avoided, for a considerable period and as much as they could,

[1] *Notices of archaeological publications*; *The illustrated archaeologist*; *Archaeologia Oxoniensis* (1893), part iii, p. 188.

the representation in carving, not only of figures, but even of foliage, and confined themselves of set purpose to geometrical forms in which they could use the axe instead of the chisel, to such an extent that in a structure of the celebrity of Ernulf's and Conrad's choir at Canterbury (1096–1130) they used the former exclusively: 'Ibi arcus et caetera omnia plana, utpote sculpta secure et non scisello.'[1]

Fig. 685. Southwell Cathedral. West end (12th century)

OXFORD CATHEDRAL.—Ethelred II's monastery was refounded after the appointment by Roger, bishop of Salisbury (1107–1139), in 1111 of Prior Guimund, chaplain to Henry I (1100–1135), who provided a large endowment. Prior Robert of Cricklade (1141–1180) obtained from Pope Hadrian IV (1154–1159) a confirmation of the new privileges of his priory (1158). In 1180 the translation of the body of St. Frideswide took place, and in 1190 the church suffered from a fire: 'Combusta est ecclesia Sanctae Frideswide.'[2] With the last event we conclude the history of the church, so far as it has reached us, as being all that is of immediate interest for our purpose.

Oxford Cathedral contains no new element which can contribute to an exposition of the development of Lombardo-Norman architecture in Great Britain. But we may well spend a short time over a church situated in so ancient and celebrated a seat of culture and learning, especially as more has been written about it to lead students astray than to guide them along the path of truth.

The oldest parts of the building show three separate constructions, and it is with reference to their respective dates that the erroneous opinions have been formulated which we shall endeavour as briefly as possible to refute.

We have already spoken of the scanty remains of Ethelred's church, incorporated in the new one erected by Prior Guimund about 1111, the walls of which are constructed of rubble faced with courses of dressed stone. The similarity between the construction

[1] *Rolls Series*, 73, *Gervasii monachi Cantuariensis opera historica*, vol. i, p. 27.
[2] DUGDALE, op. cit., vol. ii, p. 136; *Rolls Series*, 36, *Annales Monastici*, vol. iv, *Annales de Oseneia et chronicon Thomae Wykes*, pp. 39, 43; *Rolls Series*, 52, *Willelmi Malm. gesta pontificum Anglorum*, p. 316.

of these walls and those of the church of Bernay (1013) (we say nothing of that of Fécamp, of the year 990, which is also adduced in evidence, because we showed that there is no existing trace of it above ground) has given rise to the suggestion that they belong to the days of Ethelred. But this does not take into account the difference between the condition of Normandy at the beginning of the eleventh century—a prosperous, well-governed country, under the influence of the artistic and intellectual movement created by William of Volpiano and his fellow labourers, and that of England bleeding from the wounds inflicted by wars and invasions, not to speak of the vengeance, accentuated by famine, that the massacre of St. Brice's day had brought on the unhappy country.

Fig. 686. Southwell Cathedral. Capital in
the crossing (12th century)

Fig. 687. Oxford Cathedral. Opening in
quasi-triforium (12th century)

Nor does the theory consider that, from the time of Wilfrid (634–709) to that of Edward the Confessor (1041 or 1042–1066), no English dated church exhibits masonry of this kind.

That it really belongs to Guimund's work is clearly proved by two things. The first is the presence of the much discussed pair of openings from the old quasi-triforium in the south arm of the transept, with their bulbous based shafts, their capitals with two scallops on each face, and their plain arches (fig. 687). St. Albans Cathedral (1077–1088) was the first building of certain date to show capitals of the kind. There is no trace of a quasi-triforium of this sort before that in Chester Cathedral, founded in 1093. It is impossible, therefore, that Ethelred's church can have exhibited these features, which had not been thought of in his time.

The second is the presence of thick cylindrical piers in Ethelred's reputed work, but really that of Guimund. These piers have obviously been altered, but we are not without information as to the kind of capital they possessed, for in the south choir aisle two of Guimund's time remain, with their capitals showing stiff, plain leaves at the angles. But English churches of large size did not contain stout cylindrical piers before Aldwine's application of them in Malvern Priory Church (1085), though the School of

Lanfranc had used them in the crypt of Winchester Cathedral and the chapel of the Tower of London, but of smaller dimensions.

Guimund's church did not remain long intact, perhaps on account of defects in construction, which would explain the new facing with which it was invested; or, it may be, owing to injury received when Stephen burned Oxford in 1152. Certain it is that the structure was remodelled, partly by rebuilding, partly by alterations, partly by facing the old work with new. All this was carried out by Prior Robert of Cricklade, after the confirmation of 1158 had put him in a position to do so, and very probably about 1170; so that the work was quite finished in 1180 when the translation of St. Frideswide took place, an event which must have been subsequent to the renewal of the church. As long ago as 1762 Thomas Warton[1] had fixed on 1180 as the date of Christ Church.

The no less discussed capitals in the choir (fig. 688), though much decayed, are additional evidence as to the date of this restoration. They are decorated with crocket leaves, others bent as if blown by the wind, palmetto leaves, and interlaced stalks completely undercut. All are worked with a sure and vigorous hand, and have a suggestion of the Pointed style. The treatment of the foliage indicates a date contemporary with that of similar work in Canterbury Cathedral, of 1175 to 1184. The partial damage shown by their surface may be explained by some injury suffered, perhaps in the fire of 1190, involving their being scraped over.

Fig. 688. Oxford Cathedral. Choir (12th century)

PETERBOROUGH CATHEDRAL[2] was destroyed by fire in 1115, and two years later Abbot John of Séez (1114–1125) took in hand its rebuilding. After his death the work made slow progress, his successor, Henry of Anjou (1128–1133), if we are to believe the account of him in the Anglo-Saxon Chronicle, not being the person best fitted for the task. It was not till 1140 or 1143 that the monks took possession of the new choir which had been completed by Abbot Martin of Bec (1133–1155). The works were continued under Abbots William of Waterville (1155–1175), who erected the transept and the

[1] *Essay on Gothic Architecture* in *Observations on the Faerie Queene of Spenser* (2nd ed., 1802), p. 4.
[2] [The architectural history of Peterborough Cathedral has been worked out with great skill by Sir C. R. PEERS in the *Victoria County History of Northamptonshire*, iii, as part of the topographical account of the city and its buildings. (H. T.)]

three lower stages of the lantern tower, and Benedict (1177–1193), who constructed the nave as far as the west end. The last additions were the western transept and west front, and the church was dedicated in 1237 under Abbot Walter of Bury St. Edmunds (1233–1245).[1]

In later times, from the thirteenth century onwards, the bell-tower was erected, the windows altered, the central tower rebuilt in the Pointed style keeping only two of

Fig. 689. Peterborough Cathedral. South arm of transept (12th century)

the supporting arches and the piers, recently reconstructed on the old lines. Further, a porch was added to the west front, and the eastern end of the choir was concealed by a new structure. In 1541 the abbey church became a cathedral.

Choir, transept (figs. 689, 690), and nave (fig. 691) were designed with wooden ceilings, but the aisles had from the beginning unraised ribbed cross vaulting (fig. 692). The date of the painted ceiling of the nave has been the subject of much controversy.[2]

[1] SPARKE, op. cit., *Chronicon Angliae per Johannem abbatem Burgi S. Petri*, p. 107; *Hugonis Candidi coenobii Burgensis historia*, p. 117.

[2] [The usual view of the date of the nave ceiling is that it is a reconstruction of the Norman ceiling at the period mentioned in the text, but with little alteration

I have examined it, especially from under the roof, and have come to the conclusion that it belongs to the fourteenth century, when the lantern of the central tower and its eastern and western arches were rebuilt, and the original flat ceiling was replaced by a new one which fitted the new pointed western arch of the tower. Moreover, we cannot

Fig. 690. Peterborough Cathedral. North arm of transept (12th century)

imagine that there would have been any question of so rich a ceiling at a time when the nave which it covered showed such poverty of decoration.

Peterborough Cathedral tells the same story as the one preserved by the Chronicle and History of the monastery to which we have referred. The work of John of Séez

of general design. The flat transept ceilings, now without colour, may be reasonably assigned to the 12th century, and show a similar pattern of lozenge-shaped panelling. (H. T.)]

includes the apsidal end of the choir with its perfectly plain arches, and the choir aisles west of the apse, where again the capitals are absolutely plain. To Abbot Martin are to be assigned the upper story of the choir aisles, which shows a larger amount of ornament and embellished capitals, and also the eastern side of the transept. William of Waterville is responsible for the completion of the transept and the erection of the first two bays of the nave and aisles, where the tympana of the triforium arches repeat the decoration found in the choir and transept. Benedict extended the nave to the west end.

Fig. 691. Peterborough Cathedral. Nave (12th century)

The unraised ribbed cross vaulting in the choir aisles should be noted. It is original and not the result of alterations in the course of which the diagonal ribs were added, as has been mistakenly suggested. This I was able to verify for myself when the central tower was being rebuilt. This vaulting was unquestionably constructed between 1117 and 1125, and it provides a fixed point for the history of Lombardic ribbed cross vaulting in England.

DURHAM CATHEDRAL,[1] erected and dedicated in 998 by Bishop Aldhun (990–1019),

[1] [The architectural questions relating to the construction of Durham Cathedral are fully treated by J. BILSON, The Beginnings of Gothic Architecture (Journ. R.I.B.A., 3rd ser., vi. 259–69, 289–319); and Durham Cathedral, The Chronology of its Vaults (Archaeol. Journal (1922), lxxix. 101–60). These papers,

was rebuilt by Bishop William of Saint-Calais (1080–1096), first a secular priest of the church at Bayeux, and then monk and prior of the convent of Saint Carilef (Saint-Calais). The first stone was laid in 1093. How much of the building he erected we do not know precisely. All we are told is that, after a vacancy of three years in the see, William's successor, Rannulf Flambard (1099–1129), found that the work of the late bishop and the monks reached as far as the nave. These works, which must have included the two easternmost bays of the nave aisles, as the cross vaulting is of the same character as that in the choir aisles and transept, were not completed; for we hear that at the translation of the relics of St. Cuthbert in 1104 the choir was still blocked up with the timber used for the construction of the recently finished vaulting.

Fig. 692. Peterborough Cathedral. South aisle (12th century)

Between 1129 and 1133, when there was another vacancy in the see, the monks completed the nave, that is to say, they roofed it with vaulting, as we are told in a well-known passage relating to Rannulf's work: 'His namque sumptibus navem ecclesiae circumductis parietibus ad sui usque testudinem erexerat'—'muros navis novae ecclesiae Dunelmensis fabricavit.'[1]

Durham Cathedral, though deprived of its original east end, replaced by the secondary transept in the thirteenth century, with the central tower almost entirely rebuilt, the west front altered and partially concealed by the present Galilee, the western towers raised by four arcaded stories, and changes effected in other ways, still remains on the whole such as it was when erected between 1093 and 1133 (fig. 693). The plan is that of a Latin cross with choir, nave, and aisles, terminating originally in an apse with minor apses at the sides. The choir aisles (fig. 694) have ribbed cross vaulting of parabolic form springing from alternately larger and smaller supports. The choir itself (fig. 695) has thirteenth-century vaulting replacing the earlier vaulting which threatened to collapse. In the transept (fig. 696), both the aisles and the central space are also covered with ribbed cross vaulting. We observe here corbels with semi-human heads recalling those we noticed in Saint Étienne at Caen. Later they will be

though their main conclusions have been contested by some foreign writers, notably R. de Lasteyrie, may fairly be said to prove the case for the priority of the use of ribbed vaulting at Durham to any employment of it in France, where shortly afterwards it made such rapid progress. The view of the date of the vaults expressed in Signor Rivoira's minute description does not differ materially from that of Mr. Bilson, and, as noted on p. 262, was foreshadowed by Dr. Greenwell in his well-known handbook to the cathedral. On the other hand, the theory which regards the Durham vaulting as a unique example for its date of the

employment of Lombardic methods outside Italy is difficult to explain, considering the distance of Durham from such influence, and the contemporary progress which Romanesque art was making in the intervening districts. (H. T.)]

[1] *Rolls Series*, 75, *Symeonis monachi historia Eccl. Dunelm.*, vol. i, p. 129; *Rolls Series*, 75, *Symeonis monachi hist. Eccl. Dunelm. continuatio*, vol. i, p. 139; *Rolls Series* 52, *Willelmi Malm. monachi gesta pontificum Anglorum*, pp. 272, 276; Leland, *De rebus Britannicis collectanea*, vol. ii, tom. i, p. 332.

used to ornament the apex of hood-mouldings above pointed arches in naves. These heads sometimes have the tongue protruding, the source of the equally characteristic monster heads with the tongue curled over the roll moulding, which occur in English doorways of the twelfth century, for instance at Lincoln and Southwell Cathedrals. They are rude work, but vigorously treated; and an experienced eye can see that the original heads in the south arm of the transept are artistically somewhat superior to those in the north.

The nave is separated from the aisles by arches resting on compound piers alternating with cylindrical piers (fig. 697). Its cross vaulting is ribbed, and sustained by transverse arches of pointed form springing from corbel heads like those just described, but

Fig. 693. Durham Cathedral (11th and 12th centuries)

artistically more elementary than the similar ones which ornament the apex of the hood-mouldings above the pointed arches in the nave of Malmesbury Abbey, erected some time after 1153. The fact that these corbel heads are a later addition shows that the architect of the nave intended merely to throw transverse arches across it, and cover it with a wooden roof. The ribbed cross vaulting in the two easternmost bays of the nave aisles has plain ribs, as in the choir and transept aisles and in the north arm of the transept. In the case of the other bays the diagonal ribs have the zigzag moulding, which shows that Rannulf Flambard took up the work at the second bay.

Intersecting blank arcading is freely used on the ground floor of the church. There is a triforium, with a clerestory passage above. The west front is also decorated with intersecting arcading. The archivolts of the central portal are ornamented with zigzags, foliage, medallions with human and animal figures. The jambs are left plain. The simple treatment of this doorway as compared with the two elaborately decorated ones near the west end of the aisles (fig. 698), the shallow relief, and flat, clumsy character of its carving, show that there is an interval of several years between them. The aisle doorways may very well belong to the time of that great builder, Bishop Hugh Pudsey (1153–1195).

In the original parts of the cathedral the Lombardic cubico-spherical capital and the scalloped capital predominate. The only exceptions are the Corinthianesque specimens on the internal doorway near the south arm of the transept, and four others of the same type which occur in the blank arcading of the nave aisles. For bases the prevailing forms are (1) the Norman type found in Saint Étienne and Saint Nicholas at Caen, consisting of two hollow chamfers, so shallow that they appear almost like a single straight chamfer; (2) that formed by one or two slight hollow chamfers and an ovolo; and (3) that moulded into a hollow between two very flat ovolos.

Fig. 694. Durham Cathedral. North choir aisle
(11th century)

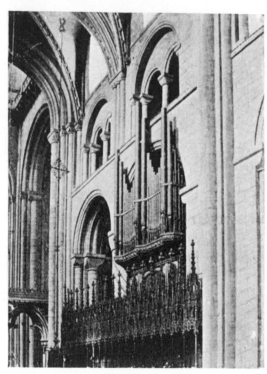

Fig. 695. Durham Cathedral. Choir (11th and
12th centuries)

Durham Cathedral presents three peculiar features worth attention.

First and foremost is the intersecting blank arcading in the choir aisles.[1] It is the earliest specimen outside Italy: previously there had been nothing but small intersecting arches such as are carved on a capital in the crypt of Lastingham Church (about 1078). It was an Anglo-Norman invention, but whether derived from the large arches intersecting two smaller ones in the great Mosque at Cordova (785–900), or from the intersecting arches used in carving by the Romans and the Lombard gilds, it is impossible to say. Certain it is that it did not appear before the last quarter of the eleventh century.

Then there is the decorative treatment of various forms applied to the cylindrical piers with the object of relieving their ponderous appearance, and removing the monotony of the effect. The feature appears frequently elsewhere in England.

[1] [In *Moslem Architecture* (pp. 315 ff.), where the subject is fully discussed, the author corrected the above statement by his discovery that blank arcading in the church of El Cristo de la Luz at Toledo dates from 980.]

Thirdly, there are the pairs of openings enclosed by a single arch, in the Ravennate fashion.

But the great importance of the building consists in the ribbed cross vaulting, with transverse arches of round or pointed form, which it contains. Much has been written about this vaulting, and the discussion is still going on. It is argued on the one side that it is a later addition, because it is to France that belongs the credit of the invention of this form of vaulting, the principal factor of the Pointed style; while, on the other side, the view is maintained that it is of the same date as the rest of the structure, in which case the credit of the discovery will fall to England.

Fig. 696. Durham Cathedral. South arm of transept
(11th and 12th centuries)

Unfortunately the champions of the two parties have hitherto confined their researches to too restricted a field; and it has never struck them that, while they were arguing whether ribbed cross vaulting appeared about the end of the eleventh century or at the beginning of the twelfth (although, as Dehio[1] rightly observes, the Lombards had already made use of the ribbed cross vault with buttresses effecting the same object as those developed later in France), this very same form had already attained a respectable antiquity in Italy. The proof of this statement depends on my discovery of the facts in San Flaviano at Montefiascone (1032). Those facts make the existence of cross vaulting with diagonal arches in Durham Cathedral, as early as the time of its rebuilder, William of Saint-Calais, easy to understand. And we must not forget that when he went to Rome as an envoy from the Conqueror, he may well have had the opportunity of inspecting the new form in San Flaviano itself, for Montefiascone was one of the regular halting places on the road to the Eternal City. Moreover, the Normans were brought into direct contact with South Italy after their countrymen, by the victory of Civitella (1053), and the investiture conferred by Pope Leo IX (1049–1055), had obtained a firm footing there; and, as we have seen, vaulting of this form existed in Campania. Nor is it conceivable that cross vaulting of this type was invented straight off at Durham, far away as it was from the very rare examples of intersecting vaults with visible ribs left by the Romans. In architecture, when it comes to essential elements, the idea is one thing and its execution another.[2]

The Durham ribbed cross vaults are not ordinary intersecting vaulting to which ribs

[1] *Repertorium für Kunstwissenschaft*, 1896, p. 172. *Die Anfänge des gothischen Baustils.*

[2] *Rivista d'Italia* (October, 1908, p. 670). U. GNOLI, *Le origini dell'architettura Lombarda.*

have been added afterwards, for the latter are quite independent of the vaulting cells, and are thus constructed on the Lombardic principle. Nor is it a case of ribbed replacing groined cross vaulting, the idea being disproved by the vaulting shafts at the angles where the choir and transept aisles meet. The clumsy way in which the vaulting is set must be ascribed, over and above the fact that it was a first attempt on the part of the

Fig. 697. Durham Cathedral. Nave (11th and 12th centuries)

English builders, to the absence of the logical Lombardic arrangement of compound supports and plain arches.

The ribbed cross vaulting in the transept aisles and the first two bays of the nave aisles is of the same period, and belongs to the years between 1093 and 1099. The whole of it may be credited to English workmen, now emancipated from Norman tuition. The Normans had no previous experience of this type of roofing in their own country.

The choir itself as well as its aisles had cross vaulting. In the clerestory walls may still be seen traces of its springing marked by the junction between the original work and that of the thirteenth century. Further, the existence in the set-back face of the triforium of groups of three wall shafts above the main arch piers suggests that each bay contained two quadripartite vaults with transverse visible arches springing only from the half-piers. What form this vaulting took we cannot say. It need not have been ribbed merely because that in the aisles is so, for the churches of Rivolta d'Adda and Sant' Ambrogio at Milan have simple cross vaulting in the aisles and the ribbed form or barrel vaults in the nave. Semicircular arches, intended to receive the thrust of the vaulting, cross the triforium at intervals corresponding to the half-piers and the groups of vaulting shafts. In 1235 the original vaulting of the choir threatened to fall in,[1] and its reconstruction was carried out in 1242 by Bishop Nicholas of Farnham (1242–1248), for such must be the meaning of Leland's[2] words, 'fecit testudinem templi'; the choir vaulting with the corbels for the diagonal ribs being in the Pointed style, which is not the case with the vaulting of the nave.

Fig. 698. Durham Cathedral. Portal in north aisle (12th century)

The builders of the church had a further intention, as has been observed,[3] of vaulting the transept, for the triforium on the east side contains the regular buttress arches set in relation to the half-piers and pairs of wall-shafts. But in the course of the work they changed their minds. On the western side they omitted the pairs of wall-shafts on the face of the quasi-triforium from which the ribs of the cross vaulting were to start, and in the clerestory, on the west side of the south arm of the transept, a range of continuous arcading was constructed, evidently implying a flat ceiling. The explanation of this change is perhaps to be found in fears for the stability of the western sides, devoid of the support of the cross vaulting in the aisles and of the buttress-arches of the triforium, in view of the weight of the vaulting. However, they soon gained fresh courage and decided on the construction of vaulting, beginning with the north arm of the transept. The absence of the pairs of vaulting shafts in the triforium stage was made up for by the insertion of corbels. The plainness of the ribs suggests that they are of the same date as the cross vaulting of the choir aisles, of the transept, and of the two first bays of the nave aisles; but the carved corbels from which the ribs spring, besides being a later insertion, show an artistic advance beyond the capitals of the old door near the south arm of the transept, inserted not later than 1099, and are certainly subsequent to 1104: therefore the cross vaulting must be of the same date. The

[1] RAINE, *Saint Cuthbert* (Durham, 1828), p. 99. [3] [BILSON in *Journal of R.I.B.A.*, 3rd ser., vi,
[2] *De rebus Britannicis collectanea*, vol. i, p. 122. pp. 259–69, 289–319.]

vaulting in the south arm of the transept shows the same characteristics as that in the northern, but the ribs are ornamented with zigzag mouldings, and it is therefore later.

The nave was designed for a wooden ceiling, and crossed by transverse arches to give it stability. Some interval must have elapsed before it was begun, for the 'Ravennate' openings of the triforium cease in this part. The construction of the vaulting involved an alteration of the clerestory, as some arches will be noticed which have been blocked up to give room for the vaulting.[1] It is of quadripartite form, with round diagonal arches springing from corbels, single, or in pairs, and carried on transverse arches of pointed form. Its construction shows a marked advance beyond that of the transept, and this progress is also exemplified by the form of the arched buttresses in the triforium (taking the place of the simple pilasters backing the arch piers), which are not round as before, but ramping, and counteract the thrust of the vaulting. But in spite of this difference there is a close analogy between the ribbing here and that in the transept cross vaults, so that we may very well ascribe all of them to the work of the same builders.

It has been suggested[2] that the nave vaulting, and indeed all the ribbed cross vaulting in the church with the possible exception of the choir aisles, is not earlier than 1133. I do not know at what date to fix this except in the years 1129–1133. For, on the one hand, we find in the vault construction, beginning with the choir aisles and ending with the nave, that undoubted sequence in order of time which has been noticed,[3] corresponding too, as it does, with the historical account left by Simeon and his continuator; a sequence both in construction and decoration confirmed in addition by the artistic progress shown by the corbel heads. While, on the other hand, in the series of works carried out between 1134 and 1195 under Bishops Geoffrey Rufus (1133–1140) and Hugh Pudsey (1153–1195), we meet with a more advanced style, which differentiates them from the nave.

These conclusions I had reached in 1896. Later study of the building has only strengthened them, and I have found that, on the whole, the story of the vaulting as told above, and foreshadowed as early as 1879,[4] may be accepted as the truth.

Accordingly, in default of further discoveries, Durham Cathedral must have the credit of forming the connecting link between Lombardic and Pointed architecture, in which every constituent element of the former was to gain fresh vitality and increased opportunity, while the style itself having reached a perfect development was destined by a natural process to give place to a new form.

Before concluding the present chapter a short space may be devoted to a church which contains carving of importance for purposes of comparison: I mean

MALMESBURY ABBEY CHURCH.[5]—The contradictory statements of William of Malmesbury leave it uncertain whether the church of St. Mary erected by Aldhelm, abbot of Malmesbury (680–705) and bishop of Sherborne (705–709), was rebuilt or at any rate restored by Elfric, who became abbot after 970 and bishop of Crediton in 977. Thus while in his life of Athelstan (925–940) he speaks of it as 'postea regis Edgari diebus sub abbate Elfrico aedificata'[6]—this Elfric being a well-known builder—in his 'Gesta

---

[1] [Dr. BILSON points out that there seems to be some confusion here, as the statement in the text is true of the south transept, but not of the nave.]

[2] DE LASTEYRIE, *Quelques considérations sur les origines de l'architecture gothique* (*Bulletin de la Société des Antiquaires de Normandie*, tome xxii, 1900 et 1901 (Caen, 1902), p. 64).

[3] BILSON, op. cit.

[4] GREENWELL, *Durham Cathedral*, pp. 23–50.

[5] [For Malmesbury see Sir HAROLD BRAKSPEAR, *Malmesbury Abbey* (*Archaeologia*, lxiv (1912–13), pp. 399–436). (H. T.)]

[6] *Rolls Series*, 90, *Willelmi Malmesberiensis monachi de gestis Regum Anglorum*, vol. ii, p. 154.

pontificum Anglorum' he ascribes it instead to the efforts of Aldhelm. Richard of
Cirencester[1] says it was built by Elfric, and repeats William's words. In any case, the
church was still standing in William's days (he seems to have died about 1143): 'Nam
tota maioris ecclesiae fabrica celebris et illibata nostro quoque perstitit aevo.'[2]

Further, there is no documentary evidence as to the precise date of its rebuilding
in the twelfth century. Every probability, however, is in favour of the years which
followed the death of William the
historian; and the new construction may
be connected with the independence
recovered by the monastery in 1140,
and the treaty which put an end to the
civil war in 1153, for no small part of
the struggles which disturbed the reign
of Stephen (1135–1154) took place in
the neighbourhood of Malmesbury,
making it unlikely that while they lasted
the monks would venture on an enterprise of this scale. As a matter of fact,
all the characteristic features of the
surviving parts of the building which
have not been subjected to later alteration point to the third quarter of the
twelfth century; and I do not think
that there is any one with experience
in such matters who can possibly fix
upon any date but, approximately, the
one suggested above (fig. 699).

After this preface let us pass to the
carving on the porch, as being the
subject in which we are immediately
interested.

The porch projects from the south
aisle of the church, and its sides are
decorated internally with arcading which
has lost some of its members, and two
sculptured lunettes. It is entered from
the outside through a portal cased in a

Fig. 699. Malmesbury Abbey Church. Nave
(12th century)

construction of the fourteenth century. This portal is decorated with scroll-work,
interlaced lozenges, foliage, and other ornamental forms. But more important are
the figure subjects (fig. 700) on the second, fourth, and sixth orders. From the
description of these sculptures by an anonymous writer who visited the church in
1634, we learn that all the subjects (except a very few which had disappeared) were
taken from the Old and New Testaments.[3] Some of those that are least decayed can
still be identified.

Each of the two lunettes (fig. 701) on either side of the porch contains a group of six

[1] *Rolls Series*, 30, *Ricardi de Cirencestria speculum
historiale de gestis Regum Angliae*, vol. ii, p. 75.
[2] *Rolls Series*, 52, *Willelmi Malmesberiensis de gestis
Pontificum Anglorum*, p. 361.

[3] E. W. BRAYLEY, editor, *The Graphic and Historical
Illustrator* (1834), pp. 411–12. (*A Relation of a short
Survey of Twenty-six Counties*, 1634.)

Fig. 700. Malmesbury Abbey Church.   Carving from outer portal
(12th century)

Fig. 701. Malmesbury Abbey Church. Lunette in the porch
(12th century)

figures seated in a row on a bench, and undoubtedly representing the Apostolic College, with angels floating in the air above them. The Apostles, mostly bearded figures, are seated in various attitudes, looking some to the right and some to the left, or with the head resting on the shoulder, and have about them a certain air of solemnity. The mantles in which they are wrapped are draped in numerous folds which fall in various arrangements. The shapeless feet are the only part treated without distinction in a uniform, monotonous manner.

The doorway (fig. 702) which leads into the church has the orders decorated with lozenges and branching scroll-work. At the top they enclose a tympanum containing a figure of Christ in the act of blessing, seated in a vesica supported by two angels.

Fig. 702. Malmesbury Abbey Church. Inner door in porch (12th century)

Fig. 703. Lincoln Cathedral. Carvings in the west front (12th century)

It appears to me that all these sculptures, treated without undercutting, are the production of one school and one date, though the work of three different hands. Thus, the decorative treatment of the two doorways is the creation of a single mind, but it is noticeable that on the outer one both ornaments and figures are modelled with higher artistic skill than those of the arch within. The carving of the two doorways must, then, be assigned to two distinct artists. Again, the drapery of the figures in the lunettes and tympanum is closely related, but, on the other hand, the figures in the latter are more artistic and better proportioned than those in the lunettes at the sides. These must accordingly be assigned to a different chisel.

We may remark at this point that all this carving, whether it consists of ornament or figures, is to be distinguished from that on the capitals in Archbishop Roger's (1154–1181) crypt in York Minster, belonging to the first years of his episcopate. The carving at York, consisting of scrolls, plants with pellets, palm leaves, intersecting arches, bunches of grapes, and eight men in tunics grasping a cable which runs below the abacus, are correct in drawing so far as regards the decorative motives, but the figures show no sense of proportion.

As we stand before the carvings of the porch at Malmesbury, forming a collection which, with the exception of the important reliefs on the west front of Lincoln Cathedral, is unrivalled among English twelfth-century monuments, we cannot but regret that the

3274.2

relentless hand of time, the mischief wrought by man, and the quality of the stone employed, have combined to reduce so much of it to the mutilated and decayed condition in which we see it to-day. But in spite of this, it is of assistance in fixing the date of other works which have given rise to differences of opinion, and of these we will select a few of the best known.

Let us begin with the reliefs which decorate the west front of Lincoln Minster. Various views have been put forward by those who have studied the subject, and it has even been suggested, owing to the way in which they are inserted in the wall, that they belong to the Anglo-Saxon age and are not in their original place—ignoring the fact that this unsymmetrical decorative treatment of church fronts was not, during the

Fig. 704. Lincoln Cathedral. Font (12th century)

Fig. 705. Winchester Cathedral. Font (12th century)

Middle Ages, effected by the adaptation of sculptures brought from elsewhere, but was a regular form of decoration, reduced to a system by the Lombard gilds, who made their principal display of it in San Michele Maggiore at Pavia (see vol. i, p. 277).

The Lincoln sculptures, here and there renewed, are treated in bas-relief, and have sacred subjects (fig. 703). The human figures are fairly proportioned and moulded, but generally stiff, awkward in their movements, and expressionless in feature, while the drapery is very rigid. The scene of the damned being carried off by devils, where the carving is untouched, should be specially noticed. While these reliefs display an art considerably more advanced than that of the 'storied' capitals at Southwell (1108–1114), it is less developed than that exhibited by the Apostles at Malmesbury, and the last years of Alexander's episcopate (1123–1148) suit them perfectly.

The black Tournai marble font[1] in the nave (fig. 704), recalling the one at Winchester (fig. 705), is the product of another school of artists.

Let us pass to the so-called 'Prior's Door' in Ely Cathedral. The jambs and the archivolts are enriched with scroll-work, foliage, flowers, pellets, human beings,

[1] [The fonts at Lincoln and Winchester belong to a group of which there are five other members, viz. three in Hampshire (East Meon, St. Mary Bourne, and St. Mary's, Southampton), one in Lincolnshire (Thornton Curtis), and one in Suffolk (St. Peter's, Ipswich). See C. H. EDEN, *Black Tournai Fonts in England* (London, 1909). (H.T.)]

quadrupeds, birds, fishes, monsters, all treated with freedom, and in deep relief, though without undercutting. On the whole it shows a more skilful arrangement and better distribution of parts than any other specimen, with the exception of the porch at Malmesbury. The tympanum contains the figure of Christ blessing within a vesica held up by two angels. These figures are rather flat and not at all undercut, but the drapery is richer than that at Malmesbury, and the hair is treated more artistically. I think we shall not be far wrong if we place them in the first years of Bishop Geoffrey Ridel (1174–1189).

To the same period, that is to say, to the years subsequent to the fall of the central tower (1175), may be assigned the well-known carvings (where untouched) on the capitals in St. John's Chapel, opening out of the south arm of the main transept of Worcester Cathedral (fig. 706). These carvings, consisting of scroll-work, a winged dragon with a serpent's tail, and the winged head of an angel, exhibit an art obviously of the same period as that of the Ely doorway.

Fig. 706. Worcester Cathedral. Chapel of St. John. Capitals (12th century)

Next comes the door in the west front of Rochester Cathedral,[1] reputed to be of the time of Henry I (1100–1135), but really later than the fire of 1179. Its decoration comprises foliage (sometimes treated with a flavour of the Pointed style), scroll-work, the figure of Christ in a vesica held by two angels and surrounded by the emblems of the Evangelists, the figures of a king and a woman, human heads, and realistic or imaginary animal heads. All is well designed and modelled, treated with vigour, and sometimes completely undercut. The king in particular, though damaged, shows fine drapery and treatment. One would look in vain for carving of this character in England, not merely in the time of Henry I, but even at the beginning of the second half of the twelfth century.

Compared with that at Malmesbury the carving on the portal at Rochester shows advance both in the decorative parts and in the figures; the animals, too, are more successfully treated than those in the crypt at Canterbury, not to say those on the door at Ely. Moreover, the composition which fills the tympanum shows progress beyond the similar feature of the doors at Malmesbury and Ely, the latter being derived from

---

[1] [The doorway at Rochester bears a close affinity to the French doorways of which the Porte Royale of Chartres Cathedral and the south doorway of the nave at Le Mans are conspicuous instances, and must therefore be dated not earlier than the second half of the 12th century. The 13th-century date suggested in the text seems too late, but it may well be work of c. 1180. (H. T.)]

the former. We shall be correct in placing it in the first years of the thirteenth century in the time of Bishop Gilbert de Glanville (1185–1214), when a good deal of work was carried out in the monastery at Rochester. We cannot accept the view of those who would see a foreign hand in the doorway on account of the absence of billets, for this detail is equally wanting on the doors at Ely and Malmesbury. The Anglo-Saxon artists had been roused from their traditional inertia by the Norman Conquest. The carvers, whom preference for the axe and the rarity of employment had rendered almost incapable of executing the finer work, were reinvigorated by the new artistic influence, and slowly but surely began to advance along the road of the revival which was stirring Western Europe. The figure in the act of blessing, to be seen on the outside of the north transept of Norwich Cathedral (fig. 707), the 'storied' capitals at Southwell, and the figure capitals at Tewkesbury, are so many stages on the road leading to the Lincoln reliefs, the capitals in Roger's crypt at York, and the sculptures at Malmesbury.

Fig. 707. Norwich Cathedral. Sculptured figure on north arm of transept (12th century)

Earlier than the carving of the Rochester door is the less advanced work on the capitals of St. Peter's, Northampton. It consists of foliage, real or imaginary creatures, pearls, birds, grapes, complicated interlacing, &c. The foundation of the church was about 1160: the date 1190 must be that of the completion of the building.[1]

Two works not much later than the Rochester door are the sculptured stone panels which were found concealed behind the choir stalls in the last century, and are now built into the wall of the south choir aisle of Chichester Cathedral (fig. 708). This church was consecrated in 1108, severely damaged by fire in 1114, repaired by Bishop Ralph de Luffa (1091–1123), reconsecrated in 1184, injured again and still more seriously by the fire of 1187, and dedicated in 1199 under Bishop Seffride II (1180–1204), though the works of the second restoration were still in progress. The panels represent Jesus meeting Mary and Martha at Bethany, and the Raising of Lazarus (figs. 709, 710). The treatment of the figures is superior to that of any which we have seen hitherto. The peculiar care and variety with which the hair and beards are treated should be noticed. The hands and faces, though not yet of the right proportions, are none the less executed with a certain naturalness. A peculiar feature are the cavities representing the eyeballs.[2]

These reliefs, together with the contemporary fragments discovered during the restoration of the cathedral, in spite of the merits to which we have called attention, are immature both in composition and details, and therefore less advanced than the figures at Rochester. Accordingly, they will find their place in the last decade of the twelfth century during the episcopate of Seffride II. Many persons, it is true, believe that they came from Selsey, whence the see was moved to Chichester in 1075; and the latest dates allowed to them are the eleventh century (and before 1075), or some time in the

[1] SERJEANTSON, *A History of the Church of St. Peter, Northampton*, &c. (Northampton, 1904), p. 17.
[2] [The cavities were originally filled with glass or paste. Compare note on the altar of Ratchis (i, p. 118, note 1). (R.)]

twelfth.[1] The formless figure sculpture of that date in England refutes any such attribution.

All the reliefs which we have examined may be ascribed to English hands. The art of carving in the countries most likely to provide artists for such a purpose, viz. France and Italy, was at that time far more advanced than that exhibited by these sculptures.

A date later than that of the Rochester doorway must be assigned to the two well-known figures of angels built into the walls of St. Laurence's Church, Bradford-on-

Fig. 708. Chichester Cathedral (12th century)

Avon.[2] Their greater purity of line and freedom of movement show that they are later than the works which we have previously examined, though the execution is still rough. They might well belong to the early years of the thirteenth century if we found them in one of the more progressive artistic centres of England. But seeing that they are in an out-of-the-way locality, even though the monastery was connected with a rich and powerful abbey like Shaftesbury, it is impossible to date them within any but very uncertain limits, but in any case later than the twelfth century.

[1] [Cf. F. M. BOND, *English Cathedrals*, p. 43; E. HERON ALLEN, *Selsey Bill* (London, 1911), p. 101. For a late Saxon date see CLAPHAM, op. cit., p. 138. (A.)]

[2] [For the angels at Bradford-on-Avon see note 3 on p. 185. The view expressed here may seriously be questioned, as there is no reason to consider them a late insertion in their surroundings, and they bear no resemblance in technique to any early 13th-century sculpture. CLAPHAM (op. cit., pp. 137 ff.) agrees. (H. T.)]

Fig. 709. Chichester Cathedral. Sculpture
(12th century)

Fig. 710. Chichester Cathedral. Sculpture
(12th century)

Fig. 711. Bari. Crypt of San Nicola (11th century)

It has been supposed by some writers on these subjects that the Lombardo-Norman basilica was the model from which that found in the Norman conquests in South Italy and Sicily was derived. They even describe as 'Norman' the style of the numerous churches erected in those lands in the eleventh and twelfth centuries.

But, as a matter of fact, an examination of these edifices reveals, at the most, two occasional characteristics inspired by the Lombardo-Norman church, viz. the plan

Fig. 712. Canosa. Sepulchral chapel of
Bohemond (12th century)

Fig. 713. Santa Maria Capua Vetere. Tomb
called 'La Conocchia'

and the intersecting arcading. None of the following features can be regarded as Norman importations.

(1) The somewhat sharply pointed roofs which occasionally occur, e.g. in San Nicola at Bari (1087–1098–1105). The form was not demanded by local climatic conditions, but depended on the aesthetic consideration of giving greater elegance to the outline of the gable by making it less depressed.

(2) The indication on the façade of the internal arrangement of the church. This idea, which originated at Ravenna, had been embodied as early as the sixth century in the church of Bagnacavallo.

(3) The Lombardic arrangement of supports alternately larger and smaller,

exemplified in the nave of San Nicola. It had appeared as far back as 985 in SS. Felice e Fortunato, near Vicenza, and was of Roman origin.

(4) Bell-towers flanking the choir. We saw the origin of these in our account of the Duomo of Ivrea, and we shall learn more when we come to deal with the old cathedral of Cologne.

(5) The capitals, revealing influences of all kinds (fig. 711)—Roman, Ravennate,

Fig. 714. Athens. Choragic monument of Lysicrates (335 B.C.)

Byzantine, Pre-Lombardic, Lombardic, Apulian, Calabrian, Campanian, Sicilian—everything except Norman—where they are not Roman, and brought from elsewhere; or of Byzantine origin, like the basket capitals with figures, probably of the sixth century, in the crypt of the twelfth-century cathedral of Otranto.

(6) Cupolas having the drum of polygonal form externally, with engaged shafts at the angles, as shown in the sepulchral chapel of Bohemond, Prince of Antioch († 1111), at Canosa (fig. 712). This is a motive of Campanian origin. For instance, on the Via Appia outside Santa Maria Capua Vetere stands a Roman tomb popularly known as 'La Conocchia' (fig. 713), where the drum of the cupola has blank arches like large round-headed windows, separated by columns.[1] Drums encircled on the outside

[1] [See *Roman Architecture*, p. 162.]

by columns had been seen before this, e.g. the Choragic monument of Lysicrates (the 'Lantern of Demosthenes') at Athens (335 B.C.) (fig. 714), or the tomb of the Gallo-Roman period at Saint Remy, where the open drum has a conical covering but has not sham windows between the columns. The Byzantines did not introduce this feature before the eleventh century. The drum of the cupola belonging to the

Fig. 715. Bari. Cathedral. Window in the apse (12th century)

convent church of Myrelaion at Constantinople (919–945) has still only ordinary buttresses.

(7) The portal, which was a Lombardic creation, the prototype being that of Sant' Andrea at Montefiascone (about 1032).

(8) Windows made in the form of the Lombardic portal, of which such a fine example occurs in the cathedral of Bari (fig. 715), erected after the destruction of the city (1156) by the troops of William I the Bad (1154–1166). The claim of the Lombardo-Apulian School to the authorship of this design cannot be denied.

(9) Rose windows, an Italian creation of the twelfth century. We noticed this point when describing the church at Vézelay and San Pietro at Toscanella.

(10) External arcaded galleries, which are of Lombardic origin, as we showed in our account of Sant' Ambrogio at Milan.

(11) The motive of several blank arches enclosed by a single arch, to be seen e.g. on the exterior of San Nicola at Bari. The idea of a large arch containing smaller ones had

Fig. 716. Cefalù. Cathedral (12th century)

been applied by the builders of Ravenna as long ago as the fifth century in the interior of the baptistery of Neon.

(12) Arched corbel courses. This form was known to the Romans, as we stated in our account of the chapel of San Pier Crisologo at Ravenna, and from them it descended to the Ravennate and Lombard gilds.

With regard to the plan of the Lombardo-Norman basilica, it was certainly taken as their model (with modifications) by the builders of the Duomo of Acerenza (1080), the second abbey church of the Trinità at Venosa (eleventh century), the cathedral of Cefalù (fig. 716) founded in 1131,[1] and that of Monreale, the first stone of which was laid in 1174 in the reign of William II (1166–1189).[2] The radiating chapels which appear in some of these churches were not of Norman origin, for this arrangement

[1] Duca di Serradifalco, *Del duomo di Monreale* (Palermo, 1838), p. 29.   [2] Ibid., pp. 5, 60.

originated in Touraine, where it was applied for the first time in Saint Martin at Tours in the first quarter of the eleventh century.

There only remains to consider the characteristic intersecting blank arcading used for decorative purposes. The oldest dated specimen known to me occurs on the interior

Fig. 717. Palermo. Cathedral (12th century)

of the choir aisles in Durham Cathedral, begun in 1093.[1] This was followed by the example in Norwich Cathedral, where, before 1119, Herbert Losinga introduced the motive in the transept. Such churches must have been the source from which the creators of the cathedrals of Cefalù, Monreale, and Palermo (fig. 717)—the last founded in 1185 by William the Good—derived the motive which they applied in such an elegant form to the exteriors of their buildings, unless, indeed, further discoveries give some support to the idea that the Sicilian craftsmen arrived at it independently under Moorish influence.

[1] [But see note on p. 258 *supra*.]

V

THE EARLY CHRISTIAN MONUMENTS OF IRELAND[1]

THE following pages contain a summary of the results of a recent study of the early Christian architecture and sculpture of Ireland. I set them out here in the hope that they may contribute, in outline at least, towards a more rational classification of the interesting and characteristic medieval monuments of the island.

Let us begin with the sculptured crosses. One of the most celebrated is the wheel-head cross of Muiredach (fig. 718), as the name is given on one of its faces, in the churchyard at Monasterboice, which contains three such monuments. Its carvings comprise religious subjects, representations of animals, panels filled with the cable pattern and intestinal interlacing, bosses, &c.

To connect it with Muiredach, abbot of Armagh, who died in 922,[2] is a complete mistake.[3] The evidence of the large number of medieval carvings which I have seen and studied convinces me that in the tenth century there was no artist in existence, even the most celebrated of Italy, France, or Germany, capable of producing work of this kind, far surpassing, as it does, both in design and execution, the best results which these countries have to show right up to the close of the eleventh century. It is equally impossible to ascribe it to an Eastern hand, for the Eastern sculptors of the Middle Ages did not produce squat figures of this type. To the same period and school belongs the other and more imposing cross at Monasterboice (fig. 719), about 27 ft. high, wrongly assigned to the tenth century.[4]

Rather later is the remarkable tall and slender cross at Tuam (fig. 720),[5] for though the figure of Christ is flattened, the anatomy and the treatment of the beard show an advance over the best figures at Monasterboice. It was set up by O'Hoisin, that is to say, the famous Archbishop Aedna Oissin (1150–1161),[6] whose period was distinguished by activity in building.[7] It was then that the celebrated stone-built castle was

---

[1] [The additional notes in this chapter are due to Dr. R. A. S. Macalister, Professor of Celtic Archaeology in the National University, Dublin; and this opportunity is taken of thanking him for the generous way in which he has placed his knowledge of Irish antiquities at the service of this edition.]

[2] *Annals of the Kingdom of Ireland by the Four Masters*, vol. ii, p. 611.

[3] [A Muiredach, with a similar patronymic (son of Domhnall), was vice-abbot or rather abbot-successor designate at Armagh at the same time. Some of the annalists treat these two as one, but the Four Masters separate them and give 924 as the obit of the Armagh Muiredach; ibid., p. 615. It must be admitted that the inscription does not specify that the Muiredach of the cross was an abbot, in Monasterboice or anywhere else; also that Muiredach was by no means an uncommon name. But the dating of the cross to the abbot's time, and by inference to the abbot's patronage, is confirmed by the testimony of the very similar cross at Clonmacnois. This is certainly a work of the same school, and quite probably of the same hand, as the Monasterboice cross; and it bore an inscription, legible when Dr. Petrie copied it about a hundred years ago, but now unfortunately defaced.

The few traces which remain confirm Petrie's transcript (*Christian Inscriptions in the Irish Language*, vol. i, p. 42), which states that the cross was erected by Colman, abbot of Clonmacnois, in memory of Flann, king of Ireland: this Flann was a generous friend and benefactor of Clonmacnois; and shared with Colman the task of building the cathedral there. Now, Flann died in A.D. 914 and Colman in A.D. 924: the date of this cross must therefore be between those dates. (M.)]

[4] MARGARET STOKES, *Early Christian Art in Ireland*, ed. of 1928, part ii, pp. 7, 15, 20.

[5] [As to the Tuam cross, it is in the first place not certain that the existing head really belongs to the shaft. A glance at the figure on p. 278 will show that it is a misfit. The shaft comes to an abrupt end, and a cross with much smaller horizontal dimensions has been placed on the top of it as a substitute for the original head, which is lost. (M.)]

[6] Sir JAMES WARE, *Archiepiscoporum Casseliensium et Tuamensium Vitae* (Dublin, 1626), pp. 34–5.

[7] [The association of the cross with the archbishop named is stated in an inscription upon the cross itself. The date is further narrowed down by the additional statement that the cross was set up under the auspices

erected at Tuam: 'Rodericus O'Conner rex Conatiae castrum lapideum Tuamae construxit, quod tanquam novum et inusitatum apud Hibernos, *castri mirifici* nomine iis temporibus innotuit.'[1] And to the same age belongs, if not the completion, at any rate the foundation or refoundation of the three churches consecrated on the occasion of the General Synod held at Tuam in 1172.[2]

Of about the same date as the cross of Tuam is the small cross preserved in the chapel of St. Kevin at Glendalough. Three of its sides are covered with intestinal interlacing, and in front is a draped figure of Christ, of similar character to the one on the cross at Tuam. The no less elaborate crosses at Clonmacnoise must also be put in the twelfth century.

To sum up, all these wheel-head crosses, a characteristic feature of which is the gabled structure, representing the Holy Sepulchre, by which they are crowned, and on which the Irish carvers seem to have concentrated all the artistic force inspired by their religious enthusiasm, are later than the Norman conquest of England (1066). They are also subsequent to the time of Archbishops Lanfranc (1070–1089) and Anselm (1093–1109), when the Danish coast-towns of Ireland acknowledged the spiritual supremacy of Canterbury and Rome. Patrick, who in 1074 succeeded Donatus (Dunan) in the see of Dublin (1038–1074), was consecrated by the English primate in St. Paul's at London.[3]

They were the result of a national artistic revival produced by the renewal of relations with Western Europe after the long period of isolation in which Danish invasions and struggles, and disastrous internal conflicts, had plunged the unfortunate country. This

Fig. 718. Monasterboice. Cross of Muiredach (12th century)[4]

of Toirdelbach ua Conchobair (Turloch O'Connor), king of Ireland, who died in 1156.

This dating makes it all the more impossible to assign the Monasterboice-Clonmacnois group to a date so late as the second half of the 12th century. Their technique and style of ornament is totally different: they are much less zoomorphic in detail, and their figure subjects belong to a much older iconographic tradition. For example Christ is represented beardless more often than not.

The cross at Dysert O'Dea, Co. Clare, which is not mentioned in this chapter, is of the same type and doubtless of the same date, as the Tuam cross; and it shows the same peculiarity of large figures standing out in relief from the face of the stem as is seen on the Glendaloch cross here quoted. As the figure of

Christ here shows the same peculiarities as that in the substituted head on the Tuam cross—with a *bowed* head, bearded and crowned—the date of the substituted cross-head at Tuam cannot be much later than that of the shaft on which it is set.

There is a second cross-shaft at Tuam, bearing the same names and similar ornament. (M.)]

[1] WARE, *De Hibernia et antiquitatibus eius, disquisitiones*, 2nd edition, 1658, p. 111.

[2] *Annals of the Four Masters*, vol. iii, p. 9.

[3] Sir JAMES WARE, *De Hibernia et antiquitatibus eius . . .*, 1654, p. 118.

[4] The illustrations to this chapter (except figs. 721 and 724) are from photographs kindly provided by the Dublin Museum.

revival, accordingly, was a reflex of the potent influence exercised by the art of Italy and by the Papacy, in the era following the epoch of 1000, on so many countries of both East and West.

So far as carving is concerned this revival cannot have become effective till considerably after the beginning of the eleventh century. The school of artists which in that

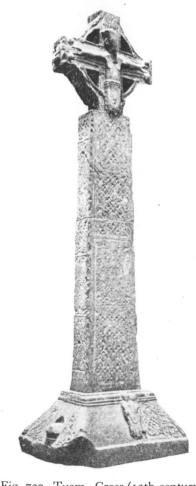

Fig. 719. Monasterboice. Cross (12th century)

Fig. 720. Tuam. Cross (12th century).
(From a cast in the Dublin Museum)

century produced the barbarous capitals of the church of St. Flannan at Killaloe, built by King Brian Boroimhe (1002–1013), could never have executed the crosses which we have described. And, besides, the infantile geometrical incised ornament of Irish churches before the eleventh century bears witness to the want of skill which characterized the school.[1]

[1] [It is not possible to use the churches and the crosses together in an argument. All the evidence available tends to show that the principal churches were of wood: the less important were of stone, and were decorated with carving only after the Romanesque style had made its way into the country from the Continent. The churches and the crosses represent parallel but wholly distinct art schools. Very rarely is the specifically 'Celtic' ornamentation of the crosses (key-patterns, interlacements, and the like) applied to the decoration of churches. The Nunnery Church at Clonmacnois and the outer order of the west doorway at Clonfert present exceptions. (M.)]

Let us now turn to the buildings, beginning with the important ecclesiastical centre of Glendalough, the town of the Seven Churches.[1] Among its ancient buildings the churches of the Rock, of Reefeart, of Our Lady, Trinity Church, the Cathedral and its tower, and the oratory and cell of St. Kevin, are believed to belong wholly or partially to the time of Kevin, who died in 618.[2] Let us take them one by one.

I. Of the church of the Rock, said to be the oldest of Kevin's foundations, nothing is left but the scanty remains (restored) of an aisleless nave.

II. Of the little church of Reefeart, so called as being the burial-place of the kings of this territory, who belonged to the family of Ui Tuathail (O"Toole), there exist the ruins of the aisleless nave measuring about 30 ft. by 18 ft., with a rectangular chancel at the east, built of roughly hewn stones of various sizes, and of rubble with a great deal of mortar.

This church probably stands on the site of a 'beautiful church' erected on the shore of the lake, according to the life of the saint in *Acta Sanctorum Hiberniae*, for the purpose of tempting him to quit the almost inaccessible rock-shelf overhanging the lake upon which he had established himself. The round-headed chancel arch is enough to show that the existing church cannot be so old as St. Kevin's time.

III. The Lady Church is represented by the remains of the nave and square chancel. The latter is the result of an alteration carried out when the building was dedicated to the Virgin, which, according to Petrie,[3] took place not before the twelfth century, because before that time no church in Ireland was dedicated to the Mother of God or to non-Irish saints. The round-headed window, decorated on the outside by a carved band springing from two heads, exactly suits the twelfth century. Its erection must have taken place after the fire of 1163.[4] On the same occasion the window with a hood mould was inserted in the south wall of the nave. The church is said to have been built by Kevin's orders, with the direction that he was to be buried in it;[5] but this is a mere tradition, and another points out an oratory or small chapel as his burial-place.[6]

IV. Of Trinity Church we have the ruins of the nave and rectangular sanctuary, with a square chamber opening out from the west end of the nave, once surmounted by a round tower. The oldest part is the nave. The chancel and porch are later additions.

V. Of the Cathedral there remain the ruins of the nave, considerably larger than that of any other of the Glendalough churches, 48 ft. long and about 30 ft. wide, and those of the chancel which is the result of an alteration probably carried out when the abbey of Glendalough was erected into a bishopric under Pope Alexander III (1159–1181).

Within the same enclosure stands the ancient, picturesque, round tower. Both cathedral and tower are believed by Petrie[7] to have been erected by Gobhan Saer (about 610), on account of the analogies between them and the church and tower of Kilmacduagh which tradition ascribes to him.[8]

VI. The two-storied Oratory of St. Kevin is preserved almost intact. In the course

---

[1] [See *Historical and Descriptive Notes with ground plans, elevations, sections, and details of the ecclesiastical remains at Glendalough*, published (1911–12) by the Board of Public Works of Ireland.]

[2] *Rolls Series*, 46, *Chronicum Scotorum*, pp. 75, 77. [No responsible person believes that any of the churches whose ruins are now to be seen are as old as St. Kevin's time. All the original buildings were made of wood or of wattle-work. (M.)]

[3] Petrie, *The Transactions of the Royal Irish Academy*, vol. xx.—*An inquiry into the origin and uses of the round towers of Ireland*, p. 173.

[4] *Annals of the Four Masters*, vol. ii, p. 1151.

[5] *Antiquarian Handbook Series*, no. 1—*Dunsany, Tara, and Glendalough*.

[6] O'Hanlon, *Lives of Irish Saints*, vi, p. 72.

[7] Petrie, op. cit., p. 385.

[8] [Petrie's work was excellent in its day but some of his theories it would be better to forget: among them his dating of this tower and its attribution to the mythical Gobhan Saer. (M.)]

of time there were added to it the chancel, which has disappeared, and the round tower and sacristy which still exist.

VII. St. Kevin's Cell, believed to have been the first monastic cell erected by him, consists of the remains of a structure of beehive form.[1]

In all these buildings the windows are narrow, and sometimes square-edged, but usually splayed on the inside. The doorways in some cases diminish in width towards the top. Those in the Cathedral and St. Kevin's Oratory have also a tympanum above them, while the one in the Lady Church has the opening framed, with a cross carved on the architrave.

In view of the almost uniform masonry of the roughly constructed walls, and the excessive poverty of the architectural decoration, confined as it is to two rude lunettes, and considering the almost entire absence of artistic ornament, consisting merely of a poor moulding round a door and a cross, the problem of fixing the date of these structures is by no means easy. We will, however, attempt to solve it, and we may begin by classifying them under three heads. To the first belong the churches of the Rock, of Reefeart, of Our Lady, the Trinity, and the Cathedral; all of them built of masonry, but without solid roofs. A second category is formed by the vaulted buildings, represented by the tower of the Cathedral and the Oratory of St. Kevin. Kevin's beehive cell forms a class by itself.

It appears to me that the monuments of the first class are the oldest, but still not so old as the time of St. Kevin. We have already seen that the churches erected in the 'Celtic' or 'Scottish' manner in England by the missionaries sent forth from Iona and Lindisfarne or its daughter monasteries were constructed of wood (it is even suggested that they may have been of osiers plastered with mud), and originally covered with reeds or thatch, and afterwards with lead. It was a style of building carried even to Italy by Columban, as the church of the Virgin at Bobbio showed. In Ireland the adoption of masonry in place of timber for ecclesiastical buildings must have been a consequence of the burnings due to the Danes who invaded the island from 794 onwards,[2] not to speak of those caused by the Irish themselves. It is true that the Annals of Ulster mention under the year 788 a stone chapel at Armagh, to which Petrie refers.[3] But one swallow does not make a summer. Inveterate customs are very reluctantly abandoned, and only under the stress of dire necessity.

The earliest record of Glendalough suffering from devastating fires at the hands of the Irish and Danes[4] occurs in the year 770. A similar calamity happened in 835.[5] From this we may infer that the sacred structures were in the interval hastily rebuilt of wood. It must have been only after the second destruction that it was decided to replace the timber construction by masonry, 'iuxta Romanorum morem' as Bede describes it.[6] It

---

[1] [There is a small circular stone fort and circular dry-stone hut, on the shore of the upper Lake, enumerated as no. VII. It is possible that these are earlier than the monastery, or even than Christianity in Ireland. The connexion of the hut with St. Kevin is traditional but not verifiable. Three buildings have been omitted from the enumeration: the so-called 'Priest's House', a rectangular building, 14 ft. 8 in. by 7 ft. 9 in., with an interesting carved tympanum over the entrance, and a fine Romanesque archway at the east end; St. Ciaran's church, a rectangular nave, 18 ft. 10 in. by 14 ft. 6 in., with a chancel, 9 ft. 4 in. by 8 ft. 10 in.; and St. Saviour's church, a nave, 40 ft. 11 in. by 20 ft. 3 in., with a domestic building of about the same size beside it, and a chancel, 17 ft. 4 in. by

11 ft. 6 in., decorated with interesting Romanesque sculpture. (M.)]

[2] *Annals of the Four Masters*, vol. i, p. 401, footnote.

[3] PETRIE, op. cit., p. 144.

[4] *Annals of the Four Masters*, vol. i, pp. 375, 453, note 4.

[5] Ibid. [The following dates are collected from various authorities in the description published by the Irish Board of Works (see above, p. 279, n. 1): A.D. 770, 830, 833, 835, 866, 977, Glendaloch destroyed by Scandinavians; 983, termon lands pillaged by Irish; 1176, ravaged by Anglo-Normans; 1398, final destruction by English forces. (M.)]

[6] *Historia abbatum*, 5 (*supra*, p. 141, n. 4).

was under these circumstances that the churches of the Rock, of Reefeart, Our Lady, the Trinity, and the Cathedral, may have been erected with stone walls and roofed with reeds or some kind of thatch. It was a form of construction which was an improvement on the use of wood only, for if it happened to be burned it was capable of being repaired, instead of requiring an entirely new erection.[1] The Cathedral was, perhaps, somewhat

different, as it may have possessed a timbered roof covered with sheets of lead, like the great church at Armagh, which was also constructed of stone with a lead roof, and was burned with its bell-tower and bells in 1020.[2] As we have seen, this type of roof had been adopted for the cathedral of Lindisfarne between 687 and 697.

Fig. 721. Glendalough. Cathedral. Round tower (10th or 11th century)

I have mentioned both systems of roofing because they are both 'Celtic', and also because the gables of these Irish churches show no traces of a junction with a stone roof. And, in any case, the width of the cathedral forbade the construction of a solid covering. The annalists, moreover, confirm the theory that the Glendalough churches as a rule had neither vaulting nor stone roofs. Thus, in 835 the Danes burned the 'oratorium', which must mean the monastery church. In 1020 they burned 'the oratories'. In 1061 the 'churches' were accidentally consumed by fire, and again in 1084. And in 1163 the 'House of Kevin' ('Cro-Chaeimhghin') was burned together with the 'church of the two Sinchells'.[3] This 'House of Kevin' must have been the abbot's residence, for it is not conceivable that an ordinary dwelling, liable to be destroyed by fire, should have been preserved intact through all the series of disasters which befell Glendalough from 770 onwards.

This system of building in stone with a roof of combustible material remained in vogue. Thus we hear that in the eleventh century—to be precise, in 1058 and 1060 respectively— 'Imlech-Ibhair was entirely burned, both stone church and steeple', and 'Cenannus was altogether burned, together with its stone church'.[4]

After the reign of Edward the Elder (901–925), when, as we noticed at the time, the efforts of the Anglo-Saxons against the Danes in England were accompanied by the construction of strongholds with towers as an effective method of successfully opposing

[1] [But in times of stress wooden buildings have this *advantage* over stone buildings, that they can be so easily and quickly replaced. The Norman bretesches —wooden towers—along the marches of Wales were in working order again six months after they were burned down. To replace a stone building would have been a very different matter.

The roofs were probably in many cases wooden *shingles*. Such a form of covering seems to be indi-cated by the treatment of the 'roofs' on the tops of the carved crosses. Compare also the representation of Solomon's Temple in the *Book of Kells*. (M.)]

[2] *Rolls Series*, 54, *The Annals of Loch Cé*, vol. i, p. 21.

[3] *Annals of the Four Masters*, vol. ii, p. 1157.

[4] *Rolls Series*, 54, *The Annals of Loch Cé*, vol. i, pp. 55, 57.

the barbarians, and as an echo of the great building era in England which distinguished the reign of Edgar (959–975), and, perhaps too, in consequence of fresh disasters which befell Glendalough in 977, 982, 984, and 985, the erection of the cathedral tower must have taken place.

This tower (fig. 721), which is some 100 ft. high from base to summit, constructed of roughly hewn stones of all sizes and rubble set in mortar, covered by a circular vault,

Fig. 722. Antrim. Round tower (10th or 11th century)

and originally divided internally into floors, the holes for the beams being still visible all round, served for the various purposes of a bell-tower, an outlook, and a stronghold and place of refuge for the lives and property of the monastic body. This fact was first brought out by Petrie,[1] who is only mistaken in the date of this and similar Irish towers which he ascribed to the centuries between the fifth and thirteenth.[2] That it was intended for ringing bells is shown by the four openings at the summit.[3] The purpose of defence and refuge is indicated by the entrance being placed at the height of some yards above the ground. It was reached by a ladder. The existence of wooden floors inside is proved not only by the holes for the beams, but also by the fact that another tower, that of Telachard (Tullyard or Steeplestown, Co. Neath), was burned in 1171 with all the unfortunate people who had taken refuge in it.[4]

The painful experience of the past was, no doubt, the convincing argument in favour of the adoption of this form of structure, impervious as it was to any attempt of an enemy to set it on fire. But I do not believe that it could have taken place until the Irish builders had obtained considerable practice in masonry construction, and had erected some vaulted buildings. The vault of the tower—and the tower is so solidly built that the wind was able to tear off the conical roof without damaging the rest—though forming a cupola on a circle of only about 8 ft. in diameter, must have demanded a Herculean effort of constructive science on their part. The difficulty arose from the fact that they were not accustomed to vaulting; and that, by making their chancels rectangular, they had avoided the constructive difficulties inherent in the circular form of apses and half-domes, requiring as they do specially prepared materials and a higher degree of skill.

The typical form of the Glendalough tower, related as it is to the bell-towers of Ravenna and also to the staircase towers with their conical cupolas in San Vitale, was undoubtedly an importation from Italy. If we could fix with certainty the date of the foundation of the Irish Colony at Poggio de' Berni in the district of Sant' Arcangelo

[1] PETRIE, op. cit., p. 367.

[2] [The dates of the towers certainly lie between the 5th and the 13th centuries: in this Petrie is correct. The mistake lies in the limits being too wide, the first date being too early, the second too late. The 10th–12th centuries may be reasonably given as limits. It should be noticed that the Glendaloch tower is unusual in having had its wooden floors supported on beams resting in holes in the wall: as a rule there were offsets at intervals in the inner face of the circular wall, upon which offsets the floors were supported. (M.)]

[3] [The only bells used were hand-bells, rung by hand out of the window. There is no trace of bell-hangings in any of the round towers. (M.)]

[4] *Annals of the Four Masters*, vol. ii, p. 1181.

(Forlì), which is described as 'Podium Hibernorum' and said to be of ancient origin,[1] some interesting light might be thrown on this importation. In any case, Continental influence on Irish architecture from the fifth to the seventeenth century has been admitted, even by recent writers.[2]

To about the same date as that at Glendalough belong the towers of Monasterboice and Antrim (fig. 722). To a later period, but before the erection by Ua Maeleoin of the tower at Clonmacnoise (finished in 1124: its top was destroyed by lightning in 1135),[3] which has a finished facing and is built with regular courses of carefully laid oblong blocks of stone, will belong the round towers of Disert Aengus (fig. 723), Scattery Island, and Holy Island in Lough Derg, the masonry of which, though still rough, is more regular than that of the towers described above.

Fig. 723. Disert Aengus. Round tower (11th century)

These round towers continued to be erected in Ireland for a long time. Thus, the one at Ardmore, about 108 ft. in height, built of oblong blocks of stone and with the exterior marked off into zones by stringcourses, is not older than the erection of the church, that is to say the end of the twelfth century.[4] This need not cause surprise, seeing that the Danes who had established themselves in Leinster before 851[5] were not finally annihilated till 1171, when the Anglo-Normans vanquished the fleet of Asgall and put him to death,[6] and that disastrous internal struggles had not ceased to rage in the island.

About the same date as the tower of Glendalough is the oratory of St. Kevin known as 'St. Kevin's House' or 'St. Kevin's Kitchen' (fig. 724). This is a chamber (22 ft. 8 in. by 14 ft. 7 in.) of two stories, one of which has a barrel and the other a pointed-arched vault. The upper supports the gabled masonry roof, covered with stones which form a continuous structure with the vault. The walls are built of stones of all sizes and rubble set in mortar. To this chamber there was added later a rectangular chancel, now destroyed, flanked by a sacristy which survives. Over the west end rises a round bell-turret which breaks the vault of the roof. Three holes for the bell ropes are pierced in the barrel vault of the lower story.

This chamber was not built for the double purpose of an oratory below and a dwelling-room above, as has been suggested. The opening now existing in the barrel vault, intended to form a communication between the two stories, is the result of an alteration. The upper vault, too, was not constructed to provide a tiny dwelling with a water-tight covering, but to carry the sloping sides of the heavy roof, and provide something to intercept the weight and take the pressure off the barrel vault below.

The constructive and statical knowledge here displayed—something quite exceptional among the builders of Ireland—with the object of making the structure as safe as possible from the assaults of time and the violence of man, points to workmen about contemporary with those who built the cathedral tower. The presence of a lunette

[1] CALINDRI, Saggio statistico storico del Pontificio Stato (Perugia, 1829), p. 371.

[2] A. S. GREEN, The making of Ireland and its undoing, p. 241.

[3] Annals of the Four Masters, vol. ii, pp. 1019, 1051.

[4] EARL OF DUNRAVEN, Notes on Irish architecture (2 vols. 1875), vol. ii, p. 149.

[5] WARE, De Hibernia et antiquitatibus eius . . . (1654), pp. 105–6.

[6] Annals of the Four Masters, vol. ii, p. 1185.

over the west door (indicative of Pre-Lombardic influence), and the care taken to secure the building as far as possible from injury, suggest that it had a very sacred character, viz. that of an oratory erected on the site of the primitive wooden dwelling of the saint, which had perished by fire, thus confirming the popular title of 'House' or 'Kitchen of St. Kevin' which is believed to have its source in the ancient tradition that he lived there for the last years of his life.[1] At a later date the oratory was converted into a church. The saint's dwelling must have been the one erected in the monastery 'of the valley of the two lakes', which was Kevin's last foundation: 'Post hec venerabilis pater insignissimum monasterium, quod Vallis duorum stagnorum dicitur, illic construxit.'[2]

Fig. 724. Glendalough. Oratory of St. Kevin (10th or 11th century)

Of the same type as this building is the well-known 'St. Colum-Cille's House', near Kells, i.e. the oratory of St. Columba, the apostle of Caledonia, who died in 597[3] (fig. 725). It, too, must have been built as an oratory[4] and earlier than the one at Glendalough, because the doorway is without a tympanum. These two buildings must be older than the equally well-known church of St. Flannan (fig. 726), close to Killaloe Cathedral, which was erected by Donnell More O'Brien (†1194), king of Limerick[5] The foundation of this church is ascribed to the year 1007 and the agency of Brian Boroimhe,[6] whose reign lasted from 1002 to 1014.[7]

The type of these three structures was reproduced in the celebrated and singular

[1] O'HANLON, op. cit., vol. vi, p. 69.
[2] *Acta SS. Hiberniae—Acta S. Caimgini*, col. 840.
[3] STOKES, *Ireland and the Celtic Church*, p. 129.
[4] [It must have been more than 'an oratory' for it was in at least three stories—a wooden floor (now gone) being interposed between the ground and the vault above it. Here, at least, there is evidence that some practical use was made of the chamber above the vault (probably as a dormitory). (M.)]
[5] DUNRAVEN, op. cit., ii. 70 ; PETRIE, op. cit., p. 277

(date of St. Flannan).
[6] Ibid., p. 390 (date of Brian Boroimhe).
[7] *Annals of the Four Masters*, vol. ii, pp. 747, 773. [The doorway of the chapel (fig. 726) is obviously 12th century in date, and not Irish in character. It may be a later insertion, but Mr. H. G. Leask (Inspector of Ancient Monuments under the Irish Board of Works) thinks that this is very doubtful, and that the whole building may be of the 12th century.]

Chapel of Cormac on the Rock of Cashel, built in the Lombardo-Norman style with a groundwork of Irish character (figs. 727, 728).[1] It has square towers flanking the east end of the aisleless nave, a rectangular chancel, from which projects an altar recess of the same form, and recessed openings of Lombardic type but Norman decoration. It has been said that it was the work of Cormac MacCullenan (†908); but it was really built by Cormac MacCarthy in 1127, and consecrated in 1134[2] or 1130,[3] or, according to another account, in 1135.[4] The presence of the Lombardic cubical capital, which made its earliest appearance in 1013 in Sant' Abondio at Como, makes a tenth-century date impossible. Moreover, the Lombardic openings, the enriched blank arcading of

Fig. 725. Kells. Oratory of St. Columba (10th century)   Fig. 726. Killaloe. Church of St. Flannan (12th century)

both interior and exterior, the figure corbels, and the quality of the vaulting of the ground floor, demonstrate undeniable Lombardo-Norman influence of considerably later date than 1066.

We have still to discuss the Cell of St. Kevin. Its date is not an easy problem to solve, but it must belong to a period subsequent to the first Danish invasions, for it is not likely that monastic cells were being built of masonry at a time when churches were constructed of wood.[5]

[1] [Cormac's Chapel is of an unusual type in Ireland, and unquestionably has been influenced by the Romanesque of the Rhineland: to apply Lombardo-Norman to it as a term is misleading. See C. McNeill, *The Affinities of Irish Romanesque Architecture, Journal, Royal Society of Antiquaries of Ireland*, 1912, p. 140. 1135 was the date of the consecration of the chapel: the building probably occupied the preceding years. (M.)]

[2] Petrie, op. cit., p. 186.

[3] *Rolls Series*, 46, *Chronicum Scotorum*, p. 335.

[4] *Rolls Series*, 54, *The Annals of Loch Cé*, vol. i, p. 135.

[5] [Beehive cells are found attached to monastic structures elsewhere, as High Island off the Galway Coast and Skellig Michael. It is not quite sound to say, 'it is not likely that monastic cells were being built of masonry at a time when churches were constructed of wood'. Wood was the normal building material, and in my own recollection part of the valley of Glendaloch was thickly forested, although it has been much thinned out now. Quite elaborate churches

In Ireland 'beehive' structures start with the tomb chambers in tumuli, like those of New Grange, Dowth, and Knowth, the first being the finest.[1] These are of circular plan and beehive section, constructed with rough dry-stone walling, which gradually converges so as to form the vault above. Others are found, of ancient date, constructed either with or without mortar, which served as oratories or dwellings. Beehive cells of very early date exist on Skellig Michael, one of which has formed a chapel. But they are not so old as is generally supposed. The first planting of this monastic colony on the Great Skellig was surely subsequent to St. Aubert's foundation of Mont Saint Michel (about 708), which in its turn was derived from San Michele on the Monte Gargano. The founder is said to have been the abbot St. Suibhneus, but we do not know his date.

Fig. 727. Cashel. Chapel of Cormac (12th century)

Destroyed in 812 by the Danes, who starved the monks to death, it was rebuilt in 860. Subsequently, an abbot, Flann macCellaig († 885), is recorded. The date of the removal of the house to Ballineskellig is not known. In any case, the oldest structures of Skellig Michael are later than the rebuilding of 860. Their form is to be explained by the fact that it was easier for the monks to procure stone than timber.

Of the same type is the well-known Oratory of Gallerus (fig. 729), entirely constructed without mortar, and with the vault almost resting on the ground. Its date is not known, but the greater skill displayed shows that it is later than the structures on the Great Skellig. Perhaps it belongs to the end of the ninth century, or the first half of the tenth; but it is certainly not of the age preceding the apostolate of St. Patrick (432–461),[2] as Petrie[3] imagined. The method of construction may well be due to the difficulty of procuring mortar, and reasons of economy.

might have been built of wood, while miserable make-shift shelters were made of beehive dry-stone huts, perhaps covered with mud. Cf. R. A. S. MACALISTER, *Ireland in pre-Celtic Times* (1921), pp. 259, 261. (M.)]

[1] *The Transactions of the Royal Irish Academy*, vol. xxx (1892–6), pp. 1–96. GEORGE COFFEY, *On the tumuli and inscribed stones at New Grange, Dowth,* *and Knowth*, p. 2; id., *The Origins of pre-historic Ornament in Ireland* in *Journal of the Royal Society of Antiquaries of Ireland*, series v (1894–7), vol. iv, pp. 349–79; vol. v, pp. 16–29; vol. vi, pp. 34–69; vol. vii, pp. 28–52.

[2] BURY, *Life of St. Patrick*, pp. 59, 206.

[3] PETRIE, op. cit., pp. 163, 164.

Later than the type of building represented by the oratory of Gallerus is the one exemplified by the chapel on St. Macdara's Island, in which the low side walls of the nave, projecting beyond the line of the front and end, originally carried a high-pitched stone roof, the junction of which with the gables may still be traced. For it was one thing to raise a converging vault from the firm ground, and quite another matter to cover a space with a heavy roof of masonry high up.

From a combination of these two types was evolved a third, viz. that with two vaulted stories, the earliest examples being the oratories of Kells, Glendalough, and the church at Killaloe. This type, together with that of St. Macdara's oratory, went on being improved through the eleventh and twelfth centuries.

Fig. 728. Cashel. Chapel of Cormac (12th century)

Before leaving the subject of Ireland I may notice that the crypt of Christ Church (Trinity) Cathedral, Dublin, is thought to represent with its vaulted construction (though its form has been changed) the original church founded by King Sihtric († 1041 or 1042) and the first (Danish) bishop, Donatus or Dunan (1038–1074), about the year 1038, or that, at any rate, it preserves the exact plan of that erection. This idea is based on a passage of the 'Liber niger' of Christ Church: 'Sitricus . . . dedit S. Trinitati et Donato primo episcopo Dublin(ensi) locum ad aedificandum ecclesiam S. Trinitatis, ubi fornices sive voltae sunt fundatae.'[1]

An examination of the structure has convinced me that the remodelled crypt is the result of the rebuilding of the church carried out about 1170 in the time of Strongbow and Archbishop Laurence O'Toole (1162–1180).[2] In

Fig. 729. Gallerus. Oratory (9th or 10th century)

the first half of the eleventh century no church of this size and form could have been

[1] ARCHDALL, *Monasticon Hibernicum* (Dublin, 1879), vol. i, p. 324. WARE, *De Hibernia et antiquitatibus eius* (2nd edition, 1658), p. 308.

[2] [An inscription upon a stone in Christ Church Cathedral has been asserted to be the epitaph of an Italian master-mason, who has consequently been credited with the design of the church. See *Archaeological Journal*, lvii (1900), 295, and 338 (facsimile). There is, however, nothing in the text of the inscription to warrant this statement, and its date is at least a century later than the original design of the building. It probably commemorates an Italian merchant, his

erected in Dublin. Neither the Danes in Ireland, nor the Irish themselves, accustomed as they were to ecclesiastical buildings of quite another type, and to the erection of structures of very modest dimensions, would have been capable of performing the task. Nor, for that matter, would English builders of the time have been in any better position. And there is no record that Sihtric during his pilgrimages to Rome in 1030 and 1035[1] engaged the services of Italian workmen capable of carrying out his intentions. Nor could the constructive skill then to be found in Normandy, thanks to William of Volpiano and his pupils, have been utilized for the occasion, for it is out of the question to suppose that the Benedictines would have placed their services at the disposal of Bishop Dunan, who had handed over his cathedral to secular canons.

wife and family. The word which describes his profession is unfortunately imperfect, but has no obvious relation to any branch of mason craft. (H.T.)]

[1] ARCHDALL, op. cit., p. 325.

VI

THE ECCLESIASTICAL ARCHITECTURE OF GERMANY[1]

FROM CONSTANTINE TO THE ELEVENTH CENTURY

IN the lands comprised within the German Empire of to-day the list of surviving churches belonging to the centuries between Constantine's grant of peace to the Christians (313) and the fatal catastrophe of the Roman Empire, long tottering under the weight of its own greatness and its inherent vices, and from that gigantic upheaval down to the reign of Charles the Great (768–814), is confined to a single building, the cathedral of Trier, and that not in its original condition. Moreover, it was never a structure erected as a whole for its purpose, being merely the result, in the first instance of an adaptation, and then of a restoration.

THE CATHEDRAL OF TRIER was formed by Agricius (who, according to Gams,[2] held the see from 314 to 332) in the hall of a Roman building[3] supported by four lofty columns united by arches, which he dedicated to St. Peter. This adaptation of a building of no great size, instead of the erection of a spacious basilica, must, considering the importance of Trier, have been due to the fact stated by Harnack[4] that at the beginning of the fourth century the number of members of the local church was still small. The cathedral was damaged by the Franks, and restored by Bishop Nicetius (526–535–566).[5]

On the north side of the church some remains of the Roman building may be seen (fig. 730). The construction is of stone with courses of brick, and there may be noticed a continuous band of tiles which follows the line of the alternate triangular and rounded heads of the niches and openings on the ground floor of the building. It looks as if it were intended to break the plainness of the wall, which is quite devoid of ornaments in relief. The structure may be assigned to the times of Diocletian (284–305), Maximian (286–310), and Constantine (306–337), the period of the city's greatest splendour;[6] or, more probably, to the reign of the last, and not long before its conversion into a church by Agricius. It certainly is not as late as the year 370, as Dehio and Von Bezold[7] and others imagine; for that date conflicts with the account in the 'Gesta Treverorum', and its masonry is evidently contemporary with that of the three-lobed structure belonging to the Baths[8] (fig. 731). This is also faced with bands of stone alternating with bands of brick, and is ascribed to the age of Constantine; rightly, I think, on account of the window arches, which, though they have not the comparative finish of the time of Diocletian, show no signs of the marked decadence of the post-Constantinian epoch.

The recent restoration has thrown light on the original construction of the interior

---

[1] [R. SCHULTZE in his *Basilika* (Berlin and Leipzig, 1928) endeavours to prove that the plans and dimensions of the German churches were derived from the remains of Roman basilicas that had survived the Barbarian invasions. Fully illustrated by plans, which are useful. (R.)]

[2] Op. cit., p. 317.

[3] [KRÜGER (*Die Trierer Römerbauten*, p. 13) dates it under Gratian by coins found in the walls, and thinks it was erected as a Christian baptistery. (A.) Cp. F. OELMANN, *Zur Deutung des römischen Kernes im Trierer Dom* (*Bonner Jahrb.*, 1922, 130 ff.).]

[4] Op. cit., ii, p. 268.

[5] *Mon. Germ. Hist. Script.*, vol. viii, p. 159. *Gesta Treverorum*. BROWERUS, *Antiquitates et Annales Trevirenses*, vol. i, pp. 310, 323. [*Congrès Archéologique de France, Rhénanie*, 1922, pp. 45, 76 ff.]

[6] BROWERUS, op. cit., vol. i, pp. 196, 197, 204.

[7] Op. cit., vol. i, p. 46.

[8] [The so-called imperial palace has been ascertained to be in reality a large set of baths, and belongs to the period between Diocletian and Constantine. E. KRÜGER and D. KREUCKER, *Abhandlungen der Preussischen Akademie*, 1915, no. 2, p. 64. (A.)]

of the cathedral, where the round arches are outlined by a ring of bricks laid horizontally, whereas those belonging to the adaptation are copied from the old ones, but without the ring of bricks.

Fig. 730. Trier. Cathedral. Roman work on north side (4th century)

Fig. 731. Trier. Remains of baths (4th century)

To the alterations of Nicetius belong two capitals (fig. 732), now built into the wall, which formerly surmounted two of the four supports of the central quadrangular space. They are imitations of the antique, of Corinthian pattern, with plain, stiff leaves, and are rude and poor work. They would be of interest if they were made on the spot, as providing evidence about the state of carving in the sixth century in an important artistic centre such as Trier was under Roman rule, and as showing the type of capital in vogue there at the time. But as we know from a letter of Ruffus, bishop of Turin (560–570), to Nicetius that the latter invited craftsmen from Italy to repair the damage inflicted on the churches of Trier by the barbarians ('artifices de partibus Italiae accitos . . . ad vos, Domino ducente, transmisi'[1]), probably they were responsible for the capitals.

We have already given a brief sketch of the ecclesiastical architecture of the Frankish Empire under Charles the Great in Italy, Dalmatia, and France. We will now extend our survey to the German lands, beginning with the most celebrated of the Carolingian buildings, the palace chapel of Aachen. The restoration in progress enabled me to examine it stripped of all accretions, and to penetrate the inmost secrets of its organic structure.

Fig. 732. Trier. Cathedral. Capital (6th century)

THE PALACE CHAPEL AT AACHEN was erected by Charles the Great between 796 and 804, and dedicated to the Virgin by Pope Leo III early in 805.[2] The plan is that of a polygon with sixteen sides, four of which are taken up by the sanctuary, the narthex, and the staircase towers. On the ground floor the arches, strengthened by substantial sub-arches, which open out of the central space (fig. 733) are carried on piers of broken outline, recalling (in section) that of the piers in San Vitale at Ravenna,[3] which, in their turn, present a striking analogy to others of the Roman period, e.g. those of an octagonal building near Pozzuoli, the plan of which has been preserved by Montano.[4] These arches, together with the blank wall-arches resting on powerful wall-piers (which have no buttresses corresponding to them outside, the outer face of the walls being unbroken, and the walls themselves over 5 ft. thick), sustain a continuous series of unraised tripartite and quadripartite cross vaults, some 2 ft. 4 in. thick at the crown (fig. 734).

This system of thrusts met by the outer walls, strengthened on the inside by pilasters or even columns (either engaged or set against the wall), is sometimes described as 'Byzantine'. As a matter of fact the Byzantines borrowed it from the Rome of the first three centuries of the Empire. The city and its environs still contain the proofs of this for any one who cares to ascertain the facts, in the shape of tombs, the Thermae, the Basilica Nova or Basilica of Constantine (310–312), not to speak of the abundant evidence provided by old drawings.

The original presbytery was in two stories, and of rectangular plan.[5] Two spiral staircases, formed in the towers which flanked the narthex and Imperial tribune, lead to the latter, the gallery, and the corridor communicating with the Imperial Palace. These staircases have rude vaulting, and terminate at the height of the roof, and below the raised part of the wall, in a round vault as in San Vitale at Ravenna. Of the same kind, but only intended to provide access to the roof, were the two staircase towers,

[1] *Mon. Germ. Hist., Epistolae Merowingici et Karolini aevi*, p. 133.

[2] *Mon. Germ. Hist. Script.*, vol. ii, p. 452. EINHARDUS, *Vita Karoli imperatoris*; *Mon. Germ. Hist. Script.*, vol. xxiv, p. 22, *Annales Tielenses*; JAFFÉ, *Regesta pontificum Romanorum*, vol. i, p. 312.

[3] [See RIVOIRA, *Roman Architecture*, p. 267.]

[4] Op. cit., libro ii, tav. 17. [HÜLSEN (*Il libro di Giuliano da San Gallo*, p. 13) compares with it the unknown building *supra*, fig. 423. (A.)]

[5] [Plan in DE LASTEYRIE, op. cit., fig. 758; CLAPHAM, op. cit., fig. 47. Cp. M. AUBERT in *Congrès archéologique, Rhénanie*, 1922, 518 ff. (R.)]

circular after the Ravennate type, in the front of the abbey church of St. Gall. The tribune is of rectangular shape with a rounded end, and has a barrel vault constructed, like the walls, and, indeed, the whole of the interior facing of the building, of dressed stone brought from Verdun ('De quadris autem lapidibus dirutae civitatis [Virdunicae] Aquisgrani capella extructa est'[1]). The jambs of the two doors leading into it have long

Fig. 733. Aachen. Palace Chapel (796–804)

and short work, while the voussoirs of the arch are of white and grey stone alternately. Two low doors lead into the gallery.

When discussing Saint Bénigne at Dijon (1002–1018) we remarked that the Eastern origin ascribed by so many writers to galleried basilicas is quite arbitrary.

The arches of the gallery are carried by piers of the same form as those below. Each arch contains a screen of two tiers of columns, which are not original. Of all the old capitals belonging to the gallery and tribune (derived from earlier buildings like the columns themselves: 'Ad cuius structuram cum columnas et marmora aliunde habere

---

[1] BOUQUET, *Recueil*, vol. v, p. 373. *Mon. Germ. Hist. Script.*, viii. 351.

non posset, Roma atque Ravenna devehenda curavit'[1]) there survive in the whole gallery only three of Corinthian form and late Roman date; and they have been restored. The idea of filling up the arch openings with screens of isolated columns is of Roman origin. It appeared frequently in the Thermae of Rome under the Empire.

From the piers and the pilasters of the outer walls, which are about 3 ft. 3 in. in thickness, spring rude visible transverse arches with voussoirs of various kinds of stone brought from elsewhere, like all the arches in the building. Upon these arches are turned barrel vaults alternating with vault cells (fig. 735). These vaults, like those of the

Fig. 734. Aachen. Palace Chapel. Vaulting of aisle (796–804)

Fig. 735. Aachen. Palace Chapel. Vaulting in the gallery (796–804)

ground floor, the staircases, the Imperial tribune, and the dome, are roughly and coarsely constructed of pieces of limestone set radiating, with above them a bed of concrete composed of lime, sand, gravel, and pounded bricks, of the kind used at Rome and Ravenna.

The two original windows exposed by the restoration are round-headed and splayed on the inside, where the jambs have the long and short work which we noticed in the entrances to the tribune, and also to be seen in the original openings of the staircase towers. Whence we may reasonably infer that all or most of the openings of the rotunda were constructed on the inside in just the same way.

Above the arches of the gallery rises the octagonal drum, and upon that the cupola of the same shape. It is conical in form, about 3 ft. 3 in. thick at the crown, and originally covered by a roof which, with the walls of the drum, was raised in height in the thirteenth century. The blank arcading of this addition has spurred bases to the shafts. Perhaps these were the source of the erroneous statement (for which the study of books instead of the monuments themselves is responsible) that this detail first appeared on bases in

[1] *Mon. Germ. Hist. Script.*, vol. ii, p. 457, EINHARDUS, *Vita Karoli imperatoris.*

Roman times, and next in the rotunda of Aachen. As a matter of fact, its creation is not earlier than the tenth century.

Unlike the lower octagon the drum (fig. 736) is strengthened close to the salient angles of the exterior, and almost up to its summit, by buttresses surmounted by capitals rudely

Fig. 736. Aachen. Palace Chapel (796–804)

carved with foliage. This device must have been chosen in preference to angle buttresses, with the object of increasing the field of resistance.

The rotunda was approached through a large cloister court or quadriporticus, remains of the foundations of which have been discovered.[1] On the north side of the great frontal recess or niche (fig. 737) there remains one of the original windows of the barrel-vaulted corridor which connected the gallery of the rotunda with the Imperial residence. The architrave of the lunette of this window is supported by an ill-formed

[1] BUCHKREMER, *Zur Wiederherstellung des Aachner Münsters* (Aachen, 1904), pp. 16–20.

fluted pier with moulded base and capital, the outer face of which has now been turned inwards, and the present outer one has been re-worked.

The Minster of Aachen as a whole is not so much an original creation as an imitation of San Vitale at Ravenna, an edifice which Charles had had an opportunity of admiring during his visit to the city in 787.[1] It belonged to a style which, though it had obtained

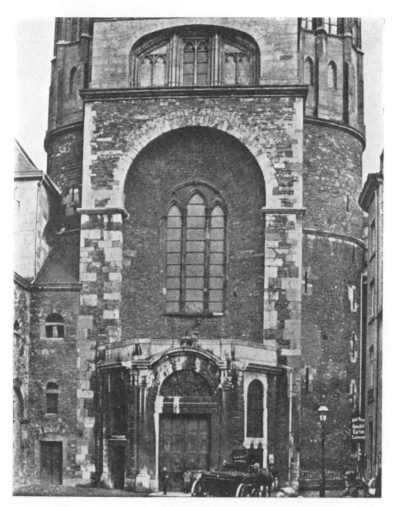

Fig. 737. Aachen. Palace Chapel. Façade (796–804)

recognition in Italy, at Ravenna and Milan, had encountered an obstacle to its wider acceptance in the shape of the ancient basilica plan on which the Latin Church had set the seal of its approval. We therefore cannot imagine that the Emperor, who was surely not unaware of the reasons which had hitherto prevented the spread of the Byzantino-Ravennate style in Italy, though still the most civilized country of Western Europe, and containing the powerful Lombard gild of the builders as well as the ancient and still fairly active school of craftsmen at Ravenna, would have cherished the vain hope, as some believe, that the erection of a building in that style would produce throughout the vast Frankish Empire, as if by a touch of a magic wand, craftsmen with the skill to

[1] *Mon. Germ. Hist.*, Agnellus, *Liber pontificalis*, p. 383.

develop and diffuse a type of construction so contrary to the artistic traditions both of its inhabitants and of the Latin Church of which, willing or unwilling, they were the faithful adherents.

The fact is, this style, in which the vault is applied only to ground plans of a certain form, the principal being the circle, the square, and the polygon, and of which the

Fig. 738. Constantinople. St. Irene (8th century)

primary source is the dome, was not successful, or very rarely so, in gaining a footing in Italy and Northern Europe. And when in the eleventh century a new age demanded a new style of architecture, it was neither the Byzantino-Ravennate, nor the Byzantine style pure and simple, which presented itself as best suited to the tastes and needs of Western Europe, but the Lombardic, born in the West, originating in the application of the vault to the Latin basilica, created by the gilds of Lombardy, and fashioned by the Benedictine Order into the forms which we find in the countries north of the Alps.

No information has reached us as to the architect of this celebrated church or the builders who worked under him. But there are grounds for believing that it was erected from the designs and under the superintendence of Byzantine architects, and carried out by Italian masons assisted by Frankish workmen.[1]

The Byzantine School is revealed in the statical principles exhibited by the structure, and also by the heaviness of the internal construction, the latter being a characteristic feature of Byzantine churches of the eighth century. This may be seen from St. Irene at Constantinople (figs. 738, 739), which is not the church rebuilt by Justinian I (527–565), but a reconstruction begun by Leo III the Isaurian (717–740), after its destruction

Fig. 739. Constantinople. St. Irene (8th century)

by the earthquake of 739;[2] not a mere restoration as is generally believed. I have formed this conclusion after making, under great difficulties, a thorough examination of the building. The Ionic capitals, with pulvins belonging to the eight columns which support the galleries under the dome, are poor work and certainly not of the age of Justinian. Further, it is enough to look at the cupola, not lighted by small windows like St. Sophia and SS. Sergius and Bacchus at Constantinople, and not springing from a low drum like that of St. Mary Diaconissa in the same place, built by the patriarch Cyriacus in the reign of the Emperor Maurice (582–602),[3] but rising from a high drum, strengthened by buttresses outside, and lighted by lofty and wide windows like those

---

[1] [A late 9th cent. MS. quoted by SCHLOSSER, *Schriftquellen f. Gesch. d. Karolingischen Kunst* (p. 28), records Odo (Eudes) of Metz as the architect. Cp. M. AUBERT in *Congrès arch. Rhén.*, pp. 519, 526. (H. T.)]

[2] DU CANGE, *Historia Byzantina, Constantinopolis*

Christiana; VAN MILLINGEN, *Byzantine Churches in Constantinople*, p. 89 (Van Millingen gives 740 as the date of the earthquake, Bury 739); BURY, *A History of the later Roman Empire*, 1st ed., vol. ii, p. 423.

[3] DU CANGE, op. cit., p. 58.

in the Nymphaeum of the Licinian Gardens (253–268) and the Imperial Mausoleum (fifth century) by St. Peter's at Rome.[1]

With regard to the actual masons, we know that, of all the countries then subject to the rule of Charles the Great, Italy was the most capable of providing them. The guard-house of Theodoric's palace at Ravenna (eighth century), and especially Santa Maria in Valle at Cividale (762–776), are convincing evidence of the capacity of the builders of Ravenna in the eighth century. And again, the structures erected in the Lombard part of Italy in the course of that century by the Lombard gilds, as well as the fact that Hadrian I asked Charles to send him a master mason ('prius nobis unum dirigite magistrum'[2]) to renew the timber roof of the Vatican Basilica, are so many testimonies to the ability of the gilds in matters of construction.

We may suppose that the 'master' referred to came from one of these gilds, seeing that, during the period of great constructive activity which comprised the pontificates of Hadrian I (772–795) and Leo III (795–816), the Lombard gilds left undoubted traces of their presence both in Rome and in other towns of the Roman Duchy as it existed in the time of Charles the Great. Another consideration is the fact that the gilds in question were better known than any others among the Emperor's subjects.

Nevertheless, the Ravennate and Lombard craftsmen, with few exceptions and those of early date, familiar only with the easy field of the old Roman basilica design, cannot but have been dismayed when brought face to face with the problems of scientific construction, and with the practical task of building a vaulted structure of the type of the Imperial chapel. It is a reasonable inference that the direction of the work was not entrusted to any of these master masons, though at the same time it is natural that their services should be engaged for its execution (with the assistance of Frankish workmen for the simpler parts), whereby the great expense of hiring Byzantine craftsmen, as some think was the case, would be avoided. That masons of Ravenna did take part in the work is shown by the use of mortar of the Roman and Ravennate kind. On the other hand, the long and short work in the openings reveals the share of Frankish workmen.[3] The fact that the dome was covered by a timbered roof makes the presence of Eastern builders doubtful, and rather points to those of Ravenna, whose predecessors had treated the cupola of San Vitale in the same way.

This employment of Italian workmen on the largest and most perfect of Charles's buildings, though it had not the marked direct effect on the Lombardic and derived styles that has been often attributed to it, still exercised an influence which, though indirect, was considerable. In the course of its erection the Lombard gilds gained a familiarity with vaulting construction such as they had never been able to do before. On their return home, fortified by the lessons they had learned and the experience they had acquired, after some further practice, in co-operation with the masters of Ravenna, in buildings of this type on the coast of Dalmatia, they devoted themselves to the researches and experiments which resulted in the creation of the Lombardic vaulted basilica.

Strzygowski[4] believed that Charles the Great's church followed Eastern models then to be found in the Gallo-Frankish lands. Having made it my practice to base my opinions on the evidence of wholly or partially existing buildings, or of those which have come down to us through drawings or descriptions, I regret that I am unable to

---

[1] [*Roman Architecture*, figs. 222, 223. For St. Irene see W. S. GEORGE, *Church of St. Irene*, Byzantine Research Fund, 1912.]

[2] DUCHESNE, *Historiae Francorum scriptores* (Paris, 1641), *Epistolae summorum pontificum ad principes et reges Francorum*, vol. iii, p. 780 A.

[3] [But see note 5, p. 144 *supra*.]

[4] *Der Dom zu Aachen und seine Entstellung* (Leipzig, 1904), p. 24.

accept this hypothesis. And I can only hope that German scholars, devoted as they are to facts, will not blame me for so doing. The Gallo-Frankish countries contain no such types. Unless, indeed, we were to make the mistake of regarding as one the three-lobed vaulted Roman structure at Trier, the similarity of whose plan with that of a hall in Hadrian's Villa at Tivoli (125–135) has been already pointed out.[1] It belongs to a type of vaulted construction absolutely unconnected with a Hellenic-Oriental origin, and essentially Roman. As a matter of fact the East, so far as is known, does not contain a single example of this kind of building earlier than the age of Hadrian. Whereas instances of these three-lobed structures, sometimes provided with external buttresses, can be found in the works of Montano,[2] Bramantino,[3] Serlio,[4] and among the drawings in the Uffizi at Florence.[5] In the same way, the East was not the birthplace of the circular buildings with annular vaulted aisles, which we discussed in connexion with the Holy Sepulchre.

It is usually thought that Einhard designed and carried out the most important of Charles the Great's buildings, from the palaces of Ingelheim and Aachen to the wooden bridge at Mainz, reaching their culmination in the rotunda of Aachen. This idea has been universally accepted, based as it was on the authority of Mabillon (1632–1707);[6] and its truth was investigated only by a few, among whom were Pertz,[7] Springer,[8] Dohme,[9] and Delisle,[10] for almost every writer on Carolingian art has simply taken it for granted without verification. As it seems to require correction I will investigate it in my turn, though well aware how difficult it is to get new ideas accepted when the attempt involves the displacement of old ones.[11]

About Einhard we know that he was brought up in the palace school, that he held the offices of royal steward or treasurer and of Crown notary, and that Charles the Great sent him (806) on a mission to Leo III (795–816) in order to obtain the Pope's assent to the act of partition of his dominions among his sons.[12] There is no documentary evidence to prove that he was also an architect. It is one thing to be Minister or Treasurer of the Household ('qui regalium aedificiorum praefectus erat'[13]—'operum regalium exactor constitutus'[14]), and quite another matter to be the architect of the royal buildings. It requires a strong effort of the imagination to interpret the words of the epitaph composed by Hrabanus Maurus,[15]

Quem Carolus princeps propria nutrivit in aula,
per quem et confecit multa salis opera,

and

ac multis arte fuit utilis

---

[1] DEHIO and VON BEZOLD, op. cit., vol. i, p. 51. Cf. *Roman Architecture*, figs. 162–64.

[2] MONTANO, op. cit., lib. iii, plates 17, 39, 43; [*Roman Architecture*, figs. 163, 164].

[3] BRAMANTINO, op. cit., plate 21.

[4] SERLIO, op. cit., lib. iii, p. 74, fig. E.

[5] [The origins of the three-lobed or trefoil plan are discussed in Mr. O. M. DALTON's *East Christian Art* (Oxford, 1925), p. 108, who inclines to an Eastern, or even (as Strzygowski) Armenian source. (R.)]

[6] *Annales Ord. S. Benedicti*, vol. ii, p. 572 A.

[7] *Mon. Germ. Hist. Script.*, vol. ii, pp. 426 ff. EINHARDUS, *Vita Karoli imperatoris*.

[8] *De artificibus monachis et laicis medii aevi*, pp. 10, 18.

[9] *Kunst und Künstler Deutschlands und der Niederlande bis gegen die Mitte des achtzehnten Jahrhunderts*, vol. i, p. 10.

[10] *De Eginhardo Caroli Magni notario.*

[11] [Although it may well be doubted whether Einhard was an architect, the passages on which comment is made here are very much more definite in statement than those which are accepted in this volume as proving the architectural skill of William of Volpiano and Lanfranc (see Appendix to Chapter I, *supra*, p. 46). It is quite clear, I think, that Einhard acted as Charlemagne's 'clerk of the works', i.e. minister of public works, which exactly meets the phrase in the pentameter from Hrabanus Maurus. (H. T.)]

[12] *Annales Ord. S. Benedicti*, vol. ii, p. 379.

[13] Ibid., p. 572 A.

[14] *Mon. Germ. Hist. Script.*, vol. ii, p. 427, EINHARDUS, *Vita Karoli imperatoris*.

[15] MIGNE, *Patr. Lat.*, vol. cxii, col. 1669, Epitaphium Einhardi.

as referring to any duties of Einhard as architect and superintendent of the Imperial buildings. Nor can such duties be any better inferred from the passage in the Fontanelle (Saint Wandrille) Chronicle: 'Heinhardo abbate viro undecunque doctissimo,'[1] or from Alcuin's well-known letter to Charles,[2] or Einhard's to his own son Vussinus.[3] The notice from Fulda of the sending to Einhard by Abbot Ratger of Brun Candidus, 'variarum artium doctorem peritissimum,'[4] tells us no more, for the latter was a painter and a man of letters, but not an architect. Again, even if we make the language of Walahfrid Strabus's flowery eulogy on Einhard

Beseleel fabre primum qui percipit omne
artificum praecautus opus[5]

mean that he superintended the workmen engaged on the Imperial buildings, there is nothing about his having designed them, and in particular the famous rotunda.

Nor is it any good to say, as Dohme does, that, as the plans and the construction of the chapel at Aachen demanded exceptional mathematical knowledge on the part of the architect, Einhard must have been the architect because Alcuin tells us that he possessed such knowledge. In the West, during the Dark Ages, vaulted buildings were not designed or erected on the basis of calculations, but on a ground-work of experience, by means of community of efforts, with the help of traditions of construction, and of the study of buildings surviving from the ancient world. Such are the conclusions at which I have arrived, and I have only been confirmed in them during my laborious researches into the subject of the experiments made for the gradual evolution of the Lombardic vaulted basilica by the most important of the medieval gilds, I mean the Lombard corporations.

Now what traditions and what experience in the art of building did Einhard possess, when, at the age of twenty-five (Dohme and Springer date his birth approximately in 770; Pertz at the end of Pippin's reign (752–768) or the beginning of that of Charles the Great (768–814)), he took in hand the design, and in 796 the execution, of the most celebrated edifice of that age either in East or West? Those tasks demanded not only a study of its original, San Vitale (a filiation noticed long ago by Hübsch),[6] by one who was familiar with the problem, but also profound technical and statical knowledge which is not acquired off-hand. My answer is that he had none. It is true that Adhemar tells us that after the conquest of Lombardy (774), Charles brought from Italy singers and organists, as well as accomplished teachers of grammar and arithmetic or calculation, of whom there was a deficiency in his own country: 'Ante ipsum enim dominum regem Karolum in Gallia nullum studium fuit liberalium artium.'[7] In this way Einhard, after he had grown up, had an opportunity of devoting himself to the study of these subjects, and we have testimony that his application was not without result. But there is a great difference between that and producing the design for the Imperial rotunda, or even having a predominant share in the preparation of the plans and the conduct of the works, especially when it comes to vaulting. His literary productions do not seem to suggest the powerful brain which gave birth to the Palatine Chapel.

Moreover, had he been the architect and master of the works, it would be difficult to explain the silence of the chronicles about the fact (while the names of several

[1] D'ACHERY, op. cit., *Chronicon Fontanellense*, vol. ii, p. 279.
[2] MIGNE, *Patr. Lat.*, vol. c, *Epistolae*.
[3] DUCHESNE, *Historiae Francorum Scriptores*, *Eginhardi, abbatis epistolae*, vol. ii, p. 761 C.
[4] *Mon. Germ. Hist. Script.*, vol. xiii, p. 272, *Catalogus abbatum Fuldensium*.
[5] MIGNE, *Patr. Lat.*, vol. cxiv, *Carmina, De Einharto magno Eginhardo*.
[6] Op. cit., p. 109.
[7] *Mon. Germ. Hist.*, ADEMARUS, *Historiae*, p. 118.

contemporary architects are preserved), and also his own; whereas he does not fail
to mention the church which he built at Seligenstadt, and insist on its importance:
'non indecori operis.'[1] It would be incomprehensible that, when he laid aside his courtly
robes as Minister of the Imperial Household and Crown notary in order to assume the
humble garb of a presbyter and abbot, he should have forgotten all the science, un-
equalled at the time, displayed in the great rotunda, and have exhibited so limited and
mean a substitute for it in the churches which we know he founded. This consideration
has peculiar force in the case of the one at Seligenstadt, erected to receive the precious
relics of SS. Peter and Marcellinus, so coveted and venerated by the founder, and also
to form the resting-place of his own mortal remains. For even without raising an edifice
too grand for the pecuniary resources of himself and his wife Emma—and they were not
contemptible—he might well have built one proportioned to his means, and yet of a
character to form a monument of the remarkable and precocious architectural attainments which have been ascribed to him.

We conclude, then, that Einhard's claim to be the architect of the chapel at Aachen
cannot survive the test of sound criticism. His name is never connected with it either
as designer or executor. The Monk of St. Gall, who has left us the least incomplete
account of the rotunda, makes no allusion to him in this connexion.[2] All that we can
say is that, being young and without experience in the difficult art of vault construction,
he may have had the opportunity of initiation into its secrets owing to the fact that the
Emperor had summoned to Aachen for the purpose masons from Italy and France.
The craftsmen of Piedmont and Lombardy were the best known and most skilful in the
Empire. Two centuries before, their services had been engaged by Nicetius, bishop of
Trier, as we learn from the letter of Bishop Ruffus of Turin, who must have been
referring to workmen of his own or neighbouring dioceses. And my belief is that it
was to them and to workmen from other parts of Italy and from Transalpine Gaul, that
the monk alluded in the words: 'ad cuius fabricam de omnibus cismarinis regionibus
magistros et opifices omnium id genus artium advocavit.'[3] Springer, too, thought that
these master masons came from Italy and Gaul.

Having said so much let us turn to the churches of Steinbach and Seligenstadt, which
are very instructive from the evidence which they afford as to the type of building
adopted by Einhard in his own foundations, and to his capacity as an architect.

THE CHURCH OF STEINBACH NEAR MICHELSTADT is believed to have been built by
Einhard († 844) some time after Louis the Pious (814–840) had made him and his wife
Emma a grant of Michelstadt (815) in the Odenwald, where a small wooden church
existed, and before 819, the year in which the husband and wife transferred the chapel
at Michelstadt to the abbey of Lorsch.[4] The dedication took place in 821.[5] In it were
deposited the relics of SS. Peter and Marcellinus, stolen from Rome (826–827), and
later enshrined in the apse of the church at Seligenstadt.[6]

Of the original structure, of T cross plan with nave and aisles terminated by apses,
there remain the nave (figs. 740, 741) and the north arm of the transept with their

[1] Mon. Germ. Hist. Script., vol. xv, part i, p. 240,
Translatio et miracula sanctorum Marcellini et Petri.

[2] Mon. Germ. Hist. Script., vol. ii, pp. 744, 755,
NOTKERUS BALBULUS, De gestis Karoli Magni imperatoris.

[3] Mon. Germ. Hist. Script., vol. ii, p. 744,
NOTKERUS BALBULUS, De gestis Karoli Magni imperatoris.

[4] Mon. Germ. Hist. Script., vol. xxi, pp. 357, 359,
360, Chronicon Laureshamense.

[5] Mon. Germ. Hist. Script., vol. iii, p. 117, Annales
Fuldenses antiqui.

[6] Mon. Germ. Hist. Script., vol. xv, part i, pp. 241–2,
EINHARDUS, Translatio et miracula sanctorum Marcellini et Petri.

respective apses. In its present condition the nave measures about 79 ft. by 24 ft. The arches, barely 4½ ft. wide, and now walled up, formerly opened into the aisles. They rest on quadrangular piers. The walls carried by the arches contained originally a corresponding number of narrow round-headed windows, splayed on the inside. The main apse, starting directly from the transept wall and of semicircular form, is lighted

Fig. 740. Steinbach near Michelstadt. South side of church (815–819)

by three similar windows. The gable and wall above the frontal arch of the apse is pierced by three round windows, two of which were intended to light the transept, and the third to give light and air to the roof. It seems that the use of round windows, derived as we suggested in our account of Norwich from a Roman source, was widely spread at this time in Germany, for we find them even represented in illuminated manuscripts. I may refer to the pictures of two aisled churches which I have noticed in the St. Gall 'Psalterium aureum' (ninth century),[1] where they appear in the nave and aisles.

---

[1] Library of the ancient abbey of St. Gall.

So far as one may judge from what is left, the arms of the transept were entered through two arches, barely 4½ ft. wide, with moulded imposts. The way in which the north arm of the transept is shut off suggests that it was used as a chapel. The apse which opens out of it has lost its original appearance.

With the exception of the apses, the whole building is roofed with timber. Underneath

Fig. 741. Steinbach near Michelstadt. Church (815–819)

the choir, crossing, and part of the nave, extends a crypt, the whole of which is under-ground and consists of barrel-vaulted passages.

So far as may be inferred from what mutilations, alterations, and extensions in the past have spared, and also from Einhard's allusions, of the same type though of larger dimensions was the church of SS. Peter and Marcellinus at Seligenstadt (827), previously known as Mulinheim and already containing a small stone church, which was given by Louis the Pious to Einhard and Emma in 815. Here he erected his new church dedicated to the martyrs, and in it he finally enshrined their relics previously deposited at Steinbach and in St. Martin's at Ostheim.[1]

[1] *Mon. Germ. Hist., Chronicon Laureshamense,* p. 359[15]; *Mon. Germ. Hist.,* EINHARDUS, *Translatio et miracula sanctorum Marcellini et Petri,* pp. 243, 244, 245.

The church of Seligenstadt consisted of a nave and aisles, the former being about 33 ft. wide, and the latter only half as much, separated by nine quadrangular piers on either side, which an excavation in the modern facing has shown to measure some 28 in. by 32 in. and to be constructed of bricks taken from Roman buildings. They have moulded imposts.

It is easy to see that the plan of both of Einhard's churches, with its T cross form, was derived from that of the Vatican Basilica.[1] But they are rough work, almost devoid of architectural decoration, and roofed, with the exception of the terminal recess, with wood. These facts are difficult to reconcile with the idea that the man who designed them was the creator and constructor of the principal buildings erected by Charles the Great.

After Charles the Great's conquest of Lombardy had brought Italy into direct relations with his northern dominions, architecture made a brilliant appearance in the German lands with the rotunda of Aachen; but this appearance was as ephemeral as the Empire which its founder was unable to endow with permanent vitality. It was ephemeral, too, because the architectural awakening brought about by the Emperor in the lands beyond the Alps was the result of his personal influence, and not the effect of a long period of preparation and, at the same time, the expression of the spirit and the needs of the age. In fact, all the buildings of his reign and vast Empire which are of importance for their vaulted construction were due to his personal will, and intended to promote his own glory and self-satisfaction. Thus, in addition to the great rotunda, another royal chapel of similar form was attached to his palace at Casseneuil,[2] which was destroyed by the Normans in 879. Other buildings, too, if not erected by his orders, were aided by his contributions, such as Theodulf's church at Germigny des Prés (801–806).

Moreover, art is dependent on public prosperity, and this was certainly not assured by the successors of Charles, whose incapacity is the theme of the historical records of two centuries. The first was Louis the Pious (814–840), born to wear the tonsure rather than the crown. In the course of a few years he fatally undermined the inheritance of the Pippins, Charles Martel, and Charles the Great, more particularly by the weakness of his conduct towards his wife Judith, and his youngest son Charles the Bald. His reign was disturbed by domestic and civil strife, fomented not so much by the indifference of his subjects, who were disgusted by his weakness, as by the discord between the Latin and the German element; in addition to which there came the incursion of Danes or Normans and Saracens. Under his successors, Lothair (840–855), Louis the German (843–876), Charles the Bald (843–877), and Pippin the Younger (838–846), the anarchy inherited from their father and grandfather respectively was intensified by the internal struggles to which we have referred, and by the abandonment of any attempt to resist the Northern barbarians and the Saracens; and at length the partition of Verdun (843) dissolved the fabric of the Empire.

This partition was succeeded by years of fruitless effort to diminish, if it was not possible to prevent, the raids within the divided realm of the barbarian hordes which left a trail of blood and ruin wherever they passed. The war against invaders was

---

[1] [R. SCHULTZE (*Basilika*, Berlin and Leipzig, 1928) would derive this and other features of the plan of early German churches from local Roman models. The earliest example of the transept at the end of the nave is to be found in the 3rd-century basilica at Ladenburg (on the Neckar), where the nave, separated from the aisles by arcades springing from piers, opens at either end with a large arch into a transept (p. 55). It only required the addition of an apse on the outer side of the transept to produce the plan of St. Peter's. (R.)]

[2] CORDERO, op. cit., p. 89.

supplemented by the one between Louis II and Charles the Bald. Finally, the death of Lothair (855) broke the last formal tie which still united the Empire of Charles the Great. It was followed by new family and civil wars, with the usual accompaniments of incursions and rebellions, until with Charles the Fat (881–887) the legitimate branch of the Imperial race became extinct in Germany.

Thereupon the eastern Franks elected as king the brave Arnulf of Carinthia (887–899), bastard son of Carloman, king of Bavaria (865–880). He succeeded in breaking the insolence of the Normans at Louvain (891), in suppressing the revolt of his vassals, and, finally, in assuming the Imperial diadem at Rome (896). His son, Louis the Child,

Fig. 742. Fulda. Church of St. Michael (818–822)

was elected as his successor (899–911), but his weak rule was troubled by civil wars and barbarian raids. With his death even the illegitimate German line of the descendants of Charles the Great came to an end.

Some idea of the conditions of ecclesiastical architecture in the German lands during the age of the heirs of Charles the Great is afforded by three churches, of which two are still in existence while we possess the plans of the third. It may be, too, that there is a fourth, of which a drawing exists. Let us see what they were like.

THE ROUND CHURCH OF ST. MICHAEL AT FULDA was built by Eigil, fourth abbot of Fulda, between the years 818 and 822,[1] as we are told in his Life, written by the monk Brun Candidus;[2] and it is known that it was not finished in 819, for Haistulf, archbishop of Mainz (813–826), did not dedicate it till 822.[3] Any one who reads this Life (in verse as well as prose) will find a clear and definite statement about the primary intention of the building, and also a description of its original form, corresponding to that of the existing structure. It was a cemetery church, of circular plan, with an annular aisle, supported by a circle of eight columns, covered with a dome of masonry, and

[1] *Mon. Germ. Hist., Annales Fuldenses antiqu*, p. 95.   vol. ii, p. 108, xv, *De vita Aegili versibus explicata.*
[2] *Mon. Germ. Hist. Script.*, vol. xv, part i, p. 229[40],   [3] BROWERUS, *Fuldenses antiquitates* (ed. 1612),p.118.
Vita Eigilis abbatis Fuldensis; *Poetae lat. aevi Carolini*,

having a crypt beneath with its vaulting supported by a central column. The actual building (figs. 742, 743) contains eight arches on the ground floor with columns surmounted by four capitals of Roman origin, three of which are Corinthian and one Composite, and by four plain cubical funnel-shaped capitals with deep abaci. An apsidal sanctuary projects at the east.

Fig. 743. Fulda. Church of St. Michael (818–822)

The building was altered in the eleventh century[1] by removing the vaulting and raising the height of the church as we now see it. A triforium gallery was constructed with openings, each of which was divided in two by a shaft carrying a cubical funnel-shaped capital and a corbel pulvin, hollow chamfered, recalling the prototypes of this kind at Mettlach (987), and curled over at the ends. Eight windows were also inserted, and the whole was roofed with wood. At the west a nave was added, approached through a tower porch, the two-light openings of which have Lombardic cubico-spherical capitals with pulvins like those just described. This nave, and two other additions on the north and south, have given the rotunda a cruciform appearance.

[1] LÜBKE, *Geschichte der deutschen Kunst* (Stuttgart, 1890), p. 42.

Beneath is a crypt. The middle part has a roughly constructed concentric barrel vault springing from a central column (a fragment of ancient origin), provided with a rude Ionic capital, and an inverted funnel-shaped capital for base. The annular aisle also has a barrel vault, which has been cut by the insertion of cross walls. Originally it was lighted by very narrow windows.

It is obvious that Eigil, the architect of the sepulchral rotunda of the abbey of Fulda ('Eigil . . . aliam aecclesiam in cymiterio rotundam mira arte typice composuit'[1]),

Fig. 744. Trier. Porta Nigra (3rd or 4th century)

derived his idea from the round tombs of ancient Rome. The annular rotunda, with its dome and barrel vault, reproduces on a smaller scale the mausoleum of Santa Costanza (fourth century). The circular vault of the central part of the crypt is modelled on the crypt of the mausoleum in the Villa of the Gordians on the Via Praenestina which belongs to the time of Diocletian. Below it is a beautifully constructed crypt, turning round a central mass which serves as a support for the whole structure.[2] This tomb provided the suggestion for the architect of the mausoleum of Romulus († 309), the son of Maxentius, standing in the midst of a spacious arcaded court close to the Circus of Maxentius by the old Via Appia,[3] though he gave the central block a more developed form by taking out of it eight semicircular recesses corresponding to those

[1] *Mon. Germ. Hist. Script.*, vol. xiii, pp. 272–4, *Catalogus abbatum Fuldensium.*

[2] [*Roman Architecture*, p. 179, n. 1 and fig. 219.]

[3] [Ibid., fig. 266.]

in the outer wall. In all these tombs the vaulted crypt is derived from the typical form found in the 'tholos' tombs of Volterra. Thus the Inghirami Tomb (Archaeological Museum at Florence),[1] dated from the middle of the fourth to the middle of the third century B.C., has a central pier supporting an elementary annular vault.

In the rotunda at Fulda the Roman cubical funnel-shaped capitals should be noticed.

Fig. 745. Turin. Porta Palatina (29 B.C.–A.D. 14)

They are derived directly from those of the Porta Nigra at Trier (fig. 744) belonging to the second half of the fourth century, or more precisely to the reign of Valentinian I (364–375),[2] under whom the city was much embellished[3] and put in a better state of defence against the Germans. The capitals of the gate at Trier are the oldest specimens of the kind that we have seen. It was on this form of capital, together with the Ravennate pulvin, that the Byzantines afterwards modelled their cubical funnel capitals of

[1] [MILANI, *Museo Archeologico di Firenze*, vol. i, p. 285.]

[2] [See ANDERSON, SPIERS, and ASHBY, *The Architecture of Ancient Rome* (London, 1927), p. 121. For a date under Constantine cp. *Congrès arch. Rhénanie*, p. 32. The Roman capitals may have been copied in the 9th century, but it should be noted that they are unfinished ('les chapiteaux ne sont qu'é bauchés', ibid., p. 25). Cp. vol. i, p. 235, n. 2. (R.)]

[3] BROWERUS, *Antiquitates Trevirenses*, vol. i, p. 251.

quadrangular shape with swelling sides, which in their simplest form may be seen in the cistern of Binbir-direk at Constantinople (sixth century).[1]

In connexion with the Gate of Trier we may observe in passing that the Gallo-Roman peoples gave exceptional importance to their city gates. In addition to this one, we may mention as proof the Porta Palatina of Turin (fig. 745),[2] erected under Augustus (29 B.C.–A.D. 14), and the Porta dei Borsari at Verona (third century).[3]

Though Eigil's church, like that at Aachen, betrays its Italian origin, the type of its original capitals indicates the work of northern craftsmen. In Italy at the time this form was rarely used, the preference being given to the Pre-Lombardic cubical pattern. The vaulted roof is to be explained by the fact that the church was erected very shortly after the completion of the great works at Aachen, and under their influence; and, indeed, some of the builders there employed may have been engaged on it.

THE ABBEY CHURCH OF ST. GALL was rebuilt by Abbot Gotzpertus (816–837) from the designs of the two monks Winiharius and Isenricus. It took seven years to finish (822–829).[4]

In studying the original of the very important plan[5] of the abbey drawn on parchment, which is dated about 820, we found that the church presents three notable features, viz. the apses facing one another at the east and west ends, the semicircular aisle round the western apse, and the towers which flank the latter.

The first of these peculiarities we discussed in our account of Abingdon Abbey (675); and we dealt with the subject of ambulatories, with or without arcades, in connexion with the cathedral of Ivrea and Saint Bénigne at Dijon. Western towers we know were designed to contain the staircases belonging to the façade, after the fashion of Ravenna. Their function here is made clear by the legend on the plan, 'Ascensus per cocleam ad universa super inspicienda.'

THE CATHEDRAL OF COLOGNE.—We possess a written account of the general form of the church erected by Archbishop Hildebold (785–819), and restored or completed by Archbishop Willibert (870–889), who dedicated it in 873. It was of basilica plan, with a choir apse at either end and crypts underneath them. Two wooden bell-towers flanked the western apse, each containing an altar. It was lighted by round windows in addition to others of rectangular form, some larger (of which three were in the eastern gable) and some smaller.

We are not told who restored or rebuilt Willibert's church after its injury in the terrible fire from which Cologne suffered at the hands of the Normans in 882. We only know, on the authority of Gelenius,[6] that in 1080, when Sigewin was archbishop (1079–1089), the easternmost part of the cathedral was suddenly burned.

A certain amount of light is thrown on the subject by the important eleventh-century

---

[1] [*Supra*, i. 67 and fig. 91.]

[2] [See *Roman Architecture*, pp. 48 ff.]

[3] [The lower part of it, at any rate, is now believed to belong to the 1st century: the inscription upon it refers to a restoration of the walls by Gallienus (STRONG, *Art in Ancient Rome* (London, 1929), vol. i, p. 151.) (A.)]

[4] MABILLON, *Annales Ord. S. Benedicti*, vol. ii, p. 530 C; *Mon. Germ. Hist. Script.*, vol. ii, pp. 65, 66, *Ratpertus Casus S. Galli*; KELLER, *Bauriss des Klosters St. Gallen vom Jahr 820*, pp. 9–11.

[5] [It is possible that the plan of St. Gall is not an actual representation of the monastery, but a drawing intended to show a typical plan, like the typical description of a monastery at the opening of the *Disciplina Farfensis* (MIGNE, *P. L.* cl). (H. T.)] [SCHULTZE reproduces (taf. 13, p. 80) DEHIO's reduction of the drawing to the terms of a modern plan in his *Kirchliche Baukunst des Abendlandes* (taf. 47). The original, in the Library of St. Gall, was first published by MABILLON (*Annales Ord. S. Benedicti*, vol. iii, 570); again by Prof. R. WILLIS (*Arch. Journal*, v (1848), 85). (R.).]

[6] *De admiranda, sacra et civili magnitudine Coloniae Claudiae Agrippinensis Augustae Ubiorum urbis* (Cologne, 1645), p. 231 D.

Fig. 746. Cologne. Cathedral Treasury. Illuminated leaf of 11th-century
Evangelistarium with representation of the old cathedral

Fig. 747. Trier. Basilica (3rd or 4th century)

Evangelistarium executed by the brothers Burchard and Conrad 'ad altare Sancti Petri infra muros Coloniae' for Illinus, canon of the cathedral,[1] in which may be seen (fol. 16 v.) a picture of the donor presenting the book to St. Peter seated in a chair, and above them a representation of the metropolitan church (fig. 746). Granted, always, that it is certain that the volume is earlier than 1080. For in that case we have an illustration (if only approximately accurate) of the cathedral of Cologne in its restored or new form after 882, showing the transepts belonging to the choirs at either end of the building.[2] The two towers rising at the east end—evidently bell-towers, as the openings in the highest stage show—must be earlier than the bell-towers of the cathedral at Ivrea (973–1001 or 1002), and are therefore the prototype of this arrangement. In the present case it is very probable that it was suggested by the staircases formed in the outer angles at the end of some building of the Roman period. Such, for instance, is the Basilica at Trier (fig. 747), thought to belong to the age of Constantine (311–337),[3] but which, considering its grand dimensions, and the character of its brick facing, together with the enclosing arches round the windows, which are original, may well be dated in the time of those great builders, Diocletian (284–305) and Maximian (286–310).

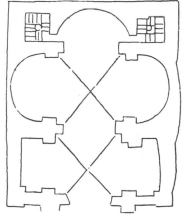

Fig. 748 Plan of a Roman
three-lobed building

I may mention here that a three-lobed building, the plan of which by Fra Giocondo is preserved among the drawings in the Uffizi, shows two staircases flanking one of its apses (fig. 748).[4]

THE SEPULCHRAL CHAPEL OF LORSCH is of rectangular shape, and its eastern and western sides (fig. 749) are decorated with a range of arches and blank triangular-headed arcading. The walls are constructed with polychrome polygonal stone checkers in imitation of Roman polychrome 'opus reticulatum' such as may be seen in the amphitheatre at Assisi. It always had, as now, a wooden roof of very high pitch.

The interior (fig. 750) contains a sarcophagus found in the old cloister of the neighbouring abbey of St. Nazarius. It is ornamented with pilasters and Ionic capitals exactly like those of the triangular-headed arcading on the chapel itself, and probably formed the coffin of Emperor Louis III the Saxon.

Many writers, Adamy[5] among them, believe that this structure (now known as the Michaelskapelle) was the old vestibule of the atrium of the abbey church of St. Nazarius, founded by King Pippin in 764,[6] and later rebuilt on a larger scale by the monk Adalbert (1144–1151). I think there is no doubt that it really is the burial chapel erected by Louis III the Saxon (876–882) near the abbey of Lorsch, as has been stated by others.[7]

---

[1] Cologne. Treasury of the Cathedral.

[2] [SCHULTZE (*Basilika*, p. 78) says that the tops of towers on the south side, seen above the roof, must belong to porches or chapels on this front, where probably the main access to the church lay. The tower shown against the north-west transept is the old sacristy and treasury, which occupied the space between the city wall and the transept. See plan, taf. 13. (R.)]

[3] [KRÜGER (*Das römische Trier*, p. 45) is in favour of the Constantinian date. (A.)]

[4] [A. BARTOLI, op. cit., vol. i, tav. lx, fig. 92.]

[5] *Die fränkische Thorhalle und Klosterkirche zu Lorsch, Historischer Verein für das Grossherzogthum Hessen* (Darmstadt, 1891), p. 7.

[6] *Mon. Germ. Hist., Chronicon Laureshamense,* p. 341.

[7] SAVELSBERG, *Deutsches Kunstblatt, herausgeg. von Eggers*; FÖRSTER, *Denkmale deutscher Baukunst,* vol. i, p. 11.

The chronicle of Lorsch says that Louis III buried his father Louis II the German (843–876), the founder of the national dynasty, in the abbey of Lorsch ('patrem in Laureshamensi monasterio tumulavit'), and that afterwards he himself was buried near his father in a church which he had built, known in the days of the chronicler as 'the variegated church': 'Ludowico rege Germanico, filio Ludowici, defuncto et iuxta patrem apud Lauresham in Ecclesia quae dicitur Varia, quam ipse huius rei gratia construxerat, sepulto.' Later, in 1053, this chapel was dedicated to the Virgin, the Apostles, and All Saints.[1]

Fig. 749. Lorsch. Sepulchral chapel. West side (876–882)

Now the existing Michaelskapelle is, as a matter of fact, 'varia' owing to its polychrome facing. That it cannot be the original porch leading to the atrium in front of St. Nazarius (according to Adamy's imaginary design) is proved by the fact that the terrible fire of 1090 destroyed the whole church, which had a wooden roof,[2] and would certainly not have spared the atrium and its vestibule. It is also proved, and still more convincingly, by the absence of any trace of the junction between the existing polychrome structure and the spacious cloister court which is supposed to have existed.

Moreover, in the Frankish realm capitals were of quite a different type and execution in the time of Pippin, under whom the building of St. Nazarius was begun, and this we learn from the crypt of the church at Flavigny (755–768). Again, edifices of the age of Charles the Great, when the works at Lorsch were finished, had no external

[1] *Mon. Germ. Hist., Chronicon Laureshamense,* op. cit., pp. 372, 375, 412.

[2] Ibid., p. 421[45]; Helwichius, *Antiquitates Coenobii Laurishamensis* (in Joannis, *Scriptores Historiae Moguntinensis,* tom. novus, Frankfort, 1727), p. 65. [De Lasteyrie (op. cit., 168) thought the chapel later than this fire. (R.)]

architectural decoration, as we know from the rotunda of Aachen and the churches of Germigny des Prés (801–806) and Steinbach (815–819). And that this was still the case in the days of Louis the Pious the round church at Fulda (818–822) bears witness.

The sepulchral chapel of Lorsch is to be regarded as the earliest instance of a building decorated with ranges of blank triangular-headed arcading, a design of German origin. For although at an earlier date the baptistery at Poitiers (seventh century) had exhibited the decorative use of pediments and blank arcading alternately triangular and round-headed, the chapel at Lorsch is the first dated building that displayed this particular form of treatment. This characteristic feature may be traced back to the

Fig. 750. Lorsch. Sepulchral chapel (876–882)

Ravennate and Pre-Lombardic blank arcading with round arches; while the substitution of triangular for round heads may have been suggested by some building such as the baptistery of Poitiers. It may even have been derived from the pedimented colonnading on sarcophagi of the Early Christian period, of which examples are to be found in the Lateran Museum. Or, again, it may have its source in some building of the Roman age. It was afterwards copied by the architect of the abbey church of Gernrode (968). And it was Lorsch and Gernrode which furnished the pattern to those who carried triangular-headed arcading to England.

I may mention here that in the tenth-century manuscript of Boethius 'De institutione arithmetica' at Bamberg[1] I have noticed the front of a building with triangular-headed arcading on its upper part, the heads forming part of a lozenge-shaped decoration; while the 'Evangelistarium of Essen', believed to be of the eighth or ninth century, and earlier than 834,[2] shows triangular-headed arcading formed of interlacing bands and scrolls.

I think that the capitals at Lorsch are the work of French chisels. We shall see presently how different were the knowledge and handiwork of the German artists.

[1] Bamberg. State Library.
[2] HUMANN, *Die Kunstwerke der Münsterkirche zu Essen* (Düsseldorf, 1914), p. viii.

On the death of Louis the Child (899–911), Conrad I of Franconia was raised to the throne, but his reign (911–918) was disturbed by perpetual civil wars and barbarian invasions. The elevation, however, of the illustrious Henry I the Fowler (918–936), the victor of Merseburg (933), saw the restoration of order and security in Germany.

THE CRYPT OF THE CHURCH OF ST. WIPERTUS NEAR QUEDLINBURG.—The church of St. Wipertus was erected by Henry I and his consort Matilda († 968). A passage in her life fixes the date as 936.[1]

The crypt (fig. 751) is all that is left of the original building. It has the form of a small basilica ending in a semicircular apse. Every part is covered with barrel vaulting, and

Fig. 751. Quedlinburg. Crypt of St. Wipertus (936)[2]

it is surrounded by an ambulatory. The pillars have roughly-made capitals formed by an inverted ovolo, a hollow moulding, and a roll, with a rude abacus. The bases have two bulbous rolls separated by a hollow moulding.

This crypt, above which must have stood the apse and presbytery of the original church, is important on account of its vaulted ambulatory, perhaps suggested by the one in Constantine's Lateran Basilica as enlarged by Pope Sergius II (844–845), which I carefully examined before its destruction in 1884. We have here, in fact, the oldest example of a crypt of this form to be found either in Italy or beyond the Alps.

The crypt of St. Wipertus recalls the ancient basilica of the SS. Annunziata at Prata, near Avellino. Of the primitive church there survives the interesting and, on account of its architectural form, important apse, pierced by round-headed windows instead of arches (fig. 752). In it is recessed a niche for the bishop's seat, a Pagan and Roman idea, for in the back of a nymphaeum in the 'Palace' of Hadrian's villa at Tivoli[3]

[1] *Mon. Germ. Hist. Script.*, vol. iii, p. 54[35], *Annales Quedlinburgenses*; KNACKFUSS, *Deutsche Kunstge-schichte* (Leipzig, 1888), vol. i, p. 71; *Mon. Germ. Hist. Script.*, vol. iv, p. 288, *Vita Mahthildis reginae.*

[2] The illustrations belonging to Quedlinburg and Gernrode are from photographs by Herr E. Kliche.

[3] REINA E BARBIERI, *Rilievo planimetrico e altimetrico di villa Adriana* (Rome, 1906), plate iii. [*Bull. Com.* lv (1927), p. 204, plates i, iii.]

a semicircular niche occurs. In the fourth century it was introduced in the basilica of St. Petronilla between the Via Ardeatina and the Via Ostiensis,[1] and also in that of the Martyrs Simplicius, Faustinus, and Viatrix (382), on the Via Portuensis near Rome.[2]

The spiral terra-cotta shafts (made for their places) which support some of the arched openings in the apse at Prata have capitals carved with very rude, stiff, plain leaves, and cauliculi like ram's horns, slightly curved at the top. These capitals enable us to fix, more precisely than has hitherto been done, the unknown date of the apse of the Annunziata, which some[3] regard as belonging to the earliest Christian age, while others[4] put it between the seventh and tenth centuries. By a process of elimination its date will be, approximately, that which followed the Lombard conquest and the scourge of pestilence and famine which afflicted Italy about 566, the period which saw the artistic awakening initiated by Theodelinda (590–625); in other words, the first half of the seventh century. Before the descent of Alboin (568) and after the reign of Rotharis (636–652), Italy never saw such degraded work as these capitals (especially the round one), even though produced in remote places and by local carvers.

Fig. 752. Prata near Avellino. Apse of the church of the SS. Annunziata (7th century)

The date which we have suggested explains the arcaded form of the apse, a plan which was in favour from the end of the fourth century to about the second half of the sixth both at Rome and Naples; so much so that in the latter century Bishop Vincentius (554–577) was still employing it in San Giovanni Maggiore at Naples ('Hic fecit praefulgidam basilicam. . . . Quem amplis aedificiis in gyro distinxit'[5]), while at Rome Pope Felix IV (526–530) adopted it for SS. Cosma e Damiano.

THE CRYPT AND CHURCH OF ST. SERVATIUS IN THE CASTLE AT QUEDLINBURG.—The erection of the castle church of Quedlinburg was begun by Matilda at the wish of her husband Henry I, shortly before his death in 936, as we are told in the Life of the Empress. In that year the crypt must have been finished, for it received the tomb of the great Emperor. In 997 the church was rebuilt by the second Matilda († 999), daughter of Otto I the Great (936–973); but it was not finished till 1021, as in that year a second

[1] Bull. di arch. cristiana, 1874, p. 123. DE ROSSI, Pianta della basilica di Santa Petronilla nel cimitero di Domitilla.

[2] DE ROSSI, La Roma sotterranea cristiana (Rome, 1877), vol. iii, p. 651, plate 52, La piccola basilica damasiana dedicata a Simplicio, Faustino, Viatrice, martiri storici del cimitero di Generosa.

[3] Archivio storico per le provincie napoletane, 1878, p. 133. TAGLIALATELA, Dell'antica basilica e della catacomba di Prata in Princ. Ulter. e di alcuni monumenti avellinesi.

[4] BERTAUX, op. cit., vol. i, pp. 85, 86.

[5] Mon. Germ. Hist., Scriptores rerum langobardicarum, p. 411, Gesta episcoporum neapolitanorum.

dedication took place.[1] In 1070 the town was burned ('Quindelincburg exusta est'[2]), and with it the church, which was rebuilt and reconsecrated in 1129.[3]

The crypt of the original building, which was discovered in the last century below the floor of the apse in the present crypt, belonging to the reconstruction after the fire of 1070, is surrounded by a range of recesses separated by engaged shafts which carry a continuous architrave; the whole being composed of stucco, and of rude workmanship (figs. 753, 754). That this is the crypt of the primitive church is proved by the existence at its west end of the tombs of Henry I, of his wife Matilda ('sepultaque est coram altari Christi presulis Servacii iuxta seniorem suum'[4]), and of their

Fig. 753. Quedlinburg. Old crypt of St. Servatius (936)

granddaughter, the Abbess Matilda, who in 999 was interred 'iuxta tumulos regum, avi et aviae suae Heinrici et Mechtildis'.[5]

Of a later date than this crypt, and probably forming part of the works carried out between 997 and 1021, is the underground apsidal chapel beneath the south aisle of the church. One of the side walls contains three arches with two shafts bearing quasi-Composite capitals, above which are corbel pulvins also carved with foliage, like some of those at Mettlach (997). The bases are of bulbous form, and rest on tall moulded plinths. The carving recalls that on the capitals and pulvins at Mettlach, though it is not so advanced.

The constructional supports in the crypt of St. Wipertus and the decorative ones in the crypt of St. Servatius found an echo in England. As a matter of fact we have already seen how, not earlier than the reign of Edgar (959–975), spiral shafts and inverted truncated pyramid capitals made their appearance in the crypt and apse of Repton; while several buildings contain bases with disproportionate, clumsy rolls, or of

[1] *Mon. Germ. Hist. Script.*, vol. iii, p. 74[1], *Annales Quedlinburgenses*; *Mon. Germ. Hist. Script.*, vol. iii, p. 436, Widukindus, *Res gestae Saxonicae*; *Mon. Germ. Hist. Script.*, vol. iv, pp. 288, 289, *Vita Mahthildis reginae*.
[2] *Mon. Germ. Hist. Script.*, vol. iii, p. 6, *Annales*

Corbeienses.
[3] Knackfuss, op. cit., vol. i, p. 73.
[4] *Mon. Germ. Hist. Script.*, vol. iii, p. 749, Thietmarus, *Chronicon.*
[5] *Mon. Germ. Hist. Script.*, vol. iii, p. 75, *Annales Quedlinburgenses.*

the bulbous form, and show the influence of the outlandish and barbarous mouldings of the supports in the church at Quedlinburg. This influence must be connected with the monastic intercourse which from the days of St. Gall († about 630) and St. Boniface († 755) had been going on between England and Germany with the other Teutonic lands, and was only intensified by the marriage of the pious Edith (929–946), daughter of Edward the Elder (901–925), with Otto the Great as his first wife.

In connexion with the two important monuments which we have examined at Quedlinburg I think it opportune to mention that bulbous bases, sometimes resting on a plinth formed like a church, are represented in abundance in German manuscripts, e.g. the 'Isidori Etymologiae' (tenth century), the 'Psalterium Folchardi' (ninth century), and the 'Vita S. Columbae' (ninth century), in the Library of St. Gall.

In the next place, these structures are evidently the work of Saxon hands, no doubt the best that could be procured, considering the importance of the place where they are found, the rank of the founders, and the royal use for which one of them was intended. They give an idea of the state of building, carving, and stucco work in Germany at a time when the local craftsmen had been forced to rely on their own attainments without help from outside. And this confirms the opinion we expressed about the carvers of the capitals in the chapel at Lorsch.

Let us now turn to the existing crypt (fig. 755) and the cathedral church of Quedlinburg which rises above it. The crypt under the choir (rebuilt in the Pointed style) and transept of the present church consists of a central space, divided into nave and aisles by pillars and terminating in an apse, and two lateral arms with small apses at their extremities. The unraised cross vaulting springs from capitals ornamented with stiff, plain leaves, palmetto leaves and other kinds of foliage, cauliculi, crosses, interlacing bands ending in a sort of

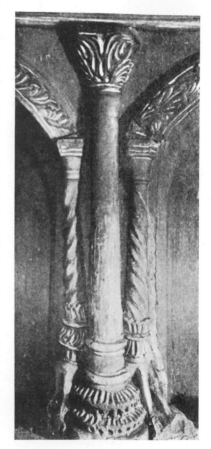

Fig. 754. Quedlinburg. Shaft in old crypt of St. Servatius (936)

Ionic volutes (fig. 756), pine cones, demons' heads with serpents coming out of their mouths and biting their ears (fig. 757), and eagles. Three are of a curious stepped form.

The church consists of nave and aisles separated by arches with columns, between every two of which comes a pier. The columns have characteristic bases with two rolls and a broad hollow moulding between them, while the capitals are of cubico-spherical form, carved, like the deep abaci, with animals (fig. 758), human figures, birds, foliage, interlacing, scroll-work, monsters, animal heads, &c. From an artistic point of view, both in the crypt and the church the foliage and other decorative elements are fairly well treated, while the representations of living beings are almost uniformly of barbarous character.

With the exception of the two minor apses in the transept, which have half-domes, the surviving portions of the church of 1070–1129 are roofed with timber. At the west end is the narthex with unraised cross vaulting and visible vaulting arches, above which is a gallery with pairs of openings, covered by a wooden roof. It is flanked by two towers, rebuilt like the gallery for the bells which unites them in their upper part.

The artistic features in the crypt are of the same date as those in the nave and transept, and the continuous cross vaulting in the central part of the crypt is contemporary with that constructed with wall and transverse arches in the lateral portions and in the narthex. The view, then, of those who regard the crypt as belonging to a different date from the church, falls to the ground. The date in question belongs to the years between the fire of 1070 and the reconsecration of 1129; for, in spite of what is believed in some

Fig. 755. Quedlinburg. Crypt of St. Servatius (1070–1129)

quarters to the contrary, there does not survive one stone upon another of the new structure of 997 that meets the eye. The quality of the builders and artists of the Harz district in the second half of the tenth century is revealed by the rough irregular vaulting in the eastern crypt of St. Cyriacus at Gernrode, and by the rude capitals and bases of the pillars, as well as by the decoration of the apse at the east end and of the western towers.

On the other hand, the capitals both in the crypt and the church at Quedlinburg present forms unknown to the West, and still more to the East, before the epoch of about 1000. I refer to the Lombardic cubico-spherical capitals which appear for the first time in Sant' Abondio at Como (1013–1095), and do not show themselves in Germany till after 1015, in St. Michael's at Hildesheim. Moreover, the Lombardic figure capitals, no longer showing the merely symbolic figures of Early Christian art, and going beyond the representations on the capitals of the eighth to the tenth century, did not show much progress before the first half of the eleventh, and only reached their culmination by the addition of scenes of writhing and struggling monsters in the second half of the eleventh and the following century.

I may notice here that the capitals at Quedlinburg have obvious analogies in style,

Fig. 756. Quedlinburg. Capital in crypt of St. Servatius (1070–1129)

Fig. 757. Quedlinburg. Capital in crypt of St. Servatius (1070–1129)

Fig. 758. Quedlinburg. Church of St. Servatius. Capital (1070–1129)

Fig. 759. Ilsenburg. Capital in the church (1087)

modelling, and execution, with those in the church of Ilsenburg (fig. 759), erected in 994 and rebuilt after the injuries it suffered during the disturbed reign of Henry IV (1056–1106) by Burchard II, bishop of Halberstadt (1059–1088), who consecrated it in 1087.[1] Compared with them the capitals at Quedlinburg show a more advanced stage of art, a fact to be explained by the earlier date of the church of Ilsenburg.

[1] *Mon. Germ. Hist. Script.*, vol. iii, p. 106, *Annales Hildesheimenses.* JACOBS, *Urkundenbuch des in der* *Graftschaft Wernigerode belegenen Klosters Ilsenburg,* vol. vi, p. 8.

They have similar analogies with the capitals in the church at Drübeck (fig. 760), which was in existence in 877 when Louis III (876–882) conferred rights of immunity on the monastery.[1] We have no information about it between 1058 and 1130, but it is believed to have been rebuilt in the early years of the twelfth century. The capitals at Quedlinburg are differentiated from these by more artistic arrangement of the foliage, so that those at Drübeck may very well belong to the end of the eleventh or the beginning of the twelfth century.[2]

Over and above the reasons given for this conclusion there is the fact that crypts of basilica plan, embracing not only the area of the apse and presbytery, as in the parish church of San Leo (881–882), but that of the transept as well, with cross vaulting sustained by pillars, did not make their appearance until the eleventh century was well advanced. The two earliest dated examples are the one in the cathedral of Speyer of 1030, and that under the existing cathedral of Parma. The latter crypt (fig. 761) belongs to the church rebuilt by Bishop Cadalus (1046–1071), and consecrated in 1106. For though the church of Steinbach has a crypt which extends not only to the crossing but also under part of the nave, it consists of mere underground passages with *arcosolia* like the Roman Catacombs.

Fig. 760. Drübeck. Capital in the church (11th or 12th century)

Further, we must remember that portals of the Lombardic type only came into existence about 1032 with that of Sant' Andrea at Montefiascone: consequently, an entrance of this kind could not have been used for the abbey church of Quedlinburg in 997.

Before leaving the church we may notice that the characteristic bases in the nave have their counterparts in the architectural decoration found in the illuminated manuscripts from the eighth or ninth to the eleventh century. Instances are the 'Concordia Evangeliorum' (ninth century) and the 'Psalterium Aureum' (ninth century) at St. Gall;[3] the Evangelistarium written for the Emperor Henry IV (Cat. 78 A. 2), and the Gospels of the abbey of Abdinghof (eleventh century) at Berlin;[4] the 'Alcuin Bible' of the eighth to ninth century at Zurich;[5] the 'Sacramentarium S. Gregorii Papae' written at Freising (1052–1078), now at Bamberg;[6] and the 'Evangelistarium of Illinus' in Cologne Cathedral (see p. 311).

Just as in former days the conquest of the Lombard kingdom by Charles the Great (774), so now the descent upon Italy (951) of Otto the Great (936–973), with the double object of comforting the lovely and not inconsolable widow of Lothair (946–950), Adelaide of Burgundy, and of renewing and strengthening the Carolingian claims to the Imperial dignity, consummated by his coronation as King of Italy (961) and Emperor (962), was the opening for Germany of an era of building activity, though not so brilliant as the first. It derived its sustenance from the free and direct communications re-established with Italy, an intercourse which continued through the reigns of Otto II (973–983) and Otto III (983–1002), with the latter of whom we conclude this section,

[1] Jacobs, *Urkundenbuch des in der Graftschaft Wernigerode belegenen Klosters Drübeck*, vol. v, p. 1.
[2] Kugler, *Kleine Schriften und Studien zur Kunstgeschichte*, vol. i, p. 614.
[3] St. Gall. Library of the ancient abbey.
[4] Berlin. State Library of Art.
[5] Zurich. Cantonal Library.
[6] Bamberg. State Library.

as we have devoted a separate chapter to the ecclesiastical architecture of Germany subsequent to the epoch of 1000.

THE ABBEY CHURCH OF ST. CYRIACUS AT GERNRODE was built by the powerful Margrave Gero († 968), born in 890.[1] It was quite complete in 968 (some say in 961[2]), so that the founder on his return from Rome, where he had deposited his armour near the altar of the Prince of the Apostles, and had received from the pope a relic of St. Cyriacus, was able to install the first abbess.[3]

Fig. 761. Parma. Crypt of the Duomo (1046–1071)

The plan is that of a T-shaped basilica with nave and aisles having apsidal endings, the transept being very short, as in the early Roman basilicas. It has an apse at either end. That at the west was rebuilt in its present form in the twelfth century,[4] but originally, no doubt, was of the modest type of the western apse at Drübeck (877), which seems to have been rebuilt between the eleventh and twelfth centuries. It is flanked by two towers.

The skeleton of the outer walls of the original church remains, here and there rebuilt, and altered by the subsequent construction of the triforium, when the arcades of the nave with their pillars were remade and the windows altered.

In the interior, the eastern apse has a semi-dome, while the presbytery, like all the rest of the church except the minor apses, western apse, and both crypts, has a wooden ceiling.

Under the chancel is the crypt, roofed with a combination of rough unraised cross

[1] PUTTRICH, *Denkmale der Baukunst des Mittelalters in Sachsen* (4 vols., Leipzig, 1836–1852), vol. i, p. 30.
[2] LÜBKE, op. cit., p. 75.
[3] *Mon. Germ. Hist. Script.*, vol. iii, p. 749, THIET-MARUS, *Chronicon*. [SCHULTZE (*Basilika*, p. 76) refers to the account of the church in A. ZELLER'S *Kirchenbauten Heinrichs I und der Ottonen* (Berlin, 1916).]
[4] DOHME, op. cit., vol. i, p. 76.

vaulting and continuous barrel vaulting springing directly from the outer walls, and supported in the centre by four piers with clumsy bases and rude moulded capitals.

The floor of the transept was raised by the insertion of an arcaded and vaulted gallery. The nave is now separated from the aisles by four arches on either side supported by two columns with a pier between them. The piers have moulded capitals; the columns, on the other hand, are crowned by Corinthianesque capitals with stiff, plain foliage with occasionally heads coming out of it (fig. 762). They have curious bases made up of rolls and hollow mouldings.

Under the western choir apse is a crypt with continuous cross vaulting supported by columns with bases which in some cases have spur-leaves at the angles, recalling those in St. Michael and St. Godehard at Hildesheim; while the capitals are of the Lombardic

Fig. 762. Gernrode. Church of St. Cyriacus.
Capital (12th century)

Fig. 763. Gernrode. Church of St. Cyriacus.
Pulvin (12th century)

cubical type, ornamented on the plane surfaces with concentric grooving and pairs of semicircles, or with foliage. The capitals are sometimes replaced by corbel pulvins, chamfered and curled over at the ends.

The triforium has, on the nave side, columns with piers between them bearing similar corbel pulvins (fig. 763), the prototypes of which are to be found at Mettlach; while at the two ends it has pairs of openings with plain or foliated funnel-shaped capitals.

The original windows are round-headed and splayed on both sides. The exterior of the eastern apse is marked off into two horizontal zones by a rude stringcourse, and into three vertical compartments by pilasters and engaged shafts.

Whether the western towers (fig. 764) were originally intended for staircases or for the bells, is impossible to say, as the highest stage with its two-light openings is the result of an alteration. The lowest part, like the eastern apse, is marked out by thick lesenas. The next stage, however, is decorated with arcading, both triangular and round-headed. Both stages are lighted by single rectangular openings with triangular or arched tops. The western apse with its blind gallery and west front have replaced the original arrangement.

The masonry and artistic details of the church indicate three separate series of building operations. Of the first of these, characterized by the rude art of some of the mouldings, and an entire absence of ornament, we have already spoken. To the second should, in my opinion, be assigned the triforium galleries with the new arcades which support them, the galleries in the transept, and the reconstruction of the apsidal west front. The artistic details presented by these portions are separated by a considerable interval from those of the age of Gero, and are occasionally superior to the results at

Fig. 764. Gernrode. Church of St. Cyriacus (10th and 12th centuries). NW. end

Quedlinburg. This second period may be placed at about the middle of the twelfth century, and with it we may associate the font. I append an illustration of one of its panels (fig. 765).

To the third, that is to say to the second half of the twelfth and the beginning of the

following century, will belong the gallery for the nuns on one of the sides, on account of the way in which the cross vaulting is constructed, and the greater artistic refinement shown in the capitals of its supports.

Gernrode is the earliest existing example in Germany of a church with an apse at either end. A still older one, however, was the abbey church of Fulda, the rebuilding of which was begun between 790 and 792 by Abbot Baugolf (779–802), continued by his successor Ratger (802–818) ('sapiens architectus'[1]), and finished by Eigil (818–822). It was dedicated in 819, and destroyed by fire in 937.[2] We learn that it was formed by two basilicas set end to end but separated by a transept,[3] and that each apse had a crypt beneath it: 'In eadem vero ecclesia duas cryptas magnifico opere conlocavit, unam quae respicit solis ortum, alteram quae solis occasum intendit.'[4] We are even told the name of the architect of these crypts, the monk Racholfus: 'Racholfo dictante magistro et monacho.'[5]

Fig. 765. Gernrode. Church of St. Cyriacus. Detail of font (12th century)

Other earlier instances were the abbey church of St. Gall (822–829), the cathedral of Cologne as built by Hildebold (785–819) and finished or restored by Willibert (870–889), and the cathedral of Hildesheim, erected by Bishop Alfred (851–874), and dedicated in 872,[6] which had a crypt at either end and therefore two apses facing one another.[7] In other countries a very early example was to be found at Abingdon Abbey (675); and it may very well be that the architect of Fulda was influenced by the English Benedictine model, just as later the designer of St. Cyriacus may have derived his plan from St. Gall, which also suggested the round towers on either side of the western apse.

In addition to this it contains the earliest dated double-splayed windows in Germany. Those in the round church at Fulda (818–822) are not original. This form of opening, the history of which we traced in our account of Bagnacavallo (sixth century), and to which a wide extension had been given by the Lombard gilds, had already made its appearance north of the Alps, in the Frankish Empire in the apse at Germigny des Prés (801–806); and also in England in St. Michael's Church, St. Albans (about 950).

Gernrode further affords the first instance for Germany of towers treated with a scheme of architectural decoration in the Lombardic manner, the prototype being the campanile of San Satiro at Milan (876), and likewise of apses marked off into horizontal

[1] *Mon. Germ. Hist. Script.*, vol. xiii, p. 272, *Catalogus abbatum Fuldensium.*

[2] *Mon. Germ. Hist. Script., Annales Fuldenses antiqui*, p. 95; *Mon. Germ. Hist. Script.*, vol. iii, p. 57, LAMBERTUS, *Annales*; *Mon. Germ. Hist. Script.*, vol. iii, p. 118, *Annales Sancti Bonifacii*; *Mon. Germ. Hist. Script.*, vol. iii, p. 56, *Annales Hildesheimenses.*

[3] BROWERUS, *Fuldenses Antiquitates*, pp. 105 ff. (ed. 1605).

[4] *Mon. Germ. Hist. Script.*, vol. xv, part i, p. 229, BRUN CANDIDUS, *Vita Eigilis abbatis Fuldensis.*

[5] *Mon. Germ. Hist. Script.*, vol. ii, p. 168, BRUN CANDIDUS, *De vita Aegili versibus explicata.* [For the plan of Ratger's church as revealed by excavations (1908–1913 and 1919–1924) see SCHULTZE, *Basilika*, fig. 46, p. 71. It appears to agree generally with the descriptions mentioned in the text. (R.)]

[6] *Mon. Germ. Hist. Script.*, vol. iii, p. 48, *Annales Hildesheimenses.*

[7] BERTRAM, *Geschichte des Bisthums Hildesheim* (Hildesheim, 1899), p. 44.

Fig. 766. Mettlach. Abbey Church (987)

zones and divided vertically into compartments by lesenas and wall-shafts. All of them were ideas imported from Italy, but carried out with such taste and ability as the Teutonic craftsmen possessed. The fact is, the lesenas and shafts are applied to the apse not merely as buttresses, as they were in Roman times, but for decorative reasons.

Italian churches of that age provided numerous instances of apses embellished with one or two tiers of lesenas and corbel arches. Some of the earliest, to which we have called attention, are those at Arliano (712–744), Toscanella (739), and San Leo (881–882); which last was, no doubt, seen by Otto the Great when, after a long and desperate resistance, he stormed the fastness, and probably also by his right-hand man, the valiant Gero.

No country outside Italy exhibited towers embellished with lesenas, arched corbel courses, and blank arcading, older than those at Gernrode. And though the scheme applied was of foreign origin, a partly Teutonic character was given to it, suggested by the ranges of arcading on the sepulchral chapel of Lorsch.

Fig. 767. Mettlach. Gallery (987)

THE ABBEY CHURCH OF METTLACH was erected by Lutwinus the first abbot, afterwards archbishop of Trier (695–713), in honour of the Virgin. It was rebuilt by Hezzel on the model of the monastery church of St. Maximin, in the time of Archbishop Egbert (977–993), and soon afterwards reconstructed by Lioffinus (987) (fig. 766) in imitation of Charles the Great's rotunda: 'et Aquisgrani palacium mittens et exinde similitudinem sumens, turrim, que adhuc superest, erexit.'[1]

In the upper story or triforium may be noticed Pre-Lombardic cubical capitals hollowed out at the angles, and with a flower or other ornament on a console projecting from the abacus. Others have the form of a simple cube (fig. 767), or are shaped like an inverted truncated cone. These capitals, decorated with conventionalized vine branches, foliage, and interlacing, fairly successfully treated though of monotonous design and

[1] *Mon. Germ Hist. Script.*, vol. xiv, p. 99, *De rebus Trevirensibus saec. VII–X libellus*; *Mon. Germ. Hist. Script.*, vol. xv, part ii, pp. 1264, 1265, *Ex miraculis S. Liutwini, auctore monacho Mediolacensi*; SAMMARTHANUS, &c., *Gallia cristiana, Ecclesia Trevirensis, Mediolacus*, vol. xiii, pp. 569 E, 570 A; HONTHEIM, *Historia Trevirensis diplomatica et pragmatica*, vol. i, p. 74 (citing MABILLON, *Annales Ben.*, i, pp. xviii, no. 38).

frigid execution, carry very depressed corbel pulvins carved with foliage, or in some cases plain and curled over at the ends. The carvings on the pulvins recall those in the underground apsidal chapel of St. Servatius at Quedlinburg (997–1021).

A noticeable feature in the church are the corbel pulvins with rudely curled ends. They are derived from the crutch-shaped pulvins, a Lombard creation of the tenth century, which make their first appearance in the towers of the cathedral of Ivrea (973–1001 or 1002). These are the oldest dated examples that I know, and are important for purposes of comparison, being earlier than the chamfered specimens at Gernrode or those of similar form in the round church at Fulda.

Fig. 768. Essen. Abbey Church Trilateral choir (1039–1056)

TRILATERAL CHOIR AND CRYPT IN THE ABBEY CHURCH AT ESSEN.

—The abbey church of Essen was founded by Alfred, bishop of Hildesheim (851–874), between 858 and 863, and was finished in 873.[1] We may infer from what survives that it consisted of a basilica with nave and aisles, a very short transept, and central and lateral apses.

The date at which the well-known three-sided choir at the west end with its façade was added is not known. It is generally believed to have been in the time of the Abbess Matilda (973–1011); but my view is that it was constructed when the convent was rebuilt by the Abbess Theophanu (1039–1056). Her memory remained closely connected with the convent of Essen: 'unde ibidem eius memoria semper in benedictione erit.'[2] On the same occasion the crypt was altered and extended eastwards. It was consecrated in 1051 by Hermann II, archbishop of Cologne (1036–1055).[3]

The three sides of the choir (fig. 768) have on the ground floor arches springing from piers copied from those in the rotunda at Aachen. The capitals in the gallery above are Corinthian (ancient, and taken from Roman structures), Corinthianesque with stiff, plain leaves and a dentilated course round the top, and freely treated Ionic. Contemporary specimens of the Corinthianesque type are to be found on the exterior (fig. 769),

[1] HUMANN, *Die Kunstwerke der Münsterkirche zu Essen*, pp. 1–2; LEIBNITIUS, *Scriptores Brunsvicensia illustrantes, Chronica episcoporum Hildensheimensium, necnon abbatum monasterii Sancti Michaelis* (Hanover, 1710), vol. ii, p. 785.

[2] *Mon. Germ. Hist. Script.*, vol. xi, p. 399, *Brunwilarensis monasterii fundatio.*

[3] HUMANN, op. cit.

which also contains examples of the Lombardic cubico-spherical pattern: a fact which connects together the eastern part of the crypt, the west front, and the atrium through which it is approached.

The crypt under the eastern choir is the work of two distinct periods. To the first belongs the central part with its plain piers, to the second the two ends which have their

Fig. 769. Essen. Abbey Church. Trilateral choir (1039-1056)

supports embellished with angle shafts and fluting. The greater amount of ornament on the eastern supports is explained by their proximity to the altar.

The earlier of these periods corresponds to the time of the Abbess Matilda. As a matter of fact we know that, after the fire of 944 or 946, which must have necessitated some restoration, a dedication of the crypt took place.[1] The second period will be that of the Abbess Theophanu. Any one who compares the carving on the capitals of the piers at the east end with the Ionic capitals and bead-and-reel moulding in the gallery of the western choir will at once see such intimate relationship both in design and execution that they may be regarded as contemporary. This point established, these carvings cannot belong to the epoch of about 1000 for the three following reasons:

[1] Humann, *Der Westbau des Münsters zu Essen*, p. 30.

(1) The form of cubical capital on the piers at the east end of the crypt is decisive against that date, for the Lombardic cubico-spherical capital did not appear in Germany till later. The date of its appearance at Essen is given by the capitals in the western atrium of the church which forms part of the great works of Theophanu.

(2) The form of the capitals in the rotunda at Mettlach, and the type of their ornamentation, are evidence of the way in which capitals were treated in Germany at the end of the tenth century. This manner is quite different from that of the Ionic, Corinthianesque, and cubico-spherical specimens, to be found in the crypt, west front, and atrium of the church of Essen.

(3) The west front of the three-sided choir exhibits an arched corbel course. The earliest example of such a feature (either in the continuous form or divided into sections by lesenas) in Germany is to be found in the abbey church of Limburg (1024–1045–1058). One might suspect that it was due to Italian builders, who, according to some,[1] were responsible for the whole structure. We cannot, however, admit that Italian craftsmen had any share in the work, for the methods of construction and the treatment of capitals in Italy at the end of the tenth century were not of this character.

We must accordingly date this carving, and consequently the alteration of the crypt and the erection of the three-sided choir and west front, in a period subsequent to the time of Abbess Matilda, in other words in the days of Theophanu, about whose works of restoration and enlargement we possess definite information: 'E quibus, Theophanu, virum se moribus agens, Asidense monasterium cum universis eius officiis iam partim vetustate collapsis, ab ipsis fundamentis novo erigens opere, mirabiliter amplificavit.'[2] These works must have included the whole of the conventual buildings, and necessarily, or rather essentially, the church as well; for it is notorious that in the Chronicles 'monasterium' has the meaning of 'church'.

[1] HUMANN, *Die Kunstwerke der Münsterkirche zu Essen*, p. 16.

[2] *Mon. Germ. Hist. Script.*, vol. xi, p. 399, *Brunwilarensis monasterii fundatio.*

VII

THE LOMBARDO-RHENISH STYLE

WHILE the Lombard gilds in Italy were seeking by repeated experiments to give an embodiment to their conception of a vaulted church, and while in France the Benedictine Order was striving after a solution of the problem how to cover every part of churches of large size with cross vaulting, the master builders of Germany were concentrating their efforts, one may say exclusively, on the creation of a peculiar ground plan. That plan, taken together with the severe character and imposing form of the structure raised upon it, was intended to endow with an Imperial dignity the Lombardo-Rhenish basilica, the highest expression of German architecture in the eleventh and twelfth centuries. It was an outward and visible sign of the Imperial idea, brought back to life among the Teutonic peoples by Otto the Great (936–973), and not only affirmed but also made good in a greater or less degree by his successors.

No one can look on the imposing towered piles of the cathedrals of Mainz, Speyer, and Worms, or the solemn naves of their interiors, without being immediately impressed by this fact. And so forcible is the result that, had the original conceptions been carried through, and had their authors been able to combine grandeur of architectural form with the wealth of ornament exhibited by contemporary buildings in Italy, and also with the constructive and statical knowledge of the Lombard gilds, there is no ecclesiastical edifice of the eleventh and twelfth centuries which would have stood the test of comparison with them; excepting always the church of Abbot Hugo at Cluny (1089–1130), standing unrivalled in its consummate majesty and pride.

Satisfied, however, with a single aim, the northern builders of the grandest German churches, though in direct contact with Italy and considerably influenced by Italian architecture, and though at times availing themselves of the services of her craftsmen, took absolutely no interest in a rational and original solution of the problem how to cover their structures with cross vaulting. By such a solution they might have contributed towards the development and completion of the architecture which immediately precedes the Pointed style, and was its source and origin.

Hence it is only at the beginning of the second thirty years of the twelfth century that we find them making their first attempts to substitute cross vaulting for flat ceilings over the wider spaces. An exception must be made in the case of the abbey church at Laach, where the vaulting of the main spans must be explained as an imitation, which was unique, of the Cluniac abbey of Vézelay (1096–1104). And this at a time when the Lombardic style had attained its completion in San Michele Maggiore at Pavia, erected after the earthquake of 1117, and when Durham had seen between 1129 and 1133 the combination of the pointed arch with diagonally-ribbed cross vaulting, and while in France the Transition, which opened the way for the Pointed style, had already made its appearance. The latter was soon moulded by the German School after its own fashion and to its own glory, reaching its culmination in the new cathedral of Cologne (1248). All which forms the subject of the present chapter.

THE ABBEY CHURCH OF ST. MICHAEL AT HILDESHEIM was begun by Bishop Bernward (993–1022), but the precise year is not known. In 1015 the crypt was ready, and was dedicated. The church was consecrated by the bishop in the year of his death, but it was only completed by his successor, Godehard (1022–1038), who performed the dedication in 1033. In 1034 it was struck by lightning ('monasterium S. Michaelis archangeli fulmine combustum et miserabiliter est deterioratum'),[1] and restored by Godehard with a fresh consecration in the next year, which shows that the damage done was inconsiderable. Injured by another fire, and beginning to suffer from the

Fig. 770. Hildesheim. Crypt of St. Michael's (about 1010–1015 and 1171–1186)[2]

effects of time, it was repaired and altered by Abbot Diedrich II in the days of Bishop Adelogus (1171–1190), who in 1186 consecrated it once more.[3]

The church as originally designed had a nave with aisles, separated by a transept from the apse at either end. The transepts were flanked by staircase turrets, and over either crossing rose a large tower. Beneath the western choir apse is a crypt where the capitals of the piers which support its roof are formed of a fillet and hollow moulding

[1] *Mon. Germ. Hist. Script.*, vol. iii, p. 99, *Annales Hildesheimenses.*

[2] The illustrations of Hildesheim are from photographs taken by Herr F. H. Bödeker.

[3] *Mon. Germ. Hist. Script.*, vol. vii, pp. 852, 857, *Chronicon Hildesheimense*; *Mon. Germ. Hist. Script.*, vol. iv, pp. 778, 779, THANGMARUS, *Vita Bernwardi*

episcopi Hildesheimensis; *Mon. Germ Hist. Script.*, vol. xi, p. 195, WOLFERIUS, *Vitae Godehardi episcopi Hildesheimensis*; LEIBNITIUS, op. cit., *Chronica episcoporum Hildensheimensium*, pp. 787, 788; BERTRAM, *Geschichte des Bisthums Hildesheim*, pp. 69, 71, 80, 94, 187.

or an ovolo (fig. 770). The two columns with Lombardic cubico-spherical capitals on either side of the present outer doorway come from the upper church. In its midst lies the limestone sarcophagus which the founder had ordered for himself during his lifetime. The bas-reliefs which decorate the coped cover should be noticed, especially those of living creatures, among which only the lamb with the cross on one of the gable

Fig. 771. Hildesheim. St. Michael's. North arm of western transept (about 1015–1035)

ends is fairly successful. The angels between tongues of flame or clouds on the sides of the cover are very rude work.

The western choir apse is the result of a reconstruction attributed to Adelogus. The north arm of the transept is occupied by a platform supported by rude unraised continuous cross vaulting, above which are two galleries one over the other (fig. 771). In them may be seen cubico-spherical capitals surmounted by deep abaci or rude corbel pulvins.

This cross vaulting with that in the crypt brings to mind the beautiful contemporary vaulting with visible arches in the crypt of San Miniato al Monte near Florence (1013),[1]

[1] *Supra*, vol. i, p. 231.

and shows what a far higher level the art of vaulting had reached in Italy in the eleventh century than in Germany, or indeed in any country north of the Alps.

This transept communicates with the north aisle by two arches supported by a column with a Lombardic cubical capital. The south arm of the transept has lost its end and staircase turret, but it has kept the two arches separating it from the

Fig. 772. Hildesheim. South aisle of St. Michael's (about 1015-1035 and 1171-1186)

corresponding aisle (fig. 772). The three arches which divide it from the crossing are not original.

The eastern choir has disappeared, together with the subordinate lateral apses, but the transept in front of it remains. Four great arches carry the central tower, which has been altered. In the south arm of the transept the capital of the column supporting the two arches leading into the aisle has its faces and angles ornamented with spear heads.

The nave is separated from the aisles by columns, between every two of which comes a quadrangular pier. The piers are original. Of the columns only two still retain their original cubico-spherical capitals and unspurred bases. The others have capitals of the time of Adelogus (figs. 773, 774), which, with their abaci, are elaborately ornamented with scroll-work, foliage, sacred and profane figures, animals, &c. Their bases are provided with the characteristic spur leaves at the angles, which occur so often in Germany.

Except for the vaulted platforms in the transepts (and no doubt the half-domes of the apses) the whole church had wooden ceilings.

St. Michael's (fig. 775) is not only an important monument for the history of art, but also contains more than one characteristic feature. Some of these—certainly the Lombardic cubico-spherical capital—had an important share in the formation of the Lombardo-Rhenish style; and this is why we include the church in our list of Rhenish buildings, though it belongs geographically to Old Saxony.

Fig. 773. Hildesheim. Capital in the nave of
St. Michael's (1171–1186)

Fig. 774. Hildesheim. Capital in the nave of
St. Michael's (1171–1186)

We notice, in the first place, the plan of a double transept flanked by staircase turrets, with a central tower over each crossing. Other churches before Bernward's had been erected with two transepts, and one or even two central towers; for instance, Saint Riquier (Centula) (793–798), and Saint Remi at Rheims (eighth and ninth centuries). But these had not the flanking towers with which St. Michael's was provided.

Next, we notice the arrangement of an arcaded platform or portico at the end of the transept. It had been introduced in the case of the great transept of Constantine's Vatican Basilica (fig. 776). In the portico to the right Pope Damasus (366–384) constructed his baptistery, while the one to the left contained chapels and the tomb of Urban II (1088–1099). In Bernward's church, however, these transept porticoes were surmounted by galleries.

The arrangement in St. Peter's influenced at a later date the architect of Cerisy la Forêt (1030–1066), from which it was copied in other Lombardo-Norman churches. It was also present to the mind of the patriarch Poppo (1017 or 1019–1042 or 1045) when building his cathedral at Aquileia, for the two arches still existing in either arm of the transept were evidently intended originally not only to strengthen the lofty transept walls but also to support two loggias which probably disappeared in the restoration and alteration of the church by the patriarch Marquard between 1365 and 1381.

Another feature is the alternation of piers with columns, not in this case an advance in the direction of the Lombardic church, but merely providing a firmer support for the lofty and substantial nave walls. This expedient (an early instance occurs in St. Demetrius at Salonica (fifth century)) we have discussed in our account of Jumièges. It was introduced at Hildesheim under the influence of the Lombardic movement, at that time specially active in Italy and France. Shortly before, it had been employed in SS. Felice e Fortunato near Vicenza (985). And while St. Michael's was in course of erection, a far more advanced scheme was being embodied in San Miniato al Monte near Florence (1013) in the form of an alternation of columns and compound piers

Fig. 775. Hildesheim. St. Michael's (about 1015–1036 and 1171–1186)

from which started longitudinal and transverse arches. The result was a sound and well-thought-out concatenation of the entire structure.

Then we have to remark the presence of the Lombardic cubico-spherical capital. Its introduction here must be later than 1015, for in that year only the crypt of Bernward's church was finished and dedicated, and the capital does not appear in it.

I ought to notice here that the date of 1001 as the beginning of the constructive works at Hildesheim is wrong. They cannot have been started earlier than about 1010, for it is inconceivable that the foundations took so long to construct. Certain it is that the choir above the crypt, the body of the church, and the eastern choir, must have been erected between 1015 and 1022, for it was only then that they were dedicated, and it was the dedication of an unfinished building: 'et ex parte dedicavit.'[1] The church was not finally completed till 1033, when a fresh consecration took place.[2]

[1] *Mon. Germ. Hist. Script.*, vol. vii, p. 852, *Chronicon Hildesheimense.*

[2] *Mon. Germ. Hist. Script.*, vol. xi, p. 195, WOLFFRIUS, *Vita Godehardi episcopi Hildesheimensis.*

We discussed the origin of the cubico-spherical capital when dealing with Sant' Abondio at Como. We may refer here to its rapid diffusion in the German lands, where it kept the carvers busy for two whole centuries, and was only dispossessed by the Pointed style. And it preserved its form unaltered, it being very rare to find in Germany the scalloped type. In German illuminated manuscripts I have never come across any

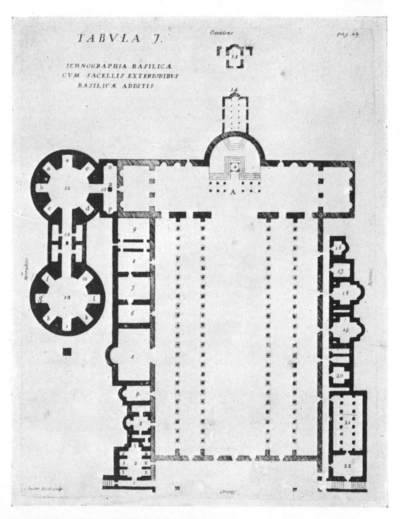

Fig. 776. Rome. Plan of Old St. Peter's (4th century). From BONANNI, *Templi Vaticani Historia*, founded on that of Alfarano (p. 166, n. 8, above)

representation of the cubico-spherical capital till well on in the eleventh century. I may refer to the 'Sacramentarium S. Gregorii Papae' (1052–1078) in the State Library at Bamberg, where it is depicted in an arcade.

Before leaving this interesting church, I should like to say a few words about various important works of art ascribed to the school founded at Hildesheim by Bernward, and carried on under his direction. The productions of this school appear to me to be in part the result of arbitrary attributions; and it is desirable that they should be subjected to a fresh examination by some one who has made a special study of the subject, and would treat them as a whole with the aid of new criteria and a comparative method

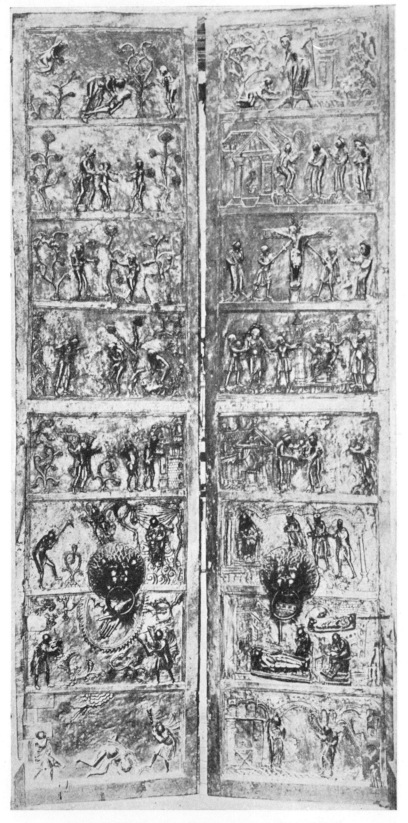

Fig. 777. Hildesheim. Bronze doors of the cathedral

based on immediate knowledge of contemporary work of the same class both Eastern and Western. Meanwhile I shall confine myself to some observations on the celebrated bronze doors of the narthex of the cathedral, and the equally celebrated portion of a candelabrum (figs. 777, 778) of the same metal (with a new top added in the last century) which is in the church.

It is suggested that Bernward derived his idea for the doors, with the story of Adam and Eve on the left side and scenes from the life of Christ on the right, from those of Santa Sabina at Rome, also having subjects from the Old and New Testament, which he must have seen and admired when, in 1001, he was the guest of the Emperor Otto III in his castle on the Aventine. In the same way, the candelabrum, with its spiral band of scenes, was inspired by the Column of Trajan.[1] Unfortunately there is no mention of these works (which, it has been recently noticed,[2] show such different treatment of the figures) by Thangmarus, the bishop's contemporary biographer and tutor; nor is it stated that the doors made by Bernward, and afterwards set up in the cathedral by Godehard,[3] are identical with those before us. We might just as well assert, and with more foundation, that the spiral candelabrum, the supposed 'columna aenea' of Bernward,[4] is one of the 'duo candelabra longa' which Adelogus gave to his cathedral.[5]

Nor must we put too much reliance on the inscription on the two middle bands of the doors, put there it is not clear when, for it is improbable that they would have been cast and fixed in place in 1015 when St. Michael's was not yet built. I believe that this inscription is of a piece with the one on the great bell at Rivolta d'Adda (eleventh century) stating that the bell-tower was added to the church in the tenth century, when the latter was not in existence.

Any one who compares the reliefs on the doors and candelabrum with the carvings on Bernward's tomb in the crypt of St. Michael's will not fail to realize the enormous interval between the artists responsible for the bronze work and the sculptor of the sarcophagus, or to be convinced of the impossibility of their being all of one date and the products of a single school. Not to speak of the fact, which no one has yet noticed, that the candelabrum was designed with figures at the angles of the base, though such appendages to the lower torus of a column base did not reach Germany from Italy, where they originated in the tenth century, before the second half of the eleventh century in the simple form of claws.

Fig. 778. Hildesheim. Candelabrum in the cathedral (about 12th century)

[1] GRISAR, *Analecta Romana*, vol. i, pp. 460, 461.
[2] HUMANN, *Zur Beurtheilung mittelalterlicher Kunstwerke in Bezug auf ihre zeitliche und örtliche Entstehung.*
[3] *Mon. Germ. Hist. Script.*, vol. xi, p. 195, WOLFERIUS, *Vita Godehardi.*
[4] LEIBNITIUS, op. cit., *Chronicon coenobii S. Michaelis in Hildesheim*, vol. ii, p. 399.
[5] *Mon. Germ. Hist. Script.*, vol. vii, p. 858, *Chronicon Hildesheimense.*

The monuments show that it was not used by the School of Hildesheim till the twelfth century. On the other hand, the rude carvings of the sarcophagus ill consort with the far more advanced reliefs on the bronze doors; and it is not likely that the feeblest member of the school would be selected to execute the tomb of its founder.

If I may hazard an opinion, taking account of the figures on Adelogus's capitals in St. Michael's, which are less advanced than those of the candelabrum, and still less so than those on the cathedral doors, and bearing in mind the numerous eleventh- and twelfth-century carvings and stucco work which we have examined in Germany, I am inclined to think that the candelabrum, if executed by German artists at all, belongs, at the earliest, to the last years of Adelogus's episcopate, and that the doors were not cast before the twelfth century, in view, among other things, of the treatment of the nude showing an advanced stage of art.[1]

Fig. 779. Strasbourg Cathedral. Choir (12th century)

STRASBOURG CATHEDRAL, rebuilt by Bishop Werinherus of Hapsburg (1001–1029) in 1015, but only finished after his death, about the year 1031,[2] would have furnished, had it survived, an important link in the chain of monuments which produced the Lombardo-Rhenish style. As it is, the reconstruction following on the repeated conflagrations between 1130 and 1176 spared next to nothing of that bishop's church; that is to say, merely building materials used, for instance, in the oldest part of the crypt. It is true that it has been suggested that a portion of the eleventh-century structure may be recognized in the crypt under the choir (fig. 779), planned like a miniature basilica with nave and aisles separated by cruciform piers alternating with columns, with a barrel vault over the central part, and cross vaulting in the aisles. There is, however, no truth in this, for not only is the system of vaulting against it, but even more, the artistic features of the supports. In fact the Lombardic capitals with scroll-work and well-rounded figures treated in high relief are obviously later than the carving in San Flaviano at Montefiascone (1032); and I feel sure that no one familiar with the decorative carving of the first centuries after the epoch of 1000 would date these figure capitals in the age of Bishop Werinherus. Moreover, we shall presently see what was the manner of carving capitals both in crypts and churches, in the Rhine lands, in and about the bishop's time.

[1] [The latest authority, R. HAMANN, *Geschichte der Kunst* (Berlin, 1933), p. 908, maintains that both doors and candlestick are of the time of Bernward. (R.)]

[2] *Mon. Germ. Hist. Script.*, vol. xvii, pp. 87, 88, *Annales Argentinenses*; DACHEUX, *La cathédrale de Strasbourg*. [The traditional date is 1028 (KRAUS, *Das Münster von Strassburg* from *Kunst und Alterthum in Elsass-Lothringen*, 1877, p. 16). (A.)]

THE ABBEY CHURCH OF LIMBURG was due to the Emperor Conrad II (1024–1039), who entrusted Abbot Poppo (1020–1048) with its erection. There are conflicting notices as to the date of foundation, with the result that Trithemius[1] puts it in 1024, Würdtwein[2] in 1030, Bucelinus[3] in about 1031, and Browerus[4] in 1034. The choir altar was dedicated in 1039, and in 1040 the high altar in front of the choir. In 1041 the crypt was finished and three altars consecrated in it.[5] The church was completed under Henry III (1039–1056);[6] or rather in 1045[7] or 1058,[8] when it was dedicated. The architect was the monk Gumbertus († about 1036).[9]

Fig. 780. Limburg. Abbey Church. North arm of transept (1024-1045-1058)

We will select the date 1024 for the foundation, as best suiting the conditions of ecclesiastical architecture in Germany in the first quarter of the eleventh century, when churches on a large scale still had wooden roofs for the aisles, whereas shortly afterwards they were occasionally, in the Rhine lands, covered with cross vaulting.

Nothing more than ruins of the abbey survives. The church had a cruciform plan with nave and aisles, the former terminating in a square chancel flanked by two apses projecting from the transept (fig. 780). At the west end was a narthex between two towers, to each of which a round staircase turret was attached. The nave was separated from the aisles by two rows of columns with Lombardic cubico-spherical capitals, ending with two massive cruciform piers which, with the responds of the chancel walls, carried the square central tower.

A restoration of the basilica which has been published[10] shows an octagonal cupola rising above the crossing. It is due to the author's imagination, for the nave and aisles, transept, and even the chancel, had wooden roofs, as is obvious to any observer, and therefore the lantern tower over the crossing can only have had a similar covering. An octagonal cupola carried on pendentives would have been an impossibility with the construction of the church such as it was.

It is true, indeed, that an erroneous interpretation of a passage in an incomplete description of the church printed in Würdtwein,[11] has given rise to the idea that the aisles had barrel vaults. There is, however, not the least trace of an impost course on the

[1] *Opera historica* (Frankfurt, 1601), *Chronica insignis monasterii Hirsaugiensis*, part ii, p. 49[10].

[2] WÜRDTWEIN, *Monasticon Palatinum chartis et diplomatibus instructum, notitiis authenticis illustratum* (6 vols., Mannheim, 1793–1796), vol. i, p. 27.

[3] *Germania topo-chrono-stemmato-graphica sacra et profana* (Augsburg, 1655), vol. i, p. 54.

[4] *Antiquitates et Annales Trevirenses*, vol. i, p. 517.

[5] WÜRDTWEIN, op. cit., vol. i, p. 41.

[6] *Mon. Germ. Hist. Script.*, vol. xvii, p. 82, *Annales Spirenses.* [7] WÜRDTWEIN, op. cit.

[8] *Mon. Germ. Hist., Deutsche Chroniken, Limburger Annalen*, p. 111[5].

[9] SACKUR, op. cit., vol. ii, p. 399. MANCHOT, *Kloster Limburg an der Haardt*, p. 8.

[10] MANCHOT, op. cit., plate ii.

[11] Op. cit., *Limburgum ad Hartam monasterium Ord. S. Benedicti*, vol. i, p. 42.

aisle walls, and they are not provided with the supports for the transverse arches which would have crossed the vault at intervals and given it stability.

Underneath the chancel was a crypt with cross vaulting (fig. 781). The whole building was decorated with blank arcading, lesenas, and arched corbel courses.

The distinctive feature of the church is the arrangement of western towers with staircase turrets attached; an idea apparently derived from Saint Riquier, where the two central towers had similar adjuncts. The transept apses, not set exactly in the line of prolongation of the aisles, are copied from the normal Lombardo-Norman basilica. They had already appeared at Bernay. Lombardic influence is suggested by the decorative use of the arched corbel course. This is its earliest dated appearance in Germany.

Fig. 781. Limburg. Abbey Church. Crypt (1024–1045–1058)

THE CHURCH OF ST. MARIA IM CAPITOL AT COLOGNE, founded about the year 700 by Plectrudis,[1] consort of Pippin II († 714), was rebuilt in the first half of the eleventh century, and consecrated by Leo IX (1049–1055) in 1049.[2] The latter fact is confirmed by the actual presence of the Pope in Cologne at the time, and also by a Bull of Leo's in a register among the archives of the church, granting indulgences to it.

The rebuilding must have taken place in the period intermediate between the erection of the abbey of Limburg (1024) and that of the cathedral of Speyer (1030), on account of the form of the supports and the vaulting of the aisles.

As designed in the eleventh century, the church consisted of a basilica with nave and aisles, a three-lobed choir surrounded by ambulatories and a western tower flanked by staircase turrets. The original outline is shown by the uniform character of the masonry in the portions of the old facing to be seen in the western towers, nave, transept, and apses.

The arrangement of the western towers must have been just then the fashion in

[1] SCHAEFER, *Beiträge zur Kölner Topographie und Kirchengeschichte* (*Römische Quartalschrift* (1904), vol. xvii, pp. 84–99, 163–73).

[2] GELENIUS, op. cit., p. 323 D; SCHAEFER, *Das Alter der Parochie S. Maria im Kapitol* (*Annalen des hist. Vereins f. d. Niederrhein*, 1902, Heft 4, p. 53 ff.);

BOARD, *S. Maria im Kapitol zu Köln*, Heidelberg, 1904, pp. 4, 6. [See also H. RAHTGENS, *Die Kirche St. Maria im Kapitol* (Düsseldorf, 1913); DE LASTEYRIE, op. cit., p. 803; *Congrès arch. Rhénanie* (1922), 429 ff.]

Cologne, for we read in Gelenius[1] that Archbishop Anno II (1056–1075) built two towers at the west end of Great St. Martin's.

The nave arcades (fig. 782) have rectangular piers with engaged columns. The roof was originally of wood, but it has been replaced by vaulting. The aisles, strengthened on the outside by buttresses connected at the top by arches, have unraised cross

Fig. 782. Cologne. St. Maria im Capitol. Nave (1049)

vaulting. At the ends of the aisles are two polygonal towers, originally quadrangular at the base and polygonal in the upper part, flanking the old nuns' choir, which was rebuilt after the fall of the western tower in 1637, and partially enclosing the bell-tower in the middle of the west end. This tower, closely bonded in its lower part into the nave walls, formed the narthex from which the nuns' choir was entered through two doors in the staircase towers, now blocked up. We may conjecture that it was raised in 1170, and so would be the bell-tower which, according to Gelenius,[2] collapsed through decay in 1637.

The three-lobed choir (fig. 783) has suffered from alteration which has affected the

[1] Op. cit., p. 375 D.   [2] Op. cit., p. 325 D.

whole of the sanctuary and the upper part of the transept, to which vaulting has been added. It had, from the first, an ambulatory forming a continuation of the aisles, and covered with cross vaulting which is old in the transept but reconstructed in the sanctuary. Whether it had a crypt from the beginning is not known. The present one contains, indeed, supports just like those in the church, but it is impossible to say with certainty whether the cross vaulting is of the eleventh century or the twelfth.

It has been suggested[1] that all this eastern part of the church was at first designed with cross vaulting in the ambulatory, half-domes for the apses, barrel vaulting for the presbytery and transept, and a cupola rising immediately from the arches of the crossing.

Fig. 783. Cologne. St. Maria im Capitol. Choir (1049 and 12th century)

The nave would have had a wooden roof. The tampering to which this part of the church has been subjected does not allow of any certain decision about such theories. To form one would necessitate an inter-comparison of all the vaulting in the church, based on tests of the masonry made in the different parts.

Meanwhile we are unable to explain why the architect vaulted the larger and more complex part of the church, while giving a wooden roof to the smaller, which was the easiest to deal with. All the more as this was not a case of extending the choir into the transept in order to find room for the stalls of a great crowd of monks, which might have been a reason for not confining a solid roof to the chancel.

Further, it looks as if the ability displayed by the designer of the rational system of vaulting in the three-lobed part was something superior to the ordinary constructive and statical knowledge current among the German builders in the first half of the eleventh century. Nor need we wonder at the application of simple barrel vaulting to a choir in the second half of the twelfth century (to which the result in question is attributed), seeing that in Great St. Martin's (Cologne), consecrated in 1172, it was

[1] BOARD, op. cit.

used not only for the rectangular bays in a choir of the same plan as that of St. Maria, but also for the first bay of the nave, as can still be seen. In St. Martin's we cannot say whether the crossing originally had, as now, a cupola resting on triangular pendentives, for in 1373 the tower suffered from a fire in which the bells were melted, and was restored a century and a half later.[1] If it had, the system of barrel vaulting in St. Maria, flanking a cupola of exactly the same form, may have been suggested by St. Martin's.

Finally, the later strengthening of the wall-piers, from which spring the transverse arches of the present barrel vaulting, is a reason for suspecting that the latter is a

Fig. 784. Cologne. St. Maria im Capitol. Choir (1049 and 12th century)

subsequent addition, and that originally the transverse arches merely supported the wooden roof.

It is not known when the changes took place which gave the church its best architectural decoration, though some would place them at the end of the twelfth century or the beginning of the next. We will confine ourselves to noticing that the external open gallery at the summit of the eastern apse (fig. 784), with shafts in twos and fours, presents a close analogy with the one in the three-lobed choir of Great St. Martin's, belonging to the rebuilding after the memorable fire of 1149, and that the date of St. Martin's may roughly correspond to that of St. Maria. All the more as the foliated capitals of Pointed style in the blank arcading on the apse of the latter exhibit a less advanced art than those in the same position in the Church of the Apostles at Cologne, erected after 1199.

St. Maria is the earliest instance of the aisles prolonged into the choir and enclosing it on all sides. The plan was soon after adopted in Saint Remi at Rheims (1036–1044), and rather later in Winchester Cathedral (1079–1093).

Dehio and Von Bezold have before now instituted the proper comparisons between the church and various Roman three-lobed structures of either simple or colonnaded

[1] GELENIUS, op. cit., p. 376 A.

form. We will only repeat what we mentioned before in our accounts of the Church of the Nativity at Bethlehem (327) and of the Palatine Chapel at Aachen (796–804),[1] that the three-lobed choir plan, derived from numerous ancient Roman examples, is of Latin origin.[2] Before its adoption by Justinian (527–565) for the Church of the Nativity it had been used in the celebrated basilica of St. Paulinus at Nola (end of the fourth or beginning of the fifth century), the idea being taken from the small tri-apsidal basilicas (third century) in the Cemetery of Calixtus, dedicated respectively to SS. Xystus and Caecilia, and to St. Soteris, the illustrious ancestress of St. Ambrose, or perhaps from the 'cella trichora' of St. Symphorosa on the Via Tiburtina (third century).[3]

We will conclude our discussion of St. Maria by remarking that the three towers of the west front may later have provided a suggestion for Hezilo, bishop of Hildesheim (1054–1079), who rebuilt Alfred's cathedral (851–874). The most striking feature of his new church was the great bell-tower of three stories at the west end, flanked by two staircase turrets, between which on the ground floor was an apse facing east, opposite to the main apse which faced the west; the whole corresponding in width to the nave and aisles. The tower was demolished in the course of the last century as it threatened to fall.[4]

THE CATHEDRAL OF SPEYER.—The most generally accepted date for its foundation by order of the Emperor Conrad II is 1030. By 1039 the crypt was ready, for we learn from various sources that in that year the founder was buried in it. The works went on under Henry III (1039–1056),[5] and they must have made considerable progress by 1071, for the church was dedicated to the Virgin in that year by Gundecar II, bishop of Eichstädt.[6] The notices about its completion differ, some giving the credit to Henry III or Henry IV (1056–1106),[7] others to his successor Henry V (1106–1125).[8]

Damaged more than once by fire, it was largely destroyed by the French in 1689. A drawing in the possession of Herr Schwartzenberger, the author of a recent book on the cathedral, executed before the restoration began in 1756, shows that the only parts then standing were the choir, eastern transept, the nave as far as the fifth bay, and the narthex. Another view in the Museum shows that other parts were missing, viz. the upper portions of the transept with its towers, and the whole of the cupola over the narthex. The western end of the church must have been in such a ruined state that most of it had to be taken down to save it from falling; thus, for instance, only the lowest part of the towers is original, as the facing shows. From another drawing in the Museum, showing the church as it was at the beginning of the seventeenth century, we learn that the cupola of the narthex was octagonal, and that the towers had three stages, with openings of several lights as in the eastern transept. The restorations and reconstructions from 1756 to 1858 have brought the cathedral to its present state.[9]

Beneath the choir and eastern transept is the imposing crypt. The beautiful cross vaulting springs from columns bearing cubico-spherical capitals with a half-round in relief on each face (fig. 785). Beyond it is the new Imperial sepulchral crypt, in which

[1] *Supra*, pp. 18, 299.

[2] [For an Eastern origin see DALTON, op. cit., p. 108, and M. AUBERT in *Congrès arch. Rhénanie*, p. 436. (R.)]

[3] STEVENSON, op. cit., p. 24.

[4] *Mon. Germ. Hist. Script.*, vol. iii, p. 104, *Annales Hildesheimenses*; BERTRAM, *Geschichte des Bisthums Hildesheim*, vol. i, p. 115.

[5] *Mon. Germ. Hist. Script.*, vol. xi, p. 274, WIPO,

Vita Chuonradi II imperatoris.

[6] *Mon. Germ. Hist. Script.*, vol. vii, p. 247, GUNDECHARUS, *Liber pontificalis Eichstetensis.*

[7] *Mon. Germ. Hist. Script.*, vol. xvii, p. 82, *Annales Spirenses*; *Mon. Germ. Hist. Script.*, vol. iii, p. 104, *Annales Hildesheimenses.*

[8] *Mon. Germ. Hist. Script.*, vol. xxii, p. 256, GOTIFREDUS VITERBIENSIS, *Pantheon.*

[9] [*Congrès arch. Rhénanie*, pp. 220–34.]

may be seen remains of the first Merovingian church, and the bases of two of the piers in the upper church, showing how the original form has been altered by the addition on the nave side of a half-pier with engaged column, the base of which has simple spurs at the angles.

Both arms of the transept have ribbed cross vaulting. At the north and south ends are arcades containing chapels, taken out of the thickness of the walls. Two apses project from the eastern side outside the lines of prolongation of the aisles. The western arch of the crossing is strengthened by a sub-arch, involving an addition to the piers, apparently inserted when the cupola was built. Above the crossing is an octagonal cupola carried, with its drum, on niches which form the transition from the square base to the octagon.

Fig. 785. Speyer Cathedral. Crypt (11th century)

The body of the church (fig. 786) is divided into nave and aisles by arches supported on piers alternately larger and smaller. Originally they were of uniform section and size: cruciform, with two engaged shafts. The alternate ones were modified when it was decided to replace the wooden roof with vaulting. The shafts of the untouched piers have cubico-spherical capitals: those on the enlarged piers (when original) are Corinthianesque with the leaves treated in a Byzantine manner, recalling those on the outer faces of the large windows.

The nave, one bay of which corresponds to two in the aisles, has raised cross vaulting, carried on wall and transverse arches. The aisles retain their original unraised cross vaults.

To pass to the exterior (fig. 787), the apse is embellished with blank arcading. One of the shafts is carved in relief with two animals, men mounted and on foot, trees, cauliculi, and intertwined snakes; the whole very rude both in design and execution (fig. 788). The summit is encircled by an open gallery, where the capitals reveal more advanced skill and a different artistic feeling from those in the blank arcading below. The bases here, as in all the external open galleries, are spurred. The gallery extends along the side walls of the presbytery. The rebuilt gable at the east end contains another open gallery, stepped so as to follow the line of the roof, and also continued at the sides. In these extensions the arches are compound and not simple as in the apse and its immediate neighbourhood.

The towers flanking the presbytery have the characteristic helmed tops (a German creation), the gables being pierced with triplets enclosed by a trefoiled arch, a feature already introduced at Laach. The tops are a later addition, as is shown by the masonry.

The eastern transept has buttresses at the angles of each arm, and another in the middle of the walls. The carving round the large windows, more advanced in the south than the north arm, is superior to the relief we noticed in the apse. There is the usual

Fig. 786. Speyer Cathedral. Nave (11th and 12th centuries)

open gallery under the eaves, continued along the nave and round the west front. Above it runs a cornice band of foliage and flowers, in part original.

In the north arm of the transept the western buttress contains at the top a two-light opening with a shaft supporting a lion. The capital is cubico-spherical, and the base is formed by a similar capital turned upside down. The idea of making a base out of an inverted capital is of great antiquity, as is proved by a Phoenician carving in the British Museum, of which I append an illustration (fig. 789).

Above the windows in the aisles runs a corbel course with lesenas at intervals; while the nave walls, as we have said, are crowned by the usual open gallery, with which even the octagonal cupola at the east end is provided.

In the angle between the north aisle and transept the chapel of St. Afra was erected by Henry IV between 1103 and 1106; otherwise it was constructed about 1097, when Herimannus, bishop of Augsburg (1096–1133), gave the emperor a relic of St. Afra. In any case it was finished by 1106, when the emperor was buried in it. Opposite to it on the south side of the church is the chapel of St. Emmerammus (1088–1091). At present it is used as a baptistery (fig. 790).

Let us now proceed to question the Sphinx of the Rhine, and compel her to reveal the main facts of her story in the eleventh and twelfth centuries. The result we shall subject to the tests of historical, architectural, and artistic criticism.

Fig. 787. Speyer Cathedral. North side (11th and 12th centuries)

We have already seen that the crypt was finished in 1039, and that the cathedral was consecrated in 1071. How much of it was really complete at that moment we cannot say. But we do know that most of it had been constructed when Henry IV, learning that the stability of the structure was being endangered by its proximity to the Rhine, commissioned (1082–1084) Benno II, bishop of Osnabrück (1068–1090), to take the necessary measures, which consisted in increasing the thickness of the walls and piling up a bulwark of large blocks of stone.[1] The type of church that Benno found in existence is easy to realize. It was a basilica with a wooden roof over nave and transept, and vaulted aisles. The design showed an intelligent step forward in the development of the Lombardo-Rhenish basilica, for at Limburg (1024–1045–1058) the aisles were still separated from the nave by cylindrical piers, and had wooden roofs. In short, it was a structure of the type of the almost contemporary St. Maria im Capitol at Cologne, though Speyer has the merit of more developed, i.e. cruciform supports in the nave, instead of the simple T form.

It is true that Schwartzenberger, who in his book[2] has invented a chronology of architecture and art, mostly of a fanciful kind, believes that the nave was vaulted as well as the aisles, on account of the form of its compound supports. All the evidence of actual buildings is against this. Thus, for instance, at San Miniato al Monte (1013) a half-column rises from the cruciform piers merely to carry a transverse arch of the nave, which, like the aisles, has a timbered roof. Again, at Mont Saint Michel (rebuilt in 1020), Cerisy la Forêt (1030–1066), Saint Étienne (1066–1086) and Saint Nicholas

---

[1] *Mon. Germ. Hist. Script.*, vol. xii, p. 76, NORBERTUS, *Vita Bennonis II episcopi Osnabrugensis.*
[2] *Der Dom zu Speyer* (Neustadt, 1903).

(1080–1093) at Caen, the compound piers give rise to a vaulting shaft, the original function of which was to carry, not the vaulting but the tie beams of the timbered roof of the nave. And, without going as far as Italy or France, the architect of the cathedral of Mainz, as rebuilt by Henry IV after the fire of 1081, carried up vaulting shafts in the nave to support a wooden ceiling.

Further, we saw that, in the first half of the eleventh century, no basilica of large size had a complete system of cross vaulting, even in the countries which had made most progress in vault construction. And, from another point of view, it is out of the question that the builders of Speyer should have begun by providing it with vaulting (a view shared, by the way, even by Choisy[1]), and then have taken the fancy to pull this down and rebuild it either on the old lines or on a more intelligent system. Lastly, we cannot imagine an architect so incapable as to design a nave of such width with cross vaulting (which in that age was very heavy), and at the same time prepare to receive it nothing more than vaulting shafts barely 2 ft. in diameter.

Fig. 788. Speyer Cathedral. Carving from the exterior of the apse (11th century)

Apart from the stone bulwark, Benno's work is apparent in the enormous thickness of the outer walls of the crypt, produced by the new facing. This is characterized by the different spirit in which the exterior of the sanctuary and transept is treated as compared with that of the body of the church, which has not been altered. The two parts are entirely devoid of that intimate connexion which marks a building constructed all of a piece. Its absence may be noticed in the blank arcading round the apse, where the inner arches, which ought to be the most elaborate, have plain Lombardic cubico-spherical capitals (which occur in all the oldest parts of the cathedral), while the outer ones have Corinthianesque capitals, and one of them is even ornamented with carving.

It might be suggested that, in the course of the operations carried out by the bishop of Osnabrück, the cross vaulting in the crypt was reconstructed. It is a fact that this vaulting is of a distinct character, and superior to the nearly contemporary work of the kind in St. Maria im Capitol at Cologne, and still more that in St. Michael's at Hildesheim. But the men who worked at Speyer were recruited from all parts ('fabros et cementarios aliosque opifices regni sui, vel etiam de aliis regnis in opere ipso habens'),[2] and the hands of master masons from Italy, especially from the North, may explain the fine quality of the cross vaulting. However this may be, the supports are the original ones, resting on bases without angle spurs (a feature which I have not found in Germany before 1052, in the Minster of Schaffhausen), whereas this detail appears in the parts of the cathedral which have been subjected to alteration.

In the matter of vaulting, Benno added it, or intended to add it, only in the transept, as is indicated, I think, by the flat buttresses on the exterior of this part of the church. What its nature was we cannot say.

Meanwhile, the completion of the great pile progressed somewhat slowly owing to the negligence and fraud of the builders. The emperor accordingly decided to send to

---

[1] *Histoire de l'architecture*, vol. ii, p. 225.
[2] *Mon. Germ. Hist. Script.*, vol. xii, pp. 750, 751, HERBORDUS, *Dialogus de vita Ottonis episcopi Babenbergensis.*

Speyer (1097) Otto, afterwards bishop of Bamberg (1103–1139), who was to put a stop to this state of things and assume the supreme direction of the works. He set things in order, and on this occasion he suggested an alteration in the windows.[1] The results of these modifications are obvious in the transept, e.g. the windows with cable mouldings and spiral shafts, elaborately decorated with carving, and ill according with the bareness of the recessed windows in the apse or the absolutely plain ones in the nave.

Fig. 789. British Museum.
No. 517. Phoenician carving

Fig. 790. Speyer Cathedral. Chapel of St. Emmerammus
(Baptistery) (11th century)

The carvings which frame these transept windows display a higher grade of art than the capitals in the blank arcading round the exterior of the apse, and must be ascribed to some constructive and decorative enterprise of a later date than Benno. Perhaps it may be connected with the erection of the chapel of St. Afra, that is to say the period of Bishop Otto's supervision, for the carvings in either case are obviously of the same date.

    The bishop of Bamberg did not confine himself to restoring order among the workmen and regularity in the works, or to providing more light for the choir: he also gave a great impetus to the completion of the church, as the following passage from his Life shows: 'Non facile dici potest, quanta conservatio rerum facta sit, et quanta structurae

[1] *Mon. Germ. Hist Script.*, vol. xii, pp. 750, 751, HERBORDUS, *Dialogus de vita Ottonis episcopi Baben-* bergensis; *Mon. Germ. Hist. Script.*, vol. xii, pp. 825, 826, EBO, *Vita Ottonis episcopi Babenbergensis.*

promotio.'[1] The finishing touches were given, according to Godfrey of Viterbo, in the reign of Henry V.

The notices of Herbordus and Godfrey are the latest transmitted to us by medieval writers concerning the building of the cathedral, which, as the original parts show, certainly does not remain in the state in which it was left by the last-named emperor. We will endeavour to supply this gap, if only in an approximate way, on the sure basis of monumental evidence.

As we said, the cathedral was originally designed to have the main spaces covered with wooden roofs. The question arises, when were these replaced by vaulting? My belief is that the change was made after the fire of 1137, which was most serious: 'Ecclesia quoque Spirensis maior, cum parte non modica ciuitatis, et oppidum Goslari-ense, eodem die quo et Moguntia, igne consumptae sunt.'[2] And it was before 1146 when St. Bernard preached the Crusade in the church. It cannot have been after the fire of 1159, for the artistic features of the old parts of the building show none of the charac-teristics of the third quarter of the twelfth century; for instance, spurred column bases with leaves of Pointed character, and capitals of similar character like those in the three-lobed choir of Great St. Martin at Cologne, which belongs precisely to that period.

At the time when the works of Benno and Otto were in progress at Speyer the Lombard gilds were putting the finishing touches to the constructive and statical revolution which had for its object the perfection of their vaulted basilica type, by the completion of the church at Rivolta d'Adda and the Ambrosian Basilica at Milan, achieved, the former under Urban II (1088-1099), the latter about 1098. Having accomplished this they went on to create and apply an essential feature of both the Lombardic and the Lombardo-Rhenish church; I mean the elaborate open galleries running round the exterior. Next, in the first quarter of the twelfth century, they had succeeded in covering wide spaces of great extent with the cupola of their creation, brought to perfection and in an embellished form; and this we saw in our account of the baptistery of Galliano. Outside Italy, Hezzel, the reputed architect of the great church at Cluny (1089–1130), had confined himself to covering the ground floor of each of the two octagonal towers in the main transept, which was only about 33 ft. wide, with an octagonal vault resting on hood-shaped pendentives. The Italian examples must have encouraged some able architect, called in to repair the damage suffered by the cathedral of Speyer in 1137, to suggest some safer form of roofing, and one more in keeping with the conditions of ecclesiastical architecture at the time. And it seems that this suggestion was acted upon.

While, however, the structure of the transept, after Benno's alterations, with the walls strengthened by buttresses, admitted of the erection of vaulting, that of the nave was unequal to such a burden. Recourse accordingly was had to the ingenious expedient which I will now describe. Every alternate pier was strengthened by the addition of a half vaulting pier, as may be seen in the crypt, in order to produce the Lombardic alternation of larger and smaller supports, and provide starting-points for the transverse arches and cross vaulting; the latter being of the raised form in order to reduce the thrust, in the manner adopted as early as the eleventh century in the aisles of San Babila at Milan, and both nave and aisles at Rivolta d'Adda and Sant' Ambrogio. The bases of these additions to the piers had rude claws instead of the leaves, some-times of Pointed character, or animal heads to be seen in other German buildings of the second half of the twelfth century. The engaged shafts in two cases have original

[1] *Mon. Germ. Hist.*, HERBORDUS, op. cit., p. 751[5].
[2] TRITHEMIUS, op. cit., *Chronica insignis monasterii Hirsaugiensis*, part ii, p. 126[50].

Corinthianesque-capitals of Byzantine character, recalling the manner of some of those in the transept windows.

The cross vaulting of the nave has been dated shortly before the end of the twelfth century. But the form which it took in the naves of the Rhenish cathedrals at that time was very different from this, in proof of which one has only to study the nave vaulting at Worms, the old parts of which were constructed by Bishop Conrad II (1171–1192), or that at Mainz (1183–1200) with its moulded ribs and pointed transverse arches. And the same was the case in other German cathedrals, e.g. that of Bamberg, which, after its consecration in 1012, was twice burned with its wooden roof, and rebuilt with vaulting between 1185 and 1237.

From the original smaller piers and the larger ones resulting from this alteration arches were sprung against the old walls to carry an additional facing of the upper part of the walls on the inside; and these walls were also raised in height to enable them to resist the thrust of the vaulting. In the lunette wall spaces thus produced small windows were formed to make up for the very moderate amount of light admitted by the openings below, instead of enlarging these at the expense of the stability of the nave walls. The walls, thus heightened and increased in thickness, could now admit of the formation of the external open galleries.

At the same time, after first raising the height of the outer walls, the transept was covered with ribbed cross vaulting, supposing that the existing ribs are not a later addition to strengthen the vault. This raising in height was carried all round the top of the building and the apse; and hence the most ornamented capitals in all the open galleries are evidently of the same date. As part of the same operations the eastern gable, with its stepped gallery, was raised, and the helmed tops of the towers, with their gables and triplet openings, erected. It was these gables that gave rise to the helmed roof, so dear to the German builders, who must certainly be credited with its invention, though, so far as I know, there is no specimen in existence older than the twelfth century. Some people, indeed, have fancied that an example belonging to the Anglo-Saxon age exists in the tower of Sompting Church (twelfth century), but it is not of such an early date as that, though undoubtedly an importation from abroad.

The last step was to add the octagonal cupolas over the transept and the narthex. Some writers[1] think that the former was part of the original design. I am unable to share this opinion. Given a basilica planned for wooden roofs in nave and transept, the crossing could only admit of a lantern tower roofed in the same way, just like the central towers of all the Lombardo-Norman churches which we have examined.

The ground plan of Speyer Cathedral represents the normal plan of the Lombardo-Rhenish basilica, with its eastern and western pairs of towers and octagonal cupolas over the crossings. The conception of a church confined by four towers, two at the front and two over prolongations of the aisles beyond the crossing, might have been suggested to the architect by San Lorenzo Maggiore at Milan 'edita in turribus'. The suggestion may also have come to him from two sources in the following way: the eastern towers from the cathedral of Ivrea (973–1001 or 1002) (unless it can be proved that they were introduced still earlier in Cologne Cathedral), or Sant' Abondio at Como (1013–1095); the western from St. Cyriacus at Gernrode (968).

The cupola over the centre of the narthex or western transept must have been suggested by Angilbert's church of Saint Riquier (793–798), or by Saint Remi at Rheims (eighth and ninth centuries), or, again, by Cologne Cathedral, supposing that Willibert's church is represented in the illumination to which we called attention,

---

[1] LÜBKE, op. cit., p. 95.

showing two towers (no doubt of wood) which must belong to the transepts. Or, lastly, the source may have been St. Michael's at Hildesheim.

THE CATHEDRAL OF TRIER.—As the old church of Agricius and Nicetius threatened to fall, it was restored by Archbishop Poppo (1015–1047), who also designed to lengthen it by a third towards the west, and took personal charge of the works. Death, however, overtook him when the walls had just risen above the ground. The new structure was continued by his successor, Eberhard (1047–1066), but how far we do not know, and finished by Udo (1066–1068–1078).[1] The excavations made by Wilmowsky[2] showed that the extension was terminated by a plain west front. From this Archbishop Bruno (1102–1124) threw out the western choir apse, and dedicated it in 1121 to the Trinity and St. Nicholas.[3]

Fig. 791. Trier. Western apse of the cathedral (1121)

The part of the cathedral which is of interest for our purpose is precisely this apse (fig. 791), where the recent restoration uncovered blank arcading round the interior, while the outside is decorated with arched corbel courses broken up into sections by lesenas, but is not encircled by an open gallery. Now, given the importance of the primatial church of Gallia Belgica, and considering Bruno's acquaintance with Italy, whither he had gone in 1104 or 1106 to receive the pallium from Paschal II (1099–1118), we may safely say that the reason why the latter feature did not appear in the apse was that, although by this time diffused throughout Italy, the land of its birth, it had not yet reached Germany, where, in my belief, it was seen for the first time at Speyer, after 1137, and at Bonn in the days of Pope Innocent II (1130–1143) and the provost Gerhard von Are (1126–1169). We may, therefore, until the contrary is proved, relegate to the domain of fable the theory which would at all costs assign a Rhenish origin to this decorative motive, and give it a vogue in Northern Europe before it found its way south of the Alps.

A noteworthy apse is that of St. Castor at Coblenz in the diocese of Trier, dedicated in 1208 by Archbishop John (1190–1212) (fig. 792).[4] Round the base is a range of blank trefoil arcading; and above this another range of arches springing from attached shafts, four of which rest on the backs of lions which the original specimens show to have been of rude design and execution. An open gallery crowns the whole, formed with isolated

[1] *Mon. Germ. Hist. Script.*, vol. viii, p. 183, *Gesta Treverorum.*

[2] *Der Dom zu Trier in seinen drei Hauptperioden* (1874), pp. 48, 52 and plate i (*Romanische Periode*).

[3] *Mon. Germ. Hist. Script.*, vol. viii, p. 198, *Gesta Treverorum.*

[4] *Mon. Germ. Hist. Script.*, vol. xv, pp. 1281–2, *Notae dedicationum dioceseos Treverensis.*

shafts interrupted at regular intervals by piers with attached shafts, an arrangement suggested by the alternation of single and grouped shafts in the open galleries of the apses at Cologne of about the same date.

I may mention here that the apse of St. Castor, which must have been rebuilt in the last years of the twelfth century, and the eastern choir apse of Worms Cathedral

Fig. 792. Coblenz. Church of St. Castor. Apse (1208)

furnish the prototypes in Germany of ranges of blank or open arches ornamented at the base with animal forms.

THE CATHEDRAL OF MAINZ.—The new church of St. Martin, erected by Archbishop Willigis (975–1011), was burned down on the day fixed for its consecration (1009).[1] The reconstruction was taken in hand by his successors, Erkenbald (1011–1021) and Aribo (1021–1031), while Bardo (1031–1051) added the panelled ceiling ('a tecto aedificare coepit, sicque domum Dei laquearibus, pavimento, et parte fenestrarum, parietibus dealbatis, dedicationis consecrationi preparavit'), and the church was

[1] *Mon. Germ. Hist. Script.*, vol. ii, p. 242, *Annales Wirziburgenses*; *Mon. Germ. Hist. Script.*, vol. iii, p. 93, *Annales Hildesheimenses.*

consecrated in 1036 or 1037.[1] That it was not complete at that date is shown by the fact that the high altar was not dedicated till 1049.[2]

After another fire in 1081, the Emperor Henry IV (1056–1106) began the rebuilding, but did not live to see its completion.[3] We are not told how the work went on after his death, but it must have been brought to an end by Archbishop Adelbert I (1111–1137), for he is stated to have erected a magnificent wooden roof which was burned in 1137: 'nec mora, civitas una cum principali templo quod ipse magnifico tecto munierat,

Fig. 793. Mainz Cathedral (11th, 12th, and 13th centuries)

igne cremata est.'[4] Damaged again by fire in the disturbances of 1160, when Bishop Arnold (1153–1160) met a violent death,[5] it was restored in the second episcopate of Conrad (1161–1165, 1183–1200), who saw his cathedral once more burned in 1190.[5] To him are attributed, with good ground, the nave vaulting, now partly reconstructed, and the rebuilding of the eastern choir. We also know that he began a new work, thought to be the western choir, the completion of which he was prevented from seeing by death. The final touches were given by Sigfried III (1230–1249), who consecrated the cathedral in 1239[6] (fig. 793).

[1] *Mon. Germ. Hist. Script.*, vol. xi, p. 321, Vulculdo, *Vita Bardonis archiep. Moguntini*; *Mon. Germ. Hist. Script.*, vol. v, pp. 555, 556, 557, Marianus Scottus, *Chronicon.*

[2] *Mon. Germ. Hist. Script.*, vol. vii, p. 347, Adam, *Gesta Hammaburgensis Ecclesiae pontificum.*

[3] *Mon. Germ. Hist. Script.*, vol. xii, p. 270, *Vita Heinrici IV imperatoris*; *Mon. Germ. Hist. Script.*, vol. v, p. 7, *Annales Ottenburani.*

[4] *Mon. Germ. Hist. Script.*, vol. xvi, p. 79, *Annales Palidenses.*

[5] Jaffé, *Bibliotheca rerum Germanicarum, Monumenta Moguntina*, vol. iii, pp. 666–72, 694.

[6] Joannis, *Rerum Moguntiacarum* (3 vols., Frankfurt, 1722–7), vol. i, p. 599; Schneider, *Der Dom zu Mainz* (Berlin, 1886), p. 28.

The oldest portions of the building are the lower parts of the restored eastern towers. They have been assigned[1] to Willigis, or at latest to Bardo. The simple and rude external decoration might point to the age of the former, but the fine internal construction would lead one to ascribe it to the time of the latter.

Next comes the body of the church, where the nave (fig. 794), with the exception of the vaulting, still represents the rebuilding of Henry IV. The aisle walls were cut

Fig. 794. Mainz Cathedral. Nave and eastern choir (11th and 12th centuries)

through in the thirteenth and fourteenth centuries for openings to chapels, and there is nothing left here save two original supports with cubico-spherical capitals in the north aisle.

The width of the nave is about 50 ft. between the piers, which are of quadrangular shape and uniform size, and provided alternately with one and two half-columns. The half-columns towards the aisles correspond to similar members on the outer walls, so that we may reasonably infer that the aisles were vaulted from the beginning (fig. 795). The half-columns of the alternate piers on the nave side form awkward imposts for the

[1] SCHNEIDER, op. cit., p. 8, and plates i and iii. [Cp. *Congrès arch. Rhénanie*, 166, 174.]

cross vaulting, which has moulded ribs and slightly pointed arches, and belongs to the second half of the twelfth century, or more precisely to the second episcopate of Conrad, who, as we saw, restored the church. Though these half-columns do not form a structural part of the piers, and seem to be a later insertion, nevertheless the piers are all of a piece, for the material used is the same, and so is the construction. We may add that the expedient was adopted for economy in stone, a fact familiar to every one acquainted with the practical side of building. Above the impost cornice of each nave pier rises a broad pilaster supporting the arcade which carries the clerestory. The idea was originally suggested by Saint Philibert at Tournus (1008–1019).

It has been thought that the half-columns carried up from the alternate piers show that the nave was originally designed for vaulting, and that afterwards, when this was found to be unsuitable, it was replaced by the present vaulting; though we know for an undoubted fact that Henry IV's church had wooden roofs over the main spaces. The half-columns were really carried up, either to support transverse arches, supposing that their present cubical capitals are original; or else, as I believe, to sustain the principal beams of the roof, in which case the half-columns were reduced in height, when the cross vaulting was constructed in the twelfth century.

I have already pointed out, in connexion with Speyer, what a

Fig. 795. Mainz Cathedral. South aisle (11th and 12th centuries)

mistake it is to suppose that a particular form of compound pier proves the existence of a system of vaulting. The nave at Mainz was so little adapted for receiving vaulting that it had to wait for the advent of a system of cross vaulting, the thrust of which was lightened so as to make up for the defective and unsuitable organic structure of the building, that is to say, the system of raised cross vaulting here employed.

The cathedral of Mainz teaches a fact of primary importance for the history of German architecture, viz. that an edifice commissioned by Henry IV, the reputed Imperial patron of the Rhenish revival, was designed with a wooden ceiling for the nave. This is fatal to the theory that, in his reign, at Speyer and Mainz vaulting was erected over the main spans, only to be taken down and rebuilt at the end of the twelfth century.

An interesting feature is the Chapel of St. Godehard, to the north of the cathedral, built by Adelbert I. Its altar was consecrated in 1137 or 1138 by Burchard II (1120–1149), bishop of Worms.[1] It is derived from San Flaviano at Montefiascone (1032), and, like it, is surrounded by an aisle with a gallery over it. Both parts have ordinary continuous unraised cross vaulting (fig. 796).

Before concluding our account of this cathedral we will call attention to a carving (fig. 797), of the time of Conrad's second tenure of the see, from the eastern choir which he rebuilt and caused to be decorated with paintings, as a specimen of the state of carving in Germany in the second half of the twelfth century.

Fig. 796. Mainz Cathedral. Gallery of Chapel of St. Godehard (12th century)

THE ABBEY CHURCH OF LAACH was founded in 1093 by the Count Palatine Henry II, with the co-operation of his wife Adelaide. After his death the works were at first neglected by his step-son Sigfried, but in 1112 he started them again with a generous contribution. On his death in the next year, the Countess Hedwig devoted herself to the progress of the building, which was finished in the time of Abbot Fulbert (1152–1178), and consecrated in 1156 by Illinus, archbishop of Trier (1152–1169), under the invocation of the Trinity, the Virgin, and St. Nicholas.[2]

The plan is that of a basilica with nave and aisles, and a transept and choir apse at either end. The presbytery is flanked by two square towers, and the arms of the western transept are terminated by two round ones. Over the principal or eastern crossing rises an octagonal cupola, while the western one supports a large square tower (fig. 798).

The nave is separated from the aisles by compound piers of uniform size (fig. 799). The capitals on the shafts are either of cubico-spherical form, or Corinthianesque carved with birds, foliage, flowering plants, monsters, billets, studs, interlacing, and other ornaments. All is in moderate relief, and of indifferent design and execution; but we must remember that the stone used is not very suitable for carving.

The crypt has a nave and aisles separated by supports with spurred bases and capitals, either cubico-spherical, or Corinthianesque with foliage, interlacing, roses, &c. Others have already remarked[3] that the cross vaulting in the presbytery, main transept, and crypt, is more advanced than that in the nave. Perhaps the church was at first designed without a crypt, and, like San Michele Maggiore at Pavia for instance, with barrel vaulting in the presbytery and eastern transept. Later, the changes were made which gave the church its present appearance.

The narthex or western transept is in two stories, and has an apse. The atrium in

[1] SCHNEIDER, op. cit., p. 21.
[2] BROWERUS, op. cit., vol. ii, p. 61; TRITHEMIUS, op. cit., *Chronica insignis monasterii Hirsaugiensis*, part ii, p. 108[20]; BUCELINUS, *Germania sacra et profana* p. 51. [*Congrès arch. Rhénanie*, 118 ff.]
[3] DEHIO and VON BEZOLD, op. cit., vol. ii, p. 473.

front of it is a subsequent addition. With the exception of the semi-domes of the two apses, unraised cross vaulting is used in every part of the building. The exterior of the eastern apse and transept is treated with blank arcading. Throughout, except on the eastern apse, arched corbel courses occur, of larger or smaller dimensions, and either continuous or broken up by lesenas.

Fig. 797. Mainz Cathedral. Carving in the eastern choir (12th century)

Fig. 798. Laach. Abbey Church (11th and 12th centuries)

It is generally thought that when the works were resumed in 1112, it was intended to vault the whole church, including the nave. The point seems to me beyond the range of doubt. What is decisive is the fact that the architect of the nave at Laach, which is only about 25 ft. wide between the bases of the piers, carried up pilasters about 4 ft. across to support the roof. Whereas the authors of the naves of Speyer and Mainz, which are about 51 ft. and 50 ft. wide respectively, contented themselves with shafts of under 2 ft. in diameter for the same purpose; and this makes clear the different conception which they had before them in the erection of their naves; for it was their intention to cover the main spaces with wooden ceilings, while the architect of Laach was all the time thinking of cross vaulting.

Nevertheless the church was not the product of a progressive study tending towards the evolution of a new architectural organism, but the result of an imitation. The

Fig. 799. Laach. Abbey Church (11th and 12th centuries)

absence from the eastern apse of the arcading which forms the principal decorative feature of the rest of the edifice shows (as has been apparent to other observers besides myself) that this is the earliest part, the remainder being assignable to the resumption of the work in 1112. Now, by that year, there had come into existence another Benedictine church, with nave and aisles covered with unraised cross vaulting springing, as at Laach, from compound piers of uniform size: I mean the church of Vézelay (1096–1104) as erected by Abbot Artald. Any one can see the striking resemblance which exists between the first experiment of the School of Cluny in the way of constructing cross vaulting over a nave of large size, and the church of Laach. In spite of its German ground plan, the decoration of the latter is Lombardic; and in the disposition of the nave and aisles with their vaulting, it is a copy of the church at Vézelay.

It was just because it was the result of an imitation that Laach constituted an isolated example in the German lands at the beginning of the twelfth century. A long time will have to elapse before the German architects design a great church planned from the outset, like that of Laach, for a complete system of cross vaulting.

But apart from its being an importation and an isolated instance, the fact remains that at the time of its conception with its unraised cross vaulting, the churches of Rivolta d'Adda and Sant' Ambrogio at Milan were already in existence with their raised cross vaulting, partially ribbed as well; while San Michele Maggiore at Pavia was about to be begun, and mark the completion of the normal Lombardic basilica.

We should observe at Laach the absence of an open gallery round the apse of 1093, which is only embellished with ordinary blank arcading. We have already seen, while discussing the cathedral of Trier, that such galleries had not made their appearance in Germany in 1121.

THE MINSTER AT BONN.—The ancient collegiate church of SS. Cassius and Florentius was rebuilt by the provost Gerhard von Are (1126–1169), no doubt after its property had been confirmed to it by Pope Innocent II (1130–1143).[1]

Fig. 800. Bonn. Crypt of Minster (12th century)

It is generally believed that nothing is left of his reconstruction except the apse and its two bell-towers. The transept and the rest of the church are ascribed by some to a rebuilding after the injuries suffered by the church during the war between Philip of Suabia (1198–1208) and Otto IV of Brunswick (1198–1212); by others to Gerhard himself, who, in the course of his long tenure of the provostship, was able to give his works the stamp of the different styles which the church exhibits. One need, however, only glance at the cross vaulting of the nave at Mainz, which we know was constructed in the last years of the twelfth century, in order to feel sure that the similar vaulting of the nave at Bonn, the supports of which were evidently planned to carry it from the beginning, is not earlier than the thirteenth century.

[1] *Neues Archiv der Gesellschaft für ältere deutsche Geschichtskunde*, vol. xiii (1888), p. 149, PERLBACH, *Aus einem verlorenen Codex traditionum der Bonner Münsterkirche St. Cassius und Florentius.*

The Minster is a basilica with nave and aisles, of Latin cross plan, with a choir apse at either end. In front of the eastern apse is a presbytery of three bays. Though there has been a good deal of alteration and reconstruction, there undoubtedly survive of Gerhard's work, in a modified condition, the eastern apse with the towers beside it, the presbytery, and the crypt beneath it. The apse is covered with a semi-dome. In the bay

Fig. 801. Bonn. Eastern choir of the Minster (12th century)

immediately in front of it, flanked by the towers, the vaulting has been reconstructed. The other two bays have been given a new dress in the Pointed style, but the skeleton is the original one, as the exterior shows.

The crypt (fig. 800) under this part of the church extends to the towers, and thus has a cruciform plan. It is divided into aisles by piers and columns, some of which have cubico-spherical capitals with indentations at the angles, or are hung with plain festoons and slightly undulated below, suggesting the scalloped capital which is very rare in Germany.

I believe this crypt to be, on the whole, the work of Gerhard, but it has been altered in the part under the sanctuary, the floor of which was raised when the bodies of

SS. Cassius and Florentius were exhumed, and the translation of other relics recorded under the year 1166 took place.[1]

The apse (fig. 801) is decorated with arcading, and at the top is an open gallery with single shafts, between every two of which are coupled shafts. The gable above is not original. The towers, the tops of which have been altered, are covered with blank

Fig. 802. Cologne. Nave of Great St. Martin's (12th and 13th centuries)

arcading, arched corbel courses, and lesenas. Here there occur capitals with crocket leaves, the earliest which I have met with in Germany.

An examination of the side walls of the presbytery shows at once that they were altered when the transept and present nave were built. Their structure is on the whole original.

The element in the Minster at Bonn which has most interest for us is the open gallery round the apse, the dated prototype (together with those in the cathedral at Speyer) of this feature for Germany, and marking the first step in the progressive history of the motive in the diocese of Cologne. The second is to be found in Great St. Martin's[2] in

[1] *Neues Archiv*, loc. cit., vol. xiii, p. 169.   [2] [*Congrès arch. Rhénanie*, pp. 458 ff.]

the same city, believed to have been founded in the eighth century, destroyed by the Saxons and the Normans in turn, restored by Archbishop Bruno (953–965), and rebuilt by Archbishop Warinus (976–984).[1] Anno II (1056–1075) added two towers at the west end.[2] Destroyed by fire in 1049, the church was rebuilt and consecrated in 1172 by Archbishop Philip von Heinsberg (1167–1191), and finished by Abbot Simon between 1206 and 1211.[3] The marked difference of style observable in the interior of the three-lobed choir and the first barrel vaulted bay of the nave, in which all the arches are round and the original capitals have occasionally a suggestion of the Pointed style, as compared with the western part of the nave (fig. 802) belonging to the Transi-

Fig. 803. Cologne. Font in Great St. Martin's
(about 13th century)

tional style, with capitals of well-developed thirteenth-century type, provides an excellent reason for believing that the body of the church was remodelled by Abbot Simon after the fire of 1185.[4]

The church of the time of Philip von Heinsberg must be supposed to have had barrel vaulting only in the first bay of the nave, where the two vault-shafts which carried the transverse arch may still be seen. Its object was to resist on this side the thrust of the cupola over the choir. The other bays had a wooden roof. Indeed, the piers in this part of the nave are not designed for vaulting; so that when Abbot Simon wanted to construct its cross vaults he was obliged to resort to the expedient of corbelling out high up the shafts on which they were carried.

I may notice in passing that the octagonal font (fig. 803) at the west end of the north aisle, ornamented with scroll-work, roses, and lions' heads, and traditionally regarded as a gift from Pope Leo III (795–816), is a work which I should describe as coming from an Italian hand, but not earlier than the thirteenth century.

The same stage in the history of the external gallery is illustrated by the three-lobed choir of the Church of the Apostles at Cologne (fig. 804), rebuilt by Archbishop Heribert (999–1021), and finished by his successor Piligrimus (1021–1036), but reconstructed afresh by Adolphus I (1193–1205) after the fire of 1199.[5] Here, just as in Great St. Martin's, the open gallery round the apse has a series of two piers, each with two engaged shafts, alternating with a pier with four engaged shafts.

Another instance at Cologne is the apse of St. Gereon, where there is said to have been a church since the fourth century.[6] The present structure is to be ascribed (1) to Archbishop Anno II (1056–1075), who threw out from the old round church a long choir flanked by towers, with a crypt below consecrated in 1068, the church being dedicated in the following year; (2) to a remodelling of this choir and its crypt in the last part of the twelfth century, completed in 1191, as we know that in 1190 the relics

[1] *Mon. Germ. Hist. Script.*, vol. xxix, p. 338, *Catalogi archiepiscoporum Coloniensium*; *Mon. Germ. Hist. Script.*, vol. ii, pp. 214–15, *Chronicon Sancti Martini Coloniensis.*

[2] GELENIUS, op. cit., p. 375 D.

[3] BOCK, *Rheinlands Baudenkmale*, series II, cap. II.

[4] *Mon. Germ. Hist. Script.*, vol. xvi, p. 625[30], *Annales Floreffienses.*

[5] GELENIUS, op. cit., p. 296.

[6] Ibid., p. 258 C.

of the martyrs were deposited in the new crypt under the altar of St. Gereon, which altar was consecrated in 1191 by Bertoldus, bishop of Metz (1180–1212). (3) Finally came the construction of the decagon forming the body of the church, which was finished in 1227.[1]

Of Anno's work there remains intact the western part of the crypt (fig. 805), where

Fig. 804. Cologne. Church of the Apostles (13th century)

the unraised continuous cross vaulting is carried on short columns with unspurred bases and cubico-spherical capitals. The eastern portion of the crypt, the 'nova cripta' of the Annals of St. Gereon, forms part of the operations which were brought to an end by the dedications of 1190 and 1191. It has raised cross vaulting with visible arches,

[1] *Mon. Germ. Hist. Script.*, vol. xvi, p. 734, *Annales Sancti Gereonis Coloniensis*; *Mon. Germ. Hist. Script.*, vol. xiii, p. 723, *Notae Sancti Gereonis Coloniensis*; *Mon. Germ. Hist. Script.*, vol. xi, p. 491, *Vita Annonis II archiep. Coloniensis, auctore monacho Sigbergensi*. [*Congrès arch. Rhénanie*, pp. 408 ff.]

and bases with angle spurs of either simple or elaborate character. To the same date belongs the apse encircled by its open gallery (fig. 806). The apse is clumsily connected with the lower part of Anno's towers; and though here we find three light supports alternating with one heavy one, the gallery is closely related to those of St. Martin's and the Apostles.

It ought to be mentioned that the arrangement of light and heavy supports in the apse galleries at Cologne is derived from the arcaded galleries interrupted by piers on the exterior of the Duomo at Modena (1099–1106) and the apse of San Pietro in Ciel d'Oro at Pavia (1132), where, however, the galleries are not continuous.

Fig. 805. Cologne. Church of St. Gereon. Western part of the crypt (11th century)

THE CATHEDRAL OF WORMS was in existence as early as the reign of Dagobert, and was struck by lightning and burned in 872. The subsequent misfortunes of the city retarded and impeded the efforts of various bishops to rebuild the church, until Burchard I (1000–1025) demolished what had been erected by his predecessors as being unsuitable and mean, and began the construction of a new cathedral in 1008. The unfinished structure, which was nearly ready for its roof ('iam pene ad culmen eductum stabat'), was dedicated in the presence of the Emperor Henry II in 1016.

The western part of Burchard's church fell in 1018, a fact not difficult to understand when we remember that it had been built so hastily that the bishop's biographer thought it rose as if by magic. By 1020 this portion was rebuilt on solid foundations, and beneath it a crypt was formed, in which the founder was buried.

In 1033 Bishop Azzecho (1025–1044) erected the chapel of St. Maurice as an adjunct to the church. Bishop Eppo expended large sums in completing the unfinished works, and at last the consecration took place (1110) in the presence of the Emperor Henry V. Trithemius gives the date as 1118.

Bishop Conrad II (1171–1192) repaired the building, which showed signs of falling, and a fresh consecration took place in the presence of the Emperor Frederick I in 1181. In the fifteenth century the north-west tower fell and was rebuilt, and in 1689 the cathedral was burned by the French.[1]

[1] SCHANNAT, *Historia episcopatus Wormatiensis*, vol. i, pp. 213, 336, 348, 360; manuscript Chronicle of the monastery of Kirschgarten in the Archives of the City of Worms; TRITHEMIUS, op. cit., *Chronica insignis monasterii Hirsaugiensis*, part ii, p. 109[30]; *Mon. Germ. Hist. Script.*, vol. iv, pp. 837, 839, 846, *Vita Burchardi episcopi*. [M. AUBERT in *Congrès arch. Rhénanie*, pp. 235 ff.]

Such, in brief, is the story of the vicissitudes through which the cathedral has passed. Some[1] have thought that our church of SS. Peter and Paul is still, on the whole, the one begun by Burchard I (the western towers being his), continued through the eleventh century, and consecrated in 1110. Others are of opinion that the body of the church,

Fig. 806. Cologne. St. Gereon. East end (11th and 12th centuries)

with the exception of the nave vaulting, which they think was subsequently reconstructed, belongs to Burchard; the eastern choir apse, with the transept and cupola, to Eppo; and the western choir to a rebuilding in the early years of the thirteenth century.

Each of these views when analysed falls to pieces. The nearest to the truth are Dehio and Von Bezold,[2] who argue that Conrad II rebuilt the church with the exception of two towers, and that the western choir was rebuilt on Burchard's foundations in the thirteenth century. My belief is that, with the exception of the western choir, which belongs to the early thirteenth century, the previous one being apsidal, the

[1] LÜBKE, op. cit., pp. 163, 164.　　　　　　[2] Op. cit., vol. ii, p. 474.

cross vaulting of the nave, different in type and execution from that in the presbytery, aisles, and transept, and perhaps the interior of the eastern apse, the church as we now see it is due to Conrad II (1171–1192). His work must have consisted, not in mere restoration of a ruinous building ('basilicam principem ruinas hinc inde minitantem maximis sumptibus in priorem statum reduxit'[1]), but in its reconstruction.

Fig. 807. Worms Cathedral. Nave looking east (12th century)

An experienced eye will readily see the constructive and decorative unity of the church, always excepting the western portion, which, apart from the towers, one of which has been rebuilt, is later than the works of Conrad. Thus, arched corbel courses (each arch being recessed), some continuous, some broken by embellished lesenas or buttresses, occur on every part of the exterior. Everywhere the openings are in groups, and the stringcourses are generally of saw-tooth design. Everything points to its being a structure of one date, including the Lombardic cupola over the crossing with its different masonry.

[1] SCHANNAT, op. cit., p. 360.

The eastern cylindrical towers cannot be assigned to Burchard's period, at any rate so far as regards the stages of the old part (with their arched corbel courses broken by lesenas, and saw-tooth mouldings) which rise above the lofty basements of the towers. The early eleventh century is not the period which suits the recessed arches of the corbel courses, separated by lesenas which are no longer plain but moulded, and in some cases supported by human heads, occasionally of fantastic character. In fact, one might search in vain for such arched courses with figure corbels on any Western building of known date belonging to the early years of the eleventh century.

Further, these towers are clearly contemporary with the choir which they flank, as is shown not only by the masonry, consisting at the base of roughly-dressed stones, with higher up a facing of carefully-dressed blocks of varying dimensions, but also by its decorative treatment; and, thirdly, by the carvings of living creatures, seeing that, on more than one ground, we may regard as contemporary the carved heads on the towers, the figures in the windows, those which project below the open gallery round the apse, and the carving on one of its shafts of a man with an animal gnawing at his head.

Fig. 808. Worms. Carving in the cathedral (12th century)

The polygonal exterior of the choir may be regarded as a casing over of the old semicircular apse inside belonging to the church of the eleventh century. Now, for the reasons given in our discussion of Speyer and Trier, the gallery round the choir, and also that round the cupola over the crossing, cannot be earlier than the twelfth century. Moreover, the Lombardic portal on the north side, with its foliage occasionally suggesting the Pointed style, and its figure sculpture, indicate a date not earlier than that century. The same may be said of the canopy which formerly surmounted it; for Lombardic portals or porches with a canopy, or niche, or arcade above them are not earlier than the erection of the cathedral of Modena (1099–1106). In any case the Lombardic portal did not appear in its developed form and elaborate dress before the twelfth century, as we made clear in our account of Saint Guilhem du Désert.

To turn now to the interior (fig. 807), the Lombardic arrangement of piers alternating with piers having engaged shafts suggests a date which is not that of Burchard I. It is inconceivable that such an important step towards the completion of the Lombardo-Rhenish basilica should have been taken at Worms between 1008 and 1016, and that afterwards, in 1030, a retrograde one should have been made at Speyer when Conrad II built St. Mary's to serve as the Imperial tomb house, and another again at Mainz in 1081 when Henry IV's cathedral was erected.

But there are other reasons for excluding the age of Burchard. There are the spurred bases of the half-columns, whereas these adjuncts do not appear in St. Michael's, Hildesheim, which was built in his lifetime, or in the later St. Maria im Capitol at Cologne, or in Speyer Cathedral. There are the ram's heads at the angles of some of the bases in the transept, indicating a stage of art which cannot be paralleled in any Western monument of the early eleventh century. There are the vaulting shafts, some

4 ft. in breadth, arranged to receive the cross vaulting of the nave; whereas we know that in the naves of German cathedrals of the eleventh century only single shafts were carried up to support the wooden roofs. Speyer and Mainz are examples. Then there are the well-known and original carvings on the wall-piers in the presbytery, one of which, signed by Otto, represents a woman holding the Devil by his horns while an angel pierces him with a lance, and another has projecting heads and scroll-work (fig. 808). No one could possibly ascribe such work to German artists of the early eleventh century, seeing that at the end of the eleventh they had only attained to the sort of carving found in the eastern choir of Mainz. And, lastly, there is the cupola over the crossing, carried on hood-shaped pendentives, first used for such a purpose north of the Alps in Hugo's church at Cluny (1089–1130) and Saint Etienne at Nevers (1097).

The slow evolution of the Lombardo-Rhenish basilica as compared with the Lombardic was not an isolated and merely local phenomenon, but was common to all the contemporary German Schools, and to those of the neighbouring German parts of Switzerland. We may set out the evidence in the form of a review of some of the best-known and dated churches of the period in these countries.

THE ABBEY CHURCH OF HERSFELD was rebuilt after the fire of 1038 by Poppo von Stablo, and the crypt was dedicated in 1040.[1] It was not finished till 1144.[2] The plan[3] was that of a Latin cross, the nave and aisles being separated by columns with cubico-spherical capitals, and Attic, unspurred bases. It had wooden roofs.

THE MINSTER OF SCHAFFHAUSEN was founded by Count Eberhard and his wife Ida. The choir must have been ready by 1052, for in that year Pope Leo IX consecrated the principal altar. The church was dedicated by Rumoldus, bishop of Constanz, in 1064. It was erected from the plans, and with the advice of the priest, Liutbald: 'prefiguratione atque adiutorio cuiusdam Liutbaldi.'[4]

It is of cruciform plan, with nave and aisles separated by columns, and a rectangular chancel. The aisles are prolonged beyond the transept in the Lombardo-Norman fashion. The columns have cubico-spherical capitals and spurred bases. With the exception of the semi-domes of the two small apses in the transept, the whole of the church is roofed with timber.

This appears to be the earliest church of Germany or German Switzerland with spurred bases for its supports. In those countries the spurs had from the beginning the form of rudimentary claws, or of leaves. It was only in the twelfth century, after the Lombardic School had produced forms so advanced as to be almost anticipations of those of the Pointed style, e.g. in San Michele Maggiore at Pavia, that the German chisels began to elaborate them with heads, paws of animals, leaves, sometimes curling over, as on the original bases in the cloister of the abbey church of Schwarzach (twelfth or thirteenth century),[5] and other ornamental forms.

If we were to accept the dates fixed by some writers for St. Ursula at Cologne (fig. 809), according to whom the oldest parts of the church go back to the rebuilding by Archbishop Heribert (999–1020) and Richeza, Queen of Poland († 1063), and its

[1] *Mon. Germ. Hist. Script.*, vol. iii, p. 101, LAMBERTUS, *Annales*.

[2] LÜBKE, op. cit., p. 89.

[3] [DE LASTEYRIE, op. cit., figs. 147, 148.]

[4] *Mon. Germ. Hist. Script.*, vol. v, p. 388, *Annales*

Scafhusenses; *Mon. Germ. Hist. Script.*, vol. xiii, pp. 721, 722[10], *Notae S. Salvatoris Scafhusensis*.

[5] SAUER, *Die Abteikirche in Schwarzach (Freiburger Diöcesan-Archivs, Freiburg im Breisgau*, New Series, v (1904), pp. 361–6, fig. 7).

completion by Anno II (1059–1075), who, we are told, used to spend much time in prayer before the relics of the Virgins,[1] in that case the half-columns in the aisles would have been provided with their spurred bases in the early years of the eleventh century. But the existence in these aisles of cubico-spherical capitals, some ornamented with foliage or other forms, and also of spurred bases, whereas in St. Maria im Capitol and Anno II's crypt at St. Gereon the capitals of this type are left plain, and the bases are devoid of any ornament at the angles, affords good ground for suspecting that the nave

Fig. 809. Cologne. St. Ursula. Nave looking west (11th century)

and transept of St. Ursula have absolutely no connexion with Heribert; and that though Queen Richeza may really have laid the foundations of a new church, she never saw it rise above the ground. This suspicion is confirmed by the abundant and varied architectural decoration of the exterior of the nave and transept, which can still be seen on the north side. It consists of arched corbel courses, either continuous or broken by lesenas at various intervals, and blank arcading. Whereas the exterior of St. Maria im Capitol has merely a range of blank arches in the aisles, and the original external face of the presbytery in St. Gereon, one of Anno's works, only two tiers of blank arcading.

Accordingly, I feel that all that is visible of the nave and transept of St. Ursula,[2] built as they were for wooden roofs, though the aisles have unraised cross vaulting, must

[1] GELENIUS, op. cit., p. 334.
[2] [M. AUBERT (Congrès arch. Rhén., p. 477) thinks that the new building followed the great discovery of relics in 1106. (R.)]

be assigned to a date not earlier than the last years of Anno, and when the choir of St. Gereon was already in existence (1069).

THE CATHEDRAL OF CONSTANZ.—The old church having fallen in 1052, Bishop Rumoldus (1051–1069) undertook its re-erection, according to Kraus in 1054, and was buried in it. The consecration took place in 1089 under Bishop Gebhard III (1084–1110).[1]

The original form was that of a basilica with arcades and a wooden roof. The substantial columns rest on Attic bases with rude leaf spurs. They are surmounted by characteristic capitals, neither cubico-spherical nor scalloped, but spherico-polygonal, crowned by an octagonal abacus (fig. 810).

Fig. 810. Constanz. Capital in the cathedral (11th century)

THE CATHEDRAL OF HILDESHEIM.—The original church, built by Bishop Alfred (851–874) and consecrated in 872, was burned down (1046) in the time of Bishop Azelinus (1044–1054), who in 1047 began the re-erection which he did not live to see finished. His successor, Hezilo (1054–1079), contined the work, and the consecration was performed in 1061. Bishop Bertholdus I (1119–1130) finished or added the apse.[2]

Hezilo's basilica, of Latin cross form, was designed, like St. Michael's, for a wooden roof, and had its nave separated from the aisles by columns, between every two of which came a quadrangular pier. Modern stucco capitals conceal the old ones. The bases are Attic, and without spurs.

Hezilo erected another cruciform church in honour of St. Maurice, replacing an older one of Bishop Godehard's (1022–1038), viz. the church of Moritzberg near Hildesheim. It had a wooden roof. Here again, the capitals of the columns are concealed by stucco. The bases rest on plinths rounded off at the angles for convenience. The water-leaf capitals in the crypt, being of the type in vogue at Hildesheim in Hezilo's days, suggest that the now concealed original capitals in the upper church, as well as those in the nave of the cathedral, are of the same pattern.

He also built the Church of the Holy Cross at Hildesheim. It has a triforium, and quadrangular piers in the nave. The main portions have wooden ceilings, but the aisles are covered by rough barrel vaulting. The latter is to be explained by the existence of the triforium; otherwise the wooden ceilings would have been extended to the aisles. Indeed, well on in the twelfth century at Hildesheim, both nave and aisles in the Church of St. Godehard were provided with ceilings (figs. 811, 812).

St. Godehard's is a church of considerable interest. Bernward I (1130–1153) laid the first stone in 1133; while Adelogus (1171–1190) carried up the towers at the west end, where he consecrated a chapel of St. Mary Magdalen, built the western apse, and finally consecrated the church afresh in 1172.

In the nave there is again the arrangement of two columns alternating with a quad-

[1] *Die Kunstdenkmäler des Grossherzogthums Baden* (Freiburg, 1887), pp. 106–10, *Die Kunstdenkmäler des kreises Konstanz.*

[2] BERTRAM, *Geschichte des Bisthums Hildesheim*, pp. 43, 44, 102, 114, 145; Id., *Zur Kritik der ältesten Nachrichten über den Dombau zu Hildesheim* (reprinted from *Zeitschrift für Christliche Kunst* (1899)), pp. 5–18; *Mon. Germ. Hist. Script.*, vol. iii, p. 48, *Annales Hildesheimenses*; *Mon. Germ. Hist. Script.*, vol. vii, pp. 851, 853, 855, *Chronicon Hildesheimense.*

rangular pier. The angles of the column bases have the upturned claws (also in Adelogus's work in St. Michael's), characteristic of the Hildesheim School of the twelfth century. Earlier it did not make use of this feature, as may be seen from the old bases in St. Michael's, as well as those in the cathedral and at Moritzberg. In one case four animal paws are introduced. The capitals (fig. 813), are of cubico-spherical form, richly decorated with foliage, cauliculi, scroll-work, flowers, disks, real or fanciful creatures, and scenes from sacred history. They are characterized by the same artistic

Fig. 811. Hildesheim. Church of St. Godehard (12th century)

quality as that of the capitals in St. Michael's, executed for Adelogus before 1186, and suggest that his munificence was not confined to the cases mentioned by the chroniclers.

THE ABBEY CHURCH OF ST. AURELIUS, HIRSAU, was begun in 830 by Count Erlefried and his son Notingus, bishop of Vercelli (827–830), and completed in 837. As it gave signs of weakness, its reconstruction was begun by Count Adelbert and his wife Wiltrudis in 1059, and in 1071 the dedication took place.[1] It consisted of a nave and aisles (fig. 814) separated by short columns (monoliths of local stone), two western towers with a narthex between them, and aisles prolonged beyond the transept, as in a Lombardo-Norman basilica. To each of the isolated columns corresponds a wall shaft standing on a continuous plinth. The capitals are of cubico-spherical form. There is

[1] TRITHEMIUS, op. cit., *Chronica insignis monasterii Hirsaugiensis*, part ii, p. 4[30, 50]; *Mon. Germ. Hist.* *Script.*, vol. xiv, pp. 254–5, *Historia monasterii Hirsaugiensis*.

Fig. 812. Hildesheim. Nave of the Church of St. Godehard (12th century)

Fig. 813. Hildesheim. Church of St. Godehard. Capitals (12th century)

cross vaulting in the narthex, but the nave had a wooden ceiling, though the aisles had unraised cross vaulting.

Before leaving Hirsau let us cross the stream which flows near the church, and climb the hill opposite to get a view of the tower (fig. 815) which is all that is left of the church of the great monastery of St. Peter, begun by William, abbot of Hirsau, in 1082, and finished in 1091 by the unaided hands, it is said, of the monks and lay brothers.[1]

This tower is regarded, and rightly, as of the twelfth century;[2] that is to say, after the monks had recovered from the losses inflicted on them by Henry IV for having taken the side of Gregory VII, and when they were in a condition to finish the works of St. Peter's, which cannot have been entirely complete in 1091.

An interesting feature of the tower is the band of carving round the base of the third stage. It contains atlantes supporting lesenas (fig. 816), and beside them animals, a

Fig. 814. Hirsau. Abbey Church of St. Aurelius (1059-1071)

human being, and the wheel of Fortune. In spite of their rudeness, these reliefs betray a more skilful hand than that which produced the carving we noticed on the exterior of the apse at Speyer, and clearly reveal Lombardic influence. They form a piece of demonstrative evidence that the well-known reliefs with the Legend of St. Vincent, and the arcaded altar front with pairs of Apostles in each arch, built into a wall in Basel Cathedral, are not, as has been thought, coeval with its erection (1014-1019)[3] under Bishop Adalbert II (999-1021), but must be dated not earlier than the end of the twelfth century. And the date will be the same, even if they are regarded as works of Italian or French origin.

THE CHURCH OF ST. JAMES AT BAMBERG was begun under Bishop Hermann I (1065-1075), and the crypt was consecrated in 1072. The dedication of the church took place in 1109.[4]

It is of cruciform plan with a choir apse at either end (the eastern one having been

[1] TRITHEMIUS, op. cit., *Chronica insignis monasterii Hirsaugiensis*, part ii, p. 77; *Mon. Germ. Hist. Script.*, vol. xiv, p. 257, *Historia monasterii Hirsaugiensis*.
[2] LÜBKE, op. cit., p. 100.
[3] ROBERT, *Gallia Christiana* (Beauvais, 1626), vol. i, col. 259 (for the dedication of the church in

1019); GAMS, op. cit., p. 260.
[4] *Mon. Germ. Hist. Script.*, vol. xvii, p. 637, *Notae Sancti Jacobi Babenbergensis*; JAFFÉ. *Bibliotheca rerum Germanicarum, Monumenta Bambergensia*, vol. v, p. 546.

Fig. 815. Hirsau. Tower of the Abbey Church of St. Peter
(12th century)

Fig. 816. Hirsau. Carving on tower of the Abbey
Church of St. Peter (12th century)

rebuilt in the Pointed style) and wooden ceilings. The nave (fig. 817) is separated from the aisles by columns with cubico-spherical capitals and Attic unspurred bases.

The much altered church of St. Gangolph in the same town, erected by Bishop Günther (1057–1065),[1] which now has clumsy vaulting, also originally had a wooden ceiling.

THE CHURCH OF ST. JUSTINUS AT HÖCHST ON THE MAIN.—As the old church was in a dangerous condition it was demolished and rebuilt in 1090 by Adelmann,

Fig. 817. Bamberg. Church of St. James (11th and 12th centuries)

abbot of the monastery of St. Albanus, in the days of Ruthardus, archbishop of Mainz (1088–1109).[2]

The church is of cruciform plan, with wooden ceilings (fig. 818). An interesting feature are the Corinthianesque capitals, surmounted by Ravennate pulvins of inverted truncated pyramid form. This is the earliest instance of the occurrence of such pulvins in any German building.

THE CHURCH OF ALPIRSBACH, erected in 1095, is of Latin cross plan, with the nave and aisles separated by columns with cubico-spherical capitals. It has a wooden roof.

THE ABBEY CHURCH OF PAULINZELLE.—We learn that it was founded in the time of

[1] JAFFÉ, *Bibliotheca rerum Germanicarum, Monumenta Bambergensia*, vol. v, pp. 39, 546; *Mon. Germ.*

Hist. Script., vol. iv, p. 794, ADALBERTUS, *Vita et miracula Henrici II imperatoris.*
[2] JOANNIS, op. cit., vol. i, p. 526.

the Emperor Henry IV by St. Paulina († 1107), who was buried there before the altar of the Holy Cross, and completed in 1119. A fire in the seventeenth century, and the abandonment of the church, have reduced it to the ruined state which it now presents. The nave and aisles were roofed with wood. The columns dividing them have cubico-spherical capitals with pairs of semicircles on the faces, and spurred bases.

Fig. 818. Höchst am Main. Church of St. Justinus (1090)

THE LIEBFRAUENKIRCHE AT HALBERSTADT, begun by Bishop Arnulfus (996–1023), and consecrated in 1005, was still in course of construction in 1020. Bishop Dietmarus (1089) bequeathed all his property for the completion of the church. Bishop Rudolfus (1136–1149) rebuilt it, and performed the consecration in 1145.

It is of cruciform plan, with a very short transept. Square piers separate the nave from the aisles; and, with the exception of the apse, the whole church was designed for wooden ceilings. The cross vaulting in the transept and presbytery was constructed after the damage suffered at the time of the destruction of the town by Henry the Lion in 1179.[1]

[1] LUCANUS, *Die Liebfrauenkirche zu Halberstadt* (Halberstadt, 1871), p. 4.

Of its four towers, the western pair, embellished with arched corbel courses, have German helmed tops.

I conclude with the expression of a wish that the new and wide field which I have opened up in the domain of Monumental Archaeology may find a worker with the will and the ability to cultivate it so that it may produce more fruit. Such an enterprise would be worthy both of the cause of knowledge and of the investigator; because the greatest of all the arts—Architecture—is the one which, by its creations, preserves in the most tangible form the memory of great nations all through the ages.

ADDENDA

By G. McN. RUSHFORTH

Vol. i, p. 6; cp. ii, 12; vol. i, pp. 95, 98. *Ravenna, Basilica Ursiana, and the Basilica of Emmaus*.

The Christian Basilica recently excavated at Emmaus (Amwâs) in Palestine has a principal apse curvilinear within but polygonal without, flanked by subordinate apses at the ends of the aisles (see PP. VINCENT ET ABEL, *Emmaus, sa basilique et son histoire*, Paris, 1932). If the date claimed for it by Père Vincent in the first quarter of the third century could be substantiated, the origin of these features would have to be put in a different period and region from those maintained in the text. For the present, however, it must be treated with considerable reserve, as it depends on inferences and not on any direct evidence.

Vol. i, p. 62. *S. Vitale, Ravenna.*

The recent restoration of this church, fully described and illustrated by Dr. R. Bartoccini in *Felix Ravenna*, 1931, pp. 77–101, and 1932, pp. 133–65, has resulted in considerable changes in the interior, which now, it is claimed, presents more or less of its original appearance. The floor of the octagon has been lowered about 80 cm., thus restoring the original proportions of the building, and revealing the bases of the columns and piers, together with remains of the sixth-century mosaic pavement (designs of acanthus and scroll-work springing from a vase), the two best-preserved sections of which have been re-set with the sixteenth-century pavement in place of two inferior sections made in 1702. The chancel has also been lowered to its original level, and the marble screens or transennae which stood in front of the altar, and for which no suitable place could be found, have been removed to the Museum. The altar itself has been stripped of later additions, the *mensa* being now supported on five shafts of verde antico; but it was not thought desirable to attempt to reconstruct the ciborium, the marble columns of which probably exist in the two monuments framing the ancient thrones of Neptune on either side of the sanctuary (see vol. i, fig. 84).

Vol. i, p. 95, note 4; vol. ii, pp. 61, note 1, 299, note 5. *Strzygowski's Iranian Theory.*

Professor Strzygowski's later theories of Iranian influence on Christian architecture and art, developed in his *Origin of Christian Church Art* (Oxford, 1923), are based on (1) the idea that through Mithraism and Manichaeism the Roman Empire was flooded with Persian religious beliefs (Mazdaism), which brought in their train Iranian culture and art-forms; and (2) the fact that, before the age of Constantine, Christian churches were built in Mesopotamia and other districts within the sphere of Persian influence. It is true that we know nothing about them, but from the later Armenian domed churches of central plan and the barrel-vaulted Mesopotamian and Persian buildings we may infer the types which were introduced into the Mediterranean world, replacing the timber-roofed basilica. Mazdaism was also the source of the non-representational element in Christian art, as in that of Islam; and it was allied with Northern art of similar character, Ostrogothic, Lombardic, Scandinavian, and Irish (*Origin*, p. 18).

Professor Karl Künstle in his *Ikonographie der christlichen Kunst*, vol. i (Freiburg im Breisgau, 1928), pp. 51 ff. (cp. also pp. 38, 41, 45, 47), has summarized some of the arguments against these views, as follows:

1. Strzygowski's picture of a Mazdean mission and a Mazdean art permeating the Western world is imaginary. The influence of Mithraism and Manichaeism in the Roman Empire though widespread was limited and not universal, and they were opposed and beaten by the Christian Church, so that it is improbable that such movements would have influenced Christian architecture and art, even if they had had any art of their own, and for that the evidence is lacking, as Strzygowski himself admits (*Origin*, pp. 19, 116, &c.).

2. Strzygowski's dating of the Mesopotamian and Armenian monuments, which he uses as evidence, is uncertain or incorrect (see S. GUYER in *Repertorium für Kunstwissenschaft*, xxxv. 483; xxxviii. 193; cp. Fr. MACLER in *Syria*, 1920, fasc. 4), and in any case they are too late to have had the

influence on Western architecture and art which Strzygowski claims for them. He asserts that the decisive influence in the dissemination of Iranian art 'seems to have been that exercised by the mass migrations of the Goths westwards from the Black Sea. This people, and the craftsmen who went with them, built vaulted structures', &c. (*Origin*, p. 77, cp. 81). But the Goths did not enter the Empire till towards the end of the fourth century or the beginning of the fifth, i.e. a century after the erection of S. Costanza at Rome, whose mosaic decorations Strzygowski compares with Central Asiatic designs. His attempt to make Cassiodorus another agent in diffusing Mesopotamian culture in the West is equally unsuccessful (Künstle, p. 52; cp. *Origin*, pp. 53, 138, 249).

The discovery at Dura on the Euphrates of wall-paintings of the Parthian and Roman periods, including Christian subjects, all not later than the 3rd century A.D., has provided new evidence, so far as pictorial art is concerned, which has hardly yet been estimated. Some account of it will be found in Prof. M. Rostovtzeff's *Caravan Cities* (Oxford, 1932), pp. 185, 189 ff., 213 ff., plates xxxiii, xxxiv. See also J. H. Breasted, *Oriental Forerunners of Byzantine Painting* (University of Chicago Oriental Institute Publications, vol. i, 1924).

Vol. i, pp. 244 ff., 269 ff. *Etruscan Influence in Early Medieval Italian Art.*

Dr. B. Nogara, Director of the Vatican Museum, in his recent book on the Etruscans (*Gli Etruschi e la loro Civiltà*, Milan, 1932: two of the lectures were given at Oxford and Cambridge respectively), refers with approval to Rivoira's comparisons between features of Etruscan construction and decorative art and similar forms in Lombardic architecture, and says that the discoveries of the last decade have only confirmed his inferences (op. cit., p. 311). He mentions particularly the projecting heads on arches (as at Deerhurst, vol. ii, p. 184), and conventional animals at the portals of churches (vol. i. 244 ff., 268 ff.).

Vol. ii, p. 177. *Westminster Abbey.*

A recent excavation on the south side of the nave has given some information about the western part of the Confessor's church. The bases of the piers were found to be alternately cruciform and square, the latter no doubt supporting cylindrical columns, so that the arrangement must have been similar to that in the nave of Jumièges (vol. ii, p. 85). Remains were also found of the south-west tower, immediately within the existing west front. A report by Messrs. A. W. Clapham and L. Tanner will appear in *Archaeologia*, vol. lxxxiii (1933).

Vol. ii, p. 242, note 1. *Rome, Tomb of Eurysaces.*

See further Mrs. Strong's statement in the *Cambridge Ancient History*, vol. ix (1932), pp. 822 and 835 (vol. of plates, iv, 72 and 100), where Mr. Ian Richmond's new interpretation of the round openings as mixing bowls for dough is referred to.

Vol. ii, p. 311. *Chapel at Lorsch.*

A late 8th century date is supported by the results of excavations in 1927. 'Die Ausgrabungen im Kloster Lorsch', *Zeitschrift für Denkmalpflege*, iii (1928–9), p. 20.

Vol. ii, p. 361. *Bonn.*

A full account of recent excavations in and around the Minster has appeared in the *Bonner Jahrbücher*, 1932 (pp. 1–216), 'Baugeschichtliche Untersuchungen am Bonner Münster' by H. Lehner and W. Bader. The following are the chief results. An Early Christian church, enlarged in Carolingian times, was replaced by a new Romanesque church on a different orientation in the eleventh century. The western part of the crypt of the eastern choir may be dated about 1060–70 by comparison with the crypts of St. Gereon at Cologne (see vol. ii, p. 364 and fig. 805) and the abbey of Siegburg (consecrated 1066). Between 1143 and 1152 Gerhard von Are destroyed the old apse and lengthened the choir towards the east, adding the towers and a cloister. About 1190–1200 the walls of the choir were heightened, and the transept was rebuilt. The nave dates from about 1225. Cp. P. Clemen, *Die Romanische Monumental Malerei in den Rheinlanden* (1916), p. 434 f.

INDEX OF PLACES

The numbers in heavy type refer to the illustrations.
The first number generally gives the most important reference to a subject.

3274.2

3 E

GENERAL INDEX

Printed in U.S.A. by
NOBLE OFFSET PRINTERS, INC.
NEW YORK, N.Y. 10003

Gary Jennings
Azteca

Colección Bestseller Mundial

AZTECA

GARY JENNINGS

Traducción de María de los Ángeles Correa E.

PLANETA

Título original: Aztec

© Gary Jennings, 1980
© por la traducción, María de los Ángeles Correa E., 1981
© Editorial Planeta, S. A., 1998
    Córcega, 273-279, 08008 Barcelona (España)
Diseño cubierta: Marc Panero
Primera edición en esta presentación: julio de 1997
Segunda edición: noviembre de 1997
Tercera edición: enero de 1998
Reimpresión: mayo de 1998 (especial para Planeta Internacional)
Depósito Legal: B. 23.738-1998
ISBN 84-08-02199-0
Impresión: Liberduplex, S. L.
Encuadernación: Eurobinder, S. A.
Printed in Spain - Impreso en España

Ediciones anteriores:

En Colección Contemporánea
1.ª a 9.ª ediciones: de enero de 1981 a junio de 1994
En Colección Planeta Bolsillo
1.ª a 3.ª ediciones: de noviembre de 1994 a febrero de 1997

Para Zyanya

*Ustedes me dicen, entonces, que tengo que perecer
como también las flores que cultivé perecerán.
¿De mi nombre nada quedará,
nadie mi fama recordará?
Pero los jardines que planté, son jóvenes y crecerán...
Las canciones que canté, ¡cantándose seguirán!*

HUEXOTZÍNCATZIN
Príncipe de Texcoco, 1484

Corte de Castilla
Valladolid

Al Legado y Capellán de Su Majestad,
Fray Juan de Zumárraga, recientemente
presentado Obispo de la Sede de Mexico (1),
a su cargo:

Deseamos informarnos de las riquezas, de las creencias y ritos y ceremonias que tuvieron en tiempos ya pasados, los naturales habitantes en esa tierra de la Nueva España. Es nuestra voluntad ser instruidos en todas estas materias concernientes a la existencia de los indios en esa tierra antes de la llegada de nuestras fuerzas libertadoras, evangelistas; de nuestros embajadores y colonizadores. Por lo tanto, es nuestra voluntad que seáis informado en persona, por indios ancianos (a quienes debéis hacer jurar para que lo que digan sea verdadero y no falso) de todo lo concerniente a la historia de su tierra, sus gobernantes, sus tradiciones, sus costumbres, etcétera. Añadiendo a esa información la que aporten testigos, escritos, tablillos u otros registros de esos tiempos ya idos, que puedan verificar lo que se dice, y enviad a vuestros frailes a que busquen e indaguen sobre esos escritos entre los indios.

Os mando atender dicha instrucción y servicio con la mayor prontitud, cuidado y diligencia, porque éste es un asunto muy importante y necesario para la exoneración de nuestra real conciencia, y que dicho relato sea escrito con mucho detalle.

(ecce signum)   CAROLUS R ✠ I

Rex et Imperator
Hispaniae Carolus Primus
Sacri Romani Imperi Carolus Quintus

---

(1) A petición del autor, y para una mayor comprensión de las lenguas indias, en la traducción española se han acentuado todas las palabras indígenas conforme a su pronunciación. *(N. del t.)*

I H S

✠

S. C. C. M.

Santificada, Cesárea, Católica Majestad,
el Emperador Don Carlos, nuestro Señor Rey:

Que la gracia, la paz y la misericordia de Nuestro Señor Jesucristo sea con Vuestra Majestad Don Carlos, por la gracia divina eternamente Augusto Emperador y que con vuestra estimada madre la Reina Doña Juana que, junto con Vuestra Majestad, por la gracia de Dios, Reyes de Castilla, de León, de Aragón, de las dos Sicilias, de Jerusalén, de Navarra, de Granada, de Toledo, de Valencia, de Galicia, de Mallorca, de Sevilla, de Cerdeña, de Córdoba, de Córcega, de Murcia, de Jaén, de las Islas Caribes, de Algecira, de Gibraltar, de las Islas de Canaria, de las Indias, Islas y Tierra Firme del Mar Océano; Condes de Flandes y del Tirol, etcétera.

Muy afortunado y Excelentísimo Príncipe: desde esta ciudad de Tenochtitlan-Mexico, capital de su dominio de la Nueva España, a doce días después de la Asunción, en el año del nacimiento de Nuestro Salvador Jesucristo, de mil quinientos veinte y nueve, os saludo.

Solamente hace diez y ocho meses, Vuestra Majestad, que nos, el más humilde de vuestros vasallos, en atención a vuestro mandato, asumimos este cargo por triple folio nombrado: el primer Obispo de Mexico, Protector de los Indios e Inquisidor Apostólico, todo en uno en nuestra pobre persona. En los primeros nueve meses desde nuestra llegada a este Nuevo Mundo, hemos encontrado mucho y muy arduo trabajo por hacer.

De acuerdo con el real mandato de este nombramiento, nos, nos hemos esforzado celosamente «en instruir a los indios en el deber de tener y de adorar al Único y Verdadero Dios, que está en el cielo, y por Quien todos viven y se mantienen», y además «para instruir y familiarizar a los indios en la Muy Invencible y Católica Majestad, el Emperador Don Carlos, quien por mandato de la Divina Providencia, el mundo entero debe servir y obedecer».

Inculcar estas lecciones, Señor, no ha sido fácil para nos. Hay un dicho aquí entre nuestros compañeros españoles, que ya existía mucho antes de nuestra llegada: «Los indios no oyen más que por sus nalgas.» Sin embargo, tratamos de tener en mente que estos indios —o aztecas, como actualmente la mayoría de los españoles llaman a esta tribu o nación en particular— miserables y empobrecidos espiritualmente, son inferiores al resto de la humanidad; por consiguiente, en su insignificancia merecen toda nuestra tolerante indulgencia.

10

Además de atender a la instrucción de los indios de que únicamente hay Un Solo Dios en el cielo y el Emperador en la tierra, a quien deben servir todos ellos, que han venido a ser vuestros vasallos, y además de tratar otros muchos asuntos civiles y eclesiásticos, nos, hemos intentado cumplir el mandato personal de Vuestra Majestad: preparar prontamente una relación de las condiciones de esta *terra paena-incognita*, sus maneras y modos de vida de sus habitantes, sus costumbres, etcétera, que anteriormente predominaban en esta tierra de tinieblas.

La Real Cédula de Su Más Altiva Majestad especifica a nos, que para poder hacer la crónica requerida seamos informados personalmente «por indios ancianos». Esto ha sido causa de una pequeña búsqueda puesto que, a la total destrucción de la ciudad por el Capitán General Hernán Cortés, quedaron muy pocos indios ancianos de quienes poder tener una historia oral verídica. Incluso los trabajadores que actualmente reconstruyen la ciudad son en su mayor parte mujeres, ancianos decrépitos que no pudieron tomar parte en las batallas, niños y zafios campesinos traídos a la fuerza de los alrededores. Todos ellos estúpidos.

Sin embargo, pudimos rastrear a un indio anciano (de más o menos sesenta y tres años) capacitado para ayudarnos con esta crónica. Este *mexícatl* —pues él niega los apelativos de azteca e indio— tiene para los de su raza un alto grado de inteligencia, es poseedor de la poca educación que se daba en tiempos pasados en estos lugares y ha sido en su tiempo escribano de lo que pasa por ser escritura entre estas gentes.

Durante su vida pasada tuvo numerosas ocupaciones aparte de la de escribano: guerrero, artesano, mercader viajante e incluso una especie de embajador entre los últimos gobernantes de este lugar y los primeros libertadores castellanos. Debido a esa tarea, pudo absorber pasablemente parte de nuestro lenguaje. A pesar de que rara vez comete faltas en castellano, nos, por supuesto, deseamos precisar todos los detalles. Así es que hemos traído como intérprete a un joven que tiene bastantes conocimientos en náhuatl (que es como los aztecas llaman a su lenguaje gutural de feas y alargadas palabras). En la habitación dispuesta para estos interrogatorios, hemos reunido también a cuatro de nuestros escribanos. Estos frailes son versados en el arte de la escritura veloz con caracteres conocidos como puntuación tironiana, que se usa en Roma cada vez que el Santo Padre habla para su memoranda y también para anotar los discursos de muchas gentes a la vez.

Nos, pedimos al azteca que se siente y nos relate su vida. Los cuatro frailes garrapatean afanosamente con sus caracteres tironianos, sin perder ni una sola de las palabras que saltan de los labios del indio. ¿*Saltar*? Sería mejor decir que las palabras llegan a nosotros como el torrente de una cascada, alternativamente repugnantes y corrosivas. Pronto vos veréis lo que deseamos decir, Señor. Desde el primer momento en que abrió la boca, el azteca mostró una gran irreverencia por nuestra persona, nuestro hábito y nuestro oficio como misionero, que su Reverenda Majestad escogió personalmente para nos, y consideramos que esta falta de respeto es un insulto implícito a nuestro Soberano.

Siguen a esta introducción, inmediatamente después, las primeras páginas de la narración del indio. Sellado para ser visto solamente por vuestros ojos, Señor, este manuscrito saldrá de Tezuitlan de la Vera Cruz pasado mañana, a la salvaguarda del Capitán Sánchez Santoveña, maestre de la carabela *Gloria*.

Dado que la sabiduría, sagacidad y distinción de Su Cesárea Majestad son conocidas universalmente, podemos dar pesadumbre a Vuestra Imperial Majestad, atreviéndonos a hacer un prefacio a estas páginas unidas con *caveat*, pero, en nuestra calidad episcopal y apostólica, sentimos que estamos obligados a hacerlo. Nos, estamos sinceramente deseosos de cumplir con la Cédula de Vuestra Majestad, en mandar una relación verdadera de todo lo que vale la pena de conocer de esta tierra. Otros aparte de nos, os dirán que los indios son criaturas miserables en las cuales apenas se pueden encontrar vestigios de humanidad; que ni siquiera tienen un lenguaje escrito comprensiblemente; que nunca han tenido leyes escritas, sino solamente costumbres y tradiciones bárbaras; que siempre y todavía son adictos a toda clase de intemperancias, paganismo, ferocidad y lujuria; que hasta recientemente torturaban y quitaban la vida violentamente a causa de su diabólica «religión».

No creemos que una relación válida y edificante pueda ser obtenida de un informante como este azteca arrogante o de cualquier otro indígena, aunque ésta sea clara. Tampoco podemos creer que nuestro Santificado Emperador Don Carlos no se sentirá escandalizado por la iniquidad, la lascivia y la impía charlatanería de este altanero ejemplar de una raza despreciable. Los papeles anexados son la primera parte de la crónica del indio, como ya hemos referido. Nos, deseamos fervientemente y confiamos en que también por órdenes de Vuestra Majestad sea la última.

Que Nuestro Señor Jesucristo guarde y preserve la preciosa vida y muy real persona y muy católico estado de Vuestra Majestad por largo tiempo, con mucho más acrecentamientos de reinos y señoríos, como vuestro real corazón desea.

De S.C.C.M., por siempre fiel vasallo y capellán,

(ecce signum) Fr. JUAN DE ZUMÁRRAGA
Obispo de Mexico
Inquisidor Apostólico
Protector de los Indios

INCIPIT

Crónica relatada por un indio viejo de la tribu llamada comúnmente azteca, cuya narración fue dirigida a Su Ilustrísima, el Muy Reverendo Don Juan de Zumárraga, Obispo de la Sede de Mexico y anotada *verbatim ab origine* por

        FRAY GASPAR DE GAYANA J.
        FRAY TORIBIO VEGA DE ARANJUEZ
        FRAY JERÓNIMO MUÑOZ G.
        FRAY DOMINGO VILLEGAS E YBARRA
        ALONSO DE MOLINA, *interpres*

Mi señor.

Perdóneme, mi señor, de que no conozca su formal y digno tratamiento honorífico, pero confío en no ofender a mi señor. Usted es un hombre y jamás ningún hombre entre todos los hombres que he conocido en mi vida se ha resentido por haber sido llamado señor. Así que, mi señor.

O, Su Ilustrísima, ¿no es así?

Ayyo, un tratamiento todavía más esclarecido, lo que nosotros llamaríamos en estas tierras un *ahuaquáhuitl*, un árbol de gran sombra. Su Ilustrísima, así lo llamaré entonces.

Estoy muy impresionado, Su Ilustrísima, de que un personaje de tan alta eminencia haya llamado a una persona como yo, para hablar en su presencia.

Ah, no, Su Ilustrísima, no se moleste si le parece que le estoy adulando, Su Ilustrísima. Corre el rumor por toda la ciudad, y también sus servidores aquí presentes me lo han manifestado en una forma llana, de cuán augusto es usted como hombre, Su Ilustrísima, mientras que yo no soy otra cosa más que un trapo gastado, una migaja de lo que fui en otro tiempo. Su Ilustrísima está adornado con ricos atavíos, seguro de su conspicua excelencia, y yo, solamente soy yo.

Sin embargo, Su Ilustrísima desea escuchar lo que fui. Esto, también me ha sido explicado. Su Ilustrísima desea saber lo que era mi gente, esta tierra, nuestras vidas en los años, en las gavillas de años, antes de que le pareciera a la Excelencia de su Rey liberarnos con sus crucíferos y sus ballesteros de nuestra esclavitud, a la que nos habían llevado nuestras costumbres bárbaras.

¿Es esto correcto? Entonces lo que me pide Su Ilustrísima está lejos de ser fácil. ¿Cómo en esta pequeña habitación, proviniendo de mi pequeño intelecto, en el pequeño tiempo de los dioses... de Nuestro Señor, que ha permitido preservar mis caminos y mis días... cómo puedo evocar la inmensidad de lo que era nuestro mundo, la variedad de su pueblo, los sucesos de las gavillas tras gavillas de años?

Piense, Su Ilustrísima; imagíneselo como un árbol de gran sombra. Vea en su mente su inmensidad, sus poderosas ramas y los pájaros que habitan entre ellas; el follaje lozano, la luz del sol a través de él, la frescura que deja caer sobre la casa, sobre una familia; la niña y el niño que éramos mi hermana y yo. ¿Podría Su Ilustrísima comprimir ese árbol de gran sombra dentro de una bellota, como la que una vez el padre de Su Ilustrísima empujó entre las piernas de su madre?

Yya, *ayya*, he desagradado a Su Ilustrísima y consternado a sus escribanos. Perdóneme, Su Ilustrísima. Debí haber supuesto que la copulación privada de los hombres blancos con sus mujeres blancas debe ser diferente, más delicada, de como yo los he visto copular a la fuerza con nuestras mujeres en público, y seguramente la cristiana copulación de la cual fue producto Su Ilustrísima, debió de haber sido aún mucho más delicada que...

Sí, sí, Su Ilustrísima, desisto.

Sin embargo, Su Ilustrísima puede darse cuenta de mi dificultad. ¿Cómo hacer posible que Su Ilustrísima, de una sola ojeada, pueda ver la diferencia entre nuestro *entonces* inferior a su *ahora* superior? Tal vez baste una pequeña ilustración para que usted no necesite molestarse en escuchar más.

Mire Su Ilustrísima a sus escribanos; en nuestro idioma se les llama «los conocedores de palabras». Yo también fui escribano y bien me acuerdo de lo difícil que era transmitir al papel de fibra, o de cuero de venado, o de corteza de árbol, los esqueletos de las fechas y sucesos históricos y eso con poca precisión. A veces, incluso a mí me era difícil leer mis propios dibujos en voz alta sin tartamudear, unos cuantos momentos después de que los colores se hubieran secado.

Sin embargo, sus conocedores de palabras y yo hemos estado practicando mientras esperábamos la llegada de Su Ilustrísima, y estoy asombrado, estoy maravillado de lo que cualquiera de sus reverendos escribanos puede hacer. Pueden escribir y leerme no solamente la substancia de lo que hablo, sino cada una de las palabras y con todas las entonaciones, las pausas y las expresiones de mi discurso. Yo pensaría que esto es una capacidad extraordinaria de memoria y de imitación, nosotros también teníamos nuestros *memoristas* de palabras, pero me dicen, me demuestran, me comprueban que todo aparece escrito en sus hojas de papel. Me felicito a mí mismo, Su Ilustrísima, por haber aprendido a hablar su idioma con la poca perfección que han podido alcanzar mi pobre cerebro y mi pobre lengua, pero su escritura estaría fuera de mi alcance.

En nuestra escritura pintada los propios colores hablaban, cantaban o lloraban, los colores eran necesarios. Teníamos muchos: rojo-sangre, rojo-magenta, oro-ocre, verde-*ahuácatl*, azul-turquesa, *chocólatl*, gris-barro, negro de medianoche. A pesar de eso, no eran adecuados para captar cada palabra individual, por no mencionar los matices y el hábil uso de las frases. Sin embargo, cualquiera de sus conocedores de palabras puede hacer precisamente eso: anotar para siempre cada parte de palabra con sólo una pluma de ganso, en lugar de un manojo de cañas y pinceles. Y lo que es más maravilloso, con *un solo color*, la decocción del negro óxido que me dicen que es tinta.

Pues bien, Su Ilustrísima, en resumidas cuentas ahí tiene en una bellota la diferencia entre nosotros los indios y ustedes los hombres blancos, entre nuestra ignorancia y sus conocimientos, entre nuestros tiempos pasados y su nuevo día. ¿Satisfaría a Su Ilustrísima el simple hecho de que una pluma de ganso ha demostrado el derecho de su pueblo para gobernar, y el destino de nuestro pueblo para ser gobernado? Ciertamente eso es todo lo que Su Ilustrísima desea de nosotros los *indios*: la confirmación de la conquista victoriosa que fue decretada, no por sus armas y artificio, ni siquiera por su Dios Todopoderoso, sino por su innata superioridad sobre las criaturas menores que somos nosotros. Ninguna palabra más que yo dijese podría respaldar los juicios astutos de Su Ilustrísima acerca de la situación pasada o presente. Su Ilustrísima no necesita más de mí o de mis palabras.

Mi esposa es vieja y enferma y no hay quien la cuide, y aunque no puedo fingir que lamenta mi ausencia, sí le molesta. Achacosa e irascible, no es bueno que ella se disguste, no me conviene. Por lo que con sincero agradecimiento a Su Ilustrísima por la forma tan benévola con que su Ilustrísima recibió a este viejo miserable, ya me voy.

Le ruego que me disculpe, Su Ilustrísima. Como usted ya lo ha hecho notar, no tengo permiso de Su Ilustrísima de irme cuando me dé la gana. Estoy al servicio de Su Ilustrísima por todo el tiempo que...

Mis disculpas, otra vez. No me había dado cuenta de que había estado repitiendo «Su Ilustrísima» más de treinta veces durante este breve coloquio, ni que lo he estado diciendo en un tono especial de voz. Sin embargo, no puedo contradecir la anotación escrupulosa de sus escribanos. De ahora en adelante intentaré moderar mi reverencia y mi entusiasmo hacia su título honorífico, Señor Obispo, y mantener un tono de voz irreprochable. Y como usted lo ordena, continúo.

Pero ahora, ¿qué voy a decir? ¿Qué le gustaría escuchar?

Como nuestra vida está medida, la mía ha sido larga. No morí durante mi infancia como pasa con muchos de nuestros niños. No morí en la guerra o en el campo de batalla, ni fui sacrificado en alguna ceremonia religiosa, como le ha sucedido a muchos por su propia voluntad. No sucumbí por el exceso de bebida, ni por el ataque de un animal salvaje o la lenta descomposición del Ser Comido por los Dioses, esa terrible enfermedad que ustedes llaman lepra. No morí por contraer ninguna de las otras muchas enfermedades terribles que ustedes trajeron con sus barcos, a causa de las cuales tantos miles de miles han perecido. Yo sobreviví aun a los dioses, los que para siempre serían inmortales. He sobrevivido a más de una gavilla de años, para ver, hacer, aprender y recordar mucho. Pero ningún hombre puede saberlo todo, ni siquiera lo de su propio tiempo, y la vida en esta tierra empezó inmensurables años antes que la mía. Solamente de mi vida puedo hablar, solamente de la mía, que puedo hacer volver como una sombra de vida por medio de su tinta negra...

¡Había un esplendor de lanzas, un esplendor de lanzas!

Un anciano de nuestra isla de Xaltocan siempre empezaba de este modo sus historias sobre batallas. A nosotros, los que le escuchábamos, nos cautivaba al instante y seguíamos su narración absortos, aunque describiera una de las batallas menos importantes, y una vez que había contado los sucesos precedentes y los que estaban por venir, quizá resultara un cuento frívolo que no valiera la pena de ser narrado. Sin embargo, tenía la habilidad de llegar inmediatamente al momento más dramático de su relato, para luego ir entretejiendo alrededor de su narración. A diferencia de él, yo no puedo hacer otra cosa más que empezar desde el principio y pasar a través del tiempo exactamente como lo viví.

Todo lo que ahora declaro y afirmo, ocurrió. Yo narro solamente lo que pasó, sin inventar y sin falsedad. Beso la tierra. Eso quiere decir: lo juro.

✠

Oc ye nechca —como ustedes dirían: «Érase una vez»— cuando en nuestra tierra nada se movía más rápido de lo que nuestros mensajeros-veloces podían correr, excepto cuando los dioses se movían y no había ningún ruido más fuerte que el que podían hacer nuestros voceadores-a-lo-lejos, excepto cuando los dioses hablaban. En el día que nosotros llamamos Siete Flor, en el mes del Dios Ascendente en el año Trece Conejo, el dios de la lluvia, Tláloc, era el que hablaba más fuerte, en una tormenta resonante. Esto era poco usual, ya que la temporada de lluvias debía haber terminado. Los espíritus tlaloque que atendían al dios Tláloc estaban golpeando con sus tenedores de luz, rompiendo las grandes cáscaras de nubes, despedezándolas con gran rugido de truenos y escupiendo violentamente sus cascadas de lluvia.

En la tarde de ese día, en medio del tumulto causado por la tormenta, en una pequeña casa en la isla de Xaltocan, nací de mi madre para empezar a morir.

Como ustedes pueden ver, para hacer su crónica más clara, me tomé la molestia de aprender su calendario. Yo he calculado que la fecha de mi nacimiento debió de ser el vigésimo día de su mes llamado septiembre, en su año numerado como mil cuatrocientos sesenta y seis. Esto fue durante el reinado de Motecuzoma Illuicamina, en su idioma el Furioso Señor que Dispara sus Flechas Hacia el Cielo. Él era nuestro Uey-Tlatoani o Venerado Orador, nuestro título de lo que vendría a ser para ustedes rey o emperador. Pero el nombre de Motecuzoma o de cualquier otro no significaba entonces mucho para mí.

En aquel momento, todavía caliente de la matriz, es indudable que estaba mucho más impresionado al ser inmediatamente sumergido en una tinaja de agua fría. Ninguna comadrona me ha explicado la razón de esta práctica, pero supongo que es debida a la teoría de que, si el recién nacido podía sobrevivir a ese espantoso choque, podría hacerlo también a todas las enfermedades que generalmente se padecen en la infancia. De todas maneras, me debí quejar a pulmón abierto, mientras la comadrona me fajaba y mi madre se desataba de las cuerdas nudosas que la habían sostenido hincada, cuando me expelía hacia el suelo, y mientras mi padre enrollaba con cuidado, a un pequeño escudo de madera que él había tallado para mí, el trozo de cordón umbilical que me habían cortado.

17

Más tarde, mi padre daría ese objeto al primer guerrero mexícatl que encontrara y a éste se le confiaría la tarea de enterrarlo en algún lugar del próximo campo de batalla al que fuera destinado. Entonces mi *tonali* (destino, fortuna, suerte o como ustedes quieran llamarlo) siempre debería estar incitándome a ser un guerrero, la ocupación más honorable para nuestra clase de gente, y también para morir en el campo de batalla; ésta era la muerte más honrosa para nosotros. Dije «debería», porque aunque mi *tonali* frecuentemente me ha impelido o mandado hacia varias direcciones, incluso dentro del combate, nunca me sentí atraído a pelear y morir con violencia antes de tiempo.

También debo mencionar que, de acuerdo con la costumbre, el cordón umbilical de mi hermana Nueve Caña fue enterrado, poco más o menos dos años antes, bajo el hogar de la casa en donde nacimos. Su hilo había sido amarrado alrededor de un huso delgadito de barro, con lo que se esperaba que al crecer fuera una buena, hacendosa y aburrida esposa. No fue así. El *tonali* de Nueve Caña fue tan indócil como el mío.

Después de mi inmersión y de ser fajado, la comadrona me habló directamente con voz solemne, si es que yo la dejaba ser escuchada. Creo que no necesito decirles que no estoy repitiendo de memoria nada de lo que se dijo o se hizo cuando nací, pero conozco todos estos rituales. Lo que la comadrona me dijo aquella tarde, lo he escuchado decir a muchos recién nacidos, como siempre fue dicho a todos nuestros infantes varones. Éste ha sido uno de los muchos ritos por siempre recordado y nunca olvidado desde tiempos anteriores a los tiempos. Por medio de nuestros ancestros muertos ha mucho tiempo, nos fueron transmitidos a los vivos su sabiduría desde el momento de nuestro nacimiento.

La comadrona me dio por nombre Siete Flor. Este nombre del día de nacimiento sería el mío hasta haber pasado los peligros de la infancia, o sea hasta que tuviera siete años, en cuya edad se podía suponer que podría vivir lo suficiente para poder crecer, y entonces me sería dado un nombre de adulto más distintivo.

Ella dijo: «Siete Flor, mi muy amado y tierno niño que he recibido, he aquí la palabra que nos fue dada hace mucho tiempo por los dioses. Tú has nacido de esta madre y este padre solamente para ser guerrero y siervo de los dioses. Este lugar en el que acabas de nacer, no es tu verdadero hogar.»

Y ella dijo: «Siete Flor, tu deber más importante es dar a beber al sol la sangre de tus enemigos y alimentar la tierra con los cadáveres de tus oponentes. Si tu *tonali* es fuerte, estarás por muy poco tiempo con nosotros y en este lugar. Tu verdadero hogar estará en la tierra de nuestro dios-sol Tonatíu.»

Y ella dijo: «Siete Flor, si tú creces hasta morir como un *xochimiqui*, uno de los muy afortunados que alcanzan el mérito suficiente de tener una Muerte Florida, en la guerra o en el sacrificio, vivirás otra vez, eternamente feliz en Tonatiucan, el otro mundo del sol y servirás a Tonatíu por siempre y para siempre y te regocijarás en su servicio.»

Puedo ver recular a Su Ilustrísima. Yo también lo habría hecho si entonces hubiera podido comprender esa triste bienvenida a este mundo, o las palabras que después pronunciaron nuestros *capuli*, vecinos y parientes, que apretujándose en la pequeña estancia habían venido a ver al recién nacido. Cada uno de ellos, inclinándose hacia mí, dijo el saludo tradicional: «Has venido a sufrir. A sufrir y a perseverar.» Si todos los recién nacidos pudieran entender este saludo se retorcerían dolientes, volviéndose hacia la matriz, consumiéndose en ella como una semilla.

No hay duda de que venimos a este mundo a sufrir y a perseverar. ¿Qué ser humano no lo ha hecho? Sin embargo, las palabras de la comadrona acerca de ser guerrero y sobre el sacrificio, no eran más que la repetición del canto del *censontli*. Yo he escuchado otras muchas arengas tan edificantes como ésas, de mi padre, de mis maestros, de nuestros sacerdotes y de los suyos, todas ellas ecos insensatos de lo que a su vez ellos escucharon de generaciones pasadas a través de los años. Por mi parte, he llegado a creer que los que murieron hace mucho tiempo no eran en vida más sabios que nosotros, y que con sus muertes no añadieron ningún lustre a su sabiduría. Las palabras pomposas de los muertos siempre las he considerado, como nosotros decimos *yca mapilxocóitl*, con mi dedito meñique, o como ustedes dicen: «como un granito de sal».

Crecemos y miramos hacia abajo, envejecemos y miramos hacia atrás. *Ayyo*, pero qué era ser un niño... ¡ser un niño! Tener todos los caminos y los días ensanchados a lo lejos, adelante, hacia arriba. Todavía ninguno de ellos desperdiciado, perdido o del que podernos arrepentir. Todo era nuevo y novedoso en el mundo, como una vez lo fue para nuestro Señor Ometecutli y nuestra Señora Omecíhuatl, la Primera Pareja, los primeros seres de toda la creación.

Sin ningún esfuerzo recuerdo los sonidos recogidos en mi memoria, que llegan otra vez nebulosamente a mis oídos envejecidos. Los sonidos que escuchaba al amanecer en nuestra isla de Xaltocan. Muchas veces me despertó el reclamo del Pájaro Tempranero, Papan, gritando sus cuatro notas: «¡Papaquiqui!, ¡papaquiqui!», invitando al mundo a «¡elevarse, cantar, danzar, ser feliz!» Otras veces me despertaba un sonido todavía más temprano; era mi madre moliendo el maíz en el *métlatl* de piedra, torteando y dando forma a la masa del maíz, para luego convertirla en los grandes panes delgados y redondos, los deliciosos *tlaxcali*, que ustedes conocen por tortillas. Incluso hubo mañanas en que me desperté más temprano que todos, con excepción de los sacerdotes del dios-sol Tonatíu. Acostado en la oscuridad los podía escuchar soplando las caracolas marinas, que emitían balidos roncos y ásperos, en lo alto del templo de la modesta pirámide de nuestra isla, en el momento en que quemaban el incienso y cortaban ritualmente el pescuezo de una codorniz (porque esta ave está moteada como una noche estrellada) y cantaban en un rítmico son a su dios: «Ve como la noche ha muerto. Ven ahora y muéstranos tu obra bondadosa, oh joya única, oh encumbrada águila, ven ahora a alumbrar y a dar calor al Único Mundo...»

Sin ningún esfuerzo, sin ninguna dificultad, recuerdo los mediodías calientes, cuando Tonatíu el sol blandía fieramente, con todo su primitivo vigor, sus flameantes lanzas mientras se levantaba y estampaba sobre el techo del universo. En aquella deslumbrante luz azul-dorada del mediodía, las montañas que rodeaban el lago de Xaltocan parecían estar lo suficientemente cerca como para poderlas tocar. De hecho, éste es mi más antiguo recuerdo; no tendría más de dos años y todavía no había en mí ningún sentido de la distancia, el día y el mundo a mi alrededor eran jadeantes y sólo quería tocar algo fresco. Todavía recuerdo mi infantil sorpresa cuando al estirar el brazo hacia afuera *no* pude sentir el azul del bosque de la montaña que se veía enfrente de mí tan cerca y claramente.

Sin ningún esfuerzo, recuerdo también el terminar de los días, cuando Tonatíu se cubría con su manto de brillantes plumas para adormecerse, dejándose caer sobre su blanda cama de pétalos coloreados y sumergirse en el sueño. Él se había ido de nuestro lado, hacia Mictlan, el Lugar de la Oscuridad. De los cuatro mundos adonde iríamos a habitar después de nuestra muerte, Mictlan era el más profundo; era la morada de la muerte total e irredimible, el lugar en donde *nada* pasa, jamás ha pasado y jamás pasará. Tonatíu era misericordioso ya que, por un tiempo (un pequeño espacio de tiempo en el que nos podíamos dar cuenta de cuán pródigo era con nosotros) prestaría su luz (una pequeña luz, solamente atenuada por su sueño) al Lugar de la Oscuridad, de la muerte irremediable y sin esperanza. Mientras tanto, en nuestro Único Mundo, en Xaltocan, de todos modos el único mundo que yo conocía, neblinas pálidas y azulosas surgían del lago de tal manera que las negruzcas montañas que le circundaban parecían flotar sobre ellas, en medio de aguas rojas y purpúreos cielos. Entonces, exactamente por encima del horizonte, por donde Tonatíu había desaparecido flameando allí todavía un momento, Omexóchitl, Flor del Atarceder, la estrella vespertina, aparecía. Esta estrella, Flor del Atardecer, venía, siempre venía para asegurarnos que a pesar de la oscuridad de la noche no debíamos temer que *esa* noche se oscureciera para siempre en las tinieblas totales y negras del Lugar de la Oscuridad. El Único Mundo vivió y volvería a vivir en un rato más.

Sin ningún esfuerzo recuerdo las noches y una en particular. Metztli, la luna, había terminado su comida mensual de estrellas y estaba llena y satisfecha, tan ahíta en su redondez y brillantez que la figura del conejo-en-la-luna estaba grabada tan claramente como una escultura tallada del templo. Esa noche, supongo que tendría tres o cuatro años de edad, mi padre me cargó sobre sus hombros y sus manos sostuvieron fuertemente mis tobillos. Sus grandes zancadas me llevaron de una fresca claridad a una oscuridad todavía más fresca: la claridad veteada de luces y sombras que proyectaba la luna por debajo de las ramas extendidas de las emplumadas hojas de los «más viejos de los viejos árboles», los *ahuehuetque*, cipreses.

Para entonces, era lo suficientemente mayor como para haber oído hablar de las terribles asechanzas que nos aguardan en la oscuridad de la noche, ocultas a la visión de cualquier persona. Allí estaba Chocacíhuatl, La Llorona, la primera de todas las madres que murió al dar a luz; por siempre vagando, por siempre lamentando la muerte de su hijo y la pérdida de su propia vida. Allí estaban las calaveras descarnadas y separadas de sus cuerpos, que flotaban a través del aire, cazando a aquellos viajeros que habían sido atrapados por la oscuridad de la noche. Si algún mortal llegaba a vislumbrar algunas de estas cosas, sabía que era para él un presagio seguro de muerte o de infortunio.

Había otros habitantes de las tinieblas, pero no eran tan pavorosos. Por ejemplo, estaba el dios Yoali Ehécatl, Viento de la Noche, que soplaba fuertemente a lo largo de los caminos nocturnos, intentando agarrar a cualquier hombre incauto que caminara en la oscuridad. Sin embargo, Viento de la Noche era tan caprichoso como cualquier otro viento. A veces agarraba a alguien y luego lo dejaba libre, y cuando esto pasaba, a la persona se le concedía incluso algún deseo que ansiara su corazón y una vida larga para gozarlo. Así es que, con la esperanza de tener al dios siempre en ese indulgente estado de ánimo, hace mucho tiempo nuestra gente construyó bancos de piedra en varias de las encrucijadas de la isla, en donde Viento de la Noche pudiera descansar de sus ímpetus. Como ya dije, yo era lo suficientemente mayor como para saber acerca de los espíritus de las tinieblas y temerles. Pero aquella noche, sentado sobre los anchos hombros de mi padre, estando temporalmente más alto que cualquier hombre, siendo mi pelo cepillado por las frondas mohosas de los cipreses y mi rostro acariciado por los rayos veteados de la luna, no sentía ningún miedo.

Sin esfuerzo recuerdo esa noche, porque por primera vez se me permitió presenciar la ceremonia de un sacrificio humano. Era un rito menor, un homenaje a una deidad muy pequeña: Atlaua, el dios de los cazadores de aves. (En aquellos días, el lago de Xaltocan rebosaba de patos y gansos que en sus temporadas discurrían pausadamente allí para descansar, comer y alimentarnos a nosotros.) Así es que en esa noche de luna llena, al principio de la temporada de caza de aves acuáticas, solamente un *xochimiqui*, un hombre solamente, sería ritualmente sacrificado para la grandeza de la gloria del dios Atlaua. El hombre no era, esta vez, un guerrero cautivo yendo a su Muerte Florida con regocijo o con resignación, sino un voluntario avanzando tristemente hacia la muerte.

«Yo ya casi estoy muerto —había dicho a los sacerdotes—. Me ahogo como un pez fuera del agua: Mi pecho hace un gran esfuerzo para poder tomar más y más aire, pero el aire ya no me nutre. Mis miembros se están debilitando, mi vista está nublada, mi cabeza me da vueltas, estoy extenuado y me caigo. Prefiero morir de una vez, en lugar de aletear como un pez fuera del agua, hasta que al final me ahogue.»

Ese hombre era un esclavo de la nación de los chinanteca, situada lejos hacia el sur. Este pueblo estaba, y todavía está, aquejado de una curiosa enfermedad que parece correr indudablemente por el linaje de ciertas familias. Ellos y nosotros le llamamos la Enfermedad Pintada y ustedes, los españoles, ahora llaman a los chinanteca, el Pueblo Pinto, porque la piel del que la aflige está manchado de un azul lívido. De alguna manera, el cuerpo se ve imposibilitado de hacer uso del aire que respira, así es que se muere por sofocación de la misma forma en que un pez muere al ser sacado del elemento que lo sustenta.

Mi padre y yo llegamos a la orilla del lago, en donde, un poco más allá, habían dos postes gruesos hincados en la arena. La noche que nos rodeaba estaba iluminada con el fuego de las urnas, pero nebulosamente por el humo de los incensarios en donde se quemaba el *copali*. A través del humo se podía ver bailar a los sacerdotes de Atlaua: hombres viejos, totalmente negros, sus vestiduras negras, sus caras negras y sus largos cabellos enmarañados y endurecidos por el *óxitl*, la resina negra del pino con que nuestros cazadores de aves se embarraban sus piernas y la parte posterior de su cuerpo para protegerse del frío, cuando vadeaban en las aguas del lago. Dos de los sacerdotes tocaban la música ritual con flautas fabricadas con huesos de pantorrillas humanas, mientras otro golpeaba un tambor. Éste era un tipo especial de tambor que convenía para la ocasión: una calabaza gigante y vacía por dentro, parcialmente llena de agua, de manera que flotaba medio sumergida en la superficie del lago. Golpeada con huesos del muslo, el tambor de agua producía un rataplán de extrañas resonancias, que hacían eco contra las montañas, ahora invisibles, al otro lado del lago.

El *xochimiqui* fue llevado hacia el círculo de luz, en donde se desprendía el humo. Estaba desnudo, no traía ni siquiera el *máxtlatl* básico que normalmente cubre las caderas y las partes privadas. Aun a la luz parpadeante del fuego podía ver que su cuerpo no tenía el color de la piel manchado de azul, sino un azul de muerto con un toque aquí y allá de color carne. Fue tendido entre los dos postes y amarrado de un tobillo y una muñeca a cada uno de ellos. Un sacerdote ondulaba una flecha en la mano, como lo haría el que dirige un coro de cantantes, mientras entonaba una invocación:

«El fluido de la vida de este hombre te lo damos a ti, Atlaua, mezclado con el agua de vida de nuestro amado lago de Xaltocan. Te lo damos a ti, Atlaua, para que tú a cambio te dignes enviarnos tus parvadas de preciosas aves hacia las redes de nuestros cazadores...» Y así seguía.

Esto continuó lo suficiente como para aburrirme, si es que no aburrió también a Atlaua. Entonces, sin ningún ritual florido, sin ningún aviso, el sacerdote bajó la flecha de repente y la clavó con todas sus fuerzas tirando después hacia arriba, retorciéndola, dentro de los órganos genitales del hombre azul. La víctima, por mucho que hubiera deseado aliviarse de esta vida, dio un grito. Aulló y ululó un grito tan agudo y penetrante que destacó sobre el sonido de las flautas, del tambor y del canto. Gritó sí, pero no por mucho tiempo.

El sacerdote, con la flecha ensangrentada, marcó una cruz a manera de blanco sobre el pecho del hombre, y todos los sacerdotes empezaron a bailar alrededor de él en círculo, cada uno llevando un arco y muchas flechas. Cada vez que uno de ellos pasaba frente al *xochimiqui*, clavaba una flecha en el pecho jadeante del hombre azul. Cuando la danza terminó y todas las flechas fueron usadas, el hombre muerto parecía una especie de animal que nosotros llamamos el pequeño verraco-espín.

La ceremonia no consistía en mucho más. El cuerpo fue desamarrado de las estacas y sujetado con una cuerda a la parte de atrás de un *acali* de cazador, que había estado esperando en la arena. El cazador remó en su canoa hacia el centro del lago, fuera del alcance de nuestra vista, remolcando el cadáver hasta que éste se hundió por la acción del agua al penetrar dentro de los orificios naturales y los producidos por las flechas. Así recibió Atlaua su sacrificio.

Mi padre me colocó otra vez sobre sus hombros y regresó con sus grandes zancadas a través de la isla. A medida que me bamboleaba en lo alto, sintiéndome a salvo y seguro, me hice un voto pueril y arrogante. Si alguna vez mi *tonali* me seleccionaba para la Muerte Florida del sacrificio, aun para un dios extranjero, no gritaría, no importa lo que me fuese hecho, ni el dolor que sufriera.

Niño tonto. Creía que la muerte sólo significaba morir cobardemente o con valentía. En aquel momento de mi joven vida, segura y abrigada, siendo llevado en los hombros fuertes de mi padre hacia la casa para disfrutar de un sueño dulce del que sería despertado en el nuevo día por el reclamo del Pájaro Tempranero, ¿cómo podía saber lo que realmente significa la muerte?

En aquellos días creíamos que un héroe muerto al servicio de un señor poderoso o sacrificado en homenaje de una alta divinidad, aseguraba una vida sempiterna en el más esplendoroso de los mundos del más allá, en donde sería recompensado y agasajado con bienaventuranzas por toda la eternidad. Ahora, el cristianismo nos dice que *todos* podemos tener la esperanza a un espléndido cielo similar, pero consideremos. Aun el más heroico de los hombres muriendo por la más honorable de las causas, aun el más devoto de los cristianos muriendo mártir con la certeza de alcanzar el Cielo, nunca volverán a sentir las caricias que los rayos lunares dejarán caer sobre sus rostros, en sombras de luz, mientras caminan bajo las ramas de los cipreses de este mundo. Un placer frívolo, tan pequeño, tan simple, tan ordinario, pero ya jamás volverán a disfrutar. Eso es la muerte.

Su Ilustrísima demuestra impaciencia. Discúlpeme, Señor Obispo, mi vieja mente me impulsa algunas veces fuera del camino recto, hacia el laberinto de una senda descarriada. Yo sé que algunas cosas que he dicho y algunas otras que diré no

23

serán consideradas por usted como una información estrictamente histórica. Sin embargo, rezo para alcanzar su indulgencia, ya que no sé si tendré otra oportunidad para contar estas cosas. Y por todo lo que cuento, no cuento lo que podría contarse...

Retrocediendo otra vez hacia mi infancia, no puedo pretender que ésta haya sido extraordinaria en ningún sentido, para nuestra época y lugar, puesto que yo era ni más ni menos que un niño ordinario. El número del día y el del año de mi nacimiento no fueron ni afortunados ni desafortunados. No nací durante algún portento ocurrido en el cielo, como por ejemplo un eclipse mordiendo a la luna, que podría haberme roído un labio en forma parecida, o haber dejado una sombra permanente en mi cara, una marca oscura de nacimiento. No tuve ninguna de esas características físicas que nuestra gente consideraba como feos defectos en un hombre: no tuve pelo rizado; ni orejas en forma de asa de jarro; ni barba partida o doble; ni dientes protuberantes de conejo; ni nariz muy achatada, pero tampoco pronunciadamente picuda; ni ombligo saltón; ni lunares visibles. Afortunadamente para mí, mi pelo creció lacio, sin ningún remolino que se levantara o que se rizara.

Mi compañero de infancia, Chimali, tenía uno de esos remolinos encrespados y durante toda su juventud, prudentemente y aun con miedo, lo conservó muy corto y aplastado con *óxitl*. Recuerdo una vez, cuando éramos niños, que él tuvo que llevar una calabaza sobre su cabeza durante todo un día. Los escribanos sonríen; es mejor que lo explique.

Los cazadores de aves de Xaltocan agarraban patos y gansos de la manera más práctica y en buen número, poniendo largas redes sostenidas por varas clavadas aquí y allá en las partes poco profundas sobre las aguas del lago; entonces, haciendo un gran ruido, asustaban a las aves, de tal manera que éstas empezaban a volar repentinamente, quedando atrapadas en las redes. Sin embargo, nosotros, los niños de Xaltocan, teníamos nuestro propio método, verdaderamente astuto. Cortábamos la parte de arriba de una calabaza y la dejábamos hueca, haciéndole un hoyo por el cual podíamos ver y respirar. Nos poníamos dicha calabaza sobre la cabeza y, chapoteando como perritos, nos acercábamos al lugar en donde los patos y los gansos nadaban plácidamente en el lago. Como nuestros cuerpos eran invisibles dentro del agua, las aves no parecían encontrar nada alarmante en una o dos calabazas que se aproximaban flotando lentamente. Nos acercábamos lo suficiente como para agarrar las patas del ave y de un rápido tirón la metíamos dentro del agua. No siempre era fácil; hasta una cerceta pequeña podía presentar batalla a un niñito, pero generalmente podíamos mantener a las aves sumergidas hasta que éstas se sofocaban y se debilitaban. La maniobra rara vez causaba perturbación en el resto de la parvada que nadaba cerca.

Chimali y yo pasábamos el día en ese deporte y para cuando nos sentíamos cansados y desistíamos de seguir, teníamos amontonados en la orilla de la playa un respetable número de patos. Fue en ese momento cuando descubrimos que con el baño se le disolvía a Chimali el *óxitl* que usaba para aplacar su remolino, y su pelo quedaba detrás de la cabeza como si fuera un penacho. Estábamos al lado de la isla más lejano de nuestra aldea, lo que significaba que Chimali tendría que cruzar todo Xaltocan.

«*¡Ayya, pochéoa!*», se quejó. Esta expresión solamente se refiere a una ventosidad maloliente y apestosa, pero de haber sido escuchada por un adulto le hubiera valido una buena tunda de azotes con una vara espinosa, pues era una expresión demasiado vehemente para un niño de ocho o nueve años.

«Podemos volver por el agua —le sugerí— y nadar alrededor de la isla, si nos quedamos lo suficientemente alejados de la orilla.»

«Quizá tú puedas hacerlo —me dijo Chimali—. Yo estoy tan lleno de agua y tan sin aliento que me hundiría en seguida. Mejor que esperemos a que anochezca para regresar a casa caminando.»

Me encogí de hombros. «Durante el día corres el riesgo de que un sacerdote vea tu remolino y dé la noticia de ello, pero en la oscuridad corres el riesgo de encontrarte con algún monstruo más terrible, como Viento de la Noche. Yo estoy contigo, así es que tú decides.»

Nos sentamos a pensar un rato y mientras, inconscientemente, nos pusimos a comer hormigas. En esa temporada del año las había por todas partes y sus abdómenes estaban llenos de miel. Así es que, cogíamos a los insectos y les mordíamos el trasero para tomar una gotita de miel, pero destilaban tan poquita que por muchas hormigas que comiéramos no aplacábamos nuestra hambre.

«¡Ya sé! —dijo Chimali al fin—. Llevaré puesta mi calabaza durante todo el camino de regreso a casa.»

Y eso fue lo que hizo. Por supuesto que no podía ver muy bien por el agujero de su calabaza, así es que yo le guiaba, aunque los dos veníamos considerablemente cargados con el peso de nuestros patos muertos. Esto significaba que Chimali tropezaba continuamente, cayéndose entre las raíces de los árboles o en las zanjas del camino. Por fortuna nunca se hizo pedazos su calabaza. Sin embargo, me reí de él durante todo el camino, los perros le ladraban y como el crepúsculo se nos echó encima antes de llegar a la casa, Chimali hubiera podido asustar y aterrorizar a cualquier persona, que viajando al anochecer lo hubiese visto.

Por otra parte, eso no debía haber sido motivo de risa. Había una buena razón para que Chimali fuera siempre cauto y cuidadoso con su indómito pelo. Y es que, como verán ustedes, cualquier niño con remolino era especialmente preferido por los sacerdotes cuando necesitaban de un joven para sus sacrificios. No me pregunten por qué. Ningún sacerdote me dijo jamás el porqué. Pues ¿cuándo un sacerdote ha dado alguna vez una buena razón para imponernos las reglas irracionales que nos hace vivir, o por hacernos sentir el miedo, la culpa o la vergüenza que tenemos que sufrir cuando algunas veces las violamos?

Eso no significa que quiera dar la impresión de que cualquiera de nosotros, jóvenes o viejos, viviéramos en constante aprensión. Excepto por unos cuantos caprichos arbitrarios, como esa predilección de los sacerdotes por los muchachos con remolinos en su pelo, nuestra religión y los sacerdotes que la interpretaban, no nos cargaban con muchas demandas onerosas. Ninguna de las otras autoridades lo hicieron tampoco. Debíamos obediencia a nuestros soberanos y gobernadores, por supuesto, teníamos ciertas obligaciones para los *pipiltin* nobles y prestábamos atención a los consejos de nuestros *tlamatintin*, hombres sabios. Yo había nacido en la clase media de nuestra sociedad, los *macehualtin*, «los afortunados», llamados así porque estábamos libres de las pesadas responsabilidades de las clases altas, como éramos igualmente libres también de ser maltratados como frecuentemente lo eran las clases bajas.

En nuestro tiempo habían solamente unas pocas leyes, deliberadamente pocas, para que cada hombre pudiera guardarlas, todas, en su corazón y en su cabeza, y no tuviera ninguna excusa para quebrantarlas aduciendo ignorancia. Por eso, nuestras leyes no estaban escritas como las suyas, ni eran pegadas en sitios públicos como ustedes lo hacen, así un hombre no tenía que estar consultando continuamente la larga lista de edictos, reglas y regulaciones, para poder así medir hasta su más pequeña acción de «si debería» o «no debería». Conforme a sus normas, nuestras pocas leyes les pueden parecer ridículas y vagas, y los castigos por sus infracciones les parecerán indebidamente rigurosos. Nuestras leyes fueron hechas para el bien de todos y todos las obedecían, conociendo de antemano las espantosas consecuencias de no acatarlas. Aquellos que no lo hicieron, desaparecieron.

Por ejemplo, de acuerdo con las leyes que ustedes trajeron de España, un ladrón es castigado con la muerte. También para nosotros era así. Sin embargo, por sus leyes un hombre hambriento que roba algo de comer es un ladrón. Esto no era así en nuestro tiempo. Una de nuestras leyes decía que en cualquier campo sembrado de maíz a la vera de los caminos públicos, las cuatro primeras hileras de varas eran accesibles a los caminantes. Así cualquier viajero podía tomar de un tirón cuantas mazorcas de maíz necesitara para su panza vacía. Pero el hombre que por avaricia, buscando enriquecerse, saqueara aquel campo de maíz para colectar un saco, ya sea para atesorarlo o para comerciar con él, si era atrapado, moría. De este modo esa ley encerraba dos cosas buenas: que el ladrón sería curado para siempre de robar y que el hombre hambriento no muriera de hambre.

Nuestras vidas, las de los *macehualtin*, eran regidas más por costumbres y tradiciones que por leyes. Conservadas por largos años, muchas de ellas gobernaban la conducta de los adultos o de las tribus o de comunidades enteras. Aun cuando como niño todavía no había crecido más allá del apelativo de Siete Flor, ya me había dado cuenta de la insistencia tradicional de que un varón debe ser valiente, fuerte, galante, trabajador y honesto y de que una mujer debe ser modesta, casta, gentil, trabajadora y humilde.

Todo el tiempo que no pasé jugando con mis juguetes —la mayoría de ellos eran miniaturas de armas de guerra o réplicas de los aperos de trabajo usados por mi padre— y todo el tiempo que no pasé jugando con Chimali, con Tlatli y con otros niños de mi edad, lo pasé en compañía de mi padre, cuando él no estaba trabajando en la cantera. Aunque yo le llamaba Tata, como todos los niños llaman infantilmente a sus padres, su nombre era Tepetzalan, que significa Valle, como el valle que está entre las montañas de la tierra firme, en donde él había nacido. Como creció muy por encima de la estatura normal de nuestros hombres, ese nombre que se le había dado a los siete años fue después ridículo. Todos nuestros vecinos y sus compañeros en la cantera le llamaban con apodos referentes a su alta estatura: como Toca Estrellas, Cabeza Inclinada y otros parecidos.

Por cierto que él tenía que agachar mucho la cabeza cuando me dirigía las pláticas tradicionales de padre a hijo. Si por casualidad me veía imitando descaradamente el caminar arrastrado del viejo jorobado Tzapátic, el hombre que recolectaba la basura de nuestra aldea, mi padre me decía severamente:

«Ten cuidado, Chapulin (él siempre me llamaba con apodos cariñosos), de no burlarte de los ancianos, de los enfermos, de los incapacitados o de cualquier persona que haya caído en algún error o transgresión. Ni los insultes ni los desprecies, más bien humíllate ante los dioses y tiembla, no sea que ellos dejen caer sobre ti las mismas miserias.»

O si yo no mostraba interés en lo que mi padre trataba de enseñarme acerca de su oficio, ya que cualquier niño *macehuali* que no aspirara a la vida de guerrero, se esperaba que siguiera los pasos de su padre, él se agachaba y me decía sinceramente:

«No huyas de cualquier labor que los dioses te asignen, hijo, sino que debes estar contento. Rezo para que ellos te otorguen méritos y buena fortuna, pero cualquier cosa que te den, recíbela con gratitud. Aunque te den solamente un pequeño don, no lo desdeñes, porque los dioses pueden quitarte lo poco que tienes. En caso de que la dádiva que recibas sea muy grande, quizá un gran talento, ni seas orgulloso ni te vanaglories, más bien recuerda que los dioses deben haber negado ese *tonali* a otra persona, para que tú lo pudieras tener.»

Algunas veces, sin instigación alguna y con su cara grande ligeramente sonrojada, mi padre me echaría un pequeño sermón que no tendría ningún significado para mí. Algo así como:

«Vive limpiamente y no seas disoluto, Chapulin, o los dioses se enojarán y te cubrirán de infamia. Contrólate, hijo, hasta que conozcas a la joven que los dioses han destinado para que sea tu esposa, porque ellos saben arreglar todas las cosas con propiedad. Sobre todo, nunca juegues con la esposa de otro hombre.»

Eso me parecía una recomendación innecesaria, porque yo vivía limpiamente. Como todos los demás mexica, a excepción de nuestros sacerdotes, me bañaba dos veces al día en agua caliente y jabonosa, nadaba frecuentemente en el lago y periódicamente sudaba los restantes «malos humores» en la casita de vapor de la aldea. Me limpiaba mis dientes por la mañana y por la noche con una mezcla de miel y cenizas blancas. En cuanto a «jugar», yo no conocía a ningún hombre en la isla que tuviera una esposa de mi edad, y de todos modos nosotros, los muchachos, no incluíamos a las niñas en nuestros juegos.

Todas estas prédicas de padre a hijo eran nada más que recitaciones de loro transmitidas a través de generaciones, palabra por palabra, como el discurso de la comadrona en el momento de mi nacimiento. Sólo en estas ocasiones mi padre Tepetzalan hablaba largamente; por lo demás, él era un hombre taciturno. El ruido que había en la cantera no daba lugar para pláticas y en casa la cháchara incesante y quejosa de mi madre no le daba oportunidad de decir ni siquiera una palabra. A Tata no le importaba. Él siempre había preferido la acción a las palabras, y me enseñó más con su ejemplo que con sus arengas de loro. Si a mi Tata de veras le faltaban algunas de las cualidades que se esperaban de nuestros hombres, fuerza, valentía y todo eso, ese defecto consistía solamente en dejarse intimidar e insultar por mi Tene.

Mi madre era una de las hembras menos típicas entre todas las *macehualtin* de Xaltocan: la menos modesta, la menos dócil, la menos humilde. Era una pendenciera consumada, la tirana de nuestra pequeña familia y la que atosigaba a todos nuestros vecinos. Sin embargo, creyéndose un modelo de perfección, había caído en un estado de insatisfacción perpetuo y enojoso hacia todo lo que la rodeaba. Si aprendí algo útil de mi Tene, fue el estar algunas veces insatisfecho *conmigo mismo*.

Me acuerdo de haber sido castigado por mi padre, corporalmente, solamente en una ocasión, cuando lo merecía plenamente. Nosotros, los niños de Xaltocan, teníamos permiso y aun éramos alentados a matar a las aves que, como los cuervos y mirlos, picoteaban las cosechas de nuestras *chinampa*, lo que hacíamos con unas cervatanas de caña que expulsaban unas bolitas de barro. Un día, por cierto tipo de perversidad traviesa, soplé una bolita contra la pequeña codorniz domesticada que teníamos en nuestra casa. (La mayoría de las casas tenían una de estas aves como mascota, para controlar a los alacranes y otras clases de bichos.) Entonces, para aumentar mi crimen, traté de culpar a mi amigo Tlatli de la muerte del ave. A mi padre no le costó mucho averiguar la verdad. El asesinato de la inofensiva codorniz podría haber sido castigado moderadamente, pero no así el pecado estrictamente prohibido de *mentir*. Mi Tata tuvo que inflingirme el castigo prescrito por «hablar escupiendo flemas», que era así como le llamábamos a una mentira. Él se sintió mal cuando lo hizo. Atravesó mi labio inferior con una espina de maguey, dejándola ahí hasta que me llegó el tiempo de ir a dormir. ¡*Ayya ouiya*, el dolor, la mortificación, el dolor, las lágrimas de mi arrepentimiento, el dolor!

Ese castigo me dejó una huella tan profunda, que yo a mi vez lo he dejado grabado en los archivos de nuestra tierra. Si ustedes han visto nuestra escritura-pintada, habrán observado pinturas de personas o de otros seres con un pequeño símbolo enroscado como un pergamino emanando de ellos. Ese símbolo representa un *náhuatl*, que significa una lengua, un lenguaje, un discurso o sonido. Esto indica que la figura está hablando o emitiendo algún sonido. Si el *náhuatl* está enroscado más de lo ordinario y elaborado con el glifo que representa una mariposa o una flor, significa que la persona está recitando poesía o está cantando. Cuando llegué a ser escribano, agregué otra figura a nuestra escritura-pintada: el *náhuatl* atravesado por una espina de maguey y pronto todos los demás escribanos lo adoptaron. Así cuando vean ese glifo antes de una figura sabrán que se está viendo la pintura de alguien que miente.

Los castigos que más frecuentemente nos daba mi madre eran infligidos sin tardanza, sin compasión y sin remordimiento; yo sospecho que incluso con algo de placer en dar una pena, además que corregir. Ésos, quizá, no dejaron legado en la historia-pintada de esta tierra como la lengua atravesada por una espina, pero ciertamente afectaron la historia de nuestras vidas: la de mi hermana y la mía. Recuerdo haber visto a mi madre golpear una noche a mi hermana con una manojo de ortigas hasta dejarle rojas las nalgas, porque la muchacha había sido culpable de inmodestia. Debo decirles que inmodestia no tiene el mismo significado para nosotros que para ustedes, los hombres blancos; entendemos por inmodestia una indecente exposición de alguna parte del cuerpo que debe estar cubierta por la ropa.

En cuestiones de ropa, nosotros los niños de ambos sexos íbamos totalmente desnudos, lo que permitía la temperatura, hasta que teníamos la edad de cuatro o cinco años. Después cubríamos nuestra desnudez con un largo rectángulo de tela tosca que atábamos a uno de los hombros y plegábamos el resto alrededor de nuestro cuerpo, hasta la mitad del muslo. Cuando éramos considerados adultos, o sea a la edad de trece años, los varones empezábamos a usar el *máxtlatl*, taparrabos, bajo nuestro manto exterior. Más o menos a esa misma edad, dependiendo de su primer sangrado, las niñas recibían la tradicional blusa y falda de las mujeres, además de una *tozotzomatli*, una ropa interior muy parecida a lo que ustedes llaman bragas.

Perdonen si mi narración está llena de pequeños detalles, pero trato de establecer el tiempo de la paliza dada a mi hermana. Nueve Caña había recibido el nombre de Tzitzitlini un poco antes —que quiere decir «el sonido de campanitas tocando»—, así es que ella ya había pasado de los siete años. Sin embargo, yo vi sus partes inferiores ser golpeadas hasta ser desolladas, lo que quiere decir que todavía no usaba bragas, por lo tanto aún no había cumplido los trece años. Considerando todas estas cosas estimo que tendría diez u once años. Y lo que ella había hecho para merecer esa paliza, la única cosa de la que era culpable, había sido el murmurar, soñadora: «Oigo tambores y música tocando. Me pregunto en dónde están bailando esta noche.» Para nuestra madre eso era una falta de inmodestia. Tzitzi estaba anhelando una frivolidad cuando debería estarse aplicando en el telar o en alguna otra cosa igualmente tediosa.

¿Conocen ustedes el *chili*? ¿Esa vaina vegetal que usamos en nuestra cocina? Aunque hay diferentes grados de picante entre las distintas variedades, todos los *chiltin* son tan picantes al paladar, pero *tan* picantes, que no es de extrañar que el nombre «chili» derive de nuestras palabras «afilar» y «aguzar». Como toda cocinera, mi madre utilizaba los *chiltin* en la forma usual, pero también tenía otro uso para ellos, que casi titubeo en mencionar, puesto que sus inquisidores tienen ya suficientes instrumentos de tortura.

Un día, cuando tenía cuatro o cinco años, me senté con Tlatli y Chimali en la puerta de nuestro patio, jugando *patli*, «el juego de los frijoles». Éste no era el mismo juego que los hombres mayores jugaban, apostando con exceso. Un juego que en ocasiones había causado la ruina de una familia o la muerte de alguien en una riña. No, nosotros, los tres niños, simplemente habíamos dibujado un círculo en la tierra y cada uno puso un *choloani*, frijol-saltarín, en el centro. El objeto del juego era ver cuál de los frijoles, calentados por la acción del sol, sería el primero en saltar fuera del círculo. El mío tenía la tendencia a flojear y yo gruñí alguna imprecación, quizá dije «¡*pocheoa!*» o algo por el estilo.

De repente estaba pies para arriba, suspendido sobre la tierra. Mi Tene me había agarrado con violencia de los tobillos. Vi las caras invertidas de Chimali y Tlatli, sus ojos y sus bocas abiertas por la sorpresa, antes de haber desaparecido dentro de la casa hasta las tres piedras del hogar. Mi madre cambió la forma de asirme, de tal manera que con una mano arrojó un puñado de *chili* rojo y seco en la lumbre. Cuando estuvo crujiendo y lanzó hacia arriba un humo denso, amarillento, mi Tene me tomó otra vez por los tobillos y me suspendió cabeza abajo sobre ese acre humo. Dejo a su imaginación los siguientes momentos, pero creo que estuve a punto de morirme. Recuerdo que mis ojos lloraban continuamente medio mes después y no podía aspirar ni superficialmente sin sentir como si inhalara llamas y lajas.

Después de eso me sentí muy afortunado, pues nuestras costumbres no dictaban que un niño pasase mucho tiempo en compañía de su madre y ya tenía una buena razón para no estar en su compañía. Por esa causa huía de ella, como mi amigo Chimali, el del pelo hirsuto, huía de los sacerdotes de la isla. Aunque ella viniera a buscarme para ordenarme alguna tarea o recado, siempre me podía refugiar en la seguridad de la colina en donde estaban los hornos para quemar la cal. Los canteros tenían la creencia de que no se le debía permitir a ninguna mujer acercarse jamás a los hornos, o la calidad de la cal se echaría a perder, y ni siquiera una mujer como mi madre se atrevería a hacerlo. Sin embargo, la pobrecita de Tzitzitlini no tenía tal refugio.

De acuerdo con la costumbre y con su *tonali*, una mujer tenía que aprender el trabajo de mujer y esposa: cocinar, hilar, tejer, coser, bordar; así es que mi hermana debía pasar la mayor parte del día bajo los ojos vigilantes y la ágil lengua de nuestra madre. Su lengua no perdía ninguna oportunidad para decir a mi hermana una de las tradicionales arengas de madre a hija. Cuando Tzitzi me repitió algunas, estuvimos de acuerdo en que habían sido confeccionadas, por algún lejano antepasado, más para el beneficio de la madre que de la hija.

«Debes atender siempre, hija, al servicio de los dioses y a dar comodidad a tus padres. Si tu madre te llama no te esperes a que te hable dos veces, ve siempre al instante. Cuando te ordene una tarea, no contestes insolentemente y no demuestres renuencia para hacerla. Lo que es más, si tu Tene llama a otro y aquél no va rápidamente, ve tú misma a ver qué es lo que desea y hazlo tú y hazlo bien.»

Otros sermones eran consejos típicos sobre la modestia, la virtud y la castidad, y ni siquiera Tzitzi y yo pudimos encontrar error en ellos. Sabíamos que desde que ella cumpliera los trece años hasta que tuviera más o menos veintidós años y estuviera casada adecuadamente, ningún hombre podría ni siquiera hablarle en público, ni ella a él.

«Si en un sitio público te encuentras con un joven que te guste, no lo demuestres, no des señal alguna, no sea que vayas a inflamar sus pasiones. Ten cuidado de no tener familiaridades impropias con los hombres, no cedas a los impulsos primitivos de tu corazón o enturbiarás de suciedad tu carácter como lo hace el lodo con el agua.»

Probablemente Tzitzitlini nunca hubiera desobedecido esa única prohibición razonable, pero cuando tenía doce años empezó a sentir, seguramente, las primeras sensaciones sexuales y alguna curiosidad acerca del sexo. Tal vez para ocultar lo que ella consideraba sentimientos impropios e indecibles, trató de darles salida privada y solitariamente. Lo único que sé es que, un día nuestra madre regresó del mercado inesperadamente a casa y encontró a mi hermana recostada en su esterilla desnuda de la cintura hacia abajo, haciendo un acto que yo no entendí hasta mucho después. La había encontrado jugando con sus *tepili*, partes, y utilizando un pequeño uso de madera para ese propósito.

Oigo que Su Ilustrísima murmura en voz baja y veo que recoge las faldas de su hábito de una manera casi protectora. ¿Le ofendí en alguna forma contándole con toda franqueza lo que sucedió? He tratado de no utilizar palabras vulgares para narrarlo. Supongo, que dado que esas palabras vulgares abundan en nuestros respectivos idiomas, los actos que describen no son extraños entre nuestros pueblos.

Para castigar la ofensa que Tzitzitlini hizo contra su propio cuerpo, nuestra Tene tomó el frasco que contenía el polvo de *chili* seco y tomando un puño lo frotó violentamente, quemando la expuesta y tierna *tepili*. Aunque ella sofocaba los gritos de su hija tapándole la boca con la colcha, los oí, fui corriendo y le pregunté entrecortadamente: «¿Debo de ir a traer al *tícitl*?» «¡No, no un físico! —me gritó nuestra madre violentamente—. ¡Lo que tu hermana ha hecho es demasiado vergonzoso para que se sepa más allá de estas paredes!»

Tzitzi sorbía su llanto y también ella me rogó: «No estoy muy lastimada, hermanito, no llames al físico. No menciones esto a nadie, ni siquiera a nuestro Tata. Es más, procura olvidar que sabes algo acerca de esto, te lo ruego.»

Quizás hubiera ignorado mi tirana madre, pero no a mi querida hermana. Aunque entonces yo no sabía la razón por la cual ella rehusaba una ayuda, la respetaba y me fui de ahí para preocuparme y preguntarme solo.

¡Ahora pienso que debí haber hecho *algo*! Y no hacer caso a ninguna de las dos, por lo que sucedió más tarde, ya que la crueldad infligida por nuestra madre en esa ocasión, en la que trató de desalentar las urgencias sexuales que apenas se despertaban en Tzitzi, tuvo un efecto totalmente contrario. Creo que desde entonces las partes *tepili* de mi hermana se quemaban como una garganta ampollada con *chili*, calientes y sedientas, clamando por ser apagadas. Creo que no hubieran pasado muchos años antes de que mi querida hermana Tzitzitlini se hubiera ido a «ahorcajarse al camino», como nosotros decimos de una ramera depravada y promiscua. Ésa, era la profundidad más sórdida en la que una joven decente *mexicatl* podría caer, o por lo menos así lo pensaba hasta que conocí el destino aún más terrible en que finalmente cayó mi hermana.

Cuál fue su conducta, lo que ella llegó a ser y cómo la llegaron a llamar, lo contaré a su debido tiempo. Sin embargo, quiero decir solamente una cosa aquí. Quiero decir que para mí, ella siempre fue y siempre será Tzitzitlini, «el sonido de campanitas tocando».

I H S

✠

S. C. C. M.

Santificada, Cesárea, Católica Majestad,
el Emperador Don Carlos, nuestro Señor Rey:

Que la serena y benéfica luz de Nuestro Señor Jesucristo caiga eternamente sobre Vuestra Majestad Don Carlos, por la gracia divina nombrado Emperador, etcétera, etcétera.

Muy Augusta Majestad: desde esta ciudad de Mexico, capital de la Nueva España, en la fiesta de San Miguel Arcángel y de Todos los Ángeles, en el año de Nuestro Señor de mil quinientos veinte y nueve, os saludo.

Vuestra Majestad ordena que continuemos enviando porciones adicionales de la llamada Historia Azteca «tan pronto como las páginas sean recopiladas». Señor, esto sorprende y ofende gravemente a vuestro bien intencionado capellán. Nos, ni por todos los reinos del dominio de Vuestra Majestad, soñaríamos con disputar los deseos y las decisiones de nuestro soberano. Pero creíamos que habíamos expuesto claramente en nuestra carta anterior, la objeción a esta crónica que a diario va siendo más detestable y habíamos esperado que la recomendación del Obispo delegado de Vuestra Majestad no hubiera sido desdeñada tan fácilmente.

Somos conscientes de la preocupación de Vuestra Graciosa Majestad por el deseo de informarse lo más minuciosamente posible acerca, inclusive, de sus remotos súbditos para poder gobernarlos más sabia y benéficamente. De hecho, hemos respetado esa valiosa y meritoria preocupación desde el primer mandato de Vuestra Majestad, que personalmente nos encomendó: la exterminación de las brujas de Navarra. Desde esa sublime y prodigiosa purificación por fuego, aquella provincia, una vez disidente, ha sido entre todas las demás la más obediente y subordinada a la soberanía de Vuestra Majestad. Vuestro humilde servidor intenta igualar esta asiduidad y arrancar los viejos demonios de estas nuevas provincias, metiendo en cintura al vicio y espoleando la virtud, para llevar igualmente a estas tierras a someterse a Vuestra Majestad y a la Santa Cruz.

Seguramente que nada puede ser intentado en el servicio de Vuestra Majestad, que no sea bendecido por Dios. Y, ciertamente Vuestra Muy Poderosa Señoría, debería tener conocimiento de lo que concierne a esta tierra, porque es tan ilimitada y maravillosa, que Vuestra Majestad bien puede llamarse Emperador sobre ella con no menos orgullo con que lo hace de Alemania, que por la gracia de Dios también es ahora posesión de Vuestra Majestad.

Sin embargo, al supervisar la transcripción de esta historia de lo que ahora es la Nueva España, solamente Dios sabe cuánto hemos sido atormentado, injuriado y molestado por las emanaciones nauseabundas e inextinguibles del narrador. Este azteca es un Acolus con una bolsa inacabable de vientos. No podríamos quejarnos de eso si se limitara a lo que nosotros le hemos pedido: una relación a la manera de San Gregorio de Tours y de otros historiadores clásicos: nombres de personajes distinguidos, sumarios breves sobre sus carreras, fechas prominentes, lugares, batallas, etcétera.

Sin embargo, no es posible restringir a esta catarata humana de sus divagaciones sobre los aspectos más sórdidos y repelentes de su historia y de la de su pueblo. Estamos de acuerdo en que este indio era un pagano hasta su bautismo hace solamente unos pocos años. Debemos conceder con caridad que las atrocidades infernales que cometió y de las que fue testigo durante su vida pasada fueron hechas o condonadas en la ignorancia de la moral cristiana, pero ahora, que por lo menos se llama cristiano, uno esperaría de él que, si es que *tiene* que concentrarse en los episodios más bestiales de su vida y de su tiempo, por lo menos manifestara una contrición humilde y decente, de conformidad a los horrores que describe con esos detalles tan lascivos.

Él no lo hace. No siente ningún horror ante esas enormidades. Ni siquiera enrojece ante las muchas ofensas a Nuestro Señor y ante a la decencia común contra la cual está golpeando constantemente los oídos de nuestros frailes escribanos: idolatría, pretensiones de magia, supersticiones, sed y deseo de sangre, obscenidades y actos contra natura, y otros pecados tan viles que nos abstenemos de mencionarlos aquí. Excepto por la orden de Vuestra Majestad de «que todo sea expuesto con mucho detalle», no permitiríamos a nuestros escribanos poner parte de la narración del azteca en lo escrito en el pergamino.

Sin embargo, este humilde siervo de Vuestra Majestad nunca ha desobedecido una orden real. Intentaremos contener nuestra náusea y considerar las murmuraciones perniciosas del indio simplemente como la evidencia de que, durante su vida, el Enemigo le presentó muchas clases de tentaciones y pruebas, que Dios permitió para aumentar la fuerza del alma del azteca. Esto nos recuerda que no es pequeña la evidencia de la grandeza de Dios, porque Él escoge no a los sabios y a los fuertes, sino a los humildes y débiles para ser, igualmente, instrumentos y beneficiarios de Su Misericordia. La Ley de Dios nos recuerda y nos obliga a extender una medida más de tolerancia hacia aquellos quienes todavía no han apagado su sed en las fuentes de la Fe, más que aquellos que habiendo ya saciado su sed, están acostumbrados a ella.

Así es que trataremos de contener nuestro disgusto. Retendremos al indio con nosotros y le dejaremos continuar vomitando sus inmundicias hasta recibir la opinión de Vuestra Majestad acerca de las siguientes páginas de su historia. Afortunadamente, en este momento en particular, no tenemos ningún trabajo urgente para sus cinco asistentes. La única recompensa que recibe esta criatura es que le dejamos compartir nuestra comida y le hemos puesto en un cuarto de la despensa que ya no se utiliza una esterilla de paja en donde dormir, aquellas noches que no las pasa atendiendo a su esposa, aparentemente achacosa, a quien lleva las sobras de nuestra merienda.

Confiamos en que pronto nos veremos libres de él y de la miasma asquerosa que le rodea. Estamos seguros de que cuando vos leáis las páginas siguientes, Señor —indescriptiblemente más horripilantes que las anteriores—, compartiréis nuestra repulsión y gritaréis: «¡No más de esta suciedad!», como David gritó: «¡No lo publiquéis, no sea que los descreídos se regocijen!»

Anhelantes y ansiosamente esperamos la orden de Vuestra Estimada Majestad, en el siguiente barco-correo, de que todas las páginas recopiladas en el ínterin sean destruidas y así poder echar fuera de nuestros recintos a este bárbaro reprensible.

Que Dios Nuestro Señor sostenga y preserve a Vuestra Más Excelentísima Majestad por muchos años en Su santo servicio.

De S.C.C.M., fiel siervo y capellán orante,

(ecce signum) ZUMÁRRAGA

ALTER PARS

¿Que no va a asistir hoy Su Ilustrísima, señores escribanos? ¿Debo continuar, entonces? Ah, ya veo. Él leerá mis palabras en sus hojas de papel, a su placer. Muy bien. Entonces permítanme dejar, por el momento, la crónica excesivamente personal de mi familia y la mía.

Para que ustedes no tengan la impresión de que yo y algunos otros que he mencionado vivíamos separados del resto de la humanidad en algún tipo de aislamiento, les daré una visión más amplia. Iré hacia atrás y lejos en mi mente, en mi memoria, para hacerles ver mejor como un todo nuestra relación con nuestro mundo. A éste nosotros le llamábamos Cem-Anáhuac, que quiere decir El Único Mundo.

Sus exploradores pronto descubrieron que éste está situado entre dos océanos ilimitados al este y al oeste. Las húmedas Tierras Calientes a las orillas de los océanos no se extienden mucho tierra adentro, sino que se inclinan hacia arriba para convertirse en sierras desmesuradamente altas, teniendo entre sus cadenas de sierras, orientales y occidentales, una alta meseta. Ésta está tan cerca del cielo que el aire es ligero, limpio y de una claridad deslumbrante. Nuestros días aquí son siempre suaves como en la primavera, aun durante la temporada de lluvias en mitad del verano, hasta que llega el seco invierno, cuando Títitl, el dios de los días más cortos del año, elige algunos de estos días para hacerlos fríos o incluso dolorosamente fríos.

La parte más poblada de todo El Único Mundo es esa depresión en forma de cuenca que está en la meseta y que actualmente ustedes lo llaman el Valle de Mexico. Ahí se encuentran los lagos que hacen de este área un lugar muy atractivo para la vida humana. En realidad, solamente hay un lago enorme, apretado por la tierra en dos lugares de manera que hay tres grandes cuerpos de agua conectados por unos estrechos más angostos. El lago más pequeño, que está más al sur, es alimentado por arroyos claros formados por las nieves derretidas de las montañas. El lago que está más al norte y de tamaño mediano, donde yo pasé mis primeros años, es de agua rojiza y salada, demasiado astringente para ser potable, porque está rodeado de tierras minerales que dejan sus sales en el agua. El lago central, Texcoco, mucho más grande que los otros dos juntos y mezclado con aguas salinas y frescas, tiene una calidad ligeramente áspera.

A pesar de que hay solamente un lago, o tres, si ustedes quieren, siempre los hemos dividido por cinco nombres. El lago de Texcoco, de color turbio, es el único que tiene un solo nombre. El lago más pequeño y cristalino, que está al sur, se llama el lago de Xochimilco en su parte alta: El Jardín de las Flores, porque es el vivero de las plantas más preciosas de todas las tierras alrededor. En su parte inferior, el lago es llamado Chalco, por la nación chalca que vive en su orilla. El lago que está más al norte, aunque también es un solo cuerpo de agua, está dividido asimismo. El pueblo que vive en Tzumpanco, que significa Isla en Forma de Calavera, le llama a su mitad el lago Tzumpanco. El pueblo donde nací, Xaltocan, que significa Isla de los Cuyos, llama a su porción el lago de Xaltocan.

En un sentido, yo podría comparar a estos lagos con nuestros dioses —nuestros antiguos dioses—. He escuchado a ustedes, los cristianos, quejarse de nuestra «multitud» de dioses y diosas, quienes tenían soberanía sobre cada faceta de la naturaleza y del comportamiento humano. Los he escuchado lamentarse de que nunca han podido entender ni comprender el funcionamiento de nuestro atestado panteísmo. Sin embargo, yo he contado y comparado. Yo no creo que nosotros dependiéramos de tantas deidades mayores y menores, por lo menos no tanto como ustedes —el Señor Dios, Su Hijo Jesús, el Espíritu Santo, la Virgen María, además de todos los otros Seres Altos a quienes ustedes llaman Ángeles y Apóstoles y Santos; cada uno de ellos patrón gobernante de alguna faceta única de *su* mundo, de sus días, de sus *tonalin* y aun de cada uno de los días de su calendario—. En verdad, creo que nosotros reconocíamos menos deidades, pero a cada una de las nuestras les encargábamos diferentes funciones a la vez.

Para un geógrafo, hay un solo lago en el valle. Para un barquero remando su *acali* laboriosamente, hay tres cuerpos anchos de agua conectados entre sí. Para la gente que vive sobre o alrededor de los lagos hay cinco separados y distinguidos por sus nombres. De la misma manera, ninguno de nuestros dioses y diosas tenía una sola cara, una sola responsabilidad, un solo nombre. Como nuestro lago de tres lagos, un solo dios podía incorporar una trinidad de aspectos...

¿Eso les pone ceñudos, reverendos frailes? Muy bien, un dios podía tener *dos* aspectos o cinco. O veinte.

Dependiendo de la estación del año: la temporada de lluvias o la temporada seca, días largos o cortos, temporadas de siembra o de cosecha, y dependiendo de las circunstancias: períodos de guerra o de paz, de abundancia o de hambre, de gobernantes benévolos o crueles, las obligaciones de un solo dios variaban y también su actitud hacia nosotros; por lo tanto, también variaba nuestro modo de reverenciarlo, celebrarlo o aplacarlo. Para verlo de otra manera, nuestras vidas podrían ser como los tres lagos: amargo, dulce o blandamente indiferente, como él lo eligiera.

Mientras tanto, ambos, los estados de ánimo del dios y los sucesos ocurridos en nuestro mundo, podían ser vistos de muy diferente manera por los diversos seguidores de ese dios. La victoria de un ejército es la derrota de otro, ¿no es verdad? Así el dios, o la diosa podía ser visto simultáneamente como premiando o castigando, exigiendo o dando, haciendo bien o mal. Si ustedes pudieran abarcar todas las infinitas combinaciones de circunstancias, comprenderían la variedad de atributos que nosotros veíamos en cada dios, la cantidad de aspectos que cada uno asumía y aun la mayor cantidad de nombres que les dábamos: en reverencia, en agradecimiento, en respeto o por temor.

Sin embargo, no voy a insistir en eso. Permítanme regresar de lo místico a lo físico. Hablaré de cosas demostradas por los cinco sentidos que aun los animales irracionales poseen.

La isla de Xaltocan es realmente casi una roca gigantesca asentada en medio del lago salado y bastante retirada de la tierra firme. Si no hubiera sido por los tres manantiales naturales de agua fresca que salían burbujeando de la roca, la isla nunca hubiera sido poblada, pero en mi tiempo sostenía quizás a unas dos mil personas distribuidas entre veinte aldeas. La roca era nuestro apoyo en más de un sentido, porque era *tenéxtetl*, piedra caliza, un producto por demás valioso. En su estado natural, esta clase de piedra es bastante suave y fácil de ser tallada, aun con nuestros toscos aperos de madera, piedra, cobre despuntado y obsidiana quebradiza, tan inferiores a los suyos de hierro y acero.

Mi padre Tepetzalan era un maestro cantero, uno de los muchos que dirigían a los trabajadores menos capacitados. Recuerdo una ocasión en que él me llevó a su cantera para enseñarme sobre su trabajo.

«Tú no lo puedes ver —me dijo—, pero aquí... y aquí... corren las fisuras y estrías naturales de este estrato en particular de *tenéxtelt*. Aunque son invisibles al ojo inexperto, tú aprenderás a adivinarlas.»

Yo nunca pude hacerlo, pero él no perdió la esperanza. Yo observaba mientras él marcaba la cara de la piedra con brochazos de *óxitl* negro. Luego vinieron otros obreros para martillar cuñas de madera dentro de las pequeñas grietas que mi padre había marcado; tenían sus rostros pálidos por el sudor y el polvo mezclado. Después de que mojaran esas cuñas con agua, regresamos a casa y pasaron algunos días, durante los cuales los obreros conservaban bien húmedas las cuñas para que se hincharan y ejercieran una creciente presión dentro de la piedra. Entonces mi padre y yo volvimos otra vez a la cantera. Nos paramos en su borde y miramos hacia abajo. Él me dijo: «Observa ahora, Chapulin.»

Pareció como si la piedra sólo hubiera estado aguardando la presencia de mi padre y su permiso, porque de repente, y por su propia voluntad, la cara de la cantera emitió un crujido que hendió el aire y se partió. Parte de ella se vino abajo rodando en inmensos trozos como cubos, otras partes se partían en forma de tablas cuadradas y planas, y todos ellos cayeron intactos dentro de unas redes hechas de cuerda, que habían sido extendidas para recibirlos antes de que pudieran hacerse pedazos contra el piso de la cantera. Fuimos hacia abajo y mi padre inspeccionó todo con satisfacción.

«Solamente un poco de tallado con las azuelas —dijo—, un poco de pulido de obsidiana y agua, y éstos —y él apuntó los bloques de piedra caliza— serán perfectos para la construcción, mientras que éstas —y señaló las tablas tan grandes como el piso de nuestra casa y tan delgadas como mi brazo— serán los paneles de las fachadas.»

Froté la superficie de uno de los bloques que me llegaba hasta la cintura. Sentí su tacto, como la cera y polvoriento a la vez.

«Oh, al principio, cuando se separan de la piedra madre, están demasiado suaves para cualquier uso —dijo mi padre. Pasó la uña de su pulgar por la piedra y dejó una marca profunda—. Después de algún tiempo de estar expuestos al aire, se hacen más sólidos, duros y tan imperecederos como el granito. Pero mientras todavía está suave, nuestra *tenéxtetl* piedra, puede ser esculpida con cualquier piedra más dura o ser cortada con una sierrecilla de obsidiana.»

La mayor parte de la piedra caliza de nuestra isla era enviada a tierra firme o a la capital, para ser usada en paredes, pisos y techos de edificios. Sin embargo, debido a la facilidad con que se trabajaba en ella, había también muchos escultores trabajando en las canteras. Esos artistas escogían los bloques de piedra caliza de más fina calidad y cuando todavía estaban muy suaves los tallaban, convirtiéndolos en estatuas de nuestros dioses, gobernantes y otros héroes. Utilizando las más perfectas tablas de piedra, las tallaban y labraban en bajorrelieves y frisos con los que se decorarían palacios y templos. También utilizaban los trozos descartados de piedra para esculpir las figurillas de dioses domésticos que en todas partes las familias acostumbraban a atesorar. En nuestra casa, por supuesto, teníamos las de Tonatíu y Tláloc, y la diosa del maíz, Chicomecóatl, y la diosa del hogar, Chantico. Mi hermana Tzitzitlini incluso tenía para sí una figura de Xochiquétzal, diosa del amor y de las flores, a la cual todas las jóvenes rezaban pidiendo un esposo amante y adecuado.

Las astillas y otros desperdicios de las canteras eran quemados en los hornos que ya mencioné, de los que sacábamos polvo de cal, otro producto valioso. Este *tenextli* es esencial para unir los bloques de un edificio. También se usa para dar una apariencia mejor a aquellos edificios que están hechos con materiales más baratos. Mezclada con agua, la cal se utiliza con los granos de maíz que nuestras mujeres suelen moler convirtiéndolos en masa para las *tlaxcaltin*, tortillas, y para otros alimentos. La cal de Xaltocan era inclusive usada por cierta clase de mujeres como cosmético; con ella blanqueaban su pelo oscuro o pardo hasta lograr un tono de amarillo, poco natural, como el que tienen algunas de sus mujeres españolas.

Por supuesto, los dioses no daban nada absolutamente gratis, y de vez en cuando exigían un tributo por la gran cantidad de piedra caliza que excavábamos de Xaltocan. Por casualidad yo estaba en la cantera de mi padre el día en que los dioses decidieron tomar un sacrificio.

Varios cargadores arrastraban un inmenso bloque de *tenéxtetl* recientemente cortado hacia arriba por el largo declive que, a semejanza de una tabla encorvada y escarpada, ascendía en forma de caracol entre el fondo y la cima de la cantera. Eso lo hacían a base de pura fuerza muscular, teniendo cada hombre alrededor de su frente una banda de tela que se amarraba a la red hecha de cuerda que arrastraba el bloque. En algún lugar muy arriba de la rampa, el bloque se deslizó demasiado hacia la orilla o se inclinó por alguna irregularidad del camino. Sea lo que fuere, giró lenta e implacablemente de lado y cayó. Hubo muchos gritos y si los cargadores no se hubiesen arrancado de sus frentes las bandas de tela, hubieran caído por la orilla junto con el bloque. A causa del ruido de la cantera, un hombre que estaba abajo no oyó los gritos, así es que el bloque le cayó encima y uno de sus filos, como una azuela de piedra, lo partió en dos exactamente a la altura de la cintura.

El bloque de piedra había hecho una muesca tan profunda en el piso de tierra de la cantera, que se quedó allí balanceándose sobre sus ángulos. Así que mi padre y todos los demás hombres que corrieron precipitadamente al lugar, pudieron sin mucha dificultad hacerlo caer a un lado. Se quedaron pasmados cuando vieron que la víctima de los dioses estaba todavía viva y aún consciente. Pasando desapercibido por la excitación de los demás, me acerqué y vi al hombre, que estaba dividido en dos partes. Desde la cintura para arriba, su cuerpo desnudo y sudoroso estaba intacto y sin ninguna herida, pero su cintura estaba comprimida en una forma ancha y plana, de tal manera que su cuerpo parecía una azuela o un cincel. La piedra lo había cortado instantánea (piel, carne, estómago, columna vertebral) y limpiamente y le había cerrado la herida, de tal modo que no había ni una gota de sangre. Él hubiera podido ser un muñeco de trapo cortado por la mitad y luego cosido por la cintura. Su mitad inferior, con su taparrabo, yacía separada de él, con el borde igualmente cortado y sin sangrar, aunque las piernas se movían espasmódica y ligeramente y esa mitad de su cuerpo estaba orinando y defecando copiosamente.

La herida parecía haber entumecido todos los nervios cortados de tal manera que el hombre ni siquiera sentía dolor. Levantando su cabeza miró, un poco extrañado, su otra mitad. Para evitarle ese espectáculo, los otros hombres rápida y tiernamente transportaron a cierta distancia de ahí lo que quedaba de él y lo apoyaron contra la pared de la cantera. Él flexionó sus brazos, cerró y abrió sus manos, movió su cabeza de un lado a otro y dijo con voz admirada:

«Todavía me puedo mover y hablar. Os puedo ver a todos vosotros, compañeros. Puedo extender la mano, tocaros y sentiros. Oigo los martillos golpeando y huelo el polvo áspero del *tenextli*. Estoy vivo todavía. Esto es maravilloso.»

«Sí, lo es —dijo mi padre con voz ronca—. Pero no puede ser por mucho tiempo, Xícama. No tiene caso ni siquiera mandar traer un *tícitl*. Tú querrás un sacerdote. ¿De qué dios, Xícama?»

El hombre pensó un momento. «Cuando ya no pueda hacer nada más, pronto saludaré a todos los dioses, pero mientras todavía pueda hablar es mejor que hable con La Que Come Suciedad.»

La llamada fue transmitida a lo alto de la cantera y de allí un mensajero fue corriendo velozmente para traer un *tlamacazqui* de la diosa Tlazoltéotl o La Que Come Suciedad. A pesar de que su nombre no era bello, era una diosa muy compasiva. Era a ella a quien los hombres moribundos confesaban todos sus pecados y malos hechos —a menudo los hombres vivos también lo hacían, cuando se sentían particularmente angustiados o deprimidos por algo que habían hecho—, así Tlazoltéotl se podía tragar todos sus pecados y éstos desaparecían como si nunca hubiesen sido cometidos. Así los pecados de un hombre no irían con él, para contar en su contra o para ser un fantasma en su memoria, a cualesquiera de los mundos del más allá adonde fuera enviado.

Mientras esperábamos al sacerdote, Xícama apartaba los ojos de sí mismo, de su cuerpo que parecía estar dentro de una hendidura del piso de roca y hablaba tranquila y casi alegremente con mi padre. Le dio recados para sus padres, para su futura viuda y para sus hijos, que pronto quedarían huérfanos, e hizo sugestiones acerca de las disposiciones sobre la pequeña propiedad que poseía, y se preguntaba en voz alta qué sería de su familia cuando su proveedor se hubiera ido.

«No preocupes tu mente —dijo mi padre—. Es tu *tonali* que los dioses tomen tu vida a cambio de la prosperidad de nosotros, los que nos quedamos. Para dar gracias por el sacrificio consumado en ti, nosotros y el Señor Gobernador daremos una compensación adecuada a tu viuda.»

«Entonces ella tendrá una herencia respetable —dijo Xícama aliviado—. Ella todavía es una mujer joven y hermosa. Por favor, Cabeza Inclinada, persuádela para que se vuelva a casar.»

«Así lo haré. ¿Alguna otra cosa?»

«No —dijo Xícama. Miró alrededor y sonrió—. Nunca pensé que me sentiría apesadumbrado al ver por última vez esta cantera funesta. ¿Sabes, Cabeza Inclinada, que aun en estos momentos esta fosa de piedra se ve bonita y atrayente? Con las nubes blancas allá arriba, el cielo tan azul y aquí la piedra blanca... como nubes encima y abajo del azul. Si aún pudiera, me gustaría ver los árboles verdes más allá de la orilla...»

«Los verás —prometió mi padre—, pero después de que hayas terminado con el sacerdote. Sería mejor no moverte hasta entonces.»

El *tlamacazqui* llegó, en el todo de su negro, sus vestiduras negras flotando al viento, su pelo negro endurecido con sangre seca y su cara cenicienta que jamás se lavaba. Él era la única oscuridad y sombra que manchaba el límpido azul y blanco del cual Xícama lamentaba despedirse. Todos los demás hombres se alejaron para darles privacía. (Y mi padre, que me descubrió entre ellos, se enojó y me ordenó que me fuera; eso no era para ser visto por un muchachito.) Mientras Xícama estaba ocupado con el sacerdote, cuatro hombres recogieron su apestosa mitad inferior, todavía estremeciéndose, para transportarla arriba de la cantera. Uno de ellos vomitó en el camino.

Evidentemente Xícama no había llevado una vida muy vil, ya que no le tomó mucho tiempo confesarse con La Que Come Suciedad de lo que se arrepentía de haber hecho o dejado por hacer. Cuando el sacerdote le había absuelto por parte de Tlazoltéotl, y después de haber dicho todas las palabras rituales y todos los gestos, se hizo a un lado. Cuatro hombres levantaron y tomaron cuidadosamente el pedazo viviente que era Xícama y lo llevaron lo más rápidamente que pudieron, sin zarandearlo, por el declive, hacia arriba de la cantera.

Tenían la esperanza de que viviera el tiempo suficiente para poder llegar a su aldea y despedirse personalmente de su familia y presentar sus respetos a aquellos dioses que él personalmente hubiera preferido. Pero en algún lugar, en lo alto del caracol, su cuerpo dividido empezó a abrirse dejando escapar su sangre y su desayuno, además de otras substancias. Ya no pudo hablar y dejó de respirar, sus ojos se cerraron para siempre y nunca llegó a ver, otra vez, los árboles verdes.

Una parte de la piedra caliza de Xaltocan había sido utilizada hace mucho tiempo para la construcción de la *icpac tlamanacali* y *teocaltin* de nuestra isla, nuestra pirámide con sus templos diversos, como ustedes les llaman. Una parte de la piedra excavada siempre fue reservada para los impuestos que pagábamos a la tesorería de la nación y para nuestro tributo anual al Venerado Orador y a su Consejo de Voceros. (El Uey-Tlatoáni Motecuzoma había muerto cuando yo tenía tres años de edad y en aquel mismo año el gobierno y el trono habían sido entregados a su hijo Axayácatl, Cara de Agua.) Otra parte de la piedra era reservada para el provecho de nuestro *tecutli*, o gobernador, para algunos otros nobles de rango y también para los gastos de la isla: construcción de canoas para el transporte, compra de esclavos para los trabajos menos agradables, pago de los sueldos de los canteros y cosas parecidas. Sin embargo, siempre sobraba mucho de nuestro producto mineral para la exportación y para trueque.

Gracias a esto, Xaltocan pudo importar y cambiar mercancías, que nuestro *tecutli* repartía entre sus súbditos, según su nivel social y sus méritos. Además permitía a toda la gente de la isla construir sus casas con esa piedra caliza tan a la mano, a excepción, claro, de los esclavos y otras clases bajas. Por eso, Xaltocan era diferente de la mayoría de las otras comunidades de estas tierras, en donde las casas eran construidas frecuentemente con ladrillos de barro secados al sol, o con madera, o con cañas, en donde muchas familias vivían apretadas en un solo edificio comunal e inclusive en cuevas en el flanco de algún cerro. Aunque nuestra casa tenía solamente tres cuartos, sus pisos también eran de losas de piedra caliza, lisa y blanca. No había muchos palacios en El Único Mundo que pudieran sentirse orgullosos de haber sido construidos con materiales tan finos. El uso de nuestra piedra para la construcción, significó también que nuestra isla no quedó desnuda de sus árboles, como sucedió en muchos otros lugares poblados del valle.

En mi tiempo, el gobernador de Xaltocan era Tlauquéchotltzin, el Señor Garza Roja, un hombre cuyos lejanos antepasados habían sido de los primeros colonizadores mexica en la isla y el hombre que ocupaba el rango más alto entre la nobleza local. Eso garantizaba su cargo como nuestro *tecutli* de por vida, como era la costumbre en la mayoría de los distritos y comunidades, y como representante nuestro ante el Consejo de Voceros encabezado por el Venerado Orador y como gobernador de la isla, de sus canteras, el lago que le circundaba y cada uno de sus habitantes, excepto en cierta medida de los sacerdotes, quienes mantenían que sólo debían lealtad a los dioses.

No todas las comunidades tenían tanta suerte con su *tecutli* como la nuestra en Xaltocan. Se esperaba que un miembro de la nobleza viviera a la altura de su posición social, o sea, *ser noble*, pero no todos lo eran. Ningún *pili* nacido dentro de la nobleza podía ser rebajado a una clase más baja, sin importar cuán innoble fuese su conducta. Sin embargo, si su conducta era inexcusable, podía ser cesado de su puesto o aun ser sentenciado a muerte por sus camaradas. También debo mencionar que la mayoría de los nobles lo eran por haber nacido de padres nobles, pero no era imposible para un simple plebeyo ganar el derecho a esa clase superior.

Recuerdo a dos hombres de Xaltocan quienes habían sido elevados a la nobleza y se les había dado un ingreso estimable de por vida. Uno era Colótic-Miztli, un viejo guerrero que en otro tiempo había cumplido con su nombre de Fiero Cugar de la Montaña, haciendo algún hecho de armas en alguna guerra ya olvidada contra algún antiguo enemigo. Esto le había costado tantas cicatrices que era horrible verlo, pero había ganado así el codiciado sufijo de -tzin a su nombre: Miztzin, Señor Cugar de la Montaña. El otro era Quali-Améyatl, o Fuente Buena, un joven arquitecto de buenas maneras que no hizo otra cosa más notable que diseñar unos jardines en el palacio del gobernador. Pero Améyatl era tan bien parecido como Miztzin era repugnante, y durante su trabajo en el palacio había ganado el corazón de una joven que se llamaba Ahuachtli, Gota de Rocío, quien por casualidad era la hija del gobernador. Cuando se casó con ella, vino a ser Améyatzin, el Señor Fuente.

Como creo que ya indiqué, nuestro Señor Garza Roja era un *tecutli* jovial y generoso, pero sobre todo un hombre justo. Cuando su propia hija Gota de Rocío se cansó de su Señor Fuente, plebeyo de nacimiento y fue sorprendida en adulterio con un *pili* noble de nacimiento, Garza Roja ordenó que ambos fueran sentenciados a muerte. Muchos otros nobles le pidieron que perdonara la vida de la joven mujer y que en su lugar la desterrara de la isla. Incluso el esposo juró a su suegro que él ya había perdonado el adulterio de su esposa y que tanto él como Gota de Rocío se irían a alguna nación lejana. Aunque todos sabíamos cuánto amaba a su hija, el gobernador no se dejó influenciar.

Dijo: «Me llamarían injusto si por mi propia hija no obedezco una ley que se hace cumplir a mis súbditos.» Y dijo a su yerno: «La gente dirá algún día que tú perdonaste a mi hija en deferencia a mi puesto y no por tu propia y libre voluntad.» Y ordenó que todas las mujeres y jovencitas de Xaltocan fueran a su palacio para ser testigos de la ejecución de Gota de Rocío.

«Especialmente las núbiles y las doncellas —dijo él—, porque son muy excitables y quizás se inclinen a simpatizar con la infidelidad de mi hija e inclusive envidiarla. Dejemos, pues, que se sobresalten con su muerte, para que en su lugar se concentren en la severidad de las consecuencias.»

Así es que mi madre fue a la ejecución y llevó consigo a Tzitzitlini. Mi madre dijo que la vil Gota de Rocío y su amante habían sido estrangulados con sogas disfrazadas de guirnaldas de flores a la vista de toda la población, y que la joven mujer aceptó muy mal su castigo, con súplicas, luchas y terrores, y que Fuente Buena, su traicionado marido, lloró por ella, pero que el Señor Garza Roja había estado observando sin ninguna expresión en su rostro. Tzitzi no hizo ningún comentario sobre el espectáculo, pero me contó que en el palacio conoció al joven hermano de la mujer condenada, Pactli, el hijo de Garza Roja.

«Él me miró largamente —dijo ella con un escalofrío— y me sonrió enseñando sus dientes. ¿Puedes creer tal cosa en un día semejante? Fue una mirada que me puso la carne de ganso.»

Yo apostaría que Garza Roja no sonrió aquel día. Sin embargo, creo que ustedes pueden comprender por qué toda la gente de la isla estimaba tanto a su gobernador siendo tan justo e imparcial. De verdad, todos esperábamos que el Señor Garza Roja viviera muchos años, ya que no nos sentíamos felices ante la idea de llegar a ser gobernados por su hijo Pactli. El nombre significaba Alegría, un nombre mal dado como ningún otro, pues el joven Alegría era malo y despótico por naturaleza mucho antes de que llegara a usar el *máxtlatl* de la edad adulta. Ese retoño odioso de un padre tan cortés, no se asociaba libremente con ningún muchacho de la clase media, como Tlatli, Chimali y yo, y de todas maneras era uno o dos años mayor. Sin embargo, cuando mi hermana empezó a florecer en belleza y Pactli empezó a manifestar un gran interés por ella, mi hermana y yo llegamos a compartir un odio especial hacia él, pero eso todavía estaba en el futuro.

Mientras tanto, nuestra comunidad era próspera, confortable y tranquila. Nosotros, que teníamos la buena fortuna de vivir allí, no nos veíamos obligados a afanar nuestras energías y espíritus sólo para poder subsistir. Podíamos contemplar horizontes más allá de nuestra isla y aspirar a alturas mayores de las que habíamos nacido. Podíamos soñar, como lo hacían mis amigos Tlatli y Chimali. Sus padres eran escultores en la cantera y ellos, los dos, a diferencia mía, aspiraban seguir sus pasos, dentro de ese arte, aunque más ambiciosamente que ellos.

«Quiero llegar a ser el *mejor* escultor», dijo Tlatli, raspando un fragmento de piedra blanda que empezaba realmente a parecerse a un halcón, animal del cual había recibido su nombre.

Él siguió: «Las estatuas y los frisos esculpidos aquí en Xaltocan se van sin firma, en las grandes canoas de carga, y sus artistas no son reconocidos. Nuestros padres no reciben mayor crédito que el que podría recibir una esclava que teje el *pétlatl*, tapete, con las cañas del lago. ¿Y por qué? Porque las estatuas y ornamentos que hacemos aquí se distinguen tan poco como el *petlame* de caña-tejida. Cada Tláloc, por ejemplo, se ve exactamente igual que cada Tláloc que ha sido esculpido en Xaltocan desde que los padres de los padres de nuestros padres, los esculpían.»

Yo dije: «Entonces es que ellos deben ser como los sacerdotes de Tláloc quieren que sean.»

«*Ninotlancuícui in tlamázque* —gruñó Tlatli—. Limpio mis dientes en los sacerdotes. —Él podía ser tan impasible e inmóvil como cualquier figura de piedra—. Yo intento hacer esculturas diferentes a todas las que se han hecho antes. Y ni siquiera dos, hechas por mí, parecerán iguales. Pero mis obras serán tan fáciles de reconocer que la gente exclamará: "*¡Ayyo*, una estatua hecha por Tlatli!" Ni siquiera tendré que firmarlas con mi glifo de halcón.»

«Tú quieres hacer un trabajo tan fino como el de la Piedra del Sol», le sugerí.

«Más fino todavía que el de la Piedra del Sol —dijo obstinadamente—. Limpio mis dientes en la Piedra del Sol.» Y pensé que eso era realmente tener audacia, porque yo había visto la Piedra del Sol.

Sin embargo, nuestro mutuo amigo Chimali tenía una meta todavía más alta que a la que aspiraba Tlatli. Quería refinar el arte de la pintura, de tal manera que fuera independiente de cualquier escultura. Él sería pintor de cuadros en paneles y de murales en las paredes.

«Oh, yo daré color a las toscas estatuas de Tlatli, si él quiere —dijo Chimali—. Pero la escultura requiere sólo colores uniformes, ya que por su forma y modelado da luz y sombra a los colores. También estoy harto de cómo son invariablemente usados por otros pintores y muralistas. Trato de mezclar nuevas variedades: colores que puedan mudar en cuanto a matiz y tono, de tal manera que los colores por sí mismos den una ilusión de profundidad. —Y hacía vehementes gestos modelando al aire—. Cuando veáis mis cuadros, pensaréis que tienen forma y substancia, aun cuando no lo tengan, cuando no tengan más que la dimensión del panel mismo.»

«Pero, ¿con qué objeto?», pregunté.

«¿Qué objeto tiene la trémula belleza y la forma del colibrí? —preguntó—. Mira. Imagínate que eres un sacerdote de Tláloc. En lugar de arrastrar una gran estatua del dios de la lluvia dentro de la pequeña habitación de un templo, restringiendo aún más el espacio, los sacerdotes de Tláloc simplemente me podrían encargar pintar sobre el muro un retrato del dios, como yo lo imagine, y con un paisaje sin límite extendiéndose atrás de él, bañado de lluvia. La habitación parecerá mucho más grande de lo que en realidad es. —Y triunfalmente concluyó—. *Ésa* es la ventaja de las pinturas planas y delgadas sobre las esculturas voluminosas y macizas.»

«Bueno —dije a Chimali—, un escudo normalmente *es* bastante delgado y plano.» Yo le estaba haciendo una broma; Chimali significa escudo y el mismo Chimali era flaco y largirucho.

Yo sonreía indulgentemente ante las grandiosas jactancias y ante los ambiciosos planes de mis amigos; o quizás con un poco de envidia porque ellos sabían lo que querían llegar a ser, mientras que yo no. Mi mente todavía no había concebido alguna noción ·propia y ningún dios había tenido a bien mandarme alguna señal. Solamente estaba seguro de dos cosas. Una era que *no* quería labrar y arrastrar piedra en una cantera ruidosa, polvorosa y amenazada por los dioses. La otra, que cualquier carrera que escogiera, *no* intentaría ejecutarla en Xaltocan ni en ningún otro lugar atrasado de la provincia.

Si los dioses me lo permitían, yo correría el riesgo en el lugar más desafiante, pero también el más potencialmente remunerador del Único Mundo, en la ciudad-capital del Uey-Tlatoani, en donde la competencia entre los hombres ambiciosos era la más despiadada y en donde solamente los más dignos podían sobresalir con distinción, en la espléndida, maravillosa y pasmosa ciudad de Tenochtitlan.

✠

Si todavía no sabía cuál sería el oficio de mi vida, por lo menos sí sabía *dónde* iba a practicarlo. Esto lo supe desde mi primer viaje allí, la visita que había sido un regalo de mi padre en mi cumpleaños número siete, el día en que me dieron mi nuevo nombre.

Antes de eso, mis padres, a quienes yo seguía, habían ido a consultar al *tonalpoqui* residente de la isla —o conocedor del *tonáltamatl*, el libro tradicional de nombres—. Después de desdoblar las capas de páginas hasta lograr la completa longitud del libro, usando la mayor parte del piso de su cuarto, el viejo vidente dio un escrutinio prolongado, moviendo los labios cada vez que hacía mención a los símbolos de las estrellas y a las actividades más relevantes de los dioses en el día Siete Flor, en el mes del Dios Ascendiente del año Trece Conejo. Luego inclinó la cabeza, volvió a doblar el libro con reverencia, aceptó sus honorarios consistentes en un rollo de tela fina, me roció con agua especial para las celebraciones y proclamó que mi nombre sería Chicome-Xóchitl-Tliléctic-Mixtli, para conmemorar la tormenta que había asistido a mi nacimiento. Desde entonces y en adelante yo sería conocido formalmente como Siete Flor Oscura Nube y llamado informalmente Mixtli.

Estaba muy complacido con mi nombre, un nombre varonil, pero no quedé muy impresionado con el ritual para seleccionarlo. Incluso a la edad de siete años, yo, Nube Oscura, tenía algunas opiniones propias. Dije en voz alta que cualquiera lo hubiera podido hacer, *yo* lo hubiera podido hacer más rápido y más barato, por lo que me callaron severamente.

En la mañana temprano de mi importante cumpleaños, me llevaron al palacio del *tecutli* y el Señor Garza Roja nos recibió personalmente con amabilidad y ceremonia. Me palmeó ligeramente la cabeza y dijo paternalmente con buen humor: «Otro *hombre* ha crecido para la gloria de Xaltocan, ¿verdad?» Con su propia mano dibujó los símbolos de mi nombre: siete puntos, el símbolo de los tres pétalos de flor, la burbuja gris que significa la nube oscura, en el *tocayámatl*, el registro oficial de todos los habitantes de la isla. Mi página quedaría allí por todo el tiempo que viviera en Xaltocan, para ser quitada únicamente si moría, si era expulsado por algún crimen monstruoso o si me iba a vivir permanentemente a otro lugar. Me pregunto: ¿cuánto tiempo hace que la página de Siete Flor Nube Oscura no está en aquel libro?

Hubiera habido una gran celebración del día-de-nombre, como lo había habido en el de mi hermana. Todos los vecinos y nuestros familiares llegando con regalos, mi madre cocinando y sirviendo un gran festín con platillos especiales, los hombres fumando *pocíetl* en tubos de caña, los viejos emborrachándose con *octli*. Pero no me importó perder todo eso, porque mi padre me había dicho: «Un cargamento de frisos para templos sale hoy para Tenochtitlan y hay espacio en el bote para ti y para mí. También he oído que una gran ceremonia se celebrará en la capital, la de una nueva conquista o algo por el estilo, y éste será el festejo de tu día-de-nombre, Mixtli.» (Nunca más me volvió a llamar Chapulin.) Así es que, después un beso de felicitación en la mejilla, por parte de mi madre y de mi hermana, seguí a mi padre hacia abajo, hasta el muelle de cargamento de las canteras.

Todos nuestros lagos tenían un tráfico constante de canoas, yendo y viniendo en todas direcciones, como hordas de insectos tejedores. La mayoría de ellas eran los *acaltin* pequeños, para uno o dos hombres, de los pescadores y cazadores de aves, hechos de un solo tronco de árbol vaciado por dentro y con la forma de una vaina de ejote. Sin embargo había otros que alcanzaban hasta el tamaño de las gigantescas canoas de guerra para sesenta hombres y nuestro *acali* de carga consistía en ocho botes casi de ese tamaño, unidos por las regalas. Nuestro cargamento de paneles de piedra tallados había sido apilado cuidadosamente dentro del lanchón, cada piedra envuelta en pesadas esterillas de fibra para su protección.

Con tal carga a bordo en una nave tan difícil de gobernar, era lógico que avanzáramos muy despacio, a pesar de los veinte hombres, entre ellos mi padre, que estaban remando o empujando con varas gruesas en donde el agua no era profunda. Debido a que la ruta no era recta —al sudoeste por el lago de Xaltocan, al sur dentro del lago de Texcoco y desde ahí al sudoeste otra vez hasta la ciudad— teníamos que cubrir algo así como siete distancias que llamábamos a cada una «una carrera larga», una de las cuales vendría a ser aproximadamente el equivalente a lo que ustedes los españoles llaman «una legua». Como quien dice, siete leguas de camino y nuestro gran lanchón casi nunca avanzaba más rápido de lo que un hombre podría caminar. Dejamos la isla de Xaltocan mucho antes del mediodía, pero estaba bien entrada la noche cuando llegamos al muelle de Tenochtitlan.

Por un tiempo, el paisaje no era nada fuera de lo común, el mismo lago rojizo que yo conocía tan bien. Luego, conforme nos deslizábamos sobre el estrecho del sur, la tierra nos encerró por los dos lados y el agua fue perdiendo color gradualmente hasta adquirir un tono parduzco cuando emergimos al vasto lago de

Texcoco. Éste se extendía tan lejos hacia el este y hacia el sur que la tierra de más allá no era más que una mancha oscura y dentada en el horizonte.

Nos movimos hacia el suroeste durante un tiempo, pero Tonatíu, el sol, se cubría lentamente en el resplandor de su vestido de dormir en el momento en que nuestros remeros retrocedían en el agua para poder llevar nuestro desmañado lanchón hacia el Gran Dique y detenerse. Esta barrera es una doble palizada de troncos de árboles clavados dentro del fondo del lago, el espacio entre las hileras paralelas de leños está sólidamente relleno con tierra y roca. Tiene como propósito el evitar que las ondas del lago, agitadas por el viento del oriente, inunden la isla-ciudad. El Gran Dique tiene pesados portalones insertados en intervalos con objeto de permitir el paso a los barcos y los hombres que trabajan en El Dique dejan esos portalones abiertos casi todo el tiempo. Por supuesto que el tráfico del lago que se dirigía hacia la capital era considerable y por ese motivo nuestro lanchón tuvo que esperar en línea, por un tiempo antes de poder pasar los portones.

Al mismo tiempo, Tonatíu tiró los oscuros cobertores de la noche sobre su cama y el cielo se tornó púrpura. Las montañas al oeste, directamente enfrente de nosotros, se vieron de pronto como si sus perfiles hubieran sido cortados en papel negro, perdiéndose sus dimensiones. Sobre ellas, hubo un centelleo tímido y luego una chispa valiente de luz: Flor del Atardecer, la estrella vespertina, llegó una vez más, asegurándonos que ésta era solamente una de tantas noches, no la última y eterna.

«¡Abre bien los ojos ahora, hijo Mixtli!», gritó mi padre desde su lugar en los remos.

Como si Flor del Atardecer hubiera dado una señal, una segunda luz apareció, ésta a un nivel muy por debajo de la línea dentada de las negras montañas. Entonces llegó otro punto de luz, y otro y otros veinte de veinte más. Así vi Tenochtitlan por primera vez en mi vida: no como una ciudad de torres de piedra, de ricos enmaderados y pinturas brillantes, sino como una ciudad de luz. Según se iban encendiendo las lámparas, linternas, velas y antorchas, por las aberturas de las ventanas, en las calles, a lo largo de los canales, en las terrazas, cornisas y tejados de los edificios, los puntitos separados de luz se hicieron grupos, los grupos se mezclaron para formar líneas de luz y las líneas de luz dibujaron los contornos de la ciudad.

Los edificios en sí, desde esa distancia, estaban oscuros y sus contornos borrosos, pero las luces, *¡ayyo, las luces!* Amarillas, blancas, rojas, *jácinth*, en todos los colores variados del fuego y aquí y allá una verde o azul, en donde el fuego del altar de algún templo había sido rociado con sal o con filigranas de cobre. Cada uno de esos grupitos y bandas de luz como cuentas relucientes, brillaban dos veces pues cada una tenía su reflejo brillante en el lago. Aun las calzadas elevadas y empedradas que saltan entre la isla y tierra firme, aun éstas, portaban linternas en palos a intervalos en toda su extensión, a través del agua. Desde nuestro *acali* podía ver solamente las dos calzadas que salían de la ciudad hacia el norte y hacia el sur, pero cada una parecía ser una brillante y delgada cadena de joyas a través del cuello de la noche, un espléndido pendiente de brillante joyería en el seno de la noche.

«Mexico-Tenochtitlan, Cem-Anáhuac Tlali Yoloco —murmuró mi padre—. Es realmente El Corazón y el Centro del Único Mundo.» Yo había estado tan transportado por el encanto, que no me había dado cuenta de que él estaba a mi lado. «Mira todo lo que puedas, hijo Mixtli. Tú puedes ver esta maravilla y muchas otras más de una vez, pero siempre y por siempre habrá sólo una primera vez.»

Sin parpadear o mover los ojos del esplendor al que nos acercábamos con demasiada lentitud, me recosté sobre una esterilla de fibra y miré y miré hasta que, me avergüenza decirlo, mis párpados se cerraron por sí solos y me quedé dormido. No tengo ni una noción en mi memoria del ruido considerable, de la conmoción y del bullicio que debió de producirse cuando desembarcamos, ni recuerdo cuando mi padre me cargó hasta una cercana posada para barqueros, donde pasamos la noche.

Desperté en un jergón en el piso de un cuarto común, donde mi padre y otros pocos hombres más, estaban todavía acostados roncando en sus jergones. Al darme cuenta de que estábamos en una posada y de dónde estaba la posada, brinqué para asomarme por la abertura de la ventana, y por un momento me sentí mareado al ver la altura sobre el empedrado. Era la primera vez que estaba dentro de un edificio que estaba encima de otro. Yo pensé que era así hasta que mi padre me enseñó más tarde, desde afuera, que nuestro cuarto estaba en el piso superior de la posada.

Dirigí mis ojos hacia la ciudad que estaba más allá de la zona de los muelles. Brillaba, pulsaba, resplandecía de blanco a la luz temprana del sol. Eso hizo que me sintiera orgulloso de mi isla natal, porque los edificios que no habían sido construidos con la blanca piedra caliza estaban aplanados con el yeso blanco, y yo sabía que la mayor parte de aquel material llegaba de Xaltocan. Aunque los edificios estaban adornados con frescos, franjas y paneles con pinturas de vívidos colores y mosaicos, el efecto dominante era el de una ciudad tan blanca que casi parecía plateada y tan resplandeciente que casi lastimaba mis ojos.

En esos momentos, las luces de la noche anterior ya estaban totalmente extinguidas y sólo desde alguna parte el fuego quieto de un templo enviaba una cinta de humo hacia el cielo. Entonces vi una nueva maravilla: en la cumbre de cada azotea, de cada templo, de cada palacio de la ciudad, de cada una de las partes más sobresalientemente altas, se proyectaba un asta y en cada una flotaba un estandarte. Éstos no eran cuadrados, triangulares o rectangulares como las insignias de batalla; eran mucho más largos y anchos. Totalmente blancos excepto por la insignia de colores que portaban. Algunas de éstas las pude reconocer, como la de la ciudad, la del Venerado Orador Axayácatl, las de algunos dioses; pero otras no me eran familiares, deberían de ser las insignias de los nobles locales y de los dioses particulares de la ciudad.

Las banderas de sus hombres blancos son siempre pedazos de tela, muy a menudo con blasones muy elaborados, pero que no dejan de ser simples hilachos que cuelgan flojamente de sus astas, o tremolean y chasquean al viento como la ropa lavada por una mujer rústica y tendida a secar sobre las espinas de los cactos. Por contraste, estas banderolas increíblemente largas de Tenochtitlan estaban entretejidas con plumas, plumas a las que se les habían quitado los cañones y solamente se había utilizado para el tejido la parte más suave de ellas. No estaban ni pintadas ni teñidas. Las banderas estaban tejidas intrincadamente con plumas de colores naturales: de garzas blancas para la parte del fondo de las banderas, y para los diseños de las insignias los variados tonos de rojo de las guacamayas, cardenales y papagayos, los diversos azules de los grajos y las garzas, los amarillos de los tucanes y de las tángaras. *Ayyo*, ustedes oyen la verdad, beso la tierra, habían allí todos los colores e iridiscencias que solamente se pueden encontrar en la naturaleza viva y no en las mezclas de pinturas que hacen los hombres.

Lo más maravilloso era que estas banderolas no se combaban ni aleteaban, sino que flotaban. No soplaba el viento esa mañana, solamente el movimiento de la gente en las calles y de los *acaltin* en los canales hacían la suficiente corriente de aire como para sostener esos pendones tan grandes y tan ligeros a la vez. Como grandes pájaros reacios a volar lejos, contentos de flotar soñando, los estandartes estaban suspendidos, totalmente extendidos en el aire. Las miles de banderas emplumadas ondulaban, gentil y silenciosamente como por arte de magia, sobre las torres y los pináculos de esa mágica ciudad-isla.

Teniendo la osadía de apoyarme demasiado peligrosamente afuera de la ventana, podía ver a lo lejos, por el sudeste, los picos de los dos volcanes llamados Popocatépelt e Ixtaccíhuatl (1), la montaña del Incienso Ardiendo y la montaña de la Mujer Blanca. A pesar de que ya estábamos en la estación seca y los días eran calurosos, las dos montañas estaban coronadas de nieve, la primera que veía en mi vida, y el candente incienso que se hallaba en las profundidades del Popocatépetl producía un penacho de humo azul que flotaba sobre su cumbre, tan perezosamente como las banderolas flotaban sobre Tenochtitlan. Desde la ventana insté a mi padre para que se levantara. Debía de estar cansado y deseoso de dormir más, pero se levantó sin ninguna queja, con una sonrisa de comprensión hacia mi deseo de salir.

El desembarcó y entrega de nuestro cargamento era responsabilidad del jefe encargado de fletes del lanchón, así es que mi padre y yo teníamos todo el día para nosotros. Él traía solamente el encargo de comprar algunas cosas para mi madre, por lo que dirigimos nuestros pasos hacia el norte, hacia Tlaltelolco.

Como ustedes saben, reverendos frailes, esta parte de la isla

(1) Traducción literal del náhuatl. *(N. del t.)*

que ahora ustedes llaman Santiago está separada de la parte sur solamente por un extenso canal atravesado por varios puentes. Sin embargo, Tlaltelolco fue por muchos años una ciudad independiente, con sus propios gobernantes, y trató siempre, osadamente, de aventajar a Tenochtitlan, pretendiendo ser la primera ciudad mexica. Las ilusiones de superioridad de Tlaltelolco fueron por mucho tiempo toleradas humorísticamente por nuestros Venerados Oradores. Pero cuando su último gobernante Moquíhuix tuvo el descaro de construir la pirámide-templo más alta de todas las que había en los cuatro distritos de Tenochtitlan, el Uey-Tlatoáni Axayácatl, justificadamente, se sintió humillado. Así es que ordenó a sus hechiceros hostigar a ese vecino ya intolerable.

Si la historia es cierta, a Moquíhuix le habló la cara de una pared de piedra labrada que estaba en la sala del trono. Lo que le dijo acerca de su virilidad fue tan insultante que Moquíhuix, agarrando una cachiporra de guerra, pulverizó el grabado. Después, cuando Moquíhuix fue a la cama con su real compañera, los labios de sus *tepili*, partes, también le hablaron, menospreciando su virilidad. Esos sucesos, aparte de dejar impotente a Moquíhuix incluso con sus concubinas, le asustaron muchísimo, pero aun así no rindió vasallaje al Venerado Orador. Por lo que al principio del mismo año en que yo había hecho la visita del día de mi nombre, Axayácatl tuvo que tomar Tlaltelolco por las armas. El mismo Axayácatl, personalmente, lanzó a Moquíhuix desde lo alto de su propia pirámide, dejándole sus sesos bien destrozados. Unos cuantos meses después de aquel suceso, cuando mi padre y yo visitamos Tlaltelolco y aunque seguía siendo una ciudad muy bella de templos, palacios y pirámides, se sentía satisfecha de ser el quinto distrito de Tenochtitlan, y un lugar de mercado dependiente de la ciudad.

Su inmensa área de mercado abierto me pareció que era tan grande como toda nuestra isla de Xaltocan, más rica, más llena de gentes y mucho más ruidosa. Esa área estaba separada por amplios corredores limitados en cuadros en donde los mercaderes extendían su mercancía sobre mesas o lienzos, y cada uno de esos cuadros estaban designados a diferentes clases de mercancías. Allí había secciones para los forjadores de oro y plata; para los que trabajaban las plumas; para los vendedores de verduras y condimentos; de carne y animales vivos; de artículos de cuero y ropa; de esclavos y perros; de cerámica y trastos de cobre; de medicinas y cosméticos; de cuerdas, reatas y fibras; de estridentes pájaros, changos y otras mascotas. Ah, bueno, este mercado ha sido restaurado y sin duda ustedes ya lo conocen. Aunque mi padre y yo fuimos temprano, el lugar ya estaba lleno de una muchedumbre de compradores. La mayor parte de ellos eran *macehualtin* como nosotros, pero también había señores y damas *pipiltin*, apuntando imperiosamente hacia los artículos que deseaban y dejando que sus esclavos regatearan el precio.

Fuimos muy afortunados por haber llegado temprano, o por lo menos yo lo fui, ya que en uno de los puestos del mercado se estaba vendiendo un artículo tan perecedero que se hubiera acabado antes de media mañana, y entre todos los alimentos que se vendían era el más exótico y delicado. Era nieve. Había sido traída a diez carreras largas desde la cumbre del Ixtaccíhuatl hasta aquí, por relevos de mensajeros veloces corriendo a través del frío de la noche. El mercader la guardaba en unas jarras de grueso barro cocida, tapadas con montones de esterillas de fibra. Un cono de nieve costaba veinte semillas de cacao. Éste era el jornal promedio de un día completo de trabajo de cualquier obrero en la nación mexica. Por cuatrocientas semillas de cacao se podía comprar para toda la vida un esclavo bastante fuerte y saludable. Así es que la nieve era, por peso, la mercancía más cara de todo el mercado, incluyendo las joyas más costosas en los puestos de los forjadores de oro. Sólo unos cuantos de los *pipiltin* podían comprar ese raro refresco. No obstante, nos dijo el hombre de la nieve, vendía siempre toda su provisión en la mañana, antes de que ésta se derritiera.

Mi padre se quejó: «Yo recuerdo el año Uno Conejo, cuando del cielo estuvo "nevando nieve" por seis días seguidos. La nieve no solamente fue gratis para el que la quisiera, sino que también fue una calamidad.» Pero se apaciguó y dijo al vendedor: «Bueno, porque es el cumpleaños *chicoxíhuitl* del niño...»

Desligando su morral del hombro contó veinte semillas de cacao. El mercader examinó una por una para estar seguro de no entrar una falsificación hecha de madera o una semilla agujereada y rellena de tierra. Entonces destapó una de sus jarras, sacó un cucharón colmado de esa preciosa golosina y con pequeños golpes la acomodó dentro de un cono hecho con una hoja enroscada, luego lo roció con una especie de jarabe dulce y me lo entregó.

Golosamente tragué un poco y estuve a punto de escupirlo de lo frío que estaba. Me destempló los dientes y me dio dolor de cabeza y, sin embargo, fue una de las cosas más deliciosas que probé en mi infancia. Lo sostuve para que mi padre lo probara y aunque le dio una lamida que obviamente saboreó tanto como yo, pretendió que no quería más. «No lo muerdas, Mixtli —me dijo—. Chúpalo, así te durará más.»

Cuando mi padre hubo comprado todo lo que mi madre le había encargado, y después de haberlo enviado con un cargador a nuestra embarcación, fuimos otra vez hacia el sur, hacia el centro de la ciudad. La mayoría de los edificios de Tenochtitlan eran de dos y algunas veces hasta de tres pisos de alto, y muchos de ellos se veían todavía más altos porque estaban construidos sobre pilares para evitar la humedad. La isla en sí no era más alta que la estatura de dos hombres por encima de las aguas del lago de Texcoco. Así es que en aquellos días había tantas calles como canales cruzando la ciudad. En algunas partes, los canales y las calles corrían paralelos, así la gente que caminaba podía platicar con la que iba en las canoas. En algunas esquinas, frente a nosotros, podíamos ver gente apretujada alborotando de un lado a otro; en otras, solamente el destello de las canoas al pasar. Algunas de ellas eran embarcaciones de alquiler para pasajeros, para llevar a aquellas personas que tenían prisa, a través de la ciudad, de una manera más rápida de lo que ellos pudieran caminar. Otras, eran los *acaltin* privados de los nobles, que estaban muy decorados y pintados con toldos arriba para protegerlos del sol. Las calles estaban fuertemente apisonadas y planas con una superficie de barro; los canales tenían bancos de mampostería. El agua de muchos canales estaba casi al mismo nivel de las calles, de tal manera que los puentes para transeúntes podían girar sobre sí mismos, hacia un lado, mientras pasaba una canoa.

Con la red de canales, el lago de Texcoco prácticamente venía a ser parte de la ciudad, así como también las tres calzadas principales hacían que la ciudad formara parte de la tierra firme. Al final de la isla, aquellas calles anchas se convertían en amplios caminos-puentes de piedra, por los cuales un hombre podía encaminarse a cinco ciudades diferentes de la tierra firme, hacia el norte, el oeste y el sur. Había otro tramo que no era una calzada sino un acueducto. Éste sostenía una gamella de curvadas baldosas, tan ancha y espesa que los dos brazos de un hombre no la podrían estrechar y que hasta nuestros días surte de agua fresca a la ciudad, desde el manantial de Chapultépec en la tierra firme, por el sudoeste.

Debido a que tanto los caminos como las rutas acuáticas de los lagos convergían a Tenochtitlan, mi padre y yo mirábamos desfilar el constante comercio, tanto de la nación mexica como el de otras naciones. Por todas partes, cerca de nosotros, había cargadores agobiados bajo el peso de la carga que soportaban sobre sus espaldas, ayudados por las bandas de tela que usaban en sus frentes. Por todas partes había canoas de todos los tamaños, transportando productos en pilas altas que eran llevados y traídos al mercado de Tlaltelolco o los tributos de los pueblos subordinados, yendo hacia los palacios o a la casa del tesoro o a los almacenes de depósito de la nación.

Solamente las multicolores canastas de frutas podían dar una idea de cuán extendido estaba el comercio. Allí había guayabas y chirimoyas de las tierras Otomí, hacia el norte; piñas de las tierras Totonaca, hacia el mar del este; papayas amarillas de Michihuacan, hacia el oeste; papayas rojas de Chiapán, lejos hacia el sur, y de las tierras Tzapoteca, del cercano sur, las frutas tzapotin que dan su nombre a la región.

También de la nación tzapoteca venían bolsas de pequeños insectos secos que servían para teñir, produciendo diferentes tonalidades de rojos. Del cercano Xochimilco traían toda clase de flores y plantas que yo no creía que existieran. De las selvas del lejano sur venían cajas llenas de pájaros de gran colorido o fardos llenos de sus plumas. De las Tierras Calientes, tanto del este como del oeste, llegaban bolsas de cacao para hacer *chocólatl* y bolsas llenas de vainas de orquídeas negras con las cuales se hace la vainilla. De las costas de la tierra Olmeca, en el sureste, venía el producto que le dio nombre a su pueblo: *oli*, largas tiras de goma que luego serían trenzadas para convertirse en las duras pelotas usadas en nuestro antiguo juego de *tlachtli*. Incluso Texcala, la nación perennemente enemiga de nosotros los mexica, nos mandaba su precioso *copali*, la aromática resina con la que hacíamos perfumes e inciensos.

De todas partes llegaban sacos y fardos de maíz, rijol y algodón, y hacinados y graznando los *huaxolome* vivos (esa ave doméstica negra y esponjada que ustedes llaman gallipavo) y canastas de sus huevos; jaulas de los comestibles *techichi*, perros, pelones y mudos; ancas de venados, de conejos y carne de verraco; jarras llenas del agua dulce y clara de la savia del maguey o de la fermentación blanca y espesa de ese jugo, la bebida que emborracha, llamada *octli*...

Cuando mi padre me estaba haciendo notar esas cosas y diciéndome sus nombres, una voz lo interrumpió: «Por sólo dos semillas de cacao, mi señor, te diré los caminos y los días que moran más allá del día-de-nombre de tu hijo Mixtli.»

Mi padre se volvió. A la altura de su codo, y no más alto que éste, estaba parado un hombre que parecía una semilla de cacao. Sólo llevaba puesto un *máxtlatl*, taparrabo, andrajoso y sucio y su piel era exactamente del color del cacao, de un pardo oscuro. Su rostro, también como el cacao, estaba surcado de arrugas. Quizás fue más alto en otro tiempo, pero entonces estaba encorvado, encogido y arrugado y nadie hubiera podido precisar su edad. Ahora que lo pienso, se veía más o menos como yo ahora. Extendiendo su mano con la palma hacia arriba como lo haría un chango, volvió a decir: «Sólo dos cacaos, mi señor.»

Mi padre negó con la cabeza y cortésmente le dijo: «Para conocer el futuro iría a un *tlachtopaitoani*, un vidente-que-ve-en-la-lejanía.»

«¿Has visitado alguna vez a uno de esos videntes-que-ven-en-la-lejanía —preguntó el hombrecillo— y ha podido reconocer en ti, inmediatamente, a un maestro cantero de Xaltocan?»

Mi padre lo miró con sorpresa y farfulló: «Tú *eres* un vidente. Tienes la verdadera visión. Entonces, ¿por qué...?»

«¿Por qué voy lleno de harapos con mi mano extendida? Porque digo la verdad y la gente hace poco aprecio de ésta. Los videntes comen los hongos sagrados y sueñan sueños para ti, porque ellos pueden cobrar más por sueños. Mi señor, el polvo de la cal está incrustado en las coyunturas de tus dedos, pero tus palmas no están encallecidas por el uso del martillo o del cincel del escultor. ¿Ya ves? La verdad es tan barata que hasta la podría regalar.»

Yo me reí y mi padre también, y le dijo: «Eres un viejo embaucador y divertido, pero nosotros tenemos muchas cosas que hacer en otra parte...»

«Esperad», dijo insistiendo el hombrecillo. Se agachó para escudriñar mis ojos, aunque no necesitaba encogerse mucho. Yo le miré fijamente.

Estoy seguro de que el viejo pordiosero y embaucador había estado cerca de nosotros cuando mi padre me compró el cono de nieve y, habiendo escuchado la mención de mi significativo séptimo cumpleaños, nos tomó por rústicos campesinos en la gran ciudad, fáciles de ser timados por él. Sin embargo, mucho más tarde, los sucesos me hicieron recordar las palabras exactas que dijo...

Escudriñó mis ojos y murmuró: «Cualquier vidente puede ver muy lejos a través de los caminos y los días. Aun cuando él vea algo que va a pasar verdaderamente, está remoto en distancia y tiempo y nada beneficia o amenaza al vidente mismo. Sin embargo, el *tonali* de este niño es ver las cosas y hechos de este mundo, verlas cerca y llanamente, así como el significado que encierran.»

Se enderezó. «Al principio eso parecerá un impedimento, niño, pero esa clase de corta visión podría hacerte discernir las verdades que los videntes que ven en la lejanía no distinguen. Si pudieras sacar ventaja de ese talento, te harías rico y poderoso.»

Mi padre suspiró pacientemente y buscó dentro de su morral.

«No, no —le dijo el hombre—. No he profetizado riquezas o fama a tu hijo. No le he prometido la mano de una bella princesa o la fundación de un linaje distinguido. El niño Mixtli verá la verdad, sí. Desafortunadamente para él, *dirá* también la verdad de lo que vea y esto acarrea más frecuentemente la calumnia que la recompensa. Por una predicción tan ambigua, mi señor, no pido gratificación.»

«Toma esto de todas formas, viejo —dijo mi padre, presionando sobre su mano una semilla de cacao—. Solamente para que ya no nos predigas nada más.»

En el centro de la ciudad había poco tránsito comercial, pero todos los ciudadanos no ocupados en negocios urgentes habían empezado a congregarse en la gran plaza, para la ceremonia de la que mi padre había oído hablar. Preguntó a un transeúnte de qué se trataba y éste le respondió: «La dedicatoria a la Piedra del Sol, por supuesto, para celebrar la dependencia de Tlaltelolco.» La mayoría de la gente congregada allí eran plebeyos como nosotros, pero había también bastantes *pipiltin* como para haber poblado una gran ciudad sólo con nobles puros. De todas formas, mi padre y yo habíamos llegado a propósito temprano. Aunque había tanta gente en la plaza como pelos tiene un conejo, no llegaban a llenar totalmente esa área tan amplia. Teníamos suficiente espacio en el cual movernos y mirar hacia varios puntos.

En aquellos días, la plaza central de Tenochtitlan —In Cem-Anáhuac Yoyotli, El Corazón del Único Mundo— no tenía ni la mitad del bellísimo esplendor que llegaría a ver en mis visitas posteriores. El Muro de la Serpiente no había sido construido todavía para circundar esa área. El Venerado Orador Axayácatl todavía vivía en el palacio que había sido de su difunto padre Motecuzoma, mientras uno nuevo sería construido para él, diagonalmente, al otro lado de la plaza. La Gran Pirámide nueva, empezada por el primer Motecuzoma estaba todavía sin terminar. Sus muros de piedra inclinados y las escaleras con pasamanos de serpientes, terminaban bastante por encima de nuestras cabezas y más arriba aún se podía atisbar la pequeña pirámide primitiva, que más tarde sería totalmente cubierta y agrandada.

Sin embargo, la plaza era lo suficientemente maravillosa para un niño campesino como yo. Mi padre me dijo que una vez él la había cruzado en línea recta, la había medido pie sobre pie y que medía casi seiscientos pies de hombre desde el norte hacia el sur y desde el este hacia el oeste. Tenía el piso de mármol, una piedra más blanca que la piedra caliza de Xaltocan y estaba tan pulida y brillante como un *téxcatl*, espejo. Mucha de la gente que estaba allí ese día, tuvo que quitarse las sandalias y andar descalza, porque éstas eran de una clase de piel muy fina y resbaladiza.

Las tres amplias avenidas, que eran lo suficientemente anchas como para que caminaran veinte hombres, hombro con hombro, partían de allí, de la plaza, y se perdían a lo lejos hacia el norte, el oeste y el sur, para convertirse en los tres caminos-puentes, igualmente anchos, que se dirigían hacia la tierra firme. La plaza, en aquel entonces, no estaba tan llena de templos, altares y monumentos como lo estaría años más tarde, pero ya había modestos *teócaltin* conteniendo estatuas de los dioses principales. También estaban allí las cremalleras en donde se mostraban las calaveras de los más distinguidos *xochimique* que habían sido sacrificados a uno o a otro de esos dioses. En aquel lugar estaba la plazoleta privada del Venerado Orador, en donde se jugaba a los juegos rituales de *tlachtli*.

Ya estaba también la Casa de Canto, que contenía habitaciones confortables y cuartos para prácticas musicales para los más distinguidos músicos, cantantes y danzantes que durante los festivales religiosos representaban en la plaza. La Casa de Canto no fue totalmente destruida como otros de los edificios de la plaza y del resto de la ciudad. Fue restaurada y es ahora, por lo menos hasta que su iglesia catedral de San Francisco sea terminada, la residencia de su Obispo y su principal centro diocesano. En donde estamos sentados en este momento, mis señores escribanos, era una de las habitaciones de La Casa de Canto.

Mi padre supuso muy correctamente que a la edad de siete años no estaría extasiado con las reliquias religiosas o arquitectónicas, así es que me llevó al edificio despatarrado que estaba en la esquina sudeste de la plaza. Éste daba morada a la colección de animales y pájaros salvajes del Uey-Tlatoani, aunque todavía no contaba con una colección tan extensa como la tuvo en años posteriores. Había sido empezada por el difunto Motecuzoma, quien tenía intención de exhibir públicamente un especimen de cada uno de los animales de tierra y aire que se pudieran encontrar en todas estas tierras. El edificio fue dividido en incontables habitaciones; unas eran meros cubículos y otras, grandes cámaras. Una gamella mantenía una continua corriente de agua para vaciar los excrementos fuera de las habitaciones. Cada habitación se abría sobre un pasillo, para los visitantes, pero había una separación hecha por una red o en algunos casos tenían fuertes barras de madera como medida de protección. Había una habitación individual para cada criatura o para aquellas especies que, aunque distintas, podían convivir amigablemente.

«¿Acostumbran a hacer tanto ruido?», le pregunté a mi padre, gritando entre los rugidos, chillidos y gritos.

«No lo sé —me dijo—. pero en este momento algunos de ellos están muy hambrientos, porque deliberadamente no se les ha dado de comer por algún tiempo. Va haber sacrificios en la ceremonia y los despojos serán enviados aquí, como comida para los felinos, los *cóyotin* y los *tzopílotin*.»

En esos momentos estaba viendo al animal más grande de nuestras tierras: el tapir, feo, voluminoso y perezoso, que meneaba su hocico prensible hacia mí, cuando una voz familiar dijo: «Maestro cantero, ¿por qué no le enseña al niño la parte de los *téquantin*?»

Era el hombrecillo pardusco y encorvado con el que nos habíamos encontrado antes en la calle. Mi padre le echó una mirada exasperada y le preguntó: «¿Nos viene siguiendo, viejo molón?»

Se encogió de hombros. «Solamente arrastré mis ancianos huesos hasta aquí, para ver la dedicación de la Piedra del Sol.» Entonces, gesticulando hacia una puerta cerrada que estaba al final del pasillo, me dijo: «Ahí, mi niño, hay un verdadero espectáculo. Animales humanos, mucho más interesantes que estos meros brutos. Una mujer *tlacaztali*, por ejemplo. ¿Sabes qué es una *tlacaztali*? Es una persona completamente blanca, piel, pelo y todo, a excepción de sus ojos que son rojizos. Y también hay ahí un enano que tiene solamente media cabeza, que come...»

«¡Chist! —dijo mi padre severamente—. Éste es un día de regocijo para el niño. No quiero que se ponga enfermo viendo a esos desgraciados monstruos.»

«Ah, bueno —dijo el viejo—. Hay quienes disfrutan viendo a los deformados y mutilados. —Sus ojos brillaron al mirarme—. Pero los *téquantin* estarán todavía aquí, joven Mixtli, para cuando tú hayas madurado y seas lo suficientemente superior como para mofarte de ellos y embromarlos. Y me atrevería a decir que habrá más curiosidades para entonces en la parte de los *tequani*, sin duda mucho más entretenidos y divertidos para ti.»

«¿Quiere callarse?», rugió mi padre.

«Perdona, mi señor —dijo el viejo encorvado, encogiéndose todavía más—. Déjame enmendar mi impertinencia. Es casi mediodía y la ceremonia empezará muy pronto. Si vamos ahora y encontramos buenos lugares, quizá pueda explicaros a ti y al niño algunas cosas que de otra manera probablemente no entenderíais.»

La plaza estaba desbordantemente llena y las gentes se rozaban hombro con hombro. Nunca hubiéramos llegado tan cerca de la Piedra del Sol, si no hubiera sido porque cada vez y en último momento llegaban más y más nobles altivos, en sillas de manos de dorada tapicería, cargadas por sus esclavos. La muchedumbre de clase media y baja se dividía, sin ningún murmullo, para dejarles pasar, y el viejo, audazmente, se pegaba como una anguila a ellos siguiéndolos, con nosotros detrás, hasta que estuvimos casi al frente de la hilera de notables palaciegos. No habría podido ver nada, si mi padre no me hubiese levantado y acomodado en uno de sus hombros. Él miró abajo, hacia nuestro guía y le dijo: «También a usted lo puedo alzar, viejo.»

«Gracias por tu consideración, mi señor —dijo, medio sonriendo—, pero soy más pesado de lo que parezco.»

La Piedra del Sol, era el centro de atención de todas las miradas, y se asentaba para esa ocasión en la terraza, en medio de las dos amplias escaleras, de la inacabada Gran Pirámide. Estaba cubierta a nuestra vista por un manto de algodón de deslumbrante blancura. Así es que me dediqué a admirar a los nobles que llegaban, sus sillas de mano y sus trajes eran algo digno de verse. Hombres y mujeres, por igual, llevaban mantos completamente entretejidos de plumas, algunos eran multicolores y otros solamente de un resplandeciente color. El cabello de las mujeres estaba teñido de púrpura, como era la costumbre en un día como ése y sostenían sus manos en alto para lucir los brazaletes y los anillos que festonaban sus dedos. Aún así, los hombres llevaban más adornos que las mujeres. Todos llevaban diademas o borlas de oro y ricas plumas sobre sus cabezas. Algunos llevaban medallones de oro colgados al cuello con eslabones y brazaletes de oro en los brazos y en las pantorrillas. Otros llevaban tapones de oro de ornato y joyas que atravesaban los lóbulos de sus orejas, o de sus narices, o el labio inferior o todos a la vez.

«Aquí llega el Gran Tesorero —dijo nuestro guía—. Ciuacóatl, Mujer Serpiente, quien es el segundo en mando después del Venerado Orador.»

Me giré, ansioso por ver la Mujer Serpiente, a quien supuse una curiosidad como esos «animales humanos» que no me habían dejado ver, pero no era más que otro *pili*, un hombre que sólo se distinguía por estar ataviado mucho más vistosamente que los demás nobles. El pendiente que atravesaba su labio inferior era tan pesado que tiraba de éste hacia abajo, dándole una expresión a su rostro como si estuviera haciendo pucheros. Era un pendiente taimado: una miniatura de una serpiente en oro, hecha de tal manera que meneaba y sacaba su pequeña lengua cada vez que el Señor Tesorero se sacudía en su silla.

Nuestro guía se rió de mí; él había notado mi desilusión. «Mujer Serpiente es solamente un título, niño, no una descripción —me dijo—. Cada Gran Tesorero siempre ha sido llamado Ciuacóatl, aunque probablemente ninguno de ellos podría decirte el porqué. Mi teoría es que ambas, serpientes y mujeres, se enroscan apretadamente a cualquier tesoro que puedan retener.»

Entonces el gentío congregado en la plaza que hasta entonces había estado murmurando, dejó de hacerlo; el Uey-Tlatoani en persona acababa de aparecer. De alguna manera había llegado sin ser visto o había estado escondido de antemano en algún lugar, porque de repente apareció parado a un lado de la velada Piedra del Sol. El rostro de Axayácatl estaba oscurecido por los adornos; tapones en los lóbulos de las orejas, tapón en la nariz y ensombrecido por el gran penacho de plumas rojo fuego de guacamaya, que ceñía totalmente su cabeza y que le caía de hombro a hombro. Tampoco era muy visible el resto de su cuerpo. Su manto de plumas verde-oro de papagayo le caía totalmente hasta los pies. En su pecho llevaba un medallón grande y laboriosamente intrincado, su *máxtlatl* era de rica piel roja, en sus pies llevaba sandalias aparentemente de oro puro, atadas hasta la altura de las rodillas con lazos dorados.

La costumbre era que todos los que estábamos congregados en la plaza debíamos saludarle con *tlalqualiztli*, el gesto de arrodillarse tocando con un dedo la tierra y luego llevarlo a nuestros labios, pero simplemente no había suficiente espacio para hacerlo; el gentío emitió una especie de fuerte murmullo en imitación de sonidos de beso. El Venerado Orador Axayácatl devolvió el saludo silenciosamente, inclinando el espectacular penacho de plumas rojas y levantando hacia lo alto de su mazo de caoba y oro.

Entonces fue rodeado por una horda de sacerdotes, quienes con sus vestiduras sucias y negras, sus rostros ennegrecidos e incrustados de mugre y sus largos cabellos ensangrentados y enmarañados, hacían un sombrío contraste con la grandiosidad de las vestiduras de Axayácatl. El Venerado Orador nos explicó el significado de la Piedra del Sol, mientras los sacerdotes cantaban oraciones e invocaciones cada vez que él hacía una pausa para respirar. No puedo recordar ahora las palabras de Axayácatl y probablemente no las entendí todas en aquel momento, pero la esencia era ésta: aunque la Piedra del Sol tenía grabado al dios-sol Tonatiú, éste tenía que compartir los honores con el dios principal de Tenochtitlan, Huitzilopochtli, Chupamirto del Sur.

Ya he dicho cómo nuestros dioses podían tener nombres y aspectos diferentes. Pues bien, Tonatiú *era* el sol, y el sol es indispensable, ya que toda vida en la tierra perecería sin él. Nosotros los de Xaltocan y las gentes de muchas otras comunidades, estábamos satisfechos de venerarlo *como* el sol. Sin embargo, parece obvio que el sol necesita nutrirse para tener fuerza y así poder continuar en sus labores diarias —¿y qué podríamos darle para vitalizarlo e inspirarlo más, que estuviera a la altura de lo que él nos daba? Solamente la misma vida humana. Por lo tanto el bondadoso dios-sol tenía otro aspecto de ferocidad, el dios de la guerra Huitzilopochtli, quien nos guiaba a nosotros los mexica en todas nuestras batallas para saquear y procurar prisioneros para ese necesario sacrificio. Era bajo este aspecto austero de Huitzilopochtli, como el dios era más reverenciado aquí en Tenochtitlan, porque aquí era donde todas nuestras guerras se planeaban, se declaraban y donde se reunían todos los guerreros. Bajo otro nombre, el de Tezcatlipoca, Espejo Humeante, el sol era el dios principal de nuestra nación vecina de los acolhua. Yo he llegado a sospechar que en otras naciones innumerables, que nunca he visitado e incluso en algunas más allá del mar de donde ustedes los españoles llegaron, veneran igualmente a este mismo dios-sol, naturalmente llamándole por algún otro nombre de acuerdo a como ellos lo ven, sonriente o ceñudo.

Mientras el Uey-Tlatoani iba hablando, mientras los sacerdotes seguían cantando una monodia y cierto número de músicos empezaron a tocar las flautas, huesos hendidos y tambores de cuero, nuestro viejo guía, el hombre de color cacao, nos contaba privadamente la historia de la Piedra del Sol:

«Al sudeste de aquí está la nación de los chalca. Cuando fue sometida por el difunto Motecuzoma y hecha nación vasalla, hace veintidós años, los chalca fueron, naturalmente, obligados a pagar tributo a los victoriosos mexica. Dos jóvenes chalca, que eran hermanos, se ofrecieron voluntariamente a tallar una pieza cada uno, para ser colocada aquí en El Corazón del Único Mundo. Escogieron piedras parecidas, pero diferentes temas y trabajaron aparte; nadie más que ellos vio su propio trabajo.»

«Seguro que sus esposas lo verían furtivamente», dijo mi padre que tenía esa clase de mujer.

«Nadie echó ni siquiera una mirada —repitió el viejo— durante todos esos veintidós años, cada uno de ellos esculpió y pintó su propia piedra, y también durante ese tiempo ellos llegaron a la edad madura y Motecuzoma se fue al mundo del más allá. Luego, cuando terminaron sus obras, separadamente las envolvieron con heno y esterillas de fibra y el Señor de los chalca reunió unos mil cargadores forzudos para transportar las piedras hasta aquí, a la capital.»

Gesticuló hacia el objeto que, todavía cubierto, estaba en lo alto de la terraza. «Como podéis ver, la Piedra del Sol es inmensa: más de dos veces la estatura de dos hombres, y terriblemente pesada: el peso de trescientos veinte hombres juntos. La otra piedra era más o menos igual. Fueron traídas aquí a través de sendas escabrosas y hasta por donde no habían senderos. Fueron deslizadas sobre rodillos de troncos, moviéndose despacio sobre varaderas y transportadas en grandes balsas a través de los ríos. Pensad sólo en el trabajo, en el sudor, los huesos rotos y en la cantidad de hombres que cayeron muertos cuando ya no pudieron jalar más o soportar los látigos de los capataces que los fustigaban.»

«¿Dónde está la otra piedra?», pregunté, pero me ignoró.

«Al fin llegaron a los lagos, de Chalco y de Xochimilco, que cruzaron en balsas, hasta llegar al camino-puente que corre hacia el norte de Tenochtitlan. Desde allí, no había más que un camino ancho y recto de no más de dos carreras largas, hasta aquí. Los escultores suspiraron con alivio. Tanto ellos como otros muchos hombres habían trabajado muy duro; sin embargo, esos monumentos tan difícilmente transportados ya estaban a la vista de su destino...»

La muchedumbre que nos rodeaba hizo un ruido. El grupo de hombres que ofrecería su sangre vital en ese día de la consagración de la Piedra del Sol estaban en filas en ese momento, y el primero de ellos ya ascendía los escalones de la pirámide. No parecía ser un guerrero enemigo cautivo; era un hombre medio rechoncho, más o menos de la edad de mi padre, que llevaba puesto un blanquísimo taparrabo y a pesar de verse macilento e infeliz, iba voluntariamente desatado y sin que los guardias tuvieran que empujarle. Allí, parado en la terraza, miró estoicamente, mientras los sacerdotes columpiaban sus incensarios humeantes y hacían los gestos rituales con sus manos y sus bastones. Entonces, uno de los sacerdotes tomó al *xochimiqui*, gentilmente lo volteó y le ayudó a acostarse de espaldas sobre el bloque de piedra que estaba enfrente del monumento velado. El bloque era una simple piedra a la altura de las rodillas, en forma más o menos como de una pirámide en miniatura, así es que cuando el hombre se acostó, estirado sobre la piedra, su cuerpo se arqueó de tal manera que su pecho sobresalió como si estuviera deseoso del cuchillo.

Él estaba tendido, a nuestra vista, de costado y a lo largo, y sus brazos y piernas eran asidos por cuatro sacerdotes-ayudantes, mientras que atrás de él estaba el sacerdote principal, el ejecutor, sosteniendo el cuchillo de obsidiana negra, ancho y de forma casi plana. Antes de que el sacerdote hiciera algún movimiento, el hombre alzó su cabeza colgante y dijo algo. Se cruzaron algunas otras palabras entre ellos en la terraza y entonces el *tlamacazqui*, entregando el cuchillo a Axayácatl cambió de lugar con él. La multitud hizo un ruido de sorpresa y perplejidad. Esa víctima en particular, por alguna razón, se le concedió el gran honor de ser sacrificado por el Uey-Tlatoáni en persona.

Axayácatl no titubeó ni tentaleó. Tan experto como cualquier sacerdote, apuñaló el pecho del hombre exactamente sobre el lado izquierdo, justo debajo de la tetilla y entre las dos costillas, luego hizo un tajo con el filo del cuchillo, girando la parte ancha de éste para separar las costillas y poder hacer la herida mucho más ancha. Con la otra mano buscó dentro de la herida sangrante, sacó el corazón completo, todavía palpitante, y lo desgarró, perdiendo el entrelazado de sus vasos sanguíneos. No fue sino hasta entonces, que el *xochimiqui* profirió su primer quejido de dolor, un sollozo gimoteante, el último sonido de su vida.

Mientras el Venerado Orador sostenía en lo alto ese reluciente objeto rojo-púrpura, que todavía goteaba, un *tlamacazqui*, sacerdote, dio un tirón a un cordón oculto en alguna parte, el velo que cubría la Piedra del Sol cayó y la multitud dio un grito concentrado de admiración: «¡Ay-yo-o-o-o!» Axayácatl se volvió, levantando en lo alto el corazón de la víctima y lo colocó en el centro exacto de la piedra circular, dentro de la boca tallada de Tonatíu; machacó y restregó el corazón hasta que no quedó nada de él en su mano y no fue más que una mancha más sobre la piedra.

Los sacerdotes me habían contado que una persona sacrificada generalmente vivía lo suficiente como para ver lo que pasaba con su corazón, pero ese hombre no pudo ver mucho. Cuando Axayácatl terminó, la sangre y los pedazos de carne difícilmente eran visibles, pues la cara tallada del sol estaba pintada de un color semejante a la sangre del corazón.

«Estuvo bien hecho —dijo el hombre encorvado que estaba al lado de mi padre—. He visto corazones que laten tan vigorosamente que han saltado de los dedos de los ejecutores, pero creo que este corazón en particular, ya estaba roto.»

El *xochimiqui* yacía inmóvil, excepto por su piel que se con-

traía aquí y allá, como la piel de los perros cuando son atormentados por las moscas. Los sacerdotes quitaron sus despojos
de la piedra y los dejaron tirados en la terraza, sin ninguna ceremonia, mientras la segunda víctima ascendía bregando los escalones. Axayácatl no hizo más honor a ningún otro de los *xochimique*, sino que les dejó el resto a los sacerdotes. Como la
procesión continuó, con cada corazón extraído de cada hombre para ungir la Piedra del Sol, yo miré atentamente ese objeto impotente para poder describírselo a mi amigo Tlatli, quien
ya había empezado a practicar para llegar a ser un escultor,
tallando pequeños trozos de madera para convertirlos en muñecos.

Yyo ayyo, reverendos frailes, ¡si sólo hubieran podido contemplar la Piedra del Sol! Ya veo por sus caras que desaprueban la ceremonia de la dedicación, pero si ustedes hubieran podido ver esa piedra, aunque hubiera sido solamente una vez, se
darían cuenta de que valió todo lo que costó en esfuerzo, años
y vidas humanas.

La pura entalladura estaba más allá de lo que se pueda creer,
pues ésta era de pórfido, una piedra tan dura como el granito.
En el centro estaba el rostro de Tonatíu, sus ojos miraban fijamente, su boca estaba abierta y a cada uno de los lados de
su cabeza había unas garras apretando los corazones humanos
que lo nutrían. Después, y en círculo, estaban los símbolos de
las cuatro épocas del mundo, las cuales precedían a la era en
que ahora vivimos, y alrededor de éstos, en otro círculo, se
encontraban los de nuestros veintidós nombres de los días, y
alrededor de ellos los glifos alternativos de piedrajade y turquesa, las gemas más preciadas de todas las encontradas en
nuestras tierras. Alrededor, se encontraba otro círculo con los
rayos del sol diurno alternando con las estrellas nocturnas, todo
esto cercado en su totalidad por dos esculturas de la Serpiente
de Fuego del Tiempo, con sus colas rematando la parte de arriba de la piedra, sus cuerpos enroscándose alrededor de ella y
sus cabezas encontrándose en su base. En una sola piedra, ese
artista único había plasmado todo nuestro universo, todo nuestro tiempo.

Estaba pintada en colores bien delineados, meticulosamente
aplicados en aquellos lugares precisos a los que correspondía
cada uno. Sin embargo, la destreza real del pintor era más evidente en donde no había color. El pórfido es una piedra com-
puesta por muchos fragmentos de otras y éstas incluyen mica,
feldespato y cuarzo, que por sí mismas poseen diversos resplandores o intensifican cualquier color cerca de ellas. Dondequiera
que estuviera empotrado uno de estos pedacitos cristalinos de
roca, el artista lo dejó sin pintar. En aquel momento, cuando la
Piedra del Sol estuvo en el resplandor del mediodía de Tonatíu,
esas joyas pequeñitas y cristalinas parpadeaban hacia nosotros
como una luz solar saliendo del brillante colorido. Ese gran objeto parecía, no tanto como si estuviera coloreado, sino más bien
totalmente iluminado.

Sin embargo, supongo que para creerlo tendrían que haberlo

visto en toda su gloria original. O a través de los límpidos ojos y la clara luz con que yo lo gocé en aquellos días. O quizá, bajo el influjo de la mente de un niñito pagano, todavía impresionable e ignorante...

De todas formas, volví mi atención hacia nuestro guía, quien continuaba su interrumpida historia acerca de los penosos problemas para hacer llegar las piedras:

«Nunca antes el camino-puente de Coyohuacan había sostenido un peso tan grande. Debido a esto fue cuando las poderosas piedras de los dos hermanos llegaron deslizándose sobre sus rodillos, una detrás de otra; repentinamente, el camino-puente se venció bajo el peso de la primera y la piedra envuelta fue a dar al fondo del lago de Texcoco. Los cargadores de la segunda, la Piedra del Sol que está aquí, se detuvieron a muy poca distancia de la orilla del puente roto. La Piedra del Sol fue puesta otra vez en una balsa y transportada por agua, alrededor de la isla, hasta la plaza. Ésta es la única que se salvó, para ser admirada por nosotros esta mañana.»

«¿Y la otra? —preguntó mi padre—. Después de todo ese trabajo, ¿no pudieron hacer un pequeño esfuerzo más?»

«Oh, así fue, mi señor. Los más expertos nadadores se sumergieron una y otra vez, pero el fondo del lago de Texcoco es fangoso y quizás insondable. También utilizaron largas estacas para sondear, pero nunca pudieron localizarla. La piedra, como haya sido esculpida, debe haber caído de lado.»

«¿Como haya sido esculpida?», repitió mi padre.

«Sólo el artista posó sus ojos sobre ella. La piedra pudo haber sido mucho más grandiosa que ésta —el viejo señalaba la Piedra del Sol—, pero nunca lo sabremos.»

«¿Y nunca dijo el artista cómo había sido?», pregunté.

«No, nunca.»

Persistí: «Bueno, ¿y no podría hacerla otra vez?» El trabajo de veintidós años se me antojaba en aquel entonces algo menos de lo que me parecería ahora.

«Quizás la hubiera podido hacer, pero ya nunca lo hará. Tomó ese desastre como una evidencia de su *tonali*, como un signo de que los dioses rechazaban su ofrenda. Él fue al que el Venerado Orador acaba de honrar, dándole la Muerte Florida por su propia mano. El artista rechazado se dio a sí mismo para ser la primera víctima en sacrificio a la Piedra del Sol.»

«Para la obra de su hermano —murmuró mi padre—. ¿Y mientras tanto, qué es de su hermano?»

«Él recibirá honores, ricos presentes y el -tzin para su nombre —dijo nuestro guía—. Sin embargo, él y todo el mundo se preguntará por siempre: ¿No será la piedra que yace en el fondo del lago de Texcoco, sin haber sido nunca vista, una obra mucho más sublime que esta Piedra del Sol?»

En verdad que con el tiempo, el mito que engrandece lo desconocido llega a ser un tesoro mucho más grande que la realidad tangible. La escultura perdida llegó a ser conocida con el nombre de In Huehuetótetl: la Piedra Más Venerable. Y la Piedra del Sol llegó a ser vista, solamente, como su substituto. El hermano que sobrevivió, jamás esculpió otra obra. Llegó a ser uñ borrachín de *octli*, una ruina lamentable, pero tuvo el suficiente respeto por sí mismo como para ofrecerse también en sacrificio en una ceremonia, antes de que cayera sobre su nuevo título de noble la vergüenza irremediable. Cuando llegó a su Muerte Florida su corazón tampoco saltó de los dedos del ejecutor.

Por cierto que la Piedra del Sol también se perdió hace ocho años, enterrada bajo los escombros, cuando El Corazón del Único Mundo fue demolido por las lanchas guerreras, con sus cañones de balas, sus arietes y sus flechas de fuego. A lo mejor algún día su Ciudad de Mexico será arrasada a su vez y la Piedra del Sol será descubierta brillando entre las ruinas. Incluso —¿*aquin ixnetla?*— quizás algún día también, será la Piedra Más Venerable.

Mi padre y yo volvimos a casa esa noche en nuestro *acali* vuelto a cargar con las mercancías de trueque, conseguidas por el encargado de los fletes. Y así les he narrado los sucesos más importantes acaecidos ese día de la celebración de mi séptimo cumpleaños y de mi nuevo nombre. De todos mis cumpleaños, y he tenido más de los normales, creo que ése ha sido el que más he disfrutado.

☩

Me alegro de haber visto entonces Tenochtitlan, porque nunca volví a verlo otra vez igual. No me refiero solamente al hecho de que la ciudad creció y cambió, ni que cuando regresé a ella estaba hastiado y no era ya un muchachito impresionable. Quiero decir que literalmente nunca volví a ver *nada* tan claramente con mis dos ojos.

Ya antes, les he narrado cómo había podido distinguir el diseño cincelado del conejo-en-la-luna, la Flor del Atardecer en el crepúsculo, los detalles de las banderolas de Tenochtitlan y los intrincados dibujos de la Piedra del Sol. Cinco años después de mi séptimo cumpleaños ya no podía ver la Flor del Atardecer, ni aunque un dios celestial hubiera extendido un hilo desde la estrella hasta mis ojos. Metztli la luna, en toda su redondez y brillantez, vino a ser para mí solamente una blanca o amarillenta burbuja borrosa, su círculo que antes había podido ver bien marcado, fue una mancha indistinta en el cielo.

En suma, desde la edad de los siete años empecé a perder mi vista. Esto me convirtió en una especie de rareza, aunque en ningún sentido envidiable. Casi toda nuestra gente posee la aguda visión de las águilas y de los *tzopilotin*, a excepción de unos cuantos que han nacido ciegos o aquellos que han llegado a serlo por alguna herida o enfermedad. Ésa era una condición prácticamente desconocida entre nosotros, y yo, que me avergonzaba de ello, no quería hablar de eso y trataba de mantenerlo como un secreto doloroso. Cuando alguien apuntaba algo y decía: «¡Mira ahí!», yo exclamaba: «¡Ah, sí!», aunque no sabía si debía entornar los ojos o escabullirme.

La decreción rápida de mi clara visión no llegó de repente; sobrevino gradual, pero inexorablemente. Cuando tenía nueve o diez años podía ver tan claramente como cualquiera, pero, quizás a la distancia de dos brazos solamente. Más allá de esa distancia las cosas empezaban a ser confusas, como si las viera a través de un espejo de agua, pero distorsionado —digamos, como cuando veía desde lo alto de una colina a través del paisaje—; los contornos individuales se empañaban tanto que los objetos se fundían y confundían y el paisaje no era más que una masa amorfa de color, como el excéntrico diseño de un sarape. Sin embargo, por lo menos, con un campo claro de visión hasta la distancia de dos brazos de largo, podía moverme con libertad sin caer encima de las cosas. Cuando necesitaba buscar algo en alguno de los cuartos de nuestra casa, lo podía encontrar sin tener que tentalear, pero el alcance de mi visión continuó disminuyendo quizás a la distancia de un brazo de largo cuando cumplí los trece años y ya no pude disimular lo suficiente como para que este hecho pasara inadvertido a otros. Supongo que en un principio mi familia y mis amigos me consideraban simplemente torpe, desmañado o quizás estúpido, pero en aquel tiempo, con la perversa vanidad de la adolescencia, deseaba pasar más como un patán que como un inválido, aunque inevitablemente llegó a ser obvio para todos que estaba perdiendo el más importante de los cinco sentidos. Mi familia y mis amigos se portaron de distintas formas ante esa revelación sorprendente.

Mi madre le echó la culpa de mi condición a la familia de mi padre. Parece ser que hubo una vez un tío que mientras estaba bebiendo *octli*, tomó otra olla por error que contenía un líquido blanco similar y se lo tragó todo antes de darse cuenta de que era el poderoso cáustico *xocóyatl*, que se usaba para limpiar y blanquear la piedra caliza del cieno nocivo. Sobrevivió y nunca volvió a beber, pero quedó ciego para el resto de su vida y, de acuerdo con la teoría de mi madre, esa herencia lamentable había caído sobre mí.

Mi padre no culpó a nadie, ni especuló, sino que trató de consolarme, aunque demasiado cordialmente: «Bien, siendo un maestro cantero tu trabajo estará cercano, Mixtli, y no te dará trabajo mirar con atención los detalles, las grietas delgadas y las hendiduras.»

Aquellos que eran de mi edad —y los niños que como alacranes clavaban sus aguijones instintiva y salvajemente— me gritaban: «¡Mira ahí!»

Yo, achicando los ojos, decía: «Ah, sí.»

«¿Verdad que es algo fantástico?»

Yo forzaba mi vista desesperadamente y decía: «Claro que lo es.»

Entonces ellos estallaban de risa y gritaban burlonamente: «¡No hay nada que ver ahí, Tozani!»

Otros, mis amigos íntimos como Chimali y Tlatli, también

hablaban algunas veces sin consideración: «¡Mira!» Aunque rápidamente añadían: «Un mensajero veloz va corriendo hacia el palacio del Señor Garza Roja y lleva el manto verde de las buenas noticias. Debe de haber habido una batalla victoriosa en alguna parte.»

Mi hermana Tzitzitlini dijo poco, pero decidió acompañarme cuando tenía que ir a alguna distancia o a lugares que no me eran familiares. Ella tomaba mi mano como si fuera solamente el gesto cariñoso de una hermana mayor, pero con discreción y presteza guiaba mis pasos alrededor de cualquier obstáculo que hubiera en mi camino.

Sin embargo, como eran más los niños y como persistían en llamarme Tozani, pronto los adultos también lo hicieron, irreflexivamente y sin crueldad, hasta que finalmente todos, excepto mi padre, mi madre y mi hermana, me llamaron así. Incluso cuando ya me había adaptado a esa desventaja y me las arreglaba para no ser tan torpe, otras personas que en realidad no se habían dado cuenta de mi poca visión, me herían lanzándome ese apodo. Yo creí que el nombre que me habían dado, Mixtli, que significaba Nube, irónicamente me había quedado mejor que antes, pero Tozani fui.

El *tozani* es un animalito al que ustedes llaman topo, que prefiere pasar su vida bajo la tierra, en la oscuridad. Cuando infrecuentemente emerge, es cegado por la luz del día que cierra sus ojitos parpadeantes. Ni ve, ni le importa ver.

Sin embargo, a mí sí me importaba mucho, y por un largo tiempo de mi joven vida me compadecí a mí mismo. Nunca llegaría a ser un *tlachtli*, jugador de pelota con la esperanza de tener algún día el gran honor de jugar en la cancha personal del Venerado Orador el juego ritual dedicado a los dioses. Si llegaba a ser un guerrero, nunca tendría la esperanza de ganar el título de campeón. De hecho, me podría sentir protegido por algún dios si conservaba mi vida en el primer día de batalla. En cuanto a ganarme la vida y sostener a mi propia familia... bueno, *no* quería ser cantero, ¿pero de qué otro trabajo sería capaz?

En mi mente, jugueteé anhelante con la posibilidad de llegar a ser alguna clase de trabajador viajero; esto me podría llevar eventualmente hacia el sur, hacia la lejana tierra de los mayas, pues había oído que los físicos mayas conocían remedios milagrosos hasta para las dolencias de los ojos más desesperadas. Quizás allí podría ser curado y regresar a casa otra vez con los ojos brillantes de triunfo, como un invencible *tlachtli* ganador o un héroe guerrero, incluso como campeón de alguna de las tres órdenes.

Entonces la oscuridad que me invadía pareció disminuir y detenerse a la distancia del largo de mi brazo. En realidad no lo hizo, pero después de los primeros años la disminución fue menos perceptible. Hoy día, sin la ayuda para mi ojo, no puedo distinguir el rostro de mi esposa más allá de la distancia de mi mano. Ahora que estoy viejo, poco importa, pero sí me importaba mucho cuando era joven.

A pesar de todo, muy despacio y resignándome, me adapté a mis limitaciones. Aquel extraño hombrecillo en Tenochtitlan había dicho la verdad cuando predijo que mi *tonali* era mirar de cerca, ver las cosas de cerca y llanamente. Por necesidad tuve que andar despacio y detenerme frecuentemente, así yo escudriñaba en lugar de ver. Cuando otros se apuraban, yo esperaba; cuando otros tenían prisa, yo me movía deliberadamente despacio. Aprendí a diferenciar entre el movimiento premeditado y la mera moción, entre la acción y la mera actividad. Donde otros, impacientes, veían una aldea, yo advertía a su gente. Donde otros veían gente, yo contemplaba a las personas. Donde otros echaban un vistazo a un extranjero, yo me aseguraba de verlo de cerca y después poder hacer un dibujo de cada línea de su rostro, tanto que hasta un artista tan diestro como Chimali exclamaba: «¡Por los dioses, Topo, has retratado al hombre en vivo!»

Empecé a notar cosas que creo que pasan desapercibidas a la mayoría de la gente, que no tiene ojos perspicaces. ¿Nunca han notado *ustedes*, señores escribanos, que el maíz crece más rápido de noche que de día? ¿Han advertido alguna vez que cada mazorca de maíz tiene un número par de hileras de granos? O casi cada mazorca, pero encontrar una con un número impar de hileras es mucho más raro que encontrar un trébol de cuatro hojas. ¿Han observado alguna vez que ni siquiera dos dedos —ni de ustedes ni de toda la raza humana— tienen precisamente el mismo molde de espirales y de líneas arqueadas infinitesimalmente grabadas en las yemas? Mis estudios pueden comprobarlo. Si no me creen, compárense a sí mismos. Compárense unos a otros. Yo esperaré.

Oh, yo sé que no hay significancia o provecho en que haya notado esas cosas. Fueron solamente detalles triviales en los que ejercité mi nueva disposición de ver de cerca y examinar atentamente todas las cosas. Sin embargo, la necesidad hace virtud, y la combinación de mi aptitud para copiar exactamente las cosas que veía me llevaron a interesarme finalmente por la escritura-pintada de nuestro pueblo. No había escuela en Xaltocan donde yo pudiera instruirme en esa recóndita materia, pero recogía cada pedacito de escritura que podía encontrar y lo estudiaba luchando por comprender sus significados.

Pienso que la escritura numérica puede ser descifrada por cualquiera con facilidad. El glifo concha, cero; los puntos o dedos, unos; las banderas, veintes, y los arbolitos, cientos, pero recuerdo la emoción que sentí el día que llegué a descifrar la primera *palabra* pintada.

Mi padre me llevó consigo al palacio, un día que tenía que arreglar algunos negocios allí; para tenerme entretenido mientras hablaban en una sala privada, el gobernador dejó que me sentara en la entrada del vestíbulo y mirara el libro de registro de todos sus súbditos. Primero volví las páginas hasta encontrar la mía. Siete puntos, el símbolo de la flor, la nube gris. Luego cuidadosamente volteé otras páginas. Algunos nombres que me eran familiares los podía comprender tan fácilmente como

el mío. No lejos de mi página estaba la de Chimali y naturalmente reconocí los tres dedos, los dos zarcillos entrelazados que
representan humo, levantándose de un disco orlado con plumas:
Yei-Ehécatl-Pocuía-Chimali, Tres Viento Humeante Escudo.

Las pinturas que se repetían más frecuentemente eran fáciles
de interpretar. Después de todo, sólo teníamos veinte nombres
de días. Sin embargo, me encontré de repente con que no había
una repetición evidente de elementos en el nombre de Chimali
y en el mío. En una página casi al final, que había sido pintada recientemente, había seis puntos, luego una forma como
de lágrima y luego el símbolo del pico de pato, después una cosa
con tres pétalos. *¡Pude leerlo!* ¡Sabía lo que significaba! Seis Lluvia Viento Flor, la hermana pequeña de Tlatli que había celebrado su cumpleaños de dar-nombre no hacía más de una se-
mana.

Entonces, con menos cautela, empecé a voltear las tiesas páginas dobladas, hacia atrás y hacia delante, viéndolas por ambos lados, buscando más repeticiones y símbolos conocidos que
pudiera unir. El gobernador y mi padre regresaron en el momento exacto en que acababa de descifrar, aunque laboriosamente,
otro nombre o por lo menos eso creí. Con una mezcla de timidez
y orgullo dije:

«Discúlpeme, mi Señor Garza Roja. ¿Podría ser tan amable
de decirme si estoy en lo cierto? ¿Está escrito en esta página
el nombre de alguien llamado Dos Caña Amarillo Colmillo?»

Él miró y me dijo que no, que no decía eso. Debió de darse
cuenta de mi decepción porque pacientemente me explicó:

«Ahí dice Dos Caña Amarilla Luz, que es el nombre de una
de las lavanderas del palacio. El Dos y la Caña son obvios y
Amarillo, Cóztic, es fácil pues se indica usando simplemente el
mismo color, como lo adivinaste, pero Tlanixtélotl, "Luz", o para
expresarlo con más claridad, el elemento de la vista, es más
difícil. ¿Cómo se puede hacer un dibujo de algo tan insubstancial? En lugar de eso, hice el dibujo de un diente, *tlanti*, para
representar no lo que significa, sino el sonido del *tlan* al principio de la palabra y después el dibujo de un ojo, *ixtelólotl*, que
sirve para hacer más claro todo el significado. ¿Lo entiendes ahora? Tlanixtélotl. Luz.»

Asentí con la cabeza sintiéndome desilusionado y tonto. Había
algo más en la escritura-pintada que el reconocer, solamente, el
dibujo de un diente. Por si no me había dado cuenta todavía, el
gobernador lo explicó más claramente:

«La escritura-pintada y la lectura son para aquellos que han
sido adiestrados en esas artes, hijo de Tepetzalan —y me dio
una palmada de hombre a hombre en el hombro—. Requiere de
mucho trabajo y mucha práctica, y sólo los nobles tienen suficiente tiempo de ocio para esa clase de estudio, pero admiro tu
iniciativa. Cualquiera que sea la ocupación a la que te vayas
a dedicar, joven, la llegarás a desempeñar muy bien.»

Supongo que el hijo de Tepetzalan debería haber tomado en
cuenta la clara insinuación del Señor Garza Roja y seguido los
pasos de Tepetzalan. Deshabilitado y con la vista débil, no po-

día ambicionar demasiado o pensar siquiera en alguna ocupación venturosa. Podría, eso sí, afanarme en un trabajo aburrido como el de cantero, pero con la barriga siempre llena, como el de un verdadero topo. Quizá hubiera sido una vida mucho menos satisfactoria de la que yo obstinadamente persistía en encontrar, pero que me hubiese llevado por senderos más lisos y días más tranquilos de aquellos que encontré cuando me fui por mi propio camino. En este momento, mis señores, yo podría haber sido empleado en ayudar a construir su Ciudad de México y, si el Señor Garza Roja hubiera tenido razón al estimar mis habilidades, posiblemente haría una ciudad mucho mejor de la que están haciendo sus arquitectos importados y sus albañiles.

Pero dejémoslo pasar, dejémoslo pasar, como yo mismo dejé pasar todo, haciendo caso omiso a la orden insinuada por el Señor Garza Roja; haciendo caso omiso del orgullo genuino de mi padre por su trabajo y de sus intentos por enseñármelos y haciendo caso omiso de la censura de mi madre, quien se quejaba de que estaba tratando de subir en mi vida muy por encima de la posición social decretada.

De entre las insinuaciones hechas por el gobernador, había una que no podía ignorar. Me había revelado que una palabra-pintada no siempre significaba lo que representaba como dibujo, sino también lo que simbolizaba como sonido. Nada más eso, pero fue lo suficientemente revelador e interesante como para que siguiera buscando en pequeños fragmentos de escritura, en las paredes de los templos, en los rollos de tríbulo de la isla, en el palacio o en cualquier papel que llevara algún mercader viajante, tratando y trabajando laboriosamente para descifrarlos.

Incluso fui a ver al anciano *tonalpoqui* que me había dado mi nombre, cuatro años antes, y le pedí que me dejara mirar su venerable libro-de-dar-nombres cuando no lo estuviera usando. Si le hubiera pedido a una de sus nietas como concubina en los ratos en que ella no estuviera ocupada, no hubiera reculado tan violentamente. Me corrió con la información de que el arte de conocer el *tonálmatl* estaba reservado para los descendientes de los *tonalpoque* y no para mocosos desconocidos y presuntuosos. Quizás eso fuera así, pero apuesto a que él recordaba mi declaración de que yo hubiera podido darme mi propio nombre tan bien o mejor de como él lo había hecho; en otras palabras, que él era un viejo asustadizo y tramposo que no podía leer el *tonálmatl* mejor de lo que yo lo hubiera podido hacer en aquel entonces.

Una tarde, me encontré con un extranjero. Chimali, Tlatli, algunos otros muchachos y yo habíamos estado jugando juntos toda la tarde, así es que Tzitzitlini no estaba con nosotros. En una playa bastante distante de nuestra aldea encontramos el casco de un *acali* viejo y putrefacto y estuvimos tan absortos jugando a los remeros, que nos sorprendió Tonatíu cuando con su cielo enrojecido dio su llamada de advertencia de que se estaba preparando para irse a dormir. Teníamos que recorrer un largo camino hasta llegar a casa y Tonatíu se apresuraba a su cama más rápido de lo que nosotros podíamos caminar, así es que los otros muchachos echaron a correr. A la luz del día yo hubiera podido seguirlos, pero en la semioscuridad del atardecer me vi forzado a moverme más despacio y a caminar con más cuidado. Probablemente los otros nunca me echaron de menos; como sea, pronto se perdieron en la distancia.

Llegué al cruce de dos caminos en donde había una banca de piedra. Hacía algún tiempo que no pasaba por allí, pero recordé que la banca tenía varios símbolos grabados y me olvidé de todo. Me olvidé de que ya estaba casi oscuro como para que pudiera ver los grabados, ya no digamos descifrarlos. Me olvidé de por qué estaba allí la banca. Olvidé todas las cosas que me acechaban y que podrían caer sobre mí en cuanto sobreviniera la noche. Incluso oí cercano el grito de un búho y no presté atención a ese presagio de mal agüero. Había algo que leer allí y no podía seguir adelante sin tratar de hacerlo.

La banca era lo suficientemente larga como para que un hombre pudiera tenderse en ella, si es que podía acomodar sus espaldas en las aristas de la piedra tallada. Me incliné sobre las marcas y me fijé en ellas, trazándolas tanto con mis dedos como con mis ojos; me fui moviendo de un lugar a otro, hasta que casi me dejé caer sobre las piernas de un hombre que estaba allí sentado. Di un salto hacia atrás, como si hubiese quemado y murmuré una disculpa:

«*M-mixpantzinco*. En su augusta presencia...»

Con la misma cortesía, pero cansadamente, él me dio la respuesta acostumbrada: «*Ximopanolti*. A su conveniencia...»

Durante un momento nos miramos fijamente. Supongo que lo único que él vio fue a un muchachito desaliñado y cegato de unos doce años. Yo no podía distinguirlo en detalle, parte porque la noche había caído sobre nosotros y parte porque había saltado lejos de él, pero me pude dar cuenta de que era un forastero o por lo menos lo era para mí, ya que su manto de buena tela estaba manchado por el viaje; sus sandalias gastadas por el mucho caminar, y su piel cobriza, polvorienta por la tierra del camino.

«¿Cómo te llamas muchacho?», me preguntó al fin.

«Bueno, me dicen Topo...», empecé.

«Puedo creer eso, pero ése no es tu nombre.»

Antes de que pudiera contestarle, me hizo otra pregunta.

«¿Qué estabas haciendo hace un momento?»

«Estaba leyendo, Yanquicatzin —realmente no sé qué había en él, que me hizo darle el título de *Señor* Forastero—. Estaba leyendo lo escrito en la banca.»

«¿De veras —lo dijo cansada e incrédulamente—. Nunca te hubiera considerado un joven noble educado. ¿Y qué es lo que dice la escritura?»

«Dice: "del pueblo de Xaltocan para que el Señor Viento de la Noche descanse".»

«Alguien te dijo eso.»

«No, Señor Forastero. Discúlpeme, pero... ¿ve? —Me moví

lo suficientemente cerca para apuntar—. Este pico de pato aquí significa viento.»

«No es un pico de pato —dejó caer el hombre—. Es una trompeta por la cual el dios sopla los vientos.»

«¡Oh! Gracias por decírmelo, mi Señor. De todas formas, significa *ehécatl*. Y esta otra marca de aquí... todos estos párpados cerrados, significan *yoali*. Yoali Ehécatl, Viento de la Noche.»

«De veras sabes leer, ¿eh?

«Muy poco, mi señor. No mucho.»

«¿Quién te enseñó?»

«Nadie, Señor Forastero. No hay nadie en Xaltocan que enseñe este arte. Es una lástima, porque me gustaría aprender más.»

«Entonces debes ir a otra parte.»

«Supongo que sí, mi señor.»

«Te sugiero que lo hagas ahora mismo. Estoy cansado de oírte leer. Ve a otra parte, muchacho a quien llaman Topo.»

«Oh. Sí. Por supuesto, Señor Forastero. *Mixpantzinco.*»

«*Ximopanolti.*»

Volteé una vez más la cabeza para verlo por última vez, pero él estaba más allá del alcance de mi corta vista o había sido tragado por la oscuridad o simplemente se había ido.

Encontré en mi casa un coro formado por mi padre, mi madre y mi hermana, que expresaba una mezcla de preocupación, alivio, consternación y enojo por haber estado tanto tiempo solo en la peligrosa oscuridad, pero hasta mi madre se quedó callada cuando le expliqué cómo había sido detenido por el inquisitivo forastero. Ella estaba quieta y callada, y tanto ella como mi hermana miraban a mi padre con los ojos muy abiertos, quien a su vez me contemplaba con esa misma expresión.

«Te encontraste con él —dijo mi padre roncamente—. Te encontraste con el dios y él te dejó ir. El dios Viento de la Noche.»

Desvelado toda la noche, traté sin ningún éxito de ver como un dios al brusco viajero, polvoriento y cansado. Aunque si él había sido Viento de la Noche, entonces por tradición se me concedería el deseo de mi corazón. Solamente había un problema. Aparte de desear aprender a leer y a escribir correctamente, no sabía cuál *era* el deseo de mi corazón. O no lo supe hasta que se me concedió, si es que eso fue así.

✠

Ocurrió un día cuando estaba trabajando como aprendiz en la cantera de mi padre. No era un trabajo pesado; se me había nombrado vigilante de la gran fosa durante el tiempo en que todos los trabajadores, dejando sus aperos, iban a sus casas para la comida del mediodía. No es que hubiera allí mucho riesgo de robo por parte de humanos, pero si se dejaban los aperos sin vigilancia, los pequeños animales salvajes iban a roer las asas y mangos, salados por la absorción del sudor de los trabajadores. Un pequeño verraco-espín podía roer totalmente una pesada barra de ébano, durante la ausencia de los hombres. Por fortuna, mi sola presencia era suficiente para que esas criaturas buscaran su sal en la playa, ya que una manada de ellos hubiera podido invadir el lugar, pululando ante mí sin ser vistos por mis ojos de topo.

Ese día, como siempre, Tzitzitlini corrió fuera de casa para traerme mi *itácatl*, mi comida del mediodía. De un puntapié se quitó sus sandalias y se sentó a mi lado sobre la hierba de la orilla de la cantera, parloteando alegremente mientras yo me comía mi ración de pescaditos deshuesados y blancos del lago, enrollados en una tortilla caliente. Habían venido envueltos en una servilleta de algodón y todavía estaban calientes del fuego. Noté que mi hermana estaba también acalorada, aunque el día era frío. Su rostro estaba sonrojado y abanicaba el pecho con el escote cuadrado de su blusa.

Los rollos de pescado tenían un ligero saber agridulce poco común. Me pregunté si Tzitzi los había preparado en lugar de mi madre y si era por eso que estaba parloteando tan volublemente a fin de que no la embromara por su falta de pericia en la cocina. Sin embargo, el sabor no era desagradable, yo tenía mucha hambre y quedé completamente lleno cuando terminé de comer. Tzitzi me sugirió que me recostara y digiriera mi comida cómodamente; ella vigilaría para que no entrara ningún verraco-espín.

Me recosté sobre mi espalda y miré hacia arriba, hacia las nubes que antes podía ver claramente dibujadas contra el cielo; en ese momento no eran más que manchas blancas sin forma en medio de desdibujadas manchas azules. Para entonces ya me había acostumbrado, pero en un momento algo le pasó a mi vista que vino a perturbarme. El blanco y el azul empezaron a girar como un torbellino, al principio despacio y después más rápido, como si un dios allá arriba empezara a menear el cielo con un molinillo para *chocólatl*. Sorprendido, traté de sentarme. pero de pronto me sentí tan mareado que me caí de espaldas otra vez sobre el césped.

Entonces sentí una sensación muy extraña y debí de hacer algún ruido raro porque Tzitzi se inclinó sobre mí y miró mi rostro. A pesar de estar confundido, tuve la impresión de que ella estaba *esperando* que algo sucediera. La punta de su lengua se asomaba entre sus blancos dientes y sus ojos rasgados me miraron como buscando alguna señal. Luego sus labios sonrieron traviesamente, se pasó la lengua por sus labios y sus ojos se agrandaron con una luz casi de triunfo. Ella se veía en mis propios ojos y su voz parecía un extraño eco venido de muy lejos.

«Tus pupilas se han puesto muy grandes, mi hermano —dijo, pero como seguía sonriendo no me sentí alarmado—. Tus iris están apenas parduzcos, casi enteramente negros. ¿Qué ves con esos ojos?»

«Te veo a ti, hermana —dije y mi voz era torpe—. De alguna manera te ves diferente. Te ves...»

«¿Sí?», dijo sugestivamente.

«Te ves tan bonita», dije, pues no pude evitar decir eso.

Como cualquier otro muchacho de mi edad, se esperaba que

despreciara y desdeñara a las muchachitas, si es que me dignaba mirarlas, y por supuesto que a la propia hermana se la desdeñaba más que a cualquier otra muchacha. Sin embargo, yo me había dado cuenta desde hacía mucho que Tzitzi iba a ser muy bonita, aunque no lo hubiera oído comentar por los adultos, hombres y mujeres por igual, quienes detenían el aliento en cuanto lo notaban. Ningún escultor podría haber captado la gracia sutil de su joven cuerpo, porque la piedra o la arcilla no se mueven y ella daba la impresión de estar siempre en un movimiento continuo y ondulante, aun cuando estuviera estática. Ningún pintor podría mezclar los colores oro-cervato de su piel, ni el color de sus ojos: ojos de gacela delineados con oro...

Sin embargo, en aquel momento algo mágico había sido agregado y fue por eso que no pude rehusar a dar crédito a su belleza, aunque no lo deseara. La magia estaba visible alrededor de ella, como esa áurea neblina de joyas de agua, que, cuando sale el sol, inmediatamente después de llover, se ve en el cielo.

«Hay colores —dije con mi voz curiosamente torpe—. Tiras de colores, como la neblina de joyas de agua. Todas alrededor de tu cara, mi hermana. La incandescencia del rojo... y afuera de éste un púrpura encendido... y... y...»

«¿Sientes placer cuando me ves?», me preguntó.

«Sí, eso. Tú me lo das. Sí. Placer.»

«Entonces cállate, mi hermano, y deja que te dé placer.»

Jadeé. Su mano estaba debajo de mi manto. Recuerden que todavía me faltaba un año para usar el *máxtlatl*, taparrabo. Debí haber pensado que el gesto de mi hermana era muy atrevido, una afrentosa violación de mi intimidad, pero por alguna causa no me lo pareció y de cualquier modo me sentía demasiado torpe para levantar mis brazos y rechazarla. Casi no sentía nada, solamente me pareció que una parte de mi cuerpo estaba creciendo, una parte que nunca antes había notado que creciera. Había cambiado también, del mismo modo, el cuerpo de Tzitzi. Sus pechos jóvenes se veían ordinariamente como modestos montecillos debajo de su blusa, pero ahora podía ver sus pezones contraídos golpeando contra la fina tela que los cubría, como si fueran pequeñas yemas de dedos, ya que ella estaba arrodillada sobre mí.

Me las arreglé para levantar mi cabeza, que sentía muy pesada, y contemplé aturdido mi *tepule*, que ella manipulaba con su mano. Nunca antes se me había ocurrido que mi miembro pudiera salirse tan lejos de su vaina de piel y ésa fue la primera vez, pues antes solamente había visto su punta y la boquita lloriqueante, pero en ese momento al resbalar su piel hacia atrás, se convirtió en una columna rojiza con una terminación bulbosa. Se parecía más a un pequeño hongo lustroso que brotaba de la mano de Tzitzi, que lo asía apretadamente.

«*Oéya, yoyolcatica* —murmuró ella, con su rostro casi tan rojo como mi miembro—. Está creciendo, empieza a tener vida. ¿Ves?»

«*Toton... tlapeztia* —dije sin aliento—. Se está poniendo enardecidamente caliente...»

Con su mano libre, Tzitzi se levantó su falda y ansiosamente desenredó su *tzotzomatli*, bragas. Tuvo que abrir las piernas para quitarse esa ropa interior y yo vi su *tepili* lo suficientemente cerca como para poderlo distinguir claramente. Siempre había tenido entre sus piernas nada más que una especie de hoyuelo cerrado o plegado, que incluso era casi imperceptible pues estaba cubierto por un ligero vello de finos cabellos. Sin embargo, en ese momento su hoyuelo se estaba abriendo por sí mismo, como...

Ayya. Fray Domingo ha tumbado y roto su tintero. Vaya, y ahora se va. Sin duda se ha de sentir afligido por el accidente.

Aprovecho esta interrupción, para mencionar que algunos de nuestros hombres y mujeres tienen un vestigio de *ymaxtli*, que es el vello que cubre las partes privadas entre las piernas. Sin embargo, a la mayor parte de la gente de nuestra raza no les crece ni el más mínimo vello en esos lugares, ni en ninguna otra parte del cuerpo, a excepción del pelo exuberante de la cabeza. Incluso nuestros hombres casi no tienen barba y la abundancia de ésta en el rostro es considerado como una fea desfiguración. Las madres bañaban diariamente a sus bebés varones escaldándoles la cara con agua caliente con cal y generalmente, como en mi caso por ejemplo, este tratamiento abatía el crecimiento de la barba, en toda la vida de un hombre.

No regresa Fray Domingo. ¿Continúo mis señores o espero?

Muy bien. Entonces regreso a lo alto de aquella colina, tan distante y tan lejana, en donde yacía aturdido y maravillado, mientras mi hermana trabajaba afanosamente para tomar ventaja de mi condición.

Como decía, su *tepili* estaba abierto por sí mismo, desdoblándose como una flor, destacando sus pétalos rojizos suaves contra el perfecto color cervato de su piel, y los pétalos, incluso, relucían como si hubieran sido mojados con rocío. Para mí, la flor, por primera vez abierta de Tzitzitlini, daba una suave fragancia almizcleña como la de la llamada caléndula. Mientras tanto, todo alrededor de mi hermana, alrededor de su cara, de su cuerpo y de sus partes descubiertas, en toda ella, estaba todavía pulsando y reflejándose aquellas inexplicables listas y oleadas de varios colores.

Arrojó a un lado mi manto para que no le estorbara y levantó una de sus piernas para sentarse por encima de mi cuerpo. Se movía con urgencia, pero con el temblor de la nerviosidad y de la inexperiencia. Con una de sus pequeñas manos, sostenía trémulamente mi *tepule* apuntándolo hacia ella y con la otra parecía tratar de abrir lo más posible los pétalos de su *tepili* flor. Como ya he dicho anteriormente, Tzitzi ya había tenido práctica utilizando un huso de madera, como en ese momento me estaba utilizando a mí, pero su *chitoli*, membrana, todavía estaba muy cerrada. En cuanto a mí, mi *tepule*, por supuesto, no era todavía del tamaño del de un hombre, aunque

ahora sé que gracias a las manipulaciones de Tzitzi llegó a tomar más rápidamente las dimensiones de la madurez o más
allá de ésa, si es que otras mujeres me han dicho la verdad. De
todos modos, Tzitzi era todavía virgen y mi miembro por lo
menos era más grande que cualquier huso pequeño y delgado.

Hubo un momento de angustia y frustración. Los ojos de mi
hermana estaban apretados y respiraba como un corredor en
plena competición; se desesperaba porque pasara algo. Yo hubiera ayudado de saber qué era lo que se suponía que debía pasar y si no hubiese estado tan entorpecido en todo mi cuerpo
a excepción de esa parte. Entonces, abruptamente, la entrada
dio paso. Tzitzi y yo gritamos simultáneamente, yo por la sorpresa y ella, quizás, de placer o de dolor. Para mi gran pasmo
y de una manera que todavía no podía entender completamente,
yo *estaba dentro de mi hermana*, envuelto, calentado y humedecido por ella, y de pronto, cuando ella empezó a mover su
cuerpo hacia adelante y hacia atrás en un suave ritmo, me estaba dando gentilmente masaje.

Me sentía aturrullado, la sensación de mi *tepule* calientemen-
te asido y lentamente frotado se diseminaba por todas las partes de mi ser. La neblina de joyas de agua alrededor de mi hermana parecía crecer y brillar más, incluyéndome también a mí.
Podía sentir la vibración y el hormigueo en todo mi cuerpo. Mi
hermana estrechó algo más esa pequeña extensión de mi carne;
me sentía totalmente absorbido por ella, dentro de Tzitzitlini,
dentro del sonido de campanitas tocando. El placer creció hasta
tal grado que creí no poder soportarlo por más tiempo; entonces culminó con un pequeño estallido mucho más delicioso, una
especie de explosión suave, como las asclepias que al impulso del
viento desparraman y avientan sus esponjosas motas blancas. En
ese mismo instante, Tzitzi dejó de jadear y lanzó un gemido
suave y prolongado, y aun yo en mi gran ignorancia, en la media inconsciencia de mi propio y dulce delirio, comprendí que
provenía de su delicioso relajamiento.

Ella se desplomó a mi lado, y su cabello largo y sedoso cayó
como una oleada sobre mi rostro. Descansamos así por un tiempo, los dos jadeando con fuerza. Lentamente me di cuenta de
que los extraños colores se desvanecían y desaparecían, y que
en lo alto el cielo dejaba de girar. Sin levantar su rostro para
mirarme, apoyada sobre mi pecho, mi hermana me preguntó tímida y quedamente: «¿Te arrepientes, mi hermano?»

«¡Arrepentirme!», exclamé, espantado y haciendo volar a una
codorniz que se paseaba por el césped, cerca de nosotros.

«¿Entonces lo podemos hacer otra vez?», murmuró, todavía
sin mirarme.

Pensé acerca de eso. «¿Es que se puede hacer otra vez?»,
interrogué. La pregunta no era tan estúpidamente jocosa como
sonaba; dije eso en una ignorancia comprensible. Mi miembro
se había deslizado fuera de ella y yacía en ese momento mojado
y frío y había regresado a su tamaño natural. No se me puede
ridiculizar por haber pensado que quizás a un hombre sola-

mente le estaba permitido tener *una* experiencia como ésa en toda su vida.

«No quiero decir que en este momento —dijo Tzitzi—. Los obreros regresarán de un momento a otro. Pero, ¿lo podemos hacer otro día?»

«¡*Ayyo*, si podemos, todos los días!»

Levantándose sobre sus codos y mirándome a la cara, sus labios sonrieron de nuevo traviesamente. «¿Y tendré que engañarte la próxima vez?»

«¿Engañarme?»

«Los colores que viste, el mareo y el entorpecimiento. Cometí un gran pecado, mi hermano. Robé uno de los hongos de su urna en el templo de la pirámide y lo cociné con tus pescados.»

Ella había hecho algo osado y peligroso, aparte de pecaminoso. Los pequeños hongos negros eran llamados *teonanácatl*, «carne de los dioses», lo que indicaba cuán escasos y preciosos eran. Los conseguían, a un gran precio, en alguna montaña sagrada en lo más profundo de las tierras Mixteca y eran para que los comieran ciertos sacerdotes y adivinos profesionales, y solamente en aquellas ocasiones muy especiales en que fuera necesario ver el futuro. Seguramente hubieran matado a Tzitzi en el mismo lugar de haberla sorprendido hurtando algo tan sagrado.

«No, nunca vuelvas a hacer esto —le dije—. ¿Por qué lo hiciste?»

«Porque quería hacer... lo que acabamos de hacer y... temía que tú te resistieras si te dabas cuenta claramente de lo que estábamos haciendo.»

Ahora me pregunto si lo hubiera hecho. No me resistí entonces ni tampoco ni una sola vez después, y cada una de las experiencias subsecuentes fue igualmente maravillosa para mí, aun sin el encanto de los colores y el vértigo.

Sí, mi hermana y yo copulamos innumerables veces durante los años siguientes, mientras estuve viviendo todavía en mi hogar, cada vez que teníamos oportunidad, durante el tiempo de la comida en la cantera, en partes despobladas en la playa, dos o tres veces en nuestra casa cuando sabíamos que nuestros padres se ausentarían por un tiempo conveniente. Los dos aprendimos mutuamente a no ser tan desmañados en el acto, pero naturalmente los dos éramos inexpertos, ninguno de nosotros hubiera pensado en hacer estos actos con ninguna otra persona, así es que no sabíamos mucho cómo enseñarnos el uno al otro. No fue sino hasta mucho más tarde que descubrimos que lo podíamos hacer conmigo arriba y después de eso inventamos otras posiciones, numerosas y variadas.

Así, pues, mi hermana se deslizó fuera de mí y se desperezó lujuriosamente. Nuestros vientres estaban húmedos y manchados con un poco de sangre de la ruptura de su *chitoli* y con otro líquido, mi *omícetl*, blanco como el *octli*, pero más pegajoso. Tzitzi arrancó un poco de zacate seco y lo metió en la jarra de agua que había traído con mi comida y me lavó y se lavó hasta que quedamos limpios, para que no hubiera ningún rastro delator en nuestras ropas. Luego volvió a ponerse sus bragas, arregló nuevamente su ropa arrugada, me besó en los labios y diciéndome «gracias» —que debí haber pensado en decir yo primero— acomodó la jarra entre la servilleta del *itácatl*, y se fue corriendo por el herboso declive, brincando alegremente, como la niña que en realidad era.

Allí, entonces y de esa manera, mis señores escribanos, terminaron los caminos y los días de mi niñez.

I H S

✠

S. C. C. M.

Santificada, Cesárea, Católica Majestad,
el Emperador Don Carlos, nuestro Señor Rey:

Muy Eminente Majestad: desde esta Ciudad de Mexico, capital de la Nueva España, en este día de la Fiesta de la Circuncisión y primer día del Año de Nuestro Señor, mil quinientos
veinte y nueve, os saludo.

Por requerimiento de Vuestra Majestad, envío otra parte de
la historia del azteca.

Este vuestro siervo, necesariamente obediente aunque todavía
renuente, os suplica que le permitáis citar a Varius Géminus,
cuando en una ocasión él se acercó a *su* emperador con alguna
vexata quaestio: «Quien se atreve a hablar delante de ti, oh Cé-
sar, no conoce tu grandeza; quien no se atreve a hablar delante
de ti, no conoce tu bondad.»

Corriendo el riesgo de daros afrenta y de recibir de vos una
represión, os rogamos, Señor, que deis vuestro consentimiento
para abandonar este proyecto pernicioso.

En vista de que Vuestra Majestad ha leído recientemente, en
la porción previa de este manuscrito entregado en vuestras reales manos, la confesión casual del indio de haber cometido el
abominable pecado de incesto —un acto prohibido inclusive por
la escasa *lex non scripta* observada por sus propios compañeros
bárbaros; un acto proscrito en todo el mundo, lo mismo el civilizado que el incivilizado; un acto abjurado inclusive por gentes
degeneradas como los vascos, los griegos y los ingleses; un acto
imposible de condonar aunque fue cometido antes de que este
despreciable pecador tuviera conocimiento de la moral cristiana—, por todas estas razones, nos, confiadamente esperamos que
Vuestra Pía Majestad estuvieseis lo suficientemente asqueado
como para ordenar la inmediata suspensión del discurso del azteca, si es que no al azteca mismo.

Sin embargo, este humilde clérigo de Vuestra Majestad jamás
ha desobedecido una orden dada por su soberano. Así es que
nos, estamos añadiendo las páginas recolectadas desde nuestro
último envío. Continuaremos manteniendo a nuestros escribanos
e intérprete en esa ocupación obligada y odiosa para seguir añadiendo más páginas, hasta que llegue el día en que nuestro Muy
Estimado Emperador se digne poner fin a esto. Nos, solamente
os suplicamos y urgimos, Señor, para que cuando hayáis leído
la siguiente parte de la narración del azteca, que contiene epi-

sodios que podrían asquear a Sodoma, Vuestra Majestad reconsidere la orden de continuar con esta crónica.

Que la luz de Nuestro Señor Jesucristo ilumine y guíe por siempre los pasos de Vuestra Majestad, es el devoto deseo del misionero y legado de Su S.C.C.M.,

(ecce signum) ZUMÁRRAGA

TERTIA PARS

Durante el tiempo del que he estado hablando, cuando recibí el nombre de Topo, iba todavía a la escuela. Todos los días al atardecer, cuando se terminaba el día de trabajo, yo y todos los demás niños mayores de siete años de todas las aldeas de Xaltocan, íbamos o a la Casa del Desarrollo de la Fuerza o, junto con las niñas, a la Casa del Aprendizaje de Modales.

En la primera, los muchachos aguantábamos rigurosos ejercicios físicos y éramos instruidos en el *tlachtli*, juego de pelota, y en los rudimentos del manejo de las armas de guerra. En la segunda, nosotros y las niñas de nuestra edad recibíamos alguna instrucción un poco superficial acerca de la historia de nuestra nación y de otras tierras; una educación algo intensiva sobre la naturaleza de nuestros dioses y los numerosos festivales dedicados a ellos, como también se nos instruía en las artes del canto ritual, la danza y la ejecución de instrumentos musicales para la celebración de todas esas ceremonias religiosas.

Era solamente en esas *tepolchcaltin* o escuelas elementales, donde podíamos asociarnos de igual a igual con los niños de la nobleza y aun con unos pocos niños esclavos que habían demostrado poseer una inteligencia lo suficientemente brillante como para ser educados. Esta enseñanza elemental que comprendía cortesía, devoción, gracia y destreza, se consideraba un estudio más que suficiente para nosotros, los jóvenes de la clase media, y un alto honor para el corto número de niños esclavos que fueran considerados dignos y capaces de cualquier enseñanza.

Sin embargo, ningún niño esclavo, como tampoco ninguna niña aunque ésta perteneciera a la nobleza y muy pocos de nosotros los muchachos de la clase media podíamos aspirar a una mayor educación de la que nos era dada en las Casas de Modales y Fuerza. Los hijos de nuestros nobles usualmente dejaban la isla para ir a una de las *calmécactin*, ya que no había esta clase de escuelas en Xaltocan. Estas instituciones de alto aprendizaje estaban formadas por grupos de sacerdotes especiales dedicados a la enseñanza y sus estudiantes aprendían a ser sacerdotes, funcionarios gubernamentales, escribanos, historiadores, artistas, físicos o profesionales en cualquier otra rama. Entrar a un *calmécac* no estaba prohibido para cualquier muchacho de la clase media, pero la asistencia y pensión eran demasiado costosas para la mayoría de las familias, a menos que el niño fuera aceptado gratis o pagando muy poco, por haber demostrado una gran distinción en la escuela elemental.

Tengo que confesar que yo no me distinguí en lo más mínimo en ninguna de las dos Casas, ni en la de Modales, ni en la de Fuerza. Recuerdo que al entrar por primera vez en la clase de música de la Escuela de Modales, el Maestro de los Niños me pidió que, para poder juzgar la calidad de mi voz, cantara el verso de alguna canción que conociera. Así lo hice y él me dijo: «Verdaderamente es algo pasmoso de oír... aunque eso no es cantar. Probaremos con un instrumento.»

Cuando comprobó que yo era igualmente incapaz de arrancar una melodía a la flauta de cuatro hoyos o cualquier clase de armonía a los tambores de varios tonos, el exasperado maestro me puso en una clase en la que se estaba aprendiendo danza para principiantes, la danza de la Serpiente Estruendosa. Cada danzante da un pequeño salto hacia adelante, lanzando una patada, entonces brinca y gira a la vez para caer hincado sobre una rodilla, se voltea de nuevo en esa posición y luego da otro brinco y lanza otra vez una patada. Cada vez que patea produce un ruido y cuando una línea considerable de niños y niñas hace esto progresivamente, el sonido es un ondulante y continuo estampido y el efecto visual es el de una larga serpiente deslizándose en su camino de sinuosas curvas. O así debería ser.

«¡Es la primera vez que veo a una Serpiente Estruendosa torcida!», gritó la Maestra de las Niñas.

«¡Sal de la fila, Malinqui!», bramó el Maestro de los Niños.

Desde entonces, para él, yo fui Malinqui, el Torcido y desde ese momento mi única contribución a las clases de música y danza en la escuela fue golpear un tambor de concha de tortuga con un par de pequeños cuernos de venado o producir un «clic» con un par de pinzas de cangrejo, una en cada' mano. Afortunadamente mi hermana era la que mantenía en alto el honor de nuestra familia en aquellos eventos, ya que siempre se la escogía para bailar en solitario. Tzitzi podía danzar hasta sin música y hacer creer al espectador que oía música a su alrededor.

Empezaba a sentir que no poseía ninguna identidad, o que tenía tantas que no sabía cuál escoger para mí. En casa había sido Mixtli, la Nube; para el resto de Xaltocan había sido conocido generalmente como Tozani, el Topo; en la Casa del Aprendizaje de Modales, era Malinqui, el Torcido, y en la Casa del Desarrollo de la Fuerza, pronto llegué a ser Poyaútla, Perdido en Niebla.

Para mi buena fortuna no tenía ninguna deficiencia muscular, como la tenía en la música, pues había heredado de mi padre su estatura y solidez. Cuando tenía catorce años era más alto que mis compañeros dos años mayores que yo. Supongo que un hombre tan ciego como una piedra podría hacer los ejercicios de estirar, brincar, levantar pesas e incluso encontrar los dedos de sus propios pies para tocarlos con las manos sin doblar las rodillas; así es que el Maestro de Ejercicios Atléticos no encontró ningún defecto en mi ejecución hasta que empezamos a participar en deportes de equipo.

Si en el juego de *tlachtli* se hubiese permitido usar las manos y los pies, hubiera podido jugar, porque las manos y los pies se mueven casi por instinto, pero a la dura pelota de *oli* solamente se le podía pegar con las rodillas, las caderas, los codos o las nalgas, y cuando por casualidad podía ver la pelota, ésta no era más que una masa indistinta cuya velocidad hacía aún más borrosa. Consecuentemente y a pesar de que los jugadores llevábamos puestos protectores para la cabeza, fajas alrededor de las caderas, mangas de cuero grueso en las rodillas y en los codos y una gruesa colchoneta de algodón encima del resto de nuestros cuerpos, era constantemente golpeado por los rebotes de la pelota.

Peor todavía. Eran pocas las veces en que podía distinguir entre mis propios compañeros de equipo y los jugadores contrarios. Cuando, infrecuentemente, lograba pegarle a la pelota con la rodilla o con la cadera, no era extraño que la mandara a través del arco de piedra incorrecto, que estaba a la altura de la rodilla y que, según las reglas del complicado juego, se llevaban continuamente arrastrando de un lado a otro de los extremos de la cancha. Si meter la pelota a través de uno de los anillos de piedra colocados verticalmente y muy hacia arriba, en la línea media de cada una de las dos paredes que encerraban la cancha —lo que indicaba un triunfo inmediato a cualquiera de los dos equipos sin importar los puntos acumulados— era muy difícil para un jugador experto, para un perdido en la niebla como yo, hubiera sido un milagro.

No pasó mucho tiempo antes de que el Maestro de Ejercicios Atléticos me echara como participante. Fui encargado de la jarra de agua, del cucharón de los jugadores, de las espinas para picar y las cañas para succionar, con las cuales después de cada juego el físico de la escuela mitigaba el rigor de los jugadores, sacando la sangre negra y remolida de sus magulladuras.

Luego vinieron los ejercicios de guerra y la instrucción sobre las armas, bajo la tutela de un avejentado y cicatrizado *quáchic*, una «vieja águila», que era el título que se le daba a aquel cuyo valor ya había sido probado en el campo de batalla. Su nombre era Extli-Quani, o Glotón de Sangre, y tenía más o menos cincuenta años. Para estos ejercicios, a nosotros los muchachos no nos estaba permitido usar ninguna de las plumas, pinturas y otro tipo de decoraciones que utilizaban los verdaderos guerreros. Sin embargo usábamos escudos de madera o de cuero duro hechos a nuestro tamaño y trajes a nuestra medida iguales a los que usaban los verdaderos guerreros. Esas vestiduras estaban hechas de grueso algodón acojinado, endurecidas por haber sido empapadas en salmuera y nos cubrían del cuello a las muñecas y a los tobillos. Permitían una razonable libertad de movimiento y se suponía que debían darnos protección contra las flechas, por lo menos aquellas que eran lanzadas desde alguna distancia, pero, ¡ayya!, eran demasiado calientes, irritantes y sudorosas, como para tenerlas puestas más de un rato.

«Primero vais a aprender los gritos de guerra —decía Glotón de Sangre—. En el combate, por supuesto, estaréis acompañados por los trompeteros de conchas y por el batir de los tambores de trueno y de los tambores gimientes, pero hay que añadir a éstos vuestras propias voces gritando por la matanza y el sonido de los puños y armas golpeando los escudos. Yo sé por experiencia, mis muchachos, que un clamoreo ruidoso y aplastante puede ser un arma en sí. Puede sacudir la mente de un hombre, convertir en agua su sangre, debilitar sus tendones e inclusive vaciar su vejiga y sus tripas. *Vosotros* tenéis que hacer ese ruido y veréis que tiene un efecto doble: alentar la propia resolución hacia el combate y atemorizar al enemigo.»

Y así, semanas antes de que pudiéramos contemplar siquiera un arma simulada, gritábamos los chillidos del águila, los ásperos gruñidos del jaguar, los prolongados gritos del búho y el ¡alalalala! del perico. Aprendimos a brincar en fingido afán por la batalla, a amenazar con gestos amplios y con muecas, a golpear nuestros escudos en un tamborileo unido hasta que éstos estuvieron manchados con la sangre de nuestras manos.

Otras naciones tenían diferentes armas de las de nosotros, los mexica, y algunas de nuestras unidades de guerreros usaban armas para algunos propósitos en particular e incluso un individuo podía escoger siempre aquella arma en la que tuviera más habilidad. Éstas incluían la honda de cuero para arrojar rocas, el hacha de piedra despuntada, la cachiporra pesada cuya bola estaba tachonada de obsidiana dentada, la lanza de tres puntas hecha de huesos con púas a los extremos para desgarrar la carne, o la espada formada simplemente con la mandíbula del pez-espada. Sin embargo, las armas básicas de los mexica eran cuatro.

Para la primera escaramuza con el enemigo, a larga distancia, usábamos las flechas y el arco. Nosotros, los estudiantes, practicábamos mucho tiempo con los arcos y las flechas, guarnecidas por bolitas de hule suave.

«Supóngase que el enemigo está en aquel matorral de *nópaltin*. —Y el maestro indicaba lo que para mi nebulosa visión era solamente una mancha verde a unos cien pasos más allá de donde estaba—. Quiero un fuerte estirón a la cuerda y que las flechas tengan un ángulo hacia arriba de exactamente la mitad del camino entre donde se encuentra el sol y el horizonte debajo de él. ¿Listos? Tomad una posición estable. Apuntad hacia la nopalera. Dejadlas volar.»

Hubo un ruido silbante seguido por un gruñido general de todos los muchachos allí reunidos. Las flechas, arqueándose, habían caído en un agrupamiento razonable a una distancia de cien pasos del lugar donde se encontraba la nopalera y eso gracias a las instrucciones de Glotón de Sangre de estirar y de medir el ángulo. Todos los muchachos gruñían porque todos por igual habían errado el blanco; las flechas se habían ido a incrustar bastante lejos, a la izquierda de la nopalera. Nos volvimos para ver al maestro, esperando que nos dijera por qué habíamos fallado tan miserablemente.

Él señaló hacia las insignias de guerra que, rectangulares y cuadradas, estaban en sus estacas, clavadas aquí y allá en el terreno cerca de nosotros. «¿Para qué sirven esas banderas de tela?», preguntó.

Nos miramos unos a otros. Luego Pactli, el hijo del Señor Garza Roja contestó: «Son banderolas guías que son llevadas por nuestros diferentes jefes de unidades en el campo de batalla. Si nos separamos durante una batalla, las banderolas nos indicarán dónde reagruparnos nuevamente.»

«Correcto, Pactzin —dijo Glotón de Sangre—. Bien, y aquella otra de plumas, ¿para qué sirve?»

Hubo de nuevo otros intercambios de miradas y un largo silencio hasta que Chimali tímidamente aventuró: «La llevamos para demostrar lo orgullosos que estamos de ser mexica.»

«Ésa no es la contestación correcta —dijo el maestro—, pero al menos es una respuesta varonil y por eso no te doy una paliza. Sin embargo observad, muchachos, cómo flota ese pendón sobre el viento.»

Todos miramos hacia allí. No había suficiente aire ese día para sostener erguida la banderola. Colgaba en un ángulo hacia el suelo y...

«¡Está flotando a nuestra izquierda! —gritó otro muchacho con gran excitación—. ¡Nosotros *no* apuntamos mal! ¡El viento llevó nuestras flechas lejos del blanco!»

«Si no dieron en el blanco —dijo el maestro, secamente— es porque sí apuntasteis mal. Echar la culpa al dios del viento no os excusa. Al apuntar, debéis tener en cuenta todas las condiciones prevalecientes. Una de ellas es la fuerza y la dirección en la cual Ehécatl está soplando su trompeta de viento. Para este propósito está el pendón de plumas. Hacia el lado que éste cuelgue, os indicará hacia dónde llevará el viento vuestras flechas. La altura en que esté os dirá con cuánta fuerza las llevará el viento. Solamente con una larga práctica podréis aprender a juzgar. Quiero que todos marchéis hacia allá y recuperéis vuestras flechas. Cuando lo hayáis hecho, os giráis hacia acá, formáis una línea y me disparáis. El primero que me dé un golpe de flecha será eximido por diez días hasta de las palizas de las que sea merecedor.»

No caminamos sino que jubilosamente corrimos a recoger nuestras flechas y disparamos, pero ninguno de nosotros dio en el blanco.

Para pelear a una distancia más corta del alcance del arco y la flecha, teníamos la jabalina, una angosta y afilada hoja de obsidiana montada en un palo corto. Sin plumas, su exactitud y su poder de penetración dependían en ser lanzada con la mayor fuerza posible.

«Por eso la jabalina no se lanza sin ayuda —dijo Extli-Quani—, sino con este palo *atlatl* para aventar. Al principio este método os parecerá incómodo, pero después de mucha práctica sentiréis el *atlatl* como lo que en realidad es: una extensión del propio brazo y un redoblamiento de la propia fuerza. A una distancia de más o menos treinta pasos largos, se puede guiar la jabalina para agujerear limpiamente un árbol tan grueso como un hombre. Imaginaos, muchachos, lo que pasará cuando la lancéis contra un *hombre*.»

También teníamos la lanza larga, cuya punta terminaba en una obsidiana ancha y afilada y que se usaba para arrojar, para punzar, clavar y agujerear al enemigo antes de que éste estuviera demasiado cerca de uno. Pero para la inevitable lucha cuerpo a cuerpo usábamos la espada llamada *maquáhuitl*. Su nombre sonaba bastante inocentemente, «la madera hambrienta», pero era una de las armas más terribles y letales con que contábamos.

La *maquáhuitl* era una estaca plana de la madera más dura, de una longitud equivalente al brazo de un hombre y la anchura de la mano, y a todo lo largo de sus dos orillas estaban insertadas agudas hojas de obsidiana. El puño de la espada era lo suficientemente largo como para permitir que el arma se esgrimiera con una mano o con ambas, y estaba tallado de tal manera que los dedos del que lo sostenía se acomodaban con facilidad. Los fragmentos cortantes no estaban simplemente acuñados dentro de la madera, sino que como la espada dependía tanto de ellos, se les había agregado magia. Las cuchillas de obsidiana estaban sólidamente pegadas con un líquido encantado hecho de hule y de la preciosa *copali*, resina perfumada, mezclada con la sangre fresca donada por los sacerdotes del dios de la guerra, Huitzilopochtli.

Siendo tan brillante como el cristal de cuarzo y tan negra como Mictlan, el mundo de ultratumba, la obsidiana lucía inicua en la punta de una flecha, de una lanza o en el filo de una *maquáhuitl*. Apropiadamente convertida en hojuela, la piedra es tan afilada que puede cortar sutilmente como lo hace algunas veces una brizna de pasto o partir tan profundamente como lo hace un hacha. El único defecto de la piedra es que es muy quebradiza; puede hacerse pedazos contra el escudo o la espada del oponente. Sin embargo, en las manos de un guerrero experto, el filo de obsidiana de una *maquáhuitl* puede acuchillar carne y hueso tan limpiamente como un matorral de cizaña... y en toda gran guerra, como Glotón de Sangre nunca dejó de recordarnos, el enemigo no es otra cosa más que cizaña que debe ser abatida.

Así como nuestras flechas, jabalinas y lanzas de práctica eran cubiertas con hule en las puntas, nuestras *maquáhuime* de imitación eran inofensivas. Estaban hechas con madera ligera y flexible, para que la espada se rompiera antes de asestar un golpe demasiado fuerte. En lugar de los filos de obsidiana, las orillas estaban guarnecidas sólo con mechones de plumas suaves. Antes de que dos estudiantes libraran un duelo a espada, el maestro mojaba estas plumas en pintura roja, así es que cada golpe recibido se registraba tan vívidamente como una herida real y la marca duraba casi tanto tiempo como duraría la de una herida. En muy poco tiempo estuve tan pintado por estas marcas en cara y cuerpo, que me avergonzaba de verme así en público. Fue entonces cuando solicité una audiencia privada con nuestro *quáchic*. Era un anciano recio, duro como la obsidiana y probablemente sin más preparación en otra cosa que no fuera la guerra, pero no era un necio estúpido.

Me agaché para hacer el gesto de besar la tierra y todavía arrodillado dije: «Maestro Glotón de Sangre, usted ya sabe que mi vista es mala. Siento que usted está malgastando su tiempo y su paciencia tratando de enseñarme cómo ser un guerrero. Si estas marcas fueran heridas reales hace mucho que estaría muerto.»

«¿Y? —dijo él fríamente. Se agachó en cuclillas para alcanzarme—. Perdido en Niebla, te contaré acerca de un hombre a quien conocí una vez en Quatemalan, el país del Bosque Enmarañado. Esa gente, como quizá tú sepas, siempre está temerosa de morir. Ese hombre en particular corría a la menor señal de peligro; evitaba los riesgos más naturales de la existencia. Se refugiaba como un animalito en su madriguera, abrigado y protegido. Se rodeaba de sacerdotes, físicos y brujos. Comía solamente los alimentos más nutritivos y todas las pociones vivificantes de las que hubiese oído hablar. Nunca antes hombre alguno había cuidado tanto de su vida. Él vivía únicamente para seguir viviendo.»

Yo esperaba que siguiera hablando, pero no dijo nada más, así es que pregunté: «¿Y qué fue de él, Maestro Quáchic?»

«Murió.»

«¿Y eso es todo?»

«¿Qué más le puede pasar a cualquier hombre? Ni siquiera recuerdo su nombre. Nadie recuerda nada sobre él, excepto que vivió y finalmente murió.»

Después de otro silencio dije: «Maestro Glotón de Sangre, yo sé que si muero en una guerra mi muerte nutrirá a los dioses y ellos me recompensarán ampliamente en el otro mundo y quizá mi nombre no sea olvidado, pero ¿no podría estar en algún servicio en *este* mundo un poco antes de lograr mi muerte?»

«Nada más toma parte en una buena batalla, muchacho. Entonces si te matan en el próximo momento, habrás hecho *algo* con tu vida, mucho más de lo que hacen todos aquellos hombres que se afanan por seguir existiendo, hasta que los dioses se cansan de ver su futilidad y los echan al lugar del olvido. —Glotón de Sangre se levantó—. Aquí, Perdido en Niebla, está mi propia *maquáhuitl*, que por mucho tiempo me ha dado un buen servicio. Nada más siente su peso.»

Debo admitir que noté un estremecimiento cuando por primera vez tuve en mis manos una verdadera espada, y no el arma de juguete hecha de madera-balsa y plumas. Era atrozmente pesada, pero su propio peso parecía decir: «Yo soy *poder.*»

«Veo que la levantas y la giras con una mano —observó el maestro—. No muchos muchachos de tu edad podrían hacer eso. Ven acá, Perdido en Niebla. Éste es un *nopali* fuerte, tírale un golpe a matar.»

El *nopali* era viejo y grande casi del tamaño de un árbol, sus pencas verdes y espinosas parecían remos y su tronco parduzco era tan grueso como mi cintura. Con mi mano derecha solamente balanceé la *maquáhuitl* experimentando, dejándola caer y el filo de obsidiana mordió dentro del cacto con un hambriento *¡tchunk!* Saqué la cuchilla meneándola, la agarré con las dos manos y balanceándola muy por arriba y atrás de mi cabeza, la dejé caer con todas mis fuerzas. Esperaba que la espada rajaría más profundamente dentro del tronco, pero me llevé una verdadera sorpresa cuando lo cortó limpiamente, salpicando con su savia como una sangre incolora. El *nopali* titubeó un momento sobre su base desunida antes de derrumbarse hacia la tierra, y tanto el maestro como yo tuvimos que brincar rápidamente para evitar la nube de espinas agudas que se nos venía encima.

«¡*Ayyo*, Perdido en Niebla! —dijo Glotón de Sangre admirado—. A pesar de los atributos que te faltan, sí tienes la fuerza de un guerrero nato.»

Enrojecí de orgullo y de placer, sin embargo tuve que decir: «Sí, Maestro, puedo golpear y matar, pero piense en mis ojos, en mi mala visión. Suponga que hiriera erróneamente a uno de nuestros propios hombres.»

«Ningún *quáchic* al mando de guerreros novatos te pondría nunca en una situación así. En una guerra de conquista, tal vez estarías asignado a los acuchilladores de la retaguardia, cuyos cuchillos dan el misericordioso alivio a aquellos compañeros y enemigos que hayan sido dejados atrás, heridos, cuando la batalla ha avanzado. O, en una guerra florida, tu *quáchic* probablemente te asignaría a los amarradores, quienes llevan las cuerdas para amarrar a los prisioneros enemigos con objeto de poderlos traer para ser sacrificados.»

«Acuchilladores y amarradores —murmuré—. Obligaciones muy escasamente heroicas como para ganarme una recompensa en el otro mundo.»

«Tú hablaste de *este* mundo —me recordó el maestro severamente—, y de servicio, no de heroísmo. Aun el más humilde puede servir. Recuerdo cuando marchamos dentro de la ciudad insolente de Tlaltelolco para anexionarla a nuestra Tenochtitlan. Por supuesto que los guerreros de esa ciudad pelearon contra nosotros en las calles, pero sus mujeres, niños y ancianos decrépitos se apostaban en las azoteas y nos tiraban grandes rocas, avisperos llenos de enfurecidas avispas y aun plastas de sus propios excrementos.»

Aquí, debo aclarar, mis señores escribanos, que de entre las diferentes clases de guerras que peleábamos nosotros los mexica, la batalla contra Tlaltelolco fue un caso excepcional. Nuestro Venerado Orador Axayácatl simplemente se encontró en la necesidad de subyugar a esa arrogante ciudad, privarla de un gobierno independiente y por fuerza hacer que su pueblo rindiera lealtad a nuestra gran capital de Tenochtitlan. Como regla general, nuestras guerras contra otros pueblos no eran de conquista, no en el sentido en que sus ejércitos han conquistado toda esta Nueva España para hacerla una abyecta colonia de su Madre España.

No. Puede ser que venciéramos y doblegáramos a otra nación, pero no la borrábamos de la tierra. Peleábamos para probar nuestra propia fuerza y para exigir tributo de los menos fuertes. Cuando una nación se sometía y nos rendía lealtad a nosotros los mexica, ésta daba una porción de sus recursos y productos nativos —oro, joyas, especies, cacao, hule, plumas, lo que fuere—, los cuales se entregarían en lo sucesivo cada año en cantidades especificadas a nuestro Venerado Orador. Tendría también que mandar a sus guerreros a pelear junto con los mexica, cuando y en el caso en que fuera necesario.

Sin embargo, esa nación retendría su propio nombre y soberanía, su propio gobernante, su forma nativa de vida y su religión. Nosotros no imponíamos ninguna de nuestras leyes, costumbres o dioses. Nuestro dios de la guerra, Huitzilopochtli, por ejemplo, era nuestro dios y bajo su apoyo los mexica éramos un pueblo separado de los otros y por encima de ellos, y no compartíamos ese dios, ni lo *dejábamos* compartir. Todo lo contrario. En muchas naciones conquistadas encontramos nuevos dioses o diferentes manifestaciones de nuestros dioses ya conocidos, y, si parecían atractivos, nuestros guerreros traían copias de sus estatuas para ponerlas en nuestros propios templos.

Debo decirles también que existían naciones de las cuales jamás *pudimos* arrancar ni tributo ni lealtad. Por ejemplo, contigua a nosotros por el oriente estaba Cuautexcalan, la Tierra de los Riscos del Águila, usualmente llamada simplemente Texcala: los Riscos. Por alguna razón ustedes los españoles optaron por llamarla Tlaxcala, lo que a nosotros los mexica nos causa risa, porque esa palabra significa tortilla.

Aunque estaba totalmente rodeada por naciones aliadas con nosotros los mexica, y por lo tanto obligada a vivir como una isla cerrada, Texcala rehusó obstinadamente someterse en cualquier forma. Esto significó que tuvo que reducir muchas de las importaciones más necesarias para la vida. Si los texcalteca, aunque de mala gana, no hubieran trocado con nosotros su sagrada *copali*, resina, que era abundante en sus bosques, no hubieran tenido ni siquiera sal para dar sabor a sus comidas, ni hule para sus *tlachtli*, pelotas.

Entonces, nuestro Uey-Tlatoáni restringió severamente la cantidad de comercio entre nosotros y los texcalteca, siempre con la esperanza de dominarlos, así es que los tercos texcaltecas sufrían perpetuamente privaciones humillantes. Tuvieron que hacer bastar su magra cosecha de algodón, por ejemplo, lo que significaba que incluso sus nobles tenían que llevar mantos tejidos únicamente de una traza de algodón mezclado con cáñamo grueso o fibra de maguey; prendas que en Tenochtitlan serían llevadas solamente por esclavos o niños. Ustedes pueden comprender bien que Texcala abrigaba un odio duradero hacia nosotros los mexica y, como ustedes saben, finalmente tuvo fatales consecuencias para nosotros, para los texcalteca y para todo lo que es en este momento la Nueva España.

«Mientras tanto —me dijo el Maestro Glotón de Sangre en aquel día que conversamos— nuestros ejércitos, mantienen en este momento una pugna desfavorable con alguna otra obstinada nación del oeste. El Venerado Orador, que intentó la invasión de Michihuacan, la Tierra de los Pescadores, ha sido rechazado ignominiosamente. Axayácatl esperaba una fácil victoria, dado que los purémpecha siempre han estado armados con cuchillos de cobre, pero éstos han repelido y vencido a nuestros ejércitos.»

«¿Cómo, Maestro? —pregunté—. Una raza pacífica, con armas de cobre suave. ¿Cómo podrían oponerse a nosotros, los invencibles mexica?»

El viejo guerrero se encogió de hombros. «Puede ser que los purémpecha sean pacíficos, pero pelean con suficiente fiereza para defender su nativo Michihuacan de lagos, ríos y tierras de labranza bien regadas. También se dice que han descubierto algún metal mágico que mezclan con su cobre mientras está todavía fundido. Cuando la mezcla se forja en hojas, se convierte en un metal tan duro que nuestra obsidiana se quiebra contra de él como si fuera papel de corteza.»

«Pescadores y agricultores —murmuré— venciendo a los guerreros profesionales de Axayácatl...»

«Oh, lo intentaremos otra vez, puedes apostarlo —dijo Glotón de Sangre—. Axayácatl solamente quería tener acceso a esas aguas ricas en peces y a esos valles llenos de árboles frutales, pero ahora él querrá tener el secreto del metal mágico. Desafiará a los purémpecha otra vez y cuando lo haga, sus ejércitos requerirán de cada hombre que pueda marchar. —El maestro hizo una pausa y luego añadió significativamente—: Incluso los viejos inválidos *quáchictin* como yo, incluso aquellos que sólo pueden servir como acuchilladores y amarradores, incluso los incapacitados y los perdidos en niebla. Nos es menester estar adiestrados, endurecidos y listos, muchacho.»

Pero Axayácatl murió antes de poder armar otra invasión sobre Michihuacan, la nación que ahora forma parte de lo que ustedes llaman la Nueva Galicia. Bajo el mando de los subsiguientes Venerados Oradores, nosotros los mexica y los purémpecha logramos vivir dentro de una especie de respeto mutuo. No necesito recordarles, reverendos frailes, que su comandante Beltrán de Guzmán, que más bien parece un carnicero, sigue *todavía* tratando de subyugar a las intransigentes bandas de purémpecha alrededor del lago de Chapalan y en otros remotos rincones de Nueva Galicia, que aún se niegan a someterse a su Rey Carlos y a su Señor Dios.

He estado hablando de nuestras guerras de conquista tal y como fueron. Estoy seguro que aun su sanguinario Guzmán puede comprender ese tipo de guerra, aunque también creo que jamás podría concebir una guerra, como la mayoría de las nuestras, que dejara sobrevivir independiente a la nación derrotada. Pero ahora les hablaré de nuestras Guerras Floridas, porque parece que son incomprensibles para cualquiera de los hombres blancos. «¿Cómo? —he oído que ustedes preguntan—, ¿podía haber tantas guerras inmotivadas e innecesarias entre naciones *amigas*? ¿Guerras en las cuales ninguno de los dos bandos ni siquiera trató de ganar?»

Trataré de explicarlo.

Naturalmente, cualquier tipo de guerra, daba placer a nuestros dioses. Cada guerrero vertía al morir su sangre vital, la más preciosa ofrenda que podría hacer un humano. En una guerra de conquista, el objetivo era la victoria decisiva y por eso ambas partes peleaban para matar o ser matados. El enemigo era, como dijo mi viejo maestro, cizaña para ser abatida. Comparativamente, sólo tomábamos unos cuantos prisioneros que guardábamos para un sacrificio ceremonial más tarde. Sin embargo, no importaba cómo llegase a morir el guerrero, ya en el campo de batalla o en el altar del templo, su muerte se consideraba como una Muerte Florida, honrable para sí mismo y satisfactoria para los dioses. El único problema era, si lo ven ustedes desde el punto de vista de los dioses, que estas guerras de conquista eran más o menos infrecuentes. Aunque proveían muchas Muertes Floridas, mucha sangre para nutrir a los dioses y mandaban a muchos guerreros al más allá para servirles, esas guerras eran esporádicas. Entre tanto los dioses tenían que esperar muchos años pasando hambre y sed. Esto les desagradó y en el año Uno Conejo, nos lo dejaron saber.

Eso debió de suceder unos doce años antes de que yo naciera, pues mi padre lo recordaba vívidamente y lo comentaba con frecuencia, moviendo tristemente la cabeza. En aquel año, los dioses mandaron a toda esta planicie el más crudo invierno de que se haya tenido noticia. Aparte de un frío álgido y de vientos penetrantes, que mataron a muchos infantes, ancianos débiles, a nuestros animales domésticos e incluso a los animales salvajes, nevó durante seis días, lo que acabó con todas las siembras invernales. Entonces se vieron misteriosas luces en el cielo nocturno: bandas verticales de luces frías y coloreadas que oscilaban y que mi padre describía como «los dioses caminando ominosamente por los cielos, nada de ellos era visible, solamente sus mantos tejidos con plumas de garzas blancas, verdes y azules».

Eso fue solamente el principio. La primavera no sólo puso fin al frío sino que trajo un calor insoportable. Luego llegó la temporada de lluvias, pero éstas no vinieron y la sequía acabó con nuestras siembras y con nuestros animales que no habían muerto ya con las nevadas, y ni siquiera acabó todo ahí. Los siguientes años fueron igualmente crueles, sin lluvias y en sus alternativos fríos y calores. Con el frío nuestros lagos se congelaban, con el calor se hacían tibios, se convertían en sal amarga y así nuestros peces morían y flotaban vientre arriba llenando todo el aire con su hedor.

Continuó así durante cinco o seis años y la gente mayor, en mi juventud, todavía se refería a ello como los Tiempos Duros. *Yya ayya*, debieron de ser unos tiempos en verdad terribles, porque nuestra gente, nuestros orgullosos y honrados *macehualtin* se vieron reducidos a venderse a sí mismos como *tlatlácotin*, esclavos. Pues verán ustedes que las otras naciones más allá de esta planicie, en las sierras del sur y en las Tierras Calientes de las costas, no fueron destruidas por aquel clima catastrófico. Entonces ofrecieron en trueque parte de sus abundantes cosechas, pero esto no fue generosidad pues sabían que nosotros casi no teníamos nada que cambiar más que a nosotros mismos. Esos otros pueblos, especialmente los más inferiores y hostiles a nosotros, se complacían en comprar a «los fanfarrones mexica» como esclavos y a humillarnos todavía más, pagando por nosotros una cantidad mísera y cruel.

El trueque establecido fue de quinientas mazorcas de maíz por un hombre en edad de trabajar y cuatrocientas por una mujer en edad de aparearse. Si una familia tenía un niño que se pudiera vender, ese muchacho o muchacha era cedido para que el resto de la familia pudiera comer. Si la familia sólo tenía infantes, el padre se vendía a sí mismo. ¿Pero por cuánto tiempo podría una familia sobrevivir con cuatrocientas o quinientas mazorcas de maíz? Y cuando éstas se acabaran ¿quién o qué quedaría para ser vendido? Aun si los Buenos Tiempos regresaban de repente, ¿cómo podría sobrevivir una familia sin tener al padre para trabajar? De todas formas, los Buenos Tiempos no regresaron...

Todo eso ocurrió durante el reinado del primer Motecuzoma y él vació tanto su tesoro personal como el de la nación y luego abrió todos los almacenes y graneros de la capital, en un intento de aliviar la miseria de su pueblo. Cuando las sobras se acabaron, cuando no quedó nada excepto los agobiantes Tiempos Duros que todavía imperaban, Motecuzoma y su Mujer Serpiente reunieron su *tlatocan*, Consejo de Voceros de los ancianos, y también llamaron a los adivinos y profetas para que les aconsejaran. No puedo jurarlo, pero se dice que la conferencia fue así:

Un mago venerable que se había pasado meses estudiando el problema, echando los huesos y consultando los libros sagrados, anunció solemnemente: «Mi Señor Orador, los dioses nos han hecho pasar hambres para demostrar que *ellos* tienen hambre. No ha habido ninguna guerra desde nuestra última incursión a Cuautexcalan y eso fue en el año Nueve Casa. Desde entonces, no hemos hecho más que escasas ofrendas de sangre a los dioses; unos cuantos prisioneros de guerra guardados en reserva, el ocasional violador de la ley y de vez en cuando un adolescente o una virgen. Los dioses nos están pidiendo claramente más alimento.»

«¿Otra guerra? —meditó Motecuzoma—. Aun nuestros mejores guerreros están demasiado débiles en este momento como para poder marchar a una frontera enemiga, ya no digamos para abrir brecha en ella.»

«Es cierto, Venerado Orador, pero hay una manera de arreglar un sacrificio en masa...»

«¿Masacrando a nuestra gente antes de que se acabe de morir de hambre? —preguntó Motecuzoma sarcásticamente—. Toda la gente está tan delgada y seca que, probablemente, ni utilizando toda la nación se llenaría una taza completa de sangre.»

«Es cierto, Venerado Orador y en todo caso éste sería un gesto de mendicidad tan cobarde, que los dioses probablemente no lo aceptarían. No, Venerado Orador, es necesaria una guerra, pero una *clase diferente* de guerra...»

Más o menos fue así como me lo contaron y creo que éste fue el origen de las Guerras Floridas, y la primera de ellas se preparó así:

Como los más grandes poderes y los mejores estaban ubicados en el centro del valle, constituyeron una Triple Alianza: nosotros los mexica con nuestra capital Tenochtitlan en la isla, los acolhua con su capital Texcoco en la orilla oriental del lago y

los tecpaneca con su capital Tlacopan en la orilla oeste. Había
tres naciones menores hacia el sureste: los texcalteca, de quienes
ya he hablado, con su capital Texcala; los huéxotin con su capital Huexotzinco, y los una vez poderosos tya nuu o mixteca,
como los llamábamos, cuyos dominios se habían reducido hasta
constituir poco más de su capital, la ciudad de Chololan. Los primeros, eran nuestros enemigos; los otros dos hacía ya bastante
tiempo que nos pagaban tributo y, queriendo o no, eran nuestros aliados ocasionales. Sin embargo, estas tres naciones, así
como también las tres de nuestra alianza, habían sido devasta-
das por los Tiempos Duros.

Después de la conferencia de Motecuzoma con su Consejo
de Voceros, también conferenció con los gobernantes de Texcoco
y Tlacopan. Los tres juntos elaboraron y enviaron una proposición a los tres gobernantes de las ciudades de Texcala, Chololan
y Huexotzinco. En esencia decía algo así:

«Hagamos una guerra para que todos podamos sobrevivir.
Somos pueblos diferentes, pero todos sufrimos igualmente con
los Tiempos Duros. Los hombres sabios dicen que sólo tenemos
una esperanza de sobrevivir: saciar y aplacar a los dioses con
sacrificios de sangre. Por lo tanto, proponemos que los ejércitos
de nuestras tres naciones se enfrenten en combate con los ejércitos de sus tres naciones, en la llanura neutral de Acatzinco, a
una distancia segura de todas nuestras tierras, al sureste. La batalla no será de conquista, no para obtener territorios o soberanía, ni por matanza, ni por saquear, sino sencillamente para tomar prisioneros a quienes será otorgada la Muerte Florida.
Cuando todas las fuerzas que participen hayan capturado un
número suficiente de prisioneros para ser sacrificados a sus dioses, será comunicado mutuamente entre los jefes y se pondrá
fin inmediatamente a la batalla.»

Esa proposición, que ustedes los españoles dicen que es increíble, fue aceptada por todos, incluyendo los guerreros que
ustedes llaman «estúpidos suicidas» porque ellos peleaban por
un fin no aparente, a excepción del fin probable y repentino de
sus propias vidas. Pero dígame, ¿cuál de sus soldados profesionales rehusaría con cualquier excusa tomar parte en una batalla, prefiriendo las obligaciones tediosas del cuartel? Por lo
menos nuestros guerreros tenían el estímulo de saber que, si
morían combatiendo o en un altar extraño, ganarían la gratitud
de la gente por haber complacido a los dioses, así como también
merecerían de éstos el regalo de una vida de bienaventuranza en
el más allá. Y, en aquellos Tiempos Duros, cuando tantos morían
de hambre y sin gloria, un hombre tenía todavía más razón para
preferir morir por la espada o por el cuchillo de sacrificio.

Así fue como se llevó a efecto la primera batalla y la lucha
se desarrolló tal como se había planeado, aunque, por supuesto,
fue una marcha larga y melancólica desde cualquier parte hacia
la llanura de Acatzinco, así es que los seis ejércitos tuvieron que
descansar por un día o dos antes de recibir la señal para iniciar
las hostilidades. A pesar de que las intenciones eran otras, un
buen número de hombres fue muerto; unos inadvertidamente,

otros por casualidad y algunos por accidente; también porque algunos de ellos o sus oponentes pelearon con mucho ardor, ya que es muy difícil para un gucrrillero adiestrado para matar abstenerse de hacerlo. La mayoría, sin embargo, de común acuerdo golpeó con la parte ancha de la *maquáhuitl* y no con la orilla de obsidiana. Los hombres que quedaban atontados no eran matados por los acuchilladores, sino rápidamente atados por los amarradores. Después de dos días, solamente, los sacerdotes principales que marchaban con cada ejército, decretaron que ya se habían tomado suficientes prisioneros para satisfacer a los dioses y a ellos. Uno tras otro, los jefes desplegaron las banderolas que ya tenían preparadas, para avisar a los hombres que todavía estaban diseminados por la llanura. Los seis ejércitos se reunieron y marcharon penosamente a sus lugares de origen, llevando consigo a sus todavía más fatigados cautivos.

Aquella primera tentativa de Guerra Florida tuvo lugar a la mitad del verano que también era, normalmente, la temporada de lluvias, pero en esos Tiempos Duros era otra temporada seca interminablemente calurosa. Se había llegado asimismo a otro acuerdo entre los seis gobernantes de las seis naciones: todos ellos sacrificarían a sus prisioneros el mismo día en sus respectivas capitales. Nadie recuerda exactamente cuántos fueron, pero supongo que varios miles de hombres murieron aquel día en Tenochtitlan, en Texcoco, en Tlacopan, en Texcala, en Chololan y en Huexotzinco. Llámenlo coincidencia si ustedes quieren, reverendos frailes, ya que por supuesto Nuestro Señor Dios no estuvo implicado en eso, pero aquel día los cascos de las nubes se rompieron al fin, sus sellos se abrieron y llovió a cántaros en toda la gran planicie y los Tiempos Duros terminaron al fin.

Precisamente ese día, mucha gente en las seis ciudades se regocijó, por primera vez en muchos años, llenando sus panzas, cuando comieron los restos de los *xochimique* sacrificados. Los dioses se sentían satisfechos con ser alimentados debidamente, con la sangre de los corazones extraídos que se amontonaban en sus altares; los restos de los cuerpos de sus víctimas no eran usados por ellos, pero sí lo fueron por el pueblo hambriento allí reunido. Así, cuando el cuerpo todavía caliente de cada *xochimique* rodaba escalera abajo de la pirámide de cada templo, los carniceros que esperaban al pie lo tomaban para cortarlo en partes y distribuirlas a la ansiosa multitud apiñada en cada plaza.

Los cráneos fueron rotos y los sesos extraídos; los brazos y piernas cortados en partes manuables; los genitales y las nalgas, los hígados y riñones fueron cortados y separados. Estas porciones de comida no se arrojaron solamente a un populacho, no, fueron distribuidas en una forma admirablemente práctica a un pueblo que esperó con elogiable paciencia. Por razones obvias, los sesos se reservaron para los sacerdotes y los sabios; los brazos y piernas musculosos para los guerreros; las partes genitales para los matrimonios jóvenes; las nalgas y tripas menos significativas para las mujeres embarazadas, las madres que estaban amamantando y las familias con muchos niños. Los restos de cabezas, manos, pies y torsos, más huesos que comida, se pusieron a un lado para ser convertidos en fertilizantes para los sembrados y *chinampa*.

Realmente no sé si esta fiesta de carne fresca fue o no fue una ventaja adicional prevista por los que planearon la Guerra Florida. Todos los diferentes pueblos en estas tierras han estado por mucho tiempo comiendo cada animal de caza existente y cada ave o perro domesticado para ese fin. Habían comido lagartos, insectos y cactos, pero jamás a alguno de sus parientes o vecinos muertos durante los Tiempos Duros. Podía haber sido un desperdicio inconsciente de alimento disponible, pero en cada nación la gente hambrienta dispuso que sus compañeros muertos a causa del hambre fueran sepultados o quemados según sus costumbres. En aquel momento, sin embargo, gracias a la Guerra Florida, tenían una cantidad abundante de cuerpos de enemigos desconocidos —aunque fuesen enemigos solamente por exagerada definición— y por lo tanto no había por qué sentir remordimiento en comérselos.

En las siguientes guerras, nunca más se volvió a hacer una matanza tan inmediata ni un llenadero de panza como en esa ocasión. Pues desde entonces, jamás ha habido tanta gente hambrienta cuyo voraz apetito se debía mitigar. Así fue cómo los sacerdotes impusieron reglas y rituales para formalizar el acto de comer los cuerpos de los cautivos. Los guerreros victoriosos solamente comían un bocado sabroso, de algunas partes musculares, y lo tomaban muy ceremoniosamente. La mayor parte de la carne era repartida entre la gente muy pobre, generalmente los más humildes esclavos, o era para alimentar a los animales en aquellas ciudades que, como Tenochtitlan, mantenían una colección pública de animales salvajes.

La carne humana diestramente preparada, sazonada y cocinada, es, como la de cualquier otro animal, un platillo muy sabroso, y en donde no hay otra clase de carne ésta puede ser un sustento adecuado. Pero así como se ha podido comprobar que de los matrimonios cercanos entre los *pípiltin* no resulta una descendencia superior, sino todo lo contrario, yo creo que también se puede demostrar que los que comen carne humana tienden a una degeneración similar. Si la línea sanguínea de una familia mejora con un matrimonio que no se efectúa entre parientes, así la sangre del hombre tendrá más fuerza por la ingestión de la carne de otros animales. Por lo tanto, después de haber pasado los Tiempos Duros, la práctica de comer a los *xochimique* sacrificados vino a ser para todos, excepto para los pobres, los desesperados y degenerados, una observancia religiosa y además de las menores.

Como esa primera Guerra Florida tuvo tanto éxito, coincidencia o no, las mismas seis naciones siguieron guerreando a intervalos regulares, como una salvaguarda contra cualquier disgusto que los dioses pudieran sentir y para que éstos no volvieran a recurrir a los Tiempos Duros. Me atrevería a decir que nosotros los mexica teníamos muy poca necesidad de esa estratagema, porque Motecuzoma y los Venerados Oradores que le sucedieron no dejaron pasar grandes lapsos de tiempo entre las guerras de conquista. Era muy rara la vez que no teníamos un ejército en el campo de batalla, extendiendo nuestro dominio. Sin embargo, los acolhua y los tecpaneca, que tenían muy pocas ambiciones de esa clase, dependían de las Guerras Floridas para ofrecer Muertes Floridas a sus dioses. Así, pues, como Tenochtitlan había sido el instigador, seguía participando complaciente; la Triple Alianza contra los texcalteca, los mixteca y los huéxotzin.

A los guerreros no les importaba. En una guerra de conquista o en una Guerra Florida un hombre podía igualmente morir o tener la oportunidad de llegar a ser aclamado como héroe o ser incluso distinguido con una de las órdenes de campeonato, por haber dejado un número notable de enemigos muertos en el campo de batalla o por traer una gran cantidad de cautivos de la llanura de Acatzinco.

«Recuerda esto, Perdido en Niebla —dijo el Maestro Glotón de Sangre en aquel día que estuve hablando con él—. Ningún guerrero, ya sea en una guerra de conquista o en una Guerra Florida, espera contarse entre los que caen o entre los que son capturados. Tiene la esperanza de vivir durante toda la guerra y salir de ella como un héroe. Oh, no creas que te engaño, muchacho; claro que puede morir, sí, y mientras está todavía dominado por esta intensa emoción, pero si él entrara en la batalla *sin* esperar la victoria para su bando y la gloria para él, con toda seguridad moriría.»

Tratando de no parecer pusilánime quise convencerle de que no temía a la muerte, pero de que tampoco estaba muy ansioso de buscarla. De cualquier modo y en cualquier guerra estaría destinado, evidentemente, para cargos insignificantes como los acuchilladores o amarradores y esa clase de obligación, como le hice notar, podía ser asignada más bien a mujeres. «¿No sería mejor para la nación mexica y para la humanidad entera, que se me dejaran ejercer mis otros talentos?», le pregunté.

«Otros talentos, ¿cuáles?», respondió Glotón de Sangre.

Eso me hizo pensar de momento, pero luego sugerí que si, por ejemplo, yo tenía éxito y lograba la maestría en la escritura pintada, podría acompañar al ejército como historiador de campaña. Podría sentarme aparte, quizás en una colina desde la cual pudiera dominar todo el panorama y escribir la descripción de la estrategia de cada batalla, sus tácticas y sus progresos, para la futura ayuda de otros jefes.

El viejo guerrero me miró sardónicamente. «Primero me dices que no puedes ver a un oponente ni para pelear cara a cara y ahora que abarcarás de una mirada toda la confusa acción del choque entre dos ejércitos. Perdido en Niebla, si quieres ser una excepción para no tomar parte en las prácticas de armas de esta escuela, no te esfuerces. No te excusaría aunque pudiera. En tu caso hay un cargo impuesto sobre mí.»

«¿Un cargo? —dije perplejo—. ¿Un cargo de quién, Maestro?»

Me miró ceñudo, enfadado, como si lo hubiese cogido en un desliz y gruñó: «Un cargo que me he impuesto a mí mismo. Creo sinceramente que un hombre debe experimentar una guerra, o al menos una batalla, durante su vida. Porque, si sobrevive, todos los sabores de la vida vendrán a ser más ricos y más queridos. ¡Y ya basta! Espero verte mañana al atardecer en el campo, como de costumbre.»

Entonces me fui y volví a ir a los ejercicios y lecciones de combate en los días y meses que siguieron. No sabía lo que el destino me reservaría, pero sí sabía una cosa. Si iba a ser destinado a alguna obligación indeseable había sólo dos medios para evadirla: o demostrando ser incapaz de realizarla o mostrándome demasiado inteligente para eso. Y como los buenos escribanos, por lo menos, no somos cizaña para ser abatida por la obsidiana, mientras asistía sin quejas a las dos Casas de Modales y de Fuerza, en privado seguía trabajando más intensa y fervientemente para descifrar los secretos del arte de conocer las palabras.

✠

Haría el gesto de besar la tierra, Su Ilustrísima, si todavía se observara esa costumbre. En su lugar, enderezaré simplemente mis viejos huesos para levantarme en señal de saludo, tal como lo hacen sus frailes.

Es un honor tener de nuevo la graciosa presencia de Su Ilustrísima entre nuestro pequeño grupo y oírle decir que ha leído mi historia en las páginas recolectadas ya hace tiempo. Sin embargo, Su Ilustrísima busca ciertas respuestas a algunos sucesos anotados allí y debo confesar que sus preguntas me hacen bajar los párpados embarazosamente, aun con cierta vergüenza.

Sí, Su Ilustrísima, mi hermana y yo continuamos gozándonos mutuamente, durante todas las ocasiones que tuvimos en esos años de nuestro desarrollo, como ya lo dije hace poco. Sí, Su Ilustrísima, nosotros sabíamos que pecábamos.

Probablemente Tzitzitlini lo sabía desde el principio, pero como yo era más joven, me vine a dar cuenta gradualmente de que lo que estábamos haciendo era incorrecto. A través de los años, he ido comprendiendo que siempre nuestras mujeres conocen más acerca de los misterios del sexo y adquieren ese conocimiento antes que cualquier hombre. Sospecho que lo mismo sucede con las mujeres de todas las razas, incluyendo las suyas. Pues desde muy jóvenes se inclinan a susurrar entre ellas y a intercambiar secretos relativos a sus cuerpos y a los cuerpos de los hombres, y se juntan con las viudas y las viejas alcahuetas, quienes —quizá porque ya se les secaron sus jugos hace mucho tiempo— están regocijada y maliciosamente ansiosas de instruir a las doncellas jóvenes en las artes mujeriles de la astucia, las trampas y la impostura.

Lamento no tener todavía suficiente conocimiento de mi nueva religión cristiana, para saber todas sus reglas y censuras sobre este asunto, aunque he llegado a deducir que ninguna manifestación sexual es aprobada, excepto la ocasional copulación entre una pareja cristiana con el único propósito de producir un niño cristiano. Sin embargo, aun nosotros los paganos observábamos algunas leyes y muchas tradiciones, tratando de llegar a una conducta sexual aceptable.

Una doncella necesitaba permanecer virgen hasta que se casaba, a menos de que escogiera no hacerlo y formar parte de las *auyanime* que daban servicio a nuestros guerreros, lo cual era una ocupación legítima para cualquier mujer, aunque no exactamente muy honorable. También, ya sea por su propia voluntad o por haber sido violada, y por lo tanto descalificada para el matrimonio, podía llegar a ser una *maátitl* e ir a horcajadas por el camino. Había también algunas muchachas que mantenían estrictamente su virginidad para poder ganar el honor de ser sacrificadas en alguna ceremonia que necesitara de una virgen, otras porque deseaban servir durante toda su vida, al igual que sus monjas, asistiendo a los sacerdotes de los templos, aunque siempre había mucha especulación acerca de la naturaleza de esa asistencia y de la duración de su virginidad.

La castidad antes del matrimonio no era muy demandada a nuestros hombres, porque ellos tenían a su disposición las complacientes *máatime* y las mujeres esclavas, bien dispuestas o a la fuerza; y, claro, la virginidad de un hombre es difícil de comprobarse o refutar. Debo decirles que tampoco la virginidad de una mujer se puede comprobar o refutar, según me contó Tzitzi, si tiene suficiente tiempo para prepararse para la noche de bodas. Hay ancianas que crían pichones a los que alimentan con unas semillas rojas de una flor que sólo ellas conocen y venden los huevos de esas aves a las muchachas que quieren fingir ser vírgenes. Un huevo de pichón es lo suficientemente pequeño como para poder ser guardado fácilmente en lo más profundo de una mujer y su cáscara es tan frágil que un novio excitado puede romperla sin darse cuenta, y la yema de ese huevo en especial es del color exacto de la sangre. También las alcahuetas venden a las mujeres un ungüento astringente hecho del *tepetómatl*, que ustedes llaman gayula, que fruncirá el orificio más flojo y bostezante a la estrechez de una adolescente...

Como usted lo ordena, Su Ilustrísima, trataré de refrenarme y no dar tantos detalles específicos.

La violación de una mujer era un crimen muy poco usual entre nuestra gente, por tres motivos. Uno, era muy difícil, por no decir imposible, cometerlo sin ser pescado, puesto que nuestras comunidades eran muy pequeñas y todo el mundo se conocía, y los forasteros eran extremadamente notorios. También era un crimen un tanto innecesario, porque había muchas *máatime* y esclavas que podían satisfacer a un hombre realmente necesitado. Y por último, se castigaba con la muerte. También el adulterio se castigaba igual y el *cuilónyotl*, que es el acto entre hombres, y el *patlachuia*, que es el acto sexual entre mujeres. Pero esos crímenes, aunque probablemente no eran raros, casi nunca se descubrían, porque se necesitaba sorprender a la pareja en pleno acto. Esos pecados, como la virginidad, son de otra forma muy difícil de comprobar.

Quiero hacer notar, que aquí solamente estoy hablando de esas prácticas que entre nosotros los mexica estaban prohibidas o que rehuíamos. Excepto por la libertad y ostentación sexual específicamente permitidas en algunas de nuestras ceremonias de fertilidad, nosotros los mexica éramos remilgados y austeros en comparación con otros pueblos. Yo recuerdo que cuando viajé por primera vez entre los mayas, lejos de aquí hacia el sur, me escandalizó el aspecto indecente de algunos de sus templos, cuyos desagües para la lluvia en los tejados, tenían la forma de un *tepule* de hombre y durante toda la temporada de lluvias estuvieron orinando continuamente.

Los huaxteca, quienes viven al noroeste, en las playas del mar del este, son excepcionalmente groseros en materia de sexo. He visto en sus palacios frisos tallados con representaciones de las muchas posiciones en que un hombre y una mujer pueden hacer el acto sexual. Cualquier huaxtécatl hombre que tenga un *tepule* más grande que lo ordinario, lo lleva colgando sin cubrirlo con el taparrabo, aun en público e incluso cuando visita lugares más civilizados. Esa jactancia altanera de los hombres huaxteca, les da una reputación de desenfrenada virilidad, que quizás puedan merecer o no. Sin embargo, en aquellas ocasiones en que un grupo de guerreros huaxteca era capturado y puesto a la venta en el mercado de esclavos de Azcapotzalco, he visto a nuestras mujeres de la nobleza mexica, veladas y subrepticiamente paradas a un lado de la multitud, haciendo señas a sus sirvientas para hacer una oferta sobre tal o cual huaxtécatl en el lugar de la venta.

Los purémpecha de Michihuacan, hacia el oeste de aquí, son más indulgentes o relajados en materia de sexo. Por ejemplo, el acto entre dos hombres no solamente no es castigado, sino que es perdonado y aceptado. Incluso ha sido representado en su escritura-pintada. ¿Sabían ustedes que el glifo de las partes *tepili* de una mujer está representado por una concha de caracol? Bueno, pues los purémpecha ilustraban sin ninguna vergüenza el acto del *cuilónyotl* con un dibujo de un hombre desnudo con una concha de caracol cubriendo sus propios órganos.

En cuanto al acto entre mi hermana y yo, la palabra que usted usa ¿es incesto? Sí, Su Ilustrísima, creo que esta relación estaba prohibida por todas las naciones conocidas. Sí, corríamos el riesgo de que nos mataran si éramos sorprendidos haciéndolo. Las leyes prescribían unas formas particularmente espantosas de ejecutar, por copulación entre un padre y su hija, madre e hijo, tío y sobrina, tía y sobrino y demás. Pero estas uniones sólo nos estaban prohibidas a nosotros los *macéhualtin*, quienes constituíamos la mayor parte de la población. Como ya hice notar antes, había familias nobles que se esforzaban en preservar lo que ellos llamaban la pureza de su linaje, efectuando matrimonios solamente entre los parientes de consaguinidad más cercana, aunque nunca fue evidente que esto mejorara las generaciones subsiguientes. Y por supuesto, ninguna ley, ninguna tradición, ninguna gente en general hizo mención de lo que pasaba entre la clase esclava: rapto, incesto, adulterio, lo que ustedes quieran.

Ah, pero usted me pregunta que cómo mi hermana y yo

pudimos evitar ser descubiertos durante nuestra larga complacencia en ese pecado. Bueno, pues habiendo sido castigados por nuestra madre muy severamente por cosas más insignificantes, ambos habíamos aprendido a ser en extremo discretos. Llegó un tiempo en que tuve que partir por varios meses lejos de Xaltocan y deseé a Tzitzi y ella me deseó. Pero cada vez que regresaba a casa, le daba un beso fraternal en la mejilla y nos sentábamos uno aparte del otro, escondiendo nuestro fuego interior, mientras yo contaba a mis padres y a otros parientes y amigos deseosos de noticias, mis andanzas en el mundo más allá de nuestra isla. Podían pasar uno o varios días antes de que por fin Tzitzi y yo pudiéramos tener una oportunidad para estar juntos en privado, en secreto y fuera de todo peligro. Ah, pero entonces era el desnudarse rápido, las frenéticas caricias, el primer relajamiento como si los dos descansáramos sobre la ladera de nuestro propio volcán; pequeño, secreto y en erupción, y después las caricias más lentas, las más suaves y exquisitas explosiones...

Sin embargo, mis ausencias de la isla llegaron después. Mientras, mi hermana y yo no fuimos sorprendidos ni una sola vez en el acto. Claro que se nos hubiera echado una calamidad encima si, como los cristianos, hubiéramos concebido una criatura en cada copulación. Yo nunca había pensado ni siquiera en esa posibilidad, pues, ¿qué muchacho puede imaginarse siendo padre? Sin embargo, Tzitzi era una mujer y sabía mucho respecto a estas cosas y así había tomado precauciones contra esa contingencia. Todas esas viejas de las que he hablado vendían secretamente a las doncellas, como nuestros boticarios lo vendían abiertamente a las parejas casadas que no querían tener un niño cada vez que iban a la cama, un polvo molido del *tlatlaohuéhuetl*, que es un tubérculo semejante al *camotli*, pero cien veces mayor; lo que ustedes llaman en español el barbasco. Cualquier mujer que diariamente tome una dosis del polvo del barbasco no corre el riesgo de concebir un indeseado...

Perdóneme, Su Ilustrísima. No tenía idea de que estaba diciendo algo sacrílego. Por favor, siéntese usted otra vez.

Debo decir que, por mucho tiempo, estuve personalmente corriendo un gran riesgo, aun estando a una distancia segura de Tzitzi. Durante nuestras clases guerreras en la Casa del Desarrollo de la Fuerza, un grupo de seis a ocho muchachos eran mandados regularmente al atardecer, a tomar sitio en los campos o bosques en una supuesta «guardia para prevenir un ataque por sorpresa contra la escuela». Ésa era una obligación muy aburrida, así es que generalmente nos entreteníamos jugando *patoli* con los frijoles saltarines.

Uno de los muchachos, no recuerdo quién era, descubrió el acto solitario y ni corto ni perezoso, no siendo egoísta con su descubrimiento, inmediatamente nos mostró ese arte a todos los demás. Desde entonces los muchachos jamás volvieron a llevar sus frijoles *choloani* a la guardia, para jugar llevaban ya su equipo unido a sus cuerpos. Hacíamos competiciones y cruzábamos apuestas sobre la cantidad de *omícetl* que cada uno de nosotros podía eyacular, el número de veces que lo podíamos hacer sucesivamente y el tiempo que necesitábamos para tener un nuevo resurgimiento de potencia. Igual que cuando éramos más jóvenes y competíamos sobre quién podía escupir u orinar más lejos o más copiosamente. Sin embargo, esta nueva competición era muy peligrosa para mí.

Verán, generalmente llegaba a esos juegos poco después del prolongado abrazo de Tzitzi y como ya se pueden imaginar, mi reserva de *omícetl* se había ya vaciado, por no mencionar mi capacidad de erección. Así es que mis eyaculaciones eran muy pocas y con un débil goteo en comparación con las de los otros muchachos, y frecuentemente no conseguía la erección de mi *tepule*. Por un tiempo, mis compañeros me ridiculizaron y se burlaron de mí, pero más tarde empezaron a mirarme con preocupación e incluso con lástima. Algunos de los muchachos más compasivos me sugirieron varios remedios como comer carne cruda, sudar mucho en la casa de vapor; cosas como ésas. Mis dos amigos, Tlatli y Chimali, habían descubierto que podían alcanzar unas sensaciones más excitantes si cada uno de ellos manipulaba el *tepule* del otro. Así es que ellos me sugirieron...

¿Suciedad? ¿Obscenidad? ¿Sus oídos se sienten lastimados al oírme? Estoy muy apenado si perturbo a Su Ilustrísima y a ustedes, señores escribanos, pero no estoy relatando estos sucesos triviales y lascivos nada más porque sí. Todos ellos formaron parte de otros más importantes, que llegaron más tarde como resultado de éstos. ¿Podrían escucharme hasta el final?

Finalmente algunos de los muchachos mayores tuvieron la idea de poner sus *tépultin* en donde debían. Unos cuantos de nuestro compañeros, incluyendo a Pactli, el hijo del gobernador, fueron a explorar una aldea que estaba muy cerca de nuestra escuela. Allí encontraron y contrataron a una mujer esclava de unos veintitantos años o quizá treinta. De alguna manera su nombre fue muy apropiado, pues se llamaba Teteo-Temacáliz, que quiere decir Regalo de los Dioses. De un momento a otro, ella llegó a ser un regalo para los puestos de guardia, que visitaba diariamente.

Pactli tenía la autoridad para ordenarle presentarse, pero no creo que hubiese sido necesario de que le ordenara nada, pues demostró ser muy complaciente e incluso una participante vigorosa en los juegos sexuales. *Ayya*, supongo que la pobre perra tenía razón. Era desaliñada, regordeta, sus muslos eran un amasijo y tenía una protuberancia cómica por nariz, así es que ella no tenía muchas esperanzas de casarse ni siquiera con un hombre de su propia clase *tlacotli*. Así fue como tomó su nueva ocupación de *maátitl* con un abandono lujurioso.

Como ya he dicho, éramos de seis a ocho muchachos acampando cada tarde en nuestros puestos de guardia. Cuando Regalo de los Dioses había ya servido a cada uno de éstos, el primero de la fila volvía a empezar y daban la vuelta otra vez. Regalo de los Dioses era tan insaciablemente lujuriosa que hubiera podido seguir así toda la noche, pero después de un rato de esa actividad estaba tan llena de *omícetl*, tan pegajosa y babosa, dando ya un hedor como de pescado enfermo, que los mismos muchachos de común acuerdo la mandaban a su casa. Aunque de todos modos, la siguiente tarde volvía allí otra vez completamente desnuda, mostrándose ampliamente abierta y ansiosa por comenzar.

Yo no había tomado parte en esas cosas, pues no había hecho otra cosa más que mirar; hasta que una tarde cuando Pactli había terminado de usar a Regalo de los Dioses, le susurró algo a ella y levantándose se acercó a donde yo estaba sentado.

«Tú eres Topo, ¿verdad? —me dijo mirándome con lascivia—. Pactzin me dice que tienes un problema.» Hizo movimientos tentadores con sus partes *tepili* sueltas y empapadas, exactamente enfrente de mi cara sonrojada. «Quizá tu lanza estaría más feliz si estuviera dentro de mí y no en tu puño.» Masculé que no la necesitaba para nada en ese momento, pero no podía protestar demasiado con seis o siete compañeros parados a mi alrededor y sonriendo maliciosamente de mi turbación.

«¡*Ayyo*! —exclamó ella, después de que con sus manos había aventado mi manto y desamarrado mi taparrabo—. ¡De veras que el tuyo es magnífico, joven Topo! —Lo sopesó en la palma de su mano—. Aun sin despertar es más grande que los *tépultin* de todos los muchachos grandes. Es mayor aun que el del noble señor Pactzin.» Mis compañeros se reían y se codeaban unos a otros. No levanté a ver al hijo de Garza Roja, pero sabía que Regalo de los Dioses me acababa de ganar un enemigo.

«Claro —dijo ella— que un benigno *macehuali* no le negará un placer a una humilde *tlacotli*. Deja armar mi guerrero con tu lanza.» Ella cogió mi miembro entre la masa de sus grandes pechos, apachurrándolos juntos con un brazo y empezando a darme masaje con ellos. No pasó nada. Entonces me hizo otras cosas, atenciones con las que no había favorecido ni siquiera a Pactli. Él se volvió y con cara furiosa se alejó altivamente. Pero no pasó nada...

Sí, sí, ya me apresuro a terminar con este episodio.

Regalo de los Dioses por fin se dio por vencida. Aventó mi miembro contra mi vientre y dijo con petulancia: «El orgulloso cachorro de guerrero guarda su virginidad sin duda para una mujer de su propia clase.» Y dando una patada en el suelo me dejó abruptamente agarrando a otro muchacho y dejándose caer a tierra con él, empezó a caracolear como un venado picado por una avispa...

¡Ay de mí! Su Ilustrísima me pidió que hablara de sexo y *pecado*, ¿no es así, reverendos frailes?, pero parece que no puede escuchar por mucho tiempo sin ponerse tan encarnado como su sotana y sin que huya fuera de aquí. Por lo menos me hubiera gustado que supiera hacia dónde se dirigía mi cuento. Aunque naturalmente se me olvidaba que Su Ilustrísima puede leerlo cuando esté en calma. Entonces, ¿puedo proseguir, mis señores?

Chimali se vino a sentar junto a mí y me dijo: «Yo no soy de los que se ríen de ti, Topo, a mí tampoco me excita.»

«No es tanto por lo fea que es», dije a Chimali y le expliqué lo que mi padre me había dicho recientemente acerca de esa enfermedad llamada *nanaua* que puede venir de una práctica sexual sin higiene, esa enfermedad que aflige tanto a sus soldados españoles y que tan fatalmente llaman «el fruto de la tierra».

«A las mujeres que hacen una carrera decente de su sexo no hay motivo alguno para temerlas —le dije a Chimali—. Las *auyanime* de nuestros guerreros, por ejemplo, siempre se conservan limpias y son revisadas periódicamente por los físicos del ejército. Sin embargo es mejor evitar a las *máatime* que se acuestan con cualquiera y con gran cantidad de hombres. La enfermedad proviene de que esas partes íntimas no se conservan limpias, y observa ahí a esa mujer, ¿quién puede saber con cuántos esclavos escuálidos se ha acostado antes de llegar a nosotros? Si alguna vez te llegas a infectar con el *nanaua*, no tendrás curación. Puede pudrir tu *tepule* hasta que se caiga por sí mismo y puede infectar tu cerebro hasta convertirte en un idiota tarado y tartamudo.»

«¿Es verdad todo eso, Topo? —preguntó Chimali con el rostro ceniciento. Luego miró al muchacho y a la mujer que, sudorosos, se revolcaban en el suelo—. Y yo que pensaba acostarme con ella, nada más que para que no se mofaran de mí, pero prefiero pasar por afeminado a llegar a ser un idiota.»

Y se fue inmediatamente a informar a Tlatli. Ellos debieron de correr la voz, porque desde esa tarde la fila para putear disminuyó considerablemente y, en la casa de vapor, vi muy seguido a mis compañeros examinándose a sí mismos para ver si no tenían síntomas de putrefacción. Así fue como la mujer llegó a ser llamada por una variante de su nombre: Teteo-Tlayo, Desecho de los Dioses. A pesar de todo esto, algunos cachorros siguieron acostándose con ella y uno de ésos fue Pactli. Mi desprecio por él debió de ser tan obvio como su disgusto por mí, pues un día se me acercó y me dijo amenazadoramente:

«¿Así es que el Topo es tan cuidadoso de su salud como para no revolcarse en la tierra con una *máatitl*? Sé que sólo es una simple excusa para tu miserable impotencia, pero ha implicado una crítica a *mi* conducta y te prevengo de no calumniar a tu futuro hermano. —Bostecé notoriamente—. Sí, antes de que se me pudra como tú has predicho, pienso casarme con tu hermana y aunque llegue a ser un idiota tarado, ella no podrá rehusar a un *pili*. Claro que prefiero que llegue a mí por su propia voluntad. Así es que te lo advierto, mi futuro hermano, nunca le digas a Tzitzitlini mi diversión con Desecho de los Dioses o te mataré.»

Se alejó a grandes zancadas sin esperar mi respuesta, que, en cualquier caso no se la hubiese podido dar en ese momento, pues me quedé mudo del susto. No es que le tuviera miedo a Pactli, ya que yo era el más alto de los dos y probablemente el más fuerte, pero aunque él hubiese sido un débil enano enfermizo era el hijo de nuestro *tecutli* y me había ganado su inquina. De hecho había estado viviendo con miedo desde que los muchachos empezaron primero con sus juegos sexuales solitarios y luego a aparearse con Desecho de los Dioses. Mi ínfima actuación y las burlas de que fui objeto, esas vergüenzas, no hirieron tanto mi pueril vanidad sino más bien pusieron el miedo en mi corazón. En verdad, tenía que pasar como un impotente y por un afeminado. Pactli no era muy listo, pero si hubiera llegado a sospechar que la verdadera razón de mi aparentemente débil sexualidad se debía a que la estaba prodigando en algún otro lado, no hubiera sido tan estúpido como para no imaginarse en dónde y sobre todo, en nuestra pequeña isla, no le hubiera tomado mucho tiempo averiguar de que no me estaba citando con ninguna mujer excepto...

Tzitzitlini había notado por primera vez el interés de Pactli cuando ella era solamente un capullo en flor, cuando había visitado el palacio para asistir a la ejecución de su hermana, la princesa adúltera. Más recientemente, Pactli había visto a Tzitzi bailar en la primavera, en la fiesta del Gran Despertar; ella había ido a la cabeza de los danzantes en la plaza de la pirámide y él quedó tontamente prendado y enamorado de ella. Desde entonces, él trató varias veces de encontrarse con ella en público y de hablarle, una violación a las costumbres que no se permitía a ningún hombre, aunque fuera un *pili*. También había inventado excusas para visitar nuestra casa, dos o tres veces, «para discutir con Tepetzalan asuntos relacionados con la cantera», y así poder entrar. Sin embargo, la fría recepción que le daba Tzitzitlini y su visible aversión hacia él, hubiera sido suficiente para que cualquier hombre joven con buenos sentimientos se alejara voluntariamente.

Y en esos momentos el vil Pactli me decía que se iba a *casar* con Tzitzi. Cuando regresé a casa aquella noche, después de que todos nos sentamos alrededor de nuestra cena y de que nuestro padre delante de nosotros dio gracias a los dioses por la comida, solté bruscamente.

«Pactli me dijo que piensa tomar a Tzitzitlini por esposa. No puntualizó si ella lo aceptaba o si la familia daba su consentimiento, sino que afirmó que iba a hacerlo.»

Mi hermana se envaró y me miró con fijeza. Pasó su mano ligeramente a través de su rostro, como siempre lo hacen todas nuestras mujeres cuando algo inesperado ocurre. Nuestro padre pareció incómodo, pero nuestra madre siguió comiendo plácidamente y con la misma placidez dijo: «Él ha hablado sobre eso, Mixtli, sí. Pactzin pronto terminará su *telpochcali*, escuela, pero todavía tendrá que pasar varios años en la *calmécac*, escuela, antes de que pueda tomar esposa.»

«Él no puede tomar a Tzitzi —dije—. Pactli es estúpido, avaricioso y malvado.»

Nuestra madre, inclinándose a través del mantel, me abofeteó el rostro con fuerza. «Esto es por hablar irrespetuosamente de nuestro futuro gobernador. ¿Quién eres tú? ¿En dónde está tu alta clase social como para que te atrevas a difamar a un noble?»

Tragándome peores palabras dije: «No soy el único en esta isla que sabe que Pactli es un ser depravado y vil...»

Ella me volvió a pegar. «Tepetzalan —dijo nuestra madre—. Si este joven desobediente dice una palabra más, tendrás que corregirlo. —Y a mí me dijo: Cuando el hijo *pili* del Señor Garza Roja se case con Tzitzitlini, todos nosotros seremos también *pípiltin*. ¿En dónde están tus grandes proyectos? Sólo tienes la intil pretensión de estudiar las palabras-pintadas ¿y crees acaso que con eso podrás brindar tanta eminencia a tu familia?»

Nuestro padre se aclaró la garganta y dijo: «No me importa mucho el -tzin para nuestros nombres, pero no me gusta la descortesía y la infamia. El rehusar a un hombre noble una petición, especialmente declinando el honor que Pactli nos hace al pedir la mano de nuestra hija, sería un insulto para él, una desgracia para todos nosotros con la que no podríamos vivir, y si es que nos dejaban vivir, todos nosotros tendríamos que irnos de Xaltocan.»

«No, no todos nosotros —por primera vez Tzitzi habló y lo hizo con firmeza—. Me iría yo sola. Si esa bestia degenerada de Pactli... No, no levantes la mano contra mí, madre. Ya soy una mujer y te devolvería el golpe.»

«¡Tú eres mi hija y ésta es mi casa!», gritó nuestra madre.

«Hijos, ¿pero qué ha pasado con vosotros?», suplicó mi padre.

«Solamente digo esto —continuó Tzitzi—. Si Pactli me pide y tú aceptas, ni tú ni él me volveréis a ver. Me iré de la isla para siempre. Si no puedo conseguir prestado o robar un *acali*, me iré nadando. Si no alcanzo a llegar a tierra firme, me ahogaré. Ni Pactli ni ningún otro hombre me tocará excepto aquel al que *yo* me quiera entregar.»

«En todo Xaltocan —refunfuñó nuestra madre— no hay otra hija tan desagradecida, tan desobediente y desafiante, tan...»

Esta vez mi padre no la dejó terminar cuando dijo, y lo hizo en forma solemne: «Tzitzitlini, si tus palabras han sido escuchadas fuera de estas paredes, ni siquiera yo podría perdonarte o evitar el castigo que mereces. Serías desnudada, golpeada y tu cabeza rapada. Si yo no lo hiciera, lo harían todos nuestros vecinos como un ejemplo para sus propios hijos.»

«Lo siento, padre —dijo ella en tono más bajo de voz—. Tienes que escoger entre una hija desobligada o no tener hija.»

«Le doy gracias a los dioses porque no tengo por qué hacerlo esta noche. Como tu madre ya dijo, faltan todavía algunos años para que el joven Señor Alegría pueda casarse. Así es que no hablemos más del asunto, ni con ira ni en ninguna otra forma. Muchas cosas pueden pasar de aquí a entonces.»

Nuestro padre tenía razón: muchas cosas podían pasar. Yo no sabía si Tzitzi pensaba realmente hacer todo lo que dijo y no tuve oportunidad de interrogarla esa noche ni al día siguiente. Sólo ósábamos intercambiar miradas anhelantes y preocupadas de vez en cuando, pero cualquier cosa que ella decidiera el respecto era desolador para mí. Si huía de Pactli, yo la perdería, si se sometía y se casaba con él, yo la perdería. Si iba a su tálamo, no importaba ya que conocía las artes para convencerlo de que era virgen, pero si antes de eso, mi conducta hacía que Pactli sospechara que otro hombre ya la había poseído y de todos los hombres, *yo*, su rabia sería monumental y su venganza inconcebible. Cualquiera que fuera la forma más horripilante que escogiese para matarnos, Tzitzi y yo ya no estaríamos más juntos.

Ayya, muchas cosas sucedieron y una de ellas fue la siguiente. Cuando al atardecer del día siguiente fui a la Casa del Desarrollo de la Fuerza encontré en la lista de guardia mi nombre y el de Pactli, como si hubiese sido dispuesto por un dios irónico. Cuando todo nuestro grupo llegó al lugar asignado entre los árboles, Desecho de los Dioses ya nos estaba esperando, desnuda, abierta de piernas y lista. Para pasmo de Pactli y de nuestros otros compañeros, inmediatamente arrojé lejos mi taparrabo y me eché encima de la mujerzuela.

Mi comportamiento fue lo más torpe que pude y mi actuación lo suficientemente calculada como para hacer creer a los demás muchachos que ésa era mi primera experiencia, y con ello no di a la puta más placer que a mí. Cuando juzgué que ya era suficiente me preparé para desunirme, pero entonces la repugnancia me ganó y vomité copiosamente sobre la cara y el cuerpo desnudo de la mujer. Los muchachos rodaron por el suelo muertos de risa y aun la desventurada. Desecho de los Dioses fue capaz de reconocer un insulto. Tomó su ropa y se alejó corriendo y nunca más regresó.

✠

No mucho después de este incidente, cuatro cosas más sucedieron en rápida sucesión. Por lo menos, así es como recuerdo.

Sucedió que nuestro Uey-Tlatoani Axayácatl murió, muy joven, a causa de las heridas recibidas en las batallas contra los purémpecha y su hermano Tíxoc, Otra Cara, lo sucedió en el trono de Tenochtitlan.

Sucedió que yo, junto con Chimali y Tlatli, terminamos nuestros estudios en la *telpochcali* de Xaltocan. Ya se me podía considerar como «educado».

Sucedió que el gobernador de nuestra isla mandó un mensajero a nuestra casa una tarde, citándome a mí personalmente, para presentarme inmediatamente en su palacio.

Y sucedió por último, que tuve que partir lejos de mi hermana, de Tzitzitlini, de mi amor.

Pero será mejor que cuente más detalladamente estos sucesos y en el orden en que ocurrieron.

El cambio de gobernante no afectó mucho nuestras vidas en la provincia. En verdad, hubo muy poco que recordar del reinado de Tíxoc, aun en Tenochtitlan a excepción de que como sus dos predecesores continuó trabajando para levantar la Gran Pirámide en el Corazón del Único Mundo. Además Tíxoc agregó un toque arquitectónico propio a la plaza. Ordenó a sus albañiles cortar y tallar la Piedra de la Batalla, un gran cilindro de piedra volcánica que yacía como una inmensa pila de tortillas entre la pirámide todavía sin terminar y el sitio del pedestal de la Piedra del Sol. Esta Piedra de la Batalla tenía más o menos la altura de un hombre y su diámetro era aproximadamente el de cuatro grandes zancadas. Alrededor de la orilla había bajorrelieves tallados que representaban a guerreros mexica, Tíxoc destacándose entre ellos, trabados en combate y sujetando cautivos. La plataforma, plana y redonda, estaba en la cima de la piedra y era utilizada para un tipo de duelo público, del cual tendré la oportunidad de hablar más tarde, mas no en este momento.

Lo que más me preocupaba en aquellos momentos era la terminación de mis estudios formales. No perteneciendo a la nobleza, no tenía derecho a ir a una *calmécac*, escuela de alto aprendizaje. Con la notoriedad que había adquirido en las escuelas de Xaltocan —como Malinqui, el Torcido, en una y como Payoútla, Perdido en Niebla, en la otra—, sería mucho pedir que alguna de las altas escuelas de tierra firme me invitara a asistir gratuitamente.

Lo que particularmente me amargó fue que, mientras yo me moría de las ganas de tener una oportunidad para aprender algo más que los triviales conocimientos recibidos en nuestras *tepóchcaltin*, mis amigos Chimali y Tlatli, a quienes les importaba muy poco cualquier tipo de educación formal, *recibieran* cada uno de ellos una invitación para ir a diferentes *calmécactin*, las dos en la ciudad de Tenochtitlan, adonde siempre había soñado con ir. Durante los años en la Casa del Desarrollo de la Fuerza, ambos se habían distinguido como jugadores *tlachtli* y como cachorros de guerreros. Aunque un noble podría sonreír ante el «garbo» que esos dos muchachos habían adquirido en la Casa del Aprendizaje de Modales, también se habían distinguido como artistas, diseñando trajes originales y escenarios para las representaciones ceremoniales en los días de festivales.

«Es una lástima que no puedas venir con nosotros, Topo —dijo Tlátli con sinceridad, aunque esto no menguó la alegría que sentía por su buena fortuna—. Hubieras podido asistir por nosotros a todas las lecciones aburridas y así nosotros quedaríamos libres para dedicarnos a nuestro trabajo en el taller artístico.»

Según los términos de su aceptación, los dos muchachos, aparte de estudiar con los sacerdotes de las *calmécactin*, iban a instruirse como aprendices con los artistas de Tenochtitlan: Tlatli con un maestro escultor y Chimali con un maestro pintor. Estoy seguro de que a ninguno de los dos les importaba en absoluto las lecciones de historia, lectura, escritura, aritmética y demás, que eran las que más me interesaban a mí. De todas maneras, antes de que se fueran, Chimali me dijo: «Tengo este regalo de despedida para ti, Topo. Son mis pinturas, cañas y pinceles. Tendré unos mejores en la ciudad y a ti te pueden servir para tu práctica de la escritura.»

Sí, todavía seguía persistiendo en ese estudio que nadie me enseñaba, el arte de leer y de escribir, aunque el llegar a ser un buen conocedor de las palabras parecía en esos momentos una esperanza muy remota y mi traslado a Tenochtitlan un sueño que jamás sería realidad. Mi padre también se desesperaba porque no llegaba a dedicarme como cantero y ya era demasiado mayor para sentarme solamente a espantar a los animales en la fosa vacía. Así es que en los últimos tiempos había estado trabajando como peón de horticultor, para contribuir al sostenimiento de mi familia.

Xaltocan, por supuesto, no era lugar de labranza. Solamente tenía una capa de tierra para arar y no era lo suficiente como para asegurar la indispensable cosecha de maíz, que requiere tierra profunda para alimentarse. Así es que Xaltocan, como todas las demás islas, hacía crecer la mayor parte de su agricultura en las amplias *chinampa*, por siempre extensas, las cuales llaman ustedes «jardines flotantes». Cada *chinámitl* es una balsa entretejida de troncos y ramas de árboles, atracadas a la orilla del lago, dentro de la cual se echan capa tras capa de tierra fina, traída de la tierra firme. Cuando, temporada tras temporada, la siembra extiende sus raíces, otras nuevas van creciendo como tirabuzones hacia abajo sobre las viejas, hasta que finalmente llegan al fondo del lago y agarrándose a él aseguran la balsa firmemente en el lugar. Otras *chinampa* se construían afianzándolas unas junto a otras. Así, en todos los lagos, cada isla habitada, incluyendo Tenochtitlan, ostentaba un ancho anillo u orla de esas balsas cubiertas de verdor. En algunas islas más fértiles es difícil saber dónde termina la tierra creada por los dioses y dónde empiezan los campos hechos por los hombres.

No se necesitaba más de la vista de un topo, o el intelecto de un topo, para atender unas *chinampa*, así es que tomé a mi cargo aquellas que pertenecían a mi familia y a los vecinos de mi barrio. El trabajo no exigía mucho esfuerzo; tenía bastante tiempo libre. Me apliqué, con las pinturas que me regaló Chimali, al dibujo de palabras pintadas, tratando siempre y asiduamente de hacer que los símbolos más complicados se vieran más sencillos, más estilizados y más pequeños. Aunque parecía inverosímil todavía seguía alimentando la secreta esperanza de que la educación que estaba adquiriendo por mí mismo llegaría a mejorar mi posición en la vida. Ahora sonrío compasivamente cuando me acuerdo de mí mismo sentado allí en la balsa sucia, entre el hedor de los fertilizantes hechos con entrañas de animales y cabezas de pescados, mientras, ausente a todo esto, garrapateaba mis prácticas de escritura y soñaba quimeras maravillosas.

Por ejemplo, jugué con la ambición de llegar a ser un *pochtécatl*, mercader viajero, y viajar hacia las tierras de los mayas, en donde algún maravilloso curandero o físico restauraría mi vista, mientras me hacía rico mediante un trueque continuo a lo largo del camino. Oh, cómo urdía planes para convertir una bagatela de mercancía en una fortuna; planes ingeniosos que estaba seguro de que a ningún otro mercader se le habían ocurrido. El único obstáculo para asegurar mi éxito, como me lo hizo notar Tzitzi con mucho tacto cuando le conté algunas de mis ideas, era que carecía hasta de la más insignificante cantidad como capital para poder empezar.

Y entonces, una tarde después de haber terminado mi día de trabajo, uno de los mensajeros del Señor Garza Roja apareció en la puerta de nuestra casa. Llevaba puesto un manto de color neutral, lo que significaba que no traía ni buenas ni malas noticias, y dijo a mi padre cortésmente: «*Mixpantzinco.*»

«*Ximopanólti*», dijo mi padre, indicándole con un gesto que entrara.

El joven, que era más o menos de mi edad, dijo dando un paso adentro: «El *tecutli* Tlauquécholtzin, mi señor y el de ustedes, requiere la presencia de su hijo Chicome-Xóchtil Tliléctic Mixtli en el palacio.»

Mi padre y mi hermana estaban sorprendidos y turbados. Y supongo que yo también. Mi madre, no. Ella se lamentaba: «*Yya ayya*, ya sabía que algún día el muchacho ofendería a los nobles o a los dioses o... —Se interrumpió para preguntarle al mensajero—: ¿Qué diablura ha hecho Mixtli? No es necesario que el *tecutli* se moleste en propinarle personalmente una paliza o lo que sea que haya decretado. Estaremos muy contentos de darle su castigo.»

«Yo no sé que nadie haya hecho nada —dijo el mensajero mirándola con recelo—. Solamente obedezco una orden. Llevarlo conmigo inmediatamente.»

E inmediatamente lo acompañé, prefiriendo cualquier cosa que me esperara en el palacio, a lo que pudiera concebir la imaginación de mi madre. Sentía curiosidad, pero no podía pensar en ninguna razón por la que pudiera echarme a temblar. Si ese emplazamiento hubiera llegado algún tiempo antes, me habría sentido muy preocupado pensando que el malicioso Pactli había instigado algún cargo contra mí. Pero el joven Señor Alegría no estaba, dos o tres años antes se había ido a una *calmécac* a Tenochtitlan en la que solamente se aceptaban a los vástagos de las familias que gobernaban y que a su vez serían gobernantes. Y Pactli regresaba a Xaltocan solamente en las cortas vacaciones escolares. Durante esas visitas, había buscado pretextos para venir a nuestra casa, pero siempre cuando yo no estaba en casa sino trabajando, así es que no había vuelto a verlo desde aquel día en que tan brevemente compartimos a Desecho de los Dioses.

Respetuosamente, el mensajero se quedó unos cuantos pasos detrás de mí, cuando entré a la sala del trono del palacio y me incliné para hacer el gesto de besar la tierra. Junto al Señor Garza Roja estaba sentado un hombre al que jamás había visto antes en la isla. Aunque el forastero estaba sentado en una silla más baja, como era lo adecuado, disminuía considerablemente el aire de importancia que usualmente ostentaba nuestro gobernador. Aun con mi vista de topo, pude darme cuenta de que llevaba un manto de brillantes plumas y adornos de una riqueza tal que ningún *pili* en Xaltocan hubiera podido exhibir.

Garza Roja dijo al visitante: «La petición había sido: hagan un hombre de él. Bien, nuestras Casas del Desarrollo de la

Fuerza y del Aprendizaje de Modales hicieron lo mejor que pudieron. Aquí está.»

«Tengo ordenado hacer una prueba», dijo el forastero. Sacó un rollito de papel de corteza y me lo alargó.

«*Mixpantzinco*», dije a los dos nobles, antes de desenrollar el papel. No traía nada que yo pudiera reconocer como una prueba; solamente una simple línea de palabras-pintadas y que yo ya había visto antes.

«¿Puede usted leerlo?», me preguntó el forastero.

«Ah, se me olvidó mencionarle eso —dijo Garza Roja como si él me hubiese enseñado personalmente—. Mixtli puede leer algunas cosas sencillas con una medida justa de comprensión.»

«Puedo leer esto, mis señores. Dice...»

«No importa —me interrumpió el forastero—. Solamente dígame: ¿qué significa la figura con pico de pato?»

«Ehécatl, el viento, mi señor.»

«¿Nada más?»

«Bien, mi señor, con la otra figura de párpados cerrados dice Viento de la Noche, pero...»

«¿Sí? Hable joven.»

«Si mi señor me perdona la impertinencia, esta figura no representa el pico de un pato. Es la trompeta del viento por la cual el dios sopla...»

«Basta. —El forastero se volvió a Garza Roja—. Él es, Señor Gobernador. ¿Tengo entonces su autorización?»

«Claro, claro —dijo Garza Roja casi obsequiosamente. Volviéndose hacia mí, me dijo—: Te puedes levantar, Mixtli. Éste es el Ciaucoátl, el Señor Hueso Fuerte, Mujer Serpiente ·de Nezahualpili, Uey-Tlatoáni de Texcoco. El Señor Hueso Fuerte trae una invitación personal del Venerado Orador para que vayas a residir, estudiar y servir a la corte de Texcoco.»

«¡Texcoco!», exclamé. Nunca antes había estado allí o en cualquier otro lugar de la nación Acolhua. No conocía a nadie allí y ningún acólhuatl podía saber nada de mí, ciertamente no el Venerado Orador Nezahualpili, quien en todas estas tierras era el segundo en poder y prestigio después de Tíxoc, el Uey-Tlatoani de Tenochtitlan. Estaba tan asombrado que sin pensarlo y con gran descortesía pregunté: «*¿Por qué?*»

«No es una orden —dijo con brusquedad el Mujer Serpiente de Texcoco—. Está usted invitado y puede aceptar o declinar la invitación. Pero no está usted invitado a hacer preguntas sobre este ofrecimiento.»

Murmuré una disculpa y el Señor Garza Roja vino en mi ayuda diciendo: «Perdone al joven, mi señor. Estoy seguro que se encuentra tan perplejo, como yo lo he estado durante todos estos años, de que un personaje tan ensalzado como Nezahualpili haya puesto su mirada sobre este joven de entre tantos macéhualtin.»

El Ciaucóatl solamente gruñó, por lo que Garza Roja continuó: «Nunca se me ha dado una explicación acerca del interés de su señor por este plebeyo en particular y siempre me contuve de preguntar. Por supuesto que recuerdo a su anterior soberano, que era un árbol de gran sombra, el sabio y bondadoso Nezahuelcóyotl y de que acostumbraba a viajar solo a través de estas tierras, disfrazada su identidad, en busca de personas estimables que merecieran su favor. ¿Es que su ilustre Nezahualpili continúa con esa benigna tradición? Y si es así, ¿puedo saber qué fue lo que vio en este nuestro joven súbdito Tliléctic-Mixtli?

«No puedo decirlo, Señor Gobernador.» El altivo noble le dio a Garza Roja una respuesta casi tan ruda como la que me había dado a mí.

«Nadie pregunta al Venerado Orador cuáles son sus impulsos y sus intenciones. Ni siquiera yo, su Mujer Serpiente. Y tengo otras obligaciones aparte de la de estar esperando a que este mozalbete indeciso se decida a aceptar este prodigioso honor. Joven, regreso a Texcoco mañana en cuanto se levante Tezcatlipoca. ¿Viene usted conmigo o no?»

«Por supuesto que sí, mi señor —dije—. Sólo tengo que empaquetar algunas ropas, mis papeles, mis pinturas. A menos de que haya algo en especial que deba llevar.» Osadamente agregué esto último con la esperanza de que me sugiriera alguna idea sobre el *porqué* iba a ir y *por cuánto* tiempo iba a estar.

Pero solamente dijo: «Le será dado todo lo necesario.»

Garza Roja dijo: «Preséntate aquí en el palacio, Mixtli, un poco antes de que se levante Tonatíu.»

El Señor Hueso Fuerte miró fríamente al gobernador, después a mí y me dijo: «Es mejor, joven, que desde este momento vaya aprendiendo a llamar al dios-sol por Texcatlipoca.»

¿Desde ese momento y *para siempre*?, me preguntaba, cuando me apresuraba a llegar a casa. ¿Era que iba a ser un acólhuatl adoptado para el resto de mi vida y convertido a los dioses acolhua?

Mi familia me había estado esperando, así es que cuando llegué les conté todo lo que había pasado y mi padre me dijo excitadamente: «¡Viento de la Noche! ¡Cómo te lo dije, hijo Mixtli! Fue el dios Viento de la Noche que encontraste en el camino hace algunos años. Y es por Viento de la Noche que se te cumplirá el deseo de tu corazón.»

Tzitzi me miró preocupada y dijo: «Pero supongamos que es un ardid. Supongamos que en Texcoco simplemente necesitan a un *xochimiqui* de cierta edad y talla para algún sacrificio especial...»

«No —dijo mi madre clarividentemente—. Mixtli no es guapo, ni gracioso, ni lo suficientemente virtuoso para haber sido escogido para ninguna ceremonia, no que yo sepa.» Parecía disgustada de que estos asuntos no hubieran estado bajo su dirección.

«Sin embargo, hay algo ciertamente sospechoso en todo esto. Dedicándose a los libros pintados y chapoteando perezosamente en las *chinampa*, Mixtli no ha hecho nada para atraer a un tratante de esclavos, mucho menos para llamar la atención de la corte real de Texcoco.»

Yo la ignoré y dije: «Por las palabras que escuché en el palacio y por el pedacito de papel escrito que traía el Señor Hueso Fuerte, creo que puedo adivinar algo. Aquella noche en el cruce de caminos no me encontré con un dios, sino con un viajero acólhuatl, quizás algún palaciego enviado por Nezahualpili al que nosotros supusimos Viento de la Noche. A través de los años, desde entonces, por alguna razón que desconozco, Texcoco siguió al tanto de mi vida. De todas maneras, parece que podré asistir a una *calmécac* en Texcoco, en donde se me enseñará el arte de conocer las palabras. Seré escribano como siempre lo había deseado. Por lo menos —terminé, encogiéndome de hombros— esto es lo que supongo.»

«Tú llamas a todo esto coincidencia —dijo mi padre firmemente—. Lo más probable, hijo Mixtli, es que realmente te encontraste con Viento de la Noche y lo tomaste por un mortal. Los dioses, como los hombres, pueden viajar disfrazados sin ser reconocidos. Además saliste ganando con el encuentro. No te haría ningún daño darle las gracias a Viento de la Noche.»

«Tienes razón y así lo haré, padre Tepetzalan. Puede ser que esté o no Viento de la Noche envuelto en esto, pero él *es* el que concede los deseos del corazón a aquella persona que él escoge y éste *es* el deseo de mi corazón y estoy a punto de realizarlo.»

«Pero solamente uno de los deseos de mi corazón —le dije a Tzitzitlini, cuando al fin tuvimos un momento para estar a solas—. ¿Cómo puedo alejarme del sonido de las campanitas tocando?»

«Si tuvieras un poco de seso te alejarías de aquí cantando alegremente —me dijo femeninamente práctica, pero sin alegría en su voz—. Mixtli, no puedes pasar toda tu vida sembrando semillas, e inventando fútiles ambiciones como la de llegar a ser un tratante. Ahora que ha sucedido esto, ya tienes un futuro, un futuro más brillante al que jamás había sido ofrecido a ningún *macehúali* de Xaltocan.»

«Pero si Viento de la Noche o Nezahualpili o quien quiera que sea, me envió esta oportunidad, quizá me mande otras y mejores. Siempre soñé con ir a Tenochtitlan, no a Texcoco. Todavía puedo declinar este ofrecimiento, según lo dijo el Señor Hueso Fuerte, y esperar, ¿por qué no?»

«Porque tienes buen sentido, Mixtli. Cuando estuve en la Casa del Aprendizaje de Modales, la Maestra de las Niñas nos dijo que si Tenochtitlan es el brazo fuerte de la Triple Alianza, Texcoco es el cerebro. Hay más que pompa y poder en la corte de Nezahualpili. Allí hay una herencia de años de poesía, cultura y sabiduría. También nos dijo la maestra que de todas las tierras en donde se habla el náhuatl, es la gente de Texcoco la que lo hace con más pureza. ¿Qué mejor destino para quien aspira a ser un erudito? Debes ir e irás. Estudiarás, aprenderás y serás el mejor. Si de veras has ganado el apoyo del Venerado Orador, ¿quién puede saber los altos planes que tiene para ti? Cuando hablas de rehusar su invitación, sabes bien que dices tonterías. —Su voz se hizo más queda—. Y todo por mi causa.»

«Por nuestra causa.»

Ella suspiró. «Algún día tendremos que madurar.»

«Siempre tuve la esperanza de que lo haríamos juntos.»

«Todavía no hay por qué perder la esperanza. Volverás a casa los días festivos y entonces estaremos juntos. Y cuando tus estudios concluyan serás rico y poderoso. Podrías, también, llegar a ser Mixtzin y un *pili* puede casarse con quien quiera.»

«Espero llegar a ser un cumplido conocedor de palabras, Tzitzi. Esa ambición es suficiente para mí y muy pocos escribanos hacen algo como para ganarse el título de -tzin.»

«Bueno... quizás seas enviado a trabajar a alguna aldea remota de los acolhua en donde no se sepa que tienes una hermana. Simplemente envías por mí y yo iré. Seré la novia escogida de tu isla nativa.»

«Para entonces habrán pasado muchos años —protesté—. Y ya estás en edad de casarte. Mientras tanto, el detestable Pactli también vendrá a Xaltocan en los días festivos. Tú sabes lo que él quiere y lo que él quiere, él lo demanda y lo que él demanda no se le puede negar.»

«Negar no, pero aplazarlo posiblemente —dijo—. Haré todo lo posible para desanimar al Señor Alegría. Quizás él sea menos insistente en sus demandas —me sonrió valerosamente— ahora que tengo un pariente y protector en la poderosa corte de Texcoco. ¿Ya ves?, tienes que ir. —Su sonrisa se hizo trémula—. Los dioses han arreglado que por un tiempo estemos separados, para que nunca más lo estemos.» Su sonrisa vaciló, cayó y se quebró en sus labios, y ella lloró.

✠

El *acali* del Señor Hueso Fuerte era de caoba, ricamente tallado y cubierto con un toldo orlado, decorado con insignias de piedrajade y pendones de plumas que proclamaban su rango. Después de cruzar la ciudad de Texcoco, que ustedes los españoles llaman ahora San Antonio de Padua, y de seguir como una carrera-larga más allá, hacia el sur, un cerro de tamaño mediano surgía directamente de las aguas del lago, el Ciaucoatl dijo: «Texcotzinco», la primera palabra que me dirigía durante toda la mañana de viaje desde Xaltocan. Entrecerré los ojos para poder observar con atención el cerro, que como ya sabía era el lugar en el que se encontraba el palacio campestre de Nezahualpili.

La gran canoa se deslizó hacia un atracadero de piedra bien construido y sólido, aunque en esos momentos estaba desierto, al pie del cerro de Texcotzinco. Los remeros soltaron sus remos y los ayudantes saltaron a la orilla para amarrar la canoa. Esperé mientras el Señor Hueso Fuerte era ayudado a descender por sus remeros, entonces salté al muelle, cargando mi cesto de mimbre en donde había puesto mis pertenencias. El lacónico Mujer Serpiente apuntó a una ancha escalera de piedra que sinuosamente iba desde el atracadero hasta lo alto del cerro y me dijo: «Por ese camino, joven», las otras palabras que me dirigió ese día. Yo vacilaba, preguntándome si sería más cortés esperarlo, pero él estaba supervisando a los hombres que descargaban del *acali* todos los regalos que el Señor Garza Roja había enviado al Uey-Tlatoani Nezahualpili. Así es que me eché al hombro mi canasto y empecé la caminata solo, escalera arriba.

Algunos de los escalones eran trozos de piedra cortados y encajados, otros estaban escarbados en la roca viva del cerro. Al llegar al escalón número trece, me encontré con un descansillo de piedra, ancho, en donde había una banca y una pequeña estatua de un dios, que no pude identificar, y el siguiente tramo de escalera subía en un ángulo desde ese descansillo. Otra vez trece escalones y otra vez un rellano. Así subí serpenteando por el cerro y al llegar al escalón cincuenta y dos me encontré en una amplia terraza, un lugar muy vasto cortado al ras de la inclinada ladera. Estaba bulliciosamente llena de flores de diferentes matices, formando un lozano jardín. Este escalón cincuenta y dos me puso sobre un sendero, el cual seguí deliberadamente, vagando a través de lechos de flores y bajo árboles espléndidos, pasando tortuosos arroyuelos borboteantes y pequeñas cascadas, hasta que el sendero volvió a convertirse en escalera. Otra vez trece escalones y un descansillo con su banca y su estatua...

El cielo se había empezado a nublar desde hacía un rato y en ese momento vino la lluvia, en la manera usual en que caía en la temporada de lluvias; una tormenta como si se fuera a acabar el mundo: muchas varas trinchadas de luces, retumbar de truenos y un diluvio que parecía que nunca tendría fin. Pero éste siempre llegaba en menos tiempo del que le llevaría a un hombre tomar una siesta y a tiempo para que Tonatíu, o Tezcatlipoca, volviera a brillar en un mundo reluciente y mojado, saturándolo de vapor para secarlo y calentarlo antes de ponerse. En el momento en que llegó la lluvia, me había refugiado en uno de los descansillos de la escalera que tenía una banca con su techo enramado. Mientras estaba al resguardo de la tormenta, medité acerca del significado numérico de la escalera serpenteante y sonreí ante la ingenuidad del que la diseñó.

Nosotros en estas tierras, al igual que ustedes los hombres blancos, vivíamos bajo un calendario anual basado en la travesía del sol en el cielo. Así nuestro año solar, como el de ustedes, consistía en trescientos sesenta y cinco días y utilizábamos este calendario para todas nuestras ocupaciones ordinarias: para saber cuándo sembrar determinadas semillas, cuándo esperar la temporada de lluvias y demás. Dividimos el año solar en dieciocho meses de veinte días cada uno, además de los *nemontemtin* —los «días inanimados», los «días vacíos»—, los cinco días que se necesitaban para completar los trescientos sesenta y cinco días del año.

Pero también teníamos otro calendario alternado que no giraba en torno a las excursiones diurnas del sol, sino que estaba basado en la aparición nocturna de la estrella brillante a quien dábamos el nombre de nuestro anciano dios Quetzalcóatl o Serpiente Emplumada. Algunas veces, Quetzalcóatl venía a ser como

Flor del Atardecer, que llameaba inmediatamente después del crepúsculo; otras, se movía al otro lado del cielo, donde sería la última estrella visible cuando el sol se levantara y borrara las demás estrellas. Cualesquiera de nuestros astrónomos podría explicarles a ustedes todo esto con hábiles diagramas, pues yo nunca he llegado a conocer bien la astronomía. Sé que los movimientos de las estrellas no son tan fortuitos como parecen y nuestro calendario alternativo ceremonial se basaba de alguna forma en los movimientos de la estrella Quetzalcóatl. Ese calendario era muy útil, incluso para nuestra gente más ordinaria, quienes basándose en él daban los nombres a sus niños recién nacidos. Nuestros escribanos e historiadores lo utilizaban para fechar los sucesos más notables y la duración de los reinados de nuestros soberanos. Sobre todo, nuestros *tlachtopaitóantin*, videntes, lo usaban para poder adivinar el futuro, para prevenirnos contra las amenazadoras calamidades y para seleccionar los días favorables para los acontecimientos importantes.

El calendario adivinatorio constaba de doscientos sesenta días por año. Para nombrar esos días se les añadían números del uno al trece a cada uno de los veinte signos tradicionales: conejo, caña, cuchillo y demás, y a cada año solar se le nombraba de acuerdo al número y signo del primer día en que comenzaba: por ejemplo, el año de mi nacimiento era Trece Conejo. Como ustedes pueden darse cuenta, nuestros dos calendarios, el solar y el ceremonial, siempre se fueron turnando entre los dos, uno adelantándose o retrasándose del otro. Sin embargo, si tienen la paciencia de hacer una cuenta aritmética, se darán cuenta de que ellos llegaban a balancearse con igual número de días al llegar a un período de cincuenta y dos años, del año solar ordinario. El año en que nací fue Trece Conejo y ningún otro año llevaría ese nombre otra vez, hasta llegar a mi cumpleaños número cincuenta y dos.

Así es que para nosotros ese número cincuenta y dos era expresivo, y le llamábamos «una gavilla de años». Era significativo porque tal número era simultáneamente reconocido por los dos calendarios y porque también eran más o menos los años que se esperaba que un hombre viviera desde su nacimiento hasta su muerte, salvo accidente, enfermedad o guerra. Por lo tanto, la escalera de piedra que subía sinuosa por el cerro de Texcotzinco, con sus trece escalones entre los descansos, representaba los trece números rituales. Cada jardín, que llegaba a la altura de los cincuenta y dos escalones, representaba una gavilla de años. Cuando finalmente llegué a la cumbre del cerro, había contado, incluyendo los descansillos y los jardines, quinientos veinte escalones. Todos juntos, denotaban dos años ceremoniales de doscientos sesenta días cada uno y simultáneamente denotaban diez gavillas de cincuenta y dos años cada una. Sí, muy ingenioso.

Cuando dejó de llover seguí subiendo. No ascendí el resto de esos quinientos veinte escalones de un tirón, aunque estoy seguro de que hubiera podido hacerlo en aquellos días lejanos de mi vigor juvenil. Me detuve en cada uno de los descansillos res-

114

tantes, solamente el tiempo suficiente para ver si podía identificar al dios o a la diosa cuya estatua se encontraba en cada uno de ellos. Conocía, quizás, la mitad de ellos: Tezcatlipoca, el sol, dios principal de los acolhua; Quetzalcóatl, de quien ya he hablado; Ometecutli y Omecíuatl, nuestra Primera Pareja...

Me detuve más tiempo en los jardines. Allí, en la tierra firme, la tierra es profunda y el espacio ilimitado, y obviamente Nezahualpili era un gran amante de las flores, porque las había por todos lados. Los jardines en la ladera estaban divididos con esmero en cuadros, pero como las terrazas no estaban limitadas por bardas, las flores se desparramaban generosamente por las orillas y diferentes variedades de enredaderas colgaban sus brillantes corolas tan abajo del cerro que casi llegaban a la terraza anterior. Sé que allí estaban todas las flores que había visto antes en mi vida, además de las incontables clases que jamás había contemplado y que muchas de ellas debían de haber sido trasplantadas, a muy alto precio, desde lejanos países. También yo comprendí de manera gradual que los numerosos estanques de nenúfares, los espejos de agua, los arroyuelos y pequeñas cascadas susurrantes constituían un sistema de riego alimentado por una caída de agua que probablemente estaba más arriba del cerro.

Si el Señor Hueso Fuerte venía subiendo detrás de mí, nunca lo vi. Pero al llegar a una de las terrazas más altas, encontré a un hombre recostado indolentemente sobre una banca de piedra. Cuando me acerqué lo suficientemente para verlo más o menos con claridad, recordé haberlo conocido antes. Su piel arrugada era del color del cacao y por única prenda llevaba un harapiento *máxtlatl*. Él se levantó, por lo menos hasta alcanzar la extensión de su encorvada y encogida estatura. Para entonces yo había crecido más que él.

Le saludé con la cortesía tradicional, pero luego le dije en una forma quizás más ruda de lo que deseaba: «Pensé que usted era un mendigo de Tlaltelolco, viejecito. ¿Qué hace usted aquí?»

«Un hombre sin hogar tiene su hogar en cualquier parte del mundo —dijo, como si fuera algo de lo que enorgullecerse—. Estoy aquí para darte la bienvenida a la tierra de los acolhua.»

«¡Usted!», exclamé, porque el grotesco anciano parecía aún más una excrecencia, en este frondoso jardín, de lo que me lo había parecido entre la muchedumbre abigarrada del mercado.

«¿Esperabas ser recibido por el Venerado Orador en persona? —preguntó, con una sonrisa burlona que mostraba una dentadura incompleta—. Bienvenido al palacio de Texcotzinco, joven Mixtli. O joven Tozani, joven Malinqui, joven Poyaútla, como quieras que te llame.»

«Usted conoció mi nombre hace ya mucho tiempo y ahora conoce todos mis apodos.»

«Un hombre que tiene talento para escuchar, puede incluso oír cosas que aún no se han dicho. Tú tendrás otros nombres todavía, en los tiempos por venir.»

«Entonces, ¿es que realmente es usted un adivino, anciano? —pregunté, haciendo eco inconscientemente de las palabras pronunciadas por mi padre hace años—. ¿Cómo supo que venía para acá?»

«Ah, que venías acá —dijo ignorando mi pregunta—. Me siento orgulloso de haber tenido una pequeña parte en este arreglo.»

«Pues usted sabe mucho más que yo, anciano. Le agradecería sumamente que me aclarara un poco el asunto.»

«Entérate, entonces, que nunca te vi antes de aquel día en el mercado de Tlaltelolco, cuando oí casualmente que era el día de tu nombre. Simplemente por curiosidad aproveché la oportunidad para observarte más de cerca. Cuando inspeccioné tus ojos, me di cuenta de tu inminente e incrementada pérdida de larga visión. Esa afección es lo suficientemente rara para que la forma distinta del globo del ojo afectado facilite un fácil diagnóstico. Podía decir con certeza que era tu destino ver las cosas de cerca y verlas como son verdaderamente.»

«Usted también dijo que yo *hablaría* con la verdad de esas cosas.»

Se encogió de hombros. «Me pareciste lo suficientemente listo, aun siendo un mocoso, como para predecir con seguridad que crecerías con una inteligencia pasable. Un hombre que se ve forzado por su mala vista a mirar todo lo de este mundo a corta distancia y con un buen sentido, también está generalmente inclinado a describir el mundo realmente como es.»

«Usted *sí* que es un tramposo muy diestro —le dije sonriéndome—. Pero, ¿qué tiene que ver todo eso con haber sido llamado a Texcoco?»

«Cada soberano, príncipe y gobernador se rodea de palaciegos serviles y de sabios egoístas, quienes dirán lo que él quiere oír, o lo que ellos quieren que oiga. Un hombre que dice únicamente la verdad es una rareza entre los cortesanos. Yo tenía fe de que llegaras a ser una de esas rarezas y que tus facultades serían apreciadas en una corte algo más noble que la de Xaltocan. Así es que dejé caer una palabra aquí y otra allá...»

Dije con incredulidad: «¿Usted es escuchado por un hombre como Nezahualpili?»

Me miró de una manera que me hizo sentir mucho más pequeño que él. «Ya te lo dije hace mucho tiempo, ¿todavía no lo he demostrado?, que yo también digo la verdad y eso en mi propio detrimento, cuando fácilmente podría hacerme pasar por un omnisciente mensajero de los dioses. Nezahualpili no es tan cínico como tú, joven Topo. Él sabe escuchar al más humilde de los hombres, si ese hombre le habla con la verdad.»

«Le pido disculpas —le dije después de un momento—. Debería estar agradeciéndole, anciano, no dudando de usted. Y verdaderamente le estoy agradecido por...»

Hizo eso a un lado. «No lo hice tanto por ti. Generalmente recibo un buen pago por mis descubrimientos. Simplemente ocúpate de dar un servicio leal al Uey-Tlatoani y ambos habremos ganado nuestros premios. Anda, vete.»

«Pero, ¿adónde? Nadie me ha dicho dónde ni a quién debo

presentarme. ¿Voy simplemente a atravesar este cerro y esperar a que me reconozcan?»

«Sí. El palacio está al otro lado y serás recibido con hospitalidad. Lo que yo no te podría decir es si el Venerado Orador te reconocerá la próxima vez que te encuentre.»

«Si nunca nos hemos encontrado —me quejé—. No es posible que me reconozca.»

«¿Oh? Bueno. Te aconsejo que te congracíes con Tolana Tecíuapil, la Señora de Tolan, porque ella es la esposa favorita de las siete que tomó en matrimonio Nezahualpili y según la última cuenta también tiene en su haber cuarenta concubinas. Así es que en el palacio hay aproximadamente unos sesenta hijos y unas cincuenta hijas de Nezahualpili. Yo creo que ni él mismo sabe cuál es la última cuenta, así es que puede ser que te tome por una consecuencia ya olvidada de una de sus peregrinaciones; un hijo que acaba de llegar a casa. Pero no temas, joven Topo, serás recibido con hospitalidad.»

Ya me iba, pero me volví de nuevo hacia él. «Pero antes de irme, ¿podría hacerle algún servicio, venerable anciano? Tal vez pueda ayudarle a llegar a la cima del cerro.»

«Gracias por tu amable ofrecimiento, pero descansaré aquí un rato todavía. Es mejor que acabes de subir el cerro solo, porque todo el resto de tu vida te espera al otro lado.»

Eso me sonó muy portentoso, pero vi una pequeña falacia en él y sonreí de mi perspicacia. «Seguramente que mi vida me espera en cualquier parte que yo vaya desde aquí, solo o no.»

El hombre de color cacao sonrió también, aunque irónicamente. «Sí, a tu edad esperan muchas clases de vida. Puedes ir en la dirección que escojas. Puedes ir solo o acompañado. Los compañeros quizás caminarán contigo una distancia larga o corta. Pero al final de tu vida, no importa cuán llenos hayan estado tus caminos y tus días, habrás tenido que aprender lo que todos aprenden. Será entonces demasiado tarde para comenzar de nuevo, demasiado tarde para todo, excepto el remordimiento. Así es que apréndelo en este momento. Ningún hombre ha vivido jamás más que una vida y ésa ha sido escogida por él mismo y la mayor parte la vive solo. —Hizo una pausa y sus ojos se fijaron en los míos—. Entonces, Mixtli, ¿qué camino vas a tomar desde aquí y en compañía de quién?»

Di la vuelta y seguí subiendo el cerro, solo.

I H S

✠

S. C. C. M.

Santificada, Cesárea, Católica Majestad,
el Emperador Don Carlos, nuestro Señor Rey:

Nuestra más Virtuosa Majestad y Sagaz Monarca: desde la Ciudad de Mexico, capital de la Nueva España, en este Día de Fiesta de la Circuncisión y en el Año de Nuestro Señor mil quinientos veinte y nueve, os saludo.

Con el corazón apesadumbrado, pero con mano sumisa, vuestro capellán os envía nuevamente, según vuestra nueva orden, otra recopilación más de los escritos dictados hasta la fecha por nuestro azteca, o Asmodeo, como esté siervo de Vuestra Majestad tiende con más frecuencia a considerarlo.

Este vuestro humilde clérigo puede simpatizar con el comentario irónico de Vuestra Majestad, de que la crónica del indio «contiene mucha más información que las fanfarronadas que recibimos incesantemente del recientemente titulado Marqués, el señor Cortés, quien actualmente nos hace el favor de asistir a la Corte». Y aun un Obispo entristecido y malhumorado es capaz de percibir el chiste irónico cuando vos escribís que «las comunicaciones del indio son las primeras que hemos recibido de la Nueva España que *no* intentan sonsacar con maña un título, o una vasta asignación de las tierras conquistadas, o un préstamo.»

Sin embargo, Señor, estamos estupefactos cuando vos relatáis que vuestra real persona y *vuestros cortesanos* estáis «completamente cautivados en la lectura en voz alta de estas páginas». Nos, confiamos en que no sean tomados de una manera superficial nuestros empeños como vasallo de Su Más Eminente Majestad, pero, por nuestros otros juramentos, nos vemos obligados a amonestar lo más solemnemente y *ex officio* contra una indiscreta mayor difusión de esta historia asquerosa.

Su Aguda Majestad debe de haberse dado cuenta seguramente, de que en las páginas anteriores han sido tratados, indiferentemente, sin compunción ni arrepentimiento, tales pecados *inter alia* como homicidio, infanticidio, suicidio, antropofagia, incesto, tortura, prostitución, idolatría y violación al Mandamiento de honrar al padre y a la madre. Si, como se dice, los pecados son las heridas del alma, la de este indio debe de estar sangrando por cada poro.

Pero, por si acaso las insinuaciones más furtivamente deslizadas escapasen a la atención de Vuestra Majestad, permítanos señalar que el procaz azteca se ha atrevido a sugerir que su pueblo se jacta de alguna línea vaga de descendencia de una Primera Pareja, una parodia pagana de Adán y Eva. Sugiere también, que *nosotros los cristianos* somos idólatras de un panteísmo comparable a la hirviente multitud de demonios que adoraba su pueblo. Con una blasfemia igual, ha sugerido que los Sagrados Sacramentos como el bautismo y la absolución por medio de la confesión y aun la petición de gracia antes de las comidas, eran ya observadas en estas tierras, anterior e independientemente de cualquier conocimiento acerca de Nuestro Señor y Su otorgamiento de los Sacramentos. Pero quizá su más vil sacrilegio es asegurar, como pronto Vuestra Majestad leerá, que uno de sus gobernantes anteriores, un idólatra, ¡nació de una virgen!

También Vuestra Majestad hace una pregunta incidental en esta última carta. Aunque nosotros mismos hemos asistido de vez en cuando a las sesiones de la narración del indio, y continuaremos haciéndolo si el tiempo lo permite para hacer preguntas específicas o exigir una explicación sobre algunos de sus comentarios que hemos leído, debemos respetuosamente recordarle a Vuestra Majestad, que el Obispo de Mexico tiene otras obligaciones urgentes que impiden verificar o refutar personalmente cualquiera de las jactancias y aseveraciones de este parlanchín.

Sin embargo, Vuestra Majestad nos pide información sobre una de sus más escandalosas afirmaciones y esperamos sinceramente que esta averiguación sea solamente una chanza humorística de nuestro jovial soberano. En cualquier caso, tenemos que responder: No, Señor, no sabemos nada acerca de las propiedades que el azteca atribuye a la raíz llamada barbasco. No podemos confirmar que «valdría su peso en oro» como un medio de comercio español. Nos, no sabemos nada acerca de esto que pudiera «silenciar la cháchara de las damas de la Corte». La simple sugestión de que Nuestro Señor Dios hubiera creado un vegetal que evitara la concepción de la cristiana vida humana, es repugnante a nuestra sensibilidad y una afrenta a...

Perdonadme, Señor, la mancha de tinta. Nuestra agitación aflige a nuestro mano. Pero *satis superque...*

Como lo ordena Vuestra Majestad, los frailes y el joven lego seguirán anotando estas páginas hasta que —con el tiempo, rezamos— Vuestra Majestad nos ordene que seamos relevados de este deber tan deplorable. O hasta que los mismos frailes ya no puedan aguantar más este trabajo. Creemos que no violamos la confianza del confesionario si solamente mencionamos que en estos últimos meses, las confesiones de dichos hermanos han sido extremadamente fantasmagóricas, espeluznantes de escuchar y necesitadas de las más exigentes penitencias para recibir la absolución.

Que nuestro Señor Jesucristo, Redentor y Maestro, sea siempre el consuelo y la defensa de Vuestra Majestad, contra todas las asechanzas de nuestro Adversario, es la constante oración del capellán de Su S.C.C.M.,

(ecce signum) Zumárraga

QUARTA PARS

El otro lado del cerro era todavía más bello que el que daba hacia el lago de Texcoco. Allí la inclinación era suave por lo que no había terrazas en declive. Los jardines ondulaban hacia abajo y lejos, variadamente regulares e irregulares, con estanques para peces, fuentes y lugares para bañarse, todos ellos destellando. Había amplias extensiones de prados verdes en donde rumiaban algunos venados domesticados; arboledas sombreadas y ocasionalmente un árbol aislado que había sido recortado y podado hasta convertirlo en la estatua de algún animal. Al pie del cerro había muchos edificios, grandes y pequeños, pero todos agradablemente bien proporcionados y construidos a distancias confortables unos de otros. Creí inclusive poder distinguir —ya que vi unos puntos brillantes moviéndose— a algunas personas ricamente vestidas ir de acá para allá en los caminos entre los edificios. En Xaltocan el palacio del Señor Garza Roja había sido un edificio cómodo y bastante grandioso, pero el palacio del Uey-Tlatoani Nezahualpili en Texcotzinco era una *ciudad* completa e idílica.

En lo alto del cerro, había una gran cantidad de los «más viejos de los viejos» cipreses, algunos tan gruesos que unos doce hombres con los brazos extendidos no hubieran podido rodear sus troncos, y tan altos que sus emplumadas hojas gris-verde emergían entre el azul claro del cielo. Miré alrededor y divisé, aunque inteligentemente ocultas por la vegetación, las grandes tuberías de barro que surtían de agua a esos jardines y a la ciudad de abajo. Por lo que podía juzgar, las tuberías se perdían en la distancia hacia una montaña aún más alta, al sureste, en donde indudablemente había un manantial de agua pura que se distribuiría dejándola alcanzar su propio nivel.

Como no había podido resistir el vagar admirado entre los diversos jardines y parques a través de los cuales venía bajando, se acercaba ya el crepúsculo cuando por fin llegué a los edificios al pie del cerro. Errante, caminé por los blancos senderos de grava bordeados de flores, encontrándome con mucha gente: hombres y mujeres nobles con ricos mantos, campeones con penachos de plumas y ancianos de apariencia distinguida. Cada uno de ellos, de la manera más amable, me dirigió una palabra o inclinó la cabeza en señal de saludo, como si yo perteneciera a ese lugar; sin embargo, no me sentía con el suficiente valor como para preguntar a cualquiera de esas personas tan distinguidas, dónde me correspondía estar exactamente. Entonces me encontré con un joven más o menos de mi edad, quien parecía no estar ocupado en algo urgente. Se encontraba parado al lado de un venado de pocos años, al cual le empezaban a crecer los cuernos, y le estaba rascando inconscientemente las protuberancias. Quizá éstas al crecer den comenzón, como sea, aquel venado parecía gozar con esa atención.

«*Mixpantzinco*, hermano —me saludó el joven. Supuse que era uno de los hijos de Nezahualpili que me confundía con otro. Entonces notó el canasto que cargaba y dijo—: Tú eres el nuevo Mixtli.»

Le dije que sí y contesté a su saludo.

—Yo soy Huexotzinca —dijo él. (*Huézotl* significa sauce.) Y continuó—: Ya tenemos por lo menos otros tres Mixtli por aquí, así es que tendremos que pensar en otro nombre diferente, para ti.»

Sintiendo que no tenía todavía una gran necesidad de adoptar otro nombre, cambié de tema: «Nunca había visto a los venados caminar entre la gente, afuera de las jaulas y sin miedo.»

«Los recibimos cuando son cervatillos. Los cazadores los encuentran generalmente cuando se ha matado a una cierva y los traen para acá. Siempre hay una nodriza por aquí con los senos llenos, pero sin bebé de momento y ella da de mamar al cervatillo. Pienso que todos crecen creyendo que *son* personas. ¿Acabas de llegar, Mixtli? ¿Quieres comer o descansar?»

Dije sí, sí y sí. «En realidad todavía no sé qué es lo que se supone que debo hacer aquí, ni adónde ir.»

«La Primera Señora de mi padre lo sabrá. Ven, te llevaré con ella.»

«Gracias, Huéxotzincatzin», dije, llamándole por Señor Sauce ya que obviamente había adivinado correctamente: era un hijo de Nezahualpili y por lo tanto un príncipe.

Mientras caminábamos por los extensos terrenos del palacio, con el venado trotando entre nosotros, el joven príncipe me fue diciendo qué eran los numerosos edificios que pasábamos. Un inmenso edificio de dos pisos rodeaba por sus tres lados un patio central con jardín. El ala izquierda, me dijo Huexotzinca, contenía las habitaciones de él y de los demás hijos reales. En el ala derecha moraban las cuarenta concubinas de Nezahualpili. En la parte central estaban los departamentos de los consejeros y sabios del Venerado Orador, que siempre estaban con él, ya residiera en su ciudad capital o en su palacio campestre, y para otros *tlamatínime*: filósofos, poetas, hombres de ciencia, cuyos trabajos eran fomentados por el Orador. Alrededor de los edificios grandes había pabellones con columnas de mármol, en los cuales un *tlamatini* se podía retirar cuando quisiera a escribir, inventar, predecir o meditar en soledad.

Finalmente llegamos al palacio, que era un edificio gigante y con una decoración tan hermosa como cualquier palacio de Tenochtitlan. De dos pisos de alto y por lo menos unos mil pasos de hombre en la fachada, contenía la sala de trono, las cámaras del Consejo de Voceros, salas de baile para los espectáculos de la corte, cuarteles para los guardias, la corte de justicia en donde el Uey-Tlatoani regularmente se entrevistaba con la gente de su pueblo que tuviera problemas o quejas que exponer delante de él. Estaban también las habitaciones del mismo Nezahualpili y las de sus siete esposas contraídas en matrimonio.

«En total, trescientas habitaciones —dijo el príncipe y después me confió con una sonrisa—: y toda clase de recónditos pasillos y escaleras para que mi padre pueda visitar a una esposa u otra sin que las demás se pongan celosas.»

Ahuyentó al venado y entramos por el gran portón central, donde a cada lado estaban haciendo guardia dos nobles señores, que en saludo al príncipe enderezaron sus lanzas cuando pasamos. Huexotzinca me guió por una antecámara espaciosa adornada con tapicería hecha de plumas, luego por una escalera ancha de piedra y a lo largo de una galería alfombrada por tapetes de junco, hasta las habitaciones elegantemente amuebladas de su madrastra. Así es que la segunda persona que conocí fue aquella Tolana-Tecíuapil que el anciano me había mencionado en el cerro, la Primera Señora y la más noble entre todas las mujeres nobles de los alcolhua. Ella estaba conversando con un hombre joven y cejijunto, pero se volvió hacia nosotros y nos sonrió dándonos la bienvenida e indicándonos con una seña que entráramos.

El príncipe le dijo quién era yo y me agaché para hacer el gesto de besar la tierra. La Señora de Tolan, con su propia mano, me levantó gentilmente de mi posición de rodillas y me presentó al otro joven: «Mi hijo mayor, Ixtlil-Xóchitl.» Caí inmediatamente para besar de nuevo la tierra, porque esta tercera persona a quien desde tan lejos había venido a conocer, era el Príncipe Heredero Flor Oscura, sucesor legítimo de Nezahualpili, al trono de Texcoco. Empezaba a sentirme un poco mareado y no solamente por haber estado subiendo y bajando. Allí estaba yo, el hijo de un simple cantero, conociendo en un momento a tres de los personajes más eminentes en El Único Mundo. Flor Oscura inclinó sus oscuras cejas hacia mí y después salió de la habitación con su medio hermano.

La Primera Señora me miró de arriba a abajo, mientras yo la observaba discretamente. No pude adivinar su edad, pero para tener un hijo de la edad del Príncipe Heredero Ixtlil-Xóchitl, por lo menos debía de tener unos cuarenta años, aunque su rostro no presentaba arrugas sino que era bello y benévolo.

«Tú eres Mixtli, ¿verdad? —preguntó—. Pero ya tenemos tantos Mixtli entre los jóvenes y oh, *soy* tan mala para recordar nombres.»

«Algunos me apodan Tozani, mi señora.»

«No, eres mucho más grande que un topo. Eres un joven alto y todavía lo serás más. Te llamaré Cabeza Inclinada.»

«Como usted quiera, mi señora —dije, con un suspiro interno de resignación—. Así es como también apodan a mi padre.»

«Entonces ambos podremos recordarlo, ¿verdad? Ahora, ven y te mostraré tus habitaciones.»

Ella debió de haber tirado de algún cordón para llamar, porque cuando salimos de la habitación nos esperaba una silla de manos portada por dos esclavos musculosos. Bajaron la silla para que ella entrara y se sentara, luego la alzaron y cargaron a lo largo de la galería; descendieron la escalera (manteniendo la silla cuidadosamente horizontal) saliendo del palacio en la oscuridad profunda de la noche. Un esclavo corría al frente cargando una antorcha de tea y otro detrás portando la bandera que indicaba el rango de la señora. Yo trotaba al lado de la silla. Llegamos al edificio de tres lados que Huexotzinca ya me había señalado, y dentro del cual me condujo la Señora de Tolan, que subiendo la escalera, hizo un 'largo recorrido dando varias vueltas, muy hacia dentro del ala izquierda.

«Aquí es», dijo, abriendo una puerta hecha de cuero extendido sobre un marco de madera y barnizado hasta quedar bien duro. La puerta no se recargaba en su lugar, estaba montada sobre pivotes por arriba y por abajo. El esclavo cargó la antorcha hacia adentro para iluminar mi camino, pero únicamente asomé la cabeza y dije sorprendido: «Parece que está vacío, mi señora.»

«Por supuesto. Son tus habitaciones.»

«Yo pensé en una *calmécac*, donde todos los estudiantes duermen amontonados en una habitación común.»

«No lo dudo, pero ésta es una parte del palacio y es aquí donde vas a vivir. Mi Señor Esposo desdeña esas escuelas y a sus sacerdotes-maestros. No estás aquí para asistir a una *calmécac*.»

«¡No asistir...! ¡Pero mi señora, yo creí que había venido a estudiar...!»

«Y así lo harás y muy duramente, en verdad, pero junto con los niños del palacio, los hijos de Nezahualpili y de sus nobles. Nuestros hijos no sin instruidos por sacerdotes sucios, fanáticos y medio locos, sino por sabios escogidos por mi Señor Esposo. Cada maestro ha sido reconocido por su *propio* trabajo en la materia que enseña. Aquí tal vez no aprendas muchas brujerías o invocaciones a los dioses, Cabeza Inclinada, pero sí serás instruido en esas cosas auténticas, verdaderas y útiles que harán de ti un hombre valioso para el mundo.»

Si para entonces no estaba boquiabierto enfrente de ella, lo estuve poco después, cuando vi al esclavo andar con su antorcha prendiendo las velas hechas de cera de abejas, metidas en candeleros pegados a las paredes. Jadeé: «¿Toda una habitación para mí solo?» Luego el hombre pasó a través de un arco a *otra* habitación y yo dije: «¿Dos habitaciones? Pues mi señora ¡esto es casi tan grande como la casa entera de mi familia!»

«Ya te acostumbrarás a la comodidad —dijo y sonrió. Casi tuvo que empujarme para que entrara—. Éste es tu cuarto de estudio. Aquél es el dormitorio. Más allá está el retrete. Me imagino que querrás utilizarlo primero para lavarte después de tu viaje. Sólo tienes que tirar del cordón-campana para que venga un siervo a asistirte. Espero que comas bien y duermas tranquilo, Cabeza Inclinada. Volveré a verte pronto.»

El esclavo la siguió fuera de la habitación y cerró la puerta. Yo me sentí triste al ver salir a una señora tan amable, pero también me alegré, pues entonces podría corretear aquí y allá en mis habitaciones, como un verdadero topo, mirando con mis ojos cegatos todos sus muebles y accesorios. El cuarto para estudiar tenía una mesa baja y una *icpali*, silla, baja con cojín, para sentarse; un cofre de mimbre donde podría guardar mi ropa y mis libros; un brasero de piedra de lava donde ya estaban puestos los *mizquitin*, leños; bastantes velas para que pudiera estudiar cómodamente aun después del oscurecer, y un espejo de *téxcatl* pulido —el cristal raro que da un reflejo definido, no el barato de clase oscura que refleja una imagen débil y muy poco visible—. Había una ventana con una cortina de varitas de caña que podía enrollarse y desenrollarse por medio de unos cordones. La ventana daba al edificio principal del palacio y en ese momento se podía distinguir la antorcha de la silla de la señora que regresaba hacia allá.

El cuarto de dormir no tenía ninguna alfombrilla de *pétlatl*, palma tejida, sino una elevada plataforma de madera y encima de ésta unas diez o doce cobijas gruesas, aparentemente rellenas de plumas; de cualquier modo, formaban una pila que se sentía tan suave como una nube. Cuando estuviera listo para dormir, podría deslizarme entre las cobijas a cualquier nivel, dependiendo del calor que deseara y de cuánta suavidad quisiera debajo.

El retrete, sin embargo, no lo pude comprender tan fácilmente. Había en el piso una depresión cubierta de azulejos para sentarse y bañarse, pero no se veían jarras de agua por ningún lado. Había asimismo un recipiente donde sentarse y efectuar las funciones necesarias, pero éste estaba firmemente fijado al piso y obviamente no podría ser vaciado después de cada uso. La bañera y el lugar para los residuos tenían cada uno de ellos un tubo de forma curiosa que se proyectaba encima, en la pared, pero ninguna de estas tuberías arrojaba agua ni hacía otra cosa según pude descubrir. Bueno, pues nunca pensé que tendría que pedir instrucciones para bañarme o evacuar, pero después de estudiar por un rato y con bastante desconcierto el pequeño cubículo, fui a tirar del cordón-campana que estaba encima de mi cama y esperé con un poco de embarazo la llegada del *tlacotli* que me habían asignado.

Se presentó un muchachito de rostro fresco, que llegó en seguida a mi puerta y dijo graciosamente: «Soy Cózcatl, mi amo, tengo nueve años de edad y sirvo a todos los jóvenes señores en los seis departamentos a este extremo del corredor.»

Cózcatl quiere decir Collar de Joyas, lo que era un nombre demasiado elegante para uno como él, pero no me reí ya que ningún *tonalpoqui* dador de nombres condescendería a consultar sus libros adivinatorios para un niño nacido de esclavos, aunque los padres pudieran pagarlo. Ninguno de esos niños tendría nunca un nombre verdadero, así es que sus padres escogían simplemente uno a su antojo y éste podría ser tan exageradamente impropio como lo prueba Regalo de los Dioses. Cózcatl parecía estar bien alimentado y no llevaba marcas de golpes, ni reculaba frente a mí; vestía un manto corto absolutamente blanco, además del taparrabo que era generalmente la única prenda que llevaba un esclavo. Así es que supuse que también entre los alcólhua o por lo menos en las cercanías del palacio, las clases más humildes eran tratadas con justicia.

El niño cargaba con las dos manos un gran recipiente de cerámica que contenía agua hirviendo, por lo que me hice rápidamente a un lado. La vació en la bañera hundida y luego me salvó de la humillación de tener que preguntarle acerca del funcionamiento del retrete. Aunque Cózcatl me hubiera tomado por un noble, muy bien podía haberse imaginado que cualquier noble de la provincia no estaría acostumbrado a tales lujos y hubiera tenido razón. Así es que sin esperar a que se lo preguntara me explicó:

«Puede enfriar así el agua de la bañera hasta la temperatura que usted prefiera, mi amo.» Señaló la tubería de barro que se proyectaba en la pared. Ésta tenía cerca de un extremo otra corta tubería introducida, que la atravesaba verticalmente. Él, simplemente torció aquel tubo más corto y salió agua limpia y fría.

«La tubería larga trae agua de nuestros abastecimientos principales. Estaría corriendo dentro de su bañera, todo el tiempo, sino fuera porque el tubo más corto le cierra el paso. Pero el tubito tiene un solo agujero en un lado y cuando uno lo mueve de manera que el agujero encare con el tubo largo, el agua puede correr según se necesite. Cuando usted termine de bañarse, mi amo, sólo tiene que quitar el tapón de hule que hay en el fondo y el agua usada se escurrirá por otro tubo.»

Después me indicó el lugar para residuos curiosamente inmóvil y dijo: «El *axixcali* funciona de la misma manera. Cuando usted haya hechos sus necesidades dentro de él, tiene simplemente que torcer esa tubería más corta que está arriba y una corriente de agua se llevará los residuos por la abertura del fondo.»

Yo ni siquiera había notado antes esa abertura y pregunté estúpidamente: «¿Y que los terrones de *cuítlatl* caigan en el cuarto de abajo?»

«No, no, mi amo. Como el agua de la bañera, van a dar a una tubería que los lleva lejos de aquí. Llegan a un estanque en donde los hombres que manejan el estiércol dragan fertilizante para los terrenos de los agricultores. Bien, ordenaré la cena de mi amo, para que le esté esperando cuando haya terminado su baño.»

Me iba tomar algún tiempo el dejar de jugar el papel de rústico y aprender los modales de la nobleza, reflexionaba mientras estaba sentado en mi propia mesa, en mi propio cuarto. Cenaba conejo a la parrilla, frijoles, tortillas y un taco frito de flor de calabaza... *con una bebida de chocólatl*. De donde yo venía, el *chocólatl* había sido un deleite especial, que era tomado una o dos veces al año. Allí, la espumosa bebida roja —hecha del precioso cacao, con miel de abeja, vainilla, especias y las semillas carmesíes del *achíyotl*, todo molido y batido hasta convertirse en una espesa espuma— se podía pedir con tanta facilidad como el agua del manantial. Me preguntaba cuánto tiempo me tomaría perder mi acento de Xaltocan para poder hablar el náhuatl preciso de Texcoco y «acostumbrarme a la comodidad» según la frase de la Primera Señora.

Con el tiempo, me di cuenta de que ningún noble, ni siquiera uno honorario o provisional como yo, jamás tenía que hacer algo por sí mismo. Cuando un noble levantaba la mano para desabrochar el broche del hombro de su magnífico manto de plumas, simplemente lo soltaba y éste nunca llegaba al suelo; algún sirviente estaba allí, listo para tomarlo de sus hombros, *y el noble sabía que siempre habría alguien allí*. Si un noble doblaba las piernas para sentarse, nunca miraba atrás, aunque se desplomara por haber tomado *octli* en exceso, pues nunca caería al suelo; una *icpali* siempre sería deslizada debajo de él, *y él sabía que la silla estaría allí*.

Por un tiempo yo me preguntaba si la gente noble nacía con ese alto grado de aplomo o si podría yo adquirirlo por medio de la práctica. Sólo había una manera de saberlo. A la primera oportunidad que tuve, no recuerdo en qué ocasión, entré en una sala llena de señores y señoras, hice los saludos apropiados y me senté con aplomo y sin mirar atrás. La *icpali* estaba allí. Ni siquiera eché una mirada atrás para ver de dónde había venido. Para entonces ya sabía que una silla, o cualquier cosa que yo deseara y esperara de mis inferiores, siempre estaría allí. Ese pequeño experimento me enseñó una cosa que jamás olvidé. Para poder exigir el respeto, la deferencia y los privilegios reservados a la nobleza, lo único que tenía que hacer era osar *ser* un noble.

A la mañana siguiente a mi llegada, el esclavo Cózcatl llegó con mi desayuno y una cantidad considerable de ropa nueva para mí, más de la que me había puesto y gastado durante toda mi vida anterior. Me trajo unos taparrabos y mantos de brillante algodón blanco, hermosamente bordados. También sandalias de ricos y moldeables cueros, incluyendo un par doradas para ser usadas en las ceremonias y que se ataban casi hasta las rodillas. La Señora de Tolan incluso me había enviado un broche de piedra de heliotropo, para mis mantos que hasta entonces había llevado solamente anudados sobre mi hombro.

Cuando me hube vestido con uno de esos trajes estilizados, Cózcatl me condujo de nuevo por los terrenos ilimitados del palacio, indicándome las salas de estudio. Había muchas más materias de estudio disponibles allí que en cualquier *calmécac*. Naturalmente las que más me interesaban eran las relacionadas con el conocimiento de las palabras, como historia, geografía y demás. Pero podría también, si así lo decidía, asistir a las lecciones de poesía, orfebrería en oro y plata, hechura de plumaje, recorte de gemas y otras artes diversas.

«Las lecciones que no requieren aperos y bancos únicamente tienen lugar dentro de un edificio durante el mal tiempo —dijo mi pequeño guía—. Los días agradables, como éste, los Señores Maestros y sus estudiantes prefieren trabajar al aire libre.»

Podría ver a los grupos sentados sobre el césped o alrededor de los pabellones de mármol. Cada maestro en cada grupo era un hombre ya entrado en años, que llevaba el manto amarillo que le distinguía, pero sus alumnos eran diversos: hombres y muchachos de diferentes edades, incluso aquí y allá una muchacha o un esclavo, sentados a corta distancia.

«¿Los estudiantes no son clasificados según sus edades?», pregunté.

«No, mi señor, lo son por su capacidad. Algunos han avanzado más en una materia que en otra. La primera vez que usted asista, será interrogado por cada Señor Maestro para determinar en qué grupo de estudiantes sería conveniente que usted estuviera; por ejemplo, entre los principiantes, los aprendices o los avanzados y demás. El Señor Maestro lo clasificará según los conocimientos que usted ya tenga y según a lo que a su juicio sea usted más apto para aprender.»

«¿Y las muchachas? ¿Y los esclavos?»

«Cualquier hija de un noble tiene permiso a asistir desde el primero hasta el más alto grado, si demuestra la capacidad y el deseo. La mayoría de ellas estudian sólo hasta poder conversar inteligentemente sobre algunos temas, para que si se llegan a casar con esposos estimables, no avergonzarlos cuando asistan a las reuniones de la Corte. Los esclavos tienen permitido estudiar hasta donde sea compatible con sus empleos individuales.»

«Tú mismo hablas muy bien para ser un *tlacotli* tan joven.»

«Gracias, mi amo. Estudié hasta llegar a aprender a hablar buen náhuatl y el comportamiento y los rudimentos del manejo de la casa. Cuando tenga más edad, me aplicaré para recibir un mayor adiestramiento, con la esperanza de llegar a ser algún día Maestro de las Llaves en alguna casa de la nobleza.»

Dije grandiosa, expansiva y generosamente: «Cuando llegue a tener una casa noble, Cózcatl, te prometo ese puesto.»

No dije «si», dije «cuando». Ya no soñaba ociosamente con elevarme rápidamente al estado de noble, lo estaba ya vislumbrando. Me quedé allí parado en aquel parque tan bello, con mi sirviente al lado y me enderecé en toda mi estatura dentro de mis ropas nuevas y finas, y sonreí al pensar en el gran hombre que llegaría a ser. Ahora, en este momento que estoy sentado aquí entre ustedes, mis reverendos amos, encorvado y consumido en mis harapos, sonrío al pensar en el joven jactancioso y pretencioso que fui.

El Señor Maestro de Historia, Neltitica, quien parecía ser lo suficientemente viejo como para haber *experimentado* toda la historia, anunció al grupo de estudiantes: «Hoy tenemos entre nosotros un nuevo *píltontli*, estudiante, un mexícatl quien será conocido por el nombre de Cabeza Inclinada.»

Me sentía tan contento de ser presentado como un «joven noble» estudiante, que no reculé esta vez por el apodo.

«Quizá sería usted tan amable, Cabeza Inclinada, en darnos una breve historia de su pueblo mexica...»

«Sí, Señor Maestro», dije confiadamente. Me paré y cada rostro del grupo se volvió hacia mí para mirarme fijamente. Aclaré la voz y dije lo que me habían enseñado en la Casa del Aprendizaje de Modales en Xaltocan:

«Sepan, entonces, que originalmente mi pueblo habitaba una región muy al norte de estas tierras. Era Aztlan, El Lugar de las Garzas Níveas, y en aquel entonces mi pueblo se llamaba a sí mismo los aztlantlaca o los azteca, la Gente Garza. Sin embargo, Aztlan era un país duro y su dios principal, Huitzilopochtli, habló a mi pueblo acerca de una tierra generosa que encontrarían hacia el sur. Dijo que sería un viaje largo y difícil, pero que reconocerían su nueva patria cuando encontraran en ella un *nopali* en el que estuviera parada un águila dorada. Así es que todos los azteca abandonaron todo: sus finos hogares, sus palacios, sus pirámides, sus templos, sus jardines y se encaminaron hacia el sur.»

A alguien del grupo de estudiantes se le escapó una risita.

«El viaje duró gavilla tras gavilla de años y tuvieron que pasar por las tierras de muchos otros pueblos. Algunos les fueron hostiles; pelearon con ellos e intentaron que los azteca regresaran. Otros fueron hospitalarios y dejaron que descansaran entre ellos, algunas veces por corto tiempo, otras por muchos años, y estos pueblos fueron pagados con el ser instruidos en el noble lenguaje, las artes y las ciencias únicamente conocidas por los azteca.»

Alguien del grupo murmuró y otro rió ahogadamente.

«Cuando los azteca llegaron finalmente a este valle fueron recibidos amablemente por los tecpanecas, la gente de la orilla occidental del lago, quienes les cedieron Chapultépec como lugar de descanso. Los aztecas vivieron en aquella colina del Chapulin mientras sus sacerdotes seguían vagando por el valle en la búsqueda del águila en el *nopali*. El *nopali* en el lenguaje tecpaneca era llamado *tenochtli*, así es que ese pueblo llamó a los azteca los tenoch-ca y con el tiempo los azteca también tomaron ese nombre para ellos mismos: la Gente Cacto. Como Huitzilopochtli había prometido, los sacerdotes encontraron la señal, un águila dorada parada sobre un *nopali* y la encontraron en una isla del lago que no estaba poblada. Todos los tenochca-azteca inmediatamente y gozosamente se trasladaron de Chapultépec a esa isla.»

Alguien del grupo se rió abiertamente.

«En la isla construyeron dos grandes ciudades, una que se llama Tenochtitlan, Lugar de la Gente Tenochtli Cacto, y la otra se llama Tlaltelolco, Lugar de Roca. Mientras ellos construían sus ciudades, los tenochca notaron que cada noche podían ver desde su isla a la luna Metztli reflejada en las aguas del lago. Así es que también llamaron a su nuevo lugar de residencia Metztli-Xictli, que significa En Medio de la Luna. Con el tiempo lo acortaron a Mexitli y luego a Mexico, finalmente llegaron a llamarse a sí mismos los mexica. Por signo adoptaron el águila posada en el *nopali*, y ésta agarrando con el pico el glifo parecido a un listón que simboliza la guerra.»

Aunque un buen número de mis nuevos compañeros se estaban riendo en ese momento, perseveré.

«Entonces, los mexica empezaron a extender su influencia y su dominio y muchos pueblos se beneficiaron, lo mismo como mexica adoptivos o como aliados o socios mercantiles. Aprendieron a adorar a nuestros dioses o a variaciones de ellos y nos dejaron apropiarnos de los suyos. Aprendieron a contar con nuestra aritmética y marcar el tiempo con nuestros calendarios. Nos pagan tributo con bienes y con moneda por el miedo a nuestros invencibles ejércitos. Hablan nuestro lenguaje en deferencia a nuestra superioridad. Los mexica han construido la más poderosa civilización que se haya conocido en este mundo, y Mexico-Tenochtitlan se levanta en su centro... *In Cem-Anáhuac Yoyotli*, El Corazón del Único Mundo.»

Besé la tierra en saludo al anciano Señor Maestro y me senté. Todos mis compañeros estaban levantando la mano, pidiendo permiso para hablar, mientras organizaban un gran clamor que iba desde las risas hasta los gritos de mofa. El Señor Maestro hizo un gesto imperioso y el grupo se quedó quieto y silencioso.

«Gracias, Cabeza Inclinada —dijo cortésmente—. Me preguntaba cuál sería la versión que estaban enseñando las *telpochcaltin* mexica en estos días. En historia, usted no conoce casi absolutamente nada, joven señor, y lo poco que sabe está equivocado en casi todo.»

Enrojecí como si hubiera sido abofeteado. «Señor Maestro, usted me pidió una historia breve. Puedo ampliarla con más detalle.»

«Sea usted tan amable de no hacerlo —dijo—, y en compensación le haré el favor de corregir sólo uno de los detalles ya ofrecidos. Las palabras mexica y mexico no derivan de Metztli, la luna.» Señaló con un movimiento de su mano para que me sentara y se dirigió a todos los estudiantes.

«Jóvenes señores y señoras, esto esclarece lo que con frecuencia les he dicho de la historia del mundo que probablemente escucharán, porque algunas narraciones están tan llenas de imposibles invenciones como de vanidad. Es más, nunca he encontrado a un historiador o a ninguna clase de profesional erudito, que pudiera poner en su trabajo la más mínima traza de humor, de picardía o de jovialidad. No he hallado a ninguno que no considerara su materia en particular como la más vital y digna de estudio. Ahora bien, sí concedo importancia a esas obras eruditas, pero, ¿es necesario que la importancia ponga siempre una cara larga de severa solemnidad? Quizá los historiadores sean hombres serios y la historia sea a veces tan solemne que entristezca. Sin embargo, la historia está hecha por *gente* y ésta frecuentemente comete travesuras o da cabriolas mientras la hace. La verdadera historia de los mexica lo confirma.»

Me habló directamente a mí, otra vez. «Cabeza Inclinada, sus antepasados azteca no aportaron nada a este valle: ninguna sabiduría antigua, ningún arte, ninguna ciencia, ninguna cultura. Lo único que trajeron fueron sus propias personas: un pueblo nómada, furtivo, lamentablemente armado, que llevaban pieles raídas repletas de sabandijas y que adoraban a un dios repulsivamente bélico ansioso de matanzas y de derramamiento de sangre. Ese populacho fue odiado y repelido por todas las demás naciones ya instaladas en este valle. ¿Podría algún pueblo civilizado dar la bienvenida a una invasión de groseros mendigos? Los azteca no se establecieron en aquella isla de la ciénaga, en medio del lago, porque su dios les diera una señal y no fueron hasta allí alegremente. Se quedaron en aquel lugar porque no había otro a donde ir, y nadie más había tenido interés en apropiarse de ese pedazo de tierra rodeado de pantanos.»

Mis compañeros me observaban con el rabillo del ojo. Intenté no demostrar ninguna angustia ante las palabras de Neltitica.

«Los azteca no construyeron inmediatamente grandes ciudades ni ninguna otra cosa; tuvieron que utilizar todo su tiempo y energía en encontrar algo para comer. No tenían permitido pescar, porque los derechos de pesca pertenecían a las naciones que los rodeaban. Así es que durante mucho tiempo sus antepasados subsistieron con gran dificultad comiendo cosas repugnantes como gusanos, insectos acuáticos, los huevos viscosos de esos bichos asquerosos y la única planta comestible que crecía en esa miserable ciénaga. Ésta era el *mexixin*, el mastuerzo común, una hierba áspera y de sabor amargo. Sin embargo, si sus ascendientes no tenían otra cosa, Cabeza Inclinada, sí poseían un mordaz sentido del humor. Dejaron de usar el nombre de azteca y se llamaron a sí mismos, con una mofa irónica, los mexica.»

El solo nombre produjo más risas entre los estudiantes bien informados. Neltitica continuó:

«Con el tiempo, los mexica inventaron el sistema *chinámitl* de cultivar cosechas adecuadas, pero aun entonces sólo laboraban para sí mismos un mínimo de alimentos básicos, como el maíz y el frijol. Sus *chinampa* se usaban principalmente para sembrar los vegetales y hierbas menos usuales como jitomates, salvia, cilantro y camotes que sus vecinos más elegantes no se molestaban en cultivar. Y los mexica trocaban esas golosinas por los utensilios que necesitaban: aperos, materiales de construcción, telas y armas, que de otra manera las naciones de tierra firme no les hubieran dado voluntariamente. Desde entonces y en adelante, progresaron rápidamente hacia la civilización, la cultura y el poder militar. Pero nunca olvidaron aquella hierba amarga que les había sostenido al principio, el *mexixin*, y no abandonaron el nombre que habían adoptado de ésta. Mexica es un nombre que ha venido a ser conocido, respetado y temido por todo nuestro mundo, pero solamente quiere decir...»

Hizo una pausa intencionada y sonrió; yo enrojecí de nuevo al escuchar gritar a todo el grupo en coro:

«¡*La Gente de la Mala Hierba!*»

«Entiendo, joven señor, que usted ha hecho algunos ensayos tratando de aprender por sí mismo algo de lectura y escritura —me dijo ásperamente el Señor Maestro de Conocer-Palabras, como si creyera que tal educación de hágalo-usted-mismo fuera imposible—. Tengo entendido que ha traído una muestra de su trabajo.»

Respetuosamente le entregué una larga tira plegada de papel de corteza, de la cual me sentía muy orgulloso. La había dibujado con mucho cuidado y pintado con los colores brillantes que me había dado Chimali. El Señor Maestro tomó el compacto libro y comenzó a desdoblar lentamente sus páginas.

Era una narración de un incidente famoso en la historia de los mexica, cuando acababan de llegar al valle y cuando la nación más poderosa era la de los culhua. El soberano de los culhua era Cóxcox, quien había declarado la guerra al pueblo de Xochimilco e invitado a los recién llegados mexica a combatir como sus aliados. Cuando se había obtenido la victoria, los guerreros cúlhua regresaron con sus prisioneros xochimilca, en cambio los guerreros mexica regresaron sin ninguno y Cóxcox los tachó de cobardes. Entonces los guerreros mexica abrieron los sacos que cargaban y los vaciaron, dejando salir montones de orejas, todas del lado izquierdo, que habían cortado a la multitud xochimilca que habían vencido. Cóxcox se quedó pasmado y a la vez contento, y desde ese momento los mexica fueron contados y reconocidos como muy buenos guerreros.

Pensé que había trabajado muy bien el episodio con las palabras-pintadas, sobre todo en la meticulosidad con que describí las innumerables orejas y la expresión de pasmo en la cara de Cóxcox. Esperaba, casi congratulándome a mí mismo, la apreciación del Señor Maestro por mi brillante trabajo.

Sin embargo, él estaba ceñudo mientras daba rápidos vistazos a las páginas del libro, que pasaba mirando de un lado a otro de las tiras plegadas; finalmente me preguntó: «¿En qué dirección se supone que se debe leer esto?»

Perplejo le dije: «En Xaltocan, mi señor, desdoblamos las páginas a la izquierda. Es decir, para que podamos leer cada tira de izquierda a derecha.»

«¡Sí, sí! —dijo severamente—. *Todos* acostumbramos a leer de izquierda a derecha, pero tu libro no tiene ninguna indicación de que se deba de leer así.»

«¿Indicación?», dije.

«Supongamos que se te ordena escribir en una inscripción que se tendrá que leer en otra dirección, en el friso de un templo o en una columna, por ejemplo, en donde la arquitectura requerirá que sea leído de derecha a izquierda o incluso de arriba hacia abajo.» Nunca se me había ocurrido esa posibilidad y así se lo dije.

«Naturalmente que cuando un escribano tiene que pintar a dos personas o a dos dioses conversando, éstos deben ser pintados cara a cara —me dijo con impaciencia—. Sin embargo, hay una regla básica. La mayoría de los individuos *tienen que mirar de cara hacia la dirección en que la escritura se deberá leer.*»

Creo que tragué saliva ruidosamente.

«¿Nunca te diste cuenta de esta regla tan simple de escritura? —dijo con disgusto—. ¿Tienes el descaro de mostrarme esto? —Y me lo lanzó sin ni siquiera tomarse la molestia de volverlo a doblar—. Cuando mañana asistas a tu primera clase de conocer-palabras, únete al grupo que está allá.»

Apuntó a través del prado hacia un grupo que estaba tomando su lección alrededor de uno de los pabellones. Me sentí descorazonado y todo mi orgullo se evaporó. Incluso a esa distancia podía darme cuenta de que todos los estudiantes tenían la mitad de mi estatura y de mi edad.

Era muy mortificante sentarme entre *infantes*, para empezar desde el principio en ambas materias de historia y de conocimientos de palabras, como si nunca se me hubiera enseñado nada, como si nunca me hubiera esforzado por aprender nada. Así es que me sentí muy contento al descubrir que en el estudio de la poesía, por lo menos, había sólo un grupo de estudiantes, que no estaban divididos en principiantes, aprendices y avanzados, y por este motivo no quedé rezagado en la clase. Entre los estudiantes se encontraban dos príncipes de los alcolhua, el joven Huexotzinca y su medio hermano mayor, el Príncipe Heredero Ixtlil-Xóchitl; había otros nobles que casi rayaban en la ancianidad y también hijas y mujeres de los *pípiltin*; también asistían más esclavos de los que había visto en otras materias.

Parece que no importaba mucho el autor del poema ni el tema, tanto si era la alabanza a un dios o a un héroe, la narración de un hecho histórico, una canción de amor, una lamentación o una composición satírica; ese poema no se tomaría en consideración por la edad del poeta, su sexo, su posición social, su educación o su experiencia. Un poema simplemente lo es o no lo es. Vive o no existe. Se hacía y era recordado o se olvidaba tan rápidamente como si nunca se hubiese compuesto. Y en esa clase sólo me contentaba con sentarme y escuchar, temeroso de intentar mis propios poemas. No fue sino hasta que pasaron muchos años que pude componer uno y desde entonces lo he escuchado recitar aun a forasteros. Así es que ese poema vivió, pero es tan pequeño que no puedo llamarme poeta por eso.

Recuerdo muy vívidamente la primera vez que asistí a la lección de poesía. Un visitante distinguido había sido invitado por el Señor Maestro a leer sus composiciones y estaba a punto de empezar cuando yo llegué y me senté sobre el pasto, al final del numeroso grupo. No podía verlo bien a esa distancia, pero sí me di cuenta de que era medianamente alto y bien constituido, tenía más o menos la edad de la Señora de Tolan, llevaba un manto de algodón bordado sujeto con un ·broche de oro y no portaba ningún adorno que hiciera notar su clase social o su oficio. Así es que juzgué que era un poeta profesional, con el talento suficiente como para haber sido recompensado con una pensión y un lugar en la Corte.

Él arregló varias hojas de papel de corteza que tenía en su mano y dio una al esclavo que estaba sentado a sus pies con las piernas cruzadas, sosteniendo sobre ellas un tamborcillo. Entonces el visitante anunció, con una voz que aunque suave se escuchaba bien: «Con permiso del Señor Maestro, mis señores estudiantes, hoy no recitaré ninguna de mis composiciones, sino que recitaré las de un poeta más grande y más sabio. Mi padre.»

«*Ayyo*, con mi permiso y *placer*», dijo el Señor Maestro moviendo benignamente la cabeza. Los estudiantes murmuraron colectivamente *ayyo* en señal de aprobación, como si cada uno ya conociera los poemas del padre del poeta.

Por todo lo que les he contado acerca de nuestra escritura-pintada, reverendos frailes, ya se habrán dado cuenta de que es inadecuada para la poesía. Nuestros poemas o se transmitían oralmente, o no se conservaban. Cualquiera que escuchaba un poema y le gustaba podía memorizarlo y transmitirlo a otra persona, que a su vez hacía lo mismo. Para ayudar a memorizarlo a los que escuchaban, un poema usualmente era construido de tal manera que las sílabas de sus palabras tenían un ritmo regular y los sonidos eran repetidos en los finales de sus líneas.

Los papeles que el visitante traía tenían solamente las palabras-pintadas para asegurar su memoria y no olvidar u omitir alguna línea, para recordar aquí o. allá la importancia de alguna palabra o algún pasaje que su padre, el poeta, hubiese trabajado en un tono especial. El papel que le daba a su esclavo cada vez que empezaba a recitar un nuevo poema, tenía marcado los compases a seguir. En cada papel había rayas de pintura, unas cortas y otras más largas; varias unidas y otras espaciadas. Éstas señalaban al esclavo qué ritmo debía golpear con su mano en el tambor para acompañar la recitación del poeta: algunas veces murmurante, otras con un riguroso énfasis en las palabras y otras como el suave palpitar de un corazón, entre las pausas de las líneas.

Los poemas que el visitante recitó y cantó aquel día fueron felizmente expresados en una cadencia dulce, pero todos tenían un dejo de triste melancolía, como cuando un otoño prematuro penetra calladamente en medio del verano. Después de tantas gavillas de años y sin tener las palabras-pintadas para ayudar a mi memoria, sin ningún tambor que marque sus tiempos y sus pausas, todavía puedo repetir uno de ellos:

> *Hice una canción en alabanza de la vida,*
> *un mundo tan brillante como de un* quétzal *la pluma:*
> *de cielos turquesa y dorada luz solar,*
> *torrentes de piedrajade, jardines brotar...*
> *Pero el oro puede fundirse, las joyas se romperán.*
> *Las flores se marchitan, sus pétalos se esparcen;*
> *desposeídos de sus hojas, los árboles se entristecen.*
> *El sol se va, las sombras espantosas llegarán.*

Ve la belleza perderse, nuestros amores enfriados.
Los dioses desamparan sus altares desgastados.
¿Por qué mi canción de repente me acribilla?

Cuando el recital concluyó, la multitud que escuchaba respetuosa y atentamente se levantó y se separó. Unos vagaban a solas repitiendo, una y otra vez, uno o varios poemas, hasta fijar las palabras en su memoria. Yo era uno de ésos. Otros rodearon al visitante y, besando la tierra delante de él, lo agasajaban dándole las gracias y felicitándolo. Yo estaba caminando en círculos sobre el pasto con la cabeza inclinada, repitiéndome a mí mismo el poema que acabo de recitarles a ustedes, cuando se me aproximó el joven príncipe Huexotzinca.

«Te he estado escuchando, Cabeza Inclinada —me dijo—. Yo también creo que ése es el mejor poema de todos. Y ése me inspiró un poema que está bulliéndome en la mente. ¿Quieres ser tan amable de escucharlo?»

«Me honra en ser el primero», dije y él recitó este poema:

Ustedes me dicen, entonces, que tengo que perecer
como también las flores que cultivé perecerán.
¿De mi nombre nada quedará,
nadie mi fama recordará?
Pero los jardines que planté, son jóvenes y crecerán...
Las canciones que canté, ¡cantándose seguirán!

Le dije: «Pienso que es un poema muy bueno, Huexotzíncatzin, y muy real. Seguro que el Señor Maestro te dará su aprobación.» Y no estaba adulando servilmente al príncipe, pues como ustedes pueden comprobar, he recordado también ese poema, durante toda mi vida.

«De hecho —continué—, pudiera haber sido compuesto por el gran poeta cuyas composiciones acabamos de escuchar.»

«*Yya*, no, Cabeza Inclinada —me increpó—. Ningún poeta de nuestro tiempo podrá igualarse con el incomparable Nezahualcóyotl.»

«¿Quién?»

«¿No lo sabes? ¿No reconociste a mi padre cuando recitaba? Él leía las composiciones de *su padre*, mi abuelo, el Venerado Orador Cóyotl Ayuno.»

«¿Cómo? ¿El hombre que recitó era Nezahualpili? —exclamé—. Pero no llevaba ninguna insignia de su dignidad. Ninguna corona o manto emplumado, ningún cayado o bandera...»

«Oh, él tiene sus excentricidades. Excepto en las reuniones de estado, mi padre jamás se viste como cualquier Uey-Tlatoani. Cree que un hombre sólo debe ostentar las muestras de sus hazañas. Medallas ganadas o cicatrices, no cosas adquiridas por herencia, compradas o en matrimonio. ¿Pero quieres decir que no has sido todavía presentado a él? ¡Ven!»

Sin embargo, parecía que Nezahualpili tenía también cierta aversión a que su gente le demostrara abiertamente su aprecio, porque cuando el príncipe y yo nos abrimos paso a codazos entre la multitud de estudiantes, él ya se había ido.

La Señora de Tolan no me había engañado cuando me dijo que tendría que trabajar muy duro en la escuela, pero no quiero aburrirlos, reverendos frailes, contándoles mi quehacer diario, ni los sucesos mundanos de mis días o las gavillas de trabajo que llevaba a mis habitaciones al final de cada jornada. Solamente les diré que aprendí aritmética, cómo llevar libros de cuentas y cómo calcular el cambio entre las varias monedas que existían. Estudié también la geografía de estas tierras, si bien en aquel tiempo no se *conocía* mucho acerca de las que estaban mucho más allá de las nuestras, y que más tarde descubrí explorándolas personalmente. Mientras tanto gozaba y adelantaba cada vez más en mis estudios del conocimiento de las palabras, siendo cada vez más hábil en lectura y escritura. Creo que también progresé mucho con las lecciones de historia, aun cuando éstas refutaran las más fomentadas alabanzas y creencias de los mexica. El Señor Maestro Neltitica compartía generosamente su tiempo con nosotros, incluso dándonos a algunos lecciones privadas. Me acuerdo de una de ellas, cuando se sentó conmigo y con otro muchacho mucho más joven llamado Póyec, hijo de un noble de Texcoco.

«Desgraciadamente hay una brecha en la historia mexica —dijo el maestro— como una grieta ancha hecha en la tierra por un terremoto.»

Y mientras disertaba, se iba preparando un *poquíetl* para fumar. Era como tubo hueco y delgado hecho sustancialmente de hueso o de piedrajade, decorativamente tallado, con una boquilla al final de uno de sus lados. En el lado opuesto, que también está abierto, se insertaba un pedacito seco de caña o papel enrollado, firmemente relleno con hojas secas y finamente picadas de la planta *picíetl*. Algunas veces se mezclaba con hierbas y especias para añadir así sabor y fragancia. El que la usa debe sostener el tubo entre sus dedos y prender fuego, en el extremo opuesto, a la caña o al papel. Su contenido empieza a convertirse lentamente en cenizas humeantes, mientras el que la usa chupa una pizca del humo, lo inhala y, puff, lo hecha fuera otra vez.

Después de darle lumbre con un carbón del brasero, Neltitica dijo: «Solamente hace unas cuantas gavillas de años que el Venerado Orador de los mexica, Itzcóatl, Serpiente de Obsidiana, fraguó la Triple Alianza: mexica-acolhua-tepaneca, siendo por supuesto los mexica la parte dominante. Teniendo segura la eminencia de su pueblo, Serpiente de Obsidiana decretó entonces que se quemaran todos los libros de los días pasados y se escribieran nuevas narraciones para glorificar el pasado de los mexica, para dar a éstos una antigüedad espuria.»

Miré al azuloso humo que se levantaba de su *poquíetl* y murmuré: «Libros... quemados...» Era difícil creer que un Uey-Tlatoani tuviera el corazón de quemar algo tan precioso, irreparable e inviolable como los libros.

«Serpiente de Obsidiana hizo eso —continuó el Señor Maestro— para que su gente creyera que ellos habían sido y siempre serían los verdaderos guardianes del arte y la ciencia, y por lo tanto hacerles creer que su destino era imponer su civilización a cualquier otro pueblo inferior. Sin embargo, ni los mexica podían ignorar la evidencia de que habían existido mucho tiempo antes de su llegada aquí otras civilizaciones avanzadas y civilizadas así es que tuvieron que urdir fantásticas leyendas para ajustarse a esa evidencia.»

Póyec y yo pensamos en eso y el muchacho sugirió: «¿Quiere usted decir cosas como Teotihuacan? ¿El Lugar En Donde Los Dioses Se Reunieron?»

«Ése es un buen ejemplo, joven Póyectzin. Esa ciudad se está cayendo, está desierta y las hierbas crecen entre sus ruinas en este momento, pero obviamente un día fue una ciudad mucho más grande y populosa de lo que Tenochtitlan jamás llegara a ser.»

Yo dije: «A nosotros nos enseñaron, Señor Maestro, que había sido construida por los dioses cuando ellos se reunieron y decidieron crear la tierra, la gente y las cosas vivientes...»

«Por supuesto que les enseñaron eso. Ninguna cosa grandiosa que no haya sido hecha por los mexica, puede atribuirse a otros hombres. —Arrojó una voluta de humo por sus narices y continuó—. Aunque Serpiente de Obsidiana borró todo el pasado histórico de los mexica, no pudo quemar las bibliotecas de Texcoco ni de otras ciudades. Nosotros todavía tenemos archivos que nos dicen cómo era este valle mucho tiempo antes de la llegada de los azteca-mexica. Serpiente de Obsidiana no podía cambiar toda la historia de El Único Mundo.»

«¿Y hasta dónde llegan esas historias inalteradas?», pregunté.

«No lo suficientemente lejos. Nosotros no pretendemos tener una información que data desde la Primera Pareja. Ustedes conocen las leyendas. Esos dos fueron los primeros habitantes de la tierra y después todos los demás dioses y luego la raza de los gigantes. —Neltitica dio dos chupadas meditativas a su *poquíetl*—. Esa leyenda acerca de los gigantes quizá sea verdad. Todavía se conserva en Texcoco un hueso muy antiguo descubierto por un agricultor cuando cavaba, yo lo he visto, y los cirujanos *tíciltin* dicen que definitivamente es un hueso humano de la cadera. Y es tan grande como mi estatura.»

El pequeño Póyec dijo riéndose impertinentemente: «No me importaría conocer a un hombre con una cadera así.»

«Bien, dioses y gigantes son cosas para ser ponderadas por los sacerdotes. A mí me interesa la historia de los hombres, especialmente la de los primeros hombres de este valle, los hombres que construyeron ciudades como Teotihuacan y Tolan. Porque todo lo que tenemos lo heredamos de ellos. Todo lo que sabemos lo aprendimos de ellos. —Dio una última chupada y quitó del agujero los residuos quemados de su *picíetl*, caña—. Quizá nunca lleguemos a saber por qué desaparecieron o cuándo, pero las vigas chamuscadas de sus edificios en ruinas sugieren que fueron asaltados por merodeadores que les hicieron huir. Probablemente los salvajes chichimeca, la Gente Perro. Lo poco que hemos podido leer en los murales que se conservan, en tallas esculpidas y en su escritura-pintada, ni siquiera nos dicen el nombre de ese pueblo desaparecido. Sin embargo, sus cosas están ejecutadas con tanto arte, que nosotros, con respeto, nos referimos a sus constructores como los tolteca: los Maestros Artistas, y por muchas gavillas de años hemos estado tratando de igualar sus conocimientos.»

«Pero —dijo Póyec— si los tolteca se fueron hace tanto tiempo, no veo cómo pudimos aprender de ellos.»

«Porque unos cuantos individuos pudieron sobrevivir, aun cuando la masa de ellos, como nación, desapareció. Debió de haber algunos supervivientes que se internaron en los altos riscos y en lo profundo de las florestas. Esos tolteca que no murieron debieron de sufrir en su escondrijo, aun conservando parte de sus libros y de sus conocimientos, con la esperanza de que su cultura pasara a sus hijos y a los hijos de sus hijos, cuando se mezclaron en matrimonio con otras tribus. Desafortunadamente, los únicos pueblos que había en aquel entonces eran totalmente primitivos: los insensibles otomi, los frívolos purémpecha y, por supuesto, los por siempre presentes, la Gente Perro.

«Ayya —dijo el joven Póyec—. Los otomi todavía no aprendían el arte de escribir. En cuanto a los chichimeca, por aquellos días todavía comían su propio excremento.»

«Sin embargo, aun dentro de los bárbaros pudo haber un puñado de especímenes extraordinarios —dijo Neltitica—. Debemos suponer que los tolteca escogieron cuidadosamente a sus compañeras y que sus hijos y nietos hicieron lo mismo, y así se pudo mantener por lo menos un poco de sangre superior. Cada recuerdo de los antiguos conocimientos tolteca, transmitidos de padres a hijos, debió de haber sido un sagrado depósito de familia. Hasta que, finalmente, empezaron a llegar a este valle otros pueblos del norte, también primitivos, pero capaces de reconocer, apreciar y utilizar ese tesoro de conocimientos. Pueblos nuevos deseosos de mantener vivo el rescoldo por tanto tiempo bien guardado, para convertirlo nuevamente en flama.

El Señor Maestro hizo una pausa para poner una nueva caña en el agujero de su *picíetl*. Muchos hombres fumaban el *poquíetl* porque decían que el fumar les conservaba sus pulmones limpios y saludables. Yo también tuve ese hábito cuando fui más viejo y para mí fue una gran ayuda para la meditación, pero Neltitica fumaba más que cualquier hombre, más que todos los que yo conocí en mi vida. Quizá por ser tan adicto a eso, logró conservar una sabiduría excepcional y una vida larga.

Él continuó: «Los primeros que llegaron del norte fueron los chulhua. Los acolhua, mis antepasados y los suyos, Póyectzin. Después de ellos todos los demás que se han asentado en el lago: los tecpaneca, los cochimilca y demás. Entonces como ahora se llamaban a sí mismos por diferentes nombres y sólo los dioses saben de dónde vinieron originalmente, pero todos esos emigrantes llegaron aquí hablando uno u otro dialecto del lenguaje náhuatl. Una vez establecidos en este lago, empezaron a aprender de los descendientes de los desaparecidos tolteca, lo que éstos recordaban de sus artes y oficios.»

«Esto no pudo haber sido hecho en un solo día —dije—. O en una gavilla de años.»

«No, y quizá no en pocas gavillas de años —dijo Neltitica—. Pero durante la mayor parte de este largo aprendizaje, tomado de esos tenues retazos de información, ensayado con errores y hecho por imitación, la mayoría de los pueblos se comprometieron a compartir este aprendizaje y el más rápido en aprender era cumplimentado por todos los demás. Afortunadamente, esos culhua, acolhua, tecpaneca y todos los demás se podían comunicar en un lenguaje común, así es que todos trabajaron juntos. Mientras tanto, fueron echando gradualmente a los pueblos inferiores lejos de esta región. Los purémpecha se fueron hacia el oeste; los otomi y los chichimeca, hacia el norte. Las naciones que hablaban náhuatl se quedaron y crecieron en conocimientos y perfección dentro de una misma paz. Cuando estos pueblos alcanzaron un cierto grado de civilización, dejaron de ayudarse mutuamente y empezaron a competir entre ellos por la supremacía. Fue entonces cuando llegaron los todavía primitivos azteca.»

El Señor Maestro me miró.

«Los azteca o mexica se asentaron en medio de una sociedad que ya estaba bien desarrollada; sin embargo, esa sociedad se encontraba entonces dividida en facciones rivales. Los mexica se las ingeniaron para poder sobrevivir hasta que Cóxcox, el gobernante de los culhua, condescendió en nombrar a uno de sus nobles, llamado Acamapichtli, como el primer Uey-Tlatoani de los azteca. Acamapichtli introdujo a los mexica en el arte de conocer las palabras, y después en todos aquellos conocimientos que ya habían sido salvados y compartidos por todas las naciones asentadas aquí desde hacía muchos años. Los mexica estaban ávidos de aprender y ya sabemos qué uso dieron a ese aprendizaje. Instigaron a las facciones rivales de estas tierras a luchar entre ellas, asegurándoles su lealtad primero a unas y luego a otras, hasta que finalmente consiguieron la supremacía en conocimientos militares, por encima de todas las demás naciones.»

El pequeño Póyec de Texcoco me lanzó una mirada como si yo tuviese la culpa de la agresividad de mis ancestros, pero Neltitica siguió hablando desapasionadamente como un historiador destacado:

«Todos sabemos cómo han crecido y prosperado los mexica desde entonces. Han dejado atrás en riqueza e influencia a todas esas otras naciones que una vez los consideraron insignificantes. Su Tenochtitlan es la ciudad más rica y opulenta que se ha construido desde los días de los tolteca. Aunque se hablan incontables lenguas en Él Único Mundo, los ejércitos, mercaderes y exploradores mexica, que han llegado muy lejos, hacen de nuestro náhuatl una segunda lengua entre todos los pueblos desde los desiertos del norte hasta las selvas del sur.»

Él debió de ver mi sonrisa de satisfacción porque concluyó:

«Pienso que esas adquisiciones deberían ser suficientes para que los mexica se sintieran satisfechos, pero no, han seguido insistiendo en conseguir más honores. Volvieron a escribir sus libros tratando de persuadirse, y de convencer a los demás, de que siempre han sido la nación más notable de esta región. Los mexica se pueden engañar a sí mismos y puede ser que defrauden a los historiadores de las próximas generaciones, pero creo que he demostrado ampliamente que los usurpadores mexica *no* son los grandes tolteca reencarnados.»

La primera Señora de Tolan me invitó a tomar *chocólatl* en sus habitaciones y acudí ansioso, pues una pregunta bullía en mi mente. Cuando llegué, su hijo el Príncipe Heredero estaba allí y guardé silencio mientras discutían pequeños detalles concernientes al funcionamiento del palacio. En cuanto hicieron una pausa en su coloquio, intrépidamente dejé caer la pregunta.

«Usted nació en Tolan, mi señora, que una vez fue una ciudad tolteca. ¿Entonces es usted una toltécatl?»

Ambos, ella y Ixtlil-Xóchitl me miraron sorprendidos; después ella sonrió: «Cualquier persona en Tolan, Cabeza Inclinada; cualquier persona en cualquier parte, se sentiría orgullosa de poder proclamar que tiene tan sólo una gota de sangre tolteca. Pero honestamente, *ayya*, yo no puedo. Durante todo el tiempo que podemos recordar, Tolan siempre ha sido parte del territorio de los tecpaneca, así es que yo vengo de estirpe tecpaneca, si bien sospecho que hace mucho tiempo en nuestra familia hubo uno o dos otomí antes de que esa raza saliera del valle.»

Dije decepcionado: «¿Entonces *no* hay ninguna huella de los tolteca en Tolan?»

«En la gente, ¿quién puede decirlo con certeza? En el lugar, sí. Están las pirámides, las terrazas empedradas y las amplias plazas amuralladas. Las pirámides han sido deslavadas por la erosión, las terrazas están sumidas y agrietadas y las paredes se han caído en algunos lugares. Sin embargo, los exquisitos patrones en donde sus piedras habían estado asentadas, son todavía discernibles, como también, aquí y allá, los bajorrelieves tallados y los fragmentos de sus pinturas. Sus muchas e impresionantes estatuas son las que están menos deterioradas.»

«¿De los dioses?», pregunté.

«No, no lo creo, porque todas tienen la misma cara. Son del mismo tamaño y forma, esculpidas de manera simple y natural, no en el estilo complejo de nuestro tiempo. Son columnas cilíndricas, como si alguna vez hubieran soportado algún techo imponente. Estas columnas están esculpidas en forma de seres humanos, parados; si puedes imaginarlos casi tres veces más altos que cualquier otro.»

«Quizá sean los retratos de los gigantes que vivieron en la tierra después de los dioses», sugerí, recordando el monstruoso hueso de la cadera del que me había hablado Neltitica.

«No, yo creo que representan a los mismos tolteca, sólo que en proporciones mayores a su tamaño real. Sus rostros no son severos, ni brutales, ni arrogantes, como se podría esperar de los dioses o de los gigantes. Tienen una expresión de sosegada vigilancia. Muchas de sus columnas yacen derrumbadas y esparcidas alrededor, abajo en la tierra, pero otras todavía están en lo alto de las pirámides, mirando a través de la campiña como si esperaran paciente y tranquilamente.»

«¿Y qué supone usted que están esperando?»

«Quizá el regreso de los tolteca. —Había sido Ixtlil-Xóchitl quien contestó, añadiendo una risa seca—: Emergiendo de donde han estado escondidos durante todas estas gavillas de años. Regresando con poder y furia a conquistarnos a nosotros los intrusos; a rescatar estas tierras que una vez fueron de ellos.»

«No, mi hijo —dijo la Señora de Tolan—. Ellos nunca fueron

138

un pueblo guerrero, ni lo querían ser, y eso fue su ruina. Si alguna vez pudieran regresar, lo harían en paz.»

Ella sorbió su *chocólatl* e hizo una mueca; se le había acabado la espuma. Tomó de una mesa colocada a su lado el batidor de grandes y pequeños anillos de madera, que se entremezclaban sueltos y ligeramente colgantes en su base cóncava, tallado hábilmente en una sola pieza alargada de cedro aromático. Lo metió en su taza, y agarrando el palo entre las dos manos lo frotó vigorosamente, haciendo girar los anillos del batidor, hasta que el líquido rojizo se esponjó, quedando otra vez espumoso. Después de otro sorbo, lamió la espuma de su labio superior y me dijo:

«Ve alguna vez a la ciudad de Tenochtitlan, Cabeza Inclinada, y contempla los murales que quedaron allí. Solamente uno de ellos muestra a un guerrero, y éste solamente está jugando a la guerra. Su espada no tiene filo, sólo un penacho de plumas en la punta y sus flechas están guarnecidas por bolitas de hule, como las que se usan para enseñar a los muchachos el tiro al arco.»

«Sí, mi señora, yo he utilizado esas flechas cuando practicaba los juegos de guerra.»

«Al ver otros murales, suponemos que los tolteca nunca ofrecieron sacrificios humanos a sus dioses, sino solamente mariposas, flores, codornices y cosas semejantes. Los tolteca fueron un pueblo pacífico porque sus dioses eran bondadosos. Uno de ellos fue, y es, ese Quetzacóatl que todavía es adorado por todas las naciones cercanas y lejanas. El concepto que los tolteca tenían de la Serpiente Emplumada nos dice mucho acerca de *ellos*. ¿Quién sino un sabio y benévolo pueblo nos hubiera podido legar un dios que mezcla tan armoniosamente el señorío y la belleza? La más pavorosa y más graciosa de todas las criaturas, la víbora, cubierta no de escamas duras, sino del suave y bello plumaje del pájaro *quetzaltótotl*.»

Dije: «Me enseñaron que la Serpiente Emplumada realmente vivió una vez en estas tierras y que algún día regresará otra vez.»

«Sí, Cabeza Inclinada, de lo que podemos entender de los restos de la escritura tolteca, es verdad que vivió una vez. Fue hace mucho tiempo Uey-Tlatoani, o como los llamaran los tolteca, y debió de haber sido un gobernante muy bueno. Se dice que Quetzacóatl, el hombre no el dios, inventó la escritura, los calendarios, los mapas de las estrellas y los números que usamos. También se dice que nos dejó la receta del *ahuacamoli* y de todas las otras *moli*, salsas, aunque realmente no puedo imaginarme a Quetzalcóatl haciendo el trabajo de un cocinero.»

Se sonrió y sacudió su cabeza, luego se puso seria otra vez. «Se dice que durante su reinado, en todos los terrenos agrícolas crecían no sólo el algodón blanco, sino también algodón de todos los colores como si ya hubiesen sido teñidos, y que un hombre sólo podía cargar una sola mazorca de maíz. Se dice también que no había desiertos en aquel tiempo, sino árboles frutales y flores creciendo por doquier, en gran abundancia, y el aire estaba perfumado de todas esas fragancias, entremezcladas...»

Yo pregunté: «¿Usted cree, mi señora, que es posible que él regrese otra vez?»

«Bien, él se fue lejos antes de que lo hiciera su pueblo, y se fue solo. Las leyendas dicen que después de haber hecho mucho bien a su pueblo, Quetzalcóatl, de alguna manera y sin quererlo, cometió un pecado tan pavoroso, o hizo *algo* que violentó tanto sus propias y elevadas normas de conducta, que voluntariamente abdicó su trono. Se fue hacia la orilla del mar oriental y construyó una balsa, unos dicen que la hizo con plumas tejidas entrelazadas, otros que la construyó entretejiendo víboras vivas. En sus últimas palabras a los afligidos tolteca, les juró que regresaría algún día. Remó lejos y se desvaneció más allá de la orilla oriental del océano. Desde entonces, Serpiente Emplumada ha sido el único dios reverenciado por cada nación y cada pueblo que conocemos. Sin embargo todos los tolteca han desaparecido desde entonces y Quetzalcóatl todavía no ha regresado.»

«Pero puede ser que ya lo hubiera hecho, puede ser que sí —dije—. Según nuestros/sacerdotes, los dioses caminan frecuentemente entre nosotros sin ser reconocidos.»

«Como mi Señor Padre —dijo Ixtlil-Xóchitl riéndose—, pero yo creo que sería muy difícil que no reconociéramos a Quetzalcóatl. La reaparición de un dios ciertamente debería hacer mucho ruido. Ten la seguridad, Cabeza Inclinada, de que si alguna vez regresa Quetzalcóatl, con o sin comitiva tolteca, lo reconoceremos.»

Abandoné Xaltocan cerca de la temporada de lluvias en el año Cinco Cuchillo y a excepción de anhelar la presencia de Tzitzitlini, había estado tan absorto en mis estudios y en los deleites de la vida de palacio, que apenas me había dado cuenta del rápido transcurrir del tiempo. Francamente me sorprendí cuando mi compañero de escuela, el príncipe Huexotzinca, me informó que en dos días más sería el primero de los *nemontemtin*, los cinco días muertos. Tuve que contar con mis dedos para poder creer que ya había estado fuera de mi casa más o menos un año entero y que éste se acercaba a su fin.

«Todas las actividades serán interrumpidas durante los días huecos —dijo el joven príncipe—. Así es que este año tendremos la oportunidad de movilizar toda la Corte hacia nuestro palacio de Texcoco, y celebrar allí el mes de Cuáhuitl Ehua.»

Ése era el primer mes de nuestro año solar. Su nombre significa El Árbol Es Levantado y se refiere a las numerosas y elaboradas ceremonias durante las cuales las gentes de todas las naciones tenían la costumbre de suplicar al dios de la lluvia, Tláloc, que el siguiente verano fuera abundante en lluvias.

«Como estoy seguro de que querrás estar con tu familia en esta ocasión —continuó Huexotzinca—, te pido que aceptes que mi *acali* personal te lleve hasta allá. Lo enviaré otra vez por ti cerca del Cuáhuitl Ehua, para que te reúnas con nosotros en la Corte de Texcoco.»

Todo eso sucedió muy repentinamente, pero acepté mostrándole mi gratitud por su amabilidad.

140

«Solamente te pido una cosa —dijo—. ¿Podrías estar listo para partir mañana temprano? Comprende, Cabeza Inclinada, que mis remeros querrán estar de vuelta a sus hogares de la playa, sanos y salvos antes de que empiecen los días muertos.»

✠

¡Ah, el Señor Obispo! Una vez más estoy contento y me siento muy honrado de que Su Ilustrísima adorne con su presencia nuestra pequeña reunión. Y una vez más, mi señor, su indigno siervo se atreve a darle la bienvenida saludándolo respetuosamente.

...Sí, entiendo, Su Ilustrísima. Usted dice que hasta estos momentos no he hablado lo suficiente sobre los bárbaros ritos religiosos de mi pueblo y que usted en persona quiere oír especialmente acerca de nuestro temor supersticioso por los días huecos y que también desea escuchar mi narración sobre los ritos paganos de petición al dios de la lluvia. Entiendo, mi señor, y no se preocupe usted, que diré todo lo que sus oídos desean escuchar. En el caso de que mi viejo cerebro vague en sus recuerdos o de que mi lengua ya vieja pase demasiado superficialmente sobre algunos detalles pertinentes, por favor, Su Ilustrísima, no vacile usted en interrumpirme con preguntas o demandas para su esclarecimiento.

Sepan ustedes que fue en el día seis antes del último día del año Seis Casa, cuando el endoselado *acali* tallado, y con banderolas del príncipe Huexotzinca, me dejó en el embarcadero de Xaltocan. La espléndida nave con seis remeros que me habían prestado, avergonzó un poco a la canoa descubierta de dos remos del Señor Garza Roja, quien ese mismo día regresaba con su hijo de la escuela, para el mes ceremonial de Cuáhuitl Ehua. Incluso yo iba mucho mejor vestido que ese principito de provincia, y Pactli inclinó la cabeza involuntariamente congraciándose conmigo, antes de reconocerme; al hacerlo, su rostro se heló.

En mi casa se me dio una bienvenida como a un héroe que regresara de una guerra. Mi padre puso sus manos sobre mis hombros, que ya habían alcanzado casi la misma estatura de los suyos y también su anchura. Tzitzitlini me envolvió con sus brazos, apretándome de una manera que hubiera parecido propia de una hermana para alguien que no hubiera visto cómo sus uñas se clavaban sugestivamente en mi espalda. Hasta mi madre estaba admirada, especialmente por mi traje. Yo llevaba, deliberadamente, mi manto más bellamente bordado, sosteniéndolo con mi broche de hematita al hombro y calzaba mis sandalias doradas que se ataban casi hasta la rodilla.

Amigos, familiares y vecinos se arremolinaban a mi alrededor, para mirar embobados al viajero que había regresado. Me sentí muy feliz al ver entre ellos a Tlatli y a Chimali, quienes habían tenido que mendigar el viaje desde Tenochtitlan, en unos de los *acaltin* cargadores de cantera que regresaban a la isla

141

para ser amarrados en el embarcadero durante los cinco días muertos. Los tres cuartos y el zaguán de mi casa, que parecían haberse contraído curiosamente, se desbordaban de visitantes. No atribuyo eso a mi popularidad personal, sino al hecho de que a la medianoche, empezarían los días huecos, durante los cuales no habría ninguna reunión social.

Pocas personas entre las allí reunidas, a excepción de mi padre y de algunos otros canteros, habían salido de nuestra isla y naturalmente estaban ansiosos de oír acerca del mundo exterior. Sin embargo, hicieron pocas preguntas, parecían estar muy contentos escuchándonos a Chimali, a Tlatli y a mí intercambiar las experiencias vividas en nuestras respectivas escuelas.

«¡Escuelas! —resopló Tlatli—. Es bien poco el tiempo precioso que tenemos para trabajos escolares. Cada día los viles sacerdotes nos levantan en la madrugada para barrer y limpiar nuestros cuartos y todos los demás del edificio. Luego tenemos que ir al lago a atender las *chinampa* de la escuela y a recoger maíz y frijol para la cocina, o ir por todo el camino de la tierra firme a cortar madera para los fuegos sagrados y a partir y llenar bolsas con espinas de maguey.»

Dije: «La comida y la leña lo puedo entender, pero ¿para qué las espinas?»

«Para penitencia y castigo, amigo Topo —gruñó Chimali—. Violas la menor regla y un sacerdote te obliga a pincharte repetidas veces. En los lóbulos de las orejas, en los pulgares y brazos, incluso en las partes privadas. Estoy punzado en todas partes.»

«También sufren hasta los que se comportan muy bien —agregó Tlatli—. Un día sí y otro no, parece que hay una fiesta para algún dios, incluyendo a muchos de los que jamás he oído hablar, y cada muchacho tiene que verter su sangre para la ofrenda.»

Uno de los que escuchaba preguntó: «¿Y cuándo tenéis tiempo de estudiar?»

Chimali hizo una mueca. «El poco tiempo que nos queda no nos rinde mucho. Los maestros sacerdotes no son hombres instruidos. No saben nada excepto lo que está en los libros de texto y éstos están ya tan viejos y manchados que se cae a pedazos la corteza.»

Tlatli dijo: «Chimali y yo tenemos suerte, aunque sea en dos aspectos. Nosotros no fuimos a aprender-libros, así es que la falta de esto no nos preocupa, además, pasamos la mayor parte de los días en los talleres de nuestros maestros de arte, quienes no pierden el tiempo en esas boberías religiosas. Nos hacen trabajar muy duro, así es que *aprendemos* lo que *nosotros* fuimos a aprender.»

«Lo mismo les sucede a algunos otros muchachos —dijo Chimali—. Aquellos que como nosotros son aprendices de físicos, trabajadores en pluma, músicos y demás; pero siento piedad hacia los que fueron a aprender las materias del arte del conocimiento de palabras. Cuando no están ocupados en ritos y en su propia mortificación o en labores serviles, son instruidos por sacerdotes que son tan ignorantes como cualquiera de los estudiantes. Puedes alegrarle, Topo, de no haber podido entrar en un *calmécac.* Hay poco que aprender en uno de ellos, a no ser que hubieras deseado ser sacerdote.»

«Y nadie —dijo Tlatli con un estremecimiento— desearía ser un sacerdote de ningún dios, a menos de que nunca quisiera practicar el sexo, ni tomar un trago de *octli* o ni siquiera bañarse una vez en su vida. A menos de que disfrute verdaderamente inflingiéndose daño a sí mismo, tanto como viendo a la demás gente sufrir.»

Una vez había sentido envidia de Tlatli y de Chimali, cuando ellos se vistieron con sus mejores mantos y se fueron a sus respectivas escuelas, y sin embargo, en esos momentos, allí estaban con sus mismos mantos y siendo ellos, entonces, los que me envidiaban. No tuve que decir una palabra acerca de la vida lujosa que gozaba en la Corte de Nezahualpili. Quedaron suficientemente impresionados cuando hice notar que nuestros textos eran pintados sobre piel de cervato para que duraran más, cuando mencioné la ausencia de interrupciones religiosas, las escasas reglas y poca rigidez, así como también la buena voluntad de los maestros para instruirnos en sesiones privadas.

«¡Imagínense ustedes! —murmuró Tlatli—. Maestros que han trabajado en lo que enseñan.»

«Textos en piel de cervato», murmuró Chimali.

Hubo una conmoción entre las personas que estaban cerca de la puerta y de repente entró Pactli, como si deliberadamente hubiera planeado su llegada para demostrar ser una obra superior del más selecto y prestigioso tipo de *calmecac*. Numerosas personas se agacharon a besar la tierra en saludo al hijo de su gobernador, pero no había espacio suficiente para que todos lo hicieran.

«*Mixpatzinco*», le saludó mi padre con inseguridad.

Desairándolo, sin molestarse en contestar la tradicional respuesta, Pactli me habló directamente: «Vengo a pedir tu ayuda, joven Topo. —Me tendió una tira de papel de corteza y dijo con camaradería—: Tengo entendido de que tus estudios se concentran en el arte del conocimiento de las palabras y te ruego que me des tu opinión acerca de este intento mío, antes de que regrese a la escuela y lo someta a la crítica de mi Señor Maestro.» Pero mientras me hablaba, sus ojos se desviaban hacia mi hermana. Debió de haberle costado un tormento al Señor Alegría, pensé, el haber tenido que servirse de *mí* como una excusa para poder visitar a Tzitzi antes de que la medianoche hiciera su visita imposible.

A Pactli en realidad le importaba muy poco mi opinión sobre su escrito, ya que en esos momentos miraba a mi hermana abiertamente, así es que lo ojeé y dije con aburrimiento: «¿En qué dirección se supone que tengo que leer esto?»

Algunas personas se escandalizaron por el tono de mi voz y Pactli gruñó como si le hubiese abofeteado. Me miró con ira y dijo entre dientes: «De izquierda a derecha, Topo, como tú bien sabes.»

«Usualmente de izquierda a derecha, sí, pero no siempre —dije—. La primera y más básica regla de escritura, que apa-

143

rentemente usted no ha comprendido, es que la mayoría de sus caracteres pintados deben encararse en la dirección hacia donde la escritura debe ser leída.»

Debí de haberme sentido muy orgulloso de mis finas vestiduras y también por haber llegado recientemente de una corte mucho más culta que la de Pactli y de ser el centro de atención de una casa llena de amigos y parientes, porqué si no, probablemente no me habría atrevido a violar las reglas convencionales del servilismo. Sin molestarme en examinar más el papel, lo doblé y se lo devolví.

¿Alguna vez ha notado, Su Ilustrísima, cómo la rabia puede hacer que diferentes personas adquieran distintos colores? La cara de Pactli estaba casi morada; la de mi madre, casi blanca. Tzitzi se llevó la mano a la boca, de la sorpresa, pero luego se rió, lo mismo que Tlatli y Chimali. Pactli desvió su mirada ominosa de mí a ellos y luego la deslizó por toda la concurrencia, de la cual la mayoría de las personas parecían querer volverse aun de otro color: el color invisible del aire. Mudo de coraje, el Señor Alegría comprimió el papel encerrándolo en su puño y salió a grandes zancadas empujando rudamente con los hombros a los que no pudieron cederle inmediatamente el paso.

La mayoría de los demás concurrentes también se fueron casi de inmediato, como si de esa manera pudieran desasociarse de mi insubordinación. Usaron el pretexto de que sus casas estaban más o menos lejos de la nuestra y que querían apurarse en llegar antes del oscurecer y así asegurarse de que ninguna ascua quedara accidentalmente encendida en sus hogares. Mientras la gente se salía, Tlatli y Chimali me lanzaron sonrisas de aprobación, Tzitzi me apretó la mano, mi padre se veía afligido y mi madre tenía una expresión helada. Sin embargo, no todos se fueron. Se quedaron algunos de los huéspedes que fueron lo suficientemente fieles o lo suficientemente necios como para no sentirse aterrorizados por mi manifiesta rebeldía, rebeldía que había ostentado precisamente en la vigilia de los días huecos.

Verán ustedes, durante esos cinco días que estaban por llegar, *cualquier cosa* era considerada como una imprudencia, patentemente infructífera y posiblemente arriesgada. Los días no eran realmente días; eran solamente un intervalo hueco necesario entre el último mes de Xiutecutli y el próximo mes del año de Cuáhuitl Ehua; los días existían tanto como existe un vacío. Por lo que nosotros tratábamos de mantener nuestra propia existencia lo más imperceptiblemente posible. Ésa era la época del año en que los dioses flojeaban y se adormecían; incluso el sol, Tonatíu, estaba pálido, frío y débil en el cielo. Ninguna persona razonable haría nada por estorbar la languidez de los dioses y exponerse a sus iras.

Así es que durante esos cinco días vacíos, todo el trabajo se interrumpía. Todas las actividades cesaban, excepto los trabajos más esenciales e inevitables. Todos los fuegos de los hogares, de las antorchas y de las lámparas eran extinguidos. No se cocinaba y solamente se servían comidas magras y frías. La gente no viajaba, ni visitaba, ni se reunía. Los esposos refrenaban su relación sexual. (También lo hacían y tomaban precauciones nueve meses antes de los *nemontemtin*, porque un niño nacido durante esos días huecos rara vez sobrevivía a ellos.) En todas nuestras tierras, la gente se quedaba dentro de sus casas y se ocupaba en pasatiempos triviales como afilar sus aperos, componer sus redes o simplemente sentarse desanimadamente.

Supongo que puesto que los días huecos eran por sí mismos de tan mal agüero, era lógico que las visitas que se quedaron en nuestra casa aquella noche, conversaran sobre el tema de augurios y presagios. Tlatli, Chimali y yo nos sentamos aparte y seguimos comparando nuestras respectivas escuelas, pero alcanzaba a oír retazos de las pláticas de nuestros mayores:

«Fue hace un año que ella pisó a su pequeña que estaba gateando en el piso de la cocina. Debí haberle dicho lo que ella estaba haciendo al *tonali* de la niña. Ésta no ha crecido ni dos dedos en un año entero desde que la pisó; va a ser una enana, esperad y lo veréis.»

«Antes me burlaba, pero ya no, porque sé que son verdad las viejas historias sobre los sueños. Una noche soñé que una jarra de agua se había roto y al día siguiente mi hermano Xícama moría accidentado en la cantera, como recordaréis.»

«Algunas veces los resultados calamitosos no suceden hasta pasado mucho tiempo y uno incluso puede haber olvidado cuál fue la acción descuidada que los provocó. Como aquella vez, hace ya años, en que avisé a Teoxihuítl para que tuviera cuidado con su escoba, pues la vi barrer encima del pie de su hijo que jugaba en el piso. Efectivamente, cuando el muchacho creció, se casó con una viuda casi tan vieja como su madre Teoxihuítl, lo que hizo de él el hazmerreír de la aldea.»

«Una mariposa voló en círculos encima de mi cabeza, y hasta un mes más tarde no supe que en ese mismo día mi única hermana, Cueponi, había muerto en su casa de Tlacopan. Pero debería haberlo sabido por la mariposa, pues ella era mi más querida hermana y mi familiar más cercano.»

No pude evitar el reflexionar en dos cosas. Una era que todo el mundo en Xaltocan, realmente hablaba de una manera muy poco refinada comparado con el náhuatl con el cual me había llegado a acostumbrar últimamente; la otra, que todos los augurios a que nuestras visitas se referían, parecían solamente presagiar nada más que mala fortuna, privaciones, miserias o adversidad. En ese momento me distrajo Tlatli diciéndome algo que había aprendido de su Señor Maestro de Escultura.

«Los humanos son las únicas criaturas que tienen narices. No, no te rías, Topo. De todas las cosas vivientes que esculpimos, solamente los hombres y las mujeres tienen narices que no son solamente parte de un hocico o de un pico, sino que se proyectan de la cara. Así que, como elaboramos nuestras estatuas con tantos detalles decorativos, mi maestro me ha enseñado a esculpir siempre a un humano con una nariz algo exagerada. De este modo cualquier persona viendo hasta la estatua más complicada y aun siendo un ignorante en arte, puede saber a primera vista que representa a un ser humano y no a un jaguar o a una serpiente o incluso a la cara de rana de la diosa del agua Chalchihuitlicue.»

Asentí y guardé esa idea en mi memoria. Desde entonces hice lo mismo con mi escritura-pintada y muchos otros escribanos imitaron mi práctica de dibujar siempre a los hombres y a las mujeres con narices prominentes. En el caso de que nuestra gente esté condenada a desaparecer de la tierra, como los tolteca, confío en que nuestros libros sobrevivirán. Los futuros lectores de nuestra pintura escritura-pintada podrán interpretar que todos los habitantes de estas tierras eran aguileños como los maya, pero no tendrán ningún problema en distinguir entre un rasgo humano y el de un animal, o el de los dioses con aspecto de animales.

«Gracias a ti, Topo, he ideado una firma única para mis pinturas —dijo Chimali sonriendo tímidamente—. Otros artistas firman sus obras con los glifos de sus nombres, pero yo uso esto.» Me mostró una tabla de más o menos el tamaño de una sandalia, con innumerables astillas pequeñitas de aguda obsidiana incrustada en toda su superficie. Me sobresalté y me sentí horrorizado cuando golpeó fuertemente su mano izquierda abierta contra la tabla, entonces, todavía riéndose, la mantuvo abierta para que viera la sangre que se escurría de su palma y de cada uno de sus dedos. «Puede ser que haya otros artistas llamados Chimali, pero fuiste tú, Topo, quien me enseñó que no hay dos manos iguales. —La suya estaba en esos momentos completamente cubierta de sangre—. Por lo tanto, tengo una firma que nunca podrá ser imitada.» Apretó con su mano izquierda el barro de la gran jarra que servía de depósito de agua para la casa, que estaba allí cerca. Sobre su opaca superficie de arcilla pardusca quedó una brillante huella roja.

Viaje usted por estas tierras, Su Ilustrísima, y verá esa misma firma en muchos de los murales de los templos y en las pinturas de los palacios. Chimali dejó una cantidad prodigiosa de sus obras antes de abandonar el trabajo.

Él y Tlatli fueron los últimos invitados en dejar nuestra casa esa noche. Los dos se quedaron a propósito hasta que se escucharon los tambores y las trompetas de concha, que desde el templo de la pirámide anunciaban el comienzo de los *nemontemtin*. Mientras mi madre se apresuraba alrededor de la casa apagando las luces, mis amigos también corrían para llegar a sus hogares antes de que los toques de tambor y los roncos sonidos dejaran de oírse. Era arriesgado para ellos, ya que si los días huecos eran malos, sus noches sin luz eran peor; pero el hecho de que mis dos amigos se quedaran hasta tan tarde, me salvó del castigo que me esperaba por haber insultado al Señor Alegría. Ni mi padre, ni mi madre, podrían encargarse de algo tan serio como un castigo durante los días que seguían y ya para cuando los *nemontentin* terminaron el asunto había sido totalmente olvidado.

Sin embargo, esos días no estuvieron exentos de acontecimientos notables para mí. Durante uno de ellos, Tzitzi me llevó aparte para susurrarme urgentemente. «¿Es que tengo que ir a robar otro hongo sagrado?»

«Hermana impía —le siseé, pero no con ira—. El acto del *ahuilnemíliztl* está prohibido en este tiempo aun a los esposos.»

«*Solamente* a los esposos, para ti y para mí está prohibido siempre, así es que no corremos un riesgo excepcional.»

Antes de que yo pudiera decir algo más, se alejó de mí y fue hasta la enorme jarra, que le llegaba a la cintura y que contenía la provisión de agua para toda la casa; aquella que llevaba la huella de sangre de Chimali. La empujó con todas sus fuerzas volcándola y rompiéndola, y el agua se vertió en cascada por el piso de piedra. Nuestra madre se precipitó dentro del cuarto y soltó una de sus diatribas contra Tzitzitlini. «Moza torpe... la jarra tomó todo un día para llenarse... se suponía que tenía que durar todo el tiempo de los *nemontemtin*... no tenemos ni una gota de agua en la casa y ningún otro recipiente de ese tamaño.»

Sin alterarse, mi hermana dijo: «Mixtli y yo podemos ir al manantial con las jarras más grandes y entre los dos traer lo más que podamos en un viaje.»

Nuestra madre no estimó mucho esta sugestión por lo que siguió chillando durante un buen rato, pero realmente no tenía otra alternativa y finalmente nos dejó ir. Cada uno de nosotros salió de la casa cargando una jarra de barriga grande asida por sus asas, pero a la primera oportunidad las dejamos en el suelo.

La última vez describí a Tzitzi como era en los primeros años de su adolescencia, pero ya para entonces tenía veinte años y por supuesto sus caderas y nalgas se habían llenado para convertirse en las graciosas curvas de una mujer. Cada uno de sus senos había crecido más allá del hueco de mi mano. Sus pezones eran más eréctiles, sus aureolas tenían un diámetro más grande y un color pardo-bermejo más oscuro que resaltaba contra la piel color de cervato que los rodeaba. Tzitzi era también, si es posible, cada vez más rápida en sus arrobamientos, y sus respuestas y movimientos eran más frenéticos. Sólo en el breve intervalo que nos permitimos entre la casa y el manantial, ella llegó al éxtasis por lo menos tres veces. Su creciente capacidad para la pasión y una notable madurez en su cuerpo, me dio el primer indicio de un aserto que mis experiencias con otras mujeres, en años posteriores, sirvieron para confirmar siempre. Así es que no lo considero un aserto, sino más bien, como una teoría comprobada y es ésta:

La sexualidad de una mujer está en proporción directa con el diámetro de la aureola de su seno. No importa cuán bello sea su rostro, ni cuán graciosa su figura; no importa lo accesible o lo alejada que parezca ser. Esas características pueden despistar, inclusive deliberadamente por su parte. Sin embargo, sea una noble astuta, una esclava ingenua o una virgen tímida del templo, existe ese único signo digno de confianza indicador de la sensualidad de su naturaleza y para el ojo conocedor ningún arte cosmético puede esconderlo ni falsificarlo. Una mujer con un área grande y oscura alrededor de su pezón, invariablemente es de sangre caliente, aunque ella desee ser diferente. Una que sólo tiene el pezón sin el disco alrededor, como el vestigio del pezón de un hombre, inevitablemente es fría, aunque ella crea honestamente ser otra, o incluso comportarse de una manera desvergonzada con el objeto de parecer diferente. Por supuesto hay grados intermedios; la medida solamente se puede llegar a aprender por la experiencia. Por lo tanto lo único que necesita un hombre es procurar lanzar una sola mirada al pecho descubierto de una mujer, y sin perder su tiempo y sin tener la necesidad de desilusionarse, puede juzgar lo pasional que será ella.

¿Su Ilustrísima desea que termine con este tema? Ah, bien. No dude de que si me entretuve en ello es porque es *mi* teoría. Siempre le he tenido cariño y me ha gustado comprobarla, y ni una sola vez le he encontrado refutación alguna. Antes pensaba que debería ser señalada a los muchachos tan pronto como entraran en la Escuela del Aprendizaje de Modales. Sigo creyendo que la correlación entre la sexualidad de una mujer y su aureola debería tener una aplicación más útil de la que corresponde solamente a la alcoba.

¡Yyo ayyo! Sabe usted, Su Ilustrísima, se me acaba de ocurrir que su Iglesia podría interesarse en usar mi teoría, como una rápida y sencilla prueba para escoger a las muchachas que, por su naturaleza, fueran las más apropiadas para ser monjas en sus...

Desisto, sí, mi señor.

Solamente mencionaré que cuando Tzitzi y yo regresamos por fin a la casa, casi tambaleándonos bajo el peso de las cuatro jarras de agua, nuestra madre nos regañó por haber estado tanto tiempo al aire libre en tal día. Mi hermana, quien hacía solamente muy poco tiempo era un joven y salvaje animalito sacudiéndose, jadeando y rasguñándome en sus éxtasis, mentía en esos momentos tan fácil y fríamente como cualquier sacerdote:

«No nos puedes regañar por haber flojeado ni haraganeado. Había otros que querían agua del manantial y dado que el día prohíbe congregarse, Mixtli y yo tuvimos que esperar nuestro turno a una distancia y acercarnos unos pasos cada vez. No perdimos el tiempo.»

Al final de esos días huecos, lúgubres y melancólicos, todos lanzamos un gran suspiro de alivio. No sé exactamente lo que usted quiere decir, Su Ilustrísima, cuando bisbisea acerca de «una parodia de la Cuaresma», pero en el primer día del mes El Árbol Es Levantado comenzó una ronda de alegría general. A través de los días siguientes hubo celebraciones privadas que tenían lugar en las casas más grandes de los nobles y en las de los plebeyos prósperos, como también en los templos locales de las diversas aldeas. Estas fiestas servían en parte como pretexto para que los anfitriones y los invitados, los sacerdotes y los devotos, se emborracharan agradablemente con *octli* y para que se permitieran el placer de otros excesos de los que se habían privado durante los *nemontemtin*.

Puede ser que los festivales anteriores durante ese año hubieran sido algo deprimentes, porque recibimos la noticia de la muerte de nuestro Uey-Tlatoani Tíxoc. Sin embargo, su reinado había sido uno de los más cortos en la historia de los gobernantes mexica y uno de los menos notables. Por cierto que corrió el rumor de que había sido envenenado, quizá por los ancianos de su Consejo que se impacientaban por la falta de interés que demostraba en preparar nuevas campañas de conquista, o por su hermano Auítzotl, Monstruo de Agua, que era el siguiente en la línea para el trono y quien ambiciosamente deseaba demostrar cuán brillantemente podía gobernar. De todas maneras, Tíxoc había sido una figura tan desvaída que no fue ni extrañado ni lamentado. Así es que los festivales de nuestra isla no se suspendieron, ni se entristecieron, sino que por el contrario fueron dedicados a celebrar el ascenso del nuevo Venerado Orador, Auítzotl.

Los ritos no empezaban hasta que Tonatíu se hubiera sumergido en su lecho occidental para dormir, no fuera que ese dios de calor viera los honores ofrecidos a su dios hermano de la humedad y se pusiera celoso. Entonces empezaban a reunirse en los límites de la plaza abierta y en los declives que se levantaban a su alrededor, cada uno de los habitantes de la isla, a excepción de aquellos demasiado viejos, demasiado jóvenes, demasiado enfermos o incapacitados, y quienes tenían que quedarse en casa para atenderlos. Tan pronto como se ocultó el sol, la plaza, la pirámide y el templo que estaba en su cumbre, se vieron llenos de sacerdotes vestidos de negro que revoloteaban ocupados en los últimos preparativos para prender una multitud de antorchas, los fuegos de las urnas que habían sido coloreados artificialmente y los quemadores de incienso que humeaban dulcemente. La piedra de los sacrificios todavía estaba allí asentada, oscura y sombría, pero no se iba a utilizar esa noche. En su lugar, una inmensa bañera de piedra llena de agua hechizada previamente con encantamientos especiales había sido traída y asentada al pie de la pirámide en donde cada espectador pudiera ver dentro de ella.

A medida que se hacía más oscuro, las arboledas que estaban atrás y a un lado de la pirámide se iluminaron con innumerables lamparitas parpadeantes como si esos árboles hubieran anidado todas las luciérnagas del mundo y sus ramas empezaron a balancearse, llenas de niños de ambos sexos que, aunque muy pequeños, eran muy ágiles y que llevaban unos trajes hechos con cariño por sus madres. Algunas de las niñitas estaban envueltas en globos construidos con papel rígido y pintados para representar frutas diversas; otras llevaban pliegues ondulantes o faldas de papel cortado y pintado que representaban diferentes flores. Los niñitos iban vestidos en una forma más ostentosa; algunos estaban cubiertos de plumas encoladas para tomar el papel de aves, otros llevando alas translúcidas de papel impregnado en aceite para actuar como las abejas y las mariposas. Durante todos los eventos subsiguientes de la noche, los niños-aves y los niños-insectos aleteaban acrobáticamente de rama en rama, fingiendo «sorber el néctar» de las niñas-frutas y de las niñas-flores.

Cuando la noche ya había caído y toda la población de la isla se hallaba reunida, el sacerdote principal de Tláloc apareció en lo alto de la pirámide. Sopló repentina y penetrantemente en su trompeta de concha, luego levantó autoritariamente sus brazos y el bullicio de la muchedumbre empezó a desaparecer. El *tlamacazqui* de Tláloc sostuvo sus brazos en lo alto hasta que la plaza quedó en un silencio absoluto. Entonces dejó caer los brazos y en ese mismo instante Tláloc habló: ¡*ba-ra-ROOM!* Un trueno ensordecedor resonó y reverberó. El ruido sacudió verdaderamente las hojas de los árboles, el humo del incienso, las flamas de los fuegos y el aire que habíamos aspirado dentro de nuestros pulmones. No era Tláloc, por supuesto, sino el poderoso «tambor de truenos», llamado también «el tambor que arranca el corazón». Su parche rígido de gruesa piel de serpiente era golpeado con frenesí por otro sacerdote que utilizaba unas baquetas de hule. El sonido del tambor de truenos se podía escuchar a una distancia de dos largas carreras, así es que ya pueden ustedes imaginarse el efecto que tuvo en nosotros, los que estábamos allí agrupados.

Esa trepitación de algún modo pavorosa, continuó hasta que nuestra carne se estremecía tanto que sentíamos que se iba a separar de nuestros huesos. Entonces fue disminuyendo gradualmente, aquietándose y callándose cada vez más, hasta que emergió de su sonido la pulsación del «tambor dios» que era tamborileado por otro sacerdote. El tambor dios, que era tocado con las manos, servía para representar a cualquier dios cuya ceremonia se celebrara; esa noche por supuesto, su cilindro de madera tenía puesto la máscara gigante, tallada en madera, del dios Tláloc. Con el murmullo del tambor dios como acompañamiento, el sacerdote principal empezó a cantar las salutaciones e invocaciones tradicionales a Tláloc. A intervalos hacía pausas para que nosotros, la multitud, respondiera a coro —como lo hacen sus devotos diciendo «amén»— con el prolongado grito del búho de «hoo-oo-ooo»... Otras veces se detenía mientras sus sacerdotes menores, dando un paso hacia adelante, metían las manos dentro de sus vestidos, sacando pequeñas criaturas acuáticas: una rana, un *axólotl* —salamandra—, una víbora y las levantaban ondulándolas para luego tragárselas vivas y enteras.

El sacerdote principal terminó su canto de introducción con las antiquísimas palabras rituales, gritando lo más que pudo: «¡*Tehuan tiezquíaya in ahuéhuetl, in póchotl, TLALOCTZIN!*», que quiere decir: «¡Quisiéramos estar debajo de los cipreses, debajo del árbol de la ceiba, Señor Tláloc!», que equivale a decir: «Pedimos tu protección, tu dominio sobre nosotros.» Y al terminar ese grito, todos los sacerdotes en todas partes de la plaza aventaron sobre los fuegos de las urnas, harina de maíz finamente pulverizada que estalló con un crujido agudo y una chispa deslumbrante com si un tenedor de luz hubiera caído entre nosotros. Luego el ¡ba-ra-ROOM! del tambor de truenos nos golpeó nuevamente y siguió haciéndolo hasta que nuestros dientes parecieron aflojarse en nuestras mandíbulas.

Sin embargo otra vez se apaciguó y cuando al fin pudimos volver a oír, escuchamos la música tocada por una flauta de arcilla en forma de un boniato; de las «calabazas suspendidas» de diferentes tamaños que daban diferentes sonidos cuando eran tocadas con palos; de la flauta construida con cinco cañas de diferentes longitudes, unidas unas con otras; mientras, destacándose por encima de éstas, el ritmo se mantenía con «el hueso fuerte», la mandíbula dentada de un venado que era raspado con una vara. Junto con la música llegaron los danzantes de ambos sexos, interpretando la Danza de las Cañas en círculos concéntricos. En sus tobillos, rodillas y codos tenían amarradas vainas secas de semillas, que sonaban, susurraban y murmuraban cuando se movían. Los hombres llevaban trajes color azul-agua, cada uno cargando un pedazo de caña del grueso de su muñeca y tan largo como su brazo. Las mujeres iban vestidas con blusas y faldas del color verde pálido de la caña tierna y Tzitzi iba a la cabeza.

Los bailarines, hombres y mujeres, se entremezclaron deslizándose graciosamente al compás de la alegre música. Las mujeres balanceaban los brazos sinuosamente arriba de sus cabezas y se podían ver las cañas mecidas por la brisa. Cuando los hombres agitaban sus pesadas cañas se oía el seco susurro que producían al ser movidas por el suave viento. Entonces la música se hizo más fuerte y las mujeres se agruparon en el centro de la plaza, danzando en un solo lugar mientras los hombres formaban un círculo alrededor de ellas, fingiendo lanzar sus gruesas cañas. Al hacer esto, de éstas salieron una serie de cañas, más y más delgadas, una después de otra. Así cada vez que los hombres hacían el movimiento de lanzar, todas las cañas interiores salían deslizándose y se convertían en una línea larga, cónica y encorvada cuya punta tocaba las puntas de todas las demás cañas. Las bailarinas estaban enramadas por una frágil cúpula de cañas y la muchedumbre de espectadores lanzó otra vez un «hoo-oo-ooo», de admiración. Luego, con un movimiento rápido y corto de sus muñecas, los hombres hicieron que todas aquellas cañas regresaran, deslizándose una dentro de la otra. El ingenioso truco se repitió una y otra vez en diversos diseños, como aquel en que los hombres formaron dos líneas y cada uno de ellos lanzó su larga caña hasta tocar la del hombre de enfrente y las cañas formaron un túnel arqueado a través del cual bailaron las mujeres...

Cuando la Danza de las Cañas hubo terminado, siguió un interludio cómico. Dentro de la plaza iluminada por las flamas se arrastraron y cojearon todos aquellos ancianos que padecían enfermedades incurables de los huesos y articulaciones. Esta dolencia, que los tiene siempre encorvados y lisiados, algunos más y otros menos, por alguna razón es especialmente dolorosa durante los meses lluviosos. Así que esos viejos y viejas se esforzaban durante esa ceremonia para bailar ante Tláloc con la esperanza de que, llegada la temporada de aguas, él les tuviera compasión y disminuyera su dolor.

Se mantenían muy serios en su intento, pero como la danza era grotesca debido a sus enfermedades, los espectadores comenzaron a reír entre dientes, luego en voz alta, hasta que los mismos bailarines comprendieron su apariencia ridícula. Uno tras otro empezaron a hacer payasadas, exagerando lo absurdo de su cojera o traba. Finalmente todos brincaban a cuatro patas como ranas, o se tambaleaban de lado como los cangrejos, o escarbaban como las tortugas de mar atrapadas en la playa, o encorvaban sus cuellos el uno al otro como grullas durante la época de celo, y la muchedumbre que los observaba gritaba desternillándose de risa. Los ancianos bailarines se entusiasmaron tanto que prolongaron sus cabriolas feas e hilarantes hasta tal punto que los sacerdotes se vieron obligados a sacarles a la fuerza de la escena. Puede que le interese saber, Su Ilustrísima, que esos suplicantes esfuerzos nunca influyeron en Tláloc a que beneficiara a un solo inválido, muy por el contrario, muchos de ellos quedaban encamados para siempre a partir de aquella noche, pero aquellos viejos tontos que todavía podían caminar seguían yendo a bailar año tras año.

Después vino la danza de las *auyanime*, aquellas mujeres cuyos cuerpos ningún hombre a excepción de un guerrero o un campeón podían tocar. Eran especialmente escogidas por su belleza y gracia; adiestradas en las artes del amor y se decía que podían hacer levantar a un guerrero muerto sólo con los jugueteos previos a su acto de amor. La danza que interpretaban se llamaba el *quequezcuícatl*, «la danza de las cosquillas», porque despertaba tantas sensaciones entre los espectadores, ya fueran hombres o mujeres, jóvenes o viejos, que frecuentemnte era necesario refrenarlos para que no corrieran hacia las bailarinas e hicieran algo execrable e irreverente. La danza era tan explícita en sus movimientos que, aunque las *auyanime* bailaban solas y cada una de ellas bastante retirada de las otras, usted juraría que tenían compañeros desnudos e invisibles con quienes...

Sí. Muy bien, Su Ilustrísima.

Después de que las *auyanime* hubieron dejado la plaza jadeando, sudando, con sus cabellos revueltos, sus piernas débiles e inestables, trajeron, al hambriento retumbar del tambor dios, a un niño y a una niña de más o menos cuatro años de edad, en una silla de manos cargada por varios sacerdotes. Como al Venerado Orador Tíxoc, ya difunto y no lamentado, le había faltado entusiasmo para hacer la guerra, no había niños cautivos de alguna otra nación disponibles para el sacrificio de esa noche, por lo que los sacerdotes habían tenido que comprar aquellos a unas familias de esclavos locales. Los cuatro padres estaban sentados muy hacia el frente de la plaza y observaban con orgullo, que posiblemente estaba teñido de melancolía, cómo sus hijos desfilaban varias veces enfrente de ellos durante las varias vueltas que dieron a la plaza.

Tanto los padres como los niños tenían razón para enorgullecerse, porque el niñito y la niñita habían sido comprados antes, con suficiente tiempo como para haber estado bien cuidados y alimentados, indudablemente mejor de lo que jamás lo habían sido en sus vidas o lo hubieran estado de seguir viviendo. En esos momentos se les veía gorditos y animados, saludando felices a sus padres y a todos los demás que dentro de la multitud los saludaban. Iban tan bien vestidos como nunca lo hubieran podido estar, pues llevaban trajes que representaban a los espíritus tlatloque, quienes atienden al dios de la lluvia. Sus pequeños mantos eran del más fino algodón, de un color verde-azul con dibujos de gotas plateadas de lluvia y llevaban en sus espaldas unas alas de papel aceitado que parecían nubes blancas.

Como ya había sucedido en otras ceremonias anteriores en honor de Tláloc, los niños se comportaban de una manera que no era la que se esperaba de ellos. Se deleitaban tanto por el ambiente festivo, por el colorido, las luces y la música, que brincaban riendo y rebosaban de alegría tan radiantemente como el sol, que era por supuesto todo lo contrario de lo que debería ser. Entonces, como de costumbre, los sacerdotes más cercanos a su silla de manos tenían que extender sus manos furtivamente y pellizcarles las nalgas. Al principio los niños se desconcertaban, pero luego se sentían verdaderamente doloridos. El niño y la niña empezaron a quejarse, luego a llorar y a gemir como era lo apropiado. Cuanto más llanto, más truenos; cuantas más lágrimas, más lluvia.

La multitud participó en los llantos, como era lo usual en esa ceremonia. Incluso los hombres grandes y los guerreros lloraban, hasta que las montañas de los alrededores retumbaban con los ecos producidos por los gruñidos, los sollozos y el sonido de la gente golpeándose los pechos. Todos los tambores e instrumentos musicales estaban sonando en esos momentos, aumentando así el ruido de la pulsación del tambor dios y los sollozos de la muchedumbre, mientras los sacerdotes bajaban la silla de manos hacia el otro lado de la gran bañera de piedra llena de agua, cerca de la pirámide. Ese ruido combinado era tan increíblemente fuerte que ni siquiera el sacerdote principal podía escuchar sus propias palabras, que cantaba sobre los dos niños cuando los sacó de la silla y los levantó uno por uno para que Tláloc pudiera verlos y diera su aprobación.

Entonces se acercaron dos sacerdotes, uno con un recipiente pequeño y el otro con un cepillo. El sacerdote principal se agachó encima del niño y de la niña y aunque nadie podía oírle, todos sabíamos qué les estaba diciendo, les explicaba que iba a ponerles una máscara para que el agua no entrara en sus ojos mientras nadaban en el tanque sagrado. Todavía lloriqueaban, no sonreían, sus mejillas estaban mojadas por las lágrimas, pero no protestaron cuando el sacerdote cepilló abundantemente el hule líquido sobre sus caras, dejando libres solamente los labios como botones de flor. No podíamos ver sus expresiones cuando el sacerdote les dio la espalda para cantar hacia la muchedumbre, todavía sin que pudiera oírsele, la última apelación para que Tláloc aceptara este sacrificio, y a cambio de él el dios mandara una temporada abundante en lluvia y demás.

Los asistentes levantaron a los niños por última vez y el sacerdote principal embadurnó rápidamente el pesado líquido de hule en las partes inferiores de sus caras, cubriéndoles sus bocas y sus narices y casi al mismo tiempo los asistentes dejaron caer a los niños dentro del estanque, donde el agua fría cuajó el hule instantáneamente. Como ven, la ceremonia requería que los sacrificados murieran *en* el agua, pero no *a causa* de ella. Así es que no se ahogaron; se sofocaron lentamente bajo la gruesa máscara de hule inamovible e irrompible, mientras, se sacudían desesperadamente en el agua y se hundían y volvían a salir y se volvían a hundir de nuevo, en tanto que la muchedumbre sollozaba sus lamentaciones y los tambores e instrumentos continuaban gritando a su dios con su cacofonía. Los niños chapotearon cada vez más débilmente, hasta que, primero la niña y después el niño, dejaron de moverse debajo del agua, con las alas blancas flotando, extendidas, inmóviles en la superficie.

¿Que fue un asesinato a sangre fría, Su Ilustrísima? Pero si eran niños esclavos. De otra manera hubieran tenido una vida de brutos; quizá cuando hubieran crecido se habrían emparejado y engendrado más brutos. Y al morir lo habrían hecho sin ningún propósito y habrían languidecido durante una eternidad pesada y aburrida en la oscuridad y la nada de Mictlan. En cambio, murieron en honor de Tláloc y para beneficio de nosotros, los que seguíamos viviendo, y con su muerte ganaron una vida feliz para siempre en el mundo lujuriosamente verde de Tláloc.

¿Que es una superstición bárbara? Sin embargo la siguiente temporada de lluvias fue tan copiosa, tanto como un cristiano la hubiera implorado, y nos dio una bella cosecha.

¿Cruel? ¿Atroz? ¿Desgarrador? Bueno, sí... Sí, por lo menos así lo recuerdo, porque ésa fue la última ceremonia feliz que Tzitzitlini y yo pudimos gozar juntos.

✠

Cuando el *acali* del príncipe Huexotzinca vino a recogerme, no llegó a Xaltocan hasta después de mediodía, porque era temporada de fuertes vientos y los remeros habían tenido una travesía turbulenta. El regreso también fue agitado, el lago se enturbiaba con olas revueltas de las que el viento arrancaba y lanzaba una espuma que escocía, así es que no llegamos al embarcadero de Texcoco hasta que el sol, Tezcatlipoca, estaba medio dormido.

Aunque los edificios y las calles de la ciudad empezaban allí, en el área de los muelles, aquel distrito realmente no era más que un suburbio de industrias y moradas, a la orilla del lago; astilleros, talleres para tejer redes, sogas, ganchos y todo lo demás, y las casas de los barqueros, de los pescadores y de los cazadores de aves. El centro de la ciudad estaba a una distancia de una gran carrera hacia el interior. Ya que nadie del palacio había venido a recogerme, los remeros de Huexotzinca voluntariamente se ofrecieron a caminar conmigo parte del camino, ayudándome a cargar los bultos que llevaba: alguna ropa adicional, otra serie de pinturas que me había regalado Chimali, una canasta de dulces garapiñados cocinados por Tzitzi.

Mis acompañantes me dejaron, uno por uno, al llegar a sus

respectivas casas. Sin embargo el último me aseguró que si seguía en línea recta, no podía dejar de reconocer el palacio que se encontraba en la gran plaza central. Para entonces ya estaba completamente oscuro y no había mucha gente caminando en esa noche en que el viento soplaba con ráfagas violentas, pero las calles estaban iluminadas. Cada casa parecía estar bien provista de lámparas con aceite de coco o de *ahuácatl* o de aceite de pescado o cualquier otro combustible que los propietarios podían adquirir. Sus luces escapaban fuera, a través de los huecos de las ventanas de las casas, aun de aquellas que estaban cubiertas por contraventanas o cortinas de tela o celosías de papel encerado. Además, había una antorcha ardiendo en cada esquina: altos palos rematados por canastas de cobre en donde ardían astillas de pino, de las que se desprendían al impulso del viento pedacitos de resina hirviente. Algunos de esos postes estaban colocados en los huecos que habían sido taladrados a través de los puños de las estatuas de piedra, erguidas o agachadas, que representaban a diversos dioses.

No había caminado mucho cuando empecé a sentirme cansado, pues iba cargado con muchos bultos y el viento me golpeaba continuamente. Sentí un gran alivio al ver en la oscuridad de la calle una banca de piedra asentada bajo un árbol *tapachini* brillando en el rojo de sus flores. Me senté un rato agradecido, disfrutando al ser levemente golpeado por los pétalos escarlata del árbol arrancados por el viento. Entonces me vine a dar cuenta de que en el banco en el que estaba sentado, había una desigualdad debido a un dibujo tallado. Sólo tuve que empezar a trazarlo con mis dedos, ni siquiera tuve que mirarlo en la oscuridad, sabía que era una escritura-pintada y lo que decía.

«Un lugar de descanso para el Señor Viento de la Noche», leí en voz alta, sonriéndome.

«Estás leyendo exactamente lo mismo que cuando nos conocimos, en la otra banca, hace ya algunos años», dijo una voz desde la oscuridad.

Di un salto por la sorpresa, luego traté de distinguir la figura al otro lado de la banca. Otra vez llevaba un manto y sandalias de buena calidad, pero gastadas por el viaje. Otra vez estaba cubierto por el polvo del camino y sus facciones cobrizas eran indistintas. Pero para entonces yo ya había crecido considerablemente y estaba probablemente tan lleno de polvo como él, así es que me maravillé de que me hubiera podido reconocer. Cuando pude recobrar la voz le dije:

«Sí, Yanquícatzin, es una extraordinaria coincidencia.»

«No deberías llamarme Señor Forastero —gruñó tan malhumorado como yo lo recordaba—. Aquí *tú* eres el forastero.»

«Es verdad, mi señor —dije—. Y aquí he aprendido a leer más que los simples glifos de las bancas de los caminos.»

«Eso espero», dijo secamente.

«Sí, y gracias al Uey-Tlatoani Nezahualpili —expliqué—. Que por su generosa invitación he podido disfrutar de varios meses de alto aprendizaje en las escuelas de su Corte.»

«¿Y qué has hecho para ganar ese favor?»

«Bien, *haría* cualquier cosa, pues le estoy muy agradecido a mi benefactor y estoy ansioso por pagárselo, pero todavía no he conocido al Venerado Orador y nadie más me ha dado alguna otra cosa que hacer, a excepción de mis tareas escolares. Me siento incómodo de pensar que soy solamente un parásito.»

«Quizá Nezahualpili sólo esté esperando ver si pruebas ser una persona digna de confianza y también, para oírte decir que tú harías *cualquier cosa* por él.»

«Sí que lo haría. Cualquier cosa que él me pidiera.»

«Me atrevería a decir que con el tiempo te pedirá algo.»

«Eso espero, mi señor.»

Nos quedamos sentados por algún tiempo en silencio, excepto por el sonido del viento gimiendo entre los edificios, como Chocacíualt, La Llorona, por siempre vagando. Finalmente el hombre cubierto de polvo dijo sarcásticamente:

«Estás ansioso por ser útil en la Corte, pero permaneces sentado aquí y el palacio está allá.» Señaló en dirección de la calle.

Me estaba despidiendo tan secamente como la otra vez. Me levanté y recogí mis bultos diciendo con algo de resentimiento: «Como me lo sugiere mi impaciente señor, me voy. *Mixpantzinco.*»

«*Ximopanolti*», me dijo con indiferencia, arrastrando la palabra. Me paré debajo del alto poste de la antorcha en la próxima esquina y miré hacia atrás, pero la luz no llegaba lo suficientemente lejos como para iluminar el banco. Si el forastero sucio por el camino todavía estaba sentado allí, yo no podía distinguirlo. Todo lo que veía era un pequeño remolino rojo hecho por los pétalos del *tapachini*, que danzaban a lo largo del camino arremolinados por el viento de la noche.

Finalmente encontré el palacio y hallé también a mi esclavo Cózcatl esperándome para mostrarme mis habitaciones. Ese palacio de Texcoco era mucho más grande que el de Texcotzinco, debía tener miles de cuartos; aunque en el centro de la ciudad no había tanto espacio para que sus anexos necesarios se extendieran y se acomodaran alrededor. De todas maneras, los terrenos del palacio de Texcoco eran extensos y aun en medio de su ciudad principal a Nezahualpili no se le había negado, evidentemente, sus jardines, arboledas, fuentes y demás.

Había también allí un laberinto viviente que ocupaba un terreno lo suficientemente grande como para que fueran necesarias veinte familias para cultivarlo. Había sido plantado por alguno de sus reales antepasados hacía ya mucho tiempo, y desde entonces había estado creciendo, aunque estaba recortado primorosamente. Para entonces era una avenida paralela de impenetrables arbustos espinosos, dos veces la altura de un hombre, que se torcía, se bifurcaba y se doblaba sobre sí misma. Había una sola abertura en la pared verde del exterior y se decía que cualquier persona que entrara por allí podría, después de dar muchas vueltas, encontrar un camino que conducía a un pequeño claro en el centro del laberinto, pero le sería imposible encontrar la ruta de regreso. Solamente el viejo jardinero de palacio sabía el camino para salir de él; un secreto, incluso para el Uey-Tlatoani, que había sido guardado tradicionalmente a través de su familia. Así es que a nadie le estaba permitido entrar allí sin el viejo jardinero como guía, excepto como un castigo. El ocasional convicto violador de alguna ley era sentenciado a ser llevado desnudo, a punta de espada si fuera necesario, y dejado solo dentro del laberinto. Después de un mes aproximadamente, el jardinero iba y recogía lo que hubiera quedado del cuerpo, rasgado por las espinas, picoteado por las aves y comido por los gusanos.

Un día, después de mi regreso, estaba esperando a que mi lección empezara cuando el joven príncipe Huexotzinca se me acercó. Después de darme la bienvenida por mi regreso a la Corte, me dijo por casualidad: «Mi padre estará muy contento de verte en la sala del trono cuando tengas tiempo, Cabeza Inclinada.»

¡Cuando tenga tiempo! Con cuánta cortesía el más alto de los acolhua citaba a su presencia a este forastero inferior, que había estado engordando bajo su hospitalidad. Naturalmente abandoné la sala de estudio y fui, casi corriendo a todo lo largo de las galerías del edificio, así es que estaba casi sin aliento cuando al fin caí sobre una rodilla en el umbral del gran salón del trono, haciendo el gesto de besar la tierra y diciendo débilmente: «En su augusta presencia, Venerado Orador.»

«*Ximopanolti*, Cabeza Inclinada. —Como me quedé inclinado en mi humilde posición, me dijo—: Puedes levantarte, Topo.» Cuando me levanté, como me quedé parado en donde estaba, me dijo: «Puedes venir aquí, Nube Oscura. —Así lo hice, despacio y respetuosamente, y él me dijo sonriendo—: Tienes tantos nombres como el de un pájaro que vuela sobre todas las naciones del mundo y que es llamado por diferentes nombres por cada pueblo. —Con un espantamoscas que empuñaba en la mano me indicó una de las varias *icpaltin* que estaban en fila, formando un semicírculo ante el trono y dijo—: Siéntate.»

La silla de Nezahualpili no era ni mucho más grande ni mucho más impresionante que la *icpali* de patas cortas en la que yo estaba sentado, pero se encontraba colocada sobre un tablado, así es que tenía que alzar la cabeza para mirarlo. Él estaba sentado con sus piernas, no formalmente cruzadas bajo de sí o con las rodillas enfrente, sino lánguidamente extendidas a lo largo cruzándolas sobre los tobillos. Si bien el salón del trono tenía colgando de sus paredes tapices trabajados en pluma y paneles pintados, no había más muebles, a excepción del trono, que esas sillas bajas para los visitantes y, directamente enfrente del Uey-Tlatoani, estaba colocada una mesa baja de ónix negro en la cual reposaba, dándole la cara, una calavera de blancura fulgurante.

«Mi padre, Nezahualcóyolt la puso ahí —dijo Nezahualpili al notar que mis ojos estaban posados sobre ella—. No sé por qué. Pudo haber sido algún enemigo desaparecido, sobre el cual se deleitara en mirar de mala manera. O alguien muy amado cuya pérdida jamás dejó de lamentar. O quizá la conservó por la misma razón que yo, para aclarar mis pensamientos, mis palabras y mis decisiones.»

Yo pregunté: «¿Y cómo lo hace usted, Señor Orador?»

«Vienen a este salón mensajeros portando amenazas de guerra u ofrecimientos de paz. Vienen aquí demandantes cargados de agravios; pedigüeños pidiendo favores. Cuando se dirigen a mí, sus rostros se tuercen de ira o se deprimen por la miseria o sonríen fingiendo devoción, pero sus labios siempre se mueven rápidos ya que tienen que echar fuera sus discursos, ensayados previamente, en el tiempo asignado a cada audiencia. Así, mientras los escucho, no veo sus rostros sino a la calavera.»

Solamente pude preguntar: «¿Por qué, mi señor?»

«Porque es el rostro más limpio y más honesto del hombre. Ningún gesto de engaño, ningún guiño astuto, ninguna sonrisa servil. Solamente fija una sonrisa burlona y eterna, como una mofa a cada una de las preocupaciones del hombre por las urgencias de la vida. Cuando cualquier visitante aboga porque el Uey-Tlatoani dé un fallo aquí, en ese momento yo contemporizo, disimulo, fumo un *poquíetl* o dos, mientras miro largamente a la calavera. Esto me recuerda que las palabras que digo a un embajador o a un pedigüeño, muy bien pudieran ser las últimas de mi vida, quedando en pie tanto como mis decretos, ¿y qué efectos tendrían sobre aquellos que todavía viven? *Ayyo*, esta calavera muchas veces me ha servido para prevenirme en contra de la impaciencia o de las decisiones impulsivas. —Nezahualpili desvió su mirada de la calavera hacia mí y rió—. Cuando la cabeza vivió, por todo lo que sé, no era más que la de un idiota parlanchín, sin embargo, muerta y silenciosa, en verdad que es un sabio consejero.»

Dije: «Creo, mi señor, que el consejero más sabio sería de poca utilidad, excepto para un hombre que fuera lo suficientemente sabio como para considerar su consejo.»

«Tomo eso como un cumplido, Cabeza Inclinada, y te doy las gracias. Dime entonces, ¿fui lo suficientemente sabio como para traerte aquí desde Xaltocan?»

«No lo puedo decir, mi señor. Porque desconozco por qué lo hizo.»

«Desde los tiempos de Nezahualcóyolt, la ciudad de Texcoco ha ido ganando fama como un centro de conocimientos y cultura, pero este lugar no se perpetúa necesariamente a sí mismo. Las familias nobles pueden engendrar tontos y haraganes, yo puedo nombrar algunos que engendré, así es que no dudamos en importar talentos de cualquier parte e incluso infundir sangre extranjera. Tú parecías un prospecto prometedor, así es que aquí estás.»

«¿Para quedarme, Señor Orador?»

«Eso depende de ti, de tu *tonali* y de las circunstancias, que ni tú ni yo lo podemos prever. Sin embargo, tus maestros me han dado buenos informes de ti, en el período de prueba que ya pasaste entre nosotros. Así es que creo que ya es tiempo de que vengas a ser un participante más activo en la vida de la Corte.»

«He tenido la esperanza de poder llegar a compensar su generosidad, mi señor. ¿Quiere usted decir que se me dará un empleo en el que pueda ser útil?»

«Si esto es de tu agrado. Durante tu reciente ausencia tomé otra esposa. Su nombre es Chalchiunénetl, Muñeca de Jade.»

No dije nada, pero pensaba confusamente si él por alguna razón había cambiado de tema. Sin embargo, Nezahualpili continuó:

«Es la hija mayor de Auítzotl. Un regalo de él para señalar su ascensión como nuevo Uey-Tlatoani de Tenochtitlan. Así es que ella es mexícatl como tú. Tiene quince años de edad, y con esa edad podría ser tu hermana mayor. Nuestra ceremonia de matrimonio ha sido celebrada debidamente, pero por supuesto la consumación física se ha pospuesto hasta que Muñeca de Jade crezca y sea más madura.»

Me quedé callado aunque bien hubiera podido decir, incluso al sabio Nezahualpili, algo acerca de las capacidades físicas de las doncellas adolescentes mexica.

Él continuó: «Como era lo adecuado, se le ha dado un pequeño ejército de damas de compañía y el ala este entera para sus habitaciones y para sus criados; cocina privada y demás, un palacio en miniatura, así es que ella no carecerá de nada tocante a comodidad, servicio y compañía femenina. Sin embargo me pregunto si tú querrás consentir, Cabeza Inclinada, en unirte a su comitiva. Sería bueno para Chalchiunénetl tener por lo menos la compañía de un hombre, siendo éste un hermano mexícatl. Al mismo tiempo me podrías servir a mí, instruyendo a la muchacha en nuestras costumbres, enseñándole el estilo de hablar de Texcoco, preparándola para ser una consorte de la cual me pueda sentir orgulloso.»

Dije desconsolado: «Quizá Chalchiunénetzin no considerará en una forma muy bondadosa el hecho de que sea nombrado su guardián, Señor Orador. Una muchacha joven puede ser voluntariosa, irreprimida y celosa de su libertad...»

«Bien que lo sé —suspiró Nezahualpili—. Tengo dos o tres hijas alrededor de esa misma edad. Siendo Muñeca de Jade princesa, hija de un Uey-Tlatoani y reina y esposa de otro, es muy probable que incluso sea más arrebatada. No condenaría ni a mi peor enemigo a ser el *guardián* de hembras jóvenes y briosas. Pero creo, Topo, que por lo menos encontrarás agradable el verla.»

Debió de tirar de algún cordón de campana escondido un poco antes, porque me hizo una seña para que mirara hacia la puerta. Me giré y vi a una muchacha delgada, ricamente ataviada con la falda y blusa ceremonial y un tocado en la cabeza, que venía caminando despacio de un modo regio, hasta el entablado. Su rostro era perfecto, su porte altivo y sus ojos modestamente bajos.

«Querida —dijo Nezahualpili—, éste es Mixtli, de quien ya te he hablado. ¿Quieres tenerle en tu comitiva como compañero y protector?»

«Si mi señor marido así lo desea y el joven Mixtli está conforme, me sentiré muy complacida de considerarlo como mi hermano mayor.»

Levantó sus largas pestañas y me miró, y sus ojos eran como lagunas insondables y pequeñas en lo profundo de los bosques. Después averigüé que ella se ponía habitualmente dentro de los ojos unas gotas del jugo de la hierba *camopalxíhuitl*, que agranda mucho las pupilas y eso hacía que sus ojos brillaran como joyas. Pero también era la causa de que evitara las luces brillantes y aun la luz del día, pues con sus pupilas tan dilatadas veía tan poco cómo yo.

«Muy bien», dijo el Venerado Orador, frotándose las manos con satisfacción. Yo me preguntaba con cierto recelo cuánto tiempo había estado en conferencia con su calavera consejera, antes de decidir ese arreglo. A mí me dijo:

«Sólo te pido que le des la dirección y el consejo que le ofrecería un hermano, Cabeza Inclinada. No espero que corrijas o castigues a la Señora Muñeca de Jade. En cualquier caso, sería una ofensa capital que un plebeyo levantara su mano o su voz contra de una mujer noble. Tampoco espero de ti que juegues a ser su carcelero o espía o el chismoso de sus confidencias. Me sentiría muy satisfecho, Topo, si dedicaras a tu señora hermana todo el tiempo libre que te quede de tus estudios y trabajos escolares. Que le sirvieras con la misma devoción y discreción con la que me sirves a mí o la Primera Señora Tolana Tecíuapil. Ya os podéis ir, jóvenes; *xinopanólti*, y familiarizaros el uno con el otro.»

Hicimos las reverencias adecuadas y dejamos el salón del trono. En el corredor, Muñeca de Jade me sonrió dulcemente y me preguntó: «¿Cuántos nombres tienes?»

«Mi señora me puede llamar como le guste.»

Ella sonrió aún más dulcemente y puso su delicado dedito sobre su pequeña barbilla. «Creo que te llamaré... —Sonrió todavía de forma más dulce y dijo con la misma dulzura del jarabe empalagoso del maguey—: ¡Te llamaré Qualcuíe!»

Esa palabra es la segunda persona del singular del imperativo del verbo «traer» y siempre se pronuncia con energía y con voz de mando: «¡Trae!» Mi corazón sintió un gran peso. Si mi último nombre iba a ser ¡Trae! mis recelos acerca de ese arreglo parecían estar justificados. Y no me equivocaba. Aunque seguía hablando con esa voz empalagosa como jugo de maguey, la joven reina perdió toda expresión de modestia, docilidad y sumisión y dijo en una forma verdaderamente regia:

«No necesitas interrumpir ninguna de tus tareas escolares durante el día ¡Trae! Pero quiero que estés disponible por las tardes y si es necesario cuando te llame durante la noche. Hazme el favor de transportar todos tus efectos personales al departamento que está directamente enfrente del mío.» Y sin esperar de mí una palabra de aquiescencia, sin decir una palabra cortés de despedida, se dio la vuelta y se alejó por el vestíbulo.

Muñeca de Jade. Ella llevaba el nombre del mineral *chalchíhuitl*, el cual, si bien no es raro ni tiene ningún valor intrínseco, es muy apreciado por nuestra gente porque tiene el color del

Centro del Todo. A diferencia de ustedes los españoles, que sólo conocen las cuatro direcciones de lo que ustedes llaman el compás, nosotros percibimos cinco y a cada una de ellas le asignamos un color diferente. Como ustedes, tenemos el este, el norte, el oeste y el sur, y nos referimos a ellos respectivamente como las direcciones de color: rojo, negro, blanco y azul, pero también tenemos el verde para marcar el centro del compás o circunferencia; en otras palabras, el lugar en el cual un hombre se para en cualquier momento dado y todo el espacio comprendido arriba de ese sitio, hasta los cielos y hacia abajo tan lejos como Mictlan, el mundo de ultratumba. Así es que el color verde era importante para nosotros y la piedra *chalchíhuitl*, que es verde, nos era preciosa y solamente una criatura de noble linaje y de alta graduación podría ser llamada apropiadamente por Muñeca de Jade.

Como el jade, esta niña-reina era un objeto que se tenía que manejar cuidadosamente y con el mayor respeto. Estaba exquisitamente hecha como una muñeca, era inefablemente bella, era el trabajo divino de un artífice. Pero al igual que una muñeca, no tenía ninguna conciencia o remordimiento humano. Y, aunque no me di cuenta inmediatamente de mi premonición, ella estaba destinada a romperse como una muñeca.

✠

Debo admitir que estaba regocijado con la suntuosidad de mis nuevas habitaciones. *Tres* cuartos y el retrete conteniendo mi propio baño de vapor. La cama tenía un mayor número de cobijas, sobre la que se extendía una enorme cubierta hecha de cientos de pedacitos blancos, cosidos unos con otros, de piel de ardilla. Encima de todo estaba suspendido un toldo ribeteado y de él colgaban unas cortinas casi invisibles que parecían redes finas y suaves, y que podía correr alrededor de la cama para estar a salvo de los mosquitos y las palomillas de noche.

El único inconveniente de ese apartamente era que estaba muy distante de los otros que atendía el esclavo Cózcatl, pero cuando le mencioné este hecho a Chalchiunénetl, ella habló unas cuantas palabras con el mayordomo de palacio y el pequeño Cózcatl quedó relevado de todas sus otras obligaciones para atenderme sólo a mí. El chico estaba muy orgulloso de esta promoción. Incluso yo me llegué a sentir como un joven señor mimado. Sin embargo, después, cuando Muñeca de Jade y yo caímos en desgracia, estuve muy contento de haber tenido a Cózcatl conmigo, siempre fiel y en todo momento dispuesto a atestiguar en mi favor.

Pronto me di cuenta de que si Cózcatl era mi esclavo, yo también lo era de Muñeca de Jade. En aquella primera tarde, cuando una de sus criadas me admitió en la gran estancia, las primeras palabras de la joven reina fueron:

«Estoy muy contenta de que me pertenezcas, ¡Trae!, porque me empezaba a aburrir inefablemente enjaulada en este lugar apartado, como un animal raro.» Yo traté de hacer alguna objeción a la palabra «pertenecer» pero ella me hizo callar. «Pitza me ha dicho —y señaló a la sirvienta entrada en años que estaba parada detrás de la banca acojinada en la que ella estaba sentada— que tú eres un experto en capturar el parecido de una persona en papel.»

«Me congratulo, mi señora, de que la gente se ha reconocido a sí misma y a los demás en mis dibujos, pero hace algún tiempo que no practico este arte.»

«Practicarás conmigo. Pitza, cruza el vestíbulo y haz que Cózcatl traiga todos los utensilios que ¡Trae! necesitará.»

El muchachito me trajo algunos palitos de tiza y varias hojas de papel de corteza, las pardas, que son las más baratas porque no están cubiertas con cal, y ésas eran las que usaba para mis toscos dibujos de escritura pintada. A un gesto mío el niño se acomodó en cuclillas en un rincón de la gran habitación.

Dije disculpándome: «Como no tengo buena vista, mi señora, ¿puedo tener su permiso para sentarme cerca de usted?»

Moví una pequeña *icpali*, silla, al otro lado de la banca y Chalchiunénetl sostuvo su cabeza inmóvil y firme, con sus gloriosos ojos sobre mí, mientras yo bosquejaba el dibujo. Cuando hube terminado le extendí el papel, pero ni siquiera le echó una mirada, sino que se lo dio a su sirvienta por encima de su hombro.

«Pitza, ¿soy yo?»

«Hasta el hoyuelo que tiene en la barbilla, mi señora. Y nadie se podría equivocar al ver esos ojos.»

Y después de oír esto, Muñeca de Jade se dignó examinarlo e inclinándose hacia mí me sonrió dulcemente. «Sí, soy yo. Soy muy bella. Gracias, ¡Trae! Bueno, ¿también puedes dibujar cuerpos?»

«Bien, sí. Las articulaciones de los miembros, los pliegues de las vestiduras, los emblemas e insignias...»

«No estoy interesada en esos adornos superficiales. Quiero decir el cuerpo. A ver, pinta el mío.»

Pitza, la sirvienta, dio un chillido apagado y Cózcatl se quedó con la boca abierta cuando Muñeca de Jade se levantó y, sin ningún recato o vacilación, se quitó todas sus joyas y brazaletes, sus sandalias, su blusa, su falda y finalmente hasta la única prenda *tzotzomatli* que le quedaba. Pitza se fue lejos y enterró su cara sonrojada entre las cortinas de la ventana; Cózcatl parecía incapaz de moverse. La reina se volvió a reclinar en la banca, en una pose de total abandono.

En mi agitación, dejé caer algunos de los materiales para dibujar que tenía en mis rodillas, pero me las arreglé para decir con voz severa: «Mi señora, eso es de lo más indecoroso.»

«*Ayya*, el pudor típico del plebeyo —dijo riéndose de mí—. Debes aprender, ¡Trae!, que una mujer noble no siente nada al ser vista desnuda o bañándose o haciendo cualquier función delante de los esclavos. Hembras o machos, siempre serán como mascotas o codornices o mariposillas nocturnas en un cuarto.»

«Yo no soy un esclavo —dije inflexiblemente—. Ver a mi señora desnuda, la Señora del Uey-Tlatoani, sería considerado como una ofensa capital y una libertad criminal. Y los esclavos hablarían.»

«No los míos. Temen más mi ira que cualquier ley o cualquier señor. Pitza, enséñale tu espalda a ¡Trae!»

La sirvienta, sollozando y sin volverse, deslizó su blusa lo suficiente como para que yo viera las señales en carne viva, que le habían sido inflingidas por alguna especie de látigo. Miré a Cózcatl para asegurarme de que él también lo había visto y entendido.

«Bien —dijo Muñeca de Jade, mostrando su sonrisa de jarabe de maguey—. Ven todo lo cerca que quieras, ¡Trae!, y dibújame completa.»

Y así lo hice, pero mi mano temblaba tanto que frecuentemente tenía que borrar y volver a delinear. Mi temblor no se debía solamente a mi miedo y aprensión. El ver a Chalchiunénetl completamente desnuda creo que haría temblar a cualquier hombre. Debía haberse llamado Muñeca de Oro, pues dorado era el color de su cuerpo, y cada una de sus curvas, la suavidad de su piel, sus articulaciones y hoyuelos parecían haber sido hechos por un hacedor de muñecas toltécatl. Debo mencionar también, que sus pezones y aureolas eran generosamente grandes y oscuras.

La dibujé en la pose que ella había adoptado: completamente extendida por encima de la banca acojinada, con una pierna negligentemente colgando por la orilla hacia el suelo; sus brazos, detrás de su cabeza, daban un toque de erección más alta a sus pechos. Si bien no podía evitar el ver, por no decir memorizar, ciertas partes de ella, debo confesar que mi sentido mojigato de buenos modales me hizo emborronar algunas partes del dibujo y Muñeca de Jade se quejó de ello cuando le di el dibujo terminado.

«¡Estoy toda tiznada en medio de las piernas! ¿Es que eres demasiado escrupuloso, ¡Trae!, o simplemente un ignorante de la anatomía de la mujer? La parte más sacrosanta de mi cuerpo merece ser tratada con más detalle.»

Se quedó inmóvil encima de la banca con las piernas abiertas encima de mí, que estaba sentado en mi silla baja. Con un dedo buscó lo que en ese momento ella quería mostrar afanosamente, mientras describía: «¿Ves? Estos labios tiernos y rosas se juntan aquí en el frente, para envolver el pequeño *tacapili*, el cual parece una perla rosa y que... ¡ooh!... responde fácilmente al más ligero roce.»

Yo estaba respirando pesadamente. Pitza, la sirvienta, se encontraba prácticamente envuelta en las cortinas y Cózcatl parecía permanentemente paralizado, agachado en su rincón.

«Bueno, ¡Trae!, no pongas esa cara de agonizante gazmoño —dijo la joven reina—. No estoy tratando de seducirte, lo único que quería era comprobar si eras un artista. Tengo una tarea para ti.»

Se volvió para gritar a la criada: «¡Pitza, deja de estar escondiendo la cabeza! Ven y vísteme otra vez.»

Mientras la sirvienta cumplía con su cometido, le pregunté: «¿Quiere mi señora que dibuje el retrato de alguna persona?» «Sí.»

«¿De quién, mi señora?»

«De cualquiera —dijo y yo parpadeé con inquietud—. Verás, cuando camino alrededor de los terrenos del palacio o voy a la ciudad en mi silla de manos no sería de dama señalar con el dedo a un hombre y decir *ése*. También mis ojos podrían quedar deslumbrados si tratara de ver bien a alguien realmente atractivo. Me refiero a hombres, por supuesto.»

«¿Hombres?», le hice eco estúpidamente.

«Lo que quiero, simplemente, es que lleves tus papeles y tus tizas a cualquier parte que vayas. En donde encuentres a un hombre guapo, dibuja su rostro y su figura para mí. —Hizo una pausa para reír ahogadamente—. No necesita tener ropa encima. Quiero muchos dibujos diferentes, tantos como hombres puedas encontrar. Sin embargo, no quiero que nadie sepa qué estás haciendo, ni para quién. Si te preguntan, diles simplemente que estás practicando tu arte. —Me devolvió los dos dibujos que acababa de hacer—. Eso es todo. Puedes irte, ¡Trae!, y no regreses hasta que no tengas para enseñarme un buen haz de hojas dibujadas.»

No era tan tonto como para no sentir un presagio en la orden que Chachiunénetl me estaba dando. Sin embargo, deseché eso fuera de mi mente, para concentrarme en mi tarea con la mayor habilidad. El gran problema consistía en tratar de adivinar lo que a una muchacha de quince años pudiera parecer «guapo» en un hombre. No habiéndome dado ningún criterio en que basarme, confiné en mis subrepticios dibujos a príncipes, campeones, guerreros y otros hombres valerosos. Cuando me presenté otra vez ante Muñeca de Jade, con Cózcatl cargado con mi montón de papeles de corteza, puse encima extravagantemente un dibujo hecho de memoria del hombre encorvado color cacao quien seguía tan extrañamente apareciendo en mi vida.

Ella resopló sorprendida diciéndome: «¡Te crees muy chistoso, ¡Trae!; pero he oído murmurar entre las mujeres que se siente un verdadero placer al ser poseída por un enano jorobado y encorvado e incluso... —y ella echó una mirada a Cózcatl—, al ser poseída por un niñito con su *tepule* como el lóbulo de una oreja. Algún día cuando ya me haya cansado de lo ordinario...»

Pasó rápidamente los papeles, entonces se detuvo y dijo: «¡*Yyo ayyo!* Éste, ¡Trae!, tiene unos ojos pardos muy intrépidos. ¿Quién es él?»

«Es el Príncipe Heredero, Flor Oscura.»

Ella hizo un lindo gesto de desagrado. «No, éste podría causarme complicaciones. —Ella siguió viéndolos, estudiando atentamente cada dibujo, luego dijo—: ¿Y quién es éste?»

«No sé su nombre, mi señora. Es un mensajero-veloz al que a veces he visto correr llevando mensajes.»

«Ideal —dijo, con esa su sonrisa. Puso el dibujo a un lado y apuntándolo dijo—: ¡Trae!» Ella no sólo se estaba refiriendo a mi nombre, sino también al otro significado posible, o sea: «¡Tráelo!»

Con cierto temor yo ya había anticipado algo como esto, pero a pesar de ello, empecé a sudar frío. De una manera en extremo tímida y formal le dije:

«Mi Señora Muñeca de Jade, me ha sido ordenado servirle a usted y se me ha prevenido de no corregirla o criticarla. Sin embargo, si no es que estoy interpretando erróneamente sus intenciones, le suplico que las reconsidere. Usted es la princesa virgen del más grande señor en todo El Único Mundo y también la reina virgen de otro gran señor. Será demandada por dos Venerados Oradores y por su propia nobleza, si usted juguetea con algún otro hombre antes de ir al lecho conyugal con su Señor Esposo.»

Yo estaba esperando que en cualquier momento me golpeara como lo hacía con sus esclavos, pero me escuchó hasta el final y luciendo su empalagosa e irritante sonrisa me dijo:

«Podría decirte que tu impertinencia puede ser castigada, pero solamente quiero hacerte notar que Nezahualpili es más viejo que mi padre y que su virilidad ha sido minada, aparentemente, por la Señora de Tolan y por todas sus otras esposas y concubinas. Él me tiene aquí secuestrada, en tanto, y sin duda, trata desesperadamente de erguir, con medicinas y encantamientos, su viejo *tepule* marchito. Pero ¿por qué tengo que desperdiciar mis estímulos, mis jugos y mi belleza en flor, mientras espero a su conveniencia o a su capacidad? Si él necesita aplazar sus deberes de marido, en verdad que yo me las arreglaré para que sean largamente pospuestos. Y entonces, cuando él y yo estemos listos, puedes tener la seguridad de que soy capaz de convencer a Nezahualpili de que llego a él como una doncella timorata, prístina y sin experiencia.»

Traté otra vez de convencerla. En verdad que hice todo lo que pude por disuadirla, aunque yo no pensé que hubiera alguien que lo creyera después.

«Mi Señora, recuerde quién es usted y el linaje del cual desciende. Usted es la bisnieta del venerado Motecuzoma y él *nació* de una virgen. Su padre tiró una gema dentro del jardín de su amada y ella la tomó y se la puso en su flor y en ese momento concibió al niño Motecuzoma, antes de que ella jamás se hubiera casado o acoplado con su padre. Así usted tiene una herencia de pureza y virginidad que no debería de mancillar con...»

Ella me interrumpió riéndose. «¡Trae, yo no soy virgen! Para tu conocimiento. Me debiste haber reprendido cuando tenía nueve o diez años de edad. Entonces *era* virgen.»

Se me ocurrió tardíamente el girarme y decirle a Cózcatl: «Es mejor que te... Ya te puedes ir, niño.»

Muñeca de Jade dijo: «¿Conoces esas esculturas que hacen los bestiales huaxteca? ¿Las estatuas de madera que les sobresale un miembro de hombre? Mi padre Auítzotl conserva una colgada en una pared de nuestro palacio, como una curiosidad

165

para divertir y pasmar a sus amigos. También interesa a las mujeres. Ésta ha sido restregada, alisada y abrillantada por todas aquellas que lo han manipulado admiradas al pasar. Mujeres nobles, sirvientas, mozas y yo misma.»

Le dije: «No creo que yo debiera escuchar...», pero ella ignoró mis protestas y continuó.

«Tenía que arrastrar contra la pared un gran arcón de madera que servía para almacenar cosas, en el cual me subía para poder alcanzar esa figura. Me tomó muchas semanas de sufrimiento, porque después de cada uno de mis primeros intentos tenía que esperar y descansar por un tiempo, hasta que mi inadecuada *tepili* dejaba de dolerme. Pero persistí, restregándome cada vez más fuerte y llegó el día del triunfo cuando finalmente me las arreglé para meterme la punta de esa cosa tremenda. Poquito a poquito fui penetrándomelo cada vez más. Desde entonces, quizá he estado con unos cien hombres, pero ninguno de ellos me ha dado jamás la sensación que gocé en aquellos días en que frotaba mis partes contra la cruda talla de los huaxteca.»

Supliqué: «No debería saber estas cosas, mi señora.»

Se encogió de hombros. «No estoy excusando mi naturaleza. Esa clase de relajamiento es algo que debo tener y debo tener seguido y *tendré*. Hasta podría usarte para ese propósito, ¡Trae! No eres intrépido y no dirías nada en contra mía, pues sé que obedecerás el mandato de Nezahualpili de no ser chismoso. Pero eso no impediría que confesaras tu *propia* culpa por nuestro acoplamiento y sería la ruina para los dos. Así...»

Me tendió el dibujo que había hecho del sencillo mensajero-veloz y un anillo que se quitó del dedo. «Dale esto. Es el regalo de bodas de mi Señor Esposo y no hay otro anillo como éste.»

Era de oro rojo con una gran esmeralda de valor incalculable. Esas raras piedras eran traídas por mercaderes que se aventuraban muy lejos, hasta la tierra de Quautemalan, el límite más lejano hacia el sur de nuestras rutas comerciales, y las esmeraldas ni siquiera venían de allí, sino de alguna tierra de nombre desconocido, a una distancia también desconocida más allá del sur de Quautemalan. El anillo era de esos cuyo diseño estaba hecho para ser sostenido verticalmente en la mano, porque contenía un círculo colgante de pendientes de jade, que solamente se podían mostrar bien cuando el que lo portaba levantaba la mano. El anillo estaba hecho a la medida del dedo de en medio de Muñeca de Jade. Yo solamente podía ponérmelo apretadamente en mi dedo pequeño.

«No, no debes llevarlo puesto —dijo la joven previniéndome—. Ni él tampoco. Este anillo puede ser reconocido por cualquier persona que lo vea. Es solamente para que él lo lleve escondido y lo muestre al guardia de la puerta este, esta medianoche. A la vista del anillo el guardia lo dejará pasar. Pitza lo estará esperando un poco adentro para conducirlo hasta aquí.»

«¿Esta noche? —dije—. Pero debo encontrarlo antes, mi señora. Quizás haya sido enviado con algún mensaje. Y quién sabe adónde.»

«Esta noche —dijo ella—. Ya he estado por bastante tiempo privada de eso.»

No sé lo que Chalchiunénetl me hubiera hecho de no haber podido encontrar al hombre, pero pude localizarlo y me acerqué a él como si yo fuera un joven noble y le llevara un mensaje para ser entregado por él. Deliberadamente, no le di mi nombre pero él me dijo: «Yo soy Yeyac-Netztlin, a las órdenes de mi señor.»

«A las órdenes de una señora —le corregí—. Ella desea que te presentes a medianoche en el palacio para atenderla.»

Él me miró preocupado y dijo: «Es muy difícil llevar un mensaje corriendo a cualquier distancia en la noche, mi señor...» Pero entonces su mirada cayó sobre el anillo que tenía en la palma de mi mano y abriendo mucho los ojos dijo: «Por *esa* señora, por supuesto que sí. Ni la medianoche o Mictlan podrían impedirme hacerle un servicio.»

«Éste es un servicio que requiere discreción —dije con un sabor amargo en la boca—. Enseña este anillo al guardia de la puerta este para que te deje pasar.»

«Oigo y obedezco, mi señor. Estaré allí.»

Y sí estuvo. Yo permanecí despierto, escuchando detrás de la puerta hasta que oí a Pitza, que guiaba a Yeyac-Neztlin, llamar con las puntas de los dedos a la puerta del otro lado del corredor. Después de eso no oí nada más, así es que no supe cuánto tiempo estuvo ni cómo se fue. Y no quise volver a escuchar sus siguientes visitas, así es que no supe cuántas fueron. Sin embargo pasó un mes antes de que Muñeca de Jade, bostezando aburrida, me pidiera que empezara a dibujar nuevos retratos, así es que aparentemente Yeyac-Netztlin la satisfizo por ese espacio de tiempo. Como el nombre del mensajero-veloz significaba apropiadamente «Piernas Largas», quizá también estuviera bien dotado de algún otro miembro.

Aunque Chalchiunénetl no había pedido nada de mi tiempo durante ese mes, eso no quería decir que yo no tuviera preocupaciones. El Venerado Orador venía cada ocho o nueve días para corresponder a las invitaciones que le hacía la mimada y supuestamente paciente princesa-reina. Con frecuencia, yo tenía que estar presente en las habitaciones y me esforzaba por no sudar visiblemente en esas entrevistas. Sólo me preguntaba el porqué, en nombre de todos los dioses, Nezahualpili no podía notar o darse cuenta de que estaba casado con una mujer madura y lista para ser saboreada inmediatamente por él. O por cualquier otro hombre.

Todos los joyeros que trabajan el jade dicen que este mineral es fácil de encontrar entre las piedras comunes del campo, porque proclama su propia presencia y actividad. Ellos dicen que sólo se tiene que ir al campo cuando empieza a salir el sol y se pueden ver varias piedras aquí o allá que están exhalando un lánguido pero inconfundible vapor que anuncia orgullosamente: «Hay jade dentro de mí. Ven y tómalo.» Como la preciada piedra de la cual lleva su nombre, Muñeca de Jade emanaba un indefinible nimbo, esencia o vibración que decía a cada hombre: «Aquí estoy. Ven y tómame.» ¿Podría ser que el Uey-Tlatoani fuera el único hombre en toda la creación que no sintiera sus ardores y su disposición? ¿O sería realmente impotente como decía la joven reina?

No. Cuando los vi y los escuché juntos, comprendí que él estaba manifestando una consideración caballerosa y reprimiéndose. Pues Muñeca de Jade en su reluctante perversidad de tener sólo un amante, había hecho que *él* no viera a la doncella casadera y núbil, sino a una adolescente delicada e inmadura que en último momento había sido dada en un matrimonio político.

Durante sus visitas no era la Muñeca de Jade que tan bien conocíamos sus esclavos y yo, y también presumiblemente Yeyac-Netztlin. Llevaba vestidos que escondían sus curvas provocativas y que la hacían tan delgada y frágil como una niña. De algún modo ella suprimía esa aureola de flagrante sexualidad, por no mencionar su usual arrogancia e irascibilidad. Jamás usó en aquellos momentos el rudo apodo de ¡Trae! cuando se refería a mí. De alguna forma escondía a la verdadera Muñeca de Jade —*topco petlacalco*— «en una bolsa, en una caja», como diríamos nosotros de un secreto.

En presencia de su señor, ni se recostaba lánguidamente, ni se sentaba siquiera en una silla. Se arrodillaba a sus pies, con las rodillas rectamente juntas, sus ojos modesta y castamente bajos y hablaba aniñadamente entre murmullos. Ella incluso me hubiera engañado a mí, haciéndome creer que no tenía más de diez años, si no hubiera sido porque sabía perfectamente que ya había pasado de esa edad.

«Espero que encuentres tu vida menos constreñida, ahora que tienes la compañía de Mixtli», dijo Nezahualpili.

«*Ayyo*, sí, mi señor —dijo ella mostrando los hoyuelos de sus mejillas—. Él es un acompañante inapreciable. Mixtli me muestra muchas cosas y me las explica. Ayer me llevó a la biblioteca de poesías de tu estimado padre y me recitó algunos de sus poemas.»

«¿Y te gustaron?», preguntó el Uey-Tlatoani.

«Oh, sí. Aunque creo que me gustaría más oír alguno de los tuyos, mi Señor Marido.»

De acuerdo con esto, Nezahualpili dijo con bastante modestia: «Por supuesto, suenan mejor cuando mi tamborcillo me acompaña», y recitó y cantó algunas de sus composiciones. Una de ellas en la que alababa la caída del sol, concluía:

...*Como un ramo de brillantes flores*
nuestro Dios radiante, nuestro encendido dios
el sol, se introduce en un vaso de esplendorosas joyas,
y el día así, ha concluido.

«Precioso —suspiró Muñeca de Jade—. Me hace sentir un poco melancólica.»

«¿La puesta del sol?», preguntó Nezahualpili.

«No, mi señor. El mencionar a los dioses. Yo sé que con el tiempo llegaré a familiarizarme con todos los de tu pueblo, pero mientras tanto, no tengo aquí conmigo ninguno de mis viejos dioses a los que estoy tan acostumbrada. ¿Sería impertinente si te pidiera permiso, mi Venerado Esposo, para poner en estas habitaciones algunas estatuas de mis dioses familiares favoritos?»

«Mi querida Muñequita —dijo él con indulgencia—. Puedes hacer o tener todo lo que te haga feliz, para que no eches de menos tu hogar. Te mandaré a Píxquitl, el escultor que reside en el palacio, y tú le darás instrucciones para que talle aquellos dioses que tu querido corazón desea.»

Cuando en esa ocasión Nezahualpili dejó las habitaciones, me hizo una seña para que lo acompañara. Fui, aunque silenciosamente ordenándoles todavía a mis poros mojados que dejaran de sudar, porque estaba completamente seguro de que Nezahualpili me iba a preguntar acerca de las actividades de Chalchiunénetl, cuando ella no estaba visitando las bibliotecas. Mas con gran alivio de mi parte, el Venerado Orador me preguntó acerca de mis propias actividades.

«¿No es para ti una gran carga, Topo, dedicar tanto tiempo a tu señora hermana?», me preguntó con amabilidad.

«No, mi señor —mentí—. Ella es muy considerada ya que no se entremete en mi tiempo de estudio. Es solamente en las tardes cuando conversamos o paseamos alrededor del palacio o vagamos por la ciudad.»

«En cuanto a conversación —dijo él—, quisiera pedirte que hicieras algún esfuerzo por tratar de corregir su acento mexícatl. Tú aprendiste muy rápido nuestra manera de hablar en Texcoco. Anímala a que hable más elegantemente, Cabeza Inclinada.»

«Sí, mi señor. Lo intentaré.»

Él continuó: «Tu Señor Maestro de Conocimientos de Palabras me dijo que has hecho progresos rápidos y admirables en el arte de la escritura-pintada. ¿Podrías disponer un poco más de tiempo para poner en práctica esta habilidad?»

«¡Estoy seguro, mi señor! —exclamé ansiosa y ardientemente—. *Haré* tiempo.»

Y así, al fin inicié mi carrera de escribano y fue en gran parte gracias al padre de Muñeca de Jade, Auítzotl. Inmediatamente después de haber sido coronado como Uey-Tlatoani de Tenochtitlan, Auítzotl había demostrado dramáticamente sus hazañas como gobernante, declarando la guerra a los huaxteca de la costa noreste. Conduciendo personalmente un ejército combinado de mexica, acolhua y tecpaneca, atacó y ganó la guerra en menos de un mes. Los ejércitos trajeron mucho botín y las tierras conquistadas tuvieron, como siempre, que pagar el tributo anual. El saqueo y la recaudación del tributo eran divididos entre las Tres Alianzas como se acostumbraba: dos quintas partes para Tenochtitlan, dos quintas partes para Texcoco y una quinta parte para Tlacopan.

El trabajo que Nezahualpili me encargó era dibujar en el libro de cuentas las partidas del tributo recibido y esperado de los huaxteca, y también dar entrada a varios artículos como turquesas, cacao, mantos, faldas, blusas de algodón y algodón en crudo, que debía anotar en otros libros en donde se llevaban las cuentas de las mercancías de los almacenes de Texcoco. Era una tarea con la que ejercitaba dos conocimientos: la aritmética y la escritura-pintada y me lancé a ese trabajo con gran placer y la consciente determinación de hacerlo bien.

Pero como ya he dicho, también Muñeca de Jade se valía de mi talento y me llamó de nuevo para ordenarme reanudar la búsqueda y los bosquejos de «hombres guapos». Aprovechó también la oportunidad para quejarse con malhumor acerca de la *falta* de talento del escultor de palacio.

«Como mi Señor Esposo me lo permitió, ordené esta estatua y le di instrucciones precisas a ese viejo escultor tonto, que él me mandó. Pero mira, ¡Trae! Una monstruosidad.»

Era la figura de un hombre en tamaño natural esculpido en barro, pintada en color de piel natural y cocida hasta adquirir mucha dureza. No representaba a ningún dios de los mexica que yo pudiera reconocer, pero había algo en ella que me era familiar.

«Se supone que los acolhua son expertos en las artes —continuó diciendo la joven con desdén—. Entérate de esto, ¡Trae! Su muy renombrado maestro escultor es un inepto, comparado con algunos artistas sin renombre cuyos trabajos he visto en mi tierra. Si Píxquitl no hace mi siguiente estatua mejor que ésta, mandaré traer de Tenochtitlan a esas nulidades para avergonzarlo. ¡Ve y dile eso!»

Tenía la sospecha de que la joven señora solamente estaba preparando alguna excusa para poder importar no a unos artistas, sino a algunos de sus amantes anteriores que recordaba con afecto. Sin embargo como ella me lo mandó, fui a ver al escultor a quien encontré en su estudio de palacio. Había gran estrépito producido por los martillos y los cinceles de sus estudiantes y aprendices, y por el rugido del fuego del horno, así es que necesité gritar para que él pudiera oír las quejas y la amenaza de Muñeca de Jade.

«Hice lo mejor que pude —dijo el anciano artista—. La señora ni siquiera me dijo el nombre del dios que había escogido para poder así contemplar otras estatuas o pinturas de éste. Todo lo que tenía para guiarme era esto.»

Y me enseñó un dibujo a tiza en papel de corteza: éste era el que yo mismo había hecho de Yeyac-Netztlin. Me sentí perplejo. ¿Por qué Muñeca de Jade había ordenado una estatua de un dios, cualquier dios, hecho a la semejanza de un simple y mortal mensajero-veloz? Aunque nunca se lo pregunté, ya que estaba seguro que me gruñiría diciendo que no me metiera en lo que no me importaba.

La siguiente vez que le entregué mis dibujos, deliberadamente incluí con un poco de espíritu jocoso uno de su legítimo esposo, el Venerado Orador Nezahualpili. Dando un resoplido desdeñoso, tanto al dibujo como a mí, lo empujó a un lado. La pintura que escogió esta vez fue la de un joven jardinero asistente del palacio llamado Xali-Otli, y fue a él a quien le di su anillo al día siguiente con las consabidas instrucciones. Él, como su predecesor, era solamente un plebeyo, pero hablaba el náhuatl con el acento de Texcoco y yo confiaba, ya que volvería a estar libre por un tiempo de la obligación de atender a la joven, que *él* podría continuar perfeccionando su forma de hablar, como lo deseaba Nezahualpili.

Cuando terminé de asentar el tributo de los huaxteca, entregué el libro de cuentas al subtesorero que se hacía cargo de esas cosas, quien alabó grandemente mi trabajo ante su superior el Mujer Serpiente, y el Señor Hueso Fuerte a su vez fue lo suficientemente amable como para dar un buen informe de mí a Nezahualpili. Después de lo cual el Venerado Orador envió a por mí para preguntarme si me gustaría intentar precisamente el mismo trabajo que ustedes están haciendo, reverendos frailes. O sea, anotar por escrito las palabras habladas en la cámara en donde el Uey-Tlatoani se reunía con su Consejo o en la Corte de Justicia, cuando daba audiencia a los ciudadanos de Texcoco quienes presentaban sus demandas o sus quejas.

Naturalmente, me encargué del trabajo con alegre entusiasmo y aunque al principio no fue fácil y cometí muchos errores, con el tiempo también recibí congratulaciones por ese trabajo. Debo decir sin mucha modestia que había logrado bastante fluidez, habilidad y precisión en hacer mis pinturas. Así es que tuve que aprender a hacer los glifos *rápidamente,* si bien, y por supuesto, nunca llegué a ser un escribano tan rápido como cualquiera de ustedes, mis señores. En esas asambleas del Consejo y recepciones de pedigüeños, rara vez había un momento en que no hablara alguien, cuyo discurso debía ser anotado, y casi siempre hablaban varias personas al mismo tiempo. Afortunadamente para mí, el sistema que empleaba era como el suyo, tener dos o más escribanos experimentados trabajando simultáneamente, así lo que a uno se le pasaba el otro probablemente lo había anotado.

Pronto aprendí a anotar las palabras más importantes del discurso de una persona y sólo bosquejándolas. Después en mis ratos libres, recordaba lo substancial y lo insertaba entre ellas, luego hacía una copia en limpio de todo, añadiéndole los cololes que la harían totalmente comprensible. Así es que este método no sólo mejoró mi velocidad en escribir, sino también mi memoria.

Asimismo encontré muy útil inventar un número de palabras, a las que llamé glifos breves, en las que podía comprimir una procesión completa de palabras. Por ejemplo, dibujaba sólo un pequeño círculo representando una boca abierta, por el largo prefacio con el que cada mujer y cada hombre empezaban su conversación con el Uey-Tlatoani: En su augusta presencia, *mixpantzinco*, mi Señor Venerado Orador Nezahualpili...» Si alguien hablaba refiriéndose simultáneamente a sucesos recientes y pasados, yo los diferenciaba unos de otros dibujando alternativamente los simples glifos que representaban a un bebé y a un buitre. El bebé, verán ustedes, representaba lo «nuevo» e identificaba los sucesos recientes. El buitre, siendo calvo, simbolizaba lo «viejo» e identificaba los sucesos pasados.

Ah, bueno. Creo que todas esas reminiscencias podrían interesar profesionalmente a algunos compañeros escribanos como ustedes, mis reverendos frailes, aunque la verdad es que si hablo de estas cosas es porque soy reacio a hablar de otras, como la siguiente vez que fui llamado a las habitaciones de la Señora Muñeca de Jade.

«Necesito otra cara nueva —me dijo abruptamente, si bien los dos sabíamos que no era cualquier *cara* la que exigía—. Y no quiero esperar mientras tú coleccionas una nueva serie de dibujos. Déjame ver otra vez los que ya tienes hechos.» Se los llevé y ella los hojeó rápidamente, dándoles una simple mirada hasta que cogiendo uno dijo: «Éste. ¿Quién es?»

«Un esclavo que vi cerca de palacio —le dije—. Creo que está empleado como portador de literas.»

«¡Trae!», ordenó, entregándome el anillo de esmeralda.

«Mi señora —protesté—. ¿Un esclavo?»

«No soy demasiado melindrosa cuando tengo urgencia —dijo—. Además, los esclavos generalmente son muy buenos. Los desgraciados no osan negarse a cumplir ni las más humillantes demandas que se les haga. —Sonrió con su dulzona sonrisa—. Y cuanta menos espina dorsal tenga un hombre, más podrá contorsionarse como un reptil y retorcerse sobre sí mismo.»

Antes de que yo pudiera hacer más objeciones, Muñeca de Jade me guió a una pared de su alcoba y me dijo: «Mira esto. Es el segundo dios que he ordenado a ese mal llamado maestro escultor Píxquitl.»

«Ése no es un dios —dije, estupefacto, mientras miraba fijamente la nueva estatua—. Ése es el jardinero Xali-Otli.»

Dijo con una voz fría y amenazante: «Por lo que a ti y a todos los de Texcoco concierne, éste es un dios no muy conocido adorado por mi familia en Tenochtitlan. Pero no importa. Por lo menos tú lo reconociste y apuesto que nadie más lo haría a excepción quizá de su madre. Ese viejo Píxquitl es desesperadamente incompetente. He mandado traer a esos artistas mexica que ya te mencioné. Estarán aquí inmediatamente después del festival de Ochpanitztli. Ve y dile a Píxquitl que quiero que prepare un estudio separado y privado para ellos, con todos los materiales que puedan necesitar. Después encuentra a ese esclavo y dale mi anillo y las instrucciones usuales.»

Cuando me enfrenté de nuevo con el viejo escultor, dijo malhumoradamente: «Sólo puedo volver a insistir que hice lo mejor que pude con el dibujo que me dieron. Por lo menos esta vez también me dio una calavera para que trabajara con ella.»

«¿Qué?»

«Oh, sí. Es mucho más fácil esculpir una buena semejanza cuando uno tiene como base real los huesos, encima de los cuales poder moldear el barro.»

Sin poder creer lo que debería haber comprendido antes, balbuceé: «Pero... pero, maestro Píxquitl, no es posible que alguien posea la calavera de un dios.»

Me miró largamente con sus viejos ojos de párpados cansados. «Lo único que sé es que se me proporcionó la calavera de un hombre adulto, muerto hacía poco, y que la estructura de ésta se aproximaba a las características faciales del dibujo, y que me dijeron que éste era el de algún dios menor. No soy un sacerdote para poner en duda su autenticidad y no soy tan tonto como para preguntarle a una reina imperiosa. Mientras haga el trabajo que me pide podré conservar mi propia calavera intacta. ¿Entiendes?»

Asentí con la cabeza. Sí, al fin entendía y demasiado bien.

El maestro continuó: «Prepararé el estudio para los nuevos artistas que están por llegar. Aunque debo decir que no envidio a ninguna persona empleada por la Señora Muñeca de Jade. Ni a mí. Ni a ellos. Ni a ti.»

Yo tampoco envidiaba mi situación —alcahuete de una asesina—, pero ya estaba demasiado involucrado para encontrar la manera de salir de ese enredo. Fui y encontré al esclavo cuyo nombre era Niez-Huéyotl, que en la patética y presuntuosa forma de los nombres de los esclavos quería decir: Yo Seré de la Grandeza. Aparentemente no pudo sobrevivir a su nombre, porque no pasó mucho tiempo antes de que Muñeca de Jade me volviera a llamar.

«Tenías razón, ¡Trae! —dijo— Un esclavo puede ser un error. Aquél efectivamente empezó a imaginarse a sí mismo como un ser humano. —Ella se rió—. Bien, será un dios en poco tiempo, que es más de lo que jamás habría esperado. Pero esto me ha hecho darme cuenta de algo. Mi Señor Esposo puede empezar a preguntarse, eventualmente, por qué nada más tengo estatuas de dioses en mis habitaciones. Debería tener por lo menos una diosa. La última vez que me enseñaste tus dibujos, vi el de una mujer muy bella. Ve y tráemelo.»

Así lo hice aunque afligido. Me arrepentía de haber mostrado a Muñeca de Jade aquel bosquejo. No lo había hecho por alguna razón encubierta, sino impulsivamente, como un gesto de admiración hacia la joven mujer, cuando ésta atrajo mi atención. Por cierto que atraía las miradas de muchos hombres y llenaba sus ojos de especulación y deseo. Sin embargo, Nemalhuili era una mujer casada; la esposa de un próspero artesano en pluma del mercado de artistas de Texcoco. Su belleza no residía sólo en su rostro vivaz y luminoso. Sus movimientos eran siempre fluidos y gentiles; su porte, regio, y sus labios tenían una sonrisa para todos. Nemalhuili exhalaba una inextinguible alegría y su nombre era el más apropiado puesto que significaba: Algo Delicado.

Muñeca de Jade estudió el dibujo y para mi alivio, dijo: «No te puedo mandar a por ella, ¡Trae! Eso sería una gran violación a las costumbres y podría causar una conmoción indeseable. Mandaré a por una de mis esclavas.»

Aunque como yo lo había esperado, no terminó así mi complicidad porque lo siguiente que me dijo la joven reina fue: «La mujer Nemalhuili estará aquí esta noche. ¿Podrás creer que ésta es la primera vez que tendré placer con una de mi propio sexo? Así es que quiero que asistas con tus materiales de pintura y tomes nota de esta aventura, para poder ver después las cosas que estuvimos haciendo.»

Por supuesto que la idea me aterró, por tres razones: Primera, y la más importante, estaba enojado conmigo mismo por haber involucrado inadvertidamente a Algo Delicado, pues aunque sólo la conocía de vista, por su reputación la tenía en alta estima. Segunda, y pensando egoístamente, después de esa noche jamás podría proclamar que no sabía con certeza, qué clase de cosas pasaban en las habitaciones de mi señora. Tercera, sentía algo de repugnancia ante la idea de ser obligado a ser testigo de un acto que debería ser privado; pero no podía rehusar y debo admitir que entre mis emociones se mezclaba una perversa curiosidad. Había escuchado la palabra *patlachuia*, pero no podía imaginarme cómo dos hembras podían hacer ese acto juntas.

Algo Delicado llegó, tan alegre y luminosa como siempre, aunque comprensiblemente un poco perpleja de esa cita clandestina a medianoche. Estábamos en verano y el aire afuera no era frío, pero a pesar de eso llevaba un *quexquémetl*, chal, sobre sus hombros. Quizá se le había ordenado disimular su rostro con el chal durante el camino hacia el palacio.

«Mi señora», dijo cortésmente inquiriendo con la mirada primero a la reina y luego a mí, que estaba sentado con un montón de hojas de papel de corteza sobre mis rodillas. No había encontrado la manera de ocultar mi presencia discretamente, ya que mi vista requería que me sentara lo más cerca posible, para poder dibujar todo lo que iba a ocurrir.

«No hagas caso del escribano —dijo Muñeca de Jade—. Sólo préstame atención a mí. Primero quiero estar segura de que tu marido no sabe nada acerca de esta visita.»

«Nada, mi señora. Él estaba durmiendo cuando lo dejé. Su criada me dijo que no debía decirle nada a él, así es que no lo hice, porque pensé que usted me necesitaría para alguna cosa... para... bueno, para alguna cosa que no tuviera que ver con los hombres.»

«Precisamente —dijo su anfitriona sonriendo con satisfacción. Y cuando los ojos de Nemalhuili se desviaron otra vez hacia mí, Chalchiunénetl le gritó—: Dije que ignoraras a éste. Él es un mueble. Ni oye, ni ve; no existe. —Entonces bajó la voz a un simple murmullo persuasivo—: Me han dicho que eres una de las mujeres más bellas de Texcoco. Como ves querida, yo también lo soy. Se me ocurrió que podríamos compartir gozosamente nuestras bellezas.»

Y al mismo tiempo y con sus propias manos le quitó el *quexquémetl* a Nemalhuili. Por supuesto, la visitante se mostró sorprendida de que la reina personalmente le quitara su chal. Sin embargo su expresión cambió a un desconcertante sobresalto cuando Muñeca de Jade le levantó la larga blusa por encima de

174

su cabeza y quitándosela la dejó desnuda de la cintura para arriba.

Sólo sus grandes ojos se movían. Rápidamente se volvieron otra vez hacia mí, como los de una cierva asustada que balando suplica ayuda a uno de los cazadores que la cercan. Pero yo pretendí no ver, hice que mi cara se viera impasible; aparentemente tenía los ojos puestos en el dibujo que acababa de empezar y no creo que Nemalhuili me volviera a ver. Desde ese momento, ella evidentemente se las arregló para hacer lo que se le había pedido: creer que yo no estaba presente, más aún, que no existía. Yo creo, que si la pobre mujer no hubiera sido capaz de borrarme de su conciencia, se hubiera muerto de vergüenza esa misma noche.

Mientras la mujer se quedó parada enfrente, los senos desnudos, tan rígida como una estatua, Chalchiunénetl se quitó su blusa, despacio, seductoramente, como si lo estuviera haciendo para excitar a un hombre que no respondía. Entonces se acercó hasta que los dos cuerpos casi se tocaron. Algo Delicado era quizá diez años mayor que la reina-niña y más alta, como la anchura de una mano.

«Sí —dijo Muñeca de Jade—, tus pechos son muy hermosos. Excepto que —y simuló hacer pucheros de desilusión— tus pezones son tímidos, se mantienen plegados hábilmente. ¿Es que no pueden empujarse hacia afuera como los míos? —Ella se paró de puntillas, con la parte superior de su cuerpo un poco hacia adelante y exclamó—: ¡Mira, ellos se tocan exactamente, querida! ¿Se podría acomodar también el resto de nuestros cuerpos?»

Apretó sus labios contra los de Namalhuili. La mujer no cerró los ojos ni cambió la expresión de su rostro en lo más mínimo, pero las mejillas de Muñeca de Jade se hundieron. Después de un momento, echó su cara hacia atrás sólo lo suficiente como para decir con deleite: «¡Ah, mira! Tus pezones *pueden* crecer. ¡Lo sabía! ¿No los sientes desdoblándose sobre los míos?» Se inclinó hacia adelante para poder probar otro beso y esta vez Algo Delicado sí cerró los ojos, como si tuviera miedo de que algo involuntario pudiera mostrarse en ellos.

Se quedaron así, inmóviles el tiempo suficiente para que yo captara una pintura de ellas; Muñeca de Jade todavía de puntillas, las dos solamente tocándose los labios y los pechos. Luego la muchacha movió los dedos hasta buscar la falda de la mujer y hábimente la desabrochó, de modo que ésta cayó al piso. Yo estaba lo suficientemente cerca como para poder ver la perceptible crispación de sus músculos, cuando apretó sus largas piernas de una manera protectora. Después de un momento Muñeca de Jade desabrochó su propia falda y la dejó caer a sus pies. No tenía nada puesto debajo de ella, de manera que quedó completamente desnuda, a excepción de sus sandalias doradas. Pero cuando apretó todo su cuerpo contra el de Algo Delicado, se dio cuenta de que la mujer, como cualquier mujer decente, todavía llevaba puesto su *tzotzomatli*, ropa interior.

Chalchiunénetl dio un paso atrás y la miró con una mezcla

de diversión, cariño y ligero enojo, y le dijo dulcemente: «No te quitaré esa última ropa, Nemalhuili. Ni siquiera te pediré que lo hagas. Haré que lo *desees*.»

La joven reina tomó la mano de la mujer y tiró de ella con fuerza haciéndola caminar y cruzaron la habitación hacia la gran cama endoselada de suaves cobertores. Se recostaron sobre ella sin cubrirse y yo me acerqué con mis tizas y mis papeles.

Pues, sí, Fray Jerónimo, hay más. Después de todo, yo estaba allí, lo vi todo y no he olvidado nada. Por supuesto que si así usted lo desea, queda disculpado de oír esto.

Permítanme decirles al resto de ustedes, que se quedaron, señores escribanos, que he sido testigo de diversas violaciones durante mi vida. He visto a nuestros soldados y a los suyos atacar violentamente a las mujeres cautivas. Pero en toda mi vida jamás he visto a una hembra ser violada tanto en su alma como en sus partes sexuales, como lo fue Algo Delicado. Violada tan insidiosa, tan cabal y espantosamente por Muñeca de Jade. Y lo que más se ha grabado en mi memoria, resaltándolo completamente más que cualquier otra violación hecha por un hombre a una mujer, fue el hecho de que la joven manipuló a la mujer casada no por la fuerza o por una orden, sino con suaves toqueteos y caricias hasta que finalmente llevó a Algo Delicado a un punto de paroxismo, que después del cual ya no fue responsable de su conducta.

Creo que sería apropiado decir aquí que, cuando nosotros hacemos mención acerca de la seducción de una mujer, en nuestro lenguaje decimos: «la acaricio con flores...»

La mujer se quedó indolente e indiferente por un rato y sólo se movía Muñeca de Jade. Utilizando solamente sus labios, la lengua y las simples yemas de sus dedos. Los usó en los párpados cerrados de Nemalhuili y en sus pestañas, en los lóbulos de sus orejas, en el hueco de su cuello, en medio de sus pechos, a lo largo y a lo ancho de su cuerpo expuesto, en el hoyuelo de su ombligo, de arriba abajo de sus piernas. Repetidas veces usó la punta de su dedo o de su lengua para trazar lentas espirales alrededor de los senos de la otra mujer, antes de pellizcar al fin, y de lamer los endurecidos y erectos pezones. No volvió a besar apasionadamente a Nemalhuili, pero entre sus otras actividades daba lengüetazos atormentadores a través de la boca cerrada de la mujer. Y gradualmente los labios de Nemalhuili, como sus tetas, se pusieron hinchados y rubicundos. Su piel de color cobre pálido, al principio lisa, se puso por todas partes como piel de ganso y empezó a temblar en varias partes.

Muñeca de Jade ocasionalmente cesaba sus manipulaciones y apretaba fuertemente contra Algo Delicado su cuerpo convulsionado. Nemalhuili, aun con los ojos cerrados, no podía evitar sentir y saber lo que le estaba pasando a la joven. Solamente una estatua de piedra se hubiera quedado quieta sin sentirse afectada por ello, pero aun la mujer más virtuosa, reacia y asustada no es ninguna estatua. Cuando Muñeca de Jade se detuvo de nuevo y empezó a temblar desvalidamente, Algo Delicado emitió un sonido parecido a un arrullo, como una madre hubiera podido hacerlo con un niño angustiado. Movió las manos para levantar de su pecho la cabeza de Chalchiunénetl y la llevó a su cara, y por primera vez le plantó un beso. Sus besos obligaron a los de la joven a abrirse y sus mejillas se ahuecaron profundamente, y un lloriqueo amortiguado salió de ambas bocas que estaban aplastadas una contra la otra. Sus cuerpos palpitaron juntos y en ese momento Nemalhuili dejó caer una de sus manos para arrancarse su ropa íntima.

Después de eso, Algo Delicado se quedó otra vez tranquila y cerró sus ojos de nuevo; mordió la parte de atrás de su mano lo cual no evitó que se le escapara un sollozo. Cuando su jadeo aminoró, Muñeca de Jade empezó a moverse otra vez y era la única que lo hacía en la cama de cobijas arrugadas. Como en esos momentos Nemalhuili estaba también desnuda, todas sus partes estaban expuestas vulnerablemente y Muñeca de Jade tenía a su disposición más lugares en donde centrar su atención. Durante un tiempo, Algo Delicado mantuvo las piernas bien apretadas, pero luego, lentamente, como si no tuviera nada que ver con ello, dejó que sus músculos se aflojaran y que sus piernas se relajasen y se abrieran un poco, un poquito más...

Muñeca de Jade escondió su cabeza entre ellas, buscando lo que una vez me había descrito como «la pequeña perla rosa». Así estuvo por un tiempo y la mujer, como si la estuvieran torturando, emitió muchos sonidos y finalmente tuvo un movimiento violento. Cuando se recuperó debía ya de haber decidido que, al fin y al cabo, podía abandonarse totalmente ya que no podría degradarse más, y entonces Nemalhuili comenzó, aunque con menos facilidad y pericia, a hacerle a Muñeca de Jade lo que la joven le había estado haciendo a ella. Esto ocasionó una variedad de acoplamientos. A veces estaban apretadas en un abrazo como hombre y mujer, besándose las bocas mientras sus pelvis se frotaban. Otras veces se acostaban con las cabezas invertidas, cada una estrechando las caderas de la otra mientras usaban la lengua, como un modelo en miniatura, pero mucho más ágil, simulando al miembro masculino. A veces se sentaban cara a cara, pero reclinándose hacia atrás sobre sus brazos, para que sus muslos se extendieran y se tocaran en las partes inferiores de sus cuerpos, esforzándose en friccionarse mutuamente sus perlitas rosas.

En esa posición me recordaron la leyenda que relata cómo se creó la raza humana. Se decía que, después de la época en que la tierra había estado poblada primero por los dioses y después por los gigantes, aquéllos decidieron legar el mundo a los seres humanos. Sin embargo, no los había todavía y los dioses tuvieron que crearlos, y lo hicieron así: crearon algunos hombres y un número igual de mujeres, pero los diseñaron mal, porque aquellos primeros seres humanos tenían cuerpos que se terminaban debajo de la cintura con un tipo de protuberancia lisa. Según la leyenda, los dioses tenían la intención de ocultar modestamente los genitales de la gente, aunque es difícil de creer, ya que los dioses y las diosas no se destacaban precisamente por su modestia sexual.

Sea como fuere, aquella primera gente podía brincar por todas partes sobre los tocones de sus cuerpos y gozar de toda la belleza del mundo que habían heredado, pero no eran capaces de gozarse los unos a los otros. Y tenían ganas de hacerlo porque ocultos o no, sus sexos se atraían respectivamente. Felizmente para el futuro de la humanidad, esa primera gente se las ingenió para superar su impedimento. Rebotaban alto una mujer y un hombre juntos y en el aire fusionaban las partes inferiores de sus cuerpos, como algunos insectos se aparejan en pleno vuelo. La leyenda no nos dice exactamente cómo lo lograban, ni cómo las mujeres daban a luz los bebés que así concibieron. Sin embargo, lo lograron y la siguiente generación llegó completa con piernas y órganos genitales accesibles. Al observar a Muñeca de Jade y a Algo Delicado en esa posición en que frotaban con urgencia sus *tepili*, no pude evitar en pensar en esos primeros humanos y en su impulso por copular a pesar de las dificultades.

Debo mencionar que la mujer y la muchacha aunque asumían las más intrincadas posiciones y se acariciaban ávidamente, no se sacudían ni brincaban tanto como lo hubieran hecho un hombre y una mujer ocupados en ese mismo acto. Sus movimientos eran sinuosos, no angulados; graciosos, no toscos. Muchas veces, aunque algunas de sus partes indudablemente estaban ocupadas, las dos mujeres parecían estar tan quietas como si durmieran. Entonces una o ambas se estremecían, o se endurecían, o brincaban o se contorsionaban. Perdí la cuenta, pero sé que las dos llegaron aquella noche a muchas más culminaciones de lo que cualquiera de ambas hubiera podido lograr con el hombre más varonil e infatigable.

En medio de esas pequeñas convulsiones, se quedaban en varias posturas el tiempo suficiente como para que yo hiciera muchos dibujos de sus cuerpos; separados o entrelazados. Si algunas de las pinturas estaban manchadas o dibujadas con una línea temblorosa, no fue por culpa de las modelos, excepto en cuanto a que sus actividades agitaban al artista. Yo tampoco era una estatua. Varias veces, observándolas fui atormentado por estremecimientos simpáticos y dos veces mi miembro ingobernable...

También nos deja precipitadamente Fray Domingo. Es curioso ver cómo un hombre puede ser afectado adversamente por algunas palabras y otros hombres por otras. Creo que las palabras evocan diferentes imágenes en distintas mentes. Incluso en las de los escribanos impersonales, quienes tienen por deber oírlas sólo como sonidos y registrarlas solamente como marcas en el papel.

Quizá por eso, debo refrenarme y no relatar con detalle todas las demás cosas que hicieron la muchacha y la mujer durante aquella larga noche. Bueno, finalmente se separaron, exhaustas, y se quedaron respirando profundamente una al lado de la otra.

Sus labios y *tepili*, partes, estaban excesivamente hinchadas y rojas; sus pieles brillaban con sudor, saliva y otras transpiraciones, y sus cuerpos estaban moteados como la piel del jaguar por las marcas de mordiscos y de besos.

Silenciosamente me levanté de mi lugar al lado de la cama y con manos temblorosas recogí mis dibujos tirados alrededor de mi silla. Cuando me había retirado a un rincón del cuarto, Algo Delicado también se levantó y moviéndose fatigada y débilmente, como alguien que apenas se está recuperando de una enfermedad, se vistió lentamente. Evitó mirarme, pero yo podía ver que había lágrimas corriendo por su rostro.

«Desearás descansar —le dijo Muñeca de Jade y tiró del cordón-campana colocado encima de la cama—. Pitza te conducirá a una habitación privada.» Nemalhuili todavía lloraba calladamente cuando la adormilada esclava la guió fuera del cuarto.

Dije con voz insegura: «Suponga que se lo cuenta a su esposo.»

«No podría soportar el hacerlo —dijo Muñeca de Jade con seguridad—. Y no lo hará. Déjame ver los dibujos. —Se los entregué y los estudió minuciosamente, uno por uno—. Así es como nos veíamos. Exquisito. Y yo que pensaba que había experimentado todo tipo de... Qué lástima que mi Señor Nezahualpili me haya provisto únicamente de sirvientas viejas y feas. Creo que mantendré a mano a Algo Delicado por bastante tiempo.» Me sentí indeciblemente feliz de oír eso, porque sabía el destino que le esperaba a la mujer y cuán rápido sería. La muchacha me devolvió los dibujos, luego se estiró y bostezó voluptuosamente. «Sabes, ¡Trae!, ¡verdaderamente creo que ha sido lo mejor de todo lo que he gozado desde que utilizaba a aquel viejo objeto huaxteca!»

Parecía razonable, pensé al regresar a mis habitaciones. Una mujer debe saber mejor que cualquier hombre cómo juguetear con el cuerpo de otra de su mismo sexo. Sólo una mujer podría conocer más íntimamente todos los más tiernos y secretos escondrijos, las superficies más y menos excitables de su propio cuerpo, y en consecuencia, también los del cuerpo de cualquier otra. Por consiguiente si un *hombre* sabía esas mismas cosas, podría mejorar sus talentos sexuales e intensificar su propio goce y el de cada una de las mujeres con quienes se apareara. Así es que pasé mucho tiempo estudiando los dibujos y grabando en mi memoria las intimidades de las cuales había sido testigo y que los dibujos no podían describir tan gráficamente.

No estaba orgulloso con la parte que me había tocado desempeñar en la degradación de Algo Delicado, pero siempre he pensado que un hombre debe aprovechar y mejorar sus experiencias aun viéndose mezclado en los sucesos más lamentables.

⚜

No quiero decir que la violación de Algo Delicado fue el suceso más lamentable que presencié en mi vida. Otro me esperaba cuando regresé a casa otra vez, a Xaltocan, para el festival de Ochpanitztli.

Esa palabra significa El Barrido de la Calle, y se refiere a los ritos religiosos que se llevaban a efecto en demanda de una extraordinaria cosecha de maíz. El festival se celebraba en nuestro mes once, aproximadamente a mediados de su mes de agosto, y consistía en varios ritos complicados que culminaban en el día exactamente ordenado para el nacimiento del dios del maíz, Centéotl. Ésta era una época ceremonial completamente entregada a las mujeres; todos los hombres, incluyendo a la mayoría de los sacerdotes, eran simples espectadores.

Empezaba cuando las más venerables esposas y las viudas más virtuosas de Xaltocan barrían, con sus escobas hechas especialmente de plumas, todos los templos y otros lugares sagrados de la isla. Entonces, bajo la dirección de nuestras mujeres que atendían los templos, todas las demás llevaban a cabo el canto, baile y ejecución de la música durante la noche climática. Una virgen escogida de entre todas las muchachas de la isla tomaba el papel de Teteoínan, la madre de todos los dioses. La parte más importante de la fiesta era el acto que hacía en la cima de la pirámide, completamente sola sin pareja masculina, pretendiendo ser desflorada y fecundada y luego sufrir los dolores del parto y dar a luz. Después de eso era atravesada hasta morir por las flechas lanzadas por arqueros femeninos, quienes cumplían su trabajo con una dedicación intensa, pero con muy poca destreza, así es que generalmente la muchacha no moría rápidamente, sino tras una prolongada agonía.

Por supuesto que siempre había una sustitución de último momento, pues nunca sacrificábamos a una de nuestras doncellas, a no ser que por alguna razón singular ésta insistiera en ofrecerse voluntariamente. De ese modo no era realmente la virgen que representaba a Teteoínan quien moría, sino una esclava disponible o una prisionera capturada de otro pueblo. Para el simple papel de morir no era necesario que fuera una virgen y a veces era una mujer vieja la despachada al otro mundo esa noche.

Cuando la mujer finalmente moría después de haber sido zafiamente destrozada y perforada por innumerables flechas, unos sacerdotes participaban por primera vez. Salían del templo de la pirámide, detrás de la cual se habían ocultado, y todavía casi invisibles en la oscuridad de sus negras vestiduras, arrastraban el cuerpo adentro del templo. Allí, rápidamente despellejaban la piel de uno de sus muslos. Un sacerdote se ponía ese gorro cónico encima de su cabeza y salía saltando del templo acompañado por una explosión de música y canto. El joven dios del maíz, Centéotl acababa de nacer. Bajaba brincando las escaleras de la pirámide, juntándose con las bailarinas y todos danzaban el resto de la noche.

Si cuento todo esto es porque supongo que la ceremonia de aquel año debió de ser igual a la de todos los anteriores. Tengo que suponerlo porque no me quedé para verla.

El generoso príncipe Huexotzinca me prestó otra vez su *acali* y remeros y llegué a Xaltocan para encontrar que los otros,

Pactli, Chimali y Tlatli, también habían llegado para esa fiesta desde sus distantes escuelas. De hecho, Pactli había regresado definitivamente, habiendo concluido hacía poco su educación en la *calmécac*. Eso me preocupaba, porque ya no tendría nada que hacer a excepción de esperar a que muriera su padre Garza Roja y le dejara el trono libre. Mientras tanto, Pactli podría concentrar todo su tiempo y fuerza en asegurarse la esposa que él deseaba: mi hermana, quien no quería serlo; y contaba con la ayuda de su más leal aliada: mi madre, la codiciosa de títulos.

Sin embargo, me encontré con una preocupación más inmediata. Tlatli y Chimali se sentían tan anhelantes por verme, que me estaban esperando en el muelle cuando mi canoa atracó y, brincando excitadamente, comenzaron a hablar, a gritar y a reír antes de que yo hubiera puesto el pie en tierra.

«¡Topo, la cosa más maravillosa!»

«¡Nuestro primer encargo, Topo, para hacer obras de arte en el extranjero!»

Me costó un poco de tiempo y unos cuantos gritos antes de poder darme cuenta y comprender lo que me querían decir. Cuando lo comprendí quedé horrorizado. Mis dos amigos eran los artistas mexica de quienes me había hablado Muñeca de Jade. No regresarían a Tenochtitlan después de la fiesta, sino que irían conmigo a Texcoco.

Tlatli dijo: «Yo voy a hacer las esculturas y Chimali las va a colorear para que parezcan vivas. Así lo dijo el mensajero que la señora Chalchiunénetl nos envió. ¡Imagínate! La hija de un Uey-Tlatoani y la esposa de otro. Ciertamente ningún otro artista de nuestra edad ha sido tan honrado anteriormente.»

Chimali dijo: «¡No teníamos idea de que la señora Muñeca de Jade hubiera visto alguna vez las obras que hacíamos en Tenochtitlan!»

Tlatli dijo: «Que las haya visto y admirado lo suficiente como para llamarnos y para viajar a tantas largas carreras. La señora debe tener muy buen gusto.»

Dije sutilmente: «La señora tiene numerosos gustos.»

Mis amigos se dieron cuenta de que no compartía su entusiasmo y Chimali me dijo, casi disculpándose: «Éste es nuestro primer trabajo verdadero, Topo. Las estatuas y pinturas que hicimos en la ciudad, no eran más que adornos para el nuevo palacio que se está construyendo para Auítzotl, y no estábamos ni mejor vistos ni mejor pagados que los albañiles. El mensaje también decía que nos estaba esperando un estudio particular totalmente equipado. Es natural que estemos contentos. ¿Hay alguna razón para que no sea así?»

Tlatli dijo: «¿Es que la señora es de esa clase de mujeres tiranas que nos va a hacer trabajar hasta morir?»

Yo podría haberle dicho a Tlatli que lo había expresado sucintamente, cuando habló de llegar a trabajar «hasta morir»; pero en lugar de eso le dije: «La señora tiene algunas excentricidades. Hay mucho tiempo para platicar sobre ella. En estos momentos estoy muy cansado por mi propio trabajo.»

«Por supuesto —dijo Tlatli—. Permítenos cargar tu equipaje,

Topo. Saluda a tu familia, come y descansa. Y después tienes que contarnos todo acerca de Texcoco y de la Corte de Nezahualpili. No queremos aparecer allá como unos ignorantes provincianos.»

En el camino hacia mi casa, los dos siguieron parloteando alegremente acerca de sus perspectivas, pero yo permanecía silencioso pensando profundamente sobre... sus perspectivas. Bien sabía yo que los crímenes de Muñeca de Jade serían algún día descubiertos, y cuando eso sucediera Nezahualpili se vengaría de todos los que habían ayudado o encubierto los adulterios de la joven, sus asesinatos para ocultar las infidelidades y las estatuas que se mofaban de los asesinados. Yo tenía la débil esperanza de ser absuelto, ya que había actuado estrictamente según las órdenes de su mismo esposo. Los otros, los sirvientes y asistentes habían actuado según las órdenes recibidas de *ella*. No hubieran podido desobedecerla, pero ese hecho no les ganaría ninguna misericordia de parte del deshonrado Nezahualpili. Sus cuellos ya estaban adentro del lazo cubierto de guirnaldas. Pitza, el guardián de la puerta, tal vez el maestro Píxquitl y pronto Tlatli y Chimali...

Mi padre y mi hermana me recibieron calurosamente con grandes abrazos, mi madre con abrazo poco animado, disculpándose con la explicación de que sus brazos estaban debilitados y cansados por haber esgrimido la escoba durante todo el día en diversos templos. Siguió hablando con mucho detalle sobre las actividades de las mujeres de la isla, en preparación de la ceremonia de Ochpanitztli, poco de lo cual oí, ya que buscaba algún pretexto para alejarme con Tzitzi en busca de algún lugar solitario. No sólo estaba ansioso por demostrarle algunas de las cosas que había aprendido observando a Muñeca de Jade y Algo Delicado, sino que también deseaba contarle mi equívoca posición en la Corte de Texcoco y pedirle su consejo sobre lo que debía hacer, si es que se podía hacer algo para evitar la ida inminente de Tlatli y Chimali.

La oportunidad nunca llegó. Sobrevino la noche y nuestra madre seguía aún quejándose de la cantidad de trabajo relacionado con El Barrido de la Calle. La noche negra llegó y con ella los sacerdotes de vestiduras negras. Eran cuatro de ellos e iban por mi hermana.

Sin siquiera decir un «*mixpantzinco*» al jefe de la casa, pues los sacerdotes siempre habían sido desdeñosos a las cortesías más elementales, uno de ellos preguntó sin dirigirse a nadie en particular: «¿Es aquí donde vive la doncella Chiucnaui-Acatl Tzitzitlini?» Su voz era torpe y hablaba emitiendo un ruido como el del gallipavo, y con trabajo le pudimos entender. Ése era el caso de muchos sacerdotes, porque una de sus penitencias favoritas era llenarse la lengua de agujeros y de vez en cuando romperla aún más, haciendo más ancho el agujero al pasar por él cañas, cuerdas o espinas.

«Mi hija —dijo nuestra madre, con un gesto de orgullo señalándola—. Nueve Caña El Sonido De Campanitas Tocando.»

«Tzitzitlini —dijo el viejo mugroso dirigiéndose directamente a ella—. Venimos a informarte que has sido escogida para tener el honor de actuar en el papel de la diosa Teteoínan en la última noche de Ochpanitzli.»

«No», dijo mi hermana moviendo los labios aunque de ellos no salió ningún sonido. Miró azorada a los cuatro hombres vestidos con sus raídos mantos negros y pasó una mano temblorosa sobre su cara. Su piel de color cervato había adquirido el del pálido ámbar.

«Vendrás con nosotros en este momento —dijo otro sacerdote—. Hay algunas formalidades preliminares.»

«No», dijo Tzitzi otra vez, pero esta vez en voz alta. Se giró hacia mí y yo casi me tambaleé por el impacto de su mirada. Sus ojos estaban agrandados por el terror, tan insondablemente negros como los de Muñeca de Jade cuando usaba la droga que dilata la pupila. Mi hermana y yo sabíamos lo que eran las «formalidades preliminares», un examen físico llevado a cabo por los asistentes femeninos de los sacerdotes, para indagar que la doncella que había sido honrada, lo era en verdad. Como ya he dicho, Tzitzi conocía los medios para parecer una virgen impecable y convencer al más suspicaz examinador. Pero no había sido avisada de esa llegada repentina y precipitada de los sacerdotes para llevársela, por lo tanto no había tenido necesidad de prepararse y en esos momentos ya no podía hacerlo.

«Tzitzitlini —dijo mi padre reprendiéndola—. Nadie rechaza a un *tlamacazqui*, ni la orden que él trae. Sería descortés al sacerdote, mostraría desdén por la delegación de mujeres que te ha conferido ese honor y mucho peor, sería un insulto a la misma diosa Teteoínan.»

«También molestaría a nuestro estimado gobernador —terció mi madre—. Se le ha dicho ya al Señor Garza Roja quién ha sido la virgen seleccionada para este año, y también a su hijo Pactzin.»

«¡Nadie me avisó a mí!», dijo mi hermana con una última chispa de brío.

Ella y yo sabíamos para entonces *quién* la había propuesto para el papel de Teteoínan sin consultarla y sin pedirle permiso, y también sabíamos el *porqué*. Así nuestra madre podría tener un crédito indirecto por la ejecución de su hija; para que nuestra madre pudiera enorgullecerse en medio del aplauso aprobador de toda la isla; para que la pantomima pública del acto sexual, que representaría su hija, inflamara todavía más la lascivia del Señor Alegría, y para que estuviera más que nunca dispuesto a elevar a toda nuestra familia a la nobleza a cambio de la muchacha.

«Mis Señores Sacerdotes —dijo Tzitzi suplicando—, verdaderamente no les convengo. No puedo actuar en el papel. No en ese papel. Sería torpe y la gente se reiría. Deshonraría a la diosa...»

«Eso es totalmente falso —dijo uno de los cuatro—. Te hemos visto bailar, muchacha. Ven con nosotros en este momento.»

«Los preliminares llevan muy poco tiempo —dijo nuestra madre—. Anda, Tzitzi y cuando regreses discutiremos sobre la hechura de tu traje. Serás la más reluciente Teteoínan que haya dado a luz al bebé Centéotl.»

«No —dijo mi hermana otra vez, pero débil y desesperadamente buscando algún otro pretexto—. Es que... es que no es el tiempo adecuado de la luna para mí...»

«¡No es posible decir no! —ladró uno de los sacerdotes—. No hay pretextos aceptables. O vienes muchacha o te llevamos a la fuerza.»

Ni ella ni yo tuvimos la oportunidad de despedirnos, pues consideramos que estaría ausente solamente por un corto espacio de tiempo. Mientras Tzitzi caminaba hacia la puerta y los cuatro viejos malolientes la rodeaban, me lanzó una última mirada desesperada. Casi me la perdí, porque entonces yo miraba alrededor del cuarto buscando un arma o cualquier cosa que pudiera servir como tal.

Les juro que si hubiera tenido la *maquáhuitl* de Glotón de Sangre a mano, me habría abierto paso a cuchilladas a través de los sacerdotes y de mis padres, hierbas malas para ser abatidas, y nosotros dos hubiéramos huido hacia algún lugar seguro, en cualquier parte. Pero no había nada afilado ni pesado a mi alcance y hubiera sido inútil por mi parte atacar desarmado. Para entonces yo ya tenía veinte años y era un hombre, y hubiera podido con los cuatro sacerdotes, pero mi padre, templado por su trabajo, podía haberme detenido sin ningún esfuerzo. Además, habrían sospechado, con toda seguridad, interrogado, verificado y el destino se hubiera vuelto contra de nosotros dos...

Desde entonces me he preguntado muy frecuentemente: ¿no hubiera sido eso preferible a lo que sucedió? Un pensamiento como ése pasó como un relámpago por mi mente en aquel momento, pero en mi indecisión vacilé. ¿Fue porque sabía, en algún rincón cobarde de mi mente, que yo no estaba directamente involucrado en la difícil situación de mi hermana Tzitzi; y que probablemente no lo estaría, por lo que fui indeciso, por lo que vacilé? ¿Fue porque tenía una esperanza desesperada de que ella todavía pudiera convencer a las examinadoras; que ella no estaba realmente en peligro de desgracia, lo que me hizo detener? ¿Fue simplemente mi inmutable e inestable *tonali*, o el de ella, lo que me hizo vacilar, lo que me hizo detener? Jamás lo sabré. Todo lo que sé es que vacilé, me detuve y el momento de actuar se fue, como Tzitzi se fue con su guardia de honor de rapaces sacerdotes, dentro de la oscuridad de la noche.

Ella no regresó a casa esa noche.

Nos quedamos sentados esperando, hasta mucho después del tiempo normal de acostarse, hasta mucho después del trompetazo de la concha del templo a la medianoche. Sin hablar nada. Mi padre se veía preocupado, sin duda por su hija y por la causa de ese inusitado alargamiento de las «formalidades preliminares». Mi madre se veía preocupada, sin duda acerca de la posibilidad de que su proyecto tan cuidadosamente elaborado para su propia exaltación, de alguna manera se hubiera desbaratado. Pero finalmente se rió y dijo: «Claro. Los sacerdotes no mandarán a

Tzitzi a casa en la oscuridad. Las vírgenes del templo le habrán dado un cuarto allá para que pase la noche. Somos unos tontos de estarla esperando despiertos. Vayamos a dormir.»

Fui a mi esterilla, pero no dormí. Me inquietaba al pensar que si las examinadoras descubrían que Tzitzi no era virgen, ¿y cómo iban a descubrir otra cosa?, los sacerdotes podrían aprovecharse rapazmente de eso. Todos los sacerdotes de nuestros dioses habían hecho ostensiblemente un juramento de celibato, pero ninguna persona inteligente creía que lo cumplían. Las mujeres del templo sostendrían, con verdad, que Tzitzi llegó a ellas ya desprovista de su *chitoli*, membrana, y por lo tanto de su virginidad. De esa condición sólo se la podía culpar a ella por su propio desenfreno anterior. Cuando saliera de nuevo del templo, cualquier cosa que le hubiera pasado en el ínterin no podría achacárseles a los sacerdotes ni probar ningún cargo en contra de ellos.

Me revolvía angustiado sobre mi esterilla, imaginando a esos sacerdotes utilizándola durante la noche, uno tras otro, y regocijadamente llamando a todos los demás de los otros templos de la isla. No porque ellos estuvieran hambrientos sexualmente, pues se suponía que usaban a las mujeres del templo a voluntad. Sin embargo el tipo de mujeres que dedicaban sus vidas al servicio del templo, como ustedes reverendos frailes tal vez hayan observado entre sus propias religiosas, casi nunca eran de facciones o figura como para volver delirante de deseo a un hombre normal. Los sacerdotes debían estar llenos de alegría esa noche al recibir el regalo de carne nueva y joven en la más deseable y bella muchacha de todo Xaltocan, en aquel entonces.

Los veía caer como rebaños sobre el indefenso cuerpo de Tzitzi, en tropeles como buitres sobre un cadáver desamparado. Agitándose como buitres, graznando como buitres, con sus garras de buitres, negros como buitres. Observaban también otro juramento: nunca desvestirse en toda su vida después de haber hecho el juramento sacerdotal. Sin embargo aun violando ese juramento para caer desnudos encima de Tzitzi, sus cuerpos estarían todavía negros, escamosos y fétidos, por no haberse bañado desde que abrazaron el sacerdocio.

Tenía la esperanza de que todo fuera producto de mi imaginación febril. Tenía la esperanza de que mi bella y amada hermana no pasara aquella noche como una carroña desgarrada por los buitres. Pero ningún sacerdote habló jamás de su estancia en el templo, ni para afirmar ni para negar mis temores, pues Tzitzi no volvió a casa por la mañana.

Un sacerdote de los cuatro que se la habían llevado la noche anterior, vino y su cara estaba exenta de toda expresión cuando dijo simplemente: «Su hija no es idónea para representar a Teteoínan en las ceremonias. En algún momento ha conocido carnalmente por lo menos a un hombre.»

«¡*Yya ouiya ayya!* —solloçó mi madre—. ¡Esto lo arruina todo!»

«No lo entiendo —murmuró mi padre—. Siempre fue tan buena muchacha, no puedo creerlo...»

«Quizás —dijo el sacerdote blandamente— ahora les gustaría más ofrecer a su hija voluntariamente para el sacrificio.»

Yo le dije al sacerdote entre dientes: «¿En dónde está ella?»

Indiferentemente me dijo: «Cuando las examinadoras la juzgaron incompetente, naturalmente comunicamos al palacio del gobernador que era necesario buscar otra candidata. Al recibir la noticia, el palacio pidió que Nueva Caña Tzitzitlini fuera llevada allá hoy por la mañana para una entrevista con...»

«Pactli», dije abruptamente.

«Estará desolado», dijo mi padre, sacudiendo la cabeza con tristeza.

«¡Estará furioso, tonto! —escupió mi madre—. ¡Todos sufriremos su ira a causa de la perra de tu hija!»

«Iré al palacio inmediatamente», dije.

«No —respondió el sacerdote con firmeza—. La corte no duda en apreciar su interés, pero el mensaje fue muy específico: que sólo la hija de esta familia sería recibida. Dos de nuestras mujeres del templo la están conduciendo para allá. Ninguno de ustedes puede pedir audiencia, solamente irán en el caso de ser llamados.»

Tzitzi no vino a casa tampoco ese día y nadie más volvió a visitarnos, ya que para entonces toda la isla debía tener conocimiento de nuestra desgracia familiar. Ni siquiera las mujeres que organizaban el festival pasaron a por mi madre para que ésta cumpliera con su barrido del día. Y esa evidencia de ostracismo hacia ella por parte de las mujeres que pronto esperaba mirar como inferiores, la hizo más vociferante y chillona de lo normal. Pasó todo ese día melancólico regañando a mi padre por haber dejado que su hija «creciera en estado salvaje» y regañándome a mí también, pues estaba segura de que le había presentado a algunos de mis «malvados amigos» y había dejado que algunos de ellos la sedujera. La acusación era absurda, pero me dio una idea.

Salí disimuladamente de la casa y fui a buscar a Tlatli y a Chimali. Me recibieron con algo de embarazo y con palabras desmañadas de conmiseración.

Dije: «Uno de vosotros puede ayudar a Tzitzitlini, si quiere.»

«Si hay algo que podamos hacer, por supuesto que lo haremos —dijo Tlatli—. Dinos, Topo.»

«Vosotros sabéis cuánto tiempo el insufrible Pactli ha estado acosando a mi hermana. Todo el mundo lo sabe. También todo el mundo sabe en estos momentos, que mi hermana ha preferido a otro en lugar del Señor Alegría, así es que ha quedado ante todos como un amante desairado y bobo por haber estado persiguiendo a una muchacha que lo desdeñaba. Sólo para salvar su orgullo herido vengará esa humillación en ella y lo hará de la forma más horrible. Uno de vosotros podría evitar que lo hiciera.»

«¿Cómo?», preguntó Tlatli.

«Casándose con ella», dije.

Nadie sabrá jamás qué dolor tan grande me costó decirlo, porque lo que quería decir con eso era: «Renuncio a ella. Llévatela.» Mis dos amigos se sobresaltaron ligeramente y me miraron confusos y pasmados.

«Mi hermana ha cometido un error —continué—. No puedo negarlo, pero vosotros dos la conocéis desde siempre y seguramente sabéis que ella no es una prostituta disoluta. Si podéis perdonarle su mal paso y creer que ella sólo lo hizo para alejar de sí la perspectiva indeseada de su matrimonio con el Señor Alegría, entonces sabréis que no se podría encontrar a otra esposa más casta, leal y protectora. No necesito agregar que probablemente no encontraréis tampoco una tan bella como ella.»

Los dos intercambiaron una mirada inquieta. Difícilmente podría censurarlos. Esa proposición radical debió de haberles golpeado, aturdiéndoles tan abruptamente como un rayo deslumbrador mandado por Tláloc.

«Vosotros sois la única esperanza de Tzitzi —dije con urgencia—. Pactli la tiene en estos momentos en su poder, como una doncella que se suponía virgen y que sorprendentemente no lo era. Él puede acusarla de haberse ido a horcajarse en el camino. Incluso puede pedir un juicio mintiendo al decir que era su prometida en matrimonio y que deliberadamente lo engañó, lo que vendría a ser tanto como un adulterio y podría incluso persuadir al Señor Garza Roja de que la condenase a muerte. *Pero no puede hacer eso a una mujer debidamente casada o que sea pedida en matrimonio.*»

Miré con energía a los ojos de Chimali y luego a los de Tlatli. «Si alguno de vosotros diera ese paso y públicamente pidiera su mano... —Abatieron sus ojos desviándolos de los míos—. Oh, ya lo sé. Se necesitaría tener algo de valentía y sería objeto de burla. El que lo hiciera sería tomado por el que la sedujo por primera vez, pero el matrimonio borraría esto y ella sería rescatada de cualquier cosa que quisiera hacerle Pactli. Esto la salvaría, Chimali. Sería una hazaña en verdad noble, Tlatli. Os suplico que me hagáis este favor.»

Los dos me volvieron a mirar y realmente había pesadumbre en sus rostros. Tlatli habló por los dos:

«No podemos, Topo. Ninguno de los dos.»

Me desilusionaron profundamente y me hirieron, pero más que eso me dejaron perplejo. «Si me dijerais que no queréis lo podría comprender, pero... ¿qué no podéis...?»

Se pararon lado a lado enfrente de mí; Tlatli, rechoncho, y Chimali, flaco como una caña. Me miraron con piedad y luego se volvieron el uno al otro, y no podría decir qué había en sus mutuas miradas. Titubeando, cada uno de ellos levantó su mano para tomar la del otro y sus dedos se entrelazaron. Parados allí, enlazados, forzados por mí a confesar un vínculo que yo ni remotamente había sospechado, se volvieron de nuevo hacia mí. Sus miradas proclamaban un orgullo desafiante.

«¡Oh! —exclamé, deshecho. Después de un momento les dije—: Perdonadme. No debí insistir cuando rehusasteis.»

Tlatli dijo: «No nos importa que lo sepas, Topo; pero sí nos preocuparía que se chismorreara.»

Volví de nuevo a la carga: «¿Entonces no sería para uno de

vosotros una ventaja el casarse? Quiero decir solamente llevar a efecto la ceremonia. Después de todo...»

«Yo no podría —dijo Chimali, con serena obstinación— y no dejaría que Tlatli lo hiciera. Sería una debilidad, una mancha en nuestros sentimientos. Tienes que verlo de esta manera, Topo. Suponte que alguien te pidiera que te casaras con alguno de nosotros.»

«Bueno, eso sería contrario a nuestras leyes y costumbres y además escandaloso. En cambio no lo es si alguno de vosotros toma por esposa a Tzitzi. Sólo *de nombre*, Chimali, y luego...»

«No —dijo él inflexiblemente y luego añadió quizás sinceramente—: Lo sentimos, Topo.»

«Yo también», dije suspirando y dándome la vuelta me fui.

Sin embargo tomé la determinación de que regresaría y persistiría en mi propósito. Tenía que convencer a alguno de los dos de que eso nos beneficiaría a todos. Salvaría a mi hermana del peligro, calmaría cualquier tipo de conjetura sobre las relaciones entre Tlatli y Chimali y entre Tzitzi y yo. Ellos se la podrían llevar abiertamente a Texcoco cuando se marcharan allí y yo secretamente la podría tener conmigo, para mí. Cuanto más pensaba en eso, más parecía el plan ideal para todos nosotros. Tlatli y Chimali *no podrían* seguir rehusando ese matrimonio con la excusa egoísta de que empañaría de alguna manera sus lances amorosos. Los persuadiría, si fuera necesario con la brutal amenaza de exponerlos como *cuilontin*. Sí, regresaría a ver a Tlatli y a Chimali.

Pero las cosas sucedieron de tal manera que ya no pude hacerlo, puesto que se me había ocurrido demasiado tarde.

Esa noche Tzitzi tampoco vino a casa.

A pesar de todo me dormí y no soñé con buitres, sino con Tzitzi y conmigo y con la inmensa jarra que contenía el agua para la casa, que llevaba la huella de sangre de Chimali. En mi sueño, volví a aquellos días de nuestras vidas en los que Tzitzi había encontrado una excusa para salir de la casa juntos. Ella había tirado y roto la jarra de agua. El agua fluía por todo el piso y salpicaba tanto que llegaba hasta mi cara. Me desperté en plena noche y encontré mi rostro bañado en lágrimas.

A la mañana siguiente llegaron las órdenes del palacio del gobernador y no eran para mi padre Tepetzalan como debía esperarse, siendo él el jefe de la casa. El mensajero anunció que los señores Garza Roja y Alegría requerían la presencia inmediata de mi madre. Mi padre se quedó sentado sufriendo mansamente en silencio, su cabeza agachada, evitando mis ojos, todo el tiempo en que esperamos a que ella regresara.

Cuando lo hizo, su rostro estaba pálido y sus manos se movían sin parar alrededor del chal que llevaba sobre sus hombros; pero a pesar de eso sus maneras eran sorpresivamente animadas. No era ya la mujer iracunda que había sido privada de un título y no se parecía en nada a una madre afligida. Nos dijo: «Parece que perdimos una hija, pero no lo hemos perdido todo.»

«Perderla, ¿cómo?», pregunté.

«Tzitzi nunca llegó al palacio —dijo mi madre sin mirarme—. Se escapó de las mujeres del templo que la conducían y corrió lejos. Por supuesto, el pobre Pactzin está casi loco por el curso que han tomado los acontecimientos. Cuando las mujeres avisaron de que ella había escapado, él ordenó su búsqueda por toda la isla. Un cazador avisó que le faltaba su canoa. Ya te acordarás —dijo mi madre dirigiéndose a mi padre— que tu hija una vez amenazó con hacer exactamente eso. Robar un *acali* y bogar hasta la tierra firme.»

«Sí», dijo él lentamente.

«Bien, parece que lo ha hecho. Nadie ha podido decir qué dirección tomó, así es que Pactli renuentemente ha cejado de continuar la búsqueda. Está tan angustiado como nosotros. —Ésa era una mentira tan clara, que mi madre continuó precipitadamente antes de que yo pudiera hablar—. Debemos ver la partida de Tzitzi como una pérdida por el bien de nosotros. Se ha fugado como dijo que haría. Para siempre. Ella lo hizo por su propio gusto, nadie la empujó a ello. Y no se atreverá a volver otra vez por Xaltocan.»

Yo dije: «No creo nada de esto.» Pero ella me ignoró y continuó dirigiéndose a mi padre:

«Como Pactli, el gobernador comparte nuestro dolor, pues no nos culpa de la mala conducta de nuestra indócil hija. Él me dijo: "Siempre he respetado a Cabeza Inclinada y me gustaría hacer algo para ayudar a mitigar su desilusión y su aflicción." Y me preguntó: "¿Cree usted que Cabeza Inclinada querría aceptar su ascenso como jefe de canteras a cargo de *todas* éstas?"»

La cabeza de mi padre se levantó con fuerza y exclamó: «¿Qué?»

«Ésas fueron las palabras de Garza Roja. Que estuvieras a cargo de todas las canteras de Xaltocan. Él me dijo: "No puedo borrar la vergüenza que ha sufrido, pero esto demostrará nuestra simpatía hacia él."»

Volví a decir: «No creo nada de esto.» El Señor Garza Roja nunca antes se había referido a mi padre como Cabeza Inclinada y dudo mucho que él hubiera conocido el apodo de Tepetzalan.

Mi madre siguió ignorando mis intervenciones, y dijo a mi padre: «Hemos sido desafortunados con nuestra hija, pero somos afortunados en tener esta clase de *tecutli*. Cualquier otro nos hubiera podido desterrar a todos nosotros. Considerando que el hijo de Garza Roja ha sido burlado e insultado por nuestra propia carne y sangre, y él te ofrece esta muestra de compasión.»

«Jefe de cantera —murmuró mi padre, mirándonos como si hubiera sido golpeado en la cabeza por una de las piedras de su propia cantera—. Sería el más joven que jamás...»

«¿Lo aceptarás?», preguntó mi madre.

Mi padre balbuceó: «Pero... pero... es una pequeña recompensa por haber perdido a una hija tan amada, no importa cuál haya sido su error...»

«¿Lo aceptarás?», repitió mi madre más severamente.

«Pues... sí. Debo aceptar. Lo aceptaré. No puedo obrar de otra forma. ¿O podría?»

«¡Vaya! —dijo mi madre mucho más complacida. Se restregó las manos como si hubiera terminado alguna sucia y desagradable tarea—. Nunca seremos *pípiltin*, gracias a esa mozuela cuyo nombre jamás volveré a pronunciar, pero hemos dado un paso hacia arriba entre los *macehualtin*. Y mientras el Señor Garza Roja esté deseoso de mitigar nuestra desgracia, todos los demás también lo estarán. Todavía podemos levantar nuestras cabezas, no bajarlas con vergüenza. Bueno —concluyó vigorosamente—, debo salir otra vez. Las mujeres me están esperando para ir con ellas a barrer el templo de la pirámide.»

«Iré contigo parte del camino, querida —dijo mi padre—. Creo que echaré un vistazo a la cantera occidental mientras los trabajadores están en sus casas. Tengo la sospecha, desde hace algún tiempo, de que el maestro cantero encargado de ésta, ha encontrado una capa de roca importante...»

En el momento en que se iban juntos hacia la puerta, mi madre se volvió para decirme: «Oh, Mixtli, ¿quieres empaquetar las pertenencias de tu hermana y acomodarlas en algún lado? Quién sabe, quizás algún día mande a alguien por ellas.»

Yo sabía que ella jamás lo haría o podría, pero hice lo que me mandó y empaqueté dentro de varios canastos todo lo que pude reconocer como sus pertenencias. Sólo dejé de empaquetar su pequeña figurita de Xochiquétzal que estaba a un lado de su esterilla; la diosa del amor y de las flores, la diosa a quienes todas las muchachas rezaban para que les concediera una feliz vida matrimonial.

Solo en la casa, solo con mis pensamientos, saqué la versión real de la historia de mi madre, de lo que estaba seguro que debía de haber pasado. Tzitzi no había escapado de las mujeres que la vigilaban. Éstas la entregaron debidamente a Pactli en el palacio, y él en su furia, de alguna manera que no quiero ni imaginarme, la mandó matar. Su padre podría haber estado estúpidamente de acuerdo con la ejecución, pero era un hombre notablemente juicioso y no podía perdonar un crimen cometido a sangre fría, sin ningún proceso, juicio y condenación. El Señor Garza Roja tuvo que escoger entonces entre llevar a su propio hijo a juicio o encubrir todo el asunto. Así que él y Pactli, y sospecho que también mi madre, la conspiradora de Pactli, urdieron la historia de la huida de Tzitzi en una canoa robada. Y para hacer las cosas más fáciles e incluso más verosímiles, y para que nadie se animara a preguntar o a reanudar la búsqueda de la muchacha, el gobernador le arrojó a mi padre un mendrugo.

Después de haber ordenado las pertenencias de Tzitzi, empaqueté las que yo había traído de Texcoco. La figurita de Xochiquétzal fue lo último que puse dentro de mi ligero canasto de mimbre. Entonces me lo eché al hombro y dejé la casa para nunca más volver. Cuando caminaba hacia los muelles una mariposa me acompañó por un rato y varias veces revoloteó en círculos alrededor de mi cabeza.

Fui lo suficientemente afortunado de encontrar a un pescador que estaba irreverentemente decidido a trabajar durante el festival de Ochpanitztli y que aún se estaba preparando para partir, esperando sólo el crepúsculo, que era cuando los *amilotlin*, peces blancos, subían. Estuvo de acuerdo en remar todo el camino hacia Texcoco, por un precio excesivo tomando en consideración lo que hubiera podido ganar en una tarde de pesca.

Cuando íbamos en camino le pregunté: «¿Ha escuchado si algún pescador o cazador ha perdido su canoa recientemente? ¿O si alguien ha visto algún *acali* flotando lejos? ¿O si alguno ha sido robado?»

«No», dijo.

Miré atrás hacia la isla, pacífica y lozanamente verde en esa tarde de verano. Extendida sobre las aguas del lago como siempre lo había estado y como siempre lo estaría, pero ya nunca más se volvería a escuchar «el sonido de las campanitas tocando» ni a tener quizás un pensamiento hacia esa pequeña pérdida. El Señor Garza Roja, el Señor Alegría, mi madre y mi padre, Tlatli y Chimali, todos los demás habitantes de Xaltocan estaban de acuerdo en olvidar.

Pero yo no.

«¡Ah, pero si es Cabeza Inclinada! —exclamó la Señora de Tolan, la primera persona con quien me encontré en mi camino hacia mis habitaciones de palacio—. Has acortado tus vacaciones y regresado más pronto de tu casa.

«Sí, mi señora. Ya no siento a Xaltocan como mi casa. Y tengo muchas cosas que hacer aquí.»

«¿Quieres decir que sentías nostalgia por Texcoco? —me dijo sonriendo—. Entonces te hemos enseñado a querernos. Estoy encantada de pensar en eso, Cabeza Inclinada.»

«Por favor, mi señora —dije roncamente—, no me llame más así. Ya estoy harto de ser Cabeza Inclinada.»

«¡Oh! —dijo y su sonrisa desapareció al estudiar mi rostro—. ¿Qué nombre prefieres entonces?»

Pensé en todas las cosas variadas que había hecho y dije: «Tliléctic-Mixtli es el nombre que me fue dado del libro de adivinación y profecías. Llámeme por lo que yo soy. Nube Oscura.»

I H S

✠

S. C. C. M.

Santificada, Cesárea, Católica Majestad,
el Emperador Don Carlos, nuestro Señor Rey:

Nuestra Más Alta y Poderosa Majestad, nuestro Real Soberano, desde la Ciudad de Mexico, capital de la Nueva España, en
la Fiesta de Nuestra Señora de los Dolores, en el Año de Nuestro Señor de mil quinientos treinta, os saludo.

Nos, sentimos mucho no poder incluir en estas últimas páginas recolectadas del manuscrito, los dibujos que Vuestra Majestad nos pide en su carta reciente: «esos dibujos de personas,
especialmente de mujeres, hechos por el narrador, a los que se
ha referido anteriormente en esta crónica». Cuando le pregunta-
mos al indio viejo sobre el paradero de éstos, se rió ante la idea de
que esos apuntes triviales e indecentes se hubieran podido guardar aquí o allá en todos estos años, aun si hubiesen tenido algún valor, pues no hubieran podido sobrevivir a través de tantos años.

Nos, nos abstenemos de deplorar las obscenidades que esos
dibujos intentarían reproducir, ya que estamos seguros de que
si estuvieran disponibles, no conducirían a nada a Vuestra Majestad. Sabemos que el sentido de apreciación de nuestro Imperial Soberano está basado en las obras de arte como las del
maestro Matsys, en cuyo retrato de Erasmo, por ejemplo, puede
sin ningún error reconocerse el rostro de éste. Las personas re-
tratadas en la forma de pintarrajear de estos indios, no se podrían reconocer ni siquiera como seres humanos, a excepción de
algunos pocos de sus más representativos murales y bajorrelieves.

Su Más Alta Majestad ha ordenado anteriormente a su capellán asegurarse con «escritos, tablillas u otros registros» la
substancia de las historias narradas en estas páginas. Pero podemos asegurarle, Señor, que el azteca exagera desatinadamente
cuando habla de escritura y lectura, de dibujo y pintura. Estos
salvajes nunca han creado, poseído o preservado algunas memo-
rias de su historia, aparte de algunos papeles plegados, pieles o
artesonados representando multitudes de figuras primitivas tales
como las que hacen los niños. Estas representaciones vienen a
ser inescrutables para cualquier ojo civilizado y fueron usadas
por los indios solamente como un conjunto de preceptos de sus
«hombres sabios», que lo garrapateaban para utilizarlo como un
estímulo para su memoria, cuando ellos repetían la historia oral
de sus tribus o clanes. Una clase de historia bastante dudosa
por cierto.

Antes de que este vuestro siervo llegara a estas tierras, los frailes franciscanos enviados cinco años antes por Su Santidad, el último Papa Adriano, ya habían rastreado toda la tierra adyacente a esta ciudad capital. Estos buenos hombres habían recolectado, de cada edificio que todavía estaba en pie, todo aquello que podían considerar como un depósito de registro; muchos miles de «libros» indios, pero no habiendo recibido ninguna disposición para ellos, están pendientes hasta recibir alguna orden de la alta directiva.

Sin embargo, como Obispo delegado de Su Majestad, nosotros mismos examinamos esa voluminosa «biblioteca» y no encontramos ninguno que no tuviera más que figuras chillonas y grotescas. La mayoría de éstas eran seres de pesadilla: bestias, monstruos, falsos dioses, demonios, mariposas, reptiles y otras cosas vulgares de la naturaleza. Algunas de las figuras tenían como propósito representar a seres humanos, pero en ese estilo de arte absurdo que los boloneses llaman *caricatura*, y los humanos no se distinguían de los puercos, asnos, gárgolas o cualquier otra cosa que la imaginación pudiera concebir.

Puesto que no había ni una sola palabra que no fuera una fétida superstición y engaños inspirados por el Demonio, nos, hemos ordenado que con los miles y miles de volúmenes y rollos se hiciera una pila en medio de la plaza del mercado de Tlaltelolco y fueran quemados hasta convertirse en cenizas. Nos, esperamos que éste haya sido el fin adecuado a esos archivos paganos y dudamos que hayan quedado algunos otros en todas las regiones de la Nueva España que ya han sido exploradas.

Tomad nota, Señor, que los indios que contemplaban esa hoguera, y que casi todos ellos ahora son cristianos *profesos*, demostraban sin ninguna vergüenza una gran aversión apesadumbrada y una gran angustia; incluso lloraban mientras miraban la pila ardiente, como si hubieran sido *verdaderos* cristianos viendo la profanación y la destrucción de las Santas Escrituras. Nos, hemos considerado eso como una evidencia de que estas criaturas no han sido convertidas de todo corazón al Cristianismo como nosotros y la Madre Iglesia desearíamos. Es por esto que este humilde siervo de Vuestra Muy Piadosa y Devota Majestad, todavía tiene y tendrá muchas obligaciones episcopales urgentes, pertinentes a una más intensa propagación de la Fe.

Pedimos a Vuestra Majestad que comprenda que estas obligaciones deben estar por encima de nuestra actuación como auditor y amonestador de la locuacidad del azteca, excepto en nuestros momentos libres que son cada vez menos. Nos, suplicamos también a Vuestra Majestad que comprenda la necesidad de que mandemos ocasionalmente el paquete de páginas sin una carta de comentario y algunas veces sin leerlas previamente.

Que Nuestro Señor Dios preserve la vida y acreciente el reino de Su Sacra Majestad por muchos años más, es la sincera oración de su S.C.C.M. Obispo de Mexico.

(ecce signum) ZUMÁRRAGA

QUINTA PARS

Mi pequeño esclavo Cózcatl me dio la bienvenida con genuino deleite y alivio, porque, según me dijo, Muñeca de Jade había estado excesivamente irritable en mi ausencia y había dejado caer su mal humor sobre él. A pesar de que ella tenía un gran grupo de mujeres que le servían, se había apropiado también de Cózcatl y lo había tenido trabajando sin descanso para ella, corriendo o trotando, o estando quieto para ser azotado, durante todo el tiempo que yo estuve fuera.

Me sugirió parte de algunas bajezas en mandados y trabajos que tuvo que hacer para ella, y a mi insinuación, me contó finalmente que la mujer llamada Algo Delicado había bebido el corrosivo *xoyócatl* un poco antes del siguiente encuentro en las habitaciones de la señora y había muerto allí, echando espumajos por la boca y convulsionada por el dolor. Después del suicidio de Nemalhuili, que de alguna forma no se había conocido fuera de esos recintos, Muñeca de Jade tuvo que depender, para sus entretenimientos, de compañeros conseguido por Cózcatl y las criadas. Deduzco que esos compañeros fueron menos satisfactorios que los que hasta entonces yo le había procurado. La señora no me presionó inmediatamente a volver a su servicio ni envió un esclavo a través del corredor para mandarme un saludo o dar alguna señal de que ella sabía o le importaba mi retorno. Estaba muy ocupada con las festividades de Ochpanitztli, que por supuesto se estaban llevando a efecto en Texcoco como en todas partes.

Poco después, cuando terminó el festival, Tlatli y Chimali llegaron al palacio según lo previsto y Chalchiunénetl se ocupó personalmente en conseguirles alojamientos, asegurándose de que su estudio tuviera suficiente arcilla, utensilios y pinturas, y dándoles instrucciones detalladas sobre el trabajo que tenían que realizar. Deliberadamente yo no estuve presente a su llegada. Cuando me los encontré accidentalmente, dos o tres días después en los jardines del palacio, sólo los saludé brevemente y ellos respondieron con un tímido murmullo.

Desde entonces me los encontraba con frecuencia, ya que su estudio estaba situado en los sótanos existentes bajo el ala del palacio donde estaban las habitaciones de Muñeca de Jade, pero sólo inclinaba la cabeza al pasar. Para entonces ellos ya habían tenido varias entrevistas con su señora y me podía dar cuenta de que el entusiasmo que habían sentido anteriormente por su trabajo se había disipado considerablemente. Se veían nerviosos y temerosos y era obvio que deseaban discutir conmigo la precaria situación en que se encontraban, pero les miraba con tanta frialdad que no les daba lugar a ningún acercamiento.

Estaba muy ocupado con mi propio trabajo, haciendo un dibujo particular que intentaría presentar a Muñeca de Jade cuando ésta finalmente me llamara a su presencia, y era un proyecto difícil que me había impuesto a mí mismo. Éste debería ser el dibujo de un joven irresistiblemente guapo, el más guapo que yo hubiera dibujado, pero al mismo tiempo tenía que parecerse a un joven que realmente existía. Hice y rompí muchísimos bosquejos y cuando al fin logré uno que me satisfaciera, pasé todavía mucho tiempo retocándolo y elaborándolo hasta finalizar el dibujo, confiando en que éste fascinaría a la reina-niña. Y así fue.

«¡Pero si él es más que guapo, es hermoso! —exclamó ella cuando se lo alargué. Lo estudió un poco más y murmuró—: Si él fuera mujer, sería como Muñeca de Jade.» Y ella no hubiera podido decir mayor cumplido. «¿Quién es él?»

«Su nombre es Alegría.»

«¡*Ayyo*, y debería de serlo! ¿Dónde lo encontraste?»

«Es el príncipe heredero de mi isla nativa, mi señora. Pactzin, hijo de Tlauquécholtzin, el *tecutli* de Xaltocan.»

«Y cuando lo volviste a ver, pensaste en mí y lo dibujaste. ¡Qué detalle tan delicado, Trae! Casi te perdono el haberte ido por tantos días. Ahora ve y tráelo para mí.»

Le dije la verdad: «Me temo que él no querrá atender mi requerimiento, mi señora. Páctli y yo sentimos una inquina mutua. Sin embargo...»

«Entonces no haces esto para beneficiarlo —me interrumpió la joven—. Me pregunto por qué haces esto por mí. —Sus profundos ojos me miraron suspicazmente—. Es verdad que nunca te he maltratado, pero tampoco te he dado motivo para sentir afecto por mí. Entonces, ¿por qué esta repentina y espontánea generosidad?»

«Trato de anticiparme a las órdenes y a los deseos de mi señora.»

Sin ningún comentario y entrecerrando ahora sus ojos, ella tiró del cordón-campana y cuando la criada se presentó ordenó que llamaran a Chimali y Tlatli. Ellos llegaron, mirando atemorizados y aprensivos, y Muñeca de Jade les mostró el dibujo. «Vosotros dos venís también de Xaltocan. ¿Reconocéis a este joven?»

Tlatli exclamó: «¡Pactli!», y Chimali dijo: «Sí, es el Señor Alegría, mi señora, pero...»

Le lancé una mirada que le hizo cerrar la boca antes de que pudiera decir: «Pero el Señor Alegría no es tan fino como aquí.» Y no me importó que Muñeca de Jade interceptara mi mirada.

«Ya veo —dijo ella arqueando las cejas como si me hubiera comprendido—. Podéis iros. —Cuando Chimali y Tlatli dejaron la habitación, me dijo—: Mencionaste una inquina. Seguramente alguna mezquina rivalidad romántica y supongo que el joven noble fue preferido a ti. Así es que sagazmente arreglaste una última cita para él, *sabiendo* que sería la última.»

Dirigiendo significativamente mi mirada por encima de ella, a las estatuas del mensajero-veloz Yéyac-Netztlin y del jardinero Xali-Otli, hechas por el maestro Píxquitl y con una sonrisa de conspirador le dije: «Prefiero pensar que estoy haciendo un favor a todos nosotros. A los tres: a mi señora, a mi señor Pactli y a mí.»

Ella se rió alegremente. «Entonces así será. Me atrevería a decir que ahora te debo un favor. Pero debes hacer que venga.»

«Me tomé la libertad de preparar una carta —dije, mostrándosela—, en la real fina piel de cervato. Con las instrucciones usuales: a medianoche por la puerta este. Si mi señora pone su firma en ella e incluye el anillo, casi puedo garantizarle que el joven príncipe vendrá en la misma canoa que llevará el mensaje.»

«¡Mi listo Trae!», dijo ella, tomando la carta y poniéndola sobre una mesa en donde había un pomo de pintura y una caña de escribir. Siendo una joven mexícatl, por supuesto que no sabía ni leer ni escribir, pero, al ser una noble, por lo menos sabía cómo escribir el glifo de su nombre. «Tú sabes en dónde está atracado mi *acali* privado. Lleva esto al jefe de los remeros y dile que salga al amanecer. Quiero mi Alegría mañana por la noche.»

Tlatli y Chimali estaban esperándome al acecho afuera en el corredor y Tlatli me dijo con vez temblorosa: «¿Sabes lo que estás haciendo, Topo?»

Chimali dijo con voz insegura: «¿Sabes cuál será el depósito del señor Pactli? Ven y mira.»

Los seguí abajo por la sinuosa escalera de piedra a su estudio. Éste estaba bien orientado, pero al estar bajo el suelo tenía que ser alumbrado de día y de noche por lámparas y antorchas, que le hacían parecer como una mazmorra. Los artistas habían estado trabajando simultáneamente en varias estatuas, dos de las cuales reconocí. Una era del esclavo Yo Seré de la Grandeza, que ya había sido esculpida en tamaño natural y que Chimali había empezado ya a pintar la arcilla con la mezcla de sus colores especiales.

«Un gran parecido —dije, y lo pensaba de veras—. La señora Muñeca de Jade lo aprobará.»

«Oh, bueno, captar la semejanza no fue difícil —dijo Tlatli con modestia—, pudiendo sobre todo trabajar con tu magnífico dibujo y moldear la arcilla sobre su calavera.»

«Pero mis dibujos no tienen colores —dije—, y aun el maestro escultor Píxquitl no fue capaz de captar éstos. Chimali, aplaudo tu talento.»

Y también sentía lo que decía. Las estatuas de Píxquitl habían sido pintadas con los colores usuales lisos: un color cobre pálido y uniforme para la piel, un invariable negro para el pelo y todo más o menos igual. Los colores que usó Chimali para la piel, variaban como los de un ser humano vivo: la nariz y las orejas eran un poquito más oscuras que el resto de la cara; las mejillas, un poquito más rojizas; incluso el negro del pelo tenía destellos parduzcos aquí y allá.

«Se verán todavía mejor cuando se hayan cocido en el horno —dijo Chimali—. Los colores se funden mejor juntos. ¡Ah, y mira esto, Topo!» Me guió alrededor de la estatua, atrás y apuntó; en la parte inferior del manto de arcilla del esclavo, Tlatli había grabado su glifo del halcón y debajo de éste estaba la huella rojo-sangre de Chimali.

«Sí, fácilmente reconocible —dije sin ninguna inflexión. Me moví hacia la siguiente estatua—. Y ésta será Algo Delicado.»

Tlatli dijo molesto: «Uh, yo creo que será mejor para nosotros no saber los nombres de los modelos, Topo.»

«Era más que su nombre», dije más para mí que para él.

Sólo la cabeza y los hombros de Nemalhuili habían sido modelados en arcilla, pero éstos se encontraban a la misma altura que habían tenido en vida, pues estaban soportados por huesos, sus huesos articulados, su propio esqueleto sostenido por detrás por una pértiga.

«Estoy un poco contrariado con ésta», dijo Tlatli como si estuviera hablando de un pedazo de piedra en el cual hubiera encontrado una grieta insospechada. Él me enseñó el dibujo que yo había hecho del rostro de Algo Delicado, aquel que había bosquejado en el mercado, el primero que enseñé a Muñeca de Jade. «Tu dibujo y la calavera me fueron muy útiles para modelar la cabeza. Y el *colotli*, la armadura, me da las proporciones lineales del cuerpo, pero...»

«¿La armadura?», pregunté.

«El soporte interior. Cualquier escultura de barro o de cera debe ser soportada por una armadura, así como el cacto pulposo es sustentado por su leñoso esqueleto interior. Para la estatua de una figura humana, ¿qué mejor armadura que su propio esqueleto original?»

«¿De verás? —dije—. Pero dime, ¿cómo obtienes el esqueleto original?»

Chimali respondió: «La señora Chalchiunénetl nos los proporciona de su cocina privada.»

«¿De su *cocina*?»

Chimali alejó su vista de mí. «No me preguntes cómo ha podido persuadir a sus cocineros y a los esclavos de la cocina. Pero ellos desollan la carne, vacían las entrañas y cortan la carne del... del modelo... sin desmembrarlo. Después cuecen lo que queda en unas tinas grandes con agua de cal. Necesitan sacarlos a tiempo antes de que los ligamentos y los tendones se disuelvan, por eso nosotros tenemos que raspar algunos fragmentos de carne que todavía quedan. Pero recibimos el esqueleto completo. Oh, a veces se pierde un hueso de un dedo o alguna costilla, pero...»

«Pero desafortunadamente —dijo Tlatli—, aún el esqueleto completo no me da una indicación de cómo era el cuerpo exterior, de cómo estaba relleno o curvado. Puedo inferir la figura de un hombre, pero no la de una mujer que es diferente. Tú sabes, los pechos, las caderas, las nalgas.»

«Eran sublimes —murmuré recordando a Algo Delicado—. Venid a mis habitaciones. Os daré otro dibujo que muestra a vuestra modelo de cuerpo entero.»

En mi departamento, ordené a Cózcatl que hiciera *chocólatl* para todos nosotros. Tlatli y Chimali correteaban por las tres habitaciones, profiriendo exclamaciones de admiración acerca de la fineza y lujo de éstas, mientras yo extraía del montón de mis hojas de dibujos uno en el que Nemalhuili estaba de cuerpo entero.

«Ah, completamente desnuda —dijo Tlatli—. Éste es ideal para mis propósitos.» Parecía como si estuviese dando una opinión pasajera acerca de una buena muestra de arcilla amargosa.

Chimali también vio el dibujo de la mujer muerta y dijo: «En verdad, Topo, que tus dibujos están detallados con destreza. Si pudieras dejar de hacer solamente *líneas* y aprender a trabajar con luz y sombras en pintura, podrías llegar a ser un verdadero artista. Tú también podrías dar belleza al mundo.»

Me reí ásperamente. «¿Como las estatuas construidas sobre esqueletos cocidos?»

Tlatli sorbió su *chocólatl* y dijo defendiéndose: «Nosotros no matamos a esa gente, Topo. Tampoco sabemos por qué la joven reina quiere conservarlos. Pero piensa que si ellos hubieran sido simplemente enterrados o quemados, se desintegrarían en moho o cenizas. Por lo menos nosotros los hacemos duraderos. Y sí, trabajamos lo mejor que podemos para hacer de ellos, objetos de belleza.»

Yo dije: «Yo soy un escribano. No doy belleza a la palabra. Sólo la describo.»

Tlatli sostuvo en alto el dibujo de Algo Delicado. «Tú hiciste esto y esto es una clase de belleza.»

«Desde ahora en adelante, sólo dibujaré palabras-pintadas. He hecho el último retrato y nunca más volveré a dibujar otro.»

«El del Señor Alegría —adivinó Chimali. Miró alrededor para asegurarse de que mi pequeño esclavo no pudiera oírlo—. Debes saber que estás poniendo a Pactli en riesgo de acabar en las tinas de cal de la cocina.»

«Eso es lo que espero fervientemente —dije—. No dejaré impune la muerte de mi hermana. —Lancé a Chimali sus propias palabras—: Podría parecer una debilidad, una mancha que caería sobre nosotros, sobre lo que sentíamos el uno por el otro.»

Los dos tuvieron al fin la delicadeza de bajar sus cabezas durante algunos momentos de silencio antes de que Tlatli hablara:

«Nos pones a todos en peligro de ser descubiertos, Topo.»

«Ya estáis en peligro. Yo lo he estado por mucho tiempo. Debí haberos avisado de esto antes de que vinieseis. —Hice un gesto en dirección a su estudio—. ¿Pero habríais creído lo que hay ahí abajo?»

Chimali protestó: «Ésos son solamente ciudadanos corrientes y esclavos, y quizá nunca sean echados de menos. ¡Pactli es el Príncipe Heredero de una provincia mexica!»

Sacudí la cabeza. «El marido de la mujer del dibujo, he oído que se ha vuelto medio loco, y que está tratando de descubrir qué pasó con su amada esposa. Nunca volverá a estar en sus cabales otra vez. Y aun los esclavos no pueden desaparecer así como así. El Venerado Orador ya ha mandado guardias para buscar y averiguar acerca de estas personas tan diferentes que se han esfumado misteriosamente. Descubrirlo es cuestión de tiempo. Ese tiempo puede ser pasado mañana, si Pactli es puntual.»

Sudando visiblemente, Tlatli dijo: «Topo, no podemos dejar que tú...»

«No podéis detenerme, y si tratáis de huir o de prevenir a Pactli o a Muñeca de Jade, lo sabré al instante y en seguida me presentaré ante el Uey-Tlatoani.»

Chimali dijo: «Él tomará tu vida como la de cada uno de nosotros. ¿Por qué nos haces esto a Tlatli y a mí, Topo? ¿Por qué te lo haces a ti mismo?»

«La muerte de Tzitzi no tiene que caer sólo sobre la cabeza de Pactli. Yo estuve comprometido y vosotros también. Estoy preparado para expiar con mi propia vida si ése es mi *tonali*. Vosotros también podéis tener vuestra oportunidad.»

«¡Oportunidad! —Tlatli levantó las manos—. ¿Qué oportunidad?»

«Una muy buena. Sospecho que la señora tiene la idea de no matar al príncipe mexica. Sospecho que jugará con él por un tiempo y luego lo mandará a su casa con los labios sellados por una promesa.»

«Cierto —murmuró Chimali bastante aliviado—. Ella querrá un cortejo peligroso, pero no un suicidio. —Se volvió hacia Tlatli—. Y mientras él está aquí, tú y yo podremos terminar las estatuas ya ordenadas. Entonces intentaremos hallar algún trabajo urgente en alguna otra parte...»

Tlatli sorbió su *chocólatl* y de un salto se levantó de su silla y dijo a Chimali: «¡Ven! Trabajaremos de día y de noche. Debemos terminar todo lo que tenemos a mano y así tendremos una razón para pedir permiso de partir, antes de que nuestra señora se canse de nuestro príncipe.»

Y con esa nota de esperanza me dejaron, con esa patética y vana esperanza.

No les había mentido, sólo fui negligente en mencionarles un detalle en mis arreglos. Dije la verdad cuando les sugerí que Muñeca de Jade no pensaba castigar con la muerte al príncipe invitado. Ésa era una posibilidad real y por esa misma razón para ese huésped en particular hice un pequeño cambio en las instrucciones usuales de la invitación. Como nosotros decimos para aquel que merece castigo: «Él sería destruido con flores.»

Aunque se supone que los dioses saben todos nuestros planes y conocen sus finales antes de sus principios, los dioses son traviesos y se deleitan en incomodar a los hombres en sus planes. Ellos prefieren con frecuencia complicar esos planes como pudieran enredar las redes de los cazadores, o frustrarlos de tal manera que los planes nunca lleguen a resultar. Muy rara vez los dioses intervienen para un propósito mejor, pero creo que en esa ocasión al ver mi plan se dijeron entre ellos: «Este oscuro proyecto con el que está contribuyendo Nube Oscura, es tan irónicamente bueno que vamos a hacerlo irónicamente mucho mejor.»

Al día siguiente a la medianoche, mantuve mi oído pegado a mi puerta hasta que oí llegar a Pitza y al huésped, y entrar al departamento de enfrente del corredor. Entonces entreabrí suavemente mi puerta para oír mejor. Me esperaba alguna exclamación o blasfemia de Muñeca de Jade cuando comparara la brutal cara de Pactli con mi dibujo idealizado. Lo que no esperaba fue lo que oí de la muchacha: un grito penetrante de verdadero horror y luego un chillido histérico llamándome: «¡Trae! ¡Ven aquí inmediatamente! *¡Trae!*»

Eso parecía una reacción por demás extrema, aun para cualquiera que por primera vez conociera al horrible Señor Alegría. Abrí la puerta y salí para encontrarme con un guardia parado junto a ella portando una lanza y otro a través del vestíbulo junto a la puerta de mi señora. Ambos hombres enderezaron sus lanzas respetuosamente cuando pasé y ninguno trató de impedir mi entrada al otro departamento.

La joven reina estaba parada apenas adentro. Su cara estaba torcida y fea, y casi blanca de la sorpresa, aunque gradualmente se fue tornando casi púrpura de la furia cuando empezó a gritarme: «¿Qué clase de comedia es ésta, tú, hijo de perro? ¿Te crees que puedes hacer sucias bromas a mis expensas?»

Ella continuó así a gritos. Me volví hacia Pitza y al hombre que ella había traído, y aun con todos mis sentimientos entremezclados, no pude impedir el soltar una carcajada grande y sonora.

Se me había olvidado por completo la droga que Muñeca de Jade usaba y que le producía tener cortedad de vista. Debió de venir corriendo a través de todos los cuartos y vestíbulos de su departamento, para abrazar al tan ansiosamente esperado Señor Alegría y debió de haber llegado tan directamente sobre su visitante antes de que su visión pudiera distinguirlo claramente. Verdaderamente había motivo suficiente para sentirse sacudido y forzar un grito, a cualquier persona que no lo hubiera visto antes. Su presencia fue para mí también una increíble sorpresa, aunque yo reí en lugar de gritar, a pesar de haber tenido la ventaja de haber reconocido al viejo encorvado y engarruñado, de color cacao-parduzco.

Había escrito la carta para Pactli de tal manera, que estaba seguro que su llegada no sería clandestina. Pero no tenía ni la menor idea de cómo o por qué ese viejo vagabundo había venido en lugar de Pactli y no parecía el momento más apropiado como para preguntárselo. Además no podía dejar de reír.

«¡Desleal! ¡Despreciable! ¡Nunca te lo perdonaré!», y mientras la muchacha estaba chillando sobre mis carcajadas y Pitza estaba tratando de esconderse en las cercanas cortinas, el viejo balanceaba mi carta de piel de cervato y decía: «Pero es su propia firma, ¿no es así, mi señora?»

Ella dejó caer todo su vilipendio de mí a él al gruñirle: «¡Sí! ¿Pero ni aun tú puedes pensar que iba a ir dirigida a un miserable y medio desnudo pordiosero? ¡Ahora cierra tu asquerosa boca sin dientes! —Ella se volvió hacia mí—. ¡Tiene que ser una broma, Trae, desde el momento en que te mueres de risa! Confiesa y sólo serás apaleado hasta quedar en carne viva. Sigue riéndote así y te juro que...»

«Y por supuesto, mi señora —el hombre persistió—, reconozco en la carta la escritura-pintada de mi viejo amigo Topo, que está aquí.»

«¡Dije *silencio*! Cuando el lazo de flores esté alrededor de tu gaznate, desearás de todo corazón haber ahorrado todo el aire que estás gastando. Y su nombre es ¡Trae!»

«¿En estos momentos? Parece muy idóneo. —Sus ojos entrecerrados se deslizaron sobre mí con una mirada no del todo amistosa y mi risa se apaciguó—. Pero la carta dice claramente, mi señora, que yo esté aquí a la medianoche, y llevando este anillo puesto y...»

«¡No, no llevando el anillo puesto! —chilló ella imprudentemente—. Tú, pretencioso viejo ratero, pretendes aun saber leer. El anillo era para ser ¡llevado escondido! Y tú lo has traído ostentándolo por todo Texcoco... *¡yya ayya!* —Rechinando los dientes se volvió otra vez hacia mí—. ¿Te das cuenta a lo que tu broma puede conducir, tú, execrable bufón? *¡Yya ouiya*, pero morirás en la más lenta de las agonías!»

«¿Cómo que es una broma, mi señora? —preguntó el hombre encorvado—. De acuerdo con esta invitación, usted debía de haber estado esperando a alguien. Y usted vino corriendo tan alegremente a recibirme...»

«¡A ti! ¿A recibirte a ti? —gritó la joven, alzando sus brazos como si estuviera materialmente arrojando lejos toda precaución—. ¿Podría la puta más barata y hambrienta de todo Texcoco acostarse *contigo*? —Una vez más ella se volvió hacia mí— ¡Trae! ¿*Por qué hiciste esto*?»

«Mi señora —dije hablando por primera vez y haciéndolo con duras palabras, pero gentilmente—. He pensado muy a menudo que su Señor Esposo no dio suficiente peso a sus palabras cuando me ordenó servir a la Señora Muñeca de Jade y servirla sin ninguna pregunta. Sin embargo estaba obligado a obedecer. Como una vez usted me hizo notar, mi señora, no podía por mí mismo traicionar su debilidad sin desobedecer a ambos, a usted y a él. Finalmente tuve que engañarla, para que usted se traicionara a sí misma.»

Dio un paso hacia atrás y su boca se abrió silenciosamente, mientras su cara enrojecida por la ira se tornaba pálida otra vez. Las palabras tardaron en salirle. «Tú... ¿me engañaste? Esto... ¿esto no es una broma?»

«En todo caso no es su broma, sino la mía —dijo el encorvado—. Yo estaba a un lado del lago cuando un joven señor, muy bien vestido, untado y perfumado desembarcó del *acali* privado de mi señora, y descaradamente inició su camino con este anillo altamente visible y reconocible sobre el dedo pequeño de su gran mano. Parecía una flagrante indiscreción, si no ya una transgresión. Llamé a unos guardias para quitarle el anillo y luego la carta que portaba. Yo traje estas cosas en su lugar.»

«¿Tú... tú... pero con qué autoridad... cómo te atreves a entrometerte? —farfulló—. ¡Trae! Este hombre ha confesado ser un ladrón. ¡Mátalo! Te ordeno matar a este hombre, aquí, delante de mí.»

«No, mi señora —dije todavía gentilmente, porque casi empezaba a sentir piedad de ella—. Esta vez voy a desobedecerla. Yo creo que por fin usted ha revelado su propia verdad a otra persona, así es que creo que estoy libre de toda obligación de obediencia y también creo que usted ya no matará a nadie más.»

Ella se volvió velozmente y abrió la puerta de un tirón hacia el corredor. Quizás pensaba huir, pero cuando el centinela que estaba afuera se volvió hacia ella impidiéndole el paso, le dijo severamente: «Guardia, aquí tengo a un ladrón y a un traidor. Ese pordiosero lleva puesto mi anillo robado, y este plebeyo ha desobedecido mis órdenes directas. Quiero que tome a los dos y...»

«Perdón, mi señora —murmuró el guardia—. Yo ya tengo mis órdenes del Uey-Tlatoani. Órdenes diferentes.»

Ella se quedó con la boca abierta.

Yo dije: «Guardia, présteme su lanza un momento.»

Dudó por un instante, pero luego me la alargó. Caminé hacia el nicho que estaba en su aposento y que tenía la estatua del jardinero Xali-Otli y con toda mi fuerza aventé la lanza apuntándola sobre la barbilla de la estatua. La cabeza pintada se rompió, pegó contra el piso y rodó, su arcilla se quebró y se desmoronó. Cuando la cabeza rebotó y se detuvo contra la pared al otro lado de la habitación, era una calavera pelada, blanca y reluciente, el rostro más limpio y honesto del hombre. El pordiosero parduzco miró todo sin expresión, pero las inmensas pupilas de Muñeca de Jade parecían haberse tragado sus ojos por entero. Eran líquidos charcos negros de terror. Devolví el arma al guardia y le pregunté:

«¿Cuáles son sus órdenes, entonces?»

«Usted y su esclavo deben permanecer en su departamento. La Señora-Reina y la mujer que le sirve deben permanecer aquí en éste. Todos ustedes quedan en custodia y bajo vigilancia mientras sus habitaciones son registradas y hasta que sean citados ante la presencia del Venerado Orador.»

Dije al hombre de cacao: «¿Quizás usted quiera venir por un rato a mi cautiverio, venerable anciano y tomar una taza de *chocólatl*?»

«No —dijo él, arrancando su vista de la expuesta calavera—. Tengo ordenado referir todos los sucesos de esta noche. Creo que el Señor Nezahualpili ahora ordenará una búsqueda más exhaustiva... en los estudios de escultura y en otros lugares.»

Hice el gesto de besar la tierra. «Entonces les deseo buenas noches a usted anciano y a usted, mi señora.» Ella se volvió hacia mí, pero no creo que me viera.

Regresé a mi departamento para encontrarme con que había sido registrado por el Señor Hueso Fuerte y por algunos otros ayudantes confidenciales del Venerado Orador. Ellos ya habían encontrado mis dibujos de Muñeca de Jade y de Algo Delicado.

✠

Dice usted, mi Señor Obispo, que asiste a esta sesión porque está interesado en oír cómo eran llevados a efecto nuestros procesos judiciales. Pues no es indispensable que yo le describa el juicio de Muñeca de Jade. Su Ilustrísima puede encontrarlo minuciosamente asentado en los archivos de la Corte de Texcoco, si se toma la molestia de examinar esos libros. Su Ilustrísima también puede encontrarlo escrito en las historias de otras tierras, y aun oírlo en los cuentos regionales que explica la gente plebeya, porque el escándalo que causó todavía es recordado y relatado, especialmente por nuestras mujeres.

Nezahualpili invitó a los gobernantes de cada nación vecina y a todos sus *tlamatínime*, hombres sabios, y a todos los *tecutlin* de cada una de las provincias, para asistir al juicio. Incluso los invitó a traer a sus esposas y a las mujeres nobles de sus cortes. Él hizo esto en parte para demostrar públicamente, que aun una mujer nacida de ilustre cuna no podía pecar impunemente, y en parte para demostrar su implacable determinación de castigar la perfidia de Muñeca de Jade en contra de él. Sin embargo, había todavía otra razón. La adúltera a juzgar era la hija del más poderoso gobernante de todas estas tierras, el Venerado Orador Auízotl, el bilioso y belicoso Uey-Tlatoani de los mexica. Al invitarlo a él y a los altos oficiales de las otras naciones, Nezahualpili procuró también demostrar que los procedimientos serían conducidos con absoluta justicia. Fue quizás que por esta razón, por la que Nezahualpili se sentó a un lado durante el juicio. Él delegó la responsabilidad de preguntar a los acusados y testigos a dos partes desinteresadas: su Mujer Serpiente, el Señor Hueso Fuerte y a un *tlamatini*, juez, llamado Tepíztic.

La sala de justicia de Texcoco estaba llena en toda su capacidad. Debió de ser la reunión más grande de gobernantes (unos amigos, otros neutrales y otros enemigos), convocada hasta entonces en un mismo lugar. Sólo Auízotl estaba ausente. Naturalmente no quiso exponerse a sí mismo a la desgracia de ser mirado con escarnio y lástima mientras la vergüenza de su propia hija era inexorablemente revelada. En su lugar, mandó al Mujer Serpiente de Tenochtitlan. Sin embargo, entre los otros muchos señores que sí asistieron, estaba el gobernador de Xaltocan, Garza Roja, el padre de Pactli. Se sentó y sufrió su humillación con la cabeza inclinada durante todo el juicio. Las pocas veces que levantó sus viejos ojos entristecidos y legañosos, fue para fijarlos en mí. Yo creo que él estaba recordando la observación que había hecho hacía ya mucho tiempo, cuando comentó acerca de mis ambiciones juveniles: «Cualquiera que sea la ocupación a la que te dediques, joven, la harás muy bien.»

Las interrogaciones hechas a todas las personas que se vieron involucradas fueron lentas, detalladas, tediosas y muy seguido repetidas. Solamente recuerdo las preguntas y respuestas más pertinentes, para contarlas a Su Ilustrísima. Las dos personas acusadas principalmente eran, por supuesto, Muñeca de Jade y el Señor Alegría. Él fue el primero en ser llamado y llegó pálido y tembloroso a prestar juramento. Entre las muchas otras preguntas hechas por los interrogadores estaban éstas:

«Usted fue visto por los guardias del palacio, Pactzin, en los terrenos del ala del palacio destinada a la muy real señora Chalchiunénetzin. Es una ofensa capital que cualquier hombre no autorizado entre con cualquier razón o bajo cualquier pretexto, en los terrenos reservados a las señoras de la Corte. ¿Sabía usted esto?»

Él tragó saliva fuertemente y dijo con voz débil: «Sí», y selló su sentencia.

Muñeca de Jade fue la siguiente y entre las numerosas preguntas que le hicieron, una de sus respuestas produjo conmoción en la audiencia. El juez Tepítztic dijo:

«Usted ha admitido, mi señora, que fueron los trabajadores de su cocina privada los que mataron y prepararon los esqueletos de sus amantes, para hacer la base de sus estatuas. Nosotros pensamos que ni el más degradado de los esclavos habría hecho ese trabajo, a menos que estuviera bajo un maltrato excesivo. ¿Cuál fue la persuasión que usted utilizó?

En su dulce voz de niñita, ella dijo: «Mucho tiempo antes, puse mis propios guardias en la cocina para ver que los trabajadores no tomaran nada de comida, ni siquiera probaran la que cocinaban para mí. Los tuve muriéndose de hambre hasta que estuvieron dispuestos... en hacer cualquier cosa que yo les ordenara. Una vez que ellos cumplieron mis órdenes por primera vez y después de alimentarlos muy bien otra vez, ya no necesitaron de más persuasión o de ser tratados de otra manera o vigilados por los guardias...»

El resto de sus palabras se perdió por la conmoción general. Mi pequeño esclavo Cózcatl estaba vomitando y tuvo que ser sacado de la sala por un rato. Yo sabía lo que él sentía y mi estómago también se revolvió ligeramente, pues nuestros alimentos habían venido de esa misma cocina.

Como cómplice principal de Muñeca de Jade, fui llamado en seguida. Narré todas mis actividades a su servicio sin omitir nada. Cuando llegué a la parte correspondiente a Algo Delicado, fui interrumpido por un alboroto que venía de la sala. El viudo demente de Nemalhuili tuvo que ser detenido por los guardias para que no se precipitara sobre mí y me ahorcara, y fue sacado de la sala gritando y echando espuma por la boca. Cuando llegué al final de mi narración, el Señor Hueso Fuerte me miró abiertamente con desprecio y dijo:

«Al menos una confesión franca. ¿Tiene algo que decir en su defensa o para mitigar su sentencia?»

Dije: «No, mi señor.»

Con lo cual una voz se dejó oír: «Si el escribano Nube Oscura declina defenderse a sí mismo —dijo Nezahualpili—, ¿puedo decir algunas palabras de atenuación, mis señores jueces?» Los dos examinadores asintieron de mala gana, pues obviamente no deseaban que se me exculpara, pero no les era posible rehusarse a su Uey-Tlatoani.

Nezahualpili dijo: «Durante su asistencia a la señora Chalchiunénetl este joven estuvo actuando, aunque muy tontamente, bajo mis órdenes expresas de servir a la señora sin ninguna pregunta y obedeciendo cada una de sus órdenes. Admito que mis órdenes fueron mal expresadas. También ha quedado demostrado que finalmente Nube Oscura aprovechó la única manera posible de divulgar la verdad acerca de la adúltera y asesina señora. Si él no lo hubiera hecho, mis señores jueces, es muy posible que todavía estuviéramos sufriendo las muertes de muchas otras víctimas.»

El juez Tepítztic gruñó: «Nuestro Señor Nezahualpili, sus palabras generosas serán tomadas en consideración en el recuento de nuestras deliberaciones. —Me miró fija y severamente otra vez—. Sólo tengo otra pregunta más para el demandado. ¿Se acostó *usted*, Tlilétic-Mixtli, alguna vez con la señora Muñeca de Jade?»

Yo dije: «No, mi señor.»

Era evidente que ellos esperaban cogerme en una mentira aborrecible, porque los examinadores llamaron a mi esclavo Cózcatl y le preguntaron: «¿Sabes si tu amo tuvo alguna vez relaciones sexuales con la señora Chalchiunénetl?»

Él dijo con su vocecita musical: «No, mis señores.»

Tepítztic persistió: «Pero él tuvo muchas oportunidades.»

Cózcatl dijo inflexiblemente: «No, mis señores. Cuantas veces mi amo estuvo en compañía de la señora por el espacio de tiempo que fuera, yo siempre estuve presente a su servicio. No, ni mi amo ni ningún otro hombre de la Corte se acostó con la señora, excepto uno y eso fue durante la ausencia de mi amo en la fiesta, una noche cuando la señora no pudo encontrar un compañero de fuera.»

Los jueces se inclinaron hacia él. «¿Algún hombre del palacio? *¿Quién?*»

Cózcatl dijo: «Yo», y los jueces oscilaron hacia atrás.

«*¿Tú?* —dijo Hueso Fuerte, sin poder creerlo—. ¿Cuántos años tienes, esclavo?»

«Acabo de cumplir los once, mi señor.»

«Habla más fuerte, muchacho. ¿Nos estás tratando de decir que tú serviste como compañero sexual de la acusada adúltera? ¿Que tú efectivamente tuviste acoplamiento con ella? ¿Que tú tienes un *tepule* capaz de...»

«¿Mi *tepule*? —gritó Cózcatl conmocionado, cometiendo la impertinencia de interrumpir al juez—. ¡Mis señores, ese miembro solamente es para hacer las aguas! Yo serví a mi señora con la boca, como ella me dijo que era lo apropiado. Yo nunca tocaría a una señora noble con algo tan sucio como un *tepule*...»

Si él dijo alguna otra cosa, fue ahogado por las carcajadas de los espectadores. Aun los dos jueces hicieron el esfuerzo de mantener sus caras impasibles. Éste fue el único momento jovial de aquel día horrible.

Tlatli fue el último cómplice en ser llamado. Había olvidado mencionar que, en las noches en que los guardias de Nezahualpili invadieron el estudio, Chimali, por alguna razón fortuita, había estado ausente. No había habido motivo para que Nezahualpili o sus ayudantes sospecharan la existencia de un segundo artista. Aparentemente ningún otro de los acusados se tomó la molestia de mencionar a Chimali y así Tlatli había podido pretender que él había estado trabajando solo.

Hueso Fuerte dijo: «Chicuace-Cali Ixtac-Tlatli, usted ha admitido que ciertas estatuas que se han presentado como evidencia, fueron hechas por usted.»

«Sí, mis señores —dijo él firmemente—. Difícilmente podría negarlo. Ustedes verán en ellas mi firma: el glifo de la cabeza del halcón grabado y abajo la marca sangrienta de mi mano.» Sus ojos buscaron los míos, suplicando silencio como diciendo: «Perdona a *mi mujer*», y yo guardé silencio.

Finalmente los dos jueces se retiraron a una habitación privada para sus deliberaciones. Todos los demás que estaban en la sala de justicia dieron gracias de poder salir de esa grande pero mal ventilada habitación, para disfrutar un poco de aire fresco o fumar un *poquíetl* afuera, en los jardines. Nosotros los demandados nos quedamos, cada uno con un guardia armado y alerta parado a nuestro lado y cuidadosamente evitábamos cruzar nuestras miradas.

No pasó mucho tiempo antes de que los jueces regresaran y la sala se volviera a llenar. El Mujer Serpiente, Señor Hueso Fuerte hizo el prefacio de rutina anunciando:

«Nosotros, los examinadores, hemos deliberado únicamente sobre las evidencias y testimonios presentados aquí, y hemos llegado a nuestras decisiones sin ninguna malicia o favor, sin la intervención de ninguna otra persona, con la asistencia solamente de Tónantzin, la gentil diosa de la ley, la misericordia y la justicia.»

Sacó una hoja de papel fino y basándose en ella pronunció primero: «Nosotros encontramos que el escribano acusado, Chicome-Xóchitl Tlilétic-Mixtli, merece la absolución, porque sus acciones, aunque culpables, no fueron mal intencionadas y además están mitigadas por sus otros servicios prestados a la Corte. Sin embargo... —Hueso Fuerte lanzó una mirada al Venerado Orador y después a mí—. Recomendamos que para su absolución sea desterrado de este reino como un forastero que ha abusado de su hospitalidad.»

Bueno, no podría decir que eso me agradó, pero Nezahualpili hubiera podido fácilmente dejar que los jueces se ocuparan de mí, como se ocuparon de los otros. El Mujer Serpiente se enfrascó otra vez en el papel y pronunció: «Las siguientes personas han sido encontradas culpables de varios crímenes, entre éstos: acciones nefandas, perfidias y otras detestables a la vista de los dioses.» Y leyó la lista de los nombres: el Señor Alegría, la Señora Muñeca de Jade, los escultores Píxquitl y Tlatli, mi esclavo Cózcatl, los dos guardias que hacían alternativamente el servicio de noche en la puerta este del palacio, Pitza la criada de Muñeca de Jade y otras mujeres a su servicio, todos los cocineros y trabajadores de su cocina. El juez concluyó su monótona locución: «En vista de que estas personas han sido encontradas culpables, nosotros no hacemos ninguna recomendación, ni en severidad ni en suavidad y sus sentencias deberán ser dictadas por el Uey-Tlatoani.»

Nezahualpili se levantó lentamente. De pie, por un momento, pensó profundamente, luego dijo: «Como mis señores recomiendan, el escribano Nube Oscura será exiliado para siempre de Texcoco y de todas las provincias de los acolhua. Al esclavo convicto, Cózcatl, le doy mi perdón en consideración a su tierna edad, pero él también será desterrado de estas tierras. Los nobles Pactzin y Chalchiunénetzin serán ejecutados en privado y dejaré que la forma de su ejecución sea determinada por las nobles señoras de la Corte de Texcoco. Todos los demás que han sido encontrados culpables por los señores jueces, son sentenciados a ser ejecutados públicamente por medio del *icpacxóchitl*, sin el auxilio previo de Tlazoltéotl. Ya muertos, sus cuerpos serán juntados con los residuos de sus víctimas y quemados en una pira común.»

Me alegré de que el pequeño Cózcatl fuera perdonado, pero sentí compasión por los otros esclavos y plebeyos. El *icpacxóchitl* era el lazo-guirnalda de la horca, que ya era bastante malo, pero Nezahualpili les había negado también el consuelo de la confesión con el sacerdote de Tlazoltéotl. Eso significaba que sus pecados no serían engullidos por la diosa La Que Come Suciedad y, puesto que ellos serían incinerados junto con sus víctimas, cargarían con sus culpas todo el camino hacia el otro mundo al que fueran y continuamente seguirían sufriendo un intolerable remordimiento por toda la eternidad.

Cózcatl y yo fuimos escoltados de regreso a nuestras habitaciones y allí uno de los guardias gruñó: «¿Qué es esto?» Afuera de la puerta de mi apartamento, a la altura de mi cabeza, había una señal, la marca impresa de una mano ensangrentada, silencioso recordatorio de que yo no había sido el único inculpado que había salido con vida ese día, y entonces me empecé a preocupar de si Chimali intentaría vengar su propia pérdida.

«Alguna broma de mal gusto —dije, encogiéndome de hombros—. Mi esclavo la limpiará.»

Cózcatl tomó una esponja y una jarra de agua y salió al corredor, mientras yo esperaba escuchando detrás de la puerta. No pasó mucho tiempo antes de que oyera llegar a Muñeca de Jade, también custodiada. No podía distinguir el sonido de sus pequeños pies entre las pesadas pisadas de su escolta, pero cuando Cózcatl volvió a entrar con su jarra de agua teñida de sangre, dijo:

«La señora viene llorando, mi amo. Y con sus guardias viene un sacerdote de Tlazoltéotl.»

Yo murmuré: «Si ella ya confesó sus pecados para ser engullidos, significa que ya no le queda mucho tiempo.» Y en verdad que le quedaba ya muy poco tiempo, pues poco después volví a oír cómo se abría su puerta cuando ella fue llevada a la última cita de su vida.

«Amo —dijo Cózcatl tímidamente—. Usted y yo estamos desterrados, ¿verdad?»

«Sí», suspiré.

«Como estamos desterrados... —Y él retorcía sus manitas ásperas por el trabajo—, ¿me llevará con usted? ¿Como su esclavo y sirviente?»

«Sí —le dije después de pensar unos momentos—. Tú me has servido con lealtad y no te abandonaré, pero en verdad, Cózcatl, no tengo ni idea de adónde iremos.»

El muchacho y yo estuvimos confinados, no fuimos testigos de ninguna de las ejecuciones, aunque después supe los detalles de los castigos infligidos al Señor Alegría y a la Señora Muñeca de Jade y estos detalles pueden interesar a Su Ilustrísima.

El sacerdote de la diosa La Que Come Suciedad, ni siquiera dio a la muchacha la oportunidad de confesarse completamente con Tlazoltéotl. Pretendiendo bondad, le ofreció una bebida de *chocólatl* —«para calmar tus nervios, hija mía»— en el que él había mezclado una infusión de la planta *toloatzin*, que es una droga soporífera de gran poder. Muñeca de Jade estaba probablemente inconsciente antes de haber contado incluso las fechorías de sus diez años, así es que ella fue hacia su muerte cargada todavía de muchas de sus culpas.

Fue llevada al laberinto del palacio del cual ya he hablado, totalmente desnuda. Entonces el viejo jardinero que era el único que conocía la salida secreta, la arrastró hasta el centro del laberinto, en donde yacía el cuerpo de Pactli.

El Señor Alegría había sido enviado antes a los trabajadores convictos de la cocina, a quienes se les había ordenado que hicieran un último trabajo antes de ser ejecutados. Si ellos mataron a Pactli piadosamente, no lo sé; pero lo dudo, ya que tenían muy poca razón para sentir algo de bondad hacia él. Desollaron todo su cuerpo, a excepción de su cabeza y sus genitales y le quitaron los intestinos y toda la carne de su cuerpo. Cuando todo lo que quedó fue su esqueleto y no un esqueleto muy limpio, ya que todavía estaba festonado con pedazos de carne viva, usaron algo para sostener su tepule erecto, quizás insertaron un pedazo de caña. Ese cadáver espantoso fue llevado al laberinto mientras Muñeca de Jade todavía estaba con el sacerdote en sus habitaciones.

La muchacha despertó en plena noche, en medio del laberinto, encontrándose desnuda y con su *tepili* confortablemente empalado, como en sus tiempos felices, en el tumefacto órgano del hombre. Sus dilatadas pupilas se fueron habituando muy rápidamente a la luz pálida de la luna, así es que ella vio esa cosa horrorosa y lúgubre que estaba abrazando.

Lo que pasó después sólo puede ser conjeturado. Seguramente Muñeca de Jade saltó de horror y gritando, huyó de ese último amante. Ella debió de haber corrido por todo el laberinto, una y otra vez, aunque los senderos tortuosos siempre la llevarían de vuelta a encontrarse con la cabeza, los huesos y el *tepule* erecto de lo que una vez fue el Señor Alegría. Y cada vez que ella regresara, lo debería de encontrar más lleno de hormigas, moscas y escarabajos. Al fin, él debió de estar tan lleno de pululantes gusanos que debió parecerle a Muñeca de Jade, que el cadáver se estaba contorsionando en un intento de levantarse y perseguirla. Cuántas veces corrió, cuántas veces se arrojó contra los muros de recias espinas, cuántas se encontró a sí misma tropezando con la carroña del Señor Alegría, nunca lo sabrá nadie.

Cuando el viejo jardinero la sacó afuera a la siguiente mañana, ya no era ninguna belleza. Su rostro y su cuerpo estaban desgarrados y ensangrentados por las espinas. Se había arrancado las uñas y se podían ver partes de su cráneo, pues se había arrancado mechones de pelo. La droga que le había agrandado los ojos, se había consumido y sus pupilas eran unos puntos invisibles en sus ojos fijos y saltones. Su boca permanecía abierta en un grito silencioso. Muñeca de Jade, que siempre se había sentido muy orgullosa y había sido muy vanidosa de su belleza, se hubiera sentido ultrajada y mortificada de lo horrible que se veía, pero en esos momentos a ella ya no le importaba. En algún momento de la noche, en alguna parte del laberinto, su aterrorizado y golpeante corazón había finalmente estallado.

Cuando todo terminó, y Cózcatl y yo fuimos liberados de nuestro arresto, los guardias nos dijeron que no podíamos ir a clases, ni mezclarnos o conversar con ninguno de nuestros conocidos del palacio y yo no regresaría a mi trabajo en la sala del Consejo de Voceros. Sólo podíamos esperar tratando de pasar lo más desapercibidamente posible, hasta que el Venerado Orador decidiera cuándo y adónde mandarnos al exilio.

Así pasé algunos días sin hacer nada más que vagar a lo largo de la orilla del lago, pateando guijarros, sintiendo lástima de mí mismo y recordando con dolor las grandes ambiciones con las que me había entretenido cuando llegué a esa tierra. En uno de esos días, ensimismado en mis pensamientos, dejé que el crepúsculo me alcanzara muy lejos, a lo largo de la ribera, y me volví para regresar a toda prisa al palacio antes de que la oscuridad cayera. A la mitad del camino hacia la ciudad, llegué hasta donde se encontraba un hombre sentado en una roca, él no estaba allí cuando pasé antes. Se seguía viendo igual como en las otras dos ocasiones anteriores en que me lo había encontrado. Llevaba sus sandalias de viaje, la piel pálida y sus facciones con una capa de polvo alcalino de la orilla del lago.

Después de intercambiar los saludos corteses de rigor, dije: «Otra vez llega usted al atardecer, mi señor. ¿Viene usted de muy lejos?»

«Sí —dijo él sobriamente—. De Tenochtitlan, en donde la guerra se está preparando.»

Dije: «Lo dice usted como si la guerra fuera a ser en contra de Texcoco.»

«No ha sido declarada exactamente en ese sentido, pero será así. El Uey-Tlatoani Auítzotl ha acabado al fin de construir la Gran Pirámide y tiene entre sus planes la ceremonia más impresionante y espectacular que jamás se haya visto antes, y para eso desea incontables prisioneros para un sacrificio en masa. Así es que ha declarado otra guerra en contra de Texcala.»

Esto no me sonó muy fuera de lo usual. Dije: «Entonces los ejércitos de la Triple Alianza pelearán lado a lado una vez más. ¿Pero por qué dice usted que es una guerra contra Texcoco?»

El hombre polvoriento dijo tristemente: «Auítzotl clama que casi todas las fuerzas de los mexica y de los tecpaneca están todavía ocupadas en pelear al oeste, en Michihuacan, y no pueden ser enviadas hacia el este contra Texcala, pero es sólo una excusa que trata de ser convincente. Auítzotl se sintió muy afrentado con el juicio y la ejecución de su hija.»

Yo le dije: «Él no puede negar que ella se lo merecía.»

«Lo cual le hace sentirse más enojado y vengativo. Así es que él ha acordado que Tenochtitlan y Tlacopan envíen sólo un puñado de hombres en contra de los texcalteca y que Texcoco deba contribuir con la mayor parte del ejército. —Sacudió su cabeza—. De todos los guerreros que pelearán y morirán para asegurar los prisioneros para el sacrificio de la Gran Pirámide, quizás noventa y nueve de cada cien serán acolhua. Ésta es la forma en que Auítzotl vengará la muerte de Muñeca de Jade.»

Yo le dije: «Cualquiera puede ver que es una injusticia que los acolhua lleven toda la carga del combate. De seguro que Nezahualpili podrá rehusarse.»

«Sí, él podría hacerlo —dijo el viajero con voz fatigada—. Pero eso podría romper la Triple Alianza e incluso provocar al irascible Auítzotl a declarar *abiertamente* la guerra contra Texcoco. —Con una voz todavía más melancólica él continuó—: También Nezahualpili debe sentir que tiene que hacer alguna expiación por haber ejecutado a esa muchacha.»

«¿Qué? —dije con indignación—. ¿Después de lo que ella le hizo?»

«A pesar de eso, pues quizás él debe de sentir alguna responsabilidad por haber sido negligente con ella. Pudiera ser que algunos otros también sientan responsabilidad. —Sus ojos me miraron y de repente me sentí incómodo—. Para esta guerra, Nezahualpili necesitará a cada hombre que puede conseguir. Sin duda él será bondadoso con los voluntarios y probablemente rescindirá cualquier deuda de honor que ellos deban.»

Tragué saliva y dije: «Mi señor, hay algunos hombres que no pueden ser útiles en una guerra.»

«Entonces pueden morir en ella —dijo fríamente—. Por gloria, por penitencia, en pago de una deuda, por una vida feliz en el mundo del más allá de los guerreros, por cualquier razón. Una vez te escuché hablar acerca de tu gratitud para con Nezahualpili y tu disposición de demostrársela.»

Hubo un gran silencio entre los dos. Después, como si por casualidad hubiera cambiado de tema, el hombre polvoriento dijo como conversando: «Se rumorea que pronto dejarás Texcoco. Si pudieras escoger, ¿adónde irías?»

Pensé en eso por bastante tiempo y la oscuridad nos envolvía alrededor, el viento de la noche empezaba a gemir a través del lago y al fin dije: «A la guerra, mi señor. Iría a la guerra.»

✠

Era un espectáculo digno de verse, el gran ejército formándose en el terreno vacío al este de Texcoco. La llanura quebrándose en resplandores de lanzas de brillantes colores, y por todos lados el sol reluciendo sobre las espadas y las puntas de obsidiana. Debían de haber unos cuatro o cinco mil hombres juntos, pero como el viajero había dicho, los Venerados Oradores Auítzotl de los mexica y chimalpopoca y de los tecpaneca, habían mandado sólo unos cientos de hombres cada uno, y esos guerreros difícilmente hubieran podido ser los mejores, pues la mayoría de ellos eran veteranos de edad avanzada y reclutas novatos.

Con Nezahualpili como jefe de batalla, todo era organización y eficiencia. Enormes banderas de plumas designaban a los contingentes principales entre los miles acolhua y los pocos cientos de tenochtitlan y tlacopan. Banderas de tela multicolores, marcaban las diferentes compañías de hombres bajo las órdenes de varios campeones. Las banderolas más pequeñas señalaban las unidades menores al mando de los oficiales *quáchictin*. También había allí otras banderas alrededor, bajo las cuales se agrupaban las fuerzas no combatientes: aquellos que eran responsables de transportar la comida, el agua, las corazas y las armas de reserva; los físicos, los cirujanos y los sacerdotes de diversos dioses; las bandas de tambores y trompetas que marchaban con el ejército; los destacamentos que limpiaban el campo de batalla, o sea los acuchilladores y amarradores.

Había sido desterrado de los dominios de Texcoco y amonestado en el aspecto de no tener nada que ver con sus asuntos. Aun así me dije que pelearía por Nezahualpili, y no obstante estaba avergonzado de la poca participación de los mexica en esa guerra, pues después de todo ellos eran mi gente. Así es que fui a ofrecer mis servicios voluntarios a su guía, el único mexícatl que comandaba el campo, un Campeón Flecha llamado Xococ. Xococ me miró de arriba abajo y me dijo cínicamente: «Bien, por muy poca experiencia que tengas, por lo menos pareces mejor constituido físicamente que cualquiera de los que mandan aquí excepto yo. Preséntate con el Quáchic Extli-Quani.»

¡El viejo Extli-Quani! Estaba tan contento de volver a escuchar su nombre que corrí directamente hacia la banderola en donde él estaba parado enfrente de un grupo de jóvenes guerreros que parecían muy infelices. Llevaba un penacho de plumas, una astilla de hueso incrustada en medio de su nariz y sostenía un escudo pintado con los glifos que denotaban su nombre y su rango. Cuando me aproximé, me arrodillé y rocé la tierra en un gesto superficial de besarla, luego, con el mismo movimiento precipitado, me levanté y lo abracé como si él hubiera sido un pariente por largo tiempo perdido, gritando contentísimo: «¡Maestro Glotón de Sangre! ¡Cuánto me alegro de volverle a ver!»

Los otros guerreros miraban con ojos muy abiertos. El viejo *quáchic* se puso colorado y empujándome rudamente, farfulló: «¡No me ponga las manos encima!» Por los huevos de piedra de

Huitzilopochtli, vaya si ese guerrero había cambiado desde la última vez que lo vi en la escuela. Gruñón y lleno de espinillas como un mozalbete y luego ¡esto! «¿Están todos los *cuilontin* preparados ya? —dijo—. ¿Listos para hacer que el enemigo sea *besado* por la muerte?»

«¡Soy yo, maestro! —grité—. El Campeón Xococ me dijo que me reuniera con su grupo.» Me tomó algún tiempo el darme cuenta de que Glotón de Sangre debía de haber enseñado a cientos de muchachos de su tiempo de maestro. A él le tomó algunos momentos también, buscarme en su memoria y finalmente encontrarme en algún remoto rincón de ella.

«¡Por supuesto, Perdido en Niebla! —exclamó, si bien no con tanta alegría como yo había demostrado—. ¿Estás destinado a mi grupo? ¿Entonces, ya estás curado de tus ojos? ¿Ya puedes ver bien?»

«Bueno, no», tuve que admitir.

Él le dio una patada feroz a una pequeña hormiga. «Mi primera acción activa en diez años —jadeó—, y me pasa esto. Quizá los *cuilontin* serían preferibles. Ah, bien, Perdido en Niebla, entra con el resto de mis ratones.»

«Sí, Maestro Quáchic —dije con fragilidad militar. Entonces sentí que tiraban de mi manto y recordé a Cózcatl, quien había estado durante todo este tiempo pegado a mis talones—. ¿Y qué órdenes tiene usted para el joven Cózcatl?»

«¿Para quién? —dijo perplejo, mirando en derredor. No fue sino hasta que· inclinó la cabeza que su mirada cayó sobre el muchachito—. ¿Para él?», estalló.

«Él es mi esclavo —le expliqué—. Mi sirviente personal.»

«¡Silencio en las filas!», voceó Glotón de Sangre, tanto a mí, como a sus guerreros, quienes empezaron a reír ahogadamente. El viajo *quáchic* caminó por un tiempo en círculo, apaciguadamente. Finalmente vino y pegó su gran cara cerca de la mía. «Perdido en Niebla, hay aquí algunos campeones y nobles quienes tienen un relativo servicio a sus órdenes. Tú eres un *yaoquizqui*, un recluta nuevo, el rango más bajo que existe. No sólo te presentas tranquilamente con tu sirviente como si fueras un campeón *pili*, ¡sino que además me traes a este renacuajo humano!»

«No puedo abandonar a Cózcatl —le dije—. Pero él nunca será un estorbo. ¿No le podría usted asignar con los sacerdotes o con algunos otros guardias de la retaguardia, en donde pudiera ser útil?»

Él rugió: «Y yo que creí que había escapado de esa escuela para entrar en esta bella y tranquila guerra. Está bien. Renacuajo, preséntate en donde está aquella banderola negra y amarilla. Dile al jefe que Extli-Quani te ordenó hacer el trabajo de pinche. Bien, Perdido en Niebla —dijo dulce y persuasivamente—, si el ejército mexica está arreglado a tu entera satisfacción, déjanos ver si recuerdas algunos de los ejercicios de batalla. —Y vociferó haciéndonos saltar a mí y a todos los demás—: *¡Todos vosotros, infelices desgraciados, formad una fila de cuatro al frente!*»

Había aprendido en la Casa del Desarrollo de la Fuerza, que el adiestramiento para ser un guerrero era muy diferente de jugar a serlo. Sin embargo en esos momentos aprendí que ambos, el adiestramiento y el juego eran pálidas imitaciones de una guerra real. Solamente mencionaré una de las cosas más duras de soportar, que los narradores de gloriosas historias de guerra, fastidiosamente omitían: la suciedad y el mal olor. Ya sea jugando o en la escuela, después de un día de duros ejercicios, yo siempre había tenido el placentero alivio de un buen baño y sudar ampliamente en la casa de vapor. Allí, no había tales facilidades. Al final de un día de instrucciones y ejercicios, estábamos sucios y así nos quedaríamos, apestando. Tuvimos que cavar hoyos para nuestras funciones excretorias; me repugnaba mi propio olor fétido de sudor seco y de ropa sin lavar, tanto como el ambiente maloliente a pies y a heces. Yo miraba la suciedad y el hedor como uno de los peores aspectos de la guerra. En aquel tiempo, por lo menos, antes de que *hubiera* estado realmente en la guerra.

Y había otra cosa también. Oí a los viejos guerreros quejarse de que, aun en la estación normalmente seca, un guerrero podía caer en la cuenta de que Tláloc maliciosamente haría de cualquier batalla y de cada una de ellas, la más difícil y miserable con una lluvia que empaparía totalmente a un hombre y le haría arrastrar los pies en el fango. Bien, pues estábamos en temporada de aguas y Tláloc nos enviaba una lluvia intermitente. Todos los días que pasamos familiarizándonos con nuestras armas y practicando los diferentes ejercicios y maniobras que esperábamos utilizar en el campo de batalla, seguía lloviendo y nuestros mantos parecían pesos muertos de lo mojado que estaban, nuestras sandalias se llenaban de fango y nuestro humor era detestable cuando al fin salimos para Texcala.

Esa ciudad estaba a trece largas carreras hacia el este y el sureste. Con buen tiempo hubiéramos podido hacer ese recorrido en dos días a marcha forzada, pero habríamos llegado fatigados y sin aliento para dar la cara al enemigo, que no tenía nada que hacer más que sentarse a descansar mientras nos esperaban. Considerando todas esas circunstancias, Nezahualpili ordenó que hiciéramos la caminata más despacio y la alargamos a cuatro días de camino, así por lo menos llegaríamos más o menos descansados.

Los dos primeros días marchamos directamente hacia el este, así es que nada más tuvimos que escalar y cruzar las más pequeñas cimas de las sierras de los volcanes que están hacia el sur; los altos picos llamados Tlaloctépetl, Ixtaccíhuatl y Popocatépetl. Entonces nos desviamos al sureste en dirección directa hacia la ciudad de Texcala. Todo el camino fuimos chapoteando entre el fango, excepto cuando nos resbalábamos y deslizábamos en el mojado terreno rocoso. Ése era el lugar más lejano en que jamás había estado antes y me habría gustado ver el paisaje, pero aunque mis ojos no hubieran estado limitados por mi corta visión, no habría podido verlo debido al perpetuo velo de lluvia. En aquella jornada no vi más que los pies de los hombres que caminaban delante de mí, arrastrándolos lentamente en el fango.

No íbamos caminando bajo el solo peso de la coraza de batalla. Además de nuestro traje usual, cargábamos un pesado traje llamado *tlamaitl*, el cual usábamos para el tiempo frío o utilizábamos como abrigo en la noche. Cada hombre llevaba también una bolsa con *pinoli* hecho de maíz endulzado con miel y otra de cuero llena de agua. Cada mañana antes de empezar la marcha y en el descanso del mediodía, mezclábamos el maíz con el agua para hacer una nutritiva comida de *atoli*, aunque muy ligera. En la parada de cada noche, teníamos que esperar a que los que cargaban las pesadas provisiones nos alcanzaran. Entonces el jefe encargado del aprovisionamiento de tropas proveería a cada hombre con una substanciosa comida caliente, incluyendo una taza del pesado *chocólatl*, alimento nutritivo y reconfortante.

Sin importar cuáles fueran sus otras obligaciones, Cózcatl siempre me servía mi comida de la noche con sus propias manos y se las arreglaba para conseguirme un poco más de la porción normal o deslizaba alguna golosina robada. Algunos de los otros hombres de la compañía de Glotón de Sangre gruñían o se mofaban por la forma en que él me cuidaba, así es que yo trataba débilmente de rehusar las cosas extras que Cózcatl me traía.

Él me amonestaba diciendo: «No es necesario que actúe noblemente y se niegue a sí mismo estas cosas, mi amo. Usted no está despojando a sus compañeros guerreros. ¿No sabe que los hombres mejor alimentados del ejército son aquellos que están más lejos del combate? Los cargadores, los cocineros, los que llevan los mensajes y también son ellos los que más alardean de su valor. Yo sólo quisiera que pudiera conseguir de alguna manera un cántaro lleno de agua caliente y traerlo aquí. Perdóneme, mi amo, pero usted apesta atrozmente.»

Poco después, en la tarde lluviosa y gris del cuarto día, cuando todavía estábamos como a una larga carrera de Texcala, nuestros exploradores que habían tomado la delantera para espiar a las fuerzas texcalteca que nos esperaban, regresaron rápidamente para dar su parte a Nezahualpili. El enemigo nos estaba esperando con toda su fuerza al otro lado del río que tendríamos que cruzar. En tiempo seco el río no era más que un arroyo poco profundo de aguas mansas, pero después de todos esos días de lluvias continuas era un obstáculo formidable. Si bien no tendría más de una cadera de profundidad, corría de orilla a orilla a mucha velocidad y muy rudamente, tanto como el disparo de una flecha. La estrategia del enemigo era obvia. Mientras nosotros intentábamos vadear el río, con aguas arrastrando nuestras piernas, seríamos un buen blanco de movimientos lentos, incapaces de utilizar nuestras armas y de evitar las del enemigo. Con sus flechas y sus *atlatl*, lanza jabalinas, los texcalteca esperaban diezmarnos y desmoralizarnos, si es que no destruirnos completamente, antes de que pudiéramos siquiera alcanzar la otra parte del río.

Se dice que Nezahualpili sonrió y dijo: «Muy bien. La trampa ha sido tan bien preparada tanto por el enemigo como por Tlátloc, que no debemos desilusionarlos. Por la mañana caeremos en ella.»

Dio órdenes al ejército de hacer alto por la noche y permanecer en donde estaba, a una buena distancia todavía del río y llamó a todos los comandantes *tlamahuichíhuantin*, campeones, y *cuachictin*, oficiales, para reunirse con él y escuchar sus instrucciones para el día siguiente. Nosotros éramos simples guerreros sentados, agachados o recostados sobre el terreno empapado, mientras el jefe de cocineros empezada a preparar nuestra comida de la noche, una especialmente abundante, ya que no tendríamos tiempo de comer ni siquiera *atoli* a la mañana siguiente. Los encargados de las armas las desembalaron y las colocaron a mano, para irlas distribuyendo al día siguiente conforme se fueran necesitando. Los tamborileros retiraron los cueros de sus tambores, que se habían reblandecido por la humedad. Los físicos y los sacerdotes capellanes prepararon respectivamente sus medicinas e instrumentos de operación, sus inciensos y sus libros de encantamientos, así ellos estarían listos mañana, lo mismo para atender las heridas como para escuchar, en favor de La Que Come Suciedad, las confesiones de los moribundos.

Glotón de Sangre regresó de la gran conferencia cuando apenas se nos acababa de servir nuestra comida y *chocólatl*. Él nos dijo: «Cuando hayáis comido, os pondréis vuestros trajes de batalla y cogeréis las armas. Luego cuando la oscuridad haya caído, nos moveremos para asignar las posiciones y dormiremos allí, ya que debemos de estar despiertos temprano.»

Después de comer, nos explicó el plan de Nezahualpili. Al amanecer, una tercera parte del ejército, en formación precisa acompañada de tambores y trompetas, marcharía hacia el río y daría la cara al enemigo como si ignorara cualquier peligro que le esperara al otro lado del río. Cuando el enemigo atacara, nuestros guerreros se dispersarían y chapotearían alrededor, para dar la impresión de sorpresa y confusión. Cuando la lluvia de proyectiles se volviera intolerable, nuestros guerreros se volverían y huirían hacia el lugar de donde habían partido, pareciendo indisciplinados y cobardemente vencidos. Nezahualpili creía que los texcalteca serían engañados con eso y los perseguirían tratando de dar caza incautamente al enemigo, excitados por su triunfo aparentemente fácil, de tal manera que no les dejaría pensar en la posibilidad de un engaño.

Mientras tanto, lo que quedaba de su ejército estaría esperando escondido entre las rocas, arbustos y árboles a los dos lados del camino que corría a todo lo largo hacia el río. Ninguno de sus hombres, sin embargo, se dejaría ver o utilizaría su arma hasta que nuestras fuerzas «en retirada» hubiesen atraído completamente a todo el ejército texcalteca a través del río. Los texcalteca correrían a lo largo de ese corredor, como lo harían, entre murallas de guerreros escondidos. Entonces Nezahualpili, que estaría vigilando desde un lugar alto, daría la señal a sus tamborileros y los tambores nos avisarían con sus estampidos. Nuestros hombres emboscados a ambos lados del camino se levantarían y las paredes del corredor serían cerradas, atrapando al enemigo en medio de ellas.

Un viejo guerrero de pelo gris de nuestra compañía preguntó: «¿Y nosotros en dónde seremos apostados?»

Glotón de Sangre gruñó tristemente: «Hasta el final. Casi tan atrás y seguros como los cocineros y los sacerdotes.»

«¿Qué? —exclamó el veterano— ¿Venir por todo este horrible camino para no estar ni siquiera lo suficientemente cerca como para *oír* el choque de la obsidiana?»

Nuestro *quáchic* se encogió de hombros: «Bien, tú sabes cuán pocos somos, vergonzosamente. Difícilmente podremos culpar a Nezahualpili que nos niegue compartir esta batalla, considerando que él está peleando la batalla de Auítzotl, en su lugar. Nuestro campeón Xococ le suplicó que por lo menos nos dejara marchar al frente, dentro del río y ser el señuelo para los texcalteca, nosotros estaríamos contentos de morir valientemente, pero Nezahualpili nos rehusó incluso esa oportunidad de gloria.»

Personalmente yo estaba muy contento de escuchar eso, pero el otro guerrero todavía estaba disgustado. «¿Entonces nosotros los mexica sólo nos sentaremos aquí como fardos, y luego esperaremos para servir de escolta a los victoriosos acolhua y a sus cautivos, de regreso a Tenochtitlan?»

«No del todo —dijo Glotón de Sangre—. Pudiera ser que también nosotros tomáramos uno o dos prisioneros. Pudiera ser que algunos de los texcalteca atrapados pudieran romper y pasar a través de las cerradas paredes de los guerreros acolhua. Nuestras compañías mexica y tecpaneca se extenderán como un abanico de uno a otro lado, de norte a sur, como una red para atrapar a los que eludan la emboscada.»

«Tendríamos mucha suerte si atrapáramos tantos como un conejo —gruñó el guerrero de pelo gris. Se puso de pie y dijo al resto de nosotros—: Todos aquellos *yaoquizque* que combatís por primera vez, es bueno que sepáis esto. Antes de poneros la coraza, id hacia los arbustos y evacuar hasta que quedéis bien vacíos. En cuanto los tambores empiecen a sonar se removerán vuestras tripas y no tendréis la oportunidad de quitaros esos apretados trajes acolchados.»

Él se fue lejos a seguir su propio consejo y yo le seguí. Cuando estaba agachado oí que murmuraba cerca de mí: «Casi olvido esto.» Yo miré por encima de su hombro. Él sacó de su morral un pequeño objeto envuelto en un papel. «Un hombre orgulloso de ser padre por primera vez, me dio esto para que lo enterrara en el campo de batalla —dijo—. El cordón umbilical de su hijo recién nacido y un pequeño escudo de guerra.» Lo dejó caer a sus pies, lo enterró bien en el fango, luego se puso de cuclillas y orinó y defecó sobre él copiosamente.

«Bien —pensé para mí—, es mucho para el *tonali* de un niñito.» Me preguntaba si mi propio escudo y cordón habían corrido la misma suerte.

Mientras la mayoría de nosotros nos poníamos nuestros trajes acolchados, los campeones se ponían los suyos llamativos que les hacían verse espléndidos. Había tres órdenes de *tlamahuichí-huantin*: la del Jaguar, la del Águila y la de la Flecha. Un guerrero podía scr distinguido con las dos primeras cuando él a su vez había descollado en muchas batallas, y a la de la Flecha sólo pertenecían aquellos que habían obtenido el campeonato de tiro con arco o jabalina, matando a muchos enemigos con esas armas inexactas.

El campeón Jaguar llevaba una verdadera piel de jaguar como una especie de capa, con la cabeza del gran gato como yelmo; la calavera por supuesto había sido quitada, pero los colmillos curvos seguían pegados en su lugar, así es que éstos colgaban sobre la frente del campeón y los de abajo sobresalían de su barbilla. La coraza que cubría su cuerpo estaba moteada como la piel de ese animal: tinta con manchas ovaladas pardo-oscuro. Un campeón Águila llevaba un yelmo de imitación, más o menos, del tamaño de la cabeza de un águila, hecho de papel pesado y hule cubierto con verdaderas plumas de águila, con el gran pico sobresaliendo sobre su frente y debajo de su barbilla. La coraza también estaba cubierta con plumas de águila y en sus sandalias llevaba unas garras artificiales que sobresalían de los dedos de sus pies, su manto de plumas era más o menos como unas alas plegadas. Un campeón Flecha llevaba un yelmo hecho como la cabeza de cualquier pájaro que él escogiera, tan grande como lo fuera una cría de águila, y su coraza estaba cubierta con las mismas plumas que él utilizara para empenachar sus flechas.

Todos los campeones llevaban escudos de piel, madera o mimbre cubiertos con plumas, pero éstas estaban trabajadas en forma de mosaicos de gran colorido y cada campeón llevaba diseñado el glifo de su nombre en su escudo. Muchos campeones habían adquirido tal renombre por su heroísmo y valor, que llegaban a ser conocidos aun por los guerreros de las naciones enemigas. Así es que era un acto de osadía el que ellos fueran a la batalla ostentando sus nombres en sus escudos, ya que éstos podían ser vistos por cualquier guerrero enemigo, quien estaría ansioso de enaltecer su propio nombre como «el hombre que aventajó al gran Xococ» o el que fuere. Nosotros los *yaoquizque* portábamos escudos sin adorno y nuestra coraza era uniformemente blanca, hasta que llegaba a ser uniformemente fangosa. No se nos permitía llevar blasones, pero algunos de los hombres más viejos se ponían brillantes plumas entre sus cabellos o veteaban sus caras con listas pintadas para significar que por lo menos ésa no era su primera batalla.

Una vez dentro de nuestras corazas, yo y otros numerosos guerreros novatos marchamos hacia la retaguardia, con los sacerdotes, a quienes jorobaríamos con nuestras confesiones, necesariamente breves, a Tlazoltéotl, y después ellos nos dieron una medicina que se suponía que era para prevenir nuestra patente cobardía en la próxima batalla. Yo en realidad no creía que cualquier cosa que tragara podría apaciguar el miedo que existía en mi recalcitrante cabeza y en mis pies, pero obedientemente tomé mi sorbo de poción: agua fresca de lluvia mezclada con arcilla blanca, poderosa amatista, hojas de cáñamo, flores de matacán, planta del cacao y orquídea campana. Cuando regresamos a reunirnos con el grupo bajo la bandera de Xococ, el campeón mexica nos dijo:

«Sepan esto. El objeto de la batalla de mañana es tomar prisioneros para ser sacrificados a Huitzilopochtli. Golpearemos con las partes planas de nuestras armas, como debe ser. Heriremos, atontaremos, para poder tomar al hombre vivo. —Hizo una pausa y luego dijo siniestramente—: Sin embargo, mientras que para nosotros ésta es solamente una Guerra Florida, para los texcalteca no lo es. Ellos pelearán por sus vidas y lo harán para matarnos. Los acolhua sufrirán más, o ganarán el mayor honor. Pero quiero que todos ustedes, mis hombres, recuerden: si se encuentran con un enemigo que huye, sus órdenes son capturarlo. Las órdenes de él serán matarlos a ustedes.»

Con este no muy inspirado discurso nos dejó, en medio de la oscuridad lluviosa. Cada uno de nosotros estaba armado con una lanza y una *maquáhuitl* y nuestra posición estaba hacia el norte en ángulo directo a la previa línea de marcha, dejando intervalos entre las diferentes compañías de hombres a lo largo del camino. La compañía de Glotón de Sangre fue la primera en ser movilizada y cuando los otros ya habían sido destacados, el *quáchic* nos hizo una última y pequeña indicación:

«Los que ya habéis luchado antes y tomado anteriormente un prisionero enemigo, sabéis que debéis tomar el siguiente sin la ayuda de nadie o esto no será considerado como un ascenso de rango, por el contrario será considerado de poca hombría. Sin embargo, vosotros los nuevos *yaoquizque*, sí tenéis la oportunidad de coger a vuestro primer cautivo, tenéis permitido llamar pidiendo ayuda hasta cinco de vuestros compañeros y todos compartiréis equitativamente el crédito de la captura. Por supuesto, cuantos menos seáis más alto será el honor para cada uno. Ahora, seguidme... Aquí hay un árbol. Tú, sube y escóndete entre sus ramas... Tú ahí, agáchate entre ese montón de rocas... Perdido en Niebla, tú debajo de ese arbusto...»

Y así fuimos esparcidos a lo largo de una amplia línea hacia el norte y nuestros lugares estaban separados por cien pasos largos o más. Incluso cuando la luz del día llegara, ninguno de nosotros podría ver al siguiente hombre, pero sí podríamos llamarnos a la distancia. Dudo mucho de que alguno de nosotros durmiera esa noche, a excepción quizás de los veteranos viejos y endurecidos. Yo no pude, pues el arbusto en el que estaba solamente me ofrecía escondite estando en cuclillas. La lluvia continuaba cayendo en una fina llovizna. Mi *tlamaitl*, sobremanto, estaba totalmente empapado y también mi coraza, hasta sentirla tan pegajosa y pesada que dudaba que alguna vez me fuera posible levantarme y enderezarme otra vez.

Después de lo que me pareció una gavilla de años de miseria, escuché indistintos sonidos hacia el sur, hacia mi derecha. El cuerpo principal de las tropas de los acolhua se estaría preparando para movilizarse, algunos emboscándose y otros para hacer frente a los texcalteca. Lo que escuché fue el canto del gran sacerdote de Huitzilopochtli, entonando la oración que pre-

218

cede a la batalla, si bien solamente parte de ella me era audible a esa distancia.

«Oh, poderoso Huitzilopochtli, dios de la guerra, una batalla está por comenzar... Escoge en estos momentos, oh gran dios, a aquellos que deben matar, a aquellos que deben morir, a aquellos que deben ser tomados como *xochimique* de los cuales tú beberás la sangre de sus corazones... Oh señor de la guerra, nosotros te suplicamos que sonrías sobre aquellos que morirán en este campo o en tu altar... Déjalos llegar derecho hacia la casa del sol, para vivir otra vez amados y glorificados, entre los valientes que les precedieron...»

¡Ba-ra-ROOM! Entumecido como estaba, me sacudí violentamente con el retumbar combinado de los diferentes «tambores que rompen el corazón». Ni siquiera el ruido de la continua lluvia pudo silenciar el tembloroso retumbido y mucho menos el temblor de los huesos. Tenía la esperanza de que ese sonido aterrorizador, no asustara a los guerreros texcalteca haciéndoles huir antes de que pudieran ser atraídos al cebo que les tenía reservado Nezahualpili. El rugido de los tambores se unió a los largos clamores, gemidos y balidos de las trompetas de concha, entonces todo ese tumulto empezó a disminuir, conforme los músicos fueron guiando a la parte del ejército que sería el señuelo, lejos de mí, a lo largo del camino que guiaba hacia el río y hacia el enemigo que esperaba.

Cubierto por nubes de lluvia a todo lo largo de un brazo sobre nuestras cabezas, el día empezó con nada que se le pareciera a una alborada, pero ya había luz perceptible. Suficiente luz, de todas maneras, para que yo pudiera ver que el arbusto bajo en el cual había estado agachado toda la noche era un mustio y casi sin hojas *huixachi,* en el cual no se hubiera podido esconder ni siquiera una ardilla de tierra. Tenía que buscar un lugar mejor para refugiarme y tenía suficiente tiempo para eso. Me levanté con un crujido de huesos llevando mi *maquáhuitl* y arrastrando mi lanza para que no fuera visible al sobresalir de entre los arbustos de los alrededores. Así me fui moviendo lo más agachado posible.

Lo que no podría decirles aún hasta este día, reverendos frailes, ni aunque me pusieran bajo las persuasiones inquisitoriales, es por qué fui en la dirección en que lo hice. Para encontrar otro escondite, pude moverme hacia la retaguardia o a cualquiera de los dos lados y todavía estaría a la distancia de un grito de los otros hombres de mi compañía. Pero me dirigí hacia el este, hacia el lugar en donde la batalla pronto empezaría. Lo único que puedo conjeturar es que algo dentro de mí me estaba diciendo: «Nube Oscura, estás al margen de tu primera guerra, quizá la única guerra en la que tomarás parte. Sería una lástima que permanecieras al margen, que no experimentaras todo lo que puedes.»

Sin embargo no llegué cerca del río en donde los acolhua se enfrentaban con los texcalteca. Ni siquiera escuché ruidos de lucha hasta que los acolhua, pretendiendo consternación, regresaron huyendo del río y del enemigo, que como Nezahualpili había esperado, se precipitaba sobre ellos con toda su fuerza. Entonces escuché los bramidos y la algarabía de los gritos de guerra, los alaridos y las maldiciones de los hombres heridos y, por encima de todo, los silbidos de las flechas y el suave susurro del vuelo de las jabalinas. Todas nuestras armas de imitación en la escuela no hacían ningún ruido distintivo, pero lo que escuchaba en aquellos momentos eran verdaderas armas de guerra, aguzadas y cortantes con afilada obsidiana, y, como si se sintieran alegres en su intento y habilidad de repartir la muerte, *cantaban* cuando volaban por el aire. Después de eso, siempre que yo dibujaba una historia en la cual estuviera incluida una batalla, pintaba las flechas, lanzas y jabalinas con el glifo curvo y en espiral del canto.

No estuve más cerca que no fuera solamente del ruido de la batalla, llegando enfrente a mi derecha, en donde los acolhua y los texcalteca se habían encontrado en el río, luego progresivamente más lejos hacia mi derecha, como si los acolhua huyeran y el ejército texcala les diera caza. Entonces, a una señal de Nezahualpili, el abrupto retumbar de los tambores hizo que las paredes del corredor se cerrasen, y en el tumulto de la batalla los sonidos se multiplicaron y crecieron en volumen: el choque de las armas al quebrarse unas con otras, los ruidos sordos de las armas contra los cuerpos, los gritos de guerra inspiradores de miedo como el aullido del coyote, el gruñido del jaguar, los chillidos del águila y los gritos del búho. Podía imaginarme a los acolhua tratando de refrenar su vehemencia y su empuje, mientras que los texcalteca peleaban desesperadamente con todas sus fuerzas y destreza matando sin ningún remordimiento.

Me hubiera gustado verlo, pues hubiera sido una instructiva exhibición de la destreza guerrera de los acolhua. Por la naturaleza de la batalla, su destreza *tenía* que ser un gran arte. Pero había un declive enfrente de mí y el lugar de la batalla, los arbustos y las copas de los árboles, una cortina gris de lluvia y por supuesto mi corta visión. Estaba pensando en si podría tratar de ir más cerca, pero fui interrumpido en mis pensamientos por un golpecito trémulo dado en mi hombro.

Aun estando protectoramente agachado, giré con rapidez y levanté mi lanza y por poco agujereo a Cózcatl antes de reconocerlo. El muchacho estaba también agachado a un lado, con un dedo sobre sus labios previniéndome. Con el aire que me quedaba jadeé o más silbé: «¡Maldita sea, Cózcatl! ¿Qué estás haciendo aquí?»

Él susurró: «Siguiéndolo a usted, mi amo. He estado cerca de usted toda la noche. Pensé que necesitaría un par de ojos mejores.»

«¡Majadero impertinente! Todavía no tengo...»

«No, amo; no todavía —dijo—. Pero en estos momentos, sí. Un enemigo se aproxima. Él le hubiera visto antes de que usted pudiera verlo a él.»

«¿Qué? ¿Un enemigo?» Me agaché todavía más.

«Sí, mi amo. Un campeón Jaguar con todas sus insignias. Debió de haber escapado a la emboscada —dijo Cózcatl arriesgándose a levantar la cabeza lo suficiente como para echar una mirada—. Yo creo que piensa rodear en un círculo y caer sobre nuestros hombres en una dirección inesperada.»

«Mira otra vez —dije con urgencia—. Dime exactamente dónde está y hacia dónde se dirige.»

Mi pequeño esclavo se alzó y se agachó otra vez rápidamente y dijo: «Está quizás a cuarenta largos pasos en línea directa de su hombro izquierdo y el río, mi amo. Se está moviendo muy lentamente, bien agachado, aunque no parece estar herido sino más bien tomando precauciones. Si continúa en la misma dirección, pasará entre los dos *mízquitin*, árboles, que están a diez pasos largos directamente enfrente de usted.»

Con esas instrucciones hasta un ciego podía interceptarlo. Dije: «Yo iré adonde están esos árboles. Tú quédate aquí vigilándolo discretamente. Si él se da cuenta de mis movimientos o tropiezo con uno de los arbustos, tú lo notarás. Grita y luego corre hacia la retaguardia.»

Dejé mi lanza y mi sobremanto tirado allí y sólo tomé mi *maquáhuitl*. Arrastrándome lo más pegado a la tierra como lo haría una serpiente, me moví directamente hacia el tronco de uno de los árboles que se alzaban a través de la lluvia. Los dos *mízquitin* se levantaban en medio de una alta maleza y bajos arbustos, si bien una casi imperceptible vereda de venado estaba claramente marcada. Supuse que el fugitivo texcaltécatl estaba siguiendo esa senda. No escuchando ninguna señal de aviso por parte de Cózcatl, pensé que estaba en una posición desapercibida para el enemigo y me puse en cuclillas en la base de un árbol, conservando ésta entre su posición y la mía. Sosteniendo mi *maquáhuitl* con los dos puños, la llevé hacia atrás y abajo de mi hombro, paralela a la tierra, sosteniéndola equilibradamente.

A través del ruido de la llovizna, sólo oí el débil rozamiento de hierbas y ramas. Luego el chapotear de unas sandalias fangosas, el suave rasguñar de las garras del jaguar que se escuchaban en la tierra directamente enfrente del lugar en donde yo estaba escondido. Un momento después, un pie y luego otro estuvo junto a éste. El hombre se puso al amparo entre los árboles, debió de haber corrido el riesgo de levantarse totalmente y mirar alrededor para ver cuál era su posición.

Balanceé la hoja alada de mi espada como ya una vez la había balanceado sobre el tronco del *nopali*, y el campeón, como el cacto, pareció estar suspendido y vacilante en el aire un momento antes de que se estrellara completamente sobre la tierra. Sus pies dentro de sus sandalias se quedaron sosteniéndose en el lugar en donde él había estado, cortados abajo de los tobillos. En un momento estuve sobre él, pateando lejos su *maquáhuitl* que él todavía empuñaba y extendiendo la parte no afilada de mi espada contra su garganta, mientras jadeaba diciendo las palabras rituales de un captor a su cautivo. En mi tiempo, nosotros no decíamos ninguna cosa tan cruda como: «Usted es mi prisionero.» Siempre decíamos cortésmente, como yo le dije en aquellos momentos al campeón caído: «Usted es mi hijo muy amado.»

Él gruño con encono: «¡Entonces se testigo de que maldigo a todos los dioses y todo lo que ellos han conseguido!» Sin embargo, su explosión era fácilmente comprensible. Después de todo, él era un *tlamahuichíhuani* de la selecta orden del Jaguar y había sido cortado por los pies, en su único momento de descuido, por un joven guerrero obviamente bruto y no adiestrado, un *yaoquizqui*, el rango más inferior. Yo sabía eso. Si nos hubiéramos encontrado cara a cara, él hubiera podido desmenuzarme a su placer, parte por parte. Él también lo sabía y su cara estaba púrpura y rechinaba los dientes. Pero al fin su afrenta y humillación decrecieron hacia la resignación y contestó las palabras tradicionales del que se rendía: «Usted es mi reverendo padre.»

Quité mi arma de su cuello y él se sentó, mirando pétreamente la sangre que manaba de sus muñones y a sus dos pies que todavía se sostenían pacientemente, casi sin sangrar uno al lado del otro sobre la vereda de venado, enfrente de él. Su traje de campeón Jaguar, si bien mojado por la lluvia y manchado por el fango, era todavía una cosa digna de verse. La piel moteada que colgaba del yelmo, que era la cabeza del animal, estaba confeccionada de tal manera que las piernas y patas fronteras del animal servían de mangas, bajando por los brazos del hombre en donde las garras sonaban sobre sus muñecas. Al caer no se había roto la correa que sostenía sobre su antebrazo izquierdo el escudo redondo de brillantes plumas.

Hubo otro sonido en la hierba y Cózcatl se nos unió, diciendo suavemente, pero con orgullo: «Mi amo acaba de tomar su primer prisionero de guerra, sin ninguna ayuda.»

«Y no quiero que muera —dije, todavía jadeante por la excitación y no por el esfuerzo—. Está sangrando gravemente.»

«Quizás los muñones puedan ser atados fuertemente», sugirió el hombre, con su pesado acento náhuatl de Texcala.

Cózcatl rápidamente se desató las correas de sus sandalias y yo las ligué fuertemente alrededor de cada una de las piernas del prisionero, por abajo de sus rodillas. El sangrado disminuyó a un goteo. Me levanté entre los árboles y miré y escuché como el campeón lo había hecho. Quedé algo sorprendido de lo que oí, lo cual no era mucho. El griterío de la batalla, hacia el sur, había disminuido ahora a no más de un murmullo como el de una multitud en la plaza de un mercado, entremezclado con algunos gritos de mando. Obviamente, durante mi pequeña escaramuza, la batalla principal había concluido.

Le dije al triste guerrero, a modo de condolencia: «Usted no es el único que ha sido hecho prisionero, mi amado hijo, parece que todo su ejército ha sido derrotado. —Él solamente gruñó—. Bueno, lo llevaré para que sus heridas sean atendidas. Creo que puedo cargarlo.»

«Sí, ya peso menos», dijo él sardónicamente.

Me agaché de espaldas a él y tomé sus piernas cortadas en mis brazos. Él dejó caer sus brazos alrededor de mi cuello y su escudo blasonado cubrió mi pecho como si éste fuera mío. Me levanté y me tambaleé ligeramente. Cózcatl ya había traído mi manto y mi lanza y en esos momentos estaba recogiendo mi escudo de mimbre y mi *maquáhuitl* cubierta de sangre. Tomando todas esas cosas bajo sus brazos, él recogió los pies amputados llevando cada uno en una mano y me siguió, mientras yo me bamboleaba a través de la lluvia. Caminé afanosamente hacia el sur, hacia los murmurantes sonidos, en donde la batalla finalmente había terminado y en donde se suponía que nuestro ejército estaría poniendo en orden la confusión resultante, haciendo que sus unidades se volvieran a formar, juntando a los cautivos texcalteca, ajustando las contingencias de ambos lados, disponiendo de los muertos y en general disponiéndose para regresar en desfile triunfal. A medio camino de ahí, encontré a varios miembros de mi compañía, ya que Glotón de Sangre los había estado llamando, haciéndoles salir de los lugares en donde habían estado en la noche, para marchar atrás del cuerpo principal del ejército.

«¡Perdido en Niebla! —me gritó el *quáchic*—. ¿Cómo te atreviste a desertar de tu puesto? ¿En dónde has...? —Entonces sus rugidos se callaron, pero su boca permaneció abierta tanto como sus ojos—. ¡Que sea condenado a Mictlan! ¡Mirad lo que el tesoro de mi estudiante ha traído! ¡Debo informar al comandante Xococ!» Y dando la vuelta se fue.

Los otros guerreros, mis compañeros me miraban a mí y a mi trofeo con pasmo y envidia. Uno de ellos me dijo: «Te ayudaré a cargarlo, Perdido en Niebla.»

«¡No!», jadeé y fue la única palabra que pude decir. Nadie reclamaría compartir el crédito de mi captura.

Y así, yo, llevando al taciturno campeón Jaguar, seguido por el jubiloso Cózcatl, escoltado por Xococ y Glotón de Sangre, orgullosamente dando grandes zancadas uno a cada lado de mí, llegué finalmente al cuerpo principal de los dos ejércitos, al lugar en donde la batalla había concluido. De un palo alto estaba colgando la bandera de rendición de los texcalteca: un cuadrado ancho de malla de oro, que parecía una pieza de red dorada para coger peces.

La escena no era de celebración, ni siquiera de tranquilo regocijo por la victoria. Aquellos guerreros, de ambos ejércitos, que no habían sido heridos o que estaban ligeramente heridos, yacían alrededor en posturas de extrema extenuación. Otros, tanto acolhua como texcalteca, no estaban acostados sino retorciéndose y contorsionándose y de ellos salía un coro desigual de gitos y lamentos de «*Yya, yyaha, yya ayya ouiya*», mientras los físicos se movían alrededor de ellos con sus medicinas y ungüentos, y mientras que los sacerdotes murmuraban sus oraciones. Unos cuantos hombres capaces estaban asistiendo a los físicos, mientras otros recogían por los alrededores las armas esparcidas, los cuerpos de los muertos y pedazos de partes de los cuerpos: manos, brazos, piernas y aun cabezas. Hubiera sido muy difícil para una persona ajena a esa batalla decir quiénes, allí, en aquella tierra de despojos y carnicería, eran los vencedores y quiénes los vencidos. Todo eso adornado con el olor mezclado de la sangre, el sudor, la fetidez de los cuerpos, los orines y las heces.

Cargado como iba, miraba con cuidado alrededor buscando a alguien con la suficiente autoridad a quien poder entregar mi cautivo. Sin embargo la noticia había llegado antes que yo y de repente me encontré frente a frente del jefe supremo, Nezahualpili. Estaba vestido como debía estarlo un Uey-Tlatoani, con un inmenso penacho de plumas en abanico y una larga capa de plumas multicolores, pero debajo de todo eso él llevaba la coraza acolchada y emplumada del campeón Águila y ésta estaba salpicada con manchas de sangre. Él no había estado solamente dirigiendo la batalla, sino que se había unido a ella para pelear. Xococ y Glotón de Sangre respetuosamente se quedaron a unos pasos detrás de mí, cuando Nezahualpili me saludó con una mano en alto.

Con gran alivio deposité a mi cautivo en tierra e hice un gesto cansado de presentación diciendo con lo último que me quedaba de aliento: «Mi señor, éste... éste es mi... muy amado hijo.»

«Y éste —dijo el campeón Jaguar con ironía, inclinando su cabeza hacia mí—, éste es mi reverendo padre. *Mixpantzinco*, Señor Orador.»

«Bien hecho, Mixtli —dijo Nezahualpili—. *Ximopanolti*, campeón Jaguar Tlaui-Cólotl.»

«Yo te saludo, viejo enemigo —dijo mi prisionero a mi señor—. Ésta es la primera vez que nosotros no nos encontramos con la obsidiana relampagueando entre nosotros en la batalla.»

«Y la última vez, según parece —dijo el Uey-Tlatoani, arrodillándose junto a él compasivamente—. Es una lástima. Te extrañaré. ¡Ah, qué duelos tan portentosos tuvimos tú y yo! En verdad no puedo recordar alguno que no haya terminado en empate o interrumpido por alguno de nuestros inferiores. —Suspiró—. A veces es tan triste perder a un buen adversario, que ha llegado a ser un héroe, tanto como perder a un buen amigo.»

Yo escuchaba esta conversación con cierto asombro. No se me había ocurrido antes notar la divisa de plumas trabajadas en el escudo de mi prisionero: Tlaui-Cólotl. Su nombre, que quería decir Escorpión-Armado, no significaba nada para mí, pero obviamente era famoso en el mundo profesional de los guerreros. Tlaui-Cólotl era uno de esos campeones de los que ya he hablado: un hombre cuyo renombre era tanto que lo traspasaba al hombre que finalmente lo vencía.

Escorpión-Armado le dijo a Nezahualpili: «Maté a cuatro de tus campeones, viejo enemigo, peleando abiertamente en tu fatal emboscada. Dos Águilas, un Jaguar y un Flecha, pero si hubiera sabido lo que mi *tonali* me tenía reservado... —y me dirigió una mirada de marcado desdén— me hubiera dejado capturar por uno de ellos.»

«Podrás pelear con otros campeones antes de morir —le dijo el Venerado Orador, tratando de consolarlo—. Yo me encargaré de eso. Atenderemos inmediatamente tus heridas.» Él se volvió y gritó a un físico que estaba atendiendo a un hombre cerca de ahí.

«Sólo un momento, mi señor», dijo el físico quien agachado sobre un guerrero acolhua trataba de acomodarle nuevamente la nariz que le había sido cortada, y afortunadamente recuperada, aunque un poco machacada y sucia por haber sido pisoteada. El cirujano la había cosido en el hoyo que había quedado en la cara del guerrero, usando una espina de maguey como aguja y uno de sus largos cabellos como hilo, pero las restitución se veía más espantosa que la herida inflingida. Entonces el físico, lanzando apresuradamente y con descuido una pasta de miel y sal sobre la nariz recién cosida, llegó rápidamente donde estaba mi prisionero.

«Desata esas correas de sus piernas —dijo al guerrero que le estaba ayudando y a otro—: Saca del fuego del brasero que está allá, unas brasas calientes.» Los muñones de Escorpión-Armado empezaron a sangrar lentamente otra vez, después a chorrear y luego a sangrar copiosamente cuando el ayudante regresó cargando un comal ancho y bajo lleno de brasas calientes al rojo vivo, sobre las cuales las llamas parpadeaban.

«Mi señor físico —dijo Cózcatl tratando de ayudar—. Aquí están sus pies.»

El físico resopló con exasperación: «Llévatelos lejos. Los pies no pueden ser pegados otra vez como las narices. —Al hombre herido le preguntó—: ¿Uno cada vez o los dos al mismo tiempo?»

«Como usted quiera —dijo con indiferencia Tlaui-Cólotl. Él jamás había gritado o gemido de dolor y tampoco lo hizo entonces, cuando el físico tomó cada uno de los muñones en cada una de sus manos y los metió al mismo tiempo dentro del comal de ardientes brasas. Cózcatl se volvió para no ver. La sangre siseó y formó una nube rojiza de vapor maloliente. La carne crepitó al quemarse y formó un humo azul que fue menos maloliente. Escorpión-Armado no emitió ningún sonido y miró todo el proceso con la misma calma con que lo hizo el físico, quien quitó de las brasas los muñones chamuscados y ennegrecidos. La quemadura cerró las heridas y cauterizó las venas cercenadas dejando totalmente de sangrar. El físico aplicó a los muñones bastante ungüento cicatrizante hecho de cera de abeja mezclada con yemas de huevos de pájaros, jugo de corteza de aliso y raíz de barbasco. Entonces se levantó y dijo: «El hombre no está en peligro de morir, mi señor, pero pasarán algunos días antes de que pueda recuperarse de la debilidad por haber perdido tanta sangre.»

Nezahualpili dijo: «Preparen una silla de manos para él. El eminente Tlaui-Cólotl encabezará la columna de prisioneros.» Luego se volvió a Xococ, lo miró fríamente y dijo:

«Nosotros los acolhua hemos perdido muchos hombres hoy y muchos más morirán antes de llegar a nuestra tierra. El ejército de Texcala perdió tantos como nosotros, pero los prisioneros supervivientes llegan a miles. Su Venerado Orador Auítzotl deberá estar muy contento del trabajo que los acolhua hemos realizado en lugar de él y por su dios. Si él y Chimalpópoca de Tlacopan hubiesen enviado verdaderos ejércitos, habríamos podido conquistar y anexionar toda la tierra completa de Quautexcálan.

—Él se encogió de hombros—. Ah, bien. ¿Cuántos prisioneros capturaron ustedes los mexica?»

El campeón Xococ arrastró sus pies, carraspeó y apuntando a Tlaui-Cólotl murmuró: «Mi señor, usted está viendo el único. Quizá los tecpaneca agarraron unos pocos extranjeros más, pero todavía no lo sé. Pero de los mexica —y él me apuntó con un dedo—, sólo este *yaoquizqui*...»

«Pues como usted sabe bien, ya no es más un *yaoquizqui* —dijo Nezahualpili mordazmente—. Su primera captura lo ha convertido en un *iyac* en rango. Así es que este único cautivo, el que ustedes oyeron decir por sí mismo que mató a cuatro campeones acolhua; pues permítanme decirles esto: Escorpión-Armado jamás se tomó la molestia de contar sus víctimas a menos que se trataran de campeones. Sin embargo, en su existencia es probable que pueda contar cientos de acolhua, mexica y tecpaneca.»

Glotón de Sangre estaba lo suficientemente impresionado como para murmurar: «Perdido en Niebla es un verdadero héroe.»

«No —dije—. No fue tanto el golpe de mi espada como un golpe de buena suerte y no lo hubiera podido hacer sin Cózcatl y...»

«Pero lo hiciste —dijo Nezahualpili silenciándome. Y dirigiéndose a Xococ, continuó—: Su Uey-Tlatoani debería de recompensar a este joven con algo más alto que el rango de *iyac*. En este encuentro, él sólo ha sostenido la reputación de valor e iniciativa de los mexica. Yo sugiero que usted lo trate con más respeto y que personalmente lo presente con Auítzotl, junto con una carta que personalmente yo le escribiré.»

«Como usted lo ordene, mi señor —dijo Xococ, casi literalmente besando la tierra—. Estamos orgullosos de nuestro Perdido en Niebla.»

«¡Entonces llámenle por otro nombre! Y basta de perder el tiempo. Ponga a sus tropas en orden, Xococ. Primero usted y luego los acuchilladores y amarradores. ¡Muévanse!»

Xococ sintió como si le abofeteara la cara, que en realidad así era, pero tanto él como Glotón de Sangre se fueron trotando obedientemente. Como ya lo he dicho antes, los amarradores eran los que ataban o se hacían cargo de los prisioneros, así ninguno de ellos podría escapar. Los acuchilladores fueron alrededor del área de batalla y más allá, buscando y dando muerte a aquellos heridos que estaban más allá de todo alivio. Cuando eso estuvo hecho, juntaron los cuerpos y los quemaron, aliados y enemigos juntos, cada uno de ellos con un pedacito de jade en su boca o en su mano.

Por unos momentos Nezahualpili y yo nos quedamos solos. Él dijo: «Hoy has hecho una hazaña como para sentirse orgulloso... y también avergonzado. Tú rendiste sabiéndote conservar salvo y sano al hombre más temido de todos nuestros oponentes en este campo de batalla. Y tú trajiste a este noble campeón al más innoble fin. Aun cuando Escorpión-Armado alcance el destino de los héroes en el más allá, su felicidad eterna tendrá eternamente un sabor agrio, ya que todos sus compañeros sabrán que fue vencido ridículamente por un inexperto y cegato recluta.»

«Mi señor —dije—. Yo solamente hice lo que pensé que era correcto.»

«Como siempre lo has hecho antes —dijo y suspiró—. Dejando a otros los sabores amargos. No te culpo, Mixtli. Hace mucho tiempo que se profetizó que tu *tonali* era conocer la verdad acerca de las cosas de este mundo y hacer conocer la verdad. Quisiera pedirte sólo una cosa.»

Incliné la cabeza y dije: «Mi señor no pide nada a un plebeyo. Él ordena y es obedecido.»

«Lo que te voy a pedir no puede ser ordenado. Mixtli, te voy a suplicar que seas gentil, aun más, que seas cauteloso en la forma en que manejas la rectitud y la verdad. Estas cosas pueden cortar tan cruelmente como una hoja de obsidiana. Y, como una hoja, también, puede cortar al hombre que las empuña.»

Él se alejó de mí abruptamente y llamando a un mensajero-veloz le dijo: «Ponte un manto verde y trenza tu pelo en la manera que significa que llevas buenas noticias. Toma un escudo nuevo y una *maquáhuitl* limpia. Corre a Tenochtitlan y en tu camino hacia el palacio, corre blandiendo el escudo y la espada por todas las calles que puedas, así la gente se regocijará y arrojarán flores a tu paso. Deja saber a Auítzotl que ha obtenido la victoria y los prisioneros que él quería.»

Y las últimas palabras que dijo Nezahualpili no fueron para el mensajero, sino para él mismo. «Así la vida y la muerte y aun el mismo nombre de Muñeca de Jade, será olvidado.»

✠

Nezahualpili y su ejército se separaron allí mismo de nosotros y partieron por el mismo camino de regreso por el cual habían venido. Los contingentes mexica y tecpaneca, además de la larga columna de prisioneros, nos dirigimos directamente hacia el oeste por un ruta más corta, hacia Tenochtitlan, a través del paso entre los picos del Tlaloctépelt y el Ixtaccíhuatl, y desde allí a todo lo largo de la costa sur del Lago de Texcoco. Fue una caminata lenta ya que muchos de los heridos cojeaban o como Tlaui-Cólotl, tenían que ser cargados, pero no fue una jornada difícil. Por una parte, la lluvia había cesado y al fin disfrutábamos de días soleados y noches templadas. Por otra parte, a lo largo del nivel salino que bordea la ribera del lago, con las aguas serenas y murmurantes a nuestra derecha y las pendientes suaves de espesos bosques que susurraban a nuestra izquierda.

¿Les sorprende a ustedes, reverendos frailes, oírme hablar acerca de bosques tan cerca de la ciudad? Ah, sí. No hace todavía mucho tiempo en que este Valle de Mexico deslumbraba enteramente con el verdor de sus árboles: los cipreses, los dulces castaños, acacias, álamos temblones, laureles, mimosas. Yo no sé nada acerca de su país, España, mis señores, o de su provincia de Castilla, pero deben de ser tierras secas y desoladas. Yo he visto a sus guardabosques despojar cada una de nuestras colinas de su verdor, para tener madera o leña. Ellos las han desnudado de todo su verdor y de todos sus árboles que han crecido por gavillas de años. Entonces se hacen hacia atrás y miran admirados la tierra gris y yerma que ha quedado y suspiran nostálgicamente diciendo: «¡Ah, Castilla!»

Nosotros llegamos al fin al promontorio que estaba entre los lagos de Texcoco y Xochimilco, lo que fue en otros tiempos las extensas tierras de los culhua. Nosotros ajustamos nuestra formación de marcha para representar un verdadero espectáculo, mientras cruzábamos por el pueblo de Ixtapalapan y cuando salimos del pueblo, Glotón de Sangre me preguntó: «¿Hace algún tiempo que no has visto Tenochtitlan, no es así?»

«Sí —dije—. Más o menos catorce años.»

«La encontrarás cambiada. Quizá más que nunca. Será visible desde la próxima elevación del camino.» Cuando alcanzamos esa elevación, él extendió su brazo en un gesto expansivo y dijo: «¡Vela ahí!» Por supuesto que pude ver la gran isla-ciudad más allá, brillando de blancura como la recordaba, pero no pude darme cuenta de ningún otro detalle o de algún cambio excepto, cuando entrecerrando los ojos esforzadamente, me pude dar cuenta que parecía quizá más luminosamente blanca. «La Gran Pirámide —dijo reverentemente Glotón de Sangre—. Debes sentirte orgulloso de haber contribuido con tu valor a su dedicación.»

Deslizándonos por el promotorio llegamos al pueblo de Mexicaltzinco y desde allí al camino-puente que se extendía hacia el oeste a través del agua, hacia Tenochtitlan. La ancha avenida de piedra artesonada que cruzaba el lago era tan amplia que podían caminar veinte hombres juntos, unos a un lado de los otros, confortablemente, pero nosotros alineamos a nuestros prisioneros de cuatro en cuatro, con guardias caminando a lo largo en intervalos. No hicimos eso para que nuestro desfile fuese más impresionante o para alargar la fila, sino que fue completamente necesario, ya que el puente estaba totalmente abarrotado de gente que nos saludaba en nuestra entrada triunfal. La muchedumbre nos vitoreaba, nos ovacionaba y nos arrojaba flores como si la victoria hubiera sido lograda totalmente por nosotros, los pocos mexica y tecpaneca.

A la mitad del camino hacia la ciudad el camino-puente se ampliaba en una vasta plataforma sobre la cual estaba la fortaleza de Acachinanco, como una defensa en contra de cualquier invasor que tratara de llegar a Tenochtitlan por esa ruta. La fortaleza, sostenida totalmente por pilones, eran tan grande como casi los dos pueblos que acabábamos de pasar a través de la tierra firme. La guarnición de sus guerreros también se unió a darnos la bienvenida, con tambores y trompetas, con gritos guerreros, golpeando sus espadas sobre sus escudos, pero yo los miré con desdén porque ellos no estuvieron con nosotros en la batalla.

Cuando los otros y yo que íbamos al frente de la columna entramos a paso largo en la gran plaza central de Tenochtitlan, la cola de nuestra formación de prisioneros salía apenas marchando de Mexicaltzinco, dos y media largas carreras atrás de nosotros. En la plaza, El Corazón del Único Mundo, nosotros los mexica salimos de la columna y dejamos a la izquierda a los guerreros tecpaneca. Ellos hicieron que los prisioneros giraran hacia la izquierda y marcharan a lo largo de la avenida hacia el camino-puente del oeste que se dirige hacia Tlacopan. Los cautivos serían acuartelados en algún lugar de la tierra firme fuera de la ciudad, hasta el día señalado para la dedicación de la pirámide.

La pirámide. Me volví a verla y me quedé boquiabierto como lo había hecho cuando era un niño. Durante mi vida, en algunos lugares, vi más grandes *icpac* tlamanacaltin, pero nunca tan luminosamente brillantes y nuevos. Éste era el edificio más alto de Tenochtitlan y dominaba toda la ciudad. Debía de ser un espectáculo digno de verse para aquellos que tenían buenos ojos; contemplarlo a lo lejos a través de las aguas, ya que los templos gemelos se asentaban allí en su cumbre orgullosos, arrogantes, espléndidos en su altura, por encima de todo lo visible a través de la ciudad hasta las montañas de la tierra firme. Sin embargo, tuve muy poco tiempo para echarle una mirada o darme cuenta de cualquier otra nueva edificación desde la última vez que había estado en El Corazón del Único Mundo. Un joven de palacio se abrió paso a codazos entre el gentío, preguntando ansiosamente por el Campeón Flecha Xococ.

«Yo soy», dijo Xococ, dándose importancia.

Él dijo: «El Venerado Orador Auítzotl le ordena que se presente ante él inmediatamente, mi señor y que traiga con usted al *iyac* llamado Tliléctic-Mixtli.»

«Oh —dijo Xococ, ceñudo y de mala gana—. Muy bien. ¿En dónde estás, Perdido en Niebla? Quiero decir Iyac Mixtli. Ven conmigo.»

Yo pensé que antes deberíamos darnos un baño e ir a una casa de vapor y vestir ropas limpias antes de presentarnos ante el Uey-Tlatoani, pero sin ninguna protesta lo acompañé. Mientras el joven nos conducía a través de la multitud, Xococ me dio instrucciones: «Haz tus reverencias humilde y graciosamente, pero después discúlpate y retírate, así el Venerado Orador podrá escuchar mi relato sobre la victoria.»

Alrededor de la plaza se distinguía el nuevo Muro de la Serpiente, rodeándola. Construido con piedra, aplanado con argamasa de yeso blanco, se levantaba dos veces más alto que la estatura de un hombre y en su elevada orilla ondulaban las curvas de una serpiente. El muro, tanto por dentro como por fuera, estaba adornado con un diseño de piedras que sobresalían, cada una de ellas tallada y pintada representando la cabeza de una serpiente. Estaba dividido en tres lugares de donde partían las tres grandes avenidas, hacia el norte, el oeste y el sur, fuera de la plaza. A intervalos había unos portones grandes de madera que conducían hacia los edificios más grandes que estaban afuera de su recinto. Uno de éstos era un palacio nuevo construido para Auítzotl, más allá de la esquina noreste del Muro de la Serpiente. Era mucho más grande que cualquiera de los que habían tenido los anteriores gobernantes de Tenochtitlan, mucho más que el palacio de Nezahualpili en Texcoco y naturalmente más lujoso y bien elaborado. Ya que había sido construido recientemente, estaba decorado con todos los últimos estilos de arte y contenía casi todas las conveniencias modernas. Por ejemplo, en los pisos altos, las habitaciones tenían techos móviles que se deslizaban para abrirse y dejar entrar la luz del día cuando el tiempo era bueno.

Quizás lo más notable de todo era la cavidad abovedada y cuadrada que había sido tallada y que formaba parte del palacio mismo, construida sobre uno de los canales de la ciudad. Así se podía entrar en el edificio desde la plaza, a través del portón del Muro de la Serpiente o se podía entrar por canoa. Un noble desocupado podía pasear en su acojinado *acali* o un botero plebeyo, llevando una carga de *camotes*, podía tomar también esta deliciosa y hospitalaria ruta de agua, a cualquier lado que él se dirigiera. En su camino, guiaría su canoa a ravés de un corredor subterráneo deslumbrante de nuevos murales pintados, luego a través de los lujuriosos jardines de la terraza del palacio de Auítzotl, para seguir por otro paraje cavernoso lleno de estatuas talladas, nuevas e impresionantes, antes de emerger otra vez hacia el canal público.

El joven nos guió, casi corriendo, a través del portón del Muro de la Serpiente hacia el palacio, después a lo largo de galerías y alrededor de pasillos, hacia una habitación cuyos únicos adornos consistían en armas de caza y guerra colgados de las paredes. Las pieles de jaguares, ocelotes, cuguares y caimanes, se utilizaban como tapetes para el piso y cubrían las bancas y las sillas bajas. Auítzotl, un hombre de cuerpo, cabeza y cara cuadrados, estaba sentado sobre un elevado trono adoselado. Estaba completamente cubierto con una afelpada y pesada piel de uno de los osos gigantes que habitaban en las montañas del norte, muy lejos de estas tierras; la fiera que ustedes los españoles llaman oso pardo o parduzco. Su maciza cabeza alzábase sobre la del Uey-Tlatoani y su abierto hocico gruñón mostraba unos colmillos del tamaño de mis dedos. El rostro de Auítzotl justamente abajo, tenía un gesto igualmente fiero.

El joven, Xococ y yo nos arrodillamos haciendo el gesto de besar la tierra. Cuando Auítzotl ásperamente nos ordenó levantarnos, el campeón Flecha dijo: «Como usted lo ordenó, Venerado Orador, traje al *iyac* de nombre...»

Auítzotl le interrumpió bruscamente: «También traes una carta de nuestro hermano gobernante Nezahualpili. Dánosla. Cuando regreses a tu cuartel de mando, Xococ, marca en tu lista que el Iyac Míxtli ha sido elevado, por nuestro mandato, al rango te *tequíua*. Puedes retirarte.»

«Pero, mi señor —dijo Xococ, herido en su amor propio—. ¿No desea usted escuchar el relato de la batalla en Texcala?»

«¿Qué puedes saber acerca de ella? ¿Excepto que marchaste de aquí y regresaste a casa otra vez? Lo escucharemos de Tequíua Míxtli. He dicho que te retires, Xococ. Vete.»

El campeón me miró con odio y se deslizó hacia atrás de la habitación sin dar la espalda, haciendo el gesto de besar la tierra todo el tiempo. No presté mucha atención a eso, estando de algún modo deslumbrado. Después de haber servido al ejército por menos de un mes, había sido promovido a un nivel al cual la mayoría de los hombres debían pelear en muchas batallas para obtenerlo. El rango de *tequíua,* que quiere decir «animal de rapiña», era generalmente otorgado solamente a aquellos que mataban o capturaban por lo menos cuatro enemigos en una batalla.

Yo asistí a esa entrevista sintiéndome bastante nervioso, no sabiendo qué esperar de ella, ya que había estado tan estrechamente relacionado a la hija difunta del Uey-Tlatoani y a su caída. Sin embargo, parecía ser que él no me asociaba a ese escándalo; quizá porque después de todo había alguna ventaja en tener un nombre tan común como Mixtli. Me sentí aliviado cuando él me miró tan benignamente como su severo semblante se lo permitía. También estaba intrigado por su forma de expresarse. Era la primera vez que escuchaba a un hombre solo que cuando se refería a sí mismo, utilizaba el «nosotros» y el «nuestro».

«La carta de Nezahualpili —dijo, después de que la hubo leído— es considerablemente más lisonjera para ti, joven guerrero, que para nosotros. Él sugiere sarcásticamente que la próxima vez le enviemos varias compañías de beligerantes escribanos como tú, en lugar de flechas desafiladas como Xococ —Auítzotl sonrió tanto como él podía, pareciéndose más a la cabeza de oso que estaba sobre su trono—. Él sugiere también, que con suficientes refuerzos, esta guerra finalmente hubiera subyugado la tierra de los turbulentos texcalteca. ¿Estás de acuerdo?»

«Difícilmente no estaría de acuerdo, mi señor, con un comandante tan experimentado como el Venerado Orador Nezahualpili. Yo sé que sus tácticas derrotaron totalmente al ejército texcala. Si hubiéramos podido presionar el sitio, cualquier otra defensa subsecuente hubiera venido a ser demasiado débil.»

«Tú eres conocedor de palabras —dijo Auítzotl—. ¿Podrías escribir para nosotros una narración detallada de las posiciones y movimiento de las diversas fuerzas envueltas? ¿Con mapas comprensibles?»

«Sí, mi Señor Orador. Puedo hacerlo.»

«Hazlo. Tienes seis días antes de que la ceremonia de dedicación al templo se lleve a efecto, cuando todo trabajo será interrumpido y tú tendrás el privilegio de presentar a tu ilustre prisionero a su Muerte-Florida. Joven, haz que el mayordomo de palacio lleve a este hombre a sus habitaciones y que le provea de todo lo necesario para su trabajo. Puedes retirarte, Tequíua Mixtli.»

Mis habitaciones eran tan cómodas y confortables como las que había disfrutado en Texcoco. Como éstas estaban en un segundo piso, tenía la ventaja de un tragaluz movible. El mayordomo del palacio me ofreció un sirviente, pero yo mandé al criado a por Cózcatl para que éste me sirviera en su lugar y después envié a Cózcatl a conseguir para cada uno de nosotros ropas, mientras me bañaba y tomaba vapor restregándome varias veces.

Primero dibujé el mapa. Ocupaba varias páginas dobladas que se extendían considerablemente. Empecé con el glifo de la ciudad de Texcoco, luego con las marcas de pequeñas huellas negras de pies, indicando la ruta de nuestra jornada desde allí hacia el este, con estilizados dibujos de montañas y una marca en cada lugar en que nos detuvimos para pasar la noche, y finalmente el glifo del río en el cual la batalla se llevó a efecto. Allí asenté el símbolo universalmente reconocido de opresión en una conquista: el dibujo de un templo ardiendo en llamas, aunque por supuesto no habíamos destruido, ni siquiera visto un *teocali*. Luego dibujé el símbolo de la toma de prisioneros: un dibujo de un guerrero agarrando a otro por los cabellos. Después dibujé las huellas de pies, alternativamente en rojo y negro para indicar quiénes eran los captores y quiénes los cautivos, trazando nuestra marcha hacia el oeste, hacia Tenochtitlan.

Sin salir para nada de mis habitaciones y tomando todos mis alimentos allí, terminé el mapa en dos días. Entonces empecé con la más completa narración de las estrategias y tácticas de los texcalteca y de los acolhua, por lo menos tanto como yo lo había podido observar y entender. Un mediodía Cózcatl vino a mi soleada habitación de trabajo y me pidió permiso para interrumpirme.

Me dijo: «Amo, una gran canoa ha llegado de Texcoco y atracado en el canal de los jardines de palacio. El jefe de los remeros dice que trae sus pertenencias.»

Me sentí muy feliz al oír eso. Tiempo atrás, cuando dejé el palacio de Nezahualpili para unirme a las tropas, no creí correcto tomar conmigo ninguno de los trajes finos y otros regalos que me habían dado antes de ser desterrado. De todas maneras, difícilmente los hubiera podido llevar conmigo a la guerra. Así, después de que Cózcatl pudo conseguir ropa prestada para los dos, al regresar de la guerra tanto él como yo no poseíamos nada más que nuestros mantos, taparrabos y sandalias extremadamente desgastados y deshonrosos, y nuestros pesados *tlamitin* que habíamos llevado a la guerra y regresado con ellos. Le dije al muchacho: «Éste es un gesto muy solícito y probablemente debemos dar las gracias a la Señora de Tolan por ello. Espero que también te hayan mandado tu ropa. Consigue al *tamemi* de palacio para que te ayude a traer nuestros bultos aquí.»

Cuando regresó, venía acompañado del jefe de remeros y de toda una hilera de *tamémine*, cargadores, y mi sorpresa fue tanta que olvidé totalmente mi trabajo. Nunca había poseído la cantidad de cosas que los portadores habían traído y amontonado en mis habitaciones. Me eran reconocibles un bulto largo y otro pequeño diestramente atados y protegidos con esterillas. Mis ropas y otras cosas que me pertenecían estaban en el grande, incluyendo el recuerdo de mi hermana desaparecida, su pequeña figurita de la diosa Xochiquétzal. Las ropas de Cózcatl estaban en el bulto más pequeño. Pero los otros fardos y bultos no los podía considerar míos, así es que protesté diciendo que debía de haber algún error en la entrega.

El jefe de remeros me dijo: «Mi señor, cada uno viene rotulado. ¿No es éste su nombre?»

Efectivamente. Cada fardo o bulto por separado llevaba atada una hoja de papel de corteza en la cual iba escrito mi nombre. Había bastantes Mixtli en ese lugar y no pocos Tliléctic-Mixtli, pero cada rótulo llevaba mi nombre completo: Chicome-Xóchitl Tliléctic-Mixtli. Les pedí a cada uno de los presentes que me ayudaran a deshacerlos, así, si el contenido probaba que había algún error en la entrega los mismos trabajadores podrían ayudarme a empaquetarlos de nuevo para ser devueltos.

Un fardo de fibra de esterilla al ser abierto reveló que contenía, diestramente acomodados, cuarenta mantos para hombre del más fino algodón, ricamente bordados. Otro contenía el mismo número de faldas de mujer, teñidas en color carmesí con la pintura que se extraía arduamente de los insectos. Otro bulto mostraba el mismo número de blusas para mujer, laboriosamente trabajadas a mano en una tela como filigrana, tanto que parecían casi totalmente transparentes. Había también otro fardo que contenía un rollo de algodón tejido, que si se extendía, tendría unos dos brazos de ancho por más o menos doscientos pasos de largo. A pesar de que el algodón era blanco y sin ningún adorno, estaba hecho de una sola pieza, sin costura y por lo tanto principesco e inapreciable, sólo por ese tipo de trabajo; posiblemente años de labor de algún tejedor amante de su trabajo. El bulto más pesado de todos contenía pedazos en bruto de *itztétl* y pedazos de roca de obsidiana sin trabajar. Los tres bultos más ligeros eran los de más valor, ya que en ellos habían mercancías en moneda corriente. Uno era un saco que contenía de doscientas a trescientas piezas de estaño y cobre en forma cruciforme y cada pieza valía ochocientas semillas de cacao. El tercero era un hato de cuatro cañas de plumas, cada una de ellas traslúcidas, cubiertas con pedacitos de *óli*, hule, para poder cubrirlas con un filo centellante de oro puro en polvo.

Yo le dije al botero: «Hubiera deseado que esto no fuera un error, pero claramente lo es. Devuélvalo. Esta fortuna debe de pertenecer al tesoro de Nezahualpili.»

«No es así —dijo él obstinadamente—. Fue el mismo Venerado Orador quien me ordenó traer esto y él personalmente vio que todo se cargara en mi embarcación. Lo único que tengo que llevar de regreso, es un mensaje diciendo que todo fue entregado adecuadamente. Por favor, mi señor, tiene usted que poner aquí el glifo de su firma.»

Yo aún no podía creer lo que mis ojos veían ni lo que mis oídos escuchaban, pero me era difícil protestar más. Todavía deslumbrado, firmé la nota que me tendía y él y los cargadores se fueron. Cózcatl y yo nos quedamos estáticos mirando las riquezas desembaladas. Finalmente el muchachito dijo:

«Solamente puede ser un último regalo del Señor Nezahualpili, mi amo.»

«Pudiera ser —concedí—. Él me adiestró para llegar a ser un palaciego y después tuvo que mandarme flotando a la deriva. Y él es un hombre de conciencia. Así es que ahora, quizá, me provee de las cosas con las cuales podría dedicarme a alguna otra ocupación.»

«¡Ocupación! —chilló Cózcatl—. ¿Quiere decir trabajar, mi amo? ¿Por qué habría usted de trabajar? Aquí hay todo lo suficiente para mantenerle confortablemente por todo lo que le queda de vida. A usted, a una esposa, a una familia y a un esclavo fiel. —Agregó esto traviesamente, pero no del todo en chanza—: Usted un día me dijo que construiría una mansión de noble y me haría Maestro de las Llaves.»

«Detén tu lengua —le dije—. Si todo lo que deseara fuera holgazanear, muy bien hubiera podido dejar que Escorpión-Armado me enviara a *mí* al más allá. Y en este momento tengo el propósito de hacer muchas cosas. Lo único que tengo que decidir es qué es lo que prefiero hacer.»

Cuando terminé el relato de la batalla, un día antes de la ceremonia de la dedicación de la pirámide, bajé encaminándome hacia la sala de trofeos de caza de Auítzotl, en donde me había entrevistado con él por primera vez. Pero el mayordomo del palacio, medio borracho, me interceptó y tomó mi relato en lugar de Auítzotl.

«El Venerado Orador está ocupado como anfitrión de los muchos nobles que han venido desde tierras lejanas para la ceremonia —dijo el hombre con voz estropajosa—. Todos los palacios alrededor de la plaza están atestados de gobernantes forasteros y de sus comitivas. No sé dónde ni cómo podremos acomodar más. Sin embargo, estaré al pendiente de que Auítzotl tenga esta narración suya cuando él la pueda leer con tranquilidad. Él le volverá a llamar para otra entrevista cuando ya todo se haya aquietado otra vez.» Y se fue bulliciosamente llevándose mis papeles.

Ya que por casualidad me encontraba en la planta baja, me pregunté si esas habitaciones eran accesibles al público para admirar su arquitectura y decorado. Finalmente me encontré en los amplios corredores de estatuas, a través y en medio de los cuales fluía el canal. Las paredes y el techo relumbraban como lentejuelas por los reflejos de luz del agua. Varios botes de carga pasaron mientras yo estaba allí; sus remeros admiraban, tanto como yo lo estaba haciendo, las diversas esculturas de Auítzotl y de sus principales esposas, la del dios protector Huitzilopochtli y las de otros numerosos dioses y diosas. La mayoría de ellos estaban muy bien hechos y diestramente trabajados, como debían ser: cada uno llevaba grabado el glifo del halcón del ya desaparecido escultor Tlatli.

Como él anteriormente lo había predicho, años atrás, su trabajo casi no necesitaba de firma; sus estatuas de los dioses eran en verdad muy diferentes de aquellas que a través de generaciones habían sido imitadas y hechas en réplica por escultores menos imaginativos. Su visión particular quizás había sido más evidente en su concepción de Coatlicue, la diosa madre del dios Huitzilopochtli. El pesado objeto de piedra se alzaba más o menos tres veces más alto de lo que yo era y, mirándolo hacia arriba, sentí que mis cabellos se erizaban del miedo imponente que inspiraba.

Ya que Coatlicue era, después de todo, la madre del dios de la guerra, la mayoría de los artistas anteriores la habían representado con un gesto ceñudo, pero en su forma siempre había sido representada como una *mujer*. No así en la concepción de Tlatli. Su Coatlicue no tenía cabeza, en su lugar, sobre sus hombros sobresalían dos grandes cabezas de serpientes que se encontraban como si se besaran, para formar su cara: el único ojo visible de cada serpiente daba a Coatlicue dos ojos feroces, sus bocas al juntarse daban a Coatlicue una boca ancha llena de colmillos sonriendo en una mueca horrible. Llevaba un collar del que pendía una calavera, sus manos entreabiertas contenían corazones humanos desgarrados. Sus ropas inferiores eran hechas completamente por culebras retorciéndose y sus pies semejaban los talones y las garras de alguna bestia inmensa. Era la imagen de una deidad femenina que aunque horrenda era única y original, y yo creo que sólo un hombre que no podía amar a las mujeres, pudo haber tallado una diosa tan titánicamente monstruosa.

Seguí por el canal fuera del recinto, bajo los sauces llorones que colgaban del jardín del patio de palacio y hacia la cámara al otro lado de éste, en donde las paredes estaban cubiertas por murales; la mayoría eran pinturas de hazañas militares y acciones cívicas hechas por Auítzotl antes y después de su ascensión al trono: él como el más prominente y activo participante en varias batallas, él supervisando personalmente los últimos toques de los dos templos en lo alto de la Gran Pirámide. Sin embargo, las pinturas parecían vivas, no estáticas; estaban hechas con todo detalle y coloreadas con arte. Como ya lo esperaba, los murales eran mejores que cualquier otra pintura moderna que yo hubiera podido ver antes. Como ya me lo había imaginado, cada uno llevaba en la parte más baja del rincón derecho la firma de Chimali; la huella rojo-sangre de su mano.

Me pregunté a mí mismo si él habría regresado ya a Tenochtitlan, si nos encontraríamos y cómo lo haría él para matarme, si lo hacía. Así es que con este pensamiento fui en busca de mi pequeño Cózcatl y le di instrucciones:

«Tú conoces de vista al artista Chimali y sabes que él tiene una razón para desear mi muerte. Yo tengo la obligación de presentarme mañana, así es que no puedo estar viendo por encima y atrás de mi hombro para pescar un asesino. Quiero que circules entre el gentío y luego me vengas a prevenir si ves a Chimali. Mañana, entre la muchedumbre y la confusión, él tendrá la oportunidad de poderme acuchillar sin ser observado y huir sin dejar sospecha.»

«Él no hará eso si yo lo veo primero —dijo Cózcatl adictamente—. Y le prometo que si él se presenta, yo lo veré. ¿No he sido útil para usted, mi amo, siendo sus ojos anteriormente?»

Le dije: «En verdad que sí lo has sido, mi pequeño, y tu vigilancia y lealtad no quedarán sin recompensa.»

✠

Sí, Su Ilustrísima, yo sé que usted está interesado particularmente en nuestras ceremonias religiosas, ya que está usted aquí presente en esta ocasión. Sin embargo yo nunca fui sacerdote, ni mucho menos amigo de sacerdotes, así es que explicaré la dedicación a la Gran Pirámide en la forma y en el significado que mejor pueda.

Si esa ceremonia no fue la más elaborada, popular y que valiera la pena de verse en toda la historia de los mexica, fue ciertamente la más grandiosa a la que asistí en mi tiempo. El Corazón del Único Mundo estaba lleno de una masa compacta de gente, del colorido de los vestidos, del olor de los perfumes, del esplendor de las plumas, del oro, del calor de los cuerpos, de joyas deslumbrantes, de sudor. Una de las razones de tal aglomeración era que se tenía que mantener un camino abierto, con cordones hechos por guardias que unían sus brazos para poder resistir el empuje del tumulto, para que la línea de prisioneros pudieran caminar hacia la pirámide y ascender al altar del sacrificio. Pero también los espectadores estaban más apretujados por el hecho de que la superficie de la plaza había sido reducida por las construcciones, hechas a través de los años, de numerosos templos nuevos, sin mencionar la gradual extensión que la Gran Pirámide había ido adquiriendo.

Ya que Su Ilustrísima jamás la vio, quizá sea bueno describirle ese *icpac* tlamanacali. Su base estaba hecha en forma de cuadrado; ciento cincuenta pasos de una esquina a otra, sus cuatro muros en declive se alzaban hasta llegar a medir setenta pasos a la cumbre de la pirámide. La escalera ascendía de frente e inclinada ligeramente hacia el oeste dividiéndose en dos, por un lado se ascendía y por el otro se descendía, separados por un pequeño canal de desagüe ornamentado, por el cual escurría la sangre hacia abajo. Había un descansillo al llegar a los primeros cincuenta y dos escalones, que angostos se elevaban hacia una terraza que circulaba en una tercera parte de altura a la pirámide. Después se levantaban otros ciento cuatro escalones que culminaban en la plataforma de la cumbre, en donde se encontraban los templos y sus dependencias. A cada lado de cada trece escalones, había en la escalera una imagen de piedra de algún dios mayor o menor, en cuyo puño sostenía un asta con una bandera de plumas blancas. Banderas blancas que impulsadas por el viento, flotaban como grandes nubes.

Para un hombre que estuviera al pie de la Gran Pirámide las estructuras que se encontraban en su cumbre le eran invisibles, pues desde abajo él sólo podría ver las dos extensas escaleras ascendentes, viéndose muy angostas y pareciendo alzarse más alto de lo que en realidad se elevaban, hacia el cielo azul o hacia el sol. Un *xochimiqui* subiendo afanosamente las escaleras hacia su Muerte-Florida, debía de haber sentido que en realidad subía hacia los altos cielos de los dioses.

Al alcanzar la cumbre, lo primero que encontraría sería la pequeña piedra triangular para sacrificios, en medio de los dos templos. En un sentido, esos *teocaltin* representaban la guerra y la paz, ya que el de la derecha pertenecía a Huitzilopochtli, el responsable de nuestras hazañas guerreras, y el de la izquierda era el de Tláloc, el responsable de nuestras cosechas y de nuestra prosperidad en tiempos de paz. Quizá debería de haber habido con todo derecho un tercer *teocali* para el sol Tonatíu; sin embargo, él ya tenía un santuario separado en una modesta pirámide, en alguna parte de la plaza, como otros dioses importantes. También había en la plaza el *coateocali*, en el cual estaban en fila las imágenes de numerosos dioses de las naciones conquistadas.

Los templos nuevos de Tláloc y Huitzilopochtli, en la cumbre de la nueva Gran Pirámide, no eran más que dos habitaciones cuadradas, conteniendo cada una la estatua hueca del dios hecha de piedra, con su boca ancha bien abierta para recibir su alimento. Sin embargo cada templo se veía más alto e impresionante porque su techo de forma piramidal terminaba en una torre de piedra, con los incisos de Huitzilopochtli en diseños angulares y pintados de rojo, y los incisos de Tláloc en diseños redondos y pintados de azul. El resto de la pirámide, como ya lo he mencionado, estaba predominantemente en yeso blanco que deslumbraba tanto como plata, pero las dos serpenteantes balaustradas, que flanqueaban a cada lado de la doble escalera, estaban pintadas de rojo, azul y verde, simulando escamas de reptiles y terminadas en grandes cabezas de serpientes, que sobresalían hacia fuera del nivel del piso, completamente recamadas de oro batido.

Cuando la ceremonia comenzó, al primer rayo de luz del día, los principales sacerdotes de Tláloc y Huitzilopochtli, con todos sus asistentes, estaban agrupados o se movían inquietos alrededor de los templos en lo alto de la pirámide, haciendo aquellas cosas que los sacerdotes hacen en el último momento. En la terraza que circundaba la pirámide estaban los más distinguidos huéspedes: el Venerado Orador de Tenochtitlan, Auítzotl, con el Venerado Orador de Texcoco, Nezahualpili, y el Venerado Orador de Tlacopan, Chimalpopoca. También estaban allí los gobernantes de otras ciudades, provincias y naciones, que venían de los más lejanos dominios de los mexica, desde las tierras de los tzapoteca, de los mixteca, de los totonaca, de los huaxteca y de algunas naciones cuyos nombres ni siquiera conocía. Por supuesto que no estaba presente nuestro implacable enemigo, el gobernante de Texcala, Xicotenga, pero el Yquígare de Michihuacan sí estaba allí.

Piense en esto, Su Ilustrísima. Si su Capitán General Cortés hubiese llegado a la plaza en ese día, hubiera podido consumar nuestra ruina con una matanza rápida y fácil de todos nuestros legítimos gobernantes. Él hubiera podido proclamarse, allí y entonces, como el señor de todo lo que ahora es practicamente la Nueva España, y nuestros pueblos, ya sin gobernantes, difícilmente le hubieran disputado su derecho. Ellos hubieran sido como un animal degollado al que se le puede tironear o azotar fútilmente. Hubiéramos sido esparcidos y ahora me doy cuenta de que eso nos hubiera ahorrado entonces toda la miseria y sufrimientos que tuvimos que soportar después. Pero en aquel día, *¡yyo ayyo!*, en aquel día en que celebrábamos el poderío mexica, ni siquiera teníamos una sospecha de la existencia del hombre blanco. En aquel entonces creíamos que nuestros caminos y nuestros días estaban guiados más allá de un ilimitado futuro. En verdad que nosotros todavía tuvimos muchos años de vigor y gloria antes de la llegada de ustedes. Y es por eso que estoy contento, a pesar de lo que ahora me doy cuenta, de que ningún intruso echara a perder ese espléndido día.

Las primeras horas de la mañana fueron dedicadas a entretenimientos. Había mucho canto y baile realizado por los artistas de esta Casa de Canto en la cual estamos ahora sentados, Su Ilustrísima, y estaban mucho mejor adiestrados profesionalmente que otros artistas que yo había visto o escuchado en Texcoco o en Xaltocan, si bien ninguno de ellos igualaba en gracia a mi perdida Tzitzitlini. Allí estaban los instrumentos que me eran familiares: el sencillo tambor de trueno, los diversos tambores de dioses, los tambores de agua, la calabazas suspendidas, las flautas de caña y de hueso de canilla y las flautas de *camote*. Pero los cantantes y danzantes estaba acompañados por el conjunto de otros instrumentos que yo no había visto en ninguna otra parte. Uno era llamado «las aguas murmurantes», era una flauta de agua que lanzaba unas notas gorgojeantes al bullir, con un efecto de eco. Había ahí también otra flauta hecha de barro, cortada en forma de un disco delgado y el que la tocaba no movía ni los labios ni los dedos, movía su cabeza alrededor mientras soplaba dentro de la boquilla, así una bolita de barro que había dentro de la flauta giraba alrededor del círculo hasta detenerse en uno o en otro agujero. Y por supuesto, había muchos de esos mismos instrumentos, una multitud de ellos. La música que producían debía de ser audible para todas las personas que estaban en sus casas, en cada una de las comunidades alrededor de los cinco lagos.

Los músicos, cantantes y danzantes hicieron sus interpretaciones en los escalones más bajos de la pirámide y en un espacio abierto directamente enfrente de ella. Cuando se cansaban, eran reemplazados por acróbatas. Hombres muy fuertes que levantaban piedras prodigiosamente pesadas, o que se lanzaban unos a otros bellas muchachas escasamente vestidas, como si éstas fueran plumas. Acróbatas que excedían a los conejos y saltamontes en sus brincos, volteretas y fantásticos saltos mortales. O ellos se colocaban sobre los hombros de otros, diez, luego veinte, luego cuarenta hombres al mismo tiempo, para formar una representación humana de la Gran Pirámide. Cómicos enanos haciendo pantomimas grotescas e indecentes. Malabaristas cuyos juegos eran increíbles, con *tlachtli*, pelotas, lanzándolas al aire de una mano a otra, en intrincados y entrelazados diseños...

No, Su Ilustrísima, no quiero dar a entender que toda la mañana se ocupaba en entretenimientos como simples diversiones (como usted quiere dar a entender) para alumbrar el horror que seguía (como quiere usted decir), y yo no sé lo que usted quiere decir por «carne de circo». Su Ilustrísima no debe deducir que estos regocijos eran en ningún momento irreverentes. Cada uno de los que representaban sus trucos o talentos en particular lo hacía para honrar a los dioses en ese día. Si las representaciones no eran tristes sino alegres, se debía a que se quería lisonjear a los dioses y tenerlos en buena disposición para recibir con gratitud nuestras ofrendas posteriores.

Todo lo que se hizo esa mañana estaba de alguna manera conectado con nuestras creencias religiosas, costumbres o tradiciones, aunque esa relación no podría ser evidente inmediatamente para un observador extranjero como Su Ilustrísima. Por ejemplo, allí estaban los *tocotine*, que habían venido invitados por los totonaca, cuyas tierras estaban a un lado del océano y cuyo arte distintivo lo habían inventado ellos o quizá lo había inspirado su dios. Su representación requería la erección de un tronco de árbol excepcionalmente alto, que se sostenía metiéndose en un hoyo excavado especialmente en el mármol de la plaza. Un pájaro vivo era puesto dentro del hoyo y masacrado cuando el tronco era insertado en él, así su sangre sería la que les daría fuerza a los *tocotine* para que ellos pudieran volar. Sí, volar.

El palo eregido alcanzaba una altura tan aterradora como la de la Gran Pirámide. En la punta se colocaba una delgada plataforma de madera, no más grande de lo que pueden encerrar los brazos de un hombre. Enroscados alrededor del tronco estaban los cabos sueltos de unas sogas muy fuertes. Cinco hombres trepaban hasta su cumbre, uno de ellos llevando un tambor pequeño y una flauta atados a su taparrabo, los otros cuatro sin ninguna carga, excepto por una profusión de brillantes plumas. De hecho, estaban totalmente desnudos a excepción de esas plumas pegadas a sus brazos. Llegando a lo alto de la plataforma, los cuatro hombres emplumados de alguna forma se sentaban en la orilla de ese pedazo de madera, mientras el quinto caminaba sobre ella muy despacio y con precaución hasta llegar a su centro.

Allí, en ese lugar tan constreñido, se paraba, vertiginosamente alto, y entonces movía un pie y luego el otro y después empezaba a bailar, acompañándose con el tamborcillo y la flauta. Tamborileaba y golpeaba el tamborcillo con una mano, mientras que con la otra manipulaba los agujeros de la flauta al soplar por ella. Para todos los que observábamos desde abajo de la plaza, silenciosamente deteniendo el aliento, la música llegaba con un sonido sordo y ligero. Mientras tanto, los otros cuatro hombres estaban haciendo algo con mucha precaución, se estaban amarrando las puntas de las sogas que colgaban del palo a sus cinturas, aunque nosotros no podíamos verlos, pues estaban demasiado alto. Cuando ellos estuvieron listos, el bailarín hizo cierta señal a los músicos de la plaza.

¡Ba-ra-ROOM! Sonaron los tambores de trueno y hubo una estruendosa conjunción de música y tambores que hizo saltar a los espectadores, y, en el mismo instante, los cuatro hombres en lo alto del palo también saltaron hacia el espacio. Ellos quedaron colgando y extendieron a todo lo largo sus emplumados brazos. Cada hombre llevaba las plumas de diferentes pájaros, las rojas

de la guacamaya, las azules del pájaro pescador, las verdes del perico y las amarillas del tucán. Sus brazos eran como las alas extendidas de esos pájaros. Ese primer salto los llevó a cierta distancia de la plataforma, sin embargo, las sogas alrededor de sus cinturas les dieron un pequeño tirón. Todos ellos hubieran podido estrellarse contra el palo, si no fuera por la forma tan ingeniosa en que estaban enroscadas las cuerdas. El salto inicial los hizo girar en un círculo, despacio, alrededor del tronco, cada hombre equidistante de los otros y cada uno de ellos en la grácial postura de alas desplegadas, como pájaros aleteando.

Mientras el hombre que estaba en la cumbre seguía danzando y los músicos abajo seguían tocando, vibrando, cantando en acompañamiento, los cuatro hombres-pájaros continuaban volando en círculo conforme las sogas se iban desenredando del tronco, y cada vez que se desenredaban el círculo se hacía más grande y la vuelta más despacio, mientras empezaban a bajar lentamente. Pero los hombres estaban tan habituados a volar, que, como los pájaros, podían batir sus brazos emplumados de tal manera que se levantaban y descendían, y se remontaban y bajaban en su vuelo, pasándose unos a otros como si también ellos danzaran en toda la dimensión del cielo.

La soga de cada hombre se iba desenredando trece veces alrededor y hacia abajo a todo lo largo del tronco. En su último circuito, cuando sus cuerpos se estaban moviendo en el más ancho y más prolongado círculo, casi tocando las piedras de la plaza, ellos arquearon sus cuerpos y plegaron sus alas contra el viento, exactamente en la forma en que los pájaros descienden, y así fue como tocaron el suelo con sus pies y mientras las sogas se aflojaban ellos corrieron a detenerlas. Los cuatro hicieron eso al mismo tiempo. Entonces uno de ellos sostuvo su soga fuertemente tirante para que el quinto hombre se deslizara a través de ella hasta el suelo.

Si Su Ilustrísima ha leído algunas de las explicaciones previas de nuestras creencias, se habrá dado usted cuenta de que el arte de los *tocotine* no era un simple juego acrobático, sino que cada aspecto de éste tenía un significado. Los cuatro voladores estaban en parte emplumados y en parte desnudos, como Quetzalcoátl, la Serpiente Emplumada. Los cuatro hombres que circunvolaron y el hombre que danzaba en la cumbre, representaban nuestros cinco puntos de alcance: norte, este, oeste, sur y centro. Las trece vueltas de cada soga correspondían a los trece días y número de años de nuestro calendario ceremonial. Y cuatro veces trece, por supuesto, es igual a cincuenta y dos, el número de años de una gavilla de años. Había otras aplicaciones más sutiles, la palabra *tocotine* significa «los sembradores», pero no me extenderé en estas cosas, porque me doy cuenta de que Su Ilustrísima está ansioso por escuchar la parte correspondiente a los sacrificios de dedicación de la ceremonia.

La noche anterior, después de que todos los prisioneros se habían confesado con los sacerdotes de La Que Come Suciedad, nuestros prisioneros texcalteca fueron movilizados hacia una parte de la isla divididos en tres grupos, así ellos podrían caminar hacia la Gran Pirámide a lo largo de las anchas avenidas que conducían a la plaza. El primer prisionero en aproximarse, bien separado del resto, fue el mío: Tlaui-Cólotl. Él había declinado arrogantemente el ser conducido en una silla de manos a su Muerte Florida, pero llegó pasando sus brazos sobre los hombros de dos campeones, solícitos en hermandad quienes por supuesto eran mexica. Escorpión-Armado se balanceaba en medio de los dos, los restos de sus piernas colgaban como raíces roídas. Yo estaba al pie de la pirámide, cuando me uní a ellos y los acompañé escaleras arriba hacia la plataforma en donde todos los nobles estaban esperando.

A mi amado hijo, Auítzotl le dijo: «Como nuestro *xochimiqui* de más alto rango y mayor distinción, Escorpión-Armado, usted tiene el privilegio de ser el primero en ir a su Muerte-Florida. Sin embargo, como campeón Jaguar de reputación grande y notable, puede usted escoger luchar por su vida en la plataforma de Piedra de Batalla. ¿Qué es lo que usted prefiere?»

El prisionero suspiró: «Yo ya no tengo más vida, mi señor. Sin embargo sería bueno para mí pelear por última vez. Si puedo escoger, prefiero la Piedra de Batalla.»

«La decisión de un guerrero valeroso —dijo Auítzotl—. Y usted será honrado con oponentes igualmente valientes, nuestros campeones de más alto rango. Guardias, ayuden al estimado Tlaui-Cólotl en su camino hacia la piedra y denle una espada para que combata mano a mano.»

Lo seguí para poder observar. La Piedra de Batalla, como ya he dicho antes, había sido la única contribución del desaparecido Uey-Tlatoani Tixoc para la plaza: esa ancha roca volcánica, gruesa y en forma de círculo que estaba situada entre la pirámide y la Piedra del Sol. Estaba reservada para cualquier guerrero de gran mérito que escogiera la distinción de morir como había vivido, guerreando. Pero el prisionero que escogiera el duelo en la Piedra de Batalla, se veía obligado a pelear con más de un oponente. Si, con astucia y valentía, vencía a un hombre, otro campeón mexica tomaba su lugar, y luego otro y otro, hasta que fueran cuatro en total. Uno de éstos debía matarlo o por lo menos así habían acabado todos los duelos antes.

Escorpión-Armado fue vestido con la coraza acojinada de algodón de batalla, además de su vestimenta de campeón, su yelmo y piel de jaguar. Después fue conducido hacia la piedra y acomodado allí, ya que sin pies él no podía pararse. Su oponente, armado con una espada de obsidiana *maquáhuitl*, tendría la ventaja de poder atacar desde cualquier dirección, saltar o moverse por el pedestal. A Tlaui-Cólotl se le habían dado dos armas para defenderse, pero éstas eran insignificantes. Una era una simple vara de madera para ponerse en guardia y para parar los golpes de su atacante. La otra era una *maquáhuitl*, pero de juguete, un arma inofensiva de las que se usaban para enseñar a los guerreros novatos: sus filos de obsidiana habían sido reemplazados por penachos de plumas.

Él se sentó cerca de la orilla de la piedra, en una postura de casi relajada anticipación, con la espada sin filo en su mano derecha y la vara de madera débilmente agarrada con su mano izquierda que descansaba sus rodillas. Su primer oponente fue uno de los dos campeones Jaguares que lo habían ayudado a llegar a la plaza. El mexícatl saltó dentro de la Piedra de Batalla por el lado derecho de Escorpión-Armado; esto era del lado en que él tenía su arma más ofensiva, la *maquáhuitl*. Sin embargo, Escorpión-Armado sorprendió al hombre. Él ni siquiera movió la *maquáhuilt*, en su lugar usó la vara como defensa. La balanceó fuertemente, formando con ella un amplio arco. El mexícatl, quien difícilmente hubiera podido esperar ese ataque con una simple vara, fue alcanzado en la barbilla. Su mandíbula se rompió y perdió totalmente el conocimiento con el golpe. Parte de la multitud murmuró con admiración y otros lo ovacionaron con el grito del búho. Escorpión-Armado simplemente se quedó sentado, con la vara de madera ahora descansando lánguidamente sobre su hombro izquierdo.

El adversario número dos fue el otro campeón Jaguar que ayudó a Escorpión-Armado. Naturalmente supuso que si el prisionero había ganado, se debía sólo a un golpe de suerte y también se acercó a la piedra por el lado derecho de Escorpión-Armado, con su hoja de obsidiana apuntando al frente, sus ojos fijos en la *maquáhuitl* del hombre sentado. Esta vez, Escorpión-Armado lo azotó con su vara defensiva, pasándola sobre su mano, levantándola por encima de la mano del campeón y luego moviéndola de tal manera que la vara se incrustó en medio de las orejas de la cabeza-yelmo de jaguar del mexícatl. El hombre cayó hacia afuera de la Piedra de Batalla, con el cráneo fracturado y murió antes de que cualquier físico pudiera atenderlo. Los murmullos y gritos de los espectadores aumentaron de volumen.

El oponente número tres era un campeón Flecha y fue mucho más precavido acerca de la vara, aparentemente inofensiva, del texcaltécalt. Subió a la piedra por el lado izquierdo y lanzó su espada al mismo tiempo. Escorpión-Armado otra vez levantó su vara, pero sólo para desviar la espada hacia un lado. Entonces también utilizó su *maquáhuitl* aunque en una forma muy poco usual. Pinchó con fuerza, dirigiéndola hacia arriba, con la afilada punta para matar y lo hizo con todas sus fuerzas, atravesando la garganta del campeón Flecha; le traspasó ese prominente cartílago que ustedes los españoles llaman «la nuez de Adán». El mexícatl cayó en agonía y se asfixió hasta morir, allí mismo en la Piedra de Batalla.

Mientras los guardias recogían el despojo y lo llevaban fuera de la piedra, la multitud alborotaba con gritos y ovaciones de aliento, no para sus propios guerreros mexícalt, sino para el texcaltécalt. Incluso los nobles en lo alto de la pirámide estaban discutiendo acerca de eso y conversando excitadamente. En la memoria de ninguno de los presentes había un prisionero, incluso un prisionero con el uso de sus pies, que hubiera vencido hasta entonces a tres de sus oponentes en duelo.

Pero el siguiente oponente era el que con toda seguridad lo mataría, porque el cuarto era nuestro más raro peleador zurdo.

Prácticamente casi todos los guerreros eran por naturaleza diestros, habían aprendido a pelear con la mano derecha y habían guerreado en esta forma toda su vida. Así, como es bien conocido, cuando un guerrero diestro se enfrenta en combate con un zurdo, se queda perplejo y confundido. Se siente totalmente desvalido contra este efecto, que es como una imagen sorprendente de un espejo.

El hombre zurdo, un campeón de la Orden Águila, se tomó su tiempo para escalar la Piedra de Batalla. Llegó pausadamente hacia el duelo, sonriendo cruel y confiadamente. Escorpión-Armado seguía sentado, su vara en su mano izquierda y su *maquáhuitl* naturalmente en su mano derecha. El campeón Águila, con su espada en la mano izquierda, se movía despacio hacia atrás y hacia adelante en la orilla de la piedra, estimando su mejor ángulo de ataque. Muy precavido, amagó un movimiento y después saltó hacia el prisionero. Cuando lo hizo, Escorpión-Armado repentinamente se ladeó moviéndose como cualquier acróbata de la mañana y con un movimiento rápido lanzó al aire su vara y su *maquáhuitl* cambiándolas de mano. El campeón mexícatl ante ese inesperado despliegue ambidiestro, frenó su estocada como si quisiera ganar tiempo y reconsiderar, pero no tuvo esa oportunidad.

Escorpión-Armado atrapó entre su vara y su espada la muñeca izquierda del campeón, retorciéndosela y la *maquáhuitl* del hombre voló de su mano. Sosteniendo fuertemente la muñeca del mexícaltl prendida entre sus armas de madera, como el poderoso pico de un loro, Escorpión-Armado se movió por primera vez de su posición sentada, hasta arrodillarse sobre sus rodillas y muñones. Con una fuerza increíble, le retorció todavía más sus dos armas y el campeón Águila tuvo que torcerse con ellas y cayó sobre sus espaldas. El texcaltécatl inmediatamente soltó la aprisionada muñeca y puso la orilla de su espada de madera a través de la garganta expuesta del hombre. Colocando cada una de sus manos en las respectivas orillas del arma, se arrodilló todavía más apoyándose sobre él pesadamente. El hombre forcejeaba bajo de él y Escorpión-Armado levantó su cabeza mirando hacia la pirámide, a los nobles.

Auítzotl, Nezahualpili, Chimalpopoca y todos los demás que estaban en la terraza conferenciaban y sus gestos expresaban admiración y asombro. Entones Auítzotl se paró a la orilla de la plataforma y levantando la mano hizo un gesto con ella. Escorpión-Armado dejó de apretar y quitó su *maquáhuitl* del cuello del hombre caído. Éste se sentó, tembloroso y frotándose la garganta, miráronse ambos perplejos y confundidos.

Tanto él como Escorpión-Armado fueron llevados juntos a la terraza. Yo los acompañé, inflamado de orgullo por mi bienamado hijo. Su cuerpo no tenía ninguna marca de combate, no tenía más que el brillo del sudor y ni siquiera respiraba agitadamente. Auítzotl le dijo:

«Tlaui-Cólotl, usted ha hecho algo jamás visto. Ha peleado por su vida en la Piedra de Batalla, con un impedimento con el que ningún otro duelista lo ha hecho y ha vencido. Este fanfarrón que fue el último que usted derrotó, tomará su lugar como *xochi-miqui* en el primer sacrificio. Usted queda libre para regresar a su casa, a Texcala.»

Escorpión-Armado negó firmemente con su cabeza. «Aunque pudiera caminar hacia mi casa, mi Señor Orador, no lo haría. Un prisionero que es cogido, es un hombre destinado por su *tonali* y por los dioses a morir. Avengonzaría a mi familia, a mis compañeros campeones, a todo Quautexcalan, si yo regresara deshonrosamente vivo. No, mi señor, yo he obtenido lo que pedí, una última batalla y ésta ha sido muy buena. Deje que su campeón Águila viva. Un guerrero zurdo es demasiado raro e invaluable para ser descartado.»

«Si es éste su deseo —dijo el Uey-Tlatoani—, entonces él vivirá. Nosotros deseamos concederle cualquier otro deseo que usted quiera. Solamente tiene que hablar.»

«Que sea enviado a mi Muerte-Florida y al mundo del más allá de los guerreros.»

«Concedido —dijo Auítzotl y entonces magnánimamente agregó—. El Venerado Orador Nezahualpili y yo tendremos el honor de enviarlo a ese mundo.»

Escorpión-Armado habló solamente una vez más, a su captor, a mí, pues era la costumbre hacer la pregunta de rigor: «¿Tiene mi reverendo padre algún mensaje que le gustaría que yo entregara a los dioses?»

Yo sonreí y dije: «Sí, mi bienamado hijo. Dígale a los dioses que solamente deseo que usted sea recompensado en muerte tanto como lo merecía en vida. Que usted viva en riqueza en otras vidas, siempre y por siempre.»

Él inclinó su cabeza asintiendo y luego poniendo sus brazos alrededor de los hombros de los dos Venerados Oradores subió los ciento cuatro escalones restantes hasta la piedra de los sacrificios. Los sacerdotes, casi con un frenesí deleitante por los buenos auspicios de los sucesos acaecidos en ese primer día de sacrificio, hicieron un gran espectáculo, moviendo los incensarios alrededor, haciendo que saliera humo de colores de las urnas y cantando invocaciones a los dioses. Al guerrero Escorpión-Armado se le otorgaron dos últimos honores. El mismo Auítzotl sostuvo el cuchillo de obsidiana y el que arrancó su corazón fue Nezahualpili, quien lo llevó dentro de un cucharón al templo de Huitzilopochtli y lo dejó caer dentro de la boca abierta del dios.

Con esto terminaba mi participación en la ceremonia, por lo menos hasta que llegaran las festividades nocturnas, así es que descendí de la pirámide y me quedé a un lado de ella. Después de haber terminado con Escorpión-Armado, todo lo demás vino a ser insignificante, a excepción de la absoluta magnitud del sacrificio: miles de *xochimique*, más de los que jamás antes habían sido llevados a su Muerte-Florida en un solo día.

El Uey-Tlatoani Auítzotl transportó el corazón del segundo prisionero hasta meterlo en la boca de la estatua del dios Tláloc, luego él y Nezahualpili descendieron otra vez a la terraza de la pirámide. Ellos y sus compañeros gobernantes cuando se cansaron de observar los procedimientos, se pusieron a platicar ociosamente dc esas cosas que los Venerados Oradores acostumbran a hablar. Mientras tanto, las tres largas hileras de prisioneros se iban mezclando hasta formar una sola conforme convergían de las avenidas Tlacopan, Ixtapalapan y Tepeyaca, dentro del Corazón del Único Mundo y en medio de las filas cerradas y aprisionadas por los espectadores, uno tras otro detrás, subiendo la escalera de la pirámide.

Los corazones arrancados de los primeros cientos de *xochimique*, quizá doscientos, fueron ceremoniosamente puestos dentro de las bocas de Tláloc y Huitzilopochtli, hasta que los hoyos de las estatuas estuvieron totalmente llenos y no pudieron caber más. Los labios de piedra de los dioses babeaban y chorreaban de sangre. Por supuesto, que en siguientes celebraciones esos corazones, que llenaban las cavidades de las estatuas, con el tiempo se hubieran podrido convirtiéndose en cieno, si así se requería. Pero ese día, como los sacerdotes tenían una sobreabundancia de corazones los últimos fueron arrancados e inceremoniosamente arrojados en tazones preparados anticipadamente. Cuando éstos estuvieron llenos de montones de corazones, todavía húmedos y débilmente palpitantes, los ayudantes de los sacerdotes los tomaron y con prisa descendieron de la Gran Pirámide, hacia la plaza y las calles del resto de la isla. Ellos entregaron estas sobras generosas a cada una de las otras pirámides, templos y estatuas de dioses, tanto en Tenochtitlan como en Tlaltelolco, y, al caer la tarde, también a los templos de las ciudades de la tierra firme.

Los prisioneros que iban a ser sacrificados ascendían por el lado derecho de la escalera, mientras que los cuerpos acuchillados de sus predecesores eran arrojados y rodaban dando saltos y volteretas hacia abajo por el lado izquierdo, pateados por jóvenes sacerdotes colocados a intervalos, y mientras, el desagüe entre las dos escaleras llevaba un continuo arroyo de sangre que se agitaba entre los pies de la multitud de la plaza. Después de los doscientos *xochimique*, más o menos, los sacerdotes abandonaron todos sus esfuerzos por pretender una ceremonia. Los que estaban recostados a un lado de sus incensarios, de sus banderas y de sus sagradas insignias, cesaron sus cantos y ayudaron, trabajando rápida e indiferentemente como los acuchilladores en el campo de batalla, dando a entender que no podían trabajar muy diestramente.

La rapidez con que se metían los corazones dentro de las estatuas había salpicado de sangre el interior de los dos templos, las paredes, los pisos y aun los techos estaban cubiertos con sangre ya seca. El exceso de sangre corría hacia afuera de las puertas, mientras que la piedra de sacrificios también la chorreaba, hasta que en toda la plataforma se chapoteaba en ella. También, muchos de los prisioneros que iban al encuentro de su destino, aunque lo hacían complacientes, involuntariamente vaciaban sus vejigas o intestinos en el momento de acostarse bajo del cuchillo. Los sacerdotes, quienes por la mañana se habían puesto sus vestimentas negras como buitres, dejando su pelo largo suelto y sin lavar, se movían entonces sobre sus ropas de color rojo y pardusco, rígidas por la sangre coagulada, los mocos secos y las plastas de excremento. En la base de la pirámide, los carniceros trabajaban frenéticamente. De Escorpión-Armado y de un buen número de otros campeones texcalteca habían cortado las cabezas, para ser cocidas hasta que sólo quedaran sus calaveras, que serían acomodadas en la vara punteada, especial para colgar las calaveras de los *xochimique* de más distinción y que se encontraba en la plaza. De esos mismos cuerpos cortaban también sus muslos, para ser asados para el festín nocturno reservado a los guerreros victoriosos. Cuanto más y más cadáveres llegaban dando tumbos hacia los carniceros, éstos cortaban sólo aquellas porciones escogidas y los restos eran enviados inmediatamente al zoológico de la plaza para alimento de los animales, o eran convertidos en cecina o ahumados para ser almacenados para posterior alimento de las fieras o para cualquier gente pobre que estuviera en la miseria o para los esclavos eficientes a quienes les era concedida esta distribución.

La multitud de cuerpos mutilados fueron apresuradamente cargados por los muchachos ayudantes de los sacerdotes hasta el cercano canal, el que fluía hacia la avenida Tepeyaca. Fueron puestos dentro de grandes canoas de carga, y cuando todos estuvieron cargados, éstas fueron enviadas a diversos puntos de la tierra firme, hacia los viveros de flores de Xochimilco, para los huertos o las hortalizas que se encontraban alrededor de los lagos, en donde los restos de los cuerpos serían enterrados y utilizados como fertilizantes. Un pequeño *acali* acompañaba aparte a toda la flota de chalanas. Éste cargaba fragmentos y pedacitos de jade, pedacitos tan pequeños que no tenían ningún valor y cada uno de ellos sería puesto en la boca o en el puño de cada hombre muerto antes de ser enterrado. Nosotros nunca negábamos a nuestros enemigos vencidos ese talismán de piedra verde, el cual era necesario para su admisión en el más allá.

Y todavía la procesión de prisioneros seguía adelante. Desde la cumbre de la Gran Pirámide, la mezcla de sangre y de otras substancias corrían como torrentes, tanto que después de un rato, el desagüe dispuesto en la escalera no podía evacuarlo todo. Esa cascada, como un viscosa caída de agua, empapaba los escalones hacia abajo, cayendo y agitándose sobre los cuerpos de los muertos y bañando los pies de la gente viva, llenándolos y haciendo que muchos de ellos resbalaran y cayeran. Fluía también hacia abajo de las paredes lisas de la pirámide por los cuatro costados. Esa sangre se esparció a través y se extendió completamente por El Corazón del Único Mundo. Aquella mañana, la Gran Pirámide estaba relucientemente blanca como la nieve que coronaba el pico del Popocatépetl, pero por la tarde se veía como un plato lleno de corazones de aves silvestres, al que un cocinero le hubiese puesto encima profusamente una pesada y roja *moli*, salsa. Parecía realmente lo que se estaba proveyendo: una gran comida para dioses de gran apetito.

¿Una abominación, Su Ilustrísima?

Lo que le provoca tan horror y náuseas, creo yo, es el número de hombres matados de una sola vez. Sin embargo, mi señor, ¿cómo puede usted tratar de medir la muerte, cuando es una entidad que no se puede evitar? ¿Cómo puede usted multiplicar una nadería por cualquier número conocido en aritmética? Cuando un solo hombre muere, es como si todo el universo viviente dejara de existir, en cuanto a lo que a él concierne. Asimismo, cada otro hombre o mujer dejan de existir para él; los que son amados y los desconocidos; cada criatura, cada flor, cada nube o brisa, toda sensación y emoción. Su Ilustrísima, el mundo y cada pequeña cosa muere todos los días, por alguien.

¿Pero qué dioses demoníacos, pregunta usted, podrían apoyar la matanza de tantos hombres, destruyéndolos indiscriminadamente? Bien, su propio Señor Dios, por una...

No, Su Ilustrísima, yo no creo que esté blasfemando, o por lo menos no deliberadamente. Simplemente repito lo que me fue dicho por sus frailes misioneros, cuando me instruyeron en los rudimentos de la historia Cristiana. Si ellos dijeron la verdad, su Señor Dios una vez estuvo muy disgustado por la corrupción inclemente de los seres humanos que Él había creado, así es que Él los ahogó a todos con un gran diluvio. Y no sólo a los hombres culpables, sino también a toda cosa viviente y sin embargo inocente. Él dejó con vida, sólo, a un navegante y a su familia y una cantidad de criaturas para que repoblaran la tierra. Yo siempre he pensado que el Señor Dios seleccionó de una forma bastante curiosa a los humanos que preservó, ya que el navegante tenía inclinación a ser borracho, y yo juzgo muy peculiar la conducta de sus hijos y de toda su progenie que siempre estaban riñendo por cualquier rivalidad.

Pero no importa.

Nuestro Mundo también fue una vez totalmente destruido y tome nota de que también lo fue por una calamitosa inundación de agua, cuando los dioses estuvieron insatisfechos de los hombres que entonces lo habitaban. Sin embargo, nuestras historias se remontan más hacia atrás que las de ustedes, ya que nuestros sacerdotes nos han contado que este mundo ha sido previamente limpiado, arrasando a toda la raza humana en otras tres ocasiones: la primera vez fueron todos devorados por jaguares; la segunda, destruidos por tornados y huracanes; la tercera, por una lluvia de fuego que cayó del cielo. Estos cataclismos pasaron hace muchos eones de años, por supuesto, y aun el más reciente de todos, la gran inundación, fue hace tanto tiempo que ni siquiera nuestros más sabios *tlamatinime* pueden calcular la fecha precisa.

Así es que los dioses han creado Nuestro Único Mundo cuatro veces, poblándolo con seres humanos y cuatro veces han declarado que la creación ha tenido algún error, borrándola y haciéndola otra vez. Nosotros aquí, todos nosotros los que vivimos, tratamos de contener el quinto experimento de los dioses. Pero de acuerdo a lo que dicen los sacerdotes, nosotros vivimos tan precariamente como vivieron aquellos infortunados, ya que los dioses algún día decidirán poner fin al mundo y volverlo a hacer de nuevo, así es que la próxima vez será devastado por medio de terremotos.

Y así como nosotros no sabemos cuándo será el próximo fin del mundo por los terremotos, tampoco sabemos cuándo atrajeron los hombres por primera vez en la tierra la furia de los dioses en la forma de jaguares, vientos, fuego e inundaciones. Sin embargo, parece seguro que ellos fallaron en alguna cosa, en dar suficiente honor y adoración y en ofrecer suficientes ofrendas de nutrimento a sus creadores. Es por eso que nosotros, en nuestro tiempo, tratamos lo mejor que pudimos por no ser mezquinos en esos aspectos.

Así es, sí, nosotros matamos miles de *xochimique* en honor a Tláloc y Huitzilopochtli en aquel día de la dedicación de la Gran Pirámide. Pero trate usted de verlo desde nuestro punto de vista, Su Ilustrísima. Ningún hombre puede dar más que su propia vida. Cada uno de esos miles de hombres que murieron esa vez, hubieran muerto de todas maneras en algún otro tiempo. Y al morir como lo hicieron, sucumbieron por una causa buena, una causa noble y ellos lo sabían. Si me puedo referir a esos frailes misioneros otra vez, Su Ilustrísima, si bien no recuerdo sus palabras con exactitud, parece ser que entre los Cristianos hay unas creencias similares. De que ningún hombre puede manifestar más grande amor que dar su vida por sus amigos.

Sin embargo, gracias a la instrucción de sus misioneros, nosotros los mexica ahora sabemos esto, aunque cuando estábamos haciendo las cosas correctas, las llevamos a cabo por razones erróneas. Aunque me apena recordar a Su Ilustrísima que todavía hay otras naciones en estas tierras, que todavía no han sido subyugadas y absorbidas por el Cristianismo en los dominios de la Nueva España, en donde los no iluminados continúan creyendo que la víctima sacrificada sufre un breve dolor en su Muerte-Florida, antes de entrar a gozar de la felicidad, las delicias y la eternidad al más allá. Estos pueblos no saben nada del Señor Dios Cristiano, Quien no limita nuestra miseria en nuestras breves vidas en esta tierra, sino que también inflinge el mundo del más allá llamado Infierno, en donde el dolor jamás termina, sino que es una agonía eterna.

Oh, sí, Su Ilustrísima, yo sé que el Infierno es sólo para la multitud de hombres débiles que merecen el tormento eterno, y que solamente son seleccionados unos pocos hombres rectos para ir a la gloria sublime llamada Cielo. Pero sus misioneros predican aun para los Cristianos, que el maravilloso Cielo es un lugar estrecho y difícil para entrar, mientras que el terrible Infierno es muy amplio y fácil de entrar. De todas formas, yo he asistido a muchos servicios religiosos en iglesias y misiones desde que fui convertido, y, si Su Ilustrísima excusa mi insólita sugestión, he llegado a pensar que el Cristianismo podría llegar a ser más atractivo para los paganos si sus predicadores pudieran describir los placeres del Cielo tan vívida y sabrosamente como presentan los horrores del Infierno.

Aparentemente a Su Ilustrísima no le importa escuchar mis opiniones, ni siquiera refutarlas o debatirlas, y en lugar de eso prefiere irse. Ah, bueno, yo no soy más que un Cristiano novato y probablemente presuntuoso al querer dar opiniones todavía inmaduras. Dejaré a un lado el tema de la religión para seguir hablando de otras cosas.

El festín de los guerreros se llevó a efecto en lo que entonces era la sala de banquetes en esta misma Casa de Canto, en la noche de la dedicación de la Gran Pirámide, y que tenía cierta relación indirecta religiosa, pero de las menores. Era una creencia que cuando nosotros los vencedores comíamos un pedazo de carne asada de los prisioneros sacrificados, entonces de alguna manera ingeríamos parte de la fuerza y del espíritu combativo de los hombres muertos. Pero estaba prohibido que cualquier «reverendo padre» comiera de la carne de su «bienamado hijo». Por tanto, ninguno podía comer de la carne de ningún prisionero que hubiera capturado, porque en términos religiosos esto sería tan irreverente como una relación incestuosa entre un verdadero padre y su hijo. Así es que, si bien todos los otros huéspedes se esforzaron por apoderarse de una tajada de carne del incomparable Escorpión-Armado, yo me tuve que contentar con un pedazo de muslo de algún campeón texcalteca de menos mérito.

¿La carne, mis señores? Pues, estaba deliciosamente bien cocinada, con buenas especias y servida en abundancia en platos que llevaban a un lado frijoles, tortillas, jitomates asados y como bebida *chocólatl* y...

¿La carne les da *náuseas*, mis señores? ¡Es todo lo contrario! Es la más sabrosa, suave y deliciosa al paladar. Y ya que este tema excita su curiosidad, les diré que la carne humana cocinada tiene casi el mismo sabor que la carne del animal que ustedes llaman puerco, la carne cocinada de los animales que ustedes han importado como cerdos. En verdad, que tienen una gran similitud en textura y sabor, lo cual ha extendido el rumor de que ustedes los españoles y sus cerdos están consanguíneamente relacionados, que ambos, españoles y puercos, propagan sus especies por mutuo intercurso, si no en un casamiento legítimo.

¡*Yya* no pongan esas caras, reverendos frailes! Yo nunca he creído ese rumor, pues me he dado cuenta de que sus cerdos son sólo animales domesticados en comparación con nuestros *coyametin*, jabalíes salvajes, de estas tierras, y yo no creo que ni siquiera un español podría copular con un *coyámetl*. Por supuesto que la carne de sus puercos es mucho más sabrosa y suave que la áspera y correosa de nuestros indómitos jabalíes. Pero la similar coincidencia de la carne de puerco y la humana es probablemente la razón por la cual la gente de la clase baja ha estado comiendo la de puerco con tanta avidez, y el porqué de que ellos le dieran la bienvenida a la introducción de los cerdos con más entusiasmo que, por ejemplo, la introducción de su Santa Iglesia.

Había muy poca concurrencia. Los invitados al banquete consistían la mayoría en campeones acolhua y guerreros que habían venido a Tenochtitlan con la comitiva de Nezahualpili. Había unos pocos campeones tecpaneca y nosotros los mexica éramos solamente tres: yo y mis inmediatos superiores en el campo de batalla, el *quáchic* Glotón de Sangre y el campeón Flecha Xócoc. Uno de los soldados acolhua que estaba presente era aquel soldado a quien le habían cortado la nariz en la batalla y cosido después, pero entonces se le había vuelto a caer. Él nos dijo, tristemente, que la operación del físico no había tenido éxito; la nariz se fue poniendo gradualménte negra y finalmente se cayó. Todos nosotros le aseguramos que no se veía mucho peor sin ella que cuando la tenía, sin embargo él era un hombre cortés y se sentó bien apartado del resto de nosotros para no estropear nuestro apetito.

Para cada invitado había una *auyanimi*, mujer seductoramente vestida, para servirnos golosinas de los platones de comida, llenar las cañas para fumar *piciétl* y encenderlas por nosotros, llenar continuamente nuestros tazones de *chocólatl* y *octli* por nosotros y después retirarse con nosotros hacia unas pequeñas alcobas con cortinas que estaban alrededor de la sala principal, para el *ahuilnemiliztli*. Sí, puedo ver sus expresiones de desagrado, mis señores escribanos, pero eso era un hecho. El festín de carne humana y el subsecuente disfrute de copulación casual tuvieron lugar aquí exactamente, en estos muros ahora santificadamente diocesanos.

Debo confesar de que no recuerdo todo lo que ocurrió, porque yo fumé por primera vez un *poquíetl* esa noche, y más que cualquier otro bebí mucho *octli.* Antes yo había probado tímidamente el jugo fermentado del maguey, pero ésa fue la primera vez que fui lo suficientemente indulgente para embotar mis sentidos. Recuerdo que los guerreros ahí congregados se vanagloriaban mucho de sus hazañas en esa guerra reciente y en batallas pasadas, y que hubo muchos brindis por mi primera victoria y rápida promoción hacia un rango superior. En algún momento, nuestros Venerados Oradores Nezahualpili, Auítzotl y Chimalpopoca nos honraron con una breve aparición y brindaron con una copa de *octli* con nosotros. Tengo la vaga reminiscencia de haberle dado las gracias a Nezahualpili, borracho, servil y posiblemente incoherentemente, por su regalo en mercancías y moneda corriente, si bien no recuerdo su respuesta, si es que hubo alguna.

Finalmente, y sin ninguna vacilación, gracias quizás al *octli*, me retiré a una de las alcobas con una de las *auyanime* y recuerdo que ella era una mujer joven y hermosa con el pelo artificialmente coloreado de rojo-oro jacinto por el teñido de las semillas de *achíyotl*. Era excepcionalmente competente y lo era, después de todo, porque ésa era la ocupación de su vida: dar placer a los guerreros victoriosos. Así es que, aparte de los actos usuales, ella me enseñó algunos artificios y métodos completamente nuevos para mí y debo decir que sólo un guerrero en su primer vigor y agilidad podría haber mantenido su actuación por tanto tiempo o aguantar la que ella. En compensación «yo la acaricié con flores», eso es, le enseñé algunas de las habilidades de que había sido testigo durante la seducción de Algo Delicado. La *auyanimi* obviamente disfrutó de esas atenciones y se maravilló mucho de ellas, ya que, teniendo que copular siempre y solamente con hombres, y la mayoría de las veces hombres rudos, ella jamás había sentido esas sensaciones particularmente placenteras, y estoy seguro de que estuvo muy contenta de aprenderlas y de añadirlas a su propio repertorio.

Al fin, saciado de sexo, comida, bebida y *poquíetl*, decidí que me gustaría estar solo un rato. La sala de banquetes estaba oscura y se respiraba un aire rancio, había una capa de humo, combinado con los olores de restos de comida, sudor de los hombres, la resina que se quemaba en las antorchas, todo lo cual hizo que mi estómago sintiera náuseas. Salí afuera de Casa de Canto y caminé inestablemente hacia El Corazón del Único Mundo. Allí mi nariz percibió un olor aún más repugnante y mi estómago se volvió a agitar. La plaza estaba llena de esclavos que raspaban y fregaban las costras de sangre pegadas por todas partes. Así es que no entré en ella, sino que la bordeé, fuera del Muro de la Serpiente, hasta que me encontré en la puerta del zoológico que había visitado con mi padre, una vez, hacía ya mucho tiempo.

Una voz dijo: «No está cerrado. Todos los inquilinos están en sus jaulas y de todas formas están ahítos y adormilados. ¿Entramos?»

A pesar de que pasaba de la medianoche, apenas me sorprendió ver al hombrecillo encorvado y encogido de color cacao-pardusco, que también había estado en el zoológico en aquella ocasión, y en mi vida varias veces más desde entonces. Murmuré alguna clase de saludo con voz estropajosa y él dijo:

«Después de pasar un día disfrutando de los ritos y las delicias de los seres humanos, tengamos una comunión con los que nosotros llamamos bestias.»

Yo le seguí hacia adentro y vagamos a lo largo del pasillo entre las jaulas y los cubículos. Todos esos animales carnívoros habían sido bien alimentados con la carne de los sacrificios, pero el constante correr del agua de los desagües se había llevado rápidamente todo vestigio y olor de allí. Aquí y allá un coyote o jaguar o una gran serpiente constrictora abrían soñolientamente sus ojos para luego volverlos a cerrar. Sólo unos cuantos animales nocturnos estaban despiertos, murciélagos, zorras, monos aulladores, pero también ellos estaban lánguidos y solamente daban débiles chillidos y gruñidos.

Después de un rato mi acompañante dijo: «Has andado un largo camino en muy poco tiempo, ¡Trae!»

«Mixtli», le corregí.

«Mixtli, otra vez entonces. Siempre te encuentro con un nombre diferente y siguiendo una carrera distinta. Tú eres como el mercurio que usan los artífices en oro. Adaptable a cualquier forma, pero sin ser confinado a ninguno por un largo tiempo. Bien, pues ya que has tenido experiencia en la guerra, ¿piensas dedicarte a ser un guerrero profesional?»

«Claro que no —le dije—. Usted sabe que no tengo buena visión para eso, ni tampoco, creo yo, buen estómago.»

Él se encogió de hombros: «Oh, un guerrero adquiere dureza con unas cuantas batallas y su estómago no vuelve más a revolverse.»

«No me refiero a no tener estómago para la pelea, sino después, en las celebraciones. En este momento tengo bastante...» Y eructé fuertemente.

«Tu primera borrachera —dijo él riéndose—. También un hombre se llega a acostumbrar a eso, te lo puedo asegurar. Muchas veces hasta lo disfruta y aun llega a necesitarlo.»

«En lo que respecta a mí, no —dije—. Recientemente he tenido demasiadas experiencias por primera vez y demasiado rápidas también. En estos momentos me gustaría tener un poco de tiempo de reposo, estancarme si usted lo prefiere, así, libre de incidentes, de excitaciones y de molestias. Creo que puedo convencer a Auítzotl para que me acoja como escribano de palacio.»

«Papel y botes de pintura —dijo él desdeñosamente—. Mixtli, esas cosas las puedes hacer cuando estés tan viejo y decrépito como yo. Guárdalas para el momento en que sólo tengas energía para asentar en ellas tus reminiscencias. Hasta entonces, corre aventuras y experiencias que puedas recordar. Realmente te recomiendo que hagas un viaje. Ve a lejanos lugares, conoce gente nueva, comidas exóticas, *ahuilnema*, mujeres de todas clases, ve paisajes desconocidos y cosas nuevas. Eso me recuerda que la otra vez que estuviste aquí, no pudiste ver los *tequantin*. Ven.»

Abrió la puerta y entramos a la cámara de los «animales humanos», los fenómenos y monstruos. Éstos no estaban en jaulas como los verdaderos animales. Cada uno de ellos vivía en lo que bien podría ser un simpático, pequeño y privado apartamento, a excepción de que no había una cuarta pared y así los espectadores como nosotros podíamos mirar y ver a los *tequani* en cualquier actividad que ellos pudieran estar haciendo para llenar sus vidas inútiles y sus días vacíos. En aquellos momentos de la noche, todos los que vimos al pasar estaban dormidos en sus esterillas. Allí estaban los hombres y las mujeres blancos, blancos de la piel y de los cabellos, viéndose tan impalpables como el viento. Allí había concorvadas otras formas humanas retorcidas y todavía más horribles, y enanos encorvados y retorcidos.

«¿Cómo es que están aquí?», pregunté en un discreto murmullo. El hombre dijo sin tomarse la molestia de bajar su voz: «Ellos vienen por sí mismos cuando han sufrido algún accidente, o son traídos por sus padres, si nacieron en forma grotesca. Sí, los *tequani* se venden a sí mismos, la cantidad que se paga por ellos es para sus padres o para aquellas personas que ellos designen. Y el Venerado Orador paga magníficamente. Hay padres que verdaderamente rezan pidiendo que les nazca un monstruo; así ellos llegan a ser ricos. Los *tequani* no utilizan esas riquezas para sí mismos, por supuesto, ya que aquí tienen todas las comodidades necesarias para el resto de sus vidas. Algunos de ellos, los más raros en extremo, cuestan grandes fortunas. Como ese enano, por ejemplo.»

Éste estaba durmiendo y yo me sentí muy contento de no verlo despierto, porque solamente tenía la mitad de la cabeza. Desde sus dientes sobresalientes que colgaban de su quijada hasta sus clavículas, no había nada más, ni mandíbula más baja, ni piel, nada más una tráquea blanca y expuesta, rojos músculos, venas rojizas y el gaznate, la abertura baja detrás de sus dientes, entre sus hinchados y pequeños carrillos de roedor. Él estaba acostado con su horrible mitad de cabeza tirada hacia atrás, respirando con un resoplido silbante.

«No puede masticar ni tragar —dijo mi guía—, así es que su comida debe ser empujada hacia dentro, hacia abajo hasta su gaznate. Ya que él tiene que inclinar su cabeza hacia atrás para poder ser alimentado, no puede ver qué es lo que le están dando y muchos visitantes le juegan bromas crueles. Pueden darle un fuerte purgante o una fruta espinosa o alguna otra cosa peor. En muchas ocasiones ha estado casi a punto de morir, pero es tan goloso y estúpido que sigue echando su cabeza hacia atrás a cualquiera que le haga un gesto de ofrecimiento.»

Me estremecí y fui hacia el siguiente apartamiento. El *tequani* no parecía que estuviera durmiendo, ya que su único ojo estaba abierto. Mientras que en donde debía estar su otro ojo, no había más que una piel lisa y plana. Su cabeza no tenía pelo, ni tampoco cuello, su piel resbalaba directamente sobre sus angostos hombros y entonces se extendía sobre una especie de cono que formaba su torso, sobre el que se sentaba como en una base hinchada tan sólida como una pirámide, puesto que no tenía piernas. Sus brazos eran bastante normales, excepto por los dedos de ambas manos que estaban pegados juntos, como las patas de las tortugas verdes.

«Ésta es llamada la mujer-tapir —dijo el hombre arrugado y yo le hice un movimiento para que hablara más bajo—. Oh, no necesitamos vigilar nuestras maneras —dijo—. Ella probablemente está profundamente dormida. El ojo liso está permanentemente cerrado y el otro perdió su párpado. De todas formas, estos *tequantin* pronto se acostumbran a ser objeto de discusiones en público.»

No tenía la menor intención de discutir sobre ese objeto espantoso digno de compasión. Me podía dar cuenta de por qué se referían a ella con el nombre de tapir, y era a causa de su hocico prensible, ya que la nariz de la mujer era muy parecida a una trompa que colgaba como un pendiente sobre su boca escondida, si es que tenía boca; pero yo no hubiera podido reconocer ninguna forma de mujer si no se me hubiera dicho. Su cabeza no era como la de una mujer, ni siquiera parecía humana. Cualquier tipo de pechos serían indistinguibles entre los rollos de carne como hule que componían su cuerpo de pirámide inmóvil. Eso me miraba por detrás de mí, con su único ojo abierto.

«El enano sin quijada nació en esa triste condición —dijo mi guía—. Pero ésta era ya una mujer cuando fue mutilada por alguna clase de accidente. Se supone, por la falta de piernas, que en el accidente estuvo implicado algún instrumento cortante, y, por el resto de ella, que también estuvo envuelta en fuego. La carne no siempre se quema con el fuego, sabes. Algunas veces sólamente se ablanda, se extiende o se funde, como...»

Mi estómago enfermo se revolvió y le dije: «Por piedad, no hable así enfrente de eso. Enfrente de ella.»

«¡Ella! —gruñó el viejo, divertido—. Tú siempre eres muy galante con las mujeres, ¿no es así? —Parecía estar censurándome—. Casi acabas de venir del abrazo de una bella *"ella"*. —Él señaló a la mujer-tapir—. ¿Te gustaría tener *ahuilnema* con esta otra cosa que describes como *ella*?»

No me pude contener más. Me doblé sobre mí mismo y allí, enfrente de aquellos monstruos reunidos, vomité hasta haber echado todo lo que comí y bebí aquella noche. Cuando al fin quedé vacío y recobré el aliento, eché una mirada apenada hacia ese ojo que me miraba. Ya sea que estuviera despierta o que el ojo simplemente goteara, no lo sé, pero una sola lágrima rodó hacia abajo de su mejilla. Mi guía ya se había ido y no lo volví a ver otra vez, así es que salí del zoológico.

Aquella noche me estaba reservada todavía otra cosa desagradable, aunque para entonces ya era la madrugada. Cuando llegué al portal del palacio de Auítzotl, el guardia me dijo: «Perdóneme, Tequíua Mixtli, pero el físico de la Corte ha estado esperando su regreso. ¿Puede usted ser tan amable de pasar a verlo antes de que se vaya a sus habitaciones?»

El guardia me guió a las habitaciones de palacio del físico, llamé y lo encontré despierto y completamente vestido. El guardia nos saludó a ambos y se retiró a su puesto. El físico me miró con una expresión extraña. Parecía una mezcla de curiosidad, piedad y unción profesional. Por un momento pensé que él me había estado esperando para recetarme un remedio para la náusea que todavía sentía, pero me dijo: «El muchacho llamado Cózcatl es su esclavo, ¿no es así?»

Le dije que sí, y le pregunté que si se había puesto enfermo.

«Ha sufrido un accidente. No un accidente mortal, por lo que me siento muy contento de poder decirlo, pero tampoco uno trivial. Cuando el gentío de la plaza empezó a dispersarse, fue encontrado tirado e inconsciente junto a la Piedra de Batalla. Parece que estuvo demasiado cerca de los combatientes.»

No había pensado en Cózcatl, ni siquiera una vez, desde que le ordené que estuviera vigilante a las asechanzas de Chimali. En esos momentos mi estómago se sentía todavía más vacío y enfermo. Yo le dije: «¿Entonces fue herido, señor físico?»

«Mal herido —dijo él—, y cortado en forma extraña.»

Desvió su mirada de mí y tomó de una mesa un pedazo de tela manchada y la desplegó para que viera lo que contenía: un miembro masculino inmaduro y sus bolsas de *ololtin*, pálidas, flexibles y sin sangre.

«Como el lóbulo de una oreja», murmuré.

«¿Cómo dice?», preguntó el físico.

«¿Usted dice que no es una herida mortal?»

«Bueno, usted y yo lo podemos considerar así —dijo el físico secamente—. Pero el muchacho no morirá por esto, no. Él perdió bastante sangre y apareció con magulladuras y otras marcas en su cuerpo, como si hubiera sido rudamente maltratado, quizás por los empujones del populacho. Sin embargo vivirá y esperemos que no lamente mucho la pérdida de lo que él nunca tendrá la oportunidad de apreciar su valor. La herida fue hecha limpiamente. Sanará totalmente, en menos tiempo del que le tomará a él recobrarse de la pérdida de sangre. He tenido que arreglar esa herida, cosiéndola de tal manera para que quede una pequeña abertura necesaria. Él está en su apartamento en estos momentos, Tequíua Mixtli, y me tomé la libertad de acomodarlo en la suave cama de usted, en lugar de su esterilla.»

Le di al físico las gracias y subí las escaleras de prisa. Cózcatl estaba acostado sobre sus espaldas en medio de mi cama bien acolchada, el cubrecama lo tapaba. Su rostro estaba enrojecido por un poco de fiebre y su respiración era ligera. Con mucho cuidado para no despertarlo, levanté la orilla del cubrecama. Estaba desnudo excepto por el vendaje que tenía entre las piernas, sostenido en ese lugar por una tira de algodón muy delgada alrededor de sus caderas. Había unas magulladuras en su hombro en donde una mano lo había agarrado fuertemente mientras la otra manipulaba el cuchillo. Sin embargo el *tícitl* había también mencionado «marcas» y yo no vi ninguna hasta que Cózcatl, probablemente sintiendo frío con el aire nocturno, murmurando entre sueños, se giró y expuso ante mí su espalda.

«Tu vigilancia y lealtad no quedarán sin recompensa», le había dicho al muchacho, sin sospechar ni remotamente la clase de recompensa que tendría. El vengativo Chimali realmente había estado entre el gentío, eso era evidente. Sin embargo, yo, la víctima señalada, estuve todo el tiempo en un lugar tan prominente que él no había podido atacarme furtivamente. Así, habiendo reconocido a mi esclavo, lo atacó en vez de a mí. ¿Pero, por qué? A menos de que el deseo de venganza hubiera vuelto loco a Chimali, ¿por qué atacar a aquel pequeño sirviente, comparativamente sin ningún valor?

Entonces recordé la curiosa expresión del físico y me di cuenta del porqué; él había estado pensando lo mismo que Chimali había tenido en mente. Chimali había supuesto que el muchacho venía a ser para mí lo que Tlatli fue para él. Había atacado al muchacho, no para privarme de un esclavo comprado, sino que lo había castrado suponiendo que era mi *cuilontli*. Era la forma mejor calculada para que recibiera un choque, y así poder mofarse de mí.

Todo esto me vino a la mente cuando vi, estampada en mitad de la delgada espalda de Cózcatl, la familiar huella roja de Chimali, solamente que esta vez no con su propia sangre.

Puesto que ya era muy tarde o demasiado temprano, ya que por el tragaluz abierto empezaba a entrar una pálida luz, y puesto que tanto mi cabeza como mi estómago me dolían horriblemente, me senté en la cama a un lado de Cózcatl, no tratando siquiera de dormir, sino intentando pensar.

Yo recordaba al degenerado Chimali en los años anteriores,

ios tiempos en que todavía éramos amigos, antes de que llegara a ser un vicioso. Él tendría más o menos la edad de Cózcatl, en aquella memorable tarde en que lo guié a través de Xaltocan hasta su casa, llevando una calabaza en su cabeza para esconder su remolino. Yo recordaba como había tenido conmiseración de mí, cuando él se fue al *calmecac* y yo no pude ir; cuando él me regaló toda su serie especial de pinturas...

Eso me llevó a pensar en el regalo tan inesperado que había recibido hacía apenas unos cuantos días. Todo lo que contenía ese regalo era de gran valor a excepción de una cosa, que por lo menos no tenía ningún valor aquí en Tenochtitlan. Era el bulto que contenía los gruesos pedazos de obsidiana no trabajados, que eran muy fáciles y baratos de adquirir de una fuente cercana, en el lecho del cañón del Río de los Cuchillos, a una jornada no muy larga al noroeste de aquí. Sin embargo, esos pedazos en bruto tendrían un valor tan grande como el jade en las naciones lejanas del sur, quienes no tenían de donde obtener la obsidiana con la cual fabricar sus aperos y armas. Ese único bulto sin nigún valor, me hizo recordar algunas de mis ambiciones con las que me había entretenido y las ideas que había urdido en aquellos lejanos días en que ociosamente soñaba, trabajando en la *chinampa* de Xaltocan.

Cuando la mañana ya estaba llena de luz, sin hacer ruido me lavé, limpié mis dientes y me cambié de vestidos. Bajé las escaleras y encontrándome con el mayordomo del palacio, le pedí una entrevista con el Uey-Tlatoani lo más pronto posible. Auítzotl fue lo suficientemente amable en acceder y no tuve que esperar mucho para ser introducido ante su presencia, en aquel salón del trono con trofeos de caza colgando.

Lo primero que él me dijo fue: «Nosotros oímos que ayer su pequeño esclavo estuvo en un lugar en donde el filo de una espada lo hirió.»

Yo le dije: «Así parece, Venerado Orador, pero se aliviará.»

No tenía la menor intención de denunciar a Chimali o demandar su búsqueda, ni siquiera mencionar su nombre. Me vería obligado a hablar de cosas ya pasadas y encerradas por la ley, acerca de los últimos días de la hija de Auítzotl, revelaciones en las que estábamos envueltos Cózcatl y yo, tanto como Chimali. Se podrían volver a inflamar la angustia y la ira paternal del Uey-Tlatoani, pudiéndonos ejecutar a mí y al muchacho aun antes de que él mandara buscar a Chimali.

Él me dijo: «Lo sentimos mucho. Accidentes como éstos son muy frecuentes entre los espectadores de los duelos. Nosotros estaríamos muy contentos de ofrecerle otro esclavo mientras el suyo está incapacitado.»

«Muchas gracias, Señor Orador, pero en realidad no necesito de ninguna asistencia. Vine para pedirle otra clase de favor. Habiendo llegado a poseer una pequeña herencia, me gustaría invertir todo en mercancías y tratar de tener éxito como comerciante.»

Me pareció ver sus labios torcerse. «¿Un comerciante? ¿Con un puesto en el mercado de Tlaltelolco?»

«No, no, mi señor. Un *pochtécatl*, un mercader viajero.»

Se recargó sobre su piel de oso, mirándome en silencio. Lo que yo estaba pidiendo era una promoción cn una posición civil relativamente y aproximadamente igual a la que se me había concedido dentro del rango militar. Aunque los *pochteca* eran todos técnicamente plebeyos como yo, pertenecían a la clase más elevada de plebeyos. Podían, si eran afortunados y astutos en sus tratos, llegar a ser tan ricos como los *pípiltin*, nobles, y tener casi tantos privilegios. Estaban exentos de casi todas nuestras leyes comunes y sujetos principalmente a las suyas, decretadas y ejecutadas por ellos mismos. Incluso tenían su propio dios principal, Yacatecutli, El Señor Que Guía. Y eran celosos al seleccionar a sus nuevos socios y en el número de ellos. No admitían como *pochtécatl* a cualquiera que solamente quisiera serlo.

«Usted acaba de ser recompensado con el rango de comandante —dijo al fin Auítzotl, bastante malhumorado—. ¿Sería usted tan negligente como para ponerse sus sandalias de camino, empaquetar sus chucherías y cargárselas a las espaldas? ¿Necesito recordarle a usted, joven, de que nosotros los mexica somos una nación que hemos hecho historia como guerreros conquistadores y no como lisonjeros tratantes?»

«Quizá la guerra exceda más de lo que sus utilidades le deja, Señor Orador —dije desafiando su disgusto—. Verdaderamente creo que nuestros mercaderes tratantes están haciendo en estos momentos mucho más que todos nuestros ejércitos; extendiendo la influencia mexica y trayendo riquezas a Tenochtitlan. Ellos tienen un intercambio comercial con naciones tan distantes que no son fáciles de conquistar, pero que son ricas en mercancías y géneros que de buena gana trocan o venden...»

«Usted hace que el comercio suene muy fácil —me interrumpió Auítzotl—. Deje que le digamos que es tan peligroso como ser guerrero. Las expediciones de los *pochteca* salen de aquí cargadas con mercancías de considerable valor. Muy a menudo son robados por salvajes o bandidos antes de que puedan llegar a sus destinos o sus mercancías generalmente son simplemente confiscadas y no reciben nada a cambio de ellas. Por estas razones, nosotros tenemos que enviar una tropa adecuadamente armada con ellos para proteger cada una de esas expediciones. Así es que dígame, ¿por qué motivo nosotros hemos de continuar despachando tropas de protección en lugar de utilizarlas para conquistar?»

«Con todo respeto, yo creo que Venerador Orador ya sabe el porqué —dije—. Porque en esa tropa llamada de protección, Tenochtitlan sólo coopera con los hombres armados y nada más. Los *pochteca* llevan, aparte de sus mercancías para tratar, la comida y las provisiones de cada jornada o las compran a lo largo del camino. A diferencia del ejército, no tienen que buscar forraje, ni robar, ni hacer nuevos enemigos por donde ellos pasan. Así es que llegan sanos y salvos a sus destinos, hacen sus comercios o tratos provechosos y luego ellos y sus hombres armados regresan a casa otra vez y pagan pródigos impuestos al tesoro de su Mujer Serpiente. Cada expedición que regresa hace más fácil la jornada para las siguientes. Los pueblos de lejanas tierras aprenden que un comercio pacífico es tan ventajoso para ellos como para nosotros. Los asaltantes que se apostan a lo largo de las rutas aprenden dolorosas lecciones y dejan de cazar en las rutas comerciales. Yo creo que con el tiempo los *pochteca* no necesitarán más del apoyo de sus tropas.»

Auítzotl me preguntó con petulancia: «¿Y qué vendrá a ser de nuestros guerreros, cuando Tenochtitlan cese de extender sus dominios? ¿Cuando los mexica no se esfuercen más por crecer en fuerza y poderío, sino que simplemente se sienten a engordar sobre su creciente comercio? ¿Cuando los una vez respetados y temidos mexica hayan llegado a ser un enjambre de buhoneros regateando sobre pesos y medidas en Tlaltelolco?»

«Mi señor exagera al hablar así —dije haciendo patente una gran humildad—. Deje a sus guerreros pelear y a sus mercaderes comerciar. Deje que sus ejércitos se ocupen de pelear entre aquellas naciones que estén fácilmente a su alcance, como Michihuacan. Deje a los mercaderes amarrar y anudar a nosotros a las naciones lejanas con tratos comerciales en lugar de subyugarlas. Entre ellas, Venerado Orador, nunca habrá necesidad de poner un límite al mundo ganado y sostenido por los mexica.»

Auítzotl me miraba otra vez, a través de un silencio todavía más largo. Así, él parecía más feroz que la cabeza de oso que colgaba arriba de su trono. Entonces dijo: «Muy bien. Usted nos acaba de decir cuáles son las razones por las que admira tanto la profesión de mercader viajante. ¿Puede usted decirnos algunas razones por las que esa profesión se beneficiaría si usted se uniera a ella?»

«La profesión, no —dije francamente—. Pero puedo sugerir algunas razones por las cuales el Uey-Tlatoani y su Mujer Serpiente pudieran tener algún beneficio.»

Él levantó sus espesas cejas. «Entonces, dígalo.»

«Yo he sido adiestrado como escribano, mientras que la mayoría de los mercaderes, no. Ellos sólo saben de números y llevar las cuentas. Como el Venerado Orador se ha podido dar cuenta, soy capaz de hacer mapas exactos y descripciones detalladas con palabras-pintadas. Puedo regresar de mis viajes con libros completos sobre datos de otras naciones, como sus depósitos de armas y almacenes, sus puntos defensivos y vulnerables...»

Sus cejas se habían vuelto a bajar mientras yo iba hablando. Con mi mayor sentido de humildad le dije: «Claro que para que yo pueda realizar eso, primero debo persuadir a los *pochteca* a fin de que me califiquen para ser aceptado dentro de su distinguida y selecta sociedad...»

Auítzotl dijo secamente: «Nosotros dudamos que ellos puedan obstinarse por largo tiempo en no recibir a un candidato propuesto por el Uey-Tlatoani. ¿Entonces es todo lo que usted pide? ¿Que nosotros seamos su aval como *pochtécatl?*»

«Si es del agrado de mi señor, me gustaría llevar dos acompañantes. No pido que me sea asignada una tropa de guerreros, sino el *quáchic* Extli-Quani, como nuestro defensor militar. Sólo ese hombre; aunque sé que es viejo, creo que es el más adecuado.

También le pido llevar conmigo al muchacho Cózcatl. Él estará listo para viajar cuando yo parta.»

Auítzotl se encogió de hombros. «El *quáchic* ha sido retirado de servicio activo por órdenes mías. Él, de todos modos, es ya muy viejo para otras cosas que no sea ayudante o maestro. En cuanto a su esclavo, es suyo y está sujeto a sus órdenes.»

«Quisiera que no lo fuera más, mi señor. Me gustaría ofrecerle su libertad como una pequeña restitución al accidente que sufrió ayer. Yo le pido a usted, Venerado Orador, que oficialmente lo eleve del estado social de *tlacotli* al de *macehuali* libre. Él me acompañará no como esclavo, sino como socio libre, compartiendo las ganancias.»

«Concedido —dijo Auítzotl, con un fuerte suspiro—. Nosotros haremos que un escribano prepare el papel de manumisión. Mientras tanto, nosotros no podemos dejar de hacer notar que ésta es la más curiosa expedición mercantil que jamás ha salido de Tenochtitlan. ¿Hasta dónde piensa llegar en su primer viaje?»

«Iré por todo el camino que lleva a las tierras maya, Señor Orador, y regresaré otra vez si los dioses lo permiten. Extli-Quani ya ha estado en esas tierras antes, es ésta una de las razones por las cuales quiero que venga. Tengo también la seguridad de que regresaré con bastante información, interesante y de gran valor para mi señor.»

Lo que no le dije fue que también tenía la ferviente esperanza de regresar con mi visión restaurada. La reputación de los físicos maya era la verdadera razón de haber escogido esa nación como nuestro destino.

«Su petición es aceptada —dijo Auítzotl—. Usted esperará a ser citado a comparecer en la Casa de los Pochteca para ser examinado. —Él se levantó de su trono de piel de oso pardo, para indicar que la entrevista había terminado—. Será muy interesante volver a hablar con usted otra vez, Pochtécatl Mixtli, cuando usted regrese, si es que lo hace.»

Fui hacia arriba, hacia mi departamento y encontré a Cózcatl despierto, sentado sobre la cama con sus manos cubriendo su rostro y llorando como si su vida se hubiera acabado. Bueno, parte de ella sí se había terminado, pero cuando entré y él levantó su rostro para verme, en su cara se reflejó primero un gran susto y después de reconocerme, una gran alegría, entonces brilló a través de sus lágrimas una radiante sonrisa.

«¡Pensé que usted estaba muerto!», gimió quitándose el cubrecama y viniendo hacia mí cojeando dolorosamente.

«¡Vuelve a la cama!», le ordené, alzándolo y llevándolo hasta allí, mientras él insistía en contarme:

«Alguien me cogió por detrás antes de que yo pudiera huir o gritar. Cuando desperté después y el físico me dijo que usted no había regresado al palacio, supuse que usted estaría muerto. Yo pensé que había sido herido sólo para no poder prevenirle a usted. Y después cuando desperté en su cama hace un rato y vi que usted todavía no estaba aquí, *supe* que usted...»

«Calma, muchacho», le dije, mientras lo metía bajo del cubrecama.

«Pero le fallé, mi amo —dijo sollozando—. Dejé que su enemigo pasara sobre mí.»

«No, no lo dejaste. Yo estoy a salvo gracias a ti. Chimali por esta vez se sintió satisfecho en herirte a ti en lugar de a mí. Te debo mucho y yo veré que la deuda sea pagada. Ésta es una promesa: cuando llegue el tiempo en que otra vez tenga en mi poder a Chimali, tú decidirás cuál será el castigo adecuado para él. ¿Sabes —dije tristemente— cuál fue la herida que te infirió?»

«Sí —dijo el muchacho, mordiéndose los labios para detener su temblor—. Cuando sucedió, yo sólo sentí un dolor espantoso y me desmayé. El buen físico me dejó así mientras él... mientras él hacía lo que debía hacer. Pero después me dio a oler algo muy fuerte y yo volví en mí y estornudé. Y yo vi... en donde él me había cosido.»

«Lo siento mucho», dije y fue todo lo que se me ocurrió decir.

La mano de Cózcatl bajó dentro del cubrecama, cautelosamente tocándose a sí mismo y preguntó tímidamente: «¿Esto quiere decir... quiere decir que ahora soy una muchacha, mi amo?»

«¡Qué idea tan ridícula! —dije—. Claro que no.»

«Yo creo que sí —dijo él lloriqueando—. Yo ya sé lo que hay entre las piernas de la única mujer desnuda que vi, la señora que fue nuestra última ama en Texcoco. Cuando el físico me revivió y me vi... ahí abajo... antes de que él me pusiera el vendaje... y se me veía exactamente igual que las partes privadas de *ella*.»

«¡Tú no eres una muchacha! —dije severamente—. Estás muy lejos de ser una hembra, mucho más lejos que el vil Chimali que te hirió por detrás como sólo lo hubiera hecho un marica. Ha habido muchos guerreros que han sufrido ese mismo tipo de herida en combate, Cózcatl, y han seguido siendo guerreros de gran hombría, fuerza y ferocidad. Algunos han llegado a ser más fuertes y han tenido fama, aun después de eso, como héroes famosos.»

Él persistió: «¿Entonces por qué el físico, por qué usted amo, me miran con esas caras tan largas?»

«Bien —dije y pensé acerca de ello hasta donde mi cabeza todavía dolorida me lo permitía—. Es que eso significa que tú nunca podrás ser padre.»

«¡Oh! —exclamó él y para mi sorpresa parecía muy contento—. Eso no tiene importancia. A mí nunca me ha gustado ser un niño, difícilmente me gustaría tener otros. Pero... ¿eso también significa que yo nunca podré ser un esposo?»

«No..., no necesariamente —dije con incertidumbre—. Tú solamente tendrás que encontrar o buscar la esposa adecuada para eso. Una mujer comprensiva. Aquella que pueda aceptar la clase de placer que como esposo tú podrás darle. Y tú le diste placer a esa señora que no debes nombrar, en Texcoco, ¿no es así?»

«Ella dijo eso. —Él empezó a sonreír otra vez—. Gracias por devolverme la confianza, mi amo. Puesto que soy un esclavo y no puedo ser más que un esclavo, me *gustaría* tener alguna esposa algún día.»

«Desde este momento, Cózcatl, tú ya no eres un esclavo y yo ya no soy más tu amo.»

Su sonrisa desapareció y un gesto de alarma se reflejó en su rostro. «¿Qué ha pasado?»

«Nada, excepto que ahora tú eres mi amigo y yo soy tu amigo.»

Él dijo con voz trémula: «Pero un esclavo sin amo, no vale nada amo. Es como una cosa desarraigada y desamparada.»

Yo le dije: «No cuando él tiene un amigo con quien compartir su vida y sus bienes. Tengo ahora una pequeña fortuna, Cózcatl, tú la has visto. Y tengo planes para acrecentarla en cuanto tú estés en condiciones de viajar. Iremos hacia el sur, a tierras extranjeras, como *pochteca*. ¿Qué piensas de eso? Los dos prosperaremos juntos y tú nunca serás pobre, o una cosa desarraigada y desamparada. Acabo de pedir al Venerado Orador autorización para nuestra empresa. También le he pedido un papel oficial en el que diga que Cózcatl no es más un esclavo sino el socio y amigo de Tliléctic-Mixtli.»

De nuevo sonrió y lloró al mismo tiempo. Dejó caer una de sus pequeñas manos sobre mi brazo, la primera vez que él me tocaba sin una orden o sin permiso, y dijo: «Los amigos no necesitan papeles en los que se digan que lo son.»

✠

La comunidad de mercaderes de Tenochtitlan no hacía muchos años antes que había construido el edificio que servía como depósito de mercancías en donde se acumulaban las de todos sus miembros, un vestíbulo o sala para sus reuniones, oficinas contables, bibliotecas de archivo y cosas semejantes. La Casa de los Pochteca estaba situada no lejos de El Corazón del Único Mundo y, aunque era más pequeña que un palacio, lo parecía en sus aposentos. Había una cocina y un comedor en donde se servían bebidas a los miembros de la comunidad y a mercaderes visitantes; arriba habían alcobas para que durmieran esos visitantes que venían desde muy lejos para pasar una noche o más. Habían muchos sirvientes, uno de ellos me introdujo altaneramente el día en que fui admitido para mi cita y me guió hacia una habitación lujosa en donde tres ancianos *pochteca* estaban sentados, esperando para entrevistarme.

Yo había ido preparado a esa augusta junta para ser recibido con deferencia como era lo adecuado, pero no para ser intimidado por ellos. Después de decir *Mixpatzinco* y de hacer el gesto usual de besar la tierra a los examinadores, me enderecé y sin mirar atrás, desabroché el adorno que sostenía mi manto y me senté. Ninguno de los dos, ni el manto ni yo caímos sobre el piso. El sirviente, a pesar de la sorpresa que le causó el gesto de ese arrogante plebeyo, se las arregló de alguna forma para que simultáneamente pudiera coger mi manto y deslizar bajo de mí una *icpali*.

Uno de los hombres me devolvió el saludo y ordenó al sirviente que trajera *chocólatl* para todos. Después los tres se sentaron y me miraron por un tiempo, como queriendo tomarme la medida con sus ojos. Los hombres llevaban mantos sencillos, sin ningún adorno, ya que la tradición *pochteca* era pasar desapercibidos, sin ostentación, incluso guardando secreto acerca de la riqueza y la posición social. Sin embargo, la falta de ostentación en el vestir no llegaba a disimular su posición, ya que los tres hombres estaban cebados en la gordura que da la buena comida y el fácil vivir. Dos de ellos fumaban *poquíetin* en un tubo de oro con agujeros.

«Usted llega con excelentes recomendaciones», dijo agriamente uno de los viejos, como si sintiera no poder rehusar mi candidatura inmediatamente.

«Sin embargo, usted debe de tener un capital adecuado —dijo otro—. ¿A cuánto asciende éste?»

Le alargué la lista que había hecho de las diversas mercancías y monedas de cambio que poseía. Mientras nosotros sorbíamos nuestro *chocólatl*, en esa ocasión aromático por la fragancia de la flor de magnolia, ellos se pasaron la lista de una mano a otra.

«Estimable», dijo uno.

«Pero no opulento», dijo otro.

«¿Cuántos años tiene?», me preguntó el tercero.

«Veintiuno, mis señores.»

«Es demasiado joven.»

«Pero eso no es ningún impedimento, espero —dije—. El gran Nezahualcóyotl tenía solamente dieciséis años cuando llegó a ser el Venerado Orador de Texcoco.»

«Suponiendo que usted no aspira al trono, joven Mixtli, ¿cuáles son sus planes?»

«Bien, mis señores, creo que la ropa más fina; los mantos, las faldas y blusas bordadas, serían muy difíciles de ofrecer a la gente de cualquier otra nación. Los venderé a los *pípiltin* aquí en la ciudad, quienes pagarán los precios adecuados. Después invertiré la ganancia en géneros más sencillos y prácticos: en cobertores de pelo de conejo, en cosméticos y preparaciones medicinales; los productos que sólo se consiguen aquí. Los llevaré al sur y los cambiaré por cosas que solamente pueden conseguirse en aquellas naciones.»

«Eso es lo que todos hemos estado haciendo durante años —dijo uno de los hombres, no muy impresionado—. Usted no ha mencionado los gastos de viaje. Por ejemplo, parte de sus inversiones serán para alquilar un grupo de *tamémime*.»

«No tengo pensado alquilar cargadores», dije.

«¿De verdad? ¿Tiene usted suficientes acompañantes como para transportar y hacer el trabajo ellos mismos? Usted está pensando en una economía tonta, joven. Usted pagaría a los *tamemi* alquilados por día. Si lleva amigos tendrá que compartir con ellos todas sus ganancias.»

Yo dije: «Solamente vendrán conmigo otros dos amigos para compartir esta aventura.»

«¿Tres hombres? —dijo el más viejo burlándose. Le dio un pequeño golpe a mi lista—. Simplemente con el bulto de obsidiana cargado entre usted y sus dos amigos, les dará un colapso antes de llegar al final del camino-puente que va hacia el sur.»

Pacientemente les expliqué: «Yo no intento cargar nada ni alquilar ningún cargador, porque compraré esclavos para ese trabajo.»

Los tres movieron sus cabezas con conmiseración. «Por el precio de un esclavo magro, usted podrá pagar toda una tropa de *tamémime*.»

«Y además —yo les hice notar—, hay que darles calzado, comida y ropa. Todo el camino hacia el sur y también de regreso.»

«¿Entonces sus esclavos van a ir sin comer, desnudos y sin sandalias? Realmente joven...»

«Si he dispuesto que las mercancías sean acarreadas por esclavos, es porque después puedo venderlos. Seguro que darán buenos precios por ellos en esas tierras de donde nosotros hemos capturado o enrolado muchos de sus trabajadores nativos.»

Los ancianos me miraron con sorpresa, ésa era una idea nueva para ellos. Sin embargo uno de ellos dijo: «Y ahí estará usted, en lo más profundo de las selvas del sur, sin cargadores ni esclavos que le ayuden a traer sus adquisiciones a casa.»

Yo dije: «Pienso traer sólo esas mercancías que no den trabajo en acarrearse, que puedan colocarse en pequeños bultos o su peso sea ligero. No haré lo que muchos *pochteca*, traer jade, conchas de tortuga o pieles pesadas de animales. Los mercaderes viajeros han traído todo lo que se les ofrece, simplemente porque han tenido los cargadores a quienes pagar y alimentar y deben regresar igualmente cargados como fueron. Yo conseguiré solamente cosas como los colorantes rojos y las más raras plumas. Esto requerirá un viaje más largo y más tiempo para encontrar esas cosas especiales, pero aun yo solo puedo regresar a casa cargando una bolsa completa del precioso colorante o un bulto compacto de plumas de *quétzal tótotl* y este solo cargamento me recompensará toda mi inversión miles de veces.»

Los tres se miraron entre ellos y luego se volvieron a mí, con un respeto quizás envidioso. Uno de ellos concedió: «Usted ha pensado bastante en esta empresa.»

Yo dije: «Bueno, soy joven. Tengo fuerza para una jornada dura y cuento con todo el tiempo disponible.»

Uno de ellos se rió secamente: «Ah, entonces usted piensa que nosotros siempre hemos sido viejos, obesos y sedentarios.» —Arrojó a un lado su manto y me enseñó cuatro cicatrices fruncidas sobre su costado derecho—. Las flechas de los huíchol cuando me aventuré dentro de sus montañas al noroeste, tratando de compar sus talismanes Ojo-de-Dios.»

Otro dejó caer su manto sobre el suelo para mostrarme que sólo tenía un pie. «Una serpiente *nauyaka* en las selvas de Chiapa. Su veneno mata antes de que uno pueda respirar diez veces. Tuve que amputármelo inmediatamente, con mi *maquáhuitl* y por mi propia mano.»

El tercer hombre se inclinó de tal manera que yo pudiera ver la parte alta de su cabeza. Lo que había tomado por un total crecimiento de pelo blanco, en realidad sólo era una franja alrededor de su cabeza, en el centro había una cicatriz roja y sinuosa. «Yo fue hacia el desierto del norte, buscando el *péyotl*, cacto, que hace soñar y que crece allí. En mi camino pasé a través de la Gente Perro, los chichimeca; a través de la Gente-Perro-Salvaje, los teochichimeca, y aun a través de la Gente-Perro-Rabioso, los zacachichimeca. Sin embargo, al final caí entre los yaki y toda la gente-perro comparada con esos bárbaros no son más que simples conejos. Pude escapar con vida, pero un yaki salvaje en estos momentos está luciendo un cinturón con mi pelo y festonado con los cabellos de otros muchos hombres.»

Con humildad les dije: «Mis señores, estoy maravillado de sus aventuras y asombrado de su valor, y sólo espero que algún día pueda yo estar a la altura de las hazañas de los *pochteca*. Me sentiré muy honrado con ser contado como el más pequeño dentro de su sociedad y estaré muy agradecido de poder participar de sus conocimientos y experiencias tan difícilmente ganados.»

Los tres hombres intercambiaron otra mirada. Uno de ellos murmuró: «¿Qué piensan ustedes?» Y los otros dos movieron sus cabezas afirmativamente. El anciano escalpado me dijo:

«Su primera jornada mercantil será la prueba real y necesaria para su aceptación. Ahora sepa esto: no todos los *pochteca* regresan de su primera correría. Nosotros haremos todo lo posible por prepararlo adecuadamente. Lo demás quedará en sus manos. Pero si usted sobrevive, con o sin ganancia, quedará formalmente iniciado dentro de nuestra sociedad.»

Dije: «Gracias, mis señores. Haré cualquier cosa que ustedes sugieran y tomaré en cuenta la menor observación que deseen hacerme. Si ustedes desaprueban mi plan concebido...»

«No, no —dijo uno de ellos—. Es recomendablemente audaz y original. Deje que parte de la mercancía transporte al otro resto. Je, je.»

«Nosotros solamente enmendaremos su plan en su extensión —dijo otro—. Usted tiene razón; su mercancía de lujo debe ser vendida aquí en donde los nobles pueden pagarla bien, pero no debe perder el tiempo vendiéndola pieza por pieza.»

«No, no pierda su tiempo —dijo el tercero—. A través de una larga experiencia y después de consultar a adivinos y refraneros, hemos encontrado que la mejor fecha auspiciada para emprender una expedición es el día Uno-Serpiente. Hoy es Cinco-Casa, así es que, déjeme ver, el día Uno-Serpiente estará en el calendario exactamente dentro de veintitrés días. Éste será el único Uno-Serpiente en este año durante la estación seca, la cual, créame, es la única adecuada para viajar hacia el sur.»

El primer hombre volvió a hablar. «Traiga aquí con nosotros todo su surtido de ricos géneros y ropa. Calcularemos su valor y le daremos a cambio lo justo en la mercancía más adecuada. Algodones sencillos, cobertores y otros géneros, como usted mencionó. Nosotros podemos disponer de la mercancía lujosa localmente y con suficiente tiempo. Sólo le deduciremos una pequeña fracción a cambio, como su contribución inicial para nuestro dios Yacatecutli y para mantener las facilidades que proporciona la sociedad.»

Quizá dudé un momento. Él levantó sus oscuras cejas y dijo: «Joven Mixtli, usted tendrá otros gravámenes que sostener. Todos los hemos tenido. No tema un engaño en la competencia comercial de sus colegas. A menos de que cada uno de nosotros sea escrupulosamente honesto, no tendremos ganancias e incluso no podremos sobrevivir. Nuestra filosofía es así de simple. Y sepa también esto, usted debe ser igualmente honesto en sus tratos con el salvaje más ignorante en las más lejanas tierras. Porque, a cualquier parte que usted viaje, algún otro *pochtécatl* ya ha estado antes o llegará después. Solamente si cada uno de los tratos comerciales son justos, puede el siguiente *pochtécatl* ser aceptado en esa comunidad... o dejarlo salir con vida.»

Me acerqué al viejo Glotón de Sangre con cierta precaución, casi esperando que él eructara alguna maldición por la proposición de llegar a ser «la niñera» de un inexperimentado perdido en niebla *pochtécatl* y de un muchachito convaleciente. Para mi sorpresa y alegría, él se mostró entusiasmado.

«¿Yo? ¿Tu única escolta armada? ¿Confiaríais vuestras vidas y fortuna en este viejo saco de huesos y aire? —Pestañeó varias veces, resopló e hizo un ruido armonioso con su mano puesta en la nariz—. ¿Cómo puedo declinar este voto de confianza?»

Dije: «No te lo hubiera propuesto si no te considerara algo más que un saco de huesos y viento.»

«Bueno, los dioses lo saben, no quiero volver a tomar parte en alguna otra ridícula campaña como aquella de Texcala. Y mi única alternativa es, ¡*ayya!*, es enseñar otra vez en la Casa del Desarrollo de la Fuerza. Pero, ¡*ayyo!*, volver a ver esas tierras lejanas otra vez... —Miró hacia el horizonte, hacia el sur—. ¡Por los huevos de granito del Gran Huitzi, sí! Te doy las gracias por tu ofrecimiento y lo acepto con gusto, joven Perdido en Nie... er... ¿patrón?»

«Socio —dije—. Tú, yo y Cózcatl vamos a compartir por partes iguales cualquier cosa que traigamos de vuelta. Y espero que me llames Mixtli.»

«Entonces, Mixtli, permíteme hacer la primera tarea para prepararnos. Déjame ir a Azcapotzalco para comprar allí esclavos. Yo tengo una mano vieja para juzgar la carne del hombre y conozco a esos tratantes que hacen algunas trampas astutas. Por ejemplo, cebando con una mezcla de cera de abejas disolviéndola sobre la piel de un pecho flaco.»

Exclamé: «¿Pero con qué objeto?»

«La cera da endurecimiento y abulta los músculos pectorales de un hombre como los de un *tocotini* volador, o da a una mujer unos pechos como los de aquellas legendarias y diversas perlas que habitan en La Isla de las Mujeres. Claro que si vas en un día caluroso, las tetas de las mujeres caerán hasta sus rodillas. Oh, no te preocupes; no compraré ninguna esclava. A menos de que las cosas en el sur hayan cambiado drásticamente, no nos harán falta voluntarias como cocineras, lavanderas y también quien nos caliente la cama.»

Así es que Glotón de Sangre tomó mis plumas de oro fundido y fue al mercado de esclavos de Azcapotzalco, en la tierra firme, y después de cuatro días de elegir y cerrar tratos volvió con doce hombres fuertes y magros. Ninguno de ellos pertenecía a la misma tribu ni tampoco habían sido de un mismo vendedor; ésa era una precaución que Glotón de Sangre había tomado, con el fin de que ninguno de ellos fueran amigos o *cuilontin*, amantes, quienes pudieran conspirar un amotinamiento o una huida. Cada uno de ellos llegó con su nombre, pero nosotros no nos tomamos la molestia de memorizarlos y simplemente los llamábamos como Ce, Ome, Yeyi y así; esto es: número Uno, Dos, Tres, hasta el Doce.

Durante esos días de preparativos, el físico de palacio había permitido a Cózcatl dejar la cama cada vez por un período más largo y finalmente le quitó las puntadas y los vendajes, recetándole ejercicios para su total restablecimiento. Pronto el muchacho estuvo tan saludable y contento como antes, y lo único que le recordaba la herida que había sufrido era que ahora para orinar, se tenía que poner en cuclillas como las mujeres para no mojarse.

Mientras tanto yo ya había hecho el cambio en la Casa de los Pochteca, dando mis mercancías de alta calidad y recibiendo a cambio cerca de dieciséis veces su valor en mercancías más sencillas. Después necesité seleccionar y comprar el equipo y las provisiones para nuestra expedición y los tres ancianos que me habían examinado estuvieron muy gustosos de ayudarme en eso también. Sospecho que gozaron siendo delegados para esa tarea o reviviendo viejos tiempos, discutiendo sobre cuál sería la fibra más fuerte y comparando la de maguey con la de yute para *mayácatl*, debatiendo las respectivas ventajas de llevar el agua en bolsas de piel de venado (en las que no se pierde ni una gota) o llevarla en jarras de barro (en las que se evapora algo de agua, pero ésta se conserva mucho más fresca), instruyéndome con mapas rudos e imprecisos que me dieron e impartiéndome toda clase de consejos adquiridos en sus años de experiencia.

«La única comida que se transporta a sí misma son los *techichi*, perros. Lleva un gran hato de ellos contigo, Mixtli. Ellos mismos buscarán su comida y agua, y son demasiados tímidos para volverse salvajes. Naturalmente la carne de perro no es de lo más sabrosa, pero tú estarás muy contento de tenerlos a mano cuando escasee la caza de animales salvajes.»

«Cuando caces un animal salvaje, Mixtli, no necesitas cargar y guardar la carne hasta que pierda su suavidad y su buen sabor. Envuélvela en hojas de árbol de papaya y te durará suave y sabrosa por más de una noche.»

«Si necesitas papel para llevar tus cuentas, arranca hojas de cualquier parra. Escribe en ellas con cualquier ramita afilada y las líneas blancas que quedarán en las hojas verdes, durarán tanto como en papel pintado.»

«Ten cuidado con las mujeres en aquellas tierras en donde los ejércitos mexica han sido invasores. Algunas han sido tan maltratadas por nuestros guerreros y guardan tanto rencor, que después, ellas han dejado que sus partes íntimas sean infectadas, deliberadamente, por la terrible enfermedad *nanaua*. Cualquiera de ellas se acostará con cualquier viajero mexica para vengarse, y así éste finalmente llegará a sufrir la podredumbre de su *tepule* y de su cerebro.»

Muy temprano en la mañana del día Uno-Serpiente, dejamos Tenochtitlan Cózcatl, Glotón de Sangre, yo y nuestros doce esclavos cargados bajo el peso de sus fardos y el hato de perros gordos que retozaban cerca de nuestros pies. Nos encaminamos a lo largo de la avenida que nos llevaría hacia el sur a través del lago. A nuestra derecha, al oeste, en el lugar más cercano a la tierra firme, se levantaba el monte de Chapultépec. En la superficie de sus rocas, el primer Motecuzoma hizo tallar su retrato en un tamaño gigantesco y cada uno de los Uey-Tlatoani que le sucedieron siguieron su ejemplo. De acuerdo con eso, el inmenso retrato de Auítzotl estaba casi terminado; sin embargo, nosotros no nos pudimos dar cuenta de ninguno de los detalles de los rasgos de la escultura, porque el monte no estaba todavía iluminado por la luz del día. Era nuestro mes *panquetzaliztli*, que vendría a ser a mediados de su noviembre, cuando el sol se levanta tarde y hacia el sureste, exactamente detrás del pico del Popocatépetl.

Cuando empezamos a caminar sobre el camino-puente, no había nada que verse en esa dirección a excepción de la neblina usual, coloreada por la luz opalina del inminente amanecer. Pero muy despacio la neblina fue disminuyendo y gradualmente la simétrica y maciza forma del volcán llegó a ser discernible, como si él se estuviera moviendo de su eterno lugar y viniendo a nuestro encuentro. Cuando el velo de la niebla se disipó totalmente, la montaña era visible en toda su magnitud. Su cono cubierto de nieve irradiaba detrás de él en un halo glorioso de sol. Entonces, pareciendo como si saliera del mismo cráter, Tonatíu se levantó y el día llegó; el lago resplandecía, todas las tierras alrededor se veían bañadas de una pálida luz dorada y de pálidas sombras purpúreas. Al mismo instante, el incienso hirviente del volcán exhaló una voluta de humo azul que se levantó y tomó la forma de un gigantesco hongo. Eso tenía que ser un buen augurio para nuestra jornada: el sol llameando sobre la cresta nevada del Popocatépetl y haciéndola brillar como ónix blanco incrustado con todas las joyas del mundo, mientras la montaña a su vez nos saludaba con un humo que se elevaba perezosamente, diciendo:

«Ustedes parten, gente mía, pero yo quedo, como siempre me he quedado y siempre me quedaré, como un faro para guiarlos de regreso sanos y salvos.»

I H S

✠

S. C. C. M.

Santificada, Cesárea, Católica Majestad,
el Emperador Don Carlos, nuestro Señor Rey:

Real e Imperial Majestad, nuestro Muy Reverendo Gobernante, desde esta ciudad de Mexico capital de la Nueva España, en el segundo día después del Domingo de Rogaciones, en el año de· Nuestro Señor mil quinientos treinta, os saludo.

De acuerdo con la petición de Vuestra Estimada Majestad en su reciente carta, nos, debemos confesar que somos incapaces de señalar a Vuestra Majestad el número exacto de indios prisioneros sacrificados por los aztecas en esa ocasión, hace ya más de cuarenta años, de la dedicación a su Gran Pirámide. Hace mucho tiempo que la Gran Pirámide desapareció, así es que no queda ninguna anotación sobre la cantidad de víctimas en ese día, si es que alguna vez la hubo.

Aun nuestro cronista azteca, que estuvo presente en aquella ocasión, es incapaz de mencionar un número exacto, sino que nada más llega a la aproximación de «miles», aunque es muy probable que el viejo charlatán exagere con el objeto de hacer parecer ese día (y ese edificio) más importante históricamente. Nuestros precursores, los misioneros franciscanos, han calculado el número de víctimas de ese día entre cuatro mil y *ochenta* mil. Pero esos buenos hermanos deben de haber aumentado excesivamente la cifra, también, quizás inconscientemente influidos por la fuerte repulsión que sentían hacia ese hecho, o quizá para impresionarnos a nosotros, su recién llegado Obispo, con la inherente bestialidad de la población nativa.

No, difícilmente necesitamos utilizar la exageración para tratar de persuadiros que los indios han nacido salvajes y depravados. Ciertamente que podríamos creer eso, ya que contamos con la evidencia diaria del narrador, cuya presencia debemos soportar por las órdenes de Vuestra Muy Magnífica Majestad. A través de estos meses, sus pocas aportaciones que pudieran contener algún valor o interés, han sido hechas a un lado por sus divagaciones viles y venenosas. Adrede nos ha causado náusea, al interrumpir sus relatos de ceremonias solemnes, viajes significativos y sucesos casuales, sólo para detenerse en algún pasaje de algún hecho transitorio lascivo, ya sea de su vida o de la de otro, y describir en la forma más minuciosamente detallada el placer que éste daba, en todas las formas físicas posibles y en una manera muy a menudo repugnante y sucia, incluyendo aquella perversión de la cual San Pablo decía: «No dejéis que eso sea nombrado entre vosotros.»

En cuanto a lo que hemos aprendido sobre el carácter del azteca, nos, podríamos realmente creer que los aztecas de buena gana hubieran matado ochenta mil hombres en su Gran Pirámide y en un solo día, excepto que esa matanza fue del todo imposible. Aunque sus sacerdotes-ejecutores hubieran trabajado incesantemente las veinticuatro horas del día, habrían tenido que matar cincuenta y cinco hombres por minuto durante todo ese tiempo, casi un hombre por segundo. Y aun el número menor de víctimas que se estima, es difícil de creer. Teniendo nosotros mismos alguna experiencia en ejecuciones masivas, nos es muy difícil creer que esa gente tan primitiva podría haber dispuesto de miles de cadáveres antes de que empezara la putrefacción y con ello engendrara la peste dentro de la ciudad.

Sin embargo, ya sea que la cifra de hombres muertos en aquel día haya sido ochenta mil o solamente diez, cientos o miles, de todas maneras esa cantidad sería execrable para cualquier Cristiano y un horror para cualquier ser civilizado, ya que tantos murieron en nombre de una religión falsa y para la gloria de unos ídolos demoníacos. Por este motivo, a vuestra orden e instigación, Señor, en los diecisiete meses desde nuestra llegada aquí, han sido destruidos quinientos treinta y dos templos de diferentes tamaños; desde estructuras elaboradas en las altas pirámides hasta simples altares erigidos dentro de cuevas naturales. Han sido destruidos más de veintiún mil ídolos de diferentes tamaños, desde monstruosos monolitos tallados hasta pequeñas figuras caseras hechas de arcilla. Para ninguno de ellos se volverá a hacer un sacrificio humano y nos, continuaremos buscando y destruyendo los que vayan quedando, conforme se vayan expandiendo las fronteras de la Nueva España.

Aunque ésta no fuera la función y la orden de nuestro oficio, siempre seguiría siendo nuestro mayor esfuerzo, el buscar hasta encontrar y destruir al Demonio en cualquier disfraz que él asuma aquí. En vista de esto, nos, deseamos llamar la atención de Vuestra Majestad, particularmente en la última parte de la crónica de nuestro azteca, en las páginas anexadas, en donde él dice que ciertos paganos al sur de esta Nueva España, ya han reconocido a una especie de Dios Único Todopoderoso y tienen un símbolo gemelo al de la Santa Cruz, mucho antes de la llegada de cualquiera de los misioneros de nuestra Santa Iglesia. El capellán de Vuestra Majestad se inclina a tomar esa aseveración con cierta duda, francamente por la mala opinión que tenemos del informante.

En España, Señor, en nuestros oficios de Inquisidor Provincial de Navarra y como Guardián de los descreídos y mendigos de la Institución de Reforma de Abrojo, hemos conocido a tantos réprobos incorregibles como para no reconocer a otro más, sin importar el color de su piel. Éste, en los raros momentos en que no está obsesionado por el demonio de la concupiscencia, evidencia las otras faltas y debilidades del común de los mortales, aunque en este caso algunas de ellas más perversas. Nos, lo consideramos con tanta doblez como esos despreciables judíos «marranos» de España quienes se someten al bautismo, que van a nuestras iglesias y que incluso comen carne de cerdo, pero que todavía mantienen y practican en secreto las ceremonias de su prohibido judaísmo.

A pesar de nuestras suspicacias y reservas, nos, debemos de mantener una mente abierta. Así es que si este viejo odioso no está mintiendo caprichosamente o mofándose de nosotros, entonces, esa nación que está hacia el sur y que proclama devoción a un ser más alto y que tiene como sagrado el símbolo cruciforme, debe ser considerada como una anomalía genuina para el interés de los teólogos. Por esta razón, nos, hemos enviado una misión de frailes Dominicos a esa región para que investiguen dicho fenómeno y nos, haremos llegar los resultados a Vuestra Majestad en cuanto los tengamos.

Mientras tanto, Señor, que Nuestro Señor Dios junto con Jesús Su Único Hijo, derrame todo género de bendiciones sobre Vuestra Inefable Majestad, que os dejen prosperar en todas vuestras empresas y que os vean tan benéficamente como vuestro S.C.C.M., leal siervo,

(ecce signum) ZUMÁRRAGA

SEXTA PARS

Creo que recuerdo todos los incidentes de cada uno de los días de aquella primera expedición, de ida y de vuelta. En las últimas jornadas no llegué a darle importancia a las menores calamidades y aun a algunas mayores, como los pies ampollados y las manos encallecidas, al tiempo enervantemente caliente o dolorosamente frío, o algunas veces a las náuseas provocadas por los alimentos que comí y las aguas que bebí y que también me provocaron retortijones, o a la no poca frecuente necesidad de no poder encontrar ni comida ni agua. Aprendí a insensibilizarme, como un sacerdote drogado en trance, para endurecerme hasta tal grado que no llegara ni siquiera a notar la cantidad de días tristes y caminos en los cuales nada pasaba en lo absoluto; cuando no había nada que hacer más que seguir adelante a través del campo, en donde no había ningún interés de color o variedad.

Pero en esa primera jornada, simplemente porque *era* la primera, cada uno de los objetos o cualquier cosa que ocurriera tuvo interés para mí, aun las fatigas e incomodidades usuales y concienzudamente anotaba cada noche, con mis palabras-pintadas, todo lo que acontecía en la expedición. Tengo la esperanza de que esos papeles de corteza doblados fueran útiles y aprovechables al Venerado Orador Auítzotl a quien se los entregué cuando regresamos. Seguramente que encontró porciones de ellos difíciles de descifrar, debido a que sufrieron los embates del tiempo, inmersiones en las corrientes que vadeábamos y siendo muy a menudo ensuciados por mi propio sudor. Puesto que Auítzotl tenía considerablemente más experiencia como viajero que yo en aquel tiempo, probablemente también debió de haber sonreído ante muchas de mis narraciones ingenuamente ensalzadas más de lo ordinario y obviamente elaboradas.

Sin embargo, aquellas tierras extranjeras y sus gentes ya han empezado a cambiar, incluso hace mucho tiempo, cuando las incursiones de los *pochteca* y otros exploradores llevaron a ellos artículos, trajes, ideas y palabras que ellos jamás habían conocido antes. Hoy en día, con sus soldados españoles, sus colonos, sus misioneros destruyendo todo por todas partes, no dudo que esas regiones y sus culturas hayan cambiado tanto que ni ellos mismos podrían reconocerse. Así, me sentía muy feliz al pensar que esas cosas ya poco duraderas que yo verifiqué en mi vida pasada, las he dejado registradas para los futuros estudiosos; de cómo eran esas otras tierras, y cómo era su gente en los años en que ellos todavía eran completamente desconocidos para el resto del mundo.

Si al contarles esta primera jornada, mis señores, encuentran algunas de las descripciones o paisajes, personas o sucesos fastidiosamente insubstanciales y con vagos detalles, ustedes pueden achacarlo a mi limitada vista. Si por otro lado, vívidamente les describo algunas otras cosas que pueden suponer que yo no podría haber visto, entonces se darán cuenta de que estoy dando detalles que recolecté en viajes posteriores a lo largo de esa misma ruta, cuando tuve la oportunidad y facilidad de ver más de cerca y más claramente.

En una larga jornada, siguiendo caminos difíciles y fáciles, una hilera de hombres cargados podían hacer por término medio cerca de cinco largas carreras entre el amanecer y el oscurecer. Nosotros cubrimos sólo la mitad de esa distancia en nuestro primer día de marcha, simplemente cruzando el largo camino hacia Coyohuacan, hacia el sur de la tierra firme y deteniéndonos allí para pasar la noche antes de que el sol se ocultara, ya que al día siguiente la caminata no sería fácil. Como ustedes saben, esa parte del lago yace en una cuenca cóncava; para poder salir de allí hacia cualquier dirección, se tiene que escalar y bajar sobre sus laderas. Y las montañas hacia el sur, más allá de Coyohuacan, son las más escabrosas de todas las que circundan esa cuenca.

Hace algunos años, cuando los primeros soldados españoles llegaron a esta nación y yo había logrado por primera vez entender y hablar un poco de su lenguaje, uno de ellos, viendo una fila de *tamémine* fatigados bajo el peso de su carga sostenida en sus espaldas por las bandas colocadas alrededor de sus frentes, me preguntó: «¿Por qué, en nombre de Dios, vosotros, estúpidos brutos, no habéis pensado nunca en inventar una rueda?»

Entonces yo no estaba muy familiarizado con el «nombre de Dios», pero sabía perfectamente lo que era una rueda. Cuando era un niñito tuve un armadillo de juguete hecho de barro, del que tiraba con un cordón. Puesto que las piernas del armadillo no se podían hacer de tal manera que éste pudiera caminar, el juguete estaba montado sobre cuatro ruedecitas de madera para que pudiera moverse. Le dije eso al español y él me preguntó: «¿Entonces, por todos los diablos, ninguno de vosotros utiliza ruedas para transportar, como las de nuestros cañones y arcones?» Yo pensé que ésta era una pregunta bastante tonta y se lo dije, y recibí un golpe en mi cara por insolente.

Sí conocíamos la utilidad de las ruedas, ya que habíamos movido cosas extremadamente pesadas como la Piedra del Sol, rodándolas sobre troncos puestos debajo y encima de ellas, pero aun en nuestros pocos caminos bien aplanados o en nuestros pocos caminos mejor pavimentados, esa clase de ruedas hubieran sido inútiles para el trabajo de los lanchones. Tampoco había en estas tierras ninguna clase de animales como sus caballos, mulas, bueyes y burros que pudieran tirar de los vehículos con ruedas. Nuestras únicas bestias de carga éramos nosotros mismos y un *tamemi* bien musculoso podía cargar cerca de la mitad de su propio peso por una distancia larga sin fatigarse. Si él hubiera puesto su carga sobre ruedas, para empujarla, simplemente hubiera agregado un peso extra a su carga con las ruedas y éstas hubieran venido a ser un gran estorbo en terreno abrupto.

Ahora, por supuesto, sus españoles han hecho muchos más caminos y sus animales hacen el trabajo mientras los conductores de yuntas cabalgan o caminan sin ninguna carga, siendo muy fácil para ellos. Yo les concedo que una procesión de veinte vagones pesados tirados por cuarenta caballos vale la pena de verse. Nuestro pequeño grupo de tres mercaderes y doce esclavos, seguramente que no se vería tan impresionante, pero nosotros transportábamos todas nuestras mercancías y la mayoría de las provisiones que necesitábamos para la jornada, sobre nuestras propias espaldas y piernas al menos con dos ventajas: no teníamos que cuidar y alimentar a un hato de animales voraces y nuestro medio de transporte *nos* hacía más fuertes cada día.

En verdad, la dura guía de Glotón de Sangre nos hizo a todos endurecernos más de lo necesario para nuestras diligencias. Aun antes de dejar Tenochtitlan y cada noche cuando hacíamos un alto a lo largo del camino, él guiaba a los esclavos, a Cózcatl y a mí cuando no estábamos ocupados en otras cosas, a practicar con las jabalinas y las hondas, que todos llevábamos. Él mismo portaba un formidable arsenal personal de hondas, lanza larga, jabalina y tira dardos; una larga *maquáhuitl* y un cuchillo corto, un arco y una aljaba llena de flechas. No fue difícil para Glotón de Sangre convencer a los esclavos de que serían mejor tratados por nosotros que por cualquier bandido que quisiera «liberarlos» y que por esa buena razón debían ayudarnos a repeler a los que pudieran atacarnos, y les enseñó cómo.

Después de haber pasado la noche en Coyohuacan, nos volvimos a poner en marcha muy temprano a la mañana siguiente, porque Glotón de Sangre había dicho: «Debemos cruzar las tierras malas de Cuicuilco antes de que el sol esté en lo alto.» Ese nombre significa El Lugar Del Dulce Cantar y quizás fuera así ese lugar en algún tiempo, pero ya no lo era. Ahora es un estéril lugar de roca gris-negra, de olas que se agitan en su lecho pedregoso y se hinchan sobre la porosa roca marcada. Por su apariencia pudo haber sido una espumosa cascada que se volvió dura y negra por la maldición de un hechicero. En la actualidad es un torrente seco de lava del volcán Xitli, que ha estado muerto por tantas gavillas de años que sólo los dioses saben cuándo hizo erupción y borró El Lugar Del Dulce Cantar. Se ve que obviamente fue una ciudad de algún tamaño, pero nadie sabe qué gente la construyó y vivió allí. El único edificio visible que queda es una pirámide la mitad de la cual está enterrada bajo la profunda orilla de la lava lisa. No está hecha sobre un cuadrado como esas que nosotros los mexica y otras naciones han construido (en franca imitación de las de los tolteca). La pirámide de Cuicuilco, o lo que se alcanza a ver de ella, es una pila cónica circundada por terrazas.

La expuesta superficie negra, cualquier que haya sido su dulzura y su canción alguna vez, no es ahora un lugar como para pasar mucho tiempo durante el día, ya que sus rocas porosas de lava succionan el calor del sol y exhalan dos o tres veces más ese calor. Incluso en el frío tempranero de aquella mañana, hace ya mucho tiempo, esa tierra hacia el occidente no era un lugar placentero para ser atravesado. Nada, ni siquiera hierbajos, crecían allí, no se escuchaban los trinos de los pájaros y lo único que se oía era el clamor de nuestros pasos, fuerte y reverberante, como si camináramos sobre una gran jarra de agua vacía, que fuera partida por gigantes.

Pero por lo menos, durante esa parte de la jornada, caminamos en línea recta. El resto del día lo pasamos subiendo la montaña, encorvados por el esfuerzo, o bajándola por su costado para luego volver a escalarla y encorvarnos nuevamente para subir la siguiente montaña. Y la siguiente y la siguiente. Por supuesto que no había ningún peligro o una dificultad verdadera a nuestro paso por esas primeras extensiones, ya que estábamos en la región en que iban todas las rutas de comercio que convergían al sur de Tenochtitlan, y multitudes de viajeros anteriores habían dejado su trazo bien marcado y firmemente estampado. Sin embargo, para una persona inexperta como yo, allí estaba el sudor escurriendo, el dolor de espalda, los pulmones esforzándose en esa desagradable faena. Cuando al fin nos detuvimos para pasar la noche en el valle alto del pueblo de los Xochimilca, aun Glotón de Sangre estaba tan fatigado que sólo nos obligó a hacer una práctica superficial de armas. Luego él y los otros comieron sin mucho apetito y se acostaron sobre sus petates.

Yo lo hubiera hecho también, excepto por el hecho de que un grupo de *pochteca* que, de regreso a casa, pasaba también allí la noche y parte de sus jornadas habían sido a lo largo de algunos caminos que yo intentaba tomar, así es que sostuve mis párpados abiertos el tiempo suficiente como para conversar con el *pochtécatl* que estaba al mando del grupo, un hombre de mediana edad, pero todavía fuerte. Su grupo componía una de las mayores expediciones, con cientos de cargadores y protegidos por una cantidad igual de guerreros mexica, así es que estoy seguro de que miró el nuestro con tolerante desdén, pero fue lo suficientemente bondadoso con un principiante como yo. Me dejó desdoblar mis rudos mapas y corrigió muchos detalles de ellos, que eran vagos o que contenían errores, y marcó en ellos los lugares en donde podríamos encontrar agua potable y otras cosas igualmente útiles. Entonces me dijo:

«Nosotros hicimos un comercio muy provechoso por cierta cantidad del precioso colorante carmín de los tzapoteca, pero oí un rumor de un colorante todavía más raro. El púrpura. Algo descubierto últimamente.»

Yo le dije: «No hay nada de nuevo acerca del color púrpura.»

«Un bello y *permanente* púrpura —dijo él pacientemente—. Uno que no se decolora o se vuelve de un verde feo. Si este colorante verdaderamente existe, será reservado únicamente para la alta nobleza. Vendrá a tener más valor que el oro o las plumas de *quétzal tótotl*.»

«Ah, un púrpura permanente —dije, inclinando la cabeza—. Es cierto, nunca antes se ha conocido. En verdad que podrá ser vendido a cualquier precio que uno pida. ¿Pero usted no buscó de dónde provenía ese rumor?»

Él negó con la cabeza: «Es una de las desventajas de un grupo numeroso. No puede alejarse prácticamente de las rutas ya conocidas y seguras, o separarse en porciones a la aventura. Hay un gran peligro substancioso en ir a cazar lo insubstancial.»

«Mi pequeño grupo podría ir hasta ese lugar», insinué.

Él me miró por un espacio de tiempo, luego se encogió de hombros: «Pasará mucho tiempo antes de que yo vuelva a esos lugares otra vez. —Se inclinó sobre mi mapa y apuntó con su dedo un lugar en particular cerca de la costa del gran océano del sur—. Fue aquí, en Tecuantepec, en donde un mercader tzapotécatl me habló sobre ese nuevo colorante. No me dijo mucho, sólo mencionó un pueblo llamado los chóntaltin, gente feroz e inaccesible. Su nombre significa solamente Los Desconocidos ¿y qué clase de pueblo podría llamarse a sí mismo Los Desconocidos? Mi informante también mencionó caracoles. ¡Caracoles! Yo le pregunto a usted: ¿caracoles y desconocidos, tiene eso algún sentido? Pero si quiere correr el riesgo con tan pequeña evidencia, joven, le deseo muy buena suerte.»

A la siguiente tarde llegamos a un pueblo que era, y todavía es, el más bello y hospitalario de las tierras tlahuica. Está situado en una planicie alta y sus edificios no están construidos confusamente, sino separados unos de otros por árboles, arbustos y otra clase de plantas muy bellas, por esta razón el pueblo era llamado Rodeado de Floresta o Quaunáhuac. A este nombre melodioso, sus compatriotas, con su lenguaje turbio, lo distorsionaron al ridículo y derogativo Cuernavaca, y espero que la posteridad nunca se lo perdone.

El pueblo, las montañas que lo circundaban, el aire puro y su clima, todo esto había sido una invitación para que Quaunáhuac fuera siempre el lugar de veraneo favorito de los opulentos nobles de Tenochtitlan. El primer Motecuzoma mandó construir para él un modesto palacio de campo en las cercanías y otros gobernantes mexica sucesivamente lo fueron alargando y agregando más edificios al palacio, hasta que en tamaño y lujo llegó a rivalizar con cualquiera de la capital y mucho más que ellos en la extensión de sus bellos jardines y prados. Tengo entendido que su Capitán General Cortés se ha apropiado de él, para hacer su propia residencia señorial. Quizá sea yo disculpado por ustedes, reverendos frailes, si hago notar malignamente que el solo hecho de que él se haya asentado en Quaunáhuac sea la única razón legítima por la cual se ha falseado el nombre del lugar.

Ya que nuestro pequeño grupo había llegado un poco antes de la puesta del sol, no pudimos resistir la tentación de quedarnos y pasar la noche entre las flores y las fragancias de Quaunáhuac. Sin embargo nos levantamos antes que el sol, y con prisa dejamos atrás lo que quedaba de esa sierra.

En cada uno de los lugares en que nos detuvimos, encontramos posada para los viajeros, en donde nosotros, los tres que guiábamos el grupo, o sea Glotón de Sangre, Cózcatl y yo, nos habían dado cuartos separados para dormir, moderadamente confortables, mientras que nuestros esclavos eran amontonados en un largo dormitorio lleno ya de otros cargadores roncando; nuestros bultos de mercancía eran guardados dentro de habitaciones aseguradas y bien custodiadas y nuestros perros eran dejados en el patio de atrás de la cocina, en donde se tiraban los desperdicios para que allí encontraran su comida.

Durante los cinco días que llevábamos viajando, todavía estábamos dentro del área en que las rutas comerciales hacia el sur convergían hacia o fuera de Tenochtitlan, así es que había muchos albergues situados convenientemente para cuando los viajeros se detuvieran a pasar la noche. Además de proveer refugio, provisiones, baños calientes y aceptables comidas, cada una de esas posadas también alquilaba mujeres. No habiendo tenido ninguna mujer por más de un mes más o menos, hubiera podido estar interesado en ese servicio, pero todas esas *maátime* eran tan feas que no me interesaron y de todas formas ellas no deseaban acostarse conmigo, sino que dedicaban sus guiños y sugestivos gestos a los miembros de las caravanas que regresaban.

Glotón de Sangre me explicó: «Ellas esperan seducir a los hombres que han estado por largo tiempo viajando por los caminos y a quienes ya se les ha olvidado cómo es un mujer bonita, y que además ya no pueden esperar a llegar a Tenochtitlan para conseguir a las más bellas mujeres. Tú y yo quizás estemos lo suficientemente desesperados como para tener una *maátitl* de éstas a nuestro regreso, pero por ahora yo sugiero que no gastemos ni nuestro dinero ni nuestra energía. Habrá mujeres a donde vamos y ellas venderán sus favores por cualquier chuchería y muchas de ellas son muy bellas. ¡*Ayyo*, espera poder regocijar tus ojos y tus sentidos con las mujeres de la Gente Nube!»

En la mañana número seis de la jornada, nos encontramos en el área en donde las rutas comerciales convergen. En algún momento de aquella misma mañana cruzamos una invisible frontera y entramos en las tierras empobrecidas de los mixteca o los tya nüü, como ellos mismos se llamaban, Hombres de la Tierra. Si bien esa nación no era enemiga de los mexica, tampoco se inclinaba a proteger a los viajeros *pochteca* ni advertía a su gente de no tomar una ventaja criminal sobre las caravanas mercantiles.

«Estamos en una nación en la que tenemos la posibilidad de encontrarnos con bandidos —previno Glotón de Sangre—. Ellos se ocultan en las cercanías de los caminos esperando emboscar a las caravanas cuando van o regresan hacia Tenochtitlan.»

«¿Por qué aquí? —pregunté—. ¿Por qué no más hacia el norte en donde las rutas se juntan y las caravanas son más numerosas?»

«Por esa misma razón. Más atrás, las caravanas muy a menudo viajan en gran compañía y son demasiado grandes para ser atacadas, a menos de que lo sean con un pequeño ejército. En cambio aquí, las caravanas que van hacia el sur se dividen y las que regresan no se encuentran ni se mezclan con las otras. En todo caso, nosotros somos una caza pequeña, pero un grupo de ladrones no nos ignorará.»

Así es que Glotón de Sangre se adelantó lejos de nosotros como una vanguardia. Cózcatl me dijo que sólo podía ver al viejo guerrero a la distancia, cuando cruzábamos lugares extremadamente anchos y llanos, libres de arbustos o árboles. Pero nuestro explorador no nos gritó ningún aviso para prevenirnos contra algún peligro y así pasó la mañana, mientras caminábamos detrás de él, casi oculto por el polvo del camino. Con nuestros mantos tratábamos de cubrirnos las narices y la boca a fin de protegernos del polvo, pero éste hacía que nos lloraran los ojos y nuestra respiración fuera difícil. Luego el camino se elevó hacia un montecillo y allí encontramos a Glotón de Sangre esperándonos sentado a la mitad de ese camino, con sus armas diestramente a ambos lados de él, sobre la hierba polvorienta, listas para ser usadas.

«Deteneos aquí —dijo quedamente—. Ellos ya se han dado cuenta por la nube de polvo de que vosotros os estáis acercando, pero todavía no saben cuántos somos. Son ocho tya nuü y no son unos tipos muy delicados que digamos. Están agachados a la derecha del camino por donde éste pasa entre unos árboles y hierba alta. Les daremos once de los nuestros, ya que si fuéramos menos no habríamos podido levantar esa nube de polvo y podrían sospechar algún truco con lo cual sería muy difícil manejarlos.»

«¿Manejarlos, cómo? —pregunté—. ¿Y qué quieres decir con darles once de los nuestros?»

Él hizo un movimiento para indicar silencio, fue hacia lo alto de la elevación, se dejó caer en el suelo y reptó para mirar un momento, luego se arrastró hacia atrás otra vez, se levantó y vino a juntarse con nosotros.

«Sólo se pueden ver cuatro, ya —dijo y resopló desdeñosamente—. Un truco muy viejo. Es mediodía, así es que los cuatro pretenderán ser humildes viajeros mixteca descansando a la sombra de los árboles y preparando un bocado para la comida del mediodía. Cortésmente nos invitarán a compartir su comida y cuando todos seamos muy amigos, sentados juntos en su compañía cerca del fuego con nuestras armas yaciendo a un lado, los otros cuatro escondidos en las inmediaciones se acercarán y... *¡yya ayya!*»

«¿Entonces qué es lo que vamos a hacer?»

«Exactamente eso mismo. Imitar su emboscada, pero desde una distancia mucho mayor. Quiero decir que algunos de nosotros lo haremos. Déjame ver. Cuatro, Diez y Seis, vosotros sois los más grandes y los que utilizáis mejor las armas. Quitaos los bultos y dejadlos aquí. Traed sólo las lanzas y venid conmigo.» Glotón de Sangre también dejó sus otras armas en el suelo y solamente tomó su *maquáhuitl*. «Mixtli, tú y Cózcatl y todos los demás id derechos hacia la trampa, como si no hubiérais sido prevenidos. Aceptad su invitación, descansad y comed. Solamente no parezcáis *muy* estúpidos y confiados o también sospecharán.»

Glotón de Sangre suavemente les dio ciertas instrucciones que no pude oír a los tres esclavos. Luego Diez y él desaparecieron rodeando por un lado el montecillo y Cuatro y Seis por el otro lado. Yo miré a Cózcatl y nos sonreímos para darnos mutua confianza. A los nueve esclavos que quedaban les dije: «Ya lo oísteis. Simplemente haced lo que os ordene y no habléis ni una sola palabra. Vamos.»

Caminamos en una sola hilera subiendo y bajando la cuesta hacia el otro lado. Levanté un brazo en señal de saludo cuando vimos a los cuatro hombres. Estaban alimentando con astillas un fuego recién prendido.

«¡*Quali potin zanenenque!* —nos dijo uno de ellos al aproximarnos—. ¡Bien venidos, compañeros viajeros! —Él habló en náhuatl y sonrió amigablemente—. Dejadme deciros que hemos venido caminando muchas largas-carreras a lo largo de este camino y éste es el único lugar con sombra. ¿Querréis compartirlo con nosotros y quizá también un poco de nuestra humilde comida?» Sostenía por las orejas dos conejos muertos.

«Descansaremos con mucho gusto —le dije haciendo un movimiento para que el resto se acomodara como quisiera—. Pero esos animales tan flacos difícilmente podrán alimentaros a vosotros cuatro. Varios de mis otros cargadores están cazando por los alrededores en este momento. Quizás nos traigan suficiente caza como para hacer una comida suculenta, que vosotros podréis compartir con nosotros.»

El que había hablado cambió su sonrisa por una mirada ofendida y dijo reprochándome: «Nos tomas por bandidos ya que tan pronto hablas del número de tus hombres. Y ésa no es una forma muy amigable de hablar. Nosotros somos los que deberíamos estar preocupados, ya que sólo somos cuatro contra once. Sugiero que todos nosotros pongamos nuestras armas a un lado.» Y pretendiendo la más pura inocencia desligó y lanzó lejos la *maquáhuitl* que llevaba. Sus tres compañeros sonrieron e hicieron lo mismo.

Yo también sonreí amigablemente y apoyé mi jabalina contra un árbol, haciendo una señal a mis hombres. Éstos también pusieron ostensiblemente sus armas fuera de su alcance. Me senté cerca del fuego que habían hecho los cuatro mixteca, dos de los cuales estaban en esos momentos acomodando los cuerpos pelados de los conejos a través de ramas verdes y acomodándolos apropiadamente sobre las llamas.

«Dime, amigo —dije al que parecía ser el jefe—. ¿Cómo está el camino desde aquí hasta el sur? ¿Hay algún peligro del que nos podáis prevenir?»

«¡En verdad que sí! —dijo con sus ojos brillantes—. Hay bandidos en las inmediaciones. La gente pobre como nosotros no tiene que temer nada de ellos, pero me atrevería a decir que vosotros lleváis mercancías de mucho valor. Deberías contratarnos para que os protegiéramos.»

Dije: «Gracias por la oferta, pero no soy lo suficientemente rico como para pagar una escolta armada. Mis cargadores y yo nos podemos proteger.»

«Los cargadores no son buenos como guardias. Y sin guardias es seguro que os robarán. —Dijo eso con toda franqueza exponiendo un hecho, pero luego habló con una voz engañosamente persuasiva—. Tengo otra sugerencia. No arriesguéis vuestras mercancías por el camino, dejadlas con nosotros para su salvaguarda, mientras vosotros viajáis sin ser molestados.»

Yo me reí.

«Yo creo, mi joven amigo, que nosotros podemos persuadirte de que esto sería lo mejor para tu propio interés.»

«Y yo creo, amigo, que ahora es tiempo de llamar a mis cargadores que andan de cacería.»

«Hazlo —se burló él—. O permíteme llamarlos en tu lugar.»

Yo le dije: «Gracias.»

Por un momento me miró un poco perplejo, pero debió de haber decidido que todavía yo tenía la esperanza de escapar de su trampa con una simple bravata. Dio un fuerte grito y al mismo tiempo él y sus tres compañeros tomaron sus armas. También en ese momento Glotón de Sangre, Cuatro, Seis y Diez aparecieron simultáneamente en el camino, pero todos desde diferentes direcciones. Los tya nuü se quedaron helados por la sorpresa, con sus espadas en alto, como si fueran unas de tantas estatuas de guerreros en acción.

«¡Una buena cacería, amo Mixtli! —tronó Glotón de Sangre—. Y veo que tenemos huéspedes. Bien, traemos para dar y repartir.» Dejó caer lo que traía cargando y lo mismo hicieron los esclavos. Cada uno de ellos dejó caer una cabeza humana cortada.

«Venid amigos, estoy seguro de que podréis reconocer una buena comida en cuanto la veáis —dijo Glotón de Sangre jovialmente a los bandidos que quedaban, quienes habían tomado una posición defensiva de espaldas a un árbol grande, aunque nos miraban temblando—. Tirad vuestras armas y no seáis tímidos. Venid y comed hasta hartaros.»

Los cuatro hombres miraban nerviosos alrededor. Para entonces nosotros también ya estábamos armados. Brincaron del susto cuando Glotón de Sangre elevó su voz a un rugido: «¡Dije que tirarais las espadas! —Ellos lo hicieron—. ¡Dije que vinierais! —Ellos se aproximaron hasta que los restos quedaron a sus pies—. ¡Dije que comierais! —Ellos retrocedieron y después de recoger los restos de sus compañeros muertos se dirigieron hacia el fuego—. ¡No, sin cocinar! —rugió despiadamente Glotón de Sangre—. El fuego es para los conejos y los conejos son para nosotros. Dije ¡comed!»

Así es que los cuatro hombres se pusieron en cuclillas en donde estaban y empezaron a roer miserablemente. En una cabeza no cocinada hay muy poco que masticar, excepto los labios, las mejillas y lengua.

Glotón de Sangre dijo a nuestros esclavos: «Tomad sus maquáhuime y destruidlas, después registrad sus bolsillos a ver si llevan algunas cosas de valor que nos puedan servir.» Seis tomó las espadas y cada una a su tiempo las golpeó contra una roca hasta que las orillas de obsidiana quedaron hechas polvo. Diez y Cuatro buscaron entre las pertenencias de los bandidos, incluso dentro de la ropa que llevaban puesta. No había nada excepto las cosas más indispensables para viajar: aperos de ocote y musgo seco para hacer fuego, varitas para limpiarse los dientes y cosas por el estilo.

Glotón de Sangre dijo: «Esos conejos parecen estar ya listos. Empieza a trincharlos, Cózcatl. — Se volvió hacia los tya nüü que roían—. ¡Y vosotros! Es descortés dejarnos comer solos. Así es que seguid comiendo todo el tiempo en que nosotros lo hacemos.»

Los cuatro desdichados ya habían vomitado varias veces mientras comían, pero hicieron lo que se les mandó, tirando con sus dientes los restos cartilaginosos de lo que habían sido orejas y narices. Ese espectáculo era suficientemente repugnante como para que Cózcatl y yo perdiéramos el apetito que pudiésemos haber sentido, pero el viejo y duro guerrero y nuestros doce esclavos cayeron sobre los conejos comiéndolos con avidez.

Finalmente, Glotón de Sangre vino a donde estábamos sentados Cózcatl y yo dando la espalda a los que comían, y limpiándose con su mano callosa la boca grasienta, dijo: «Podemos tomarlos como esclavos, pero alguien tendrá siempre que estarlos vigilando contra cualquier alevosía que nos puedan hacer. En mi opinión, no vale la pena.»

Yo le dije: «Por lo que más quieras, mátalos. Se ven muy cerca de morir en estos momentos.»

«No —dijo pensativamente Glotón de Sangre, chupándose un diente—. Yo sugiero que los dejemos ir. Los bandidos no emplean corredores-veloces o llamadores-a-lo-lejos, pero tienen sus sistemas para intercambiar información acerca de las tropas que se deben evitar y de los viajeros que están listos para ser robados. Si estos cuatro quedan libres para ir a esparcir su historia en todas partes, otra banda de ladrones se lo pensará al menos dos veces antes de atacarnos.»

«Vaya que si se lo pensarán», dije al hombre que no hacía mucho tiempo se había descrito a sí mismo como un saco de huesos y viento.

Así es que recuperamos los bultos de Cuatro, Seis y Diez y las armas esparcidas de Glotón de Sangre y continuamos nuestro camino. Los tya nüü no se escaparon inmediatamente poniendo más distancia entre nosotros, sino que enfermos y exhaustos se quedaron simplemente sentados en donde nosotros los dejamos, demasiado débiles hasta para tirar lejos de sí las ensangrentadas y peludas calaveras cubiertas de moscas que todavía sostenían sobre sus rodillas.

Ese día, a la caída del sol, nos encontramos en medio de un valle verde, placentero y totalmente inhabitado. Ahí no se veía ni una aldea o posada, ni siquiera un refugio hecho por la mano del hombre.

Glotón de Sangre nos hizo seguir andando hasta que llegamos a un riachuelo de agua fresca y allí nos enseñó cómo acampar. Por primera vez en toda la jornada, usamos nuestros aperos y yesca para encender fuego y en él cocinamos nuestra comida de la noche o por lo menos lo hicieron los esclavos Diez y Tres. Luego sacamos de nuestros bultos las cobijas para hacer nuestras camas sobre el terreno. Todos estábamos conscientes de que allí no había muros alrededor del campamento y ningún tejado sobre él; que no éramos ningún ejército numeroso para protegernos, mutuamente, que allí sólo estaba la noche y sus criaturas, todas ellas alrededor de nosotros, y que esa noche el dios Viento de la Noche soplaba fríamente.

Después de haber comido, me paré a la orilla del círculo de luz que daba nuestro fuego y miré hacia la oscuridad; ésta era tan profunda que aun si yo hubiera podido ver, no habría visto nada. No había luna y sí alguna estrella, aunque eran imperceptibles para mí. No era como mi única campaña militar, en la que los sucesos nos habían llevado a mí y a otros a tierras extranjeras. A ese sitio yo había ido por mi propia voluntad y allí sentí que estaba vagando sin saber el camino, sin consecuencia, y que de mi parte era más temerario que intrépido. Durante mis noches en el ejército, siempre había habido un tumulto de voces, ruidos y conmoción, el movimiento de una multitud alrededor, En esos momentos, teniendo detrás de mí la luz de un simple fuego de campamento, solamente escuchaba la palabra ocasional y el sumiso sonido que los esclavos hacían lavando los utensilios, alimentando el fuego y quitándoles el polvo a nuestros petates de dormir; el ruido provocado por los perros que se peleaban por los desperdicios de nuestra comida.

Delante de mí, en la oscuridad, no había traza de actividad ni de seres humanos. Yo podría haber mirado tan lejos como la orilla del mundo y no ver ningún otro ser humano o alguna evidencia de que alguno hubiese estado allí. Y lejos en la noche, delante de mí, el viento trajo a mis oídos solamente un sonido, quizás el más solitario que uno pueda oír, la audible y única ululación que se puede percibir desde muy lejos, el gemido del coyote que parece lamentar la pérdida de algo muerto o perdido.

Rara vez en mi vida he sentido la soledad aun estando completamente solo, pero aquella noche parado allí me sentí solo, tratando deliberadamente de soportar y sufrir lo que viniere, con mi espalda hacia el único pedazo alumbrado y caliente del mundo y con mi rostro vuelto al destino negro, vacío y desconocido.

En esos momentos, escuché que Glotón de Sangre nos ordenaba: «Dormid completamente desnudos, como si estuvièrais en casa o en cualquier habitación. Quitaos toda la ropa o podéis estar seguros de que *verdaderamente* sentiréis el frío de la mañana.»

Cózcatl habló, tratando de que el sonido de su voz fuera como si estuviera bromeando: «Pero suponte que viene un jaguar y que tengamos que correr.»

Mirándolo fijamente, Glotón de Sangre le dijo: «Si viene un jaguar, muchacho, te puedo garantizar que correrás sin darte cuenta de si estás vestido o desnudo. De todos maneras, un jaguar comerá tus vestidos con el mismo gusto con que comería la tierna carne de muchachito. —Quizás vio que a Cózcatl le temblaban los labios, porque el viejo guerrero, apiadándose y riendo entre dientes, le dijo—: No te preocupes. Ningún gato se acerca al fuego de un campamento y yo estaré pendiente de que éste siga ardiendo. —Suspiró y añadió—: Es un hábito que no he podido dejar atrás a través de muchas campañas. Cada vez que el fuego disminuye me despierto y lo alimento.»

No me encontré muy incómodo el enrollarme dentro de mis dos cobijas con solamente algo áspero y mezquino apilado entre mi cuerpo desnudo y el suelo frío y duro, porque en el último mes en mis habitaciones de palacio, había estado durmiendo sobre el *pétlatl* ligeramente acojinado de Cózcatl. Durante ese mismo tiempo, Cózcatl había dormido en mi cama bien acojinada, caliente y suave, y era evidente que se había acostumbrado a la comodidad. Aquella noche, mientras ronquidos y jadeos salían de las formas abultadas alrededor del fuego, lo oí que cambiaba de posición sin poder dormir y volteándose de un lado a otro tratando de encontrar una posición que le permitiera reposar, gimiendo suavemente cuando no podía encontrarla. Así es que al fin le susurré por encima: «Cózcatl, trae tus cobijas aquí.»

Él vino agradecido, y con sus cobijas y las mías hicimos una cama más gruesa y doble para cubrirnos. Esa actividad hizo que nuestros cuerpos desnudos expuestos al frío tuvieran un violento temblor, nos apresuramos a meternos dentro de la cama improvisada, arrebujándonos juntos como si fuéramos platos sobrepuestos; la espalda de Cózcatl arqueándose sobre mi cuerpo enconchado y mis brazos alrededor de él. Gradualmente se nos fue quitando el temblor y Cózcatl murmuró: «Gracias, Mixtli», y pronto cayó en la respiración regular que da el sueño.

Pero entonces *yo* no podía dormir. Mi cuerpo calentando el suyo, hizo volar mi imaginación, pues no era como descansar al lado de otro hombre, en la forma en que los guerreros se amontonan unos contra otros para mantenerse calientes y secos como en Texcala. Y tampoco era como acostarse con una mujer, como yo lo había hecho la última noche en el banquete de los guerreros. No, era como en los tiempos en que yo me había acostado con mi hermana, en los primeros días en que nos explorábamos, nos descubríamos y nos sentíamos el uno al otro, cuando ella no era más grande que ese muchacho. Yo había crecido mucho desde entonces, en muchos sentidos, pero el cuerpo de Cózcatl, tan pequeño y suave, me recordaba lo que había sentido con Tzitzi cuando se presionaba contra mí, en aquellos tiempos en que ella era todavía una niña. Mi *tepuli* creció y empezó a empujarse hacia arriba contra las nalgas del muchacho. Severamente tuve que recordarme a mí mismo que aquél *era* un muchacho y de la mitad de mi edad.

Sin embargo, mis manos también recordaban a Tzitzi y sin mi consentimiento, se movieron reminiscentes a lo largo del cuerpo del muchacho; los contornos todavía no musculosos o angulares, tan parecidos a los de una joven; la piel todavía no encallecida; la leve cintura y el regordete abdomen infantil; la suave división de las caderas; las piernas delgadas. Y allí, en medio de las piernas, no había la protuberancia esponjosa o dura de las partes masculinas, sino algo liso invitando hacia adentro. Abracé a Cózcatl otra vez contra de mí, sus nalgas acomodadas en mis ingles, mientras mi miembro se escondía entre sus muslos, entre el tejido del surco dejado por la suave cicatriz que muy bien pudiera haber sido un *tepili* cerrado. Para entonces ya estaba demasiado excitado para poder contenerme de lo que hice después. Esperanzado de hacerlo sin despertarle, empecé muy, pero muy suave a moverme.

«¿Mixtli?», susurró él muy sorprendido.

Yo detuve mi movimiento y me reí, quieta pero trémulamente susurré: «Después de todo quizá debí haber traído una esclava.»

Él movió su cabeza y dijo soñoliento: «Si puedo servirte para ese uso...», y se pegó más íntimamente contra mí, apretando sus muslos sobre mi *tepuli*, y yo reanudé mi movimiento.

Después, cuando los dos nos dormimos todavía enconchados, soñé con el ensueño enjoyado de Tzitzitlini y creo que hice eso otra vez durante aquella noche; en el sueño con mi hermana, en la realidad con el muchachito.

Creo que puedo entender por qué Fray Toribio ha salido tan abrupta y atropelladamente. Él ha de ir a enseñar el catecismo a la gente joven, ¿no es así?

Me preguntaba a mí mismo si desde aquella noche llegaría a ser un *cuilontli* y si en lo sucesivo sólo anhelaría muchachitos, pero esa preocupación no persistió por mucho tiempo. Al final de la caminata del siguiente día, llegamos a una aldea llamada Tlancualpican, que ostentaba una posada rudimentaria que ofrecía comidas, baños y dormitorios adecuados, pero sólo les quedaba uno vacío para dormir.

«Yo dormiré con los esclavos —dijo Glotón de Sangre—. Tú y Cózcatl tomad la habitación.»

Yo sabía que mi rostro estaba colorado, porque me di cuenta de que debió de haber oído algo de lo que pasó la noche anterior: quizás el insistente crujido de nuestro petate. Él vio mi cara y soltó una sonora carcajada, después, dejando de reír, me dijo:

«Así que es la primera vez que el joven viajero está largo tiempo fuera de casa. ¡Y en estos momentos él duda de su hombría! —Movió su cabeza gris y rió otra vez—. Déjame decirte una cosa, Mixtli. Cuando se necesita una mujer y no hay ni una disponible o ninguna que te guste, usa cualquier sustituto que quieras. Tengo experiencia en ese aspecto, en nuestras marchas militares a través de las aldeas, los hombres que vivían allí enviaban a sus mujeres a esconderse, así es que nosotros usábamos como mujeres a los guerreros capturados.»

No sé exactamente qué expresión tendría en aquellos momentos, pero él se rió de nuevo y me dijo:

«No me mires así. Mira, Mixtli, he conocido guerreros que han estado tan privados realmente de eso, que han utilizado animales que han sido dejados por el enemigo. Como cachorros o cualquier clase de perros. Una vez en las tierras maya, uno de mis hombres clamó que había gozado con un tapir hembra que había encontrado vagando en la selva.»

Supongo que para entonces me veía lo suficientemente aliviado, aunque todavía sonrojado, porque él concluyó:

«Puedes sentirte contento de tener a tu pequeño compañero si él es de tu gusto y si él te ama lo suficiente como para ser complaciente. Yo te puedo asegurar que la próxima vez que una mujer cruce por tu camino, encontrarás que tus urgencias naturales no han disminuido.»

Sólo para estar seguro, hice la prueba. Después de haberme bañado y comido en la hostería, vagué hacia arriba y hacia abajo por dos o tres calles de Tlancualpican hasta que vi a una mujer asomada a la ventana y vi que volteaba la cabeza cuando yo pasaba de largo. Regresé y me acerqué lo suficiente para ver si ella me estaba sonriendo, y sí lo estaba; aunque no era bonita, ciertamente que no era repugnante. No mostraba las señales que deja la enfermedad *nanaua*: no tenía salpullido en su rostro, su cabello era abundante y no ralo, no tenía la boca llagada ni ninguna otra parte de su cuerpo, según pude verificar pronto.

Llevaba conmigo, para ese propósito, un pendiente barato de jade. Se lo di y ella me ayudó a saltar por la ventana, ya que su esposo estaba en la otra habitación durmiendo la mona completamente borracho, y así nos dimos cada uno más de una medida generosa de placer. Regresé a la hostería seguro de dos cosas. Una, que no había perdido ninguna de mis capacidades: ni la de desear a una mujer, ni la de saber darle placer. Y la otra, de que en mi estimación, una mujer capaz e indulgente estaba mucho mejor equipada para el *ahuilnemíliztli* que el más bello e irresistible muchacho.

Oh, Cózcatl y yo muchas veces dormimos juntos después de aquella primera vez, siempre que nos encontrábamos en una posada en donde las habitaciones eran limitadas o cuando acampábamos al aire libre y nos juntábamos para darnos mutua comodidad. Sin embargo, las veces subsecuentes que lo utilicé sexualmente fueron muy infrecuentes. Lo hice sólo en aquellas ocasiones cuando, como dijo Glotón de Sangre, verdaderamente tenía urgencia de ese servicio y no había ninguna mujer o pareja preferible. Cózcatl ideó varias formas de hacer el acto conmigo, probablemente porque su pasiva participación hubiera venido a ser aburrida para él. De esos actos no hablaré y de todas formas las ocasiones finalmente cesaron, pero él y yo nunca dejamos de ser amigos íntimos durante los días de su vida, hasta que él decidió dejar de vivir.

✠

La estación seca era buena para viajar, con días cálidos y noches despejadas, si bien cuanto más nos aproximábamos hacia el sur, las noches se hacían lo suficientemente cálidas como para dormir a la intemperie sin cobijas y los mediodías eran tan calurosos que hubiéramos deseado andar sin ropa y dejar todo lo que cargábamos.

Aquellas tierras que cruzamos eran muy hermosas. Algunas mañanas nos despertábamos en un campo de flores en las cuales las gotas del rocío del amanecer todavía brillaban, un campo de joyas relucientes que se extendía hasta el horizonte en todas direcciones. Había flores de profusas variedades y colores o sólo de una misma clase; algunas veces había esas flores altas y amarillas, grandes y esponjosas que siempre vuelven sus corolas hacia el sol.

Conforme la alborada daba paso al día, nos movíamos a través de cualquier clase de terreno imaginable. Algunas veces era una floresta tan lujuriosamente cubierta de frondosas hojas y crecida maleza que nos intimidaba, cuyo suelo estaba tapizado de suave hierba y en donde los troncos de los árboles estaban espaciados tan primorosamente como si un maestro jardinero los hubiese plantado en el jardín de un noble. O atravesábamos por un mar frío de helechos emplumados. O, invisibles unos de otros, atravesábamos pasando por grupos de cañas doradas y verdes o de una maleza verde y plateada que crecía más alta que nuestras cabezas. Ocasionalmente, teníamos que escalar alguna montaña y desde su cumbre se podían ver a lo lejos otras montañas, disminuidos sus colores por la distancia, que iban desde el verde claro hasta el azul paloma.

Sin importar quien fuera el hombre que encabezaba nuestra marcha, éste siempre se espantaba por los signos de vida, repentinos e insospechados, que existían alrededor de nosotros. Un conejo podía estar agazapado como una piedra sin movimiento, hasta que nuestro guía casi lo pisaba y entonces, rompiendo su inmovilidad, huía lejos. O el hombre que guiaba podía alterarse similarmente con un *chachaláctli*, faisán, que volando en silbante vuelo casi rozaba su rostro. O podía verse afectado por una bandada de codornices o palomas o por un pájaro correcaminos que se alejaría lejos sobre sus patas, con largo paso peculiar. Muchas veces un armadillo acorazado eludiría nuestro camino o un lagarto se reavivaría a través de nuestro paso... y cada vez que nos encontrábamos más hacia el sur, los lagartos se convertían en iguanas y algunas de ellas eran tan largas como lo alto de Cózcatl, con crestas coronadas de brillantes colores en rojo, verde y púrpura.

Casi siempre había un halcón volando silenciosamente sobre nuestras cabezas, en círculos, observando ansiosamente por si algún pequeño gamo se asustaba a nuestro paso, moviéndose vulnerablemente. O un *zopílotl*, buitre, trazando silenciosos círculos, con la esperanza de que abandonáramos alguna cosa comestible. En los bosques, las ardillas voladoras se deslizaban desde las ramas altas a las más bajas, pareciéndose en su vuelo a los halcones y buitres, pero no tan silenciosas, pues nos chillaban enojadas. En la floresta o en la pradera, siempre habían, revoloteando y aleteando alrededor de nosotros, brillantes papagayos, chupamirtos que parecían gemas, abejas de aguijones negros y una multitud de mariposas de extravagantes colores.

Ayyo, siempre había color, color por todas partes, y los mediodías eran los que tenían más colorido, ya que llameaban como cofres llenos de tesoros que eran abiertos otra vez; llenos de cada piedra y cada metal, apreciado tanto por los dioses como por los hombres. En el cielo, que era una turquesa, el sol flameaba como un escudo redondo de oro batido. Su luz brillaba sobre las peñas, rocas y guijarros ordinarios, transformándolos en topacios o jacintos; o en ópalos, a los que nosotros llamábamos piedras luciérnagas; o en plata; o en amatistas; o en *téxcatl*, la piedra espejo; o en perlas, las cuales no son en realidad piedras sino los corazones de las ostras; o en ámbar, que tampoco es una piedra sino espuma sólida. Todo el verdor que nos rodeaba se convertía en esmeraldas, glauconita y jade. Si estábamos en la floresta, en donde la luz del sol abigarraba el follaje en esmeralda, nosotros caminábamos inconscientemente con cuidado y delicadeza, para no hollar los preciosos discos, platos y fuentes dorados, sembrados bajo nuestros pies.

En el crepúsculo todos los colores empezaban a perder su brillo. Los colores calientes se enfriaban, aun los rojos y los amarillos se suavizaban hasta tornarse en un color azul, luego púrpura y finalmente gris. Al mismo tiempo, una neblina opaca empezaba a levantarse y salir de las grietas y cavidades de la tierra alrededor de nosotros, hasta que sus vahos se juntaban como formando una cobija por la que teníamos que caminar afanándonos en patear sus pelusas y penachos. Los murciélagos y los pájaros nocturnos empezaban a volar como dardos alrededor, atrapando insectos invisibles en su vuelo y arreglándoselas mágicamente para no chocar nunca con nosotros, o con ninguna de las ramas de los árboles, o chocar unos con otros. Muchas veces nos envolvió la oscuridad completa, cuando todavía estábamos admirando la belleza del campo, aunque ya no pudiéramos verla. Muchas noches dormimos inhalando el fuerte perfume de esas flores cuyas corolas parecen lunas-blancas, que *solamente* en la *noche* abren sus pétalos y lanzan al aire sus dulces suspiros.

Si la caída de la noche coincidía con nuestra llegada a una comunidad de los tya nüü, pasábamos la noche bajo techo y con muros que podrían ser de ladrillo de barro, o de madera en los lugares más poblados, o simplemente de cañas y paja en los más pequeños. Podíamos comprar comida decente y algunas veces escoger las golosinas peculiares de la vecindad y alquilar mujeres para cocinar y servirnos. También se podía comprar agua caliente para bañarnos e incluso en algunas ocasiones alquilar una casita-vapor de alguna familia, en donde existiera una. En las comunidades lo suficientemente grandes y por un pago insignificante, Glotón de Sangre y yo, usualmente podíamos encontrar una mujer para cada uno y también, algunas veces, podíamos conseguir una esclava para ser compartida entre nuestros hombres.

Sin embargo, muchas noches la oscuridad nos cogió en alguna tierra desierta entre los lugares poblados. Aunque para entonces ya todos nos habíamos acostumbrado a dormir en el suelo y a no temer a la oscuridad que nos rodeaba, aquellas noches eran por supuesto menos agradables. Nuestra cena sólo consistía en frijoles, *atoli* espeso y agua para beber. Pero si bien esto no era realmente una privación, en cambio sí lo era la falta de baño: yéndonos todos a dormir costrudos por la suciedad del día y escocidos por las picaduras de los insectos. No obstante, a veces teníamos la suficiente suerte como para poder acampar junto a un arroyo o un estanque de agua, en donde por lo menos podíamos tomar un baño de agua fría. Y otras veces, también, nuestra comida incluía la carne de algún animal salvaje cazado, por supuesto, por Glotón de Sangre.

A Cózcatl le había dado por cargar el arco y las flechas de Glotón de Sangre y ociosamente disparaba contra los árboles o cactos a lo largo del camino, hasta que llegó a utilizarlos con cierta habilidad. Como tenía la tendencia infantil de disparar sobre cualquier cosa que se moviera, generalmente traía criaturas que eran demasiado pequeñas para poder alimentarnos a todos, un conejo o una ardilla terrestre y cosas por el estilo, pero una vez nos hizo correr a todos en todas direcciones cuando hirió a un *épatl*, zorrillo rayado blanco-pardusco, con las consecuencias que ya pueden ustedes imaginarse. Sin embargo, un día explorando por delante del grupo encontró a un venado que estaba descansando y le lanzó una flecha y corrió detrás de la bestia hasta que ésta se bamboleó, cayó y murió. Él lo estaba descuartizando torpemente con su pequeño cuchillo de obsidiana cuando lo encontramos y Glotón de Sangre le dijo:

«Ni te tomes la molestia, muchacho. Déjalo para festín de los *cóyotin* y buitres. Mira, has agujereado los intestinos. Así es que todo lo que contenían sus tripas se ha regado dentro de la cavidad de su cuerpo y toda la comida estará completamente infectada. —Cózcatl miró alicaído, pero asintió cuando el viejo guerrero le enseñó—: Cualquiera que sea el animal, trata de dar en el blanco aquí... o aquí... en el corazón o en los pulmones. Eso hará que le des una muerte más piadosa y nos producirá mayor comida.» El muchacho aprendió la lección y algunas veces nos brindó un buen manjar con la carne del venado que él había matado limpia y adecuadamente.

En cada parada que hacíamos en la noche, ya sea en una aldea o en la selva, yo dejaba que Glotón de Sangre, Cózcatl y los esclavos hicieran el campamento o los arreglos necesarios para hospedarnos. Lo primero que hacía era sacar mis pinturas y papel de corteza y sentarme a anotar el curso de ese día: un mapa de la ruta haciéndolo lo más perfecto que podía, señalando los límites, la naturaleza del terreno y cosas parecidas; además de una descripción de cualquier paisaje extraordinario que hubiéramos visto o de cualquier otro suceso notorio que nos hubiera ocurrido. Si no me alcanzaba el tiempo para hacer eso antes de que faltara totalmente la luz, lo terminaba temprano a la mañana siguiente mientras que los demás levantaban el campamento. Siempre procuraba asentar la crónica lo más pronto posible, mientras todavía podía recordar cada cosa pertinente. El hecho fue que, en esos años de juventud, esa práctica hizo que mi memoria se ejercitara tan asiduamente que vengo a caer en la cuenta de que ahora en mis años débiles, todavía puedo recordar muchas cosas con claridad... incluyendo un número de ellas que podría desear que desaparecieran o se oscurecieran.

En aquella jornada, como en las siguientes, aumenté mi conocimiento de palabras. Me esforzaba en aprender nuevas palabras de las tierras por las que íbamos viajando y el modo en que ésas se unían, para juntarse como su gente las hablaba. Como ya he dicho, mi náhuatl nativo era el lenguaje común en las rutas comerciales, y en casi todas las pequeñas aldeas los *pochteca* mexica podrían encontrar a alguien que lo hablara adecuadamente. Muchos mercaderes que viajaban se sentían satisfechos de encontrar a esos intérpretes, y hacer todos sus tratos por medio de ellos. Probablemente nadie podría decir cuántas lenguas diferentes se hablaban fuera de las tierras de la Triple Alianza, pero un simple tratante en su carrera podía llegar a traficar con personas que hablaban cada una de ellas. Ese tratante ocupado con todas las cosas concernientes al comercio, rara vez se inclinaba a molestarse en aprender cualquier lengua extranjera, dejándolas todas a un lado.

Yo me sentía tan interesado que me tomé ese trabajo, porque consideraba que el conocimiento de las palabras era una ocupación más importante que el comercio. También parecía que poseía un don especial, por la facilidad con que aprendía nuevos lenguajes sin mucha dificultad... posiblemente porque había estado estudiando palabras toda mi vida, quizá por la temprana revelación de diferentes dialectos y acentos del náhuatl hablado en Xaltocan, en Texcoco, en Tenochtitlan y aun el conciso de Texcala. Los doce esclavos de nuestro grupo hablaban sus diversas lenguas nativas, además de fragmentos de náhuatl que habían aprendido durante su cautiverio. Y así fue como empecé mi aprendizaje de nuevas palabras, con ellos, señalando a lo largo de nuestras jornadas, tal o cual objeto.

No quiero pretender que llegué a dominar cada una de esas lenguas extranjeras que encontré durante esa expedición. No hasta después de muchos otros viajes, podría decir esto. Pero aprendí lo suficiente del lenguaje de los tya nuü, de los tzapoteca, de los chiapa y maya, de tal manera que por lo menos podía entenderme en casi todos los lugares que pasamos y a nuestro regreso todavía más. Esta habilidad para comunicarme, también me facilitó el aprender las costumbres locales y sus maneras, y conforme a éstas, ser aceptado más hospitalariamente por cada pueblo. Además de hacer mi viaje más agradable y prolífero en experiencias, esa mutua aceptación me procuró mejores tratos comerciales, más que si hubiera sido el usual «sordomudo» mercader tratando de ajustar sus ventas por medio de un intérprete.

Les ofrezco un ejemplo. Cuando nosotros cruzamos la orilla de una sierra, nuestro esclavo llamado Cuatro, que ordinariamente era muy lerdo, empezó a demostrar una viveza que no le caracterizaba, una cierta clase de alegre agitación. Le pregunté con lo que había aprendido de su lenguaje y me contestó que su aldea natal de Ynochixtlan no estaba lejos, delante de nosotros. Él la había dejado algunos años atrás para ir en busca de fortuna fuera de su mundo, pero habiendo sido capturado por bandidos había sido vendido a un noble Chalca, siendo revendido varias veces más, hasta que finalmente vino a ser incluido en una ofrenda de tributo a Tenochtitlan y así había venido a dar al grupo de esclavos en donde Glotón de Sangre lo había encontrado.

Yo hubiera llegado a saber todo esto muy pronto, aun sin conocer nada de su lenguaje. Porque al llegar a Ynochixtlan, nos encontramos con el padre, la madre y los dos hermanos de Cuatro que habían venido a recibir y saludar con lágrimas y sonrisas, al que habían perdido hacía ya tiempo. Ellos y el *tecutli* de la aldea, o *chagóola*, que es como llaman en aquellos lugares a un pequeño gobernante, me suplicaron que les vendiera al hombre. Yo les expresé que estaba de acuerdo con sus sentimientos y con buena disposición para llegar a un acuerdo, pero les hice notar que Cuatro era el más grande de nuestros cargadores y el único que podía con el pesado saco de ruda obsidiana. Ante eso, el *chagóola* me propuso comprar al hombre y a la obsidiana, innegablemente útil para su pueblo que no tenía roca para construir sus aperos. Él sugirió como un trato justo, una cantidad de chales tejidos que eran el único producto de la aldea.

Admiré debidamente los chales que me enseñó, ya que eran bellos y prácticos. Sin embargo, tuve que decir a los aldeanos que yo estaba sólo en la tercera parte de mi camino para terminar mi jornada, que todavía no estaba buscando hacer tratos, por lo que no me interesaba adquirir nuevas mercancías que tendría que cargar todo el camino hacia el sur y luego de regreso a casa otra vez. Yo podría haber dejado ese argumento fuera, pues había determinado en mi interior, dejar a Cuatro en su familia aun teniéndolo que perder, pero para mi agradable sorpresa, su madre y su padre se pusieron a mi lado.

«*Chagóola* —dijeron ellos respetuosamente al hombre que era la cabeza de la aldea—. Mira al joven mercader. Tiene una cara bondadosa y es simpático. Él no quiere dejar que nuestro hijo se vaya otra vez. Pero nuestro hijo es legalmente de su propiedad y seguro que él pagó un alto precio por un hijo como el de nosotros. ¿Vas a estar regateando sobre el precio de libertad de uno de tu propia gente?»

No tuve necesidad de decir más. Simplemente me quedé allí mirando bondadosa y simpáticamente, mientras la familia vociferante de Cuatro hacía que su líder reconociera su mezquino ajuste de precio. Finalmente, con la cara enrojecida de vergüenza, estuvo de acuerdo en abrir el tesoro del pueblo y me pagó con moneda corriente en lugar de mercancías. Por el hombre y su carga me dio semillas de cacao, pedacitos de estaño y cobre, mucho menos difíciles de cargar y más fáciles de negociar que los pedazos de obsidiana. En suma, recibí un precio justo por los pedazos de roca y *dos* veces el precio de lo que había pagado por el esclavo. Cuando el cambio fue hecho y Cuatro volvió a ser otra vez un ciudadano libre de Ynochixtlan, toda la aldea se regocijó y declaró un día de fiesta e insistieron en darnos alojamiento allí aquella noche y un verdadero festín que incluía *chocólatl* y *octli*, todo eso completamente gratis.

La celebración continuaba cuando nosotros, los viajeros, nos retiramos a las chozas que nos haban asignado. Ya estando desvestidos para dormir, Glotón de Sangre eructó y me dijo: «Yo siempre pensé que era rebajarse mucho reconocer que la forma de hablar de los extranjeros fuera un lenguaje humano. Y pensaba que eras un necio en perder tu tiempo, Mixtli, cuando tomabas tus pinturas para aprender nuevas palabras de los bárbaros. Pero en estos momentos tengo que admitir...» Él tuvo otro ventrudo eructo y se quedó dormido.

Quizás sea del interés de usted, en su calidad de intérprete, joven señorito Molina, saber que cuando usted aprendió el náhuatl probablemente aprendió la más fácil de todas las lenguas nativas. No quiero decir con esto que le dé escasa importancia a sus conocimientos, usted habla el náhuatl admirablemente para ser un extranjero, pero si alguna vez quiere ensayar con otros de nuestros lenguajes, los encontrará considerablemente más difíciles.

Para citar nada más uno, por ejemplo, usted sabe que casi siempre en nuestro náhuatl los acentos caen sobre la penúltima parte de la palabra, como parece serlo también en español. Ésta pudiera ser una de las razones por las cuales yo no encontré su español insuperable, si bien en otros aspectos es muy diferente del náhuatl. Por contraste, nuestros vecinos más cercanos con diferente lenguaje, los purémpecha, acentúan casi siempre cada una de sus palabras en la tercera parte antes de la última. Ustedes lo habrán observado porque todavía quedan lugares llamados: Pátzkueario, Kerétaro y otros. El lenguaje de los otomí se habla más al norte de aquí y es todavía más difícil porque ellos acentúan sus palabras *en donde sea*. Debo decir que de todos los lenguajes que he escuchado, incluyendo el de ustedes, el otomite es el más difícil de aprender. Solamente como una ilustración, ésta tiene diferentes palabras para la risa de un hombre y la de una mujer.

Toda mi vida he tenido que soportar el ser llamado por diferentes nombres. Entonces, cuando llegué a ser mercader viajero y era llamado en diferentes lenguajes, adquirí más nombres todavía, porque naturalmente Nube Oscura se decía diferente en todas partes. La gente tzapoteca, por ejemplo, traducían mi nombre náhuatl de Tliléctic-Mixtli a Zaa Nayàzú o Nube Que Es Oscura. Aun después de que hube enseñado a la muchacha Zyanya a hablar con soltura el náhuatl como cualquier mujer mexica, ella siempre me llamaba Zaa. Podía con facilidad pronunciar la palabra Mixtli, pero invariablemente me llamaba Zaa y hacía de su sonido un encarecimiento que viniendo de sus labios era el nombre que más me gustaba de todos los que siempre he llevado...

Pero de eso hablaré a su tiempo.

Veo que usted, Fray Toribio, hace pequeñas anotaciones después de que ya ha escrito, tratando de indicar la forma en que el sonido se levanta y vuelve a descender en ese nombre de Zaa Nayàzú. Sí, el sonido sube y baja, casi como una canción y no sé cómo se las arreglará para hacerlo notar en su escritura, tanto como en la nuestra.

Sólo el lenguaje de los tzapoteca se habla así y es el más melodioso de todos los lenguajes Del Único Mundo, así también como los hombres tzapoteca son los más bellos y sus mujeres las más sublimes. Asimismo debo decir que la palabra tzapoteca es como los otros pueblos los llaman por la fruta del *tzapote* que crece abundantemente en sus tierras. El nombre que ellos se dan es más evocativo de las cumbres en que casi todos viven: Be'n Zaa, la Gente Nube.

Ellos llaman a su lenguaje lóochi. Comparado con el náhuatl tiene sólo un tronco de unos cuantos sonidos y éstos están compuestos en palabras mucho más cortas que las del náhuatl. Pero esos pocos sonidos tienen una infinidad de significados, de acuerdo a la forma en que ellos hablen: llanamente o cantando hacia arriba o vocalizando hacia abajo. El efecto musical que producen no es solamente un sonido dulce, sino que éste es indispensable para la comprensión de las palabras. En verdad, el canto es una de las partes más importantes de su lenguaje, ya que un tzapotécatl puede componer con sonido *hablado* y transmitir su significado, hasta el tamaño de un simple mensaje por lo menos, zumbando o silbando solamente su melodía.

Así fue como supimos cuándo nos aproximábamos a las tierras de la Gente Nube y así también ellos lo supieron. Oímos un silbido penetrante que salía de la montaña que se veía enfrente de nuestro camino. Era un gorgojeo largo como ningún pájaro podría haberlo hecho y, después de un momento, fue repetido por alguien más adelante de nosotros y el mismo silbido exactamente. Después de otros momentos el silbido se repitió idénticamente y casi inaudible a la distancia, muy lejos, delante de nosotros.

«Los vigías tzapoteca —explicó Glotón de Sangre—. Ellos se comunican con silbidos en lugar de gritos como lo hacen nuestros llamadores-a-lo-lejos.»

Yo le pregunté: «¿Por qué tienen vigías?»

«Nosotros estamos en la tierra llamada Uaxyácac y esta tierra ha sido disputada por los mixteca, los olmeca y los tzapoteca. En algunos lugares ellos se han mezclado y viven amigablemente unos junto de otros; en otros, se molestan y se roban unos a otros. Así es que todos los que llegan deben ser identificados. Este mensaje a base de silbidos, probablemente en estos momentos esté llegando al palacio de Záachila y sin duda está diciéndole a su Venerado Orador que nosotros somos mexica, que somos mercaderes *pochteca*, cuántos somos y quizás aun el tamaño y forma de nuestros bultos.»

Quizás uno de sus soldados españoles montando a caballo y viajando veloz, cruzando a través de nuestras tierras cada día, encontraría cada aldea en la que parara cada noche muy distinta y diferente de la aldea en que pasó la noche anterior. Pero nosotros que viajábamos despacio a pie, no encontrábamos cambios abruptos de un lugar a otro. Además nos dimos cuenta de que al sur del pueblo de Quaunáhuac, todos parecían andar descalzos excepto cuando se vestían para algún festival local, y no notamos una gran diferencia entre una comunidad y otra. La apariencia física de la gente, sus costumbres, su arquitectura, todas esas cosas, sí cambiaban, sí, pero el cambio era usualmente gradual y únicamente perceptible a intervalos. Oh, nosotros pudimos observar aquí y allá, especialmente en las aldeas en donde todos sus habitantes se habían mezclado por generaciones, que un pueblo se diferenciaba de otro solamente porque unos eran más altos que otros, de piel más clara o más oscura, su carácter más jovial o gruñón que el de los otros. Pero generalmente la gente tendía a confundirse indistinguiblemente de un lugar a otro.

En todas partes los hombres que trabajaban llevaban nada más que un taparrabo blanco y se cubrían con un manto blanco en sus ratos de ocio. Las mujeres llevaban la familiar blusa blanca, la falda y presumiblemente la ropa interior usual. La ropa de esa gente estaba avivada en su blancura por bellos bordados y tanto los diseños como los colores variaban de un lugar a otro. También los nobles de diferentes regiones tenían gustos distintos sobre sus mantos de plumas y sus penachos, sus tapones de nariz, sus aretes, sus pendientes, sus brazaletes, los adornos para las pantorrillas y otra clase de aderezos. Pero esas variaciones rara vez eran notadas por los viajeros que cruzaban sus tierras, como nosotros; se necesitaría una larga residencia en una aldea para reconocer a simple vista a un visitante de la aldea vecina a lo largo del camino. Ni siquiera los lenguajes cambiaban bruscamente, ni siquiera en las fronteras de cada nación. La manera de hablar de una nación se mezclaba y emergía dentro del lenguaje de la siguiente y sólo después de varios días de camino se venía a dar cuenta el viajero que estaba escuchando una lengua totalmente nueva.

Ésta había sido una de nuestras experiencias en toda nuestra jornada, hasta esos momentos en que entramos en la tierra de Uaxyácac, la que ustedes se contentan con llamar Oaxaca, en donde el primer silbido melodioso de la bella y única lengua lóochi nos hizo notar que estábamos de repente entre gente completamente diferente a la que nos habíamos encontrado antes.

Pasamos la primera noche en Uaxyácac en una aldea llamada Texitla y no había nada especialmente notable acerca de aquélla en particular. Las casas estaban construidas como todas las que nos habíamos acostumbrado a ver desde hacía algún tiempo, con varas sacadas del alma de las hojas de la palmera y con tejados hechos por sus hojas. Los baños y las cabañas de vapor estaban hechos de barro cocido, como todos los otros que habíamos visto recientemente. La comida que compramos era muy parecida a la que nos había sido servida en noches anteriores. Lo que era diferente era la gente de Texitla.

«¡Pero si son muy bellos!», exclamó Cózcatl.

Glotón de Sangre no dijo nada ya que él había estado antes en esos lugares. El viejo veterano solamente miró alrededor con afectación y aires de propietario, como si personalmente hubiera arreglado la existencia de Texitla con el único propósito de sorprendernos a Cózcatl y a mí.

Nunca antes había estado en una comunidad en donde toda

la gente era tan uniformemente bella y que incluso sus ropas de diario tuvieran un colorido tan alegre. Los hombres eran altos y musculosos, y sin embargo no se mostraban arrogantes ni se envanecían de su fuerza; eran alegres y reían y jugaban con sus hijos como si ellos también fueran niños. Las mujeres eran también altas para su sexo, ligeras y gentiles, sus ojos sonreían cuando sus labios lo hacían. Tanto los hombres como las mujeres hacían que los viajeros como nosotros nos sintiéramos bien recibidos, aunque como ya lo explicaré, los tzapoteca no tenían muchos motivos para ser amistosos con nosotros los mexica. A pesar de eso y de que la aldea era pequeña, yo hubiera podido tener una mujer aun y a pesar de que todas las mujeres núbiles parecían estar felizmente casadas.

Sin embargo, Texitla no era el único lugar aislado en donde había gente hermosa, como descubrimos al llegar a la populosa ciudad capital de Záachila y como confirmamos durante nuestra travesía por todo el resto de Uaxyácac. Era una tierra en donde toda la gente era bien parecida y sus maneras tan brillantes como sus vestidos. El gusto de los tzapoteca por los colores brillantes era fácilmente comprensible, ya que esa nación producía los más finos colorantes. Era también el lugar más al norte en el recorrido de papagayos, guacamayos, tucanes y otros pájaros tropicales de esplendorosos plumajes. La razón por la cual los tzapoteca llegaron a ser tan notables especímenes humanos era evidente. Así es que después de un día o dos en Záachila, le dije a un anciano de la ciudad:

«Su pueblo parece ser muy superior a otros pueblos que he conocido. ¿Cuál es su historia? ¿De dónde vinieron ustedes?»

«¿De dónde venimos?», preguntó él con un dejo de desdén en su voz ante mi ignorancia. Él era uno de los habitantes de la ciudad que hablaba náhuatl y que regularmente servía de intérprete a los viajeros *pochteca* y él fue el que me enseñó las primeras palabras que aprendí en lóochi. Su nombre era Gíigu Nashinyá que quiere decir Río Rojo y su rostro parecía un peñasco curtido por los elementos. Me dijo:

«Ustedes los mexica cuentan que sus ancestros llegaron de un lugar muy lejano hacia el norte de sus dominios actuales. Los chiapa dicen que sus antepasados eran originarios de un lugar que estaba a una inmensurable distancia hacia el sur de su tierra actual. Y todos los demás pueblos también dicen que sus orígenes provienen de algún otro lugar, lejos del actual en el que viven. Sí, todos los demás pueblos excepto nosotros los be'n zaa. No nos llamamos a nosotros mismos así por una razón tonta. Nosotros *somos* la Gente Nube... nacidos de las nubes, los árboles, las rocas y las montañas de esta tierra. Nosotros no llegamos aquí. Nosotros siempre hemos estado aquí. Dígame, joven, ¿usted ya ha visto y olido la *gie lazhido*, la flor-corazón?»

Yo le dije: *Keá, Gíigu zhibi»*, que en el lenguaje tzapoteca quiere decir: «No, Señor Río.»

«Ya las verá. Los hacemos crecer en los jardines de nuestras casas. La flor es llamada así porque su botón cerrado tiene la forma de un corazón humano. Las amas de casa sólo cortan un botón cada vez, porque una sola flor aunque todavía no esté abierta, llenará de perfume toda la casa. Otra de las distinciones de la flor-corazón es que originalmente creció salvaje en las montañas que ve usted a lo lejos, y creció sólo en estas montañas y no en ningún otro lado. Como nosotros los be'n zaa llegamos a existir solamente aquí y como nosotros todavía florece aquí. Es un regocijo oler y ver a la flor-corazón, como siempre lo ha sido. Y los be'n zaa son gente vigorosa y fuerte, como siempre lo han sido.»

Haciendo eco de lo que Cózcatl había dicho, cuando por primera vez él vio a esa gente, yo murmuré: «*Líi skarú...* Gente muy bella.»

«Sí, tan bella como alegre —dijo el anciano sin falsa modestia—. La Gente Nube ha permanecido así, manteniéndose como Gente Nube pura. Nosotros purificamos cualquier impureza que crece o se arrastra.»

Yo dije: «¿Qué? ¿Cómo?»

«Si un niño nace malformado o intolerablemente feo o da evidencias de tener alguna deficiencia mental, no lo dejamos crecer. Oh, nosotros no somos asesinos, como algunas otras tribus bárbaras que no solamente matan a sus infantes, sino que además los devoran. Al infortunado infante sólo se le niega la teta de la madre y se consume y muere en el buen tiempo que los dioses señalen. También desechamos a nuestros ancianos, cuando ellos ya están muy feos para ser vistos o demasiado débiles para cuidarse a sí mismos, o cuando sus mentes empiezan a decaer. Por supuesto, la inmolación de los viejos generalmente es voluntaria y hecha en beneficio público. Yo, también, cuando sienta que mis sentidos o mi vigor empiezan a menguarse, me despediré de todos e iré a la Casa Santa y nunca más volveré a ser visto.»

Dije: «Eso me parece bastante cruel.»

«¿Es cruel desarraigar el jardín? ¿Podar las ramas muertas de un huerto?»

«Bueno, pues...»

Él dijo sardónicamente: «Usted admira los efectos, pero deplora los medios. Que nosotros escojamos desechar lo inútil y lo que ya no sirve para nada, y que de otra manera vendría a ser una carga para sus compañeros. Que nosotros escojamos dejar morir a los defectuosos y de esa manera prevenir una generación todavía más defectuosa. Joven moralista, ¿usted también condena que nosotros rehusemos engendrar mestizos?»

«¿Mestizos?»

«Hemos sido repetidamente invadidos por los mixteca y los almeca en tiempos pasados, y por los mexica en tiempos más recientes, y sufrimos continuas infiltraciones de tribus más pequeñas alrededor de nuestras fronteras, pero jamás nos hemos mezclado con ninguno de ellos. Si bien los extranjeros se mueven entre nosotros y aun viven entre nosotros, siempre les prohibiremos mezclar su sangre con la nuestra.»

Yo le dije: «No sé cómo pueden hacerlo. Hombres y mujeres siempre serán lo que son, y difícilmente podrán permitir un intercurso social con los forasteros y tener la esperanza de prevenir un contacto sexual con ellos.»

«Oh, nosotros somos humanos —concedió él—. Nuestros hombres voluntariamente prueban las mujeres de otras razas y algunas de nuestras mujeres voluntariamente van a horcajarse al camino. Pero si alguno de la Gente Nube formalmente toma a un extranjero por marido o por esposa, en ese momento deja de ser Gente Nube. Este hecho es suficiente para que usualmente descorazone a aquellos que desean casarse con extranjeros. Pero hay otra razón por la cual estos matrimonios no son comunes. Seguro que usted podrá darse cuenta de ello.»

Yo negué inciertamente con la cabeza.

«Usted ha viajado a través de otros pueblos. Mire a nuestros hombres. Mire a nuestras mujeres. ¿En qué otra nación fuera de Uaxyácac podrían encontrar parejas tan cerca de lo ideal para cada uno de ellos?

Yo ya lo había notado y su pregunta no tenía respuesta. Privilegiadamente yo había conocido en otros tiempos ejemplares humanos en exceso favorables de otros pueblos: mi bella hermana Tzitzi, que era mexícatl; la Señora de Tolan, que era tecpanécatl; el pequeño y bello Cózcatl, quien era acolhua. Y privilegiadamente ninguno de los especímenes tzapoteca tenía ningún defecto. No podía negar que casi todas sus gentes tenían un rostro y una figura tan superiores como para hacer que la mayoría de los otros pueblos se vieran como los primeros experimentos fallidos de los dioses.

Entre los mexica a mí se me consideraba como una rareza por mi estatura y mi musculatura, pero casi todos los hombres tzapoteca eran tan fuertes y altos como yo y tenían ambas cosas, fuerza y sensibilidad en sus rostros. Casi todas las mujeres estaban ampliamente dotadas con las curvas femeninas, pero eran flexibles como las cañas y sus rostros habían sido hechos en imitación de una diosa: ojos grandes y luminosos, nariz recta, boca hecha para besar, piel traslúcida y sin manchas. Zyanya era un vaso simétrico de cobre barnizado lleno hasta el borde de miel y puesto al sol. Tanto los hombres como las mujeres se paraban altivos y se movían con gracia y hablaban su melodiosa lengua lóochi con voces suaves. Los niños eran exquisitos, más allá de toda descripción y educados con muy buenos modales. Me sentí muy contento de no poder salir de mí mismo para compararme con ellos. Pero los otros forasteros que vi en Uaxyácac, la mayoría de ellos inmigrantes mixteca, se veían entre la Gente Nube terrosos en un color lodoso y en comparación muy imperfectos.

Hasta estos momentos todavía no lo puedo creer. Como nosotros decimos, considero con mi dedito el cuento del viejo intérprete Gíigu, de cómo había sido creada su gente... espontánea, espléndida y completamente. Yo no puedo creer que, ya completamente formada, la Gente Nube brotó de esas montañas como la flor-corazón. Jamás ninguna otra nación habló de un origen tan tontamente imposible. Todos los pueblos *deben* venir de algún otro lado, ¿no es así?

Sin embargo puedo creer, porque lo vi con mis propios ojos, que los tzapoteca se negaron orgullosa y obstinadamente a mezclarse con los extranjeros, y que habían preservado su línea sanguínea original, aun cuando eso significara una crueldad hacia los que amaban. Como quiera que haya sido el verdadero origen de la Gente Nube, ellos se conformaron solamente con ser la mejor nación. Puedo creer eso porque yo estaba allí, caminando entre ellos, los hombres admirables y las mujeres deseables. ¡*Ayyo*, mujeres notables, irresistibles y atormentadoramente deseables!

✠

Ah, Su Ilustrísima, en nuestra práctica aquí, el señor escribano me acaba de leer la última frase que dije para recordarme en dónde me había quedado en nuestra última sesión. ¿Podría atreverme a suponer que Su Ilustrísima se ha unido hoy con nosotros para poder escuchar cómo violé a toda la población femenina de Záachila?

¿No?

Si como usted dice, no se sorprendería de oír tal cosa, pero no desea escucharlo, entonces, permítame realmente sorprender a Su Ilustrísima. Aunque nosotros pasamos varios días en Záachila y sus alrededores, no toqué ni siquiera a una mujer ahí. Sí, como Su Ilustrísima lo hace notar, ésa no era una de mis características, aunque no puedo clamar el haber gozado de una repentina redención en mi manera libertina de ser. Más bien, yo estaba en esos momento afligido por una nueva perversidad. Yo no deseaba a ninguna de las mujeres que podía tener, porque las *podía* tener. Esas mujeres eran adorables, seductoras y sin duda muy diestras —Glotón de Sangre se revolcó en el prostíbulo todo el tiempo que estuvimos allí—, pero la sola facilidad de tenerlas me hizo declinarlas. Lo que yo quería, lo que deseaba con lujuria y que insistía en tener, era una verdadera mujer de la Gente Nube, quiero decir una mujer que pudiera recular de horror ante un forastero como yo. Ése era el dilema. Yo deseaba lo que no podía tener y no quería nada más que eso. Así es que no tuve a ninguna mujer y por eso no puedo decirle nada a Su Ilustrísima acerca de las mujeres de Záachila.

Permítame en su lugar hablar un poco acerca de Uaxyácac. Esa tierra es un caos de montañas, picos y peñascos; montañas junto a montañas, montañas sobre montañas. Los tzapoteca, contentos con la protección y el aislamiento que reciben de sus montañas, rara vez se han tomado la molestia de aventurarse más allá de esas murallas. Así, también rara vez le dan la bienvenida a otras personas adentro. Para otras naciones, han llegado a ser «la gente encerrada».

Sin embargo, el primer Motecuzoma había determinado extender las rutas comerciales de los mexica hacia el sur y más allá del sur y decidió hacerlo empleando la fuerza y no por negociaciones diplomáticas. En el año de mi nacimiento, él guió a un ejército dentro de Uaxyácac y después de causar una gran devastación y muerte entre los tzapoteca, decidió finalmente tomar a Záachila por asalto. Él exigió libre paso a los viajeros *pochteca* mexica y, por supuesto, puso a la Gente Nube bajo el tributo de Tenochtitlan. Pero careció de un ejército más grande para apoyar las fuerzas de ocupación, y cuando regresó a su tierra llevando consigo la mayor parte de su ejército, dejó sólo una pequeña guarnición para amparar al gobernador mexica y a los recaudadores de impuestos. En cuanto él estuvo fuera de la vista, los tzapoteca mataron con toda naturalidad a toda la guarnición y reanudaron su forma de vida, y jamás pagaron por tributo algo más que una mezquina cantidad de algodón.

Esto hubiera atraído una nueva y punitiva invasión por parte de los mexica, quienes hubieran destruido esa nación, ya que a Motecuzoma no se le llamaba el Señor Furioso sin ninguna razón. Pero hubo dos cosas que lo impidieron: los tzapoteca fueron lo suficientemente sabios como para mantener su promesa de dejar a los mercaderes mexica viajar por sus tierras sin ser molestados, y en ese mismo año Motecuzoma murió. Su sucesor, Axayácatl, estuvo satisfecho con la concesión que le daban al comercio mexica y lo suficientemente consciente de las dificultades que acarrearía el conquistar y sostener una nación tan lejana, así es que no mandó más ejércitos. Aunque no había mucha amistad entre las dos naciones, sí se estableció una tregua mutua y tratos comerciales, que prevalecieron durante los veinte años antes de mi llegada y por algunos años después de ella.

El centro ceremonial y la ciudad más venerada de Uaxyácac era la antigua ciudad de Lyobaan, a una corta jornada hacia el este de Záachila, a la cual Gíigu nos llevó un día a Cózcatl y a mí, para conocerla. (Glotón de Sangre se quedó en Záachila divirtiéndose en la *auyanicali*, casa de placer.) El nombre de la ciudad, Lyobaan, significa El Hogar Santo, pero nosotros los mexica la conocíamos desde hacía ya mucho tiempo por Mictlan, porque aquellos mexica que la habían visto, de verdad creían que era la entrada terrestre hacia la oscuridad y hacia el horrendo lugar de ese mundo del más allá.

Es una ciudad muy hermosa y bien conservada para su antigüedad. Hay muchos templos con muchas habitaciones, una de las cuales era la más grande que jamás había visto en mi vida, con un techo que sólo hubiera podido estar soportado por un bosque de pilares. Las paredes de los edificios, tanto afuera como adentro, estaban adornadas con diseños profundamente labrados, que parecían tejidos petrificados, repetidos infinitamente en mosaicos blancos de piedra caliza, perfectamente bien acomodados. Como a Su Ilustrísima difícilmente necesita que le digan, esos numerosos templos de El Hogar Santo evidenciaban claramente que la Gente Nube, como nosotros los mexica y ustedes los Cristianos, rendía homenaje a una hueste completa de deidades. Allí estaba la virgen diosa luna Beu y el dios jaguar Béezye y la diosa del amanecer Tangu Yu y no sé cuántos más.

Pero a diferencia de nosotros los mexica, la Gente Nube cree, como ustedes los Cristianos, que todos esos dioses y diosas están subordinados a un gran señor todopoderoso que creó el universo y que gobierna sobre todas las cosas. Como sus ángeles santos y demás, esos dioses menores no podrían hacer uso de sus varias y separadas funciones, y en verdad ni siquiera hubieran podido existir, sin el permiso y la supervisión del dios más alto de toda la creación. Los tzapoteca lo llaman Uizye Tao, que quiere decir El Aliento Poderoso.

Sin embargo, esos grandes templos austeros están construidos solamente en el nivel más alto de Lyobaan. Fueron construidos especialmente sobre aberturas terrestres que llevan a cuevas naturales, túneles y cavernas, en lo más profundo de la tierra, dando lugar a los tzapoteca para enterrar a sus muertos por años incontables. A esa ciudad siempre han sido llevados sus nobles, altos sacerdotes y héroes guerreros muertos, para ser ceremoniosamente enterrados en cuartos ricamente decorados y amueblados, directamente debajo de los templos.

Pero también había y hay habitación para los plebeyos en esas criptas profundas. Gíigu nos contó que no se conocía el final de esas cuevas; se comunicaban y corrían bajo el suelo por incontables largas-carreras, y que había festones de piedra colgando de sus techos y pedestales de piedra surgiendo de sus suelos, que había cortinas y drapeados de piedra con diseños naturales, maravillosos y sobrenaturales como si fueran cascadas petrificadas o como los temerosos mexica imaginaban los portones de Mictlan.

«Y no sólo los muertos vienen a El Hogar Santo —dijo él—. Como ya les dije, cuando sienta que mi vida ya no sirve para nada, vendré aquí para desaparecer.»

De acuerdo a lo que él decía, cualquier hombre o mujer, plebeyos o nobles, quien estuviera baldado por la ancianidad, o cargado por sufrimientos o pesares, o cansado de vivir por alguna razón, podía demandar a los sacerdotes de Lyobaan un entierro voluntario en El Hogar Santo. Él o ella, provistos con una antorcha de palo de pino, pero sin nada para comer, sería dejado en una de las cuevas que se cerraría a su espalda. Entonces, vagaría a través de los pasajes hasta que la luz o su fuerza se agotaran, o encontrara una caverna conveniente, o diera con un lugar que por instinto le dijera que alguno de sus antepasados yacía allí y era un lugar agradable para morir. Entonces el nuevo habitante se acomodaría y esperaría con calma a que su espíritu partiera a cualquier destino que le estaría reservado.

Una de las cosas que me tenía perplejo de Lyobaan era que ese lugar sagrado estuviera enclavado sobre plataformas de piedra al nivel del piso, y no hubiera sido elevado, con todo y sus templos, sobre una pirámide. Le pregunté al viejo el porqué.

«Los ancestros construyeron así este lugar para que tuviera solidez para resistir el *zyuiùù*», dijo, usando una palabra que yo no conocía. Pero en un momento tanto Cózcatl como yo supimos a lo que se refería, porque lo sentimos, como si nuestro guía lo hubiera citado especialmente para instruirnos.

«*Tlalolini*», dijo Cózcatl, con una voz que resonó, como todo lo que nos rodeaba.

Nosotros lo llamamos en náhuatl, *tlalolini*; los tzapoteca lo llaman *zyuüù*; ustedes lo conocen por temblor de tierra. Yo ya había sentido a la tierra moversc antes en Xaltocan, pero su movimiento era un moderado bailoteo hacia arriba y hacia abajo, y nosotros sabíamos que era solamente un acomodamiento de la isla, para estar más confortablemente asentada en el fondo inestable del lago. Allí, en El Hogar Santo, el movimiento era diferente; un bamboleo rodante de lado a lado, como si la montaña hubiera sido un bote pequeño en un lago enfurecido. Exactamente como lo había sentido algunas veces en aguas turbulentas, y en ese momento tuve náuseas. Varias piezas de piedra se salieron de su lugar en la parte alta de un edificio y llegaron fuertemente rodando hacia abajo un poco más allá.

Gíigu, apuntando hacia ellas, dijo: «Los antepasados construyeron fuertemente, pero rara vez pasa un día sin que haya un *zyuüù* en Uaxyácac, moderado o fuerte. Así, nosotros generalmente construimos las casas menos fuerte. Una casa hecha con el alma de la hoja de palma y tejado de palma o paja, no puede dañar mucho a sus habitantes si los techos se caen encima de ellos y se puede reconstruir con facilidad.»

Yo asentí con la cabeza, pues mi estómago estaba tan revuelto que tuve miedo de abrir la boca. El viejo sonrió comprensivamente.

«Esto ha afectado sus tripas, ¿verdad? Le apuesto a que afectará además, a otro de sus órganos.»

Y así fue. Por alguna razón, mi *tepuli* se puso erecto y se estiró en toda su longitud y grosor.

«Nadie sabe el porqué —dijo Gíigu—, pero el *zyuüù* afecta a todos los animales, de preferencia a los humanos. Los hombres y las mujeres se excitan sexualmente y en ocasiones, en un gran terremoto, se exaltan de tal manera que hacen cosas inmorales y en público. Cuando un temblor es realmente violento o prolongado, aun los muchachos pequeños eyaculan involuntariamente y las muchachas pequeñas llegan al orgasmo, como si fueran los adultos más sensuales y por supuesto que se descarrían por lo ocurrido. Algunas veces, mucho antes de que la tierra se mueva, los perros y los *coyotin* empiezan a lloriquear y a aullar y los pájaros revolotean alrededor. Sabemos por su conducta cuándo un temblor verdadero y peligroso está por sentirse. Nuestros mineros y canteros corren a lugares seguros, los nobles abandonan sus palacios de piedra, los sacerdotes dejan sus templos de piedra. Aun estando prevenidos, una convulsión muy fuerte puede causar mucho daño y muerte. —Para mi sorpresa, él se sonrió otra vez—. A pesar de todo, nosotros tenemos que conceder que un temblor de tierra nos da más vida de las que arrebata. Después de cada temblor fuerte, cuando tres cuartas partes del año han transcurrido, una gran cantidad de bebés nacen con solamente unos días de diferencia unos de otros.»

Podía creerlo, pues mi rígido miembro se había levantado de repente como un garrote y se negaba a apaciguarse. Envidié a Glotón de Sangre quien estaba haciendo que ese día fuera, probablemente, recordado para siempre en la *auyanicali*. Si yo hubiera estado en cualquiera de las calles de Záachila, habría podido romper la tregua entre los mexica y los tzapoteca y desnudar y violar a la primera mujer que encontrara...

No, no necesito platicar sobre eso. Pero quiero decir a Su Ilustrísima, que aunque un temblor de tierra produce temor a los animales menores, a los humanos les inspira temor y excitación sexual.

En la primera noche en que nuestro grupo acampó al aire libre, al principio de aquella larga jornada, por primera vez sentí el impacto del miedo hacia la oscuridad, el vacío y la soledad durante la noche en la selva y después me embargó un sentimiento que me empujaba con urgencia a copular. Tanto el animal humano como cualquier otro animal irracional, sentimos miedo al enfrentarnos a cualquier aspecto de la naturaleza que no podemos comprender ni controlar. Sin embargo, las criaturas inferiores no saben lo que es sentir miedo a la muerte, porque ellas no saben lo que *es* la muerte. Nosotros los humanos sí lo sabemos. Un hombre puede afrontar cara a cara una muerte honorable en el campo de batalla o en un altar. Una mujer puede afrontar el riesgo de una muerte honorable al dar a luz. Pero nosotros no podemos afrontar una muerte que llega de un modo diferente, como el soplo que apaga la llama de una lámpara. Nuestro miedo más grande proviene de ser extinguidos de una manera caprichosa y sin sentido. Y en el momento en que sentimos ese gran pavor, nuestro impulso instintivo nos hace hacer la única cosa que sabemos hacer en preservación de la vida. Algo muy profundo dentro de nuestro cerebro nos grita con desesperación: «¡*Ahuilnéma*! ¡Copula! Si no puedes salvar tu vida, puedes hacer otra.» Y así el *tepuli* del hombre se levanta por sí solo, las *tepili*, partes de la mujer, se abren incitadoras, sus jugos genitales empiezan a fluir...

Bueno, ésta es solamente una teoría, y una teoría solamente mía. Sin embargo, Su Ilustrísima, y también ustedes reverendos frailes, eventualmente tendrán la oportunidad de verificar o desaprobar lo que les digo. Esta isla de Tenochtitlan-Mexico está asentada en una forma todavía más incómoda que la de Xaltocan sobre el fondo fangoso del lago, y ha cambiado su posición varias veces antes y algunas de ellas muy violentamente. Tarde o temprano, ustedes sentirán un convulsivo temblor de tierra, y entonces podrán verificar por sí mismos lo que sienten sus reverendas partes.

✠

No había ninguna razón verdadera para que nuestro grupo se quedara en Záachila y en sus alrededores por tantos días, como nosotros hicimos, excepto porque era el lugar más agradable para descansar antes de que emprendiéramos la larga y pesada caminata ascendente a través de las montañas, y también por el hecho de que, por todos los días grises que Glotón de Sangre había vivido, parecía determinado a no dejar desatendida a ni una sola de las accesibles y bellas tzapoteca. Por lo tanto, yo me dediqué a ver los bellos paisajes de la comarca y ni siquiera me esforcé en concertar algún trato comercial, por una simple razón, la mercancía local más apreciada era el famoso colorante y éste estaba agotado.

Ustedes llaman a ese colorante cochinilla y quizá sepan que se obtiene de cierto insecto, el *nocheztli*. Esos insectos viven por millones en inmensas plantaciones de una variedad especial de *nopali*, cactos, de los que se alimentan. Todos los insectos maduran en la misma estación y sus cultivadores los toman de los cactos y los introducen en bolsas para luego matarlos, ya sea metiendo las bolsas en agua hirviendo, colgándolas en las casas de vapor o dejándolas secar al sol. Los insectos se secan hasta que quedan como semillas arrugadas y entonces son vendidos por su peso. El color que se desprende de ellos, depende de la forma en que hayan sido matados —cocidos, por vapor o asados— y cuando han sido aplastados su colorante puede ser jacinto amarillo-rojo o escarlata brillante o un carmín particularmente luminoso, que no se puede obtener de ninguna otra fuente. Si yo les explico todo esto es porque la última cosecha de los tzapoteca había sido vendida en su totalidad a un mercader mexica, el mismo con el que había conversado tiempo atrás en la nación de los xochimilca, y ya no había más colorante durante ese año, pues ni aun a los insectos más mimados se les puede apurar para que se reproduzcan.

Como recordaba lo que ese mercader me había dicho acerca de un colorante nuevo y aún más raro, un púrpura permanente que de alguna manera estaba relacionado con caracoles y un pueblo llamado Los Desconocidos, le pregunté sobre eso a mi intérprete y a varios de sus amigos mercaderes lo que pudieran saber sobre el particular; pero lo único que conseguí de todos fue un gesto vago de ignorancia y una respuesta como un eco: «¿Púrpura? ¿Caracoles? ¿Desconocidos?» Así es que sólo hice una transacción en Záachila y no fue ese tipo de negocio que un típico *pochtécatl* hubiera podido hacer.

El viejo Gíigu arregló para mí una entrevista de cortesía con Kosi Yuela, el Bishosu Ben Záa, que quiere decir Venerado Orador de la Gente Nube y ese gentilhombre tuvo la amabilidad de agasajarme, invitándome a conocer su palacio para que pudiera admirar sus muebles lujosos. Me interesé en la adquisición de dos de ellos. Uno, fue la reina del Bishosu, Pela Xila, una mujer que hacía que a cualquier hombre se le hiciera agua la boca, pero me contenté con hacer el gesto de besar la tierra delante de ella. Sin embargo, cuando vi un bellísimo tapiz trabajado en pluma decidí que lo tendría.

«Ha sido hecho por uno de sus compatriotas», dijo mi anfitrión y su voz sonó como si yo hubiera sido un impertinente en detenerme a admirar el trabajo de un mexícatl, en lugar de admirar los productos de su pueblo, la Gente Nube. Por ejemplo, las tapicerías abigarradas e interesantes del salón del trono, hechas por apretados nudos coloreados, luego otra vez anudados y vueltos a colorear y así por varias veces más.

Señalando con mi cabeza el tapiz, le dije: «Déjeme adivinar, mi señor. Ese trabajo de pluma es de un artista que vino de muy lejos, llamado Chimali.»

Kosi Yuela sonrió. «Tiene razón. Estuvo aquí por un tiempo haciendo bosquejos de los mosaicos de Lyobaan, y después no tuvo con qué pagar al posadero excepto con este tapiz. El posadero lo aceptó, aunque no muy contento, y luego vino a quejarse conmigo. Así es que yo le retribuí, porque confío en que el artista vuelva otra vez y lo redima.»

«Estoy seguro de que él lo hará —le dije—. Pero yo conozco a Chimali desde hace mucho tiempo y probablemente lo vea antes que usted. Si me lo permite, mi señor, estaré encantado de pagar su deuda y de asumir esto en prenda.»

«Sería muy amable de su parte —dijo el Bishosu—. Un favor muy generoso tanto para su amigo como para nosotros.»

«No se fije usted en eso —le dije—. Sólo le pago a usted la bondad que ha tenido para con él. Y de todas maneras —y recordé el día que guié al asustado Chimali a su casa, llevando una calabaza en la cabeza—, ésta no será la primera vez que he ayudado a mi amigo en alguna dificultad temporal.»

Chimali debió de haber vivido muy bien durante su estancia en la posada, pues me costó un bulto completo de pedacitos de estaño y cobre para liquidar su deuda. Sin embargo, el tapiz fácilmente valdría diez o veinte veces más. Ahora, probablemente su valor sería de cien veces más, ya que casi todos nuestros trabajos de pluma han sido destruidos y no se han hecho más en estos últimos años. Ya sea porque también los artistas que trabajan la pluma hayan sido destruidos o porque hayan perdido el deseo de su corazón para crear belleza. Así que es muy probable que Su Ilustrísima nunca haya visto uno de esos trabajos deslumbrantes.

El trabajo de pluma es mucho más delicado, difícil y lleva más tiempo que cualquier clase de pintura, escultura o joyería. El artista empieza a trabajar con una pieza del más fino algodón, fuertemente estirada sobre un panel o marco de madera. Sobre la tela dibuja suavemente las líneas del motivo que ya tenía en mente, luego, cuidadosamente llena todos los espacios con plumas de colores, quitando el cañón a cada una para utilizar la parte más suave de ésta. Pega, quizá, miles y miles de plumas, una por una, con gotas diminutas del líquido del hule. Algunos que se llamaban a sí mismos artistas, negligente y suciamente falseaban el trabajo utilizando solamente plumas blancas de pájaros, las cuales teñían con pinturas y colorantes según lo iban requiriendo y ajustando sus formas para llenar los lugares más intrincados del diseño. Sin embargo, los verdaderos artistas usaban sólo las plumas de colores naturales y con mucho cuidado escogían exactamente el matiz correcto en todos los grados de colores y usaban plumas largas o cortas, rectas o curvas según lo pedía el dibujo. Dije «largas», sí, pero rara vez había en cualquiera de esos trabajos una pluma más grande que el pétalo de una violeta y la más pequeña era más o menos del tamaño de una pestaña humana. Un artista debía separar cuidadosamente, comparar y seleccionar de entre un bulto de plumas tan grande que podría llenar este cuarto en el que nosotros estamos sentados.

No sé por qué Chimali, por esta vez, hizo a un lado su pintura y en lugar de ello escogió el trabajo de pluma para hacer la escena de un paisaje. Lo hizo con la perfección de un maestro con muchos años de experiencia en ese tipo de trabajo. En el claro de un bosque bañado por el sol, un jaguar yacía descansando entre flores, mariposas y pájaros. El dibujo de cada pájaro estaba hecho con las plumas de su especie, cada pájaro azulejo, por ejemplo, había requerido que Chimali buscara las más pequeñitas plumas azules de cientos de verdaderos azulejos. El verdor no era solamente masas de plumas verdes; cada hoja individual de hierba o de un árbol, era una pluma separada en diferente tono de verde. Conté más de treinta plumas minúsculas que componían el diseño de una pequeña mariposa en color pardo-amarillo. La firma de Chimali era la única parte del paisaje hecha en un solo color sin matiz, con las plumas rojizas de la huacamaya y la huella era mucho más pequeña como de la mitad de su tamaño real.

Tomé el tapiz, lo llevé a nuestra posada y se lo di a Cózcatl diciéndole que sólo dejara en la tela la marca escarlata de la huella de la mano. Cuando él hubo quitado cada una de las plumas del tapiz, yo las apiñé por separado, mezclándolas confusamente dentro de la tela otra vez. La enrollé y la até fuertemente y la llevé de nuevo al palacio. Kosi Yuela no estaba, pero su reina Pela Xila me recibió y le entregué a ella el paquete atado, diciendo:

«Solamente en caso de que el artista Chimali regrese por este camino antes de que yo lo encuentre, mi señora, tenga la bondad de decirle que esto es una prueba de amistad... que todas sus deudas serán pagadas similarmente.»

El único camino hacia el sur de Záachila era a través de las altas hileras de montañas llamadas Tzempuüla y ése fue el que seguimos; a través de ellas, día tras día interminablemente. A menos de que usted haya escalado alguna montaña, Su Ilustrísima, no sé cómo podría expresarme para que supiera lo que es escalar una. No sé cómo podría hacerle sentir los músculos en tensión y la fatiga, las magulladuras y los arañazos, el sudor chorreante y la tierra que se mete en las sandalias, el vértigo de las alturas y la sed insaciable durante los días cálidos, la necesidad continua de vigilar cada uno de nuestros pasos, las veces que el corazón se nos paraba en un instante de miedo, dos resbalones por cada tres pasos que dábamos hacia arriba y el descenso casi tan arduo y peligroso... y después de sufrir todo eso, ni siquiera encontrábamos una tierra llana en donde poder negociar, sino otra montaña...

Cierto que había una vereda, así es que no perdíamos nuestro camino. Había sido hecha por y para los fuertes hombres de la Gente Nube, aunque eso no quería decir que a ellos les gustara viajar por allí. No había ninguna vereda que permaneciera firme o fuertemente hollada, pues continuamente se estaban desprendiendo pedruscos de las montañas. En algunas partes, el camino se encontraba lleno de pequeños fragmentos de pedazos de roca que se deslizaban metiéndose en nuestras sandalias y nos amenazaba con despeñarnos en cualquier momento. En otros lugares, la vereda cruzaba por una zanja honda causada por la erosión y de su fondo salíamos con los tobillos torcidos por las rocas que se volteaban y los restos de tierra podrida que se desmoronaba. En otros, se tornaba en una estrecha escalera en espiral de roca, cuyos escalones eran lo suficientemente anchos como para que nuestros dedos de los pies se pudieran afianzar. En otros, era sólo un desfiladero suspendido en el flanco de la montaña, con una pared de roca escarpada de un lado, que parecía ansiosa de querer empujarnos a todos sobre el profundo abismo que yacía del otro lado.

Muchas de las montañas eran tan altas que nuestra ruta nos llevó algunas veces por encima de los bosques. Allí arriba, no había ninguna vegetación, excepto los pocos líquenes que crecían entre las grietas o que se apretujaban siempre verdes y retorcidos por el viento, ya que había muy poca tierra para que cualquier otra planta pudiera echar raíces. Esos pasos habían sido erosionados desde la base de la roca; muy bien pudimos estar escalando a lo largo de una de las expuestas costillas del esqueleto de la tierra. Tan pronto como subíamos y bajábamos esos picos, jadeábamos como si estuviéramos compitiendo entre nosotros por el poco aire insustancial que allí había.

Los días eran todavía calientes, demasiado calientes para un ejercicio tan riguroso. Pero las noches eran tan frías en aquellas alturas como para herirnos hasta la médula de los huesos. Si hubiéramos podido escoger, habríamos viajado solamente de noche para que el ejercicio nos hubiera mantenido calientes, y habríamos dormido durante el día en lugar de esforzarnos bajo el peso de nuestros bultos, sudando y palpitando hasta caer casi desfallecidos. Pero ningún ser humano hubiera podido moverse a través de esas montañas en la oscuridad, sin romperse por lo menos una pierna y probablemente también el cuello.

Solamente dos veces durante esa parte de la jornada, nos encontramos con aldeas pobladas. Una fue Xalapan, una aldea de la tribu huave, que son oscuros de piel, feos y desagradables. Nos recibieron con grosería y nos impusieron un precio exorbitante que nosotros tuvimos que pagar. La comida que nos dieron fue abominable; un grasoso estofado de riñones de zorra, que por lo menos ayudó a que nuestras provisiones no disminuyeran. Las chozas de paja que nos cedieron olían mal y estaban llenas de lombrices, pero por lo menos nos mantuvieron resguardados del viento nocturno de la montaña. La otra aldea fue Nejapa, en donde fuimos más cordialmente recibidos y agradablemente tratados con hospitalidad, nos alimentaron bien e incluso nos vendieron algunos huevos de sus aves, para llevárnoslos cuando nos fuéramos. Desafortunadamente, la gente de esa aldea eran chinanteca, quienes, como ya mencioné hace bastante tiempo, padecían la enfermedad que ustedes llaman pinto. Aunque todos sabíamos que no era contagiosa, excepto quizá por acostarse con sus mujeres y a ninguno de nosotros se nos ocurrió hacerlo, el solo hecho de ver todos aquellos cuerpos manchados de azul, nos hizo sentirnos casi tan sarnosos e inconfortables en Nejapa como lo estuvimos en Xalapan.

En muchas partes que pasamos, tratamos de seguir las instrucciones del rudo mapa que yo llevaba y así pudimos acampar cada noche en una cañada entre dos montañas. Usualmente encontrábamos por lo menos un arroyo de agua fresca, crecimientos de *mexixin*, mastuerzo, coles de pantano u otras verduras comestibles. La ventaja que había en las tierras bajas era que un esclavo no necesitaba pulverizar la yesca durante media noche para encender un fuego, como lo haría en el aire delgado de las alturas, antes de que pudiera generar suficiente calor para prender la mecha y conseguir un fuego para el campamento. Sin embargo, ya que ninguno de nosotros, a excepción de Glotón de Sangre, nunca antes habíamos viajado por esa ruta, y ya que él no siempre podía acordarse exactamente de todas las subidas y las bajadas, la oscuridad, frecuente y maliciosamente, nos cogía mientras nosotros ascendíamos o descendíamos por una montaña.

Una de esas noches, Glotón de Sangre me dijo con disgusto: «Ya estoy cansado de comer carne de perro y frijoles; después de todo sólo nos quedarán tres perros esta noche. Éste es el país de los jaguares. Mixtli, tú y yo estaremos despiertos para tratar de cazar alguno.»

Glotón de Sangre buscó algunos troncos que estuvieran cerca de nuestro campamento, hasta que al fin encontró uno hueco y muerto, lo socavó haciendo un cilindro del largo de su antebrazo. Tomó la piel que le habían quitado al perrito, que el esclavo Diez estaba asando en esos momentos, y la extendió sobre el hueco del tronco atándola al final del mismo, en donde él la anudó con un cordón, como si fuera un rudo tambor. Después le hizo un agujero en medio y a través de él dejó pasar una tira de cuero crudo y también la anudó para que no se deslizara. Así la tira quedó vertical y firme dentro del tambor y Glotón de Sangre metió su mano por la abertura que éste tenía del otro lado. Cuando él pellizcó la fluctuante tira pasando al mismo tiempo su calloso dedo a lo largo de la piel del tambor improvisado, éste sonó como un gruñido áspero, exactamente igual al de un jaguar.

«Si por aquí cerca o en los alrededores hay un gato —dijo el viejo guerrero—, su primitiva curiosidad le llevará a investigar la luz del fuego de nuestro campamento; pero se aproximará contra el viento y no muy cerca. Tú y yo, también iremos contra el viento hasta encontrar un lugar confortable en el bosque. Tú te sentarás y rascarás el tambor, Mixtli, mientras yo me esconderé con una hilera de lanzas a mano. El humo de la hoguerra, esparcido por el viento cubrirá lo suficiente nuestro olor y tu llamada hará que se vuelva lo suficientemente curioso como para venir directamente hacia nosotros.»

No estaba muy entusiasmado que digamos, con la idea de jugar a incitar a un jaguar, pero dejé que Glotón de Sangre me mostrara cómo trabajar en su invento, haciendo ruidos a diestro y siniestro, a irregulares intervalos, gruñidos cortos y largos. Cuando terminamos de comer, Cózcatl y los esclavos se envolvieron en sus cobijas, mientras Glotón de Sangre y yo nos internábamos en la oscuridad de la noche.

Cuando el fuego de nuestro campamento era sólo un resplandor en la distancia, pero podíamos todavía oler débilmente el humo, nos detuvimos en lo que Glotón de Sangre dijo que era un claro, aunque muy bien hubiera podido ser una de las cuevas de El Hogar Santo, por todo lo que yo podía ver. Me senté en una roca mientras él iba hacia algún lugar detrás de mí, quebrando ramas a su paso y cuando todo estuvo en silencio empecé a aporrear la tira de cuero crudo del improvisado tambor... un gruñido, una pausa, un gruñido y un rugido, una pausa, tres ásperos gruñidos...

El sonido era casi tan exacto al que hacía un gato grande mientras vagaba gruñendo caprichosamente, que hasta mi propia espalda se erizó. Sin desearlo realmente, recordé algunas historias acerca del jaguar que había escuchado de cazadores experimentados. El jaguar, decían ellos, nunca tiene que estar muy cerca de su presa. Tiene la habilidad de hipar violentamente y su aliento dejará incapacitada a su víctima, entorpeciéndola, pasmándola, aun a la distancia. Un cazador que utilice flechas debe siempre tener cuatro en su mano, porque el jaguar también es notorio en su habilidad de saber esquivar las flechas y después, como un insulto, las toma entre sus dientes y las convierte en astillas. Así es que un cazador debe disparar las cuatro flechas una detrás de otra, con la esperanza de que por lo menos una surta efecto, porque es bien sabido que él no podrá tomar más de cuatro flechas antes de que el hipo del gato lo alcance.

Yo traté de distraer mis pensamientos haciendo algunas variaciones e improvisaciones con los gruñidos de mi tambor; rápidos gruñidos como cloqueos engañadores, largos e indecisos gemidos como los que haría un gato al bostezar. Hasta llegué a creer, en verdad, que estaba llegando a ser un maestro en eso, especialmente cuando de alguna manera producía un gruñido después de haber dejado de rascar la tira de cuero crudo y me preguntaba si sería bueno introducir ese invento como un nuevo instrumento musical y conmigo como único maestro en todo el mundo, en alguna ceremonia de un festival...

En esos momentos llegó hasta mis oídos otro gruñido y desperté rápidamente de mi ensueño horrorizado, pues tampoco había producido ese otro gruñido. También llegó hasta mi nariz un cierto olor a orines y a mi visión, disminuida como estaba, una sensación de algo oscuro que se movía furtivamente en la oscuridad, a un lado de mí, hacia la izquierda. El gruñido que provenía de la oscuridad se dejó oír otra vez, fuertemente, y como inquiriendo algo. Aunque estaba casi totalmente paralizado, volví a rasgar la tira de cuero con un gruñido, que tenía la esperanza de que sonara como si fuera una bienvenida. ¿Qué otra cosa podía hacer?

Desde mi izquierda, casi al frente, se volvieron hacia mí dos luces frías y amarillas. Y me preguntaba qué podía hacer en esos momentos, cuando de repente un viento afilado pasó silbando muy cerca de mi mejilla. Pensé que era el hipo letal del jaguar, pero las luces amarillas parpadearon y luego salió de su garganta un grito desgarrador, como los que lanza un mujer sacrificada bajo el cuchillo tosco de un inepto sacerdote. El grito se quebró y se oyó, entonces, un ruido ahogado y burbujeante, acompañado por el sonido de un cuerpo al arrastrarse, que evidentemente arrancaba los arbustos a su paso.

«Siento mucho haber dejado que se acercara tanto a ti —dijo Glotón de Sangre a mi lado—. Pero tuve que esperar a ver el brillo de sus ojos para poder afinar mi puntería.»

«¿Qué cosa es?», pregunté, con aquel grito pavoroso como el de una mujer todavía sonando en mis oídos y temiendo que hubiéramos cazado a una mujer.

Como el ruido de arrastre había cesado, Glotón de Sangre fue a investigar. Él dijo triunfalmente: «Exactamente en los pulmones. No estuvo mal para disparar casi a la ventura.» Después debió de haberse caído sobre el cuerpo muerto, porque le oí murmurar: «Que me condene en Mictlan...», y yo esperé que confesara haber disparado sobre una pobre mujer chinantécatl perdida en la oscuridad de los bosques. Pero lo único que dijo fue: «Ven y ayúdame a arrastrar esto hacia el campamento.» Así lo hice, y si era una mujer, ésta pesaba tanto como yo y tenía las patas traseras como las de un gato.

Todos los que estaban en el campamento se habían envuelto totalmente en sus cobijas, como era de suponer, para no escuchar esos ruidos pavorosos. Glotón de Sangre y yo dejamos caer nuestra presa y por primera vez pude ver a un gato enorme, pero no era moteado sino leonado.

El viejo guerrero dijo jadeando: «Debo de estar... perdiendo mi habilidad... pues hice la llamada del jaguar. Pero éste es un cuguar, un león de la montaña.»

«No importa —jadeé—. La carne es igual de buena. Su piel servirá para que te hagas un buen manto.»

Naturalmente que ya nadie durmió en lo que restaba de la noche. Glotón de Sangre y yo nos sentamos a descansar, siendo admirados por los otros y yo lo felicité por su hazaña y él a mí por mi invencible paciencia. Entretanto algunos esclavos le quitaban la piel al animal, mientras otros raspaban la superficie interior de ésta y otros cortaban el cadáver en piezas convenientes para ser transportadas. Cózcatl cocinaba el desayuno para todos nosotros: *atoli* de maíz que nos daría energía durante el día, pero también nos preparó un festín para celebrar nuestro éxito en la cacería. Sacó los huevos que con tanto cuidado habíamos cargado desde Nejapa y con una ramita hizo un hoyo en cada cáscara y revolvió con ella la yema y la clara, luego los asó brevemente en los rescoldos del fuego y nosotros nos comimos su rico contenido, por el agujero.

En la parada que hicimos dos noches después, nos dimos un festín con la carne del gato, que era en extremo sabrosa. Glotón de Sangre le dio la piel del cuguar al más gordo de los esclavos, a Diez, para que la llevara como capa, y mientras la ablandaría sobándola continuamente con las manos. Pero como nosotros no nos tomamos la molestia de encontrar algo para curtir la piel, ésta pronto empezó a apestar nauseabundamente, así es que hicimos que Diez caminara a una buena distancia lejos de nosotros. Como él también tenía que utilizar frecuentemente sus cuatro extremidades para poder escalar la montaña, muy raras veces tuvo las manos libres para poder suavizar la piel. El sol caía de lleno sobre el pobre Diez, hasta que pareció que traía una puerta de piel barnizada incrustrada sobre su espalda. Sin embargo, Glotón de Sangre con obstinación murmuró algo acerca de hacer de la piel un escudo para él y se negó a que Diez dejara de andar con ella, y así anduvo con nosotros, todo el camino a través de las montañas de Tzempuüla.

✠

Estoy muy contento de que el Señor Obispo no esté hoy con nosotros, mis señores escribanos, porque debo contarles un encuentro sexual que estoy seguro de que Su Ilustrísima lo juzgaría sórdido y repulsivo. Él, probablemente, se pondría colorado otra vez. En verdad, a pesar de que han pasado como cuarenta años desde aquella noche, todavía me siento incómodo cuando lo recuerdo y omitiría el episodio sino fuera porque el contarlo es necesario para poder entender los incidentes todavía más significativos que derivaron de él.

Cuando por fin los catorce que formábamos nuestra comitiva descendimos de la última y larga hilera de montañas de Tzempuüla, fuimos a dar otra vez dentro del territorio tzapoteca, a una ciudad más o menos grande asentada a la orilla de un gran río. Ustedes ahora la llaman Villa de Guadalcázar, pero en aquellos días la ciudad, el río y todas las tierras que se extendían alrededor, se llamaban en el lenguaje lóochi, Layú Beezhù o El Lugar del Dios Jaguar. Pero como era un lugar muy concurrido por ser el cruce de caminos de diferentes rutas comerciales, la mayoría de su gente hablaba náhuatl como un segundo lenguaje y con frecuencia usaban el nombre que los viajeros mexica le habían dado al lugar: Tecuantépec o simplemente La Colina del Jaguar. Pienso que ninguna persona, ni antes ni después, a excepción mía, se dio cuenta jamás de lo ridículo que era aplicar ese nombre de Colina del Jaguar, tanto a la corriente ancha del río como a las tierras excepcionalmente planas que lo circundaban.

La ciudad estaba sólo a unas cinco largas-carreras desde donde el río escupía sus aguas dentro del mar del sur, así es que había atraído a inmigrantes de otras varias naciones del área de la costa: los zoque, los mexitzo, algunos huave y aun algunos grupos desplazados de los mixteca. En sus calles, uno se podía encontrar con gran variedad de diferentes colores de tez, apariencias físicas, trajes y acentos. Sin embargo, y afortunadamente, los nativos, la Gente Nube, predominaban, así es que la mayoría de las gentes de la ciudad eran superlativamente guapos y corteses como los de Záachila.

En la tarde en que llegamos, mientras nuestro pequeño grupo

estaba ansioso por cruzar el puente de cuerdas que colgaba sobre el río, a pesar de que veníamos dando traspiés y fatigados, Glotón de Sangre dijo con voz enronquecida por el polvo y la fatiga: «Hay excelentes posadas más allá de Tecuantépec.»

«Las excelentes pueden esperar —dije roncamente—. Nosotros nos detendremos en la *primera* que encontremos.»

Y así, cansados y hambrientos, como unos sacerdotes andrajosos, sucios y malolientes, nos detuvimos en la entrada de la primera posada que encontramos en la ciudad y que estaba a un lado del río. Y por esa impulsiva decisión mía, justamente como las volutas de humo se desenrollan dando varias vueltas al encenderse un fuego, así, inevitablemente se desplegaron los sucesos de los restantes caminos y días de mi vida, y de los de la vida dc Zyanya y las vidas de otras personas que ya he mencionado y de otras que nombraré, y aun, la de una que nunca tuvo nombre.

Pues bien, reverendos frailes, todo empezó así:

Cuando todos nosotros, incluyendo a los esclavos, nos bañamos y estuvimos en la casa de vapor y luego nos volvimos a bañar y después de vestirnos con trajes limpios, pedimos que nos sirvieran de comer. Los esclavos comieron afuera en el patio a la luz del crepúsculo, pero a Cózcatl, a Glotón de Sangre y a mí, nos pusieron un mantel en una habitación alumbrada por antorchas y alfombras con un *pétlatl*. Nos hartamos con las delicias frescas del cercano mar: ostiones crudos, rosados camarones cocidos y un pescado rojo de gran tamaño.

Cuando el hambre que sentía mi estómago fue mitigada, noté la extraordinaria belleza de la mujer que nos servía y recordé que también era capaz de otros apetitos. También advertí otra extraordinaria circunstancia. El propietario de la posada pertenecía a una de las razas de inmigrantes; era chaparro, gordo y de piel untuosa. Sin embargo, la mujer que nos servía y a quien él gritaba órdenes con brusquedad, era obviamente una be'n zaa; alta y flexible, con una piel que resplandecía como el ámbar y un rostro que rivalizaba con la reina de su pueblo, la primera señora Pela Xila. Estaba fuera de todo pensamiento que ella pudiera ser la esposa del propietario. Y ya que ella muy difícilmente podría haber nacido esclava o comprada como tal en propia nación, supuse que alguna desgracia la había obligado, por algún contrato, a trabajar para ese posadero extranjero y grosero.

Era muy difícil juzgar la edad de cualquier mujer adulta de la Gente Nube, porque los años eran bondadosos con ellas, especialmente una tan bella y grácil como aquella sirvienta. Si hubiera sabido que ella era lo suficientemente vieja como para tener aproximadamente mi edad, es posible que ni siquiera le hubiera dirigido la palabra. Probablemente no lo hubiera hecho de todas formas, si no hubiera sido porque Glotón de Sangre y yo, habíamos estado acompañando nuestra comida con copiosos tragos de *octli*. Sea lo que fuere, el caso es que cuando la mujer se volvió a acercar la miré con atrevimiento y le pregunté:

«¿Cómo es que una mujer Nube como tú, trabaja con ese imbécil inferior?»

Ella echó una mirada temerosa alrededor para asegurarse de que el posadero no estaba en esos momentos en la habitación. Entonces se arrodilló para decirme al oído la siguiente pregunta en náhuatl, y por cierto que una pregunta sorprendente.

«¿Joven señor *pochtécatl*, desea una mujer para la noche?» Mis ojos debieron de abrirse tanto, que ella se puso colorada como amapola y bajó los ojos. «El propietario —dijo ella— le puede proporcionar una *maátitl* común de las que se van a horcajarse al camino desde aquí hasta la playa de los pescadores, en la costa. Permíteme, joven señor, que ofrezca a mí misma en lugar de una de ellas. Mi nombre es Gie Bele, que en su lenguaje quiere decir Flor Flameante.»

Debí de haber estado, tontamente, con la boca abierta porque ella se enderezó y parándose frente a mí, me dijo casi fieramente: «Yo seré una *maátitl* pagada, pero todavía no lo soy. Ésta será la primera vez desde la muerte de mi esposo, yo nunca antes... ni siquiera con un hombre de mi propia gente...»

Me sentí tan impresionado por su embarazosa necesidad, que tartamudeé: «Yo... yo estaré encantado.»

Gie Bele volvió a mirar alrededor y dijo: «No se lo diga al posadero. Él exige parte del pago a sus mujeres y me pegaría por tratar de engañarlo con un cliente. Yo estaré esperándolo afuera a la caída de la noche, mi señor, e iremos a mi cabaña.»

Y empezó rápidamente a recoger los utensilios vacíos, para parecer ocupada, cuando el propietario, dándose gran importancia y alborotando, entró en la habitación. Glotón de Sangre, que no había podido impedir el escuchar el ofrecimiento de la mujer, me miró de reojo y me dijo sarcásticamente:

«Siempre la primera vez. Desearía tener una semilla de cacao cada vez que una mujer me dijera eso. Y me cortaría uno de los testículos cada vez que pudiera probar que es verdad.»

El posadero vino hacia nosotros, jovial, frotándose sus manos gordas, para preguntarnos en náhuatl si deseábamos algún dulce para terminar la cena. «Quizás un dulce para gozar en sus ratos de ocio, mis señores, mientras ustedes descansan en las esterillas de sus habitaciones.»

Yo le dije que no. Glotón de Sangre me miró y luego vociferó al hombre gordo: «¡Sí. Yo sí quiero probar un poco de ese dulce! ¡Por Huitztli, que también quiero el dulce de él! —Y me señaló con el dedo—. ¡Mándeme las dos a mi cuarto! ¡Y tenga cuidado de enviarme las dos más sabrosas que tenga!»

El posadero murmuró admirado: «Un señor con noble apetito», y se escurrió hacia afuera. Glotón de Sangre todavía enardecido me miró y dijo con exasperación:

«¿No sabes, imbécil baboso, que ése es el *segundo* engaño que las mujeres aprenden en este comercio? Llegarás a su cabaña para encontrarte que ella todavía tiene a su hombre, probablemente dos o tres más, todos ellos zafios pescadores y encantados de conocer a este nuevo pez que ella ha puesto en el anzuelo. Te robarán y te dejarán tan plano y machacado como una tortilla.»

Cózcatl dijo con timidez: «Sería una lástima que nuestra expedición terminara antes de tiempo en Tecuantépcc.»

Yo no escuchaba. Estaba embrutecido no solamente por el *octli*. Creía firmemente que aquella mujer era de la clase que yo había deseado en Záachila y que por supuesto no había podido conseguir; de esa clase honesta que no desearía ensuciarse con uno como yo. Aun si, como había expresado Gie Bele, yo sería sólo el primero de muchos otros amantes que pagarían por tener sus favores, yo seguiría siendo el primero. Y todavía, borracho como estaba de bebida, deseo, y aun imbécil, tenía el suficiente sentido como para preguntarme: ¿por qué yo?

«Porque tú eres joven —dijo ella, cuando nos encontramos afuera—. Tú eres lo suficientemente joven como para no haber tenido y conocido a muchas mujeres de la clase que te infectarían. Tú no eres tan guapo como mi difunto esposo, pero casi puedes pasar como un be'n zaa. También eres un hombre de propiedad, quien puede pagar por sus placeres.» Después de que hubimos caminado un poco más en silencio, me preguntó con voz débil: «¿Me pagarás?»

«Claro», le dije con voz estropajosa. Mi lengua estaba tan tan hinchada por el *octli*, como mi *tepuli* lo estaba por la anticipación.

«Alguno debe ser el primero —dijo ella, no quejándose como una mártir, sino como exponiendo un hecho de la vida—. Estoy contenta de que seas tú. Lo único que desearía es que todos fueran igual. Soy una viuda desamparada con dos hijas y nosotras nos tenemos que contar entre los esclavos y mis niñas tendrán maridos decentes entre la Gente Nube. Si hubiera sabido cuál sería su *tonali*, habría retenido mi leche y dejado morir cuando eran bebés, pero ahora es ya muy tarde para desear sus muertes. Si tenemos que vivir, debo hacer esto y ellas deben aprender a hacerlo también.»

«¿Por qué?», pregunté con dificultad, pues estaba caminando haciendo eses y ella me tomó de un brazo para guiarme a través de las oscuras callejuelas del barrio pobre de la ciudad.

Gie Bele señaló sobre su hombro con su mano libre y dijo tristemente: «Antes esa posada era nuestra, pero mi esposo se aburría de la vida de posadero y siempre estaba en busca de aventuras, con la esperanza de encontrar alguna fortuna que nos dejara libres de ese negocio. Encontró algunas cosas raras y singulares, pero ninguna de valor, y mientras se fue endeudando cada vez más con el tratante que prestaba y cambiaba dinero. En su última expedición, mi esposo vio algo que dijo que podía comprar muy barato y sacar un buen provecho de ello. Así es que para tener el dinero necesario empeñó el mesón, dejándolo en prenda de pago. —Ella se encogió de hombros—. Nunca regresó. Como el hombre que persiguió el fantasma trémulo de Xtabai en el pantano y desapareció dentro de las arenas movedizas. Eso fue hace ya cuatro años.»

«Y ahora el tratante es el propietario», murmuré.

«Sí. Él pertenece a la tribu de los zoque y su nombre es Wáyay. Pero la propiedad no ha sido suficiente como para redimir toda la deuda. El *bishosu* de la ciudad es un hombre bueno, pero cuando la demanda fue presentada delante de él no pudo hacer nada. Entonces fui obligada a trabajar desde el amanecer hasta el anochecer. Y puedo dar gracias de que por lo menos mis niñas no han trabajado así. Se ganan lo que pueden cosiendo, bordando o lavando ropa ajena, pero la mayoría de la gente que puede pagar este tipo de trabajo, tienen hijas o esclavos para que lo hagan.»

«¿Y por cuánto tiempo más tienes que trabajar para Wáyay?»

Ella suspiró. «De alguna manera la deuda parece que nunca disminuye. He tratado de vencer mi repulsión y ofrecerle a *él* mi cuerpo en parte del pago, pero es un eunuco.»

Yo gruñí perversamente divertido.

«Él era sacerdote de algún dios de los zoque y en el éxtasis de un hongo sagrado se cortó sus partes y las dejó en el altar. Sintió mucha pesadumbre e inmediatamente dejó la orden, aunque para entonces ya había reunido para sí, de las ofrendas de los creyentes, lo suficiente como para tener un negocio.»

Y gruñí otra vez.

«Las niñas y yo vivimos de la manera más sencilla posible, pero cada día es más difícil para nosotras. Si de todas maneras tenemos que vivir, pues... —Entonces enderezó sus hombros y dijo con firmeza—: Les he explicado qué es lo que debemos hacer. Esta noche se lo demostraré. Ya llegamos, es aquí.»

Me precedió haciendo a un lado la cortina de encaje que cubría la puerta de una choza desvencijada de madera y palma. Tenía solamente un cuarto con piso de tierra apisonada, alumbrado por la débil luz de una lámpara alimentada con aceite de pez y pobremente amueblada; había una esterilla en la que sólo podía ver una cobija, un brasero de carbón flameaba débilmente y unos cuantos artículos femeninos estaban colgados en una cuerda amarrada a los delgados troncos de las paredes.

«Mis hijas», dijo ella, indicando a dos muchachas que estaban recargadas de espaldas contra la pared, al otro lado del cuarto.

Yo había estado esperando ver a dos pequeñas rapaces desaliñadas, que mirarían atemorizadas al extranjero que de repente su madre había llevado a casa. Pero una de ellas era casi de mi edad, tan alta y tan bella como su madre, tanto en su cuerpo como en sus facciones; la otra era unos tres años más joven e igualmente bonita. Las dos me miraban con pensativa curiosidad. Estaba sorprendido y perturbado, pero traté de hacer el gesto de besar la tierra delante de ella, y me hubiera ido de bruces si la más joven no me hubiera detenido.

Ella se rió ahogadamente y yo también, pero luego me callé y las miré confundido. Muy pocas mujeres tzapoteca muestran su edad hasta que son verdaderamente viejas. Pero esa muchacha que no tendría más de dieciséis o diecisiete años, ya tenía en su pelo negro un mechón estremecedoramente blanco, como un rayo de luz que partía de su frente en medio de la noche.

Gie Bele me explicó: «Un escorpión la picó ahí cuando era apenas una niña que gateaba. Estuvo muy cerca de morir, pero el último efecto fue ese mechón de pelo, por siempre blanco.»

«Ella es... las dos son tan bellas como su madre», murmuré

galantemente. Pero mi rostro debió mostrar consternación y pena al descubrir que la mujer era lo suficientemente vieja como para ser *mi* madre, porque ella me miró preocupada o casi espantada y dijo:

«No, por favor, no piense en tomar a una de ellas en mi lugar.»

Rápidamente se quitó la blusa por encima de su cabeza e instantáneamente enrojeció tanto que sus pechos desnudos se encendieron. «¡Por favor, mi joven señor! Yo sola me ofrecí para usted. Mis niñas todavía no...» Ella pareció entender mal mi torpe silencio de indecisión; otra vez con premura se desanudó tanto su falda como sus bragas y las dejó caer al piso, quedando completamente desnuda enfrente de mí y de sus hijas.

Yo las miré incómodo y sin duda, con los ojos bien abiertos, tanto como los de las muchachas y debí haberle parecido a Gie Bele que estaba comparando la mercancía. Implorando todavía: «¡Por favor, no mis muchachitas! ¡Úseme a *mí*!» me cogió forzándome a acostarme a su lado en la esterilla. Estaba demasiado sorprendido como para resistirme, mientras ella arrojaba mi manto a un lado y me arrancaba el taparrabo, diciéndome jadeante: «El posadero pide cinco semillas de cacao por una *maátitl* y él se queda con dos. Así es que yo sólo le pediré tres. ¿Verdad que es un precio justo?»

Estaba demasiado apenado como para contestar. Nuestras partes privadas estaban expuestas a la vista de las muchachas, quienes las contemplaban como si no *pudieran* mirar hacia otra parte, y su madre en esos momentos estaba tratando de ponerme sobre ella. Quizá las muchachas no estaban acostumbradas a ver el cuerpo de su madre o quizá nunca antes habían visto un órgano masculino erecto, pero de lo que sí estoy seguro es de que nunca antes habían visto a dos personas juntas. A pesar de estar borracho, protesté: «¡Mujer! ¡Mujer! ¡La luz de la lámpara, las muchachas! Por lo menos mándalas afuera mientras nosotros...»

«¡Déjalas que miren! —casi me gritó—. ¡Ellas tendrán que hacer lo mismo aquí en otras noches!» En esos momentos su rostro estaba lleno de lágrimas y al fin me pude dar cuenta de que no estaba tan resignada a ser una prostituta como había tratado de pretender. Miré a las muchachas y les hice un gesto para ahuyentarlas. Asustadas, desaparecieron rápidamente tras la cortina de la puerta. Pero Gie Bele no lo notó y gritó llorando otra vez, como si quisiera humillarse más todavía: «¡Dejemos que vean lo que pronto ellas estarán haciendo!»

«¿Tú quieres que otros vean, mujer? —la regañé—. ¡Pues dejemos que vean a más y mejor!»

En lugar de quedarme extendido sobre ella, rodé sobre mis espaldas cogiéndola al mismo tiempo y sentándola a través de mí, y la penetré hasta lo más profundo. Después de ese primer dolor, Gie Bele se relajó lentamente y yació quieta entre mis brazos, aunque podía sentir sus lágrimas que se escurrían continuamente sobre mi pecho desnudo. Bueno, todo sucedió muy rápido y potentemente para mí y ciertamente que ella sintió mi *omícetl* dentro de sí misma, pero no trató de separarse con violencia como lo hubiera hecho un mujer comprada.

313

Ya para entonces, su propio cuerpo estaba pidiendo que se le satisfaciera y creo que ni siquiera se dio cuenta de si las muchachas estaban o no en el cuarto, por la demostración detallada que estaba dando nuestra posición o por el ruido húmedo de succión hecho por el movimiento de mi *tepuli* que se introducía y se salía de ella. Cuando Gie Bele alcanzó el éxtasis, se alzó y se recostó sobre sus espaldas, los pezones puntiagudos, su largo pelo rozando mis rodillas, sus ojos cerrados apretadamente, su boca abierta como en un mudo llanto como el de los cachorros del jaguar. Después se desplomó suavemente sobre mi pecho, su cabeza junto a la mía y yació así tan quietamente que hubiera pensado que estaba muerta, excepto porque respiraba con cortos jadeos.

Después de un rato, cuando me hube recobrado y estando un poco más sobrio por la experiencia, me di cuenta de que otra cabeza estaba cerca de la mía, al otro lado. Me volví para ver unos inmensos ojos pardos, muy abiertos bajo sus pestañas negras y exuberantes; el bello rostro de una de las hijas. En algún momento había entrado de nuevo en la habitación y se arrodilló a un lado de la esterilla y en esos momentos me estaba mirando intensamente. Yo dejé caer mi manto sobre mi desnudez y la de su madre, que todavía estaba sin moverse.

«*Nu shishá skarú...*», empezó a susurrar la muchacha. Pero entonces viendo que no la comprendía, habló suavemente en un náhuatl incorrecto y, con una risita sofocada, me dijo sintiéndose culpable: «Nosotras estuvimos observando por las hendiduras de la pared.» Yo gruñí de vergüenza y turbación, y todavía me pongo colorado cuando lo recuerdo. Pero, luego me dijo pensativamente seria: «Siempre pensé que eso sería una cosa muy fea, pero sus rostros se veían tan agradables; como si fueran felices.»

Como no estaba en vena de filosofar después de eso, le dije quietamente: «Nunca he creído que esto sea una cosa fea. Pero es mucho mejor cuando lo haces con una persona a la que amas. —Y añadí—: Y en privado, sin tener ratones mirando por las rendijas de las paredes.»

Empezó a decir algo más, pero de repente su estómago gruñó más fuerte que su voz. Me miró patéticamente mortificada y trató de pretender que nada había pasado, retirándose un poco de mí.

Yo exclamé: «¡Tienes hambre, niña!»

«¿Niña? —Ella levantó la cabeza con petulancia—. Tengo casi su edad, y soy lo suficientemente grande para... para hacer *eso*. No soy una niña.»

Moví a su adormecida madre y le dije: «Gie Bele, ¿cuándo comieron tus hijas por última vez?»

Se incorporó y me dijo con voz suave: «A mí se me permite comer las sobras que quedan en la posada, pero no puedo traer mucho a casa.»

«¡Y estás pidiendo tres semillas de cacao!», dije enojado.

Le podría haber hecho notar que era más justo que yo pidiera un salario, por haber representado ante una audiencia o instruido a las jóvenes, pero busqué mi taparrabo en la oscuridad y busqué la bolsa cosida en él. «Toma —le dije a su hija, quien extendió sus manos y puse en ellas unas veinte o treinta semillas de cacao—. Tú y tu hermana vais a comprar comida y leña para encender un fuego. Y cualquier otra cosa que queráis, todo lo que podáis conseguir con esas semillas.»

Ella miró sus manos como si yo las hubiera llenado de esmeraldas. Impulsivamente se inclinó y me dio un beso en la mejilla, luego se levantó y salió de la cabaña. Gie Bele se recargó sobre un codo y me miró.

«Eres bondadoso con nosotras... después de que me porté tan mal contigo. Por favor, ¿podría darte placer ahora?»

Yo le dije: «Ya me diste lo que vine a comprar. No estoy tratando de comprar tu afecto.»

«Pero yo quiero dártelo», insistió ella. Y empezó a acariciarme en una forma en que solamente lo haría para un hombre de la Gente Nube.

En verdad que eso es mucho mejor cuando se hace amorosamente y en privado. Y en verdad que era una mujer tan atractiva que difícilmente un hombre podría quedar harto de ella. Sin embargo, ya estábamos vestidos cuando las muchachas regresaron, cargadas de comida: un pavo enorme, entero y desplumado, una canasta llena de tortillas, verduras y muchas cosas más. Parloteando alegremente entre ellas encendieron el fuego del brasero, y después la mayor nos preguntó cortésmente si comeríamos con ellas.

Gie Bele les contestó que nosotros ya habíamos comido en la posada. Entonces me dijo que me guiaría de regreso a la posada y encontraría alguna otra cosa en que ocuparse en lo que restaba de la noche, porque si ella se dormía ahora, era seguro que no se despertaría al levantarse el sol. Así es que deseé a las muchachas buenas noches y las dejamos comiendo lo que fue, según supe después, su primera comida decente desde hacía cuatro años. Mientras la mujer y yo caminábamos tomados de las manos por calles y callejuelas, que entonces parecían más oscuras todavía, yo iba pensando en las muchachas hambrientas, en la viuda y desesperada mujer, en el avaro acreedor zoque... y por fin dije abruptamente:

«¿Me venderías tu casa, Gie Bele?»

«¿Qué? —Ella se sorprendió tanto que nuestras manos se desunieron—. ¿Esa choza desvencijada? ¿Para qué la quieres?»

«Oh, pues para reconstruirla mejor, por supuesto. Si continúo dentro del comercio, ciertamente que volveré a pasar por aquí, quizás muy seguido y preferiría un lugar propio a donde llegar que a una posada llena de gente.»

Ella se rió de lo absurdo de mi mentira, sin embargo pretendió tomarlo en serio y preguntó: «¿Y en dónde viviremos nosotras?»

«En algún lugar mucho mejor. Pagaré un buen precio, lo suficiente como para que vosotras podáis vivir otra vez confortablemente, como lo merecéis. Y —dije con firmeza— para que las niñas o tú, no tengáis la necesidad de ir a horcajarse en el camino.»

«¿Cuánto... cuánto quieres ofrecer en pago?»

«Ahora mismo lo vamos a arreglar. Ya estamos en la posada. Por favor lleva luces a la habitación en donde cenamos. Y materiales para escribir... papel y tiza también. Mientras tanto, dime cuál es la habitación del eunuco gordo. Y deja de estarme mirando con miedo; no estoy más trastornado de lo usual.»

Sonrió nerviosa y fue a hacer lo que le ordené, mientras yo tomaba una lámpara para encontrar el cuarto del propietario e interrumpí sus ronquidos con una patada en sus amplias nalgas.

«Levántese y venga conmigo —dije, mientras él farfullaba violentamente, todavía atontado por el sueño—. Tenemos negocios que tratar.»

«Es medianoche. Usted está borracho. Váyase.»

Casi tuve que cogerlo de los pies y me tomó algún tiempo convencerlo de que estaba sobrio y en mis sentidos, pero al fin lo arrastré conmigo, todavía forcejeando por anudarse el manto, hacia la habitación que Gie Bele había alumbrado para nosotros. Cuando ya casi lo había empujado adentro, ella empezó a salir.

«No te vayas, quédate —dije—. Esto nos concierne a los tres. A ver, viejo gordo, traiga acá todos los papeles pertinentes al título de propiedad de esta posada y a la deuda que pesa sobre ella. Yo estoy aquí para redimirla.»

Tanto él como ella me miraron igualmente atónitos y Wáyay después de farfullar algo, me dijo: «¿Es para esto por lo que me sacó de la cama? ¿Usted quiere comprar este lugar, hijo de perra? Todos podemos volver a la cama. No tengo ninguna intención de vender.»

«No puede venderlo, porque no es suyo —dije—. Usted no es el propietario, sino el tenedor de derecho de retención. Cuando yo pague la deuda con todos sus intereses, usted será el transgresor. Vaya y traiga los documentos.»

Había tenido cierta ventaja sobre él mientras todavía estaba confundido por el sueño; pero, cuando nos sentamos enfrente de las columnas de puntos, banderas y arbolitos, que significaban números, volvió a ser tan astuto y exigente como siempre lo había sido en sus profesiones de cambista y sacerdote. No voy a deleitarles, mis señores, con todos los detalles de nuestra negociación. Sólo quiero afirmar que yo *conocía* el arte de trabajar con números y la astucia posible que hay en ese arte.

Cuando el difunto marido explorador había pedido el préstamo, en mercancía y moneda corriente, solicitó una cantidad apreciable. Sin embargo, el interés que había quedado de acuerdo en pagar por el préstamo no era excesivo, o por lo menos no debía de haberlo sido, excepto por el método muy sagaz que empleó el prestamista. No recuerdo las cantidades, por supuesto, pero puedo explicarles un ejemplo simplificado. Si yo le presto a un hombre cien semillas de cacao por un mes, tengo derecho a que me sean pagadas ciento diez o si a él le toma dos meses pagarme, entonces serán ciento veinte semillas de cacao. Por tres meses, ciento treinta y así. Pero lo que Wáyay había hecho era agregar las diez semillas de cacao como interés al final del mes y luego tomar en cuenta el total de ciento diez semillas como base para calcular el siguiente interés, así al finalizar los dos meses él había conseguido ciento *veintiuna* semillas de cacao. La diferencia puede parecer trivial, pero sumado proporcionalmente cada mes y en una cantidad cuantiosa, la suma puede llegar a ser alarmante.

Por lo tanto, exigí un nuevo cálculo desde el principio, o sea desde que Wáyay dio el primer crédito sobre la hostería. *Ayya*, chilló él como seguramente hizo cuando despertó después de haber comido aquel hongo en sus días de sacerdote. Pero, cuando con toda calma le sugerí que podía llevar el asunto al *bishosu* de Tecuantépec para que él lo juzgara, rechinó los dientes y empezó a hacer las cuentas de nuevo, mientras yo lo observaba de cerca. Hubo muchos otros detalles que discutir, tales como, por ejemplo, los gastos y las ganancias de la hostería mientras él la estuvo administrando. Pero finalmente, cuando empezaba a alborear, llegamos a un acuerdo sobre una fuerte suma devengada y quedé que la pagaría totalmente en moneda corriente y no con mercancías. La cantidad era muy superior a lo que yo tenía en aquellos momentos en polvo de oro, cobre, estaño y semillas de cacao, pero no dije nada. En lugar de eso hablé blandamente:

«Usted ha olvidado una pequeña partida. Le debo el pago del hospedaje de mi grupo.»

«Ah, sí —dijo el gordo viejo timador—. Usted es muy honesto por recordármelo.» Y agregó eso al final.

Como si súbitamente hubiera recordado algo, le dije: «Oh, otra cosa.»

«¿Sí?», preguntó expectante con la tiza lista para agregar algo más.

«Substraiga de ahí, cuatro años de salario devengado de la mujer Gie Bele.»

«¿Qué? —dijo mirándome espantado. Ella también me miró, pero llena de admiración—. ¿Salario? —dijo mofándose—. Esta mujer quedó obligada a trabajar para mí como una *tlacotli*.»

«Si su contabilidad hubiera sido honesta, ella no se hubiera visto obligada a ello. De acuerdo con la revisión que usted mismo ha hecho, el *bishosu* le hubiera concedido la *mitad* del interés sobre la hostería. Usted no sólo ha contribuido a estafar a Gie Bele, sino que también ha conspirado a avasallar a un ciudadano libre, convirtiéndolo en esclavo.»

«Está bien, está bien. Déjeme hacer la cuenta. Dos semillas de cacao por día...»

«Ése es el salario de un esclavo. Usted ha tenido el servicio de la formal propietaria de la posada. El salario que gana un hombre libre por día, es de veinte semillas de cacao. —Él se tiró de los cabellos aullando. Yo añadí—: Usted es solamente un forastero apenas tolerado en Tecuantépec. Ella es de los be'n zaa, al igual que el *bishosu*. Si nosotros vamos a verle...»

Entonces, dejó su acceso de cólera y empezó furiosamente a escribir de prisa, dejando caer gotas de sudor sobre el papel de corteza. Entonces, volvió a aullar.

«¡Más de veintinueve mil! ¡No hay tal cantidad de semillas de cacao en todas las plantas de todas las Tierras Calientes!»

«Transfiéralo a cañas de polvo de oro —sugerí—. No aparecerá entonces como una suma tan grande.»

«¿No? —bramó él, luego, cuando lo hubo hecho dijo—: Pues si accedo a la demanda de salario, pierdo hasta mi propio taparrabo en toda la transacción. ¡Si yo substraigo esta cantidad quiere decir que usted me pagará menos de la *mitad* de la suma original que presté!» Su voz se había hecho tan aguda como un chillido y sudaba como si estuviera recibiendo una infusión.

«Sí —dije—. Está de acuerdo con mi propio cálculo. ¿Cómo lo quiere usted? ¿Todo en oro, o algo en estaño o en cobre?» Yo había hecho traer mi fardo de la habitación que todavía no había ocupado, y para entonces lo estaba abriendo.

«¡Esto es una extorsión! —gritó con rabia—. ¡Un robo!»

En el fardo también había una pequeña daga de obsidiana. La tomé y la apunté directamente contra la segunda o tercera papada de Wáyay.

«Sí, era extorsión y robo —le dije fríamente—. Usted engañó a una mujer indefensa para quedarse con su propiedad, luego la hizo trabajar en las cosas más desagradables durante cuatro largos años y yo sé a qué caminos tan desesperados hubiera llegado. Pero aquí está lo que usted mismo calculó, y yo se lo sostengo. Le pagaré la última cantidad a la que usted llegó...»

«¡Esto es la ruina! —ladró—. ¡La devastación!»

«Me va a extender un recibo y en él va a escribir que este pago anula toda la demanda sobre esta propiedad y sobre esta mujer, en estos momentos y para siempre. Después, mientras yo lo veo, romperá el viejo papel en prenda, firmado por el difunto esposo. Luego, recogerá todas aquellas cosas personales que son de su propiedad y se irá de estas posesiones.»

Él hizo el último intento de oponerse: «¿Y si rehúso?»

«Lo llevaré a punta de espada a ver al *bishosu* y ya sabe usted los cargos. El castigo por robo es la muerte a garrote con lianas floridas. ¿Qué es lo que sufrirá antes por haber esclavizado a una persona libre? No puedo decirlo, ya que no conozco los refinamientos de tortura de esta nación.»

Desplomándose al fin derrotado, dijo: «Aleje de mí ese puñal. Cuente el dinero. —Levantó su cabeza para gritar a Gie Bele—: Traiga papel nuevo... —luego cambiando de parecer y utilizando un tono untuoso—: Por favor, mi señora, traiga papel, pinturas y cañas para escribir.»

Yo conté cañas de polvo de oro y un montón de pedacitos de estaño y cobre poniéndolos en el mantel que había entre nosotros y después de haber hecho eso, quedó un pequeño bulto en el fardo. Le dije: «Haga el recibo a mi nombre. En el lenguaje de este lugar, me llamo Zaa Nayàzú.»

«Nunca hubo un hombre con un nombre tan de mal agüero y tan bien puesto», murmuró, mientras empezaba a hacer las palabras pintadas y las columnas con glifos de números. Él lloraba mientras trabajaba, lo juro.

Sentí la mano de Gie Bele sobre mi hombro y la miré. Había trabajado muy duro durante todo el día anterior y también había pasado una noche sin dormir, por no mencionar algunas otras cosas, pero estaba allí parada con garbo, los bellos ojos le brillaban y todo su rostro resplandecía.

Yo le dije: «Esto no tomará mucho tiempo. ¿Por qué no vas y traes a las niñas? Tráelas a su casa.»

Cuando mis socios despertaron y llegaron para desayunar, Cózcatl se veía descansado y sus ojos brillaban de nuevo, pero Glotón de Sangre se veía alicaído. Él ordenó un desayuno consistente sólo en huevos fritos, luego dijo a la mujer: «Mándeme al propietario. Le debo diez semillas de cacao. —Y agregó para su coleto—: Soy un libertino manirroto y a mi edad.»

Ella le sonrió y le dijo: «Por esa diversión, para usted, no hay ningún cargo mi señor», y se fue.

«¿Eh? —gruñó Glotón de Sangre, viéndola salir—. Ninguna hostería ofrece este servicio gratuito.»

Yo le recordé: «Cínico viejo raboverde, tú dijiste que no había primeras veces. Quizás sí.»

«Puedes estar loco y ella también, pero el propietario...»

«Desde la noche pasada, ella *es* la propietaria.»

«¿Eh?», dijo otra vez abruptamente. Y dos veces más volvió a decir «¿eh?». Primero cuando su desayuno fue llevado por la bellísima muchacha, casi de mi edad, y otra vez cuando su espumoso *chocólatl* fue servido por la no menos bella joven, del mechón de luz sobre su pelo.

«¿Qué ha pasado aquí? —preguntó confundido—. Nos detenemos en la primera hostería que encontramos, un establecimiento inferior, con un zoque grasiento y una esclava...»

«Y durante la noche —terminó Cózcatl por él, con voz sorprendida—, Mixtli lo convirtió en un templo lleno de diosas.»

Así es que nuestro grupo se quedó otra noche en la hostería y cuando todo estuvo en silencio, Gie Bele se metió furtivamente en mi habitación, más radiante que nunca, en la nueva felicidad que había encontrado y esta vez nuestro amoroso abrazo no fue disminuido, ni forzado, ni de ninguna manera distinto del mutuo y verdadero acto de amor.

Cuando cargamos nuestros bultos, listos para partir temprano, a la siguiente mañana, ella y luego cada una de sus hijas me abrazaron fuertemente y cubrieron mi rostro con besos húmedos por las lágrimas, dándome las gracias de todo corazón. Miré hacia atrás varias veces, hasta que no pude ya distinguir a la hostería dentro de la masa confusa de los otros edificios.

No sabía cuándo regresaría, pero había plantado semillas allí, y en el futuro, sin importar cuán lejos o por cuánto tiempo vagara, nunca volvería a ser un extranjero entre la Gente Nube, nunca mientras las más altas tijeretas trepadoras de las enredaderas se pudieran sostener de sus raíces, en la tierra. Eso era todo lo que sabía. Lo que no podía saber o siquiera soñar, era qué fruto de esas semillas probaría... qué agradable sorpresa o estrujante tragedia, o cuánta riqueza y cuánta pobreza, o cuánta alegría y cuánta miseria. Pasaría mucho tiempo antes de que yo pudiera probar el primero de esos frutos y mucho tiempo antes de que todos ellos maduraran a su tiempo y uno de esos frutos no lo he probado completamente, todavía, hasta la semilla amarga de su corazón.

✠

Como ustedes saben, reverendos frailes, esta tierra que ahora es la Nueva España, está circundada en toda su longitud, en ambos lados, por grandes mares que se extienden desde sus costas hasta el horizonte. Ya que esos mares están más o menos al este y oeste de Tenochtitlan, nosotros los mexica siempre nos hemos referido a ellos como a los océanos del este y del oeste. Sin embargo, de Tecuantépec en adelante, la masa de tierra se tuerce hacia el este, así·es que esas aguas son llamadas allí, más adecuadamente, los océanos del norte y del sur y la tierra que los separa es un istmo bajo y delgado. No quiero decir con esto, que un hombre puede pararse en medio del istmo y escupir sobre el océano que él escoja. El ancho del istmo es de más o menos cincuenta largas-carreras de norte a sur y cerca de diez días de camino, pero de un camino fácil, porque la mayor parte de esa tierra es lisa y llana.

Pero nosotros no cruzamos de una costa a otra. Viajamos hacia el este sobre esa tierra plana, mal llamada La Colina del Jaguar, con el océano del sur no muy lejos a nuestra derecha, aunque no era visible a nuestro paso. Entonces fueron las gaviotas las que revoloteaban más a menudo sobre nuestras cabezas, en lugar de los buitres. Excepto por el calor opresivo de esas tierras bajas, nuestra caminata fue fácil, casi monótona, sin nada que ver más que la hierba amarilla y los bajos arbustos grises. Marchamos con gran rapidez y encontramos fácil y abundante caza para comer, conejos, iguanas, armadillos, y como el clima era agradable para acampar en la noche, no dormimos en ninguna de las aldeas de la Gente Mixe, cuyas tierras estábamos atravesando.

Tenía una buena razón para tratar de llegar lo antes posible a nuestro destino, que eran las tierras de los maya, en donde finalmente empezaríamos a cambiar las mercancías que llevábamos por otras de mucho más valor, para transportarlas después a Tenochtitlan. Por supuesto que mis socios se habían dado cuenta de algunas de las extravagancias en que había caído últimamente, pero nunca les había dado todos los detalles y los precios que había pagado por ellas. Mucho más atrás, había hecho un negocio bastante ventajoso a lo largo del camino, cuando había vendido al esclavo Cuatro a sus parientes, pero eso había sido bastante tiempo atrás. Desde entonces había hecho solamente otras dos transacciones, las dos costosas y ninguna de ellas con una ganancia visible o inmediata, para nosotros. Había comprado el tapiz de plumas de Chimali sólo para darme la dulce venganza de destruirlo. A un precio mucho mayor, había comprado la hostería por el placer de darla. Si había sido reticente con mis socios, era porque sentía cierta vergüenza de no haberme mostrado todavía como un *pochtécatl* sagaz.

Después de varios días de viajar fácil y rápidamente a través de las llanuras coloreadas y brunas, vimos el azul pálido de las montañas que se empezaban a levantar hacia nuestra izquierda y que gradualmente se destacaron enfrente de nosotros, en un color verde-azul oscuro y de nuevo volvimos a escalar, aquella vez dentro de un espeso bosque de pinos, cedros y enebros. De allí en adelante, empezamos a encontrar las cruces que siempre han sido consideradas sagradas por las diversas naciones del lejano sur.

Sí, mis señores, la cruz de ellos es prácticamente igual a su cruz Cristiana. Como ésta, el palo principal es un poco más largo que el que la cruza, la única diferencia es que en la parte de arriba y a ambos lados, los remates son en forma comba y tallados como una hoja de trébol. Para esos pueblos, el significado religioso de esa cruz es la simbolización de los cuatro puntos y el centro del compás. Sin embargo, también tenía un uso práctico. En cualquier lugar despoblado de la selva en donde encontráramos esa cruz de madera pesada y larga, sabíamos que ésta no demandaba: «¡sed reverentes!», sino: «¡estad contentos!», porque ella marcaba la presencia cercana de agua clara y fresca.

Las montañas cada vez se fueron haciendo más escarpadas y más escabrosas, hasta que llegaron a ser tan grandes como aquellas que habíamos dejado atrás en Uaxyácac, pero aunque para entonces ya habíamos llegado a ser unos montañistas experimentados, no las hubiéramos encontrado tan atemorizantes, excepto porque además del frío usual de las alturas sufrimos un repentino frente frío. Bueno, en aquellas tierras sureñas era aún invierno y para entonces estábamos a mitad de esa estación y el dios Títitl de los días-cortos fue excepcionalmente duro con nosotros durante ese año.

Nos pusimos cuanta ropa llevábamos y empezamos a subir fatigados bajo el peso de nuestra carga y envolvimos nuestras sandalias con trapos bien atados, a lo largo de nuestros pies y piernas. Pero el viento penetraba como una hoja de obsidiana aun a través de esa protección, y en los picos más altos el viento arrastraba nieve, como si fueran delgadas astillas. Entonces, nos sentimos realmente muy contentos de estar rodeados por pinos, ya que juntábamos la savia que manaba de ellos y la cocinábamos hasta que sus aceites irritantes se evaporaban y quedaba solamente un espeso y pegajoso óxitl negro que repelía tanto al frío como a la humedad. Después nos desvestíamos y nos untábamos el óxitl por todo nuestro cuerpo y nos volvíamos a vestir. A excepción de nuestros ojos y bocas, el resto de nosotros era de un color negro-noche, como siempre había sido pintado el ciego dios Itzcoliuqui.

Para entonces, ya nos encontrábamos en la nación de los chiapa y cuando empezamos a llegar a las aldeas más apartadas de la montaña, nuestra apariencia grotesca causó cierta sorpresa. Los chiapa no usaban el óxitl negro, pues estaban acostumbrados a cubrir sus cuerpos con sebo de jaguar, cuguar o tapir, como una protección similar contra el mal tiempo. Sin embargo, la gente era casi tan oscura como nosotros lo estábamos; no negra, por supuesto, pero el tono de su piel era del más oscuro pardo-cacao que yo había visto en todas las naciones en que habíamos estado. La tradición de los chiapa cuenta que sus más lejanos ancestros habían emigrado de su tierra original, que estaba mucho más al sur, y su tez venía a confirmar esa leyenda. Obviamente habían heredado el color de sus antepasados, quienes habían sido bien requemados por la fiereza del sol.

Nosotros con gusto hubiéramos pagado por un solo rayo de aquel sol. Cuando nos afanábamos a través de los valles y barrancas protegidos del viento, sólo sufríamos el entumecimiento y el letargo provocado por el tiempo helado, pero cuando se cruzaba una montaña en nuestro camino o paso, el viento cortante silbaba a nuestro alrededor, como flechas disparadas todas a un mismo tiempo, a través de un túnel cavado. Y cuando no había una vereda o un paso, cuando teníamos que escalar todo el camino hacia arriba y a lo largo de la montaña, estaría todo cubierto con nieve o aguanieve cayendo con violencia en su cumbre o nos encontraríamos con nieve vieja ya endurecida en el suelo, que teníamos que vadear o hender para podernos afianzar. Todos nos sentíamos desgraciados, pero uno de nosotros se sentía todavía más miserable que los demás: el esclavo Diez que se sentía agobiado por alguna dolencia.

Como nunca se había quejado o rezagado, ni siquiera sospechamos que se estaba encontrando mal, y ya habían pasado varios días sintiéndose así, hasta que una mañana él cayó bajo el peso de su carga, como si una mano pesada lo hubiera empujado. Trató con todas sus fuerzas de levantarse, pero no pudo y se desplomó cuan largo era sobre el suelo. Cuando nosotros le desligamos la banda que llevaba en la frente y lo despojamos de su carga, volteamos su rostro y descubrimos que estaba tan caliente por la fiebre que el *óxitl* que llevaba pegado se había cocido en su cuerpo como una costra seca incrustada en él. Cózcatl le preguntó solícitamente si él se sentía afectado en alguna parte específica de su cuerpo. Diez le contestó, en su náhuatl incorrecto, que sentía como si en su cabeza le clavaran una *maquáhuitl*, que sentía su cuerpo cubierto de fuego y que le dolían cada una de las articulaciones, pero que por lo demás, nada le molestaba en particular.

Le pregunté si había comido algo fuera de lo común o si había sido picado o mordido por alguna criatura venenosa. Él me contestó que sólo había comido los alimentos que todos habíamos compartido y que el único encuentro que había tenido con una criatura era con una completamente inocua, siete u ocho días antes, cuando trató de cazar un conejo para nuestro estofado. Lo había cogido, pero el conejo lo había mordido y había escapado. Me enseñó la marca de los dientes del roedor en su mano y luego rodó lejos de mí y vomitó.

Glotón de Sangre, Cózcatl y yo nos sentíamos realmente apenados por eso, pues de todos nosotros el que tuvo que caer enfermo fue Diez, a quien todos queríamos. Nos había ayudado fielmente para salvarnos de los bandidos tya nuü y él era el que más seguido se había ofrecido para desempeñar la tarea femenina de cocinar para todos. Él era el más fuerte de todos los esclavos, después del forzudo Cuatro a quien habíamos vendido y que había cargado el bulto más pesado en aquel entonces. También, había estado llevando sumisamente la piel pesada e insalubre del cuguar; y de hecho él todavía la llevaba encima, pues obstinadamente Glotón de Sangre no quería desecharla.

Todos descansamos, hasta que el mismo Diez fue el primero en ponerse de pie para continuar. Toqué su frente y me pareció que la fiebre había disminuido bastante. Miré más de cerca su rostro oscuro y le dije: «Matlactli, te conozco por más de una gavilla de días, pero hasta ahora no caigo en la cuenta. Tú perteneces a esta nación chiapa. ¿No es así?»

«Sí, amo —dijo débilmente—. Soy de la ciudad capital de Chiapán. Es por lo que me urge llegar. Espero que usted sea lo suficientemente bondadoso como para venderme allá.»

Así es que él levantó su bulto, deslizó otra vez la banda alrededor de su frente y todos continuamos, pero a la caída de la tarde de ese mismo día se tambaleaba de una manera tan lastimosa que era muy difícil que pudiera continuar, pero aun así, siguió insistiendo en seguir caminando y rehusó nuestras sugerencias de hacer otro alto o de aligerar su carga; no lo hizo hasta que encontramos un valle protegido por el viento, con una cruz marcando un arroyo helado que corría a través de él, y allí acampamos.

«No hemos matado ningún gamo últimamente —dijo Glotón de Sangre— y ya se nos han acabado los perros. Sin embargo, Diez debe tener algún alimento nutritivo y fresco, no solamente *atoli* y ventosos frijoles. Que se pongan Tres y Seis a prender el fuego y mientras ellos lo encienden, pues les costará bastante hacerlo, yo voy a ver qué pesco por ahí.»

Él encontró una vara en forma de horquilla y con los pedazos de nuestras ropas gastadas fabricó una red y fue al arroyo para probarla. Regresó después de un rato diciendo: «Cózcatl lo hubiera podido hacer. Estaban entumecidos por el frío», y nos mostró un manojo de peces verde-plata, ninguno más largo de una mano ni más grueso de un dedo, pero lo suficiente para hacer nuestro puchero. Aunque cuando los vi, no estaba muy seguro de quererlos comer y así se lo dije.

Glotón de Sangre hizo a un lado mi objeción: «No importa que sean feos, son muy sabrosos.»

«Pero si se ven tan raros —se quejó Cózcatl—. ¡Cada uno tiene cuatro ojos!»

«¡Sí, es muy listo este pez... estos peces! Flotan apenas bajo de la superficie del riachuelo, con los ojos de encima buscan insectos en el aire y con los de abajo están alerta para pescar alguna presa bajo el agua. Quizás puedan dar a nuestro enfermo Diez un poco de su propia vitalidad.»

Si se la dieron fue sólo para que no pudiera tener el sueño tranquilo que tanto necesitaba. Desperté varias veces oyendo al hombre enfermo agitarse y toser arrojando flemas y murmurando incoherencias. Una o dos veces me di cuenta de que murmuraba una palabra que parecía sonar como «binkizaka» y a la mañana siguiente llevé a Glotón de Sangre aparte para preguntarle si tenía alguna idea de lo que eso significaba.

«Sí, es una de las pocas palabras extranjeras que conozco —dijo con altanería, como si con eso le confiriera mucha importancia—. Los *binkizaka* son criaturas mitad humanas y mitad animales, que habitan en las alturas de las montañas. Me han contado que son los hijos detestables y horrorosos de las mujeres que se han apareado en forma no natural, con jaguares, o monos, o cualquier otro animal. Cuando oigas un ruido como de un trueno en las montañas y que no haya tormenta, lo que oyes es a un *binkizaka* haciendo diabluras. Personalmente creo que esos ruidos son provocados por caídas y deslizamientos de rocas, pero ya conoces la ignorancia de los extranjeros. ¿Por qué lo preguntas? ¿Has escuchado ruidos extraños?»

«Sólo he oído a Diez hablando en sueños, creí que estaba delirando. Y creo que está mucho más enfermo de lo que suponemos.»

Así es que desoyendo sus muchas protestas, tomamos su carga y la dividimos entre el resto de nosotros y solamente le dejamos a él la piel del león de la montaña, para que la llevara ese día. Ya sin carga, caminaba bastante bien, pero podía darme cuenta cuando sentía un escalofrío, porque se encogía bajo la piel dura arrebujándose en ella para cubrir su tosco taparrabo. Después, cuando el escalofrío pasaba y la fiebre lo atormentaba, se quitaba la piel y aun abría sus vestiduras para que por ellas penetrara el aire frío de la montaña. También respiraba con un sonido burbujeante, cuando no estaba tosiendo o carraspeando, y escupía esputos excepcionalmente malolientes.

Íbamos escalando una montaña de considerable altura, pero cuando llegamos a su cumbre nos encontramos con el camino cortado. Nos detuvimos al borde de un cañón que corría de norte a sur, uno de los más profundos que jamás había visto antes. Estaba cortado a filo en hileras, como si un dios enojado hubiera dejado caer desde el cielo una *maquáhuitl* del tamaño del dios. Era una vista que quitaba el aliento por lo impresionante, bella y engañosa, todo a un mismo tiempo. Aunque un frío helado soplaba en donde nosotros estábamos parados, era evidente que éste nunca penetraba en el cañón, porque las cercanas paredes perpendiculares estaban festonadas por flores colgantes de todos los colores. En lo más profundo de su fondo, en donde se veían florestas, árboles floridos y suaves praderas, un hilo de plata cruzaba y parecía, desde donde nosotros estábamos parados, un simple arroyo.

Afortunadamente, no tratamos de descender hacia las invitadoras profundidades, sino que volviéndonos hacia el sur, seguimos la orilla del cañón hasta que ésta gradualmente se fue deslizando hacia abajo. Ya había caído la tarde cuando llegamos a la orilla de aquel «arroyo», que fácilmente podría medir cien pasos de orilla a orilla. Después supe que aquel arroyo, el río Suchiapa, es el más ancho, profundo y rápido de todos los Del Único Mundo. Ese cañón que cruza cortando las montañas de Chiapa, también es único en todo El Único Mundo, por su longitud: cinco largas-carreras de largo y de la orilla al fondo tiene cerca de media larga-carrera de profundidad.

Llegamos a una planicie en donde el aire era caliente y el viento más suave. También llegamos a una aldea, aunque pobre. Era llamada Toztlan, apenas era lo suficientemente grande como para llevar un nombre y la única comida que los aldeanos nos pudieron ofrecer fue un cocido de carne de búho tan desagradable, que me produce asco sólo el recordarlo. Sin embargo, Toztlan tuvo una choza lo suficientemente grande como para que todos pudiéramos dormir, por primera vez en varias noches, bajo techo. La aldea también tenía cierta clase de físicos.

«Yo solamente soy doctor en hierbas —dijo él disculpándose en su mal hablado náhuatl, después de haber examinado a Diez—. Le he dado al paciente una purga y no puedo hacer más por él. Pero mañana ustedes llegarán a Chiapán y allí encontrarán a muchos doctores-de-pulso famosos.»

No sabía qué clase de doctores-de-pulso podrían ser, pero al día siguiente lo único que podía esperar es que fuera un doctor de hierbas, pero más avanzado.

Antes de llegar a Chiapán, Diez se desmayó y tuvimos que cargarlo sobre la piel del cuguar, que llevó puesta todo el tiempo. Lo cargamos en turnos de cuatro, cogiendo la improvisada litera por las patas de la piel, mientras Diez acostado en ella se quejaba, entre espasmos y toses, de que varios *binkizaka* estaban sentados en su pecho y no lo dejaban respirar.

«Uno de ellos también me está mordiendo. ¿No lo ven?» Y levantaba su mano. Lo que nos mostraba era sólo el lugar en donde el conejo lo había mordido, pero que por alguna razón se había ulcerado convirtiéndose en una llaga abierta. Nosotros, que lo cargábamos, tratábamos de decirle que no veíamos a nadie sentado sobre él ni mordiéndolo y que su problema había sido el aire enrarecido de aquella alta llanura. A nosotros mismos nos costaba tanto trabajo respirar, que ninguno lo podía cargar por mucho tiempo sin tener que ser relevado.

Chiapán no se parecía en nada a una ciudad capital. No era más que cualquier otra aldea situada a la orilla de un tributario del río Suchiapa, y yo supuse que era la capital en virtud de que era la más grande de todas las demás aldeas de la nación chiapa. También, algunos de sus edificios eran de madera o de adobe, en lugar de ser como los otros, chozas de troncos y paja. Además había los restos en ruinas de viejas pirámides.

Llegamos a la aldea caminando vacilantes por la fatiga y preguntando por un doctor-de-pulso. Una persona que pasaba, bondadosamente se detuvo a escuchar nuestros incomprensibles, aunque obvios gritos de urgencia y se aproximó a ver a Diez, quien estaba inconsciente. Entonces exclamó: «¡Macoboö!», y gritó algo más en su lenguaje, lo que hizo que se acercaran corriendo dos o tres personas más que por allí pasaban. Después nos hicieron gestos con la cabeza para que los siguiéramos a la casa del doctor, quien sabía hablar en náhuatl, según entendimos por sus gestos.

Para cuando llegamos allí, íbamos seguidos por una excitada y parlanchina multitud. Parece que los chiapa no tienen totalmente nombres individuales, como nosotros los mexica. Aunque cada persona tiene, naturalmente, uno que le distingue, es también conocida por el nombre de su familia, como los apellidos de ustedes los españoles, que no sufren cambio a través de muchas generaciones. El esclavo al cual llamábamos Matlactli o Diez, pertenecía a la familia Macoböö de Chiapán y el ciudadano que lo había reconocido, había gritado a alguien para que fuera corriendo a avisar a sus familiares de que había regresado al pueblo.

Desgraciadamente Diez no estaba en condiciones de reconocer a ninguno de los otros Macoböö que llegaron, y el doctor, quien visiblemente se sentía satisfecho de tener a toda esa clamorosa multitud a su puerta, no pudo dejarlos entrar a todos. Cuando los cuatro que cargábamos a Diez, lo hubimos dejado sobre el piso de tierra, el anciano físico insistió en que todo el mundo saliera a excepción hecha de su vieja esposa que lo asistía, el paciente y yo, a quien él explicaría el tratamiento a seguir. Se presentó a sí mismo como el doctor Maäsh y me explicó en un náhuatl no muy bien hablado, la teoría del doctorado-en-pulso.

Él sostuvo la muñeca de Diez mientras llamaba por su nombre a todos los dioses, buenos y malos, en los que creían los chiapa. Me explicó que cuando gritara el nombre del dios que afligía al paciente, el corazón de Diez golpearía y su pulso se aceleraría. Después, ya sabiendo qué dios era el responsable de la dolencia, se sabría con exactitud qué sacrificio ofrecer al dios para persuadirlo de que dejara de molestar. Él, también, sabría entonces qué medicinas se debían administrar para reparar el daño que de algún modo hubiese causado el dios.

Diez yacía sobre la piel de cuguar, sus ojos cerrados y hundidos en sus cuencas y su pecho afanándose por respirar, y el viejo doctor Maäsh, sosteniendo su muñeca, se inclinó sobre él y le gritó en el oído:

«¡Kakal, el dios brillante!», después una pausa para esperar la respuesta en el pulso, luego: «¡Tótick, dios de la oscuridad!», y luego una pausa, y: «¡Teo, diosa del amor!», y «¡Antún, dios de la vida!», y «¡Hachakyum, dios poderoso!», y así siguió nombrando los dioses y diosas de los chiapa, de los cuales no me puedo acordar. Al fin, se levantó de sus cuclillas y murmuró aparentemente derrotado: «El pulso es tan débil que no puedo estar seguro de la respuesta en *ningún* nombre.»

De repente Diez graznó, sin abrir los ojos: «¡*Binkizaka* me muerde!»

«¡Ajá! —exclamó el doctor Maäsh, muy contento—. No se me había ocurrido sugerir al bajo *binkizaka*. ¡Y de veras que hay un agujero en su mano!»

«Perdóneme, señor doctor —aventuré—. No fue ningún *binkizaka*. Fue un conejo lo que le mordió.»

El físico levantó su cabeza tanto que casi incrustó su nariz en mi cara. «Joven, yo estaba sosteniendo su muñeca cuando él dijo "binkizaka" y yo conozco el pulso cuando lo siento. ¡Mujer!» Yo pestañeé, pero él le estaba hablando a su esposa. Después de un rato me explicó lo que le había dicho a ella: «Tendré que tener una plática con un experto en seres menores. ¡Fue a buscar al doctor Kamé!»

La vieja corrió fuera de la choza, pasando a fuerza de codazos entre la apretada multitud y en unos pocos momentos se nos juntó otro viejo. Los doctores Kamé y Maäsh se alborotaron y murmuraron, luego sosteniendo por turnos la muñeca fláccida de Diez, gritaban en su oído «¡*Binkizaka*!». Después volvían a alborotarse y se consultaban más, por fin llegaron a un acuerdo. El doctor Kamé dio otra orden a la vieja y ella salió con prisa otra vez. El doctor Maäsh me dijo:

«Es inútil hacer un sacrificio al *binkizaka*, ya que son mitad bestias y no comprenden los ritos de propiciación. Éste ha sido un caso de emergencia, mi colega y yo hemos tenido que decidir en la medida radical de sacar la aflicción del paciente, quemándola. Hemos mandado traer la Piedra del Sol, el más sagrado tesoro de nuestro pueblo.»

La mujer regresó seguida de dos hombres cargados con lo que parecía ser a simple vista un cuadrado de piedra. Después vi que en la superficie superior habían sido incrustados fragmentos de jade en forma de cruz. Sí, muy similar a su cruz Cristiana. En los cuatro espacios entre los brazos de la cruz, la roca había sido completamente horadada y en cada uno de esos agujeros se había colocado un pedazo de *chipilotl*, cuarzo. Sin embargo, y eso es importante para entender lo que siguió, mis señores, cada uno de esos cuarzos cristalinos habían sido tallados y pulidos de tal manera que su circunferencia era perfectamente redonda y uniformemente convexa por sus dos lados. Cada uno de aquellos vidrios transparentes de la Piedra del Sol eran como pelotas achatadas o como conchas extremadamente simétricas.

Mientras los dos hombres recién llegados sostenían la Piedra del Sol sobre Diez, que en esos momentos yacía totalmente inconsciente, la vieja tomó una escoba y con el palo hizo unos agujeros en el techo de paja, dejando entrar por cada uno de ellos un rayo de sol, hasta que al fin hizo uno que dejó caer un rayo de sol directamente sobre el paciente. Los dos doctores corrieron la piel del cuguar para ajustar la posición de Diez con relación al rayo de sol y a la Piedra del Sol. Entonces sucedió la cosa más maravillosa y yo me acerqué para poder observar mejor.

Bajo la dirección de los doctores, los dos hombres sostuvieron la pesada piedra alisada, ajustándose de tal manera que un rayo de sol pasara a través de uno de los cristales de cuarzo, cayendo directamente sobre la mano ulcerada de Diez. Después, moviendo la piedra hacia arriba y hacia abajo a través del rayo de sol, concentraron todo el poder de esa luz sobre un *punto*, que caía directamente sobre la llaga. Los dos doctores sostenían la mano en ese lugar, mientras los otros dos hombres concentraban más la luz en ella, y, créanme o no, como ustedes prefieran, un poco de humo salió de la horrible llaga. Después de un momento, se escuchó un sonido siseante y se vio una pequeña llama allí, casi invisible al reflejo de esa luz intensa. Los doctores movieron con mucho cuidado la mano, de tal manera que el sol formara una llama alrededor de la llaga.

Por fin, uno de ellos dijo algo y los dos hombres se llevaron la Piedra del Sol afuera de la choza, la vieja volvió a acomodar el techo de paja con su escoba y el doctor Maäsh se movió para que me inclinara y mirara. La úlcera había sido cauterizada limpia y totalmente como si hubiera sido hecho con una varilla de cobre al rojo vivo. Felicité a los dos físicos sinceramente, ya que nunca antes había visto algo parecido. También felicité a Diez por haber soportado esa quemada sin ninguna queja.

«Es triste decirlo, pero él no sintió nada —dijo el doctor Maäsh—. El paciente está muerto. Lo hubiéramos podido salvar todavía si usted nos hubiera dicho todo lo referente al *binkizaka* y evitar la rutina innecesaria de llamar a todos los dioses mayores. —Aun hablando mal el náhualt, su tono era de crítica agria—. Todos ustedes son iguales cuando necesitan un tratamiento médico, guardan un silencio obstinado acerca de los más importantes síntomas. Insisten en que el físico primero tiene que *adivinar* la enfermedad y *entonces* curarla y si no, él no ha ganado su salario.»

«Estaré muy complacido en pagar todos los salarios, señor doctor —dije también agriamente—. ¿Sería usted tan amable de decirme qué es lo que ha curado?»

En esos momentos fuimos interrumpidos por una mujercita ajada de piel oscura, quien se había deslizado dentro de la choza y tímidamente dijo algo en el lenguaje local. El doctor Maäsh tradujo de mala gana.

«Ella ofrece pagar todos los gastos, si usted consiente en venderle el cuerpo en lugar de comérselo, como ustedes los mexica acostumbran a hacer con los esclavos muertos. Ella es... ella era su madre.»

Yo rechiné los dientes y dije: «Por favor, infórmele que los mexica no hacemos tales cosas, que le devuelvo a su hijo sin cobrarle nada y que sólo siento no poder ofrecérselo vivo.»

El rostro lleno de angustia de la mujer fue cambiando mientras el físico hablaba. Entonces ella le hizo otra pregunta.

«Es nuestra costumbre —tradujo él— enterrar a nuestros muertos junto con la esterilla en la que fallecen. Ella quiere comprarle esa piel maloliente de león de montaña.»

«Es de ella —dije, y por alguna razón mentí—. Su hijo mató a la bestia.» El doctor podría ganar su salario como intérprete, pero nada más, pues le conté toda la historia de cómo había matado al animal, solamente dándole a Diez el lugar de Glotón de Sangre, y haciendo parecer como que Diez había salvado mi vida de un eminente peligro casi a costa de la suya. Al final de la historia el rostro de la mujer brillaba de orgullo maternal.

Claramente se veía que le costaba mucho esfuerzo al disgustado doctor, pero tradujo la última frase de ella. «Ella dice que si su hijo fue tan leal al joven señor, es porque usted es un hombre bueno y digno. Los Macoboö están en deuda con usted para siempre.»

Entonces, ella dijo algo y cuatro hombres más penetraron en la habitación, probablemente de la misma familia, y se llevaron a Diez sobre la maldita piel de la que ya nunca más se despegaría. Yo salí de la choza después de ellos y me encontré con que mis socios habían estado escuchando por la ventana. Cózcatl estaba lloriqueando, pero Glotón de Sangre me dijo sarcásticamente:

«Eso fue muy noble. ¿Pero no se le ha ocurrido, a mi joven señor, que esta llamada expedición comercial está dando más de sí, en valor, de lo que ha adquirido todavía?»

«Acabamos de adquirir algunos amigos», dije.

Y así fue. La familia Macoboö, que era muy numerosa, insistió en que todos nosotros fuéramos sus invitados durante nuestra estancia en Chiapán y nos prodigaron hospitalidad y adulación. No había cosa que pidiéramos que no se nos fuera dada completamente gratis, como yo había dado al esclavo muerto, devolviéndolo a su familia. Creo que lo primero que pidió Glotón de Sangre, después de un buen baño y de una buena comida, fue a una de las bellas primas; recuerdo que también a mí me ofrecieron una y muy bella, pero después, pues el primer favor que les pedí a los Macoboö fue que me buscaran a una persona de Chiapán que hablara y comprendiera el náhuatl. Y cuando me llevaron a ese hombre, la primera pregunta que le hice fue:

«Esos cristales de cuarzo que tiene la Piedra del Sol, ¿no podrían ser utilizados para producir fuego, en lugar de nuestros tediosos aperos?»

«Naturalmente —dijo él, sorprendiéndose de que le hiciera una pregunta tan innecesaria—. Nosotros siempre los usamos para eso.»

«¿Los que están en la Piedra del Sol?»

«Oh, no, ésos no. La Piedra del Sol se utiliza sólo para prender los fuegos de los altares ceremoniales y cosas parecidas. O para curar. Quizás usted haya notado que los cristales de la Piedra del Sol son tan grandes como el puño de hombre. Un cuarzo tan claro y de ese tamaño es extremadamente raro y naturalmente los sacerdotes se apropian de éstos y los proclaman sagrados. Sin embargo, simples fragmentos sirven también para prender fuegos, cuando están adecuadamente pulidos y cortados.»

Él buscó entre su manto y extrajo de la orilla de su taparrabo un cristal con la misma convexidad de una concha de mar, pero no más grande que la uña del pulgar.

«No necesito decirle, joven señor, que esto solamente funciona como instrumento para encender cuando el dios Kakal arroja sus rayos de luz a través de él. Sin embargo, aun en la noche o en un día nublado esto tiene un segundo uso... para ver de cerca cosas pequeñas. Déjeme enseñarle.»

Utilizando el bordado de la orilla de su manto para ese propósito, él me lo demostró sosteniéndolo a una distancia adecuada entre el objeto y el ojo, yo casi salto de la sorpresa, cuando el diseño del tejido se aumentó tanto, que podía contar cada uno de los hilos coloreados en él.

«¿En dónde consiguen estos cristales?», pregunté, tratando de que mi voz no sonara muy ansiosa por adquirirlos.

«El cuarzo es una piedra muy común en estas montañas —dijo

con franqueza—. En cualquier parte de nuestras tierras todos nos podemos tropezar con un buen puñado de cuarzo, o con un pedacito y lo guardamos hasta que podemos traerlo aquí a Chiapán. Aquí vive la familia Xibalbá y sólo ellos conocen por generaciones el secreto de cómo transformar la piedra en bruto, en estos útiles cristales.»

«Oh, no es un secreto muy profundo —dijo el maestro Xibalbá, a quien todos recurrían para ese menester—. No son como los conocimientos en hechicería o profecía. —Mi intérprete nos había presentado y una vez que hubo traducido, el artesano en cristal continuó—: Es solamente cuestión de conocer cómo dar la curvatura apropiada y luego tener la paciencia de afilar y pulir cada cristal con exactitud.»

Teniendo la esperanza de que mi voz sonara igualmente inexpresiva, dije: «Son cosas muy interesantes y útiles también. Me pregunto si no habrán sido ya vistos y copiados por los artesanos de Tenochtitlan.»

Mi intérprete me hizo notar que probablemente nunca antes los habían visto, ya que la Piedra del Sol jamás se había exhibido a los ojos de ninguna persona de Tenochtitlan. Después tradujo el comentario del maestro Xibalbá:

«Dije, joven señor, que no es un gran secreto hacer cristales. No dije que fuera fácil de imitar. Uno debe saber, por ejemplo, cómo conservar la piedra centrada con precisión para poder afilarla. Mi bisabuelo Xibalbá aprendió el método de la Gente Jaguar, quienes fueron los primeros en vivir aquí en Chiapán.»

Dijo eso con orgullo y parecía ser una simple conversación casual acerca de los secretos de su profesión, pero estoy seguro de que nunca antes había revelado esos secretos más que a su propia progenie. Y eso me cayó como anillo al dedo: que los Xibalbá fueran los únicos guardianes de ese conocimiento; que los cristales no fueran fácilmente imitables; que me dejara comprar los suficientes de ellos...

Pretendiendo incertidumbre, dije: «Yo pienso... yo creo... quizás pudiera vender estas cosas como curiosidades en Tenochtitlan o Texcoco. No estoy completamente seguro... pero sí, quizás los escribanos, para una mayor exactitud en los detalles de sus palabras-pintadas...»

Los ojos del maestro brillaron traviesos y me preguntó directamente: «¿Cuántos cree usted, joven señor, que pudiera requerir casi con seguridad?»

Yo sonreí y dejé caer mi proposición: «Eso depende de cuántos me podría usted proveer y a qué precio.»

«Usted puede ver aquí toda la cantidad que tengo de material para trabajar en estos momentos.» Se movió hacia una de las paredes de su cuarto de trabajo, que estaba llena de anaqueles desde el piso hasta el techo; en cada tabla, acomodados en nichos de tela de algodón, estaban los cuarzos en bruto. Eran objetos blancos, opacos, distinguiéndose por sus ángulos de seis lados, como eran encontrados en la tierra, y se alineaban a lo largo por tamaños que iban desde la falange de un dedo, hasta el tamaño de una mazorca.

«Aquí está lo que he pagado por este material —continuó el artesano, alargándome un papel de corteza lleno de columnas de números y glifos. Estaba sacando la cuenta mentalmente, cuando él dijo—: Con él puedo hacer seis veintenas de cristales, terminados en diferentes tamaños.»

Le pregunté: «¿Y cuánto tiempo tomaría en hacerlos?»

«¿Veinte días?»

«¡Veinte días! —exclamé—. ¡Pensé que *un solo* cristal le llevaría todo ese tiempo!»

«Nosotros los Xibalbá hemos tenido cientos de gavillas de años de práctica —dijo—. Y tengo siete hijos aprendices para ayudarme. También tengo cinco hijas, pero por supuesto que ellas tienen prohibido tocar las piedras, no vaya a ser que siendo mujeres las arruinen.»

«Seis veintenas de cristales —medité, repitiendo su manera provinciana de contar—. ¿Y cuánto me cobraría por ellas?»

«Lo que usted ve allí», dijo, indicando el papel de corteza.

Perplejo, hablé con el intérprete. «¿No entendí bien? ¿No dijo él que esto era lo que había pagado por todo el material? ¿Por la piedra en bruto?» El intérprete asintió y después a través de él me dirigí al artesano:

«Esto no tiene sentido. Aun una vendedora de tortillas pide más por ellas que por lo que pagó por el maíz. Usted no recibe nada de utilidad. Ni siquiera un mes de salario por su trabajo y el de sus siete hijos.» Los dos, el intérprete y el artesano sonrieron indulgentes y menearon sus cabezas. «Maestro Xibalbá —persistí—, vine aquí preparado para comerciar, sí, pero no para robar. Le puedo decir honestamente que estoy dispuesto a pagar ocho veces este precio, y sería muy feliz de pagar seis y estaría encantado de pagar cuatro.»

Me contestó inmediatamente: «Y yo me vería obligado a rehusar.»

«En el nombre de todos los dioses, suyos y míos, ¿por qué?»

«Usted ha probado ser un amigo de los Macoboö. Así es que usted es amigo de todos los chiapa, y nosotros los Xibalbá somos chiapa también. No, no proteste más. Váyase. Disfrute de su estancia entre nosotros. Déjeme volver a trabajar y regrese en un mes por sus cristales.»

«¡Entonces nuestra fortuna ya está hecha! —se regocijó Glotón de Sangre, mientras jugaba con una muestra de cristal que me había dado el artesano—. No necesitamos viajar más. ¡Por el gran Huitztli, cuando regresemos, podemos vender estas cosas a cualquier precio que pidamos!»

«Sí —dije—. Pero tenemos que esperar un mes y todavía nos quedan otras mercancías para tratar y tengo razones personales para visitar a los maya.»

Él gruñó: «Aunque estas mujeres de Chiapán son de piel oscura, son fantásticas en comparación con las que encontraremos entre los maya.»

«Viejo sinvergüenza, ¿no puedes pensar en otra cosa que no sea mujeres?»

331

Cózcatl, quien no pensaba en lo absoluto en mujeres, suplicó: «Sí, continuemos adelante. Hemos venido desde tan lejos para no ver la selva.»

«También pienso en la comida —dijo Glotón de Sangre—. Estos Macoboö nos han extendido un amplio mantel de comida, que la selva no hará. Además, perdimos a nuestro único cocinero capaz cuando murió Diez.»

Dije: «Tú y yo seguiremos adelante, Cózcatl. Dejemos que este anciano flojo se quede aquí, si es lo que él desea, y que viva de la fama de su nombre.»

Glotón de Sangre gruñó un poco más, pero como yo ya sabía su deseo de viajar era más fuerte que cualquier otro. Pronto se fue al mercado a comprar las cosas que necesitaría para nuestra travesía por la selva. Mientras tanto, yo fui otra vez con el maestro Xibalbá para invitarlo a que tomara de nuestras mercancías aquellas que llamaran su atención, como un anticipo al pago que le haría posteriormente en moneda corriente. Él, otra vez, mencionó su numerosa progenie y estuvo muy contento de seleccionar una cantidad de mantos, taparrabos, blusas y faldas. Ese trueque me dejó a mí también muy satisfecho, ya que esas mercancías eran las más pesadas de cargar. Su selección me dejó a dos esclavos sin carga y no tuve ningún problema en encontrarles comprador entre los chiapa, quienes me pagaron con polvo de oro.

«Visitaremos otra vez al físico —dijo Glotón de Sangre—. Hace mucho tiempo que yo recibí protección contra la mordedura de cualquier serpiente, pero tú y el muchacho todavía no han sido tratados.»

«Gracias por tus buenas intenciones —dije—. Pero no creo que pudiera confiar en el doctor Maäsh, ni siquiera para tratarme un granito en mi trasero.»

Él insistió: «Cualquier tonto puede hacer lo necesario, pero sólo un doctor puede tener todos los colmillos necesarios para hacerlo. La selva hierve en serpientes venenosas. Cuando pises una, desearás haber visitado la choza del doctor Maäsh primero. —Y él empezó a contar con sus dedos—: Allí encontraremos a la serpiente barbilla-amarilla, la coralillo, la *nauyaka*...»

Cózcatl se puso pálido y yo recordé al viejo mercader de Tenochtitlan, contando cómo había sido mordido por una *nauyaka* y cómo se había tenido que cortar su propia pierna para no morir. Así es que capitulé y Cózcatl y yo fuimos a ver al doctor Maäsh, quien utilizó los colmillos de cada una de las serpientes que Glotón de Sangre había mencionado y de tres o cuatro más. Con cada uno de esos colmillos nos picó la lengua, nada más lo suficiente como para que saliera una gota de sangre.

«Hay un poquito de veneno seco en cada uno de estos colmillos —explicó—, esto hará que a los dos les salga una roncha suave. Ésta desaparecerá en unos cuantos días y entonces ustedes quedarán a salvo de la mordedura de cualquier serpiente conocida. Sin embargo, hay otra precaución que se debe tener en cuenta. —Sonrió maliciosamente y dijo—: Desde este momento y para siempre, *sus* dientes son tan letales como los de cualquier serpiente. Así es que tengan mucho cuidado de a quién muerden.»

Así, nosotros dejamos Chiapán tan pronto como nos pudimos escabullir de la insistente hospitalidad de los Macoboö, y especialmente de las dos primas, jurando que pronto regresaríamos y volveríamos a ser sus invitados otra vez. Para continuar hacia el este tuvimos que escalar otra hilera de montañas, sin embargo, para entonces el dios Títitl había restaurado el clima cálido propio de aquellas regiones, así es que nuestra caminata no fue tan dura a pesar de estar muy por encima de los bosques.

Por el otro lado de la montaña, desde las rocas con líquenes de las alturas hasta donde empezaba la línea de los árboles, la bajada era muy pronunciada; después un escarpado descenso entre una floresta de pinos, cedros y enebros. Desde allí, los árboles que me eran familiares empezaron a escasear, pues estaban rodeados por otras clases que nunca antes había visto y todos parecían estar luchando por sus vidas contra las lianas y enredaderas que trepaban y se enredaban alrededor de ellos.

Lo primero que descubrí en la selva, fue que la cortedad de mi vista no era allí un gran inconveniente, ya que las distancias no existían; todo estaba muy cerca entre sí. Extraños árboles contorsionados, plantas verdes de gigantescas hojas, altos y empenachados helechos, monstruosos y esponjados hongos, todos ellos creciendo cerca nos apresaban y nos rodeaban por todas partes, casi sofocándonos. El endoselado del follaje sobre nuestras cabezas era como una nube verde que nos cubría; caminando entre la selva, aun al mediodía, siempre nos encontrábamos dentro de un crepúsculo verde. Cada cosa que crecía, incluso los pétalos de las flores, parecía exudar una humedad caliente y viscosa. Aunque aquella era la estación seca, el aire en sí era denso, húmedo y pesado para respirar, como una niebla clara. La selva olía a especias, a almizcle, un olor maduro dulzón de raíces: todos los olores del desenfrenado crecimiento de raíces podridas.

Desde las copas de los árboles, sobre nosotros, los monos aulladores y los monos araña chillaban, e incontables variedades de papagayos gritaban indignadas por nuestra intromisión, mientras otros pájaros de inconcebibles colores relampagueaban de un lado a otro como flechas de advertencia. El aire que nos rodeaba estaba lleno de chupamirtos no más grandes que una abeja, y abanicado por revoloteantes mariposas tan grandes como murciélagos. Bajo nuestros pies, en la hierba, se escuchaba un sonido susurrante de criaturas activas o huidizas. Quizás algunas eran serpientes venenosas, pero la mayoría eran criaturas inofensivas: el pequeño lagarto *itzam* que corre en sus patas traseras; los sapos con dedos prensiles que trepaban los árboles huyendo de nosotros; las iguanas con papadas y crestas multicolores; el lustroso *jaleb*, quien escapaba sólo un corto trecho y luego volviéndose nos miraba fijamente. Aun los animales más grandes y feos, nativos de esas selvas, temían a los humanos: el pesado tapir, el peludo *capybara*, el oso hormiguero con sus formidables garras. A menos de que uno pisara dentro de un arroyo sin precaución, encontraría cocodrilos y caimanes acechando, pero aun esas bestias masivas no eran peligrosas. Nosotros éramos más una amenaza para aquellas criaturas de lo que ellas eran para nosotros. Durante el mes que estuvimos en la selva, las flechas de Glotón de Sangre nos proveyeron de las diversas carnes de *jaleb*, iguanas, de *capybaras* y del tapir. ¿Comestibles, mis señores? Ya lo creo. La carne del *jaleb* no se distingue mucho de la de la zorra; la carne de la iguana es tan blanca y suave como la del cangrejo de río que ustedes llaman langosta; el *capybara* sabe igual al más tierno conejo y la carne del tapir es muy similar a la de su puerco.

Al único de los animales grandes que teníamos que temer era al jaguar. En aquellas selvas del sur, los gatos son más numerosos que en todas las tierras templadas. Por supuesto, que sólo un jaguar demasiado viejo o demasiado enfermo para cazar una presa más ágil atacaría a un hombre ya desarrollado sin ninguna provocación. Sin embargo, el pequeño Cózcatl podía ser una tentación irresistible, así que nunca lo dejábamos fuera del grupo protector de adultos. Y cuando caminábamos por la selva en una hilera, Glotón de Sangre nos hacía llevar nuestras espadas cortas apuntando hacia arriba, derecho sobre nuestras cabezas, porque la manera favorita de cazar del jaguar de la selva es simplemente descolgarse desde la rama de un árbol y dejarse caer sobre su inadvertida víctima, al pasar por debajo.

Glotón de Sangre había comprado en Chiapán dos cosas para cada uno de nosotros y creo que no hubiéramos podido sobrevivir en la selva sin ellas. Una era una delicada tela mosquitera en la cual nos enrollábamos aun cuando caminábamos durante el día, tan pestilentes eran los insectos voladores; otra, una cama llamada *gishe*, también conocida por hamaca de cuerdas, que se colgaba entre dos árboles. Era mucho más cómoda que las esterillas o petates, así es que en todos mis viajes siguientes llevé conmigo una *gishe* y siempre la utilizaba en donde había árboles.

Nuestras camas elevadas nos ponían fuera del alcance de las serpientes y las mosquiteras por lo menos disuadían a los murciélagos chupadores de sangre, a los escorpiones y a otras plagas con algo de iniciativa. Pero nada podía mantener lejos a las más ambiciosas criaturas; por ejemplo, a las hormigas, éstas usaban las cuerdas de nuestras *gishes* como puentes y hacían túneles bajo nuestras mosquiteras. Si alguna vez quieren saber lo que se siente con la picadura de una hormiga roja, reverendos frailes, sostengan uno de los cristales del maestro Xibalbá entre el sol y su carne.

Sin embargo, había cosas todavía más horrorosas. Una mañana desperté sintiendo que algo oprimía mi pecho, cautelosamente levanté mi cabeza para ver una mano gruesa, peluda y negra yaciendo en él, una mano dos veces más ancha que la mía. «Un mono me está agarrando —pensé somnoliento—, debe de ser de una nueva raza desconocida, más grande que un hombre.» Entonces caí en la cuenta de que aquella cosa pesada era una tarántula «come-pájaro» y que sólo había un delgado mosquitero entre mi carne y sus mandíbulas segadoras. En ninguna otra mañana de mi vida me levanté con tanto celo, aventando el mosquitero y corriendo más allá de las cenizas del fuego del campamento, todo a la vez y gritando de tal manera que puse en pie a todos los demás, casi con tanta urgencia.

Debo decir, también, que no todo en la selva es feo, amenazante o pestilente. Para un viajero que toma razonables medidas de precaución, la selva puede ser hospitalaria y bella a la vez. La caza es fácil para tener carne comestible; muchas de las plantas son muy nutritivas; incluso algunos de los hongos parduscos que crecen allí son deliciosos. Hay en la selva una rama de liana muy gruesa que parece tan costrosa y seca como el barro cocido, pero si se corta un pedazo tan largo como un brazo, se puede ver que adentro es tan porosa como un panal de abejas, y si se pone por encima de la cabeza escurrirá una generosa bebida, tan fresca, dulce y fría como el agua. En cuanto a la belleza que la selva encierra, no puedo describir las flores tan brillantes que vi allí, solamente puedo decir que de miles y miles que había, no recuerdo dos similares en forma y color.

Los pájaros más hermosos que vimos eran de las numerosas variedades del *quétzal*, de vívidos colores y crestas y plumajes diferentes. Pero sólo dos o tres veces vislumbramos el más primoroso de todos los pájaros, el *quétzal tótotl*: el único con una cola de plumaje esmeralda tan larga como las piernas de un hombre. Ese magnífico pájaro está tan orgulloso de su plumaje como cualquier noble que use sus plumas más tarde. O por lo menos eso me dijo una muchacha maya llamada Ix Ikoki. Me explicó que el *quétzal tótotl* hace su nido en forma globular y que éste es único entre los demás pájaros, porque tiene dos agujeros de entrada. Así el pájaro puede entrar por uno y salir a través del otro sin tener que dar la vuelta por dentro y correr el riesgo de romper una de las espléndidas plumas de su cola. También me dijo Ikoki, que el *quétzal tótotl* come solamente pequeños frutos que arranca de los árboles al pasar volando y los come mientras vuela en lugar de pararse cómodamente en una rama de árbol, para asegurarse que el jugo no gotee ni manche sus plumas colgantes.

Ya que mencioné a la muchacha Ix Ikoki, debo decir también, que en mi opinión ni ella ni ningún otro ser humano de los que vivían allí, añadió ninguna belleza apreciable a la selva de aquellas tierras.

De acuerdo con todas las leyendas, los maya una vez tuvieron una civilización poderosa, rica y resplandeciente, a la que nosotros los mexica jamás nos hemos aproximado, y las ruinas vivientes de lo que fueron una vez sus ciudades, nos dan una poderosa evidencia para sostener tales leyendas. Es evidente, también, que los maya aprendieron todas sus artes y oficios directamente de los incomparables tolteca, antes de que esos magníficos artesanos desaparecieran. Por un lado, los maya tuvieron muchos de los mismos dioses de los tolteca, los mismos que nosotros los mexica nos apropiaríamos más tarde. Al benevolente Serpiente Emplumada, Quetzalcoatl, ellos lo llaman Kukulkán. El dios de la lluvia a quien nosotros llamamos Tláloc, ellos lo llaman Chak.

En ese viaje y en los sucesivos, he visto lo que queda de las muchas ciudades maya y nadie puede negar que debieron de haber sido magníficas en su principio. En sus plazas vacías y en sus patios, todavía se pueden ver estatuas admirables, tallados paneles de piedra, fachadas ricamente ornamentadas e incluso pinturas en las que los vívidos colores no se han despintado a través de gavillas sobre gavillas de años, desde que fueron pintadas por primera vez. Yo, particularmente, me di cuenta de un detalle en los edificios maya —las aberturas de las puertas están rematadas graciosamente en forma piramidal— lo que nuestros modernos arquitectos todavía no han podido hacer o quizás nunca han podido imitar.

Les llevó a los arquitectos, artistas y artesanos maya, muchas generaciones, cuidadoso trabajo y amor para construir y embellecer aquellas ciudades. Pero ahora están vacías, abandonadas y olvidadas. No hay trazas de que alguna vez hayan sido sitiadas por ejércitos enemigos, o que hayan sufrido algunos de los más insignificantes desastres de la naturaleza; a pesar de eso, sus habitantes, que se contaban por millares, las abandonaron por alguna razón. Y los descendientes de aquellos habitantes son ahora tan ignorantes y tan despegados de su historia que no pueden decir, ni siquiera aventurar una opinión plausible, del *porqué* sus ancestros evacuaron aquellas ciudades, mientras que a la selva se le está permitido reclamarlas y destruirlas. En esos días los maya no podían decir por qué *ellos*, que habían heredado toda esa grandeza, vivían resignadamente en aldeas de chozas de paja a la vera de las ciudades fantasma.

Los dominios vastos y unificados de los maya, formalmente regidos desde su ciudad capital llamada Mayapán, han venido a ser divididos geográficamente de norte a sur. Para entonces, mis compañeros y yo estábamos viajando por la parte más importante: la lujuriosa selva del país llamado Tamoán Chan, La Tierra de las Tinieblas, cuyas extensiones sin límites corrían hacia el este desde las fronteras del territorio de los chiapa. Hacia el norte, por donde viajé en otra ocasión, se extiende la gran península a lo largo del océano del norte, el lugar en donde sus exploradores españoles tocaron tierra por primera vez. Yo hubiera pensado que después de echar una mirada a esas tierras infecundas e inhospitalarias, ellos debieron haber vuelto a España, para no regresar aquí jamás. Pero en lugar de eso, le dieron a aquella tierra un nombre todavía más absurdo que el de Cuernos de Vaca por Quaunáhuac o el de Tortilla por lo que debía ser Texcala. Cuando aquellos primeros españoles tocaron tierra y preguntaron: «¿Cómo se llama este lugar?», los habitantes, que nunca antes habían oído hablar castellano, naturalmente replicaron: «*Yectetán*», que quiere decir solamente: «No entiendo.» De ahí sacaron esos exploradores el nombre de Yucatán y supongo que la península será llamada así para siempre. Pero no debería reír, ya que el nombre que los maya le dieron a esa tierra: Uluümil Kutz o Tierra de Plenitud, era igual de ridículo o quizás irónico, pues la mayor parte de esa península es desgraciadamente infértil e inhóspita.

Así como dividieron su tierra, los maya ya no son un solo pueblo regido por un solo gobernante. Ellos se han fraccionado dentro de una profusión de tribus teniendo a la cabeza despreciables caciques y todos ellos son insolentes y discordes. La mayoría de los maya están tan desanimados y sumidos en letargo que viven en lo que sus ancestros debían de haber considerado como una repugnante inmundicia. Y todavía, cada una de esas tribus insignificantes, pretende ser la única y verdadera descendiente de la gran raza maya. Personalmente creo que los antiguos maya desconocerían toda relación con cualquiera de ellos.

Esos zafios ni siquiera pueden decir los nombres de lo que fueron las grandes ciudades de sus ancestros, sino que las llaman como les da la gana. Una de esas ciudades, que ahora está casi ahogada por el crecimiento de la selva, todavía muestra una pirámide que se levanta hacia el cielo, un palacio con torreones y numerosos templos, pero sin ninguna imaginación ellos la llaman por Palemké, la palabra maya para denominar cualquier «lugar santo». En otra ciudad abandonada, las galerías que todavía no han sido invadidas por raíces y lianas destructivas, muestran en sus paredes murales diestramente pintados con escenas de guerreros en plena batalla, ceremonias cortesanas y cosas parecidas. Cuando les pregunté a los descendientes de esos guerreros y cortesanos qué sabían del lugar, se encogieron de hombros con indiferencia, llamándolo por Bonampak, que sólo quiere decir: «paredes pintadas».

Uluümil Kutz es una ciudad casi destruida por la erosión y muy bien podría haber sido conocida por El Lugar en Donde el Hombre Creó Belleza, por la arquitectura intrincada y todavía delicada de muchos de sus edificios, sin embargo, es solamente llamada Uxmal, que significa «tres edificios». Otra ciudad que está situada magníficamente en lo alto de una colina, mirando hacia un ancho río, en lo profundo de la selva, tiene las ruinas o cimientos de por lo menos cien grandes edificios construidos con trozos de cantera verde, que yo conté y creo que ha de haber sido el más majestuoso de *todos* los centros antiguos maya. Sin embargo, los campesinos que viven ahora en sus alrededores lo conocen por Yaxchilán, que quiere decir que es un lugar en donde hay algunas «piedras verdes».

Oh, debo de reconocer que algunas tribus, como la notable de los xíu al norte de la península y los tzotxil de las selvas del sur, todavía manifiestan alguna inteligencia y vitalidad y se preocupan por su perdida herencia. Reconocen clases de acuerdo al nacimiento y condición social: noble, clase media, clase baja y esclavos. Todavía mantienen algunas de las artes de sus antepasados; sus sabios saben medicina y cirugía, aritmética y astronomía y llevan un calendario. Cuidadosamente preservan los incontables libros escritos por sus predecesores, aunque el hecho de que ellos conozcan tan poco de su propia historia me hace dudar de que aun sus sacerdotes mejor educados puedan leer esos libros o se tomen la molestia de hacerlo.

Sin embargo, también los antiguos maya, civilizados y cultos, observaban algunas costumbres que nosotros los modernos debemos considerar muy extravagantes y es una lástima que sus descendientes hayan escogido perpetuar esas excentridades mientras dejan a un lado acciones mucho más dignas. Para un forastero como yo, lo más notablemente grotesco es lo que los maya consideran como bello, dentro de su propia apariencia.

Por la evidencia de las antiguas tallas y pinturas, los maya siempre tuvieron narices de pico de halcón y puntiagudas barbillas, y por siempre se empeñaron en aumentar esa semblanza con las aves de presa. Lo que quiero decir es que, tanto los antiguos maya como los actuales, han deformado a sus hijos desde el nacimiento. Una tabla lisa es puesta sobre la frente del recién nacido y dejada allí durante toda la infancia. Cuando al fin se le quita, el niño tiene una frente tan puntiaguda como su barbilla, y eso hace que la prominencia natural de su nariz parezca más como un pico. Y eso no es todo. Un niño o una niña maya pueden ir desnudos hasta una edad en que su desnudez es positivamente indecente. Sin embargo, aunque desnudos, ellos siempre llevarán unas bolitas de arcilla o resina suspendidas por un cordón que llevan alrededor de la cabeza, de tal manera que cuelguen directamente entre los ojos. Esto es con la intención de que el niño crezca bizco, lo cual, los maya de todas las tierras y clases juzgan como otro rasgo de gran belleza. Algunos hombres y mujeres maya son tan bizcos que pienso que si no fuera porque tienen de por medio su nariz ganchuda, los ojos se les juntarían. Ya he dicho que hay muchas cosas bellas en las selvas del país de Tamoán Chan, pero no incluiría a la población humana entre ellas.

Probablemente hubiera ignorado a todas esas mujeres con cara de halcón si no hubiera sido porque, en la primera aldea que pasamos la noche y eso fue entre los limpios tzotxil, una muchacha parecía mirarme con determinación anhelante y yo deduje que ella se había sentido herida de pasión por mí a primera vista. Así es que ni corto ni perezoso me presenté a ella con mi último nombre: Nube Oscura que en su lenguaje es Ek Muyal y ella me confió tímidamente que se llamaba Ix Ikoki o sea Estrella del Atardecer. No fue sino hasta que estuve bastante cerca de ella, que me di cuenta de que era excesivamente bizca, por lo que llegué a la conclusión de que no me había estado viendo en absoluto. Incluso en ese momento en que estábamos cara a cara, podría haber estado mirando al árbol de detrás mío, o a sus propios pies desnudos, o quizás a los dos al mismo tiempo, nunca lo pude determinar.

Eso me desconcertó de alguna manera, pero la curiosidad me impelió a persuadir a Ix Ikoki para que pasara la noche conmigo. Y con esto no quiero decir que estuviera encendido por una curiosidad lasciva, acerca de que una muchacha bizca pudiera ser interesantemente peculiar en otros de sus órganos. Simplemente fue que por algún tiempo me había estado preguntando cómo se podría copular, con *cualquier* mujer o cómo sería el acto realizado en una hamaca. Tengo el gusto de comunicarles que no sólo lo encontré factible sino también delicioso, como si lo hiciera en el aire, en una libertad sin restricciones, profunda como el agua. En verdad, me sentí tan transportado que no me di cuenta, sino hasta que descansamos consumidos y sudorosos uno junto al otro en el vaivén de la *gishe*, que había dado varias mordidas de amor a Ix Ikoki y por lo menos una de ellas tenía una gota de sangre.

Por supuesto que eso me hizo recordar las palabras de advertencia del doctor Maäsh, después de habernos administrado el tratamiento contra las mordeduras de serpientes y no pude pegar un ojo en toda la noche, sufriendo la agonía de la aprensión.

Estuve esperando que Ix Ikoki cayera en convulsiones o poco a
poco se fuera poniendo tiesa y fría a mi lado, y me preguntaba
cuál sería el terrible castigo que los tzotxil daban a los asesinos de
sus mujeres. Sin embargo, Ix Ykoki no hizo otra cosa más alarmante que roncar toda la noche por su gran nariz, y a la mañana
siguiente se sentó con ligereza a la orilla de la hamaca, con sus
ojos bizcos radiantes.

Naturalmente que estaba muy contento de no haber matado a
la muchacha, pero también ese hecho me perturbó y me llenó de
ira. Si el viejo chapucero del doctor-de-pulso, quien nos dijo que
desde aquel momento nuestros dientes estaban llenos de veneno,
sólo estaba repitiendo una más de las estúpidas supersticiones de
su pueblo, quería decir que era seguro que Cózcatl y yo no estábamos protegidos contra el indudable veneno de las serpientes, o
que Glotón de Sangre jamás lo estuvo. Así es que advertí a mis
socios y desde entonces pusimos más precaución al ver en dónde
poníamos nuestros pies y manos cuando regresamos otra vez a
través de la selva.

Poco después fui a ver a otro físico, pero de la clase que había
deseado por tanto tiempo y que desde tan lejos había ido a ver:
uno de esos doctores maya famosos por su habilidad en tratar las
dolencias de los ojos. Su nombre era Ah Chel y era de la tribu de
los tzotxil, y *tzotxil* quiere decir Gente Murciélago, lo que tomé
por un buen augurio ya que los murciélagos son las criaturas que
pueden ver mejor en la oscuridad. El doctor Ah Chel tenía otras
dos cualidades que me lo hacían más recomendable: hablaba fluidamente el náhuatl y no era bizco. Creo que no hubiera tenido mucha confianza en un doctor bizco.

No se puso a oír mi pulso o a llamar a algún dios o a utilizar
algún otro tipo místico de diagnóstico. Empezó con toda franqueza
a ponerme unas gotas del jugo de la hierba *camopalxihuitl* en mis
ojos, para engrandecer mis pupilas y así poder ver adentro de
ellas. Mientras esperábamos que la droga surtiera efecto, me puse
a platicar, quizá por el ansia de mi propio nerviosismo, y le conté
acerca del doctor Maäsh y las circunstancias de la enfermedad y la
muerte de Diez.

«La fiebre del conejo —dijo el doctor Ah Chel, asintiendo—.
Deben estar muy contentos de que ninguno de ustedes contrajo
también esa enfermedad del conejo. La fiebre no mata por sí misma, pero debilita tanto a la víctima que ésta sucumbe por contraer otra enfermedad, una que hace que se le llenen los pulmones
de un líquido espeso. Pudiera ser que su esclavo todavía estuviera
vivo, si usted lo hubiera bajado de las alturas a un lugar en donde
hubiera podido respirar un aire más pesado y rico. Bien, ahora
déjeme verlo.»

Él utilizó un cristal exactamente igual a los del maestro Xibalbá y sin duda hecho por aquel gran artesano. Lo acercó a cada
uno de mis ojos mirando con atención, después se echó para atrás
y dijo llanamente:

«Joven Ek Muyal, usted no tiene nada que aflija a sus ojos.»

«¿*Nada?*», exclamé. Y me pregunté que si después de todo, Ah
Chel era tan charlatán como Maäsh. Entre dientes le dije: «No

hay nada malo en mis ojos, excepto que no puedo ver más allá de lo largo de mi brazo. ¿Y a eso es a lo que usted le llama *nada*?»

«Lo que quiero decir es que usted no tiene ninguna enfermedad o perturbación en su visión que yo o cualquier otro doctor pudiera tratar.»

Eché una de las maldiciones de Glotón de Sangre, con la esperanza de que eso hiciera que el gran dios Huitzilopochtli pateara sus partes privadas. Ah Chel me hizo un gesto para que le acabara de escuchar.

«Usted ve las cosas borrosas por la *forma* de sus ojos y esto es de nacimiento. Esa forma poco común del globo del ojo distorsiona la visión precisamente como lo hace esta pieza de cuarzo poco común. Sostenga este cristal cerca entre su ojo y una flor y usted ve bien la flor, pero sostenga el cristal entre su ojo y un jardín distante y solamente verá un manchón de colores.»

Yo dije afligido: «¿Entonces no hay medicina para esto, ni operación...?»

«Lamento decirle que no. Si usted tuviera la ceguera de la enfermedad provocada por la mosca negra, sí, yo podría lavar sus ojos con medicamentos. Si estuviera afligido de lo que nosotros llamamos la cortina blanca, sí, yo podría cortarla y darle mejor visión, aunque no perfecta. Pero no existe ninguna operación que haga que el globo del ojo sea más pequeño, no sin destruirlo totalmente. Nosotros nunca llegaremos a conocer un remedio para su condición, al igual que ningún hombre conocerá el secreto del lugar en donde los cocodrilos viejos van a morir.»

Sintiéndome todavía más miserable, murmuré: «¿Entonces debo vivir todo el resto de mi vida en niebla, cegato como un topo?»

«Bien —dijo él, sin simpatizar con mi autocompasión—. Usted también puede vivir dándole gracias a los dioses por *no* estar completamente ciego por la cortina o por las moscas o por cualquier otra causa. Usted verá a muchos que lo están. —Él hizo una pausa y luego me hizo notar—: Ellos nunca lo verán a usted.»

Quedé tan deprimido por el veredicto del físico que pasé el resto del tiempo en Tamoán Chan de un humor negro y temo que no fui muy buena compañía para mis socios. Cuando un guía de la tribu de los pokomán, de la lejana selva sur, nos mostró los maravillosos lagos de Tziskao, los miré tan fríamente como si el dios de la lluvia maya, Chak, los hubiera creado sólo para afrentarme personalmente. Esos lagos son aproximadamente sesenta cuerpos diferentes de agua, que no están conectados unos con otros por corrientes y no tienen ninguna visible que los provea, aunque nunca disminuyen de agua en la estación seca, ni se desbordan en la estación de lluvias. Pero lo verdaderamente notable acerca de ellos es que ni siquiera dos de sus cuencas son del mismo color.

Desde la altitud en donde estábamos mirando seis o siete de esas cuencas, nuestro guía, apuntando hacia ellas, dijo con orgullo: «¡Contemple usted, joven viajero Ek' Muyal! Aquélla es de un azul-verde oscuro; esa otra, de color turquesa; aquélla, verde brillante como una esmeralda; la de allí, verde oscuro como el jade, y ésa, azul pálido como el cielo en invierno...»

Yo gruñí: «Pueden ser rojas como la sangre, por lo que a mí respecta.» Y por supuesto esto no era realmente la verdad. La verdad era que yo estaba viendo todo y a todos a través de mi negro desaliento.

Por un tiempo muy breve, acaricié una idea optimista tratando algunos experimentos con el cristal del maestro Xibalbá. Sabía que era para ver cosas de cerca, más de cerca y claramente, pero aun así traté de todas formas, sosteniéndolo cerca de mi ojo, a la distancia de un brazo mientras miraba unos árboles distantes, luego poniéndolo cerca de las ramitas de un arbusto y retrocediendo hasta que difícilmente podía ver el mismo cristal. De nada sirvió. Cuando lo apuntaba hacia las cosas a la distancia de una mano, el cuarzo hacía que todo se viera indistinto más de lo que lo veían mis ojos sin ayuda. Y esos experimentos me deprimieron todavía más.

Aun con los compradores maya estuve irritado y taciturno, pero afortunadamente había tanta demanda por nuestras mercancías que mi conducta desagradable fue tolerada. Bruscamente rehusé el canje de sus pieles de jaguar, ocelotes y otro animales, y las plumas de guacamaya, de tucán y de otros pájaros. Lo que yo quería era polvo de oro o moneda corriente, pero esas cosas casi no circulaban en aquellas tierras incivilizadas. Así es que les dejé saber que canjearía nuestras mercancías: telas, vestidos, joyería y chucherías, medicinas y cosméticos, solamente por plumas de *quétzal tótotl*.

Debo hacer notar que, en teoría, cualquier cazador que adquiera esas plumas verde-esmeralda del largo de una pierna estaba obligado, bajo pena de muerte, a presentarse inmediatamente al cacique de la tribu, quien las utilizaría ya sea como adorno o como moneda corriente en sus tratos con otros caciques maya y los más poderosos gobernantes de otras naciones. Pero en la práctica, creo que no tengo mucha necesidad de decirles que los cazadores daban a sus caciques sólo unas pocas de esas raras plumas y guardaban para sí la mayor parte de ellas, para su enriquecimiento. Ya que yo rehusé tratos que no fueran más que con plumas de *quétzal tótotl*, los clientes ofrecieron sus pieles y otras cosas entre sus propios compañeros, haciendo apresurados tratos... y yo obtuve las plumas del *quétzal tótotl*.

Conforme fuimos canjeando nuestras mercancías, fui vendiendo los esclavos que las cargaban. En esa tierra de débiles, ni siquiera los nobles tenían mucho trabajo para los esclavos y pagaban poco por ellos. Sin embargo, cada cacique tribal estaba ansioso de vanagloriarse de su superioridad sobre los otros rivales y tener más esclavos, aunque más bien fueran una carga para su despensa, eso constituía un legítimo lujo del que se podían envanecer. Así es que, en muy buen polvo de oro vendí nuestros diferentes esclavos en una forma imparcial, dos por jefe, a los caciques de los tzotxil, quiché y tzeltal y solamente nos acompañaron de regreso a la tierra de los chiapa los dos que nos quedaron. Uno cargaba el gran bulto, aunque ligero, de las plumas de *quétzal tótotl*, y la carga del otro consistía en aquellas mercancías que todavía no habíamos vendido.

Como lo había prometido, el artesano Xibalbá había terminado los cristales que estaban listos cuando regresé a Chiapán —ciento veintisiete de ellos, en varios tamaños—, y gracias a que había vendido los esclavos, pude pagarle en polvo de oro como le había prometido. Mientras él envolvía cada cristal por separado, cuidadosamente, y luego los acomodaba todos juntos en una tela haciendo un solo paquete, yo le dije por medio del intérprete:

«Maestro Xibalbá, estos cristales hacen que un objeto se vea más grande. ¿Alguna vez ha inventado usted cristales que hagan que las cosas se vean más pequeñas?»

«Oh, sí —dijo sonriendo—. Hasta mi bisabuelo trató de hacer algunas otras cosas aparte de los cristales para encender fuego. Todos lo hemos hecho. Yo también, sólo por diversión.»

Le platiqué cuán limitada era mi visión y añadí: «Un doctor maya me dijo que mis ojos estaban formados de tal manera que parecía que siempre estaba mirando a través de uno de esos cristales de aumento. Yo me pregunto si podría encontrar una cosa como cristal reducido y si al mirar a través de él...»

Él me miró con interés, se frotó la barbilla, dijo «hum» y se fue a su cuarto de trabajo que estaba atrás de la casa. Regresó trayendo un cajón de madera con varios departamentos pequeños y en cada uno de ellos había un cristal. Ninguno de ellos era como el cristal simétricamente convexo como una concha de mar; todos ellos eran de diferentes formas, incluso algunos eran pirámides en miniatura.

«Guardo esto sólo como una curiosidad —dijo el artesano—. No tienen ningún uso práctico, pero algunos de ellos tienen raras características. Éste por ejemplo. —Él levantó un pedacito con tres lados planos—. Éste no es un cuarzo, sino una clase de piedra caliza transparente, lo crea o no. Y yo no corté ni pulí esta piedra, sus partes son planas por naturaleza. Sosténgala más allá en el sol, y vea la luz que arroja en su mano.»

Así lo hice, esperando a medias un dolor causado por una quemada. En lugar de eso exclamé: «¡La neblina de joyas de agua!» La luz del sol al pasar por el cristal hacia mi mano se transformaba; era una banda de colores, partiendo desde el rojo oscuro en un extremo, hasta el amarillo, el verde, el azul y el púrpura profundo; un pequeño simulacro del arco coloreado que surge en el cielo después de la lluvia.

«Pero usted no anda buscando cosas para jugar —dijo el hombre—. Usted quiere un cristal de disminución. Aquí está.» Y él me dio una pieza redonda que no tenía su superficie convexa sino cóncava; lo que quiere decir que se veía como si tuviera dos platos juntos pegados en el fondo.

Yo lo sostuve sobre la orilla bordada de mi manto y el diseño se encogió a la mitad de su tamaño. Levanté mi cabeza todavía deteniendo el cristal enfrente de mí y miré al artesano. Las facciones del hombre, que habían estado borrosas antes, de repente tuvieron forma y se pudieron distinguir, pero su rostro era tan pequeño que parecía como si él se hubiera alejado de mí, como si estuviera en la plaza.

«Es maravilloso —dije temblando. Dejé el cristal y me froté el ojo—. Puedo *verle*... pero muy lejos.»

«Ah, entonces su disminución es demasiado poderosa. Ellos tienen diferentes grados de intensidad. Trate éste.»

Aquél era cóncavo sólo por un lado; la otra cara era perfectamente plana. Lo levanté con precaución...

«Puedo ver —dije y lo hice como una plegaria de gratitud hacia el más benéfico de los dioses—. Puedo ver de cerca y de lejos. Hay manchas y ondulaciones, pero todo lo demás es claro y distinto como cuando era un niño. Maestro Xibalbá, usted ha hecho algo que los célebres doctores maya admiten que no pueden hacer. ¡Usted ha hecho que vea otra vez!»

«Y durante todas esas gavillas de años... nosotros pensamos que estas cosas eran inservibles... —murmuró muy asombrado consigo mismo. Después habló alegremente—: Así es que se necesita un cristal con una superficie plana y con una curva en su interior. Pero usted no puede ir alrededor, sosteniendo siempre esa cosa lejos, enfrente de usted así. Eso sería como si estuviera atisbando por el agujero de un canuto. Trate de acercarlo lo más posible a su ojo.»

Así lo hice y grité y me disculpé diciendo: «Pensé que mi ojo se salía de su cuenca.»

«Todavía muy poderoso. Debe ser rebajado. Pero hay manchas y ondulaciones según dice usted. Así es que debo buscar una piedra más perfecta y sin los defectos del más fino cuarzo. —Sonrió y se frotó las manos—. Usted me ha puesto la primera tarea nueva que los Xibalbá han tenido por generaciones. Regrese mañana.»

Me consumía por la excitación y la espera, pero no dije nada a mis compañeros, en caso de que ese experimento lleno de esperanza terminara en la nada. Tanto ellos como yo volvimos a residir con los Macoböö para nuestra gran comodidad y para el regocijo de las dos primas y esta vez nos quedamos seis o siete días. Yo sostuve que todos necesitábamos un buen reposo antes de emprender la larga jornada de regreso y Cózcatl y Glotón de Sangre no pusieron objeciones. Mi verdadera razón era que estaba visitando varias veces al día al maestro Xibalbá, mientras él trabajaba sobre el cristal más escrupulosamente exacto, haciendo una labor que nunca antes le había sido pedida por nadie.

Había conseguido un pedazo de topacio claro y maravilloso, que estaba empezando a graduar dándole la forma de un disco plano a una circunferencia, que cubría mi ojo desde la ceja hasta la mejilla. El cristal quedaba plano en la parte de afuera, pero en su parte cóncava interior precisaba de cierto espesor y curvatura que solamente podía determinar experimentando sobre mi visión, para irlo graduando lentamente.

«Puedo irlo adelgazando y haciendo mayor la curvatura del arco, poco a poco —dijo él—, hasta que acertemos con el poder exacto de reducción que usted requiere. Pero necesitaremos saberlo con precisión, si corto demasiado se arruina.»

Así es que estuve yendo a las pruebas y cuando uno de mis ojos se puso rojo por el esfuerzo cambié al otro y luego otra vez al primero. Finalmente, para mi indecible regocijo, llegó el día, y el momento de ese día, en que pude sostener el cristal en cualquiera de mis dos ojos y ver perfectamente. Todo en el mundo era ya claro y bien delineado, desde un libro sostenido para leer hasta los árboles de las montañas más allá del horizonte de la ciudad. Estaba extasiado y el maestro Xibalbá se sentía casi igual, lleno de orgullo por su creación sin precedentes.

Le dio al cristal una pulida final con una pasta húmeda de cierta clase de arcilla roja, muy fina. Después alisó la orilla del cristal y lo montó sobre un fuerte arillo de cobre forjado para sostenerlo con seguridad. Este anillo tenía un mango corto con el cual podía sostenerlo enfrente de cada uno de mis ojos y el mango estaba atado a una correa de piel tan larga que podía tenerla siempre alrededor de mi cuello, listo para usarse y asegurado para no perderse. Cuando el instrumento estuvo terminado lo llevé a casa de los Macoboö, pero no se lo enseñé a nadie sino que esperé una oportunidad para sorprender a Glotón de Sangre y a Cózcatl.

A la caída del crepúsculo, nos sentamos en el atrio con nuestros anfitriones, la madre del difunto Diez y algunos otros miembros de la familia, siendo todos los hombres maduros fumábamos después de nuestra comida de la tarde. Los chiapa no fuman *poquíetl*, en lugar de eso ellos usan una jarra de arcilla a la que se le hacen varios agujeros; luego la rellenan con *picíetl* y hierbas olorosas acomodándolas para ser fumadas; después cada uno de los participantes inserta en cada hoyo de la jarra una larga caña hueca y toda la comunidad goza fumando.

«Allá viene un muchacha muy bonita», murmuró Glotón de Sangre apuntando con su caña hacia la calle.

Lo único que podía vislumbrar a la distancia era algo pálido que se movía en la oscuridad, sin embargo dije: «Pídeme que la describa.»

«¿Eh? —gruñó el viejo guerrero levantando sus cejas, y usando sarcásticamente mi apodo formal me dijo—: Bien, Perdido en Niebla, descríbela... como tú la ves.»

Puse mi cristal en el ojo izquierdo y vi a la muchacha claramente a pesar de la escasa luz. Con entusiasmo, como si hubiera sido un tratante de esclavos en su puesto, enumeré todos los detalles físicos de su cuerpo... el color de su piel, lo largo de sus trenzas, cómo eran sus pies desnudos, las facciones regulares de su rostro, que en verdad era muy bonito. Añadí que el bordado de su blusa era de los llamados diseños de cerámica. «También lleva —concluí—, un fino velo sobre su pelo en donde han quedado atrapados unos cuantos *kukaji*, cocuyos. Un adorno muy atractivo.» Después solté la carcajada al ver las expresiones de las caras de mis socios.

Como nada más podía utilizar un solo ojo al mismo tiempo, había cierto apocamiento, una carencia de extensión en todo lo que veía. A pesar de ello, pude otra vez ver *casi* todo tan claramente como cuando era un niño y eso era suficiente para mí. Debí haber mencionado que el topacio era de un color amarillo pálido; cuando veía a través de él, todo parecía estar iluminado por el sol, aun en los días grises, es por eso que quizá yo vi al mundo mucho más hermoso de lo que otros lo vieron. Sin embargo, pude descubrir al mirar un espejo de *tézcatl*, que el uso de mi cristal no me hacía verme muy hermoso, ya que el ojo que lo cubría se veía más chico que el otro. También, como para mí era más fácil sostener el cristal con mi mano izquierda mientras tenía ocupada la derecha, por un tiempo sufrí de jaquecas. Pronto aprendí a sostenerlo alternativamente en los dos ojos y esa molestia desapareció.

Comprendo, reverendos escribanos, que deben de estar aburridos de mi cháchara entusiasta acerca de este instrumento que para ustedes no es ninguna novedad. Nunca había visto un invento como ése hasta muchos años después, cuando tuve mi primer encuentro con los primeros españoles que llegaron. Uno de los frailes capellanes que desembarcaron con el Capitán General Cortés llevaba dos de esos cristales, uno en cada ojo, sostenidos por un cordón de piel atado alrededor de su cabeza.

Pero, para mí y para el artesano en cristales, mi topacio fue una invención nunca vista antes. De hecho, él rehusó todo pago por su trabajo y aun por el topacio, que debió de ser muy costoso. Insistió en que se sentía bien pagado por el simple orgullo de haber hecho una cosa, que aun los maestros artesanos de la Gente Jaguar jamás soñaron. Así es que en vista de que no quiso aceptar nada de mí, dejé con la familia Macoboö, para que se las entregaran, una cantidad de plumas de *quétzal tótotl* suficiente como para hacer que el maestro Xibalbá fuera probablemente uno de los hombres más ricos en Chiapán, pues yo sentía que él merecía serlo.

Aquella noche, miré las estrellas.

Como había estado por tanto tiempo deprimido, de pronto y muy comprensiblemente me sentía muy feliz, así es que les dije a mis socios: «Ahora que puedo ver, ¡me gustaría contemplar el océano!» Y estuvieron tan contentos con mi cambio de temperamento, que no pusieron ninguna objeción y pronto dejamos Chiapán yendo hacia el sur y luego hacia el este, aunque tuvimos que volver a atravesar gran cantidad de montañas, en las que había varios volcanes en movimiento. Sin embargo, salimos de esa sierra sin ningún incidente y llegamos a la orilla del mar, en las Tierras Calientes, habitadas por la Gente Mame. A esa región llana se la conoce por Xoconochco y los mame se dedican a trabajar en la producción de algodón y sal, que comercian con otras naciones. El algodón crece en una tierra ancha y fértil que queda entre las montañas rocosas y las playas arenosas. En aquel tiempo estábamos en invierno y por eso no había nada distintivo en esos campos, pero volví a visitar Xoconochco en la estación caliente, cuando las motas de algodón son tan grandes y profusas que las ramas verdes que las sostienen desaparecen de la vista; todo el campo parece blanqueado por una pesada nieve, a pesar de que caían bajo el peso del calor agobiante del sol.

La sal se recoge cada año, construyendo diques en las partes poco profundas de las lagunas a lo largo de la costa y dejando secar sus aguas para después cerner la sal de la arena. Como aquélla es tan blanca como la nieve, es muy fácil de distinguir en la arena, pues todas las playas del Xoconochco son de un color negro opaco; están formadas por el cascajo, el polvo y las cenizas de los volcanes que se encuentran tierra adentro. La espuma de las rompientes del mar del sur tampoco es blanca, sino que se ve de un color gris sucio ocasionado por las arenas oscuras siempre en movimiento.

Como la cosecha de algodón y la recolección de la sal son dos faenas muy fatigantes, los mame estuvieron muy contentos de pagarnos un buen precio, en polvo de oro, por los dos últimos esclavos que nos acompañaban, y también nos compraron las últimas mercancías que nos quedaban. Así, tanto Cózcatl, Glotón de Sangre y yo nos quedamos sin carga, solamente con nuestros bultos de viaje, un pequeño fardo de cristales para encender lumbre y un fardo voluminoso pero ligero de plumas que podíamos cargar sin ayuda. De regreso a casa, ya no nos molestaron más bandidos, quizás porque no parecíamos ser una caravana de mercaderes o quizás porque todos los que existían habían oído acerca de nuestro primer encuentro, cuando pasamos por allí.

Nuestra ruta al noroeste fue fácil a todo lo largo de la costa, por tierras llanas todo el camino, teniendo a nuestra izquierda lagunas tranquilas o un mar murmurante, y a nuestra derecha las altas montañas. El clima era tan agradable que sólo buscamos refugio en dos aldeas: Pijijía entre la Gente Mame y Tonalá entre la Gente Mixe, y solamente para darnos el lujo de tomar un baño de agua fresca y gozar de las delicias que el mar local nos ofrecía: huevos crudos de tortuga y carne cocida de ese mismo animal, camarones cocidos, toda clase de mariscos cocidos o crudos, y aun filetes asados de un pez llamado *yeyemichi*, que nos dijeron que era el más grande del mundo y puedo decir que es uno de los más sabrosos.

Al fin nos encontramos caminando afanosos directamente hacia el este y otra vez sobre el istmo de Tecuantépec, pero ya no nos detuvimos en esa ciudad, porque antes de llegar allí nos encontramos con otro mercader que nos dijo que si nos desviábamos un poco hacia el norte de la ruta este, que llevábamos, encontraríamos un camino más fácil a través de las montañas de Tzempuülá, diferente del que habíamos tomado antes. A mí me hubiera gustado mucho volver a ver a mi preciosa Gie Bele, no tanto por visitarla simplemente, sino también para poder inquirir acerca de esas personas misteriosas que guardaban el colorante púrpura. Pero después de todo nuestro vagabundear, creo que me sentía impelido de volver a casa urgentemente. Como sabía que mis compañeros también se sentían igual, me dejé convencer para desviarnos hacia el norte, hacia el camino sugerido por el mercader. Esa ruta también nos llevó por un largo camino, a través de otra parte de Uaxyácac por la que no habíamos pasado antes, aunque no quisimos detenernos para nada, hasta que llegamos otra vez a la ciudad capital de Záachila.

Igual como lo hicimos al empezar nuestra expedición, también había ciertos días del mes que se consideraban propicios para regresar. Así es que como ya estábamos muy cerca de casa, pasamos un día completo de ocio en el placentero pueblo de Quaunáhuac, que está en la montaña. Cuando por fin habíamos escalado la última altura, los lagos y la isla de Tenochtitlan estuvieron a la vista y me fui deteniendo en el camino para poder admirarla a través de mi cristal. Quizás viéndola a través de un solo ojo se haya perdido la dimensión de la ciudad, pero de todas maneras era algo muy consolador de ver: los edificios blancos, los palacios brillando a la luz del sol primaveral, los coloridos destellos de sus jardines en las azoteas, las volutas de humo azul de sus templos y fogones, sus banderas de plumas flotando casi sin movimiento en el aire suave, y luego la inmensa pirámide con sus templos gemelos dominándolo todo.

Con una mezcla de orgullo y alegría, cruzamos finalmente el camino-puente de Coyohuacan y entramos en la poderosa ciudad la tarde del día de buen augurio Uno-Casa, en el mes llamado El Gran Despertar, en el año Nueve-Cuchillo. Habíamos estado fuera por ciento cuarenta y dos días, más de siete meses nuestros, y habíamos vivido muchas aventuras y conocido muchos pueblos y lugares maravillosos, pero era muy agradable regresar al centro de la majestad mexica, El Corazón del Único Mundo.

✠

Estaba prohibido a todo *pochtécatl* que entrara, en plena luz del día, dentro de la ciudad con toda su caravana, o que desfilara ostentosamente a su entrada, sin importar el éxito que hubiera obtenido y cuanta utilidad pudiera traer la expedición. Aun sin que hubiera existido esa ley de moderación, cada uno de los *pochtécatl* se daba cuenta de que debía regresar a casa con prudencia y discreción. No todas las personas en Tenochtitlan se daban cuenta de cómo dependía de los intrépidos mercaderes viajeros toda la prosperidad mexica, pues mucha gente se resentía de la legítima utilidad que los mercaderes percibían por la prosperidad que brindaban. La clase noble reinante en particular, ya que ellos obtenían su riqueza del tributo pagado por las naciones vencidas e insistían en que el comercio pacífico derogaba su porción devengada del botín de guerra, y estaban en contra del «simple comercio».

Así es que cada uno de los *pochtécatl* que regresaban, entraba a la ciudad con vestidos sencillos, escondidos bajo una capa de polvo, y dejaba que los portadores de su tesoro lo siguieran en uno o dos hombres. Cuando un mercader construía su casa debía ser muy modesta, aunque en sus armarios, arcones y bajo los pisos, fuera acumulando gradualmente una riqueza que le permitiría construir un palacio que rivalizaría con el del Uey-Tlatoani. Mis socios y yo no tuvimos ningún problema al entrar en Tenochtitlan; no llevábamos ninguna caravana de *tamémime* y nuestra carga consistía sólo en unos cuantos bultos polvorientos; nuestras ropas estaban manchadas y gastadas y ninguno de nosotros fue a su propia casa, sino que llegamos a una posada común para viajeros.

A la mañana siguiente, después de baños consecutivos de agua y vapor, me puse mi mejor ropa y me presenté en el palacio del Venerado Orador Auítzotl. Como no era un desconocido para el mayordomo de palacio, no tuve que esperar mucho tiempo para ser recibido en audiencia. Besé la tierra frente Auítzotl aunque me abstuve de utilizar mi cristal para verlo claramente, ya que no estaba seguro de lo que el Señor pudiera objetar al ser visto así. De todas maneras, conociéndolo como lo conocía, puedo asegurar que él lucía tan mal encarado como siempre y tan fiero como la piel de oso que adornaba su trono.

«Estamos muy complacidos y también muy sorprendidos de verte regresar intacto, *pochtécatl* Mixtli —dijo con aspereza—. ¿Entonces, tu expedición fue un éxito?»

«Creo que dejará buena utilidad, Venerado Orador —repliqué—. Cuando los viejos *pochteca* hayan evaluado la mercancía, usted podrá juzgar por la parte que le corresponderá a su tesoro. Mientras tanto, mi señor, espero que usted encuentre esta crónica interesante.»

A lo cual entregué a uno de sus asistentes los libros maltratados por el viaje que tan fielmente había escrito. Contenían muchas de las cosas que les he estado narrando, reverendos frailes, con la excepción de haber omitido muchas insignificancias, como mis encuentros con mujeres, aunque, considerablemente incluía más descripciones del terreno, de las comunidades y sus gentes, aparte de muchos mapas que había dibujado.

Auítzotl me dio las gracias y me dijo: «Nosotros y nuestro Consejo de Voceros, los examinaremos atentamente.»

Yo le contesté: «En caso de que alguno de sus consejeros sea muy viejo o falto de vista, Señor Orador, encontrará esto muy útil —y le alargué uno de los cristales para encender lumbre—. Traje un buen número para vender, pero el más grande y brillante lo traje como un regalo para el Uey-Tlatoani.»

Él no se sintió muy impresionado hasta que le pedí permiso para acercarme y demostrarle cómo podía utilizarlo, tanto para el escrutinio en la lectura de palabras-pintadas como para cualquier otra cosa. Después lo guié hacia una ventana abierta y utilizando un pedazo de papel de corteza le enseñé cómo podía utilizarlo también para encender un fuego. Entonces quedó encantado y me dio las gracias efusivamente.

Mucho tiempo después, me dijeron que Auítzotl siempre llevaba su piedra de hacer lumbre a todas las campañas guerreras en las que tomaba parte, pero que se divertía más en darle un uso menos práctico en tiempos de paz. Ese Venerado Orador ha sido recordado hasta nuestros días por su carácter irascible y sus caprichos crueles; su nombre ha venido a ser parte de nuestro lenguaje, pues cualquier persona que cause problemas, ahora es llamada *auítzotl*. Pero al parecer, el tirano tenía también un rasgo infantil para hacer travesuras. En conversación con cualquiera de sus más dignos sabios, se las arreglaba para llevarlo hacia una ventana y sin que el sujeto se diera cuenta, sostenía su cristal de tal manera que los rayos del sol pasaran a través sobre la espalda o la rodilla desnuda del hombre quemándolo y luego se moría de risa al ver al viejo sabio saltando como un conejo joven.

Del palacio regresé a la posada para recoger a Cózcatl y Glotón de Sangre, ambos también limpios y bien vestidos, y por nuestros dos fardos de mercancías. Los llevamos a la Casa de los Pochteca e inmediatamente fuimos recibidos por los tres viejos que nos habían ayudado en nuestra partida. Mientras nos servían tazas de *chocólatl* con esencia de magnolia, Cózcatl abrió el más grande de nuestros bultos para que su contenido fuera examinado.

«¡*Ayyo!* —exclamó uno de los viejos—. Ha traído solamente en plumas una respetable fortuna. Lo que debe hacer es conseguir a los nobles más ricos y ofrecérselas en subasta, por polvo de oro. Cuando se alcance el precio más alto, *sólo hasta entonces*, deje que el Venerado Orador sepa acerca de la existencia de esta mercancía. Simplemente para mantener su propia supremacía, él pagará muy por encima del precio más alto de postura.»

«Como ustedes lo aconsejen, mis señores», dije estando de acuerdo y luego hice otra señal a Cózcatl para que abriera el bulto más pequeño.

«¡*Ayya!* —dijo otro de los viejos—. Me temo que en esto usted no ha estado muy atinado. —Y movía tristemente entre sus dedos, dos o tres cristales—. Están muy bien pulidos y cortados, pero me apena decirle que no son joyas. Son simples cuarzos, cuyo valor intrínseco es mucho menor al del jade y no tiene ninguna relación religiosa como la que le da tan insólito valor a éste.»

Cózcatl no pudo evitar una risita, ni tampoco Glotón de Sangre una sonrisa de conocimiento. Yo también sonreí cuando dije: «Sin embargo, observen, mis señores», y les mostré las dos propiedades de los cristales e inmediatamente se excitaron.

«¡Increíble! —dijo uno de los viejos—. ¡Usted ha traído algo completamente nuevo a Tenochtitlan!»

«¿Dónde los encontró? —dijo otro—. No, no piense ni siquiera en contestarme. Discúlpeme por preguntarle eso. Un tesoro único que sólo puede ser del que lo descubrió.»

El tercero dijo: Ofreceremos los más grandes a los nobles más altos y...»

Le interrumpí haciéndole notar que todos los cristales, chicos y grandes tenían la misma propiedad por igual, de agrandar los objetos y de encender fuegos, pero él me hizo callar con impaciencia.

«No importa eso. Cada *pili* querrá un cristal de acuerdo a su alto rango y a su sentido de propia importancia. Ahora bien, un ornamento tallado artísticamente en jade vale dos veces su peso, en polvo de oro. Por éstos, sugiero que empecemos a ofrecerlos a ocho veces el valor de su peso. Con los *pípiltin* ofreciendo cada vez más, usted obtendrá mucho más.»

Jadeé perplejo: «Pero mis señores, ¡eso nos haría ganar

mucho más de mi peso en oro! Aun después de haber contribuido con la parte correspondiente a el Mujer Serpiente, a esta honorable sociedad y aun dividido en tres partes... ¡nos colocaría entre los tres hombres más ricos de Tenochtitlan!»

«¿Y por qué pone usted algún reparo en eso?»

Yo tartamudeé: «Es que... no me parece muy correcto... tener una ganancia tan inmensa en nuestra primera aventura... y viniendo de un cuarzo común como ustedes dicen... y sobre todo de un producto que puedo suplir en grandes cantidades. Porque, yo podría proveer de cristales para encender a cada una de las más humildes amas de casa en todos los dominios de la Triple Alianza.»

Uno de los viejos dijo cortante: «Quizás usted pueda, pero tendrá el buen sentido de no hacerlo. Usted nos ha dicho que el Venerado Orador ahora posee una de estas piedras mágicas. Sólo los dioses saben cuántos *pípiltin* existen en estas tierras. Sin embargo y de momento, solamente ciento veintiséis de ellos pueden poseer un cristal similar. Mira, muchacho, ¡ellos pagarán cualquier precio por muy extravagante que sea, aunque estas cosas estuvieran hechas de cieno compacto! Después, naturalmente, tú puedes ir a conseguir más, para ser vendidos a otros nobles, pero nunca más de esta cantidad a un mismo tiempo...»

Cózcatl estaba radiante de felicidad y se veía a Glotón de Sangre más que divertido. Yo me encogí de hombros y dije: «Por supuesto que no voy a objetar nada por ganar una riqueza substancial.»

«Oh, ustedes tres gastarán inmediatamente parte de ella —dijo uno de los viejos—. Usted ha mencionado las partes correspondientes al tesoro de Tenochtitlan y de nuestro dios Yacatecutli, pero quizás no sepan acerca de nuestra tradición; cada *pochtécatl* que regresa a casa, si lo hace con una gran utilidad, da un banquete a todos los demás *pochteca* que están en la ciudad, en esos momentos.»

Yo miré a mis socios y ellos asintieron sin vacilación, así es que dije: «Para nosotros será un placer, mis señores. Pero, somos nuevos en esto...»

«Nos sentiremos muy contentos de poderlos ayudar —dijo el mismo anciano—. Hagamos el banquete pasado mañana en la noche. Pondremos a su disposición todas las facilidades que para esa ocasión les brinda el edificio. También nosotros nos encargaremos de todo lo relativo al banquete: comida, bebida, músicos, danzantes, mujeres y, por supuesto, invitaremos a todos los *pochteca* calificados y accesibles, mientras que ustedes pueden invitar a aquellas personas que deseen. Ahora —y movió su cabeza como un gallo—, el banquete puede ser modesto o extravagante de acuerdo a sus gustos y generosidad.»

Otra vez consulté silenciosamente con mis socios y luego dije expansivamente: «Es el primero. Tiene que estar a la altura de nuestro éxito. Si fueran ustedes tan amables, me gustaría pedirles que cada plato, cada bebida, cada invitación sean de lo más fino posible y sin mirar el costo. Hagamos que este banquete sea recordado.»

Yo por lo menos, lo recuerdo vívidamente.

Anfitriones e invitados vestíamos de lo mejor. Como ya formábamos parte de los prósperos y emplumados *pochteca*, a Cózcatl, a Glotón de Sangre y a mí se nos estaba permitido usar cierta cantidad de ornamentos de oro y joyas, para señalar nuestra nueva posición en la vida. Aunque nosotros solamente utilizamos unas pocas chucherías modestas. Yo sólo llevaba el broche de oro y piedra-sangre que la Señora de Tolan me había dado hacía ya mucho tiempo y una pequeña esmeralda en la aleta derecha de mi nariz, pero mi manto era del más fino algodón bordado; mis sandalias, de lo más fino y con lazos hasta la rodilla; mi pelo, que me lo había dejado crecer durante el transcurso de mi viaje, estaba recogido en la nuca con un anillo de piel roja trenzada.

En los patios del edificio se asaban tres venados sostenidos y volteados por varas, sobre una inmensa zona de brasas y toda la comida era incomparable en calidad y en cantidad. Los músicos tocaban, pero no tan fuerte como para molestar la conversación. Había muchas bellas mujeres circulando entre la multitud y muy seguido alguna de ellas ofrecía una graciosa danza acompañada por la música. Tres de los esclavos del establecimiento fueron puestos a nuestro servicio y cuando no estaban ocupados en eso, se colocaban detrás de nosotros tres, dándonos aire con grandes abanicos de plumas. Nos presentaron a toda una procesión de mercaderes y escuchamos sus relatos sobre sus más notables excursiones y adquisiciones. Glotón de Sangre había invitado a cuatro o cinco de sus compañeros, viejos guerreros, y muy pronto todos ellos estuvieron alegremente borrachos. Como Cózcatl y yo no conocíamos a nadie en Tenochtitlan, no tuvimos a quien invitar, pero de pronto apareció un huésped inesperado, que hubiera podido ser un invitado mío.

Una vez a mi lado dijo: «Topo, tú nunca dejas de sorprenderme.» Cuando me volví para ver quién era, me encontré con el viejo color cacao que varias veces había aparecido en otros momentos significativos de mi vida. En esa ocasión estaba menos sucio y mejor vestido, por lo menos llevaba manto encima de su taparrabo.

Le dije sonriendo: «No más topo», y levanté mi topacio para verlo con más claridad. Al hacer eso, de alguna forma tuve la sensación de encontrar algo muy familiar en él, pero a la vez diferente, como si me recordara a alguien más.

Él sonrió casi con maldad, diciendo: «Siempre te encuentro de diferentes maneras: primero como una insignificancia, luego como un estudiante, un escribano, un cortesano, un villano perdonado, un héroe guerrero... y ahora, un próspero mercader, mirando malignamente a través de un ojo dorado.»

Yo le dije: «Usted mismo, venerable, me sugirió que viajara. Bien venido a la fiesta, diviértase.»

«*Ayya*, yo no puedo, si tú no puedes.»

Levanté las cejas. «¿Y por qué no habría de gozar de mi banquete, para celebrar el éxito de mi empresa?»

«¿De tu empresa? —preguntó mofándose—. ¿Todas tus hazañas pasadas, han sido por tu propia voluntad? ¿Sin ayuda? ¿Tú solo?»

«Oh, no —dije, con la esperanza de que mi negación desviara los golpes de las oscuras implicaciones, que se desprendían de sus preguntas—. Usted será presentado a mis socios, que tomaron parte en esta empresa.»

«En esta empresa. ¿Y hubiera sido posible ésta sin el regalo inesperado de mercancías y capital que invertiste?»

«No —dije otra vez—. Y espero darle las más cumplidas gracias a la persona que me lo donó y compartir con...»

«Es muy tarde —me interrumpió—. Ella ha muerto.»

«¿Ella?», dije haciendo eco en el vacío, porque naturalmente yo estaba pensando en mi formal benefactor, Nezahualpili de Texcoco.

«Tu difunta hermana —dijo—. El regalo misterioso fue la herencia de Tzitzitlini.»

Moví la cabeza negando. «Mi hermana está muerta, viejo, como usted acaba de decir, pero ciertamente que ella nunca me dejó esa fortuna.»

Siguió hablando como distraídamente: «El Señor Garza Roja de Xaltocan también murió durante tu viaje hacia el sur. Naturalmente que él llamó a su cabecera al sacerdote de la diosa Tlazoltéotl y como la confesión que hizo fue tan sensacional, difícilmente se pudo mantener en secreto. Sin duda muchos de tus invitados distinguidos tienen conocimiento de esa historia, aunque por supuesto, son lo suficientemente corteses como para no hablarte de ello.»

«¿Qué historia? ¿Qué confesión?»

«El encubrimiento de Garza Roja a la última atrocidad que su hijo Pactli cometió con tu hermana.»

«Nunca fue lo suficientemente encubierta para mí —dije con un gruñido—. Y todo el mundo sabe cómo me vengué de él.»

«Excepto que Pactli no mató a Tzitzitlini.»

De pronto sentí que todo me daba vueltas y sólo pude jadear.

«El Señor Alegría la torturó y la mutiló a fuego y navaja con una insana habilidad, pero no fue su *tonali* que muriera en el tormento. Luego, con el permiso tácito de su padre y con, por lo menos, la muda aquiescencia de los padres de la muchacha, la echó fuera de la isla. Eso fue lo que Garza Roja confesó a La Que Come Suciedad, y cuando el sacerdote hizo esto público causó un rugir en todo Xaltocan. Me aflige decirte también, que el cuerpo de tu padre fue hallado al pie de la cantera; al parecer saltó desde la orilla. Tu madre cobardemente huyó. Nadie sabe a donde, lo que es una fortuna para ella. —Él empezó a irse diciendo con indiferencia—: Creo que son todas las nuevas que han ocurrido desde que te fuiste. Bien, ¿podemos ahora divertirnos...?»

«¡Espera! —dije fieramente, cogiéndolo del nudo que sostenía su manto en el hombro—. ¡Tú, fragmento con patas de las tinieblas de Mictlan! ¡Cuéntame el resto! ¿Qué fue de Tzitzitlini? ¿Qué quieres decir con eso de que el regalo me lo envió ella?»

«Ella te dejó todo el dinero que recibió y Auítzotl le pagó un buen precio cuando ella se vendió a sí misma para su zoológico, aquí en Tenochtitlan. Ella no pudo o no quiso decir de dónde venía o quién era, sólo fue popularmente conocida por la mujer-tapir.»

Si no hubiera sido porque lo estaba deteniendo de su hombro, me hubiera caído. Por un momento, todo y todos desaparecieron alrededor de mí, mientras veía a través del largo túnel de mi memoria. Yo contemplaba otra vez a Tzitzitlini, a la que yo había adorado; ella, la del rostro amado, la del cuerpo bello y movimiento flexible. Luego vi aquel objeto repugnante e inmóvil del zoológico, en la parte de los monstruos, me vi vomitando de horror y vi, otra vez, aquella lágrima de pena que resbaló de su único ojo.

Mi voz sonó hueca en mis oídos, como si de verdad estuviera parado en un túnel largo, cuando le dije acusándolo: «*Tú lo sabías*. Viejo vil, tú lo sabías antes de que Garza Roja confesara. Y tú hiciste que yo me parara enfrente de ella y mencionaste que había estado acostado con una mujer... y me preguntaste si me hubiera gustado...» Me estremecí, y estuve a punto de vomitar otra vez nada más de acordarme.

«Era bueno que por lo menos la vieras por última vez —dijo él con un suspiro—. Ella murió un poco después. Piadosamente en mi opinión, aunque Auítzotl quizás se haya enojado mucho, habiendo pagado tan pródigamente...»

Volví en mí y me di cuenta de que lo estaba sacudiendo con violencia y diciendo con demencia: «Nunca hubiera comido la carne de tapir en la selva, de haberlo sabido. Pero tú lo has sabido todo el tiempo. *¿Cómo lo sabías?*»

Él no contestó, sólo dijo suavemente: «Se creía que la mujer-tapir no podía mover esa masa de carne chamuscada, pero de alguna manera se volvió cara abajo, y su hocico de tapir quedó obstruido hasta que murió sofocada.»

«¡Bien, pues ahora es tu turno de morir, maldito adivino de los demonios! —No creo que para entonces estuviera borracho, sino más bien fuera de mí por la pena, la rabia y repulsión—. ¡Regresarás a Mictlan adonde perteneces!» Caminé violentamente entre la multitud de huéspedes y sólo con ofuscación, le oí decir detrás de mí:

«Los guardianes del zoológico todavía insisten en que la mujer-tapir no hubiera podido morir sin la ayuda de alguien. Era lo suficiente joven como para haber vivido en esa jaula por muchos años, muchos años más.»

Encontré a Glotón de Sangre y con rudeza lo interrumpí en la conversación que sostenía con uno de sus amigos. «Necesito un arma y no tengo tiempo de ir por una. ¿Llevas tu daga?»

Buscó bajo su manto en la banda de atrás de su taparrabo y dijo con un hipo: «¿Es que tú vas a cortar la carne?»

«No —le dije—. Quiero matar a alguien.»

«¿Tan pronto? —sacó su corta daga de obsidiana y pestañeó para poder verme mejor—. ¿Vas a matar a alguien que yo conozca?»

«No —le dije—. Sólo a un sórdido hombrecillo, pardusco y tan arrugado como una semilla de cacao. Poca pérdida para cualquiera. —Alargué la mano—. La daga, por favor.»

«¡Poca pérdida! —exclamó Glotón de Sangre sin soltar el cuchillo—. ¿Tú quieres asesinar al Uey-Tlatoani de Texcoco? ¡Mixtli debes de estar tan proverbialmente borracho como los cuatrocientos conejos!»

«Seguro que alguien lo está —grité—. ¡Deja ya de parlotear y dame el cuchillo!»

«Nunca. Vi al hombre pardusco hablando contigo y reconocí su disfraz peculiar —Glotón de Sangre se guardó la daga otra vez—. Él nos honra con su presencia aunque escoja venir disfrazado. Cualquiera que sea tu imaginario disgusto para con él, no dejaré que tú...»

«¿Disfrazado? —le interrumpí—. ¿Disfraz?» Glotón de Sangre había hablado con la suficiente frialdad como para calmarme un poco.

Uno de los guerreros, amigo de él, me dijo: «Quizás sólo nosotros, que hemos combatido con frecuencia con él, nos damos cuenta de ello. Nezahualpili le gusta ir así a veces, de esa manera puede observar a los demás desde su propio nivel y no desde las gradas del trono. Aquellos de nosotros que lo hemos conocido lo suficiente como para reconocerlo, no lo hacemos notar.»

«Todos estáis lamentablemente embrutecidos —dije—. Yo también conozco a Nezahualpili y sé que él tiene todos sus dientes.»

«Un pedacito de *óxitl* puede ennegrecer dos o tres de ellos —dijo Glotón de Sangre hipando—. Líneas hechas con *óxitl* pueden parecer arrugas en una cara oscurecida con aceite de nuez. Y él tiene talento para que su cuerpo parezca tosco y ajado, y sus manos nudosas como las de un hombre muy viejo...»

«Pero en realidad él no necesita de marcas y contorsiones —dijo el otro—. Simplemente puede empolvarse todo el cuerpo con la tierra del camino y parecer totalmente un extranjero. —El guerrero hipó en su turno y sugirió—: Si usted quiere matar al Venerado Orador esta noche, joven anfitrión, vaya y busque a Auítzotl y luego oblíguenos a todos nosotros también.»

Me fui de allí sintiéndome tonto y confuso, pero por encima de todos esos sentimintos estaba la angustia, la rabia y... bien eran muchos y tumultuosos...

Volví otra vez a buscar al hombre que era Nezahualpili... o un adivino o un dios del mal... ya no con la intención de matarlo sino para arrancarle las respuestas a muchas más preguntas. No lo encontré. Se había ido, como también se fue mi apetito por el banquete, por la compañía y por el regocijo. Me deslicé afuera de la Casa de los Pochteca, regresé a la hostería y empecé a recoger las cosas más esenciales para viajar en una bolsa pequeña. La pequeña figurita de Tzitzi, la diosa del amor Xochiquétzal, llegó a mis manos, pero separé éstas rápidamente como si hubiera tocado fuego. No la puse adentro de mi bolsa.

«Vi que te fuiste y te seguí —dijo el joven Cózcatl desde la puerta del cuarto—. ¿Qué pasó? ¿Adónde vas?»

Dije: «No tengo corazón para contarte todo lo que ha pasado, pero parece que es del dominio público. Pronto sabrás todo. Es por eso que me iré por un tiempo.»

«¿Adónde, Mixtli?»

«No lo sé. Solo... por ahí vagando...»

«¿Puedo ir contigo?»

«No.»

La expresión ansiosa de su rostro decayó, así es que le dije: «Creo que será mejor que esté solo por un tiempo, para pensar qué voy a hacer del resto de mi vida. Y no te estoy dejando como un indefenso esclavo sin amo, como una vez temiste. Tú eres tu propio amo y rico a la vez. Tendrás tu parte en nuestra fortuna, tan pronto como los ancianos hagan el trueque. Te encargo que guardes segura la mía y estas otras pertenencias hasta que regrese.»

«Por supuesto, Mixtli.»

«Glotón de Sangre será otra vez llamado a cuartel. Quizás tú y él podáis comprar una casa... o cada uno una casa. Puedes terminar tus estudios o aprender algún arte o poner un negocio. Y yo regresaré otra vez, algún día. Si tú y nuestro viejo protector todavía tienen espíritu para viajar, podemos hacer otros viajes juntos.»

«Sí, alguna vez —dijo él tristemente, luego enderezó sus hombros—. Bien, ¿te puedo ayudar en algo, en esta abrupta ida tuya?»

«Sí, sí puedes. En mi bolsa para colgar al hombro y en la bolsa cosida dentro de mi *máxtlatl* llevaré una cantidad pequeña de dinero para mis gastos, pero también quiero llevar oro por si acaso encuentro alguna mercancía excepcional, como cuando encontré el cristal para encender lumbre, y quisiera llevar el polvo de oro escondido en donde nigún bandido pueda fácilmente encontrarlo.»

Cózcatl pensó por un momento y después dijo: «Algunos viajeros meten el oro en cáscaras de nuez y luego las esconden en el recto.»

«Es un truco que todos los ladrones conocen muy bien. No, mi pelo ha crecido bastante largo y creo que lo puedo utilizar para eso. Mira, he sacado todo el oro en polvo de sus cañitas y lo he puesto en esta tela. Haz un bultito apretado con él, Cózcatl, e inventaremos alguna manera segura de acomodarlo en la parte de atrás de mi cuello, como si fuera una cataplasma, escondida bajo el pelo.»

Mientras yo terminaba de preparar mi bolsa, él dobló la tela meticulosamente una y otra vez. Hizo un rollo flexible casi del tamaño de una de sus manitas, pero era tan pesado que lo tuvo que levantar con ambas manos. Me senté, arqueé la cabeza y él me lo acomodó a través de la nuca.

«Ahora... para que se sostenga ahí... —murmuré—. Déjame ver...»

Lo acomodó en el lugar con dos fuertes cordeles atados a cada lado de sus puntas, corriendo detrás de mis orejas y cruzando sobre mi cabeza. Eso quedaba mucho más seguro y escondido si me ponía una tela doblada a través de mi frente, como las que utilizábamos para la carga y amarrándola atrás. Muchos viajeros llevaban eso para mantener su pelo y el sudor fuera de sus ojos.

«Es bastante invisible, Mixtli, a menos de que sople el viento, pero entonces podrías hacer una capucha con tu manto.»

«Sí, gracias, Cózcatl. Y —lo dije rápidamente no queriendo prolongar la despedida— hasta pronto.»

No tenía miedo de La Llorona, ni de ningún otro de los espíritus malévolos que se suponía que cazaban en la oscuridad a los incautos que se aventuraban por las calles, como yo. En verdad, que resoplé desdeñosamente cuando pensé en Viento de la Noche... y en el extranjero cubierto de polvo con el que me había encontrado frecuentemente, en otras noches. Caminé vigorosamente fuera de la ciudad y llegué pronto al camino sur que conduce a Coyohuacan. A la mitad del camino, en el fuerte de Acachinánco, los centinelas se mostraron más que sorprendidos de ver a alguien caminando durante la noche. Pero como venía vestido de fiesta, no me detuvieron con la sospecha de que fuera un ladrón fugitivo, sino que sólo me hicieron una o dos preguntas para asegurarse de que no iba borracho y de que estaba perfectamente consciente de lo que estaba haciendo y me dejaron proseguir.

Un poco más allá, giré a mi izquierda para tomar el camino de Mexicaltzinco, pasé por ese pueblo dormido y continué hacia el este caminando toda la noche. Cuando llegó la aurora y otros viajeros tempraneros en el camino me empezaron a saludar con precaución mientras me miraban extrañados, me vine a dar cuenta de que presentaba un espectáculo poco común: un hombre vestido casi como un noble, con sandalias amarradas hasta las rodillas, con un broche enjoyado en el manto y una esmeralda de adorno en su nariz, pero con un bulto de mercader, un morral al hombro y una banda en la frente. Me quité las joyas y las escondí dentro de mi bolsa, volteé mi manto hacia dentro para esconder el bordado. El bultito que llevaba en la cabeza, al principio fue muy molesto, pero al fin llegué a acostumbrarme a usarlo y sólo me lo quitaba cuando dormía, o tomaba un baño de agua o vapor, en privado.

Aquella mañana me encaminé de prisa hacia el este, mientras el sol se levantaba y calentaba rápidamente, no sintiendo ninguna fatiga ni necesidad de dormir; mi mente era todavía un tumulto de pensamientos y recuerdos. (Eso es lo peor de sentir pena: el modo en que invita a acumular recuerdos de días felices, en comparación acerca de la presente miseria de uno.) Durante la mayor parte de ese día seguí otra vez por el camino que un día marché, a lo largo de la costa sur del Lago de Texcoco, con el ejército victorioso que regresaba de la guerra con Texcala. Sin embargo, después de un rato ese camino divergió del mío y dejé la orilla del lago para adentrarme en un país en donde nunca había estado antes.

✠

Vagué por más de un año y medio a través de muchas tierras nuevas para mí, antes de alcanzar algo que pareciera destino. Durante la mayor parte de ese tiempo, estuve tan fuera de mi mente que en estos momento no puedo contarles, mis señores escribanos, todas las cosas que vi y que hice. Yo creo que si no hubiera sido por eso, todavía recordaría muchas palabras que aprendí en los lenguajes de esos lejanos lugares; incluso se me hace difícil traer a mi memoria la ruta general que seguí. Sin embargo, todavía recuerdo unos cuantos paisajes y sucesos, tantos como los pocos volcanes de esas tierras del sur, yacen todavía sobre sus suelos.

Entré a grandes zancadas y con audacia en Quautexcalan, La Tierra de los Peñascos del Águila, la nación en la que una vez había entrado con el ejército invasor. No hay duda, de que si me hubiera anunciado como mexícatl, nunca más hubiera salido de ella. Y estoy muy contento de no haber muerto en Texcala, porque la gente de allí tiene una idea religiosa tan simple como ridícula. Ellos creen que cuando un noble muere, vivirá otra vida gozosa en el mundo del más allá; cuando cualquier plebeyo muere, vivirá otra vez una vida miserable. Los nobles muertos, hombres y mujeres, simplemente cambian sus cuerpos mundanos y regresan como nubes flotantes o pájaros de radiantes plumajes o joyas de un valor fabuloso. Los plebeyos que mueren regresan como sucios escarabajos, o comadrejas furtivas o como mofetas apestosas.

De todas maneras, no morí en Texcala, ni siquiera fui reconocido como uno de los odiados mexica. Aunque los texcalteca siempre han sido nuestros enemigos, físicamente no son diferentes de nosotros los mexica; ellos hablan el mismo lenguaje y me fue muy fácil imitar su acento para pasar como uno de ellos. La única cosa que me hizo un poco conspicuo en su tierra fue que yo era un hombre joven y saludable, lleno de vida y no mutilado. La batalla en la cual yo había tomado parte, había diezmado la población masculina, entre las edades de la pubertad y la senectud. Sin embargo, todavía quedaba una nueva generación de jóvenes desarrollándose. Ellos crecieron aprendiendo un odio todavía más profundo hacia los mexica, jurando vengarse de nosotros y cuando los españoles llegaron ellos ya eran adultos y ustedes saben en qué forma se vengaron.

Sin embargo, en aquel tiempo de vagabundeo ocioso a través de Quautexcalan, todo eso estaba en el futuro. El haber sido uno de los pocos adultos y un hombre apropiado, no me causó ningún problema, al contrario, fui muy bienvenido por las numerosas y seductoras viudas texcalteca, cuyas camas hacía mucho tiempo que estaban frías.

De allí, me dirigí hacia el sur, a la ciudad de Chololan, capital de los tya nuü y, de hecho, la única concentración grande que

357

quedaba de esos Hombres de la Tierra. Era evidente que los mixteca, como todos los llamaban a excepción de ellos mismos, habían creado y mantenido una vez una cultura refinada y envidiable. Por ejemplo, en Chololan yo vi unos edificios de gran antigüedad, primorosamente adornados con mosaicos que parecían tejidos petrificados y sólo podían haber sido los modelos originales de los templos construidos supuestamente por los tzapoteca, en el Hogar Santo de Lyobaan, de la Gente Nube.

También hay una montaña en Chololan, que en aquellos días tenía en su cumbre un magnífico templo dedicado a Quetzalcóatl, un templo de lo más artísticamente embellecido con tallas coloreadas de la Serpiente Emplumada. Sus españoles lo arrasaron, aunque, aparentemente, tomaron prestado algo de la santidad de ese lugar, pues he oído decir que han construido una iglesia Cristiana en su lugar. Déjenme decirles: esa montaña no es tal; es una pirámide de ladrillos cocidos al sol, hecha por los hombres y tiene muchos más ladrillos que los pelos que tiene un hato de venados, cubiertos de cieno y hierbas desde tiempos antes de los tiempos. Nosotros creemos que es la pirámide más antigua de todas estas tierras; sabemos que ha sido la más gigantesca que se ha construido. Puede ser que ahora se vea como cualquier otra montaña cubierta de árboles y de arbustos y puede ser que sirva para exaltar y elevar su nueva iglesia, pero no dejo de pensar que su Señor Dios debe de sentirse muy incómodo por haber usurpado esas alturas que fueron levantadas para el servicio de Quetzalcóatl y no para otro.

La ciudad de Chololan estaba gobernada no por un hombre sino por dos, con igual poder. Ellos eran llamados por Tlaquíach, el Señor De Lo Que Está Encima, y Tlalchíac, el Señor De Lo Que Está Abajo, significando que reinaban, por separado, sobre las cosas espirituales y materiales respectivamente. Me fue dicho que los dos hombres tenían diferencias con frecuencia y que incluso llegaron a los golpes, pero en aquel entonces ellos estaban, por lo menos temporalmente, unidos en una enemistad contra Texcala, la nación por la que acababa de pasar. Ya olvidé cuál era la pendencia, pero, al poco tiempo de mi llegada a Chololan, había arribado también una comisión de cuatro nobles texcalteca, mandados por su Venerado Orador, Xicotenca, para discutir y resolver la disputa.

Los Señores Tlaquíach y Tlalchíac rehusaron, incluso, dar audiencia a los enviados; en lugar de eso, ordenaron a los guardias de su palacio que los cogieran y los mutilaran, haciéndolos regresar a su tierra a punta de espada. Los cuatro nobles tenían la piel de su caras completamente desollada y antes de que regresaran a Texcala bamboleantes y gimiendo, sus cabezas parecían hechas de carne cruda con bolas de ojos y sus rostros parecían colgajos pendiendo sobre sus pechos. Creo que todas las moscas de Chololan los siguieron por el camino del norte, fuera de la ciudad. Puesto que yo sólo podía ver como resultado de ese ultraje una guerra, y como que no quería que se me llamara a filas para pelear, también salí apresuradamente de Chololan, y me dirigí hacia el este.

Después de haber cruzado otra frontera invisible y ya estando en la nación Totonaca, me detuve un día y una noche en una aldea y desde la ventana de la posada podía ver al poderoso volcán llamado Citlaltépetl, Estrella de la Montaña. Estaba muy satisfecho de verlo desde esa respetable distancia, usando mi cristal de topacio. Podía ver su picacho helado y humedecido por las nubes, desde la aldea por siempre caliente, verde y llena de flores.

El Citlaltépetl es la montaña más alta de todo el mundo conocido, tan alta que la nieve cubre su cono enteramente más arriba de su tercera parte, excepto cuando su cráter arroja grumos mezclados de lava y ceniza y hace que la montaña se vea roja en su cumbre en lugar de blanca. Me han dicho que éste fue el primer punto visible que avistaron sus barcos desde alta mar. En el día, sus vigías veían la nieve de su cono y por la noche el resplandor de su cráter, mucho antes de que pudieran vislumbrar cualquier otra cosa de la Nueva España. El Citlaltépetl es tan viejo como el mundo; sin embargo, hasta ahora ningún hombre, nativo o español, ha podido escalarlo hasta su cumbre. Y si alguno lo hizo, es muy probable que las estrellas al pasar le hayan arañado el trasero.

Luego llegué a otro límite de las tierras Totonaca, la playa del océano del este; a una bahía encantadora llamada Chachihuahuecan, que significa El Lugar En Donde Abundan Cosas Bellas. Si menciono esto es solamente porque constituye una pequeña coincidencia, si bien yo no lo sabía entonces. En otra primavera, otros hombres pusieron sus pies en ella, reclamando para España esa tierra, plantando en sus arenas una cruz de madera y una bandera de colores sangre y oro y llamando a ese lugar por el de la Vera Cruz.

Las playas de ese océano eran mucho más bonitas y hospitalarias que las costas a lo largo del Xoconochco. Las bahías no eran de tierra negra volcánica, sino de fina arena blanca y amarilla y algunas veces tenían el color rojizo del coral. El océano no era turbulento y en color verde sucio, sino de un cristalino turquesa, gentil y murmurante. Rompía sobre las arenas con una espuma blanca y susurrante y en muchos lugares se inclinaba tanto playa adentro y el agua estaba tan baja, que podía vadear casi fuera de la vista de la tierra, antes de que el agua me llegara a la cintura. Al principio, la costa del océano me guió casi directamente hacia el sur, pero después de varias largas-carreras, esa costa se curvaba en un gran arco. Así es que casi imperceptiblemente me encontré viajando hacia el sureste, luego hacia el este y finalmente hacia noreste. Como ya dije antes, lo que nosotros en Tenochtitlan llamábamos el océano del este, es más apropiadamente el océano del norte.

Por supuesto que esas playas no son todas sólo arenas festoneadas por palmeras, pues las hubiera encontrado monótonas si así fueran. A lo largo de mi camino, muchas veces me encontré con ríos desembocando en el mar y necesité acampar a la espera de algún pescador o barquero que me cruzara en su canoa hueca, de tronco de árbol. En otros lugares, me encontré con que las arenas secas se humedecían bajo mis sandalias y luego las mojaba y de pronto estaba dentro de aguas cenagosas; los insectos infestaban esos pantanos, mientras desaparecían las graciosas palmeras para dar paso a los árboles de mangle con raíces nudosas, que sobresalían como las viejas piernas de un hombre. Para poder salir de esos pantanos, a veces acampaba y esperaba que alguna barca de pescador pasara para que me llevara bordeando su orilla. Sin embargo, otras veces rodeaba tierra adentro hasta que los pantanos disminuían a flor de tierra y se disipaban en tierra seca, por la cual podía transitar.

Recuerdo que la primera vez que lo hice me llevé un buen susto. La noche me cogió en la húmeda orilla de una de esos pantanos y pasé un rato amargo tratando de encender un fuego. De hecho, éste fue tan pequeño y daba tan poca luz, que cuando levanté los ojos pude ver, a través del heno que colgaba más allá, en los mangles, un fuego mucho más brillante que el mío, pero que ardía con una flama azul que no era natural.

«¡La Xtabai!», pensé inmediatamente, habiendo oído historias del fantasma de una mujer que camina por esas regiones, envuelta en unas vestiduras que emiten una luz atemorizante. De acuerdo con esas historias, cualquier hombre que se aproxime a ella se dará cuenta de que su vestido es solamente una caperuza para esconder la cabeza, y que el resto de su cuerpo está desnudo y es seductoramente bello. Él, inevitablemente, se verá tentado a acercarse más, pero ella seguirá tratando de esquivarlo y de repente se encontrará caminando sobre arenas movedizas, de las que por desgracia no podrá salir. Mientras él es tragado por ellas y antes de que su cabeza desaparezca, la Xtabai por fin dejará caer su capucha para revelar que su rostro es sólo una calavera sonriendo perversamente.

Llevando mi cuchillo de obsidiana, me moví agachándome hasta donde estaban las raíces y los árboles de mangle y después me arrastré sobre ellos. La llama azul me esperaba. Probaba cada parte del terreno antes de poner completamente mi pie con todo su peso y si bien me llegué a mojar hasta las rodillas y mi manto se desgarró con las espinas de los arbustos circundantes, nunca llegué a hundirme. La primera cosa que noté fue un olor poco usual. Por supuesto, todo el pantano era lo suficientemente fétido; con aguas estancadas, raíces podridas y mohosos hongos venenosos, pero ese nuevo olor era horrible: como de huevos podridos. Yo pensé para mí: «¿Cómo es posible que un hombre persiga aun a la más bella Xtabai, si ella apesta tanto?» Sin embargo proseguí y, finalmente me paré enfrente de la luz, pero no era un fantasma de mujer en lo absoluto. Era una llama sin humo, que perdiendo altura brotaba directamente del suelo. No sé qué la mantenía viva, pero obviamente se alimentaba de aquel aire nocivo que se colaba de alguna fisura del pantano.

Quizás otros fueron atraídos a sus muertes por la luz, pero la Xtabai es completamente inocente de eso. Y nunca he podido descubrir por qué ese aire maloliente puede prender una llama cuando un aire ordinario no lo hace. Sin embargo después, en varias ocasiones me volví a encontrar con el fuego azul, siempre con el mismo hedor y la última vez me tomé la molestia de investigar, y encontré otro material tan extraordinario como el aire que lo enciende. Cerca de la llama de la Xtabai me paré sobre una clase de vegetal viscoso e instantáneamente pensé: «Esta vez las arenas movedizas me *han agarrado*.» Pero no; fácilmente pude librarme y cogí un puñado apretado de ese cieno y regresé con él al campamento.

Era negro como el *óxitl* que se extrae de la savia del pino, aunque más pegajoso, como goma. Cuando lo examiné enfrente del fuego, un pedacito cayó sobre las llamas causando un fuego más alto y más caliente. Muy contento de ese descubrimiento accidental, tiré todo el puñado sobre el fuego y éste ardió brillantemente toda la noche, sin que yo tuviera que poner más ramas. Desde entonces cada vez que tenía que acampar cerca de un pantano, no me tomaba la molestia en juntar ramas secas, buscaba el cieno negro, ciertas clases de burbujas y fango, y siempre hacía un fuego mucho más caliente y brillante del que podría haber hecho cualquiera de los aceites que acostumbrábamos para el uso de nuestras lámparas.

Para entonces, estaba en las tierras de la gente que nosotros los mexica llamábamos indiscriminadamente los olmeca, simplemente porque ese pueblo era nuestro principal suministrador de *oli*. Por supuesto, sus gentes estaban divididas en varias naciones: Coatzacuali, Coatlícamac, Cupilco y otras, pero toda esa gente era muy parecida. Muchos hombres iban inclinados bajo el peso de sus nombres y las mujeres y los niños iban constantemente masticando. Es mejor que me explique.

En los árboles originarios de esa nación, hay dos clases que cuando su corteza se corta, gotea una savia que se solidifica hasta cierto grado. Un árbol produce el *oli* que nosotros usamos en su forma más líquida como goma de pegar y en su forma más dura, en nuestras elásticas pelotas *tlachtli*. La otra clase de árbol, produce una goma más suave de sabor dulce llamada *tzictli*. No tiene absolutamente ningún uso excepto ser mascada. No quiere decir comida; nunca se traga; cuando pierde su sabor o elasticidad se escupe y otro pedazo se pone en la boca y se masca, se masca y se masca. Sólo las mujeres y los niños hacen eso; en los hombres se consideraría afeminado. Sin embargo, gracias a los dioses, ese hábito no ha sido introducido en ninguna otra parte, porque hace que las mujeres olmeca, que por otro lado son muy atractivas, se vean tan faltas de animación y tan bobas, como la cara llena de bolas de un manatí eternamente rumiando las cañas de un río.

Puede ser que los hombres no masquen *tzictli*, pero ellos tienen una costumbre igual de imbécil. En algún tiempo de su pasado, empezaron a usar distintivos para su nombre. En su pecho un hombre colgaba un pendiente de cualquier material que pudiera conseguir; cualquier cosa desde una concha marina hasta oro, llevando su nombre en glifo para que cualquier persona que pasara lo leyera. Así, si un extranjero preguntaba algo, podría dirigirse a él por su nombre. Quizás era innecesario, pero en aquellos días el distintivo del nombre se usaba solamente para incrementar la cortesía.

A través de los años, sin embargo, ese simple pendiente acabó siendo muy elaborado. Ya que ahora se le agrega también el símbolo de la ocupación del que lo lleva: un puño de plumas, por ejemplo, si él se dedica a ese comercio, y también indicación de su rango: si pertenece a la nobleza o los plebeyos; también distintivos adicionales con los glifos de los nombres de sus padres, abuelos y aun los más distantes antepasados; y chucherías de oro, plata o piedras preciosas como una ostentación de su riqueza; y para aclarar cuál es su estado civil, enmarañados listones de colores para demostrar si es soltero, casado, viudo o padre de tantos hijos; además, otra señal de sus proezas militares, varios discos llevando los glifos de las campañas en las cuales tomó parte. Puede traer muchas más de esas chucherías colgando de su cuello hasta las rodillas. Así hasta nuestros días, cada hombre olmeca se inclina y casi se esconde bajo la aglomeración de preciosos metales, joyas, plumas, listones, conchas y coral. Y así, ningún extranjero *tiene* que hacerle preguntas; cada hombre lleva la respuesta a cualquier cosa que otro quiere saber de él o acerca de él.

A pesar de esas excentricidades, no todos los olmeca son tontos que se dedican durante toda su vida a cortar la corteza de los árboles. Son también aclamados y con justicia por sus artes, antiguas y modernas. Esparcidas aquí y allá, a lo largo de las tierras costeras, están las antiguas ciudades desiertas de sus antepasados y algunas de esas reliquias que quedan son sorprendentes.

Particularmente me sentí impresionado con las tremendas estatuas talladas en basalto, ahora medio hundidas en la tierra y cubiertas de hierbas. Todo lo que se puede ver de ellas son sus cabezas. Presentan una expresión vívida de truculencia alerta y todos sus cascos tienen una semejanza a las piezas de cuero protectoras para la cabeza de nuestros jugadores de *tlachtli*, por lo que es posible que las tallas representen a los dioses que inventaron ese juego. Digo dioses y no hombres, porque cualquiera de esas cabezas, por no mencionar sus cuerpos enterrados que van más allá de toda imaginación, es tan inmensamente grande, que puede caber en ella la casa de un ser humano.

Hay allí también, muchos frisos, columnas y cosas parecidas de piedra, incisos con figuras de hombres desnudos, algunos *muy* desnudos y *muy* machos, que parecen que están danzando, bebiendo o convulsionándose, por lo que yo presumo que los ancestros de los olmeca eran gente muy alegre. Y allí también hay figuritas de jade con detalles preciosos y soberbiamente terminadas, aunque es muy difícil distinguir las antiguas de las modernas, ya que aún quedan muchos artesanos entre los olmeca, quienes hacen trabajos increíbles en el tallado de piedras preciosas.

En la tierra llamada Cupilco, en su ciudad capital Xicalaca, bellamente situada en un delgado y largo pedazo de tierra, con el océano azul pálido a un lado y con una laguna verde claro al otro lado, encontré a un artesano llamado Tuxtem cuya especialidad era hacer peces y pájaros pequeñitos, no más grandes que la falange de un dedo, y cada una de las infinitesimales plumas y escamas de esas criaturas estaban hechas alternativamente en oro y plata. Más tarde yo llevé algunos de sus trabajos a Tenochtitlan y aquellos españoles que vieron y admiraron las pocas piezas que me quedaban dijeron que ningún artesano en ninguna parte de lo que ellos llamaban el Viejo Mundo, jamás había hecho nada tan maravilloso.

Yo continué siguiendo la costa, que entonces me guiaba hacia el norte a lo largo de la península maya de Uluúmil Kutz. Ya les he descrito brevemente esa tierra monótona, mis señores, y no gastaré más palabras para hacerlo, excepto para mencionar que en su costa del oeste recuerdo solamente un pueblo, lo suficientemente grande para ser llamado pueblo, Kimpéch; y en la costa del norte otro, Tihó; y en la costa del oeste otro, Chaktemal.

Para entonces había estado ausente de Tenochtitlan durante más de un año. Así es que en una forma general me encaminé a casa otra vez. Desde Chaktemal me dirigí a tierra, hacia el oeste, cruzando a lo ancho de la península. Llevé conmigo bastante *atoli*, *chocólatl* y otras raciones de comida para viajar, además de cierta cantidad de agua. Como ya he dicho, es una tierra árida, con un clima maligno y no tiene una estación de lluvia bien definida. Crucé esas tierras en lo que podía ser su mes de junio, que es el mes dieciocho del año maya, llamado Kumkú, Trueno; no lo llamaban así porque trajera tormentas o por lo menos una llovizna, sino porque ese mes es tan seco que las tierras de por sí secas hacen el ruido de un trueno artificial, gimiendo y crujiendo, como si ellas se encogieran y se arrugaran.

Quizás ese verano fue mucho más seco y caliente de lo usual porque hice un extraño y valioso descubrimiento, según supe después. Un día llegué a un pequeño lago que parecía estar formado del cieno negro, que ya antes había encontrado en los pantanos de los olmeca, y que había utilizado para prender los fuegos de mis campamentos. Tiré una piedra en el lago, pero ésta no se hundió; rebotó en la superficie como si el lago hubiera sido de *oli* duro. Con mucho cuidado puse un pie en su negra superficie y me encontré con que ésta sostenía perfectamente bien mi peso. Era *chapopotli*, un material parecido a resina dura, pero negro. Derretido es usado para hacer que las antorchas ardan más brillantemente, para rellenar las grietas de los edificios, como un ingrediente en varias medicinas y como una pintura que no deja pasar el agua. Sin embargo, jamás había visto un lago lleno de eso.

Me senté en su orilla para comer un poco, contemplando ese descubrimiento. Mientras estaba allí sentado, el calor del Kumkú que todavía estaba haciendo que el campo retumbara y estallara alrededor de mí, hizo que de pronto se resquebrajara el *chapopotli* del lago. Su superficie se abrió en todas direcciones, como si hubiera estado hecha de telaraña, después, se separó en pedazos negros y dentados, que fueron arrojados a un lado, mientras que de su fondo sobresalían unas cosas largas negroparduscas que parecían ser las ramas y los brazos de un árbol, por mucho tiempo enterrado.

Me felicité a mí mismo por no haberme aventurado en el lago, en el momento en que éste crujió, pues probablemente hubiera sido herido en su convulsión. Pero, para cuando acabé de comer, todo estaba quieto otra vez. El lago ya no era liso; estaba agrietado con un revoltijo de fragmentos lustrosamente negros, sin embargo, no parecía que fuera otra vez a agitarse y tenía mucha curiosidad acerca de los objetos que habían sido arrojados fuera de la superficie. Así es que, cautelosamente volví a aventurarme por el lago, y cuando comprobé que no me hundía, caminé con cuidado a través de los pedazos y protuberancias agrietadas, y me encontré con que esas cosas eran huesos.

Aunque ya no estaban blancos, como generalmente lo están los huesos viejos, pues habían perdido su color durante el tiempo que estuvieron enterrados, éstos eran de un tamaño inconcebible, y entonces recordé que una vez nuestras tierras estuvieron habitadas por gigantes. Pero, aunque reconocí una costilla y un hueso de muslo allí, también me di cuenta de que no pertenecían a un gigante humano, sino a algún animal monstruoso. Lo único que puedo suponer es que, mucho tiempo antes, el *chapopotli* debió de haber estado líquido y que, alguna criatura sin fijarse pisó dentro de él y fue atrapado y succionado hacia adentro. Después, a través de las gavillas de años el líquido se solidificó a su presente consistencia.

Luego encontré dos huesos mucho más grandes que los otros, por lo menos así lo pensé. Cada uno era tan largo como mi estatura y cilíndrico, pero en uno de sus extemos era tan ancho como mi muslo y en su otro extremo terminaba en una punta áspera, tan ancha como mi dedo pulgar. Hubieran sido todavía más largos si no fuera porque habían crecido curvos en forma gradual, retorciéndose en su punta en una media espiral. Como los otros, estaban de un color negropardusco por el *capopotli*, en el que habían estado enterrados. Estuve meditando por algún tiempo antes de ponerme en cuclillas y rascar su superficie con mi cuchillo, hasta encontrar su color natural: un blanco perla lustroso y suave. Esas cosas eran colmillos, unos colmillos inmensos como los de un jabalí. Sin embargo, pensé para mí, que si ese animal atrapado había sido un jabalí, en verdad debió de ser de la era de los gigantes.

Me levanté y consideré el asunto. Había visto pendientes, nariceras y otras chucherías similares, talladas en colmillos de osos, de tiburones, de jabalíes y eran vendidos por su peso, al mismo precio del oro. Lo que me preguntaba era: ¿qué podría hacer un maestro escultor como el difunto Tlatli, con un material como el de esos colmillos?

Como el país estaba escasamente habitado, cosa que no era sorprendente en vista de su destemplanza, tuve que andar hasta las tierras verdes y dulces de Cupilco, antes de llegar a la aldea de una oscura tribu olmeca. Todos los hombres se dedicaban a sacar la goma de los árboles, pero entonces no era la estación de recolectar la savia, así es que estaban sentados sin trabajar. No necesité ofrecer demasiada paga para que cuatro de los más fuertes trabajaran para mí, como cargadores. Aunque casi los perdí cuando se dieron cuenta de hacia dónde nos dirigíamos. El lago negro, me dijeron, era al mismo tiempo sagrado y pavoroso, y un lugar al que se deba evitar; así es que tuve que aumentar el precio prometido, antes de seguir adelante. Cuando llegamos allí y les mostré los colmillos, se dieron prisa en sacarlos; dos hombres para cada colmillo y luego, a pesar de lo pesados que eran, corrieron alejándose lo más rápido posible.

Los guié a través de Cupilco y hacia la orilla del océano a lo largo de esa franja de tierra, hacia la ciudad capital de Xicalanca, para llegar al taller del maestro Tuxtem. Él miró sorprendido y no muy complacido, cuando mis cargadores se acercaron bamboleándose bajo el peso de lo que parecían ser unos troncos. «No soy tallador de madera», dijo él, inmediatamente. Pero yo le expliqué lo que creía que eran, cómo los había encontrado y cuán raros debían de ser. Él tocó el lugar que yo había raspado y su mano que primero se detuvo expectante, lo acarició después y en sus ojos surgió un brillo.

Despedí a los cansados cargadores dándoles las gracias y pagándoles un poco más. Entonces, le dije al artista Tuxtem qué quería que él hiciera con mi descubrimiento.

«Quiero algunas tallas para vender en Tenochtitlan. Usted puede cortar los colmillos ajustándolos a sus conveniencias. De las partes más largas, quizás pueda hacer figuritas talladas de dioses y diosas mexica. De las piezas más chicas, quizá pueda hacer tubos para *poquíetl*, peines, dagas ornamentales. Aun de los fragmentos más pequeñitos puede hacer pendientes y cosas parecidas. Pero lo dejo a su gusto, maestro Tuxtem, a su juicio artístico.»

«De todos los materiales con que he trabajado en mi vida —dijo solemnemente—, éste es único. Me proporciona una oportunidad y un desafío que seguramente nunca volveré a tener. Antes de sacar la más pequeña muestra con que experimentar, pensaré larga y profundamente qué aperos y qué sustancias debo utilizar para darles el pulido final... —Hizo una pausa y luego dijo casi desafiante—. Es mejor que le diga lo siguiente: De mí y de mi trabajo simplemente demando lo mejor. Éste no será un trabajo de un día, joven señor Ojo Amarillo, ni de un mes.»

«Claro que no —convine—. Si usted me hubiera dicho lo contrario, yo hubiera tomado los trofeos y me hubiera ido. De todas maneras, no tengo ni idea de cuándo volveré a pasar por Xicalanca, así es que tome usted todo el tiempo que requiera. Ahora, en cuanto a su paga...»

«Sin duda soy un tonto por decir esto, pero estimo que el mayor precio que se me pueda pagar es la promesa de que usted dará a conocer que las piezas fueron esculpidas por mí y dirá mi nombre.»

«Tonto de la cabeza, maestro Tuxtem, si bien lo digo admirando la integridad de su corazón. Ya sea que usted ponga un precio o no, ésta es mi oferta. Usted tomará una vigésima parte, por peso, del trabajo terminado que usted hará para mí o del material en bruto, para hacerlo a su gusto.»

«Una oferta magnífica. —Él inclinó la cabeza en señal de aquiescencia—. Ni aun siendo el más ambicioso de los hombres, me hubiera atrevido a pedir un pago tan extravagante.»

«Y no tema —añadí—. Yo escogeré a los compradores tan cuidadosamente como usted escogerá sus aperos. Solamente serán personas capaces de comprender el valor de estas cosas. Y a cada una de ellas se les dirá: esta pieza fue hecha por el maestro Tuxtem de Xicalanca.»

Si en la península de Uluümil Kutz el tiempo había sido seco, en Cupilco era la temporada de lluvias, una temporada muy molesta para viajar en esas Tierras Calientes, en donde casi todo era selva desparramándose. Así es que me dirigí de nuevo hacia las playas abiertas, caminando hacia el oeste, hasta que llegué al pueblo de Coatzacoalcos, al que ustedes ahora llaman Espíritu Santo, y en donde terminan las rutas comerciales del norte al sur, a través del angosto istmo de Tecuantépec. Pensé, que como ese istmo era una tierra llana, de pocos bosques y con un buen camino, podría hacer una jornada fácil aunque la lluvia me cogiera con frecuencia. Y, también, que al otro lado del istmo había una posada hospitalaria, en donde estaba mi adorable Gie Bele de la Gente Nube, y en donde podría tener un agradable descanso antes de continuar hacia Tenochtitlan.

Así es que de Cotzacoalcos me desvié hacia el sur. Algunas veces caminé en compañía de caravanas de *pochteca* o con mercaderes individuales y pasamos a muchos otros yendo en dirección contraria. Pero un día en que iba viajando solo por un camino solitario, cuando llegué a su cumbre, vi a cuatro hombres sentados debajo de un árbol al otro lado. Estaban andrajosos y parecían bestiales; lentamente y con expectación se levantaron cuando yo me aproximé. Recordé a los bandidos con los cuales nos habíamos encontrado antes, y puse mi mano sobre mi cuchillo de obsidiana que traía en la banda de mi taparrabo. No podía hacer otra cosa más que caminar y tener la esperanza de pasar con un simple intercambio de saludos. Sin embargo, aquellos cuatro hombres no pretendieron invitarme a compartir su comida, o pedir compartir mis raciones o siquiera hablar, solamente cayeron sobre mí.

✠

Desperté. O desperté lo suficiente como para darme cuenta de que estaba desnudo sobre una esterilla, con una cobija abajo y otra encima de mi desnudez. Me encontraba en una choza aparentemente vacía, sin ningún otro mueble y a oscuras, excepto por la luz del día que se filtraba a través de las hendeduras de las paredes y del tejado de paja. Un hombre de mediana edad estaba arrodillado a mi lado y por sus primeras palabras comprendí que era un físico.

«El paciente vuelve en sí —dijo a alguien que estaba detrás de él—. Temí que nunca se recobrara de ese prolongado estupor.»

«¿Entonces, vivirá?», preguntó una voz femenina.

«Bien, por lo menos puedo empezar a aplicarle el tratamiento, que no hubiera sido posible si se hubiera quedado insensible. Yo diría que él llegó apenas a tiempo con ustedes.»

«Estaba tan mal, que casi lo echamos fuera. Sin embargo, a través de la sangre y la tierra, lo reconocimos como Zaa Nayàzú.»

Ese nombre no me sonó muy bien. Por un momento y de alguna manera, yo no podía ni recordar mi nombre, pero tenía la intuición de que era un poco menos melodioso de como lo pronunció, cantando, esa voz de mujer.

Mi cabeza me dolía atrozmente y sentía como si todo su contenido me lo hubieran sacado y en su lugar me hubieran puesto brasas al rojo vivo, y también me dolía todo el cuerpo. Mi memoria estaba en blanco y no recordaba muchas cosas más, además de mi nombre, pero estaba lo suficientemente consciente como para saber que no me había enfermado o algo por el estilo, sino que de alguna manera había sido golpeado o herido. Deseaba preguntar dónde estaba, cómo había llegado hasta allí y quién me estaba atendiendo, pero no pude hablar.

El doctor le decía a la mujer que yo no alcanzaba a ver: «Quienes hayan sido los ladrones, intentaron darle un golpe de muerte. Si no hubiera sido por esa pesada banda que lo protegió, ahora lo estaría; su cuello se habría roto o su cabeza se habría partido como una calabaza. Sin embargo, el golpe fue un choque muy fuerte para su cerebro, eso es evidente por la gran hemorragia nasal. Y ahora que sus ojos están abiertos, observe, una pupila está más grande que la otra.»

Una muchacha se inclinó por el hombro del doctor y me miró. A pesar de la triste condición en que estaba, pude darme cuenta de que su rostro era muy bello y que del pelo negro que lo enmarcaba partía desde su frente un mechón blanco, hacia atrás. Tuve la vaga impresión de haberla visto antes y para mi perplejidad, también parecía encontrar algo familiar con el simple hecho de mirar hacia el techo de paja.

«Si sus pupilas no son iguales —dijo la muchacha—, ¿es eso un mal síntoma?»

«Sí, en extremo —dijo el doctor—. Una indicación infalible de que algo anda mal dentro de su cabeza. Así es que, además de tratar de fortalecer y nutrir su cuerpo, de curar sus contusiones y magulladuras, debemos tener cuidado de que su cerebro esté libre de todo esfuerzo y excitación. Manténgalo caliente y sin luz. Dele caldo y sus medicinas cada vez que despierte, pero por ningún motivo lo deje sentarse y trate de que no hable.»

De la manera más tonta, traté de decirle al físico que estaba totalmente incapacitado para hablar. Entonces, de repente, la choza se hizo más oscura y yo tuve la desagradable sensación de ir cayendo rápidamente en las tinieblas profundas.

Me dijeron más tarde que estuve así por muchos días y muchas noches, que mis períodos de consciencia eran solamente esporádicos y breves, y que, entre esos períodos, yacía en un estupor tan profundo que tenía muy preocupado al doctor. En mis momentos de consciencia, algunas veces solamente, recordaba cuando había estado el físico, pero siempre se encontraba allí la muchacha. Siempre estaba dejando caer sobre mis labios, con cuidado, un caldo sabroso y caliente o una amarga poción, o lavaba con una esponja aquellas partes de mi cuerpo que podía sin cambiarme de posición, o me ponía un ungüento que olía a flores. Su rostro era siempre el mismo, bello, preocupado, sonriendo con ánimo hacia mí; pero extrañamente, o por lo menos así le parecía a mi mente ofuscada, a veces tenía el mechón blanco y a veces no.

Debí de haber estado entre la vida y la muerte, y debí de haber escogido entre presentarme ante los dioses o dejar eso más tarde a mi *tonali*. Sin embargo, llegó el día en que desperté con mi mente un poco más clara, miré al techo y me pareció singularmente familiar, miré a la muchacha que estaba cerca de mí, miré su mechón blanco y me las arreglé para gruñir: «Tecuantépec.»

«*Yaa* —dijo ella en náhuatl y luego siguió—: *Quema*», y sonrió. Era una sonrisa cansada, después de una vigilia de día y de noche atendiéndome. Traté de preguntar, pero ella me puso un dedo frío sobre mis labios.

«No hables. El doctor dijo que no debías hacerlo por un tiempo. —Ella hablaba el náhuatl de forma vacilante, aunque mejor de lo que yo recordaba haberlo oído hablar anteriormente en aquella choza—. Cuando estés bien, nos podrás contar todo lo que recuerdes de lo que te sucedió. Ahora, yo te contaré lo poco que sabemos.»

Había estado limpiando un pavo en el patio de la posada, una tarde, cuando una persona llegó allí tambaleándose, no venía por donde pasan las rutas comerciales que van del este al oeste, sino que se acercaba por el norte, a través de los campos vacíos que están en la ribera del río. Hubiera huido adentro de la posada y atrancado la puerta, si el susto que se llevó la hubiera dejado moverse con más rapidez y por eso pudo reconocer algo familiar en el hombre desnudo, sucio y cubierto de sangre cuajada, que tenía enfrente. A pesar de haber estado casi al borde de la muerte, el instinto de conservación debió de obrar en mí, para poder recordar dónde estaba la posada. Mi cara abatida parecía una máscara y mi pecho estaba cubierto de sangre que todavía manaba de mi nariz. Tenía el resto de mi cuerpo lleno de rojos arañazos hechos por espinas, con marcas de contusiones por los golpes y las caídas. Las plantas de mis pies desnudos estaban abiertas, incrustadas de polvo y piedrecillas. Pero ella me reconoció como el benefactor de su madre y me ayudó. No me llevaron a la hostelería, porque no hubiera podido descansar apaciblemente. Para entonces era un lugar próspero y de continuo movimiento, muy favorecido por los *pochteca* mexica como yo que, según me dijo ella, le habían ayudado a mejorar su conocimiento del náhuatl.

«Por lo tanto, creímos que era mejor traerte aquí, a nuestra antigua casa, en donde podríamos atenderte sin ser molestado por las continuas idas y venidas de los huéspedes. Y después de todo, es tuya, recuerda que tú se la compraste a mi madre. —Ella hizo un movimiento para que yo no hablara y continuó—: Supimos que te atacaron unos bandidos, pues llegaste desnudo y sin ningún bulto.»

De pronto me sentí alarmado al recordar algo. Con un esfuerzo ansioso levanté mi brazo dolorido y lo dejé caer sobre mi pecho, mientras mis dedos encontraban el topacio que todavía estaba colgando de su correa y di un gran suspiro de alivio. Aun aquellos ladrones tan rapaces, debieron de pensar que era el símbolo de algún dios, y supersticiosamente se abstuvieron de robarlo.

«Sí, sólo *traías* eso puesto —dijo la muchacha al ver mi movimiento—. Y esa cosa pesada, que no sé qué es.» Sacó por debajo de mi esterilla el pesado bultito con sus cordones y la banda que servía para sujetarlo a la frente.

«Ábrelo», dije, y mi voz sonó ronca después de no haber hablado en tanto tiempo.

«No hables», me repitió, pero me obedeció y cuidadosamente fue desdoblando capa tras capa de tela. Al quedar al descubierto el polvo de oro, que por alguna causa se había endurecido por la transpiración, era tan brillante que casi iluminaba el interior oscuro de la cabaña, y ponía chispas doradas en sus ojos oscuros.

«Siempre supusimos que eras un joven rico —murmuró, luego pensó por un instante y dijo—: Pero, tú te preocupaste primero por el pendiente. Antes que el oro.»

No sabía si podía hacerle entender mi explicación sin palabras, pero le hice un guiño y con otro esfuerzo alcancé el cristal y esa vez lo llevé a mi ojo y la miré a través de él, por todo el tiempo que pude sostenerlo allí. Y entonces me quedé sin habla aunque hubiera podido hablar, de lo bella que era. Mucho más bella de lo que pensaba o recordaba. Y entre otras cosas, no podía recordar su nombre.

El mechón claro cautivó mi ojo, pero no era necesario para cautivar el corazón. Sus largas pestañas eran como las alas del más pequeño chupamirto. Sus cejas tenían la curvatura de las alas de las gaviotas al levantar el vuelo. Sus labios se elevaban en sus junturas, también, como alas desplegadas, en las que parecía atesorar una sonrisa secreta. Cuando sonreía, como inconfundiblemente lo estaba haciendo en aquellos momentos, quizá por la expresión intrigada de mi rostro, aquellas alas se profundizaban hasta convertirse en unos hoyuelos encantadores y su rostro resplandecía más que mi oro. Si la choza hubiera estado llena de gente desgraciada, afligida por un duelo o por las almas sombrías de los sacerdotes, se hubieran sentido impelidos por su sonrisa, a sonreír a pesar de ellos mismos.

Me sentí muy feliz por haber vuelto a Tecuantépec y haber encontrado a aquella muchacha, aunque habría deseado llegar saludable y fuerte, con todo el éxito de un joven *pochtécatl*. En lugar de eso, yacía postrado en una cama, casi sin vida y fláccido y no era un espectáculo muy agradable de ver, cubierto como estaba con las costras de numerosos arañazos y cortes. Me sentía muy débil todavía como para comer por mí mismo o tomar mis medicinas, excepto por su mano. Y si, además, no olía mal, era porque me tenía que someter a aque ella me lavara todo el cuerpo.

«Eso no es conveniente —protesté—. Una doncella no debe lavar el cuerpo desnudo de un hombre.»

Ella dijo con calma: «Ya te hemos visto desnudo antes. Y debiste de haber venido desnudo a través de la mitad del istmo. Además —y en aquellos momentos su sonrisa era atormentadora—, aun una doncella puede admirar el cuerpo de un hombre joven y guapo.»

Creo que me ruboricé en toda la extensión de mi cuerpo, pero por lo menos la debilidad me ahorró la mortificación de que uno de mis órganos estuviera impelido a responder a su contacto y quizás hacerla huir de mi presencia.

No había pensado en las ventajas del matrimonio desde los sueños poco prácticos que Tzitzitlini y yo habíamos compartido. Pero no necesitaba pensar mucho para decidir que nunca encontraría en ninguna otra parte o nunca más, quizás, una novia tan deseable como aquella muchacha de Tecuantépec. A pesar de que la herida de mi cabeza aún estaba en proceso de curación, mi cerebro todavía retenía en su memoria algunas de las tradiciones tzapoteca; que la Gente Nube tenía muy pocas razones y deseos para casarse con forasteros y si alguno de ellos lo hacía, quedaba para siempre proscrito. A pesar de ello, cuando el doctor me dijo que ya podía hablar, traté solamente de decir aquellas palabras que me hicieran atracivo a los ojos de la muchacha. Aunque sólo era un mexícatl despreciable, y en aquellos momentos un espécimen ridículo y desdichado, hice gala de todo el encanto de que era capaz. Le di las gracias por su bondad para conmigo, la cumplimenté también por su belleza y le dije muchas lisonjas y palabras persuasivas. Pero dentro de mis más floridos discursos, me las arreglé para mencionar la considerable fortuna que, a tan temprana edad, había ya amasado, y los planes que tenía para engrandecerla más; también le hice ver claramente que si se casaba conmigo no le faltaría nada. Aunque me abstuve de hablar abruptamente y aun de insinuar una proposición, hice alusiones al respecto, como:

«Me sorprende mucho que una muchacha tan bonita como tú, no se haya casado.»

Ella sonreía y decía algo como: «Ningún hombre me ha cautivado lo suficiente como para perder mi independencia.»

Otra vez le dije: «Pero seguramente eres cortejada por muchos pretendientes.»

«Oh, sí. Desafortunadamente, los jóvenes de Uaxyácac tienen muy poco que ofrecer. Yo creo que están más interesados en tener la parte que me corresponde de la hostería, que en tenerme a mí.»

En otra ocasión dije: «Debes de conocer a muchos hombres elegibles, entre el constante tráfico de huéspedes de tu posada.»

«Bien, ellos me dicen que son elegibles. Pero tú sabes que la mayoría de los *pochteca* son viejos, muy viejos para mí, y además extranjeros. Sin embargo, me hacen la corte ardientemente, aunque siempre he sospechado que tienen una esposa en casa y no me sorprendería que tuvieran otras esposas al final de cada una de las rutas en que viajan.»

Yo me atreví a decir: «Yo no soy viejo. No tengo esposa en ninguna parte. Si alguna vez tengo una, será ella sola y para el resto de mi vida.»

Me miró largamente y después de cierto silencio dijo: «Quizá te hubieras casado con Gie Bele. Mi madre.»

Repito, mi mente no estaba todavía bien del todo, como debiera de estar. Hasta ese momento, había olvidado por completo que me había acostado con su madre —¡a)ya, qué vergüenza!— y en su propia presencia. Dadas las circunstancias, debió de haber pensado que era el más salaz sinvergüenza, cortejando de repente a la hija de esa mujer.

Sólo pude murmurar con un embarazo muy grande: «Gie Bele... ya recuerdo... lo suficientemente mayor como para ser mi madre...»

A lo cual la muchacha me volvió a mirar largamente, sin decir nada y yo pretendí quedarme dormido.

Quiero reiterarles, mis señores escribanos, que mi mente había sido afectada tremendamente por el golpe recibido, y que con verdadero tormento volvía lentamente a su entendimiento. Ésta es la única excusa que tengo por los desatinos que dije. El peor de todos, el más triste y que me trajo las más largas y últimas consecuencias, fue el que hice una mañana, cuando le dije a la muchacha:

«Me he estado preguntando cómo lo haces y por qué.»

«¿Cómo hago qué?», preguntó ella, mostrando su sonrisa.

«Algunos días tu pelo tiene ese mechón blanco, maravilloso en toda su longitud. Otros, como en estos momento, no lo tienes.»

Involuntariamente, con un gesto femenino de sorpresa, pasó su mano a través de su rostro, que por primera vez vi desanimarse. Y por primera vez, también, aquellos rincones de su boca, como alas levantadas, decayeron. Se quedó parada y nos quedamos mirándonos el uno al otro por un buen rato. Estoy seguro de que la expresión de mi rostro era la de un sinvergüenza. Cuál era la emoción que ella sentía, no puedo decirlo, pero cuando por fin habló, había un ligero temblor en su voz.

«Yo soy Beu Ribé —dijo ella e hizo una pausa como si estuviera esperando que yo hiciera algún comentario—. En tu lenguaje quiere decir: Luna que Espera.» E hizo otra pausa, y yo le dije de todo corazón:

«Es un nombre muy bello, y te queda a la perfección.»

Evidentemente estaba esperando oír otra cosa, pues me dijo: «Gracias —pero lo dijo mitad enojada y mitad dolida—. Es mi hermana menor, Zyanya, la que tiene un mechón blanco en su pelo.»

No me había dado cuenta, estúpidamente, de que eran dos

muchachas igualmente bellas, las que me atendían en días alternados. Había caído apasionadamente enamorado de lo que, en mi confusión, había tomado por una sola y bella doncella. Y había sido capaz de eso, solamente porque de la manera más tonta había olvidado que una vez por lo menos estuve un poco enamorado de su madre... de la madre de ambas. Si me hubiera quedado más tiempo en Tecuantépec en mi primera visita, esa intimidad hubiera culminado en haber llegado a ser el padrastro de las muchachas. Lo más espantoso de todo fue que durante esos días de mi lenta convalecencia, había estado, indiscriminadamente, simultáneamente y con imparcial ardor, cortejando a ambas, a ellas que hubieran podido ser mis hijastras.

Deseé morir. Deseé haber muerto en los eriales del istmo. Deseé no haber salido nunca del estupor en el que había estado por tanto tiempo. Pero lo único que pude hacer fue esquivar su mirada y no decir nada más. Beu Ribé hizo lo mismo. Siguió atendiendo a mis necesidades tan apta y tiernamente como siempre, pero conservaba su rostro alejado del mío y cuando no tenía otra cosa que hacer por mí, se iba sin ninguna ceremonia. En sus siguientes visitas durante aquel día, trayendo comida o medicinas, permaneció silenciosa y reservada.

El siguiente día le correspondía a la hermana menor, la del mechón blanco, y yo la saludé con un: «Buenos días, Zyanya», sin hacer ninguna mención acerca de mi indiscreción del día anterior, pues tenía la esperanza de poder pretender que había estado bromeando y que siempre había notado la diferencia entre las dos muchachas. Pero, como era lógico, ella y Beu Ribé desde un principio debían de haber discutido la situación, así es que a pesar de mis brillantes esperanzas, no la engañé más de lo que ustedes esperaban. Me miró de reojo largamente mientras yo parloteaba, aunque su expresión parecía ser más divertida que enojada o resentida. Quizás haya sido la forma en que las muchachas acostumbraban a mirar, como atesorando una secreta sonrisa.

Con verdadera pena, tengo que comunicarles que todavía no acababa de cometer desatinos, o de quedar desolado por las nuevas revelaciones. De pronto se me ocurrió preguntar: «¿Es que tu madre atiende todo el tiempo la posada, para que vosotras tengáis que cuidarme? Yo pensé que Gie Bele podría disponer de un momento para venir a...»

«Nuestra madre murió», me interrumpió y por un momento su rostro se nubló.

«¿Qué? —exclamé—. ¿Cuándo? ¿Cómo?»

«Hace más de medio año. En esta casa, ya que no podía pasar su confinamiento en la hostería entre los huéspedes.»

«¿Confinamiento?»

«Mientras esperaba la llegada de su bebé.»

Si no hubiera estado acostado, me hubiera caído. Dije débilmente: «¿Tuvo un bebé?»

Zyanya me miró con cierta preocupación. «El físico dijo que no

372

debías causar problemas a tu mente. Te contaré todo cuando estés más fuerte.»

«¡Que los dioses me condenen en Mictlan! —erupté, con mucho más vigor del que pensé que tendría—. Debió de ser *mi* bebé, ¿no es así?»

«Bien... —dijo ella y dejó escapar un profundo suspiro—. Tú fuiste el único hombre con quien se acostó después de la muerte de mi padre. Estoy segura de que ella sabía cómo tomar las debidas precauciones, porque cuando *yo* nací ella sufrió muchísimo y el doctor la previno de que debía ser la última criatura. De ahí mi nombre. Pero como habían pasado tantos años, debió pensar que ya no estaba en edad de concebir. De todas maneras —Zyanya retorció sus dedos—, sí, ella estaba preñada por un extranjero mexícatl y tú sabes cuáles son los sentimientos de la Gente Nube, acerca de esas relaciones. No hubiera pedido ser atendida por un físico de los be'n zaa.»

«¿Entonces, ella murió por negligencia? —demandé—. Solamente porque la testaruda de su gente rehusó a asistirla...?»

«No lo sé. Quizás hubieran rehusado, pero ella no les preguntó. Había un joven viajero mexícatl en la posada, que había estado por un mes o más. Él fue muy solícito con ella por su condición y se ganó su confianza hasta que ella le contó todas las circunstancias, y él la comprendió con tan buen corazón, como ninguna otra mujer lo hubiera hecho. Él dijo que había estudiado en una *calmécac*, escuela, y que ahí había recibido clases rudimentarias en el arte de la medicina. Así es que cuando le llegara su tiempo, él estaría aquí para ayudarla.»

«¿Ayudarla? ¿Cómo, si ella murió?», dije, maldiciendo silenciosamente al entremetido.

Zyanya se encogió de hombros con resignación. «Ella había sido prevenida del peligro. Fue un parto muy difícil y que llevó mucho tiempo. Tuvo una gran hemorragia y mientras el hombre trataba de contenerla, el bebé se estranguló con el cordón umbilical.»

«¿Los dos murieron?», sollocé.

«Lo siento. Tú insististe en saber. Espero que no vaya a provocarte una recaída.»

«¡Que me condene en Mictlan! —maldije otra vez—. El bebé... ¿qué fue?»

«Un niño. Ella pensaba... si hubieran vivido... ella decía que lo iba a llamar Zaa Nayàzú, como tú. Pero por supuesto no hubo ceremonia de nombre.»

«Un niño. Mi hijo», dije rechinando los dientes.

«Por favor, Zaa, trata de tener calma —dijo ella, utilizando mi nombre por primera vez, con agradable familiaridad, y añadió compasivamente—: No hay a nadie a quien culpar. No creo que ninguno de nuestros doctores lo hubiera hecho mejor, de como lo hizo ese extranjero bondadoso. Como ya te dije, tuvo una gran hemorragia. Nosotras limpiamos la casa, pero todavía quedan algunos rastros indelebles. ¿Ves?»

Levantó la cortina que cubría la puerta dejando pasar un rayo de luz, y me enseñó en el marco de la puerta, la mancha rojiza que dejó el hombre al estampar allí su firma, la huella sangrienta de su mano.

No sufrí una recaída. Continué mejorando, mi cerebro gradualmente se fue despojando de sus telarañas y mi cuerpo recobró su fuerza y su peso. Beu Ribé y Zyanya continuaron cuidándome alternativamente y ninguna de ellas dio lugar a ningún avance amoroso de mi parte, y por supuesto tuve mucho cuidado de no mencionarles nada más que pudiera tomarse por un cortejo. En verdad, me maravillaba de su tolerancia para atenderme en todo y prodigarme tantos cuidados, considerando que fui la causa primordial de la muerte de su madre. En cuanto a mis sueños, la esperanza de ganarme la voluntad de alguna de las muchachas y casarme con ella, aunque sincera y perversamente amaba a las dos por igual, estaba fuera de todo pensamiento. La posibilidad de que ellas alguna vez hubiesen sido mis hijastras, fue sólo una especulación. Sin embargo, el que yo había engendrado a su medio hermano, de tan corta vida, era un hecho inalterable.

Llegó el día en que me sentí lo suficientemente bien, como para seguir mi camino. El doctor me examinó y dijo que mis pupilas estaban normales otra vez, pero insistió en que diera un poco de tiempo a mis ojos para que éstos se fueran acostumbrando poco a poco a la plena luz del día, y así lo hice yendo afuera de la puerta primero y luego más lejos cada día. Beu Ribé sugirió que estaría más cómodo si pasaba ese tiempo de convalecencia en la posada, ya que había una habitación vacía en aquel momento. Así es que accedí y Zyanya me trajo algunas ropas de su difunto padre. Por primera vez, en no sé cuántos días, me puse un manto y un taparrabo otra vez. Las sandalias que me prestaron eran demasiado pequeñas para mí, así es que le di a Zyanya un poquito de polvo de oro y fue corriendo al mercado a comprarme un par de mi talla. Después, con pasos vacilantes, pues no estaba tan fuerte como había pensado, dejé aquella choza para siempre.

No era difícil de ver que la posada se había convertido en un lugar favorecido por los *pochteca* y otros viajeros. Cualquier hombre con buen sentido y buena vista se sentiría complacido en pernoctar allí, sólo por tener el privilegio de estar cerca de las bellas y casi gemelas anfitrionas. Sin embargo, la hostería también ofrecía habitaciones limpias y cómodas, alimentos de buena calidad y sirvientes atentos y corteses. Las muchachas habían hecho esas mejoras deliberadamente, pero, sin calcularlo conscientemente, también habían saturado el aire de todo el establecimiento con sus sonrisas y buen humor. Con suficientes sirvientes para hacer las faenas pesadas y el fregado, las muchachas tenían sólo que supervisar, así es que siempre andaban vestidas de la mejor manera y para realzar el doble impacto de sus bellezas se vestían como gemelas, siempre igual. Aunque al principio me resentí de la forma en que los huéspedes masculinos las miraban y de cómo bromeaban con ellas, después me sentí agradecido de que estuvieran tan ocupados en enamorarlas, ya que no se dieron cuenta, como yo lo hice un día, de algo mucho más sorprendente acerca de la ropa de las muchachas.

«¿En dónde conseguisteis esas blusas?», pregunté a las hermanas sin que me oyeran los otros viajeros y mercaderes.

«En el mercado —dijo Beu Ribé—. Pero eran todas blancas cuando las compramos. Nosotras las decoramos.»

La decoración consistía en un diseño que bordeaba el escote cuadrado de las blusas y el borde del dobladillo. Era de lo que nosotros llamamos «diseño de cerámica», del que he escuchado decir a algunos de sus arquitectos españoles, con cierta sorpresa al verlo, «el diseño de las grecas griegas», aunque no sé qué es una greca griega. Y esa decoración no estaba bordada, sino pintada en color, y el color era de un púrpura vivo y profundo.

Yo pregunté: «¿Dónde conseguisteis ese colorante?»

«Ah, esto —dijo Zyanya—. Es bonito ¿verdad? Entre los efectos de mi madre, encontramos un pequeño recipiente de cuero que tenía un colorante de este color. Mi padre se lo dio poco antes de que él desapareciera. Como sólo había lo suficiente para teñir estas dos blusas, no pudimos pensar qué otro uso darle. —Luego me dijo vacilante y casi con desazón—: ¿Tú crees que hicimos mal, Zaa, al apropiárnoslo para una frivolidad?»

Dije: «De ninguna manera. Todas las cosas bellas deberían estar reservadas solamente a las personas bellas. Pero, decidme, ¿habéis lavado ya esas blusas?»

Las muchachas me miraron perplejas: «Pues, sí, varias veces.»

«Entonces el color no se corre, ni se decolora.»

«No, es un buen colorante —respondió Beu Ribé y entonces me dijo lo que había estado tratando de averiguar—. Esto es por lo que perdimos a nuestro padre. Él fue al lugar en donde se encuentra el colorante, para comprar una gran cantidad y hacer una fortuna con esto, y nunca más regresó.»

Dije: «Eso fue hace años. ¿No erais vosotras demasiado jóvenes como para recordar si vuestro padre mencionó adónde había ido?»

«Hacia el suroeste, a lo largo de la costa —dijo frunciendo el ceño por la concentración—. Él habló de un lugar salvaje con grandes rocas, en donde el océano ruge y se estrella.»

«En donde vive una tribu ermitaña que se llama Los Desconocidos —agregó Zyanya—. Oh, también mencionó, ¿recuerdas Beu?, dijo algo acerca de caracoles. Nos prometió traernos conchas pulidas para hacernos un collar.»

Tratando de no parecer demasiado ansioso, pregunté: «¿Podría alguna de vosotras guiarme cerca del lugar en donde creéis que él fue?»

«Cualquiera puede —dijo la hermana mayor, haciendo un gesto vago hacia el oeste—. La única costa con rocas en estas partes es allá.»

«Pero el lugar exacto del colorante debe de ser un secreto bien guardado. Nadie más lo ha encontrado desde que vuestro padre fue a buscarlo. Una de vosotras podría recordar, mientras vamos hacia allá, algunas otras alusiones que haya dejado caer.»

«Es posible —dijo la más joven—. Pero, Zaa, tenemos que encargarnos de la hostería.»

«Por mucho tiempo, mientras me estuvisteis atendiendo, os turnasteis como hosteleras. Seguro que alguna de vosotras podría tomarse unas vacaciones. —Ellas se miraron con incertidumbre y yo persistí—: Estaréis persiguiendo el sueño de vuestro padre. Él no fue un tonto. Allí *hay* una fortuna en colorante púrpura.» Alcancé una maceta cerca de allí y corté de la planta dos pajitas, una corta y una larga y las sostuve en mi puño de tal manera que sobresalieran al mismo nivel. «Escoged. La que tome la pajilla corta se gana unas vacaciones y una fortuna que los tres podemos compartir.»

Las muchachas vacilaron sólo un momento, luego estiraron sus manos y escogieron. De eso hace más o menos cuarenta años, mis señores, y hasta este día no puedo decirles quién de los tres ganó o perdió al escoger. Lo único que puedo decirles es que Zyanya tomó la más corta. Y así, como un eje pequeño y trivial da vueltas, nuestras vidas dieron vuelta en ese instante.

✠

Mientras las muchachas cocinaban y secaban comida de *pinoli* y molían y mezclaban *chocólatl* para nuestras provisiones, fui al mercado de Tecuantépec para comprar otras cosas que necesitaríamos en el viaje. En la tienda del armero sopesé y balanceé varias armas, finalmente seleccioné una *maquáhuitl* y una lanza corta que se acomodaba mejor a mi brazo.

El armero dijo: «¿Se está preparando el joven señor para enfrentarse a algún peligro?»

Respondí: «Voy a la tierra de los chóntaltin. ¿Ha oído hablar de ellos?»

«*Ayya*, sí. Esa gente horrible que vive en la costa. Chóntaltin es por supuesto la palabra en náhuatl. Nosotros los llamamos zyú, pero quiere decir lo mismo: Los Desconocidos. Actualmente, todos son huave, una de las tribus de los huave más bestiales y escuálidas. Quizá sepa que los huave no tienen realmente tierra propia. Nosotros los toleramos viviendo en pequeños grupos aquí y allá, en tierras que no nos son aptas.»

Yo dije: «Arriba, en las montañas de Tzempuüla, una vez pasé la noche en una de sus aldeas. No eran gente muy sociable.»

«Bueno, si durmió entre ellos y despertó vivo, conoció a una de las tribus huave más benigna. No encontrará a los zyú de la costa tan hospitalarios. Oh, ellos le darán una bienvenida calurosa, quizá demasiado calurosa. A ellos les gusta asar y comerse a los visitantes, para cambiar un poco su monótona dieta de pescado.»

Yo estuve de acuerdo con él, en que ellos eran encantadores, pero le pregunté cuál era el camino más fácil y expedito para llegar.

«Usted puede ir directamente de aquí hacia el suroeste, pero hay una cadena de montañas volcánicas por ese camino. Le sugiero que siga el río que corre hacia el sur hasta el océano, luego a lo largo de las playas. O hacia nuestro puerto pesquero de Nozibe, donde podrá encontrar a un barquero que lo llevará todavía más rápido por el mar.»

Y eso fue lo que Zyanya y yo hicimos. Si hubiera estado viajando solo, no me hubiera puesto a pensar en escoger una ruta tan fácil, pero quería ahorrarle a la muchacha la mayor cantidad posible de rigores e incomodidades. Sin embargo, después descubrí que ella era una buena compañera, dura para viajar; nunca se quejó del mal tiempo, o de acampar al aire libre o si comía comida fría o ninguna, o si estaba rodeada por la selva y por animales salvajes. Pero ése fue un viaje pausado y cómodo. Fue un solo día de camino, un paseo agradable, a través de las llanuras paralelas al río hasta el puerto de Nozibe. Ese nombre sólo significa Salinas y el «puerto» consistía en unos cuantos postes con techos de hojas de palma, en donde los pescadores podían sentarse a la sombra. La playa estaba llena de redes tendidas para secarse y para remendarse; había un gran movimiento de canoas hechas de troncos huecos, yendo y viniendo a través de las rompientes o arrastradas en la arena por los hombres.

Encontré a un pescador que estuvo algo reacio en admitir que en algunas ocasiones había visitado a los zyú al otro lado de la costa, que algunas veces había completado su pesca comprándoles algunos pescados y que hablaba un poco de su lengua. «Pero de mala gana, me permiten que les hable —Y luego me previno—. Un forastero que se aproxime a ellos va hacia su propia muerte.» Tuve que subir mi oferta de pago hasta un precio exorbitante, para que estuviera de acuerdo en llevarnos, de ida y vuelta, en su bote, a lo largo de la costa de esa nación, y servirme como intérprete allí, si es que me daban la oportunidad de decir algo. Mientras tanto, Zyanya había encontrado un refugio de palma desocupado y extendido, sobre la arena suave, las cobijas que habíamos traído de la hostería. Así es que aquella noche, dormimos castamente retirados el uno del otro.

Nos pusimos en camino al amanecer. El bote estaba cerca de la playa, exactamente en la línea en donde el agua rompía y el botero remó en un silencio moroso, mientras Zyanya y yo parloteábamos alegremente, haciéndonos notar el uno al otro los maravillosos paisajes tierra adentro, que parecían enjoyados. La extensión de la playa se veía como un polvo de plata, pródigamente esparcido entre la turquesa del mar y la esmeralda de las palmeras, de las que prorrumpían frecuentemente bandadas de aves color rubí y pájaros dorados. Sin embargo, conforme nos íbamos alejando hacia el oeste, la arena blanca gradualmente se fue oscureciendo hasta llegar a ser gris y luego negra; de las verdes palmeras se levantaba una hilera de volcanes. De repente, algunos de ellos echaban humo. Las erupciones violentas y los temblores de tierra, me dijo Zyanya, ocurrían con mucha frecuencia en esa costa.

A la mitad de la tarde, nuestro botero rompió su silencio. «Ahí está la aldea zyú a la que voy a llamar», y con sus remos hizo girar nuestro bote hacia un montón de chozas que estaban en una playa negra.

«¡No! —exclamó Zyanya, de repente y con excitación—. Tú me dijiste, Zaa, que podría recordar algunas otras cosas que mi padre dijo. ¡Y así es! ¡Él mencionó la montaña que camina en el agua!»

«¿Qué?»

Y ella apuntó enfrente de la proa del bote. Más allá de la aldea zyú, las arenas se terminaban abruptamente en un formidable peñasco, como una montaña que se hubiera salido de la hilera de volcanes que estaban tierra adentro. Se levantaba como una muralla a lo largo de la playa y se extendía mar adentro. Aun a la considerable distancia en que estábamos, podía ver, con mi cristal de topacio, los chorros de agua emplumada que se estrellaban muy alto, contra la falda del gigantesco peñasco.

«¡Ve qué rocas tan grandes forman esa montaña! —dijo Zyanya—. ¡Ése es el lugar en donde se encuentra el colorante púrpura! ¡Ahí es donde debemos ir!»

Yo le aclaré: «Ahí es a donde yo debo ir, muchacha.»

«No —dijo el barquero negando con su cabeza—. La aldea ya es bastante peligrosa.» Tomé mi *maquáhuitl* y la sostuve de tal manera que él la pudiera ver y acaricié su orilla inicua de obsidiana negra y dije: «Usted dejará a la muchacha aquí en la playa. Dirá a los nativos que no la molesten, que regresaremos por ella al oscurecer. Luego usted y yo iremos a la montaña que camina en el agua.»

Él gruñó y predijo cosas espantosas, pero movió su bote hacia la playa. Supongo que todos los hombres zyú debían de estar pescando, porque sólo unas cuantas mujeres salieron de las chozas, cuando nosotros desembarcamos. Eran unas criaturas sucias, con los pechos desnudos, descalzas y vestidas con faldas harapientas. Oyeron impasibles todo lo que les dijo el barquero y miraban de fea manera a la muchacha bonita que se quedaba desamparada entre ellas, pero no hicieron ningún movimiento siniestro, mientras estuvimos al alcance de la vista. No me sentía muy feliz de dejar a Zyanya allí, pero eso era preferible a llevarla a un peligro mayor.

Cuando el botero y yo estuvimos otra vez fuera de la playa, hasta un hombre acostumbrado a vivir en la tierra como yo, podía ver que era casi imposible aproximarse al declive de la montaña. Sus peñascos irregulares, muchos de ellos tan grandes como un palacio de Tenochtitlan, se extendía alrededor como un obstáculo insalvable. El océano rompía sobre esas rocas de riscos y torres, dejando caer toda su fuerza en columnas de agua blanca. Éstas se levantaban increíblemente altas y como se suspendieran un momento y luego se dejaran caer con fuerza con un rugido estruendoso, como si todos los rayos de Tláloc tronaran al mismo tiempo, y después, se deslizan otra vez adentro, haciendo remolinos que engullían y succionaban tan poderosamente, que incluso algunos de aquellos peñascos del tamaño de una casa se estremecían a simple vista.

La agitación del mar era tan fuerte que el barquero tuvo que utilizar toda su destreza para que pudiéramos desembarcar sin zozobrar en una playa al este de la montaña. Cuando hubimos arrastrado la canoa por la arena fuera del alcance de las garras del mar, y cuando al fin dejamos de toser y de escupir el agua salada, sinceramente lo felicité:

«Si usted se puede enfrentar tan valerosamente a este mar borrascoso, no debe temer a esos viles zyú.»

Mis palabras parecieron infundirle cierto valor, así es que le di mi lanza para que la llevara y le hice una seña para que me siguiera. A grandes zancadas atravesamos la playa hacia la pared de la montaña, y encontramos un declive por el cual pudimos subir. Éste nos llevó a cierta altura de la montaña, como la mitad del camino entre el nivel del mar y la cumbre, y desde esa altura podíamos ver la interrumpida playa que continuaba hacia la parte oeste. Dimos la vuelta hacia la izquierda siguiendo la orilla, hasta que llegamos a un promontorio muy por encima de esa hilera de grandes rocas desparramadas y de la furia de las grandes olas. Estaba en el lugar del que habló el padre de Zyanya, pero no parecía el sitio más adecuado para encontrar el precioso colorante púrpura o los frágiles caracoles o cosa parecida.

Lo que encontré fue un grupo de cinco hombres que escalaban hacia nosotros. Obviamente eran sacerdotes zyú pues estaban tan sucios y con el pelo tan enredado como los sacerdotes mexica y para añadir algo más a su falta de elegancia, no llevaban vestiduras harapientas, sino andrajosas pieles de animal, cuyo olor llegaba hasta nosotros. Los cinco hombres nos miraban hostilmente y cuando el que parecía ser el más importante de ellos dijo algo en la lengua huave, también sonó hostil.

«Dígales y dígaselo rápido —dije al botero—, que vengo a ofrecerles oro a cambio de comprarles un poco de su colorante púrpura.»

Antes de que él pudiera hablar, uno de los hombres gruñó: «No necesito él. Yo hablo lóochi. Yo sacerdote de Tiat Ndik, dios del mar, y éste es su santuario. Ustedes morirán por poner pies aquí.»

Yo traté de convencerlos con simples palabras lóochi, de que no hubiera tenido que introducirme en terreno santo, si hubiera podido hacer mi proposición en cualquier otro lugar o de otra manera. Pedí su indulgencia por mi presencia y que considerara mi oferta. Aunque sus cuatro subordinados seguían mirándome con miradas asesinas el sacerdote principal pareció un poco más apaciguado y sus maneras fueron más obsequiosas. O por lo menos, su siguiente amenaza a mi vida no fue tan ruda.

«Váyase ahora, Ojo Amarillo, quizá pueda salir con vida.»

Traté de sugerir que, ya que de todas maneras había profanado esos santos recintos, sólo tomaría un poco más de tiempo el que pudiéramos intercambiar mi oro, por su colorante.

Él dijo: «Colorante santo para dios del mar. Ningún precio lo puede comprar. —Y volvió a repetir—: Váyase ahora, quizá pueda salir con vida.»

«Muy bien. Pero antes de que me vaya, ¿puede usted satisfacer mi curiosidad? ¿Qué tienen que ver los caracoles con el colorante púrpura?»

«¿*Chachi*?» Él hizo eco de la palabra lóochi de caracoles, sin comprender, y se volvió hacia el barquero para que tradujera, quien estaba perceptiblemente temblando de miedo.

«Ah, el *ndik diok*», dijo el sacerdote comprendiendo. Vaciló por un momento, pero se volvió y me hizo señas para que lo siguiera. El botero y los otros cuatro hombres se quedaron allí en lo alto, mientras el sacerdote principal y yo descendíamos hacia el mar. Fue un largo camino, las paredes resonaban, los chorros de agua blanca rompían cada vez más arriba y más arriba, alrededor de nosotros rociándonos con una espuma fría. Al fin, llegamos a una depresión abrigada por grandes peñascos y en ella había un estanque de agua que sólo chapoteaba de un lado a otro, mientras afuera el resto del océano se estrellaba rugiendo.

«Lugar santo de Tiak Ndik —dijo el sacerdote—. Donde el dios nos deja escuchar su voz.»

«¿Su voz? —dije—. ¿Quiere usted decir, algún ruido del océano?»

«¡Su voz! —insistió el hombre—. Para oír, tiene que poner cabeza adentro.»

Sin dejar de verlo y sin soltar mi *maquáhuitl*, me arrodillé e incliné mi cabeza de lado, hasta que uno de mis oídos descansó sobre el agua que chapoteaba. Al principio sólo pude oír el latido de mi propio corazón, que pulsaba en mi oído, era un sonido atemorizante; luego, escuché uno todavía más extraño; empezó suavemente, pero lentamente se fue haciendo más audible. Pudo haber sido algún silbido bajo el agua —si es que alguien puede hacerlo bajo el agua— y silbaba una melodía mucho más sutil de la que podría cualquier músico en la tierra. Aun ahora, no puedo compararlo con ningún otro sonido que haya escuchado en toda mi vida. Mucho después, decidí que debió de haber sido el viento que corría a través de las grietas y hendiduras de aquellas rocas, silbaba y simultáneamente al entrar al agua, emitía un sonido diferente. Ese silbido engañador, sin duda llegaba de algún otro lado, y el estanque sólo lo revelaba como una música que no era terrenal. Pero en ese momento y bajo esas circunstancias, estaba dispuesto a aceptar la palabra del sacerdote, de que *era* la voz de un dios.

Mientras tanto él se estaba moviendo alrededor del estanque y observándolo desde varios puntos, finalmente metió el brazo hasta su hombro. Buscó por un momento y luego sacando su mano la abrió ante mí, diciendo: «*Ndik diok.*» Me atrevería a decir que tenía cierta relación con el caracol de tierra, pero el padre de Zyanya se había equivocado al prometerle un collar de pulidas conchas. Aquella criatura era una babosa viscosa del largo de mi dedo. El liso caracol no tenía ninguna concha en su espalda y no se distinguía en nada que yo pudiera ver.

El sacerdote inclinó su cabeza cerca de la babosa que tenía en su mano y la apretó fuertemente. Evidentemente eso molestó a la criatura, porque orinó o defecó en su mano; era una pequeña substancia amarillo-pálido. El sacerdote con cuidado volvió a dejar al animal en una roca dentro del agua, luego sostuvo la palma de su mano ante mí para que observara y yo me retiré un poco, por el olor de pescado podrido que despedía aquella substancia. Sin embargo y para mi sorpresa, empezó a cambiar de color; del amarillo al verde, del verde al azul, del azul al rojo y luego se fue haciendo de color más profundo y más intenso hasta llegar al fin a un púrpura vibrante.

Sonriendo, el hombre levantó la mano y restregó la substancia en mi manto. La mancha brillante seguía oliendo de forma horrible, pero sabía que su colorante jamás se desteñía o se borraba. Él me volvió a hacer un gesto para que lo siguiera y nosotros ascendimos entre las rocas dando traspiés mientras que con una combinación de señas y su lóochi lacónico, el sacerdote me explicó todo lo referente al *ndik diok*:

Los hombres zyú exprimen a los caracoles solamente dos veces al año, en los días santos que son seleccionados por una complicada adivinación.

Aunque hay miles de caracoles marinos adheridos a las rocas, de cada uno de ellos se extrae una cantidad diminuta de segregación. Así es que para colectarlo, los hombres tienen que nadar entre el agua de rompientes tumultuosas y sumergirse entre ellas, en busca de caracoles que exprimir, poniendo sus substancias en redecillas de hilo de algodón o en recipientes de cuero y volviendo a dejar a las criaturas ilesas. Los caracoles se tienen que mantener vivos hasta la siguiente extracción, sin embargo, los hombres no son tan indispensables; en cada uno de esos rituales de medio año, cuatro o cinco se ahogan o se estrellan contra las rocas.

«¿Pero cómo es posible que usted rehúse un beneficio, después de tantos trabajos y de tanto sacrificio de su gente?», pregunté arreglándomelas para hacerme comprender por el sacerdote. Él volvió a hacer señas con la cabeza y me guió todavía más lejos, hacia una gruta viscosa y me dijo con orgullo:

«Nuestro dios del mar a quien escuchó, Tiat Ndik.»

Era una estatua en bulto hecha sin maestría, que solamente consistía en una pila de rocas redondas: un gran peñasco para el abdomen, uno más pequeño para el pecho y uno, todavía más pequeño, para la cabeza. Sin embargo, toda esa cosa —ese montón de inútiles rocas inanimadas— estaba coloreada de un púrpura brillante.

Alrededor del Tiat Ndik habían recipientes y redecillas de algodón llenas de colorante; un tesoro de incalculable valor enterrado ahí.

Cuando regresamos al punto de partida, el disco rojo encendido de Tonatíu se estaba hundiendo a lo lejos en el océano, al oeste y bullendo entre nubes vaporosas. Luego el disco desapareció y por un momento vimos la luz de Tonatíu brillando fuera del mar, allí en la orilla tenue del mundo, un destello verde esmeralda, brillante, breve y nada más. El sacerdote y yo regresamos hacia donde habíamos dejado a los otros, mientras él seguía tratando de convencerme de que las ofrendas del colorante púrpura eran necesarias, ya que si no se halagaba con ellas a Tiat Ndik, los zyú no tendrían más peces en sus redes.

Yo argüí: «Por todos esos sacrificios y ofrendas, su dios del mar los deja vivir en una existencia miserable, comiendo pescado. Déjeme llevar su púrpura al mercado y yo les traeré el suficiente oro como para que puedan comprar una *ciudad*. La ciudad de una nación agradable y honesta, llena hasta el borde de mejores alimentos que el pescado y con esclavos que les sirvan.»

Él continuó obstinadamente: «El dios nunca lo permitiría. El púrpura no se puede vender. —Después de un momento añadió—: Algunas veces nosotros no comemos pescado, Ojo Amarillo.»

Él sonrió y señaló a los cuatro sacerdotes que estaban alrededor de un fuego. Estaban asando dos muslos humanos acabados de cortar, utilizando mi lanza para eso. No había ninguna señal del resto del barquero. Tratando de no aparentar en mi rostro el temblor que sentía, tomé de mi *máxtlatl* el bultito de polvo de oro y lo tiré al suelo entre el sacerdote y yo.

«Ábralo con cuidado —dije—, no sea que se lo lleve el viento. —Mientras él se arrodillaba y empezaba a desdoblar la tela, yo continué—: Si yo pudiera llenar mi canoa del púrpura, regresaría con el bote casi lleno de oro. Pero le ofrezco esta cantidad de oro sólo por la cantidad de recipientes que yo pueda cargar con mis brazos.»

Para entonces ya había abierto la tela, el montón de polvo brillaba a la luz del ocaso, los otros cuatro sacerdotes se acercaron a echar una mirada sobre su figura encogida. Él dejó parte del polvo correr entre sus dedos, luego, sosteniendo la tela con sus dos manos, la sopesó con suavidad para juzgar su peso. Sin mirarme me dijo: «Usted da todo este oro por el púrpura. ¿Cuánto da por la muchacha?»

«¿Qué muchacha?», pregunté y el corazón me dio un brinco.

«La que está detrás de usted.»

Yo lancé una mirada rápida hacia atrás. Zyanya estaba exactamente detrás de mí, se veía infeliz, y un poco más atrás de ella había seis o siete hombres de los zyú, quienes veían con ansiedad a ella, a mí y al ojo de oro. El sacerdote todavía estaba arrodillado sopesando el oro, cuando yo me volví otra vez y dejé caer mi *maquáhuitl*. La tela y sus manos cortadas cayeron en el suelo, aunque el sacerdote solamente se tambaleó, azorado y estremecido por la sangre que manaba de sus muñecas.

Los otros sacerdotes y los pescadores saltaron hacia él, no sé si fue para agarrar el oro que se escapaba o para ayudar a su jefe mutilado, pero exactamente en el mismo instante giré rápidamente, asiendo a Zyanya por la mano, y a golpazos y patadas me abrí paso entre el círculo cerrado de hombres y tiré de ella, encabezando una carrera a todo lo largo del risco y bajando hacia el lado este. En breve estuvimos fuera de la vista de los aporreados zyú y yo me desvié abruptamente, para escabullirme entre algunos peñascos que estaban más altos, sobre nuestras cabezas.

Los zyú nos darían caza y naturalmente esperaban que saliéramos disparados hacia nuestra canoa en la playa. Sin embargo, aunque hubiéramos podido alcanzarla y hacernos al mar, yo no tenía ninguna experiencia en el arte de remar y conocer el mar; los perseguidores probablemente nos hubieran cogido con sólo vadear adelante de nosotros.

Algunos de ellos pasaron corriendo y gritando en aquellos momentos cerca de nuestro escondite improvisado, corriendo con dirección de la playa, como yo lo había esperado. «¡Ahora, vamos colina arriba!», dije a Zyanya y no perdió aliento en preguntar el porqué, sino que subió conmigo. La mayor parte de aquel promontorio era roca desnuda y nosotros teníamos que escalar con mucho cuidado a través de las hendiduras y grietas para no ser visibles a los de abajo. Más arriba crecían en la montaña, árboles y arbustos en los que nos hubiéramos podido esconder con más facilidad, pero aquella parte estaba todavía a un largo trecho de distancia, y también estaba preocupado acerca de los pájaros, pues con sus chillidos podían descubrir nuestra posición. Cada paso que dábamos, parecía como si se levantaran en vuelo toda una bandada de gaviotas, pelícanos y cuervos marinos.

Sin embargo, luego me di cuenta de que los pájaros estaban revoloteando no sólo alrededor de nosotros, sino en todas partes de la montaña; también habían aves de tierra: papagayos, palomas, mirlos; volando alrededor a la ventura y graznando o chillando con aparente agitación. Y no solamente las aves, animales usualmente tímidos y nocturnos huían singularmente; armadillos, iguanas, ardillas, víboras y hasta un ocelote pasó brincando sin mirarnos y todos los animales, como nosotros, se movían montaña arriba. Entonces, a pesar de que todavía faltaba un buen rato para que estuviera completamente oscuro, oí el aguzado lamento del coyote desde algún lugar, y adelante de nosotros en las alturas, no muy lejos una hilera sinuosa de murciélagos salió como escupida de una grieta, y entonces supe lo que se aproximaba: una de las convulsiones tan comunes en aquella costa.

«Rápido —urgí a la muchacha—. Ahí arriba. Donde salen los murciélagos. Debe de haber una caverna. Entremos en ella.»

La alcanzamos exactamente cuando los últimos murciélagos salían, era un túnel en la roca, lo suficientemente ancho como para que nos acurrucáramos en él, lado a lado. Qué tan profunda era, nunca lo averigüé, pero de todas maneras debió de ser una caverna muy grande por la incontable multitud de murciélagos que salieron de ella y, porque mientras yacíamos en el túnel, hasta nosotros llegaba más allá de su interior, el olor de guano acumulado. De repente, todo quedó en silencio afuera de nuestra madriguera; los pájaros debieron de haber volado muy lejos y los animales estarían ya sanos y salvos en la tierra; aun se calló el usual chillido continuo de las cigarras.

El primer temblor fue corto pero también sin ruido. Oí a Zyanya susurrando asustada: «Zyuüu», y yo la abracé protectora y fuertemente contra mí. Después oímos un rumor largo, sordo como un gruñido que venía desde algún lugar tierra adentro. Uno de los volcanes de aquella sierra estaba vomitando, si es que no en erupción, tan violentamente que hacía temblar toda la tierra, tan lejos que llegaba hasta aquí.

El segundo y tercer temblor, y no puedo recordar cuántos más llegaron intensificándose con gran rapidez, con una mezcla de movimientos oscilatorios y simultáneamente rotatorios, de golpazos y meneos. Parecía como si la muchacha y yo hubiéramos sido puestos dentro de un tronco y luego haber sido lanzados sobre los rápidos de un río y entonces oímos el ruido, tan ensordecedoramente fuerte y prolongado que hubiéramos podido estar, igualmente, dentro de un tambor que rompe corazones, siendo tocado por un sacerdote demente. El ruido era producido por la montaña que se rompía en pedazos, haciendo que todas las rocas de ese gran peñasco se extendieran más sobre el mar.

Yo me preguntaba en qué momento Zyanya y yo estaríamos entre esos fragmentos, después de todo, los murciélagos habían huido de allí, pero ya no podíamos escurrirnos fuera del túnel, aunque tuviéramos pánico, ya que estábamos siendo fieramente sacudidos. Tratamos de acurrucarnos un poco más adentro del túnel, cuando de repente, la boca de éste se oscureció; un pedazo gigantesco había caído de lo alto de la montaña y había rodado exactamente allí. Afortunadamente para nosotros, siguió rodando y dejó que la luz entrara nuevamente aunque con una nube de polvo que llegó hasta nosotros haciéndonos toser.

Entonces mi boca quedó todavía más seca, pero fue de terror, al oír un sordo retumbido atrás de nosotros, que salía de *dentro* de la montaña. El vasto agujero de la caverna de los murciélagos era sacudido desde dentro; su techo, como una cúpula, se caía a pedazos atrayendo hacia sí, probablemente, todo el peso de la montaña. Yo esperaba que nuestro túnel se rompiera lanzándonos a los dos de pies adentro de ese colapso total y crujiente del mundo inmediato. Cubrí a Zyanya con mis brazos y puse mis piernas alrededor de ella, sosteniéndola todavía más apretadamente, con la pobre esperanza de que mi cuerpo le diera alguna protección, cuando los dos fuéramos arrojados dentro de las entrañas pulverizadas de la tierra.

Sin embargo, nuestro túnel se sostuvo firme y ése fue el último temblor alarmente. Lentamente el movimiento y los ruidos se aquietaron, hasta que no oímos más que unos cuantos ruidos afuera de nuestro refugio: el de piedras pequeñas que caían y guijarros que seguían detrás de las rocas más grandes, montaña abajo. Yo me moví, tratando de sacar mi cabeza hacia afuera para ver qué había quedado de la montaña, pero Zyanya me detuvo por la espalda.

«No, todavía no —me previno—. Todavía hay más temblores. O puede haber algún peñasco oscilando sobre nosotros, listo para caer. Espera un rato.» Por supuesto que ella tenía razón de ser prudente, aunque nunca le pregunté francamente si ésa fue la única razón por la que me detuvo.

Ya he mencionado los efectos que un temblor de tierra tiene sobre un ser humano fisiológica y emocionalmente. Yo sé que Zyanya podía sentir mi *tepuli* erecto contra sus pequeñas partes. Y aun teniendo puesta su blusa y yo mi manto, podía sentir la erección insistente de sus pezones contra mi pecho.

Al principio murmuró: «Oh, no, Zaa, no debemos...»

Luego dijo: «Por favor, no, Zaa. Tú fuiste el amante de mi madre...»

Y luego dijo: «Tú fuiste el padre de mi hermanito. Tú y yo no podemos...»

Si bien su aliento estaba acelerado, siguió diciendo: «Esto no está bien...», hasta que al fin dijo, con lo que le restaba de aliento: «Bien, tú me salvaste amorosamente de esos salvajes...», después de lo cual, jadeó silenciosamente hasta que los gritos y gemidos de placer empezaron. Luego un poquito más tarde, ella susurró: «¿Lo hice bien?»

Si hay algo bueno que decir de un temblor, debo hacer notar que su singular movimiento ayuda a una muchacha virgen a disfrutar su desfloración, que rara vez se consigue de otra manera. Zyanya se deleitó tanto con eso que me retuvo hasta que nos entregamos el uno al otro dos veces más y tanto vigor me había dado el temblor, que en todo ese tiempo no nos desunimos. Después de cada eyaculación mi *tepuli* naturalmente se encogía, pero entonces el pequeño círculo de músculos que Zyanya tenía allí, lo apretaba tan atormentadoramente que mi miembro se volvía a alargar. Hubiéramos podido seguir así por más tiempo sin ninguna pausa, pero la boca del túnel se oscureció en esos momentos en un singular color gris-rojizo y como deseaba saber cuál era nuestra situación antes de que cayera la noche, nos escurrimos hacia afuera y nos pusimos de pie. Era después del ocaso, pero el volcán o el temblor había lanzado una nube de polvo hacia el cielo y en ella todavía se reflejaban los rayos de Tonatíu, desde Mictlan, o desde donde se encontraba en ese momento. El cielo, que había estado azul oscuro, estaba entonces luminosamente rojo y coloreaba de rojo el mechón que Zyanya tenía en el pelo. También reflejaba la suficiente luz para que nosotros pudiéramos ver alrededor.

El océano estaba bullendo y agitándose espumosamente, alrededor de un área mayor de rocas. El camino que habíamos tomado para escalar la montaña ya no era reconocible; en muchas partes tenía montones de cascajo, en otras se había abierto en profundas y anchas grietas. A un lado de nosotros la montaña se había hundido formando un agujero negro, exactamente en donde había estado la caverna de los murciélagos.

«Parece —reflexioné—, que las rocas al deslizarse aplastaron a todos nuestros perseguidores y quizá también su aldea desapareció. Si no fue así, seguro que nos culparán del desastre y tratarán de vengarse más.»

«¿*Culparnos?*», exclamó Zyanya.

«Yo profané el lugar sagrado de su poderoso dios. Supondrán que provoqué su ira. —Pensé acerca de eso interrogándome, y dije—: A lo mejor lo hice. —Después volví a la realidad—. Pero si pasamos aquí la noche en este lugar escondido, y mañana nos levantamos temprano y nos vamos antes del amanecer, creo que podemos poner bastante distancia a cualquier tipo de persecución. Cuando otra vez tengamos a la vista a Tecuantépec...»

«¿Podremos regresar, Zaa? No tenemos provisiones, ni agua...»

«Todavía tengo mi *maquáhuitl*. He cruzado peores montañas de las que hay de aquí a Tecuantépec. Cuando regresemos... Zyanya, ¿querrás casarte conmigo?»

Se sorprendió de mi abrupta proposición pero no exactamente por ese hecho. Ella dijo suavemente: «Yo supuse que ya había contestado antes de que tú me lo preguntaras. Quizá sea inmodesto de mi parte lo que voy a decir, pero no puedo culpar totalmente al *zyuüu* por... lo que pasó.»

Dije sinceramente: «Le doy las gracias al *zyuüu*, por haber hecho esto posible. Sin embargo, desde hace mucho tiempo te quiero, Zyanya.»

«¡Está bien, entonces!», dijo ella, y sonrió hermosamente haciendo un gesto con sus brazos, como diciendo, está hecho. Yo negué con mi cabeza, dando a entender de que no era tan fácil y su sonrisa desapareció para dejar paso a cierta ansiedad.

Dije: «Para mí, tú eres el más grande tesoro que jamás tuve la esperanza de encontrar. Para ti, yo no lo soy. —Ella empezó a hablar, pero yo moví otra vez mi cabeza—. Si tú te casas conmigo, serás proscrita para siempre de tu gente, la Gente Nube. No es un pequeño sacrificio el ser relegado por este pueblo unido, orgulloso y admirable.»

Ella pensó un momento, luego me preguntó: «¿Me creerías si te dijera que eres una persona de mucho valor?»

«No —dije—, porque estoy mejor informado de mi valor o de mi falta de valor, más de lo que tú sabes.»

Ella asintió como si ya esperara una respuesta parecida. «Entonces lo único que puedo decir es que amo más a un hombre llamado Zaa Nayàzú, que lo que amo a la Gente Nube.»

«¿Por qué, Zyanya?»

«Pienso que te he amado siempre... pero no hablemos de lo pasado. Solamente te digo que te amo hoy y que te amaré mañana. Porque el pasado se ha ido. Los hoy y los mañanas serán todos los días que podrán ser. Y en cada uno de estos días te diré, te amo. ¿Puedes creer eso, Zaa? ¿Puedes tú decir lo mismo?»

Yo le sonreí. «Puedo, y más que puedo, lo haré. Te amo, Zyanya.»

Ella me devolvió la sonrisa y dijo de una manera traviesa: «No sé por qué estamos discutiendo eso. De todas maneras, parece que estamos marcados por nuestros destinos, por tu *tonali*, o por el mío o por los dos.» Y ella apuntó su pecho y el mío. El colorante que el sacerdote me había embarrado estaba todavía húmedo cuando nos acostamos juntos. Así es que, en esos momentos, cada uno de nosotros tenía una mancha púrpura idéntica, ella en su blusa y yo en mi manto.

Y luego dije tristemente: «He estado mucho tiempo enamorado de ti, Zyanya, y ahora que tenemos promesa de ser esposo y esposa quisiera preguntarte lo que nunca pensé preguntarte, ¿qué significa tu nombre?»

Cuando me lo dijo, yo creí que bromeaba y solamente después de su solemne insistencia, la pude creer.

Como seguramente ya se habrán dado cuenta hasta ahora, mis señores, todas las gentes de todas las naciones tenían nombres que tomaban prestados de alguna cosa de la naturaleza, o de alguna cualidad natural o alguna combinación de los dos. Esto se evidencia en mi propio nombre de Nube Oscura y de otros de los que ya he hablado: Algo Delicado, Glotón de Sangre, Estrella del Atardecer, Flor Llameante. Así es que me costó mucho trabajo creer que una muchacha tuviera un nombre que no significaba absolutamente *nada*. Zyanya es sólo una palabra común y corriente y no significa nada en el mundo más que siempre.

Siempre.

I H S

✠

S. C. C. M.

Santificada, Cesárea, Católica Majestad,
el Emperador Don Carlos, nuestro Señor Rey:

Muy Laudable Majestad, nuestro Mentor y Monarca, desde esta Ciudad de Mexico, capital de la Nueva España, en este día de San Próspero, en el año de Nuestro Señor Jesucristo de mil quinientos treinta, os saludo.

Como de costumbre, Señor, va anexado aquí la última emanación del azteca que reside entre nosotros, y también, como de costumbre: muy poco de *vis* y mucho de *vomitus*. Por la carta más reciente de Vuestra Majestad, es evidente que nuestro Soberano todavía considera esta historia lo suficientemente entretenida, como para que cinco hombres útiles continúen sujetos a escuchar y a transcribir.

Quizá, Vuestra Delicada Majestad, también pueda estar interesado en saber que los misioneros dominicos que nos, enviamos, han regresado sanos y salvos del sur, de la región llamada Oaxaca, para dar testimonio a nuestro azteca que clamaba que esos indios han estado adorando por mucho tiempo a un solo y omnipotente dios de dioses, extravagantemente conocido por el Aliento Poderoso, y que también han estado utilizando la cruz como un símbolo santo.

El hermano Bernardino Minaya y sus compañeros frailes han atestiguado que vieron en ese país muchas cruces similares a las Cristianas, por lo menos cruces en forma heráldica llamada *croix botonée*. Sin embargo, éstas no se utilizan para un fin religioso, sino que tienen un uso práctico, puesto que solamente sirven para marcar los lugares en donde hay agua fresca. Así es que el vicario de Vuestra Majestad se ha visto inclinado a considerar esas cruces con escepticismo agustino. Según nuestra apreciación, Señor, no son más que una manifestación más, astutamente maligna, del Adversario. Claramente anticipándose a nuestra llegada a la Nueva España, el Diablo debió de enseñar apresuradamente a cierto número de idólatras, una imitación profana de varias creencias, ritos y objetos sagrados Cristianos, con la esperanza de frustrar y confundir la Verdadera Fe, que más tarde nos, introduciríamos.

También, como los dominicos pudieron comprobar (aunque tuvieron dificultades lingüísticas), el Aliento Poderoso no es un dios sino un gran brujo (o sacerdote, o alguien como nuestro cronista) que tiene dominio sobre las criptas subterráneas, en las ruinas de esa ciudad llamada Mitla, considerada formalmente por los nativos como su Hogar Santo. Los frailes informados por nos, acerca de esos entierros paganos y de esos suicidios criminales o inmolaciones de vida voluntarios, en ese lugar, obligaron al brujo a permitirles acceso a esas criptas.

Como Teseo se aventuró en el Laberinto de Dédalo, fueron desenrollando un cordón detrás de ellos, mientras caminaban a la luz de las antorchas a través de las diferentes cuevas y de los tortuosos pasajes subterráneos. Fueron embestidos por la pestilencia de la carne corrompida y caminaron sobre los huesos de incontables esqueletos que yacían plácidamente allí. Desdichados y a diferencia de Teseo, perdieron su valor antes de haber podido caminar algunas leguas. Cuando se encontraron ante ratas y víboras gigantes y gordas, y otras clases de alimañas, su determinación se disolvió en horror y huyeron de la manera más indigna.

Una vez afuera, ordenaron que las entradas de los túneles fueran permanentemente tapadas y selladas con muchas piedras, «para poner un muro y esconder para siempre esa puerta trasera del Infierno», según la frase de Fray Bernardino. Eso se llevó a efecto, a pesar de las protestas y lamentaciones de los indios. La acción, por supuesto, estaba justificada y aunque ya ha pasado mucho tiempo y sin querer rebajar en la comparación, nos recuerda a Santa Catalina de Siena, quien rogaba que su cuerpo impecable fuera arrojado al Pit, para que así no hubiera más pobres pecadores que se arrojaran sobre sus aguas. No obstante, nos apena que nunca lleguemos a saber, ahora, la total extensión de esas cavernas talladas bajo tierra, y ya nunca podremos recobrar los tesoros que de seguro tenían en sus tumbas los personajes de alto rango de ese pueblo. Y lo que nos, más tememos, lo peor de todo, es que la acción impetuosa de los dominicos, ha hecho que los indios de esa región sean menos perceptibles a la Fe o que sientan muy poco amor hacia nosotros, que se la llevamos.

También con pena, tenemos que deciros que nos, personalmente, no somos mucho más amados por nuestros compañeros españoles, aquí en la Nueva España. Los encargados del Real Archivo de las Indias de Vuestra Majestad, quizás hayan recibido ya algunas cartas de personas que se quejan de nuestra «interferencia» en asuntos seculares. Dios sabe que ellos se han quejado lo suficiente con nosotros, sobre todo los hacendados, quienes emplean un gran número de trabajadores indígenas en sus granjas, ranchos y plantaciones. Esos señores propietarios han hecho un juego de palabras con nuestro nombre y ahora, irreverentemente, se dirigen a nos, como el Obispo Zurriago, «el Azote». Es por esto, Señor, que nosotros nos atrevimos a denunciar desde el púlpito sus prácticas de hacer trabajar a los indios literalmente hasta morir.

«¿Y por qué no lo hemos de hacer? —preguntan ellos—. Todavía quedan en estas tierras unos quince mil hombres rojos por cada hombre blanco. ¿Qué hay de malo en reducir esa peligrosa disparidad, especialmente si podemos forzar a trabajar a esos desgraciados, como lo hacemos?»

Los españoles que sostienen esa actitud, dicen que tienen una buena justificación religiosa para ello, *viz.*: porque como nosotros los cristianos rescatamos a esos salvajes de su adoración al demonio y de su inevitable condenación, y porque nosotros les trajimos la esperanza de su salvación, por eso, los indios deben estar eternamente agradecidos a nosotros, sus redentores. El capellán de Vuestra Majestad, no puede negar que hay cierta lógica en ese argumento, pero nosotros no creemos que el agradecimiento de los indios los obligue a morir indiscriminada y arbitrariamente, por golpes, por marcas de hierro, por falta de alimentación y otros malos tratos, y ciertamente, antes de que hayan sido bautizados y totalmente confirmados dentro de la Fe.

Ya que los datos recopilados por el censo y catastro de la Nueva España, todavía tienden a ser, necesariamente, irregulares e incompletos, nos, sólo podemos ofreceros un cálculo imperfecto sobre el número de la población nativa, pasada y presente. Sin embargo, hay razón para creer que aproximadamente seis millones de hombres rojos vivían en tiempos pasados dentro de los confines de lo que hoy es la Nueva España. Naturalmente, las guerras de conquista acabaron con una considerable cantidad de ellos. También, desde entonces y desde hace nueve años, se ha estimado que dos millones y medio de indios han muerto, bajo la autoridad española, de diferentes enfermedades, y sólo Dios sabe cuántos más están muriendo aún en las regiones no conquistadas y en todas partes, en gran número.

Aparentemente agrada a Nuestro Señor el que esa raza roja sea peculiarmente vulnerable a ciertas enfermedades que parece que no existían antes en estas tierras. Mientras que la pestilencia de la sífilis era conocida aquí (cosa que no es de sorprender en vista de su gente licenciosa), parece que las plagas de la fiebre bubónica, del cólera morbus, de viruelas negras, de viruelas blancas y del sarampión, no lo eran. Ya sea que esas enfermedades hayan hecho su aparición por coincidencia con la derrota de estos pueblos, o que sean un castigo que Dios en Su Juicio dejó caer sobre ellos, éstas han devastado a los indios con mucha más virulencia que a los europeos.

Pero aun así, esa pérdida de vidas, aunque es una calamidad de gran magnitud, como sea es debido a una causa natural, a un acto de Dios inescrutable y por lo tanto nuestros compatriotas no están obligados a sentirse afectados por ello. Sin embargo, nos, debemos poner un alto, como lo haremos, a la matanza de hombres rojos que deliberadamente cometen nuestros compatriotas. Vuestra Majestad nos dio otro oficio aparte del de Obispo e Inquisidor y nos, sostendremos ese título de Protector de los Indios, aunque eso signifique llevar sobre nos, el odioso título de Azote puesto por nuestros compañeros.

Si los indios nos ofrecen un trabajo barato y útil, debe esto considerarse desde un punto secundario para poder salvar sus almas paganas. Nuestro éxito en esta noble tarea se ve disminuido cada vez que un indio muere sin ser Cristiano. Si muchos de ellos mueren así, el nombre de la Iglesia sufrirá menoscabo. Además, si todos esos indios mueren, ¿quiénes construirán nuestras catedrales e iglesias, nuestras capillas y monasterios, nuestros conventos y claustros, nuestros santuarios y casas de retiro y todos los demás edificios Cristianos? ¿Quiénes constituirán, entonces, la mayor parte de nuestra congregación y quiénes van a trabajar para contribuir en el sostenimiento de los siervos de Dios, en la Nueva España?

Que Nuestro Señor Dios preserve a Vuestra Más Renombrada Majestad, ejecutor de muchas obras buenas, y que vos gocéis de los frutos de esas obras en Su Santa Gloria.

(ecce signum) ZUMÁRRAGA

SEPTIMA PARS

¿Es que Su Ilustrísima viene hoy a acompañarnos para escuchar cómo fue mi vida de casado?

Pienso que usted encontrará esta narración sin muchos incidentes... y tengo la esperanza de que sea menos molesta para la sensibilidad de Su Ilustrísima que los tiempos tempestuosos de mi primera juventud. Aunque tengo que decirle con pesadumbre que la ceremonia efectiva de mi boda con Zyanya estuvo nublada por la tempestad y la tormenta; sin embargo, estoy muy contento de poder decir que la mayor parte de nuestra vida marital fue alegre y tranquila. No quiero decir que ésta haya sido siempre insípida; con Zyanya experimenté muchas otras aventuras y estímulos; en verdad, su sola presencia llenó de entusiasmo cada uno de mis días. También en los años que siguieron a nuestro matrimonio, los mexica alcanzaron el pináculo de su poder creciendo en vigor y en algunas ocasiones me vi envuelto en acontecimientos, que ahora me doy cuenta de que tenían una pequeña importancia. Pero al mismo tiempo, ellos fueron para Zyanya y para mí —y sin duda también para la mayoría de la gente común como nosotros— sólo como una clase de figuras en movimiento de un mural pintado, en frente del cual vivíamos nuestras vidas privadas, nuestros pequeños triunfos y nuestra pequeña felicidad insignificante.

Oh, no quiere decir que *nosotros* miráramos cualquier pequeño aspecto de nuestro matrimonio como insignificante. Hace algún tiempo, pregunté a Zyanya cómo lo hacía para contraer trémulamente el pequeño círculo de músculos de su *tepili*, que hacía nuestro acto de amor tan excitante. Enrojeció de tímido placer y murmuró: «Es lo mismo que si me preguntaras cómo parpadeo. Lo hago así, simplemente. ¿No lo hacen todas las mujeres?»

«No conozco a todas las mujeres —dije—, y no deseo conocerlas ahora que tengo la mejor de todas.» Me abstuve de mencionar que ninguna de las mujeres que *había* conocido, incluyendo a su propia madre, nunca había manifestado ese talento particular. Pero creo que Su Ilustrísima no está interesado en estos detalles hogareños. Pienso que lo mejor que puedo hacer para que usted vea y aprecie a Zyanya, es compararla con la planta que nosotros llamamos *metl*, aunque por supuesto, el *metl* no es tan bello como ella era y no ama, ni habla, ni ríe.

El *metl*, Su Ilustrísima, es la planta del tamaño de un hombre, verde o azul, que ustedes nos han enseñado a llamar maguey. Bienhechor, generoso y aun bello de mirar, el maguey es el vegetal más útil que crece en cualquier parte. Sus hojas largas y curvas se pueden cortar y colocarse de tal manera extendidas, que pueden formar el techo de una casa, protegiéndola contra la lluvia. O las hojas se pueden golpear hasta hacerlas pulpa y prensadas y secas convertirse en papel. O las fibras de sus hojas ser separadas y torcerse para dar forma a cualquier tipo de cordón, desde cuerda hasta hilo, y éste se puede tejer para hacer una tela ruda, pero útil. Las duras y aguzadas espinas que están en los bordes de las hojas, pueden servir como agujas, alfileres o clavos. Éstas sirven a nuestros sacerdotes como instrumento de tortura, mutilación y automortificación.

Sus raíces, que crecen casi al ras de la tierra, son blancas y suaves, y se pueden cocinar para hacer un dulce delicioso. O se pueden poner a secar, y sirven para alimentar un fuego sin que eche humo, y las cenizas blancas que quedan son usadas para todo, desde alisar papel de corteza hasta hacer jabón. Si se corta la hoja del maguey por el centro, se puede hacer un hoyo hasta su corazón para extraerse una savia clara. Ésta es una bebida sabrosa y nutritiva. Embarrada sobre la piel, previene arrugas, salpullidos y la deja sin defectos; nuestras mujeres lo usan mucho para eso. Nuestros hombres prefieren dejar fermentar el jugo del maguey hasta convertirse en el emborrachador *octli*, o pulque, como ustedes lo llaman. Nuestros niños lo prefieren cocido hasta convertirse en un jarabe, que llega a ser tan pesado y dulce como la miel.

Para acabar, el maguey ofrece cada una de las partes y partículas de su ser, para el bien de nosotros que lo hacemos crecer y lo cuidamos. Y Zyanya era como él, aunque incomparablemente mejor. Poseía el bien en cada una de sus partes, en su manera de ser, en cada una de sus acciones, y no sólo para mí. Aunque, por supuesto, yo gozaba lo mejor de ella, nunca conocí a una persona que no la amara, la estimara y la admirara. Zyanya no era solamente siempre, ella era todo.

Sin embargo, no debo de malgastar el tiempo de Su Ilustrísima en sentimentalismos. Déjeme recordar las cosas en el orden en que éstas sucedieron.

Después de haber escapado de los asesinos zyú y de haber sobrevivido en ese fiero temblor de tierra, nos tomó a Zyanya y a mí siete días para regresar a Tecuantépec por la ruta de tierra. Ya fuera que el temblor había aniquilado a los salvajes o que éstos pensaran que había acabado con nosotros, no lo sé, el caso fue que ninguno de ellos nos persiguió y de esa manera no tuvimos ningún obstáculo al cruzar las montañas, excepto por la sed y el hambre ocasionales. Hubiera podido cazar algún animal con mi *maquáhuitl*, pero hacía mucho tiempo que había perdido mi cristal para encender fuegos en manos de los ladrones del istmo y no llevaba nada que me sirviera para encender, y nunca llegamos a tener tanta hambre como para comer la carne cruda. Encontramos suficientes bayas, frutas silvestres y huevos de aves, lo que podíamos comer crudo y todo eso nos proporcionaba suficientes jugos como para sostenernos hasta encontrar alguno de los arroyos poco frecuentes en la montaña. Por la noche, apilábamos montones de hojas secas y dormíamos entrelazados en ellas, para darnos mutuo calor y otras satisfacciones.

Quizá los dos estábamos un poco más delgados cuando llegamos a Tecuantépec; aunque ciertamente andrajosos, descalzos y con los pies lastimados, pues nuestras sandalias se habían quedado entre las rocas de las montañas. Llegamos al patio de la hostería tan cansados y tan agradecidos, como cuando mis compañeros y yo llegamos por primera vez a ese lugar; Beu Ribé salió corriendo a darnos la bienvenida, su rostro expresaba una mezcla de preocupación, exasperación y gran alivio.

«¡Pensé que habíais desaparecido, como nuestro padre, y que nunca más regresaríais! —dijo ella, mitad riendo, mitad regañándonos, después de haber abrazado apretadamente, primero a Zyanya y después a mí—. En el momento en que os perdísteis de vista, pensé que era una aventura tonta y peligrosa...»

Su voz decayó, en tanto nos miraba a Zyanya y a mí y vi perder su sonrisa otra vez. Pasó su mano ligeramente a través de su rostro y repitió: «Tonta... peligrosa...» Sus ojos se agrandaron cuando vieron más de cerca a su hermana y su mirada fue de enojo al dirigirla a mí.

A pesar de haber vivido muchos años y de haber conocido muchas mujeres, todavía no puedo saber cómo una de ellas puede percibir intensamente y con seguridad cuando otra se ha acostado con un hombre por primera vez. Luna que Espera miró a su hermana con sorpresa y decepción y a mí con ira y resentimiento.

Dije rápidamente: «Nos vamos a casar.»

Zyanya dijo: «Tenemos la esperanza de que tú lo apruebes, Beu. Tú eres, después de todo, la cabeza de familia.»

«¡Entonces, debíais habérmelo dicho antes! —dijo la muchacha mayor, con voz sofocada—. Antes de que tú... —Parecía estar ofendida por eso. Entonces sus ojos no miraban enojados, sino llameantes—. Y no con *cualquier* extranjero, sino con un bruto mexícatl lujurioso que continuamente está en celo, sin ninguna discriminación. ¿Cómo pudiste hacer eso, Zyanya? Si no hubieras sido tan convenientemente disponible —su voz se hizo más fuerte y más desagradable— es probable que hubiese regresado con una hembra mugrosa de los zyú, haciéndole la corte para que su largo e insaciable...»

«¡Beu! —jadeó Zyanya—. Nunca te he escuchado hablar así. ¡Por favor! Yo sé que esto es muy repentino, pero te puedo asegurar que Zaa y yo nos amamos.»

«¿Repentino? ¿Asegurarme? —dijo violentamente Luna que Espera y dejó caer su rabia sobre mí—. ¿Estás seguro? ¡Tú todavía no has probado a todas las mujeres de esta familia!»

«¡Beu!», volvió a rogar Zyanya.

Traté de conciliarlas, pero solamente me intimidé. «No pertenezco a la nobleza *pípiltin*. Sólo me puedo casar una vez en mi vida.» Eso me ganó que Zyanya me mirara tan tiernamente como su hermana. Así es que añadí rápidamente: «Quiero a Zyanya por esposa. Me sentiría muy honrado, Beu, si te pudiera llamar hermana.»

«¡Sí! —dijo ella casi regañándome—. Pero sólo el tiempo necesario para decirle a tu hermana adiós. Cuando te vayas te deberás llevar a tu... a tu *escogida* contigo. Gracias a ti, ella no tendrá aquí ni honra, ni respeto, ni nombre, ni hogar. Ningún sacerdote de los be'n zaa querrá casaros.»

«Ya sabemos eso —dije—. Iremos a Tenochtitlan a casarnos.

—Mi voz sonó firme—: Pero no será una ceremonia clandestina o vergonzosa. Nos casará uno de los sacerdotes más altos de la corte del Uey-Tlatoani de los mexica. Tu hermana ha escogido un forastero, sí, pero no un inútil vagabundo. Y ella se casará conmigo, con tu consentimiento o sin él.»

Hubo un gran intervalo de tenso silencio. Las lágrimas resbalaban por los rostros igualmente apesadumbrados y casi idénticamente bellos de las muchachas y el sudor corría por el mío. Los tres estábamos como en los vértices de un triángulo atado por invisibles tiras de *oli* extendiéndose cada vez más y más, en una increíble tensión. Pero antes de que cualquiera de ellas se rompiera, Beu relajó la tensión. Su rostro perdió energía y sus hombros se hundieron y dijo:

«Lo siento. Por favor, perdóname, Zyanya, y tú también, hermano Zaa. Por supuesto que tenéis mi consentimiento, mis más que amantes deseos por vuestra felicidad. Y os suplico que olvidéis las otras palabras que dije. —Trató de reírse de sí misma, pero su risa se quebró—. Esto ha sido tan repentino, como tú dijiste. Tan inesperado. No todos los día pierdo... una hermana tan querida. Pero ahora entrad. Bañaos, comed y descansad.»

Luna que Espera me odió desde ese día hasta ahora.

Zyanya y yo estuvimos más o menos diez días en la hostería, pero guardando una distancia discreta entre los dos. Como antes, ella compartió la habitación de su hermana y yo dispuse de una para mí, y tuvimos mucho cuidado de no hacer demostraciones públicas de afecto. Mientras nos reponíamos de nuestra infructuosa excursión, Beu parecía recobrarse del disgusto y de la melancolía que·nuestro regreso le había causado. Ayudó a Zyanya a elegir entre sus cosas personales y sus posesiones mutuas, unas pocas cosas relativamente queridas e irreemplazables que ella llevaría consigo.

Como otra vez me encontré sin suficientes semillas de cacao, tomé prestado una pequeña cantidad del dinero de las muchachas, para gastos de viaje y una cantidad adicional, que mandé con mensajero-veloz a Nozibe, para ser entregada a la familia que hubiera podido dejar el desventurado botero. También informé del incidente al Bishosu de Tecuantépec, quien dijo que él a su vez iba a informar al señor Kosi Yuela, de esa última salvajada cometida por los despreciables huave zyú.

En la víspera de nuestra partida, Beu nos sorprendió con una fiesta, como ella la hubiera hecho si Zyanya se hubiera casado con un hombre de los be'n zaa. Tuvo la asistencia de todas las personas que estaban hospedadas y había algunos invitados entre la gente del pueblo. Había alquilado músicos y danzantes en espléndidos trajes, que bailaban el *genda lizaa*, que es la tradicional danza «de espíritu de compañerismo» de la Gente Nube.

Con una apariencia por lo menos de buenos sentimientos entre nosotros, Zyanya y yo nos despedimos de Beu a la mañana siguiente, con besos solemnes.

No fuimos inmediata o directamente a Tenochtitlan. Cada uno de nosotros cargando un bulto, nos encaminamos hacia el norte, a través de las tierras llanas del istmo, el camino por el que había llegado a Tecuantépec. En esa jornada, ya que tenía que pensar en otra persona, fui especialmente precavido con los villanos que acechaban en los caminos. Llevaba mi *maquáhuitl* lista en la mano y miraba atentamente el terreno cuando éste tenía algún arbusto en donde se podría esconder alguien.

No habíamos caminado más de una larga-carrera, cuando Zyanya dijo simplemente, pero con una animación anticipada en el rostro: «Nada más piensa. Voy tan lejos de casa como nunca antes lo había estado.»

Esas pocas palabras envanecieron mi corazón y me hicieron amarla mucho más. Se estaba aventurando confiadamente en lo que era para ella un vasto territorio desconocido, solamente porque yo la cuidaba. Yo me sentía orgulloso y agradecido porque su *tonali* y el mío nos hubieran unido. Toda la gente que formó parte de mi vida fue dejada atrás en los ayeres y en los años pasados, pero Zyanya fue de algún modo siempre el *ahora*, fresca y nueva, sin ser trivial en la intimidad.

«¡Nunca hubiera creído —dijo ella, extendiendo sus brazos ampliamente— que pudiera *haber* tanta tierra, nada más que tierra!»

Aun siendo el paisaje árido en las tierras del itsmo, podía exclamar eso y hacer que compartiera con ella su sonrisa y su entusiasmo. Así sería a través de todos nuestros ahoras y mañanas juntos. Tuve el privilegio de darle a conocer cosas que para mí eran prosaicas, pero que para ella eran nuevas y extrañas. Y ella, en su incansable regocijo, hacía que yo viera esas cosas, también, como si fueran brillantemente novedosas y exóticas.

«Mira esa planta, Zaa. ¡Está viva! Y tiene miedo, pobre. ¿Ves?, cuando le toco una rama, ella enrosca sus hojas y sus flores apretadamente y saca sus espinas como si fueran blancos colmillos.»

Ella hubiera podido ser una joven diosa, tardíamente nacida de Teteoínan, la madre de los dioses, y enviada nuevamente del cielo a la tierra para trabar conocimiento con ella. Pues encontraba misterio, maravillas y delicias en cada pequeño detalle de este mundo, aun incluyéndonos a mí y a ella misma. Estaba tan llena de vida y centelleante, como la chispa encerrada en una esmeralda. Continuamente me sorprendía con sus actitudes inesperadas hacia cosas que yo consideraba ordinarias.

«No, no nos desvistamos —dijo, en nuestra primera noche de camino—. Haremos el amor, oh, sí, pero vestidos, como lo hicimos en las montañas.» Naturalmente protesté, pero se mantuvo firme y me explicó el porqué. «Déjame tener una pequeña y última modestia hasta nuestra boda, Zaa. Y entonces, el estar desnudos por primera vez, será como si todo fuera nuevo y diferente, como si nunca lo hubiéramos hecho antes.»

Le repito, Su Ilustrísima, que la narración completa de nuestra vida marital debe de ser muy poco dramática, porque sentimientos como la alegría y la felicidad son mucho más difíciles de expresarse en palabras que los simples sucesos. Sólo puedo decirle que en ese entonces, yo tenía veintitrés años y Zyanya veinte, y los amantes de esa edad son capaces de los mayores extremos y de una adhesión que nunca más conocerán. De cualquier modo, ese primer amor entre nosotros nunca disminuyó; creció en profundidad e intensidad, pero no puedo decirle el porqué.

Ahora que estoy recordando, creo que Zyanya pudo haber estado muy cerca de decirlo en palabras, hace ya mucho tiempo, en aquel día que partimos juntos. Uno de esos cómicos pájaros correcaminos huyó veloz de nuestro lado, fue el primero que ella vio en su vida, y me dijo pensativamente: «¿Por qué un pájaro prefiere la tierra al cielo? Yo no lo preferiría si tuviera alas para volar. ¿Lo preferirías tú, Zaa?»

Ayyo, su espíritu tenía alas y yo participaba de la alegría de sus sueños. Desde el principio, fuimos compañeros que compartíamos cada aventura encubierta. Nosotros amábamos la aventura y nos amábamos el uno al otro. Ningún hombre ni ninguna mujer hubieran podido pedir más de lo que los dioses nos habían dado a Zyanya y a mí, excepto quizá la promesa de su nombre: que fuera para siempre.

El segundo día nos encontramos con una caravana de mercaderes tzapoteca que viajaban hacia el norte, cuyos portadores iban cargados de conchas de tortugas de donde se consigue el carey. Éstas serían vendidas a los artesanos olmeca, para ser calentadas y torcidas y aprovechadas en la confección de ornamentos e incrustraciones ornamentales. Fuimos bien recibidos por los mercaderes y aceptados en su caravana y aunque Zyanya y yo hubiéramos podido viajar más rápido por nuestra cuenta, por seguridad seguimos en esa compañía hasta su destino, el pueblo de Coatzacoalcos, que está en el cruce de las rutas comerciales.

Apenas habíamos llegado al mercado de ese lugar y Zyanya revoloteaba excitadamente entre los puestos de apiladas mercancías y de ropa, cuando una voz familiar me gritó: «¡Vaya, no estás muerto entonces! ¿Es que hicimos ahorcar a aquellos desgraciados por nada?»

«¡Glotón de Sangre! —exclamé contento—. ¡Y Cózcatl! ¿Qué es lo que os ha traído hasta estos lugares tan distantes?»

«Oh, qué fastidio», dijo el viejo guerrero con voz aburrida.

«Él quiere decir que estábamos preocupados por ti», dijo Cózcatl, quien había dejado de ser un muchachito, para convertirse en un adolescente todo rodillas, huesos y ángulos.

«No, no estaba preocupado, sino *fastidiado* —insistió Glotón de Sangre—. Mandé construir una casa en Tenochtitlan, pero la supervisión de albañiles y yeseros no es un trabajo muy edificante. También los albañiles me hicieron notar que estarían mejor sin mis ideas. Y Cózcatl encontró los estudios de su escuela más o menos insípidos después de todas las aventuras que pasó. Así es que el muchacho y yo decidimos seguir tus huellas y averiguar qué habías estado haciendo durante estos dos años.»

Cózcatl dijo: «No estábamos seguros de estar siguiendo la ruta correcta hasta que llegamos aquí y nos encontramos con cuatro hombres que trataban de vender algunas cosas de valor. Nosotros reconocimos tu broche de piedra-sangre para el manto.»

«No pudieron dar una razón satisfactoria por la posesión de

esos artículos —dijo Glotón de Sangre—, así es que los llevamos ante el tribunal del mercado. Fueron juzgados, convictos y muertos por garrote. Ah, bueno, estoy seguro que ellos lo merecían por alguna otra fechoría. Como sea, aquí tienes tu broche, tu cristal para encender fuego y la turquesa para tu nariz...»

«Hicisteis bien —dije—. Ellos me robaron, me golpearon y me dejaron por muerto.»

«Así lo pensamos, pero teníamos la esperanza de que no lo estuvieras —dijo Cózcatl—. Y ya que no teníamos otra cosa que hacer desde entonces nos dedicamos a explorar estas costas de arriba y abajo. ¿Y tú, Mixtli, qué has estado haciendo?»

«También explorando —dije—. Buscando un tesoro, como simpre.»

«¿Encontraste alguno?», gruñó Glotón de Sangre.

«Bueno, encontré una esposa.»

«Una esposa. —Él carraspeó y escupió en la tierra con desprecio—. Y nosotros que temíamos que sólo estuvieras muerto.»

«El mismo viejo gruñón —dije riendo—. Pero cuando la veáis...»

Miré alrededor de la plaza, la llamé y en un momento ella estuvo con nosotros, parecía una reina como Pela Xila o la Señora de Tolan, pero infinitamente más bella. En ese pequeño espacio de tiempo, ella había comprado una blusa, una falda, sandalias y se las había puesto en lugar de sus vestidos manchados por el viaje y traía lo que nosotros llamamos una joya viva —escarabajos iridiscentes de muchos colores— prendida en su brillante mechón blanco. Creo que yo también me quedé con la boca abierta de admiración, como lo hicieron Cózcatl y Glotón de Sangre.

«Tenías razón en refunfuñar, Mixtli —concedió el viejo—. *Ayyo*, una doncella de la Gente Nube. En verdad, ella es un tesoro que no tiene valor.»

«Yo la reconozco a usted, mi señora —dijo Cózcatl galantemente—. Usted era la joven diosa de un templo disfrazado de hostería.»

Después de que los hube presentado, y que mis dos viejos amigos, creo yo, quedaron instantáneamente enamorados de Zyanya, dije: «Estoy muy contento por nuestro encuentro. Iba en camino hacia Xicalanca, en donde me espera otro tesoro. Creo que no será necesario que alquile portadores si nosotros cuatro podemos transportarlo.»

Así es que fuimos caminando tranquilamente, a través de esas tierras en donde las mujeres mascaban como manatíes y los hombres caminaban inclinados bajo el peso de sus identificaciones, hacia Cupilco, la ciudad capital y de allí al taller del maestro Tuxtem, quien nos enseñó los artículos que había confeccionado de los colmillos gigantes. Ya que sabía algo sobre la calidad del material que le había dado para trabajar, no me sorprendí tanto como lo hicieron Zyanya, Cózcatl y Glotón de Sangre, cuando vimos lo que él había hecho.

Como yo se lo había pedido, él había tallado figuritas de diosas y dioses mexica, algunos de ellos del tamaño de mi antebrazo, y dagas talladas, peines y otras cosas que también le había sugerido. Pero además, él había hecho unas calaveras más o menos del tamaño de la cabeza de un niño, que tenían grabadas intrincadas escenas de antiguas leyendas. También había hecho cajitas trabajadas artísticamente con tapas adecuadas, y redomas para perfume de *copali* con tapones del mismo material. Había tallado medallones, broches para mantos, silbatos y prendedores en forma de pequeños jaguares, búhos, pericos; exquisitas figuras de mujeres desnudas, flores, conejos, peces y caritas sonrientes.

En muchas de esas cosas, los detalles eran tan pequeñitos que solamente los pude apreciar bajo el escrutinio de mi cristal de aumento. Incluso se podía ver el *tepili* de una mujer desnuda, en un ornamento no mayor que una espina de maguey. Siguiendo mis instrucciones, Tuxtem no había desperdiciado ni un pequeño fragmento, ni una astilla: había hecho también adornos para la nariz, las orejas, pendientes y delicados palillos para los dientes y para los oídos. Todas esas cosas, pequeñas y grandes, brillaban bajo un blanco aperlado, como si poseyeran una luz interior propia, como si hubieran sido talladas por la luna. Eran tan agradables al tacto como a la vista; el artesano había hecho las superficies tan lisas como los pechos de Zyanya. Como su piel, ellos parecían decir: «Tócame, acaríciame, desliza tus manos sobre mí.»

«Usted me prometió, joven señor Ojo Amarillo —dijo Tuxtem— que sólo personas conocedoras podrían poseer una de estas cosas. Permítame la presunción de escoger a la primera de estas personas.»

Diciendo esto se arrodilló a besar la tierra ante Zyanya, luego se levantó y colgó alrededor de su cuello una cadena de delicados y sinuosos eslabones, que le debía de haber costado incontable tiempo de esculpido de una parte larga y dura del colmillo. Zyanya sonrió con una sonrisa radiante y dijo: «De verdad que el maestro Tuxtem me hace un honor. Nunca podrá haber otro trabajo como éste. Debería ser reservado para los dioses.»

«Yo solamente creo en lo creíble —dijo él irreverentemente—. Una mujer bella y joven, con una luz en su pelo, y un nombre en lóochi que sé que significa siempre, es una diosa más creíble que cualquiera.»

Tuxtem y yo dividimos los artículos como habíamos acordado y después dividí mi parte, otra vez, en cuatro y envolví cuidadosamente cada objeto en algodón. Las piezas trabajadas eran mucho menos pesadas y hacían menos bulto que lo que pesaban los colmillos anteriormente, así es que los fardos resultaron lo suficientemente ligeros como para que mis tres compañeros y yo los pudiéramos llevar, sin utilizar cargadores. De allí nos fuimos primero a una hostería en Xicalanca, en donde alquilamos cuartos para descansar, bañarnos y comer.

Al día siguiente, seleccioné una de nuestras nuevas adquisiciones: una pequeña daga con estuche, que tenía esculpida la escena de Quetzalcóatl remando fuera de la playa en su bote hecho de serpientes emplumadas. Después me vestí de lo mejor y mientras Cózcatl y Glotón de Sangre llevaban a Zyanya a conocer Xicalanca, yo fui al palacio a solicitar una audiencia con el noble gobernante de Cupilco, el Tabascoöb, como le llaman allí. De ese título, no sé por qué, ustedes los españoles le han concedido un nuevo nombre a toda esa tierra que antes era Cupilco.

El señor me recibió con mucha cortesía. Como casi todas las personas de otras naciones, él probablemente no sentía una afección prodigiosa hacia nosotros los mexica. Pero nosotros éramos los que teníamos más mercaderes y su tierra vivía del comercio.

Yo dije: «Señor Tabascoöb, uno de sus artesanos locales, el maestro Tuxtem, me hizo hace poco un trabajo artístico, único en su clase, con el cual espero conseguir una buena utilidad. Sin embargo, considero que es conveniente que la primera muestra sea presentada al señor de estas tierras. Así es que le ofrezco esta prenda como un regalo en nombre de mi propio señor, el Uey-Taltoani Auítzotl de Tenochtitlan.»

«Un gesto atento y un regalo generoso —dijo él, examinando la funda de la daga con gran admiración—. Un trabajo muy, muy bello. Nunca he visto otro igual.»

El Tabascoöb me dio las gracias efusivamente, también una pequeña caña con polvo de oro para el maestro Tuxtem y en una caja, con una colección de criaturas del mar, en baño de oro para su preservación y para añadirles más belleza, como un regalo recíproco para el Venerado Orador Auítzotl. Dejé el palacio con la sensación de que, por lo menos, había ayudado un poco en las buenas relaciones futuras entre Cupilco y Tenochtitlan.

Tenía la intención de mencionarle eso a Auítzotl, cuando inmediatamente después de nuestra llegada, al corazón y al Centro del Único Mundo, fui llamado a su presencia. Tenía la esperanza de que el regalo de buena voluntad enviado por el Tabascoöb pudiera inducir al Venerado Orador a favorecerme con una petición: que Zyanya y yo fuéramos casados por un sacerdote del palacio de impecable rango y condición. Sin embargo Auítzotl solamente me lanzó una mirada de sus ojos enrojecidos y gruñó:

«¿Cómo se atreve a venir a solicitar de nosotros un favor, después de haber desobedecido nuestras órdenes expresas?»

Honestamente no entendí y dije: «¿Desobedecido, mi señor?»

«Cuando nos trajo la narración de su primera expedición hacia el sur, nosotros le dijimos que permaneciera usted disponible para una discusión posterior. En lugar de eso, usted desapareció y privó a los mexica de una posible e invaluable oportunidad de conquista. Ahora regresa usted, dos años más tarde, dos años demasiado tarde, ¡sonsacando con regalos nuestro padrinazgo en una cosa tan frívola como una boda!»

Todavía perplejo, dije: «Le aseguro, Señor Orador, que yo nunca me hubiera ido si hubiera sospechado que estaba desobedeciendo. Pero... ¿qué oportunidad fue la que se perdió?»

«En sus palabras pintadas contaba cómo su caravana había sido acosada por bandidos mixteca. —Levantó la voz por la ira—. Nosotros, nunca hemos dejado que un ataque a nuestros *pochteca* viajeros, quede sin venganza. —Él estaba obviamente más enojado conmigo que con los bandidos—. Habiendo estado disponible para hacer presión sobre ese agravio, nosotros hubiéramos tenido una buena excusa para mandar un ejército contra los mixteca. Pero, sin tener al demandante...»

Yo murmuré mis disculpas y bajé la cabeza en señal de humildad, pero al mismo tiempo hice un gesto deprecatorio. «Los miserables mixteca, mi señor, poseen muy poco para ser conquistados. Sin embargo, esta vez regreso del extranjero con noticias de un pueblo, que sí posee algo de bastante valor, y que también ellos merecen castigo y yo puedo ofrecer la misma excusa válida para ser castigados. Yo fui tratado con más violencia por ellos.»

«¿Por quiénes? ¿Cómo? ¿Qué es lo que ellos poseen? ¡Hable! Pudiera ser que usted todavía se pueda redimir en nuestra estimación.»

Le narré cómo había descubierto la montaña de rocas en el mar, que servía de parapeto y habitación a los chóntaltin o los zyú o Los Desconocidos, esa rama de la tribus huave aislada y perniciosa. Le conté cómo esa gente es la única que sabe cómo, en dónde y cuándo bucear para encontrar los caracoles marinos y cómo hacer que esas feas babosas produzcan un hermoso colorante, púrpura profundo, que nunca se corre ni se decolora. Sugerí que ese producto único tendría un valor inmensurable en el mercado. Le dije cómo mi guía tzapoteca había sido asesinado por Los Desconocidos y cómo Zyanya y yo habíamos escapado con dificultad del mismo destino. Durante mi narración, Auítzotl había dejado el trono de piel de oso y empezó a dar grandes zancadas, excitadamente alrededor de la habitación.

«Sí —dijo él, sonriendo vorazmente—. El ultraje contra uno de nuestros pochteca puede justificar una invasión punitiva y el colorante solo, muy bien puede reparar éste. ¿Pero por qué nada más avasallar esa tribu de los miserables huave? La tierra de Uaxyácac tiene muchos más tesoros para ser adquiridos. Hace mucho tiempo, desde los días del reinado de mi padre, los mexica no han humillado a esos altivos tzapoteca.»

«Quiero recordar al Venerado Orador —dije rápidamente— que ni siquiera su padre Motecuzoma pudo mantener por mucho tiempo como vasallo de Tenochtitlan a ese pueblo que está tan lejos. Para poder hacer eso, se necesita una guarnición considerable y permanente en ese país. Y para sostener tal guarnición se requiere extender las líneas de suministro, siempre vulnerables de ser cortadas. Aunque fuera impuesto y mantenido un gobernante militar, éste nos costaría mucho más de lo que pudiéramos esperar de cualquier botín y tributo.»

Auítzotl gruñó:

«Usted siempre parece tener un argumento en contra de los hombres que quieren guerrear.»

«No siempre, mi señor. En este caso, yo le sugeriría que usted adhiera a los tzapoteca por aliados. Ofrézcales el honor de pelear al lado de sus tropas cuando usted caiga sobre los bárbaros huave. Después ponga usted a esa tribu costera bajo tributo, no directamente de usted, sino del Señor Kosi Yuela de Uaxyácac para que le entreguen a él todo ese colorante púrpura desde entonces y para siempre.»

«¿Qué? ¿Combatir una guerra y renunciar a sus frutos?»

«Déjeme terminar, Venerado Orador. Después de su victoria, usted haga un trato por el cual Uaxyácac se compromete a vender el púrpura a nadie más que a nuestros mercaderes mexica. De esa forma las dos naciones tendrán beneficios, aunque por supuesto nuestros *pochteca* revenderán el colorante a un precio mucho más elevado. Así usted atará a los tzapoteca a nosotros con los vínculos de un comercio creciente... y *por* haber peleado al lado de los mexica por primera vez, en una mutua aventura militar.»

Su mirada fija en mí empezó a ser especulativa. «Y si ellos pelean una vez como nuestros aliados, lo podrían hacer otra vez. Y otra vez. —Él me regaló con una mirada casi amistosa—. La idea es buena. Daremos la orden de marchar tan pronto como nuestro *tonalpoqui* haya escogido un día propicio para eso. Esté listo, Tequíua Mixtli, para tomar el mando de los guerreros que se le conferirán.»

Yo protesté: «Mi señor, pero si voy a casarme.»

Él rezongó: «*Xoquíui* —lo cual es una baja blasfemia—. Usted puede casarse en cualquier tiempo, pero un guerrero está siempre sujeto a ser llamado, especialmente uno que tiene un rango de mando. También, usted es otra vez la parte demandante en este asunto. Usted es nuestra excusa para invadir las fronteras Uaxyácac.»

«Mi presencia física no es necesaria, Señor Orador. La excusa ya la he dejado bien preparada.» Y le conté cómo había informado de las acciones perversas de Los Desconocidos al noble gobernante de Tecuantépec y a través de él al Señor Bishosu de aquellas tierras. «Ninguno de los tzapoteca siente afecto por esa advenediza tribu huave, así es que su camino hacia ellos no será impedido. En verdad es muy probable que Kosi Yuela no necesite ningún halago en lo absoluto, para unirse a usted en esa incursión de castigo, mi señor. —Hice una pausa y luego dije con modestia—: Espero haber hecho lo correcto, en la presunción de suavizar un avance entre los asuntos de sus señores, sus ejércitos y sus naciones.»

Por un corto espacio de tiempo, no hubo más sonido en la habitación que el tamborileo de los dedos de Auítzotl sobre la tapicería del respaldo de la banca, que sospecho que era de piel humana. Por fin dijo:

«Nos han dicho que su futura novia es incomparablemente bella. Muy bien. Ningún hombre que haya hecho ejemplares servicios por su nación debe pedírsele que anteponga los placeres de la guerra a los placeres de la belleza. Usted se casará aquí, en el salón de baile de la corte, que nosotros hemos mandado decorar recientemente. Un sacerdote de palacio oficiará... nuestro sacerdote de la diosa del amor Xochiquétzal, creo, no el dios de la guerra Huitzilopochtli... y todos nuestros criados darán el servicio. Invite a todos sus compañeros *pochteca*, sus amigos, cualquier persona que usted quiera. Mientras tanto, usted y su mujer vayan alrededor de la ciudad y escojan algún lugar que les guste para fijar su residencia, un lugar que todavía no esté ocupado o que su propietario quiera vender y ése será el regalo de bodas de Auítzotl.

✠

A su debido tiempo, en la tarde del día de mi boda, me aproximé nervioso a la entrada del salón de baile, que estaba atestado de gente y ruidoso, y me detuve lo suficiente para inspeccionar a la multitud a través de mi cristal; después, lejos de toda vanidad, lo guardé dentro de mi rico y nuevo manto, antes de poner un pie en la habitación. Había visto la nueva decoración del vasto vestíbulo, pinturas murales que podía reconocer aun sin firma... y que en esa multitud de nobles, cortesanos y plebeyos privilegiados, había un hombre alto que, aunque me daba la espalda en esos momentos, podía reconocer como el artista Yei-Ehécatl Pocuía-Chimali.

Me abrí paso entre la gente; algunos estaban parados, platicando locuazmente y bebiendo en copas doradas; otros, la mayoría mujeres nobles de la corte, ya estaban arrodilladas o sentadas alrededor de incontables manteles bordados con hilos de oro, que se habían extendido sobre el piso alfombrado. La mayoría de la gente se movía para darme una palmada en la espalda o para esestrechar mi mano, sonriendo y murmurando palabras de felicitación. Sin embargo, como lo requería la tradición, yo no decía o no hacían ningún gesto de reconocimiento. Fui a la parte de enfrente del salón, en donde se había extendido el más elegante mantel de todos sobre un elevado tablado y en donde un número de hombres me esperaban, entre ellos el Uey-Tlatoani Auítzotl y el sacerdote de Xochiquétzal. Después de que me saludaron, los artistas de la Casa de Canto empezaron a tocar una música.

En la primera parte de la ceremonia, en la que sería introducido a la edad viril, había pedido a los tres viejos *pochteca* que me hicieran ese honor, y en aquellos momentos estaban sentados en el tablado. Ya que sobre el mantel se habían puesto platones llenos de *támaltin* calientes y potentes *octli* y como estaba prescrito que los padrinos se fueran después de ese primer ritual, los tres viejos se habían despachado a sí mismos, a tal extremo que era completamente notorio que se encontraban ahítos, borrachos y medio dormidos.

Cuando se hizo silencio en todo el salón y sólo la música se podía oír, Auítzotl, el sacerdote y yo nos paramos juntos. Quizá supongan ustedes que un sacerdote de una diosa llamada Xochiquétzal, por lo menos, podría ser limpio en sus hábitos, pero aquél estaba tan profesionalmente mugroso, desgreñado y hediondo como cualquier otro. Y como cualquier otro, se aprovechó de la ocasión para hacer su discurso tediosamente largo, más lleno de advertencias horrorosas acerca de las trampas del matrimonio, que la mención de cualquiera de sus placeres. Finalmente terminó y Auítzotl habló dirigiéndose a los tres viejos sentados a sus pies, quienes sonreían borrachos y sentimentales, unas cuantas palabras directas:

«Señores *pochteca*, su compañero mercader desea tomar espo-

sa. Miren este *xeloloni* que les doy. Éste es el signo de que Chico-
me Xóchitl Tliléctic-Mixtli desea terminar por sí mismo, con
los días de su irresponsable soltería. Tómenlo y déjenlo libre para
ser un hombre en toda su virilidad.»

.El viejo que no tenía pelo aceptó el *xeloloni*, que era una pequeña hacha casera. Siendo yo un plebeyo común en su ceremonia
de casamiento, el *xeloloni* hubiera sido un simple utensilio de
mango de madera y cabeza de pedernal, pero aquél tenía un mango de plata sólida y un filo de fino jade. El viejo lo blandió en
su mano, eructó sonoramente y dijo:

«Hemos oído, Venerador Orador, nosotros y todos los presentes hemos oído el deseo del joven Tliléctic-Mixtli: que de aquí en
adelante sobrellevará todos los deberes, las responsabilidades y
privilegios de la virilidad. Como usted y él lo desean, que así sea.»

Borracho como estaba, hizo un dramático movimiento con el
xeloloni y estuvo a punto de cortar el pie que le quedaba a su
colega cojo. Después, los tres hombres se levantaron y se fueron,
llevándose el hacha simbólica, el hombre cojo iba saltando sobre
su pie entre los otros dos y todos ellos se bamboleaban al ir saliendo de la habitación. No hacía mucho que se habían ido, cuando oímos el clamor de la llegada de Zyanya al palacio, la multitud de plebeyos de la ciudad, que se apiñaban fuera del edificio,
le gritaban: «¡Muchacha feliz! ¡Muchacha afortunada!»

Todos los arreglos habían sido hechos a su debido tiempo,
porque ella había llegado exactamente cuando el sol se ocultaba,
como era lo apropiado. El salón de baile, que se había ido quedando gradualmente oscuro durante la ceremonia preliminar, entonces empezó a iluminarse de luces doradas, conforme los sirvientes fueron prendiendo, alrededor, las antorchas de madera de
pino en los ángulos que a intervalos se encontraban en las paredes pintadas. Cuando el vestíbulo estaba resplandeciente de luz,
Zyanya cruzó la entrada, escoltada por dos damas de palacio. Estaba permitido a una mujer en su boda, sólo esa vez en su vida,
embellecerse en extremo utilizando todas las artes en afeites de
las *auyanimi*, cortesanas: coloreando su pelo, aclarando su piel,
enrojeciendo sus labios. Pero Zyanya no necesitaba de tales artificios y no había utilizado ninguno. Llevaba una simple blusa
y falda de un virginal amarillo pálido, y había seleccionado para
esa ocasión los tradicionales festones de plumas a lo largo de sus
brazos y pantorrillas, las largas plumas blanquinegras de un pájaro, obviamente para resaltar el blanco mechón en su largo y
flotante pelo negro.

Las dos mujeres la guiaron hasta el entablado, a través de la
multitud que murmuraba de admiración, y ella y yo nos paramos uno enfrente del otro. Ella se veía tímida y yo solemne, como
lo requería la ocasión. El sacerdote tomó de uno de sus asistentes
dos objetos y nos dio uno a cada uno de nosotros; una cadena
de oro de la que pendía una bola de oro perforada, en cuyo interior se quemaba un poco de *copali*, incienso. Yo levanté mi cadena y balanceé la bola alrededor de Zyanya, dejando una voluta
olorosa de humo azul flotante alrededor de sus hombros. Después
me incliné un poco y ella hizo lo mismo parada en las puntas de

sus pies. El sacerdote nos recogió los dos incensarios y nos pidió que nos sentáramos lado a lado.

En ese momento, deberían de haber salido de entre la multitud nuestros parientes y amigos trayéndonos regalos. Como ninguno de los dos teníamos, solamente se acercaron Glotón de Sangre, Cózcatl y la delegación de la Casa de los Pochteca. Todos ellos, cada uno en su turno, besaron la tierra delante de nosotros y dejaron enfrente sus diversos regalos; los de Zyanya eran vestiduras: blusas, faldas, chales y cosas por el estilo, todas ellas de la más fina calidad; para mí, también cierta cantidad de ropa, además de una cantidad estimable de armas: una *maquáhuitl* bien labrada, una daga, un haz de flechas.

Después, cuando los donantes se habían retirado, llegó el momento en que Auítzotl y una de las mujeres nobles que había escoltado a Zyanya, por turnos nos cantaran la rutina de consejos paternales y maternales acerca del matrimonio. En una voz monótona y sin emoción, Auítzotl me previno, entre otras cosas, de no seguir acostado después de haber escuchado el canto del Pájaro Tempranero, Papan, sino levantarme inmediatamente y ponerme a trabajar. La madrina de Zyanya le recitó un copioso catálogo de obligaciones maritales, y a mí me pareció que dijo absolutamente todo, incluyendo su receta favorita para hacer *támaltin*. Como si eso hubiera sido una señal, un sirviente llegó portando un platón vaporoso de maíz y rollos de carne fresca y lo puso delante de nosotros.

El sacerdote hizo un gesto y Zyanya y yo tomamos un pedacito de *tamali* caliente y nos lo dimos mutuamente, que, por si ustedes nunca lo han tratado, les diré que no es una acción fácil de hacer. Mi barbilla quedó bien engrasada y la nariz de Zyanya corrió la misma suerte, pero cada uno de nosotros, por fin, llegó a comer un poquito de las otras ofrendas. Mientras hacíamos esto, el sacerdote empezó con otra arenga larga y rutinaria, con la cual no los aburriré. Todo terminó cuando él se inclinó hacia nosotros, tomando una punta de mi manto y otra punta de la blusa de Zyanya, las amarró juntas.

Estábamos casados.

La suave música de pronto sonó fuerte y festiva y gritos de alegría se propagaron entre los invitados allí reunidos, y desde esos momentos toda esa rígida ceremonia podía relajarse dentro de la jovialidad. Los sirvientes se movían con rapidez por todo el salón, repartiendo entre los manteles, platones de *támaltin* y jarras de *octli* y *chocólatl*. Cada uno de los invitados esperaba, para entonces, poder engullir y emborracharse hasta que las antorchas fueran apagadas al amanecer o hasta que los hombres cayeran inconscientes y fueran llevados a casa por sus mujeres y sus esclavos. Zyanya y yo comeríamos, sí, pero delicadamente, y luego seríamos guiados discretamente —todo el mundo pretendería que éramos invisibles— a nuestra recámara de bodas, que estaba escaleras arriba en una parte del palacio, dispuesta por Auítzotl para nosotros. Sin embargo en esos momentos, yo rompí la tradición.

«Discúlpame un momento, querida», le susurré a Zyanya y me

levanté para cruzar el salón, el Venerado Orador y el sacerdote me vieron con perplejidad y sus bocas se abrieron dejando ver pedazos de *tamali* a medio masticar.

Sin duda, en mi larga vida he sido odiado por muchas personas, ni siquiera sé por cuántas, pues nunca me he preocupado en contarlas o recordarlas. Pero en esos momentos tenía, en esa noche, en ese mismo salón, un enemigo mortal, un enemigo declarado e implacable y con sus manos ya manchadas de sangre. Chimali había mutilado y matado a varias personas que me eran queridas. Su próxima víctima sería, antes que yo, Zyanya. El haber asistido a nuestra boda era su modo de amenazar y su desafío a que hiciera algo por detenerlo.

Mientras caminaba en busca de Chimali, dando vueltas alrededor de los cuatro ángulos que componían los grupos de invitados sentados, éstos empezaron a dejar de parlotear hasta que se hizo un silencio expectante. Incluso los músicos bajaron el sonido de sus instrumentos para prestar atención. Al fin el silencio que imperaba en la habitación fue roto por un sonido colectivo, cuando con mi mano golpeé y mandé muy lejos, el vaso dorado que Chimali se llevaba a los labios, estrellándose musicalmente contra sus pinturas murales.

«No bebas mucho —le dije y todos lo oyeron—. Necesitarás una mente clara en la mañana. Al amanecer, Chimali, en el bosque de Chapultépec. Solamente nosotros dos, pero con cualquier clase y número de armas que tú quieras. A muerte.»

Me miró con una mezcla de disgusto, desprecio y cierta diversión, luego miró a sus vecinos que engullían a su alrededor. En privado, hubiera podido rehusar ese desafío, o poner condiciones e incluso evitarlo humillándose. Pero como ese desafío fue acompañado de un golpe insultante, que había sido visto y oído por cada uno de los ciudadanos más importantes de Tenochtitlan, él se encogió de hombros, alcanzó la copa de *octli* de otra persona, la levantó en un saludo perverso y dijo claramente: «Chapultépec. Al amanecer. A muerte.» Se lo bebió de un trago, se levantó y salió orgullosamente del salón.

Cuando regresé al tablado, la multitud empezó a murmurar y a platicar otra vez, detrás de mí, pero de algún modo su charla se oía como sojuzgada y atemorizada. Zyanya me miró con perplejidad, pero no me preguntó nada, ni se quejó de que hubiera convertido una ocasión tan feliz en otra cosa. El sacerdote, sin embargo, me vio con una mirada funesta de mal de ojo y empezó:

«Muy poco auspiciable, joven...»

«¡Cállese! —gruñó entre dientes el Venerado Orador, y el sacerdote cerró la boca. Auítzol me dijo a través de los dientes—: Su repentina entrada a la madurez y el desposorio ya le han trastornado.»

Yo dije: «No, mi señor. Estoy cuerdo y tengo una buena razón para...»

«¡Razón! —dijo interrumpiéndome sin levantar la voz, lo cual hacía que ésta sonara todavía más iracunda que si estuviera gritando—. ¿Una razón como para hacer un escándalo público en el día de su boda? ¿Una razón como para haber echado a perder una ceremonia arreglada para usted, como si fuera nuestro propio hijo? ¿Una razón como para agredir a nuestro palaciego e invitado personal?»

«Siento mucho si he ofendido a mi señor —dije, pero añadí con obstinación—: Mi señor hubiera pensado aún más mal de mí, si yo hubiera pretendido no darme cuenta de la burla que un enemigo me hacía con su presencia.»

«Sus enemigos son su problema. El artista de palacio es nuestro y usted lo ha amenazado de muerte. Y, mire allá, él todavía no ha terminado de decorar toda una pared de este salón.»

Yo dije: «Puede ser que la termine todavía, Señor Orador. Chimali era un luchador mucho más capacitado que yo, cuando los dos estuvimos juntos en la Casa del Desarrollo de la Fuerza.»

«Así es que en lugar de perder a nuestro artista de palacio, nosotros perderíamos entonces al consejero por cuyo consejo y al demandante por cuyo patrocinio, nosotros estamos preparándonos para marchar dentro de una nación extranjera. —Y todavía en esa media voz baja y amenazante me dijo—: Le prevengo ahora, y una prevención del Uey-Tlatoani Auítzotl no es como para tomarse a la ligera. Si cualquiera de los dos muere mañana; ya sea nuestro valioso pintor Chimali o Mixtli quien ocasionalmente nos ha dado valiosos consejos, será Mixtli a quien culpemos. Será Mixtli quien pagará, aunque él fuese el que muriera.»

Muy despacio, para que no pudiera equivocarme de lo que quería decir, volvió sus ceñudos ojos hacia Zyanya.

«Deberíamos de estar rezando, Zaa», dijo Zyanya con suavidad.

«*Estoy* rezando», le dije honesta y fervientemente.

Nuestra recámara contenía todos los muebles necesarios, excepto la cama, que no nos sería entregada hasta cuatro días después de la ceremonia. Los días y las noches intermedias se suponía que debíamos pasarlas ayunando, refrenándonos los dos en alimentación y en la consumación de nuestra unión, mientras rezábamos a nuestros dioses favoritos para que fuéramos buenos el uno con el otro y para que nuestro matrimonio llegara a ser un matrimonio feliz.

Pero yo estaba silencioso y devotamente empeñado en otra clase muy diferente de plegaria. Sólo estaba pidiendo a todos los dioses existentes, que Zyanya y yo pudiéramos sobrevivir a la mañana siguiente para poder *tener* un matrimonio. Antes, ya había pasado en situaciones muy precarias, pero nunca como ésa, de la cual era muy posible que no pudiera salir adelante, sin importar lo que hiciera. Si por una proeza o buena fortuna, o porque mi *tonali* así lo destinara, pudiera acertar a matar a Chimali, entonces podría escoger entre dos cosas. Podría regresar al palacio y dejar que Auítzotl me ejecutara por haber instigado el duelo. O podría huir y dejar a Zyanya para ser castigada, sin duda, en una forma horrible. La tercera circunstancia previsible, era que Chimali me pudiera matar, por su conocimiento superior en armas, o porque yo contuviera mi brazo al tratar de matarlo o, porque su *tonali* era más fuerte. En cuyo caso, yo estaría más allá del castigo de Auítzotl y él dejaría caer su furor sobre mi querida Zyanya. El duelo terminaría en una de esas tres eventualidades, y cada una de ellas era como para no pensarse. Pero no, había otra posibilidad: que simplemente no me presentara en el bosque de Chapultépec al amanecer...

Mientras pensaba en lo impensable, Zyanya quietamente estaba desempaquetando el pequeño equipaje que habíamos traído. Su exclamación de júbilo me hizo despertar de mi lóbrego ensueño. Levanté mi cabeza de entre mis brazos para ver que había encontrado en uno de mis cestos, la antigua figurita de barro de Xochiquétzal, la que yo había guardado desde la desgracia de mi hermana.

«La diosa que nos veía cuando nos casamos», dijo Zyanya, sonriendo.

«La diosa que te hizo para mí —dije—. Ella, la que gobierna toda belleza y amor. Deseaba que su estatua fuera un regalo de sorpresa para ti.»

«Oh, sí lo es —dijo ella fielmente—. Tú siempre me estás sorprendiendo.»

«Temo que no todas mis sorpresas han sido placenteras para ti. Como mi desafío con Chimali esta noche.»

«No conozco su nombre, pero me parece haberlo visto antes. O a alguien parecido a él.»

«Fe a él al que viste, aunque me imagino que él no se vestía como un elegante cortesano, en aquella ocasión. Déjame explicarte y tengo la esperanza de que tú comprenderás por qué tuve que echar a perder nuestra ceremonia de bodas, por qué no pude posponer lo que hice... y lo que tengo que hacer todavía.»

Mi explicación instantánea de la figurita de Xochiquétzal, unos momentos antes —que había deseado que fuera un recuerdo de nuestra boda— fue una mentira blanca que le conté a Zyanya. Sin embargo, en esos momentos en que le contaba mi vida pasada, entonces sí fui culpable de algunas omisiones deliberadas. Empecé con la primera traición de Chimali, cuando él y Tlatli se negaron a ayudar a salvar la vida de Tzitzitlini y dejé algunos huecos en mi narración, como el porqué de que la vida de mi hermana había estado en peligro. Yo le conté cómo Chimali, Tlatli y yo nos habíamos encontrado otra vez en Texcoco y, omitiendo algunos de los detalles más horribles, cómo había disimulado para poder vengar la muerte de mi hermana. Cómo, por cierta piedad o cierta debilidad, había quedado satisfecho con dejar caer la venganza sólo en Tlatli, dejando escapar a Chimali. Y cómo desde entonces, él continuamente me había pagado ese favor, molestándome a mí y a los míos. Y al final dije: «Tú misma me contaste cómo pretendió ayudar a tu madre cuando...»

Zyanya jadeó: «Él fue el viajero, quien atendió... quien *mató* a mi madre y a tu...»

«Él es —dije, cuando ella discretamente hizo una pausa—. Y porque ha pasado todo eso, cuando lo vi sentado arrogantemente en nuestra fiesta de bodas, determiné que él no mataría más.»

Ella dijo, casi con fiereza: «En verdad que debes enfrentártele. Y superarlo, no importa lo que el Venerado Orador dijo o lo que él haga. ¿Pero y si los guardias no te dejan salir del palacio al amanecer?»

«No. Auítzotl no conoce todo lo que te he dicho, él cree que es un asunto de honor. Él no me detendrá. Te detendrá a ti en mi lugar. Y es por esto que mi corazón sufre... no por lo que me pudiera pasar a mí, sino por lo que tú pudieras sufrir por mi impetuosidad.»

Zyanya pareció resentir eso último. «¿Piensas que soy menos valerosa que tú? Cualquier cosa que pase en el campo de duelo y cualquier cosa que venga después, yo estaré esperando con gusto. ¡Ya lo he dicho! Ahora, que si tú detienes tu mano, Zaa, es que lo estás utilizando como una excusa. Y no podría vivir contigo después.»

Yo sonreí tristemente. Así es que la cuarta y última elección no fue escogida por mí. Meneé mi cabeza y la tomé tiernamente entre mis brazos. «No —dije con un suspiro—. No detendré mis mano.»

«Nunca pensé que lo harías —dijo ella, como si fuera un hecho de que al casarse conmigo se hubiera casado con un campeón Águila—. Ahora no queda mucho tiempo para el amanecer. Recuéstate un rato y apoya tu cabeza en mí. Duerme mientras puedas.»

Parecía que apenas había puesto mi cabeza sobre su pecho suave, cuando escuché unos golpecitos discretos en la puerta y la voz de Cózcatl llamándome: «Mixtli, el cielo palidece. Es tiempo.»

Me levanté, mojé mi cabeza en una vasija de agua fría y arreglé mis vestidos arrugados.

«Él acaba de partir desde el atracadero —me dijo Cózcatl—. Quizás intenta tenderte una emboscada.»

«Entonces, sólo necesitaré armas para pelear de cerca, no para arrojar —dije—. Trae mi lanza, mi daga y mi *maquáhuitl*.»

Cózcatl corrió y yo pasé unos momentos amargos y dulces diciéndole adiós a Zyanya, mientras ella me decía palabras para darme valor y asegurarme de que todo iba a salir bien. Le di un último beso y bajé la escalera en donde Cózcatl me estaba aguardando con las armas. Había esperado que Glotón de Sangre también se presentara, pero él no estaba. Ya que él había sido el Maestro Quáchic, que nos enseñara a ambos, a Chimali y a mí, en la Casa del Desarrollo de la Fuerza, no hubiera sido bien visto que él diera consejos o aun apoyo moral a ninguno de los dos, cualesquiera que fueran sus sentimientos acerca del duelo.

Los guardias de palacio no hicieron nigún movimiento para impedirnos salir fuera de la puerta que conducía, a través del Muro de la Serpiente, dentro del Corazón de Único Mundo. El sonido de nuestras sandalias sobre el piso de mármol hacía eco de ida y vuelta desde la Gran Pirámide hasta los numerosos edificios menores. La plaza se veía mucho más inmensa que de ordinario, en esa temprana mañana; entre la luz aperlada y la soledad, no había más gente que unos pocos sacerdotes renqueando a sus deberes, en el amanecer. Dimos vuelta a la izquierda, en el portón del lado oeste del Muro de la Serpiente y fuimos a través de calles y sobre puentes de canales a la orilla de la isla, más cercana a la tierra firme. En el atracadero ordené que me dieran una de las canoas reservadas al palacio y Cózcatl insistió en remar y llevarme a través de esa extensión no muy ancha de agua, para que yo pudiera conservar la fuerza de mis músculos.

Nuestro *acali* golpeó la orilla, al pie de la colina llamada Chapultépec, en el lugar en que el acueducto se arquea desde la colina hasta la ciudad. Arriba de nuestras cabezas, los rostros esculpidos de los Venerados Oradores Auítzotl, Tixoc, Azayácatl y el primer Motecuzoma, nos miraban desde lo que antes había sido una roca natural. Otra canoa ya estaba allí, su cuerda amarrada estaba sostenida por un paje de palacio, quien apuntando hacia arriba y hacia un lado de la colina dijo cortésmente: «Él le espera en el bosque, mi señor.»

Yo dije a Cózcatl: «Tú espera aquí con el otro paje de armas. Pronto sabrás si te necesito más tarde o no.» Puse la daga de obsidiana en la cintura de mi taparrabo, tomé mi espada de filo de obsidiana en mi mano derecha y en la izquierda la lanza con punta de obsidiana. Fui a la cumbre del risco y miré hacia abajo, hacia el bosque.

Auítzotl había empezado a hacer un parque de lo que en toda forma había sido un bosque silvestre. Ese proyecto no sería terminado por varios años, todavía; los baños, las fuentes, las estatuas y demás, pero la floresta ya había sido cortada en su densidad para dejar solamente en pie los incalculablemente viejos y grandes *ahuehuetque*, cipreses, y la alfombra de pasto y flores silvestres que crecían en sus profundidades. Como yo estaba en esos momentos en la parte alta del risco, esa alfombra era casi invisible para mí y los poderosos cipreses parecían pararse sin raíces, mágicamente, en la neblina azul pálida que se proyectaba en el suelo, mientras Tonatíu se levantaba. Chimali hubiera podido pasar igualmente invisible para mí, si se hubiera escondido en cualquier parte, bajo esa neblina. En lugar de eso, en cuanto utilicé mi topacio, vi que había escogido yacer desnudo a lo largo de una rama gruesa de un ciprés, la cual colgaba horizontalmente, como a la mitad de mi estatura, más arriba del nivel del suelo. De momento eso me confundió. ¿Cómo era posible una emboscada tan sencilla? ¿Por qué estaba sin ropa?

Cuando capté su intención, creo que debí de haber sonreído como un *cóyotl*. En la recepción de la noche anterior, Chimali no me había visto ni una vez utilizar mi cristal para ver, y era obvio que nadie le había informado que tenía ese objeto artificial para mejorar mi visión. Se había quitado su ropa de brillantes colores, para que su cuerpo se confundiera con el color pardo oscuro del ciprés. Creía que de esa manera sería invisible a su viejo amigo Topo, su compañero de estudios Perdido en Niebla, mientras que yo iría tentaleando y buscando entre los árboles. Lo único que tenía que hacer, era esperar allí a salvo hasta que, entre mis tanteos vacilantes y cegatones, pasara al fin debajo de él. Luego balanceando su *maquáhuitl* hacia abajo, de un solo golpe, yo estaría muerto.

Por un instante, sentí que había sido casi injusto de mi parte tener la ventaja de mi cristal, con el cual había descubierto dónde estaba, pero luego pensé: «Debe de estar muy contento de que yo haya estipulado que nos encontráramos aquí.» Después de haberme despachado, él se vestiría y regresaría a la ciudad para contar cómo nos habíamos enfrentado cara a cara, bravamente, y cómo habíamos tenido un duelo salvaje y caballeroso, antes de que al fin me hubiera vencido. Conociendo bien a Chimali, estaba seguro de que incluso se haría unos cortes pequeños para hacer su historia más verídica. Así es que ya no tuve ni el menor remordimiento de lo que iba a hacer. Volví a poner el topacio dentro de mi manto, dejé caer mi *maquáhuitl* en el suelo y con ambas manos tomé el mango nivelado de mi lanza y me adentré en la niebla del bosque.

Caminé despacio y astutamente, como él esperaría del inepto luchador Perdido en Niebla; mis rodillas flexionadas, mis ojos como ranuras, como los de un topo. Por supuesto que no fui directamente hacia su árbol, sino que empecé a dar vueltas a uno que estaba a un lado, buscando entre una hilera de árboles a la misma distancia, después me volví a lo largo de otra hilera. Cada vez que yo me aproximaba a un árbol, buscaba lo más lejos posible dando golpes de ciego con mi lanza, alrededor del lado opuesto del tronco, antes de moverme más lejos. Sin embargo, había tomado nota mentalmente del lugar en donde se escondía y la posición de la rama en que yacía. Cuando, inevitablemente, me acerqué a ese lugar, empecé gradualmente a levantar mi lanza de su posición horizontal, hasta que la llevé completamente derecha enfrente de mí, apuntando hacia arriba, como Glotón de Sangre me había enseñado en la selva, para desanimar a los jaguares que yacían en las ramas esperando para dejarse caer, exactamente como Chimali lo estaba haciendo en esos momentos. Con mi arma en esa posición, me aseguré de que él no pudiera deslizarse enfrente de mí; él tenía que esperar hasta que la punta de mi lanza y yo pasáramos un poco más allá, debajo de él y luego golpearme en la parte de atrás de mi cabeza o en el cuello.

Me aproximé a su árbol como lo había hecho con los otros, agachado y despacio, andando a hurtadillas, continuamente volviendo mi rostro ceñudo y atisbando de lado a lado, manteniendo mi mirada cegatona al mismo nivel, sin mirar nunca hacia arriba. En el momento en que llegué bajo su rama, sostuve mi arma con las dos manos y al pasar la lancé hacia arriba y hacia atrás con todas mis fuerzas. Hubo un momento en que mi corazón dejó de latir, ya que la punta de mi lanza nunca lo tocó, se detuvo antes de haber tocado su carne, pues cayó con un ¡*crac*! sobre la rama e hizo que con el golpe mis brazos se sintieran entorpecidos. Sin embargo, Chimali debió de estar balanceando su *maquáhuitl* en ese mismo momento, ya que simultáneamente perdió el equilibrio. Por el golpe que le di a la rama él salió disparado, cayendo exactamente detrás de mí, y sobre sus espaldas.

411

El aire de sus pulmones se salió mientras su *maquáhuitl* saltaba de su mano. Me volteé con rapidez y lo golpeé en la cabeza con el mango de mi lanza, dejándolo inanimado.

Me incliné sobre él para darme cuenta de que no estaba muerto, pero de que sí estaría inconsciente por un tiempo. Así es que simplemente recogí su espada y volví hacia el risco, en donde recuperé mi espada y me volví a juntar con los dos jóvenes pajes de armas. Cózcatl dio un pequeño grito de alegría cuando me vio cargando el arma de mi oponente: «¡Sabía que lo matarías, Mixtli!»

«No, no lo hice —dije—. Lo dejé sin sentido, pero cuando despierte lo peor que puede sufrir será un dolor de cabeza. Si es que despierta. Una vez te prometí, hace mucho tiempo, que cuando llegara el momento de ejecutar a Chimali, tú decidirías en qué forma se haría.» Saqué mi daga de la banda de mi cintura y se la entregué. El paje nos miraba con fascinación horrorizada. Guié a Cózcatl hacia el bosque. «Tú lo encontrarás con facilidad. Ve y dale lo que se merece.»

Cózcatl asintió con la cabeza y con la daga en la mano se alejó de mi vista, risco abajo. El paje y yo esperamos. Su rostro estaba descolorido y contorsionado y tragaba saliva en un esfuerzo por no sentirse enfermo. Cuando Cózcatl regresó, antes de que llegara lo suficiente cerca como para hablar, pudimos ver que su daga ya no estaba lustrosamente negra, sino brillantemente roja.

Sin embargo él denegó con su cabeza, al aproximarse y dijo: «Lo dejé vivir, Mixtli.»

Yo exclamé: «¿Cómo? ¿Por qué?»

«Anoche escuché las palabras amenazantes del Venerado Orador —dijo disculpándose—. Estuve tentado a hacerlo, teniendo a Chimali indefenso delante de mí, pero no lo maté. Ya que él todavía vive, el Señor Orador no puede desahogar demasiado su ira contra ti. Sólo le quité esto a Chimali.»

Él tenía su puño convulsivamente apretado, hasta que lo abrió para que yo pudiera ver dos glóbulos relucientes y viscosos y una cosa blanda rojiza cortada más o menos a la mitad de su extensión.

Le dije al miserable paje que hacía esfuerzos por no vomitar: «Ya oíste. Él vive. Sin embargo necesitará de tu ayuda para regresar a la ciudad. Ve y trata de detener su hemorragia y espera a que recobre el sentido.»

«Así es que el hombre Chimali vive —dijo Auítzotl con frialdad—. Si es que usted puede llamarle a eso vida. Así es que usted cumplió con nuestra prohibición de no matarlo, por lo menos de no matarlo completamente. Así es que usted espera con alegría, que nosotros no nos sintamos ofendidos y no nos venguemos como lo prometimos. —Yo no dije nada prudentemente—. Nosotros le concedemos que usted obedeció nuestra palabra, pero no comprendió muy bien lo que nosotros dijimos en silencio. ¿Y qué de eso? ¿Qué uso mundano podemos darles a ese hombre en la condición presente?»

Para entonces ya me había resignado a ser, en todas las entrevistas con el Uey-Tlatoani, el foco de su mirada beligerante. Otros temblarían y se desanimarían bajo el influjo de esa horrible mirada, pero yo ya lo tomaba como una cosa usual.

Yo le dije: «Quizás, si el Venerado Orador quisiera escuchar mis razones por las que tuve que desafiar al artista de palacio, mi señor pudiera sentirse inclinado a ver con más benevolencia el trágico duelo que tuvo lugar.»

Él sólo gruñó, y tomé eso como permiso para que hablara. Le conté mucho de la misma historia que le había contado a Zyanya, sólo que esta vez omití mencionar todo lo relacionado con Texcoco, ya que todo eso había estado íntimamente ligado con su difunta hija. Cuando concluí con la narración de cómo Chimali había matado a mi hijo recién nacido, y de ahí mis temores por mi recién adquirida esposa, Auítzotl gruñó otra vez, luego meditó sobre el asunto —o por lo menos fue lo que supuse ante su hosco silencio —y al fin dijo:

«Nosotros no empleamos al artista Chimali por su vil amoralidad o a pesar de ella, o por sus peculiares propensiones sexuales, su naturaleza vengativa o su tendencia a la traición. Nosotros sólo lo empleamos por sus pinturas, que él las hace mucho mejor que cualquier otro pintor en nuestros días y en épocas pasadas. Por supuesto que usted no mató al hombre, pero ciertamente que usted mató al artista. Ya que le han sacado las ojos de las cuencas, no podrá pintar más. Ya que su lengua fue cortada, él ni siquiera puede decir a ningún otro de nuestros artistas, el secreto de la composición de esos colores únicos que él inventó.»

Yo me quedé callado, pensando solamente y con satisfacción, que tampoco podría el mudo y ciego Chimali revelar jamás al Venerado Orador, que yo había sido quien causó la desgracia pública y la ejecución de su hija mayor.

Él continuó, como si estuviera resumiendo el caso a favor y en contra de mí. «Nosotros todavía estamos encolerizados con usted, pero debemos aceptar como una mitigación las razones que nos ha dado por su conducta. Debemos aceptar que era un asunto de honor ineludible. Tenemos que aceptar que usted obedeció nuestra palabra, dejando que el hombre viviera, y nosotros sostendremos también nuestra palabra. Usted queda libre de todo castigo.»

Yo dije sincera y agradecidamente: «Gracias, mi señor.»

«Sin embargo, ya que nosotros hicimos nuestra amenaza en público y toda la población lo sabe en estos momentos, *alguien* debe expiar por la pérdida de nuestro artista de palacio.» Detuve el aliento, pensando en que seguramente sería Zyanya, pero sólo dijo con indiferencia: «Bien, ya pensaremos en eso. La culpa caerá sobre alguna nulidad disponible, pero todos sabrán que nuestras amenazas no se las lleva el viento.»

Dejé salir mi aliento retenido. Él tenía razón. Aunque sonaba inhumano, realmente no podía sentir pena o culpa a favor de esa víctima desconocida, quizás un esclavo rebelde, que moriría por el capricho de ese tirano orgulloso.

Auítzotl concluyó diciendo: «Su viejo enemigo será expulsado de palacio tan pronto como el *tícitl* haya terminado de vendar sus heridas. Chimali tendrá que vivir en un basurero como cualquier pordiosero callejero, en el futuro. Usted ha tenido su venganza, Mixtli. Cualquier hombre preferiría estar muerto a estar como usted dejó a ese hombre. Ahora salga de mi vista, antes de que me arrepienta. Vaya con su mujer, que probablemente debe de estar muy preocupada por su bienestar.»

Sin duda que ella lo estaba, tanto por mí como por ella, pero Zyanya era una mujer de la Gente Nube, y no dejaría ver su preocupación a ningún sirviente de palacio que pasara. Cuando entré a nuestra recámara, ella estaba de rodillas rezando con su rostro tan grácilmente sereno como su postura, y su expresión no cambió hasta que le dije: «Está hecho. Él está acabado y yo estoy perdonado.» Entonces lloró y rió y volvió a llorar y me abrazó apretadamente, sosteniéndome en sus brazos como si nunca más me quisiera dejar ir, otra vez.

Cuando le conté todo lo que había pasado, ella me dijo: «Debes de estar casi muerto de fatiga. Acuéstate otra vez y...»

«Me acostaré —dije—, pero no para dormir. Debo decirte algo. El escapar escasamente de un peligro, parece que tiene cierto efecto sobre mí.»

«Ya lo sé —dijo ella sonriendo—. Puedo sentirlo. Pero, Zaa, se supone que debemos de estar rezando todavía.»

Yo dije: «No hay una forma más sincera de rezar que amar.»

«No tenemos cama.»

«El suelo alfombrado es más suave que una gruta en la montaña. Y estoy ansioso de que cumplas la promesa que me hiciste.»

«Ah, sí, recuerdo», dijo ella. Y despacio, sin resistencia y atormentadoramente, se desvistió para mí, quitándose todo lo que tenía puesto, excepto el collar de eslabones blanco-perla, que el artesano Tuxtem le había colgado al cuello en Xicalanca.

¿Les he contado ya, mis señores, que Zyanya era como un vaso simétrico de cobre quemado, brillando como miel puesta al sol? La belleza de su rostro la había conocido desde hacía algún tiempo, pero la de su cuerpo, la había conocido al tacto. En esos momentos en que lo estaba viendo, tuvo razón en su promesa, ya que pareció como si hubiera sido nuestro primer contacto. Literalmente sentí dolor al poseerla.

Cuando se paró desnuda frente a mí, todas sus partes femeninas parecían presionar hacia adentro y hacia afuera, en un ofrecimiento ardiente de sí mismas. Sus pechos se mantenían altos y firmes, en sus esferas de pálido cobre, sus aureolas coloreadas de cacao sobresalían como pequeños globos y sus pezones se extendían, pidiendo ser besados. Su *tepili* se levantaba también alta y hacia afuera; aun cuando estuviera parada con las piernas unidas modestamente, sus suaves labios se abrían ligeramente en la parte alta, en donde se juntaban, para permitir una mirada a la perla rosa de su *xacapili*, que en aquel momento estaba húmeda, como una perla acabada de salir del mar...

Es suficiente.

Aunque Su Ilustrísima no está presente en estos momentos, para callarme con su habitual repulsión, no les voy a contar lo que pasó entonces. He sido francamente explícito acerca de mis relaciones con otras mujeres, pero Zyanya fue mi amada esposa y creo que seré el avaro más miserable con su recuerdo. De todo lo que he poseído en mi vida, sólo me quedan mis recuerdos. En verdad, pienso que los recuerdos son el único tesoro verdadero que cualquier ser humano tiene la esperanza de poseer para siempre. Y ése fue su nombre. Siempre.

Pero estoy divagando. La delicia de hacer el amor no fue el último suceso notable de ese día todavía más notable. Zyanya y yo estábamos abrazados, nuestra respiración para entonces era suave y yo me empezaba a dormir, cuando oímos unos golpecitos en la puerta, como los que había hecho Cózcatl un poco antes. Entre la niebla del sueño, tuve la esperanza de no ser citado a pelear en otro duelo; con un esfuerzo me puse de pie, me eché el manto encima y fui a investigar. Era uno de los sirvientes de palacio.

«Perdone que interrumpa sus devociones, señor escribano, pero un mensajero-veloz trae un requerimiento urgente de su joven amigo Cózcatl. Le pide que vaya lo más rápido posible a la casa de su viejo amigo Extli-Quani. Parece que el hombre se está muriendo.»

«Tonterías —dije con incredulidad—. Se deben de haber equivocado en el mensaje.»

«Ésa sería una esperanza, mi señor —dijo él con obstinación—, pero me temo que no sea así.»

«Tonterías», me dije a mí mismo, otra vez, pero empecé a vestirme apresuradamente mientras le explicaba el recado a mi mujer. «Tonterías —me seguía diciendo—, Glotón de Sangre no puede estar muriendo.» La muerte no podría clavar sus dientes en el pellejo curtido y robusto del viejo guerrero. La muerte no podría chupar, hasta secar, sus jugos todavía vitales. Podría ser que él fuera viejo, pero un hombre como él, todavía lleno de apetitos vitales no era lo suficientemente viejo como para morir. De todas maneras fui lo más rápido que pude y ya el sirviente me esperaba en un *acali* en el embarcadero de la corte, para llegar lo antes posible al cuartel Moyotlan de la ciudad.

Cózcatl me estaba esperando en la puerta de la casa, que todavía no estaba acabada de construir, retorciéndose las manos con ansiedad. «El sacerdote de La Que Come Suciedad está en estos momentos con él, Mixtli —dijo sollozando asustado—. Tengo la esperanza de que conserve suficientes alientos como para decirte adiós.»

«¿Entonces, sí *está* muriendo? —gemí—. ¿Pero de qué? Estaba en lo mejor de su vida en el banquete de la noche pasada. Comió como una bandada entera de buitres, y se la pasó poniendo su mano sobre las faldas de todas las muchachas que servían. ¿Qué pudo golpearlo tan de repente?»

«Supongo que los guerreros de Auítzotl siempre golpean de repente.»

«¿Qué?»

«Mixtli, yo creí que los cuatro guardias de palacio habían venido por mí, por lo que le hice a Chimali, pero ellos me hicieron a un lado con violencia y cayeron sobre Glotón de Sangre. Él tenía a mano su *maquáhuitl*, como siempre lo hace, así es que no sucumbió sin pelear y tres de los cuatro hombres estaban sangrando copiosamente cuando partieron. Sin embargo una de las lanzas alcanzó al viejo y lo hirió profundamente.»

Ese hecho hizo que mi cuerpo entero temblara de horror y de pena. Auítzotl había prometido ejecutar a una nulidad disponible en mi lugar; debió de haberlo escogido mientras decía eso; había descrito, una vez, a Glotón de Sangre como una nulidad, por ser demasiado viejo y no servir para otra cosa que no fuera ayudante o maestro, o como para hacer el papel de «nana» en mis expediciones mercantiles. Y había dicho que *todos* debían de saber que sus amenazas no se las llevaba el viento. Bien, entre esos todos estaba incluido yo. Me había felicitado a mí mismo por haber sido liberado del castigo, lo había celebrado alegremente con Zyanya y en ese mismo momento *eso* se estaba llevando a efecto. No se había hecho eso sólo para horrorizarme y agraviarme, eso se había hecho también para que desechara toda noción que pudiera concebir de ser indispensable y para prevenirme de que nunca más volviera a menospreciar los deseos del implacable y déspota Auítzotl.

«El anciano te lega la casa y todas sus posesiones, muchacho —dijo una nueva voz. Era del sacerdote, que estaba ya parado en la puerta, dirigiéndose a Cózcatl—. Ya me he hecho cargo de su testamento, pero necesitaré un testigo...»

Me moví para pasar al sacerdote y anduve a través de los cuartos de enfrente hasta llegar al de atrás. Sus paredes de piedra, que todavía estaban sin aplanar, se veían salpicadas de sangre y mi viejo amigo que yacía sobre su esterilla, estaba empapado en ella, aunque no vi ninguna herida en él. Tenía puesto sólo su taparrabo y estaba extendido sobre su vientre, su cabeza encanecida estaba vuelta hacia mí, sus ojos estaban cerrados.

Me dejé caer en la esterilla, a su lado sin fijarme en la sangre coagulada y dije apremiante: «¡Maestro Quáchic, soy su estudiante Perdido en Niebla!»

Abrió sus ojos lentamente. Luego uno de ellos se cerró otra vez, brevemente, en un guiño acompañado de una débil sonrisa. Sin embargo, las señales de la muerte estaban allí: su mirada, una vez viva y penetrante, se había ido y un color cenizo estaba alrededor de sus pupilas; su nariz, una vez carnosa, se había convertido en delgada y aguda como la de un mosquito.

«Siento mucho esto», dije con voz sofocada.

«No lo sientas —dijo lánguidamente y continuó con pequeños jadeos forzados—: Peleé antes de morir. Hay peores maneras de morir, y yo me las he ahorrado. Te deseo... un fin tan bueno como éste. Adiós, joven Mixtli.»

«¡Espera! —grité, como si hubiera podido ordenarle a la muerte—. Fue Auítzotl quien ordenó esto, porque peleé con Chimali, pero tú no tenías nada que ver con este asunto. Ni siquiera tomaste partido por ninguno. ¿Por qué el Venerado Orador se vengó en *ti*?»

«Porque yo fui —dijo él con trabajo— quien os enseñó a los

dos a matar. —Sonrió otra vez, mientras cerraba sus ojos—. Os enseñé bien, ¿no es así?»

Ésas fueron sus últimas palabras y nadie pudo haber pronunciado un epitafio mejor. Pero yo me rehusaba a creer que no pudiera hablar más. Pensé que quizá la posición en que estaba no lo dejaba respirar bien y que si lo giraba, descansaría mejor sobre su espalda. Desesperadamente, lo sostuve levantándolo para girarlo y al hacerlo todas sus entrañas se le salieron.

✠

Aunque tuve duelo por Glotón de Sangre y sentía que me hervía la sangre de ira ante su asesinato, me consolé pensando que Auítzotl nunca sabría cuánta pena me causó. Y aun así, de golpe a golpe, yo todavía tenía prioridad sobre él. Yo le había privado de una hija. Así es que hice un gran esfuerzo por tragarme mi bilis y mi pena, por dejar el pasado atrás y por empezar esperanzado a prepararme para un futuro libre de más derramamientos de sangre, de dolor, de rencor y de riesgos. Y así Zyanya y yo ocupamos nuestras energías en la construcción de un hogar. El sitio que elegimos, como ustedes recordarán, fue comprado por Auítzotl como un regalo de bodas para nosotros. Esa vez no decliné el ofrecimiento y hubiera sido muy poco político de mi parte desdeñarlo después de nuestras mutuas hostilidades, pero en verdad, yo no necesitaba de regalos.

Los viejos *pochteca* habían vendido las mercancías de mi primera expedición, de plumas y cristales, con un beneficio tan grande que, aun después de dividir la utilidades entre Cózcatl y Glotón de Sangre, yo era lo suficientemente opulento como para llevar una existencia cómoda, sin tener que desempeñar nunca más algún comercio, o levantar mi mano para hacer cualquier otro trabajo. Pero más tarde, la segunda entrega de mercancías foráneas había incrementado astronómicamente mi riqueza. Si los cristales para prender lumbre habían sido un notable éxito comercial, los artículos tallados de los colmillos habían causado una positiva sensación y entre la nobleza se había sobrepujado frenéticamente por ellos. Los precios que esos objetos alcanzaron nos hicieron lo suficientemente ricos a Cózcatl y a mí como para establecernos, y si lo hubiéramos deseado, habríamos llegado a ser tan entumecidos, complacientes y sedentarios como nuestros viejos de la Casa de los Pochteca.

El lugar que Zyanya y yo habíamos escogido para nuestro hogar estaba en Ixacualco, uno de los lugares más residenciales de la isla, pero entonces estaba ocupado por una casa pequeña y parda, de adobe. Contraté un arquitecto y le dije que la derribara y construyera en su lugar un sólido edificio de piedra caliza que pudiera ser un hogar lujoso y un placer para la vista de los que pasaban, pero sin ostentación en ninguno de los dos aspectos. Ya que el lugar era, como todos los de la isla, alargado y estrecho, le dije que lo hiciera de dos pisos. Especifiqué que quería un jardín azotea, una habitación dentro de la casa para el sanitario, con todos los aditamentos necesarios, y una pared falsa en uno de los cuartos, con un lugar amplio, entre muros, para poder esconder cosas.

Mientras tanto, sin haberme mandado llamar para otra consulta, Auítzotl marchaba hacia el sur, hacia Uaxyácac, aunque no llevaba un inmenso ejército, sino una pequeña tropa con los guerreros más experimentados; a lo sumo quinientos hombres. Dejó a su Mujer Serpiente en el trono temporalmente, pero llevó con él, como lugarteniente militar a un joven cuyo nombre les es familiar a ustedes los españoles. Era Motecuzoma Xocóyotzin, lo que quiere decir El Joven Señor Motecuzoma; de hecho, él era un año más joven que yo. Era sobrino de Auítzotl, hijo del anterior Uey-Tlatoani Axayácatl, por lo tanto nieto del primer y gran Motecuzoma. Hasta entonces él había sido un alto sacerdote del dios de la guerra Huitzilopochtli, pero aquella expedición era su primera prueba en una guerra real. Él tendría muchas más, porque dejó el sacerdocio para convertirse en un guerrero profesional y, por supuesto, en un comandante de alto rango.

Más o menos un mes después de que la tropa partió, mensajeros veloces de Auítzotl, empezaron a llegar a intervalos a la ciudad y el Mujer Serpiente hizo públicos sus mensajes. Por las primeras noticias que trajeron sus mensajeros, era obvio que el Venerado Orador estaba siguiendo el consejo que yo le había dado. Había enviado con anticipación un aviso de su llegada, y como yo se lo había predicho, el Bishosu de Uaxyácac había dado la bienvenida a sus tropas y contribuido con un número igual de guerreros. Esas fuerzas combinadas de mexica y tzapoteca, invadieron las playas y las madrigueras de Los Desconocidos, haciendo un trabajo rápido entre ellos, matando suficientes hombres entre los que se rindieron y dejando una leva permanente para tomar como tributo su colorante púrpura, por tanto tiempo guardado.

Sin embargo, los mensajeros que llegaron después no trajeron tan buenas noticias. Los victoriosos mexica se habían acuartelado en Tecuantépec, mientras que Auítzotl y el gobernante Kosi Yuela conferenciaban sobre asuntos de estado. Como esos guerreros por mucho tiempo habían estado acostumbrados a su derecho de pillaje, en cualquier nación que vencieran se pusieron muy enojados e iracundos cuando supieron que su jefe había cedido el único y visible botín, el precioso púrpura, al gobernante de esa nación. Los guerreros mexica pensaron que habían estado en combate sólo para beneficiar al gobernante de esa nación. Ya que Auítzotl no era de esa clase de hombres que justifican sus acciones ante sus inferiores y así consiguen apaciguarlos, los mexica simplemente se rebelaron contra cualquier contención militar. Rompieron filas, no respetaron la disciplina y corrieron salvajemente por todo Tecuantépec saqueando, violando y quemando.

Ese motín hubiera podido romper las delicadas negociaciones que se llevaban a efecto de una alianza entre nuestra nación y Uaxyácac, pero por fortuna, antes de que los desenfrenados mexica pudieran matar a alguien de importancia y antes de que las tropas tzapoteca se interfirieran, lo que hubiera significado una pequeña guerra, el orgulloso Auítzotl metió en orden a su horda y les prometió que, inmediatamente después de su regreso a Tenochtitlan, personalmente le pagaría a cada *yaoquizqui*, de su tesoro personal, una suma mucho más alta de lo que hubieran podido esperar como botín de esa nación. Como los guerreros sabían que Auítzotl era un hombre de palabra, eso fue suficiente para poner fin al motín. El Venerador Orador también pagó a Kosi Yuela y al Bishosu de Tecuantépec, una indemnización considerable por el daño que había sido causado.

Las noticias de los estragos hechos en la ciudad natal de Zyanya, naturalmente que nos preocuparon a ella y a mí. Ninguno de los mensajeros-veloces nos pudo dar noticias acerca de si la posada de nuestra hermana Beu Ribé había estado dentro del área del pillaje. Así es que esperamos hasta que Auítzotl y su tropa regresaron y entonces hice algunas indagaciones discretas entre sus oficiales, pero ni así pude tener la certeza de que algo le hubiera pasado a Luna que Espera.

«Estoy muy preocupada por ella, Zaa», dijo mi esposa.

«Pues parece que no se puede indagar nada, excepto yendo a Tecuantépec.»

Ella dijo vacilante: «Yo podría estar aquí y continuar con la dirección de la construcción de nuestra casa, si tú consideras...»

«No necesitas ni siquiera pedírmelo. De cualquier modo ya tenía en mente volver a visitar esos lugares.»

Ella parpadeó de la sorpresa: «¿Qué tú tenías en mente? ¿Por qué?»

«Un negocio que no he concluido —le dije—. Podría haber esperado un poco más, pero el no tener noticias de Beu significa que tengo que ir ahora.»

Zyanya comprendió rápidamente y jadeó: «¡Tú quieres ir otra vez a la montaña que camina en el agua! ¡No debes de ir, mi amor! ¡Esos bárbaros zyu casi te matan la última vez...!»

Yo puse mi dedo, suavemente, a través de sus labios. «Yo voy al sur en busca de noticias de nuestra hermana y ésa es la verdad, y ésa es la única verdad que tú debes decir a cualquier persona que te pregunte. Auítzotl no debe oír ningún rumor acerca de que yo pudiera tener otro objetivo.»

Ella asintió, pero me dijo con tristeza: «Ahora me tengo que preocupar por dos personas a las que amo.»

«Regresaré sano y salvo y también sabré de Beu. Si ha sido agraviada, veré lo que se puede hacer. O si ella lo prefiere puede acompañarme cuando yo regrese. Y también me traeré otras cosas preciosas.»

Por supuesto que Beu Ribé era lo que más me preocupaba y la razón inmediata para regresar a Uaxyácac. Pero también podrán percibir, reverendos frailes, que estaba cerca de consumar el plan que con mucho cuidado había preparado. Cuando le había sugerido al Venerado Orador que invadiera a Los Desconocidos y que llegara al acuerdo de tomar como tributo todo el colorante púrpura que ellos pudieran recolectar para siempre, no le mencioné el vasto tesoro que había en la cueva del Dios del Mar. Por las preguntas que hice a los guerreros que regresaron, sabía que, aun vencidos, Los Desconocidos no habían hecho alguna alusión acerca de la existencia de su colorante. Pero yo sí lo sabía y sabía de la gruta en la cual estaba escondido, y había arreglado que Auítzotl dominara lo suficientemente a los zyú, como para que me fuera posible ir y conseguir para mí esas fabulosas riquezas.

Hubiera llevado a Cózcatl conmigo, pero estaba muy ocupado, también, en terminar de construir la casa que había heredado de Glotón de Sangre, así es que sólo le pedí permiso para tomar prestadas algunas armas del viejo guerrero. Después fui alrededor de la ciudad y reuní a siete de los viejos amigos y guerreros de Glotón de Sangre. Como él, pasaban de la edad de servicio y estaban retirados de las armas, pero, como él, todavía estaban fuertes y vigorosos. También estaban enfadados con su aburrido retiro. Cuando, después de hacerles jurar que guardarían el secreto, les expliqué lo que tenía en mente, estuvieron muy ansiosos por la aventura.

Zyanya me ayudó a propagar la historia de que iba a saber qué había pasado con su hermana y que mientras estuviera viajando, también aprovecharía para hacer una expedición comercial. Así es que cuando los siete y yo nos encaminamos hacia el sur por el camino-puente de Coyohuacan, no causamos comentarios o curiosidad. Por supuesto, que si alguien nos hubiera observado de cerca, se hubiera preguntado por qué habría yo escogido a unos cargadores tan viejos y por qué todos ellos tenían cicatrices o narices u orejas cortadas. Si hubieran inspeccionado los bultos que los hombres cargaban, aparentemente llenos de mercancías para el trueque, hubieran encontrado que contenían, aparte de las raciones de comida y las cañas de polvo de oro, solamente escudos de piel y toda clase de armas que fueran más fáciles de manejar que la lanza larga; varias pinturas de guerra, plumas y otras insignias guerreras en miniatura.

Continuamos a lo largo del camino que nos llevaría por la ruta del sur, pero sólo hasta más allá de Quaunáhuac. Luego, abruptamente nos desviamos hacia la derecha, a lo largo de un camino que casi no se utilizaba y que conducía hacia el oeste, la ruta más corta hacia el mar. Ya que esa ruta nos llevaba, la mayor parte de nuestro camino, a través de la orilla sur de Michihuacan, nos hubiéramos visto en problemas si alguien nos hubiera *desafiado* y examinado nuestros fardos. Nos hubieran tomado por espías mexica y nos hubieran ejecutado instantáneamente o quizá no tan instantáneamente. Todas las veces que nuestro ejército mexica intentó invadir esa tierra, en tiempos pasados, siempre fue rechazado gracias a las armas superiores de los purémpecha, hecha con algún metal misteriosamente duro y agudo. Por supuesto, que cada purempe estaba siempre en guardia en contra de cualquier mexícatl que entrara en sus tierras, con cualquier motivo.

Debo hacer notar que Michihuacan, Tierra de Pescadores, era como nosotros los mexica la llamábamos, a lo que ustedes los españoles ahora le llaman la Nueva Galicia, sea lo que sea su significado. Para los nativos tenía varios nombres en sus diversas áreas —Xalisco, Nauyar Ixú, Kuanáhata y otros—, pero en su mayor parte lo llamaban Tzintzuntzani, En Donde Hay Chupamirtos, como su ciudad capital que lleva el mismo nombre. A su lenguaje se le llama poré y durante aquella jornada y las siguientes, aprendí lo más que pude de él, o mejor debería decir de ellos, ya que el poré tiene muchos y diversos dialectos locales, como los tiene el náhuatl. Por lo menos tengo suficientes conocimientos de poré como para preguntarme el porqué de que ustedes los españoles insistan en llamar a los purémpecha, los tarasca. Al parecer, ustedes tomaron ese nombre de la palabra poré *taraskue*, que los purémpecha usan para designarse a sí mismos, prudentemente, en una «relación distante» con los otros pueblos vecinos. En fin, no importa; yo he tenido más que suficientes y diferentes nombres. Y en esa tierra tuve otro: Anikua Pakápeti, que es el equivalente de Nube Oscura.

Michihuacan era y es una nación rica y vasta, tan rica como nunca lo ha sido el dominio de los mexica. Su Uandákuari o Venerado Orador, reinaba, o por lo menos cobraba tributo, sobre una región que se extendía desde los huertos frutales de Xichú, al este de las tierras Otomí, hasta el puerto mercante de Patámkuaro, en el océano sur.

Aunque los purémpecha estaban constantemente en guardia y contra una intrusión militar de nosotros los mexica, no estaban en contra del comercio, así que intercambiaban sus riquezas con nosotros. Incluso enviaban mensajeros-veloces diariamente para llevar pescado fresco a las mesas de nuestros nobles, a cambio, se permitía a nuestros mercaderes viajar por todo Michihuacan sin ser molestados, como lo hicimos mis siete presuntos cargadores y yo.

Si realmente hubiéramos pensado comerciar a lo largo del camino, habríamos podido conseguir muchas cosas de valor: perlas del corazón de las ostras; cerámica de rico cristal; utensilios y ornamentos hechos de cobre, plata, nácar y ámbar; objetos de brillante lacado que sólo se pueden encontrar en Michihuacan.

Esos objetos lacados le pueden tomar a un artesano, meses o años de trabajo, ya que varían en tamaño, desde una simple bandeja hasta un inmenso biombo.

Nosotros, los viajeros, podíamos adquirir cualquier producto local excepto el misterioso metal del que ya he hablado. A ningún extranjero le estaba permitido siquiera echar una mirada sobre él: incluso las armas hechas de ese material se mantenían guardadas, para ser distribuidas entre los guerreros sólo cuando las necesitaran. Ya que nuestros ejércitos mexica nunca habían podido ganar una simple batalla contra esas armas, ninguno de nuestros guerreros había podido recoger del campo de batalla ni siquiera un daga purempe tirada.

Bien, no comerciamos, pero mis hombres y yo probamos algunas comidas nativas que eran nuevas para nosotros o que rara vez estaban disponibles, por ejemplo, el licor de miel de Tlachco. Las ásperas montañas que circundaban esa nación, literalmente *zumbaban* todo el día. Puedo imaginarme que lo que oía era la vibración producida por los hombres, que bajo el suelo excavaban en busca de plata, pero arriba, en el exterior definitivamente podía oír el zumbido de enjambres y nubes de abejas entre las incontables flores. Y, mientras los hombres excavaban para desenterrar la plata, sus mujeres e hijos trabajaban en la recolección y elaboración de la miel dorada que producían esas abejas. Algunas veces, sólo se tenían que estirar las manos para tomar ese dulce sólido y claro; otras, lo tenían que dejar secar al sol, hasta que estuviera lo suficientemente dulce y cristalino. Alguna de esa miel, la convertían, por medio de un método tan celosamente guardado en secreto como el del metal, en una bebida que ellos llamaban *chápari*. Ésta era mucho más potente en sus efectos que el viscoso *octli* que nosotros los mexica conocíamos tan bien.

Ya que el *chápari*, como el metal, nunca se había exportado fuera de Michihuacan, mis hombres y yo tomamos todo lo que pudimos mientras estuvimos allí. También nos dimos un festín con los pescados, las ancas de rana y las anguilas de los lagos y los ríos de Michihuacan, cada vez que pasábamos la noche en una hostería. De hecho, pronto nos llegamos a cansar de comer pescado, pero esas gentes tenían una manera peculiar de pensar en contra de la matanza de cualquier animal disponible para la caza. Un purempe no cazaría un venado porque cree que éste es una manifestación del sol, y esto es debido a su creencia de que las astas de los venados machos se asemejan a los rayos del sol. Ni siquiera las ardillas pueden ser atrapadas o cazadas con dardos, porque a los sacerdotes purémpecha, tan sucios y desgreñados como los nuestros, los llaman *tiuîmencha*, y esta palabra quiere decir «ardillas negras». Así es que casi todas las comidas que tomamos en las hosterías eran a base de pescado o aves salvajes o domésticas.

Muy seguido, se nos daba a escoger *después* de que hubiéramos comido otro tipo de ofrecimientos. Creo que ya les he mencionado las actitudes que asumían los purémpecha acerca de las prácticas sexuales. Un forastero podía llamar a ésas un alivio perverso o ideas muy liberales y tolerantes, dependiendo de su propia actitud, pero de hecho se daba gusto a los más inconcebibles. Cada vez que terminábamos de comer, el posadero nos preguntaba a mí y luego a mis cargadores: «*Kaukukuárenti Kuézetzi iki Kuirarani?* ¿Qué prefiere usted para putear, un hombre o una mujer?» Yo no respondía por mis hombres; les pagaba lo suficiente como para que ellos escogieran por sí mismos. Sin embargo, ahora que tenía a Zyanya esperándome en casa, no me sentía inclinado a probar cada uno de los ofrecimientos de cada nación nueva que visitaba, como lo había hecho en mis tiempos de soltero. Invariablemente replicaba al posadero: «Ninguno de los dos, gracias», y el posadero siempre persistía pestañando o enrojeciendo: «*¿Imákani kezukezúndini?*», que traducido literalmente significa: «¿Entonces, usted come fruta verde?», que quiere decir lo que ustedes pueden suponer.

Para un viajero que buscara placer, realmente era necesario que especificara con claridad qué clase de *maátitl* deseaba —un hombre o una mujer ya madura o una jovencita o un jovencito— porque en Michihuacan a veces es difícil para un extranjero distinguir entre un sexo y otro, pues los purémpecha observan otra práctica peculiar. Todos aquellos que pertenecen a una clase más alta de las de los esclavos, depilan de sus cuerpos todo cabello o vello removible. Se rasuran o restregan, o de alguna otra forma se quitan todo cabello de sus cabezas, de sus cejas y hasta el más ligero trazo de vello debajo de sus brazos o en medio de sus piernas. Hombres, mujeres y niños no tienen absolutamente nada de cabello y vello a excepción de sus pestañas. Y en contraste con cualquiera de los actos deshonestos que pudieran hacer durante la noche, de día van modestamente vestidos por varias capas de mantos y blusas, y es por eso que es tan difícil de decir quiénes son las mujeres y quiénes los hombres. En un principio, supuse que la práctica de llevar el cuerpo liso y lustroso representaba para los purémpecha tanto una singular noción de la belleza como una afectación pasajera de la moda, aunque muy bien podría ser una razón de obsesión sanitaria. En mi estudio de su lenguaje, descubrí que el pore tiene por los menos ocho palabras diferentes para caspa y muchas más para despiojar.

Llegamos a la costa del mar, que era como un inmenso refugio azul protegido por dos brazos de tierra abrigadores, contra las tormentas marítimas y las fuertes marejadas. Allí estaban situados el puerto y la aldea de Patámkuaro, llamado así por sus habitantes y Acamepulco por nuestros visitantes mercaderes mexica; ambos nombres, en poré y en náhuatl, fueron dados por las grandes extensiones en donde crecían juncos y cañas. Acamepulco era un puerto pesquero por sus propios derechos, y también un centro de mercado para las gentes que vivían a lo largo de la costa, hacia el este y hacia el oeste, quienes llegaban en canoas para vender sus mercancías procedentes tanto del mar como de la tierra: pescados, tortugas, sal, algodón, cacao, vainilla y otros productos tropicales de esas Tierras Calientes.

Entonces, no tuve la intención de alquilar sino que quise comprar cuatro canoas amplias con sus remos, para que los ocho pudiéramos ir y venir remando, sin tener testigos observando. Sin embargo, eso era más fácil de intentar que de llevar a efecto. La canoa usual que se utilizaba en nuestros lagos, el *acali*, se hacía fácilmente de la madera suave del pino que crecía allí. Pero la canoa de mar, o *chékakua*, estaba construida con la madera pesada, dura y formidable de un árbol tropical llamado caoba y hacer una canoa llevaba meses de trabajo. Casi la mayoría habían sido usadas en Acamepulco a través de generaciones por una misma familia y ninguna deseaba vender, ya que eso significaría una suspensión temporal de toda utilidad proporcionada por la caza y la pesca mientras se construía una nueva. Pero finalmente pude adquirir las cuatro que necesitaba, aunque me costó todo mi poder de persuasión, frustrantes días de negociación y una cantidad mayor en polvo de oro de la que tenía en mente gastar.

No fue tan fácil como había supuesto, el remar a lo largo de la costa hacia el sureste, con dos de nosotros en cada *chékakua*. Aunque todos teníamos una gran experiencia en canoas de lago y las aguas de éstos algunas veces eran movidas tempestuosamente por los vientos, no estábamos acostumbrados a los tumbos de esas aguas de olas fluctuantes aun con el tiempo calmado que gracias a los dioses tuvimos en todo nuestro viaje por mar. Varios de esos fuertes y viejos guerreros cuyos estómagos jamás se habían revuelto ante los horrores nauseabundos de la guerra, se encontraron muy mal en los dos primeros días de viaje; yo no quizás porque ya había estado antes en el mar.

Pronto aprendimos a no navegar muy cerca de la costa en donde el movimiento del agua era más violento e impredecible. Aunque todos nos sentíamos como si estuviéramos en un gran columpio sobre el Único Mundo, nos lo pasábamos bastante bien más allá de las primeras olas rompientes, solamente remando hasta que el sol se ponía, para pasar las noches agradablemente sobre la arena suave de la playa.

Esa playa, como ya la había visto antes, se iba oscureciendo gradualmente de un blanco brillante a un gris total y luego a un negro profundo de arenas volcánicas, y de repente, la playa se interrumpió por un alto promontorio que se internaba en el mar; la montaña que camina en el agua. Gracias a mi topacio, pude espiar con facilidad la montaña desde lejos, y estando ya cerca el ocaso, di instrucciones para desembarcar en la playa.

Cuando estuvimos sentados alrededor del fuego de nuestro campamento, les repetí a mis hombres las acciones planeadas para nuestra misión en la mañana, y añadí: «Alguno de vosotros podría tener alguna reserva para levantar la mano en contra de un sacerdote, aunque éste lo fuera de un dios extranjero. No lo tengáis. Esos sacerdotes pueden parecer desarmados, simplemente molestos ante nuestra intrusión y desamparados ante nuestras armas; pero no lo están. A la primera oportunidad que les demos, nos matarán a cada uno de nosotros, luego nos ensartarán como a verracos y nos comerán a su placer. Mañana cuando todo esté listo, nosotros los mataremos sin piedad o correremos el riesgo de que nos maten. Recordad eso y recordad mis señales.»

Así, cuando a la mañana siguiente nos volvimos hacer a la mar, no éramos ya un joven *pochtécatl* con su siete viejos cargadores. Éramos un destacamento de siete temibles guerreros mexica guiados por uno no tan viejo, un *quáchic* «vieja águila». Habíamos deshecho nuestros fardos, poniéndonos nuestras insignias de guerra y nos habíamos armado.

Yo llevaba el escudo insignia *quáchic*, el bastón de mando y el yelmo *quáchic* de Glotón de Sangre. Lo único distintivo que me faltaba de ese rango era un hueso atravesado en la nariz, pero nunca me había perforado el puente de la nariz para poder utilizarlo. Los siete guerreros, como yo llevaban una dura armadura de blanco impoluto; se habían puesto sus plumas guerreras, sostenidas en lo alto de sus cabezas con una cinta de tal modo que formaran un abanico y se habían pintado de diferentes colores, fieros diseños en sus caras. Cada uno de nosotros llevábamos una *maquáhuitl*, una daga y una jabalina.

Nuestra pequeña flota remó descaradamente hacia el promontorio de la montaña, sin tratar de ocultarse, sino con la intención deliberada de que los guardianes nos vieran llegar. Y así fue, ellos nos estaban esperando a un lado de la montaña, por lo menos doce de esos malvados sacerdotes zyú, con sus vestiduras de pieles harapientas y parcheadas. No dirigimos nuestras canoas hacia la playa para desembarcar con facilidad, sino que remamos directamente hacia ellos.

No sé si porque era una estación diferente del año o porque nos aproximamos por el lado oeste de la montaña, el océano estaba mucho menos agitado de lo que había estado en aquel entonces, cuando el difunto botero tzapotécatl y yo llegamos por el lado este. De todas formas, el mar estaba lo suficientemente enojado y agitado como para que unos marineros tan inexpertos como nosotros, nos hubiéramos estrellado contra las rocas, de no ser porque algunos sacerdotes vinieron a nuestro encuentro para ayudarnos a desembarcar sanos y salvos. Naturalmente que lo hicieron gruñendo y solamente porque conocían y temían las costumbres de nuestros guerreros mexica, con lo que ya había contado.

Nosotros nos dimos maña para atracarlas allí y dejé a uno de los guerreros para vigilarlas. Entonces vadeé hacia las rocas haciendo un gesto para que me siguieran tanto mis hombres como los sacerdotes y todos empezamos ascender brincando de roca en roca a través de los tumbos y chorros de agua, a través de nubes de espuma de mar, hasta alcanzar el declive principal de la montaña. El sacerdote principal del Dios del Mar estaba parado allí, tenía sus brazos cruzados a través de sus pechos, intentando esconder sus muñones sin manos. Él no me reconoció inmediatamente bajo mi traje de batalla. Nos gritó algo en su dialecto huave. Cuando levanté mis cejas, en señal de que no comprendía lo que decía, él utilizó el lóochi diciendo con jactancia:

«¿A qué más vienen ustedes los mexica? Nosotros sólo somos los guardianes del color del dios y ustedes ya lo tienen.»

«No lo tenemos todo», dije en el mismo lenguaje.

Él pareció temblar ligeramente ante la brusca seguridad con que hablé, sin embargo insistió: «*Nosotros* no tenemos más.»

«No —me mostré de acuerdo con él—. Pero tiene uno que es mío. Un púrpura por el que pagué mucho oro. ¿Recuerda? En el día en que yo hice *esto*.» Con la parte plana de mi *maquáhuitl* separé sus brazos, de tal manera que los muñones de sus muñecas fueron visibles. Entonces me reconoció y su rostro malvado se veía todavía más horrible por la rabia y el odio impotente. Los otros sacerdotes que estaban a ambos lados de él se desparramaron alrededor de mí y de mis guerreros en un amenazante círculo. Había dos para cada uno de nosotros, sostuvimos nuestra lanza en un círculo de puntas levantadas. Yo dije al sacerdote principal: «Guíenos hacia la cueva del dios.»

Su boca se movió por un momento, probablemente intentando otras mentiras, antes de decir: «Su ejército dejó vacía la cueva de Tiat Ndik.»

Hice un movimiento hacia el guerrero que tenía a mi derecha. Éste clavó profundamente su jabalina en las entrañas del sacerdote que estaba parado a la izquierda del jefe. El hombre se dobló, cayó y rodó por el suelo, cogiéndose el abdomen y gritando continuamente.

Yo dije: «Esto es para demostrarles que estamos impacientes. Es para que vean que tenemos prisa.» Hice otro gesto y el guerrero punzó de nuevo al hombre caído, esa vez atravesándolo en el corazón y él dejó de gritar. «Ahora —dije al sacerdote principal— iremos a la cueva.»

Él tragó saliva y no dijo nada más; esa demostración había sido suficiente. Conmigo y mi jabalina a su espalda, y con mis guerreros apuntando a los restantes sacerdotes, nos guió todo el camino entre un montón de rocas y después por el hueco protector hasta la cueva. Sentí un gran alivio al encontrar que la gruta del dios no había sido devastada o enterrada por el temblor de tierra.

Cuando estuvimos enfrente del montón de piedras embadurnadas de púrpura que simulaban una estatua, señalando los recipientes de cuero y las redecillas de colorante que estaban amontonados por todas partes, dije al sacerdote principal: «Dígales a sus ayudantes que empiecen a llevar todo esto a nuestras canoas. —Él volvió a tragar saliva, pero no dijo nada—. Dígaselo —repetí—, o lo que le cortaré en seguida serán sus codos y luego sus hombros y así seguiré.»

Él dijo apresuradamente algo en su lenguaje que no entendí, pero que fue lo bastante convincente. Sin palabras, pero dirigiéndome miradas asesinas, los desgreñados sacerdotes empezaron a levantar y a acarrear los recipientes y los fardos de hilaza de algodón. Mis hombres los acompañaban de ida a los botes y de vuelta a la cueva, durante los muchos viajes que les tomó el llevar todo ese tesoro de un lugar a otro. Mientras tanto, el sacerdote manco y yo estábamos a un lado de la estatua, inmovilizado por la punta de mi lanza puesta bajo su barbilla. Hubiera podido utilizar ese tiempo en obligarlo a que me devolviera el oro que me había robado aquella otra ocasión, pero no lo hice. Preferí dejarlo como pago por lo que estaba haciendo, así no me sentía un ladrón, sino más bien un comerciante que está concluyendo una transacción ligeramente retrasada, pero legítima.

No fue sino hasta que los últimos recipientes fueron llevados afuera de la cueva, que el sacerdote principal habló otra vez, con odio en su voz: «Usted ya antes ha profanado este lugar santo. Usted hizo que Tiat Ndik se enojara tanto que él mandó el *zyuúú* como castigo. Él volverá a hacer eso o algo peor. No le perdonará este insulto y esta pérdida. El Dios del Mar no dejará que usted se vaya libremente con su púrpura.»

«Oh, quizás sí —dije tranquilamente—, si le dejo un sacrificio de otro color.» Y al decir esto, empujé mi jabalina hacia dentro y la punta pasó a través de la quijada, la lengua y el paladar hasta los sesos del hombre. Cayó totalmente sobre su espalda, un chorro de sangre manó de su boca y yo tuve que apoyar mi pie contra su barbilla para sacar el mango de mi lanza.

Oí un grito de inquietud y consternación atrás de mí. Mis guerreros acababan de llegar con los otros sacerdotes a la gruta y ellos habían visto caer a su jefe. Sin embargo, no necesité dar ninguna señal u orden a mis hombres; antes de que los sacerdotes pudieran recobrarse de esa estremecedora sorpresa, para pelear o huir, todos estaban muertos.

Yo dije: «Prometí un sacrificio al montón de rocas que está aquí. Acomodad todos los cadáveres enfrente y a su alrededor.»

Cuando eso fue hecho, la estatua del dios no se veía ya púrpura sino de un rojo brillante y la sangre manaba sobre el suelo de toda la cueva. Yo creo que Tiat Ndik debió de haber quedado muy satisfecho con esa ofrenda. No hubo ningún temblor de tierra mientras íbamos hacia nuestras canoas. Nada interfirió en contra de nuestro precioso cargamento o al echar al agua otra vez nuestros pesados botes. Ningún Dios del Mar agitó con violencia su elemento para evitar que nosotros pudiéramos remar libremente lejos, bien lejos de ese mar y de los alrededores de esas rocas cubiertas de agua hasta las partes más altas de su promontorio, fuera del territorio de Los Desconocidos. Sin ningún obstáculo remamos hacia el este directamente a la costa y nunca más volví a poner mis pies y mi mirada sobre la montaña que camina en el agua.

Sin embargo, todos nosotros seguimos llevando puestos nuestros trajes mexica de batalla en los siguientes días, mientras estuvimos todavía en aguas huave y tzapoteca, pasando Nozibe y otras aldeas costeras y hasta nos alejamos del istmo de Tecuantépec y llegamos al Xoconochco, la nación del algodón. Allí, desembarcamos por la noche en un lugar apartado y quemamos nuestros trajes y otras insignias, enterrándolo todo a excepción de unas cuantas armas. Luego volvimos a hacer nuestros fardos para poder transportar, entonces, los recipientes de cuero y las madejas de algodón con colorante.

Cuando nos hicimos a la mar al día siguiente, íbamos vestidos otra vez como un *pochtécatl* y sus cargadores. Desembarcamos en la tarde de ese mismo día, abiertamente, en el pueblo mame de Pijijía, y allí vendí nuestras canoas, aunque desgraciadamente a precio muy bajo ya que los pescadores de ese lugar, como los de todos los demás pueblos de la costa, tenían ya todos los botes que necesitaban. Como habíamos estado navegando por tanto tiempo, cuando mis hombres y yo tratamos de caminar lo hicimos balanceándonos ridículamente. Así es que pasamos dos días en Pijijía para acostumbrarnos otra vez a caminar en terreno sólido, lo que aproveché para tener unas conversaciones muy interesantes con los ancianos de los mame, antes de que volviéramos a tomar nuestros fardos y partir tierra adentro.

Usted me pregunta, Fray Toribio, por qué nos habíamos tomado tanto trabajo en hacer primero un viaje tan largo disfrazados como comerciantes, luego como guerreros y después otra vez como comerciantes.

Bien, la gente de Acamepulco sabía que un comerciante había comprado para él y para sus cargadores, cuatro canoas y la gente de Pijijía sabía que un grupo similar había vendido unas canoas similares y puede ser que a los dos pueblos les haya parecido una circunstancia extraña. Sin embargo, esos pueblos estaban tan lejos uno del otro que hubiera sido imposible que intercambiaran impresiones y ambos estaban tan distantes de las capitales tzapoteca y mexica que temía muy poco que sus chismes llegaron a los oídos del Bishosu Kosi Yuela o del Uey-Tlatoani Auítzotl.

Era inevitable que los zyú descubrieran pronto el asesinato de sus sacerdotes y la desaparición del púrpura acumulado en la cueva del dios. Aunque nosotros habíamos silenciado a todos los testigos del saqueo, era casi seguro que hubiera habido otros zyú en la playa que nos hubieran visto aproximarnos a la montaña sagrada o alejarnos de ella. Ellos *levantarían* un clamor que tarde o temprano llegaría a oídos de Kosi Yuela y de Auítzotl y que enfurecería a los dos Venerados Oradores. Pero los zyú sólo podrían imputar el hurto a un grupo de guerreros mexica, vestidos con sus atavíos de guerra. Kosi Yuela podría sospechar que Auítzotl le había jugado sucio para asegurarse ese tesoro, pero Auítzotl podría honestamente decir que él no sabía nada acerca de unos mexica que fueron en busca de botín por esa área. Por eso había estado vagando, para que hubiera una confusión tal que los guerreros nunca se podrían relacionar con los comerciantes y que ninguno de los dos grupos se pudiera nunca relacionar conmigo.

Mi plan requirió que fuera desde Pijijía a través de la hilera de montañas hacia la nación chiapa. Como mis portadores estaban con cargas muy pesadas, no vi la necesidad de que escalaran esas montañas. Así es que nos pusimos de acuerdo en el día y el lugar en que nos volveríamos a encontrar, en los eriales del istmo de Tecuantépec, y eso les daría tiempo suficiente para viajar con calma. Les dije que evitaran las aldeas y los encuentros con otros viajeros, pues un grupo de cargados *tamémime* sin el mercader que los guiaba podría provocar comentarios e incluso su detención para una investigación. Así es que cuando estuvimos bastante lejos de Pijijía, mis siete hombres se dirigieron hacia el oeste, quedándose en las tierras bajas del Xoconochco, mientras yo me dirigía hacia el norte, adentrándome en las montañas.

Al fin salí de ellas, para entrar en la magra ciudad capital de Chiapán y fui inmediatamente al taller del maestro Xibalbá.

«¡Ah! —dijo encantado—. Pensé que regresaría, así es que he estado coleccionando todo el cuarzo posible y haciendo nuevos cristales para encender lumbre.»

«Sí, se venden muy bien —le dije—. Pero esta vez insisto en pagarle el valor total de la mercancía y de su trabajo.» También le dije que mi topacio que ayudaba mi vista había enriquecido mucho mi vida, por lo cual le estaba profundamente agradecido.

Cuando terminé de arreglar mi fardo de cristales envueltos en algodón, quedé casi tan cargado como cada uno de mis portadores ausentes. Pero esa vez no me quise quedar y descansar en Chiapán, pues no me hubieran permitido quedarme en otro lado que no fuera la casa de los Maçaboö, y allí habría tenido que rechazar los avances amorosos de las dos primas, lo cual habría sido muy descortés por parte de un invitado. Así es que le pagué al maestro Xibalbá con polvo de oro y me apresuré a encaminarme hacia el oeste.

Varios días después, y tras haber buscado un poco entre los alrededores, encontré el lugar en donde me esperaban mis hombres, sentados alrededor de un fuego de campamento y rodeados de desechos de huesos de iguanas, armadillos y demás, lejos de toda área habitada. Allí nos quedamos sólo el tiempo suficiente como para que yo echara un sueño y para que uno de los viejos compañeros me cocinara la primera comida caliente que probé desde que los había dejado: un faisán *chachálatl* asado sobre el fuego.

Cuando llegamos a la ciudad de Tecuantépec a través del camino del este, pudimos ver los estragos hechos por los mexica, a pesar de que la mayoría de las áreas quemadas ya habían sido reconstruidas. De hecho, la ciudad había mejorado en muchas partes. Se habían construido casas decentes y fuertes en el lugar en donde antes había un área escuálida, en donde sólo se habían visto cabañas de gente miserable, incluyendo aquella que dejó una huella imborrable en mi vida. Cuando cruzamos la ciudad hacia la orilla oeste, encontramos que, aparentemente, los guerreros amotinados no habían llegado tan lejos en su violencia. La hostería que me era familiar, todavía estaba allí. Dejé a mis hombres en el patio, mientras que yo entraba vociferando a todo pulmón:

«¡Hostelera! ¿Tiene cuartos para un *pochtécatl* cansado y para sus cargadores?»

Beu Ribé salió de alguna habitación interior; estaba tan saludable, tan juiciosa y tan bella como siempre, aunque su único saludo fue:

«En estos días, los mexica no son muy populares en los alrededores.»

Yo le dije, tratando todavía de ser cordial: «Seguro, Luna que Espera, que tú harás una excepción con tu hermano, Nube Oscura. Tu hermana me mandó desde tan lejos, nada más para estar segura que estás bien. Estoy muy contento de ver que quedaste a salvo de todos esos problemas.»

«A salvo —dijo con voz cortante—. Yo también estoy muy contenta de que tú lo estés, ya que tú fuiste quien hizo que esos guerreros mexica vinieran aquí. Todo el mundo sabe que ellos fueron enviados por tus desventuras con los zyú y de cómo fallaste en apoderarte del colorante púrpura.»

Admití que todo eso era verdad. «Pero no me puedes culpar por...»

«¡Tengo bastante culpa que compartir contigo! —casi me escupió—. ¡Se me culpa, en primer lugar, de haberte dado siempre albergue en esta hostería! —Y luego, de repente, pareció desistir—. Aunque desde hace mucho tiempo he sido tratada con desprecio, ¿no es así? ¿Por qué me he de preocupar por la poca estimación que perdí? Sí, puedes tener una habitación y ya sabes dónde acomodar a tus cargadores. Los criados te atenderán.»

Ella me dio la espalda y se fue. Pensé para mis adentros que había sido una bienvenida un tanto tumultuosa, aun viniendo de una hermana. Sin embargo, los sirvientes acomodaron a mis hombres, pusieron las mercancías en un lugar y prepararon una comida para mí. Cuando terminé de comer y estaba fumando un *poquíetl*, Beu entró en la habitación y habría pasado de largo si no la hubiera detenido cogiéndola de la muñeca.

«No creas que me engaño a mí mismo, Beu —le dije—. Yo sé que no te caigo bien y los recientes desenfrenos de los mexica han servido para que tú me quieras todavía menos...»

Ella me interrumpió y sus cejas se levantaron con altivez: «¿Caerme bien? ¿Quererte? Ésas son emociones. ¿Qué derecho tengo de sentir cualquier emoción por ti, *esposo* de mi hermana?»

«Está bien —dije con impaciencia—. Despréciame. Ignórame. ¿Pero es que no le vas a mandar a Zyanya unas palabras, cuando yo regrese?»

«Sí. Dile que me violó un guerrero mexícatl.»

Aturdido, le solté la muñeca. Traté de pensar en algo que decir, pero ella se rió y continuó:

«Oh, no me digas que lo sientes mucho. Creo que todavía puedo decir que soy virgen, porque él era excepcionalmente inepto. En su deseo de avergonzarme, sólo confirmó la opinión tan baja que ya tenía de los arrogantes mexica.»

Le dije tratando de que mi voz se oyera: «Dame su nombre. Si no ha sido ejecutado todavía, veré que lo hagan.»

«¿Es que supones que él se presentó a sí mismo? —dijo riendo otra vez—. Creo que él no era un guerrero de rango común, aunque no conozco sus insignias militares y el cuarto estaba oscuro. Pero sí reconocí el traje que me hizo vestir para la ocasión. Me forzó a cubrir mi cara con hollín y a ponerme las vestiduras negras y tristes que usan las mujeres que atienden los templos.»

«¿Qué?», dije estupefacto.

«No tuvimos mucha conversación, pero me pude dar cuenta de que mi simple virginidad no era suficiente para excitarlo. Comprobé que sólo podía tener erección, si pretendía que estaba violando algo santo e intocable.»

«Nunca he oído hablar de tal...»

Ella dijo: «No trates de disculpar a tus paisanos. Y no necesitas tener lástima de mí. Ya te dije que ni siquiera podía ser un violador de mujeres. Su... creo que vosotros lo llamáis *tepuli*... su *tepuli* era nudoso, retorcido y doblado como un gancho. El acto de penetración...»

«Por favor, Beu —dije sintiéndome incómodo—. Lo que me estás contando no debe de ser muy placentero para ti.»

«La experiencia tampoco lo fue —dijo tan fríamente como si estuviera hablando de otra persona—. Una mujer que tiene que sufrir el ser víctima de una violación, por lo menos debería ser bien violada. Su *tepuli* defectuoso sólo podía penetrar hasta su cabeza o bulbo o como sea que llaméis a *eso*. Y a pesar de todos sus esfuerzos y gruñidos, ni siquiera lo pudo mantener allí. Cuando al fin emitió su jugo, éste simplemente goteó sobre mi pierna. No sé si hay diferentes grados de virginidad, pero *creo* que todavía me puedo llamar virgen. Pienso también, que ese hombre se sintió más humillado y avergonzado que yo. Ni siquiera me pudo mirar a los ojos mientras me desvestía otra vez, para que pudiera recoger esas horribles vestiduras de templo y llevárselas con él.»

No pude evitar decir: «Realmente no me suena como si fuera...»

«¿Como si fuera el típico mexícatl, sanguinario y muy macho? ¿Como Zaa Nayàzú? —Bajando la voz me susurró—: Dime la verdad, Zaa, ¿ha quedado mi hermana *realmente* satisfecha en su lecho conyugal?»

«Por favor, Beu. Eso es vergonzoso.»

Ella soltó una blasfemia: «¡*Gì zyabà!* ¿Qué puede ser vergonzoso para una mujer ya degradada? ¿Si tú no me lo dices, por qué no me lo demuestras? Pruébame que eres un marido adecuado. Oh, no te pongas colorado o te vayas. Recuerda que yo te vi una vez haciéndolo con mi madre, pero nunca nos dijo después si habías sido *bueno* para eso o no. Estaré muy contenta de saberlo por experiencia propia. Ven a mi cuarto. ¿Por qué has de tener escrúpulos en tomar a una mujer que ya ha sido utilizada? Aunque no mucho, por supuesto, pero...»

Cambié de tema con firmeza: «Le dije a Zyanya que te llevaría conmigo a Tenochtitlan si estabas sufriendo o en algún peligro. Tenemos una casa con bastantes habitaciones. Te lo pregunto, Beu, si encuentras tu situación intolerable aquí, ¿te vendrías con nosotros?»

«Imposible —gritó—. ¿Vivir bajo tu mismo techo? ¿Cómo puedo ignorarte allí, como has sugerido?»

Sin poder contenerme por más tiempo, le grité: «He hablado con cortesía, con contrición, con simpatía y con el cariño de un hermano. Te he ofrecido que empieces otra vez en un buen hogar, en una ciudad diferente, en donde puedas levantar la cabeza y olvidar el pasado. Pero tú sólo me contestas con burlas, despectivamente y con malicia. Me iré por la mañana, mujer, ¡y puedes venir conmigo si quieres!»

Ella no quiso.

Llegamos a la ciudad capital de Záachila, para seguir en mi papel de comerciante. Otra vez visité al Bishosu be'n zaa quien me recibió en audiencia y le conté mi mentira: como había estado vagando por la nación chiapa y como hasta hacía muy poco había sabido sobre los sucesos del mundo civilizado, le dije:

«Como el Señor Kosi Yuela·debe de haber adivinado, fue por mi instigación que Auítzotl trajo a sus hombres a Uaxyácac. Así es que me siento en la necesidad de pedir algunas disculpas.»

Él hizo un gesto como no dándole importancia. «Cualesquiera que hayan sido las intrigas en las que nos vimos envueltos, no tienen la menor importancia. Estoy muy contento de que su

Venerado Orador viniera con buenas intenciones y estoy satisfecho de que la larga animosidad que había entre nuestras naciones, haya cedido finalmente, además de que no tengo nada que objetar en recibir un tributo tan rico como el púrpura.»

Yo le dije: «Sin embargo los hombres de Auítzotl tuvieron una conducta reprobable en Tecuantépec. Simplemente como un mexícatl debo pedir disculpas por eso.»

«No culpé a Auítzotl. Ni siquiera culpo mucho a sus hombres.»

Debí de mostrar mi sorpresa, porque me explicó: «Su Venerado Orador se movió con rapidez para detener los ultrajes. A los peores los mandó matar por medio del garrote y a los demás los aplacó con promesas, que estoy seguro de que cumplirá. Luego pagó para expiar esos estragos o por lo menos lo más que se hubiera *podido* pagar por ellos. Nuestras naciones, probablemente, estarían en estos momentos en guerra si no hubiera sido porque actuó rápida y honorablemente. No, Auítzotl estaba ansiosamente humilde por restaurar las buenas relaciones.»

Era la primera vez que oía describir al colérico Monstruo del Agua con el apelativo de humilde.

«Sin embargo, había otro hombre, un hombre joven, su sobrino. Uno que estaba al mando de los mexica mientras nosotros conferenciábamos y fue cuando empezó el tumulto. Ese joven lleva un nombre que nosotros la Gente Nube detestamos por una razón histórica, él se llama Motecuzoma, y creo que ha heredado el deseo sanguinario de su tocayo. También creo que él vio como un signo de debilidad la alianza que Auítzotl concertó con nosotros. Pienso que desea a los be'n zaa como vasallos de los mexica y no como iguales. Tengo la fuerte sospecha de que él fomentó ese motín, con la esperanza de que nos degolláramos los unos a los otros, otra vez. Si usted puede hacerse oír de Auítzotl, joven mercader, le sugiero que le insinúe unas palabras para prevenirle acerca de su sobrino. Enaltecido de repente, este nuevo Motecuzoma, si llega a tener cualquier tipo de posición en el poder, podría arruinar todo el bien que su tío pudiera buscar para su satisfacción.»

✠

En el camino-puente hacia Tenochtitlan, en donde la ciudad iba apareciendo ante nosotros, luminosamente blanca contra el crepúsculo rojizo como el color de la tórtola, mandé a mis hombres adelante de dos en dos. La noche ya había caído cuando puse un pie en la isla y la ciudad estaba iluminada por las llamas de las antorchas, de los candiles y las lámparas. A través de esa parpadeante iluminación, pude ver que mi casa ya estaba terminada y que tenía una fachada muy bonita, pero no pude apreciar todos los detalles exteriores; ya que había sido construida sobre pilares más o menos de mi estatura, tuve que subir una pequeña escalera para entrar. Fui admitido por una mujer de mediana edad, que obviamente era una nueva esclava, ya que nunca antes la había visto. Ella se presentó como Teoxíhuitl, o Turquesa, y dijo: «Cuando los portadores llegaron, mi señora subió al piso de arriba, para que usted pudiera hablar en privado con los hombres sobre sus negocios. Ella le esperará en la alcoba, mi amo.»

La mujer me guió hacia una habitación que estaba en la planta baja, en donde mis siete compañeros estaban devorando una comida fría, que ella tuvo que preparar con precipitación. Después de que me dio a mí también un plato de comida y de que todos apaciguamos nuestra hambre, los hombres me ayudaron a mover la pared falsa del cuarto secreto y a guardar nuestros fardos allí, en donde ya habían sido almacenadas otras mercancías. Luego, les pagué el salario que les correspondía de regreso y les di más de lo que les había prometido, ya que se habían portado admirablemente. Todos besaron la tierra ante mí cuando se fueron, después de hacerme jurar que los citaría otra vez si concebía otros proyectos que fueran del agrado de siete viejos guerreros, que de otra forma estarían en el ocio de la paz y del aburrimiento.

En el piso de arriba, encontré el cuarto sanitario exactamente como le había dicho al arquitecto que lo quería: tan completo y eficiente como aquellos que se vaciaban solos y que había utilizado en los palacios. En el cuarto de vapor adyacente, la esclava Turquesa ya había colocado y calentado las piedras al rojo vivo y cuando terminé mi primer baño, dejó caer agua sobre ellas para producir una nube de vapor. Sudé allí por un rato y luego regresé al estanque de baño otra vez, hasta que estuve seguro de que todo el polvo, la suciedad y el mal olor del viaje estaban fuera de mis poros.

Cuando pasé desnudo de allí a la recámara, encontré a Zyanya igualmente desnuda y recostada sobre los suaves cobertores de la cama en una posición invitadora. Sólo había en la habitación la pequeña luz roja de un brasero, pero era suficiente para alumbrar su mechón de pelo pálido y delinear sus pechos puntiagudos. Cada uno de ellos era una bella semiesfera simétrica, en cuyas cumbres se encontraban sus pequeñas aureolas como otras esferitas, exactamente como ustedes pueden ver a través de la ventana el perfil del Popocatépetl, mis señores frailes; un cono sobre otro cono. No, por supuesto que no tengo necesidad de explicarles estos detalles. Sólo quería decirles qué fue lo que alteró mi pulso, mientras me encaminaba hacia Zyanya.

Yo le dije: «Tengo noticias que darte, pero pueden esperar.»

«Entonces deja que esperen», respondió ella con un susurro de voz y sonrió alargando su mano para alcanzarme.

Después le di las noticias que traía sobre Beu Ribé; de que estaba sana y salva, pero que era muy infeliz. Me alegro de que hubiéramos hecho primero el amor, ya que le proporcioné a Zyanya la languidez usual que da al último el placer satisfecho, con lo cual tenía la esperanza de que las palabras que dijera fueran o resultaran más suaves. Le conté el encuentro infortunado que Beu Ribé tuvo con el oficial mexica y traté de que se pareciera, tal como Beu lo había hecho, más a una farsa que a una tragedia.

Concluí diciéndole: «Pienso que es su orgullo obstinado el que hace que se quede allí, atendiendo la hostería. Tiene la determinación de no tomar en cuenta lo que la gente del pueblo pudiera pensar de ella, ya sea que sientan vergüenza o simpatía por ella. No dejará Tecuantépec por ninguna buena razón o por una vida mejor, porque eso sería tomado como un signo de debilidad por parte de ella.»

«Pobre Beu —murmuró Zyànya—. ¿Hay algo que podamos hacer por ella?»

Reprimiendo mi propia opinión acerca de la «pobre Beu», medité y dije al fin: «No puedo pensar en otra cosa, más que *tú* sufras una desgracia. Si tú, que eres su única hermana, la necesitaras con desesperación, creo que vendría a verte. Pero no provoquemos a los dioses. No dejemos que un infortunio nos ponga a prueba.»

Al día siguiente, cuando Auítzotl me recibió en su horrible salón del trono, otra vez conté la historia que había inventado; que había ido a ver si la hermana de mi esposa no había sufrido ningún percance en el saqueo de Tecuantépec, y que mientras estuve allí aproveché la oportunidad para ir un poco más hacia el sur, para procurarme más cristales para encender. Otra vez, ceremoniosamente le regalé uno y él me dio las gracias entusiasmado. Entonces, antes de traer a colación un tema que estaba seguro que se le saltarían los ojos y pondría su irascibilidad al rojo candente, le dije algo que aplacaría su carácter.

«En mis viajes, Señor Orador, he llegado hasta la costa de la tierra del Xonocochco, desde donde proviene la mayor parte de nuestro algodón y de nuestra sal. Pasé dos días entre la Gente Mame, en su aldea principal de Pijijía y los ancianos me llevaron a su consejo. Deseaban que yo trajera un mensaje al Uey-Tlatoani de los mexica.»

Él se encogió de hombros con indiferencia: «Dígame el mensaje.»

Yo dije: «Sepa usted, mi señor, que el Xoconochco no es una nación, sino simplemente una vasta extensión de tierra fértil, habitada por varios pueblos: Los mame, los mixe, los comiteca y otras tribus aún más pequeñas. Sus territorios se encuentran en esa extensión de tierra y están aliados por medio de esas tribus de ancianos como la de Pijijía. El Xoconochco no tiene una capital principal o un cuerpo de gobierno, ni un ejército.»

«Interesante —murmuró Auítzotl—. Pero no mucho.»

Continué sin dejarme apabullar: «Al este del Xoconochco, que es rico en huertos frutales, está la selva improductiva de la nación de Quautemalan, El Bosque Enmarañado. Sus nativos, los quiché y lacandón, son descendientes degenerados de los maya. Son pobres, sucios y flojos y en tiempos pasados fueron considerados como muy despreciables. Sin embargo, recientemente han sacado energías para salir de Quautemalan e invadir los territorios del Xoconochco. Esos desgraciados amenazan con hacer sus correrías más frecuentes, hasta convertirlas en una guerra continua, a menos de que los pueblos del Xoconochco estén de acuerdo en pagarles un gran tributo en algodón y sal.»

«¿Tributo? —gruñó Auítzotl, al fin interesado—. ¡*Nuestro* algodón y *nuestra* sal!»

«Sí, mi señor. Pues bien, es difícil poder esperar que un puñado de recolectores de sal y algodón, y simples pescadores puedan defender fieramente sus tierras. Sin embargo, han tenido las suficientes agallas como para encolerizarse ante esas demandas arrogantes. No están dispuestos a darles a los quiché y lacandón lo que nos han estado vendiendo formalmente y con provecho a nosotros los mexica. Ellos piensan que nuestro Venerado Orador debería sentirse igualmente ultrajado ante esta idea.»

«Ahorre su énfasis en lo que es obvio —rezongó Auítzotl—. ¿Qué es lo que sus ancianos proponen? ¿Que nosotros entremos en guerra con Quautemalan por ellos?»

«No, mi señor. Ellos ofrecen darnos el Xoconochco.»

«¿Qué?» Él se tambaleó honestamente sorprendido.

«Si el Uey-Tlatoani acepta las tierras del Xoconochco como un nuevo dominio, sus pequeños gobernantes abandonarán sus puestos y todas sus tribus dejarán a un lado sus identidades y todas sus gentes jurarán lealtad a Tenochtitlan, como mexica voluntarios. Sólo piden dos cosas: que les sea permitido seguir viviendo y trabajando como siempre lo han hecho, sin que se les moleste, y que continúen recibiendo un pago por su trabajo. Los mame, hablando por todas las demás tribus, quieren pedir que un noble mexícatl sea enviado como gobernante y protector del Xoconochco y que una fuerte guarnición de tropas mexica se establezca y sea mantenida allí permanentemente.»

Viéndose muy complacido y hasta deslumbrado por el cambio, Auítzotl murmuró para sí: «Increíble. Una tierra rica, libre para ser tomada. Dada libremente. —Dirigiéndose hacia mí, me dijo mucho más calurosamente de lo que nunca antes se había dirigido a mí—: No *siempre* nos traes problemas y molestias, joven Mixtli.»

Yo callé modestamente.

Él continuó pensando en voz alta: «Éste sería el dominio más lejano de la Triple Alianza. Si ponemos un ejército allí, el Único Mundo tendría un amplio dominio de mar a mar, entre dos mandíbulas. Las naciones que quedaran cercadas por éstas siempre se lo pensarían antes de causarnos problemas, pues esas quijadas se cerrarían y las aplastarían. Vivirían siempre con temor, sumisas y serviles...»

Yo volví a hablar: «Puedo hacerle notar otra ventaja, Señor Orador. Ese ejército, aunque esté muy lejos de aquí, no necesita ser mantenido por Tenochtitlan. Los ancianos de los mame me prometieron que lo mantendrían y lo aprovisionarían sin restricción. Los guerreros vivirán muy bien en la abundancia del Xoconochco.»

«¡Por Huiztli que lo haremos! —exclamó Auítzotl—. Por supuesto que nosotros presentaremos esta proposición a nuestro Consejo de Voceros, pero sólo será una formalidad.»

Yo dije: «También, mi señor, podría decir al Consejo de Voceros que una vez que la guarnición esté establecida, las familias de los guerreros podrían ir a reunírseles. Proveedores y comerciantes podrían seguirlos, y quizás otros mexica que quisieran dejar estas tierras del lago, ya muy abarrotadas de gente y asentarse en las amplias tierras del Xoconochco. La guarnición llegaría a ser una semilla de colonización, y aunque más pequeña que Tenochtitlan, quizás algún día llegue a ser la segunda gran ciudad de los mexica.»

Él dijo: «Sus sueños no son pequeños, ¿verdad?»

«Quizás me tomé una libertad, Venerado Orador, al mencionar esta posibilidad de colonización al Consejo de Ancianos de los mame. Sin embargo, lejos de objetar, ellos me dijeron que se sentirían muy honrados si su tierra llegara a ser con el tiempo, por decirlo así, la Tenochtitlan del sur.»

Él me miró con aprobación y tamborileó con sus dedos por un momento antes de hablar. «En su condición civil, usted no es más que un mercader contando semillas de cacao y en el rango militar un simple *tequíua*...»

«Por la cortesía de mi señor», dije humildemente.

«Y todavía sobre eso, usted, un don nadie, viene a darnos toda una nueva provincia, mucho más valiosa que cualquier otra anexada por tratado o por conquista, desde la época reinante de nuestro estimado padre Motecuzoma. También este hecho debe ser presentado a la atención de nuestro Consejo de Voceros.»

Yo dije: «La mención de Motecuzoma, mi señor, me recordó algo.» Y le dije lo que me costaba tanto trabajo repetir: las palabras ásperas y suspicaces del Bishosu Kosi Yuela acerca de su sobrino. Como ya lo esperaba, Auítzotl empezó a bufar, a resoplar y a ponerse colorado visiblemente, pero su ira no estaba dirigida a mí. Él dijo en un tono de exasperación:

«Ahora comprendo. Como sacerdote, el joven Motecuzoma era muy celoso de dos cosas. Una, prestarle una infatigable obediencia a cada una de las más triviales e imbéciles supersticiones, impuestas por los dioses, y otra trataba siempre de abolir cualquier falla o debilidad en él mismo, como en los otros. Nunca rabiaba o echaba espuma por la boca, como muchos de nuestros sacerdotes lo hacen; sino que siempre permanecía frío e inalterable. Una vez que dijo algo que le pareció que no era del agrado de los dioses, se perforó la lengua y pasó a través de ella un hilo en el que estaban anudadas unas veinte espinas de maguey. Lo mismo hacía cuando un mal *pensamiento* cruzaba por su mente; se agujereaba en la base de su *tepuli* y se castigaba de la misma manera con un hilo de espinas. Bien, ahora que ha llegado a ser un militar, parece ser que es igualmente fanático en la manera de hacer una guerra. Parece que al tener el mando por primera vez, el cachorro de *cóyotl* ha doblado la fuerza de sus músculos, en contra del orden y del buen gobierno...»

Auítzotl hizo una pausa. Cuando continuó, pareció como si otra vez pensara en voz alta. «Sí, naturalmente que desearía vivir sobre el nombre de su abuelo, El Señor Furioso. El joven Motecuzoma no está contento con que reine la paz entre nuestra nación y las otras, ya que así no tendrá muchos adversarios a quienes desafiar. Quiere ser respetado y temido como a un hombre de puño duro y voz fuerte, pero un hombre debe ser algo más que eso, o se humillará cuando se enfrente a un puño más duro o una voz más fuerte.»

Yo me aventuré a decir: «Tengo la impresión, mi señor, de que el Bishosu de Uaxyácac tiene terror a la posibilidad de que Motecuzoma El Joven llegue a ser algún día el Uey-Tlatoani de los mexica.»

En esos momentos Auítzotl me miró directamente y dijo con frialdad: «Kosi Yuela estará muerto mucho antes de que tenga que preocuparse por unas nuevas relaciones con algún otro Uey-Tlatoani. Nosotros sólo tenemos cuarenta y tres años y pensamos vivir mucho más. Antes de que nosotros muramos o chocheemos, dejaremos saber al Consejo de Voceros quién será nuestro sucesor. Aunque nosotros hemos olvidado cuántos de nuestros veinte hijos son varones, es seguro que entre ellos debe de encontrar otro Auítzotl. Tenga en mente Tequíua Mixtli, que el tambor más ruidoso es el más hueco y que su único servicio o función es estar en pie para ser golpeado. Nosotros no pondremos sobre el trono a un tambor hueco como nuestro sobrino Motecuzoma. *¡Recuerde mis palabras!*»

Las recordé. Las recuerdo con tristeza.

Le tomó algún tiempo al Venerado Orador tranquilizarse de su momentánea indignación. Después dijo con suavidad: «Le damos las gracias, Tequíua Mixtli, por la oportunidad de establecer esa guarnición en el lejano Xoconochco. Será la siguiente asignación para el joven Señor Furioso. Recibirá la orden de salir inmediatamente hacia el sur, para construir, establecer y tomar el mando en ese distante lugar. Sí, tendremos a Motecuzoma ocupado y a salvo, lejos de nosotros, o si no, pudiera ser que nosotros nos sintiéramos tentados a utilizar nuestro puño en contra de los que llevan nuestra propia sangre.»

Pasaron algunos días, y el tiempo que no estuve en la cama, familiarizándome con mi esposa, lo pasé acostumbrándome a mi primera casa. Su exterior estaba hecho con la piedra caliza de Xaltocan, deslumbrantemente blanca y decorada modestamente con algunas filigranas talladas, ninguna de ellas embellecidas por el color. Para los transeúntes, no era más que la casa típica de un *pochtécatl* con éxito, pero no *demasiado* próspero. Adentro, sin embargo, sus acabados eran mucho más finos y olía a nuevo y no al humo, a la comida, al sudor y a viejas rencillas, como olía con sus anteriores habitantes. Todas las puertas eran de hermoso cedro tallado, y se movían sobre pivotes puestos arriba y abajo, teniendo también una cerradura de aldaba con un broche de picaporte. Los huecos de las ventanas daban hacia los muros de enfrente y de atrás, y todas ellas tenían celosías de tablitas que se enrollaban.

El piso de abajo —que no descansaba en el suelo como ya he dicho— tenía una cocina, otra habitación separada para el comedor y otra todavía más grande, en la cual podíamos entretener a un grupo de invitados o podía atender mis negocios con los socios que me visitaran. Como allí no había suficiente espacio como para hacer un cuarto para criados, Turquesa simplemente se enrollaba en una cobija y se acostaba sobre su *pétlatl*, alfombrilla, en la cocina, después de que nosotros nos habíamos ido a la cama. En el piso de arriba se encontraba nuestra estancia y otra para las visitas, cada una de ellas con su sanitario y su baño de vapor; había también otra más pequeña a la que de momento no hallé ningún propósito, hasta que Zyanya me dijo sonriendo tímidamente: «Algún día puede haber un niño, Zaa. Quizás niños. Así, esta habitación es para ellos y su niñera.»

La azotea de la casa era plana, circundada por una balaustrada de piedras y cemento con un diseño calado, más o menos de la altura de mi cintura. Toda la superficie ya había sido preparada con la rica tierra de labranza de los chinampa, lista para plantar las flores, los arbustos de sombra y las hierbas de cocina. Nuestra casa estaba rodeada por otros edificios más altos, así es que no teníamos vista al lago, pero podíamos contemplar los dos templos gemelos en lo alto de la Gran Pirámide, los picos de los volcanes, el humeante Popocatépetl y el dormido Ixtaccíhuatl. Zyanya había amueblado todos los cuartos, tanto arriba como abajo, con las cosas más necesarias; las camas con sus varios cobertores, guardarropas de mimbre, unas cuantas *icpaltin*, sillas bajas, y bancas. Así es que en los cuartos cualquier sonido producía eco por lo vacíos que estaban, sus pisos de madera brillaban pues no tenían alfombras todavía, y sus lisos muros encalados estaban sin adornar.

Ella dijo: «Pienso que los muebles más importantes, los ornamentos y tapices para colgar en las paredes, debe escogerlos el hombre de la casa.»

«Visitaremos los talleres y los mercados juntos —dije—. Sólo iré para estar de acuerdo con lo que tú escojas, y para pagar.»

Con la misma deferencia, ella había comprado la única esclava, y Turquesa era suficiente para ayudar a Zyanya en el trabajo de la casa. Sin embargo, decidí adquirir otra mujer para compartir las labores diarias de cocinar, limpiar y demás, y también un esclavo que hiciera el trabajo duro, atendiera el jardín-azotea, llevara recados y cosas por el estilo. Para ese trabajo pesado, adquirimos un esclavo no muy joven, pero todavía fuerte y aparentemente listo, llamado según la patética manera grandilocuente de la clase de los *tlacotli*, Citlali-Cuicani, o sea Estrella Cantadora; también conseguimos a una joven criada llamada, contrariamente a la costumbre de los esclavos, Quequelmiqui, que quiere decir Cosquillosa. Quizá mereció ese nombre, porque constantemente se estaba riendo de la manera más tonta y sin motivo.

Inmediatamente, en sus ratos libres, mandamos a los tres, a Turquesa, a Estrella Cantadora y a Cosquillosa, a estudiar a la nueva escuela fundada por mi joven amigo Cózcatl. Su más grande ambición, en aquellos días en que era un niño esclavo, había sido aprender todos los rudimentos necesarios para atender el puesto doméstico más alto en la casa de un noble, o sea el de mayordomo. Pero para entonces se había elevado considerablemente sobre su posición, poseyendo una casa estimable y una fortuna propia. Así es que Cózcatl había convertido su casa en una escuela para adiestrar sirvientes, es decir, para hacer de ellos los mejores sirvientes.

Él me dijo con orgullo: «Por supuesto que he contratado a los mejores maestros para enseñar los trabajos básicos como cocina, jardinería, bordado; cualquier cosa en que los estudiantes quieran sobresalir. Pero soy yo quien les enseña a tener maneras elegantes, que de otra manera sólo podrían aprender a lo largo de mucho tiempo de experiencia, si es que lo aprenden. Ya que he trabajado en dos palacios, mis estudiantes prestan mucha atención a mis enseñanzas, aun cuando la mayoría de ellos son mucho mayores que yo.»

«¿Maneras elegantes? —dije—. ¿Para simples criados?»

«Así *no* serán simples criados, sino valiosos miembros de la casa. Les enseño cómo comportarse con dignidad, en lugar de la actitud servil y obsequiosa usual, y también cómo anticiparse a los deseos de sus amos antes de que ellos se los digan. Un mayordomo, por ejemplo, aprende a tener siempre preparado el *poquíetl*, para que su amo fume. La mujer que está al mando de la casa, aprende a avisar a su ama cuáles son las flores que están floreciendo en su jardín; así su señora puede pensar con anticipación qué arreglos florales quiere en sus habitaciones.»

Yo dije: «Con toda seguridad, un esclavo no podría pagar tus enseñanzas.»

«Pues, no —admitió—. Como todos mis estudiantes están trabajando como domésticos, como los que tú me trajiste, los que pagan son sus amos. Sin embargo, al estudiar aumentarán sus habilidades y su valor, de tal manera que ganarán promociones entre sus amos, o podrán ser vendidos por más dinero, lo que quiere decir que necesitarán reemplazarlos, por lo que puedo ver una gran demanda de graduados de mi escuela. Eventualmente, podré comprar esclavos en el mercado, adiestrarlos, buscarles colocación y cobrarles de los salarios que ganen.»

Yo asentí y dije: «Eso sería una cosa muy buena para ti, para ellos y para las personas que los empleen. Es una idea ingeniosa, Cózcatl. No solamente has encontrado tu lugar en el mundo, sino que has tallado un nicho, completo y nuevo, en donde nadie cabe tan bien como tú.»

Él dijo con humildad: «Pero nunca lo hubiera podido hacer si no hubiera sido por ti, Mixtli. Si no nos hubiéramos aventurado juntos, probablemente todavía estaría trabajando muy duro, en algún palacio de Texcoco. Y mi buena suerte se la debo al *tonali*, ya sea al tuyo o al mío, que unió nuestras vidas.»

Y yo también, pensé mientras caminaba lentamente hacia mi casa, estaba en deuda con un *tonali* que una vez juzgué caprichoso y hasta maligno. Ese *tonali* me había causado problemas, pérdidas y desdichas, pero también me había hecho un hombre de propiedad, un hombre rico, un hombre que se había elevado de la posición social que por derecho de nacimiento le correspondía, un hombre casado con una de las mujeres más deseables y un hombre todavía lo suficientemente joven como para seguir explorando y haciendo descubrimientos en el futuro.

Mientras me encaminaba a mi cómoda casa y hacia el abrazo

de bienvenida de Zyanya, estaba contento por haber echado a volar mi gratitud hacia el cielo, supuesta residencia de los dioses mayores. «Dioses —dije, no en voz alta sino en mi mente—, si existen los dioses y si ésos sois vosotros, os doy las gracias. Algunas veces, me habéis quitado con una mano mientras me dabais con la otra. Pero en la cuenta total, me habéis dado más de lo que me habéis tomado. Beso la tierra ante vosotros, dioses.» Y los dioses debieron de sentirse contentos con mi gratitud, pues no perdieron el tiempo en componer las cosas, de tal manera, que cuando entré a la casa me encontré con un paje de palacio que me estaba esperando para que me presentara ante Auítzotl. Sólo me entretuve lo suficiente como para darle un beso de saludo y despedida a Zyanya y luego seguí al muchacho a través de las calles Del Corazón del Único Mundo.

Era bastante noche cuando regresé a casa otra vez y llegué vestido de muy diferente manera y más que ligeramente borracho. Cuando nuestra criada Turquesa me abrió la puerta, perdió toda la serenidad que pudo haber aprendido durante su primer día en la escuela de Cózcatl. Me miró, a mí y mi profusión de plumas desordenadas, y dando un grito penetrante, huyó hacia la parte de atrás de la casa. Zyanya vino mirando con ansiedad.

Ella dijo: «¡Zaa, estuviste tanto tiempo afuera...! —Entonces también dio un grito y reculó exclamando—: ¿Qué te hizo ese monstruo de Auítzotl? ¿Por qué está sangrando tu brazo? ¿Qué traes en tus pies? ¿Qué es eso que llevas en la cabeza? ¡Zaa, *di algo!*»

«Hola», murmuré estúpidamente, hipando.

«¿Hola? —repitió haciendo eco, sorprendida ante ese saludo absurdo. Entonces dijo enojada—: Sea como sea, estás borracho.» Y se fue hacia la cocina. Me dejé caer con cuidado sobre una *icpali*, silla, pero me puse de pie rápidamente, otra vez, y quizás a bastante altura sobre el suelo, cuando Zyanya dejó caer una jarra de agua, estremecedoramente fría, sobre mi cabeza.

«¡Mi yelmo!», grité, cuando dejé de temblar y de farfullar.

«¿Es un yelmo? —dijo Zyanya, mientras yo forcejeaba por quitármelo y secarlo antes de que el agua lo echara a perder—. A mí me pareció como si estuvieras agarrado por el pico de un ave gigante.»

«Mi señora esposa —dije con la augusta sobriedad del que está medio borracho—, podrías haber arruinado esta noble cabeza de águila. Y en estos momentos estás parada en una de mis garras. Y mira... mira nada más, mis pobres plumas desaliñadas.»

«Ya lo veo. Ya lo estoy viendo», dijo ella, con voz ahogada y entonces me di cuenta de que estaba tratando con todas sus fuerzas de no soltar la carcajada. Me dijo con frases cortas, tratando de mantener firme la voz, después de cada una: «Zaa, quítate ese traje tonto. Ve al cuarto de vapor. Suda un poco del *octli* que tienes adentro. Límpiate la sangre de tu brazo. Y luego, por favor, ve a la cama y explícame... explícame todos los...» No pudo contener más la risa, que brotó a carcajadas.

«Como un traje tonto —dije, tratando de que mi voz se oyera a la vez, presuntuosa y herida—. Sólo una mujer puede ser tan insensible ante una insignia de tan alto honor. Si fueras un hombre, te arrodillarías en reverencia y admiración, y me felicitarías. Pero no. He sido ignominiosamente empapado y te has reído de eso.» Después de lo cual, me volví y subí majestuosamente las escaleras, aunque con algunas cuantas caídas ocasionales, debido a mis sandalias de largas garras, y fui a remojarme el mal humor al cuarto de vapor.

Si tuve una conducta tan lúgubremente colérica se debió a que tuve un recibimiento de regocijada indulgencia en el día que debió ser el más solemne de mi vida. Ni diez o veinte mil de mis compatriotas llegarían a ser jamás lo que yo llegué a ser en ese día, un Tlamahuichihuani Cuaútlic, o sea un Campeón de la Orden del Águila, de los mexica.

Más tarde, me sentí mortificado conmigo mismo, por haberme quedado dormido en el cuarto de vapor, y porque de alguna manera Zyanya y Estrella Cantadora tuvieron que llevarme a la cama totalmente inconsciente. Así es que no fue sino hasta la siguiente mañana, cuando me desperté ya tarde, que le pude contar a Zyanya coherentemente lo que había pasado en palacio, mientras sorbía en la cama una taza de *chocólatl* caliente, con el objeto de disminuir el poderoso peso de mi jaqueca.

Auítzotl estaba solo en el salón del trono cuando llegué, siguiendo al paje, y me dijo con brusquedad: «Nuestro sobrino Motecuzoma dejó Tenochtitlan esta mañana, guiando una fuerza considerable que será la guarnición del Xoconochco. Como se lo prometimos, nosotros mencionamos ante el Consejo de Voceros el admirable papel que usted desempeñó en la adquisición de ese territorio y se decidió que usted fuera recompensado por ello.»

Hizo una seña al paje y éste se fue; un momento después la habitación se empezó a llenar con otros hombres. Había esperado que fueran el Mujer Serpiente, varios de los viejos *tlamatínime* y otros miembros del Consejo de Voceros, pero cuando miré a través de mi topacio me quedé sorprendido, pues todos ellos eran viejos guerreros —los más grandes guerreros—, todos ellos campeones Águila, con sus trajes de batalla, completamente emplumados, sus yelmos de cabeza de águila, sus alas plegadas a sus brazos y sus sandalias de garras en sus pies.

Auítzotl me presentó con cada uno de ellos, los más grandes jefes capitanes de la Orden del Águila y dijo: «Ellos han votado, Mixtli, por unanimidad, para elevarlo del grado insignificante de *tequíua*, al más alto grado de su orden, el campeonato.»

Y por supuesto, hubo varios rituales que se llevaron a efecto. Como me había quedado mudo de la sorpresa, tuve que hacer un esfuerzo para encontrar mi voz y poder hacer todos los juramentos: que sería fiel y pelearía hasta morir por la Orden del Águila, por la supremacía de Tenochtitlan, por el poder y el prestigio de la nación mexica, por la preservación de la Triple Alianza. Tuve que hacer un corte en mi antebrazo, pues los campeones lo hacían así, para poder restregar mi antebrazo con los otros y así mezclar nuestra sangre en hermandad.

Luego me dieron mi traje acojinado con todos sus adornos,

así es que mis brazos se convirtieron en anchas alas, mi cuerpo se cubrió de plumas y mis pies, con las fuertes garras del águila. La culminación de la ceremonia fue el momento de mi coronación con el yelmo: una cabeza de águila hecha de madera, papel endurecido y plumas pegadas con goma. Su ancho pico se abría, sobresaliendo por encima de mi frente y bajo mi barbilla, y sus ojos brillantes de obsidiana quedaban en alguna parte atrás de mis oídos. Me dieron, también, otros emblemas de mi nuevo rango: un escudo de cuero muy fuerte, con el glifo de mi nombre trabajado en plumas al frente; un brillante gallardete sobre un asta, que llevaría como banderola para reunir a mis hombres a mi alrededor en el campo de batalla; las pinturas que harían que mi cara se viera más feroz, y el pendiente de oro que llevaría en la nariz, cuando me la agujereara para eso...

Después, cargado con todos esos atavíos abrumadores, me senté junto a Auítzotl y con los otros campeones, mientras los sirvientes de palacio servían un banquete opulento y muchas jarras del mejor *octli*. Tuve que pretender que comía bastante, ya que para entonces estaba tan borracho y excitado que casi no tenía apetito. No hubo manera, pues, de eludir tanta bebida en respuesta a los numerosos y vociferantes brindis: por mí, por los campeones Águila allí presentes, por los campeones Águila que habían muerto espectacularmente en el pasado, por nuestro comandante supremo Auítzotzin, para que perdurara el gran poderío de los mexica... Después de un rato, no supe ni por qué brindábamos. Por todo esto, cuando al fin me dejaron salir del palacio estaba algo más que mareado y mi nuevo y espléndido traje, algo más que desarreglado.

«Estoy orgullosa de ti, Zaa y también muy feliz por ti —dijo Zyanya, cuando terminé de contarle todo—. En verdad que es un gran honor. Y ahora, mi guerrero esposo, ¿qué gran hazaña piensas hacer? ¿Cuál será tu primera muestra de valor, como un campeón Águila?»

Yo dije débilmente: «¿No tenemos que ir hoy a comprar las flores, cuando la flota de canoas llegue de Xochimilco? ¿Flores para plantar en nuestro jardín-azotea?»

Mi cabeza me dolía tanto como para que me esforzara más, así es que ni siquiera traté de comprender por qué Zyanya, como lo había hecho la noche anterior, soltó la carcajada.

✠

Nuestra nueva casa significó una nueva vida para todos los que la habitábamos, puesto que todos teníamos mucho trabajo que hacer. Zyanya continuó muy ocupada en la interminable y necesaria tarea de visitar los puestos del mercado y los talleres de los artesanos, en busca de «exactamente el diseño *correcto* del *pétlatl*, alfombrilla, para el cuarto de los niños» o «una figurita preciosa, de alguna diosa, para el nicho de arriba de la escalera» o alguna otra cosa que parecía que siempre se le escapaba.

Mis contribuciones para la casa no siempre fueron recibidas

con aclamaciones de júbilo, como por ejemplo, cuando llevé a casa una pequeña estatua de piedra, para el nicho de la escalera y Zyanya dijo que era «horrible». Bueno, sí lo era. Pero la compré porque me di cuenta de que era exactamente igual al viejo pardusco-cacao, arrugado y encorvado; el disfraz que había usado Nezahualpili cada vez que me encontraba. De hecho, era la figurita que representaba a Huehuetéotl, el Viejo Más Viejo de los Dioses, que eso era lo que él era. Aunque ya no era adorado en demasía, el viejo y arrugado Huehuetéotl, de sonrisa enigmática, era todavía venerado como el primer dios reconocido por estas tierras y conocido desde tiempos inmemoriales, mucho antes que Quetzalcóatl o de cualquier otro dios adorado posteriormente. Como Zyanya no me dejó ponerlo en un lugar en donde lo vieran los invitados, lo coloqué a un lado de nuestra cama.

Nuestros tres sirvientes, en los pocos meses que llevaban con nosotros, asistieron a la escuela de Cózcatl para tomar lecciones en sus ratos libres, con notables adelantos. La pequeña criada Cosquillosa, dejó de reírse tontamente cada vez que alguien le hablaba, y sólo sonreía modesta y servicial. Estrella Cantadora se volvió tan atento que casi todo el tiempo, cuando me sentaba, me tenía listo un *poquíetl* para fumar, y, para no rechazar su solicitud, fumé mucho más de lo que deseaba.

Mis negocios consolidaban mi fortuna. Caravanas de *pochteca* habían ido llegando, desde hacía un tiempo, a Tenochtitlan desde Uaxyácac, trayendo recipientes con el colorante púrpura y madejas de algodón púrpura, que habían comprado legítimamente al Bishosu Kosi Yuela. Por supuesto, habían pagado un precio exorbitante por ello, y, por supuesto, ellos pedían un precio mucho mayor cuando lo distribuían entre los mercaderes de Tlatelolco. Sin embargo, los nobles mexica, especialmente sus esposas, estaban tan ávidos de poseer ese colorante único, que pagaban lo que les pidieran. Y, una vez que el púrpura adquirido legítimamente fue puesto en el mercado, pude, discretamente y sin ningún peligro, introducir el mío, poco a poco, dentro del mercado.

Vendí lo que tenía atesorado por una moneda mucho más fácil de esconder: jade labrado, unas cuantas esmeraldas y otras gemas, joyería de oro y cañas de polvo de oro. Pero Zyanya y yo guardamos el suficiente para nuestro uso, tanto que creo que teníamos más trajes bordados de púrpura que el Venerado Orador y todas sus esposas. Por lo menos, *sé* que nuestra casa era la única en todo Tenochtitlan que tenía en las ventanas cortinas con púrpura fijo, aunque éstas eran solamente admiradas por nuestros invitados, puesto que las que daban hacia la calle estaban hechas con un material menos suntuoso.

Nos visitaban con frecuencia los viejos amigos: Cózcatl, entonces ya conocido apropiadamente por el maestro Cózcatl; mis socios de la Casa de los Pochteca; uno o varios de los compañeros de Glotón de Sangre, quienes me habían ayudado a conseguir el púrpura. Sin embargo, también habíamos hecho muchos amigos entre nuestros vecinos de la clase alta, en nuestra zona de Ixacualco y entre los nobles que habíamos conocido en la corte, muy en particular cierto número de mujeres nobles que se sintieron cautivadas por el encanto de Zyanya. Una de ellas era la Primera Señora de Tenochtitlan, o sea la primera esposa de Auítzotl. Cuando venía de visita, muy a menudo traía consigo a su hijo mayor, Cuautémoc, Águila Que Cae Sobre Su Presa, el joven señor que sería el último sucesor al trono de su padre. Aunque los mexica no consideraban la sucesión de padres a hijos como en algunas otras naciones, el primer candidato considerado por el Consejo de Voceros en la muerte de un Uey-Tlatoani, era el hijo mayor cuando no le sobrevivía ningún hermano. Así es que Zyanya y yo tratábamos a Cuautémoctzin y a su madre con la debida deferencia; no daña en lo absoluto estar en buenas relaciones con alguien que, quizás algún día, sea llamado Venerado Orador.

De tiempo en tiempo durante aquellos años, un mensajero militar o el portador de un mercader llegaba desde el sur y desviándose a nuestra casa, nos traía algún mensaje de Beu Ribé. El mensaje siempre era el mismo; que todavía no se casaba, que Tecuantépec seguía siendo Tecuantépec, que la hostería seguía progresando, y mucho más ahora, por el aumento de tráfico de ida y vuelta al Xoconochco. Pero esas escasas noticias eran por demás deprimentes, pues Zyanya y yo sólo podíamos asumir que si Beu permanecía soltera, no era por inclinación, sino por falta de pretendientes. Y al pensar en eso, siempre venía a mi mente el exilado Motecuzoma, porque yo estaba seguro de que él había sido el oficial mexícatl, de extrañas propensiones, que había destruido la vida de Beu; aunque nunca mencioné esto a nadie, ni siquiera a Zyanya. Sólo por lealtad familiar, supongo que debía sentir animosidad hacia ese Motecuzoma El Joven. Sólo por lo que me habían dicho Beu y Auítzotl, debía sentir desdén por un hombre que había estropeado tanto sus partes privadas como sus apetitos. Pero ni yo, ni ningún otro, podría negar que él hizo el trabajo de guarnición, para acrecentar y sostener el Xoconochco, para nosotros.

Colocó a su guarnición armada casi prácticamente en la frontera con Quautemalan y vigiló personalmente el proyecto y la construcción del fuerte, que los vecinos quiché y lacandón observaron desalentados, sin duda, conforme se iban levantando sus muros, y las patrullas comenzaban a hacer sus rondas. Esa gente desgraciada, nunca más volvió a salir de sus selvas para otras correrías, nunca más volvió a amenazar o a echar bravatas o a demostrar de alguna otra manera otro signo de ambición. Volvieron a ser lo que habían sido, gente escuálida y apática, y, hasta donde yo sé, siguen siendo así.

Sus primeros soldados españoles, que viajaron dentro del Xoconochco, se sorprendieron al encontrar allí, a una distancia tan lejana de Tenochtitlan, tantas gentes que sin ninguna relación con nosotros los mexica —los mame, mixe, comiteca y demás— hablaban nuestro náhuatl. Sí, ésa fue la tierra más lejana en la que uno se podía parar y decir: «Ésta es tierra mexica.» Era también, a pesar de la distancia entre ella y El Corazón del Único Mundo, quizá la provincia más leal, y eso se debía al hecho de que muchos mexica se habían ido a vivir al Xoconochco después de su anexión.

Mucho antes de que la guarnición de Motecuzoma estuviera terminada, otros empezaron a establecerse en aquella área, y a construir casas, puestos de mercado, hosterías rudimentarias e incluso *auyanicaltin*, casas de placer. Eran inmigrantes mexica, acolhua y tecpaneca cn busca de horizontes más amplios y de oportunidades que nunca podrían encontrar en las tierras atestadas de la Triple Alianza. Para cuando la guarnición estuvo totalmente construida, armada y organizada, ésta dejó caer su sombra protectora sobre un pueblo de considerables dimensiones. El pueblo tomó el nombre náhuatl de Tapachtlan, Lugar de Coral, y aunque nunca se aproximó en tamaño y esplendor a Tenochtitlan, la ciudad que le dio su origen, es todavía una de las comunidades más grandes y de más tráfico al este del istmo de Tecuantépec.

Muchos de los que llegaron del norte, después de haber estado un poco de tiempo en Tepachtlan o en cualquier otra parte del Xoconochco, se fueron todavía más lejos. Nunca he viajado tan lejos, pero sé que más al este de la selva de Quautemalan hay unas tierras altas muy fértiles y tierras costeras. Y más allá de ellas, hay otro istmo, mucho más angosto que el de Tecuantépec, en un recodo entre los océanos del norte y del sur, aunque nadie puede decir qué lejos está. Algunos insisten en que en algún lugar de ésos hay un río que conecta a los dos océanos. Su Capitán General Cortés fue a buscarlo, mas en vano, pero quizás algunos otros españoles puedan encontrarlo todavía.

Aunque los inmigrantes fueron llegando progresivamente, eran sólo exploradores individuales o a lo mucho grupos de familias que se esparcieron por esas tierras lejanas; sin embargo, me han contado que dejaron huellas indelebles entre los nativos de esos lugares. Tribus que jamás, y ni remotamente, se hubieran emparentado con nosotros, ahora tienen nuestros mismos rasgos; hablan nuestro lenguaje náhuatl, aunque en dialectos adulterados; han adoptado y perpetuado muchos trajes y artesanías mexica; han vuelto a darles nombres náhuatl a sus aldeas, sus montañas y sus ríos.

Varios españoles que han viajado muy lejos, me han preguntado: «¿Era verdaderamente tan vasto, el imperio azteca, como para que sus confines llegaran hasta el imperio inca, en el gran continente hacia el sur?» Aunque no comprendía totalmente su pregunta, siempre les decía: «No, mis señores.» No estoy muy seguro de lo que quiere decir un imperio, o un continente, o un inca, pero sé que nosotros los mexica —o aztecas, si así lo desean ustedes— nunca llevamos nuestras fronteras más allá del Xoconochco.

Sin embargo, en aquellos años, no todos nuestros ojos e intereses estaban puestos hacia el sur. Nuestro Uey-Tlatoani no ignoraba los otros puntos del compás. Me sentí muy contento de poder romper la rutina diaria doméstica, cuando un día Auítzotl me mandó llamar a su palacio para preguntarme si podía hacerme cargo de una misión diplomática en Michihuacan.

Él dijo: «Usted trabajó tan bien para nosotros en Uaxyácac y en el Xoconochco, que, ¿cree que podría conseguirnos una relación mejor que la actual con la Tierra de los Pescadores?»

Le dije que podría intentarlo. «Pero ¿por qué, mi Señor? Los purémpecha permiten a nuestros viajeros y mercaderes paso libre a través de sus tierras. Comercian libremente con nosotros. En cuanto a relaciones, ¿qué más podemos pedirles?»

«Oh, piense en algo —dijo alegremente—. Piense en algo que pueda justificar su visita a su Uandákuari, el viejo Yquíngare.»

Debí de mirarlo con perplejidad, porque me explicó: «Sus supuestas negociaciones diplomáticas sólo serían una máscara para encubrir su verdadera misión. Queremos que nos traiga el secreto de cómo consiguen ese soberbio y duro metal, con el cual destruyen nuestras armas de obsidiana.»

Respiré profundamente y tratando de parecer razonable en lugar de aprensivo, dije: «Mi señor, probablemente los artesanos que saben cómo forjar ese metal deben de estar a buen recaudo, lejos del encuentro con cualquier extranjero que pudiera hacerles traicionar su secreto.»

«Y las armas han de estar guardadas, con toda seguridad, lejos de la vista de cualquier curioso —dijo Auítzotl con impaciencia—. Nosotros sabemos eso, pero también sabemos que hay una excepción dentro de esa política. Los consejeros más cercanos y la guardia personal de Uandákuari, *siempre* van armados con esas armas de metal para protegerlo contra cualquier atentado. Vaya a su palacio y tendrá la oportunidad de hacerse de una espada, un cuchillo, o algo parecido. Eso es todo lo que necesitamos. Si nuestros forjadores de metales pudieran tener una muestra para su estudio, podrían encontrar la composición de éste. Le hemos dado nuestras órdenes directas, Campeón Águila Mixtli.»

Yo suspiré y dije: «Como mi señor lo ordene. Un campeón Águila debe hacerlo.» Y pensé en las dificultades que me esperaban con esa tarea y luego sugerí: «Si sólo voy allí para robar, en verdad que no necesito la complicada excusa de negociaciones diplomáticas. Podría ser sólo un enviado, llevando un regalo de amistad del Venerado Orador Auítzotl al Venerado Orador Yquíngare.»

Auítzotl también pensó en eso, enfurruñado. «Pero, ¿por qué? —dijo—. Hay tantas cosas preciosas en Michihuacan como las hay aquí. Tendría que ser algo invaluable para él, algo único.»

Yo dije tímidamente: «Los purémpecha son muy dados a extrañas diversiones sexuales. Pero, no. El Uandákuari es un hombre viejo. Sin duda ya ha probado todos y cada uno de los placeres sexuales e indecentes y está más allá de...»

«¡*Ayyo*! —gritó Auítzotl triunfante—. Hay un dulce que no es posible que él haya probado, uno que no podrá resistir. Un nuevo *tequani* que nosotros acabamos de comprar para nuestro zoológico humano.» Estoy seguro de que yo me tambaleé a simple vista, pero él no pareció darse cuenta, ya que estaba enviando a un criado a traer eso, lo que fuera.

Traté de imaginarme qué clase de monstruo humano podría hacer que se levantara el *tepuli* del viejo más licencioso y sinvergüenza, cuando Auítzotl dijo: «¡Mire esto, Campeón Mixtli! Aquí están.» Y yo levanté mi topacio.

Eran dos muchachas tan comunes en sus rostros como las que siempre había visto, así es que difícilmente podía llamarlas monstruos, sin faltar a la caridad. Quizás fueran una cosa poco usual, sí, ya que eran gemelas idénticas. Calculé que debían tener unos catorce años y que debían de pertenecer a alguna tribu olmeca, pues las dos estaban mascando *tzictli* tan plácidamente como un par de rumiantes manatíes. Estaban paradas hombro con hombro, ligeramente vueltas una hacia la otra, y cada una dejaba descansar su brazo alrededor del hombro de la otra. Llevaban una simple manta drapeada, alrededor de sus cuerpos, desde sus pechos hasta el piso.

«Todavía no han sido mostradas al público —dijo Auítzotl— porque nuestra costurera de palacio aún no ha terminado las blusas y faldas especiales que ellas requieren. Mozo, quíteles la manta.»

Él lo hizo así, y mis ojos se abrieron por la sorpresa cuando vi a las muchachas desnudas. No eran solamente gemelas; parecía como si algo las hubiera pegado juntas de sus entrañas. Desde sus sobacos hasta sus caderas, las dos estaban unidas por una piel mutua y tan apretadamente, que era obvio que no podían pararse, sentarse, caminar o acostarse más que dando media cara la una a la otra. Por un momento pensé que sólo tenían tres pechos, pero cuando me acerqué, vi que el pecho de en medio era en realidad dos pechos normales, pero apretadamente juntos, pues podía dividirlos con mi mano. Miré a las muchachas por todos lados; cuatro pechos enfrente, dos pares de nalgas atrás. Excepto porque no tenían rostros bellos ni inteligentes, no podía ver alguna otra deformidad a excepción hecha de la parte de piel que compartían.

«¿No podrían ser divididas? —pregunté—. Cada una de ellas tendría una cicatriz, pero podrían vivir separadas y normales.»

«¿Con qué objeto? —gruñó Auítzotl—. ¿Qué uso mundano se les podría dar a estas hembras olmeca, mascadoras de *tzictli* y de caras feas? Juntas son una novedad valiosa y pueden gozar de la vida de *tequani*, placenteramente ociosa. De todas formas, nuestros *tíciltin*, cirujanos, las han examinado y han llegado a la conclusión de que no pueden ser separadas. Por dentro de esa tira colgante de piel, comparten venas y arterias vitales y quizás hasta uno o dos órganos. Sin embargo, y esto es lo que seducirá al viejo Yquíngare, cada una de las muchachas tiene su propio *tepili* y ambas son vírgenes.»

«Es una lástima que no sean bonitas —dije pensativo—. Pero tiene usted razón, mi señor. La única novedad que ellas ofrecen se debe a esa tira de piel. —Me dirigí entonces a las gemelas—: ¿Tenéis nombres? ¿Podéis hablar?»

Ellas dijeron en lengua coatlícamac y casi al unísono: «Yo soy Izquierda.» «Yo soy Derecha.»

Auítzotl dijo: «Teníamos la intención de presentarlas al público como la Señora Pareja. El nombre de la diosa Omecíuatl. Una clase de broma, como ve.»

Yo dije: «Si un regalo poco común puede hacer que el Uandá-kuari sea más amigable con nosotros, la Señora Pareja sería ese regalo y yo estaré muy contento de llevarlo. Sólo una recomendación, mi señor, para hacerlo todavía más atractivo. Mande que les afeiten, a las dos, todo el vello, el cabello y las cejas. Ésa es la moda purempe.»

«Una moda muy singular —dijo Auítzotl admirado—. El cabe-

447

llo es lo único atractivo que tienen éstas, pero así se hará. Esté listo para partir cuando hayan terminado el guardarropa de ellas.» «Estaré listo en el lugar señalado, Señor Orador. Y tengo la esperanza de que la presentación de la Señora Pareja cause la suficiente excitación en la corte como para que pueda hurtar una de sus armas de metal en la conmoción, sin que ellos se den cuenta.» «No quiero solamente la esperanza —dijo Auítzotl—. ¡Hágalo!»

«¡Ah, pobres muchachas!», exclamó Zyanya próxima a llorar, cuando le presenté a la Señora Pareja. Me sorprendí de que alguien expresara piedad por ellas, ya que todos los que estaban implicados con Izquierda y Derecha, o se reían o bostezaban de ellas, o como Auítzotl, las miraban como un lujo puesto a la venta en el mercado, como la carne de un animal raro. Sin embargo, Zyanya maternalmente las trató con ternura a todo lo largo de la jornada a Tzintzuntzaní y continuamente les estuvo asegurando —como si ellas tuvieran el suficiente cerebro como para darse cuenta— que viajaban al encuentro de una nueva vida maravillosa, de libertad y lujo. Bueno, supongo que estarían mucho mejor en la libertad comparable de un palacio, aunque fueran una especie de concubina doble, que siendo un objeto al que siempre se apunta y se ríe, confinadas en el zoológico de la ciudad.

Zyanya había venido conmigo, porque cuando le conté de esa última y rara embajada que había caído sobre mí, había insistido en ir también. En un principio dije un fuerte no, porque sabía que ninguno de los que me acompañaran podrían vivir por mucho tiempo en el momento en que me cogieran tratando de robar una de las sacrosantas armas de metal, como sería lo más probable. Sin embargo, Zyanya me probó persuasivamente que, si podíamos disipar las sospechas de nuestro anfitrión con anticipación, tendría una gran oportunidad para irme acercando a tal arma y llegarla a poseer sin ser descubierto.

«¿Y qué puede ser menos sospechoso —preguntó— que un hombre y su esposa viajando juntos? Y yo *quiero* ver los paisajes de Michihuacan, Zaa.»

Su idea del hombre y su esposa, tenía cierto mérito, reflexioné, aunque no exactamente el mérito que ella le daba. Para ellos, el ver a un hombre viajando con su propia compañera, la compañera común y corriente de cada día, en una nación en donde con sólo preguntar uno podía tener otra compañera u otra clase de compañía o cierto número de compañías, eso en verdad enmudecería a los purémpecha. Me desdeñarían y me mirarían como demasiado impotente, tonto, sin imaginación y letárgico como para ser un ladrón, un espía o cualquier otra cosa peligrosa. Así es que le dije que sí a Zyanya y ella empezó inmediatamente a preparar el equipaje para el viaje.

Auítzotl me mandó llamar, cuando las gemelas tuvieron listo su guardarropa para partir, por lo que me presenté en el palacio. *¡Ayya!*, me quedé horrorizado cuando vi por primera vez cómo habían rapado a las muchachas. Sus cabezas se parecían a sus pechos desnudos —cónicas, rematadas en una punta— y me preguntaba si mi recomendación no habría sido un espantoso error. Una cabeza rapada podría ser la cumbre de la belleza para un purempe, pero, ¿lo sería una punta de cabeza rapada? Ellos conservaban la punta con pelo. Bien, era muy tarde para poner remedio; tenían que quedarse rapadas como estaban.

También fue entonces cuando descubrimos que una silla de manos ordinaria no serviría para Izquierda y Derecha y que se necesitaba construir una especial para sus peculiares necesidades, lo que retrasó nuestra partida unos cuantos días. Sin embargo, Auítzotl estaba determinado a no ahorrar gastos en esa expedición, y así, cuando al fin salimos, éramos una gran caravana.

Dos guardias de palacio iban al frente, desarmados visiblemente, aunque yo sabía que los dos eran expertos en combate mano a mano. Yo sólo llevaba el escudo emblasonado que me identificaba como un campeón Águila y una carta de presentación, firmada por el Uey-Tlatoani Auítzotl. Caminaba al lado de la silla de Zyanya, sostenida por cuatro hombres, actuando en mi papel de marido domesticado, llamando la atención de ella, hacia algún que otro paisaje. Detrás de nosotros venía la silla de manos de las gemelas, cargada por ocho hombres, y seguían a éstos otros que los reemplazarían en cargar la pesada silla, puesta sobre pértigas. Esa silla de manos había sido construida en una forma especial, así es que no era un simple asiento, sino que estaba techada como una pequeña choza y tenía cortinas que se podían recorrer en dos lados. Cerraban nuestra caravana numerosos *tamemime* que cargaban nuestros fardos, canastos y provisiones.

Después de tres o cuatro días de camino, llegamos a un pueblo llamado Zitákuaro, en donde en un lugar custodiado, de sus orillas, estaba marcada la frontera con Michihuacan. Allí hicimos un alto, mientras los guardias purémpecha de la frontera examinaban cuidadosamente y con respeto la carta que les presenté, y luego con precipitación, pero sin abrirlos, pincharon varios de nuestros fardos. Parecían sorprendidos cuando vieron la silla de manos, demasiado grande y dentro de ella a las dos muchachas rapadas e idénticas, sentadas lado a lado, en una posición que parecía la más incómoda. Sin embargo, no hicieron ningún comentario. Se hicieron a un lado cortésmente para dejarnos pasar a través de Zitákuaro a mí, a mi esposa y a toda la comitiva.

Después de eso ya no nos volvieron a detener o a provocar, pero ordené que las cortinas del entoldado de la silla de manos de la Señora Pareja fueran corridas para que ellas no fueran visibles a ninguno de los nativos, a nuestro paso. Sabía, para entonces, que un mensajero-veloz estaría en aquellos momentos informando al Uandákari de nuestra llegada, pero deseaba que su regalo se mantuviera en el misterio y sin descripción, el mayor tiempo posible, hasta nuestra llegada a palacio. Zyanya pensó que eso era una crueldad por mi parte: dejar que las gemelas recorrieran todo el camino sin poder ver nada, sobre el nuevo país en el que iban a vivir. Así es que cada vez que le mostraba a *ella* algo de interés, detenía toda la caravana y cuando no se veía ningún viajero en el camino, iba personalmente a ver a las gemelas y descorriendo las cortinas les mostraba lo que hubiera despertado mi interés. Siguió haciendo eso a través de todo nuestro camino por Michihuacan, para mi más grande exasperación, ya que Izquierda y Derecha eran totalmente apáticas e indiferentes acerca de lo que les rodeaba. La primera cosa que excitó la curiosidad de Zyanya en la gente, fue, por supuesto, la preponderancia de cabezas lustrosas por falta de cabello. Ya le había hablado sobre esa costumbre, pero no es lo mismo decir que ver. Cuando poco a poco se acostumbró a ello, se quedaba mirando fijamente a algún joven y murmuraba: «Ése es un muchacho. No, una muchacha...» Y yo debo admitir que ellos la miraban con la misma curiosidad. Los purémpecha estaban acostumbrados a ver a otras gentes con pelo —viajeros extranjeros, su gente de clase baja y quizás algunos excéntricos—, pero nunca antes habían visto a una bella mujer con un cabello tan largo y abundante, y que partiendo de su frente tenía un vívido mechón blanco, así es que también ellos la miraban fijamente y luego murmuraban.

Había otras maravillas, aparte de la gente. La parte de Michihuacan que por aquel entonces estábamos cruzando, tenía montañas, como cualquier otra tierra, pero éstas parecían estar asentadas en el horizonte, siendo un simple marco a las llanuras o a la nación suave y ondulante que encerraban. Algunas partes de ese territorio eran florestas, algunas otras praderas cubiertas de zacate y flores silvestres. Pero la mayor parte consistía en generosas tierras de labranza, anchas y extendidas, y granjas productivas. Allí había campos inmensurables de maíz, frijol, *chilis*, huertos de *ahuácatin* y de frutos dulces. Aquí y allá se levantaban en medio de los campos los graneros de adobe, en donde se almacenaban la semilla y el producto. Éstos estaban hechos en forma cónica, como una reminiscencia de las cabezas puntiagudas de la Señora Pareja.

En esas regiones, hasta las casas más humildes se veían agradables. Todas estaban hechas de madera, ya que ésta abundaba allí, sus tablas y vigas estaban puestas ingeniosamente sobre apretadas muescas, todas juntas, sin mortero o cuerdas que las amarraran. Cada casa tenía un alto tejado puntiagudo, cuyas alas caían circundando la casa, pues ese tipo de construcción era la mejor para dar sombra durante la estación caliente y para dejar caer el agua en la estación húmeda, y algunos de los tejados estaban hechos con imaginación, de tal manera que sus cuatro esquinas quedaran levantadas en puntas ornamentales. Ésa era la estación de las golondrinas y en ninguna parte había tantas como en Michihuacan —volando, revoloteando, aleteando, deslizándose por todas partes—, sin duda porque esos amplios aleros eran muy adecuados para hacer sus nidos.

Con sus bosques y sus corrientes de agua, Michihuacan era un hogar hospitalario para toda clase de pájaros. Los ríos reflejaban los colores centelleantes y brillantes de los papagayos, los pájaros musicapa y los pájaros pescadores. En las florestas, los pájaros carpinteros hacían constantemente su ruido peculiar de clavar y tamborilear. En el lago, las golondrinas se posaban sobre las garzas blancas y azules, e incluso sobre el gran pájaro *kuinko*. El *kuinko* tiene un pico en forma de cuchara; su cara es tan fea que causa risa, sus patas y su forma son desmañadas, pero el *kuinko* es soberbio en su plumaje de colores de crepúsculo y cuando una bandada de ellos levanta el vuelo al mismo tiempo, es como si el viento se hiciera visible y en un color rosa.

La única concentración humana de Michihuacan, en aquellos días, estaba en la multitud de aldeas que bordeaban el gran Lago de Juncos, Pátzkuaro, o asentadas en las muchas islas pequeñas del lago. Aunque cada una de las aldeas de los alrededores vivían de la caza de aves y de la pesca, cada una tenía, por órdenes de su Uandákuari, que proveer localmente algún producto en especial o algún servicio que pudiera ser cambiado entre las demás. Una comunidad trabajaba la madera, otra tejía ropa, otra trenzaba los juncos para convertirlos en alfombrillas *pétlatin*, otra se dedicaba al lacado y así todas. En la aldea que llevaba el nombre del lago, Pátzkuaro, estaba el mercado en donde se ofrecían todas esas cosas. En una isla en medio del lago, llamada Xarákuaro, se habían construido todos los templos, altares y plazas, y era el centro ceremonial para todos los habitantes de las aldeas. Tzintzuntzaní, que quiere decir En Donde Hay Colibríes, era la capital, el centro y el corazón de toda esa actividad. Por sí misma no producía otra cosa más que las decisiones, acciones y órdenes con que se gobernaba a la nación entera. Estaba construida a base de palacios y totalmente habitada por sus nobles y sus familias, por cortesanos, sacerdotes y sirvientes.

Conforme se iba aproximando nuestra caravana, el primer objeto hecho por el hombre que podíamos ver, sobre el camino, desde varias largas-carreras, era la anciana *iyákata*, como se le dice en poré a una pirámide, que se alzaba sobre las alturas, al este de los palacios de los nobles. Más allá de toda imaginación, esa *iyákata*, no muy alta pero extravagantemente alargada, era una curiosa mezcla de plazas y de edificios redondos, que se habían llegado a convertir en un majestuoso montón de piedras, pues hacía ya mucho tiempo que habían perdido toda su cubierta de yeso y colorido; se estaban rompiendo en partes y la hierba crecía por todos lados.

Los numerosos palacios de En Donde Hay Colibríes estaban todos construidos de madera, y aunque pudieran ser mucho menos impresionantes que los de piedra de Tenochtitlan, eran totalmente diferentes, así es que tenían su propia grandeza. Bajo los aleros desplegados de sus altos techos puntiagudos, terminados en un rizo, había dos pisos y el alto estaba totalmente circundado por una galería exterior. Los poderosos troncos de cedro que sostenían esos edificios, las columnas, los remates y los pilares, las innumerables vigas visibles bajo sus aleros, todos ellos estaban trabajados laboriosamente y tallados con rizos y filigranas. Sus puertas eran más a menudo tablas que se deslizaban, que las familiares para nosotros sostenidas sobre pivotes. Cualesquiera que fueran los artistas que los consiguieron, y en algunos palacios debieron de haber utilizado mano de obra importada, los ricos lacados debieron de haber sido trabajados a mano. Cada palacio tenía bellos ornamentos que brillaban de color y de oro batido, pero por supuesto el palacio del Uandákuari hacía que los otros parecieran insignificantes.

Los mensajeros-veloces habían tenido a Yquígare informado

de nuestra aproximación, así es que nuestra llegada era esperada y una multitud de nobles con sus esposas nos estaba aguardando para recibirnos. Un poco antes de nuestra llegada, la comitiva se había desviado hacia el lago, y buscando un lugar solitario, todos nos bañamos y nos pusimos nuestros trajes más finos. Llegamos a la entrada del palacio, sintiéndonos frescos y altivos; ordené que dejaran las sillas de manos, junto a una pared que tenía un jardín colgante, sombreado por altos árboles. Despedí a nuestros guardias y cargadores, quienes fueron conducidos a las habitaciones de los criados. Sólo Zyanya, la Señora Pareja y yo fuimos a través del jardín hacia el gran edificio del palacio. En la confusión general que provocaron los que nos daban la bienvenida, la manera singular de caminar de las gemelas pasó desapercibida.

Entre la alegría y los murmullos de bienvenida, aunque no pude comprender todo lo que decían, fuimos conducidos a través de los portales de troncos de cedro dentro de una terraza también de cedro, luego atravesamos una gran puerta abierta y pasamos por un corredor al salón de recepciones de Yquígare. Era inmensamente largo y ancho y con dos pisos de alto: como el patio interior del palacio de Tenochtitlan, pero cubierto. A cada lado había unas escaleras que terminaban en un pasillo circular interior, sobre el que se abrían los cuartos superiores. El Uandákuari estaba sentado sobre su trono, que no era otra cosa más que una *icpali*, silla baja, sin embargo, de la entrada del salón al lugar en donde él se encontraba, la distancia era tan grande que claramente se veía que había sido proyectada en esa forma para que el visitante se sintiera como un pedigüeño.

A pesar de lo grande que era el vestíbulo, éste estaba completamente lleno de señoras y señores vestidos elegantemente, pero se hicieron hacia atrás, a ambos lados, para que pudiéramos pasar cómodamente, primero yo, luego Zyanya y después la Señora Pareja. Caminamos despacio en procesión, solemnemente, hacia el trono y yo levanté mi topacio sólo el tiempo suficiente como para echarle una buena mirada a Yquíngare. Antes, solamente lo había visto una vez, en la dedicación a la Gran Pirámide, y en aquellos días no lo había podido ver con claridad. Ya entonces era viejo y ahora lo era más: un manojito arrugado de hombre. Debió de haber sido su calvicie la que había inspirado esa moda entre su pueblo, aunque él no necesitaba usar una hoja de obsidiana para raparse. Era tan desdentado como pelón y casi sin voz: nos dio la bienvenida con un susurro desmayado, como el sonido que hace un pomito de semillas al ser agitado. Aunque me sentía contento de desembarazarme de la lerda Señora Pareja, sentí cierto remordimiento al ponerla, aunque fuera rara, dentro de los dedos como tijeretas de aquella vieja semilla retorcida y marchita.

Le extendí la carta de Auítzotl y el Uandákuari a su vez se la dio a su hijo mayor, ordenándole con impertinencia que la leyera en voz alta. Siempre había concebido a los príncipes como hombres jóvenes, pero si ese Príncipe Heredero Tzímtzicha se hubiese dejado crecer el cabello, éste hubiera sido gris, sin embargo, su padre todavía le jadeaba órdenes, como si él no llevara un taparrabo bajo su manto.

«Un regalo para mí, ¿eh? —graznó el padre cuando el hijo acabó de leer la carta en poré. Fijó sus ojos legañosos sobre Zyanya, que estaba parada a un lado de mí, y se relamió las encías—. Ah. Puede ser una novedad, sí. Que la rapen toda, menos el mechón blanco...»

Zyanya, horrorizada, se puso atrás de mí. Rápidamente le dije: «Éste es el regalo, mi Señor Yquíngare», y me acerqué a la Señora Pareja. Las hice detener exactamente enfrente del trono y les arranqué su vestidura de una sola pieza, color púrpura, que las cubría del cuello a los pies. La multitud allí reunida lanzó un grito por haber destruido esa pieza hecha de un material tan fino y luego dieron otro de sorpresa, cuando la tela cayó al piso y las mellizas quedaron desnudas.

«¡Por los huevos emplumados de Kurkauri!», resolló el viejo, usando el nombre poré de Quetzalcóatl. Él continuó diciendo algo, pero su voz se perdió entre el parloteo de sus cortesanos, que seguían con sus exclamaciones de sorpresa, y de lo único que me pude dar cuenta era de que le estaba babeando la barbilla. Obviamente el regalo había tenido mucho éxito.

A todos los presentes, incluyendo a las diversas esposas coronadas y concubinas del Uandákuari, se les dio la oportunidad de acercarse a empujones, para ver de cerca a la Señora Pareja. Algunos hombres y también unas pocas mujeres se acercaron descaradamente y con sus manos hicieron caricias en alguna parte de la Señora Pareja. Cuando la curiosidad de todos quedó satisfecha, Yquíngare graznó una orden que dejó vacío todo el salón de recepciones, con excepción de él, de nosotros, del Príncipe Heredero y de unos cuantos guardias impasibles, parados en los rincones.

«Ahora, aliméntenme —dijo el viejo, restregándose sus manos secas—. Debo prepararme para darme un buen agasajo, ¿eh?»

El príncipe Tzímtzicha pasó la orden a uno de los guardias, quien salió. En un momento, empezaron a llegar sirvientes trayendo un mantel para la comida, que depositaron allí mismo y después de que Zyanya terminó de vestir a las gemelas, con su vestido desgarrado, nos sentamos los seis. Yo inferí que de ordinario no se le permitía al Príncipe Heredero comer al mismo tiempo que su padre, pero como él hablaba correctamente el náhuatl, se le podría utilizar como intérprete cuando el viejo y yo ni pudiéramos entendernos. Mientras tanto, Zyanya ayudaba a comer a la Señora Pareja con una cuchara, ya que de otra manera, ellas hubieran tomado aun la espuma del *chocólatl* con sus dedos y a manos llenas, masticando con sus bocas abiertas y provocando náuseas a todos los presentes en general. Sin embargo, sus modales no eran peores que los del viejo.

Cuando nos sirvieron a nosotros el delicioso pescado blanco, que sólo se puede encontrar en el lago de Pátzkuaro, él nos dijo con su sonrisa desdentada: «Coman, disfruten. Yo sólo puedo tomar leche.»

«¿Leche? —repitió Zyanya, preguntando cortésmente—: ¿Leche de gacela, mi señor?»

Entonces ella levantó sus cejas de la sorpresa. Una mujer muy larga y muy rapada, llegó, se hincó a un lado del Uandákuari, se levantó la blusa y le presentó un pecho muy, muy grande, que si hubiera tenido rostro habría podido ser su cabeza rapada. Durante el resto de la comida, cuando Yquíngare no estaba haciendo preguntas acerca de las peculiaridades de la Señora Pareja, su origen y su adquisición, estaba succionando ruidosa e indistintamente de un pezón al otro.

Zyanya evitaba el verlo, lo mismo que el Príncipe Heredero; ellos simplemente movían su comida de un lado a otro, en sus platos lacados de oro. Las gemelas comían hasta por los codos porque siempre lo hacían así, y yo comía abundantemente porque estaba prestando muy poca atención a las vulgaridades que estaba haciendo Yquíngare, ya que estaba viendo algo atrás de él. Cuando por primera vez entré en la habitación, me pude dar cuenta de que los guardias llevaban lanzas, cuyas puntas eran de cobre, pero de un peculiar cobre oscuro. En esos momentos, pude percibir que tanto el Uandákuari como su hijo, llevaban dagas cortas del mismo metal, colgadas de sus cinturas y aseguradas con unas presillas de cuero.

El viejo me estaba endilgando un discurso, dándole vueltas con el claro objeto de que al llegar al final me preguntaría si también le podría conseguir un par de adolescentes varones unidos, cuando Zyanya, como si ya no pudiera seguir escuchando más, lo interrumpió para preguntarle: «¿Qué *es* esta bebida deliciosa?»

El Príncipe Heredero pareció muy contento por esa interrupción, e inclinándose a través del mantel, le dijo que era *chápari*, un producto hecho de la miel de abeja, muy, muy potente y que sería bueno que no bebiera demasiado, esa primera vez.

«¡Qué maravilloso! —exclamó, empinando la taza lacada—. Si la miel puede emborrachar tanto, ¿por qué las abejas no están siempre ebrias?» Ella hipó y se quedó pensativa, evidentemente acerca de las abejas, porque para cuando el Uandákuari trató de resumir la cháchara de su pregunta, Zyanya dijo en voz alta: «A lo mejor lo están. ¿Quién puede saberlo?» Y se sirvió otra taza, y luego otra a mí, tirando un poco de su contenido.

El viejo suspiró, chupó por última vez la teta baboseada de su nodriza y le dio un sonoro manotazo en una nalga, en señal de que la horrorosa comida había terminado. Zyanya y yo nos apresuramos a beber nuestras segundas tazas de *chápari*. «Bien», dijo Yquíngare, mascando con su boca, de tal manera que su nariz y su barbilla se juntaban varias veces. Su hijo saltó detrás de él, para ayudarlo a ponerse en pie.

«Un momento, mi señor —dije—, sólo un momento; voy a dar algunas instrucciones a la Señora Pareja.»

«¿Instrucciones?», dijo él con suspicacia.

«Para que cumplan —dije sonriendo como lo haría un alcahuete—. Como son vírgenes, pueden ser rudas al acariciar.»

«¿Ah? —dijo roncamente, sonriéndome también—. ¿Son también vírgenes? Sí, que cumplan, por todos los medios que cumplan.»

Tanto Zyanya como Tzímtzicha me lanzaron por un igual una mirada de desprecio, cuando me llevé a las gemelas aparte y les di instrucciones, instrucciones urgentes que en ese momento se me ocurrieron. Fue bastante difícil, porque tenía que hablar muy bajo y en una mezcla de náhuatl y de coatlícamac y ellas eran *tan* estúpidas, pero al fin, las dos asintieron aunque con cierta clase de lerda comprensión, y encogiéndome de hombros, de esperanza y desesperación, las llevé hacia el Uandákuari. Sin protestar, ellas lo acompañaron escalera arriba ayudándolo a subir y de hecho parecía como si un cangrejo ayudara a una araña. Un poco antes de alcanzar el piso alto, la araña se volvió y gritó algo a su hijo en poré, tan carrasposamente que no pude entender una palabra. Tzímtzicha asintió obedientemente, luego se volvió y me preguntó que si yo y mi señora estábamos listos para retirarnos. Ella sólo hipó, así es que yo contesté que pensaba que sí lo estábamos, pues había sido un día muy largo. Seguimos al Príncipe Heredero escaleras arriba, al otro lado del vestíbulo.

Así como pasó todo, allí en Tzintzuntzaní, por primera y única vez en nuestra vida de casados, Zyanya y yo nos acostamos con otras gentes. Sin embargo, les suplico que recuerden, reverendos frailes, que tanto ella como yo, estábamos un poco borrachos por el *chápari*. De todas formas, no fue exactamente como suena, y lo explicaré de la mejor manera posible.

Antes de salir de casa, traté de explicarle a Zyanya la predilección de los purémpecha, por inventar prácticas sexuales voluptuosas y aun perversas. Así es que estuvimos de acuerdo en no demostrar sorpresa o disgusto ante cualquier tipo de hospitalidad de esa naturaleza que nos pudiera ofrecer nuestro anfitrión, sino declinarla de la mejor manera posible. O por lo menos eso fue lo que habíamos determinado, pero cuando esa hospitalidad nos fue brindada y cuando nos dimos cuenta de lo que se trataba, ya estábamos tomando parte en ella. Si nosotros no reculamos ante ello, fue porque, aunque no pudimos decidir después qué había sido perverso y qué inocuo, fue innegablemente delicioso.

A medida que nos guiaba por el piso superior, Tzímtzicha se volvió e imitando mi sonrisa de alcahuete, preguntó: «¿Querrán el señor campeón y su señora habitaciones separadas? ¿Camas separadas?»

«Naturalmente que no», dije y lo dije fríamente, antes de que me preguntara: «¿Quieren otros amantes?», o alguna otra indecencia.

«Entonces, una cámara conyugal, mi señor —me dijo estando de acuerdo—. Pero, algunas veces —volvió sobre lo mismo, casual, como conversando—, después de un día agotador de viaje, hasta la pareja más bien avenida puede estar fatigada. La Corte de Tzintzuntzaní, se juzgaría negligente si sus huéspedes se sintieran demasiado fatigados, como para poderse complacer el uno al otro. Por lo tanto, les ofrecemos un servicio llamado *atanatanárani*. Éste engrandece al hombre adecuadamente y a la mujer la hace más receptiva, quizás hasta un extremo del que ninguno de ustedes ha disfrutado jamás.»

La palabra *atanatanárani*, hasta donde pude desenmarañar sus elementos, sólo significaba «juntarse a un mismo tiempo». Antes de poder averiguar acerca de cómo se puede engrandecer cualquier cosa, juntándola a un mismo tiempo, él se había inclinado ante nosotros, dentro de nuestras habitaciones y dándose la vuelta cerró tras de sí la puerta lacada.

La habitación alumbrada por lámparas, tenía una de las camas más grandes, más suaves y con más gran profusión de cobijas que yo nunca había visto antes. También nos estaban esperando dos esclavos ya de edad: un hombre y una mujer. Yo los miré con cierta aprensión, pero sólo me pidieron permiso para preparar nuestros baños. Junto a la recámara había dos baños completos, para cada uno de nosotros, incluyendo su bañera y su cuarto de vapor, ya listo. Mi sirviente me ayudó a bañarme con esponja y luego me frotó vigorosamente con piedra pómez, en el cuarto de vapor, pero no hizo nada más, nada que me molestara. Pensé que los esclavos, el baño de agua y de vapor, era lo que el Príncipe Heredero había querido decir por: «un servicio llamado *atanatanárani*». Si era eso, no era sino una cosa agradable y civilizada, nada obscena y que había funcionado muy bien. Me sentía fresco, con la piel hormigueante y mucho más «adecuado» para, como dijo Tzímtzicha, poder «satisfacer» a mi mujer.

Su esclava se inclinó al mismo tiempo que mi esclavo, antes de salir y ella y yo salimos de los baños para encontrar que la cámara principal estaba completamente oscura. Los cortinajes estaban corridos y las lámparas de aceite apagadas, así es que nos tomó algún tiempo encontrarnos en ese inmenso cuarto, y otro momento más para encontrar la inmensa cama. Era una noche calurosa; sólo la cobija de encima había sido doblada. Nos deslizamos en ella y descansamos uno junto al otro, sobre nuestras espaldas, contentos de momento con poder disfrutar de una suavidad de nube bajo de nosotros.

Zyanya murmuró adormilada: «Sabes, Zaa, todavía me siento borracha como una abeja. —Entonces, súbitamente dio un pequeño respingo y jadeó—: ¡*Ayyo*, estás muy ardiente! Me cogiste por sorpresa.»

Yo estuve a punto de exclamar lo mismo. Me toqué abajo, donde una manita me manoseaba con gentileza suavemente; había supuesto que era su mano y exclamé asombrado: «¡Zyanya!» Casi al mismo tiempo ella dijo:

«Zaa, puedo sentirlo... es un *niño* que está aquí abajo. Jugando con mi... jugando conmigo.»

«También yo tengo uno —dije todavía muy sorprendido—. Nos estaban esperando bajo los cobertores. ¿Qué vamos a hacer ahora?»

Yo esperaba que ella dijera: «¡patear!» o «¡gritar!» o que hiciera ambas cosas, pero en lugar de eso, dio otro pequeño respingo, rió sofocada y repitió mi pregunta: «¿Qué vamos a hacer? ¿Qué está haciendo el tuyo?»

Le dije lo que estaba haciendo.

«El mío, lo mismo.»

«No es desagradable.»

«No, decididamente no.»

«Deben de estar adiestrados para esto.»

«Pero no para su propia satisfacción. Éste, por lo menos, parece demasiado joven.»

«No. Lo hacen sólo para aumentar nuestro placer, como dijo el príncipe.»

«Ellos pueden ser castigados, si nosotros los rechazamos.»

Ahora, yo hago estos comentarios con voz fría y desapasionada, pero no fue así. Estábamos hablándonos con voces roncas y frases entrecortadas por involuntarios jadeos y movimientos.

«El tuyo, ¿es niño o niña? No puedo estirarme lo suficiente como para...»

«Yo tampoco. ¿Tiene importancia?»

«No. Pero estoy palpando un rostro que me parece bello. Las pestañas son lo suficientemente largas como para... ¡ah!, ¡sí!, ¡con las pestañas!»

«Están bien adiestrados.»

«Oh, exquisitamente. Me pregunto si cada uno de ellos fue enseñado especialmente para... quiero decir...»

«Cambiémoslos y veremos.»

Los dos niños no objetaron nada por cambiar de lugar y su ejecución no disminuyó en lo más mínimo. Quizás la boca juguetona de éste, era más caliente y mojada, acabando de hacer lo que...

Bueno, no quiero entretenerme mucho en este episodio; Zyanya y yo pronto caímos en un frenesí, besándonos cada vez más apasionadamente, agarrándonos y arañándonos; haciendo otras cosas arriba de la cintura, mientras los muchachos estaban más ocupados que nunca abajo. Cuando ya no me pude contener más, nos apareamos como jaguares copulando y los muchachos, apretándose fuera de nosotros, bullían sobre nuestros cuerpos, deditos aquí, lengüecitas allá.

Esto no sucedió sólo una vez, fueron más veces de las que me puedo acordar. Después de cada eyaculación, los niños descansaban un ratito contra nuestros cuerpos jadeantes y sudorosos, y luego, muy delicadamente, se nos volvían a insinuar y empezaban a importunarnos y a acariciarnos. Se movían hacia atrás y hacia adelante de Zyanya a mí, algunas veces individualmente y otras juntos, de tal manera que entonces podía ser atendido por los dos y por mi esposa y luego, ambos muchachos y yo podíamos concentrarnos en ella. No terminó esta actividad, hasta que ella y yo ya no pudimos más y nos hundimos en un sueño profundo. Nunca averiguamos ni el sexo, ni la edad o apariencia de nuestros *atanatanárani* acompañantes. Cuando despertamos muy temprano en la mañana, ya se habían ido.

Lo que me despertó fue un arañazo en la puerta. Estando sólo medio consciente, me levanté y abrí. No vi nada más que la oscuridad que precede a la aurora a través del balcón, y la gran fuente que estaba más allá del vestíbulo, hasta que un dedo arañó mi pierna. Sentí un estremecimiento y miré hacia abajo y allí estaba la Señora Pareja, tan desnudas como yo. En ellas todo se veía doble, todo cuatros, o más bien debería de decir ochos. Las dos estaban sonriendo lascivamente, engarruñadas entre mis piernas.

«Cosa muy agradable», dijo Izquierda.

«La de él, también», dijo Derecha, sacudiendo su cabeza en dirección a la recámara del viejo, según supuse.

«¿Qué hacéis aquí?», les pregunté tan ferozmente como se podía hacer en un susurro.

Una de sus ocho extremidades se levantó y puso en mi mano la daga de Yquíngare. Investigué el oscuro metal, mucho más oscuro en las tinieblas y dejé correr mi pulgar a lo largo de su filo. En verdad que era afiloso y puntiagudo.

«¡Lo hicisteis!», dije, sintiendo una intempestiva gratitud, casi afecto, por ese monstruo agachado a mis pies.

«Fácil», dijo Derecha.

«Él puso ropas a un lado cama», dijo Izquierda.

«Él puso eso en mí —dijo Derecha, picando mi *tepuli* y haciéndome saltar otra vez—. Agradable.

«Yo me aburrí —dijo Izquierda—. Nada que hacer. Sólo vaivén. Yo busqué entre ropas, sentí algo redondo, encontré cuchillo.»

«Ella sostuvo cuchillo mientras yo tenía diversión —dijo Derecha—. Yo sostuve cuchillo mientras ella tenía diversión. Ella sostuvo cuchillo mientras...»

«¿Y ahora?», la interrumpí.

«Él ronca al fin. Nosotras trajimos cuchillo. Ahora nosotras despertarlo. Tener más diversión.»

Como si les hubiera sido muy difícil esperar, antes de que pudiera darles las gracias, las gemelas se fueron a paso acelerado como lo haría un cangrejo, a lo largo del pasillo oscuro. En lugar de darles las gracias a ellas, se las di a las propiedades aparentemente fuertes de la leche mamada y entré otra vez a la recámara, para esperar la salida del sol.

Los cortesanos de Tzintzuntzaní no parecían ser muy madrugadores. Sólo el Príncipe Heredero Tzímtzicha se nos unió en el desayuno a Zyanya y a mí. Le dije al viejo príncipe que mi cortejo y yo debíamos de ponernos en camino. Que parecía obvio que su padre estaba gozando de su regalo, así es que no deseábamos haraganear por los alrededores y hacer que él interrumpiera su placer, sólo para entretener a unos huéspedes que no habían sido invitados. El príncipe dijo con suavidad:

«Bien, si ustedes sienten que deben de partir, no los detendremos, excepto por una formalidad. Un registro de sus personas, de sus posesiones, fardos y de cualquier cosa que ustedes se lleven. Puedo asegurarles que no intentamos insultarlos; yo también tengo que sufrir esto cada vez que viajo a cualquier parte.»

Me encogí de hombros con tanta indiferencia como cuando uno lo rodea un grupo de guardias armados. Discretamente y con respeto, pero también cabalmente, ellos golpearon ligeramente todas las partes de nuestras vestiduras, tanto mías como de Zyanya; después nos pidieron que nos quitáramos por un momento nuestras sandalias. En el jardín que estaba enfrente de palacio hicieron lo mismo con nuestros guardias y cargadores, deshicieron todos nuestros fardos, incluso tocaron todos los cojines y las cortinas de las sillas de manos. Para entonces, otras gentes ya se habían levantado y andaban por los alrededores, la mayoría eran niños del palacio que observaban todos esos procedimientos con ojos brillantes y conocedores. Miré a Zyanya. Estaba mirando de cerca a los niños, tratando de saber cuál de ellos... Cuando me vio sonriéndole, se puso tan colorada como la pequeña hoja de metal, que ya sin su mango de madera llevaba escondida en mi cuello, bajo mi cabello.

Los guardias le dijeron a Tzímtzicha que no llevábamos nada que no hubiéramos traído. Su mal humor cambió inmediatamente, y mostrándose amigable, dijo: «Entonces, por supuesto que nosotros insistimos en que usted le lleve *algo*, como un regalo recíproco, a su Uey-Tlatoani. —Él me alargó un pequeño saco de piel, y más tarde vi que contenía una cantidad de las más finas perlas, corazones-de-ostiones—. Y —continuó él— algo todavía más precioso, que podrá caber en esa litera tan grande que ustedes traen. No sé lo que hará mi padre sin ella, ya que es su posesión más preciada, pero ésa ha sido su orden.» Y diciendo eso nos dio a la tremenda mujer rapada que había alimentado al viejo en la cena de la noche anterior.

Era por lo menos dos veces más pesada que las gemelas juntas, y en todo el camino de regreso a casa, los cargadores se tuvieron que turnar continuamente para poder sobrevivir, y toda la comitiva se detenía más o menos cada larga-carrera y esperábamos impacientes, mientras la nodriza sin ninguna vergüenza se sacaba la leche con los dedos para aliviar la presión. Zyanya rió todo el camino de regreso y siguió riendo aun cuando Auítzotl mandó que me dieran garrote allí mismo, cuando le presenté su regalo. Entonces, rápidamente, le expliqué lo que aparentemente podía hacer por el viejo marchito de Yquíngare; él la miró apreciativamente y canceló la orden de estrangularme, y Zyanya siguió riendo tanto que al Venerado Orador y a mí no nos quedó más remedio que unirnos a su risa.

Si Auítzotl consiguió tener un vigor mayor con ella, la mujer-lechera fue el botín más valioso que lo que llegó a ser la daga de metal asesino. Nuestros forjadores de metales mexica la estudiaron ansiosamente, raspándola profundamente, tomando limaduras de ella y por último llegaron a la conclusión de que estaba hecha con una mezcla de cobre y estaño. Pero por más que trataron, nunca pudieron encontrar las proporciones adecuadas, las temperaturas o algo por el estilo, así es que nunca tuvieron éxito en copiar la aleación del metal.

Sin embargo, como el estaño no existía en estas tierras, a excepción hecha de los pedacitos cruciformes que usábamos como moneda corriente para canjear y ya que éstos nos llegaban a través de las rutas comerciales del sur, desde algún país lejano y desconocido, pasando de mano en mano, Auítzotl pudo por lo menos ordenar una confiscación inmediata y continua de todos ellos. Así es que el estaño desapareció como moneda circulante y ya que no teníamos otro uso que darle, supongo que Auítzotl solamente lo apiló en algún lugar, fuera de la vista.

En cierto modo ése fue un gesto interesado: si nosotros los mexica no podíamos tener el secreto del metal, nadie más lo podría tener. Pero para entonces los purémpecha ya tenían suficientes armas como para que Tenochtitlan jamás se sintiera animado a declararles la guerra, y al detener los envíos de estaño, por lo menos preveníamos que siguieran haciendo más armas adicionales, las suficientes como para que se envalentonaran y nos declararan la guerra. Así es que supongo que puedo decir que mi misión en Michihuacan no fue del todo inútil.

✠

Más o menos por el tiempo en que regresamos de Michihua-can, Zyanya y yo cumplimos los siete años de casados, y me atrevería a decir que mis amigos nos miraban como una vieja pareja, y tanto ella como yo veíamos nuestra vida en común fija en su curso, no susceptible de cambios o rompimientos, y éramos lo suficientemente felices el uno con el otro, que nos sentíamos satisfechos de estar así. Pero los dioses lo quisieron de un modo diferente y Zyanya me lo dejó saber de la siguiente manera:

Una tarde habíamos estado de visita con la Primera Señora en sus alcobas de palacio. Cuando ya nos íbamos, vimos en el corredor a ese animal-lechero de mujer traído de la Corte de Tzintzuntzaní. Sospecho que Auítzotl simplemente la dejaba vivir en palacio, como una sirvienta en general, pero en aquella ocasión hice un comentario jocoso acerca de la «nodriza-mojada», esperando que Zyanya se riera. En lugar de eso, ella me dijo en un tono demasiado cortante para ella:

«Zaa, no debes hacer bromas vulgares acerca de la leche. Acerca de la leche de las madres. Acerca de las madres.»

«No si eso te ofende. Pero, ¿por qué habría de ofenderte?»

Tímida, ansiosa y aprensivamente ella dijo: «En algún tiempo, al término de este año, yo... yo seré... yo seré un animal de leche.»

Me la quedé mirando. Me tomó un tiempo comprender y antes de que pudiera responder, ella añadió: «Lo había sospechado desde hace poco tiempo, pero hace dos días que nuestro *tícitl*, físico, me lo confirmó. He estado tratando de pensar de qué manera te lo podía decir con palabras suaves y dulces. Y ahora —lloriqueó sintiéndose infeliz— sólo sé soltártelo así. Zaa, ¿adónde vas? *¡No me dejes, Zaa!*»

Me fui corriendo, sí, y de una manera poco digna, pero sólo para conseguir una silla de manos de palacio, para que ella no caminara de regreso a casa. Ella rió y dijo: «Eso es ridículo —cuando insistí en levantarla para ponerla sobre los cojines de la silla—. Pero, ¿quiere decir esto, Zaa, que estás contento?»

«¡Contento! —exclamé—. ¡Contentísimo!» Y me solté hablando mientras caminaba saltando a un lado de su silla. Ya olvidé cuáles fueron exactamente mis palabras, pero ellas expresaban placer, deleite y preocupación por ella.

Al llegar a nuestra casa, Turquesa abrió la puerta y miró preocupada cómo asistía a Zyanya que protestaba, a subir los pocos escalones. Pero le grité: «¡Vamos a tener un bebé!», y ella lanzó un grito alegre. A tanto ruido, Cosquillosa vino corriendo de algún lado y yo ordené: «¡Cosquillosa, Turquesa, id en este instante a dar una buena limpieza al cuarto de los niños! Haced todos los preparativos necesarios. Comprad todo lo que necesitamos. Una cuna. Juguetes. Flores. ¡Poned flores por todas partes!»

«Zaa, ¿quieres callarte? —dijo Zyanya, medio divertida, medio apenada—. Todavía faltan meses. El cuarto puede esperar.»

Sin embargo, las dos esclavas ya habían corrido escalera arriba, obedientes y bulliciosas. Y, a pesar de haber reanudado sus protestas, también ayudé a Zyanya a subir la escalera, e insistí que descansara un poco, después del esfuerzo hecho en su visita a palacio. Al fin ella accedió —me imagino que solamente para poderse librar de mí— y yo fui escaleras abajo para felicitarme a mí mismo con un brindis de *octli* y una fumada de *picíetl* y a sentarme en el crepúsculo, satisfecho en mi soledad.

Poco a poco, mi eufórica satisfacción cayó dentro de una meditación seria y empecé a percibir las razones por las cuales Zyanya había vacilado al comunicarme este acontecimiento. Ella había dicho que eso ocurriría en el término de ese año. Yo conté con los dedos hacia atrás, y me di cuenta de que nuestro bebé debió de haber sido concebido durante aquella maravillosa noche en el palacio del viejo Yquíngare, cuando nosotros habíamos disfrutado con la colaboración de los *atanatanárani*. Yo cloqueé de gusto por eso. Sin duda Zyanya estaba un poco turbada por ese hecho; hubiera preferido concebir al niño en unas circunstancias más sosegadas. Bien, pensé, es mucho mejor concebir un hijo en el paroxismo del éxtasis, como nosotros lo habíamos hecho, que en una adormecida conformidad, por obligación o inevitablemente, como la mayoría de los padres lo hacen. Pero no pude cloquear cuando me vino a la mente el siguiente pensamiento. El niño podría tener una deficiencia desde el momento de su nacimiento, porque era casi seguro que heredaría mi mala visión. Aunque él no tendría que ir dando traspiés y andar a tientas como yo lo hice por muchos años, antes de haber descubierto el cristal para ver, me daría mucha lástima un niño que tendría que aprender a sostener un topacio ante su ojo, antes de aprender cómo llevar la cuchara a su boca, y que sin ese objeto sería patéticamente incapaz de caminar con pasos seguros por los alrededores, en sus excursiones infantiles, y que sería llamado cruelmente Ojo Amarillo o algo parecido por sus compañeros de juegos...

Si el bebé era una niña, esa visión corta no sería mucha desventaja. Ni los juegos de su infancia, ni sus ocupaciones como adulta serían vigorosas y osadas o tendrían que depender de la agudeza de sus sentidos físicos. Las mujeres no competían entre ellas hasta que llegaban a la edad de merecer, entonces lo harían por los maridos más deseables y entonces sería mucho menos importante, como vería mi hija a cómo ella se vería. Sin embargo, me atormentaba un pensamiento, ¡la suposición de que viera como yo, y que se pareciera a mí, ambas cosas! Un hijo estaría contento de heredar mi estatura de cabeza inclinada. Una hija estaría desolada y ella podría odiarme y yo probablemente renegaría al verla. Me imaginaba que nuestra hija se veía exactamente igual a esa mujer-lechera tan tremenda...

Ese pensamiento me trajo una preocupación mayor. Durante muchos días antes de la noche en que concebimos al niño, ¡Zyanya había estado íntimamente cerca de la monstruosa Señora Pareja! Estaba bien probado que incontables niños habían nacido deformados o deficientes cuando sus madres se vieron afectadas bajo el influjo de horrorosas influencias. Pero eso no era todo, lo peor era que Zyanya había dicho: «más o menos al terminar el año». ¡Y precisamente en ese momento serían los cinco días *nemontemtin*! Un niño nacido durante esos días sin vida y sin nombre, sería de tan mal agüero como sus padres lo esperaran, aun dejándose persuadir a dejarlo morir de hambre. No era tan supersticioso como para hacer eso, cualesquiera que fueran las presiones que me trajera. Pero entonces, ¿qué carga, o monstruo o malhechor llegaría a ser ese niño cuando creciera...?

Fumé *picíetl* y bebí *octli* hasta que Turquesa llegó y al verme en la condición en que estaba me dijo: «¡Qué vergüenza, mi señor amo!», y llamó a Estrella Cantadora para que me ayudara a llegar a mi cama.

«Seré una ruina temblorosa antes de que llegue el momento —dije a Zyanya, a la mañana siguiente—. Me pregunto si todos los padres pasan por estas molestas preocupaciones.»

Ella sonrió y dijo: «Creo que no tanto como las que tiene una madre. Pero una madre sabe que no puede hacer absolutamente nada más que esperar.»

Suspiré y dije: «Tampoco veo otra salida para mí. Sólo puedo dedicar cada uno de mis momentos a cuidarte, atenderte y ver que no tengas ni la más pequeña desgracia o aflicción...»

«¡Haz eso y *yo* seré una ruina! —gritó ella y lo decía de verdad—. Por favor, querido, encuentra alguna otra cosa en que ocuparte.»

Molesto y empequeñecido por el rechazo, fui cabizbajo a darme mi baño matutino. Sin embargo, después de haber bajado la escalera y de haber desayunado, una desviación del asunto se hizo presente, en la persona de Cózcatl, que me llamaba.

«*Ayyo*, ¿cómo pudiste enterarte tan pronto? —exclamé—. Ha sido muy amable por tu parte venir a vernos tan pronto.»

Mi saludo pareció sorprenderlo. Él dijo: «¿Enterarme de qué? De hecho he venido a...»

«¡Pues de que vamos a tener un niño!»

Su rostro se ensombreció por un momento, antes de decir: «Estoy muy contento por ti, Mixtli, y por Zyanya. Le pido a los dioses que os bendigan con un niño bien favorecido. —Luego él murmuró—: Es sólo que esta coincidencia me sorprendió por un momento, porque he venido a pedirte permiso para casarme.»

«¿Para casarte? ¡Pero si ésa es una noticia maravillosa como la mía! —Yo moví la cabeza reminiscente—. Increíble... el muchachito Cózcatl ya está en edad de tomar esposa. Muchas veces no me doy cuenta de cómo pasan los años. ¿Pero qué quieres decir con pedir mi permiso?»

«Mi futura esposa no es libre para casarse, es una esclava.»

«¿Sí? —Yo seguía sin entender—. Seguro que puedes comprar su libertad.»

«Sí puedo —dijo él—. Pero ¿me la venderás? Quiero casarme con Quequelmiqui y ella se quiere casar conmigo.»

«¿Qué?»

«Fue por ti que la conocí y confieso que muchas de mis visitas aquí han sido en parte un pretexto, así ella y yo podíamos estar un poco de tiempo juntos. Mucho de nuestro noviazgo ha tenido lugar en tu cocina.»

Yo estaba pasmado: «¿Cosquillosa? ¿Nuestra criadita? ¡Pero si es casi una adolescente!»

Él me recordó con suavidad: «Ella lo era cuando la compraste, Mixtli. Los años *han* pasado.»

Pensé en ellos. Cosquillosa podría ser uno o dos años más joven que Cózcatl, y él tenía, déjenme pensar, andaba por los veintidós. Le dije magnánimamente:

«Tienes mi permiso y mis felicitaciones. ¿Pero comprarla? Ciertamente que no. Ella será uno de nuestros primeros regalos de boda. No, no, no escucharé ninguna protesta; insisto en ello. Si ella no hubiera sido enseñada por ti, la muchacha nunca hubiera llegado a considerarse lo suficientemente valiosa como para ser una esposa. La recuerdo cuando por primera vez llegó aquí. Riéndose.»

«Entonces te doy las gracias, Mixtli, como también lo hará ella. También quería decirte —se sonrojó otra vez— que por supuesto le he hablado de mí mismo. Acerca de la herida que sufrí. Ella comprende que nosotros nunca podremos tener niños, como tú y Zyanya.»

Entonces me di cuenta de que con mi abrupta noticia debió de haber decaído mucho su entusiasmo. Sin saberlo y sin mala intención lo había herido, pero antes de que yo le pudiera decir algunas palabras de disculpa, continuó:

«Quequelmiqui me jura que me quiere y que me acepta como soy, pero quiero estar seguro de que ella lo comprende perfectamente bien, en toda su capacidad. Nuestras caricias, en la cocina, nunca llegaron hasta el punto de...»

Como se sentía tan incómodo y se interrumpía mucho, traté de ayudarlo: «Quieres decir que vosotros todavía no habéis...»

«Ella nunca me ha visto desnudo —me dijo abruptamente—. Y es virgen, inocente en cuanto a todo lo relacionado entre un hombre y una mujer.»

«Es responsabilidad de Zyanya, como su ama, de sentarse con ella y tener una conversación de mujer a mujer. Estoy seguro de que Zyanya podrá instruirla en los aspectos más íntimos del matrimonio.»

«Eso será muy bondadoso de su parte —dijo Cózcatl—. Pero después de eso, ¿podrías hablar también con ella, Mixtli? Tú me has conocido por mucho tiempo y... más bien que Zyanya. Tú podrías especificarle a Quequelmiqui, qué es lo que ella realmente *puede* esperar de mí, como cónyuge. ¿Harías eso?»

Dije: «Haré por ti todo lo que pueda, Cózcatl, pero quiero prevenirte. Una muchacha virgen e inocente sufre dudas y miedos aun para tomar un esposo común, con los atributos físicos ordinarios. Cuando le diga llanamente lo que ella puede esperar de este matrimonio y lo que no puede esperar, es muy probable que se asuste.»

«Ella me ama —dijo Cózcatl sonoramente—. Ella me ha dado su promesa. Yo conozco su corazón.»

«Entonces, tú eres único entre los hombres —le dije secamente—. Yo sólo sé esto. Una mujer piensa del matrimonio en términos de flores, cantos de pájaros y mariposas revoloteando. Cuando le hable a Cosquillosa en términos de carne, órganos y tejidos, será una desilusión para ella. Lo peor que podría pasar es que huyera sintiendo pánico de casarse contigo o con cualquier otro. No me darás las gracias por eso.»

«Sin embargo, lo haré —dijo él—. Quequelmiqui merece algo mejor que una sorpresa espantosa en su noche de bodas. Si ella rehúsa a casarse conmigo, es mejor que sea ahora y no después. Oh, eso me destruirá, sí. Si la buena y amante Quequelmiqui no me tiene por esposo, jamás me tendrá ninguna otra mujer. Me alistaré en la tropa de algún ejército e iré a la guerra a algún lugar y pereceré en ella. Pero cualquier cosa que pase, Mixtli, no lo tendré en tu contra. Todo lo contrario, te ruego que me hagas este favor.»

Así, cuando él partió, informé a Zyanya acerca de esta noticia y de lo que él nos pedía. Ella llamó a Cosquillosa que estaba en la cocina y la muchacha vino colorada, temblando y retorciéndose sus dedos en la bastilla de su blusa. Nosotros la abrazamos y la felicitamos por haber sabido conquistar el cariño de un joven tan fino. Luego Zyanya, tomándola maternalmente por la cintura, la llevó escaleras arriba mientras yo me sentaba abajo, con mis pomos de pinturas y papel de corteza. Cuando terminé de escribir el papel de manumisión, fumé nerviosamente una *poquíetl*... varias de ellas, antes de que Cosquillosa volviera a bajar.

Si ella había estado colorada antes, ahora relucía como un brasero y temblaba visiblemente. Su agitación quizás la hacía verse mucho más bonita que lo usual, pero en verdad que ésa era la primera vez que yo me daba cuenta de ese hecho; era una muchacha muy atractiva. Supongo que uno nunca le presta mucha atención a los muebles de su casa hasta que otro viene de fuera y le halaga esa pieza en particular.

Le alargué el papel doblado y ella dijo: «¿Qué es esto, mi señor amo?»

«Un documento en el que dice que la mujer libre Quequelmiqui nunca más volverá a llamar a nadie amo. Trata, en su lugar, de ver en mí a un amigo familiar, porque Cózcatl me ha pedido que te explique algunas cosas. —Fui derecho al asunto y temo que no con mucha delicadeza—. La mayoría de los hombres, Cosquillosa, tienen una cosa llamada *tepuli*...»

Ella me interrumpió, aunque sin levantar su cabeza inclinada. «Sé lo que es eso, mi señor. Tengo hermanos en mi familia. Mi señora ama dice que el hombre pone eso dentro de una mujer... aquí. —Ella apuntó modestamente en su falda—. O lo hace si él tiene uno. Cózcatl me explicó cómo había perdido el suyo.»

«Y con eso perdió para siempre su capacidad de hacerte madre. También está privado de algunos de los placeres del matrimonio, pero no quiere decir eso que él no tenga el deseo de que tú goces de esos placeres o la habilidad para dártelos. Aunque él no tiene *tepuli* para que os unáis, hay otras maneras de hacer el acto de amor.»

Me retiré un poco de ella, con el objeto de ahorrarnos a ambos la molestia de verla sonrojarse y traté de hablar con voz llana y en tono aburrido, como un maestro de escuela, cuando le describí las numerosas cosas estimulantes y satisfactorias que se pueden hacer en los pechos, *tepili* y especialmente en el sensitivo *xacapili* de una mujer, utilizando los dedos, la lengua, los labios y aun las pestañas. Bien, las instrucciones básicas las pude decir con una voz de maestro de escuela, pero no pude evitar el recordar todas aquellas que yo había empleado y gozado, en tiempos recientes y pasados, y mi voz tendió a ser inconsecuente, por lo que me apresuré a concluir:

«Una mujer puede encontrar esos placeres casi tan satisfactorios como el acto normal. Muchos de ésos serán mucho más placenteros que el solo hecho de ser penetrada. Algunas mujeres lo hacen incluso con otras mujeres, y ni siquiera piensan en la ausencia del *tepuli*.»

Cosquillosa dijo: «Eso suena... —y lo dijo con una voz tan trémula, que me giré para mirarla—. Eso se debe sentir... —Ella se sentó con su cuerpo tenso y rígido, sus ojos y puños fuertemente cerrados—. Eso debe de ser... —su cuerpo entero se sacudió— ¡ma-ra-vi-llo-so!» La palabra fue dicha así, largamente, como si la estuvieran atormentando. Pasó un poco de tiempo antes de que abriera sus puños y sus ojos. Entonces los levantó hacia mí, y eran como lámparas humeantes.

«Gracias por... por decirme esas cosas.»

Recordé cómo Cosquillosa acostumbraba a reír sin ningún motivo. ¿Sería posible que ella pudiera excitarse en otra forma, sin ser tocada o aun desvestida?

Yo dije: «Solamente quiero pedirte otra cosa. Ya no te puedo ordenar y esto es una impertinencia, a la que tú puedes rehusarte, pero me gustaría ver tus senos.»

Sus ojos se abrieron inocentemente y vaciló un momento, pero luego, lentamente se levantó la blusa. Sus pechos no eran muy grandes, pero estaban bien formados y sus pezones se contrajeron sólo con mi mirada, sus aureolas eran oscuras y grandes, casi tan grandes como para que la boca de un hombre las pudiera circundar. Suspiré y le hice una señal para que se fuera. Tenía la esperanza de estar en un error, pero mucho temí que Cosquillosa no *siempre* estaría satisfecha con algo que no fuera la copulación normal, y que Cózcatl se estaba arriesgando a ser uno de tantos maridos infelices.

Fui arriba y encontré a Zyanya parada en la puerta del cuarto de los niños, sin duda contemplando todos los arreglos que se habían hecho en él. No le dije nada acerca de mis presentimientos, en cuanto a la prudencia del matrimonio de Cózcatl, o de la probabilidad de su fracaso. Sólo le hice notar:

«Cuando Cosquillosa se vaya, nosotros nos quedaremos sin una sirviente. Turquesa no puede encargarse de toda la casa y cuidarte al mismo tiempo. Cózcatl encogió un momento inoportuno para declararnos sus intenciones. Muy desafortunado para nosotros.»

«¡Desafortunado! —exclamó Zyanya, con una gran sonrisa—.

Una vez me dijiste, Zaa, que si necesitaba ayuda, podríamos persuadir a Beu para que viniera con nosotros. La partida de Cosquillosa es una pequeña desgracia, gracias a los dioses, pero que nos da una excusa. Nosotros *necesitaremos* otra mujer en la casa. ¡Oh, Zaa, preguntémosle si quiere venir!»

«Una idea inspirada —dije. No estaba exactamente muy contento con la idea de tener cerca a la agria Beu, especialmente durante ese tiempo de tensión, pero cualquier cosa que Zyanya quisiera se lo daría—. Le mandaré una invitación tan implorante que no podrá rehusarse.»

La envié con los mismos siete guerreros que una vez habían ido al sur conmigo, así Luna que Espera tendría una escolta protectora, si es que estaba de acuerdo en venir a Tenochtitlan. Y así lo hizo, sin ninguna protesta o resistencia. De todos modos le llevó algún tiempo hacer todo los arreglos necesarios para dejar la hostería en manos de los empleados. Mientras tanto, Zyanya y yo hicimos una gran ceremonia de bodas para Cózcatl y Cosquillosa y ellos se fueron a vivir a su casa.

Había empezado el invierno cuando los siete viejos guerreros llevaron a Beu Ribé a la puerta de nuestra casa. Para entonces yo me sentí tan honestamente ansioso y contento de verla, como lo estaba Zyanya. Mi esposa se había puesto muy gorda, alarmante en mi opinión, y había empezado a sufrir jaquecas, estaba irritable y padecía síntomas de angustia. A pesar de que ella, con impertinencia, seguía asegurando que esas cosas eran completamente naturales, me preocupaban y me desvivía por ella, tratando de ayudarle asiduamente, pero lo único que conseguía era aumentar su mal humor.

Ella gritó: «¡Oh, Beu, gracias por venir! ¡Le doy gracias a Uizhe Tao y a cada uno de los dioses porque llegaste! —Y cayó en los brazos de su hermana como si estuviera abrazando a su libertadora—. ¡Tú puedes salvar mi vida! ¡Me han estado mimando hasta morir!»

El equipaje de Beu fue puesto en la habitación para las visitas, preparada para ella, pero pasó la mayor parte de ese día con Zyanya en nuestro cuarto, del cual había sido excluido por la fuerza, para vagar abatido por el resto de la casa enfadado y sintiéndome descartado. Hacia el crepúsculo, Beu bajó sola y mientras tomábamos una taza de *chocólatl* juntos, me dijo como si conspirara:

«Zyanya estará pronto en la etapa de su embarazo en que debes de dejar a un lado tus... tus derechos de marido. ¿Qué harás durante ese tiempo?»

Estuve a punto de decirle que eso no era de su incumbencia, pero sólo contesté: «Me imagino que sobreviviré.»

Ella persistió: «Sería indecoroso que recurrieras a una extranjera.»

Encarándome a ella, me puse de pie y dije inflexiblemente: «Quizás no goce con la abstinencia, pero...»

«Pero, ¿quizás, no tengas la esperanza de encontrar otra sustituta como Zyanya?»

Ella hizo un gesto, como si en verdad esperara una respuesta. «¿No podrías encontrar en todo Tenochtitlan a una mujer tan bella como ella? ¿Así es que por eso me mandaste traer desde Tecuantépec, desde tan lejos? —Sonrió y se levantó acercándose mucho a mí, sus senos rozaban mi pecho—. Me parezco tanto a Zyanya, que pensaste que yo sería una sustituta satisfactoria, ¿no es así? —Jugó maliciosamente con el broche de mi manto, como si fuera a desabrocharlo—. Pero Zaa, aunque Zyanya y yo somos hermanas, y físicamente muy parecidas, no quiere decir que seamos iguales. En la cama podrías darte cuenta de que somos muy diferentes...»

Con firmeza la alejé de mí. «Te deseo una estancia feliz en esta casa, Beu Ribé. Espero que si no puedes esconder el desagrado que sientes por mí, por lo menos, ¿no podrías dejar de mostrar esa coquetería maliciosa y tan poco sincera? ¿No podríamos arreglarnos de tal manera, que simplemente nos ignoremos el uno al otro?»

Cuando me alejé a grandes zancadas, su rostro estaba tan colorado como si la hubiese sorprendido haciendo algún acto indecente, y se restregaba la mejilla como si le hubiese dado un cachete.

✠

Señor Obispo Zumárraga, es un honor y es una lisonja para mí que usted se reúna nuevamente con nosotros. Su Ilustrísima ha llegado en el momento preciso en que iba a anunciar, tan orgullosamente como lo anuncié hace ya muchos años, el nacimiento de mi amada hija.

Todas mis aprensiones, y estoy muy contento de decirlo, fueron infundadas. La niña demostró una clara inteligencia aun antes de emerger a esta vida, porque esperó prudentemente en el vientre hasta que pasaron los *nemontemtin,* días sin vida, e hizo su aparición en el día Ce-Malinali, o Uno-Hierba, del primer mes del año Cinco-Casa. Para entonces yo tenía treinta y un años, un poco viejo para empezar una familia, pero me pavoneé y contoneé tan absurdamente como lo hacen los hombres muy jóvenes, como si yo sólo hubiera concebido, cargado y entregado al infante.

Mientras Beu se quedaba a un lado de la cama con Zyanya, el *tícitl* y la partera vinieron inmediatamente a decirme que el bebé era una niña y a contestar mis ansiosas preguntas. Debieron de haber pensado que estaba loco cuando, estrujándome las manos, les dije: «Decidme la verdad. Lo puedo soportar. ¿Son dos niñas en un solo cuerpo?» No, me dijeron, no era ninguna clase de gemelas, sino sólo una hija. No, ella no era extraordinariamente larga. No, no era un monstruo ni nada que se le pareciera y no tenía marcas de ningún portento. Cuando insté al físico acerca de la agudeza de su vista, él me replicó con cierta exasperación que a los recién nacidos no se les notaba una visión de águila o por lo menos ellos no se vanagloriaban de ello. Debía esperar hasta que ella pudiera hablar y me lo dijera por sí misma.

Me dieron el cordón umbilical de la niña, y luego regresaron al cuarto de los niños para sumergir a Uno-Hierba dentro del agua fría, para fajarla y someterla a la arenga instructiva y prudente de la comadrona. Yo fui escaleras abajo, y con dedos temblorosos enredé el cordón umbilical alrededor de un huso de cerámica y murmurando unas pocas oraciones silenciosas y dándoles las gracias a los dioses, lo enterré debajo de las piedras del centro de la cocina. Después corrí hacia arriba otra vez, para esperar con impaciencia a que me admitieran, para ver por primera vez a mi hija.

Besé a mi descolorida y sonriente esposa, y con mi topacio examiné la carita de enano que se escondía en el recoveco de su codo. Había visto otros recién nacidos, así es que no me sorprendí mucho, pero me desilusioné un poco al ver que mi hija no era en ningún modo superior. Estaba tan roja y arrugada como una vaina de *chopini chili*, tan calva y fea como un viejo purempe. Traté de sentir un amor arrollador por ella, pero no lo conseguí. Todos los presentes me aseguraron que en verdad era hija mía, pero también les habría creído si me hubieran dicho que ese nuevo pedazo de raza humana era un mono aullador recién nacido y sin pelo todavía. De todas formas, estaba aullando.

No necesito decir que la niña parecía más humana cada día, y que la llegué a ver con más afecto y solicitud. La llamé Cocoton, un apodo cariñoso y muy común entre las niñas, que quiere decir migaja que cae de un gɪan pedazo de pan. Poco tiempo después, Cocoton empezó a parecerse a su madre y naturalmente a su tía, lo que significa que rápidamente fue más bonita que cualquier otro bebé. Su cabello creció rizado. Aparecieron sus pestañas, con la misma abundancia, pero en miniatura, que las alas del colibrí, como las de Zyanya y Beu. Sus cejas salieron y tenían el mismo arco alado de las de Zyanya y Beu. Empezó a sonreír con más frecuencia que a chillar, y era la misma sonrisa de Zyanya, reflejándola a su alrededor. Aun Beu, que en los últimos años había estado tan amargada, con frecuencia volvía a sonreír gozosa al impacto de aquella sonrisa.

Pronto, Zyanya se levantó, aunque sus actividades se concentraron por un tiempo sólo en Cocoton, quien insistía que su leche animal estuviera disponible a tiempo. La presencia de Beu había hecho que yo no tuviera necesidad de ver por el bienestar de Zyanya y de nuestro bebé, y muy seguido me desairaban ambas mujeres y aun la pequeña, cuando alguna vez sugería algo o tenía atenciones con ellas que no me habían solicitado, pero en ocasiones insistía en que me obedecieran, simplemente por ser el hombre de la casa. Cuando Cocoton tenía cerca de dos meses y ya no necesitaba con tanta frecuencia a su proveedora de leche, Zyanya empezó a dar muestras de desasosiego.

Había estado encerrada en la casa por meses, sin ir más allá que el jardín de la azotea, para bañarse con los rayos de Tonatíu y a recibir la brisa de Ehécatl, el viento. Para entonces, ella deseaba salir a pasear, según me dijo, y me recordó que pronto sería la ceremonia de Xipe Totec en El Corazón del Único Mundo. Zyanya quería asistir, pero yo se lo prohibí terminantemente.

Yo le dije: «Cocoton nació sin marcas, sin ser un monstruo y a simple vista aparentemente intacta gracias a su *tonali* o a los nuestros o al buen deseo de los dioses. No la pongamos ahora en peligro. Todo el tiempo que ella esté mamando, debemos tener cuidado de que ninguna influencia maligna pueda llegar a tu leche, por medio de un susto y de una contrariedad ante la vista de algo desagradable. No puedo pensar en algo que te llegue a horrorizar más que la celebración de Xipe Totec. Iremos a cualquier parte que tú quieras, mi amor, pero no allí.»

Oh, sí, Su Ilustrísima, ya antes había visto varias veces los honores a Xipe Totec, ya que era uno de los rituales religiosos más importantes observados por nosotros los mexica y por muchos otros pueblos. La ceremonia era impresionante, y hasta podría decir que inolvidable, pero aun en esos días, no puedo creer que ninguno de los participantes o de los espectadores *gozara*. Aunque ya han pasado muchos años desde que vi por última vez morir a Xipe Totec y volver a la vida otra vez, todavía no puedo tolerar el describir de qué manera lo hacía, y mi repulsión no tiene nada que ver con el haber llegado a ser Cristiano y civilizado. Sin embargo, si Su Ilustrísima está tan interesado e insiste tanto...

Xipe Totec era nuestro dios de las siembras y éstas se efectuaban durante nuestro mes de Tlacaxipe Ualiztli, que más fácilmente se puede traducir por El Desollador Benévolo. Era la estación en que los tocones y hierbas muertas de la cosecha del año anterior se quemaban, o se arrancaban o se escarbaban, así la tierra quedaba limpia y lista para recibir las nuevas siembras. La muerte abriendo paso a la vida, como pueden ver, incluso como lo hacen los Cristianos, cuando en cada época de siembra Jesús muere y resucita. Su Ilustrísima no tiene necesidad de protestar, la similitud impía no va más allá.

Me abstendré de describir todos los preliminares públicos y los acompañamientos: las flores, la música, la danza, el colorido, las costumbres y procesiones y el retumbar del tambor rompe corazones. Seré tan piadosamente breve como pueda.

Sepan entonces, que un joven o una joven eran seleccionados de antemano para actuar en el honroso papel de Xipe Totec, que quiere decir El Desollador Amado. El sexo del que desempeñaba ese papel no era importante, lo era más el hecho de que, ya sea él o ella, fueran vírgenes. Por lo general, era un extranjero noble, capturado en alguna guerra cuando todavía era un muchacho y al que se le guardaba especialmente para representar al dios, cuando creciera. Jamás era un esclavo comprado para ese propósito, ya que Xipe Totec merecía y demandaba una persona joven que siempre fuera de la más elevada clase social.

Algunos días antes de la ceremonia, el joven era hospedado en el templo de Xipe Totec y tratado con mucha bondad y se le permitía cualquier goce, prodigándole todo placer, ya fuese en comida, en bebida y en diversión. Una vez que la virginidad de la joven era comprobada, podía perderla inmediatamente. A él o a ella, se le estaba permitido toda licencia sexual, y no sólo se le animaba a ello, sino que aun se le forzaba cuando era necesario, pues eso era una parte vital en el papel que jugaba el dios de la fertilidad de la primavera. Si el *xochimique* era un joven, podía nombrar a todas las mujeres o muchachas de la comunidad que él deseara, fueran solteras o no. Suponiendo que esas mujeres consintieran, como muchas aun siendo casadas hacían, se las llevaban a él. Si el *xochimique* era una muchacha, podía nombrar, citar y acostarse con todos los hombres que quisiera.

Sin embargo, algunas veces un joven seleccionado para ese honor, sentía aversión sobre ese aspecto. Si era una joven y si trataba de declinar la oportunidad de revolcarse, entonces era desflorada a la fuerza por uno de los altos sacerdotes de Xipe Totec. En el caso de un joven muy casto, era atado y sobre él se ponía a horcajadas una mujer de las que atendían el templo. Si una vez que era introducido al placer, la joven persona seguía siendo recalcitrante, tenía que sufrir repetidas violaciones, ya sea por parte de las mujeres o de los sacerdotes del templo, o cuando ellos ya estaban hartos, cualquier gente común podía hacerlo si lo deseaba, y siempre había muchos de ésos: el devoto quien como un esclavo copulaba con el dios o la diosa, el que era un simple sinvergüenza, el curioso, las mujeres estériles o los hombres impotentes quienes tenían las esperanzas de quedar, unas embarazadas y los otros rejuvenecidos, por la deidad. Sí, Su Ilustrísima, todo eso tenía lugar dentro del templo e incluía todo exceso sexual, que la fantasía de Su Ilustrísima pueda vislumbrar, a excepción hecha de la copulación de un dios con un hombre, o una diosa con una mujer, pues esos actos van en contra de la fertilidad, y hubieran sido repugnantes a Xipe Totec.

El día de la ceremonia, después de que la multitud allí reunida se había divertido con las muchas representaciones de enanos, malabaristas, *tocotine* y demás, Xipe Totec hacía su aparición pública. Él o ella iba vestido como el dios, en un traje que combinaba las viejas mazorcas de maíz desgranándose y la cosecha verde, nueva y brillante, con un gran penacho de plumas de bellos colores, con un manto flotante y sandalias doradas. Al joven se le llevaba varias veces alrededor de El Corazón del Único Mundo, en una elegante silla de manos, con mucha pompa y música ensordecedora, mientras dejaría caer semillas o granos de maíz sobre la multitud alegre y cantadora. Luego la procesión llegaría a la pirámide baja de Xipe Totec, en una esquina de la plaza, y cesaría todo ruido producido por los tambores, por la música y los cantantes, y la multitud se apaciguaría, mientras quien personificaba al dios era puesto a los pies de la escalera del templo.

Dos de los sacerdotes le ayudarían a desvestirse, quitándose pieza por pieza, hasta que estuviera completamente desnudo ante los ojos de todos los que estaban en la plaza, algunos de los cuales habían conocido en privado cada parte de su cuerpo. Los sacerdotes le darían un haz de veinte flautitas de caña y volviendo la espalda a la multitud, con un sacerdote de cada lado, subiría despacio hasta donde se encontraba el altar de piedra, dentro del templo. Tocaba unos trinos con cada flauta en cada uno de los veinte escalones ascendentes y luego rompía esa flauta entre sus manos. En el último escalón, tocaba la última flauta, quizás más triste y más prolongadamente, pero los sacerdotes de escolta no permitirían ninguna pérdida de tiempo y ellos mismos romperían la flauta, si trataba de prolongar la canción indebidamente. Se requería que la vida de Xipe Totec terminara cuando los trinos de la última flauta se apagaran.

Luego, los otros sacerdotes que esperaban en lo alto de la pirámide, lo llevarían y lo acomodarían sobre la piedra, y dos sacerdotes dejarían caer con fuerza sus cuchillos de obsidiana. Mientras uno abría el pecho y sacaba el corazón todavía palpitante, el otro cortaba de un tajo la cabeza cuyos ojos pestañaban todavía y cuya boca murmuraba. En ninguna otra de nuestras ceremonias, la víctima sacrificada era decapitada y aun en los ritos de Xipe Totec, esto no tenía ningún significado religioso, ya que el *xochimiqui* era decapitado sólo por una razón práctica: es más fácil quitar la piel a una persona muerta cuando la cabeza y el cuerpo están separados.

Se le desollaba a la vista de toda la multitud, siendo los sacerdotes muy diestros en eso, y luego los dos pedazos del cuerpo eran arrastrados rápidamente dentro del templo. La piel de la cabeza era cortada desde atrás, de la nuca a la coronilla; el cuero cabelludo y la piel de la cara se desprendían de la calavera y los párpados eran cortados. Al cuerpo también se le hacía una incisión por detrás, desde el ano hasta el cuello, pero quitaban la piel tan cuidadosamente que los brazos y piernas no quedaban desgarrados, sino como tubos vacíos. Si el *xochimiqui* había sido una mujer, la carne suave que rellenaba sus pechos y nalgas, se dejaba allí intacta para preservar su forma. Si había sido un joven, su *tepuli* y *ololtin* se dejaban allí colgando.

Siempre había un sacerdote pequeño de estatuta entre los de Xipe Totec, y éste se quitaba con rapidez sus vestiduras y, desnudo, se ponía las dos piezas como traje. Como todavía la piel del cuerpo estaba húmeda y resbaladiza, no tenía ninguna dificultad en deslizar sus piernas y brazos por los tubos correspondientes. Los pies del muerto se cortaban, para que no interfirieran en la danza del sacerdote, pero las manos se dejaban colgando para que golpearan a un lado de las del sacerdote. Por supuesto que la piel del torso estaba abierta por detrás, pero había sido perforada con espinas y se ataba por medio de cordones, fuertemente al cuerpo. Después, el sacerdote se ponía el cabello y la piel de la cara del muerto, de tal manera que pudiera ver a través de los agujeros y cantar a través de los labios despegados y eso también se amarraba por detrás. Se lavaba cualquier rastro de sangre, para que no se viera en el traje.

Todo eso lo hacían en muy poco tiempo, en menos tiempo del que me toma a mí narrarlo, Su Ilustrísima. Parecía a los espectadores que Xipe Totec apenas acababa de morir en la piedra del altar, cuando nuevamente reaparecía en la puerta del templo. Aparecía encorvado, pretendiendo ser un viejo y usando los únicos huesos que se utilizaban en la ceremonia, del cuerpo del *xochimiqui*. Mientras los tambores rugían para darle la bienvenida, El Desollador Amado se iba estirando lentamente, como lo haría un viejo que se volviera joven otra vez. Danzaba bajando la escalera de la pirámide y luego saltaba como un maniático por toda la plaza, blandiendo los huesos limpios de los muslos y usándolos para dar un golpecito de bendición, a todos aquellos que estuvieran lo suficientemente cerca.

Antes de la ceremonia, el pequeño sacerdote siempre se emborrachaba y comía mucho de los hongos llamados la carne de los dioses, para entrar en delirio. Tenía que hacerlo, pues a él le correspondía la parte más ardua. Tenía que bailar frenéticamente y sin cesar, excepto en los períodos en que caía inconsciente, por cinco días y sus noches. Por supuesto que su danza iba perdiendo lentamente los movimientos salvajes con que la iniciaba, conforme la piel se iba secando y apretándole. Hacia el final de los cinco días, la piel estaba encogida y crujiente, como constreñida, y el sol y el aire la habían tornado de un color amarillo enfermizo, razón por la cual era llamada la Vestidura de Oro, y olía tan horriblemente que nadie en la plaza se podía aproximar lo suficiente para que Xipe Totec le bendiciera con golpecito de su hueso...

La forma en que Su Ilustrísima salió, tan agitadamente, me inclina a hacer notar, si esto no es una irreverencia, señores escribanos, que Su Ilustrísima tiene una facultad asombrosa para reunirse con nosotros siempre que hay que escuchar las cosas que más molestan y disgustan al oír.

En los últimos años, y lo digo con profunda pena, hubiera deseado no haberle negado jamás cualquier cosa a Zyanya; debí dejar que ella hiciera, viera y experimentara todo aquello que le interesara y que sus ojos se regocijaran con esas maravillas; nunca debí poner, ni siquiera una vez, un obstáculo a su natural entusiasmo, por cada cosa pequeña del mundo que la rodeaba. Aunque no puedo reprocharme nada, al no dejar que ella presenciara la ceremonia de Xipe Totec.

De todas maneras, puedo afirmar que tuve razón, ya que ninguna pestilencia cayó en la leche de Zyanya. La pequeña Cocoton se desarrolló bien mamándola, y creció y creció cada vez más bonita, como una miniatura de su madre y de su tía. Yo estaba loco por ella, pero no era el único. Un día Zyanya y Beu llevaron a la niña al mercado y un *totonácatl* que iba pasando vio a Cocoton que sonreía desde el rebozo, en donde la llevaba colgando Beu, y pidió permiso a las mujeres para plasmar esa sonrisa en barro. Era uno de esos artistas ambulantes, que hacían cantidades de moldes de figuritas de terracota y después viajaban continuamente fuera del país para venderlas, muy baratas, a los campesinos pobres. En el mismo lugar, con rapidez y destreza, esculpió el rostro de Cocoton en arcilla, y después, cuando hubo sacado el molde para hacer los duplicados, le regaló el original a Zyanya. Sus rasgos no estaban muy bien hechos, y él había esculpido sobre su cabeza un tocado totonaca, pero inmediatamente pude reconocer la amplia y contagiosa sonrisa de mi hija, incluyendo sus hoyuelos. No sé cuántas copias hizo, pero por mucho tiempo se vieron niñitas por todas partes jugando con esas muñecas. Incluso, hubo algunos adultos que las compraron bajo la impresión de que representaba al risueño y joven dios Xochipili, Señor de las Flores o a la diosa feliz Xilonen, Joven Madre del Maíz. No me sorprendería mucho si aún hubiera algunas de esas figuritas aquí y allá, todavía sin romperse, pero mi corazón se sentiría lacerado si encontrara una ahora y volviera a ver otra vez la sonrisa de mi hija y de mi esposa.

Cuando a la niña le había brotado su primer granito de maíz de diente, cerca de su primer año de vida, fue destetada a la vieja usanza de las madres mexica. Cuando lloraba porque quería mamar, sus labios se encontraban cada vez más seguido no con el dulce pecho de Zyanya, sino con una taza de té amargo, uno de esos astringentes, hecho con hojas de maguey y que hace que la boca se arrugue. Poco a poco, Cocoton se dejó convencer para tomar en lugar de eso un suave potaje de *atoli*, hasta que al fin abandonó el pecho para siempre. Fue entonces cuando Beu nos dijo que debía regresar a su hostería, pues ya no la necesitábamos más, ya que Turquesa podría cuidar con facilidad a la niña, cuando Zyanya estuviera cansada u ocupada en otras cosas.

Otra vez le proporcioné una escolta; los siete mismos viejos guerreros, a quienes había llegado a considerar como mi ejército privado, y los acompañé hasta el camino-puente.

«Esperamos que regreses otra vez, hermana Luna que Espera», le dije, aunque habíamos pasado la mayor parte de esa mañana diciéndonos adiós, le habíamos dado muchos regalos y las dos mujeres habían llorado a placer.

«Volveré cada vez que me necesitéis... o que lo deseéis —dijo ella—. Ahora que ya he salido por primera vez de Tecuantépec, será mucho más fácil para mí viajar en lo sucesivo. Aunque no creo que deseéis verme o que me necesitéis muy seguido. Por mucho tiempo no he querido reconocer mi error, Zaa, pero la honestidad me obliga. *Eres* un buen marido para mi hermana.»

«No me cuesta mucho trabajo serlo —dije—. El mejor marido es el que esté casado con la mejor esposa.»

Ella dijo, en esa forma tan molesta que tenía para hablar: «¿Cómo lo sabes? Sólo te has casado una vez. Dime, Zaa, ¿nunca sientes, aunque sea una atracción pasajera hacia... hacia cualquier otra mujer?»

«Oh, sí —dije, riéndome de mí mismo—. Soy humano y las emociones humanas pueden ser indomables y siempre hay otras mujeres bellas. Como tú, Beu. Incluso puedo sentirme atraído por mujeres mucho menos bonitas que Zyanya y tú... simplemente por curiosidad acerca de otros atributos posibles, que puedan encerrar bajo sus vestidos o detrás de sus mentes. Pero en casi nueve años, mis pensamientos nunca se han hecho realidad y al acostarme con Zyanya, pronto desaparecen, así es que no me ruborizo de ellos.»

Me apresuro a asegurarles, reverendos frailes, que mis catequistas cristianos me educaron en forma diferente: me enseñaron que el entretenerme con una idea puede ser tan pecaminoso como la más lasciva fornificación. Pero entonces yo todavía era un idólatra, todos lo éramos, y las fantasías que no compartí ni cometí, no me causaban ningún problema, como no lo causaron a nadie más.

Con sus bellísimos ojos, Beu me echó una larga mirada y dijo: «Ya eres un campeón Águila. Solamente falta que seas honrado con el -tzin en tu nombre. Siendo un noble, no necesitarás sofocar hasta tus más secretos anhelos. Zyanya no podría objetar nada en ser la Primera Esposa entre las otras. Podrías tener todas las esposa que desearas.»

Sonreí y dije: «Ya tengo todas las que deseo, su nombre es Siempre.»

Beu asintió, luego se giró y sin volver a mirar hacia atrás, marchó a lo largo del camino-puente, hasta desaparecer de mi vista.

Ese día, había hombres trabajando en donde la isla terminaba, en el camino-puente por el que había cruzado Beu, y otros trabajaban también a lo largo de su curso, hasta la mitad del camino del fuerte de Acachinanco, y otros más, trabajaban en la tierra firme hacia el sudeste. Los hombres estaban construyendo las dos últimas partes de un nuevo acueducto de piedra y mortero que traería una cantidad mayor de agua fresca a la ciudad.

Por mucho tiempo, las comunidades en las tierras comprendidas en el distrito del lago habían crecido en población con tanta rapidez, que todas las naciones de la Triple Alianza habían llegado a estar intolerablemente superpobladas. Tenochtitlan, por supuesto, era la más afectada, por la simple razón de que era una isla sin capacidad de expansión. Ése fue el motivo por el cual, muchos mexica que residían en la ciudad tomaron sus familias y sus pertenencias y se fueron a establecer al Xoconochco, cuando éste fue anexado. Esa migración voluntaria fue lo que le dio al Uey-Tlatoani la idea de emprender otras renovaciones.

Para entonces, llegó a ser evidente que la guarnición de Tapachtlan impediría para siempre la invasión de cualquier enemigo extranjero en el Xoconochco; entonces, Motecuzoma El Joven fue relevado de su cargo. Como ya expliqué, Auítzotl tenía sus razones para mantener lejos a su sobrino, pero era lo suficientemente sagaz como para aprovechar la ya probada habilidad de éste para organizar y administrar. En seguida mandó a Motecuzoma a Teloloapan, que era una aldea insignificante entre Tenochtitlan y el océano del sur, y le ordenó levantar allí otra comunidad tan fortificada y próspera como la de Tepachtlan.

Para ello, se le dio a Motecuzoma una gran cantidad de tropas y un número considerable de civiles. Quizás algunas de esas familias o individuos vivían contentos o quizás insatisfechos en Tenochtitlan o en sus alrededores, pero cuando el Venerado Orador dijo: «Ustedes irán», ellos tuvieron que ir. Cuando Motecuzoma repartió entre ellos una estimable cantidad de tierra en los alrededores de Teloloapan, y cuando ellos se hubieron asentado bajo su gobierno, esa aldea miserable se convirtió en un pueblo respetable.

Así, tan pronto como Teloloapan tuvo lista su guarnición y empezó a alimentarse con sus propias cosechas, Motecuzoma El Joven fue otra vez relevado de su cargo y enviado a algún otro lugar, para hacer lo mismo. Auítzotl lo mandó de una aldea insignificante a otra, siempre con la misma orden; fueron varias aldeas: Oztoman, Alahuiztlan; bueno, he olvidado sus nombres, pero todas ellas estaban situadas en las fronteras más lejanas de la Triple Alianza. En cuanto esas colonias remotas se multiplicaron y crecieron, se resolvieron tres problemas y esto llenó de satisfacción a Auítzotl. Hubo un éxodo cada vez mayor, que vino a resolver el exceso de población, tanto en Texcoco, en Tlacopan y en otras ciudades del lago, como Tenochtitlan. Quedamos provistos de fuertes puestos fronterizos. Y la continuidad en ese proceso de colonización, mantuvo a la vez a Motecuzoma ocupado provechosamente y lejos de cualquier posibilidad de intrigar en contra de su tío.

Sin embargo, las emigraciones y renovaciones sólo pudieron detener el continuo *incremento* de población en Tenochtitlan; nunca llegaron más que a disminuir el gentío y a dejar suficiente espacio a los que quedaban. Por ese motivo, la ciudad principal de la isla, necesitaba más agua fresca. Un suministro regular de agua nos llegaba desde que el Primer Motecuzoma se había preocupado por mandar construir un acueducto, que partía de los manantiales de agua dulce de Chapultépec, más o menos una gavilla de años antes, y por esas mismas fechas mandó construir el Gran Dique para proteger a la ciudad contra las inundaciones provocadas por los vientos. Sin embargo, no se pudo persuadir al chorro de Chapultépec para que creciera, solamente porque se necesitaba más agua. Eso se comprobó; un número de nuestros sacerdotes y adivinos, utilizaron todos los medios de persuasión, pero fracasaron.

Fue entonces cuando Auítzotl determinó encontrar una nueva fuente de agua y envió a esos mismos sacerdotes y adivinos, y también a unos cuantos de sus sabios del Consejo de Voceros, a explorar algunas regiones de la tierra firme. Cualesquiera que fueran los significados de la adivinación, el caso es que ellos dieron con un manantial que nunca antes había sido descubierto, y el Venerado Orador empezó inmediatamente el plan para construir el nuevo acueducto. Ya que esa corriente recién encontrada estaba cerca de Coyohuacan, y puesto que traía mucha más fuerza que la que venía de Chapultépec, Auítzotl planeó también unas fuentes borboteantes para El Corazón del Único Mundo.

Esa idea, sin embargo, no causó entusiasmo en toda la gente y uno de los que le aconsejaron precaución, fue el Venerado Orador Nezahualpili de Texcoco, cuando por invitación de Auítzotl inspeccionó el nuevo manantial y los trabajos que apenas se habían comenzado sobre el lugar en donde se ubicaría el nuevo acueducto. Yo no escuché la conversación con mis propios oídos, ya que no había razón por la cual estuviera allí presente; probablemente estaba en esos momentos jugando con mi pequeña. Sin embargo, puedo reconstruir la conversación que tuvieron los dos Venerados Oradores, por lo que me contaron sus asistentes mucho después del suceso.

Entre otras cosas, Nezahualpili le llegó a prevenir: «Mi amigo, usted y su ciudad tendrán que escoger entre tener muy poca agua o tener demasiada», y recordó a Auítzotl varios hechos históricos.

Esta ciudad es ahora, como lo ha sido durante gavillas de años, una isla rodeada de agua, pero no siempre fue así. Cuando los primeros ancestros de nosotros los mexica llegaron a este valle y se asentaron permanentemente aquí, ellos *caminaron* hasta aquí. Sin duda fue un camino resbaladizo e incómodo, pero no tuvieron que nadar. Toda esta área que ahora contiene agua, desde aquí hasta la tierra firme, por el oeste, el norte y el sur, era en aquellos días sólo un pantano húmedo con lodo, cieno y juncos, y éste era el único lugar con tierra firme y seca que sobresalía de esa extensa ciénaga.

A través de los años en que se construyó esta ciudad, esos primeros pobladores, también hicieron veredas más firmes para tener más fácil acceso a la tierra firme. Las primeras, no fueron más que montones de tierra apretada y apilada un poco más alto que el pantano. Pero, eventualmente, los mexica llegaron a acomodar allí una doble hilera de pilotes que rellenaron con cascajo, y sobre esa construcción colocaron el pavimento empedrado y los parapetos de los tres caminos que hasta hoy en día existen. Éstos impidieron a las aguas del pantano correr libremente, más allá del lago y así las aguas bloqueadas empezaron a elevarse perceptiblemente.

Eso contribuyó a un aprovechamiento considerable bajo previas circunstancias. El agua cubrió la ciénaga maloliente y también los juncos que lastimaban las piernas, y los lodazales del pantano en donde se criaban multitud de mosquitos. Por supuesto que si las aguas hubieran seguido subiendo, al final habrían llegado a cubrir toda la isla e inundar las calles de Tlácopan y de otras ciudades de tierra firme. Sin embargo, los caminos-puentes estaban construidos con aberturas de madera puestas a intervalos, y la isla en sí estaba excavada por muchos canales para dar paso a las canoas. Esas espuertas permitían que hubiera un continuo desagüe de aguas hacia el lago de Texcoco, sobre el lado este de la isla, así que la laguna creada artificialmente no levantaba mucho su cauce, por lo menos no demasiado.

«Todavía no se ha elevado excesivamente el nivel del agua —dijo Nezahualpili a Auítzotl—. Pero ahora que usted se propone traer más de la tierra firme, ésta debe desaguarse en algún sitio.»

«Pero si será consumida por nuestra gente en la ciudad —dijo Auítzotl con petulancia—. Para ser bebida, para bañarse, para lavar...»

«El agua que se *consume*, siempre es muy poca —dijo Nezahualpili—. Aunque su pueblo bebiera durante todo el día, tendrían que orinar exactamente igual. Por eso repito: el agua debe desaguarse en algún sitio. ¿Y en dónde será, sino en alguna maldita parte del lago? Su nivel se podría elevar más rápido de lo que se pudiera desaguar a través de los canales y de los caminos-puentes, más allá del lago de Texcoco.»

Empezando a ponerse enojado y colorado, Auítzotl preguntó: «¿Sugiere usted que nosotros ignoremos este manantial, recién encontrado, que es un regalo de los dioses? ¿Que nosotros no hagamos nada por aliviar la sed de Tenochtitlan?»

«Eso sería lo más prudente. Por lo menos le sugiero a usted que construya su acueducto de tal manera, que el chorro de agua pueda ser disminuido y controlado, e incluso cortado si fuera necesario.»

Auítzotl dijo gruñendo: «Con el paso de los años, viejo amigo, usted ha llegado a ser tan temeroso como una vieja. Si nosotros los mexica hubiéramos escuchado siempre a aquellos que nos decían que no hiciéramos tal o cual cosa, nunca habríamos hecho nada.»

«Usted me ha pedido mi opinión, viejo amigo, y yo se la he dado —dijo Nezahualpili—. Pero la responsabilidad final es suya y —él sonrió— su nombre es Monstruo de Agua.»

El acueducto de Auítzotl quedó terminado, más o menos un año después de eso, y los adivinos de palacio tuvieron grandes problemas para escoger el día más favorable para su inauguración, dejando correr la primera agua. Recuerdo muy bien la fecha de ese día, Trece-Viento, porque su nombre vivió siempre en nuestra memoria.

La multitud empezó a reunirse mucho antes de que empezara la ceremonia, pues era un suceso tan importante como la dedicación a la Gran Pirámide que se había llevado a efecto doce años antes. Por supuesto que a toda esa gente no se la hubiera dejado entrar en el camino-puente de Coyohuacan, en donde se estaban llevando a cabo los ritos ceremoniales. La multitud de plebeyos se aglomeraban al final de la isla-ciudad, hacia el sur, apretujándose y repantigándose para poder echar un vistazo a Auítzotl, a sus esposas, a su Consejo de Voceros, a los altos nobles, sacerdotes, campeones y otros personajes que habían llegado en sus canoas desde el palacio, para tomar sus lugares en el camino-puente, entre la ciudad y el fuerte de Acachinanco. Desafortunadamente, yo tuve que estar entre esos altos dignatarios, con mi uniforme completo y con toda la compañía de campeones Águila. Zyanya también quería asistir llevando con ella a Cocoton, pero yo la disuadí otra vez.

«Aunque pudiera conseguir que te acercaras lo suficiente como para poder ver algo —le dije esa mañana, mientras bregaba por ponerme mi traje de plumas acojinado—, el viento del lago te golpearía y la brisa te mojaría. También, en medio de esa multitud aplastante, podrías caer o desmayarte y la niña podría ser pisoteada.»

«Creo que tienes razón —dijo Zyanya sin sentirse muy desilusionada. Impulsivamente tomó a la pequeña en sus brazos y la abrazó fuertemente—. Y Cocoton es muy bonita para ser apretada por alguien más que por nosotros.»

«¡No apretar!», se quejó Cocoton, pero con dignidad. Luego zafándose de los brazos de su madre se fue haciendo pinitos hacia el otro lado del cuarto. A la edad de dos años, nuestra hija tenía un vocabulario considerable, pero no era parlanchina como una ardilla; rara vez utilizaba más de dos palabras a la vez.

«Cuando nació Migajita creí que iba a ser muy fea —dije mientras me vestía—. Pero ahora creo que es tan bonita, que no es posible que llegue a serlo más. De aquí en adelante se va a ir poniendo fea y es una lástima. Para cuando la querramos casar, va a parecer una verraca salvaje.»

Estando de acuerdo conmigo, Cocoton dijo desde su rincón: «Verraca salvaje.»

«No es cierto —dijo Zyanya firmemente—. Cuando un niño es muy bonito, alcanza casi su máxima belleza a los dos años y sigue siendo muy bonito, con sutiles cambios por supuesto, hasta alcanzar, a los seis años, su máxima belleza infantil. La belleza de los niños se detiene ahí, pero las niñas...»

Yo gruñí.

«Quiero decir que los niños dejan de ser *bonitos*, para llegar a ser guapos, agradables, varoniles, pero no *bellos*. O por lo menos no deberían desearlo. A la mayoría de las mujeres no les gustan los hombres bonitos, ni tampoco a los hombres.»

Le dije entonces que estaba contento de haber crecido siendo feo y cuando ella no me desmintió, adopté una mirada melancólica.

«Luego —continuó ella—, las niñitas alcanzan otro grado de belleza cuando llegan más o menos a los doce años, dependiendo de su primer sangrado. Durante la adolescencia, generalmente son tan nerviosas y malhumoradas, como para ser admiradas en lo absoluto. Sin embargo, después vuelven a florecer y a los veinte más o menos, sí, como a los veinte, diría yo, una muchacha llega a ser tan bella como nunca antes lo fue y como no lo volverá a ser otra vez.»

«Lo sé —dije—. Tú tenías veinte años cuando yo me enamoré de ti y me casé contigo. Y desde entonces no tienes edad.»

«Eres un adulador y un mentiroso —me dijo ella, pero sonriendo—. Tengo arrugas en las orillas de mis ojos, mis pechos no son tan firmes como entonces, hay marcas en mi abdomen y...»

«No importa —dije—. La belleza de tus veinte años causó tal impresión en mi mente, que se ha quedado ahí indeleblemente grabada. Nunca podré verte de otra manera, aunque la gente algún día diga: "Viejo tonto, no estás viendo más que una vieja", yo no podré creerles.»

Hice una pausa para pensar un momento, pero luego dije en su lengua nativa: «*Rizalazi Zyanya chuüpa chíi, chuüpa chíi zyanya*», era un juego de palabras, que más o menos quería decir: «Recuerda, Siempre, que los veinte te dejaron en veinte siempre.»

Ella preguntó tiernamente: «¿Siempre?»

Y yo le aseguré: «Siempre.»

«Eso será muy hermoso —dijo ella con una mirada nublada por las lágrimas—, pensar que por todo el tiempo que esté a tu lado, seré siempre una muchacha de veinte años. Incluso, aunque nos tengamos que separar algunas veces, sin importar en qué parte del mundo estés, yo seguiré siendo para ti una muchacha de veinte años. —Parpadeó con sus largas pestañas, hasta que sus ojos brillaron otra vez y sonriendo me dijo—: Debí de haberlo mencionado antes, Zaa... tú no eres realmente feo.»

«Realmente feo», dijo mi adorada y adorable hija.

Eso nos hizo reír a los dos, rompiendo ese momento de encanto.

Tomando mi escudo dije: «Debo irme.» Zyanya me dio un beso de despedida y dejé la casa.

Era muy temprano en la mañana. El lanchón recolector de basura se abría paso por el canal contra el viento, al final de nuestra calle, recogiendo los desperdicios apilados en la noche. La recolección de los desperdicios de la ciudad era el trabajo más bajo de Tenochtitlan, y sólo los más desafortunados desgraciados eran empleados en eso, tullidos sin esperanza, borrachos incurables y demás. Me volví para no ver ese cuadro depresivo y caminé en otra dirección, calle arriba hacia la plaza principal y sólo había caminado un poco, cuando oí que Zyanya me llamaba por mi nombre.

Me volví y levanté mi topacio para ver. Había salido a la puerta de la casa para decirme otra vez adiós, con la mano y para decirme algo más antes de volver a entrar en la casa. Pudo haber sido algo que sólo las mujeres pueden decir, como: «Luego me dices qué llevaba puesto la Primera Señora.» O algo que sólo puede decirlo una esposa, como: «Ten cuidado de no llegar muy mojado.» O algo que salía del corazón, como «Recuerda que te amo.» Cualquier cosa que fuera, no la oí, pues en aquellos momentos llegó el viento, un viento, y él se llevó sus palabras.

✠

Ya que el manantial de Coyohuacan formaba parte de la tierra firme, éste se encontraba un poco más alto que el nivel de las calles de Tenochtitlan, así es que el acueducto se deslizaba pendiente abajo desde allí. Era tan ancho y vasto, que un hombre no lo podía encerrar entre sus dos brazos, y de casi dos largas-carreras de longitud. Su punto de unión en el camino-puente era en donde se encontraba, exactamente, el fuerte de Acachinanco y haciendo un ángulo, partía de allí paralelo al parapeto del camino-puente, derecho hacia la ciudad. Una vez en ella, se dividía en ramificaciones, para alimentar los canales que tenían menos agua y que corrían por Tenochtitlan y Tlaltelolco, llenando también los estanques de abastecimiento, puestos en cada manzana en lugares convenientes y las diversas fuentes recién construidas en la plaza principal.

En cierto modo, Auítzotl y sus constructores habían tenido en cuenta la advertencia de Nezahualpili, acerca de controlar el agua del manantial. En el ángulo en donde el acueducto corría paralelo al camino-puente y en otro punto, ya casi entrando en la ciudad, se le habían hecho a las gamellas de piedra unas ranuras verticales, en las cuales estaban semiintroducidas unas tablas, hechas siguiendo la misma forma de la gamella, que cerrarían el paso del agua. Lo único que se tenía que hacer era dejar caer esas tablas para cortar el chorro de agua, si eso fuera necesario.

La nueva estructura debía ser dedicada a la diosa de los estanques, corrientes y otras aguas, la cabeza de rana Chalchihuitlicué y ella no exigía demasiados ofrecimientos humanos, como algunos otros dioses. Así es que los sacrificados en ese día iban a ser sólo los necesarios. En donde se iniciaba el acueducto, en el manantial, fuera del alcance de nuestra vista, estaba otro contingente de nobles y sacerdotes y un número de guerreros guardando a los prisioneros. Ya que nosotros los mexica estábamos muy ocupados en esos momentos, como para entrar en alguna otra Guerra Florida, la mayoría de esos prisioneros eran bandidos comunes que Motecuzoma El Joven había encontrado en sus idas y venidas de un lado a otro, y que los había capturado y enviado a Tenochtitlan sólo para ese propósito.

En el camino-puente en donde estaba Auítzotl, junto conmigo y con otros cientos de personas, todos tratábamos de conservar nuestros penachos de plumas y las plumas que pasaban por alas de nuestro traje, al abrigo del viento del este. Había rezos, cantos e invocaciones, mientras los sacerdotes menores mataban cierta cantidad de ranas, *axololtin* y otras criaturas acuáticas, para complacer a Chalchihuitlicué. Luego encendieron un fuego y espolvorearon en él una sustancia sacerdotal y secreta para que se elevara una voluta de humo azul. Aunque el soplo del viento rompió esa columna de humo, alcanzó a subir lo suficiente como para dar la señal al otro grupo ceremonial que se encontraba en el manantial de Coyohuacan.

Allí, los sacerdotes acostaron al primer prisionero sobre la gamella, al comienzo del acueducto, y abriéndolo en canal dejaron su cuerpo allí, mientras la sangre corría. Luego otro prisionero fue puesto allí e hicieron lo mismo con él. En cuanto un cuerpo se empezaba a secar, era arrojado a un lado y se ponía otro, así siempre había sangre fresca corriendo. No sé cuántos *xochimique* mataron y desangraron, antes de que la primera sangre, que escurría suavemente, llegara a la vista de Auítzotl y de sus sacerdotes, quienes dieron un grito de alabanza cuando la vieron. Otra sustancia fue arrojada al fuego produciendo un humo rojo: la señal para que los sacerdotes que estaban junto al manantial dejaran de matar.

Entonces llegó el momento en que Auítzotl haría el sacrificio más importante, y le entregaron a la víctima más adecuada: una pequeñita de cuatro años, vestida con un traje azul-agua que tenía cosido por todas partes gemas verdes y azules. Era la hija de un cazador de aves que se había ahogado cuando su *acali* se volcó en el agua, un poco antes de que ella naciera y ésta había nacido con una cara muy parecida a una rana, o a la diosa

Chalchihuitlicué. La viuda había considerado esas coincidencias relacionadas con el agua, como una señal de la diosa y había ofrecido a su hija voluntariamente para la ceremonia.

Con un gran acompañamiento de cantos y graznidos por parte de los sacerdotes, el Venerado Orador levantó a la niña sobre la gamella que estaba detrás de él, mientras que los sacerdotes se balanceaban a un lado del fuego. Auítzotl acostó a la niña sobre el acueducto y tomó de su cintura su cuchillo de obsidiana. El humo de la urna cambió a un color verde; otra señal para que los sacerdotes en la tierra firme, al otro lado del acueducto, dejaran correr el agua por éste. No sé exactamente cómo lo hicieron, si quitaron alguna clase de obstáculo que obstruía el agua, o si rompieron el último dique de tierra o si sólo rodaron algún peñasco. El caso es que el agua, que un principio había llegado coloreada de rojo, no vino chorreando como la sangre.

Con la fuerza que le daba su largo declive desde la tierra firme, llegó rugiendo como una inmensa lanza líquida, cuya punta estaba empenachada de hirviente espuma rosa. No toda el agua pudo tomar la curva de la gamella, sino que la que venía más atrás se levantó y rompió sobre el parapeto con la fuerza de una ola del océano. Así, aunque no toda el agua entró en la gamella, la que sí lo hizo entró con tal fuerza que tomó por sorpresa a Auítzotl. Él acababa de abrir el pecho de la niña y de sacar el corazón, pero todavía no lo había roto, cuando el agua rugiente arrastró el cuerpo de la niña, llevándoselo lejos de allí. Ya sin su pequeño corazón, pues Auítzotl todavía lo tenía en la mano mirando pasmado cómo el cuerpo de la niña salía disparado hacia la ciudad, como lo haría una bolita lanzada a través de una cerbatana.

Todos los que estábamos en el acueducto, nos quedamos como estatuas, sin ningún movimiento a excepción de los de nuestros penachos, mantos y banderas zarandeados por el viento. Luego me di cuenta de que estaba mojado hasta los tobillos, como lo estaban todos los demás, y las mujeres de Auítzotl empezaron a gritar de aflicción. El pavimento bajo nuestros pies se empezaba a anegar, con rapidez. El agua seguía saltando sobre el ángulo del parapeto y todo el fuerte de Acachinanco se estremecía bajo su impacto.

A pesar de ello, gran parte del agua continuaba corriendo por la gamella hacia la ciudad, con tal fuerza que cuando llegó golpeando en donde se ramificaban los canales, rompió como una batiente en la playa. A través de mi cristal, podía ver a la apretada multitud de espectadores, que en esos momentos eran revolcados por el espumoso golpe de agua, y luchaban por huir y dispersarse. A través de toda la ciudad, más allá de nuestra vista, los nuevos canales y los depósitos de agua se derramaban, mojando las calles y vaciándose sobre los canales. En la plaza, las fuentes nuevas estaban lanzando chorros de agua tan fantásticamente altos que el agua no volvía a caer sobre los estanques de drenaje puestos alrededor de cada una, sino que se desparramaban totalmente a través del Corazón del Único Mundo.

Los sacerdotes de Chalchihuitlicué rompieron en balbucientes plegarias, suplicando a la diosa que abatiera su abundancia. Auítzotl rugió para que se callaran, luego empezó a vociferar nombres: «¡Yólcatl! ¡Papaquilíztli!», los de aquellos hombres que habían descubierto el nuevo manantial. Aquellos que estaban presentes, obedientemente chapotearon con el agua hasta las rodillas y sabiendo perfectamente bien para qué habían sido llamados, se acostaron, uno por uno sobre el parapeto. Auítzotl y los sacerdotes, sin palabras o gestos rituales, abrieron los pechos de los hombres, arrancaron sus corazones y los sumergieron en las aguas turbulentas. Ocho hombres fueron sacrificados en ese acto de desesperación, dos de ellos fueron miembros, ancianos augustos, del Consejo de Voceros, y sin embargo, eso no sirvió de nada.

Así es que Auítzotl gritó: «¡Dejen caer la puerta de la gamella!» Y varios campeones Águila treparon al parapeto. Trataron de acomodar la tabla de madera, que estaba designada para cortar el chorro de agua, deslizándola a través de las hendiduras de la gamella, pero por más esfuerzos que hicieron, combinando su fuerza y peso, los campeones sólo la pudieron empujar un poco. Tan pronto como su orilla curva entró en el agua, la poderosa corriente la empujó de las ranuras y ladeándola la inmovilizó en ese punto. Por un momento, todo fue silencio en el acueducto a excepción del ruido producido por el agua borboteante, el sonido silbante y suspirante del viento, el crujido del oprimido fuerte de madera y los sordos gritos que nos llegaban desde la isla, de la multitud que huía con rapidez. Viéndose al fin derrotado, con todas sus plumas empapadas y caídas, el Venerado Orador dijo lo suficientemente fuerte como para que todos lo oyéramos:

«Debemos regresar a la ciudad, para ver todo el daño que ha sido causado y para ver si podemos reprimir el pánico. Los campeones Flecha y Jaguar vengan conmigo. Ustedes se harán cargo de todos los *acaltin* de la isla, para que salgan inmediatamente hacia Coyohuacan. Esos tontos todavía deben de estar celebrando allí. Hagan todo lo que puedan para detener o desviar el agua de su curso. Los campeones Águila quédense aquí —Él apuntó el lugar en donde el acueducto se juntaba con el camino-puente—. ¡Rómpanlo ahí! ¡*Ahora!*»

Hubo cierta confusión cuando los diversos grupos se dispersaron. Auítzotl, sus esposas con su acompañamiento, los sacerdotes y los nobles, los campeones Flecha y Jaguar, todos ellos, se fueron bregando hacia Tenochtitlan, tan rápido como les permitía el agua que les llegaba ya cerca de los muslos. Nosotros, los campeones Águila nos quedamos contemplando la pesada piedra y el mortero firme de la gamella. Dos o tres campeones le pegaron a la piedra con sus *maquáhuime*, haciendo que cayera sobre el resto de nosotros una lluvia de astillas y de obsidiana quebrada. Después, mirando disgustados sus espadas arruinadas, las tiraron en el lago.

Luego uno de los campeones de más edad caminó por un trecho del acueducto y echó una mirada sobre el parapeto. Nos llamó y preguntó: «¿Cuántos de ustedes saben nadar? —y casi todas nuestras manos se levantaron. Él apuntó y dijo—: Exactamente aquí, en donde el acueducto se desvía, la fuerza del agua que cambia de dirección hace que los pilotes se resientan. Quizás podamos cortarlos o romperlos lo suficiente, como para que la estructura se caiga por sí misma.»

Eso fue lo que hicimos. Yo y ocho de los campeones, nos quitamos nuestros trajes mojados y sucios, mientras nos conseguían unas *maquáhuime*, luego saltamos sobre el parapeto hacia las aguas del lago. Como ya he dicho, las aguas hacia el oeste del camino-puente no eran muy profundas, pues si hubiéramos tenido que nadar, habría sido imposible cortar los pilotes, pero el agua sólo nos llegaba al hombro en ese lugar. A pesar de ella, no fue un trabajo fácil. Esos tres troncos de soporte, habían sido impregnados con *chapopotli* para que resistieran a la putrición y eso también los hacía muy resistentes a nuestras espadas. La noche había llegado y se había ido, y el sol estaba ya en lo alto cuando uno de los pesados pilotes se sacudió y dio un tremendo ¡*crac!* Yo estaba bajo el agua en ese momento, y la conmoción casi me hace perder el sentido, pero salí a la superficie a tiempo de oír a uno de nuestros compañeros, gritando a todos que volviéramos a trepar al camino-puente.

Apenas trepamos a tiempo. La parte del acueducto en donde formaba ángulo con el camino-puente, se estremecía violentamente. Con un sonido de resquebrajamiento, se rompió en donde se curvaba lanzando agua en todas direcciones. Esa parte de la estructura que al fin caía, parecía la cola cascabelera de una *coacuechtli*, serpiente. Luego, una sección como de diez pasos de largo se ladeó, cuando los pilotes que habíamos cortado cedieron bajo su peso y se rompió con un gran gemido, cayendo con un poderoso chapoteo. La parte dentada de la gamella que todavía quedaba en pie, se veía como una cascada que caía sobre el lago, pero al agua ya no corría hacia Tenochtitlan. Incluso, mientras nosotros estábamos todavía allí, el agua que estaba en el camino-puente empezó a menguar.

«Regresemos a casa —dijo uno de nuestros hermanos campeones, suspirando— y esperemos haber salvado algunos hogares, a los cuales poder regresar.»

Hogar. Déjenme hacer a un lado, por un momento, mi narración de cómo regresé a mi hogar.

El agua había corrido sobre Tenochtitlan la mayor parte del día y toda la noche, habiendo inundado algunas partes de la ciudad a la profundidad de la estatura de ocho hombres. Algunas casas que habían sido construidas a ras de tierra y que no eran de piedra se habían derrumbado por la inundación e incluso otras construidas sobre pilotes; mucha gente había resultado herida y cerca de veinte, la mayoría de ellos niños, se había ahogado o habían sido aplastados o muertos de alguna otra manera. Sin embargo, el daño se había limitado a aquellas partes de la ciudad en donde las ramificaciones de canales y los estanques de aprovisionamiento se habían derramado y esa agua se había drenado hacia los otros canales, mucho antes de que nosotros los campeones Águila hubiéramos cortado el acueducto.

Sin embargo, antes de que esa pequeña inundación se hubiera escurrido totalmente, llegó una segunda y mucho más grande. Nosotros sólo habíamos roto el acueducto, pero no habíamos detenido el agua y los campeones que Auítzotl había mandado a la tierra firme, no pudieron detener el agua del manantial. Éste continuó lanzando sus aguas en el lago, en la parte que estaba entre los caminos-puente del este y del sur. Mientras tanto, el viento continuaba soplando desde el este, impidiendo que el exceso de agua fuera drenado hacia el gran lago de Texcoco, por los pasajes del camino-puente y por los canales que cruzaban la ciudad hacia ese lado. Así es que los canales se llenaron hasta los topes desbordándose y el agua subió sobre la isla, y Tenochtitlan llegó a ser un gran enjambre de edificios empujados de un lado a otro de la isla por una fuerte sábana de agua.

Inmediatamente después de haber regresado de la inconclusa ceremonia de dedicación, Auítzotl envió un remero a Texcoco y Nezahualpili llegó inmediatamente, en respuesta a su llamada de auxilio. Había traído consigo a un grupo de trabajadores, que dándose prisa se dirigían directamente hacia el manantial inextinguible de Coyohuacan, y como todos lo habíamos esperado, ideó la manera de desviar las aguas. Nunca he visitado ese sitio, pero sé que está a un lado de una colina y supe que Nezahualpili dirigió un sistema de excavaciones de zanjas y fortificaciones para poder desviar la corriente del manantial hacia el otro lado de la colina, en donde podía correr sin daño sobre una tierra vacía. Cuando se terminó de hacer eso, el manantial fue domado y una vez que las aguas de la inundación se dispersaron totalmente, el acueducto pudo ser reparado y puesto en uso nuevamente. Nezahualpili diseñó unas compuertas, que conforme lo necesitara la ciudad dejarían correr poca o mucha agua. Así, hasta este día, todavía estamos bebiendo de esas aguas dulces.

Pero la operación salvadora de Nezahualpili, no se efectuó en una noche. Mientras sus hombres trabajaban, esa segunda inundación continuó y su ola se mantuvo cuatro días enteros. Aunque hubo poca gente que pereció en ella, por lo menos dos terceras partes de la ciudad fueron destruidas y la reconstrucción total de Tenochtitlan tomó por lo menos unos cuatro años. La inundación no hubiera causado mucho daño si las aguas sólo hubieran cubierto las calles yaciendo quietamente. En lugar de eso, se movían furiosamente de un lado a otro; se movían hacia un lado por la fuerza que las impelía a buscar un nivel uniforme; se movían hacia el otro lado a empuje del malicioso viento del este. La mayor parte de los edificios de Tenochtitlan estaban sostenidos por pilotes o por cualquier otra clase de cimientos, sobre el nivel de la calle, pero eso era sólo para elevarlos de la humedad de la tierra. Sus cimientos nunca habían sido construidos para soportar las corrientes batientes que sufrieron, así es que la mayoría de ellos no se pudieron sostener. Las casas de adobe simplemente se disolvieron en el agua; las de piedra, pequeñas y grandes, cayeron cuando sus pilotes fueron corroídos por las aguas y se rompieron en los mismos bloques con que fueron construidas.

Mi casa resultó ilesa, probablemente porque era una construcción relativamente nueva, y eso la hizo más fuerte que otras. En El Corazón del Único Mundo, las pirámides y templos también quedaron en pie, sólo la barra dentada para las calaveras, comparativamente frágil, se vino abajo. Sin embargo, exactamente a un lado y afuera de la plaza, cayó un palacio completo —el más nuevo y el más magnífico de todos—, el palacio del Uey-Tlatoani Auítzotl. Ya les he contado que éste estaba construido cruzando a horcajadas uno de los principales canales de la ciudad, de tal manera que el público que pasaba a través, podía admirar su interior. Cuando ese canal, como todos los otros, se desbordó, primero inundó los pisos bajos del palacio y luego arremetió con gran fuerza sobre las paredes bajas exteriores, con lo que el gran edificio se vino abajo ruidosamente.

De momento yo no supe todos esos acontecimientos, ni siquiera sabía que era lo suficientemente afortunado como para tener todavía mi propia casa, no lo supe hasta que las aguas menguaron. En esa segunda y más terrible inundación, las aguas no se elevaron tan rápidamente, dando tiempo para que la ciudad fuera evacuada. A excepción de Auítzotl, de otros nobles gobernantes, de la guardia de palacio de algunas tropas de guerreros y de cierto número de sacerdotes que perplejos seguían rezando, por la intervención de la diosa, prácticamente toda la gente había huido de Tenochtitlan, cruzando el camino-puente del norte para encontrar refugio en las ciudades de Tepeyaca y Atzacoalco, en la tierra firme, incluyéndome a mí, a mis dos sirvientes y a lo que me quedaba de familia.

Volvamos a ese lejano día, a esa madrugada, cuando regresé a casa arrastrando mi traje sucio y empapado de campeón Águila...

Conforme me iba aproximando, era obvio que mi barrio de Ixacualco había sido uno de los distritos que más había sufrido con la primera inundación. Todavía podía ver la marca húmeda y alta, que el agua había dejado en los edificios, tan alta como mi cabeza, y aquí y allá una casa de adobe yacía oblicuamente. La arcilla fuertemente apisonada de mi calle estaba resbaladiza con una capa de moho; había lodo y escombros, y también algunos objetos de valor que aparentemente fueron dejados caer por la gente que huía. En aquel momento no había ni un alma en la calle, sin duda estaban dentro de sus casas, en la incertidumbre de si la ola de la inundación volvería a regresar; sin embargo, la calle desacostumbradamente vacía, me hizo sentir desasosegado. Estaba demasiado cansado para correr, pero arrastré los pies lo más rápido que pude y mi corazón volvió a latir cuando vi mi casa todavía en pie, sin marcas a excepción de una capa de limo sobre los escalones de la entrada.

Turquesa vino corriendo hacia la puerta de la entrada exclamando: «¡*Ayyo*, es nuestro señor amo! ¡Gracias sean dadas a Chalchihuitlicué por haberle permitido vivir!»

Cansado, pero de todo corazón, le dije que deseaba que esa diosa en particular estuviera en Mictlan.

«¡No hable así! —suplicó Turquesa y las lágrimas resbalaban por las arrugas de su rostro—. ¡Nosotros también temimos haber perdido a nuestro amo!»

«¿También? —jadeé, y una banda invisible apretó dolorosamente mi pecho. La vieja esclava rompió a llorar violentamente y no pudo responder. Dejé caer las cosas que llevaba y la zarandeé por los hombros—. ¿La niña? —pregunté. Ella movió su cabeza, pero no les podría decir si fue para negar o para asentir. La zarandeé de nuevo fieramente y dije—: ¡Habla, mujer!»

«Fue nuestra señora Zyanya —dijo otra voz detrás de ella; era el sirviente Estrella Cantadora, quien había llegado a la puerta estrujándose las manos—. Yo lo vi todo. Traté de detenerla.»

No dejé que se fuera Turquesa o hubiera caído. Sólo pude decir: «Cuéntamelo, Estrella Cantadora.»

«Entonces sepa mi amo que ayer, al atardecer, en el momento en que las antorchas de las calles son encendidas usualmente, aunque por supuesto no las encendieron pues la calle parecía una catarata. Sólo vino un hombre, era arrastrado por la corriente y golpeado contra los postes de las antorchas y contra los escalones de las casas. Él trataba por todos los medios de poner pie en algo o de cogerse de algo para detenerse, pero aun cuando él estaba a bastante distancia, pude ver que era un baldado y que él no...»

Tan ásperamente como me lo permitió mi agonía y debilidad, le dije: «¿Qué tiene que ver todo eso con mi esposa? ¿En dónde está?»

«Ella *estaba* en la ventana de enfrente —dijo él apuntando y continuó con deliberado enojo—. Ella había estado todo el día allí, preocupada y esperando su regreso, mi señor. Yo estaba con ella cuando el hombre llegó, golpeado y azotado calle abajo y ella me gritó que debíamos de salvarlo. Naturalmente que yo no estaba muy ansioso de meterme en las aguas rugientes y le dije: "Mi señora, puedo reconocerlo desde aquí. Es sólo un viejo desgraciado, que últimamente ha estado trabajando en las canoas de la basura, que dan servicio a este barrio. No vale la pena que nadie se tome la molestia por él."»

Estrella Cantadora hizo una pausa, tragó saliva y dija roncamente: «No me quejaré si mi amo me pega, o me vende o me mata, porque debí haber ido a salvar al hombre, pues mi señora lanzándome una mirada de indignación, fue por sí misma. Se dirigió hacia la puerta y bajó la escalera, mientras yo miraba desde esa ventana, e inclinándose sobre la corriente lo pescó.»

Él volvió a hacer una pausa y yo dije irritado: «¿Y bien? ¿Si los dos están a salvo...?»

Estrella Cantadora denegó con la cabeza. «Eso es lo que no comprendo. Claro, que los escalones estaban mojados y resbaladizos, mi señor, pero parece que... parece que mi señora habló con el hombre y empezó a alejarse de él, pero entonces... entonces el agua se los llevó. Se llevó a los dos ya que él la estaba agarrando. Sólo pude ver cómo un bulto era arrastrado ante mi vista, ya que los dos estaban juntos. Entonces corrí hacia fuera y me metí en la corriente detrás de ellos.»

«Estrella Cantadora casi se ahoga, mi señor —dijo Turquesa sollozando—. Él trató, él realmente trató...»

«No había ni señal de ellos —resumió miserablemente—. Hacia el final de la calle, cierto número de casas de adobe se acababan de caer... quizás sobre ellos, creo yo. Sin embargo, estaba ya muy oscuro para poder ver y las maderas que flotaban me habían golpeado y estaba casi sin conocimiento. Me agarré a la puerta de una casa, cogiéndome con fuerza y así pasé toda la noche.»

«Llegó a la casa cuando las aguas bajaron esta mañana —dijo Turquesa—. Después los dos fuimos afuera y buscamos.»

«¿Y no encontrasteis nada?», gruñí.

«Sólo encontramos al hombre —dijo Estrella Cantadora—. Medio enterrado bajo los ladrillos caídos, como yo lo había sospechado.»

Turquesa dijo: «Todavía no le hemos dicho nada a Cocoton acerca de su madre. ¿Quiere mi señor ir con ella ahora, allá arriba?»

«¿Y decirle lo que ni yo mismo puedo creer? —gemí. Hice acopio de mi última reserva de energía, para enderezar mi cuerpo doblegado y dije—: «No, no lo haré. Ven, Estrella Cantadora, busquemos otra vez.»

Más allá de mi casa, la calle se deslizaba en un declive suave conforme nos aproximábamos al puente que cruzaba el canal, así es que las casas allí abajo, naturalmente, habían sido golpeadas con más violencia por la muralla de agua. También allí era en donde estaban las casas más pobremente construidas, de madera y adobe. Como había dicho Estrella Cantadora, ya no existían más casas allí; solo había montones de ladrillos de lodo y paja, medio rotos, medio disueltos, astillas de tablones y pedazos de muebles. El sirviente apuntó a un bulto de tela que sobresalía entre ellos y dijo:

«Ahí está ese desgraciado. No ha sido ninguna pérdida para nadie. Vivía vendiéndose a sí mismo, a los hombres que trabajaban en las chalupas recolectadoras de basura. Aquellos que no tenían con que pagar una mujer lo utilizaban a él, pues sólo cobraba una semilla de cacao.»

Él yacía boca abajo. Era una cosa con harapos sucios y pelo gris, largo y enmarañado. Usé mi pie para voltearlo boca arriba y lo miré por última vez. Chimali me miraba con sus cuencas vacías y con su boca abierta.

No fue en ese momento, sino más tarde cuando pude pensar, cuando recordé las palabras de Estrella Cantadora; de que el hombre había estado últimamente a bordo de las chalupas de recolección de basura, de nuestro vecindario. Me preguntaba: ¿Había descubierto Chimali, recientemente, en dónde vivía yo? ¿Había llegado buscándome, tanteando ciegamente, con la esperanza de tener otra oportunidad para infligirme un daño a mí o a los míos? ¿Le había dado la inundación una oportunidad, como para hacerme el daño más doloroso y a la vez haberlo puesto más allá y para siempre, del alcance de mi venganza? ¿O toda la tragedia había sido una maquinación lúgubre y alegre de los dioses? Parece que ellos se divierten en disponer una concatenación de sucesos que de otra forma vendrían a parecer inverosímiles, inexplicables e increíbles.

Nunca lo sabré.

En ese momento, sólo sabía que mi esposa había desaparecido, que no podía aceptar su desaparición y que tenía que buscarla. Así es que le dije a Estrella Cantadora: «Si este hombre maldito está aquí, también tiene que estar Zyanya. Moveremos cada uno de todos estos millones de adobes. Yo empezaré ahora mismo, mientras tú vas a conseguir más manos para que nos ayuden. ¡Ve!»

Estrella Cantadora salió corriendo y yo me incliné para levantar y poner a un lado una viga de madera y así continué, agachándome y lanzando todo hacia atrás de mí.

La tarde ya había caído cuando recobré el conocimiento en mi cama; los dos sirvientes se inclinaban solícitos sobre mí. Lo primero que pregunté fue: «¿La encontrasteis? —Y los regañé cuando los dos negaron tristemente con la cabeza—. ¡Os dije que removierais cada ladrillo!»

«Amo, no se puede hacer —sollozó Estrella Cantadora—. El agua volvió a subir. Yo regresé y lo encontré a usted apenas a tiempo, de no ser por eso, usted se habría ahogado.»

«Nos preguntábamos si debíamos volverle en sí —dijo Turquesa con manifiesta ansiedad—. El Venerado Orador ha ordenado que toda la ciudad sea evacuada antes de que el agua la cubra totalmente.»

Y así me senté esa noche a un lado de la colina sin poder dormir, en medio de una multitud de fugitivos dormidos. «Mucho andar», había dicho Cocoton, durante el camino. Ya que sólo la gente que salió primero de Tenochtitlan encontró alojamiento en la tierra firme, los que llegaron después simplemente se detuvieron en cualquier lugar en donde se pudieran acostar, a campo abierto. «Noche oscura», dijo mi hija muy apropiadamente. Nosotros cuatro ni siquiera encontramos un árbol bajo el cual guarecernos, pero Turquesa había llevado cobijas. Ella, Estrella Cantadora y Cocoton se envolvieron y durmieron abrigados, pero, yo me senté con la cobija sobre mis hombros y miré hacia abajo, hacia mi hija, mi migajita, el remanente único y precioso de mi esposa y sentí dolor.

Hace algún tiempo, mis señores frailes, yo traté de describir a Zyanya comparándola con la generosa y útil planta del maguey, pero hay algo que se me olvidó decirles acerca de él. Una vez en su vida, sólo una, le crece una simple vara cubierta totalmente de flores amarillas de dulce fragancia y luego el maguey muere.

Esa noche, traté con todas mis fuerzas de hallar alivio a mi pena, recordando las aseveraciones untuosas de los sacerdotes, que siempre decían: la muerte no debe ser motivo de aflicción o de tristeza. La muerte, decían los sacerdotes, es solamente el despertar del sueño en que uno ha vivido. Quizás sí. Sus sacerdotes Cristianos dicen cosas parecidas. Sin embargo, esas palabras no me confortaban mucho, a mí que había quedado atrás de ese sueño, vivo, solo, triste. Así es que pasé esa noche acordándome de Zyanya y del tiempo, demasiado breve, que pasamos juntos antes de que su sueño terminara.

Todavía recuerdo...

Una vez, cuando fuimos a Michihuacan, ella vio una flor que nunca había visto, que crecía en la grieta de una peña, algo más arriba de nuestras cabezas, y a ella le gustó mucho y dijo que le gustaría tener una de ésas para plantarla en el jardín de nuestra casa; yo habría podido trepar fácilmente y arrancarla para ella...

Otra vez, oh, no fue en ninguna ocasión en particular, ella pasó el día enamorada, cosa muy frecuente en Zyanya, y compuso una pequeña canción y luego hizo la melodía y pasó todo el día cantándola por lo bajo, hasta que la grabó en su memoria, luego me preguntó que si le podría comprar una de esas flautas de arcilla, de las que eran llamadas agua murmurante, para poder tocar en ella su canción. Yo le dije que sí, que lo haría la próxima vez que viera a un músico conocido mío y que lo iba a persuadir para que me hiciera una, pero se me olvidó y ella, viendo que tenía otras cosas en mi mente, nunca me lo recordó.

Y otra vez...

Ayya, cuántas otras veces más...

Oh, yo sé que ella nunca dudó de que la amara, pero ¿por qué dejé pasar la más pequeña oportunidad para demostrárselo? Yo sé que ella perdonaba mis lapsos ocasionales de descuido y mis negligencias triviales; probablemente las olvidaba al instante, lo que yo nunca he podido hacer. Desde entonces, a través de todos los años de mi vida, he estado recordando ese o aquel tiempo en que debí haber hecho eso o aquello y no lo hice, y que nunca volvería a tener la oportunidad de hacerlo. Mientras que las cosas que quisiera recordar persisten en no llegar a mi memoria. Oh, si pudiera recordar las palabras de aquella pequeña canción que ella compuso cuando se sentía tan feliz, o tan sólo la melodía, podría susurrrarlas algunas veces para mí. O si supiera qué fue lo que me dijo cuando el viento se llevó sus palabras, la última vez que la vi...

Cuando al fin regresamos a la isla, la mayor parte de la ciudad estaba en ruinas, tanto que los primeros escombros que se apilaron en nuestra calle no se distinguían de los que habían caído después. Trabajadores y esclavos ya estaban quitando los despojos, salvando los bloques de piedra caliza que no se habían roto y que se podrían utilizar otra vez, y nivelando los cimientos para volver a construir. Pero el cuerpo de Zyanya nunca se encontró, no se halló ni una huella de ella; ni siquiera uno de sus anillos o una sandalia. Ella se desvaneció tan completa e irreparablemente como aquella cancioncita que una vez compuso. Sin embargo, mis señores, yo sé que ella todavía está aquí en algún lado, aunque desde entonces dos nuevas ciudades se han construido sucesivamente sobre su tumba perdida. Yo lo sé, porque ella no llevó consigo el pedacito de jade que asegura su pasaje hacia el mundo del más allá.

Muchas veces, ya muy de noche, he caminado por esas calles llamándola suavemente. Lo hice en Tenochtitlan y también lo he hecho en esta Ciudad de Mexico; un hombre viejo duerme muy poco en la noche. Aunque he visto muchos aparecidos, ninguno ha sido ella.

Solamente me he encontrado con espíritus desgraciados o malvados y ninguno de ellos ha sido Zyanya, en eso no puedo equivocarme, ya que ella fue feliz toda su vida y murió mientras trataba de hacer el bien. Yo he visto y reconocido a muchos guerreros mexica muertos; la ciudad está llena de esos espectros abrumados de angustia. He visto a La Llorona; ella es como una voluta de niebla arrastrada por el viento, pero con forma de mujer; he escuchado su aullido lastimero. Sin embargo no me ha asustado, antes al contrario, siento piedad por ella porque también he conocido lo que es perder a un ser querido, pero, cuando ella no me asustaba con su aullido, huía de mis palabras de consuelo. Una vez, me pareció que me encontré y conversé con dos dioses vagabundos, Viento de la Noche y El Más Viejo de Todos los Dioses. De todas formas, eso fue lo que ellos dijeron ser, pero no me hicieron ningún daño, juzgando que ya había bastante en mi vida.

Algunas veces, en calles completamente oscuras y desiertas, me pareció escuchar la alegre risa de Zyanya. Hubiera podido ser un producto de mi imaginación senil, pero cada vez la risa estuvo acompañada por un reflejo de luz en la oscuridad, muy parecido al mechón blanco que tenía en su pelo negro. Pudiera haber sido también un truco de mi vista débil, pues la visión desaparecía cada vez que me llevaba, desmañadamente, mi topacio hacia el ojo. De todas maneras, yo sé que ella está aquí, en alguna parte y no necesito de ninguna evidencia, por mucho que la desee.

He estado considerando este asunto y me pregunto: ¿Sólo me encuentro con esos dolientes y misántropos ciudadanos de la noche, porque me parezco mucho a ellos? ¿Es posible que las personas que tienen un carácter mejor y un corazón alegre, puedan percibir con más facilidad a los fantasmas más gentiles? Yo les suplico, mis señores frailes, si alguno de sus hombres buenos llegara a encontrarse con Zyanya, alguna noche, ¿me lo dirían? La reconocerán inmediatamente y no se espantarán ante un fantasma de tanta belleza. Ella seguirá pareciendo una muchacha de veinte años, como lo era entonces, pues la muerte por lo menos le ahorró las enfermedades y la marchitez que trae consigo la vejez. Ustedes reconocerán su sonrisa, ya que no podrán dejar de sonreírle a su vez. Y si ella hablara...

Pero no, ustedes no comprenderán lo que ella diga. Solamente tengan la bondad de decirme que la vieron. Ella sigue caminando por estas calles, yo lo sé. Ella está aquí y lo estará por siempre.

I H S

✠

S. C. C. M.

Santificada, Cesárea, Católica Majestad,
el Emperador Don Carlos, nuestro Señor Rey:

Real y Temible Majestad, nuestro Rey Supremo: desde esta Ciudad de Mexico, capital de la Nueva España, en el día de San Papahnutius, mártir, en el año de Nuestro Señor de mil quinientos treinta, os saludo.

Es una atención típica de Nuestro Compasivo Soberano que os apiadéis del Protector de los Indios de Vuestra Majestad y que pidáis más detalles sobre los problemas y obstáculos que nos, diariamente afrontamos en nuestro oficio.

En tiempos pasados, Señor, era una práctica muy común entre los españoles a quienes se les concedieron tierras y haciendas, en estas provincias, que también se apropiaran de muchos indios que vivían en los alrededores de ellas y acostumbraban marcarlos con hierros en las mejillas con una «G» de «guerra», proclamándolos como prisioneros de guerra, tratándolos cruelmente y explotándolos a la vez. Por lo menos esa práctica se ha mejorado a tal grado, que a los indios ya no se les puede sentenciar a ser esclavos, a menos de que se les hallen culpables de algún crimen por las autoridades seculares o eclesiásticas.

También, la ley de la Madre España se aplica ahora más estrictamente en esta Nueva España, así es que los indios aquí, como los judíos allá, tienen los mismos derechos como cualquier español cristiano y no pueden ser condenados por un crimen sin ser procesados, juzgados y convictos. Naturalmente que el testimonio de un indio, como el de un judío y aun el de un converso cristiano, no se le puede permitir tener el mismo peso del de un cristiano que lo ha sido durante toda su vida. De aquí que, si un español desea adquirir como esclavo a algún robusto hombre rojo o a alguna mujer roja de buena presencia, todo lo que tiene que hacer para conseguirlo es dejar caer sobre ese indio cualquier acusación que sea capaz de inventar.

Porque nos, tenemos la convicción de que muchos de los cargos contra los indios son falsos, y porque nos, tememos por las almas de nuestros compatriotas, quienes aparentemente se están engrandeciendo a sí mismos y a sus propiedades por medios tortuosos, impropios de Cristianos, nos, que sentimos tristeza, hemos actuado. Utilizando la influencia de nuestro título de Protector de los Indios, nosotros hemos tenido éxito en persuadir a los jueces de la Audiencia de que todos los indios que tengan que ser marcados, en el futuro deben ser registrados bajo nuestro cargo. Por eso es que desde ahora los hierros de marcar están encerrados en una caja que se debe abrir con dos llaves y una de éstas está en nuestra posesión.

Ya que ningún indio convicto puede ser marcado sin nuestra colaboración, firmemente, nosotros hemos rehusado en esos casos que son flagrantes abusos de la justicia y esos indios han sido liberados a la fuerza. El ejercer esa autoridad propia de nuestro oficio de Protector de los Indios, nos ha ganado el odio de muchos de nuestros compatriotas, pero podemos sobrellevarlo con ecuanimidad, sabiendo que actuamos para el bien de todos los que están involucrados en eso. Sin embargo, la prosperidad económica de toda la Nueva España podría resentirse (y disminuiría el quinto correspondiente a las riquezas del Rey) si también nos, duramente obstruyéramos el reclutamiento de esclavos de labor, de donde depende la prosperidad de estas colonias. Así es que ahora, cuando un español desea adquirir algún indio como esclavo, no hace uso del arma secular; los cargos que él hace en contra del indio, siendo éste un cristiano converso, es que ha cometido algún *lapsus fidei*. Ya que nuestro oficio de Defensor de la Fe está muy por encima de nuestros otros oficios y de sus problemas, en esos casos nosotros no detenemos el hierro marcador.

Con eso hemos hecho que se cumplieran tres cosas simultáneamente y que estamos seguros que hallarán favor a los ojos de Vuestra Majestad. *Primus*, prevenimos efectivamente la negligencia legal en la ley civil. *Secundus*, firmemente protegemos el dogma de la Iglesia, para que no se deje de observar por los conversos. *Tertius*, no impedimos el mantenimiento de una labor proveedora, firme y adecuada.

Incidentalmente, sepa Vuestra Majestad, que el hierro marcador de mejilla, no lleva más la «G», que impone el deshonor al vencido en guerra. Ahora nosotros, aplicamos las iniciales del nuevo propietario del esclavo (a menos que el convicto sea una bella mujer, cuyo amo no quiera desfigurar). Aparte de que la marca sirve para identificar al propietario y al esclavo que huye, esa clase de señal sirve también para distinguir a esos esclavos desesperados que se rebelan, e incapaces de trabajar. Muchos de esos descontentos intratables, habiendo cambiado varias veces de amo, llevan ahora en sus caras numerosas iniciales sobrepuestas, como si sus pieles fueran un palimpsesto.

Hay un toque evidente de buen corazón, en vuestra última carta, cuando Vuestra Compasiva Majestad hace mención de nuestro cronista el azteca, en lo concerniente a la muerte de su mujer: «Aunque es de una raza inferior, parece un hombre con emociones humanas, capaz de sentir felicidad y dolor tan vehementemente como nosotros.» Vuestra simpatía es muy comprensible, ya que el amor continuo de Vuestra Majestad para vuestra joven Reina Isabel y vuestro hijito Felipe, es un cariño notorio y tierno, muy admirado por todos.

Sin embargo, nos, muy respetuosamente sugerimos que Vos no extendáis demasiado vuestra compasión sobre esas personas que Vuestra Majestad no puede conocer tanto como nos, y especialmente sobre ese que una y otra vez demuestra ser indigno de ello. Éste, ocasionalmente en algún tiempo, pudo sentir emoción o se entretuvo, ocasionalmente, con un pensamiento humano, que no disminuye ante el de un hombre blanco. Sin embargo, Vuestra Majestad habrá notado que aunque él profesa ahora como Cristiano, el viejo chocho murmuró mucho acerca de que su hembra muerta todavía anda vagando por este mundo y ¿por qué? ¡Porque ella no llevaba encima cierto guijarro verde cuando murió! También, como Vuestra Majestad podrá percibir, el azteca no se dejó abatir por mucho tiempo por esa aflicción. En estas siguientes páginas de su narración, él se divierte otra vez como un coloso y vuelve a las antiguas andanzas.

Señor, no hace mucho tiempo, oímos a un sacerdote más sabio que nos, decir esto: «Que ningún hombre puede reír sin reservas, mientras todavía esté vivo y navegando sobre el mar incierto de la vida. Ni él ni ningún otro, puede saber si podrá sobrevivir a todas las tempestades que le acechan y a los arrecifes ocultos y a los cantos perturbadores de las sirenas, para llegar a salvo al puerto. Ese hombre puede considerarse justamente glorificado, cuando Dios sea su guía, de tal manera que él pueda finalizar sus días en el puerto de la Salvación, pues la *Gloria* es cantada solamente al final.»

Quiera Nuestro Señor Dios seguir sonriendo sobre y a favor de Vuestra Imperial Majestad, cuyos reales pies son besados por vuestro capellán y siervo,

(ecce signum) ZUMÁRRAGA

OCTAVA PARS

Mi tragedia personal eclipsó naturalmente todo lo que me rodeaba en el mundo, pero no pude evitar el darme cuenta de que la nación mexica había sufrido también una tragedia, más grande que la demolición de su ciudad capital. La súplica frenética y poco característica de Auítzotl a Nezahualpili, para detener el chorro del manantial, fue su último acto como Uey-Tlatoani. Él estaba dentro de su palacio cuando éste se vino abajo y aunque eso no lo mató, es muy probable que él lo hubiera preferido, ya que fue golpeado en la cabeza por una viga y desde entonces —como me lo contaron, ya que nunca lo volví a ver vivo— quedó tan falto de entendimiento como el madero que lo golpeó. Vagaba sin objeto por los alrededores, hablando incoherentemente consigo mismo, mientras un asistente seguía al que una vez fue un gran estadista y guerrero, por todas partes que fuera, para poder cambiarle el taparrabo que continuamente ensuciaba.

La tradición prohibía que Auítzotl fuera destituido de su título de Venerado Orador, mientras viviera, aunque sólo pudiera decir incoherencias y no pudiera ser venerado más de lo que podría serlo un vegetal ambulante. En lugar de eso, tan pronto como fue factible, el Consejo de Voceros convino en elegir a un regente que guiara a la nación, durante la incapacidad de Auítzotl. Sin duda por venganza, ya que Auítzotl había matado a dos de sus ancianos durante el pánico en el camino-puente, esos viejos rehusaron considerar al candidato más lógico, el primogénito Cuautémoc. Escogieron como regente a su sobrino, Motecuzoma El Joven, porque ellos anunciaron: «Motecuzoma Xocóyotzin ha probado sucesivamente su habilidad como sacerdote, comandante militar y administrador colonial. Como ha viajado mucho, conoce a conciencia todas las tierras más lejanas de los mexica.»

Yo recordé las palabras de Auítzotl, cuando una vez me vociferó: «¡Nosotros no sentaremos sobre este trono a un tambor hueco!» Si Auítzotl hubiera muerto en forma correcta, o sea, con sus cinco sentidos, él habría subido de los abismos más profundos de Mitlan y habría sentado su cadáver sobre el trono en lugar de Motecuzoma. Como llegaron a ponerse las cosas, casi hubiera sido mejor para los mexica, tener a un muerto por gobernante. Un cuerpo, por lo menos se puede mantener en una posición firme.

Pero en aquel tiempo, yo no estaba interesado en absoluto en intrigas de la Corte; yo mismo me estaba preparando para abdicar por un tiempo, por varias razones. Una era que mi casa se había convertido en un lugar de recuerdos dolorosos, del que quería escapar. Incluso el contemplar a mi hija me causaba dolor, porque en su rostro veía mucho de Zyanya. Otra razón era que tenía que inventar algo, de tal manera que Cocoton no sintiera demasiado la pérdida de su madre. Y todavía había otra, que cuando mi amigo Cózcatl y su esposa Quequelmiqui vinieron a confortarme y a darme sus condolencias, dejaron caer la noticia de que estaban sin hogar, ya que su casa había sido una de las que se cayeron con la inundación.

«No estamos tan alicaídos como deberíamos estarlo —dijo Cózcatl—. A decir verdad, nos estábamos sintiendo apretados e incómodos, ya que ambos, nuestro hogar y la escuela, estaban bajo un mismo techo. Ahora que por fuerza tenemos que volver a construir, haremos dos edificios separados.»

«Y mientras tanto —dije— ésta será vuestra casa. Viviréis aquí. De todas maneras yo estoy a punto de partir, así es que la casa y los sirvientes serán todos vuestros. Sólo os pido un favor de compensación. ¿Podréis los dos sustituir a la madre y al padre de Cocoton por el tiempo que yo esté ausente? ¿Podréis jugar a Tene y a Tata para una criatura huérfana?»

Cosquillosa dijo: «¡*Ayyo*, qué idea tan maravillosa!»

Cózcatl dijo: «Lo haremos con mucho gusto... no, con agradecimiento. Será la única vez que nosotros tendremos familia.»

Yo dije: «La niña no da problemas. La esclava Turquesa atiende a sus necesidades diarias. Vosotros no tendréis que hacer nada, más que darle la seguridad de su presencia... y demostrarle afecto de tiempo en tiempo.»

«¡Por supuesto que lo haremos!», exclamó Cosquillosa, y había lágrimas en sus ojos.

Yo continué: «Ya le he explicado a Cocoton, quiero decir que le he mentido, la ausencia de su madre durante estos días pasados. Le dije que su Tene había ido al mercado a comprar las cosas que necesitamos, ella y yo, para el largo viaje que tenemos que hacer. La niña sólo asintió con la cabeza y dijo: "largo viaje", pues para ella, a su edad, significa muy poco. Pero, si vosotros continuáis recordándole a Cocoton que su Tata y su Tene están viajando por lugares lejanos... bien, tengo la esperanza de que se haya acostumbrado a estar sin su madre para cuando yo regrese, así ella no se sentirá demasiado acongojada cuando le diga que su Tene no regresó conmigo.»

«Pero también se acostumbrará a no estar contigo», me previno Cózcatl.

«Supongo que sí —dije resignadamente—. En lo único que puedo confiar, cuando regrese, es que ella y yo nos volvamos a familiarizar. Mientras tanto, yo sé que Cocoton está bien cuidada y que es amada...»

«¡Sí lo será! —dijo Cosquillosa dejando caer su mano sobre mi brazo—. Nosotros viviremos aquí con ella todo el tiempo que sea necesario. Y no dejaremos que te olvide, Mixtli.»

Se fueron a preparar el traslado de las posesiones que habían podido salvar de las ruinas de su casa, y esa misma noche yo hice un fardo de viaje ligero y compacto. Muy temprano, a la mañana siguiente, fui al cuarto de la niña, desperté a Cocoton y le dije a la somnolienta niñita:

«Tu Tene me pidió que te dijera adiós por los dos, Migajita, porque... porque ella no puede dejar a nuestra caravana de cargadores o ellos se escaparían corriendo como unos ratoncitos.

Pero éste es un beso de despedida de parte de ella. ¿No te supo exactamente como a un beso de ella? —Para mi sorpresa, así fue, por lo menos para mí—. Ahora, Cocoton, con tus dedos toma el beso de tu Tene de tus labios y guárdalo en tu mano, así, para que tu Tata pueda besarte también. Ahora pon el mío con el suyo y guarda ambos apretadamente en tu mano, mientras te vuelves a dormir. Cuando te levantes, pon los besos en algún lugar seguro y guárdalos para que nos los vuelvas a dar cuando regresemos.»

«Regresemos», dijo ella adormilada y sonrió y su sonrisa era la de Zyanya y cerró sus ojos, los ojos de Zyanya.

Abajo, Turquesa lloriqueaba y Estrella Cantadora se sonó varias veces las narices mientras nos despedíamos, y entonces les encargué que atendieran bien la casa, y les recordé que hasta mi regreso debían obedecer a Cózcatl y a Quequelmiqui, como su amo y ama.

Me detuve sólo una vez antes de salir de la ciudad, en la Casa de los Pochteca, y dejé un mensaje para que lo llevara la próxima caravana de mercaderes que fuera en dirección de Tecuantépec. El papel doblado era para avisar a Beu Ribé, con las palabras-pintadas menos dolorosas que pude componer, la muerte de su hermana y la forma en que murió. No se me ocurrió pensar que el flujo normal del comercio mexica había sido considerablemente roto, y que mi mensaje tardaría en poder ser entregado.

La franja de *chinampa* que circundaba Tenochtitlan había quedado bajo el agua durante cuatro días, en la estación en que las semillas de maíz, frijol y otras verduras estaban justamente germinando. Aparte de inundar esas plantas, el agua también había invadido los almacenes de semillas, que se conservaban para emergencias, y había arruinado todos los alimentos secos abodegados en ellos. Así es que, durante muchos meses, los *pochteca* mexica y sus cargadores estuvieron solamente ocupados en proveer a la devastada ciudad. Eso los mantuvo viajando constantemente, pero sin separarse mucho de los caminos principales y fue por eso que Luna que Espera no recibió el aviso de la muerte de Zyanya hasta un año más tarde.

Yo también estuve viajando constantemente durante ese tiempo, vagando como una flor de brisa, dejándome llevar hacia donde el viento soplara, o a cualquier parte en donde algún paisaje maravilloso me atrajese, o siguiendo cualquier camino que encontrara y que fuera lo suficientemente tentador, como si por siempre me estuviera diciendo: «Sígueme. Exactamente en el siguiente recodo está la tierra del olvido, en donde los corazones pueden descansar.» Por supuesto que ese lugar no existía. Un hombre puede caminar hasta el final de todos los caminos existentes y hasta el final de sus días, pero no puede deshacerse de su pasado, ni alejarse de él, ni dejar de echar una mirada atrás.

Muchas de mis aventuras durante ese tiempo no valen la pena de ser contadas y no busqué comercio, ni me cargué con nuevas adquisiciones y si hubiera habido algunos descubrimientos fortuitos, como el del colmillo gigante que encontré en otro tiempo, cuando trataba de alejarme de la miseria, pasé sin verlos. La única aventura memorable que tuve, y que caí en ella por accidente, fue la siguiente:

Estaba cerca de la costa del oeste, en la tierra de Nauyar Ixú, una de las provincias o dependencias más remotas hacia el noroeste de Michihuacan. Había estado vagando por allí con el único deseo de ver el volcán que había estado en continua y visible erupción casi por espacio de un mes, y amenazaba con no parar nunca. Al volcán le llaman el Tzebóruko, que quiere decir, El que Bufa con Ira, pero estaba haciendo más que eso: estaba rugiendo con rabia, como una inundación guerrera bajando a las profundidades de Mictlan. Un humo gris negruzco se levantaba por encima de él, lanzando llamas de fuego color jacinto que se elevaban hacia el cielo y había estado así durante tantos días, que el cielo entero estaba sucio y en todo Nauyar Ixú, durante todo el día, pareció como un crepúsculo. De esa nube llovía constantemente una ceniza gris, suave, caliente y acre. Desde el cráter llegaba el incesante gruñido rabioso de la diosa del volcán, Chántico, que lanzaba gotas de fiera lava roja, que desde la distancia parecían piedrecitas que salían disparadas hacia arriba y arrojadas muy lejos, pero eran inmensos peñascos arrojados con violencia.

El Tzebóruko se alzaba exactamente enfrente de un río que cruzaba un valle, y vertía su efusión sobre el cauce de ese río, pero las aguas eran poco profundas, así es que no podían enfriar, endurecer y detener la roca líquida; el agua simplemente chisporroteaba un instante al primer contacto con la lava, luego levantaba una nube de vapor antes de desaparecer bajo el empuje de ésta. Cada ola caliente de ardiente lava, vomitada por el cráter, se deslizaba embravecida a un lado de la montaña, bajando directamente sobre el valle, luego se movía más despacio, hasta que sólo chorreaba enfriándose y tornándose oscura. Pero al endurecerse se convertía en una superficie lisa por la que pasaría la siguiente ola, que llegaría más lejos antes de detenerse. Así, para cuando yo llegué a ver el espectáculo, la lava, como una larga lengua roja, se extendía a lo lejos sobre el río, cuyas aguas cubría. El calor que desprendía la roca fundida y las nubes de vapor eran tan intensos, que no me podía aproximar a ninguna parte de la montaña. Nadie podía, ni nadie lo deseaba. La mayoría de la gente de los alrededores, estaban recogiendo tristemente sus pertenencias para poderse ir lejos. Me explicaron que erupciones pasadas habían desvastado totalmente el río hasta tan lejos que habían alcanzado la costa, quizás unas veinte largas-carreras de largo.

Y esa erupción fue así. Trataré de explicarles, reverendos escribanos, la furia de la erupción, pues es la única forma de que ustedes me crean, cuando les cuente cómo me lanzó finalmente fuera de El Único Mundo, hacia lo desconocido.

No teniendo nada que hacer, pasé algunos días andando alrededor del río de lava, o lo más cerca que pude a un lado de su calor chamusqueante y de sus humos irrespirables, mientras que implacablemente hacía hervir el agua del río, llenando todo su lecho de orilla a orilla. La lava se movía como una ola de cieno, a una velocidad como la del paso de un hombre caminando despacio, así cuando cada noche instalaba mi campamento en algún lugar más alto, comía algo de mis provisiones y me enrollaba en mi cobija para dormir, a la mañana siguiente, cuando despertaba, encontraba que la lava se había movido ya tan lejos de mí que tenía que apurarme para alcanzarla. Pero aunque el Tzebóruko disminuía la distancia detrás de mí, no dejaba de escupir lava, así es que continué acompañando su chorro, sólo para ver hasta dónde *podría* llegar. Después de varios días de continuar así, llegué al océano del oeste.

El valle se estrechaba allí, entre dos tierras altas, y el río desembocaba en las aguas de una playa larga, profunda y ondulante, que formaba una gran bahía de agua color azul turquesa. Allí habían varias cabañas hechas de cañas, pero no se veía a nadie por los alrededores; claramente se notaba que los pescadores, como la gente que vivía tierra adentro, habían huido; pero algunos dejaron sobre la playa varios *acali* de mar con sus remos. Eso me dio la idea de remar mar adentro para poder ver desde la bahía, a una distancia prudente, cómo la lava hacía contacto con el mar. El río, poco profundo, había sido incapaz de resistir el avance de la lava, pero yo sabía que las aguas inextinguibles del océano la detendrían. El encuentro, pensé, debía de ser algo que valiera la pena verse.

Sin embargo, tuve que esperar hasta el siguiente día y para entonces había puesto mi bulto de viaje dentro de una canoa, había remado más allá de las rompientes y estaba exactamente en medio de la bahía. Podía ver a través de mi topacio cómo esa lava sofocante se extendía y arrastraba a través de la playa, avanzando en un ancho frente, hacia la línea del agua. Tierra adentro, casi nada era visible, sólo podía darme cuenta, a través del humo oscuro y de las cenizas que caían, de los relámpagos rojizos y los centelleos refulgentes y ocasionales del Tzebóruko, que seguía vomitando desde las entrañas de Mictlan.

Luego ese cieno rojo ardiente y ondulante, al llegar al agua, pareció vacilar y fruncirse, y en lugar de arrastrarse, chocó ferozmente con el océano. Durante aquellos primeros días, allá en donde estaba el río, cuando la roca fundida y el agua fría se encontraban, el sonido que producían era casi como un chillido humano y un convulsivo jadeo, pero en el mar, el sonido era como un bramido poderoso, lanzado por un dios herido inesperadamente, un dios ultrajado y sorprendido. Fue un tumulto compuesto por dos sonidos: el océano que hirvió tan de repente que estalló en vapor, y la lava que chisporroteó al endurecerse tan repentinamente que saltó en fragmentos a todo lo largo de la orilla del mar. El vapor subió tan alto, como un peñasco hecho de una nube, y una llovizna caliente empezó a caer sobre mí, y mi *acali* bailoteó tan abruptamente que casi me caigo de él. Me cogí de sus laterales y por eso dejé caer los remos por la borda.

La caona continuó caracoleando hacia atrás, conforme el océano reculaba ante ese cieno tan poco amigable. Luego el mar se recobró de su aparente sorpresa, y volvió a romper sobre la playa otra vez, pero la roca fundida seguía avanzando todavía; el clamor era ininterrumpido y la nube se elevaba como si tratara de alcanzar el cielo, que era el lugar al que las nubes pertenecían; y el océano, sintiéndose agraviado, reculaba nuevamente. Esa vasta bahía se movía hacia atrás y hacia adelante cada vez, por una cantidad de veces que no pude ni contar, pues estaba mareado de tanto vaivén. Aunque por lo menos me pude dar cuenta de que esos movimientos me llevaban cada vez más lejos de tierra, mar adentro. En las agitadas aguas que estaban alrededor de mi canoa, que hacía cabriolas, había peces y otras criaturas marinas sobre la superficie, las más de ellas, panza arriba.

Todo el día, hasta cuando el crepúsculo se tornó todavía más oscuro, mi canoa continuó moviéndose, una ola hacia la playa, tres mar adentro. Con la última luz del día, vi que estaba precisamente entre las dos puntas de tierra que le daban entrada a la bahía, pero demasiado lejos para nadar hacia alguna de ellas y más allá estaba el vacío ilimitado del océano. No podía hacer nada, excepto dos cosas. Me incliné sobre la canoa y cogí del agua cuantos pescados muertos pude alcanzar y los amontoné en una de las esquinas de mi canoa. Luego me acosté con mi cabeza sobre mi bulto empapado y me dormí.

Cuando desperté a la mañana siguiente, pude haber pensado que había soñado todo aquel tumulto, excepto porque todavía estaba a merced de las olas en un *acali* y la playa estaba tan lejos que sólo alcanzaba a reconocer sus contornos, por los perfiles dentados de las montañas azul claro. Pero el sol se levantaba sobre un cielo despejado, no había ni señal de humo ni de cenizas, y no se podía ver al Tzebóruko eruptando entre las montañas distantes; el océano estaba tan quieto como el lago de Xaltocan en un día de verano. Usando mi topacio, fijé mi ojo en la línea de tierra y traté de imprimir su perfil en mi visión. Luego cerré mis ojos por unos momentos antes de volverlos a abrir otra vez, para ver si algo había cambiado en la visión que recordaba. Después de haber hecho esto varias veces, me pude dar cuenta de que las montañas que estaban más cerca se movían pasando a las que estaban más atrás, de izquierda a derecha. Entonces, era obvio que había sido arrastrado por una corriente oceánica que me estaba llevando hacia el norte, pero atemorizantemente lejos de la playa.

Traté de desviar la canoa hacia la tierra, intentando remar con mis manos, pero pronto me olvidé del asunto. Había una aleta rondando en la superficie quieta del agua, y algo golpeó tan fuertemente mi canoa, que ésta dio un brinco. Cuando miré hacia ese lado, vi que habían quedado unos profundos arañazos en la fuerte caoba y una aleta vertical, como un escudo de guerra ovalado, cortaba el agua cerca de mí. Le dio la vuelta a mi canoa dos o tres veces antes de desaparecer, con un poderoso giro dentro del agua y desde entonces tuve buen cuidado de no poner ni un dedo fuera de ese refugio protector de madera.

«Bien —me dije—, he escapado de cualquier peligro que me amenazaba en el volcán. Ahora no tengo nada que temer, excepto ser devorado por los monstruos del mar, o morir de hambre o arrugado por el sol y la sed, o perecer ahogado cuando el mar se encrespe.» Pensé acerca de Quetzalcóalt, aquel lejano gobernante de los tolteca, quien de forma parecida había flotado mar adentro en el otro océano del este, y que posteriormente llegó a ser el más querido de todos los dioses, el único dios adorado por pueblos muy distantes unos de otros, que no tenían nada en común. Por supuesto, me recordé a mí mismo, que una multitud de sus respetuosos vasallos habían ido a la playa para verlo partir, y que lo lloraron cuando él no regresó, y después fueron a informar a los otros pueblos de que Quetzalcóatl el hombre debía ser reverenciado como Quetzalcóatl el dios. En cuanto a mí, ni siquiera una simple persona me había visto en la playa, o sabía algo acerca de mí, y era casi seguro que si nunca más volvía, no habría una demanda popular para elevarme a la calidad de dios. «Así —me dije a mí mismo—, ya que no tengo la esperanza de convertirme en un dios, debo hacer lo mejor que puedo para que lo que queda de este hombre, dure el mayor tiempo posible.»

Tenía veintitrés peces, de los que reconocí a diez como pertenecientes a especies comestibles. Dos de ésos los limpié con mi daga y me los comí crudos, aunque no totalmente, por lo menos estaban un poco cocidos por aquella bahía que parecía una caldera. Los otros trece peces, que no sabía si eran comestibles o no, los destripé y haciéndolos tiras los exprimí dentro de mi cuenco para extraer cada gota de su jugo. Guardé en mi bulto de viaje el cuenco y los ocho pescados comestibles que me quedaban, para que no estuvieran expuestos directamente a los rayos del sol. Todavía pude comer dos peces más al día siguiente, pues aún no estaban del todo echados a perder. Pero al tercer día, en verdad que me tuve que forzar a comer dos más, tratando de tragar los pedazos sin masticarlos, de lo resbaladizos y babosos que estaban y tuve que tirar los que me quedaban por la borda. Por algún tiempo, después de eso, mi único alimento, aparte de lamer mis labios dolorosamente agrietados, fue un pequeño sorbo, de vez en cuando, del jugo de pescado contenido en mi cuenco.

Creo que también fue en ese tercer día en el mar, cuando vi por última vez el pico de una montaña, y El Único Mundo desapareció tras el horizonte del este. La corriente me había llevado totalmente fuera de la vista de la tierra y no había ni un lugar alrededor en donde poner pie, y créanme, que nunca antes había tenido esa clase de experiencia en toda mi vida. Me preguntaba si al fin sería arrojado a Las Islas de las Mujeres, de las que había oído muchas historias, aunque ninguno de los que me las contó había estado allí personalmente. De acuerdo con las leyendas, ésas eran unas islas habitadas solamente por mujeres, que pasaban todo el tiempo buceando para encontrar ostras, y luego extraían las perlas-corazón que en esas ostras crecían muy grandes. Sólo una vez al año, las mujeres veían hombres, cuando un número de éstos iban en canoas desde la tierra para hacer un trueque con ellas, de algodón y otras cosas necesarias, a cambio de las perlas recolectadas, y mientras estaban allí, ellos copulaban con las mujeres. De los bebés que luego nacían de ese breve acoplamiento, las mujeres sólo conservaban a las niñas, y a los niños los ahogaban. Por lo menos eso decían las historias que se contaban. Yo medité acerca de lo que me pasaría si desembarcaba en Las Islas de las Mujeres, sin que me esperaran y sin ser invitado. ¿Me matarían inmediatamente o sufriría cierto tipo de violación masiva, a la inversa? Pero nunca llegué a esas islas imaginarias ni a ninguna otra.

Fui impulsado y mecido miserablemente a través de aquellas aguas sin fin. El océano me rodeaba por todas partes y yo me sentía de lo más infeliz, como una hormiga que hubiera caído en el fondo de una urna azul, con paredes tan resbaladizas que era imposible escalar. Las noches no eran tan enervantes, si dejaba a un lado mi topacio y no miraba la profusión abrumadora de estrellas. En la oscuridad, podía imaginarme que estaba en algún lugar a salvo, en cualquier lugar sólido, en un bosque en tierra firme y aun dentro de mi casa. Podía pretender que el movimiento del bote era el de una *gishe*, hamaca, y así quedaba profundamente dormido.

Al paso de los días, sin embargo, ya no pude pretender que estaba en ningún lado que no fuera exactamente en medio de esa inmensidad aterradoramente azul, caliente y sin sombra. Afortunadamente para mi salud mental había algunas cosas que ver durante la luz del día, además de esa extensión de agua sin fin e inhóspita. Aunque algunas de esas otras cosas tampoco eran muy particularmente agradables, me obligué a mí mismo a mirarlas a través de mi cristal, y a examinarlas de cerca, tanto como las circunstancias me lo permitían y a especular acerca de su naturaleza.

Algunas de las pocas cosas que vi, sabía qué eran, aunque nunca las había visto antes. El pez espada de un color azul plata, más grande que yo, que le gustaba brincar fuera del agua y por un momento bailar sobre su cola. También había allí otro tipo de pez espada, todavía más grande, plano y pardo, con aletas planas a lo largo de su cuerpo, como las alas ondulantes de las ardillas voladoras. Yo reconocí a esos peces por sus trompas inicuas, pues los guerreros de algunas tribus de la costa las usaban como armas. Temí que algunos de esos peces pudieran destrozar mi *acali* con sus espadas o trompas, pero ninguno lo hizo.

Otras de las cosas que vi, mientras flotaba en el océano del oeste, eran totalmente desconocidas para mí. Había incontables criaturas pequeñas, con largas aletas que usaban como alas, pues saltaban del agua y se elevaban a distancias prodigiosas. Yo las hubiera tomado por cierta clase de insectos acuáticos, pero uno de ellos cayó en mi canoa, y yo lo agarré y me lo comí casi al instante y sabía a pescado. Había unos grandes peces de un azul grisáceo, inmensos, que me miraban con ojos inteligentes y me sonreían, y eran más simpáticos que amenazantes. Un gran número de ellos acompañaron a mi *acali* por largos períodos y me entretenían haciendo acrobacias en el agua, que practicaban al unísono.

Sin embargo, había un pez al que le tenía mucho miedo; el más grande de todos: unos grises muy grandotes, que de vez en cuando emergían, uno o dos, o muchos de ellos, y por medio día, podían flotar perezosamente, alrededor de mí, como si imploraran un poco de aire fresco y un poco de sol, que es una conducta muy rara en un pez. Y lo que todavía hacían que se parecieran menos a un pez, era su tamaño y forma, pues eran las criaturas más grandes de todas las que yo había visto en mi vida. No los culpo, reverendos frailes, si no me creen, pues cada uno de esos monstruos era tan largo como de un extremo al otro de la plaza que está más allá de esta ventana, y cada uno de ellos era ancho y voluminoso, proporcionado a su longitud. Una vez, cuando estaba en el Xoconochco, muchos años antes, me sirvieron una comida que contenía un pescado llamado *yeyemichi*, y el cocinero me dijo que el *yeyemichi* era el pescado más grande del océano. Lo que yo comí en esa ocasión, en verdad que sólo fue un pedacito de esas grandes pirámides nadadoras que veía entonces en el océano del oeste, y ahora siento de todo corazón no haber buscado y conocido, para expresarle mi admiración, a ese hombre heroico o al ejército de hombres, que capturaron y arrastraron a través de las olas, a ese pez.

Cualquiera de esos *yeyemichtin*, que acostumbraban a jugar en parejas, chocando uno con el otro, hubiera podido desbaratar a mi *acali* y a mí, sin siquiera darse cuenta de ello, pero no lo hicieron. Y no me ocurrió ninguna desventura y en el día seis o siete de mi viaje involuntario, justo a tiempo, porque ya había agotado mi última gota de jugo de pescado y estaba lleno de ampollas, flaco y sin fuerzas, llegó la lluvia, un lluvia que parecía un velo gris que avanzaba por el océano, a un lado de mi bote, y llegó sobre mí, mojándome todo. Me sentí mucho más fresco, y llené mi cuenco y bebí en él dos o tres veces hasta vaciarlo y volverlo a llenar. Entonces empecé a preocuparme un poco, pues la lluvia trajo un viento y éste empezó a levantar las olas del mar. Mi canoa se balanceaba y se movía como si fuera un pedacito de madera, y muy pronto me vi obligado a utilizar mi cuenco para echar toda el agua que había, tirándola por la borda. A pesar de esto, sentí una ligera esperanza, por el hecho de que la lluvia y el viento llegaron detrás de mí, del sudoeste, y acordándome de dónde había estado el sol en aquel momento, juzgué, que por lo menos ya no era empujado mar adentro.

No me importaba mucho en dónde fuera a desembocar, pensé con cansancio, pues aparentemente tenía que desembarcar al fin. Ya que el viento y la lluvia continuaban sin ninguna pausa, y que el océano hacia que mi *acali* continuara bailando, no pude dormir, ni siquiera descansar, pues necesitaba seguir achicando el bote. Estaba tan débil, que mi cuenco me pesaba tanto como si fuera una gran jarra de piedra, cada vez que lo llenaba, lo levantaba y lo vaciaba por la borda. Aunque no pude dormir, poco a poco fui cayendo en una especie de sopor, así es que ahora no les puedo decir cuántos días y cuántas noches pasé así, pero evidentemente durante todo ese tiempo, continué vaciando el bote, como si hubiera llegado a ser un hábito que no se puede romper. Lo que sí recuerdo, es que ya hacia el final, mis movimientos eran cada vez más lentos y el nivel del agua iba subiendo más rápidamente dentro del bote de lo que yo lo podía vaciar. Cuando al fin sentí que el fondo de mi canoa tocaba tierra, supe que al fin había zozobrado y sólo pude medio maravillarme de no sentir que el agua me envolviera, o a los peces jugando con mis cabellos.

Entonces debí de haber perdido todo sentido de consciencia, porque cuando volví en mí, la lluvia había terminado, el sol brillaba en el cielo azul y yo miré a mi alrededor maravillado. En verdad que había zozobrado, pero no a una gran profundidad. El agua me llegaba sólo a la cintura, pues la canoa había tocado fondo en una especie de playa de grava que se extendía a la vista en ambas direcciones, pero no había ningún signo de vida humana. Todavía débil, entumido y empapado, vadeé hacia la playa; allí había palmeras con cocos pero estaba demasiado débil para trepar o para poder tirar uno, o para buscar otro tipo de comida. Traté de hacer un esfuerzo para sacar lo que había en mi bulto, para ponerlo a secar al sol, pero sólo pude gatear hasta la sombra de una palmera y allí volví a quedar inconsciente.

Desperté cuando todo estaba oscuro, y me tomó algunos momentos darme cuenta de que ya no estaba bamboleándome en el mar. No tenía ni la menor idea de dónde *estaba*, pero parecía que no me encontraba solo, pues alrededor de mí oía un ruido misterioso y atemorizante. Era un clic-clic que venía de todas partes y de ningún lado en particular, no era un clic muy fuerte, sino un conjunto de sonidos, como el crujiente crepitar del fuego de una floresta, que avanzaba hacia mí. O hubiera podido ser una multitud de gente, tratando de pasar a hurtadillas sobre mí, pero no totalmente de puntillas, pues se oía como que hollaran cada piedrecita de la playa o rompieran cada varita de las que hubieran.

Empecé a levantarme y mi movimiento hizo que todo ese clic-clic cesara instantáneamente, pero cuando me volví a acostar, ese crujido siniestro se dejó oír de nuevo. El resto de la noche, cada vez que me movía, ese sonido cesaba y luego volvía a empezar. No había usado mi cristal para encender un fuego, cuando todavía estaba consciente y cuando aún había sol, así es que no tenía medios para encenderlo en esos momentos. No pude hacer otra cosa más que yacer inquieto y despierto, y esperar que algo saltara de repente sobre mí, hasta que la primera luz de la aurora me mostró la causa de ese ruido.

A primera vista, hizo que se me pusiera la piel de ganso. Toda la playa, a excepción del pequeño pedazo en que yo yacía, estaba llena de cangrejos verde-parduscos, del tamaño de mi mano, que se movían desmañada y bruscamente, reptando sobre la arena y unos sobre los otros. Eran incontables y de una especie que nunca antes había visto. Los cangrejos nunca han sido criaturas bonitas, pero aquellos que yo conocía por lo menos tenían una forma simétrica. Éstos, no; sus tenazas no eran iguales. Una era larga, pesada y moteada en un color rojo azulado brillante; la otra era larga y plana del color del cangrejo, y era tan delgada que parecía una varita. Cada cangrejo usaba su tenaza delgada a guisa de palo de tambor y la otra tenaza como un tambor, aunque el sonido era muy aburrido y no tenía nada de musical.

El amanecer pareció ser la señal para que cesaran su ridícula ceremonia; la numerosa horda empezó a desaparecer, conforme iban escarbando sus escondrijos en la arena. Sin embargo, yo me las arreglé para agarrar algunos de ellos, sintiendo que me debían algo por haberme hecho pasar una noche llena de ansiedad y de temor, sin poder dormir. Sus cuerpos eran pequeños y contenían muy poca carne bajo sus caparazones, pero sus largas tenazas, que asé en un fuego antes de abrirlas, fueron un delicioso desayuno.

Sintiéndome completamente lleno por primera vez en mucho tiempo y un poco más vivo, me paré frente al fuego y eché un vistazo a mi situación. Estaba de vuelta en El Único Mundo, y ciertamente estaba todavía en su costa oeste, pero incalculablemente mucho más al norte de lo que nunca había estado antes. Como siempre, el mar se extendía al oeste, a todo lo largo del horizonte, pero curiosamente tenía menos oleaje que los mares que había conocido en el sur: no tenía grandes olas retumbantes, ni siquiera una espumosa marejada, sino suaves olas lamiendo la playa. Hacia la otra dirección, hacia el este, más allá de la línea de palmeras y de árboles, se elevaba una cadena de montañas. Se veían formidablemente altas, pero eran agradables a la vista por el verdor de sus bosques, no como esas feas hileras de dos volcanes de roca negra y pardusca en las que hacía poco había estado. No tenía ninguna manera de averiguar cuánto al norte había sido llevado por la corriente oceánica y por la tormenta, pero sabía que si caminaba hacia el sur, a lo largo de la costa, alguna vez llegaría otra vez a la bahía, cerca del Tzebóruko, y allí me encontraría en una nación que me era familiar. Continuando a través de la playa, no tendría tampoco que preocuparme por la comida y la bebida, pues podría vivir de esos cangrejos toca tambores y del agua del coco, si no podía conseguir otra cosa.

Sin embargo, la realidad era que estaba completamente hastiado del océano y quería perderlo de vista. Esas montañas tierra adentro eran totalmente desconocidas para mí, y probablemente estaban habitadas por tribus salvajes que jamás había visto antes. Aun así, no eran más que montañas y yo ya había viajado mucho, y había vivido muy bien con lo que ellas me proporcionaron. Lo que más me atrajo en realidad, fue el hecho de saber que la montaña ofrecía una gran variedad de paisajes, mientras que el mar o la playa no cambiaban nunca. Así es que nada más me quedé en la playa lo suficiente como para reponer mis fuerzas y descansar, durante dos o tres días. Después volví a hacer mi bulto de viaje y me encaminé hacia el este, hacia la primera línea de esas montañas.

Era a mediados de verano, lo que fue una fortuna para mí, pues aun en esa estación las noches eran heladas en aquellas alturas. Las pocas prendas que llevaba y la cobija ya estaban muy maltratadas por el hecho de haber estado mucho tiempo empapada de agua salada. Pero si yo me hubiera aventurado en esas montañas en el invierno, en verdad que habría sufrido mucho, pues los nativos me contaron que los inviernos son tan fríos que entumecen y que cae tanta nieve que se apila hasta alcanzar la estatura de un hombre.

Sí, al fin me encontré con alguna gente, aunque no fue sino hasta después de haber estado en la montaña por varios días, y para entonces yo me preguntaba si El Único Mundo había sido totalmente despoblado por la erupción del Tzebóruko o por algún otro desastre acaecido mientras yo estaba en el mar.

Las personas que encontré pertenecían también a un pueblo muy peculiar. Ellos se llamaban rarámuri, y supongo que siguen llamándose así, una palabra que significa Pies Veloces, y tenían una buena razón para llamarse de tal forma, como ya les contaré. Me encontré al primero de ellos cuando estaba en la cumbre de un peñasco, descansando de una ascensión que me quitó el aliento y admirando una vista como para dejarle a uno boquiabierto. Miraba una barranca completamente vertical y profundamente bella, cuyas laderas estaban festonadas de árboles emplumados. En su fondo corría un río que era alimentado por una cascada que borboteaba de una hendidura en la cumbre de la montaña, al otro lado del cañón en donde yo estaba parado. La cascada debía de haber medido una media larga-carrera hacia abajo, y empezaba en una poderosa columna de agua blanca y terminaba en el fondo con un poderoso penacho de espuma blanca. Estaba admirando ese espectáculo cuando oí un grito:

«¡Kuira-ba!»

Yo me sorprendí de momento, porque era la primera voz humana que oía después de mucho tiempo, pero como sonó lo suficientemente alegre, yo lo tomé por un saludo. El que había gritado era un hombre joven y venía sonriendo hacia mí, a lo largo de la orilla del peñasco. Su rostro era hermoso, con la misma hermosura de un halcón, y estaba bien constituido aunque era un poco más bajo de estatura que yo. Estaba vestido decentemente, aunque descalzo, pero para entonces yo iba igual, pues mis sandalias hacía mucho tiempo que se habían deshecho. Además de su taparrabo de piel de cuero de venado, él llevaba un manto de la misma piel alegremente pintado, en un estilo nuevo para mí, porque tenía mangas largas para que diera más calor.

Conforme iba subiendo hacia mí, yo le devolví el saludo de «Kuira-ba». Él indicó la catarata que yo estaba admirando y sonriendo tan orgulloso como si él fuera su dueño, dijo: «Basaséachic», que yo tomé por Agua que Cae ya que a una cascada no se le puede llamar por otro nombre. Yo repetí esa palabra, pero la repetí con mucho sentimiento, para convencerlo de que yo pensaba que esa agua era maravillosa, y que su caída era impresionante. El joven, apuntándose a sí mismo, me dijo: «Tesdisora», obviamente su nombre, y que significaba, según supe después, Tallo de Maíz. Yo también me apunté y dije «Mixtli», y apunté a una nube del cielo. Él asintió con la cabeza, luego golpeándose ligeramente el pecho dijo: «Raramurime», luego indicándome a mí, dijo: «Chichimecame.»

Yo negué enfáticamente con mi cabeza, y golpeando mi pecho desnudo dije: «¡Mexícatl!», a lo cual, él sólo movió la cabeza asintiendo otra vez, con indulgencia, como si yo sólo hubiera especificado una de las numerosas tribus de los chichimeca, la Gente Perro. Hasta mucho más tarde, no comprendí que los rarámuri jamás habían oído hablar de nosotros los mexica, ni de nuestra civilizada sociedad, ni de nuestros conocimientos y poder, ni de nuestros extensos y lejanos dominios, y creo que les hubiera importado muy poco, si hubieran oído hablar de todo eso. Los rarámuri llevaban una vida muy cómoda dentro de sus escondidas montañas, bien alimentados y con bastante agua, contentos con ellos mismos, muy raras veces viajaban más lejos. Así es que no conocían a otros pueblos, más que a sus vecinos, quienes ocasionalmente hacían alguna correría por sus territorios, o buscaban alimento, o simplemente vagaban como yo lo había hecho.

Al norte de su territorio, vivían los terribles yaki, y ningún pueblo en sus cinco sentidos deseaba tener alguna familiaridad con ellos. Yo recordé a los yaki por lo que me había contado aquel viejo *pochtécatl*, a quien le habían quitado el cuero cabelludo. Cuando más tarde pude entender mejor el lenguaje de Tes-disora, éste me contó más sobre ellos: «Los yaki son tan salvajes como las fieras más terribles. Por taparrabos, ellos usan el cabello de otros hombres. Antes de matar a un hombre, primero le quitan el cuero cabelludo, luego lo matan, lo desmembran y lo devorán. Mira, si ellos lo matan primero, entonces sus cabellos no tienen ningún valor y no vale la pena usarlos. Y el cabello de las mujeres no tiene ningún valor. Las mujeres que ellos capturan, sólo sirven para comer, por supuesto después de haberlas violado tantas veces que ya se parten por sí mismas, y cuando ya no sirven para eso, entonces se las comen.»

Al sur de las montañas de los rarámuri, viven otras tribus más pacíficas, relacionadas con ellos por similares lenguajes y costumbres. A lo largo de la costa del mar del oeste, habitan tribus de pescadores que casi nunca se aventuran tierra adentro. Todas esas tribus, si no se les podía llamar lo que se dice civilizadas, por lo menos eran limpias de cuerpo y aseadas en sus vestiduras. Los únicos vecinos de los rarámuri que eran desaliñados y sucios eran los chichimeca, las tribus que habitan los desiertos del este.

Estaba tan quemado por el sol como cualquier chichimécatl, que residía en el desierto y casi tan desnudo. A los ojos de ese rarámuri, solamente podía haber pertenecido a esa despreciable raza, aunque quizás un raro espécimen por haberme tomado la molestia de escalar las alturas de la montaña. Creo que en nuestro primer encuentro, por lo menos Tes-disora se dio cuenta de que yo no apestaba. Gracias a la gran abundancia de agua en esas montañas, me había podido bañar diariamente, y como los rarámuri, lo continué haciendo. Pero a pesar de mi evidente gentileza, a pesar de mi insistencia acerca de que era un mexícatl, a pesar de mi reiterada glorificación hacia esa nación tan lejana, nunca persuadí ni siquiera a una sola persona entre los rarámuri de que no era un «chichimecame» del desierto, fugitivo.

Bueno, no importa. Si ellos me creyeron o no, si ellos sólo pensaron que yo estaba pretendiendo ser de otra nación, de todas maneras los rarámuri me dieron la bienvenida hospitalariamente. Me quedé por un tiempo entre ellos, no por otra cosa, sino porque tenía curiosidad y me intrigaba su género de vida y disfrutaba compartiéndola con ellos. Me quedé lo suficiente como para aprender bastante de su lenguaje, como para sostener una conversación por lo menos con la ayuda de muchos gestos, por mi parte y por la de ellos. Por supuesto que durante mi primer encuentro con Tes-disora *toda* nuestra comunicación fue a base de gestos.

Después de habernos dicho nuestros nombres, usó sus manos sobre su cabeza para indicar un refugio —supuse que con ello, quería significar una aldea— y dijo: «Guagüey-bo», y apuntó hacia el sur. Luego él indicó a Tonatíu en el cielo, llamándolo «Ta-tevarí», o Abuelo Fuego, e hizo que comprendiera que llegaríamos a la aldea de Guagüey-bo en una jornada que duraría tres soles. Yo hice gestos con mis manos y mi rostro de agradecimiento ante su invitación, y fuimos en esa dirección. Para mi sorpresa Tes-disora empezó a trotar a largos pasos, pero cuando vio que yo estaba cansado, sin aliento y no podía seguir corriendo, él trotó hacia atrás y desde entonces caminó a mi paso. Por lo visto acostumbraba a cruzar montañas y cañones trotando de aquella manera, y aunque yo tenía piernas largas nos tomó cinco días caminando a mi paso, en lugar de tres, llegar a Guagüey-bo.

Durante el camino, antes de llegar, Tes-disora me dio a entender que él era uno de los cazadores de la aldea. Por medio de gestos yo le pregunté que cómo era eso posible, si él no llevaba nada en las manos. ¿Dónde estaban sus armas? Él sonrió e hizo que dejara de andar, me hizo señas para que nos agacháramos bajo unos arbustos. Sólo esperamos, allí en la floresta, un momento, luego Tes-disora me dio un codazo y me señaló un lugar, yo sólo pude ver vagamente una sombra veteada que se movía entre unos árboles. Antes de que pudiera levantar mi cristal, Tes-disora saltó de repente de donde estaba, y salió disparado como una flecha lanzada desde el arco.

El bosque era tan espeso, que ni aun con la ayuda de mi topacio pude seguir cada momento de la «cacería», pero vi lo suficiente como para quedarme con la boca abierta, sin poder creer lo que veía. Esa forma veteada era una joven gacela que había huido, casi al mismo instante que Tes-disora había salido en persecución de ella. La gacela corría muy rápido, pero él lo era todavía más. Corrió zigzagueante todo el tiempo, pero de algún modo, él se anticipaba a cada uno de sus movimientos, de su desesperada carrera. En menos tiempo del que yo tardo en contarlo, él se acercó a la gacela, cayó sobre ella de un brinco y le rompió el cuello con sus propias manos.

Mientras comíamos la carne de uno de los animales cazados, por medio de gestos le demostré a Tes-disora mi asombro ante su rapidez y agilidad. Él me respondió igualmente, con modestia, que era uno de los corredores menos ágiles de los Pies Veloces, pues había otros cazadores que corrían mucho más rápido, y que en todo caso, una gacela no era un reto comparado con un venado totalmente desarrollado. Entonces, él a su vez, me demostró por gestos, su asombro ante el cristal que había usado para encender el fuego para cocinar. Él me dio a entender que nunca había visto un instrumento tan útil y maravilloso en posesión de ningún otro bárbaro.

«¡Mexícatl!», repetí varias veces muy enojado. Él sólo asintió con su cabeza y dejó de hablar, tanto con la boca como con las manos, ocupando éstas en comer con gran apetito la suave carne asada.

✠

Guagüey-bo estaba situada en otra de las espectaculares barrancas de aquella nación, y era una aldea, en el sentido de que abrigaba a varias veintenas de familias, quizás unas trescientas personas, pero sólo tenía una residencia visible, una pequeña casa muy limpia, hecha de madera, en donde vivía el Si-ríame. La palabra significa: jefe, brujo, doctor y juez, pero no quiere decir que sean cuatro personas; en una comunidad rarámuri todos esos oficios eran investidos a una sola persona. La casa del Si-ríame y varias otras estructuras —unas casitas de vapor con techo de arcilla, algunos refugios enramados que hacían las veces de bodega, una plataforma con el piso de laja, para ceremonias comunitarias— se encontraban en el fondo del cañón, a lo largo de la ribera de una corriente de agua clara, que lo cruzaba. El resto de la población de Guagüey-bo vivía en cuevas, ya sean naturales o excavadas en las paredes que se elevaban a ambos lados de la inmensa hondonada.

El hecho de que los rarámuri habitaran en cuevas, no quiere decir que fueran primitivos o débiles, sino más bien prácticos. Si todos ellos lo hubieran querido, habrían podido tener casas, tan buenas como la del Si-ríame. Pero las cuevas estaban disponibles o fáciles de excavar, y sus ocupantes las convertían en viviendas muy agradables. Dividían una estancia muy amplia de roca, en varios cuartos y cada uno tenía una abertura para dejar entrar luz y aire. Cubrían el suelo con olorosas ramitas de pino, que parecía una alfombra, y diariamente renovaban esas ramitas. Las aberturas exteriores se cubrían con cortinas y sus paredes estaban decoradas con pieles de venados pintadas en vívidos dibujos. Esas habitaciones-cuevas eran tan cómodas, confortables y bien orientadas como muchas de las casas de la ciudad en las que había estado.

Tes-disora y yo llegamos a la aldea, moviéndonos con toda la rapidez que nos permitía la percha que teníamos entre los dos. Quizá suene increíble, pero esa misma mañana, muy temprano, él había corrido detrás de un gran venado matándolo, de una gacela y de un verraco de buen tamaño. Les quitamos las tripas a todos los animales y después de desmembrarlos, nos apuramos para llegar a Guagüey durante la mañana, cuando todavía hacía fresco. La aldea rebosaba de comida que sus cazadores y recolectadores de frutas habían llevado, porque, según me informó Tes-disora, el festival *tes-güinápuri* estaba por llegar. Silenciomente me felicité a mí mismo por haber tenido la buena suerte de encontrar a ese rarámuri, en un momento en que todos ellos se sentían hospitalarios. Sin embargo, luego me di cuenta de que solamente por una verdadera casualidad no hubiera podido encontrar a ningún rarámuri gozando de una festividad, o preparándose para una, o descansando de una. Sus ceremonias religiosas no eran solemnes, sino muy alegres —la palabra *tes-güinápuri* puede ser traducida como «ahora, pongámonos borrachos»— y en total esas ceremonias ocupaban la tercera parte de un año completo de los rarámuri.

Ya que sus bosques y ríos les daban gratis caza y comida, cueros y pieles, fuego y agua, los rarámuri no tenían necesidad como otros pueblos de trabajar para poder suplir las necesidades de la vida. Lo único que ellos cultivaban era el maíz, pero la mayor parte de él no era para comer, sino para hacer el *tesgüino*, un brebaje fermentado que de alguna manera era más embriagador que el *octli* que nosotros los mexica bebíamos, y un poquito menos que el *chápari*, el licor de miel de abeja de los purémpecha. Al este de las montañas, en las tierras más bajas, los rarámuri recolectaban un pequeño cacto muy potente, que se podía masticar y al que llamaban *jípuri*, que quiere decir «la luz de Dios», por razones que luego explicaré. Teniendo tan poco trabajo que hacer y tanto tiempo libre, ese pueblo tenía muy buena razón para pasar una tercera parte del año alegremente borrachos con *tesgüino* y dichosamente drogados con *jípuri* y placenteramente dándoles gracias a los dioses por su bondad.

En el camino a la aldea, yo aprendí de Tes-disora algunas palabras de su lenguaje y después tanto él como yo nos comunicamos con más facilidad. Así es que dejaré de mencionar nuestros gestos y muecas y sólo contaré la substancia de nuestras siguientes conversaciones. Cuando hubimos entregado nuestra cacería a unas viejas que se encargaban de los grandes fuegos para cocinar, que estaban a un lado del río, él me sugirió que fuéramos a sudar a una de las casas de vapor, para bañarnos. También me sugirió con cierta delicadeza, que después de bañarme me proveería de ropa limpia, si no me importaba tirar los harapos que traía al fuego. Yo estaba encantado de complacerlo.

Una vez que nos desvestimos a la entrada de la casa de vapor, me llevé una ligera sorpresa al ver a Tes-disora desnudo pues observé que le crecían unos mechones de pelo abajo de los sobacos y otro entre las piernas, e hice un comentario al respecto. Tes-disora sólo se encogió de hombros, y apuntando su vello dijo: «Raramurime», y luego apuntando mi carencia de vello dijo: «Chichimecame.» Lo que quiso decir fue que él no era una rareza; a los rarámuri les crecía abuntante *ymaxtli* alrededor de los genitales y bajo sus brazos; a los chichimeca, no.

«Yo no soy de los chichimeca», le contesté, pero lo dije abstraído, pues estaba pensando. De todos los pueblos que había conocido, sólo a los rarámuri les crecía ese pelo superfluo. Supuse que eso se debía al tiempo extremadamente frío que tenían que soportar durante parte del año, ya que no había visto ese vello en los lugares en donde esa protección contra el frío no era necesaria. Y entonces se me ocurrió otro pensamiento y le pregunté a Tes-disora:

«¿Vuestras mujeres tienen ese mismo vello?»

Él se rió y dijo que claro que lo tenían. Me explicó que la presencia de ese *ymaxtli*, vello, era uno de los primeros signos de que la niñez se aproximaba a la juventud. Lo mismo en los hombres que en las mujeres, ese vello se convertía en cabello, no un cabello largo y no era una molestia ni un impedimento, pero sin lugar a dudas, era pelo. También había observado, en los breves momentos que llevaba en la aldea, que la mayor parte de las mujeres rarámuri, aunque muy musculosas, eran muy bien formadas y muy bellas de cara. Lo que quiere decir que yo ya las había encontrado atractivas, aun antes de saber esa distintiva peculiaridad, lo que me hacía preguntarme: ¿qué se sentirá al copular con una mujer cuyo *tepili* no fuera del todo visible, o sólo velado por un fino vello, sino totalmente obscurecido y atormentadoramente escondido tras un pelo como el de su cabeza?

«Fácilmente lo puedes averiguar —dijo Tes-disora, como si él hubiera podido adivinar mi pensamiento—. Durante los juegos de *tes-güinápuri*, simplemente caza a una mujer, corre detrás de ella y así podrás verificar por ti mismo ese hecho.»

Cuando entré en Guagüey-bo, fui objeto de ciertas miradas, muy comprensibles, de preocupación y desprecio por algunos de los aldeanos, pero cuando salí peinado, limpio y vistiendo un taparrabos y un manto de mangas largas, de piel de venado, no me miraron ya más con desdén. Desde entonces, y a excepción de las risitas que se echaban cuando yo cometía grandes errores al hablar en su lenguaje, los rarámuri fueron muy corteses y amistosos conmigo. Y mi estatura excepcional, atrajo sobre mí algunas miradas especulativas y aun de admiración de parte de las muchachas y las solteras de la aldea. Me pareció que había algunas entre ellas que estarían muy gustosas de correr para darme caza.

Casi siempre estaban corriendo, a cualquier parte, *todos* los rarámuri, hombres o mujeres, jóvenes o viejos. Excepto los que estaban en edad de hacer pinitos o en la edad senil, todos los demás corrían durante todo el tiempo del día, a menos que estuvieran inmovilizados por hacer alguna tarea o llenos de *tesgüino* o deslumbrados con la luz del dios, el *jípuri*, ellos corrían. Cuando no estaban corriendo en parejas o en grupos, lo hacían solos, hacia un lado y otro del cañón, o hacia arriba y hacia abajo de la barranca. Los hombres corrían usualmente, golpeando con los pies una pelota, ésta era totalmente redonda y cuidadosamente pulida, hecha de dura madera y del tamaño de la cabeza de un hombre. Las mujeres corrían usualmente, también, llevando en sus manos un aro hecho de mimbre, que empujaban con un palito, una lo tiraba primero lo más lejos que podía, y los otras corrían compitiendo para poder alcanzar el aro y lanzarlo a su vez. Todo ese movimiento frenético e incesante me pareció que tenía muy poco objeto hasta que Tes-disora me explicó:

«En parte es para mantenernos alegres y conservar nuestra energía animal, pero es algo más que eso. Es una ceremonia incesante con la cual, después de hacer ese ejercicio y de sudar mucho, rendimos homenaje a nuestros dioses Ta-tevarí, Ka-laumarí y Ma-tinierí.»

Difícilmente podía imaginarme a cualquier dios que necesitara ser nutrido con sudor en lugar de sangre, pero los rarámuri habían escogido esos que Tes-disora había nombrado, y cuyos nombres significaban Abuelo Fuego, Madre Agua y Hermano Venado. Quizás la religión reconozca a otros dioses, pero ésos son los únicos tres que nunca antes había oído mencionar. Considerando las pocas necesidades de los habitantes de la floresta, los rarámuri, supongo que ésos eran suficientes.

Tes-disora dijo: «Nuestras continuas carreras son para demostrar a nuestros dioses creadores que la gente que ellos crearon todavía están vivos, felices y muy agradecidos de ser así. También mantiene a nuestros hombres en buen estado para los rigores de la caza. También es una práctica para los juegos que vas a ver, o a tomar parte en ellos, espero, durante este festival. Y esos juegos son solamente una práctica.»

«Ten la bondad de decirme —le dije suspirando, y sintiéndome cansado sólo de oírle hablar de tanto ejercicio—, ¿practicar para qué?»

«Para la *verdadera* carrera, por supuesto. El *ra-rajípuri*. —Sonrió ante la expresión de mi rostro—. Ya lo verás. Es el gran final de toda celebración.»

El *tes-güinápuri* tuvo lugar al día siguiente, cuando toda la población de la aldea se reunió a un lado del río, en la casa de madera esperando a que el Si-ríame saliera y ordenara que las festividades empezaran. Todo el mundo estaba vestido con sus mejores trajes, los más finos y mejor decorados en colores; la mayoría de los hombres con mantos y taparrabos de piel de venado y las mujeres con faldas y blusas de la misma piel. Muchos de los aldeanos, habían pintado sus rostros con puntos y rayas onduladas en color amarillo brillante, y muchos llevaban plumas en sus cabellos, aunque los pájaros de esas regiones no tienen plumas muy deslumbrantes. Muchos de los cazadores veteranos de Guagüey-bo ya estaban sudando, pues llevaban puestos trofeos que ya habían ganado: trajes largos hasta los tobillos hechos con piel de cuguar o chaquetas de pieles pesadas o gruesas del gran saltador, de cuernos grandes, de la montaña.

El Si-ríame salió de la casa, su traje estaba hecho totalmente con brillantes pieles de jaguar, llevaba un gran bastón rematado en su punta por una bola de plata en bruto. Estaba tan asombrado, que levanté mi topacio para estar seguro de lo que veía. Habiendo oído que el jefe debía ser sabio, brujo, juez y doctor, naturalmente había esperado que toda esa maravilla estuviera en la persona de un hombre viejo y de cara solemne. Pero no era un hombre, no era viejo, no era solemne. Ella no era más vieja que yo, y era muy bonita y todavía me lo pareció más cuando sonrió.

«¿Vuestro Si-ríame es una mujer?», exclamé cuando empezaban a rezar sus oraciones ceremoniales.

«¿Y por qué no?», dijo Tes-disora.

«Nunca había oído de un pueblo que escogiera a un gobernante que no fuera un hombre.»

«Nuestro último Si-ríame fue un hombre. Pero cuando un Si-ríame muere, cualquier otra persona madura de la aldea, ya sea hombre o mujer, puede ser elegida para sucederle. Todos nos reunimos, masticamos mucho *jípuri* y nos ponemos en trance. Vemos visiones y unos corren salvajemente, mientros otros tienen convulsiones. Pero esta mujer fue la única bendecida por la luz-del-dios, o por lo menos fue la primera en despertar y decirnos que había visto y hablado con el Abuelo Fuego, con la Madre Agua y con el Hermano Venado. Indudablemente que la luz-del-dios resplandeció sobre ella, y ése es el único y supremo requisito para llegar a ser el Si-ríame.»

La bella mujer terminó su canto, sonrió otra vez y elevó sus bien formados brazos en una bendición general, luego dándose la vuelta volvió a entrar en la casa, mientras la multitud la aplaudía con afecto respetuoso.

«¿Ella se queda recluida?», pregunté a Tes-disora.

«Durante los festivales, sí —dijo, y luego riéndose entre dientes continuó—: Algunas veces durante el *tes-güinápuri*, nuestra gente tiene muy mala conducta. Se pelean entre ellos, cometen adulterios o algunas otras travesuras. La Si-ríame es una mujer sabia. Lo que ella no ve o no oye, no lo castiga.»

Yo no sabía qué era lo que ellos llamaban travesuras, pero lo que yo tenía intención de hacer era: cazar, coger y copular con el más deseable y disponible ejemplar femenino de los rarámuri. Pero como las cosas sucedieron, no hice eso exactamente... y, lejos de castigarme, fui recompensado de alguna manera.

Primero lo que ocurrió fue que, como todos los aldeanos, me convertí en un glotón, comiendo toda clase de carne de venado, *atoli* de maíz y bebí el pesado *tesgüino*. Luego, demasiado pesado para ponerme de pie y demasiado borracho para poder caminar, traté de unirme a algunos de los hombres en su juego pateador-de-pelota, pero de todas maneras hubiera estado fuera de poder competir con ellos aunque hubiera estado en la mejor condición física. Eso no me importó. Así que me dejé caer al suelo para observar el juego de las mujeres que corrían tras el aro, con su palito, y cierta muchachita núbil que estaba entre ellas atrajo mi ojo. Y digo un ojo, porque si no cerraba uno veía a dos muchachitas en lugar de una. Caminé bamboleante hacia ella, moviéndome desmañadamente y preguntándole con lengua estropajosa que si quería dejar al grupo para tomar parte en un juego diferente.

Sonrió condescendiente, pero eludió mi mano que quería agarrarla. «Tienes que cazarme primero», dijo y volviéndose echó a correr a lo largo del cañón.

Aunque no esperaba sobresalir entre los corredores rarámuri, sí estaba seguro que podría correr tras cualquier mujer, pero detrás de aquélla no lo pude hacer, aunque sospecho que ella detuvo adrede su paso para hacerme la carrera más fácil. Quizás hubiera podido hacerlo mejor, de no estar tan ahíto de comida y de bebida, especialmente de bebida. Con un ojo cerrado es muy difícil de medir las distancias, y aunque la muchacha hubiera estado sin moverse enfrente de mí, probablemente hubiera fallado al tratar de agarrarla. Y con mis dos ojos abiertos, todo a mi paso se veía doble... raíces, rocas y todas esas cosas... y siempre que trataba de pasar entre esas dos cosas, invariablemente tropezaba con una de ellas. Después de nueve o diez caídas, traté de saltar el siguiente doble obstáculo, una larguísima piedra, y caí a través de ella sobre mi barriga, tan pesadamente que todo el aire se me salió del cuerpo.

La muchacha me había estado observando por encima de su hombro y pretendiendo huir siempre, pero cuando me caí, ella se detuvo y regresó a donde yo estaba y parándose sobre mi cuerpo aporreado dijo con cierta exasperación:

«A menos de que me cojas, podremos jugar el otro juego. Tú sabes a lo que me refiero.»

Ni siquiera pude jadear pues estaba doblado dolorosamente, tratando de aspirar aire, y me sentía incapaz de jugar cualquier tipo de juego. Ella me miraba ceñuda y enfurruñada, y probablemente compartía la baja opinión que tenían de mí, pero de pronto sus ojos se iluminaron y me dijo:

«No pensé en preguntártelo. ¿Mascaste tu parte de *jípuri*?»

Yo negué débilmente con la cabeza.

«Eso lo explica todo. No es que seas inferior, lo que pasa es que los otros hombres tienen la ventaja de haber reforzado su fuerza y vigor. ¡Ven! ¡Debes mascar un poco de *jípuri*!»

Yo todavía estaba doblado como una pelota, pero ya había empezado a respirar otra vez, y no pude rehusarme a obedecer su imperiosa orden. Así es que dejé que me tomara de la mano y me llevara otra vez al centro de la aldea. Ya sabía qué era el *jípuri* y qué efectos producía, pues se importaba también a Tenochtitlan, en pequeñas cantidades, en donde se llamaba *péyotl* y era reservado exclusivamente para los sacerdotes adivinos. El *jípuri* o *péyotl* es un pequeño cacto, que, en forma muy engañosa, parece muy insignificante. Es redondo y parece una pelotita, crece muy pegado al suelo y rara vez alcanza el tamaño de la palma de la mano y está dividido en gajos o bulbos, parece una calabaza muy fina de un color verde grisáceo. Para poder aprovechar su efecto más potente, se debe mascar cuando está recién cortado. Sin embargo, se puede secar al sol y guardarse indefinidamente, colgándose y amarrándose de unas cuerdas, y en la aldea de Guagüey-bo había muchos de esos cordones colgando de las varas de sus enramados lugares de almacenaje. Iba a coger uno, cuando mi acompañante me dijo:

«Espera. ¿Alguna vez has mascado *jípuri?*»

Otra vez, negué con mi cabeza.

«Entonces tú eres un *ma-tuane*, un hombre que busca por primera vez la luz-del-dios y eso requiere una ceremonia de purificación. No, no suspires así. Eso no hará que nuestro... nuestro juego tenga que esperar. —Ella miró en derredor y vio que los aldeanos todavía estaban comiendo o bebiendo o danzando o corriendo—. Todo el mundo está demasiado ocupado como para participar, pero la Si-ríame no está haciendo nada. Ella estará muy contenta en administrarte la purificación.»

Así es que fuimos a la simple casa de madera y la muchacha tiró de un cordón de conchas que estaba colgado a un lado de la puerta. La mujer-jefe, todavía llevando su traje de piel de jaguar, levantó la cortina de piel de venado y dijo:

«*Kuira-ba*», y nos hizo un gracioso gesto para que entráramos.

«Si-ríame —dijo mi compañera—, éste es el chichimecame llamado Mixtli, que ha venido a visitar nuestra aldea. Como tú puedes ver él ya tiene cierta edad, pero es muy mal corredor aun para su edad. No me pudo coger cuando trató de hacerlo. Yo creo que el *jípuri* puede dar agilidad a sus viejas piernas, pero él dice que nunca antes ha buscado la luz-del-dios, así es que...»

Los ojos de la mujer-jefe brillaron divertidos, mientras me miraba de extraña manera, durante ese discurso tan poco ceremonioso. Yo murmuré: «No soy un chichimecame», pero me ignoró y dijo a la muchacha:

«Y por supuesto, tú estás ansiosa de que él tenga su iniciación de *ma-tuane* lo más pronto posible. Bien, lo haré con mucho gusto.» Ella me miró de arriba abajo apreciativamente, y su mirada dejó de ser divertida para dar paso a otra cosa. «Sin importar cuántos años tenga, este Mixtli parece ser muy buen espécimen, considerando especialmente su bajo origen. Y voy a darte un pequeño consejo, que nunca escucharás de nuestros hombres. Aunque tú esperas, de la mejor manera, admirar la media pierna, digámoslo así, de un hombre en una carrera, compitiendo, con lo cual demostraría mejor su hombría, yo puedo decirte que aun el mejor miembro cae en desuso, cuando el hombre dedica toda su atención en desarrollar todos los músculos a excepción de ése. Así es que no desdeñes tan rápido a un corredor mediocre, antes de examinar sus demás atributos.»

«Sí, Si-ríame —dijo la muchacha con impaciencia—. Tengo la intención de que él desarrolle algo muy parecido.»

«Lo podrás intentar después de la ceremonia, así es que te puedes ir, querida.»

«¿Irme? —protestó la joven—. ¡Pero si no hay ningún secreto en la iniciación de un *ma-tuane*! ¡Toda la aldea mira siempre!»

«Pero no vamos a interrumpir la celebración de *tes-güinápuri*. Y este Mixtli es extraño a nuestras costumbres. Él puede sentirse embarazado ante esa horda de mirones.»

«¡Yo no soy una horda! ¡Y yo soy quien lo ha traído a su purificación!»

«Lo tendrás otra vez cuando la purificación esté hecha. Entonces podrás juzgar por ti misma si valió la pena el que te tomaras la molestia. Te he dicho que te vayas. —Mirándonos furiosa la muchacha se fue y la Si-ríame me dijo—: Siéntate, invitado Mixtli, mientras yo mezclo un poco de hierbas para aclarar tu cerebro. No debes emborracharte cuando vayas a mascar *jípuri*.»

Me senté en el piso de tierra alfombrado por ramitas de pino. Ella puso una hierba a hervir a fuego lento, en el hogar que estaba en un rincón, y luego volvió con una pequeña jarra. «Es el jugo de la planta sagrada *urá*», y ella la describió luego utilizando una pluma como pincel, me pintó en las mejillas y en la frente unos círculos, espirales y puntos con un color amarillo brillante.

«Bien —dijo ella después de haberme dado a beber el brebaje, que como por arte de magia, me quitó el atontamiento—. No sé qué quiere decir exactamente Mixtli, pero como un *ma-tuane* en busca de la luz-del-dios por primera vez, debes escoger un nombre nuevo.»

Casi solté la carcajada. Hacía ya tanto tiempo que había perdido la cuenta de todos los nombres viejos y nuevos que había tenido que llevar durante mi vida, pero solamente dije: «Mixtli significa esas cosas que cuelgan en el cielo y creo que los rarámuri llaman *kurú*.»

«Ése es un buen nombre, pero necesita una descripción adicional. Nosotros te llamaremos Su-kurú.»

Y no me reí. Su-kurú significa Nube Oscura y no me explicó cómo pudo saber que ése *era* mi verdadero nombre. Sin embargo, luego recordé que la Si-ríame tenía reputación, entre otras cosas, como adivina y supuse que su luz-del-dios podría enseñarle verdades ocultas a las demás gentes.

«Y ahora, Su-kurú —dijo ella—, debes confesar todos los pecados que has cometido durante tu vida.»

«Mi Señora Si-ríame —dije sin ningún sarcasmo—, probablemente no me alcanzaría toda la vida que tengo para contarlos.»

«¿De veras? ¿Tantos son? —me miró pensativamente y luego dijo—: Bien, como la verdad de la luz-del-dios sólo reside en nosotros los rarámuri y a nosotros nos corresponde el compartirlo, entonces sólo confiesa los pecados que has hecho mientras has estado con nosotros. Dime ésos.»

«No he cometido ninguno. O por lo menos ninguno que yo sepa.»

«Oh, no necesitas haber hecho alguno. Desear haberlo hecho es lo mismo. Sentir ira u odio, o desear vengarse o haberte entretenido con pensamientos o emociones que no son buenos. Por ejemplo, tú querías dejar caer toda tu lujuria sobre esa muchacha, pues claramente querías cazarla con ese propósito.»

«No, no con lujuria, mi señora, sino con curiosidad.»

Ella me miró perpleja, así es que le expliqué todo acerca del *ymaxtli*, el pelo que nunca antes había visto en otros cuerpos y las urgencias que eso despertó en mí. Ella soltó la carcajada.

«¡Vaya con este bárbaro, intrigado por una cosa que una persona civilizada halla tan natural! ¡Podría apostar, que sólo hace unos cuantos años que vosotros los salvajes, habéis dejado de mistificaros con fuego!»

Después de que se rió y se mofó de mí todo lo que pudo, hasta que las lágrimas corrieron por sus mejillas, me dijo con más simpatía:

«Bien, Su-kurú, entérate de que nosotros los rarámuri somos física y moralmente muy superiores a los pueblos primitivos y por eso nuestros cuerpos reflejan nuestras más finas sensibilidades, así como nuestra gran modestia. Así es como ha crecido naturalmente en nuestros cuerpos ese pelo que tú encuentras tan poco común. Así nuestros cuerpos se aseguran de que aunque estemos desnudos, nuestras partes privadas estarán cubiertas discretamente.»

Yo dije: «Yo creo que ese pelo, lejos de hacer que vuestras partes pasen desapercibidas, más bien las hacen destacar. No modestamente, sino inmodestamente provocativas.»

Sentado como estaba, cruzado de piernas, no podía esconder lo que se evidenciaba bajo mi taparrabo y la Si-ríame difícilmente podría pretender que no lo veía. Ella movió la cabeza maravillada y murmuró no para mí sino para ella misma:

«Simple cabello entre las piernas... tan común y tan poco evidente como las hierbecitas que crecen entre las hendiduras de las rocas... y eso excita a un forastero. Y sólo con tener esta conversación hace que esté consciente de mí... —Luego dijo con ansiedad—: Nosotros aceptaremos tu curiosidad como un pecado confesado. Ahora toma, y masca rápido el *jípuri.*»

Me presentó una canasta con los pequeños cactos, verdes y frescos, no secos. Yo escogí uno que tenía muchos gajos.

«No, toma uno con cinco gajos —dijo ella—. Los que tienen muchos gajos son para todos los días, para ser masticados por nuestros corredores, los que tienen que correr más largas distancias, o para los ociosos que sólo desean sentarse y caer en visiones. Pero el *jípuri* de cinco gajos, el más raro y difícil de encontrar, es el que te acerca más a la luz-del-dios.»

Así es que le di un mordisco al cacto que ella me tendía, que dejó un sabor agrio y astringente en mi boca, seleccionó otro para ella y dijo: «No masques tan rápido como yo lo hago, *matu-ane* Su-kurú. Tú sentirás el efecto más rápido porque es la primera vez que lo pruebas y necesita haber paz entre nosotros.»

Ella tenía razón. Apenas había tragado un poquito del jugo cuando con gran perplejidad, empecé a ver que las paredes de la casa se disolvían alrededor de mí. Se volvieron transparentes, luego desaparecieron y vi a todos los aldeanos que estaban afuera, ya sea entretenidos con los juegos o festejando el *tes-güinápuri.* No podía creer que estaba viendo, en esos momentos, a través de las paredes, las figuras de las gentes tan claramente definidas, pues no estaba usando mi topacio; el haber visto tan claramente, fue una ilusión provocada por el *jípuri.* Pero después ya no estuve tan seguro de lo que me pasaba. Me pareció que estaba flotando en el lugar en donde me había sentado, que me elevaba hasta el techo... o hasta donde había estado el techo... y la gente se veía tan lejos y tan pequeñita mientras yo me remontaba hasta las ramas más altas de los árboles. Involuntariamente, exclamé: «¡Ayya!» La Si-ríame, desde alguna parte detrás o a un lado de mí, gritó: «¡No tan rápido! ¡Espérame!»

Dije que gritó, pero en realidad yo no la oí. Quiero decir que sus palabras no llegaron a mis oídos, sino de alguna manera a mi propia boca y yo las saboreé, suaves, deliciosas como *chocólatl*, y de alguna manera me di cuenta de ese sabor. En verdad que parecía como si todos mis sentidos hubieran cambiado sus funciones usuales. Podía *oír* el aroma de los árboles y el humo de los fuegos de la aldea, que se levantaba entre las copas de los árboles, llegando hasta donde yo estaba. En lugar de despedir un aroma a hojas, el follaje de los árboles hacía un ruidito metálico; el humo hacía un sonido apagado, como el de un tambor tocado muy suavemente. No veía los colores alrededor de mí, los *olía*. El verde de los árboles no parecía un color, sino una fragancia fría y húmeda que llegaba a mi nariz; las flores de pétalos rojos que había en las ramas, no eran rojas sino que daban un olor a especias; el cielo no era azul sino que olía a fresco y limpio como los senos de una mujer.

Entonces percibí que mi cabeza estaba realmente entre los senos de una mujer, entre unos senos muy amplios. Mis sentidos de tacto y gusto no habían sido afectados por la droga. La Si-ríame me había cogido y puesto entre su blusa abierta y se había unido a mí hasta su fondo y así nos elevamos juntos hasta las nubes. Puedo decir que una parte de mi cuerpo se estaba elevando más rápidamente que las otras. Mi *tepuli* ya se había levantado antes, pero para entonces lo sentía más largo, más tieso, más caliente y me palpitaba con urgencia, como si un temblor de tierra hubiera sucedido sin que yo me diera cuenta. La Si-ríame soltó una risa alegre, y yo la saboreé, era como frescas gotas de rocío y sus palabras me supieron a besos.

«Ésta es la mayor bendición de la luz-del-dios, Su-kurú, su calor y su brillo se añade al acto de *ma-rákame*. Combinemos los fuegos que el dios nos ha dado.»

Ella tiró lejos su falda de piel de jaguar y yació desnuda, o por lo menos tan desnuda como lo puede estar una mujer rarámuri, porque en verdad que tenía un triángulo de pelo en la parte baja de su abdomen, y entre sus muslos podía ver la forma de ese colchoncito excitante y su textura rizada, pero su color negro como todos los otros colores hasta ese momento, no era un color sino un aroma. Me incliné cerca para inhalarla y era una fragancia cálida, húmeda y almizcleña...

Cuando copulamos por primera vez, sentí que su *ymaxtli* me picaba y me hacía cosquillas en mis partes lampiñas como si restregara la parte baja de mi cuerpo sobre las frondas de un lujurioso helecho. Pronto, nuestros jugos fluyeron tan rápido, que su pelo se tornó húmedo y suave, y si yo no hubiera sabido que lo tenía no me habría dado cuenta. Sin embargo, puesto que lo sabía, sentí que mi *tepuli* era abrazado más que por carne, que era agarrado por primera vez por una densa y afelpada *tepili*, y el acto tuvo un nuevo sabor para mí. Sin duda les he de parecer que estoy delirando cuando cuento todo esto, pero en realidad estaba delirando. Me sentía aturdido por estar en aquellas alturas, fuera ilusión o realidad; e igualmente por la sensación que producían en mi boca los gritos, las palabras y los gemidos de la mujer, como también, por la sensación que me producía cada parte de su cuerpo, cada curva y los matices de su color que llegaban a mí en fragancias distintas y sutiles. Y los efectos del *jípuri* enriquecían cada una de esas sensaciones, como también cada movimiento que hacíamos y cada uno de nuestros contactos.

Supongo que debí de haber sentido un poco de miedo también, y el miedo hace que cualquier sensación humana sea más aguda, cada emoción más vívida. Ordinariamente los hombres no vuelan hasta las alturas, más a menudo caen de una de esas alturas y generalmente esas caídas son fatales. Sin embargo, la Si-ríame y yo estábamos suspendidos sobre un piso que no se podía ver y sin ningún soporte bajo de nosotros. Y como no teníamos ningún soporte, ni ninguna traba, nosotros nos movíamos tan libremente y tan ligeros, como si hubiéramos estado bajo el agua, pero pudiendo respirar con facilidad. Esa libertad que gozábamos en todas las dimensiones nos permitió tomar algunas posiciones muy placenteras, con contorsiones y torsiones, que de otra manera no hubieran sido posibles. En cierto momento, la Si-ríame jadeó algunas palabras y éstas me supieron a su *tepili* empenachado. «Ahora sí creo que has cometido más pecados de los que puedes contar.» No tengo ni idea de cuántas veces ella alcanzó el orgasmo, ni cuántas veces eyaculé durante el tiempo que la droga nos hizo elevarnos y extasiarnos, pero para mí fueron muchas más veces de las que he gozado en tan poco tiempo.

Me pareció que había pasado muy poco tiempo. Me empecé a dar cuenta de que estaba oyendo y no saboreando los sonidos cuando ella suspirando dijo: «No te preocupes, Su-kurú, si nunca llegas a ser un buen corredor.»

Para entonces, yo veía los colores otra vez, en lugar de olerlos; olía los olores en lugar de oírlos; y descendía de las alturas y de la exaltación. No lo hice como si fuera un pedazo de plomo, sino que bajé despacio, suavemente, como una pluma que cae. La Si-ríame y yo estábamos otra vez dentro de su casa y a un lado de nosotros estaban nuestras ropas arrugadas. Ella yacía de espalda, completamente dormida y con una sonrisa en su rostro. El pelo de su cabeza se desparramaba alrededor, pero el de su *ymaxtli* ya no estaba rizado ni negro; estaba mate y claro pintado por mi *omícetl* blanco. Había otras sustancias secas entre sus pesados pechos y en algunas otras partes. También yo estaba lleno de emanaciones y de mi propio sudor seco, y también estaba terriblemente sediento, sentía la boca como si tuviera un estropajoso *ymaxtli* que me estuviera creciendo adentro; más tarde supe que ésos eran los efectos posteriores del *jípuri.*

Moviéndome en silencio y con cuidado para no despertar a la Si-ríame, me vestí para ir fuera de la casa a buscar un trago de agua. Antes de partir eché un último vistazo apreciativo, con mi topacio, a la bella mujer que yacía totalmente relajada sobre la piel de jaguar. Era la primera vez, reflexioné, que había tenido relaciones sexuales con una soberana. Y me sentí muy orgulloso de mí mismo, aunque no por mucho tiempo.

Cuando salí de la casa, me encontré con que el sol todavía brillaba en lo alto y que las celebraciones continuaban. Después de haber bebido mucho, al levantar mis ojos de la jícara mojada que tenía en la mano, me encontré con la mirada acusadora de la muchacha que había tratado de cazar. Le sonreí lo más inocentemente que pude y le dije:

«¿Corremos otra vez? Ahora ya puedo mascar *jípuri*, pues he sido adecuadamente iniciado.»

«No necesitas vanagloriarte de eso —dijo hablando entre dientes—. Por haber tenido medio día, toda una noche, y casi otro día de iniciación.»

Me quedé con la boca abierta estúpidamente, pues no podía creer que había pasado tanto tiempo cuando a mí me pareció muy poco, y me sonrojé cuando la muchacha continuó diciéndome acusadoramente:

«*Siempre* consigue a los primeros y mejores *ma-rákame* que quieran iniciarse en la luz-del-dios. ¡Eso no es justo! Y no me importa si dicen que soy rebelde e irreverente. Ya lo he dicho antes y lo vuelvo a repetir, que sólo *pretendió* recibir la luz-del-dios del Abuelo, de la Madre y del Hermano. *Mintió* para que la escogieran como Si-ríame, pues así ella podía tener derecho sobre todos los primeros *ma-tuane* que fueran a pedirle ese favor.»

Eso de alguna manera bajó la alta estimación en que me había tenido unos momentos antes, por haberme acostado con una soberana ungida, para darme cuenta que no era en ningún modo superior a cualquier mujer de las que van a horcajarse en el camino. Mi propia estimación sufrió todavía más, pues durante todo el tiempo que me quedé en la aldea, la Si-ríame no me ordenó presentarme ante ella otra vez. Evidentemente sólo deseaba lo «primero y lo mejor» que cada hombre podría ofrecer bajo la influencia de la droga.

Pero por lo menos fui lo suficiente capaz como para apaciguar a la enojada muchacha, después de haber dormido y recuperado mis energías. Su nombre era, según supe, Vi-rikota que quiere decir Tierra Santa, que también es el nombre de aquella nación que está en las montañas del este y donde se consigue el *jípuri*.

Las celebraciones duraron muchos días más y yo persuadí a Vi-rikota para que me dejara cazarla otra vez, pero entonces tuve buen cuidado de no comer demasiado ni tomar excesivo *tesgüino*, y creo que la capturé muy bien.

Cogimos varios *jípuris* secos que estaban en las ramadas y nos separamos de los otros para ir a un claro del bosque, muy agradable. Tuvimos que mascar una gran cantidad de ese cacto menos potente para aproximarnos a los efectos que yo había disfrutado en casa de la Si-ríame, pero después de un rato, sentí que mis sentidos empezaban a cambiar sus funciones. Esa vez, los colores de las mariposas y de las flores que estaban alrededor de nosotros *cantaban.*

Por supuesto que Vi-rikota también tenía ese medallón de *ymaxtli* entre sus piernas, que en su caso era un colchoncito menos encrespado y más blando, y como seguía siendo una novedad para mí, otra vez me provocó una extraordinaria energía. Sin embargo, ella y yo nunca alcanzamos el éxtasis que yo conocí durante mi iniciación. Nunca tuvimos la ilusión de estar ascendiendo hacia el cielo, pues todo el tiempo estuvimos conscientes de la suave hierba en donde yacíamos. También, Vi-rikota era demasiado joven y aun pequeña de cuerpo para su edad, y una mujer-niña simplemente no puede extender totalmente sus muslos, como para que el cuerpo grande de un hombre, pueda estar lo suficientemente cerca, como para penetrar totalmente su *tepuli.* Además de eso, nuestra copulación *tuvo* que ser menos memorable que la de la Si-ríame porque Vi-rikota y yo no tuvimos acceso a la *verdadera* luz-del-dios, o sea a ese *jípuri* verde y fresco de cinco gajos.

No obstante, nos entendimos tan bien que no intercambiamos otros compañeros durante todo el festival y muchas veces hicimos el acto del *ma-rákame* y sentí una verdadera pena al tener que separarme de ella, cuando el *tes-güinápuri* concluyó. Nos separamos sólo porque mi anfitrión Tes-disora insistió: «Ha llegado el momento de la *verdadera* carrera, Su-kurú, y debes verla. El *ra-rajípuri* es la competición entre nuestros mejores corredores y los de Guacho-chi.»

Yo le pregunté: «¿Y dónde están ellos? No he visto a ningún extranjero.»

«No todavía. Ellos llegarán después de que nosotros nos hayamos ido, y llegarán corriendo. Guacho-chi está bastante lejos de aquí, hacia el sudeste.»

Él me dijo la distancia, en la forma en que los rarámuri contaban, pero ya lo he olvidado, aunque recuerdo que calculé a unas quince largas-carreras de los mexica o quince leguas españolas. Sin embargo, él estaba hablando de esa distancia en línea recta, pero una carrera en esa nación tan desigual de terreno, tendría que llevarse a efecto siguiendo un curso tortuoso, con vueltas y revueltas a través de barrancos y montañas. Calculé que la distancia total a correr entre Guagüey-bo y Guacho-chi debía de ser de cerca de cincuenta y una largas-carreras. Luego Tes-disora dijo casualmente:

«Correr de una aldea a la otra, de ida y de vuelta, pateando la pelota de madera durante todo el camino, le toma a un buen corredor un día y una noche.»

«¡Imposible! —exclamé—. ¿Cien largas-carreras? Pero si eso es lo que le tomaría a un hombre correr, desde la ciudad de Tenochtitlan hasta la lejana ciudad de Kerétaro. —Yo negué con mi cabeza enfáticamente—. ¿Y la mitad de ese camino, durante la oscuridad de la noche? ¿Y sobre eso, pateando una pelota? ¡Imposible!»

Por supuesto que Tes-disora no sabía nada acerca de Tenochtitlan o Kerétaro, y de la distancia que mediaba entre esas ciudades. Él se encogió de hombros y dijo: «Si tú crees que es imposible, Su-kurú, entonces debes venir con nosotros para verlo por ti mismo.»

«¿Yo? ¡Yo sé que es imposible para mí!»

«Entonces sólo ven parte del camino y luego nos esperas para regresar con nosotros. Tengo un par de sandalias fuertes, de piel de verraco, que tú puedes llevar. Y ya que no eres uno de los corredores de nuestra aldea, no será una trampa si no corres en el *ra-rajípuri* descalzo con nosotros.»

«¿Trampa? —dije más que asombrado—. ¿Quieres decir que hay reglas en este juego?»

«No muchas —dijo con toda seriedad—. Nuestros corredores saldrán de aquí en la tarde, exactamente en el preciso instante en que el Abuelo Fuego —y él lo señaló— toque con su arco la orilla más alta de esa montaña. La gente de Guacho-chi tiene una forma similar para juzgar el momento exacto y sus corredores partirán también. Nosotros correremos hacia Guacho-chi y ellos correrán hacia Guagüey-bo. Entre esos puntos, en alguna parte del camino, nos pasaremos unos a otros gritándonos saludos, maldiciones e insultos amistosos. Cuando los hombres de Guacho-chi lleguen aquí nuestras mujeres les ofrecerán algo con qué refrescarse y tratarán astutamente de entretenerlos lo más que puedan, y lo mismo harán las suyas con nosotros, pero puedes estar seguro de que no les haremos caso, sino que nos daremos la vuelta inmediatamente y continuaremos corriendo, hasta nuestras respectivas aldeas. Para entonces, Abuelo Fuego estará otra vez tocando esa montaña o desapareciendo detrás de ella, o un poco arriba de ella y así podremos determinar el tiempo y duración de nuestra carrera. Los hombres de Guacho-chi harán lo mismo y enviaremos mensajeros para intercambiar los resultados y así sabremos quién ha ganado la carrera.»

Le dije: «Al ver el consumo de tiempo y esfuerzo, espero que el premio para el ganador sea algo que valga la pena.»

«¿Premio? No hay premio.»

«¿Qué? ¿Hacéis todo eso por nada, ni siquiera un trofeo? ¿Ni tampoco por una meta que alcanzar y obtener? ¿Sin ninguna aspiración al final más que llegar exhausto a vuestras propias casas y mujeres de nuevo? ¿A nombre solamente de sus tres dioses? *¿Por qué?»*

Se encogió de hombros nuevamente. «La hacemos porque es lo mejor que sabemos hacer.»

No dije nada más porque sabía que es inútil discutir cualquier asunto razonable con personas irrazonables. Sin embargo, más tarde le presté más atención a la contestación que Tes-disora me dio en aquella ocasión y entonces ya no me pareció tan insensata. Si alguien me hubiera preguntado el porqué de mi preocupación de toda la vida, por el arte de conocer las palabras, no hubiera podido dar una respuesta tan adecuada.

Únicamente seis hombres robustos acreditados como los mejores corredores de Guagüey-bo fueron los verdaderos participantes en el *ra-rajípuri*. Los seis, uno de los cuales era Tes-disora, se habían hartado de *jípuri* para aliviar la fatiga antes de que comenzara la carrera y cada uno cargaba un pequeño saco con agua así como una bolsita de *pinoli*, ambos alimentos se podían consumir casi sin necesidad de disminuir su velocidad, al ir corriendo. También sujetados a las cinturas de sus taparrabos llevaban unos pequeños sacos de piel seca, que tenían una piedrecita cuyo ruido les ayudaba a no caer dormidos.

El resto de los corredores del *ra-rajípuri* eran todos los hombres físicamente hábiles de Guagüey-bo, desde los adolescentes hasta hombres mayores que yo, y su trabajo consistía en ayudar a levantar el ánimo de los corredores. Muchos se habían adelantado desde temprano en la mañana. Eran hombres capaces de correr asombrosamente rápido por poco tiempo, pero tendían a debilitarse en largas distancias. Se fueron deteniendo a diferentes intervalos del camino entre las dos aldeas. Y cuando los corredores escogidos pasaban por cada uno de esos intervalos, éstos corrían a su lado para animar a los participantes a dar lo más posible de sí mismos.

Otros hombres que no estaban dentro de la competencia cargaban pequeñas ollas de carbones calientes y antorchas de astillas de pino, estas últimas serían encendidas al oscurecer para poder iluminar el camino de los corredores durante la noche. Había otros hombres que cargaban más manojitos de *jípuri* junto con sacos de agua y de *pinoli*. Los más jóvenes y los más viejos no cargaban nada pues su trabajo consistía en mantener un continuo griterío para animar a los corredores. Todos los hombres estaban pintados en la cara, el pecho desnudo, en la espalda y con diseños de puntos, ruedas y espirales con un *urá*, pigmento, de un tono amarillo vivo. Yo sólo estaba pintado en la cara, ya que a mí se me permitió ponerme mi manto con mangas.

En cuanto al Abuelo Fuego, se levantó sobre la montaña designada, al atardecer. La Si-ríame salió sonriente a la puerta de su casa, vestida con pieles de jaguar, y cargando un bastón con puño de plata en una mano y una bola de madera del tamaño de la cabeza de un hombre en la otra. Se paró mirando oblicuamente al sol, mientras los corredores y todos sus compañeros se pararon cerca de ella, inclinándose un poco hacia adelante, preparándose a partir. En el momento en que el Abuelo Fuego tocó la cima de la montaña, la Si-ríame sonrió ampliamente y lanzó la pelota desde el umbral de su puerta hacia los pies descalzos de los seis corredores. Cada habitante de Guagüey-bo dio un jubiloso grito y los seis corredores partieron, jugueteando con la pelota, pateándola de uno a otro mientras corrían. Los otros participantes los siguieron a cierta distancia, y yo también. La Si-ríame aún sonreía cuando la vi por último, y la pequeña Virikota seguía brincando tan alegre como una llama que está a punto de apagarse.

Había esperado que toda esa multitud de corredores me dejarán atrás en un momento, pero debí suponer que no utilizarían todas sus energías al principio de la carrera. Partieron trotando a paso moderado que hasta yo pude sostener. Nos fuimos por la orilla del cañón y los gritos de las mujeres de la aldea, los niños y los viejos desaparecieron detrás de nosotros y nuestros propios animadores comenzaron a vociferar. Como los corredores naturalmente evitaban tener que patear la pelota al subir las montañas, cuando esto fuera posible, continuamos por el fondo del cañón hasta que los lados de éste se inclinaron y bajaron lo suficiente como para permitir que nosotros pudiéramos salir de él fácilmente y así penetrar en el bosque situado al sur.

Me siento orgulloso de poderles decir que continué con los corredores por lo que yo calculo que fue la tercera parte del camino de Guagüey-bo a Guacho-chi. Tal vez el crédito debe llevárselo el *jípuri* que mastiqué antes de salir, pues varias veces me encontré corriendo más rápido de lo que jamás corrí en toda mi vida, antes y después de esa carrera. Era entonces cuando alcanzábamos a los corredores principales y hacíamos lo posible por igualar su velocidad. Y varias veces pasamos ante los corredores de Guacho-chi, que estaban parados, sin correr todavía, colocados en espera de sus propios competidores que venían en dirección contraria. Éstos nos gritaron alegremente nombres burlones, en el momento de nuestra pasada.

«¡Cojos! ¡Flojos!» y otros nombres por el estilo, especialmente a mí, porque para entonces yo ya me encontraba a la cola del contingente de Guagüey-bo.

Correr a toda velocidad entre bosques y en las orillas de los barrancos con un suelo lleno de piedras sueltas, que hacían falsear los tobillos, era algo a lo que no estaba acostumbrado, pero logré hacerlo mientras había suficiente luz. Cuando el brillo de la tarde comenzó a desaparecer, tuve que correr con mi topacio pegado al ojo, y por lo tanto mi paso disminuyó considerablemente. Al oscurecer aún más, empecé a ver las luces-guía que se prendían y brillaban adelante de mí, en donde se encontraban los portadores de las antorchas, pero naturalmente, ninguno de esos hombres iba a regresar para compartir su luz con uno que no estaba tomando parte en la carrera, así es que cada vez me fui quedando más rezagado, detrás de la multitud que corría y sus gritos disminuían en la distancia.

Luego, cuando la oscuridad total me rodeó, vi un destello rojo en el suelo, delante de mí. Los bondadosos rarámuri no habían olvidado ni dejado a un lado, a su compañero extranjero Su-kurú. Uno de los que portaban las antorchas, después de haber encendido la suya, había dejado bien acomodado, en un lugar donde yo lo pudiera ver fácilmente, su pequeño brasero de barro. Me detuve en ese lugar y prendí fuego de campamento y me recosté para pasar allí la noche. Debo admitir que, a pesar de haber ingerido *jípuri*, estaba lo suficientemente cansado como para haber caído dormido, pero sólo de pensarlo sentí vergüenza, pues todos los hombres de los alrededores estaban ocupados en ese ejercicio. También, hubiera sido intolerablemente humillado y lo mismo la aldea que me estaba dando asilo, si cuando los corredores rivales de Guacho-chi pasaran a lo largo del camino, se encontraran allí a «un hombre de Guagüey-bo» yaciendo dormido. Así es que comí un poco de *pinoli* remojado en agua, que traía en un cuero, y masqué un poco de *jípuri* que había traído conmigo, y eso me revivió bastante. Me pasé toda la noche sentado, tirando ocasionalmente unas ramitas al fuego sólo para sentirme un poco cómodo, pero no lo suficientemente caliente como para dormirme.

Se suponía que debía ver dos veces a los corredores de Guacho-chi antes de volver a ver a Tes-disora ·y a sus compañeros. Después de que los dos contingentes se cruzaron en sus caminos, más o menos a la mitad de su curso, los corredores rivales aparecieron por el sudeste y llegarían a mi campamento más o menos a medianoche. Después ellos llegarían a Guagüey-bo y volverían por el noroeste, pasando delante de mí otra vez por la mañana. Tes-disora y sus compañeros no llegarían a mi campamento hasta que el sol estuviera a la mitad de su camino, y entonces regresaría con ellos.

Bien, mi cálculo acerca del primer encuentro fue correcto. Con la ayuda de mi topacio continué mirando a las estrellas, y de acuerdo a ellas, *era* medianoche cuando vi unas luces que se movían viniendo del sudeste. Decidí pretender que era uno de los corredores de avanzada de Guagüey-bo, así es que me puse en pie, mirando alerta, antes de que el primero de esos corredores que pateaban la pelota, llegara a mi vista, y entonces empecé a gritar: «¡Cojos!» «¡Flojos!» Los competidores y los portadores de antorchas no me contestaron; estaban demasiado ocupados en mantener sus ojos en la pelota de madera, cuya pintura se había caído y estaba más que astillada y desmenuzada, pero todos los que seguían a los corredores de Guacho-chi me devolvieron mis mofas, gritando: «¡Vieja!» y «¡Calienta tus huesos cansados!» y cosas por el estilo... entonces comprendí que el haber encendido un fuego era ante los ojos de los rarámuri de muy poca hombría, pero ya era demasiado tarde para apagarlo y ellos pasaron demasiado rápido, hasta que sólo pude ver, otra vez, las luces que parpadeaban y desaparecían por el noroeste.

Después de un tiempo muy largo, el cielo empezó a clarear hacia el este y al fin, el Abuelo Fuego hizo su aparición, y pasó todavía más mientras, tan lentamente como lo haría un abuelo humano, él trepó una tercera parte de su camino por el cielo. Era el tiempo del desayuno, y según mis cálculos, también para que los hombres de Guacho-chi estuvieran de regreso hacia su aldea. Me volví hacia el noroeste, hacia donde los había visto la última vez. Como era de día, no vería las luces de las antorchas avisándome su regreso, así es que agudicé el oído para escucharlos, antes de que los tuviera al alcance de la vista. No oí nada y no vi nada.

Pasó mucho más tiempo. Así es que volví a contar en mi mente para ver si no había calculado mal, pero no encontré ningún error. Pasó más tiempo. Traté de acordarme si Tes-disora me habría dicho algo acerca de que los corredores tomarían otro camino para regresar. Pasó más tiempo, pero naturalmente, ninguno de esos hombres y el sol estaba exactamente arriba de mi cabeza, cuando escuché un grito:

«¡*Kiura-ba!*»

Era uno de los rarámuri, que traía puesto un taparrabo de

corredor, un cuero de agua a la cintura, y diseños amarillos pintados en piel desnuda, pero no recordé haberlo visto antes, así es que lo tomé por uno de los corredores de avanzada de Guacho-chi. Evidentemente él me tomó a mí por una avanzada de los Guagüey-bo, porque después de que le hube devuelto su saludo, él se aproximó a mí, con una sonrisa amistosa, aunque ansiosa y me dijo:

«Vi tu fuego en la noche, así es que dejé mi lugar y vine a verte. ¿Me puedes decir, confidencialmente. amigo, cómo se las arregla tu gente para detener a nuestros corredores en la aldea? ¿Vuestras mujeres los están esperando, ya totalmente desnudas y yaciendo listas para complacerlos?»

«Bueno, ésa sería una visita muy agradable, como para entretenerse —dije—. Pero no creo que lo hagan, no que yo sepa. Yo también me preguntaba, si no sería posible que tus corredores hubieran regresado por otro camino.»

Él empezó a decir: «Sería la primera vez que ellos...», cuando se interrumpió. Ambos oímos otro grito de «¡Kiura-ba!» y nos volvimos para ver a Tes-disora y a sus cinco compañeros, aproximarse a nosotros. Estaban tan fatigados que venían haciendo eses y la pelota que descuidadamente pateaban, había quedado reducida al tamaño de mi puño.

«Nosotros... —dijo Tes-disora dirigiéndose al hombre de Guacho-chi, y haciendo una pausa para tomar aire. Luego jadeó con dificultad—: Nosotros todavía no... nos hemos encontrado con sus corredores. ¿Qué clase de trampa...?»

El hombre le interrumpió diciendo: «Precisamente nos estábamos preguntando, este corredor de ustedes y yo, qué habrá pasado con ellos.»

Tes-disora nos miró a los dos, respirando pesadamente. Otro de los hombres también jadeó, con una voz en donde se notaba la incredulidad:

«¿Que ellos... todavía no... han pasado por aquí?»

Para entonces toda la compañía de corredores estaba con nosotros. Yo les dije: «Le pregunté al forastero, que si ellos no habrían tomado otra ruta. Y él me preguntó, que si vuestras mujeres no habrían contribuido mucho para detenerlos en su aldea.»

Todas las cabezas hicieron gestos de negación, luego se movieron más despacio y los hombres empezaron a mirarse los unos a los otros, con preocupación.

Algunos de ellos dijo en voz baja y preocupada: «Nuestra aldea.»

Algún otro dijo, más fuerte y ansiosamente: «Nuestras mujeres.»

Y el forastero dijo, con voz aguda: «Nuestros mejores corredores.»

Entonces hubo una mirada de terrible comprensión y de angustia en todos los ojos, incluyendo los del hombre de Guachochi. Todos esos ojos muy abiertos, se volvieron hacia el noroeste y por un momento los hombres contuvieron el aliento antes de dejarme repentinamente, ya que todos ellos rompieron a correr

como nunca antes lo habían hecho y alguno de ellos sólo dijo una palabra:
«¡Yaki!»

No, no los seguí hacia Guagüey-bo. Nunca más regresé allí. Yo era un forastero y hubiera sido presuntuoso de mi parte, juntarme con los rarámuri para lamentar sus pérdidas. Me imaginé lo que encontrarían: que los asesinos yaki y los corredores de Guacho-chi, debieron de llegar al mismo tiempo a Guagüey-bo, y que los corredores estarían muy cansados para poder presentar batalla adecuada a esos salvajes. Todos los hombres de Guacho-chi debieron de haber perdido su cuero cabelludo antes de morir. Qué fue lo que la Si-ríame, la pequeña Vi-rikota y las otras mujeres de Guagüey-bo tuvieron que sufrir antes de morir, no quiero ni pensarlo. Presumo que los hombres supervivientes de los rarámuri, finalmente volvieron a repoblarse, dividiendo las mujeres de los Guacho-chi entre ellos, pero realmente nunca lo sabré.

Y jamás vi a un yaki, ni entonces, ni hasta este día. Me hubiera gustado, si me las hubiera podido arreglar para que los yaki no me vieran a mí, ya que deben de ser los animales humanos más fieros que existen y por lo tanto una cosa que vale la pena de verse. En todo lo que tengo de vida, sólo he conocido a un hombre que se encontró con los yaki y que vivió para contarlo, y ése fue aquel viejo de la Casa de los Pochteca, que no tenía pelo en la coronilla. Tampoco ninguno de sus españoles se ha encontrado con los yaki. Sus exploradores todavía no se han aventurado tan al norte y al oeste. Creo que hasta podría sentir piedad por alguno de sus españoles que se encontrara entre los yaki.

Cuando esos hombres afligidos se fueron corriendo, yo me quedé mirándolos hasta que desaparecieron en el bosque. Y seguí mirando hacia el noroeste, por un rato más, después de que ellos desaparecieron totalmente de mi vista, diciéndoles un silencioso adiós. Después me puse en cuclillas e hice una comida con el *pinoli* y agua y masqué *jípuri* para mantenerme despierto el resto del día. Eché tierra sobre las brasas que quedaban del fuego, y poniéndome en pie miré hacia donde estaba el sol y a grandes zancadas me dirigí hacia el sur. Había disfrutado mi estancia con los rarámuri, y me apesadumbraba el tenerlos que dejar así. Sin embargo, traía puesta buena ropa de piel de venado, fuertes sandalias de piel de verraco, un saco de cuero con agua y comida y una hoja de pedernal en mi cintura, también mi cristal para ver y mi cristal para encender fuego. Así es que no había dejado nada atrás, en Guagüey-bo, sólo los días que había vivido con ellos. Pero aun ésos los llevaba conmigo, guardados en mi memoria.

I H S

✠

S. C. C. M.

Santificada, Cesárea, Católica Majestad,
el Emperador Don Carlos, nuestro Señor Rey:

Más Sublime y Augusta Majestad, desde esta Ciudad de México, capital de la Nueva España, en el día de San Ambrosio, en el año de Nuestro Señor Jesucristo de mil quinientos treinta, os saludo.

En nuestras últimas cartas, Señor, nosotros nos extendíamos sobre nuestras actividades como Protector de los Indios. Permitidnos detenernos aquí sobre nuestra principal función, la del Obispo de Mexico, y sobre nuestra labor de propagar la Verdadera Fe entre estos indios. Como Vuestra Percipiente Majestad puede discernir en las siguientes páginas de la crónica de nuestro azteca, su gente siempre ha sido despreciablemente supersticiosa, viendo siempre malos agüeros y portentos, no solamente en donde hombres razonables pueden verlos —como en un eclipse de sol, por ejemplo—, sino también en cualquier simple coincidencia, en cualquier fenómeno común de la naturaleza. Esa tendencia hacia la superstición y la credulidad, ambas cosas, nos han ayudado, e impedido a la vez, a continuar con nuestra campaña de hacer que la adoración al demonio se troque en Cristianismo.

Los conquistadores españoles, en sus primeras matanzas en estas tierras, hicieron una admirable labor, destruyendo sus templos mayores, sus ídolos y poniendo en esos lugares la Cruz de Cristo y la imagen de la Virgen. Nosotros y nuestros hermanos de hábito, hemos continuado y mantenido esa destrucción y erigido en esos mismos sitios más iglesias Cristianas, en donde de otra manera se estuvieran adorando a todos los diablos y diablesas. Gracias a que los indios prefieran obstinadamente congregarse para hacer sus adoraciones en los viejos sitios en que acostumbraban a hacerlo, ahora han encontrado esos lugares libres de seres deseosos de sangre como sus Huichilobos y Tlaloque, y en lugar de ellos han encontrado a Jesús Crucificado y a su Bendita Madre.

Para citaros sólo alguno de los muchos ejemplos, el Obispo de Tlaxcala está construyendo una iglesia a Nuestra Señora, en lo alto de esa pirámide gigantesca de Cholula —que era como la arrogante Torre de Babel de Shina —y en donde se rendía adoración a Quetzalcóatl, La Serpiente Emplumada. Aquí, en la capital de la Nueva España, nuestra casi totalmente construida iglesia-catedral de San Francisco, ha sido deliberadamente edificada (como casi lo pudo determinar el arquitecto García Bravo) en el sitio en donde una vez estuvo la Gran Pirámide de los aztecas. Nos, creemos que incluso se utilizaron algunas de las piedras con que estaba construido ese monumento de atrocidad, ya demolido. En un punto de la tierra llamada Tepeyaca, al norte de aquí y al otro lado del lago, había un lugar en donde los indios adoraban a Tónatzin, una especie de Madre Diosa, y nos, hemos mandado construir allí un santuario a la Madre de Dios. A petición del Capitán General Cortés, le hemos dado el mismo nombre de Santuario de Nuestra Señora de Guadalupe, como el que está situado en el lugar de donde él proviene, la provincia de Extremadura en España.

Quizás a algunos les pueda parecer indecoroso que nos, construyamos nuestros Cristianos tabernáculos sobre las ruinas de esos templos paganos que todavía están manchados con sangre derramada en esos sacrificios sacrílegos. Sin embargo, nos, sólo emulamos a esos primeros evangelistas Cristianos, que levantaron sus altares en donde los romanos, griegos, sajones, etcétera, etcétera, habían estado adorando a Júpiter, Pan y a Eostras, etcétera... para que esos demonios fueran echados fuera por la divina presencia de Cristo Crucificado, y esos lugares que una vez fueron sitios de abominación e idolatría, han llegado a ser lugares santificados, en donde el pueblo puede ser inducido, de una manera más rápida, por los ministros del Verdadero Dios, a adorarlo conforme a su Alta Divinidad.

En eso, Señor, las supersticiones de los indios nos han ayudado mucho. Sin embargo, en otras cosas que hemos emprendido, no; porque además de estar muy ceñidos a ellas, son tan hipócritas como los fariseos. Muchos de nuestros aparentes conversos, incluso aquellos que dicen ser devotos creyentes de la Fe Cristiana, todavía viven con un temor supersticioso hacia sus viejos demonios. Ellos piensan que son muy prudentes al conservar *cierta* reverencia hacia Huichilobos y toda la demás horda; así, ellos lo explican con toda solemnidad, pueden evitar toda posibilidad de que esos demonios celosos tomen venganza por haber sido suplantados.

Ya os hemos mencionado acerca de nuestro éxito, durante nuestro primer año o algo así, en esta Nueva España, al encontrar y destruir miles de ídolos que los conquistadores habían visto. Cuando al fin, ya no estaba a la vista ninguno de ellos y cuando los indios juraron antes nuestros Inquisidores que ya no había ni uno en lugares escondidos, nos, no obstante, sospechamos que los indios todavía seguían venerando a esas viejas deidades prohibidas, en privado. Así es que, nos, predicamos más estrictamente e hicimos que nuestros sacerdotes y misioneros hicieran lo mismo, ordenando que ningún ídolo, ni siquiera el más pequeño, ni siquiera un amuleto ornamental, debería existir. Y así, confirmando nuestras sospechas, los indios empezaron a traer otra vez, humildemente, a nos, y a otros sacerdotes, gran número de figuras de barro y cerámica y ante nuestra presencia renunciaron a ellas y las rompieron en pedazos.

Nosotros, nos sentimos muy satisfechos de haber vuelto a descubrir y destruir, otra vez, tantos objetos sacrílegos... hasta que, después de algún tiempo, nos dimos cuenta de que los indios sólo buscaban apaciguarnos y mofarse de nos. Esto no tiene la menor importancia, ya que en ese caso, lo mismo nos hubiera ofendido su impostura. Parece que nuestros severos sermones, provocaron una verdadera industria entre los artesanos indígenas, ya que apresuradamente fabricaron esas figuras, sólo con el único propósito de que fueran mostradas y rotas delante de nos, en una aparente sumisión ante nuestras amonestaciones.

Al mismo tiempo, para nuestra mayor pena y afrentamiento, nos, supimos que numerosos ídolos verdaderos, o sea las antiguas estatuas no las falsas, habían sido escondidas a los ojos de nuestros frailes. ¿Y dónde supondríais vos, Señor, que las escondieron? Ellos las escondieron en los cimientos de nuestros santuarios, de nuestras capillas y de otros monumentos Cristianos, ¡que fueron construidos por trabajadores indios! Esos hipócritas salvajes, escondieron sus impías imágenes en esos lugares santos, creyendo que nunca se descubrirían. Y peor todavía, creían que podrían adorar allí a esas monstruosidades escondidas, mientras *aparentaban* rendir homenaje a la cruz, o a la Virgen o a cualquier santo que estuviera visiblemente representado allí.

Nuestra repulsión hacia esas revelaciones horribles, solamente se vio un poco mitigada por haber tenido la satisfacción de decirles a todas nuestras congregaciones —y del placer de ver cómo se sentían avasallados cuando se los dije— que el Demonio y otros Adversarios del Verdadero Dios, sufrían una angustia indescriptible con la proximidad de la cruz Cristiana y de otros objetos santos de la Fe. Desde entonces, y sin ninguna incitación, esos indios albañiles, que habían ayudado a esconderlos, resignadamente revelaron dónde estaban los ídolos, y muchos de ellos, no los hubiéramos podido encontrar sin su ayuda.

Temiendo tantas evidencias de que tan sólo unos pocos indios han despertado totalmente del sueño de su error —a pesar de todos nuestros esfuerzos y de los esfuerzos de otros—, nos, tememos que sólo pueden ser despertados con una sacudida, como lo fue Saulo en las afueras de Damasco. O quizás ellos se puedan inclinar más suavemente a tomar el *salvatio omnibus* por medio de un milagro como aquel que hace mucho tiempo nos dio a la Santa Patrona de Vuestra Majestad y principal Patrona de Cataluña en el reino de Aragón: el descubrimiento milagroso de la imagen negra de la Virgen de Montserrat, a no más de cien leguas de donde nosotros nacimos. Sin embargo, no podemos rezar para que la Virgen Bendita nos conceda otro milagro, o incluso la repetición de uno en que Ella se manifieste a sí misma.

Queremos dar las gracias a Vuestra Generosa Majestad por vuestro regalo, que ha sido traído por la última carabela: los muchos injertos de rosas que nos habéis mandado de vuestro Real Invernadero para suplir aquellas que nos trajimos en un principio. Los injertos serán concienzudamente distribuidos entre los jardines de todas nuestras propiedades eclesiásticas. Quizás interese saber a Vuestra Majestad que nunca antes crecieron rosas en estas tierras, y que las que nos plantamos, han florecido tan exuberantemente como nunca antes nos lo hemos visto, ni siquiera en los jardines de Castilla. El clima aquí es tan saludable como el de una eterna primavera, y por eso las rosas florecen abundantemente durante todo el año, incluso en este mes (que es diciembre cuando nos os escribimos) que de acuerdo a nuestro calendario es mitad del invierno. Y nos, nos consideramos muy afortunados en tener a un jardinero altamente capaz, en la persona de nuestro fiel Juan Diego.

A pesar de su nombre, Señor, él es un indio como lo son todos nuestros domésticos y como todos *nuestros* domésticos, es un Cristiano de una piedad y una convicción intachable (no como esos de los que hemos hablado en párrafos anteriores). Ese nombre bautismal le fue dado algunos años atrás por el capellán que acompañaba a los conquistadores, el Padre Bartolomeo Olmedo. El Padre Bartolomeo tenía una forma muy práctica de bautizar a los indios; no lo hacía individualmente sino que los juntaba a todos en grandes multitudes, para que así fueran muchos los que recibieran la gracia de este sacramento lo más pronto posible. Y naturalmente, por conveniencia, él daba a cada indio, aunque fueran cientos de ellos, de ambos sexos, el nombre del santo que correspondía a ese día en particular. Habiendo una multitud de San Juanes en el calendario de la Iglesia, ahora parece, para nuestra confusión y aún molestia, que en la Nueva España, de cada dos indios Cristianos, uno se llama Juan o Juana.

Quitando eso, nosotros estamos muy complacidos con nuestro Juan Diego. Él camina entre las flores, con un carácter servicial y humilde, y con sincera devoción por el Cristianismo y por nosotros.

Que Vuestra Real Majestad, a quien nos servimos, sea bendecida con la continua benignidad de Nuestro Dios a Quien ambos servimos, es la oración incesante de Vuestro S.C.C.M., respetuoso vicario y legado,

(ecce signum) ZUMÁRRAGA

NONA PARS

He llegado al punto de la historia de nosotros los mexica en que habiendo escalado por tantas gavillas de años la montaña de la grandeza, finalmente llegamos a su cumbre, lo que significa que sin saberlo, comenzamos a descender al otro lado.

Ya de regreso a casa, después de unos meses más de viajar a la aventura por el occidente, me detuve en Tolocan, un pueblo agradable encima de una montaña en las tierras de los matlalzinca, una de las tribus menores aliadas a la Triple Alianza. Me hospedé en una hostería, y después de bañarme y cenar, me dirigí a la plaza de la ciudad para comprarme nuevas vestimentas para mi llegada y un regalo para mi hija. Mientras me encontraba entretenido en esto, un mensajero-veloz llegó corriendo desde Tenochtitlan. Atravesó la plaza de Tolocan y llevaba puestos dos mantos. Uno era blanco, que representaba duelo, porque ese color corresponde al occidente, hacia donde van los muertos. Encima de ése, llevaba un manto color verde, el color que significa buenas noticias. Así que no fue una sorpresa para mí cuando el gobernador de Tolocan hizo el siguiente anuncio públicamente: que el Venerado Orador Auítzotl, quien se encontraba muerto de mente desde hacía ya dos años, había muerto finalmente en cuerpo; y que el señor regente, Motecuzoma El Joven, había sido elevado oficialmente por el Consejo de Voceros al exaltado rango de Uey-Tlatoani de los mexica.

La noticia me puso de un humor como para dirigir mi espalda en dirección a Tenochtitlan y encaminarme otra vez hacia lejanos horizontes. Pero no lo hice. Muchas veces en mi vida me he burlado de la autoridad y he sido irresponsable en mis acciones, pero no siempre me he comportado como un cobarde o un tonto. Seguía siendo un mexícatl, sujeto por lo tanto al Uey-Tlatoani, quienquiera que fuera, sin importar lo lejos que vagara. Es más, yo era un campeón Águila que había jurado fidelidad incluso hasta un Venerado Orador a quien en lo personal no podía venerar.

Sin haberlo conocido jamás, sentía antipatía y desconfianza por Motecuzoma Xocóyotzin; por su intento en frustrar la alianza de *su* Venerado Orador con los tzapoteca, hacía años, así como por la manera tan perversa con la cual había violado a Beu, la hermana de Zyanya. Pero Motecuzoma posiblemente jamás había oído hablar de mí y no podría saber lo que yo sabía acerca de él, y por lo tanto no tenía razón para tenerme antipatía. Hubiera sido un tonto como para darle tal razón al hacer mis sentimientos evidentes o buscar la manera de que él se fijara en mí. Si por ejemplo, a él se le ocurriera tomar en cuenta a los campeones Águila presentes en su inauguración, tal vez se sentiría insultado por la ausencia imperdonable de un campeón llamado Nube Oscura.

Así que me dirigí hacia el este de Tolocan, bajando los empinados cerros que van desde allí hacia el lago y a las ciudades que yacen allí. Al llegar a Tenochtitlan, me dirigí hacia mi casa, donde se me recibió con júbilo por parte de los esclavos Turquesa y Estrella Cantadora, así como por mi amigo Cózcatl, y con menos entusiasmo por parte de su esposa, quien me dijo con lágrimas en los ojos: «Ahora nos quitarás a nuestra querida y pequeña Cocoton.»

Le contesté: «Ella y yo siempre te seremos fieles, Quequelmiqui, y nos podrás visitar tan seguido como quieras hacerlo.»

«Pero no será lo mismo que *tenerla.*»

Le dije a Turquesa: «Dile a la niña que su padre está en casa. Dile que venga a verme.»

Bajaron la escalera cogidas de la mano. A los cuatro años, Cocoton aún estaba en edad de andar desnuda por la casa, y eso hizo que el cambio sufrido en ella fuera inmediatamente obvio para mí. Me dio gusto ver que como había dicho su madre, aún era bella; es más, su parecido físico a Zyanya era más pronunciado. Pero ya no era regordeta sin forma y con miembros como pequeños tronquecillos. Ahora parecía un ser humano en miniatura, con brazos y piernas de verdad y en proporción a su cuerpo. Me había ausentado por dos años, un lapso de tiempo en el cual un hombre entre los treinta años puede pasarlos sin darse cuenta. Pero en ese tiempo mi hija había doblado su edad, tiempo durante el cual se había transformado mágicamente de infante en una encantadora pequeña. De pronto me sentí mal por no haber estado presente para observar su florecimiento, como el desdoblar de un lirio de agua en la noche. Me reproché el haberme privado de esto y me hice una promesa silenciosa de no volver a hacerlo.

Turquesa nos presentó con un gesto de orgullo: «Mi pequeña ama Ce-Malinali llamada Cocoton. Aquí tienes a tu Tata Mixtli, por fin con nosotros. Salúdalo con respeto, tal como se te ha enseñado.»

Agradable fue mi sorpresa al observar que Cocoton cayó graciosamente al suelo para hacerme el gesto de besar la tierra. No alzó la cabeza de esa postura de obediencia hasta que la llamé por su nombre. Fue entonces cuando yo le hice una señal para que se acercara y me regaló una de sus hermosas sonrisas y corrió hacia mis brazos y me dio un tímido y húmedo beso y me dijo: «Tata, estoy contenta de que hayas regresado de tus aventuras.»

Le dije: «Estoy muy contento de encontrar una damita tan bien educada esperando mi regreso. —A Cosquillosa le dije—: Gracias por cumplir tu promesa de mantenerme vivo en su recuerdo.»

Cocoton, moviéndose entre mis brazos para mirar a su alrededor, dijo: «Tampoco me olvidé de mi Tene. Quiero saludarla también.»

Todos los que estaban en el salón dejaron de sonreír y discretamente empezaron a irse. Tomando un fuerte aliento le dije:

«Debo decirte con tristeza, mi pequeña, que los dioses necesitaban la ayuda de tu madre para algo en un lugar muy lejos a donde yo no podía acompañarla, un lugar de donde no puede regresarse; tú y yo debemos hacer nuestras vidas sin ella. Pero no por eso vas a olvidarte de tu Tene.»

«No», me contestó la niña solemnemente.

«Pero para ayudarte a que no la olvides, tu Tene te mandó esto.» Le di el collar que había comprado en Tolocan. Estaba hecho con veinte pequeñas piedras fosforecentes ensartadas en un fino hilo de plata. Dejé que Cocoton lo tomara en sus manos por un momento y las acariciara, luego lo abroché atrás de su delgado cuello. Viendo a la niñita allí, sin más ropa que un collar de ópalos, me hizo sonreír, pero las mujeres exclamaron de gusto y Turquesa corrió a traer un *téxcatl*, espejo.

Dije: «Cocoton, cada una de estas piedras resplandece como lo hacían los ojos de tu madre. En cada uno de tus cumpleaños, vamos a poner una cada vez más grande. Con todas esas luciérnagas brillando alrededor de ti, su luz te recordará siempre a tu Tene Zyanya, y así nunca la olvidarás.»

«Tú sabes que ella nunca la olvidará —dijo Cózcatl y apuntando a Cocoton, quien se estaba admirando en el espejo que sostenía Turquesa, dijo—: Lo único que necesita hacer para recordar a su madre es mirarse en un espejo. Y tú, Mixtli, lo único que necesitas hacer, es ver a Cocoton. —Y como si se sintiera un poco incómodo por haber dado muestras de sentimentalismo, aclarando su voz dijo a Cosquillosa, poniendo cierto énfasis en su voz—: En estos momentos, yo creo que los padres *temporales* deben irse.»

Era obvio que Cózcatl estaba ansioso por dejar mi casa, para irse a vivir a su nueva casa, en donde le sería más fácil supervisar su escuela para sirvientes, pero era igualmente obvio que Cosquillosa, quien había llegado a sentir un gran amor por Cocoton, ahora se sentiría como una madre sin hijos. Ese día que se fueron, tuvimos que esforzarnos por separarla, casi físicamente, pues la mujer no quería quitar sus brazos de alrededor de mi hija. Durante los días siguientes, cuando Cózcatl, Cosquillosa y sus cargadores hicieron repetidos viajes para llevarse todas sus pertenencias, fue Cózcatl quien dirigió la mudanza, ya que cada viaje era para su esposa una excusa para «pasar un último momentito» con Cocoton.

Aun después de que Cózcatl y su esposa ya se habían establecido cómodamente en su propia casa y de que ella debía de estarle ayudando a dirigir la escuela, Cosquillosa todavía inventaba algunas cosas que tenía que hacer cerca de nuestro barrio, para visitar a mi hija. De hecho yo no podía quejarme, pues comprendía que mientras yo me estaba ganando el amor de Cocoton, Cosquillosa estaba tratando de renunciar a él. Yo estaba tratando por todos los medios de que la niña aceptara como su Tata, a un hombre que le era casi totalmente desconocido, así es que simpatizaba con la pena de Cosquillosa, que tenía que dejar de ser su Tene después de haberlo sido por dos años, y naturalmente necesitaba tiempo para ello.

Tuve mucha suerte de que en esos primeros días de mi regreso a casa no fuera llamado a ningún servicio, así es que pasé ese tiempo libre en renovar mi familiaridad con la niña. A pesar de que el Venerado Orador Auítzotl había muerto dos días antes de mi regreso, su funeral —y la coronación de Motecuzoma— no se podía llevar a efecto sin la presencia de cada gobernador, noble y personaje notable de todas las naciones de El Único Mundo, y muchos de ellos tenían que venir desde muy lejos. Mientras todas esas gentes se reunían, el cuerpo de Auítzotl fue preservado cubriéndolo con la nieve que era traída por mensajeros-veloces, desde los picos de los volcanes.

Pero al fin llegó el día del funeral, y yo, con mi traje e insignias de campeón Águila, me encontraba entre toda la multitud que llenaba la plaza, llorando el grito del búho cuando los portadores llevaban a nuestro difunto Uey-Tlatoani en su última jornada, hacia el mundo del más allá. Toda la isla parecía retumbar con nuestro largo y vibrante lamento «¡hoo-oo-ooo!» de despedida. El difunto Auítzotl estaba sentado en su silla, pero encorvado ya que sus rodillas estaban unidas a su pecho, por medio de sus brazos. Su Primera Viuda y sus otras viudas habían lavado el cuerpo en agua de esencia de clavo y de otras hierbas dulces, y lo habían perfumado con *copali*. Sus sacerdotes lo habían vestido con diecisiete mantos, pero de un algodón tan fino, que no hacían bulto. Aparte de todo ese ritual, Auítzotl llevaba una máscara y un manto para darle el aspecto de Huitzilopochtli, dios de guerra y el más grande dios de nosotros los mexica. Ya que el color que distinguía a Huitzilopochtli era el azul, también lo era el traje que llevaba Auítzotl, aunque no estaba pintado ni teñido. La máscara que llevaba sobre su rostro tenía delineadas sus facciones ingeniosamente por medio de pedacitos de turquesa unidos en oro; para los ojos utilizaron obsidiana y nácar y sus labios estaban delineados con piedras-sangre, hematites. Su manto estaba cuajado de fragmentos de jade, que habían sido cosidos, aunque se habían escogido aquellos que se veían más azules que verdes.

Todos los que formábamos parte de la procesión, nos colocamos en orden de prioridad y muchas veces dimos la vuelta al Corazón del Único Mundo, con los tambores tocando suavemente haciendo contrapunto a nuestro canto fúnebre. Auítzolt, en su silla, abría la procesión, que era seguida por el «hoo-oo-ooo» de la multitud. A un lado de su silla caminaba su sucesor, Motecuzoma, pero no caminaba triunfalmente, sino llorando doliente, como lo demandaba la ocasión. Iba descalzo y no llevaba puesto nada ostentoso, sino sólo sus vestiduras harapientas y negras de su época de sacerdote. Su cabello colgaba enmarañado y desgreñado, había puesto polvo de cal en sus ojos para enrojecerlos y para hacerlos llorar continuamente.

Después iban todos los gobernantes de otras naciones y entre ellos algunos conocidos míos como Nezahualpili de Texcoco, Kosi Yuela de Uaxyácac y Tzímtzicha de Michihuacan que se había presentado en representación de su padre Yquíngare, pues éste era demasiado viejo para viajar. Por esa misma razón, el viejo y ciego Xicotenca de Texcali había enviado a su hijo y heredero, El Joven Xicotenca. Esas dos naciones, como ya lo he mencionado tiempo atrás, y como ustedes lo saben, eran rivales y enemigas de Tenochtitlan, pero la muerte de un gobernante de cualquier nación imponía una tregua y obligaba a todos los demás gobernantes a reunirse en público duelo en su funeral, aunque en muchos de sus corazones no existiera tal dolor sino la alegría por su muerte. De todas maneras, ellos y sus nobles podían entrar y salir de la ciudad a salvo de ser asesinados o cualquier otra clase de traición, pues eso estaba completamente fuera de todas las mentes, en el funeral del gobernante de cualquier nación.

Atrás de todos los dignatarios visitantes venía la familia de Auítzotl: La Primera Señora y sus hijas, luego las otras esposas legítimas y sus hijos y al final sus numerosas concubinas con sus todavía más numerosos hijos. El heredero reconocido de Auítzotl, su hijo mayor Cuautémoc, llevaba amarrado a una cadena de oro un perrito que acompañaría al hombre muerto en su jornada al mundo del más allá. Algunos otros de sus hijos, llevaban aquellos artículos que Auítzol deseaba o necesitaría: sus varias banderas, bastones, penachos y otras insignias de su oficio, incluyendo una gran cantidad de joyas; sus uniformes de batalla, sus armas y escudos; algunas otras pertenencias simbólicas que no eran oficiales, pero que él estimaba, incluyendo aquella horrible piel y cabeza de oso gris, que había adornado su trono por tantos años.

Atrás de la familia caminaban todos los hombres viejos del Consejo de Voceros y otros hombres sabios consejeros del Venerado Orador, y sus brujos, sus visionarios, y sus repetidores-de-palabras. Luego venían todos los más altos nobles de su corte y aquellos nobles que habían venido con las delegaciones extranjeras. Detrás de ellos, marchaban la guardia de palacio de Auítzotl, los viejos guerreros que habían servido bajo sus órdenes cuando él todavía no era Uey-Tlatoani y algunos de sus sirvientes y esclavos favoritos, por supuesto las tres compañías de campeones: Águila, Jaguar y Flecha. Yo lo había arreglado todo para que Cózcatl y Cosquillosa pudieran estar al frente de la hilera de espectadores, llevando con ellos a Cocoton, así ella podría verme desfilar con mi uniforme en esa digna compañía aunque fue un poco embarazoso, ya que al pasar frente a ella, su vocecita sobresalió por entre el canto, los tambores y los «hoo-oo-ooo» de la multitud, al gritar alegremente con admiración: «¡Ése es mi Tata Mixtli!»

El cortejo debía cruzar el lago, ya que se había decidido que Auítzotl yaciera al pie del peñasco de Chapultépec, exactamente abajo del lugar en donde se había tallado en la roca magníficamente su semblanza. Como prácticamente cada *acali*, desde el elegante y privado de un cortesano, hasta los lanchones de carga, los de los cazadores de aves y los pescadores, se estaban utilizando para transportar todo el cortejo fúnebre, muchos de los ciudadanos de Tenochtitlan no nos pudieron seguir. Sin embargo, cuando alcanzamos la tierra firme, nos encontramos con que una multitud igual de Tlácopan, Coyohuacan y otras ciudades se había reunido allí para rendir su último homenaje.

Todos caminamos hacia la tumba abierta al pie de la colina de Chapultépec y nos quedamos allí parados, acalorados y sudando bajo el peso de nuestros trajes ceremoniales, mientras los sacerdotes susurraban a Auítzotl sus últimas y largas instrucciones para que pudiera cruzar el terreno prohibido que había entre nuestro mundo y el del más allá.

En estos últimos años, yo he escuchado a Su Ilustrísima el Obispo y a algunos pocos más padres Cristianos, prorrumpir en sus sermones en invectivas contra nuestras bárbaras costumbres funerales, de que cuando un alto personaje muere, nosotros matamos a una gran cantidad de sus esposas y esclavos para que ese personaje sea adecuadamente atendido en el otro mundo. Esa crítica siempre me ha dejado perplejo. Yo estoy completamente de acuerdo en que esa práctica debería de ser condenada, pero me pregunto de dónde sacarían esa idea los padres Cristianos. Yo creo que estoy bastante familiarizado con todas las naciones, gentes y costumbres de todo El Único Mundo, y nunca he sabido que haya ocurrido un entierro en masa de esa clase.

Auítzotl fue el único noble de alto rango que me tocó ver enterrar, pero si algún otro gran personaje hubiera llevado una gran compañía a su muerte, se hubiera sabido. Yo he visto muchos lugares de enterramiento de otras tierras: viejas tumbas sin cubrir en las desiertas ciudades maya, las antiguas criptas de la Gente Nube en Lyobaan, y en ellas solamente he visto los restos de un solo ocupante, como es lo correcto. Por supuesto que cada uno de ellos ha llevado consigo sus insignias de nobleza y prestigio, sus joyas y cosas parecidas, pero ¿esposas y esclavos? No. Esa práctica no sólo hubiera sido más que bárbara, sino también tonta. Quizás un noble agonizante hubiera deseado la compañía de sus familiares y sirvientes, pero aun así, nunca lo hubiera decretado, porque tanto él como ellos y como todo el mundo, sabían que las personas inferiores cuando mueren van a un mundo totalmente diferente al que él va.

La única criatura que murió ese día, en la tumba de Auítzotl fue el perrito que llevaba el Príncipe Cuautémoc y aun para esa pequeña muerte había una razón. El primer obstáculo que se interponía entre el mundo y el más allá, o por lo menos eso era lo que nos decían, era un río negro que corría a un lado de una nación negra y la persona que moría siempre llegaba a ese río en la oscuridad de la noche negra. Solamente lo podría cruzar cogiéndose de un perro que oliera la distante playa y nadara directamente hacia ella, pero ese perro tenía que ser de un color medio. Si era blanco se rehusaría a esa tarea diciendo: «Amo, ya estoy muy limpio por haber estado mucho tiempo en el agua y no me bañaré otra vez.» Si era negro, también declinaría diciendo: «Amo, usted no me podrá ver en la oscuridad. Si no me ve, usted no podrá agarrarse de mí y por lo tanto se perderá.» Así es que Cuautémoc había conseguido un perro de color jacinto, tan rojo como el oro de la cadena de oro rojo que lo sujetaba.

Había también muchísimos obstáculos más allá de ese río

negro, pero ésos los debería vencer Auítzotl por sí mismo. Tendría que pasar entre dos grandes montañas, que en intervalos impredecibles se contraerían juntas y se extenderían. Tendría que escalar otra hecha de pedacitos de cortante obsidiana. Tendría que caminar entre un bosque impenetrable de banderas flotantes, en donde éstas se moverían obstaculizando el sendero y tremolando sobre su rostro para cegarlo y confundirlo; y de allí a una región en donde la lluvia nunca cesaba y en donde cada gota sería como una punta de flecha. En medio de esos dos lugares, tendría que luchar o escabullirse de serpientes, cocodrilos y jaguares que le acecharían ansiosos de comer su corazón.

Y una vez venciendo todo eso, llegaría al fin a Mictlan, en donde el Señor y la Señora que lo gobernaban esperarían su llegada. Allí él tomaría de su boca el jade con que había sido enterrado si no había gritado cobardemente durante su trayecto y lo había perdido en alguna parte. Cuando él alargara esa piedra a Mictlantecutli y a Mictlancíuatl, el Señor y la Señora le sonreirían dándole la bienvenida y lo mandarían hacia el mundo que él merecía, en donde viviría con lujo y felicidad eternas.

Era ya muy tarde cuando los sacerdotes terminaron sus largas instrucciones y sus oraciones de despedida y entonces Auítzotl fue colocado en su tumba junto con el perrito de color oro rojo, la tierra cayó sobre ellos, y fue fuertemente apisionada, mientras los albañiles colocaban una simple piedra para cubrirla. Ya estaba oscuro cuando nuestra flota de *acaltin* atracó otra vez en Tenochtitlan, en donde nos reagrupamos para formar la procesión y marchar otra vez hacia El Corazón del Único Mundo. Para entonces la plaza estaba vacía, pero nosotros tuvimos que permanecer en nuestras filas mientras los sacerdotes rezaban más oraciones a la luz de las antorchas en lo alto de la Gran Pirámide, luego quemaron un incienso especial en las urnas que estaban alrededor de la plaza y por último acompañaron ceremoniosamente al harapiento y descalzo Motecuzoma dentro del templo de Tezcatlipoca, El Espejo Ardiente.

Debo decirles que el haber escogido el templo de ese dios, no tenía ninguna significación especial, pues aunque Tezcatlipoca era considerado en Texcoco y en otros lugares como el más grande de todos los dioses, en Tenochtitlan era mucho menos glorificado. Lo que pasaba era que ese templo era el único en la plaza que tenía su propio patio amurallado. En cuanto Motecuzoma entrara en ese patio, los sacerdotes cerrarían las puertas detrás de él y por cuatro noches y días, el que fue escogido Venerado Orador estaría allí solo ayunando, sin beber y meditando, siendo quemado por el sol o mojado por la lluvia, conforme lo escogieran los dioses, durmiendo sobre la dura piedra del patio, sin ninguna cobija y solamente en ciertos intervalos especificados iría dentro del templo a rezar a todos los dioses —uno por uno— para que lo guiaran en el cargo que en muy poco tiempo desempeñaría.

Todos los demás, arrastramos nuestros cansados pies hacia los palacios, hosterías, casas y cuarteles, agradecidos de no tener que aguantar otro largo día en nuestros trajes, hasta que Motecuzoma saliera de su retiro.

Yo arrastré pesadamente mis sandalias de garras sobre los escalones de entrada de mi casa, y si no hubiese estado tan cansado, me habría sorprendido de que Cosquillosa me abriera la puerta en lugar de Turquesa. Una solitaria lámpara de débil llama, ardía en la entrada del vestíbulo.

Le dije: «Ya es muy tarde. Espero que Cocoton ya esté dormida en su cama. ¿Por qué tú y Cózcatl no os habéis ido a vuestra casa?»

«Cózcatl se fue a Texcoco a tratar un asunto de la escuela. En cuanto se desocupó un *acali* después del funeral, él lo contrató para ir allá. Así es que aproveché esa oportunidad para pasar un rato más con mi... con tu hija. Turquesa te está preparando tu baño y el cuarto de vapor.»

«Bien —dije—. Déjame llamar a Estrella Cantadora para que te alumbre todo el camino hasta tu casa y yo me apresuraré a ir a la cama, para que los sirvientes se puedan acostar también.»

«Espera —dijo nerviosa—. No me quiero ir.» Su rostro de un color cobre claro se había encendido a un color cobre rojizo, como si la débil flama de la lámpara que estaba en el vestíbulo no estuviera atrás de ella sino dentro de su cuerpo. «Cózcatl no estará de vuelta hasta mañana en la noche, lo más pronto. Esta noche me gustaría estar contigo en tu cama, Mixtli.»

«¿Qué significa esto? —dije pretendiendo que no había comprendido—. ¿Pasa algo malo en tu casa, Cosquillosa?»

«¡Sí, y tú sabes qué es! —Su color se encendió todavía más—. Tengo veintiséis años y he estado casada durante cinco y todavía no sé lo que es sentir realmente a un hombre.»

Yo le respondí: «Si te hace sentirte mejor, te diré que tengo una buena razón para creer que nuestro flamante Venerado Orador está tan impedido en ese aspecto como tu esposo Cózcatl.»

«Eso es muy difícil de creer —dijo—, ya que en cuanto se le dio la regencia a Motecuzoma, éste tomó *dos* esposas.»

«Y que presumiblemente han de estar tan insatisfechas como tú lo estás.»

Cosquillosa denegó impacientemente con la cabeza. «Por lo menos es lo suficientemente adecuado como para embarazar a sus esposas. Cada una de ellas tiene un niño, ¡y es más de lo que yo puedo esperar! Si fuera la esposa del Venerado Orador, por lo menos pariría un hijo. Pero no he venido aquí para hablar de las esposas de Motecuzoma. ¡No me importan las esposas de Motecuzoma!»

Yo dejé caer inmediatamente: «¡Ni a mí! ¡Pero les alabo que sigan estando en sus propias camas conyugales, en lugar de venir a asediar la mía!»

«No seas cruel conmigo, Mixtli —dijo—. Si sólo supieras lo que he sufrido. ¡Cinco años, Mixtli! Cinco años de sumisión y de pretender que me siento satisfecha. He rezado y he hecho ofren-

das a Xochiquétzatl, suplicándole que me ayude a estar contenta
con las atenciones de mi esposo. Pero no ha dado resultado. Todo
el tiempo me pregunto: ¿Cómo será en realidad, con un hombre normal? Ese preguntarme, y luego la tentación, la indecisión
y finalmente el tener que humillarme al pedírtelo a ti.»

«Así es que me lo pides a mí, de entre todos los hombres,
a mí, para que traicione a mi mejor amigo. Para poner a la
esposa de mi mejor amigo y a mí a riesgo del garrote.»

«Pues por eso te lo he pedido, porque tú eres su amigo.
Tú nunca te estarías sugiriendo como otro hombre lo haría.
Y aunque Cózcatl se diera cuenta, él nos ama lo suficiente a
ambos como para denunciarnos. —Ella hizo una pausa y luego
añadió—: Si el mejor amigo de Cózcatl no hace esto, entonces
le hace un gran perjuicio. Te digo la verdad. Si tú no me aceptas, no me humillaré más pidiéndoselo a algún otro conocido,
alquilaré a un hombre por una noche o se lo pediré a algún
forastero en alguna hostería. Piensa en lo que eso sería para
Cózcatl.»

Yo pensé. Y recordé que un día él había dicho que si esa
mujer no lo quería, él acabaría con su vida de algún modo. Yo
le creí entonces y también creí que él haría lo mismo si llegaba a saber que ella lo traicionaba.

Le dije: «Dejando todas esas consideraciones a un lado, Cosquillosa, en estos momentos estoy tan fatigado que no serviría
para ninguna mujer. Has esperado cinco años, así es que yo
creo que puedes aguardar hasta que me haya bañado y haya
dormido, sobre todo si dices que tenemos todo el día de mañana. Así es que ve a tu casa y piensa un poco más sobre esto
y si mañana todavía estás determinada a...»

«Así lo hare, Mixtli. Y vendré mañana otra vez.»

Llamé a Estrella Cantadora y él encendió una antorcha, y
él y Cosquillosa salieron a la noche. Estaba tomando mi baño
cuando le oí regresar, y fácilmente me hubiera quedado dormido, de no haber sido porque el agua estaba demasiado fría, y
me forzó a salir. Me tambaleé hacia mi habitación y me dejé
caer sobre la cama, cogí las cobijas y me quedé profundamente
dormido, sin tomarme siquiera la molestia de apagar la lámpara que Turquesa había dejado encendida.

Sin embargo, aun en medio de mi sueño pesado, debí de
estar anticipando y temiendo el regreso impetuoso de la impaciente Cosquillosa, porque abrí los ojos cuando la puerta se
abrió. La luz de la lámpara era pobre y débil, pero por la ventana entraba una gris claridad, la primera luz del amanecer y
lo que vi me hizo estremecer.

De abajo no había llegado ningún sonido que me previniera
de esa aparición increíble e inesperada... y estaba seguro de que
si Turquesa o Estrella Cantadora hubieran visto a ese fantasma
en particular, habrían proferido un grito. Aunque ella estaba
vestida para viajar, con un chal en la cabeza y un pesado manto
de piel de conejo y aunque la luz era débil, mi mano tembló al
levantar el topacio enfrente de mi ojo para ver... ¡a Zyanya
parada enfrente de mí!

«Zaa —dijo en un susurro deliciosamente audible, pues era la voz de Zyanya—. No estás dormido, Zaa.»

Pero debí de estarlo, estaba seguro de eso, pues estaba viendo lo imposible y eso sólo lo había visto en sueños.

«Sólo tenía la intención de mirar. No deseaba despertarte», dijo ella, todavía susurrando; manteniendo su voz baja para que no me espantara, por lo menos eso supuse.

Traté de hablar, pero no pude, una experiencia que también había tenido en sueños.

«Iré a la otra habitación», dijo ella. Su chal se movió al impulso de su movimiento, y empezó a caminar tan despacio, como si estuviera muy cansada habiendo viajado por un largo, inimaginable largo camino. Pensé en todos los obstáculos, en esas montañas que se cerraban juntas, en el río negro de la noche negra, y temblé de miedo.

«Cuando mandé mi mensaje para avisar de mi llegada —dijo ella—, tenía la esperanza de que no me esperaras dormido.» Sus palabras no tenían ningún sentido para mí, hasta que su chal resbaló de su cabeza y entonces vi que no había ningún mechón blanco en su pelo. Beu Ribé continuó: «Por supuesto, que sería muy agradable saber que al recibir mi mensaje de llegada, éste te excitó tanto que no pudiste dormir. Estaría muy contenta de saber que estabas tan ansioso de verme.»

Por fin encontré mi voz y ésta sonó áspera: «¡No recibí ningún mensaje! ¿Cómo te atreves a entrar a hurtadillas en mi casa? ¿Cómo puedes pretender que...?» Pero me reprimí, pues no era justo acusarla de parecerse tanto a su difunta hermana, como si ella lo hiciera a propósito.

Ella pareció genuinamente abatida y empezó a balbucear tratando de explicar: «Pero yo mandé a un muchacho... Le di una semilla de cacao para que trajera el mensaje. ¿Entonces no vino? Pero si allá abajo... Estrella Cantadora me recibió muy cordialmente. Y te encontré despierto, Zaa...»

Yo gruñí: «Ya antes Estrella Cantadora me invitó a que le diera una buena azotaina. Tendré que hacerlo esta vez.»

Hubo un corto silencio, en el cual yo estaba esperando que mi corazón dejara de latir fuertemente, por el miedo, la alarma y la alegría. Beu se sintió vencida por el aturdimiento y reprochándose su intrusión dijo por fin, demasiado humildemente para ella: «Iré a dormir al cuarto que antes ocupé. Quizás mañana estés menos enojado porque yo estoy aquí...» Y salió de la habitación antes de que yo pudiera responder.

Por un breve momento en la mañana, respiré un poco del sentimiento que tenía de verme asediado por mujeres. Fui a desayunar solo, a excepción de los dos esclavos que me servían, pero empecé el día gruñendo: «No me agradan las sorpresas que llegan en la madrugada.»

«¿Sorpresas, mi amo?», dijo Turquesa sin saber de lo que yo hablaba.

«No me avisasteis de la llegada de la señora Beu.»

Ella dijo todavía más perpleja: «¿La señora Beu está aquí? ¿En la casa?»

«Sí —dijo Estrella Cantadora—. También fue una sorpresa para mí, amo, pero supuse que a usted se le había olvidado informarnos.»

Por lo tanto, el muchacho que Beu había enviado, nunca avisó de su inminente llegada. El primer aviso que tuvo de eso Estrella Cantadora fue cuando unos golpecitos en la puerta de la calle, lo despertaron. Como Turquesa seguía durmiendo, él se levantó para dejar entrar a la visitante y ella le había dicho que no me molestara.

«Como la señora Luna que Espera llegó con bastantes cargadores —dijo él—, yo supuse que ya la estaba usted esperando. —Eso explicaba por qué él no se había asustado al verla, pensando erróneamente como yo lo hice, que era el fantasma de Zyanya—. Ella me dijo que no lo despertara a usted, y que no hiciera ningún ruido, ya que ella conocía la casa, podía ir escaleras arriba. Sus cargadores trajeron mucho equipaje, mi amo, y yo acomodé todos sus bultos y canastos en el cuarto de enfrente.»

Bueno, por lo menos podía dar gracias de que ninguno de los sirvientes se había dado cuenta de mi perturbación ante la presencia repentina de Beu y que Cocoton no se había despertado y asustado, así es que olvidé el asunto. Seguí tomando mi desayuno con tranquilidad, aunque no por mucho tiempo. Estrella Cantadora, aparentemente temeroso de que me volviera a enojar con nuevas sorpresas, vino a anunciarme con toda formalidad de que tenía otra visitante, pero que a ésta no la había admitido más allá de la puerta de la entrada. Sabiendo de antemano quién era, terminé mi *chocólatl* y suspirando fui hacia la entrada.

«¿Nadie me va a invitar a pasar? —dijo Cosquillosa en broma—. Éste es un lugar muy público, Mixtli, para lo que nosotros va...»

«Debemos olvidar todo lo que hablamos —la interrumpí—. La hermana de mi difunta esposa llegó de visita. Tú recuerdas a Beu Ribé.»

Por un momento Cosquillosa me miró desconcertada. Luego dijo: «Bueno, si no lo podemos hacer aquí, entonces ven a mi casa.»

Dije: «Entiende, querida, que es la primera visita de Beu en tres años. Sería muy descortés por mi parte el dejarla sola y muy difícil de explicar el porqué.»

«¡Pero Cózcatl regresará esta noche!», gimió.

«Entonces temo que hemos perdido nuestra oportunidad.»

«¡Debemos tener otra! —dijo desesperadamente—. ¿Cómo podemos arreglar otra y cuándo?»

«Probablemente nunca —dije, no muy seguro de sentir pena o alivio ante esa delicada situación, que se resolvía de esa manera—. De hoy en adelante, habrán aquí muchos ojos y oídos. No podremos evitarlos. Es mejor que te olvides de...»

«¡Tú sabías que ella iba a llegar! —se encendió Cosquillosa—.

¡Sólo estabas aparentando cansancio anoche, para que me fuera y luego tener una verdadera excusa para rehusarte!»

«Cree lo que quieras —dije cansado y no estaba aparentándolo—. Pero debo rehusar.»

Ella pareció desplomarse. Desviando sus ojos de mí, dijo suavemente: «Por mucho tiempo tú has sido mi amigo, y por más lo has sido de mi esposo, pero lo que estás haciendo en estos momentos, Mixtli, no es de amigos. Para ninguno de los dos.» Y ella bajó despacio la escalera y muy lentamente se alejó a lo largo de la calle.

Cuando volvía al interior de la casa, Cocoton estaba tomando su desayuno, así es que llamé a Estrella Cantadora e inventando un mandato totalmente innecesario en el mercado de Tlatelolco, lo mandé sugiriendo que llevara a la niña consigo. Cuando ella terminó de desayunar, se fueron los dos y yo esperé no muy contento que Beu hiciera su aparición. La confrontación con Cosquillosa no había sido fácil para mí, pero por lo menos había sido breve, cosa que no esperaba con Luna que Espera. Ella durmió hasta tarde y bajó la escalera al mediodía, con la cara hinchada y líneas marcadas en su rostro, debido a un sueño ligero. Yo me senté en el lado opuesto de la mesa y cuando Turquesa la hubo servido y se retiró a la cocina, le dije:

«Siento mucho haberte recibido con tanta aspereza, hermana Beu. No estoy acostumbrado a recibir visitas tan temprano y mis modales no son los mejores, hasta haber pasado un tiempo considerable después de la aurora, y de todos los visitantes que yo esperara, el último serías tú. ¿Puedo preguntarte por qué estás aquí?»

Ella me miró con incredulidad, casi sorprendida: «¿Y necesitas preguntármelo, Zaa? Entre nosotros, la Gente Nube, los lazos familiares están fuertemente unidos. Yo pensé que podría ser de alguna ayuda, de alguna utilidad, aun un consuelo para el viudo de mi hermana y para su criatura huérfana.»

Le dije: «En cuanto al viudo, he estado fuera de la nación desde la muerte de Zyanya. He ido muy lejos, y por lo menos he sobrevivido a mi aflicción. En cuanto a Cocoton, ella ha sido muy bien atendida durante estos dos años. Mis amigos Cózcatl y Quequelmiqui han sido unos adorables Tata y Tene. —Y añadí secamente—: Durante esos dos años, tu aparente solicitud no ha sido muy evidente.»

«¿Y de quién es la culpa? —me demandó enojada—. ¿Por qué no me mandaste un mensajero-veloz para que me contara la tragedia? No fue sino hasta hace un año que recibí, casi por casualidad, tu carta arrugada y tiznada, que me fue entregada por un mercader que pasaba. ¡Mi hermana llevaba muerta más de un año cuando lo supe! Y después me tomó casi la mayor parte del año para encontrar alguien que me comprara la hostería, para arreglar todos los detalles de la venta y para prepararme para venir a Tenochtitlan a vivir permanentemente. Entonces supimos que el Venerado Orador Auítzotl había vuelto de su locura y que pronto había muerto, lo que significaba que nuestro Bishosu Kosi Yuela, naturalmente, tendría que asistir a la ceremonia aquí. Así es que esperé hasta poder viajar con su escolta, para mi conveniencia y protección. Sin embargo me detuve en Coyohuacan, no queriendo tener que pasar entre el gentío que había en la ciudad, durante el funeral y fue por eso que le di un cacao a aquel muchacho para que te viniera a avisar de que pronto estaría aquí. No fue sino hasta cerca de la madrugada que pude procurar cargadores para mis pertenencias. Te pido que me disculpes por haber llegado en ese momento y en la forma en que llegué, pero...»

Ella se detuvo para respirar y yo, que me sentía bastante avergonzado conmigo mismo, le dije sinceramente: «Yo soy quien debo pedirte disculpas, Beu. Has llegado en el mejor momento posible. Los padres que había tomado prestados para Cocoton, han regresado a sus propios asuntos, así es que la niña sólo me tiene a mí, y debo reconocer tristemente que tengo muy poca experiencia como padre. Cuando te digo que eres bien venida, no te estoy diciendo sólo una formalidad. Como madre sustituta para mi hija, seguro que tú serás la mejor después de Zyanya.»

«La mejor, después», repitió ella no demostrando gran entusiasmo por mi cumplido.

«En muchos sentidos —dije—, tú podrás enseñarle a hablar el lenguaje lóochi tan fluido como nuestro náhuatl. Tú puedes hacer que ella sea tan encantadora y cortés como esos niños de la Gente Nube que tanto admiré. De verdad, que solamente tú podrás enseñarle *todas* esas cosas que Zyanya era. Este mundo será mejor cuando haya otra Zyanya.»

«Otra Zyanya. Sí.»

Yo concluí: «Puedes considerar esta casa, desde ahora y para siempre, como tu hogar y a la niña como tu pupila y los esclavos están a tus órdenes. Daré órdenes en este momento de que tu cuarto sea totalmente vaciado, limpiado y vuelto a amueblar a tu gusto. Cualquier cosa que necesites o desees, no necesitas preguntar, hermana Beu, sólo tienes que decirlo. —Pareció como si ella fuera a decir algo, pero cambió de idea. Yo seguí—: Y en estos momentos... llega Migajita del mercado.»

La niñita entró a la habitación, radiante en su manto de un amarillo dorado. Ella miró largamente a Beu Ribé y movió su cabeza como si estuviera recordando dónde había visto ese rostro antes. Yo no pude saber si ella se daba cuenta de que lo había visto muy seguido en sus espejos.

«¿No me quieres hablar? —dijo Beu, casi sin voz por la emoción—. He esperado tanto tiempo...»

Cocoton dijo tímidamente y deteniendo el aliento: «¿Tene...?»

«¡Oh, querida!», exclamó Luna que Espera, y las lágrimas asomaron a sus ojos, cuando ella se arrodilló y extendió sus brazos hacia la niñita, que feliz se dejó envolver por ellos.

«¡Muerte! —rugió el alto sacerdote de Huitzilopochtli, desde lo alto de la Gran Pirámide—. Fue la muerte la que dejó caer el manto del Venerado Orador sobre tus hombros, Señor Motecuzoma Xocóyotl y a su debido tiempo la muerte vendrá por ti,

543

y entonces tendrás que dar cuenta a los dioses, por la manera en que llevaste ese manto y ejerciste tu alto oficio.»

Él continuó así, en la forma usual en que los sacerdotes menosprecian a sus sufridos oyentes, mientras yo y mis compañeros campeones, los nobles mexica, los dignatarios extranjeros y sus nobles, mientras todos nosotros sufríamos abotagados bajo nuestros yelmos, plumas, pieles, armaduras y otros trajes llenos de color y esplendor. Los varios miles de otros mexica que se apiñaban en El Corazón del Único Mundo, no llevaban más que los engorrosos mantos de algodón por lo que espero que disfrutaran más de la ceremonia de inauguración que nosotros.

El sacerdote dijo: «Motecuzoma Xocóyotzin, desde este día tu corazón debe ser como el de un viejo: solemne, serio y severo. Tienes que saber, mi señor, que el trono de un Uey-Tlatoani no está acojinado para yacer en él, en el ocio y el placer, sino para yacer en él en sufrimiento, trabajo y preocupación.»

Yo dudo que Motecuzoma estuviera sudando como todos nosotros, a pesar de llevar puestos dos mantos, uno negro y otro azul, los dos bordados de calaveras y otros símbolos, para recordarle que aun hasta un Venerado Orador muere algún día. Incluso dudo que Motecuzoma sudara alguna vez. Por supuesto que nunca puse ni un dedo sobre su piel, pero siempre parecía tan frío y seco.

El sacerdote siguió: «Desde este día, mi señor, debes convertirte en un árbol de gran sombra para que la multitud pueda encontrar refugio entre sus ramas y se apoyen en la fuerza de tu tronco.»

Aunque la ocasión era solemne y bastante impresionante, lo fue menos que en otras coronaciones anteriores durante mi vida, aunque no fui testigo de ellas, como las de Axayáctl, Tixoc y Auítzotl, ya que Motecuzoma fue nada más confirmado en el oficio en que ya había trabajado por dos años.

Y el sacerdote dijo: «Mi señor, usted debe gobernar y defender a su pueblo y tratarlo con justicia. Usted debe castigar al débil y corregir al desobediente. Usted debe ser diligente en procurar todas las guerras que sean necesarias. Usted debe dar una especial atención a los requerimientos de los dioses, a sus templos y a sus sacerdotes, que no les falten ofrendas y sacrificios. Así los dioses se sentirán contentos y mirarán por usted y por su pueblo, y todos los asuntos de los mexica prosperarán.»

Desde donde yo estaba, las banderas de plumas, que suavemente se movían, se alineaban a lo largo de la escalera de la Gran Pirámide y parecían convergir hacia las alturas, como una flecha apuntando las figuras distantes y pequeñas de nuestro nuevo Venerado Orador y del viejo sacerdote que en ese momento ponía sobre su cabeza la corona de piel enjoyada. Al fin se calló el sacerdote y Motecuzoma habló:

«Grande y respetuoso sacerdote, tus palabras pudieron haber sido dichas por el mismo y poderoso Huitzilopochtli. Tus palabras me han dado mucho en qué reflexionar. Y rezo para poder llegar a efectuar el sabio consejo que me has dado. Gracias por tu fervor y aprecio el amor con que has hablado. Si he de llegar a ser el hombre que mi pueblo desea que sea, debo recordar siempre tus palabras sabias, tus advertencias, tus amonestaciones...»

Listos hasta para destrozar las mismas nubes del cielo cuando Motecuzoma terminara su discurso de aceptación, las hileras de sacerdotes tenían ya en sus manos las conchas trompetas, los músicos levantaban sus baquetas y tenían listas sus flautas.

Y Motecuzoma siguió: «Estoy muy orgulloso de volver a poner en el trono el nombre estimado de mi venerado abuelo. Estoy orgulloso de llamarme Motecuzoma El Joven. Y en honor de la nación que voy a guiar, una nación todavía más poderosa que en los tiempos de mi abuelo, mi primer decreto en este cargo que ya ocupo, es no volver a llamar a los Venerados Oradores de los mexica por ese título, sino por otro todavía más adecuado.

—Él se volvió para dar la cara a la multitud que llenaba la plaza y levantando su bastón de oro, gritó—: Desde estos momentos, mi pueblo, serás gobernado, defendido y guiado hasta alcanzar las más grandes alturas por Motecuzoma Xocóyotzin, ¡Cem-Anáhuac Uey-Tlatoani!»

Si a todos los que estábamos en la plaza nos hubieran arrullado hasta dormir, con todos esos discursos que tuvimos que aguantar por medio día, tendríamos que haber despertado con ese grito resonante que pareció hacer que toda la isla trepitara. Y en ese mismo instante se dejó oír el sonido producido por las flautas, los trinos, los broncos bramidos de las conchas y el increíble retumbar de unos veinte tambores que arrancan el corazón, todos a un mismo tiempo. Pero creo que los músicos, también podrían haber estado dormidos y que sus instrumentos hubieran permanecido mudos, si no hubiera sido por el impacto que las últimas palabras de Motecuzoma produjeron en todos nosotros.

Entre nosotros los campeones Águila, nos intercambiamos miradas y pude ver cómo los numerosos gobernantes extranjeros se intercambiaban gestos de desagrado. Aun la gente del pueblo se mostraba sorprendida por el anuncio del nuevo señor, y nadie estaba muy complacido ante esa audacia. Cada uno de los gobernantes anteriores, en toda la historia de nuestra nación, se habían sentido satisfechos con ser llamados solamente Uey-Tlatoani de los mexica. Pero Motecuzoma acababa de extender su dominio hasta los horizontes más lejanos, en todas direcciones.

Se acababa de conferir un nuevo título: Venerado Orador de todo el Único Mundo.

✠

Cuando arrastrando los pies llegué a mi casa esa noche, otra vez estaba ansioso por quitarme todo el plumaje que llevaba, y meterme en una nube de limpio vapor, así es que hice un simple saludo a mi hija, en lugar de cargarla y aventarla hacia arriba de mi cabeza para luego abrazarla, como acostumbraba a hacer. Estaba sentada en el piso, sin ropa y arqueaba el cuerpo hacia atrás, mientras sostenía un *tézcatl*, espejo, tras su cabeza, tratando de mirarse su espalda desnuda y estaba demasiado absorta en eso, como para tomar en cuenta mi llegada. Encontré a Beu en la habitación de al lado y le pregunté qué estaba haciendo Cocoton.

«Está en la edad de hacer preguntas.»

«¿Acerca de espejos?»

«Acerca de su propio cuerpo —dijo Beu y añadió con desprecio—. Su Tene Cosquillosa le contó un sinnúmero de ignorantes conjeturas. ¿Sabes que una vez Cocoton le preguntó que por qué a ella no le colgaba nada enfrente, como lo que tenía su compañerito de juegos? ¿Y sabes lo que le dijo Cosquillosa? Que si Cocoton era buena en este mundo, ella sería recompensada en la otra vida, al reencarnarse siendo un niño.»

Como estaba muy cansado y malhumorado, y no muy contento con la carga de mi propio cuerpo, sólo murmuré: «Nunca sabré por qué las mujeres pueden pensar en que sea una *recompensa* el nacer hombre.»

«Es exactamente lo que le dije a Cocoton —dijo Beu con afectación—. Que una mujer es muy superior. También está más bien hecha, no teniendo una excrecencia como ese colgajo de enfrente.»

«¿Y está tratando de ver si en su lugar no le crece una cola por detrás?», pregunté, indicando a la niña que trataba de verse la parte baja de su espalda, con el espejo.

«No. Es sólo que se dio cuenta de que cada uno de sus compañeros de juego tiene la *tlacihuitztli*, y me preguntó si ella también tenía una, pues no se había dado cuenta. Así es que está tratando de examinarla.»

Quizás ustedes, reverendos frailes, como todos los españoles que han llegado recientemente, no estén familiarizados con la *tlacihuitztli*, marca, pues tengo entendido que los niños blancos no la tienen. Y si es que aparece en los cuerpos de sus negros, supongo que no se notará. Pero todos nuestros infantes nacen con ella: una mancha oscura como si fuera un moretón en la parte baja de la espalda. Puede ser tan grande como un platito o tan pequeña como una uña y no puede tener ninguna función, aunque gradualmente disminuye hasta borrarse pues a los diez años más o menos, desaparece totalmente.

«Le dije a Cocoton —continuó Beu— que cuando la *tlacihuitztli* desapareciera, ella sería una pequeña señora.»

«¿Una señora a los diez años de edad? No le des unas ideas tan caprichosas.»

Beu dijo con altivez: «¿Como algunas ideas tontas que tú le das, Zaa?»

«¿Yo? —exclamé perplejo—. Yo siempre he contestado a sus preguntas de la manera más honesta que he podido.»

«Cocoton me dijo que un día que la llevaste a pasear al nuevo parque de Chapultépec, ella te preguntó por qué el pasto era verde y que tú le respondiste que para que ella no caminara en el cielo por error.»

«Oh —dije—. Bueno, fue la respuesta más honesta que pude encontrar. ¿Sabes alguna otra mejor?»

«El pasto es verde —dijo Beu autoritariamente— porque los dioses han decidido que sea así.»

Yo dije: «*Ayya*, eso nunca se me hubiera ocurrido. Tienes razón. —Asentí con la cabeza—. No hay duda de eso. —Ella sonrió complacida de su sabiduría y de sus conocimientos—. Pero dime, ¿por qué los dioses escogieron el *verde* en lugar del rojo, o el amarillo o algún otro color?»

Ah, Su Ilustrísima llega a tiempo para esclarecerme algo. En el tercer día de la Creación, ¿no es así? Según usted ha recitado las palabras de nuestro Señor Dios. «A cada cosa que se arrastra por la tierra, Yo le he dado cada una de las hierbas verdes.» Uno difícilmente podría diferir de eso. Que la hierba es verde es evidente hasta para uno que no es Cristiano y por supuesto nosotros los Cristianos sabemos que nuestro Señor Dios la hizo así. Yo simplemente me pregunto, todavía, después de todos los años que han pasado desde que mi hija lo inquirió, ¿por qué nuestro Señor Dios la hizo *verde* en lugar de...?

¿Motecuzoma? ¿Que cómo era?

Ah, ya entiendo. A Su Ilustrísima le interesa oír cosas más importantes: usted se impacienta, con mucha razón, al escuchar trivialidades como el color de la hierba, y esas pequeñas y queridas cosas, que a través de los años recuerdo de mi pequeña familia. No obstante, el gran Señor Motecuzoma, en cualquier lugar que yazca olvidado ahora, no es más que una tiznada materia descompuesta enterrada, y quizás solamente discernible por la hierba que crece, brillantemente verde, en el lugar en que él yace. Para mí, parece que el Señor Dios tomó más cuidado en mantener Su hierba verde, que lo que Él se preocupa por mantener verde el recuerdo de los grandes nobles.

Sí, sí, Su Ilustrísima. Cesaré ya en mis vanas reflexiones. Echaré mi mente hacia atrás para satisfacer su curiosidad acerca de la naturaleza del hombre, Motecuzoma Xocóyotzin.

Y ese hombre era solamente eso, un simple hombre. Como ya lo he dicho, él era aproximadamente un año más joven que yo, lo que quiere decir que cuando él tomó el trono de los mexica, o de todo el Único Mundo, como lo haría, tenía treinta y cinco años. Tenía el promedio de estatura de los mexica, pero su cuerpo era tan delgado y su cabeza tan chica, que esta desproporción le hacía parecer mucho más chaparro de lo que en realidad era. Su complexión era fina, de un color de cobre pálido, sus ojos tenían un brillo frío y hubiera podido ser guapo, si no hubiera sido por su nariz que era demasiado chata, pues sus aletas se extendían muy abiertas.

En la ceremonia de coronación, cuando Motecuzoma se quitó los mantos negro y azul, que significaban humildad, estaba envuelto en unas vestiduras que sobrepasaban toda riqueza, que allí mismo quedó establecido la clase de gusto con que se favorecería a partir de entonces. En cada una de sus apariciones en público, cada uno de sus trajes era diferente de los otros en diseño y en cada detalle, pero su suntuosidad era siempre más o menos como la que voy a describir:

Usaba, ya sea un *máxtlatl* de suave piel roja o de algodón ricamente bordado, cuyos extremos le colgaban hasta las rodillas, adelante y atrás. Ese taparrabo tan amplio, sospecho que lo había adoptado para prevenir que alguna postura accidental pusiera al descubierto la malformación de sus genitales, y trataba de evitarlo. Sus sandalias eran doradas y algunas veces, si solo aparecía delante del pueblo y no tenía que caminar mucho, las suelas eran de oro sólido. Utilizaba toda clase de adornos, como una cadena de oro con medallón, sobre el pecho, que lo cubría casi totalmente; un pendiente para su labio inferior, hecho de cristal que envolvía una pluma del pájaro pescador; orejeras de jade y turquesa en la nariz. Su cabeza estaba coronada por una diadema de oro, de donde partía un penacho de largas plumas o uno maravilloso con plumas del *quétzotl tótotl* y cada una de ellas era del largo de un brazo.

Sin embargo, lo que más sobresalía de su vestimenta era su manto, que siempre era del mismo largo, de los hombros a los tobillos, y siempre hecho con las más bellas plumas de los pájaros más raros y más preciosos, primorosamente trabajadas. Tenía mantos hechos con todas las plumas escarlatas, con todas las plumas amarillas, todas en azul o en verde, o algunos de plumas combinadas en diversos colores. Pero el que recuerdo más y el más bello, era un manto voluminoso hecho con miles de plumas multicolores, iridiscentes y centelleantes, de colibríes. Si le recuerdo a usted que la pluma de un colibrí, es un poco más grande que las cejas afelpadas y pequeñas de un insecto grande, Su Ilustrísima, es para que usted pueda apreciar el talento, el trabajo y el ingenio de los artesanos en plumas, para hacer ese manto y el inestimable valor de esa verdadera obra de arte.

Durante los dos años de su regencia, Motecuzoma no hizo notorio sus gustos por demás lujosos, mientras vivía Auítzotl o medio vivía. Motecuzoma y sus dos esposas habían vivido sencillamente, ocupando sólo algunos rincones del viejo palacio, bastante abandonado, construido por su abuelo Motecuzoma El Viejo. Se había vestido modestamente y había evitado toda pompa y ceremonia, incluso se había refrenado de ejercer todo su poder en los asuntos inherentes a la regencia. No había promulgado ninguna ley nueva, no había fundado ninguna guarnición en una nueva frontera, no había instigado ninguna guerra. Había centrado su atención, sólo en aquellos asuntos cotidianos de los dominios de los mexica, que no requerían importantes decisiones o pronunciamientos.

Sin embargo, en el momento de su coronación como Uey-Tlatoani, cuando Motecuzoma se quitó esas sombrías vestiduras negra y azul, en ese mismo momento, él echó fuera toda humildad. Creo que podría ilustrarle mejor sobre esto, contándole mi primera entrevista con ese hombre, algunos meses después de su ascensión, cuando él empezó a llamar, para entrevistarlos uno por uno, a todos sus nobles y campeones. Expresó su deseo de llegar a ser familiar a aquellos subordinados que sólo conocía por nombre o en la lista oficial, pero yo creo que su verdadera intención era impresionarnos con su nuevo aire de majestad y magnificencia y que le llegáramos a temer. Bueno, el caso es que cuando él terminó de entrevistar a todos los cortesanos, nobles, hombres sabios, sacerdotes, brujos y adivinos, llegó por fin a los campeones Águila y sólo fue cuestión de tiempo que me llamara a su presencia, así es que una mañana me presenté en palacio. Llegué, otra vez sintiéndome incómodo bajo el resplandor de mi uniforme emplumado, cuando el mayordomo de palacio que estaba afuera del salón del trono me dijo:

«¿Sería usted tan amable, mi señor Campeón Águila Mixtli, en despojarse por sí mismo de su uniforme?»

«No —dije llanamente—, me costó mucho trabajo *ponérmelo.*»

«Mi señor —dijo tan nervioso como un conejo—. Ésta es una orden que dio personalmente el Venerado Orador. Si usted es tan amable de quitarse el yelmo de cabeza de águila, el manto y las sandalias de garras, usted puede cubrir la armadura acojinada con esto.»

«¿Con estos harapos? —exclamé, cuando él me alargó una vestimenta informe, hecha con tela de fibra de maguey que nosotros usábamos para costales—. ¡Hombre, no soy un mendigo ni un suplicante! ¿Cómo se atreve usted a esto?»

«Por favor, mi señor —me suplicó, retorciéndose las manos—. Usted no es el primero en resentirse. De aquí en adelante, ésta será la vestimenta con que todo el mundo aparecerá enfrente del Venerado Orador, deberán verlo descalzos y vestidos como mendigos. No puedo dejarlos pasar en otra forma o me costará la vida.»

«Esto es una tontería», gruñí, pero para ayudar al pobre conejo me quité el yelmo y todo lo que llevaba, y dejando también el escudo a un lado, me puse ese saco encima.

«Bueno, cuando usted entre en...», empezó a decir el hombre.

«Gracias —le dije encrespado—, pero sé muy bien cómo comportarme en la presencia de altos personajes.»

«Es que ahora hay otras reglas para el protocolo —dijo el desgraciado—. Le ruego, mi señor, que no se enoje ni deje caer su desagrado en mí. Yo sólo digo las órdenes que me dan.»

«Dígamelas», dije rechinando los dientes.

«Hay tres marcas de cal en el piso entre la puerta y la silla del Venerado Orador. En cuanto usted entre, la primera marca está un poco más allá del umbral. Allí se para usted y hace el gesto de *tlalqualiztli,* un dedo al piso y a sus labios, diciendo: "Señor." Camine hacia la segunda marca, haga otra vez la reverencia y diga: "Mi señor." Camine hacia la tercera marca, bese la tierra otra vez y diga: "Mi gran Señor." Y no se levante hasta que él se lo autorice y no se mueva de esa tercera marca, para aproximarse más a su persona.»

«Esto es increíble», dije.

Desviando la mirada, el mayordomo continuó: «Sólo le dirigirá la palabra al Venerado Orador cuando él le pregunte algo directamente. Nunca levante la voz, más allá de un discreto murmullo. La entrevista concluirá cuando el Venerado Orador lo diga. En ese momento, haga el *tlalqualiztli* en donde usted está, luego camine hacia atrás...»

«Esto es una locura.»

«Camine hacia atrás, siempre dando su cara respetuosamente al trono, besando la tierra en cada marca y continúe hacia atrás hasta que esté afuera de la puerta, otra vez en este corredor. Entonces podrá tomar otra vez sus vestiduras y su rango...»

«Y mi dignidad humana», dije con acritud.

«*Ayya*, se lo suplico mi señor —dijo el aterrorizado conejo—. No vaya a decir ninguna clase de broma como ésa, en su presencia. Caminará hacia atrás, pero por partes.»

Cuando me hube aproximado al trono, en la forma humillante en que lo habían prescrito, diciendo en los intervalos apropiados: «Señor... mi señor... mi gran señor», Motecuzoma me dejó allí inclinado por un tiempo largo, antes de que condescendiera a hablarme, arrastrando las palabras: «Se puede levantar, Campeón Águila Chicome-Xochitl Tliléctic-Mixtli.»

Formados en hilera detrás de su trono, estaban todos los ancianos del Consejo de Voceros, la mayoría de ellos, por supuesto, habían formado parte de este consejo en reinados anteriores, pero había dos o tres caras nuevas. Una de ellas, era el recién nombrado Mujer Serpiente, Tlácotzin. Todos los hombres estaban descalzos y en lugar de los mantos amarillos que los distinguían, no llevaban más que el saco pardusco que yo tenía puesto y todos ellos se sentían infelices. El trono del Venerado Orador era sólo una baja *icpali*, silla, que ni siquiera estaba sobre una tarima, pero la elegancia de sus vestiduras, especialmente en contraste con las ropas que vestían los demás, contradecía toda pretensión de modestia. Tenía algunos papeles desdoblados sobre sus rodillas y otros esparcidos a su alrededor en el suelo y evidentemente acababa de leer mi nombre completo en uno de ellos. Después consultó otros diferentes, varios de ellos, y dijo:

«Parece que mi tío Auítzotl tenía la idea de elevarlo a usted al Consejo de Voceros, Campeón Mixtli. Pero yo no tengo semejante idea.»

«Gracias, Venerado Orador —respondí, y lo dije en serio—. Nunca he aspirado a...»

Él me interrumpió con una voz que parecía un mordisco: «Usted sólo hablará cuando yo se lo indique por medio de una pregunta.»

«Sí, mi señor.»

«Y no le he hecho ninguna pregunta. La obediencia no necesita ser expresada, se da por sentado.»

Estudió los papeles otra vez, mientras yo me quedaba allí parado, mudo y muerto del coraje. Una vez había pensado que Auítzotl era tontamente pomposo, hablando siempre de sí mismo como «nosotros», pero viéndolo retrospectivamente, entonces me pareció humano y hasta campechano comparándolo con ese sobrino suyo, tan frío y tan distante.

«Sus mapas y las rutas de sus viajes son excelentes, campeón

Mixtli. Este de Texcala será utilizado inmediatamente ya que planeo una nueva guerra que pondrá fin a todas las provocaciones de esos texcalteca. También tengo aquí sus mapas de rutas comerciales del sur, todo el camino hasta la nación mayà. Todo soberbiamente detallado. Muy buen trabajo, en verdad. Hizo una pausa y después dejó caer su mirada fría sobre mí—. Debe de decir "gracias" cuando su Venerado Orador le cumplimente.»

Como era debido dije: «Gracias», y Motecuzoma continuó:

«Tengo entendido que en los siguientes años en que presentó a mi tío estos mapas, hizo usted otros viajes. —Él esperó un momento y como vio que yo no contestaba, me ladró—: ¡Hable!»

«No me ha hecho ninguna pregunta, mi señor.»

Sonriendo sin ningún sentido del humor, dijo con mucha precisión: «¿Hizo usted, también, durante esos viajes siguientes otros mapas?»

«Sí, Señor Orador, ya sea durante el camino o inmediatamente al volver a mi casa, mientras todavía tenía frescos en mi memoria todos los detalles del paisaje.»

«Debe entregar todos esos mapas aquí, en el palacio. Podré utilizarlos cuando alguna vez haga la guerra en otros lugares, después de Texcala. —Yo no dije nada: la obediencia se daba por sentada. Él continuó—: Tengo entendido también que usted domina admirablemente los lenguajes de muchas provincias.»

Él esperó otra vez. Yo dije: «Gracias, Señor Orador.»

Él me regañó: «¡Eso no era un cumplido!»

«Usted dijo admirable, mi señor.»

Algunos miembros del Consejo de Voceros levantaron sus ojos al techo y otros los cerraron con fuerza.

«¡Deje de insolentarse! ¿Cuántas lenguas habla?»

«¡Del náhuatl, hablo el culto y el popular que se usa aquí en Tenochtitlan. Incluso el más refinado náhuatl de Texcoco y varios de los rudos dialectos que se hablan en naciones extranjeras como Texcala. —Impacientemente Motecuzoma tamborileó con sus dedos en su rodilla—. Hablo fluidamente el lóochi de los tzapoteca, y no tan fluidamente muchos de los dialectos poré de Michihuacan. También puedo hacerme entender en el lenguaje de los maya y en numeroso dialectos que derivan del maya. Sé algunas palabras en otomite y...»

«Es suficiente —dijo Motecuzoma cortante—. Quizás le dé una oportunidad para que practique sus talentos cuando haga la guerra en aquellas naciones en donde no sé cómo se diría "rindanse". Pero de momento sus mapas son suficientes. Dese prisa en entregarlos.»

Yo no dije nada, la obediencia se daba por sentada. Algunos de los ancianos, estaban moviendo sus labios silenciosamente hacia mí, con urgencia y yo me preguntaba el porqué hasta que Motecuzoma casi me gritó: «¡Puede irse, Campeón Mixtli!»

Caminé fuera de la sala del trono como me habían dicho que hiciera; ya en el corredor me quité el saco de mendigo y dije al mayordomo: «Ese hombre está loco. Pero no sé qué es, ¿un *tlahuele* o sólo un *xolopitli*?» Esas dos palabras en náhuatl se usan para un hombre loco: *xolopitli* sólo significa un inocuo retrasado mental y *tlahuele* significa que es un maniático delirante y peligroso. Cada una de estas palabras hizo brincar del susto al mayordomo conejo.

«Por favor, mi señor, baje su voz. —Luego gruñó—: Debo concederle a usted, que él tiene sus peculiaridades, ¿sabe usted? Sólo come una comida al día, por la tarde, pero para prevenir lo que él pueda ordenar, se preparan unas veintenas de platos, aun cientos, todos diferentes, así, cuando llega el tiempo para su comida él puede solicitar cualquier alimento que le apetezca en aquel instante. De la comida que se ha preparado, él sólo devora un platito y delicadamente prueba dos o tres de los otros.»

«¿Y el resto se desperdicia?», pregunté.

«Oh, no. Cada vez que come invita a todos los nobles de más alto rango que sean sus favoritos y que están al alcance de sus mensajeros. Y los señores vienen, por veintenas y aun por cientos, aunque eso haya significado dejar sus propias meriendas y sus familias y comer lo que el Uey-Tlatoani ha desdeñado.»

«Extraordinario —murmuré—. Nunca me hubiera imaginado a Motecuzoma como a un hombre que le guste tener mucha compañía y mucho menos en el momento de su comida.»

«Bueno, regularmente no. Los otros señores comen en el mismo gran comedor, pero la conversación está prohibida y nunca le pueden echar ni una mirada al Venerado Orador. Un gran biombo se pone alrededor del rincón en el que él acostumbra merendar, así es que se sienta allí sin ser visto, ni molestado. Los otros señores ni siquiera notarían su presencia, a no ser porque de vez en cuando, cuando Motecuzoma se siente especialmente complacido con algún platillo, lo manda alrededor del comedor y todos deben probarlo.»

«Ah, entonces él no está loco —dije—. Recuerde que siempre se ha murmurado que el Uey-Tlatoani Tíxoc murió envenenado. Lo que usted acaba de decir puede sonar excéntrico y extravagante, pero también puede ser que el astuto Motecuzoma se esté asegurando de no irse como se fue su tío Tíxoc.»

Mucho antes de conocer personalmente a Motecuzoma, había concebido una gran antipatía hacia él, pero mientras me alejaba del palacio ese día, tuve un nuevo sentimiento hacia él, un sentimiento de indulgente piedad. Sí, piedad. Para mí un gobernante debe inspirar a otros a exaltar su eminencia, no debe de exaltarla él mismo; que los otros deben besar la tierra en su presencia, porque él lo merece no porque él lo exige. Para mi mente, todo ese protocolo, ritual y panoplia con que se había rodeado Motecuzoma era menos majestuoso que pretencioso y aun patético. Era como todos los adornos que usaba en sus vestiduras, simples adornos de supuesta grandeza, asumidos por un hombre impertinente, inseguro de sí mismo e indeciso, que no tenía nada de grandeza en lo absoluto.

Llegué a casa para encontrarme con Cózcatl, que me había estado esperando para contarme las últimas noticias sobre su escuela. Mientras me empezaba a desvestir de mi traje de campeón Águila, para ponerme otra ropa más cómoda, restregándose las manos y en muy buen estado de humor, me anunció:

«El Venerado Orador Motecuzoma me ha llamado para decirme que quiere que adiestre a todo el personal de palacio, desde los más altos mayordomos hasta los ayudantes de cocina. Todos, sirvientes y esclavos.»

Eran unas noticias tan buenas, que llamé a Turquesa para que nos trajera una jarra de *octli* frío para poder celebrarla. Estrella Cantadora vino corriendo también, para ofrecernos y encendernos nuestros *poquíetl.*

«Pues acabo de regresar del palacio —le dije a Cózcatl— y me llevé la impresión de que Motecuzoma ya tiene bien adiestrados a sus sirvientes, o por lo menos servilmente acobardados, desde su Consejo de Voceros hasta la última persona conectada con su Corte.»

«Oh, sus criados sirven bastante bien —dijo Cózcatl. Aspiró su pipa y lanzó al aire un anillo de humo azul—. Pero él quiere que los pula y los haga más refinados, igual a todo el personal que tiene Nezahualpili en Texcoco.»

Yo dije: «Parece que nuestro Venerado Orador tiene más sentimientos de envidia y rivalidad que verdaderos deseos de tener sirvientes refinados como los de la Corte de Texcoco. Hasta podría decir que abriga sentimientos de animosidad. Motecuzoma me dijo esta mañana que se propone lanzarse a una nueva guerra contra Texcala, cosa que no es como para sorprenderse. Lo que él no me dijo, pero que yo escuché por ahí, es que trató de ordenarle a Nezahualpili que guiara personalmente el asalto y que las tropas acolhua formaran el cuerpo principal del ejército. También oí que Nezahualpili denegó ese honor de la manera más firme, y me alegro pues después de todo él ya no es un joven. Pero parece ser que a Motecuzoma le gustaría hacer lo que Auítzotl hizo en nuestros días de guerra, Cózcatl. Diezmar a los acolhua y aun forzar a Nezahualpili a caer en el combate.»

Cózcatl dijo: «Muy bien pudiera ser, Mixtli, que Motecuzoma tenga la misma razón que tuvo Auítzotl.»

Bebí un reconfortante trago de *octli* y dije: «¿Quieres decir lo que temo oír?»

Cózcatl asintió: «Aquella niña-novia que una vez fuera esposa de Nezahualpili y que su nombre no debe mencionarse jamás. Siendo la hija de Auítzotl, era la prima de Motecuzoma... y quizás algo más que una prima para él. Porque es mucha coincidencia que inmediatamente después de su ejecución, él tomara las vestiduras negras del sacerdocio y del celibato.»

Yo dije: «Una coincidencia que en verdad invita a hacer especulaciones —y me acabé mi copa de *octli*, lo que me animó lo suficiente como para decir—: Bien, hace ya mucho tiempo que él dejó el sacerdocio y en estos momentos tiene dos esposas legales y tendrá más. No perdamos la esperanza de que al fin deje a un lado su animosidad hacia Nezahualpili. Y esperemos que él nunca llegue a averiguar la parte que nos correspondió, a ti y a mí, en la caída de su prima.»

Cózcatl dijo alegremente: «No te preocupes por eso. El buen

Nezahualpili siempre ha guardado silencio acerca de nosotros. Auítzotl nunca nos relacionó con ese asunto. Motecuzoma tampoco, o si no él no estaría patrocinando mi escuela con tanto empeño.»

Yo dije con alivio: «Probablemente tienes razón. —Luego reí y continué—: Parece que en estos momentos nada te afecta, estás más allá de toda preocupación y aun de dolor. —Y apunté con mi *poquíetl*—. ¿No te das cuenta de que te estás quemando?»

Aparentemente no se había dado cuenta de que la mano que sostenía su caña encendida, la había bajado de tal manera que las brasas ardientes estaban en contacto directo sobre su otro brazo. Cuando le hice notar eso, él tiró lejos su *poquíetl* y miró con mal humor la roja ampolla que se levantaba en su piel.

«Algunas veces mi atención se concentra tanto en algo —murmuró— que no me doy cuenta de... de estas pequeñeces.»

«¿Pequeñeces? —dije—. Eso debe de dolerte más que una picadura de avispa. Déjame llamar a Turquesa para que traiga un ungüento.»

«No, no, no lo hagas... no me duele en lo absoluto —contestó él y se puso de pie—. Te veré pronto, Mixtli.»

Él iba saliendo de la casa, cuando Beu Ribé regresaba de algún mandado. Como de costumbre, Cózcatl la saludó efusivamente, pero ella pareció inquieta al sonreírle y cuando él se fue, ella me dijo:

«Me encontré con su esposa en la calle y conversamos un rato. Quequelmiqui debe saber que yo estoy informada de todo acerca de Cózcatl; su herida y la clase de matrimonio que llevan; sin embargo, estaba radiante de felicidad y me miró con cierto desafío para ver si me atrevía a decirle algo.»

Un poco amodorrado por el *octli*, le pregunté: «¿Y qué tenías que atreverte a decirle?»

«Acerca de su embarazo. Que es bastante obvio a los ojos de cualquier mujer.»

«Te debes de haber equivocado —le dije—. Tú sabes que eso es imposible.»

Me miró con impaciencia. «Pudiera ser imposible, pero no me he equivocado. Hasta una solterona puede darse cuenta de eso. No pasará mucho tiempo antes de que su marido lo note. ¿Y entonces qué?»

No tenía respuesta para aquella pregunta y Beu se fue de la habitación sin esperar que respondiera, dejándome allí, sentado y pensando. Debí de haberme dado cuenta de que, cuando Cosquillosa vino a suplicarme para tener una experiencia conmigo que no podía tener con su marido, lo que en realidad quería era que yo le diera algo más duradero que una simple experiencia. Lo que deseaba era un hijo, una Cocoton, pero suya. ¿Y quién podría dárselo mejor que el querido padre de Cocoton? Seguro que Cosquillosa había venido a verme después de haber comido carne de zorro o hierba *cihuapatli* o cualquier otra de esas especies que se supone que aseguran el embarazo en una mujer. Bien, casi sucumbí a sus demostraciones de afecto, y si no hubiera sido por la llegada inesperada de Beu, no habría tenido ninguna excusa para rehusar. Así es que yo no era el padre, ni tampoco Cózcatl, pero alguno lo era. Cosquillosa me había dicho claramente que si yo no aceptaba ella buscaría la forma con otros hombres. Me dije a mí mismo: «Cuando le dije que se fuera, ella tuvo todo el día para...»

Sin duda debí de haber estado más preocupado acerca de ese asunto, pero entonces estaba trabajando muy duro, obedeciendo la orden de Motecuzoma de que buscara todos los mapas que hice durante mis viajes. Y eso era lo que estaba haciendo, aunque me tomé algunas libertades al interpretar su orden. No mandé al palacio mis mapas originales, sino que me puse a hacer copias de todos ellos, y los fui mandando uno por uno, conforme los iba terminando. Expliqué el retraso dando la excusa de que muchos mapas estaban en fragmentos y manchados por el viaje, algunos hechos con papel muy corriente y otros simplemente garrapateados en hojas de árbol, y que quería que mi Señor Orador tuviera unos dibujos bien hechos, claros y duraderos. Esa excusa en sí no era del todo una mentira, pero la verdadera razón por la que quería guardar los originales era que éstos representaban para mí preciosos recuerdos de mis viajes, algunos de los cuales había hecho en compañía de mi adorada Zyanya y por tanto deseaba conservarlos.

También, quizás alguna vez quisiera volver a viajar por esos caminos otra vez, y seguir caminando, sin querer volver, si el reinado de Motecuzoma hacía de Tenochtitlan un lugar incómodo para mí. Teniendo en mente esa posible emigración, omití algunos detalles significativos en las copias que le mandé al Uey-Tlatoani. Por ejemplo, no hice mención, ni puse una marca en el lugar en donde estaba el lago negro en el que había encontrado aquellos colmillos gigantes de jabalí, pues si había algún otro tesoro allí, algún día podría necesitarlo.

Cuando no estaba trabajando, pasaba el mayor tiempo posible con mi hija. Había adquirido la agradable costumbre de contarle cuentos cada tarde, y por supuesto le contaba aquellos que a mí me hubieran interesado mucho cuando tenía su edad: historias repletas de acción, violencia y aventuras. De hecho, muchas de esas historias eran verdaderas experiencias, por las que yo había pasado: ligeramente adornada la verdad o ligeramente atenuada, según el caso. Esa clase de cuentos requerían que frecuentemente tuviera que rugir como un jaguar enloquecido o chillar como lo haría un mono-araña enojado o aullar como un coyote melancólico. Cuando Cocoton temblaba ante algunos de los sonidos que hacía, me sentía muy orgulloso por el talento que tenía para contar una aventura tan vívidamente que un oyente podía casi compartirla. Pero un día en que la niñita vino en el tiempo acostumbrado para que la entretuviera, me dijo casi solemnemente: «¿Podríamos hablar, Tata, como personas mayores?»

Yo estaba muy divertido ante esa grave formalidad con la que me hablaba una niña de escasos seis años, pero le contesté casi tan gravemente: «Podemos hacerlo, Migajita. ¿Qué me quieres decir?»

«Quiero decirte que no creo que esas historias que me cuentas sean las más adecuadas para una niña.»

Un poco sorprendido y aun herido, dije: «A ver, dime tus quejas sobre esas historias tan poco adecuadas.»

Ella dijo, como si estuviera apaciguando a un chiquillo petulante más joven que ella: «Estoy segura de que son muy buenas historias. Estoy segura de que un niño estaría encantado de oírlas. Yo pienso que a los niños les gustan que los asusten. Mi amigo Chacalin —y movió su manita en dirección de la casa de los vecinos— algunas veces hace ruidos de animales y sus *propios* ruidos le espantan, que hasta se pone a llorar. Si quieres, Tata, lo traeré todas las tardes para que él oiga tus cuentos en mi lugar.»

Yo dije, quizás un poco enojado: «Chacalin tiene su propio padre para que le cuente historias. Y sin duda muy emocionantes, acerca de sus aventuras como comerciante en cerámica, en el mercado de Tlaltelolco, pero, Cocoton, nunca he notado que tú llores cuendo te cuento una historia.»

«Oh, no lo haría. No enfrente de ti. Lloro en la noche, cuando estoy sola en mi cama. Entonces recuerdo los jaguares, las serpientes y los bandidos y en la oscuridad se ven como si estuvieran vivos, y sueño que tratan de agarrarme.»

«Oh, mi niñita querida —exclamé atrayéndola hacia mí—. ¿Por qué no me habías dicho nada antes?»

«No soy muy valiente —dijo escondiendo su cara en mi hombro—. No con animalotes, ni con papás grandes tampoco.»

«De ahora en adelante —le prometí— voy a tratar de parecer más pequeño. Y no te contaré más cuentos de bestias y bandidos. ¿Qué clase de cuentos prefieres?»

Lo pensó seriamente y luego me preguntó tímidamente: «¿Tata, alguna vez has tenido alguna aventura *fácil*?»

No pude pensar en una respuesta inmediata. Ni siquiera podía imaginarme lo que quería decir por «una aventura fácil», a menos de que se refiriera a algunas que le pudieran haber pasado al padre de Chacalin, como vender un cacharro rajado sin que el cliente se hubiera dado cuenta. Pero entonces recordé algo y le dije:

«Una vez tuve una aventura muy *tonta*. ¿Tú crees que ésa sería aceptable?»

Ella dijo: «¡*Ayyo*, sí, me divierten los cuentos tontos!»

Me acosté en el suelo y levanté las rodillas, y apuntando a ellas le dije: «Ése es un volcán, un volcán que se llama Tzebóruko, que quiere decir El que Resopla con Ira. Pero te prometí que no resoplaría. Siéntate aquí arriba, exactamente en su cráter.»

Una vez que se hubo acomodado en mis rodillas, yo empecé con el tradicional «*Oc-ye-necha*», y le conté cómo la lava del volcán me había empujado mar adentro, por haber estado, estúpidamente, en medio de la bahía. Durante toda mi historia, me contuve de hacer los ruidos que hacía el volcán al eruptar la lava y los que hacía el vapor, pero cuando llegué a la parte más importante de mi narración, de repente grité: «¡*Uiuiuóni!*» y bajé y subí las rodillas rápidamente. «¡Y *o-o-ompa*! ¡Me fui con el mar!» Con ese movimiento y al decir *ompa*, Cocoton brincaba de tal manera que se resbalaba por mis muslos hasta caer en mi barriga, sacándome todo el aire, lo que hacía que gritara y riera con placer.

Parecía que al fin había atinado con una historia y en la forma de contarla más adecuada para una niñita. Desde entonces y por mucho tiempo, cada tarde jugábamos al volcán haciendo erupción. Aunque le narraba otras historias que no la asustaban, Cocotón siempre insistía en que le contara también y le demostrara cómo el Tzebóruko me había arrojado una vez fuera del Único Mundo. Y se lo contaba una y otra vez, siempre con su participación trémulamente agarrada a mis rodillas, mientras yo arrastraba y alargaba las palabras preliminares para darle más emoción, y luego gritando alegremente cuando la balanceaba, y riéndose fuertemente cuando al fin la dejaba caer sobre mí, sacándome todo el aire. El volcán haciendo erupción, siguió con sus erupciones todos los días hasta que Cocoton creció lo suficiente como para que Beu desaprobara «esa conducta que no era la de una señora», y cuando Cocoton también encontró el juego «muy infantil». Yo estaba para entonces un poco triste de verla crecer, y salir de su infancia, pero también estaba cansado de que me brincara en la barriga.

Llegó el día en que, inevitablemente, Cózcatl vino a verme otra vez, y en un lamentable estado: sus ojos tenían rojas ojeras, su voz se oía ronca y sus manos se retorcían y entrelazaban como si estuvieran peleando la una con la otra.

Yo le pregunté con suavidad. «¿Has estado llorando, amigo mío?»

«No dudes de que tengo razón para ello —dijo gravemente—. «Pero no, no he estado llorando. Lo que pasa es que... —y él separó sus manos en un gesto distraído— desde hace tiempo, mis ojos y mi lengua parece como si estuvieran... como si los sintiera hinchados o más gruesos... como si tuvieran una capa de algo encima.»

«Lo siento mucho —le dije—. ¿No has visto a un físico?»

«No. Pero no vine a hablar de eso. ¿Mixtli, fuiste tú?»

No pretendí hipócritamente que no sabía nada, así es que le dije: «Sé de lo que me estás hablando, Beu me dijo algo acerca de eso hace algún tiempo, pero no, yo no fui.»

Él asintió con la cabeza y dijo sintiéndose miserable: «Te creo. Pero eso solamente lo hace más difícil de sobrellevar. Nunca sabré quién fue. Aunque la mate a palos, ella nunca me lo dirá, y además no podría pegarle a Quequelmiqui.»

Yo reflexioné por un momento y luego le dije: «Te diré que ella *deseaba* que yo fuera el padre.»

Él asintió otra vez, temblando como un viejo: «Lo había supuesto. Ella debió de haber querido un niño lo más parecido posible a tu hija. —Después de una pausa, dijo—: Si tú lo hubieras hecho, me hubiera sentido herido, pero lo habría podido soportar...»

Con su mano se restregó una mancha pálida muy curiosa que

tenía en su mejilla, casi de un color plateado. Me preguntaba si no se habría quemado otra vez, sin darse cuenta. Luego noté que los dedos de las manos que tanto se estrujaba, casi no tenían color en sus puntas. Él continuó hablando: «Mi pobre Quequelmiqui. Creo que ella hubiera podido soportar un matrimonio con un hombre sin sexo, pero después de haber llegado a sentir tan grande amor de madre por tu hija, ya no pudo sufrir un matrimonio sin frutos.»

Miró a través de la ventana y se sintió infeliz; mi hijita estaba jugando en la calle con algunos de sus amigos.

«Yo tenía la esperanza... yo traté de darle alguna satisfacción en ese aspecto a ella. Empecé a darles clases especiales a los hijos de los sirvientes que ya tenía a mi cargo, preparándolos para que siguieran dentro del mismo servicio doméstico de sus padres. Mi verdadera razón era que tenía la esperanza de distraerla de su anhelo a ver si podía aprender a amar a esos niños. Pero como ellos eran los hijos de otras gentes... y ella no los quería desde que eran pequeños como Cocoton...»

«Mira Cózcatl —le dije—. El niño que ella lleva en su vientre no es tuyo, no puede serlo, pero a excepción de la semilla es *su* hijo. Y ella es tu amada esposa. Suponte que te casaste con una viuda madre de una criatura, dime, ¿sufrirías estos tormentos si ése hubiera sido el caso?»

«Ella ya ha tratado ese argumento conmigo —dijo con aspereza—. Pero en ese caso, como tú lo puedes ver, yo no tendría por qué sentirme traicionado, como me siento ahora después de todos esos años de felicidad conyugal. Bueno, por lo menos yo era feliz.»

Recordé los años durante los cuales Zyanya y yo habíamos sido completamente el uno para el otro, y traté de imaginarme cómo me habría sentido si ella me hubiese sido infiel, y al fin le dije: «Amigo mío, sinceramente te comprendo. Sin embargo ese niño será el hijo de tu esposa, y ella es una mujer muy hermosa, por lo que es casi seguro que el niño también lo será. Casi te puedo asegurar que pronto lo aceptarás e incluso lo llegarás a amar. Yo sé cuán bondadoso eres y sé que puedes amar a una criatura sin padre, tan profundamente como amaste a mi hija cuando perdió a su madre.»

«No exactamente sin padre», refunfuñó.

«Será el hijo de tu esposa —persistí—. Tú eres su marido. Tú serás su padre. Si ella no ha dicho quién es el padre, ni siquiera a ti, es muy difícil que se lo diga a otra persona. ¿Y quién conoce las condiciones físicas en que te encuentras? Beu y yo, sí, pero puedes estar seguro de que nunca diremos una palabra, acerca de eso. Glotón de Sangre hace ya mucho tiempo que murió, lo mismo que aquel viejo físico de palacio, que atendió tu herida. No puedo pensar en ninguna otra persona que...»

«¡Yo sí! —me interrumpió ásperamente—. El hombre que *es* el padre. Que muy bien pudiera ser un borracho de *octli*, que en meses pasados se ha estado vanagloriando de su conquista, en todas las casas para beber que hay en la isla. Quizás algún día se presente en nuestra casa y venga a demandar...»

Yo dije: «Uno debe de suponer que Cosquillosa fue discreta y escogió bien al hombre», aunque personalmente yo no estaba muy seguro de eso.

«Y hay otra cosa también —continuó Cózcatl—. ¿Tú crees que volverá a estar satisfecha, por mucho tiempo, con la clase de sexo que yo le ofrezco? ¿Tú crees que no volverá a buscar a un *hombre* otra vez? ¿Ahora que ella ha disfrutado el... el sexo normalmente?»

Yo le dije con severidad: «Te estás ahogando en una taza de agua, probablemente todas esas posibilidades nunca lleguen a suceder. Ella deseaba un hijo, eso es todo, ahora ella lo tendrá. Puedo asegurarte que las nuevas madres tienen muy poco tiempo de ocio para dedicarse a la promiscuidad.»

«*Yya ouiya* —se quejó roncamente—. Desearía que *tú* fueras el padre, Mixtli. Si supiera que el que había hecho eso era mi viejo amigo... oh, claro que hubiera tomado tiempo, pero habría llegado a estar en paz conmigo mismo...»

«¡Basta, Cózcatl!» Él me estaba haciendo sentir doblemente culpable, porque *casi* me acuesto con su esposa y porque *no* me había acostado con ella.

Pero no había quien lo hiciera callar. «Además hay otras consideraciones —dijo él vagamente—, pero no tienen la menor importancia. Si ese niño fuera tuyo, yo podría aguantar... podría haber sido su padre por algún tiempo más, por lo menos...»

Me dio la impresión de que estaba divagando y busqué desesperadamente algunas palabras para hacerlo volver a su mente, pero de repente se echó a llorar, con ese llanto seco, áspero, desapacible, como lloran los hombres; nada parecido al llanto suave, blando, casi musical de las mujeres... y luego salió corriendo de la casa.

Nunca lo volví a ver. El resto es tan desagradable que lo contaré rápidamente. Esa misma tarde, Cózcatl huyó de su casa, de su escuela, de sus estudiantes, dejando incluso a todos los sirvientes de palacio que estaban a su cargo. Se fue y se alistó en el ejército de la Triple Alianza que peleaba contra Texcala y de allí marchó directamente a la punta de una espada enemiga.

La forma abrupta en que se fue y su repentina muerte causó tanta perplejidad como pena entre sus amigos y asociados, sin embargo la impresión general fue que él había hecho eso, porque no había podido quedar bien con su patrón, el Venerado Orador. Ni Cosquillosa, ni Beu, ni yo, quisimos desvirtuar esa impresión, e igualmente nunca dijimos nada acerca de la creencia general de que el niño que esperaba su esposa fue engendrado por él antes de irse tan de improviso a la guerra. Por mi parte, nunca dije a ninguno de mis conocidos, ni siquiera a Beu, nada de lo que sospechaba. Recordaba algunas de las frases inconclusas de Cózcatl: «Yo podría aguantar... podría haber sido su padre por algún tiempo más, por lo menos...» Y recordaba que las brasas del *poquíetl* le habían quemado y él no lo había sentido, su voz pesada, sus ojos legañosos y ojerosos, aquella mancha plateada en su cara...

Los servicios funerarios se hicieron sobre su *maquáhuitl* y su escudo, que habían sido traídos del campo de batalla. En aquella ocasión y en compañía de incontables dolientes, le di a su viuda mis condolencias fríamente y después evité el volverla a ver, deliberadamente. En lugar de eso, busqué al guerrero mexícatl que había traído las reliquias de Cózcatl y que había estado presente en el entierro. Le hice la pregunta con toda franqueza y después de un momento de vacilación, al fin me contestó:

«Sí, mi señor. Cuando el físico del ejército rompió su armadura acojinada alrededor de la herida de ese hombre, encontró que éste tenía como unos granos y una gran parte de la piel de su cuerpo tenía unas manchas escamosas. Usted adivinó bien, mi señor. Él estaba enfermo de *teococoliztli*.»

Esa palabra significa El Ser Comido Por Los Dioses. Claro que esa enfermedad también es conocida en el Viejo Mundo, de donde ustedes vienen, porque cuando los primeros españoles que llegaron aquí vieron a ciertos hombres y mujeres sin dedos de las manos y de los pies, sin nariz, pues en las etapas finales de esta enfermedad se cae casi toda la cara, ellos dijeron: «¡Lepra!»

Los dioses se comen a sus escogidos *teocócox*, rápida o gradualmente, y pueden hacerlo muy despacio o vorazmente o de diferentes maneras, pero ninguno de los comidos por los dioses, se han sentido muy honrado por haber sido escogido. Al principio, algunas partes de su cuerpo pierden toda sensibilidad, como en el caso de Cózcatl, cuando él no sintió cómo se quemaba su brazo. Sienten también que los tejidos de adentro de sus ojos, nariz y garganta se hacen más gruesos, como si se hincharan, así es que el que lo padece se ve afectado de su vista, su voz se enronquece y traga y respira con dificultad. La piel de su cuerpo se seca y se cae como si fuera trapo viejo o pueden salirle granos que se convierten en incontables nódulos que se rompen por la supuración, convirtiéndose en llagas. La enfermedad es invariablemente fatal, pero lo más horrible de todo es que usualmente toma mucho tiempo comerse a la víctima completamente. Las extremidades más pequeñas del cuerpo, como los dedos, la nariz, las orejas, el *tepuli*, era lo primero que se comían, dejando en su lugar solamente hoyos o viscosos muñones. La piel de la cara se tornaba como cuero, cogía un color gris plateado y se caía de tal manera que la piel de la frente de una persona podía caer dentro del hoyo en donde una vez había estado su nariz. Sus labios se hinchaban y el de abajo lo hacía tanto que pendía tan pesadamente que su boca estaba por siempre abierta.

Sin embargo, aun así los dioses continuaban comiendo ese alimento, sin ninguna prisa. Podía ser sólo cuestión de meses o tomaba años, antes de que un *teocócox* estuviera incapacitado de ver, caminar, hablar o sin poder hacer uso de ninguno de sus miembros carcomidos. Y todavía así, seguía viviendo; encamado, inútil, maloliente por la putrefacción, sufriendo esa miseria horrible por muchos años más, antes de que muriera por sofocación. Pero no todos los hombres o las mujeres que lo sufrían deseaban vivir esa media vida y aunque la pudieran soportar sus seres queridos no podían sufrir por tanto tiempo las náuseas y el horror que les provocaba al atender las funciones de sus cuerpos y sus necesidades. La mayoría de los escogidos para ser comidos por los dioses, sólo vivían hasta que ellos dejaban de parecer seres humanos, luego se mataban tomando un trago de veneno, estrangulándose o con una daga, o encontrando la manera de lograr la muerte más honorable de todas, la Muerte-Florida, como lo hizo Cózcatl.

Él sabía lo que le esperaba, pero amaba tanto a su Quequelmiqui, que pudo haber sufrido y desafiado el ser comido por los dioses por el mayor tiempo posible, o el que ella hubiera podido soportar sin recular a su vista. Aunque se hubiera dado cuenta de que su esposa lo traicionó hubiera esperado a ver al niño y habría sido su padre por lo menos por un tiempo, como él me lo había dicho, si ese niño hubiera sido mío. Pero no lo era, y su esposa le había sido infiel con un extraño. Así es que no tenía deseo o razón para posponer lo inevitable y fue derecho a enterrarse en la espada de un texcalteca.

Sentí más que pena y aflicción cuando perdí a mi amigo Cózcatl. Después de todo yo había sido responsable de él durante mucha parte de su vida, desde que tenía nueve años y era mi esclavo en Texcoco. Desde entonces mi comportamiento con él no fue de lo mejor, pues casi hago que lo ejecuten al haberlo involucrado en mi venganza contra el Señor Alegría. Después él perdió su virilidad mientras trataba de protegerme contra Chimali. Y si no le hubiera pedido a Cosquillosa que fuera la madre de Cocoton, ella nunca habría deseado tan ávidamente llegar a serlo. Y en cuanto a su adulterio, si no me vi realmente involucrado en él fue debido a las circunstancias y no a mi rectitud o a mi fidelidad hacia Cózcatl, y aun así, le causé un perjuicio. Si yo me hubiera acostado con Cosquillosa y la hubiera dejado embarazada, Cózcatl habría vivido por un poco más de tiempo y quizás hasta dichoso, antes de ser totalmente comido por los dioses...

Pensando en todo eso, me he preguntado muchas veces por qué Cózcatl siempre me llamó *amigo*.

La viuda de Cózcatl todavía dirigió la escuela y al grupo de maestros por unos cuantos meses más, hasta que le llegó el tiempo de parir a su maldito bastardo. Y en realidad fue maldecido, porque nació muerto; ni siquiera recuerdo haber oído de qué sexo fue. Cuando Cosquillosa pudo caminar, ella también, como Cózcatl, dejó la isla para siempre alejándose de Tenochtitlan y nunca más regresó. La escuela fue toda confusión y los maestros a quienes no se les había pagado amenazaron con irse también. Así que Motecuzoma, sintiéndose vejado con la idea de recibir a sus sirvientes a medio educar, ordenó que la propiedad abandonada fuera confiscada. Puso a cargo de ella a unos maestros-sacerdotes sacados de una *calmécac* y la escuela siguió existiendo por todo el tiempo que existió la ciudad.

✠

Llegó por fin el día en que mi hija Cocoton cumplió los siete años, y por supuesto que todos dejamos de llamarla Migajita.

Después de pensarlo mucho, de escoger y descartar, decidí agregar a su nombre de nacimiento Uno-Hierba el nombre adulto de Zyanya-Nochipa, que quiere decir Siempre Siempre, la primera palabra en el lenguaje de su madre, el lóochi y la segunda en náhuatl. Pensé que ese nombre, aparte de ser a la memoria de su madre, también era un hábil uso de las palabras. Zyanya-Nochipa podría significar «siempre y por siempre», como un encarecimiento al ya bello nombre de su madre. O se podría interpretar por «siempre Siempre», significando que la madre vivía en la persona de su hija.

Con la ayuda de Beu, arreglé una gran fiesta de celebración para ese día, invitando al vecinito Chacalin y a todos los demás compañeros de juegos de mi hija, con sus respectivos padres. Antes, por supuesto, Beu y yo llevamos a la niña para que fuera registrada con su nuevo nombre en el registro de ciudadanos de esa edad. No fuimos a ver al hombre que se encargaba del registro de toda la población en general. Ya que Zyanya-Nochipa era la hija de un campeón Águila, fuimos a ver al *tonalpoqui* de palacio, quien se encargaba de registrar a los ciudadanos más selectos.

El viejo archivero gruñó: «Es mi obligación y mi privilegio usar el libro *tonálmatl* adivinatorio y con mi talento interpretar el nombre que le corresponde a la criatura. Las cosas han llegado a ser tan agraviantes, que los padres creen que simplemente pueden venir aquí y *decirme* qué nombre debo ponerle al nuevo ciudadano. Eso ya es bastante indecoroso, Señor Campeón, y para colmo usted todavía quiere ponerle a la pobre criatura dos palabras exactamente iguales aunque están en diferentes lenguas, pero que además no quieren decir *nada*. ¿No podría llamarla por lo menos Siempre Enjoyada o algo más comprensible que eso?»

«No —dije con firmeza—. Ella será Siempre Siempre.»

Él preguntó con exasperación: «¿Por qué no Nunca Nunca? ¿Cómo espera que yo dibuje en la página que le corresponde del registro, un nombre que simboliza sólo palabras abstractas? ¿Cómo puedo hacer el dibujo de sonidos que no significan nada?»

«Eso de que no significan nada no es cierto —dije con sentimiento—. Sin embargo, Señor Tonalpoqui, ya me anticipé a tal objeción, pues me jacto de poder trabajar con palabras-pintadas. Verá usted, en mis tiempos yo también fui escribano.» Le di el dibujo que había hecho, que mostraba una mano agarrando una flecha en la cual estaba posada una mariposa.

Leyó en voz alta las palabras, mano, flecha y mariposa: «*Noma, chichiquili, papálotl*. Ah, veo que usted está familiarizado con la manera útil de dibujar el significado de una cosa únicamente por el sonido. Sí, en verdad que los primeros sonidos de las tres palabras hacen que se lea *no-chi-pa*. Siempre.»

Aunque lo dijo con admiración, parecía como si le hubiera costado un gran esfuerzo decirlo. Entonces caí en la cuenta de que el viejo sabio temía que no se le pagara su salario completo, ya que no le dejé más trabajo que hacer, que copiar el nombre. Así es que le pagué una cantidad en polvo de oro que hubiera tenido que ganar en varias semanas de estudiar sus libros adivinatorios. Cuando hice eso, dejó de gruñir y se puso a trabajar inmediatamente. Ceremoniosamente y con gran cuidado, utilizando más pinceles y cañas de los que en realidad necesitaba, pintó los símbolos utilizando toda la hoja completa del registro: un punto, el glifo afelpado, la hierba y luego los símbolos que yo había dibujado de Siempre, dos veces. Así mi hija quedó registrada con el nombre de: Ce-Malinali Zyanya-Nochipa, para ser llamada familiarmente por Nochipa.

En el tiempo en que Motecuzoma subió al trono, su capital Tenochtitlan apenas se había medio recobrado de la devastación producida por la gran inundación. Miles de sus habitantes todavía estaban viviendo amontonados, con los familiares que habían tenido la suerte de conservar sus casas, o habitaban en cabañas construidas con los pedazos de piedras dejados por la inundación o hechas con las hojas de los magueyes que estaban en la tierra firme, o viviendo en un estado todavía más miserable en canoas atadas bajo los soportes de los caminos-puentes de la ciudad. Se necesitaron dos años más antes de que la adecuada reconstrucción de viviendas de Tenochtitlan fuera terminada bajo la dirección de Motecuzoma.

Y ya que estoy hablando de eso, él se mandó construir un palacio nuevo, a la orilla del canal que da al lado sur en El Corazón del Único Mundo. Era un palacio inmenso, de lo más lujoso y elaboradamente decorado y amueblado, un palacio sin igual, como nunca se había visto en estas tierras, mucho más grande que toda la ciudad y nación completa de Nezahualpili. De hecho, Motecuzoma, imitando a Nezahualpili, mandó construir también un elegante palacio campestre, en la falda de la bellísima montaña en el pueblo de Quaunáhuac, al que ya he mencionado varias veces con admiración. Como ustedes saben, mis señores escribanos, si alguna vez han visitado ese palacio desde que su Capitán General Cortés se apropió de él, para convertirlo en su residencia, habrán visto que sus jardines son los más vastos y los más magníficos, con plantas exóticas que estoy seguro que ustedes jamás las han visto en ninguna otra parte.

La reconstrucción de Tenochtitlan hubiera sido más rápida y en todos los dominios mexica se habría podido asegurar una mayor prosperidad, si no hubiera sido porque Motecuzoma, desde que ascendió al trono, se pasó de una guerra a otra, cuando no estaba supervisando dos al mismo tiempo. Como ya dije, se lanzó inmediatamente sobre Texcala, en una nueva guerra contra esa nación frecuentemente acosada, aunque por siempre obstinada. Aunque naturalmente eso ya era de esperarse. Todo nuevo Uey-Tlatoani que se instalaba en el trono, casi siempre empezaba su reinado ejercitando sus músculos contra esa tierra, ya que ésta tenía la gran ventaja de la cercanía y su estólida enemistad la hacía la víctima más natural; sin embargo, muy poco valor hubiera tenido para nosotros si alguna vez la *hubiéramos* conquistado.

Sin embargo, en ese mismo tiempo Motecuzoma había empezado a trazar los jardines en sus tierras y él escuchó de cierto viajero una historia sobre un árbol singular que solamente crecía en una pequeña región al norte de Uaxyácac. El viajero, sin ninguna imaginación, le llamaba sólo por «el árbol de las flores rojas», pero la descripción que hizo de él intrigó al Venerado Orador. Las flores de ese árbol, dijo el hombre, estaban formadas de tal manera que parecían una réplica exacta, pero en miniatura, de las manos humanas, cuyos pétalos parecían dedos con su respectivo pulgar. Desgraciadamente, dijo el viajero, el único lugar en donde crecía ese árbol era en la tierra de una miserable tribu de los mixteca. Su jefe o cacique, hombre viejo llamado Suchix, había reservado ese árbol de flores rojas para sí mismo, y tres o cuatro árboles grandes crecían alrededor de su escuálida cabaña, manteniendo continuamente a sus hombres en busca de nuevos brotes, para arrancarlos hasta las raíces pues no permitía que crecieran en ningún otro lado.

«No es que sólo tenga una gran pasión por tener posesiones en exclusiva —afirmaron que dijo el viajero—. Esa flor en forma de mano es una medicina muy buena que cura las enfermedades del corazón, que no pueden ser curadas por medio de otros tratamientos. El viejo Suchix lo vende a todos aquellos que padecen esas enfermedades, en todas las tierras de los alrededores y a precios abusivos. Es por eso que desea con todas sus ansias que esos árboles sean una rareza y que sean sólo para él.»

Dicen que Motecuzoma sonrió indulgentemente. «Ah, es sólo una cuestión de codicia, lo único que tengo que hacer es ofrecerle más oro del que sus árboles y él podrán obtener en toda su vida.»

Y mandó a un mensajero-veloz que hablara mixteca, corriendo hacia Uaxyácac, llevando con él una fortuna en oro con las instrucciones de comprar esos árboles y pagar cualquier precio que pidiera Suchix. Pero dentro de ese viejo jefe mixteca debió de haber algo más que avaricia; debió de haber algún rasgo de orgullo o integridad natural, pues el mensajero regresó a Tenochtitlan con toda esa fortuna en polvo de oro y las noticias de que Suchix arrogantemente declinó compartir ni una astilla. Así es que lo siguiente que Motecuzoma mandó fue una tropa de guerreros, llevando obsidiana esta vez y Suchix y toda su tribu fue exterminada, y ahora ustedes pueden ver esos árboles cuyas flores parecen manos, creciendo afuera de los jardines de Quaunáhuac.

Pero el Venerado Orador no sólo se preocupaba por los sucesos acaecidos en el extranjero. Cuando no estaba proyectando sus jardines, o tratando de provocar una nueva guerra, o dirigiendo la construcción de sus palacios, o disfrutando al guiar personalmente un ejército en un combate entonces se quedaba en casa y se preocupaba por la Gran Pirámide. Si esto les parece inexplicablemente excéntrico, reverendos frailes, lo mismo nos sucedió a muchos de nosotros, sus súbditos, cuando Motecuzoma concibió una muy peculiar preocupación al decidir que la pirámide estaba «mal colocada». Parece que lo que estaba mal era que en dos días en todo el año, uno en primavera y otro en el otoño, cuando el día y la noche son exactamente iguales, se proyectaba una sombra casi imperceptible sobre uno de sus lados, exactamente al mediodía. De acuerdo con Motecuzoma, el templo no debería de tener ninguna sombra en lo absoluto en esos dos instantes, en el año. «Eso hace —decía él tratando de dar a entender que la Gran Pirámide había sido construida negligentemente, quizá sólo en la anchura de uno o dos dedos— que su oblicuidad no guarde la adecuada proporción con relación al curso de Tonatíu cuando cruza por el cielo.»

Bueno, la Gran Pirámide había estado asentada allí, plácidamente por diecisiete o dieciocho años desde su terminación y dedicación y por más de cien años, cuando Motecuzoma El Viejo empezó su construcción. Y durante todo ese tiempo ni el sol-dios, ni ningún otro dios dio muestras de estar enojado por ello. Sólo Motecuzoma El Joven parecía tener problemas con esa sombra, tan pequeña como el filo de un hacha. Se le podía ver muy seguido parado y observando ceñudo al inmenso edificio, como si sólo hubiera ido para darle una patada irritada con la que corrigiera uno de sus ángulos incorrectamente construidos. Por supuesto que la única forma posible de enmendar el error del arquitecto era tirando totalmente la Gran Pirámide y volviéndola a construir desde sus cimientos hasta la cumbre, un proyecto como para desanimar a cualquiera. No obstante, creo que Motecuzoma la habría llevado a efecto, si no hubiera sido porque su atención se vio desviada, forzosamente, hacia otros problemas.

Fue precisamente en ese tiempo cuando una serie de alarmantes presagios empezaron a ocurrir: los extraños sucesos que ahora todos estamos firmemente convencidos de que presagiaban la ruina de los mexica y la caída de todo el mundo civilizado que florecía en estas tierras, la muerte de todos nuestros dioses y el fin de El Único Mundo.

Un día, ya para finalizar el año Uno-Conejo, un paje de palacio vino corriendo a decirme que debía presentarme inmediatamente ante el Uey-Tlatoani. Si menciono el año, es porque fue siniestro por sí mismo, como lo explicaré más tarde. Motecuzoma no me ahorró el ritual de besar la tierra repetidas veces cuando entré en el salón del trono, pero impacientemente tamborileaba con sus dedos una de sus rodillas, como si quisiera que me aproximara con más rapidez.

El Venerado Orador estaba solo en esa ocasión, pero noté dos cosas nuevas en la habitación. A cada lado de su *icpali*, trono, colgaban de un marco de madera, por medio de cadenas, unos grandes discos de metal. Uno era de oro y el otro de plata; cada disco tenía tres veces más de diámetro que un escudo de guerra; los dos tenían escenas de los triunfos de Motecuzoma grabados y en relieve, con palabras pintadas que explicaban esas escenas. Aunque los dos discos eran de incalculable valor, sólo por la cantidad que contenían de esos preciosos metales, eran todavía más valiosos por el trabajo artístico grabado en ellos. No fue sino hasta mucho tiempo después, que supe que esos discos no eran simples ornamentos. Motecuzoma podía golpear con su puño cualquiera de ellos y resonaría con un sonido profundo y hueco por todo el palacio. Cada uno de ellos producía un sonido adecuadamente diferente; cuando golpeaba el disco de plata debía ir corriendo el jefe de mayordomos, y cuando lo hacía en el de oro se presentaba enseguida toda una tropa de guardias armados.

Sin saludarme formalmente esta vez, sin un ápice de sarcasmo y con mucha menos de su calma fría, Motecuzoma me dijo: «Campeón Mixtli, ¿está usted familiarizado con las tierras de los maya y con su gente?»

Yo dije: «Sí, Señor Orador.»

«¿Consideraría usted a ese pueblo como nervioso e inestable?»

«No, mi señor, en absoluto, más bien todo lo contrario, porque en nuestros días ellos son tan flemáticos como lo son los tapires y los manatíes.»

Él dijo: «Muchos de nuestros sacerdotes son así, pero eso no es ningún obstáculo para que vean visiones portentosas. ¿Y en ese respecto, cómo son los maya?»

«¿Sobre ver visiones? Bueno, mi señor, me atrevería a decir que los dioses muy bien pueden enviar una visión aun al más lerdo de los mortales. Especialmente si se embriaga con algo así como los hongos carne-de-los-dioses. Sin embargo, los patéticos descendientes de los maya, escasamente se dan cuenta del mundo real que les rodea, dejando a un lado todo lo que pudiera ser extraordinario. Quizás si mi señor me diera una idea más clara acerca de lo que estamos discutiendo...»

Él dijo: «Un mensajero-veloz de los maya llegó corriendo, aunque no sé exactamente de qué tribu o lugar. Pasó con tanta rapidez por la ciudad, nada lerdo por cierto, y se detuvo sólo el tiempo necesario para jadearle un mensaje al guardia que está en la puerta de palacio. Luego corrió en dirección a Tlácopan antes de que el mensaje me fuera transmitido o antes de que hubiera podido detenerle para interrogarlo. Parece ser que los maya mandan a todos sus mensajeros-veloces a través de todas estas tierras, para contar sobre unas cosas maravillosas que se han visto hacia el sur. Hay una península llamada Uluümil Kutz, que queda en el océano del norte. ¿La conoce usted? Muy bien. Hace poco los maya que residen en esa costa se sintieron amenazados y asustados por dos objetos que nunca antes habían visto y que se acercaron a sus playas. —Él no pudo resistir la tentación de hacer una pausa, para dejarme en suspenso un momento—. Algo tan grande como una casa que flotaba en el mar. Algo que se deslizaba suavemente con la ayuda de anchas alas desplegadas. —No pude evitar sonreír y el siguió diciendo ceñudo—: No me venga ahora con que los maya ven visiones dementes.»

«No, mi señor —dije todavía sonriendo—. Pero creo que sé lo que ellos vieron. ¿Puedo hacerle una pregunta? —Hizo un breve gesto de asentimiento—. Esas cosas que mencionó, la casa que flota y el objeto con alas, ¿son una sola cosa o dos objetos separados?»

Motecuzoma más ceñudo y más cortante dijo: «El mensajero ya se había ido antes de que pudiéramos obtener más detalles. Él dejó dicho que dos cosas se habían visto. Supongo que una podría ser la casa flotante y el otro, el objeto con alas. Sea lo que sean, dijo que estaban bastante retirados de la playa, así es que parece que nadie pudo observarlos bien, como para dar una descripción adecuada. ¿Y puedo saber por qué tiene usted esa maldita sonrisa?»

Traté de reprimirla y dije: «Esas gentes no pueden haber imaginado esas cosas, Señor Orador. Son demasiado débiles como para investigar. Si alguno de esos que estaban observando hubiera tenido la iniciativa y el coraje de nadar cerca, habría podido reconocer que eran criaturas marinas, maravillosas y quizá poco comunes de ver, pero no un profundo misterio, y los mensajeros maya no estarían en estos momentos regando una alarma innecesaria.»

«¿Quiere decir que *usted* ha visto esas cosas? —dijo Motecuzoma mirándome casi con temor—. ¿Una casa que flota?»

«No una casa, mi señor, pero sí un pez literal y *honestamente* tan grande como una casa. Los pescadores del océano le llaman *yeyemichi*.» Y le conté cómo una vez había estado a la deriva en el mar en mi canoa, y cómo una horda de esos monstruos habían flotado lo suficientemente cerca de mi frágil canoa como para ponerla en peligro. «El Venerado Orador quizá no lo crea, pero si la cabeza de un *yeyemichi* topara con este cuarto, su cola se sacudiría entre los restos de lo que en otro tiempo fue el palacio del finado Orador Auítzotl, exactamente al otro lado de la gran plaza.»

«¿Tan grande es? —murmuró asombrado Motecuzoma, mirando por la ventana. Luego volviéndose hacia mí, preguntó otra vez—: ¿Y durante su estancia en el mar, usted también se encontró con criaturas con alas?»

«Sí, mi señor. Volaban por enjambres alrededor de mí y en un principio los tomé por insectos marinos de inmenso tamaño. Pero uno de ellos cayó en mi canoa y yo lo cogí y me lo comí. Sin lugar a dudas era un pez, pero también sin lugar a dudas tenía alas con que volar.»

La postura rígida de Motecuzoma se relajó un poco y claramente se vio que respiró con alivio. «Sólo un pez —murmuró—. ¡Que los estúpidos maya sean condenados a Mictlan! Pueden provocar el pánico en todas las poblaciones con esos cuentos disparatados. Yo veré que la verdad sea contada amplia e instantáneamente. Muchas gracias, Campeón Mixtli. Su explicación ha sido de lo más útil. Usted merece una recompensa. Por lo tanto le invito a usted y a su familia para que formen parte de las pocas personas seleccionadas que ascenderán conmigo a la Colina de Huixachi, para la ceremonia del Fuego Nuevo, el próximo mes.»

«Me sentiré muy honrado, mi señor», dije, y de veras era así. El Fuego Nuevo era encendido sólo una vez, en el promedio de la vida de un hombre y ordinariamente ese hombre nunca se podría acercar lo suficiente para ver esa ceremonia, pues la Colina de Huixachi podía acomodar sólo unos cuantos espectadores además de los sacerdotes que oficiaban.

«Un pez —volvió a decir Motecuzoma—. Pero usted los vio mar adentro. Si ahora ellos se acercaron a la playa lo suficiente como para que los mayas los vieran, por primera vez, eso puede constituir algún presagio de consecuencia...»

No necesito hacer hincapié en lo que es obvio; sólo me queda sonrojarme cuando recuerdo mi impetuoso escepticismo. Esos dos objetos vistos por los maya de la costa, lo que yo consideré fatuamente como un pez gigante y un pez con alas, eran por supuesto las embarcaciones españolas que navegaban a toda vela. Ahora que conozco todos los detalles de esos sucesos que hace tanto tiempo pasaron, sé que eran los barcos de sus exploradores, Solís y Pinzón, que inspeccionaban la costa, pero que no desembarcaron en Uluümil Kutz.

Ahora sé que estaba equivocado y que en verdad era un presagio.

Esa entrevista con Motecuzoma se llevó a efecto al final del año, cuando los *nemontemtin*, días huecos, se aproximaban. Y, lo repito, fue el año Uno-Conejo, aunque para ustedes era el año de mil quinientos seis.

Durante los vacíos días sin nombre, cuando cada año solar tocaba a su fin, como ya lo he contado, nuestra gente vivía en la aprensión de que los dioses pudieran castigarlos con algún desastre, pero nunca antes nuestra gente había vivido con tan mórbida aprensión como entonces. Porque el año Uno-Conejo era el último que componía los cincuenta y dos años del *xiumolpili* o gavilla de años, lo que provocaba que nosotros temiéramos los peores desastres imaginarios: la completa destrucción de la raza humana. De acuerdo con nuestros sacerdotes, nuestras creencias y nuestras tradiciones, los dioses habían previamente, durante cuatro veces, purgado al mundo limpiándolo de los hombres, y lo podrían hacer otra vez cuando ellos lo escogieran. Era natural que nosotros pensáramos que los dioses, si se decidían a exterminarnos, escogerían el tiempo adecuado, como esos últimos días del último año con el que se cerraba una gavilla de años.

Y así, durante esos cinco días, entre el final del año Uno-Conejo y el comienzo de su sucesor Dos-Caña, que suponíamos que podríamos vivir para ver llegar ese año de Dos-Caña, y con el que empezaría una nueva gavilla de años, había tanto temor como obediencia religiosa, que hacía que la gente adoptara una conducta sumisa y silenciosa. La gente casi literalmente caminaba de puntillas. Todos los sonidos eran acallados, todas las conversaciones eran susurradas, toda risa estaba prohibida. Los ladridos de los perros, los gorgoteos de las aves domésticas, los chillidos de los bebés eran silenciados lo más pronto posible. Todos los fuegos y luces de los hogares eran apagados durante los días vacíos, cuando terminaba un año solar ordinario, y todos los *demás* fuegos eran extinguidos también, incluyendo los de los templos, los de los altares y urnas puestas enfrente de las estatuas de los dioses. Incluso el fuego que estaba sobre la Colina de Huixachi, el único fuego que se había conservado siempre ardiendo, durante los últimos cincuenta y dos años, aun ese se apagó. En todas estas tierras no hubo ni un vislumbre de luz durante esas cinco noches.

Cada familia, noble o humilde, rompía todas sus vasijas de barro, las que se usaban para cocinar, las que estaban guardadas y las que estaban en los comedores; enterraban o tiraban al lago todas sus *metlatin*, piedras para moler el maíz, y otros utensilios de piedra, cobre y metales preciosos; quemaban sus cucharas de madera, sus platos, sus batidores para *chocólatl* y otros utensilios parecidos. Durante esos días no se cocinaba y de todas formas se comía muy poco, y se usaban las hojas del maguey como platos y los dedos como cucharas, para comer la comida fría de *camotin* o *atoli* que se había preparado con anticipación. No se viajaba, no se comerciaba ni se llevaba a efecto ninguna clase de negocio, no había reuniones sociales, no se utilizaban joyas o plumas, sólo se usaba el traje sencillo. Nadie, desde el Uey-Tlatoani hasta el más bajo esclavo, hacía nada más que esperar, y pasar lo más desapercibidamente posible mientras aguardaban.

Como nada pasó durante esos días sombríos, nuestra tensión y aprensión aumentó comprensiblemente cuando Tonatíu fue a su cama la tarde del día número cinco. Solamente podíamos preguntarnos: ¿se levantaría nuevamente y nos traería un nuevo día, un nuevo año, otra gavilla de años? Puedo decir que la gente común sólo podía esperar con sus preguntas ya que era tarea de los sacerdotes utilizar toda su persuasión, toda la que tenían en su poder. Poco después de que el sol se había ido, cuando la noche estaba completamente en tinieblas, una completa procesión de ellos, los sacerdotes principales de cada dios y diosa, mayor y menor, todos con el traje, la máscara y pintados con la semblanza de su dios en particular, caminaban desde Tenochtitlan, a lo largo del camino-puente del sur hacia la Colina de Huixachi. Eran seguidos por el Venerado Orador y sus invitados, todos vestidos con aquellas vestiduras humildes como sacos, con las que no se podrían reconocer como señores de alto cargo, hombres sabios, adivinos, o lo que fueran. Entre ellos estaba yo, llevando de la mano a mi hija Nochipa.

«Sólo tienes ahora diez años —le había dicho—, y podrías tener una buena oportunidad de vivir, para volver a ver el *próximo* Fuego Nuevo, pero es muy posible que no seas invitada a ver de cerca esa ceremonia. Así es que eres muy afortunada de poder observar ésta.»

Ella estaba muy entusiasmada con la idea, pues era una de las primeras y mayores celebraciones religiosas, que por primera vez asistía. Si no hubiera sido una ocasión tan solemne, ella habría brincado feliz y alegre a mi lado. En lugar de eso, caminaba despacio, como era lo adecuado, llevando una ropa pardusca y una máscara de hoja de maguey confeccionada por mí. Mientras seguíamos a los demás, en procesión a través de la oscuridad solamente atenuada por el pálido rayo de la luna plateada, yo recordaba que ya hacía mucho tiempo había acompañado muy entusiasmado a mi padre a través de Xaltocan para ver la ceremonia en honor del dios de los cazadores de aves, Atlaua.

Nochipa llevaba una máscara que escondía totalmente su rostro, porque en esa noche en especial, la más insegura de todas las noches, los niños debían ir así. La creencia —o la esperanza— era que si los dioses decidían borrar a la raza humana de la faz de la tierra, se podían equivocar y pensar que los jóvenes disfrazados eran otra clase de criaturas y dejarlos sobrevivir, y así, por lo menos, ellos volverían a perpetuar nuestra raza. Los adultos no tratábamos de utilizar esa débil simulación, pero tampoco nos dormiríamos resignadamente ante lo inevitable. En todas partes de esas tierras sumidas en las tinieblas, nuestras gentes pasarían esa noche en los tejados y en las azoteas, pellizcándose y moviéndose unos a otros para mantenerse despiertos, con sus miradas fijas hacia donde estaba la Colina de Huixachi, rezando para que se levantara otra vez la llama del Fuego Nuevo, que les diría que los dioses también esta vez habían diferido el último desastre.

La colina que en nuestro lenguaje llamábamos Huixachtlan estaba situada en un promontorio entre los lagos de Texcoco y Xochimilco al sur del pueblo de Ixtapalapan. Su nombre le venía de los frondosos arbustos *huixachi* que crecían allí, y que en esa estación del año empezaban a abrir sus florecitas amarillas cuya gran fragancia dulce era desproporcionada a su tamaño. Esa colina no se distinguía mucho, ya que era un simple grano comparada con las grandes montañas que se elevaban atrás. Sin embargo, se elevaba abruptamente del terreno plano que circundaba los lagos, y era lo suficientemente alta y estaba lo suficientemente cerca de todas las comunidades del lago, como para que todos sus habitantes —desde Texcoco al este hasta Xaltocan al norte— pudieran verla, y ésa había sido la razón por la que se había seleccionado, hacía ya bastante tiempo en nuestra historia, para que tuviera lugar la ceremonia del Fuego Nuevo.

Mientras subíamos por el sendero que ascendía suavemente en espiral hasta la cumbre, estando cerca de Motecuzoma escuché que él murmuraba preocupado a uno de sus consejeros: «Las *chiquacéntetl aparecerán* esta noche, ¿no es así?»

El sabio, un anciano, pero con muy buenos ojos todavía para ser un astrónomo, se encogió de hombros y dijo: «Siempre lo han hecho, mi señor. Nada de lo que indican mis estudios puede probar que no lo hagan siempre así.»

Chiquacéntetl significa grupo de seis. Motecuzoma se estaba refiriendo a ese grupo cerrado de seis imperceptibles estrellas, cuya ascensión en el cielo habíamos ido a ver, o teníamos la esperanza de ver. La voz del astrónomo, cuya función era calcular y predecir todo lo referente a los movimientos de las estrellas, sonó con tal confianza que disipó los temores de todos nosotros. Por otro lado, ese viejo sabio era notoriamente irreligioso y de opiniones muy atrevidas. Había enfurecido, más de una vez, a muchos sacerdotes al decir con gran llaneza, como lo dijo entonces: «Ningún dios, ni todos los dioses que nosotros conocemos, jamás han demostrado ningún poder para interrumpir el curso ordenado de los cuerpos celestiales.»

«Si los dioses los pusieron ahí, viejo incrédulo —le dijo un adivino—, los dioses pueden quitarlos. Ellos simplemente no lo han hecho en todo el tiempo de nuestra vida en que hemos estado observando el cielo. Sin embargo, la cuestión no es si las *chiquacéntetl* ascenderán en el cielo, sino si este grupo de seis estrellas estarán en el lugar exacto en el cielo, exactamente a la medianoche.»

«Que no es mucho decir de los dioses —dijo secamente el astrónomo—, y en cuanto llegue el tiempo de que el sacerdote sople su trompeta porque es medianoche, puedo apostar que ya para entonces estará borracho. Y a todo esto, amigo adivino, si todavía sigue usted basando sus profecías sobre ese grupo de seis estrellas, no me sorprendería mucho que sus cálculos estuvieran equivocados. Nosotros los astrónomos, hace mucho tiempo que lo reconocemos por *chicóntetl*, el grupo de siete estrellas.»

«¿Se atreve usted a refutar los libros de adivinación? —farfulló el adivino—. Todos ellos dicen y siempre han dicho *chiquacéntetl.*»

«Así es como la mayoría de la gente lo conoce, por el grupo de las seis. Se necesita un cielo claro y buenos ojos para verlas a todas, en verdad que son siete estrellas pálidas, las que forman este grupo.»

«¿Nunca cesará en sus calumnias irreverentes? —gruñó el otro—. Usted simplemente trata de confundirme, de poner en duda mis predicciones y ¡de difamar mi venerable profesión!»

«Sólo con hechos, venerable adivino —dijo el astrónomo—. Sólo con hechos.»

Motecuzoma se rió entre dientes ante esa discusión, sin preocuparse más por lo que la noche nos traería y entonces los tres hombres se adelantaron, quedando fuera del alcance de mi oído, en el momento en que llegamos a la cumbre de la Colina de Huixachi.

Un buen número de sacerdotes jóvenes nos habían precedido y ya lo tenían todo listo. Había preparada una pila de antorchas sin encender y una pequeña pirámide de ocotes y leños que servirían para encender el fuego. También había allí otros combustibles: yesca, unos palitos secos, papel de corteza finamente picado, ocotes y madejas de algodón empapadas en aceite. El *xochimique* escogido para esa noche era un joven guerrero de pecho amplio, que recientemente había sido capturado en Texcala, y quien yacía desnudo sobre la piedra de sacrificio. Ya que era esencial que él estuviera sin moverse durante toda la ceremonia, le habían dado a beber alguna droga sacerdotal. Así es que yacía completamente relajado, sus ojos cerrados, sus miembros colgando y respirando apenas perceptiblemente.

Las únicas luces venían de las estrellas y de la luna que se levantaba sobre nuestras cabezas y el reflejo de los rayos de la luna hacía brillar el lago abajo de nosotros. Para entonces, nuestros ojos ya se habían habituado a la oscuridad y podíamos ver los surcos y contornos de la tierra que rodeaba la colina; las ciudades y los pueblos parecían muertos y desiertos, pero en realidad estaban esperando bien despiertos y casi se podían percibir sus latidos de aprensión. Había un grupo de nubes en el horizonte del este, y pronto llegaría el tiempo de que las tan esperadas estrellas, por las que todo mundo rezaba, se hicieran visibles en el cielo. Y al fin llegaron: el grupo de seis estrellas pálidas, y después de ellas, una brillante y roja que siempre las seguía. Esperamos mientras ellas recorrían, muy lentamente, su viaje por el cielo, y esperamos conteniendo el aliento, pero ninguna se desvaneció o se separó del resto, ni cambiaron su curso acostumbrado. Al fin, ante un suspiro colectivo de alivio, quedaron exactamente arriba de la colina atestada, cuando el sacerdote que llevaba la cuenta arrancó un sonido a su concha-trompeta, para señalar que era la medianoche. Varias gentes dijeron: «Llegaron exactamente al lugar, en el preciso momento», y el principal sacerdote de todos los sacerdotes presentes, el gran sacerdote de Huitzilopochtli, rugió ordenando: «*¡Encendamos el Fuego Nuevo!*»

Un sacerdote colocó sobre el pecho del postrado *xochimique*, un madero hueco con yesca, luego cuidadosamente acomodó los pedacitos de ocote. Otro sacerdote, que estaba al otro lado de la piedra de sacrificios, se acercó e inclinó con un palito seco y empezó a darle un movimiento giratorio con las palmas de sus manos. Todos nosotros, los espectadores, esperábamos ansiosos; los dioses todavía nos podían negar esa chispa de vida. Pero entonces surgió un destello de llama humeante. El sacerdote detuvo con una mano el madero y con la otra alimentó y animó la llamita luminosa, con madejas de algodón con aceite, pedacitos de papel seco, que produjeron una pequeña, parpadeante pero definitiva llama. Pareció que eso despertó bastante al *xochimique*, quien abrió sus ojos lo suficiente como para ver el despertar del Fuego Nuevo en su pecho, pero no lo vio por mucho tiempo.

Uno de los sacerdotes movió cauteloso hacia un lado el madero que sostenía el fuego. Otro sacó un cuchillo y apuñaló al joven tan diestramente, que éste apenas sí se movió. Cuando el pecho estuvo bien abierto, otro sacerdote se aproximó y extrajo el corazón que había dejado de palpitar y lo levantó, mientras otro acomodaba el madero con el fuego en la herida abierta, luego rápidamente, pero con destreza, acomodó más ocote, papeles y algodón. Cuando ya la llama se levantaba lo suficiente del pecho de la víctima, que todavía se movía débilmente, otro sacerdote depositó con cuidado el corazón en medio del fuego. Las llamas cesaron por un momento mojadas por el corazón sangrante, pero se volvieron a levantar otra vez con nuevo vigor y el corazón hacía un ruido audible al asarse.

Un grito salió de todos los presentes: «*¡El Fuego Nuevo se ha encendido!*», y la multitud inmóvil hasta ese momento, empezó a moverse de un lado a otro. Uno tras otro, por orden de rango, los sacerdotes tomaron sus antorchas de la pila y tocaron con ellas el pecho del *xochimique*, que se achicharraba rápidamente, para encenderlas con el Fuego Nuevo y luego corrían con ellas. El primero utilizó su antorcha para encender la pila de leña que estaba en la colina, para que todos al mirar la Colina de Huixachi vieran esa gran hoguera y supieran que todo peligro había pasado, que todo sería igual en El Único Mundo. Me imaginé que podía oír los gritos de alegría, las risas y los sollozos de felicidad, de todas las gentes que miraban desde sus azoteas alrededor de los lagos. Después los sacerdotes corrieron por el sendero de la colina, mientras sus antorchas ondulaban detrás de ellos inflamando el aire. En la base de la colina otros sacerdotes estaban esperando, que venían de todas las comunidades, cercanas y lejanas. Tomaron las antorchas y corrieron para llevar ese precioso fragmento del Fuego Nuevo, a los templos de las diferentes ciudades, pueblos y aldeas.

«Puedes quitarte tu máscara, Nochipa —le dije a mi hija—. Ya estamos a salvo, quítatela para que puedas ver mejor.»

Ella y yo estuvimos parados al lado norte de la colina, mirando cómo esas lucecitas brillaban alejándose de nosotros y se desparramaban en todas direcciones. Luego hubo unos estallidos silenciosos. Ixtapalapan, el pueblo más cercano, fue el primero en encender la urna de su templo principal, el siguiente pueblo fue Mexicaltzinco. En cada templo había esperando un sinnúmero de habitantes, portando sus propias antorchas para encenderlas en los fuegos de los templos y llevarlas corriendo a casa para encencender los fuegos de sus hogares y los de sus vecinos. Así es que cada antorcha que se alejaba de la Colina de Huixachi, primero brillaba como un punto en la distancia, luego brillaba en la urna de un templo y luego se desparramaba por las calles, dejando tras de sí destellos centelleantes en movimiento. La secuencia se repitió una y otra vez en Coyohuacan, en la gran Tenochtitlan, en las comunidades, las lejanas y las más apartadas, hasta que toda esa vasta cuenca, de lagos y tierras, rápidamente se llenó de luz y de vida. Había alegría, entusiasmo y regocijo a simple vista, y yo traté con todas mis fuerzas de imprimirlo entre mis recuerdos felices, porque no tenía esperanzas de volver a ver eso.

Como si estuviera leyendo mis pensamientos, mi hija me dijo suavemente: «Oh, tengo la esperanza de vivir hasta que sea una vieja. Me gustaría tanto volver a ver esta maravilla la próxima vez, padre.»

Cuando Nochipa y yo volvimos a donde se encontraba la gran hoguera, cuatro hombres estaban agachados cerca de ella, en ansiosa consulta: el Venerado Orador Motecuzoma, el sacerdote principal de Huitzilopochtli, el astrónomo y el adivino de los que ya he hablado antes. Todos ellos estaban discutiendo qué palabras debería decir el Uey-Tlatoani en su discurso, el siguiente día, para proclamar lo que el Fuego Nuevo había prometido en los años por venir. El adivino, inclinado sobre algunos diagramas que había dibujado en la tierra con un palito, evidentemente acababa de decir una profecía, que el astrónomo consideraba como excepcional, pues le estaba diciendo burlonamente:

«No más sequías, no más miserias, una larga y fructífera gavilla de años. Muy consolador, amigo adivino. ¿Pero usted no ve un presagio inminente que aparece en el cielo?»

El adivino le dijo: «Los cielos son sus asuntos. Usted hace los mapas y yo me encargaré de leer lo que hay en ellos.»

El astrónomo gruñó: «Puede ser que usted encontrara más inspiración si de vez en cuando usted mirara las estrellas y en lugar de esos tontos círculos y ángulos que usted dibuja. —Y apuntó los garabatos hechos en la tierra—. ¿Entonces, usted no lee ningún amenazante *yqualoca*?»

La palabra significa eclipse. El adivino, el sacerdote y el Uey-

Tlatoani, todos ellos repitieron al mismo tiempo y con inquietud: «¿Eclipse?»

«De sol —dijo el astrónomo—. Hasta este viejo fraudulento podía preverlo, si alguna vez leyera el pasado de la historia, en lugar de pretender conocer el futuro.»

El adivino tragó saliva y se quedó sin palabras. Motecuzoma se le quedó mirando. El astrónomo continuó:

«Está registrado, Señor Orador, que los maya del sur vieron un *yqualoca* dándole un hambriento mordisco a Tonatíu el sol, en el año Diez-Casa. El próximo mes, en el día Siete-Lagarto, se cumplirán exactamente dieciocho años solares y once días desde que eso ocurrió. De acuerdo a los registros llevados por mí y por mis predecesores, de las tierras del norte y del sur, esos oscurecimientos solares regularmente pasan en alguna parte de El Único Mundo, en intervalos de esa duración. Confiadamente puedo predecir que Tonatíu se volverá a eclipsar por una sombra en el día Siete-Lagarto. Desafortunadamente, como no soy adivino, no puedo decir qué severo será ese *yqualoca* ni en qué tierra será visible. Pero todos aquellos que lo vean, lo tomarán como el presagio más maléfico, inmediatamente después de haber pasado el Fuego Nuevo. Sugeriría, mi señor, que todos los pueblos deben ser informados y prevenidos, para que no se asusten tanto.»

«Tiene razón —dijo Motecuzoma—. Enviaré mensajeros-veloces a todas las tierras. Aún a aquellas que son nuestras enemigas, para que no crean que ese presagio significa el debilitamiento de nuestro poder. Gracias, señor astrónomo. En cuanto a usted... —Se volvió fríamente hacia el tembloroso adivino—. El más experto y sabio adivino puede estar propenso a cometer un error, y eso se puede perdonar, pero un total inepto es un verdadero peligro para la nación y eso no lo puedo tolerar. Cuando regresemos a la ciudad, se presentará a la guardia de palacio para que lo ejecuten.»

En la mañana del siguiente día, Dos-Caña, primer día del año nuevo Dos-Caña, el gran mercado de Tlaltelolco, como todos los mercados en El Único Mundo, estaba lleno de gente que compraba todos los utensilios para sus casas, para reemplazar los viejos que habían destruido. A pesar de que la gente casi no había dormido después del alumbramiento del Fuego Nuevo, todos estaban alegres y charlatanes, y mucho se debía a que estrenaban ropas nuevas y joyas, y por el hecho de que los dioses estuvieran dispuestos a dejarlos seguir viviendo.

Al mediodía, desde lo alto de la Gran Pirámide, el Uey-Tlatoani Motecuzoma hizo el tradicional discurso a su pueblo. En parte, él dijo lo que el finado adivino había predicho —buen clima, buenas cosechas, y todo eso—, pero prudentemente diluyó en mieles los presagios, diciendo que los dioses continuarían dándonos sus beneficios, mientras ellos estuvieran satisfechos con nosotros los mexica. Por lo tanto, dijo Motecuzoma, todos los hombres deberían trabajar duro, todas las mujeres deberían ser ahorrativas, todas las guerras deberían pelearse con vigor, todas las ofrendas apropiadas y sacrificios deberían hacerse en ocasiones ceremoniales. En esencia, se le dijo al pueblo que la vida continuaría como siempre había sido. No hubo ninguna revelación o algo nuevo en el discurso de Motecuzoma, a excepción de su anuncio —como si fuera una casualidad que había arreglado para un entretenimiento público— del próximo eclipse solar.

Mientras él oraba en lo alto de la pirámide, sus mensajeros veloces ya habían partido desde Tenochtitlan hacia todos los puntos del horizonte. Ellos llevaban la noticia del inminente eclipse a todos los gobernantes, gobernadores, caciques de todas partes, e hicieron énfasis en el hecho de que los dioses habían dado a nuestros astrónomos la primera noticia de ese suceso, por lo tanto no causaría nada, ni bueno ni malo, y no debería ser causa de preocupación. Pero una cosa es decirle a la gente que no preste atención a un fenómeno del que hay que temer, y otra, que la gente no quede expuesta a él.

Incluso yo, que fui el primero en oír acerca de ese *yqualoca* amenazante, cuando éste tuvo lugar no lo pude mirar bostezando con calma, sino que tuve que pretender que lo veía con calma e interés científico, por Nochipa, Beu Ribé y los criados que estaban conmigo en el jardín-azotea el día de Siete-Lagarto y tuve que darles un ejemplo de serenidad.

No sé cómo se vio en otros lugares de El Único Mundo, pero aquí en Tenochtitlan pareció como si Tonatíu hubiera sido totalmente tragado. Y probablemente fue sólo por un breve momento, pero para nosotros pareció una eternidad. Ese día estaba bastante nublado, así es que el sol era solamente un disco pálido como la luna sin brillantez y podíamos mirarlo directamente. Se pudo observar el primer mordisco que le dieron en su orilla, como si hubiera sido una tortilla, y luego vimos cómo se iban comiendo su cara poco a poco. El día se oscureció, el calor de la primavera desapareció y un viento helado sopló por todo el mundo. Los pájaros volaban sobre nuestra azotea en confusión y podíamos oír aullar a los perros de nuestros vecinos.

El mordisco que estaba recibiendo Tonatíu, se fue haciendo más y más grande, hasta que al final toda su cara fue tragada y se puso tan oscura como la cara parduzca de un nativo de Chiapa. Por un instante, el sol estuvo más oscuro que las nubes que le rodeaban, como si viéramos a través de un pequeño hoyo del día hacia la noche. Cuando las nubes, el cielo y todo el mundo se oscureció con la misma oscuridad de la noche, Tonatíu quedó totalmente fuera de nuestra vista.

Las únicas luces reconfortantes que podíamos ver desde nuestras azoteas, eran los pocos fuegos parpadeantes que ardían fuera de los templos y el humo rojizo que salía del interior del Popocatépetl y que se sostenía encima de él. Los pájaros dejaron de volar y uno de ellos, un pájaro muscícapa de cabeza roja, revoloteó entre Beu y yo y fue a pararse en uno de los arbustos de nuestro jardín, poniendo su cabeza dentro de su ala y echándose a dormir aparentemente. En esos largos momentos en que el día era noche, casi deseé poder esconder mi propia cabeza. De las otras casas y de las calles, podía oír gritos, gemidos y oraciones, pero Beu y Nochipa se mantuvieron en silencio y Estrella Cantadora y Turquesa sólo gimoteaban suavemente, así es que supuse que mi actitud de serenidad tuvos los efectos deseados.

Luego una rayita delgada de luz volvió a aparecer en el cielo y muy despacio se fue ensanchando y brillando. El arco del tragador *yqualoca* se deslizaba reluctante, dejando que Tonatíu saliera de sus labios. El medio sol creció, el mordisco disminuyó hasta que Tonatíu fue un disco otra vez, entero, el mundo se volvió a iluminar con su luz. El pájaro que estaba en la rama, a un lado de mí, levantó su cabeza y se nos quedó mirando con una perplejidad casi cómica y echó a volar. Mis familiares y los sirvientes volvieron sus rostros pálidos hacia mí y me sonrieron trémulamente.

«Eso es todo —dije con autoridad—. Se ha acabado.» Y todos bajamos las escaleras para volver a nuestras actividades respectivas.

Con razón o erróneamente, mucha gente dijo después que el Venerado Orador había dicho una mentira deliberadamente, cuando él había asegurado que el eclipse no sería un mal presagio, porque sólo unos cuantos días después, todo el distrito del lago se vio sacudido por un temblor de tierra. Era un simple temblor comparado con el *zyuiíù* que Zyanya y yo habíamos vivido una vez, y, aunque mi casa se estremeció como las demás, quedó en pie tan firmemente como lo hizo en el tiempo de la gran inundación. Pero, por muy simple que yo lo cuente, el temblor fue uno de los peores que habían sacudido esas tierras, y muchos edificios se cayeron en Tenochtitlan, en Tlácopan, en Texcoco y en otras pequeñas comunidades y cuando esos edificios se cayeron mataron a muchos de sus ocupantes. Creo que murieron unas dos mil personas y los que les sobrevivieron levantaron un gran clamor en contra de Motecuzoma, así es que a éste no le quedó más remedio que prestar atención a él. No quiero decir que él pagara algún daño o que hiciera alguna reparación, sino que lo que hizo fue invitar a toda la gente al Corazón del Único Mundo, para que vieran morir por garrote, públicamente, al astrónomo que había predicho el eclipse.

Pero eso no hizo que se acabaran los presagios, porque eran presagios. Y algunos de ellos, pienso que francamente no lo eran. Como por ejemplo, en ese simple año de Dos-Caña, se vieron caer del cielo nocturno más estrellas de las que jamás se habían visto caer antes, más que todas las estrellas juntas que se habían registrado durante *todos* los años, por nuestros astrónomos. Durante esos dieciocho meses, cada vez que caía una estrella, cualquier persona que la veía podía ir a palacio o a mandar un mensaje. Motecuzoma no vio personalmente esa obviamente errónea aritmética que se estaba llevando a efecto, y ya que su orgullo no le permitía volver a correr el riesgo de otra acusación de engañar a su pueblo, hizo anuncios públicos de ese diluvio de estrellas, ya que las sumas eran alarmantes.

Para mí y para otros, la razón de ese total sin precedentes de estrellas muriendo era evidente; después del eclipse más gente empezó a mirar al cielo más aprensivamente, y cada uno de ellos estaba ansioso por anunciar cualquier hecho sobrenatural que viera. En cualquier noche de cualquier año, un hombre parado en la puerta de su casa mirando al cielo, en el tiempo que le llevaría fumar un *poquíetl*, vería a dos o tres de las más pálidas estrellas, perder su débil sostén en el cielo y caer seguida de una cola-mortaja de chispas. Sin embargo, si un gran número de personas lo ve y aunque sólo dos o tres de ellas den aviso de haberlo visto, los datos recogidos parecerán como si cada noche hubiera una continua y amenazadora lluvia de estrellas. Y eso es lo que más recuerda nuestra gente de ese año Dos-Caña. Si eso hubiera sido cierto, el cielo se habría quedado totalmente vacío de estrellas para siempre.

Ese juego ocioso de coleccionar estrellas caídas hubiera seguido adelante, excepto que el siguiente año, Tres-Cuchillo, la atención de la gente se vio desviada hacia otro presagio, uno que involucraba más directamente a Motecuzoma. Su hermana soltera Pápantzin, la Señora Pájaro Tempranero, escogió ese tiempo para morir. No hubo nada extraordinario en su muerte, sólo que era muy joven y se supuso que murió de una típica enfermedad femenina que nadie hizo mención. Lo siniestro fue que, dos o tres días después de su entierro, numerosos ciudadanos de Tenochtitlan afirmaron haber visto a la señora caminando por la noche, retorciéndose las manos y lanzando un lamento. De acuerdo con lo que dijeron esos que la encontraron —y que se multiplicaron en una noche— la Señora Papan había dejado su tumba para traer un mensaje, y éste era que desde el mundo del más allá, ella había visto un gran ejército conquistador que avanzaba hacia Tenochtitlan, por el sur.

Yo particularmente llegué a la conclusión de que los que decían eso, lo único que habían visto era el familiar y bastante cansado viejo espíritu de La Llorona, que por *siempre* se lamentaba y estrujaba sus manos, y también ellos habían equivocado tercamente y mal interpretado su cansado lamento. Pero Motecuzoma no podría negar con facilidad el supuesto fantasma de su hermana. La única forma de poder apaciguar a ese fantasma que salía de su tumba, era ordenando que el sepulcro de Papan fuera abierto en la noche, para poder probar que ella yacía tranquilamente allí y no andaba vagando en la noche por toda la ciudad.

Yo no estaba con aquellos que hicieron esa excursión en la noche, pero la lúgubre historia de lo que pasó fue conocida en todas estas tierras. Motecuzoma fue en compañía de algunos sacerdotes, cortesanos y testigos. Los sacerdotes cavaron la tierra de la tumba y la abrieron, luego quitaron la espléndida mortaja que cubría el cadáver, mientras Motecuzoma estaba parado a un lado, agitado y nervioso. Los sacerdotes descubrieron la cabeza de la mujer muerta para su positiva identificación, y la encontraron no muy corrompida, así es que ella era la Señora Pájaro Tempranero y ciertamente que estaba muerta.

Se dice que entonces Motecuzoma dio un alarido terrible, tan terrible que hasta los más impasibles sacerdotes se asustaron, cuando de las cuencas de los ojos de la señora brilló una luz verde-blanquecina sobrenatural. De acuerdo con esa historia, ella fijó esa mirada directamente en su hermano, y él, en el colmo del horror le dirigió un largo, aunque incoherente discurso. Unos dijeron que se estaba disculpando por haber abierto su tumba perturbando sus restos; otros dijeron que fue una confesión de culpabilidad y esos mismos luego afirmaron que la enfermedad de la hermana soltera de Motecuzoma, fue supuesta, pues en realidad había muerto de un mal parto.

Poniendo a un lado al fantasma, los testigos que estaban presentes dijeron que el Venerado Orador, finalmente se dio la vuelta y huyó lejos de la tumba abierta. Huyó demasiado pronto como para ver que los ojos blanqui-verdes brillantes del cuerpo se empezaron a mover, y luego se extendieron y se escurrieron por la arrugada mejilla. No era nada sobrenatural, era solamente un *petlazolcoatl*, un ciempiés feo y que como las luciérnagas son peculiarmente luminosos y brillantes en la oscuridad. Dos de esas criaturas, evidentemente, se habían introducido en el cadáver, por las puertas más fáciles de comer y se habían enroscado en cada una de las cuencas de los ojos, para vivir cómodamente y comer a su placer la cabeza de la señora. Esa noche, molestos por toda esa conmoción, lenta y ciegamente se arrastraron fuera de donde estaban y retorciéndose entre los labios del cadáver, desaparecieron otra vez.

Después de eso, ya no se recordó que Pápantzin hiciera más apariciones públicas, pero otros sucesos extraños se dejaron oír por los alrededores, causando tanta conmoción que el Consejo de Voceros nombró investigadores especiales para que buscaran la verdad en todos ellos. Sin embargo, que yo recuerde, ninguno fue corroborado y los más de ellos fueron considerados como presagios hechos por adivinos que querían llamar la atención o por alucinaciones de borrachos.

Entonces, cuando ese hético año terminó, cuando los días vacíos ya habían pasado y el año Cuatro-Casa empezaba, el Venerado Orador Nezahualpili llegó de Texcoco inesperadamente. Se dijo que él había venido a Tenochtitlan sólo para disfrutar de nuestra celebración de El Árbol Se Levanta, pues por muchos años había estado viendo una versión de esa celebración en Texcoco. La verdad era que él había venido para consultar secretamente con Motecuzoma, pero los dos gobernantes se habían encerrado juntos, sólo por un pequeño tiempo en la mañana, antes de mandar llamar a otra persona que necesitaban consultar. Para mi gran sorpresa fue a mí a quien mandaron llamar.

Con el vestido de saco puesto, hice mi entrada al salón del trono, aunque esta vez mis reverencias fueron más humildes de lo que exigía el protocolo, ya que en la sala había dos Venerados Oradores esa mañana. Yo estaba bastante sorprendido de ver que Nezahualpili estaba casi calvo y que el pelo que le quedaba era gris. Cuando al fin me puse de pie enfrente de los dos *icpaltin*, tronos, que estaban lado a lado entre los dos discos de oro y plata, el Uey-Tlatoani de Texcoco al fin me reconoció y dijo casi alegremente:

«¡Mi formal cortesano, Cabeza Inclinada! ¡Mi una vez escribano y conocedor de palabras, Topo! ¡Mi una vez heroico guerrero, Nube Oscura!»

«En verdad, que Nube Oscura —gruñó Motecuzoma. Ése fue su único saludo, acompañado de una mirada enojada—. ¿Entonces usted conoce a este desgraciado, mi amigo?»

«*Ayyo*, hubo un tiempo en que estuvimos muy unidos —dijo Nezahualpili, sonriendo ampliamente—. Cuando usted me habló de un campeón Águila llamado Mixtli, no lo relacioné con él, pero debí pensar que se elevaría de título tras título. —Dirigiéndose a mí, dijo—: Le saludo y lo felicito, campeón de la Orden del Águila.»

Tengo la esperanza de que contesté adecuadamente, pues estaba ocupado en ver que el saco me cubriera bien las rodillas, pues éstas me temblaban visiblemente.

Motecuzoma preguntó a Nezahualpili: «¿Ha sido siempre este Mixtli un embustero?»

«Nunca un embustero, mi amigo, le doy mi palabra. Mixtli siempre ha dicho la verdad, conforme la ha visto. Desgraciadamente, sus visiones no son siempre cómodamente acordes con las de otras gentes.»

«Ni tampoco las de un embustero —dijo Motecuzoma entre dientes. Y a mí me dijo casi gritándome—: Usted nos hizo creer a todos nosotros que no había nada que temer de...»

Nezahualpili le interrumpió diciendo calmadamente: «¿Me permite, señor amigo? ¿Mixtli?»

«¿Sí, Señor Orador?» respondí roncamente, sin saber en qué problema me hallaba, pero sintiéndome totalmente seguro de que estaba en un problema.

«Hace poco más de dos años, los maya enviaron mensajeros-veloces a todas estas tierras, para avisar que habían visto extraños objetos, casas flotantes, dijeron, en las playas de la península de Uluúmil Kutz. ¿Recuerda aquella ocasión?»

«Vívidamente, mi señor —dije—. Yo interpreté ese mensaje, como que ellos habían visto un pez gigante y cierto pez alado.»

«Sí. Ésa fue la explicación que se esparció por orden de su Venerado Orador, y creo que toda la gente la escuchó con alivio.»

«Para mi muy considerable vergüenza», dijo ceñudo Motecuzoma.

Nezahualpili hizo un gesto para aplacarlo y luego continuó preguntándome: «Parece que algunos de los maya que vieron esas apariciones hicieron algunos dibujos, joven Mixtli, pero sólo hasta ahora llegó uno de esos dibujos a nuestro poder. ¿Puede usted todavía decir, si estos objetos pintados son un pez?»

Me alargó un pedazo de papel de corteza, pequeño, cuadrado y andrajoso, que yo observé atentamente. Era un típico dibujo maya, tan pequeño y tan mal hecho que no me quedó otro remedio que casi adivinar qué era lo que en realidad quería representar. Sin embargo tuve que decir: «Debo confesar, mis señores, que esto se asemeja más a una casa que a un pez inmenso. Yo me confundí.»

«¿O el pez volador?», preguntó Nezahualpili.

«No, mi señor. Las alas del pez se extienden a ambos lados.

Todo lo que puedo decirle es que, en estos objetos las alas parece que están directamente encima de ellos, sobre sus espaldas o sus azoteas.»

Él hizo notar: «Y esos puntos que están en fila, entre las alas y el tejado o azotea, ¿qué cree usted que son?»

Sintiéndome algo molesto dije: «Es casi imposible de asegurar por este dibujo tan mal hecho, pero puedo aventurar que parecen las cabezas de los hombres que se asoman.»

Sintiéndome miserable, levanté los ojos del papel para mirar directamente a cada uno de los Oradores. «Mis señores, me desdigo de mi anterior interpretación. Sólo puedo decir que no había recibido la información adecuada. Ahora puedo decir que Uluümil Kutz fue visitado por unas inmensas canoas que de alguna manera se mueven con alas y van llenas de hombres. No podría decir de qué nación son esos hombres ni de dónde vienen, excepto que son extranjeros y que obviamente tienen muchos conocimientos. Si ellos pueden construir esa clase de canoas, muy bien pueden hacer la guerra y quizás una guerra de lo más atemorizante, como nunca la hemos visto.»

«¡Ah, lo ve! —dijo Nezahualpili con gran satisfacción—. Aun a riesgo de desagradar a su Venerado Orador, Mixtli no titubea en decir la verdad como él la ve... cuando él la ve. Mis adivinos y oráculos, cuando vieron este dibujo maya, leyeron en él ese mismo portento.»

«Si ese presagio hubiera sido leído correctamente y pronto —murmuró Motecuzoma— hace más de dos años que hubiera fortificado y enviado hombres a las costas de Uluümil Kutz.»

«¿Con qué propósito? —preguntó Nezahualpili—. Si los extranjeros escogen ese sitio para golpear, deje que los maya que están allí reciban el golpe. Pero si es como parece, ellos nos pueden invadir por el ilimitado mar, hay innumerables playas en donde ellos puedan desembarcar, al este o norte, al oeste o al sur. Ni los guerreros de todas las naciones juntas, alcanzarían para proteger todas las playas vulnerables. Es mejor que usted concentre su defensa, en un apretado círculo, alrededor de su nación.»

«¿Yo? —exclamó Motecuzoma—. ¿Y usted qué?»

«Ah, yo estaré muerto para entonces —dijo Nezahualpili arrellenándose regaladamente en su silla—. Los adivinos me han asegurado eso, y estoy muy contento, porque así podré pasar mis últimos años en paz y reposando. De ahora en adelante no haré más la guerra, hasta que muera. Ni tampoco la hará mi hijo Flor Oscura, quien será mi sucesor en el trono.»

Yo estaba parado enfrente del trono, sintiéndome bastante incómodo, pero aparentemente les tenía sin cuidado y se habían olvidado de mí, ni siquiera me dijeron que me fuera.

Motecuzoma miró a Nezahualpili, y su rostro se fue ensombreciendo. «¿Me está usted dando a entender que Texcoco y su nación alcohua dejan de pertenecer a la Triple Alianza? Señor amigo, aborrezco hablar sobre traición y cobardía.»

«Pues entonces no hable sobre eso —dejó caer Nezahualpili—. Lo que quiero decir es que nosotros... que nosotros debemos... reservar todos nuestros guerreros para la invasión que ha sido profetizada. Y cuando digo nosotros, me estoy refiriendo a *todas* las naciones de estas tierras. No debemos gastar más nuestras fuerzas y nuestros guerreros combatiendo entre nosotros. Los feudos y rivalidades deben ser suspendidas y todas nuestras energías, todos nuestros ejércitos juntos deben luchar para repeler al invasor. Así es como yo lo veo a la luz de los presagios y a la interpretación que de ellos dieron mis sabios. Es por eso que pasaré los días que me quedan y Flor Oscura lo seguirá haciendo después de mí, en trabajar para conseguir una tregua y la solidaridad entre todas las naciones, para que todos presentemos un frente unido cuando los extranjeros lleguen.»

«Todo eso está muy bien para usted y para su dócil y disciplinado Príncipe Heredero —dijo Motecuzoma en una forma insultante—. Pero nosotros ¡somos los mexica! Desde que hemos implantado nuestra supremacía en El Único Mundo, ningún extranjero ha puesto un pie dentro de nuestros dominios sin nuestro consentimiento. Y siempre será así, si debemos pelear solos contra todas las naciones conocidas o no conocidas, aunque *todos* nuestros aliados deserten o se vuelvan contra nosotros.»

Sentí un poco de pena al ver que el Señor Nezahualpili no se resentía ante esa demostración abierta de desprecio. Él dijo casi con tristeza:

«Entonces le contaré una leyenda, señor amigo. Quizá ha sido olvidada por ustedes los mexica, pero todavía se lee en nuestros archivos de Texcoco. De acuerdo con esa leyenda, cuando sus ancestros azteca se aventuraron por primera vez fuera de su tierra de Aztlán, al norte de aquí, e hicieron esa larga caminata que les tomó varios años hasta llegar aquí, ellos no sabían los obstáculos que podrían encontrar en su camino. Todo lo que sabían era que se encontrarían en tierras prohibidas, y con pueblos tan hostiles a ellos, que pudieran juzgar preferible retroceder en sus caminos y regresar a Aztlán. Para prevenir esa contingencia, hicieron todos los arreglos para poder tener una rápida y segura retirada. En siete u ocho de los lugares en que se detuvieron entre Aztlán y este distrito del lago, ellos recolectaron y escondieron grandes cantidades de armas y provisiones. Si ellos se veían forzados a retroceder a su tierra otra vez, lo harían a su propio paso bien nutridos y bien armados. O podrían detenerse en cualquiera de esas posiciones ya preparadas.»

Motecuzoma bostezó; claramente se veía que él no había escuchado ese cuento antes, ni yo tampoco. Nezahualpili continuó:

«Por lo menos eso dice esa leyenda. Desgraciadamente no dice dónde estaban ubicados esos siete u ocho lugares. Respetuosamente le sugiero, señor amigo, que mande usted exploradores hacia el norte, a través de las tierras desiertas para buscarlos. Podría utilizarlos o mandar hacer una nueva línea de aprovisionamiento, pues si usted no desea tener como aliado a ninguna nación vecina ahora, llegará el tiempo en que ninguna de ellas lo será y entonces usted podrá necesitar una ruta de escape. Nosotros los acolhua preferimos rodearnos de amigos.»

Motecuzoma estuvo en silencio por largo tiempo, encogido en su silla como si estuviese confundido ante la aproximación de una tormenta. Luego se sentó derecho, levantó sus hombros y dijo: «Suponga que esos extranjeros nunca lleguen. Usted se encontrará tranquilamente acostado, sin más propósito que el caer en la trampa de cualquier *amigo* que se sienta lo suficientemente fuerte.»

Nezahualpili movió su cabeza y dijo: «Los extranjeros vendrán.»

«Usted parece muy seguro de ello.»

«Lo suficientemente seguro como para hacerles la guerra —dijo Nezahualpili casi jovial—. Señor amigo, lo reto a usted. Juguemos al *tlachtli* en el patio ceremonial. Sin jugadores, sólo usted y yo, digamos tres juegos. Si pierdo, tomaré ese presagio como contradictorio. Me retractaré de todas mis tristes predicciones y pondré todas las armas acolhua, todos sus ejércitos y recursos a su disposición. Si usted pierde...»

«¿Qué?»

«Concédame sólo esto. Me dejará a mí y a mis acolhua libres y fuera de todos sus futuros enredos, para que podamos pasar así nuestros últimos días en paz, dedicados a otras cosas más placenteras.»

Motecuzoma dijo al instante: «De acuerdo. Tres buenos juegos», y sonrió malignamente.

Él debió de haber sonreído así porque no era el único que pensaba que Nezahualpili debía de estar loco al retarlo a jugar. Por supuesto, nadie excepto yo —que había jurado guardar el secreto— sabía en esos momento que el Venerado Orador de Texcoco acababa de apostar su porvenir. Para los ciudadanos de Tenochtitlan, así como para los visitantes, la contienda sería otro simple entretenimiento para ellos o un honor más para Tláloc, durante las celebraciones de la ciudad, de El Árbol Se Levanta. Pero no era un secreto que Motecuzoma era por lo menos veinte años más joven que Nezahualpili, ni que ese juego de *tlachtli* era un juego brutal, jugado solamente por jóvenes fuertes y robustos.

Todo alrededor y más allá de las paredes exteriores del patio de pelota y El Corazón del Único Mundo, estaba lleno de gente, tanto nobles como plebeyos, que se apretujaban hombro con hombro, aunque ni siquiera uno de cien pudiera haber tenido la esperanza de echarle una simple mirada al juego. Sin embargo, cuando el juego hacía que los espectadores que estaban adentro del patio, gritaran un «¡*Ayyo!*» de alabanza, o un «¡*Ayya!*» como gemido, o un «*hoo-oo-ooo*» piadoso, toda la gente que estaba afuera en la plaza, lo repetía como un eco, sin ni siquiera saber el porqué.

Las hileras de escalones de piedra inclinadas, que se desprendían de las paredes de mármol del patio interior, estaban pletóricas de altos nobles de Tenochtitlan y de Texcoco —los que habían venido con Nezahualpili—. Posiblemente en compensación o como soborno a mi silencio, los dos Venerados Oradores me habían asignado uno de los preciosos asientos allí. Siendo sólo un campeón Águila, yo era la persona de más bajo rango en toda esa augusta reunión, a excepción de Nochipa, a quien había llevado para sentarla en mis piernas.

«Mira, hija, y recuerda —le dije al oído—. Esto es algo que nunca se volverá a ver. Dos de los hombres más notables y con mayor señorío en todo El Único Mundo, compitiendo en público espectáculo. Mira y recuérdalo para toda tu vida. Nunca volverás a ver un espectáculo como este.»

«Pero, padre —dijo ella—, ese jugador que trae un yelmo azul es un *viejo*.» Y apuntó discretamente con su barbilla a Nezahualpili, quien estaba parado en el centro del patio, un poco aparte de Motecuzoma y del principal sacerdote de Tláloc, el sacerdote que se encargaba de todas las ceremonias durante ese mes.

«Bueno —le dije—, el jugador que tiene un protector de cabeza de color verde, es más o menos de mi edad, por lo tanto no es tan juvenil.»

«Parece que estás más a favor del viejo.»

«Espero que grites de alegría por él, cuando yo lo haga. He apostado una pequeña fortuna a su favor.»

Nochipa se movió en mis piernas para poder mirarme a la cara. «Oh, eres muy tonto, padre. ¿Por qué?»

Yo le dije: «No lo sé realmente. —Y en verdad no lo sabía—. Ahora quédate quieta. Ya eres bastante pesada sin moverte.»

Aunque mi hija acababa de cumplir los doce años y ya había tenido su primer sangrado, por lo que llevaba los vestidos de mujer, y se empezaba a formar muy bien, con las curvas y las formas de la mujer, no había heredado —gracias a los dioses— la estatura de su padre, o no hubiera soportado tenerla encima y estar sentado sobre la piedra dura.

El sacerdote de Tláloc recitó invocaciones y oraciones especiales y quemó incienso, todo ello demasiado largo y tedioso, hasta que al fin lanzó muy alto la pelota para que el primer juego empezara. No intentaré, mis señores escribanos, contarles cada bote y rebote de la pelota, pues ustedes desconocen las complejas reglas del *tlachtli* y no podrían, por lo tanto, apreciar las partes más importantes del juego. El sacerdote se escurrió fuera del patio como un negro escarabajo, dejando solos a Nezahualpili y a Motecuzoma, y a los dos encargados de las metas, cada uno al lado opuesto del patio, pero esos hombres se mantenían inmóviles, excepto cuando el juego requería que ellos movieran los yugos para marcar puntos.

Esas cosas, los bajos arcos movibles por donde los jugadores debían tratar de pasar la pelota, no estaban hechos de piedra como de ordinario lo eran en todos los patios de juego de pelota. Los yugos, como los anillos verticales que pendían de las paredes, estaban hechos del más fino mármol, al igual que las paredes. Tanto los anillos como los yugos estaban elaboradamente esculpidos, pulidos y pintados con brillantes colores. Incluso la pelota había sido trenzada especialmente para esa contienda, con las tiras del más ligero *oli*, cuyas tiras se entrelazaban en los colores verde y azul.

Cada uno de los Venerados Oradores llevaba un yelmo de cuero acolchado que cubría su cabeza y sus orejas, asegurado por unos cordones que cruzaban su cabeza y se remataban en la barbilla; pesadas rodilleras y coderas de piel en forma de discos; un apretado taparrabo acolchado y voluminoso que llevaba a la altura de las caderas un ceñidor de piel. Como ya he mencionado, los protectores que llevaban en la cabeza tenían los colores de Tláloc —azul para Nezahualpili y verde para Motecuzoma—, pero, aun sin esa distinción y sin la ayuda de mi topacio, no hubiera tenido ninguna dificultad en distinguir a los dos oponentes. Entre todas esas cosas acojinadas, se podía ver el cuerpo liso, firme y musculoso de Motecuzoma. En cambio, Nezahualpili estaba flaco, encorvado y se le veían las costillas. Motecuzoma se movía con facilidad, con la misma elasticidad de las tiras de *oli* y la pelota fue de él desde el momento en que el sacerdote la lanzó. Nezahualpili se movía tosca y desmañadamente; era una pena verlo tratar de dar caza a su adversario que huía, tratando de agarrarlo como si fuera la sombra de Motecuzoma. Sentí un codazo en mi espalda; me volví para ver al Señor Cuitláhuac, el hermano más joven de Motecuzoma y el comandante de todos los ejércitos mexica. Él me sonrió burlonamente; él era uno con los que había apostado una fuerte cantidad en polvo de oro.

Motecuzoma corría, saltaba, flotaba, volaba. Nezahualpili se afanaba siguiéndolo jadeante, su calva estaba cubierta de sudor bajo su yelmo. La pelota rebotaba con violencia de un lado a otro, pero siempre de Motecuzoma a Motecuzoma. De un lado a otro del patio, lanzaba la pelota hacia la pared en donde estaba parado con indecisión Nezahualpili, quien nunca era lo suficientemente rápido como para interceptarla, y la pelota rebotaba sobre la pared y aunque parezca imposible, sin importar en donde cayera, Motecuzoma siempre estaba allí para pegarle con un codo, o la rodilla o la cadera. Lanzaba la pelota como si fuera una flecha a través del yugo, como una jabalina o como un dardo, y siempre que pasaba al través, nunca tocaba sus lados de piedra, todas las veces anotando un golpe contra Nezahualpili, todas las veces levantando una ovación de todos los espectadores, con excepción hecha de mí, de Nochipa y de los cortesanos de Nezahualpili.

El primer juego lo ganó Motecuzoma. Él trotó por el patio como si fuera un joven venado, sin experimentar cansancio, sintiéndose invencible, y se dirigió hacia sus masajistas que después de atenderlo le dieron un refrescante *chocólatl*, después de lo cual él se quedó allí parado orgullosamente, listo para el siguiente juego, cuando el fatigado y sudoroso Nezahualpili apenas había alcanzado su asiento para descansar, entre sus masajistas. Nochipa se volvió hacia mí y me preguntó: «¿Nos vamos a quedar pobres, padre?» Y el Señor Cuitláhuac, que la oyó, soltó una carcajada, pero en cuanto se reanudó el juego, él ya no volvió a reír más.

Mucho tiempo después, los jugadores veteranos de *tlachtli* todavía seguían discutiendo varias explicaciones contradictorias, por lo que ocurrió después. Unos decían que el primer juego le había servido a Nezahualpili para calentar sus miembros. Otros decían que Motecuzoma había jugado sin prudencia en el primer juego, esforzándose demasiado y cansándose prematuramente. Y había muchas más teorías acerca de eso y por supuesto yo tenía la mía. Yo conocía a Nezahualpili por mucho tiempo y muy a menudo lo había visto así, como un patético viejo, raquítico, encorvado, un hombre como una semilla de cacao y con ese mismo color. Yo creo que lo que yo vi, en ese día del juego de *tlachtli* fue que Nezahualpili pretendió en el último momento esa decrepitud, cuando en son de burla le dio a Motecuzoma el primer juego.

Pero ninguna teoría, incluyendo la mía, podría considerar la maravilla que ocurrió entonces. Motecuzoma y Nezahualpili se encontraron cara a cara para el segundo juego y como Motecuzoma había ganado el anterior, le tocaba lanzar la pelota. Con su rodilla la mandó bien alto, en el aire y ésa fue la última vez que él tocó la pelota.

Naturalmente que como él había ganado antes, todos los ojos estaban puestos en Motecuzoma, esperando que se moviera en un instante y estuviera exactamente en el lugar en donde iba a caer la pelota, antes de que su viejo oponente pudiera moverse haciendo crujir sus huesos. Sin embargo, Nochipa, por alguna razón estaba observando a Nezahualpili y fue su grito de entusiasmo lo que hizo que todos los espectadores se pusieran de pie, todos gritando y alborotando como si hubiera sido un volcán en erupción. La bola estaba bailando alegremente dentro del aro de mármol que colgaba en la pared norte del patio, como si se hubiera detenido allí lo suficiente como para ser admirada y luego cayó del otro lado, al lado opuesto de Nezahualpili, quien la había lanzado allí con uno de sus codos.

Había un alboroto y un regocijo que fue del patio a las gradas de piedra y de allí continuó todavía más lejos. Motecuzoma se apresuró en abrazar a su oponente para felicitarlo, los guardametas y los masajistas se arremolinaban en torno a él saltando gustosos. El sacerdote de Tláloc llegó, danzando y brincando, al patio moviendo sus brazos delirante, proclamando probablemente que eso había sido un buen augurio de Tláloc, aunque sus palabras se perdieron por el griterío. Algunos espectadores, alegremente saltaron hacia el patio. El «¡Ayyo!» vociferante se oyó todavía más fuerte, tan fuerte que parecía romper los oídos, cuando la multitud reunida en la gran plaza, supo lo ocurrido en el patio del juego de pelota. Ya deben de haber comprendido ustedes, reverendos frailes, que Nezahualpili ganó el segundo juego; el haber hecho pasar la pelota por el anillo vertical del muro le hizo ganar, sin importar cuántos puntos pudo haber acumulado Motecuzoma.

Deben ustedes comprender que los espectadores estaban verdaderamente conmovidos, no sólo porque la pelota pasó por el aro, sino también por el hombre que hizo eso. Eso había sido una cosa tan rara, tan increíblemente rara, que realmente no sé cómo puedo explicarles lo raro que fue. Imagínense que ustedes tienen una pelota de duro *oli* del tamaño de sus cabezas, y un anillo de piedra cuyo diámetro es un poquito más grande que el de la pelota; ese anillo está tan alto como dos veces más la estatura de ustedes y puesto verticalmente. Traten de hacer pasar la pelota por ese agujero, sin usar las manos, sólo utilizando sus caderas, sus rodillas, sus codos o sus muslos. Un hombre puede tratar de hacerlo por días, sin hacer otra cosa, sin ser interrumpido o distraído y nunca lo logrará. En un juego, con los movimientos rápidos y la confusión, el que hace eso, realmente consigue una cosa milagrosa.

Mientras la multitud dentro y fuera del patio continuaba aplaudiendo salvajemente, Nezahualpili tomaba un poco de *chocólatl* y sonreía modestamente, mientras Motecuzoma lo hacía aprobadoramente. Él pudo mandarle esa sonrisa porque lo único que tenía que hacer era ganar el siguiente juego, y la pelota que entró en el aro —sin importar que lo hubiera hecho su oponente— le podía asegurar que el día de su victoria sería recordado para siempre, y en ambas partes: en los archivos de deportes y en la historia de Tenochtitlan.

Y fue recordado, todavía se recuerda, pero no con alegría. Cuando todo el tumulto se hubo apaciguado, los dos contrincantes comenzaron de nuevo el juego, esta vez tirando la pelota Nezahualpili. Él la mandó al aire de un rodillazo, hacia uno de los ángulos del patio, y en el mismo momento se movió rápidamente a donde él sabía que iba a caer la pelota y allí volvió a usar sus rodillas, una y otra vez, con gran precisión, hacia arriba y al través del aro de piedra que estaba arriba. Todo pasó tan rápido que yo creo que Motecuzoma no tuvo tiempo ni de moverse, y hasta Nezahualpili parecía no poder creer lo que había hecho. Esa pelota pasada otra vez por el anillo, dos veces seguidas, era más que una cosa maravillosa, más de lo que se había hecho en todos los anales de la historia del juego, era una consumación perfecta, real y extraordinaria.

Esa vez no se oyó ni un ruido de parte de los espectadores. Nosotros, ni siquiera nos movíamos, ni aun los ojos que los teníamos fijos, maravillados, sobre el Venerado Orador. Después, entre los espectadores se oyeron murmullos circunspectos. Algunos nobles murmuraban cosas llenas de esperanza, como que Tláloc estaba tan complacido con nosotros que él mismo había metido sus manos en el juego. Otros gruñían suspicaces: que Nezahualpili había hechizado los juegos y había ganado por obra de magia. Los nobles de Texcoco refutaban esa acusación, pero no en voz alta. Parecía como si nadie quisiera hablar en voz alta, y aun Cuitláhuac no gruñó audiblemente cuando me tendió un saquito de piel, muy pesado, lleno de polvo de oro. Nochipa me miraba muy solemnemente, como si sospechara que yo había adivinado secretamente las cosas que iban a suceder.

Sí, ese día gané una gran cantidad en oro, gracias a mi intuición, o a un vestigio de lealtad, o a cualquiera que fuera el motivo indefinible que hizo que pusiera mis apuestas sobre el que una vez fue mi señor. Pero daría todo ese oro si lo tuviera ahora, daría más que eso, *ayya*, miles y miles de veces más, si lo tuviera por *no* haber ganado ese día.

Oh, no, señores escribanos, no sólo porque la victoria de Nezahualpili dio validez a sus predicciones sobre la invasión, que tarde o temprano llegaría por el mar. Yo ya creía en la posibilidad de ello, el rudo dibujo de los maya me había convencido. No, la razón por la cual siento una pesadumbre tan amarga, fue que por el de haber ganado Nezahualpili esa contienda, cayó sobre mí y sobre los míos una inmediata tragedia.

Me vi envuelto en el problema, otra vez, casi inmediatamente después de que Motecuzoma furioso dejó el patio a grandes zancadas. De alguna manera, para cuando la gente empezó a dejar los asientos vacíos y la plaza en ese día, ellos sabían que en esa contienda estaban más que involucrados los dos Venerados Oradores, que había sido para probar las fuerzas de sus respectivos adivinos y oráculos. Todos se dieron cuenta de que la victoria de Nezahualpili dio crédito a sus profecías, y sabían cuáles eran ésas. Probablemente alguno de los cortesanos de Nezahualpili hizo saber esas cosas, tratando de apaciguar los rumores acerca de que su señor había ganado el juego por medio de hechicería. Lo único que sé con toda certeza, es que la verdad salió a relucir y que no fui yo quien lo hizo.

«Si usted no fue quien lo hizo —dijo Motecuzoma con voz fría y enojada—, si usted no ha hecho nada para merecer un castigo, entonces, claramente se ve que no lo estoy castigando.»

Nezahualpili acababa de dejar Tenochtitlan y dos guardias de palacio me habían llevado ante el trono casi a la fuerza y el Venerado Orador me acaba de decir lo que me tenía reservado.

«Pero mi señor me ordena que guíe una expedición militar —protesté, haciendo a un lado todo el protocolo establecido en el salón del trono—. Y si eso no es un castigo, entonces es un destierro y yo no he hecho nada para...»

Él me interrumpió: «La orden que le he dado Campeón Águila Mixtli, es un experimento. Todos los presagios indican que las fuerzas que nos han de invadir, si es que llegan, lo harán por el sur. Necesitamos que usted fortalezca nuestras defensas del sur. Si su expedición tiene éxito, enviaré a otros campeones guiando otros grupos de emigrantes en esas áreas.»

«Pero mi señor —persistí—, no sé nada acerca de cómo fundar y fortificar una colonia.»

Él dijo: «Yo tampoco sabía cómo, hasta que se me ordenó hacer eso mismo en el Xoconochco, muchos años atrás. —No podía contradecirlo, yo había sido hasta cierto punto responsable de eso. Él continuó—: Usted llevará consigo a unas cuarenta familias, aproximadamente doscientas personas entre hombres, mujeres y niños. Todos ellos son campesinos que simplemente no disponen de suficientes tierras aquí, en medio de El Único Mundo. Usted establecerá a sus emigrantes en alguna tierra nueva al sur, y organice la construcción de una aldea decente y sus defensas. Aquí está el lugar que he escogido para eso.»

El mapa que me mostró era uno de los que yo había dibujado, pero el área que apuntaba estaba sin ningún detalle, y nunca antes había visitado ese lugar.

Yo dije: «Mi Señor Orador, ese lugar está en las tierras de la gente teohuacana. Quizás ellos se resientan si son invadidos por una horda de extranjeros.»

Sonriendo sin ningún humor, él me contestó: «Su viejo amigo Nezahualpili nos aconsejó que nos hiciéramos amigos de todos nuestros vecinos, ¿no es así? Una de sus tareas será convencer a los teohuacana de que usted llega como un buen amigo, dispuesto a defender celosamente su nación como la suya propia.»

«Sí, mi señor», dije sintiéndome infeliz.

«El Venerado Orador Chimalpopoca de Tlácopan es quien amablemente le proveerá de una escolta militar. Usted estará al mando de un destacamento de cuarenta guerreros tecpaneca.»

«¿Ni siquiera mexica? —dejé caer desanimado—. Mi Señor Motecuzoma, una tropa tecpaneca ¡es seguro que estará muy descontenta por estar a las órdenes de un campeón mexícatl!»

Él lo sabía tanto como yo, pero era parte de su malicia, la parte de castigo que recibía por haber sido amigo de Nezahualpili. Con voz suave continuó:

«Los guerreros les darán protección en todo el viaje hasta Teohuacán y allí se quedarán para proteger el fuerte que usted mandará construir. Usted también se quedará allí, Campeón Mixtli, hasta que todas las familias estén ya bien asentadas y puedan mantenerse de sus propias cosechas. A ese lugar usted le llamará simplemente por el nombre de Yanquitlan, Lugar Nuevo.»

Me aventuré a preguntar: «¿Me permitiría usted, por lo menos, llevar conmigo a unos cuantos veteranos mexica, mi señor, como mis ayudantes? —Él probablemente hubiera dicho que no, inmediatamente, pero yo añadí—: Son unos hombres ya viejos que yo conozco y que hace ya tiempo fueron puestos a un lado, por ser demasiado viejos.»

Él resolló con desdén y dijo: «Si necesita guerreros adicionales para poder sentirse a salvo, usted tendrá que pagarlos.»

«Estoy de acuerdo, mi señor —dije con rapidez, ansioso de estar fuera de allí antes de que cambiara de idea, y me dejé caer a besar la tierra murmurando al mismo tiempo—: ¿Tiene algo más que mandarme el Señor Orador?»

«Que parta usted inmediatamente para que se encaminen lo más rápidamente posible hacia el sur. Los guerreros tecpaneca y el grupo de familias se están reuniendo en estos momentos en Ixtapalapan. Quiero que estén en su nueva comunidad de Yanquitlan a tiempo de echar la siembra de primavera. Vaya y hágalo.»

«Iré inmediatamente», dije, y arrastré mis pies desnudos hacia atrás, hacia la puerta.

✠

Aunque Motecuzoma me mandó como su pionero colonial, simplemente por vengarse de mí, no me podía quejar mucho ya que yo había sido el primero en presionar sobre esa idea de colonización, hacía ya bastantes años, a Auítzotl. Además, y para ser honesto, hacía tiempo que me había estado aburriendo con ser sólo un hombre rico y ocioso y había estado yendo frecuentemente a la Casa de los Pochteca, con la esperanza de escuchar algo acerca de alguna mercancía extraña que me llevara fuera de la nación. Hubiera aceptado de buena gana esa asignación para guiar el grupo de emigrantes, si no hubiera sido porque Motecuzoma insistió en que me quedara en el nuevo sitio establecido hasta que éste echara raíces firmemente. Tanto como yo podría estimar, estaría dentro de los muros de Yanquitlan por todo un año, si es que no dos o más. Cuando yo era joven, cuando mis caminos y mis días parecían ilimitados e incontables, no hubiera echado de menos todo ese tiempo que sería substraído de mi vida, pero a los cuarenta y dos años me repugnaba la idea de pasar siquiera uno de mi vida atado a un trabajo insípido en una insípida aldea campesina, mientras, quizás, otros horizontes más luminosos me estuvieran llamando por todas partes.

No obstante, preparé esa expedición con la mayor organización posible y entusiasmo. Primero llamé a las mujeres de mi casa y a los criados y les hice saber mi misión.

«Soy lo suficientemente egoísta como para no desear estar lejos de mi familia durante ese año o más, y también creo que el tiempo se puede usar con ventaja. Nochipa, hija mía, tú nunca has viajado más allá de Tenochtitlan a excepción de la tierra firme que está cerca de los caminos-puentes, y eso rara vez. Quizas este viaje sea riguroso para ti, pero, si quieres acompañarme, creo que te beneficiaría mucho el ver y conocer más de esas tierras.»

«¿Y crees que tienes que preguntármelo? —exclamó encantada, batiendo las palmas de sus manos. Luego se puso seria y dijo—: Pero, ¿y mis clases, padre, en la Casa del Aprendizaje de Modales?»

«Simplemente dile a tu señora maestra que sales fuera, hacia el extranjero. Que tu padre garantiza que aprenderás más en los caminos abiertos, que dentro de unos muros. —Entonces me volví hacia Beu Ribé—. Me gustaría mucho si tú también vinieras, Luna que Espera, si ése es tu deseo.»

«Sí —dijo ella inmediatamente, y sus ojos brillaron—. Estaré muy contenta de ir, Zaa, si tú ya no quieres caminar solo. Si puedo ser...»

«Sí puedes serlo. Una doncella de la edad de Nochipa no debe ir sin que la cuide una mujer de edad madura.»

«Oh», dijo ella, y sus ojos dejaron de brillar.

«La compañía de guerreros y de gente de clase baja puede ser muy ruda. Me gustaría mucho que tú siempre estuvieras a un lado de Nochipa y compartieras con ella su esterilla cada noche.»

«Su esterilla», repitió Beu.

Yo les dije a los criados: «Turquesa y Estrella Cantadora, vosotros ocuparéis de la casa y estaréis pendientes de ella y de custodiar nuestras pertenencias.» Ellos dijeron que así lo harían y me prometieron que encontraría todo en perfecto orden cuando regresara, sin importar cuánto tiempo estuviéramos fuera. Les dije que no dudaba de ello. «Y ahora mismo tengo un encargo para ti, Estrella Cantadora.»

Lo mandé para que citara a los siete viejos guerreros que habían sido mi pequeño ejército en otras expediciones. Me entristecí, aunque no me sentí muy sorprendido, cuando al regresar me dijo que tres de ellos ya habían muerto desde la última vez que requerí sus servicios.

Los cuatro que aún vivían vinieron, y ya se veían de edad cuando yo los conocí como los amigos de Glotón de Sangre, sin embargo, aunque ya no eran nada jóvenes acudieron sin vacilar. Llegaron ante mi presencia con bravura, esforzándose por caminar con apostura y pisando fuerte, para desviar mi atención hacia sus músculos flojos y sus coyunturas nudosas. Llegaron alborotando con voces fuertes y carcajadas de alegría y entusiasmo por la próxima partida, y así sus arrugas y los pliegues de sus rostros podrían haber pasado como las líneas producidas por el buen humor. Sin embargo, no los insulté haciéndoles notar que sólo simulaban juventud y vigor; si ellos habían venido tan contentos, ésa era la prueba suficiente de que todavía eran hombres capaces, y yo los habría llevado conmigo, aunque hubieran llegado sosteniéndose sobre bastones. Les expliqué la misión y luego me dirigí hacia el más viejo de ellos, Qualanqui, cuyo nombre quería decir Siempre Enojado:

«Nuestros guerreros tecpaneca y los doscientos civiles nos están esperando en Ixtapalapan. Ve para allá, amigo Enojado, y asegúrate de que todos estén listos para empezar la caminata cuando nosotros lo estemos. Sospecho que te vas a encontrar con que no están preparados para viajar, en muchos aspectos, pues no están acostumbrados a hacerlo. El resto de tus hombres que vayan a comprar todo lo que vamos a necesitar, incluyendo las provisiones; todo lo que necesitaréis vosotros cuatro, mi hija, mi señora hermana y yo.»

Me sentía más preocupado porque los emigrantes pudieran terminar esa larga jornada que por el recibimiento hostil que pudiera recibir en Teohuacán. Como la misma gente que yo estaba guiando, los teohuacana eran también agricultores y eran muy pocos, además de nada belicosos. Casi podía esperar que hasta nos dieran la bienvenida, pues nosotros significábamos para ellos gente nueva con quien mezclar y casar a sus retoños.

Cuando hablo diciendo Teohuacán y los teohuacana, por supuesto estoy utilizando el nombre náhuatl que les dábamos. Los teohuacana son una rama de los mixteca o tya nüü, quienes se llaman a sí mismos y a su nación por Tya Nya. Esa tierra nunca había sido sitiada por nosotros los mexica ni puesta bajo tributo, porque a excepción de sus productos agrícolas tenían sólo unas cuantas cosas que ofrecer como tesoros. Lo único que podían aportar eran sus manantiales de aguas calientes y minerales, una cosa bastante difícil de confiscar, y de todas manera, los tya nya comerciaban libremente con nosotros las ollas y recipientes conteniendo esas aguas, que por otra parte se compraban nada más como tónico, pues olían y sabían horrible; también muchos físicos muy a menudo ordenaban a sus pacientes ir a Tya Nya a tomar baños en esas aguas calientes y apestosas. Debido a eso, los nativos habían hecho un buen negocio al construir lujosas hosterías junto a los manantiales. En suma, yo no esperaba tener muchos problemas en una nación de agricultores y hosteleros.

Siempre Enojado regresó al día siguiente para decirme: «Tenías razón, Campeón Mixtli. Esa banda de patanes había traído todos sus utensilios de piedra para moler el maíz y todas las imágenes de sus dioses favoritos, en lugar de llevar el mismo peso en semillas para plantar y las raciones necesarias de polvo de *pinoli* para viajar. Por supuesto que gruñeron mucho, pero les hice que dejaran aquí todo impedimento que podrá ser reemplazado.»

«¿Y crees, Qualanqui, que toda esa gente podrá bastarse a sí misma, como una comunidad?»

«Yo creo que sí. Aunque casi todos ellos son agricultores, también hay albañiles, carpinteros, ladrilleros y demás. Pero se quejan de que les falta algo muy importante para viajar, que no les han provisto de sacerdotes.»

Yo dije malhumorado: «Nunca he sabido de una comunidad que crezca como la hierba, pero esa plenitud de sacerdotes parece como si brotaran de la tierra, siempre pidiendo ser alimentados, temidos y venerados.» No obstante mandé un recado a palacio sobre eso y nuestra compañía tuvo seis o siete *tlamacazque* jóvenes y novicios de diferentes dioses y diosas, esos sacerdotes eran tan jóvenes que sus vestidos negros todavía no estaban lo suficientemente mugrientos y costrosos de sangre.

Nochipa, Beu y yo cruzamos el camino-puente al atardecer del día que habíamos planeado para partir y pasamos la noche en Ixtapalapan, así podría a la primera luz de la mañana pasar revista y ver que todos los bultos habían sido repartidos equitativamente entre todos los hombres disponibles, mujeres y muchachos, para poder estar en el camino lo más pronto posible. Mis cuatro ayudantes gritaron a todos los guerreros tecpaneca para que se pusieran en fila y yo pasé revista utilizando para ello mi topacio. Eso causó muchas risas solapadas entre las filas y desde entonces todos ellos se referían a mí aunque se suponía que yo no debía darme por enterado, como Mixteloxixtli, una forma bastante ingeniosa de entremezclar mi nombre con otras palabras, pues traducido en una forma simple quería decir: Mixtli Ojo Orinador.

Los civiles que formaban la comitiva, es seguro que me llamaban con nombres menos lisonjeros, ya que siempre se estaban lamentando y la queja principal era que ninguno de ellos jamás había tenido la más remota intención o deseo de llegar a emigrar. Motecuzoma tuvo buen cuidado en no decirme que todos ellos no iban como voluntarios, sino que él los había escogido como «el sobrante de población» y que habían sido obligados por sus guardias. Así es que ellos se sentían, y con cierta justificación, como si hubieran sido desterrados injustamente a un desierto. Y los soldados se sentían igualmente desgraciados, ya que no les gustaba el trabajo que se les había encomendado, de ser los guardianes de esa comunidad y marchar lejos de sus hogares de Tlácopan, no para pelear en el campo de batalla, sino para estar por tiempo indefinido en la aburrida obligación de guarnición. Si yo no hubiera llevado a mis cuatro veteranos para mantener el orden, me temo que el Campeón Águila Ojo Orinador no hubiera podido contener un amotinamiento o deserción.

Ah, bueno, yo también deseé por mucho tiempo poder desertar. La jornada fue horrible, los soldados por lo menos sabían cómo marchar, pero los civiles se rezagaban, se extraviaban, les dolían los pies, gruñían y lloraban. Ni siquiera dos de ellos descansaban al mismo tiempo; las mujeres exigían que nos paráramos para poder darles el pecho a sus bebés; el sacerdote de tal o cual dios hacía que nos detuviéramos a cada determinado tiempo del día para rezar una oración ritual. Si ordenaba caminar a paso vivo, la gente floja se quejaba de que los estaba haciendo correr hasta morir, si los hacía ir despacio, en beneficio de los flojos, los otros se quejaban de que iban a morir de ancianidad antes de terminar la jornada.

Mi hija Nochipa fue la única persona que hizo que esa caminata fuera agradable para mí. Como su madre Zyanya, en *su* primer viaje fuera de casa, Nochipa exclamaba jubilosa ante el paisaje que por primera vez se revelaba a cada vuelta del camino. El paisaje en sí era de lo más ordinario, pero algo en él alegraba sus ojos y su corazón. Estábamos siguiendo la ruta principal de comercio hacia el sur, y aunque ésta tenía bellas vistas yo ya estaba acostumbrado a ellas, como también lo estaban Beu y mis ayudantes, y en cuanto a los emigrantes, éstos eran incapaces de exclamar ante algo que no fueran sus miserias. Pero hubiéramos podido estar atravesando por los desiertos muertos de Mictlan y Nochipa habría encontrado algo nuevo y maravilloso.

Algunas veces ella rompía a cantar, como lo hacen los pájaros, sin ninguna razón, sólo por el hecho de tener alas y de sentirse felices por eso. (Como mi hermana Tzitzitlini, Nochipa había ganado muchos honores en su escuela, por su talento en el canto y en la danza.) Cuando ella cantaba, hasta los más odiosos descontentos dejaban de gruñir para escucharla. También, cuando no estaba muy cansada después de la caminata diaria, Nochipa nos iluminaba las noches oscuras bailando para nosotros, después de la comida de la tarde. Uno de mis hombres sabía cómo tocar una flauta de arcilla, que llevaba con él, así es que acompañaba a Nochipa en su danza y esas noches en que ella danzaba, todos se iban a dormir sobre el duro suelo con menos lamentaciones de las que acostumbraban.

Además de que Nochipa nos iluminó todo ese camino largo y cansado, sólo recuerdo otro incidente que me impresionó más de lo ordinario. Una noche en que habíamos acampado, caminé a cierta distancia de la luz de la fogata para orinar junto a un árbol y casualmente pasé por allí un poco más tarde y vi a Beu —ella no me vio— haciendo una cosa singular. Estaba hincada a un lado de ese lugar y recogía un poco de fango sobre el que yo había orinado. Pensé que quizás ella estaba tratando de preparar una cataplasma para calmar los dolores de alguien que se hubiera hecho una ampolla o torcido un tobillo, así es que no la interrumpí, ni más tarde le mencioné ese hecho.

Sin embargo, debo contarles a ustedes, señores escribanos, que entre nuestra gente había ciertas mujeres, usualmente muy viejas, y que ustedes llaman brujas, quienes conocían ciertas artes secretas. Una de sus capacidades era hacer un muñeco con la imagen de un hombre, con el fango del lugar en donde ese hombre hubiera orinado recientemente, y luego sometían ese muñequito a ciertas indignidades, haciendo que el hombre sufriera dolores y penas inexplicables, y aun locura, deseos desordenados, pérdida de la memoria y de todas sus posesiones hasta quedar en la miseria más absoluta. Sin embargo, yo no tenía ninguna razón para sospechar que Luna que Espera hubiera sido una bruja toda su vida, pues nunca me había dado cuenta de eso, así es que consideré lo que estaba haciendo esa noche como una simple coincidencia y me olvidé de eso hasta que lo recordé más tarde.

Después de unos veinte días de haber salido de Tenochtitlan —que hubieran sido doce para un viajero experto y sin trabas— llegamos a la aldea de Huajuapan, que yo ya conocía, y después de pasar la noche allí, cambiamos totalmente nuestro rumbo desviándonos hacia el noreste, hacia otra ruta comercial, pero era un camino menor que ninguno de nosotros conocía. La vereda nos llevó a través de verdes y hermosos valles en donde ya se veía una temprana primavera, rodeados por bajas y bellas montañas azules que nos guiarían hacia la capital Tya Nya, que además de ser llamada así, era llamada por Teohuacán. Pero no llegamos hasta allá; después de cuatro días a lo largo de esa ruta, nos encontramos ante un inmenso valle en donde tuvimos que vadear la corriente de un arroyo, ancho, pero no profundo. Me arrodillé y tomé en mi mano un poco de esa agua, la olí, y luego la probé.

Siempre Enojado se paró junto a mí y me preguntó: «¿Qué piensas?»

«Bien, no proviene de uno de esos manantiales típicos de Teohuacán —le dije—. El agua no está amarga, ni maloliente, ni caliente. Es buena para regar y para beber. La tierra parece ser buena también, y no veo otros habitantes o plantaciones. Yo pienso que éste es el lugar para nuestra Yanquitlan. Diles eso.»

Qualanqui se volvió y bramó para que todos pudieran oírle: «¡Dejad los bultos! ¡Hemos llegado!»

Yo dije: «Dejadlos descansar por lo que queda del día. Mañana empezaremos a...»

«Mañana —me interrumpió uno de los sacerdotes, tocando mi codo repentinamente— y al día siguiente, y al día siguiente de ese día nos dedicaremos a consagrar esta tierra. Con su permiso, por supuesto.»

Yo le dije: «Ésta es la primera comunidad que yo he fundado, joven señor sacerdote, y no estoy familiarizado con las formalidades, lo que quiere decir que usted haga todo lo que los dioses requieran.»

Sí, dije esas palabras exactas sin darme cuenta de cómo serían interpretadas, al dar mi permiso a una ilimitada licencia religiosa, sin prever la forma en que serían tomadas por los sacerdotes y la gente, sin sospechar ni remotamente que por todo el resto de mi vida sentiría una gran angustia por la forma tan casual con que me expresé.

La iniciación ritual, la consagración del terreno, llevó tres días enteros de oraciones, invocaciones, incienso y todas esas cosas. Algunos de esos ritos eran hechos por los sacerdotes solamente, pero otros requerían la participación de todos nosotros. A mí no me importó, pues tanto los guerreros como la gente necesitaba de unos días de descanso y diversión, hasta Nochipa y Beu estaban muy contentas, por supuesto, de que las ceremonias les dieran la ocasión de ponerse mejores ropas, más femeninas y más adornadas que los trajes de viaje que tuvieron que llevar por tanto tiempo.

Y eso hizo que también otros de los colonizadores tuvieran otra diversión... diversión que yo compartí, ya que yo me divertí observando. La mayoría de los hombres del grupo tenían esposas y familia, pero entre ellos había tres o cuatro viudos con familia, así es que durante esos días de consagración tuvieron la oportunidad de hacerle la corte a Beu, uno tras otro. También había entre los hombres muchachos o jóvenes ya en la edad de hacer la corte, toscamente, a Nochipa. No podía culparlos, ya fueran jóvenes o viejos, ya que Nochipa y Beu eran infinitamente más bellas, refinadas y deseables que esas mujeres y muchachas del pueblo, con sus cuerpos cuadrados, sus rostros ordinarios, sus pies feos de agricultoras.

Beu Ribé los rechazaba arrogantemente, a cualquiera de ellos que viniera a solicitarle formar pareja con ella, en alguno de los bailes ceremoniales o con cualquier pretexto para estar cerca de ella, pero lo hacía así, solamente cuando creía que yo no la observaba. Pero algunas veces, cuando sabía que yo estaba cerca de ella, dejaba al pobre estúpido allí parado por un rato, mientras ella coqueteaba y se sugería de mal modo, con una sonrisa y una mirada tan atrayente, que el pobre desgraciado empezaba a sudar. Claramente ella se estaba mofando de mí, tratando de que yo me diera cuenta de que ella era todavía una mujer atractiva. No necesitaba que me lo recordara; Luna que Espera tenía en verdad un rostro y un cuerpo tan bello como lo había tenido Zyanya, pero yo, a diferencia de esos hombres que la adulaban servilmente, ya estaba acostumbrado a sus astucias, primero provocando tentación y luego rechazando. Yo solamente sonreía y asentía, como un hermano benevolente que aprobaba lo que hacía su hermana y sus ojos cambiaban su mirada de atrayente a fría y su dulce voz se tornaba agria y el pretendiente desdeñado quedaba en total confusión.

Nochipa no hacía esa clase de juegos; ella era tan casta como siempre habían sido sus danzas. Cada vez que un joven se aproximaba a ella, lo miraba tan sorprendida, casi perpleja, que el joven luego, después de pronunciar algunas palabras tímidas, se escurría intimidado ante su mirada, con el rostro colorado y pateando el suelo. Su mirada eran tan inocente que se proclamaba a sí misma inviolable, tan inocente que aparentemente hacía que todo pretendiente se sintiera embarazado y avergonzado de sí mismo, como si se hubiera mostrado deshonesto. Yo me mantenía aparte, sintiendo dos clases de orgullo por mi hija; sentía orgullo porque era tan bonita que podía atraer a muchos hombres; orgullo por saber que ella esperaría al hombre que amara. Muchas veces desde entonces, he deseado que los dioses me hubieran abatido en ese mismo instante, castigando mi orgu-

594

llo complaciente, pero los dioses conocían otros castigos más crueles.

La tercera noche, cuando los sacerdotes exhaustos anunciaron que la consagración había terminado y que ya se podía empezar el trabajo de acomodamiento para la nueva comunidad, pues se suponía que ahora la tierra sería buena y hospitalaria, yo le dije a Siempre Enojado:

«Mañana las mujeres empezarán a cortar ramas para hacer las cabañas y hierba para formar los techos, mientras que sus hombres empezarán a limpiar todo el terreno del lado del arroyo, para prepararlo para la siembra. La orden de Motecuzoma es que se siembre lo más pronto posible y la gente sólo necesitará albergues mientras se hace eso, después, antes de que lleguen las lluvias, nosotros trazaremos las calles y los lugares en donde quedarán permanentemente las casas. También, como los guerreros no tienen nada que hacer y como supongo que las noticias de nuestra llegada ya deben de haber alcanzado la capital, creo que debemos darnos prisa en visitar al Uey-Tlatoani o como los teohuacana llamen a su señor gobernante, para dejarle saber nuestras intenciones. Llevaremos con nosotros a todos los guerreros, pues son lo suficientemente numerosos como para evitar que nos maten o ser repelidos, y por otro lado, no son tantos como para que crean que llegamos como conquistadores.»

Qualanqui asintió y dijo: «Informaré a los campesinos que mañana empieza el trabajo y tendré listos a los tecpaneca para viajar.»

En cuanto él se fue, me volví a Beu Ribé y le dije: «Tu hermana, mi difunta esposa, una vez utilizó su encanto para ayudarme a influir sobre otro gobernante extranjero, el hombre más horrible que he conocido en todas estas tierras. Si yo llego a la corte de Teohuacán acompañado igualmente por una bella mujer, eso hará que también esta misión parezca más amistosa que audaz. ¿Podría pedirte, Luna que Espera que...?»

«¿Que vaya contigo, Zaa? —preguntó ansiosamente—. ¿Como tu consorte?»

«Sí, aparentando eso. No necesitamos revelar que tú eres solamente mi señora hermana. Considerando nuestra edad, no habrá ningún comentario si pedimos habitaciones separadas.»

Me sorprendió al decir encolerizada: «¡A nuestra edad! —Pero en seguida se calmó y murmuró—: Por supuesto, no diremos nada. Si eso es lo que tú ordenas, seré solamente tu hermana.»

Yo le dije: «Gracias.»

«Sin embargo, señor hermano, tú me diste la orden, anteriormente, de que no me separara de Nochipa, para protegerla de esta compañía ruda. Sí, yo voy contigo, ¿y Nochipa?»

«Sí, ¿y yo padre? —preguntó mi hija, cogiéndome mi manto por el otro lado—. ¿También yo iré, padre?»

«No, tú te quedarás aquí, mi niña —le dije—. Realmente no espero encontrarme en un lío en el camino o en la capital, pero siempre existe ese riesgo. Aquí estarás a salvo entre la multitud. A salvo con la presencia de los sacerdotes, que cualquier persona hostil vacilaría en atacar, por un temor religioso. Estos rudos campesinos estarán trabajando tan duro, que no tendrán tiempo de molestarte y estarán tan cansados en la noche, que los jóvenes ni siquiera tendrán ganas de coquetear contigo. En todo caso, he observado, mi hija, que tú tienes suficiente capacidad como para descorazonarlos. Estarás a salvo aquí, Nochipa, más que en los caminos abiertos, y de todas formas, no estaremos fuera por mucho tiempo.»

Sin embargo, ella me miró tan alicaída que añadí: «Cuando regrese tendremos mucho tiempo de ocio y toda esa nación para recorrer. Te prometo que lo veremos todo. Sólo tú y yo, Nochipa, viajando juntos, a todo lo largo y lo ancho.»

Le brillaron los ojos y me dijo: «Sí, eso será mucho mejor. Sólo tú y yo. Me quedaré aquí de buena gana padre, y en la noche, cuando la gente esté cansada de sus labores, quizá pueda hacerles olvidar su cansancio. Danzaré para ellos.»

Aun sin tener que arrastrar un grupo de colonizadores, nos llevó otros cinco días alcanzar la capital, a Beu, a mí y·a mis cuarenta y cuatro hombres de escolta. Es todo lo que recuerdo, y recuerdo también que fuimos muy bien recibidos en el pueblo de Teohuacán o Tya Nya, por su señor gobernante, aunque no recuerdo su nombre ni el de su señora, ni recuerdo tampoco cuántos días estuvimos allí como sus huéspedes, en el edificio destartalado que ellos llamaban palacio. Recuerdo que él me recibió diciendo:

«Esa tierra que usted ha ocupado, Campeón Águila Mixtli, es uno de nuestros pedazos de terreno más fértiles y placenteros. —A lo cual añadió rápidamente—: Pero no tenemos suficiente gente para separar de sus labores agrícolas o de otras ocupaciones, para ir a trabajar allí. Sus colonizadores son bien venidos y también le damos la bienvenida a usted. Toda nación necesita de nueva sangre para su cuerpo.»

Él dijo mucho más y en ese mismo sentido, y me dio unos regalos a cambio de los que yo le llevé de parte de Motecuzoma. Y recuerdo que muy a menudo nos daban un festín y nos trataron muy bien, tanto a mis hombres como a Beu y a mí, y que nos vimos forzados a beber de esa horrible agua mineral, de la que los teohuacana están tan orgullosos, y hasta nos relamimos los labios pretendiendo que era muy sabrosa. Y recuerdo que nadie se asombró cuando pedí habitaciones separadas para mí y Beu, aunque también recuerdo muy vagamente que ella vino a mi cuarto una de esas noches. Dijo algo, suplicó algo, y yo le contesté con aspereza y ella seguía suplicando. Creo que la golpeé en la cara... pero ahora no puedo recordar...

No, mis señores escribanos, no me miren así. No es que mi memoria de pronto haya fallado. Si todas esas cosas han estado nebulosas en mi mente durante todos estos años desde que pasaron, es porque otra cosa sucedió muy poco tiempo después y ese suceso quedó tan grabado en mi cerebro que quemó todos los recuerdos de los sucesos anteriores. Recuerdo que nos despedimos de nuestros anfitriones en Tya Nya, intercambiando mutuas expresiones de cordialidad y amistad, y que la gente del pueblo salió a las calles a despedirnos alegremente, y que sólo Beu no parecía muy contenta del éxito de nuestra embajada. Y supongo que nos llevó otros cinco días regresar sobre nuestra ruta...

El crepúsculo caía cuando llegamos al río, a la orilla opuesta de Yanquitlan. No parecía que hubieran trabajado mucho durante nuestra ausencia; aun utilizando mi topacio sólo pude ver unas cuantas cabañas construidas en donde iba a quedar la aldea. Pero en cambio estaban celebrando nuevamente algo y muchos fuegos ardían altos y brillantes, aunque la noche todavía no cerraba. No empezamos a vadear inmediatamente el río, sino que nos detuvimos para escuchar los gritos y las risas que provenían del otro lado de las aguas, pues era la primera vez que oíamos un verdadero sonido de alegría, viniendo de ese grupo de rústicos. Entonces un hombre, uno de los viejos agricultores, surgió inesperadamente de las aguas del río, delante de nosotros. Vio nuestra tropa parada allí y vino hacia nosotros chapoteando, y saludándome respetuosamente dijo:

«¡*Mixpantzinco!* En su augusta presencia Campeón Águila, y sea bienvenido de regreso. Temíamos que usted se perdiera toda la ceremonia.»

«¿Qué ceremonia? —pregunté—. No conozco ninguna ceremonia en que a los participantes se les permita ir a nadar.»

Se rió y dijo: «Oh, ésa fue una idea mía. Me sentía tan caliente por estar danzando y tomando parte de la fiesta, que deseé refrescarme un poco. Pero ya me han bendecido con el hueso.»

No pude ni hablar, y él debió de tomar mi mutismo por incomprensión, pues me explicó: «Usted mismo les dijo a los sacerdotes que hicieran todas aquellas cosas que los dioses requerían. De seguro que usted se dio cuenta de que el mes de Tlacaxipe Ualiztli ya había pasado cuando usted nos dejó y el dios todavía no había sido invocado para bendecir la tierra ya lista para la siembra.»

«No», dije o más bien grazné. No le estaba desmintiendo, sabía la fecha. Solamente estaba tratando de rechazar el pensamiento que hizo que mi corazón se sintiera agarrado por un fuerte puño. El hombre continuó, como si se sintiera muy orgulloso de ser el primero en decírmelo:

«Algunos querían esperar hasta que usted regresara, Campeón Águila, pero los sacerdotes se dieron prisa en terminar todas las preparaciones y las actividades preliminares. Usted sabe que no tenemos con qué festejar a la persona escogida, ni tenemos los instrumentos adecuados para la música, pero cantamos muy fuerte y quemamos mucho *copali*. También, como no teníamos ningún templo para copular, como lo requiere la ceremonia, los sacerdotes santificaron un pedazo de hierba suave que estaba rodeado por unos arbustos, y no faltaron voluntarios, muchos de ellos lo hicieron muchas veces. Ya que todos estuvimos de acuerdo de que debíamos de honrar a nuestro campeón, aun en su ausencia, todos escogimos por unanimidad a la que representaría al dios. Y ahora usted ha llegado a tiempo para ver al dios representado por...»

Él dejó de hablar abruptamente, porque yo había balanceado

mi *maquáhuitl* dejándola caer sobre su cuello, clavándola limpiamente en el hueso de atrás. Beu dio un grito corto y los guerreros que estaban atrás de ella, estiraron mucho sus cuellos y abrieron mucho los ojos. El hombre se tambaleó por un momento, mirándome perplejo cabeceó, su boca se abría y cerraba silenciosamente, mientras su labio inferior lleno de sangre caía sobre su barbilla. Luego su cabeza se echó hacia atrás, la herida se abrió totalmente y un chorro de sangre manó de ella y el hombre cayó a mis pies.

Beu dijo horrorizada: «¿Por qué? ¿Por qué has hecho eso, Zaa?»

«¡Cállate, mujer! —gritó Siempre Enojado. Luego me tomó por el brazo, con lo cual impidió que yo también cayera y dijo—: Mixtli, puede ser que todavía estemos a tiempo de evitar el procedimiento final...»

Negué con mi cabeza. «Tú lo oíste. Ya había sido bendecido con el hueso. *Todo* se ha hecho como lo requieren los dioses.»

Qualanqui suspiró y me dijo roncamente: «Lo siento.»

Uno de sus ancianos compañeros me tomó por el otro brazo y dijo: «Todos lo sentimos, joven Mixtli. ¿Prefieres esperar aquí mientras nosotros... mientras nosotros cruzamos el río?»

Yo dije: «No. Todavía estoy al mando. Yo mandaré lo que se debe hacer en Yanquitlan.»

El viejo asintió, luego levantó la voz y les gritó a los guerreros que estaban hacinados en el camino: «¡Vosotros, hombres! Romped filas y desparramaos a lo largo de la orilla del río, para hacer una escaramuza. ¡Moveos!»

«¡Dime qué pasó! —gritaba llorando Beu y retorciéndose las manos—. ¡Dime qué vamos a hacer!»

«Nada —grazné—. Tú no vas a hacer nada, Beu. —Y traté de tragar el nudo que tenía en la garganta y parpadeé con fuerza para dejar mis ojos sin lágrimas e hice todo lo posible por pararme derecho y ser fuerte—. Tú no harás nada más que quedarte aquí, en este lado del río. Cualquier cosa que oigas desde aquí, sin importar el tiempo que pase, no te muevas hasta que venga por ti.»

«¿Que me quede aquí sola? ¿Con eso?», y apuntó el cadáver del hombre.

Yo le dije: «No temas a ése, más bien siente felicidad por él. Fui muy rápido en mi primer impulso de cólera. A éste le di un descanso rápido.»

Siempre Enojado gritó: «¡Hombres, avanzad en línea de escaramuza y cruzad el río! De ahí en adelante no hagáis ningún ruido. Cerraos en un círculo sobre el área de la aldea. No dejéis que nadie escape, sino que rodead y luego esperad órdenes. Vamos, Mixtli, si piensas que debes venir.»

«Debo ir», dije y fui el primero que vadeé el río.

Nochipa había dicho que bailaría para la gente de Yanquitlan y era eso lo que ella estaba haciendo, pero no era esa danza bella y modesta que siempre le había visto hacer. En el crepúsculo color púrpura, entre el atardecer y la luz de los fuegos, podía verla totalmente desnuda bailando sin gracia, con sus piernas indecente y groseramente abiertas, mientras movía por encima de su cabeza las dos varas blancas, que ocasionalmente dejaba caer sobre alguna persona que hiciera cabriolas cerca de ella.

Aunque no lo deseaba, levanté mi topacio para verla más claramente. Lo único que llevaba puesto era el collar de topacios que le había regalado cuando tenía cuatro años, y al que le había añadido una nueva piedra luciérnaga en cada uno de sus ocho cumpleaños siguientes, los pocos, muy pocos cumpleaños que ella tuvo. Su cabello usualmente brillante, colgaba en sus espaldas enmarañado y opaco. Sus pechos se veían como pequeños montecillos y sus caderas todavía no estaban bien formadas, pero entre sus muslos, en donde su *tipili* de doncella debía estar casi invisible, había una abertura en su piel y de ella sobresalían colgando flojamente un *tepuli* de hombre y se zarandeaban sus bolsitas de *ololtin*. Las varas blancas que movía, eran sus propios huesos, los de sus muslos, pero las manos que los agarraban eran de hombre y sus propias manos medio cortadas colgaban golpeando las muñecas de él.

Un grito de alegría salió de la gente, cuando yo me paré en medio de ellos, que bailaban alrededor de esa cosa danzante que había sido mi hija. Ella había sido una niña, una niña que parecía un destello de luz, y ellos la habían convertido en una carroña. Esa efigie de Nochipa vino danzando hacia mí, con un hueso brillante extendido hacia mí, como si me quisiera dar un golpecito de bendición antes de que yo la abrazara, con el abrazo de un padre amante. Esa cosa obscena se fue acercando lo suficientemente hasta que pude ver que sus ojos no eran los de Nochipa. Entonces sus pies que danzaban vacilaron y finalmente se detuvieron ante mi mirada de rabia y repulsión, y cuando se detuvo, lo mismo hizo toda la alegre multitud, dejando de moverse, de hacer cabriolas, cesando todo ruido de alegría y la gente empezó a mirar con miedo, a mí y a los guerreros que cercaban el sitio. Esperé hasta que nada podía oírse, excepto el ruido producido por los fuegos ceremoniales. Entonces dije, sin dirigirme a nadie en particular:

«Coged a esta asquerosa criatura... pero cogedla con suavidad, pues lleva los restos de lo que una vez fue una niña viva.»

El pequeño sacerdote que llevaba puesta la piel de Nochipa, me miraba parpadeando sin poder creerlo, luego dos de mis guerreros lo cogieron. Los otros cinco o seis sacerdotes de la caravana, vinieron hacia mí, abriéndose paso a codazos entre la multitud y gritando enojados porque había interrumpido la ceremonia. Yo los ignoré y dije a los hombres que tenían agarrado al que representaba al dios:

«La piel de su rostro fue separada de su cabeza. Tomad esa piel del rostro de éste, con mucho cuidado, y llevadla reverentemente hacia el fuego que está allá, rezad una pequeña oración porque ella un día le dio belleza y quemadla. Traedme el collar de ópalo que llevaba puesto.»

Yo volví mi rostro mientras hacían eso. Los otros sacerdotes volvieron a gritar de rabia, cada vez más indignados, hasta que Siempre Enojado les gritó tan amenazadoramente que se quedaron quietos y tan dóciles como la multitud inmóvil.

«Ya está hecho, Campeón Mixtli», dijo uno de mis hombres, alargándome el collar, algunas de cuyas piedras estaban manchadas con la sangre de Nochipa. Me volví otra vez hacia el sacerdote cautivo. Ya no mostraba las facciones de mi hija ni su pelo, sino su propia cara crispada por el miedo.

Yo dije: «Tendedlo sobre el suelo con los brazos y las piernas extendidos y tened cuidado de no poner vuestras rudas manos sobre la piel de mi hija. Clavad con estacas sus manos y sus pies al suelo.»

Él era, como todos los demás sacerdotes, un hombre joven y gritó como un niño cuando la primera estaca entró dentro de su mano izquierda. Gritó las cuatro veces, mientras los otros sacerdotes y la gente de Yanquitlan se movían y murmuraban aprensivamente, y con razón, sobre el destino que les estaba reservado, pero todos mis guerreros tenían listas sus armas y ninguno de ellos se atrevió a ser el primero en huir. Yo miré hacia la grotesca figura que yacía en el suelo, retorciéndose bajo las cuatro estacas que mantenían bien abiertas sus extremidades. Los jóvenes pechos de Nochipa levantaban sus pezones puntiagudos hacia el cielo, pero los genitales del hombre sobresalían de entre sus piernas, fláccidos y arrugados.

«Preparad agua con cal —dije—. Usad bastante cal, para que se concentre bien y empapad la piel con ella. Seguid mojando la piel toda la noche, hasta que quede bien penetrada de cal. Luego esperaremos a que el sol salga.»

Siempre Enojado asintió aprobando. «¿Y los otros? Esperamos sólo tus órdenes, Campeón Mixtli.»

Uno de los sacerdotes, impelido por el terror, se echó hacia adelante, hacia nosotros y, cayendo de rodillas delante de mí con sus manos llenas de sangre cogiendo la orilla de mi manto, dijo: «Campeón, fue con su permiso que nosotros celebramos esta ceremonia. Cualquier otro hombre aquí, se hubiera sentido feliz porque su hijo o hija hubiera sido escogido para esa personificación, pero era la suya la que mejor reunía todas las cualidades. Una vez que ella hubiera sido escogida por toda la población y aprobada por los sacerdotes del pueblo, *usted no habría podido rehusar ceder* su hija para la ceremonia.»

Yo me le quedé mirando y él bajó su mirada, pero luego dejó caer: «Por lo menos... en Tenochtitlan... usted no habría podido rehusar.» Él se cogió de mi manto otra vez y dijo implorante: «Ella era virgen, como se requería, pero también era lo suficientemente madura como para funcionar como mujer, como ella hizo. Usted mismo me dijo, Jefe Campeón: haga todas las cosas que los dioses requieran. Así es que ahora la Muerte-Florida de su hija ha bendecido a su pueblo, a su nueva colonia y ha asegurado la fertilidad de esta tierra. Usted no hubiera podido impedir esa bendición. Créame, Jefe Campeón, ¡sólo deseábamos honrar a... Xipe Totec, a su hija... y a usted!»

Le di un golpe que le hizo caer de lado, luego dije a Qualanqui:

«¿Estás familiarizado con todos los *honores* que tradicionalmente se le ofrecen a Xipe Totec?»

«Lo estoy, amigo Mixtli.»

«Bien, entonces tú sabes todo lo que le hicieron a la pura e inocente Nochipa. Que les hagan a todos estos mugrosos las cosas que ellos le hicieron a Nochipa. Hazlo a tu manera, como más te plazca, tienes suficientes guerreros para ello. Déjalos que se diviertan todo lo que quieran, no hay prisa. Déjalos que inventen cosas y que hagan todo a su placer. Pero cuando terminen, no quiero a nadie... *nada*... vivo en Yanquitlan.»

Ésa fue la última orden que di allí. Siempre Enojado se hizo cargo de todo. Él se volvió y ladró órdenes específicas y la multitud aulló como si ya estuviera en agonía, pero los guerreros se movieron con rapidez para cumplir con las instrucciones. Varios de ellos reunieron rápidamente a un grupo de hombres adultos, separándolos del resto y los mantuvieron así a punta de espada. Los otros guerreros dejaron sus armas, se desvistieron y empezaron a trabajar... o a jugar... y cuando alguno de ellos se cansaba, cambiaba su lugar con otro de los que hacían guardia.

Yo miré durante toda la noche, pues los grandes fuegos mantuvieron la noche iluminada hasta el amanecer. Sin embargo, no veía realmente lo que estaba sucediendo ante mis ojos, ni sentía orgullo por ello, ni satisfacción ante mi venganza. No estaba prestando atención a los gritos, bramidos y gemidos y otra clase de sonidos líquidos ocasionados por las violaciones y la destrucción; sólo veía y oía a Nochipa que danzaba grácilmente enfrente del fuego, que cantaba melodiosamente como sólo ella sabía hacerlo, acompañada por una sola flauta.

Lo que Qualanqui había ordenado, lo que realmente ocurrió fue esto. Todos los niños muy pequeños, y los bebés, fueron cortados en pedacitos por los guerreros, mientras sus padres eran obligados a observar, llorando, maldiciendo y bramando. Luego toda la población, niños, jóvenes, adultos y ancianos, de ambos sexos, fueron violados hasta morir. Mientras unos eran violados los otros observaban, y cuando unos ya no servían, eran dejados a un lado agonizantes, mientras otros eran utilizados. He mencionado que los sacerdotes eran también jóvenes, así es que sirvieron a los guerreros igualmente. El único sacerdote que estaba estacado en el suelo, miraba, gemía y veía con terror sus partes privadas expuestas; pero aun dentro de esa turbulenta lascivia, los tecpaneca comprendían que ese hombre no debía ser tocado, así es que no lo hicieron.

Todo eso fue hecho con cierto orden, pues los guerreros primero utilizaron a todos los jóvenes, luego de una forma u otra vaciaron todo lo que les quedaba de apetito, al violar a las mujeres adultas y aun a dos o tres abuelas que habían hecho el viaje. Los hombres mientras tanto, eran obligados a observar como eran violadas hasta morir sus esposas, hijas, hermanas, hermanos, hijos, madres. Al día siguiente, cuando el sol ya estaba en todo lo alto, Siempre Enojado ordenó que soltaran al grupo de hombres que tenían cercado. Ellos, los esposos, los padres, los tíos, de esas ruinas humanas, fueron alrededor del campo dejándose caer sobre tal o cual cuerpo desnudo, roto, cubierto de sangre, de babas y de *omícetl*. Algunos todavía vivían y vivieron para ver cómo los guerreros, a otra orden de Qualanqui, agarraban otra vez a sus padres, esposos y tíos. Entonces los tecpaneca utilizaron sus cuchillos de obsidiana, amputando, y haciendo que los hombres abusaran de sí mismos con sus partes amputadas, mientras yacían sangrando hasta morir.

Mientras tanto, el sacerdote estacado había estado muy quieto, esperanzado quizás, a ser olvidado. Pero cuando el sol se levantó un poco más, comprendió que le esperaba una muerte mucho más horrible de la que tuvieron todos los demás, pues la piel de Nochipa empezó a tomar venganza. La piel, totalmente saturada con agua de cal, empezó a contraerse al secarse lenta pero inexorablemente. Lo que habían sido los pechos de Nochipa, gradualmente se fue aplanando, conforme la piel se apretaba abrazando el pecho del sacerdote. Empezó a jadear y a ahogarse, y quizás hubiera deseado expresar su terror por medio de un grito, pero trataba de agarrar todo el aire que podía inhalar, sólo para poder vivir un poquito más.

Y la piel continuó estrechándose inexorablemente y empezó a impedir el movimiento de la sangre en el cuerpo. Lo que había sido el cuello, las muñecas, y los tobillos de Nochipa, estrecharon sus aberturas agarrotándolo lentamente. La cara, las manos y los pies del hombre se empezaron a hinchar y a ponerse negros y en un feo color púrpura. Por sus labios extendidos salió al fin un sonido: «ugh... ugh... ugh...», y se fue ahogando gradualmente. Mientras tanto, lo que había sido la pequeña *tipili* de Nochipa, se constriñó más virginalmente, apretándose fuertemente a los genitales del sacerdote. Su saco de *ololtin* se hinchó, hasta tener el tamaño de una pelota de *tlachtli* y su *tepuli* engordó tanto y se puso tan largo y tieso, que era más grande que mi antebrazo.

Los guerreros vagaban alrededor del área, inspeccionando cada cuerpo para asegurarse de que estaba muerto o agonizante. Los tecpaneca no mataron piadosamente a los que estaban vivos, sino que solamente se aseguraron de que morirían cuando los dioses lo quisieran, para no dejar nada, ni nadie, vivo en Yanquitlan, como yo lo había ordenado. Nada nos detenía más allí, como no fuera quedarnos a ver cómo moría el sacerdote que quedaba. Así es que mis cuatro viejos compañeros y yo nos pusimos a observar cómo agonizaba, cada movimiento de estiramiento, cada jadeo de su pecho, mientras la piel que le constreñía hacía que su torso y sus miembros se tornaran cada vez más flacos, y sus extremidades visibles cada vez se vieran más largas. Sus manos y sus pies parecían pechos negros, pero llenos de tetas también negras, su cabeza parecía una negra calabaza ya sin forma. Él encontró todavía un poco de aire, como para dar un último y fuerte grito, cuando su rígido *tepuli* no pudo contener más la presión y estalló rompiendo su piel, quedando en pedazos y saliéndole sangre negra.

Aunque todavía vivía, de hecho ya estaba acabado y nuestra venganza concluida. Siempre Enojado ordenó a los tecpaneca prepararlo todo para empezar el viaje, mientras los otros tres viejos vadeaban el río conmigo, para regresar a donde habíamos dejado a Beu Ribé que nos estaba esperando. Silenciosamente le mostré los ópalos manchados de sangre. No sé qué fue lo que ella oyó, o vio o adivinó, y tampoco sé qué aspecto presentaba yo en ese momento, pero ella me miró con ojos llenos de horror, piedad, reproche y pena, pero sobre todo horror, y por un instante retrocedió ante la mano que le tendía.

«Ven, Luna que Espera —dije con dureza—. Te llevaré a casa.»

I H S

✠

S. C. C. M.

Santificada, Cesárea, Católica Majestad,
el Emperador Don Carlos, nuestro Señor Rey:

Muy Perspicaz y Magistral Príncipe, desde esta Ciudad de Mexico, capital de la Nueva España, dos días después de la Fiesta de la Purificación, en el año de Nuestro Señor Jesucristo, mil quinientos treinta, os saludo.

Soberano Señor, nos, sólo podemos expresar nuestra admiración ante las reflexiones profundas y osadas de nuestro Soberano en el campo especulativo de la hagiología y nuestro asombro más genuino por vuestra brillante conjetura, propuesta en la última carta de Vuestra Majestad. *Viz.*, que la deidad más amada por todos estos indios y que tan frecuentemente alude nuestro azteca en su narración, Quetzalcóatl, pudo muy bien haber sido el *Apóstol Tomás*, que visitó estas tierras hace quince siglos, con el propósito de traer el Evangelio a estos idólatras.

Por supuesto que, ni aun siendo el Obispo de Mexico, nos podemos dar una cédula episcopal a esta hipótesis extraordinaria e intrépida, Señor, sin ponerla antes a consideración de la más alta jerarquía de la Iglesia. Sin embargo, nos, podemos afirmar que sí existe un cuerpo circunstancial de evidencias para sostener la nueva teoría de Vuestra Majestad.

Primus: La llamada Serpiente Emplumada ha sido el único ser sobrenatural, reconocido por todas las naciones conocidas en la Nueva España y cuyas religiones varían, aunque ha sido llamado por diferentes nombres como, Quetzalcóatl entre la gente que habla nahuátl, Kukulkán entre la gente que habla maya, Gukumatz entre los pueblos que están todavía más hacia el sur, etcétera.

Secundus: Todos esos pueblos están de acuerdo en sus tradiciones en asegurar que Quetzalcóatl fue al principio un ser humano mortal, que encarnado como rey o emperador vivió y caminó sobre la tierra durante el breve tiempo de su vida, antes de su transmutación en una deidad inmortal e insubstancial. Ya que el calendario de los indios es exasperantemente inútil y ya que no existen más los libros de historias místicas, será muy difícil declarar la fecha del tiempo de reinado de Quetzalcóatl. No obstante, él muy bien *pudo* ser contemporáneo de Santo Tomás.

Tertius: Todos esos pueblos también están de acuerdo en que Quetzalcóatl no fue como esos gobernantes, o tiranos, como la mayoría de sus gobernantes han sido, sino que fue un maestro y predicador y no por casualidad, y guardó el celibato por convicción religiosa. A él se le atribuyen las invenciones o introducciones de numerosas cosas, como costumbres, creencias, etcétera, que perduran hasta la fecha.

Quartus: Entre las incontables deidades de estas tierras, Quetzalcóatl fue uno de los muy pocos que no demandó ni apoyó el sacrificio humano. Todos los ofrecimientos hechos a él, siempre fueron inocuos: pájaros, mariposas, flores y cosas parecidas.

Quintus: La Iglesia sostiene como un hecho histórico, que Santo Tomás viajó a las tierras de la India del Este y que allí convirtió a muchas gentes al Cristianismo. Es por eso que Vuestra Majestad sugiere: «¿No sería razonable suponer que el Apóstol pudo haber hecho eso mismo en las Indias desconocidas del Oeste?» Sin embargo, pudiera haber algún réprobo materialista que hiciera notar que Santo Tomás tuvo la ventaja de haber viajado sobre la ruta terrestre, de Tierra Santa a las Indias Orientales, pero que probablemente él hubiera encontrado alguna dificultad en cruzar el Mar Océano quince siglos antes del desenvolvimiento de la navegación y de la construcción de carabelas, facilidades con que cuentan ahora nuestros modernos exploradores. Pero, cualquier cavilación acerca de la falta de habilidades de uno de los Doce Apóstoles sería tan imprudente como la duda que una vez expuso el propio Tomás, y por la que fue amonestado por Cristo resucitado.

Sextus et mirabile dictu. Un soldado común español llamado Díaz, quien ocupaba sus ratos libres en explorar ociosamente las viejas ruinas, recientemente visitó la ciudad abandonada de Tolan o Tula. Los aztecas le han revelado que allí fue donde se estableció un pueblo legendario llamado los toltecas, y cuyo gobernante fue ese rey que luego se convirtió en dios, Quetzalcóatl. Entre las raíces de un árbol que crecía en una hendidura de una de las viejas paredes de piedra, Díaz encontró una caja de ónix labrado, de manufactura indígena, pero de edad indeterminada y dentro de ésta halló cierto número de obleas blancas y delicadas, de pan, muy diferentes al pan hecho por estos indios. Díaz inmediatamente reconoció lo que eran, y nosotros, cuando él nos las trajo, verificamos que eran hostias. ¿Cómo fue que esas obleas sacramentales llegaron a ese lugar y dentro de un copón de manufactura indígena? ¿Por cuántos siglos se conservó secretamente allí, y cómo es que no se rompieron, se secaron o dejaron de existir, desde hace mucho tiempo? Nadie puede adivinarlo. ¿Podría ser que Vuestra Erudita Majestad nos haya dado la respuesta? ¿Pudieron haber sido dejadas esas obleas de Comunión, por el Evangelista Tomás como un recuerdo?

Nos, en este día, estamos relatando todas estas cosas, en comunicación directa con la Congregación de la Propagación de la Fe, y dando todo el crédito posible a la inspiración con que Vuestra Majestad ha contribuido, por lo que esperamos ansiosos la opinión de los teólogos de Roma, que son mucho más sabios que nosotros.

Que Nuestro Señor Dios siga sonriendo y favoreciendo las empresas de Vuestra Imperial Majestad, a quien vuestros súbditos y vasallos rinden y profesan infinita admiración, no menos que vuestro S.C.C.M., capellán y siervo,

(ecce signum) ZUMÁRRAGA

DECIMA PARS

Por la misma razón por la que no me acuerdo de los sucesos anteriores a la extinción de Yanquitlan, no me acuerdo claramente de las cosas que sucedieron inmediatamente después. Beu, nuestra escolta y yo, marchamos otra vez hacia el norte, hacia Tenochtitlan, y me imagino que el viaje no tuvo nada en especial, ya que casi no me acuerdo de nada, excepto dos breves conversaciones.

La primera fue con Beu. Ella había estado llorando todo el camino mientras caminaba, desde que le había hablado acerca de la muerte de Nochipa, pero un día, en algún lugar del camino, se detuvo de repente y dejando de llorar, miró a su alrededor como alguien que acaba de despertar de un sueño y me dijo:

«Me dijiste que me llevarías a casa, pero vamos hacia el norte.»

Le dije: «Naturalmente, ¿adónde querías ir?»

«¿Por qué no hacia el sur? Hacia Tecuantépec.»

«No tienes ya nada allí —le dije—. Ni familia, ni tal vez amigos. Ya han pasado, ¿cuántos?, ocho años desde que te fuiste de allí.»

«¿Y qué tengo en Tenochtitlan?»

Pude haberle dicho que un techo bajo el cual dormir, pero sabía a qué se refería en realidad. Así es que simplemente le dije: «Tienes lo que yo tengo, Luna que Espera. Recuerdos.»

«Que no son muy agradables, Zaa.»

«Eso también lo sé —le dije sin compasión—. Son los mismos que yo tengo. Y los tendremos en donde quiera que vaguemos o en el lugar que llamemos hogar. Por lo menos en Tenochtitlan puedes pasar duelo y pena cómodamente, pero nadie te está llevando a la fuerza. Tú puedes escoger en venir con nonosotros o tomar tu propio camino.»

Seguí sin mirar para atrás, por eso no sé cuánto tiempo tardó en decidirse, pero cuando levanté nuevamente la mirada, saliendo de mis contemplaciones interiores, Beu caminaba otra vez a mi lado.

La otra conversación la tuve con Siempre Enojado. Por muchos días, los hombres me habían dejado solo, encerrado en mi silencio meditativo, pero uno de esos días él me alcanzó y caminando a mi lado me dijo:

«Perdona que interrumpa tu dolor, amigo Mixtli, pero ya estamos cerca de Tenochtitlan y hay algunas cosas que debes saber. Algunas cosas que nosotros los cuatro ancianos hemos discutido y hemos llegado a la conclusión, de que se han de arreglar entre nosotros. Hemos inventado una historia y les hemos dicho a los tecpaneca que cuenten esa historia. Es ésta. Mientras que todos nosotros, tú, nosotros y los guerreros, hacíamos esa embajada a la corte de Techuacán, necesitando ausentarnos por fuerza, unos bandidos se apoderaron de la colonia y robaron y masacraron a toda la gente. A nuestro regreso de Yanquitlan, como es natural, enfurecidos salimos en busca de los asesinos, sin encontrar ni huellas de ellos. No encontramos ni siquiera una flecha que nos pudiera indicar por sus plumas, a qué nación pertenecían. Esa inseguridad de identidad, detendrá a Motecuzoma de declarar la guerra inmediatamente a los inocentes teohuacana.»

Asentí y dije: «Diré exactamente lo que me acabas de contar. Es una buena historia, Qualanqui.»

Él carraspeó y dijo: «Desgraciadamente, no es lo suficientemente buena como para que tú la cuentes, Mixtli. Por lo menos no enfrente de Motecuzoma. Aunque la creyera, no dejaría de echarte la culpa por el fracaso de esa misión. Si es que por casualidad estuviera de buen humor y no te mandara estrangular inmediatamente con la guirnalda de flores, podría darte otra oportunidad, pero eso significaría que te encargaría conducir a otro grupo de colonizadores y probablemente a ese mismo lugar execrable.»

Negué con la cabeza. «No podría ni querría hacerlo.»

«Lo sé —me dijo—, y además, tarde o temprano la verdad saldrá a relucir. Al llegar a Tlácopan, sanos y salvos, cualquiera de estos guerreros tecpaneca, es seguro que presumirá de la parte que tuvo en la masacre. Cómo violó y cómo mató a seis niños y a un sacerdote, o cualquier cosa parecida. Eso llegará a oídos de Motecuzoma y estarás atrapado en una red de mentiras, que con toda seguridad te llevará al garrote, si no a algo peor. Yo pienso que es mejor que dejes eso en nuestras manos, en nosotros los viejos, porque ante Motecuzoma sólo somos asalariados y por lo tanto estamos en menos peligro que tú. También pienso que no deberías regresar a Tenochtitlan, por lo menos, no por un tiempo, ya que tu futuro allí sólo puede ofrecerte dos cosas, o el exilio a Yanquitlan o la pena de muerte.»

Asentí nuevamente. «Tienes razón. He estado penando los días oscuros y los caminos que han quedado atrás de mí, sin mirar los que tengo por delante. Hay un viejo dicho que afirma que nacemos para sufrir y aguantar, ¿no es cierto? Y un hombre siempre debe pensar en aguantar, ¿no es así? Gracias, Qualanqui, buen amigo y consejero, meditaré en tus consejos.»

Cuando llegamos a Quaunáhuac y pasamos la noche en una hostería, Beu, mis cuatro viejos amigos y yo cenamos aparte. Cuando acabamos de comer, tomé de mi banda-cinturón mi saco lleno de polvo de oro y lo dejé caer sobre el mantel, diciendo:

«Ahí está el pago por vuestros servicios, amigos míos.»

«Es demasiado», dijo Siempre Enojado.

«No, no lo es por todo lo que vosotros habéis hecho por mí. Tengo otro saco con pedacitos de cobre y semillas de cacao, más que suficiente para lo que ahora voy a hacer.»

«¿Ahora vas hacer?», repitió uno de los ancianos.

«Esta noche abdico al mando y éstas serán mis últimas instrucciones para vosotros. Amigos guerreros, desde aquí iréis a la frontera occidental de los lagos, para entregar las tropas tecpaneca a Tlácopan. De allí, atravesaréis el camino-puente hacia Tenochtitlan y escoltaréis a la señora Beu a mi casa, antes de presentaros ante el Venerado Orador. Contadle la historia que habéis inventado, pero agregad también que yo mismo me he castigado por haber fracasado en esa expedición. Decidle que voluntariamente me he exiliado.»

«Así se hará, Campeón Mixtli», dijo Siempre Enojado y los otros tres ancianos estuvieron de acuerdo.

Sólo Beu me preguntó: «¿Adónde vas, Zaa?»

«Voy en busca de una leyenda», le contesté y les conté la historia que hacía poco Nezahualpili le había contado a Motecuzoma delante de mí, y concluí: «Retrocederé por la ruta que siguieron nuestros antepasados, cuando todavía se llamaban a sí mismos los aztecas. Iré hacia el norte, siguiendo su pista conforme la pueda reconstruir y llegando lo más lejos que pueda... hasta su tierra de Aztlán, si es que tal lugar aún existe o existió. Y si ellos enterraron en realidad sus provisiones y armas a intervalos, las encontraré y marcaré su ubicación en un mapa. Ese mapa será de gran valor militar para Motecuzoma. Trata de mencionarle esto cuando te presentes ante él, Qualanqui. —Sonreí sin humor—. Tal vez así me dé la bienvenida con flores en lugar de una guirnalda de flores, cuando regrese.»

«Si es que regresas», dijo Beu.

Y ante eso no pude sonreír, y dije: «Parece que mi *tonali* siempre me obliga a regresar, pero cada vez más solo. —Después de un momento dije entre dientes—: Algún día en algún lugar me encontraré con un dios y le preguntaré: "¿Por qué los dioses nunca me abaten cuando he hecho tantas cosas para merecer su ira? ¿Por qué siempre dejan caer su ira sobre las personas que están cerca de mí, cuando ellas no han hecho nada para merecer ese castigo?"»

Los cuatro ancianos se inquietaron ante mi amargo lamento y parecieron tranquilizarse cuando Beu dijo: «Viejos amigos, ¿seríais tan amables en dejar que Zaa y yo pudiéramos hablar a solas un momento?»

Se pusieron de pie, haciendo el gesto de cortesía de besar la tierra y cuando se fueron a sus habitaciones le dije bruscamente a Beu: «Si me vas a pedir que te deje acompañarme, Beu, es mejor que no lo hagas...»

No lo hizo. Permaneció callada por bastante tiempo y sus ojos estaban puestos sobre sus dedos, los cuales retorcía. Por fin me habló y sus primeras palabras no tenían nada que ver con lo que habíamos estado hablando.

«Cuando yo cumplí siete años, me pusieron el nombre de Luna que Espera y solía preguntarme por qué, pero un día me di cuenta y llevo años sabiéndolo, y por eso creo que Luna que Espera ya ha esperado bastante.» Fijó su hermosa mirada en mí, mirándome suplicante en lugar de burlona como era su costumbre, y hasta se sonrojó como una doncella cuando me dijo: «Zaa, casémonos por fin.»

Con que eso era, me dije, recordando en aquel momento la

vez que ella había recogido subrepticiamente el barro en donde yo había orinado. Antes y por un breve lapso de tiempo, me pregunté si ella habría hecho con eso una imagen mía, para poder maldecirme y que la desgracia cayera sobre mí y también me pregunté si debido a eso yo había perdido a Nochipa. Sin embargo, esa sospecha fue sólo pasajera y me avergoncé de ella. Sabía que Beu había querido intensamente a mi hija y con su llanto me demostró un dolor tan genuino, como el mío sin lágrimas. Por eso me había olvidado del muñeco de barro, hasta que sus propias palabras me revelaron que sí lo había hecho y el porqué. No lo había moldeado para dañar mi vida, sino que sólo quería debilitar mi voluntad, para que no pudiera rechazar esa proposición supuestamente impulsiva, pero en realidad largamente planeada. No contesté inmediatamente, sino que esperé un poco, mientras ella dejaba caer sus argumentos cuidadosamente reunidos.

«Hace un momento, Zaa, tú comentaste que cada vez estabas más y más solo. Tú bien sabes que yo también lo estoy. Los dos lo estamos ahora. Ya nadie nos queda, sólo quedamos nosotros.»

Y siguió: «Era aceptable que viviera contigo en tu casa mientras fuera la encargada y la compañía de tu hija, huérfana de madre, pero ahora que Nochipa... bueno ahora que mi posición ya no es la de una tía, no se verá bien que una mujer soltera y un hombre solo compartan la misma casa.»

Y me dijo, volviéndose a sonrojar: «Sé que nada podrá reemplazar a nuestra querida Nochipa, pero sí podría haber... yo no estoy *tan* vieja como para...»

Y allí dejó de hablar, con una buena imitación de modestia al no continuar hablando. Me esperé y sostuve su mirada hasta que su cara estuvo tan sonrojada que parecía cobre caliente y fue entonces cuando le dije:

«No deberías haberte molestado en hacer tantas conjeturas y en buscar tantos argumentos para convencerme, Beu. Tenía la intención de pedirte eso mismo esta noche. Y como parece que estás de acuerdo conmigo, mañana nos casaremos en cuanto podamos despertar a un sacerdote.»

«¿Cómo?», me dijo con voz apagada.

«Como tú acabas de decir, ahora estoy completamente solo. También, soy un hombre con cierta riqueza y si muero sin heredero, mi propiedad será confiscada por la tesorería de la nación. Preferiría que no fuera a dar a manos de Motecuzoma. Por eso mañana el sacerdote hará un documento afirmando tu herencia, así como el documento que atestigüe nuestra boda.»

Lentamente Beu se puso de pie y mirando hacia abajo, hacia mí, tartamudeó: «Eso no era... nunca pensé que... Zaa, lo que yo trataba de decir...»

«Y te he echado a perder el espectáculo —le dije sonriendo—. Todos esos argumentos y toda esa labor de convencimiento no eran necesarios, pero no los consideres inútiles, Beu. Esta noche tuviste una práctica muy buena, que podrás utilizar en el futuro; quizás cuando seas una viuda rica, pero solitaria.»

«¡Basta, Zaa! —exclamó—. Te niegas a escuchar lo que tan seriamente he estado tratando de decirte. Es difícil para mí, porque esas cosas no le corresponde a la mujer decirlas...»

«Por favor, Beu —dije, haciendo un gesto de desagrado—. Hemos vivido demasiado tiempo juntos y por lo tanto estamos ya acostumbrados a la rudeza de nuestros caracteres. Hablar con suavidad a estas alturas sería un gran esfuerzo para cualquiera de los dos y probablemente asombraríamos a todos los dioses. Pero por lo menos de mañana en adelante, el aborrecimiento que sentimos el uno por el otro será consagrado de manera formal y para no ser diferentes a todas las demás personas casadas...»

«¡Qué cruel eres! —me interrumpió—. Eres inmune a todo sentimiento tierno y no tomas en cuenta la mano que se te tiende.»

«Demasiadas veces he sentido la palma dura de tu tierna mano, Beu. ¿Y acaso no estoy a punto de sentirla otra vez? ¿No te vas a reír ahora y a decirme que tus palabras de matrimonio no eran más que otra de tus bromas burlonas?»

«No —contestó—. Te lo decía en serio. ¿Y tú?»

«Yo también. —Y alzando en lo alto mi copa de *octli*, dije—: Que los dioses tengan piedad de nosotros.»

«Qué proposición tan elocuente —me dijo—, pero así la aceptaré, Zaa. Me casaré contigo mañana.» Y corrió a su cuarto.

Seguí sentado, bebiendo con melancolía mi *octli*, mientras observaba a los demás huéspedes de la hostería. La mayoría de ellos eran *pochteca* en camino a Tenochtitlan, que celebraban las ganancias y el éxito de sus viajes, así como el haber regresado sanos y salvos, emborrachándose, ayudados por las numerosas mujeres disponibles que abundaban en la hostería. El hostelero, que se había dado cuenta de que había pedido cuartos separados para Beu y para mí, viendo que ella se había ido sola, se me acercó y me preguntó:

«¿No se le antojaría al Señor Campeón un dulce con el cual terminar su comida? ¿Qué le parecería una de nuestras encantadoras *maátime*?»

Gruñí: «Son muy pocas las que se ven excepcionalmente encantadoras.»

«Ah, pero ver no lo es todo. Mi señor debe saber eso, ya que el comportamiento de su bella acompañante parece ser algo frío. La gracia y el encanto yace en otros atributos además de la cara y el cuerpo. Por ejemplo, observe a aquella mujer.»

Él apuntó a una mujer que parecía ser la menos atractiva de todo el establecimiento. Sus facciones y su pecho estaban tan caídos como el barro húmedo, y su pelo, a causa de haber sido teñido tantas veces, parecía hierba picuda y seca como la alfalfa enredada. Hice un gesto de asco, pero el hostelero sólo se rió y dijo:

«Lo sé, lo sé. Contemplar a esa mujer es como para querer tener un muchacho en lugar de ella. A primera vista la tomaría por una abuela, pero yo sé que apenas llega a los treinta años. ¿Y me creerá usted, Señor Campeón? *Cada hombre* que alguna vez ha tratado a Quequelyehua *siempre* la pide la siguiente vez

610

que viene a visitarnos. Cada uno de sus clientes, se convierte en un cliente regular y no aceptará a ninguna otra *maátitl*. Yo nunca la he probado, pero sé de buena fuente que ella sabe hacer cosas extraordinarias para deleitar a un hombre.»

Levanté mi topacio y observé más detalladamente a aquella bruja de pelo horrible y mirada aguardentosa. Pudiera haber apostado que era la enfermedad de *nanaua* ambulante y que el hostelero afeminado lo sabía tan bien, que con gusto malicioso trataba de echarla a todo individuo ingenuo.

«Todas las mujeres se parecen en la oscuridad, mi señor, ¿no es cierto? Bueno, también todos los muchachos, por supuesto, ¿pero no son otras consideraciones lo que importan? Aunque lo más probable es que la altamente cotizada Quequelyehua ya tenga una lista de espera esta noche, pero un Campeón Águila puede exigir preferencia sobre unos simples *pochteca*. ¿Mando llamar a Quequelyehua, mi señor?»

«Quequelyehua —repetí, pues el nombre me traía un recuerdo—. Una vez conocí a una muchacha muy bella llamada Quequelmiqui.»

«¿Cosquillosa? —dijo el hostelero y se rió—. A juzgar por su nombre debió de haber sido una concubina bastante divertida, ¿no?, pero ésta ha de ser más, porque su nombre es La Que Hace Cosquillas.»

Sintiéndome mal le dije: «Gracias por su recomendación, pero no, gracias. —Tomé un largo trago de *octli*—. ¿Y qué me dice de esa muchacha delgada que está tan quieta, sentada en aquel rincón?»

«¿Lluvia Neblinosa? —dijo el hostelero con indiferencia—. Así le dicen porque llora todo el tiempo que está, humm... trabajando. Es nueva, pero lo suficientemente competente, según me han dicho.»

Yo le dije: «Mándeme ésa a mi cuarto. Yo iré en cuanto esté lo suficientemente borracho.»

«A sus órdenes, Señor Campeón Águila. A mí me da lo mismo las preferencias de mis clientes, pero a veces siento algo de curiosidad. ¿Podría saber por qué mi señor escogió a Lluvia Neblinosa?»

Yo dije: «Simplemente porque no me recuerda a ninguna mujer que he conocido.»

La ceremonia de matrimonio fue pequeña, sencilla y quieta, por lo menos hasta que terminó. Mis cuatro guerreros fueron los testigos y el hostelero preparó *tamaltin* para la comida ritual. Algunos de los huéspedes más madrugadores se unieron como invitados. Como Quaunáhuac es la comunidad principal del pueblo tlahuica, había conseguido un sacerdote de la deidad más importante de los tlahuica, el buen dios Quetzalcóatl. Y el sacerdote, al observar que la pareja parada ante él estaba un poco más allá del primer florecimiento de la juventud, inteligentemente omitió de su servicio las advertencias acostumbradas, que se les dan a las doncellas, supuestamente inocentes, como las acostumbradas exhortaciones que se le dan a un novio supuestamente ansioso. Por lo tanto su arenga fue muy pequeña y sencilla.

Sin embargo, a pesar de ese ritual tan simple, Beu Ribé demostró bastante emoción o pretendió hacerlo. Derramó unas cuantas lágrimas virginales y entre ellas, sus labios sonreían trémulamente. Debo reconocer que su actuación embelleció más su impresionante belleza, belleza que nunca he negado, ya que era igual a la hermosura de su difunta hermana y aun indistinguible. Beu vestía de una manera incitante y, cuando la vi sin mi cristal, parecía tan joven como mi joven Zyanya, eternamente de veinte años. Fue por esa razón, que durante la noche utilicé repetidas veces a la muchacha Lluvia Neblinosa, pues no quería correr el riesgo de desear a Beu, aunque fuera sólo físicamente, y así agoté cualquier posibilidad de excitarme, aun en contra de mi voluntad.

El sacerdote por fin giró su incensario de *copali* humeante alrededor de nosotros, por última vez. Luego nos miró mientras dábamos un mordisco a los *tamaltin* calientes, luego hizo un nudo de unión con mi manto y la orilla de la falda de Luna que Espera y por último nos deseó la mejor de las suertes en nuestra nueva vida.

«Gracias, Señor Sacerdote —le dije, entregándole su salario—. Gracias, sobre todo por sus buenos deseos. —Deshice el nudo que me ataba a Beu—. Voy a necesitar de la ayuda de todos los dioses hacia donde voy ahora.» Colgué al hombro mi morral de viaje y le dije adiós a Beu.

«¿Adiós? —repitió con voz aguda—. Pero, Zaa, éste es el día de nuestra boda.»

Le dije: «Te dije que me iría. Mis hombres te llevarán a salvo a casa.»

«Pero... pero yo pensé... yo pensé que te quedarías por lo menos otra noche. Para... —Miró a su alrededor, a los invitados que solamente veían y escuchaban con atención. Poniéndose muy colorada, levantó la voz—: ¡Zaa, ahora soy tu esposa!»

La corregí: «Estás casada conmigo tal y como me lo pediste, y serás mi viuda y heredera. Zyanya fue mi esposa.»

«*¡Zyanya lleva diez años muerta!*»

«Su muerte no ha roto nuestro lazo. No puedo tener otra esposa.»

«¡Hipócrita! —me gritó—. Tú no has practicado el celibato durante estos diez años. Tú has tenido más mujeres. ¿Por qué no tienes a la mujer con la que te acabas de casar? ¿Por qué no quieres tenerme?»

A excepción del hostelero que veía todo eso riéndose con malicia, la mayoría de las personas que se encontraban en la habitación se mostraban inquietas e incómodas. También el sacerdote se sentía así, tanto que se sintió obligado a decir: «Mi señor, después de todo ésa es la costumbre, sellar los votos con un acto de... bueno, conocerse uno al otro más íntimamente...»

Yo le dije: «Su preocupación es muy loable, Señor Sacerdote, pero sepa que ya conozco a esta mujer bastante íntima mente.»

Beu dejó caer sorprendida: «¡Pero qué mentira tan horrible dices! Nosotros jamás...»

«Y jamás lo haremos. Luna que Espera, te conozco demasiado bien en otros aspectos. También sé que el momento más vulnerable en la vida de un hombre es cuando se acuesta con una mujer. No quiero correr el riesgo de que un día me rechaces desdeñosamente, o que te burles y rías de mí, o que me hagas de menos, empleando cualquiera de los medios que por tanto tiempo llevas practicando y perfeccionando.»

Ella lloriqueó: «¿Y qué es lo que tú me estás haciendo en este momento?»

«Lo mismo —estuve yo de acuerdo—, pero sólo por esta vez, querida, me he adelantado. Ahora el día corre y debo estar en camino.»

Cuando me fui, Beu estaba secando sus lágrimas con la esquina arrugada de la falda, que había sido nuestro nudo matrimonial.

✠

No era necesario que retrocediera la marcha de mis ancestros desde su término en Tenochtitlan, ni tenía que ir a ninguno de los lugares que anteriormente habían habitado en el área del lago, ya que esos sitios no tenían ningún secreto escondido de los azteca. Sin embargo, según las antiguas leyendas, uno de los lugares habitados por los azteca antes de que encontraran el lago y el valle, había sido un lugar al norte de los lagos; un lugar llamado Atlitalacan. Por eso, desde Quaunáhuac viajé hacia el noroeste, luego al norte, después al noroeste, desviándome en círculo para quedar bastante afuera de los dominios de la Triple Alianza, hasta que me encontré en la tierra que está más allá de Oxitipan, la ciudad fronteriza más lejana con guarnición de guerreros mexica. En ese territorio poco conocido, con pequeñas aldeas y escaso movimiento de viajeros, comencé preguntando por el camino hacia Atlitalacan, pero las únicas respuestas que conseguí fueron miradas en blanco y gestos indiferentes, pues tenía dos dificultades. Una de ellas era que no tenía ni idea de lo que *era* o había sido Atlitalacan. Pudo haber sido una comunidad establecida durante el tiempo en que los azteca permanecieron allí, pero que pudo haber dejado de existir desde entonces, o haber sido simplemente un lugar hospitalario para poder acampar —una vereda, o un campo— al cual los azteca le habían dado ese nombre sólo temporalmente. Mi otra dificultad fue que había penetrado en la parte sur del pueblo otomí, o para ser más preciso, era la tierra a la que el pueblo otomí, de mala gana, se había ido cuando poco a poco los fueron echando de sus tierras en el lago, a la llegada de los culhua, acolhua, azteca, y demás oleadas de invasores de habla náhuatl. Así que en esa tierra fronteriza tenía el problema del lenguaje. Algunas personas que encontraba, hablaban aceptablemente la lengua náhuatl o en su defecto en el poré de sus vecinos del occidente, pero todos los demás sólo hablaban otomí, idioma que yo no dominaba, y también había quienes hablaban una extraña mezcla de los tres idiomas. Y aunque mi constante interrogar a aldeanos, agricultores y caminantes, me ayudó a adquirir un vocabulario aceptable de palabras otomí para poder explicar mi misión, no pude encontrar a nadie que me pudiera orientar hacia el perdido Atlitalacan.

Tenía que encontrarlo por mí mismo y así lo hice. Afortunadamente, el nombre en sí era una pista, pues quiere decir: «en donde el agua brota», y un día llegué a una aldea pequeña, limpia y ordenada llamada D'ntado Dehé, que quiere decir casi lo mismo en otomí. La aldea se encontraba allí, porque había una fuente de agua dulce que brotaba de unas piedras y era el único manantial en un área considerablemente extensa y árida. Parecía un lugar adecuado para que los azteca se hubieran detenido, ya que había un camino viejo que llegaba a la aldea por el norte y seguía hacia el sur, en dirección del lago Tzumpanco.

La gente de esa pobre población de D'ntado Dehé, como es natural me miraban de soslayo, pero una viuda ya vieja, demasiado pobre como para darse el lujo de tener demasiados recelos, me alojó durante unos días en la bodega, ya casi vacía, de su choza de una sola pieza. Durante esos días, traté sonriendo de congraciarme con los taciturnos otomí, halagándolos para sacarles algo de conversación, pero fracasé; por lo que empecé, a las afueras de la aldea, a buscar cualquier cosa que mis antepasados pudieran haber escondido allí, aunque tenía la sospecha de que una búsqueda como ésta sería inútil. Si los azteca *hubieran escondido* provisiones y armas a lo largo de su marcha, debieron estar seguros de que los depósitos no serían encontrados por los residentes locales, o por gentes que pasaran por allí. Debieron de marcar esos escondites con alguna señal desconocida para todos, excepto para ellos. Y ninguno de sus descendientes mexica, incluyéndome, teníamos ninguna noción de lo que pudo haber sido esa señal.

Sin embargo, corté un palo largo y fuerte, le afilé la punta y con él piqué profundamente en cada surco, o línea del terreno, que me pareciera que no había estado allí desde la creación del mundo; todo lo que hacía un bulto aislado en la tierra, bosque de hierba sin limpiar y los restos de edificios antiguos. No sé si mi comportamiento hizo que los aldeanos se divirtieran o sintieran lástima por el pobre extranjero loco o simple curiosidad, el caso fue que al fin me invitaron a sentarme y a explicar mis acciones a dos de sus ancianos más venerados.

Esos ancianos contestaron a mis preguntas, utilizando las menos palabras posibles. No, me dijeron, jamás habían oído hablar de un lugar llamado Atlitalacan, pero si el nombre quería decir lo mismo que D'nte Dehé, era el mismo lugar, pues era cierto que según sus padres, los padres de sus padres y los padres de éstos, hacía mucho tiempo que una tribu de extranjeros rudos, andrajosos y verminosos había acampado cerca de la fuente, permaneciendo allí durante algunos años, antes de seguir adelante y desaparecer hacia el sur. Cuando pregunté diplomáticamente acerca de posibles excavaciones y depósitos dentro de esa área, los dos ancianos movieron sus cabezas. Ellos decían siempre: «n'yéhina», que quiere decir «no», y también dijeron algo que tuvieron que repetir varias veces antes de que los pudiera entender.

«Los azteca estuvieron aquí, pero no trajeron nada con ellos y no dejaron nada cuando partieron.»

Unos pocos días después, dejé esas regiones en donde se hablaba el último vestigio de esa mezcla de náhuatl y poré y penetré en el territorio solamente habitado por los otomí o gente de habla otomí. No viajé en línea recta, pues hubiera tenido que caminar sobre colinas sin veredas, escalar peñascos formidables y luchar con bosques de cactos, que estaba seguro de que los inmigrantes azteca no hicieron. Por el contrario, pensaba que éstos habían seguido los caminos que encontraron, si los hubo, y las numerosas veredas bien definidas. Eso hizo que mi camino fuera muy tortuoso y lento, pero siempre me dirigía hacia el norte.

Todavía estaba en la alta meseta que se extendía entre las cadenas de poderosas montañas que invisibles se alzaban al este y al oeste, pero a medida que avanzaba por esa meseta, poco a poco se inclinaba hacia abajo, delante de mí. Cada día bajaba un poco más de las tierras altas, en donde el aire era limpio y fresco y esos últimos días de primavera empezaron a calentarse tanto que hasta llegaron a molestarme, pero las noches eran tranquilas y suaves. Eso estuvo muy bien, porque no había posadas en esas tierras otomí y las aldeas y rancherías en donde pedía alojamiento estaban muy separadas unas de otras, así es que la mayor parte de las noches, las pasaba a campo raso y aun sin mi cristal alcanzaba a distinguir la estrella Tlacpac, situada en lo alto del horizonte, hacia el norte, adonde me dirigía otra vez al amanecer.

La falta de hosterías y de lugares en donde comer, no significó una gran carestía para mí. La timidez de la gente en esa región, hacía que los animales fueran menos huidizos que en otros lugares más poblados; conejos y ardillas se sentaban en el pasto, sin miedo, para verme pasar; de vez en cuando, un pájaro correcaminos caminaba a mi lado tranquilamente y al anochecer algún armadillo o zorra venía a investigar el fuego de mi campamento. Aunque no llevaba ningún arma más que mi *maquáhuitl*, que no era muy adecuada para la caza menor, lo único que tenía que hacer usualmente para procurarme una buena comida, era darle un golpe a algún animalito. También, si deseaba variar mi comida o acompañar la carne con otra cosa, había un sinfín de vegetales creciendo por todas partes.

Otomí es el nombre de esa nación que está al norte, pero es sólo un apócope de un término mucho más largo y difícil de pronunciar, que quiere decir algo así como «los hombres cuyas flechas bajan pájaros de un ala», aunque me hacía pensar que el tiempo en que fueron cazadores ya había pasado hacía mucho tiempo. Hay muchas tribus entre los otomí, pero todas ellas viven de la agricultura, cultivando campos de maíz, *xitomatin* y otras verduras, o recolectando frutas de los árboles y cactos, así como también extrayendo la savia dulce de las plantas de maguey. Sus campos y hortalizas eran tan productivos que podían enviar muchos alimentos frescos al mercado de Tlaltelolco y a otros mercados extranjeros, y nosotros los mexica llamábamos a su tierra Atoctli, la Tierra Fértil. Sin embargo, para indicar la forma tan baja en que nosotros mirábamos a esa gente, habíamos calificado nuestro licor *octli* en tres grados de calidad: fino, ordinario y otomí.

Las aldeas otomí tienen nombres casi imposibles de pronunciar, por ejemplo, la más grande de todas se llama N't Tahí, a la que uno de sus exploradores de la región norte, no sé por qué, la llama por Zelalla. Pero en ninguna de esas comunidades, tan difíciles de nombrar, pude encontrar los almacenamientos secretos de los azteca o algún rastro que me indicara que ellos habían pasado alguna vez por esos lugares. Solamente en unas pocas aldeas pude encontrar algún anciano de los que contaban las historias y tradiciones de su pueblo, que haciendo un gran esfuerzo de memoria recordaba que la tradición decía que hacía ya muchas gavillas de años, había pasado, efectivamente, una caravana de nómadas arrastrando sus pies doloridos, o habían pernoctado allí, en aquella región. Y cada anciano agregaba: «No traían nada con ellos y no dejaron nada cuando partieron.» Eso era desalentador, pero entonces pensaba que yo era un descendiente directo de esos vagabundos y como ellos, no llevaba nada. Sólo una vez durante mi viaje a través de esas tierras otomí, pude haber *dejado* algo muy pequeño...

Los hombres otomí son bajos de estatura, gordos y, como la mayoría de los agricultores, de disposición cortante y cerrada. Las mujeres también son bajas de estatura, pero delgadas de cuerpo y mucho más vivarachas que sus hombres tristes. Hasta puedo decir que son bellas, de la rodilla para arriba, aunque me doy cuenta de que es un extraño cumplido, pero lo que quiero decir es que sus pechos, cinturas, caderas, traseros y muslos, están muy bien formados, pero debajo de la rodilla sus piernas son demasiado flacas y sin forma, y como sus pies son muy pequeños, eso les da un aspecto de renacuajitos equilibrándose sobre sus pequeñas colas.

Otra cosa peculiar de los otomí es que embellecen su aspecto, o por lo menos eso creen, por medio de un arte que llaman *n'detade*, que quiere decir pintarse con colores *permanentes*. Se pintan sus dientes de negro o rojo, o alternativamente de negro y rojo. Adornan sus cuerpos con unos diseños en color azul, picándose la piel con espinas de tal manera que los diseños les quedan grabados para siempre. Algunos solamente se hacen pequeñas decoraciones en la frente o en las mejillas, pero otros continúan haciéndose el *n'detade* tan frecuentemente como pueden soportar el dolor, por toda la piel de todo su cuerpo.

Parece como si estuvieran detrás del extraordinario tejido de una araña que hubiese utilizado hilo azul.

Tanto como yo me di cuenta, los hombres otomí no mejoraron ni empeoraron con esos adornos. Por un tiempo, pensé que era una pena que esas mujeres, que de otra manera se hubieran visto muy hermosas, oscurecieran su belleza detrás de esos tejidos, espirales y diseños que ya nunca podrían borrar. Sin embargo, conforme me fui acostumbrando a ver el *n'detade*, debo confesar que empecé a verlo como un disfraz sutil. Esa máscara hacía que las mujeres parecieran hasta cierto punto inaccesibles, con un no sé qué de desafiante y un no sé qué de tentador...

Al extremo norte de esas extensas tierras otomí, hay una aldea llamada M'boshte, cruzada por un río, y allí conocí a una de las aldeanas que se llamaba R'zoöno H'donwe, que quiere decir Flor de Luna. Y en verdad que ella estaba toda florida; cada parte visible de su cuerpo, adornada con pétalos, hojas y frondas pintadas en azul. Detrás de ese jardín artificial, ella mostraba un hermoso rostro y una bella figura, excepto por sus feas piernas. Al verla por primera vez, sentí el deseo de quitarle sus ropas y ver hasta dónde era pétalos floridos, y luego abrir mi camino entre esa floresta hasta llegar a la mujer que se escondía atrás.

Flor de Luna también se sintió atraída por mí, y sospecho que casi del mismo modo: con el deseo de disfrutar de una rareza, ya que mi alta estatura y la amplitud de mis hombros, que sobresalía aun entre los mexica, me hacía parecer un gigante entre los otomí. Ella me dijo que en aquel momento no estaba unida a ningún hombre. Había quedado viuda hacía poco, cuando su esposo había muerto en el R'donte Sh'mboi o sea en el Río de la Laja, el arroyo que cruzaba la aldea. Ya que el agua no era más profunda que el ancho de una mano y casi tan angosto que se podía cruzar de un salto, le hice notar que su marido debería de haber sido un hombre muy, *muy*, pequeño para haberse ahogado en él. Ella se rió de eso y me contó que su marido se había caído al cruzar el río y se había roto la nuca.

Así es que la única noche que estuve en M'boshte, la pasé con Flor de Luna. No puedo decir lo mismo de todas las mujeres otomí, pero esa mujer estaba decorada en toda la superficie de su cuerpo, por todas partes excepto sus labios, sus párpados, las puntas de sus dedos y sus pezones. Yo recuerdo el haber pensado lo muchísimo que debía de haber sufrido cuando el artista local le pinchó los diseños de flores, exactamente a un lado de las membranas de su suave *tepili*. Porque verán ustedes, durante el transcurso de esa noche, yo vi todas las flores que tenía. El acto de copular se llama en otomite *agui n'degue* y empieza —o por lo menos Flor de Luna prefería que así empezara— examinando, trazando, acariciando y, bueno, probando cada pétalo de cada flor que había en todo el jardín que tenía su cuerpo. De veras que llegué a sentirme como un venado alimentándose en una floresta dulce y abundante, y entonces decidí que el venado debería de ser uno de los animales más felices.

Cuando estuve listo para partir, a la siguiente mañana, Flor de Luna me dio a entender que tenía la esperanza de haber quedado embarazada, lo que su difunto esposo jamás pudo hacer. Eso me hizo sonreír pensando que ella me estaba dando un cumplido, pero luego me explicó la razón por la cual ella tenía la esperanza de tener un hijo o una hija de mí. Como yo era un hombre grandote, el niño también sería de buen tamaño, así es que si él crecía así, tendría bastante piel para embellecer de una manera prodigiosa, con innumerables dibujos de n'detade, así es que sería una rareza que haría que M'boshte fuera la envidia de otras comunidades otomí. Yo suspiré y me fui.

Todo el tiempo que seguí el curso de las aguas del R'donte Sh'mboi, la tierra que le rodeaba estaba cubierta de verdor, llena de hierba y de flores rojas, amarillas y azules, en gran cantidad. Sin embargo, tres o cuatro días después, el Río de la Laja se desviaba hacia el oeste, lejos del rumbo norte que yo llevaba y con él se llevó todo el colorido, el verdor y la frescura. Sabía que conforme fuera avanzando, iría dejando atrás los árboles y los arbustos, hasta que éstos dejaran su lugar al desierto, casi estéril, abierto y cocido por el sol.

Por un momento me detuve, tentado a regresar hacia el río y a quedarme en la temperatura agradable de las tierras otomí, pero no tenía ninguna excusa para hacer eso. La única razón del viaje que estaba haciendo era seguir las huellas de los azteca, y, tanto como yo sabía, ellos habían venido de un lugar mucho más allá, del desierto o más allá del desierto, si es que allí había algo. Así pues, llené en el río mi bolsa de agua, respiré lo más profundo que pude el aire fresco del río y me encaminé hacia el norte. Le di la espalda a las tierras llenas de vida y caminé hacia las tierras vacías, hacia las tierras quemadas, hacia las tierras de huesos muertos.

El desierto es una selva que cuando los dioses no la ignoran totalmente, se dedican a atormentarla.

Coatlicue, la diosa de la tierra y su familia, no hace nada para darle interés al terreno tan monótono y casi uniformemente llano, con su arena gris amarillenta, su grava gris pardusca y sus peñascos negruzcos. Coatlicue ni siquiera se digna molestar esa tierra con un temblor, ni Chántico ha arrojado allí algunos volcanes, ni Tmazcaltoci escupe sobre ella los chorros de agua caliente y vapor. Tepeyólotl, el dios de la montaña, permanece en sus dominios, muy lejos de allí. Con la ayuda de mi topacio apenas podía percibir los perfiles bajos de las montañas, muy a lo lejos, tanto al este como al oeste; eran montañas picudas de un granito gris blancuzco, pero siempre permanecieron allí, infinitamente distantes, jamás se acercaron a mí ni yo a ellas.

Todas las mañanas, el sol-dios Tonatíu se levantaba enojado de su cama, sin su acostumbrada ceremonia, que hacía al amanecer, de escoger sus arcos y flechas para ese día. Todas las tardes caía sobre su cama sin ponerse su lustroso manto de plumas o abriendo ampliamente su cobija de flores multicolores. Entre esos despertares y esas caídas de noche tan abruptos, Tonatiú era sólo una mancha blancoamarillenta, más brillante, en ese cielo también de ese mismo tono —soleado, malhumorado, chupándole el aliento a esa tierra—, quemando a su paso el cielo abrasado, poco a poco y laboriosamente, como yo también cruzaba arrastrándome esas arenas abrasadas.

Aunque ya era tiempo de lluvias, Tláloc, el dios de la lluvia, no prestaba ni la menor atención a ese desierto. Sus vasijas de nubes con frecuencia se juntaban, pero sólo sobre las montañas de granito que se encontraban al este y al oeste. Las nubes se inflaban y se posaban muy arriba, sobre el horizonte, y luego se oscurecían preñadas de lluvia y los espíritus tlaloque golpearían con sus tenedores de luz, produciendo el ruido del tambor, que llegaba hasta mí como un suave murmullo. Sin embargo, el cielo arriba y delante de mí, siempre permaneció inmutable con ese color blanco amarillento. Ni las nubes, ni los espíritus tlaloque se aventuraron sobre el calor calcinante del desierto. Dejaron caer su lluvia, como velos azul grisáceos, a la distancia sobre las grises montañas, tan lejanas. Y por ningún lado pude ver jamás a la diosa de las corrientes, Chalchihuitlicué.

Ehécatl, el dios del viento, soplaba de vez en cuando, pero sus labios estaban tan abrasados como la tierra desierta y su aliento era tan caliente y seco, que pocas veces alcanzaba a hacer ruido, ya que casi no tenía nada en contra de qué soplar. Eso sí, algunas veces lo hacía tan fuerte que parecía silbar y era entonces cuando la arena se movía y se levantaba, arremolinándose a través de la tierra, con nubes tan fuertes como el polvo de obsidiana que los escultores utilizaban para suavizar la piedra sólida.

Los dioses de las criaturas vivientes tienen muy poco que hacer en esa tierra tan caliente, dura y árida, sobre todo Mixcóatl, el dios de los cazadores. Claro que veía u oía un coyote de vez en cuando, pues ese animal parece poder vivir en cualquier lugar. Y también había conejos, aunque me imagino que era sólo para que los coyotes pudieran comer. Había reyezuelos y búhos, y éstos casi del tamaño de los reyezuelos y vivían en orificios hechos en los cactos. Tampoco podía faltar un buitre o dos, que volando alto circulaba sobre mí, pero todos los demás habitantes del desierto eran reptiles, ya que vivían debajo de la tierra o debajo de las piedras, como las venenosas serpientes de cascabel, lagartos como látigos, lagartijas con granos y cuernos y escorpiones del tamaño de mi mano.

Por lo visto, nuestros dioses de las cosas que crecen, no tienen ningún interés en el desierto. Es cierto que en el otoño hasta los *nopali*, cactos, dan sus rojos y dulces *tónaltin*, frutos, y el gran cacto *quinámetl* ofrece sus dulces y purpurinos frutos *pitaaya*, al final de sus brazos levantados, pero a la mayoría de los del desierto, sólo les crecen púas y espinas. En cuanto a árboles, únicamente se ve de vez en cuando un torcido *mizquitl*, la yuca de hojas como lanzas, el *quamátlatl* de color raro, ya que sus hojas, ramas y hasta su tronco son de un verde brillante. Los arbustos más pequeños incluyen al *chiyáctic*, que es muy útil porque su savia es como un aceite y facilita el encendido de una fogata, y el *quauxeloloni*, cuya madera es más dura que el cobre y por lo tanto casi imposible de cortar y tan pesada que se hundiría en el agua, si es que la hubiera por allí.

Sólo una diosa bondadosa se atreve a caminar entre ese horrible desierto, para meterse entre las garras de esas plantas tan feas y suavizar su naturaleza tan mala, con su caricia. Ésta es Xochiquétzal, la diosa del amor y de las flores, la diosa más amada por mi ya ha muchos años difunta hermana Tzitzitlini. Cada primavera, aunque sólo por poco tiempo, la diosa embellece hasta el más feo de los arbustos y de los cactos. Durante el resto del año, le parecerá a cualquier viajero que Xochiquétzal ha abandonado el desierto y lo ha condenado a una continua fealdad, pero no es así, pues yo hice lo que había hecho en mi lejana infancia, cuando sólo podía ver las cosas de cerca, esas cosas que no llamarían la atención de las personas que tienen una visión normal, y encontré flores en el desierto, para cada estación, que sobresalían entre las enredaderas, largas y espesas, que se arrastraban sobre la tierra. Eran flores muy pequeñas, casi invisibles a menos que uno las buscara, pero eran flores y por eso sabía que Xochiquétzal estaba allí.

Aunque una diosa pueda existir en el desierto con facilidad y sin peligro, no es un medio adecuado para un ser humano. Todo lo que hace la vida tolerable escasea allí o no existe en absoluto. Si un hombre ignorante de la naturaleza del desierto trata de cruzarlo sin prepararse para ello, pronto encontrará la muerte y ésta no será rápida ni fácil. Para mí, aunque ésa fue mi primera aventura en el desierto, no desconocía lo que éste era e iba preparado. Cuando había estado en la escuela, en donde se nos enseñaba cómo ser guerreros, el Quáchic Glotón de Sangre había insistido en incluir ciertas enseñanzas para poder sobrevivir en un desierto.

Por ejemplo, gracias a sus enseñanzas jamás me faltó agua. La fuente más común es el cacto *comitl*, y es por lo que se llama *comitl*, jarra. Escogía un cacto grande y le ponía una rueda de ramitas alrededor de su tronco, las encendía y esperaba hasta que el calor lanzara la humedad del *comitl* hacia su interior. Después sólo tenía que cortar la parte superior de ese cacto, moler la pulpa y exprimir el agua que salía de ella sobre mi bolsa de cuero. Todas las noches, solía cortar también uno de los cactos más altos, de tronco recto, y acostarlo con su punta recargada sobre una piedra, para que se doblara por en medio. A la mañana siguiente toda la humedad se encontraba en medio y sólo tenía que cortar allí y dejar que el agua escurriera sobre mi cuero.

Pocas veces tuve carne para asar sobre mi fogata nocturna, salvo alguna que otra lagartija que sólo servía para dos bocados, aunque una vez tuve un conejo que todavía estaba pataleando cuando se lo quité al buitre que lo acababa de atrapar. Pero la carne no es indispensable para el sostenimiento de la vida. En el transcurso del año, el árbol de *mizquitl* está festonado de semillas, unas verdes y otras parduscas; las verdes son las nuevas y las pardas las que sobraron del año anterior. Las semillas verdes se pueden cocer en agua caliente hasta que quedan tiernas y luego se aplastan para hacer de ellas una pulpa comestible. Las semillas secas que están dentro de las vainas viejas, se pueden moler entre dos piedras hasta que tengan una consistencia harinosa. Ese polvo se puede llevar como *pinoli* y cuando no se cuenta con un alimento más fresco, éste puede mezclarse con agua y hervirse.

Bueno, sobreviví y caminé por ese desierto horrible durante todo un año, pero no es necesario que lo describa más, ya que cada larga-carrera era igual a la anterior. Sólo agregaré, por si ustedes, reverendos frailes, todavía no alcanzan a imaginarse toda su grandeza, extensión y soledad, que estuve caminando en él aproximadamente un mes entero sin encontrarme a otro ser humano.

De lejos, porque tenía el color de la tierra del desierto, creí que era tan sólo una extraña colinita de arena, pero al acercarme vi que era un ser humano sentado. Muy contento, pues llevaba mucho tiempo sin ver a nadie, le grité, pero no me contestó. Conforme me iba acercando, le gritaba, pero ni así recibí respuesta, pero para entonces ya estaba lo suficientemente cerca como para ver que la boca del extraño estaba abierta, como si estuviera gritando.

Entonces, me detuve sobre la figura de una mujer desnuda sentada sobre la arena y cubierta con una ligera capa de arena. Si es que alguna vez gritó, ya no podía hacerlo, pues estaba muerta, con sus ojos y su boca bien abiertos. Estaba sentada con sus piernas extendidas y abiertas, con sus manos recargadas sobre la tierra, como si se hubiera muerto mientras trataba de levantarse. Toqué sus hombros arenosos, su piel era suave y todavía no estaba fría, lo que indicaba que había muerto hacía poco. Apestaba, pues estaba muy sucia, pero sin duda yo olía igual, y su pelo largo estaba lleno de pulgas de arena, que si no hacían que éste se moviera, era porque estaba muy enredado. Sin embargo, con un buen baño, ella habría sido bastante bonita, tanto de cara como de cuerpo, y era más joven que yo, sin tener signos de enfermedad o de lesión, así es que yo estaba perplejo ante la causa de su muerte.

Durante el último mes, había caído en el hábito de hablar conmigo mismo a falta de otra persona, así es que me dije con tristeza: «Este desierto está abandonado de los dioses o los dioses me han abandonado a mí. Tuve, por un lado, la suerte de encontrarme con lo que tal vez fuera la única persona existente en todo este desierto, y que resultó ser una mujer. Ella hubiera sido la compañera ideal para viajar, pero por desgracia ya es un cadáver. Si hubiera llegado un día antes, tal vez hubiera aceptado compartir mi viaje, mi cobija y mis atenciones, pero como está muerta, la única atención que le puedo dar es la de enterrarla antes de que lleguen los buitres.»

Solté mi morral y mi bolsa de cuero con agua y comencé a excavar un hoyo en la arena con mi *maquáhuitl*, pero sentía como si me mirara con reproche, por lo que decidí que sería mejor acostarla para que descansara, mientras yo excavaba su tumba. Dejé caer mi espada y tomé a la mujer de los hombros para acostarla de espaldas, pero me llevé una gran sorpresa. Resistió la presión de mis manos e insistió en permanecer en esa postura, como si fuera una muñeca cosida por en medio, para poder conservar esa posición. No podía entender la renuencia del cadáver, pues sus músculos no estaban tiesos todavía, lo comprobé al levantar uno de sus brazos y encontrarlo bastante flexible. Traté otra vez de moverla y su cabeza cayó sobre uno de sus hombros, pero su torso no se movió. Entonces pensé algo muy loco, ¿acaso los habitantes del desierto al morir, echaban raíces para quedarse en un solo lugar? ¿Acaso esos habitantes no se convertían, poco a poco, en esos gigantescos cactos con figuras humanas?

Retrocedí un poco para examinar el cadáver, que incomprensiblemente había resultado ser tan terco y me volví a sorprender, cuando algo me picó fuertemente en la espalda. Me volví y me encontré en medio de un semicírculo de flechas, todas apuntándome. Cada una de ellas estaba colocada sobre la cuerda tensa de un arco, cada arco la sostenía un hombre ceñudo y enojado, y cada hombre vestía solamente un taparrabo muy sucio de piel desgarrada, una capa de mugre y unas cuantas plumas en su pelo sin brillo. Eran nueve hombres. Debo admitir que como había estado tan preocupado con ese hallazgo tan peculiar, y como ellos se esforzaron en rodearme tan silenciosamente, ni siquiera los olí mucho antes de que se acercaran, pues apestaban igual que la mujer muerta, pero multiplicado por nueve.

«¡Chichimeca!», exclamé para mí o quizás lo hice en voz alta. Lo que sí les dije fue: «Acabo de encontrar a esta infeliz mujer y sólo trataba de ayudarla.»

Como eso lo dije lo más rápido que pude, con la esperanza de detener sus flechas antes de que las lanzaran, hablé en mi propia lengua, pero a la vez acompañé mis palabras con gestos comprensibles hasta para unos salvajes y aun en ese momento tan tenso, pensé que si llegaba a vivir lo suficiente, tendría que aprender otra nueva lengua. Pero grande fue mi sorpresa, cuando uno de los hombres que me había picado con la punta de su flecha, un hombre casi de mi estatura y casi de mi tamaño, me contestó en comprensible náhuatl.

«La mujer es mi esposa.»

Tragué saliva y le dije con un tono de condolencia, como cuando uno tiene que dar una mala noticia: «Siento decirle que *era* su esposa. Parece ser que murió hace un rato. —La flecha del chichimeca, mejor dicho, las nueve flechas, seguían apuntándome. Rápidamente agregué—: Yo no fui la causa de su muerte. Ya la encontré así. Y no tenía ninguna intención de molestarla, aun si la hubiera encontrado viva.»

El hombre se rió roncamente, sin humor.

«Es más —continué diciendo—, estaba a punto de hacerle el favor de enterrarla antes de que los buitres la despedazaran.» E indiqué el lugar en donde estaba mi *maquáhuitl.*

El hombre contempló el hoyo que había empezado a excavar, luego hacia arriba, en donde ya rondaban los buitres y por último me miró fijamente y su expresión de dureza se relajó un poco. Él me dijo: «Es usted muy amable, forastero», y bajó su flecha aflojando la tensión de su arco.

Los otros ocho chichimeca hicieron lo mismo, y metieron sus flechas entre sus cabellos enredados. Uno de los hombres se empinó para recoger mi *maquéhuitl* y la examinó detenidamente, mientras otro empezó a registrar el contenido de mi morral. Quizás me robaran lo poco que llevaba, pensé, pero por lo menos parecía que no me iban a matar inmediatamente, por ser un intruso. Tratando de seguir aparentando amabilidad le dije al viudo:

«Siento mucho su pena. Su esposa era joven y bonita. ¿De qué murió?»

«De ser una mala esposa —me contestó melancólicamente. Luego dijo—: La mordió una serpiente de cascabel.»

No vi ninguna relación entre esas dos frases y sólo pude contestar: «Qué extraño, no parecía estar enferma.»

«No, si se restableció del veneno —gruñó el hombre—, pero antes, pensando que iba a morir, se confesó con La Que Come Suciedad, delante de mí. Lo único que confesó a Tlazoltéotl fue que se había acostado con un hombre de otra tribu y luego tuvo la desgracia de no morir de la picadura.»

Movió su cabeza sombríamente y yo hice lo mismo. Él continuó:

«Esperamos a que se recuperara, porque no estaría bien ejecutar a una mujer enferma. Cuando se alivió y estuvo fuerte otra vez, la trajimos aquí. Esta mañana. Para morir.»

Observé los restos, preguntándome qué clase de ejecución se le pudo dar a la víctima, sin que dejara ninguna huella, sólo los ojos muy abiertos y también la boca, en un grito silencioso.

«Ahora veníamos a quitarla de aquí —concluyó el viudo—. Un buen lugar para ejecutar es muy difícil de encontrar en el desierto, así que no profanamos éste al dejar la carroña, para atraer a los buitres y a los coyotes. Fue muy gentil de su parte, forastero, el haber apreciado eso. —Dejó caer su mano amigablemente sobre mi hombro—. Pero nosotros atenderemos a nuestro difunto y después tal vez quiera compartir nuestra comida en el campamento.»

«Con gusto», le dije y mi estómago vacío gruñó, pero lo que luego presencié me quitó el apetito.

El hombre se acercó a donde estaba sentada su esposa y la movió de un modo que a mí jamás se me hubiera ocurrido. Yo traté de acostarla, pero él la sujetó por debajo de las axilas y la alzó. Aun así vi que se resistía y él tuvo que hacer un gran esfuerzo. Entonces, se oyó un ruido horrible como cuando algo se destapa y se desgarra, como si la parte de abajo de la mujer efectivamente hubiera *echado* raíces en la tierra, y se desprendió de la estaca sobre la que había estado empalada.

Entonces, comprendí por qué el hombre había dicho que un lugar de ejecución no era fácil de encontrar en el desierto. Tenía que haber un árbol con la medida justa, que creciera derecho y sin raíces que obstruyeran. Ese palo había sido un pequeño *mizquitl*, del grueso de mi brazo y cortado a la altura de mi rodilla, y luego punteado hasta hacer una punta filosa en la parte de arriba, pero sin pulir la madera. Me pregunté si sería el esposo quien tan delicadamente había posado a su esposa en ese artefacto y si lo había hecho poco a poco o de un solo empujón para que no sufriera mucho. Seguí pensando en eso, pero no hice ni una pregunta.

Al llevarme a su campamento, los nueve hombres trataron de que me sintiera a gusto allí y me trataron con amabilidad todo el tiempo que permanecí entre ellos. Habían inspeccionado detenidamente mis pertenencias, pero no robaron nada, ni siquiera mi bultito de pedacitos de cobre. Sin embargo, creo que su comportamiento habría sido otro si hubiera llevado algo de valor o si hubiera llegado con un grupo de cargadores. Después de todo, esos hombres eran chichimeca.

Siempre que nosotros los mexica pronunciábamos ese nombre, lo hacíamos con desprecio, burla y odio, de forma parecida a cuando ustedes los españoles hablan de los «bárbaros» y de los «salvajes». El nombre chichimeca viene de la palabra *chichine*, una de nuestras palabras que significa perro. Cuando decimos chichimeca, nos referimos a esa gente como la Gente Perro y en esos momentos me encontraba entre ellos, entre esa gente sin hogar, sucia, siempre vagando en el desierto, no lejos de las tierras otomí. (Ésa fue la razón por la que me indigné tanto, cuando diez años atrás los rarámuri me tomaron por un chichimécatl.) Despreciábamos bastante a los chichimeca que se encontraban en esas tierras, al norte, pero era una creencia popular que todavía los había de un nivel más bajo. Se creía que todavía más al norte de donde habitaba esa Gente Perro, había tribus desérticas, aún más bravas, a las que les pusimos el nombre de teochichimeca, o como dirían ustedes, «Gente aún más perra». Y en la región del extremo norte, supuestamente vivían tribus todavía más peligrosas a las que nosotros llamábamos los zacachichimeca o como quien dice, «la más depravada Gente Perro».

Sin embargo, debo decirles que después de haber viajado a través de todas esas tierras desérticas, jamás encontré esas tribus inferiores o superiores entre sí. Todos eran igual de ignorantes, sin sensibilidad y con frecuencia inhumanamente crueles, pero ese cruel desierto era el que los había hecho así. Todos vivían en una suciedad tal que repugnaría a cualquier persona civilizada o a un Cristiano, y comían alimentos que revolverían el estómago a un hombre de la ciudad. No tenían casas, comercio o artes, porque continuamente se veían en la necesidad de vagar para arrancar del desierto el poco alimento que éste les daba. Aunque las tribus chichimeca entre las que viajé hablaban un náhuatl comprensible o algún dialecto parecido, no sabían el conocimiento-de-palabras ni tenían otro tipo de educación, y las costumbres y los hábitos de algunas de ellas eran repugnantes. Sin embargo, mientras que habrían horrorizado a cualquier comunidad civilizada si alguna vez la hubieran visitado, debo decir que los chichimeca se habían adaptado admirablemente a vivir en ese desierto inclemente, y sé de muy pocos hombres civilizados que hubieran podido hacerlo.

El primer campamento que visité, el único hogar que esa gente conocía, era un pedazo más del desierto del que se habían apoderado, porque sabían que había una corriente de agua subterránea que les era accesible al excavar un poco en esa parte de arena. El único aspecto hogareño que tenía el campamento eran las fogatas prendidas para cocinar y alimentar a las dieciséis o dieciocho familias de la tribu. A excepción de las ollas y utensilios muy rudimentarios, no tenían muebles. Amontonadas cerca de la fogata se encontraban todas las armas que poseía la familia, para cazar, así como todos sus aperos: un arco, flechas, una jabalina con su *atlatl*, un cuchillo para pelar, un hacha para cortar carne y demás utensilios. Pocas eran las armas que estaban bien punteadas o tenían filo de obsidiana, ya que esa piedra era muy difícil de encontrar en aquellas regiones. La mayoría de las armas estaban hechas de madera de *quauxeloloni* ya que ésta era tan dura como el cobre, y los chichimeca ingeniosamente le daban con fuego forma y filo.

Por supuesto que no había casas de construcción maciza, sólo dos pequeñas chozas temporales, que estaban construidas con palos de madera seca y sin mucho cuidado. Según me dijeron, en cada choza se encontraba una mujer embarazada esperando su alumbramiento, razón por la que ese campamento era más permanente que otros. Por permanencia entendían que podrían permanecer allí durante varios días, en lugar de una noche solamente. El resto de la tribu no necesitaba de ningún albergue. Tanto hombres como mujeres y niños, hasta los más pequeños, dormían en el suelo, como yo lo había estado haciendo en los últimos tiempos, pero en lugar de acostarse sobre una cobija de suave piel de conejo, como la que yo tenía, sólo usaban pieles de venado, viejas y sucias. También la poca ropa que llevaban puesta era de diferentes pieles de animales: taparrabos para los hombres, blusas sin forma para las mujeres, hasta el largo de la rodilla y los niños no llevaban ningún tipo de vestiduras, aunque ya estuvieran casi completamente desarrollados.

Sin embargo, la cosa más fea de ese campamento era su olor, que a pesar de que se encontraba en campo abierto era muy fuerte y penetrante y esa pestilencia era despedida por la misma Gente Perro, pues cada uno de ellos era mucho más sucio que cualquier perro. Se podía creer que uno no tendría por qué ensuciarse en el desierto, pues la arena era tan limpia como la nieve, pero esa gente estaba sucia de su propia mugre, de su propio excremento, de su propia negligencia. Dejaban que el sudor se secara en sus cuerpos y éste se incrustaba en las otras grasas y humores que el cuerpo normalmente despide, en capas casi invisibles. Cada arruga y curva de sus cuerpos era un patrón de mugre oscura: dedos, puños, cuellos, codos, las partes de atrás de las rodillas. Su pelo caía como en pedazos, no como hilos, y pulgas y piojos caminaban entre toda esa pestilencia. La ropa de cuero que cubría sus cuerpos estaba impregnada de olores adicionales de humo de leña, sangre seca y grasa rancia de animal. El olor que representaba todo ese conjunto era algo agobiante y aunque llegué a acostumbrarme a él, durante mucho tiempo me quedé con la opinión de que los chichimeca eran la gente más sucia que he conocido y además la que menos interés tenía por su limpieza personal.

Todos tenían nombres muy sencillos, como Zoquitl, Nacatl y Chachapa, que quieren decir Cieno, Carne y Tormenta, nombres que con lástima veía que no tenían nada de común con sus dueños; tal vez ellos los escogían para poder soñar y olvidar. Carne era el nombre del viudo que me había invitado al campamento. Él y yo nos sentamos cerca de una fogata atendida por varios hombres solteros y apartada de las de los grupos familiares. Carne y sus compañeros ya sabían que yo era un mexícatl, pero yo tenía la inquieta inseguridad de cómo referirme a su raza. Así que mientras uno de los hombres utilizaba un cucharón hecho de una hoja de yuca para servirnos un caldo indistinguible, sobre un pedazo de hoja de maguey, dije:

«Carne, no sé si sabes que nosotros los mexica tenemos la costumbre de llamar chichimeca a toda la gente que habita en el desierto, pero sin duda os debéis llamar a vosotros mismos de otra manera.»

Indicando el montón de fogatas dijo: «Los que estamos aquí somos la tribu tecuexe. Hay muchas tribus en el desierto, la pame, janambre, hualahuise y muchas otras más, pero efectivamente, todos somos chichimeca, ya que pertenecemos a la raza de piel roja.» Pensé que más bien, tanto él como los demás miembros de su tribu, eran de un color gris-mugre. Carne, tomando otro bocado del caldo agregó: «Tú también eres un chichimécatl. No tienes nada que te diferencie de nosotros.»

Me había dolido que los rarámuri me llamaran así, pero era aún más insultante que un salvaje del desierto reclamara parentesco con un mexícatl civilizado, aunque lo dijo de una manera tan casual que me di cuenta de que no lo había dicho con presunción. Era cierto que, debajo de su mugre, tanto Carne como los otros tecuexe eran de complexión bronceada parecida a la mía y a la de todos los que yo conocía. Las tribus y los indivuduos de nuestra raza pueden variar en tono de color, desde el más pálido de rojo bronceado hasta el pardo oscuro del cacao, pero por lo general, piel roja era la descripción más adecuada. Así que entendía cómo esa gente ignorante, sucia y nómada, obviamente creía que el nombre de chichimeca era derivado no del *chichine*, perro, sino de la palabra *chichíltic*, que quiere decir rojo. Para aquel que creyera eso, chichimeca no era un nombre despectivo, sino que sólo describía a cada ser humano que viviera en el desierto, en la selva, en cada ciudad civilizada de El Único Mundo.

Seguí alimentando a mi estómago agradecido y aunque el caldo estaba lleno de arena me supo muy sabroso, y meditaba sobre los lazos entre las diferentes gentes. Era obvio que los chichimeca en algún tiempo habían tenido un contacto positivo con la civilización. Carne había mencionado la confesión imprudente de su esposa con Tlazoltéotl en su lecho de enferma, por lo que me daba cuenta de que conocían a esa diosa. Más tarde supe que también adoraban a la mayoría de nuestros dioses, pero dentro de su aislamiento e ignorancia habían inventado un solo dios para ellos. Tenían la cómica creencia de que las estrellas son mariposas hechas de obsidiana y que la luz que brilla sobre ellas es sólo el reflejo de la luz de la luna sobre sus alas de piedra brillante. Así es que habían concebido una diosa: Itzpapálotl, Mariposa de Obsidiana, a quien consideraban la más grande entre todos los dioses. Bueno, debo reconocer que las estrellas son espectacularmente brillantes en el desierto, y que sí parecen aletear como las mariposas casi al alcance de la mano.

Aunque los chichimeca tengan algunas cosas en común con los pueblos más civilizados, y aunque interpretan el mismo nombre de chichimeca para implicar que toda la gente de piel roja está relacionada una con otra, eso no les impide el no tener compasión y de vivir a expensas de esos parientes lejanos o cercanos. Esa primera noche que cené con la tribu tecuexe, el caldo tenía pedazos de carne blanca y muy tierna, tan tierna que sus delicados huesos se deshacían y no podía reconocerla como de lagarto o conejo o alguna otra criatura que hubiera visto en el desierto, así es que le pregunté:

«Carne, ¿qué carne estamos comiendo?»

Él gruñó: «Bebé.»

«¿Qué bebé?»

Él repitió: «Bebé —y se encogió de hombros—. Comida para los tiempos difíciles. —Como vio que yo seguía sin entender, me explicó—: Algunas veces nos salimos del desierto para atacar aldeas otomí, y nos llevamos, entre otras cosas, a sus bebés. O peleamos con otra tribu chichimeca aquí en el desierto abierto. Cuando se aleja la tribu vencida, abandona aquellos niños que por ser tan pequeños no pueden correr. Como esos cautivos no nos sirven para nada, los matamos, les sacamos las entrañas y los curamos al sol o los asamos sobre un fuego de *mizquitl*, para que puedan durar mucho tiempo sin echarse a perder. Pesan muy poco, así que cada una de nuestras mujeres puede cargar con facilidad tres o cuatro a la vez, colgados de un cordón amarrado a su cintura. Se llevan, se preparan y se sirven, cuando, como este día, Mariposa de Obsidiana no nos manda animales para nuestras flechas.»

En sus caras, reverendos frailes, leo que esto lo ven como un crimen reprobable, aunque debo confesarles que aprendí a comer *cualquier* cosa comestible, con casi tanta satisfacción y con tan poco asco como cualquier chichimécatl, porque a lo largo de mi viaje por el desierto no conocí otra ley más grande que las del hambre y la sed. No obstante, no deseché del todo los modales y gustos diferentes del ser civilizado, ya que los chichimeca tenían otras costumbres alimenticias tales que ni la más grande privación me hubiera podido hacer participar.

Acompañé a Carne y a sus compañeros durante el tiempo en que sus vagabundeos los llevaron hacia el norte, la ruta que yo llevaba. Luego, cuando los tecuexe decidieron desviarse hacia el este, Carne, amablemente me llevó al campamento de otra tribu, los tzacateca y me presentó a un amigo con el que había sostenido batallas, un hombre llamado Verdoso. Así que me fui con los tzacateca mientras éstos se dirigieron hacia el norte, hasta que también nuestros caminos se desviaron y Verdoso, a su vez, me presentó a otro amigo llamado Banquete, de la tribu hua. Así pasé de tribu en tribu, con la toboso, la iritila, la mapimí, en el transcurso de todas las estaciones comprendidas en un año entero y pude observar algunas de las costumbres más repugnantes de los chichimeca.

En la última parte del verano y a principios del otoño, los diversos cactos del desierto dan sus frutos. He mencionado el gran cacto *quinámetl*, que se parece a un gran hombre verde, con muchos brazos levantados. Da la fruta llamada *pitaaya*, que es reconociblemente sabrosa y nutritiva, pero creo que se le aprecia tanto porque es muy difícil de obtener. Como no hay hombre que pueda escalar el *quinámetl* por la gran cantidad de espinas que tiene, la fruta sólo se puede obtener con la ayuda de un palo o garrote, muy largo, o lanzándole piedras. De todos modos, la *pitaaya* es una de las golosinas predilectas de los habitantes del desierto, un lujo tal que se come *dos* veces.

Un chichimécatl, ya sea hombre o mujer, se comerá rápidamente esos frutos redondos, enteros y con toda su pulpa, jugo y semillas negras, y luego espera lo que esa gente llama por el *ynic ome pixquitl*, o «segunda cosecha». Esto es cuando los que comieron esa fruta la digieren y segregan el residuo, entre el cual se encuentran las semillas de *pitaaya* no digeridas. En cuanto alguien ha vaciado sus intestinos, examina su excremento y busca en él las semillas, y las recoge para comérselas otra vez con muchísimo gusto, masticándolas y saboreándolas, para sacarles todo el sabor y valor nutritivo que les queda. Si un hombre o una mujer, encuentra algún excremento en el desierto en esa estación, ya sea de algún animal o buitre o algún otro ser humano, correrá a examinarlo y a buscar entre esa suciedad, con la esperanza de encontrar alguna semilla de *pitaaya* para apropiarse de ella y comérsela.

Esa gente tiene otra costumbre que encontré todavía más repugnante, pero para poder explicársela debo decir algo antes. Cuando llevaba en el desierto cerca de un año y llegó la primavera, yo me encontraba en ese tiempo entre las gentes de la tribu iritila, entonces vi que Tláloc sí escupe algo de su lluvia en el desierto, pues por espacio de un mes, de veinte días, llueve. Hay tanta lluvia durante algunos de esos días, que los charquitos ya secos se convierten en torrentes de agua, pero la gracia de Tláloc no dura más que un mes al año, y la tierra rápida-

mente absorbe el agua. Por lo tanto, el desierto florece brevemente durante esos veinte días, con flores en los cactos y en los
arbustos secos. También, es cuando la tierra permanece lo suficientemente húmeda como para que el desierto dé una planta
que no se ve en ninguna otra época del año: el hongo llamado
chichinanácatl; es un honguito rojo de tallo delgado con granitos blancos encima.

Las mujeres iritila recogían con rapidez esos hongos, pero
jamás los cocinaban con los otros alimentos que preparaban y
se me hizo muy raro no verlos. Durante esa misma primavera
húmeda, el jefe de los iritila dejó de orinarse en el suelo como
los demás hombres. Durante ese lapso de tiempo, una de sus
esposas siempre llevaba a todos lados una vasija especial de
barro. Cuando el jefe sentía necesidad de vaciar sus riñones,
ella colocaba la vasija y él orinaba allí. También, durante esa
temporada hubo otro detalle raro: todos los días algunos hombres iritila estaban tan ebrios que no podían ir de cacería o a
robar, y yo no podía imaginarme qué brebaje habían encontrado
y dónde, para poder estar así. Pasó un poco de tiempo antes
de que pudiera descubrir la conexión entre esos dos raros
detalles.

En realidad no había ningún misterio. Los hongos se guardaban para que solamente el jefe de la tribu los comiera; y quien
lo hace tiene una combinación de borrachera y de deliciosas
alucinaciones, como el efecto que da el *peyotl*. Ese efecto del
chichinanácatl sólo disminuye un poco al ser comido y digerido,
cualquiera que sea la magia que posee, atraviesa el cuerpo humano directamente hasta llegar a su vegija. Mientras el jefe se
encontraba en un estado de constante alucinación, con frecuencia orinaba en su recipiente y su orina era casi tan potente y
embriagadora como los mismos hongos.

El primer recipiente lleno de orina se le daba a los sabios
y a los brujos de la tribu. Cada uno se alborozaba por beber
de allí y poco después se tambaleaban o se tiraban al suelo con
una expresión de absoluta dicha. El siguiente recipiente lleno
se repartía entre los amigos más cercanos del jefe; el siguiente
era para los guerreros más grandes de la tribu y así sucesivamente. Antes de que transcurrieran muchos días, el recipiente estaba circulando entre los ancianos y hombres de menor importancia y finalmente hasta entre las mujeres. Al fin, casi todos
los iritila disfrutaban un momento de dicha, antes de volver a
esa existencia tan monótona que tenían que sufrir durante el
resto del año. Hasta a mí me pasaron el recipiente, como un
gesto hospitalario con un forastero, pero con mucho respeto rehusé de tal delicia y nadie se sintió insultado o enojado de que
no bebiera mi porción de esa preciosa orina.

A pesar de las muchas privaciones que tenían los chichimeca, debo decir que esa gente del desierto no es del todo depravada y detestable. En primer lugar, poco a poco me di cuenta
de que si estaban sucios, llenos de parásitos y apestosos, no era
porque *quisieran* estar así. Durante los diecisiete meses del año,
cada gota de agua que se pudiera sacar del desierto, si no se

bebía luego por bocas ávidas y sedientas, la que sobraba se debía almacenar para el día en que no hubiera ni siquiera un cacto semihúmedo y había muchos días como ésos. La temprana temporada de primavera, escasa y fugaz, es el único tiempo en que el desierto proporciona agua suficiente como para darse el lujo de tomar un baño. Siguiendo mi ejemplo, cada miembro de la tribu iritila aprovechó esa oportunidad para bañarse tan frecuentemente como les fue posible. Y ya sin la mugre habitual que les cubre, los chichimeca se parecen a cualquier gente civilizada.

Recuerdo que vi algo muy hermoso. Era casi el anochecer y vagaba a cierta distancia del campamento iritila, cuando encontré a una mujer joven tomando lo que obviamente era su primer baño en un año. Se encontraba parada en medio de un pequeño estanque de agua formado por la lluvia en la cavidad de una roca, y estaba sola, sin duda queriendo disfrutar del agua pura, antes de que los demás también la encontraran y quisieran compartirla y ensuciarla. No hice ningún ruido, pero la observé con mi vidrio, mientras se enjabonaba con la raíz de un planta de *amoli* y se enjugaba repetidas veces, despacio, como saboreando el novedoso placer de ese acto. Detrás de la muchacha, Tláloc estaba preparando una tormenta hacia el este, construyendo un muro de nubes tan oscuras como una pizarra. Al principio, la muchacha casi se perdía entre ese muro, de tan oscura que estaba por tanta mugre, pero mientras se enjabonaba y enjuagaba capa tras capa, su color natural aparecía más y más claro. Tonatíu se ponía en el oeste, y sus rayos acentuaban el dorado bronceado de su cuerpo. En ese vasto paisaje, que se extendía llano y vacío hasta donde se encontraba la pared de nubes oscuras, en el horizonte, la mujer era lo único brillante. Las curvas de su cuerpo desnudo estaban delineadas por gotas brillantes de humedad, su pelo limpio relucía y el agua que se salpicaba, se rompía en gotas que centelleaban como joyas. Sobre el fondo de ese cielo tormentoso, ella se distinguía entre los últimos rayos del ocaso, tan bella como un pequeño pedazo de ámbar sobre una tabla oscura.

Había pasado mucho tiempo desde que me había acostado con una mujer, y aquélla tan limpia y bella fue una poderosa tentación, pero me acordé de otra mujer empalada en una estaca, y no me acerqué a su charco hasta que con verdadera pena de mi parte, la muchacha se fue.

Durante todos mis vagabundeos con las diversas tribus chichimeca, me cuidé mucho de no jugar con sus mujeres y de no desobedecer las pocas leyes que tenían, ni de ofenderles de algún otro modo, pues siempre me trataron como a un compañero nómada igual a ellos. Jamás me asaltaron o maltrataron, me daban mi porción de lo poco que había para comer y de la poca comodidad que sacaban del desierto, a excepción, por supuesto, de las golosinas ocasionales que yo había declinado, como el elixir de orina. El único favor que les pedía era información: lo que pudieran saber acerca de los antiguos azteca y de su viaje hecho hacía mucho tiempo, y del rumor acerca de las provisiones o aprovisionamientos que habían enterrado durante su larga jornada.

Carne, de la tribu tecuexe; así como Verdoso, de la tribu tzacateca, y Banquete, de la tribu hua, me dijeron: «Sí, es sabido que tal tribu en una ocasión atravesó estas tierras. No sabemos nada acerca de ella, excepto que, como nosotros los chichimeca, llevaba poco consigo y no dejaba nada detrás.»

Era la misma respuesta desalentadora que había escuchado desde el principio de mi búsqueda y que seguí oyendo cuando les hice esa misma pregunta a los toboso, a los iritila y todas las tribus con las que viajé. No fue sino hasta mi segundo verano en ese maldito desierto —para entonces ya estaba harto de él y también de mis ancestros azteca— que mi pregunta recibió una respuesta un poco diferente. Me encontraba en compañía de la tribu mapimí y su lugar de residencia era la región más caliente y seca de todas las que hasta entonces había atravesado. Estaba tan al norte de las tierras vivas, que hubiera jurado que ya *no* podía haber *más* desierto, pero en verdad que sí lo había, y según me dijeron los mapimí era un terreno ilimitado y todavía más terrible de todos los que yo había visto. Naturalmente que esa información me llenó de angustia, así como también las palabras del hombre que contestaba mi ya vieja y cansada pregunta sobre los azteca.

«Si, Mixtli —me dijo—. Hubo una vez esa tribu e hicieron el viaje que describes, pero no traían nada consigo...»

«Y no dejaron nada atrás, cuando partieron», terminé amargamente.

«A excepción de nosotros», me contestó el hombre.

Durante un momento me quedé mudo tratando de asimilar esa información.

El hombre me sonrió con su boca desdentada. Se llamaba Patzcatl, que quiere decir Jugo, por lo que su nombre parecía una ironía; era el jefe de los mapimí y era un hombre muy anciano, encorvado y seco por el sol. Él me dijo:

«Hablaste del viaje de los azteca, que partieron desde su tierra desconocida llamada Aztlán y hablaste de cómo llegaron a su último destino muy al sur de aquí. Nosotros los mapimí y los demás chichimeca, durante todas esas gavillas de años, hemos habitado estos desiertos y hemos oído rumores de esa ciudad y de su grandeza, pero jamás ninguno de nosotros ha llegado lo suficientemente cerca como para verla. Así que piensa, Mixtli, ¿no te parece raro que nosotros los salvajes, tan lejos de su Tenochtitlan y tan ignorantes de todo lo que lo representa, a pesar de eso, hablemos el náhuatl que vosotros habláis?»

Pensé en lo que me decía y contesté: «Sí, Jefe Patzcatl. Me sorprendió y alegró ver que podía conversar con tantas tribus diferentes, pero no me detuve a pensar el porqué de eso. ¿Tú tienes alguna teoría que podría ayudarme a encontrar la respuesta?»

«Más que una teoría —me contestó con cierto orgullo—. Soy un anciano y vengo de una larga línea de padres que han llegado a vivir mucho tiempo. Pero tanto ellos como yo no siempre fuimos viejos, y en nuestra juventud éramos muy curiosos. Cada uno de nosotros hicimos preguntas y no olvidamos las respuestas. Así que todos aprendimos y repetimos a nuestros hijos lo que habíamos conservado en nuestra memoria sobre el origen de nuestra gente.»

«Debo de agradecerle, venerado jefe, que quiera compartir su sabiduría conmigo.»

«Quiero que sepas entonces —dijo el viejo Patzcatl— que las leyendas hablan de *siete* tribus diferentes, entre las que se encontraban tus azteca, que partieron hace mucho de esta tierra del Aztlán, El Lugar de las Garzas Níveas, en busca de un lugar mejor para vivir. Todas las tribus tenían los mismos lazos de sangre, hablaban el mismo idioma, reconocían los mismos dioses, observaban las mismas costumbres y durante mucho tiempo esa gente viajó junta amistosamente. Sin embargo, como puedes imaginarte, entre tanta gente y un viaje tan largo, surgieron fricciones y diferencias de opinión. A lo largo del camino, algunos se salieron de la caravana; familias, *capuli*, clanes enteros y hasta toda una tribu. Unos discutieron y se fueron, otros se detuvieron del cansancio tan grande y algunos se quedaron en algún lugar de su agrado. Me es imposible decir quiénes se fueron a tal o cual parte. Desde entonces, a través de los años, esas mismas tribus rebeldes se han desunido más y se han separado. Se ha sabido que tus azteca continuaron su camino hasta donde ahora se encuentra su Tenochtitlan, y tal vez otros hayan llegado tan lejos como vosotros. Pero nosotros no estábamos entre ellos, nosotros quienes ahora somos los chichimeca; por eso digo esto. Cuando tus azteca cruzaron las tierras desérticas, no dejaron ningún aprovisionamiento que pudieran utilizar en el futuro, no dejaron ninguna huella, no dejaron nada detrás de ellos, más que nuestro pueblo.»

Su narración bien podía ser cierta y resultaba tan desconcertante como la afirmación de mi compañero Carne, quien dijo que el término chichimeca era para nombrar a todos aquellos pueblos que tenían el mismo color de piel. La implicación era de que en lugar de encontrar algo de posible valor, como las supuestas provisiones y armas escondidas, sólo había encontrado una chusma horrible que buscaba parentesco con mis primos. Rápidamente hice a un lado esa espantosa posibilidad y dije con un suspiro:

«De todas maneras, me gustaría encontrar la tierra del Aztlán.»

El jefe Patzcatl movió la cabeza y dijo: «Queda bastante lejos de aquí. Como ya te dije, las siete- tribus llegaron desde su tierra, que está muy lejos, antes de empezar a separarse.»

Miré hacia el norte, hacia lo que se me había dicho que era el desierto aún más terrible y sin fin, y gruñí: «*Ayya*, quiere decir que debo continuar a través de esa maldita tierra...»

El anciano miró en aquella dirección y después con expresión perpleja me preguntó: «¿Por qué?»

Probablemente yo también le miré extrañado ante una pregunta tonta, sobre todo viniendo de un hombre a quien consideraba bastante inteligente. Le dije: «Los azteca vinieron del norte. ¿Adónde más podría ir?»

«Norte no es un *lugar* —me explicó, como si yo fuera un tonto—. Es una dirección y una dirección bastante vaga. Tú has venido demasiado al norte.»

«¿Entonces el Aztlán está *atrás* de mí?»

Se rió ante mi desconcierto. «Atrás, a un lado y más allá.»

Con impaciencia dije: «¡Y me está hablando de direcciones vagas!»

Riéndose aún, continuó: «Al seguir en el desierto durante todo tu camino, siempre te moviste en dirección noroeste, pero no lo suficientemente hacia el oeste. Si no te hubieras dejado llevar por la idea de *norte*, posiblemente habrías encontrado el Aztlán desde hace mucho, sin tener que soportar el desierto y sin tener que dejar las tierras vivas.»

Hice un ruido como si me estuvieran estrangulando y el jefe continuó:

«Según los padres de mis padres, *nuestro* Aztlán se encontraba al suroeste de este desierto, cerca del mar, a orillas de un gran mar, y con seguridad nunca hubo más de un Aztlán. Pero desde allí, nuestros antepasados y los tuyos vagaron en círculos durante todos esos años. Es muy probable que la última caravana de los azteca, como lo recordarán tus leyendas mexica, efectivamente *sí* los llevaron directamente del norte a lo que es ahora Tenochtitlan. Sin embargo, Aztlán se debe de encontrar casi directamente al noroeste de aquí.»

«Así que tendré que regresar de nuevo... hacia el suroeste desde aquí...», murmuré, acordándome de todos aquellos largos y tediosos meses, de la pestilencia y miseria que sin necesidad había tenido que soportar.

El viejo Patzcatl se encogió de hombros. «Yo no te digo que *tienes* que hacerlo, pero si *quieres* continuar en eso, no te aconsejaría ir más al norte. Aztlán no se encuentra allí. Al norte sólo hay más desierto, un desierto más terrible, un desierto sin misericordia, en el que ni nosotros los fuertes mapimí podemos vivir. Sólo los yaki de vez en cuando penetran brevemente en ese desierto, porque sólo ellos son más crueles que el desierto mismo.»

Con tristeza recordé lo que había pasado hacía diez años y dije: «Sé cómo son los yaki. Regresaré, Jefe Patzcatl, tal y como me aconseja.»

«Dirígete hacia allá.» Señaló hacia el sur, y hacia donde Tonatíu se caía, sin su manto, a una cama sin cobijas, detrás de las montañas gris blancuzcas que habían caminado conmigo, aunque guardando siempre su distancia, a través de todo mi camino en ese desierto. «Si deseas encontrar el Aztlán, debes ir hacia esas montañas, escalarlas, atravesarlas. Debes de ir más allá de esos montes.»

✠

Y eso fue lo que hice. Me dirigí al suroeste, hacia, sobre, a través y más allá de las montañas. Durante más de un año había contemplado aquellos cerros remotos y pálidos, y esperaba tener que escalar paredes de granito, pero al acercarme comprobé que era sólo la distancia lo que me había hecho creerlo. Las faldas de las montañas, que se levantaban del suelo desértico, estaban cubiertas con unos cuantos arbustos, los típicos del desierto, pero el pasto se hacía más denso y más verde al ir ascendiendo. Al llegar a las montañas verdaderamente altas, me encontré con verdaderas florestas y tan hospitalarias como los bosques de la tierra de los rarámuri. Es más, al atravesar aquellos cerros encontré aldeas en cuevas cuyos habitantes se parecían a los rarámuri incluso en la cuestión del pelo, y oí que hablaban un idioma similar hasta que me dijeron que efectivamente eran parientes de los rarámuri, cuya tierra se encontraba mucho más al norte, sobre esa misma cordillera.

Cuando por fin bajé de las alturas, del otro lado de la cordillera, me encontré en otra playa, muy al sur de aquella otra a la que había llegado después de haber hecho mi viaje involuntario por mar, hacía más de diez años. Esa costa se llama Sinalobola, según me dijo la gente de una tribu pesquera, cuya aldea encontré en los alrededores. Esa gente, los kaíta, no se mostraron hostiles, pero tampoco eran muy hospitalarios, simplemente eran indiferentes y sus mujeres olían a pescado. Por lo tanto, no me quedé por mucho tiempo en su aldea y me fui hacia el sur, por Sinalobola, esperando que fuera cierta la afirmación del Jefe Patzcatl de que el Aztlán estaba en algún lado sobre la costa del gran mar.

Durante la mayor parte de mi camino, me mantuve a la altura de las arenas de la playa, con el mar a mi derecha. Había veces que tenía que meterme un poco tierra adentro para evitar una laguna grande o un pantano en la costa o una selva enredada de mangles, y otras veces tenía que esperar en las orillas de los ríos, llenos de cocodrilos, hasta que un lanchero kaíta pasaba por allí y me llevaba al otro lado, en contra de su voluntad. Sin embargo, me movía usualmente con rapidez, sin detenerme y sin contratiempos. Una brisa fresca procedente del mar se mezclaba con el calor del sol, y después del ocaso las arenas de la playa retenían algo de ese calor, por lo que era muy cómodo dormir en ellas.

Mucho después de haber dejado las tierras de los kaíta, y no encontrado más aldeas en donde poder comprar algo de pescado, pude comer de nuevo aquellos cangrejos tamborileros tan raros que me habían asustado la primera vez que los encontré, años atrás. También, el movimiento de la marea me llevó a descubrir otro alimento marino, que puedo recomendar como un platillo delicioso. Me fijé que, cuando las aguas se retiraban, los estrechos de lodo o arena no se quedaban completamente quietos. Aquí y allá se veían pequeños chisguetes y fuentecillas de agua que brotaban del suelo en esos lugares. Llevado por la curiosidad, me dirigí hacia esos sitios y esperé a ver esos pequeños chisguetes, escarbé con mis manos hasta hallar lo que ocasionaba ese movimiento. Me encontré con una concha azul, de forma ovalada y lisa, una almeja tan grande como la palma de mi mano.

Me imagino que el chorrito de agua era su modo de toser y sacarse la arena de la garganta o lo equivalente a la garganta de una almeja. De todos modos, escarbando en esos estrechos, recogí una carga de almejas y me las llevé a la playa, con la intención de comérmelas crudas.

Entonces se me ocurrió una idea. Excavé un hoyo no muy profundo en la arena seca y coloqué allí las almejas, pero antes envolví cada una con hierba del mar húmeda para evitar que alguna arena o basura entrara, luego puse una capa de arena encima. Encima de eso encendí una fogata con hojas muertas de palmera y dejé el fuego fuerte durante un tiempo, después hice a un lado sus cenizas y desenterré mis almejas. Sus conchas habían servido como casas de vapor en miniatura, cociéndose en sus propios jugos salados. Abrí las conchas y me las comí, calientes, tiernas, deliciosas, y luego me tragué el líquido que contenía la concha y les digo que pocas veces he disfrutado de un alimento tan sabroso, ni siquiera en la cocina de palacio.

Sin embargo, mientras continuaba mi marcha hacia abajo sobre aquella costa interminable, las mareas ya no se alejaban de los estrechos lisos y accesibles, dentro de los cuales podía meterme a recoger almejas. Las mareas, sencillamente se levantaban o bajaban al nivel del agua, en los ilimitados pantanos que de pronto se cruzaron en mi camino. Éstos eran selvas de mangles, enredados unos con otros por el heno que colgaba de sus ramas y que se alzaban fastidiosamente encima de sus muchas raíces. Cuando la marea estaba baja, el pantano era una masa de lodo pegajoso y charcos apestosos. Cuando la marea subía, se cubría de agua mala. Continuamente, esos pantanos estaban calientes, húmedos, pegajosos, apestosos y llenos de voraces mosquitos. Traté de ir hacia el este para encontrar un camino alrededor de los pantanos, pero las ciénagas parecían extenderse hacia adentro, hasta llegar a la cordillera. Así es que atravesé aquel lugar lo mejor que pude; cuando era posible brincaba de un pedazo de tierra seca a otro, pero la mayor parte del tiempo tuve que vadear, incómodamente, el agua fétida y el cieno.

No recuerdo cuántos días me arrastré despacio entre ese pedazo de tierra, que sin duda fue el más feo, impenetrable y desagradable que jamás me había encontrado hasta entonces. Subsistí principalmente de hojas de palmera y *mexixin* y algunas otras hierbas que sabía que eran comestibles. Para dormir, cada noche escogía un árbol lo suficientemente alto como para estar fuera del alcance de los cocodrilos y de las neblinas nocturnas. Acojinaba mi lugar con todo el gris *paxtli*, heno, que podía reunir y me acomodaba sobre él. No me extrañó no encontrar a ningún otro ser humano, porque sólo el más torpe y tonto de los humanos hubiera aguantado vivir en aquella selva tan nociva. No tenía ni idea de qué nación sería la dueña de esa tierra, o si alguna se había molestado en reclamarla. Sabía que para entonces estaba más al sur del Sinalobola de los kaíta y supuse que me estaba acercando a la tierra de Nauyar Ixú, pero no podía estar seguro hasta que escuchara hablar a alguien en esa lengua.

Luego, una tarde, en medio de ese pantano miserable, me encontré con otro ser humano. Un hombre joven, con taparrabo, que estaba parado a la orilla de un estanque de agua lodosa, observándolo y sosteniendo una lanza primitiva hecha con tres huesos afilados. Me sorprendí tanto al ver a alguien y me sentí tan contento, que hice algo imperdonable, le grité muy fuerte en el preciso momento en que dejaba caer su lanza dentro del agua. Levantó la cabeza con rapidez, me miró con enojo y me replicó ladrando:

«¡Me hiciste fallar!»

Quedé asombrado, no por sus bruscas palabras, pues tenía razón de sentirse resentido al haberle hecho fallar su puntería, sino por no haber hablado, como yo había esperado, en algún dialecto poré.

«Lo siento», le grité menos fuerte. Él sólo volvió a mirar hacia el agua, sacando su lanza que había quedado atrapada en el lodo, mientras que yo me acercaba esta vez sin hacer ruido para no perturbarlo. Al llegar a su lado, dejó caer de nuevo su lanza y sacó una rana atrapada en una de las puntas.

«Hablas náhuatl», le dije. Gruñó y tiró la rana, junto a otras que estaban en un cesto mal hecho de enredaderas tejidas. Pensando en que a lo mejor había encontrado a un descendiente de los antepasados del jefe Patzcatl, de aquellos que se habían quedado en tierra nativa, le pregunté: «¿Eres chichimécatl?» Claro que me habría sentido muy sorprendido si me hubiera contestado que sí lo era; pero lo que me dijo fue todavía más asombroso:

«Soy un aztécatl. —Y se empinó sobre el estanque mugroso otra vez, y colocando su lanza en posición, agregó—: Y estoy ocupado.»

«Y tienes una manera muy descortés de saludar a un forastero», le dije. Su mal modo me dejó sin el asombro y la extrañeza que hubiera sentido de otro modo, al descubrir lo que aparentemente era un verdadero y actual descendiente de los azteca.

«La cortesía no debe ser desperdiciada en cualquier forastero que se extravíe tanto como para llegar hasta aquí —gruñó y ni siquiera se giró para mirarme. El agua sucia chapoteó al impulso de la lanza al pescar otra rana—. En todo el mundo, sólo un tonto visitaría a esta pestilente inmundicia, ¿no es cierto?»

Le hice notar: «Cualquier tonto que vive aquí, tiene muy poca razón para insultar a quien sólo viene de visita.»

«Tienes razón —dijo con indiferencia y tiró la rana dentro de su canasto—. ¿Y por qué estás aquí dejándote insultar por otro tonto?»

Dije con firmeza: «He viajado durante dos años y he caminado miles de largas-carreras en busca de un lugar llamado Aztlán. Tal vez tú puedas decirme...»

«Lo acabas de encontrar», me interrumpió con tono indiferente.

«¿Aquí?», exclamé perplejo.

«Un poco más allá —me dijo, indicando con un dedo detrás de su hombro, todavía sin molestarse en levantar la vista de aquel estanque podrido de ranas—. Sigue el camino que da a la laguna, y luego grita para que una lancha te cruce.»

Me alejé un poco de él y miré, y *sí* había un camino que atravesaba la fétida maleza, me dirigí hacia él apenas atreviéndome a creer que...

Pero luego me acordé que no le había dado las gracias al joven, así es que regresé a donde estaba parado, apuntando su lanza hacia el charco. «Gracias», le dije y con un pie le metí zancadilla y cayó sobre el agua pestilente. Cuando su cara salió de la superficie llena de viscosas hierbas vacié el contenido del cesto sobre él. Dejándolo escupiendo el agua de su boca y maldiciéndome, además de buscar por donde salir, me dirigí nuevamente hacia el Lugar de las Garzas Níveas, el perdido y legendario Aztlán.

No sé realmente, qué era lo que esperaba o tenía la esperanza de encontrar. ¿Quizás una versión menos suntuosa y más primitiva de Tenochtitlan? ¿O una ciudad de pirámides, templos y torres, aunque no tan moderna en su diseño? Realmente no lo sé. Pero lo que encontré era para dar lástima.

Seguí el camino seco entre el pantano y los árboles cada vez estaban más lejos uno de otro, el lodo de cada lado estaba más mojado. Finalmente, las raíces colgantes dejaron lugar a las ramas colgantes sobre el agua. Allí terminaba el camino y me encontré a orillas de un lago bañado de rojo-sangre por la puesta del sol. Era una gran extensión de agua negra, pero no era muy honda, a juzgar por las ramas y cañaverales que sobresalían de su fondo y las garzas blancas que se veían por todas partes. Directamente enfrente de mí, había una isla tal vez a dos tiros de flecha de distancia y levanté mi cristal para ver mejor el lugar, al que esas garzas le habían dado el nombre.

Aztlán era una isla sobre un lago, como Mexico-Tenochtitlan, pero ése era el único parecido. Parecía una joroba de tierra seca de poca altura, a pesar de la ciudad construida sobre ella, porque no se veía ningún edificio que tuviera más de un piso de alto. No había ninguna pirámide, ni un templo lo suficientemente grande como para distinguirse entre los demás edificios. Lo rojo del ocaso se veía entre el humo azul del fuego de los hogares. Alrededor del lago, navegaban muchas canoas hacia la isla y le grité a la que estaba más cerca de mí.

El hombre la impulsaba con un palo, ya que el lago no era lo suficientemente profundo como para poder usar remos. Él hizo deslizar la canoa hacia las cañas en donde yo estaba parado, luego mirándome con suspicacia, gruñó una grosería y dijo: «Tú no eres el... Tú eres un forastero.»

«Y tú eres otro aztécatl mal educado», pensé, pero sin decir nada. Me subí a la canoa antes de que pudiera alejarse y le dije: «Si venías por un cazador de ranas, dice que está ocupado y yo creo que así es. Hazme el favor de llevarme a la isla.»

A excepción de repetir la majadería, no protestó y no demostró ninguna curiosidad, ni me dijo nada mientras me transportaba a través del agua. Dejó que me bajara a orillas de la isla y luego se fue por uno de los varios canales que cruzaban la isla, el otro único parecido con Tenochtitlan, según pude ver. Caminé por las calles por un rato. Además de una calle ancha que circundaba la orilla de la isla, sólo había cuatro más, dos que iban a lo largo de la isla y dos que la atravesaban, todas pavimentadas de manera primitiva, con conchas de ostiones y almejas machacadas. Las casas y chozas estaban pegadas unas con otras, por las calles y canales, y aunque me imagino que tenían bases de madera, éstas estaban cubiertas con lo que parecía ser también polvito de concha.

La isla era de forma ovalada y bastante grande, como del tamaño de Tenochtitlan, sin su distrito norte de Tlaltelolco. Tal vez tenía la misma cantidad de edificios, pero como sólo eran de un piso, no había la misma cantidad de gente que habitaba en Tenochtitlan. Desde el centro de la isla podía ver el resto del lago que la rodeaba y comprobar que éste estaba a su vez circundado por todos lados por el mismo pantano fétido por el que había venido. Cuando menos, los azteca no eran tan degradados como para vivir *dentro* de ese pantano horrible, pero era como si vivieran en él, puesto que las aguas del lago no detenían las neblinas nocturnas del pantano ni tampoco la pestilencia, y mucho menos los mosquitos que caían sobre la isla. Aztlán no era un lugar adecuado para vivir, y me sentí contento de que mis antepasados hubieran tenido el buen sentido de abandonarlo.

Pensé que los habitantes actuales eran los descendientes de aquellos que habían sido demasiado débiles e indiferentes para dejarlo, y salir en busca de un lugar mejor en donde vivir. Y por lo que podía ver, los descendientes de los que se habían quedado no habían adquirido más iniciativa o creatividad en todas las generaciones transcurridas desde entonces. Parecían estar abatidos y vencidos por el medio deprimente que los rodeaba, y aunque lo resentían, se resignaban a él. La gente caminaba por la calle y me miraba sabiendo que era un forastero y sin lugar a dudas un recién llegado debía ser algo raro en ese lugar, pero nadie comentó con otro mi presencia. Nadie me saludó o gentilmente me preguntó si tenía hambre como obviamente se veía, ni siquiera se burlaron de mí por ser un intruso.

Llegó la noche y las calles empezaron a quedarse vacías y lo único que penetraba la oscuridad era el débil brillo que salía de las casas de los fuegos nocturnos de los hogares y las lámparas de aceite de coco. Había visto suficiente la ciudad y de todos modos ya era muy poco lo que se podía ver, por lo que en cualquier momento podía correr el peligro de caerme dentro de algún canal. Así pues intercepté a alguien que por lo visto llegaba tarde y trataba de pasar desapercibido, y le pregunté dónde podría encontrar el palacio del Venerado Orador de la ciudad.

«¿Palacio? —repitió sin entender—. ¿Venerado Orador?»

Debí de haber comprendido que algo como un palacio era inconcebible para esos habitantes de chozas. Y debí de haber recordado, que ningún Venerado Orador de los azteca había adoptado ese título hasta mucho después, cuando llegaron a ser los mexica. Así es que rectifiqué mi pregunta:

«Busco a su gobernante. ¿Dónde vive?»

«Ah, el Tlatocapili», dijo el hombre y Tlatocapili no quiere decir más que jefe de tribu, como el jefe de cualquier gentuza bárbara del desierto. El hombre rápidamente me dio instrucciones y luego dijo: «Ahora llegaré tarde para comer», y se perdió en la oscuridad. Por tratarse de gente aislada, en medio de ningún lugar y con tan poco en qué ocuparse, se mostraba muy estúpido pretendiendo llevar mucha prisa y tener mucha actividad.

Aunque los azteca de Aztlán hablaban náhuatl, usaban muchas palabras que me supongo fueron dejadas a un lado por los mexica hacía ya mucho tiempo, y otras que obviamente habían adoptado de las tribus vecinas, porque reconocí algunas de ellas como kaíta y un poré mal hablado. Por otro lado, los azteca no conocían muchas de las palabras náhuatl que yo usaba, palabras que supongo entraron en la lengua después de la migración, inspiradas por cosas y circunstancias del mundo exterior de las que éstos no sabían nada. Después de todo, nuestro lenguaje aún cambiaba para amoldarse a las nuevas situaciones. Tan sólo en los últimos años, por ejemplo, ha incorporado palabras como *cahuayo* por caballo, *Crixtanóyotl* por Cristiandad, *caxtilteca* por castellanos y españoles en general y *pitzome* que quiere decir puercos...

El «palacio» de la ciudad era cuando menos una casa decentemente construida, cubierta de yeso de concha reluciente y tenía varias habitaciones. A la entrada me encontré a una joven que me dijo ser la esposa del Tlatocapili. No me permitió entrar, pero nerviosamente me preguntó qué quería.

«Quiero ver al Tlatocapili —le contesté, con lo último que me quedaba de paciencia—. He venido desde muy lejos, sólo para hablar con él.»

«¿De veras? —me preguntó mordiéndose un labio—. Pocos vienen a verlo y él tiene menos interés en ver a alguien. De todos modos no ha llegado a casa.»

«¿Podría pasar y esperarlo?», le pregunté con impaciencia.

Lo pensó y haciéndose a un lado dijo decidida: «Pues sí podría, pero llegará hambriento y no querrá hablar con nadie antes de comer.» Empecé a decir que a mí no me disgustaría algo por el estilo, pero ella continuó: «Quería comer ancas de rana, esta noche, por lo que tuvo que ir a la tierra firme, ya que el lago es demasiado salado para que ellas vivan en él. Y no habrá encontrado muchas porque se le ha hecho muy tarde.»

Casi salgo corriendo de la casa, pero luego pensé: «¿El castigo por echar a un Tlatocapili al agua puede ser peor que pasar toda la noche tratando de evitarlo y vagando en esta isla miserable entre mosquitos voraces?» La seguí a un cuarto en donde una cantidad de niños pequeños y unos ancianos estaban sentados comiendo hierbas del pantano. Todos se sorprendieron al ver a un forastero, pero no dijeron nada y no me ofrecieron un lugar en su mantel. Ella me llevó a un cuarto vacío, en donde agradecido me senté en una tosca silla *icpali*. Le pregunté:

«¿Cómo se dirige uno al Tlatocapili?»

«Su nombre es Tliléctic-Mixtli.»

Casi me caigo de la silla baja, ya que esa coincidencia era estremecedora. Si él también era Nube Oscura, entonces ¿cómo debería llamarme? Seguramente que el hombre a quien había empujado al agua, me tomaría por un burlón si me presentara con *su* nombre. En ese preciso momento, del cuarto anterior me llegó el ruido de su llegada y su timorata esposa corrió a encontrar a su amo y señor. Cambié mi cuchillo a la parte de atrás de mi banda-cinturón, para que no se viera, y mantuve mi mano derecha sobre él.

Oí el murmullo de la voz de la mujer, luego el grito del esposo: «¿Que un visitante quiere verme? ¡Que se vaya a Mictlan! ¡Me muero de hambre! ¡Prepara estas ranas mujer, las tuve que pescar dos veces!» Su esposa murmuró suavemente otra vez y él gritó todavía más fuerte: «¿Qué? ¿Un forastero?»

De un tirón salvaje hizo a un lado la cortina del umbral del cuarto en donde yo estaba sentado. Efectivamente era el mismo joven y aún llevaba algunas de las hierbas del estanque en el pelo y estaba cubierto de lodo de la cintura para abajo. Me miró por un instante y luego vociferó: «¡*Tú!*»

Me incliné de la silla para besar la tierra, pero hice el gesto con la mano izquierda, ya que tenía la derecha sobre el cuchillo, cuando cortésmente me puse de pie. Entonces para mi gran sorpresa, el hombre soltó una gran carcajada y se lanzó para abrazarme fraternalmente. Su esposa y algunos de los parientes más jóvenes y ancianos se asomaron por el umbral, con sus ojos llenos de asombro.

«¡Bien venido, forastero! —gritó y siguió riéndose—. Por las piernas desplegadas de la diosa Coyolxáuqui, qué gusto me da volverte a ver. ¡Mira lo que me hiciste, hombre! Cuando al fin salí de ese pantano, todas las canoas se habían ido. Tuve que vadear a través del lago.»

Cautelosamente le pregunté: «¿Y eso te parece chistoso?»

Le dio más risa: «¡Te juro por la *tepili* seca de la diosa luna que sí! En toda mi vida dentro de este hoyo de agua, agobiante y deprimente, éste ha sido el primer suceso inesperado y fuera de lo común y te agradezco que hayas hecho algo fuera de lo usual, para romper este abismo de monotonía. ¿Cómo te llamas forastero?»

Yo dije: «Mi nombre es, hum, Tepetzalan», y utilicé el nombre de mi padre por esa vez.

«¿Valle? —dijo—. Jamás he visto un valle tan alto. Bueno Tepetzalan, no temas un castigo por lo que hiciste. Te juro por los pechos aguados de la diosa, que es un placer al fin, encontrar a un hombre con testículos debajo del taparrabo, porque si los hombres de mi tribu tienen algunos, sólo se los enseñan a sus mujeres. —Se volvió para gritarle a su mujer—: Hay suficientes ranas para mi amigo y para mí. Prepáralas mientras me quito algo de esta lama con vapor. Amigo Tepetzalan, ¿no te gustaría tomar un baño refrescante?»

Mientras nos desnudábamos en la choza de vapor, detrás de la casa, me di cuenta de que su pecho carecía de pelo como el mío, y el Tlatocapili dijo:

«Me imagino que eres alguno de nuestros primos del lejano desierto. Porque ninguno de nuestros vecinos habla nuestro lenguaje.»

«Creo que sí soy primo tuyo —le dije—, pero no soy del desierto. ¿No has oído hablar de la nación mexica? ¿Ni de la gran ciudad de Tenochtitlan?»

«No —contestó con indiferencia, como si no tuviera de qué avergonzarse por su ignorancia. Incluso dijo—: De entre todas las diversas aldeas miserables de estas tierras, la única ciudad es Aztlán. —Yo no me reí y él continuó—: Aquí nos enorgullecemos de nuestra propia suficiencia, por lo que pocas veces viajamos o traficamos con otras tribus. Sólo conocemos a nuestros vecinos más cercanos, pero no nos interesa mezclarnos con ellos. Por ejemplo, al norte de estos pantanos se encuentran los kaíta. Ya que vienes de esa dirección te habrás dado cuenta de que sólo hay una aldea, Yakóreke, y ésta es insignificante.»

Me alegré al oír eso. Si Yakóreke era la comunidad más cercana hacia el sur, entonces estaba más cerca de casa de lo que había pensado. Yakóreke era una aldea fronteriza de las tierras Nauyar Ixú, súbditas a la nación purémpecha, y desde cualquier punto de Nauyar Ixú no había una distancia demasiado grande a Michihuacan, y más allá estaban los territorios de la Triple Alianza.

El joven continuó: «Al este de estos pantanos están las montañas grandes, donde viven los cora y los huichol. Más allá de esas montañas está un desierto seco en donde han vivido, durante mucho tiempo en exilio, nuestros parientes más pobres. Pasan grandes períodos de tiempo antes que uno de ellos encuentre el camino hacia acá, hacia el hogar de sus antepasados.»

«Conozco a tus parientes pobres del desierto —le dije—, pero te repito que yo no soy uno de ellos, y también sé que no todos tus parientes lejanos son pobres. De aquellos que hace mucho se fueron de aquí en busca de fortuna en el mundo exterior, algunos sí la encontraron y una fortuna que va más allá de tu imaginación.»

«Me alegro de oír eso —dijo indiferentemente— y el abuelo de mi esposa también se alegrará, pues él es el Recordador de la Historia de Aztlán.»

Ese comentario me indicó que obviamente los azteca no conocían la escritura-pintada. Nosotros los mexica la adquirimos mucho después de emigrar. Por lo tanto, no podían tener ningún libro de historia o alguna clase de archivos. Si dependían solamente de un anciano, como depositario de su historia, quería decir que él era el último de un largo linaje de ancianos que habían transmitido esa historia a través del tiempo, de boca en boca.

El otro Mixtli continuó: «Los dioses saben que esta abertura en las nalgas del mundo no es un lugar agradable en donde vivir. Pero seguimos aquí porque tenemos todo lo necesario para sobrevivir. Las mareas nos traen mariscos, sin que tengamos que ir a buscarlos; el coco nos ofrece dulces y aceite para nuestras lámparas y su líquido se puede fermentar hasta hacer con él una bebida deliciosamente embriagadora; otra clase de palmera nos da fibras, con las que tejemos nuestra ropa; otra, harina, otra su fruta *coyacapuli*. Por eso no tenemos la necesidad de hacer trueques con ninguna otra tribu, y los pantanos nos protegen para no ser molestados por nuestros vecinos...»

Me siguió enumerado, sin ningún entusiasmo, la larga lista de las horribles ventajas naturales que tenía el Aztlán, pero yo dejé de escucharle. Me sentía un poco mareado, pues me daba cuenta del *poco* parentesco que en realidad existía entre mi «primo», que llevaba mi mismo nombre, y yo. Probablemente, nosotros los dos Mixtli, nos pudimos haber sentado y buscado entre nuestros antepasados hasta encontrar uno mutuo, pero nuestro diferente desarrollo nos separaba en ese aspecto. Nos distanciaba una inmensurable disparidad, en educación y criterio, ya que bien se podría decir que mi primo Mixtli vivía en el Aztlán de la antigüedad, el que sus ancestros no habían querido dejar, pues Aztlán seguía igual desde entonces; la cuna de seres sin ambición de aventuras y apáticos. Sin conocimientos en el arte de la escritura-pintada, eran igual de ignorantes en toda clase de enseñanzas: matemáticas, geografía, arquitectura, comercio, conquista. Eran más ignorantes que los primos que tanto despreciaban, los chichimeca del desierto, quienes por lo menos se habían atrevido a aventurarse un *poco* más allá de los horizontes restringidos del Aztlán.

Gracias a que mis antepesados habían dejado atrás ese pedazo de nada y habían encontrado un lugar en donde florecía el arte de las palabras, yo había tenido acceso a las bibliotecas de sabiduría y experiencias acumuladas durante toda una secuencia de gavillas de años por los azteca-mexica, por no mencionar todas las artes y ciencias de civilizaciones aún más antiguas. Cultural e intelectualmente, yo era tan superior a mi primo Mixtli, como lo sería un dios para mí, pero decidí no presumir de esa superioridad, pues no era su culpa el haber estado privado por la apatía de sus antepasados de las ventajas que yo había gozado, y en realidad sentía lástima por él. Haría lo que pudiera por convencerlo para que saliera de su maldito Aztlán y entrara en el mundo civilizado.

Canaútli, el abuelo de su esposa, el historiador anciano, se sentó con nosotros, mientras cenábamos. El viejo era una de las personas que había visto sentada comiendo, un rato antes, las repugnante hierbas del pantano y nos miraba con envidia, a nosotros los Mixtlis, mientras saboreábamos nuestro exquisito platillo de ancas de rana. Creo que el viejo Canaútli prestó más atención al movimiento de nuestras bocas al masticar que a lo que yo estaba diciendo. A pesar del hambre que tenía, entre bocado y bocado, pude relatar brevemente qué había sido de los azteca que habían salido del Aztlán; cómo se habían dado a conocer primero como los tenochca, más tarde como los mexica y por último como los amos y señores de El Único Mundo. El anciano y el joven movían de vez en cuando la cabeza con admiración o tal vez con incredulidad, mientras contaba hazaña tras hazaña, tanto en el campo de la guerra, como en el de la cultura y el comercio.

El Tlatocapili me interrumpió sólo una vez, para murmurar: «Te juro por los seis fragmentos de la diosa, que si en verdad los mexica son así de grandes y poderosos, tal vez sería mejor cambiar el nombre de Aztlán. —Pensándolo, farfulló dos o tres nombres—: El lugar de origen de los mexica... Primera nación dc los mexica...»

Seguí dando una pequeña biografía del Uey-Tlatoani de los mexica y luego una descripción lírica de su capital Tenochtitlan. El anciano abuelo suspiró y cerró sus ojos, como si quisiera ver en su imaginación lo que yo describía.

Yo dije: «Los mexica no hubieran podido progresar tanto ni tan rápido, si no se hubieran valido del arte de conocer las palabras. —Y delicadamente les sugerí—: Tlatocapili Mixtli, tú también podrías hacer del Aztlán una ciudad mejor y más grande, lograr que tu pueblo iguale a sus primos mexica, si aprendes a conservar la palabra hablada por medio de imágenes ilustradas y duraderas.»

Se encogió de hombros y dijo: «No veo que hayamos sufrido por no tener esos conocimientos.»

No obstante, su interés pareció despertar cuando le mostré cómo se podía grabar su nombre para siempre, para lo cual utilicé un hueso delgado de rana, dibujándolo en la dura tierra del piso.

«De veras, parece una nube —me concedió—, pero ¿cómo puede decir Nube Oscura?»

«Simplemente la iluminas con pintura oscura, ya sea gris o negro. Una simple figura puede ser usada en infinidad de variaciones. Pinta esta misma figura de azul verdoso, por ejemplo, y tienes el nombre de Nubes de Jade.»

«¿No me digas? —me dijo y luego me preguntó—: ¿Y qué es el jade?» Y un abismo se volvió a interponer entre nosotros. Jamás había oído hablar del jade o ni siquiera había visto ese mineral tan sagrado para todos los pueblos civilizados.

Murmuré algo sobre lo tarde que era y que les contaría más al día siguiente. Mi primo me ofreció una esterilla para acostarme esa noche, si no tenía inconveniente en dormir en un cuarto lleno de otros hombres, posibles parientes míos. Le di las gracias y acepté, y terminé mi relato explicándoles cómo había llegado a Aztlán: retrocediendo el viaje hecho por mis antepasados, tratando de verificar una leyenda. Me dirigí hacia el anciano Canaútli y dije:

«Venerado Recordador de Historia, quizá tú lo sepas. Al irse de aquí ¿se llevaron las suficientes provisiones y armas para poderlas utilizar en el caso de que regresaran sobre sus pasos?»

No me contestó. El venerable recordador de historia se había quedado profundamente dormido.

Al día siguiente me dijo: «Tus antepasados casi no se llevaron nada al irse de aquí.»

Había almorzado junto con toda la «familia de palacio», y habíamos comido unos pescaditos y hongos, asados juntos, y una bebida procedente de una hierba. Luego mi tocayo había salido, pues tenía unos asuntos cívicos pendientes, dejándome con el historiador anciano; esta vez fue Canaútli quien habló.

«Si todos nuestros recordadores han dicho la verdad, esa gente que partió sólo se llevó las pertenencias que pudieron preparar a toda prisa y unas pocas raciones de comida para su jornada. Y llevaban la imagen de su nuevo y perverso dios; era una imagen tallada rudamente en madera, acabada de hacer a toda prisa, por la urgencia de su partida, pero según nos contaron, eso ocurrió hace muchas gavillas de años. Me atrevería decir que tu gente ha fabricado desde entonces unas estatuas mucho más finas. Nosotros, la gente del Aztlán tenemos una deidad principal, diferente a la vuestra, y sólo tenemos una imagen de ella. Claro que reconocemos a todos los otros dioses y recurrimos a ellos cuando es necesario. Tlazoltéotl, por ejemplo, nos limpia de nuestras malas acciones; Atlaua llena las redes de nuestros cazadores y así con los otros, pero solamente uno es el dios supremo. Ven primo, permíteme enseñártelo.»

Me llevó afuera de la casa y caminamos a lo largo de las calles hechas de conchas de la ciudad. Mientras andábamos, su negros ojitos de pájaro me miraban de soslayo entre sus nidos de arrugas, era una mirada astuta y humorística, y él me dijo:

«Tepetzalan, has sido muy cortés o por lo menos discreto. No nos has dado la opinión que tienes acerca de nosotros, los azteca que quedamos aquí. No obstante, permíteme que lo adivine. Apostaría que nos consideras las piltrafas que fueron dejados en el Aztlán, cuando los más fuertes y superiores se fueron.»

En verdad que ésa era mi opinión, pero hubiera agregado algo para que no pareciera tan dura, pero él continuó:

«Tú crees que nuestros antepasados eran demasiado débiles y holgazanes o tímidos como para levantar su mirada ante una visión de gloria. Crees que temieron tomar ese riesgo y así perdieron su oportunidad. Crees que tus propios ancestros, por lo contrario, se aventuraron valerosamente lejos de aquí porque sabían con seguridad que estaban destinados a ser exaltados por encima de todas las naciones del mundo.»

«Bueno...», dije yo.

«Aquí está nuestro templo —me interrumpió Canaútli y se detuvo a la entrada de un edificio de construcción baja hecha con yeso de concha machacada, pero con muchas conchas buenas incrustadas, así como otras diferentes criaturas del mar—. Es nuestro único templo y es humilde, pero si gustas pasar...»

Lo hice y con mi topacio vi lo que estaba allí y dije: «Ésa es Coyolxaúqui— y con sinceridad y admiración agregué—: Es un trabajo excelente.»

«Ah, la reconoces —y el anciano pareció sorprenderse—. Hubiera creído que tu gente ya se había olvidado de ella.»

«Le confieso, venerable anciano, que ahora sólo se le considera como una diosa menor, entre todos nuestros dioses, pero su leyenda es una de las más antiguas y aún se recuerda.»

Para acabar pronto, reverendos frailes, la leyenda es ésta. Coyolxaúqui, cuyo nombre quiere decir adornada con Campanas, era una de las hijas de la diosa principal Coatlicue, pues cuentan que esta diosa, aunque ya había sido madre muchas veces, quedó encinta otra vez, cuando un día cayó sobre ella una pluma del cielo. (No me puedo explicar cómo se podría embarazar a una mujer de esa manera, pero cosas como ésa suceden en muchos cuentos viejos. Y al parecer la hija-diosa Coyolxaúqui también dudó de esa historia cuando su madre se la contó.) Coyolxaúqui juntó a sus hermanos y hermanas y les dijo: «Nuestra madre ha dejado que la vergüenza caiga sobre su cabeza y sobre las de nosotros, sus hijos. Por lo tanto, tendremos que matarla.» Sin embargo, el niño que estaba en las entrañas de Coatlicue era el dios de la guerra Huitzilopochtli. Al oír esas palabras, salió al instante del viente de su madre, completamente desarrollado y armado ya con una *maquáhuitl* de obsidiana, mató a su hermana Coyolxaúqui, haciéndola pedazos y tiró éstos al cielo, donde la sangre los fijó en la luna. Hizo lo mismo con sus otros hermanos y hermanas, lanzándolos también al cielo y desde entonces han sido estrellas, que no se distinguen de las que ya habían. Ese dios de la guerra recién nacido, Huitzilopochtli, fue desde entonces un dios principal de nosotros los mexica y ya no le dimos ninguna importancia a Coyolxaúqui. No le construimos ninguna imagen, ni templos, ni siquiera le dedicamos un día de fiesta.

«Para nosotros —me dijo el historiador del Aztlán— Coyolxaúqui siempre ha sido la diosa de la luna y siempre lo será, y la veneramos como tal.»

Como no lo entendí, se lo hice saber: «¿Por qué adoran a la luna, venerado Canaútli? Se lo pregunto con el mayor respeto, ya que la luna no es de ningún beneficio para la humanidad, a excepción de su luz nocturna, pero ni aun en sus mejores momentos es muy brillante.»

«Por las mareas —me explicó el anciano—, y ésas *sí* que nos benefician. Este lago nuestro está separado del océano nada más que por una barrera pequeña y baja de rocas, en la punta occidental. Cuando la marea sube, arroja peces, cangrejos y almejas en nuestro lago y todo eso se queda aquí cuando la marea baja. Atrapar esas criaturas necesarias para nuestra subsistencia es mucho más fácil de hacer aquí en el lago que es poco profundo, que en el profundo océano. Estamos profundamente agradecidos porque se nos provee con tanta prodigalidad y tan escrupulosamente.»

«Pero ¿qué tiene que ver la luna? —le pregunté extrañado—. ¿Usted cree que la *luna*, de alguna manera, causa las mareas?»

«¿Causar? No lo sé. Pero la luna sí que nos permite saber de las mareas. Cuando la luna está en su punto más delgado y luego cuando está completamente redonda, sabemos que en determinado tiempo después, la marea estará en lo más alto y escupirá peces de la manera más generosa. Con seguridad la diosa luna tiene algo que ver con eso.»

«Así parece», le dije y miré la imagen de Coyolxaúqui con más respeto.

No era una estatua. Era un disco de piedra tan redondo como la luna llena y casi tan grande como la gran Piedra del Sol de Tenochtitlan. Coyolxaúqui estaba tallada en relieve como ella debió de verse después de ser desmembrada por Huitzilopochtli. Su tronco ocupaba el centro de la piedra, o la luna, sus pechos estaban desnudos y colgaban sueltos, su cabeza degollada se encontraba de perfil en el centro superior de la luna, y llevaba un penacho de plumas y en la mejilla tenía marcado el símbolo de la campana, de la cual toma su nombre. Sus brazos y piernas, cortados, se encontraban distribuidos alrededor, adornados con pulseras para las muñecas y los tobillos. Por supuesto que no había escritura-pintada para ilustrar de algún modo la piedra, que aún tenía restos de la pintura original; un azul pálido en el fondo de la piedra, un amarillo pálido en algunas de las partes de la diosa. Pregunté qué antigüedad tenía.

«Sólo la diosa lo sabe —dijo Canaútli—. Lleva aquí desde mucho antes de que se fueran tus antepasados, desde antes del tiempo que se puede recordar.»

«¿Y cómo le rinden homenaje? —le pregunté mirando alrededor del cuarto, que obviamente estaba vacío, a excepción de un fuerte olor a pescado—. No veo ninguna señal de sacrificio.»

«Quieres decir que no ves sangre —me dijo el viejo—. Tus antepasados también buscaban sangre y por eso se fueron de aquí. Coyolxáuqui jamás ha exigido cosas como el sacrificio humano. Sólo le ofrecemos las criaturas más insignificantes, cosas del mar y de la noche. Búhos, garzas que vuelan en la noche y las grandes mariposas de luz. También hay un pequeño pez, tan grasoso que se puede secar y quemar como una vela. Los adoradores encienden esos animales cuando sienten la necesidad de comulgar con la diosa.»

Cuando salíamos de aquel templo maloliente a pescado, otra vez en la calle, el anciano continuó: «Quiero que sepas, primo Tepetzalan, lo que nosotros los Recordadores hemos conservado en la memoria. En un tiempo muy lejano, nosotros los azteca no estábamos confinados nada más en esta simple ciudad. Ésta era la capital de un dominio considerable, que se extendía desde estas costas hasta muy arriba, en las montañas. Los azteca estaban constituidos en muchas tribus, divididas en numerosos clanes, *capultin*, y todos bajo el mando de un solo Tlatocapili que no era como mi nieto por matrimonio lo es, un jefe de nombre nada más. Eran gente fuerte, pero apacible, contenta de lo que tenía y se daban por bien servidos con el cuidado que les prodigaba la diosa.»

«Hasta que algunas gentes mostraron más ambición», sugerí.

«¡Hasta que algunos mostraron debilidad! —dijo con voz cortante el anciano—. Las historias nos narran cómo algunos de ellos, que estaban cazando en las altas montañas, un día se encontraron con un forastero de lejanas tierras. Aquél se rió burlándose al saber la vida tan sencilla que llevaban y de esa religión que nada les exigía. El forastero dijo: "De todo el sinfín de dioses que hay, ¿por qué escogísteis adorar a la más débil, a la diosa que mereció ser humillada y degollada? ¿Por qué no veneráis al que se apoderó de ella, el fuerte, el bravo, el viril dios Huitzilopochtli?"»

Me preguntaba quién podría haber sido ese forastero. ¿Tal vez uno de los tolteca de los tiempos antiguos? No, porque si un toltécatl hubiera querido separar a los azteca de su adoración por Coyolzaúqui, habría puesto en su lugar al bondadoso dios Quetzalcóatl.

Canaútli continuó: «Ésos fueron los primeros de nuestro pueblo que se dejaron influenciar por la maldad de un extranjero y empezaron a cambiar. "Alimentad a Huitzilopochtli con sangre", dijo el extraño, y así lo hicieron. Y según nuestros Recordadores, ésos fueron los primeros sacrificios humanos hechos por gente que no se consideraba del todo salvaje. Celebraban ceremonias secretas en las siete cuevas grandes de las montañas, y tenían cuidado de derramar sólo la sangre de huérfanos indefensos y de ancianos. El extraño dijo: "Huitzilopochtli es el dios de la guerra, dejad que os guíe para conquistar tierras más ricas." Y más y más de nuestra gente escuchaba y atendía lo que les decía y ofrecían más y más sacrificios. El extraño les urgía: "Alimentad a Huitzilopochtli, hacedlo más fuerte todavía y él os dará una vida mucho mejor de la que podríais soñar." Y los incrédulos crecían en cantidades más y más numerosas, estando cada vez más insatisfechos con sus viejas formas de vida, pero cada vez más deseosos y ávidos de sangre.»

Dejó de hablar y se quedó callado un momento. Vi a mi alrededor a los hombres y las mujeres que pasaban por la calle. Era lo que quedaba de los azteca. «Vístelos un poco mejor —pensé—, y bien podrían ser ciudadanos mexica en cualquier calle de Tenochtitlan. No, vístelos un poco mejor y dales más fuerza de voluntad.»

Canaútli siguió narrando: «Cuando el Tlatocapili supo lo que estaba pasando en esas regiones fronterizas de su dominio, se dio cuenta de *quiénes* serían las próximas víctimas de ese nuevo dios de la guerra. Serían los azteca que seguían siendo pacíficos y que estaban contentos con su pacífica diosa Coyolzaúqui. ¿Y por qué no? ¿Qué conquista podría ser más fácil para los seguidores de Huitzilopochtli? Bueno, el Tlatocapili no contaba con un ejército, pero sí tenía un cuerpo de guardias, leales y valerosos. Todos ellos se fueron a las montañas y cayeron sobre los incrédulos, los sorprendieron y mataron a muchos de ellos. A los quedaron vivos, les quitaron todas las armas que poseían. El Tlatocapili los maldijo echándolos de su propia nación por traidores, tanto a hombres como a mujeres y les dijo: "Así es que queréis seguir a vuestro horrible y nuevo dios, ¿no? ¡Entonces, lleváoslo junto con vuestras familias e hijos y seguid a vuestro dios lejos de aquí! Tenéis hasta mañana para salir de aquí o seréis ejecutados." Y cuando llegó el amanecer, partieron en cantidades que ahora ya nadie puede recordar.» Después de una pausa, agregó: «Me alegra saber por ti, que ya no llevan el nombre de azteca.»

Me quedé callado y asombradísimo, hasta que se me ocurrió preguntar: «¿Y qué fue del forastero culpable de todo ese exilio?»

«Oh, naturalmente que ella estuvo entre los primeros que mataron.»

«¿*Ella?*»

«¿No mencioné que el forastero era una mujer? Sí, todos nuestros Recordadores han mantenido en su memoria que era una yaki fugitiva.»

«¡Pero eso es increíble! —exclamé—. ¿Qué podría saber una

yaki de Huitzilopochtli o Coyolxaúqui o de cualquier otro dios azteca?»

«Cuando ella llegó aquí, ya había viajado mucho y sin duda también había oído mucho. Con seguridad acababa de aprender nuestro lenguaje, y algunos de nuestros Recordadores han sugerido que también pudo haber sido una bruja.»

«Aún así —insistí—, ¿por qué había de predicar la adoración de Huitzilopochtli, que ni siquiera era su dios?»

. «Ah, en esto sólo podemos hacer suposiciones. Pero bien se sabe que los yaki viven principalmente de la caza de venados y que su dios principal es el que les proporciona esos venados, es el dios que *nosotros* llamamos Mixcóatl. Cuando los cazadores yaki observan que las manadas de venados disminuyen, llevan a cabo una ceremonia especial. Cogen a la mejor de sus mujeres y la atan como si fuera una venado vivo atrapado y bailan como acostumbran a bailar después de una cacería provechosa, luego le sacan las entrañas, la desmembran y se la comen como si fuera un venado. Es su creencia, sencilla y salvaje, que esa ceremonia convence a su dios de la caza a surtir con abundancia las manadas de venados. De todos modos, ya se sabe que los yaki se comportaban así ya en la antigüedad. Tal vez no sean tan salvajes ahora.»

«Creo que lo siguen siendo —le dije—. Pero no veo cómo eso causó lo que pasó aquí.»

«La mujer había huido de su gente, escapando a ese destino que le esperaba. Te repito que sólo son suposiciones, pero nuestros Recordadores siempre han supuesto que la mujer deseaba con toda su ansia que los hombres sufrieran de igual modo. Cualquier hombre, ya que su odio por ellos era indiscriminado y aquí encontró su oportunidad. Nuestras propias creencias tal vez le dieron la idea, porque no olvides que Huitzilopochtli había matado y desmembrado a Coyolxaúqui sin más remordimiento que el mostrado por un yaki. Así que esa mujer, al aparentar admiración y exaltación por Huitzilopochtli, esperaba que los hombres pelearan entre sí, matándose y derramando la sangre y las entrañas del otro, como se hubieran derramado las suyas si no hubiera podido escapar.»

Estaba tan horrorizado de oír eso que sólo pude exclamar: «¿Una mujer? ¿Entonces fue una *mujer* sin nombre ni importancia la que concibió la idea de un sacrificio humano? ¿La ceremonia que ahora se practica en todas partes?»

«Aquí no se practica —me recordó Canaútli—. Y nuestra suposición muy bien puede no ser la correcta. Después de todo, eso fue hace muchísimo tiempo, pero tiene todas las trazas de una idea femenina de venganza, ¿no es cierto? Y por lo visto dio resultado, porque *tú* has mencionado que, en el mundo exterior, el hombre no ha dejado de acabar con su prójimo, en nombre de un dios u otro, durante todas las gavillas de años que han transcurrido desde entonces.»

No dije nada. No podía ni pensar qué decir.

«Así que como puedes ver —continuó el anciano— aquellos azteca que se fueron del Aztlán no eran ni de los mejores ni de los más valerosos. Eran de los peores y menospreciados y se fueron porque se les echó de aquí a la fuerza.»

Como seguía sin decir nada, terminó así:

«Dices que buscas los aprovisionamientos que tus antepasados pudieron haber escondido en su ruta de aquí a tu tierra. Pues da por terminada esa búsqueda, primo. Es inútil. Aunque se les hubiera permitido a esa gente llevarse algunas posésiones cuando se fueron de aquí, no las pudieron haber escondido en caso de un posible regreso a lo largo de esa ruta. Sabían que jamás podrían regresar.»

No estuve muchos días más en Aztlán, aunque creo que mi primo, el otro Mixtli, quería que me quedara algunos meses más. Había decidido que deseaba aprender el conocimiento de palabras y escritura-pintada y trató de convencerme dándome una choza y a una de sus hermanas menores para que me hiciera compañía. Ella no se podía comparar en absoluto con una hermana llamada Tzitzitlini, pero sí era una muchacha bonita y una compañera lo suficientemente sumisa y que podía disfrutar. No obstante tuve que desengañar a su hermano diciéndole que el conocimiento de palabras no era algo que se podía aprender tan rápidamente como, por ejemplo, el arte de atrapar ranas. Le enseñé cómo representar cosas físicas dibujando figuras simplificadas de ellas y luego le dije:

«Para aprender cómo utilizar estas figuras y construir el lenguaje escrito necesitarás un maestro dedicado a tal enseñanza, y yo no lo soy. Algunos de los mejores están en Tenochtitlan, y te aconsejaría que fueras allí. Ya te he dicho dónde se encuentra.»

Gruñó como solía hacerlo al principio. «Te juro por los músculos tiesos de la diosa que lo que pasa es que ya te quieres ir de aquí. Y yo no lo puedo hacer. No puedo dejar a mi gente sin jefe, sin ninguna excusa más que mi deseo repentino de recibir un poco de educación.»

«Hay una excusa mucho mejor que ésa —le dije—. Los mexica han extendido sus dominios a lo lejos y a lo ancho, pero aún no tienen una colonia en esta costa norteña del mar occidental. Al Uey-Tlatoani le gustaría mucho saber que tiene primos ya establecidos aquí. Si te presentaras ante Motecuzoma llevando un regalo adecuado de introducción te podrías encontrar como el jefe oficial de una provincia nueva e importante de la Triple Alianza, una provincia que valdría más la pena de gobernar que ésta que ahora tienes.»

«¿Y dime qué regalo le podría ofrecer? —me preguntó burlón—: ¿Un pescado? ¿Unas ranas? ¿Una de mis hermanas?»

Fingiendo que apenas en ese momento se me había ocurrido, le dije: «¿Por qué no le llevas la piedra de Coyolxaúqui?»

Se tambaleó de la sorpresa. «¿Nuestra única imagen sagrada?»

«Motecuzoma tal vez no estime a la diosa, pero sí apreciará los trabajos de arte bien hechos.»

Jadeó: «¿Regalar la Piedra de la Luna? ¡Pero si lo único que conseguiría es que me odiaran y despreciaran más que a aquella bruja yaki de quien habla el abuelo Canaútli!»

«Todo lo contrario —le dije—. Ella causó la disolución de los azteca. Tú estarías efectuando su reconciliación, y mucho más que eso. Yo diría que la escultura sería un precio pequeño a cambio de las ventajas en reunir nuevamente a la nación más grande de toda la tierra conocida. Piénsalo.»

Así que al irme, cuando me despedía de mi primo Mixtli, de su bella hermana y del resto de su familia, sólo murmuraba: «Yo solo no podría rodar la Piedra de la Luna de aquí hasta Tenochtitlan, tengo que convencer a otros...»

Ya no tenía ninguna razón válida para seguir explorando, pues sólo estaría vagando por vagar. Ya era tiempo de que regresara de nuevo a casa, y Canaútli me dijo que llegaría más pronto cruzando en línea recta los pantanos hasta donde terminaban, y luego atravesando las montañas de los cora y huichol. Pero no les contaré mi trayecto a través de esas montañas, porque solamente eran más montañas, o de las diferentes gentes que me encontré allí, porque solamente eran montañeses, y a decir verdad me acuerdo de muy poco de esa parte de regreso a casa, porque estaba demasiado ocupado con mis pensamientos, acordándome de todas las cosas que había visto y aprendido... y desaprendido. Por ejemplo:

La palabra chichimeca no necesariamente tenía que significar «salvajes» aunque eso es lo que son. La palabra bien podría significar «gente roja», o sea, toda la raza a la que todos los humanos y yo pertenecíamos. Nosotros los mexica podríamos presumir de la acumulación de años de civilización y cultura, pero eso no quería decir que fuéramos superiores a aquellos salvajes. Los chichimeca, sin lugar a dudas eran nuestros primos. También nosotros los mexica, orgullosos y presuntuosos, habíamos bebido nuestra propia orina y comido nuestro propio excremento.

Muchas historias ostentosas acerca de nuestro linaje sin duda estaban tan llenas de errores que daban lástima o risa. Nuestros antepasados no habían salido del Aztlán para buscar osada y heroicamente un poco de grandeza. Simplemente habían sido unos crédulos ingenuos víctimas de los deseos de venganza de una mujer loca o bruja, ¡y un espécimen de una de las razas más inhumanas que hayan existido! Pero aun si esa legendaria mujer yaki nunca hubiera existido, quedaba el hecho de que nuestros antepasados se volvieron tan bestiales y tan odiosos para su propia gente que no pudieron tolerar más su presencia. Nuestros antepasados salieron del Aztlán a punta de espada, arrastrándose en la oscuridad de la noche, con vergüenza y desprestigio. La mayoría de ellos seguían siendo rechazados por cualquier sociedad decente, resignados en su exilio perpetuo, en ese destierro vacío. Sólo unos pocos de alguna forma habían vagado hasta llegar a la región civilizada de los lagos, y se les había permitido establecerse lo suficiente como para aprender, crecer, prosperar y poseer por sí mismos las riquezas de la civilización. Fue sólo gracias a esa buena suerte el que ellos... que nosotros... que *yo*... y todos los demás mexica no estuviéramos viviendo una vida sin porvenir, vagando en la selva, vestidos con cueros apestosos, manteniéndonos vivos al comer carne de bebé secada al sol o algo peor.

Por mucho tiempo caminé cabizbajo y despacio hacia el este, meditando en esos molestos y denigrantes descubrimientos. La mayor parte de ese tiempo, sólo podría ver que nosotros los mexica no éramos más que el fruto de un árbol sembrado en el lodo del pantano y alimentado con abono humano. Pero poco a poco llegué a una nueva conclusión, que las gentes no son una planta, no están fijadas a ninguna raíz, ni dependen de ella; la gente es móvil y libre de ir desde donde nacieron hasta muy lejos si eso les satisface, y subir en la vida si tienen la ambición y habilidad suficiente para ello. Los mexica por mucho tiempo nos habíamos enorgullecido de nosotros, y de pronto me sentía avergonzado de ello; pero ambas actitudes eran igual de tontas; nuestros antepasados no tenían la culpa ni eran responsables de que nosotros fuéramos lo que éramos.

Habíamos *aspirado* a algo mejor que la vida en los pantanos y lo habíamos logrado. Nos habíamos trasladado de la isla del Aztlán a otra de iguales posibilidades, y habíamos hecho de ella la ciudad más resplandeciente jamás vista; la capital había adquirido un dominio nunca alcanzado hasta entonces, era el centro de una civilización que continuamente se extendía a tierras que hubieran sido pobres y humildes de no mediar nuestra influencia. Sean cuales fueran nuestros orígenes o las fuerzas que nos habían motivado, *habíamos* escalado una altura jamás lograda por ningún otro pueblo, y no teníamos por qué discutir, explicar o justificar nuestros principios, nuestro arduo viaje a través de las generaciones, y haber alcanzado la cima que al fin ocupábamos. Para obtener el respeto de cualquier otro pueblo, bastaba con que nosotros solamente dijéramos: *¡somos los mexica!*

Enderecé mis hombros, levanté la cabeza y con orgullo me dirigí al Centro del Único Mundo.

✠

Sin embargo me di cuenta de que no podría mantener por mucho tiempo ese paso firme y orgulloso. Durante todo el transcurso del viaje había estado retrocediendo, descubriendo y deduciendo la historia pasada de las tierras antiguas y de sus gentes. Cuanto más me acercaba a casa, más me parecía que todas esas cosas de la antigüedad, que había estado escuchando, penetraban en mi mente, en mis músculos y en mis huesos. Sentía como si trajeran sobre mí el peso de cada una de esas gavillas de años que habían transcurrido desde el comienzo de la historia, y no creo que simplemente me hubiera estado imaginando ese peso. Caminaba más despacio y menos derecho de lo que acostumbraba y al escalar las colinas más altas me quedaba sin aliento, y cuando subía algún monte muy inclinado mi corazón latía, quejándose, como si se quisiera salir de entre mis costillas.

Porque llevaba ese sentimiento de portar encima el peso del mundo, no quise entrar a Tenochtitlan cuando me aproximé a la ciudad, sino que me desvié a un lado, pues era demasiado moderna para el humor que tenía. Decidí ir primero a un lugar más antiguo, un lugar que nunca antes había visitado, aunque sólo queda un poco al este de donde había nacido. Quería ver el lugar que había sido habitado por primera vez en toda la región, el sitio en donde se fundó la primera civilización que llegó a florecer aquí. Rodeé el valle hacia el norte y luego al sureste, permaneciendo en tierra firme, y por fin llegué a la antigua ciudad de Teotihuacan, El Lugar En Donde Los Dioses Se Reunieron.

No se sabe cuántas gavillas de gavillas de años ha permanecido en ese silencio soñador. Sólo quedan ruinas en Teotihuacan, aunque éstas son majestuosas, y ha estado así durante toda la historia escrita que se ha podido recordar de todos los pueblos que ahora habitan esta región. El pavimento de sus anchas avenidas hace mucho que quedó enterrado bajo la hierba y el polvo, y de sus templos no quedan más que las bases de sus cimientos. Sus pirámides todavía levantan sus cumbres sobre la tierra, pero sus puntas están achatadas, sus líneas y sus ángulos se han suavizado y desmoronado bajo la presión de los años y de los elementos. Los colores que brillaron alguna vez en esa ciudad, se han perdido; el resplandor del yeso blanco, el fulgor del oro batido, la brillantez de las múltiples pinturas e inscripciones, y sólo quedan las grises piedras de sus construcciones. De acuerdo con la tradición mexica, la ciudad fue construida por los dioses para reunirse allí mientras hacían sus planes para crear el resto del mundo, y por eso le dábamos ese nombre. Pero según la teoría del anciano Señor Maestro de Historia, de Texcoco, esa leyenda era sólo una idea romántica y errónea, ya que la ciudad había sido construida por hombres. Aun así, sigue siendo asombrosa, pues sus moradores fueron los ya desaparecidos tolteca y esos maestros artesanos hacían construcciones maravillosas.

Como yo vi Teotihuacan por primera vez —en un atardecer lleno de un colorido singular, con su pirámide levantándose sobre la tierra llana y el sol cubierto con una nueva capa de oro rojo, destacándose luminoso contra el púrpura de las montañas distantes, bajo el azul profundo del cielo— era algo tan maravilloso que uno podría creer que en verdad la ciudad fue construida por los dioses, o si fue hecha por hombres éstos se asemejaban a los dioses.

Entré a la ciudad por el ángulo norte y dirigí mis pasos entre los bloques de piedras caídas que estaban tiradas alrededor de la base de la pirámide que según nuestros sabios mexica había sido dedicada a la luna. Esa pirámide había perdido como una tercera parte de su altura, su cima ya se había desgastado, y sus escaleras ascienden a través de un sinfín de piedras sueltas. La Pirámide de la Luna está rodeada de columnas, caídas o en pie, y paredes cuyos edificios debieron de haber sido de dos o tres pisos de altura. A uno de esos edificios lo llamamos el Palacio de las Mariposas, por la abundancia de esas alegres criaturas pintadas en los muros interiores, todavía visibles.

Sin embargo, no me detuve allí. Caminé hacia el sur por la avenida principal de la ciudad, que es tan larga y ancha como un valle de buen tamaño, aunque muy bien nivelada. La llamamos

In Micoaotli, o sea la Avenida de los Muertos y, aunque está llena de hierbas por donde se arrastran las víboras y los conejos saltan, aún permite un paseo agradable. Tiene la longitud de una larga-carrera y está bordeada a ambos lados por las ruinas de templos hasta que uno llega al centro. Allí la hilera de templos a mano izquierda se interrumpe para dejar lugar a la increíble e inmensa masa del *icpac tlamanacali* que nuestros hombres sabios decidieron que era la Pirámide del Sol.

Si digo que toda la ciudad de Teotihuacan es impresionante, pero que la Pirámide del Sol hace que todo lo demás parezca insignificante, tal vez así tendrán una idea de su tamaño y de su majestuosidad. En todas sus dimensiones, fácilmente es casi el doble de grande de la Gran Pirámide de Tenochtitlan, y jamás he visto otra tan grande. Es más, nadie sabe realmente el verdadero tamaño de la Gran Pirámide del Sol, porque gran parte de su base está bajo la tierra depositada por el viento y la lluvia durante las edades desde que Teotihuacan fue abandonada. Pero lo que es visible y se puede medir, es impresionante. A nivel del suelo, cada uno de sus cuatro lados mide unos doscientos treinta pasos de esquina a esquina, y la construcción sube a la altura de unas veinte casas de tamaño regular, puestas una sobre otra.

La superficie total de la pirámide es tosca y desigual, porque las tablas lisas de pizarra con las que se recubría, ya se han aflojado de los remaches de piedra que alguna vez las sostuvieron. Y mucho antes que esas pizarras cayeran para convertirse en una mezcla de cascajo en el suelo, me imagino que ya se les había caído su capa de yeso blanco así como los colores de su pintura. La estructura se divide en cuatro niveles y cada uno de éstos se inclinan hacia arriba en diferentes ángulos que no están colocados así por una razón lógica, excepto que ese diseño sutil engaña la vista y produce un efecto de grandeza mayor de la que tiene el edificio en realidad. Por lo tanto, hay tres terrazas anchas alrededor de los cuatro lados, y hasta arriba hay una plataforma cuadrada sobre la cual debió de haber en alguna época un templo. Pero creo que sería un templo muy pequeño y poco adecuado para las ceremonias de sacrificio humano. Las escaleras que subían por el frente de la pirámide, ahora están en tan malas condiciones que los escalones casi no se distinguen.

La Pirámide del Sol da hacia el occidente, hacia el ocaso, y su frente flameaba como oro cuando llegué a él, pero en esos momentos las sombras alargadas de los demás templos, del otro lado de la avenida, empezaron a arrastrarse frente de esa pirámide y parecían unos dientes rotos queriendo morderla. Rápidamente empecé a subir lo que quedaban de los escalones, manteniéndome en la luz del sol durante toda la subida, justamente arriba y enfrente de los dientes de sombra.

Llegué a la plataforma de la cima en el mismo momento que el último rayo de sol dejó la pirámide, y me senté cansado, recuperando el aliento. Una mariposa nocturna subió volando de algún lugar y se posó cerca de mí en la plataforma, era una mariposa negra muy grande y movía sus alas delicadamente como si también estuviera recobrando el aliento después de la subida.

Para entonces, el crepúsculo caía sobre todo Teotihuacan y un poco después una neblina pálida comenzó a levantarse del suelo. La pirámide donde me había sentado, a pesar de su grandeza y tamaño, parecía flotar sobre la tierra. La ciudad que había estado resplandeciendo bajo los rojos y amarillos, se oscureció bajo azul y plata. Todo estaba somnoliento y apacible. Se notaba su antigüedad. Se veía más vieja que el tiempo, pero tan sólida que se sostendría así hasta cuando todos los tiempos se hayan ido.

Observaba la ciudad de punta a punta, a esa altura era posible usando mi topacio y podía ver los numerosos hoyos y cavidades en la tierra llena de hierbas que se extendía a lo lejos, a ambos lados de la Avenida de los Muertos; lugares en donde antes se habían encontrado más habitaciones que en Tenochtitlan. Y luego vi algo más que me sorprendió: a lo lejos unos pequeños fuegos brillaban. ¿Era que la ciudad muerta estaba volviendo a la vida otra vez? Pero entonces percibí que eran luces de antorcha, una larga fila doble de ellas, que se aproximaban por el sur. De pronto me molesté por no hallarme solo en la ciudad, aunque sabía que solían ir peregrinos con frecuencia, solos o en grupos, de Tenochtitlan, de Texcoco y otra partes para hacer ofrendas u oraciones en aquel lugar donde en un tiempo se habían reunido los dioses. Incluso, hasta había lugar especial para acampar y acomodar a esos visitantes; era una pradera en forma rectangular y encogida que se hallaba en el extremo sur de la avenida principal. Se creía que originalmente había sido el mercado de Teotihuacan, y que bajo tanto pasto y hierba seguramente se hallaban las paredes que lo encerraban así como su plaza empedrada.

La noche ya había caído para cuando la procesión de antorchas llegó a ese lugar, y durante un tiempo vi cómo algunas de las antorchas se detuvieron y se quedaron en un círculo, mientras que otras se movían por ahí y por allá, sus portadores ocupados con la tarea de levantar un campamento. Luego, al estar seguro de que ninguno de los peregrinos se alejaría adentrándose en la ciudad antes de que amaneciera, me giré en la plataforma para mirar hacia el este y ver el ascenso temprano de la luna. Era luna llena y ésta era tan perfectamente redonda y benignamente bella como la piedra de Coyolxaúqui en Aztlán. Cuando se encontró bien situada sobre los perfiles ondulantes de las montañas distantes, volví la vista para mirar a Teotihuacan, bañada en su luz. La suave brisa de la noche había despejado la neblina del suelo, y muchos de los edificios se veían bien delineados, hasta el más mínimo detalle por la luz azul-blanca de la luna, y proyectaban sobre el suelo azul, sombras tan negras como la muerte.

Casi todos los caminos y los días de mi vida habían estado plenos y llenos de sucesos, sin muchos intervalos de ocio, y esperaba que siguieran siendo así hasta el final. Sin embargo, me senté allí lleno de serenidad y fue como un tesoro para mí que incluso me motivó a componer un poema, el único que compuse en toda mi vida llena de acontecimientos o de historias; fue inspirado solamente por la belleza de la luz de la luna, por el silencio y la tranquilidad del lugar y del tiempo. Cuando había compuesto mi poema mentalmente, me paré erguido sobre esa imponente Pirámide del Sol y recité el poema, en voz alta, a la ciudad vacía:

Una vez, cuando nada era más que noche,
se reunieron en tiempos ya olvidados
todos los dioses más grandes, poderosos
para crear el amanecer del día y de la noche,
acá... en Teotihuacan.

«Muy bonito», dijo una voz que no era la mía, y me sobresalté tanto que casi me caí de la pirámide. La voz me recitó mi poema, palabra por palabra, lentamente como saboreándolo, y reconocí la voz. He oído cómo ese pequeño esfuerzo mío ha sido recitado por otras personas aun en tiempos recientes, pero nunca más por el Señor Motecuzoma, Xocóyotl, Cem-Anáhuac Uey-Tlatoani, Venerado Orador del Único Mundo.

«Muy bonito —dijo nuevamente—. Sobre todo porque a los Campeones Águila no se les conoce por ser un tanto poéticos.»

«Ni tampoco algunas veces por su valentía y caballerosidad», contesté con algo de pena sabiendo que él me había reconocido también.

«No se asuste, Campeón Mixtli —me dijo, sin ninguna emoción aparente—. Sus viejos compañeros pagados asumieron toda la responsabilidad por el fracaso de la colonia Yanquitlan. Se les ejecutó debidamente. Ya no queda pendiente ninguna deuda. Y antes de partir con guirnaldas de flores, me hablaron de la expedición que intentaba. ¿Cómo le fue?»

«No mejor que en Yanquitlan, mi señor —dije deteniendo un suspiro por los amigos que habían muerto en mi lugar—. Solamente comprobé que los legendarios aprovisionamientos de los azteca no existen y jamás existieron.» Le di una versión muy resumida de mi viaje, y de mi encuentro con el legendario Aztlán, y terminé con las palabras que había escuchado en varios idiomas por todos lados. Motecuzoma movió la cabeza atento y repitió las palabras, mirando hacia la noche como si pudiera ver ante él todas las tierras de su dominio, y la manera en que dijo las palabras sonaron macabras, como las de un epitafio:

«Los azteca estuvieron aquí, pero nada trajeron consigo, y nada dejaron atrás.»

Después de un silencio un poco incómodo, yo dije: «Durante más de dos años no he recibido noticias de Tenochtitlan o de la Triple Alianza. ¿Cómo van los asuntos aquí, Venerado Orador?»

«Tan desalentadores como usted descubre los asuntos del triste Aztlán. Nuestras guerras no son productivas. Nuestros territorios no han aumentado ni la palma de una mano, malos agüeros se multiplican, cada vez más misteriosos y amenazando con un desastre futuro.»

Me favoreció con un pequeño resumen de los eventos más recientes. Jamás había dejado de molestar y tratar de avasallar la terca independencia de la nación vecina de Texcala, pero sin mucho éxito. Los texcalteca seguían siendo independientes y más enemigos que nunca de Tenochtitlan. Las únicas batallas recien-

655

tes que Motecuzoma podía llamar modestamente productivas habían sido sólo saqueos vengativos. Los habitantes de un pueblo llamado Tlaxiaco, en algún lugar de la tierra mixteca, habían estado interceptando y robando las riquezas de tributo enviadas por las ciudades más al sur de Tenochtitlan. Motecuzoma personalmente había llevado sus tropas hacia allá y había convertido la ciudad de Tlaxiaco en un charco de sangre.

«Pero los asuntos de estado no han estado tan descorazonadores como las hazañas de la naturaleza —continuó—. Una mañana, hace como año y medio, todo el lago de Texcoco de pronto se puso tan turbulento como un mar tormentoso. Durante un día y una noche se movía, espumaba y se derramaba en las áreas bajas. Y sin ninguna razón, porque no había tormenta, ni viento, ni siquiera un temblor que pudiera ser el culpable de haber levantado las aguas. Y luego, el año pasado inexplicablemente, el templo de Huitzilopochtli se incendió y se quemó hasta quedar totalmente en ruinas. Se ha restaurado desde entonces, y el dios no ha dado muestras de ira. Pero ese incendio, encima de la Gran Pirámide, se podía ver por todos lados alrededor del lago, y aterrorizó a todos los que lo vieron.»

«Qué raro —contesté—. ¿Cómo pudo haberse encendido un templo de piedra, aun si algún loco le hubiera puesto una antorcha? La piedra no se quema.»

«Pero la sangre coagulada sí —dijo Motecuzoma—, y el interior del templo estaba lleno de pesadas costras de ella. La pestilencia permaneció por toda la ciudad muchos días después. Pero esos sucesos, sea lo que hayan pretendido ser, ya están en el pasado. Ahora viene esta maldita cosa.»

Apuntó hacia el cielo, y levanté el vidrio para mirar hacia arriba y gruñí sin querer cuando lo vi. Jamás había contemplado algo parecido; y tal vez ni lo hubiera notado si uno de mis ojos débiles no se hubieran fijado; pero lo reconocí como lo que nosotros llamamos una estrella humeante. Ustedes los españoles lo llaman una estrella con cola o cometa. Pero realmente era muy bella —como un pelito pequeño y luminoso de pelusa deshaciéndose entre las demás estrellas—, pero sabía claramente que era algo que debería verse con miedo, pues era una segura precursora de mal.

«Los astrólogos de la corte la espiaron hace como un mes —dijo Motecuzoma—, cuando aún era demasiado pequeña como para verse a simple vista. Ha seguido apareciendo en el mismo lugar en el cielo todas las noches desde entonces, pero siempre más y más grande y brillante. Mucha de nuestra gente no sale de sus casas por la noche, y hasta los más valientes se aseguran de que sus hijos permanezcan adentro, para no ver esa luz nociva.»

«¿Entonces esa estrella humeante obliga a mi señor a venir en busca de una comunión con los dioses de esta ciudad sagrada?»

Suspiró y dijo : «No. Bueno, no totalmente. Esa aparición en sí es problemática, pero no le he contado todavía la profecía más reciente y más peligrosa. Por supuesto que usted sabe que el dios principal de esta ciudad de Teotihuacan era la Serpiente

Emplumada, y que durante mucho tiempo se ha creído que él y sus tolteca tarde o temprano regresarían para reclamar estas tierras.»

«Conozco esas historias antiguas, Venerado Orador; Quetzalcóatl construyó una especie de canoa mágica y se fue lejos por el mar del este, jurando regresar algún día.»

«¿Y recuerda, Campeón Mixtli, que hace unos tres años usted, yo y el Venerado Orador Nezahualpili de Texcoco, hablábamos de un dibujo sobre un papel traído de las tierras maya?»

«Sí, mi señor —dije incómodo, de que se me recordara ese incidente—. Una casa de gran tamaño que flotaba sobre el mar.»

«Sobre el mar del *este* —dijo con énfasis—. En el dibujo, la casa flotante parecía llevar ocupantes. Nezahualpili y usted les llamaron hombres. Extranjeros, forasteros.»

«Lo recuerdo, mi señor. ¿Acaso nos equivocábamos en llamarlos extranjeros? ¿Quiere decir que ese dibujo representaba el regreso de Quetzalcóatl trayendo a sus tolteca de la Tierra de los Muertos?»

«No lo sé —me dijo, con una humildad poco común en él—, pero acabo de recibir noticias de que una de esas casas flotantes apareció de nuevo por la costa maya, y se hundió en el mar, como una casa que se derrumba de lado en un temblor, y dos de sus ocupantes fueron encontrados a orillas del agua, casi muertos. Si había otros en esa casa, se han debido ahogar. Pero estos dos supervivientes revivieron después de un tiempo, y ahora se encuentran en una aldea que se llama Tiho. Su jefe es un hombre que se llama Ah Tutal, y éste envió un mensajero-veloz para preguntarme qué hacer con ellos, porque él afirma que son dioses, y él no está acostumbrado a convivir con los dioses. Por lo menos no dioses vivos, visibles y palpables.»

Conforme escuchaba me iba quedando más asombrado. Y se me escapó el decir: «Y bien mi señor, ¿qué son dioses?»

«No lo sé —dijo de nuevo—. El mensaje era típicamente maya, inepto, histérico e incoherente, que no puedo decir si aquellas dos personas son hombres o mujeres, o una de cada uno, como el Señor y la Señora Pareja, pero la descripción, tal y como está, para mi experiencia no describe nada que se parezca a una mujer. Sólo dice que son de una piel increíblemente blanca, muy peludos de cara y cuerpo, y hablando un lenguaje incomprensible hasta para los más sabios de esas regiones. Seguramente que los dioses deben de ser diferentes y hablar también de forma distinta ¿no es así?»

Lo pensé y por fin contesté: «Me imagino que los dioses podrían asumir el aspecto que quisieran. Y podrían hablar cualquier lengua humana que gustaran, si realmente quisieran comunicarse. Algo que me impide creer esa teoría es que no creo que siendo dioses dejaran hundir su casa flotante casi ahogarse ellos también, como cualquier humano. Pero, dígame, Venerado Orador, ¿qué les ha aconsejado?»

«Primero, que guarden silencio hasta que hayamos verificado qué clase de gente son. En segundo lugar, que se les dé la mejor alimentación y bebida, junto con toda clase de lujos, y con la compañía del sexo opuesto si así lo desean, para que su descanso pueda ser placentero en Tiho. En tercer lugar, y más importante todavía, mantenerlos allí bien *encerrados* y sin que los vea más gente de la que ya les haya visto, para que su existencia sea lo menos conocida. La apatía de los maya posiblemente no se verá muy afectada por este hecho, pero si las noticias llegan entre la gente más inteligente y sensitiva, podría haber un disturbio y no quiero eso.»

«Ya he visitado Tiho —le dije—, y es más que una aldea, es más bien un pueblo de tamaño regular, y sus habitantes son la gente xiu, y de un intelecto muy superior al del resto de los maya. Estoy seguro de que obedecerán sus órdenes, Venerado Orador. Que ellos mantendrán el asunto en secreto.»

A la luz de la luna pude ver que Motecuzoma giraba su cara y su cabeza se inclinó fuertemente hacia mí, mientras decía: «Usted habla la lengua maya.»

«Sí, mi señor, hablo el dialecto xiu aceptablemente.»

«Y usted rápidamente aprende lenguas exóticas —continuó antes de que pudiera hacer algún comentario, pero parecía que estaba hablando consigo mismo—. Vine a Teotihuacan, la ciudad de Quetzalcóatl, esperando que éste o algún otro dios me diera alguna señal, alguna indicación de cómo debía afrontar esta situación. ¿Y qué me encuentro en Teotihuacan? —Se rió, aunque la risa se oía forzada, y otra vez se dirigió a mí—. Podría hacer méritos por delitos cometidos en el pasado, Campeón Mixtli, si se ofreciera hacer algo que está más allá de las capacidades de otros hombres, aun hasta de los más altos sacerdotes. Si pudiera ser emisario de los mexica, de toda la humanidad, nuestro emisario a los dioses.»

Dijo esas últimas palabras incrédulamente, como si por supuesto él no creyera que lo fueran, aunque los dos sabíamos que bien podría ser la verdad. La idea era como para quitar el aliento: el que yo bien podría ser el primer hombre en hablar —no predicar, como lo hacían los sacerdotes o conferir por medio de alguna ceremonia mística— realmente con seres que quizá no eran humanos, quienes tal vez eran eminentemente más grandes y superiores que los humanos. Que podría hablar y oír las palabras de... sí... de los *dioses*...

La impresión era tan grande que en ese momento me quedé sin hablar y Motecuzoma se rió otra vez de mi mudez. Se puso de pie, erguido sobre la punta de la pirámide, e inclinándose para poner su mano en mi hombro, me dijo alegremente: «¿Demasiado débil para decir sí o no, Campeón Mixtli? Bueno, mis sirvientes deben de haber preparado una buena comida. Venga y sea mi huésped y permítame alimentar su decisión.»

Así pues, bajamos con mucho cuidado por el lado iluminado por la luna. Una bajada casi tan difícil como la subida, y caminamos hacia el sur por la Avenida de los Muertos hasta llegar al campamento, que daba hacia la tercera y más pequeña pirámide de Teotihuacan, donde se hallaban las fogatas, y se estaba preparando la comida, y las esterillas cubiertas con telas para mosquitos se estaban colocando por cien o más sirvientes, sacerdotes, campeones y demás cortesanos que habían acompañado a Motecuzoma. Allí encontramos al sacerdote principal, quien, según recordé, había sido el que había oficiado en la ceremonia del Fuego Nuevo, cinco años antes. Sólo me miró de pasada y empezó a decir con pomposa importancia:

«Venerado Orador, para las peticiones de mañana a los antiguos dioses de este lugar, yo le sugiero el primer rito de...»

«No se moleste —lo interrumpió Motecuzoma—, Ahora ya no hay necesidad de hacer esa petición. Regresaremos a Tenochtitlan en cuanto nos levantemos mañana.»

«Pero, mi señor —protestó el sacerdote—. Después de venir hasta acá, con toda su caravana y augustos invitados...»

«Algunas veces, los dioses voluntariamente nos dan su bendición antes de que se lo pidamos —dijo Motecuzoma y dejó caer sobre mí una mirada inequívoca—. Claro, que nunca podemos estar seguros si ese gesto es en son de burla o seriamente.»

Dicho esto, él y yo nos sentamos a comer entre un círculo formado por sus guardias de palacio y otros campeones, muchos de los cuales me reconocieron y me saludaron. Aunque yo vestía de forma harapienta, estaba sucio y me sentía fuera de lugar entre esa asamblea llena de colorido alhajado y emplumado, el UeyTlatoani me hizo sentar en el cojín de honor, que estaba a su derecha. Mientras comíamos y yo trataba heroicamente de contener mi hambre voraz, el Venerado Orador habló por un tiempo sobre mi próxima «misión a los dioses». Me sugirió algunas preguntas que podía hacerles cuando ya dominara su lenguaje, y otras que sería mejor que evitara. Esperé a que estuviera masticando un bocado de codorniz asada, y entonces me atreví a decirle:

«Mi señor, quisiera hacerle una petición. ¿Podría ir a casa por lo menos por un corto tiempo, antes de emprender el viaje nuevamente? Comencé este último en pleno vigor de vida, pero le confieso que siento que he regresado a casa a la edad de los nuncas.»

«Oh, sí —me dijo comprensivo el Venerado Orador—. No tiene por qué disculparse; es el destino normal del hombre. Todos llegamos siempre a la *ueyquin ayquic.*»

Por sus expresiones, reverendos escribas, me doy cuenta de que no entienden el significado del *ueyquin ayquic,* «la edad de los nuncas». No, no, mis señores, no quiere decir que sea una edad específica en años. A algunas personas les llega antes y a otras después. Tomando en cuenta que entonces tenía cuarenta y cinco años, bien entrados en la madurez, había eludido sus garras más tiempo que la mayoría de los hombres. La *ueyquin ayquic* es la edad en que un hombre empieza a murmurarse a sí mismo. «*Ayya,* los montes nunca me habían parecido tan altos...», o «*Ayya,* mi espalda nunca me había dolido antes...», o «*Ayya,* nunca antes me había encontrado una cana en el pelo...»

Ésa es la edad de los nuncas.

Motecuzoma continuó: «Por supuesto, Campeón Mitxtli, tome el tiempo necesario para recobrar sus fuerzas antes de partir hacia el sur. Y esta vez no irá a pie ni solo. Un emisario enviado por los mexica debe ir con pompa, sobre todo si va a conferenciar con los dioses. Le proporcionaré una majestuosa silla de manos con fuertes cargadores y una guardia armada, y llevará puesto un rico traje de campeón Águila.»

Mientras nos preparábamos para dormirnos a la luz de la luna y de las fogatas que se iban apagando, Motecuzoma mandó llamar a uno de sus mensajeros-veloces. Le dio instrucciones, y el corredor salió inmediatamente para Tenochtitlan, a avisar a mi casa de mi próxima llegada. Me pareció un gesto gentil y bien intencionado de parte del Venerado Orador, el que mis sirvientes y mi esposa Beu Ribé tuvieran tiempo de preparar una recepción a mi llegada, pero el verdadero efecto de esa recepción casi me mata y casi mato a Beu.

Al mediodía del día siguiente caminaba ya por las calles de Tenochtitlan. Y como casi parecía un leproso limosnero cualquiera e iba inmodestamente desnudo como cualquier huaxtécatl orgulloso de sus genitales, la gente que pasaba, o me rodeaba ampliamente o ostentosamente se recogían sus mantos para evitar el contacto conmigo. Pero al llegar a mi barrio en Izacualco me empecé a encontrar con vecinos que me recordaban y me saludaban con suficiente cortesía. Entonces vi mi casa y a su ama parada, con la puerta abierta, sobre los escalores de la calle, y levanté mi topacio para verla, y casi me caigo allí mismo en la calle. Era Zyanya esperándome.

Estaba parada bajo la brillante luz del día vestida solamente con una blusa y una falda, su hermosa cabeza descubierta y su único y hermoso mechón blanco se distinguían claramente en su pelo agitado por el viento. La impresión de esa ilusión fue como la de un golpe recibido en todos mis sentidos y mis órganos. De pronto parecía como si viera, dentro del agua en medio de un vórtice, las casas de la calle, y la gente se movía como en círculos a mi alrededor. Mi garganta se obstruyó y mi aliento ni entraba ni salía. Mi corazón latió primero de alegría y luego frenéticamente protestando por la presión: me golpeaba mucho más fuerte de lo que lo había hecho últimamente durante el extenuante ascenso a las montañas. Me tambaleé y tuve que cogerme de un poste de antorcha que estaba cerca.

«¡Zaa! —gritó ella, cogiéndome. No la había visto correr hacia mí—. ¿Estás herido? ¿Estás enfermo?»

«¿Eres de verdad Zyanya?», alcancé a decirle con una voz débil que apenas podía salir de mi garganta. La calle según mi vista se había oscurecido, pero aún podía ver el brillo de aquel mechón de pelo blanco en su cabeza.

«¡Querido mío! —fue todo lo que ella dijo—. Mi viejo... y querido... Zaa...», y me apretó contra su pecho suave y caliente.

Dije lo que era obvio a mi mente turbada. «Entonces no estás aquí. Yo estoy allá. —Me reí de la dicha de estar muerto—. Me has esperado durante todo este tiempo... en la frontera de ese lejano país...»

«No, no, no estás muerto —me susurró—. Sólo estás cansado. Y yo fui una imprudente. Tenía que haber aplazado la sorpresa.»

«¿Sorpresa?», pregunté. Recobrando mi visión, levanté los ojos de su pecho a su cara. Era la cara de Zyanya, y era tan bella que estaba por encima de la belleza de otras mujeres, pero no era la Zyanya de veinte años que yo recordaba. Su rostro era tan viejo como el mío, y los muertos no envejecen. En alguna parte, Zyanya aún era joven, y Cózcalt más joven todavía, y el anciano Glotón de Sangre seguía sin envejecer más, y mi hija Nochipa sería siempre una niña de doce años. Sólo yo, Nube Oscura, había quedado en este mundo para tolerar la edad más oscura y nublada de los nuncas.

Beu Ribé debió de ver algo terrorífico en mis ojos. Me soltó y con cautela caminó hacia atrás. El loco latir de mi corazón y todos los demás síntomas provocados por la impresión habían cesado, sólo sentía frío por todas partes. Me paré bien derecho y dije con aspereza:

«Esta vez lo pretendiste deliberadamente. Esta vez lo hiciste a propósito.»

Seguía alejándose despacio y me dijo con una voz que temblaba: «Pensé... tenía la esperanza de agradarte, que si tu esposa se veía otra vez como tú la habías amado a ella... —Cuando su voz llegó a un susurro, aclaró su garganta para decir—: Zaa, tú sabías que la única diferencia visible entre nosotros era su cabello.»

Dije entre dientes: «¡La única diferencia!» Y descolgué de mi hombro mi bolsa de agua, vacía.

Beu continuó desesperadamente: «Así que anoche, cuando el mensajero me informó de tu regreso, preparé agua de cal y me pinté este mechón. Yo pensé que así... me aceptarías... por lo menos por un tiempo...»

«¡Pude haber muerto! —le grité—, y lo hubiera hecho con gusto, ¡pero no por ti! Te prometo que éste será el último de tus malditos trucos, de las hechicerías e indignidades que has dejado caer sobre mí.»

Tomé con mi mano derecha las correas de mi bolsa de cuero y con la izquierda cogí a Beu por la muñeca y se la retorcí hasta que la hice caer en tierra.

Ella gritó absurdamente: «¡Zaa, ahora tú también tienes canas en tu pelo!»

Nuestros vecinos y algunos transeúntes se detuvieron en la calle sonrientes, cuando vieron a mi esposa correr a abrazar al viajero que regresaba a casa, pero dejaron de hacerdo cuando empecé a golpearla. En verdad que habría podido matarla a golpes si hubiera tenido la fuerza suficiente para hacerlo, pero estaba cansado, como ella misma había dicho; yo ya no era joven como ella había hecho notar.

Aun así, las correas como látigos desgarraron la delgada tela de su ropa, convirtiéndola en tiras y esparciéndola alrededor, de tal manera que ella quedó allí casi desnuda, a excepción de unos cuantos jirones que le colgaban del cuello. Su cuerpo, de un cobre amielado, que pudo haber sido el de Zyanya, quedó marcado con rojos latigazos, pero no tuve suficientes fuerzas como para abrirle la piel y sacarle sangre. Cuando ya no pude azotarla más, ella ya se había desmayado por el dolor. La dejé allí tirada, desnuda, a la vista de todo el que la quisiera ver, y tambaleando subí la escalera de mi casa, otra vez sintiéndome medio muerto.

La vieja Turquesa, más anciana aún, observaba amedrentada desde la puerta. Como no me quedaba voz, sólo pude gesticular para que fuera a atender a su ama. De algún modo pude subir al segundo piso de la casa y me encontré con que sólo estaba preparada una recámara: la que había sido mía y de Zyanya. La cama estaba cubierta de suaves cobijas y la de encima estaba desdoblada por ambos lados. Maldiciendo, me arrastré al cuarto de los huéspedes e hice un gran esfuerzo para sacar y desenrollar las cobijas guardadas ahí, para luego tirarme de cabeza en ellas. Me sumí en el sueño, como algún día caeré en la muerte y dentro de los brazos de Zyanya.

Dormí hasta el mediodía del día siguiente y cuando desperté la vieja Turquesa se encontraba espiando ansiosamente, fuera de mi puerta; la de la recámara principal estaba cerrada y no se oía ningún ruido. No pregunté por la salud de Beu, sino que le ordené a Turquesa que preparara mi baño y las piedras para el cuarto de vapor, que sacara ropa limpia y que empezara a cocinar, pero que cocinara una comida abundante. Cuando por varias veces me bañé y sudé alternativamente, me vestí, bajé y me senté a beber y a comer como por tres hombres.

Mientras la sirvienta me servía un segundo plato y tal vez una tercera taza de *chocólatl*, le dije: «Voy a necesitar la armadura acojinada, las insignias y las armas de mi traje de campeón Águila. Cuando termines de servirme, sácalos de donde estén guardados y encárgate de que sean desempolvados y de que todas sus plumas estén arregladas y acomodadas, y que todo esté en orden. Pero ahora mándame a Estrella Cantadora.»

Con voz temblorosa me dijo: «Siento decirle, mi amo, que Estrella Cantadora murió de frío el invierno pasado.»

Le dije que me entristecía saberlo. «Entonces tendrás que hacerlo tú, Turquesa, antes de que arregles mi traje. Irás al palacio...»

Me interrumpió reculando: «¿Yo, mi amo? ¿Ir al palacio? ¡Pero los guardias ni siquiera me dejarán acercarme a la gran puerta!»

«Si les dices que vas de mi parte te dejarán pasar. —Y agregué con impaciencia—: Debes darle un recado al Uey-Tlatoani y a nadie más.»

Me interrumpió otra vez: «¿Al Uey...?»

«¡Calla, mujer! Esto es lo que debes decirle. Memorízalo. Sólo esto. "El emisario del Venerado Orador no requiere de más descanso. Nube Oscura ya está preparado para empezar su misión, tan pronto como el Señor Orador pueda tener lista su escolta."»

Y así sin haber visto a Luna que Espera otra vez, fui al encuentro de los dioses que esperaban.

I H S

✠

S. C. C. M.

Santificada, Cesárea, Católica Majestad,
el Emperador Don Carlos, nuestro Señor Rey:

Muy Altiva Majestad, Preeminente entre Príncipes, desde esta
Ciudad de Mexico, capital de la Nueva España, en la fiesta de
Corpus Christi, en el año de Nuestro Señor Jesucristo, de mil
quinientos treinta y uno, os saludo.

Nos, escribimos con tristeza, ira y contrición. En nuestra última carta, nos, expresamos con alegría la observación sabia de
nuestro Soberano acerca del posible, no posible, sino aparentemente irrefutable, parecido entre la deidad de los indios llamada Quetzalcóatl y nuestro Cristiano Santo Tomás. ¡Ay! Con mucha pena y embarazo nos, debemos daros algunas malas noticias.

Nos apresuramos a decir que en ningún momento se ha puesto en duda la brillante teoría *per se*, expuesta por Vuestra Muy
Benevolente Majestad. Sin embargo, nos, debemos deciros que
vuestro devoto capellán fue demasiado impetuoso en aducir
evidencias para sostener esa hipótesis.

Lo que a nosotros nos pareció una prueba *indudable* de la
suposición de nuestro Monarca, fue por otra parte la presencia
extraordinaria, aquí, de las hostias escondidas en ese copón hecho por los nativos, en la antigua ciudad de Tula. Hace poco,
nos, supimos por medio de la narración de nuestro azteca, como
Vuestra Majestad lo podrá saber también al leer las siguientes
páginas, adjuntas y transcritas, que nos, fuimos engañados con
lo que no fue más que un acto supersticioso de los indios, cometido hace relativamente pocos años. Y ellos fueron inducidos
a eso por un sacerdote español, evidentemente fracasado o após-
tata, que antes de ese hecho se atrevió a un indecible acto de
hurto. Por lo tanto, nos, hemos escrito con verdadera pena a la
Congregación de Propagación de la Fe, confesando nuestra credulidad y pidiendo que ignoren esa falsa evidencia. Ya que todos los demás y aparentes lazos de unión entre Santo Tomás
y la mística Serpiente Emplumada fueron puramente circuns-
tanciales, es de esperarse que la Congregación hará a un lado,
por lo menos hasta que reciba pruebas más convincentes, la sugerencia de Vuestra Majestad de que la deidad indígena pudiera
haber sido, realmente, el Apóstol Tomás haciendo un viaje evan-
gélico a este Nuevo Mundo.

Nos apena mucho tener que daros esta desconsoladora noticia, pero nos, sostenemos que no fue nuestra culpa, ya que sólo
tuvimos el afán de hacer más evidente la sagacidad de Nuestra

Admirada **Majestad**, sino que *¡toda la culpa la tiene ese pedazo de mono que es el azteca!*

Él sabía que había llegado a nuestro poder ese copón, conteniendo el Sacramento, que se mantenía fresco e intacto, según nosotros, más o menos por quince siglos. Él sabía que ese hecho había engendrado, en todos y cada uno de los Cristianos de estas tierras, una conmoción maravillosa y asombrada. Entonces fue cuando el indio debió decirnos cómo llegó ese objeto al lugar en donde se encontró. Él pudo evitar todas nuestras exclamaciones injustificadas sobre ese descubrimiento, los muchos servicios eclesiásticos que se llevaron a efecto para celebrarlo y la gran reverencia que se le dio a esa aparente reliquia divina. Y por encima de todo, pudo haber evitado, que nos, hiciéramos el ridículo al informar, tan apresurada y erróneamente, ese asunto a Roma.

Pero, no. El odioso azteca observó toda esa conmoción y ese júbilo, y estoy seguro que escondiendo su maliciosa alegría, sin decir ni una palabra para sacarnos de nuestro equivocado regocijo. No fue sino hasta después, hasta que ya fue demasiado tarde, que siguiendo el orden cronológico de su narración dejó caer, como por casualidad, el verdadero origen de esas hostias de comulgar ¡y por qué habían estado escondidas en Tula! Nosotros nos sentimos bastante humillados, sabiendo de antemano cómo se mofarán o disgustarán nuestros superiores en Roma, habiendo sido víctimas de un engaño. Sin embargo, nosotros nos sentimos inmensamente contritos porque, en nuestra prisa por informar a la Congregación, pareció como si nos, hubiéramos imputado un engaño similar a nuestro Muy Respetado Emperador y Rey, aunque el acto fue cometido con la mejor intención de dar a Vuestra Majestad la fama merecida por lo que *debió* de haber sido una razón de regocijo para todos los Cristianos del mundo.

Nos suplicamos y esperamos que vos hagáis recaer la culpa y nuestras mutuas vergüenzas sobre quien verdaderamente la tiene: ese indio falso y traicionero, cuyo silencio, tan evidente ahora, puede ser tan ultrajante como algunas de sus expresiones. (En las siguientes páginas, si es que vos podéis creerlo cuando lo leáis, Señor, utiliza la noble lengua castellana como una excusa para decir palabras que, seguramente, ¡jamás han sido inflingidas deliberadamente en los oídos de ningún Obispo en ninguna parte del mundo!) Quizás ahora, nuestro Soberano pueda tomar conocimiento de que cuando esa criatura tan descaradamente hace mofa del Vicario de Vuestra Majestad, indiscutiblemente y por extensión se mofa también de vos, y no del todo sin intención. Ahora, quizás, Señor, estaréis por lo menos de acuerdo, en que ya han pasado considerablemente más días de los debidos y que nos, podríamos ser dispensados de ser empleados para ese viejo bárbaro depravado, cuya presencia no es bien recibida y cuyas nocivas declaraciones, nos, hemos tenido que soportar por más de un año y medio.

Por favor, Señor, perdonad la brevedad, aspereza y descortés concisión de esta comunicación. En estos momentos, nosotros

nos sentimos demasiado vejados y turbados para poder escribir
más extensamente o con la mansedumbre que requiere nuestro
santo oficio.

Que toda la bondad y virtud que brillan en Vuestra Radiante
Majestad, continúe iluminando al mundo, es la ferviente oración
de Vuestro S.C.C.M., devoto (y afligido) capellán,

(ecce signum) ZUMÁRRAGA

UNDECIMA PARS

¡Ayyo! Después de habernos desdeñado por tanto tiempo, Su Ilustrísima se reúne otra vez con nosotros. Pero creo que puedo adivinar la razón. Ahora voy a empezar a hablar de esos dioses recién llegados y claro está que los dioses son de gran interés para un hombre de Dios. Nos sentimos muy honrados con su presencia, mi Señor Obispo, y para no tomar demasiado del tiempo invaluable de Su Ilustrísima, me apresuraré a contar mi encuentro con esos dioses. Solamente me saldré un poco del asunto para contar mi encuentro, en el camino, con un ser pequeño e insignificante, porque ese ser demostró más tarde no ser tan pequeño.

Dejé Tenochtitlan un día después de mi regreso a casa y lo hice con gran estilo. Ya que la estrella humeante no se veía durante el día, había muchas gentes en las calles, quienes echaban miradas de soslayo a mi cortejo, mientras salía de la ciudad. Llevaba puesto mi feroz yelmo de pico de águila y mi armadura emplumada de campeón Águila y llevaba también mi escudo con el símbolo de mi nombre, trabajado en plumas. Sin embargo, tan pronto como hube cruzado el camino-puente, me quité mi traje y se lo encargué al esclavo que llevaba la bandera con mi rango y mis otras insignias. Me puse una ropa más cómoda para viajar y no me volvía a poner mi fina vestimenta, excepto cuando llegábamos a una que otra comunidad importante a lo largo del camino, y yo deseaba impresionar con mi importancia a los gobernantes locales.

El Uey-Tlatoani me había provisto con una silla de manos dorada y enjoyada, en la cual podía viajar cómodamente cuando estaba cansado de caminar y otra silla de manos llena de regalos para el jefe xiu, Ah Tutal, además de otros regalos que debía presentar a los dioses, si éstos no los despreciaban y si probaban serlo. Además de los hombres que cargaban las sillas de mano y de los cargadores que llevaban nuestras provisiones de viaje, me acompañaba una tropa que Motecuzoma escogió entre los hombres más altos, robustos e imponentes de su guardia de palacio, y todos ellos iban magníficamente vestidos y armados.

Creo que no necesito decir que ningún bandido o villano se atrevió a atacar nuestra caravana; tampoco necesito decir la gran hospitalidad con que fuimos recibidos y regalados cada vez que paramos a lo largo de nuestra ruta. Sólo contaré lo que pasó una noche en que nos detuvimos en Coatzacoalcos, un pueblo-mercado que está en la costa norte, sobre esa tierra angosta comprendida entre los dos océanos.

Llegamos casi a la puesta del sol, en uno de esos días que parecían ser uno de los de más movimiento en el mercado, y por eso no llegamos hasta el centro de la población en donde hubiéramos sido alojados como huéspedes distinguidos. Sólo levantamos un campamento en un lugar para ello, fuera del pueblo, en donde otras caravanas que llegaron más tarde estaban haciendo lo mismo. Una de ellas, la que estaba más cerca de nosotros, era la de un mercader de esclavos que llevaba un considerable número de hombres, mujeres y niños, para venderlos en el mercado. Después de que todos hubimos comido, yo vagué por el campamento de esclavos, medio pensando que quizás podría encontrar uno bueno para reemplazar a mi difunto siervo, Estrella Cantadora, y que quizás pudiera hacer un trato al comprar uno de ellos antes de que los hombres fueran subastados públicamente en el mercado del pueblo, al día siguiente.

El mercader me dijo que había conseguido todo ese hato de seres humanos de dos en dos, en las tierras interiores de Coatlícamac y Cupilco. El cordón de hombres que traía era en realidad un cordón, puesto que viajaban, descansaban, comían y aun dormían, atados unos a otros por una larga cuerda, que cada hombre llevaba atravesada por una argolla que le colgaba del puente de la nariz. Las mujeres y las niñas, sin embargo, andaban libres para poder trabajar en los quehaceres del campamento, prendiendo hogueras, cocinando, acarreando agua y leña y cosas por el estilo. Mientras caminaba por los alrededores, ociosamente poniendo mis ojos sobre la mercancía, una muchachita que llevaba un cántaro de agua con una pequeña jícara, se aproximó tímida y me preguntó con dulce voz:

«¿Le gustaría a mi Señor Campeón Águila refrescarse con un trago de agua fresca? En el lado más lejano de este campo hay un arroyo claro que corre hacia el mar y metí mi cántaro lo suficiente como para que todas las impurezas se asentaran en el fondo.»

Yo la miré, a través de la jícara mientras bebía. Era una muchacha sencilla del campo, pequeña de estatura y delgada, no muy limpia y vestía una blusa larga hasta la rodilla de tela corriente. Sin embargo no era de complexión oscura ni tosca, era bastante bonita, en la forma en que puede serlo una adolescente cuyas líneas todavía son suaves y no están bien formadas. Ella, a diferencia de todas las demás mujeres del campamento, no estaba mascando *tzictli* y obviamente no era una ignorante, como se hubiera esperado.

«Me hablas en náhuatl —le dije—. ¿Cómo llegaste a aprenderlo?»

La muchacha, con una expresión de tristeza, murmuró: «Una viaja mucho, siendo, repetidamente, comprada y vendida. Por lo menos así se educa de cierta manera. Yo nací hablando la lengua de Coatlícamac, mi señor, pero he aprendido algunos dialectos maya y la lengua de los mercaderes, el náhuatl.»

Yo le pregunté cómo se llamaba y ella me respondió: «Ce-Malinali.»

«¿Uno-Hierba? —dije—. Eso es sólo la fecha del calendario, por lo tanto sólo medio nombre.»

«Sí —dijo ella suspirando trágicamente—. Hasta los hijos de los esclavos reciben un nombre en su cumpleaños número siete, pero yo no. Yo estoy todavía más abajo de un esclavo nacido de esclavos, Señor Campeón. He sido huérfana desde mi nacimiento.»

Y me lo explicó. Su desconocida madre había sido una mujerzuela que había quedado embarazada de alguno de los hombres con quien se había ido a horcajar al camino. La mujer había dado a luz en el surco de un campo de labranza, un día, mientras trabajaba allí, y luego, como si hubiese simplemente defecado, había dejado a la recién nacida allí, sin importarle en lo más mínimo, como si sólo hubiera dejado su excremento. Otra mujer, con más corazón o quizás porque ella misma no podía tener hijos, encontró al bebé abandonado antes de que pereciera, se lo llevó a su casa y lo socorrió.

«Pero ya no me acuerdo de quien tan bondadosamente me recogió —dijo Ce-Malinali—. Yo era muy pequeña cuando ella me vendió, por maíz, para poder comer, y desde entonces he pasado de amo en amo. —Ella me miró como quien ha sufrido mucho, pero ha perseverado—. Sólo sé que nací el día Uno-Hierba del año Cinco-Casa.»

Yo exclamé: «Vaya, ése fue el mismo día y año en que mi hija nació en Tenochtitlan. Ella también fue Ce-Malinali hasta que recibió el nombre de Zyanya-Nochipa a la edad de siete años. Tú eres muy pequeña para tu edad, niña, pero tienes exactamente la edad que ella...»

La muchacha me interrumpió con excitación: «¡Entonces, quizás usted me compre, Señor Campeón, para ser la criada personal y la compañía de su joven y señora hija!»

«*Ayya* —dije con pena—. Esa otra Ce-Malinali... murió... hace casi tres años...»

«Entonces cómpreme para ser una sirviente en su casa —me urgió—. O para esperar por usted, en la casa, como su hija lo hubiera hecho. Lléveme con usted cuando regrese a Tenochtitlan. Haré cualquier clase de trabajo, o —y ella bajó modestamente los ojos— si mi señor *no* desea de mí ningún servicio como hija, puede utilizar mi agujero. —Como en ese momento estaba tomando otra vez un sorbo de agua, lo eché fuera. Ella continuó con rapidez—: O puede revenderme en Tenochtitlan, mi señor, quizás entre los viejos raboverdes.»

Yo dejé caer: «Bribonzuela impertinente, la mujer que yo desee ardientemente, ¡no necesito comprarla!»

No se sintió afectada ante mis palabras, sino que dijo con ardor: «¡Yo tampoco deseo ser vendida nada más por mi cuerpo, Señor Campeón! Tengo otras cualidades, yo lo sé, y anhelo tener la oportunidad para hacer uso de ellas. —Se agarró de mi brazo para enfatizar su ruego—. Deseo ir a donde sea apreciada, no solamente por ser mujer; deseo probar fortuna en una gran ciudad. Tengo ambiciones, mi señor, tengo sueños, pero serán vanos si estoy condenada a ser una esclava para siempre en estas secas provincias.»

Yo dije: «Un esclavo es siempre un esclavo, aun en Tenochtitlan.»

«No siempre, no necesariamente para siempre —insistió ella—. En una ciudad, con hombres civilizados, quizás mi valía, mi inteligencia y mis aspiraciones podrán ser reconocidas. Un señor podría elevarme a la posición de concubina y aún más, podría hacerme una mujer libre. ¿No han dado algunos señores la libertad a sus esclavos, cuando éstos han demostrado merecerlo?»

Le dije que sí, que inclusive yo lo había hecho una vez.

«Sí —me dijo, como si hubiera arrancado una concesión de mí. Y oprimiendo mi brazo, con voz persuasiva me dijo—: Usted no necesita una concubina, Señor Campeón. Usted es un hombre fuerte y bien parecido, lo suficiente como para no tener que comprar una mujer, pero hay otros hombres, viejos o feos, quienes deben hacerlo y lo hacen. Usted me puede vender a uno de ellos en Tenochtitlan y sacar una buena ganancia.»

Supongo que debía de haber sentido simpatía por esa muchacha, pues yo también había sido joven una vez y también había estado lleno de ambición y anhelando probar fortuna en la más grande de todas las ciudades. Pero había algo tan duro y tan intenso en la forma en que Ce-Malinali trataba de congraciarse, que me dio la impresión de que ella no suplicaba. Así es que le dije: «Parece que tienes una gran opinión de ti misma y una opinión muy baja de los hombres.»

Se encogió de hombros. «Los hombres siempre han usado a las mujeres para tener placer. ¿Por qué una mujer no habría de usar a los hombres para avanzar en la vida? Por otra parte, a mí no me gusta el acto sexual, pero puedo pretender que sí lo disfruto, y aunque todavía no he sido usada muy a menudo, puedo llegar a ser muy buena en eso. Si ese talento me puede ayudar a salir de la esclavitud... bueno... He oído que una concubina de un gran señor puede llegar a gozar de más privilegios y poder que su legítima primera esposa. Y aun al Venerado Orador de los mexica le gusta coleccionar concubinas, ¿no es así?»

Yo me reí: «Ah, pequeña perra, sí que tienes grandes ambiciones.»

Ella dijo agriamente: «Yo sé que puedo ofrecer más de un agujero entre mis piernas, aunque todavía esté lo suficientemente suave y cerrado. ¡Un hombre puede comprar una perra *techichi* y tener también eso!»

Me liberé de la garra que apretaba mi brazo. «Recuerda esto, muchacha. Algunas veces un hombre conserva a un perro sólo por el afecto de su compañía. No puedo ver ninguna capacidad de afecto en ti. Un *techichi* puede ser también un alimento nutritivo. Tú no estás limpia ni eres lo suficientemente apetitosa como para cocinarte. Solamente eres una rapaz de una región apartada, sin nada que ofrecer a excepción de tus ventosas jactancias, una codicia bien escondida y una idea patética de tu propia importancia. Tú misma admites que ni siquiera te *gustaría* emplear ese agujero apretado del que tanto haces gala y que es la única cosa por la que vales. En lo único en que tú estás por encima de tus hermanas esclavas es solamente en tus vanas presunciones.»

Me dijo con rabia: «¡Podría ir adonde está el río y bañarme hasta estar más que limpia, podría también hacerme apetitosa y tú no podrías rechazarme! ¡Con ropa fina podría pasar perfectamente como una señora! ¡Puedo pretender tanto afecto que hasta tú lo creerías! —Hizo una pausa y entonces se burló sonriendo—: ¿Qué otra mujer pudo haber hecho algo más por ti, mi señor, cuando ella aspiraba a ser algo más que el recipiente de tu *tepuli*?»

Mis dedos se crisparon con el deseo de castigar su impertinencia, pero aquella esclava desaliñada ya era lo suficientemente grande como para ser golpeada como una niña y demasiado joven para ser azotada como una mujer. Así es que sólo puse mis manos sobre sus hombros, pero las sostuve allí lo más fuerte que pude para causarle daño y le dije entre dientes:

«Es verdad que he conocido a otras mujeres como tú; venales, falsas y llenas de perfidia, pero he conocido a otras que no lo fueron. Una de ellas fue mi hija, que nació con el mismo nombre que tú llevas y si ella hubiera vivido se habría hecho un nombre del que hubiese estado orgullosa.» No pude reprimir la ira que me llegaba como oleadas y mi voz se levantó al decir: «¿Por qué ella tuvo que morir, mientras tú estás viva?»

Sacudí tan fieramente a Ce-Malinali que ella dejó caer su cántaro de agua, que se rompió entre el ruido del barro y el agua, pero no presté atención a ese hecho de mala suerte. Grité tan fuerte que varias cabezas se volvieron hacia donde estábamos y el mercader de esclavos llegó corriendo para suplicarme que no maltratara la mercancía. Creo que en ese momento, se me concedió por un breve tiempo la visión de los adivinos-que-ven-a-lo-lejos, pues como si viera el futuro le grité:

«¡Tú harás que ese nombre sea vil, sucio y despreciable y toda la gente al pronunciarlo escupirá en él!»

Noto la impaciencia de Su Ilustrísima porque me he detenido en ese encuentro que parecía no significar nada, pero ese episodio aunque breve, no es trivial. Quién era esa muchacha, lo que ella llegó a ser cuando fue adulta y por último a qué la llevó su precoz ambición, todas esas cosas son de lo más significativo. Si no hubiera sido por esa muchacha, podría ser que Su Ilustrísima, no fuera ahora nuestro ilustre Obispo de Mexico.

Sin embargo, cuando me fui a dormir esa misma noche, bajo la estrella humeante de mal agüero que colgaba arriba en el cielo negro, ya había olvidado totalmente a la muchacha. Al día siguiente nuestra caravana se puso en camino, más allá de Coatzacoalcos y manteniéndonos sobre la costa pasamos las ciudades de Xicalanca y Kimpech, y por último llegamos al lugar en donde se suponía que nos esperaban los dioses, el pueblo llamado Tiho, capital de los xiu, una tribu maya que estaba al extremo norte de la península de Uluümil Kutz. Llegué en todo el esplendor de mi traje de campeón Águila e insignias, y por supuesto que fuimos respetuosamente recibidos por la guardia personal del jefe xiu, Ah Tutal, y conducidos en solemne procesión a través de todas las calles de esa ciudad blanca, hasta su palacio. No era realmente un palacio, ya que no se puede esperar mucho de esos descendientes de los maya, pero sus edificios de adobe, de una sola planta y con techos de palma tejida, como todos los demás del pueblo, relucían con su cubierta de cal blanca, y los edificios del palacio estaban distribuidos en un cuadrado alrededor de un patio interior.

Ah Tutal era un señor noble más o menos de mi edad, completamente bizco, quien quedó adecuadamente impresionado con los regalos que le mandó Motecuzoma, y como era lo debido me recibió con un festín; mientras comíamos conversamos acerca de su salud, de la mía, de todas nuestras relaciones y de nuestros amigos. No nos hubiéramos preocupado lo más mínimo por esos intercambios triviales, pero el propósito de eso era medir mis conocimientos en su dialecto maya. Cuando más o menos habíamos determinado la extensión de mi vocabulario en xiu, empezamos a hablar sobre la razón de mi visita.

«Señor Madre —le dije, pues ése era el título (ridículo) adecuado para dirigirse a cualquier jefe de cualquier comunidad en esos lugares—, dígame usted, ¿esos forasteros recién llegados, son dioses?»

«Campeón Ek Muyal —dijo el Madre, utilizando mi nombre en el lenguaje maya—, cuando mandé avisar a su Venerado Orador, estaba seguro de que lo eran, pero ahora...» Y puso cara de incertidumbre.

Le pregunté: «¿Cree usted que alguno de ellos pueda ser el dios Quetzacóatl, quien se fue hace mucho tiempo, prometiendo que regresaría; el dios que ustedes llaman en estas tierras Kukulkán?»

«No. De ningún modo, ninguno de esos forasteros tiene la forma de la Serpiente Emplumada. —Luego suspiró y encogiéndose de hombros dijo—: De todas maneras, si no hay un aspecto exterior como para maravillarnos, ¿cómo podemos reconocer a un dios? Estos dos parecen humanos en apariencia, aunque tienen mucho pelo y más largo de lo normal. Son más altos que nosotros.»

Yo dije: «De acuerdo con la tradición, otros dioses han adoptado cuerpos humanos para visitar el mundo de los mortales. Ellos, comprensiblemente, podrían adoptar cuerpos con apariencia estremecedora.»

Ah Tutal continuó: «Fueron cuatro los que llegaron en esas extrañas canoas y que fueron arrojados a nuestras playas, más al norte. Pero cuando fueron traídos en sillas de manos a Tiho, descubrimos que dos de ellos estaban muertos. ¿Pueden los dioses morir?»

«Morir... —dije reflexionando—. ¿No podría ser que ellos no *estuvieran todavía vivos*? Quizás traían esos dos cuerpos de repuesto, así cuando desearan un cambio podrían mutar de cuerpos.»

«Nunca se me ocurrió eso —dijo Ah Tutal sintiéndose incómodo—. Claro que sus hábitos y apetitos son muy peculiares y su lenguaje es incomprensible. ¿Qué dioses se toman la molestia de aparecer como mortales, y no la de hablar como los humanos?»

«Aquí hay muchos y diversos lenguajes humanos, Señor Madre.

Pudieron haber escogido un lenguaje que no sea comprensible en estas regiones, pero que quizás yo pueda reconocer por los muchos viajes que he hecho en todas partes.»

«Señor Campeón —dijo el jefe un poco impertinente—, usted tiene tantos argumentos como cualquier sacerdote. ¿Pero usted puede darme alguna razón por la cual esos dos seres rehúsan *bañarse*?»

Pensé acerca de eso. «¿Quiere decir, en agua?»

Se me quedó mirando como si se preguntara si Motecuzoma no le habría mandado como emisario al bufón de su corte. Él dijo, pronunciando con mucha precisión: «Sí, en agua. ¿Qué otra cosa cree usted que quise decir por bañarse?»

Carraspeé disculpándome y dije: «¿Y cómo sabe usted si los dioses no están acostumbrados a bañarse más que en puro aire? ¿O quizás sólo con luz del sol?»

«¡Porque ellos apestan! —dijo Ah Tutal, triunfalmente y disgustado a la vez—. Sus cuerpos huelen a viejos humores, a sudor, a aliento rancio y a suciedad pegada. Y como si eso no fuera poco, y ya bastante malo, parecen contentarse en vaciar sus vejigas y tripas por una ventana que está en la parte de atrás de sus cuartos, y muy contentos también en dejar que esa porquería se acumule allí con el hedor insoportable que eso despide. Parece que los dos no están familiarizados con la limpieza, ni con la libertad, ni con la buena comida que les servimos.»

Dije: «¿Qué quiere usted decir con eso de que no están familiarizados con la libertad?»

Ah Tutal apuntó a través de una de las ventanas, que estaban en el lado opuesto de la sala del trono, indicando otro edificio bajo que estaba del otro lado del patio. «Ellos están allí. Permanecen siempre allí.»

Exclamé: «¿Seguro que usted no tiene a los *dioses* en cautividad?»

«¡No, no, no! Ellos así lo desean. Le digo a usted que sus conductas son de lo más excéntrico. Desde que se les ofreció esos cuartos, desde su llegada, no han salido de ellos.»

Yo dije: «Perdone usted la pregunta, Señor Madre, pero ¿no serían tratados con rudeza cuando llegaron?»

Ah Tutal me miró ofendido y dijo fríamente: «Desde un principio ellos han sido tratados con cordialidad, consideración y aun reverencia. Como ya le dije, dos de ellos ya estaban muertos cuando llegaron aquí, o por lo menos convencieron a nuestros mejores físicos de que estaban totalmente muertos. Así es que, de acuerdo a nuestra costumbre civilizada, les rendimos a cada uno de ellos un funeral honroso y devoto, incluyendo la ceremonia de cocinar y comer las partes más estimables y sus órganos. Fue entonces cuando los otros dos dioses vivos corrieron a encerrarse a sus cuartos y desde entonces han estado allí tercamente.»

Yo me aventuré a decir: «Quizás se molestaron porque ustedes dispusieron rápidamente de lo que pudieron haber sido sus cuerpos de repuesto.»

Ah Tutal dejó caer sus manos en un gesto de exasperación y dijo: «Pues bien, su propio confinamiento hubiera hecho que los cuerpos que *ahora llevan* se hubieran muerto de hambre, si yo no les hubiese mandado regularmente sirvientes llevando comida y bebidas. Aun así, sólo han comido muy frugalmente; frutas, vegetales y maíz, pero no han comido ninguna clase de carne, ni siquiera la deliciosa carne del tapir y del manatí. Campeón Ek Muyal, créame que he tratado continuamente de averiguar sus preferencias en todas las cosas, pero debo confesarle que me siento frustrado. Por ejemplo, tome en cuenta el asunto de las mujeres...»

Le interrumpí: «¿Usan a las mujeres como los demás hombres?»

«Sí, sí, sí —dijo con impaciencia—. De acuerdo con lo que dicen las mujeres, son humanos y hombres en todo excepto por su pelo excesivo. Y me atrevería a decir que cualquier dios que tiene todo lo que tiene el hombre, va a ocupar eso en la misma forma en que lo hace el hombre. Si usted piensa acerca de ello, Señor Campeón, convendrá conmigo, en que ni siquiera un *dios* podrá utilizar eso en otra forma diferente.»

«Por supuesto que usted tiene razón, Señor Madre. Continúe usted.»

«Pues les he estado mandando continuamente mujeres y muchachas, dos al mismo tiempo, pero hasta ahora los forasteros no han retenido a ninguna de ellas por más de dos o tres noches consecutivas. Las han seguido echando afuera, para que yo siga mandándoles otras, por lo menos eso es lo que supongo y eso es lo que he estado haciendo. Parece que ninguna de nuestras mujeres satisface a ninguno de ellos por largo tiempo. Si con eso están sugiriendo o tienen la esperanza de que les mande alguna *clase* de mujer particular o peculiar, no tengo la forma de saber qué clase sería y dónde la podría conseguir. Una noche les mandé dos muchachos muy bonitos y los huéspedes provocaron una conmoción aterradora, les pegaron y los arrojaron fuera. Y ahora no quedan más mujeres a quienes echar mano, aquí en Tiho ni en los alrededores, para poder mandárselas. Ellos ya han tenido a todas las esposas e hijas de la mayoría de los xiu, a excepción de mi familia y de las de otros nobles. Y para colmo, estoy corriendo el riesgo de que todas nuestras mujeres se rebelen, ya que tengo que usar la fuerza bruta para obligar hasta a la esclava más baja a entrar en esa fétida caverna. Las mujeres dicen que la peor cosa que tienen esos forasteros, y la más innatural, es que hasta en sus *partes privadas* tienen pelo y que los forasteros huelen todavía peor ahí, en esas partes, que lo que huelen sus sobacos y sus alientos. Oh, yo sé que su Venerado Orador dice que me debo considerar altamente favorecido y muy honrado por hospedar a esos dos dioses o lo que sean, pero yo quisiera que Motecuzoma estuviera aquí, tratando de utilizar toda su habilidad para custodiar a estos huéspedes tan pestilentes. Créame, Campeón Ek Muyal, cuando le digo que he llegado a considerar ese honor ¡como una desgracia y un fastidio! ¿Y por cuánto tiempo vamos a seguir así? Ya no los quiero más aquí, pero no me atrevo echarlos fuera. Les doy gracias a todos los demás dioses porque se me ocurrió darles a esos dos mugrosos esas habitaciones al otro lado del patio de palacio, pero aun así, al capricho del dios del viento, me llegan los tufos de esos seres desagradables, tan fuertemente que casi me hacen caer al suelo. Un día o más, el hedor no necesitará del viento para venir arrastrándose hacia acá. En estos precisos momentos, algunos de mis cortesanos están horriblemente enfermos de una enfermedad, que los físicos dicen que antes jamás se había visto en estas tierras. Personalmente, yo creo que todos nos estamos intoxicando al oler la pestilencia de esos extranjeros sucios. Y tengo la fuerte sospecha de que la razón por la que Motecuzoma me mandó tantos regalos es porque tiene la esperanza de que yo mantenga a estos dos, bien lejos de su limpia ciudad. Y además de eso, podría decir...»

«Usted lo ha hecho todo muy bien, Señor Madre —le dije rápidamente, para poder detener toda esa recitación de quejas—. Por mucho tiempo usted ha sobrellevado esa responsabilidad y todo el honor debe recaer sobre usted, pero ahora que yo estoy aquí podría ayudarle con algunas sugestiones. Primero que nada, antes de que yo sea presentado formalmente a esos seres, me gustaría tener una oportunidad para escuchar cómo hablan, sin que ellos lo sepan.»

«Eso es muy fácil —refunfuñó Ah Tutal—. Sólo cruce el patio, y párese junto a una de las ventanas en donde ellos no lo puedan ver, pues durante el día lo único que hacen allí es charlar incesantemente como si fueran monos. Lo único que le aconsejo es que se tape la nariz.»

Yo sonreí indulgentemente mientras me disculpaba por dejar su presencia, pues pensaba que el Señor Madre estaba exagerando en ese respecto, como en algunas otras de sus actitudes enojadas hacia los extranjeros, pero estaba equivocado. Cuando me acerqué a sus cuartos, el olor nauseabundo casi hace que devuelva toda la comida que acababa de ingerir. Estornudé para limpiar mi nariz y luego tapándomela con mis dedos, me escurrí con prisa contra la pared del edificio. Había voces murmurando y yo me pegué lo más cerca que pude a la abertura de la puerta, para poder distinguir las palabras ininteligibles. Como ya habrá supuesto Su Ilustrísima, en aquel tiempo los sonidos de la lengua española no significaban nada para mí, como muy pronto lo verifiqué, pero como yo sabía que ese momento sería histórico, me paré traspasado por cierto temor, para oír, memorizar y recordar hasta hoy, las palabras enfáticas de ese ser, nuevo y extraño que muy bien pudiera ser un dios.

«Os juro por Santiago, ¡que ya estoy harto de chingar con estas putas lampiñas!»

Y la otra voz dijo...

¡Ayya!

Usted me espantó, Su Ilustrísima. Saltó con tanta agilidad para un hombre que ya ha llegado a la edad de los nuncas, que francamente le envidio.

Con todo mi respeto, Su Ilustrísima, tengo que decirle con pena que no puedo retractarme de esas palabras, ni pedir disculpas por ellas, ya que yo no las pronuncié. Yo sólo las memoricé ese día, como lo haría un perico, repitiendo los sonidos. Un perico sería inocente al repetir esas palabras, aun en su iglesia catedral, Su Ilustrísima, porque un perico no puede saber lo que significan. Hasta el perico más inteligente no podría saberlo, porque, verá usted, una perica no posee lo que usted adecuadamente llamaría...

Muy bien, Su Ilustrísima, no insistiré más sobre este asunto y me cuidaré mucho de repetir los sonidos exactos, hechos por el otro forastero. Pero éste también, como el otro, dijo que echaba de menos y por mucho tiempo, los servicios de una buena puta castellana, con bastante pelo en sus partes inferiores. Y fue todo lo que pude oír, pues me sentí muy enfermo por el olor y temí que mi presencia fuera descubierta. Corrí lo más rápido que pude a la sala del trono, para tomar un poco de aire fresco cuando entré, y una vez all le dije al jefe Ah Tutal:
«Verdaderamente usted no exageró al hablar de sus fragancias, Señor Madre. Debo verlos y tratar de hablar con ellos, pero de veras que prefiero hacerlo en lugar abierto.»
Él dijo: «Puedo ponerles alguna droga en su próxima comida y sacarlos de ese fétido lugar cuando estén dormidos.»
«No es necesario —le dije—. Mis guardias pueden sacarlos ahora mismo.»
«¿Y pondrán sus manos sobre los dioses?»
«Bueno, si al tocarlos les dejan caer un rayo de luz y los matan —dije— por lo menos sabremos al fin que *son* dioses.»
Ellos no hicieron eso. Aunque forcejearon y dieron chillidos, cuando fueron sacados por la fuerza de sus cuartos, al patio abierto, los dos forasteros no se sintieron tan disgustados como lo estaban mis guardias, quienes con mucha dificultad detenían sus vómitos. Cuando sus captores musculosos los soltaron, ninguno de los dos saltó enojado o hizo algunos sonidos amenazantes o alguna hechicería que se pudiera reconocer; simplemente cayeron de rodillas delante de mí y empezaron a farfullar patéticamente e hicieron extraños gestos con sus manos, primero entrelazándolas enfrente de sus caras, luego moviéndolas como repitiendo un cierto patrón. Por supuesto que ahora ya sé que lo que estaban haciendo era recitar una oración Cristiana en latín con sus manos entrelazadas, y luego hicieron frenéticamente el signo de la cruz Cristiana, de su frente a su pecho y luego hacia sus hombros.
Tampoco me tomó mucho tiempo el adivinar que ellos se habían estado escondiendo todo ese tiempo, sintiéndose seguros en sus cuartos, porque se habían asustado ante las buenas intenciones de los xiu, para con sus dos compañeros muertos. Si los fo-

rasteros se habían sentido aterrados por los xiu, que son gente sencilla de costumbres simples, ya se pueden ustedes imaginar que casi cayeron medio muertos del susto cuando de repente se enfrentaron conmigo y mis mexica, todos ellos hombres altos y malencarados, guerreros fieramente adornados con sus trajes de batalla, sus yelmos, plumas y armas de obsidiana.

Por un tiempo, yo solamente los observé a través de mi cristal, lo que hizo que temblaran más notoriamente. Ahora ya estoy más acostumbrado y resignado a la apariencia tan desagradable de los hombres blancos, pero en aquel entonces no lo estaba y ambos me intrigaron y me repugnaron a la vez, por la blancura de cal de la piel de su rostro, pues en nuestro Único Mundo, blanco era el color de la muerte y del luto. Ningún ser humano era de ese color, excepto por los muy poco frecuentes monstruos tlacaztali. Bueno, esos dos tenían por lo menos ojos pardos o negros, de humano, o pelo negro o pardo aunque feamente rizado y de arriba de sus cabezas el pelo les crecía, de la misma manera, en sus mejillas, sobre sus labios, en sus barbillas y gargantas. Lo demás de ellos estaba escondido por lo que parecía ser un montón de ropas en desorden, aunque ahora sé que eran camisas, justillos, calzones, guanteletes, botas y cosas por el estilo, pero aun así, me parecía que sus ropas eran excesivamente pesadas, ceñidas y probablemente muy incómodas en comparación con la que acostumbraban a utilizar a diario nuestros hombres, el simple taparrabo y el manto, ambos muy ligeros.

«Desvestidlos», ordené a los guardias, quienes me miraron con indignación y refunfuñaron antes de cumplir mi orden. Los dos forasteros, otra vez, forcejearon y chillaron aún más fuerte, como si los estuvieran desollando en lugar de quitarles las ropas de tela y cuero. Nosotros, los que observábamos, éramos los que deberíamos habernos quejado, pues cada ropa mugrosa que era quitada nos traía un nuevo olor todavía más repugnante. Y cuando les quitaron las botas —¡yya ayya!—, cuando las botas salieron, todos los que estábamos en el patio del ·palacio, incluyéndome a mí, nos retiramos lo más rápido que pudimos y lo más lejos también, de tal manera que los dos forasteros quedaron, vilmente desnudos, en el centro de un círculo extremadamente amplio y distante de espectadores.

Ya antes les he hablado con desprecio de la mugre y la miseria de los chichimeca, los moradores del desierto, pero también les expliqué que su suciedad era el resultado de las circunstancias en que vivían, pero ellos se bañaban, peinaban y arreglaban cuando tenían las facilidades para hacerlo. Así que los chichimeca olían a flores de jardín en comparación con los hombres blancos, quienes parecían *preferir* su repulsión y *temían* la limpieza como un signo de debilidad o afeminamiento. Por supuesto, que sólo hablo de los soldados blancos, Su Ilustrísima, quienes todos ellos, desde el de rango más bajo hasta su comandante Cortés, compartían esa vergonzosa excentridad. No estoy muy bien familiarizado con los hábitos de limpieza de las clases más altas, como Su Ilustrísima, pero muy pronto me di cuenta de que esos caballeros, utilizan con liberalidad perfumes y pomadas para disimular el olor del sudor, queriendo dar la *impresión* de que se bañan frecuentemente.

Los dos extranjeros no eran gigantes, como Ah Tutal los había descrito y como yo había esperado. Sólo uno de ellos era un poco más alto que yo y el otro era más o menos de mi estatura, lo que significaba que en realidad ellos eran más altos que el promedio de hombres de estas tierras. Sin embargo, estaban parados allí, encorvados y temblorosos, como niños que esperaran una tunda de azotes y protegían sus genitales con las dos manos, como si fueran un par de doncellas temerosas de ser violadas, así es que la altura de sus cuerpos quedaba muy menguada. Y lo que es más, se veían miserablemente debiluchos, pues la piel de sus cuerpos era todavía más blanca que la de sus caras.

Le dije a Ah Tutal: «Nunca podré acercarme lo suficiente para interrogarles, Señor Madre, hasta que ellos no se hayan bañado. Si no lo hacen por sí mismos, entonces nosotros debemos hacerlo por ellos.»

Él me dijo: «Francamente le diré, Campeón Ek Muyal, que en la forma en que huelen, así desvestidos, tengo que declinar el honor de permitir que utilicen las tinas de baño y las casas de vapor. Créame usted que tendría que destruirlas y volverlas a construir.»

«Estoy completamente de acuerdo con usted —le dije—. Simplemente dé la orden a sus esclavos de que traigan agua y jabón y los bañen aquí mismo.»

A pesar de que el jefe de los esclavos usó agua tibia, jabón de cenizas y suaves esponjas de baño, los objetos de su atención se defendían lanzando alaridos como si los hubiesen estado engrasando para asarlos o como si les escaldaran el pellejo como se le hace al verraco-espín para poder quitarle más fácilmente sus púas. Mientras todo ese estrépito se llevaba a efecto, yo hablé con cierto número de mujeres y muchachas tiho, quienes habían pasado una noche o más con los forasteros. Éstas habían aprendido algunas palabras del lenguaje de ellos y me las dijeron, pero sólo eran nuevas palabras para *tepili* y *tepuli*, el acto sexual y demás, palabras que no me eran muy útiles en un interrogatorio formal. Las mujeres también me confiaron que los miembros de los forasteros estaban proporcionados a su estatura y así es que cuando estaban en erección eran admirablemente inmensos, comparados con los miembros usuales de los xiu, pero ninguna mujer se deleitó al tener ese gran *tepuli* a su servicio, según ellas mismas me dijeron, pues estaban tan rancios por la suciedad acumulada durante toda su vida, que daban ganas de vomitar ante su vista o su olor. Como una muchacha hizo notar: «Sólo una hembra buitre podría disfrutar realmente el copular con una de esas criaturas.»

Sin embargo, aunque las mujeres sintieron repugnancia, hicieron sumisamente todo lo mejor que sabían para ofrecerles la mejor hospitalidad femenina, pero quedaron muy perplejos ante los aspavientos y los rechazos que los forasteros hacían, desaprobando algunos de esos ofrecimientos íntimos. Por lo visto, dijeron las mujeres, los extranjeros sólo sabían una manera y una posición para tomar y dar placer, y, tan vergonzosos y tercos como muchachitos, rehusaron ensayar alguna otra variación.

Aunque hubiera muchas evidencias que proclamaran que los extranjeros eran dioses, ese testimonio de las mujeres me hubiera hecho dudarlo, puesto que por lo que yo sabía de los dioses, no eran en lo más mínimo gazmoños en la manera de satisfacer sus lujurias. Así es que muy pronto sospeché que los extranjeros eran alguna otra cosa, pero no dioses, y no fue sino hasta mucho más tarde que supe que solamente eran buenos Cristianos. Su ignorancia y su inexperiencia en las diversas maneras de hacer el acto sexual, sólo reflejaba su adherencia a la moralidad Cristiana y a lo que en ella se consideraba normal, y no he conocido jamás a ningún español que se desvíe de esa estricta norma aun cuando esté cometiendo, en una forma ruda y tumultuosa, un acto de violación. Con toda verdad puedo decir que nunca vi violar a nuestras mujeres, aun por el soldado más bajo, más que por un único orificio y en la única posición permitida a los Cristianos.

Aunque se les dio a los dos forasteros tanta limpieza como fue posible, algunas de sus partes siguieron hediendo por uno o dos días más, y no eran todavía lo que se dice una agradable compañía. Los esclavos no pudieron hacer mucho, con sólo jabón y agua, para quitarles la capa verde que cubría sus dientes y mal aliento, por ejemplo, pero se les dieron mantos limpios, y la miasma de sus ropas, que casi se sostenían por sí solas de la mugre, fueron quemadas. Mis guardias guiaron a los dos hombres al rincón en donde estábamos, sentados en nuestras sillas bajas, Ah Tutal y yo, y los empujaron para que se sentaran en el suelo enfrente de nosotros.

Ah Tutal, muy inteligentemente había preparado una de esas jarras perforadas para fumar, llenas con rico *poçíetl* y otras hierbas varias olorosas. Cuando él hubo encendido esa mezcla, los dos metimos nuestras cañas por los agujeros y aspiramos, dejando salir nubes de humo aromático, con el fin de formar una cortina de olor para resguardarnos del mal olor de los sujetos a quienes íbamos a entrevistar. Cuando los vi temblando, supuse que sería por el frío causado por sus cuerpos al secarse o quizás ante el choque estremecedor al haber recibido un baño. Después supe que estaban aterrorizados al ver, por primera vez, «a hombres respirando fuego».

Bien, si a ellos no les gustaba nuestro aspecto, a mí no me gustaba en absoluto el suyo. Sus rostros estaban todavía más pálidos desde que habían perdido varias capas de mugre incrustada, y la piel que se veía a través de sus barbas, no era de una complexión lisa como la de nosotros. Uno de los hombres tenía la cara toda picada, como si hubiera sido un pedazo de roca volcánica, y la del otro estaba llena de granitos, bolas y pústulas abiertas. Cuando yo supe lo suficiente de su idioma como para hacer una pregunta discreta sobre eso, se encogieron de hombros indiferentemente y dijeron que casi toda la gente de su raza, hombres y mujeres por igual, sufrían alguna vez en su vida las «pequeñas viruelas». Algunos morían de esa enfermedad, nos dijeron, pero la mayoría no sufría más que esa desfiguración facial, y puesto que la mayoría estaba igualmente afectada por eso, no sentían que fuera denigrante para su belleza. Quizás ellos no, pero yo sí pienso que es una de las cosas más desagradables a la vista, o por lo menos lo pensé en aquellos momentos. Hasta nuestros días, cuando ahora tanta gente de mi propia raza se ve desfigurada por esos granos, como piedras volcánicas, trato de no retroceder ante su vista.

Usualmente empezaba a aprender algún lenguaje extranjero apuntando los objetos que se hallaban cerca de mí, y animando a las personas que hablaban esos lenguajes a decirme los nombres con que ellos los conocían. Había una muchacha esclava que en esos momentos acababa de servirnos nuestro *chocólatl* a Ah Tutal y a mí, así que la detuve y la atraje y levantándole la falda, apunté a sus partes femeninas y dije... dije lo que ahora sé que es la palabra menos apropiada en español. Los dos forasteros parecieron sorprenderse mucho y apenarse un poco. Luego apunté a mi propio corchete, que ahora sé que es la mejor palabra para decirla en público, aunque yo dije otra.

Entonces yo fui el que me sorprendí mucho. Los dos se enroncharon hasta sus pies, mirándome con ojos muy abiertos y aterrados. Entonces comprendí su pánico y no pude evitar el soltar la carcajada. Obviamente pensaron que si podía mandar restregarlos con tanta facilidad, también podía dar la orden de que los castraran por haberse aprovechado de las mujeres de la localidad. Todavía riéndome, negué con mi cabeza y les hice gestos para que se sosegaran. Apunté a la horquilla de la muchacha y a mi corchete y dije «*tepili*» y «*tepuli*». Después, apuntándome a la nariz, dije «*yacatl*». Los dos dieron signos de haber descansado y asintieron el uno al otro comprendiendo; uno de ellos apuntando también dijo «nariz». Ellos dieron muestras de quitarse un gran peso de encima y empezaron a enseñarme el último y nuevo lenguaje, que jamás hubiera tenido necesidad de conocer.

Esa primera sesión no terminó hasta que ya había oscurecido y cuando ellos empezaron a quedarse dormidos entre las palabras. Sin duda su vigor se había visto menguado por el baño, quizás el primero en toda su vida, así es que dejé que volvieran a sus cuartos, dando traspiés, para poder dormir. Sin embargo, los desperté muy temprano a la mañana siguiente y después de recibir su olor, les di a escoger entre bañarse ellos mismos o ser restregados a la fuerza otra vez. Aunque me miraron perplejos y disgustados, como dando a entender que nadie debería pasar por una cosa tan horrible *dos* veces en su vida, prefirieron bañarse ellos mismos. Desde entonces, lo hicieron diariamente, cada mañana, y aprendieron a hacerlo tan bien que entonces yo ya me pude sentar con ellos, durante todo el día, sin sentirme muy incómodo. Así es que nuestras sesiones duraban desde la mañana hasta la noche, e incluso intercambiábamos palabras mientras comíamos los alimentos traídos por los sirvientes de palacio. Debo también mencionar que los huéspedes finalmente empezaron a comer carne, una vez les pude explicar a qué animales pertenecían.

Algunas veces para premiar su colaboración como maestros, otras para reanimarlos cuando se quejaban continuamente por lo cansados que estaban, les daba una taza o dos del refrescante *octli*. Entre los «varios regalos para los dioses» que mandó Motecuzoma, yo había llevado varias jarras del mejor *octli* y fue el único de sus muchos regalos que yo les ofrecí. La primera vez que lo probaron, hicieron gestos y dijeron que era «cerveza fermentada», sea lo que eso signifique. Pero muy pronto les gustó y una noche, deliberadamente, hice el experimento de dejarles tomar lo que quisieran. Fue muy interesante para mí comprobar que ellos se pusieron tan desagradablemente borrachos como cualquiera de nuestra gente.

Conforme pasaban los días y yo extendía mi vocabulario, supe muchas cosas y la más importante fue ésta: los forasteros no eran dioses sino hombres, hombres ordinarios aunque sin embargo con una apariencia extraordinaria. No pretendieron ser dioses, ni siquiera algún tipo de espíritus preparando el camino para la llegada de sus dioses-maestros. Parecieron honestamente sorprendidos cuando con cautela les mencioné que nuestros pueblos esperaban que algún día los dioses regresaran a El Único Mundo. Me aseguraron ansiosamente que ningún dios había caminado por ese mundo desde más de mil cinco años, y ellos me hablaron de ese dios, como si fuera el *único* dios. Ellos mismos, me dijeron, eran sólo hombres mortales quienes, en este mundo y en el otro, habían jurado ser devotos a ese dios; mientras vivieran en este mundo, me dijeron, serían igualmente obedientes a su rey, quien era como cualquier otro hombre, pero más eminente, y que claramente venía a ser el equivalente del Venerado Orador.

Como más tarde le contaré a Su Ilustrísima, no toda nuestra gente estaba dispuesta a aceptar lo que afirmaban los mismos forasteros, o lo que yo afirmaba, de que eran simplemente hombres. Sin embargo, yo, desde mi primer contacto con ellos nunca dudé de eso y con el tiempo demostré que tenía razón. Así es que desde ahora en adelante, Su Ilustrísima, hablaré de ellos no como seres misteriosos, forasteros, extraños o extranjeros, sino como seres humanos.

El hombre que tenía los granitos y llagas era Gonzalo Guerrero, comerciante en madera y carpintería. El hombre con la cara picada era Jerónimo de Aguilar, un escribano profesional como los reverendos frailes que están aquí. Puede ser que hasta alguno de ustedes lo haya conocido en algún tiempo, porque me contó que su primera ambición había sido ser sacerdote de su dios y que había estudiado por un tiempo en una *calmécac* o como ustedes les llamen a sus escuelas para sacerdotes.

Los dos habían llegado, según me dijeron, de una tierra que está hacia el este y más allá del océano. Yo ya lo había supuesto, pero no pude comprender más aunque ellos me dijeron que esa tierra se llamaba Cuba y que ésta era sólo una colonia de la nación mucho más grande, y que estaba todavía más distante hacia el este, llamada España o Castilla, en donde con mucho poder su Rey gobierna todos los dominios españoles que se extienden hasta muy lejos. Esa España o Castilla, dijeron ellos, era una tierra en donde todos, hombres y mujeres, eran de piel blanca excepto unas cuantas personas inferiores que ellos llamaban moros, cuyas pieles eran totalmente negras. Quizás yo hubiera podido encontrar esa última declaración tan increíble, que hubiera recelado de todo lo que me contaron, pero reflexioné que si en estas tierras han nacido, ocasionalmente, los monstruos blancos *tlacaztali*, en esas tierras de hombres blancos, ¿por qué no podrían haber monstruos negros?

Aguilar y Guerrero me explicaron que habían llegado a nuestras playas sólo por mala suerte. Ellos habían estado entre unos cientos de personas, hombres y mujeres, que habían dejado Cuba en doce de esas grandes casas flotantes —ellos les llamaban barcos— bajo el mando del Capitán Diego de Nicuesa, que los llevaba consigo para formar otra colonia en la que él iba a ser el gobernador; un lugar llamado Castilla de Oro, hacia algún lugar más lejos de aquí, hacia el sur. Sin embargo, la expedición había tenido mala suerte y ellos se inclinaban a culpar de ello al «cometa con cola».

Una fiera tormenta había dispersado los barcos, y el que los llevaba a ellos acabó finalmente encallado entre unas rocas puntiagudas que rompieron su fondo, lo giraron y lo hicieron hundirse. Sólo Aguilar, Guerrero y otros hombres pudieron arreglarse para poner a flote otra embarcación, una especie de larga canoa que el barco llevaba para esas emergencias. Para su sorpresa, la canoa no estuvo mucho tiempo en el mar, antes de que éste la arrojara a las playas de esta tierra. Los otros dos ocupantes de la canoa se ahogaron entre la turbulencia de las rompientes y Aguilar y Guerrero quizás también hubieran muerto, si «los hombres rojos» no hubieran llegado corriendo a ayudarles a ponerse a salvo.

Aguilar y Guerrero expresaron su gratitud por haber sido rescatados, recibidos hospitalariamente, por haber sido alimentados muy bien y por los entretenimientos que les proporcionaron, pero estarían todavía más agradecidos, según dijeron, si nosotros los hombres rojos los podíamos guiar otra vez de regreso a la playa y a su canoa. Guerrero, que era carpintero, estaba seguro de que podría reparar cualquier daño que tuviera la canoa y hacer los remos para impulsarla adecuadamente. Él y Aguilar estaban seguros de que si su dios les daba tiempo favorable, podrían remar hacia el este hasta encontrar Cuba otra vez.

«¿Los dejo ir?», me preguntó Ah Tutal, a quien le había estado traduciendo nuestras entrevistas.

Le dije: «Si pueden encontrar desde aquí ese lugar llamado Cuba entonces no tendrán ningún problema en encontrar Uluümil Kutz otra vez. Y usted ya lo oyó: su Cuba parece estar llena de hombres blancos, ansiosos de establecer nuevas colonias en cualquier lugar que puedan alcanzar. ¿Desea usted que lleguen aquí por enjambres, Señor Madre?»

«No —dijo con preocupación—. Pero ellos podrían traer a uno de sus físicos para curar esta extraña enfermedad que esparcieron entre nosotros; los nuestros ya han utilizado cuantos remedios conocen, pero cada día caen más personas enfermas y tres ya han muerto.»

«Quizás estos mismos hombres sepan algo para remediar eso —le sugerí—. Veamos a alguna persona que esté enferma.»

Ah Tutal nos guió a Aguilar y a mí a una cabaña en el pueblo, dentro de la cual encontramos a un doctor parado, murmurando, rascándose la barbilla ceñudo e inclinado sobre la esterilla de una muchacha que yacía agitada por la fiebre con su cara brillando de sudor, sus ojos vidriosos y sin ver. Aguilar se sonrojó al recordarla como a una de las mujeres que habían visitado a Guerrero en sus cuartos.

Él dijo muy despacio, para que yo pudiera entenderle: «Siento deciros que ella tiene las viruelas pequeñas. ¿Veis? La erupción empieza a brotar en su frente.»

Traducí sus palabras al físico, quien le miraba con recelo profesional, pero dijo: «Pregúntele qué tratamiento siguen sus médicos.»

Así lo hice, pero Aguilar sólo se encogió de hombros y dijo: «Ellos rezan.»

«Evidentemente son gente muy retrasada —gruñó el doctor, pero añadió—: Pregúntele a qué dios.»

Aguilar dijo: «¡Pues, al Señor Dios!»

Eso no ayudaba en lo más mínimo, pensé yo, pero le pregunté: «¿Rezan en alguna forma a ese dios, que nosotros podamos imitar?»

Él trató de explicarlo, pero la exposición era demasiado complicada para lo poco que sabía de su lenguaje, así es que nos indicó que era mucho más fácil demostrárnoslo, y los tres, Ah Tutal, el físico y yo, le seguimos apresuradamente al patio de palacio. Él corrió a sus cuartos cuando todavía nosotros estábamos a cierta distancia y regresó con algo en cada mano.

Una de esas cosas era una cajita con una tapa muy apretada, que Aguilar abrió para mostrarnos su contenido: cierto número de pequeños discos que parecían haber sido cortados de un papel blanco y grueso. Trató de darme otra explicación que era que al parecer, según pude yo entender, había tomado ilícitamente o robado esa caja como un recuerdo de sus días en la escuela para sacerdotes, y pude comprender, hasta cierto punto, que aquellos discos eran una especie de pan muy especial y de lo más santo, el más potente de todos los alimentos, porque la persona que comía uno de ellos, podía poseer parte de la fuerza de ese poderoso Señor Dios.

El otro objeto era un cordón que contenía muchas cuentas irregularmente intercaladas con otras más grandes; todas eran de una sustancia azul que nunca antes había visto: tan azules y duras como la turquesa, pero tan transparentes como el agua. Aguilar empezó con otra explicación compleja que lo único que entendí fue que cada cuenta representaba una oración; naturalmente yo estaba recordando nuestra práctica de poner un pedacito de jade en la boca de alguien muerto y pensé que las cuentas-oraciones se emplearían similarmente y con igual beneficio en una persona que todavía no estuviera muerta, así es que interrumpí a Aguilar preguntándole con urgencia:

«¿Entonces, ustedes ponen las oraciones en la boca?»

«No, no —dijo—. Se sostienen en las manos.» Entonces él gritó protestando cuando le arrebaté la caja y las cuentas.

«Tome, señor físico —le dije al doctor, mientras rompía el cordón y le daba dos cuentas, traduciéndole lo poco que había comprendido de las instrucciones de Aguilar—. Ponga cada una de estas oraciones en las manos de la joven, que las sostenga apretadamente...»

«¡No, no! —aullaba Aguilar—. ¡Lo que estáis haciendo es un error! Se debe rezar más que...»

«¡Cállese! —le dije en su propia lengua—. ¡No tenemos tiempo para más!»

Desmañadamente tomé uno de esos papelitos de pan, que estaban en la caja y me lo puse en la boca. *Sabía* como a papel y se disolvió en mi boca sin necesidad de que yo lo masticara. No sentí que instantáneamente surgiera en mí una fuerza de dios, pero por lo menos me di cuenta de que el pan podría alimentar a la muchacha aun en su estado medio consciente.

«¡No, no! —gritó Aguilar otra vez, cuando me tragué la cosa aquella—. Eso es imperdonable, ¡usted no puede recibir el Sacramento!»

Él me miró con el mismo horror que veo ahora en el rostro de Su Ilustrísima. Siento mucho el haber sido tan impulsivo, pero recuerde que en aquel entonces yo sólo era un pagano ignorante, que se preocupaba y se apuraba por salvar la vida de aquella muchacha. Tomé algunos de los pequeños discos y los puse en la mano del doctor, diciéndole:

«Esto es comida del dios, comida mágica y fácil de ingerir. La puede poner dentro de la boca de la muchacha, sin ningún riesgo de que vaya a convulsionarse.»

Él se fue corriendo tanto como su propia dignidad se lo permitía...

Más o menos como lo acaba de hacer Su Ilustrísima.

Amistosamente puse una de mis manos sobre el hombro de Aguilar y le dije: «Perdóneme que haya tomado eso de sus manos, pero si la muchacha se cura le será reconocido y será muy honrado por estas gentes. Ahora, busquemos a Guerrero para sentarnos a charlar, quiero saber más sobre *su* gente.»

Había muchas cosas que deseaba saber de Jerónimo de Aguilar y de Gonzalo Guerrero, pues para entonces ya podíamos conversar pasablemente y aunque lo hacíamos con poca fluidez, ellos a su vez sentían una curiosidad similar por saber muchas cosas de estas tierras. Me hicieron varias preguntas, que pretendí no entender: «¿Quién es vuestro Rey? ¿Tiene muchos ejércitos a su mando? ¿Posee una gran cantidad de riquezas en oro?» Y algunas otras preguntas, que en verdad no entendí, tales como: «¿Quiénes son vuestros Duques, Condes y Marqueses? ¿Quién es el Papa de vuestra Iglesia?» Y algunas otras que me atrevo a decir que nadie podría responder: «¿Por qué vuestras mujeres no tienen vello abajo?» Así es que yo evitaba sus preguntas, preguntando a mi vez y ellos contestaban a todo sin aparente vacilación o suspicacia.

Me hubiera podido quedar con ellos por lo menos un año, perfeccionando los conocimientos sobre su lenguaje y pensando constantemente en cosas nuevas que preguntarles, pero tomé la decisión precipitada de dejar su compañía cuando dos o tres días después de nuestra visita a la muchacha enferma, el físico fue en mi busca y me hizo señas silenciosas de que lo acompañara. Lo seguí hasta esa cabaña para ver que el rostro de la muchacha muerta estaba horriblemente hinchado, tanto que no se podía ni siquiera reconocer y con un color muy feo, un tono de púrpura muy oscuro.

«Sus vasos sanguíneos se rompieron y sus tejidos se abotagaron —dijo el doctor—, incluyendo los de dentro de la nariz y de la boca. Murió tratando de respirar. —Y añadió desdeñosamente—: La comida del dios que usted me dio, no tenía ninguna magia.»

Yo le pregunté: «¿Y a cuántos pacientes ha curado usted, señor físico, sin recurrir a esa magia?»

«A ninguno —suspiró, perdiendo toda su afectación—. Ni ninguno de mis colegas ha podido salvar un solo paciente. Algunos han muerto así, por asfixia; otros, por un chorro de sangre que les llega a la boca y a la nariz, y algunos más, delirando por la fiebre. Temo que todos morirán y lo harán de forma miserable.»

Mirando los restos horrorosos de lo que había sido una vez una muchacha bastante bonita, le dije: «Esta muchacha, ella misma, me dijo que sólo una hembra buitre podría tener placer con esos hombres blancos. Ella debió de haber tenido una verdadera premonición, porque ahora los buitres se sentirán muy contentos de engullir su carroña, y ella murió a causa de los hombres blancos.»

Cuando regresé a palacio y le conté eso a Ah Tutal, él me dijo enfáticamente: «¡No quiero más aquí a estos extranjeros enfermos y sucios! —Yo no estaba muy seguro si sus ojos bizcos me estaban mirando a mí o detrás de mí, pero indiscutiblemente que lo hacían con ira—. ¿Los dejo ir en su canoa o se los lleva usted a Tenochtitlan?»

«Ninguna de las dos cosas —le dije—. Ni tampoco los va usted a matar, Señor Madre, no por lo menos sin el permiso de Motecuzoma. Le sugiero que se deshaga de ellos, regalándolos como esclavos. Regáleselos a esos jefes de tribus que estén bastante lejos de aquí; jefes que se puedan sentir muy halagados y honrados con esos regalos. Ni siquiera el Venerado Orador de los mexica tiene un esclavo blanco.»

«Hum... sí... —dijo Ah Tutal pensativamente—. Hay dos jefes que particularmente no me gustan y de quienes desconfío, y no sentiría ni la menor pena si los hombres blancos les atrajeran miserias. —Me miró más amablemente—. Pero usted fue enviado hasta acá, Campeón Ek Muyal, para ver a los forasteros. ¿Qué va a decir Motecuzoma cuando usted regrese con las manos vacías?»

«No completamente vacías —respondí—. Por lo menos me llevaré la caja con la comida del dios y las pequeñas oraciones azules y sé muchas cosa que puedo decir a Motecuzoma. —Entonces, de repente, se me ocurrió una idea—. Oh, sí, Señor Madre, puede haber otra cosa para enseñársela a él. Si algunas de las mujeres que se acostaron con esos hombres blancos resultaran preñadas y si no caen víctimas de las pequeñas viruelas, bien, si tienen alguna progenie, mándelos a Tenochtitlan. Así el Venerado Orador podría ensanchar su zoológico humano en la capital, pues creo que serán unos monstruos únicos.»

El aviso de mi regreso a Tenochtitlan me precedió con varios días de anticipación y es seguro que Motecuzoma se moría de impaciencia por conocer las noticias o los visitantes que yo pudiera llevar. Sin embargo, cuando llegué me encontré con que él seguía siendo el mismo viejo Motecuzoma, así es que no fue introducido inmediatamente a su presencia. Necesité detenerme en el corredor, afuera del salón del trono y cambiar mi traje de campeón Águila por el acostumbrado saco de suplicante y luego hacer el ritual ordinario de adulación de besar la tierra, a través del salón hasta donde estaba sentado, entre los dos discos de oro y plata. A pesar de haberme recibido fríamente y sin prisas, era obvio que deseaba ser el primero en conocer las noticias que llevaba o quizás el único que las oyera, pues los miembros de su Consejo de Voceros no estaban presentes. Lo que sí me permitió fue dejar a un lado la formalidad de hablar solamente cuando él me preguntara, así es que le conté todo lo que les he narrado a ustedes, reverendos frailes, y unas cuantas cosas más que pude averiguar de sus dos compatriotas:

«Conforme he podido calcular, Señor Orador, creo que fue hace unos veinte años cuando las primeras casas flotantes, que ellos llaman barcos, salieron de esa tierra lejana llamada España, para explorar el océano de occidente. Entonces ellos no llegaron a nuestras costas, porque parece que hay un gran conjunto de islas, grandes y pequeñas, entre esa España y aquí. Cuando desembarcaron en esas islas ya había gente viviendo en ellas, y por la descripción que me hicieron parece ser que esa gente es como los salvajes chichimeca de nuestras tierras del norte. Algunos de esos isleños pelearon contra los hombres blancos para echarlos de sus islas, pero otros permitieron mansamente esa incursión, pero ahora, todos son vasallos de los españoles y de su rey. O sea, que durante esos veinte años, los hombres blancos han estado muy ocupados en colonizar esas islas, despojando a los nativos de sus recursos y traficando entre las islas y su tierra, España. Hasta ahora, sólo unos pocos de sus barcos le han echado un vistazo a estas tierras, ya sea pasando en su recorrido de una isla a otra, o por estar explorando ociosamente, o porque el soplo del viento las ha desviado de sus rutas. Sería de esperar que los nativos tuvieran ocupados a esos hombres blancos, por muchos años, en esas islas, pero le ruego a usted que lo considere así. Aunque una isla sea muy grande, no deja de ser una isla, por lo tanto sus riquezas y la población que puede ser aprovechada, será muy limitada. También los españoles parecen ser insaciables en ambas cosas: en su curiosidad y en su rapacidad. Para estas fechas ellos ya están buscando, más allá de esas islas, nuevos descubrimientos y nuevas oportunidades. Tarde o temprano, su búsqueda los traerá a estas tierras. Entonces sucederá lo que el Reverendo Orador Nezahualpili ya dijo: una invasión a la que todos nosotros debemos prepararnos de la mejor forma.»

«¡Preparar! —gritó Motecuzoma, seguramente al sentirse aguijoneado por recordar cómo Nezahualpili había sostenido su promesa al ganar el partido en el juego *tlachtli*—. Ese viejo tonto sólo está *preparado* para sentarse y quedarse allí sentado. Ni siquiera me ha ayudado una sola vez a hacer la guerra a los insufribles texcalteca.»

No le quise recordar lo demás que había dicho Nezahualpili: que todos nuestros pueblos deberían cesar sus enemistades pasadas y unirnos contra esa invasión inminente.

«Usted dice invasión, ¿eh? —continuó Motecuzoma—, pero también dice que esos dos forasteros llegaron sin armas y totalmente indefensos. Si es que hay una invasión, significa que ésa será inusitadamente pacífica.»

Yo le dije: «No me confiaron la clase de armas que ellos perdieron al hundirse su barco. Quizás ni siquiera necesiten armas en lo absoluto, por lo menos no la clase de armas que nosotros conocemos, si pueden inflingirnos una enfermedad a la que ellos son inmunes.»

«Sí, en verdad que ésa sería un arma potente —dijo Motecuzoma—. Un arma que sólo puede ser reservada a los dioses. Y usted, todavía insiste en que no son dioses. —Meditando miró la cajita y su contenido—. Ellos traían la comida del dios. —Tomó las cuentas azules—. Ellos traían las oraciones más palpables y hechas de una piedra misteriosa. Y con todo eso, usted todavía insiste que no son dioses.»

«Sí, mi señor. Se emborracharon como lo hacen los hombres y se acostaron con mujeres igual que los demás hombres.»

«¡Ayyo! —me interrumpió triunfalmente—. Las mismas razones por las que el dios Quetzalcóatl se fue lejos de aquí. De acuerdo con todas las leyendas, una vez sucumbió y se emborrachó y cometió una mala acción sexual, y de la vergüenza abdicó como jefe de los tolteca.»

«Y también de acuerdo con las leyendas —dije—, en el tiempo de Quetzalcóatl estas tierras estaban perfumadas por flores, por todas partes y cada soplo del viento esparcía dulces fragancias. El aroma que despedían esos dos hombres que yo conocí haría que se desmayara el dios del viento. —Y pacientemente seguí insistiendo—: Los españoles no son más que hombres, mi señor. Sólo se diferencian de nosotros en que tienen la piel blanca, tienen mucho pelo y son más altos que nuestra estatura normal.»

«Las estatuas de los tolteca en Tolan son mucho *más* altas que cualquiera de nosotros —dijo Motecuzoma tercamente—, y cualquiera que hayan sido los colores con que las pintaron, ya no son perceptibles. Y por todo lo que nosotros sabemos, los tolteca eran de piel blanca. —Yo exhalé un fuerte suspiro de exasperación, aunque él no prestó atención a eso—. Haré que nuestros historiadores investiguen en cada papel archivado, así podremos encontrar y saber cómo *eran* exactamente los tolteca. Mientras tanto, haré que nuestros más grandes sacerdotes pongan esta comida-del-dios en un recipiente mucho más fino y que lo lleven reverentemente a Tolan y lo pongan en donde se encuentran esas esculturas tolteca...»

«Señor Orador —le dije—, en varias de mis conversaciones con esos dos hombres blancos les mencioné repetidas veces el nombre de tolteca y éste no significó nada para ellos.»

Él dejó caer su mirada en la comida-del-dios y en las cuentas, y luego sonrió de manera verdaderamente victoriosa. «¡Ya lo ve! Naturalmente que ese nombre no significaría nada para un tolteca genuino, nosotros los llamamos los Maestros Artesanos, *¡porque no sabemos cómo se llamaban a sí mismos!*»

Bueno, por supuesto que él tenía razón y yo me sentí muy cortado. No pude pensar en nada adecuado con que replicar a eso, así es que sólo murmuré: «Dudo mucho de que ellos se llamaran a sí mismos españoles. Esa palabra, como todo su lenguaje, no guarda ninguna relación con ninguna de las lenguas que yo he conocido en cualquier parte de estas tierras.»

«Campeón Águila Mixtli —dijo él—, esos hombres blancos pueden ser, como usted dice, seres humanos, simples hombres, y *también los tolteca*, descendientes de aquellos que desaparecieron desde hace tanto tiempo. Ese Rey del que ellos hablaron, muy bien puede ser ese dios Quetzalcóatl que se exilió a sí mismo. Puede estar listo en estos momentos, preparando su regreso como él lo había prometido, esperando más allá del mar a que sus súbditos, los tolteca, le informen si nosotros estamos satisfechos con su regreso.»

«¿Y estamos *satisfechos* de su regreso, mi señor? —le pregunté descaradamente—. ¿Está *usted* satisfecho de eso? Porque el regreso de Quetzalcóatl despojará de su gobierno a todo gobernante en estas tierras, desde los Venerados Oradores hasta el más bajo jefe de tribu. Él será el gobernante supremo.»

Motecuzoma puso una expresión de piadosa humildad. «Ese dios, cuando vuelva, seguramente estará muy agradecido con aquellos que preservaron y aun ensancharon sus dominios y sin duda él hará evidente esa gratitud. Si él me concediera, tan sólo, formar parte de su Congreso de Voceros, me sentiría altamente honrado, como ningún otro ser humano lo haya sido nunca.»

Yo le dije: «Señor Orador, yo ya he cometido errores antes. Puede ser que me equivoque de nuevo al creer que esos hombres blancos no son dioses, ni son los enviados de ningún dios. Pero ¿no estará usted cometiendo un error todavía más grande, al suponer que ellos son dioses?»

«¿Suponer? ¡Yo no lo supongo! —me contestó con severidad—. No estoy diciendo, si un dios llega o no, ¡como usted está impertinentemente asegurando! —Se levantó derecho y casi me gritó—: ¡Yo soy el Venerado Orador de El Único Mundo y no digo esto o aquello, sí o no, dioses u hombres, hasta que no haya examinado, observado, esperado y tenido una *certeza*!»

Consideré, al levantarse, que me estaba despidiendo, así que cuando terminó de hablar, caminé hacia atrás y repetidamente besé la tierra, como era el protocolo, salí de la cámara y en el corredor me quité el saco de tela y me fui a casa.

¿En cuanto a la cuestión de si eran dioses y hombres? Bien, Motecuzoma dijo que esperaría hasta tener la certeza y eso fue lo que hizo. Esperó y esperó demasiado y aun cuando ya no importaba más, él todavía no tenía la certeza. Y como él esperó indeciso, al fin murió en desgracia y la última orden que él trató de dar a su pueblo fue igualmente incierta, yo lo sé, porque yo estaba allí y oí la última palabra que Motecuzoma dijo en su vida: «¡*Mixchía*...! ¡Esperen...!»

✠

En esa ocasión, Luna que Espera no hizo nada para echar a perder mi regreso a casa. Para entonces ella tenía el pelo canoso, pero pintó o cortó lo que había quedado de aquel otro mechón blanco que tanto me ofendió. No obstante de que Beu dejó de simular que era su hermana muerta, me encontré con que había adoptado una personalidad muy diferente a la que yo había conocido durante casi media gavilla de años, desde la primera vez que la vi en la cabaña de su madre, en Tecuantépec. Durante todos esos años, cada vez que estábamos juntos, parecía que teníamos que estar peleándonos, insultándonos o en el mejor de los casos manteniendo una tregua. Pero parecía que ella había decidido que hiciéramos el papel de una pareja ya entrada en años, amigable y casada desde hacía mucho tiempo. No sé si eso fue el resultado del castigo que le había inflingido, o por el qué dirán de los admirados vecinos, o porque Beu, que había llegado a la edad de los nuncas, se había dicho resignadamente: «Nunca más tendremos animosidades abiertas entre nosotros.»

De todas maneras, su nueva actitud hizo que con facilidad me adaptara otra vez a vivir en la casa y en la ciudad. Antes, siempre, aun en los días cuando mi esposa Zyanya y mi hija Nochipa estaban vivas, siempre había regresado a casa con la idea de volver a partir pronto, en busca de nuevas aventuras, pero cuando regresé esa vez, sentí que lo hacía para quedarme en casa para el resto de mi vida. Si hubiera sido joven, pronto me habría rebelado contra ese proyecto y habría encontrado alguna razón para volver a partir, a viajar, a explorar; o si hubiera sido un hombre pobre, me habría tenido que mover para ganarme la vida, o si Beu hubiera sido la mujer colérica de otros tiempos, yo habría tenido que encontrar *alguna* excusa para tenerme que ir... hasta guiando una tropa de guerreros a algún lugar en donde hubiera guerra. Pero por primera vez en mi vida no tenía ninguna razón o necesidad para irme lejos y recorrer todos los caminos y todos los días. Hasta me persuadí a mí mismo de que *merecía* un largo descanso y la vida fácil que mi riqueza y mi esposa me podían proporcionar. Así es que gradualmente caí en una rutina que ni me exigía ni me recompensaba mucho, pero por lo menos me tenía ocupado y no muy aburrido. Y no hubiera podido hacer eso, si no hubiera sido por el cambio de carácter de Beu.

Cuando digo que ella había cambiado, me refiero a que había logrado con mucho éxito esconder el desagrado y el aborrecimiento que siempre había sentido por mí durante toda su vida. Ella jamás me dio una razón para que yo pensara que esos sentimientos habían muerto en ella, sino que solamente dejó de demostrarlos y esa pequeña ficción fue suficiente para mí. Dejó de mostrarse orgullosa e incisiva y se tornó blanda y dócil en la forma en que lo eran la mayoría de las esposas. En cierto modo, casi echaba de menos a la mujer imperiosa que había sido, pero esa pequeña pena desaparecía por el peso de encima que se me quitaba al no tener que batallar con su testarudez. Cuando Beu disimulaba la personalidad que siempre la había caracterizado y asumía esa otra personalidad de deferencia y solicitud, entonces, yo podía tratarla con la misma cortesía.

Su dedicación a la vida de casada no incluyó la sugestión desdeñosa de que al fin la utilizaría como esposa, cosa que me había estado refrenando de aprovecharme. Nunca sugirió que consumáramos nuestro matrimonio; nunca más volvió a ostentar su feminidad o a incitarme burlonamente; nunca se quejó de que tuviéramos habitaciones separadas. Y yo me alegré mucho de que no lo hiciera. Si hubiera tenido que rechazar sus avances amorosos, la nueva ecuanimidad de nuestras vidas en común se habría visto perturbada, pues habría sido muy difícil para mí el obligarme a abrazarla como esposa. El hecho triste era que Luna que Espera era tan vieja como yo y su edad estaba reflejada en ella. De esa belleza que una vez había sido igual a la de Zyanya, quedaba muy poco, sólo sus bellos ojos y yo rara vez los miraba. En su nuevo papel servicial, Beu trató siempre de permanecer modestamente en un segundo plano, y de la misma manera, siempre hablaba en voz baja. Antes, sus ojos acostumbraban a mirarme con destellos brillantes y su voz, al dirigirse a mí, había sido mordaz, burlona o desdeñosa; pero entonces, con su nuevo disfraz, cuando me hablaba, y esto era muy raras veces, lo hacía con suavidad. Cuando salía de casa por las mañanas acostumbraba a preguntarme: «¿Cuándo desea mi señor que se le sirva su comida y qué desea comer?» Cuando dejaba la casa por las tardes, me prevenía: «Puede ser que haga aire frío, mi señor, y puede enfermarse si no lleva un manto más pesado.»

Ya les he dicho que tenía una rutina diaria, y era ésta: salía de casa por las mañanas y por las tardes, para pasar el tiempo en las únicas dos maneras que pude encontrar.

Cada mañana iba a la Casa de los Pochteca y pasaba la mayor parte del día allí, conversando, escuchando y bebiendo el rico *chocólatl* que era servido por los criados. Por supuesto que los tres ancianos que me habían entrevistado en esas habitaciones, media gavilla de años antes, habían muerto hacía mucho tiempo, pero habían sido reemplazados por un buen número de hombres como ellos: viejos, gordos, calvos, complacidos y seguros de su propia importancia y de su dirección en el establecimiento. A excepción de que todavía no estaba ni calvo ni gordo y que tampoco me *sentía* viejo, supongo, hubiera podido pasar por uno de ellos, pues lo único que hacía era regodearme en el recuerdo de mis aventuras y en mi presente opulencia.

La llegada ocasional de algún mercader con su caravana, me ofrecía una oportunidad para hacerle una oferta sobre sus mercancías o por la parte de éstas que me gustara. Y antes de que el día terminara, usualmente había convencido a otro *pochtécatl* para que comprara mi mercancía, teniendo un beneficio por ella. Podía hacer eso sin tener que dejar, siquiera, mi taza de *chocólatl*, sin tener la necesidad de ver lo que había comprado y vendido. Algunas veces, había en el edificio algunos jóvenes que aspiraban a ser mercaderes, haciendo los preparativos para su primer aventura a alguna parte. Entonces, yo los detenía todo el tiempo que podía, dándoles todo el beneficio de mi experiencia en alguna ruta en particular, por lo menos todo el tiempo que escucharan sin molestarse e inventar algunos encargos urgentes.

Sin embargo, la mayoría de los días sólo había unas cuantas personas presentes, yo y algunos *pochteca* ya retirados, que no tenían otro lugar en donde pasar su tiempo de ocio. Así es que nos sentábamos juntos e intercambiábamos historias en lugar de mercancías.

Yo escuchaba sus historias de aquellos días en que ellos habían sido más jóvenes y menos ricos, pero con una ambición ilimitada; los días cuando ellos viajaban, cuando enfrentaron riesgos y peligros. Todas nuestras historias eran lo suficientemente interesantes, sin necesidad de adornarse, por lo menos yo no necesitaba exagerar las mías, pero como todos los viejos trataban de que sus cuentos fueran mejores que los de los otros, en lo único de sus experiencias y su variedad, en los peligros que habían tenido que afrontar y la forma tan difícil en que habían podido escapar a ellos, en lo notable de sus adquisiciones que tan astutamente habían conseguido... bien, pues me di cuenta de que algunos de esos hombres empezaron a adornar sus aventuras después de haber contado diez o doce cuentos...

En las tardes salía de casa, no para buscar compañía, sino porque quería estar solo para recordar, murmurar y anhelar sin ser observado. Por supuesto que no hubiera objetado nada si mi soledad se hubiera visto interrumpida por el encuentro de alguno de los ya idos. Sin embargo, como ya les he dicho, eso todavía no me ha sucedido. Así es que con serena esperanza y no con expectación, caminaba en la noche por las calles casi vacías de Tenochtitlan, de un lado a otro de la isla, recordando alguna cosa que ocurrió ahí o allí o más allá.

En el norte estaba el camino-puente de Tepeyaca, a través del cual había cargado a mi pequeña cuando habíamos huido de la inundación de la ciudad para buscar un lugar seguro en la tierra firme. En ese tiempo, Nochipa sólo había podido hablar dos palabras a la vez, pero algunas de ellas habían dicho mucho, pues en aquella ocasión ella había dicho: «Noche oscura.»

Hacia el sur, estaba el camino-puente hacia Coyohuacan y hacia las tierras lejanas del sur, el camino-puente que yo había cruzado con Cózcatl y Glotón de Sangre en mi primera expedición mercantil. En el amanecer esplendoroso de aquel día, el poderoso volcán Popocatépetl nos había visto partir y parecía que nos decía: «Vosotros os vais, mi gente, pero yo me quedo...»

En medio de la isla había dos grandes plazas. La que estaba más al sur era la de El Corazón del Único Mundo, en donde se alzaba la Gran Pirámide, tan grande, sólida y eterna en su aspecto que el que la veía podría pensar que se levantaría allí por siempre, tanto como se levantaría el Popocatépetl en el distante horizonte. Se me hacía difícil, aun a mí, pensar que era tan viejo que había visto terminar la construcción de esa pirámide, que había estado por muchos años sin terminar, cuando la vi por primera vez.

La plaza que estaba más al norte era la de Tlaltelolco, esa área de mercado amplia y extensa, por la que por primera vez había caminado cogiendo apretadamente la mano de mi padre, y cuando él había pagado generosamente un precio extravagante al comprarme la primera nieve que saboreé en mi vida, mientras le decía al vendedor: «Recuerdo los Tiempos Duros...» Fue entonces cuando me encontré por primera vez con el hombre color cacao, quien tan certeramente me predijo la vida que tenía por venir.

Al recordar eso, me sentí bastante perturbado pues me recordó que todo ese futuro que él había visto, estaba ya en mi pasado. Cosas que alguna vez había visto, ahora se convertían en recuerdos. Para entonces, estaba a punto de completar mi gavilla de años y no muchos hombres han vivido más de esos cincuenta y dos años. ¿Entonces no habría más futuro para mí? Cuando me había estado diciendo a mí mismo que al fin estaba disfrutando, como debía ser, la vida de ocio por la que había trabajado tanto, quizás sólo estaba rehusando confesarme que había sobrevivido a mi utilidad, que había sobrevivido a todas las personas que había amado y que me habían amado. ¿Estaba sólo utilizando un espacio en este mundo, en lo que era llamado a presentarme a otro?

¡No! Me rehusé a pensar en eso y para confirmarlo miré al cielo nocturno. Otra vez se veía allí la estrella humeante, como aquella que había visto cuando Motecuzoma se reunió conmigo en Teotihuacan, y también cuando encontré a la muchacha Ce-Malinali, y también estaba allí cuando me encontré con los visitantes de España. Nuestros astrónomos no se ponían de acuerdo en si era el mismo cometa que regresaba con diferente forma y brillantez y con un ángulo diferente del cielo o si por el contrario era un nuevo cometa cada vez. Pues después de aquella estrella que me había acompañado en mi viaje hacia el sur, *alguna otra* estrella humeante había aparecido en el cielo nocturno dos veces más durante dos años consecutivos y cada vez había sido visible casi por un mes. Incluso hasta los astrónomos que usualmente eran imperturbables, estuvieron de acuerdo en que era un augurio, pues tres cometas en tres años desafiaban toda explicación. Así es que algo iba a pasar en este mundo y, bueno o malo, valía la pena esperar. Quizás tendría parte en ese asunto o quizás no, pero no renunciaría a este mundo, por lo menos no todavía.

Varias cosas pasaron durante esos años y cada vez yo me preguntaba: «¿Es el portento que nos augura la estrella humeante?» Todos esos sucesos fueron notables en un aspecto u otro, y algunos fueron lamentables, pero ninguno de ellos pareció lo suficientemente portentoso como para justificar que los dioses nos enviaban advertencias siniestras.

Por ejemplo, hacía apenas unos cuantos meses que había regresado de mi encuentro con los españoles, cuando nos llegó un aviso de Uluümil Kutz de que la misteriosa enfermedad de pequeñas viruelas se había extendido, como una ola en el océano, sobre toda la península. Había caído sobre las tribus xiu, tzotxil, quiché y sobre todos los descendientes de los maya y de cada diez personas tres morían, uno de los que murieron fue mi anfitrión, el Señor Madre Ah Tutal, y cada uno de los supervivientes quedaba desfigurado para el resto de su vida por las marcas de esas viruelas.

Por mucho que Motecuzoma hubiera estado inseguro acerca de la naturaleza e intenciones de esos dioses u hombres, que nos visitaban de España, no estuvo muy ansioso de exponerse a sí mismo a cualquier enfermedad del dios, pues por una vez actuó pronta y decisivamente prohibiendo estrictamente todo comercio con las tierras maya. A nuestros *pochteca* se les prohibió ir allá y a los guardias de nuestras fronteras en el sur se les dio instrucciones de devolver todo producto y mercancía que viniera de allí. Entonces, el resto de El Único Mundo esperó con aprensión por algunos meses más, pero las pequeñas viruelas fueron contenidas con éxito dentro de las infortunadas tribus maya y si no, por lo menos no afligieron a ningún otro pueblo.

Pasaron algunos meses más y un día Motecuzoma mandó a uno de sus mensajeros para llevarme al palacio y otra vez me pregunté: «¿Será que *esto* significa que las profecías de las estrellas humeantes se han cumplido?» Pero cuando hube hecho, cubierto con mi saco de suplicante, las acostumbradas cortesías en el salón del trono, vi que el Venerado Orador sólo estaba molesto, no lleno de pánico o maravillado o mostrando alguna de esas grandes emociones. Varios de los miembros de su Consejo de Voceros, que estaban parados alrededor del cuarto, parecían más que divertidos. Me sentí aturrullado cuando dijo:

«Este hombre loco se llama a sí mismo Tlilectic-Mixtli.»

Entonces me di cuenta de que no estaba hablando de mí, sino *conmigo* y estaba apuntando a un extranjero de cara malhumorada y vestido mezquinamente, que dos guardias de palacio tenían agarrado. Levanté mi cristal para poder verlo y comprobé que no era un extraño, así que sonreí, primero a él y luego a Motecuzoma, y dije:

«Tlilectic-Mixtli es su nombre, mi señor. El nombre de Nube Oscura es muy usual entre...»

«¡Lo conoce! —dijo Motecuzoma interrumpiéndome o acusándome—. ¿Algún pariente suyo, quizás?»

«Quizás tanto suyo como mío, Señor Orador y quizás con igual nobleza.»

Él parpadeó: «Se atreve a compararme con ese mendigo tonto y sucio. Cuando los guardias de la Corte lo aprehendieron estaba demandando audiencia conmigo, porque es un dignatario visitante. ¡Pero mírelo! ¡Este hombre está loco!»

Yo dije: «No, mi señor. De donde él viene tiene un rango equivalente al de usted, sólo que los azteca no usan el título de Uey-Tlatoáni.»

«¿Qué?», dijo Motecuzoma sorprendido.

«Éste es el Tlatocapili Tlilectic-Mixtli de Aztlán.»

«¿De dónde?», gritó Motecuzoma pasmado.

Volví a sonreír a mi tocayo. «¿Entonces, trajiste la Piedra de la Luna?»

Él asintió con un gruñido abrupto y enojado y dijo: «Empiezo a desear no haberlo hecho. Pero la Piedra de Coyolxaúqui está más allá, en la plaza, custodiada por los hombres que pudieron sobrevivir a la labor de ayudarme a empujarla, arrastrarla y embarcarla hasta aquí...»

Uno de los guardias que lo sujetaba murmuró lo suficientemente audible: «Esa maldita piedrota ha deshecho el pavimento de la ciudad, desde aquí hasta el camino-puente de Tepeyaca.»

El recién llegado dijo: «Esos hombres que quedan y yo, estamos casi muertos de fatiga y de hambre. Creímos que íbamos a ser bien recibidos aquí. Nos hubiéramos sentido satisfechos con una hospitalidad común y corriente, pero en cambio he sido llamado mentiroso sólo por decir *¡mi propio nombre!*»

Me volví hacia Motecuzoma, quien todavía estaba mirando como si no lo pudiera creer. Yo le dije: «Como puede comprobar, Señor Orador, el Señor del Aztlán es capaz de explicar su nombre. También le puede decir su rango, su origen y cualquier cosa que usted desee saber de él. Encontrará que el náhuatl de los azteca es un poco anticuado, pero bastante comprensible.»

Motecuzoma volvió de su sorpresa con un sobresalto y se disculpó y saludó al hombre diciendo: «Nosotros conversaremos con usted a su conveniencia, Señor del Aztlán, después de que usted haya cenado y descansado.» Y dio órdenes a sus guardias y consejeros para que los visitantes fueran alimentados, vestidos y hospedados como se debía hacer con un dignatario. Él me hizo un gesto para que me quedara cuando todos salieron de la sala del trono, y entonces me dijo:

«Apenas puedo creerlo. Una experiencia tan inquietante como lo sería el encontrarme con mi legendario abuelo Motecuzoma. O como ver una figura de piedra desprenderse del bajorrelieve del friso de un templo. ¡Imagínese! Un aztécatl genuino y vivo. —Sin embargo, su naturaleza suspicaz pronto salió a relucir, pues me preguntó—: Pero, ¿qué hace él *aquí*?»

«Como yo le sugerí, cuando volví a descubrir el Aztlán, le trae a usted un regalo, mi señor. Si usted quiere ir a la plaza y verlo, yo creo que valió la pena que hubiera roto unas cuantas piedras del pavimento.»

«Eso haré —dijo, pero luego añadió todavía suspicaz—: Él ha de querer algo a cambio.»

Yo dije: «Pienso que la Piedra de la Luna es lo suficientemente valiosa como para que su dador tenga algunos títulos rimbombantes y también algunos mantos de plumas, algunos ornamentos enjoyados, en fin, que vaya vestido de acuerdo a su nuevo rango. Y quizás también podrían serle cedidos algunos guerreros mexica.»

«¿Guerreros?»

Le conté a Motecuzoma la idea que ya antes le había expuesto al gobernante del Aztlán: que si se renovaban los lazos familiares que unían a los mexica con los azteca, darían a la Triple Alianza lo que todavía no tenía, una fuerte guarnición en la costa del noroeste.

Él dijo con precaución: «Teniendo en cuenta todos estos augurios, éste no debe de ser el tiempo de dispersar nuestros ejércitos, pero consideraré esa idea. Y una cosa sí es segura, aunque él es más joven que usted o yo, nuestro ancestro merece un título mejor que el de Tlatocapili. Por lo menos pondré el -tzin a su nombre.»

Así que dejé el palacio ese día sintiéndome muy complacido de que un Mixtli, aunque no fuera yo, hubiese conseguido el noble nombre de Mixtzin. Lo que sucedió fue que Motecuzoma aceptó todas las sugestiones que le hice. El visitante dejó nuestra ciudad llevando el rimbombante título de Azteca Tlani-Tlatoani o Menor Orador de los Azteca. También llevó con él, una tropa considerable de guerreros armados y un buen número de familias para colonizar, seleccionadas por su destreza en el arte de la construcción y fortificación.

Sólo tuve la oportunidad de sostener una breve conversación con mi tocayo antes de que él saliera de Tenochtitlan. Me dio las gracias efusivamente por mi ayuda en darle la bienvenida, en conseguirle su nuevo título y por haberle hecho un aliado de la Triple Alianza y añadió:

«Teniendo el -tzin para mi nombre, lo pueden usar todas las personas de mi familia y mis descendientes, aun aquellos que no desciendan en la línea directa y de divergente linaje. Debes de venir otra vez al Aztlán, hermano, pues te espera una pequeña sorpresa. Encontrarás más que una ciudad nueva y mejor.»

En ese tiempo, supuse que lo que él quería decir era el arreglar alguna ceremonia para hacerme señor honorario o algo por el estilo de los azteca, pero nunca he regresado al Aztlán y no sé lo que ha llegado a ser en todos estos años, después del regreso de Mixtzin. En cuanto a la magnífica Piedra de la Luna, Motecuzoma hizo lo de costumbre, fue incapaz de decidir en qué parte de El Corazón del Único Mundo podía ser colocada. Así es que la última vez que recuerdo haberla visto, la Piedra de la Luna todavía estaba yaciendo de lado sobre el pavimento de la plaza, ahora ha quedado tan enterrada y perdida como la Piedra del Sol.

El hecho fue que pasó algo más que hizo que yo y la mayoría de la gente olvidáramos rápidamente la visita del azteca, la Piedra de la Luna que había traído consigo y los planes para hacer del Aztlán una gran ciudad marítima. Lo que sucedió fue que un mensajero llegó cruzando el lago de Texcoco y llevando puesto el manto blanco de duelo. La noticia no fue ni tan inesperada ni sorprendente, pues el Reverendo Orador Nezahualpili ya era para entonces muy viejo, pero yo me sentí desolado al oír que mi antiguo patrón y protector había muerto.

Pude haber ido a Texcoco con todos los campeones Águila, acompañando a los demás nobles mexica y cortesanos, quienes cruzaron el lago para asistir al funeral de Nezahualpili y quienes se quedarían allí o volverían a cruzar el lago, poco tiempo después, para asistir a la coronación del Príncipe Heredero Ixtlil-Xóchitl, como el nuevo Venerado Orador de la nación acolhua. Pero escogí ir sin pompa ni ceremonia, vestido completamente de duelo y como un ciudadano privado. Fui como un viejo amigo de la familia y me recibió mi viejo compañero de escuela, el Príncipe Huexotzinca, quien lo hizo tan cordialmente como la primera vez, hacía unos treinta y tres años atrás, y me saludó con el nombre que entonces yo había llevado: «¡Bien venido, Cabeza Inclinada!» No pude dejar de notar que mi antiguo compañero de escuela ya estaba viejo; traté de que no notara por mi expresión lo que había sentido, cuando lo vi con el pelo gris y su rostro surcado de arrugas, pues yo lo recordaba como aquel delgado y joven príncipe que paseaba con su venado en un jardín lleno de verdor. Pero luego pensé, incómodo: «Él no es mayor que *yo*.»

El Uey-Tlatoani Nezahualpili fue enterrado en el suelo de su palacio de la ciudad, y no en la tierra más extensa de la colina de Texcotzinco. Así es que el pequeño palacio quedó abarrotado con toda aquella gente que había ido allí para decirle adiós a ese hombre tan amado y respetado. Allí había gobernantes, señores y señoras de todas las naciones de la Triple Alianza y de todas las tierras, amigas o enemigas. Aquellos emisarios de lejanas naciones que no podían llegar a tiempo para el funeral de Nezahualpili, sin embargo, ya estaban de camino hacia Texcoco en ese momento, apurándose a llegar a tiempo para saludar a su hijo, como el nuevo gobernante. De todos los que *debían* estar al lado de su tumba, el ausente más destacado fue Motecuzoma, quien había mandado en su lugar a su Mujer Serpiente Tlácotzin y a su hermano Cuitláhuac, jefe principal de los ejércitos mexica.

El Príncipe Huexotzinca y yo estuvimos lado a lado de la tumba y no muy retirados de su medio hermano, Ixtlil-Xóchitl, heredero del trono de los acolhua. De alguna manera él hacía recordar su nombre de Flor Oscura, ya que todavía tenía las cejas tan oscuras que le hacían parecer como si siempre estuviera enfurruñado. Pero había perdido mucho de su pelo y yo pensé que parecía diez años más viejo de lo que representaba su padre cuando yo fui a la escuela por primera vez en Texcoco. Después del entierro, la multitud se dirigió hacia los salones de baile de palacio, para festejar, cantar, pensar en voz alta y contar las hazañas y méritos del difunto Nezahualpili. Pero Huexotzinca y yo nos llevamos varias jarras del mejor *octli* a sus cámaras privadas y gradualmente nos fuimos poniendo muy borrachos, conforme revivíamos los viejos días de nuestra juventud y contemplábamos los días por venir.

Recuerdo que dije: «He oído muchos murmullos acerca de la ausencia tan descortés de Motecuzoma el día de hoy. Nunca le ha perdonado a tu padre el no haberse mantenido lejos durante todos estos años pasados y particularmente el haberse rehusado a ayudarlo en sus pequeñas y despreciables guerras.»

El príncipe se encogió de hombros: «Las descortesías de Motecuzoma no le ganarán los favores de mi medio hermano. Flor Oscura es el hijo de nuestro padre y piensa como él pensaba, que El Único Mundo algún día, muy pronto, será invadido por forasteros y que nuestra única seguridad será la unión. Él continuará la política de mi padre: que nosotros los acolhua debemos conservar nuestras energías para una guerra que no será precisamente pequeña.»

«Quizás sea lo más correcto —le dije—. Pero Motecuzoma no amará a tu hermano más de lo que amó a tu padre.»

Lo siguiente que recuerdo es que miré por la ventana y exclamé: «Cómo se fue el tiempo. Ya es noche cerrada... y yo estoy desastrosamente borracho.»

«Descansa en la habitación de allá —dijo el príncipe—. Debemos de estar en pie mañana para escuchar a todos los poetas de palacio leer sus panegíricos.»

«Si duermo ahora tendré un horrible dolor de cabeza mañana —le dije—. Es mejor, con tu permiso, que primero vaya a caminar por la ciudad y deje que Viento de la Noche sople los vapores que tiene mi cerebro.»

Mi manera de caminar probablemente era digna de verse, pero no había nadie por allí que pudiera hacerlo. Las calles, en la oscuridad de la noche, estaban más vacías que de costumbre, pues todos los habitantes de Texcoco estaban de duelo adentro de sus casas. Y era evidente que los sacerdotes habían arrojado partículas de cobre entre las astillas de pino de las antorchas, que estaban en los soportes de las esquinas de las calles, pues sus llamas eran azules y sus luces se veían disminuidas y sombrías. Medio sonámbulo como iba, de alguna manera tuve la impresión de que estaba repitiendo el camino que había seguido una vez, hacía ya mucho tiempo. Esa impresión exaltó todavía más mi imaginación cuando vi, delante de mí la banca de piedra y el árbol *tapachini* de flores rojas. Me senté agradecido, por un rato, gozando al ser rociado por los pétalos escarlata del árbol, que el viento hacía volar. Entonces me di cuenta de que a cada lado de mí, estaba sentado un hombre.

Me giré hacia mi izquierda, levanté mi cristal y vi al mismo hombre encorvado, de color cacao, vestido con jirones que había visto muy seguido en mi vida. Me volví a mi derecha y vi a aquel otro mejor vestido, pero sucio y cansado, que había visto antes, aunque no tan seguido. Supongo que debí de brincar y lanzar un fuerte grito, pero sólo me reí entre dientes como un borracho, dándome cuenta de que eran simplemente visiones producidas por todo el *octli* que había ingerido. Todavía riendo me dirigí a ambos:

«Venerables señores, ¿no se han ido a la tumba con su personificador?»

El hombre de color cacao sonrió enseñando los pocos dientes que tenía: «Hubo un tiempo en que tú creías que éramos dioses. Supusiste que yo era Huehuetéotl, El Más Viejo de Todos los Viejos Dioses, el que fue más venerado en estas tierras, mucho antes de que lo fueran los otros.»

«Y yo era el dios Yoali Ehécatl —dijo el hombre sucio—. El Viento de la Noche, quien puede arrebatar a los viajeros que caminan despreocupados por la noche, o recompensarlos, de acuerdo a su voluntad.»

Yo asentí, decidido a seguirles el humor aunque ellos sólo fueran alucinaciones. «Es verdad, mis señores, de que yo una vez fui joven y crédulo. Pero luego supe que el pasatiempo favorito de Nezahualpili era vagar disfrazado por el mundo.»

«¿Y eso hace que no creas en los dioses?», me preguntó el hombre color cacao.

Yo hipé y dije: «Déjeme aclarar esto. Nunca me he encontrado con ninguno, excepto ustedes dos.»

El hombre polvoriento murmuró oscuramente: «Pudiera ser que los verdaderos dioses sólo aparecieran cuando están cerca de desaparecer.»

Yo les dije: «Entonces, será mejor que ustedes desaparezcan, y se vayan a donde deben estar. Nezahualpili no se sentirá muy contento caminando por ese horrendo camino hacia Mictlan, mientras dos de sus formas incorpóreas están todavía en este mundo.»

El hombre color cacao se rió. «Quizás no podamos dejarte, viejo amigo. Hemos seguido por tanto tiempo tu destino en *tus* diferentes personalidades: como Mixtli, el Topo, Cabeza Inclinada, ¡Trae!, como Zaa Nayàzú, Ek Muyal, Su-kurú...»

Yo le interrumpí: «Usted recuerda todos mis nombres mejor que yo.»

«¡Entonces, recuerda los nuestros! —dijo cortante—. Yo soy Huehuetéotl y éste es Yoali Ehécatl.»

«Para ser unos simples aparecidos —gruñí—, ustedes son abominablemente persistentes e insistentes. Hace mucho que no había estado tan borracho como ahora, la última vez debió de haber sido hace unos siete u ocho años. Y ahora recuerdo... que entonces dije que algún día encontraría a un dios en alguna parte y entonces le preguntaría... le preguntaría esto: ¿por qué los dioses tenían que dejarme vivir por tanto tiempo, mientras que hacían morir a todas aquellas personas que estaban cerca de mi corazón? Mi querida hermana, mi amada esposa, mi hijo recién nacido, mi adorada hija y tantos amigos cercanos, aunque fueran cariños pasajeros...»

«Eso tiene una fácil respuesta —dijo la harapienta aparición que se llamaba a sí misma El Más Viejo de Todos los Viejos Dioses—. Esas personas fueron, por decirlo así, los martillos y los cinceles con que te hemos esculpido y ellos se rompieron o fueron descartados. Tú, no. Tú has aguantado todos los golpes, las raspaduras y las asperezas.»

Yo asentí con la solemnidad de la borrachera y dije: «Ésa es la respuesta de un borracho, si es que es una respuesta.»

La polvorienta aparición que se llamaba a sí misma Viento de la Noche dijo: «De toda la gente, Mixtli, tú eres el que más sabes que una estatua o un monumento no llega ya esculpido a la cantera de piedra caliza. Debe ser cortado con hachas, alisado con polvo de obsidiana y expuesto a los elementos para que se endurezca. Y hasta que no está cortado, endurecido y pulido no se puede utilizar.»

«¿Utilizar? —dije con aspereza—. Al final de mis caminos y de mis días ya mermados, ¿para qué podría ser útil?»

Viento de la Noche dijo: «Yo mencioné un monumento. Lo único que tienes que hacer es estar en pie y derecho, pero no siempre es una cosa fácil de hacer.»

«Y no se consigue fácilmente —dijo El Más Viejo de Todos los Dioses Viejos—. Esta misma noche, tu Venerado Orador Motecuzoma ha cometido un error irreparable y cometerá otros. Una tormenta de fuego y sangre se aproxima, Mixtli. Has sido tallado y endurecido con un solo propósito, que puedas sobrevivir a ella.»

Volví a hipar y pregunté: «¿Y por qué yo?»

El Más Viejo dijo: «Hace mucho tiempo, un día tú estuviste parado al lado de una colina, no lejos de aquí, indeciso si escalarla o no. Entonces yo te dije que ningún hombre podría jamás vivir cualquier vida, que no fuera la que él escogiera. Tú escogiste subir la cuesta. Los dioses te elegimos y te ayudamos.»

Yo reí con una risa horrible.

«Oh, tú no puedes apreciar nuestras intenciones —admitió—, no más que la piedra puede reconocer los beneficios que le da el martillo y el cincel. Pero sí te ayudamos. Y ahora tienes que devolver los favores recibidos.»

«Tú sobrevivirás a la tormenta», dijo Viento de la Noche.

El Más Viejo continuó: «Los dioses te ayudaron a llegar a ser un conocedor de palabras; luego para que viajaras a muchas partes, para ver, aprender y adquirir mucha experiencia. Es por eso que tú, más que ningún otro hombre, sabrás cómo era el Único Mundo.»

«¿Era?», repetí.

El Más Viejo hizo un gesto como de barrer con su brazo delgado. «Todo esto va a desaparecer de la vista, del tacto y de cualquier otra sensación y sentido humano. Sólo existirá en la memoria. Y tú serás el encargado de recoger y transmitir esos recuerdos.»

«Tú perseverarás», dijo Viento de la Noche.

El Más Viejo cogió mi hombro y dijo con un dejo de infinita melancolía: «Algún día, cuando todo se haya ido... para nunca volverse a ver... algunos hombres levantarán las cenizas de estas tierras y ellos se maravillarán y se preguntarán. Tú tienes los recuerdos y las palabras para contar la magnificencia de El Único Mundo, para que así nunca sea olvidado. ¡Tú, Mixtli! Cuando todos los monumentos de todas estas tierras hayan caído, cuando incluso la Gran Pirámide haya caído, tú no lo harás.»

«Tú permanecerás en pie», dijo Viento de la Noche.

Yo me reí otra vez, mofándome ante la absurda idea de que la Gran Pirámide se cayera alguna vez. Todavía tratando de seguirles el humor a los dos fantasmas censores, les dije: «Mis señores, yo no estoy hecho de piedra. Sólo soy un hombre y un hombre es el más frágil de los monumentos.»

Pero no escuché ninguna respuesta o censura. Las apariciones se habían ido tan rápidamente como habían llegado y yo estaba hablando solo.

Desde la distancia en donde estaba sentado, la antorcha de la calle parpadeaba sus caprichosas llamas azules. Bajo esa luz mortecina, las flores rojas del *tapachini* que caían sobre mí se veían oscuras, de un color carmesí, como si lloviznara gotas de sangre. Me estremecí de horror, pues sentí algo que ya había experimentado una vez, mucho tiempo antes —cuando por primera vez me había parado a la orilla de la noche, a la orilla de la oscuridad—, el sentimiento de encontrarme totalmente solo en el mundo, desolado y perdido. El lugar en donde estaba sentado era sólo una pequeña isla dentro de la luz azul y opaca y todo lo que le rodeaba estaba oscuro, vacío y el suave gemido del viento nocturno, y el viento gemía: «Recuerda...»

✠

Cuando fui despertado por el guarda que hacía su ronda, apagando las antorchas de la calle, al amanecer, me reí de mi conducta de borracho, tan impropia, e incluso de mi sueño tan tonto. Caminé de regreso al palacio, entumecido por haber dormido en la banca de piedra fría, esperando encontrar a toda la corte todavía dormida. Pero había una gran excitación allí, todo el mundo estaba levantado y se movía de un lado para otro y un buen número de guerreros mexica armados estaban inexplicablemente apostados en todas las puertas del edificio. Cuando encontré al príncipe Huexotzinca y ceñudo me dio la noticia, entonces empecé a preguntarme si el encuentro de la noche pasada había sido en realidad un sueño. Pues la nueva era que Motecuzoma había hecho una cosa muy baja y jamás oída.

Ya he dicho que era una tradición inviolable que en una solemne ceremonia como el funeral de algún alto gobernante, no se echara a perder ésta con un asesinato o con algún otro tipo de traición. También he dicho que el ejército acolhua había sido dado de baja por el difunto Nezahualpili y las pocas tropas que todavía estaban bajo las armas, no estaban preparadas para rechazar invasiones. Como también les dije, Motecuzoma había enviado al funeral a su Mujer Serpiente y al jefe de su ejército, Cuitláhuac. Pero no les he dicho, porque no lo sabía, que Cuitláhuac había llevado consigo un *acali* de guerra con sesenta buenos guerreros mexica, quienes habían desembarcado secretamente, a las afueras de Texcoco.

Durante la noche, mientras en la confusión de mi borrachera estaba conversando con mis alucinaciones o conmigo mismo, Cuitláhuac y sus guerreros habían derrotado a los guardias de palacio, habían tomado el edificio y el Mujer Serpiente había citado a todos sus habitantes para que escucharan lo que iba a proclamar. El Príncipe Flor Oscura *no* sería coronado como el sucesor al trono de su padre. Motecuzoma, como jefe supremo de la Triple Alianza, había decretado que el gobernante de Texcoco sería, en lugar de él, uno de los príncipes menores, Cacama, Mazorca de Maíz, de veinte años de edad e hijo de Nezahualpili y de una de sus concubinas, que no incidentalmente era la hermana menor de Motecuzoma.

Ese despliegue de coacción era inaudito y censurable, pero indisputable. Aunque la política pacifista de Nezahualpili hubiera sido admirable en un principio, desgraciada y tristemente dejó a su pueblo incapacitado para resistir cuando los mexica se mezclaran en sus asuntos. El Príncipe Heredero Flor Oscura demostró la más furiosa y oscura indignación, pero fue todo lo que pudo hacer. El Jefe Cuitláhuac no era un hombre malo a pesar de ser hermano de Motecuzoma y de haber seguido sus órdenes, así es que expresó sus condolencias al desposeído príncipe y le aconsejó que se fuera silenciosamente lo más lejos posible, antes de que Motecuzoma pudiera tener la buena idea, muy práctica por cierto, de hacerlo su prisionero o de eliminarlo.

Así es que Flor Oscura se fue ese mismo día, acompañado por sus cortesanos, sirvientes y guardias personales y de un buen número de otros nobles, que estaban igualmente enfurecidos por lo que había sucedido, todos ellos prometiendo a viva voz que tomarían venganza por haber sido traicionados por un aliado que lo había sido durante mucho tiempo. El resto de la gente de Texcoco sólo pudo quedarse impotentemente ultrajada y preparándose para asistir a la coronación del sobrino de Motecuzoma, como Cacámatzin, Uey-Tlatoani de los acolhua.

No me quedé a la ceremonia. Yo era mexícatl y en esos momentos un mexícatl no era muy popular en Texcoco, y en verdad que no me sentía muy orgulloso de ser un mexícatl. Aun mi antiguo compañero de escuela, Huexotzinca, me miraba pensativo, probablemente preguntándose si yo había hablado veladamente de esa traición cuando le había dicho: «Motecuzoma no amará a tu hermano más de lo que amó a tu padre.» Así es que me fui y regresé a Tenochtitlan, en donde todos los sacerdotes jubilosamente estaban preparando ritos especiales en casi todos los templos, para celebrar «la estratagema tan astuta de nuestro Venerado Orador». Y Cacámatzin apenas había calentado con sus nalgas la silla del trono de Texcoco, cuando le fue anunciado que la política de su padre sería derogada, llamando a lista nuevamente a todas las tropas acolhua, para ayudar a su tío Motecuzoma a llevar a efecto otra batalla ofensiva en contra de la eternamente beligerante nación de Texcala.

Tampoco esa guerra tuvo éxito, principalmente porque el nuevo aliado de Motecuzoma, joven y belicoso, no fue de mucha ayuda para él, a pesar de que lo había seleccionado personalmente y de que era su pariente. Cacama no era ni amado ni temido por sus súbditos y su llamada a todos los guerreros fue absolutamente ignorada. Aunque en seguida él hizo una llamada severa para el reclutamiento, sólo unos pocos hombres, comparativamente, respondieron a ésta, y eso con mucha reluctancia, y demostraron ser muy negligentes en la batalla. Otros acolhua, quienes de otra manera hubieran estado ansiosos de tomar las armas, se excusaron diciendo que ya eran muy viejos para pelear o que habían caído enfermos durante los años de paz que Nezahualpili había decretado o que eran padres de una gran familia a la que no podían dejar. La verdad era que ellos eran fieles al Príncipe Heredero que debió ser su Venerado Orador.

Al dejar Texcoco, Flor Oscura se había ido a alguna otra residencia campestre de la familia real, en algún lugar al norte en las montañas y había empezado a fortificar una guarnición allí. Además de los nobles y sus familias que se habían ido, voluntariamente, al exilio con él, muchos otros acolhua se unieron a esa compañía: campeones y guerreros que habían servido bajo las órdenes directas de su padre. Había otros hombres también que aunque no podían dejar sus hogares o negocios permanentemente y que por eso se tuvieron que quedar en los dominios de Cacama, se escurrían por intervalos al reducto que Flor Oscura tenía en la montaña, para adiestrarse y practicar con las otras tropas. Todos esos hechos eran desconocidos por mí en ese tiempo, como también lo eran a la mayoría de la gente. Era un secreto muy bien guardado el que Flor Oscura se estaba preparando, despacio y cuidadosamente, para rescatar su trono de las manos del usurpador, aunque tuviera que pelear con toda la Triple Alianza.

Mientras tanto, la disposición de Motecuzoma, venenosa la mayor parte del tiempo, no había adelantado mucho. Sospechaba que había caído mucho en el ánimo y en la estima de los otros gobernantes, por su intervención dominante en los asuntos de Texcoco. Se sentía humillado por haber fallado, una vez más, en su intento de humillar a Texcala, y no estaba muy complacido con su sobrino Cacama. Entonces, como si no tuviera suficientes cosas que le causaran preocupación y fastidio, otras todavía más problemáticas empezaron a ocurrir.

La muerte de Nezahualpili casi pudo haber sido la señal para que se cumplieran sus oscuras predicciones. En el mes El Árbol Se Levanta que siguió a su funeral, un mensajero-veloz maya llegó con más noticias perturbadoras acerca de que los extraños hombres blancos habían vuelto otra vez a Uluümil Kutz y esa vez no fueron dos, sino cientos. Habían llegado en tres barcos, que echaron anclas en el puerto del pueblo de Kimpech, en la playa oeste de la península, y habían remado hacia la playa en sus grandes canoas. La gente de Kimpech, la que no había sido diezmada por las pequeñas viruelas, resignadamente los dejaron desembarcar sin molestarlos u oponerse. Sin embargo, los hombres blancos entraron en un templo, todos en grupo, y sin hacer siquiera un gesto para pedir permiso, empezaron a arrancar la ornamentación dorada del templo, a lo cual, la población local arremetió en contra de ellos.

O por lo menos lo intentaron, según dijo el mensajero, pues las armas de los guerreros kimpech se estrellaban contra los cuerpos de metal de los hombres blancos y entonces éstos habían gritado «¡Santiago!», como un grito de guerra y pelearon retrocediendo a sus barcos, con unos palos que llevaban, pero que no eran palos ni estacas. Los palos esos lanzaban truenos y luces como lo hace el dios Chak cuando está enojado, y muchos maya cayeron muertos a gran distancia por lo que escupían esos palos. Por supuesto que ahora todos sabemos lo que el mensajero estaba tratando de describir, la armadura de acero de sus soldados y sus arcabuces que matan desde lejos, pero en aquel tiempo esa historia parecía la de un demente.

Sin embargo, él había llevado consigo dos cosas para sustentar su extraña historia. Una era un papel de corteza llevando la cuenta de los que habían muerto: más de cien de los kimpech, entre hombres, mujeres y niños; cuarenta y dos de los forasteros, y una indicación de que los kimpech habían tenido que pelear muy fuerte contra esas nuevas y terribles armas. Como fuera, los defensores habían podido repeler a los invasores. Los hombres blancos se batieron en retirada hacia sus canoas y de allí a sus barcos, que extendiendo sus alas se perdieron de vista, otra vez, más allá del horizonte. La otra cosa que había traído el mensajero era la cara de un hombre blanco muerto, que había sido desollada de su cabeza, con todo su pelo y su barba, y la traía seca y tiesa dentro de una horquilla de sauce. Más tarde tuve la oportunidad de verla y se parecía mucho a las de los otros hombres que había conocido, por lo menos la misma piel color de cal, pero su pelo y su barba eran de un color todavía más extraordinario: eran tan amarillos como el oro.

Motecuzoma recompensó al mensajero por haber traído ese trofeo, pero después de que el hombre se fue, se refirió a ellos maldiciéndolos mucho, por lo tontos que eran los maya: «¡Imagínense, atacar a visitantes que bien pudieran ser dioses!» Y con gran agitación se encerró con su Consejo de Voceros, sus sacerdotes, sus adivinos, sus profetas y hechiceros. Pero a mí no me pidió que me reuniera en esa conferencia y si llegaron a alguna conclusión, yo no oí nada acerca de eso.

Sin embargo, un poco más de un año después, en el año Trece-Conejo, el año en que yo cumplí mi gavilla de años, los hombres blancos se dejaron ver de nuevo en el horizonte, pero esa vez Motecuzoma me llamó para tener una conferencia privada con él.

«Para variar —dijo—, esta noticia no ha sido traída por un maya de frente puntiaguda y cerebro pequeño; lo ha hecho un grupo de nuestros propios pochteca, que en aquellos momentos estaban comerciando a lo largo de la costa del mar del este. Se encontraban en Xicalanca cuando seis de esos barcos llegaron y ellos tuvieron el buen sentido de no sentir pánico ni dejar que éste cundiera entre la población.»

Yo recordaba muy bien Xicalanca, el bellísimo pueblo situado entre el océano azul y una laguna verde, en la nación de Cupilco.

«Así es que allí no hubo lucha —continuó Motecuzoma—, a pesar de que esta vez los hombres blancos eran doscientos cuarenta y de que los nativos estaban muy asustados. Nuestros firmes *pochteca* tomaron el mando de la situación, hicieron que todo el mundo conservara la calma e incluso persuadieron al gobernante Tabascoöb para que les diera la bienvenida a los recién llegados. Así es que los hombres blancos no causaron ningún problema, no saquearon ningún templo, no robaron nada, ni siquiera molestaron a las mujeres y se volvieron a ir, después de haber pasado el día admirando el pueblo y probando la comida nativa. Por supuesto que nadie pudo comunicarse con ellos en su propio lenguaje, pero nuestros mercaderes se las arreglaron por medio de señas para sugerirles algún trueque. Aunque los hombres blancos habían llegado a la costa, sin traer mucho con que comerciar, así lo hicieron; a cambio de unas cuantas cañas de polvo de oro, dieron ¡*esto!*»

Y Motecuzoma, con el mismo gesto que hace un adivino callejero sacando mágicamente unos dulces ante una multitud de niños, extrajo de su manto, con rápido movimiento, varios hilos de cuentas. Aunque estaban hechos de diferentes materiales y de diversos colores, tenían las mismas cuentas pequeñas separadas por otras más largas a determinados intervalos. Eran hilos de oraciones, como el que yo había conseguido de Jerónimo de Aguilar, siete años antes. Motecuzoma sonrió y su sonrisa parecía ser de vindicación, como si esperara de mí que de repente yo me rebajara ante él y le concediera: «Usted tenía razón, mi señor, los extranjeros *son* dioses.»

Pero en lugar de eso, dije: «Claramente se ve, Señor Orador, que esos hombres blancos, todos ellos, adoran o rezan de la misma manera, lo que indica que todos son del mismo lugar de origen. Pero ya hemos supuesto eso. Y estas cuentas no nos dicen nada nuevo acerca de ellos.»

«¿Y esto? —Y de detrás de su trono, sacó con el mismo aire de triunfo lo que parecía ser una olla de plata empañada—. Uno de los visitantes se la quitó de la cabeza y la cambió por oro.»

Yo examiné esa cosa. No era una olla, pues por su forma no se podía mantener inmóvil. Era de metal, de una clase del mismo color de la plata, pero no tan brillante —por supuesto que era acero— y en la parte que estaba abierta tenía amarradas unas tiras de cuero, evidentemente para ser asegurada a la barbilla del que la llevaba.

Yo dije: «Es un yelmo, como seguramente el Venerado Orador ya ha adivinado. Y muy práctico, ninguna *maquáhuitl* podría lastimar la cabeza del hombre que llevara puesto uno de éstos. Sería una cosa muy buena si nuestros propios guerreros pudieran ser equipados con...»

«¡Usted se está olvidando del punto más importante! —dijo él interrumpiéndome impaciente—. Esta cosa tiene la forma exacta de lo que el dios Quetzalcóatl habitualmente llevaba sobre *su* reverenda cabeza.»

Yo dije escéptico, pero respetuoso. «¿Cómo podemos saber eso, mi señor?»

Con otro movimiento rápido, él sacó la última de sus triunfantes sorpresas. «¡Aquí está! Mire ahí, obstinado y viejo incrédulo. Mi sobrino Cacama me lo envió de los archivos de Texcoco.

Era un texto de historia escrito en piel de venado, que narraba la abdicación y la partida del gobernante tolteca Serpiente Emplumada. Motecuzoma apuntó, con dedo tembloroso, uno de los dibujos que mostraba a Quetzalcóatl diciendo adiós en su canoa que flotaba en el mar.

«Él está vestido como nosotros —dijo Motecuzoma, con voz algo trémula—. Pero lleva en su cabeza una cosa que seguramente era la corona de los tolteca. Ahora, ¡compárelo con el yelmo que usted sostiene en este momento!»

«No, indiscutiblemente que no puede discutirse la semejanza entre los dos objetos —le dije y él dio un gruñido de satisfacción. Pero yo continué con precaución—: Aunque a pesar de todo, mi señor, debemos tener en mente que hacía mucho tiempo que todos los tolteca ya no estaban aquí cuando cualquiera de los acolhua aprendió a dibujar. Por lo tanto, el artista que dibujo esto jamás pudo *ver* cómo se vestían los tolteca y mucho menos Quetzalcóatl. Le concedo a usted que la apariencia del tocado que está en este dibujo tiene una semejanza maravillosa con el yelmo del hombre blanco. Yo sé cómo los escribanos historiadores pueden dejar volar su imaginación en su trabajo, por lo que sugiero a mi señor que esto es sólo una coincidencia.»

«*¡Yya!* —exclamó Motecuzoma como si fuera a vomitar—. ¿Nada puede convencerlo a usted? Escuche, hay una prueba todavía mayor. Como hace tiempo lo prometí, puse a todos los historiadores de toda la Triple Alianza a buscar lo que pudieran encontrar acerca de los desaparecidos tolteca. Para su sorpresa, según ellos mismos reconocieron, encontraron muchas viejas leyendas sobrenaturales, extraviadas y olvidadas. Y escuche esto: de acuerdo con esas leyendas redescubiertas, los tolteca tenían una complexión pálida muy fuera de lo común y también tenían mucho pelo, los hombres acostumbraban dejárselo crecer en sus caras, porque lo consideraban un signo de hombría. —Él se inclinó hacia mí para verme mejor—. En simples palabras, Campeón Mixtli, los tolteca eran unos hombres blancos y barbudos, exactamente iguales a estos forasteros que cada vez nos visitan más frecuentemente. ¿Qué puede usted decir a eso?»

Pude haberle dicho que nuestras historias están tan llenas de leyendas y éstas son tan diversas y elaboradas, que cualquier niño podría encontrar alguna de ellas que pudiera sostener cualquier creencia extraordinaria o cualquier teoría nueva. Pude haberle dicho que aun el historiador más dedicado, de ninguna manera hubiera desilusionado al Venerado Orador si éste estaba encaprichado con una idea irracional y demandando algo con que sustentarla. Pero me callé esas cosas y dije circunspecto:

«Cualquier cosa que sean los hombres blancos, mi señor, usted ha hecho notar correctamente que sus visitas son cada vez más frecuentes. También, cada vez vienen en número mayor. También, cada vez desembarcan más hacia el oeste: Tiho, luego Kimpech y ahora Xicalanca, cada vez más cerca de nuestras tierras. ¿Qué va a hacer mi señor acerca de eso?»

Él se levantó de su trono, como si inconscientemente sospechara que estaba sentado allí precariamente y después de haber meditado por unos momentos, contestó:

«Cuando nadie se les ha opuesto, no han causado perjuicios o daño. Es obvio que prefieren viajar siempre en sus barcos o estar cerca del mar. Usted mismo ha dicho que vienen de unas islas. Así es que quienquiera que sean... los tolteca que regresan o los verdaderos dioses de los tolteca... no parecen demostrar ninguna inclinación a internarse tierra adentro, para venir a esta región que una vez fue de ellos. —Se encogió de hombros—. Si ellos desean regresar al Único Mundo, o quedarse sólo en las tierras costeras, bueno... —Se volvió a encoger de hombros—. ¿Por qué no habríamos de vivir, ellos y nosotros, amigablemente como vecinos? —Hizo una pausa y como yo no dije nada, él me preguntó con aspereza—: ¿No está usted de acuerdo?»

Yo le dije: «Según mi experiencia, Señor Orador, uno nunca puede saber cuándo un vecino será un tesoro o una desgracia hasta que éste se ha mudado para quedarse, y para entonces será muy tarde para arrepentirse. Lo podría comparar con un matrimonio impetuoso, uno sólo puede tener la esperanza de que será un buen matrimonio.»

Un poco menos de un año después, los vecinos se mudaron para quedarse. Fue en la primavera del año Uno-Caña que otro mensajero-veloz llegó y éste era de la nación de Cupilco, pero esa vez traía un recado tan alarmante que Motecuzoma envió por mí y al mismo tiempo reunió a su Consejo de Voceros para escuchar la noticia. El mensajero era portador de unos papeles de corteza en los que se daba la triste historia en palabras-pintadas. Pero mientras los examinábamos, él mismo nos contó lo que había pasado con palabras entrecortadas y llenas de angustia. En el día Seis-Flor, unos barcos habían aparecido en la costa, otra vez, con sus alas anchas desplegadas al viento y no unos cuantos de ellos, sino toda una *flota*, bastante atemorizante, de once barcos. Según su calendario, reverendos escribanos, eso debió de haber sido el día veinticinco de marzo o el primer día de su Año Nuevo, del año de mil quinientos diecinueve.

Los once barcos anclaron en la boca del Río de los Tabascoöb, mucho más hacia el oeste que la visita anterior, y habían vomitado en la playa incontables *cientos* de hombres blancos. Todos ellos armados y cubiertos con metal, que habían desembarcado gritando «¡Santiago!», que era aparentemente el nombre de su dios de la guerra, y llegaron con la clara intención de hacer algo más que admirar el paisaje y saborear los alimentos locales. Así es que la población había reunido inmediatamente a sus guerreros, no solamente los de Cupilco sino que también juntaron a los coatzacuali, a los coatlícamac y otros más de esa región, que en total fueron unos cinco mil. Se pelearon muchas batallas en el espacio de diez días, y la gente había luchado con bravura, pero sin provecho, pues las armas de los hombres blancos eran invencibles.

Ellos tenían lanzas, espadas, escudos y armaduras de metal,

contra las cuales la obsidiana de las *maquáhuime* se rompía al primer golpe. Tenían arcos muy pequeños y con el arco muy mal hecho, pero que lanzaba pequeñas flechas con increíble destreza. Tenían esos palos que lanzaban luz y truenos y que aunque hacía unos agujeritos insignificantes en sus víctimas, eran de muerte. Tenían unos tubos de metal puestos sobre unas ruedas muy grandes, que se parecían mucho más a una tormenta furiosa enviada por el dios, pues éstos escupían todavía más luz, atronaban más fuerte y que arrojaban pedacitos de metal dentado que segaban la vida de muchos hombres al mismo tiempo, como un maizal abatido por una tormenta de granizo. Pero lo más maravilloso, increíble y aterrorizador de todo, dijo el mensajero, es que algunos de esos guerreros blancos son hombres-bestias: sus cuerpos son como venados gigantes pero sin astas, sus cuatro patas tienen cascos, con los que galopan tan rápido como un venado, mientras que sus dos armas humanas que empuñan con habilidad, ya sea la lanza o la espada, tienen efectos letales y a su sola vista, hasta los hombres más valerosos tiemblan de miedo.

Veo que sonríen, reverendos frailes, pero en aquel tiempo, ni las palabras entrecortadas del mensajero, ni los rudos dibujos de Cupilco, nos pudieron dar una idea coherente de soldados montados en unos animales mucho más grandes de los que hay en estas tierras. Por lo mismo, nos quedamos sin comprender lo que el mensajero llamaba por perros-leones, que podían correr detrás de un hombre huyendo u oler su escondite y que podía destrozarlo tan terriblemente como lo haría una espada o un jaguar. Ahora, por supuesto, todos nosotros estamos íntimamente familiarizados con sus caballos y sabuesos y de su gran utilidad en la caza o en una batalla.

Cuando todas las fuerzas juntas de los nativos habían perdido ochocientos hombres por muerte y cerca de igual número por heridas graves, dijo el mensajero, y en ese tiempo sólo habían matado catorce de los invasores blancos, el Tabascoöb los llamó para que se rindieran. Mandó unos emisarios nobles portando las banderas doradas de tregua y ellos se aproximaron a las casas de tela que los hombres blancos habían erigido en la playa. Los nobles se sorprendieron cuando vieron que podían comunicarse con ellos, sin necesidad de gesticular, puesto que uno de los hombres blancos hablaba, comprensiblemente, un dialecto maya. Los enviados preguntaron que cuáles serían las demandas de los hombres blancos para rendirse y que la paz fuera declarada. Uno de los hombres blancos, evidentemente su jefe, dijo unas palabras ininteligibles que el que hablaba maya tradujo.

Reverendos escribanos, no puedo atestiguar la exactitud de esas palabras, ya que sólo les repito a ustedes lo que el mensajero cupícatl nos dijo ese día, y él lo escuchó, por supuesto, después de que éste hubo pasado por varias bocas y en las diversas lenguas que se hablaban en esos lugares. Pero las palabras fueron éstas:

«Decid a vuestro pueblo que no hemos venido a hacer la guerra. Venimos buscando un remedio para nuestras enfermedades. Nosotros los hombres blancos sufrimos de un mal del corazón, y el único remedio es el oro.»

A eso, el Mujer Serpiente Tlácotzin mirando a Motecuzoma dijo, en una voz que quería ser estimulante: «Eso puede ser una cosa muy valiosa para nosotros, Señor Orador. Los forasteros no son invulnerables a *todo*. Ellos tienen una curiosa enfermedad que jamás ha causado problemas a los pueblos de estas tierras.»

Motecuzoma asintió vacilante, con incertidumbre. Todos los hombres viejos de su Consejo de Voceros siguieron su ejemplo y como él asintieron, como si se reservaran sus juicios. Sólo un hombre viejo que estaba en esa habitación fue lo suficientemente rudo como para dar una opinión, y por supuesto ése era yo.

«Discúlpeme por diferir con usted, Señor Mujer Serpiente —le dije—. He conocido a mucha de nuestra gente que sufre los síntomas de esa enfermedad, y es llamada avaricia.»

Ambos, Tlácotzin y Motecuzoma me miraron enojados y yo ya no hablé más. Al mensajero se le dijo que prosiguiera con su historia, de la cual ya no quedaba mucho.

El Tabascoöb, dijo él, había hecho la paz al amontonar sobre las arenas cada fragmento de oro que pudo ser traído inmediatamente a ese lugar: vasijas, cadenas, imágenes de dioses, joyas, ornamentos de oro batido y aun en polvo, pepitas y pedazos crudos del metal todavía no trabajado. El hombre blanco que obviamente era el que mandaba, preguntó casi casualmente, de dónde conseguía la gente ese oro que aliviaba el corazón. El Tabascoöb le replicó que se encontraba en diferentes partes de El Único Mundo, pero que la mayor parte lo tenía el gobernante de los mexica, Motecuzoma, pues estaba atesorado en su ciudad capital. Los hombres blancos parecían estar seducidos por esa noticia y preguntaron dónde estaba esa ciudad. El Tabascoöb les dijo que sus casas flotantes podrían acercarse más a ella si iban más hacia el oeste, siguiendo la costa y luego hacia el noroeste.

Motecuzoma gruñó: «Qué vecinos tan útiles tenemos.»

El Tabascoöb también había dado, como un regalo, al comandante blanco veinte mujeres bellas para que se las dividieran entre él y sus oficiales. Diecinueve de las muchachas habían sido escogidas por el mismo Tabascoöb, como las vírgenes más deseables de toda esa región. Ellas no se sentían muy felices cuando fueron conducidas al campamento de los extranjeros, pero la muchacha número veinte se había ofrecido a sí misma, sin ningún egoísmo, para completar la cifra de veinte para ese regalo, cuyo número ritual podría influenciar a los dioses para que ya no mandaran más visitantes a Cupilco. Así es que, concluyó el mensajero cupícatl, los hombres blancos cargaron su oro y sus mujeres dentro de sus grandes canoas y luego abordaron sus inmensas casas flotantes y como toda la gente fervientemente esperaba, las grandes casas desplegaron sus alas y salieron rumbo al oeste, el día Trece-Flor, manteniéndose lo suficientemente cerca de la costa.

Motecuzoma gruñó un poco más, mientras los viejos de su

Consejo de Voceros se mezclaban en murmurante conferencia y el mayordomo de palacio acompañaba al mensajero fuera de la habitación.

«Mi Señor Orador —dijo uno de los viejos con timidez—, éste es el año Uno-Caña.»

«Muchas gracias —dijo Motecuzoma con acritud—. Eso es algo que ya sé.»

Otro viejo dijo: «Pero quizás el posible significado de él, haya escapado a la atención de mi señor. De acuerdo con una de las leyendas, Uno-Caña fue el año en que Quetzalcóatl nació en su forma humana, para ser el Uey-Tlatoani de los tolteca.»

Y otro dijo: «Uno-Caña pudo haber sido, por supuesto, el año en que Quetzalcóatl completó su gavilla de cincuenta y dos años. Y, también fue en *ese* año Uno-Caña, según la leyenda, que su enemigo el dios Tezcatlipoca lo engañó haciendo que se emborrachara, así que sin quererlo él cometió un pecado abominable.»

Y otro dijo: «El gran pecado que él cometió, mientras estaba ebrio, fue copular con su hija. Cuando despertó a su lado, a la mañana siguiente, su remordimiento le hizo abdicar su trono e irse lejos en su canoa, más allá del mar del este.»

Y otro dijo: «Pero aunque se fue él prometió volver. ¿Lo ve usted, mi señor? La Serpiente Emplumada había nacido en el año Uno-Caña y desapareció en el siguiente año llamado Uno-Caña. Admitimos que ésta es sólo una leyenda y que las otras acerca de Quetzalcóatl citan fechas diferentes y que todo eso sucedió hace incontables gavillas de años, pero, ya que éste *es* otro año Uno-Caña, ¿no sería bueno preguntarnos...?»

Ese hombre dejó caer su pregunta en el silencio, porque la cara de Motecuzoma estaba casi tan pálida como la de cualquier hombre blanco. Se vio tan afectado que se quedó sin habla y debió de haber sido porque al recordarle esas fechas que coincidían, siguiendo su significado de cerca llegó a lo que había dicho el mensajero: que los hombres que se fueron por el mar del este, aparentemente intentarían buscar su ciudad. O quizás se había puesto pálido por la alusión directa de una semejanza entre él y el Quetzalcóatl que había dejado el trono, por haber sentido vergüenza de su propio pecado. Motecuzoma tenía por entonces varios hijos de diferentes edades, de sus diversas esposas y concubinas, y por algún tiempo se escuchó por ahí un sordo rumor acerca de sus relaciones con dos o tres de sus hijas. El Venerado Orador tenía suficientes cosas para reflexionar en ese momento, pero el mayordomo de palacio regresó otra vez, besando la tierra y pidiendo permiso para anunciar la llegada de más mensajeros.

Era una delegación de cuatro hombres que venían de la nación totonaca en la costa este, y llegaban para informar que *allí* habían aparecido once de esos barcos llenos de hombres blancos. La entrada al salón de esos mensajeros totonaca, inmediatamente después del mensajero cupícatl, fue otra coincidencia inquietante, aunque no inexplicable. Habían pasado unos veinte días entre que los barcos habían dejado Cupilco para aparecer en la costa totonaca, pero esta última nación estaba casi directamente al este de Tenochtitlan y había muy buenos caminos comerciales entre las dos, en cambio el hombre de Cupilco había tenido que venir por una ruta mucho más larga y difícil. No era sorprendente, pues, la llegada de esos mensajeros diferentes, pero esto no hizo que ninguno de los que estábamos en el salón del trono nos sintiéramos tranquilos.

Los totonaca eran gente ignorante y no conocían el arte de las palabras-pintadas, así es que no habían enviado ningún mensaje escrito. Los cuatro mensajeros eran recordadores-de-palabras y traían un mensaje memorizado de su gobernante, el Señor Patzinca, como él se los había dicho, palabra por palabra. Debo hacerles notar aquí, que en un aspecto nuestros memoristas de palabras eran casi tan útiles como los informes escritos: podían repetir lo que hubieran memorizado, una y otra vez, cuantas veces fuera necesario y sin omitir o cambiar alguna palabra. Sin embargo, tenían sus limitaciones al ser imperiosamente interrogados. Cuando se les preguntaba algo para esclarecer alguna parte del mensaje, ellos no lo podían hacer, sólo podían repetir el mensaje exactamente como se les había dado. Ni siquiera podían hacer ese mensaje más elaborado, añadiéndole sus propias opiniones o impresiones, porque la sencillez de sus mentes les impedía hacer alguna de esas cosas.

«En el día Ocho-Lagarto, mi Señor Orador», empezó uno de los totonaca y continuó recitando el mensaje mandado por Patzinca. En el día Ocho-Lagarto, once barcos se materializaron sobre el océano y se detuvieron afuera de la bahía de Chalchihuacuecan. Era un lugar que yo ya había visitado una vez, El Lugar En Donde Abundan Las Cosas Bellas, pero no hice ningún comentario, pues sabía que no se debe interrumpir a un recordador de palabras. El hombre siguió con su mensaje diciendo que al día siguiente, el día Nueve-Viento, los extranjeros blancos y barbudos empezaron a llegar a la playa, en donde construyeron casitas de tela y que además habían erigido allí un palo largo, con grandes banderas y que habían empezado a representar lo que parecía ser una ceremonia, ya que cantaban mucho y gesticulaban y se arrodillaban y se paraban y que también había varios sacerdotes, que habían reconocido porque vestían todos de negro, exactamente igual a los de estas tierras. Ésos fueron los sucesos en el día Nueve-Viento. Al siguiente día...

Uno de los ancianos del Consejo de Voceros dijo pensativamente: «Nueve-Viento. De acuerdo, por lo menos con una de las leyendas, el nombre completo de Quetzalcóatl era Nueve-Viento Serpiente Emplumada. Lo que quiere decir que él había nacido en el día Nueve-Viento.»

Motecuzoma se tambaleó a simple vista, quizás porque esa información lo había sorprendido portentosamente o quizás porque el anciano debía de haber sabido que no se debía interrumpir a un recordador de palabras ya que éste no puede coger de nuevo el hilo de la narración en donde la dejó cuando lo interrumpen, tiene que volver a empezar otra vez.

«En el día Ocho-Lagarto...»

Él recorrió todo el principio hasta llegar al punto en donde se había quedado y continuó con su informe de que no había habido ninguna batalla en la playa ni en ningún otro lado, todavía. Cosa que era de comprenderse, pues los totonaca aparte de ser ignorantes eran serviles y de todo lloriqueaban. Por años habían estado subordinados a la Triple Alianza y regularmente habían pagado su tributo anual de frutas, madera fina, vainilla y cacao para hacer *chocólatl*, *pícietl* para fumar y otros productos de las Tierras Calientes, pero siempre habían entregado su tributo lloriqueando y quejándose.

Los habitantes de El Lugar En Donde Abundan Las Cosas Bellas, había dicho el mensajero, no se habían opuesto a la llegada de los forasteros, pero habían mandado aviso a su Señor Patzinca en la ciudad capital de Tzempoalan. Patzinca envió a varios de sus nobles llevando muchos regalos a los extranjeros blancos y barbados, y también una invitación para que fueran a visitar su Corte. Así es que cinco de esos hombres blancos, presumiblemente personajes de alto rango, aceptaron su invitación, llevando con ellos una mujer que había desembarcado con ellos. Ella ni era blanca ni tenía barbas, dijo el mensajero, sino que era una hembra de alguna nación más al norte de El Único Mundo. En el palacio de Tzempoalan, los visitantes presentaron sus regalos a Patzinca: una silla de curiosa construcción, muchas cuentas de colores, un sombrero muy pesado y una tela como con pelitos color roja. Los visitantes anunciaron entonces que ellos llegaban en representación de su gobernante llamado Reidoncarlos, y de un dios llamado Nuestro Señor y una diosa llamada Nuestra Señora.

Sí, reverendos escribanos, ya sé, ya sé. Solamente repito lo que aquel ignorante totonaca había dicho.

Entonces los visitantes le hicieron muchas preguntas a Patzinca referentes a su tierra. ¿A qué dios veneraba su pueblo? ¿Había mucho oro en ese lugar? ¿Era él un rey o un simple virrey? Aunque Patzinca estaba perplejo ante los muchos términos extraños utilizados en su interrogación, contestó lo mejor que pudo. De toda la multitud de dioses que existían, él y su pueblo adoraban a Tezcatlipoca como el más grande. Él era el gobernante de todos los totonaca, pero estaba sometido a las tres naciones más poderosas que se encontraban tierra adentro y de las cuales la más fuerte era la nación mexica, gobernada por el Venerado Orador Motecuzoma. Y en ese momento preciso, les había confiado Patzinca, cinco registradores de la tesorería mexica estaban en Tzempoalan para revisar la lista de artículos que los totonaca pagaban como tributo...

«Quisiera saber —dijo de repente el viejo consejero—, ¿a qué conducía toda esa interrogación? Hemos escuchado que uno de los hombres blancos hablaba la lengua maya, pero ninguno de los totonaca puede hablar más que su propia lengua y nuestro náhuatl.»

El recordador de palabras miró confundido por un momento, luego se aclaró la garganta y empezó otra vez: «En el día Ocho-Lagarto, mi Señor Orador...»

Motecuzoma miró exasperado al desgraciado viejo que había interrumpido y entre dientes le dijo: «Ahora todos moriremos de viejos antes de que este estúpido pueda terminar su mensaje.»

El totonácatl se aclaró otra vez la garganta y empezó: «En el día Ocho-Lagarto...», y todos nos sentamos inquietos hasta que llegó de nuevo en donde se había quedado, para darnos nueva información. Cuando lo hizo, ésta fue lo suficientemente interesante como para haber valido la pena el esperar.

Los cinco arrogantes registradores de tributo mexica, le dijo Patzinca a los hombres blancos, estaban muy enojados con él porque les había dado la bienvenida a ellos, los extranjeros, sin haber pedido permiso primero a su Venerado Orador Motecuzoma. En consecuencia, ellos habían añadido al tributo la demanda de diez muchachos totonaca y diez doncellas vírgenes totonaca para ser mandados junto con la vainilla, el cacao y otros artículos a Tenochtitlan, para ser sacrificados como víctimas cuando lo requirieran los dioses mexica.

Al oír eso, el jefe de los hombres blancos hizo gestos de que sentía una gran repugnancia por eso, y colérico le dijo a Patzinca que él no debía hacer una cosa como ésa, que en lugar de esto tenía que coger a los cinco oficiales mexica y hacerlos sus prisioneros. Cuando el Señor Patzinca expresó, horrorizado, su reluctancia a poner las manos sobre los funcionarios de Motecuzoma, el jefe blanco le prometió que sus soldados blancos defenderían a los totonaca contra cualquier represalia. Así es que Patzinca, aunque sudando por la aprensión, dio la orden y los cinco registradores fueron por último vistos —por los recordadores de palabras antes de salir para Tenochtitlan— aprisionados en una jaula pequeña, atados a las barras de ésta, todos ellos amontonados como si fueran pavos llevados al mercado, con las plumas de sus mantos lamentablemente alborotadas, por no hablar del estado de sus mentes.

«¡Eso es ultrajante! —gritó Motecuzoma, olvidándose de sí mismo—. Los extranjeros tienen una disculpa pues no conocen nuestras leyes tributarias, pero ese necio de Patzinca...! —Se levantó de su trono y agarró fuertemente al totonácatl que había estado hablando—. Cinco de mis registradores del tesoro han sido tratados así ¡y te atreves a venírmelo a *contar*! Por los dioses, que te echaré vivo a los grandes gatos que hay en el zoológico, ¡a menos de que tus siguientes palabras sean para dar una explicación y una disculpa a ese loco acto de traición de Patzinca!»

El hombre tragó saliva, sus ojos se hicieron acuosos, pero lo que él dijo fue: «En el día Ocho-Lagarto, mi Señor Orador...»

«¡*Ayya ouiya*, cállate! —rugió Motecuzoma. Regresó a su trono y con desesperación se cubrió el rostro con las manos—. Me retracto, ningún gato podría sentirse muy orgulloso de comerse semejante porquería.»

Uno de los ancianos consejeros, diplomáticamente, completó

la diversión al hacerle una señal a otro de los mensajeros para que hablara. Ése, inmediatamente empezó a balbucir muy rápido y mezclando los lenguajes. Era evidente que había estado presente por lo menos en una de las conferencias entre su gobernante y los visitantes, y estaba repitiendo cada una de las palabras que habían hablado entre ellos. También era evidente que el jefe blanco hablaba en español y después otro de los visitantes lo traducía al maya y después eso era traducido al náhuatl para que lo pudiera entender Patzinca, y después de que Patzinca había contestado, era otra vez traducido al jefe blanco de la misma manera.

«Afortunadamente está usted aquí, Mixtli —me dijo Motecuzoma—. Aunque el náhuatl está muy mal hablado, por lo menos podremos coger sentido, con suficientes repeticiones. Mientras que las otras lenguas... ¿puede decirnos qué es lo que ellos quieren decir?»

Me hubiera gustado poder hacerlo con una traducción inmediata y fluida, pero en verdad entendía tan poco como todos los presentes, incluyendo al que estaba revolcando las palabras. El acento del mensajero totonaca era más que un impedimento, pero tampoco su gobernante hablaba bien el náhuatl, ya que él sólo había aprendido ese lenguaje para conversar con sus superiores. También, como el dialecto maya era una traducción de la tribu xiu y aunque yo era bastante competente en esa lengua, era muy difícil de comprender, pues aparentemente el traductor blanco no era muy ducho en esa lengua. Y entonces, por supuesto que yo no hablaba fluidamente el español, además de que había muchas palabras en español como «rey» y «virrey» que no existían en ninguno de nuestros lenguajes, y por lo tanto no se podían traducir ni en xiu ni en náhuatl. Un poco abatido tuve que confesar a Motecuzoma:

«Quizás yo también, mi señor, oyendo varias repeticiones pueda sacar algo limpio de todo esto. Pues de momento lo único que puedo decirle es que la palabra que más pronuncia en la lengua del hombre blanco es "cortés".»

Motecuzoma dijo desalentado: «Una palabra.»

«Eso quiere decir cortesía, Señor Orador, o gentil, o bien educado, o bondadoso.»

Los ojos de Motecuzoma se iluminaron un poco y dijo: «Bueno, por lo menos eso no pronostica nada malo, si los forasteros hablan de gentileza y bondad.» Me contuve de hacerle notar que los forasteros no habían tenido una conducta muy gentil cuando asaltaron las tierras de Cupilco.

Después de vacilar un momento, Motecuzoma nos dijo a mí y a su hermano, el jefe guerrero Cuitláhuac, que nos lleváramos a los mensajeros a algún lado y escucháramos todo lo que tenían que decir, tantas veces como fuera necesario, hasta que pudiéramos reducir todo el flujo de sus palabras a un informe coherente de lo que había sucedido en la nación totonaca. Así es que los llevamos a mi casa, en donde Beu nos dio suficiente comida y bebidas para todos, y dedicamos varios días completos a escucharlos. Uno de los mensajeros repitió una y otra vez el mensaje que había enviado Patzinca, los otros tres, repitieron una y otra vez toda aquella palabrería que memorizaron en las varias conferencias, en diversas lenguas, que tuvo Patzinca con sus visitantes. Cuitláhuac se concentró en las porciones recitadas en náhuatl, yo en las xiu y español, hasta que nuestros oídos y cerebros estaban bien embotados. Sin embargo, de ese flujo de palabras pudimos al fin sacar algo en limpio que yo puse en palabras–pintadas.

Cuitláhuac y yo percibimos que la situación era ésta. Los hombres blancos parecían estar escandalizados porque los totonaca o cualquier otro pueblo tuvieran que sentir temor o estar subyugados a la dominación de un gobernante «extranjero» llamado Motecuzoma. Les ofrecieron utilizar sus armas, únicas e invencibles, para «liberar» a los totonaca y a otros que desearan igualmente verse libres del despotismo de Motecuzoma, con la condición de que esos pueblos se aliaran a su Rey Don Carlos, quien todavía era más extranjero. Nosotros sabíamos que algunas naciones gustosamente se unirían para destruir a los mexica, pues ninguna de ellas había estado muy *complacida* de tener que pagar tributo a Tenochtitlan, y Motecuzoma había hecho que los mexica fuéramos todavía menos populares en todo El Único Mundo. Sin embargo, los hombres blancos habían añadido otra condición a su ofrecimiento de liberación, y la aceptación de ésta por cualquier aliado sería tanto como cometer un acto de rebelión todavía más horroroso.

Nuestro Señor y Nuestra Señora, dijeron los hombres blancos, estaban celosos de todas sus deidades y se sentían asqueados con la práctica de sacrificios humanos. Todos los pueblos que deseasen liberarse de la dominación de los mexica, debían, también, adorar al nuevo dios y a la nueva diosa. Deberían evitar toda ofrenda sangrienta, tenían que tirar o destruir todas sus estatuas y todos los templos dedicados a sus viejas deidades, y en su lugar pondrían las cruces que representaban a Nuestro Señor y las imágenes de Nuestra Señora que los hombres blancos les proporcionarían. Cuitláhuac y yo estuvimos de acuerdo en que los totonaca y cualquier otro pueblo descontento podría ver una gran ventaja en deponer a Motecuzoma y a todos sus mexica que se esparcían por doquier y ponerse de lado del Rey Don Carlos, que estaba todavía más lejos e invisible. Pero también estábamos seguros que ningún pueblo estaría dispuesto a renunciar a los antiguos dioses, inmensurablemente más atemorizantes que *cualquier* gobernante en la tierra y por lo tanto correr el riesgo de ser destruidos, ellos y hasta todo El Único Mundo, por un terremoto. Nos dimos cuenta por sus mensajeros que hasta el voluble Patzinca estaba espantado ante esa sugestión.

Así es que ésa era la narración y las conclusiones que nosotros recogimos y que llevamos al palacio. Motecuzoma puso sobre sus piernas el libro de papel de corteza que le entregué, y lo fue leyendo melancólicamente, pasando hoja por hoja, mientras yo contaba lo que había escrito, en voz alta para beneficio del Consejo de Voceros que estaba allí reunido. Pero esa reunión, como la anterior, fue interrumpida por el mayordomo de palacio que nos anunció que otros recién llegados imploraban audiencia inmediata.

Eran los cinco registradores que habían estado en Tzempoalan cuando los hombres blancos llegaron. Como todos los oficiales que viajaban recogiendo los tributos de esas tierras, ellos portaban sus más ricos mantos, sus penachos de plumas y las insignias de su oficio —para impresionar y atemorizar a los que pagaban el tributo—, pero ellos entraron en el salón del trono como pájaros que hubieran sido zarandeados por una tormenta. Estaban desgreñados, sucios, flacos y sin resuello, parte porque, como dijeron ellos, habían llegado de Tzempoalan a paso rápido, pero principalmente porque habían pasado muchos días y noches confinados en la maldita jaula prisión en donde los había encerrado Patzinca, y en donde no había facilidades sanitarias.

«¿Qué locura está sucediendo allí?», preguntó Motecuzoma.

Uno de ellos suspiró cansado y dijo: «*Ayya*, mi señor, es indescriptible.»

«¡Tonterías! —dijo Motecuzoma—. Todo lo que puede sobrevivir es descriptible. ¿Cómo se las arreglaron para escapar?»

«No escapamos, Señor Orador. El jefe de los extranjeros blancos, en secreto, nos abrió la jaula.»

Todos parpadeamos y Motecuzoma exclamó: «¿*En secreto*?»

«Sí, mi señor. El hombre blanco que se llama Cortés...»

«¿Su *nombre* es Cortés?», exclamó Motecuzoma taladrándome con la mirada, pero yo sólo pude encogerme de hombros impotente y poner una cara de confundido, igual a la de él. Aunque los recordadores de palabras habían memorizado partes de las conversaciones, con las cuales me dieron la idea de que era un nombre.

El recién llegado continuó, paciente y cansadamente: «El hombre blanco, Cortés, llegó a nuestra jaula en secreto una noche, cuando no había totonacas en los alrededores y lo hizo acompañado por dos intérpretes. Abrió la puerta de la jaula con sus propias manos. Por medio de sus intérpretes nos dijo que su nombre era Cortés y que huyéramos para salvar nuestras vidas y nos pidió que trajéramos sus respetos y saludos a nuestro Venerado Orador. El hombre blanco Cortés desea que usted sepa, mi señor, que los totonaca se quieren rebelar y que Patzinca nos puso en prisión a pesar de que Cortés le previno con urgencia de que no debía tratar así tan rudamente a los enviados del poderoso Motecuzoma. Cortés desea que usted sepa, mi señor, que ha escuchado mucho acerca del poderoso Motecuzoma y que es un ferviente admirador de usted y que él de buena gana se arriesgó a ponerse bajo la furia del traicionero Patzinca, mandándonos de regreso sanos y salvos como una muestra de simpatía. También desea que sepa que él utilizará toda su persuasión para evitar que los totonaca se levanten en contra de usted. A cambio de mantener la paz, Señor Orador, el hombre blanco Cortés sólo pide que lo invite a Tenochtitlan, así él podrá personalmente rendir homenaje al más grande gobernante de todas estas tierras.»

«Bien —dijo Motecuzoma sonriendo y sentándose muy derecho

en su trono, inconscientemente componiéndose ante esa muestra de adulación—. El hombre blanco forastero tiene un nombre adecuado, Cortés.»

Sin embargo su Mujer Serpiente, Tlácotzin, le preguntó al hombre que acababa de hablar: «¿Y usted cree lo que le dijo el hombre blanco?»

«Señor Mujer Serpiente, sólo le puedo decir lo que sé. Que fuimos hechos prisioneros por los totonaca y liberados por el hombre Cortés.»

Tlácotzin se volvió hacia Motecuzoma: «Nos han dicho los mismos mensajeros de Patzinca que éste puso las manos sobre estos funcionarios, sólo después de que se lo ordenó el jefe de los hombres blancos.»

Motecuzoma dijo con incertidumbre: «Patzinca pudo haber mentido, por algunas razones aviesas.»

«Yo conozco a los totonaca —dijo Tlácotzin desdeñosamente—. Ninguno de ellos, incluyendo a Patzinca, tiene el coraje de rebelarse o el ingenio para ser hipócrita. No sin ayuda.»

«Si me permites hablar, Señor Hermano —dijo Cuitláhuac—. Todavía no has terminado de leer el informe que preparamos el Campeón Mixtli y yo. Las palabras que repetimos ahí son las palabras exactas que se dijeron el hombre Cortés y el Señor Patzinca. Y no están de acuerdo con el mensaje que acabamos de recibir de ese tal Cortés. No hay duda de que él engañó astutamente y con maña a Patzinca para que cometiera una traición y que ha mentido desvergonzadamente a los registradores.»

«Eso no tiene sentido —objetó Motecuzoma—. ¿Por qué habría de incitar a Patzinca para que nos traicionara aprisionando a estos hombres y luego negarlo dejándolos libres por sí mismo?»

«Quería tener la seguridad de que nosotros culpáramos a los totonaca por la traición —resumió el Mujer Serpiente—. Ahora que los funcionarios han regresado, Patzinca debe estar aterrorizado y preparando su ejército en contra nuestra, esperando la represalia. Cuando ese ejército lo haya reunido sólo para defenderse, el hombre Cortés lo puede incitar fácilmente para que lo utilice no para defenderse sino para atacar.»

Cuitláhuac añadió: «Y eso *está* totalmente de acuerdo con nuestras conclusiones, ¿no es así, Mixtli?»

«Sí, mis señores —dije, dirigiéndome a todos los presentes—. El jefe blanco Cortés claramente desea *algo* de nosotros los mexica y utilizará la fuerza si es necesario. La amenaza es implícita en el mensaje que trajeron los registradores, tan astutamente puestos en libertad. El precio que pide por mantener a los totonaca tranquilos es que lo invitemos aquí. Si esa invitación se le rehúsa, él utilizará a los totonaca y quizás a otros para que los ayuden a pelear aquí.»

«Entonces nosotros podemos anticiparnos a eso —dijo Motecuzoma— extendiéndole la invitación que solicita. Después de todo, él sólo dice que desea presentar sus respetos y está bien que lo haga. Si viene sin su ejército, sólo con una escolta de sus oficiales de alto rango, ciertamente que nadie le causará daño aquí. Yo creo que lo que él desea es pedir permiso para asentar una colonia en la costa. Ya sabemos que estos forasteros son por naturaleza isleños y marineros. Si sólo desean una porción de playa cerca del mar...»

«Siento cierta vacilación al contradecir a mi Venerado Orador —dijo una voz enronquecida—, pero los hombres blancos desean algo más que una porción de playa. —El que así hablaba era uno de los registradores que habían regresado—. Antes de haber salido libres de Tzempoala, vimos el resplandor de las llamas de unos grandes fuegos en dirección del océano y uno de los mensajeros llegó corriendo de la bahía en donde los hombres blancos habían anclado sus once barcos y eventualmente oímos lo que había pasado. A una orden del hombre Cortés, sus soldados desmantelaron y quitaron cada cosa útil de diez de esos barcos y luego los quemaron hasta convertirlos en cenizas. Sólo uno de los barcos quedó, aparentemente para servir de correo entre aquí y el lugar de donde vienen los hombres blancos, cualquiera que ése sea.»

Motecuzoma dijo con irritación: «Esto cada vez tiene menos sentido. ¿Por qué habrían de destruir los únicos medios que tienen de transporte? ¿Me está tratando de decir que todos esos hombres extranjeros están locos?»

«No lo sé, Señor Orador —dijo el hombre de la voz enronquecida—. Yo sólo sé esto. Esos cientos de guerreros blancos están ahora en la costa, sin medios para regresar de donde vinieron. Al jefe Cortés ya no se le puede persuadir o forzar para que se vaya, porque con su propia acción, ya no puede. Para regresar tiene que hacerlo por el mar y no creo que piense quedarse allí donde está. Su única alternativa es caminar tierra adentro. Creo que el Campeón Águila Mixtli lo ha predicho correctamente, él marchará hacia acá, hacia Tenochtitlan.»

Pareciendo tan problemático e inseguro como el desgraciado Patzinca de Tzempoalan, nuestro Venerado Orador se negó a tomar alguna rápida decisión o a ordenar alguna acción inmediata. Nos ordenó que despejáramos el salón del trono y que lo dejáramos solo. «Tengo que pensar profundamente en esos asuntos —dijo— y estudiar de cerca esta narración recopilada de mi hermano y el Campeón Mixtli. Debo conversar con los dioses. Cuando haya determinado lo que se debe hacer, les comunicaré mis decisiones. Por ahora, necesito estar solo.»

Así que los cinco harapientos registradores se fueron para descansar al fin, el Consejo de Voceros se dispersó y yo me fui a casa. Aunque Luna que Espera y yo rara vez hablábamos mucho entre nosotros y cuando lo hacíamos sólo tratábamos asuntos de la casa, en esa ocasión sentí la necesidad de hablar con alguien. Le relaté las cosas que habían estado pasando en la costa y en la corte y las molestas aprensiones que estaban causando.

Ella dijo con suavidad: «Motecuzoma teme que sea el fin de nuestro mundo, ¿y tú, Zaa?»

Negué con la cabeza sin tener una idea clara. «No soy un adivino-que-ve-en-la-lejanía. Todo lo contrario. Sin embargo, el final de El Único Mundo ya ha sido profetizado varias veces, así como también el regreso de Quetzalcóatl, con o sin sus tolteca. Si este Cortés es sólo un merodeador nuevo y diferente, podemos pelear contra él y probablemente lo venceremos, pero si su venida es hasta cierto punto un cumplimiento de todas esas viejas profecías... bien, será como cuando llegó la inundación veinte años atrás, contra la cual ninguno de nosotros pudo hacer nada. Yo no pude, y eso que estaba en los mejores años de mi primera juventud. Ni siquiera el Orador Auítzotl, tan fuerte y tan temido, pudo hacer nada. Ahora estoy viejo y tengo muy poca confianza en el Orador Motecuzoma.»

Beu me miró pensativamente y luego dijo: «¿Estás pensando que quizás deberíamos tomar nuestras pertenencias y huir a algún lugar más seguro? Aunque hubiera cierta clase de calamidad aquí en el norte, la ciudad de Tecuantépec, mi antiguo, hogar, podría estar fuera de peligro.»

«Ya *he* pensado en eso —dije—, pero como por mucho tiempo he estado implicado en la suerte de los mexica, sentiría que estaba desertando si tuviera que partir en el momento crítico. Y quizás sea una perversidad de mi parte, pero si esto es algún tipo de final, cuando esté en Mictlan me gustaría poder decir: yo lo vi todo.»

Motecuzoma hubiera podido seguir vacilando o alargando el asunto por mucho tiempo, si no hubiera sido por lo que pasó esa misma noche. Hubo otro augurio y tan alarmante como para que Motecuzoma por lo menos se animara a mandarme llamar. Un paje del palacio vino muy perturbado a levantarme de la cama, para que lo acompañara inmediatamente al palacio.

Mientras me vestía, podía oír un alboroto que como un ronroneo venía de la calle y gruñí: «¿Y ahora qué está pasando?»

«Se lo mostraré, Campeón Mixtli —dijo el joven mensajero—, tan pronto como estemos afuera.»

Cuando lo estuvimos, él apuntó al cielo y dijo en voz baja: «Miré ahí.» Aunque ya pasaba de la medianoche, nosotros no éramos los únicos que estábamos en la calle viendo esa aparición. La calle estaba llena de gente, todos mis vecinos, escasamente vestidos con aquello que encontraron a la mano, y todos ellos miraban hacia el cielo, murmurando inquietos excepto cuando iban a despertar a otros vecinos. Levanté mi topacio y miré al cielo y al principio me maravillé como todos los demás, pero luego recordé algo que estaba en mi mente desde hacía mucho tiempo y de alguna manera eso hizo que disminuyera, por lo menos para mí, el temor que podría despertar ese espectáculo. El paje me miró de reojo, esperando quizás, a que yo hiciera alguna exclamación de miedo, pero sólo suspiré y dije:

«Esto era todo lo que nos faltaba.»

En el palacio, el mayordomo a medio vestir se apresuró en conducirme escalera arriba hacia el piso alto y luego por otra escalera hacia la azotea del gran edificio. Motecuzoma estaba sentado en una banca en su jardín y creo que estaba temblando, aunque la noche primaveral no era fría y a pesar de que estaba envuelto en varios mantos que caían pesados alrededor de él. Sin dejar de ver al cielo me dijo:

«Después de la ceremonia del Fuego Nuevo hubo un eclipse de sol; luego la caída de estrellas; luego las estrellas humeantes. Todas esas cosas que sucedieron durante los años pasados, ya eran augurios suficientemente malos, pero por lo menos los conocíamos por lo que ellos representaban. En cambio *esta* aparición jamás se había visto antes.»

Yo dije: «Discúlpeme si le corrijo, Señor Orador... ya que sólo deseo disminuir sus aprensiones. Si usted despertara a sus historiadores, mi señor, y los pusiera a buscar en los archivos, seguramente ellos encontrarían que esto ya *había* ocurrido antes. En el año Uno-Conejo que precedió a la última gavilla de años, durante el reinado de su abuelo, su tocayo.»

Él se me quedó mirando, como si de repente yo le hubiera confesado que era cierta clase de adivino. «¿Hace sesenta y seis años? Mucho antes de que usted naciera. ¿Cómo puede saberlo?»

«Recuerdo que mi padre me habló de unas luces como éstas, mi señor. Él clamaba que eran los dioses caminando en el cielo, pero que lo único visible de ellos eran sus mantos, pintados con todos estos mismos colores fríos.»

Y así era como se veían esas luces aquella noche: como si fueran unas telas drapeadas en forma singular, pendiendo de algún punto arriba del cielo y dejándose caer hacia atrás de las montañas que estaban en el horizonte y se movían y se estiraban como si un viento suave soplara sobre ellas. Pero no había ningún ruido silbante mientras se mecían. Solamente brillaban frías, con colores blancos, verdes y azul pálido. Conforme se movían esas cortinas drapeadas, suavemente ondulando, los colores sutilmente cambiaban de lugar y algunas veces emergían. Era una noche muy hermosa, pero ese espectáculo hacía que a uno se le erizara el pelo.

Mucho después, por casualidad mencioné el espectáculo de esa noche a uno de sus marineros españoles y le conté cómo nosotros los mexica habíamos interpretado eso, como el aviso de que muchas cosas espantosas iban a suceder. Él se rió y me llamó salvaje supersticioso. «Nosotros también vimos esas luces aquella noche —dijo él—, y estábamos muy sorprendidos de verlas tan al sur. Pero yo sé que eso no significa nada, ya que las he visto muchas veces cuando navegamos en los océanos fríos del norte. Es muy común ver eso en los mares enfriados por Boreas, el viento del norte. Y por eso las llamamos nosotros Luces Boreales.»

Pero aquella noche, yo sólo sabía que esas luces pálidas, bellas y atemorizantes, se habían visto por primera vez en El Único Mundo hacía sesenta y seis años y le dije a Motecuzoma: «De acuerdo con mi padre, fue el augurio que presagió el principio de los Tiempos Duros.»

«Ah, sí —asintió sombríamente Motecuzoma—. He leído la historia de esos años devastadores. Sin embargo, pienso que esos Tiempos Duros no significarán nada en comparación con los que nos esperan ahora. —Se quedó ahí sentado en silencio por un rato y pensé que se estaba adormeciendo, pero de repente me dijo—: Campeón Mixtli, deseo que usted haga otro viaje.»

Yo protesté lo más cortésmente que pude: «Mi señor, ya soy un hombre viejo.»

«Le proveeré nuevamente con una silla de manos y una escolta, y no es un camino muy riguroso de aquí a la costa totonaca.»

Protesté todavía con más fuerza: «El primer encuentro formal entre los mexica y los blancos españoles, mi señor, no debería ser confiado a personajes de menos categoría que sus nobles del Consejo de Voceros.»

«Muchos de ellos son mucho más viejos que usted y por lo tanto menos apropiados para viajar. Ninguno de ellos tiene su facilidad para registrar los hechos con palabras-pintadas o sus conocimientos sobre lenguas extranjeras. Y lo más importante, Mixtli, usted tiene bastante destreza para pintar a la gente como es en realidad. Eso es algo que nosotros no tenemos todavía, no desde la llegada de los primeros forasteros a las tierras maya... un buen retrato de ellos.»

Le dije: «Si eso es todo lo que mi señor desea, todavía puedo dibujar de memoria los rostros de los dos que visité en Tiho y le aseguro que puedo hacer un retrato bastante reconocible y pasable.»

«No —dijo Motecuzoma—. Usted mismo dijo que ellos eran sólo artesanos comunes. Deseo ver la cara de su capitán, el hombre llamado Cortés.»

Me aventuré a decirle: «¿Entonces, mi señor ha llegado a la conclusión de que Cortés es un hombre?»

Él sonrió de forma torcida: «Usted siempre ha desdeñado la idea de que él pudiera ser un dios, pero han habido muchos augurios y coincidencias. Si él no es Quetzalcóatl, si sus guerreros no son los tolteca que regresan, todavía podrían ser los enviados de los dioses. Tal vez como alguna clase de retribución.» Estudié su rostro que se veía muerto por las luces verdes que brillaban en el cielo. Me preguntaba si cuando él había hablado de retribución estaba pensando en cómo le había arrebatado el trono de Texcoco al Príncipe Heredero Flor Oscura o si estaba pensando en algunos otros pecados secretos y privados. Pero de repente se enderezó y dijo en su forma usual, tajante: «Esta parte del asunto es algo que a usted no debe interesarle. Sólo tráigame el retrato de Cortés y un recuento en palabras-pintadas de sus fuerzas, la descripción de sus armas misteriosas, la manera en que ellos pelean y cualquier otra cosa que nos ayude a conocerlos mejor.»

Traté de hacer una última objeción: «Sea lo que sea ese hombre Cortés, mi señor, juzgo que él no es ningún tonto. Él no es de la clase de hombre que permite que un escribano espía vague tranquilamente por todo su campamento, contando sus guerreros y examinando sus armas.»

«Usted no irá solo, sino acompañado de muchos nobles, ricamente ataviados de acuerdo a su rango y todos ustedes se dirigirán al hombre Cortés, tratándolo de igual a igual, como a un noble. Eso lo halagará. También llevará una caravana de cargadores portando ricos regalos, lo que apaciguará sus suspicacias y no se fijará en las verdaderas intenciones que usted lleva. Usted será un alto emisario del Venerado Orador de los mexica y de El Único Mundo, yendo al encuentro y a saludar a los emisarios del Rey Don Carlos de España. —Luego hizo una pausa y me miró—. Cada uno de ustedes debe ser un auténtico señor, representando a la nobleza mexica.»

Cuando regresé a casa, me encontré a Beu despierta. Después de haber estado viendo las luces en el cielo por un tiempo, se había puesto a hacer *chocólatl* para cuando yo regresara. La saludé de una manera un poco más efusiva de lo usual: «Ha sido una noche completa, mi Señora Luna que Espera.»

Obviamente, ella tomó eso por un cumplido y me miró asombrada y complacida, pues pienso que en todo el tiempo que llevábamos casados, jamás le había dicho una palabra de cumplido.

«Pero, Zaa —dijo enrojeciendo de placer—, si tú sólo me llamaras "esposa" eso alegraría mi corazón, pero... ¿*mi señora*? ¿Por qué esta repentina muestra de afecto? ¿Ha pasado algo...?»

«No, no, no —la interrumpí. Por tantos años había estado tan satisfecho de tener cerca a Beu, pero conteniendo sus muestras de amor, que entonces no quería que ella de repente se me pusiera sentimental—. Hablo con la debida formalidad. "Señora" es el título con que ahora se deben dirigir a ti. Esta noche el Venerado Orador me acaba de otorgar el -tzin a mi nombre, y queda conferido también a ti.»

«Oh —dijo ella como si hubiera preferido otra clase de beneficio, aunque rápidamente volvió a su manera de ser, fría y sin emoción—. Me imagino que estás complacido, Zaa.»

Yo me reí un poco irónicamente. «Cuando era joven soñaba con hacer grandes hazañas, con tener una gran riqueza y llegar a ser noble. Y hasta ahora que ya he pasado mi gavilla de años, he llegado a ser Mixtzin, el Señor Mixtli de los mexica y quizás sólo por un breve espacio de tiempo, Beu... Quizás sólo por el tiempo que *haya* señores, sólo por el tiempo en que haya mexica...»

Me acompañaron otros cuatro nobles, quienes no estuvieron muy contentos de que Motecuzoma me hubiese puesto al mando de la expedición y de la misión que teníamos que cumplir, pues yo había sido un plebeyo elevado al rango de noble, mientras que ellos lo eran de nacimiento.

«Ustedes se deben ganar la estima y atención del hombre Cortés, así como halagarlo —dijo el Venerado Orador cuando nos dio sus instrucciones—, y a todos aquellos hombres que le acompañan, que ustedes se den cuenta de que son de alto rango. Cada vez que puedan deben festejarlos. En su caravana van cocineros muy capaces que llevan un amplio surtido de las más deliciosas golosinas. Los cargadores llevan también muchos regalos, que ustedes deben presentar con pompa y gravedad, diciendo que Motecuzoma los envía como una muestra de amistad y de paz entre nuestros dos pueblos. —Hizo una pausa y luego murmuró—: Además de las otras riquezas, va suficiente oro como para mitigar todas sus enfermedades del corazón.»

«Seguro que sí», pensé. Además de los medallones, diademas, máscaras y otros adornos de oro sólido, las más bellas piezas trabajadas de su colección particular y de otros Venerados Oradores anteriores; muchas piezas de gran antigüedad e inimitable belleza, Motecuzoma estaba enviando también los dos grandes dioses de oro y plata que habían estado a un lado de su trono y que le servían de batintín para llamar a sus empleados y guerreros. También había espléndidos mantos de pluma y penachos para la cabeza; esmeraldas, ámbar, turquesas y otras joyas exquisitamente talladas, incluyendo una cantidad extravagante de nuestras piedras de jade sagradas.

«Pero, por encima de todo —dijo Motecuzoma—, desanimen a los hombres blancos para que vengan aquí o siquiera deseen venir aquí. Si ellos sólo buscan riquezas, este regalo será más que suficiente para mandarlos a buscar en otras naciones de la costa. Si no, díganles que el camino hacia Tenochtitlan es duro y peligroso y que nunca podrán salir vivos de ese viaje. Si eso falla, entonces díganles que su Uey-Tlatoani está demasiado ocupado para poderlos recibir o que es muy viejo o que está enfermo o también que no es digno de ser visitado por tan distinguidos personajes. Díganles *cualquier* cosa con tal de que pierdan el interés de venir a Tenochtitlan.»

Cuando cruzamos el camino-puente del sur, desviándonos hacia el este, yo iba en cabeza de la caravana más larga y con tantas riquezas, que ningún *pochtécatl* había guiado jamás. Nos desviamos hacia el sur rodeando la tierra de nuestros enemigos los texcalteca, para seguir hacia Chololan. Allí y en otras ciudades, pueblos y aldeas en donde descansamos a lo largo de nuestra ruta, los habitantes ansiosos nos molestaban preguntándonos acerca de los «monstruos blancos», que sabían que estaban causando disturbios cerca y de los planes que teníamos para mantenerlos a distancia. Cuando hubimos dado la vuelta a la base del poderoso volcán Citlaltépetl, empezamos a descender por la última nación montañosa, hacia las Tierras Calientes. En la mañana de ese día que nos llevaría directo a la costa, mis compañeros señores se pusieron sus trajes esplendorosos, sus penachos, sus mantos, insignias y demás, pero yo no.

Yo había decidido agregar un poco de astucia a nuestros planes e instrucciones. Por un lado, habían pasado unos ocho años desde que yo había aprendido lo poco que sabía de español y ya se me había olvidado mucho, así es que deseaba mezclarme con los españoles sin ser observado y escucharles hablar en su propio lenguaje y absorberlo lo mejor posible, para que volviera a hablarlo con cierta fluidez antes de cualquier reunión formal con nuestros señores y los suyos. También, en ese tiempo podría estar espiando y tomando nota de lo que ellos hacían y todas esas tareas las podría hacer mejor si ellos no se fijaban en mí.

«Así es que —les dije a los otros nobles— desde aquí hasta la tierra en donde los tengamos que encontrar, yo iré descalzo, llevando sólo mi taparrabo y cargando uno de los bultos más ligeros. Ustedes guiarán la caravana, saludarán a los extranjeros y cuando hayan acampado dejarán que sus portadores se dispersen y descansen en donde quieran, pues uno de ellos seré yo y quiero tener libertad para vagar. Ustedes harán el festín y las entrevistas con los hombres blancos, y yo, de tiempo en tiempo hablaré con ustedes en privado, al anochecer. Cuando tengamos toda la información que el Venerado Orador desea, yo les avisaré para que nos vayamos.»

⊞

Estoy muy contento de que usted esté otra vez con nosotros, Señor Obispo, porque sé que le gustará oír nuestra confrontación real entre su civilización y la nuestra. Por supuesto que Su Ilustrísima apreciará que muchas cosas que vi en ese tiempo eran tan nuevas y exóticas como engañosas para mí, y muchas de las que oí me sonaron como el parlotear de un mono. Pero no prolongaré mi narración repitiendo los errores tan ingenuos que cometí muy seguido, en mis primeras impresiones. No hablaré tontamente diciendo, como lo hicieron nuestros primeros observadores, que los soldados españoles tenían cuatro patas de animal. Contaré las cosas tal como las vi tiempo después, cuando comprendí claramente de qué se trataban. Las cosas que oí, se las repetiré como después las pude componer, cuando ya tenía un conocimiento más perfecto de su lenguaje.

Como pretendí ser un cargador, muy pocas veces, y siempre subrepticiamente, pude hacer uso de mi topacio para ver las cosas, pero éstas fueron las que vi primero. Como ya nos habían dicho que esperáramos ver, sólo había un barco en medio de la bahía, que estaba a cierta distancia de la playa, pero a pesar de eso era obvio que tenía el tamaño de una buena casa. Sus alas estaban aparentemente plegadas, pues desde la parte alta de su azotea sólo sobresalían unos palos muy altos, llenos de cuerdas. Aquí y allá, alrededor de la bahía, otros palos similares sobresalían un poco del agua, en donde los otros barcos habían sido quemados y hundidos. En la playa, los hombres blancos habían erigido tres señales para conmemorar el lugar en donde por primera vez habían desembarcado. Eran unas cruces muy grandes hechas de una pesada viga de madera, que había sido de uno de los barcos destruidos. Había un palo muy alto en donde tremolaba una inmensa bandera de colores sangre y oro, los colores de España, y otro palo más corto que tenía una bandera más chica, que era la insignia personal de Cortés, y era azul y blanca con una cruz roja en medio.

El Lugar En Donde Abundan Cosas Bellas, que los hombres blancos habían llamado Villa Rica de la Vera Cruz, se había convertido rápidamente en una aldea. Algunos de los albergues eran sólo unos palos que tenían una tela encima, pero otros eran las típicas cabañas costeras hechas con cañas y con tejados de palma, construidas para los visitantes por sus sumisos anfitriones, los totonaca. Pero ese día no había muchos hombres blancos por allí, ni sus animales, ni sus trabajadores totonaca, pues nos dijeron que la mayoría de ellos estaban trabajando en un lugar más al norte, en donde Cortés había decretado que se construyera lo que sería permanentemente la Villa Rica de la Vera Cruz, con casas sólidas de madera, piedra y adobe.

La aproximación de nuestra caravana había sido vista, por supuesto, por sus centinelas que fueron a avisar a los españoles, por lo que había un pequeño grupo esperándonos para saludarnos. Nuestra caravana se detuvo a respetable distancia y nuestros cuatro señores, tal como yo les había recomendado en privado, encendieron unos incensarios de *copali* y empezaron a balancearlos sobre sus cadenas, haciendo espirales de humo azul en el aire que estaba alrededor de ellos. Los hombres blancos creyeron entonces y por mucho tiempo después —y creo que hasta este día, según lo tengo entendido— que el balancear este humo perfumado era nuestra manera tradicional de saludar a los extranjeros distinguidos. Era sólo para tratar de poner un velo defensivo contra el hedor intolerable de esos extranjeros que jamás se bañaban.

Dos de los hombres se adelantaron a encontrar a nuestros señores, y estimo que los dos andaban alrededor de los treinta y cinco años. Iban bien vestidos, con lo que ahora sé que eran sombreros de terciopelo, capotes, justillos de manga larga y calzones abombados de merino, con largas y ceñidas botas de cuero. Uno de los hombres era más alto que yo, ancho de espaldas, musculoso y de una apariencia extraordinaria, pues tenía abundante cabello dorado y su barba era igual y flameaban a la luz del sol. Sus ojos eran azules y muy brillantes y aunque tenía la piel pálida, sus facciones eran fuertes. Los totonaca le habían puesto el nombre de su dios, Tezcatlipoca, por su parecido con él, en cuanto al color. Nosotros los recién llegados, naturalmente que lo consideramos el jefe de los hombres blancos, pero pronto supimos que era el segundo en mando y que su nombre era Pedro de Alvarado.

El otro hombre era más corto de estatura y mucho menos impresionante, tenía las piernas zambas y el pecho raquítico como la proa de una canoa, su piel se veía todavía más blanca que la de los otros, pues tenía el pelo y la barba negros. Sus ojos eran tan descoloridos, fríos y distantes como un cielo invernal cubierto de nubes grises. Esa persona tan poco impresionante era, según nos dijo pomposamente, el Capitán Hernán Cortés de Medellín en Extremadura, más recientemente en Santiago de Cuba y venía en representación de Alta Majestad Don Carlos, Emperador del Santo Imperio Romano y Rey de España.

En aquel tiempo, como ya les he dicho, nosotros entendimos muy poco de esa introducción y título tan largo, a pesar de que nos fue repetido en xiu y en náhuatl por los dos intérpretes, que habían venido, caminando un poco atrás de Cortés y Alvarado. Uno de ellos era un hombre picado de viruelas, vestido como usualmente lo hacían sus soldados de bajo rango. El otro era una mujer joven de nuestra propia raza, vestida con la blusa y la falda amarillas de las doncellas, pero su pelo era de un color, no natural, rojo pardusco casi tan llamativo como el de Alvarado. De todas las mujeres nativas que les regalaron a los españoles, primero por el Tabascoöb de Cupilco y más recientemente por Patzinca de los totonaca, ésa era la más admirada por los soldados españoles, porque tenía el pelo rojo y ellos decían: «Como las putas de Santiago de Cuba.»

Aunque yo luego reconocí que su pelo estaba teñido con el jugo de las semillas de *achíotl*, como también pude reconocer a ambos, al hombre y a la muchacha. Él era Jerónimo de Aguilar, aquel que había sido un huésped muy desagradable de los xiu, hacía ocho años. Antes de llegar a Cupilco y luego a estas tierras, Cortés había pasado por Tiho y habiendo encontrado a ese hombre lo había rescatado. Guerrero, el compañero náufrago de Aguilar, después de haber contagiado a toda la nación maya con las pequeñas viruelas, había muerto de esa misma enfermedad. La muchacha de pelo rojo, que para entonces tenía veintitrés años de edad, seguía siendo pequeña, bonita, era la esclava Ce-Malinali a quien había conocido en Coatzacoalcos en mi camino hacia Tiho, ocho años antes.

Cuando Cortés habló en español, fue Aguilar quien tradujo sus palabras al difícil xiu que él había aprendido durante su cautividad y fue Ce-Malinali quien las tradujo a nuestro náhuatl, y cuando nuestros señores emisarios hablaron, el proceso se invirtió. No me tomó mucho tiempo el darme cuenta de que las palabras de ambos, los dignatarios mexica y los españoles, muy a menudo eran traducidas imperfectamente y no siempre porque los intérpretes se vieran embrollados en ese sistema de tres lenguas. Sin embargo, no dije nada y ninguno de los dos intérpretes se dio cuenta de que yo estaba entre los cargadores y yo deseaba que no se dieran cuenta, por lo menos por un tiempo.

Estuve presente cuando los señores mexica presentaron ceremoniosamente los regalos que les había mandado Motecuzoma. Un brillo de avaricia iluminó los ojos opacos de Cortés, conforme cada cargador posaba su carga y desenvolvía su contenido: los grandes batintines de oro y plata, los artículos trabajados en pluma, las gemas y las joyas. Cortés dijo a Alvarado: «Llamad al lapidario de Flandes», y pronto se les unió otro hombre blanco, que evidentemente había llegado con los españoles con el solo propósito de valuar los tesoros que pudieran encontrar en estas tierras. Sea lo que sea Flandes, el caso es que él hablaba español y aunque sus palabras no fueron traducidas para nosotros, pude pescar el sentido de casi todas.

Él dijo que el oro y la plata eran de gran valor, lo mismo que las perlas, los ópalos y las turquesas. Las esmeraldas, los jacintos, los topacios y amatistas, dijo, eran todavía más valiosos, pero por encima de todo, las esmeraldas, aunque él hubiera preferido que estuvieran cortadas en facetas y no talladas como flores, animales y demás, en miniatura. Él sugirió que los mantos y penachos de pluma, podrían ser valiosos como curiosidad para algunos museos. Muchas de las piedras de jade laboriosamente trabajadas, las hizo a un lado desdeñosamente, aunque Ce-Malinali trató de explicarle que por su aspecto religioso, debían ser los regalos más respetados.

El lapidario la miró, se encogió de hombros y le dijo a Cortés: «No son como el jade de Cathay, ni siquiera como el jade falso. Sólo son piedrecillas talladas en serpentina verde, Capitán, que difícilmente valdrán un poco más que nuestras cuentas de vidrio.»

Entonces yo no sabía lo que era el vidrio y todavía no sé lo que es el jade de Cathay, pero siempre he sabido que nuestras piedras de jade sólo poseían un valor ritual. Por supuesto que hoy en día ni siquiera valen eso, ahora son cosas con las que pueden jugar los niños y que pueden chupar los infantes. Pero en aquel entonces todavía significaban algo para nosotros y yo estaba muy enojado por la forma en que los hombres blancos habían recibido nuestros regalos, poniéndole precio a todo, como si nosotros sólo fuéramos unos mercaderes importunos tratando de vender una mercancía falsa. Y lo que más nos molestó y causó pena, fue que aunque los españoles tan altaneramente valuaron todo lo que les dimos, ni siquiera supieron apreciar esas obras de arte, sino que sólo las consideraron de valor por el simple metal, pues quitaron todas las gemas de las montaduras de oro y plata y las pusieron en unos sacos, mientras que las montaduras de filigranas de oro y plata fueron rotas y aplastadas dentro de unas vasijas de piedra y luego éstas fueron puestas sobre un fuego muy caliente, ya que para avivar ese fuego tenían un extraño invento de cuero que al oprimirlo echaba mucho aire y así derritieron todo el metal. Mientras tanto, el lapidario y sus ayudantes, cavaron unas depresiones muy pequeñas en la arena húmeda de la playa y sobre ellas dejaron caer el metal derretido, hasta que éste se enfrió y endureció. Así es que eso fue todo lo que quedó del tesoro que les dimos, aun esos enormes discos, bellos e irreemplazables que le habían servido a Motecuzoma como batintín, se convirtieron en barritas de oro y plata que no tenían ninguna belleza, sino que parecían pequeños adobes.

Mientras mis compañeros hacían sus tareas señoriles, yo pasé los siguientes días yendo y viniendo, entre la masa de soldados comunes. Los conté a ellos y a sus armas, también a sus caballos y sabuesos amarrados, y otras de sus pertenencias aunque no podía adivinar para qué servían, cosas como unas bolas muy pesadas de metal que tenían almacenadas y unas sillas de cuero, curvas, muy extrañas. Tuve el cuidado de no atraer su atención al verme vagar ocioso. Como todos los demás hombres totocana, a quienes los españoles habían forzado a trabajar, yo siempre iba cargado con algo, como una tabla de madera o alguna otra cosa, para que pareciera que la estaba llevando a algún lado. Ya que había un constante tráfico de soldados españoles y cargadores totonaca entre el campamento de la Vera Cruz al pueblo que se estaba levantando de la Vera Cruz y como los españoles clamaban (como lo siguen haciendo hasta ahora) «que no les podían hacer entender a esos malditos indios que se hicieran a un lado», yo anduve desapercibido como una simple hoja de caña que se extiende a lo largo de la costa. Cualquier cosa que cargara, no interfería para que pudiera utilizar mi topacio subrepticiamente, hacer notas de las cosas y personas que conté y rápidamente describirlas con palabras pintadas.

Lo único que hubiera deseado es haber podido cargar un incensario en lugar de las otras cosas, cuando estaba entre los españoles, pero debo conceder que éstos no olían tan mal como recordaba de los otros. Aunque todavía no demostraban ninguna inclinación por limpiarse y tomar baños de vapor, por lo menos al final de un día duro de trabajo, se desnudaban mostrando su piel espantosamente blanca y quedándose sólo con su sucia ropa interior, se metían vadeando en el mar. Me di cuenta de que ninguno de ellos sabía nadar, pero chapoteaban lo suficiente como para que se les cayera el sudor que habían acumulado durante el día. No crean que eso hacía que olieran a flores, sobre todo porque luego se volvían a poner sus ropas rancias y llenas de costras, pero por lo menos no olían tan mal como su fétido aliento de buitre.

Mientras vagaba de un lado a otro, pasé varias noches lo mismo en el campamento que en el pueblo de la Vera Cruz, manteniendo mis oídos y ojos bien abiertos. Aunque rara vez pude escuchar algo que realmente me sirviera como información, pues los soldados la mayor parte del tiempo se lo pasaban hablando y gruñendo acerca de esas indias lampiñas, que no tenían ni sus horquillas ni sus sobacos llenos de cómodo vello, como sus mujeres allende el mar; y así, yo volví a comprender el español y mejoré mis conocimientos en esa lengua. También fui muy cauto, para que ninguno de los soldados me oyera cuando estaba repitiendo, para mí mismo, sus palabras y sus frases.

Para prevenir que no me fueran a coger con esa impostura, tampoco conversé con ninguno de los totonaca, así es que no pude preguntar a nadie acerca de unas cosas curiosas que había visto repetidamente y que me causaban mucha perplejidad. A lo largo de la costa y especialmente en la ciudad capital de Tzempoalan, hay muchas pirámides erigidas a Tezcatlipoca y a otros dioses, incluso hay una que no es cuadrada sino como una torre redonda, cuyas terrazas van disminuyendo de tamaño al ascender y está dedicada al dios del viento Ehécatl; esta pirámide había sido construida así para que pudiera soplar su aliento libremente, sin que éste tuviera que hacer ángulo en los rincones.

Cada una de las pirámides de los totonaca tenía un templo en la cumbre, pero todos esos templos habían sido cambiados en una forma sorprendente. Ninguno de ellos contenía ya una estatua de Tezcatlipoca o Ehécatl o cualquier otro dios. A todos se les había raspado y limpiado la sangre coagulada acumulada en ellos. A todos se les había dado por dentro una capa de agua de cal y en todos ellos sólo había una rígida cruz de madera y una simple y pequeña figurita, también de madera aunque tallada en una forma muy burda; ésta representaba a una mujer joven con su mano derecha levantada en un vago gesto admonitorio. Su cabello estaba pintado de negro sin ningún matiz, su vestido en un azul suave y sus ojos del mismo color, su piel blanca-rosada como la de los españoles, pero lo más singular de todo era que llevaba una corona circular dorada, que era tan grande para ella, que no podía sostenerse sobre su cabeza, sino que estaba atada en la parte de atrás de su pelo.

Estaba claro para mí, que aunque los españoles no buscaron ni provocaron una batalla con los totonaca, los *habían* amenazado con bravatas y espantado, como para que ese pueblo reemplazara a todos sus antiguos dioses tan poderosos, por una simple mujer pálida y plácida. Pensé que era la diosa Nuestra Señora de quien había oído hablar, pero no podía comprender qué habían visto los totonaca en ella que fuera superior a los antiguos dioses. En verdad, se veía tan insípida que seguía sin comprender qué atributos de diosa le habían visto para venerarla, incluyendo a los españoles.

Pero un día, mis vagabundeos me llevaron a una barranca cubierta de hierba, un poco tierra adentro, que estaba llena de totonaca que parados escuchaban con evidente estupidez la arenga de uno de los sacerdotes españoles que habían venido con los soldados. Esos sacerdotes, como ya les he hecho notar, no se veían tan extranjeros y fuera de lo común como los soldados; sólo el corte de sus cabellos era diferente, porque por otro lado sus vestiduras negras se parecían mucho a las de nuestros sacerdotes y olían casi como ellos, también. El que estaba sermoneando a los allí reunidos lo hacía con la ayuda de los dos intérpretes, Aguilar y Ce-Malinali, que evidentemente tomaba prestados cuando Cortés no los necesitaba. Los totonaca parecían escuchar petrificados su discurso, aunque yo sabía que no podrían entender más que dos palabras de cada diez que tradujera Ce-Malinali al náhuatl.

El sacerdote explicaba, entre otras muchas cosas, que Nuestra Señora no era exactamente una diosa, que ella había sido una mujer humana a quien llamaban la Virgen María, porque de alguna manera había quedado virgen, aunque había copulado con el Espíritu Santo del Señor Dios, quien *era* un dios, y ella había dado a luz al Señor Jesús Cristo quien era el Hijo de Dios y que podía andar por este mundo con forma humana. Bien, nada de eso era difícil de comprender, ya que nuestra propia religión tenía muchos dioses quienes habían copulado con mujeres humanas y muchas diosas que habían sido excesivamente promiscuas con ambos, dioses y hombres, quienes prolificaron muchos niños diosecitos, mientras que de alguna manera mantuvieron sin mancha su reputación y su apelativo de Virgen.

Por favor, Su Ilustrísima, estoy contando cómo veía yo esas cosas *cuando* mi mente todavía no había sido instruida en ellas.

También estuve atento a la explicación del sacerdote sobre el acto del bautismo, del que decía que todos nosotros podríamos en ese mismo día participar; aunque normalmente se imponía a los niños recién nacidos: una inmersión de agua que nos obligaría por siempre a adorar y servir al Señor Dios, a cambio de todas sus bondades, que recibiríamos durante toda nuestra vida y en el mundo del más allá. No pude ver mucha diferencia entre eso y las creencias y prácticas de la mayoría de nuestros pueblos, aunque la inmersión se hacía con diferentes dioses puestos en la mente.

Por supuesto que el sacerdote no trató en ese discurso de explicarnos todos los detalles de la Fe Cristiana, con todas sus complicaciones y contradicciones. Y aunque yo era el que mejor podía entender las palabras en español, en xiu y en náhuatl, aun yo me equivoqué en la comprensión y en el pensamiento de esas cosas. Por ejemplo, como el sacerdote habló muy familiarmente de la Virgen María y como yo ya había visto sus estatuas con piel pálida y ojos azules, pensé que Nuestra Señora era una mujer española, que quizá muy pronto cruzaría el océano para visitarnos en persona, y que tal vez trajera con ella a su niñito Jesús. También pensé que el sacerdote estaba hablando de un compatriota suyo, cuando dijo que ese día era el día de San Juan de Damasco y que todos nosotros seríamos honrados cuando se nos diera el nombre de ese santo, al ser bautizados.

Después de eso, él y sus intérpretes llamaron a todos aquellos que desearan abrazar el Cristianismo, para que se arrodillaran, y prácticamente casi todos los totonaca presentes lo hicieron, aunque como era natural ninguna de esa gente lerda tenía idea de lo que pasaba y quizás hasta pensaron que estaban allí para ser sacrificados ritualmente. Sólo unos cuantos viejos y algunos niñitos se fueron; los viejos, si es que entendieron algo, probablemente no vieron ningún beneficio en cargarse con otro dios para lo que les quedaba de vida, y los niños probablemente deseaban disfrutar de otro tipo de juegos.

Aunque el mar no estaba muy lejos, el sacerdote no llevó a toda esa gente allí para una inmersión ceremonial, sino que simplemente caminó entre las filas de los totonaca arrodillados, rociándoles agua con una varita que llevaba en una mano y con la otra dándoles a probar algo. Yo observé y cuando ninguno de los bautizados cayó muerto o presentó algún otro efecto horroroso, decidí quedarme y compartirlo yo también, ya que aparentemente no me haría ningún daño y quizá me pudiera dar alguna ventaja desconocida en mis futuros tratos con los hombres blancos. Así es que recibí unas cuantas gotas de agua en mi cabeza y tomé un poco de sal de la palma de la mano del sacerdote, aunque no era más que sal común y corriente, y algunas palabras que él murmuró sobre mí y que ahora sé que es latín, su lenguaje religioso.

Para concluir, el sacerdote cantó sobre todos nosotros un pequeño discurso en latín y nos dijo que de acuerdo a eso, todos los hombres nos llamaríamos Juan Damasceno y todas las mujeres Juana Damascena, y de esta manera la ceremonia se acabó. Por lo que puedo recordar, ése fue el primer nombre nuevo que adquirí después del de Ojo Orinador, y el último nombre que he adquirido hasta este día. Me atrevería a decir que es un nombre mejor que el de Ojo Orinador, pero debo confesar que muy rara vez he pensado en mí mismo como Juan Damasceno. Sin embargo, supongo que el nombre vivirá más que yo, porque he sido inscrito con él en todos los rollos de registro y otros papeles oficiales del gobierno de esta Nueva España, y probablemente el último registro de todos sin duda dirá que Juan Damasceno murió.

Durante una de las conferencias secretas que por la noche tenía con los señores mexica, en la casa de tela colgante que había sido erigida como morada para ellos, me dijeron:

«Motecuzoma se ha estado preguntando mucho si estos hombres blancos pudieran ser dioses o los tolteca convertidos en dioses, así es que decidimos hacer una prueba. Nosotros le ofrecimos un sacrificio a su guía, el hombre Cortés, matar para él un *xochimiqui*, quizás a alguno de los señores de los totonaca, que estuviera disponible, pero se sintió muy insultado ante nuestra sugestión. Él dijo: "Vosotros sabéis muy bien que el benevolente Quetzalcóatl nunca pidió o permitió sacrificios humanos para él. ¿Por qué habría de permitirlo yo?" Así es que ahora nosotros no sabemos qué pensar. ¿Cómo podría saber este forastero todo lo relacionado con la Serpiente Emplumada, a menos que...?»

Yo les dije: «La muchacha Ce-Malinali le pudo haber contado todas las leyendas sobre Quetzalcóatl; después de todo, ella nació en algún lugar de esta costa, desde donde Quetzalcóatl se fue.»

«Por favor, Mixtzin, no la llame por su nombre común —dijo uno de los señores, pareciendo muy nervioso—. Ella insiste mucho en que se le llame Malintzin.»

Yo le dije divertido: «Se ha elevado mucho desde la primera vez que la conocí en un mercado de esclavos.»

«No —dijo mi compañero—. Ella era noble antes de ser esclava. Era la hija del señor y la señora de Coatlícamac. Cuando su padre murió y su madre se volvió a casar, su nuevo marido celosa y traicioneramente la vendió como esclava.»

«En verdad —dije secamente— que su imaginación ha mejorado mucho desde la primera vez que la encontré, pero claro que ella me *dijo* que haría cualquier cosa para realizar sus ambiciones. Les sugiero a todos ustedes que estén en guardia de las palabras que hablen y que estén al alcance de los oídos de la *Señora Malinali*.»

Creo que fue al siguiente día cuando Cortés dispuso, para los señores, una demostración de sus armas maravillosas y de las proezas militares que sus hombres podían hacer. Por supuesto que yo estuve presente entre la multitud de nuestros cargadores y de los totonaca que también se reunieron para observar. Esos plebeyos quedaron despavoridos por lo que vieron; jadeaban a intervalos y murmuraban «¡*Ayya!*» llamando a sus dioses muy seguido. Los emisarios mexica mantuvieron sus caras impasibles, como si no estuvieran muy impresionados y yo estaba muy ocupado memorizando los diversos eventos para poder lanzar alguna exclamación. No obstante, tanto los señores como yo, varias veces brincamos ante el repentino estruendo, tan sorprendidos como cualquiera de los plebeyos.

Cortés mandó construir una burda casita hecha de madera, con algunos de los tablones que quedaron de los barcos, tan lejos sobre la playa que apenas era visible desde donde estábamos nosotros. Sobre la playa, enfrente de nosotros, mandó acomodar uno de esos tubos pesados de metal amarillo que eran portados sobre grandes ruedas...

No, llamaré a las cosas por sus nombres, adecuadamente. Ese tubo con ruedas altas... era un cañón de bronce que fue apuntado hacia la distante casa de madera. Diez o doce soldados cabalgaban, formando una hilera, sobre la húmeda y dura arena entre el cañón y la línea de la playa. Los caballos llevaban esas sillas de cuero que antes no había comprendido para qué servían, eran sillas de montar con todos sus aditamentos: bridas para guiar a los animales, faldas de un material acojinado, muy parecido al de nuestras armaduras para pelear. Otros hombres se quedaron a un lado de los caballos, con esos sabuesos gigantes que tiraban de las correas de cuero con que los detenían.

Todos los soldados vestían su traje de batalla completo, que los hacía verse muy aguerridos, con esos yelmos de acero brillando sobre sus cabezas y esos corseletes de acero brillando sobre sus justillos de cuero. Llevaban sus espadas envainadas en sus costados, pero cuando montaban sus cabalgaduras llevaban en sus manos unas armas largas muy parecidas a nuestras lanzas, excepto que sus hojas de acero además de ser puntiagudas estaban hechas de tal manera que podían desviar los golpes de cualquier enemigo, mientras cabalgaban.

Cortés sonrió a sus guerreros sintiéndose orgulloso de ellos, cuando tomaron sus posiciones. A cada lado de él estaban sus intérpretes, y Ce-Malinali también sonreía con un dejo de superioridad medio aburrida, por haber visto ya antes esa representación. Por medio de ella y de Aguilar, Cortés dijo a nuestros señores mexica: «A vuestros ejércitos les encantan los tambores, yo los he escuchado. ¿Os' gustaría que empezáramos el espectáculo con el retumbido de un tambor?»

Antes de que nadie pudiera contestar él gritó: «¡Por Santiago... ahora!» Los tres soldados que estaban a cargo del cañón hicieron algo para encender una llama en la parte de atrás del tubo y se oyó un solo retumbido, tan fuerte como jamás lo habrían podido hacer nuestros tambores que rompían el corazón. El cañón de bronce saltó, y yo también, y de su boca salió un humo del color de las nubes en tormenta y su estruendo fue como el de Tláloc y arrojó una luz más brillante que cualquiera de los tenedores de luz de los tlaloque. Después, para mi gran sorpresa, vi un objeto pequeño que iba muy rápido y muy lejos volando a través del aire. Era por supuesto la bola de hierro fundido, que cayó sobre la casa de madera haciéndola añicos.

El repentino retumbar del cañón se vio prolongado, como frecuentemente lo hace Tláloc, por un estruendo más pequeño. Era el sonido que hacían las herraduras de los caballos, al patear la arena dura, pues sus jinetes habían tirado de sus bridas para lanzarlos a un galope furioso en el momento en que el cañón había vomitado. Fueron corriendo a lo largo de la costa, lado a lado, tan rápido como un venado sin astas y los grandes perros que habían soltado al mismo tiempo, fácilmente mantenían el paso. Los jinetes llegaron hasta donde estaban las ruinas de la casa y podíamos ver a lo lejos el relampaguear de sus lanzas cuando pretendían matar a cualquier superviviente. Luego hicieron que sus monturas se dieran la vuelta y regresaron galopando hacia nosotros, otra vez. Los perros no los siguieron inmediatamente y a pesar de que mis oídos seguían zumbando, podía oír en la distancia a los sabuesos haciendo ruidos voraces y pensé que también había escuchado gritos de hombres. Cuando los perros regresaron, sus fieras quijadas chorreaban de sangre. Pudiera ser que algunos de los totonaca hubiesen escogido ese lugar, cerca de aquella casa, para observar los ejercicios o que Cortés deliberada e insensiblemente se las arregló para que ellos estuviesen allí.

Mientras tanto, los jinetes que se aproximaban ya no guardaban su formación de una línea al frente, sino que movían a sus caballos de arriba a abajo, entrecruzándose unos a otros, formando intrincados movimientos y diseños que se cruzaban, para demostrarnos el perfecto control que podían mantener aun galopando en esa forma tan temeraria. También, el hombrón aquel de barba roja, Alvarado, nos dio una representación personal mucho más temeraria. A todo galope, se descolgó de su silla de montar y sosteniéndose de ella con una sola mano, *corrió* a un lado de su animal que parecía un relámpago, conservando con facilidad su mismo paso y entonces sin detener su galope saltó por la parte de atrás de su caballo para caer sobre la silla de montar. Eso hubiera sido una hazaña admirable de agilidad hasta para los Pies Veloces raramuri, pero Alvarado lo hizo llevando puesto su traje de acero y cuero, así es que eso pesaba tanto como lo que él hizo.

Cuando los jinetes terminaron de mostrar cómo galopaban y la seguridad con que podían manejar a sus grandes animales, un número de soldados se desplegaron sobre la playa. Algunos llevaban arcabuces y otros unos arcos pequeños montados sobre una caja pesada de madera que se acomodaban contra el hombro. Algunos trabajadores totonaca pusieron unos adobes a una buena distancia a tiro de flecha, enfrente de los soldados. Entonces los hombres blancos se arrodillaron alternativamente para disparar sus arcos y arcabuces. La destreza de los arqueros era encomiable, acertando quizás a dos de cinco adobes, pero no eran muy rápidos con sus armas. Después de haber arrojado una flecha, no podían volver la cuerda del arco a su lugar con rapidez, sino que tenían que estirarla a lo largo de la caja hasta uno de los extremos en donde estaba una pequeña pieza que la fijaba.

Los arcabuces eran unas armas formidables; sólo el ruido que hacían, la nube de humo y las llamas que despedían eran suficientes como para acobardar a cualquier enemigo que las tuviera enfrente por primera vez. Pero éstas despedían más que miedo, lanzaban unas pequeñas bolitas de metal que volaban tan rápido que eran invisibles. Las pequeñas flechas de las ballestas simplemente golpeaban los adobes, pero las bolitas de metal de los arcabuces chocaban tan fuerte que los adobes volaban en pedazos.

No obstante, yo me di cuenta de que esas bolitas no volaban más lejos de lo que podrían hacerlo nuestras flechas y un hombre que lo manejara tardaba tanto en volverlo a cargar, que en ese tiempo nuestros guerreros podían haber lanzado seis o siete flechas.

Cuando la demostración se acabó, yo tenía muchos más papeles de corteza dibujados para mostrárselos a Motecuzoma y muchas cosas más que decirle, sólo me faltaba el dibujo de la cara de Cortés que me había pedido que hiciera. Muchos años antes, en Texcoco, había jurado que nunca más haría retratos, pues parecía que algún desastre caía siempre sobre las personas que retrataba, pero no sentía ningún remordimiento, si eso le causaba algún problema a los hombres blancos. Así es que la siguiente tarde, cuando los señores mexica tuvieron la última entrevista con Cortés y sus oficiales y sus sacerdotes, éramos cinco los señores. Ninguno de los españoles parecieron darse cuenta de que había uno más y ni Aguilar ni Ce-Malinali me reconocieron bajo mi traje de señor, como tampoco lo hicieron cuando andaba vestido de cargador.

Nos sentamos todos juntos para cenar, pero no haré ningún comentario acerca de los modales que tenían los hombres blancos para comer. Nosotros habíamos puesto la comida, así es que era de la mejor calidad; los españoles habían contribuido con un brebaje que llamaban vino, que llevaban en unas bolsas largas de cuero. Uno era pálido y seco, y otro oscuro y dulce, pero yo bebí muy poco porque era tan embriagador como el *octli*. Mientras mis cuatro compañeros señores se hacían cargo de la conversación, yo me senté en silencio, tratando de captar de la manera más discreta las facciones de Cortés sobre el papel de corteza, utilizando una tiza. Viéndolo de cerca por primera vez, me pude dar cuenta de que el pelo de su barba era más ralo que el de sus compañeros, que no podía esconder adecuadamente una fea cicatriz en su labio inferior y que su barbilla era casi tan puntiaguda como las de los maya, y puse todos esos detalles en el retrato. Entonces, me di cuenta de que todos los hombres se habían callado y estaban silenciosos y cuando levanté los ojos me encontré con los ojos grises de Cortés puestos en mí.

Él me dijo: «¿Así es que estoy siendo retratado para la posteridad? Dejadme verlo.» Por supuesto que él habló en español, pero su mano extendida significaba una orden fácil de comprender, así es que se lo alargué.

«Bueno, no puedo llamarlo muy halagador —dijo—, pero sí se reconoce. —Él lo mostró a Alvarado y a los otros españoles y cada uno de ellos cloqueó y asintió—. En cuanto al artista —dijo Cortés todavía mirándome—, observen *su* cara, compañeros. Si le quitaran todas esas plumas que lleva y le blanquearan la complexión, podría pasar por un hijodalgo y aun por un hombre de distinción. Si os hubieseis encontrado con él en la Corte de Castilla, un hombre de su estatura y con esas facciones tan fuertes, os hubieseis quitado vuestros sombreros, haciendo una gran reverencia. —Él me devolvió el dibujo y sus intérpretes tradujeron su siguiente pregunta—: ¿Por qué me estáis retratando?»

Uno de mis compañeros señores, pensando rápidamente, le contestó: «Ya que nuestro Venerado Orador Motccuzoma desgraciadamente no tendrá la oportunidad de conocerle, mi Señor Capitán, nos pidió que le lleváramos su retrato como recuerdo de su corta visita a estas tierras.»

Cortés sonrió con sus labios, pero no con sus ojos opacos y dijo: «Sin embargo, yo *veré* a vuestro emperador. He determinado hacerlo. Todos nosotros admiramos tanto los tesoros que nos mandó de regalo que estamos ansiosos por ver las maravillas que debe de tener vuestra ciudad capital. No pensaría en irme antes de que mis hombres y yo nos regocijemos la vista en lo que según me han dicho es la ciudad más rica de todas estas tierras.»

Cuando todo eso fue traducido, otro de mis compañeros, poniendo cara de duelo, le dijo: «*Ayya*, el señor blanco sólo hará un viaje largo y peligroso para encontrarse con una desilusión. No deseamos confesárselo, pero el Venerado Orador despojó y echó a perder la ciudad, para poderles dar estos regalos. Él escuchó que los hombres blancos que nos visitaban parecían apreciar el oro, así es que él mandó todo el oro que poseía, como también todos sus demás adornos de valor. Ahora la ciudad ha quedado pobre y fría. No vale la pena que los visitantes se molesten en verla.»

Ce-Malinali dijo, al traducir todo eso en xiu a Aguilar: «El Venerado Orador Motecuzoma les mandó esos simples regalos con la esperanza de que el Capitán Cortés estuviera satisfecho con ellos e inmediatamente se fuera de aquí. Pero de hecho sólo representa una pequeña parte de todos los tesoros inestimables que tiene en Tenochtitlan. Motecuzoma desea desanimar al Capitán, para que no vea la riqueza *real* que tiene en su ciudad capital.»

Mientras Aguilar se lo traducía a Cortés en español, yo hablé por primera vez y con voz baja a Ce-Malinali en su lengua nativa de Coatlícamac, para que sólo ella lo pudiera comprender:

«Tu trabajo es decir lo que se habla, no inventar mentiras.»

«¡Pero *él* mintió!», barbotó, apuntando a mi compañero. Entonces se sonrojó al darse cuenta de que había sido cogida en su traición, y que lo había confesado abiertamente.

Yo le dije: «Yo sé los motivos por los que miente. Me interesaría mucho conocer los tuyos.»

Ella me miró fijamente y sus ojos se abrieron mucho al reconocerme: «¡Usted!», dijo sin aliento, y espantada y desanimada a la vez.

Nuestro pequeño coloquio había pasado desapercibido para los demás y Aguilar todavía no me reconocía. Cuando Cortés volvió a hablar y Ce-Malinali tradujo, su voz era sólo ligeramente insegura.

«Le agradeceremos mucho a vuestro emperador si nos extendiera una formal invitación para visitar su magnífica ciudad. Pero decidle, mis señores embajadores, que nosotros no insistimos en ningún recibimiento oficial, ya que de todas maneras iremos, con invitación o sin ella. *Aseguradle* que iremos.»

Mis cuatro compañeros empezaron otra vez a exponerle sus razones, pero Cortés los cortó diciendo:

«Para ahora, ya les hemos explicado con mucho cuidado la naturaleza de nuestra misión, como nuestro Rey Don Carlos nos ha mandado con instrucciones muy particulares de presentar nuestros respetos a vuestro gobernante y pedirle permiso para introducir la Santa Fe Cristiana en estas tierras. Y con mucho cuidado nosotros les hemos explicado la naturaleza de esa Fe, de Nuestro Señor Dios, de Jesucristo y de la Virgen María, quienes sólo desean que todos los pueblos vivan como hermanos. También nos hemos tomado el trabajo de demostrarles las armas insuperables que poseemos, y no puedo pensar en alguna otra cosa en la que hayamos sido negligentes de aclararles. Pero antes de que os hayáis ido, ¿deseáis saber alguna otra cosa de nosotros? ¿Alguna pregunta que queráis hacer?»

Mis cuatro compañeros lo miraron molestos e indignados, pero no dijeron nada. Así es que me aclaré la garganta y hablándole directamente a Cortés en su propia lengua, le dije: «Sólo una pregunta, mi señor.»

Los hombres blancos me miraron sorprendidos porque había hablado en español y Ce-Malinali se puso envarada, temiendo sin duda que fuera a denunciarla... o quizá temiendo que fuera a quitarle su trabajo de intérprete.

«Tengo curiosidad por saber... —empecé, pretendiendo humildad e incertidumbre—. ¿Podría decirme...?»

«¿Sí?», apuró Cortés.

Todavía pareciendo tímido y vacilante, le dije: «He escuchado que sus hombres, muchos de sus hombres, hablan de que nuestras mujeres, bien..., están incompletas en cierto aspecto...»

Hubo un ruido de metal y de cuero cuando todos los hombres blancos se inclinaron hacia mí, prestando toda su atención. «¿Sí? ¿Sí?»

Entonces les pregunté como si realmente deseara saberlo, les pregunté con cortesía y solemnidad, sin demostrar la menor burla o gazmoñería: «Sus mujeres... su Virgen María, ¿tienen pelo en sus partes privadas?»

Se oyeron otros chirridos y rechinos de sus armaduras; creo que también sus bocas y ojos abiertos rechinaron, conforme todos se hicieron para atrás, boquiabiertos —más o menos como ahora lo está haciendo Su Ilustrísima—, soltando exclamaciones agitadas de «¡Locura!» y «¡Blasfemia!» y «¡Ultraje!»

Sólo uno de ellos, el grande y barbirrojo Alvarado, soltó la carcajada. Se volvió hacia los sacerdotes que estaban cenando con nosotros y poniendo sus dos manos en los hombros de dos de ellos, entre sus espasmos de risa, les preguntó: «Padre Bartolomé, Padre Merced, ¿os *han* preguntado eso antes? ¿Os enseñaron en el seminario cómo contestar adecuadamente a una pregunta como ésa? ¿Habéis pensado antes siquiera una vez en *eso*? ¿Eh?»

Los sacerdotes no hicieron ningún comentario, pero me miraron aviesamente y sonriendo me enseñaron sus dientes e hicieron la señal de la cruz para alejar al demonio. Cortés no había quitado sus ojos de mí. Observándome detenidamente con su mirada de halcón, me dijo: «Tú no eres un hijodalgo o un hombre distinguido, no, ni ninguna clase de caballero. Pero serás recordado, sí, yo te recordaré.»

. A la siguiente mañana, mientras nuestro grupo se estaba aprestando para partir, vino Ce-Malinali y con una señal imperiosa me indicó que deseaba tener una discusión privada conmigo. La hice esperar y cuando me reuní con ella, le dije:

«Debe de ser algo interesante. Habla, Uno-Hierba.»

«Por favor, no me llame con mi nombre de esclava. Debe llamarme Malintzin o Doña Marina. —Me explicó—: He sido cristianizada con el nombre de Santa Margarita Marina. Por supuesto que eso no significa nada para usted, pero le sugiero que me demuestre el debido respeto, porque el Capitán Cortés me tiene en muy alta estima y él es muy rápido para castigar la insolencia.»

Yo le dije con frialdad: «Entonces te sugiero que duermas muy estrechamente con tu Capitán Cortés, porque a una sola palabra mía cualquiera de estos totonaca que andan por aquí con mucho gusto metería una hoja de obsidiana entre tus costillas, al primer descuido que tengas. Ahora estás hablando insolentemente al Señor Mixtli, quien ha ganado el -tzin a su nombre. Esclava, puedes hacer tontos a los hombres blancos con tus pretensiones de nobleza. Puedes hacer que te deseen pintándote el pelo como una *maátitl*, pero para tu propia gente sólo serás una hija de perra con el pelo pintado de rojo que ha vendido más que su cuerpo al invasor Cortés.»

Eso la hirió y dijo como defendiéndose: «No me acuesto con el Capitán Cortés, sólo le sirvo de intérprete. Cuando el Tabascoöb nos regaló, las veinte mujeres fuimos repartidas entre los hombres blancos y a mí me tocó ese hombre. —Y apuntó a uno de los oficiales que había estado cenando con nosotros—. Su nombre es Alonso.»

«¿Y estás disfrutando de él? —le pregunté con sequedad—. Si no recuerdo mal, cuando nos vimos la última vez te estabas expresando con odio de los hombres y de la manera en que ellos usaban a las mujeres.»

«Puedo pretender *cualquier* cosa —dijo—. Todo lo que pueda servir para mis propósitos.»

«¿Y cuáles son tus propósitos? Estoy seguro de que no es la primera vez que traduces mal. ¿Por qué aguijoneaste a Cortés para que vaya a Tenochtitlan?»

«Porque *yo* deseo ir allá. Ya le había dicho eso, hace años, cuando lo encontré por primera vez. Una vez que esté en Tenochtitlan, no me importará lo que les pase a los hombres blancos. Quizás hasta sea recompensada por haberlos llevado, en donde Motecuzoma podrá aplastarlos como chinches. Bueno, de todas maneras yo estaré en donde siempre he deseado estar y seré notoria y reconocida y no me tomará mucho tiempo llegar a ser una mujer noble, tanto de hecho como de nombre.»

«Sí, y por otro lado —sugerí—, si por algún golpe de suerte los hombres blancos no llegan a ser aplastados, entonces recibirás una recompensa mejor.»

Hizo un gesto de indiferencia. «Solamente quiero pedirle...

quiero suplicarle, Señor Mixtli... que no haga nada para impedir mi oportunidad. Sólo deme el tiempo suficiente para demostrarle a Cortés cuán útil puedo ser, y así no pueda privarse de mi ayuda y consejo. Sólo déjeme llegar a Tenochtitlan. Eso puede significar muy poco para usted o para su Venerado Orador o para cualquier persona, pero significa mucho para mí.»

Me encogí de hombros y le dije: «No me voy a salir de mi camino sólo para aplastar chinches. No voy a impedir tus ambiciones, esclava, siempre y cuando éstas no causen problemas a los intereses que yo sirvo.»

Mientras Motecuzoma veía el retrato de Cortés y otros dibujos que había hecho, yo enumeraba las personas y las cosas que había contado:

«Incluyendo a él y a sus otros oficiales, eran quinientos ocho hombres para pelear. La mayoría de ellos llevaban espadas y lanzas, pero trece también portaban arcabuces, treinta y dos tenían ballestas y me atrevería a decir que todos los otros hombres eran capaces de usar esas armas especiales. Además había cien hombres más, que evidentemente eran los marineros de los diez barcos que habían quemado.»

Motecuzoma pasó las hojas de papel de corteza encima de su hombro y los ancianos del Consejo de Voceros que estaban detrás de él, en una línea, se las empezaron a pasar de un lado a otro.

Yo continué: «Hay cuatro sacerdotes blancos. Tienen muchas mujeres de nuestra propia raza que les fueron regaladas por el Tabascoöb de Cupilco y por Patzinca de los totonaca. Tienen dieciséis caballos y doce perros grandes de caza. Tienen diez cañones de largo alcance y cuatro más pequeños. Como nos dijeron, Venerado Orador, sólo se quedaron con un barco que está todavía flotando en la bahía y en donde hay hombres, pero no los pude contar.»

Dos ancianos del Consejo de Voceros, que eran físicos, estaban examinando con atención solemne el retrato de Cortés y conferenciaban en murmullos profesionales.

Concluí: «Además de todas las personas que he mencionado, prácticamente toda la población de los totonaca parece estar bajo las órdenes de Cortés, trabajando como cargadores, carpinteros, albañiles y demás... cuando no les están enseñando los sacerdotes blancos, cómo adorar ante la cruz y la imagen de la Señora.»

Uno de los dos doctores dijo: «Señor Orador, si puedo hacer un comentario... —Motecuzoma asintió—. Mi colega y yo hemos estado observando el retrato del rostro del hombre Cortés y en otros dibujos en donde se ve completo.»

Motecuzoma dijo con impaciencia: «Y supongo que, como físicos que son, declaran oficialmente que él es un hombre.»

«No sólo eso, mi señor. Hay otros signos de diagnóstico. Es imposible decirlo con certeza, a menos de que alguna vez tuviéramos la oportunidad de examinarlo en persona, pero parece que por sus facciones enclenques, su pelo ralo y lo mal proporcionado de su cuerpo, él debe de haber nacido de una madre que estaba afligida, vergonzosamente, por la enfermedad *nanaua*. Hemos visto esas características muchas veces entre la progenie de las *maátime*.»

«¿De verdad? —dijo Motecuzoma visiblemente contento—. Si eso es cierto y si el *nanaua* ha afectado su cerebro, eso podría explicar muchas de sus acciones. Sólo un loco podría haber quemado esos barcos, con los que hubiera podido retirarse a salvo. Y si un hombre consumido por el *nanaua* es el guía de esos extranjeros, los otros deben de ser unos bichos con un intelecto todavía más pobre. Y usted, Mixtzin, díganos que sus armas no son tan terriblemente invencibles como otros lo han dicho. Saben, empiezo a pensar que hemos exagerado mucho el peligro que pueden suponer esos visitantes.»

De pronto, Motecuzoma había cambiado de ánimo, de ese ánimo con que lo había visto por tanto tiempo, pero su rápido cambio, pasando de la melancolía a una alegre ligereza, no me impelió a imitarlo. Hasta entonces él había pensado en los hombres blancos como una amenaza, como dioses o mensajeros de los dioses y requiriendo de nosotros que les profesáramos todo respeto, amistad y probablemente hasta toda nuestra sumisión. Pero al oír mi información y la opinión de los doctores, estaba muy dispuesto a subestimar a los hombres blancos, como si no merecieran nuestra atención y preocupación. Esa actitud se me hacía tan peligrosa como la otra, pero como no podía decir eso con tantas palabras, sólo le dije:

«Quizá Cortés esté enfermo hasta el punto de estar loco, Señor Orador, pero un loco puede ser todavía más peligroso que un cuerdo. Hace solamente unos cuantos meses que esos bichos vencieron a unos cinco mil guerreros en las tierras de Cupilco.»

«Pero los defensores de Cupilco no tienen nuestras ventajas. —No fue Motecuzoma quien habló, sino su hermano, el jefe guerrero Cuitláhuac—. Fueron al encuentro de los hombres blancos con la antigua táctica de combate cuerpo a cuerpo. Pero gracias a usted, Señor Mixtli, nosotros sabemos ahora algo acerca de las capacidades del enemigo. Si a la mayoría de mis guerreros les doy arcos y flechas, podremos estar fuera del alcance de sus armas de metal y escapar a las descargas de sus pesadas armas de fuego y podremos vencerlos con flechas más rápidas, que no podrán contestar con sus proyectiles.»

Motecuzoma dijo con indulgencia: «Es de suponerse que un jefe de guerra hable de guerra, pero no veo en absoluto la necesidad de tener una guerra. Simplemente le mandaremos una orden al Señor Patzinca para que todos los totonaca dejen de ayudar a los hombres blancos, de proveerlos con comida, mujeres y otras comodidades. Los intrusos se cansarán muy pronto de estar comiendo sólo el pescado que puedan pescar por sí mismos, bebiendo sólo el jugo de los cocos y teniendo que sufrir un verano en las Tierras Calientes.»

Fue su Mujer Serpiente, Tláctozin, quien contestó a eso: «Patzinca no parece estar muy inclinado a rehusarles nada a los hombres blancos, Venerado Orador. Los totonaca nunca se han regocijado de ser nuestros vasallos tributarios. Ellos preferirán cambiar de amos.»

Uno de los emisarios que había ido conmigo a la costa dijo: «También, estos hombres blancos hablaron de otros hombres blancos, incontables, que viven en esas tierras de donde éstos llegaron. Si nosotros peleamos contra ellos y los vencemos o si se rinden por hambre, ¿cómo sabríamos cuándo otros más lleguen o cuántos llegarán o qué armas más poderosas traerán con ellos?»

La alegría de Motecuzoma se disipó. Sus ojos lanzaron una mirada de desasosiego alrededor, como si inconscientemente buscaran una forma de escapar, ya fuera de los hombres blancos ya de tomar una firme decisión, no lo sé. Pero su mirada cayó casualmente sobre mí, se me quedó mirando y luego me dijo: «Mixtzin, su agitación habla de impaciencia. ¿Qué es lo que usted podría decir a esto?»

Yo dije sin vacilar: «Quemar el único barco que les queda a los hombres blancos.»

Algunos de los hombres que estaban en el salón del trono exclamaron: «¿Qué?» o «¡Deshonroso!» Otros dijeron cosas como: «¿Atacar a los visitantes sin ninguna provocación?» y «¿Empezar la guerra sin mandarles siquiera nuestras insignias de declaración de guerra?» Motecuzoma con un gesto los silenció y volviéndose hacia mí sólo me dijo: «¿Por qué?»

«Antes de que nosotros dejáramos la costa, mi señor, ese barco fue cargado con todo el oro fundido y todos los demás regalos que usted les mandó. Pronto desplegará sus alas hacia ese lugar llamado Cuba o hacia el lugar llamado España o quizás irá directamente a presentarse con su Rey Don Carlos. Los hombres blancos estaban hambrientos de oro y los regalos de mi señor no los saciaron, sino que sólo excitaron más su apetito. Si le permite a ese barco partir, con la prueba de que aquí hay oro, nada nos podrá salvar de una inundación de hombres blancos, que vendrán cada vez más y más hambrientos de oro. Pero el barco está hecho de madera. Envíe sólo unos cuantos buenos guerreros mexica hacia esa bahía, mi señor, de noche y en canoas. Mientras pretenden pescar a la luz de las antorchas, se pueden aproximar lo suficiente como para prenderle fuego.»

«¿Y luego?» —dijo Motecuzoma mordiéndose un labio—. Cortés y sus hombres no podrán regresar a su tierra. Entonces, *ciertamente* que se vendrán para acá... y ciertamente que no vendrán con unas intenciones muy amistosas, no después de una acción tan hostil por nuestra parte.»

«Venerado Orador —dije con cansancio—, ellos vendrán de todas maneras, sea lo que nosotros hagamos o dejemos de hacer. Y vendrán con sus dóciles totonaca para enseñarles el camino, para que les carguen todas sus provisiones durante la jornada, para asegurarse de que podrán sobrevivir al pasar esas montañas y a los encuentros con otras gentes. Pero también eso lo podemos prevenir. He tomado, cuidadosamente, nota de todo el terreno. Hay varias formas de ascender de las costa a las tierras altas y todas ellas llevan a través de pasos y desfiladeros muy angostos. En esos lugares tan apretados, a los hombres blancos no les servirán de nada sus caballos, sus cañones, sus arcabuces y aun sus armaduras de metal no serán una defensa. Unos cuantos y buenos guerreros mexica apostados en esos pasos, sin más armas que piedras, podrían convertir a cada uno de esos hombres en una pulpa.»

Se oyó otro coro de exclamaciones horrorizadas, ante mi sugestión de que los mexica pudieran atacar escondidos como salvajes. Pero yo continué con voz más fuerte:

«Debemos detener esta invasión, aunque sea con los medios más desagradables, si eso es lo conveniente, o nunca más tendremos la esperanza de contener la invasión. Quizás el hombre Cortés al ser un loco nos facilitó el camino, sólo tenemos que quemar o destruir el barco que él no mandó quemar. Si ese barco mensajero nunca regresa a su Rey Don Carlos, si ninguno de los hombres blancos queda vivo y capacitado para hacer siquiera una balsa con que escapar, el Rey Don Carlos nunca sabrá qué pasó con esa expedición.»

Se hizo un gran silencio en el salón del trono. Nadie quería ser el primero en comentar algo y yo traté de no impacientarme. Al fin Cuitláhuac dijo: «Es un consejo práctico, Señor Hermano.»

«Es un consejo monstruoso —gruñó Motecuzoma—. Primero destruir el barco de los extranjeros y por ende empujarlos a que avancen tierra adentro y luego cogerlos indefensos en un ataque encubierto. Eso requerirá mucha meditación y consultarlo detenidamente con los dioses.»

«¡Señor Orador! —dije con desesperación—. ¡Ese barco mensajero puede estar extendiendo sus alas en este momento!»

«Lo que indicaría —dijo imperativo— que los dioses así lo desean. Y por favor no agite de esa forma sus manos enfrente de mí.»

En esos momentos mis manos deseaban estrangularlo, pero las contuve para que pareciera un gesto que indicaba que cedía resignadamente de mi propósito.

Él meditó en voz alta: «Si el Rey Don Carlos no llega a saber nada de este grupo, se imaginará que está en algún peligro y ese rey no vacilará en enviar una tropa para que los rescate o los refuerce. Quizás incontables barcos trayendo a incontables hombres blancos. Por la forma tan simple en que Cortés quemó sus diez barcos, aparentemente su Rey Don Carlos tiene una gran reserva de ellos. Me da la impresión de que Cortés es sólo la punta de una lanza que ya ha sido arrojada. Quizá lo más sabio sea tratar a Cortés con cautela y pacíficamente, por lo menos hasta que podamos determinar cuán pesada es la lanza que se apoya detrás de él. —Motecuzoma se levantó, como una señal para que nos retiráramos, y dijo mientras salíamos—: Pensaré en todo lo que se ha dicho aquí. Mientras tanto, enviaré a unos *quimíchime* a las tierras de los totonaca y a todas las tierras intermedias, para que me tengan informado de lo que los hombres blancos están haciendo.»

Quimíchime quiere decir ratón, pero esa palabra también la usábamos para decir espía. Entre toda la comitiva de esclavos que tenía Motecuzoma, estaban incluidos hombres de cada nación de

El Único Mundo y los que eran de más confianza siempre los había utilizado frecuentemente para que espiaran en las tierras de donde ellos eran nativos, pues se podían infiltrar fácilmente y en completo anonimato entre su propia gente. Por supuesto que yo también en los últimos tiempos, había hecho el papel de espía en las tierras totonaca y he hecho ese trabajo en otras ocasiones... aun en algunos lugares en donde no hubiera podido pasar por un nativo del lugar... pero sólo era un hombre. Un hato completo de ratones, como el que había enviado Motecuzoma, podía cubrir más lugares y traer mucha más información.

Motecuzoma volvió a llamar a su presencia al Consejo de Voceros y a mí, cuando regresó el primer *quimichi* para informar que la casa flotante de los hombres blancos en verdad ya había desplegado sus alas y se había ido hacia el oeste perdiéndose de vista en el mar. Aunque me sentí desanimado al oír eso, seguí escuchando el resto del informe, pues el ratón había hecho un buen trabajo escuchando y observando, incluso había oído varias conversaciones traducidas.

El barco mensajero había partido con todos aquellos marineros que necesitaba y con otro hombre que había sido separado de la fuerza militar de Cortés, posiblemente encargado de entregar tanto los regalos y el oro, como el informe oficial de Cortés a su Rey Don Carlos. Ese hombre era el oficial Alonso, el que había tenido a Ce-Malinali, pero por supuesto no se había llevado consigo a esa joven mujer tan valiosa para ellos. Como era de esperar, Malintzin, como era llamada cada vez con más frecuencia, no se había sentido en lo más mínimo afectada por ello, sino que inmediatamente se convirtió en la concubina de Cortés aparte de ser su intérprete.

Con su ayuda, Cortés les dio un discurso a los totonaca. Les dijo que el barco mensajero regresaría con la orden de su rey de elevarlo de rango, pero que él se anticiparía a ello y que de ahí en adelante no debían llamarlo solamente por Capitán, sino por Capitán General y que también anticipándose a la orden de su rey, él le daba un nuevo nombre al Cem-Anáhuac, El Único Mundo. Todas las tierras de la costa que él ya tenía y todas las tierras que él descubriera en el futuro, se llamarían en lo sucesivo como La Capitanía General de la Nueva España. Por supuesto que esas palabras en español significaban muy poco para nosotros, sobre todo cuando el *quimichi* las dijo con su acento totonaca. Pero estaba lo suficientemente claro que Cortés, aunque fuese un loco digno de lástima o un hombre audaz quien actuaba incitado por las ambiciones de su consorte, se estaba atribuyendo tierras sin límites y pueblos incontables que ni siquiera había visto, sin haberlos conquistado por combate o por algún otro medio. Las tierras sobre las que él clamaba sus dominios incluían *las de nosotros* y los pueblos sobre los que él clamaba soberanía incluía *al nuestro*, los mexica.

Casi echando espuma por la boca ante ese ultraje, Cuitláhuac dijo: «Si ésa no es una declaración de guerra, Venerado Hermano, entonces nunca he oído una.»

Motecuzoma dijo con incertidumbre: «Él no ha mandado todavía los regalos guerreros u otras insignias guerreras con esa intención.»

«¿Esperarás hasta que él descargue sus estruendosos cañones sobre tus oídos? —demandó con impertinencia Cuitláhuac—. Obviamente él ignora nuestras costumbres de declarar la guerra. Quizás el hombre blanco lo haga sólo con palabras de desafío y presunción, como él lo ha hecho. Así es que enseñémosle a ese plebeyo engrandecido algunas buenas maneras. *Mandémosle* nuestros regalos de guerra, nuestras banderas y armas. Luego vayamos a la costa y ¡echemos de ella a ese insufrible jactancioso, empujándolo al mar!»

«Cálmate, mi hermano —dijo Motecuzoma—. Todavía él no ha molestado a nadie en estos lugares excepto a esos despreciables totonaca y aun a ellos sólo les ha hecho ruido. Por lo que a mí respecta, Cortés se puede quedar en la playa pavoneándose, poner su estado allí y romper el viento por ambos lados. Mientras tanto, hasta que él no haga nada, nosotros esperaremos.»

I H S

✠

S. C. C. M.

Santificada, Cesárea, Católica Majestad,
el Emperador Don Carlos, nuestro Señor Rey:

Estimada Majestad, nuestro Patrón Real, desde esta ciudad de
Mexico capital de la Nueva España, en la vigilia de la Fiesta de
la Transfiguración, en el año de Nuestro Señor Jesucristo de mil
quinientos treinta y uno, os saludo.

Aunque nunca recibimos de Vuestra Trascendental Majestad
la orden de desistir en la copilación de esta crónica, ahora, nos,
hemos completado ésta, pues el mismo narrador, el azteca, de-
clara que ya no tiene más que contar, así es que vos encontraréis
aquí anexado, el segmento final.

Mucho de la narración del indio, acerca de la Conquista y sus
consecuencias, ya es conocido por Vuestra Eminente Majestad,
por los informes enviados durante todos estos años por el Capitán
General Cortés y otros oficiales que hicieron la crónica de esos
sucesos en los que tomaron parte. Sin embargo, la narración de
nuestro azteca más bien repudia la ostentación de la que hace
gala el Capitán General, que tediosamente repite que «sólo él y
un puñado de intrépidos soldados castellanos» conquistaron todo
este continente sin ayuda.

Está más allá de toda duda que ahora que nos y vos, Señor,
podemos contemplar toda esta historia completa, ésta no se ha de
parecer en nada a lo que Vuestra Majestad debió de haber imaginado, cuando con vuestra real cédula nos habéis ordenado princi-
piarla. Y nos, difícilmente podremos reiteraros nuestra insatisfacción por lo que probó ser. No obstante, si ha servido por lo
menos de alguna información a nuestro Soberano o le ha esclarecido algunos puntos diminutos y extraños, nos, trataremos entonces de persuadirnos que nuestra paciencia e indulgencia, así
como el trabajo desagradable y sin descanso de nuestros escribanos, no se ha perdido por completo. Nos, oramos para que Vuestra Majestad, imitando al benigno Rey del Cielo, no tomará en
cuenta estos volúmenes acumulados de valor trivial, sino que considerará la sinceridad con que nos, emprendimos este trabajo y
el espíritu con que nosotros nos esforzamos por cumplirlo, y
esperamos que Vos lo veáis y a nosotros también, desde ese aspecto indulgente.

También, deseamos preguntaros, Señor, antes de terminar aquí
con el trabajo del azteca, ¿desea Vuestra Majestad que nos, de-
mandemos a él alguna información más o que añada algo más
a su ya de por sí voluminosa narración? Si es así, nos, veremos
de que continúe a nuestra disposición, pero si Vos ya no tenéis

ningún uso que darle al indio, Señor, ¿podríais ser tan amable de dictarnos vuestra disposición acerca de él o preferiría Vuestra Majestad que nos, simplemente lo pusiéramos en las manos de Dios al terminar su trabajo?

Mientras tanto y por siempre, que la gracia santa de Nuestro Señor Dios, continúe en el alma de nuestra Loable Majestad, es la constante oración de Vuestro S.C.C.M. devoto siervo,

(ecce signum) ZUMÁRRAGA

ULTIMA PARS

Como ya les había dicho, reverendos escribanos, el nombre de nuestro mes once Ochpaniztli, quería decir el «Barrido de las calles». Ese año, el nombre tomó una importancia nueva y siniestra; fue a final del mes, la temporada de lluvias estaba ya terminando, cuando Cortés inició la marcha tierra adentro conforme los había amenazado. Dejó sus remeros y algunos de sus soldados para vigilar la población de la Villa Rica de la Vera Cruz y se dirigió hacia el oeste, camino a las montañas en compañía de cuatrocientos hombres blancos y unos mil trescientos guerreros totonaca, todos ellos armados y vistiendo sus trajes de guerra. Había otros mil hombres totonaca que servían como *tamemime* para cargar las armas de reserva, así como los cañones desarmados y sus pesados proyectiles, provisiones de viaje y demás. Entre los cargadores se encontraban algunos espías de Motecuzoma que fielmente se comunicaban con otros *quimíchime* apostados a lo largo de la ruta, y de esta manera nos mantenían informados a todos nosotros en Tenochtitlan sobre las personas que formaban el grupo de Cortés y su avance.

Cortés dirigía la marcha, según nos dijeron, llevando su armadura de metal brillante y montando el caballo que burlona pero afectuosamente llamaba la *Mula*. Su otra posesión femenina, Malintzin, portaba su estandarte y caminaba orgullosamente junto al estribo de su cabalgadura. Sólo unos cuantos de los otros oficiales llevaban a sus mujeres, porque hasta los soldados de más bajo rango esperaban que les dieran otras o conseguirlas ellos por el camino. Pero según nos informaron los *quimíchime*, sus perros y caballos se encabritaron, se mostraron tercos y les causaron problemas al llegar a las montañas. También, en esas alturas, Tláloc había prolongado su estación lluviosa; la lluvia era fría, el viento soplaba mezclado frecuentemente con aguanieve. Los viajeros caminaban empapados y ateridos, sus armaduras caían pesadamente húmedas, agobiándolos y difícilmente pudieron disfrutar de ese viaje.

«¡Ayyo! —dijo Motecuzoma muy complacido—. Vaya, ya se darán cuenta de que el interior del país no es tan hospitalario como las Tierras Calientes. Ahora les enviaré a mis hechiceros para hacerles la vida más pesada.»

Cuitláhuac dijo ceñudo: «Mejor deja que lleve a los guerreros, para hacerles la vida todavía más imposible.»

Pero Motecuzoma siguió diciendo: «No. Prefiero pretender una ilusión de amabilidad, mientras sirva a nuestros propósitos. Deja que los hechiceros maldigan y aflijan esa tropa hasta que por sí mismos desistan sin saber que fue cosa nuestra. Deja que informen a su Rey que la tierra es insana e impenetrable, para que no le den un informe malo de nosotros.»

Los hechiceros, acatando apresuradamente sus órdenes, se fueron hacia el este, disfrazados como viajeros comunes. Ahora bien, los hechiceros pueden ser capaces de hacer muchas cosas extrañas y maravillosas más allá del poder de la gente ordinaria, pero los impedimentos que pusieron en el camino de Cortés fueron tan ineficaces que daban lástima. Primero, adelante del camino por el que iban a pasar, extendieron unos hilos delgados entre los árboles, de los cuales colgaron unos papeles azules con signos misteriosos. Aunque esas barreras se suponía que debían ser impenetrables para cualquiera excepto para los hechiceros, la *Mula*, que iba al frente de la caravana, sin ningún cuidado las rompió y pasó entre ellas, y tal vez ni Cortés ni nadie se fijó en esas cosas. Los hechiceros le mandaron decir a Motecuzoma, no que habían fallado, sino que los caballos poseían cierto hechizo que había vencido esa estrategia en particular.

Lo que hicieron después de eso fue reunirse secretamente con los *quimíchime*, quienes viajaban en la caravana sin levantar sospechas, y tomaron medidas para que los espías mezclaran savia de ceiba y frutas de Tónaltiu en las raciones de los hombres blancos. Cuando alguien toma la savia del árbol de la ceiba, llega a tener un hambre tal, que come vorazmente de todo lo que tenga a su alcance, hasta que, en unos cuantos días solamente, engorda a tal punto que no puede moverse. Al menos, eso nos dicen los hechiceros; yo nunca he presenciado ese fenómeno. Pero ya se ha comprobado que el fruto del *tonal* sí hace daño, aunque de un modo menos espectacular. El *tonal* es lo que ustedes llaman la «pera espumosa» y es el fruto del *nopali*, y los primeros españoles no sabían cómo pelarlo con cuidado antes de comérselo. Con eso los hechiceros esperaban que los hombres blancos se sintieran intolerablemente atormentados por tener esas espinitas invisibles clavadas, y muy difíciles de quitar, en sus dedos, labios y lengua. El *tonal* también tiene otro efecto. La persona que come su pulpa roja, su orina se torna de color todavía más rojo, y aquel que no sepa esto pensará que está orinando sangre y se sentirá aterrorizado en la certeza de que está mortalmente enfermo.

Si la savia de la ceiba engordó a los hombres blancos, ninguno de ellos llegó a estarlo tanto como para quedar inmóvil; si los hombres blancos maldijeron las espinas del *tónaltin*, o vieron con preocupación su orina roja, eso tampoco los detuvo. Tal vez sus barbas les daban cierta protección contra las espinas, y hasta que yo sepa, *siempre* orinaban de un color rojo. Pero es casi seguro que la mujer Malintzin, sabiendo lo fácil que *sería* envenenar a sus nuevos compañeros, prestaba mucha atención a lo que comían, y les enseñó cómo comer *tónaltin*, y les dijo qué efecto esperar después. De todos modos, los hombres blancos siguieron inexorablemente su camino hacia el este.

Cuando los espías de Motecuzoma llevaron las noticias de los fracasos de sus hechiceros, portaban una noticia aún más alarmante. Cortés y su grupo estaban pasando por las tierras de muchas tribus pequeñas que habitaban en esas montañas, tribus como los tepeyahuaca, los xica y otras que nunca habían pagado los tributos de buena gana a nuestra Triple Alianza. En cada pueblo, los soldados totonaca gritaban: «¡Venid! ¡Uníos a nosotros!

¡Uníos a Cortés! ¡Nos lleva a liberarnos del detestable Motecuzoma!» Y aquellas tribus contribuyeron voluntariamente con muchos guerreros. Así que, a pesar de que varios de los hombres blancos eran llevados en camillas, por haberse herido al caer de sus caballos encabritados, y aunque muchos de esa tierra baja, totonaca, se cayeron en las orillas del camino por haberse puesto enfermos con el aire tan delgado de aquellas alturas, el grupo de Cortés en lugar de disminuir, aumentaba en fuerzas.

«¡Oíste, Venerado Hermano! —le reclamó violento Cuitláhuac a Motecuzoma—. ¡Estas criaturas, hasta se han atrevido a presumir de que vienen a enfrentarse *personalmente contigo*! Tenemos toda clase de excusas para caer sobre ellos y debemos hacerlo ahora. Como lo ha dicho el Señor Mixtli, están casi completamente indefensos en esas montañas. No tenemos por qué temerles a sus animales o a sus armas. Ya no puedes seguir diciendo *¡esperen!*»

«Digo esperen —dijo Motecuzoma imperturbable—, y tengo buena razón para decirlo. El esperar salvará muchas vidas.»

Cuitláhuac literalmente aulló: «Entonces dime: ¿*cuándo* se ha visto en toda la historia que se pueda *salvar* una sola vida humana?»

Motecuzoma disgustado contestó: «Está bien, entonces hablo de no terminar innecesariamente con la vida de un guerrero mexícatl. Quiero que sepas esto, hermano. Esos extranjeros en estos momentos se acercan a la frontera oriental de Texcala, la nación que durante tanto tiempo ha resistido los asaltos feroces, aun de nosotros los mexica. Esa nación no estará dispuesta a recibir otro enemigo de diferente color, que le llega de otra dirección. Deja que los *texcalteca* peleen con los invasores y nosotros los mexica obtendremos ganancia por lo menos en dos aspectos. Los hombres blancos y sus totonaca seguramente serán vencidos, pero también espero que los texcalteca sufran bastantes pérdidas, lo suficientemente grandes como para que nosotros podamos atacarlos inmediatamente después y, por fin, vencerlos totalmente. Si durante esa batalla llegamos a encontrar algún hombre blanco todavía vivo, lo ayudaremos y le daremos albergue. Así aparecerá que hemos peleado con el fin de rescatarlos solamente y nos ganaremos su gratitud y la de su Rey Carlos. ¿Quién nos puede decir qué beneficios nos resultarán de eso en el futuro? Por lo tanto seguiremos esperando.»

Si Motecuzoma hubiera compartido con Xicotenca, el gobernante de Texcala, lo que había sabido de las capacidades y limitaciones guerreras del hombre blanco, sabiamente los texalteca hubieran atacado a los hombres blancos en algún lugar de aquellas montañas empinadas que tanto abundan en su nación. En lugar de eso, el hijo de Xicotenca, que también era jefe de guerreros y que se llamaba Xicotenca el Joven, escogió defenderse sobre uno de los pocos terrenos planos y extensos de su tierra. Acomodó a sus tropas a la manera tradicional en preparación para una batalla normal, una en la que ambos oponentes equilibraban sus fuerzas, intercambiaban las formalidades tradicionales y luego empezaban la lucha cuerpo a cuerpo, para probar quién era el más fuerte. Xicotenca pudo haber escuchado rumores de que el enemigo nuevo poseía más que una fuerza humana, pero no tenía modo de saber que a ese nuevo enemigo no le importaba en absoluto las tradiciones de nuestro mundo y las reglas guerreras establecidas por nosotros.

Según supimos más tarde en Tenochtitlan, Cortés salió de un bosque, a orillas de esa tierra plana, al frente de sus cuatrocientos cincuenta soldados blancos seguidos por cerca de tres mil guerreros totonaca y demás tribus, para encontrarse del otro lado con una pared sólida de texcalteca, por lo menos diez mil; algunos informes dijeron que eran aproximadamente treinta mil. Aun si Cortés se encontraba enfermo, como se afirmaba, hubiera reconocido lo formidable de su adversario. Éstos vestían su armadura acojinada, *quilted*, de colores amarillo y blanco. Portaban muchas banderas de pluma, trabajadas con el águila dorada de alas extendidas de Texcala y la garza blanca símbolo de Xicotenca. Amenazantes tocaban sus tambores de guerra y las flautas guerreras de sonido silbante y agudo. Sus lanzas y *maquáhuime* lanzaban destellos brillantes en la obsidiana limpia y negra que estaba sedienta de sangre.

En ese momento, Cortés seguramente deseó tener mejores aliados que los totonaca, con sus armas rústicas hechas de pez espada y huesos puntiagudos, y con sus pesados escudos que no eran más que conchas de tortuga. Pero si Cortés estaba preocupado, tuvo suficiente calma como para mantener su arma más extraña escondida. Los texcalteca sólo lo vieron a él y aquellas de sus tropas que iban a pie. Todos los caballos, incluyendo el suyo, aún estaban en el bosque, y bajo órdenes suyas permanecieron allí, fuera de la vista y alcance de los defensores de Texcala.

Según lo demandaba la tradición, varios Señores texcalteca salieron al frente de sus filas y cruzando el terreno verde entre los dos ejércitos presentaron las armas simbólicamente, los mantos y escudos de pluma, para declarar la guerra. Cortés deliberadamente prolongó esa ceremonia preguntando el significado de ella. Debo decir que para entonces rara vez se utilizaba a Aguilar como intérprete; la mujer Malintzin había hecho un esfuerzo por aprender el español, y había progresado rápidamente; porque después de todo, la cama es el mejor lugar para aprender cualquier idioma. Así que, después de reconocer la declaración texcalteca, Cortés hizo la suya, desenvolviendo un pergamino y leyendo, mientras Malintzin traducía a los señores que esperaban. Puedo repetirlo de memoria, porque hacía la misma proclamación a la entrada de cada aldea, pueblo, ciudad y nación que se cerraba ante su llegada. Primero demandaba que se le dejara entrar sin resistencia, y luego decía:

«Pero si no obedecéis, entonces, con la ayuda de Dios, entraré a la fuerza. Haré la guerra contra vosotros con la mayor violencia, os ataré al yugo de la obediencia de nuestra Santa Iglesia y de nuestro Rey Don Carlos. Tomaré vuestras esposas e hijos, y los haré esclavos, o los venderé, según el gusto de Su Majestad. Me apoderaré de vuestras pertenencias y haré caer todo el peso de mi fuerza, dándoos el tratamiento de súbditos rebeldes que se niegan maliciosamente a someterse a las leyes de sus soberanos. Por lo tanto vosotros seréis los culpables de todo el derramamiento de sangre y calamidades que surjan a consecuencia de esto, y no culpa de Su Majestad, mía o de los caballeros que sirven bajo mi mando.»

Es de imaginarse que a los Señores texcalteca no les gustó mucho oírse llamar súbditos de un extranjero, o que se les dijera que estaban desobedeciendo a alguien al defender su propia frontera. Lo único que esas palabras orgullosas lograron fue aumentar el deseo de los texcalteca de entrar en una sangrienta batalla, y contra más sangrienta, mejor. Por lo tanto no contestaron, sino que se dieron la media vuelta y con paso largo atravesaron la gran distancia donde se encontraban sus guerreros gritando más y más fuerte y tocando sus flautas con más agudeza y sus tambores con más fuerza.

Ese intercambio de formalidades había dado a los hombres de Cortés bastante tiempo para armar y acomodar sus diez cañones de gran boca y cuatro más pequeños y para cargarlos no con esas bolas con fuerza demoledora, sino con pedazos de metal cortado, vidrio roto, grava áspera y demás. Los arcabuces estaban sobre sus soportes listos para ser disparados y las ballestas también estaban en posición. Cortés rápidamente dio órdenes y Malintzin se las repitió a los guerreros aliados, y después se apresuró a ponerse a salvo, retrocediendo por donde habían llegado. Cortés y sus hombres estaban parados o hincados mientras que otros permanecieron en el bosque montados en sus caballos. Todos esperaron pacientemente mientras ese gran muro amarillo y blanco de pronto se lanzó hacia adelante y una lluvia de flechas surgió de él y cruzó y el muro se rompió convirtiéndose en miles de guerreros, pegando sus escudos, aullando como jaguares, gritando como águilas.

Ni Cortés ni ninguno de sus hombres se movió para salir al encuentro como era tradicional hacerlo. Él solamente gritó: «¡Por Santiago!», y el rugir de los cañones hizo que los gritos y ruidos guerreros de los texcalteca sonaran como el crujir de la madera en una tormenta. Todos los guerreros que se encontraban en las primeras filas atacantes quedaron convertidos en pedacitos de hueso, trozos de carne y bañados en sangre. Los hombres que iban en las siguientes filas simplemente caían, pero lo hacían muertos y sin ninguna razón aparente, ya que las balas de los arcabuces y las pequeñas flechas de las ballestas desaparecían dentro de sus armaduras acojinadas. Y luego se escuchó un trueno diferente, cuando los jinetes salieron a toda velocidad del bosque, con los sabuesos corriendo con ellos. Los soldados blancos montaban con sus lanzas apuntadas y destrozaban al enemigo como quien junta una hilera de chiles en un hilo, y cuando sus lanzas ya no podían juntar más cadáveres, los jinetes las tiraban y sacaban sus espadas de acero y encima de sus caballos las movían de tal modo que por el aire volaban manos, brazos y hasta cabezas cercenadas. Y los perros se lanzaron mordiendo, rompiendo y desgarrando, y la armadura de algodón no era ninguna protección en contra de sus colmillos. Los texcalteca estaban comprensiblemente sorprendidos. Aterrorizados y descorazonados ante ese choque, perdieron sus ímpetus y toda su voluntad de triunfo; se arremolinaban y dispersaban, y manejaban sus armas inferiores desesperadamente, pero con poco efecto. Varias veces sus campeones y *quáchictin* los volvían a reunir y a animar para guiarlos en nuevos ataques. Pero cada vez que hacían eso, los cañones, arcabuces y ballestas ya estaban listos y soltaban sus terribles proyectiles una y otra vez contra las filas de los texcalteca, causando un daño incalculable.

Bueno, no es necesario que relate cada detalle de esa batalla tan desigual; lo que pasó ese día es bien conocido. De cualquier manera, sólo puedo describir lo que más tarde dijeron los supervivientes de ese día, si bien más tarde yo mismo presencié matanzas similares. Los texcalteca huyeron del campo, perseguidos por los guerreros totonaca de Cortés, quienes con voces fuertes y de una manera cobarde, gozaron de la oportunidad de participar en una batalla que sólo pedía de ellos el que persiguieran los guerreros que se retiraban. En ese día los texcalteca dejaron tal vez una tercera parte de todo su ejército tirado en el campo, y al enemigo sólo lo habían alcanzado a herir superficialmente. Me parece que sólo cayó un caballo y unos cuantos españoles fueron heridos por las primeras flechas lanzadas, y algunos otros fueron heridos de mayor gravedad gracias a los acertados golpes de algunas *maquáhuime*, pero no hubo ningún muerto, ni fueron puestos fuera de combate por mucho tiempo ya que cuando los texcalteca habían huido fuera del área de persecución, Cortés y sus hombres acamparon allí mismo en el campo de batalla, para curar sus pocas heridas y celebrar su victoria.

Considerando las terribles pérdidas que los texcalteca habían sufrido, es una honra para Texcala que, a pesar de eso, la nación en sí no se rindió ante Cortés, pues los texcalteca eran un pueblo valiente, orgulloso y desafiante. Pero desgraciadamente tenían una fe enorme en la infalibilidad de sus adivinos y profetas. Así es que a esos hombres sabios fue a los que el jefe guerrero Xicotenca reunió urgentemente, la tarde del mismo día en que fue derrotado, y les preguntó:

«¿Es verdad que esos extranjeros son dioses, según se rumorea? ¿Son realmente invencibles? ¿No hay alguna manera de vencer sus armas que escupen fuego? ¿Debo seguir perdiendo más hombres buenos por pelear más tiempo?»

Después de deliberar por los medios mágicos que ellos utilizaran, los profetas dijeron esto:

«No, no son dioses. Son hombres. Pero la evidencia de esa llama que despiden sus armas nos indica que de alguna manera han aprendido a emplear el poder caliente del sol. Y mientras el sol brilla, ellos tendrán la ventaja de sus armas escupefuegos, pero al bajar el sol, también bajará su poder solar. Al anochecer, sólo serán hombres ordinarios, que únicamente podrán emplear armas ordinarias. Serán tan vulnerables como todos los hombres, y estarán muy cansados de los esfuerzos de hoy. Si quieren vencerlos será necesario que los ataquen de noche. Esta noche. Esta misma noche. O cuando el sol se levante, ellos también se levantarán y arrasarán con su ejército, como quien corta hierba.»

«¿Atacar de noche? —murmuró Xicotenca—. Va en contra de todas las costumbres. Viola todas las tradiciones de un combate justo. A excepción de estado de sitio, jamás se ha peleado de noche.»

Los sabios movieron sus cabezas. «Exactamente. Los extraños blancos no estarán preparados y no estarán esperando tal asalto. Se debe hacer lo inesperado.»

Los adivinos texcalteca estaban en un error tan grande como con frecuencia sucede con los adivinos de todas partes. Evidentemente, todos los ejércitos de los blancos, sí pelean de noche con frecuencia entre ellos mismos, y tienen la costumbre de tomar precauciones contra tal sorpresa. Cortés había puesto centinelas alrededor de su campamento; esos hombres permanecían despiertos y alertas, mientras sus compañeros dormían con sus armaduras y trajes de batalla, y listos con sus armas cargadas a un lado de sus manos. Aun en la oscuridad, los centinelas de Cortés percibieron con facilidad el primer avance de los exploradores texcalteca, mientras se arrastraban de estómago a través del campo abierto.

Los centinelas no dieron ningún grito de alarma, sino que regresaron silenciosamente al campamento y despertaron a Cortés y al resto de su ejército. Ningún soldado se paró de perfil contra el cielo; ningún hombre se levantó más alto de lo que es una posición sentada o hincada; ningún hombre hizo ruido. Así que los exploradores de Xicotenca regresaron y le informaron que todo el campamento parecía estar dormido, sin defensas y vulnerable. Lo que quedaba del ejército de los texcalteca se movió en masa, a gatas, hasta encontrarse dentro del perímetro del campamento enemigo. Luego se levantaron para atacar al dormido adversario, pero no tuvieron oportunidad de dar ni siquiera un grito de guerra. En cuanto se enderezaron, y por lo tanto presentaron un blanco fácil, la noche estalló en relámpagos, truenos y silbidos de proyectiles... y el ejército de Xicotenca fue arrasado como quien corta hierba.

A la mañana siguiente, con lágrimas en sus ojos ciegos, Xicotenca el Viejo mandó una embajada de sus nobles más altos, portando un cuadro de banderas de tela dorada como señal de tregua, para negociar con Cortés las disposiciones de la rendición de los texcalteca ante él. Grande fue la sorpresa de los enviados al ver que Cortés no portaba el aire de un conquistador, los recibió con mucho calor y aparente afecto. Por medio de su Malintzin, alabó el valor de los guerreros texcalteca. Sentía que por haber confundido sus intenciones se habían visto en la necesidad de defenderse. Porque, según dijo, él no quería que Texcala se rindiera, así es que no aceptaría su rendición. Había ido a esa nación sólo con la esperanza de cultivar una amistad y de ayudarla.

«Yo sé —dijo él, sin duda bien informado por Malintzin— que durante mucho tiempo habéis tenido que tolerar la tiranía de los mexica de Motecuzoma. He liberado a los totonaca y algunas otras tribus de ese yugo, y ahora haré lo mismo por vosotros. Sólo os pido que vuestra gente se una a mí en esta santa y venerable cruzada, que me proporcionéis cuantos guerreros sea posible para aumentar mi ejército.»

Los nobles, extrañados, dijeron: «Pero si nosotros habíamos oído que tú les exigías a todos los pueblos que se doblegaran sumisamente ante tu gobernante extranjero y tu religión, y que se acabara con todos nuestros dioses, ya fueran antiguos o nuevos.»

Cortés hizo un gesto casual como haciendo a un lado todo eso. La resistencia de los texcalteca cuando menos le había enseñado a tratarlos con cierta astucia.

«Yo pido alianza, no sumisión —dijo—. Cuando estas tierras ya hayan quedado fuera de la influencia maligna de los mexica, con gusto les extenderemos las bendiciones de la Cristiandad y las ventajas de un acuerdo con nuestro Rey Don Carlos. Y luego vosotros podréis ver si queréis aceptar esos beneficios. Pero veamos los asuntos más urgentes. Preguntadle a vuestro estimado gobernante si nos concederá el honor de estrechar su mano en signo de amistad y hacer con nosotros una causa común.»

El viejo Xicotenca apenas había recibido el mensaje de sus nobles, cuando nosotros en Tenochtitlan lo habíamos escuchado por parte de nuestros espías. En el palacio, todos nos dimos cuenta, pues era obvio, que Motecuzoma se sentía asombrado, abrumado y estaba enfurecido por el resultado de todas sus predicciones; casi al borde del pánico al ver lo que irremediablemente había traído consigo ese error suyo. Era bastante malo que los texcalteca *no* hubieran detenido a los invasores blancos, ni siquiera habían sido un estorbo en su camino. Era bastante malo que Texcala no hubiera caído para que luego nosotros la venciéramos. Y lo peor de todo era que los hombres blancos de ningún modo estaban desalentados o debilitados; seguían viniendo, seguían lanzando amenazas en contra nuestra. Y para colmo, los hombres blancos ahora vendrían reforzados por la fuerza y el odio de nuestros más viejos, más feroces y más encarnizados enemigos.

Motecuzoma se recobró, tomando una decisión que cuando menos tenía más fuerza que «esperar». Mandó llamar su mensajero-veloz más inteligente y le dictó un mensaje y lo envió corriendo inmediatamente para que se lo repitiera a Cortés. Por supuesto que el mensaje era largo y lleno de un lenguaje florido, pero en esencia decía:

«Estimado Capitán General Cortés, no ponga su confianza en esos texcalteca desleales, quienes le contarán cualquier mentira para ganarse su confianza y falsamente lo traicionarán. Como podrá descubrir fácilmente, la nación de Texcala es una isla completamente rodeada y bordeada por aquellas naciones vecinas de las cuales se ha hecho enemiga. Si usted protege a los texcalteca será, como ellos, despreciado, rehuido y rechazado por todas las demás naciones. Atienda nuestro consejo, abandone a los insignificantes texcalteca y únase a la poderosa Triple Alianza de los mexica, los acolhua y los tecpaneca. Nosotros lo invitamos a que visite nuestra ciudad aliada de Chololan, una marcha sencilla hacia el sur de donde está. Allí se le recibirá con una gran ceremonia de bienvenida digna de tan distinguido visitante. Cuando haya descansado será escoltado a Tenochtitlan, tal y como lo ha deseado, donde yo, el Uey-Tlatoani Motecuzoma Xocoyotzin, lo espero ansiosamente para estrecharlo como amigo y con honor.»

Puede ser que Motecuzoma quería decir precisamente eso, que estaba dispuesto a capitular al grado de conceder una audiencia a los hombres blancos, mientras pensaba qué hacer luego. No lo sé. En aquel entonces no me confió sus planes, ni tampoco a algún miembro de su Consejo de Voceros. Pero lo que sí sé es que si yo hubiera sido Cortés, me habría reído de tal invitación, especialmente con la astuta Malintzin a su lado interpretándolo, de manera más clara y sucinta.

«Detestado enemigo: Haz el favor de despedir a tus nuevos aliados, desecha las fuerzas adicionales que has adquirido y hazle el favor a Motecuzoma de caminar estúpidamente a una trampa, de la cual jamás saldrás.»

Pero, para mi gran sorpresa, pues entonces todavía no sabía lo audaz que era ese hombre Cortés, envió de regreso al mensajero aceptando esa invitación y efectivamente *marchó* hacia el sur para hacer una visita de cortesía a Chololan, en donde fue acogido como un huésped agradable y notable. Fue recibido en las afueras de la ciudad por los dos gobernantes unidos, el Señor de lo que Está Arriba y el Señor de lo que Está Abajo, así como por la mayoría de la población civil y sin hombres armados. Esos señores Tlaquíach y Tlalchíac no habían reunido a ninguno de sus guerreros y no se veía ninguna arma; todo parecía como Motecuzoma lo había prometido, apacible y hospitalario.

Como era natural, Cortés no había cumplido todas las sugerencias de Motecuzoma; no había despedido a sus aliados antes de marchar hacia Chololan, y mientras llegaba el mensajero de Motecuzoma, el anciano Xicotenca de la vencida Texcala había aceptado el ofrecimiento de Cortés de hacer una causa común y le había puesto bajo su mando a diez mil guerreros texcalteca, sin mencionar muchas cosas: una cantidad de mujeres texcalteca más bellas y nobles para ser repartidas entre los oficiales de Cortés y hasta una gran cantidad de sirvientas para ocupar el puesto de criadas personales de la Señora Uno-Hierba, o Malintzin, o Doña Marina. Así que Cortés llegó a Chololan al frente de aquel ejército texcalteca, además de sus tres mil hombres sacados del pueblo totonaca y otras tribus, y por supuesto, de sus cientos de soldados blancos, sus caballos y perros, su Malintzin y las otras mujeres que viajaban en su compañía.

Después de saludar a Cortés debidamente, los dos señores de Chololan vieron con miedo a aquella multitud y suavemente le dijeron por medio de Malintzin: «Por orden del Venerado Orador Motecuzoma, nuestra ciudad está desarmada y sin defensa. Podemos acomodarlo a usted, Señor, y a sus tropas y sirvientes personales, cómodamente, pero, sencillamente no hay lugar para sus incontables aliados. También nos disculpará por mencionar-lo, pero los texcalteca son nuestros enemigos irreconciliables, y nos sentiríamos muy inquietos si se les permitiera entrar a nuestra ciudad...»

Así que Cortés, servicialmente, dio órdenes de que su fuerza mayor de guerreros nativos permaneciera fuera de la ciudad, pero acampando en un círculo que la rodeara completamente. Cortés seguramente se sintió lo suficientemente protegido, con todos aquellos miles de guerreros tan cerca y a su disposición si necesitara ayuda. Y sólo él y los demás hombres blancos entraron a Chololan, caminando tan orgullosamente como si en verdad fueran nobles, o montando sus caballos con elegante majestuosidad, mientras la población reunida allí gritaba y lanzaba flores a su paso.

Como se le había prometido, a los hombres blancos se les dio lujosos alojamientos; cada soldado menor era tratado tan obsequiosamente como si fuera un campeón o noble y se les proporcionaron sirvientes, asistentes y mujeres para sus camas esa noche. Chololan ya había sido avisada acerca de los hábitos personales de los hombres, así es que nadie, ni las mujeres cuyas órdenes eran copular con ellos, jamás comentaron sobre el terrible olor que despedían o de la manera tan voraz que tenían de comer, o el que jamás se quitaban sus vestimentas y botas por apestosas, o cómo rehusaban bañarse, o de su descuido por lavarse aunque fuera sólo sus manos, después de hacer sus funciones excretoras y sentarse a comer. Los hombres blancos vivieron la clase de existencia, durante catorce días, que los guerreros heroicos podrían esperar como premio en el mundo del más allá. Se les festejó, se les obsequió *octli*, y se les dejó emborrachar y portarse tan desordenadamente como querían, y gozaron a lo máximo de las mujeres que se les había asignado, se les entretuvo con música, baile y canto. Y al cabo de esos catorce días, los hombres blancos se levantaron e hicieron una matanza de cada hombre, mujer y niño en Chololan.

Recibimos esa noticia en Tenochtitlan, tal vez antes de que el humo de los arcabuces hubieran despejado la ciudad, por medio de nuestros espías, quienes se infiltraban y se escurrían en las propias filas de Cortés. Según ellos, la matanza se hizo por instigación de la mujer Malintzin. Llegó una noche al cuarto de su amo en el palacio de Chololan, donde se encontraba tomando *octli* y divirtiéndose con varias mujeres. Les gritó a las mujeres que se fueran y luego lo advirtió de una conjura que se estaba fraguando. Ella se había enterado, dijo, al mezclarse y conversar con las mujeres locales del mercado, quienes inocentemente la tomaron por una cautiva de guerra ansiosa por libertarse de sus captores blancos. Todo el propósito del entretenimiento tan profuso hacia los visitantes, dijo Malintzin, era para que éstos se confiaran y se debilitaran mientras Motecuzoma enviaba secretamente una fuerza de veinte mil guerreros mexica a rodear Chololan. Dada cierta señal, dijo ella, las fuerzas mexica caerían sobre las tropas nativas que acampaban en las afueras, mientras que los hombres dentro de la ciudad se armarían y atacarían a los hombres blancos que no estarían preparados para hacerles frente. Y ella dijo que mientras regresaba del mercado había visto a gente de la ciudad agrupándose bajo los estandartes en la plaza central.

Cortés salió corriendo del palacio, con sus oficiales menores quienes también se habían alojado allí, y sus gritos de «¡Santiago!» trajeron a los miembros de sus tropas corriendo, de otros alojamientos de la ciudad, tirando a un lado a sus mujeres, sus vasos y levantando sus armas. Como lo había advertido Malintzin, encontraron la plaza llena de gente, mucha de ella portando estandartes de pluma, todos llevando vestimentas ceremoniales que posiblemente tenían aspecto guerrero. A esa gente reunida no se le dio tiempo ni siquiera de levantar un grito de guerra o de lanzar un reto a combate, o de explicar de algún modo su presencia en ese lugar, porque los hombres blancos inmediatamente descargaron sus armas, y tan densa era la multitud, que la primera serie de balas, flechas y demás proyectiles arrasaron con ellos como si fueran hierba.

Cuando el humo se despejó un poco, tal vez los hombres blancos vieron que la plaza contenía mujeres y niños así como hombres, y tal vez hasta se preguntaron si sus actos precipitados habían sido justificados. Pero el ruido de aquello trajo a sus aliados texcalteca y a los otros, corriendo de sus campamentos a la ciudad. Fueron ellos los que con más maldad que los hombres blancos llevaron la ciudad a la ruina y acabaron con su población sin misericordia o discriminación, matando hasta a los Tlaquíach y Tlalchíac. Algunos de los hombres de Cholólan alcanzaron a correr por armas con las cuales pelear, pero eran tan pocos y estaban tan rodeados, que sólo podían hacerlo en retirada, moviéndose hacia arriba de los flancos de la pirámide-montaña de Cholólan. Se debatieron valerosamente hasta llegar a la cima de ésta y al final se encontraban acorralados dentro del gran templo de Quetzalcóatl. Así que sus atacantes simplemente colocaron leña alrededor de éste y lo encendieron, quemándolos vivos.

Eso fue hace cerca de doce años, reverendos frailes, cuando el templo fue quemado, derrumbado y su escombro regado. No quedaron más que árboles y arbustos, razón por la cual mucha de su gente, desde entonces, no ha podido creer que la montaña *no* es una montaña sino una pirámide levantada, hace mucho, por los hombres. Claro que ahora sé que tiene algo más que verdor. La cima en donde fueron abatidos Quetzalcóatl y sus adoradores esa noche, últimamente ha sido coronada en una iglesia Cristiana.

Cuando Cortés llegó a Cholólan ésta estaba habitada por cerca de ocho mil personas; cuando se fue, estaba vacía. Repito que Motecuzoma no me confió ninguno de sus planes, así es que no podría decir, *si* tenía tropas mexica caminando cautelosamente hacia aquella ciudad, y *si* había dado instrucciones a la gente de levantarse en combate cuando la trampa se hubiera puesto, pero permítanme dudarlo. La masacre ocurrió el primer día de nuestro mes quince, llamado Panquétzaliztli, que quiere decir El Florecimiento de las Banderas Emplumadas, y se celebraba en todas partes con ceremonias en que la gente llevaba estandartes emplumados.

Puede ser que la mujer Malintzin jamás hubiera asistido a alguna ceremonia de ese festival. Es posible que ella realmente creyera, o por error supusiera, que la gente concurría allí con banderas guerreras. O tal vez pudo haber inventado una «conjura», nacida de un resentimiento celoso por las atenciones que Cortés recibió de parte de las mujeres locales. Si es que ella malentendió o lo hizo sólo por pura malicia, el hecho fue lo que eficazmente impulsó a Cortés a convertir a Chololan en un desierto. Y si es que él se arrepintió, no lo estuvo por mucho tiempo, porque eso elevó su fortuna aún más de lo que lo había hecho su victoria sobre los texcalteca. He mencionado que he visitado Chololan y he visto que la gente es menos cariñosa. No tenía por qué importarme si la ciudad seguía existiendo y su repentina devastación no me causó angustia alguna, a excepción de saber que eso aumentaba la reputación de temible que cada día más iba adquiriendo Cortés. Porque a causa de las noticias de la masacre de Chololan, que se extendieron por medio de mensajeros-veloces por todo El Único Mundo, los gobernantes y jefes guerreros de las muchas otras comunidades comenzaron a considerar todos los sucesos hasta esa fecha más o menos con estas palabras:

«Primero los hombres blancos le quitaron los totonaca a Motecuzoma. Luego conquistaron Texcala, cosa que Motecuzoma ni ninguno de sus predecesores había podido hacer jamás. Luego terminaron con los aliados de Motecuzoma en Chololan, sin importarles en absoluto la ira de Motecuzoma o su carácter vengativo. Empieza a parecer que los hombres blancos son más poderosos todavía que los reconocidamente fuertes mexica. Sería más sabio por nuestra parte ponernos del lado de la fuerza superior... mientras lo podamos hacer voluntariamente.»

Un noble poderoso hizo eso sin vacilar: El Príncipe Heredero Ixtlil-Xóchitl, legítimo heredero de los acolhua. Motecuzoma debió de arrepentirse amargamente de haberle usurpado el trono a ese príncipe, tres años antes, cuando se dio cuenta de que Flor Oscura no sólo había pasado esos años quejándose, en su retiro en la montaña, sino que había estado reuniendo guerreros preparándose para reclamar su trono en Texcoco. La llegada de Cortés debió parecerle a Flor Oscura como un regalo del cielo y una ayuda oportuna para su causa. Bajó de su escondite a la ciudad devastada de Chololan, donde Cortés estaba reagrupando su multitud para preparar su marcha continua hacia el oeste. En su encuentro, Flor Oscura seguramente le habló a Cortés del mal trato que había sufrido a manos de Motecuzoma y seguramente Cortés prometió ayudarle a repararlo. De todos modos, la siguiente mala noticia que recibimos en Tenochtitlan fue que Cortés había aumentado su fuerza con la unión del vengativo Príncipe Flor Oscura y sus varios miles de guerreros acolhua soberbiamente adiestrados.

Era obvio que la innecesaria y tal vez impulsiva masacre en Chololan había sido un buen golpe para Cortés, y todo se lo debía a su mujer Malintzin, fuera cual fuese la verdadera razón que tuvo para provocarlo. Ella había demostrado una entera dedicación a su causa, su ansiedad por ayudarlo a adquirir su destino, aunque lo hiciera pisoteando los cadáveres de hombres, mujeres y niños de su propia raza. De ahí en adelante, aunque Cortés dependía todavía de ella como intérprete, la valoró aún más como su consejera principal en estrategia, su oficial menor de mayor confianza y la más leal de sus aliados. Quizás hasta llegó a amar a esa mujer; nadie jamás lo supo. Malintzin había logrado sus dos ambiciones: se había convertido en algo indispensable para su señor y además iba a Tenochtitlan, su destino soñado, con el título y los requisitos de una dama.

Aunque puede ser que todos los sucesos que pasaron, y que les he contado, hubieran sucedido de todos modos aunque la huérfana Ce-Malinali jamás hubiera nacido de aquella esclava prostituta de los coatlícamac. Y es posible que tenga un motivo personal para despreciar esa devoción rastrera que le tenía a su amo, esa deslealtad vergonzosa hacia los de su raza. Es posible que le guardara un odio especial, simplemente porque no podía olvidar que tenía el mismo nombre de nacimiento de mi difunta hija, porque era de la misma edad que Nochipa hubiera tenido, de modo que sus actos despreciables parecían, a mi modo de ver, insultar a mi indefensa y sin culpa Ce-Malinali.

Pero dejando mis sentimientos personales a un lado, ya *había* encontrado a Malintzin dos veces antes de que se convirtiera en el arma más perversa de Cortés, y en ambas ocasiones pude haber evitado que llegara a serlo. Cuando nos conocimos por primera vez en el mercado de esclavos, la pude haber comprado, y ella habría estado contenta de pasar su vida en la gran ciudad de Tenochtitlan, como miembro de la casa de un campeón Águila de los mexica. Cuando nos vimos nuevamente en tierra totonaca, aún era esclava y propiedad de un oficial de poca importancia, un simple eslabón en la cadena de interpretar conversaciones. Su desaparición en aquel entonces sólo hubiera ocasionado un mínimo alboroto y con facilidad la hubiera hecho desaparecer. Así que dos veces pude haber cambiado el curso de su vida, y tal vez también el de la historia, pero no lo hice. Sin embargo su instigación en la matanza de Chololan me hizo ver la amenaza que ella representaba, pero sabía que tarde o temprano la volvería a encontrar en Tenochtitlan, hacia donde había deseado llegar durante toda su vida, y me juré a mí mismo que me las arreglaría para que su vida terminara ahí.

Mientras tanto, inmediatamente después de recibir la noticia de la masacre de Chololan, Motecuzoma dio muestras de su indecisión, con una acción decidida, al enviar otra delegación de nobles, y esa embajada estaba dirigida por Tlácotzin, su Mujer Serpiente, El Alto Tesorero de los mexica, segundo en mando después de Motecuzoma. Tlácotzin y sus compañeros nobles iban al frente de una caravana de cargadores que llevaban otra vez oro y otras riquezas, éstas no eran con la intención de repoblar a esa desgraciada ciudad, sino para adular a Cortés.

Creo que en ese único acto, Motecuzoma reveló el mayor grado de hipocresía del que era capaz. Ya sea que la gente de Cho-lolan hubiese sido totalmente inocente, por lo que no merecían ser aniquilados, o ya sea que efectivamente *habían* planeado le-vantarse en contra de Cortés, sólo lo pudieron haber hecho obe-deciendo las órdenes secretas de Motecuzoma. Sin embargo, el Venerado Orador, en el mensaje llevado a Cortés por Tlácotzin, culpó a sus aliados de Chololan de haber creado esa dudosa «conjura» por sí mismos; afirmó no haber tenido que ver con ella y los describió como «traidores a nosotros dos»; felicitaba a Cortés por la rapidez con que había aniquilado totalmente a esos rebeldes y esperaba que ese triste suceso no pondría en peligro la amistad anticipada entre los hombres blancos y la Tri-ple Alianza.

Pienso que era muy adecuado que el mensaje de Motecuzoma fuera entregado por su Mujer Serpiente, ya que era una obra maestra, en cuanto a la forma en que se puede arrastrar una serpiente. Y el mensaje continuaba: «Sin embargo, si la perfidia de Chololan ha desalentado al Capitán General y su compañía, de aventurarse más lejos en estas tierras tan peligrosas y entre gente tan impredecible, comprenderemos su decisión de volver-se y regresar a casa, aunque sinceramente sentiremos el haber perdido la oportunidad de conocer al valiente Capitán General Cortés, cara a cara. Por lo tanto, como ya no visitará nuestra ciudad capital, nosotros los mexica le pedimos que acepte estos regalos como un pequeño sustituto de nuestro abrazo amistoso y para que los comparta con su Rey Don Carlos al regresar a su país natal.»

Más tarde supe que Cortés con dificultad pudo contener la risa cuando ese mensaje tan transparente le fue traducido por Malintzin, y que pensando en voz alta, dijo: «Cómo ansío cono-cer cara a cara a ese hombre de dos caras.» Pero la contesta-ción que le dio a Tlácotzin fue:

«Le agradezco a vuestro amo su preocupación y estos regalos de compensación que agradecidamente acepto en nombre de Su Majestad el Rey Don Carlos. Sin embargo —y aquí bostezó, se-gún nos informó Tlácotzin—, las dificultades recientes aquí en Chololan no fueron ningún problema. —Y aquí se rió—. Según nosotros, los hombres de lucha españoles, esto no fue más que como un picotazo de pulga que tuvimos que rascar. Vuestro Se-ñor no necesita preocuparse de que este acontecimiento haya disminuido nuestra determinación por continuar nuestras explo-raciones. Seguiremos viajando hacia el oeste. Bueno, tal vez nos desviemos por aquí y por allá, para visitar otras ciudades y naciones, que tal vez quieran contribuir con más fuerzas a las que ya tenemos. Pero tarde o temprano, os aseguro, nuestro viaje nos llevará a Tenochtitlan. Podéis darle a vuestro soberano nuestra solemne promesa, de que nos conoceremos. —Se rió de nuevo—. Cara a cara.»

Como era natural, Motecuzoma había previsto que los inva-sores podrían seguir resistiendo su persuasión, así que le había proporcionado a su Mujer Serpiente una hipocresía más.

«En ese caso —dijo Tlácotzin—, le agradaría a nuestro Venerado Orador que el Capitán General ya no demorara su llegada. —Eso quería decir que Motecuzoma *no* quería que Cortés anduviera vagando entre las gentes inconformes que le pagaban tributos y buscar alistar guerreros de esas naciones—. El Venerado Orador sugiere que de estas provincias incómodas y primitivas, sólo puede recibir la impresión de que nuestros pueblos son bárbaros e incivilizados. Él desea que usted vea el esplendor y magnificencia de su ciudad capital, para que pueda darse cuenta del verdadero valor y habilidad de nuestra gente. Lo invita a que venga ahora directamente a Tenochtitlan. Yo lo llevaré hasta allá, mi señor. Y como soy Tlácotzin, segundo en mando del soberano de los mexica, mi presencia, será una prueba en contra de los trucos o emboscadas de otras personas.»

Cortés hizo un amplio gesto con su brazo, señalando todas las tropas formadas y esperando alrededor de Chololan. «No me preocupo demasiado sobre posibles trucos y emboscadas, amigo Tlácotzin —dijo sutilmente—. Pero acepto la invitación de vuestro señor de ir a la capital, y vuestro gentil ofrecimiento de conducirnos. Estamos listos para marchar cuando vosotros lo estéis.»

Era cierto que Cortés tenía poco que temer ya fuera de un ataque abierto o emboscada, o que tuviera una verdadera necesidad de seguir alistando más guerreros. Nuestros espías estimaron que, cuando partió de Chololan, sus fuerzas combinadas eran de unos veinte mil y además había como ocho mil cargadores que llevaban el equipaje y provisiones del ejército. La compañía se estiraba a lo largo de dos largas-carreras de longitud, y requería una cuarta parte del día para marchar de un punto a otro. A propósito, para entonces, cada guerrero y cargador llevaba una insignia que lo proclamaba como un hombre en el ejército de Cortés. Como los españoles seguían quejándose de que «no podían distinguir a un maldito indio de otro», ya que en la confusión del combate no podían distinguir entre indio aliado y un enemigo, Cortés les había ordenado a sus tropas indígenas que adoptaran un estilo uniforme de penachos; una alta corona de hierba *mazatla*. Cuando ese ejército de veintiocho mil hombres avanzó hacia Tenochtitlan, los espías dijeron que desde cierta distancia parecía como que un gran campo ondulante y lleno de pasto se moviera por medio de magia.

Motecuzoma posiblemente consideró decirle a su Mujer Serpiente que llevara a Cortés sin rumbo fijo alrededor de la tierra montañosa, hasta que los invasores estuvieran desesperadamente fatigados e irremediablemente perdidos, para que se les abandonara allí, pero, lógicamente, había muchos hombres entre los acolhua y texcalteca y demás tropas que los acompañaban que rápidamente hubieran adivinado ese truco. Sin embargo, Motecuzoma aparentemente *sí* instruyó a Tlácotzin para que no fuera un viaje sencillo, seguramente porque seguía esperanzado a que Cortés diera por terminada la expedición por desaliento. De cualquier modo, Tlácotzin los trajo al oeste y no por uno de los caminos más sencillos a través de los valles, sino que los llevó arriba y atravesando el paso alto entre los volcanes Ixtaccíuatl y Popocatépetl.

Como ya he dicho, en esas alturas hay nieve aun en los días más calientes del verano. Para cuando la compañía terminó de cruzar, el invierno ya comenzaba. Si había algo que *pudiera* desalentar a los hombres blancos, eso hubiera sido el frío entumecedor, los vientos feroces y grandes cerros de nieve por los que tenían que pasar. Hasta este día, no sé cómo es el clima de su España natal, pero Cortés y sus soldados habían pasado años en Cuba, isla en la cual tengo entendido que es tan tórrida y húmeda como cualquiera de nuestras Tierras Calientes, de la costa. Así que los hombres blancos, como sus aliados totonaca, no estaban preparados, ni vestidos como para aguantar el penetrante frío de la ruta congelada escogida por Tlácotzin. Más tarde informó con gran satisfacción, que los hombres blancos habían sufrido terriblemente.

Sí, sufrieron y se quejaron y cuatro hombres blancos murieron, así como dos de sus caballos y varios de sus perros y también unos cien de sus guerreros totonaca, pero el resto de la caravana perseveró. Es más, diez de los españoles, para presumir su vigor y habilidad, se desviaron brevemente de la ruta con la intención declarada de escalar hasta arriba del Popocatépetl y mirar hacia adentro de su cráter humeante. No llegaron tan alto, pero hasta entonces poca de nuestra propia gente lo había llegado a hacer, o habían tenido el interés de hacerlo. Los alpinistas se reunieron a su compañía, azules y tiesos de frío, y a algunos de ellos, más tarde, se les cayeron una cantidad de dedos ya sea de la mano o de los pies. Pero fueron muy admirados por sus compañeros por haber hecho el intento, y hasta el Mujer Serpiente, tuvo que reconocer de mala gana que los hombres blancos, a pesar de su locura, eran intrépidos, valerosos y enérgicos.

Tlácotzin también nos informó de las expresiones de asombro por cierto muy humanas de los hombres blancos y la sorpresa y la alegría que sintieron cuando al fin salieron por la parte occidental del paso, y que se pararon en el declive de la montaña, desde donde se dominaba la cuenca de ese inmenso lago, y la nieve que había estado cayendo levantó brevemente su cortina para darles una vista sin obstáculos. Abajo y más allá de donde se encontraban, estaban los cuerpos de agua multicolores que se comunicaban unos con otros yaciendo en su vasta cuenca, rodeados de un follaje lujurioso y de pequeños pueblos y caminos rectos que se cruzaban. Visto así, de una manera tan repentina, después de las alturas agobiantes que acababan de atravesar, el panorama de esa tierra debió de haberles parecido como un jardín; agradable y verde en todos los tonos de verde, verdes bosques densos, verdes hortalizas bien delineadas y diferentes verdes en la *chinampa* y lugares de cultivo. Debieron de haber visto, aunque sólo en miniatura, las numerosas ciudades y pueblos que se encontraban al borde de los diversos lagos, y las comunidades de las islas pequeñas que sobresalían del agua. Aún estaban a unas veintiún largas-carreras de Tenochtitlan, pero la ciudad blanca como plata debía de brillar como una estrella. Habían estado viajando durante meses, desde las playas costeras, sobre y alrededor de un sinfín de montañas a través de barrancas empedradas y ásperos valles, mientras pasaban y veían tan sólo pueblos y aldeas insignificantes, y finalmente acometiendo por ese paso helado entre los volcanes. Entonces, repentinamente, los viajeros miraron hacia abajo viendo una escena que —se lo decían entre sí— parecía un sueño... como una maravilla salida de los viejos libros de fábulas...

Al bajar de los volcanes, por supuesto que los viajeros se encontraron en los dominios de la Triple Alianza a través de las tierras acolhua, donde fueron recibidos por el Uey-Tlatoani Cacámatzin, quien había llegado desde Texcoco con un acompañamiento impresionante de sus señores, nobles, cortesanos y guardias. Aunque Cacama, por instrucciones de su tío, hizo un discurso caluroso de bienvenida a los recién llegados, me atrevo a decir que debió de sentirse incómodo al ser visto por su medio hermano, el destronado Flor Oscura, quien en ese momento se encontraba ante él con una fuerza poderosa de guerreros acolhua que le eran leales. La confrontación entre esos dos pudo haber estallado en una batalla allí mismo, de no ser porque tanto Motecuzoma como Cortés habían prohibido estrictamente cualquier disgusto que pudiera echar a perder ese importante encuentro, así es que todo fue de lo más amistoso, y Cacama llevó a toda la caravana a Texcoco, para que se hospedaran allí y les dieron bebidas refrescantes y diversión antes de continuar hacia Tenochtitlan.

Sin embargo, no hay duda de que Cacama sintió vergüenza e ira cuando sus propios súbditos llenaron las calles de Texcoco para recibir el regreso de Flor Oscura con gritos de alegría. Eso ya era bastante insultante, pero no pasó mucho tiempo antes de que Cacama tuviera que soportar un insulto mayor, una deserción en masa. Durante ese día o en dos días más, en que los viajeros permanecieron allí, quizás unos dos mil hombres de Texcoco desenterraron las armas y armaduras acojinadas que desde hacía mucho no habían usado, y cuando los visitantes partieron, esos hombres fueron con ellos como voluntarios en la tropa de Flor Oscura. De ese día en adelante, la nación acolhua quedó desastrosamente dividida. La mitad de su población permaneció sumisa a Cacama quien *era* su Venerado Orador y reconocido como tal por sus compañeros soberanos de la Triple Alianza. La otra mitad, le entregó su lealtad a Flor Oscura, quien debía haber sido Venerado Orador, aunque muchos de ellos deploraban que él hubiera unido su suerte a la de los extranjeros blancos.

Desde Texcoco, Tlácotzin, el Mujer Serpiente, condujo a Cortés y a su multiud alrededor del margen sur del lago. Los hombres blancos se admiraron de aquel «gran mar interior»; y aún más del creciente esplendor evidente de Tenochtitlan que se veía desde varios puntos a un lado del camino, y que parecía crecer en tamaño y magnificencia al acercarse. Tlácotzin llevó a la compañía entera a su propio palacio que era bastante grande, situado en la ciudad alta de Ixtapalapan donde se alojaron mientras lustraban sus espadas, armaduras y cañones, mientras cuidaban sus caballos, mientras remendaban sus uniformes maltratados lo mejor que pudieron, para verse lo más impresionantes posible al hacer la última marcha a través del camino-puente hacia la capital.

En el transcurso de todo esto, Tlácotzin le informó a Cortés que la ciudad, por ser una isla demasiado poblada, no tenía lugar más que para alojar la parte más mínima de sus miles de aliados. El Mujer Serpiente también le aclaró a Cortés que no cometiera la imprudencia de llevar un visitante tan indeseable, como era Flor Oscura, a la ciudad, o una aglomeración de tropas, que aunque eran de nuestra raza representaban a naciones enemigas de nosotros.

Habiendo visto la ciudad, por lo menos a cierta distancia, Cortés no tenía excusa para quejarse de las limitaciones del alojamiento y estaba lo suficientemente dispuesto a ser diplomático en su elección de los que le acompañarían ahí. Pero puso algunas condiciones. Tlácotzin debería acomodar a sus hombres para que se repartieran y fueran hospedados a orillas de la isla, en un arco que se extendiera desde el camino-puente del sur hasta el camino-puente del norte, con el objeto de cubrir toda salida de la ciudad-isla. Cortés entraría a Tenochtitlan al lado de la mayoría de sus españoles, sólo unos cuantos guerreros acolhua, texcalteca y totonaca, y se le tuvo que prometer que aquellos guerreros tendrían un paso libre dentro y fuera de la isla en cualquier momento y que podría utilizarlos como mensajeros para mantenerse en contacto con sus fuerzas centrales.

Tlácotzin estuvo de acuerdo con estas condiciones, sugirió que algunas de las tropas nativas podían permanecer donde estaban, en Ixtapalapan, a mano en el camino-puente del sur; otras podrían acampar en Tlácopan cerca del camino-puente del oeste, y otras en Tepeyaca cerca del camino-puente del norte. Así que Cortés seleccionó los guerreros que utilizaría como mensajeros y mandó a los miles que restaban marchando con los guías proporcionados por Tlácotzin, y ordenó a varios de sus oficiales blancos que se pusieran al mando de cada una de las fuerzas repartidas. Cuando los enlaces regresaron de cada uno de esos destacamentos, para informarle que estaban en posición y acampando para estar a mano cuando fuera necesario, Cortés le dijo a Tlácotzin, y el Mujer Serpiente le envió el mensaje a Motecuzoma, que los emisarios del Rey Don Carlos y el Señor Dios entrarían a Tenochtitlan al día siguiente.

✠

Ese día fue el Dos-Casa en nuestro año de Uno-Caña, que significa lo mismo que su mes de noviembre, en el año que ustedes cuentan como mil quinientos diez y nueve. El camino-puente del sur había presenciado muchas procesiones en su tiempo, pero jamás una que hiciera un ruido tan desacostumbrado. Los españoles no llevaban instrumentos musicales, y no cantaban, ta-

761

rareaban o hacían ninguna otra clase de música que acompañara sus pasos. Pero había un rechinar, un tintinear y un tronar de todas las armas que llevaban, de las armaduras de acero que usaban y de los arneses de sus caballos. Aunque la procesión andaba a un paso ceremoniosamente lento, las ·patas de los caballos caían pesadamente en el pavimento empedrado y las ruedas grandes de los cañones resonaban gravemente; de modo que toda la extensión del camino-puente vibraba; y la superficie del lago, como la cabeza de un tambor, amplificaba el ruido, y éste producía eco en todas las montañas distantes.

Cortés estaba al frente, por supuesto, montado en la *Mula*, llevando en un palo alto la bandera sangre y oro de España, y Malintzin caminaba orgullosamente a su lado, llevando el banderín personal de su amo. Detrás de ellos iban el Mujer Serpiente y otros señores mexica que habían ido y vuelto de Chololan. Detrás de éstos iban los soldados españoles montados, sus lanzas en posición erecta, llevando pendones en sus puntas, y luego venía una selección de unos cincuenta guerreros de nuestra propia raza. Detrás de ellos iban los soldados españoles de a pie, con sus ballestas y arcabuces en posición de desfile, sus espadas envainadas y sus lanzas apoyadas sobre sus hombros. Siguiendo a esa compañía ordenada y profesional, marchaba empujándose una multitud de ciudadanos de Ixtapalapan y de otros pueblos de los alrededores, que miraban con curiosidad ese espectáculo sin precedente, nunca antes visto, de extranjeros de aspecto guerrero entrando sin resistencia a la ciudad de Tenochtitlan, hasta entonces impenetrable.

En medio del camino-puente en el fuerte Acachinanco, la procesión fue recibida por los primeros oficiales: el Venerado Orador Cacámatzin de Texcoco y muchos nobles acolhua que habían atravesado el lago en canoa, así como los nobles tecpaneca de Tlacopan, la tercera ciudad de la Triple Alianza. Esos señores magníficamente vestidos indicaban el camino tan humildes como esclavos barriendo el camino-puente con escobas y sembrándolo con pétalos de flores antes de que pasara el desfile, todo el camino hasta el lugar en que el camino-puente se unía a la isla. Mientras tanto, Motecuzoma había sido llevado desde su palacio en su silla de manos más elegante. Lo acompañaba una impresionante cantidad de campeones Águilas, Jaguares y Flechas y todos los señores y señoras de su corte, incluyendo al Señor Mixtli y mi Señora Beu.

Se había medido el tiempo para que nuestra procesión llegara a la orilla de la isla,. a la entrada de la ciudad, justamente en el momento en que lo hiciera la otra comitiva. Las dos caravanas se detuvieron, a una distancia de unos veinte pasos, y Cortés desmontó de su caballo, entregándole su bandera a Malintzin. En ese momento se bajó al suelo la silla de manos de Motecuzoma. Al salir de entre las cortinas bordadas, todos nos sorprendimos al ver su vestimenta. Por supuesto llevaba su manto más llamativo y largo, el que estaba hecho completamente de incandescentes plumas de colibrí, y una corona de abanico hecha con plumas de *tototl quetzal*, y muchos medallones y adornos de lo más suntuoso. Pero no llevaba sus sandalias doradas; estaba descalzo y ninguno de nosotros los mexica nos sentimos complacidos al ver nuestro Venerado Orador de El Único Mundo manifestar su humildad aunque fuera con esa pequeña prueba.

Motecuzoma y Cortés se adelantaron a encontrarse, caminando despacio por el espacio abierto que los separaba. Motecuzoma hizo la reverencia de besar la tierra y Cortés respondió con lo que ahora sé que es un saludo de mano militar de los españoles. Como era propio, Cortés presentó el primer regalo, inclinándose hacia adelante para colgar alrededor del cuello del Orador, un collar perfumado de lo que parecía ser una combinación de perlas y joyas brillantes, que más tarde comprobamos que era una cosa vulgar de mala calidad, de nácar y vidrio. Motecuzoma entonces colgó sobre el cuello de Cortés un collar doble, hecho con las conchas más raras y adornado con cientos de pendientes finamente trabajados en oro sólido, en forma de diferentes animales. Después el Venerado Orador pronunció un discurso florido y largo de bienvenida. Malintzin, quien portaba una bandera extranjera en cada mano, dio atrevidamente un paso hacia adelante al lado de su amo, para traducir las palabras de Motecuzoma, y luego las de Cortés, que eran menos.

Motecuzoma regresó a su silla de manos, Cortés montó nuevamente su caballo y la comitiva de nosotros los mexica guiaba por la ciudad a la procesión de los españoles. Los hombres de Cortés comenzaron a marchar con un poco de menos orden, empujándose y pisándose los talones mientras miraban a su alrededor, para ver a la gente bien vestida que llenaba las calles, a los elegantes edificios y los jardines colgantes de las azoteas. En El Corazón del Único Mundo los caballos mantenían dificultosamente la estabilidad en el pavimento de mármol de aquella plaza inmensa; Cortés y los demás jinetes tuvieron que desmontar y guiarlos. Pasamos por la Gran Pirámide y giramos hacia la derecha, al antiguo palacio del Axayácatl, donde un suntuoso banquete esperaba para estos cientos de visitantes y todos los cientos que los habíamos recibido. Por igual debían de haber cientos de manjares diferentes, servidos sobre miles de platos lacados en oro. Mientras ocupábamos nuestros lugares ante los manteles, Motecuzoma llevó a Cortés a la plataforma que se le tenía preparada, diciéndole:

«Éste era el palacio de mi padre, quien fue uno de mis predecesores como Uey-Tlatoani. Se ha limpiado escrupulosamente y ha sido amueblado y decorado para ser digno de huéspedes tan distinguidos. Contiene conjuntos de habitaciones para usted, para su señora —eso lo dijo con cierto disgusto— y para sus oficiales principales. Hay suficientes cuartos amplios para el resto de su compañía y un grupo completo de esclavos para servirle, cocinarle y atender sus necesidades. El palacio será su residencia durante el tiempo que usted permanezca en estas tierras.»

Creo que cualquier otro hombre que no fuera Cortés, en una situación tan equívoca como ésa, hubiera rehusado tal ofrecimiento. Cortés sabía que era un huésped porque se había invitado a sí mismo y era considerado un agresor, que no era bien recibido. Al tomar residencia en el palacio, aun con unos trescientos soldados de confianza bajo el mismo techo que él, el Capitán General estaría en una posición aún más peligrosa que su estancia en el palacio de Chololan. Aquí estaría constantemente bajo la vigilancia y alcance de Motecuzoma, y su anfitrión, quien de tan mala gana le había extendido una mano amistosa, podría en cualquier momento cerrarla, agarrarlo y apretar. Los españoles serían cautivos —desatados, pero cautivos— y en la misma ciudad de Motecuzoma, la ciudad asentada sobre una isla, la isla rodeada por un lago, el lago rodeado por todas las ciudades y la gente de la Triple Alianza. Mientras Cortés permanecía en la ciudad, sus propios aliados no podrían estar a mano, y aun si los llamara, esos refuerzos con dificultad podrían llegar a su lado. Porque Cortés seguramente notó, que a su entrada por el camino-puente del sur, los diferentes pasos para las canoas, podían moverse con facilidad y evitar así que fueran cruzados. Y pudo haber adivinado que los demás caminos-puente de la ciudad estaban construidos de una manera semejante, tal como era en realidad.

El Capitán General pudo haber dicho con tacto a Motecuzoma que prefería residir en tierra firme, y de ahí visitar la ciudad cuando lo fueran requiriendo sus varias conferencias. Pero no hizo tal cosa. Le agradeció a Motecuzoma su ofrecimiento hospitalario, y lo aceptó, como si el palacio correspondiera realmente a su posición social y como si despreciara considerar la existencia de algún peligro al habitarlo. Aunque no siento cariño por Cortés, ni admiración por su ingenio y su falacia, debo reconocer que cuando se enfrentaba al peligro siempre actuaba sin vacilar, con una audacia que desafiaba lo que otros hombres llamamos sentido común. Tal vez sentí que él y yo teníamos un temperamento semejante, porque en el transcurso de mi vida yo también tomé muchos riesgos audaces que los hombres «sensatos» hubieran considerado como locuras.

Pero aun así, Cortés no confiaba su supervivencia totalmente a la suerte. Antes de que él y sus hombres pasaran su primera noche en el palacio, ordenó que se subieran cuatro de sus cañones al techo, esto por medio de unas gruesas sogas y a base de un gran esfuerzo por subirlos, sin importarle que en el proceso se destruyese casi todo el jardín de flores que se acababa de plantar para su deleite, y colocó los cañones de modo que cubrieran toda aproximación al edificio. También, esa noche y cada noche, los soldados, portando arcabuces, se paseaban durante toda la noche alrededor del techo y alrededor del exterior del palacio.

Durante los siguientes días, Motecuzoma personalmente condujo sus huéspedes en paseos por la ciudad, acompañado por el Mujer Serpiente y otros miembros de su Consejo de Voceros, y por una cantidad de sacerdotes de la corte, quienes llevaban caras y expresiones de gran disgusto, y yo también me encontraba allí. A insistencia de Motecuzoma, siempre me hallaba en su compañía, pues le había advertido sobre la astucia de Malintzin en traducir mal. Cortés se acordó de mí, como dijo que lo haría, pero aparentemente sin rencor. Me sonrió de forma sutil cuando se nos presentó formalmente, y aceptó mi compañía de forma suficientemente amistosa, y él habló para que yo tradujera sus palabras con tanta frecuencia como las traducía su mujer. Por supuesto que ella también me reconoció y obviamente con odio, ya que jamás se dirigía a mí. Cuando su amo elegía que yo le tradujera, ella me dirigía una mirada de odio, como si sólo estuviera esperando el momento oportuno para mandarme matar. Bueno, estábamos a la par, pensé. Eso era lo que yo había planeado para ella.

En esas caminatas por la ciudad, Cortés siempre iba acompañado del segundo de su mando, el gran pelirrojo Pedro de Alvarado, por la mayoría de sus oficiales y como es natural por Malintzin y por dos o tres de sus propios sacerdotes, que mostraban expresiones tan agrias como las de nuestros sacerdotes. Por lo general, también nos seguían unos cuantos soldados comunes, aunque otros grupos estaban vagando libremente por la isla, en tanto que los guerreros indígenas de su compañía tendían a no alejarse de la seguridad de sus barracas en el palacio.

Como había dicho antes, los guerreros ahora llevaban los penachos nuevos ordenados por Cortés; parecía un mechón alto de pasto dócil que crecía sobre sus cabezas. Pero desde la última vez que había visto a los soldados españoles, éstos también habían agregado algo a su tocado, que era un adorno distintivo. Cada uno de ellos llevaba una curiosa banda de cuero descolorido, justamente en la orilla del yelmo. No era muy decorativo, y no servía a ningún propósito aparente, así que eventualmente pregunté a uno de los españoles, quien riéndose me dijo lo que era.

Durante el tumulto de Cholólan, mientras los texcalteca se encontraban matando sin distinción alguna la masa de los habitantes de esa ciudad, los españoles habían ido en busca específicamente de las mujeres con quienes se habían divertido durante sus catorce días de fiesta, y encontraron a la mayoría de estas mujeres y muchachas aún en sus habitaciones, temblando de miedo. Convencidos de que ellas sólo habían coitado para sacarles las fuerzas, los españoles les impusieron una venganza muy original. Agarraron a las mujeres y muchachas, las desnudaron y las usaron una o dos veces más. Luego, a pesar de los gritos y súplicas de éstas, los soldados las inmovilizaron de cintura hacia abajo, y con el afilado acero de sus cuchillos cortaron de la entrepierna de cada mujer un pedazo de piel del tamaño de la mano que contenía la abertura ovalada de su *tepili*. Partieron y dejaron a las mujeres mutiladas y sin sexo sangrándose hasta morir. Se llevaron las bolsitas de piel aún calientes y estiraron los labios de éstas alrededor de las perillas de sus sillas de montar. Cuando la piel se había secado, pero seguía aún dócil, colocaron las ruedas resultantes sobre sus cascos, cada una con su pequeña perlita de *xacapili* volteada hacia adelante —más bien la bolita encogida y en forma de frijol que *había sido* un tierno *xacapili*—. No sé si los soldados llevaban esos trofeos como una broma macabra o como una advertencia para todas aquellas mujeres intrigantes.

Todos los españoles observaron aprobadoramente el tamaño, la población, el esplendor y la limpieza de Tenochtitlan, y la compararon con todas las otras ciudades que habían visitado. Los nombres de éstas no significaban nada para mí, pero ustedes, reverendos frailes, tal vez las conozcan. Los visitantes dijeron que nuestra ciudad era más grande en extensión que Valladolid, que tenía más habitantes que Sevilla, que sus edificios eran *casi* tan magníficos como los de Santa Roma, que sus canales la asemejaban a Amsterdam o Venecia, y que sus calles, su aire y sus aguas eran más limpios que los de *cualquiera* de esos lugares. Nosotros, los guías, nos abstuvimos de comentar que el enorme flujo de españoles estaba disminuyendo notablemente aquella limpieza. Sí, en efecto, los recién llegados quedaron muy impresionados con la arquitectura de nuestra ciudad, con su ornamentación y su orden, ¿pero saben qué fue lo que más les impresionó? ¿Qué los llevó a lanzar las más fuertes exclamaciones de asombro y sorpresa?

Nuestros cuartos sanitarios.

Bien se veía que muchos de esos hombres habían viajado extensamente en Su Viejo Mundo, pero también estaba bastante claro que en ningún lugar habían encontrado una facilidad interior para llevar a cabo las funciones primarias de uno. De por sí se asombraron de encontrar tales cuartos en el palacio que ocupaban; pero mayor fue su sorpresa cuando los llevamos a visitar la plaza del mercado de Tlaltelolco y encontraron *facilidades públicas* al alcance de la gente del pueblo: los vendedores y los comerciantes de allí. Cuando primero se fijaron en estas cosas los españoles, cada uno de ellos, incluyendo al mismo Cortés, simplemente *tuvieron* que entrar y probarlo. Así también lo hizo Malintzin, ya que esos artefactos eran tan desconocidos en su tierra semicivilizada de Cupilco como por lo visto lo eran en España y en la Santa Roma. Mientras Cortés y su compañía permanecieron en la isla, y mientras existió la plaza, esos baños públicos fueron las atracciones más populares y solicitadas de todas las que pudiera ofrecer Tenochtitlan.

Mientras los españoles quedaban encantados con los cubículos de agua disponible, nuestros médicos mexica maldecían esos mismos objetos, porque deseaban ávidamente adquirir una muestra del excremento de Cortés. Y si los españoles se estaban comportando como niños con juguete nuevo, esos doctores lo hacían como ratones *quimíchime*, siempre detrás de Cortés o asomando las cabezas por las esquinas. Cortés no pudo más que darse cuenta de cómo esos extraños ancianos se asombraban repentinamente y lo miraban fijamente, donde quiera que fuera. Por fin le preguntó a Motecuzoma por ellos, y éste, secretamente divertido por los hechos, contestó que sólo eran doctores velando por la salud de su huésped más honrado. Cortés se encogió de hombros y no dijo más, aunque sospecho que se quedó con la impresión de que todos nuestros médicos estaban más necesitados de ayuda que cualquiera de sus pacientes. Por supuesto que lo que los doctores estaban haciendo, y no demasiado sutilmente, era tratar de verificar su conclusión anterior de que el hombre blanco Cortés estaba efectivamente afligido con la enfermedad del *nanaua*. Trataban de medir con la vista la curvatura significante de los huesos de sus muslos, tratando de acercarse lo suficiente para saber si respiraba con el ruido sorbente característico de ese mal, y trataban también de asomarse a ver si tenía las muelas y dientes con agujeros.

Hasta yo empecé a sentir que eran una vergüenza y un estorbo, porque siempre estaban espiando nuestras caminatas por la ciudad y saliendo de pronto de lugares inesperados. Un día literalmente tropecé con un doctor anciano que estaba empinado para observar mejor la pierna de Cortés; enojado lo llevé aparte y le dije: «Si no se atreve a pedir permiso para examinar a este exaltado hombre blanco, seguramente puede inventar alguna excusa para examinar a su mujer, que solamente es una de nosotros.»

«No serviría de nada, Mixtzin —dijo tristemente el doctor—. Ella no queda infectada sólo por tener contacto con ellos. El *nanaua* es contagioso sólo en las primeras etapas de esa enfermedad. Si, como sospechamos, el hombre nació de una madre enferma, entonces desde hace mucho dejó de ser una amenaza para cualquier otra mujer, aunque *sí* podría darle un hijo enfermo. Es natural que todos nosotros queramos saber ansiosamente si hemos adivinado su condición correctamente, pero no podemos estar seguros. Si no fuera porque está tan fascinado con las facilidades sanitarias, podríamos examinar su orina para buscar indicios de *chiatoztli*...»

Dije con exasperación: «Los puedo encontrar a ustedes donde sea, *menos* empinados en los sanitarios. Le sugiero, señor médico, que vaya e instruya al mayordomo de palacio, para que ordene quitar el sanitario de este hombre por unos esclavos, explicando que está tapado y mientras le pueden proporcionar una olla para su uso e instruir también a la criada para que le entregue a usted esa olla...»

«*Ayyo*, es una idea brillante», dijo el médico y rápidamente se fue. Ya no se nos molestó más durante nuestras excursiones, pero jamás supe si los doctores encontraron alguna evidencia definitiva de que a Cortés le aquejara un mal tan vergonzoso.

Debo informarles de que aquellos primeros españoles no admiraban *todo* en Tenochtitlan. Algunas de las cosas que les enseñamos, les disgustaron y hasta las despreciaron. Por ejemplo, se estremecieron violentamente al contemplar un estante de cráneos en El Corazón del Único Mundo. Veían con asco el que nosotros quisiéramos conservar aquellas reliquias de tantas personas distinguidas que habían partido a sus Muertes-Floridas en esa plaza. Pero he escuchado que sus historiadores españoles cuentan de su antiguo héroe, el Cid, cuya muerte se mantuvo en secreto para que no lo supieran sus enemigos, mientras que su cuerpo ya tieso por la muerte, era doblado para ser montado en un caballo, y así guió a su ejército para ganar la última batalla.

Como ustedes los españoles parecen atesorar ese cuento, no sé por qué Cortés y sus compañeros creían que nuestra exhibición de los cráneos de personas ilustres era más horrorosa que la preservación del cadáver del Cid después de su muerte.

Pero las cosas que más asco les daba a los hombres blancos eran nuestros templos, con la evidencia de sus muchos sacrificios, tanto recientes como pasados. Para dar a los visitantes la mejor vista posible de su ciudad, Motecuzoma los llevó a la cumbre de la Gran Pirámide, que, a excepción del tiempo en que duraban los sacrificios ceremoniales, siempre se conservaba limpia y reluciente por fuera. Los huéspedes ascendían las escaleras a cuyos lados estaban los portabanderas, admirando la gracia e inmensidad del edificio, sus pinturas tan vívidas y sus decorados en oro batido, y podían ver a su alrededor la vista de la ciudad y el lago que se extendía conforme iban subiendo. Los dos templos arriba de la pirámide también estaban brillantes por fuera, pero el interior de ellos jamás se limpiaba. Como la acumulación de sangre significaba la acumulación de nuestra reverencia, las imágenes y muros, así como los techos y pisos, estaban tiesos de sangre coagulada.

Los españoles entraron al templo de Tláloc e inmediatamente corrieron hacia afuera, con gestos y exclamaciones de náusea. Fue la primera y única vez que vi que los hombres blancos retrocedieran ante un mal olor, o hasta que percibieran uno, pero en verdad que la pestilencia de ese lugar *era* peor que la de ellos. Cuando pudieron controlar las sensibilidades de sus estómagos, Cortés, Alvarado y el sacerdote Bartolomé entraron nuevamente, y tuvieron espasmos de rabia cuando descubrieron que la imagen hueca de Tláloc se había llenado hasta el borde de su boca cuadrada y abierta con corazones humanos en estado de putrefacción. Cortés estaba tan enfurecido que sacó su espada y con ella le dio un fuerte golpe a la estatua. Sólo rompió un fragmento de sangre seca de la cara de piedra de Tláloc, pero fue un insulto que hizo que Motecuzoma y *sus* sacerdotes dieran un grito de sobresalto y consternación. Sin embargo, Tláloc no respondió con ningún trueno devastador o con un relámpago, y Cortés controló su ira. Le dijo a Motecuzoma:

«Este ídolo vuestro, no es un dios. Es una cosa del mal que nosotros llamamos un diablo. Debe ser tirado, sacado y enterrado en una oscuridad eterna. Permitidme colocar en su lugar la cruz de Nuestro Señor y una imagen de Nuestra Señora. Veréis que este demonio no se atreverá a oponerse y os daréis cuenta de que es inferior y que le teme a la Verdadera Fe, y haríais bien en hacer a un lado a seres tan malvados y en adorar a los nuestros que son bondadosos.»

Motecuzoma con seguridad dijo que la idea era inaudita, pero los españoles volvieron a sentir náuseas cuando entraron al templo adyacente de Huitzilopochtli, y otra vez cuando vieron los templos similares, en la cumbre de la pirámide menor de Tlaltelolco, y cada vez Cortés se expresaba con mayor repugnancia y palabras más fuertes.

«Los totonaca —dijo él— han limpiado su país de estos ídolos sucios y le han entregado su alianza a Nuestro Señor y Su Virgen Madre. Se ha arrasado ese templo monstruoso en la montaña de Chololan. En estos momentos, algunos de mis frailes están instruyendo al Rey Xicotenca y a su corte para recibir las bendiciones del Cristianismo. Os digo que en ninguno de esos lugares se ha escuchado aunque sea sólo un gemido por parte de esas viejas deidades diabólicas. ¡Os doy mi palabra y juramento, que tampoco lo harán cuando *vosotros* los echéis fuera!»

Motecuzoma contestó y yo traduje, tratando de imitar la frialdad de sus palabras: «Capitán General, usted está aquí como mi huésped y un huésped educado no menosprecia las creencias de su anfitrión, como tampoco se burlaría del gusto de su anfitrión en vestirse o en sus esposas. También, aunque usted sea mi huésped, la mayoría de mi pueblo resiente el tener que ser hospitalario con ustedes. Si trata de entrometerse con sus dioses, los sacerdotes levantarán sus voces en contra de ustedes, y en asuntos de religión los sacerdotes pueden mandar sobre mis órdenes. El pueblo obedecerá a los sacerdotes, no a mí, y tendrá suerte si usted y sus hombres son echados vivos de Tenochtitlan.»

Aun el impetuoso Cortés comprendió que se le estaba recordando fríamente la posición tan frágil en que se encontraban, así es que dejando el templo a un lado, murmuró unas palabras de disculpa. Ante lo cual Motecuzoma también perdió algo de su frialdad y dijo:

«Sin embargo, trato de ser un hombre justo y un anfitrión generoso. Me he dado cuenta de que ustedes los Cristianos no tienen un lugar en donde adorar a sus dioses, y no me opongo a que lo hagan. Ordenaré que el pequeño Templo Águila que está en la gran plaza se limpie y que sean quitadas las piedras de sus altares y sus imágenes, y todo aquello que pueda ser ofensivo a su religión. Sus sacerdotes pueden amueblarlo como ellos lo requieran y el templo *será* su templo por el tiempo que ustedes lo deseen.»

Naturalmente que nuestros propios sacerdotes no oyeron con agrado ni siquiera esa pequeña concesión que les había otorgado a los extranjeros, pero no hicieron más que gruñir cuando los sacerdotes blancos se apoderaron del pequeño templo. De ahí en adelante, el lugar fue más frecuentado que nunca antes. Los sacerdotes Cristianos parecían decir sus misas y demás servicios continuamente de mañana a tarde, ya fuera que los soldados blancos atendieran esos servicios o no, o para una gran cantidad de nuestra propia gente, que atraída por la simple curiosidad empezó a acercarse a esos servicios. Digo nuestra propia gente, pero en realidad se trataba principalmente de las mujeres de los hombres blancos y los guerreros aliados de otras naciones. Pero los sacerdotes usaban a la Malintzin para que ella tradujera sus sermones, y veían gustosos cuando muchos de los participantes paganos se sometían —aun no más que curiosos por la novedad de ello— a tomar la sal y a ser rociados con el agua del bautismo que les daba un nombre nuevo. De todos modos, la concesión de ese templo por parte de Motecuzoma, temporalmente distrajo a Cortés de poner sus manos violentas sobre nuestros antiguos dioses, como lo había hecho en otros lugares.

Cuando los españoles llevaban en Tenochtitlan poco más de un mes, pasó algo que pudo haberlos expulsado de allí para siempre y hasta de todo El Único Mundo. Un mensajero-veloz llegó de parte del Señor Patzinca de los totonaca, y si se hubiera entregado su mensaje a Motecuzoma, como anteriormente se había hecho, la estancia del hombre blanco hubiera terminado entonces. Sin embargo, el mensajero dio su informe al ejército totonaca acampado en la tierra firme, y fue llevado por uno de esa compañía a la ciudad para que lo repitiera en privado a Cortés. La noticia era que había sucedido algo de mucha gravedad en la costa.

Lo que había pasado era lo siguiente: Un recolector de tributos mexica llamado Cuaupopoca, al hacer su visita acostumbrada a varias naciones tributarias, acompañado por una tropa de guerreros mexica, había recogido los tributos anuales de los huaxteca, quienes también vivían en la costa, pero al norte de los totonaca. Luego, llevando una caravana de cargadores huaxteca reclutados para cargar sus propios bienes tributarios a Tenochtitlan, Cuaupopoca se había ido al sur a la tierra totonaca, como lo había estado haciendo año tras año, durante mucho tiempo. Pero al llegar a la capital Tzempoalan, grande fue su asombro e indignación al encontrarse que los totonaca no esperaban su llegada. No se había reunido nada para él; no se encontraba ningún cargador esperándolo; el gobernante Señor Patzinca ni siquiera tenía preparada la lista acostumbrada para que Cuaupopoca supiera en qué consistía el tributo.

Como venía de las tierras fronterizas del norte, Cuaupopoca no había oído nada de las desventuras que les habían sucedido a los registradores mexica quienes siempre eran enviados antes que él y no había sabido nada de lo ocurrido. Motecuzoma le pudo haber enviado un mensaje con facilidad, pero no lo había hecho. Y jamás sabré si el Venerado Orador simplemente se olvidó, por la presión de tantos otros sucesos, o si deliberadamente decidió que las recolecciones de tributos siguieran como de costumbre, sólo para ver qué *pasaba*. Bueno, Cuaupopoca trató de hacer su trabajo. Le exigió el tributo a Patzinca, quien retorciéndose las manos rehusó a entregárselo, con el argumento de que ya no era un subordinado de la Triple Alianza. Tenía nuevos amos, blancos, quienes vivían en una aldea fortificada más abajo en la playa. Patzinca, lloriqueando, le sugirió a Cuaupopoca que se dirigiera al oficial blanco encargado de allí, un tal Juan de Escalante.

Enfurecido y extrañado, pero decidido, Cuaupopoca llevó a sus hombres a la Villa Rica de la Vera Cruz, para ser recibidos con burlas en un idioma incomprensible, pero que en la forma en que era hablado se podía reconocer que era insultante. Así que él, un simple recolector de tributos, hizo lo que hasta entonces ni el poderoso Motecuzoma había hecho todavía: se opuso a ser tratado de una manera tan despectiva y se opuso de un modo extenuante, violento y decisivo. Al hacerlo, Cuaupopoca tal vez cometió un error, pero lo hizo de una manera grande, de la manera señorial esperada de los mexica. Patzinca y Escalante cometieron un error más grande al provocar esta reacción, porque debieron ser conscientes de su vulnerabilidad. Casi todo el ejército totonaca había marchado con Cortés, junto con prácticamente todos los suyos. Tzempoalan tenía pocos hombres que lo pudieran defender, y Vera Cruz no se encontraba en mejor posición, ya que la mayoría de su ejército consistía en unos remeros que se habían quedado simplemente porque no habían barcas en donde requirieran sus servicios.

Cuaupopoca, repito, sólo era un oficial menor de los mexica. Tal vez yo sea la única persona que recuerde su nombre, aunque muchos todavía recuerdan el destino que le reservó su *tonali*. Este hombre era cumplido en su deber de recolectar tributos, y ésa era la primera vez en toda su carrera que se había encontrado con que una nación tributaria lo desafiaba, y él debió de tener un temperamento fiero, como su nombre —quería decir Águila Humeante— y nada podría haberlo detenido en el cumplimiento de su misión. Dio una orden cortante a su fuerza de guerreros mexica y éstos rápidamente se pusieron en acción, porque eran hombres de guerra, aburridos de las pocas exigencias que les demandaba su deber de escolta. Alegremente aprovecharon esa oportunidad para combatir, y no se amedrentaron por los disparos de los pocos arcabuces y ballestas, tirados desde la barricada de la aldea, por los hombres blancos.

Mataron a Escalante y a los pocos soldados profesionales que Cortés había dejado encargados del mando. Los remeros, que no eran hombres de guerra, se rindieron inmediatamente. Cuaupopoca colocó guardias allí y alrededor del palacio de Tzempoalan, y le ordenó al resto de sus hombres despojar a esa nación, que había rendido. Ese año, proclamó a los totonaca aterrorizados que su tributo no comprendería una fracción de sus bienes y productos agrícolas, sino *todo*. Por lo que había sido una hazaña del mensajero Patzinca, el haber escapado del palacio vigilado, y deslizarse entre los guerreros de Cuaupopoca y llevarle la mala noticia a Cortés.

Es seguro que Cortés percibió cuán peligrosa se había convertido su propia posición y lo inseguro de su porvenir, pero no perdió el tiempo meditando. Inmediatamente se dirigió al palacio de Motecuzoma, ni sumiso ni sintiendo miedo. Se llevó al gigante pelirrojo Alvarado, a Malintzin y a una cantidad de hombres bien armados, y todos ellos hicieron a un lado a los mayordomos del palacio y sin ceremonia alguna entraron directamente al salón del trono de Motecuzoma. Cortés se enfureció, o lo simuló, mientras le contaba al Venerado Orador una versión corregida del informe que había recibido. Según lo contó, una banda de ladrones mexica sin provocación alguna había atacado a los pocos hombres que había dejado en la costa y que vivían apaciblemente, y los habían matado. Era un rompimiento grave de la tregua y amistad que Motecuzoma había prometido, ¿y qué haría éste al respecto?

El Venerado Orador sabía de la presencia de la caravana de tributos en esa área en general, así que al oír la narración de Cortés debió de suponer que se habían visto envueltos en una escaramuza que *había* causado daño a los hombres. Pero no era necesario que se apresurara a reconciliarse con Cortés; pudo haber contemporizado el tiempo suficiente como para informarse del verdadero estado de las cosas. Y la verdad era ésta: el único poblado establecido por los hombres blancos en esas tierras se había rendido a las tropas mexica, encabezadas por Cuaupopoca; el aliado más fuerte de los hombres blancos, el Señor Patzinca, se encontraba acobardado en su palacio, prisionero de los mexica. Mientras tanto, Motecuzoma tenía a casi todos los hombres blancos en su isla, una presa que fácilmente podría ser eliminada; y las demás tropas de hombres blancos de Cortés, así como sus guerreros indígenas, con facilidad se podrían detener antes de llegar a la isla, mientras los ejércitos de la Triple Alianza que se encontraban en tierra firme, se juntarían para acabar con ellos. Gracias a Cuaupopoca, Motecuzoma tenía a todos los españoles y sus aliados indefensos en la palma de su mano. Bastaba con cerrar esa mano y hacer un puño y apretar hasta que la sangre corriera entre sus dedos.

No lo hizo. Le expresó a Cortés su consternación y sus condolencias. Mandó una fuerza de sus guardias de palacio para presentar sus disculpas a Tzempoalan y Vera Cruz, y quitarle a Cuaupopoca su autoridad y con órdenes de arrestarlo a él y a sus oficiales principales y conducirlos a Tenochtitlan.

Lo que era peor, cuando Cuaupopoca, quien merecía un premio por lo que había hecho, así como sus *quáchictin*, Águilas Viejas, del ejército mexica, se hincaron con obediencia ante el trono, en donde Motecuzoma se sentaba relajado y cómodo, con Cortés y Alvarado a cada lado y con una voz nada señorial les dijo a los prisioneros:

«Ustedes han excedido la autoridad de su misión. Han avergonzado a su Venerado Orador seriamente y han puesto en peligro el honor de la nación mexica. Han roto la promesa de tregua que le había concedido a estas estimables visitas y todos sus subordinados. ¿Tienen algo que decir en su defensa?»

Cuaupopoca fue cumplido hasta el final, aunque se veía que era más hombre, más noble y más mexícatl, que la criatura en el trono, a quien se dirigió respetuosamente: «Yo lo hice solo y por mi cuenta, Señor Orador. Hice lo que creí mejor. Ningún hombre pudo haber hecho más.»

Motecuzoma dijo sin expresión: «Me ha causado un gran daño. Pero las muertes y daños han perjudicado a nuestros huéspedes. Por lo tanto... —e increíblemente el Venerado Orador del Único Mundo añadió—: Por lo tanto, cederé mi veredicto al Capitán General Cortés y dejaré que él determine qué castigo merecen.»

Evidentemente, Cortés ya había pensado en algo, porque decretó un castigo que seguramente evitaría que ningún individuo tratara de oponerse, y al mismo tiempo fue un castigo que intencionalmente se burlaba de nuestras costumbres y vejaba a nuestros dioses. Ordenó que se matara a los cinco, pero que no fuera una Muerte Florida. No se daría el corazón para alimentar a ningún dios, no se derramaría sangre para honrar algún dios, ni se despojaría a estos hombres de algún miembro de sus cuerpos, para usarse como ofrenda en algún rito de sacrificio.

Cortés mandó a sus soldados traer una cadena larga; era la más gruesa que yo había visto, como una boa redondeada y hecha de hierro; más tarde supe que era de lo que se llama una cadena de ancla, utilizada para inmovilizar sus pesados barcos. Con mucho esfuerzo por parte de los soldados y seguramente causándole mucho dolor a Cuaupopoca y a sus cuatro guerreros, los eslabones gigantescos de aquella cadena fueron puestos sobre las cabezas de los hombres condenados; para que un eslabón colgara del cuello de cada hombre. Fueron llevados al Corazón del Único Mundo, donde un gran madero se había colocado parado en la plaza... a poca distancia de aquí, enfrente de donde ahora se encuentra la catedral, y en donde ahora el Señor Obispo tiene su pilar para exponer a los pecadores en penitencia pública. La cadena se colocó alrededor de la parte superior de ese poste bromoso, de modo que los cinco hombres se encontraban parados en forma circular, dando la espalda a aquel tronco, y sujetados por el cuello. Entonces pusieron una carga de leña previamente remojada en *chapopotli* que se colocó alrededor de sus pies, a lo alto de sus rodillas, y se le prendió fuego.

Un castigo tan innovador —pues se trataba de una ejecución en que deliberadamente no se derramaba sangre— jamás se había visto antes por estas tierras, por lo que la mayoría de los habitantes de Tenochtitlan lo fueron a ver. Pero yo lo vi mientras estaba parado a un lado del sacerdote Bartolomé, y éste me confió que tales suplicios eran algo bastante común en España, y que son los más apropiados para la ejecución de los enemigos de la Santa Madre Iglesia, porque la Iglesia siempre le ha prohibido a su clero el derramamiento de sangre, hasta del pecador más grande. Es una lástima, reverendos escribanos, que su Iglesia no emplee unos métodos más misericordiosos de ejecución. Porque he visto muchas formas de matar y de morir en mis tiempos, pero creo que ninguno tan espantoso como el que Cuaupopoca y sus oficiales tuvieron que sufrir ese día.

Lo soportaron valientemente por algún tiempo, mientras las llamas primero brincaban por sus piernas. Arriba del pesado collar de hierro de los eslabones de cadena, sus caras tenían expresiones calmadas y resignadas. No estaban atados de ninguna forma al poste, pero no pateaban sus piernas ni movían sus brazos, o gesticulaban de algún modo indecoroso. Sin embargo, cuando las llamas llegaron a sus ingles y les quemaron sus taparrabos y comenzaron a quemar lo que había debajo, sus expresiones eran de agonía. Y luego el fuego ya no necesitó ser alimentado de leña o *chapopotli*; bastó con el aceite natural de sus pieles, así como el tejido grasoso inmediatamente abajo de la piel para que se extendiera. En lugar de que se les estuviera quemando a los hombres, los hombres mismos empezaron a quemarse por sí mismos y las llamas subieron tan altas que casi no distinguíamos sus caras. Pero vimos el destello más fuerte de cuando su pelo se consumió de pronto y pudimos escuchar los primeros gritos de aquellos hombres.

Después de un rato los gritos se apaciguaron hasta que sólo se escuchó un gemido delgado y agudo apenas distinguible entre el tronar de las llamas, que era más desagradable que los gritos; cuando los espectadores pudimos ver brevemente a los hombres entre las llamas, estaban todos renegridos y arrugados, pero de alguna forma todavía vivían y uno o más continuaron con ese gemido inhumano. Las llamas poco a poco penetraron debajo de su piel y comenzaron a morder sus músculos, y eso hizo que éstos se apretaran de una manera rara, pues los cadáveres de los hombres comenzaron a contorsionarse. Sus brazos se doblaron por sus codos; sus manos con los dedos quemados subieron a sus caras, o mejor dicho donde habían estado sus caras. Lo que quedaba de sus piernas lentamente se dobló a la rodilla y a la cadera; se levantaron del suelo y se encogieron contra sus estómagos.

Conforme quedaban colgados y asados se iban encogiendo, hasta que dejaron de parecer hombres, tanto en tamaño como en aspecto. Sólo sus cabezas achicharradas y sin facciones seguían siendo de tamaño normal; por lo demás parecían cinco niños, renegridos, y en una postura semejante a la de un niño cuando duerme. Y era difícil creer que dentro de esas cosas dignas de lástima todavía había vida, pues ese ruido agudo continuó hasta que sus cabezas estallaron. La leña remojada en *chapopotli* da un fuego caliente y tal calor que hace que el cerebro hierva y se vaporice hasta que el cráneo ya no lo pueda contener más. Hubo un ruido repentino como el de una olla de barro cuando se rompe y se oyó cuatro veces más, y luego no se escuchó más que el ruido de los últimos pedazos de los cuerpos, que caían al fuego, y el suave rechinar de la leña que descansaba en una suave cama de brasas.

Tardó bastante en enfriarse la cadena del ancla lo suficiente como para que los soldados pudieran desenredarla del poste quemado y dejar que los cinco pequeños cuerpos cayeran a las cenizas para quedar completamente quemados, y se llevaron la cadena para guardarla por lo que ofreciera en el futuro, aunque desde entonces no se ha hecho otra ejecución igual. Eso fue hace once años. Pero el año pasado, Cortés regresó de su visita a España donde su Rey Carlos lo ascendió a Capitán General y lo ennobleció con el título de Marqués del Valle, y Cortés mismo diseñó el emblema de su nueva nobleza. Lo que ustedes llaman su escudo de armas, ahora se puede ver por donde quiera; está marcado con varios símbolos y el escudo está rodeado por una cadena, y en los eslabones de esa cadena cuelgan cinco cabezas humanas.

Cortés pudo haber conmemorado otros de sus triunfos, pero él bien sabe que el fin del valiente Cuaupopoca marcó el principio de la conquista de El Único Mundo.

Causó mucha inquietud e incertidumbre entre nuestra gente el que la ejecución hubiera sido decretada y dirigida por los extranjeros blancos, quienes no debían ejercer tal autoridad. Pero el siguiente suceso fue aún más inesperado, increíble y extraño: Motecuzoma anunció públicamente que iba a dejar su propio palacio e ir a vivir durante un tiempo con los hombres blancos.

Los ciudadanos de Tenochtitlan se reunieron en El Corazón del Único Mundo, viendo con expresiones petrificadas el día que su Venerado Orador, caminando plácidamente, atravesó la plaza del brazo de Cortés, bajo ninguna aparente o visible presión, y entró en el palacio de su padre Axayácatl, el palacio que ocupaban los forasteros. Durante los siguientes días, hubo un tráfico constante yendo y viniendo de un lado a otro de la plaza mientras los soldados españoles ayudaban a los cargadores y esclavos de Motecuzoma a cambiar toda la corte de un palacio a otro: a sus esposas, hijos y sirvientes, su guardarropa y los muebles de todas sus habitaciones, el contenido de la sala del trono, su biblioteca y los registros de la tesorería y todo lo necesario para conducir los asuntos de la corte.

Nuestra gente no podía entender *por qué* su Venerado Orador quería ser huésped de sus huéspedes, o de hecho el prisionero de sus propios prisioneros. Pero creo saber el porqué. Hacía mucho tiempo que yo había oído describir a Motecuzoma como «un tambor hueco», y a través de los años escuché a ese tambor hacer ruidos fuertes, y la mayoría de las veces supe que éstos eran producidos por el golpear de las manos de los sucesos, de las circunstancias, sobre las cuales Motecuzoma no tenía ningún control... o cosas que sólo podía pretender controlar... o que aparentemente trataba de controlar. Si hubo alguna vez una esperanza de que algún día llegara a golpear su tambor con sus propias baquetas, por decir así, esa esperanza se desvaneció cuando le cedió a Cortés la resolución del asunto de Cuaupopoca.

Porque nuestro jefe guerrero Cuitláhuac, poco después afirmó lo que en efecto había logrado Cuaupopoca —una ventaja que pudo haber puesto a los hombres blancos, así como a sus aliados, a nuestra merced—, y Cuitláhuac no utilizó frases fraternales al contar cómo Motecuzoma de una manera tan apresurada, débil y desgraciada había desperdiciado la mejor oportunidad de salvar El Único Mundo. Esa revelación de su último y peor error, le quitó por completo cualquier fuerza o voluntad o señoría aún inherente en el Venerado Orador. Efectivamente se convirtió en un tambor hueco, demasiado flojo como para hacer algún ruido al ser tocado. Y en tanto que Motecuzoma disminuía para quedar en el letargo y la debilidad más completa, Cortés se erguía cada vez más audaz. Después de todo, él había demostrado que tenía el poder de la vida y de la muerte, aun estando dentro del cerco de los mexica. Había salvado a su puesto en la Vera Cruz y a su aliado Patzinco casi de ser extinguidos, por no mencionar a él mismo y todos los hombres que lo acompañaban. Así es que no vaciló al hacer a Motecuzoma la inaudita exigencia de que voluntariamente se sometiera a su propia captura.

«No soy un prisionero. Ustedes pueden verlo —dijo Motecuzoma la primera vez que mandó llamar a su Consejo de Voceros y a mí, junto con algunos otros señores, para que fuéramos a verlo a su nuevo salón del trono—. Aquí hay suficiente espacio para toda mi corte, cuartos cómodos para todos nosotros y suficientes facilidades que me permiten seguir conduciendo los asuntos de la nación, en los cuales les puedo asegurar que los hombres blancos no tienen ninguna voz. Su propia presencia en este momento prueba que mis señores consejeros, sacerdotes y mensajeros tienen libre acceso a mí y yo a ellos, y no necesita estar aquí ningún forastero. No van a interferir tampoco en nuestras observancias religiosas, aun en aquellas que requieren algún sacrificio. En pocas palabras, nuestras vidas seguirán exactamente como siempre. Antes de estar de acuerdo en cambiar mi residencia, hice que el Capitán General me diera esas garantías.»

«¿Pero por qué estuvo usted de acuerdo con todo lo que ellos exigieron? —preguntó el Mujer Serpiente, con voz angustiada—. Eso no está bien, mi señor. No era necesario.»

«Tal vez no era necesario, pero sí prudente —dijo Motecuzoma—. Desde que los hombres blancos entraron en mis dominios, mi propia gente o aliados, en dos ocasiones, han atentado en contra de sus vidas y propiedades, primero en Chololan y últimamente en la costa. Cortés no me echa la culpa, ya que esos intentos se hicieron como desafío o en la ignorancia de mi promesa de una tregua. Pero esas cosas podrían suceder otra vez. Yo personalmente le he advertido a Cortés que mucha de nuestra gente resiente la presencia de los hombres blancos. Cualquier cosa que haga que ese resentimiento se agrave podría hacer que nuestro pueblo olvidara su obediencia hacia mí, y se levantarían otra vez, causando un gran desorden.»

«Si Cortés está preocupado por el resentimiento que le guarda nuestra gente —dijo un consejero anciano—, con facilidad podría remediarlo. Que se vaya por donde vino.»

Motecuzoma contestó: «Exactamente le dije eso, pero por supuesto es imposible. No tiene modo de hacerlo hasta que, como espera, su Rey Don Carlos le envíe más barcos. Mientras tanto, si él y yo residimos en el mismo palacio, eso demuestra dos cosas: que confío en que Cortés no me haga daño y que confío en que mi pueblo no lo provoque para que él, a su vez, no haga daño a nadie, así estas gentes se verán menos inclinadas a causar más altercados. Y es por estas razones que Cortés me pidió que fuera su huésped aquí.»

«Su prisionero», dijo Cuitláhuac, casi despectivamente.

«*No* soy un prisionero —insistió Motecuzoma nuevamente—. Todavía soy el Uey-Tlatoani, el gobernante de esta nación y el principal aliado de la Triple Alianza. He concedido esta pequeña gracia para asegurar el mantenimiento de la paz entre nosotros y los hombres blancos, hasta que éstos se vayan.»

Yo dije: «Discúlpeme, Venerado Orador. Usted parece estar muy seguro de que se irán. ¿Cómo lo sabe usted? ¿Cuándo será eso?»

Me miró como deseando que no hubiera preguntado eso. «Se irán cuando lleguen los barcos por ellos. Y sé que se irán, porque les he prometido que se pueden llevar lo que vinieron a buscar.»

Hubo un pequeño silencio; luego alguien dijo: «Oro.»

«Sí, mucho oro. Cuando los soldados blancos ayudaron en la mudanza de mi residencia, registraron mi palacio de arriba a abajo y descubrieron los cuartos de la Tesorería, aunque había tomado la precaución de mandar tapiar las puertas, y...»

Fue interrumpido por exclamaciones de disgusto de la mayor parte de los hombres allí presentes, y Cuitláhuac le preguntó: «¿Les darás el tesoro de la nación?»

«Sólo el oro —dijo Motecuzoma a la defensiva—. Y las joyas más valiosas. Es todo lo que les interesa. No les importan las plumas, los tintes y las piedras de jade y las raras semillas de flores y demás. Eso seguirá atesorado y esas riquezas sostendrán a la nación el tiempo suficiente para que nosotros podamos trabajar, pelear e incrementar nuestras demandas tributarias hasta recuperar todo nuestro tesoro.»

«¡Pero por qué dárselo!», gritó alguien.

«Sepan esto —continuó Motecuzoma—, los hombres blancos podrían exigir eso, además de la riqueza de cada noble como precio de su partida. Podrían hacer una guerra a causa de esto y llamar a sus aliados que están en tierra firme y pedirles ayuda para que se nos despoje de todo. Prefiero evitar tal situación, ofreciéndole el oro y las joyas en un aparente gesto de generosidad.»

El Mujer Serpiente dijo entre dientes: «Aun como el Alto Tesorero de la Nación, como aparente guardián del tesoro que mi señor está regalando, debo reconocer que sería un precio pequeño que pagar con tal de expulsar a esos extranjeros. Pero le quisiera recordar a mi señor que en otras ocasiones cuando se les ha dado oro, sólo se les ha estimulado a querer más.»

«No tengo más para darles y créanme de que los he convencido de que es la verdad. A excepción del oro que está circulando como moneda o que está guardado por ciudadanos individuales, ya *no* hay más oro en las tierras mexica. Nuestro tesoro en oro representa el acumulo de gavillas y gavillas de años. Es el ahorro hecho por todos los Venerados Oradores en el pasado. Se llevaría generaciones y más generaciones para poder rasguñar y extraer de nuestras tierras una fracción más de él. También he hecho de esto un obsequio condicional. No lo tocarán hasta que se vayan de aquí y se lo deben llevar directamente a su Rey Don Carlos como un regalo personal, de mí para él, el regalo *de todo el tesoro que tenemos.* Cortés está de acuerdo, y yo también, como también lo estará su Rey Don Carlos. Cuando los hombres blancos se vayan, ya no regresarán más.»

Nadie dijo nada para contradecirle; una vez que nos hubo despedido y que habíamos pasado por la puerta del palacio hacia el Muro de la Serpiente, fue cuando comentamos mientras cruzábamos la plaza.

Alguien dijo: «Esto es intolerable. El Cem-Anáhuac Uey-Tlatoani está siendo detenido como prisionero por esos salvajes sucios y apestosos.»

Alguien más dijo: «No, Motecuzoma tiene razón. *Él* no es ningún prisionero. Los prisioneros somos el resto de nosotros. Mientras él humildemente se entrega como rehén, ningún mexícatl se atreverá ni siquiera a escupir al hombre blanco.»

Otra persona dijo: «Motecuzoma ha rendido su persona y la independencia orgullosa de los mexica, además de la mayor parte de nuestro tesoro. Si los barcos de los hombres blancos tardan en llegar, ¿quién nos puede decir qué más les podrá entregar la siguiente vez?»

Y luego alguien dijo lo que todos estábamos pensando: «En el transcurso de toda la historia de los mexica, ningún Uey-Tlatoani jamás ha sido despojado de su rango mientras viviera. Ni siquiera Auítzotl, cuando ya no fue capaz de seguir gobernando.»

«Pero se nombró a un regente para que gobernara en su nombre, y funcionó bastante bien, al mismo tiempo que unía la sucesión.»

«Cortés podría tener la ocurrencia de matar a Motecuzoma en cualquier momento. ¿Quién conoce los caprichos del hombre blanco? O Motecuzoma podría morir del propio asco que representa. Parece listo para ello.»

«Sí, el trono podría estar vacío de un momento a otro. Si tomamos la debida precaución ante esa posibilidad, podríamos tener un gobernante provisional listo... en caso de que el comportamiento de Motecuzoma fuera tal que *debiéramos* despojarlo de su título por órdenes del Consejo de Voceros.»

«Se debe decidir y arreglar en secreto. Evitémosle a Motecuzoma esa humillación, hasta que no quede otra alternativa. También, Cortés no debe tener la menor sospecha de que su rehén de un momento a otro, podría serle inútil.»

El Mujer Serpiente se dirigió a Cuitláhuac, quien hasta entonces no había comentado nada y le dijo, usando su título de nobleza: «Cuitláhuatzin, como hermano del Orador, normalmente serías el primer candidato que se podría considerar como sucesor suyo a su muerte. ¿Aceptarías el título y la responsabilidad de regente, si en un cónclave formal acordáramos llegar a eso?»

Cuitláhuac caminó unos pasos más adelante, frunciendo el ceño en meditación. Por fin dijo: «Me dolería usurpar el poder de mi propio hermano mientras él siga viviendo, pero en verdad es, mis señores, que me temo que sólo está viviendo a medias ahora, y ya ha abdicado de casi todo su poder. Si el Consejo de Voceros decide que la supervivencia de nuestra nación depende de ello y elige el momento oportuno, yo gobernaré en la capacidad que se me pida.»

Pero en la manera que todo fue sucediendo, no hubo necesidad inmediata de que Motecuzoma fuera usurpado, o que se tomara ninguna acción drástica. Es más, durante considerable tiempo pareció ser que Motecuzoma había estado en lo cierto al aconsejar que todos debíamos calmarnos y esperar. Porque los españoles permanecieron en Tenochtitlan durante aquel invierno, y si no hubiera sido porque eran tan blancos, casi no nos hubiéramos fijado en su presencia. Pudieron haber sido gente campesina de su propia raza, venidos a la gran ciudad a una fiesta, para ver sus atractivos y divertirse apaciblemente. Hasta se comportaron irreprochablemente durante nuestras ceremonias religiosas. Algunas de ellas, las que llevaban solamente música, baile y canto, eran vistas por los españoles con interés y algunas veces hasta con diversión. Cuando los ritos llevaban el sacrificio del *xochimique*, los españoles discretamente permanecían en su palacio. Nosotros, los ciudadanos, por nuestra parte, tolerábamos a los hombres blancos, tratándolos con cortesía, pero manteniéndonos a cierta distancia. Así que durante todo ese invierno no hubo fricciones entre nosotros y ellos, ningún incidente premeditado, ni siquiera se dejaron ver más augurios.

Motecuzoma, sus cortesanos y consejeros parecieron adaptarse con facilidad a su cambio de domicilio, y el gobierno de los asuntos de la nación no pareció ser afectado por el cambio del centro de gobierno. Como lo habían hecho siempre todos los demás Uey-Tlatoani, se veía con frecuencia con su Consejo de Voceros: recibía emisarios de las lejanas provincias mexica, de las otras naciones de la Triple Alianza y de naciones extranjeras, concedía audiencias a suplicantes individuales que llevaban peticiones, así como demandantes con quejas. Uno de sus visitantes más frecuentes era su sobrino Cacama, sin duda nervioso y con razón acerca de lo inseguro que estaba en su trono en Texcoco. Pero tal vez Cortés también le estaba pidiendo a sus aliados y subordinados que «tuvieran calma y esperaran». De todos modos, ninguno de ellos, ni el Príncipe Flor Oscura, impaciente por apoderarse del trono de los acolhua, hicieron algo drástico o indebido. Durante ese invierno, la vida de nuestro mundo pareció seguir, como lo había prometido Motecuzoma, exactamente como siempre.

Digo que «parecía», porque en lo personal tuve menos y menos que ver con los asuntos del estado. Rara vez se solicitaba mi presencia en la corte, excepto cuando alguna cuestión se suscitaba, sobre la cual Motecuzoma deseaba la opinión de todos sus señores residentes en la ciudad. Mi ocupación, menos señorial, de servir como intérprete también fue siendo menos necesaria y por último ya no fue necesaria, pues Motecuzoma aparentemente había decidido que, si iba a confiar en el hombre Cortés, podría confiar también en la mujer Malintzin. Se les podía ver a los tres paseando mucho tiempo juntos. Eso era difícil de evitar, ya que todos compartían el mismo techo, a pesar de lo grande del palacio. Pero el hecho fue que Cortés y Motecuzoma llegaron a disfrutar de su mutua compañía. Con frecuencia conversaban sobre la historia y el estado actual de sus diferentes países y religiones, y de sus diferentes modos de vivir. Como diversión menos solemne, Motecuzoma le enseñó a Cortés cómo jugar el juego de los frijoles, llamado *patoli*; por lo menos yo, aunque creo que era el único, tenía la esperanza de que el Venerado Orador estuviera jugando con apuestas grandes y que ganara, para que pudiera quedarse por lo menos con parte del tesoro que les había prometido a los hombres blancos.

A su vez, Cortés enseñó a Motecuzoma diferentes cosas. Mandó a la costa por una cantidad de sus marineros, los artesanos que ustedes llaman carpinteros de ribera, y trajeron consigo sus aperos de metal que iban a necesitar y ellos pusieron a sus leñadores a que cortaran unos árboles completamente derechos. y casi mágicamente convirtieron aquellos troncos en tablones, vigas, costillas y astas. Y en un tiempo sorprendentemente corto habían construido una réplica de medio tamaño de uno de sus barcos oceánicos y lo habían puesto a flote en el lago de Texcoco: el primer barco jamás visto en nuestras aguas que llevara esas alas que ellos llamaban velas. Mientras los marineros se encargaban del problema tan complicado que era guiar esa embarcación, Cortés llevó a Motecuzoma, algunas veces acompañado por miembros de su familia y de la corte, a pasear por los cinco lagos comunicados.

No sentí pena en lo absoluto por haber dejado de asistir, gradualmente, a la corte o haber dejado la traducción de los hombres blancos. Con gusto reanudé mi vida de antes de indolente retiro, para pasar otra vez algún tiempo en la Casa de los Pochteca, aunque no tanto como antes. Mi esposa no me lo pedía, pero yo sentía que debía estar en la casa más seguido en su compañía, porque parecía estar algo débil y tenía la tendencia de cansarse pronto. Luna que Espera siempre había ocupado sus ratos de ocio en labores femeninas como trabajo de bordado, pero me fijaba que ya tenía la costumbre de acercar el trabajo mucho a sus ojos. También solía coger una olla de la cocina o alguna otra cosa, para luego soltarla y romperla. Cuando le pregunté solícitamente, simplemente me contestó:

«Me estoy haciendo vieja, Zaa.»

«Sí, somos casi de la misma edad», le recordé.

Ese comentario pareció ofenderla, como si de pronto me hubiera puesto a corretear y bailar para demostrarle mi comparativa vivacidad. Beu me dijo con una voz demasiado seca para ella: «Es una de las maldiciones de las mujeres. Cada año somos más viejas que los hombres. —Y luego se suavizó y sonrió haciendo una pequeña broma de ello—. Es por eso que las mujeres tratan a sus hombres como niños. Porque jamás parecen envejecer... o crecer.»

Así que ella, ligeramente, olvidó ese asunto, pero pasó bastante tiempo antes de que yo me diera cuenta de que de hecho estaba mostrando los primeros síntomas del mal que gradualmente la llevaría a su lecho de enferma, que hasta ahora ha ocupado durante años. Beu jamás se quejó de algún malestar ni exigió alguna atención de mi parte, pero de todos modos se la di, y aunque hablábamos muy poco podía ver que ella me lo agradecía. Cuando Turquesa, nuestra vieja sirvienta, murió, llevé a casa a dos jóvenes mujeres, una para hacer el trabajo doméstico y otra para dedicarse totalmente a las necesidades y deseos de Beu. Como durante años me había acostumbrado a llamar a Turquesa cuando necesitaba dar alguna orden doméstica, me fue difícil quitarme ese hábito. Solía llamar a ambas mujeres Turquesa sin discriminación, y se acostumbraron a ello, y ahora no puedo recordar sus verdaderos nombres.

Quizás inconscientemente había adoptado el descuido con que los hombres blancos pronunciaban los nombres propios y las expresiones correctas. Durante casi ese medio año que residieron los españoles en Tenochtitlan, ninguno de ellos hizo el más mínimo esfuerzo por aprender la lengua náhuatl, o siquiera los rudimentos de la pronunciación. La única persona de nuestra raza con quienes estaban más ligados era con la mujer que se hacía llamar Malintzin, pero hasta su consorte Cortés, invariablemente pronunciaba mal ese nombre que ella había asumido, llamándola Malinche. Con el tiempo, también nuestra gente la llamó así, ya fuera por cortesía, como lo hacían los españoles, o en señal de desprecio. Porque a Malintzin siempre le enfurecía que la llamaran Malinche —era quitarle el -tzin de la nobleza—, pero difícilmente podía quejarse de que le faltaran al respeto, que pareciera que criticara la manera de hablar, tan usual, de su amo.

De todos modos, Cortés y los otros hombres eran imparciales, ya que también se equivocaban en el nombre de todos los demás. Como el sonido suave de la «sh» no existe en su lenguaje español, a nosotros los mexica nos llamaron por mucho tiempo, ya sea los mes-sica o mec-sica. Pero ustedes los españoles últimamente han preferido darnos nuestro nombre antiguo, ya que les es más fácil llamarnos los aztecas. Como Cortés y sus hombres encontraron difícil pronunciar el nombre de Motecuzoma, lo convirtieron en Montezuma, y honestamente creo que no lo hacían con descortesía, ya que incluían en ese nombre la palabra «montaña» y eso, aún se podía tomar como implicación de grandeza e importancia. El nombre del dios de la guerra Huitzilopochtli también los venció y como de todos modos odiaban a ese dios, le pusieron Huichilobos, incorporando a esa palabra el nombre que le dan a las bestias llamadas «lobos».

Bien, el invierno pasó y llegó la primavera, y con ella vinieron más hombres blancos. Motecuzoma escuchó la noticia poco antes que Cortés y por pura casualidad. Uno de sus ratones *quimíchime* aún situado en el territorio totonaca, habiéndose cansado y aburrido, había vagado una buena distancia más al sur de donde debía estar. Por lo que este espía vio, una flota de barcos anchos y con alas, a sólo una pequeña distancia de la tierra y moviéndose lentamente hacia el norte por la costa, deteniéndose en las bahías y bocas de ríos, «como si estuvieran buscando alguna traza de sus compañeros», dijo el *quimichi*, cuando llegó corriendo a Tenochtitlan, portando un papel de corteza de árbol sobre el cual había hecho un dibujo enumerando la flota.

Los otros señores y yo, y todo el Consejo de Voceros estábamos presentes en el salón del trono, cuando Motecuzoma mandó a un paje para que llamara a Cortés, quien todavía desconocía esa noticia. El Venerado Orador, aprovechando la oportunidad para pretender que sabía todo lo que sucedía en estas tierras, expuso las noticias por medio de mi traducción, de esta manera:

«Capitán General, su Rey Don Carlos ha recibido su barco mensajero y su primer informe de estas tierras y nuestros primeros regalos que le mandó, y está muy complacido con usted.»

Cortés se mostró debidamente impresionado y sorprendido. «¿Y cómo se pudo enterar de eso, Señor Don Montezuma?», preguntó.

Aún fingiendo omnipotencia, Motecuzoma dijo: «Porque su Rey Carlos está mandando una flota dos veces más grande que la suya, veinte barcos completos sólo para llevarlo a usted y a sus hombres de regreso a su país.»

«¿En verdad? —dijo Cortés, cortésmente sin demostrar escepticismo—. ¿Y dónde están?»

«Se acercan —dijo Motecuzoma misteriosamente—. Tal vez usted no esté enterado que mis adivinos-que-ven-en-la-lejanía pueden ver tanto hacia el futuro como más allá del horizonte. Ellos me hicieron este dibujo, mientras los barcos aún estaban a medio océano. —Le entregó el papel a Cortés—. Se lo enseño ahora, porque los barcos ya no tardarán en ponerse a la vista de su propia guarnición.»

«Asombroso —dijo Cortés, examinando el papel. Luego murmuró para sí—: Sí... galeones, transportes, alimentos... sí, este maldito dibujo se acerca a lo correcto. —Frunció el ceño—. Pero... ¿*veinte* de ellos?»

Motecuzoma dijo con suavidad: «Aunque todos nos hemos sentido muy honrados por su visita, y yo en lo personal he disfrutado de su compañía, me agrada el que sus hermanos hayan venido y que ya no esté usted aislado en una tierra extraña. —Agregó con algo de insistencia—: *Sí* han venido para llevarlo a casa, ¿no es cierto?»

«Así parece», dijo Cortés, aunque con una expresión ligeramente atontada.

«Mandaré abrir las habitaciones del tesoro ahora mismo», dijo Motecuzoma con voz más bien alegre, ante la inminente pobreza de su nación.

Pero en ese momento el mayordomo de palacio y algunos otros hombres entraron besando el suelo del salón del trono. Cuando dije que Motecuzoma había recibido la noticia de los barcos poco antes que Cortés, hablaba literalmente. Ya que los recién llegados eran dos mensajeros-veloces enviados por el Señor Patzinca, y habían sido llevados rápidamente de tierra firme por los campeones totonaca, a quienes se habían dirigido primero. Cortés miró incómodo alrededor del cuarto; era obvio que le hubiera gustado llevarse a los hombres e interrogarlos en privado; pero me pregunto si pudiera transmitirles a todos los presentes lo que los mensajeros tenían que decir.

El que habló primero llevaba un mensaje dictado por Patzinca: «Veinte de los barcos con alas, los más grandes vistos hasta ahora, han llegado a la bahía de la pequeña Villa Rica de la Vera Cruz. De esos barcos han desembarcado mil trescientos soldados blancos, armados y con sus armaduras. Ochenta llevan arcabuces, y ciento veinte traen ballestas, además de sus espadas y lanzas. También hay noventa y seis caballos y veinte cañones.»

Motecuzoma miró suspicaz a Cortés y dijo: «Parece que es una fuerza guerrera, mi amigo, sólo para conducirlo a casa.»

«Así parece —dijo Cortés, mostrándose menos que complacido al escuchar la noticia. Se dirigió a mí—. ¿No tienen otra cosa más que informarnos?»

Entonces el otro mensajero habló y resultó ser uno de esos buenos recordadores de palabras bastante tedioso. Repitió palabra por palabra lo que había dicho Patzinca desde su primer encuentro con los hombres blancos, pero fue una algarabía como la de un mono, pues mezclaba el totonaca y el español, de una manera incomprensible, debido a que no tenían un intérprete para poder descifrar las pláticas. Encogí los hombros y dije: «Capitán General, no entiendo nada más que la repetición continua de dos nombres. El suyo y otro que suena como Narváez.»

«¿Narváez, aquí?», dijo abruptamente Cortés, y agregó una exclamación bastante grosera.

Motecuzoma empezó nuevamente: «Mandaré traer las joyas y el oro del tesoro, en cuando su grupo de cargadores...»

«Disculpadme —dijo Cortés, recobrándose de su evidente sorpresa—. Os sugiero que mantengáis el tesoro escondido y seguro hasta que pueda verificar las intenciones de estos recién llegados.»

Motecuzoma contestó: «Pero con seguridad son sus compatriotas.»

«Sí, Don Montezuma. Pero vos me habéis dicho, cómo vuestros propios paisanos algunas veces se convierten en bandidos. Así también, nosotros los españoles debemos ser cautelosos con algunos de nuestros compañeros marineros. Vos me habéis comisionado para llevarle al Rey Don Carlos el regalo más rico que haya enviado algún monarca extranjero. No quisiera correr el riesgo de perderlo a manos de los bandidos del mar que nosotros llamamos piratas. Con vuestro permiso, iré inmediatamente a la costa e investigaré a esos hombres.»

«Por supuesto», dijo el Venerado Orador, quien no hubiera podido caber de alegría, si esos dos grupos de hombres blancos decidieran atacarse y acabar el uno con el otro.

«Debo moverme rápidamente, en una marcha forzada —continuó Cortés, haciendo sus planes en voz alta—. Solamente llevaré a mis soldados españoles y los más escogidos de nuestros guerreros aliados. Los del Príncipe Flor Oscura son los mejores...»

«Sí —dijo Motecuzoma con aprobación—. Muy bien. Muy, muy bien.» Pero dejó de sonreír al oír las siguientes palabras del Capitán General:

«Dejaré a Pedro de Alvarado, el hombre de barba roja que vuestras gentes llaman Tonatíu, para salvaguardar mis intereses aquí. —Rápidamente se retractó de esa declaración—. Quiero decir, por supuesto, que se queda a ayudarle a defender vuestra ciudad en caso de que los piratas puedan vencerme y llegar hasta acá. Como sólo puedo dejarle a Pedro una pequeña reserva de nuestros compatriotas, debo reforzarlos trayendo tropas nativas de la tierra firme...»

Las cosas quedaron así: cuando Cortés marchó hacia el este con la mayoría de sus fuerzas blancas y todos los acolhua de Flor Oscura, Alvarado se quedó al frente de cerca de ochenta hombres blancos y cuatrocientos texcalteca, todos alojados en el palacio. Fue el último insulto. Motecuzoma había estado residiendo con los hombres blancos durante el largo invierno, en una situación en sí peculiar, pero la primavera lo encontró en una posición todavía más denigrante, al vivir no sólo con los extranjeros blancos, sino también con una multitud de guerreros groseros, irascibles y nada respetuosos, quienes eran los verdaderos invasores. Si el Venerado Orador había parecido recobrar la vida y actividad ante la posibilidad de poder deshacerse de los españoles, se sintió completamente abatido bajo la desesperación más impotente y pesimista al verse como anfitrión y cautivo para el resto de su vida por los enemigos más aborrecidos y aborrecedores. Sólo hubo una circunstancia mitigante, aunque dudo que Motecuzoma encontrara mucho consuelo en ello: los texcalteca eran notablemente más limpios en sus hábitos y olían mucho mejor que una cantidad igual de hombres blancos.

El Mujer Serpiente dijo: «¡Esto es intolerable!» Éstas eran las palabras que yo escuchaba ya con más y más frecuencia por parte de más y más súbditos inconformes de Motecuzoma.

Por ese motivo hubo una reunión secreta del Consejo de Voceros, a la cual se había pedido la presencia de muchos otros campeones, sacerdotes, hombres sabios y nobles mexica, entre los que yo me encontraba. Motecuzoma no estaba presente y no supo nada.

El jefe guerrero Cuitláhuac dijo enfurecido: «Nosotros los mexica sólo en raras ocasiones hemos podido penetrar las fronteras de Texcala. *Jamás* hemos peleado hasta llegar a su capital. —Su voz se alzó para decir las siguientes palabras, hasta que estaba casi gritando—. Y ahora los detestables texcalteca están *aquí*, en la ciudad inexpugnable de Tenochtitlan, El Corazón del Único Mundo, en el palacio del soberano guerrero Axayácatl quien seguramente en estos momentos estará tratando de buscar una manera de salirse del otro mundo y regresar a éste para contestar el insulto. Los texcalteca no nos invadieron por la fuerza, están aquí por *invitación*, pero no por *nuestra* invitación, y para colmo viven en el palacio con la misma categoría y lado a lado de *¡NUESTRO VENERADO ORADOR!*»

«Venerado Orador sólo de nombre —gruñó el sacerdote principal de Huitzilopochtli—. Les digo que nuestro dios de la guerra lo desconocerá.»

«Si es el tiempo de hacerlo —dijo el Señor Cuautémoc, hijo

dcl difunto Auítzotl—. Y si lo demoramos más puede ser que jamás tengamos otra oportunidad. Quizás el hombre Alvarado brille como Tonatíu, pero tiene menos brillantez como sustituto de Cortés. Debemos atacarlo antes de que el astuto Cortés regrese.»

«¿Entonces está seguro de que Cortés regresará?», pregunté, porque no había asistido a juntas de Consejo, ya fuera públicas o secretas, desde la partida del Capitán General diez días antes, y no estaba al tanto de las últimas noticias. Cuautémoc me dijo:

«Es muy extraño lo que hemos sabido de nuestros *quimíchime* de la costa. Cortés no recibió a sus hermanos recién llegados de un modo fraternal. Los tomó por sorpresa, atacándolos por la noche. Aunque sus fuerzas eran mucho más pequeñas, yo creo que numéricamente eran menos, creo que tres por uno, sus hombres prevalecieron sobre los otros. Lo curioso es que hubo pocos heridos de ambos lados, porque Cortés había ordenado que no se hicieran más matanzas que las necesarias, y que a los recién llegados sólo se les capturara y desarmara, como si estuvieran peleando en una Guerra Florida. Y desde entonces, Cortés y el jefe blanco de la expedición nueva se han encontrado en muchas discusiones y negociaciones. No nos podemos explicar el porqué de todos estos hechos. Pero debemos suponer que Cortés está arreglando la rendición de esa fuerza a su mando, y que regresará aquí al frente de todos esos nuevos hombres y armas.»

Pueden entender, señores escribanos, por qué todos nos encontrábamos en constante zozobra por la sucesión de acontecimientos en aquellos días. Habíamos supuesto que los recién llegados venían de parte del Rey Don Carlos, a petición del mismo Cortés; y su ataque sin provocación era un misterio que no nos podíamos explicar. No fue sino hasta mucho tiempo después que pude reunir los suficientes fragmentos de informaciones y unirlos para poder llegar a darme cuenta hasta dónde llegaba el carácter fraudulento e impostor de Cortés, tanto con mi gente como con sus compatriotas.

Desde el momento de su llegada a estas tierras, Cortés se había hecho pasar por un emisario de su Rey Don Carlos, y ahora sé que no fue así. Su Rey Don Carlos jamás envió a Cortés como expedicionario aquí ni por el engrandecimiento de Su Majestad ni por el de España, ni por la propagación de la Fe Cristiana, ni por ninguna otra razón. Cuando Hernán Cortés pisó por primera vez El Único Mundo, su Rey Don Carlos ¡jamás había oído hablar de Hernán Cortés!

Hasta la fecha, hasta Su Ilustrísima Excelencia el Obispo se expresa de ese «farsante de Cortés» despectivamente de sus bajos orígenes, de su rango advenedizo, de sus ambiciones presuntuosas. Por medio de comentarios del Obispo Zumárraga y otros, ahora comprendo que Cortés fue enviado aquí originalmente, no por su Rey o por su Iglesia, sino por una autoridad mucho más pequeña, el gobernador de aquella colonia en la isla llamada Cuba. Y Cortés fue enviado con instrucciones de no hacer nada más venturoso que explorar nuestras costas, trazar mapas de ellas, y quizás un poco de comercio provechoso, cambiando sus cuentas de vidrio y otras curiosidades.

Pero hasta yo pude comprender que Cortés vio una gran oportunidad después de vencer con tanta facilidad a los guerreros del Tabascoöb en Cupilco, y especialmente después de que la gente totonaca débilmente se sometió a él sin pelear en lo absoluto. Debió de haber sido entonces cuando Cortés se propuso ser el Conquistador en Jefe, el Conquistador de todo El Único Mundo. He escuchado que algunos de sus oficiales menores, temerosos de la ira de su gobernador, se opusieron a sus planes de grandeza, y fue por esa razón que ordenó a sus seguidores más leales quemar los barcos. Aislados en estas costas, hasta los más recalcitrantes no tuvieron otra opción más que someterse al plan de Cortés.

Según he llegado a escuchar la historia, sólo hubo un incidente que brevemente amenazó con impedir el éxito de Cortés. Envió el único barco que le quedaba y Alonso, su oficial —aquel hombre quien había sido el primer dueño de Malintzin—, para entregar el primer cargamento de tesoros sacados de nuestras tierras. Se suponía que Alonso debía pasar sigilosamente por Cuba y atravesar el océano directamente hacia España y allí deslumbrar al Rey Don Carlos con los ricos regalos, para que éste diera su real bendición al proyecto de Cortés, junto con la concesión de un rango alto, para hacer legítimo su saqueo durante la conquista. Pero de alguna forma, no sé cómo, el gobernador supo que ese barco había pasado en secreto por la isla, y adivinó que Cortés estaba haciendo *algo* en contra de sus órdenes. Así que el gobernador reunió los veinte barcos y una multitud de hombres, mandando a Narváez como comandante de esa flota, a perseguir y atrapar al prófugo Cortés, despojándolo de toda autoridad para que hiciera la paz con cualquier gente que hubiera ofendido o de quien hubiera abusado, y traerlo encadenado nuevamente a Cuba.

Sin embargo, según nuestros vigilantes ratones, el prófugo había vencido al cazador. Así, mientras Alonso supuestamente estaba mostrando dorados regalos y perspectivas no menos doradas ante su Rey Don Carlos en España, Cortés estaba haciendo lo mismo en Vera Cruz, mostrándole a Narváez muestras de las riquezas de estas tierras, convenciéndolo de que estaban casi ganadas, y de que debía unirse a él y concluir la conquista, asegurándole de que no había ninguna razón para temer la ira de un simple gobernador de colonias. Pues pronto mandarían —no a su insignificante superior inmediato, sino al todo poderoso Rey Don Carlos— toda una colonia nueva y más grande en tamaño y riqueza que la Madre España y todas sus demás colonias juntas.

Aunque nosotros, los guías y los ancianos de los mexica hubiéramos sabido todas esas cosas ese día que nos reunimos en secreto, no creo que hubiéramos podido hacer más de lo que hicimos. Y eso fue que por voto formal se declaró que Motecuzoma Xocoyótzin quedaba «temporalmente incapacitado», y se nombraba a su hermano Cuitláhuatzin como regente para gobernar en su lugar, y aprobar su primera decisión en ese oficio: que rápidamente elimináramos todos los extranjeros que infestaban Tenochtitlan.

«Dentro de dos días —dijo Cuitláhuac— será la ceremonia en honor de la hermana del dios de la lluvia, Ixtocíuatl. Como ella solamente es la diosa de la sal, normalmente sería una ceremonia menor con la presencia de sólo unos cuantos sacerdotes, pero el hombre blanco no puede saber eso. Tampoco los texcalteca, quienes jamás han asistido a ninguna de las observaciones religiosas de esta ciudad —echó una risita maliciosa—; por esa razón, podemos alegrarnos de que Cortés eligiera dejar a nuestros antiguos enemigos aquí, y no a los acolhua que sí conocen bien nuestros festivales. Porque ahora iré al palacio y, pidiéndole a mi hermano no demostrar ningún asombro, le diré al oficial Tonatíu Alvarado una gran mentira. Haré hincapié de la *importancia* de nuestra ceremonia a Ixtocíuatl, y pediré su permiso de que se le permita a toda nuestra gente reunirse en la gran plaza durante ese día y noche, para hacer adoración y regocijo.»

«¡Sí! —dijo el Mujer Serpiente—. Mientras tanto, los demás de ustedes avisarán a todos los campeones y guerreros disponibles y hasta el último *yoaquizqui* que pueda portar armas. Cuando los extranjeros vean esa multitud portando inofensivamente armas en lo que parece ser solamente una danza ritual, acompañada de música y canto, sólo observarán con la misma diversión tolerante de siempre. Pero a una señal...»

«Espera —dijo Cuautémoc—. Mi primo Motecuzoma no divulgará el fraude, ya que adivinará la buena razón por lo que lo hacemos, pero nos estamos olvidando de esa maldita mujer Malintzin. Cortés la dejó como intérprete del oficial Tonatíu durante su ausencia. Y ella ha hecho por saber mucho sobre nuestras costumbres. Cuando vea la plaza llena de gente además de sacerdotes, sabrá que no es el homenaje acostumbrado para la diosa de la sal. Con toda seguridad dará la alarma a sus amos blancos.»

«Déjenme a la mujer —dije yo. Era la oportunidad que había estado esperando, ya que eso llenaría mi satisfacción personal—. Siento que estoy demasiado viejo como para pelear en la plaza, pero sí puedo deshacerme de nuestro enemigo más peligroso. Procedan con sus planes, Señor Regente. Malintzin no verá la ceremonia, ni sospechará nada, ni dirá nada. Estará muerta.»

El plan para la noche de Ixtocíuatl fue éste. Sería precedida de todo un día de bailes, cantos y combates simulados en El Corazón del Único Mundo, todo hecho por las mujeres de la ciudad, las doncellas y los niños. Sólo cuando empezara a anochecer sería cuando los hombres comenzarían a entrar de dos en dos y tomarían los lugares de las mujeres y niños bailando afuera de la plaza en pares o grupos de tres. Para entonces sería totalmente de noche y el escenario estaría iluminado por antorchas y urnas, la mayoría de los extranjeros ya estarían cansados del espectáculo y se irían a sus habitaciones, o cuando menos, en la tenue luz que dan las fogatas no se darían cuenta de que todos los participantes eran grandes de tamaño y de género masculino. Esos danzantes, cantando y gesticulando gradualmente, formarían filas y columnas que se moverían del centro de la plaza desviándose hacia la entrada del Muro de la Serpiente al palacio de Axayácatl.

La resistencia más fuerte para su asalto era la amenaza de los cuatro cañones en el techo del palacio. Uno o dos de ellos podrían arrasar casi toda la plaza abierta con sus fragmentos terribles, pero difícilmente se podían apuntar directamente hacia abajo. Y era la intención de Cuitláhuac juntar a sus hombres lo más posible contra las mismas paredes de aquel palacio antes de que los hombres blancos se dieran cuenta de que se les iba a atacar. Entonces, a una señal suya, toda la fuerza mexica se abriría paso por los portones de la guardia y pelearían en las habitaciones, patios y corredores, en donde la fuerza numérica de sus *maquahuime* de obsidiana vencerían a las espadas de acero de sus oponentes, que aunque más efectivas que sus armas, eran menos en cantidad, así como sus pesados arcabuces. Mientras tanto, otros mexica quitarían los puentes de madera extendidos sobre los tres caminos-puente de la isla, y con arcos y flechas esos hombres rechazarían a cualquiera de los soldados de Alvarado que trataran de huir cruzando o nadando por esos huecos.

Tracé mis planes con el mismo cuidado. Visité al físico que había atendido a las personas de mi casa por mucho tiempo, un hombre en el cual podía confiar, y sin vacilar, a petición mía, me dio una poción sobre la cual juraba que podía confiar totalmente. Por supuesto que era bien conocido por los sirvientes de la corte de Motecuzoma y por los trabajadores de su cocina que estaban bastante inconformes con su trabajo, así es que no tuve ninguna dificultad en obtener su cooperación en emplear la poción de la manera exacta y en el tiempo exacto que especifiqué. Entonces, le dije a Beu que quería que saliera de la ciudad durante la ceremonia de Ixtocíuatl, aunque no le dije que la causa era porque iba a haber un levantamiento y temía que la lucha se extendiera por toda la isla, y tenía la certidumbre, por la parte singular que me correspondía en todo el asunto, de que el hombre blanco, si tenía la oportunidad, dejaría caer una venganza terrible sobre mí y los míos.

Como ya lo he dicho, Beu se encontraba delicada de salud, y obviamente no sentía ningún entusiasmo por dejar nuestra casa, pero estaba al tanto de las reuniones secretas a las que había asistido, por lo que se imaginó que *algo* iba a pasar, y obedeció sin protestar. Visitaría a una amiga que vivía en Tepeyaca, en la tierra firme. Como una concesión por su estado tan débil, dejé que permaneciera en casa, descansando, hasta un poco antes que se levantaran los puentes del camino-puente. Fue por la tarde cuando la mandé en una silla de manos, con las dos Turquesas caminando de cada lado de ella.

Permanecí en la casa, solo. Ésta quedaba lo suficientemente lejos del Corazón del Único Mundo como para que se pudiera escuchar la música o alguno de los ruidos de los supuestos festejos, pero me podía imaginar cómo se iba desenvolviendo el plan mientras anochecía: los caminos-puente quedaban divididos, los guerreros armados empezarían a sustituir a las mujeres celebrantes. No contemplaba mis suposiciones con gusto, ya que mi propia contribución había sido matar a escondidas por primera vez en mi vida. Conseguí un garrafón de *octli* y una taza de la cocina, esperando que la bebida fuerte amortiguara los remordimientos de mi conciencia. Y sentándome en la penumbra de mi cuarto en la planta baja, sin prender las lámparas, traté de beber hasta quedar adormecido, esperando lo que pudiera pasar después.

Escuché el ruido de muchos pasos afuera en la calle, y luego llamaron a mi puerta; al abrirla, vi a cuatro guardias del palacio, portando las cuatro esquinas de un catre tejido con caña sobre el que estaba tendido un cuerpo delgado, tapado con una tela de algodón, fina y blanca.

«Disculpe la intrusión, Señor Mixtli —dijo uno de los guardias con un tono de voz que no era curioso—; a nosotros se nos ordenó que le pidiéramos que viera el rostro de esta mujer muerta.»

«No necesito hacerlo —dije, algo sorprendido de que Alvarado o Motecuzoma hubiera adivinado tan pronto quién había sido el responsable del asesinato—. Puedo identificar a esa hembra de coyote sin verla.»

«De todos modos, le verá usted el rostro», insistió el guardia con severidad.

Levanté la sábana que cubría su cara, al mismo tiempo que alzaba mi topacio para ver, e hice un ruido involuntario, porque era el de una joven que jamás había visto antes.

«Su nombre es Laurel —dijo Malintzin—, o mejor dicho era.» No me había dado cuenta de que una silla de manos estaba al pie de las escaleras. Sus portadores la bajaron y Malintzin salió de ella, y los guardias que llevaban el catre se hicieron a un lado para que pasara y subiera a verme. Dirigiéndose a mí me dijo: «Hablaremos adentro —y volviéndose a los cuatro guardias—: Esperen abajo hasta que baje o les llame. Si lo hago, tiren su cargamento y vengan de inmediato.»

Abrí la puerta ampliamente para que pasara y luego la cerré en las narices de los guardias. Caminé a tientas en el corredor oscuro buscando una lámpara, pero ella me dijo: «Deje la casa oscura. No nos es muy grato vernos las caras, ¿no es cierto?» Así que la llevé al cuarto de enfrente y nos sentamos uno frente al otro. Era pequeña, una figura confusa en la penumbra, pero la amenaza que ella representaba la hacía parecer más grande. Me serví y tomé otro trago grande de *octli*. Si antes deseaba estar adormecido, ante las nuevas circunstancias prefería estar paralizado o con un delirio maniático.

«Laurel fue una de las doncellas texcalteca que me dieron para que me sirviera como criada —dijo Malitzin—. Hoy le tocó probar mi comida. Es una precaución que he estado tomando desde hace tiempo, pero los sirvientes y demás ocupantes del palacio no lo saben. Así es que no tiene por qué reprocharse tan severamente su fracaso, Señor Mixtli, aunque podría alguna vez sentir un momento de remordimiento por la inocente y joven Laurel.»

«Es algo que he estado deplorando por años —dije con la gravedad del ebrio—. Siempre muere la gente equivocada; la buena, la útil, la merecedora, la inocente, pero la malvada, la que es peor, la completamente inútil, inservible y prescindible es la que sigue ocupando nuestro mundo, más allá del ciclo de vida que merecen vivir. Pero claramente, no se necesita ser un sabio para hacer esa observación. Lo mismo podría gruñir porque las tormentas de granizo enviadas por Tláloc destruyan el maíz nutritivo, pero nunca dañen un arbusto de espinas.»

En verdad que estaba divagando, diciendo lo que para mí era evidente, pero era porque alguna parte de mi mente, que todavía estaba sobria, trataba frenéticamente de concentrarse en un asunto diferente. El atentado a la vida de Malintzin, quien sin duda venía con la intención de devolverme esa atención, por lo pronto la había distraído de fijarse en los hechos, poco comunes, que estaban teniendo lugar en El Corazón del Único Mundo. Pero si acababa conmigo rápidamente y regresaba al lugar de los hechos de inmediato, *sí* se daría cuenta, y aún tendría tiempo de avisar a sus amos. Además de que no tenía muchas ganas de morir por ningún motivo, como lo había hecho la desdichada Laurel, había jurado que Malintzin no sería ningún impedimento para los planes de Cuitláhuac. Tenía que mantenerla conversando o gozando, o si fuera necesario hacer que escuchara mis súplicas cobardes para salvar mi vida hasta que la noche cayera completamente y que se escuchara el rugir de la plaza. Al oírlo sus cuatro guardias podrían correr a investigar. Y aunque lo hicieran o no lo hicieran no durarían mucho tiempo bajo las órdenes de Malintzin. Si es que podía retenerla conmigo, manteniéndola ocupada por un rato.

«Las tormentas de granizo de Tláloc también destruyen las mariposas —seguí balbuciendo—, pero que yo sepa nunca terminan con una simple mosca pestilente.»

Ella dijo cortante: «Deje de hablar como si estuviera senil, o como si yo fuera una niña. Soy la mujer que trató de envenenar y ahora estoy aquí...»

Para desviar sus siguientes palabras, que ya esperaba, hubiera sido capaz de decir cualquier cosa. Lo que dije fue: «Me supongo que es porque sigo pensando en ti como en una niña que se está convirtiendo en mujer... como sigo pensando en mi difunta hija Nochipa...»

«Pero soy lo suficientemente grande como para sancionar el que se me intente matar —dijo ella—. Señor Mixtli, si mi poder es tal que usted lo considera peligroso, también podría considerar su posible utilidad. ¿Por qué tratar de acabar con él, cuando podría tenerlo a su favor?»

Parpadeé como lo haría una lechuza, pero no la interrumpí

para preguntar qué era lo que quería decir con eso, dejé que siguiera hablando todo lo que quisiera.

Ella dijo: «Usted se encuentra exactamente igual con los mexica, como me encuentro yo con los hombres blancos. No como un ·consejero reconocido oficialmente, sin embargo, una voz a la que escuchan y atienden. Jamás nos simpatizaremos, pero sí nos podríamos ayudar. Usted y yo bien sabemos que las cosas en El Único Mundo jamás volverán a ser igual, pero nadie puede decir a quién le pertenecerá en el futuro. Si la gente de estas tierras prevalece, usted podría ser un fuerte aliado para mí. Si el hombre blanco prevalece, yo puedo ser su aliada.»

Yo hipé con ironía: «¿Sugieres que nos pongamos de acuerdo para traicionar al bando que cada uno de nosotros ha escogido? ¿Por qué no nos cambiamos de ropa y con ella de bando?»

«Sepa esto. Sólo tengo que llamar a mis guardias y usted será un hombre muerto, aunque usted no es "nadie", como Laurel. Eso pondría en peligro la tregua que nuestros dos amos han tratado de conservar. Hernán se podría sentir obligado a entregarme para ser castigada, como Motecuzoma lo hizo con Cuaupopoca. Y si no fuera así, por lo menos perdería algo de la eminencia que he logrado. Pero si no lo elimino, constantemente tendré que estar cuidándome del *siguiente* atentado que pueda usted hacer a mi vida. Eso sería una distracción, una interferencia a la concentración que necesito para mis propios intereses.»

Me reí y dije, casi con admiración auténtica: «Tienes la sangre fría de una iguana.» Y eso me hizo reír tanto que casi me caigo de la silla.

Esperó hasta que me callara, y luego continuó como si no le hubiera interrumpido: «Hagamos un pacto secreto entre nosotros. Si no de alianza, cuando menos de neutralidad. Y sellémoslo de tal forma que ninguno de nosotros jamás pueda romperlo.»

«Sellarlo, ¿cómo, Malintzin? Ambos hemos probado ser traicioneros y sin escrúpulos.»

«Nos acostaremos —dijo ella, y eso hizo que me fuera para atrás, que hasta me caí de la silla. Esperó a que me levantara nuevamente y cuando seguí sentado estúpidamente en el suelo, me preguntó—: ¿Estás borracho, Mixtzin?»

«Debo de estarlo —contesté—. Estoy escuchando cosas imposibles. Creí oír que habías propuesto que nosotros...»

«Lo hice. Que nos acostemos juntos esta noche. Los hombres blancos son aún más celosos de sus mujeres que los hombres de nuestra raza. Hernán te mataría por haberlo hecho y me mataría a mí por haberme sometido a ello. Los cuatro guardias siempre estarán disponibles para atestiguar que pasé mucho tiempo adentro contigo, en la oscuridad, y que me fui de tu casa sonriendo y no enojada y llorando. ¿No te parece hermosamente sencillo? ¿Y un lazo irrompible? Ninguno de nosotros podrá atreverse jamás a herir u ofender, por miedo a que alguno diga las palabras que sentenciarán a los dos.»

Corriendo el riesgo de enfurecerla y dejarla escapar, le contesté: «A los cincuenta y cuatro años no estoy sexualmente senil, pero ya no me acuesto con cualquier mujer que se me ofrece. No he quedado incapacitado, sino simplemente tengo unos gustos más refinados.» Quise hablar con tono altivo y digno, pero el hecho es que me dio frecuentemente hipo entre las palabras, y como las dije sentado en el suelo, disminuyó algo el efecto. «Como ya lo has mencionado, no nos gustamos. Pudiste haber usado palabras más fuertes. La repugnancia hubiera descrito mejor nuestros sentimientos.»

Ella dijo: «No quisiera que nuestros sentimientos fueran de otro modo. Sólo propongo algo para nuestra propia conveniencia. En cuanto a sus gustos refinados, ya casi está oscuro aquí. Puede hacer de mí la mujer que desea.»

«¿Debo hacer esto, con tal de retenerla aquí y lejos de la plaza?», me pregunté, y en voz alta protesté: «Si tengo la edad suficiente como para ser tu padre.»

«Entonces, pretenda que lo es —dijo con indiferencia—, si el incesto es de su agrado. —Luego se rió—. Por lo que sé, usted realmente podría ser mi padre. Y yo, yo puedo pretender *cualquier* cosa.»

«Entonces así lo harás —le dije—. Ambos pretenderemos que copulamos ilícitamente, aunque no sea así. Simplemente pasaremos el rato conversando, y los guardias podrán atestiguar que estuvimos juntos durante un lapso de tiempo lo suficiente comprometedor. ¿Te gustaría un trago de *octli*?»

Me tambaleé hasta la cocina y, después de romper algunas cosas en la oscuridad, me tambaleé de vuelta con otra taza. Mientras la servía, Malintzin dijo pensativa: «Recuerdo... usted dijo que su hija y yo teníamos el mismo nombre de nacimiento y año. Que éramos de la misma edad. —Tomé otro trago largo de *octli*, ella también bebió e inclinando su cabeza a un lado inquisitivamente, dijo—: ¿Usted y su hija jugaban alguna vez... juntos?»

«Sí —contesté con voz pastosa—, pero no lo que yo supongo que estás pensando.»

«Yo no pensaba nada —dijo ella inocentemente—. Estamos conversando, como usted lo sugirió. ¿A qué jugaban?»

«Había uno que nosotros llamábamos El Volcán Hipando... digo El Volcán Eruptando.»

«No conozco ese juego.»

«Era un juego tonto que nosotros mismos inventamos. Yo me acostaba en el suelo. Así. —No me acosté precisamente; caí cuan largo era, con gran golpe—. Y doblaba mis rodillas, ¿ves?, porque las rodillas representan el pico del volcán. Nochipa se colocaba ahí.»

«¿Así?», dijo haciéndolo. Era pequeña y ligera de peso, y en el cuarto oscuro pudo haber sido cualquiera.

«Sí —dije yo—. Entonces movía mis rodillas, el volcán despertaba, ¿entiendes?, y luego la hacía saltar...»

Lanzó una exclamación de sorpresa, y resbaló hasta caer en mi estómago. Su falda se alzó al hacer eso y cuando la sujeté para detenerla, descubrí que no llevaba nada debajo de su falda.

Suavemente, dijo: «¿Y era así como el volcán hacía erupción?»

Llevaba mucho sin una mujer, y era muy bueno tener otra de nuevo, y mi borrachera no afectó mi capacidad. Me exalté tan poderosamente y lo hice tantas veces que creo que algo de mi ingenio se derramó con mi *omícetl*. La primera vez, podría haber jurado que verdaderamente había sentido la vibración y había escuchado el rugir de un volcán en erupción. Si ella también lo sintió, no dijo nada, pero después de la segunda vez, ella gimió: «Es diferente, casi agradable. Usted es tan limpio y huele tan bien.» Y después de la tercera vez, cuando hubo recobrado de nuevo su aliento, dijo: «Si usted no dijera su edad a nadie, nadie lo podría adivinar.» Por fin, ambos nos encontrábamos exhaustos, respirando fuertemente, entrelazados, y sólo poco a poco me fui dando cuenta que en el cuarto ya había entrado la luz del día. Sentí algo de sobresalto y cierta incredulidad al reconocer que la cara que estaba junto a la mía era la de Malintzin. La actividad prolongada de la copulación había sido de lo más agradable, pero parecía ser que había salido de ella en un estado de distracción o tal vez hasta de trastorno. Yo pensé: «¿Qué estoy haciendo con *ella*? Ésta es la mujer que he detestado con tanta vehemencia durante tanto tiempo, y ahora hasta soy culpable de haber asesinado a una persona inocente...»

Pero, fueran cuales fueran mis demás pensamientos y emociones en aquel momento, antes de recobrar la conciencia y una sobriedad parcial por lo menos, sentí una curiosidad inmediata, ya que no tenía por qué haber luz en la habitación; no era posible que hubiéramos estado toda la noche haciéndolo. Giré mi cabeza hacia donde venía la 'uz, y aun sin mi cristal, pude ver que Beu se encontraba en el umbral del cuarto, sosteniendo una lámpara encendida. No tenía idea de cuánto llevaría observando. Se apoyaba en la puerta, mientras estaba allí parada, y sin ira, pero con tristeza, me dijo:

«¿Puedes hacer eso mientras están matando a tus amigos?»

Malintzin, lánguidamente se volvió para mirar a Luna que Espera. No me extrañó ver que a ella no le importaba ser encontrada en tales circunstancias, pero hubiera esperado que cuando menos lanzara alguna exclamación de desaliento al saber que sus amigos estaban siendo exterminados. En lugar de eso, sonrió y dijo:

«*Ayyo*, qué bueno. Tenemos a un testigo mucho mejor que los guardias, Mixtzin. Nuestro pacto será más comprometedor de lo que hubiera podido esperar.»

Se puso de pie, desdeñando cubrir su cuerpo húmedo y brillante. Me eché encima mi manto, pero aun en la confusión de mi vergüenza, embarazo y borrachera, tuve la suficiente presencia de ánimo para decir: «Malintzin, creo que has estado perdiendo tu tiempo y tus favores. Ningún pacto te servirá de nada ahora.»

«Creo que el que está equivocado es *usted*, Mixtzin —dijo ella, sonriendo despreocupadamente—. Pregúntele a la anciana que está ahí parada. Ella habló de la muerte de *sus* amigos.»

Me senté de repente y jadeé: «¿Beu?»

«Sí —suspiró ella—. Nuestros hombres me hicieron volver del camino-puente. Se disculparon diciendo que no podían correr el riesgo de que alguien se comunicara con los extranjeros al otro lado del lago. Por eso volví y vine por la plaza para ver las danzas. Entonces... fue horrible...»

Cerró sus ojos, se apoyó en el marco de la puerta y dijo aturdida: «Se veían relámpagos y se oían truenos que salían del techo del palacio, y los danzantes, como por arte de alguna magia horrible, se hicieron garras y pedazos. Luego los hombres blancos y sus guerreros salieron del palacio, con más fuego y ruido y brillar de metal. Zaa, ¿sabías que una de sus espadas puede cortar a una mujer por la mitad, por la cintura? ¿Y sabías que la cabeza de un pequeño puede rodar como una pelota de *tláchtli*, Zaa? Rodó hasta llegar a mis pies. Fue cuando algo picó mi mano, y huí...»

Entonces vi que había sangre en su blusa. Corría por su brazo hasta la mano que sostenía la lámpara. Brinqué hacia ella, en el mismo momento en que se desmayó y cayó. Detuve la lámpara antes de que pudieran arder los petates que cubrían el suelo. Luego la levanté en mis brazos para colocarla sobre la cama. Malintzin, tranquilamente recogió su ropa y dijo:

«¿Ni siquiera puedes detenerte un momento para darme las gracias? Aquí estoy yo, y los guardias que podemos atestiguar que estuviste en casa y no tuviste nada que ver en ningún levantamiento.»

La miré fríamente: «Tú lo sabías; durante todo el tiempo.»

«Por supuesto. Pedro ordenó que me mantuviera fuera de peligro, por eso decidí venir aquí. Tú deseabas que no viera los preparativos de tu gente en la plaza. —Se rió—. Yo quería estar segura que tú no vieras los nuestros: por ejemplo, cómo cambiábamos el emplazamiento de los cuatro cañones para que pudieran cubrir la plaza. Pero debes reconocer, Mixtzin, que no fue una velada aburrida. Y tenemos un pacto, ¿no es así? —Se rió de nuevo y con verdadera alegría—. Jamás podrás levantar tu mano en mi contra. Ahora ya no.»

No entendí en lo absoluto lo que quiso decirme, hasta que Luna que Espera estuvo consciente y pudo decírmelo. Eso fue después de que vino el físico, quien curó su mano rota, herida por lo que debieron de ser los fragmentos disparados por los cañones de los españoles. Cuando se fue, yo permanecí sentado a la orilla de la cama. Beu yacía, sin verme, su rostro más acabado y desmejorado que antes, una lágrima corría por su mejilla y durante mucho tiempo no dijimos nada. Finalmente pude decir roncamente que lo sentía. Aun sin mirarme, me dijo:

«Jamás has sido un esposo para mí, Zaa, y nunca he sido una esposa para ti. Por lo que infidelidad hacia mí o tu omisión de ella no vale la pena discutirla. Pero tu conducta hacia alguna... alguna norma propia... eso ya es otro asunto. Copular con la mujer usada por los hombres blancos ya hubiera sido bastante vil, pero tú no copulaste con ella, no en realidad. Yo estuve ahí, y lo sé.»

Entonces Luna que Espera giró la cabeza y me contempló con una mirada que cubrió el golfo de indiferencia que nos había dividido durante tanto tiempo. Por primera vez desde los años de nuestra juventud, sentí una emanación de emoción por parte de ella que sabía que no era un fingimiento o una afectación. Sino una verdadera emoción, sólo que habría deseado que hubiera sido una emoción más cordial. Porque me miró como si hubiera visto a alguno de los monstruos humanos del zoológico, y dijo:

«Lo que tú hiciste... creo que no tiene nombre. Mientras estabas... mientras estabas con ella... movías tus manos por todo su cuerpo desnudo y murmurabas con ternura. "Zyanya, mi amor", y decías "Nochipa, mi querida", y "Zyanya, mi adorada" y exclamabas ¡otra vez!, "¡Nochipa!", y así seguías. —Tragó saliva, como para no devolver el estómago—. Porque los dos nombres quieren decir lo mismo, no sé con quién pensabas que te acostabas, si con mi hermana o con tu hija, o con las dos, o alternándolas. Pero sí sé esto: las dos mujeres llamadas Siempre, tu esposa y tu hija, murieron hace años. ¡Zaa, estabas copulando con los muertos!»

Me apena, reverendos frailes, ver que mueven sus cabezas de la misma manera que lo hizo Beu Ribé, después de decirme esas palabras aquella noche.

Ah, bueno. Puede ser que, al tratar de dar una narración honesta de mi vida y del mundo en que viví, algunas veces lo que descubro de mí mismo es más de lo que mis seres más queridos llegaron a saber de mí, quizás más de lo que yo mismo hubiera deseado saber. Pero no me retractaré, ni cambiaré nada de lo que he dicho, ni les pediré que omitan algo en sus páginas. Que quede así. Algún día mi crónica podrá servir como mi confesión a la bondadosa diosa La Que Come Suciedad, ya que los sacerdotes Cristianos prefieren confesiones más cortas de lo que pudiera ser la mía, e imponen una penitencia más larga que la vida que me queda para hacerla, y no son tan tolerantes con la humana fragilidad como lo era la misericordiosa y paciente Tlazoltéotl.

Pero si les he contado mi desliz con Malintzin aquella noche, es sólo para explicarles por qué está viva hasta este día, aunque después de eso la odié más que nunca. Mi odio se inflamó más al ver la repugnancia reflejada en los ojos de Beu y la que por ende sentí por mí mismo. Sin embargo, jamás volví a intentar nada contra la vida de Malintzin, aunque tuve otras oportunidades y de ninguna manera traté de impedir sus ambiciones. Ella tampoco me hizo daño ya que no tuvo motivo para ello, pues sus ambiciones se vieron satisfechas, ya que llegó a pertenecer a la nueva nobleza de esta Nueva España, así es que yo pasé desapercibido para ella.

He dicho que Cortés quizás quiso a esa mujer porque la mantuvo a su lado durante algunos años más. No trató de esconderla ni cuando inesperadamente llegó de Cuba su esposa Doña Catalina, a quien tenía abandonada por mucho tiempo. Doña Catalina murió unos meses después, algunos lo atribuyeron a tristeza y otros a razones menos románticas; el mismo Cortés convocó un juicio formal que lo absolvía de alguna culpabilidad por la muerte de su esposa. Poco después de eso, Malintzin dio a luz a Martín, el hijo de Cortés; el niño ahora tiene unos ocho años, y tengo entendido que pronto partirá a España, para estudiar allá.

Cortés no se apartó de Malintzin hasta después de su visita a la corte del Rey Don Carlos, de donde regresó como el Marqués del Valle, trayendo con él a su recién adquirida Marquesa Doña Juana. Entonces se aseguró de que Malintzin, a quien había hecho a un lado, quedara bien establecida económicamente. En nombre de la Corona, le dio una concesión considerable de tierra, e hizo que contrajera matrimonio en una ceremonia Cristiana con un tal Juan Jaramillo, capitán de un barco. Desgraciadamente el comedido capitán desapareció en el mar, poco después. Así que hoy en día, Malintzin es conocida por ustedes, reverendos escribanos, y por Su Ilustrísima el Obispo, quien la trata con la mayor deferencia, como Doña Marina Viuda de Jaramillo, dueña de la impresionante isla en el estado de Tacamichapa, cerca del pueblo del Espíritu Santo, el pueblo que anteriormente se llamaba Coatzacoalcos, y la isla que le concedió la Corona se encuentra en el río en donde hace mucho tiempo la muchacha esclava Uno-Caña me ofreció un trago de agua.

Doña Marina vive, porque la dejé vivir, y la dejé vivir porque, por un breve tiempo, una noche, ella fue... bien, ella representó a alguien a quien yo había amado...

Ya sea que los españoles tontamente habían estado demasiado ansiosos por devastar El Corazón del Único Mundo, o deliberadamente habían escogido hacer su ataque lo más inolvidable, punitivo y cruel; porque no había caído la noche completamente cuando sonaron sus cañones y atacaron a la multitud con sus espadas, lanzas y arcabuces, matando o hiriendo horriblemente a más de mil de las mujeres, doncellas y niños que danzaban. Pues en esos momentos, cuando apenas empezaba a oscurecer, sólo unos cuantos de nuestros guerreros mexica se habían infiltrado en la actuación, por lo que sólo habían caído unos veinte o menos, y ninguno de los campeones o señores que habían concebido la idea del levantamiento. Después de lo que hicieron los españoles, ni siquiera fueron a buscar a los conspiradores principales para castigarlos; los hombres blancos, después de su salida explosiva del palacio, se volvieron a retirar de allí y no se atrevieron a salir otra vez a la ciudad, cuya gente estaba enfurecida.

Para disculparme por haber fallado en mi intento de eliminar a Malintzin, no fui en busca de Cuitláhuac, el jefe guerrero, quien me imagino que debía de estar echando pestes de rabia y frustración. En su lugar, busqué al Señor Cuautémoc, esperando que él fuera más comprensivo ante mi fracaso. Lo había conocido cuando él era un niño e iba a visitarnos con su madre, la Primera Señora, en aquellos días en que su padre Auítzotl y mi esposa Zyanya aún vivían. En aquel tiempo, Cuautémoctzin había sido el Príncipe Heredero al trono mexica, y había sido sólo por culpa del infortunio el que no fuera Uey-Tlatoani antes de que Motecuzoma fuera puesto en ese oficio. Como Cuautémoc conocía la desilusión, pensé que sería más indulgente conmigo por no haber prevenido el que Malintzin avisara a los hombres blancos.

«Nadie lo culpa, Mixtzin —me dijo, cuando le conté cómo había eludido el veneno—. Le hubiera hecho un gran servicio al Único Mundo si se hubiera podido deshacer de esa mujer traidora, pero no importa que no lo haya logrado.»

Perplejo, le dije: «¿No importa? ¿Por qué no?»

«Porque ella no nos traicionó —dijo Cuautémoc—. Ella no tuvo que hacerlo. —Hizo una mueca como de dolor—. Fue mi honrado primo. Nuestro Venerado Orador Motecuzoma.»

«¡Qué!», exclamé.

«Cuitláhuac fue a ver al oficial Tonatíu Alvarado, como recordará, y pidió y se le concedió permiso para la ceremonia a Ixtocíuatl. En cuanto Cuitláhuac se fue del palacio, Motecuzoma le dijo a Alvarado que tuviera mucho cuidado pues era un engaño.»

«¿Por qué?»

Cuautémoc se encogió de hombros. «¿Orgullo herido? ¿Despecho vengativo? Es de suponer que a Motecuzoma no le agradaría mucho la idea de un levantamiento planeado por sus inferiores, sin su conocimiento, y hecho sin su aprobación o participación. Sea cual fuera su verdadera razón, su excusa es que no consentirá en romper su tregua con Cortés.»

Lancé una maldición, que generalmente no se aplica a los Venerados Oradores. «¿Cómo se puede comparar nuestra ruptura de una tregua, con su instigación en la matanza de mil mujeres y niños de su propia raza?»

«Imaginemos, caritativamente, que esperaba que Alvarado solamente prohibiría la celebración y que él no pensó en la posibilidad de que se dispersara a los celebrantes con tanta violencia.»

«Dispersarlos con tanta violencia —gruñí—. Ésa es una manera nueva de decir matanza sin distinción. Mi esposa, un simple espectador, fue herida. Una de sus dos sirvientas fue muerta y la otra huyó aterrorizada para esconderse en algún lado.»

«Por lo menos —dijo Cuautémoc con un suspiro— el incidente ha unido a toda nuestra gente que se siente ultrajada. Antes, solamente murmuraban y gruñían, algunos desconfiando de Motecuzoma, otros apoyándolo, pero ahora todos están listos para acabar con él, pedazo por pedazo, junto con todos los que se encuentran en el palacio.»

«Muy bien —dije—; entonces hagámoslo. Aún tenemos a la mayoría de nuestros guerreros. Levantemos también a los habitantes de la ciudad, hasta los ancianos como yo, y caigamos sobre el palacio.»

«Eso sería un suicidio. Los extranjeros han levantado barricadas por dentro, detrás de sus cañones, de sus arcabuces y de sus ballestas, apuntados desde cada ventana. No nos podríamos acercar al edificio sin ser completamente aniquilados. Debemos combatirlos en lucha cuerpo a cuerpo, como se planeó originalmente y debemos esperar a tener esa oportunidad otra vez.»

«¡Esperar!», dije, lanzando otra maldición.

«Pero mientras esperamos, Cuitláhuac está llenando la isla con más guerreros. Tal vez se haya dado cuenta de un aumento en el tráfico de canoas y lancheros de carga que cruzan de la tierra firme para acá, aparentemente llevando flores, verduras y cosas por el estilo. Escondidos debajo de esos cargamentos hay hombres y armas, son las tropas acolhua de Cacama de Texcoco, tropas tecpaneca de Tlacopan. Mientras nosotros nos hacemos fuertes, nuestros enemigos pueden debilitarse. Durante la masacre, todos sus sirvientes y asistentes huyeron del palacio. Ahora, por supuesto, ni un solo vendedor mexicatl o cargador les llevará ni comida ni nada. Dejaremos que los hombres blancos y sus amigos, Motecuzoma, Malintzin, todos ellos, se queden sentados en su fortaleza y sufran un tiempo.»

Pregunté: «¿Tiene Cuitláhuac la esperanza de rendirlos por hambre?»

«No. Estarán incómodos, pero tienen las cocinas y despensas lo suficientemente llenas como para sostenerlos hasta que Cortés regrese. Cuando lo haga, no debe encontrarnos demasiado agresivos, manteniendo el palacio bajo sitio, porque todo lo que tendría que hacer sería montar un sitio de ataque similar, alrededor de toda la isla, y dejarnos morir de hambre como nosotros lo estamos haciendo con ellos.»

«¿Por qué hemos de permitir que regrese? —le pregunté—. Sabemos que viene hacia acá. Ataquémoslo abiertamente.»

«¿Se ha olvidado de la facilidad con la que ganó la batalla de Texcala? Y ahora trae muchos más hombres, caballos y armas. No, no nos enfrentaremos con él en el campo. Cuitláhuac piensa dejar que Cortés llegue hasta aquí sin oposición y que encuentre a todas sus gentes sanas y la tregua aparentemente restaurada. No sabrá que tenemos guerreros escondidos, sólo esperando. Pero cuando lo tengamos junto con *todos* sus hombres blancos dentro de nuestro territorio, *entonces* atacaremos, suicidamente si es necesario, y limpiaremos de su suciedad esta isla y todo el distrito del lago.»

✠

Quizás los dioses decidieron que ya era tiempo que Tenochtitlan tuviera un cambio bueno en su *tonali* común, porque ese último plan sí funcionó, con unas cuantas complicaciones imprevistas.

Cuando recibimos la noticia de que Cortés y la multitud de soldados que lo acompañaban, se estaban acercando, todos en la ciudad, por órdenes del regente Cuitláhuac, asumieron una apariencia exterior de tranquilidad normal, incluso los viudos, huérfanos y demás parientes de las personas que murieron. Se colocaron los puentes exactamente igual, otra vez en los tres camino-puentes, y los viajeros y cargadores caminaban y pasaban por ellos. Los barcos y las canoas que llenaban los canales de la ciudad y el lago que rodeaba la isla llevaban en verdad cargas inofensivas. Los miles de guerreros acolhua y tecpaneca que antes habían sido transportados en secreto, bajo las narices de los aliados de Cortés que se encontraban en tierra firme, estaban escondidos desde entonces. Es más, ocho de ellos estaban viviendo en mi casa, aburridos e impacientes por algo de acción. Las calles de Tenochtitlan se encontraban tan llenas como siempre, y el mercado de Tlaltelolco tenía el mismo movimiento multicolor y seguía tan ruidoso como siempre. La única parte de la ciudad que estaba casi vacía era El Corazón del Único Mundo, con su pavimento de mármol aún salpicado de sangre, su vasta extensión sólo era atravesada por los sacerdotes de los templos que estaban allí, que continuaban cada día sus funciones, orando, cantando, quemando el incienso y soplando las trompetas de concha al amanecer, al mediodía y demás.

Cortés llegó cauteloso, temiendo alguna animosidad, porque como era natural había oído acerca de aquella masacre y no expondría a su ejército, aun siendo formidable, al riesgo de una emboscada. Después de desviarse de Texcoco a una distancia prudente, llegó a orillas del lago por el sur como antes, pero no tomó el camino-puente del sur a Tenochtitlan, pues sus hombres hubieran sido vulnerables a un ataque de canoas cargadas de guerreros, si éstos desfilaban por el espacio abierto de ese largo camino-puente. Continuó alrededor del lago y por arriba de su orilla occidental, dejando al Príncipe Flor Oscura y a sus guerreros, acomodando los grandes cañones a intervalos, todos ellos apuntados a través del agua hacia la ciudad, con hombres que los atendieran. Marchó por todo el camino hacia Tlacopan, porque ese camino-puente es mucho más corto. Primero él y más o menos cien de sus jinetes lo cruzaron galopando, temiendo que les quitaran los puentes de un momento a otro. Luego sus soldados hicieron lo mismo, corriendo en grupos como de cien hombres a la vez.

Una vez que se encontró en la isla, Cortés debió de respirar con más facilidad. No había habido ninguna emboscada ni otro obstáculo a su regreso. Aunque la gente que transitaba por las calles de la ciudad no lo saludaban con una bienvenida tumultuosa, tampoco lo rechazaban; sólo inclinaban la cabeza como si él nunca se hubiera ido. Y debió de sentirse cómodamente poderoso por estar acompañado de mil quinientos de sus compatriotas, sin mencionar el respaldo de miles de guerreros aliados, acampados en un arco alrededor de la tierra firme. Tal vez se convenció de que nosotros los mexica por fin nos habíamos resignado a reconocer su supremacía. Así que, desde el camino-puente, él y sus tropas marcharon por la ciudad como conquistadores reconocidos.

Cortés no mostró ninguna sorpresa al encontrar la plaza central desierta, tal vez pensó que la habían dejado así para que él la utilizara. De todos modos, la mayor parte de su fuerza se detuvo allí, y con mucho ruido, actividad y la pestilencia de sus humores desagradables, empezaron a atar sus caballos, sacar sus cobijas, prender fogatas y, en una palabra, a acomodarse para un estancia indeterminada. Todos los texcalteca, a excepción de sus campeones, dejaron el palacio de Axayácatl y también acamparon en la plaza. Motecuzoma y un grupo leal de sus cortesanos por primera vez salieron del palacio desde la noche de Ixtocíuatl, a recibir a Cortés, pero él desdeñosamente no les hizo caso. Él y su recién llegado compañero de armas, Narváez, pasaron entre ellos y entraron al palacio.

Me imagino que lo primero que hicieron fue gritar pidiendo comida y bebida, y me hubiera gustado ver la cara de Cortés cuando le sirvieron los soldados de Alvarado y no los sirvientes, y que solamente comió frijoles viejos, puré de *atoli* y otras provisiones como ésas. También me hubiera gustado escuchar la primera conversación entre Cortés y Alvarado, cuando ese oficial con aspecto de sol le contó cómo había controlado heroicamente ese «levantamiento» de mujeres y niños desarmados, pero cómo no pudo eliminar a un puñado de guerreros mexica, quienes todavía podían ser una amenaza.

Cortés y todo su ejército habían llegado a la isla por la tarde. Evidentemente él, Narváez y Alvarado habían permanecido juntos en conferencia hasta el anochecer, pero lo que discutieron o los planes que trazaron, nadie lo supo. Lo único que sé es que en determinado momento Cortés mandó una compañía de soldados a través de la plaza al palacio de Motecuzoma, en donde con lanzas, barras de hierro y vigas echaron abajo las paredes con que Motecuzoma había tratado de sellar los cuartos del tesoro. Luego, como hormigas trabajando entre un panal de miel, los soldados, yendo y viniendo, transportaron todo el tesoro de oro y joyas al comedor del palacio donde estaba Cortés. Eso les llevó a los hombres la mayor parte de la noche, porque costaba mucho trabajo saquear, ya que no era fácil de transportar en la forma en que estaba, por ciertas razones que es mejor que explique.

Ya que nuestros pueblos creían que el oro es el excremento sagrado de los dioses, nuestros tesoreros no lo guardaban simplemente en su forma natural de polvo o piedras, no lo derretían en formas sin expresión o hacían monedas de él como hacen ustedes los españoles. Antes de llegar a nuestra tesorería pasaba por las manos expertas de nuestros orfebres, quienes aumentaban su valor y belleza, transformándolo en figuritas, alhajas incrustadas de joyas, medallones, coronas, adornos de filigrana, jarros, tazas y platos; toda clase de obras de arte, hechas en honor a los dioses. Así que mientras Cortés debía de estar radiante de felicidad al ver la pila que constantemente crecía con ese tesoro, que sus hombres estaban colocando en el corredor y casi llenando aquella sala espaciosa, también debió fruncir el ceño al ver la variedad de formas, tan poco prácticas, como para ser transportadas, ya fuese por los caballos o los cargadores.

Mientras Cortés ocupó en esta forma su primera noche de regreso a la isla, la ciudad que lo rodeaba permaneció callada, como si nadie hiciera caso de esa actividad. Cortés se acostó poco antes del amanecer, llevándose a Malintzin con él, y de la manera más despectiva dejó dicho que Motecuzoma y sus consejeros principales estuvieran listos para verlo cuando despertara y los llamara. Así que Motecuzoma, patéticamente obediente, envió mensajeros al día siguiente muy temprano para llamar a su Consejo de Voceros y a otros incluyéndome a mí. No tenía pajes de palacio a quienes pudiera enviar; fue uno de sus hijos menores quien llegó a mi casa y estaba mal vestido y sucio después de su estancia tan larga en el palacio. Todos los conspiradores estábamos esperando tal mensaje y habíamos planeado vernos en la casa de Cuitláhuac. Cuando nos reunimos, todos mirábamos expectantes al regente y jefe guerrero, y uno de los consejeros ancianos le preguntó:

«¿Obedecemos el mandato o lo ignoramos?»

«Obedecemos —respondió Cuitláhuac—. Cortés aún piensa que nos tiene indefensos por retener a nuestro complaciente gobernante en su poder. No lo desilusionemos.»

«¿Por qué no? —preguntó el alto sacerdote de Huitzilopochtli—. Estamos listos para nuestro asalto. Cortés no puede meter todo ese ejército dentro del palacio de Axayácatl, poniendo barricadas en contra de nosotros, como lo hizo Tonatíu Alvarado.»

«No tiene que hacerlo —dijo Cuitláhuac—. Si le damos la más ligera alarma, rápidamente puede convertir todo El Corazón del Único Mundo en una fortaleza tan impenetrable como lo fue el palacio. Debemos dejar que se confíe con falsa seguridad, un poco más. Iremos al palacio como se nos pidió y actuaremos como si nosotros y todos los mexica todavía fuéramos los muñecos dóciles y pasivos de Motecuzoma.»

El Mujer Serpiente señaló: «Cortés podría mandar cerrar la entrada cuando estemos allí y también nos tendría como rehenes.»

«Soy consciente de eso —dijo Cuitláhuac—. Pero todos mis campeones y *quachictin* ya tienen sus órdenes, no necesitarán de mi presencia. Una de mis consignas es que continúen haciendo los diferentes artificios y movimientos, sea cual sea el peligro en que me encuentre o en que se encuentre quien esté en el palacio en el momento de atacar. Si prefiere no compartir ese riesgo, Tlácotzin, o alguno de ustedes, en este momento les doy permiso de irse a sus casas.»

Por supuesto que ningún hombre se echó para atrás. Todos acompañamos a Cuitláhuac al Corazón del Único Mundo, y con fastidio nos abrimos paso entre la multitud apestosa de hombres, caballos, fogatas, armas amontonadas y demás cosas. Me sorprendió ver, agrupado en un área a un lado de los hombres blancos como si fueran inferiores, un contingente de hombres *negros*. Me habían hablado acerca de esos seres, pero hasta entonces nunca los había visto.

Movido por la curiosidad, dejé por un momento a mis compañeros para ver más de cerca a esos seres extraños. Usaban casquetes y uniformes idénticos a los de los españoles, pero físicamente se parecían menos a ellos que yo. No eran realmente *negros*, negros, pero sí de un pardo negruzco, como el corazón de madera del árbol de ébano. Tenían narices peculiarmente planas y grandes, labios protuberantes —en verdad se parecían a aquellas cabezas de piedra gigantescas, que una vez vi en la nación olmeca— y sus barbas sólo eran como una pelusa negra y rizada, casi invisible hasta que me acerqué. Pero entonces estuve lo suficientemente cerca para observar que uno de los hombres negros tenía la cara cubierta con granos rojos y pústulas que supuraban, como los que había visto hacía mucho tiempo en la cara del hombre blanco llamado Guerrero, y rápidamente me fui a reunir con mis señores compañeros.

Al llegar a la entrada del Muro de la Serpiente, que da paso al palacio de Axayácatl, los centinelas blancos allí apostados nos registraron, buscando armas escondidas, antes de dejarnos pasar. Pasamos por el comedor en el que, a semejanza de una montaña, se encontraban tiradas las alhajas, las joyas y el oro, que resplandecían ricamente aun en ese cuarto oscuro. Varios soldados, que se suponía que debían estar cuidando el tesoro, manoseaban algunas piezas, sonriéndoles y casi babeando sobre ellas. Subimos al salón del trono en donde nos esperaba Cortés, Alvarado y muchos españoles más, incluyendo al recién llegado Narváez. Motecuzoma se veía cercado y oprimido, ya que la mujer Malintzin era la única de su raza entre esa multitud de blancos hasta que nosotros llegamos. Todos besamos la tierra enfrente de él, pero él sólo nos saludó con una inclinación de cabeza, mientras continuaba hablando con otros hombres blancos.

«Yo no sabía cuáles eran las intenciones de la gente. Sólo sabía que planeaban una ceremonia. Por medio de su Malintzin le dije a Alvarado que sería mejor no permitir que esa reunión se llevara a efecto tan cerca de esta guarnición, que sería mejor que él ordenara que la plaza quedara libre de gente —dijo Motecuzoma y suspiró trágicamente—. Bueno, ustedes saben de qué manera tan calamitosa la dejó libre de gente.»

«Sí —dijo Cortés entre dientes. Sus ojos opacos miraron fríamente a Alvarado, quien estaba parado, retorciéndose los dedos y se veía como si hubiese pasado una noche muy mala—. Pudo haber arruinado todos mis... —Cortés tosió y en lugar de eso dijo—: Pude haberme convertido en el enemigo de toda vuestra gente, para siempre. Lo que me extraña, Don Montezuma, es que no fue así. ¿Por *qué* no? Si fuera uno de vuestros súbditos y hubiera sufrido tan mal trato, yo habría tirado por lo menos mi excremento, pero nadie en la ciudad parece mostrar ni la más mínima señal de odio, y eso me parece muy poco natural. Hay un proverbio español que dice: "Puedo evitar el torrente turbulento; que Dios me cuide de las aguas tranquilas."»

«Es porque todos me culpan a mí —dijo Motecuzoma sintiéndose desdichado—. Ellos creen que insensatamente ordené matar a mi propia gente, a todas aquellas mujeres y niños, y que cobardemente empleé a sus hombres como armas. —Para entonces, tenía lágrimas en los ojos—. Por eso todos mis criados me dejaron, disgustados y desde entonces no se ha parado por aquí ni siquiera un vendedor de gusanos fritos de maguey.»

«Sí. Qué situación tan difícil —dijo Cortés—. Debemos remediar eso. —Volvió su rostro a Cuitláhuac, e indicándome que tradujera, le dijo—: Usted es el jefe guerrero. No especularé sobre la verdadera intención de esa supuesta celebración religiosa. Hasta me disculparé humildemente por la impetuosidad de mi propio teniente, pero le recuerdo que todavía existe una tregua. Debo pensar que es responsabilidad de un jefe guerrero el procurar que mis hombres no queden segregados y aislados, privados de comida y de contacto humano con sus anfitriones.»

Cuitláhuac respondió: «Sólo estoy al frente de los guerreros, Señor Capitán General. Si la población civil prefiere esquivar este lugar, yo no tengo ninguna autoridad para ordenarles lo contrario. Ésta solamente reside en el Venerado Orador; fueron sus propios hombres los que se encerraron aquí, junto con el Venerado Orador.»

Cortés se dirigió nuevamente a Motecuzoma. «Entonces la decisión es vuestra, Don Montezuma, vos debéis aplacar a vuestra gente y convencerla de que nos surtan otra vez de provisiones y de que nos sirvan.»

«¿Cómo puedo hacerlo si no se me acercan? —preguntó Motecuzoma, gimiendo—. ¡Y si salgo a su encuentro, tal vez vaya a mi muerte!»

«Os proporcionaremos una escolta...», empezó a decir Cortés, cuando un soldado entró corriendo y lo interrumpió diciendo:

«Mi Capitán, los nativos empiezan a reunirse en la plaza. Hombres y mujeres se están juntando alrededor de nuestro campamento y vienen para acá. No traen armas, pero sus expresiones no son muy amistosas. ¿Los expulsamos? ¿Los rechazamos?»

«Dejad que lleguen —respondió Cortés y luego le dijo a Narváez—: Ve ahí y toma el mando. La orden es: no disparéis. Ni un hombre debe moverse hasta que *yo* lo ordene. Estaré en el techo donde podré ver todo lo que pasa. ¡Ven, Pedro! ¡Venga, Don Montezuma!» De hecho cogió la mano del Venerado Orador y lo tiró del trono.

Todos los que nos encontrábamos en el salón del trono los seguimos, corriendo por las escaleras hasta llegar a la azotea y pude escuchar a Malintzin que jadeando repetía a Motecuzoma las instrucciones de Cortés:

«Vuestra gente se está reuniendo en la plaza. Se dirigirá a ellos. Haga la paz con ellos, y si vos lo deseáis, podéis echar toda la culpa sobre nosotros los españoles. ¡Dígales *lo que sea* con tal de mantener la calma en esta ciudad!»

La azotea había sido un jardín poco antes de la primera llegada del hombre blanco, pero había estado sin ser atendido desde entonces y además había aguantado todo un invierno. En donde las ruedas pesadas de los cañones no habían hecho surcos, sólo quedaba un terreno seco y árido, ramas secas, arbustos pelones, cabezas de flores muertas y hojas parduscas barridas por el viento. Desde esa plataforma, desolada y sombría, Motecuzoma pronunció su último discurso.

Todos nosotros fuimos hacia el parapeto que dominaba la plaza y nos paramos en fila a lo largo de esa barda, asomándonos hacia El Corazón del Único Mundo. Fácilmente se identificaban los mil o más españoles que estaban en la plaza, por el brillo de sus armaduras, ya fuera que estuvieran parados o moviéndose inseguros, entre la multitud de mexica que casi los doblaba en cantidad, y quienes estaban llegando y convergiendo hacia nosotros. Como el mensajero había informado, había tantos hombres como mujeres, y sólo vestían su ropa de diario, y no mostraban ni interés en los soldados o en el hecho sin precedente de que un campamento armado se hubiera levantado sobre esa tierra sagrada. Solamente se abrieron camino entre ese desorden, sin prisas pero sin titubear, hasta que debajo de nosotros hubo una multitud compacta.

«El cabo tenía razón —dijo Alvarado—, no traen ninguna arma.»

Cortés le respondió con acritud: «Justamente la clase de oponentes que te gustan, ¿eh, Pedro? —y la cara de Alvarado casi se puso tan roja como su barba. Dirigiéndose a todos sus hombres presentes, Cortés dijo—: Nosotros hagámonos para atrás, que no nos vean. Dejad que el pueblo sólo vea a su soberano y a sus señores.»

Él, Malintzin y los otros retrocedieron hasta quedar en medio de la azotea. Motecuzoma se aclaró nerviosamente la garganta y luego tuvo que gritar tres veces, cada vez más fuerte, antes de que la multitud lo pudiera escuchar entre su propio murmullo y el ruido del campamento. Algunos puntos negros se convirtieron en color carne al levantar sus cabezas, hasta que finalmente todos los mexica congregados estaban mirando hacia arriba y muchas de las caras blancas también, y entonces la multitud se calló.

«Mi pueblo... —empezó Motecuzoma con voz ronca. Aclaró su garganta otra vez, y entonces dijo fuerte y con claridad—: Mi pueblo...»

«¡*Tu* pueblo!», y ese grito hostil y concentrado llegó hasta nosotros y luego un clamor de gritos confusos y enojados. «¡El pueblo que traicionaste!» «¡Tu gente son los blancos!» «¡Tú no eres nuestro Orador!» «¡Ya no eres Venerado!» Me extrañó oírlo aunque ya lo había estado esperando, sabiendo que todo había sido arreglado por Cuitláhuac y que todos los hombres de esa multitud eran guerreros temporalmente sin armas para aparentar que toda la población se reunía para hacer patente su público desprecio.

Más bien debería decir que no estaban armados con armas ordinarias, porque en ese momento todos sacaron piedras y pedazos de adobe, los hombres de debajo de sus mantos, las mujeres de debajo de sus faldas y aún gritando imprecaciones comenzaron a lanzarlos hacia arriba. La mayoría de las pedradas de las mujeres no llegaron a la azotea, sino que golpearon contra el muro del palacio, debajo de nosotros, pero bastantes piedras alcanzaron la azotea y tuvimos que evadirlas. El sacerdote de Huitzilopochtli lanzó una exclamación muy poco sacerdotal cuando una de las piedras lo golpeó en un hombro. Varios de los españoles que estaban detrás de nosotros, también maldijeron al ser alcanzados por las pedradas. El único hombre, y debo decirlo, que no se movió fue Motecuzoma. Se quedó donde estaba, erguido, levantando sus brazos en gesto conciliador, y gritó por encima del ruido: «¡Esperen!» Lo dijo en náhuatl: «*¡Mixchia...!*», y fue entonces cuando le golpeó una piedra en la frente, se tambaleó hacia atrás y cayó inconsciente.

Cortés tomó inmediatamente otra vez el mando, y me gritó: «¡Atiéndelo! ¡Haz que descanse!» Y agarrando a Cuitláhuac del manto, y apuntándole con su dedo, le dijo: «Haz lo que puedas. Di lo que sea. Hay que calmar a esa multitud.» Malintzin le tradujo a Cuitláhuac y éste estaba en el parapeto gritando, cuando yo junto con dos oficiales españoles cargamos el cuerpo flojo de Motecuzoma hacia abajo y lo llevamos nuevamente al salón del trono. Acostamos al hombre inconsciente en una banca que estaba allí y los dos oficiales salieron corriendo hacia afuera, me imagino que para ir en busca de alguno de los cirujanos de su ejército.

Me puse de pie y contemplé el rostro de Motecuzoma, relajado y tranquilo a pesar del chichón que empezaba a salir sobre su frente. Entonces pensé en muchas cosas: en los eventos y sucesos de nuestras vidas simultáneas. Recordé su desafío desleal hacia su propio Venerado Orador Auítzotl, durante la campaña en Uaxyácac... y en la forma tan innoble y miserable en que trató allí de violar a la hermana de mi esposa... y en sus muchas amenazas en mi contra en el transcurso de los años... y de su manera tan rencorosa de enviarme a Yanquitlan, en donde mi hija Nochipa murió... y en sus débiles vacilaciones desde que aparecieron los primeros hombres blancos en nuestras costas... y en su traición al intento hecho por hombres más valientes de librar a nuestra ciudad de esos hombres blancos. Sí, tenía muchas razones para hacer lo que hice y algunas de ellas eran inmediatas y urgentes, pero supongo, que sobre todo eso lo maté para vengarme de su viejo insulto a Beu Ribé, quien había sido la hermana de Zyanya y que entonces era mi esposa, aunque fuera sólo de nombre.

Estos recuerdos pasaron por mi mente en un momento. Dejé de verlo y miré alrededor del cuarto, buscando un arma. Había dos guerreros texcalteca en la habitación, a quienes habían dejado como guardias, y le hice una seña a uno de ellos para que se acercara, éste vino ceñudo hacia mí y cuando estuvo cerca le pedí que me diera la daga de obsidiana que llevaba en la cintura. Él me miró todavía más ceñudo, sin estar seguro de mi identidad, rango o intención, pero entonces se la pedí como un gran señor, con voz fuerte e inmediatamente me la entregó. La coloqué con cuidado, porque había presenciado suficientes sacrificios como para saber exactamente dónde está el corazón en un pecho humano, y entonces la empujé hasta el fondo y el corazón de Motecuzoma dejó de latir para siempre. Dejé la daga en la herida, así es que sólo un poco de sangre salió de ella. El guardia texcaltécalt se quedó viendo horrorizado, y luego él y su compañero salieron coriendo del cuarto.

Apenas lo hice a tiempo. Escuché el clamor de la multitud aunque se oía un poco más apaciguada. Entonces toda la gente que se encontraba en la azotea bajó ruidosamente las escaleras por el corredor y entraron al salón del trono. Hablaban alterados o preocupados en sus diferentes idiomas, pero de pronto se quedaron callados al pararse en el umbral de la puerta, cuando se dieron cuenta de la enormidad de mi hazaña. Se acercaron lentamente, todos juntos, los españoles y los señores mexica, sorprendidos, y muchos miraban el cuerpo de Motecuzoma, la empuñadura de la daga que salía de su pecho, a mí que estaba imperturbable parado junto al cadáver. Cortés me miró con sus ojos opacos y dijo con suavidad, peligrosamente:

«¿Qué... has... hecho?»

Contesté: «Lo que ordenó, señor, lo puse a descansar.»

«Maldita tu insolencia, hijo de puta —dijo, pero aún sin levantar la voz, con furia contenida—. Ya he escuchado tus burlas antes.»

Con calma meneé mi cabeza. «Porque Motecuzoma está descansando, Capitán General, quizás también todos nosotros podremos descansar un poco. Incluyéndolo a usted.»

Dejó caer uno de sus dedos sobre mi pecho, luego lo alzó apuntando hacia la plaza. «¡Afuera hay un levantamiento que puede terminar en guerra! ¿Y quién va a controlar ahora a esa gente?»

«Motecuzoma no lo hubiera hecho, ni vivo ni muerto, pero aquí se encuentra su sucesor, su hermano Cuitláhuac, un hombre de mano firme y un hombre que aún es respetado por esa gente.»

Cortés se volvió para mirar al jefe guerrero, aunque con ciertas dudas y yo pude adivinar lo que pensaba. Cuitláhuac podría dominar a los mexica, pero Cortés aún no dominaba a Cuitláhuac. Como si también adivinara sus pensamientos, Malintzin dijo:

«Podemos poner a prueba al nuevo soberano, Señor Hernán. Vayamos nuevamente a la azotea, mostremos el cadáver de Motecuzoma a la multitud, dejemos que Cuitláhuac proclame su sucesión y veamos si la gente obedece su primera orden: que nos vuelvan a servir y a alimentar bien otra vez en este palacio.»

«Qué idea tan astuta, Malinche —dijo Cortés—. Dale esas instrucciones precisamente. También dile que debe aclarar bien que Montezuma murió —y sacó la daga del cuerpo y, mirándome de mala manera, siguió—: que Montezuma murió a manos de su propia gente.»

Así pues, regresamos a la azotea, pero todos nos quedamos atrás mientras Cuitláhuac, tomando el cadáver de su hermano en brazos, se paró junto a la barda y gritó para atraer la atención. Mientras mostraba el cadáver y les comunicaba la noticia, el ruido que nos llegó de la plaza fue un murmullo que parecía de aprobación. Entonces sucedió otra cosa: una lluvia suave empezó a caer del cielo, como si Tláloc, y sólo Tláloc, y ningún otro ser más que Tláloc, lamentara el final de los caminos, los días y el reinado de Motecuzoma. Cuitláhuac habló lo suficientemente fuerte como para ser escuchado por la gente reunida abajo, pero de una manera tranquila y persuasiva. Malintzin le traducía a Cortés, y le aseguró: «El nuevo gobernante habla según se le indicó.»

Al fin, Cuitláhuac se volvió hacia nosotros y nos hizo un gesto con la cabeza para que todos nos acercáramos al borde de la azotea, mientras que dos o tres sacerdotes le quitaban el peso del cadáver de Motecuzoma. La gente que había estado sólidamente apretada bajo el muro del palacio se estaba separando y abriéndose camino otra vez entre la barahúnda del campamento. Como algunos de los soldados españoles estaban todavía nerviosos y ponían sus manos sobre sus armas, Cortés les gritó: «¡Dejad que vayan y vengan sin impedírselo, mis muchachos! ¡Nos traen comida fresca!» Los soldados estaban gritando alegremente cuando todos bajamos de la azotea por última vez.

Una vez que estuvimos en el salón del trono, Cuitláhuac miró a Cortés y dijo: «Tenemos que hablar.» Cortés estuvo de acuerdo: «Sí, debemos hablar», y mandó llamar a Malintzin, como si desconfiara de mi traducción sin la presencia de su propio traductor. Cuitláhuac dijo:

«El que yo le diga a la gente que soy su Uey-Tlatoani no quiere decir que lo sea. Deben observarse ciertas formalidades y en público. Comenzaremos las ceremonias de sucesión esta misma tarde, cuando aún quede algo de luz. Como sus tropas han ocupado El Corazón del Único Mundo, yo, junto con los sacerdotes y el Consejo de Voceros —con un gesto de su brazo incluyó a cada uno de los mexica que nos encontrábamos en la habitación—, nos iremos a la pirámide de Tlaltelolco.»

Cortés dijo: «Oh, pero seguramente que no lo haréis ahora. La lluvia se está convirtiendo en una tormenta. Esperad a un día más propicio, mi señor. Os invito como nuevo Venerado Orador a que seáis mi huésped en este palacio, como lo fue Montezuma.»

Cuitláhuac contestó con firmeza: «Si permanezco aquí, no seré el Venerado Orador, por lo tanto soy inútil como su huésped. ¿Qué prefiere?»

Cortés frunció el ceño; no estaba acostumbrado a oír hablar a un Venerado Orador como un Venerado Orador. Cuitláhuac continuó:

«Aun después de quedar formalmente confirmado como Uey-Tlatoani por los sacerdotes y el Consejo de Voceros, debo ganarme la confianza y la aprobación de la gente. Podría hacerlo si les dijera exactamente cuándo piensa partir el Capitán General y su compañía de este palacio.»

«Bueno... —dijo Cortés, prolongando la palabra, dejando claro que no se había tomado el tiempo de pensar en eso, y que no tenía ninguna prisa—. Le prometí a vuestro hermano que partiría cuando estuviera listo para llevarme el regalo del tesoro que ofreció donarme. Ahora ya lo tengo. Pero me llevará algo de tiempo el hacerlo derretir para poder transportarlo a la costa.»

«Eso le podría llevar años —dijo Cuitláhuac—. Nuestros orfebres rara vez trabajan con pedazos grandes de oro. Así es que usted no encontrará ninguna facilidad en esta ciudad para hacer la profanación de derretir todos esos incontables objetos de arte.»

«Y no debo quedarme aquí por años, abusando de la hospitalidad de mi anfitrión —dijo Cortés—. Así que ordenaré que se lleve el oro a tierra firme y dejaré que mis propios orfebres lo hagan más compacto.»

Groseramente, le dio la espalda a Cuitláhuac y se dirigió a Alvarado diciéndole en español: «Pedro, manda traer a algunos de nuestros artesanos. Déjame ver... que quiten estas puertas bromosas, y todas las otras que hayan en el palacio. Que se construyan unas angarillas pesadas para poder cargar todo ese oro. También ve que se hagan los arneses adecuados para que los caballos puedan tirar de las angarillas.»

Se dirigió nuevamente a Cuitláhuac: «Mientras tanto, Señor Orador, os pido vuestro permiso para que yo y mis hombres permanezcamos en la ciudad por lo menos un tiempo razonable. La mayor parte de mi compañía actual, como vos sabéis, no estuvo conmigo durante mi visita previa, y como es natural están muy ansiosos por ver los atractivos de vuestra gran ciudad.»

«Por un tiempo razonable, entonces —repitió Cuitláhuac, asintiendo con la cabeza—. Así se lo haré saber a la gente, y les pediré que sean tolerantes, hasta afables, si es que pueden serlo. Ahora, mis señores y yo los dejamos para comenzar los preparativos para el funeral de mi hermano, así como mi propia ascensión. Cuanto más pronto terminemos esas formalidades, más pronto podré ser su huésped de verdad.»

Cuando todos los que habíamos sido llamados por Motecuzoma, hubimos dejado el palacio, los soldados-carpinteros españoles estaban mirando la montaña de tesoro en el comedor de la planta baja, estimando su tamaño y peso. Pasamos por El Muro de la Serpiente a la plaza y nos detuvimos a ver la actividad allí. Los hombres blancos que se movían de un lado a otro, en sus diversas labores de campamento, se veían bastante molestos por la humedad ya que para entonces la lluvia era muy fuerte. Una cantidad igual de nuestros propios hombres se movían entre los españoles, ocupados o tratando de parecer ocupados, todos desnudos a excepción de sus taparrabos, por lo que la lluvia no les era muy molesta. Hasta ahora, el plan de Cuitláhuac estaba saliendo bien, tal y como nos lo había explicado, a excepción de la muerte de Motecuzoma que aunque imprevista, no fue desafortunada.

Todo lo que les he contado, reverendos escribanos, había sido planeado por Cuitláhuac hasta en el más mínimo detalle, mucho antes de estar ante la presencia de Cortés. Él había ordenado que ese grupo de hombres y mujeres mexica se reunieran fuera del palacio para demostrar su hostilidad. Él había ordenado que después se dispersaran y consiguieran alimento y bebida para los hombres blancos. Pero los españoles no se dieron cuenta, en la confusión, que sólo las *mujeres* de aquella multitud habían dejado la plaza, al recibir esa orden. Cuando regresaron, no entraron al campamento otra vez, sino entregaron sus bandejas, jarras y canastas a los hombres que se habían quedado. Por eso ya no había ninguna mujer en esa área de peligro, con excepción de Malintzin y sus doncellas texcalteca, cuya seguridad nos tenía muy sin cuidado. Y nuestros hombres seguían yendo y viniendo, dentro y fuera del palacio, de un lado a otro del campamento, repartiendo carne, maíz y demás alimentos, portando leña seca para las fogatas de los soldados, cocinando en las cocinas del palacio, haciendo todo aquel trabajo que podría justificar su presencia en ese lugar... y que los mantendría allí hasta que las trompetas conchas del templo señalaran la medianoche.

«A la medianoche atacaremos —nos recordó Cuitláhuac—. Para entonces, Cortés y todos éstos ya se habrán acostumbrado al tráfico constante y la servilidad aparente de nuestros hombres casi desnudos y desarmados. Mientras tanto, que Cortés escuche la música y vea el humo de incienso de lo que parece ser una jubilosa ceremonia, preliminar a mi coronación. Encuentren y junten a todos los sacerdotes posibles. Ya se les avisó que deben aguardar mis instrucciones, pero ustedes deben empujarlos, ya que ellos, al igual que los hombres blancos, han de renegar pues esta lluvia los va a dejar limpios. Reúnan a todos los sacerdotes en la pirámide de Tlaltelolco para que representen el espectáculo más ruidoso y lucido que jamás se haya hecho. También que se reúnan allí todas las mujeres y niños, todos los hombres que estén imposibilitados de pelear; así parecerá una ceremonia bastante convincente y además allí estarán seguros.»

«Señor Regente —dijo uno de los consejeros ancianos—, quiero decir, Señor Orador, ¿si los extranjeros han de morir a la medianoche, por qué presionó a Cortés para que diera una fecha de partida?»

Cuitláhuac miró fijamente al anciano; y aposté a que éste no permanecería mucho tiempo como miembro del Consejo. «Cortés no es tan tonto como usted, mi señor. Sabe que quiero deshacerme de él. Si no hubiera hablado tan enérgica e insistentemente, podría haber sospechado que lo quiero echar por la fuerza. Por el momento tengo la esperanza de que se sienta seguro, pues he aceptado aunque a disgusto su presencia. Espero fervientemente que no cambie de parecer de aquí a la medianoche.»

No cambió. Por lo visto, Cortés no sentía ninguna preocupación por su seguridad y la de los suyos, sino que estaba aparentemente mucho más ansioso de poner fuera del alcance de sus verdaderos dueños el botín del tesoro, o quizás viendo las calles mojadas decidió que eso facilitaba a los caballos el tirar de su pesada carga. De cualquier forma, a pesar de que tuvieron que trabajar bajo la molesta lluvia, para el anochecer sus soldados-carpinteros ya tenían armados y clavados dos artefactos parecidos a unos lanchones de tierra. Entonces otros soldados, ayudados por algunos de nuestros propios hombres que aún estaban prestando sus servicios a los españoles, sacaron el oro y las joyas del palacio y las distribuyeron en montones iguales dentro de esas angarillas. Mientras tanto, otros soldados utilizaron un enredo enorme de tiras de cuero para juntar cuatro caballos por carga. Aún faltaba tiempo para la medianoche cuando Cortés dio la orden de partir, y los caballos se inclinaron bajo sus telarañas de cuero, como los cargadores humanos se doblan bajo el peso de las bandas colocadas en sus frentes, y las angarillas se deslizaron con bastante facilidad a través del mármol mojado de El Corazón del Único Mundo.

Aunque la mayor parte del ejército blanco permaneció en la plaza, una escolta bastante grande de soldados armados salieron con la caravana, que era guiada por los tres españoles de mayor rango: Cortés, Narváez y Alvarado. Estoy de acuerdo en que trasladar ese inmenso tesoro era una tarea laboriosa, pero no necesitaba la atención personal de los tres comandantes, más bien sospecho que ninguno de ellos podía confiar ni siquiera por un pequeño espacio de tiempo toda esa riqueza, sin que alguno de ellos se quedara con ella a la primera oportunidad. Malintzin también acompañó a su amo, probablemente sólo con el fin de disfrutar de una refrescante excursión, después de todo el tiempo que llevaba encerrada en el palacio. Las angarillas se deslizaron hacia el oeste, cruzando la plaza y entrando en la calzada de Tlacopan. Ninguno de los hombres blancos sospechó en lo absoluto al ver que no había gente fuera de la plaza, pues podían escuchar el ruido de los tambores y la música procedente del extremo norte de la isla, y podían ver que las nubes más bajas, que estaban en esa dirección, se veían teñidas de rojo por el brillo de las luces de las antorchas y de los fuegos de las urnas.

Así como tuvimos esa oportunidad inesperada para quitar de en medio a Motecuzoma, como posible obstáculo a nuestros planes, la orden de Cortés de trasladar inesperada y repentinamente su tesoro, fue un hecho impredecible que obligó a Cuitláhuac a llevar a cabo su ataque más temprano de lo que había pensado. Y así como la muerte de Motecuzoma fue una ventaja para Cuitláhuac, ese hecho también lo fue. Mientras la caravana del tesoro se deslizaba por la calzada de Tlacopan, era obvio que estaba tomando el camino más corto para llegar a la tierra firme, por lo que Cuitláhuac podía llamar a los guerreros que había puesto para cuidar las otras dos calzadas y aumentar así su fuerza para atacar. Luego corrió la voz entre todos sus campeones y *quáchictin*: «No esperéis las trompetas de medianoche. ¡Atacad *ahora*!»

Debo hacer notar que yo me encontraba en casa con Luna que Espera durante los sucesos que ahora estoy contando, porque yo era de los hombres a quienes Cuitláhuac caritativamente había descrito como «imposibilitados de pelear»: hombres demasiado viejos o que no estaban en condiciones para tomar parte en la lucha. Por lo tanto no presencié personalmente lo que sucedió en la isla y en tierra firme, y en ese caso ningún testigo ocular pudo haber estado en todos esos lugares al mismo tiempo, pero como más tarde estuve presente para escuchar los informes de varios de nuestros campeones, es por lo que les puedo decir con bastante precisión, señores frailes, todo lo que sucedió en esa noche, que desde entonces Cortés llamó la «Noche Triste».

A la orden de atacar, el primer movimiento fue hecho por algunos de aquellos hombres que se encontraban en El Corazón del Único Mundo desde que se apedreó a Motecuzoma. Su trabajo era de soltar y dispersar a los caballos de los españoles y estos hombres debían ser valientes porque en ninguna batalla jamás se había visto que ninguno de nuestros guerreros tuviera que pelear con criaturas que no fueran humanas. Aunque algunos de los caballos se habían ido en la caravana del tesoro, aún quedaban unos ochenta, todos amarrados en un rincón de la plaza donde se encontraba el templo que se había convertido en capilla cristiana. Nuestros hombres desataron los tirantes de cuero que detenían a los caballos y prendiendo unos palos de la fogata más cercana corrieron entre los animales espantándolos. Los caballos sintieron pánico y corrieron por todas partes, galopando por el campamento, pateando los arcabuces apilados, pisoteando a varios de sus dueños y provocando que todos los otros hombres blancos corrieran en confusión, gritando y maldiciendo.

Luego la masa de nuestros guerreros armados penetraron a la plaza. Cada uno de ellos portaba dos *maquáhuime,* y el arma que llevaban de más, se la tiraban a alguno de los hombres que ya llevaban tiempo dentro de la plaza. Ninguno de nuestros guerreros llevaba la armadura acojinada, porque no era de mucha protección en un combate cuerpo a cuerpo, y hubiera restringido sus movimientos al quedar empapada por la lluvia; nuestros hombres pelearon sólo con el taparrabo. La plaza estaba iluminada tenuemente durante esa noche, ya que las fogatas para calentar la comida de los soldados habían sido protegidas contra la lluvia por escudos y demás objetos colocados alrededor o encima de ellos. Los caballos que corrían y coccaban acabaron con la mayoría de esas fogatas y desconcertaron a los soldados de tal forma que fueron tomados casi completamente por sorpresa, cuando nuestros guerreros casi desnudos salieron de las sombras, matando y cortando todo lo que alcanzaron a ver como piel blanca o caras barbudas o cualquier cuerpo portando una armadura de acero, mientras otros guerreros se abrieron paso hacia el palacio que Cortés acababa de dejar.

Los españoles al mando de los cañones que estaban en la azotea del palacio escucharon la conmoción de abajo, pero casi no podían ver lo que estaba sucediendo, y de todos modos no podían descargar sus armas en contra del campamento de sus propios compañeros. Otra circunstancia que estuvo a nuestro favor fue que los pocos españoles que pudieron apoderarse de sus arcabuces se encontraron con que estaban tan mojados que no pudieron escupir sus rayos, sus truenos y muerte. Una cantidad de soldados dentro del palacio, sí lograron utilizarlos una sola vez, pero no tuvieron tiempo de volver a cargarlos antes de que una multitud de nuestros guerreros estuvieran encima de ellos. Así que cada hombre blanco y texcaltécatl que se encontraba dentro del palacio fue aniquilado o capturado, y nuestros propios hombres sufrieron pocos daños. Sin embargo, nuestros guerreros que se encontraban peleando afuera en El Corazón del Único Mundo, no pudieron luchar tan rápido, ni obtuvieron una victoria total, pues después de todo, los españoles y sus texcaltecas eran hombres valientes y soldados adiestrados, y al sobreponerse de esa sorpresa inicial, se defendieron hábilmente. Los texcalteca tenían armas iguales a las nuestras y los blancos, aun sin sus arcabuces, tenían espadas y lanzas muy superiores a las nuestras.

Aunque yo no estuve allí, puedo imaginarme la escena, debió de haber sido como una guerra que tiene lugar en nuestro Mictlan o en su infierno. Esa inmensa plaza estaba escasamente iluminada por los restos de las fogatas, y las brasas humeantes esporádicamente estallaban en chispas cuando hombres o caballos tropezaban con ellas. La lluvia seguía cayendo y creando un velo que no permitía ver a los combatientes cómo les estaba yendo a sus compañeros en otros lugares. Todo ese espacio estaba cubierto con cobijas enredadas, los bultos de los españoles con su contenido desparramado, los restos de las cenas, muchos cadáveres tirados y mucha sangre que hacía que el mármol fuera más resbaladizo. El brillo de las espadas y hebillas de acero y las caras blancas y pálidas contrastaba con los cuerpos desnudos, pero menos visibles, de nuestros guerreros de piel bronceada. Se llevaban a efecto duelos separados en todas partes de las escaleras de la Gran Pirámide, y dentro y fuera de los muchos templos, bajo las miradas tranquilas de las innumerables calaveras sin ojos de la barra. Para hacer aún más irreal la batalla, los caballos aterrados todavía se arremolinaban, saltando, corriendo y pateando. El Muro de la Serpiente era demasiado alto como para saltarlo, pero de vez en cuando un caballo hallaba fortuitamente una de las entradas a la calzada y se escapaba por las calles de la ciudad.

Hubo un momento en donde cierta cantidad de hombres blancos retrocedieron hacia una esquina lejana de la plaza, mientras una hilera de sus compañeros, usando sus espadas con habilidad, trataban de impedir que nuestros hombres los persiguieran, y esa retirada aparente, resultó ser una táctica astuta. Aquellos que habían huido, al hacerlo se llevaron unos arcabuces y durante su breve pausa del ataque, pudieron cargar sus armas con municiones secas que llevaban en unas bolsitas a la cintura. Los espadachines se hicieron de pronto para atrás, y los que portaban los arcabuces caminaron hacia adelante y todos al mismo tiempo descargaron sus balas mortales a la multitud de guerreros que los habían estado combatiendo y muchos de nuestros hombres cayeron muertos o heridos en ese solo rugir de trueno. Pero los arcabuces no pudieron cargarse otra vez antes de que más de nuestros hombres estuvieran combatiéndolos hacia adelante. Por eso, desde ese momento, la lucha fue entre armas de piedra contra armas de acero.

No sé cómo Cortés se dio cuenta de que algo le estaba pasando al ejército que había dejado sin comandante. Tal vez uno de los caballos sueltos pasó galopando por una de las calles o quizás un soldado logró escapar de la lucha, o lo primero que escucharían sus oídos, fue el gran trueno que a un mismo tiempo soltaron los arcabuces. Lo que sí sé es que todo su grupo y él, ya habían llegado al camino-puente de Tlacopan antes de darse cuenta que algo malo estaba sucediendo. En un momento decidió lo que se debía hacer, y aunque más tarde nadie pudo repetir palabra por palabra lo que él dijo en esos momentos, lo que decidió fue: «No podemos dejar el tesoro aquí. Llevémoslo a un lugar seguro en la tierra firme, y luego regresemos.»

Mientras tanto, el ruido que habían hecho esos arcabuces, se había escuchado en todos los alrededores del lago, y por supuesto también lo habían oído las tropas de Cortés y sus aliados de la tierra firme. Aunque Cuitláhuac les había indicado a nuestras fuerzas en la tierra firme que esperaran las conchas de medianoche, al escuchar el ruido del combate tuvieron el sentido común de movilizarse inmediatamente. Por otro lado, los destacamentos de Cortés no habían recibido ninguna orden, y aunque debieron de estar alertas ante ese ruido repentino, no sabían qué hacer. De la misma forma, los hombres blancos encargados de los cañones colocados alrededor de las orillas del lago ya habían cargado y apuntado, pero no podían mandar sus proyectiles volando hacia la ciudad en donde estaban su Capitán General y la mayoría de sus compañeros. Así es que supongo que todas las tropas de Cortés en la tierra firme solamente se encontraban allí paradas, indecisas, tratando de mirar ansiosas hacia la isla que apenas se alcanzaba a ver entre la cortina de lluvia, cuando fueron atacados por detrás.

Alrededor del arco occidental de la orilla del lago, se levantaron los ejércitos de la Triple Alianza. Aunque muchos de los mejores guerreros se hallaban en Tenochtitlan peleando al lado de nuestros mexica, todavía quedaba una gran multitud de buenos luchadores en la tierra firme. Desde el extremo más al sur hasta las tierras Xochimilca y Chalca, las tropas se habían estado moviendo secretamente y reuniéndose para ese momento y cayeron encima de las fuerzas acolhua del Príncipe Flor Oscura que acampaban en los alrededores de Coyohuacan. Por los estrechos que estaban del otro lado, los culhua atacaron las fuerzas totonaca de Cortés que acampaban en un promontorio de tierra, cerca de Iztapalapan. Los tecpaneca se levantaron en contra de los texcalteca acampados en los alrededores de Tlacopan.

Casi al mismo tiempo, los españoles en estado de sitio en El Corazón del Único Mundo tomaron la sensata decisión de huir. Uno de sus oficiales brincó sobre un caballo que pasó galopando por el campamento, colgado todavía de él, comenzó a gritar en español. No puedo repetir su palabras exactas, pero la orden del oficial fue: «¡Cierren las filas y sigan a Cortés!» Eso les dio a los hombres blancos que aún sobrevivían, por lo menos un punto de destino y abriéndose camino lucharon desde los rincones de la plaza, en donde habían quedado rezagados, hasta que lograron juntarse en un apretado grupo, del cual sólo sobresalían sus afiladas puntas de acero. Como un pequeño puerco espín puede convertirse en una bola llena de espinas y desafiar aun a los coyotes a tragárselo, así ese grupo de españoles se defendían de los asaltos repetidos de nuestros hombres.

Siguiendo así, en un grupo compacto, los hombres retrocedieron tras de donde venían los gritos del único hombre montado a caballo, hasta llegar a la abertura occidental en el Muro de la Serpiente. Varios de ellos, durante esa lenta retirada, pudieron apoderarse de algunos caballos y montarlos. Cuando todos aquellos hombres blancos y texcalteca se encontraron fuera de la plaza, sobre la calzada de Tlacopan, los soldados montados formaron una retaguardia. Sus relampagueantes espadas y las coces de sus caballos detuvieron la persecución de nuestros guerreros el tiempo suficiente para que los hombres que iban a pie pudieran huir tomando la ruta que había seguido Cortés.

Cortés debió de haberlos encontrado cuando él a su vez regresaba al centro de la ciudad, pues como era de suponerse, él y toda su caravana del tesoro sólo habían llegado al primer pasaje de canoa en el camino-puente, encontrándose que el paso estaba interrumpido pues el puente de madera había sido quitado y que por lo tanto no podían cruzar. Así que Cortés volvió solo a la isla y allí se encontró con lo que quedaba de su ejército; todos los soldados desorganizados y huyendo empapados por la lluvia y la sangre y quejándose de sus heridas, pero todos huyendo para salvar sus vidas. Y escuchó no muy lejos detrás de su gente, los gritos de guerra de nuestros guerreros que los perseguían aún tratando de penetrar la barrera de jinetes.

Conozco a Cortés, y sé que no perdió tiempo pidiendo una explicación detallada de lo ocurrido. Debió de ordenarles a esos hombres que tomaran una posición firme, allí donde la calzada se unía a la isla y que resistieran al enemigo el tiempo que fuera posible, porque inmediatamente volvió por la calzada a donde Alvarado, Narváez y los demás soldados le esperaban, y les gritó que echaran todo el tesoro al lago para dejar libres las angarillas y que las dejaran caer sobre el hueco del camino-puente a guisa de puente. Me atrevo a decir que desde Alvarado hasta el soldado más insignificante levantaron un coro de protestas y me imagino que Cortés los calló con una orden como: «¡Hacedlo, o todos somos hombres muertos!»

Así que obedecieron o al menos la mayoría lo hizo. Protegidos por la oscuridad de la noche, antes de ayudar a vaciar las angarillas, muchos de los soldados vaciaron las bolsas de viaje que llevaban consigo y las llenaron, así como llenaron sus jubones y hasta las partes abiertas de sus botas, con todo el oro que pudieron robar, por muy pequeño que fuera, pero la mayor parte del tesoro desapareció en las aguas del lago. Y los caballos fueron desunidos de las angarillas, y los hombres las colocaron a través para poder unir el camino-puente.

Para entonces, el resto de su ejército entraba en el camino-puente, no completamente por voluntad propia, sino porque nuestros guerreros los empujaban a batirse en retirada. Al fin llegaron al puente, en donde Cortés y los demás esperaban, la retirada se detuvo por un momento, mientras las primeras filas de los españoles y los mexica se encontraron combatiendo en un espacio muy reducido. La razón para aquello fue que, aunque el camino-puente era lo suficientemente ancho como para que pudieran caminar por él veinte hombres lado a lado, no todos podían así pelear eficazmente. Quizá sólo los primeros doce de nuestros guerreros podían combatir con los primeros doce de los suyos, y los de atrás, sin importar cuántos fueran no nos servían de nada.

Entonces, los españoles parecieron ceder el paso de repente y se hicieron para atrás. Pero al hacerlo, retiraron también sus angarillas-puentes, dejando a nuestros guerreros de adelante tambaleándose y buscando equilibrio en la orilla de ese hueco repentino.

Una de las angarillas, varios de nuestros hombres y también algunos españoles cayeron en el lago. Sin embargo, los hombres blancos que estaban en el otro lado tuvieron poco tiempo para recobrar su aliento. Nuestros guerreros no llevaban ropa pesada y eran buenos nadadores. Empezaron a echarse deliberadamente al agua, nadando entre el hueco y subiéndose por los pilones que estaban abajo de donde estaban parados los hombres blancos. Al mismo tiempo, una lluvia de flechas cayó sobre los españoles de ambos lados. Cuitláhuac había pensado en todo y para entonces muchas canoas llenas de arqueros se acercaban al camino-puente. A Cortés no le quedó más remedio que batirse en retirada otra vez. Como sus caballos eran lo más valioso y los más grandes y por lo tanto presentaban un fácil blanco, ordenó que un número de hombres los obligaran a echarse al agua y luego que se sujetaran a ellos mientras nadaban hasta llegar a tierra firme. Sin que se le pidiera nada de eso, Malintzin saltó con ellos y agarrándose a un caballo que nadaba llegó a la otra orilla.

Luego Cortés y los hombres que quedaban hicieron lo posible por organizar la huida. Aquellos que tenían ballestas y arcabuces que podían utilizar, los descargaban sin dirección fija en la oscuridad, por ambos lados del camino-puente, esperando pegarle a alguno de los atacantes que iban en las canoas. Los demás españoles se alternaban utilizando sus espadas y deslizando la angarilla que les quedaba, deslizándose hacia atrás y tratando de alejarse del sinnúmero de guerreros que cada vez más cruzaban y subían por ese primer hueco del camino-puente, con todo éxito. Había otros dos pasajes de canoa entre Cortés y la tierra firme de Tlacopan. La angarilla le ayudó a él y a sus hombres a llegar hasta el siguiente, pero allí tuvieron que abandonar su improvisado puente porque sus perseguidores también lo habían cruzado. Al llegar al siguiente hueco, los hombres blancos simplemente pelearon caminando hacia atrás, hasta que se cayeron por el borde, al lago.

De hecho ya estaban muy cerca de la orilla de la tierra firme y el lago no era muy profundo allí, puesto que hasta un hombre que no pudiera nadar podía llegar a tierra firme por medio de una serie de brincos, manteniendo su cabeza fuera del agua, pero los hombres blancos llevaban unas armaduras muy pesadas y muchos de ellos iban cargados además de oro, todavía más pesado, y al caer al agua chapotearon desesperadamente para mantenerse a flote. Cortés y sus otros compañeros que venían detrás de ellos, no vacilaron en pisarlos tratando de saltar esa brecha. Así, muchos hombres que habían caído al agua se hundieron y los que quedaron más abajo, me imagino que lo hicieran profundamente dentro del lodo del fondo del lago. Mientras más y más españoles caían y se ahogaban, sus cadáveres se amontonaban lo suficientemente alto como para hacer un puente humano y así fue cómo los últimos españoles supervivientes pudieron cruzar.

Sólo uno de ellos pudo cruzar sin pánico, con un alarde que nuestros guerreros admiraron tanto que hasta la fecha hablan del «salto de Tonatíu». Cuando a Pedro de Alvarado lo empujaron hasta la orilla, estaba armado solamente con una espada. Les dio la espalda a sus atacantes, metió su espada entre el montón de hombres blancos, unos ahogados y otros todavía palpitantes, y dio un poderoso salto, y a pesar de llevar una pesada armadura, probablemente herido y ciertamente cansado, *saltó* a través de aquel hueco casi desde la orilla del camino-puente, hasta la otra orilla, que estaba bastante retirada... y se salvó.

Allí fue donde nuestros guerreros se detuvieron. Habían echado hasta el último extranjero fuera de Tenochtitlan, hasta el territorio tecpaneca, en donde se suponía que los que quedaban serían matados o capturados. Nuestros guerreros se volvieron por el camino-puente, en donde los barqueros ya venían con los puentes que faltaban para empezarlos a acomodar, y camino a casa hicieron la labor de acuchilladores y amarradores. Recogieron a sus propios compañeros caídos, así como aquellos hombres blancos heridos que vivirían para servir como sacrificios, y con sus cuchillos les daban un fin misericordioso y rápido a aquellos españoles que ya se encontraban a punto de morir.

Cortés y los supervivientes pudieron dejar de pelear y tuvieron la oportunidad de descansar en Tlacopan. Los tecpaneca de esa región no eran tan buenos guerreros como los texcalteca a quienes Cortés mandó luchar contra ellos, pero habían atacado con la ventaja de la sorpresa y conocían su propio terreno, así que para cuando Cortés llegó a aquella ciudad, los tecpaneca estaban echando a sus aliados texcalteca desde Tlacopan hacia el norte, hacia Azcapotzalco, y seguían huyendo. Así fue cómo Cortés y sus compañeros pudieron tener un descanso para atender sus heridas, darse cuenta de sus bajas y decidir qué hacer después.

Entre los que aún se encontraban vivos, por lo menos estaban los principales subordinados de Cortés: Narváez, Alvarado y otros, y su Malintzin, pero su ejército ya no era un ejército. Había entrado triunfalmente en Tenochtitlan con más de mil quinientos hombres blancos. Acababa de salir de Tenochtitlan con poco menos de cuatrocientos, con unos treinta caballos, algunos de los cuales habían logrado escapar de la batalla en la plaza y habían nadado desde la isla, y Cortés no tenía ni idea de dónde se encontraban sus aliados nativos, ni en qué situación estarían. El hecho era que también ellos habían sido vencidos por los ejércitos vengativos de la Triple Alianza. A excepción de los texcalteca, quienes eran empujados hacia el lado opuesto de donde él estaba, todas sus otras fuerzas, que habían estado colocadas a lo largo de la orilla del lago hacia el sur, se les estaba echando hacia el norte, hacia donde él se encontraba sentado exhausto y triste en su derrota.

Se dice que Cortés hizo eso precisamente, que se sentó como si jamás fuera a volverse a levantar. Se sentó recargado en uno de los «más viejos de los viejos» cipreses y lloró.

Claro está que realmente no sé si lloró por haber sido derrotado o por la pérdida de su tesoro. Sin embargo, hace poco se puso una cerca alrededor de ese árbol en donde Cortés lloró, para marcarlo en memoria de la «Noche Triste». Si nosotros los mexica todavía estuviéramos anotando la historia, le habríamos dado un nombre muy diferente a ese día, quizás «la noche de la última victoria de los mexica», pero como ahora son ustedes, los españoles, los que escriben la historia, supongo que esa noche sangrienta y lluviosa que por su calendario fue el día treinta del mes de junio en el año mil quinientos veinte será por siempre recordada como la «Noche Triste».

✠

En muchos aspectos, esa noche no fue tampoco muy feliz para El Único Mundo. La circunstancia más desafortunada fue que todos nuestros ejércitos no continuaron persiguiendo a Cortés y los hombres blancos que quedaban, así como a sus aliados indígenas, hasta acabar con el último hombre. Pero, como ya he dicho, los guerreros de Tenochtitlan creían que sus aliados en la tierra firme harían eso precisamente, por lo que regresaron al centro de la isla y dedicaron el resto de la noche a una celebración de lo que les pareció ser una victoria completa. Los sacerdotes de nuestra ciudad y la mayoría de la gente aún se encontraba en la ceremonia simulada en la pirámide de Tlaltelolco, y con gran alborozo se dirigieron en masa Al Corazón del Único Mundo para llevar a cabo una verdadera ceremonia para dar gracias en la Gran Pirámide. Hasta Beu y yo, al escuchar los gritos de júbilo de los guerreros que regresaban, salimos de nuestra casa para asistir, y aun Tláloc, como para ver mejor el regocijo de su gente, levantó su cortina de lluvia.

En tiempos normales, jamás nos hubiéramos atrevido a observar ninguna clase de rito en la plaza central hasta que cada piedra, cada imagen y adorno hubiera quedado completamente limpio de la más mínima señal de mugre, de cualquier imperfección, hasta que El Corazón del Único Mundo brillara deslumbrante para recibir la aprobación y admiración de los dioses, pero esa noche las antorchas y fuegos de las urnas mostraron a la enorme plaza como si fuera un basurero grande y extenso. Por todos lados se veían cadáveres, o restos de cadáveres, tanto blancos como bronceados, así como gran cantidad de entrañas regadas de color gris rosado y gris azulado, por lo tanto indistinguibles en cuanto a su origen. Por doquiera se encontraban armas rotas y abandonadas y el excremento de los caballos asustados y de hombres que continuamente habían defecado al morir, y las ropas y cobijas rancias de los españoles, así como otros de sus efectos. Sin embargo, los sacerdotes no se quejaron acerca del escenario tan sucio para la ceremonia y los celebrantes se amontonaron sin mostrar mucha repugnancia al pisar tanta suciedad. Todos confiábamos en que, por esa sola vez, los dioses no se ofenderían al ver en qué condición tan sucia estaba la plaza, ya que se trataba de sus enemigos así como de los nuestros, a los que habíamos vencido.

Sé que siempre se han angustiado, reverendos escribanos, cuando me han escuchado describir el sacrificio de cualquier ser humano, aun el de los paganos tan despreciados por su Iglesia, por lo que no les hablaré detalladamente sobre los sacrificios de sus propios compatriotas Cristianos, que comenzaron cuando el sol Tonatíu empezó a levantarse. Sólo comentaré, aunque nos crean una gente muy tonta, que también sacrificamos los cuarenta o más caballos que los soldados habían dejado atrás, porque como verán, nosotros no podíamos estar muy seguros de que también *ellos* no fueran cierta clase de Cristianos. También podría agregar que los caballos fueron a sus Muertes Floridas de una manera más noble que los españoles, quienes se resistieron mientras se les estaba desnudando, maldicieron mientras se les arrastraba por las escaleras y lloraron como niños cuando se les acostó sobre la piedra. Nuestros guerreros reconocieron a algunos de los hombres blancos que con más valentía habían luchado, por lo que después de que éstos murieron, se les cortaron los muslos para asarse y...

Pero tal vez no se muestren tan asqueados, señores frailes, cuando les asegure que la mayoría de los cadáveres sin ninguna ceremonia sirvieron de alimento a los animales del zoológico de la ciudad...

Muy bien, mis señores, vuelvo a los sucesos menos festivos de aquella noche. Mientras le estábamos dando gracias a los dioses por habernos deshecho de los extranjeros, no nos dimos cuenta de que nuestros ejércitos en la tierra firme *no* los habían aniquilado totalmente. Cortés todavía se encontraba sintiéndose triste y enojado en Tlacopan en donde tuvo que volverse a levantar ante la llegada ruidosa de sus otras fuerzas que huían. Eran los acolhua y totonaca, o más bien lo que quedaba de ellas, que huían perseguidos por los xochimilca y los chalca. Cortés y sus oficiales, junto con Malintzin, que sin duda tuvo que gritar más fuerte de lo que había hecho en toda su vida, lograron detener la derrota rotunda y restaurar alguna semblanza de orden. Entonces Cortés y sus hombres blancos, algunos de ellos montados a caballo, algunos a pie, otros cojeando y otros más en camillas, dirigieron las tropas nativas reorganizadas haciéndolas huir hacia el norte, antes de que los alcanzaran sus perseguidores. Y aquellos perseguidores, tal vez creyendo que los fugitivos serían matados y esparcidos por alguna otra fuerza de la Triple Alianza que estuvieran más allá, o tal vez ansiosos por comenzar sus propias celebraciones de victoria, dejaron escapar a los fugitivos.

En cierto momento, antes del amanecer, en el extremo norte del lago Tzumpanco, Cortés se dio cuenta de que estaba un poco detrás de nuestros aliados los tecpaneca, y ellos, un poco detrás de *sus* aliados los texcalteca. Los tecpaneca se dieron cuenta con sorpresa y disgusto que estaban en medio de dos fuerzas enemigas, y pensando que algo malo había sucedido con el plan general de batalla, éstos también abandonaron su persecución, dispersándose a ambos lados del camino y se fueron hacia sus casas en Tlacopan. Cortés, al fin, alcanzó a sus texcalteca, y todo su ejército se volvió a reunir otra vez, aunque notablemente disminuido y sumamente deprimido. Aun así, Cortés se tranquilizó al ver que sus mejores guerreros indígenas, los texcalteca, porque sí *eran* los mejores luchadores, habían sufrido pocas pérdidas. Puedo imaginarme qué debió de pasar por la mente de Cortés en aquel momento:

«Si voy a Texcala, su anciano rey Xicotenca verá que he conservado a la mayoría de los guerreros que me prestó. Por lo que no puede enojarse mucho conmigo, o considerarme un rotundo fracaso y tal vez lo pueda convencer para que nos dé un refugio a todos los demás.»

Fuera cual fuese su razonamiento, Cortés llevó efectivamente a sus miserables tropas alrededor de las tierras del lago hacia el norte, rumbo a Texcala. Varios hombres más murieron de sus heridas durante aquella marcha larga y todos ellos sufrieron terriblemente, porque tomaron una ruta que rodeaba prudentemente cualquier lugar poblado, por lo que no pudieron pedir caridad o exigir alimentos. Se vieron obligados a subsistir alimentándose de criaturas y plantas salvajes que pudieran encontrar y cuando menos una vez tuvieron que matar y comer algunos de sus valiosos caballos y perros.

Solamente una vez en el transcurso de esa larga marcha tuvieron que pelear de nuevo, pues al llegar al pie de las montañas del este, se encontraron con una fuerza de guerreros acolhua de Texcoco, aún leales a la Triple Alianza. Pero aquellos acolhua carecían tanto de guía como de incentivo para luchar, por lo que la batalla se produjo casi sin derramamiento de sangre, como una Guerra Florida. Cuando aquellos acolhua capturaron cierta cantidad de prisioneros —creo que todos eran totonaca— se retiraron del campo y se fueron a Texcoco para tener su propia celebración de «victoria». Así que lo que quedó del ejército de Cortés no fue severamente mermado entre su huida en la Noche Triste y su llegada, doce días después, a Texcala. El gobernante de aquella nación, quien se había convertido al Cristianismo, el anciano y ciego Xicotenca, recibió bien a Cortés y le dio permiso de alojar sus tropas y permanecer allí todo el tiempo que quisiera. Todos los sucesos que les acabo de contar, y que estaban en contra nuestra, nos eran desconocidos en Tenochtitlan, cuando en el amanecer radiante que siguió a la Noche Triste enviamos al primer *xichimique* español a la piedra del sacrificio, en la cima de la Gran Pirámide.

Otras cosas sucedieron durante la Noche Triste, que aunque no eran tristes, por lo menos eran singulares. Como ya lo he dicho, la nación mexica había perdido a su Venerado Orador Motecuzoma y también había muerto el Venerado Orador Totoquihuaztli de Tlacopan en aquella ciudad, durante la batalla nocturna que tuvo lugar allí. Y el Venerado Orador Cacama de Texcoco, quien había peleado con sus guerreros acolhua que había traído a Tenochtitlan, fue encontrado entre los muertos cuando nuestros esclavos hicieron el trabajo macabro de limpiar El Corazón del Único Mundo de los cadáveres e inmundicias que quedaron de esa noche. Nadie lamentó la pérdida ni de Motecuzoma ni de su sobrino Cacama, pero sí fue una coincidencia perturbadora el que *los tres* gobernantes y aliados de la Triple Alianza murieran en la tarde y en la noche de ese mismo día. Aunque Cuitláhuac ya había asumido el trono vacante de los mexica —si bien jamás pudo disfrutar de toda la pompa y ceremonia de una coronación oficial—, y aunque la gente de Tlacopan escogió un sustituto, cuando asesinaron a su Uey-Tlatoani, en la persona de su hermano Tetlapanquétzal, la elección de un nuevo Venerado Orador para Texcoco fue más difícil. Quien reclamaba ese derecho era el Príncipe Flor Oscura, quien debería ser, de todas maneras, el gobernante legítimo y a quien la mayoría del pueblo acolhua le hubiera dado la bienvenida al trono, pero como se había aliado a los hombres blancos, tan odiados, el Consejo de Voceros de Texcoco, en consulta con los nuevos Venerados Oradores de Tenochtitlan y Tlacopan, decidieron nombrar un hombre de tal insignificancia que sería aceptable por todos, y al mismo tiempo podría ser sustituido por el guia o líder que finalmente surgiera con fuerza, entre los divididos acolhua. Se llamaba Cohuanácoch y creo que era un sobrino del difunto Nezahualpili. Fue por la incertidumbre y por la división de lealtades de aquella nación, y porque tenían a un gobernante tan insignificante que los guerreros acolhua atacaron el ejército de Cortés que huía, de una forma tan desganada, cuando pudieron haber acabado con él por completo. Los acolhua jamás volvieron a manifestar la ferocidad guerrera que tanto había admirado cuando Nezahualpili los guió a ellos y a nosotros contra los texcalteca hacía tantos años.

Otro de los raros sucesos que ocurrieron esa Noche Triste fue que, en algún momento, desapareció el cadáver de Motecuzoma del salón del trono de palacio, en donde había quedado por última vez, y jamás se volvió a ver. He oído muchas suposiciones acerca de su paradero: que cuando nuestros guerreros se apoderaron del palacio lo descuartizaron y que esparcieron todos sus miembros; que sus esposas e hijos sacaron el cadáver para disponer de él de una manera más respetuosa; que sus sacerdotes leales manipularon el cadáver para conservarlo y lo escondieron, y con magia le volverían a dar vida otra vez, algún día, cuando ustedes los hombres blancos se hubieran ido y los mexica reinaran de nuevo. Yo creo que el cadáver de Motecuzoma fue mezclado con los cuerpos de los campeones texcalteca, quienes fueron aniquilados en aquel palacio y que sin ser reconocido fue a dar a donde se llevaron los otros: con los animales del zoológico. Pero una cosa sí es segura, Motecuzoma partió de este mundo tan vaga e irresolutamente como había vivido, así es que el lugar en donde descansa su cuerpo, también es tan desconocido como el lugar en donde quedó el tesoro que desapareció, durante esa misma noche.

Ah sí, el tesoro, lo que ahora llaman «el tesoro perdido de los aztecas». Me preguntaba cuándo me interrogarían acerca de eso. Cortés solía llamarme con frecuencia para ayudar a Malintzin a traducir, mientras interrogaba a muchas personas, y cada una de ellas muchas veces y de diversas maneras interesantemente persuasivas, también con frecuencia me exigía lo que *yo* pudiera saber sobre el tesoro, aunque nunca me sujetó a ninguna de esas formas persuasivas. Muchos otros españoles, además de Cortés, repetidamente me lo han preguntado, así como también otros cortesanos han deseado que les diga en qué consistía el tesoro y cuánto valía, y por encima de todo en dónde está ahora. No me creerían si les dijera algunas de las cosas que aún se me siguen ofreciendo hasta este día, sólo les diré que algunas de las personas que con más insistencia me han interrogado y que más generosas se han mostrado, han sido algunas de las más altas señoras españolas.

Ya les he dicho, reverendos frailes, en qué consistía el tesoro. En cuanto a su valor, no sé en cuánto valorarían ustedes aquellas innumerables obras de arte. Aun considerando solamente el oro y las gemas por separado, no puedo hacer la cuenta de su valor en su moneda de maravedíes y reales, pero según me han contado de la gran riqueza de su Rey Don Carlos y su Papa Clemente y otros personajes ricos de su Viejo Mundo, creo que puedo declarar que cualquier hombre que poseyera «el tesoro perdido de los aztecas» sería sin duda el más rico de los ricos de su Viejo Mundo.

¿Pero dónde está? Bueno, el antiguo camino-puente aún se extiende desde aquí hasta Tlacopan o Tacuba, como ustedes prefieran llamarlo. Aunque ese camino es más corto ahora que antes, el último pasaje de canoas del extremo occidental aún está allí, y en ese lugar es donde se hundieron muchos de los soldados españoles por el peso del oro en sus bolsas, jubones y botas. Por supuesto, se debieron de hundir mucho más adentro del fondo del lago en los últimos once años y deben de haber quedado todavía más enterrados por la tierra y la grava que se ha depositado encima en ese mismo lapso de tiempo. Pero cualquier hombre lo suficientemente avaro y lo suficientemente activo como para nadar hacia el fondo y excavar por allí, podría encontrar entre los muchos huesos blanqueados, diademas de oro e incrustadas de joyas, medallones, figuritas y demás. Tal vez no sea lo suficiente como para igualar la riqueza del Rey Don Carlos o el Papa Clemente, pero tendrá lo suficiente como para jamás volverse a sentir ambicioso y codicioso.

Desgraciadamente para aquellos buscadores de tesoros que son realmente codiciosos, la mayor parte del botín fue tirado al lago por orden de Cortés, en el primer pasaje *acali* del camino-puente, el más cercano a la ciudad. El Venerado Orador Cuitláhuac pudo haber mandado a algunos nadadores para recobrarlo más tarde, y tal vez sí lo hizo, pero tengo razones para dudar de ello. De todos modos, Cuitláhuac murió antes de que Cortés pudiera preguntárselo, ya sea cortésmente o empleando sus métodos persuasivos. Y si algunos de los nadadores mexica sacaron el tesoro de su nación, quizá también han muerto o son hombres de la más excepcional discreción.

Creo que la mayor parte del tesoro aún yace donde Cortés lo mandó tirar en aquella Noche Triste. Pero cuando Tenochtitlan fue arrasada hasta sus cimientos, más adelante y después de eso, cuando se limpió el escombro para hacer la reconstrucción de la ciudad en el estilo español, los restos inútiles de Tenochtitlan simplemente fueron amontonados a ambos lados de la isla, en parte por conveniencia de sus albañiles, en parte para aumentar el área de la superficie de la isla. Así que el camino-puente de Tlacopan se acortó gracias al relleno en los límites para alargar la isla y ahora ese pasaje de canoa está bajo la tierra y los escombros. Si estoy en lo cierto en cuanto a mi estimación de donde yace el tesoro, se encuentra en algún lugar profundamente debajo de los cimientos de los elegantes edificios señoriales que adornan su calzada llamada de Tacuba.

De todas las cosas que les he contado sobre la Noche Triste, no he mencionado un suceso que, en sí, determinó el futuro de El Único Mundo. Fue la muerte de un hombre que no tenía ninguna importancia. Si tuvo nombre, jamás lo supe. Tal vez no hizo nada que valiera la pena, ya sea bueno o malo, en todo el transcurso de su vida, excepto el hecho de finalizar sus caminos y sus días aquí y no sé cómo murió, valiente o cobardemente. Pero durante la limpieza del Corazón del Único Mundo, al día siguiente se encontró su cuerpo con una *maquahuitl* clavada y los esclavos gritaron al encontrarlo, porque no era ni un hombre blanco ni uno de nuestra raza, y ellos jamás habían visto antes una criatura como ésa. Yo sí. Era uno de esos hombres increíblemente negros que habían venido de Cuba con Narváez y éste era aquel cuyo rostro me hizo huir cuando lo vi.

Me sonrío ahora —con tristeza y menosprecio, pero sonrío— cuando veo el caminar altivo y orgulloso de Hernán Cortés, de Pedro de Alvarado, de Beltrán de Guzmán y de todos los demás veteranos españoles quienes se exaltan a sí mismos llamándose «los Conquistadores». Oh, no puedo negar que sí hicieron algunas cosas valientes y atrevidas. Por ejemplo, cuando Cortés mandó quemar su barcos al llegar por primera vez a estas tierras, hazaña que no se ha llegado a superar como una muestra de ostentosa audacia, aunque hubiera sido un capricho de los dioses.

Y hubieron más factores que contribuyeron a la caída de El Único Mundo como el hecho deplorable de que el Único Mundo se volvió contra sí mismo: nación contra nación, vecino contra vecino, llegando finalmente hasta hermano contra hermano. Pero si alguien merece ser honrado y recordado con el título de El Conquistador, ése debe ser un solo y único hombre, aquel negro sin nombre que trajo la enfermedad de las pequeñas viruelas a Tenochtitlan.

Él pudo haber contagiado esa enfermedad a los soldados de Narváez durante su viaje para acá, desde Cuba, pero no lo hizo. Les pudo haber transmitido la enfermedad a ellos, y además a las tropas de Cortés, durante su marcha hacia acá desde la costa, pero no lo hizo. Él mismo pudo haber muerto de la enfermedad antes de llegar aquí, pero vivió. Vivió para ver Tenochtitlan y traernos a nosotros la enfermedad. Tal vez fue uno de los caprichos de los dioses que le permitieran vivir y nosotros nada hubiéramos podido hacer para evitarlo. Pero quisiera que no hubieran matado al hombre negro. Habría deseado que él escapara con sus otros compañeros, así tarde o temprano los hubiera contagiado, pero no. Tenochtitlan se vio desgarrado por la viruela, y la enfermedad se extendió por toda la región del lago, hasta llegar a cada comunidad de la Triple Alianza, pero jamás alcanzó Texcala o afligió allí a ninguno de nuestros enemigos.

De hecho, nuestras gentes empezaron a caer enfermas aun antes de que recibiéramos noticias de que Cortés y su compañía habían encontrado refugio en Texcala. Ustedes, reverendos escribanos, sin duda conocen los síntomas y la forma en que la enfermedad avanza. De todos modos, hace mucho que les describí cómo había visto morir años atrás a una joven xiu de la viruela en la lejana población de Tiho. Así es que sólo tengo que decirles que nuestra gente murió de la misma forma: asfixiándose con su tejidos hinchados, dentro de sus narices y gargantas o de alguna forma igualmente espantosa; moviéndose y gritando en un delirio violento hasta que sus cerebros ya no aguantaron el tormento, o vomitando sangre hasta que sus cuerpos quedaron sin una gota de sangre, hasta que quedaron secos como una cáscara y no parecieron ya humanos. Por supuesto que yo reconocí muy pronto la enfermedad y les dije a nuestros físicos:

«Es una aflicción entre los hombres blancos y le dan poca importancia, porque raras veces mueren de ella. Le llaman las pequeñas viruelas.»

«Si éstas son sus pequeñas viruelas —dijo un doctor sin ningún sentido del humor— espero que nunca nos honren con las más grandes. ¿Qué hacen los hombres blancos para no morir de esto?»

«No hay remedio. Al menos eso dicen. Excepto rezar.» Así es que desde aquel momento nuestros templos estuvieron llenos de sacerdotes y adoradores haciendo ofrendas y sacrificios a Patécatl, el dios de la salud, así como también a todos los otros dioses. El templo que Motecuzoma les había prestado a los españoles también estaba lleno, con aquellas de nuestras gentes que se habían sometido al bautismo y que de repente tuvieron la esperanza devota de que en realidad se habían hecho Cristianos, y que por tanto tenían la esperanza de que el dios Cristiano de las pequeñas viruelas viera en ellos a unos hombres blancos simulados, y de ese modo los salvara. Prendían velas y movían sus manos trazando la cruz y murmuraban lo que recordaban de los rituales de los cuales solamente habían recibido una pequeña instrucción y de la cual habían prestado una atención aún más ligera.

Pero nada contuvo la enfermedad y la muerte que traía consigo. Nuestras oraciones fueron tan inútiles y nuestros médicos se vieron tan imposibilitados como los de los maya. No mucho después de haber empezado la enfermedad, también estuvimos a punto de morir de hambre, puesto que la epidemia no pudo mantenerse en secreto y los habitantes de la tierra firme tenían miedo de acercarse a nosotros, por lo que cesó el tráfico de *acaltin* con las provisiones tan necesarias para la subsistencia de nuestra isla.

Pero la enfermedad no tardó en aparecer también en las comunidades de la tierra firme, y una vez que se hizo evidente que toda la Triple Alianza se encontraba en el mismo peligro, los lancheros reanudaron su trabajo, o mejor dicho, los que aún no habían sido atacados por la enfermedad. Porque ésta parecía escoger sus víctimas bajo un aspecto particularmente cruel. Yo jamás enfermé, como tampoco lo hizo Beu ni ninguno de nuestros contemporáneos. Las pequeñas viruelas parecían ignorar a los de nuestra edad, así como a los que estaban enfermos de otra cosa y a aquellos que siempre habían tenido una salud débil. En lugar de todos nosotros, parecía apoderarse de los jóvenes, fuertes y saludables y no desperdiciaba su maleficencia en aquellos que por alguna razón no vivirían por mucho tiempo.

El hecho de haber sido afligidos por las pequeñas viruelas fue por lo que dudo que Cuitláhuac hiciera algo jamás por recobrar el tesoro que quedó hundido en el lago. La enfermedad nos cayó encima poco después de la llegada de los hombres blancos, sólo pocos días después de limpiar los desechos que habían dejado, antes de que empezáramos a recobrarnos de la tensión que nos había dejado esa larga ocupación, antes de que pudiéramos reanudar nuestra vida cívica que había sido interrumpida; por eso sé que el Venerado Orador no pudo prestar atención en aquel tiempo en salvar el oro y las joyas. Y más tarde, a medida que la enfermedad se convertía en una epidemia, tuvo otros motivos para dejar esa tarea a un lado. Verán ustedes, durante mucho tiempo quedamos incomunicados de toda noticia que viniera del mundo que estaba más allá de la región del lago. Comerciantes y mensajeros de otras naciones rehusaban entrar en nuestra área contaminada y Cuitláhuac les prohibió a nuestros *pochteca* y viajeros salir a algún otro lado, para que no llevaran una posible contaminación. Creo que pasaron unos cuatro meses después de la Noche Triste cuando uno de nuestros ratones *quimíchime* colocado en Texcoco tuvo el valor suficiente de venir aquí y avisarnos de lo que estaba sucediendo en ese tiempo.

«Entonces sepa, Venerado Orador —le dijo a Cuitláhuac y a

los demás, incluyéndome a mí, que ansiosos le escuchábamos—, que Cortés y su compañía pasaron algún tiempo solamente descansando y comiendo vorazmente, mientras convalecían de sus heridas y recobraban su salud en general. Pero no lo hicieron para desde allí continuar hacia la costa, abordar sus barcos y dejar estas tierras. Ellos se han estado recuperando solamente con un propósito, para acumular fuerzas y caer otra vez sobre Tenochtitlan. Ahora están otra vez de pie y activos, pues ellos y sus anfitriones texcalteca están viajando por todas las naciones hacia el este, para reunir la mayor cantidad de guerreros de todas las tribus que no son amigas de los mexica.»

El Mujer Serpiente interrumpió al ratón para decirle al Venerado Orador con urgencia: «Esperábamos haberlos aniquilado para siempre, pero como no fue así ahora debemos hacer lo que se debió haber hecho desde hace mucho. Debemos reunir a todas nuestras fuerzas y marchar a su encuentro. Matar hasta el último hombre blanco, cada uno de sus aliados y simpatizantes y a cada uno de nuestros tributarios inconformes que han ayudado a Cortés. Y debemos hacerlo *ahora*, antes de que esté lo suficientemente fuerte como para hacer lo mismo con ¡*nosotros!*»

Cuitláhuac dijo débilmente: «¿Cuáles son las fuerzas que sugieres que reunamos, Tlácotzin? Difícilmente podremos encontrar un guerrero en cualquier ejército de la Triple Alianza que pueda levantar con sus dos manos su espada.»

«Perdóneme, Venerado Orador, pero todavía tengo más que contarle —dijo el *quimichi*—. Cortés también envió a muchos de sus hombres a la costa, donde ellos junto con sus totonaca desmantelaron algunas de las barcas ancladas. Con un trabajo y dificultad inconcebible han traído muchas de esas piezas de madera y metal tan pesadas desde el mar, cruzando las montañas a Texcala. Allí, en este momento, los carpinteros de Cortés están pegando estas piezas, para hacer barcos más pequeños. Como lo que hicieron, si usted recuerda, cuando construyeron aquel pequeño barco para divertir al difunto Motecuzoma. Pero ahora están haciendo muchos de ellos.»

«¿En tierra firme? —exclamó Cuitláhuac incrédulo—. No hay aguas lo suficientemente profundas en toda la nación Texcala donde pueda flotar algo más grande que un *acali* para pescar. Me parece una locura.»

El *quimichi* se encogió de hombros con delicadeza. «Cortés pudo haber perdido la razón gracias a su reciente humillación aquí. Pero con respeto le reitero, Venerado Orador, que estoy diciendo la verdad de lo que he visto, y que yo sí estoy sano, o lo estaba hasta que aquellos hechos me parecieron lo suficientemente peligrosos como para que arriesgara mi vida en traerle estas noticias.»

Cuitláhuac sonrió: «Sano o no, fue el acto de un mexica valiente y leal, y te lo agredezco. Serás bien recompensado, y luego se te dará una recompensa mayor: mi permiso para que te alejes de esta ciudad pestilente otra vez y tan rápido como puedas.»

Así fue cómo nos enteramos de las acciones de Cortés y cuando menos de algunas de sus intenciones. He escuchado cómo muchas personas —que no estuvieron aquí en aquel tiempo— critican nuestra apatía o estupidez o nuestro confiado sentido de seguridad, porque nos aislamos y no hicimos nada para evitar la llegada de las fuerzas de Cortés, pero la razón de ello era que no podíamos hacer nada. Desde Tzumpanco, que estaba al norte, hasta Xochimilco, en el sur; desde Tlacopan, al oeste, hasta Texcoco, en el este, todo hombre y mujer que no estaba ayudando a cuidar a los enfermos se encontraba moribundo o muerto. En nuestra debilidad, sólo podíamos esperar, tener la esperanza de habernos recobrado hasta cierto grado antes de que regresara Cortés nuevamente. Acerca de eso, no teníamos ninguna ilusión; sabíamos que vendría de nuevo. Y fue durante ese triste verano de espera, que Cuitláhuac hizo un comentario, en mi presencia y en la de su primo Cuautémoc:

«Preferiría que el tesoro de la nación permaneciera para siempre en el fondo del lago de Texcoco, o que se hundiera hasta las profundidades más negras de Mictlan, para que los hombres blancos jamás lo vuelvan a tener en sus manos otra vez.»

Dudo que más tarde llegara a cambiar de opinión, porque apenas tuvo tiempo. Antes de que terminara la temporada de lluvias, ya había caído enfermo de las pequeñas viruelas, había vomitado toda su sangre y había muerto. Pobre Cuitláhuac, se había convertido en nuestro Venerado Orador sin la ceremonia debida de coronación y cuando terminó su breve reinado no fue honrado con el funeral que le correspondía por su alto rango.

Para entonces, ni al noble más alto entre los nobles se le podía otorgar un entierro con tambores dolientes y panoplia, pues hasta enterrarlo era un lujo. Sencillamente había demasiados muertos y cada día morían más. Ya no quedaban lugares disponibles en donde enterrarlos o ya no habían suficientes hombres o suficiente tiempo para excavar todas las tumbas que fueran necesarias. En lugar de eso, cada comunidad había designado una extensión de terreno que estuviera cerca, en donde sin ninguna ceremonia se amontonaban sus muertos y se quemaban hasta quedar solamente las cenizas, y aún así, no fue fácil incinerar tantos cadáveres en los días húmedos, en la temporada de lluvias. Tenochtitlan escogió un lugar para quemar a sus muertos que estaba atrás de la colina de Chapultépec, y el tráfico se incrementó mucho entre nuestra isla y tierra firme, pues los lanchones de carga se habían convertido en transportes fúnebres, cuyos remeros eran ancianos indiferentes a la enfermedad y que como rehiletes iban de una orilla a otra durante el transcurso del día y así un día tras otro. De esta manera, el cadáver de Cuitláhuac fue sólo uno de tantos entre los cientos acarreados el día en que murió.

La enfermedad de las pequeñas viruelas fue el verdadero conquistador de nosotros los mexica y de algunos otros pueblos. Y todavía hubo otras naciones que fueron abatidas o que todavía lo están siendo por enfermedades que antes jamás se habían visto en estas tierras, algunas de las cuales hicieron que nosotros los mexica casi nos sintiéramos agradecidos por haber sido visitados sólo por las pequeñas viruelas.

Hay una enfermedad que ustedes llaman la peste, en la que a la víctima le crecen unas bolas negras, en el cuello, la ingle y bajo las axilas, que la ponen en agonía y que hacen que continuamente estire su cabeza y sus extremidades, como si con gusto quisiera deshacerse de esas bolas y no sufrir más dolor. Mientras tanto, cada emanación de su cuerpo —su saliva, su orina y excremento, hasta su sudor y su mismo aliento— tienen un olor tan desagradable que ni el físico más endurecido y humanitario puede soportar estar cerca de la víctima, hasta que al fin las bolas se revientan, saliendo de ellas un chorro nauseabundo de color negro, y el enfermo muere misericordiosamente.

Hay otra enfermedad que ustedes llaman el cólera, cuyas víctimas sienten calambres en cada uno de los músculos de su cuerpo y que pueden sentirlos de vez en cuando o todos al mismo tiempo. De pronto, un hombre puede sentir que sus brazos o piernas se contorsionan en un dolor angustioso y luego se estiran como si quisiera desmembrarse a sí mismo y en el siguiente momento se vuelve a encoger hasta que todo su cuerpo se convulsiona en un nudo de tortura. Y todo el tiempo se siente atormentado también por una sed insaciable. Aunque trague torrentes enteros de agua, continuamente la echa fuera por medio de una orina y defecación incontrolable. Como no puede retener nada de agua o humedad en su cuerpo se encoge, de modo que cuando por fin muere, parece una semilla seca.

Tienen esas otras enfermedades que llaman el sarampión y la viruela loca que matan de manera menos horrible, pero tan eficaz como las otras. Su único síntoma visible son unas ronchas que provocan una comezón horrible en la cara y el torso, pero esas enfermedades invaden de una manera invisible el cerebro, por lo que la víctima primero cae en la inconsciencia y luego muere.

No les estoy contando algo que ustedes no sepan ya, señores frailes, pero ¿han pensado en eso alguna vez? Las enfermedades espantosas traídas aquí por sus compatriotas, muchas veces se han adelantado y extendido con más rapidez de lo que esos hombres han podido caminar. Algunos de esos pueblos que ellos pensaban conquistar, ya estaban conquistados y muertos antes de que ellos mismos supieran que eran objetos de conquista. Esas gentes murieron sin haber peleado jamás en contra de sus conquistadores o haberse rendido a ellos, y sin siquiera haber visto a los hombres que los mataron. Es completamente posible que todavía haya pueblos en los más remotos rincones de estas tierras; tribus como los rarámuri y los zhu huave, por ejemplo, que ni sospechan que existen tales seres como los hombres blancos. No obstante, esas gentes pueden estar agonizando horriblemente a consecuencia de las pequeñas viruelas o la peste, muriéndose sin saber siquiera que los están *matando*, ni por qué, ni quién, en estos precisos momentos.

Ustedes nos trajeron la religión Cristiana y nos aseguran que el Señor Dios nos recompensará en el cielo, cuando hayamos muerto, pero sólo aceptándolo a Él podemos salvarnos de ir al Infierno cuando muramos. ¿Por qué el Señor Dios nos mandó entonces esas enfermedades que mataron y condenaron a tantos inocentes al Infierno, antes de que ellos pudieran ver a Sus misioneros y oír hablar acerca de Su religión? A los Cristianos constantemente se les pide que alaben cada una de las obras del Señor Dios, lo cual ha de incluir el trabajo que Él hizo aquí. Reverendos frailes, si sólo nos pudieran explicar por qué el Señor Dios escogió mandar Su religión gentil y nueva tras aquellas enfermedades nuevas y cruelmente mortales, entonces nosotros, los que sobrevivimos, podríamos unirnos gozosos a sus cantos de alabanzas ante la infinita sabiduría y bondad del Señor Dios, Su compasión, Su bondad y Su amor paternal hacia todos Sus hijos, de todas partes.

Por decisión unánime del Consejo de Voceros, se dio el título de Uey-Tlatoani de los mexica al Señor Cuautémoc. Sería interesante especular sobre lo diferente que hubiera podido ser nuestra historia y nuestro destino si Cuautémoc hubiera sido el Venerado Orador, como debió ser, al morir su padre Auítzotl, dieciocho años antes. Sería interesante por supuesto, aunque inútil. «Si» es una pequeña palabra en nuestro lenguaje —tla— como lo es en el suyo, pero he llegado a creer que es la que lleva más peso sobre sí misma de todas las que componen la lengua.

La cantidad de muertos a causa de las pequeñas viruelas comenzaron a disminuir conforme terminaba el calor del verano y las lluvias se abatían, y con el primer frío del invierno la enfermedad abrió sus garras para soltar al fin, totalmente, las tierras del lago. Pero dejó a la Triple Alianza débil en todo el sentido de la palabra. Toda nuestra gente se sentía desalentada; estábamos apesadumbrados por las incontables muertes; sentíamos lástima por los que habían sobrevivido y que habían quedado horriblemente desfigurados por el resto de sus vidas; estábamos agotados por esa larga visita que nos había traído tanta calamidad; habíamos perdido, individual y colectivamente, toda fuerza humana. Nuestra población había quedado reducida más o menos a la mitad y los que quedaban eran principalmente ancianos y enfermos. Como los que habían muerto eran hombres jóvenes, sin hablar de las mujeres y los niños, nuestros ejércitos habían disminuido en más de la mitad. Ningún campeón con sentido común hubiera ordenado una acción ofensiva en contra de los numerosos extranjeros e incluso era dudosa la utilidad de ese ejército para defenderse.

Fue entonces cuando Cortés marchó en contra de la Triple Alianza, en el momento en que se encontraba más débil que nunca. Él ya no podía presumir de una ventaja muy grande en cuanto a armas superiores, porque tenía menos de cuatrocientos soldados blancos y las cantidades que fueran de arcabuces y ballestas que llevaban con ellos. Todos los cañones que había abandonado en la Noche Triste —los cuatro que se encontraban en el palacio de Axayácatl y los treinta o más que había puesto en la tierra firme— los habíamos echado al lago. Pero aún tenía más de veinte caballos, una cantidad de sabuesos y todos los guerreros que le habían seguido antes y los nuevos que acababa de reunir: texcalteca, totonaca y los de otras tribus menores, y los acolhua aún bajo el mando del Príncipe Flor Oscura. En total, Cortés contaba con unos cien mil combatientes. De todas las ciudades y tierras de la Triple Alianza, contando lugares circunvecinos como Tolocan y Cuaunáhuac, que realmente no formaban parte de la Alianza, pero que nos apoyaban, no pudimos reunir más que a una tercera parte de lo que él tenía.

Así que cuando las largas filas de Cortés llegaron procedentes de Texcala, hacia la ciudad-capital más cercana, perteneciente a la Triple Alianza, que era Texcoco, la tomaron. Podría contarles sin omitir nada de la defensa desesperada de esa ciudad debilitada y de las contingencias que sus defensores infligieron y sufrieron, y las tácticas que por último la vencieron... pero ¿para qué? Basta decir que los merodeadores la tomaron. Entre esos merodeadores estaba el Príncipe Flor Oscura de los acolhua, y pelearon contra sus propios guerreros acolhua que apoyaban al nuevo Venerado Orador Cohuanáncoh, o para hablar con la verdad, eran leales a su ciudad de Texcoco. Y así sucedió que en aquella batalla muchos acólhuatl se encontraron luchando contra otro acólhuatl que era su propio hermano.

Pero no todos los guerreros de Texcoco murieron en esa batalla, quizás unos dos mil pudieron escapar antes de quedar atrapados allí. Las tropas de Cortés habían atacado a la ciudad por el lado de la tierra firme, por lo que los defensores, cuando ya no pudieron resistir, retrocedieron lentamente hacia la orilla del lago. Allí se apoderaron de todos los *acali* que había: los de pesca, los de caza, los de pasajeros y de carga y aun los *acaltin* elegantes de la corte, y se internaron en el lago. Sus perseguidores, al no tener ninguna canoa con que perseguirlos, sólo pudieron mandar una nube de flechas detrás de ellos, pero éstas hicieron poco daño. Así que los guerreros acolhua cruzaron el lago y se unieron a nuestras fuerzas en Tenochtitlan, en donde, a causa de la muerte de tanta gente, hubo bastante lugar en donde alojarlos.

Cortés sabía, por sus conversaciones con Motecuzoma o por algún otro medio, que Texcoco era la ciudad más fuerte de nuestra Triple Alianza, después de Tenochtitlan. Y después de haber conquistado tan fácilmente la ciudad de Texcoco, confiaba apoderarse de todas las pequeñas ciudades y pueblos que estaban en las orillas de los lagos con mucha más facilidad, así es que él no designó a toda su tropa para hacer esa tarea, ni guió personalmente a la parte de su ejército que lo hizo. Para gran desconcierto de nuestros espías, mandó la mitad de su tropa de regreso a Texcala. La otra mitad la dividió en destacamentos, cada uno comandado por uno de sus oficiales: Alvarado, Narváez, Montejo, Guzmán. Algunos salieron de Texcoco hacia el norte y otros hacia el sur, y comenzaron a rodear el lago, atacando por el camino, ya fuese por separado o simultáneamente a todas aquellas comunidades pequeñas. Aunque nuestro Venerado Orador Cuautémoc había empleado la flota de canoas traída por los fugitivos acolhua para enviar a esos mismos guerreros y nuestros propios mexica en ayuda de esos pueblos sitiados, las batallas fueron tantas y los pueblos estaban tan retirados unos de otros que no pudo enviar suficientes hombres a cada una de ellas para poder cambiar el curso de los acontecimientos. Cada lugar que atacaban las fuerzas guiadas por los españoles era tomado. Lo mejor que pudieron hacer nuestros hombres fue rescatar de esos pueblos a todos los guerreros que habían sobrevivido y llevarlos a Tenochtitlan, para reforzar nuestra propia defensa, cuando nos llegara el turno.

Se supone que por medio de mensajeros, Cortés dirigió la estrategia general de sus oficiales y de sus batallones, pero él y Malintzin permanecieron en el lujoso palacio de Texcoco, en donde yo mismo había vivido, y mantuvo allí a la fuerza al desventurado Venerado Orador Cohuanácoch, como su anfitrión, o su huésped o su prisionero. Pues debo mencionar que el Príncipe Heredero Flor Oscura, quien había envejecido esperando convertirse en Uey-Tlatoani de los acolhua, jamás obtuvo la distinción de ese título.

Aun después de la toma de la capital de los acolhua, en donde las tropas de Flor Oscura habían jugado un papel importante, Cortés decretó que el inofensivo Cuahuanácoch debería permanecer en el trono. Cortés sabía que todos los acolhua, a excepción de los guerreros que durante tanto tiempo seguían a Flor Oscura, habían llegado a odiar al antes respetado Príncipe Heredero, por haber sido un traidor a su propia gente y un instrumento del hombre blanco. Cortés no podía correr el riesgo de provocar un futuro levantamiento en toda esa nación al entregar el trono al traidor, trono por el cual había traicionado a su gente. Aun cuando Flor Oscura se había rebajado a aceptar el rito del bautismo, teniendo a Cortés como padrino y con notoria zalamería tomó el nombre cristiano de Fernando *Cortés* Ixtlil-Xóchitl, su padrino cambió un poco su determinación, lo suficiente como para nombrarlo señor gobernante de tres provincias insignificantes en las tierras acolhua. Ante eso, Don Fernando Flor Oscura mostró un rasgo de su antiguo temperamento señorial protestando con ira:

«¿Me das lo que ya me pertenece? ¿Lo que siempre perteneció a mis antepasados?»

Sin embargo, no tuvo que sufrir por mucho tiempo su insatisfacción y humillación. Salió enfurecido de Texcoco para iniciar su gobierno en una de esas provincias apartadas, pero llegó al mismo tiempo que la epidemia de las pequeñas viruelas y en un mes o dos estaba muerto.

Pronto nos enteramos que los ejércitos merodeadores del Capitán General permanecían en Texcoco por otras razones además de disfrutar solamente de un descanso lleno de lujo. Nuestros *quimíchime* llegaron a Tenochtitlan para informarnos no de cosas desconcertantes, sino de que la mitad de la fuerza de Cortés que había partido, regresaba a Texcoco llevando sobre sus espaldas, o arrastrando, o rodando sobre troncos, todas las partes —cascos, palos, jarcias— y demás componentes de los trece «barcos», que se habían construido parcialmente en la tierra seca de Texcala. Cortés había permanecido en Texcoco para estar allí cuando llegaran y supervisar su construcción final y botadura en el lago.

Por supuesto que no eran tan formidables como los barcos de donde los habían sacado. Más bien eran como nuestros lanchones de carga con fondo plano y solamente con lados altos, y con velas en forma de alas que para nuestra congoja los hacían más veloces que nuestros *acaltin* de muchos remos grandes y rápidos, y mucho más ágiles que nuestros *acaltin* más pequeños. Además de los tripulantes que controlaban los movimientos del barco, cada uno de ellos llevaba veinte soldados españoles parados sobre unas tablas fijas detrás de esos lados altos. Así, ellos tenían la ventaja, muy significativa, de que en cualquier batalla en el agua podrían pelear a cierta altura sobre nuestros *acaltin* de proa baja, y además estar lo suficientemente altos como para descargar sus armas a través de nuestros caminospuentes.

El día que salieron a probar sus barcos en el lago de Texcoco, Cortés se encontraba a bordo de la nave que guiaba a las demás, que él llamaba *La Capitana*. Cierto número de nuestras más grandes canoas de guerra salieron de Tenochtitlan y pasaron por el Gran Canal, para enfrentarlos en el estrecho más ancho del lago. Cada canoa llevaba sesenta guerreros, cada uno de los cuales estaba armado con un arco y muchas flechas, un *atlatl* y varias jabalinas, pero entre las aguas agitadas del lago, las naves más pesadas de los hombres blancos eran plataformas más estables para descargar sus proyectiles, así que sus arcabuces y ballestas fueron totalmente más eficaces que los arcos sostenidos en las manos de nuestros hombres. Además sus soldados sólo exponían sus cabezas, sus brazos y sus armas, así es que nuestras flechas sólo pegaban en los lados altos de sus barcos o desaparecían sobre sus cabezas sin hacer ningún daño. Sin embargo, nuestros hombres que se hallaban en las canoas abiertas y bajas, estaban expuestos a los dardos y bolitas metálicas y muchos de ellos cayeron muertos o heridos. Así que los remeros trataban de mantener desesperadamente una distancia más segura, y eso significó una distancia demasiado grande como para que nuestros guerreros pudieran lanzas sus jabalinas. Poco tiempo después nuestras canoas guerreras regresaron ignominiosamente, y la nave enemiga desdeñó perseguirlos. Durante un rato navegaron alegremente haciendo diseños y cruzando a través del agua, como si estuvieran demostrando que ellos eran los dueños del lago, antes de regresar a Texcoco. Pero al día siguiente estaban otra vez allí y todos los días después de ése, y no hacían más que danzar sobre el agua.

Para entonces, los oficiales de Cortés y sus diferentes compañías habían marchado alrededor de todo el distrito del lago, dejando ruinas y ocupando o capturando cada comunidad que encontraban a su paso, hasta que llegó el momento en que se volvieron a unir en dos ejércitos considerables que ocuparon los promontorios que se extendían exactamente al norte y al sur de nuestra isla. Sólo les quedaba destruir o vencer a las ciudades más numerosas y pobladas, ubicadas alrededor de la costa occidental del lago, para tener a Tenochtitlan totalmente rodeada.

Lo hicieron de la manera más calmada. Mientras la otra mitad del ejército de Cortés estaba descansando en Texcoco, después de su increíble labor de trasladar aquellos botes de guerra por tierra firme, y esos mismos botes fueron de un lado a otro, en toda la extensión del lago de Texcoco al este del Gran Canal, desembarazándose de cuanta canoa encontraban. Las destrozaban o las volteaban, apoderándose, capturando o matando a los ocupantes de cada canoa que surcara las aguas, aunque éstas no fueran guerreras, sino los *acaltin* de los pescadores, los cazadores y los cargadores que apaciblemente transportaban su mercancía de un lugar a otro. Muy pronto, esos botes guerreros con alas fueron efectivamente los dueños de *todo* aquel extremo del lago. No había un pescador que se atreviera a surcar las aguas, ni para lanzar una red y así conseguir alimentos para su propia familia. Sólo en nuestro extremo del lago, dentro del dique, era donde continuaba el tráfico normal, pero no siguió así por mucho tiempo.

Al fin Cortés movió su ejército de reserva fuera de Texcoco, dividiéndolo en dos partes iguales que marcharon por separado alrededor del lago, hasta unirse con las otras dos fuerzas que se encontraban al sur y al norte de nosotros. Y mientras sus ejércitos hacían eso, sus botes de guerra se abrieron paso a través del Gran Dique. Todo lo que tuvieron que hacer fue ir matando, a lo largo del canal, con sus arcabuces y ballestas, a todos los trabajadores indefensos y desarmados quienes habían cerrado los portones del dique para impedirles el paso. Entonces los botes se deslizaron por los canales y entraron en aguas mexica. Aunque Cuautémoc inmediatamente envió guerreros que estuvieran parados hombro con hombro a lo largo de los caminos-puentes del norte y del sur, no pudieron por mucho tiempo impedir el avance de los botes, que se dirigían directamente hacia el cruce del camino-puente. Mientras algunos soldados blancos se desembarazaban de los defensores con andanadas de bolitas de metal y dardos, otros se inclinaban a los lados de los botes para poder mover los puentes de madera y dejar paso libre a sus barcos. Y así los botes de guerra pasaron las últimas barreras, y al penetrarlas hicieron lo que ya habían hecho en el lago, desembarazarse también de todo el tráfico marítimo: canoas guerreras, *acaltin* de carga, todo.

«Los hombres blancos se han apoderado de todos los caminos-puentes y también de todas las vías por agua —dijo el Mujer Serpiente—. Cuando vengan a las otras ciudades de la tierra firme, no tendremos modo de enviar a nuestros hombres para reforzar aquellas ciudades. Y lo que es peor, no tendremos modo alguno de recibir *nada* de la tierra firme. Ni fuerzas adicionales, ni armas adicionales. Ni comida.»

«Hay suficiente en las bodegas de la isla para sostenernos durante algún tiempo —dijo Cuautémoc, y agregó con amargura—: Podemos agradecer a las pequeñas viruelas que hay mucha menos gentes que alimentar de la que hubiera habido anteriormente. Y también tenemos las cosechas de la *chinampa*.»

El Mujer Serpiente dijo: «Las bodegas contienen solamente maíz seco y las *chinampas* sólo golosinas, como jitomates, chiles, cilantro y demás. Será una dieta extraña, las tortillas y el potaje de maíz que comen los hombres pobres, aderezados con los más elegantes condimentos.»

«Esa extraña dieta la recordarás con cariño —dijo Cuauhtémoc— cuando tu estómago tenga adentro, en lugar de eso, el acero español.»

Como los botes mantuvieron encerrados a nuestros guerreros dentro de la isla, las tropas de Cortés continuaron su marcha alrededor de la orilla occidental de la tierra firme, y una tras otra las ciudades se vieron obligadas a rendirse. La primera en caer fue Tepeyaca, nuestro vecino más cercano hacia el norte; luego lo hicieron las ciudades de Ixtapalapan y Mexicaltzinco; más tarde, Tenayuca, al noroeste, y Azcapotzalco; después, Coyohuacan, al suroeste. Se estaba cerrando el círculo y en Tenochtitlan ya no necesitábamos de los *quimíchime* espías para informarnos de lo que estaba sucediendo. En cuanto a nuestros aliados en la tierra firme cayeron o se rindieron y una cantidad de sus guerreros supervivientes lograron huir hasta nuestra isla, protegidos por la noche, ya fuera en *acaltin* y logrando eludir los botes de guerra que patrullaban, o deslizándose por los caminos-puentes y nadando entre los huecos, o atravesando a nado todo el estrecho de agua.

Algunos días, Cortés se los pasaba montado en la *Mula*, dirigiendo el avance implacable de sus fuerzas terrestres. Otros, estaba en su bote *La Capitana*, dirigiendo con banderas de señalización los movimientos de sus otras canoas y las descargas de sus armas, matando o dispersando cualquier guerrero que estuviera en la orilla de la tierra firme o en los caminos-puentes truncados de Tenochtitlan. Para defendernos de esas molestas canoas, los que vivíamos en Tenochtitlan ingeniamos la única defensa posible. A cada pedazo de madera útil que se encontraba en la isla se le sacó filo en uno de sus extremos y los nadadores llevaron esas estacas afiladas bajo el agua y las acomodaron firmemente, haciendo un ángulo hacia afuera justamente debajo de la superficie menos profunda alrededor de toda la isla. Si no hubiéramos hecho esto, los botes de guerra de Cortés habrían entrado por nuestros canales, directamente hacia el centro de la ciudad. Esa defensa demostró su valor cuando un día uno de los botes se acercó mucho, con la aparente intención de destruir algunas de nuestras cosechas de *chinampa*, y quedó clavado en una o más de esas estacas. Nuestros guerreros inmediatamente enviaron una lluvia de flechas y tal vez mataron a algunos de sus ocupantes, antes de que éstos pudieran zafar el barco y retirarse a la tierra firme para repararlo. De ahí en adelante, como los tripulantes no podían saber a qué distancia de la isla estaban colocadas las agudas estacas, se mantuvieron prudentemente alejados.

Fue entonces cuando las tropas de Cortés encontraron los

cañones que nuestros hombres habían tirado al lago durante la Noche Triste, ya que esos objetos tan pesados no pudieron ser arrojados muy lejos, los españoles empezaron a recuperarlos. Nosotros habíamos tenido la esperanza de que esas malditas cosas se arruinaran al ser sumergidas en el agua, pero no fue así. Sólo necesitaron que las limpiaran del cieno, que las dejaran secar y que las volvieran a cargar, y quedaron listas para usarse otra vez. Conforme se iban recuperando, Cortés mandó montar los primeros trece cañones, de uno en uno, en sus botes de guerra y esas naves tomaron posiciones a orillas del lago en las ciudades donde se hallaban peleando sus tropas y sobre ellas descargaron sus relámpagos, truenos y lluvias de proyectiles mortales. Sin poder defenderse por más tiempo, al ser acosados simultáneamente, enfrente y por un lado, las ciudades tuvieron que rendirse y cuando lo hubo hecho la ciudad Tlacopan, la capital de los tecpaneca y tercer baluarte de la Triple Alianza, las fuerzas de Cortés, que como en un abrazo habían circundado esas ciudades, se encontraron y se unieron.

Sus botes de guerra ya no necesitaban apoyar a sus tropas desde la playa, sin embargo al día siguiente estaban navegando otra vez alrededor del lago, descargando sus cañones. Los que estábamos en la isla los pudimos observar y durante un tiempo no adivinamos su intención, ya que no apuntaban ni a nosotros ni a ningún blanco en la tierra firme. Entonces, vimos y escuchamos el impacto destructivo de la bola de un cañón y fue cuando comprendimos, los proyectiles pesados golpearon primero al antiguo acueducto de Chapultépec y luego al que había mandado construir Auítzotl en Coyohuacan, rompiéndolos ambos.

El Mujer Serpiente dijo: «Los acueductos eran nuestra última conexión con la tierra firme. Ahora quedamos tan desamparados como un barco navegando sin remos sobre un mar tormentoso y lleno de monstruos malévolos. Estamos rodeados, sin protección y completamente expuestos. Todas las naciones que nos rodean y que no se han unido voluntariamente a los hombres blancos, han quedado vencidas y ahora obedecen sus órdenes. A excepción de los guerreros fugitivos que se encuentran aquí, no queda nadie más que nosotros, los mexica, solos contra todo El Único Mundo.»

«Así debe ser —dijo Cuautémoc con calma—. Si es nuestro *tonali* no ser al fin los vencedores, entonces que El Único Mundo recuerde para siempre que los mexica fuimos los últimos en ser vencidos.»

«Pero, Venerado Orador —suplicó el Mujer Serpiente—, los acueductos también fueron nuestro último vínculo con la vida. Quizás podríamos luchar durante un tiempo sin comida fresca, pero ¿cuánto tiempo podremos sobrevivir sin agua potable?»

«Tlácotzin —dijo Cuautémoc, con tanta suavidad como lo haría un maestro al dirigirse a un alumno que no hubiera entendido la lección—, hubo un tiempo, hace mucho, en que los mexica se encontraron solos, en este mismo lugar, indeseados y detestados por todos los demás pueblos; sólo tenían hierbas para comer, sólo tenían el agua pestilente del lago para beber. En esas circunstancias tan desesperadas y deprimentes, ellos pudieron haberse hincado ante los enemigos que los rodeaban, para ser esparcidos o absorbidos, y olvidados por la historia. Pero no fue así. Se sostuvieron de pie, se quedaron y construyeron todo esto. —Y movió su brazo para abarcar todo el esplendor de Tenochtitlan—. Cualquiera que sea el final, la historia no puede olvidarlos ahora. Los mexica se sostuvieron de pie. Los mexica siguen de pie. Los mexica permanecerán de pie hasta que ya no puedan sostenerse de pie.»

Después de los acueductos, nuestra ciudad fue el blanco de todos los cañones, los que se habían acomodado en la tierra firme y los que estaban montados en los botes que constantemente rodeaban la isla. Las bolas de hierro que venían de Chapultépec eran las más peligrosas y espantosas, porque los hombres blancos habían llevado algunos de sus cañones hasta la cima de aquel monte y desde allí podían enviar las bolas volando en un arco alto para que cayeran casi directamente abajo, como inmensas gotas de hierro sobre Tenochtitlan. Quisiera hacer notar que una de las primeras que cayó en la ciudad demolió el templo de la Gran Pirámide; ante esto, nuestros sacerdotes gritaron «¡desgracia!», «¡infortunio!», «¡mal agüero!» e hicieron ceremonias en donde combinaban oraciones abnegadas pidiendo perdón al dios de la guerra y oraciones desesperadas en demanda de la intercesión del dios de la guerra a nuestro favor.

Aunque los cañones continuaron ese rugir durante algunos días, sólo lo hacían a intervalos y parecía un ataque de lo más irregular, comparado con lo que sabíamos que eran capaces de *hacer* esos cañones. Creo que Cortés tenía la esperanza de que admitiéramos que estábamos abandonados, indefensos e inevitablemente derrotados, y así nos rendiríamos sin luchar, como él lo esperaría de cualquier gente sensata, sobre todo en esas condiciones. No creo que él lo estuviera haciendo así porque sintiera algún remordimiento o misericordia en matarnos, más bien creo que quería conservar la ciudad intacta, para poder presentarle a su Rey Don Carlos la colonia de la Nueva España completa con todo, incluida su capital, una capital que era muy superior a cualquier ciudad de la Vieja España.

Sin embargo, Cortés era y es un hombre impaciente. No perdió muchos días en estar esperando que nosotros tomáramos la decisión sensata de rendirnos. Mandó a sus artesanos que construyeran unos puentes de madera portátiles y ligeros, con ellos cubrió las brechas entre los caminos-puentes y envió a numerosos hombres corriendo hacia la ciudad en un ataque repentino, desde los tres caminos-puentes al mismo tiempo. Sin embargo, nuestros guerreros todavía no estaban debilitados por el hambre y las tres columnas de españoles y sus aliados, se vieron detenidos como si hubieran corrido contra una pared sólida de piedra, que circundaba toda la isla. Muchos de ellos murieron y los que quedaron se batieron en retirada, aunque no tan rápido como habían llegado, pues llevaban muchos heridos.

Cortés esperó algunos días más y luego volvió a tratar otra

vez, de la misma manera, pero con peores resultados. En esa ocasión, cuando el enemigo penetró en la isla, nuestras canoas de guerra habían partido con anterioridad y una vez que hubo pasado la primera ola de atacantes, nuestros guerreros desembarcaron de las canoas sobre los caminos-puentes detrás de ellos, quitaron los puentes portátiles y así tuvimos una buena porción de las fuerzas de ataque dentro de la ciudad, *con nosotros*. Los españoles atrapados pelearon por sus vidas, pero sus aliados nativos, sabiendo mejor lo que les esperaba, pelearon hasta caer muertos, para no ser capturados. Esa noche toda la isla estaba encendida por las antorchas y los fuegos ceremoniales de los inciensos y de los altares, en particular la Gran Pirámide estaba brillantemente iluminada, así Cortés y todos los demás hombres podrían ver, si se acercaban lo suficiente y si se tomaban la molestia de observar, lo que les esperaba a los cuarenta o más de sus compañeros que habíamos capturado vivos.

Y por lo menos Cortés sí presenció ese sacrificio en masa o cuando menos lo suficiente para que montara en cólera. Nos exterminaría a todos, aunque tuviera que pulverizar la ciudad que tanto deseaba preservar, así es que suspendió esos intentos de invasión y sometió a la ciudad a un intenso y rencoroso cañoneo. Las balas eran lanzadas tan rápido y regularmente como supongo que lo permitían los cañones sin llegar a derretirse por tan prolongado esfuerzo. Los proyectiles caían como plomo desde la tierra firme y silbaban a través del agua por los botes que la rodeaban. Nuestra ciudad empezó a derrumbarse y mucha de nuestra gente murió. Una sola bala de cañón podía arrancar un gran pedazo a un edificio, por muy macizo que fuera, tanto como la Gran Pirámide, y muchos quedaron como ésta, pues la que fue una vez una bella estructura lisa se veía entonces como una masa de pan mordida y roída por ratas gigantes. Una sola bala de cañón podía tirar toda una pared de una casa hecha de piedra y una de adobe simplemente quedaba hecha añicos.

Esa lluvia de fuego continuó por lo menos por dos meses, día tras día, deteniéndose sólo un poco durante la noche, pero aun así, los cañoneros nos mandaban dos o tres bolas retumbantes a intervalos impredecibles e irregulares, sólo para asegurarnos que nuestro sueño no sería tranquilo por no decir imposible y de que no tendríamos la oportunidad de dormir en paz. Después de un tiempo, los hombres blancos se quedaron sin sus proyectiles de hierro y tuvieron que usar piedras redondas, que juntaron. Aunque éstas eran mucho menos destructivas sobre los edificios de la ciudad, con el impacto muy seguido se partían en pedazos y sus fragmentos volaban y así eran mucho más destructoras para la piel humana.

Sin embargo los que murieron de esa manera por lo menos lo hicieron de una forma rápida, pues los demás parecíamos condenados a una muerte más lenta, infeliz y agonizante. Como los alimentos que teníamos en reserva tenían que durarnos lo más posible, los oficiales encargados repartían el maíz seco en raciones pequeñísimas, lo suficiente nada más para sostener la vida. Por un tiempo, también pudimos alimentarnos de las aves y los perros de la isla y compartíamos los peces atrapados por los hombres que a escondidas salían de noche para echar sus redes bajo los caminos-puentes y entre las raíces y el fondo de las *chinampa*. Pero llegó el día en que no quedó ni perros ni aves y los peces empezaron a alejarse de los alrededores de la isla. Entonces repartimos y nos comimos a todos los animales comestibles que estaban en el zoológico público, a excepción de los especímenes más raros y más bellos, pues sus guardianes no quisieron deshacerse de ellos. Esos animales se mantuvieron vivos, y en verdad en mejores condiciones de salud que sus guardianes, siendo alimentados con los cuerpos de nuestros esclavos que morían de hambre.

Con el tiempo, llegamos hasta atrapar las ratas, los ratones y las lagartijas. Nuestros niños, los pocos que habían sobrevivido a las pequeñas viruelas, se volvieron muy hábiles para cazar a todo pájaro que fuera lo suficientemente tonto como para acercarse a la isla. Más tarde, cortamos todas las flores de nuestras azoteas y deshojamos todos los arbustos y los árboles, y con esto preparamos ensaladas. Ya hacia el final, nosotros buscábamos todo insecto comestible en esos jardines, y le quitábamos la corteza a los árboles, y masticábamos nuestras cobijas de piel de conejo, nuestros vestidos de piel y las páginas de piel de venado de nuestros libros, buscando cualquier pedazo de carne que se hubiera escondido en ellos. Algunas personas trataban de engañar sus estómagos haciéndoles creer que habían comido y los llenaban con el cemento de cal que tomaban del escombro de los edificios destruidos.

Los peces no huyeron de los alrededodes de la isla por miedo a ser atrapados, se fueron porque nuestras aguas se habían contaminado. Aunque ya había llegado la temporada de lluvias, sólo llovía parte de las tardes, así es que poníamos cuantas ollas y cazuelas teníamos para recogerla y también colgábamos tiras de tela para que se empaparan y luego exprimirlas, pero a pesar de todos nuestros esfuerzos, pocas veces había algo más que un chorrito de agua fresca para cada boca seca. Así, aunque al principio nos repugnó, pronto nos acostumbramos a tomar el agua contaminada del lago. También, las aguas llegaron a contaminarse más, pues como ya no había manera de colectar y acarrear los desperdicios y los excrementos humanos, esas substancias fueron tiradas a los canales y de allí pasaron a las aguas del lago, y como sólo los cuerpos de los esclavos eran dados como alimento a los animales del zoológico, no teníamos manera de deshacernos de los otros cadáveres, excepto arrojándolos al mismo lago; Cuautémoc ordenó que fueran echados hacia el lado occidental de la isla, pues al lado este del lago había una extensión más amplia de agua y debido al viento del este que soplaba continuamente, esa agua se mantenía renovada y por eso esperábamos que estuviera menos contaminada. Sin embargo, llegó el momento inevitable en que los desperdicios y los cadáveres contaminaron todas las aguas alrededor de la isla. Como de todas maneras teníamos que tomar de esa agua cuando la sed nos apretaba, entonces mojábamos telas, las exprimíamos y luego hervíamos esa agua, pero aun así, retorcía nuestras entrañas con flujos y retortijones. Muchos de nuestros niños y ancianos murieron por tomar esa agua podrida.

Una noche, cuando Cuautémoc ya no pudo ver sufrir más su pueblo, citó a toda la población de la ciudad para que se reuniera en El Corazón del Único Mundo, así que todos nos reunimos en la noche, cuando los cañones no estaban tronando y creo que todo el que podía estar de pie estaba allí. Nos paramos sobre el piso lleno de baches, de lo que antes había sido mármol liso de la plaza, que estaba rodeado por los escombros cortados y picudos de lo que había sido el ondulante Muro de la Serpiente, mientras el Venerado Orador nos hablaba desde lo que quedaba de las escaleras rotas de la Gran Pirámide.

«Si Tenochtitlan ha de sobrevivir un poco más, ya no debe de ser una ciudad, sino una fortaleza y una fortaleza debe estar comandada por aquellos que aún están en posibilidad de luchar. Estoy orgulloso de la lealtad y resistencia demostrada por todo mi pueblo, pero ha llegado el momento en que con gran pena debo pediros que pongáis fin a vuestra lealtad. Todavía queda una bodega sin abrir, pero sólo una...»

La multitud allí reunida ni gritó de alegría ni hizo un clamor en demanda. Sólo murmuraba, pero ese ruido parecía el sordo rumor provocado por un inmenso estómago hambriento.

«Cuando mande abrir esa bodega —continuó Cuautémoc—, el maíz se repartirá en partes iguales entre todos los que lo pidan. Ahora bien, eso puede proporcionar a cada persona en esta ciudad, quizás, una última comida muy escasa, o, será lo suficiente para alimentar un poco mejor a nuestros guerreros, para darles más fuerzas con que pelear hasta el final, cuando llegue ese final y como llegue. Pueblo mío, no os daré ninguna orden, sólo os pido que escojáis y toméis una decisión.»

El pueblo no hizo ningún sonido.

Él terminó diciendo: «Esta noche he mandado colocar el puente sobre el camino-puente del norte. El enemigo espera con cautela al otro lado, preguntándose por qué habré hecho eso. Lo he hecho para que todos los que queráis partir, y podáis hacerlo, lo hagáis. No sé qué es lo que encontraréis en Tepeyaca, quizás comida o descanso o la Muerte Florida, pero os suplico a aquellos que ya no podáis luchar que aprovechéis esta oportunidad para dejar Tenochtitlan. Esto no será una deserción ni con ello debéis sentiros derrotados, no incurriréis en ninguna vergüenza al partir. Al contrario, de esta manera permitiréis que nuestra ciudad pueda defenderse un poco más. No diré más.»

Ninguno se fue con prisa o de buena gana, todos lo hicieron con lágrimas en los ojos y con pena, pero reconocieron lo práctico de la súplica de Cuautémoc, y en una sola noche la ciudad quedó vacía. Toda su gente, la más joven y la más anciana, sus enfermos e inválidos, sus sacerdotes y los asistentes de los templos, todos se fueron, todos los que no podían por más tiempo ser útiles en el combate. Cargando sus bultos y llevando en ellos las pocas cosas de valor que pudieron llevar al partir, se dirigieron hacia el norte a través de las calles de los cuatro barrios de

Tenochtitlan y empezaron a convergir hacia el área del mercado de Tlaltelolco, formando una columna al cruzar el camino-puente. No fueron recibidos con destellos de relámpagos y truenos al final del camino-puente, según supe después, los hombres blancos que estaban allá sólo los vieron llegar con indiferencia y en cuanto a los texcalteca que ocupaban esas posiciones, les pareció que esa gente que llegaba buscando refugio, tropezando y enfermos, eran demasiado débiles como para que valiera la pena sacrificarlos en una celebración de victoria, y la gente de Tepeyaca, aunque también ellos eran cautivos por las fuerzas de Cortés, los recibieron con comida, dándoles agua fresca y albergue.

En Tenochtitlan sólo quedó Cuautémoc, otros señores de su corte, su Consejo de Voceros, sus esposas y familias, tanto del Venerado Orador como de sus otros nobles, varios físicos y cirujanos, todos los campeones y guerreros útiles y algún que otro viejo obstinado como yo, quienes habían tenido buena salud antes del sitio y que no habíamos quedado tan debilitados a consecuencia del mismo y que aún podíamos luchar si era necesario. También permanecieron las mujeres jóvenes cuya salud y fuerza todavía era aceptable y por lo tanto eran útiles, y una vieja que a pesar de mis súplicas rehusó dejar su lecho de enferma, que ya tenía tiempo de ocupar.

«Estorbo menos aquí acostada —dijo Beu—, a que se me lleve cargada en una silla de manos por otros que apenas pueden caminar. También, hace mucho tiempo que dejó de importarme cuanto como y con facilidad puedo pasar sin ello. Si me quedo puedo morir más rápido de lo que me mataría esta larga y tediosa enfermedad. Además, Zaa, tú también ignoraste una oportunidad para ponerle a salvo, anteriormente. Podría ser una tontería, dijiste, pero tú querías ver el final de todo. —Sonrió débilmente—. Ahora, después de todas las imprudencias que he tenido que soportar de tu parte, ¿me negarás el poder compartir contigo otra imprudencia más que muy bien pudiera ser la última?»

Acertadamente, Cortés llegó a la conclusión, al ver la evacuación repentina de Tenochtitlan y el aspecto cadavérico de los que dejaron la ciudad, de que los que todavía estaban adentro, se sentirían tan débiles como los que la habían abandonado. Por lo que al día siguiente ordenó otro ataque contra la ciudad, aunque no lo hizo de una manera tan impetuosa como antes. Comenzó el día enviándonos una lluvia de proyectiles, como nunca antes habíamos sufrido, pues pareció que puso a trabajar sus cañones hasta que estuvieran a punto de fundirse. Sin duda él tenía la esperanza de que todos nosotros nos refugiáramos bajo algún lugar, sin movernos de allí mucho después de que terminara esa lluvia desvastadora, pero aun así, cuando sus cañones de la playa dejaron de trabajar, él mantuvo a sus botes de batalla dando vueltas alrededor de la isla, pero sobre todo por el lado norte, descargando esos cañones sobre esa parte de la ciudad, mientras sus soldados bregaban a lo largo del camino-puente del sur.

Pero no nos encontraron acobardados bajo ningún refugio, es más, lo que hallaron las primeras filas de hombres blancos hizo que éstas se detuvieran haciendo que se amontonaran las de atrás, ya que habíamos puesto en cada lugar en donde esperábamos que llegaran los invasores a uno de nuestros hombres más gordos, bueno, por lo menos el más lleno en comparación con los demás, y los españoles lo encontraron simplemente paseándose por allí, eructando plácidamente mientras mordisqueaba una pierna de perro o de conejo o de algún otro tipo de carne. Si los soldados se hubieran acercado lo suficiente, se habrían dado cuenta de que la carne estaba en realidad ya totalmente enlamada, por haber sido guardada mucho tiempo, sólo con el fin de hacer ese gesto de ostentación.

Sin embargo no se acercaron a verlo, porque el hombre gordo desapareció rápidamente, mientras una horda de hombres mucho más delgados se alzaron repentinamente detrás de las ruinas de los edificios que estaban cerca, y lanzaron una lluvia de jabalinas. Muchos de los merodeadores cayeron en esos momentos, otros trataron de avanzar, pero sólo para encontrarse con guerreros armados con *maquáhuime* y otros se hicieron para atrás en donde se encontraron con una lluvia de flechas. Todos los que sobrevivieron ante esa fuerte y sorprendente defensa, retrocedieron todo el camino hacia la tierra firme. Estoy seguro de que informaron a Cortés acerca de la aparición de ese hombre gordo, bien comido y que se estaba alimentando con carne, y estoy seguro de que Cortés se rió de aquel patético gesto de valentía de nuestra parte, pero ellos debieron de haberle informado también, con bastante realismo, que ahora las ruinas les estaban proporcionando una mejor defensa a los ocupantes de la ciudad, que si ésta hubiera quedado intacta.

«Muy bien —dijo el Capitán General de acuerdo con ese último informe—. Tenía la esperanza de poder salvar parte de ella, para que nuestros compatriotas se maravillaran al verla, cuando vinieran a colonizarla. Pero la arrasaremos... no dejaremos en pie ni una piedra, ni una viga... la destruiremos de tal manera que ni un escorpión pueda esconderse, para luego arrastrarse ante nosotros.»

Y por supuesto, eso fue lo que hizo. Mientras los cañones de sus barcos seguían derrumbando la parte norte de la ciudad, Cortés llevó varios de los que tenía en la playa hacia los camino-puentes del sur y del oeste; los cañones fueron arrastrados a lo largo de las calzadas seguidos por soldados, unos a pie y otros montados que a su vez eran seguidos por los sabuesos y otros hombres seguían a éstos, sólo armados con mazos, hachas, palancas de hierro y arietes. Primero los cañones fueron utilizados para barrer todo obstáculo que tuvieran enfrente y matar a los guerreros que se pudieran esconder allí, o por lo menos mantenerlos agachados sin poder pelear. Luego los soldados avanzaban dentro del área devastada y cuando nuestros guerreros se levantaban para pelear, eran coceados por los caballos y los soldados que iban a pie les caían encima. Nuestros hombres lucharon valientemente, pero ya estaban muy débiles por el hambre y medio aturdidos por los cañonazos que habían tenido que soportar, y casi todos murieron; los que pudieron escapar lo hicieron hacia el centro de la ciudad.

Algunos de ellos trataron de permanecer ocultos en sus escondites, mientras los soldados pasaban por allí, pues tenían la esperanza de matar por lo menos a uno de ellos lanzándole una jabalina o una *maquáhuitl* por detrás, pero ninguno tuvo esa oportunidad, ya que los encontraban rápidamente por medio de los perros. Esos sabuesos podían oler a un hombre desde mucha distancia, sin importar lo bien escondidos que pudieran estar y si ellos mismos no acababan con él, por lo menos descubrían su posición a los soldados. Entonces, en cuanto un área quedaba libre de peligro y de defensores, las cuadrillas de trabajadores empezaban a utilizar sus herramientas de demolición, limpiando todo a su paso. Echaron abajo casas, torres, templos y monumentos, y le prendieron fuego a todo lo que podía arder. Cuando terminaron de hacer eso, sólo quedaba una tierra lisa y llana.

Eso equivalía a un día de trabajo. Al siguiente día, los cañones podían avanzar mejor sin ningún impedimento en su camino, y luego cañoneaban otra parte de la ciudad, a lo que seguirían sus soldados, sus perros y sus demoledores. Así lo hicieron día tras día, y la ciudad iba desapareciendo poco a poco, como si fuera Comida Por Los Dioses. Nosotros, los que todavía no estábamos en esa parte de la ciudad, podíamos ver desde nuestras azoteas cómo avanzaban y cómo al nivelar la ciudad se iban acercando cada vez más a nosotros.

Recuerdo el día en que los destructores llegaron al Corazón del Único Mundo. Primero se divirtieron lanzando flechas incendiarias a aquellas inmensas banderolas de plumas, que aunque ya estaban destrozadas todavía flotaban majestuosas y tristes por encima de nuestras cabezas y esas banderas fueron desapareciendo poco a poco en medio de las llamas. Sin embargo, se requirieron muchos días para destruir esa ciudad que estaba dentro de una ciudad, sus templos, sus patios de *tlachtli*, su barra de calaveras, los palacios y los edificios de la corte. Aunque la Gran Pirámide ya era una ruina que se desmoronaba por sí sola y que difícilmente podría servir de escondite a alguien, Cortés debió de pensar que tenía que derribarla porque era el símbolo que distinguía la magnificencia de Tenochtitlan. No la pudo demoler tan fácilmente a pesar de tener trabajando en ello a cientos de obreros con sus pesadas herramientas, pero al fin fue cayendo capa tras capa, revelando las antiguas pirámides que estaban dentro de ella, cada una de ellas más pequeña y más primitiva, hasta que también éstas desaparecieron. Cortés hizo que los hombres que trabajaban en la demolición del palacio de Motecuzoma Xocóyotl lo hicieran con mucho cuidado, pues obviamente esperaba encontrar el tesoro de la nación otra vez puesto bajo las gruesas paredes de las habitaciones, pero no fue así, y al no hallarlo la destrucción fue terminada con rabia.

También recuerdo que quemó el gran zoológico, pues ese día yo estaba observando desde la azotea de una casa que se encontraba lo suficientemente cerca y podía escuchar los rugidos, los aullidos y los gritos de sus ocupantes al ser quemados vivos. Es verdad que la población del zoológico había quedado muy reducida, ya que nos tuvimos que comer a parte de sus ocupantes, pero todavía habían allí animales maravillosos, pájaros y reptiles. Algunos de ellos no los podrán nunca reponer, si alguna vez ustedes los españoles deciden poner un lugar así. Por ejemplo, en aquel tiempo el zoológico exhibía unos jaguares totalmente blancos, un tipo de animal muy raro que nosotros los mexica nunca antes habíamos visto y que nunca más se volverán a ver.

Cuautémoc, conociendo bien la debilidad de sus guerreros, les dio órdenes de que solamente lucharan en retirada, obstaculizando el avance del enemigo lo más posible y tratando de matar a la mayor parte de los invasores, pero los mismos guerreros estaban tan indignados y enfurecidos por la demolición de El Único Mundo que, desobedeciendo las órdenes y sacando fuerzas de flaqueza tomaron la ofensiva, así es que muchas veces, surgiendo de entre los escombros, golpeaban sus escudos y lanzaban sus gritos de guerra atacando. Incluso nuestras mujeres estaban tan enfurecidas por eso, que se les unieron y tiraron nidos llenos de avispas desde las azoteas de sus casas y piedras y otras cosas menos mencionables sobre las cabezas de los destructores.

Nuestros guerreros sí mataron a algunos de los soldados y de los demoledores y atrasaron en lo que pudieron su obra de destrucción, pero muchos de nuestros hombres murieron haciendo eso y cada vez tenían que retroceder más. Sin embargo, para no temer ese hostigamiento, Cortés mandó que sus cañones continuaran hacia el norte, abatiendo la ciudad por ese lado, y sus soldados, sus perros y sus obreros siguieron a los cañones, dejando el terreno liso por donde iban pasando. A que avanzaron hacia el norte se debe el que no destruyeran esta Casa del Canto en la cual estamos sentados ahora y a que dejaran algunos pocos edificios en pie, aunque no muy importantes, en la mitad del sur de la isla.

Sin embargo, no quedaron muchos edificios en pie en ninguna parte y los pocos que resistieron parecían como si fueran los últimos dientes en la boca desdentada de un anciano, y mi casa no fue de las que quedaron en pie. Supongo que debo de estar contento de que cuando mi casa fue demolida yo no estuviera adentro, pero por ese tiempo, toda la población que quedaba en la ciudad se había ido a refugiar al barrio de Tlaltelolco y en medio de él, para quedar lo más lejos posible del incesante tronar de los proyectiles de los cañones y de las flechas incendiarias que lanzaban los barcos que rodeaban la isla. Los guerreros y los supervivientes que estaban más fuertes vivían en las partes abiertas del mercado, mientras que las mujeres y la gente más débil se amontonaban en las casas, ya de por sí llenas, de la gente de ese barrio. Cuautémoc y su corte ocupaban el antiguo palacio que había sido de Moquíhuix, el último gobernante de Tlaltelolco, cuando esa ciudad todavía era independiente. Como yo formaba parte de esa corte, pues ya era un Señor, se me concedió un pequeño cuarto que compartía con Beu. Aunque había protestado otra vez en contra de ser movida de su casa, esa vez yo la cargué en mis brazos. Así, con Cuautémoc y muchos otros más, estuve parado en la pirámide de Tlaltelolco viendo cómo los demoledores de Cortés llegaban a Ixacualco, el barrio en donde yo había vivido. No pude ver, entre el humo del cañón y el polvo de la cal pulverizada, en qué momento exacto cayó mi casa, pero cuando el enemigo se retiró antes de que el día terminara, el barrio de Ixacualco era, como la mayor parte del extremo sur de la isla, un desierto vacío.

No sé si jamás Cortés llegó a saber que cada *pochtécatl* rico de nuestra ciudad tenía en su casa, al igual que yo, un cuarto en donde esconder su tesoro. Por lo visto no lo sabía entonces, porque su grupo de trabajadores tiraron todas las casas con la mayor indiferencia y entre el humo y el polvo del derrumbamiento de cada casa nadie jamás alcanzó a ver los paquetes envueltos o los bultos de oro, joyas, plumas, tintes y demás que quedaron enterrados entre el escombro y que más tarde fue hecho a un lado para dar lugar a la ampliación de la ciudad. Por supuesto que si Cortés se hubiera apoderado de todos esos objetos valiosos que tenían los *pochteca*, éstos hubieran sido sólo una fracción del tesoro perdido hasta la fecha, pero todo eso aún hubiera constituido un regalo capaz de asombrar y de alegrar a su Rey Don Carlos. Así es que observé ese día la devastación de mi casa con irónica satisfacción, aunque cuando ese día terminó, me convertí en pobre, un anciano más pobre de lo que lo fue el niñito que había visto Tenochtitlan por primera vez.

Bien, así estábamos todos los mexica que aún quedábamos vivos, incluyendo al Venerado Orador. El fin llegó poco después y cuando llegó, lo hizo rápido. Por incontables días, nosotros no habíamos tenido comida y estábamos tan débiles que no teníamos humor ni para movernos, hablarnos o escucharnos. Cortés y su ejército, tan implacable y voraz como esas hormigas que acaban con bosques enteros, llegaron al fin a la plaza y al mercado de Tlaltelolco y empezaron a demoler la pirámide, lo que significaba que nosotros los fugitivos, que nos apretujábamos en el pequeño espacio que había quedado para esconderse, difícilmente teníamos ya espacio para pararnos cómodamente. Aun así, Cuatémoc se había mantenido de pie, y lo hubiera seguido haciendo aunque sólo se hubiera parado sobre un pie, pero, después de que yo, el Mujer Serpiente y otros consejeros hubimos conferenciado privadamente fuimos hacia él y le dijimos:

«Señor Orador, si los extranjeros lo capturan, toda la nación mexica caerá con usted, pero si escapa, el gobierno de los mexica irá a donde usted vaya. Aunque cada persona en esta isla cayese muerta o capturada, Cortés no habrá vencido a los mexica.»

«¿Escapar? —dijo lentamente—. ¿Adónde? ¿Y para hacer qué?»

«A exiliarse, sólo con sus familiares más cercanos y con algunos de los señores principales. Es verdad que ya no tenemos aliados en ninguna parte en las tierras cercanas, pero hay naciones más lejanas en donde puede encontrar aliados. Puede que pase mucho tiempo antes de que usted tenga la esperanza de volver triunfalmente y con una gran fuerza, pero aun así, y sin importar el tiempo que le lleve, los mexica seguirán siendo invictos.»

«Pero ¿a qué naciones lejanas voy a ir?», preguntó sin entusiasmo.

Los otros señores me miraron y yo le dije: «A Aztlán, Venerado Orador. Regrese a donde se encuentran nuestros orígenes.»

Me miró como si me hubiera vuelto loco, pero yo le recordé que hacía relativamente poco habíamos reanudado los lazos que nos ataban con nuestros primos que habitaban en el lugar de nuestros orígenes y le di un mapa que había hecho para señalarle el camino, y agregué: «Puede tener la seguridad de que será bien recibido, Señor Cuautémoc. Cuando su Orador Tlilectic-Mixtli se fue de aquí, Motecuzoma mandó con él una fuerza de guerreros mexica y cierto número de familias adiestradas para construir allí una ciudad moderna. Posiblemente se encuentre con la existencia de una pequeña Tenochtitlan, o por lo menos esos azteca podrían ser la semilla del maíz, como una vez lo fueron antes, para crear otra nación poderosa y nueva.»

Me tomó mucho tiempo persuadir a Cuautémoc para que estuviera de acuerdo con eso, pero no les contaré todo ya que fue inútil. Todavía pienso que el plan hubiera podido tener éxito, pues estaba bien concebido, pero los dioses decretaron otra cosa y el plan no resultó. Al atardecer, cuando los botes de batalla cesaban su cañoneo después de un largo día de trabajar y empezaban a volver hacia la tierra firme, un buen número de nuestros hombres acompañó a Cuautémoc y a las personas que se habían escogido para acompañarlos, a la orilla de la isla. Todos subieron en las canoas y a una sola señal éstas se desbandaron en todas direcciones, para parecer que querían escurrirse para ponerse a salvo. El *acali* que llevaba a Cuautémoc y a su pequeña corte, se dirigió hacia una pequeña bahía que estaba entre Tenayuca y Aztcapotzalco. Como no había habitantes allí o si los había eran muy pocos, era de suponer que no habría guardias o centinelas o algún campamento de Cortés, y Cuautémoc podría con facilidad deslizarse desde allí hacia el norte, tierra adentro hacia el Aztlán.

Sin embargo, los botes de guerra se dieron cuenta de esa repentina salida de los *acaltin* desde la isla y regresaron navegando lo más rápido que pudieron para determinar si en realidad llevaban una *ruta*. Y por mala suerte, el capitán de uno de los botes fue lo suficientemente astuto como para notar que los ocupantes de cierta canoa, iban vestidos más ricamente que si fueran sólo simples guerreros. Ese barco dejó caer unos ganchos de hierro sobre la canoa y capturándola la sujetó fuertemente hacia uno de sus costados y subiendo al Venerado Orador al barco, lo llevó directamente ante el Capitán General Cortés.

Aunque no estuve presente en ese encuentro supe más tarde lo que Cuautémoc dijo a Cortés por medio de su intérprete Malintzin: «Yo no me rindo. Era por el beneficio de mi gente que los estaba eludiendo, pero como me han atrapado limpiamente —y señaló la daga que Cortés llevaba al cinto—, y puesto que estamos en guerra, yo merezco y exijo que me maten como a un guerrero. Le pido que me mate ahora, aquí en donde estoy parado.»

Magnánimo en su victoria o por lo menos untuoso, Cortés dijo: «No, vos no os habéis rendido, ni habéis cedido vuestro reino. Por lo tanto rehúso mataros e insisto en que conservéis el mando de vuestra gente, ya que tenemos mucho que hacer y rezo porque vos me ayudéis a lograrlo. Hagamos entre los dos una ciudad con mucha más grandeza, mi estimado Señor Cuautémoc.»

Cortés probablemente pronunció Guatemoc como siempre lo hizo después. Creo que ya hace algún tiempo les mencioné a ustedes, reverendos frailes, que el nombre de Cuautémoc significa Águila Que Cae Sobre Su Presa, pero supongo que era inevitable y hasta más adecuado que después de ese día, que en nuestro calendario fue Uno-Serpiente de nuestro año Tres-Casa y que en el de ustedes fue el trece de agosto de su año mil quinientos veintiuno, el nombre de nuestro último Venerado Orador fuera siempre y desde entonces traducido al español como El Águila Caída.

✠

Por algún tiempo después de la caída de Tenochtitlan, la vida no cambió mucho en El Único Mundo. Fuera del área inmediata de la Triple Alianza, ninguna otra parte de estas tierras había sido devastada de esa manera y probablemente había todavía muchos lugares en donde la gente ni siquiera se había dado cuenta de que ya no vivían en El Único Mundo, sino en un lugar llamado la Nueva España. Aunque habían sido abatidos cruelmente por esa nueva y misteriosa enfermedad, ellos casi nunca vieron a un español o a un cristiano, así es que no tuvieron nuevas leyes o dioses impuestos por ellos y siguieron con sus formas acostumbradas de vida, recogiendo la cosecha, cazando, pescando y demás, como lo habían hecho durante gavillas de años antes.

Sin embargo, aquí, en las tierras del lago, toda la vida cambió y fue difícil para nosotros, nunca se nos hizo fácil ese cambio y dudo que alguna vez lo sea. Al día siguiente de que Cuautémoc fue capturado, Cortés concentró toda su atención y energía en la reconstrucción de esta ciudad, aunque más bien debería decir *nuestra* energía. Pues decretó que, como había sido por culpa de nosotros, los imprudentes mexica, el que Tenochtitlan fuera destruida, nosotros seríamos los responsables de la restauración de dicha ciudad como la Ciudad de Mexico. Aunque sus arquitectos fueron los que hicieron los planos, sus artesanos los que supervisaron la obra y sus más brutales soldados los que movieron los látigos para que el trabajo fuera hecho, fue nuestra gente la que lo hizo, y fuimos nosotros los que proporcionamos los materiales y si queríamos comer después de nuestro trabajo, éramos nosotros los que nos teníamos que proporcionar esa comida. Así que los canteros de Xaltocan trabajaron como nunca lo habían hecho en toda su vida, y los carpinteros arrasaron con todos los bosques de las colinas del lago y cortaron vigas y tablas, y nuestros guerreros y *pochteca* se convirtieron en forrajeadores y cargadores de alimentos y de todas las demás necesidades que pudieron arrancar por la fuerza de las tierras circunvecinas; y nuestras mujeres, cuando no eran molestadas abiertamente por los soldados blancos e incluso violadas enfrente de todo el que lo quería ver, eran empleadas como cargadoras y mensajeras, y hasta a los niños pequeños se les ponía a trabajar mezclando la cal.

Por supuesto, las cosas más importantes fueron las que se

atendieron primero. Los acueductos rotos fueron reparados y se pusieron los cimientos de lo que sería su iglesia catedral, enfrente de la cual se levantó el pilar de ajusticiamiento y la horca. Ésas fueron las primeras estructuras en funcionar en esta nueva Ciudad de Mexico, pues se utilizaban con frecuencia para inspirarnos a hacer una labor más incesante y consciente. Aquellos que flojeaban en cualquier tarea eran estrangulados en la horca o se les grababa con fuego «prisionero de guerra» en las mejillas y luego eran expuestos en el pilar para que los extranjeros les lanzaran piedras y excremento de caballo o eran azotados con los látigos de los capataces. Pero los que trabajaban muy duro, morían con la misma frecuencia que los débiles a causa de que muchas veces los obligaban a cargar piedras tan pesadas que se destripaban.

Yo fui mucho más afortunado que los demás, puesto que Cortés me dio trabajo como intérprete. Con todas las instrucciones que tenían que dar los arquitectos a los albañiles, con todas las leyes nuevas, proclamas y edictos y todos los sermones que se tenían que traducir a la gente había demasiado trabajo para que Malintzin lo pudiera hacer ella sola, y el hombre Aguilar, que hubiera podido servir en alguna forma, había muerto hacía tiempo en algún lugar en alguna batalla. Por eso Cortés me empleó y hasta me pagaba un pequeño salario en moneda española, además de darnos alojamiento a mí y a Beu en su espléndida residencia, ya que se había apropiado lo que en un tiempo fue el palacio de campo de Motecuzoma, cerca de Quaunáhuac, en donde vivía en compañía de Malintzin, de sus oficiales y concubinas y en donde vigilaba a Cuautémoc, a su familia y a sus cortesanos.

Quizás deba disculparme aunque no sabría con quién, por haber dejado que el hombre blanco me empleara en lugar de desafiarlo, pero como las batallas ya habían terminado y como no había perecido en ellas, parecía que mi *tonali* había ordenado que por lo menos durante un tiempo debería luchar por no perecer. Una vez, hacía ya tiempo se me había pedido: «¡Sosténte en pie! ¡Aguanta! ¡Recuerda!» Y eso estaba determinado a hacer.

Durante un tiempo, una parte principal de mis deberes como intérprete consistieron en traducir las exigencias incesantes e insistentes de Cortés, por saber qué se había hecho del tesoro desaparecido de los mexica. Si hubiera sido más joven y hubiera estado en condiciones de trabajar en cualquier tipo de comercio, para poder mantenerme a mí y a mi esposa, que cada vez estaba más enferma, en ese mismo momento hubiera dejado ese trabajo tan humillante. Tenía que sentarme junto a Cortés y a sus oficiales, como si fuera uno de ellos, mientras ellos maltrataban e insultaban a mis compañeros señores, llamándolos «¡Indios malditos, mentirosos, ambiciosos, avarientos, traidores y codiciosos!» Me sentía todavía más avergonzado cuando tenía que traducir las preguntas que repetidas veces se le hacían al Uey-Tlatoani Cuautémoc, a quien Cortés ya no trataba con unción, ni siquiera con respeto. Ante las repetidas preguntas de Cortés, Cuautémoc sólo respondía, ya fuese porque sólo eso podía responder o sólo quería responder eso, con la siguiente respuesta:

«Que yo sepa, Capitán General, mi predecesor Cuitláhuac dejó el tesoro en el mismo lugar en donde usted lo tiró en el lago.»

A lo que Cortés respondía enojado: «He enviado a mis mejores nadadores y a los suyos y sólo han encontrado ¡lodo!»

Y Cuautémoc sólo quería o podía contestar: «El lodo es muy suave. Sus cañones hicieron que todo el lago de Texcoco temblara. Un objeto de oro es lo suficientemente pesado como para hundirse profundamente en el cieno.»

Y todavía me sentí mucho más avergonzado el día que tuve que observar cómo se «persuadía» a Cuautémoc y a dos viejos de su Consejo de Voceros que lo habían acompañado, a responder en esa sesión de preguntas. Después de que hube traducido sus mismas palabras no sé cuántas veces más, Cortés se puso furioso. Ordenó a sus soldados que trajeran de la cocina tres braseros encendidos e hizo que los tres señores mexica pusieran sus pies sobre los braseros mientras les hacía las mismas preguntas y ellos, apretando los dientes por el dolor, le dieron las mismas respuestas. Por fin, Cortés levantando sus manos en un gesto de disgusto, salió a grandes zancadas de la habitación. Los tres señores se sentaron con cuidado sobre sus sillas y sacaron los pies de las brasas y lentamente se dirigieron hacia sus cuartos. Los dos ancianos y el hombre joven tratando de ayudarse los unos a los otros lo más que podían, cojearon sobre sus pies ennegrecidos y llenos de ampollas y escuché que uno de los viejos gimió:

«Ayya, Señor Orador, ¿por qué no les dice algo diferente? Cualquier cosa. ¡Esto me duele horriblemente!»

«¡Silencio! —le dijo Cuautémoc cortante—. ¿Crees acaso que yo estuve en un lecho de flores?»

Aunque odiaba a Cortés tanto como a mí mismo por la asociación que tenía con él, me detuve de comentar o hacer cualquier cosa que pudiera enfurecerlo y poner en peligro mi situación de por sí frágil, pues en uno o dos años más habría muchos de mis compañeros que con gusto me sustituirían como intérpretes de Cortés y que lo podrían hacer perfectamente. Cada vez más y más gente mexica y de otros pueblos de la Triple Alianza, y fuera de ésta también, se estaba apresurando a aprender el español y a convertirse al Cristianismo, no lo hacía por obsequiosidad, sino por ambición y hasta por necesidad. Cortés había promulgado una ley que decía que ningún «indio» podría tener una posición mayor de la de un obrero a menos de que fuera un cristiano confirmado y hablara con soltura el lenguaje de los conquistadores.

Los españoles ya me conocían a mí como Don Juan Damasceno y a Malintzin como Doña Marina y a las concubinas de los españoles como Doña Luisa y Doña María Inmaculada y nombres por estilo, y algunos nobles habían sucumbido a la tentación de las ventajas que podían gozar siendo cristianos y hablando el español; por ejemplo, el que antes había sido el Mujer Serpiente, llegó a ser Don Juan Tlacotl Velázquez, pero como era de esperarse, muchos de los que una vez fueron pípiltin, desde Cuautémoc para abajo, desdeñaron la religión de los hombres blancos, sus lenguajes y sus nombres. Sin embargo, a pesar de lo admirable de su posición, eso fue un error, pues no les dejó nada más que su orgullo. Fue la gente de la clase baja, la de la clase media más baja y aun los esclavos de la clase *tlacotli*, los que asediaban a los frailes misioneros y capellanes para ser instruidos en el Cristianismo y para ser bautizados con nombres españoles. Ellos fueron los que aprendieron a hablar el español y los que con gusto entregaban a sus hermanas e hijas como pago a los soldados españoles que tenían la inteligencia y educación suficiente como para enseñarles.

Así fue cómo los seres más mediocres y las piltrafas de la sociedad al carecer de un orgullo nato pudieron librarse a sí mismos de esas labores pesadas y se pusieron al frente de ellas, sobre todos aquellos quienes en días pasados habían sido sus superiores, sus gobernante, hasta sus dueños. A todos esos oportunistas «blancos por imitación», como les llamábamos nosotros, se les concedieron más adelante puestos en el creciente gobierno de la ciudad, y fueron hechos jefes de los pueblos circunvecinos, y hasta de algunas provincias sin importancia. Eso pudo haberse considerado como algo digno de admiración: que un don nadie progresara y se levantara hasta llegar a la eminencia, si no fuera porque no me puedo acordar de uno solo de esos hombres que utilizara su eminencia para el bien, de todo aquel que fuera él mismo. De pronto se encontraba por encima de todos los que antes habían sido sus superiores e iguales y hasta allí llegaba toda su ambición. Ya sea que hubiera adquirido el puesto de gobernador provincial o sólo el de velador de alguna obra en construcción, se convertía en un déspota para todos los que estaban bajo su mando. El velador podía denunciar como flojo o borracho a cualquier trabajador que no se congraciara con él, o que no lo sobornara con regalos, y podría condenar a aquel obrero desde que lo marcaran en las mejillas hasta que lo ahorcaran. El gobernador humillaba a los que en un tiempo habían sido señores y señoras y que para entonces eran cargadores de basura y barrenderos de las calles, mientras que obligaba a sus propias hijas a someterse a lo que ustedes los españoles llaman «los derechos de señorío». Sin embargo, con toda justicia debo decir que la nueva nobleza de cristianos que hablaban el español, se comportaban de *igual* manera con *todos* sus paisanos. Así como humillaban y atormentaban a los que antes habían pertenecido a las clases más altas, también maltrataban a las clases bajas de las que ellos mismos provenían. Hacían la vida de todos, a excepción de las de sus superiores, mucho más miserable de lo que desde hacía años había sido el más miserable de los esclavos. Y aunque toda esa nueva sociedad puesta al revés no me afectaba en lo personal, sí me preocupaba al darme cuenta de que, como le dije a Beu: «¡Esos blancos por imitación son la gente que escribirá nuestra historia en el futuro!»

Aunque yo tenía una posición cómoda dentro de esa nueva sociedad de la Nueva España durante esos años, puedo tener una disculpa por mi renuencia a dejarla, ya que algunas veces podía utilizar mi posición para ayudar a otros además de a mí. Cuando menos de vez en cuando, si Malintzin o algún otro de los nuevos intérpretes no estaban presentes para traicionarme, podía utilizar mi traducción para enfatizar la súplica de alguna persona que buscaba un favor o mitigar el castigo de alguien acusado como malhechor. Mientras tanto, como Beu y yo gozábamos de sostenimiento y alojamiento gratis, pude guardar mi poco salario para el caso de que algún día, ya fuera por un error mío o porque Beu empeorara en su condición, se me expulsara de mi empleo y por lo tanto del palacio de Quaunáhuac.

Sin embargo, como sucedieron las cosas, dejé ese trabajo por mi voluntad y sucedió de este modo. Cerca del tercer año después de la Conquista, Cortés, que era un hombre impaciente, ya se encontraba incómodo en su papel tan poco aventurero de administrador de muchos detalles y árbitro de disputas sin importancia. Para entonces ya se había reconstruido gran parte de la Ciudad de Mexico y los edificios todavía no terminados, estaban ya muy adelantados. Entonces, como ahora, cada año llegaban unos mil hombres blancos a la Nueva España, la mayoría con sus mujeres blancas, quienes se aposentaban dentro o alrededor de la región del lago, creando sus propias pequeñas Españas en las mejores tierras y apropiándose de nuestra gente más robusta como «prisioneros de guerra», para trabajar en sus tierras. Todos los recién llegados consolidaron sus posiciones de hacendados de una manera tan firme y veloz que una insurrección en su contra era algo inconcebible. La Triple Alianza se había convertido irreparablemente en la Nueva España y según tengo entendido estaba funcionando tan bien como Cuba o cualquier otra colonia española, con su población indígena subyugada y resignada, aunque a simple vista se veía que no eran felices ni se sentían cómodos con ese vasallaje. Cortés parecía confiado de que sus oficiales y sus blancos por imitación, eran capaces de mantener el orden. Él quería conquistar nuevas tierras, o para ser más preciso, quería ver más de cerca las tierras que ya consideraba que eran suyas.

«Capitán General —le dije—, usted ya está familiarizado con la tierra que está entre las costas del este y aquí. Las tierras en este lugar y la costa occidental son casi iguales y hacia el norte son tierras áridas, que casi no vale la pena de ver. Pero hacia el sur, *ayyo*, al sur de aquí hay cordilleras majestuosas de montañas y valles verdes y bosques impresionantes, y más al sur de todo, está la selva pavorosa, virgen e infinitamente peligrosa, pero tan llena de maravillas que ningún hombre debe vivir su vida sin haber penetrado en ella.»

«¡Entonces, hacia el sur! —gritó como si ya estuviera ordenando que una tropa saliera en ese mismo momento—. ¿Tú ya has estado allí? ¿Conoces el lenguaje? ¿Conoces la tierra? —Le contesté que sí a todas sus preguntas, a lo cual me dio una orden—: Tú nos guiarás.»

«Capitán General —le dije—. Tengo cincuenta y ocho años de edad. Ése es un viaje para hombres jóvenes, de buena condición y fuerza.»

«Te proporcionaré una silla de manos y cargadores... y también unos compañeros muy interesantes», me dijo y me dejó abruptamente para ir a escoger a los soldados que irían en la expedición, así que no tuve la oportunidad de decirle nada acerca de lo poco práctico que sería una silla de manos en las faldas empinadas de las montañas o en la selva enmarañada.

Pero la idea de ir no me molestó, estaría bien hacer un último viaje largo a través de este mundo, antes de mi *último* y más largo viaje, todavía, hacia el otro mundo. Aunque Beu se quedara sola mientras yo estaba fuera, estaría en buenas manos. Los sirvientes de palacio que conocían su condición siempre la habían atendido bien, con bondad y eran muy discretos, y Beu sólo tendría que ser prudente y no llamar la atención de ninguno de los residentes españoles. En cuanto a mí, a pesar de que era un anciano según el calendario, no me sentía decrépito ni inútil. Si pude sobrevivir al estado de sitio de Tenochtitlan, como lo había hecho, me supuse que podría sobrevivir a los rigores exigidos por la expedición de Cortés. Si la suerte me favorecía, podría hacer que *se perdiera* o llevar la caravana entre la gente que estaba tan asqueada de ver a los hombres blancos, que acabarían con *todos* nosotros y así mi muerte serviría de algo.

Estaba un poco perplejo sobre lo que había mencionado Cortés, acerca de unos «compañeros muy interesantes» para mí, y en aquel día de otoño en que partimos, francamente me sorprendió ver de quiénes se trataba: los tres Venerados Oradores de las tres naciones de la Triple Alianza. Me pregunté por qué Cortés deseaba que hicieran ese viaje, si era porque tenía miedo de que en su ausencia tramaran una conspiración en su contra, o porque deseaba impresionar a la gente de las tierras del sur, al ver cómo esos personajes tan augustos seguían su caravana con mansedumbre.

Y en verdad que fueron todo un espectáculo, pues como sus elegantes sillas de manos resultaron muy molestas en muchas partes del camino, los personajes tenían que bajarse y caminar, y como Cuautémoc, después de las interrogaciones persuasivas de Cortés había quedado inválido para siempre, en muchos lugares a lo largo del camino los habitantes locales tuvieron la oportunidad de ver el espectáculo que representaba Cuautémoc, el Venerado Orador de los mexica, cojear y colgarse de los hombros de los otros dos que lo sostenían: de un lado el Venerado Orador Tetlapanquétzal de Tlácopan, y del otro, el Venerado Orador Cohuanácoch de Texcoco.

Sin embargo, ninguno de los tres se quejó jamás, aunque debieron de darse cuenta, después de un tiempo, de que deliberadamente estaba guiando a Cortés, a sus jinetes y a sus soldados por los caminos más difíciles y por una tierra que no me era familiar. Lo hice sólo en parte con la intención de hacer que esa expedición fuera la menos placentera posible para los españoles y con la esperanza de que jamás pudieran regresar. También porque ése sería mi *último* viaje, así que había decidido aprovecharlo y ver algo nuevo. Después de llevarlos por las montañas más duras de Uaxyácac y luego a través de los eriales desolados en esa tierra angosta que está entre los mares del norte y del sur, me desvié hacia el noroeste, conduciéndolos por los pantanos más profundos de la tierra de Cupilco. Y allí fue en donde por fin, asqueado de los hombres blancos, asqueado de mi asociación con ellos, me fui y los dejé.

Debo mencionar que con el fin de verificar la veracidad de mis traducciones por el camino, Cortés había llevado consigo a un segundo traductor. Para variar un poco, no era Malintzin, ya que en aquel entonces ella estaba amamantando a su pequeño Martín Cortés, y casi sentía su ausencia, porque cuando menos era agradable de ver. Quien la sustituía era también una mujer, pero una mujer con la cara, el quejido y el carácter de un mosquito. Pertenecía a la clase baja, de esos que se habían levantado y convertido en blancos por imitación al aprender a hablar el español y había tomado el nombre cristiano de Florencia. Pero como su otra lengua era el náhuatl, no era de ninguna utilidad en esos lugares extranjeros, excepto por el hecho de que cada noche complacía a los soldados españoles, cuando éstos, por medio de regalos o tratando de despertar la curiosidad, no habían podido atraer hacia sus petates a las prostitutas más jóvenes y deseables de la localidad.

Una noche, al principio de la primavera, después de haber pasado el día chapoteando entre un pantano particularmente desagradable, acampamos en un pedazo de tierra seca, a la vera de unos árboles de *amatl* y ceiba. Ya habíamos cenado y estábamos descansando alrededor de las varias fogatas de campamento, cuando Cortés se acercó a mí e inclinándose me puso amistosamente una mano sobre uno de mis hombros y me dijo:

«Mirad hacia allá, Juan Damasceno. Mirad, es una cosa digna de admiración.» Levanté mi topacio y miré hacia donde me apuntaba: los tres Venerados Oradores estaban sentados juntos, apartados del resto de los hombres. Ya los había visto sentados así en muchas ocasiones en el transcurso del viaje, supuestamente discutiendo lo poco que puede discutir un gobernante que ya no tiene a quién gobernar. Cortés dijo: «Creedme que eso es algo que se ve con muy poca frecuencia en el Viejo Mundo. Tres reyes sentados apaciblemente juntos y que tal vez no se vuelva a ver por aquí. Me gustaría un recuerdo de ellos. Dibujadme un retrato de ellos, Juan Damasceno, tal y como están, con sus rostros inclinados en atenta conversación.»

Lo tomé por una petición inocente. En verdad, tratándose de Hernán Cortés, me pareció un pensamiento poco común, por el hecho de considerar ese momento como para que valiera la pena de ser registrado. Por lo que lo complací de buena gana. Quité una tira de corteza de uno de los árboles de *amatl* y sobre la limpia superficie interior dibujé con una astilla ahumada que tomé de una fogata, el mejor dibujo que pude hacer con un material tan primitivo. Los tres Venerados Oradores se reconocían en él, individualmente, y capté la expresión solemne de sus rostros, de modo que cualquiera que viera el dibujo sabría que hablaban de cosas señoriales. No fue sino hasta la mañana siguiente, que tuve motivo para lamentar de nuevo el haber roto mi antiguo juramento de no dibujar más retratos por miedo de traerles mala suerte a quienes dibujaba.

«Muchachos, hoy no nos pondremos en camino —anunció Cortés al levantarnos—, porque en este día tendremos la desagradable tarea de llevar a efecto una corte marcial.»

Sus soldados lo miraron tan extrañados y perplejos como lo hicimos los Venerados Oradores y yo.

«Doña Florencia —dijo Cortés, con un gesto hacia la mujer que sonreía afectadamente— se ha tomado la molestia de escuchar las conversaciones entre nuestros tres huéspedes distinguidos y los jefes de las aldeas por las que hemos pasado. Ella atestiguará que estos reyes han estado tramando con la gente de estos lugares, para un levantamiento en masa en contra de nosotros. Y gracias a Don Juan Damasceno, también tengo —y mostró el pedazo de corteza— un dibujo que es la prueba convincente de que se encontraban en la más profunda de las conspiraciones.»

Los tres Oradores sólo habían mirado despectivamente a la despreciable Florencia, pero la mirada que dirigieron a mí estaba llena de tristeza y desilusión. Me adelanté con rapidez y grité: «¡No es verdad!»

Inmediatamente, Cortés sacó su espada y recargando su punta en mi cuello dijo: «Creo que tu testimonio y traducción en estos procedimientos no sería del todo imparcial. Doña Florencia servirá de intérprete y tú, ¡tú estarás en silencio!»

Por lo tanto seis de sus oficiales presidieron el tribunal y Cortés presentó los cargos y Florencia, su testigo, presentó la evidencia falsa que sostenía esos cargos. Quizás Cortés le había dado instrucciones previas, pero no creo que eso hubiera sido del todo necesario. Personas con su manera de ser tan baja, resentidas porque el mundo ni sabe ni se interesa de su existencia, se aprovecharán de cualquier oportunidad para ser reconocidas, aunque nada más sea por su maldad atroz. Así Florencia aprovechó la única oportunidad que tenía para que se fijaran en ella: denigrando a sus mayores, con aparente impunidad y ante una audiencia que aparentaba atención y fingía creerla. Manifestando la frustración que había llevado durante toda su vida, por ser una insignificancia, soltó un torrente de mentiras, invenciones y acusaciones, con la intención de que los tres señores parecieran unas criaturas más despreciables de lo que ella era.

No pude decir nada, no hasta ahora, y los Venerados Oradores tampoco dijeron nada. Despreciaron al mosquito con pose de buitre y no refutaron ninguna de sus acusaciones, ni se defendieron ni mostraron en sus rostros lo que pensaban de la burla de ese juicio. Florencia hubiera continuado así por días y meses, hasta hubiera podido inventar la evidencia de que los tres eran Diablos del Infierno, si hubiera tenido el intelecto para haber pensado eso. Pero al fin el tribunal se cansó de escuchar sus divagaciones, someramente le ordenaron callarse y de la misma manera dieron el veredicto de que los tres señores eran culpables de conspirar una revuelta en contra de la Nueva España.

Sin protestar o reclamar, sólo se intercambiaron despedidas irónicas entre ellos y luego los tres dejaron que los colocaran en fila bajo un árbol enorme de ceiba y los españoles lanzaron las cuerdas sobre una rama conveniente y los ahorcaron a los tres, al mismo tiempo. En aquel momento en que murieron los Venerados Oradores Cuautémoc, Tetlapanquétzal y Cohuanácoch, también murió lo que quedaba de la existencia de la Triple Alianza. No sé la fecha exacta del año, porque no había llevado un diario en esa jornada. Pero tal vez ustedes, reverendos escribanos, puedan calcular la fecha, porque cuando terminó la ejecución, Cortés gritó alegremente:

«Bien, muchachos, ¡vayamos de cacería, matemos algunas aves y hagamos una fiesta! ¡Hoy es último martes que podemos comer carne, el último día de Carnaval!»

Se divirtieron durante toda la noche, por lo que no me fue difícil escurrirme del campamento sin que se dieran cuenta y regresar por donde habíamos venido. En mucho tiempo menos del que habíamos empleado en la ida, regresé a Quaunáhuac, al palacio de Cortés. Los guardias estaban acostumbrados a mis idas y venidas y aceptaron con indiferencia mi explicación de que se me había enviado a que me adelantara al resto de la expedición. Fui a la habitación de Beu y le conté lo que había pasado.

«Ahora soy un fugitivo —le dije—, pero creo que Cortés no sabe que tengo una esposa o que ésta se encuentra residiendo aquí, y aunque lo supiera no creo que dejara caer mi castigo sobre tu cabeza. Debo huir y puedo esconderme mejor entre el gentío de Tenochtitlan. Quizás pueda encontrar una choza vacía en la sección de la gente baja. No quisiera que vivieras entre tanta pobreza, Luna que Espera, cuando puedes permanecer aquí y estar cómoda...»

«Ahora *somos* fugitivos —me interrumpió con voz ronca, pero decidida—. Hasta podré caminar si tú me guías hasta la ciudad, Zaa.»

Discutí y supliqué, pero no cambió de parecer; entonces hice un paquete con nuestras pertenencias, que no eran muchas, y pedí a dos esclavos que la llevaran en una silla de manos. Viajamos por la orilla de la montaña, otra vez, hacia las tierras del lago y luego cruzamos el camino-puente del sur hacia Tenochtitlan. Y aquí hemos estado desde entonces.

✠

Otra vez le doy la bienvenida a Su Ilustrísima, después de una ausencia tan larga. ¿Viene usted a escuchar la conclusión de mi narración? Bien. Ya casi lo he contado todo, a excepción de un pedacito.

Cortés regresó con su caravana casi un año después de haberla dejado yo y su primera preocupación fue la de hacer correr la falsa historia acerca de la insurrección planeada por los tres Venerados Oradores, y mostró mi dibujo como «prueba» de su confabulación, proclamando la justicia de haberlos ejecutado por traición. Eso causó una gran sorpresa entre la gente que había pertenecido a la Triple Alianza, porque yo no se lo había dicho a nadie, aparte de Beu. Por supuesto que toda la gente tuvo duelo y se celebraron servicios fúnebres en su memoria. También, como era de suponerse, murmuraron por lo bajo entre ellos, pero no tuvieron otra alternativa más que fingir que creían en la versión de ese incidente, contado por Cortés. Debo hacer notar que él no trajo de regreso a Florencia, para que apoyara su historia. No hubiera deseado correr el riesgo de que ella tratara de tener otro momento fugaz de reconocimiento, al publicar esa mentira dentro de sus otras mentiras. Dónde y cómo se deshizo de esa criatura, nadie lo supo o nadie se interesó jamás en investigarlo.

Es seguro que Cortés se enojó porque deserté de su expedición, pero esa ira debió de esfumarse durante el año que transcurrió hasta su regreso, pues nunca ordenó que se me diera caza, o por lo menos nunca supe tal cosa. Ninguno de sus hombres anduvo indagando acerca de mi paradero; ninguno de sus perros fue puesto a olfatear mi rastro. Así que Beu y yo seguimos viviendo como pudimos.

Para entonces ya se había restaurado el mercado de Tlaltelolco, aunque había quedado muy reducido de tamaño. Fui a ver qué se estaba comprando y vendiendo, por quién y a qué precios. El mercado estaba lleno de gente como en los viejos tiempos, aunque por lo menos la mitad de la aglomeración consistía en hombres y mujeres blancos. Me fijé que la mayoría de las cosas que adquiría mi propia gente era por medio de trueque, «te cambio este gallipavo por esa cazuela», pero los compradores españoles estaban pagando con monedas: ducados, reales y maravedíes. Y mientras ellos compraban comida y otras cosas necesarias, también adquirían muchas cosas de valor únicamente decorativo y sin utilidad. Al escucharlos mientras conversaban y compraban, deduje que estaban comprando «esas curiosas artesanías nativas» para guardarlas por su «valor de curiosidad» o para enviarlas a sus parientes como «recuerdos de la Nueva España».

Como usted sabe, Su Ilustrísima, muchas banderas diferentes 'han tremolado en esta ciudad durante los años, desde su reconstrucción como la Ciudad de Mexico. Se ha visto el estandarte personal de Cortés, en azul y blanco con una cruz roja, y la bandera color sangre y oro de España, y la que lleva la imagen de la Virgen María, con lo que supongo que son sus colores reales y una con un águila de dos cabezas, significando el imperio, y, otras cuyo significado me es desconocido. Aquel día en el mercado, vi cómo muchos artesanos ofrecían, obsequiosamente, la venta de esas banderas diferentes pero en miniatura, bien o mal hechas, pero ni aun las mejores reproducciones levantaban algún fervor entre los españoles que estaban comprando. Y observé que los vendedores no estaban ofreciendo alguna réplica parecida de nuestro orgulloso símbolo de la nación mexica. Quizás temían ser acusados de apoyar simpatías contrarias a la paz y el buen orden.

Bueno, yo no tenía esos temores. O mejor dicho, yo podría ser castigado por ofensas más graves, así es que no me preocupaban las triviales. Me fui a casa, a nuestra pequeña y miserable choza, hice un dibujo, me arrodillé junto al catre de Beu y lo sostuve cerca de sus ojos.

«Luna que Espera —le dije—, ¿puedes ver esto lo suficientemente claro, como para copiarlo? —Miró intensamente, mientras yo le señalaba los elementos—. Mira, es un águila, con sus alas equilibradas y está parada sobre un cacto *nopali* y en su pico sostiene el símbolo de la guerra, los listones intercalados...»

«Sí —dijo ella—. Sí, distingo los detalles con más facilidad ahora que me los has explicado; pero ¿qué quieres decir con copiarlo, Zaa?»

«Si compro los materiales, ¿podrías bordar una copia de esto, con hilos de colores, sobre un pequeño cuadro de tela? No es necesario que lo bordes tan primorosamente como solías hacerlo. Sólo café para el águila, verde para el *nopali* y tal vez rojo y amarillo para los listones.»

«Creo que sí podré hacerlo. ¿Pero para qué?»

«Si haces suficientes copias podría venderlas en el mercado, a los hombres y mujeres blancos. Parece que les gustan las curiosidades y pagarían con monedas.»

Ella dijo: «Haré uno y mientras tú me observas, para que me puedas corregir donde me vaya mal. Cuando lo haya hecho bien y pueda sentirlo con las puntas de mis dedos, podría usarlo como patrón para hacer muchos más.»

Y así lo hizo y muy bien además. Yo solicité un lugar en el mercado, se me dio un pequeño espacio en donde extendí mi manta y sobre ella acomodé las réplicas del antiguo emblema de los mexica. Ninguna autoridad vino a molestarme y a decirme que quitara mis cosas, en lugar de eso, mucha gente vino a comprar. La mayoría eran españoles, pero hasta algunos de mi raza me ofrecieron tal o cual cosa a cambio, porque habían pensado que nunca volverían a ver otra vez eso, que era lo único que quedaba de lo que éramos y de lo que fuimos.

Desde el principio muchos españoles se quejaron del diseño: «Esa serpiente que se está comiendo el águila, no se ve muy real.» Traté de explicarles que no se trataba de una serpiente, ni que el águila se lo estuviera comiendo. Pero no parecían entender lo que era, o sea palabras-pintadas y que los listones intercalados significaban fuego y humo, y por lo tanto también significaban guerra. Y guerra, les explicaba, constituía una gran parte de la historia mexica, lugar que jamás habían ocupado los reptiles. Pero sólo me decían: «Quedaría mejor con una serpiente.»

Si eso era lo que querían eso sería lo que tendrían. Hice un dibujo corregido y ayudé a Luna que Espera a hacer un bordado nuevo de ese dibujo, que después utilizó como molde. Cuando los otros vendedores del mercado, inevitablemente, copiaron ese emblema, lo copiaron con todo y serpiente, pero ninguna de las imitaciones estaba tan bien hecha como las de Beu, así es que mi negocio no sufrió mucho por ello. Al contrario, me divertía ver la calidad de las copias, comprobar que había iniciado una industria completamente nueva y saber que *ésa* era mi última contribución al Único Mundo. Había sido muchas cosas durante mi vida, aun siendo el Señor Mixtli, un hombre de estatura, riqueza y respetado. Entonces me hubiera reído si alguien me hubiera dicho: «Terminarás tus días y tus caminos como un vendedor ambulante, vendiéndolas a extranjeros altivos, pequeñas telas con copias del emblema mexica y hasta una imitación de éste.» Me hubiera reído, así es que reía mientras me sentaba en la plaza del mercado, día tras día, y aquellos que se detenían a comprar me consideraban un anciano simpático y alegre.

Pero tal como resultaron las cosas, no terminé ahí del todo, porque llegó el tiempo en que la vista de Beu se acabó completamente, también sus dedos se acabaron y ya no pudo bordar, así que tuve que cerrar mi pequeña aventura en el comercio. Desde entonces, hemos vivido de los ahorros de las monedas que ganamos, aunque Luna que Espera con frecuencia y enojo ha expresado su deseo de que la muerte la libere de su oscura prisión, de su inmovilidad y su miseria. Después de un tiempo de inactividad, de no hacer nada más que existir, yo estaba casi deseando lo mismo para mí, pero fue entonces cuando los frailes de Su Ilustrísima me encontraron y me trajeron aquí, y me pidieron que les hablara de los tiempos ya idos y eso ha sido una diversión suficiente como para sostener mi interés por la vida. Mi empleo aquí ha significado para Beu una prisión más triste y solitaria, pero la ha soportado con tal de que yo tenga alguien que me espere en casa, en las noches en que he llegado a esa choza que ahora es mi hogar. Cuando finalmente vuelva otra vez para quedarme allí, tal vez arregle las cosas de modo que no sea una estancia demasiado larga ni para ella ni para mí. Ya no tenemos más trabajo que hacer, ni ninguna excusa para permanecer en este mundo de los vivos. Y debería mencionar que en lo último en que contribuimos para El Único Mundo, ya no me divierte ahora. Vayan a la plaza de Tlaltelolco hoy y verán el emblema mexica a la venta, aun con todo y serpiente, pero lo que es peor, lo que no me divierte es que ahora también, ustedes escucharán a los narradores de cuentos profesionales, enroscando a esa serpiente entre nuestras leyendas más veneradas.

«Escuchen y sepan. Cuando nuestra gente llegó por primera vez a este lugar, en la región del lago, aún éramos los azteca y nuestro dios Huitzilopochtli le indicó a nuestros sacerdotes buscar un lugar en donde se encontrara un *nopali* y sobre él un águila posada *devorando a una serpiente...*»

Bien, Su Ilustrísima, creo que con lo contado es suficiente. Yo no puedo cambiar sus pequeñas falsedades patéticas, ni tampoco la realidad todavía más patética. Pero la historia que les he contado es la historia que he vivido, en la que he tomado parte y todo lo que he dicho es verdad. Beso la tierra, lo que quiere decir: lo juro.

Ahora, pudiera ser que en el transcurso de mi narración haya dejado unos pequeños huecos aquí o allá, y que Su Ilustrísima quisiera llenarlos, o puede haber preguntas que a Su Ilustrísima le interesara hacer, o más detalles que a Su Ilustrísima le gustaría saber sobre uno u otro tema. Pero le suplico que pospongan eso por un tiempo y que me permita un descanso en este empleo. Ahora, le pido a Su Ilustrísima permiso para irme y dejar a los reverendos escribanos y este cuarto que una vez fue de la Casa de Canto. No es porque esté cansado de hablar o porque haya dicho todo lo que había que decir, o porque crea que estén cansados de escucharme hablar. Le pido permiso para irme, porque anoche cuando llegué a mi choza y me senté junto al catre de mi esposa, sucedió algo increíble. ¡Luna que Espera me dijo que me amaba! Ella me dijo que me quería, que siempre lo había hecho y que aún me amaba. Como Beu jamás ha dicho tal cosa en toda su vida, creo que tal vez se está acercando al fin de su larga agonía y que debo estar con ella cuando llegue. Por muy desunidos que hayamos estado, ahora sólo nos tenemos a nosotros... Anoche, Beu me dijo que me amó desde el momento en que nos conocimos, hace mucho, en Tecuantépec, en los días de nuestra dorada juventud. Pero que me había perdido la primera vez y me perdió para siempre, me dijo, cuando decidí ir a buscar el colorante púrpura, cuando ella y su hermana Zyanya escogieron las pajillas para ver cuál de las dos me acompañaría. Fue entonces, me dijo, cuando me perdió, pero nunca dejó de quererme y nunca encontró a otro hombre que pudiera amar. Cuando anoche hizo esa sorprendente revelación, un mal pensamiento cruzó por mi mente. Pensé: «Si hubieras sido tú, Beu, quien hubiera ido conmigo, quien se hubiera casado conmigo después, entonces hubiera sido Zyanya quien ahora estaría conmigo.» Pero ese pensamiento fue borrado por otro: «¿Hubiera deseado que Zyanya sufriera como has sufrido tú, Beu?» Y me compadecí de esos pobres restos que yacían allí, diciéndome que me amaba y me lo decía tan triste que traté que la situación fuera un poco más ligera, así es que le comenté que ella siempre había escogido una forma muy extraña de manifestarme su cariño y le conté cómo la había visto entretenida con el arte de la magia, haciendo una imagen mía de lodo como lo hacen las brujas cuando quieren hacerle daño a algún hombre. Beu dijo, y parecía más triste todavía, que la había hecho sin intención de dañarme, que había esperado durante mucho tiempo y en vano a que compartiéramos el mismo lecho; que había hecho esa imagen para dormir con ella y así encantarme para que llegara a amarla. Entonces me senté junto a su catre, silencioso, y reflexioné sobre muchas cosas pasadas y me di cuenta de lo poco observador y distraído que había sido, durante los años que Beu y yo llevábamos compartiendo; he sido más ciego y más inválido de lo que está Beu en este momento, en su total ceguera. No es la mujer quien debe decir al hombre que lo ama y Beu siempre había respetado esa inhibición tradicional; jamás lo dijo y escondió sus sentimientos bajo una actitud impertinente, que yo obstinadamente había considerado burlona y con gazmoñería. Sólo unas pocas veces había hecho a un lado su restricción de gran señora; recuerdo una ocasión en que me dijo anhelante: «Siempre me he preguntado por qué se me habrá llamado Luna que Espera», y ni siquiera en esos momentos pude reconocer lo que pasaba por ella o me rehusé a ello, cuando todo lo que hubiera tenido que hacer era haberla tomado en mis brazos... Es cierto, yo amaba a Zyanya y hubiera seguido amándola y siempre lo seguiré haciendo, pero eso no hubiera disminuido aunque hubiera amado también a Beu. ¡*Ayya*, los años que he desperdiciado! De los que yo mismo me he privado, pues no puedo culpar a nadie más. Y lo que más lacera mi corazón es la forma tan desagradable en que también privé de esos años a Luna que Espera, quien había esperado durante tanto tiempo, hasta ahora que ya es demasiado tarde para salvar todavía un último momento de todos esos años perdidos. Si pudiera se los repondría de alguna forma, pero no puedo. Anoche la hubiera tomado entre mis brazos, yacido junto a ella y hubiera hecho el acto del amor. Quizás yo lo hubiera podido hacer, pero lo que queda de Beu no puede ya hacerlo. Así que hice la única cosa posible, que fue hablar y lo hice honestamente diciendo: «Beu, mi querida esposa, yo también te amo.» Ella no pudo contestar, porque se le salieron las lágrimas y ahogaron la poca voz que le quedaba, pero puso su mano sobre la mía. La apreté tiernamente y permanecí allí sentado sosteniéndosela y hubiera entrelazado mis dedos con los suyos, pero no pude ni siquiera hacer eso, pues ya no tiene dedos. Como ya habrán adivinado, mis señores, la causa de su larga agonía ha sido El Ser Comido Por Los Dioses y como ya les he descrito los efectos de esa enfermedad, preferiría no decirles lo que no se han comido los dioses de esa mujer, que en un tiempo fue tan bella como Zyanya. Sólo me senté a su lado y así permanecimos en silencio. No sé qué estaría pensando ella, pero yo recordaba los años que habíamos vivido juntos, sin estar juntos nunca y todo lo que había desperdiciado en esos años; nos habíamos desperdiciado el uno al otro y habíamos desperdiciado el amor, que es el desperdicio más imperdonable de todo. Amor y tiempo son las únicas dos cosas en el mundo que no se pueden comprar, sólo gastar. Anoche, Beu y yo por fin nos declaramos nuestro amor... pero tan tarde, demasiado tarde. Ya el tiempo pasó y ya no se puede recuperar. Por eso me senté y recordé todos esos años perdidos... y recordé también otros años, otros años más lejanos... recordé aquella noche cuando mi padre me cargó sobre sus hombros y cruzamos la isla de Xaltocan, bajo los «más viejos de los viejos árboles», los cipreses y cómo pasaba entre las sombras y luces veteadas de la luna. Entonces no lo podía saber, pero estaba pasando por lo que sería mi vida más tarde: luz y sombra, alternativamente, días brillantes y noches oscuras, buenos tiempos y tiempos malos. Y desde entonces he soportado mi carga de penas y angustias, tal vez más de lo que me toca, pero mi descuido imperdonable hacia Beu Ribé es la prueba suficiente de que yo también he causado sufrimientos y angustias a otros. Aun así, es inútil arrepentirse o quejarse del *tonali* de uno, pero si pusiera mi vida en una balanza resultaría que ésta ha sido más buena que mala. Los dioses me favorecieron con buena fortuna y con haber hecho cosas de valor. Si tuviera que lamentar cualquier aspecto de mi vida, sería el hecho de que los dioses me negaron la última buena fortuna: o sea el morir después de haber realizado esas obras de valor. Eso hubiera sido hace mucho tiempo, pero aún estoy vivo. Por supuesto que si así lo deseo, podría creer que los dioses han tenido sus razones para ello. Por lo menos puedo recordar aquella noche distante, cuando soñé borracho y puedo creer que los dos dioses me dieron sus razones. Me dijeron que mi *tonali* no era el ser feliz o desdichado, rico o pobre, productivo u ocioso, con buen temperamento o malhumorado, inteligente o estúpido, alegre o desolado, aunque he sido todo eso en uno u otro tiempo. De acuerdo con los dioses, mi *tonali* sólo era aceptar cada desafío y cada oportunidad que la vida me pusiera adelante para vivir mi vida tan plenamente como lo puede hacer un hombre. Y haciendo eso, he participado en muchos sucesos, grandes y pequeños, históricos y particulares. Pero los dioses dijeron, si es que eran dioses y si es que hablaron de verdad, que mi verdadera función en todos esos sucesos era sólo recordarlos y hablar de ellos a los que vinieran a buscarme, para que así esos sucesos no fueran nunca olvidados. Bien, ahora ya he hecho eso. Excepto por algunos detalles que Su Ilustrísima quiera que añada, no puedo pensar en alguna otra cosa que narrar. Como les previne desde el principio, sólo puedo contarles la historia de mi vida y toda ella es ahora pasado y si hay algún futuro no puedo verlo y pienso que no me gustaría tampoco. Recuerdo las palabras que oí muchas veces, durante mi viaje en busca del Aztlán, las palabras que Motecuzoma repitió una noche cuando estábamos en la cumbre de la pirámide de Teotihuacan a la luz de la luna, repitiéndolas como si fueran un epitafio: «Los azteca estuvieron aquí, nada traían cuando llegaron, nada dejaron cuando se fueron.» Los azteca, los mexica, como quieran ustedes llamarnos, nos estamos yendo ahora, seremos dispersados y absorbidos, y pronto, muy pronto, desapareceremos y quedará muy poco por lo que seamos recordados. Todas las otras naciones también, invadidas por sus soldados que llevan nuevas leyes, por sus señores propietarios exigiendo esclavos para laborar, por sus misioneros llevando nuevos dioses, esas naciones también desaparecerán o cambiarán tanto que no se las podrá reconocer y caerán hasta quedar decrépitas. Cortés se encuentra en estos momentos llevando a sus colonizadores a lo largo de las tierras del océano del sur. Alvarado está peleando por conquistar las tribus de las selvas de Quautemalan. Montejo pelea para vencer a los maya, los más civilizados en Uluümil Kutz. Guzmán está luchando para vencer a los desafiantes purémpecha de Michihuacan. Cuando menos todos esos pueblos, al igual que nosotros los mexica, tendrán el consuelo de que pelearon hasta el último momento. Compadezco a esas otras naciones, aun a nuestros antiguos enemigos los texcalteca, que ahora se lamentan amargamente por haberles ayudado a ustedes, los hombres blancos, empujándolos a tomar El Único

Mundo. Dije hace unos momentos que no podía ver el futuro, pero de cierta manera *sí* lo he hecho. He visto a Martín, el hijo de Malintzin, y a la creciente cantidad de niños y niñas que nacen, con un color de *chocólatl* aguado y baja calidad. *Eso* puede ser el futuro; no toda nuestra gente de El Único Mundo va a quedar exterminada, pero decaerán en una raza diluida, insípida en su debilidad, uniforme e inútil. Puede ser que esté equivocado, es más, me queda la esperanza de equivocarme. pero lo dudo. Debe de haber algunos pueblos en estas tierras, tan remotos o invencibles que puedan ser dejados en paz y que se multipliquen, y entonces... *¿aquin ixnentla? ¡Ayyo*, casi hasta me gustaría vivir para ver qué pasará! Mis ancestros no se sintieron avergonzados cuando los llamaron Gente de la Mala Hierba, pues aunque la mala hierba sea fea e indeseable, crece fuer-
· te y fiera y es casi imposible de erradicar. No fue cortada sino hasta que la civilización de la Gente de la Mala Hierba creció y floreció, pues las flores son bellas, fragantes y deseables, pero perecen. Quizás en alguna otra parte de El Único Mundo existe o existirá otro pueblo como la Gente de la Mala Hierba y tal vez su *tonali* sea que crezcan y quizás sus hombres blancos no puedan abatirlos y tal vez alguna vez alcanzarán nuestra propia eminencia. Podría pasar eso y también que cuando ellos se pongan en camino, alguno de mis descendientes marchara con ellos. No tomo en cuenta las semillas que alguna vez pude haber dejado en las lejanas tierras del sur, pues la gente allí lleva mucho tiempo degenerada y nunca serán otra cosa, ni siquiera con mi posible infusión de sangre mexica entre ellos. Pero hacia el norte, bien, entre los muchos pueblos en que vagué está todavía el Aztlán. Y hace mucho tiempo que me di cuenta del significado de la invitación que me extendió aquel Orador Menor, quien también se llamaba Tliléctic-Mixtli. Él me dijo: «Debes venir otra vez al Aztlán, hermano, pues te vas a encontrar con una pequeña sorpresa», pero no fue sino hasta mucho después que me acordé que había dormido muchas noches con su hermana y sabía cuál era la sorpresa que me estaba esperando. Muchas veces me he preguntado: ¿niño o niña? Pero sé esto, que ya sea él o ella, no se quedará, temeroso o estúpido, en el Aztlán si sale otra migración de allí. Y le deseo todo éxito en el futuro a esa joven semilla. Pero estoy divagando otra vez y Su Ilustrísima se muestra impaciente. Entonces, si me da usted su permiso, Su Ilustrísima, me iré ahora. Me iré y me sentaré junto a Beu y seguiré diciéndole que la amo, pues quiero que ésas sean las últimas palabras que ella oiga cada noche antes de que se duerma y antes de que se duerma para siempre. Y cuando ella se duerma, yo me levantaré y saldré hacia la noche y caminaré por las calles vacías.

✠

EXPLICIT

Crónica narrada por un indio anciano de la tribu comúnmente llamada azteca, como fue recopilada *verbatim ab origine* por:

FRAY GASPAR DE GAYANA J.
FRAY TORIBIO VEGA DE ARANJUEZ
FRAY JERÓNIMO MUÑOZ G.
FRAY DOMINGO VILLEGAS E YBARRA
ALONSO DE MOLINA, *interpres*

En el día de la fiesta de San Juan Apóstol, 25 de julio, 1531 D.C.

I H S

✠

S. C. C. M.

Santificada, Cesárea, Católica Majestad,
el Emperador Don Carlos, nuestro Señor Rey:

Muy Magistral Majestad, desde esta Ciudad de Mexico, capital de la Nueva España, es este día de los Santos Inocentes, en el año de Nuestro Señor Jesucristo de mil quinientos treinta y uno, os saludo.

Perdonad, Señor, el largo intervalo entre nuestra última comunicación. Como el Capitán Sánchez Santoveña puede atestiguar, su carabela correo tardó mucho en llegar aquí, al encontrarse con vientos contrarios cerca de las Azores y una gran calma en las estáticas latitudes del Mar de los Sargazos. Por este motivo acabamos de recibir la carta de Vuestra Majestad, en la que nos da vuestras instrucciones para que nos hagamos cargo de que, «como una recompensa por sus servicios prestados a la Corona», nuestro cronista el azteca sea favorecido «con una casa cómoda para él y su mujer, con un pedazo de tierra laborable y una pensión adecuada para que puedan sustentarse hasta el final de sus días».

Tengo la pena de informaros, Señor, que no podemos cumplir con eso, porque el indio ha muerto, y si su inválida viuda todavía vive no tenemos ni idea de dónde pueda estar. Ya que nos, anteriormente habíamos preguntado a Vuestra Majestad acerca de lo que deseaba que se hiciera con el azteca al terminar su trabajo y puesto que la única respuesta fue un silencio largo y ambiguo, quizás nos, podamos ser excusados por haber asumido que Vuestra Devota Majestad, compartía la creencia de este clérigo, expuesta con mucha frecuencia durante nuestra campaña en contra de las brujas de Navárra, de que «pasar por alto la herejía, es incitar la herejía».

Después de haber esperado un tiempo razonable para recibir alguna instrucción de Vos, o que expresarais vuestros deseos acerca de las disposiciones a tomar sobre este asunto, nos, tomamos una medida eminentemente justificada. Levantamos contra el azteca un cargo formal de herejía, así que fue sometido a juicio. Por supuesto, que si la carta de Vuestra Clemente Majestad hubiera llegado antes, habría constituido un tácito perdón real sobre las ofensas de ese hombre, y la acusación habría sido descartada. Sin embargo, Vuestra Majestad podría considerar que ¿no sería una indicación de la voluntad de Dios que los vientos del Mar Océano hayan retrasado el correo?

De cualquier modo, nos, recordamos bien el juramento hecho por nuestro Soberano que una vez declaró en nuestra presencia, que vos «estaréis dispuesto a poner a un lado vuestros dominios, amigos, sangre, vida y alma con tal de extinguir la herejía». Así es que nos, tenemos la confianza de que Vuestra Cruzada Majestad aprobará el que hayamos ayudado al Señor a librar al mundo de un favorito más del Adversario.

La Corte de la Inquisición fue convocada en nuestra sala de justicia el día de San Martín. Todo el protocolo y todas las formalidades fueron cuidadosamente y estrictamente observados. Estuvieron presentes además de nos, como Inquisidor Apostólico de Vuestra Majestad, nuestro vicario general actuando como Presidente de la Corte, nuestro Alguacil Mayor, nuestro Notario Apostólico y por supuesto el acusado. El proceso se llevó a efecto en la mañana de ese mismo día, puesto que nos, fuimos acusador y juez, y el acusado fue el único testigo a declarar, pues la única evidencia presentada fue una selección de las palabras citadas y extraídas de la crónica del acusado y transcritas por nuestros frailes.

De acuerdo con lo que él mismo admitió, el azteca abrazó el Cristianismo de una manera fortuita, por haber estado presente en una ceremonia de bautismo llevada a efecto por el Padre Bartolomé de Olmedo hace muchos años, y él se sometió a ello tan casualmente como durante toda su vida se sometió a cada oportunidad que tuvo para pecar. Pero sin tomar en consideración la actitud que haya asumido en aquel entonces —de frivolidad, de curiosidad o escepticismo— no hay manera de anular el Sacramento del Bautismo. El indio llamado Mixtli (entre otros muchos nombres) murió en el momento en que el Padre Bartolomé derramó sobre él las aguas bautismales, y en esos momentos él renació limpio de todo pecado original y de todos sus pecados anteriores en el *character indelibilis* de Juan Damasceno.

No obstante, durante todos los años después de su conversión y confirmación en la Fe, Juan Damasceno cometió muchas y diversas iniquidades, de las cuales las más notorias fueron sus palabras de escarnio y desprecio hacia la Santa Iglesia, que disimuladamente o descaradamente expresó en el curso de su narración en su «historia azteca». Por eso, Juan Damasceno fue condenado y juzgado como hereje en tercera categoría: *v.g.*: uno que habiendo abrazado la Fe, habiendo abjurado de todos sus pecados anteriores, cae de nuevo dentro de sus errores nefandos.

Por razones políticas, nos, hemos omitido de la acusación de Juan Damasceno algunos de sus pecados corporales que cometió después de su conversión y que admitió sin ninguna contrición. Por ejemplo, si nosotros aceptamos que estaba «casado» (por la ley existente de esta gente), en el tiempo en que él cometió fornicación con la mujer que entonces era llamada Malinche, claramente es culpable del pecado mortal de adulterio. Sin embargo, nos, juzgamos muy imprudente llamar bajo *sub poena* a la ahora muy respetable y estimada Doña Marina Vda. de Jaramillo, para atestiguar en este juicio. Además, el propósito de la Inquisición no es tanto examinar las ofensas particulares del acusado, sino indagar su tendencia incorregible y su susceptibilidad hacia *fomes peccati*, para encender «la yesca del pecado». Así es que nosotros nos contentamos con no acusar a Juan Damasceno de cualquiera de sus inmoralidades carnales, sino sólo de sus *lapsi fidei*, que eran bastante numerosos.

La evidencia se presentó en forma de letanía, con nuestro notario apostólico leyendo los pasajes seleccionados de la transcripción, sacada de las propias palabras del acusado y luego el juez respondía con la acusación adecuada: *v.g.*: «Profanación de la santidad de la Santa Iglesia.» El notario leía alguna otra frase y el juez respondía: «Vilipendio y falta de respeto al clero.» El notario leería otra vez y el juez volvería a responder: «Promulgación de doctrinas contrarias a los Santos Cánones de la Iglesia.»

Y así seguía y a través de toda la lista oficial de cargos se hizo patente que el acusado era el autor de un libro obsceno, blasfemo y pernicioso, que ha prorrumpido en invectivas en contra de la Fe Cristiana, que ha incitado a la apostasía y propuesto la sedición y lesa majestad, que ha ridiculizado el estado monástico, que ha pronunciado palabras que ningún otro cristiano piadoso y súbdito leal de la Corona jamás pronunciaría ni oiría.

A pesar de que todo esto son graves errores contra la Fe, al acusado se le dio la oportunidad de retractarse y de abjurar sus ofensas, aunque por supuesto ninguna retractación hubiera sido aceptada por la Corte, ya que todas sus observaciones herejes han sido tomadas y preservadas por escrito, lo que hace que cada cargo sea substancialmente en contra de él ya que la palabra impresa no se puede borrar. De cualquier forma, cuando el notario le leyó otra vez, uno por uno, los pasajes seleccionados de su narración como: *v.g.*: su observación idólatra de que «algún día mi crónica me servirá como una confesión a la bondadosa diosa La Que Come Suciedad», y le preguntaba después de cada frase: «Don Juan Damasceno, ¿es verdad que ésas son sus palabras?», él rápida e indiferentemente aceptaba que lo eran. No alegó nada en su defensa ni para mitigar sus ofensas, cuando el Presidente de la Corte le informó de la manera más solemne del castigo tan horrible al que se enfrentaría si era encontrado culpable, a lo que Juan Damasceno sólo hizo un comentario espontáneo:

«¿Eso quiere decir que no voy a ir al Cielo Cristiano?»

Se le dijo que en verdad ése sería su peor castigo, que podía estar seguro de que él no iría al Cielo. A lo cual, se sonrió provocando un sentimiento de horror en cada una de las almas que estaban en la Corte.

Nos, como Inquisidor Apostólico, estábamos obligados a advertirle sus derechos: aunque era imposible que se retractara de sus pecados, todavía podía confesarse y manifestar arrepentimiento, de esa manera sería recibido como penitente, reconciliado con la Iglesia y sujeto a la pena menor prescrita por los cánones de la ley civil, *viz.*, condenado a pasar el resto de su vida trabajando en las galeras de Vuestra Majestad como prisionero. Nosotros también le recitamos la ley de conjuración: «Si vos os mostráis sinceramente afligido por vuestra obstinación culpable, nos, rezaremos para el Cielo os dé el don y el espíritu de arrepentimiento y contrición. No nos deis pena al persistir en vuestro error y herejía; ahorradnos el dolor de vernos obligados a invocar las justas pero severas leyes de la Inquisición.»

Sin embargo, Juan Damasceno se mantuvo en su actitud obstinada, sin ceder a ninguna de nuestras persuasiones e incitaciones, sólo continuó sonriendo sombrío y murmurando algo acerca de que su destino había sido decretado por su *«tonali»* pagano, otra herejía más que suficiente. De ahí que el alguacil mayor lo llevó a su celda, mientras la Corte deliberaba sobre su juicio y por supuesto las pruebas fueron convincentes, así es que se pronunció el veredicto de que Juan Damasceno era culpable de herejía.

Como lo establecen las leyes del canon, al siguiente domingo su sentencia fue formalmente proclamada y publicada. Juan Damasceno fue sacado de su celda y conducido al centro de la gran plaza, en donde a todos los cristianos de la ciudad se les había ordenado ir y prestar atención. Así pues, había una gran multitud, que incluía además de los españoles e indios de nuestras varias congregaciones, a varios oidores de la Real Audiencia y a otros oficiales seculares de la Justicia Ordinaria y al provincial encargado de dar auto de fe. Juan Damasceno llegó llevando el saco de sambenito de los condenados 'y en su cabeza la corona de la infamia, hecha con las varas del corojo, y acompañado por Fray Gaspar de Gayana, quien cargaba una gran cruz.

Una plataforma muy elevada había sido erigida especialmente en la plaza, por nosotros los Inquisidores, y desde esa altura el Secretario del Santo Oficio leyó en voz alta a la multitud la lista oficial de las ofensas y de los cargos, y el juicio y veredicto de la Corte, todo lo cual fue repetido en náhuatl por nuestro intérprete Molina, para que fuera comprendido por los muchos indios que se hallaban presentes. Después nos, como Inquisidor Apostólico, dimos el *sermo generalis* de la sentencia, enviando al pecador condenado al brazo secular de castigo *debita animadversione*, y haciendo las recomendaciones rutinarias a esas autoridades para que ejercieran misericordia, al llevar a efecto el castigo.

«Nosotros nos encontramos en condiciones de declarar que Juan Damasceno es un hereje rebelde, así que lo pronunciamos como tal. Nosotros nos encontramos en condiciones de remitirlo, así que lo remitimos al brazo secular de la Justicia Ordinaria de esta ciudad, a quienes rogamos descargar la justicia sobre él, en una forma benigna.»

Después nosotros hablamos directamente a Juan Damasceno, haciendo la última súplica obligatoria para que abandonara su obstinación, para que confesara y abjurara de sus herejías, cuya penitencia le ganaría por lo menos la ejecución rápida y misericordiosa del garrote, antes de que su cuerpo fuera arrojado al

fuego. Pero él se mantuvo tan obstinado como siempre y sólo·
dijo sonriendo:

«Su Ilustrísima, una vez, cuando yo era un niñito, me juré
a mí mismo que si alguna vez era seleccionado para tener una
Muerte Florida, aunque fuera en un altar extranjero, nunca deshonraría
la dignidad de mi partida.»

Ésas fueron sus últimas palabras, Señor, y debo decir en
su favor que no trató de soltarse de sus amarras, ni suplicó
ni lloró cuando los alguaciles le echaron encima la vieja cadena
de ancla para sujetarlo a la estaca, que estaba sobre la
plataforma, ni cuando pusieron, bastante alto, alrededor de su
cuerpo, una gran gavilla de leña, ni cuando el provincial le prendió
fuego. Como Dios lo permitió y los pecados del hombre lo
merecían, las llamas consumieron su cuerpo y en ese fuego Dios
quiso que el azteca muriera.

Nos, nos subscribimos ante nuestro Gracioso Soberano, como
leal Defensor de la Fe, empeñando nuestra constancia al servicio
de Dios, para la salvación de las almas y de las naciones,

OBISPO DE MEXICO
INQUISIDOR APOSTÓLICO
PROTECTOR DE LOS INDIOS

IN OTIN IHUAN IN TONALTIN NICAN TZONQUICA

AQUÍ TERMINAN LOS CAMINOS Y LOS DÍAS

Índice